حياة الصحابة

Hayatus Sahabah

The lives of the Companions

By
Maulana Muhammad Yusuf Kandhelwi رحمة الله

Translated by
Abdul Hye, PhD

www.finalrevelation.net
Houston, Texas

حياة الصحابة
Hayatus Sahabah

Published by:
www.finalrevelation.net
a6h@yahoo.com
281- 488 - 3191
P.O. Box – 890071
Houston, TX 77289

Translated by: Abdul Hye, PhD

1st Print: April / 2008

Printed in the United States of America

Library of Congress Catalog Card Number 2008903635

ISBN 978-0-9817276-0-8

حياة الصحابة
Hayatus Sahabah

Translator's Note

One of the great achievements in these modern times of this century for the cause of Da'wah / Tabligh is the book '**Hayatus Sahabah**' compiled by a great scholar, Maulana Muhammad Yusuf Kandhelwi رحمة الله, Delhi, India. He not only dedicated his life for the cause of Da'wah / Tabligh but compiled this book as he felt the need at this time with the details about the efforts, sacrifice, and struggle of Rasulullah ﷺ and his companions. This book shows the examples of Rasulullah ﷺ and his companions in their efforts as a guide for all Muslims around the world to follow and benefit. The work of Da'wah / Tabligh is now a global effort to revive the understanding among the Muslims to take on the responsibility. When Rasulullah ﷺ said, *"Convey from me even if it is a single verse." (Bukhari)* and that he is the **last** Messenger, it is obligatory on every Muslim to do the effort of Da'wah.

The original book was written in Arabic with 3 volumes. The general Muslims who are involved in the effort of Da'wah / Tabligh do not have easy access to this great book. Sheikh Maulana Saad of Nizamuddin, New Delhi, India, recently emphasized the need for Muslims to use this book as a guiding tool in the efforts of Da'wah / Tabligh and benefit from it. In order to have this book available for the general Muslims who are involved in the efforts of Da'wah / Tabligh, the translation of all 3 complete volumes is compiled in **one** volume with easy English and a minimum number of Arabic terms so it is easy for all Muslims around the world to understand and benefit from it. All stories, subject categories, and chapters can be found in the same book. The Table of Contents lists all 19 chapters at the beginning. Since it is a big book, every effort was made to format each of the 19 chapters to easily identify titles, headings, topics, etc with their pre-set page numbers. The translation of all Qur'anic verses are in *italics* from the Noble Qur'an of Darussalam, Saudi Arabia with their locations. All references of Ahadith are inserted at the end of each Hadith in *italics* rather than at the bottom of the page in order to clearly show their sources. May Allah ﷺ help and guide all Muslims around the world to benefit most from this great book in the efforts of Da'wah / Tabligh.

Abdul Hye, PhD
finalrevelation.net
April 25, 2008

Original Arabic Edition Introduction
By Shaikh Sayyid Abul Hasan Ali Nadwi Rahmatullah

All praises be to Allah, the Rabb of the universe. May the special mercies of Allah ﷻ and peace be on our leader Muhammad ﷺ who is the last of all prophets. May Allah's mercy and peace be on his family, all his companions, and all those coming until the day of Judgment who follow him. The lifestyle and history of Rasulullah ﷺ and his companions, without a doubt, are among the most powerful sources to provide strength of Iman and love for Islam. There sources have always been inspiring sparks of Iman to the Ummah and the call towards Islam. It is by this inspiration that the embers of their hearts have been kept burning. Unfortunately, these embers are being extinguished quickly by the strong wind force of worldly attraction. Once they are extinguished, this Ummah will lose its strength, identity, and influence over others. It will then become merely a dead body which life will carry along on its shoulders.

This book presents the history of the Sahabah who accepted the call of Islam when it was presented to them. They accepted the truth sincerely from the bottom of their hearts. When they were called towards Allah and His Rasul ﷺ, they said, "*Our Rabb, Surely we have heard the caller (Rasulullah ﷺ) calling to Iman (saying), 'Believe in your Rabb!' so we believed*" (Al-Imran:193). When they placed their hands in the hands of Rasulullah ﷺ, it became easy for them to sacrifice their lives, wealth, and families. Then they began to tolerate the difficulties and hardships that afflicted them during the work of Da'wah: calling others towards Allah. In this way, strong conviction filled their hearts and gained control over their bodies and minds. They showed strong belief in the unseen with strong love for Allah and Rasulullah ﷺ, compassion for the believers, and firmness towards the disbelievers. They preferred the life of the hereafter over this world, the rewards of the hereafter over the rewards of this world, the unseen over the seen, and guidance over ignorance. They were anxious to invite people towards Islam, remove the creation (people) from their worship of the creation towards the worship of Allah alone. They saved people from the injustice of other religions and brought them into the justice of Islam. The worldly attractions and vanities were not their concern. The only aspiration was to meet Allah and enter Paradise. They showed firm determination and vision to spread Islam and deliver it to every part of the world at any cost. For this purpose, they spread themselves to every corner of the world without any limit on their part. They forgot their personal pleasures, abandoned their luxuries and comfort, left their homes, spent their lives and wealth selflessly. They continued this mission until the foundations of Islam were established; hearts of people turned towards Allah, and the winds of Iman blew strongly everywhere. An environment of Iman, good deeds was established. People became attracted towards paradise, guidance to Allah spread throughout the world, and people entered into the fold of Islam in masses.

The history books are full of their stories and records of their achievements. This has always been a source of inspiration to revive the efforts in the lives of Muslims. It is for these reasons that the efforts by the callers to Islam and reformers have intensified. These narrations and histories have always helped to revive the courage of the Muslims, rekindle the embers of Iman in their hearts, and increase their enthusiasm for Islam. But over a period of time, the Muslims grew unmindful of this history and forgot all about it. Muslim writers, lecturers and preachers then turned towards the descriptions and accounts of pious people, learned ones, and saints of the later period. Books were filled with stories about them and their miracles. People became obsessed with these descriptions and they occupied themselves with pride of those places in lectures, academic lessons and books. As far as we know to the best of our knowledge in our times, the first person who turned his attention towards the excellence of the description and lives of the Sahabah for the cause of Da'wah and reformed the religious consciousness of people was the famous preacher and great reformer Sheikh Muhammad Ilyas Kandhelwi رحمة الله (passed away in 1363 AH / 1944 CE). He recognized the great value of this treasure of reformation that was buried between the pages of books and realized the importance of its effect on the hearts of people. He dedicated himself quickly to study these accounts, teach, narrate, and discuss them to the Muslims. I have seen him personally show great interest in the stories of Rasulullah ﷺ and the Sahabah by discussing them with his students and friends. These descriptions and histories used to be recited to him every night and he would listen to them with great attention and respect. He desired that these descriptions and histories be revived, circulated, and discussed. His nephew the great scholar Sheikh Muhammad Zakariyya Kandhelwi رحمة الله (the author of **Mu'atta Imam Malik, Aujazul-Masalik**) has written a book in Urdu about the stories of the Sahabah (titled **Hikayatus Sahabah**). Sheikh Muhammad Ilyas رحمة الله was very pleased with this book and asked those engaged in Da'wah and traveling in the Path of Allah to study and teach this book. Subsequently, this book became one of the most important prescribed books for preachers and others, and enjoyed popular acceptance.

Sheikh Muhammad Yusuf رحمة الله (the compiler of this book) succeeded his esteemed father (Sheikh Muhammad Ilyas رحمة الله) in assuming leadership of those engaged in the effort of Da'wah. He also followed his father's footsteps in his deep interest in the stories of Rasulullah ﷺ and the Sahabah. He used to read these stories to his father. Even after his father passed away, he continued studying stories of Rasulullah ﷺ, books of Islamic history and the Sahabah in spite of his busy commitments to the effort of Da'wah. Personally I do not know of anyone with a deeper knowledge about the Sahabah and fine details of their lives. I do not know anyone who could quote so many stories of their lives so eloquently and connect them together so beautifully, just as pearls in a necklace. These stories inspired his listeners and caused magical impacts on the hearts of large crowds of people who then found it easy to give great sacrifices in the Path of Allah. The people were motivated to accept great hardships and difficulties in the path of Allah. During the period of his leadership, the effort of Da'wah spread throughout the Arabian Peninsula and even to places such as America, Europe, Japan, and the islands of the Indian Ocean. At that time, it became necessary to prepare a book for those who were involved in the effort of Da'wah and travel to foreign countries so that they could read to each other from that book. This was necessary to provide nourishment in their hearts and minds, to inspire their spirituality, and to encourage them to emulate the efforts of Rasulullah ﷺ and the Sahabah to spend their lives and wealth for the sake of Islam. It was necessary to encourage them to travel and migrate for the cause of Islam, to assist others doing the same, and to teach them the virtues of good deeds and build moral character. It was then necessary to read a book with such reports which would cause the reader to see how small is his efforts in front of the sacrifices of the Sahabah just as rivers lose themselves in the ocean and just as even a tall man would seem tiny in front of a tall mountain. In this way, they would begin to understand the weakness of their conviction, they would consider their efforts and sacrifices to be inadequate when compared to Sahabah, and then would give less importance to their lives in this world. This will motivate them to develop courage to make greater efforts and sacrifices.

Allah had willed to give the credit of writing such a valuable book to Sheikh Muhammad Yusuf رحمة الله who also contributed tremendously to the effort of Da'wah. Therefore, in spite of his big commitment and a busy schedule filled with travels, lectures for Da'wah, and meetings with delegations and guests; he was miraculously able to compile such a big book. He drew great courage and resolved to involve himself to write with the guidance and help of Allah. Though it was difficult to combine the life of a writer with that of a preacher, he succeeded in completing a commentary of the famous book 'Sharhu Ma'anil Athar' written by the eminent Imam Tahawi رحمة الله. This commentary, titled 'Amanil Ahbar' was completed in several volumes. With the help of Allah, he compiled this book 'Hayatus Sahabah' in 3 large volumes, collecting from many reports that were scattered in the various books of biography and history. The distinguished author initiated every section with reports from the life of Rasulullah ﷺ and then added accounts from the lives of the Sahabah. He also devoted special attention to Da'wah and spiritual reformation for the benefit of those involved in these efforts. Therefore, this book offers advice to preachers with a great provision for those engaged in Da'wah, a valuable guide to develop Iman, and conviction to the Muslim public. He has collected such reports in these 3 volumes that cannot be found in any other book because they are compiled from countless number of historical and biographical books. He has created actually an encyclopedia that shows the lives, behavior and attributes of those living during the time of Rasulullah ﷺ. The significant details mentioned in this book provide an inspirational impact that can not be felt in other books with brief accounts. As a result, the reader is always highly motivated by an environment of Iman, Da'wah, courage, virtue, sincerity, and clear description.

It is generally believed that a book is a reflection of the author - it represents the love of his life, and it expresses the dedication and spirit with which it is written. I can promise that this book is truly inspiring, powerful, and a success because the author wrote it with great passion and love for the Sahabah. Love for the Sahabah had penetrated truly in his flesh and blood in such a manner that it had dominated his personality and psychology. He has lived in the mould of their lives for a long time and continues to do so, always benefiting from the refreshing fountains of their lives. *(This introduction was written during the lifetime of Maulana Muhammad Yusuf Kandhelwi رحمة الله).*

This book does not require an introduction from someone like me because the author is an extremely eminent and sincere personality of this age. I am convinced that he is a divine gift and a gem from the gems of time with regard to the strength of his Iman, the power of his Da'wah, his devotion to Da'wah, and his sacrifice in the Path of Allah. A personality like him is born after a long period of time. He led an Islamic movement of Da'wah that is one of the most powerful, sensible, and inspiring. However, I am honored by his request to write this foreword and I have every intention to be a part of this great work. I have therefore written these few words hoping to seek nearness to Allah. May Allah accept this book and make it a means of benefit to mankind.

Abul Hasan Ali Nadwi
Saharanpur, India.
2 Rajab 1378 / 12 January 1959.

Brief Biography of Maulana Muhammad Yusuf Kandhelwi رحمة الله

Maulana Muhammad Yusuf رحمة الله was born on Tuesday the 25th of Jumadal Ula, 1335 Hijri (20th March, 1914). He was the son of Maulana Muhammad Ilya رحمة الله - the founder of the Tablighi movement, son of Maulana Muhammad Ishmael. The author of Faza'il-e-A'mal, Shaikhul Hadith Maulana Muhammad Zakariyyah رحمة الله married the sister of Maulana Muhammad Yusuf رحمة الله after the demise of his first wife. Thus, Shaikhul Hadith was the brother-in-law of Maulana Muhammad Yusuf رحمة الله. In 1353 Hijri, at the age of 18, Maulana Yusuf رحمة الله started to study under Shaikhul Hadith Maulana Muhammad Zakariyyah رحمة الله at Saharanpur. Maulana Muhammad Yusuf رحمة الله first married the eldest daughter of Shaikhul Hadith on the 3rd Muharram, 1354 Hijri. The marriage ceremony was performed by Shaikhul Islam Maulana Said Hussain Ahmad Madani رحمة الله at the annual gathering of Madrasah Mazahir-e-Ulum, Saharanpur, India. In Shawwal, 1367 Hijri, she passed away while performing sejda. She was survived by only one son, Maulana Muhammad Harun رحمة الله. In the year 1369 Hijri, Maulana Muhammad Yusuf رحمة الله married the 2nd daughter of Shaikhul Hadith. No children were born from this marriage. His father Maulana Muhammad Ilyas رحمة الله passed away in 1944. He took over the responsibility of the Tablighi movement at the age of 30 till the last day of his life. He lived only 48 years. He had 3 outstanding qualities of his father: the reality of knowledge, sincerity, and a burning enthusiasm of striving to give Da'wah. During this short life, Maulana Muhammad Yusuf رحمة الله dedicated his life for Da'wah by traveling continuously to places, giving resourceful speeches with in-depth knowledge and references on how the Prophet Muhammad ﷺ and his companions dedicated themselves on Da'wah. At the same time Maulana Muhammad Yusuf took time to write this great book **'Hayatus Sahabah'** to benefit Muslims around the world. After so many years since his departure from this world, Muslims around the world still discuss his activities, approach, speeches as a guiding tool for Da'wah.

Thoughts and Sayings of Muhammad Yusuf Kandhelwi رحمة الله

- The remedy for current unislamic influence is the unlimited movement of Tablighi activities and spreading of the 6 points.
- The purpose of the Tabligh effort is that the Muslims must be obedient to the commands of Allah. A life of obedience will result through the development of the 6 qualities.
- It is my conviction that peace and tranquility will prevail wherever Jamats will go.
- The cure and remedy for this Ummah is to involve yourselves in the effort of Sayyidina Rasulullah ﷺ. Connect the Muslims to the Masjid where Iman is explained, Talim is conducted, Dhikr is practiced, and Mashwara regarding Islamic effort takes place.
- Islam cannot be understood by remaining at one place. It is understood by movement. The Qur'an was not revealed at one place. It was revealed sometimes at home sometimes on journey and sometimes in battle.
- Success is not in wealth. If success was in wealth, the Qarun would have been successful. Success is in the control of Allah. If Allah wills, He can make a poor person successful and, if Allah wills, He can make a rich person unsuccessful.
- Our life in this world is temporary. We have to make such an effort in this short life-span that will save us from disgrace in the hereafter.
- It is wrong to think that gaining control of authority and wealth will cause Islam to prosper. In fact, political authority and wealth is causing much harm to Islam. Today's political leaders are no longer the representatives of Abu Bakr and Omar. They represent Qaisar, Kisra, Saddad and Namrud. There is no hope in them for the revival of Islam. The condition of Islam under their rule has caused the heart to cry out, 'How will Allah revive this dead corpse.' *(ref. Al-Baqarah)*
- (Referring to Ikhwanul Muslimin): When Hasan Al-Banna announced that his men should use their physical force in Egypt, I sent a message through my men, stopping him from doing so. I advised him to continue the great task of reviving Islam and not to use physical force, otherwise the government would crush his organization. Unfortunately he did not listen to my advice.
- (Addressing to a group of businessmen): Earning a living is not a part of the pillars of Islam. It is surprising that we are destroying the pillars of Islam and wasting away our lives on those activities which are not the pillars of Islam.
- (While sending Jamats to Arabia, he reminded) You (Arab communities) brought Islam to us. At that time and even presently, you are more worthy of doing the effort of Islam. The people of the world learnt Islam from you. Even now, you should continue doing the same work.
- This Ummah was formed when none supported only his own family, community, party, nation, area or language.
- Honor and disgrace is not in the hands of Russia and America, but in the control of Allah. Allah has blessed honor and disgrace on certain principles. Whenever an individual or nation or family sticks to the principles of success, Allah will make them successful. On the other hand, whoever chooses the actions of failure, Allah will destroy him.
- Allah has made the deeds produced by Sayyidina Rasulullah ﷺ more powerful than the atomic bomb. Each and every deed of his is a means of causing a complete change in the universe. (Remember) Salatul Istisqa is a means of changing the condition of drought on earth.
- The month of Ramadhan is the month of the Qur'an, guidance, and correction of deed. If we proceed in this month to make effort for Islam according to its principles, then it is hoped that Allah will open the path of guidance for all nations of the world.
- The ultimate object is to develop a natural dislike of the divine prohibitions.
- Make sure that the oppressor compensates the oppressed, though the oppressor be from one's own family, nation or country.
- Knowledge without Dhikr is darkness and Dhikr without knowledge is the door of confusion.
- Regard teaching as one of the fundamental duties. Involvement in teaching should be combined with Tabligh.
- When you listen to the recitation of the Qur'an, think: "Allah is addressing me. When you read or listen to the Ahadith, then think: Sayyidina Rasulullah ﷺ is addressing me."
- We do not send Jamats to Deoband and Saharanpur Madrasah for the sake of doing Da'wah and Tabligh amongst the Ulema. We send them with the sole purpose of bridging the gap which currently exists between the public and the Ulema. In this lies the benefit of the public.
- I undertook the journey with the intention of following the

Sunnah. It will be a bargain for me to sacrifice all my wealth in order to follow one Sunnah.

- It is better to spend as less time as possible to reach our destination. The ordinary place will take 9 hours, whereas the jet will reach the destination in approximately 3 hours.

- Whenever pious people were introduced, it was never ever said, he is the owner of so many factories, instead they were introduced in this manner, 'He is a Badri,' 'He participated in Uhud,' 'He participated in these battles,' 'He is the one who made these sacrifices for Islam.'

- The time you spend for useless pursuits should be utilized for the sake of Islam. Your entire vacation period spent in entertainment and fun should be correctly utilized in the Path of Allah. Do not forsake your studies.

- The influence of western culture can be overcome in the universal Da'wah and propagation of the Sunnah.

- Two nations have been permanent enemies of Islam. Their culture has caused much harm to Islam. It is a difficult task to rectify this harm. They have distorted the history of Islam, the life of Sayyidina Rasulullah ﷺ and the meaning of the Qur'an in such a manner that even knowledgeable persons are deceived.

- When a person makes effort to himself, he reaches a stage when Allah becomes pleased with Him. Allah then makes decisions (of favorable conditions) upon the actions of his limbs and the world falls at his feet. Today, we are chasing after the world, whereas the world is running away from us.

- Do not prepare people to attend Ijtima (convention) for the sake of meeting me or to request me to make Du'a for them. Instead, prepare them to come for the pleasure of Allah, receive rewards in the hereafter and become inviters to Islam.

- If you fulfill the right of involvement in this effort (of Da'wah), then those powers who possess atom and hydrogen bombs will become submissive to you with all their weapons. To fear the atom and hydrogen bombs is equal to the fear of the idolaters for their idols.

- The foundation of the social life of Sayyidina Rasulullah ﷺ is based on purity, simplicity and modesty. The social life of the non-Muslims is based on immodesty, extravagance and luxury. You do not prefer the social life of those who shed the blood of your pious predecessors, dishonored you and seized your land. Now they are extending their help to you in a manner like you feed chickens (for the sake of slaughtering them).

- You can spread light (of Islam) in this world if you travel with it as the sun rotates. You can acquire light through Iman, the deeds and Akhlaq (actions and character) of Sayyidina Rasulullah ﷺ and give Da'wah of Islam with sincerity. The sun has 3 qualities: (1) it rotates with light, (2) it is in continuous rotation all the time, and (3) it does not take any benefit from those upon whom it sheds its light. Your effort should be similar, travel with this light (of Islam), continuously proceed in the Path of Allah, and make this pledge as your principle: "I do not seek any reward from you for this work of Tabligh." You should not take any personal benefit from the effort of Da'wah.

- One wisdom of performing 2 sejdah in every Rakat is that we should remember our creation from sand when performing the first Sejdah. The 2nd Sejdah should remind us of the termination of our life one day and our return to sand. Standing up from Sejdah should remind us of our standing in front of Allah to render an account of our lives of this world.

- Remember, slogans like: 'my nation,' 'my country,' 'my community,' disunites the Ummah. Allah dislikes such slogans.

- Remember, the corruption of monetary and social dealings destroy the unity of the Ummah.

- Remember, Islam demands unity not individuality.

Works of Maulana Muhammad Yusuf Kandhelwi رحمة الله

➤ **Hayatus Sahabah** with 3 volumes. The first volume has 612 pages, the 2nd and 3rd volumes with about 714 pages. After the demise of Maulana Mohammad Yusuf رحمة الله, Maulana In'amul Hasan رحمة الله began reading this book after Isha Salah at Nizamuddin, India.

➤ Arabic commentary of Imam Tahawi's book, '**Sharh Ma'aniyul Athar**' 2 volumes have been published. The 1st volume consists of 376 pages and 2nd with 442 pages. Maulana was busy working on the 3rd volume when all of a sudden he passed away.

➤ The book '**Sharah Am'aniyul Athar**' of Imam Tahawi رحمة الله. First Maulana Muhammad Ilyas رحمة الله began to edit. Then Maulana Muhammad Yusuf رحمة الله continued to edit the book.

➤ Maulana Muhammad Yusuf رحمة الله wrote an Arabic booklet on 6 points of Tabligh in the light of the Ahadith.

Table of Contents

Volume – 2 / Chapter - 7

The chapter concerning the unity.................................7-1

Volume – 2 / Chapter - 8

Volume – 2 / Chapter - 10

Volume -3 / Chapter - 11

بِسْمِ اللهِ الرَّحْمنِ الرَّحِيمِ

Qur'anic Verses on the Obedience to Allah and His Rasul ﷺ

بِسْمِ اللَّهِ الرَّحْمنِ الرَّحِيمِ (1) الْحَمْدُ لِلَّهِ رَبِّ الْعَالَمِينَ (2) الرَّحْمنِ الرَّحِيمِ (3) مَالِكِ يَوْمِ الدِّينِ (4) إِيَّاكَ نَعْبُدُ وَإِيَّاكَ نَسْتَعِينُ (5) اهْدِنَا الصِّرَاطَ الْمُسْتَقِيمَ (6) صِرَاطَ الَّذِينَ أَنْعَمْتَ عَلَيْهِمْ غَيْرِ الْمَغْضُوبِ عَلَيْهِمْ وَلَا الضَّالِّينَ (7)

1. In the Name of Allah, the Most Beneficent, the Most Merciful. 2. All the praises and thanks be to Allah, the Lord of the Alameen (mankind, jinns and all that exists). 3. The Most Beneficent, the Most Merciful. 4. The Only Owner (and the Only Ruling Judge) of the Day of Recompense (i.e. the Day of Resurrection). 5. You (Alone) we worship, and You (Alone) we ask for help (for each and everything). 6. Guide us to the Straight Way. 7. The Way of those on whom You have bestowed Your Grace , not (the way) of those who earned Your, nor of those who went astray. (Al-Fatiha:1-7)

إِنَّ اللَّهَ رَبِّي وَرَبُّكُمْ فَاعْبُدُوهُ هذَا صِرَاطٌ مُسْتَقِيمٌ (51)

2. Truly! Allah is my Lord and your Lord, so worship Him (Alone). This is the Straight Path. (Al-Imran:51)

قُلْ إِنَّنِي هَدَانِي رَبِّي إِلَى صِرَاطٍ مُسْتَقِيمٍ دِينًا قِيَمًا مِلَّةَ إِبْرَاهِيمَ حَنِيفًا وَمَا كَانَ مِنَ الْمُشْرِكِينَ (161) قُلْ إِنَّ صَلَاتِي وَنُسُكِي وَمَحْيَايَ وَمَمَاتِي لِلَّهِ رَبِّ الْعَالَمِينَ (162) لَا شَرِيكَ لَهُ وَبِذلِكَ أُمِرْتُ وَأَنَا أَوَّلُ الْمُسْلِمِينَ (163)

3. Say (O Muhammad ﷺ): "Truly, my Lord has guided me to a Straight Path, a right religion, the religion of Ibrahim (Abraham), Hanifa (i.e. the true Islamic Monotheism - to believe in One God (Allah i.e. to worship none but Allah, Alone)) and he was not of Al-Mushrikoo." Say (O Muhammad ﷺ): "Verily, my Salat (prayer), my sacrifice, my living, and my dying are for Allah, the Lord of the Alameen (mankind, jinns and all that exists). He has no partner. And of this I have been commanded, and I am the first of the Muslims." (Al-An'am: 161-163)

قُلْ يَا أَيُّهَا النَّاسُ إِنِّي رَسُولُ اللَّهِ إِلَيْكُمْ جَمِيعًا الَّذِي لَهُ مُلْكُ السَّمَاوَاتِ وَالْأَرْضِ لَا إِلَهَ إِلَّا هُوَ يُحْيِي وَيُمِيتُ فَآمِنُوا بِاللَّهِ وَرَسُولِهِ النَّبِيِّ الْأُمِّيِّ الَّذِي يُؤْمِنُ بِاللَّهِ وَكَلِمَاتِهِ وَاتَّبِعُوهُ لَعَلَّكُمْ تَهْتَدُونَ (158)

4. Say (O Muhammad ﷺ): "O mankind! Verily, I am sent to you all as the Messenger of Allah - to Whom belongs the dominion of the heavens and the earth. La ilaha illa Huwa (none has the right to be worshipped but He); It is He Who gives life and causes death. So believe in Allah and His Messenger (Muhammad ﷺ), the Prophet who can neither read nor write (i.e. Muhammad ﷺ) who believes in Allah and His Words ((this Qur'an), the Taurat (Torah) and the Injeel (Gospel) and also Allah's Word: "Be!" - and he was, i.e. Iesa (Jesus) son of Maryam (Mary)), and follow him so that you may be guided." (Al-A'raf:158)

وَمَا أَرْسَلْنَا مِنْ رَسُولٍ إِلَّا لِيُطَاعَ بِإِذْنِ اللَّهِ وَلَوْ أَنَّهُمْ إِذْ ظَلَمُوا أَنْفُسَهُمْ جَاءُوكَ فَاسْتَغْفَرُوا اللَّهَ وَاسْتَغْفَرَ لَهُمُ الرَّسُولُ لَوَجَدُوا اللَّهَ تَوَّابًا رَحِيمًا (64)

5. We sent no Messenger, but to be obeyed by Allah's Leave. If they (hypocrites), when they had been unjust to themselves, had come to you (Muhammad ﷺ) and begged Allah's Forgiveness, and the Messenger had begged forgiveness for them: indeed, they would have found Allah All-Forgiving (One Who accepts repentance), Most Merciful.. (An-Nisa:64)

يَا أَيُّهَا الَّذِينَ آمَنُوا أَطِيعُوا اللَّهَ وَرَسُولَهُ وَلَا تَوَلَّوْا عَنْهُ وَأَنْتُمْ تَسْمَعُونَ (20)

6. O you who believe! Obey Allah and His Messenger, and do not

turn away from him (i.e. Muhammad ﷺ) while you are hearing. (Al-Anfal:20)*

وَأَطِيعُوا اللَّهَ وَالرَّسُولَ لَعَلَّكُمْ تُرْحَمُونَ (132)

7. And obey Allah and the Messenger (Muhammad ﷺ) so that you may obtain mercy. (Al-Imran:132)

وَأَطِيعُوا اللَّهَ وَرَسُولَهُ وَلَا تَنَازَعُوا فَتَفْشَلُوا وَتَذْهَبَ رِيحُكُمْ وَاصْبِرُوا إِنَّ اللَّهَ مَعَ الصَّابِرِينَ (46)

8. And obey Allah and His Messenger, and do not dispute (with one another) lest you lose courage and your strength departs, and be patient. Surely, Allah is with those who are patient. (Al-Anfal:46)

يَا أَيُّهَا الَّذِينَ آمَنُوا أَطِيعُوا اللَّهَ وَأَطِيعُوا الرَّسُولَ وَأُولِي الْأَمْرِ مِنْكُمْ فَإِنْ تَنَازَعْتُمْ فِي شَيْءٍ فَرُدُّوهُ إِلَى اللَّهِ وَالرَّسُولِ إِنْ كُنْتُمْ تُؤْمِنُونَ بِاللَّهِ وَالْيَوْمِ الْآخِرِ ذَلِكَ خَيْرٌ وَأَحْسَنُ تَأْوِيلًا (59)

9. O you who believe! Obey Allah and obey the Messenger (Muhammad ﷺ), and those of you (Muslims) who are in authority. If you differ in anything amongst yourselves, refer it to Allah and His Messenger (Muhammad ﷺ) if you believe in Allah and in the Last Day. That is better and more suitable for final determination. (An-Nisa:59).

إِنَّمَا كَانَ قَوْلَ الْمُؤْمِنِينَ إِذَا دُعُوا إِلَى اللَّهِ وَرَسُولِهِ لِيَحْكُمَ بَيْنَهُمْ أَنْ يَقُولُوا سَمِعْنَا وَأَطَعْنَا وَأُولَئِكَ هُمُ الْمُفْلِحُونَ (51) وَمَنْ يُطِعِ اللَّهَ وَرَسُولَهُ وَيَخْشَ اللَّهَ وَيَتَّقْهِ فَأُولَئِكَ هُمُ الْفَائِزُونَ (52)

10. The only saying of the faithful believers, when they are called to Allah (His Words, the Qur'an) and His Messenger, to judge between them, is that they say, "We hear and we obey." And such are the successful ones (who will live forever in Paradise). And whosoever obeys Allah and His Messenger, fears Allah, and keeps his duty (to Him), such are the successful. (An-Nur: 51-52)

قُلْ أَطِيعُوا اللَّهَ وَأَطِيعُوا الرَّسُولَ فَإِنْ تَوَلَّوْا فَإِنَّمَا عَلَيْهِ مَا حُمِّلَ وَعَلَيْكُمْ مَا حُمِّلْتُمْ وَإِنْ تُطِيعُوهُ تَهْتَدُوا وَمَا عَلَى الرَّسُولِ إِلَّا الْبَلَاغُ الْمُبِينُ (54) وَعَدَ اللَّهُ الَّذِينَ آمَنُوا مِنْكُمْ وَعَمِلُوا الصَّالِحَاتِ لَيَسْتَخْلِفَنَّهُمْ فِي الْأَرْضِ كَمَا اسْتَخْلَفَ الَّذِينَ مِنْ قَبْلِهِمْ وَلَيُمَكِّنَنَّ لَهُمْ دِينَهُمُ الَّذِي ارْتَضَى لَهُمْ وَلَيُبَدِّلَنَّهُمْ مِنْ بَعْدِ خَوْفِهِمْ أَمْنًا يَعْبُدُونَنِي لَا يُشْرِكُونَ بِي شَيْئًا وَمَنْ كَفَرَ بَعْدَ ذَلِكَ فَأُولَئِكَ هُمُ الْفَاسِقُونَ (55) وَأَقِيمُوا الصَّلَاةَ وَآتُوا الزَّكَاةَ وَأَطِيعُوا الرَّسُولَ لَعَلَّكُمْ تُرْحَمُونَ (56)

11. Say, "Obey Allah and obey the Messenger, but if you turn away, he (Muhammad ﷺ) is only responsible for the duty placed on him (i.e. to convey Allah's Message) and you for that placed on you. If you obey him, you shall be on the right guidance. The Messenger's duty is only to convey (the message) in a clear way (i.e. to preach in a plain way)." Allah has promised those among you who believe, and do righteous good deeds, that He will certainly grant them succession to (the present rulers) in the earth, as He granted it to those before them, and that He will grant them the authority to practice their religion, that which He has chosen for them (i.e. Islam). And He will surely give them in exchange a safe security after their fear (provided) they (believers) worship Me and do not associate anything (in worship) with Me. But whoever disbelieves after this, they are the Fasiqoon (rebellious, disobedient to Allah). And establish Salat, and give Zakat and obey the Messenger (Muhammad ﷺ) so that you may receive mercy (from Allah). (An-Nur: 54-56)

يَا أَيُّهَا الَّذِينَ آمَنُوا اتَّقُوا اللَّهَ وَقُولُوا قَوْلًا سَدِيدًا (70) يُصْلِحْ لَكُمْ أَعْمَالَكُمْ وَيَغْفِرْ لَكُمْ ذُنُوبَكُمْ وَمَنْ يُطِعِ اللَّهَ وَرَسُولَهُ فَقَدْ فَازَ فَوْزًا عَظِيمًا (71)

12. O you who believe! Keep your duty to Allah and fear Him, and speak (always) the truth. He will direct you to do righteous good deeds and will forgive you your sins. And whosoever obeys

Allah and His Messenger (Muhammad ﷺ), he has indeed achieved a great achievement (i.e. he will be saved from the Hell-fire and will be admitted to Paradise). (Al-Ahzab:70-71)

يَا أَيُّهَا الَّذِينَ آمَنُوا اسْتَجِيبُوا لِلَّهِ وَلِلرَّسُولِ إِذَا دَعَاكُمْ لِمَا يُحْيِيكُمْ وَاعْلَمُوا أَنَّ اللَّهَ يَحُولُ بَيْنَ الْمَرْءِ وَقَلْبِهِ وَأَنَّهُ إِلَيْهِ تُحْشَرُونَ (24)

13. O you who believe! Answer Allah (by obeying Him) and (His) Messenger when he calls you to that which will give you life, and know that Allah comes in between a person and his heart (to prevent evil). And verily to Him you shall (all) be gathered. (Al-Anfal:24)

قُلْ أَطِيعُوا اللَّهَ وَالرَّسُولَ فَإِنْ تَوَلَّوْا فَإِنَّ اللَّهَ لَا يُحِبُّ الْكَافِرِينَ (32)

14. Say (O Muhammad ﷺ), "Obey Allah and the Messenger (Muhammad ﷺ)." But if they turn away, then Allah does not like the disbelievers. (Al-Imran:32)

مَنْ يُطِعِ الرَّسُولَ فَقَدْ أَطَاعَ اللَّهَ وَمَنْ تَوَلَّى فَمَا أَرْسَلْنَاكَ عَلَيْهِمْ حَفِيظًا (80)

15. He who obeys the Messenger (Muhammad ﷺ) has indeed obeyed Allah, but he who turns away, then We have not sent you (Muhammad ﷺ) as a watcher over them. (An-Nisa:80)

وَمَنْ يُطِعِ اللَّهَ وَالرَّسُولَ فَأُولَئِكَ مَعَ الَّذِينَ أَنْعَمَ اللَّهُ عَلَيْهِمْ مِنَ النَّبِيِّينَ وَالصِّدِّيقِينَ وَالشُّهَدَاءِ وَالصَّالِحِينَ وَحَسُنَ أُولَئِكَ رَفِيقًا (69) ذَلِكَ الْفَضْلُ مِنَ اللَّهِ وَكَفَى بِاللَّهِ عَلِيمًا (70)

16. And whoso obeys Allah and the Messenger (Muhammad ﷺ), then they will be in the company of those on whom Allah has bestowed His Grace, of the Prophets, the Siddiqun (those followers of the Prophet who were first and foremost to believe in them, like Abu Bakr As-Siddiq ﷺ), the martyrs, and the righteous. And how excellent these companions are! Such is the Bounty from Allah, and Allah is Sufficient as All-Knower. (An-Nisa:69-70)

تِلْكَ حُدُودُ اللَّهِ وَمَنْ يُطِعِ اللَّهَ وَرَسُولَهُ يُدْخِلْهُ جَنَّاتٍ تَجْرِي مِنْ تَحْتِهَا الْأَنْهَارُ خَالِدِينَ فِيهَا وَذَلِكَ الْفَوْزُ الْعَظِيمُ (13) وَمَنْ يَعْصِ اللَّهَ وَرَسُولَهُ وَيَتَعَدَّ حُدُودَهُ يُدْخِلْهُ نَارًا خَالِدًا فِيهَا وَلَهُ عَذَابٌ مُهِينٌ (14)

17. These are the limits (set by) Allah (or ordainments as regards laws of inheritance), and whosoever obeys Allah and His Messenger (Muhammad ﷺ) will be admitted to Gardens under which rivers flow (in Paradise), to abide therein, and that will be the great success. And whosoever disobeys Allah and His Messenger (Muhammad ﷺ), and transgresses His limits, He will cast him into the Fire, to abide therein; and he shall have a disgraceful torment. (An-Nisa:13-14)

يَسْأَلُونَكَ عَنِ الْأَنْفَالِ قُلِ الْأَنْفَالُ لِلَّهِ وَالرَّسُولِ فَاتَّقُوا اللَّهَ وَأَصْلِحُوا ذَاتَ بَيْنِكُمْ وَأَطِيعُوا اللَّهَ وَرَسُولَهُ إِنْ كُنْتُمْ مُؤْمِنِينَ (1) إِنَّمَا الْمُؤْمِنُونَ الَّذِينَ إِذَا ذُكِرَ اللَّهُ وَجِلَتْ قُلُوبُهُمْ وَإِذَا تُلِيَتْ عَلَيْهِمْ آيَاتُهُ زَادَتْهُمْ إِيمَانًا وَعَلَى رَبِّهِمْ يَتَوَكَّلُونَ (2) الَّذِينَ يُقِيمُونَ الصَّلَاةَ وَمِمَّا رَزَقْنَاهُمْ يُنْفِقُونَ (3) أُولَئِكَ هُمُ الْمُؤْمِنُونَ حَقًّا لَهُمْ دَرَجَاتٌ عِنْدَ رَبِّهِمْ وَمَغْفِرَةٌ وَرِزْقٌ كَرِيمٌ (4)

18. They ask you (O Muhammad ﷺ) about the spoils of war. Say, "The spoils are for Allah and the Messenger." So fear Allah and adjust all matters of difference among you, and obey Allah and His Messenger (Muhammad ﷺ), if you are believers. The believers are only those who, when Allah is mentioned, feel a fear in their hearts and when His Verses (this Qur'an) are recited unto them, they (i.e. the Verses) increase their Faith; and they put their trust in their Rabb (Alone); who establish Salat and spend out of that We have provided them. It is they who are the believers in truth. For them are grades of dignity with their Rabb, and Forgiveness and a generous provision (Paradise). (Al-Anfal:1-4)

وَالْمُؤْمِنُونَ وَالْمُؤْمِنَاتُ بَعْضُهُمْ أَوْلِيَاءُ بَعْضٍ يَأْمُرُونَ بِالْمَعْرُوفِ وَيَنْهَوْنَ عَنِ الْمُنْكَرِ وَيُقِيمُونَ الصَّلَاةَ وَيُؤْتُونَ الزَّكَاةَ وَيُطِيعُونَ اللَّهَ وَرَسُولَهُ أُولَئِكَ سَيَرْحَمُهُمُ اللَّهُ إِنَّ اللَّهَ عَزِيزٌ حَكِيمٌ (71)

19. The believers, men and women, are Auliya (helpers, supporters, friends, protectors) of one another, they enjoin (on the people) Al-Maroof (i.e. Islamic Monotheism and all that Islam orders one to do), and forbid (people) from Al-Munkar (i.e. polytheism and disbelief of all kinds, and all that Islam has forbidden); they establish Salat and give the Zakat, and obey Allah and His Messenger. Allah will have His Mercy on them. Surely Allah is All-Mighty, All-Wise. (At-Taubah:71)

قُلْ إِنْ كُنْتُمْ تُحِبُّونَ اللَّهَ فَاتَّبِعُونِي يُحْبِبْكُمُ اللَّهُ وَيَغْفِرْ لَكُمْ ذُنُوبَكُمْ وَاللَّهُ غَفُورٌ رَحِيمٌ (31)

20. Say (O Muhammad ﷺ), "If you (really) love Allah then follow me (Muhammad ﷺ), Allah will love you and forgive you your sins. And Allah is Most Forgiving, Most Merciful." (Al-Imran:31)

لَقَدْ كَانَ لَكُمْ فِي رَسُولِ اللَّهِ أُسْوَةٌ حَسَنَةٌ لِمَنْ كَانَ يَرْجُو اللَّهَ وَالْيَوْمَ الْآخِرَ وَذَكَرَ اللَّهَ كَثِيرًا (21)

21. Indeed in the Messenger of Allah (Muhammad ﷺ) you have a good example to follow for him who hopes for (the meeting with) Allah and the Last Day, and remembers Allah much. (Al-Ahzab:21)

مَا أَفَاءَ اللَّهُ عَلَى رَسُولِهِ مِنْ أَهْلِ الْقُرَى فَلِلَّهِ وَلِلرَّسُولِ وَلِذِي الْقُرْبَى وَالْيَتَامَى وَالْمَسَاكِينِ وَابْنِ السَّبِيلِ كَيْ لَا يَكُونَ دُولَةً بَيْنَ الْأَغْنِيَاءِ مِنْكُمْ وَمَا آتَاكُمُ الرَّسُولُ فَخُذُوهُ وَمَا نَهَاكُمْ عَنْهُ فَانْتَهُوا وَاتَّقُوا اللَّهَ إِنَّ اللَّهَ شَدِيدُ الْعِقَابِ (7)

22. What Allah gave as booty to His Messenger (Muhammad ﷺ) from the people of the townships - it is for Allah, His Messenger (Muhammad ﷺ), the kindred (of Muhammad ﷺ), the orphans, the poor, and the travelers, in order that it may not become a fortune used by the rich among you. And whatsoever the Messenger (Muhammad ﷺ) gives you, take it, and whatsoever he forbids you, abstain (from it). And fear Allah, verily, Allah is Severe in punishment. (Al-Hashr:7)

Ahadith on Obedience to Rasulullah ﷺ, his Successors (Khulafa)

Abu Hurairah ﷺ narrated that Rasulullah ﷺ said, "Whoever obeys me, obeys Allah and whoever disobeys me, disobeys Allah. Whoever obeys my Amir whom I have appointed, obeys me and whoever disobeys my Amir, disobeys me." (Bukhari). Abu Hurairah ﷺ narrated that Rasulullah ﷺ said, "Everyone belonging to my Ummah shall enter paradise except those who refuse, they will not enter paradise." Someone asked, "Who are those who refuse?" Rasulullah ﷺ replied, "Those who obey me shall enter paradise while those who disobey me are the ones who refuse." (Bukhari). Jabir ﷺ narrated that few angels came to Rasulullah ﷺ while he was asleep. One of the angels addressing others said, "There is a similarity for this friend of yours. Mention this similarity." One of them said, "But he is asleep." Another responded, "Although his eyes sleep, his heart remains awake." The angels then said, "His likeness is like that of a person who built a house and then prepared a feast there. He then sent a caller to invite people. Whoever accepted the invitation of the caller entered the house and enjoyed the meal. On the other hand, those who did not accept the invitation neither entered the house nor enjoyed the meal." Some angels then said to the others, "Explain this to him (Rasulullah ﷺ) so that he may understand it." One of them said, "But he is asleep." Another responded, "Although he is in sleep with closed eyes, his heart remains awake." The angels then said, "The house is paradise and the caller is Muhammad ﷺ. Therefore, whoever obeys Rasulullah ﷺ obeys Allah and whoever disobeys Muhammad ﷺ disobeys Allah. Muhammad ﷺ sets people apart: those who obey him have obeyed Allah and will enter paradise while those who do not obey him have disobeyed Allah and will not enter paradise. *(Bukhari, Darmi)*

Abu Musa Ash'ari ؓ reported that Rasulullah ﷺ said, "The similarity of mine and Islam with which Allah has sent me is like a person who comes to his people saying, 'O my people! I have personally seen a large army approaching to attack you and I am warning you without any hidden motives. Save yourselves by leaving the town!' So a group of his people obeyed him. They left early that evening, traveled calmly and were saved. Another group of his people regarded the warning as a lie and they remained in the town. The enemy attacked them early next morning and destroyed them. This is the similarity of those people who accept my word and practice Islam I have brought and those people who disobey me and who reject Islam I have brought." *(Bukhari, Muslim)*. Abdullah bin Omar ؓ narrated that Rasulullah ﷺ said, "Every condition that afflicted the Bani Israel will certainly afflict my Ummah as well with similar conditions that it will be just as the 2 soles of a pair of shoes correspond with each other. The 2 conditions will be so close that even if a person from the Bani Israel committed open incest with his mother, there will be someone from my Ummah who will do the same. Also the Bani Israel split into 72 groups, my Ummah will split into 73. All these are headed for hellfire except one." The Sahabah asked, "Which group will this be, O Rasulullah ﷺ?" "The one that follows my ways and the ways of my Sahabah." *(Tirmidhi)*

Irbad bin Sariyah ؓ narrated that one day after leading the salah, Rasulullah ﷺ turned to the Sahabah and delivered a lecture that caused tears roll down from their eyes and their hearts trembled. Someone then said, "O Rasulullah ﷺ! This lecture appears to be a parting advice so do tell us about the things that you wish to emphasize." Rasulullah ﷺ said, "I advise you to fear Allah, listen and obey your Amir even if he is an Abyssinian slave because those coming after me shall face many disputes. During these times you should keep practicing my Sunnah and the Sunnah of my rightly guided successors (Khulafa). Hold fast to this and bite hard into it. Beware of innovations in Islam because every innovation is a Bid'ah and every Bid'ah leads to deviation from the right course." *(Tirmidhi, Abu Dawud)*. Omar ؓ narrated that Rasulullah ﷺ said, "When I asked my Rabb about the disputes to arise between my Sahabah after me, He sent revelation to me saying, 'O Muhammad ﷺ! Your Sahabah are like stars in the sky for Me. While all the stars are radiant, the radiance of some exceed those of others. When their opinions differ concerning a matter, a person following the opinion of any of them (Sahabah) will be rightly guided.'" Rasulullah ﷺ added, "My Sahabah are like stars. You will be rightly guided by following anyone of them." *(Razin)*

Hudhaifa ؓ narrates that Rasulullah ﷺ said, "I do not know how much longer I shall be with you." Making a gesture towards Abu Bakr ؓ and Omar ؓ, Rasulullah ﷺ added, "Follow these 2 after me, adopt the lifestyle of Ammar and believe whatever Ibn Mas'ood ؓ narrates from me." *(Tirmidhi)*. Bilal bin Harith ؓ narrates that Rasulullah ﷺ said, "Any person who revives any of my Sunnah who had died after me shall receive the rewards of all those who practice it without any of their rewards being decreased. On the other hand any person who introduces any misleading way with which Allah and His Rasul ﷺ are displeased with, he shall bear the sins of all those who practice it without their sins being decreased." *(Tirmidhi, Ibn Majah)*. Amr bin Awf ؓ narrates that Rasulullah ﷺ said, "Islam will recoil to Hijaz just as a snake recoils towards its hole. Islam will then make its home in Hijaz just as a mountain goat makes its home on the peak of

mountains. Islam started off as a stranger and will again become a stranger. So glad tidings to those who are regarded as the strangers because of their association with Islam. They are the ones who will rectify the distortions that people had introduced into my Sunnah." *(Tirmidhi)*

Anas ؓ reported that Rasulullah ﷺ addressed him saying, "O my son! If you can pass the day and night without any ill-feelings in your heart for anyone, then do so." Rasulullah ﷺ then added, "O my son! This practice is among my Sunnah. Whoever loves my Sunnah loves me and whoever loves me shall be with me in paradise." *(Tirmidhi)*. Abdullah bin Abbas ؓ narrates that Rasulullah ﷺ said, "Whoever holds fast to my Sunnah during the corrupt times in my Ummah shall have the rewards of 100 martyrs." *(Targheeb)*. *Bayhaqi and Tabrani have reported this Hadith from Abu Hurairah ؓ, stating that the reward will be that of one martyr.* Abu Hurairah ؓ reported that Rasulullah ﷺ said, "The person who holds fast to my Sunnah during the corrupt times in my Ummah shall have the reward of a martyr." *(Tabrani, Abu Nu'aym in 'Hilya')*. Abu Hurairah ؓ narrated that Rasulullah ﷺ said, "The person who holds fast to my Sunnah during times when my Ummah will be divided shall be like a person holding a burning charcoal." *(Hakim)*. Anas ؓ narrated that Rasulullah ﷺ said, "The person who turns away from my Sunnah has no affiliation with me." *(Muslim)*. Abdullah bin Omar ؓ narrates which begins with the words, "The person who practices my Sunnah has an affiliation with me." *(Ibn Asakir)*. Aisha ؓ narrated that Rasulullah ﷺ said, "The one who holds fast to the Sunnah shall enter paradise." *(Dar Qutni)*. Anas ؓ reports that Rasulullah ﷺ said, "Whoever revives my Sunnah, has love for me and whoever loves me shall be with me in paradise." *(Sajzi)*

Qur'anic Verses concerning Rasulullah ﷺ and the Sahabah

مَا كَانَ مُحَمَّدٌ أَبَا أَحَدٍ مِنْ رِجَالِكُمْ وَلَكِنْ رَسُولَ اللَّهِ وَخَاتَمَ النَّبِيِّينَ وَكَانَ اللَّهُ بِكُلِّ شَيْءٍ عَلِيمًا (40)

1. Muhammad ﷺ is not the father of any of your men, but he is the Messenger of Allah and the last (end) of the Prophets. And Allah is All-Aware of everything. (Al-Ahzab:40)

يَا أَيُّهَا النَّبِيُّ إِنَّا أَرْسَلْنَاكَ شَاهِدًا وَمُبَشِّرًا وَنَذِيرًا (45) وَدَاعِيًا إِلَى اللَّهِ بِإِذْنِهِ وَسِرَاجًا مُنِيرًا (46)

2. O Prophet (Muhammad ﷺ)! Verily, We have sent you as witness, and a bearer of glad tidings, and a warner, and as one who invites to Allah by His permission and as a lamp spreading light. (Al-Ahzab:45-46)

إِنَّا أَرْسَلْنَاكَ شَاهِدًا وَمُبَشِّرًا وَنَذِيرًا (8) لِتُؤْمِنُوا بِاللَّهِ وَرَسُولِهِ وَتُعَزِّرُوهُ وَتُوَقِّرُوهُ وَتُسَبِّحُوهُ بُكْرَةً وَأَصِيلًا (9)

3. Verily, We have sent you (O Muhammad ﷺ) as a witness, as a bearer of glad tidings, and as a warner, so that you (O mankind) may believe in Allah and His Messenger (ﷺ), and that you assist and honor him (ﷺ), and (that you) glorify (Allah's) praises morning and afternoon. (Al-Fath:8-9)

إِنَّا أَرْسَلْنَاكَ بِالْحَقِّ بَشِيرًا وَنَذِيرًا وَلَا تُسْأَلُ عَنْ أَصْحَابِ الْجَحِيمِ (119)

4. Verily, We have sent you (O Muhammad ﷺ) with the truth (Islam), a bringer of glad tidings (for those who believe) and a warner (for those who disbelieve). And you will not be asked about the dwellers of the blazing Fire. (Al-Baqara:119)

إِنَّا أَرْسَلْنَاكَ بِالْحَقِّ بَشِيرًا وَنَذِيرًا وَإِنْ مِنْ أُمَّةٍ إِلَّا خَلَا فِيهَا نَذِيرٌ (24)

5. Verily! We have sent you with the truth, a bearer of glad tidings, and a warner. And there never was a nation but a warner had passed among them. (Fatir:24)

وَمَا أَرْسَلْنَاكَ إِلَّا كَافَّةً لِّلنَّاسِ بَشِيرًا وَنَذِيرًا وَلَكِنَّ أَكْثَرَ النَّاسِ لَا يَعْلَمُونَ (28)

6. And We have not sent you (O Muhammad ﷺ) except as a giver of glad tidings and a warner to all mankind, but most people know not. (Saba:28)

وَمَا أَرْسَلْنَاكَ إِلَّا مُبَشِّرًا وَنَذِيرًا (56)

7. And We have sent you (O Muhammad ﷺ) only as a bearer of glad tidings and a warner. (Al-Furqan:56)

وَمَا أَرْسَلْنَاكَ إِلَّا رَحْمَةً لِّلْعَالَمِينَ (107)

8. And We have sent you (O Muhammad ﷺ) not but as a mercy for the Alameen (mankind, jinns and all that exists). (Al-Anbiya: 1O7)

هُوَ الَّذِي أَرْسَلَ رَسُولَهُ بِالْهُدَى وَدِينِ الْحَقِّ لِيُظْهِرَهُ عَلَى الدِّينِ كُلِّهِ وَلَوْ كَرِهَ الْمُشْرِكُونَ (33)

9. It is He (Allah) Who has sent His Messenger (Muhammad ﷺ) with guidance and the religion of truth (Islam), to make it superior over all religions even though the Mushrikoon (polytheists, pagans, idolaters, disbelievers) hate (it). (At-Taubah:33)

وَيَوْمَ نَبْعَثُ فِي كُلِّ أُمَّةٍ شَهِيدًا عَلَيْهِم مِّنْ أَنفُسِهِمْ وَجِئْنَا بِكَ شَهِيدًا عَلَى هَٰؤُلَاءِ وَنَزَّلْنَا عَلَيْكَ الْكِتَابَ تِبْيَانًا لِّكُلِّ شَيْءٍ وَهُدًى وَرَحْمَةً وَبُشْرَى لِلْمُسْلِمِينَ (89)

10. And (remember) the Day when We shall raise up from every nation a witness against them from amongst themselves. And We shall bring you (O Muhammad ﷺ) as a witness against these. And We have sent down to you the Book (the Qur'an) as an exposition of everything, a guidance, a mercy, and glad tidings for those who have submitted themselves (to Allah as Muslims). (An-Nahl:89)

وَكَذَلِكَ جَعَلْنَاكُمْ أُمَّةً وَسَطًا لِّتَكُونُوا شُهَدَاءَ عَلَى النَّاسِ وَيَكُونَ الرَّسُولُ عَلَيْكُمْ شَهِيدًا

11. Thus We have made you (true Muslims), a Wasat (just) (and the best) nation, that you be witnesses over mankind and the Messenger (Muhammad ﷺ) be a witness over you. And We made the Qiblah (towards Jerusalem) which you used to face, only to test those who followed the Messenger (Muhammad ﷺ) from those who would turn on their heels (i.e. disobey the Messenger). Indeed it was great (heavy) except for those whom Allah guided. And Allah would never make your faith (prayers) to be lost (i.e. your prayers offered towards Jerusalem). Truly, Allah is full of Kindness, the Most Merciful towards mankind. (Al-Baqara:143)

قَدْ أَنزَلَ اللَّهُ إِلَيْكُمْ ذِكْرًا (10) رَّسُولًا يَتْلُو عَلَيْكُمْ آيَاتِ اللَّهِ مُبَيِّنَاتٍ لِّيُخْرِجَ الَّذِينَ آمَنُوا وَعَمِلُوا الصَّالِحَاتِ مِنَ الظُّلُمَاتِ إِلَى النُّورِ وَمَن يُؤْمِن بِاللَّهِ وَيَعْمَلْ صَالِحًا يُدْخِلْهُ جَنَّاتٍ تَجْرِي مِن تَحْتِهَا الْأَنْهَارُ خَالِدِينَ فِيهَا أَبَدًا قَدْ أَحْسَنَ اللَّهُ لَهُ رِزْقًا (11)

12. Allah has prepared for them a severe torment. So fear Allah and keep your duty to Him, O men of understanding who have believed! Indeed Allah has sent down to you a Reminder (this Qur'an), (also sent to you) a Messenger (Muhammad ﷺ), who recites to you the verses of Allah (the Qur'an) containing clear explanations, that He may take out those who believe and do righteous good deeds, from the darkness (of polytheism and disbelief) to the light (of faith). And whosoever believes in Allah and performs righteous good deeds, He will admit him into gardens under which rivers flow (paradise), to dwell therein forever. Allah has indeed granted for him an excellent provision. (At- Talaq:10-11)

لَقَدْ مَنَّ اللَّهُ عَلَى الْمُؤْمِنِينَ إِذْ بَعَثَ فِيهِمْ رَسُولًا مِّنْ أَنفُسِهِمْ يَتْلُو عَلَيْهِمْ آيَاتِهِ وَيُزَكِّيهِمْ وَيُعَلِّمُهُمُ الْكِتَابَ وَالْحِكْمَةَ وَإِن كَانُوا مِن قَبْلُ لَفِي ضَلَالٍ مُّبِينٍ (164)

13. Indeed Allah conferred a great favor on the believers when He sent among them a Messenger (Muhammad ﷺ) from among themselves, reciting unto them His Verses (the Qur'an), and purifying them (from sins by their following him), and instructing

them (in) the Book (the Qur'an) and Al-Hikmah (the wisdom and the Sunnah of the Prophet ﷺ), while before that they had been in open error. (Al-Imran:164)

كَمَا أَرْسَلْنَا فِيكُمْ رَسُولًا مِّنكُمْ يَتْلُو عَلَيْكُمْ آيَاتِنَا وَيُزَكِّيكُمْ وَيُعَلِّمُكُمُ الْكِتَابَ وَالْحِكْمَةَ وَيُعَلِّمُكُم مَّا لَمْ تَكُونُوا تَعْلَمُونَ (151) فَاذْكُرُونِي أَذْكُرْكُمْ وَاشْكُرُوا لِي وَلَا تَكْفُرُونِ (152)

14. Similarly (to complete My Blessings on you) We have sent among you a Messenger (Muhammad ﷺ) of your own, reciting to you Our Verses (the Qur'an) and purifying you, and teaching you the Book (the Qur'an) and the Hikmah (i.e. Sunnah, Islamic laws), and teaching you that which you used not to know. Therefore remember Me (by praying, glorifying, etc.), I will remember you, and be grateful to Me (for My countless favors on you) and never be ungrateful to Me. (Al-Baqara:151-152)

لَقَدْ جَاءَكُمْ رَسُولٌ مِّنْ أَنفُسِكُمْ عَزِيزٌ عَلَيْهِ مَا عَنِتُّمْ حَرِيصٌ عَلَيْكُم بِالْمُؤْمِنِينَ رَءُوفٌ رَّحِيمٌ (128)

15. Verily, there has come unto you a Messenger (Muhammad ﷺ) from amongst yourselves (i.e. whom you know well). It grieves him that you should receive any injury or difficulty. He (Muhammad ﷺ) is anxious for you (to be rightly guided, to repent to Allah etc); for the believers (he ﷺ is) full of pity, kind, and merciful. (At-Taubah:128)

فَبِمَا رَحْمَةٍ مِّنَ اللَّهِ لِنتَ لَهُمْ وَلَوْ كُنتَ فَظًّا غَلِيظَ الْقَلْبِ لَانفَضُّوا مِنْ حَوْلِكَ فَاعْفُ عَنْهُمْ وَاسْتَغْفِرْ لَهُمْ وَشَاوِرْهُمْ فِي الْأَمْرِ فَإِذَا عَزَمْتَ فَتَوَكَّلْ عَلَى اللَّهِ إِنَّ اللَّهَ يُحِبُّ الْمُتَوَكِّلِينَ (159)

16. And by the Mercy of Allah, you (Muhammad ﷺ) dealt with them gently. And had you been severe and harsh-hearted, they would have broken away from you; so pass over (their faults), and ask (Allah's) Forgiveness for them; and consult them in the affairs. Then when you have taken a decision, put your trust in Allah, certainly, Allah loves those who put their trust (in Him). (Al- Imran:159)

إِلَّا تَنصُرُوهُ فَقَدْ نَصَرَهُ اللَّهُ إِذْ أَخْرَجَهُ الَّذِينَ كَفَرُوا ثَانِيَ اثْنَيْنِ إِذْ هُمَا فِي الْغَارِ إِذْ يَقُولُ لِصَاحِبِهِ لَا تَحْزَنْ إِنَّ اللَّهَ مَعَنَا فَأَنزَلَ اللَّهُ سَكِينَتَهُ عَلَيْهِ وَأَيَّدَهُ بِجُنُودٍ لَّمْ تَرَوْهَا وَجَعَلَ كَلِمَةَ الَّذِينَ كَفَرُوا السُّفْلَى وَكَلِمَةُ اللَّهِ هِيَ الْعُلْيَا وَاللَّهُ عَزِيزٌ حَكِيمٌ (40)

17. If you help him (Muhammad ﷺ) not (it does not matter), for Allah did indeed help him when the disbelievers drove him out, the second of two, when they (Muhammad ﷺ and Abu Bakr ﷺ) were in the cave, and he (ﷺ) said to his companion (Abu Bakr ﷺ), "Be not sad (or afraid), surely Allah is with us." Then Allah sent down His Sakinah (calmness, tranquility, peace, etc.) upon him, and strengthened him with forces (angels) which you saw not, and made the word of those who disbelieved the lowermost, while it was the Word of Allah that became the uppermost, and Allah is All-Mighty, All-Wise. (At-Taubah:40)

مُّحَمَّدٌ رَّسُولُ اللَّهِ وَالَّذِينَ مَعَهُ أَشِدَّاءُ عَلَى الْكُفَّارِ رُحَمَاءُ بَيْنَهُمْ تَرَاهُمْ رُكَّعًا سُجَّدًا يَبْتَغُونَ فَضْلًا مِّنَ اللَّهِ وَرِضْوَانًا سِيمَاهُمْ فِي وُجُوهِهِم مِّنْ أَثَرِ السُّجُودِ ذَلِكَ مَثَلُهُمْ فِي التَّوْرَاةِ وَمَثَلُهُمْ فِي الْإِنجِيلِ كَزَرْعٍ أَخْرَجَ شَطْأَهُ فَآزَرَهُ فَاسْتَغْلَظَ فَاسْتَوَى عَلَى سُوقِهِ يُعْجِبُ الزُّرَّاعَ لِيَغِيظَ بِهِمُ الْكُفَّارَ وَعَدَ اللَّهُ الَّذِينَ آمَنُوا وَعَمِلُوا الصَّالِحَاتِ مِنْهُم مَّغْفِرَةً وَأَجْرًا عَظِيمًا (29)

18. Muhammad ﷺ is the Messenger of Allah and those who are with him are severe against disbelievers, and merciful among themselves. You see them bowing and falling down prostrate (in prayer), seeking Bounty from Allah and (His) Good Pleasure. The mark of them (i.e. of their Faith) is on their faces (foreheads) from the traces of (their) prostration (during prayers). This is their description in the Torah. But their description in the Injeel (Gospel) is like a (sown) seed which sends forth its shoot, then makes it strong, it then becomes thick, and it stands straight on

its stem, delighting the sowers that He may enrage the disbelievers with them. Allah has promised those among them who believe and do righteous good deeds, forgiveness and a mighty reward (i.e. Paradise). (Al-Fath:29)

فَسَأَكْتُبُهَا لِلَّذِينَ يَتَّقُونَ وَيُؤْتُونَ الزَّكَاةَ وَالَّذِينَ هُمْ بِآيَاتِنَا يُؤْمِنُونَ (156) الَّذِينَ يَتَّبِعُونَ الرَّسُولَ النَّبِيَّ الْأُمِّيَّ الَّذِي يَجِدُونَهُ مَكْتُوبًا عِنْدَهُمْ فِي التَّوْرَاةِ وَالْإِنْجِيلِ يَأْمُرُهُمْ بِالْمَعْرُوفِ وَيَنْهَاهُمْ عَنِ الْمُنْكَرِ وَيُحِلُّ لَهُمُ الطَّيِّبَاتِ وَيُحَرِّمُ عَلَيْهِمُ الْخَبَائِثَ وَيَضَعُ عَنْهُمْ إِصْرَهُمْ وَالْأَغْلَالَ الَّتِي كَانَتْ عَلَيْهِمْ فَالَّذِينَ آمَنُوا بِهِ وَعَزَّرُوهُ وَنَصَرُوهُ وَاتَّبَعُوا النُّورَ الَّذِي أُنْزِلَ مَعَهُ أُولَئِكَ هُمُ الْمُفْلِحُونَ (157)

19. And ordain for us good in this world, and in the Hereafter. Certainly we have turned unto You. He said, (As to) My Punishment I afflict therewith whom I will and My Mercy embraces all things. That (Mercy) I shall ordain for those who are the Muttaqoon (pious), and give Zakat; and those who believe in Our Ayat (verses, signs and revelations, etc.); Those who follow the Messenger, the Prophet who can neither read nor write (i.e.Muhammad ﷺ) whom they find written with them in the Torah and the Injeel (Gospel), - he commands them for Al-Maroof (good belief); and forbids them from Al-Munkar (disbelief, polytheism); he allows them as lawful At-Taiyibat (all good and lawful), and prohibits them as unlawful Al-Khabaith (all evil and unlawful) he releases them from their heavy burdens (of Allah's covenant), and from the fetters (bindings) that were upon them. So those who believe in him (Muhammad ﷺ), honor him, help him, and follow the light (the Qur'an) which has been sent down with him, it is they who will be successful. (Al-A'raf:156-157)

Verses of the Qur'an concerning the Sahabah

لَقَدْ تَابَ اللَّهُ عَلَى النَّبِيِّ وَالْمُهَاجِرِينَ وَالْأَنْصَارِ الَّذِينَ اتَّبَعُوهُ فِي سَاعَةِ الْعُسْرَةِ مِنْ بَعْدِ مَا كَادَ يَزِيغُ قُلُوبُ فَرِيقٍ مِنْهُمْ ثُمَّ تَابَ عَلَيْهِمْ إِنَّهُ بِهِمْ رَءُوفٌ رَحِيمٌ (117) وَعَلَى الثَّلَاثَةِ الَّذِينَ خُلِّفُوا حَتَّى إِذَا ضَاقَتْ عَلَيْهِمُ الْأَرْضُ بِمَا رَحُبَتْ وَضَاقَتْ عَلَيْهِمْ أَنْفُسُهُمْ وَظَنُّوا أَنْ لَا مَلْجَأَ مِنَ اللَّهِ إِلَّا إِلَيْهِ ثُمَّ تَابَ عَلَيْهِمْ لِيَتُوبُوا إِنَّ اللَّهَ هُوَ التَّوَّابُ الرَّحِيمُ (118)

1. Allah has forgiven the Prophet ﷺ, the Muhajiroon (Muslim emigrants who left their homes and came to Madinah) and the Ansar (Muslims of Madinah) who followed him (Muhammad ﷺ) in the time of distress (Tabook expedition, etc.), after the hearts of a party of them had nearly deviated (from the Right Path), but He accepted their repentance. Certainly, He is unto them full of Kindness, Most Merciful. And (He did forgive also) the 3 (who did not join the Tabook expedition (whom the Prophet)) left (i.e. he did not give his judgment in their case, and their case was suspended for Allah's decision) till for them the earth, vast as it is, was straitened and their ownselves were straitened to them, and they perceived that there is no fleeing from Allah, and no refuge but with Him. Then, He accepted their repentance, which they might repent (unto Him). Verily, Allah is the One Who accepts repentance, Most Merciful. (At- Taubah:117-118)

لَقَدْ رَضِيَ اللَّهُ عَنِ الْمُؤْمِنِينَ إِذْ يُبَايِعُونَكَ تَحْتَ الشَّجَرَةِ فَعَلِمَ مَا فِي قُلُوبِهِمْ فَأَنْزَلَ السَّكِينَةَ عَلَيْهِمْ وَأَثَابَهُمْ فَتْحًا قَرِيبًا (18) وَمَغَانِمَ كَثِيرَةً يَأْخُذُونَهَا وَكَانَ اللَّهُ عَزِيزًا حَكِيمًا (19)

2. Indeed, Allah was pleased with the believers when they pledged their allegiance to you (O Muhammad ﷺ) under the tree, He knew what was in their hearts, and He sent down As-Sakinah (calmness and tranquility) upon them, and He rewarded them with a near victory. And abundant spoils that they will capture. And Allah is Ever All-Mighty, All-Wise. (Al-Fath:18-19)

وَالسَّابِقُونَ الْأَوَّلُونَ مِنَ الْمُهَاجِرِينَ وَالْأَنْصَارِ وَالَّذِينَ اتَّبَعُوهُمْ بِإِحْسَانٍ رَضِيَ اللَّهُ عَنْهُمْ وَرَضُوا عَنْهُ وَأَعَدَّ لَهُمْ جَنَّاتٍ تَجْرِي تَحْتَهَا الْأَنْهَارُ خَالِدِينَ فِيهَا أَبَدًا ذَلِكَ الْفَوْزُ الْعَظِيمُ (100)

3. And the first to embrace Islam of the Muhajirun (those who migrated from Makkah to Madinah) and the Ansar (the citizens of Madinah who helped and gave aid to the Muhajirun) and also those who followed them exactly (in faith). Allah is well-pleased with them as they are well-pleased with Him. He has prepared for them gardens under which rivers flow (Paradise), to dwell therein forever. That is the supreme success. (At-Taubah:100)

لِلْفُقَرَاءِ الْمُهَاجِرِينَ الَّذِينَ أُخْرِجُوا مِنْ دِيَارِهِمْ وَأَمْوَالِهِمْ يَبْتَغُونَ فَضْلًا مِنَ اللَّهِ وَرِضْوَانًا وَيَنْصُرُونَ اللَّهَ وَرَسُولَهُ أُولَئِكَ هُمُ الصَّادِقُونَ (8) وَالَّذِينَ تَبَوَّءُوا الدَّارَ وَالْإِيمَانَ مِنْ قَبْلِهِمْ يُحِبُّونَ مَنْ هَاجَرَ إِلَيْهِمْ وَلَا يَجِدُونَ فِي صُدُورِهِمْ حَاجَةً مِمَّا أُوتُوا وَيُؤْثِرُونَ عَلَى أَنْفُسِهِمْ وَلَوْ كَانَ بِهِمْ خَصَاصَةٌ وَمَنْ يُوقَ شُحَّ نَفْسِهِ فَأُولَئِكَ هُمُ الْمُفْلِحُونَ (9)

4. (And there is also a share in this booty) for the poor emigrants, who were expelled from their homes and their property, seeking Bounties from Allah and to please Him. And helping Allah (i.e. helping His religion) and His Messenger (Muhammad ﷺ). Such are indeed the truthful (to what they say). And those who, before them, had homes (in Madinah) and had adopted the faith, love those who emigrate to them, and have no jealousy in their hearts for that which they have been given (from the booty of Bani An-Nadeer), and give them (emigrants) preference over themselves, even though they were in need of that. And whosoever is saved from his own enviousness, such are they who will be the successful. (Al-Hashr:8-9)

اللَّهُ نَزَّلَ أَحْسَنَ الْحَدِيثِ كِتَابًا مُتَشَابِهًا مَثَانِيَ تَقْشَعِرُّ مِنْهُ جُلُودُ الَّذِينَ يَخْشَوْنَ رَبَّهُمْ ثُمَّ تَلِينُ جُلُودُهُمْ وَقُلُوبُهُمْ إِلَى ذِكْرِ اللَّهِ ذَلِكَ هُدَى اللَّهِ يَهْدِي بِهِ مَنْ يَشَاءُ وَمَنْ يُضْلِلِ اللَّهُ فَمَا لَهُ مِنْ هَادٍ (23)

5. Allah has sent down the best statement, a Book (this Qur'an), its parts resembling each other in goodness and truth, oft-repeated. The skins of those who fear their Lord shiver from it (when they recite it or hear it). Then their skin and their heart soften to the remembrance of Allah. That is the guidance of Allah. He Guides therewith whom He pleases and whomever Allah sends astray, for him there is no guide. (Az-ZOmar:23)

إِنَّمَا يُؤْمِنُ بِآيَاتِنَا الَّذِينَ إِذَا ذُكِّرُوا بِهَا خَرُّوا سُجَّدًا وَسَبَّحُوا بِحَمْدِ رَبِّهِمْ وَهُمْ لَا يَسْتَكْبِرُونَ (15) تَتَجَافَى جُنُوبُهُمْ عَنِ الْمَضَاجِعِ يَدْعُونَ رَبَّهُمْ خَوْفًا وَطَمَعًا وَمِمَّا رَزَقْنَاهُمْ يُنْفِقُونَ (16) فَلَا تَعْلَمُ نَفْسٌ مَا أُخْفِيَ لَهُمْ مِنْ قُرَّةِ أَعْيُنٍ جَزَاءً بِمَا كَانُوا يَعْمَلُونَ (17)

6. Only those believe in Our Ayat (verses, revelations, etc.), who, when they are reminded of them fall down prostrate, and glorify the Praises of their Lord, and they are not proud. Their sides forsake their beds, to invoke their Lord in fear and hope, and they spend (charity in Allah's cause) out of what We have bestowed on them. No person knows what is kept hidden for them of joy as a reward for what they used to do. (As-Sajdah:15-17)

فَمَا أُوتِيتُمْ مِنْ شَيْءٍ فَمَتَاعُ الْحَيَاةِ الدُّنْيَا وَمَا عِنْدَ اللَّهِ خَيْرٌ وَأَبْقَى لِلَّذِينَ آمَنُوا وَعَلَى رَبِّهِمْ يَتَوَكَّلُونَ (36) وَالَّذِينَ يَجْتَنِبُونَ كَبَائِرَ الْإِثْمِ وَالْفَوَاحِشَ وَإِذَا مَا غَضِبُوا هُمْ يَغْفِرُونَ (37) وَالَّذِينَ اسْتَجَابُوا لِرَبِّهِمْ وَأَقَامُوا الصَّلَاةَ وَأَمْرُهُمْ شُورَى بَيْنَهُمْ وَمِمَّا رَزَقْنَاهُمْ يُنْفِقُونَ (38) وَالَّذِينَ إِذَا أَصَابَهُمُ الْبَغْيُ هُمْ يَنْتَصِرُونَ (39)

7. So whatever you have been given is but a passing enjoyment for this worldly life, but that which is with Allah (Paradise) is better and more lasting for those who believe (in the oneness of Allah) and put their trust in their Lord. And those who avoid the greater sins, and Al-Fawahish (illegal sexual intercourse, etc.), and when they are angry, they forgive. And those who answer the call of their Lord (believe in Allah and worship none but Him Alone), and establish As-Salat, and who (conduct) their affairs by mutual consultation, and who spend of what We have bestowed

on them. And those who, when an oppressive wrong is done to them, they take revenge. (Ash-Shura:36-39)

مِنَ الْمُؤْمِنِينَ رِجَالٌ صَدَقُوا مَا عَاهَدُوا اللَّهَ عَلَيْهِ فَمِنْهُمْ مَنْ قَضَى نَحْبَهُ وَمِنْهُمْ مَنْ يَنْتَظِرُ وَمَا بَدَّلُوا تَبْدِيلًا (23) لِيَجْزِيَ اللَّهُ الصَّادِقِينَ بِصِدْقِهِمْ وَيُعَذِّبَ الْمُنَافِقِينَ إِنْ شَاءَ أَوْ يَتُوبَ عَلَيْهِمْ إِنَّ اللَّهَ كَانَ غَفُورًا رَحِيمًا (24)

8. Among the believers are men who have been true to their covenant with Allah (i.e. they have gone out for fighting and showed not their backs to the disbelievers), of them some have fulfilled their obligations (i.e. have been martyred), and some of them are still waiting, but they have never changed (i.e. they never proved treacherous to their covenant which they concluded with Allah) in the least. That Allah may reward the truthful for their truth (i.e. for their patience at the accomplishment of that which they promised with Allah), and punish the hypocrites if He will or accept their repentance by turning to them in Mercy. Verily, Allah is Oft-Forgiving, Most Merciful. (Al-Ahzab:23-24)

أَمَّنْ هُوَ قَانِتٌ آنَاءَ اللَّيْلِ سَاجِدًا وَقَائِمًا يَحْذَرُ الْآخِرَةَ وَيَرْجُو رَحْمَةَ رَبِّهِ قُلْ هَلْ يَسْتَوِي الَّذِينَ يَعْلَمُونَ وَالَّذِينَ لَا يَعْلَمُونَ إِنَّمَا يَتَذَكَّرُ أُولُو الْأَلْبَابِ (9)

9. Is one who is obedient to Allah, prostrating himself or standing (in prayer) during the hours of the night, fearing the Hereafter and hoping for the Mercy of his Lord (like one who disbelieves)? Say, "Are those who know equal to those who know not?" It is only people of understanding who will remember (i.e. get a lesson from Allah's Signs and Verses). (Az-ZOmar:9)

Description of Rasulullah ﷺ and the Sahabah in the Divine Scriptures before the Revelation of the Qur'an

Ata bin Yasar رحمة الله reports that once when he met Abdullah bin Amr bin Al Aas ؓ, he asked him, "Tell me about the description of Rasulullah ﷺ in the Torah." Abdullah bin Amr bin Al Aas ؓ replied, "Well, I swear by Allah that the Torah describes him just as the Qur'an does. Qur'an says, 'O Nabi ﷺ! Verily We have sent you as a witness, a giver of glad tidings, a warner, and a protector for the unlettered people. You are My servant and My Rasul and I have named you Mutawakkil (one who relies on Allah only). You are neither harsh, hard-hearted nor one who shouts in the marketplace. You do not resist evil with evil, but rather pardons and forgives.' The Torah continues: Allah shall never take him (Rasulullah ﷺ) from the world until people straighten their crooked religion by saying, 'La Ilaha Illalaah' ('There is none worthy of worship but Allah), due to which Allah opens closed eyes, deaf ears, and veiled hearts." (Ahmad, Bukhari, Bayhaqi)

Wahab bin Munabbih رحمة الله narrates that Allah sent the following revelation to prophet Dawood in the Zabur (Psalms), "O Dawood! A Nabi shall soon come after you whose name will be Ahmad and Muhammad ﷺ. He shall be truthful, a leader, and I shall never be angry with him. I have forgiven all his errors even before he can commit them. His Ummah shall be showered with My Mercy. I shall grant them such optional prayer (Nawafil) that I have granted only to the Ambiya and I shall make compulsory prayer (Fara'idh) for them that I have made compulsory only for the Ambiya and the Rasul. They will come to me on the Day of Judgment shining with the same light that shines the Ambiya." Allah then said to Dawood عليه السلام, "O Dawood! I have granted superiority to Muhammad ﷺ and his Ummah over all other nations." (Al-Bidayah wan Nihayah)

Said bin Abi Hilal quoted Abdullah bin Amr ؓ once asked Ka'b ؓ to describe to him the qualities of Rasulullah ﷺ and his Ummah. Ka'b ؓ said, "I have found them with the qualities described as follows in Allah's book (the Torah), 'Verily Ahmad

and his Ummah shall praise Allah abundantly who will praise Allah (by saying "Al Hamdu Lillah") during good and bad conditions. They will exalt Allah (by saying "Allahu Akbar") when ascending a high place and glorify Him (by saying "Subhanallah") when descending from a raised place. Their call (the Adhan) shall resound in the skies and during their salah they will communicate with Allah with humming (whispering) sounds like the sound of bees over a rock. They will form rows in their congregational salah just as the angels form rows and will form rows in battle as they do in salah. When they go for battle in the Path of Allah, the angels will be before and behind them with sharp spears. When they present themselves for battle in Allah's path, Allah will shade (shelter) them just as a vulture shades her nest (while saying this, Ka'b ؓ demonstrated with his hand how a vulture protects her nest by spreading her wings over it). They shall never flee from the battlefield." (Abu Nu'aym in Hilya). Another narration says, Ka'b ؓ said, "The people (the Ummah of Rasulullah ﷺ were described in the Torah) shall praise Allah abundantly (by saying "Al Hamdu Lillah") during all conditions. They will exalt Allah (by saying "Allahu Akbar") when ascending an incline. They will track the movement of sun (to determine the correct times of salah). They will perform their 5 daily salah on time even at a dusty place. They will tie their loin cloths at their waists and wash their limbs (during wudhu)." (Abu Nu'aym)

Ahadith describing Rasulullah ﷺ

Hasan bin Ali ؓ says that he once asked his uncle Hind bin Abi Halah ؓ to describe Rasulullah ﷺ because he could describe correctly. His reason for asking for a description of Rasulullah ﷺ was to imagine something of the description because Hasan bin Ali ؓ was only 7 when Rasulullah ﷺ passed away, he did not have sufficient opportunity to study the appearance of Rasulullah ﷺ in much detail. Hind bin Halah ؓ started, "Rasulullah ﷺ was of outstanding stature, highly honored in others eyes. His face used to shine brightly like the full moon at night. He was taller than the average person yet shorter than a tall person. His head was gracefully large and his hair had little curls. If his hair formed a path while combing, he would leave it that way, otherwise he never took pains to make one. When his hair would grow long, it would be below his earlobes. His complexion was radiant and his forehead was wide. His eyebrows were full and stood separately. Between the 2 eyebrows was a thin vein which would swell when he would become angry. His nose was smooth with a high bridge and had a shine on it, which made a new person think that it was large. His beard was thick, his eyes were black and his cheeks were smooth. His mouth was moderately wide; his teeth had a slight gap between the 2 front teeth. The hair of his chest formed a thin line up to the navel. Because of its smoothness and clarity, his neck appeared to be that of a carved silver statue. His body was firm and moderately built with his stomach in line with his chest. His chest and shoulders were wide; his bone joints were prominent and powerful. The uncovered parts of his body were always radiant. He had a line of hair running between his chest and navel. Although his abdomen and breasts were hairless, his arms, shoulders and upper part of the chest had hair. He had long forearms, broad palms, and his bones were well formed and straight. His hands and feet were well-built, his fingers and toes were proportionately long. The inside of his foot was deep with the upper part and so smooth that water easily flowed down them. He lifted his feet well off the ground and leaned forward when he walked. He put his steps down lightly and walked briskly, taking long strides as he went along. He walked as if he was descending from a high place.

When he turned to someone, he turned his entire body towards that person. His kept his gazes lowered and would more often look down than up. He never looked at a person straight in the face due to modesty, walked behind his people, and greeted whoever he met before they greeted him."

Hasan ؓ then asked his uncle to describe the manner in which Rasulullah ﷺ talked. His uncle said, "Rasulullah ﷺ always remained grieved concerning the life hereafter, was concerned for the plight of his Ummah forever and had no rest. He remained silent for long periods and would speak only when necessary. From beginning to end his speech was complete spoke clearly and spoke most comprehensively without wasting extra words. His words were distinct and conclusive with neither more nor less leaving no room for ambiguity. He spoke kindly without being harsh towards anyone or embarrassing anyone. Regardless of how insignificant they seemed to be, he always held favors in high esteem without belittling them or praising them excessively without showing any greed. As far as the meals are concerned, he neither scorned them nor praised them excessively. When the truth was being opposed, nothing could stem his anger until the truth was avenged. Another narration states, "Matters relating to this world never made him angry. However, whenever the truth (matters of Islam) met opposition, nothing and no one could stem his anger until the truth was avenged. He never became angry for personal reasons and never took revenge for anything affecting his personal life. Whenever he pointed towards something, he pointed with his entire hand (not by one finger) and he always turned his hands over when expressing surprise. He would sometimes move his hands when speaking and hit the palm of his right hand on the thumb of the left hand. When he was angry with someone, he would turn his face away from that person and then either ignore or forgive him. When he was happy, he would lower his gaze because of modesty. Rasulullah ﷺ smiled most of the time and when he did; his teeth would shine like hailstones." Hasan bin Ali ؓ says that he did not mention this description to his brother Husain bin Ali ؓ for some time afterwards, but when he did, he gathered that his brother had learned about this from their uncle even before he could. He also learned that his brother Husain ؓ had even enquired from their father (Ali ؓ) about the manner in which Rasulullah ﷺ entered his home, left home, and conducted his gatherings and about other manners and behavioral characteristics of Rasulullah ﷺ. It appeared that there were not details of Rasulullah ﷺ's life that Husain ؓ had not asked about.

Husain ؓ narrates further that when he asked his father Ali ؓ about the manner in which Rasulullah ﷺ entered the house, he replied, "His entry into his home was governed by (Allah's) permission and when he arrived home, he divided his time into 3 parts. There was a part reserved for Allah (for Ibadah), a part for his family to speak to them and see their needs and a part for himself. The part reserved for him was further divided between him and the people. The Sahabah closest to him would discuss matters with Rasulullah ﷺ at home and pass on whatever they heard from Rasulullah ﷺ to the public without keeping anything secret. When he allowed the Sahabah to enter into discussions with him during this time, it was his practice to give preference to the Sahabah who were most virtuous. Among them were those who had one need, others who had 2 needs, and others who had more needs. Rasulullah ﷺ would engage himself with fulfilling the needs of these people and would advise them concerning matters on their (spiritual) reformation and the reformation of the Ummah at large. Rasulullah ﷺ would enquire from those visiting him about the welfare of the Muslim public and advise them accordingly. Rasulullah ﷺ would say to those coming to see him, 'Those present here should pass the message on to those who are absent. You should communicate to me the needs of those who are unable to present themselves because they are too modest, afraid or live too far to appear in person. On the Day of Judgment, Allah will keep firm the feet of that person who informs their leader about the needs of another person who cannot do so himself.' It was important matters that were relayed to Rasulullah ﷺ and he would not discuss anything else (such as idle talk). People used to visit him in search of religious knowledge and would not leave without tasting something. Either they would not leave without receiving the knowledge they came for or they would not leave without having something to eat or drink. They would leave him after receiving guidance towards good."

Husain ؓ further narrates that he asked his father about how and when Rasulullah ﷺ left the house. Ali ؓ replied, "Rasulullah ﷺ always guarded his tongue from everything besides matters that concerned him. He always put people at ease without ever making them feel uncomfortable, always advised and censured them in a manner that never made them afraid being close to him. He always honored the noble persons of a tribe and appointed them as leaders of their tribes. He would warn people about the punishment of the hereafter and the harms they face from other elements and people. Along with warning others, he also guarded himself from the harms of others without depriving anyone of his cheerfulness and good character. He always watched over his companions and enquired about the welfare of the masses. Rasulullah ﷺ would commend anything good and encourage it. On the other hand, he condemned anything evil and discouraged it. He chose the moderate path in all matters and he was never contradictory. He was never negligent of the religious welfare of the people so that they did not grow negligent towards Islam or turn away from it altogether. He had a systematic approach of dealing with every situation without compromising on the rights of any person or transgressing them in any way. The best people were in his attendance, those whom he regarded as the most virtuous were the ones who wished the best for others. In his eyes, the highest ranking people were those who sympathized most with people and assisted them most."

Husain ؓ narrates that he further asked his father about the gatherings that Rasulullah ﷺ held. Ali ؓ replied, "Rasulullah ﷺ never sat or stood without Dhikr on his tongue. He would never reserve a place for himself in the Masjid and also forbade others from doing this. Whenever he arrived in a gathering, he sat on the edge of the gathering and instructed people to do the same. He gave equal attention to each person in the gathering so that all of them thought that they were the most honored. Whenever a person sat with him or stood with him to address an issue, Rasulullah ﷺ remained with him patiently until the person himself took leave. When anyone asked him for anything, he would give the person his need or tell the person kindly that he did not have the means to fulfill the need. Rasulullah ﷺ distributed his cheerfulness and good character generously to every person so that he was able to fulfill the rights of each one of them equally. His gatherings included patience, modesty, tolerance and confidentiality. Voices were never raised in his gatherings, reputations were never smeared and faults were never publicized. Those attending his gatherings were treated equally (no racial or social discrimination existed) and people were held in very high esteem only in relation to the level of their Taqwa. Each person respected the other and just as the elderly were shown great reverence, the youngsters were shown great compassion. The needy were helped and enquiries were made about strangers / travelers to fulfill their needs."

Husain ؓ asked his father about Rasulullah ﷺ's interaction

with the people in his gatherings. Ali ﷺ replied, "Rasulullah ﷺ always smiled and displayed a tolerant attitude and a soft nature. He was never ill-tempered, never hard-hearted, never shouted, never rude, never searched for the faults of people, and never joked excessively. Rasulullah ﷺ pretended not to be aware of things he disliked but would not make a person lose hope in receiving something he wanted, which Rasulullah ﷺ himself disliked, he would rather give the person something to satisfy him or advise him kindly. Rasulullah ﷺ avoided 3 things and also prevented people from these 3 things. These were (1) arguing, (2) speaking too much, and (3) indulging in useless talk. He never spoke ill of anyone, never insulted anyone, and never searched for the faults of any person. He only spoke when he expected rewards for his speech. Whenever Rasulullah ﷺ spoke, the Sahabah sat in the gathering with their heads bowed as if there were birds sitting on their heads, they sat without any movement. The Sahabah remained silent as he spoke and spoke only when he was silent. They never argued in his presence. Rasulullah ﷺ laughed (smiled) when the Sahabah laughed and expressed surprise when they did. He tolerated roughness and harsh manner of questioning that strangers used. The Sahabah used to bring such strangers to the gatherings when they saw that Rasulullah ﷺ did not mind the questions and because they were too respectful to ask such questions. Rasulullah ﷺ used to say, 'Help a needy person whenever you see one.' He did not tolerate anyone praising him, unless a person was expressing gratitude for a favor done to him so that people learned that they should express gratitude to others. He would never interrupt the speech of any person unless the person spoke something wrong, in which case, Rasulullah ﷺ would interrupt the speech by either stopping the person from continuing or by standing up and leaving."

Husain ﷺ states further that he even asked his father about the manner in which Rasulullah ﷺ observed silence. His father Ali ﷺ replied, "Rasulullah ﷺ observed silence on 4 occasions. These were (1) when he needed to bear with something, (2) when exercising caution, (3) when considering something and (4) when pondering about something. There were 2 things that he always considered. These were how he could (1) see all people alike and (2) hear all of them alike. There were also 2 things that he usually pondered about. These were (1) that which is everlasting (the hereafter) and (2) that which will come to an end (this world). Allah had granted Rasulullah ﷺ both the qualities of patience and courage which made him not to be so angry that he lost control of himself. *(Tirmidhi)*

Rasulullah ﷺ exercised caution with regard to 4 matters. These were (1) ensuring that he does good and (2) giving importance to those things that would benefit the Ummah in this world as well as in the hereafter (this narration mentions only 2 matters). However, the narration in *Kanzul Ummal* states, "Rasulullah ﷺ exercised caution with regard to 4 matters. These were (1) ensuring that he does good so that his example should be followed (2) avoiding evil so that others also stay away from it, (3) exerting his mind in matters that will benefit the Ummah and (4) giving importance to those things that would benefit the Ummah in this world as well as in the hereafter. *(Jam'ul Fawa'id)*

The Statements of the Sahabah concerning their Qualities

Suddi رحمة الله reported the following narration from Omar ﷺ concerning the verse,

كُنْتُمْ خَيْرَ أُمَّةٍ أُخْرِجَتْ لِلنَّاسِ تَأْمُرُونَ بِالْمَعْرُوفِ وَتَنْهَوْنَ عَنِ الْمُنْكَرِ وَتُؤْمِنُونَ بِاللَّهِ

You (true believers in Islam and followers of Muhammad ﷺ) are the best of peoples ever raised up for mankind; you enjoin Al-

Maroof (Islamic Monotheism and all that Islam has ordained) and forbid Al-Munkar (polytheism, disbelief and all that Islam has forbidden), and you believe in Allah. (Al-'Imran:110)

He reported that Omar ﷺ stated, "If Allah had willed, He would have used the word أَنْتُم (meaning "You are"), in which case the verse would have referred to all of us whether a person enjoins good and forbids evil or not. However, Allah used the word كُنْتُمْ meaning "you were" to refer specifically to the Sahabah. Therefore, whoever does as the Sahabah did enjoin good and forbids evil shall be among "the best of all nations who have been raised for the benefit of mankind." *(Ibn Jurauj, Ibn Abi Hatim)*

Qatadah رحمة الله reports that Omar ﷺ once recited the verse,

كُنْتُمْ خَيْرَ أُمَّةٍ أُخْرِجَتْ لِلنَّاسِ تَأْمُرُونَ بِالْمَعْرُوفِ وَتَنْهَوْنَ عَنِ الْمُنْكَرِ وَتُؤْمِنُونَ بِاللَّهِ

You (true believers in Islam and followers of Muhammad ﷺ) are the best of peoples ever raised up for mankind; you enjoin Al-Maroof (Islamic Monotheism and all that Islam has ordained) and forbid Al-Munkar (polytheism, disbelief and all that Islam has forbidden), and you believe in Allah. (Al-'Imran:110)

Then, Omar ﷺ said, "O people! Whoever wishes to be among this Ummah (best of nations), then he should fulfill the condition that Allah mentions in the verse (enjoin good and forbid evil)." *(Kanzul Ummal)*. Abdullah bin Mas'ood ﷺ stated, "Allah looked at the hearts of all His servants and chose that of Muhammad ﷺ. Allah then made him His messenger and granted him special knowledge from Him. Allah then again gazed at the hearts of His servants and selected companions for Rasulullah ﷺ (the Sahabah) to assist (in the propagation of) Islam and be helpers in bearing the responsibility of Rasulullah ﷺ. Therefore, whatever these Mu'mineen (the Sahabah) regard as good, is good in the eyes of Allah and whatever they regard as unacceptable, is unacceptable in the eyes of Allah." *(Abu Nu'aym in Hilya)*

Abdullah bin Omar ﷺ mentioned, "Whoever wishes to follow the ways of others, should follow the ways of those who have passed away. These were the companions of Muhammad ﷺ, who were the best people of this Ummah. Their hearts were most pious, their knowledge was deepest, and they were least in formalities. They were people whom Allah had chosen to be companions of His Nabi ﷺ and for the propagation of Islam. You people should therefore emulate their character and manners. By the Rabb of the Kabah! The Sahabah of Rasulullah ﷺ were correctly guided." *(Abu Nu'aym in Hilya)*. Abdullah bin Mas'ood ﷺ once said to the people, "Although you people fast more often, perform more salah, and make more efforts, the companions of Rasulullah ﷺ were better than you." When the people asked him the reason for this, he replied, "Because they had less concern for this world and more concern for the hereafter." *(Abu Nu'aym in Hilya)*. Abu Wa'il رحمة الله narrates that Abdullah bin Mas'ood ﷺ once heard a person saying, "Where are the people who have no concern for this world and look forward to the hereafter?" Abdullah bin Mas'ood ﷺ said to him, "They are the people of Jabiya, a place in Sham where Muslims fought the Romans during Khalifa Omar ﷺ. They were 500 Muslim men who pledged that they would be martyred in battle and not return home. According to their custom, they shaved off their hair, fought the enemy and all were martyred except one who lived to tell the story." *(Hilya)*. Abdullah bin Omar ﷺ once heard a person saying, "Where are the people who have no concern for this world and look forward to the hereafter?" Taking the person to the graves of Rasulullah ﷺ, Abu Bakr ﷺ and Omar ﷺ; Abdullah bin Omar ﷺ said to him, "Did you ask about these personalities?" *(Abu Nu'aym in Hilya)*

Abu Araka رحمة الله narrates that he once performed the Fajr salah behind Ali ؓ. After the salah, Ali ؓ turned to his right and appeared to be extremely worried. When the sun rose the length of a spear's height above the Masjid wall, he performed 2 Rakahs of salah. Then he turned his hands over and said, "By Allah! I have seen the Sahabah of Rasulullah ﷺ and do not see such people anywhere today. In the mornings, their faces were pale, their hair disheveled, their bodies covered in dust and between their eyes were the marks of prostration which resembled the marks on the knees of goats. Their nights were spent prostrating (in Sejdah) and standing before Allah (in Salah). They recited the Book of Allah (the Qur'an) and would attain comfort by standing in Salah and making Sejdah. When the mornings arrived and they engaged in Dhikr, their bodies would move as the trees do when the gentle wind blows through them. Their eyes would flow with tears until their clothing got wet. I swear by Allah by seeing such person it would reveal as if the people of our age had spent their nights in negligence." Ali ؓ stood up and was never again seen laughing by anyone after that until he was martyred by the wicked enemy of Allah, Ibn Muljim. *(Bidaya, Abu Nu'aym in Hilya)*

Dirar bin Damirah Kinani رحمة الله once came to Mu'awiya ؓ, who asked him to describe Ali. Dirar bin Damirah Kinani رحمة الله said, "Would you excuse me?" Mu'awiya ؓ replied, "You cannot be excused." Dirar bin Damirah Kinani رحمة الله continued, "If I have to say something, then I swear by Allah that Ali ؓ was a man of high objectives with honor. He was a man of tremendous strength who always spoke decisively and passed judgment with justice. Knowledge seemed to come out from his every limb, people learned something from his every word, action, and even when he was doing nothing and wisdom spread through him from every angle. He kept him away from the world and its attraction, taking comfort from the night and its darkness. By Allah! Ali ؓ shed many tears and remained in deep thought for long time. He would often turn his hands over and address himself. He liked simple clothing and coarse food. By Allah! He was just like one of us and when we met with him, he would make us sit close to him and ensured that he answered our every question. Despite him being close to us and we being close to him, we would hesitate to speak to him. When he smiled, his teeth appeared to be a string of pearls. He showed lot of respect towards learned people and he showed great love towards the poor. A powerful person never succeeded with false claims in front of him and a weak person never lost hope in his justice. Allah is Witness to the night when I once saw him sitting in his Mihrab when the night was already in and the stars had vanished. He was holding his beard and bending over displaying the distress of a person bitten by a scorpion. He wept like a grieved person and I can still hear his cries echoing in my ears as he repeated the words, 'Ya Rabbana! Ya Rabbana! (Oh our Rabb! Oh our Rabb!)' In this way, he humbled himself before Allah. He then addresses the world saying, 'O world! Are you trying to deceive me? Are you staring at me? Get away! Get away and use your charms on someone else because I have divorced you thrice. Your life is short, your company is humiliating and people easily get into trouble because of you. Oh dear! Oh dear! The provision for the hereafter journey is not enough, the journey is long and the road is scary.'" Upon hearing this, tears rolled non stop from the eyes of Mu'awiya ؓ onto his beard and he began wiping them away with his sleeve. The people present were also choked with their weeping. Mu'awiya ؓ then said, "That was indeed an accurate description of Abul Hasan (Ali ؓ). May Allah have mercy on him. O Dirar, what was your reaction to his death?"

Dirar bin Damira Kinani رحمة الله replied, "1 felt the agony of a woman whose only child is killed in her lap, whose tears neither stop nor does her grief diminish." After saying this, Dirar bin Damira Kinani رحمة الله stood up and left." *(Abu Nu'aym in Isti'ab)*. Qatadah رحمة الله reports that someone once asked Abdullah bin Omar ؓ if the Sahabah ever laughed. He replied, "Yes, but the Iman in their hearts still remained firmer than mountains." *(Abu Nu'aym in Hilya)*. Seeing the carriages of some Yemeni travelers made out of animal skin, Omar ؓ remarked, "Whoever wishes to see a similarity of the Sahabah of Rasulullah ﷺ should look at these peop1e." *(Kanzul Ummal)*

Abu Sa'eed Maqbari رحمة الله reports that when Abu Ubaidah bin Jarrah ؓ contracted a plague, he asked Mu'adh bin Jabal ؓ to lead the salah, which the latter did. When Abu Ubaidah bin Jarrah ؓ passed away, Mu'adh ؓ addressed the people saying, "O people! Sincerely repent to Allah for your sins because when any servant of Allah meets Allah after he sincerely repents for his sins, Allah's forgiveness is guaranteed." Mu'adh ؓ then continued to say, "You are grieved by the loss of a man whom I swear had a heart cleaner than any other I have seen. I have not seen anyone with a purer heart, who was further away from evil, who had very much love for the hereafter and who cared more for the well-being of the masses. Pray for mercy on him and plan to perform his funeral prayer in an open plain. I swear by Allah that you shall never have another leader like him." The people gathered and the bier of Abu Ubaidah ؓ was taken to the plain where Mu'adh ؓ led the funeral prayer. When the dead body was brought to the grave, Mu'adh ؓ, Amr bin Al Aas ؓ and Dahak bin Qais ؓ entered the grave to lay the body to rest. When they came out from the grave, they closed the grave with sand and standing at the head-side of the grave, Mu'adh ؓ addressed the deceased saying, "O Abu Ubaidah! I shall certainly praise on you a lot but will say nothing untrue because 1 fear that it may incur Allah's wrath. By Allah! As far as I know, you were certainly from among those people who engaged in the Dhikr of Allah abundantly, who walked humbly on earth, and who would greet and part from company of foolish people when they addressed you to avoid argument. You were among those who would neither be miserly nor extravagant when spending in charity, but who showed excellent moderation between the 2 extremes. By Allah! You were among those whose hearts submitted to Allah, who displayed humility, who were compassionate towards orphans and the poor, and who disliked the behavior of unfaithful and arrogant people." *(Hakim in Mustadrak)*

Rib'e bin Hirash رحمة الله narrates that Abdullah bin Abbas ؓ once sought permission to meet Mu'awiya ؓ when members of various tribes of the Quraish were with him. As Abdullah bin Abbas ؓ approached, Mu'awiya ؓ said to Sa'eed bin Al Aas ؓ who was on his right-hand side, "I shall present to Abdullah bin Abbas ؓ such questions that he will be unable to answer." Sa'eed ؓ replied; "There is none like Abdullah bin Abbas ؓ to answer your questions." When Abdullah bin Abbas ؓ sat down, Mu'awiya ؓ asked him, "What do you say about Abu Bakr ؓ?" Abdullah bin Abbas ؓ replied, "May Allah shower His mercy on Abu Bakr ؓ. By Allah! He eagerly recited the Qur'an, stayed far away from deviation, avoided arrogance, prevented people from evil, knew Islam well and feared Allah. He engaged in Ibadah during the nights, fasted during the days, not attracted by the world, and was committed to establish justice among Allah's creation. He instructed what was good and always did what was good. He was grateful to Allah under all conditions, engaged in Dhikr morning and evening, and was strict on himself in matters on reformation. He excelled ahead of his companions in terms of piety, contentment, abstinence, virtue, caution, self-discipline, and in repaying people for the good they did to him. On the Day of Judgment, may Allah's curses be on those who dishonor him."

Mu'awiya ؓ then asked, "What have you to say about Omar bin Khattab ؓ?" Abdullah bin Abbas ؓ replied, "May Allah shower His mercy on Abu Hafs (Omar ؓ). By Allah! He was a great supporter of Islam, protector of the orphans, a treasure of Iman and a shelter for the weak. By Allah! He was truly a shelter for the pious, a fort for Allah's creation, and an ally to every fall

on the person who maintains enmity with him." Mu'awiya ؓ then continued, "What do you have to say about Uthman bin Affan ؓ?" Abdullah bin Abbas ؓ replied, "May Allah shower His mercy on Uthman ؓ. By Allah! He was an extremely honorable son-in-law of Rasulullah ﷺ who kept the company of pious people and was among the most untiring soldiers. He stayed awake during Tahajjud salah for nights and wept excessively when engaging in Allah's Dhikr. Throughout the day and night he was engaged with matters of importance, always ready to do any virtuous deed and never tired of completing anything that would lead to salvation. Among his noble character was that he stood firmly against every calamity, was generous for the Muslim army especially during the Tabuk expedition and the sponsor of well which he bought Ruma well from a Jew and donated to the Muslims. After all, he was the husband of 2 of Rasulullah ﷺ's daughters. Till the Day of Judgment, may the curse of Allah fall on the person who speaks ill of him."

Thereafter, Mu'awiya ؓ asked Abdullah bin Abbas ؓ, "What do you say about Ali bin Abi Talib ؓ?" The reply was, "May Allah shower His mercy on Abu Hasan (Ali ؓ). By Allah! He was a bearer of knowledge, a fortune of piety, very intelligent, and a mountain of good. He was a light to those walking in the dark and a continuous caller to the straight path. Ali ؓ had deep knowledge of the earlier scriptures, propagated the teachings of the Qur'an, and always conveyed excellent advice. He was always holding on to the ways of guidance, stayed far away from injustice, from harming others, and from every destructive thing. He was the best of those who possessed Iman and Taqwa, and the leader of all those who dressed in sewn garments or in unstitched clothes. He was the most noble of those who performed Hajj and Sa'ee, the most generous of those who established justice and equity, the most persuasive person like the Ambiya ﷺ, and the chosen Rasul of Allah. He was also among

person. With strength and confidence in Allah, he established Islam until the time came when Allah made Islam dominant and conquered many lands. Allah's name was then mentioned in every direction, every hill, and every spring in many parts of the world. He showed exceptional tolerance when people spoke offensively. He was always grateful to Allah during times of hardship and times of ease and engaged in the Dhikr of Allah at every moment. Til the Day of Judgment, may Allah's curse

those early Muslims who performed salah facing towards both Qiblas such as the Kabah and Baytul Maqdas. Can there be anyone like him? He was extremely fortunate to marry the best woman (Fatima ؓ) and was the father of the 2 noble grandsons of Rasulullah ﷺ. My eyes have never seen anyone like him and will never see anyone like his talents until the Day of Judgment. Till the Day of Judgment may the curses of Allah and the curses of every servant of Allah be on the one who curses him."

Mu'awiya ؓ asked, "What do you say about Talha ؓ and Zubair ؓ?" Abdullah bin Abbas ؓ replied, "May Allah's mercy be showered on them. By Allah! They were both extremely virtuous and pious Muslims who remained extremely pure. They were both martyrs and exceptionally learned. Although they made an error, Allah will forgive them because of their enormous help they rendered to Rasulullah ﷺ and for the propagation of Islam, because they were among the earliest Muslims, among the earliest companions of Rasulullah ﷺ and because of many good deeds they carried out." Mu'awiya ؓ asked, "What do you say about Abbas ؓ?" Abdullah bin Abbas ؓ said, "May Allah shower His mercy on Abul Fadhl (Abbas ؓ). By Allah! He was the real brother of Rasulullah ﷺ and the joy of his eyes. He was a chosen servant of Allah, a sanctuary for all people and the leader of all the uncles of Rasulullah ﷺ. He possessed deep insight into all matters, always considered the consequences of everything, and was decorated by profound knowledge. The virtue of others fades when his virtues are mentioned, and the achievements of other families seem insignificant before the accomplishments of his family. Why should he not be such a great person when he was raised by none other than Abdul Muttalib, who was the most honorable person and the most respected of the Quraish who ever walked or rode." This is a part of a lengthy Hadith. *(Bayhaqi, Tabarani)*

Da'wah Towards Allah and His Rasul ﷺ

This chapter explains how the action of calling people towards Allah and Rasulullah ﷺ was loved more than anything else by Rasulullah ﷺ and the Sahabah. Their utmost desire was for mankind to be guided towards Islam and to enter its fold so that they may be immersed in Allah's mercy. It also focuses on their determined efforts to achieve this objective so that the creation could be linked to their Creator.

The Concern of Rasulullah ﷺ for Mankind to Accept Iman

Abdullah bin Abbas ﷺ narrates that Rasulullah ﷺ was very concerned for mankind to accept Iman and follow him. Allah revealed Qur'anic verses such as (105) فَمِنْهُمْ شَقِيٌّ وَسَعِيدٌ

Some among them (mankind) will be wretched and (others) blessed. (Hud:105)

In this verse, Allah informed Rasulullah ﷺ that people will accept Iman only if the good fortune has been destined for them. Similarly, only those people for whom ill-fortune has been destined will go astray. Allah then revealed to Rasulullah ﷺ,

لَعَلَّكَ بَاخِعٌ نَفْسَكَ أَلَّا يَكُونُوا مُؤْمِنِينَ (3) إِنْ نَشَأْ نُنَزِّلْ عَلَيْهِمْ مِنَ السَّمَاءِ آيَةً فَظَلَّتْ أَعْنَاقُهُمْ لَهَا خَاضِعِينَ (4) *It may be that you (O Muhammad ﷺ) are going to kill yourself with grief, that they do not become believers (in Islamic Monotheism). If We will, We could send down to them from the heaven a sign, to which they would bend their necks in humility. (Ash-Shuara':3-4) (Tabrani, Haythami)*

Rasulullah ﷺ Preaches to People When his Uncle Abu Talib is About to Leave the World

Abdullah bin Abbas ﷺ narrates that when Abu Talib was about to die, a group from the Quraish came to see him including Abu Jahal. They complained to Abu Talib about what his nephew (Rasulullah ﷺ) was saying and doing, including insulting their gods. They requested Abu Talib to call Rasulullah ﷺ and forbid him from what he was doing. Abu Talib sent for Rasulullah ﷺ, he promptly arrived and entered the house. Rasulullah ﷺ came to the room, there was a space for one person between the group of the Quraish and Abu Talib. Abdullah bin Abbas ﷺ states, "The accursed Abu Jahal feared that if Rasulullah ﷺ occupy the empty space next to his uncle, Abu Talib may be more pity. So he jumped to occupy the place, leaving no place for Rasulullah ﷺ near his uncle and was forced to sit near the door. Abu Talib said, 'O my nephew! Why are these people complaining that you insult their gods and tell them so many things?' Those present also started saying many things." Rasulullah ﷺ answered his uncle saying, "O my uncle! All I want these people to accept a single statement that would make all the Arabs serve them and make all the non-Arabs pay them taxes." The people exclaimed, "Only one statement! By the oath of your father, we are prepared to accept 10 such statements! What is this statement?" Abu Talib also asked, "O my nephew! What is this statement?" Rasulullah ﷺ replied, "*La Ilaha Illallah* (There is none worthy of worship but Allah)." Upon hearing this, the people stood up and said, "Does he make all our gods that we worship into one god? This is indeed something strange! Abdullah bin Abbas ﷺ states that with reference to this, Allah revealed the verses: أَجَعَلَ الْآلِهَةَ إِلَهًا وَاحِدًا إِنَّ هَذَا

لَشَيْءٌ عُجَابٌ (5) وَانْطَلَقَ الْمَلَأُ مِنْهُمْ أَنِ امْشُوا وَاصْبِرُوا عَلَى آلِهَتِكُمْ إِنَّ هَذَا لَشَيْءٌ يُرَادُ (6) مَا سَمِعْنَا بِهَذَا فِي الْمِلَّةِ الْآخِرَةِ إِنْ هَذَا إِلَّا اخْتِلَاقٌ (7) أَؤُنْزِلَ عَلَيْهِ الذِّكْرُ مِنْ بَيْنِنَا بَلْ هُمْ فِي شَكٍّ مِنْ ذِكْرِي بَلْ لَمَّا يَذُوقُوا عَذَابِ (8)

"Has he (Muhammad ﷺ) made (all) the aliha (gods) into One Ilah (God – Allah)? Verily, this is a curious thing!" And the leaders among them went about (saying), "Go on, and remain constant to your aliha (gods)! Verily, this is a thing designed (against you)! We have not heard (the like) of this among the people of these later days. This is nothing but an invention! Has the Reminder been sent down to him (alone) from among us?" Nay! but they are in doubt about My Reminder (this Qur'an)! Nay, but they have not tasted (My) Torment! (Sad:5-8) (Ahmad, Nasa'ee, Tirmidhi)

Rasulullah ﷺ Presents the Kalimah to his Uncle Abu Talib

Abdullah bin Abbas ﷺ reports that several Quraish leaders went to Abu Talib to speak about Rasulullah ﷺ. Among them were Utba bin Rabe'ah, Shaiba bin Rabe'ah, Abu Jahal bin Hisham, Umayyah bin Khalaf and Abu Sufyan bin Harb. They said, "You are well aware of the high position you hold among us. The condition of your health makes us concerned for your life. Since you know the differences that exist between us and your nephew, we ask you to call him to mediate between us so that he accepts some of our requests and we accept some of his. In this way, he can stop opposing us, we will also stop opposing him, he can leave us to our religion and we will leave him to his religion." Abu Talib sent for Rasulullah ﷺ. When Rasulullah ﷺ arrived, Abu Talib said to him, "O my nephew! These prominent leaders have come to me to offer you some of their requests and to accept from you some of your requests." Rasulullah ﷺ replied, "Very well. I ask you people to tell me a single statement which would give you control over all the Arabs and which would make the non-Arabs follow you." Hearing this, Abu Jahal exclaimed, "Certainly! By the oath of your father! We are prepared to accept 10 such statements." Rasulullah ﷺ said, "You should then say, 'La Ilaha Illallah (There is none worthy of worship but Allah) and discard everything that you worship besides Him." Those present started clapping their hands with insult saying, "Do you wish to make all our gods into one! This is indeed very strange!" Then they said to each other, "By Allah! This man will not give in to any of your requests. Let us leave and continue practicing the religion of our forefathers until Allah decides between us and him." Then they dispersed. When all left, Abu Talib said to Rasulullah ﷺ, "O my nephew, I don't think that you asked anything difficult for them." Hopeful that his uncle would accept the message of Islam, Rasulullah ﷺ said to him, "O uncle! Why don't you say it (the Kalimah) so that I may intercede for you on the Day of Judgment." Seeing the enthusiasm of Rasulullah ﷺ, Abu Talib said, "O nephew! By Allah! I would certainly utter this Kalimah to please you if it were not for my fear that me and my progeny would become targets of insults and that the Quraish would say that I said it only for the fear of death." *(Al Bidayah wan Nihayah.* Sa'eed bin Musaib رحمة الله reports from his father that Rasulullah ﷺ visited Abu Talib when he was at his death-bed and when Abu Jahal was also present. Rasulullah ﷺ said, "O my uncle! Say 'La Ilaha Illallah' so that I could defend you in the court of Allah." Abu Jahal and Abdullah bin Abi Umayyah said to Abu Talib, "Are you turning away from the religion of your father Abdul Muttalib?" The 2 of them continued speaking to Abu Talib in this manner until the final words he uttered as he passed away were, "I remain with the religion of Abdul Muttalib." Rasulullah ﷺ then said, "I shall continue seeking Allah's forgiveness for you, O my uncle until I am forbidden from doing so." Allah then revealed the verses of the Qur'an which states, مَا كَانَ لِلنَّبِيِّ وَالَّذِينَ آمَنُوا أَنْ يَسْتَغْفِرُوا لِلْمُشْرِكِينَ وَلَوْ كَانُوا أُولِي قُرْبَى

مِنْ بَعْدِ مَا تَبَيَّنَ لَهُمْ أَنَّهُمْ أَصْحَابُ الْجَحِيمِ (113)

It is not (proper) for the Prophet and those who believe to ask Allah's Forgiveness for the Mushrikun (polytheists, idolaters, disbelievers in the Oneness of Allah) even though they be of kin, after it has become clear to them that they are the dwellers of the Fire (because they died in a state of disbelief) (At-Tauba:113)

إِنَّكَ لَا تَهْدِي مَنْ أَحْبَبْتَ وَلَكِنَّ اللَّهَ يَهْدِي مَنْ يَشَاءُ وَهُوَ أَعْلَمُ بِالْمُهْتَدِينَ (56)

Verily! You (O Muhammad ﷺ) guide not whom you like, but Allah guides whom He wills. And He knows best those who are the guided. (Al-Qasas:56) (Bukhari, Muslim)

Similar report states that Rasulullah ﷺ continued presenting the Kalimah to Abu Talib as the 2 Mushrikin: Abu Jahal and Abdullah bin Abi Umayyah repeated their words to him. Eventually, Abu Talib passed away with the words, "I remain on the religion of Abdul Muttalib" without reciting, "La Ilaha Illallah." Rasulullah ﷺ then said, "Behold! I shall continue seeking Allah's forgiveness for you, O my uncle until I am forbidden from doing so." It was after this that Allah revealed the 2 verses mentioned above. *(Bukhari, Muslim)*. Abu Hurairah ﷺ narrates that Rasulullah ﷺ came to see his uncle Abu Talib when he was about to die. Rasulullah ﷺ said to him, "O my beloved uncle! Say 'La llaha Illallah' so that I may be witness to it on the Day of Judgment." Abu Talib said, "I would have certainly said it to please you if I did not fear that Quraish would ridicule me by saying, 'He said it only because he feared death.' I would have definitely said it only to please you." It was on this occasion that Allah revealed the verse,

إِنَّكَ لَا تَهْدِي مَنْ أَحْبَبْتَ وَلَكِنَّ اللَّهَ يَهْدِي مَنْ يَشَاءُ وَهُوَ أَعْلَمُ بِالْمُهْتَدِينَ (56)

Verily! You (O Muhammad ﷺ) guide not whom you like, but Allah guides whom He wills. And He knows best those who are the guided. (Al-Qasas:56) (Al Bidayah wan Nihayah)

Rasulullah ﷺ Refuses to Forsake Calling People to Allah

Aqil bin Abi Talib the son of Abu Talib narrated that once when the members of the Quraish approached Abu Talib to discuss about Rasulullah ﷺ, Abu Talib said to Rasulullah ﷺ, "O my nephew! By Allah! As you well know, I have always listened to you what you said, now I wish that you listen to me. People have come to me to complain that hurt them. If you think it appropriate, you should stop doing this." Looking towards the heavens, Rasulullah ﷺ replied, "I do not have the ability to stop doing what I have been sent to do just as any of you do not have the ability to hold a spark of fire from the sun. *(Tabrani, Bukhari)*. *Bayhaqi* reports that Abu Talib called Rasulullah ﷺ and told him that the people told him many things about what Rasulullah ﷺ was doing. Addressing Rasulullah ﷺ, he said, "Have mercy on me and on yourself and do not cast a burden on me that neither of us can bear. Stop telling the people things that they dislike." Hearing this, it appeared in Rasulullah ﷺ's mind that his uncle had changed his opinions, he would stop assisting him, he would now hand him over to the people, and he had lost courage in supporting him. Rasulullah ﷺ said, "O my uncle! Even if the sun were placed in my right hand and the moon in my left hand, I would not forsake this work of propagation until Allah makes Islam dominant or I am destroyed in the process." After saying this, the eyes of Rasulullah ﷺ were filled with tears and he began weeping. Jabir bin Abdullah ﷺ narrates that the Quraish once gathered and said, "Look for a person who is most learned in magic, teller of fortune and poetry so that he may meet this man (Rasulullah ﷺ) who has split our community, divided us and insulted our religion. When he meets Rasulullah ﷺ, he should speak to him and gauge the response." Everyone agreed

that the best person for the task was Utba bin Rabe'ah and they said to him, "Go to him, O Abu Walid!" When Utba met Rasulullah ﷺ, he asked, "O Muhammad ﷺ! Are you better than Abdullah, your father?" Rasulullah ﷺ remained silent. Utba continued, "Are you better than Abdul Muttalib, your grandfather?" When Rasulullah ﷺ remained silent for the 2nd time, Utba proceeded to say, "If you think that all these people are better than you, then remember that they worshipped the very idols that you find fault with. However, if you think that you are better than them, then say so, so that we may hear you. By Allah! We have never seen a youngster who has brought more ill-fortune to his nation than yourself! You have split our community, disunited us, insulted our gods and disgraced us among the Arabs so much so that news has spread among people that the Quraish have a magician and a fortune-teller. By Allah! We are disunited so much that we are waiting for a shout of pain like that of a pregnant woman before we begin opposing each other with swords and destroy each other. O you! If you have any financial need, we shall pool our resources for you until you become the richest man of the Quraish. If need a woman, you may choose any of the women of the Quraish and let alone one, we shall offer you to marry 10 of them." Rasulullah ﷺ said, "Have you finished?" When Utba replied in the affirmative, Rasulullah ﷺ recited the following verses of the Qur'an,

بِسْمِ اللَّهِ الرَّحْمَنِ الرَّحِيمِ

حم (1) تَنْزِيلٌ مِنَ الرَّحْمَنِ الرَّحِيمِ (2) كِتَابٌ فُصِّلَتْ آيَاتُهُ قُرْآنًا عَرَبِيًّا لِقَوْمٍ يَعْلَمُونَ (3) بَشِيرًا وَنَذِيرًا فَأَعْرَضَ أَكْثَرُهُمْ فَهُمْ لَا يَسْمَعُونَ (4) وَقَالُوا قُلُوبُنَا فِي أَكِنَّةٍ مِمَّا تَدْعُونَا إِلَيْهِ وَفِي آذَانِنَا وَقْرٌ وَمِنْ بَيْنِنَا وَبَيْنِكَ حِجَابٌ فَاعْمَلْ إِنَّنَا عَامِلُونَ (5) قُلْ إِنَّمَا أَنَا بَشَرٌ مِثْلُكُمْ يُوحَى إِلَيَّ أَنَّمَا إِلَهُكُمْ إِلَهٌ وَاحِدٌ فَاسْتَقِيمُوا إِلَيْهِ وَاسْتَغْفِرُوهُ وَوَيْلٌ لِلْمُشْرِكِينَ (6) الَّذِينَ لَا يُؤْتُونَ الزَّكَاةَ وَهُمْ بِالْآخِرَةِ هُمْ كَافِرُونَ (7) إِنَّ الَّذِينَ آمَنُوا وَعَمِلُوا الصَّالِحَاتِ لَهُمْ أَجْرٌ غَيْرُ مَمْنُونٍ (8) قُلْ أَئِنَّكُمْ لَتَكْفُرُونَ بِالَّذِي خَلَقَ الْأَرْضَ فِي يَوْمَيْنِ وَتَجْعَلُونَ لَهُ أَنْدَادًا ذَلِكَ رَبُّ الْعَالَمِينَ (9) وَجَعَلَ فِيهَا رَوَاسِيَ مِنْ فَوْقِهَا وَبَارَكَ فِيهَا وَقَدَّرَ فِيهَا أَقْوَاتَهَا فِي أَرْبَعَةِ أَيَّامٍ سَوَاءً لِلسَّائِلِينَ (10) ثُمَّ اسْتَوَى إِلَى السَّمَاءِ وَهِيَ دُخَانٌ فَقَالَ لَهَا وَلِلْأَرْضِ اِئْتِيَا طَوْعًا أَوْ كَرْهًا قَالَتَا أَتَيْنَا طَائِعِينَ (11) فَقَضَاهُنَّ سَبْعَ سَمَوَاتٍ فِي يَوْمَيْنِ وَأَوْحَى فِي كُلِّ سَمَاءٍ أَمْرَهَا وَزَيَّنَّا السَّمَاءَ الدُّنْيَا بِمَصَابِيحَ وَحِفْظًا ذَلِكَ تَقْدِيرُ الْعَزِيزِ الْعَلِيمِ (12) فَإِنْ أَعْرَضُوا فَقُلْ أَنْذَرْتُكُمْ صَاعِقَةً مِثْلَ صَاعِقَةِ عَادٍ وَثَمُودَ (13)

In the name of Allah, the Most Compassionate, the Most Merciful. Ha-Meem. A revelation from (Allah), the Most Beneficent, the Most Merciful. A Book whereof the verses are explained in detail- a Qur'an in Arabic for people who know. Giving glad tidings (of Paradise to the one who believes in the Oneness of Allah and fears Allah much (abstains from sins and evil deeds) and loves Allah much, and warning (of punishment in the Hell Fire to the one who disbelieves in the Oneness of Allah), but most of them turn away, so they hear not. And they say, "Our hearts are under coverings (screened) from that to which you invite us, and in our ears is deafness, and between us and you is a screen, so work you (on your way); verily, we are working (on our way)." Say (O Muhammad ﷺ), "I am only a human being like you. It is revealed to me that your Ilah (God) is One Ilah (God – Allah), therefore take Straight Path to Him (with true Faith) and obedience to Him, and seek forgiveness of Him. And woe to Al-Mushrikoon (the disbelievers, polytheists, idolaters). Those who give not the Zakat and they are disbelievers in the Hereafter. Truly, those who believe (in the Oneness of Allah, and in His Messenger Muhammad ﷺ) and do righteous good deeds, for them will be an endless reward that will never stop (i.e. Paradise). Say (O Muhammad ﷺ), "Do you verily disbelieve in

Him Who created the earth in 2 Days and you set up rivals (in worship) with Him? That is the Lord of the Alameen (mankind, jinns and all that exists). He placed therein (i.e. the earth) firm mountains from above it, and He blessed it, and measured therein its sustenance (for its dwellers) in 4 days equal (i.e. all these 4 days were equal in the length of time), for all those who ask (about its creation). Then He Istawa (rose over) towards the heaven when it was smoke, and said to it and to the earth, "Come both of you willingly or unwillingly." They both said, "We come, willingly." Then He completed and finished from their creation (as) 7 heavens in 2 days and He made in each heaven its affair. And We adorned the nearest (lowest) heaven with lamps (stars) to be an adornment as well as to guard (from the devils by using them as missiles against the devils). Such is the Decree of Him the All-Mighty, the All-Knower. But if they turn away, then say (O Muhammad ﷺ), "I have warned you of a Saiqah (destructive awful cry) like the Saiqah which overtook Ad and Thamud (people)." (Fussilat:1-13)

Utba exclaimed, "Enough! Don't you have anything else to say?" Rasulullah ﷺ replied, "No." Utba then left. When he met with the other members of the Quraish, he said to them, "I told him everything you wanted me to tell him." They enquired, "Did he give you a reply?" Utba started saying, "Yes," but then quickly said, "No!" He added, "By the being Who made the Kabah a place of worship! I understood nothing from what he said except that he warns us of a punishment like the punishment that afflicted the Aad and the Thamud." To this the people said, "Woe to you! A man speaks to you in Arabic and you cannot understand what he says!" Utba replied, "No I cannot help it! By Allah! I understood nothing except the mention of the punishment that afflicted the Aad and Thamud." *(Abd bin Humaid).* *Bayhaqi* have reported a narration from *Hakim* in which it is added that Utba also said to Rasulullah ﷺ, "If it is the leadership that you want, we all will anchor our flags for you as it was the tradition that leaders would have the flags anchored at their homes so that you become our leader as long as you live. This narration also adds that Utba placed his hand on the mouth of Rasulullah ﷺ when Rasulullah ﷺ reached the verse,

فَإِنْ أَعْرَضُوا فَقُلْ أَنْذَرْتُكُمْ صَاعِقَةً مِثْلَ صَاعِقَةِ عَادٍ وَثَمُودَ (13)

But if they (disbelievers) turn away, then say (O Muhammad ﷺ), "I have warned you of a Saiqah (a destructive awful cry) like the Saiqah which overtook Ad and Thamud (people)." (Fussilat:13)

He then bade Rasulullah ﷺ for the sake of their family ties so that he would not recite any more. After leaving the company of Rasulullah ﷺ, Utba stayed at home and did not venture to meet the other members of the Quraish. To this Abu Jahal commented, "O Quraish! By Allah! It appears that Utba has accepted the religion of Muhammad ﷺ and likes his food. There can be no other reason for this except that he has become poor. Let us go to see him." When they arrived to see Utba, Abu Jahal said, "We have come only because you have accepted the religion of Muhammad ﷺ and like his talk. If you have become poor, we shall collect money for you so that you don't need Muhammad ﷺ's food." Utba grew very angry when he heard this and swore by Allah that he would never again speak to Rasulullah ﷺ. He then said to them, "You know well that I am one of the wealthiest people of the Quraish." He then related the meeting with Rasulullah ﷺ and said, "I went to him and he replied with words that I swear by Allah are neither products of magic, poetry or fortune-telling. He started reciting,

بِسْمِ اللَّهِ الرَّحْمَنِ الرَّحِيمِ حم (1) تَنْزِيلٌ مِنَ الرَّحْمَنِ الرَّحِيمِ (2)

In the name of Allah, the Most Compassionate, the Most Merciful. HaaMeem. (This Qur'an is) a revelation from the Most

Compassionate, the Most Merciful. He continued reciting until he reached the verse,

فَإِنْ أَعْرَضُوا فَقُلْ أَنْذَرْتُكُمْ صَاعِقَةً مِثْلَ صَاعِقَةِ عَادٍ وَثَمُودَ (13)

But if they (disbelievers) turn away, then say (O Muhammad ﷺ), "I have warned you of a Saiqah (a destructive awful cry) like the Saiqah which overtook Ad and Thamud (people)." (Fussilat :13)

I held his mouth and asked him in the name of our family relations that he should stop reciting. You know very well that Muhammad ﷺ never lies when he speaks, so I feared that the punishment would afflict you people."*(Al Bidayah wan Nihayah)*

Abdullah bin Omar ؓ narrates that some members of the Quraish gathered to discuss about Rasulullah ﷺ when Rasulullah ﷺ was sitting in the Masjidul Haram in Makkah. Utba bin Rabe'ah said, "Let me speak to him as I shall perhaps be softer on him than the rest of you." Utba stood up and sat by Rasulullah ﷺ. He then said, "O my nephew! I have no doubts that you are certainly from the best family and enjoy the most honor from all of us. However, you have placed your people in a situation that no other has done to their people before. If it is wealth that you want by propagating your message, your people will take the responsibility to ensure that they accumulate their wealth to make you the wealthiest person. If it is position that you want, we shall all honor you until there is none more honorable than you and we shall do nothing without your approval. If you are doing this because you have been afflicted by evil spirits which you are unable to get rid of, then we shall spend all our fortunes until we become helpless to find a cure for you. If it is leadership that you want, we shall make you our leader." Rasulullah ﷺ then said, "Have you finished O Abu Walid?" When Utba replied in the affirmative, Rasulullah ﷺ recited Surah Fussilat and prostrated in Sejdah when he recited the Sejdah verse (verse 37-38). However, Utba remained sitting with his hand behind him for support. When Rasulullah ﷺ completed reciting the Surah, Utba stood up and was so astonished by the words of the Qur'an that he did not know what to tell others. When they saw him arrive, they commented, "Utba is returning with a face quit different from the one he left you with." Utba said, "O gathering of Quraish! I spoke to him as you instructed but when I had finished, he spoke to me the words that I swear by Allah, my ears have never heard before. I did not know what to say to him. O gathering of the Quraish! Listen to me once even if you disobey me forever later. Leave this man alone because I swear by Allah that he will never forsake what he is doing. Allow him to do as he pleases with the Arabs because if he is dominant over them, his honor would be yours and if they dominate him, your objective would be fulfilled without your intervention." The others said, "O Abul Walid! You have forsaken your religion." *(Al Bidayah wan Nihayah)*

Rasulullah ﷺ's Resolve on the Duty that Allah Sent Him With

Miswar bin Makhrama ؓ and Marwan ؓ have reported concerning the incident leading to the Treaty of Hudaibiyah, which is discussed later in this chapter. It states that while Rasulullah ﷺ and the Sahabah were stationed in the valley of Hudaibiyah, Budayl bin Waraqa Khuza'i arrived there along with a group of people from his Khuza'ah tribe. This tribe was from the Tihama region and was very friendly towards the Muslims. He told Rasulullah ﷺ that they had just passed by the tribes of Amir bin Luway and Ka'b bin Luway, who had camped at some of the springs of Hudaibiyah. They informed Rasulullah ﷺ that these tribes were ready to engage in battle with the Muslims and prevent them from coming to the Kabah. In fact they were so determined to fight the Muslims that they had arrived with all their resources and even those camels that were about to give birth and those that had just given birth. Rasulullah ﷺ said, "I have not come to fight anyone, but wish only to perform Umrah. It is surprising that the Quraish has weakened by the fight and caused them much harm. If they want, we are prepared to make a treaty with them for a period. During this period, they should not interfere with my efforts on the people. If I am successful over the people so that if they accept Islam, the Quraish will have the choice to enter into Islam which the others have entered. On the other hand, if people get the upper hand over me, the Quraish will have no worries about me. However, if the Quraish refuse to accept Islam and insist on fighting, then I swear by the Being in whose control my life lies, I shall fight them for the sake of Islam until either my head is separated from my neck or Islam flourishes." *(Bukhari)*. Tabrani also narrated from Miswar bin Makhrama ☺ and Marwan ☺, which ends with the words, "Woe be to the Quraish! War has certainly weakened them from previous battles. Rather why don't they allow me to continue my work among the people without interference? If the other Arabs gain the upper hand over me and finish me off, the desire of the Quraish will be fulfilled. On the contrary, if Allah grants me victory over the other Arabs, the Quraish will also can enter the fold of Islam. However, if the Quraish refuse to accept Islam and have the strength to fight me, what do they think? I swear by Allah that I shall fight them for the sake of Islam which Allah has sent me with until Allah grants me victory or my head is separated from my body." *(Ibn Is'haq)*

Rasulullah ☺ Commands Ali ☺ to Call People Towards Islam First During the Battle of Khaibar

Sahal bin Sa'd ☺ narrates that during the Battle of Khaibar, Rasulullah ☺ announced, "Tomorrow I shall give the flag to the person on whose hands Allah shall grant victory. He is a person who has love for Allah and His Rasul ☺ and whom Allah and His Rasul ☺ also love." Sahal ☺ mentioned that during the entire night, the Sahabah kept on thinking which of them would receive the flag to lead the army into battle. The following morning, all the Sahabah came to Rasulullah ☺, each one hoping that he would be the one to receive the flag. Rasulullah ☺ announced, "Where is Ali bin Abi Talib ☺?" The Sahabah replied, "O Rasulullah ☺! He is suffering from pain in his eyes." Rasulullah ☺ sent someone to call him. When he arrived, Rasulullah ☺ applied some of his blessed saliva onto Ali's eyes and prayed for him. His eyed were immediately cured and it appeared as if he had never suffered any pain at all. Rasulullah ☺ then handed the flag over to him. Ali ☺ asked, "Should I fight them until they become like us?" Rasulullah ☺ replied, "Proceed at a moderate pace until you reach their field. Then invite them to accept Islam, explaining the rights due to Allah that are compulsory for them to fulfill. By Allah! If Allah uses you to guide even a single person, it is better for you than red camels." *(Bukhari, Muslim)*

The Perseverance of Rasulullah ☺ During Invitation of Hakam bin Kaisan to Islam

Miqdad bin Amr ☺ narrates that when he took Hakam bin Kaisan prisoner during one battle, his commander wanted Hakam executed. However, Miqdad ☺ managed to persuade his commander not to execute Hakam but rather take him to Rasulullah ☺. When they brought him to Rasulullah ☺, Rasulullah ☺ started inviting him to accept Islam and spent long time speaking to him. After some time, Omar ☺ said, "O Rasulullah ☺! For what reason are you talking to him so much? By Allah! He shall never accept Islam! Allow me to execute him so that he may reach his destination in hell!" However, Rasulullah ☺ paid no attention to Omar ☺ and continued

speaking until Hakam accepted Islam. Omar ☺ says, "When I saw Hakam accept Islam, I was surrounded by thoughts of the past and future. I blamed myself for talking to Rasulullah ☺ concerning a matter about which he had more knowledge than me. Then I told myself that I had done so only for the welfare of Allah and His Rasul ☺." Later Omar ☺ said, "Hakam became a Muslim by Allah, he was an excellent Muslim who fought for the pleasure of Allah until he was martyred at Bir Ma'ona. Rasulullah ☺ was pleased with him and he has entered the gardens of Paradise." *(Ibn Sa'd)*. Zuhri narrates that Hakam asked Rasulullah ☺, "What is Islam?" Rasulullah ☺ replied, "That you worship Allah Alone Who has no partner and that you testify that Muhammad ☺ is Allah's servant and Rasul." Hakam then said, "I accept Islam." Rasulullah ☺ then turned to the Sahabah and said, "Had I listened to you just now and killed him, he would have entered the fire of hell." *(Ibn Sa'd)*

Wahshi bin Harb ☺ Accepts Islam

Abdullah bin Abbas ☺ narrates that Rasulullah ☺ sent a messenger with the invitation of Islam to Wahshi bin Harb who was responsible for killing Hamza ☺ the uncle of Rasulullah ☺. The messenger returned with a message from Wahshi stating, "O Muhammad ☺! How can you call me to Islam when you say that a murderer, disbelievers, and an adulterer shall meet with a grave punishment and this punishment will be multiplied for them on the Day of Judgment where they shall remain disgraced in it forever? *(mentioned in Al-Furqan:68-69)*. I have committed all of these crimes, so is there any way out for me?" Allah then revealed the verse,

إِلَّا مَنْ تَابَ وَآمَنَ وَعَمِلَ عَمَلًا صَالِحًا فَأُولَٰئِكَ يُبَدِّلُ اللَّهُ سَيِّئَاتِهِمْ حَسَنَاتٍ وَكَانَ اللَّهُ غَفُورًا رَحِيمًا (70)

Except those who repent and accept Iman and do righteous deeds, for those, Allah will exchange their sins into good deeds, and Allah is Oft-Forgiving, Most Merciful. (Al-Furqan:70)

In reply to this verse, Wahshi ☺ said, "O Muhammad ☺! The condition in this verse is uncompromising which states, 'Except those who repent and accept Iman and do righteous deeds.' What if I do not have the opportunity to fulfill it?" Allah then revealed the verse, إِنَّ اللَّهَ لَا يَغْفِرُ أَنْ يُشْرَكَ بِهِ وَيَغْفِرُ مَا دُونَ ذَٰلِكَ لِمَنْ يَشَاءُ

Verily, Allah forgives not that partners should be set up with Him in worship, but He forgives except that (anything else) to whom He wills. (An-Nisa:48)

To this, Wahshi ☺ replied, "This forgiveness depends on the will of Allah. I do not know whether I shall be forgiven or not. Is there any other way for me?" Allah then revealed the verse,

قُلْ يَا عِبَادِيَ الَّذِينَ أَسْرَفُوا عَلَىٰ أَنْفُسِهِمْ لَا تَقْنَطُوا مِنْ رَحْمَةِ اللَّهِ إِنَّ اللَّهَ يَغْفِرُ الذُّنُوبَ جَمِيعًا إِنَّهُ هُوَ الْغَفُورُ الرَّحِيمُ (53)

Say, "O Ibadi (My servants) who have transgressed against themselves (by committing evil deeds and sins)! Despair not of the Mercy of Allah, verily Allah forgives all sins. Truly, He is Oft-Forgiving, Most Merciful. (Az-ZOmar:53)

Upon hearing this, Wahshi ☺ said, "Yes, this is in order." He then accepted Islam. Other Muslims asked, "O Rasulullah ☺! We had also committed the sins that Wahshi committed. Does this verse apply to us as well?." Rasulullah ☺ replied, "It applies to all Muslims in general." *(Tabrani, Haythami)*

Abdullah bin Abbas ☺ reports that some disbelievers who had committed murder and adultery in abundance approached Rasulullah ☺. They said, "What you are saying and calling towards are really good. Do tell us if there is any way out for our sins?" It was on this occasion that Allah revealed the following 2 verses,

وَالَّذِينَ لَا يَدْعُونَ مَعَ اللَّهِ إِلَهًا آخَرَ وَلَا يَقْتُلُونَ النَّفْسَ الَّتِي حَرَّمَ اللَّهُ إِلَّا بِالْحَقِّ وَلَا يَزْنُونَ وَمَنْ يَفْعَلْ ذَلِكَ يَلْقَ أَثَامًا (68)

And those who invoke not any other ilah (god) along with Allah, nor kill such life as Allah has forbidden, except for just cause, nor commit illegal sexual intercourse and whoever does this shall receive the punishment. (Al-Furqan:68)

قُلْ يَا عِبَادِيَ الَّذِينَ أَسْرَفُوا عَلَى أَنْفُسِهِمْ لَا تَقْنَطُوا مِنْ رَحْمَةِ اللَّهِ إِنَّ اللَّهَ يَغْفِرُ الذُّنُوبَ جَمِيعًا إِنَّهُ هُوَ الْغَفُورُ الرَّحِيمُ (53)

Say, "O Ibadi (My servants) who have transgressed against themselves (by committing evil deeds and sins)! Despair not of the Mercy of Allah, verily Allah forgives all sins. Truly, He is Oft-Forgiving, Most Merciful. (Az-ZOmar:53) (Bukhari)

Fatima Weeps at the Pale-look of Rasulullah Caused by his Effort to Fulfill the Duty Allah has Entrusted to Him

Abu Tha'laba Khushani narrates that Rasulullah once returned from a battle and entered the Masjid to perform 2 Rakahs of salah. Whenever he returned from a journey, Rasulullah always liked to proceed first to the Masjid to perform 2 Rakahs of salah and then go to the house of Fatima, his daughter before proceeding to the homes of his wives. Consequently, he went to the house of Fatima upon returning from a journey. Welcoming him at the door, Fatima started kissing Rasulullah on his face and his eyes. She then began weeping. When Rasulullah asked her what made her to weep, she replied, "O Rasulullah! Because I see your face so pale and your clothing so torned because of the journey." Rasulullah said, "Do not weep, O Fatima. Allah has sent me with Islam by means of which He will offer honor or disgrace into every baked and unbaked home and every skin tent on the surface of the earth so that those accept Islam will have the honor while the others will have the disgrace. Islam shall reach wherever the night reaches (everywhere)." *(Tabrani, Abu Nu'aym, Hakim)*

The Hadith of Tamim Dari Concerning the Spreading of Islam

Tamim Dari narrates that he heard Rasulullah say, "This Islam shall definitely reach wherever the day and the night reach. Allah shall enter this Islam into every baked and unbaked home with either great honor or terrible disgrace. Allah will grant the honor to Islam and the people of Islam, while the disgrace will go to kufr: disbeliever and its people." Tamim Dari also says, "I saw the reality of this in my own family. Those who accepted Islam were blessed with good, honor and respect while those who remained Disbeliever suffered disgrace, humiliation and had to pay the Jizya (tax)." *(Ahmad, Tabrani)*

Omar Desires the Traitors to Return to Islam

Anas narrates that Abu Musa Ash'ari sent him to give the news of the conquest of Tustar to Omar. He says that Omar asked him about what had happened to 6 members of the Bakr bin Wa'il tribe who had forsaken Islam and proceeded to live with the disbelievers. Anas replied, "O Amirul Mu'minin! They have renounced Islam and joined the disbelievers. Their only treatment is their execution." To this Omar said, "I prefer to get them alive and well compared to all the gold and silver in the world." Anas asked, "O Amerul Mu'minin! What would you do with them if you get them alive?" Omar replied, "I would present the door from which they left so that they may re-enter it. If they accept, I would accept it from them, otherwise I would imprison them." *(Kanzul Ummal)*. Abdur Rahman Al Qari reports that Abu Musa Ash'ari once sent a person to Omar. When Omar asked the person about the condition of the

people, he replied. When Omar asked the person if there were any recent developments, he said, "Yes, O Ameerul Mu'mineen! A person who had become a Muslim, reverted to kufr." Omar asked, "What did you do with him?" The reply came, "We called him and executed him." Omar said, "Why didn't you rather imprison him for 3 days, feed him bread each day and encourage him to repent? He may then have repented and re-entered Islam. O Allah! I was not present there. I did not command it and not pleased with it now that it has come to my notice." *(Malik, Shafi'ee, Bayhaqi)* Amr bin Al Aas once wrote to Amirul Mu'mineen Omar to ask him what to do with a person who had reverted to Kufr after accepting Islam, then accepted Islam again, only to return to Kufr. The person had done several times already. Amr bin Al Aas asked, "Should his Islam be accepted from him again?" Omar wrote back, "As long as Allah accepts Islam of a person, you should do the same. You should therefore present Islam to him again. If he accepts, you should set him free, otherwise you may execute him." *(Kanzul Ummal)*

Omar Weeps Over the Efforts of a Christian Monk

Abu Imran Jowni narrates that Omar once passed by a monk and remained standing there. Someone called the monk and told him that the Amirul Mu'mineen was there. When the monk looked out, the effects of difficulty, exertion, and forsaking the world were clearly apparent on his face, he grew pale on account of his spiritual efforts. Looking at him, Omar began to weep. Someone commented, "But he is a Christian". Omar replied, "I know, but I feel sorry for him because I thought of the verse in which Allah mentions, عَامِلَةٌ نَاصِبَةٌ (3) تَصْلَى نَارًا حَامِيَةً (4)

Laboring (hard in the worldly life by worshipping others besides Allah), weary (in the Hereafter with humility and disgrace). They will enter in the hot blazing Fire. (Al-Ghashiyah:3-4)
I feel sorry for him because despite his efforts in this world, he shall still end up in hellfire." *(Bayhaqi, Ibn Mundhir, Hakim in Kanzul Ummal)*

Preaching to Individuals: Rasulullah Invites Abu Bakr to Islam

Aisha narrates that her father Abu Bakr was a close friend of Rasulullah even during the period of ignorance. One day, Abu Bakr left home to meet Rasulullah. When he met Rasulullah, he said, "O Abul Qasim! (means father of Qasim, Rasulullah's son). Why are you no longer present in the gatherings of your people'? Why do they accuse you of speaking ill of their forefathers'?" Rasulullah said, "I am the Rasul of Allah and am calling you towards Allah." As soon as Rasulullah had completed, Abu Bakr accepted Islam. When Rasulullah had left Abu Bakr, there was none between the mountains of Makkah happier than Rasulullah because Abu Bakr had accepted Islam. Abu Bakr then met Uthman bin Affan, Talha bin Ubaidullah, Zubair bin Awwam and Sa'd bin Abi Waqqas, all of whom accepted Islam. The following day, Abu Bakr met Uthman bin Madh'un, Abu Ubaidah bin Jarah, Abdur Rahman bin Awf, Abu Salma bin Abdil Asad and Arqam bin Abil Arqam, all of whom also readily accepted Islam. *(Al Bidayah wan Nihayah)*. Abu Bakr once met Rasulullah and said, "O Muhammad! Is it true what the Quraish are saying about you forsaking our gods, calling us foolish and referring to our forefathers as infidels?" Rasulullah replied, "Yes. I am Allah's Rasul and Nabi. Allah has sent me to propagate His message. With conviction I am calling you towards Allah by Allah! This is certainly the truth. O Abu Bakr! I call you towards the One Allah Who has no partner. Do not worship anyone but Him and always be obedient to Him."

Rasulullah ﷺ then recited a part of the Qur'an to Abu Bakr. Abu Bakr ؓ neither accepted the message nor rejected it. He accepted Islam, abandoned idols, renounced all partners in worship and attested to the truth of Islam. Abu Bakr ؓ returned from his meeting with Rasulullah ﷺ as a true Mu'min. *(Ibn Is'haq)*. Rasulullah ﷺ said, "Everyone I called to Islam expressed some hesitation and doubts except Abu Bakr. When I mentioned Islam to him, he neither hesitated nor expressed any doubts but accepted immediately." *(Ibn Is'haq)*. There is an error in the words of Ibn Is'haq's narration when it reads, "Abu Bakr ؓ neither accepted the message nor rejected it". Ibn Is'haq himself and other scholars have mentioned that Abu Bakr ؓ was a close friend of Rasulullah ﷺ even before Rasulullah ﷺ announced his prophethood. Abu Bakr was well aware of the truthfulness, honesty, excellent habits, and inspiring character of Rasulullah ﷺ which would not allow him to even speak a lie about the creation, let alone lie about The Creator. As soon as Rasulullah ﷺ told Abu Bakr ؓ that he was Allah's Nabi, he immediately accepted without hesitation. Bukhari narrates a Hadith in which it is reported that once when there was an argument between Abu Bakr ؓ and Omar ؓ, Rasulullah ﷺ said, "When Allah sent me as a Nabi to you people, you all said that I was lying while Abu Bakr said, 'You are speaking the truth'. He then offered me great assistance with his life and wealth. For my sake, will you people not leave this friend of mine alone and refrain from causing him any trouble?" Rasulullah ﷺ repeated this statement twice, after which no one ever caused any harm to Abu Bakr. This Hadith of Rasulullah ﷺ is a clear proof that Abu Bakr ؓ was the first to accept Islam. *(Al Bidayah wan Nihayah)*

Rasulullah ﷺ Invites Omar ؓ to Islam

Abdullah bin Mas'ood ؓ narrates that Rasulullah ﷺ once prayed to Allah saying, "O Allah! Strengthen Islam by means of either Omar bin Khattab or Abu Jahal bin Hisham." Allah accepted the Du'a in favor of Omar ؓ and made him a means to strengthen the foundations of Islam and destroy the idols. *(Al Bidayah wan Nihayah)*. Thowban narrated the suffering of Omar ؓ's sister Fatima and her husband Sa'eed bin Zaid, shall be discussed in a forthcoming chapter concerning the suffering that the Sahabah endured for Islam. It is mentioned that when Omar ؓ came to Rasulullah ﷺ after leaving his sister's home, Rasulullah ﷺ held him by his arms and shook him saying, "What do you want? Why have you come?" Omar replied, "Present to me what you are calling towards." Rasulullah ﷺ said, "That you testify that there is none worthy of worship but Allah Who is One and has no partner and that you testify that Muhammad ﷺ is Allah's servant and Rasul." Omar ؓ accepted Islam then and there. Omar ؓ then told Rasulullah ﷺ to leave the house and to perform salah openly in the Masjidul Haram without fearing the Disbeliever *(Tabrani)*. Aslam narrates that Omar ؓ once said to them, "Do you want to hear about how I came into the fold of Islam?" When those present wanted to know, Omar ؓ said, "I was one of the people most opposed to Rasulullah ﷺ. I once came to him as he sat in a house near Safa and sat before him. Taking hold of my collar Rasulullah ﷺ said, 'O son of Khattab! Accept Islam.' He then prayed for me saying, 'O Allah! Guide him.' I then said, 'I testify that there is none worthy of worship but Allah and I testify that you are the Rasul of Allah.' The Muslims present there exclaimed, 'Allahu Akbar' so loudly that it was heard in the streets of Makkah." *(Abu Nua'ym, Bazzar)*

Rasulullah ﷺ Invites Uthman ؓ to Islam

Amr bin Uthman reports that Uthman ؓ said, "I was once visiting my aunt Arwa bint Abdil Muttalib (my mother's sister) when Rasulullah ﷺ arrived there. I began to stare at him because in those days there was some mention of his prophethood. Turning to me, he asked, 'What seems to be the matter, O Uthman?' I replied, 'I am surprised that there is so much talk about you when you are such an honorable person among us.' Rasulullah ﷺ said, "*La Ilaha Illallah*'. Allah is witness to the fact that I shake at this. Rasulullah ﷺ then began reciting,

وَفِي السَّمَاءِ رِزْقُكُمْ وَمَا تُوعَدُونَ (22) فَوَرَبِّ السَّمَاءِ وَالْأَرْضِ إِنَّهُ لَحَقٌّ مِثْلَ مَا أَنَّكُمْ تَنْطِقُونَ (23)

And in the heaven is your provision, and that which you are promised. Then, by the Lord of the heaven and the earth, it is the truth (i.e. what has been promised to you), just as it is the truth that you can speak. (Adh-Dhariyat:22-23)

Thereafter, Rasulullah ﷺ stood up and left. I left after him, met him and accepted Islam." *(Mada'ini in Insti'ab)*

Rasulullah ﷺ Invites Ali bin Abi Talib ؓ to Islam

Ibn Is'haq narrates that Ali ؓ came to Rasulullah ﷺ while Rasulullah and Khadija ؓ were performing salah. Ali ؓ asked Rasulullah ﷺ, "O Muhammad ﷺ! What is this?" "This is Islam that Allah has chosen and for which He has sent His Ambiya. I call you towards the One Allah Who has no partner. I call you to worship Him Alone and to renounce both Lat and Uzza." Ali ؓ responded by saying, "I have never heard of anything like this before. I cannot decide anything until I speak to Abu Talib." Since Rasulullah ﷺ did not want his secret to be exposed until he made an open declaration to the people, he said to Ali ؓ, "O Ali! If you are not going to accept Islam, keep this a secret." Ali ؓ spent the night in this condition without telling anyone and Allah inspired him with the urge to accept Islam. Early next morning, he set out to meet Rasulullah ﷺ. When he met Rasulullah ﷺ, he said, "What was it that you presented to me, O Muhammad ﷺ?" Rasulullah ﷺ replied, "You testify that there is none worthy of worship but the One Allah Who has no partner and that you renounce Lat and Uzza and clear Him from all partners." Ali complied, accepted Islam, and would visit Rasulullah ﷺ in secret for fear of Abu Talib. He concealed his acceptance of Islam and did not make it known to anyone. *(Al Bidayah wan Nihayah)* Habba Urani narrates that he once saw Ali ؓ laugh quietly as he sat on the Mimbar (pulpit). He had never before seen Ali ؓ laugh in this manner that his teeth showed. Ali ؓ said, "I just thought about words of my father Abu Talib. He arrived suddenly one day as Rasulullah ﷺ and I were performing salah in the Valley of Nakhla. He asked, "O my nephew! What are the 2 of you doing?" Rasulullah ﷺ then invited him to accept Islam. Referring to the Sejdah posture, Abu Talib then said, "There is no harm in what you are doing but I cannot allow my buttock to ever rise above me". Ali ؓ was laughing quietly at these words of his father and then said, "O Allah! Besides your Nabi ﷺ, no servant of this Ummah has worshipped You before me." He repeated these 3 times and then said, "I performed salah 7 years before other people." *(Ahmad, Haythami, Bazzar, Tabrani)*

Rasulullah ﷺ Invites Amr bin Absah ؓ to Islam

Shaddad bin Abdullah narrates that Abu Umama ؓ once asked Amr bin Absah ؓ why he claimed to be the 4th person to accept Islam. He replied, "Even during the period of ignorance, I realized that people were astray and I had no regard for idols. When I heard about a person in Makkah who was informing about many happenings and saying many things, I rode to Makkah. Upon reaching Makkah, I realized that Rasulullah ﷺ was in hiding and that his people were shamelessly harassing him. I therefore used clever tactics and finally managed to meet him. I asked, 'What are you?' Rasulullah ﷺ replied, 'I am the Nabi of Allah.' I asked further, 'What is a Nabi?' He said, 'A Rasul of Allah.' I enquired, 'Has Allah sent you?' When he replied in the affirmative, I asked, 'What message has Allah sent you with?' Rasulullah ﷺ responded, 'Allah should be accepted as One, no partners should be ascribed to Him, the idols should be destroyed and family ties should be maintained.' I asked, 'Who are with you in this?' The reply was, 'A free man and a slave.' I saw that Abu Bakr bin Abi Quhafa ؓ was with him along with his servant Bilal. I then said, 'I shall follow you in this.' Rasulullah ﷺ said, 'You cannot do so right now. Rather go home and come to meet me when you hear that I have become influential.' I then returned home as a Muslim. Rasulullah ﷺ later migrated to Madinah and I kept making enquiries about him until a caravan from Madinah arrived one day. I asked them, 'What is the condition of the person from Makkah who has come to you people?' They replied, 'His people tried to assassinate him but were unable to do so as Allah's help came. As we left, people were flocking to him.'" Amr bin Absah ؓ continues, "I immediately mounted my camel and rode off. When I reached Madinah, I appeared before Rasulullah ﷺ and then said, "O Rasulullah ﷺ! Do you recognize me?" He replied, "Are you not the person who met me in Makkah?" I said, "Yes, I am the same person" and I added further, "O Rasulullah ﷺ! Teach me something that Allah has taught you and which I do not know." There is still a considerable portion of this Hadith still to be mentioned. (Ahmad, Ibn Sa'd). Amr bin Absah ؓ narrated yet another Hadith. He says that he once asked and Rasulullah ﷺ said, "With what message did Allah send you?" He replied, "Allah has sent me with the message that family ties should be maintained, human life should be preserved, roads should remain safe, idols should be broken and that only one Allah should be worshipped Who has no partner." I then said to him, "These teachings from Allah are indeed very fine. I make you a witness that I have accepted Iman and that I accept you as a true Nabi. May I now stay with you if you decide that this is appropriate?" He replied, "As you can see, the people regard Islam which I have brought as something very evil. You should return home and when you hear that I have reached the place of my Hijra, then you may come to me." (Ahmad, Muslim, Tabrani, Abu Nu'aym)

Rasulullah ﷺ Invites Khalid bin Sa'eed bin Al Aas ؓ to Islam

Khalid bin Sa'eed bin Al Aas ؓ was one of the first people to accept Islam. He was the first of his brothers to accept Islam. His path to Islam started with a dream that he saw that he himself was standing on the edge of a blazing fire. He mentioned that the fire was so large that only Allah knows how big it was. In the dream he saw his father pushing him into the fire while Rasulullah ﷺ was holding him back by the waist so that he would not fall. This scene frightened him so much that he woke up with the shock. When he awakened, he said to himself, "This is definitely a true dream." Thereafter, he met Abu Bakr ؓ and related the dream to him. Abu Bakr ؓ said to him, "There is good in store for you. He (Rasulullah ﷺ) is the Nabi of Allah, so do follow him. Your dream means you will follow him and enter into Islam with him. Thereafter this Islam will save you from entering the fire of the hell where your father is at the moment." Khalid bin Sa'eed ؓ then met Rasulullah ﷺ and said to him, "O Muhammad ﷺ! To what do you call me?" He replied, "I call you to the One Allah who has no partner and to believe that Muhammad ﷺ is His servant and Rasul. I call you to renounce your worship of stones that cannot hear, cannot cause harm, they cannot be of any benefit to you as they do not even know those

who worship them and those who do not worship them!" Khalid bin Sa'eed ؓ said, "I testify that there is none worthy of worship besides Allah and I testify that you are the Rasul of Allah." Rasulullah ﷺ was extremely happy when Khalid bin Sa'eed ؓ accepted Islam. Khalid bin Sa'eed ؓ then stayed away from his home. When his father discovered that he had accepted Islam, he sent someone to look for him. When the person brought him before his father, his father rebuked him very harshly and started beating him with the whip he had in his hand. He beat Khalid so severely that the whip broke as it struck his head. His father then said, "By Allah! I shall not give you anything to eat!" To this Khalid bin Sa'eed said, "If you do not give me anything to eat, then Allah shall definitely provide for me and I will pass my life." He then left and went to Rasulullah ﷺ. Thereafter he constantly remained in the company of Rasulullah ﷺ. (Bayhaqi)

Another narration says his father sent their slave Rafi to look for him along with Khalid ؓ's other brothers who had not yet accepted Islam. When they found him, they brought him to his father Abu Uhaiha. His father started to rebuke him and beat him with a whip that he carried in his hand. He beat him so severely that the whip broke on his head. His father then said, "Do you follow Muhammad ﷺ when he opposes his people and finds faults with their gods and their forefathers who have passed away?" Khalid bin Sa'eed ؓ said to his father, "By Allah! He is speaking the truth and I follow him." Thereupon his father became very angry and started swearing and saying, "You are a wicked person! Go whenever you please. I swear by Allah that I shall stop feeding you." In reply, Khalid bin Sa'eed ؓ said, "If you stop feeding me, Allah will grant me enough sustenance with which to live." His father chased him out of the house and said to all his other sons that they will receive the same treatment if they ever spoke to Khalid ؓ. Khalid bin Sa'eed ؓ then left his father and was the constant companion of Rasulullah ﷺ. (Hakim). Khalid bin Sa'eed ؓ hid from his father in the ditch of Makkah and when the second group of Sahabah migrated to Abysinia, Khalid ؓ accompanied them. (Isti'ab). When his father Sa'eed bin Al Aas bin Umayyah fell ill, he said, "If Allah removes this illness from me, the god of Ibn Abil Kabsha (Rasulullah ﷺ) will never be worshipped in the valley of Makkah." To this, Khalid bin Sa'eed ؓ said, "O Allah! Do not remove the illness from him." Later, he died with that illness. (Ibn Sa'd)

Rasulullah ﷺ Invites Dimad ؓ to Islam

Abdullah bin Abbas ؓ narrates that Dimad ؓ was from the Azd-Shanu'ah tribe who used to cure insane people and people affected with evil spirits using some words that he used to recite. He had heard some foolish people of Makkah that Muhammad ﷺ was insane. He said to them, "where is this man? Perhaps Allah will cure him at my hand." When he met Rasulullah ﷺ, he said, "I recite certain words by which I cure people. Indeed Allah has cured at my hand those people whom He wished to cure. I come to cure you as well." Rasulullah ﷺ thrice repeated the following sermon, "Verily all praise is for Allah. We praise Him and seek help from Him. There can be none to misguide the person whom Allah has guided and there can be none to guide the person whom Allah has caused to go astray. I testify that there is none worthy of worship besides the One Allah Who has no partner." Dimad ؓ said, "By Allah! I have heard the words of fortune-tellers, the words of magicians and the words of poets. However, I have never heard such words before. Give me your hand so that I may pledge allegiance to you on Islam." Rasulullah ﷺ then accepted his pledge of allegiance and said to him, "Is this pledge on behalf of your people as well?" Dimad ؓ replied, "It is for my people as well." Once some Muslim soldiers were passing the tribe of Dimad 🙵. The leader of the soldiers asked them, "Did any of you take something from these people?" One soldier replied, "Yes, I have their water jug with me." To this, the leader replied, "Then return it to them because these are the people of Dimad 🙵." According to another narration, Dimad said to Rasulullah 🙵, "Repeat those words to me because they reach the depths of the ocean of eloquence." *(Muslim, Bayhaqi, Nasa'i)*

Abdur Rahman Adawi reports that Dimad 🙵 said, "I went to Makkah to perform Umrah and was sitting in a gathering together with Abu Jahal, Utba bin Rabee'ah and Umayyah bin Khalaf. Abu Jahal said, "This man has disunited us. He makes us look foolish and claims that those of us who have passed away were misguided. He also insults our gods." Umayyah said, "There is no doubt that this man is certainly mad." Dimad 🙵 says that he said to himself, "But I am able to cure people affected with evil spirits." He then left the gathering and started looking for Rasulullah 🙵. However, after searching the entire day he was unable to find Rasulullah 🙵 anywhere. The following day he again set out to search for Rasulullah 🙵 and finally found him performing salah behind the Maqam-e-Ibrahim. Dimad 🙵 says that he then sat down. When Rasulullah 🙵 had finished the salah, Dimad 🙵 said to him, "O son of Abdul Muttalib!" Rasulullah 🙵 turned to him and replied, "What do you want?" Dimad replied, "I am able to cure people affected by evil spirits. If you wish, I can cure you as well. Do not think that your illness is of great concern because I have cured people who were even more ill than you are. I have just come from some of your people who have nothing good to say about you. They say that you are insane, you have caused disunity amongst them, and you refer to their forefathers as being misguided. They also say that you insult their gods. I have therefore come to the conclusion that only an insane person would do such things." Rasulullah 🙵 then said the following, "Verily all praise is for Allah. I praise Him and seek help from Him. I believe in Him and have complete trust in Him. There can be none to misguide the person whom Allah has guided and there can been none to guide the person whom Allah has caused to go astray. I testify that there is none worthy of worship besides the One Allah Who has no partner. I testify that Muhammad 🙵 is the servant of Allah and His Rasul." Dimad 🙵 says that he had never heard such words from anyone before. He then requested Rasulullah 🙵 to repeat the words, which Rasulullah 🙵 repeated twice. Dimad 🙵 continues the story by saying, "I asked, 'To what are you calling people?'" Rasulullah 🙵 replied, "I call people to believe in One Allah Who has no partner. I clear myself from worshipping idols and I testify that I am the Rasul of Allah." Dimad asked, "What shall I receive if I also do the same?" Rasulullah 🙵 said, "You shall receive paradise." Dimad exclaimed, "I testify that there is none worthy of worship besides the one Allah Who has no partner. I remove the idols from my neck and express that I have cleared myself from them. I also testify that you are certainly the servant and Rasul of Allah." Dimad 🙵 says further, "I started living with Rasulullah 🙵 until I had learnt many Surahs of the Qur'an. Then I returned to my people." Abdullah bin Abdir Rahman Adawi says that Rasulullah 🙵 once dispatched an army under the command of Ali 🙵. The army got some camels from a certain place and were taking them along as they went. When Ali found out that the camels were taken from the people of Dimad 🙵, he commanded that the camels be returned.

Rasulullah 🙵 Invites Hussain 🙵, the Father of Imran bin Hussain 🙵

Some members of the Quraish approached respectfully

Hussain 🙵 and said to him, "Go to this person (Rasulullah 🙵) and speak to him on our behalf because he insults our gods." These members of the Quraish proceeded with Hussain 🙵 until they reached the door of Rasulullah 🙵's house. When Hussain 🙵 sat near the door, Rasulullah 🙵 said to the many people who had already gathered there, "Make way for the respected elder." Amongst those present was the son of Hussain 🙵 whose name was Imran 🙵. Hussain 🙵 said, "What is happening here? The news has reached me that you insult our gods whereas your father was a devout and excellent man. Rasulullah 🙵 replied, "O Hussain! My father and your father are both in hellfire. O Hussain! Tell me how many gods you worship?" Hussain replied, "I have 7 gods on earth and one in the sky." Rasulullah 🙵 further asked him, "Which god do you call for when you are in difficulty?" Hussain 🙵 replied, "I call the one in the sky." Rasulullah 🙵 said, "Who do you call when your wealth gets destroyed?" He replied, "The one in the sky." Rasulullah 🙵 said, "It is strange that only this one God comes to your assistance yet you associate others as partners to him! Do you have permission from the god in the sky to associate the others as his partners? Or are you afraid of these other gods thinking that they will harm you if you do not associate them as partners?" Hussain 🙵 replied, "Neither of these 2 statements is correct" Hussain 🙵 says, "It now occurred to me that I had never spoken to such a great personality before this." Rasulullah 🙵 said further, "O Hussain! Become a Muslim and you will live in peace." Hussain responded by saying, "What about my people and my family? What would they say if I accept Islam? What do I do now?" Rasulullah 🙵 advised him to recite this du'a, "O Allah! I seek your guidance towards that which is more correct and increase me in knowledge that will benefit me." Hussain recited this Du'a and was a Muslim and he stood up from the gathering. At that instant, his son Imran immediately stood up and began kissing the head, hands and feet of his father. Rasulullah 🙵 began weeping when he saw this and said, "I am weeping because I was touched by what Imran has done. He did not stand for his father nor pay any attention to him when he entered as a Kafir. However, he fulfilled the right of his father once his father entered the fold of Islam." When Hussain 🙵 stood up to leave, Rasulullah 🙵 said to the others, "Stand up and take him home." As soon as Hussain emerged from the doorway, the people of the Quraish who had been waiting there for him saw him and said, "He has forsaken his religion." They then left him and dispersed. *(Ibn Khuzaimah)*

Rasulullah 🙵 Invites an Unnamed Man to Islam

Abu Tamima Hujaimi 🙵 narrates that he once came to meet Rasulullah 🙵. Abu Tamima 🙵 was present when the man came to Rasulullah 🙵. The man said, "Are you the Nabi of Allah?" "Yes," replied Rasulullah 🙵. He asked, "Whom do you pray to?" Rasulullah 🙵 replied, "I pray to the One Allah Who is Most Honored and Most High. He is the One Who removes your difficulty when you call to Him. It is He Who causes your crops to grow when you call to Him to remove your drought It is He Who responds to your prayer when you call Him at the time when you are lost in a rocky land without transport" The man accepted Islam and then asked for advice. Rasulullah 🙵 said, "Do not swear anything." *(Hakam)* When relating this to people, the man said that since Rasulullah 🙵 gave him the piece of advice, he has not even sworn a goat. *(Ahmad, Haythami)*

Rasulullah 🙵 Invites Mu'awiya bin Haydah 🙵 to Islam

Mu'awiya bin Haydah 🙵 narrates that once he came to

Rasulullah ﷺ and said, "O Rasulullah ﷺ! I have not come to you before this because I have sworn more times than my fingertips can count that I shall never come to you and never accept your religion." He placed his hands on top of each other as he said this to show the number of his fingertips. Now, Allah has sent me to you, so here I am with no knowledge of that which Allah has given you. I ask you in the name of Allah to tell me what Allah has sent you with." Rasulullah ﷺ replied, "Allah has sent me with Islam." "What is Islam?" was his next question. Rasulullah ﷺ said, "Islam is to say that you surrender yourself to Allah and renounce all other gods. It also wants you to establish salah and pay Zakah. Every Muslim deserves respect and every 2 Muslims are brothers to each other and help one another. When a nonbeliever accepts Islam, his deeds will be accepted from him only when he separates himself from the other nonbelievers. Why should I be holding your waists to save you from hellfire? Listen! My Rabb shall call me on the Day of Judgment and ask me, 'Did you convey the message of Islam to my servants?' I shall then be able to say, 'O my Rabb! I have certainly conveyed it.' Understand this well! Those present here must convey the message to those who are absent. Behold! You will be called forward on the Day of Judgment with your mouths sealed. The first thing to speak will be a person's thigh followed by his hands." Mu'awiya bin Haydah ؓ asked, "O Rasulullah ﷺ! Is this our Islam?" Rasulullah ﷺ replied, "This is our Islam. If you practice on it properly, it will be sufficient for you." *(Isti'ab)*

Rasulullah ﷺ Invites Adi bin Hatim ؓ to Islam

Adi bin Hatim ؓ narrates, "When I heard about the coming of Rasulullah ﷺ, I disliked it very much. So I left and found myself close to Rome. In another narration he said, "So I left and went to the Caesar". However, I disliked this place more than I disliked the coming of Rasulullah ﷺ. I then said to myself, 'By Allah! Why not I rather meet this person? If he is a liar, it will not harm me in the least. On the other hand, if he is speaking the truth, I would know it.'" Adi bin Hatim ؓ continues the story and says, "So I came to Rasulullah ﷺ. When I arrived, the people started shouting, 'Adi bin Hatim! Adi bin Hatim!' When I came before Rasulullah ﷺ, he said to me, 'O Adi bin Hatim! Accept Islam and stay in peace.' He repeated this 3 times. I said to him, 'But I already follow a religion." He replied, 'I know more about your religion than you do.'" Adi bin Hatim ؓ says further, "I said, 'You know more about my religion than I do?' He replied, 'Yes. Are you not from the Rakosiyya sect and have taken a quarter of your people's booty? I said, 'True.' He then continued, 'This is not permissible for you according to your religion.' I admitted. 'Yes, it certainly is not permissible.' After hearing this, I was humbled before him." Rasulullah ﷺ then added, "Listen. I am also well aware of the thing that prevents you from accepting Islam. You say that only simple people who have no influence follow him; people whom the Arabs have cast out. Do you know the place Hira?" Adi ؓ replied, "Though I have never seen the place, I have certainly heard about it." Rasulullah ﷺ then said, "I swear by the Being Who controls my life! Allah shall bring Islam to such places and the land will be so safe that a veiled woman shall leave from Hira all alone and perform Tawaf of the Kabah without the need of having someone accompany her. Without doubt, the treasures of Kisra bin Hurmuz shall also be conquered." In astonishment, Adi ؓ said, "The treasures of Kisra bin Hurmuz?" "Yes," replied Rasulullah ﷺ, "The treasures of Kisra bin Hurmuz. In addition to this, wealth will be so freely spent that there will be none to take it." After narrating the story, Adi ؓ said, "There is the woman from Hira performing Tawaf

without anyone to accompany her and I was among those who conquered the treasures of Kisra. I swear by the Being in whose control is my life, the 3rd prophesy shall also come true because Rasulullah ﷺ said it." *(Ahmad)*

Adi bin Hatim ؓ narrates that he and some others were at a place called Aqrab when a group of horsemen sent by Rasulullah ﷺ arrived there. They captured some people along with Adi ؓ's aunt. When they were brought before Rasulullah ﷺ and lined up before him, his aunt said, "O Rasulullah ﷺ! My wage earner has gone missing, my children are no more and I am just an old woman who cannot be of any service. Be kind to me and Allah will be kind to you." "Who is your wage earner?" Rasulullah ﷺ asked. "Adi bin Hatim" was the reply. Rasulullah ﷺ said, "The one who escaped from Allah and His Rasul." Rasulullah ﷺ showed kindness to her by setting her free and as she was leaving, a man who had been with Rasulullah ﷺ whom they believe was Ali ؓ, said to her, "Why do you not ask Rasulullah ﷺ for transport'?" When she asked for transport, Rasulullah ﷺ ordered and had it arranged for her. Adi ؓ continues the story. He says, "When my aunt came back, she said to me, 'Your father would have never done what you did deserting me like that.' Whether you like it or not, you will have to go to him (Rasulullah ﷺ).' She counted the incidents of many people who had gone to meet Rasulullah ﷺ and enjoyed a good reception. I then proceeded to meet Rasulullah ﷺ. When I came to Rasulullah ﷺ, I saw a woman and 1 or 2 children were sitting with him very close. I gathered from this that he was neither like the king Kisra nor the Caesar but easily approachable. He said to me, 'O Adi bin Hatim! What made you run away? Did the thought of saying that there is none worthy or worship but Allah make you run away? Is there anyone worthy of worship but Allah? What made you run away? Did the thought of saying Allah is the greatest make you run away? Is there anything greater than Allah, the Most High, the Most Exalted?' I accepted Islam and I saw the face of Rasulullah ﷺ light up with happiness and he said, 'Indeed those with whom Allah is angry are the Jews and those who are astray are the Christians.'" *(Fatiha)*

Adi ؓ continues, "Then some people began asking Rasulullah ﷺ for things and because he had nothing with him, Rasulullah ﷺ encouraged the Sahabah to help these people. Rasulullah ﷺ then praised Allah and said to the people, 'O people! Spend from that wealth which is extra even though it may be one Saa or even less than that; whether it may be a handful or even less than that. One narrator named Shu'ba says that Rasulullah ﷺ also added, 'Whether it may be a single date or even a piece of a date. Everyone of you will stand before Allah on the Day of Judgment and Allah will ask him exactly as I am telling you now. Allah will say, 'Did I not bless you with the faculties of hearing and seeing'! Did I not give you wealth and children'! What have you sent ahead from this'! Then a person will look in front, behind, his right, and his left but he will find nothing there. He will have nothing to save him from the hellfire besides the favors of Allah. Therefore, save yourselves from the fire of hell even though it be with a piece of the date (that you give as charity). If you do not even have this much, then do so by speaking a kind word to a beggar. Verily I do not fear poverty overcoming you as Allah will certainly assist you and will certainly bestow His bounties upon you. According to another narration he said, "Allah will grant you many conquests" Until the time comes when a veiled woman shall travel between Hira and Madinah or even a greater distance without the fear of being robbed while sitting in her carriage." *(Ahmad, Tirmidhi, Bayhaqi)*

Rasulullah ﷺ Invites Dhi Jowshin Dhababi ؓ to Islam

Dhi Jowshin Dhababi ؓ narrates, "I came to Rasulullah ﷺ after the battle of Badr and brought with me my horse Qar'ha. I said to Rasulullah ﷺ, 'O Muhammad ﷺ! I have brought for you my horse Qar'ba so that you may use it for yourself.' Rasulullah ﷺ replied, 'I have no need for it. However, if you wish to exchange it for an armor from the battle of Badr, you could have any suit you choose.' I replied, 'I am not prepared to exchange this rare breed horse today.' Rasulullah ﷺ said, 'I have no need for it. O Dhi Jowshin! Will you not accept Islam to become among the first to accept Islam!' When I replied in the negative, Rasulullah ﷺ asked, 'Why not!' I said, 'Because I see that your people are upset with you.' He asked me, 'How did you receive the news of the defeat of the disbelievers at Badr?' I said, 'All the news has reached me.' He said, 'We will have to give you guidance to Islam.' 'One condition that you take control of the Kabah and start living there.' I responded. Rasulullah ﷺ said, 'If you are alive then, you shall certainly see it.'" Rasulullah ﷺ then said to Bilal ؓ, "O Bilal! Take the man's bag and fill it with Ajwa dates as a provision for his journey." As Dhi Jowshin ؓ was leaving, Rasulullah ﷺ said to the Sahabah, "He is among the finest horsemen of the Banu Amir tribe." Dhi Jowshin ؓ continues the story when he said, "By Allah! I was with my family in a place called Ghowr when a rider arrived. I asked him, 'What have people been doing?' He replied, 'By Allah! Muhammad ﷺ has taken control of the Kabah and is living there.' When I heard this, I said to myself, 'If only my mother had lost me as a child, if only I had accepted Islam that day, if I had even asked Rasulullah ﷺ for the district of Hira then, he would have given it to me.'" Another narration says, Rasulullah ﷺ asked him, "What prevents you from Islam!" He replied, "I see that your people believe you, have exiled you from Makkah and are now at war with you. I shall now watch developments. If you get the upper hand over your people, I shall accept Islam and follow you. However, if they get the upper hand over you, I shall not be following you. *(Tabrani, Abu Dawud)*

Rasulullah ﷺ Invites Bashir bin Khasasiya ؓ to Islam

Bashir bin Khasasiya ؓ narrates that Rasulullah ﷺ invited him to accept Islam on one occasion. After he accepted lslam, Rasulullah ﷺ asked him, "What is your name?" When he replied that his name was Nadhir, Rasulullah ﷺ said, "From today your name shall be Bashir." Rasulullah ﷺ then made him stay on the platform within the Masjid called Suffa where the poor homeless Muslims stayed. It was the practice of Rasulullah ﷺ to share all the gifts he received with the men on Suffa and give them all the Sadaqa he received. One night Rasulullah ﷺ left his home and Bashir ؓ followed him. Rasulullah ﷺ went to the graveyard called Baqi and said, "Peace be on you, O home of the Mu'minin! We shall soon join you as we all belong to Allah and shall return to Him. You people have certainly met with lot of good and have been saved from many evils." Rasulullah ﷺ then turned to Bashir ؓ and asked, "Who is there'!" When Bashir ؓ gave his name, Rasulullah ﷺ said, "Does it not please you that Allah has diverted your hearing, your heart, and your sight to Islam whereas you had been from among the Rabee'ah tribe who breed fine horses and who claim that the earth would be turned upside down if it had not been for them!" Bashir replied, "Indeed. O Rasulullah ﷺ!" Rasulullah ﷺ then asked him, "What brings you here?" Bashir ؓ replied, "I followed you here because I was afraid that a calamity may befall you or that some creature may harm you." *(Ibn Asakir, Tabrani, Bayhaqi)*

Rasulullah ﷺ Invites an Unnamed Person to Islam

A person from the Baladawiya tribe narrates from his grandfather, "As I was coming to Madinah, I pitched my tent in a valley where I saw 2 persons trading. The buyer was saying to the seller, 'Make me a good deal on this purchase.' I said to myself, 'Could this not be the Hashimi who is misleading his people!' As I watched them, another man approached. He was extremely handsome with a broad forehead, slim nose, fine eyebrows, and a black line of hair running from his chest to his navel. He was wearing 2 old sheets of cloth. He greeted us with 'Asaalamu Alaikum' and we all replied to his greeting. He has just arrived when the buyer said, 'O Rasulullah ﷺ! Tell this seller to make a good deal with me.' Rasulullah ﷺ raised his hands and said, 'You people are the owners of your goods. All I want is to meet Allah on the Day of Judgment without any of you claiming from me any wealth, any blood or any honor that I may have wrongfully taken from you. Allah showers His mercy on a person who is easy when he sells, easy when he buys, easy when he takes, easy when he gives, easy when he pays his debts and easy when he asks for payment.' After saying this, Rasulullah ﷺ left. I said to myself, 'By Allah! I must certainly have to find out about this man because his words are excellent.' I therefore followed him and shouted, 'O Muhammad ﷺ!' He turned around to face me and said, 'What is it?' I asked, 'Are you the person who has misled your people, destroyed them, and stopped them from worshipping what their forefathers worshipped?' He replied, 'That is Allah.' I asked, 'To what are you calling people?' 'I am calling the servants of Allah to Allah,' he responded. 'What have you to say?' I asked further. He said, 'That you should testify that there is none worthy of worship but Allah, that Muhammad ﷺ is the Rasul of Allah, that you believe in everything revealed to me, that you renounce Lat and Uzza, and that you establish salah, and pay Zakah.' 'What is Zakah?' I asked. 'Wealth that our rich give to our poor,' came the reply. I responded by saying, 'These are excellent things you are calling towards.' Prior to this, there was no one on earth whom I hated more than Rasulullah ﷺ. However, it was not long that he became more beloved to me than even my children, my parents and all of mankind. I then said to him, 'I have understood.' 'Have you understood?' he asked. 'Yes,' I replied. He asked, 'Do you testify that there is none worthy or worship but Allah, that I Muhammad ﷺ am the Rasul of Allah, and do you believe in everything revealed to me?' 'Yes, O Rasulullah ﷺ,' I replied. I then asked him, 'There is an oasis where many people are settled. May I invite them towards that which you have invited me? I feel that they will want to follow you.' He replied, 'Yes, you may invite them.'" Later, all the men and women of the oasis accepted Islam and in appreciation and happiness, Rasulullah ﷺ rubbed the head of this Sahabi. *(Abu Ya'la, Haythami)*. Anas bin Malik ؓ narrates that Rasulullah ﷺ was once visiting a man from the Banu Najjar tribe when he said to the man, "O uncle. Say, *'La Ilaha Illalah'*." The man asked, "Am I your maternal uncle or paternal uncle?" Rasulullah ﷺ replied, "You are my maternal uncle. Please say, *'La Ilaha Illalah'*." "Will this be good for me," the man asked. "Certainly," replied Rasulullah ﷺ. *(Ahmad, Haythami)*. Anas ؓ narrates that Rasulullah ﷺ once visited a Jewish boy who used to serve him but had fallen ill. Sitting by his head, Rasulullah ﷺ said to the boy, "Accept Islam." The boy looked at his father who was also there. The father said, "Obey Abul Qasim (Rasulullah ﷺ)." The boy accepted Islam. When Rasulullah ﷺ left the house, he said, "All praise for Allah Who has used me to save him from hellfire. *(Bukhari, Abu Dawud)*. Anas ؓ narrated that Rasulullah ﷺ once said to a person, "Accept Islam and you will remain in peace."

The person said, "But I dislike it." Rasulullah ﷺ said to him, "Even though you dislike it." *(Ahmad, Abu Ya'la, Haythami)*

Rasulullah ﷺ Invites Abu Quhafa ؓ to Islam

Asma bint Abu Bakr ؓ reports that the day Muslims conquered Makkah, Rasulullah ﷺ said to Abu Quhafa ؓ, "Accept Islam and remain in peace." *(Tabrani, Haythami)*. Asma bint Abu Bakr ؓ also reports that when Rasulullah ﷺ entered Makkah and was peacefully sitting in the Masjidul Haram, Abu Bakr ؓ brought his father Abu Quhafa to him. When Rasulullah ﷺ saw him, he said, "O Abu Bakr! Why did you not leave the respected man and take me to him instead?" Abu Bakr ؓ replied, "O Rasulullah ﷺ! It is more appropriate that he comes to you rather than you go to him." Rasulullah ﷺ made the old man sit in front of him, placed his hand on the old man's heart and said, "O Abu Quhafa! Accept Islam and remain in peace." He accepted Islam and recited the testimony of Iman (the Kalima). Abu Quhafa ؓ was brought to Rasulullah ﷺ, his hair and beard were white as the 'Tugama' plant. Rasulullah ﷺ said to him, "Change the color of these hairs but stay away from black." *(Ibn Sa'd)*

Da'wah to Individuals Who did not Accept Islam: Rasulullah ﷺ Invites Abu Jahal to Islam

Mughiera bin Shu'ba ؓ narrates that the first time he came to know about Rasulullah ﷺ was when Rasulullah ﷺ met him walking with Abu Jahal in one of the roads of Makkah. Rasulullah ﷺ said to Abu Jahal, "O Abul Hakam! Come to Allah and His Rasul. I am inviting you to Allah." Abu Jahal replied, "O Muhammad ﷺ! Will you not refrain from insulting our gods? Do you want us to testify that you have conveyed the message? We then testify that you have conveyed the message. I swear by Allah that I would have certainly followed you if I knew that whatever you say is the truth." Mughiera bin Shu'ba ؓ says that when Rasulullah ﷺ had left them, Abu Jahal said to him, "By Allah! I know for sure that whatever he says is the truth. There is only one thing that prevents me from accepting as Rasulullah ﷺ belongs to the Bani Qusay family. Bani Qusay said, 'Keeping the keys to the Kabah is our duty,' we, the other families of the Quraish accepted. When they said, 'Giving water to the people performing Hajj is our duty,' we accepted. When they said, 'Conducting the public meetings is our duty,' we accepted. When they said, 'Holding the flag during times of war is our duty,' we again accepted. When they fed people, we also fed people until we were almost equal. They say, 'We have a Nabi among us.' By Allah! This I shall never accept." *(Bayhaqi, Kanzul Ummal)*.

Rasulullah ﷺ Invites Walid bin Mughiera to Islam

Abdullah bin Abbas ؓ narrates that Rasulullah ﷺ once recited a part of the Qur'an to Walid bin Mughiera who had come to him. This caused the heart of Walid to soften. When Abu Jahal heard about this, he approached Walid saying, "O uncle! Your people intend to collect money for you." Why is this?" asked Walid. "They want to give it to you because you have been to Muhammad ﷺ to get something from him," was the reply. Walid said, "But the Quraish know well that I am among the richest people I do not need money from Muhammad ﷺ." Abu Jahal said, "Then you will have to tell them something to make them know that you have nothing to do with Muhammad ﷺ." Walid said, "What should I tell them? By Allah! None of you know as much about poetry as I do. None of you know as much about poem as I do. None of you know as much about songs as I do. None of you know as much about the poetry of the Jinn as I do. By Allah! What Muhammad ﷺ says bears no resemblance to

any of these things. By Allah! What he said is extremely sweet, beautiful and attractive. What he said is a prosperous tree the top of which bears abundant fruit and the bottom of which is very green. His words shall always be lowering without being subdued. His speech crushes all other speech." Abu Jahal said to him, "Your people shall never be pleased with you until you say something against him." Walid said, "Give me time to think about it." After thinking for a while, Walid said, "This is nothing but magic recounted from tales of the past." It was with reference to Walid that Allah revealed the following verses of the Qur'an:

ذَرْنِي وَمَنْ خَلَقْتُ وَحِيدًا (11) وَجَعَلْتُ لَهُ مَالًا مَمْدُودًا (12) وَبَنِينَ شُهُودًا (13) وَمَهَّدْتُ لَهُ تَمْهِيدًا (14) ثُمَّ يَطْمَعُ أَنْ أَزِيدَ (15) كَلَّا إِنَّهُ كَانَ لِآيَاتِنَا عَنِيدًا (16) سَأُرْهِقُهُ صَعُودًا (17) إِنَّهُ فَكَّرَ وَقَدَّرَ (18) فَقُتِلَ كَيْفَ قَدَّرَ (19) ثُمَّ قُتِلَ كَيْفَ قَدَّرَ (20) ثُمَّ نَظَرَ (21) ثُمَّ عَبَسَ وَبَسَرَ (22) ثُمَّ أَدْبَرَ وَاسْتَكْبَرَ (23) فَقَالَ إِنْ هَذَا إِلَّا سِحْرٌ يُؤْثَرُ (24) إِنْ هَذَا إِلَّا قَوْلُ الْبَشَرِ (25) سَأُصْلِيهِ سَقَرَ (26)

Leave Me Alone (to deal) with whom I created Alone (without any means, i.e. Walid bin Al-Mughiera)! And then granted him resources in abundance. And children to be by his side! And made life smooth and comfortable for him! After all that he desires that I should give more; Nay! Verily, he has been stubborn and opposing Our Ayat (verses). I shall oblige him to (climb a slippery mountain in the Hell-fire called As-Saood, or to) face a severe torment! Verily, he thought and plotted. So let him be cursed: how he plotted! And once more let him be cursed, how he plotted! Then he thought. Then he frowned and he looked in a bad tempered way; then he turned back and was proud. Then he said: "This is nothing but magic from that of old; this is nothing but the word of a human being!" I will cast him into Hell-fire. (Al-Muddaththir:11-26) (Is'haq bin Rahway, Bayhaqi) According to another narration, the verse that Rasulullah ﷺ recited for Walid was:

إِنَّ اللَّهَ يَأْمُرُ بِالْعَدْلِ وَالْإِحْسَانِ وَإِيتَاءِ ذِي الْقُرْبَى وَيَنْهَى عَنِ الْفَحْشَاءِ وَالْمُنْكَرِ وَالْبَغْيِ يَعِظُكُمْ لَعَلَّكُمْ تَذَكَّرُونَ (90)

Verily, Allah enjoins Al-Adl (justice) and Al-Ihsan (to be patient in performing your duties to Allah, totally for Allah's sake and in accordance with the Sunnah of the Prophet), and giving (help) to kith and kin and forbids Al-Fahsha (all evil deeds) and Al-Munkar (all that is prohibited by Islam), and Al-Baghy (all kinds of oppression). He admonishes you, that you may take heed. (An-Nahl:90) (Al Bidayah wan Nihayah, Ibn Kathir)

Da'wah to Pairs: Rasulullah ﷺ Invites Abu Sufyan ؓ and Hind ؓ

Mu'awiya ؓ narrates that he was a young boy riding his donkey while his father Abu Sufyan ؓ was riding another animal with his wife Hind sitting behind him. They were passing by Abu Sufyan ؓ's farm when they heard the voice of Rasulullah ﷺ. Addressing his son, Abu Sufyan ؓ said, "O Mu'awiya! Get off from the donkey so that Muhammad ﷺ may ride." When Rasulullah ﷺ got on the donkey, he rode ahead for a while and then turned to the family saying, "O Abu Sufyan bin Harb! O Hind bint Utba! I swear by Allah that you will definitely die, after which you will certainly be resurrected. Thereafter, the good people will proceed to paradise while the evil ones will proceed to hell. I am telling you the absolute truth and you 2 are among the very first to be warned about Allah's punishment." Thereafter, Rasulullah ﷺ recited the verses of the Qur'an:

بِسْمِ اللَّهِ الرَّحْمَنِ الرَّحِيمِ

حم (1) تَنْزِيلٌ مِنَ الرَّحْمَنِ الرَّحِيمِ (2) كِتَابٌ فُصِّلَتْ آيَاتُهُ قُرْآنًا عَرَبِيًّا لِقَوْمٍ يَعْلَمُونَ (3) بَشِيرًا وَنَذِيرًا فَأَعْرَضَ أَكْثَرُهُمْ فَهُمْ لَا يَسْمَعُونَ (4) وَقَالُوا قُلُوبُنَا فِي أَكِنَّةٍ مِمَّا تَدْعُونَا إِلَيْهِ وَفِي

آذَانَا وَقْرٌ وَمِنْ بَيْنِنَا وَبَيْنِكَ حِجَابٌ فَاعْمَلْ إِنَّنَا عَامِلُونَ (5) قُلْ إِنَّمَا أَنَا بَشَرٌ مِثْلُكُمْ يُوحَى إِلَيَّ أَنَّمَا إِلَهُكُمْ إِلَهٌ وَاحِدٌ فَاسْتَقِيمُوا إِلَيْهِ وَاسْتَغْفِرُوهُ وَوَيْلٌ لِلْمُشْرِكِينَ (6) الَّذِينَ لَا يُؤْتُونَ الزَّكَاةَ وَهُمْ بِالْآخِرَةِ هُمْ كَافِرُونَ (7) إِنَّ الَّذِينَ آمَنُوا وَعَمِلُوا الصَّالِحَاتِ لَهُمْ أَجْرٌ غَيْرُ مَمْنُونٍ (8) قُلْ أَئِنَّكُمْ لَتَكْفُرُونَ بِالَّذِي خَلَقَ الْأَرْضَ فِي يَوْمَيْنِ وَتَجْعَلُونَ لَهُ أَنْدَادًا ذَلِكَ رَبُّ الْعَالَمِينَ (9) وَجَعَلَ فِيهَا رَوَاسِيَ مِنْ فَوْقِهَا وَبَارَكَ فِيهَا وَقَدَّرَ فِيهَا أَقْوَاتَهَا فِي أَرْبَعَةِ أَيَّامٍ سَوَاءً لِلسَّائِلِينَ (10) ثُمَّ اسْتَوَى إِلَى السَّمَاءِ وَهِيَ دُخَانٌ فَقَالَ لَهَا وَلِلْأَرْضِ ائْتِيَا طَوْعًا أَوْ كَرْهًا قَالَتَا أَتَيْنَا طَائِعِينَ (11)

In the name of Allah the Most Gracious, the Most Merciful. HaMeem. A revelation from Allah, the Most Beneficent, the Most Merciful. A Book whereof the verses are explained in detail; a Qur'an in Arabic for people who know. Giving glad tidings and fears Allah much (abstains from all kinds of sins and evil deeds) and loves Allah much (performing all kinds of good deeds which He has ordained), and warning (of punishment in the Hell), but most of them turn away, so they listen not. And they say: "Our hearts are under coverings (screened) from that to which you invite us, and in our ears is deafness, and between us and you is a screen, so work you (on your way); verily, we are working (on our way)." Say (O Muhammad ﷺ): "I am only a human being like you. It is inspired in me that your Ilah (God) is One Ilah (Allah), therefore take Straight Path to Him and obedience to Him, and seek forgiveness of Him. And woe to Al-Mushrikoon (the disbelievers). Those who give not the Zakat and they are disbelievers in the Hereafter. Truly, those who believe (in the Oneness of Allah) and do righteous good deeds, for them will be an endless reward that will never stop (i.e. Paradise). Say (O Muhammad ﷺ): "Do you verily disbelieve in Him Who created the earth in two Days and you set up rivals (in worship) with Him? That is the Lord of the Alameen (mankind, jinns and all that exists). He placed therein (i.e. the earth) firm mountains from above it, and He blessed it, and measured therein its sustenance (for its dwellers) in 4 Days equal, for all those who ask (about its creation). Then He Istawa (rose over) towards the heaven when it was smoke, and said to it and to the earth: "Come both of you willingly or unwillingly." They both said: "We come, willingly." (Fussilat:1-11)

Abu Sufyan ﷺ said, "Have you finished, O Muhammad ﷺ'?" Rasulullah ﷺ replied, "Yes" and then got off from the donkey. When Mu'awiya ﷺ got on it again, Hind turned to Abu Sufyan ﷺ and said, "Did you make my son got off for that magician'?" Abu Sufyan ﷺ replied, "I swear by Allah that he is neither a magician nor a liar." *(Kanzul Ummal, Tabrani, Haythami)*

Rasulullah ﷺ Invites Talha ﷺ and Zubair ﷺ to Islam

Yazid bin Ruman narrates that Uthman ﷺ and Talha ﷺ followed Zubair ﷺ to Rasulullah ﷺ. When Talha ﷺ and Zubair ﷺ came to Rasulullah ﷺ, he presented Islam to them, recited the Qur'an to them, informed them about the rights of Islam and promised them Allah's generosity. Both of them accepted Islam and acknowledged the message. Uthman ﷺ then said, "O Rasulullah ﷺ! I have just arrived from Sham. We were between Ma'an and Zarqa, we fell into sleep and then heard a caller announcing, 'O you sleeping ones! Get up because Ahmad had appeared in Makkah. We then heard of you when we reached." Uthman ﷺ was among the first to accept Islam even before Rasulullah ﷺ started coming to the house of Arqam. *(Ibn Sa'd).*

Rasulullah ﷺ Invites Ammar ﷺ and Suhaib ﷺ to Islam

Amar bin Yasir ﷺ narrates, "I met Suhaib bin Sanan ﷺ at the door of Arqam's house. I asked him, 'What are you doing here?' He asked me, 'What are you doing here?' I replied, 'I want to meet Muhammad ﷺ and hear what he has to say.' He then said, 'I have the same intention.' We entered the house and met Rasulullah ﷺ. He presented Islam to us and we both accepted. We then stayed there the entire day until the evening then we left silently." Amar bin Yasir ﷺ and Suhaib ﷺ accepted Islam after 30 odd people had accepted. May Allah be pleased with all of them. *(Ibn Sa'd)*

Rasulullah ﷺ Invites Sa'd bin Zurarah ﷺ and Dhakwan bin Abd Qais ﷺ to Islam

Khubaib bin Abdir Rahman ﷺ narrates that Sa'd bin Zurarah ﷺ and Dhakwan bin Abd Qais ﷺ came to Makkah to settle a dispute with Utba bin Rabee'ah. When they arrived and heard about Rasulullah ﷺ, they both went to him. Rasulullah ﷺ presented Islam, recited the Qur'an to them, and they both accepted Islam without even getting close to Utba bin Rabee'ah. Sa'd bin Zurarah ﷺ and Dhakwan bin Abd Qais ﷺ were therefore the first people from Madinah to accept Islam. *(Ibn Sa'd)*

Da'wah to Groups: The Leaders of the Quraish Dispute the Da'wah of Rasulullah ﷺ

Abdullah bin Abbas ﷺ narrates that several leaders of the Quraish gathered behind the Kabah for a meeting after sunset. Among them were Utba and Shaiba the 2 sons of Rabee'ah, Abu Sufyan bin Harb, someone from the Abid Dar tribe, Abul Bakhtari from the Banu Asad tribe, Aswad bin Abdil Muttalib bin Asad, Zam'ah bin Al Aswad, Walid bin Mughiera, Abu Jahal bin Hisham, Abdullah bin Abi Umayyah, Umayyah bin Khalaf, Aas bin Wa'il, and Nabeeh and Munabbah - the 2 sons of Hajjaj from the Banu Sahm tribe. They decided to send someone to call Rasulullah ﷺ to them to speak frankly and clear out matters so that people would know that they had made every effort to resolve matters. The message reached Rasulullah ﷺ that the leaders of his people have gathered to speak to him. Rasulullah ﷺ hurried to meet them thinking that they had changed their opinions about him and would be ready to accept Islam as he was always eager for their welfare, always desired that they be rightly guided, and always distressed by their sinful ways. When Rasulullah ﷺ sat with them, they said, "O Muhammad ﷺ! We have sent for you so that people may know that we have done our best to persuade you. By Allah! We do not know of any other Arab who has distressed his people as you have done. You have insulted our forefathers, defamed against our religion, made our leaders seem foolish, abused our gods, and disrupted our unity. In fact, you have done everything possible to spoil relations between us. If it is wealth that you want by propagating your message, we shall accumulate wealth to make you the richest person amongst us. If it is honor that you want, we shall make you our leader. If it is kingship you aspire for, we shall make you our king. If you are doing this because you have been afflicted by evil spirits that have overwhelmed you, then we shall spend all our fortunes until you are cured or until we grow helpless in finding a cure for you." Rasulullah ﷺ replied, "I seek none of the things you have mentioned. I have brought the message of Islam to you and I am not in search of your wealth nor to attain honor or kingship. Allah has sent me as a messenger to you. Allah has revealed a book to me and commanded me that I convey glad tidings to you if you accept Islam and warn you at the same time. I have therefore conveyed to you the messages of my Rabb and I have given you sound advice. If you accept what I have brought to you, you shall be fortunate in this world as well as in the Hereafter. On the other hand, if you reject this, I shall wait for the decision of Allah when He decides matters between myself and you people." After listening to him, the leaders of the Quraish said, "O Muhammad ﷺ! You would not accept any of our proposals, you know very well that there is no city more restricted than ours, no nation poorer than us, and none who lives more difficult than ours. Therefore, ask your Rabb who has sent you to move these mountains from us that have restricted us, to expand our city, to cause rivers to flow like the rivers of Sham and Iraq. In addition to this, ask Him to bring back our forefathers to life who have passed away. Amongst these He should bring back to life Qusay bin Kilab because he was a pious person. We shall then ask him whether you are truthful in your claim or not. If you fulfill all that we have asked you and if our forefathers verify what you say, then we shall believe you and acknowledge your status with Allah. We shall then acknowledge that Allah has sent you as a messenger as you claim. In response to this, Rasulullah ﷺ said, "I have not been sent for this reason. I have been sent to you people with that which Allah has sent me for and I have already conveyed to you that which Allah has sent me with. If you accept it, you shall meet good fortune in this world as well as in the next. If you reject this, I shall patiently await the command of Allah when He decides matters between yourselves and me."

The disbelievers then said, "If you do not wish to do this, then at least do this for yourself that you ask your Rabb to send an angel to verify what you say and give answers on your behalf. You should also ask Him to grant you orchards, treasures and palaces of gold and silver by which you would become independent of the things we assume you are pressing after because you merely stand in the market places and earn a living just as we do. If you do this, we shall acknowledge your high standing in the sight of your Rabb. This you would do if you are really a Nabi as you claim." Rasulullah ﷺ said to them, "I shall not do this. I am not one to ask my Rabb for such things and I have not been sent to you for this reason. However, Allah has sent me is a bearer of glad tidings and as a warner. If you accept what I say, you shall meet good fortune in this world as well as in the next. On the other hand, if you reject this, I shall patiently await the command of Allah when He decides matters between yourselves and me." Then disbelievers then said, "In that case, cause the sky to fall on us as you claim your Rabb is able to do if He pleases. We shall never believe you unless you do this." Rasulullah ﷺ said to them, "That is left to Allah. If He wills, He would make it happen." They said, "O Muhammad ﷺ! Did your Rabb not know that we will be sitting with you and asking you for these things? Could He not have informed you earlier about the questions we will be asking and the replies you ought to be giving? Could He not have told you what He would do well with us if we refused to accept what you say? The news has reached us that you have learnt everything you say from a man in Yamamah whose name is Rahman. By Allah! we shall never believe in Rahman! O Muhammad ﷺ! We have placed everything before you without leaving anything behind. By Allah! We shall never leave you alone and will keep seeking revenge for what He and you had done to us. Eventually, it will be us who will finish you off or you who will finish us off." Thereafter one of them said, "We worship the angels who are the daughters of Allah." Another said, "We shall never believe you until you bring Allah and the angels all before us." When they had said this, Rasulullah ﷺ stood up and left them. His cousin by the name of Abdullah bin Abi Umayyah bin Mughiera bin Abdullah bin Omar bin Makhzum who was the son of Rasulullah's paternal aunt Atika also stood up with him and said,

"O Muhammad ﷺ! Your people presented to you what they had to say but you refused to accept any of their proposals. Thereafter they asked you for some things they require by which they could recognize your high status in the sight of Allah, but you refused to do even this. Eventually they asked you to hasten the punishment about which you had been warning them. I swear by Allah and that I shall never believe in you until I see you set up a staircase leading to the heavens, climb it and return with an open scripture together with 4 angels who would testify that you are as you claim you are. By Allah! I think that I would not even believe you after you do this." He then turned away from Rasulullah ﷺ, leaving Rasulullah ﷺ to return to his family in a state of sadness and because not only was his wish for them to accept Islam left unfulfilled, but because he noticed that they were drifting further away from him. *(Ibn Jareer, Ibn Kathir, Al Bidayah wan Nihayah)*

Rasulullah ﷺ Invites Abil Hashim and Youths From the Banu Abdil Ash'hal to Islam

Mahmood bin Labid from the Banu Abdil Ash'hal tribe narrates that Abul Haysim Anas bin Rati and some youths from the Banu Abdil Ash'hal tribe arrived in Makkah to conclude a treaty with the Quraish on behalf of their tribe the Khazraj. Among these youths was Ilyas bin Mu'adh. When Rasulullah ﷺ heard about their arrival, he approached them and said, "Do you desire something better than that which has brought you?" They replied, "What is it'?" He said, "I am the Rasul of Allah. Allah has sent me to his servants to call them to worship Him without ascribing any partners to Him. Allah has also revealed a book to me. Rasulullah ﷺ then spoke to them about the beauty of Islam and recited a part of the Qur'an to them. Ilyas bin Mu'adh who was still a young boy said to the people, "By Allah! This is certainly better than that which has brought you here." Abul Haysim Anas bin Rafi threw a handful of pebbles into the face of Ilyas and said, "Ignore this. I swear by my life that we have come for some other purpose." Ilyas remained silent and Rasulullah ﷺ left them. The group later left for Madinah. This occurred during the period when the Aws and Khazraj tribes were fighting a prolonged battle called "Bu'ath". It was not long thereafter that Ilyas passed away. Mahmood bin Labid narrates further that the people who were with Ilyas at the time of his death informed him that they heard Ilyas reciting the words "La Ilaha Illallah", "Allahu Akbar" and "Subhanallah" until he died. There is no doubt about the fact that he died as a Muslim. He had accepted Islam as soon as he received the invitation directly from Rasulullah ﷺ. *(Kanzul Ummal, Ahmad, Tabrani, Haytham)*

The Da'wah of Rasulullah ﷺ to Large Gatherings

Rasulullah ﷺ invites his close relatives to Islam together with various tribes of the Quraish upon the revelation of a verse. Abdullah bin Abbas ؓ narrates that Rasulullah ﷺ climbed the hill of Marwah when the following verse of the Qur'an was revealed: وَأَنْذِرْ عَشِيرَتَكَ الْأَقْرَبِينَ (214)

And warn your tribe (O Muhammad ﷺ) of near relatives. (Ash-Shuara':214)

From the top of the hill, Rasulullah ﷺ called out, "O the family of Fahr! to this call, the Quraish arrived. Abu Lahab bin Abdul Muttalib said, "The Fahr tribe are present before you, so say your piece?" Rasulullah ﷺ called, "O the family of Ghalib!" So the Banu Maharib and Banu Harith tribes, who were the descendants of Fahr returned. Then Rasulullah ﷺ called, "O the family of Luway bin Ghalib!" So the Banu Taymul Adram tribe, who were the descendants of Ghalib returned. Thereafter,

Rasulullah ﷺ called, "O the family of Ka'b bin Luway!" So the Banu Amir tribe, who were the descendants of Luway returned. Then Rasulullah ﷺ called, "O the family of Murrah bin Ka'b!" So the Banu Adi bin Ka'b, the Banu Salim and the Banu Jumah bin Amr bin Husays tribes, who were all the descendants of Ka'b bin Luway returned. Then Rasulullah ﷺ called, "O the family of Kilab bin Murrah!" So the Banu Makhzum bin Yaqzah and Banu Taym tribes, who were the descendants of Murrah returned. Then Rasulullah ﷺ called, "O the family of Qusay!" So the Banu Zuhrah tribe, who were the descendants of Qusay returned. Then Rasulullah ﷺ called, "O the family of Abd Manaf!" So the Banu Abdud Dar, the Banu Asad bin Abdil Uzza and Banu Abd tribes, who were the descendants of Qusay returned. Abu Lahab then said, "The Abd Manaf tribe are present before you, so say your message?" Rasulullah ﷺ then spoke, "Allah has commanded me to warn my closest relatives and you are the closest to me from among the Quraish. I can do nothing on your behalf in the court of Allah, nor can I do anything in your favor in the Hereafter unless you say, 'La Ilaha Illallah'. If you do so, I shall testify to this in the court of your Rabb. At the same time, all the Arabs shall be in your control and the non-Arabs shall be submissive to you." Abu Lahab retorted by saying, "May you be destroyed! Have you called us for this?!" It was in response to this that Allah revealed the verses: (1) تَبَّتْ يَدَا أَبِي لَهَبٍ وَتَبَّ

Perish the 2 hands of Abu Lahab (an uncle of the Prophet), and perish him! (Al-Masad) (Kanzul Ummal)

Abdullah bin Abbas ؓ narrates that Rasulullah ﷺ climbed the hill of Safa when the following verse of the Qur'an was revealed: (214) وَأَنذِرْ عَشِيرَتَكَ الْأَقْرَبِينَ

And warn your tribe (O Muhammad ﷺ) of near relatives. (Ash-Shuara:214)

He then called out, "Ya Sabahah!" In response to this call, everyone gathered around Rasulullah ﷺ, some came themselves, while others sent representatives. Addressing them, Rasulullah ﷺ said, "O the family of Abdul Muttalib! O the family of Fahr! O the family of Ka'b! Tell me. Would you believe me if I told you that the enemy cavalry was preparing to attack you from the foot of this hill?" When they all responded in the affirmative, Rasulullah ﷺ said, "I am then warning you of a severe punishment." Abu Lahab snapped, "May you be destroyed for all the day! Have you called us for this?!" It was in response to this that Allah revealed the verses: (1) تَبَّتْ يَدَا أَبِي لَهَبٍ وَتَبَّ

Perish the 2 hands of Abu Lahab (an uncle of the Prophet), and perish him! (Al-Masad) (Ajmad, Bukhari, Muslim)

The Da'wah of Rasulullah ﷺ to Various Arab Tribes During the Hajj

Abdullah bin Ka'b bin Malik narrates that Rasulullah ﷺ gave Da'wah secretly for the first 3 years. It was during the 4th year that he openly began calling people to Islam. This continued for the next 10 years in Makkah. During this time, Rasulullah ﷺ invited people to Islam wherever people for Hajj stayed when they arrived, even at the marketplaces of Ukaz, Majina and Dhil Majaz. He used to even find out about the place where each individual tribe stayed. He requested them to grant him asylum so that he could propagate the message of Allah, with the promise of paradise in return for them. However, he found none to assist him. When he reached the Banu Amir bin Sa'sa'h tribe, they ill-treated him like no other tribe did. When he was leaving them, they actually threw stones at him. When Rasulullah ﷺ met the Banu Muharib tribe, he spoke to one of them who was 120 years old. Rasulullah ﷺ invited him to Islam and requested that they offer him asylum so that he may propagate the message of

Allah. However, the old man said, "O person! Your people know your condition better. By Allah! Whoever takes you back to their locality will return with the worst thing a person performing Hajj could return with this season. Stay away from us." All this time, Abu Lahab had been listening to the conversation. He approached the old man of the Banu Muharib and said, "If all the people this season would had been like you, he (Rasulullah ﷺ) would have forsaken the religion he practices. He is an irreligious liar." The old man said, "By Allah! You know him better for he is your brother's son and your own flesh." Addressing Abu Lahab, the old man said, "O Abu Utba! Is he perhaps not insane? We have with us a man from the tribe who will know how to cure him." Abu Lahab gave no reply. However, whenever Abu Lahab saw Rasulullah ﷺ standing with a tribe calling them to Islam he would shout out, "He is irreligious! He is a liar! *(Abu Nu'ayn in Dala'ilum Nabawa)*

Rasulullah ﷺ Invites the Banu Abs Tribe to Islam

Wabisa narrates from his grandfather that their tribe was stationed close to the first Jamara in Mina near the Masjid Khaif when Rasulullah ﷺ came to them riding. Mounted behind him on the same animal was Zaid bin Haritha ؓ. He says, "Rasulullah ﷺ invited us to accept Islam but by Allah, we failed to accept his invitation and thus committed a grave crime." He continues, "We had already heard about the message of Rasulullah ﷺ during Hajj season and when he came to us and gave us the message, we did not accept it. With us was Maysara bin Masruq Absi who said, 'I swear by Allah that it will be an excellent idea to believe this man and to take him with us to our locality and keep him with us. I swear by Allah that the words of this man shall soon be dominant and reach the entire world.' The people said to him, 'Forget this talk. Why do you present to us something that we do not have the strength to handle?'" After hearing what Maysara had to say, Rasulullah ﷺ became hopeful that he would accept Iman, so he spoke to him further. Maysara said to Rasulullah ﷺ, "What you are speaking is most excellent and extremely enlightening. However, my people are opposing me and a man has to do as his people do. If a man's own people do not support him, how can he expect his enemies to treat him?" Rasulullah ﷺ then left. As the people left, Maysara ؓ told them to proceed to Fidak because many Jews lived there and they could ask the Jews about Rasulullah ﷺ. When they approached the Jews asked about Rasulullah ﷺ), the Jews took out a book, placed it before them and read to them about Rasulullah ﷺ. It read, "The unlettered Arab Nabi shall ride a camel and shall live on very little to eat. He shall neither be too tall nor too short and his hair shall neither be very curly nor extremely straight. His eyes shall have red lines and his complexion shall be fair with tone of red." After reading this much the Jews said, "If the person who invited you fits this description, you should believe in him and adopt his religion. We shall not follow him because we are jealous of him and we shall fight battles against him on many occasions. There shall not be an Arab who does not either follow him or fight him, so you should be among those who follow him." Upon hearing this, Maysara ؓ turned to his people and said, "O people! The matter is now clear." The people said, "We shall return the following Hajj season to meet him." So they returned to their homes. However, their leaders refused to let them return for the following Hajj and therefore none of them were able to see Rasulullah ﷺ. Rasulullah ﷺ later migrated to Madinah and it was then when he performed the farewell Hajj that he met Maysara ؓ and recognized him. Maysara ؓ asked, "O Rasulullah ﷺ! By Allah! I was eager to follow you from the day you stopped your camel by us, but matters took their course as they did. As you see, Allah had decided that I become a Muslim much later. Most of those who were with me have passed away. Where have they gone to without Islam?" Rasulullah ﷺ replied, "All those who have passed away while following a religion other than Islam are in the fire of hell." Maysara ؓ said, "All praise is due to Allah who has saved me." He then accepted Islam and was a very good Muslim. He also enjoyed a respectable standing with Abu Bakr ؓ. (Abu Nu'aym, Al Bidayah wan Nihayah)

Rasulullah ﷺ Invites the Kindah Tribe to Islam

Ibn Ruman, Abdullah bin Abi Bakr ؓ and others have reported that Rasulullah ﷺ approached the Kindah tribe at their camp near the market of Ukaz. Never before he met a tribe that was so soft-spoken. When Rasulullah ﷺ realized how soft-spoken and loving they were, he addressed them saying, "I call you towards the One Allah Who has no partners and that if you protect me like you protect yourselves, you shall have your choice once I with the message of Islam become dominant." Most of the people said, "These words are excellent but we worship the gods that our forefathers used to worship." One of the youngest person said, "O my people! Hurry to receive this man before you are beaten to it. By Allah! The Ahlul Kitab have been saying that the time is close when a Nabi shall emerge from the Haram." To this, a one-eyed man from the tribe stood up and said, "Be silent and hear me! His own people have driven him out yet you want to shelter him and thus bear fighting all the Arabs! You cannot do this! I repeat: You cannot do this!" Rasulullah ﷺ then left them feeling very grieved. When the tribe returned home and informed their people about the incident, a Jew said to them, "You people have missed a golden opportunity. Had you received this man, you would have become the leaders of the Arabs. We have the description of this man in our scriptures. As he described Rasulullah ﷺ from the scriptures, those people who had seen Rasulullah ﷺ confirmed every description he gave. The Jew said further, "We have in our scriptures that he shall appear in Makkah and then migrate to Yathrib (Madinah)." The people then decided that they would meet Rasulullah ﷺ the following Hajj season, but none of them got to meet him because one of their leaders prevented them from going for Hajj that season. When the Jew passed away, he was heard accepting Rasulullah ﷺ as Allah's Nabi and believed in him. (Abu Nu'aym in Dala'ilum Nubuwa)

Rasulullah ﷺ Invites the Banu Ka'b Tribe to Islam

Abdur Rahmaan Al Amiri narrates from the elders of his tribe that they were in the marketplace of Ukaz when Rasulullah ﷺ approached them. When he asked them which tribe they belonged to, they replied that they belonged to the Banu Amir bin Sa'sa'h tribe. Rasulullah ﷺ asked, "Which family of the Banu Amir?" "The descendants of Ka'b bin Rabee'ah," came the reply. Rasulullah ﷺ asked them, "How strong are you'?" They replied, "None would dare to touch anything in our territory or even warm himself at our fireplace." Rasulullah ﷺ then said to them, "I am the Rasul of Allah. If I come to you, will you grant me protection so that I may propagate the message of my Rabb? I shall not force any of you into anything." The people asked, "To which family of the Quraish do you belong?" "To the family of Abdul Muttalib," Rasulullah ﷺ replied. They then asked, "How have the family of Abd Manaf treated you?" Rasulullah ﷺ said, "They were the first to reject me and discard me." The people said, "But we shall not discard you nor shall we believe in you. However, we shall protect you so that you may propagate the message of your Rabb." Rasulullah ﷺ then joined them with the intention to return with them to their territory. In the meantime, the tribe continued trading in the marketplace when Bujra bin Qais Qushairi came to them and said, "Who is this with you? I do not recognize him." "He is Muhammad ﷺ bin Abdullah from the Quraish," they replied. "What you people are doing with him?" Bujra asked. They said, "He claims that he is the Rasul of Allah and asked us to grant him asylum so that he could propagate the message of his Rabb." Bujra asked further, "What was your reply?" They said, "We welcomed him and told him that we shall protect him as we protect ourselves." Bujra told them, "As far as I am concerned, no one in this marketplace shall return with anything worse than that with which you shall return. You are doing something that will cause all the Arabs to shun you and wage war with you. His people know him better. Had there been any good in him, they would have considered it a privilege to support him. He is a foolish man whose people have discarded him and rejected him yet you people wish to give him shelter and assist him! Your decision is evil indeed!" Bujra then went to Rasulullah ﷺ and said, "Get up and return to your people! By Allah! Had you been among my people, I would have severed your head!" When Rasulullah ﷺ mounted his camel, the wicked Bujra stabbed the camel with a stick in its abdomen, causing it jump and throw Rasulullah ﷺ off. Subagha bint Amir bin Qurt ؓ who was one of the ladies who accepted Islam in Makkah happened to be visiting her cousins there. When she saw this, she said, "O children of Amir! None of you are like Amir to me if you do not help Rasulullah ﷺ. Can any of you do something when this has happened to the prophet of Allah right in front of you?!" In response to her request, 3 of her cousins stood up and attacked Bujra, while 2 other men stood up to defend Bujra. The 3 cousins grounded their opponents, sat on their chests and beat them up. Rasulullah ﷺ said, "O Allah! Bless these 3 cousins and curse those!" Consequently, the 3 who assisted Rasulullah ﷺ, accepted Islam and died as martyrs while the others died under the curse of Allah. The names of the 2 who helped Bujra were Hazn bin Abdullah and Mu'awiya bin Ubadah while the 3 who helped Rasulullah ﷺ were Urwa bin Abdullah ؓ and Ghitref and Ghatfan the 2 sons of Sahl. (Abu Nu'aym in Dala'ilum Nubuwah, Al Bidayah wan Nihayah)

Zuhri رحمة الله narrates that Rasulullah ﷺ met the Banu Amir bin Sa'sa'h tribe and presented Islam and himself before them to accept Islam and to assist him. Among the members of this tribe was a person named Bajira bin Firas who said, "If I could hold on to this person, I could destroy all the Arabs with him." He then said to Rasulullah ﷺ, "You say that if we support you in your effort and then Allah grants you victory over your enemies, shall we then have kingship?" Rasulullah ﷺ replied, "The decision rests with Allah. He shall grant kingship to whoever He pleases." Bajira exclaimed, "Hear! Hear! We should risk our necks in front of the Arabs and then when Allah grants you victory, others will receive kingship! We have no need for your effort." Upon this, all the members of the tribe rejected the message of Rasulullah ﷺ. When all the people left after performing Hajj, the Banu Amir tribe also left. Whenever they reached home, they would discuss their experiences to a very old man of their tribe who could not perform the Hajj with them. They told him that a Quraishi man from the family of Abdul Muttalib who claimed to be a Nabi had approached them asking for their protection, their support and to be taken back to their area. When he heard the incident, the old man held his head and said, "Oh Banu Amir! Can there be any correction for the damage done! Can you ever hold of this bird's tail again! I swear by the being in whose control lays the life of a person! To this day no descendant of Ishmael صلى الله عليه وسلم has ever made a false claim to Prophethood. His claim to Prophethood is absolutely true. Where have you lost your senses?!" *(Ibn Is'haq in Al-Bidayah wan Nihayah, Abu Nu'aym)*. Zuhri رحمة الله has also narrated that Rasulullah ﷺ met the Kindah tribe at the place where they were staying while one of their leaders by the name of Mulay was with them. Rasulullah ﷺ invited them to Allah and placed himself before them to accept Islam and to assist him. However, they refused to accept his message. *(Ibn Is'haq)*

Rasulullah ﷺ Invites the Bani Kalb to Islam

Muhammad ﷺ bin Abdur Rahman bin Hussain narrates that Rasulullah ﷺ approached a family of the Banu Kalb tribe called the Banu Abdullah at the place where they were staying. Rasulullah ﷺ invited them to Allah and placed himself before them to accept Islam and to assist him. He said to them, "Allah has given your father a wonderful name because Abdullah means "the servant of Allah" They refused to accept his message.

Rasulullah ﷺ Invites the Bani Hanifa to Islam

Abdullah bin Ka'b bin Malik ﷺ narrates that Rasulullah ﷺ approached the Banu Hanifa tribe at the place where they were staying. Rasulullah ﷺ invited them to Allah and placed himself before them to accept Islam and to assist him. However, there was an Arab tribe that rejected his message in a manner worse than they did. *(Al Bidayah wan Nihayah)*

Rasulullah ﷺ Invites the Banu Bakr to Islam

Abbas ﷺ narrates that Rasulullah ﷺ once said to him, "I do not see any help coming from you and your brother. Will you not take me to the marketplace tomorrow so that we may stop at the places where the various tribes are staying?" This was during the time when all the Arabs were gathered there in Makkah for the Hajj. They then left for the marketplace, where Abbas ﷺ showed Rasulullah ﷺ the camps of the various tribes. Continuing the narration, Abbas ﷺ says that he pointed out to Rasulullah ﷺ, "This is the Kindah tribe and those who are with them. They are the best of tribes from Yemen performing Hajj." Pointing towards the camps of other tribes, Abbas ﷺ further said, "This is the camp of the Banu Bakr bin Wa'il tribe and that is the Banu Amir bin Sa'sa'h camp. You may choose whichever tribe you like to talk." Rasulullah ﷺ started by meeting the Kindah tribe. He approached them and said, "Where do you people come from?" They replied, "From the people of Yemen." "From which tribe of Yemen?" asked Rasulullah ﷺ. "From the Kindah tribe," they responded. Rasulullah ﷺ further asked them, "Which family of the Kindah tribe do you belong?" They said, "The Banu Amr bin Mu'awiyah family." Rasulullah ﷺ then asked them, "Do you want something good?" "What is it?" they asked. Rasulullah ﷺ said to them, "That you should testify that there is none worthy of worship but Allah, that you establish salah, and that you believe in everything that has come from Allah." According to a report from the elders of the Kindah tribe, the people of Kindah then said to Rasulullah ﷺ, "If you are successful, shall we receive kingship thereafter?" Rasulullah ﷺ replied, "All kingship belongs to Allah and He shall grant it to whomsoever He pleases." The people then said, "We have no need for the message that you have brought to us." According to a report of Kalbi, they said to Rasulullah ﷺ, "Have you come to us to prevent us from worshipping our gods and so that we should oppose the Arabs? Go back to your people as we have no need for you." After leaving them, Rasulullah ﷺ approached the Banu Bakr bin Wa'il tribe. He asked them, "Where do you people come from?" They

replied, "We are from Banu Bakr bin Wa'il tribe." Rasulullah ﷺ further asked them, "From which family of the Banu Bakr bin Wa'il tribe do you belong?" "From the Banu Qais bin Tha'laba family," they responded. Rasulullah ﷺ asked them, "How large are your numbers?" "We are as many as the grains of sand," they boasted. "What authority do you have?" asked Rasulullah ﷺ. "None," they replied, "The Persians are our neighbors and we can neither defend ourselves against them nor defend anyone else against them." Rasulullah ﷺ said to them, "If you people steadfastly take it on your shoulders to recite 'Subhanallah' 33 times, 'Al Hamdulillah' 33 times and 'Allahu Akbar' 34 times, you shall see a time if Allah wishes when you would live in the homes of the Persians, marry their women and take their sons as your slaves." "Who are you?" they asked. Rasulullah ﷺ replied, "I am the messenger of Allah." Rasulullah then left them. According to a report of Kalbi, Rasulullah ﷺ's uncle Abu Lahab always followed him and said to the people, "Do not accept what he has to say." When Rasulullah ﷺ had left the people and Abu Lahab was passing by them, they asked him, "Do you know this man?" Abu Lahab replied, "Yes. He is a man of high status among us. What do you wish to know about him?" When the people informed Abu Lahab about the talk Rasulullah ﷺ had given to them and that he claimed to be Allah's Rasul; Abu Lahab laughed, "Do not even raise your head to speak to him for he is insane and speaks without thinking." The people said, "That is what we thought when he told us about the Persians." *(Al Bidayah wan Nihayah)*

Rasulullah ﷺ Invites Various Tribes to Islam at Mina

Rabe'ah bin Ibad ﷺ narrates that he was a youngster with his father at Mina when Rasulullah ﷺ stopped at the camps of various Arab tribes saying to them, "O people of this tribe! I am indeed Allah's Rasul to you, instruct you to worship Allah Alone without ascribing any partners to Him and to forsake these idols that you worship. I further direct you to believe in me, to accept me and to offer me asylum so that I may clearly express that which Allah has sent me with." Rabe'ah bin Ibad ﷺ says further that Rasulullah ﷺ was being followed by a handsome man whose hair was divided into 2 locks and who was wearing clothes from Aden. When Rasulullah ﷺ had completed his talk and the message he had to convey, this man say to the people, "O people of this tribe! This man is calling you to remove Lat and Uzza from your necks together with the Jinns of the Banu Malik bin Uqaysh who are your allies. He wants you to rather follow the new-found and misguided religion he has brought. Do not follow him and do not even listen to him." Rabe'ah ﷺ says that he asked his father, "O father! Who is this man who follows him and belies what he says?" His father replied, "That is his uncle Abdul Uzza bin Abdil Muttalib also known as Abu Lahab." *(Ibn Is'haaq in Al Bidayah wan Nihayah, Tabraani, Haythami)*

Rasulullah ﷺ Invites a Large Group to Islam at Mina

Mudrik ﷺ narrates that when he performed Hajj with his father and they found themselves amongst a large group of people, he asked his father, "What is this gathering about?" His father replied, "They have gathered for that irreligious man." When Mudrik ﷺ saw who his father was referring to, he noticed Rasulullah ﷺ standing there telling the people, "O people! Say 'La Ilaha Illallah' and you will be successful." *(Tabrani, Haythami)*. Harith bin Harith Ghamidi ﷺ narrates that he asked his father at Mina, "What is this gathering about'?" His father replied, "They have gathered for that irreligious man." When Harith ﷺ extended his neck to see who his father was referring to, he noticed Rasulullah ﷺ standing there calling the people to accept the Oneness of Allah, but they rejected his message. (Bukhari, Tabrani). Hassan bin Thabit ؓ reports that he performed Hajj during the time when Rasulullah ﷺ was still calling people to accept Islam and his companions were being tortured. He says that he happened to stop by Omar who was not yet a Muslim as he was busy torturing a slave girl of the Banu Amr bin Mu'ammil. Omar stopped by Zinnera ؓ and started torturing her. (Isabah)

Rasulullah ﷺ Invites the Banu Shaiban to Islam

Ali bin Abi Talib ؓ says, "When Allah commanded His Nabi ﷺ to present himself to the Arab tribes, Rasulullah ﷺ left for Mina with me and Abu Bakr ؓ. When we reached a gathering of Arabs, Abu Bakr ؓ would approach them first and greet them. Abu Bakr ؓ was always one to take the initiative and was very capable in his knowledge of each Arab tribe's lineage. He asked the people, 'Where are you people from?' They replied, 'From the Rabe'ah tribe.' He then asked, 'From which family of the Rabe'ah tribe?'" Ali ؓ then continues the lengthy narration until he reached the words, "We then reached a gathering filled with air of respect where there sat several elders of high status and reputation. Abu Bakr ؓ was always one to take the initiative so he approached them and greeted them. When he asked them where they came from, they replied that they were from the Banu Shaiban bin Tha'laba tribe. Abu Bakr ؓ then turned to Rasulullah ﷺ and said, 'May my parents be sacrificed for you! There are none more respectable in their tribe than these men.' Among them were Mafroq bin Amr, Hani bin Qabesah, Muthanna bin Haritha and Nu'man bin Sharek. The closest to Abu Bakr ؓ from them was Mafroq bin Amr who was also the most fluent speaker from among the tribe. He wore 2 locks of hair that fell on his chest and he sat closest to Abu Bakr ؓ." Continuing with the narration, Ali ؓ says that Abu Bakr ؓ asked Mafroq, "How large are your numbers?" Mafroq replied, "We are certainly more than a thousand and a thousand cannot be defeated easily." Abu Bakr ؓ further asked, "What authority do you have?" "We have to work very hard, but such is the condition of every nation," he responded. Abu Bakr ؓ posed a further question saying, "What are the battles like between yourselves and your enemies?" Mafroq said, "We are very angry when we fight and we fight very hard when we are angry. We love war so much that we prefer fighting horses to children and weapons to milk-yielding camels. All help is from Allah Who sometimes grants victory to us and sometimes allows others to be victorious over us. Are you not from the Quraish?" Abu Bakr ؓ said, "What if you were told that the Quraish have the Rasul of Allah and that this is him?" Mafroq said, "The news has already reached us that he claims to be Allah's Rasul." Mafroq then turned to Rasulullah ﷺ and said, "To what are you calling, O brother of the Quraish?" Rasulullah ﷺ then stepped forward and sat down. Abu Bakr ؓ stood up and shaded Rasulullah ﷺ with his clothing. Rasulullah ﷺ said, "I call you to testify that there is none worthy of worship but the One Allah and to testify that I am the Rasul of Allah. I am also asking you to grant me asylum, to protect me and to assist me so that I may convey that message which Allah has commanded me to pass on because the Quraish have joined forces against Islam, they have rejected His Rasul, have satisfied themselves with falsehood instead of the truth. But Allah is Independent, Worthy of all praise." To this, Mafruq asked further, "What else are you calling us towards, O brother of the Quraish?" To this, Rasulullah ﷺ recited the following verse of the Qur'an:

قُلْ تَعَالَوْا أَتْلُ مَا حَرَّمَ رَبُّكُمْ عَلَيْكُمْ أَلَّا تُشْرِكُوا بِهِ شَيْئًا وَبِالْوَالِدَيْنِ إِحْسَانًا وَلَا تَقْتُلُوا أَوْلَادَكُمْ مِنْ إِمْلَاقٍ نَحْنُ نَرْزُقُكُمْ وَإِيَّاهُمْ وَلَا تَقْرَبُوا الْفَوَاحِشَ مَا ظَهَرَ مِنْهَا وَمَا بَطَنَ وَلَا تَقْتُلُوا النَّفْسَ الَّتِي حَرَّمَ اللَّهُ إِلَّا بِالْحَقِّ ذَلِكُمْ وَصَّاكُمْ بِهِ لَعَلَّكُمْ تَعْقِلُونَ (151) وَلَا تَقْرَبُوا مَالَ الْيَتِيمِ إِلَّا بِالَّتِي هِيَ أَحْسَنُ حَتَّى يَبْلُغَ أَشُدَّهُ وَأَوْفُوا الْكَيْلَ وَالْمِيزَانَ بِالْقِسْطِ لَا نُكَلِّفُ نَفْسًا إِلَّا وُسْعَهَا وَإِذَا قُلْتُمْ فَاعْدِلُوا وَلَوْ كَانَ ذَا قُرْبَى وَبِعَهْدِ اللَّهِ أَوْفُوا ذَلِكُمْ وَصَّاكُمْ بِهِ لَعَلَّكُمْ تَذَكَّرُونَ (152) وَأَنَّ هَذَا صِرَاطِي مُسْتَقِيمًا فَاتَّبِعُوهُ وَلَا تَتَّبِعُوا السُّبُلَ فَتَفَرَّقَ بِكُمْ عَنْ سَبِيلِهِ ذَلِكُمْ وَصَّاكُمْ بِهِ لَعَلَّكُمْ تَتَّقُونَ (153)

Say (O Muhammad ﷺ): "Come, I will recite what your Lord has prohibited you from: Join not anything in worship with Him; be good and dutiful to your parents; kill not your children because of poverty - We provide sustenance for you and for them; come not near to Al-Fawahish (shameful sins, illegal sexual intercourse, etc.) whether committed openly or secretly, and kill not anyone whom Allah has forbidden, except for a just cause. This He has commanded you that you may understand. And come not near to the orphan's property, except to improve it, until he (or she) attains the age of full strength; and give full measure and full weight with justice. We burden not any person, but that which he can bear. And whenever you give your word (judge between men or give evidence, etc.), say the truth even if a near relative is concerned, and fulfill the covenant of Allah, This He commands you so that you may remember. And verily, this (Allah's commandments) is my Straight Path, so follow it, and follow not (other) paths, for they will separate you away from His Path. This He has ordained for you that you may become Al-Muttaqoon (the pious)." (Al-An'am:151-153)

Impressed by this, Mafruq further asked, "What else do you call us? I swear by Allah that this is not the speech of those on earth because if it were, we would have definitely recognized it." Thereafter Rasulullah ﷺ recited the following verse of the Qur'an:

إِنَّ اللَّهَ يَأْمُرُ بِالْعَدْلِ وَالْإِحْسَانِ وَإِيتَاءِ ذِي الْقُرْبَى وَيَنْهَى عَنِ الْفَحْشَاءِ وَالْمُنْكَرِ وَالْبَغْيِ يَعِظُكُمْ لَعَلَّكُمْ تَذَكَّرُونَ (90)

Verily, Allah enjoins Al-Adl (justice) and Al-Ihsan (to be patient in performing your duties to Allah), and giving (help) to kith and kin and forbids Al-Fahsha (all evil deeds), and Al-Munkar (all that is prohibited by Islam), and Al-Baghy (all kinds of oppression), He admonishes you, that you may take heed. (An-Nahl:90)

Mafruq exclaimed, "O Quraishi! I swear by Allah that you call towards the best of character and the most beautiful actions. Without doubt, any nation that rejects you and supports others against you are certain liars." Mafroq then decided to include Hani bin Qabisah in the conversation. He therefore introduced Hani by saying, "This is Hani bin Qabisah. He is our elder and in charge of our religious affairs." Thereafter, Hani addressed Rasulullah ﷺ saying, "O my Quraishi brother! I have heard what you have to say and accept every word of it. However, I feel that if we forsake our religion to follow yours, it would be a mistake and would reflect on us the weakness of our understanding and lack of thought over the matter. The reason for this is that this is only our first meeting with each other, which may not even be the last and no one knows what the future holds. Mistakes often occur because of quick decision. In addition to this, we have people at home who would dislike that we enter into any agreement without consulting them. Therefore, you should return and we shall return. You consider over your matter and we shall consider over ours." Hani then wished to include Muthanna bin Haritha into the conversation. He therefore introduced him saying, "This is Muthanna bin Haritha. He is our elder and in charge of our military affairs." Addressing Rasulullah ﷺ, Muthanna said, "O Quraishi brother! I have listened to what you have said. I like what you said for it appealed to me very much. However, my reply to you will be the same reply that Hani bin Qabisah has given. We find ourselves between the borders of 2 countries. The one is Yamamah and the other is Samawah." Rasulullah ﷺ asked him, "On which border of the 2 countries you are situated?" He replied, "On one side and we have the land, the high hills and mountains of the Arabs while on the other side we have the land of the Persians and the rivers of the Kisra. The Kisra has permitted us to live there on condition that we do not start anything new and do not support any person who starts a new movement. There is a possibility that the Persian king would not like that which you are calling us. Though the custom in the Arab land is to forgive those who will make mistake and to accept their excuse, the custom of the Persian land is that people who make mistakes are not forgiven nor are their excuses accepted. Therefore, if you wish that we take you back to our land and assist you against the Arabs, we can take this responsibility but we cannot take responsibility to oppose the Persians." Rasulullah ﷺ said to them, "Your reply is not bad because you have spoken frankly. However, the only people who can establish Islam are those who protect it from every angle." Rasulullah ﷺ then stood up taking the hand of Abu Bakr ؓ. Ali ؓ narrates further that the 3 of them then proceeded to the Aws and Khazraj tribes and left them after they had pledged their allegiance to Rasulullah ﷺ. Speaking about the Aws and Khazraj tribes, Ali ؓ says, "They were extremely truthful and preserved people. May Allah be pleased with all of them." (Abu Nu'aym in Dala'il). Another narration states that Rasulullah ﷺ said to them, "The only people who can establish Islam are those who protect it from every angle." Thereafter, Rasulullah ﷺ added, "Tell me if after a short while Allah grants you the Persians' land and their wealth and makes their women to serve you as your wives and slaves, will you then not be prepared to glorify Him and proclaim His purity?" To this, Nu'man bin Sharik said, "You have our support, a brother of the Quraish." Rasulullah ﷺ recited the verse:

يَا أَيُّهَا النَّبِيُّ إِنَّا أَرْسَلْنَاكَ شَاهِدًا وَمُبَشِّرًا وَنَذِيرًا (45) وَدَاعِيًا إِلَى اللَّهِ بِإِذْنِهِ وَسِرَاجًا مُنِيرًا (46)

O Prophet (Muhammad ﷺ)! Verily, We have sent you as witness, and a bearer of glad tidings, and a warner, and as one who invites to Allah by His permission, and as a lamp spreading light (through your instructions from the Qur'an and the Sunnah). (Al-Ahzab:45-46)

Ali ؓ says, "Rasulullah ﷺ then stood up, taking the hand of Abu Bakr ؓ. He turned to us and said, 'O Ali! How excellent are the manners of the Arabs even during the time of ignorance! How noble are they! It is because of this, they protect each other in the life of this world." The 3 of them then proceeded to the Aws and Khazraj tribes and left them only after they had pledged their allegiance to Rasulullah ﷺ. Ali ؓ says, "The Aws and Khazraj tribes were extremely truthful and preserved people. Rasulullah ﷺ was happy that Abu Bakr ؓ possessed so much knowledge about the lineage of the Arabs. Not much time had elapsed afterwards when Rasulullah ﷺ came to his companions and said, 'Praise Allah abundantly because today the Banu Rabee'ah of the Banu Shaiban tribe have defeated the Persians. They have killed the Persian leaders and defeated their armies. Allah has assisted them because of me." (Al Bidayah wan Nihayah, Abu Nu'aym, Hakim, Bayhaqi). This states that when the soldiers of the Banu Rabe'ah met the Persian army at a place called Quraqir, which was close to the Euphrates river, they used the name of Muhammad ﷺ as their codeword, because of which Allah granted them victory. After this battle, the Banu Rabe'ah entered the fold of Islam." (Hafidh Ibn Hajar in Fat'hul Bari)

Rasulullah ﷺ Invites the Aws and Khazraj Tribes to Islam

While mentioning the virtues of the Ansar that they were pioneers in Islam, Ali bin Abi Talib ؓ said, "The person who does not like the Ansar and does not recognize the rights due to them, cannot be a Mu'min. By Allah, they used their swords, their power of speech, and the their generosity of their hearts to take care of Islam just as a mare takes care in a green field. During the seasons of Hajj, Rasulullah ﷺ used to go out to call various tribes to Islam. However, none was prepared to accept his message. He used to meet various tribes at the marketplaces of Majinna, Ukaz, and Mina until he would meet the same tribes again next year. In fact, there were those tribes who used to say to him, "When will the time come for you to give up hope on us because you have been meeting with us for such a long time? Eventually the time came when the Most Powerful the Most Honored Allah decided matters in favor of the tribes of the Ansar. Rasulullah ﷺ then presented Islam to them and they readily accepted. They took Rasulullah ﷺ to their town, assisted him, and sympathized with him. May Allah reward them with the best of rewards. Thereafter, we the Muhajir came to them and took up residence in their homes. They preferred us above themselves to the extent that they would even draw lottery to decide which of them would be host to us. Eventually, they allowed us from the depths of their hearts to have greater rights than them in their very own wealth. They sacrificed their lives for the protection of Allah's Nabi. May the mercies and blessings of Allah be showered on them." (Abu Nu'aym in Dila'il).

Umm S'ad bint Sa'd bin Rabi ؓ says that Rasulullah ﷺ continued calling people to Islam when he was staying in Makkah. However, he was abused and hurt. Finally the decision of Allah demanded that the honor come to this tribe of the Ansar. Then Rasulullah ﷺ met a group of them at a place called Aqaba as they were busy shaving off their hair after performing Hajj. When one of the narrators asked Umm Sa'd ؓ who the group was, she replied, "They were 6 or 7 persons. From the Banu Najjar tribe were As'ad bin Zurarah and 2 sons of Afra." She did not name the rest of them. Rasulullah ﷺ sat down with them, conveyed the message of Allah to them and recited a part of the Qur'an to them. They accepted Allah and his Rasul ﷺ and agreed to meet him the following year. This incident is known as the **first pledge of Aqaba**. Thereafter, the **second pledge of Aqaba** took place. One of the narrators then asked Umm Sa'd ؓ, "How long did Rasulullah ﷺ stay in Makkah?" She replied, "Have you not heard the words of Abu Sirma Qais bin Abi Anas?" The narrator responded by saying, "I do not know what he said." She then quoted the following couplet:

ثَوِي فِي قُرَيْشٍ بِضْعَ عَشْرَةَ حِجَّةً يُذَكِّرُ لَوْ لَاقَى صَدِيقًا مُوَاتِيَا

"He stayed with the Quraish for a few years more than 10 advising people with the hope of meeting a suitable friend"

She then proceeded to quote an entire poem, which shall InsAllah be quoted in a Hadith of Abdullah bin Abbas ؓ in the chapter concerning the help that the Sahabah rendered to the cause of Islam. (Abu Nu'aym in Dila'il). Aqil bin Abi Talib ؓ and Zuhri narrate that one day during the period when the disbelievers started harassing Rasulullah ﷺ to a great degree, he said to his uncle Abbas bin Abdil Muttalib ؓ, "O my beloved uncle! Allah will help Islam using such people to whom the oppressive people of the Quraish would seem unimportant and who would enjoy great honor in the eyes of Allah. Take me to the marketplace of Ukaz and show me where the various Arab tribes are staying because I want to call them towards Allah and request them to protect me and grant me asylum so that I may propagate the message of Allah to humanity." Abbas ؓ said, "O my beloved nephew! Proceed to Ukaz. I shall accompany you and show you where the tribes are staying." Rasulullah ﷺ started inviting the Thaqif tribe to Islam and then continued meeting the other tribes who were there for Hajj that year. The following year when Allah commanded Rasulullah ﷺ to preach openly, Rasulullah ﷺ met 6 persons from amongst the Aws and Khazraj tribes. They were As'ad bin Zurarah ؓ, Abul Haytham bin At Tayyihan ؓ, Abdullah bin Rawaha ؓ, Sa'd bin Rabi ؓ, Nu'man bin Haritha ؓ and Ubadah bin Samit ؓ. Rasulullah ﷺ met them one night at the Jamara Aqaba during the days of Mina. Rasulullah ﷺ sat with them, invited them to believe in Allah, to worship Him and to assist him in the propagation of Islam. When they asked Rasulullah ﷺ to present to them what Allah had revealed to him, he recited the following verses of Surah lbrahim to them:

وَإِذْ قَالَ إِبْرَاهِيمُ رَبِّ اجْعَلْ هَذَا الْبَلَدَ آمِنًا وَاجْنُبْنِي وَبَنِيَّ أَنْ نَعْبُدَ الْأَصْنَامَ (35) رَبِّ إِنَّهُنَّ أَضْلَلْنَ كَثِيرًا مِنَ النَّاسِ فَمَنْ تَبِعَنِي فَإِنَّهُ مِنِّي وَمَنْ عَصَانِي فَإِنَّكَ غَفُورٌ رَحِيمٌ (36) رَبَّنَا إِنِّي أَسْكَنْتُ مِنْ ذُرِّيَّتِي بِوَادٍ غَيْرِ ذِي زَرْعٍ عِنْدَ بَيْتِكَ الْمُحَرَّمِ رَبَّنَا لِيُقِيمُوا الصَّلَاةَ فَاجْعَلْ أَفْئِدَةً مِنَ النَّاسِ تَهْوِي إِلَيْهِمْ وَارْزُقْهُمْ مِنَ الثَّمَرَاتِ لَعَلَّهُمْ يَشْكُرُونَ (37) رَبَّنَا إِنَّكَ تَعْلَمُ مَا نُخْفِي وَمَا نُعْلِنُ وَمَا يَخْفَى عَلَى اللَّهِ مِنْ شَيْءٍ فِي الْأَرْضِ وَلَا فِي السَّمَاءِ (38) الْحَمْدُ لِلَّهِ الَّذِي وَهَبَ لِي عَلَى الْكِبَرِ إِسْمَاعِيلَ وَإِسْحَاقَ إِنَّ رَبِّي لَسَمِيعُ الدُّعَاءِ (39) رَبِّ اجْعَلْنِي مُقِيمَ الصَّلَاةِ وَمِنْ ذُرِّيَّتِي رَبَّنَا وَتَقَبَّلْ دُعَاءِ (40) رَبَّنَا اغْفِرْ لِي وَلِوَالِدَيَّ وَلِلْمُؤْمِنِينَ يَوْمَ يَقُومُ الْحِسَابُ (41) وَلَا تَحْسَبَنَّ اللَّهَ غَافِلًا عَمَّا يَعْمَلُ الظَّالِمُونَ إِنَّمَا يُؤَخِّرُهُمْ لِيَوْمٍ تَشْخَصُ فِيهِ الْأَبْصَارُ (42) مُهْطِعِينَ مُقْنِعِي رُءُوسِهِمْ لَا يَرْتَدُّ إِلَيْهِمْ طَرْفُهُمْ وَأَفْئِدَتُهُمْ هَوَاءٌ (43) وَأَنْذِرِ النَّاسَ يَوْمَ يَأْتِيهِمُ الْعَذَابُ فَيَقُولُ الَّذِينَ ظَلَمُوا رَبَّنَا أَخِّرْنَا إِلَى أَجَلٍ قَرِيبٍ نُجِبْ دَعْوَتَكَ وَنَتَّبِعِ الرُّسُلَ أَوَلَمْ تَكُونُوا أَقْسَمْتُمْ مِنْ قَبْلُ مَا لَكُمْ مِنْ زَوَالٍ (44) وَسَكَنْتُمْ فِي مَسَاكِنِ الَّذِينَ ظَلَمُوا أَنْفُسَهُمْ وَتَبَيَّنَ لَكُمْ كَيْفَ فَعَلْنَا بِهِمْ وَضَرَبْنَا لَكُمُ الْأَمْثَالَ (45) وَقَدْ مَكَرُوا مَكْرَهُمْ وَعِنْدَ اللَّهِ مَكْرُهُمْ وَإِنْ كَانَ مَكْرُهُمْ لِتَزُولَ مِنْهُ الْجِبَالُ (46) فَلَا تَحْسَبَنَّ اللَّهَ مُخْلِفَ وَعْدِهِ رُسُلَهُ إِنَّ اللَّهَ عَزِيزٌ ذُو انْتِقَامٍ (47) يَوْمَ تُبَدَّلُ الْأَرْضُ غَيْرَ الْأَرْضِ وَالسَّمَوَاتُ وَبَرَزُوا لِلَّهِ الْوَاحِدِ الْقَهَّارِ (48) وَتَرَى الْمُجْرِمِينَ يَوْمَئِذٍ مُقَرَّنِينَ فِي الْأَصْفَادِ (49) سَرَابِيلُهُمْ مِنْ قَطِرَانٍ وَتَغْشَى وُجُوهَهُمُ النَّارُ (50) لِيَجْزِيَ اللَّهُ كُلَّ نَفْسٍ مَا كَسَبَتْ إِنَّ اللَّهَ سَرِيعُ الْحِسَابِ (51) هَذَا بَلَاغٌ لِلنَّاسِ وَلِيُنْذَرُوا بِهِ وَلِيَعْلَمُوا أَنَّمَا هُوَ إِلَهٌ وَاحِدٌ وَلِيَذَّكَّرَ أُولُو الْأَلْبَابِ (52)

And (remember) when Ibrahim said: "O my Lord! Make this city (Makkah) one of peace and security, and keep me and my sons away from worshipping idols. O my Lord! They have indeed led astray many among mankind. But whoso follows me, he verily is of me. And whoso disobeys me, - still You are indeed Oft-Forgiving, Most Merciful. O our Lord! I have made some of my offspring to dwell in an uncultivable valley by Your Sacred House (the Kabah at Makkah); in order, O our Lord, that they may establish salat, so fill some hearts among men with love towards them, and (O Allah) provide them with fruits so that they may give thanks. O our Lord! Certainly, You know what we conceal and what we reveal. Nothing on the earth or in the heaven is hidden from Allah. All the praises and thanks be to Allah, Who has given me in old age Ismail and Ishaque. Verily! My Lord is indeed the All-Hearer of invocations. O my Lord! Make me one who establish salat, and (also) from my offspring, our Lord! And accept my invocation. Our Lord! Forgive me and my parents, and (all) the believers on the Day when the reckoning will be established." Consider not that Allah is

unaware of that which the Zalimoon (polytheists, wrong-doers, etc.) do, but He gives them respite up to a Day when the eyes will stare in horror. (They will be) hastening forward with necks outstretched, their heads raised up (towards the sky), their gaze returning not towards them and their hearts empty (from thinking because of extreme fear). And warn (O Muhammad ﷺ) mankind of the Day when the torment will come unto them; then the wrong-doers will say: "Our Lord! Respite us for a little while, we will answer Your Call and follow the Messengers!" (It will be said): "Had you not sworn aforetime that you would not leave (the world for the Hereafter). And you dwelt in the dwellings of men who wronged themselves, and it was clear to you how We had dealt with them. And We put forth (many) parables for you." Indeed, they planned their plot, and their plot was with Allah, though their plot was a great (one, still) it would never be able to remove the mountains (real mountains or the Islamic law) from their places (as it is of no importance). So think not that Allah will fail to keep His Promise to His Messengers. Certainly, Allah is All-Mighty, All-Able of Retribution. On the Day when the earth will be changed to another earth and so will be the heavens and they (all creatures) will appear before Allah, the One, the Irresistible. And you will see the Mujrimoon (criminals, disbelievers) that Day bound together in fetters; (with their hands and feet tied to their necks with chains). Their garments will be of pitch, and fire will cover their faces. That Allah may requite each person according to what he has earned. Truly, Allah is Swift at reckoning. This (Qur'an) is a Message for mankind, in order that they may be warned thereby, and that they may know that He is the only One Ilah (God) - (none has the right to be worshipped but Allah), and that men of understanding may take heed. (Ibrahim:35-52)

Their hearts were moved by these words of the Qur'an and they accepted Islam. As they were engaged in conversation with Rasulullah ﷺ, Abbas ؓ passed by. Recognizing the voice of Rasulullah ﷺ, he said, "O my nephew! Who are these people with you?" Rasulullah ﷺ said, "These are the residents of Yathrib from the Aws and Khazraj tribes. I gave them the same Da'wah that I had given to so many other tribes before them and they accepted my message and believed what I said. They have also mentioned that they will take me back with them to their city." Abbas ؓ descended from his animal, tied it up and said, "O people of the Aws and Khazraj! This is my nephew and the person I love most. If you accept his message, believe him, and intend to take him with you to your city, I want you to make a promise so that my heart may be contented. Promise me that you will never desert him and never betray him because your neighbors are the Jews and the Jews who are his enemies. I fear that the Jews may make a scheme against him." When Abbas ؓ expressed his mistrust in As'ad bin Zurarah ؓ and his companions, As'ad ؓ felt insulted and said, "O Rasulullah ﷺ! Permit me to reply to him in such a way that will neither upset you nor appear unpleasant to you. However, the reply will confirm that we have accepted your message and it will express our Iman in you." Rasulullah ﷺ said, "You may reply to him as I have complete confidence in you." Facing Rasulullah ﷺ, As'ad bin Zurarah ؓ said, "O Rasulullah ﷺ! There is a way to every call. While some ways are easy, others are difficult. Today you have called us towards something that is both new and difficult for people to accept. You have called us to forsake our religions and to follow you in Islam. This is not an easy task. However, we have accepted your call. You have called us to severe all ties we have with both close and distant relatives by following you. This is not an easy task. However, we have accepted your call. You have invited us to Islam whereas we are a strong group living in a place that is powerful and mighty where our lives and properties are safe. No one could ever imagine that our leader shall be someone not from amongst us, whose people have disliked him and whose uncles have deserted him. This is not an easy task but we have accepted it. These things appear difficult for all except those whose welfare Allah has decided and who foresee good in its results. We have accepted your call with our tongues, our hearts, and our hands because we believe what you have conveyed to us and we accept it with conviction that has settled deep within our hearts. We pledge our commitment to you completely and we pledge it to our Rabb and your Rabb as well. Allah's hand is above ours to approve this pledge. We shall spill our blood to protect your and give our lives for your. We shall protect you as we protect ourselves, our children, and our wives. It shall be for Allah to fulfill this pledge. Should we betray this pledge, it will be betraying Allah with the cost of making us the most shameful people. O Rasulullah ﷺ! All that we have told you is the absolute truth and we seek Allah's assistance to help us fulfill the pledge." As'ad bin Zurarah ؓ then turned to Abbas ؓ saying, "You have used your words to be a barrier between Rasulullah ﷺ and us. Allah knows best what you meant by your words but you have mentioned that this is your nephew and the person whom you love the most. But we have cut ourselves off from people near and distant as well as from blood relatives. We testify that he is certainly the Rasul of Allah whom Allah has Himself sent. He is certainly not a liar and whatever he has brought does not at all resemble the words of man. As for your statement that you cannot be contented with us until we make a promise to you, we shall certainly not refuse such a request made out of concern for Rasulullah ﷺ. You may therefore take from us whatever promises you wish." Turning once again to Rasulullah ﷺ, As'ad bin Zurarah ؓ said, "O Rasulullah ﷺ! Take any promises you wish from us and make any conditions from the side of your Rabb that you wish to make." The details of their pledge of allegiance shall InsAllah be mentioned in the complete Hadith in the chapter concerning the assistance that the Ansar rendered to Islam at the very beginning. *(Abu Nu'aym in Dala'il)*

The Da'wah Rasulullah ﷺ Gave in the Marketplaces

Rabe'ah bin Ibad ؓ belonged to the Banu Deel tribe all of them accepted Islam after passing through the period of ignorance. He narrates that during the period of ignorance, he saw Rasulullah ﷺ in the marketplace of Dhul Majaz saying to those gathered around him, "O people! Say 'La Ilaha Illallah' and you will be successful." Rasulullah ﷺ was being followed by a handsome man whose hair was divided into 2 locks. He followed Rasulullah ﷺ wherever he went and said to the people, "He (Rasulullah ﷺ) is an irreligious man and a liar." Rabee'ah bin Ibad ؓ says that when he asked about the man, he was informed that the man was Abu Lahab, the uncle of Rasulullah ﷺ. *(Ahmad, Bayhaqi, Haythami, Ibn Hajar)*. According to another narration, Rasulullah ﷺ used to run away from Abu Lahab who continuously harassed him. Other narrations also mention that as people used to attack Rasulullah ﷺ, there were no one to say anything. However, he would never remain silent from talking about Islam. *(Ibn Is'haq in Al Bidayah wan Nihayah, Abdullah bin Ahmad, Tabrani, Haythami)*. Tariq bin Abdillah ؓ narrates that he was in the Dhul Majaz marketplace when a man passed by wearing a shawl with red threads. He was saying to the people, "O people! Say 'La Ilaha Illallah' and you will be successful." He was being followed by another man who had injured first man's heels and legs, causing them to bleed. The second man was saying, "O people! Do not follow him because he is a liar!" When Tariq bin Abdillah asked the people who the men were, he was told, "He (first man) is a man from the Banu Hashim who claims to be Allah's Rasul and the other is his uncle Abdul Uzza (Abu Lahab)." *(Tabrani, Haythami)*. A person from the Banu Malik bin Kinana tribe narrates that he saw Rasulullah ﷺ in the Dhul Majaz marketplace saying to the people, "O people! Say 'La Ilaha Illallah' and you will be successful." Abu Jahal threw sand into the face of Rasulullah ﷺ saying, "Do not let this man deceive you into leaving your religion. He wants you to forsake your gods. He wants you to forsake Lat and Uzza." However, Rasulullah ﷺ paid no attention to him. When the narrator was asked to describe Rasulullah ﷺ, he said, "He was wearing 2 shawls with red threads. He was of medium height with a well-built body and extremely handsome face. His hair was very black and thick and his complexion was exceptionally fair." *(Ahmad, Bayhaqi)* The Da'wah that Rasulullah ﷺ gave in the marketplace of Ukaz has already been mentioned in the chapter entitled "The Da'wah Rasulullah ﷺ gave to various Arab tribes during the Hajj Season."

Da'wah to Close Relatives: Rasulullah ﷺ Addresses Fatima ؓ and Safiya ؓ

Aisha ؓ narrates that Rasulullah ﷺ gathered his family members when Allah revealed the verse: وَأَنذِرْ عَشِيرَتَكَ الْأَقْرَبِينَ (214) *And warn your tribe (O Muhammad ﷺ) of near relatives. (Ash-Shu'ara:214)*

Rasulullah ﷺ then said, "O Fatima the daughter of Muhammad ﷺ! O Safiya the daughter of Abdul Muttalib! O children of Abdul Muttalib! Ask me whatever you wish from my wealth, but 1 can give you nothing from Allah as I cannot help you against Allah's punishment." *(Ahmad, Muslim)*

Rasulullah ﷺ Invites his Household and Relatives for a Meal to Call Towards Islam

Ali ؓ narrates that Rasulullah ﷺ gathered his family members when Allah revealed the verse: وَأَنذِرْ عَشِيرَتَكَ الْأَقْرَبِينَ (214) *And warn your tribe (O Muhammad ﷺ) of near relatives. (Ash-Shu'ara:214)*

30 of them gathered and had something to eat and drink. Thereafter, Rasulullah ﷺ asked them, "Who will assume the responsibility to pay my debts and fulfil my pledges? Whoever does this shall be my companion in paradise and my successor in my family." Someone said, "But you are an ocean of generosity and virtue. Who could possibly assume your responsibilities?" Rasulullah ﷺ then repeated the request thrice. When Rasulullah ﷺ presented the request to the members of his household, Ali ؓ said, "I am prepared." *(Ahmad)*. Ali ؓ narrates that Rasulullah ﷺ invited the family of Abdul Muttalib who were such people that each one of them could easily eat a young animal and drink the equivalent of a "faraq" (~ 20 liters) Rasulullah ﷺ prepared food weighing only a "mudd" (small quantity), from which everyone ate to their fill. The leftover food was as much as there had been at the beginning and it appeared as if it had not been touched. Then Rasulullah ﷺ sent for a small cup from which everyone drank to their fill. The leftover drink was also as much as there had been at the beginning, appearing as if it had not been touched. Thereafter, Rasulullah ﷺ addressed them saying, "O children of Abdul Muttalib! I have been sent as a Rasul to you people in particular and to all of mankind in general. You have just witnessed one of my miracles, so which of you shall pledge his allegiance to me to become my brother and companion?" No

one volunteered. Ali ﷺ says, "I then stood up although I was the youngest of all of them. Rasulullah ﷺ told me to seat and repeated himself thrice. I stood up each time and each time he told me to seat. Eventually, when this happened the 3rd time, Rasulullah ﷺ placed his hand on mine to accept my pledge of allegiance."(Ahmad). Ali ﷺ has also narrated that Rasulullah ﷺ instructed him to prepare a meal using the leg of an animal and a "saa" (~ 7lbs) of wheat flour for bread when the following verse of the Qur'an was revealed: (٢١٤) وَأَنذِرْ عَشِيرَتَكَ الْأَقْرَبِينَ

And warn your tribe (O Muhammad ﷺ) of near relatives. (Ash-Shu'ara:214)

Then Rasulullah ﷺ told Ali ﷺ to invite the Banu Hashim. During that time, the Banu Hashim numbered approximately 40 to 42 persons. Ali ﷺ continues the narration by saying, "After their guests had arrived, Rasulullah ﷺ sent for the food. When he placed the food before them, they all ate to their fill even though there were people amongst them who could eat a young animal together with gravy all by themselves. Then Rasulullah ﷺ sent for a small cup of milk. When he passed the cup around for them to drink, they all managed to drink to their fill. One of them commented, "Until today, I had never seen such magic." It is widely believed that it was Abu Lahab who said this. The following day, Rasulullah ﷺ said to Ali ﷺ, "O Ali! Prepare the leg of a goat together with a "saa" of wheat flour and a large cup of milk." Ali ﷺ says, "I did as I was told. The guests ate as they had eaten the first day and drank as they had drunk on the first day. Just as it occurred on the first day, so much food was left over as we had begun with." To this, someone commented, "Never before have we seen such magic as we have witnessed today." On the 3rd day, Rasulullah ﷺ said, "O Ali! Prepare the leg of a goat together with a "saa" of wheat flour and a large cup of milk." After doing as he was told, Rasulullah ﷺ asked Ali ﷺ to invite the Banu Hashim. He gathered them together and they ate and drank. Rasulullah ﷺ then spoke to them saying, "Which of you are prepared to settle my debts for me?" Ali ﷺ says, "I remained silent as did everyone body else. Thereafter, Rasulullah ﷺ repeated himself. I responded by saying, 'I am prepared to do so O Rasulullah ﷺ!' He said to me, 'You O Ali! You O Ali You are certainly fit for the task!'" (Bazzar, Haythami). Ibn Abi Hatim reported a similar Hadith in which Rasulullah ﷺ said to the people, which of you is prepared to settle my debts and to succeed me as head of my family after my demise? Ali ﷺ says, "Everybody remained silent including Abbas ﷺ who feared that all his wealth would be used up in settling the debts. I remained silent out of respect for Abbas ﷺ who was much elder than me. When Rasulullah ﷺ repeated his request, Abbas ﷺ again remained silent. When I saw this, I said, 'O Rasulullah ﷺ! I am prepared to accept this responsibility.' On that day, I was worse off than any of them. I was suffering from pain in my eyes, my stomach was bloated and my legs were extremely thin."' (Ibn Kathir, Bayhaqi, Ibn Jareer). A similar Hadith has already appeared in the chapter entitled "The Da'wah Rasulullah ﷺ gave to large gatherings". That Hadith has a different chain of narrators and is reported from Abdullah bin Abbas ﷺ.

During Travel: Rasulullah ﷺ Gives Da'wah During the Hijrah

Sa'd Aslami ﷺ was the guide who directed Rasulullah ﷺ through the Rakuba valley. His son Abdullah says, "My father informed us that Rasulullah ﷺ came to them, asked the shortest path to Madinah. He was accompanied by Abu Bakr ﷺ, whose daughter was then being suckled by a woman from our tribe." Sa'd ﷺ informed them, "They is a road along the valley of Rakuba but there are 2 thieves from the Aslam tribe who

are called "Muhanan". If you wish, you could use the road past them." Rasulullah ﷺ said, "Lead us to the road past them." Then they took the road and when they came close to the thieves, one of them said to the other, "Look at this person from Yemen!" Rasulullah ﷺ then gave them Da'wah and invited them to accept Islam. They both became Muslims. When Rasulullah ﷺ asked them their names, they said that they were called "Muhanan" (2 disgraceful ones). Rasulullah ﷺ said to them, "No. You 2 are 'Mukraman' (2 honored ones)." Rasulullah ﷺ then told them to join him in Madinah. The Hadith still continues after this. (Ahmad, Haythami)

Rasulullah ﷺ Invites a Villager to Islam During a Journey

Abdullah bin Omar ﷺ narrates that they were once traveling with Rasulullah ﷺ when a villager passed by. As he drew close, Rasulullah ﷺ asked him, "Where are you going?" "I am going home," he replied. Rasulullah ﷺ asked him, "Do you want to take something good with you?" "What is this good thing?" he asked. Rasulullah ﷺ replied, "That you testify that there is none worthy of worship but the One Allah and that Muhammad ﷺ is Allah's servant and Rasul." The villager asked, "Are there any witnesses to verify what you say?" Rasulullah ﷺ replied, "Yes. This tree is a witness." Rasulullah ﷺ then called the tree which stood at the edge of the valley. The tree moved through the earth as it came towards Rasulullah ﷺ. When it stood before Rasulullah ﷺ, he thrice asked to testify the truth of what he said. All 3 times, the tree testified to the truth of his words and then returned to the place where it grew. As he returned, the villager said to Rasulullah ﷺ, "If my people follow me, I shall bring them all to you. I shall come alone and live with you." (Hakim, Haythami)

Rasulullah ﷺ Invites Buraida bin Khusaib and His Companions to Islam During the Hijrah Journey

Asim Aslami ﷺ narrates that while Rasulullah ﷺ was migrating from Makkah to Madinah, Buraida bin Khusaib ﷺ met him at a place called Ghamim. When Rasulullah ﷺ invited him to accept Islam, he and about 80 families with him all accepted. Rasulullah ﷺ then led them all in the Isha salah. (Ibn Sa'd)

Travel by Foot to Convey Islam: Rasulullah ﷺ Walks to Ta'if

Abdullah bin Ja'far ﷺ narrates that after his uncle Abu Talib had passed away, Rasulullah ﷺ traveled on foot to Ta'if to invite the people to Islam. However, they did not accept his Da'wah and he had to return. On the way back, he took shade beneath a tree, performed 2 Rakahs salah and made the following Du'a:

اللَّهُمَّ إِنِّي أَشْكُوا إِلَيْكَ ضَعْفَ قُوَّتِي وَهَوَانِي عَلَى النَّاسِ يَا أَرْحَمَ الرَّحِمِينَ أَنْتَ أَرْحَمُ الرَّحِمِينَ إِلَى مَنْ تَكِلُنِي؟ إِلَى عَدُوٍّ يَتَجَهَّمُنِي أَمْ إِلَى قَرِيبٍ مَلَّكْتَهُ أَمْرِي إِنْ لَمْ تَكُنْ غِضْبَانَ عَلَيَّ فَلَا أُبَالِي غَيْرَ أَنَّ عَافِيَتَكَ أَوْسَعُ لِي أَعُوذُ بِوَجْهِكَ الَّذِي أَشْرَقَتْ لَهُ الظُّلُمَاتُ وَصَلَحَ عَلَيْهِ أَمْرُ الدُّنْيَا وَالْآخِرَةِ أَنْ يَنْزِلَ بِي غَضَبُكَ أَوْ يَحِلَّ بِى سَخَطُكَ حَتَّى تَرْضَى وَلَا قُوَّةَ إِلَّا بِاللهِ

"O Allah! Only to you do I communicate my weakness and lack of importance among people. O the most Merciful of those who show mercy, You are certainly the most Merciful of those who show mercy. To whom shall you hand me over? To an enemy who will treat me harshly or to a near one to whom You shall give control over me? If You are not angry with me, I care for nothing except that Your protection should be vast enough for me. In Your countenance by which multitudes of darkness are turned to light and by which the affairs of this world and the hereafter are remedied, I seek protection from being afflicted by Your wrath and displeasure. The causes of Your displeasure should be removed until You are pleased. There is no might but with Allah." (Tabrani, Haythami). A narration from Zuhri رحمة الله

shall be quoted in the chapter on the difficulties that were borne for the sake of Da'wah.

Da'wah Towards Islam in the Battlefield: Rasulullah ﷺ Never Fought Anyone Until he Had Invited Them to Allah

Abdullah bin Abbas ؓ narrates that Rasulullah ﷺ would never fight any nation until he had already conveyed the message of Islam to them. *(Hakim, Ahmad, Tabrani, Haythami, Bayhaqi)*

Rasulullah ﷺ Instructs the Muslim Battalion to First Gain People's Confidence and Then to Invite Them to Islam

Abdur Rahman bin Aa'idh ؓ narrates that whenever Rasulullah ﷺ dispatched a battalion, he would brief them like this, "Gain the confidence of people and do not attack them until you have called them to Islam. If you bring to me the residents of every baked and unbaked home of every city and village on earth as Muslims, it would please me more than your killing their men and bringing their women and children to me as captives." *(Ibn Mandah, Ibn Asakir in Kanzul Ummal, Tirmidhi)*

Rasulullah ﷺ Instructs the Commanders of Muslims Troops to Convey the Message of Islam

Buraida ؓ narrates that whenever Rasulullah ﷺ appointed someone as commander of Muslim troops, he would instruct him to fear Allah with regard to his personal actions and advise him to be good towards those under his command. Also, Rasulullah ﷺ would brief them with the following words: "When you face your disbelieving enemies, invite them to accept 1 of 3 options. Should they accept any of these, you may not engage them in battle. First invite them to accept Islam. If they accept, you should accept this from them and refrain from fighting them. You should then call them to move from their places to the home of the Muhajir. Inform them that if they do this, they shall enjoy the privileges of the Muhajir and will have to fulfill the same responsibilities that the Muhajir do. However, if they refuse to move and prefer their homes, inform them that they will fall in the category of the Muslim villagers. Allah's commands that apply to all Muslims shall apply to them but they will have no share in the spoils of war unless they fight together with the other Muslims. If they refuse this option, ask them to pay the Jizya (tax). Should they accept this, accept it from them and refrain from fighting them. However, if they refuse even this, seek Allah's assistance and fight them. If you siege a fort and the enemy asks you to allow them to leave on Allah's terms, do not allow it because you have no idea what Allah's terms are. You should rather allow them to leave on your terms. You may then decide what the terms should be." *(Abu Dawud, Muslim, Ibn Majah, Bayhaqi, Ahmad, Darmi, Ibn Hibban)*

Rasulullah ﷺ Commands Ali ؓ not to Fight Until he Invites the Enemy to Islam

Anas bin Malik ؓ narrates that Rasulullah ﷺ once dispatched Ali bin Abi Talib ؓ as commander of a battalion to fight a battle. Then Rasulullah ﷺ sent a messenger with instructions to draw close to Ali ؓ with the message and not to call it out from a distance. The message was that he should not engage in battle until he had invited the enemy to Islam. *(Tabrani, Haythami)*. Narrated from Ali ؓ that Rasulullah ﷺ once sent him somewhere as commander of a battalion. Rasulullah ﷺ then instructed another person like this, "Join with Ali ؓ and without calling him from behind, tell him that Nabi ﷺ commands you to wait for him and that you should not fight anyone until you have invited them to accept Islam. *(Kanzul*

Ummal). Ali ؓ has also mentioned that when Rasulullah ﷺ sent him, he said, "Never fight a nation until you have invited them to accept Islam." *(Nasbur Ra'yah)*. Sahl bin Sa'd ؓ as reported by Bukhari and others has passed in which Rasulullah ﷺ said to Ali ؓ during the battle of Khaibar, "March at a moderate pace until you reach their field.. Then invite them to accept Islam, explaining to them the rights due to Allah that are compulsory for them to fulfill. By Allah! If Allah uses you to guide even a single person, it is better for you than red camels." *(Bukhari)*

Rasulullah ﷺ Commands Farwa Ghutaifi ؓ to Convey Islam

Farwa bin Musaik Ghutaifi ؓ narrates that he came to Rasulullah ﷺ and asked, "Should I not take those of my people who have accepted Islam to fight those of them who have not accepted Islam?" Rasulullah ﷺ replied, "Why not'?" Farwa ؓ says, "I then had a second thought and said, 'No I shall be unable to fight them as they are the people of Saba and are extremely powerful and strong. However, Rasulullah ﷺ still made me the commander and instructed me to wage war against them. When I had left, Allah sent revelation to Rasulullah ﷺ concerning the people of Saba. He then said, "Where is Ghutaifi?" When Rasulullah ﷺ sent someone to my home, I had already left. The man sent me back and I appeared before Rasulullah ﷺ. When I came to Rasulullah ﷺ, I found him sitting with the Sahabah around him. Rasulullah ﷺ said to me, 'Invite the people to Islam. Receive those who accept but do not be hasty to do anything to those who do not accept until you hear from me.'" Someone then asked, "O Rasulullah ﷺ! What is Saba? Is it a place or a woman?" Rasulullah ﷺ replied, "Saba was neither a place nor a woman. He was an Arab who had 10 sons. 6 of them settled in Yemen and the other 4 settled in Sham. Those who settled in Sham were Laghm, Judham, Ghassan and Amila. Those who settled in Yemen were Azd, Kindah, Himyar, Ash'ariun, Anmar and Madh'hij." The Sahabi then asked, "O Rasulullah ﷺ! Who are the Anmar?" Rasulullah ﷺ replied, "The Anmar are those who have amongst them the Khath'am and Bajelah tribes." *(Ibn Sa'd, Ahmad, Abu Dawud, Tirmidhi, Tabrani, Hakim)*. Farwa ؓ came to Rasulullah ﷺ and asked, "Should I not take those of my people who have accepted Islam to fight those of them who have not accepted Islam?" Rasulullah ﷺ replied, "Yes. Use those who have accepted to fight those who have not accepted." When Farwa ؓ was leaving, Rasulullah ﷺ called him back and said, "Do not fight them until you have invited them to accept Islam." Farwa ؓ asked, "O Rasulullah ﷺ! Tell me about Saba. Was it a valley, a mountain or what?" Rasulullah replied, "No. He was an Arab who had 10 sons." The Hadith continues later. *(Ibn Kathir)*

Rasulullah ﷺ Instructs Khalid bin Sa'eed to Convey Islam When he was Sent to Yemen

Khalid bin Sa'eed ؓ reports that when Rasulullah ﷺ dispatched him to Yemen, Rasulullah ﷺ said to him, "If you hear the Adhan being called out among any nation you meet, leave them alone. If you pass a nation and hear no Adhan from them, you should invite them to Islam." *(Tabrani, Haythami)*

Rasulullah ﷺ Frees Captives who had not been Invited to Islam

Ubay bin Ka'b ؓ narrates that when some captives from Lat and Uzza were brought before Rasulullah ﷺ, he asked the Muslims who captured them, "Did you invite them to accept Islam?" When they said that they had not, Rasulullah ﷺ asked the captives, "Did they invite you to accept Islam?" When they confirmed that no invitation was given to them, Rasulullah ﷺ instructed, "Free them so that they may reach their place of safety." Thereafter, Rasulullah recited the following 2 extracts of the Qur'an:

يَا أَيُّهَا النَّبِيُّ إِنَّا أَرْسَلْنَاكَ شَاهِدًا وَمُبَشِّرًا وَنَذِيرًا (45) وَدَاعِيًا إِلَى اللَّهِ بِإِذْنِهِ وَسِرَاجًا مُنِيرًا (46)

O Prophet (Muhammad ﷺ)! Verily, We have sent you as witness, and a bearer of glad tidings, and a warner, and as one who invites to Allah by His permission, and as a lamp spreading light (through your instructions from the Qur'an and the Sunnah). (Al-Ahzab:45-46)

وَأُوحِيَ إِلَيَّ هَذَا الْقُرْآنُ لِأُنْذِرَكُمْ بِهِ وَمَنْ بَلَغَ أَئِنَّكُمْ لَتَشْهَدُونَ أَنَّ مَعَ اللَّهِ آلِهَةً أُخْرَى قُلْ لَا أَشْهَدُ قُلْ إِنَّمَا هُوَ إِلَهٌ وَاحِدٌ وَإِنَّنِي بَرِيءٌ مِمَّا تُشْرِكُونَ (19)

Say (O Muhammad ﷺ): "What thing is the most great in witness?" Say: "Allah (the Most Great!) is Witness between me and you; this Qur'an has been revealed to me that I may therewith warn you and whomsoever it may reach. Can you verily bear witness that besides Allah there are other aliha (gods)?" Say "I bear no (such) witness!" Say: "But in truth He (Allah) is the only one Ilah (God). And truly I am innocent of what you join in worship with Him." (Al-An'am:19)

Another narration states that when Rasulullah ﷺ dispatched a battalion to a vicinity where the idols Lat and Uzza stood, they attacked an Arab tribe living there and captured the soldiers and their families. When brought before Rasulullah ﷺ, the captives said, "O Rasulullah ﷺ! They attacked us without inviting us to Islam" When Rasulullah ﷺ questioned the battalion about this, they confirmed that it was true. Rasulullah ﷺ then said to them, "Allow them to return to their place of safety and then invite them to Islam." *(Kanzul Ummal)*

Dispatching Individuals to Give Da'wah: Rasulullah ﷺ sends Mus'ab bin Umair ﷺ to Madinah

Urwa bin Zubair ﷺ narrates that when the Ansar heard what Rasulullah ﷺ had to say, they became convinced and completely satisfied with his message, they believed in him and professed their Iman. Then they became one of the vehicles of good for mankind at large and returned to their people after promising to meet Rasulullah ﷺ the following Hajj season. They then sent a message to Rasulullah ﷺ requesting him to send someone to them who would call people towards the Book of Allah because this would cause people to accept more readily. Rasulullah ﷺ therefore sent Mus'ab bin Umair ﷺ, who belonged to the Banu Abdud Dar tribe. He stayed among the Banu Ghanam tribe with As'ad bin Zurarah ﷺ. There he taught them the sayings of Rasulullah ﷺ and recited the Qur'an to them. Later on, Mus'ab bin Umair ﷺ continued his Da'wah while staying with Sa'd bin Mu'adh ﷺ. Allah guided people at his hands until there was hardly a home of the Ansar that did not have Muslims in it. Even the leaders of the Ansar accepted Islam, including Amr bin Jamooh ﷺ. The idols of the Ansar were broken and Mus'ab bin Umair ﷺ returned to Rasulullah ﷺ with the title of "Al Muqri" (The Mentor). *(Abu Nu'aym)*. Urwa ﷺ narrated another report in which he mentions how Rasulullah ﷺ presented Islam to the Ansar. This will InsAllah be quoted in the chapter discussing the condition of the Ansar at the beginning. In this report, Urwa ﷺ mentions that when the Ansar returned to Madinah after meeting Rasulullah ﷺ during the Hajj and started calling people to Islam secretly. They informed the people about Rasulullah ﷺ, the teachings Allah had sent with him, and called them towards the Qur'an. Eventually there was hardly a home among the Ansar that did not have Muslims. They then sent a message to Rasulullah ﷺ requesting him to send someone to them who would call people towards the Book of Allah because this would

cause people to accept more readily. Rasulullah ﷺ therefore sent Mus'ab bin Umair ﷺ, who belonged to the Banu Abdud Daar tribe. He stayed among the Banu Ghanam tribe with As'ad bin Zurarah ﷺ. There he started to call people to Islam, spread Islam, and increased its supporters. This he did in secrecy. Urwa ﷺ proceeds further to mention the Da'wah Mus'ab bin Umair ﷺ gave to Sa'd bin Mu'adh and how he became a Muslim, followed by the conversion of the entire Banu Abdil Ash'al to Islam. This will InsAllah be mentioned in the chapter discussing the Da'wah of Mus'ab bin Umair ﷺ. Then the Banu Najjar tribe pressured Mus'ab bin Umair ﷺ's host As'ad bin Zurarah ﷺ and Mus'ab bin Umair ﷺ was forced to stay with Sa'd bin Mu'adh ﷺ. There he continued his Da'wah and Allah guided people at his hands until there was hardly a home of the Ansar that did not have Muslims in it. Even the leaders of the Ansar accepted Islam, including Amr bin Jamooh ﷺ. The idols of the Ansar were even broken. The Muslims became dominant in Madinah and their affairs ran smoothly. Mus'ab bin Umair ﷺ returned to Rasulullah ﷺ with the title of "Al Muqri" (The Mentor) *(Tabrani, Abu Nu'aym, Haythami)*. Another narration states that the Ansar sent Mu'adh bin Afra ﷺ and Rafi bin Malik ﷺ to Rasulullah ﷺ to send someone to them who would call people towards the Book of Allah because this would cause people to accept more readily. Rasulullah ﷺ sent Mus'ab bin Umair ﷺ. The rest of the narration is similar to the one above. *(Abu Nu'aym)*

Rasulullah ﷺ Dispatches Abu Umamah ﷺ to his Bahila Tribe

Abu Umamah ﷺ narrates that Rasulullah ﷺ sent him to invite his people to Allah and to present the command of Islam to them. When he arrived, his people had already watered their camels, milked them, and drunk the milk. When they saw him, they exclaimed, "Welcome O Suday bin Ajlan (real name)! We heard that you have defected that man." He replied, "I have rather believed in Allah and His Rasul ﷺ and Rasulullah ﷺ has sent me to present Islam and its commands to you." As they spoke, a platter of food was brought and placed before them. As they gathered around the platter to eat, they said, "Come and join us, O Suday!" He responded by saying, "Shame on you! I have just come to you from someone who forbids this sort of food except for those animals that you slaughter." They asked, "What has he to say?" Abu Umamah ﷺ told them that the following verse had been revealed in this regard:

حُرِّمَتْ عَلَيْكُمُ الْمَيْتَةُ وَالدَّمُ وَلَحْمُ الْخِنْزِيرِ وَمَا أُهِلَّ لِغَيْرِ اللَّهِ بِهِ وَالْمُنْخَنِقَةُ وَالْمَوْقُوذَةُ وَالْمُتَرَدِّيَةُ وَالنَّطِيحَةُ وَمَا أَكَلَ السَّبُعُ إِلَّا مَا ذَكَّيْتُمْ وَمَا ذُبِحَ عَلَى النُّصُبِ وَأَنْ تَسْتَقْسِمُوا بِالْأَزْلَامِ *Forbidden to you (for food) are: Al-Maytatah (the dead animals - cattle-beast not slaughtered), blood, the flesh of swine, and the meat of that which has been slaughtered as a sacrifice for others than Allah, or has been slaughtered for idols, etc., or on which Allah's Name has not been mentioned while slaughtering, and that which has been killed by strangling, or by a violent blow, or by a headlong fall, or by the goring of horns - and that which has been (partly) eaten by a wild animal - unless you are able to slaughter it (before its death) and that which is sacrificed (slaughtered) on An-Nusub (stone altars). (Forbidden) also is to use arrows seeking luck or decision, (all) that is Fisqun (disobedience of Allah and sin). (Al-Ma'ida:3)*

Abu Umamah ﷺ says that as he invited them towards Islam, they kept rejecting. He then said to them, "Shame on you! At least give me some water for I am extremely thirsty." They responded by saying, "No! We shall not give you any water but would rather leave you to die thirsty." He then tied his turban around his head and lay down on the hot sand. He narrates,

"When I fell asleep, I saw a person come to me with a crystal glass as beautiful as no one had ever seen. In the glass was a drink that no one has ever tasted a drink as delicious. He gave the glass to me and I drank from it. I woke up as soon as I had finished drinking and I swear by Allah that after that I had never been thirsty nor even known what thirst is." *(Tabrani, Haythami).* A shorter version is reported by Abu Ya'la states at the end that someone from Abu Umamah ⌘'s tribe said to the others, "One of your leaders has come to you and you could not even honor him!" The people brought some milk for him to drink, but he said, "I have no need for it now." He narrated the dream and showed them his full stomach. Everyone of them then accepted Islam. A narration of Bayhaqi in *Dala'il* states that Abu Umamah ⌘ was sent to his Bahilah tribe. *(Isaba, Tabrani, Hakim)*

Rasulullah ⌘ Sends a Person to the Banu Sa'd Tribe

Ahnaf bin Qais ⌘ narrates that he was once performing Tawaf around the Kabah when a man from the Banu Layth tribe hold his hand saying, "Shall I not give you glad tidings?" When Ahnaf bin Qais ⌘ asked to be informed, the person said, "Do you not remember the time when Rasulullah ⌘ sent me to invite your tribe to Islam? When I presented Islam to them and invited them to accept, you said to me, 'You are inviting us towards something excellent. You are instructing us with a good thing and Rasulullah ⌘ is certainly calling towards something of great merit.' When Rasulullah ⌘ heard about this, he said, 'O Allah! Forgive Ahnaf.'" It was on account of this that Ahnaf ⌘ would always say, "I have more hope in this Du'a of Rasulullah ⌘ than any good act that I have done." *(Ibn Abi Asim, Hakim).* Imam Ahmad and Tabrani have reported this Hadith like this: "Rasulullah ⌘ sent me to convey the message of Islam to your Banu Sa'd tribe. It was you who said, "Rasulullah ⌘ speaks only good" or you said, "What I am hearing is only good". When I returned and informed Rasulullah ⌘ about what you said, he prayed thus, 'O Allah! Forgive Ahnaf." It was on account of this that Ahnaf ⌘ would always say, "I have more hope in this Du'a of Rasulullah ⌘ than any good act that I have done." *(Haythami)*

Rasulullah ⌘ Sends a Person to an Influential Leader During the Period of Ignorance

Anas ⌘ narrates that Rasulullah ⌘ once sent one of the Sahabah to give Da'wah to a person who was influential during the period of ignorance. The person asked, "What is your Rabb towards whom you call? Is he made of iron? Is he made of copper? Is he made of silver? Is he made of gold?" When the Sahabi reported back to Rasulullah ⌘, Rasulullah ⌘ sent him back to invite again. However, the person repeated his remark. When the Sahabi reported back to Rasulullah ⌘ the 2nd time, Rasulullah ⌘ sent him back for the 3rd time. However, the person repeated his remark yet again. When the Sahabi again reported to Rasulullah ⌘, Rasulullah ⌘ said, "Allah has struck him with a bolt of lightning that burned him." Then this verse was revealed:

(13) وَيُرْسِلُ الصَّوَاعِقَ فَيُصِيبُ بِهَا مَنْ يَشَاءُ وَهُمْ يُجَادِلُونَ فِي اللَّهِ وَهُوَ شَدِيدُ الْمِحَالِ

And Ar-Rad (thunder) glorifies and praises Him, and so do the angels because of His Awe, He sends the thunderbolts, and therewith He strikes whom He wills, yet they (disbelievers) dispute about Allah. And He is Mighty in strength and Severe in punishment. (Ar-Ra'd:13) (Abu Ya'la, Haythami, Bazzar)

Bazzar states that the person was one of the oppressive Arab leaders and that the Sahabi said, "O Rasulullah ⌘! He is more oppressive than Fir'oun. This version of the report states that the Sahabi was still busy inviting the person to Islam for the 3rd time when Allah sent a cloud above him that started to roar with thunder. A bolt of lightning then emerged from the cloud and beheaded the man. *(Tabrani).* The narration of Khalid bin Sa'eed ⌘ has already described in the chapter entitled "Inviting towards Islam on the Battlefield". In that narration, he mentions that when Rasulullah ⌘ dispatched him to Yemen, Rasulullah ⌘ said to him, "If you hear the Adhan being called out among any nation you meet, leave them alone. However, if you pass a nation and hear no Adhan from them, you should invite them to Islam."

Rasulullah ⌘ Dispatches Different Groups to Give Da'wah

Abdullah bin Omar ⌘ narrates that Rasulullah ⌘ once asked Abdur Rahman bin Auf ⌘ and said to him, "Prepare yourself because I want to send you out with a group." The Hadith continues that Abdur Rahman bin Auf ⌘ joined with some other Sahabah. They all then left together until they reached a place called Dowmatul Jandal, a fortress between Madinah and Sham in which several villages were included. When he arrived there, Abdur Rahman bin Auf ⌘ spent 3 days inviting the people to accept Islam. On the 3rd day, their leader Asbagh bin Amr Kalbi ⌘ who was a Christian accepted Islam. Abdur Rahman bin Auf ⌘ sent a letter with a person from the Juhaina tribe called Rafi bin Makith ⌘, reporting the events to Rasulullah ⌘. Rasulullah ⌘ wrote back to him with the instruction to marry the daughter of Asbagh. He therefore married her. This daughter of Asbagh was called Tumadir from whom Abdur Rahman bin Auf ⌘ had a son called Abu Salma. *(Isabah)*

Rasulullah ⌘ Sends Amr bin Al Aas ⌘ to Banu Baliy Tribe to Encourage to Accept Islam

Abdur Rahman Tamimi ⌘ narrates that Rasulullah ⌘ sent Amr bin Al Aas ⌘ to encourage the Arabs to accept Islam. Rasulullah ⌘ sent him to the Banu Baliy tribe because the mother of Aas bin Wa'il (his father) was from this tribe and he would be able to identify with them. When he reached a watering place called Salasil (the Battle of Salasil got its name) which was situated in the territory of the Judham, he sensed danger and sent a message for Rasulullah ⌘ to dispatch reinforcements to assist him. Rasulullah ⌘ then sent a battalion of the early Muhajir under the leadership of Abu Ubaidah bin Jarrah ⌘. Among this battalion were Abu Bakr ⌘ and Omar ⌘. The Hadith continues and will be mentioned in the chapter concerning the appointment of leaders. *(Al Bidayah wan Nihayah)*

Rasulullah ⌘ Dispatches Khalid bin Walid ⌘ to Yemen

Bara bin Aazib ⌘ narrates that he was among the group that Rasulullah ⌘ dispatched to Yemen under the leadership of Khalid bin Walid ⌘ to invite the people of Yemen to Islam. They stayed there for 6 months but no one was prepared to accept Islam. Rasulullah ⌘ sent Ali ⌘ with instructions to relieve Khalid bin Walid ⌘ and send him back with his men except those who preferred to remain behind with li ⌘. Bara bin Aazib ⌘ narrates that he was the one of those who remained behind with Ali ⌘. When Ali ⌘ and the Muslims drew close to the people of Yemen, they also marched forward to meet the Muslims. Ali ⌘ stepped forward and led the Muslims in salah. Then he formed the Muslims into a single row, stepped forward in front of the Muslims and read out the letter that Rasulullah ⌘ had written. In response to this, the entire Hamdan tribe accepted Islam. Ali ⌘ wrote to Rasulullah ⌘ to inform him that the Hamdan tribe had accepted Islam. When Rasulullah ⌘ read the letter, he fell into Sejdah and lifted his head and prayed, "Peace be to the Hamdan! Peace be to the Hamdan!" *(Bayhaqi, Bukhari)*

Rasulullah ﷺ Dispatches Khalid bin Walid ؓ to Najran

Ibn Is'haq narrates that Rasulullah ﷺ once dispatched Khalid bin Walid ؓ to Najran with instructions to invite the Banu Harith bin Ka'b to Islam for 3 days before engaging them in battle. Rasulullah ﷺ told him that if the people accept Islam, he should accept it from them, otherwise he should start battle. Khalid bin Walid ؓ left Madinah and when he arrived in Najran, he sent riders in every direction to meet the people and invite them to Islam saying, "O people! Accept Islam and remain in peace." Consequently, all the people accepted Islam. Khalid bin Walid ؓ stayed with the people to teach them Islam, the Qur'an, and the Sunnah of Rasulullah ﷺ according to the directives that Rasulullah ﷺ had given to him for the people if they accept Islam without fighting. Khalid bin Walid ؓ then wrote the following letter to Rasulullah ﷺ:

The Letter Khalid bin Walid ؓ Sent to Rasulullah ﷺ

In the name of Allah the Most Kind, the Most Merciful
To Muhammad the Nabi and Rasul of Allah ﷺ
From Khalid bin Walid
May peace be to you, O Rasulullah ﷺ and the mercy and blessings of Allah. Before you, I praise Allah besides Whom there is none worthy of worship.

O Rasul of Allah - may Allah shower His special mercies on you - you sent me to the Banu Harith bin Ka'b tribe with instructions to invite them to Islam for 3 days without engaging them in battle. Your instructions were that I accept from them their conversion to Islam, after which I should teach them the commands of Islam, the Qur'an and the Sunnah of Allah's Nabi. Had they not accepted Islam, I was to engage in battle with them. When I arrived, I invited them to Islam for 3 days according to the instruction of Allah's Rasul ﷺ and sent riders among them saying, 'O Banu Harith! Accept Islam and live in peace." They all accepted Islam without a fight and I am presently among them instructing them the instructions of Allah and forbidding them from that which are forbidden. I shall teach them the commands of Islam and the Sunnah of Allah's Nabi until the Rasul of Allah ﷺ writes back to me with new instructions. May peace be to you, O Rasulullah ﷺ and the mercy and blessings of Allah.

The Letter that Rasulullah ﷺ Sent in Reply to Khalid bin Walid ؓ

In the name of Allah the Most Kind, the Most Merciful
From Muhammad the Nabi and Rasul of Allah ﷺ
To Khalid bin Walid
May peace be to you. Before you, I praise Allah besides Whom there is none worthy of worship. Your letter sent with your messenger has reached me with the news that the Banu Harith bin Ka'b tribe had surrendered without a fight and that they have accepted Islam. Your letter also informed me the excellent news that they all testify that there is none worthy of worship but Allah and that Muhammad ﷺ is Allah's servant and Rasul and that Allah has guided them by His guidance. You should give them glad tidings of paradise and warn them against hellfire. Return to Madinah together with a delegation from them. May peace be to you as well as the mercy and blessings of Allah.

Khalid bin Walid ؓ Returns to Rasulullah ﷺ with a Delegation of the Banu Harith

After receiving the letter from Rasulullah ﷺ, Khalid bin Walid ؓ returned to Rasulullah ﷺ with a delegation from the Banu Harith bin Ka'b tribe. When Rasulullah ﷺ saw them arriving in Madinah, he said, "Who are these people who resemble the people of India?" Someone said, "They are the Banu Harith bin

Ka'b tribe." When they arrived in the presence of Rasulullah ﷺ, they greeted him and said, "We testify that you are Allah's Rasul and that there is none worthy of worship but Allah." Rasulullah ﷺ said, "I also testify that there is none worthy of worship but Allah and that I am Allah's Rasul." Addressing them further, Rasulullah ﷺ asked, "Are you the people who accepted Islam when you were warned?" They all remained silent without offering a reply. Rasulullah ﷺ repeated the question a 2nd and 3rd time and still no one replied. When Rasulullah ﷺ repeated the question the 4th time, Yazid bin Abdil Madan ؓ said, "Yes, O Rasulullah ﷺ! It was us who came forward when we were warned." He repeated the reply 4 times. Thereafter Rasulullah ﷺ said, "If Khalid had not written to me with the news that you had accepted Islam without a fight, I would have cast your heads under your feet." Yazid bin Abdil Madan ؓ said, "By Allah! When we accepted Islam, we neither praised you nor Khalid." "Who then did you praise?" asked Rasulullah ﷺ. The reply was, "We praised Allah Who used you to guide us, O Rasulullah ﷺ!" Rasulullah ﷺ said, "You are quite right." Thereafter, Rasulullah ﷺ asked them, "How were you able to defeat your enemies during the period of ignorance?" They said, "We never offended and subdued our enemies." "Why not!" Rasulullah ﷺ exclaimed, "You were certainly victorious over those whom you fought." They said, "O Rasulullah ﷺ! We would defeat our enemies because we remained united and never oppressed anyone." Rasulullah ﷺ said, "You have spoken the truth." Rasulullah ﷺ then appointed Qais bin Husain ؓ as their leader. *(Al Bidayah wan Nihayah, Isaba)*

Call People To Fulfil the Fara'idh of Islam: Rasulullah ﷺ Invites Jareer ؓ Towards Iman, Recite the Shahada and Fulfils the Fara'idh

Jareer bin Abdullah ؓ narrates that Rasulullah ﷺ once sent for him and when he arrived, said to him, "O Jareer! What brings you here?" "I have come to accept Islam at your hands, O Rasulullah ﷺ!" came the reply. Rasulullah ﷺ then threw his shawl over Jareer ؓ and turned to the Sahabah and said, "Give due honor to the noble members of a community when they come to you." Rasulullah ﷺ then said, "O Jareer! I call you to testify that there is none worthy of worship but Allah, that I am Allah's Rasul, that you believe in Allah, in the Last Day, in the fate of all good and evil, that you perform Fardh salah and that you pay the Fardh zakah." Jareer ؓ says that he complied with all of them and Rasulullah ﷺ never failed to smile with him each time he saw him. *(Bayhaqi, Tabrani, Abu Nu'aym)*

Rasulullah ﷺ Teaches Mu'adh ؓ How to Call People Towards the Fara'idh of Islam as he Leaves for Yemen

Abdullah bin Abbas ؓ narrates that when Rasulullah ﷺ sent Mu'adh bin Jabal ؓ to Yemen, he said to him, "You will certainly meet people from the Ahlul Kitab. When you come to them, invite them to testify that there is none worthy of worship but Allah and that Muhammad ﷺ is Allah's Rasul. If they obey you in this, inform them that Allah has made Fardh for them the 5 salah during each day and night. If they obey you in this, inform them that Allah has made Fardh for them zakah that is taken from the wealthy amongst them and given to the poor amongst them. If they obey you, abstain from taking the best of their wealth as zakah and beware of the curses of the oppressed because there is no barrier between it and Allah." *(Bukhari)*

Rasulullah ﷺ calls Howshab Dhi Dhulaim ؓ to the Fara'idh of Islam

Howshab Dhi Dhulaim ؓ narrates that when Allah granted

authority to Rasulullah ﷺ, he sent a letter with Abd Shar and a band of 40 horsemen to Rasulullah ﷺ. When they arrived in Madinah, Abd Shar asked, "Which of you is Muhammad ﷺ?" When someone pointed Rasulullah ﷺ out to him, he asked "What have you brought to us? I am willing to follow you if it is good." Rasulullah ﷺ said to him, "You should establish salah, pay zakah, safeguard the blood of people, enjoin good and forbid from evil." Abd Shar said, "This is fine indeed. Stretch out your hands so that I may pledge my allegiance to you." Rasulullah ﷺ then asked his name. When he replied that it was Abd Shar (servant of evil), Rasulullah ﷺ said, "No, you are rather Abd Khair (servant of good)." Rasulullah ﷺ accepted his pledge of allegiance to Islam and replied to the letter of Howshab Dhi Dhulaim ﷺ, who also accepted Iman. *(Kanzul Ummal, Isaba)*

Rasulullah ﷺ Calls the Abd Qais Delegation Towards Fulfilling the Fara'idh of Islam

Abdullah bin Abbas ﷺ narrates that when a delegation from the Abd Qais tribe met Rasulullah ﷺ, he said to them, "Welcome to the people who will suffer neither regret nor humiliation in both worlds because they accepted Islam willingly." They said, "O Rasulullah ﷺ! The disbelieving tribe of Mudhar, famous war-mongers live between Madinah and us. We are therefore able to meet you only during one of the sacred months when they do not fight. We request you to inform us of something excellent that will lead us to paradise when we carry it out and towards which we may call our people who have remained behind." Rasulullah ﷺ said to them, "I command you to do 4 things and forbid you from 4 things. Things to do are to believe in Allah by testifying that there is none worthy of worship but Allah, to establish salah, to pay zakah, to fast during the month of Ramadhan and an additional thing is to pay 1/3rd of the spoils of war to the public treasury. I forbid you from the following 4 things: drinks brewed in utensils made from marrow, utensils made from hollowed trunks, utensils that are oiled and green in color, and utensils covered in tar. Drinks brewed in all these utensils cannot be consumed because they are intoxic." *(Bukhari)*.Another narration *(Tayalisi)* mentions that Rasulullah ﷺ added, "Always bear this in mind and convey the message to those of your people who remained behind."

The Hadith of Alqama ﷺ on the Reality of Iman, Da'wah Towards Iman and the Fara'idh

Alqama ﷺ narrates that he was one of 7 people from his tribe who came to meet Rasulullah ﷺ. Rasulullah ﷺ replied to their greeting and when they spoke to him, he liked what they said. Rasulullah ﷺ asked them, "What are you?" "We are Mu'minin," they replied. Rasulullah ﷺ said, "Every statement has a reality to substantiate it. What is the reality of your Iman?" They replied, "15 attributes to prove the existence of our Iman. 5 are those that you have commanded us to do, 5 are those that your messengers have commanded us to do and 5 are those that we have adopted from the period of ignorance and are still practicing until now unless you forbid us from them O Rasulullah ﷺ..Rasulullah ﷺ asked, "What are the 5 that I have commanded you to do?" They replied, "You have commanded us to believe in Allah; in His angels, His books, His Ambiya and in the fate of all good and evil." Rasulullah ﷺ asked, "What are the 5 that my messengers have commanded you to do?" They replied, "Your messengers have commanded us to testify that there is none worthy of worship but the One Allah Who has no partners and that you are Allah's servant and Rasul. Also they instructed us to establish the obligatory salah, to pay the obligatory zakah, to fast during the month of Ramadhan and to perform Hajj to the Kabah should we have the ability to do so." Rasulullah ﷺ asked, "And what are the attributes that you have adopted during the period of ignorance?" They replied, "Expressing gratitude when enjoy good fortune, exercise patience when experiencing difficulty, speak the truth during occasions of confrontation, be happy with the decrees of fate and not express pleasure when an enemy is afflicted by calamity," Addressing the Sahabah, Rasulullah ﷺ exclaimed, "Intellectuals and well--cultured people! Their manners are close to those of the Ambiya because they are so excellent." Rasulullah ﷺ smiled with them and said, "I shall advise you with another 5 attributes so that Allah may complete your excellent attributes. Never store that which you cannot eat, never build that which you cannot live in, never compete to achieve that which you shall have to leave behind tomorrow, fear that Allah to Whom you shall have to go and before Whom you shall be gathered and concern yourselves with that towards which you are heading and where you shall live forever." *(Hakim, Isaba, Abu Nu'aym)*

Suwayd bin Harith ﷺ narrates that he was one of 7 people who met Rasulullah ﷺ as a delegation. When they arrived in his presence and spoke to him, he was impressed by their manners and appearance. Rasulullah ﷺ asked them, "What are you?" They replied, "Mu'minin." Rasulullah ﷺ said, "Every statement has a reality to validate it. What is the reality of your Iman?" They replied, "15 attributes prove the existence of our Iman. 5 are those that your messengers have commanded us to believe in, 5 are those that your messengers have commanded us to carry out and 5 are those that we have adopted from the period of ignorance and are still practicing until now unless you dislike them in which case we are prepared to forsake them…" The rest of the Hadith is similar to the one mentioned above except that in place of "fate of all good and evil", he mentioned, "resurrection after death" and instead of "not expressing pleasure when an enemy is afflicted by calamity", he said, "steadfastness when enemies rejoice at our misfortunes." A Hadith has already passed earlier in which an unnamed person from the Baladawiyya tribe narrates the following conversation between his grandfather and Rasulullah ﷺ: I asked, "To what are you calling people?" "I am calling the servants of Allah to Allah," Rasulullah ﷺ responded. "What have you to say?" I asked further. He said, "You should testify that there is none worthy of worship but Allah, that Muhammad ﷺ is the Rasul of Allah, that you believe in everything revealed to me, that you renounce Lat and Uzza, and that you establish Salah and pay Zakah." "What is Zakah?" I asked. "Wealth that our rich give to our poor," came the reply. I responded, "These are excellent things you are calling towards."

Rasulullah ﷺ Dispatches the Sahabah to Far Away Places and Encourages Them to Give Da'wah and not to Fall Into Disputes

Miswar bin Makhrama ﷺ narrates that Rasulullah ﷺ once came to the Sahabah and said, "Allah has sent me as a mercy to all of mankind. Execute this responsibility on my behalf and Allah shall shower you with mercy. Isa ﷺ also placed a similar request to his disciples to propagate the message far and wide so do not fall into disputes as they fell into disputes before him. Those of them who were sent to far places disliked it while only those sent nearby were prepared to do as asked so Isa ﷺ prayed to Allah about this. The next day, Allah made each one of them speak the language of the people to whom he had been sent to propagate the religion. Isa ﷺ then addressed them saying, "Allah has made this task incumbent on you, so ensure that you carry it out." The Sahabah said, "O Rasulullah ﷺ! We shall certainly execute the responsibility on your behalf so send us wherever you like. Rasulullah ﷺ then sent Abdullah bin Hudhafa ؓ to Kisra, the Emperor of Persia while Saleet bin Amr was sent to Howdha bin Ali, the chief of Yamamah, Ala bin Hadhrami ؓ was sent to Mundhir bin Sawa the chief of Hajar and Amr bin Al Aas was sent to Jaifar and Abbad the 2 sons of Julunda who both ruled over Amman. In addition to these messengers, Dihia Kalbi ؓ was sent to the Caesar, Emperor of Rome, Shuja bin Wahab Asadi was sent to Mundhir bin Harith bin Abi Shimar Ghassani and Amr bin Umayyah Dhamri was sent to Najashi, the King of Abyssinia. All of these messengers returned before the death of Rasulullah ﷺ except Ala bin Hadhrami ؓ who was still in Bahrain when Rasulullah ﷺ passed away. (Tabarani, Haythami). Historians have mentioned that Rasulullah ﷺ also sent Muhajir bin Abi Ummayyah ؓ to Harith bin Abd Kulal while Jareer ؓ was sent to Dhul Kula, Sa'ib was sent to Musalama and Hatib bin Abi Balta'h was sent to Maqowqis, the king of Egypt. (Fat'hul Bari). Anas ؓ narrates that before his death, Rasulullah ﷺ sent letters to emperors of Persia, Rome and Abyssinia as well as to every dictator, inviting them towards Allah The Glorious and Magnificent. The king of Abyssinia referred to here was not the one who accepted Islam and for whom Rasulullah ﷺ led the funeral prayer. (Muslim). Jabir ؓ narrates that before his death Rasulullah ﷺ sent letters to the Emperors of Persia and Rome and to every other dictator. (Ahmad, Tabrani, Haythami)

The Letter Rasulullah ﷺ Sent to Najashi, the King of Abyssinia

With reference to Ja'far bin Abi Talib ؓ and other Sahabah who had migrated to Abyssinia, Rasulullah ﷺ sent the following letter with Arm bin Umayyah Dhamri ؓ to Najashi:

In the name of Allah the Most Kind, the Most Merciful
From Muhammad the Rasul of Allah ﷺ
To Najashi As'ham, the king of Abyssinia

Peace be to you. Before you I praise Allah the Supreme Sovereign, Most Pure, Giver of peace and Protector. I testify that Isa was the spirit that Allah created and His word that He cast to the chaste, pure and innocent Maryam. She bore Isa ﷺ whom Allah created from the spirit and breath from Him just as Allah created Adam by His hand and breath from Him. I call you towards the One Allah Who has no partner and to dutifully obey Him. I invite you to follow me, to believe in me and in that which I have brought because I am the Rasul of Allah. I have sent my cousin Ja'far to you together with a group of Muslims. When they arrive, treat them as your guests without arrogance.

I invite you and your forces to the worship of the Glorious and Magnificent Allah. I have conveyed my message, given you good counsel so do accept my counsel.
Peace be on the one who follows the guidance.

The Reply letter that Najashi Sent to Rasulullah ﷺ

In the name of Allah the Most Kind, the Most Merciful
To Muhammad the Rasul of Allah ﷺ
From Najaashi As'ham bin Abjar
May the peace from Allah, His mercy and blessings be showered on you, O Nabi of Allah. There is none worthy of worship but He Who has guided me to Islam.
O Rasulullah ﷺ, your letter concerning Isa has reached me. I swear by the Rabb of the heavens and the earth that Isa himself never said more than what you have mentioned. We understand the letter you have sent to us and we have entertained your cousin and his companions.
I testify that you are the true and accepted Rasul of Allah. I have pledged my allegiance to you at the hands of your cousin by

whose hand I have accepted Islam for the pleasure of Allah the Rabb of the universe. I am sending to you my son Areeha bin As'ham bin Abjar. I have control over none but my own self. O Rasulullah ﷺ! If you wish that I come to you personally, I am prepared to do so for I testify that whatever you say is the absolute truth. (Bayhaqi, Ibn Is'haq in AlBidayah wan Nihayah)

The Letter Rasulullah ﷺ Sent to Heraclius, the Emperor of Rome

Dihya Kalbi ؓ narrates that Rasulullah ﷺ sent him with a letter to the Emperor of Rome. When he arrived there and handed over the letter, the emperor's nephew who was a blue-eyed boy with a reddish complexion and straight hair was present with him. When he opened the letter, he read, "From Muhammad ﷺ the Rasul of Allah to Heraclius the Roman leader." When he read this much, the Emperor's nephew breathed out loudly and exclaimed, "This cannot be read today!" "Why not?" asked the Emperor. His nephew replied, "Because he started the letter with his name and wrote 'the Roman leader' instead of 'the Emperor of Rome.'" The Emperor instructed, "You shall definitely read it!" When the letter was read and the people dispersed from the Emperor's court, he summoned Dihya ؓ and also sent for the high priest who was his special advisor. The people had informed the high priest about what had happened and the Emperor also informed him and had the letter read out to him. The high priest said, "He (Rasulullah ﷺ) is the one whom we have been waiting for and about whom Isa ﷺ had predicted." The Emperor asked him, "What do you advise me to do?" The high priest said, "As for myself, I certainly believe him and shall follow him." The Emperor said, "As for myself, I shall lose my kingship if I do so." Thereafter, everyone left the Emperor's court. The Emperor then sent for Abu Sufyan who happened to be there at the time for trade. The Emperor asked Abu Sufyan, "Tell me about this person who has appeared in your land. How is he?" Abu Sufyan replied, "He is a young man." The Emperor asked further, "What is his lineage amongst you?" Abu Sufyan replied, "He enjoys a lineage that none can surpass." The Emperor said, "This is sure sign of Prophethood. How is his honesty?" Abu Sufyan replied, "He has never spoken a lie." The Emperor observed, "This is sure sign of Prophethood." He then asked, "Tell me about those of your people who have joined with him. Have any of them returned to you?" "None," came the reply. The Emperor again remarked, "This is sure sign of Prophethood. Is he ever defeated when he leads his companions to battle?" Abu Sufyan replied, "His people have done battle with him. Sometimes they have defeated him and at other times he had defeated them." The Emperor said, "This is sure sign of Prophethood." He then sent for Dihya ؓ and said to him, "Tell your leader that although I know well that he is a prophet, I cannot forsake my kingship."

Dihya ؓ narrates further that the people used to gather before the high priest every Sunday when he would deliver lectures to them and advise them. However, when Sunday came, he did not go out to meet the people and remained in his home until the following Sunday. Dihya ؓ says that he used to meet with the high priest who would speak to him and ask him many questions. When the next Sunday came, the people again awaited his arrival. However, he did not meet them with the pretext of being ill. This he did for several Sundays until the people eventually delivered the ultimatum and sent a message to him stating, "You will come to us otherwise we shall come to you and kill you. We have noted the change in your attitude since the Arab has arrived." The high priest then said to Dihya ؓ, "Take this letter to your leader. Greet him on my behalf and inform him that I testify that there is none worthy of worship but Allah and that Muhammad ﷺ is Allah's Rasul. I believe in Rasulullah ﷺ, accept what he says and follow him but my people dislike this. Also inform him about what you have seen." He then went to meet the people and they killed him. *(Bazzar, Haythami, Tabrani, Abu Nu'aym).* Some Hadith scholars have narrated that Heraclius said to Dihya ؓ, "O dear! I swear by Allah that I know that your leader is the right prophet and that he is the one we have been waiting for and who is described in our scriptures. However, I fear that the Romans will take my life. Were it not for this fear, I would have certainly followed him. Go to the high priest Daghatir and tell him about your leader for he is higher than me in status and more influential in Rome. When Dihya ؓ approached the high priest and informed him of matters, he said, "I swear by Allah that your leader is a right prophet. We recognize him by his description and his name." The high priest then entered his rooms, removed his clothing and wore white clothing. He then went out to meet the Roman people and testified to the true Shahada. They then attacked him and killed him. *(Ibn Is'haq, Tabari, Isaba)*

Sa'eed bin Abi Rashid narrates that it was in Hims that he once saw the man from the Tanokh tribe whom Heraclius had sent to Rasulullah ﷺ as an envoy. The man was his neighbor and had was extremely old, close to death. Sa'eed bin Abi Rashid asked the man, "Will you not tell me about the letter that Heraclius sent to Rasulullah ﷺ and the letter that Rasulullah ﷺ sent to Heraclius." He readily agreed and related that Rasulullah ﷺ was in Tabuk when he sent Dihya ؓ to Heraclius. When the letter of Rasulullah ﷺ reached Heraclius, he summoned all the priests and learned scholars of Rome to his court and had all the doors locked. He then addressed them saying, "This person has reached the place you see (Tabuk) and has sent to me a letter with 3 options. He invites me to (1) follow him in his religion, (2) to pay him our tax (Jizya) in which case we keep our land or (3) to prepare for battle. By Allah! You know from what you have read in the scriptures that he shall definitely take the land from beneath my feet. Come! Let us follow him in his religion or give him part of our wealth to keep our land." When those present heard this, they breathed out simultaneously like the breathe out of a single person and threw down their hats shouting, "Are you proposing that we forsake Christianity and become the slaves of a villager from Hijaz?!" When Heraclius sensed that they would incite a rebellion among the citizens if they left in that condition, Heraclius added, "I have said this only to test your steadfastness in your religion." Thereafter, Heraclius sent for a person from the Tujaib tribe who had been the leader of the Arab Christians and said to him, "Get me someone with a good memory who speaks Arabic so that I may send him to that man (Rasulullah ﷺ) with a reply to his letter." The narrator of this report from the Tanukh tribe says that it was he who was sent to Heraclius, who handed over to him a letter with a decoration of an animal on it. Heraclius then said to the man, "Take this letter to that person and remember everything you hear him say, take careful note of 3 things. See whether he mentions anything about the letter that he wrote to me. See whether he mentions the night when reading my letter and look carefully at his back to see for anything that puts you in doubt."

The envoy carried the letter to Rasulullah ﷺ in Tabuk and found Rasulullah ﷺ sitting with the Sahabah near a watering place. When he asked for their leader, one of the Sahabah pointed Rasulullah ﷺ out to him. The envoy walked up to Rasulullah ﷺ, sat before him and handed over the letter to him. Placing the letter in his lap, Rasulullah ﷺ asked, "Which tribe do you belong to'? When he identified himself as a member of the Tanukh

tribe, Rasulullah ﷺ asked him, "Do you wish to enter into the religion of your father Ibrahim ﷺ, which is far away from all deviation and is securely on the straight path?" The envoy replied, "I am an envoy for a nation and follow their religion, I shall not leave their religion until I first return to them."

Rasulullah ﷺ then recited the following verse of the Qur'an:

إِنَّكَ لَا تَهْدِي مَنْ أَحْبَبْتَ وَلَكِنَّ اللَّهَ يَهْدِي مَنْ يَشَاءُ وَهُوَ أَعْلَمُ بِالْمُهْتَدِينَ (56)

Verily! You (O Muhammad ﷺ) guide not whom you like, but Allah guides whom He wills. And He knows best those who are the guided. (Al-Qasas:56)

Rasulullah ﷺ then said, "O my brother from the Tanukh! I have sent a letter to Najashi (not the king of Abyssinia who accepted Islam) but he tore it up. Allah will tear him and his kingdom apart likewise. I also wrote a letter to your leader Heraclius who held on to the letter without tearing it up. Therefore, as long as good is destined in his life, people shall continue living in fear of him." The envoy narrates that he said to himself, "This is one of the 3 things that Heraclius instructed me to take note of." He therefore removed an arrow from his quiver and imprinted the words on his cover. Rasulullah ﷺ then handed over the letter to someone on his left hand side, to which the envoy asked, "Who is your scribe who reads your letters?" "Mu'awiya," came the reply. The letter contained the following: "Do you invite me to a paradise the width of which spans the heavens and the earth, which has been prepared for those who have Taqwa? If the Paradise occupies all this space then where is the fire?" Rasulullah ﷺ exclaimed, "Subhanallah! Then where is the night when the day appears?" Taking an arrow from his quiver, the envoy imprinted these words on his cover. After reading the letter, Rasulullah ﷺ said to the envoy, "You are an envoy and have a right over us. If we had anything with us, we would surely have rewarded you with it, but we are travelers whose provisions have been used up." Then someone amongst a group called out, "I shall reward him." He then opened his shoulder bag and brought a set of clothing from Safura (a place in Jordan), which he placed in the envoy's lap. When the envoy asked who the donor of the clothing was, he was told that it was Uthman ؓ. Continuing the report, the envoy says, "Rasulullah ﷺ asked the Sahabah, 'Who shall entertain the envoy?' A youth from the Ansar volunteered for the job and stood up. I stood up with him. When I was leaving the gathering, Rasulullah ﷺ called me back saying, 'O brother from the Tanukh!' I hastened back until I stood in the very place where I had been sitting before him. Rasulullah ﷺ removed the shawl from his back and said, 'Here! Come over and do what you have been ordered.' I went around to his back and saw the seal of Prophethood between his shoulder blades, which resembled the egg of a dove." *(Abdullah bin Ahmad, Abu Ya'la, Haythami Al Bidayah wan Nihayah)*

Abu Sufian and Heraclius

Abdullah bin Abbas ؓ narrates that Abu Sufyan ؓ told him that he went to Sham with a trade caravan of the Quraish during the period when Rasulullah ﷺ had extended a peace treaty to Abu Sufian and the disbelievers of the Quraish. When they were at a place called Ilyia (Baytul Maqdas) when Heraclius summoned them. When they appeared in his court in the presence of the Roman ministers, Heraclius called for an interpreter. Heraclius then asked, "Which of you is closest in lineage to the person who clams to be a prophet?" Abu Sufian replied, "I am closest to him in lineage." Heraclius then ordered that Abu Sufian be brought close to him while the others should be made to sit behind him. He then addressed the others through the interpreter saying, "I shall ask this man about that person (Rasulullah ﷺ). Point out his lies if he lies to me." Abu Sufian thought to himself, "By Allah! I would have certainly lied had I not feared being called a liar." The first question Heraclius asked was: "How is his lineage amongst you?" "He is of extremely high lineage amongst us," was the reply. Heraclius asked further, "Has anyone from amongst you made such a claim before?" Abu Sufyan replied in the negative. The next question was, "Were there any kings amongst his forefathers?" "No," replied Abu Sufian. "Is it the nobles among people who follow him or the weak ones?" Abu Sufian replied, "The weak ones." Heraclius asked, "Are his followers increasing or decreasing?" Abu Sufian replied, "They are increasing," Heraclius then asked, "Have any of them turned back to their religion out of displeasure for his religion after entering it?" Abu Sufian replied in the negative. The next question was, "Have any of you accused him of lying before he made his claim?" "No," came the reply. "And has he ever broken a treaty?" came the question. "No," replied Abu Sufyan, "But we are presently bound by a treaty with him and do not know what he will do." Abu Sufian says, "Besides this, there was nothing else I could add." Heraclius continued, "Have you ever fought against him?" "Yes," replied Abu Sufian. "Then how did you fare?" the emperor asked. Abu Sufian said, "Wars are like the bucket of a well between us. Sometimes he defeats us and sometimes we defeat him." Heraclius asked, "What does he command you to do?" "He commands us to worship the One Allah without ascribing partners to Him and to forsake what our forefathers said. He also commands us to perform salah, be truthful, remain chaste and keep family ties." Heraclius then instructed the interpreter saying, "Tell him that when I asked about his (Rasulullah ﷺ's) lineage, he maintained that he is of extremely high lineage. Such are the prophets who are of high birth. Then I asked you if anyone had made such a claim of Prophethood before him and you replied in the negative. Had anyone made such a claim before him, I would have said that he is such a man what was said before him. You again replied in the negative when I asked whether any of his forefathers were kings. Had there been kings amongst his forefathers, I would have said that he is a man seeking the kingdom of his father. Then I asked you whether any of you had ever accused him of lying before and you said that none had done so. I do realize that it is impossible for a person to abstain from lying about people and then lie about Allah. I then asked you whether it is the nobles among people who follow him or the weak and you replied that they were the weak ones. These have always been the followers of the prophets. I also asked you whether his followers are increasing or decreasing and you said that they were increasing. Such is the case with faith until it is completed. Thereafter I asked you whether anyone had returned to his former religion out of displeasure after entering into his religion and you informed me that none had done so. Such is the condition of faith when it penetrates the depths of the heart. When I asked you whether he ever broke a treaty, you said that he had not. Such are the prophets. They never break their pledges. I then asked you what he commanded and you said that he commanded you to worship the One Allah without ascribing partners to Him, that he forbade you from worshipping idols and that he commanded you to perform salah, to speak the truth and to remain chaste. If whatever you say is true then he shall seize control of the ground I stand on. Although I was expecting his appearance, I had no idea that he would appear among you people. If I knew that I could reach him, I would have burdened myself to do so and had I been in his presence, I would have washed his feet." He then called for the letter that Rasulullah ﷺ sent with Dihya ؓ to the chief of Busra, which the chief of Busra has subsequently forwarded to Heraclius. The letter read:

بِسْمِ اللّهِ الرَّحْمَنِ الرَّحِيمِ

In the name of Allah the Most Kind, the Most Merciful
From Muhammad the servant and Rasul of Allah ﷺ
To Heraclius, the Emperor of Rome
Peace be on the one who follows the guidance.
I call you with the invitation of Islam. Accept Islam, you will live in peace and Allah shall double your reward. Should you turn your back, sin of all your subjects shall be burdened on you.

قُلْ يَا أَهْلَ الْكِتَابِ تَعَالَوْا إِلَى كَلِمَةٍ سَوَاءٍ بَيْنَنَا وَبَيْنَكُمْ أَلَّا نَعْبُدَ إِلَّا اللَّهَ وَلَا نُشْرِكَ بِهِ شَيْئًا وَلَا يَتَّخِذَ بَعْضُنَا بَعْضًا أَرْبَابًا مِنْ دُونِ اللَّهِ فَإِنْ تَوَلَّوْا فَقُولُوا اشْهَدُوا بِأَنَّا مُسْلِمُونَ (64)

Say (O Muhammad ﷺ): "O people of the Scripture (Jews and Christians): Come to a word that is just between us and you, that we worship none but Allah, and that we associate no partners with Him, and that none of us shall take others as lords besides Allah. Then, if they turn away, say: "Bear witness that we are Muslims." (Al-'Imran:64)

Abu Sufian narrates further, "After Heraclius had spoken and read the letter, there was a lot of noise around and people started speaking at the top of their voices. It was then that they sent us out. When we were sent out, I said to one of my companions, 'The affair of Ibn Abi Kabsha (Rasulullah ﷺ) has grown so powerful that even the king of the yellow skins (the Romans) have begun to fear him.' Thereafter, I remained convinced that Rasulullah ﷺ would dominate until Allah blessed me with Islam." A person by the name of Ibn Natur was the governor of Ilyia, a good friend of Heraclius and the high priest of the Christians in Sham. He narrates that once when Heraclius was visiting Ilyia (Baytul Maqdas), he appeared extremely sick and restless one morning. In fact, some of his pastors even told him that he did not seem well. Heraclius was an astrologer and could read the stars so when they asked him about the reason for his ill disposition he said to them, "When I gazed into the stars, I saw that the king of the circumcised people had made his appearance. Which nation practices circumcision?" They told him, "It is only the Jews who practice circumcision, but you have nothing to fear from them. Simply circulate a command throughout your kingdom calling for all Jews to be killed." They were still busy discussing this when an envoy arrived from the governor of Ghassan, informing them about Rasulullah ﷺ. When Heraclius had questioned the envoy, he instructed the pastors to investigate whether the envoy was circumcised. When they determined that he had been circumcised, he was asked whether the Arabs practiced circumcision. When he informed them that circumcision was custOmary amongst the Arabs, Heraclius said, "It is the king of this nation who has made his appearance." Heraclius then wrote a letter to a friend in Rome who was also an expert in astrology as he was. He then left for Hims. He had not yet reached Hims when a reply came from his friend who corresponded with the opinion of Heraclius that Rasulullah ﷺ had made his appearance and that he was a prophet. Heraclius then invited the leading people of Rome to his castle in Hims and had all the doors locked. He then made an appearance and addressed them saying, "O leaders of the Roman people! Do you want to achieve success, good fortune and keep your kingdom? Simply follow this prophet." When they heard this, everyone present started to flee like wild camels and headed for the doors, which they found locked. When Heraclius noticed their disrespect and lost hope in their accepting faith, he instructed his men to bring everyone back. He then said to them, "I told you this only to test your steadfastness in adhering to your religion. I have now witnessed it." They all prostrated before him and were satisfied with him. This was the final stand of Heraclius (he never accepted Iman). *(Bukhari)*

The Letter Rasulullah ﷺ Sent to Kisra, the Emperor of Persia

Abdullah bin Abbas ؓ narrates that Rasulullah ﷺ sent a messenger with a letter addressed to Kisra, instructing the messenger to hand the letter over to the governor of Bahrain. The governor in turn had it sent to Kisra. However, Kisra tore the letter up and it was probably Ibn Musaib who narrates that Rasulullah ﷺ cursed Kisra by saying that Allah should also tear him apart completely. *(Bukhari)*. Abdur Rahman bin Abd Qari ؓ narrates that Rasulullah ﷺ stood on the pulpit one-day to deliver a sermon. After praising Allah, and reciting the Shahada, he said, "I intend to send some of you to the non-Arab kings so do not dispute before me as the Bani Israel did in front of Isa the son of Maryam عليه السلام." To this, the Muhajir said, "O Rasulullah ﷺ! We shall never ever dispute with you concerning anything. Issue the command and send us wherever you wish." Rasulullah ﷺ then sent Shuja bin Wahab ؓ to Kisra. When he arrived, Kisra had his palace decorated and gathered the leading personalities of his kingdom there before admitting Shuja ؓ. When Shuja ؓ entered, Kisra ordered that the letter of Rasulullah ﷺ should be taken from Shuja ؓ and handed over to him. However, Shuja ؓ refused to surrender the letter and insisted that he wanted to personally hand the letter to Kisra as Rasulullah ﷺ had commanded him. Kisra permitted him to draw close and when he did, he handed the letter over. Kisra then summoned one of his scribes from Hira who read the letter out. The letter read: "From Muhammad ﷺ bin Abdullah the Rasul of Allah to Kisra the Emperor of Persia." The fact that Rasulullah ﷺ begun the letter with his name first made Kisra so angry that he tore the letter to bits before being informed of what it contained. He then ordered Shuja ؓ out of his court. Mounting his conveyance, Shuja ؓ said, "By Allah! Now that I have delivered the letter of Rasulullah ﷺ, I have no concern about which of the 2 paths I am on whether Kisra is pleased or not." When Kisra's anger had decreased, he sent someone to call Shuja back, but Shuja ؓ had already left by then. The person searched for him until he reached Hira but Shuja ؓ was already far ahead. Shuja ؓ reported back Rasulullah ﷺ and informed him that Kisra had torn up the letter, Rasulullah ﷺ commented, "Kisra has torn up his kingdom." *(Al-Bidayah wan Nihayah)*

Abu Salam bin Abdur Rahman ؓ narrates that after the letter of Rasulullah ﷺ had reached Kisra and he read it and tore it up, he wrote to Badhan, the governor of Yemen instructing, "Sent 2 sturdy men to this man in Hijaz with instructions to bring him to me." In compliance with the letter, Badhan sent his chief minister Abanuh in the company of a Persian man called Jad Jamira. Abanuh was a man proficient in Persian letters and numbers. Badhan sent a letter with them to Rasulullah ﷺ, instructing Rasulullah ﷺ to leave for the court of Kisra with the 2 of them. Badhan also instructed his chief minister to inspect Rasulullah ﷺ to engage him in discussion and to report the details back to him. The 2 left and finally reached Taif where they made enquiries about Rasulullah ﷺ from some businessmen of the Quraish. They were informed that Rasulullah ﷺ was in Madinah. Realizing that the 2 men were out to take Rasulullah ﷺ to Kisra, the businessmen became overjoyed and exclaimed, "Now that Kisra has stood up against him (Rasulullah), we have nothing more to do." When the 2 reached Madinah, Abanuh spoke to Rasulullah ﷺ and said to him, "Kisra has written to Badhan with instructions to send someone to take you before him. He has sent me so that you come with me." Rasulullah ﷺ said to him, "You

may leave now and return to see me tomorrow." When the 2 arrived the next day, Rasulullah ﷺ informed them of the precise night of a particular month in which Allah has killed Kisra and handed the kingdom over to his son Sherway. The 2 men said, "Do you know what you are saying? May we write back to Badhan with this news?" "Certainly," replied Rasulullah ﷺ, "and tell him that if he accepts Islam, I shall hand back to him control of all the lands he presently rules." Rasulullah ﷺ then gave Jad Jamirah a belt decorated with gold and silver that had been given to him as a gift. When the 2 returned to Yemen and informed Badhan about the events, he said, "This is not the speech of some king. We should definitely investigate the truth of what he said." They did not have to wait long before they received a letter from Sherway which after the formalities stated, "With the support of the Persian people, I have killed Kisra with anger because he saw nothing wrong to kill Persian nobles without reason. Secure allegiance to me from all the people in Yemen and ensure that you cause no harm to the person (Rasulullah ﷺ) whom Kisra ordered you to capture." After reading the letter of Sherway, Badhan said, "This man (Rasulullah ﷺ) must certainly be a Rasul." He accepted Islam and so did all the Persians living in Yemen. *(Abu Nu'aym, Isaba)*

Ibn Is'haq narrates that Rasulullah ﷺ sent Abdullah bin Hudhafa ؓ with a letter addressed to Kisra in which Rasulullah ﷺ invited him to accept Islam. When he read the letter, he tore it up and wrote to Badhan his governor in Yemen. The rest of the Hadith is similar to the one above. However, this narration states that when the 2 men reached Madinah, Badhan spoke to Rasulullah ﷺ and told him, "Indeed the king of all kings, Kisra wrote to the governor Badhan instructing him to send someone to him who would bring you to him. If you comply by going to Kisra, I shall send a letter with you that will benefit you. However, if you refuse, Kisra shall destroy you and your people and turn your land into ruins." Rasulullah ﷺ said to him, "You may leave and return tomorrow." The rest of the Hadith is similar to the one above. *(Dala'ilum Nabuwah, Isaba)*. Zaid bin Abi Habib narrates that Rasulullah ﷺ sent Abdullah bin Hudhafa with a letter for Kisra bin Hurmuz who was the Emperor of Persia. The letter read:

In the name of Allah the Most Kind the Most Merciful
From Muhammad ﷺ, the Rasul of Allah
To Kisra, the Emperor of Persia

Peace be on the one who follows the guidance, who believes in Allah and His Rasul and who testifies that there is none worthy of worship but the One Allah Who has no partners and that Muhammad ﷺ is Allah's servant and Rasul.

I call you with the invitation of Allah ﷻ for I am the Rasul of Allah to all of mankind who warns the living so that the decree of punishment becomes binding on the disbelievers. If you accept Islam, you shall live in peace and if you refuse, then the sin of the fire-worshippers shall be on you.

Kisra tore up the letter when he read it and wrote to Badhan. The rest of the Hadith is as mentioned earlier from the narration of Ibn Is'haq. However, this report adds that when the 2 men entered the presence of Rasulullah ﷺ their faces were shaven off and their moustaches were grown very long. Rasulullah ﷺ therefore disliked even looking at them and said, "Woe to you! Who instructed you to do this?" Referring to Kisra, they said, "Our Rabb commanded us to do this." Rasulullah ﷺ said to them, "My Rabb has commanded me to let my beard grow and to trim my moustache." *(Al Bidayah wan Nihayah)*. Abu Bakr ؓ narrates that when Rasulullah ﷺ was sent to propagate the message, Kisra sent a message to his governor over Yemen and the surrounding areas of Arabia, who was called Badam. He stated in his letter, "It has reached me that a person has surfaced in your district who claims to be a Nabi. Tell him to stop what he is doing otherwise I shall send an army that will kill him and his people." When Badam's envoy conveyed the message to Rasulullah ﷺ, Rasulullah ﷺ said to him, "Had this propagation been something that I am doing of my own accord, I shall be able to stop it. However, the Glorious and Magnificent Allah has sent me to do it." The envoy stayed awhile and Rasulullah ﷺ once said to him, "My Rabb has killed Kisra and there is no Kisra after this day. My Rabb has also killed Caesar and there is no Caesar after this day." The envoy wrote down the statement the moment Rasulullah ﷺ said it, during the day in which he said it and during the month in which he said it. When he returned to Badam, he found out that Kisra had already died and the Caesar has been killed. *(Tabrani, Haythami, Ahmad, Bazzar)*

Dihya Kalbi ؓ narrates that Rasulullah ﷺ sent him with a letter addressed to the Caesar. The Hadith is similar to that mentioned under the heading "The Letter Rasulullah ﷺ sent to Heraclius, the Emperor of Rome". However, at the end of this narration of Bazzar, it is stated that when Dihya ؓ returned to Rasulullah ﷺ, he found envoys of the San'a governors with Rasulullah ﷺ. They had sent their envoys to Rasulullah ﷺ because Kisra had written a threat to the governor of San'a instructing him to deal with the person from his region (Rasulullah ﷺ) who had written to Kisra saying that he should either embrace his religion or pay Jizya. Kisra threatened the governor with death and other stern measures if he failed in his task. It was in response to this that the governor of San'a sent the 25 persons whom Dihya ؓ found with Rasulullah ﷺ. When their leader read out the letter to Rasulullah ﷺ, he gave them no reply and left them for 15 nights. When the 15 nights had passed, they came before him and when he saw them, he said, "Go to your governor and inform him that my Rabb has killed his lord (Kisra) this night." When they returned and informed the governor likewise, he said to them, "Take note of that night." He then asked them, "Tell me how you found him?" They replied, "We have not seen a king as blessed as he. He walks about freely without any fear, dresses most simply, has no bodyguards and no one raises their voice before him." Dihya ؓ said that the news later came that Kisra was killed on the night that Rasulullah ﷺ has mentioned. *(Bazzar, Haythami)*

Rasulullah ﷺ Sent a Letter to Maqoqis, the King of Alexandria

Abdullah bin Abd Qari ؓ narrates that Rasulullah ﷺ sent Hatib bin Abi Balta'h ؓ with a letter addressed to Maqoqis the king of Alexandria. When Hatib ؓ arrived with the letter, Maqoqis kissed the letter and entertained Hatib ؓ most excellently. When he sent Hatib ؓ back to Rasulullah ﷺ, he sent gifts for Rasulullah ﷺ with him that included a suit of clothing, a saddled mule and 2 slave women. The one slave woman Maria was the mother of Rasulullah ﷺ's son Ibrahim and Rasulullah ﷺ gave the other to Muhammad bin Qais Abdi ؓ *(Bayhaqi)*. Hatib bin Abi Balta'h ؓ narrates that Rasulullah ﷺ sent him to Maqoqis the king of Alexandria. When he delivered the letter, Maqoqis hosted Hatib ؓ in his palace, where he stayed awhile. Maqoqis then gathered his high priests and called for Hatib. Maqoqis said to him, "I wish to pose a few questions and want you to understand them well." "By all means," replied Hatib ؓ. Maqoqis asked, "Tell me about your leader. Is he really a prophet'?" "He certainly is the Rasul of Allah," replied Hatib ؓ. Maqoqis then asked further, "If he really is Allah's prophet, why did he then not curse his people when they drove him out of his

town Makkah?" Hatib ؓ responded by asking, "Do you not testify that Isa the son of Maryam ؑ was Allah's Rasul?" "Indeed," came the reply. "Then when his people seized him to crucify him," began Hatib ؓ, "why did he not pray to Allah to destroy them when Allah raised him to the heavens?" Maqoqis said to Hatib ؓ" "You are a wise man who has come from the company of a wise man. Here are some gifts that I am sending with you to Muhammad ﷺ. I am also sending some guards with you to protect you until you reach your place of safety." Maqoqis sent 2 slave women to Rasulullah ﷺ, one of whom was the mother of Rasulullah ﷺ's son Ibrahim. Rasulullah ﷺ gave another to Hassan bin Thabit ؓ. Besides this, Maqosqis also sent selected gifts that were highly praised in their land. *(Bayhaqi in Al Bidayah wan Nihayah, Ibn Shahin in Isaba)*

Rasulullah ﷺ Sent a Letter to the People of Najran

The grandfather of Abd Yasu who was a Christian before accepting Islam narrates that Rasulullah ﷺ sent a letter to the people of Najran before Surah "Naml" was revealed. The letter does not begin with "*Bismillahir Rahmanir Rahim*" because it was only after the revelation of this Surah that Rasulullah ﷺ started using "*Bismillahir Rahmanir Rahim*" in his letters as this Surah mentions that Sulaiman did. The letter read:

I begin in the name of the Ilah of Ibrahim ؑ, Is'haq ؑ and Ya'qub ؑ.
From Muhammad, the Nabi and Rasul of Allah
To the high priest and people of Najran
Peace be to you. Before you I praise the Ilah of Ibrahim ؑ, Is'haq and Ya'qub ؑ. I call you from the worship of Allah's slaves to the worship of Allah and from the friendship of Allah's slaves to the friendship of Allah. Should you refuse to accept Islam, you shall have to pay the Jizya and should you refuse even this, I shall have to declare war against you. Was Salam

---

When the high priest read the letter, he was alarmed and became extremely frightened. He immediately sent for a person from Najran called Shurabil bin Wada'h who hailed from Hamdan tribe. Whenever any problem arose, he was summoned even before the heroes, leaders and high-ranking people. The high priest handed over Rasulullah ﷺ's letter to Shurabil, who read it. The high priest then asked, "O Abu Maryam! What is your opinion?" Shurabil said, "You know well that Allah promised Ibrahim ؑ Prophethood in the progeny of his son Ishmail ؑ. It would come as no surprise if this is the very person who has received the promised Prophethood. I can offer no opinion in the matter of Prophethood. Had the matter been a worldly one, I would have advised you and pressed myself to assist you." The high priest then asked Shurabil to step aside and be seated, which he did. The high priest then sent for a man called Abdullah bin Shurabil who was also from Najran and belonged to the Dhu Asba branch of the Himyar tribe. When the high priest read the letter to him and asked his opinion, his reply was similar to that of Shurabil. The high priest then asked Abdullah to step aside and be seated, which he did. He then sent for a man called Jabbar bin Faidh who was also from Najran and belonged to the Banu Harith bin Ka'b branch of the Banul Himas tribe. When the high priest read the letter to him and asked his opinion, his reply was similar to that of Shurabil and Abdullah. He also took a seat when asked to do so. Once they had all agreed on the matter, the high priest called for the bells to be tolled, fires to be lit and flags to be raised in the churches. This was their practice whenever trouble developed during the day. When there was trouble during the night, they would only toll the bells and light the fires in the churches. Consequently, when the bells were tolled and the flags rose, all the people living on the top and bottom parts of the valley gathered. The valley was so long that it would take a speeding rider a complete day to pass and there were 73 villages in it comprising of 120,000 warriors. When the high priest read the letter of Rasulullah ﷺ to them, everyone agreed that Shurabil bin Wada'h from the Hamdan tribe, Abdullah bin Shurabil from the Dhu Asba tribe and Jabbar bin Faidh from the Banu Harith tribe should be sent to gather news about Rasulullah ﷺ. The delegation left and finally arrived in Madinah. There they removed their traveling clothes and wore decorative long garments made in Yemen, which they dragged along. They also wore gold rings. When they approached Rasulullah ﷺ and greeted him, he did not reply to their greeting. The entire day they sought an opportunity to speak to Rasulullah ﷺ but he refused to speak to them as long as they wore those clothes and gold rings. Then they looked for Uthman bin Affan ؓ and Abdur Rahman bin Auf ؓ who knew them and eventually found them sitting with a group of Muhajir and Ansar. They said, "O Uthman! O Abdur Rahman! Your Nabi wrote a letter to us and we have arrived in response to the letter. However, when we came to him and greeted him, he did not reply to our greeting and although we searched all day for an opportunity to speak to him, we have been unable to do so. What is your opinion? Do you think that we should return?" Ali bin Abi Talib ؓ was also in the gathering, so the 2 of them asked him, "What do you think of these people, O Abul Hasan?" Addressing Uthman ؓ and Abdur Rahman bin Auf ؓ, Ali ؓ said, "I think that they should remove these clothes and these rings and wear their traveling clothes. Thereafter they should return to Rasulullah ﷺ. When they did this and again greeted Rasulullah ﷺ, he replied to their greeting and said, "I swear by the Being Who has sent me with the truth that Satan was certainly with you when you came to me the first time." Rasulullah ﷺ then asked about them and they asked him questions. During the course of their questioning, they asked, "What have you to say about Isa عليه السلام? We are Christians and will be returning to our people. If you are a Nabi, we would be pleased to hear what you have to say about him." Rasulullah ﷺ said to them, "I have nothing much to say about him today. Stay a while longer until I am able to inform you what my Rabb has to say about Isa عليه السلام." By the following morning, the following verses of the Qur'an had been revealed:

إِنَّ مَثَلَ عِيسَى عِنْدَ اللَّهِ كَمَثَلِ آدَمَ خَلَقَهُ مِنْ تُرَابٍ ثُمَّ قَالَ لَهُ كُنْ فَيَكُونُ (59) الْحَقُّ مِنْ رَبِّكَ فَلَا تَكُنْ مِنَ الْمُمْتَرِينَ (60) فَمَنْ حَاجَّكَ فِيهِ مِنْ بَعْدِ مَا جَاءَكَ مِنَ الْعِلْمِ فَقُلْ تَعَالَوْا نَدْعُ أَبْنَاءَنَا وَأَبْنَاءَكُمْ وَنِسَاءَنَا وَنِسَاءَكُمْ وَأَنْفُسَنَا وَأَنْفُسَكُمْ ثُمَّ نَبْتَهِلْ فَنَجْعَلْ لَعْنَةَ اللَّهِ عَلَى الْكَاذِبِينَ (61)

Verily, the likeness of Isa before Allah is the likeness of Adam. He created him from dust, then (He) said to him: "Be!" and he was. (This is) the truth from your Lord, so be not of those who doubt. Then whoever disputes with you concerning him (Isa) after (all this) knowledge that has come to you, (i.e. Isa being a slave of Allah, and having no share in Divinity) say: (O Muhammad ﷺ), "Come, let us call our sons and your sons, our women and your women, ourselves and yourselves - then we pray and invoke (sincerely) the Curse of Allah upon those who lie." (Al-'Imran:59-61)

After Rasulullah ﷺ recited these verses to them, they refused to accept it rather accepted the challenge of Mubahala (when 2 parties collectively make dua to Allah that He should destroy the wrong party) offered in the last verse above Consequently, Rasulullah ﷺ arrived the following morning for the challenge with Hasan ؓ and Husain ؓ wrapped in his shawl. Behind him came Fatima ؓ and his many wives. Seeing this, Shurabil said to his 2 companions, "You know well that the people from the

entire top and bottom places of our valley always return contented with my decisions. I swear by Allah that what I see here is an extremely serious and important affair. If he is a sent Rasul, we shall be the first Arabs to be a disgrace for him and the first to oppose him. This insult will not leave his heart nor the hearts of his companions until they destroy us. We are also the closest Arabs to them and are most likely face any pending attacks. If he is a sent Rasul of Allah, then to engage him in Mubahala would even destroy the hairs and fingernails of each of us on earth." The 2 asked him, "What is then your proposal, O Abu Maryam?" Shurabil said, "I propose that we negotiate a treaty with him for I do not see him to be one who would ever make useless phrases." The 2 said to him, "We leave you to do as you see appropriate." Shurabil went to see Rasulullah ﷺ and said, "I propose something better than Mubahala." "What is that'?" asked Rasulullah ﷺ. Shurabil replied, "You have today and tonight to pass judgment and prepare the phrases of a treaty. We are prepared to accept whatever phrases you make." Rasulullah ﷺ asked him, "Perhaps there are people left behind who may criticize you for this." Shurabil said, "You may ask my 2 companions." When Rasulullah ﷺ asked them, they said, "The people from the entire top and bottom parts of our valley always return contented with the decisions of Shurabil." Rasulullah ﷺ then returned home without carrying out the Mubahala." The next day, they met Rasulullah ﷺ and wrote the following letter:

In the name of Allah the Most Kind the Most Merciful This is the treaty that the Nabi and Rasul of Allah Muhammad ﷺ has written for the people of Najran. He has determined that all their fruit crops, their gold, their silver, their produce and their slaves would remain their property on condition that they pay 2,000 sets of clothing; 1,000 every Rajab and the other 1,000 every Safar.
Other clauses are also mentioned in the narration. *(Bayhaqi in Tafseer ibn Kathir)*

A narration of *Al Bidayah wan Nihayah (Vol.5 Pg.55)* adds that the witnesses to this treaty were Abu Sufian bin Harb, Ghailan bin Amr, Malik bin Auf of the Banu Nasr tribe, Aqra bin Habis Handhali and Mughiera ؓ. Rasulullah ﷺ had the treaty written out and the 3 returned with it to Najran. Their high priest at the time was his step brother who was also his cousin. His name was Bashir bin Mu'awiya and he was commonly known as Abu Alqama. The 3 handed over the letter of Rasulullah ﷺ to the high priest. The high priest and Abu Alqama were mounted on their camels at the time and the high priest was busy reading the letter when Abu Alqama's camel tripped and fell. Abu Alqama also fell and without cutting his words, he cursed Rasulullah ﷺ as he fell. When this happened, the high priest said to him, "By Allah! You have cursed a sent prophet!" Affected by the words of the high priest, Abu Alqama said, "If he is a true prophet, then I swear by Allah that I shall not unlock my shoulder bag until I meet Rasulullah ﷺ." Saying this, he turned his camel to the direction of Madinah. The high priest also turned his camel in the same direction and said, "Understand well what I have to say. I have said what I did in fear so that the Arabs may hear from me that we have acknowledged the right of Rasulullah ﷺ, that we accepted his call and have submitted to him as the other Arabs did not even though we are the most noble of the Arabs and have the largest population." Abu Alqama said to him, "No! By Allah! I shall never accept anything coming from your head!" Abu Alqama then hit his camel and left the high priest behind. As he rode, he urged the camel on by reciting the following couplets:
O Rasulullah ﷺ, to you does the camel run with her rope shaking her belly lies her unborn child in a breeched

position Her (master's) religion is now other than Christianity

Abu Alqama met Rasulullah ﷺ, accepted Islam and lived his life with Rasulullah ﷺ until he was finally martyred. In the meantime, the 3 man delegation returned to Najran and approached a monk called Ibn Abi Shimr who lived at the top of his monastery. They told him that a prophet had been sent to the Tihama district and told him about the Najran delegation that met Rasulullah ﷺ. They also informed him that Rasulullah ﷺ had challenged them to Mubahala that they had declined the challenge and that Bashir bin Mu'awiya (Abu Alqama) left to meet Rasulullah ﷺ and had accepted Islam. The monk said, "Take me down from here before I throw myself down from this monastery." When they took him down, he took some gifts along with him and left to meet Rasulullah ﷺ. Among these gifts were the shawl that the Khulafa wore, a cup and a staff. He stayed for some while with Rasulullah ﷺ, listening to the revelation but he was not ready to accept Islam. He left Rasulullah ﷺ, promising to return shortly, but his return did not happen and Rasulullah ﷺ passed away. The high priest Abul Harith came to Rasulullah ﷺ in the company of several leaders and high-ranking persons. They stayed some time with Rasulullah ﷺ, listening to what revelation came to Rasulullah ﷺ. Rasulullah ﷺ wrote this letter to the high priest and to all the priests of Najran after him:

> In the name of Allah the Most Kind the Most Merciful
> From Muhammad ﷺ, the Rasul of Allah
> To the high priest Abul Harith, the priests, fortune-tellers and monks of Najran
> Everything they possess in large and small quantities shall enjoy the protection of Allah and His Rasul. No priest, monk or fortune-teller shall lose his position nor the rights due to him nor any authority he may be enjoying. This protection of Allah and His Rasul shall remain intact forever as long as they continue doing what is correct and remain well-wishers without supporting oppression or oppressors.

This letter was written by Mughiera bin Shu'ba.

The Letter Rasulullah ﷺ Sent to the Bakr bin Wa'il Tribe

Marthad bin Dhabian ؓ narrates that a letter from Rasulullah ﷺ reached them and that they could find no one in their tribe to read it until a man from the Dabe'ah tribe read it to them. It read:
From Rasulullah ﷺ
To the Bakr bin Wa'il tribe
Accept Islam and live in peace.*

(Ahmad, Haythami, Bazzar, Abu Ya'la, Tabrani)

The Letter Rasulullah ﷺ Sent to the Banu Judhama Tribe

Ma'bad Judhami ؓ narrates that when Rifa'h bin Zaid Judhami ؓ met with Rasulullah ﷺ, he wrote the following letter for them:
From Muhammad the Rasul of Allah
This letter has been sent through Handed to Rifa'h bin Zaid whom I have sent to his people and those included amongst them to invite towards Allah and His Rasul. Whoever accepts Iman shall be included in the legion of Allah and His Rasul. As for those who turn their backs, they shall have only two months respite. When Rifa'h ؓ came to his people, they all accepted Iman. *(Tabrani, Haythami, Istaba)*

The Character / Actions of Rasulullah ﷺ Inspired People to Accept Islam: The Conversion of Jewish Rabbi Zaid bin Su'na ؓ to Islam

Abdullah bin Salam ؓ narrates that when Allah decreed that Zaid bin Su'na ؓ should accept Islam, Zaid bin Su'na himself said, "When I looked at Muhammad ﷺ, I recognized all the signs of Nabuwat except for 2 signs that I had not tested; (1) that his self-control should outstrip his anger and (2) that his tolerance should conquer a display of extreme foolishness." Zaid bin Su'na ؓ narrates further that one day Rasulullah ﷺ had just emerged from his rooms with Ali bin Abi Talib ؓ when a rider who appeared to be a Bedouin came to him. He said, "O Rasulullah ﷺ! A few people from a certain tribe have accepted Islam because I told them that they will receive abundance in sustenance if they accepted Islam. However, no rain has fallen and they are afflicted by a drought. O Rasulullah ﷺ! I fear that they may leave the fold of Islam out of greed just as they had entered out of greed. If you agree, we could perhaps send them something to assist them." Zaid bin Su'na ؓ says, "Rasulullah ﷺ looked at the person beside him whom I assume was Ali. He said, 'O Rasulullah ﷺ! I do not think that anything is left of that wealth.' I (Zaid bin Su'na ؓ) approached Rasulullah ﷺ and said, 'O Muhammad ﷺ! Do you wish to sell to me a fixed amount of dates from the orchard of a specific tribe to be paid before a specified term?' Rasulullah ﷺ replied, 'Alright, but do not specify whose orchard it shall be.'" Zaid bin Su'na ؓ agreed and the deal was done. Zaid bin Su'na ؓ opened his bag and paid 80 Mithqal (~1lb) of gold for the specified amount of dates on a specified date. Rasulullah ﷺ handed over the money to the person and said to him, "Take this to assist them." Zaid bin Su'na ؓ narrates further that there were only 2 or 3 days left for the expiry of the term, when Rasulullah ﷺ left his home to perform a funeral prayer. With him were Abu Bakr ؓ, Omar ؓ, Uthman ؓ and several other Sahabah. When they approached a wall to sit by it, Zaid bin Su'na ؓ came to Rasulullah ﷺ and hold Rasulullah ﷺ's collar. Staring angrily into the face of Rasulullah ﷺ, he said. "O Muhammad ﷺ! When are you going to pay my dues? By Allah! All that the children of Abdul Muttalib have learnt is how to delay! By mixing with you people, I now have first-hand knowledge of this!" Zaid bin Su'na ؓ says that as he was doing this, his gaze fell on Omar ؓ. He noticed that Omar ؓ's eyes were starting to roll with anger and he stared with anger. He said, "O enemy of Allah! Do you speak to Rasulullah ﷺ like that and treat him in this manner!? Had it not been for respect of people in the company of Rasulullah ﷺ, I would have cut off your neck!" Zaid bin Su'na says that all the time Rasulullah ﷺ looked at him in a most calm and relaxed manner. Rasulullah ﷺ then said to Omar ؓ, "O Omar! All that the 2 of us need is for you to tell me to pay him quickly and to tell him to place his demands in a better manner. O Omar! Go with him and give him his dues. Also give him 20 Saa of dates extra in lieu of the threat you gave him." Zaid bin Su'na ؓ says that Omar ؓ took him along, paid him what was due and added another 20 Saa to it. When Zaid bin Su'na ؓ asked Omar ؓ what was the 20 Saa extra for, Omar ؓ said that it was the command of Rasulullah ﷺ because of the threat he had made. Zaid bin Su'na ؓ then asked, "O Omar! Do you recognize me?" "No," replied Omar. Zaid bin Su'na ؓ said, "1 am Zaid bin Sn'na ؓ." "The Rabbi?" asked Omar ؓ. "Yes, the Rabbi," was the reply. Omar ؓ asked, "But why did you behave as you did? Why did you speak as yon did?" Zaid bin Sn'na ؓ replied, "O Omar! When I looked at Muhammad ﷺ, I recognized all the signs of Nabuwat except for 2 signs that I had not tested; (1) that his self-control should outstrip his anger and (2) that his tolerance should conquer a display of extreme foolishness. I have tested both these attributes. O Omar! I make you witness that I am content with Allah as Rabb, with Islam as the true religion and with Muhammad ﷺ as the Nabi ﷺ. I also make you witness that I give half of my wealth (I am one of the wealthiest people) as charity to the Ummah of Rasulullah ﷺ." Omar ؓ said, "Say that it is for a part of the Ummah because you will be unable to give all of them." "Alright," said Zaid bin Su'na ؓ, "then for a part of the Ummah." Omar ؓ and Zaid bin Su'na ؓ then returned to Rasulullah ﷺ and Zaid bin Su'na ؓ exclaimed, "I testify that there is none worthy of worship but Allah and that Muhammad ﷺ is Allah's servant and Rasul." He then accepted Iman and pledged his allegiance to Rasulullah ﷺ. He participated in many expeditions with Rasulullah ﷺ and was martyred during the expedition to Tabuk as he was advancing and not retreating. May Allah shower His mercy on Zaid bin Su'na ؓ. *(Tabarani, Haythami, Ibn Hibban, Hakim, Abu Nu'aym)*

The Treaty of Hudaibiya: The Quraish Prevent Rasulullah ﷺ from Visiting the Kaba

Miswar bin Makhrama ؓ narrates that when Rasulullah ﷺ left Madinah for the Treaty of Hudaibiya, he said to the Sahabah when they had reached a particular place, "Khalid bin Walid and a group of horsemen have a arrived at a place called Umaym to gather intelligence. Therefore, alter your course towards the right." Miswar ؓ swears by Allah that Khalid bin Walid did not notice them until the Muslims were almost on top of him and he saw their dust fly. He then quickly returned to warn the Quraish. Rasulullah continued riding until he reached a valley that fell on the road to Makkah. It was there that his camel sat down. The camel's name was Qaswa. According to their custom, when the Sahabah shouted, "Hal! Hal!" to get her moving, she refused to move. The Sahabah started saying, "Qaswa has become stubborn! Qaswa has become stubborn!" Rasulullah ﷺ pointed out to them that she was not being stubborn for she normally never behaved in this manner. He then added, "The One who stopped the people of the elephants from entering Makkah has stopped her as well." Thereafter, Rasulullah ﷺ commented, "I swear by the Being in Whose control is my life that I shall grant the disbelievers any request they make as long as it blesses those things that Allah has made sacred." Rasulullah ﷺ then scolded his camel and she stood up again. He moved away from the road and settled at the end of the valley of Hudaibiyah where there was a spring. The spring contained so little water that the Sahabah could only draw very little. They were hardly there long enough when all the water was finished. The Sahabah complained about this to Rasulullah ﷺ, he took out an arrow from his quiver and instructed them to fix it at the spring which they did. Miswar says, "By Allah, the water of the spring gushed forth for the Sahabah until they left the place."

Budail's Meets Rasulullah ﷺ

While the Muslims camped at Hudaibiya, Budail bin Warqa Khuza'e arrived with a group of his tribesmen from the Banu Khuza. This was the tribe who were well-wishers of the Muslims from the people of Tihama. This tribe were from the Tihama region and were very friendly tribe of the region towards the Muslims. He told Rasulullah ﷺ that they had just passed by the tribes of Amir bin Luway and Ka'b bin Luway, who camped at some of the springs of Hudaibiya. They informed Rasulullah ﷺ that these tribes were ready to engage in battle with the Muslims and prevent them from coming to the Kaba. In fact they were so intent on fighting the Muslims that they had arrived with all their resources and even those camels that were close to giving birth and those that had just given birth. Rasulullah said, "I have not come to fight anyone, but wish only to perform Umrah. It is strange that the Quraish want to fight because fighting has

already weakened them and caused them much harm. If they want, we are prepared to enter into a treaty with them for a period of time. During this period, they should not interfere with my efforts on the people. If I dominate over the people if they accept Islam, the Quraish have the choice to enter into Islam which the others have entered into. On the other hand, if people get the upper hand over me, the Quraish will have no worries. However, if the Quraish refuse to accept Islam and insist on fighting, then I swear by the Being in Whose control my life lies, I shall fight them for the sake of Islam until either my head is separated from my neck or this Islam flourishes." Budail told Rasulullah ﷺ that he would convey this message to the Quraish. He then left and when he met with the Quraish, he said to them, "We have just come from that man and have heard him say something. If you wish us to convey it to you, I shall oblige." Some foolish persons present said, "We have no need to be told anything about him." However, some intelligent ones said, "Tell us what you heard." Budail then continued to tell them everything Rasulullah ﷺ had told him.

Urwa bin Mas'ood Meets Rasulullah ﷺ

Urwa bin Mas'ood then stood up and said, "O people! Am I not like a father unto you?" "Indeed," they replied. He added, "And are you not like my children?" "Certainly," they responded. He asked further, "Do you have any doubts about me?" "Of course not," they asserted. Urwa asked, "Are you not aware of the fact that I mustered the support of the people of Ukaz to assist you but when they refused, I presented myself with my family, my children and all who would obey me?" "We are well aware of that," they agreed. Urwa then said to them, "He (Rasulullah ﷺ) has presented a fine proposal. Accept it and allow me to negotiate with him." When they agreed that he negotiate with Rasulullah ﷺ, Urwa met with Rasulullah ﷺ and started the negotiation process. When Rasulullah ﷺ told Urwa what he had told Budail, Urwa said, "O Muhammad ﷺ! Have you ever heard of any Arab before you who has wiped out his family? However, if matters take the other course if the Quraish get the upper hand then I do not see a group of loyal and trustworthy people around you. I see a mixed lot around who are ready to desert you and leave you all alone." At this, Abu Bakr said to Urwa, "Go suck Lat's genitals! Did we ever desert Rasulullah ﷺ and leave him by himself!" "Who is this?" asked Urwa. "He is Abu Bakr," was the reply. Urwa responded by saying, "I swear by the Being in whose control is my life! Had it not been for a favor that I owe you and which I have not yet repaid, I would have certainly replied to you." Urwa then continued speaking with Rasulullah ﷺ and would repeatedly touch the beard of Rasulullah ﷺ as he spoke. Standing by Rasulullah ﷺ's headside was Mughiera bin Shu'ba ؓ (Urwa's nephew) who was wearing a helmet at the time and carrying a sword. When Urwa raised his hand to touch Rasulullah ﷺ's beard again, Mughiera ؓ struck Urwa's hand with the handle of his sword saying, "Keep your hand away from Rasulullah ﷺ's beard." Raising his gaze, Urwa asked, "Who is this?" When he was informed that it was Mughiera ؓ, Urwa said, "O betrayer! Have I not tolerated the burden of your betrayal?" During the period of ignorance, Mughiera ؓ had befriended some people whom he later killed and robbed of their possessions. He later came to Rasulullah ﷺ with all the stolen goods and accepted Islam. However, Rasulullah ﷺ said to him, "I shall accept your conversion to Islam but will have nothing to do with the wealth." Urwa was referring to this incident. Urwa then started observing the Sahabah very closely. He says, "By Allah! Even when Rasulullah ﷺ would spit, someone would catch it and rub it on his face and body. Whenever he issued any command, the Sahabah would immediately carry it out and when he made wudhu, they get close to fighting with each other to get the water falling off his limbs. They always lower their voices when speaking to him and do not look him in the eye out of respect for him." Urwa then returned to his people and said to them, "O people! I have been to the royal courts of Caesars, Kisra, and Najashi. I have never seen the followers of any ruler so devoted to him as the followers of Muhammad ﷺ are to him. By Allah! Even when he spits, someone would catch it and rub it on his face and body. Whenever he issues any command, the Sahabah would immediately carry it out and when he made wudhu, they get close to fighting with each other to get the water falling off his limbs. They always lower their voices when speaking to him and do not look him in the eye out of respect for him. He had indeed forwarded a fine proposal to you so accept it."

A Man from the Kinana Tribe Meets with Rasulullah ﷺ

Someone from the Kinana tribe said, "Allow me to meet him." "Go see him," the others said. When the man came to Rasulullah ﷺ and the Sahabah, Rasulullah ﷺ said, "Here comes a man belongs to a tribe that honors sacrificial animals, so put some of them in front for him." When the animals were sent forward to him and the people met him reciting the Talbiya, he said, "Subhanallah! It is not correct to prevent these people from the Kaba." When he returned to his people, he said, "I saw the sacrificial animals already garlanded and marked for sacrifice. I do not think that they should be prevented from the Kaba." Thereafter, another person by the name of Mikraz bin Hafs stood up and requested to leave to meet with Rasulullah ﷺ, which was granted. When he arrived to meet Rasulullah ﷺ, Rasulullah ﷺ said, "He is Mikraz who is an evil person." Mikraz started negotiating with Rasulullah ﷺ and was still in the process of doing so when Suhail bin Amr arrived.

Suhail bin Amr Meets with Rasulullah ﷺ and the Clauses of the Treaty

Ma'mar رحمة الله narrates from Ayub and Ikrama رحمة الله that when Suhail bin Amr arrived, Rasulullah ﷺ took a good sign from his name and said, "Allah has said, "Come, let us write a treaty between ourselves." Rasulullah ﷺ sent for a scribe and instructed him to write: بِسْمِ اللَّهِ الرَّحْمَنِ الرَّحِيمِ
"(We begin) in the name of Allah the Most Kind the Most Merciful"
To this Suhail bin Amr objected, "By Allah! We do not know what 'Ar Rahman' is. As we usually do, why do you not rather write:
"(We begin) in Your name O Allah" بِسْمِكَ اللَّهُمَّ
The Muslim protested against writing anything but:
بِسْمِ اللَّهِ الرَّحْمَنِ الرَّحِيمِ
"We begin in the name of Allah the Most Kind the Most Merciful"
However, Rasulullah ﷺ instructed the scribe to write: بِسْمِكَ اللَّهُمَّ
"We begin in Your name O Allah"

Thereafter, Rasulullah ﷺ instructed the scribe to write, "This is what Muhammad ﷺ the Rasul of Allah has decided." Suhail bin Amr again objected by saying, "By Allah! Had we known that you are truly the Rasul of Allah, we would not have prevented you from visiting the Kabah, nor would we have fought against you. Rather write, 'Muhammad ﷺ the son of Abdullah.'" To this, Rasulullah ﷺ said, "By Allah! I am certainly the Rasul of Allah even though you people deny it." Addressing the scribe, Rasulullah ﷺ said, "Write, 'Muhammad ﷺ the son of Abdullah.'" These compromises were on account of what Rasulullah ﷺ had stated earlier when he said, "I swear by the Being in Whose control is my life that I shall grant the disbelievers any request they make as long as it blesses those things that Allah has made sacred." Rasulullah then said, "The first clause is that you allow us to perform Tawaf of the Kabah." Suhail bin Amr objected by saying, "Never! By Allah, then the Arabs would say that we bowed before you. This will only be during the following year." Consequently, this was written that the Muslims will be allowed to perform Umrah during the following year. Proposing the next clause, Suhail bin Amr said, "Should any man from our ranks join you, he would be returned to us even though he follows your religion." The Muslims exclaimed, "Subhanallah! How can he be returned to the disbelievers when he has come as a Muslim?"

The Incident of Abu Jandal ﷺ

Negotiations were still underway when Abu Jandal ﷺ the son of Suhail bin Amr arrived there chained in fetters. He had just left the lower part of Makkah and joined the Muslims. Suhail bin Amr said, "O Muhammad ﷺ, this man is the first person I am demanding that you return to me in accordance with the treaty." "But we have not yet concluded the treaty," said Rasulullah ﷺ. Suhail bin Amr adamantly said, "Then I shall never negotiate any treaty with you!" Rasulullah ﷺ said, "At least leave him to me." Suhail bin Amr shouted, "I shall never leave him to you!" Rasulullah ﷺ requested, "Why not? I am sure you can." "I shall not," Suhail bin Amr said stubbornly. Mikraz however said, "We shall leave him to you." Abu Jandal ﷺ addressed the Muslim saying, "O gathering of Muslim! Why should I be returned to the disbelievers when I have come as a Muslim? Have you not seen how I have suffered?" Abu Jandal ﷺ had endured severe torture at the hands of the disbelievers. Omar then approached Rasulullah ﷺ and said, "Are you not the true Nabi of Allah?" "I am indeed," replied Rasulullah ﷺ. Omar ﷺ asked further, "Are we not on the truth and our enemies on falsehood?" "Certainly," said Rasulullah ﷺ. Omar ﷺ asked, "Then why do we have to submit?" Rasulullah ﷺ said to him, "I am certainly the Rasul of Allah. I cannot disobey Him and He is my Helper." Omar ﷺ asked, "Did you not tell us that we shall arrive at the Kabah and perform Tawaf around it?" Rasulullah ﷺ replied, "Indeed I did but did I tell you that it would be this year?" "No," said Omar ﷺ. Rasulullah ﷺ assured him, "Then you shall certainly arrive there and perform Tawaf around it." Omar ﷺ then approached Abu Bakr ﷺ and asked him, "Is he not the true Nabi of Allah?" "He is indeed," replied Abu Bakr ﷺ. Omar ﷺ asked further, "Are we not on the truth and our enemies on falsehood?" "Certainly," said Abu Bakr ﷺ. Omar ﷺ asked, "Then why do we have to submit?" Abu Bakr ﷺ said to him, "O person! He is certainly the Rasul of Allah. He cannot disobey Allah and Allah is his Helper." Omar ﷺ asked, "Did Rasulullah ﷺ not tell us that we shall arrive at the Kabah and perform Tawaf around it?" Abu Bakr ﷺ replied, "He did indeed, but did he tell you that it would be this year?" "No," said Omar. Abu Bakr ﷺ assured him, "Then you shall certainly arrive there and perform Tawaf around it." After narrating this incident, Omar ﷺ says that he later carried out many good deeds to amend for this behavior. After the treaty was written, Rasulullah ﷺ instructed the Sahabah to slaughter their animals and to shave off their hair (an indication that they would return without performing Umrah). The narrator of the Hadith says, "By Allah! No one stood up to do this even though Rasulullah ﷺ thrice repeated the instruction because they all hoped that perhaps he would reconsider the situation." When he saw that no one was prepared to carry out the command, he went to his tent where he met his wife Umm. When he informed her of the difficulty he was having, she said, "O Nabi of Allah! Why don't you rather do this? Go out there without speaking a word to anyone, slaughter your animal, call for someone to shave your hair and have it shaved off." Rasulullah ﷺ went out and did accordingly. He slaughtered his animal, called for someone to shave off his hair and had it shaved off. When the Sahabah saw, they stood up, slaughtered their animals and started shaving each others' hair. They were so sad that it appeared that they could almost kill each other out of grief. Some Muslim women arrived there to join the Muslims and the following verse was revealed:

يَا أَيُّهَا الَّذِينَ آمَنُوا إِذَا جَاءَكُمُ الْمُؤْمِنَاتُ مُهَاجِرَاتٍ فَامْتَحِنُوهُنَّ اللَّهُ أَعْلَمُ بِإِيمَانِهِنَّ فَإِنْ عَلِمْتُمُوهُنَّ مُؤْمِنَاتٍ فَلَا تَرْجِعُوهُنَّ إِلَى الْكُفَّارِ لَا هُنَّ حِلٌّ لَهُمْ وَلَا هُمْ يَحِلُّونَ لَهُنَّ وَآتُوهُمْ مَا أَنْفَقُوا وَلَا جُنَاحَ عَلَيْكُمْ أَنْ تَنْكِحُوهُنَّ إِذَا آتَيْتُمُوهُنَّ أُجُورَهُنَّ وَلَا تُمْسِكُوا بِعِصَمِ الْكَوَافِرِ وَاسْأَلُوا مَا أَنْفَقْتُمْ وَلْيَسْأَلُوا مَا أَنْفَقُوا ذَلِكُمْ حُكْمُ اللَّهِ يَحْكُمُ بَيْنَكُمْ وَاللَّهُ عَلِيمٌ حَكِيمٌ (10)

O you who believe! When believing women come to you as emigrants, examine them, Allah knows best as to their Faith, then if you ascertain that they are true believers, send them not back to the disbelievers, they are not lawful (wives) for the disbelievers nor are the disbelievers lawful (husbands) for them. But give the disbelievers that (amount of money) which they have spent (as their Mahr) to them. And there will be no sin on you to marry them if you have paid their Mahr to them. Likewise hold not the disbelieving women as wives, and ask for (the return of) that which you have spent (as Mahr) and let them (the disbelievers, etc.) ask back for that which they have spent. That is the Judgment of Allah. He judges between you. And Allah is All-Knowing, All-Wise. (Al-Mumtahanah:10)

To comply with the above verse, Omar ؓ divorced 2 of his wives whom he had married as a disbeliever. Consequently, Mu'awiya bin Abi Sufyan married one of them while the other was married to Safwan bin Umayyah.

The Incident of Abu Bashir and the 2 men who were Sent After Him

After the incident at Hudaibiyah, Rasulullah ﷺ returned to Madinah where a Muslim from the Quraish named Abu Bashir ؓ came to him. However, the Quraish had dispatched two men after him to remind Rasulullah ﷺ about the treaty. Rasulullah ﷺ therefore handed him over to the 2 men. The 2 men left with him and when they stopped to eat some dates at Dhul Hulaifa, Abu Bashir ؓ said to one of them, "By Allah! I see that you have an extremely fine sword." The man drew the sword from the sheath and said, "By Allah! It is fine indeed. I have tried it again and again." Abu Bashir ؓ said, "Let me have a look at it." When the man handed it over, Abu Bashir ؓ struck him and killed him instantly. The other person rushed for Madinah and when he came running into the Masjid, Rasulullah ﷺ commented, "It seems as if something terribly frightening has occurred to him." When the person reached the Rasulullah ﷺ, he exclaimed, "My companion has been killed and I will also be killed." Abu Bashir ؓ came close behind him following. He said, "O Rasulullah ﷺ! Allah has pardoned you of your responsibility when you returned me. Allah has now freed me from my captors." Rasulullah ﷺ said, "Oh dear! This man is a true warmonger. If only there was someone who could do something for him." Abu Bashir ؓ understood from this that Rasulullah ﷺ would return him again. He therefore left Madinah and settled along the coast.

Abu Jandal ؓ Joins up with Abu Bashir ؓ and They Attack the Caravans of the Quraish

Abu Jandal ؓ the son of Suhail bin Arm managed to escape from the Quraish and joined with Abu Bashir ؓ. Thereafter, every man who accepted Islam and left the Quraish joined with Abu Basir ؓ until they grew into a large group. The narrator states, "By Allah! Every caravan of the Quraish traveling to Sham that they heard about, they attacked, killing the people and taking their goods." The Quraish eventually became tired and sent a message to Rasulullah ﷺ, pleading him in the name of Allah and by the family ties they shared that he should call this group to Madinah. They also added that whoever came to Rasulullah ﷺ from Makkah as a Muslim afterwards would be left in peace without returning him to Makkah. Rasulullah ﷺ then called them to Madinah. It was then that Allah revealed the following verses of the Qur'an:

وَهُوَ الَّذِي كَفَّ أَيْدِيَهُمْ عَنْكُمْ وَأَيْدِيَكُمْ عَنْهُمْ بِبَطْنِ مَكَّةَ مِنْ بَعْدِ أَنْ أَظْفَرَكُمْ عَلَيْهِمْ وَكَانَ اللَّهُ بِمَا تَعْمَلُونَ بَصِيرًا (24) هُمُ الَّذِينَ كَفَرُوا وَصَدُّوكُمْ عَنِ الْمَسْجِدِ الْحَرَامِ وَالْهَدْيَ مَعْكُوفًا أَنْ يَبْلُغَ مَحِلَّهُ وَلَوْلَا رِجَالٌ مُؤْمِنُونَ وَنِسَاءٌ مُؤْمِنَاتٌ لَمْ تَعْلَمُوهُمْ أَنْ تَطَئُوهُمْ فَتُصِيبَكُمْ مِنْهُمْ مَعَرَّةٌ بِغَيْرِ عِلْمٍ لِيُدْخِلَ اللَّهُ فِي رَحْمَتِهِ مَنْ يَشَاءُ لَوْ تَزَيَّلُوا لَعَذَّبْنَا الَّذِينَ كَفَرُوا مِنْهُمْ عَذَابًا أَلِيمًا (25) إِذْ جَعَلَ الَّذِينَ كَفَرُوا فِي قُلُوبِهِمُ الْحَمِيَّةَ حَمِيَّةَ الْجَاهِلِيَّةِ فَأَنْزَلَ اللَّهُ سَكِينَتَهُ عَلَى رَسُولِهِ وَعَلَى الْمُؤْمِنِينَ وَأَلْزَمَهُمْ كَلِمَةَ التَّقْوَى وَكَانُوا أَحَقَّ بِهَا وَأَهْلَهَا وَكَانَ اللَّهُ بِكُلِّ شَيْءٍ عَلِيمًا (26)

And He it is Who has withheld their hands from you and your hands from them in the midst of Makkah, after He had made you victors over them. And Allah is Ever the All-Seer of what you do. They are the ones who disbelieved (in the Oneness of Allah), and hindered you from Al-Masjidal-Haram (the sacred mosque of Makkah) and the sacrificial animals, detained from reaching their place of sacrifice. Had there not been believing men and believing women whom you did not know, that you may kill them, and on whose account a sin would have been committed by you without (your) knowledge, that Allah might bring into His Mercy whom He will, if they (the believers and the disbelievers) should have been apart, We verily had punished those of them who disbelieved, with painful torment. When those who disbelieve had put in their hearts pride and haughtiness the pride and haughtiness of the time of ignorance, then Allah sent down His Sakina (calmness and tranquility) upon His Messenger (ﷺ) and upon the believers, and made them stick to the word of piety (none has the right to be worshipped but Allah), and they were well entitled to it and worthy of it. And Allah is the All-Knower of everything. (Al-Fath:24-26) (Bukhari, Ibn Kathir, Bayhaqi)

Rasulullah ﷺ Sends Uthman ؓ to Makkah After Setting up Camp in Hudaibiyah

Urwa ؓ narrates that the Quraish became very scared when Rasulullah ﷺ camped at Hudaibiyah. Rasulullah ﷺ decided to send one of the Sahabah to the Quraish so he called for Omar bin Khattab ؓ for this task. Omar ؓ said, "O Rasulullah ﷺ! Although I a willing to fulfill your command, I am the most disliked person in their sight and if they cause me any harm, there shall be none from my Bani Ka'b tribe who will stand up for me. Rather send Uthman ؓ because he has family in Makkah and he will be able to convey exactly what you want." Rasulullah ﷺ therefore called Uthman bin Affan ؓ and sent him to the Quraish. Rasulullah ﷺ briefed him saying, "Tell them that we have not come to fight but have come only to perform Umra. Invite them to Islam as well." Rasulullah ﷺ also instructed him to meet the Muslim men and women in Makkah and to give them the glad tidings of victory and that Allah shall soon make Islam dominant in Makkah so that none would have to keep their faith a secret. Rasulullah ﷺ sent Uthman ؓ with this message to give the Muslims courage. Uthman ⚜ left for Makkah and passed a group of the Quraish at a place called Balda. When they asked him where he was headed, he informed them that Rasulullah ⚜ had sent him to invite them towards Allah and towards Islam and to tell them that the Muslims have not come to fight but only to perform Umra. Uthman ⚜ then gave them the Da'wah to Islam as Rasulullah ⚜ had instructed him. They said, "We hear what you say. You may proceed to fulfill your task." Aban bin Sa'eed bin Al Aas then stood up, welcomed Uthman ⚜ and guaranteed his safety. He saddled his horse and allowed Uthman ⚜ to sit in front as they rode to Makkah. The Quraish sent Budail bin Waraqa and someone from the Banu Kinana to meet Rasulullah ⚜. After this, they sent Urwa bin Mas'ood Thaqafi. The Hadith still continues further. *(Ibn Asakir, Kanzul Ummal, Bayhaqi)*

The Words of Omar ⚜ Concerning the Treaty of Hudaibiyah

Abdullah bin Abbas ⚜ narrates that Omar ⚜ said, "Rasulullah entered into a peace treaty with the people of Makkah and conceded to many things. Had Rasulullah ⚜ appointed an Amir over me who did as Rasulullah ⚜ did, I would have not listened to or obeyed him. The clauses in their favor was that anyone from the disbeliever who joined the Muslims would be returned while anyone who joined the disbeliever would not have to be returned." *(Ibn Sa'd in Kanzul Ummal)*

The Words of Abu Bakr ⚜ Concerning the Treaty of Hudaibiyah

Abu Bakr ⚜ used to say, "There has never been a victory in Islam greater than the victory at Hudaibiyah but the people on that day were unable to understand what Muhammad ⚜ and his Rabb were doing. Allah does not use the hasty man as because of which matters condense to what Allah intends On the occasion of the Farewell Hajj I have seen Suhail bin Arm standing at the place where animals were being slaughtered, taking Rasulullah ⚜'s camel closer to him. Rasulullah ⚜ slaughtered it with his own hand and then called for someone who shaved off his hair. I then saw Suhail snatching up the hair of Rasulullah ⚜ and even saw him placing it on his eyes. I then thought that it was the same Suhail who on the occasion of Hudaibiyah had refused to allow the writing of بِسْمِ اللَّهِ الرَّحْمَنِ الرَّحِيمِ and had refused the writing of 'Muhammad ⚜ the Rasul of Allah'. I then praised Allah Who had guided him to Islam." *(Ibn Asakir in Kanzul Ummal)*

Amr bin Al Aas ⚜ Accepts Islam

Amr bin Al Aas ⚜ narrates that when they left the trench after the Battle of Ahzab, he gathered some people from the Quraish who usually shared his opinions and who did as he said. He said to them, "As you know, I am of the opinion that Islam of Muhammad ⚜ shall dominate all others in a very unpleasant manner. However, I see a solution so tell me what you think." When the people asked what he thought, Amr bin Al Aas ⚜ said, "I think that we should join Najashi (in Abyssinia) and remain there. If Muhammad ⚜ is victorious, we shall be with Najashi and being under his rule is better than being under the rule of Muhammad ⚜. On the other hand, if our people are victorious, then they would still know us and we can expect only god from them." "This is an excellent opinion," they all agreed. Amr bin Al Aas ⚜ then told them to collect some articles to offer as gifts to Najashi and because Najashi likes the leather most from these gifts, they collected a large amount of leather. They finally reached Najashi with the gifts. Amr bin Al Aas ⚜ narrates further, "By Allah! We had reached the court of Najashi when Amr bin Umayyah Damri arrived. Rasulullah ⚜ had sent him to Najashi to speak to him about Ja'far ⚜ and other Sahabah who

had migrated to Abyssinia earlier. Amr bin Umayyah entered Najasjhi's court and then came out again. I said to my companions, 'This is Amr bin Umayyah. If I go to Najashi and ask request that he (Amr bin Umayyah) be handed over to me so that I could kill him, the Quraish would feel that I have avenged them by killing the envoy of Rasulullah ⚜.' I then entered the court of Najashi and bowed before him as I always did. He said, 'A hearty welcome to my friend. Have you brought me any gifts from your land?' 'Yes, O King,' I replied, 'I have brought you plenty leather.' I then brought it before him. He was very pleased because it was what he liked. I then said to him, 'O King! I happened to see someone leaving your presence who is an envoy of our enemy. Hand him over to me so that I may kill him because he has caused harm to our leaders and. nobles.'" Amr bin Al Aas ⚜ says, "Najashi became extremely angry. He extended his hand and hit his nose so hard that I thought he had broken it. Had the ground opened up just then, I would have certainly dived into it out of fear. I said to him, 'O King! I would have never mentioned this had I known that you would dislike it.' The King said, 'You are asking me to hand over to you the envoy of that person who is visited by the great spirit (Jibrael 🕊) who visited Musa so that you could kill him!?' I said, 'O King! Is he really?' Najashi replied, 'Shame on you, O Amr! Listen to me. Follow him for I swear by Allah that he is certainly on the truth. He shall definitely conquer those who oppose him just as Musa the son of Imran 🕊 defeated Fir'oun and his armies." Amr bin Al Aas ⚜ then asked Najashi, "Will you accept my pledge of allegiance on his behalf?" "Certainly," replied Najashi. He then stretched out his hands and Amr bin Al Aas ⚜ pledged his allegiance to Islam. Amr bin Al Aas ⚜ then met with his companions with a changed frame of mind and kept his conversion to Islam secret. He later left to meet Rasulullah ⚜ and to accept Islam at his hands and met Khalid bin Walid who was traveling from Makkah. This occurred not long before the conquest of Makkah. Amr ⚜ asked Khalid ⚜, "Where are you heading, O Abu Salman?" Khalid ⚜ replied, "By Allah! Matters are now crystal clear. The man is certainly a Nabi. By Allah! I am going to accept Islam. Until when can we continue avoiding the issue?" Amr bin Al Aas ⚜ said, "By Allah! I have also come to accept Islam." The 2 then arrived in Madinah to meet Rasulullah ⚜. Khalid ⚜ went forward, accepted Islam and pledged his allegiance to Rasulullah ⚜. Amr bin Al Aas ⚜ then drew close to Rasulullah ⚜ and said, "O Rasulullah ⚜! May I pledge my allegiance to you on condition that all my past sins be forgiven. I am also unaware of what sins may occur in the future." Rasulullah ⚜ said to him, "O Amr! You may pledge your allegiance because Islam surely wipes out all past sins and Hijra also wipes out all past sins." Amr bin Al Aas ⚜ then pledged his allegiance to Rasulullah ⚜ and left. *(Ibn Is'haq, Ahmad, Tabrani, Haytham)*.

A more detailed narration of Bayhaqi reported from Waqidi, Amr bin Al Aas ⚜ is stated to have said, "I traveled from Abyssinia until I reached a place called Hada where I noticed 2 men not far ahead of me who were pitching camp there. One of them was inside the tent while the other was holding on to the transportation. When I looked carefully, I saw that it was Khalid bin Walid ⚜. When I asked him where he was headed, he replied, 'To Muhammad ⚜. Everyone is accepting Islam and there is none who has not. By Allah! If I were to remain a disbeliever, our necks would be grabbed just as a badger is grabbed from its hole by the neck.' I said to him, 'By Allah! I also intend to meet Muhammad ⚜ and accept Islam.' Uthman bin Talha ⚜ then emerged from the tent and welcomed me. We all then settled down together. We traveled together until we reached Madinah." Amr bin Al Aas ؤ continues the story saying, "I shall never forget the words of a person we met at Abu Utba well. Calling his slave he shouted, 'O Rabah!, O Rabah! O Rabah!' Because Rabah means success, we took a god sign from his call, which made us very happy. He then looked at us and I heard him say, 'After these 2, Makkah has already given us her leadership.' I guessed that he was referring to myself and Khalid bin Walid ؤ. He then turned and rushed towards the Masjid to give Rasulullah ﷺ the news of our arrival. It was exactly as I assumed. We then settled our camels at a place called Harra and wore the best of our clothing, the Adhan was then called out for the Asr salah and we left to meet Rasulullah ﷺ. When we reached him, his face was dazzling like the full moon and the Muslims around him were delighted that we had come to accept Islam. Khalid bin Walid ؤ went forward and pledged his allegiance to Rasulullah ﷺ. Uthman bin Talha ؤ pledged his allegiance to Rasulullah ﷺ. I then went forward and sat before him. By Allah! I was unable to lift my gaze out of respect for him. I then pledged my allegiance to him on condition that all my past sins be forgiven and that I am unaware of what sins may occur in the future. Rasulullah ﷺ said, 'Islam surely wipes out all past sins and Hijra also wipes out all past sins.' By Allah! After accepting Islam Rasulullah ﷺ never compared any of the other Sahabah with me and Khalid bin Walid ؤ when it concerned matters that worried him military matters." *(Al-Bidayah wan Nihayah)*

Khalid bin Walid ؤ Accepts Islam

Khalid bin Walid ؤ says that when Allah decided that good thing head his way, Allah created the desire within his heart to accept Islam and opened many avenues to him. He says, "I said to myself, 'I fought every battle against Rasulullah ﷺ but after each battle I got the feeling that all these efforts were useless because there was no doubt that Rasulullah ﷺ would eventually emerge victorious. When Rasulullah ﷺ arrived at Hudaibiyah, I led a contingent of disbelieving horsemen and faced Rasulullah ﷺ at a place called Usfan where we intended to launch an attack. Rasulullah ﷺ led the Sahabah in the Zuhr salah and we saw a perfect opportunity to attack. However, we were undecided and did not attack. Rasulullah ﷺ was aware of our intention through revelation and when he led the Asr salah, he performed Salatul Khowf - performed during difficult situations like the one when one group pray while another group face the enemy. This had an impact upon us and we were left saying, 'This man is certainly protected by Allah.' Rasulullah ﷺ then moved forward clear of us and took a path to the right that led away from the path of our horses." Continuing the story, Khalid bin Walid ؤ says, "Rasulullah ﷺ then entered into a treaty with the Quraish at Hudaibiyah when the Quraish managed to save their necks by opting for a treaty rather than a battle. I then said to myself, 'What is left now? Where shall I run? To Najashi? He is already a follower of Muhammad ﷺ and the Sahabah are living peacefully with him. Should I go to Heraclius where I will have to forsake my religion for Christianity or Judaism and live with foreigners? Should I rather stay at home with those left here?' I was still in this dilemma when Rasulullah ﷺ came to Makkah to perform the Umra they had missed the previous year. I made myself scarce and did not see them to enter Makkah. My brother Walid bin Walid also arrived in Makkah with Rasulullah ﷺ and looked for me. He was unable to find me and left a letter for me which read:

In the name of Allah the Most Kind the Most Merciful

I have seen nothing more astonishing than the fact that someone as intelligent as you has not yet decided to accept Islam. How can anyone remain in the dark about a religion as great as Islam? When Rasulullah ﷺ asked where you were, I told him that Allah will soon bring you. He said, "How can a person like Khalid remain unaware of a religion like Islam? It would be best for him to spend his efforts and energies with the Muslims and we shall put him ahead of others." O my brother! You have missed tremendous opportunities so please make amends.

Khalid bin Walid ؤ says, "After reading this letter, I was inspired to leave for Madinah and my inclination towards Islam increased. It pleased me to think that Rasulullah ﷺ had actually asked about me. During this time, I dreamt that I was in a thin and drought stricken land after which I went to a land that was vast and fertile. I thought this is certainly a true dream. I thought that I should definitely relate this dream to Abu Bakr ؤ when I reach Madinah. When he related it to Abu Bakr ؤ, Abu Bakr ؤ said, 'Your leaving the place was the guidance Allah gave you towards Islam and the thin place was the Shirk you had been involved with.' When I made up my mind to leave for Rasulullah ﷺ, I wondered who would accompany me. I approached Safwan bin Umayyah and said to him, 'O Abu Wahab! Don't you see the situation we find ourselves in? We are becoming fewer in numbers. Muhammad ﷺ has dominated the Arabs and non-Arabs. I feel that we should meet him and follow him so his honor shall be ours.' Safwan strongly rejected the offer and said, 'I shall never follow him even if I am the last person left!' Leaving him, I said to myself, 'Both his brother and father had been killed in the battle of Badr and that is why he is so reluctant to accept Islam.' I then met Ikrama bin Abi Jahal and told him what I had mentioned to Safwan. His response was similar to that of Safwan. However, I told him to keep it a secret and he agreed to that. I then went home and prepared my transportation. As I was riding out, I met Uthman bin Talha and said to myself, 'He is a good friend of mine. Perhaps I should tell him what I intend to do.' I then remembered that many of his relatives had been killed by the Muslims in battle and it would not be appropriate to mention it to him. However, it occurred to me that there is no harm to tell him since I am already on my way. I therefore spoke to him about the undesirable results of our efforts against the Muslims and said, 'We are just like a fox in his hole who will have to emerge as soon as a bucket of water is thrown down the hole.' I also told him what I had mentioned to my 2 friends earlier. He immediately accepted what I said. I told him that I am leaving today and that my transport is ready and waiting at a place called Faj. We then decided to meet at a place called Yajuj where I would wait for him if I arrives first, otherwise he would wait for me if he arrives first. We left our homes very early in the morning and met at Yajuj before the break of dawn. We then proceeded together from there and when we reached Hada, we met Amr bin Al Aas ؤ. After he had welcomed us and we had welcomed him, he asked us where we were heading. We asked him what had brought him from his home and he asked us the same question. We then said to him, 'We intend entering the fold of Islam and following Muhammad ﷺ.' He responded by saying, 'That is exactly what has brought me.' We then joined together until we reached Madinah where we left our transportation at a place called Harra. Rasulullah ﷺ was already informed about our arrival and was very pleased. I wore my best clothes and headed for Rasulullah ﷺ. My brother met me and said, 'Hurry! Rasulullah ﷺ has been informed about you and is pleased about your arrival. He is eagerly waiting for you." We walked hastily until we arrived and Rasulullah ﷺ smiled with me until I came in front of him. I greeted him as the Nabi of Allah and he replied to my greeting with a smiling face. I then said, 'I testify that there is none worthy of worship but Allah and that you are Allah's Rasul.'

He called me closer and said, 'All praise belongs to Allah Who has guided you; When I saw your intelligence I hoped that it would inspire you only to do good.' I then said, "O Rasulullah ﷺ! I keep thinking of the battles I fought against you in opposition to the truth. Pray to Allah to forgive me.' Rasulullah ﷺ said, 'Accepting Islam wipes out all previous sins.' I said, 'O Rasulullah ﷺ! Despite that please pray for me.' He prayed, 'O Allah! Forgive Khalid bin Walid for all the efforts he exerted to prevent people from the Path of Allah.' Thereafter, Uthman bin Talha ؓ and Amr ؓ came forward and pledged their allegiance to Rasulullah ﷺ. We had arrived in Madinah during the month of Safar, 8 years after the Hijra. By Allah! Rasulullah ﷺ never equated any of the other Sahabah with me when it concerned matters that worried him military matters." *(Al-Bidayah wan Nihayah, Kanzul Ummal)*

The Conquest of Makkah (زَادَهَا اللهُ تَشْرِيفًا) : Rasulullah ﷺ Leaves Madinah and Camps at Marruz Zahran

Abdullah bin Abbas ؓ narrates that when Rasulullah ﷺ left Madinah for Makkah, he appointed Abu Ruhm Kulthum bin Husain Ghifari ؓ as the Amir of Madinah. He left on the 10th of Ramadhan while he and the Sahabah were fasting. They broke their fasts when they reached Kudaid which was an oasis between Usfan and Amj. Rasulullah ﷺ then proceeded with the 10,000 Sahabah until they set up camp at Marruz Zahran. There were also 1,000 people from the Muzaina and Sulaim tribes and every tribe had brought provisions and weapons. Everyone of the Muhajir and Ansar left with Rasulullah ﷺ.

The Leaders of the Quraish Spy on the Muslims

When Rasulullah ﷺ reached Marruz Zahran, the Quraish were still in the dark. No news about Rasulullah ﷺ had reached them and they had no idea what he was doing. That night Abu Sufian bin Harb, Hakim bin Hizam and Budail bin Warqa left Makkah on a spying expedition to see if they could see or hear any news. Abbas ؓ had joined Rasulullah ﷺ on the road and it was also on the road from Madinah to Makkah that Abu Sufian bin Harith bin Abdul Muttalib (Rasulullah ﷺ's cousin) and Abdullah bin Abi Umayyah bin Mughiera (Rasulullah ﷺ's cousin and brother-in-law) came to meet Rasulullah ﷺ to seek permission to join him. Umm interceded on their behalf saying, "The one is your cousin (father's brother's son) and the other is your cousin (father's sister's son) as well as your brother-in-law (my brother)." Rasulullah ﷺ said, "I have no need for either of them. As for my father's brother's son, he humiliated me in Makkah and my father's sister's son and brother-in-law is the one who made insulting statements about me." When the news reached the 2, Abu Sufian who had a child with him said, "By Allah! If Rasulullah ﷺ does not permit me to join him, I will take this child in my hands and set out with him in the wilderness until we die of thirst and hunger." When Rasulullah ﷺ heard about this statement, he felt sorry and permitted them to join. They both joined the Muslims and accepted Islam.

Abbas ؓ Encourages the Quraish to Appeal for Amnesty

When the Muslims camped at Marruz Zahran, Abbas ؓ said, "The Quraish are destroyed! By Allah! If Rasulullah ﷺ were to enter Makkah by force before the Quraish seek amnesty from him, it would signal the eternal destruction of the Quraish." He then mounted the white mule belonging to Rasulullah ﷺ and set out towards Makkah until he reached a place called Arak, thinking that he may meet some woodcutter, someone milking an animal or anyone else who had come out for some need. He could inform them of where Rasulullah ﷺ was so that they could seek amnesty from him before he entered Makkah by force.

The Incident of Abu Sufian with Abbas ؓ and Omar ؓ

Abbas ؓ continues to say that he was still searching for someone when he heard the voices of Abu Sufian and Buday bin Waraqa, who were talking to each other. Abu Sufian was saying, "By Allah! To this day I have neither seen such a large concentration of camp-fires nor a large army." Budail bin Waraqa said, "By Allah! These are the camp-fires of the Khuza'h tribe. It appears as if a war has lit them." Abu Sufian commented, "By Allah! The Khuza'h tribe is smaller than this. This cannot be their fires and army." Recognizing the voice of Abu Sufian, Abbas ؓ called out, "O Abu Hanzala!" Recognizing Abbas ؓ's voice, Abu Sufian called out, "O Abul Fadhl!" When Abbas ؓ confirmed that it was he, Abu Sufian asked, "May my parents be sacrificed for you! What are you doing here?" Abbas ؓ replied, "Shame on you, O Abu Sufian! Here is Rasulullah ﷺ with the people! By Allah! The Quraish shall surely be destroyed!" Abu Sufian asked, "May my parents be sacrificed for you! What is the way out?" Abbas ؓ replied, "If Rasulullah ﷺ gets hold of you, he will surely have your head. Mount this mule with me so that I may take you to Rasulullah ﷺ to seek amnesty from him." Consequently, Abu Sufian's 2 companions returned and he mounted the mule with Abbas ؓ, who quickly took him to Rasu1ullah ﷺ. Whenever they passed by any Muslim camp-fire, people would ask, "Who goes there?" However, when they saw the mule of Rasulullah ﷺ, they would say, "The uncle of Rasu1ullah ﷺ on his mule." However, when they passed the camp-fire of Omar ؓ, he challenged, "Who goes there?" and stood up before them. When he saw Abu Sufian on the back of the mule, he called out, "The enemy of Allah! All praise belongs to Allah who has handed you over without any truce or amnesty." He then ran to Rasulullah ﷺ and Abbas urged the mule until he beat Omar as animals usually beat people on foot. Abbas ؓ then jumped from the mule and met Rasu1ullah ﷺ. Omar ؓ also arrived just then and said, "O Rasulullah ﷺ! Here is Abu Sufian. Allah has handed him over without any truce or amnesty. Allow me to execute him." Abbas ؓ intervened by saying, "O Rasulullah ﷺ! I have granted him amnesty." Abbas ؓ then sat with Rasulullah ﷺ and said, "O Rasulullah ﷺ! There was none but I who spoke in confidence with Abu Sufian tonight." As Omar ؓ increased his protests concerning Abu Sufian, Abbas ؓ said to him, "That will do. By Allah! Had he been from your tribe the Banu Adi bin Ka'b, you would have not spoken like this. You are saying these things only because you know that he belongs to the Banu Abd Manaf tribe." To this, Omar ؓ replied, "Take it easy, O Abbas! Your entry into Islam pleased me more than if my own father had accepted Islam. This was only because I knew that your entry into Islam pleased Rasulullah ﷺ more than if Khattab my father had accepted Islam." Rasulullah ﷺ then said to Abbas ؓ, "Take him to your tent and bring him back in the morning." Abbas ؓ took Abu Sufian to his tent where he spent the night. The next morning, they proceeded to Rasulullah ﷺ.

Abu Sufian Testifies About Rasulullah ﷺ and Enters into Islam

When Rasulullah ﷺ saw Abu Sufian, he said, "Shame on you, O Abu Sufian! Has not the time come for you to testify that there is none worthy of worship but Allah?" Abu Sufian replied, "May my parents be sacrificed for you! You are so noble, merciful and good towards relatives! I am now convinced that had there been any deity besides Allah, he would have surely been of some help to me." Rasulullah ﷺ then said, "Shame on you, O Abu Sufian! Has not the time come for you to testify that I am Allah's Rasul'?" Abu Sufian replied, "May my parents be sacrificed for you! You are so noble, merciful and good towards relatives! Until now, I have always had reservations about this." Then Abbas ؓ said, "Shame on you, O Abu Sufian! Accept Islam and testify that there is none worthy of worship but Allah and that Muhammad ﷺ is Allah's Rasul before you are executed." Abbas ؓ narrates that it was then that Abu Sufian testified to the true Shahada and accepted Islam.

Rasulullah ﷺ grants Amnesty on the Day the Muslims Conquered Makkah

Abbas ؓ then said, "O Rasulullah ﷺ! Abu Sufian enjoys fame, so allow him some." Rasulullah ﷺ agreed and said, "Whoever enters the house of Abu Sufian shall be safe. Whoever locks his door shall be safe. Whoever enters the Masjid shall be safe." As Abu Sufian was leaving, Rasulullah ﷺ said, "O Abbas! Keep him in the valley at the point where the mountain sticks out so that he may witness the armies of Allah marching by." Abbas ؓ says that to comply with the instruction of Rasulullah ﷺ, he took Abu Sufian to the point where the valley narrowed. Various tribes then began passing by him, each bearing their flags. When a tribe passed by, Abu Sufian asked, "Who are they, O Abbas?" "They are the Banu Sulaim tribe," came the reply. To this, Abu Sufian would say, "What I have to do with the Banu Sulaim and why should they be marching against us?" When another tribe passed, Abu Sufian asked, "Who are they, O Abbas?" When Abbas ؓ informed him that they were the Muzayna tribe. Abu Sufian said, "What I have to do with the Muzayna tribe?" This continued until all the tribes had passed. Each time a tribe passed, Abu Sufian would ask, "Who are they, O Abbas'?" When informed, Abu Sufian would say, "What I have to do with them?" Eventually Rasulullah ﷺ passed by with a large group that included the Muhajir and Ansar. Because of their armor and helmets, nothing but the whites of their eyes were visible. Abu Sufian exclaimed, "Subhanallah! Who are they, O Abbas!" Abbas ؓ replied, "That is Rasulullah ﷺ with the Muhajir and the Ansar." Abu Sufian said, "None has the power or capacity to resist them. O Abul Fadhl! I swear by Allah! The empire of your nephew has certainly become enormous." Abbas ؓ said, "O Abu Sufian! This is prophethood not the average empire of a king." Abu Sufian acknowledged this by saying, "Indeed, now that you mention it." Abbas ؓ then said to him, "Go to your people and inform them about what is happening." Abu Sufian then left and came to the people of Makkah, shouting at the top of his voice, "O Quraish! Muhammad ﷺ is on his way with an army that you have no power to restrain. Whoever enters the house of Abu Sufian shall be safe." His wife Hind bint Utba stood before him and grabbed hold of his moustache saying, "Kill this dark wretch! He brings bad news!" Abu Sufian said, "Shame on you people! Do not let this woman mislead you because Rasulullah ﷺ is certainly approaching with an army that you have no power to restrain. Whoever enters the house of Abu Sufian shall be safe." The people said, "Shame on you! Your house shall never accommodate all of us." Abu Sufian then said, "Whoever locks the door of his house shall be safe and whoever enters the Masjid shall be safe." The people then dispersed towards their homes and the Masjid. (Tabrani, Haythami, Bayhaqi).

The Manner in which Rasulullah ﷺ Entered Makkah

Ibn Asakir narrated from Waqidi a narration just like that of Abdullah bin Abbas ؓ that Tabrani narrated above. It also mentions that when Abu Sufian left the presence of Rasulullah ﷺ,

Rasulullah ﷺ said to Abbas, "Take him to the point where the valley narrows as the mountain sticks out so that he may witness the armies of Allah passing by." Abbas ؓ then left the main road and took Abu Sufian to the point where the valley narrowed as the mountain stick out. When Abbas ؓ held Abu Sufian at this point, Abu Sufian protested, "Is this betrayal, O family of Hashim?" Abbas ؓ replied by saying, "Verily, the people of Nabuwat never betray. I have brought you here for a reason." Abu Sufian said, "Then why did you not do this at the beginning and inform me that you needed to bring me here? This would have put me at ease." Abbas ؓ replied, "It did not occur to me and that you would look at it this way." Rasulullah ﷺ had already arranged the lines of the Sahabah and each tribe began passing by with their leaders. Each battalion also passed by carrying their flags. The first battalion that Rasulullah ﷺ sent forward was the Banu Sulaim tribe under the leadership of Khalid bin Walid ؓ. They numbered a 1,000 strong. They bore a small flag carried by Abas bin Mirdas as well as another carried by Khufaf bin Nudba ؓ. The large flag was held high by Hajaj bin Ilat ؓ. Abu Sufian asked, "Who are they?" "That is Khalid bin Walid," replied Abbas ؓ. "The youngster?" asked Abu Sufian. "Yes," was the response. When Khalid bin Walid ؓ drew alongside Abbas ؓ with Abu Sufian at his side, the soldiers cried out, "Allahu Akbar!" thrice before passing by. Thereafter Zubayr bin Awam ؓ passed by leading a battalion of 500 men comprising of Muhajir and many unknown people. They carried a black flag and when Zubair bin Awam ؓ passed Abu Sufian, he called out "Allahu Akbar!" thrice. His battalion echoed after him. Abu Sufian asked, "Who are they'?" "That is Zubair bin Awam," replied Abbas ؓ. "Your sister's son'?" asked Abu Sufian. "Yes," was the reply. Carrying their flag, Abu Dhar Ghifari ؓ then passed with 300 soldiers of the Ghifar tribe. According to other scholars, it was Ima bin Rahda ؓ who carried the flag. They also proclaimed, "*Allahu Akbar*!" thrice as they passed Abu Sufian. Abu Sufian asked, "Who are they, O Abul Fadhl'?" "That is the tribe of Ghifar," replied Abbas ؓ. "What have I to do with the Ghifar tribe'?" responded Abu Sufian. Next followed the Aslam tribe. They comprised of 400 soldiers and bore 2 flags. One was carried by Buraida bin Husaib ؓ while Najiya bin A'jam ؓ carried the other. They also called out "Allahu Akbar!" thrice as they passed Abu Sufian. Abu Sufian asked, "Who are they, O Abul Fadhl'?" "That is the tribe of Aslam," replied Abbas ؓ. "What have I to do with the Aslam tribe?" responded Abu Sufian, "There has never been any dispute between us." Abbas ؓ said to him, "They are a nation who have entered the fold of Islam." Then 500 men belonging to the Banu Ka'b bin Amr tribe passed by with Bishr bin Shaiban ؓ carrying their flag. Abu Sufian asked, "Who are they'?" "They are the Ka'b bin Amr tribe," replied Abbas ؓ. "O yes," acknowledged Abu Sufian, "they are the allies of Muhammad ﷺ." They also proclaimed "Allahu Akbar!" thrice as they passed Abu Sufian. The Muzayna tribe passed next. They were a 1,000 strong who included a 100 horsemen and they carried 3 flags. Their flag bearers were Nu'man bin Muqarrin, Bilal bin Harith and Abdullah bin Amr ؓ. They also cried "Allahu Akbar!" thrice as they passed Abu Sufian. Abu Sufian asked, "Who are they?" "That is the Muzayna tribe," replied Abbas ؓ. "What have I to do with the Muzayna tribe'?" responded Abu Sufian, "They have also come to me from the peaks of their mountains with their weapons rattling." The Juhaina tribe passed next with their leader. They consisted of 800 soldiers and bore 4 flags. There was a flag with Abu Zur'ah Ma'bad bin Khalid ؓ, another with Suwaid bin Sakhr, a 3rd with Rafi bin Makith ؓ and the 4th with Abdullah bin Badr ؓ. They also cried "Allahu Akbar!" thrice as they passed Abu Sufian. Thereafter, came the Kinana tribe that consisted of the Banu Laith, the Banu Dhamra and Banu Sa'd bin Bakr families. They numbered 200 and Abu Waqid Laithi ﷺ bore their flag. They also cried "Allahu Akbar!" thrice as they passed Abu Sufian. Abu Sufian asked, "Who are they?" "That is Banu Bakr tribe," replied Abbas ﷺ. Abu Sufian said, "Oh yes! By Allah! They are a tribe of misfortune. It is because of them that Muhammad ﷺ is attacking us. After the Treaty of Hudaibiya, the Banu Bakr tribe made an allegiance with the Quraish while the Banu Khuza'h aligned with the Muslims. But a joint attack on the Banu Khuza'h by the Banu Bakr and the Quraish led to the annulment of the Treaty and allowed the Muslims the opportunity to march to Makkah. Abu Sufian was referring to this incident. Swear by Allah that they (the Quraish) did not consult with me and I had no knowledge of the matter. When the news of what happened reached me, I was disgusted. The matter was predestined." Abbas ﷺ said to Abu Sufian, "Allah has destined good in this offensive of Rasulullah ﷺ against you as you all enter the fold of Islam."

Waqidi has mentioned that he was informed by Abdullah bin Amir who narrates from Abu Amr bin Himas that the Banu Laith marched all by themselves. They numbered 250 and Sa'b bin Juthama ﷺ carried their flag. They cried "Allahu Akbar!" thrice as they passed Abu Sufian. When Abu Sufian asked who they were, Abbas informed him that they were the Banu Laith tribe. The last battalion to pass was that of the Banu Ash'ja tribe who numbered 300. They had a flag carried by Ma'qal bin Sanan ﷺ and another carried by Nu'aym bin Mas'ood ﷺ. Abu Sufian remarked, "Of all the Arabs, they were the tough opponents of Muhammad ﷺ." Abbas ﷺ commented, "Allah has entered Islam into their hearts. That is the grace of Allah." Abu Sufian then remained silent for awhile. Abu Sufian then asked, "Has the battalion of Rasulullah ﷺ not passed?" Abbas ﷺ replied, "He has not yet passed. If you see the battalion of Rasulullah ﷺ, you will see only steel, horses, brave men and an army that none has the power to withstand." Abu Sufian said, "O Abul Fadhl! By Allah! I am now convinced of this. Who has the capacity to resist them?" When the battalion of Rasulullah ﷺ appeared, all that could only be seen was large masses and dust rising from the feet of horses. As they marched by in a successive chain, Abu Sufian kept asking, "Has Muhammad ﷺ not passed yet'?" Abbas ﷺ kept informing him that Rasulullah ﷺ had not yet passed. When Rasulullah ﷺ passed riding his camel Qaswa. He was between Abu Bakr ﷺ and Usaid bin Hudhair ﷺ and speaking to the 2 of them. Abbas ﷺ then said, "That is Rasulullah ﷺ amongst a powerful battalion of Muhajir and Ansar." The battalion carried many large and small flags. Every hero of the Ansar carried a large and small flag. They were dressed in steel armor and only the whites of their eyes were visible. Omar ﷺ was also covered in armor and he was busy arranging the lines of the army with his loud voice. Abu Sufian asked, "O Abul Fadhl! Who is that man talking'?" "He is Omar bin Khattab," replied Abbas. Abu Sufian remarked, "The Banu Adi (the tribe of Omar ﷺ) were very few in number and possessed little honor. By Allah! They have now assumed great positions." Abbas ﷺ said, "O Abu Sufian! Allah elevates whoever He wills as He wills. Omar ﷺ is indeed amongst those whom Islam has elevated." The narrator of this report mentions that there were 2,000 coats of armor in this battalion. Rasulullah ﷺ had given his flag to Sa'd bin Ubadah ﷺ who was at the head of the battalion. When Sa'd ﷺ passed by Abu Sufian with the flag of Rasulullah ﷺ, he shouted to Abu Sufian, "Today is the day of bloodshed! Today, the holiness of the Haram shall be lifted! Today Allah shall disgrace the

Quraish!" As Rasulullah ﷺ approached and drew alongside Abu Sufian, he called out, "O Rasulullah ﷺ! Have you commanded that your people be killed as Sa'd and those with seemed to think as they passed us? He called out saying, 'O Abu Sufian! Today is the day of bloodshed! Today, the holiness of the Haram shall be lifted! Today Allah shall disgrace the Quraish!' Taking the name of Allah, I plead with you on behalf of your people for you are the best of all people." Abdur Rahman bin Auf and Uthman ﷺ both said, "O Rasulullah ﷺ! We fear that the Quraish may suffer an attack from Sa'd." Rasulullah ﷺ then said, "O Abu Sufian! Today is a day of mercy. On this day Allah will give honor to the Quraish." Then he sent a message that Sa'd ﷺ be relieved of the post as flag-bearer and assigned the task of bearing the flag to Qais ﷺ Sa'd's son. In this way Rasulullah ﷺ intended that the flag would really not leave the hands of Sa'd ﷺ when it went to his son so he would not feel offended. However, Sa'd refused to surrender the flag until he received a signal from Rasulullah ﷺ. Then Rasulullah ﷺ sent his turban to Sa'd ﷺ, by which he acknowledged the command and handed the flag over to his son Qais ﷺ. (*Kanzul Ummal*)

Abu Layla ﷺ who reports that they were with Rasulullah ﷺ when he informed them that Abu Sufian was at a place called Arak. The Sahabah then went there and captured him. With their swords still covered, they surrounded him and brought him before Rasulullah ﷺ. Rasulullah ﷺ said to him, "Shame on you, O Abu Sufian! I have brought to you the world as well as the Hereafter. Accept Islam and live in peace." Abbas ﷺ was a friend of Abu Sufian, so he said, "O Rasulullah ﷺ! Abu Sufian loves glory, so grant him some." Rasulullah ﷺ therefore sent a crier to Makkah to announce, "Whoever locks his door shall be safe! Whoever throws down his weapons shall be safe! Whoever enters the house of Abu Sufian shall be safe!" Rasulullah ﷺ then sent Abu Sufian with Abbas ﷺ and they both sat at the edge of the valley. When the Banu Sulaim tribe marched by, Abu Sufian asked, "Who are they?" "They are the Banu Sulaim tribe," replied Abbas ﷺ. Abu Sufian then said, "What have I to do with the Banu Sulaim tribe?" Thereafter, Ali bin Abi Talib ﷺ came at the head of the Muhajir. It was when Rasulullah ﷺ arrived amongst the Ansar that Abu Sufian asked, "O Abbas! Who are they?" Abbas ﷺ said, "They are the red death who are not afraid to spill the blood of their enemies. That is Rasulullah ﷺ with the Ansar." Abu Sufian commented, "I have seen the kingdom of the Kisra and the kingdom of the Caesar but I have never seen anything like the kingdom of your nephew." Abbaas said, "This is not a mere kingdom but the greater kingdom of Prophethood." (*Tabrani, Haythami*)

Urwa ﷺ narrates that Rasulullah ﷺ left Madinah with an army of 12,000 comprising of the Muhajir, the Ansar, the Aslam tribe, the Ghifar tribe, the Juhaina tribe and the Banu Sulaim tribe. They led with horses and were so fast that they reached Marruz Zahran close to Makkah without the Quraish even knowing about them. The Quraish sent Hakim bin Hizam and Abu Sufian to Rasulullah ﷺ with instructions to either secure a peace treaty with Rasulullah ﷺ or declare war against him. Abu Sufian and Hakim bin Hizam left for Madinah. On the way they met Budail bin Waraqa and asked him to accompany them. When they reached an area of Makkah called Arak at the time of Isha, they noticed many tents and an army. They also heard the noise of horses. This frightened them and they grew scared. They said, "This is the Banu Ka'b tribe whom war has gathered here." Budail observed, "They are more than the Banu Ka'b. All of them combined cannot equal this number. Could the Hawazin tribe be searching for grass in our territory? By Allah! We cannot even say this. These numbers are like those of people performing Hajj." Rasulullah ﷺ had sent horsemen ahead of the army to capture spies. In addition to this, the Banu Khuza'h tribe lived along the road and were not allowing anyone to pass. As soon as Abu Sufian and his companions entered the Muslim army, the horsemen captured them in the darkness of the night and took them to Rasulullah ﷺ. Abu Sufian and his companions now feared that they would surely lose their lives. Omar ﷺ stood up before Abu Sufian and slapped him on his neck. The people close to Abu Sufian took him away to be presented before Rasulullah ﷺ. Abu Sufian feared that he would now be killed. Since Abbas ﷺ had been a close friend of Abu Sufian during the period of ignorance, he called out at the top of his voice, "Will you not hand me over to Abbas?" Abbas ﷺ arrived and dispersed everyone from Abu Sufian. Abbas ﷺ requested Rasulullah ﷺ to make Abu Sufian over to him. In the meantime, the news of Abu Sufian being there spread throughout the army. Abbas ﷺ mounted his animal with Abu Sufian that night and rode around the army with him until they had seen him. When he slapped Abu Sufian on his neck, Omar ﷺ told him, "By Allah! You shall die before you even draw near to Rasulullah ﷺ." He therefore sought help from Abbas ﷺ and said, "I shall surely be killed." Abbas ﷺ protected him from assaulting him. When Abu Sufian saw the large numbers of people and their great discipline, he commented, "Never before have I seen a concentration of people as I see tonight." After rescuing him from the people, Abbas said to Abu Sufian, "You will certainly be killed if you do not accept Islam and do not testify that Muhammad ﷺ is Allah's Rasul. As much as Abu Sufian wanted to say what Abbas ﷺ had told him, he could not get his tongue to do so. He then spent the night with Abbas ﷺ. As for Hakim bin Hizam and Budail bin Waraqa, they both went to Rasulullah ﷺ and accepted Islam. Rasulullah ﷺ then asked them about the people of Makkah. When the Fajr Adhan was called out, everyone gathered and waited for the salah to begin. Abu Sufian became alarmed and asked, "O Abbas! What are you people going to do'?" Abbas replied, "The Muslims are awaiting the arrival of Rasulullah ﷺ." Abbas ﷺ took Abu Sufian along with him outside. When Abu Sufian saw the Muslims, he asked, "Do they do anything that Rasulullah ﷺ commands them?" "Yes," replied Abbas, "they will even stop eating and drinking if Rasulullah ﷺ commands them." Abu Sufian then asked, "Ask him if he will forgive his people." Abbas then took him along to Rasulullah ﷺ and said, "O Rasulullah ﷺ! Here is Abu Sufian." Abu Sufian said, "O Muhammad ﷺ! I prayed to my god for help and you prayed to yours for help. By Allah! It is evident to me that you have defeated me. Had my god been true and yours false, I would have certainly defeated you." He then testified that that there is none worthy of worship but Allah and that Muhammad ﷺ is Allah's Rasul. Abbas ﷺ then requested, "O Rasulullah ﷺ! Permit me to go to your people (the Quraish in Makkah) to warn them about what is about to befall them and to invite them towards Allah and His Rasul." When Rasulullah ﷺ granted him permission, Abbas ﷺ asked, "What shall I tell them, O Rasulullah ﷺ? Give me some assurance of safety so that they may rest at ease." Rasulullah ﷺ said, "Tell them that the person will be safe who testifies that there is none worthy of worship but the One Allah Who has no partner and that Muhammad ﷺ is Allah's servant and Rasul ﷺ. The person who throws down his weapons and sits near the Kabah shall also be safe and the person who locks his door will also remain safe." Abbas ﷺ then said, "O Rasulullah ﷺ! Abu Sufian is our cousin and he wishes to return with me. Allow him something that will give him status." Rasulullah ﷺ said, "Tell the people that whoever enters the house

of Abu Sufyan will be safe and whoever enters the house of Hakim bin Hizam will also be safe." Rasulullah ﷺ said this because Abu Sufyan's house was in the upper end of Makkah and the house of Hakim bin Hizam was in the lower end. Abu Sufian understood these announcements well. Rasulullah ﷺ then gave Abbas ﷺ the white mule that Dihya Kalbi ﷺ had given him as a gift and he left on it with Abu Sufian mounted behind him. When Abbas ﷺ had left, Rasulullah ﷺ sent some of the Sahabah after him with instructions to catch up with him and call him back. Rasulullah ﷺ also informed them about his fears concerning Abu Sufian. When the messenger conveyed the message to Abbas ﷺ, he did not like to return and said, "Does Rasulullah ﷺ fear that Abu Sufian would forsake Islam to join the few people in Makkah and commit kufr after accepting Islam?" The messenger then told Abbas ﷺ to keep Abu Sufian there, which he did. When he did this, Abu Sufian asked, "Is this betrayal, O family of Hashim?" To this Abbas ﷺ replied, "We never betray anyone. I just need you to do something." "Tell me what it is so that I may do it for you," complied Abu Sufian. Abbas ﷺ responded by saying, "You will know what it is when Khalid bin Walid ﷺ and Zubair bin Awam ﷺ arrive." Abbas ﷺ waited by a narrow pass just ahead of Arak and Marruz Zahran. Abu Sufian kept the words of Abbas ﷺ in mind as Rasulullah ﷺ dispatched the various battalions of horsemen one after the other. Rasulullah ﷺ divided the horsemen into 2 sections, the 1st with Zubair bin Awam ﷺ and Khalid bin Walid ﷺ, followed by another comprising of soldiers from the Aslam, Ghifar and Qudha'h tribes. Abu Sufian asked, "O Abbas! Is this Rasulullah ﷺ?" "No," replied Abbas ﷺ, this is Khalid bin Walid ﷺ." Ahead of him, Rasulullah ﷺ had sent Sa'd bin Ubadah ﷺ together with a regiment of the Ansar. Sa'd ﷺ called out, "Today is the day of bloodshed! Today, the holiness of the Haram shall be lifted!" Thereafter, Rasulullah ﷺ arrived with the battalion of Iman, namely the Muhajir and Ansar. When Abu Sufian saw so many faces that he did not recognize, he said, "O Rasulullah ﷺ! You have given preference to these people over your people?" Rasulullah ﷺ replied, "This is the result of your people's doings. These people believed in me when you people called me a liar and it was them who assisted me when you people expelled me from Makkah."

On that day, Aqra bin Habis, Abbas bin Mirdas and Uyayna bin Hisn Fazari were with Rasulullah ﷺ. When he saw them around Rasulullah ﷺ, Abu Sufian asked, "Who are these people, O Abbas?" Abbas replied, "These are the battalion of Rasulullah ﷺ. With them is the red death. They are the Muhajir and the Ansar. Abu Sufian then said, "Come on, O Abbas! I have never seen an army or group as large as I have seen today." Zubair bin Awam ﷺ proceeded with his battalion until they reached Hajon while Khalid bin Walid ﷺ proceeded further and entered the lower end of Makkah. There he encountered some ruffians from the Banu Bakr tribe and had to fight them. Allah granted Khalid ﷺ victory over them and while some were killed at a place called Hazwara, others fled to their homes. Those who were mounted on horseback climbed the Handama hill as the Muslims followed in pursuit. Rasulullah ﷺ eventually entered Makkah with the last group of people. A crier announced, "Whoever locks himself in his house without fighting shall be safe." Abu Sufian was also calling out in Makkah, "Accept Islam and remain safe." It was really through Abbas ﷺ that Allah had protected the people of Makkah. Hind bint Utba (Abu Sufyan's wife) grabbed hold of his beard and shouted, "O family of Ghalib! Kill this madman!" He shouted at her, "Let my beard go! I swear by Allah that you will definitely be executed if you do not accept Islam. Woe to you!

Rasulullah has come with the truth. Go home and hide."
(Tabrani, Haythami, Bukhari, Bayhaqi)

Suhail bin Amr Accepts Islam and Testifies the Noble Character of Rasulullah ﷺ

Suhail bin Amr ؓ narrates that he entered his house and locked the doors when Rasulullah ﷺ arrived victoriously in Makkah. He then sent his son Abdullah bin Suhail to secure amnesty for him from Rasulullah ﷺ because he feared being killed. Abdullah went and said, "O Rasulullah ﷺ! Will you grant amnesty to my father?" "Certainly," replied Rasulullah ﷺ, "he has the protection of Allah. He may leave the house." Addressing those around him, Rasulullah ﷺ then said, "Whoever meets Suhail should not even look at him severely so that he may leave his house in peace. I swear by my life that Suhail surely possesses intelligence and esteem. Someone like him cannot be ignorant about the beauty of Islam. He has already come to know that whatever his efforts against Islam have been, they have carried no fruit." Abdullah bin Suhail reported back to his father what Rasulullah ﷺ had said. Suhail said, "By Allah! He is an excellent person in youth and in old age. Suhail would then go to and forth to meet Rasulullah ﷺ and even accompanied Rasulullah ﷺ in the Battle of Hunain as a disbeliever. He eventually accepted Islam at Jirana and Rasulullah ﷺ gave him 100 camels from the booty. *(Kanzul Ummal, Hakim)*

Rasulullah ﷺ's Speech to the People of Makkah on the Day Makkah was Conquered

Omar ؓ narrates that when Rasulullah ﷺ was in Makkah on the day that Makkah was conquered, he sent for Safwan bin Umayyah, Abu Sufian bin Harb and Harith bin Hisham. Omar ؓ then said, "Allah has given us power over them today. I shall certainly remind them of what they had done in the past." As he was still saying this, Rasulullah ﷺ said to them, "My example and yours is like that of Yusuf ؑ and his brothers." Rasulullah ﷺ then recited the following verse of the Qur'an that quotes the words Yusuf ؑ said to his brothers:

قَالَ لَا تَثْرِيبَ عَلَيْكُمُ الْيَوْمَ يَغْفِرُ اللَّهُ لَكُمْ وَهُوَ أَرْحَمُ الرَّاحِمِينَ (92)

He said: "No reproach on you this day, may Allah forgive you, and He is the Most Merciful of those who show mercy!
(Yusuf:92)

Omar ؓ says that he covered his head in embarrassment before Rasulullah ﷺ because it would look very bad if he had to say something without thinking whereas Rasulullah ﷺ had mentioned what he already did. *(Kanzul Ummal)*. Ibn Abi Husain narrates that when Rasulullah ﷺ conquered Makkah, he entered the Kabah and when he came out, he placed his hands on the frames of the door and said to the people gathered there, "What have you people to say?" Suhail bin Amr said, "We say and we anticipate good from you. You are a big-hearted brother and the son of a big-hearted brother. You now have control over us." Rasulullah ﷺ said, "I shall say as Yusuf ؑ said: لَا تَثْرِيبَ عَلَيْكُمُ الْيَوْمَ

There shall be no blame on you today (and no revenge will be taken). (Istabah)

Part of a lengthy Hadith narrated by Abu Hurairah ؓ states that Rasulullah ﷺ came to the Kabah and while holding the door-frame, asked, "What do you people have to say? What are your expectations?" The people responded, "We say that you are our nephew and a most lenient and merciful son of our uncle." This they repeated thrice. Rasulullah ﷺ said, "I shall say as Yusuf ؑ said: قَالَ لَا تَثْرِيبَ عَلَيْكُمُ الْيَوْمَ يَغْفِرُ اللَّهُ لَكُمْ وَهُوَ أَرْحَمُ الرَّاحِمِينَ (92)

He said: "No reproach on you this day, may Allah forgive you, and He is the Most Merciful of those who show mercy!
(Yusuf:92)

Abu Hurairah ؓ narrates further that the people then dispersed as if they had been revived from their graves and they accepted Islam. Imam Bayhaqi states that in a narration of this incident that Imam Shafi'e رحمة الله narrated from Imam Abu Yusuf رحمة الله. It is mentioned that when the people gathered in the Masjidul Haram, Rasulullah ﷺ asked them, "What do you think I shall do with you?" They said, "You will do only good, for you are a big-hearted brother and the son of a big-hearted brother." Rasulullah ﷺ then said to them, "Go! You are all free." *(Bayhaqi)*

Ikrama bin Abi Jabal ؓ Accepts Islam and Granted Amnesty on the Request of his Wife

Abdullah bin Zubair ؓ narrates that on the day that Makkah was conquered, Ummu Hakim bint Harith bin Hisham ؓ accepted Islam. She was the wife of Ikrama bin Abi Jahal and therefore said, "O Rasulullah ﷺ! Ikrama has run away from you to Yemen, fearing that you would execute him. Would you please grant him amnesty." Rasulullah ﷺ said, "He has amnesty." Umm Hakim ؓ therefore left in search of Ikrama with the company of her Roman slave. The slave tried to seduce her and she continuously gave him hope until they reached a tribe of the Uk from whom she asked for help. The people caught him and tied him up. She eventually managed to catch up with Ikrama who had already reached one of the Tihama coasts where he had boarded a ship. One of the sailors said to him, "Recite the words of sincerity." Ikrama asked him, "What should I say, "He replied, "Say that there is none worthy of worship but Allah." Ikrama said to him, "It is from this that I am fleeing." As they were speaking, Umm Hakim ؓ arrived and started waving a cloth to attract their attention as she shouted, "O my cousin! I have come to you from him who best maintains family ties, who is the most pious of people and the best of people. Do not destroy yourself." He waited for her until she caught up with him. She then said to him, "I have secured amnesty for you from Rasulullah ﷺ." "Have you really?" he asked. She replied, "Yes, I spoke to Rasulullah ﷺ and he granted you amnesty." Ikrama then returned with Umm Hakim ؓ when she informed him about the details of her experiences with the Roman slave. With anger he killed the slave but had not yet accepted Islam.

Ikrama ؓ Accepts Islam and Testifies to the Perfect Excellence of Rasulullah ﷺ

When Ikrama drew close to Makkah, Rasulullah ﷺ said to the Sahabah, "Ikrama, the son of Abu Jahal is coming to you as a believer and a Muhajir, so do not curse his father because cursing the dead only hurts the living without ever reaching the dead." Ikrama kept making efforts to cohabit with his wife but she refused saying, "You are disbeliever while I am a Muslim." Ikrama ؓ remarked, "Whatever prevents you from me must be something very great." When Rasulullah ﷺ saw Ikrama ؓ, he hastened towards him without wearing his upper shawl out of happiness at seeing Ikrama ؓ. Rasulullah ﷺ then sat down while Ikrama ؓ stood before him alongside his wife who was wearing a veil. Ikrama said, "O Muhammad ﷺ! This lady has informed me that you have granted me amnesty. Rasulullah ﷺ responded by saying, "She has spoken the truth. Your safety is assured." Ikrama then asked, "Towards what do you invite?" Rasulullah ﷺ replied, "I invite you to testify that that there is none worthy of worship but Allah and that I am Allah's Rasul ﷺ. I also invite you towards establishing salah and paying zakah." Rasulullah ﷺ then mentioned several other things that he needed to do. Ikrama ❀ said, "By Allah! You have invited to nothing but the truth and excellent and beautiful actions. By Allah! Even before you started inviting towards your invitation, you had been the most truthful of us and the most righteous. I testify that there is none worthy of worship but Allah and that Muhammad ❀ is Allah's servant and Rasul ❀." This pleased Rasulullah ❀ greatly. Ikrama ❀ then asked, "O Rasulullah ❀! Teach me the best thing to say." Rasulullah ❀ told him to say:

اَشْهَدُ اَنْ لَا اِلٰهَ اِلَّا اللهُ وَاَشْهَدُ اَنَّ مُحَمَّدًا عَبْدُهُ وَرَسُوْلُهُ

"I testify that there is none worthy of worship but Allah ❀ and that Muhammad ❀ is Allah's servant and messenger"

Ikrama ❀ then asked what else he could say. Rasulullah ❀ told him to say, "I make Allah and all present witness to the fact that I am a Muslim, Mujahid and Muhajir." Ikrama then said what Rasulullah ❀ told him.

The Da'wah that Rasulullah ❀ Gave to Ikrama ❀

Rasulullah ❀ then said to Ikrama ❀, "I shall grant you anything you ask for if I am able to do." Ikrama ❀ asked, "I ask you to seek forgiveness from Allah for every type of enmity I have shown towards you, for every journey I have undertaken to oppose you, for every battle I have fought against you and for every harsh word I have said in your face or behind your back." Rasulullah ❀ made Du'a, "O Allah! Forgive him for every type of enmity he has displayed and for every journey he undertook to any place with the intention of extinguishing Your light. Also forgive him for every insulting remark he has made in my face or behind my back." Ikrama ❀ remarked, "I am pleased, O Rasulullah ❀." Ikrama ❀ then said, "O Rasulullah ❀! I swear by Allah that every expense I bore opposing Islam, I shall spend double that amount in the Path of Allah. I swear also that every battle I fought opposing Islam, I shall fight double the number of battles in the Path of Allah." True to his word, Ikrama ❀ exerted every effort to fight in Jihad until he was martyred. Rasulullah ❀ upheld the marriage of Ikrama ❀ to his wife without renewing the Nikah. *Waqidi* has narrated that during the Battle of Hunain when the Muslims were suffering a temporarily defeat at the beginning, Suhail bin Amr remarked, "The Muslims have never experienced before the likes of these 2 tribes (the Thaqif and Hawazin)." To this, Ikrama ❀ responded by saying, "One should not speak like this. Everything lies in the control of Allah and Muhammad ❀ has no control over things. If he is defeated today, tomorrow shall hold promising results from Allah." Suhail mocked, "By Allah! It was not long before this that you opposed Rasulullah ❀!" Ikrama ❀ then replied by saying, "By Allah! All our previous efforts have been useless. We considered ourselves to be intelligent people, we used to worship stones that could neither harm nor give any benefit." *(Kanzul Ummal)*

Abdullah bin Zubair ❀ has also narrated their incident but in fewer words. He says that when Ikrama ❀ reached the door of Rasulullah ❀, Rasulullah ❀ was so overjoyed at his arrival that he jumped up into a standing position. A narration of Urwa bin Zubair quotes from Ikrama ❀ that when he met Rasulullah ❀ he said, "O Muhammad ❀! This woman has informed me that you have granted me amnesty." Rasulullah ❀ replied, "Indeed. You have been granted amnesty." Ikrama ❀ then said, "I testify that there is none worthy of worship but the one Allah Who has no partner and that Muhammad ❀ is Allah's servant and Rasul ❀. I also would testify that you are the best of people, the most truthful person, and one who best fulfils his promises." Ikrama ❀ says that out of embarrassment, his head was bowed as he said this. He then said, "O Rasulullah ❀! Do seek forgiveness from Allah for every type of enmity I displayed towards you and for every journey I undertook to promote Shirk." Rasulullah ❀ made the following Du'a, "O Allah! Forgive Ikrama ❀ for all the enmity he displayed towards me and for every journey he undertook with the intention of preventing people from Islam." Ikrama ❀ then said, "O Rasulullah ❀! Teach me the best that you know so that I may learn it and practice." Rasulullah ❀ advised him that together with striving in the Path of Allah, he should recite: اَشْهَدُ اَنْ لَا اِلٰهَ اِلَّا اللهُ وَاَشْهَدُ اَنَّ مُحَمَّدًا عَبْدُهُ وَرَسُوْلُهُ

"I testify that there is none worthy of worship but Allah ❀ and that Muhammad ❀ is Allah's servant and Rasul ❀"

Ikrama ❀ then said, "O Rasulullah ❀! I swear by Allah that every expense I bore to oppose Islam, I shall spend double that amount in the Path of Allah. I swear also that every battle I fought an opposing Islam, I shall fight double the number of battles in the Path of Allah."

Ikrama ❀ Strives in Jihad and is Martyred

Ikrama ❀ continued fighting in Jihad and in turn he was martyred in the Battle of Ajnadin during Khilafa of Abu Bakr ❀. Rasulullah ❀ appointed Ikrama ❀ to collect the zakah of the Hawazin tribe during the year that Rasulullah ❀ performed the farewell Hajj. When Rasulullah ❀ passed away, Ikrama ❀ was in a place called Tabalah in Yemen. *(Hakim, Tabrani)*

Safwan bin Umayyah ❀ Accepts Islam and Granted Amnesty at the request of Umair bin Wahab ❀

Abdullah bin Zubair ❀ narrates that when Makkah was conquered, the wife of Safwan bin Umayya ❀ accepted Islam. Her name was Baghom bint Mu'addal ❀ and she belonged to the Kinana tribe. Safwan bin Umayyah ❀ had run away from Makkah and reached some valley. As they sat there, he said to his slave Yasir who was alone with him, "O dear! What do you see?" Yasir replied, "That is Umair bin Wahab." "What should I do with Umair? By Allah! He has come to kill me and has helped Rasulullah ❀ against me." When Umair bin Wahab ❀ met him, Safwan bin Umayyah ❀ said, "Are you not satisfied with what you have already done to me? You placed the burden of settling your debts and caring for your family on me and now you have come to kill me?" Umair bin Wahab ❀ said to him, "O Abu Wahab! May my life be sacrificed for you! I have come to you from the best of people and the one who best maintains family ties." Before coming to Safwan ❀ Umair bin Wahab ❀ had mentioned to Rasulullah ❀, "O Rasulullah ❀! The leader of our people Safwan bin Umayyah has run away from Makkah to throw himself into the ocean fearing that you shall not grant him amnesty. May my parents be sacrificed for you! Do grant him amnesty." Because Rasulullah ❀ had granted the amnesty, Umair bin Wahab ❀ had now come to Safwan bin Umayyah ❀ to inform him that he had been granted amnesty.

Rasulullah ❀ Sends his Turban to Safwan bin Umayyah ❀ to Confirm his Amnesty

Safwan ❀ then said, "By Allah! I shall never return with you to Makkah until you bring me a sign which I may identify." When Umair ❀ returned to Rasulullah ❀ with this request, Rasulullah ❀ said, "Take this turban of mine." Umair ❀ then returned to Safwan ❀ with the turban which was actually a striped shawl that Rasulullah ❀ tied on his head as a turban on the day the Muslims conquered Makkah. Searching for Safwan ❀ the second time, Umair ❀ found him and showing him the turban said, "O Abu Wahab! I have come to you from the best of people, the one who best maintains family ties, the most righteous of people and the most tolerant. His honor is yours, his dignity is yours and his kingdom is yours for his forefathers and yours are the same. I advise you to fear Allah for your own good." Safwan ؓ said, "I fear that I shall be killed." Umair said, "Rasulullah ﷺ invites you to accept Islam. It would be best if you accept willingly. If not, you have 2 month's grace. Of all people, he best keeps his word and had even sent to you the shawl he wore as a turban when he entered Makkah. Do you recognize it?" "Certainly," replied Safwan ؓ. When Umair ؓ took out the turban, Safwan said, "That it certainly is." Safwan ؓ then returned and reached Rasulullah ﷺ as he was busy leading the Asr salah in the Masjidul Haram. While the 2 stood waiting, Safwan ؓ asked, "How many salah do the Muslims perform each day and night." When Umair ؓ informed him that they perform 5 salah daily, he asked, "Is Muhammad ﷺ leading them in salah?" "Yes," came the reply. When Rasulullah ﷺ said the Salam to end the salah, Safwan ؓ called out, "O Muhammad ﷺ! Umair bin Wahab has brought me here with your shawl and says that you have asked me to come to you. He says that it would be best if I accept Islam willingly otherwise you shall allow me 2 month's grace." Rasulullah ﷺ said, "Dismount, O Abu Wahab." "By Allah!" exclaimed Safwan ؓ, "I shall never dismount until you verify this for me." Rasulullah ﷺ said, "In fact, you may have a grace period of 4 months." Safwan ؓ then dismounted.

Safwan ؓ Marches with Rasulullah ﷺ Against the Hawazin Tribe and Accepts Islam

When Rasulullah ﷺ marched against the Hawazin tribe, Safwan ؓ marched with him while still a disbeliever. Rasulullah ﷺ sent someone to him to request that he loan some weapons to the Muslims. Safwan ؓ sent 100 coats of armor together with all the equipment that went with it and asked, "Shall this be taken with my permission or by force?" When Rasulullah ﷺ told him that it was on loan and that it would be returned, he loaned it. According to the request of Rasulullah ﷺ, he loaded it on his animal and took it to Hunain. He therefore witnessed the Battles of Hunain and Ta'if. He then accompanied Rasulullah ﷺ to Jiranah. As Rasulullah ﷺ was walking amongst the booty to have a look at it, Safwan ؓ was with him. Safwan then started looking at a valley filled with camels, goats and shepherds. Rasulullah ﷺ watched with long gaze at the scene and said to him, "O Abu Wahab! Do you like this valley?" When he replied in the affirmative, Rasulullah ﷺ said to him, "It is all yours." Safwan ؓ accepted Islam on the spot and said, "It is only be the heart of a Nabi that can be so generous. I testify that there is none worthy of worship but Allah and that Muhammad ﷺ is Allah's servant and Rasul ﷺ." (Kanzul Ummal, Al-Bidayah wan Nihayah). Another narration quotes from Safwan that Rasulullah ﷺ asked him to give some weapons on loan. He said, "Are you taking it away from me by force?" Rasulullah ﷺ answered, "I wish to borrow them and damages shall be paid back." It so happened that some of the coats of armor were destroyed. Rasulullah ﷺ therefore approached Safwan to pay for the damages. Safwan said, "O Rasulullah ﷺ! Today I have a greater desire to accept Islam than to be reimbursed." (Ahmad)

Abu Dhar ؓ Invites Huwaitib to Islam and he Accepts

Mundhir bin Jahm ؓ narrates from Huwaitib bin Abdil Uzza ؓ that he was frightened when Rasulullah ﷺ entered Makkah after it was conquered. He left his house and scattered his family in various places where they would be safe. He then hid himself in an orchard belonging to the Auf clan. He narrates, "One day, Abu Dhar ؓ suddenly arrived. We had been good friends before

and friendship always bears fruit. However, as soon as I saw him, I started to run away." Abu Dhar ؓ called out, "O Abu Muhammad ﷺ!" When Huwaitib ؓ responded, Abu Dhar ؓ asked, "What is the matter?" "Fear," replied, Huwaitib ؓ. "Have no fear," said Abu Dhar ؓ, "You have amnesty in the protection of Allah." Huwaitib ؓ then went back and greeted Abu Dhar ؓ, "You may go home," said Abu Dhar ؓ. "How can I to go home?" asked Huwaitib ؓ, "By Allah! I do not see myself returning home alive. I shall be met on the street and be killed by someone barging into my house. In addition, my family are scattered in various places." Abu Dhar ؓ said, "Then gather your family in one place and I shall escort you home." Abu Dhar ؓ then took Huwaitib ؓ home and announced, "Huwaitib ؓ has been granted amnesty and may not be harmed." When Abu Dhar ؓ went to Rasulullah ﷺ and informed him about the events, he said, "Has everyone not been granted amnesty besides those whose execution I have ordered'?" This statement put Huwaitib ؓ's heart at ease and he took his family home. Abu Dhar ؓ again came to Huwaitib ؓ and said, "O Abu Muhammad! Until when? Where to? You have participated in all the battles. Although you have lost so much good, much good is still left for you. Go to Rasulullah ﷺ and accept Islam. You will then be able to live in peace. Rasulullah ﷺ is the most righteous of people, the one who best maintains family ties and the most tolerant of all people. His honor is yours and his dignity is yours." Huwaitib ؓ then said to Abu Dhar ؓ, "I am prepared to accompany you to Rasulullah ﷺ." The 2 then met Rasulullah ﷺ at Bat'ha while Abu Bakr ؓ and Omar ؓ were with him. Huwaitib ؓ then asked Abu Dhar ؓ, "What should be said when Rasulullah ﷺ is greeted?" Abu Dhar ؓ told him to say: السلام عليك ايها النبى ورحمة الله وبركاته
"May peace, the mercy of Allah and His blessings be showered on you, O Nabi of Allah"

When Huwaitib ؓ greeted Rasulullah ﷺ with these words, Rasulullah ﷺ replied, "Peace be to you too, O Huwaitib." Huwaitib ؓ then said, "I testify that that there is none worthy of worship but Allah and that you are Allah's Rasul ﷺ." Rasulullah ﷺ then said, "All praise belongs to Allah Who has guided you." Huwaitib ؓ narrates that Rasulullah ﷺ was happy that he accepted Islam. Rasulullah ﷺ asked him for a loan and he borrowed 40,000 Dirhams. He then participated in the Battles of Hunain and Ta'if after which Rasulullah ﷺ gave him 100 camels from the booty received from the Battle of Hunain. (Hakim, Ibn Sa'd). In a narration reported by Ja'far bin Mahmood bin Muhammad bin Salma ؓ, it is mentioned that Huwaitib ؓ said, "Amongst the elders of the Quraish who remained on their religion up to the conquest of Makkah, there was none who disliked the conquest more than myself. However, whatever is predestined must take place. I was present with the disbelievers during the Battle of Badr when I witnessed many eye-opening lessons. I saw the angels descend from the heavens to the earth, kill and chain up the disbelievers. I then said to myself that Rasulullah ﷺ is a protected person, but I did not mention this to anyone. We were defeated and returned to Makkah where people gradually started accepting Islam. I was also present when the Treaty of Hudaibiyah was signed and was one of the people who took part in the negotiations until it was completed. However, it served only to promote Islam further because Allah does as He wills. Being the last witness when the treaty was signed, I said to myself, 'Although the Quraish are pleased to have forced Rasulullah ﷺ to leave, they shall be see from him only what displeases them.' Rasulullah ﷺ arrived to complete the missed Umrah and the Quraish left Makkah, Suhail bin Amr and myself were amongst those who remained behind to expel Rasulullah ﷺ

as soon as their time of 3 days expired. When the 3rd day was over, Suhail ◈ and myself approached Rasulullah ◈ and said, 'Your term has expired, so leave our town.' Rasulullah ◈ then called out, "O Bilal! Announce that no Muslim who has come with us should be in Makkah after the sun has set." *(Hakim)*

Harith bin Hisham ◈ Accepts Islam

Abdullah bin Ikrama ◈ narrates that when Makkah was conquered, Harith bin Hisham and Abdullah bin Abi Rabe'ah went to Ummu Hani ◈ the daughter of Abu Talib to seek protection. When they requested her protection, she granted amnesty to them both. Ali ◈ her brother then arrived, saw the 2 of them and drew his sword. When Ummu Hani ◈ came between them and grabbing Ali around the neck, she said, "From all people, you do this to me? You shall have to kill me before you get to them!" Ali ◈ said, "You give protection to the disbelievers!" He then left. Ummu Hani ◈ herself narrates that she then went to Rasulullah ◈ and said, "O Rasulullah ◈! From the treatment I received from my own mother's son Ali, I am unable to escape him. I granted amnesty to 2 of my disbelievers brothers-in-law and he attacked them to kill them." Rasulullah ◈ said, "He should not have done that. We shall protect whoever you protect and we grant amnesty to whoever you grant amnesty." When Ummu Hani ◈ returned and informed the 2 about this, they returned to their homes. When Rasulullah ◈ was informed that Harith bin Hisham and Abdullah bin Abi Rabe'ah were wearing saffron colored clothing and sitting without fear, he said, "You can do nothing to harm them because we have already granted them amnesty." Harith bin Hisham says that he then started feeling shy when Rasulullah ◈ saw him because he remembered that Rasulullah ◈ also saw him in all the battles the disbelievers fought against the Muslims. Thinking the kind and merciful nature of Rasulullah ◈ he met Rasulullah ◈ in the Masjid. Rasulullah ◈ met him with a smile and waited for him. He then went to Rasulullah ◈, greeted him and recited the Shahada. Rasulullah ◈ then said, "All praise is for Allah Who has guided you. It was not possible that someone like you could ever remain in the dark about Islam." Harith bin Hisham ◈ says, "By Allah! Islam can never be unknown." *(Hakim)*

Nudhair bin Harith ◈ Accepts Islam

Muhammad bin Shurabil Abdari narrates that Nudhair bin Harith ◈ was amongst the most learned of people and used to say, "All praises belong to Allah Who has honored us with Islam, has blessed us with Muhammad ◈ and saved us from dying as our forefathers died as disbelievers. I used to join myself with the Quraish in every effort against the Muslims until the year arrived when Rasulullah ◈ conquered Makkah and then went to Hunain. We left with him with the intention that should Muhammad be defeated, we would assist the enemy against him. However, we never got the opportunity. By Allah! I was still as I was planning against the Muslims when Rasulullah ◈ left for Jiranah and I saw none but he meet me with a smiling face. He asked, 'Is it Nudhair?' 'It is me,' I replied. He said, 'This opportunity is better than the one which you lost during the Battle of Hunain?' I jumped up and drew closer to him. He said, 'The time has come for you to think about your religion.' When I told him that I had been thinking about this, he said, "O Allah! Increase his dedication.' By the Being Who sent Rasulullah ◈ with the truth! The effect of this Du'a was that my heart became a rock of dedication in Islam and to assist the cause of Islam. I had just returned to my tent when a man from the Banu Duwal came to me and said, 'O Abu Harith! Rasulullah ◈ has ordered that 100 camels be given to you. Would you please give me some because I have debts.' I decided not to take the camels thinking that it was being given to me only to win me over and I would not want to be bribed to accept Islam. I then thought to myself that I had not wanted nor asked for it. So I accepted the camels and gave 10 to the man of the Banu Duwal tribe." *(Isabah)*

Rasulullah ◈ Leaves the Thaqif Tribe and Urwa bin Mas'ood ◈ Accepts Islam

Ibn Is'haq narrates that when Rasulullah ◈ left the Thaqif tribe, Urwa bin Mas'ood ◈ of Thaqif followed him and reached him just before he arrived Madinah. He accepted Islam and requested permission to take the message of Islam to his people. Rasulullah ◈ said to him, "They would kill you." Rasulullah ◈ said this because he knew from his experience with them that they were extremely proud and stubborn. Urwa bin Mas'ood ◈ said to Rasulullah ◈, "I am more beloved to them than their virgins." He was greatly loved and obeyed by the Thaqif.

Urwa bin Mas'ood ◈ Invites his People to Islam and is Martyred

Urwa bin Mas'ood ◈ left to invite his people to Islam expecting that they would not oppose him because of his high status among them. When he invited them to Islam standing on the balcony of his house and made Islam clear to them, they fired arrows at him from every angle. He was martyred when one of the arrows struck him. He was asked, "What have you to say about your blood?" He replied, "Allah has blessed me with great honor and brought to me the rank of martyrdom. I have also attained the rank of those martyrs who were killed while fighting with Rasulullah ◈ before leaving this world. Bury me with them." He was buried with those Sahabah. The Sahabah believed that it was concerning him that Rasulullah ◈ said, "His example amongst his people is like that of Surah *Ya-Seen*."

The Thaqif Tribe Sends Abd Yalil bin Amr with a Delegation to Rasulullah ◈ and is Informed of Their Arrival

Few months after the killing Urwa bin Mas'ood ◈ the Thaqif tribe consulted with each other and decided that they did not have the strength to fight all the Arabs around them who had already pledged allegiance to Rasulullah ◈ and accepted Islam. They decided to send one of their people to Rasulullah ◈. The person they sent was Abd Yalil bin Amr together with 2 persons from their allies and a 3rd person from the Banu Malik tribe. When they came close to Madinah and camped at a spring, they met Mughiera bin Shu'ba ◈ who was looking at the riding animals of the Sahabah. After meeting them, he rushed to Rasulullah ◈ to give him the glad tidings of their arrival. He first met Abu Bakr ◈ and informed him that some riders from the Thaqif had arrived and were prepared to pledge their allegiance and accept Islam if Rasulullah ◈ accepted a few of their conditions and if a letter is written to their people. Abu Bakr ◈ said to Mughiera ◈, "I ask you on oath not to go to Rasulullah ◈ before me so that I may be the first to inform him." Mughiera ◈ allowed this. Abu Bakr ◈ then went to Rasulullah ◈ and informed him about their arrival. In the meantime, Mughiera ◈ went back to the delegation and brought them together with the grazing animals. Although Mughiera ◈ taught the delegation how to greet Rasulullah ◈, they still greeted him like people greeted during the period of ignorance. When the delegation arrived at the Masjid, a tent was pitched for them. The person who conducted negotiations between them and Rasulullah ◈ was Khalid bin Sa'eed bin Al Aas ◈. Whenever he brought food to them, they would not touch it until he had eaten from it himself. It was also he who wrote the letter to their people. Amongst the conditions that they made with Rasulullah ﷺ was that he leaves their idol Lat alone for 3 years. However, Rasulullah ﷺ refused to allow this and they continued reducing the number of years until they finally requested for a single month starting from the day they arrived in Madinah. They requested for this period so that foolish people amongst them could gradually be won over. Rasulullah ﷺ refused to allow them this period and decided to send Mughiera bin Shu'ba ﷺ and Abu Sufyan bin Harb ﷺ with them to destroy their idol. Another condition was that they should not be required to perform salah and that they should not have to break their idols with their own hands. Rasulullah ﷺ said to them, "As for the breaking of your idols with your own hands, we shall overlook this since we shall send people to do it for you. However, as for the salah, there is no good in a religion without salah." They gave in saying, 'We shall grant you this even though it is humiliating."

Uthman bin Abil Aas ﷺ narrates that when the Thaqif delegation came to Rasulullah ﷺ, he accommodated them in the Masjid so that it would soften their hearts. They made the conditions that they should not be recruited for Jihad, that Ushr (zakah on crops) should not be taken from them, that they should not be required to perform salah, and that a person from outside their tribe should not be appointed as their leader. Rasulullah ﷺ said to them, "Granted that you will not be recruited for Jihad, that Ushr shall not be taken from you, and that a person from outside your tribe should not be appointed as your leader. However, there is no good in a religion without Ruku without salah, therefore not acceptable." Uthman bin Abil Aas ﷺ said, "O Rasulullah ﷺ!' Teach me the Qur'an and appoint me as a Imam of my people." (Ahmad, Abu Dawud). It also narrates that he asked Jabir ﷺ about the Thaqif delegation when they pledged their allegiance to Rasulullah ﷺ. He replied by saying that they made the conditions that they should not be required to pay zakah or to fight in Jihad. Rasulullah ﷺ accepted their conditions and Jabir ﷺ says that he later heard Rasulullah ﷺ say, "Soon when they accept Islam, they will pay zakah and wage Jihad without being told to do so." (Abu Dawud). Aws bin Hudhaifa ﷺ narrates, "We came to meet Rasulullah ﷺ with the Thaqif delegation. While the allies of the Thaqif stayed with Mughiera bin Shu'ba ﷺ, Rasulullah ﷺ accommodated the delegates of the Banu Malik tribe in one of his tent. He would meet us after Isha and address us while standing. He stood so long that he had to lean on each foot. He often told us about the treatment that he received from his Quraish tribe and would say, 'I have no grief about it. In Makkah we were regarded as the weak ones and were looked down upon. We reached Madinah, victory in battles alternated between us and the Quraish.' One night when Rasulullah ﷺ arrived later than he usually did, we asked, 'You are late tonight?' He replied, 'A part of the portion of the Qur'an I recite daily was not provided and I disliked coming to you without completing it.'"(Ahmad, Abu Dawud, Ibn Majah, Ibn Sa'd).

The Da'wah that the Sahabah Gave to Individuals: Abu Bakr ﷺ Gives Da'wah to Individuals

Ibn Is'haq narrates, "When Abu Bakr ﷺ accepted Islam and made his Islam known, he started inviting people towards Allah. He was well acquainted with the people, well liked by his people, soft-natured, and among all of the Quraish he possessed the most knowledge of their family trees, and the good and bad conditions that prevailed among them. He was a good-natured businessman of excellent character. Because of his vast knowledge about people along with business expertise and his entertaining nature, people used to come to him and disclose to him numerous matters. He therefore started calling all those people to Allah and to Islam when they came to him to meet and sat in his company. As far as I am told, the following persons accepted Islam at his hands: Zubair bin Awam ﷺ, Uthman bin Affan ﷺ, Talha bin Ubaidullah ﷺ, Sa'd bin Abi Waqqas ﷺ and Abdur Rahman bin Auf ﷺ. They all came to Rasulullah ﷺ with Abu Bakr ﷺ and Rasulullah ﷺ presented Islam to them, recited the Qur'an to them and informed them about the rights Islam had on them. They all accepted Iman. These 8 persons (5 named with Abu Bakr, Ali, Zaid bin Haritha) were the front-runners in Islam who believed in Rasulullah ﷺ and believed everything he brought from Allah." (Al-Bidayah wan Nihayah)

The Da'wah of Omar bin Khattab ﷺ

Asbaq narrates that he was a slave of Omar bin Khattab ﷺ and a Christian. Omar ﷺ used to present Islam to him saying, "If you accept Islam, I could take help from you in safeguarding my trusts because it is not permissible for me to use you to safeguard the trusts of the Muslims when you do not belong to their religion." However, when Asbaq refused to accept Islam, Omar ﷺ would say, "There is no compulsion in Islam." Asbaq narrates further, "When Omar ﷺ was on his deathbed, he freed me while I was still a Christian and said, 'You may go wherever you please." Asbaq did accept Islam afterwards (Ibn Sa'd in Kanzul Ummal, Abu Nu'aym). Aslam also a slave of Omar ﷺ narrates that when they were in Sham, he brought some water for Omar ﷺ to make wudhu. Omar ﷺ asked, "Where have you brought this water from? I have never seen any sweet water nor any rainwater as good as this." Aslam informed him that he had obtained the water from the house of an old Christian lady. When Omar ﷺ had completed his wudhu, he approached the old lady and said, "O lady! Accept Islam for Allah has sent Muhammad ﷺ with the truth." The old lady then opened her hair which was as white as the blossoms on a tree. She then said, "I am an extremely old woman and shall die at any moment." Omar ﷺ said, "O Allah! You be witness." (Kanzul Ummal)

The Da'wah that Mus'ab bin Umair ﷺ Gave to Usaid bin Hudhair ﷺ who Accepts Islam

Abdullah bin Abi Bakr bin Muhammad bin Amr bin Hazm and many others narrate that As'ad bin Zurarah ﷺ took Mus'ab bin Umair ﷺ to the locality of the Banu Abdil Ash'al and the Banu Zafar tribes. They entered one of the orchards of the Banu Zafar tribe where there was a well called Bir Maraq. The 2 of them sat in the orchard and many Muslims gathered there with them. During those days, Sa'd bin Mu'adh ﷺ and Usaid bin Hudhair ﷺ were 2 leaders of the Banu Abdil Ash'al tribe and were still disbelievers steadfast on the religion of their forefathers. Sa'd bin Mu'adh ﷺ also happened to be the cousin of As'ad bin Zurarah ﷺ. When these 2 leaders heard about the gathering, Sa'd bin Mu'adh ﷺ said to Usaid bin Hudhair ﷺ, "Have you no father or no self-respect?! Go to those 2 men who have come to our locality to make fools of our innocent people. Warn them for coming to our area. I would have done this for you had it not been for the relation I have with As'ad bin Zurarah as you know. He is my cousin and I cannot confront him." Usaid ﷺ took his spear and went to them. When As'ad ﷺ saw him coming, he said to Mus'ab ﷺ, "He is the leader of his people. He is coming to you so be sincere to Allah when speaking to him." Mus'ab ﷺ said, "I shall speak to him if he is willing to sit down." Usaid ﷺ stood in front of them and began swearing them. He said, "Why have you come to us? Have you come to make fools of our innocent people? Leave us alone if you want to save your lives!" Mus'ab ﷺ said to him, "Please seat and listen for a moment. If you like what you hear, you may accept it. Otherwise, we shall stop doing what you dislike." Usaid ﷺ said, "That is a fair proposition." He then stuck his spear into the ground and sat down. Mus'ab ﷺ then spoke to him about Islam and recited the Qur'an to him. Mus'ab ﷺ and As'ad ﷺ say that from the radiance and gentleness they saw in the face of Usaid ﷺ, they recognized that he would accept Islam before he could even mention it. Usaid ﷺ said, "How excellent and beautiful this is! What do you do when you want to enter the fold of this religion?" They said to him, "Take a bath, clean yourself well, purify your 2 upper and lower clothes, recite the Shahada of truth and perform salah." Usaid ﷺ stood up, took a bath, washed his clothes, recited the Shahada and then stood up to perform 2 Rakats salah. He then said to the 2, "Behind me is a man whom I shall soon send to you. If he follows you, not a soul from his people will fail to follow him. He is Sa'd bin Mu'adh."

Mus'ab ﷺ Gives Da'wah to Sa'd bin Mu'adh ﷺ

Usaid ﷺ then took his spear and went to the place where Sa'd bin Mu'adh ﷺ and his people were sitting in a gathering. When Sa'd bin Mu'adh ﷺ saw Usaid ﷺ approaching, he said, "I swear by Allah that Usaid is coming to you with a look that is very much different from the one he left you with." When Usaid ﷺ stopped by the gathering, Sa'd ﷺ asked, "What did you do?" Usaid ﷺ replied, "1 have spoken to the 2 men and see nothing wrong with what they say. I have also forbidden them from what they do and they accepted to do as I tell them. I have also found out that the Banu Haritha tribe have left to kill As'ad bin Zurarah because they have learnt that he is your cousin and thereby wish to insult you." Fearing the news that had reached him about the Banu Haritha, Sa'd bin Mu'adh ﷺ filled with anger. He stood up and quickly grabbed a spear saying, "By Allah! You have done nothing!" He then went to As'ad ﷺ and when he saw As'ad ﷺ and Mus'ab ﷺ sitting in peace, he realized that Usaid had wanted him to listen to them. He also stood in front of the 2 and swore them. He said to As'ad ﷺ, "O Abu Umamah! By Allah! If it were not for the relationship between you and me, you would have never thought of doing this. You dare to introduce into our locality something that we hate!" Already before his arrival, As'ad ﷺ had mentioned to Mus'ab ﷺ, "O Mus'ab! By Allah! Here comes the leader of all those behind him. Should he follow you, no 2 persons of his community would remain behind." Mus'ab ﷺ said to him, "Please seat and listen for a moment. If you like what you hear, you may accept it. Otherwise, we shall stop doing what you dislike." Sa'd ﷺ said, "That is a fair proposition." He then stuck his spear into the ground and sat down. Mus'ab ﷺ then spoke to him about Islam and recited the Qur'an to him. One of the narrators by the name of Musa bin Aqba says that Mus'ab ﷺ recited the beginning of Surah Zukhruf. Mus'ab ﷺ and As'ad ﷺ say that from the radiance and gentleness they saw in the face of Usaid ﷺ, they recognized that he would accept Islam before he could even mention it. Sa'd ﷺ said, "What do you do when you want to enter the fold of this religion?" They said to him, "Take a bath, clean yourself well, purify your 2 upper and lower clothes, recite the Shahada of truth and perform salah." Sa'd ﷺ stood up, took a bath, washed his clothes, recited the Shahada, and then stood up to perform 2 Rakats salah. He then took his spear and returned to the gathering of his people who were still in the company of Usaid bin Hudhair ﷺ.

Sa'd bin Mu'adh ﷺ Gives Da'wah to the Banu Abdil Ash'hal Tribe

When his people saw him return, they said, "We swear by Allah that Sa'd is returning to you with a look very different to the one he left you with." When Sa'd ﷺ stopped by them he said, "O Banu Abdil Ash'al! How do you rate my status amongst you?" They replied. "You are our leader, the one with the best opinions and the most far-sighted." He then said, "It is now forbidden for me to peak to any of your men or women until you all believe in Allah and His Rasul ﷺ." The narrator says, "By Allah! There was not a man or woman amongst the Banu Abdil Ash'al tribe that did not accept Islam by the evening." As'ad ﷺ and Mus'ab ﷺ then returned to As'ad ﷺ's house where Mus'ab ﷺ continued calling people to Allah. Eventually, there was not a single Ansar that was devoid of Muslim men or women. The only exceptions were the homes of the Banu Umayyah bin Zaid, the Khatma, the Wa'il and Waqif, all of whom belonged to the Aws tribe. (Al-Bidayah wan Nihayah). Tabrani and Abu Nu'aym in **Dala'ilum Nnbuwwah** have narrated a lengthy report from Urwa ﷺ mentioning the Da'wah Rasulullah ﷺ gave to the Ansar and how they accepted Islam. This will appear in the chapter concerning the condition of the Ansar at the beginning, Inshallah. The Ansar secretly invited their people to Islam and asked Rasulullah ﷺ to send someone to give Da'wah to the people. Rasulullah ﷺ complied by sending Mus'ab ﷺ. This is in the chapter entitled, "Rasulullah dispatches individuals to give Da'wah". The narration then continues to state that As'ad bin Zurarah ﷺ and Mus'ab ﷺ once came to the well of Bir Maraq or close to it. There they sat and sent a message that the people of the area should come secretly. As Mus'ab ﷺ was speaking to the people and reciting the Qur'an to them, Sa'd bin Mu'adh ﷺ was informed about them. Taking his weapons and spear along, he came and stood before them. He said, "Why have you come to us in our locality with this lonely man who is an outcast and a stranger? With falsehood he is making fools of our innocent people and inviting them. I do not want to see you 2 again in our vicinity." The people all returned. However, they returned a 2nd time to Bir Maraq or nearby. When Sa'd ﷺ was again informed about them, he gave them another warning which was less harsh than the first. When As'ad ﷺ noticed that he had somewhat softened, he said to him, "O cousin! Give him a hearing at least. If you hear anything unpleasant, O Sa'd, you may refuse to accept it from him. Another narration states, "You may refute it with something better". However, if you hear something good, then respond to this call from Allah." Sa'd ﷺ said, "What has he to say'?" Mus'ab ﷺ recited the following verses of the Qur'an:

حم (1) وَالْكِتَابِ الْمُبِينِ (2) إِنَّا جَعَلْنَاهُ قُرْآنًا عَرَبِيًّا لَعَلَّكُمْ تَعْقِلُونَ (3)

HaMeem. By the manifest Book (this Qur'an). We verily, have made it a Qur'an in Arabic, that you may be able to understand (its meanings and its admonitions). (Az-Zukhruf:1-3)

Sa'd ﷺ said, "I can certainly relate to what I hear." Allah guided him and he returned to his people without announcing his acceptance of Islam until he reached them. When he returned to his people, he invited the Banu Abdil Ash'al to Islam, thereby disclosing his acceptance of Islam. He said, "Any young or old person, male or female who has doubts should present something better and we shall readily accept it. By Allah! Such a thing had appeared before which necks are forced to bow." When Sa'd ﷺ accepted Islam and gave Da'wah to his people, the entire Banu Abdil Ash'al accepted Islam besides a negligible number of people. The Banu Abdil Ash'al was the first family of the Ansar whose members all accepted Islam. The rest of the narration is the same as appeared in the chapter entitled, "Rasulullah dispatches individuals to give Da'wah". The last part states that Mus'ab ﷺ then returned to Rasulullah ﷺ at Makkah.

Tulaib bin Umair ❀ Gives Da'wah to his Mother Arwa bint Abdil Muttalib

Muhammad bin Ibrahim bin Harith ❀ narrates that when Tulaib bin Umair ❀ accepted Islam, he went to his mother Arwa who was the daughter of Abdul Muttalib, Rasulullah ﷺ's maternal aunt. He said to her, "I have accepted Islam and I am the follower of Muhammad ﷺ." Relating the incident, he also mentioned to her, "What prevents you from accepting Islam and following Muhammad ﷺ! Even your brother Hamza has accepted Islam." She replied, "I am waiting to see what my sisters do. I shall then do as they do." Tulaih ❀ states that he then said to his mother, "In the name of Allah I beg you to go to Rasulullah ﷺ, to greet him, to believe in him and to testify that that there is none worthy of worship but Allah and that Muhammad is Allah's Rasul ﷺ." She immediately uttered:

اَشْهَدُ اَنْ لاَ اِلٰهَ اِلاَّ اللهُ وَاَشْهَدُ اَنَّ مُحَمَّدًا وَرَسُوْلُ الله

"I testify that there is none worthy of worship but Allah and that Muhammad is Allah's Rasul ﷺ."

Thereafter, she continuously assisted Rasulullah ﷺ with her words and encouraged her son to assist Rasulullah ﷺ and to establish Islam. *(Isti'ab).* Abu Salma bin Abdir Rahman ❀ narrates that Tulaib bin Umair ❀ accepted Islam in the house of Arqam. Later he went to his mother who was Arwa bint Abdil Muttalib. He said to her, "I follow Muhammad ﷺ and have submitted to Allah, the Rabb of the universe Who is most exalted." His mother said, "Your maternal uncle's son Rasulullah ﷺ is certainly most deserving of your assistance. By Allah! If we women had the strength of men, we would certainly follow him and defend him." Tulaib ❀ says that he then asked her, "O beloved mother! What is it that prevents you from accepting Islam?" The rest of the narration is the same as the one quoted above. *(Hakim, Ibn Sa'd)*

Umair bin Wahab Jumhi ❀ Gives Da'wah and his Acceptance

Urwa bin Zubair narrates that shortly after their defeat at Badr, Umair bin Wahab Jumhi was sitting with Safwan bin Umayyah in the Hatem. Umair bin Wahab used to harm Rasulullah ﷺ and the Sahabah, who suffered lot of difficulty at his hands in Makkah. His son Wahab bin Umair was also one of the captives whom the Muslims had captured during the Battle of Badr. When Umair bin Wahab mentioned what had happened to the people of the well (the well in Badr where the dead bodies of 70 disbelievers were thrown), Safwan bin Umayyah commented, "By Allah! There is no enjoyment in life after their deaths." Umair bin Wahab remarked, "That is true. By Allah! Had it not been for the debts I have which I am unable to settle, and for my family whom I fear shall be destroyed without me, I would certainly ride to Muhammad and kill him. In fact, I have an excuse to see him, my son is a captive in the hands of the Muslims." Taking advantage of the situation, Safwan bin Umayyah said, "I take the responsibility of settling your debts and I shall care for your family with my own and I shall do everything in my capacity to care for them as long as they live." Umair bin Wahab said to him, "Keep this matter a secret between us." Safwan bin Umayyah agreed and Umair bin Wahab proceeded to have his sword sharpened and poisoned. He then left on his journey until he reached Madinah. In the meantime, Omar ❀ was in the company of a group of Sahabah who were busy discussing the Battle of Badr. They spoke about the victory that Allah had blessed them and the defeat of their enemy that Allah had shown them. As they spoke, Omar ❀ noticed Umair bin Wahab settling his camel at the door of the Masjid and carrying a sword around his neck. Omar ❀ asked, "That dog and enemy of Allah Umair bin Wahab is no good. It was he who caused trouble during the Battle of Badr and who estimated our numbers for the enemy."

Umair bin Wahab ❀ with Rasulullah ﷺ

Omar ❀ came to Rasulullah ﷺ and said, "O Nabi of Allah! The enemy of Allah Umair bin Wahab has come with a sword hanging from his neck. Rasulullah ﷺ said, "Allow him to meet me." Omar ❀ grabbed the handle of Umair bin Wahab's sword and pulled him towards Rasulullah ﷺ by the collar. He then said to the men of the Ansar who were with him, "Go to Rasulullah ﷺ and sit with him. Watch this man closely for he cannot be trusted." He then brought Umair bin Wahab to Rasulullah ﷺ. When Rasulullah ﷺ saw him with Omar ❀ pulling him by the handle of his sword at his collar, Rasulullah ﷺ said, "Leave him, O Omar! You may come closer, O Umair." When Umair bin Wahab came closer to Rasulullah ﷺ he greeted with the words, "Blessed is your morning." This was the manner in which people used to greet during the period of ignorance. Rasulullah ﷺ said, "Allah has blessed us with a greeting better than your greeting, O Umair. He has blessed us with the greeting of Salam which is the greeting of the people of paradise." Umair said, "By Allah! This is new to me, O Muhammad." Rasulullah ﷺ asked, "What brings you here, O Umair?" Umair replied, "I have come regarding this prisoner that you have with you. Please be kind to him." Rasulullah ﷺ asked, "Why then the sword around your neck?" Umair cursed, "These swords! Have they ever done us any good?!" Rasulullah ﷺ said, "Tell me the truth. What have you come for?" "I have come only for this," lied Umair. Rasulullah ﷺ then said to him, "You and Safwan bin Umayyah were sitting in the Hatim and discussing what had happened to the people of the well when you said, 'Had it not been for my debts and the family I have, I would have gone to kill Muhammad.' Safwan then assumed responsibility for your debts and your family if you would kill me. However, Allah stands between you and me."

Umair bin Wahab Accepts Islam and Gives Da'wah to the People of Makkah

Umair exclaimed, "I testify that you are certainly the Rasul of Allah. O Rasulullah ﷺ! We used to treat everything as a lie that you brought to us from the heavens and the revelation that descended on you. However, this is a matter that none witnessed but Safwan and me. By Allah! I am convinced that none besides Allah could have brought you this news. All praises belong to Allah Who has guided me to Islam and has pulled me in this way." He then recited the Shahada of truth. Rasulullah ﷺ said to the Sahabah, "Educate your brother about Islam, teach him the Qur'an and free his prisoner." When the Sahabah had done as they were commanded, Umair ❀ said, "O Rasulullah ﷺ! I made tremendous efforts to extinguish the Islam of Allah and I used to cause great harm to those who followed Islam. I would now like you to permit me to go to Makkah and invite the people towards Allah, His Rasul ﷺ and Islam. Perhaps Allah will guide them. If they do not accept, I shall cause harm to them because of their religion as I used to cause harm to your companions because of Islam." Rasulullah ﷺ gave permission and he arrived in Makkah. After Umair ❀ had left for Makkah, Safwan bin Umayyah had been telling the people, "Rejoice at the news that will come to you in a few days, which will make you forget the incident of Badr." Safwan used to enquire about Umair ❀ from travelers coming from Madinah. Someone arrived and informed him that Umair ❀ had accepted Islam. Safwan then took an oath saying that he will never speak to Umair and will never do him any good turn. *(Al Bidayah wan Nihayah)*

A Large Number of People Accept Islam at the Hands of Umair ⌀

Ibn Jareer has narrated this incident from Urwa but with the addition that when Umair ⌀ arrived in Makkah, he stayed there inviting people to Islam and harassing those who opposed him. A large number of people accepted Islam at his hands. *(Kanzul Ummal, Tabarani, Haythami)*

The Comment of Omar ⌀ concerning the Conversion of Umair ⌀

Urwa bin Zubair ⌀ has reported a narration which states that the Muslims were overjoyed when Umair bin Wahab ⌀ accepted Islam. Omar used to say, "There is no doubt that I liked a pig more than him the day he arrived. However, today he is more beloved to me than some of my own children." *(Tabrani, Isaba).* Amr bin Umayyah ⌀ narrates that when Umair ⌀ returned to Makkah after accepting Islam, he proceeded straight to his house without meeting Safwan bin Umayyah. He made it public that he had accepted Islam and started inviting people to Islam. When this news reached Safwan, he said. "When he went to his family before coming to me, I knew that Umair had become involved in the very thing he feared and had forsaken his religion. I shall never speak to him again and never do a good turn to him or his family." As Safwan stood in the Hatem one day, Umair ⌀ called for him. When Safwan ignored him, Umair ⌀ said to him, "You are one of our leaders. Tell me, when we worshipped stones and sacrificed animals for them, was this any religion? I testify that there is none worthy of worship but Allah and that Muhammad ⌀ is Allah's servant and Rasul." Safwan did not utter a word in response. *(Isti'ab).* The effort Umair ⌀ made to get Safwan to accept Islam has been mentioned before.

Abu Hurairah ⌀ Gives Da'wah to his Mother and she Accepts Islam

Abu Hurairah ⌀ says that he used to invite his mother to Islam when she was still a disbeliever. One day as he was giving her the Da'wah, she told him things about Rasulullah ⌀ that he did not like. He went crying to Rasulullah ⌀ and said, "O Rasulullah ⌀! When I invite my mother to Islam, she refuses to accept. When I did so today, she told me things about you that I did not like. Pray to Allah to guide the mother of Abu Hurairah." Rasulullah ⌀ made Du'a saying, "O Allah! Guide the mother of Abu Hurairah." Abu Hurairah ⌀ narrates further, "I was happy with the Du'a of Rasulullah ⌀. I left and when I tried to open the door of the house, I found it locked. Hearing my footsteps, my mother shouted, 'Stay where you are, O Abu Hurairah.' I then heard the sound of water as my mother was taking bath to accept Islam. She then wore her clothes and hastily put on a scarf. She opened the door and said, 'O Abu Hurairah!

اَشْهَدُ اَنْ لاَ اِلهَ اِلاَّ الله وَاَشْهَدُ اَنَّ مُحَمَّدًا وَرَسُوْلُ الله

'I testify that there is none worthy of worship but Allah and that Muhammad is Allah's Rasul ⌀!'"

Abu Hurairah ⌀ says that he then returned to Rasulullah ⌀ and informed him about what had happened. Rasulullah ⌀ praised Allah and made Du'a in their favor. *(Muslim, Ahmad in Istaba).* According to another narration, Abu Hurairah ⌀ used to say, "By Allah! Whenever any male or female Muslim hears my name, they like me." "How do you know this?" the narrator asked. He then mentioned that he used to invite his mother to Islam and the narration continues like the one mentioned above. However, this narration states at the end, "I then hurried back to Rasulullah ⌀ crying out of happiness as I had been crying out of sorrow earlier. I said, 'Hear the good news. Allah has accepted your Du'a and has guided the mother of Abu Hurairah to Islam.' I

then added, 'O Rasulullah ⌀! Pray to Allah to make my mother and me be beloved to every Mu'min male and female.' Rasulullah ⌀ made Du'a saying, 'O Allah! Make this little servant of Yours and his mother beloved to every Mu'min male and female.' Whenever any male/female Muslim hears my name, they like me." *(Ibn Sa'd)*

Ummu Sulaim ⌀ Invites Abu Talha to Islam When he Proposes to her and he Accepts Islam

Anas ⌀ narrates that before he accepted Islam, Abu Talha proposed for Ummu Sulaim ⌀. She said to him, "O Abu Talha! Do you not know that the god you worship is a tree growing from the ground?" He replied, "I do indeed." She then said, "Do you not feel ashamed to worship a tree? If you accept Islam, I require no other dowry from you." Abu Talha ⌀ said that he would think over the matter and left. He later came back and said:

اَشْهَدُ اَنْ لاَ اِلهَ اِلاَّ الله وَاَشْهَدُ اَنَّ مُحَمَّدًا عَبْدُهُ وَرَسُوْلُ الله

"I testify that there is none worthy of worship but Allah and that Muhammad ⌀ is Allah's Rasul."

Ummu Sulaim ⌀ then said to her son, "O Anas! Get Abu Talha married." Anas ⌀ conducted the Nikah. *(Ahmad, Isabah)*

The Da'wah that the Sahaba Gave to Various Tribes and Arabs: The Da'wah Dimam bin Tha'laba Gave to the Banu Sa'd bin Bakr Tribe

Abdullah bin Abbas ⌀ narrates that the Banu Sa'd bin Bakr tribe sent Dimam bin Tha'laba ⌀ as their representative to Rasulullah ⌀. When he arrived in Madinah, he seated his camel at the door of the Masjid and tied it up. He then entered the Masjid where Rasulullah ⌀ was sitting with the Sahabah. Dimam ⌀ was a large, hairy, and heavily built man. He went forward and stood before Rasulullah ⌀ and the Sahabah. He then asked, "Which of you is the descendant of Abdul Muttalib?" Rasulullah ⌀ replied, "I am the descendant of Abdul Muttalib." "Are you Muhammad ⌀?" Dimam ⌀ clarified. "Yes," confirmed Rasulullah ⌀. Dimam ⌀ then said, "O descendant of Abdul Muttalib! I want to ask you some questions and I will be very blunt. So please do not take offence." Rasulullah ⌀ said, "I will not take offence. You may ask whatever you please." Dimam ⌀ said, "I ask you in the name of that Allah Who is your deity, the deity of those before you and the deity of those coming after you. Has Allah sent you to us?" Rasulullah ⌀ replied, "Yes, by Allah!" Dimam ⌀ asked further, "I ask you in the name of that Allah Who is your deity, the deity of those before you and the deity of those coming after you. Has Allah commanded you to instruct us that we should worship only He Who is The One and that we should not ascribe anyone as partner to Him?" Dimam ⌀ then enquired, "I ask you in the name of that Allah Who is your deity, the deity of those before you and the deity of those coming after you. Has Allah issued the command to you that we should perform these 5 salats?" Rasulullah ⌀ again responded by saying, "Yes, by Allah!" In this manner, Dimam ⌀ asked about each of the Fara'idh of Islam, about zakah, fasting, Hajj as well as the other injunctions of the Shari'a. Each time he asked about any Fardh injunction, he asked Rasulullah ⌀ in the name of Allah as he had done initially. When he had completed the questioning, he said: ا اَشْهَدُ اَنْ لاَ اِلهَ اِلاَّ الله وَاَشْهَدُ اَنَّ مُحَمَّدًا وَرَسُوْلُ الله

"I testify that there is none worthy of worship but Allah and that Muhammad ⌀ is Allah's Rasul."

He said further, "I shall fulfill all these Fara'idh and abstain from everything you have forbidden. Neither shall I add to this, nor reduce anything." He then went to his camel to return home. Rasulullah ⌀ commented, "If this man with 2 locks of long hair is truthful, he shall definitely enter paradise."

The Banu Sa'd Accept Islam and the Statement of Abdullah bin Abbas ◈ Concerning Dimam ◈

Dimam ◈ went to his camel, untied the rope and then rode away until he reached his people. The first thing he said was, "Lat and Uzza are most terrible!" The people said, "Do not say that Dimam! Beware of white liver! Beware of leprosy! Beware of insanity! The idols will inflict you with these diseases for saying this." Dimam ◈ said to them, "Shame on you! By Allah! These 2 idols can neither do harm nor give benefit. Allah has sent a Rasul and revealed a book to him to save you from what you are involved in. I testify that there is none worthy of worship but Allah and that Muhammad ﷺ is Allah's servant and Rasul. I have just come from him with the details of things he has commanded and those that he has forbidden." The narrator of the reports states, "By Allah! By the same evening every male and female present with Dimam became Muslim. Abdullah bin Abbas ◈ states, "We have never heard of any representative of his tribe who was nobler than Dimam bin Tha'laba ◈. A narration of Waqidi mentions that by the same evening every male and female present with Dimam ◈ was a Muslim and that they built Masajid and called out the Adhan for salah. *(Ibn Is'haq, Ahmad and Abu Dawood as quoted in Al Bidayah wan Nihayah, Hakim)*

Amr bin Murrah Juhani ◈ Gives Da'wah to his People: The Dream of Amr bin Murrah ◈ had About the Risalat of Rasulullah ﷺ

Amr bin Murrah ◈ narrates that he once performed Hajj with a group of his people during the period of ignorance. While in Makkah he had a dream in which he saw a light rising from the Kabah which extended its illumination to the mountains of Yathrib (now called Madinah) and the Ash'ar mountains in the region of the Juhaina tribe. He also heard a voice in the light saying, "Darkness has been dispersed, light has spread and the seal of the Ambiya has been sent." He then saw another light which illuminated for him the palaces of Hira and white buildings of Madain. He again heard a voice in the light which said, "Islam has become manifest, the idols are destroyed and family ties are fostered." He woke up with a fear and said to his people, "By Allah! Something astounding is going to take place amongst the tribe of the Quraish." He related the dream to them.

Ami bin Murrah ◈ Meets Rasulullah ﷺ and Accepts Islam

When Amr bin Murrah ◈ reached his locality, the news reached him that a person called Ahmad has been sent as a Rasul. He left home and came to Rasulullah ﷺ. When he informed Rasulullah ﷺ about his dream, Rasulullah ﷺ said, "O Amr bin Murrah! I am the Rasul of Allah sent to all of mankind. I invite you to Islam and command you to protect life, to foster good family ties, to worship Allah Alone, to forsake idols, to perform Hajj to the Kabah, and to fast during Ramadhan which is one of the 12 months of the year. Whoever accepts this shall have paradise and whoever disobeys shall have the fire of hell. Accept Iman, O Amr bin Murrah and Allah shall rescue you from the terror of hell." Amr bin Murrah ◈ said, "I testify that there is none worthy of worship but Allah and that you are Allah's Rasul. I believe in everything Halal and Haram that you have brought even though a great number of people reject it." The tribe of Amr bin Murrah ◈ had an idol and it was his father who used to look after it. However, Amr bin Murrah ◈ broke the idol before coming to meet Rasulullah ﷺ. After accepting Islam Amr bin Murrah ◈ then recited to Rasulullah ﷺ some couplets he had composed when he heard of Rasulullah ﷺ. These are translated:

"I testify that Allah is True and without doubt I am the first
to forsake the gods of stone I have folded up my trousers to
migrate over difficult roads and inhospitable lands.
I travel to you (O Rasulullah ﷺ!) to be in the company of
him who is the best of people in personality and lineage who
is the messenger of the King of mankind and of everything
above the heavens"

Rasulullah ﷺ congratulated him on these couplets.

Rasulullah ﷺ Sends Amr bin Murrah ◈ to Give Da'wah to People

Amr bin Murrah ◈ said to Rasulullah ﷺ, "May my parents be sacrificed for you! Do send me to my people. Perhaps Allah shall bestow His grace on them through me as He has bestowed His grace on me through you." When Rasulullah ﷺ sent him, he first advised him saying, "Always adopt gentleness and honest speech. Never be ill-tempered, proud or jealous." Amr bin Murrah ◈ then went to his people and said, "O Rifa'h or I should rather say O gathering of the Juhaina tribe! I am the messenger of the Rasul of Allah. I invite you to accept Islam and command you to protect life, to foster good family ties, to worship Allah Alone, to forsake idols, to perform Hajj to the Kabah, and to fast during Ramadhan, which is one of the 12 months of the year. Whoever accepts this shall have paradise and whoever disobeys shall have the fire of hell. O gathering of the Juhaina! Allah has made you the best of the Arab tribes. Even during the period of ignorance you disliked the evil practices which other Arab tribes liked. They used to join 2 sisters in one marriage, wage wars during the sacred months and succeed their fathers as husbands of their mothers. Accept the call of the Nabi that Allah has sent from the lineage of Luway bin Ka'b and you will attain the honor of this world and great distinction in the hereafter." Only one person came to him saying, "O Amr bin Murrah! May Allah make your life bitter! Do you command us to forsake our gods and to create divisions within ourselves? Do you command us to oppose the religion of our forefathers who were all of extremely high character and to adopt the religion towards which the person of the Quraish from the people of Tihamah is calling? We have neither love for him nor any respect. He then proceeded to say the following couplets:

"Ibn Murrah has come with a statement, a statement that
cannot be from one who wishes reformation I am sure that
the words and actions of lbn Murrah shall prove to be a
lump in the throat even though some time may elapse, he
makes fools of our noble predecessors and whoever dares to
do these can never attain success"

Amr bin Murrah ◈ said to the man, "May Allah make life bitter for the one who is lying from the 2 of us. May Allah make him dumb and blind as well." A narrator says, "By Allah! Before the man died, he lost all this teeth; he became blind, went insane and was unable to taste any food."

Amr bin Murrah ◈ Comes to Rasulullah ﷺ with his Tribe who Accepted Islam and Rasulullah ﷺ Wrote a Letter for Them

Amr bin Murrah ◈ left his locality with those of his people who accepted Islam and came to Rasulullah ﷺ. Rasulullah ﷺ greeted them and welcomed them. He also had the following letter written to their people:

In the name of Allah The Most Kind The Most Merciful
This is a letter from the Mighty Allah, expressed on the tongue of His Rasul who has come with the absolute truth and a Book that speaks the truth. It is entrusted with Amr bin Murrah and addressed to the Juhaina bin Zaid tribe. You may have for yourselves the low-lying lands and plains as well as the hills and backs of the valleys. You may also tend its crops and drink its water. All this is on condition that you pay 1/5th of booty,

perform 5 salahs, give 2 goats as zakah for every flock of sheep or goats when they are together and they number between 120 and 200 and one goat for every flock that is separate and number between 40 and 119. There shall be no zakah on animals used for ploughing fields and for drawing water. Allah and all the Muslims present are witness to this settlement between us. Qais bin Shammas ❀ wrote this letter. *(Kanzul Ummal, Al Bidayah wan Nihayah, Tabrani in Majma)*

Urwa bin Mas'ood ❀ Accepts Islam, Gives Da'wah to his People and They Kill Him

Urwa bin Zubair ❀ narrates that when the Muslims started performing Hajj during the 9th year after Hijra, Urwa bin Mas'ood ❀ came to Rasulullah ﷺ as a Muslim. When he requested permission to go back to his people to preach Islam, Rasulullah ﷺ said, "I fear that they will kill you." He said, "They have so much respect for me that if they find me asleep, they would not even wake me up." Rasulullah ﷺ permitted him and he returned to his people. It was at night when he returned and all the people of the Thaqif tribe came to greet him. However, when he started calling them to Islam, they made accusations against him, became furious at him, swore at him, and finally killed him. Rasulullah ﷺ said, "Urwa's example is like that of the person of Surah Ya-Seen who called his people towards Allah and they killed him." *(Tabrani, Haythami, Hakim)*

Urwa bin Mas'ood ❀ Becomes Happy with his Martyrdom and Advises his People

Numerous scholars have reported this narration. Their reports mention that Urwa bin Mas'ood ❀ reached home at night and went to his house. The people of the Thaqif came to his house and greeted him in the manner people greeted during the period of ignorance. He refused to accept their greeting and said, "You should adopt the greeting of the people of paradise which is Salam." The people then started abusing him and hit him but he tolerated. Then they left him and started discussing about him. After dawn, he went up to his balcony and called out the Adhan for salah. The people of the Thaqif came out of their homes and came to him from every direction. A person from the Banu Malik tribe called Aws bin Auf shot an arrow at Urwa bin Mas'ood ❀, which struck an artery. The blood would not stop flowing. When this happened, Ghailan bin Salma, Kinana bin Abd Yalil, Hakam bin Amr, and several leading figure of their allied tribes took up their arms and got together. They announced, "Either we are killed or we shall take the lives of 10 leaders of the Banu Malik tribe in retaliation." When Urwa bin Mas'ood ❀ saw the developments, he said, "Do not take any lives for my sake. I have donated my blood to the person who took it to preserve your unity. This death is a blessing that Allah has bestowed on me for he had brought martyrdom to me. I testify that Muhammad is Allah's Rasul ﷺ because he informed me that you would kill me." He then called for his family and said, "When I die you should bury me with those martyrs who were killed while fighting with Rasulullah ﷺ before he left you." They then buried him with these martyred Sahabah when he passed away. When the news of his martyrdom reached Rasulullah ﷺ, he said, "Urwa's example..." The rest of the Hadith is the same as mentioned above. The narration on how Thaqif accepted Islam is in the chapter entitled "Incidents About the character and actions of Rasulullah ﷺ that inspired people to accept Islam." *(Ibn Sa'd)*

Tufail bin Amr Dowsi ❀ Gives Da'wah to his People

Muhammad bin Is'haq says that despite the harsh treatment that Rasulullah ﷺ saw his people made to him, he exerted all his efforts to guide them and to save them from the evils they were involved in. When Allah protected from them, the Quraish started warning the Arabs about Rasulullah ﷺ when they came to meet him. Tufail bin Amr ❀ was a highly respected and intelligent poet. He narrates that when he arrived in Makkah during the time when Rasulullah ﷺ was still living there, some men from the Quraish came to him and asked, "O Tufail! You have come to our city. This person amongst us had caused us great difficulty and has disunited us. His speech has caused division between fathers and sons, between brothers and between husband and wife. We fear that you and your tribe should not suffer as we have. Do not speak to him and do not even listen to him." Tufail ❀ says, "By Allah! They did not let me go until I agreed not to hear anything Rasulullah ﷺ said and not to speak to him. I even went as far as stuffing pieces of wool in my ears when I proceeded to the Masjid the following morning, fearing that any of his words may reach me without me intentionally listening to him."

Tufail bin Amr ❀ Accepts Islam

Tufail bin Amr ❀ says, "When I went to the Masjid in the morning, Rasulullah ﷺ was standing there, performing salah near the Kabah. I stood close to him and Allah destined that I should hear some of his words. What I heard were excellent words and I said to myself, 'Shame on you! I am supposed to be an intelligent poet who can distinguish between good and bad. What prevents me from listening to what this man has to say? If what he says is good, I shall accept and if it is not, I shall ignore it.'" Tufail ❀ then waited until Rasulullah ﷺ left for home. He then followed Rasulullah ﷺ and met him when he entered his house. He then told Rasulullah ﷺ what the Quraish had told him and added, "By Allah! They were so convinced that I plugged my ears with wool so that I do not hear your words. Allah destined that I should listen to you. What I heard were excellent words indeed. Present to me your case." Rasulullah ﷺ presented Islam to him and recited the Qur'an to him. Tufail ❀ remarked, "I swear by Allah that I have never heard words more beautiful than the Qur'an nor any matter as balanced as Islam." After accepting Islam and reciting the Shahada, Tufail ❀ said, "O Rasulullah ﷺ! My people obey me so I shall return to them and invite them to Islam. Pray to Allah to grant me a sign which will assist me in inviting them." Rasulullah ﷺ made Du'a, "O Allah! Grant him a sign."

Tufail ❀ Returns to his People to Invite to Islam and Allah Helps Him with a Sign

Tufail ❀ says that he went to his people and was at a valley from which he could see the people present there when a light radiated from between his eyes like a lantern. He then prayed, "O Allah! Not on my face because my people will think that this is a form of punishment affecting my face because I had left my religion." He narrates further, "The light then moved to the top of my whip. The people present saw the light on my whip which resembled a suspended lantern as I descended the valley towards them. When I reached them it was still morning."

Tufail ❀ Invites his Father and Wife to Islam and They Both Accept

Tufail ❀ narrates that when he came to his people, his father who was an extremely old man came to him. Tufail ❀ said, "Keep away from me, O father because you are not mine and I am not yours." "Why is it, O beloved son?" his father asked. Tufail replied, "Because I have accepted Islam and am a follower of Muhammad ﷺ." His father said, "Your religion is mine." His father then took a bath, cleaned his clothes and came back to Tufail ﷺ who presented Islam to him. He accepted Islam. When his wife came to him, Tufail ﷺ said to her, "Keep away from me for I am not yours and you are not mine." "Why is it? May my parents be sacrificed for you!" Tufail ﷺ replied, "Islam has separated me from you." She also accepted Islam. Tufail ﷺ further says that when he invited the rest of the Dows tribe to Islam, they showed reluctance.

Rasulullah ﷺ Makes Du'a for the Dows Tribe and They Accept Islam and Come to Rasulullah ﷺ Along with Tufail ﷺ

Tufail ﷺ then went to Rasulullah ﷺ in Makkah and said, "O Nabi of Allah ﷺ! The Dows tribe has overpowered me. Please invoke Allah's curses on them." Instead Rasulullah ﷺ prayed, "O Allah! Guide the Dows tribe." Rasulullah ﷺ then said to him, "Return to your people, give them Da'wah and be gentle with them." Tufail ﷺ then returned to his people and continued giving them Da'wah all the time until Rasulullah ﷺ migrated to Madinah and the battles of Badr, Uhud and Khandaq were over. Thereafter, Tufail went to meet Rasulullah ﷺ together with all those from his tribe who had accepted Islam. At that time Rasulullah ﷺ was in Khaibar. Tufail ﷺ eventually reached Madinah with 70 or 80 families from the Dows tribe. (Al Bidayah wan Nihayah, Isaba). Abdullah bin Abbas ﷺ has also narrated from Tufail bin Amr ﷺ the story of how he accepted Islam, how he gave Da'wah to his father, his wife, his people, and his arrival in Makkah, just as it was mentioned in the previous narration. However, the narration of Abdullah bin Abbas ﷺ adds that Rasulullah ﷺ sent Tufail ﷺ to burn an idol called Dhul Kaffain. In addition, it also mentions that Tufail ﷺ thereafter left for Yamamah where he saw a dream and was then martyred in the battle of Yamamah. (Isti'ab)

Another narration states that when Tufail ﷺ arrived in Makkah, some people from the Quraish told him about Rasulullah ﷺ and requested him to assess Rasulullah ﷺ. He therefore went to Rasulullah ﷺ and recited some of his poetry to Rasulullah ﷺ. Rasulullah ﷺ then recited Surah Ikhlas and the *Mu'awadhatain (Surahs Falaq and Nas)* to him. He accepted Islam on the spot and then returned to his people. The narration then goes on to speak about his whip and its light. The narrator mentions further that Tufail ﷺ then invited his parents to Islam. His father accepted Islam but his mother did not. When he invited his tribesmen, it was only Abu Hurairah who accepted. Then Tufail ﷺ went to Rasulullah ﷺ and said, "Would you like a strong fort with strong defences?" He was referring to the territory of the Dows tribe which he wanted Rasulullah ﷺ to curse. But when Rasulullah ﷺ made Du'a for the Dows tribe instead, Tufail ﷺ said, "This is not what I wanted." Rasulullah ﷺ said, "There are many of them who are just like you." Amongst the Dows tribe was a person called Jundub bin Amr bin Humama bin Auf who used to say during the period of ignorance, "I know that the creation has a creator but I do not know who it is." When he heard of Rasulullah ﷺ, he went to Rasulullah ﷺ along with 75 men of his tribe and they all accepted Islam. Abu Hurairah ﷺ narrates that Jundub placed each man individually before Rasulullah ﷺ. Ali ﷺ gave to the Hamdan tribe, the Da'wah Khalid bin Walid ﷺ gave to the Banu Harith bin Ka'b tribe and the Da'wah Abu Umama ﷺ gave to his tribe.

The Sahabah Dispatch Individuals and Groups to Give Da'wah: Hisham bin Al Aas ﷺ and Others are Sent to Heraclius

Hisham bin Al Aas Umawi ﷺ narrates that during the Khilafa of Abu Bakr ﷺ, he and another person were sent with the invitation to Islam to Heraclius, the Emperor of Rome. He says that when they arrived at Ghowtha meaning Damascus, they went to see Jabala bin Aiham Ghassani who happened to be lying on his bed at the time. He sent a messenger to speak to them. When the messenger came, the Sahabah said, "By Allah! We shall never speak to a messenger for we have been sent to see the king. If he grants permission, we shall speak to him but not to a messenger." When the messenger returned to the king with the news, he permitted them to enter and to speak. Hisham bin Al Aas ﷺ spoke to him and invited him to accept Islam. The king was wearing black clothing. When Hisham bin Al Aas ﷺ asked him why he was dressed in that manner, he replied, "I have vowed never to remove this clothing until I expel you from Sham." The Sahabah said to him, "By Allah! We shall soon take from you this place where you sit and we shall also take the kingdom of your high emperor Heraclius, Inshallah! Our Rasul Muhammad ﷺ has informed us of this." The king said, "You are not those people. They will be people who fast during the day and stand in worship during the night." The narration continues further and will Inshallah be quoted in the chapter dealing with the help received from the unseen. (Bayhaqi). Musa bin Uqba narrates that Hisham bin Al Aas ﷺ, Nu'aym bin Abdullah, and another person whom the narrator did name were sent to the Emperor of Rome during the Khilafah of Abu Bakr ﷺ. Hisham ﷺ says, "We came to Jabala bin Aiham who was in Damascus and noticed that he was wearing black and that everything around him was black. He said, 'You may speak, O Hisham.'" Hisham ﷺ then spoke to him and invited him towards Allah. The Hadith proceeds in detail as will be quoted later. (Abu Nu'aym)

The Sahabah Send Letters to Invite Towards Allah and Islam: Ziyad bin Harith Sudai ﷺ Sends a Letter to His People

Ziyad bin Harith Sudai ﷺ narrates that he met Rasulullah ﷺ, accepted and pledged his allegiance to Islam at the hand of Rasulullah ﷺ. He then heard that Rasulullah ﷺ had already dispatched an army to his people. He said, "O Rasulullah ﷺ! Call the army back as I will take the responsibility of ensuring that my people accept Islam and remain obedient." When Rasulullah ﷺ told him to go and call the army back but he was forced to excuse himself because his camel was too slow. Rasulullah ﷺ then sent someone else who called them back. Ziyad ﷺ then wrote a letter to his people in response to which a delegation came to inform Rasulullah ﷺ that they had accepted Islam. Rasulullah ﷺ said to Ziyad ﷺ, "Dear Sudai brother! It appears as if your people really obey you." Ziyad ﷺ replied, "I cannot accept credit as it was Allah Who has guided them to Islam." Rasulullah ﷺ then asked, "Can I appoint you as their leader?" When Ziyad ﷺ accepted, Rasulullah ﷺ wrote a letter to confirm his appointment. Ziyad ﷺ then asked Rasulullah ﷺ to reserve a share of the zakah for them. Rasulullah ﷺ agreed and then wrote another letter in this regard. Ziyad ﷺ continues to relate that all these occurred during one of Rasulullah ﷺ's journeys. When Rasulullah ﷺ camped at a place, the people there came to him and complained about the person who was appointed to collect their zakah. They told Rasulullah ﷺ that because there was some friction between their tribe and his during the period of ignorance, he was being harsh with them. Rasulullah ﷺ asked, "Is he really doing this?" "Yes," they confirmed. Rasulullah ﷺ then turned to the Sahabah with Ziyad ﷺ amongst them and said, "There is no good for a Mu'min in being appointed as a leader." Ziyad ﷺ says that this statement lingered in his heart. Another person later came to Rasulullah ﷺ to ask for something. Rasulullah ﷺ said, "The person who begs from people despite possessing sufficient wealth, his begging shall earn him nothing besides a headache and stomach disease." The person then asked to be given from the zakah money. Rasulullah ﷺ said to him, "Allah does not sanction the command of a Nabi or anyone else regarding the distribution of zakah but issues the command Himself. Allah has distributed it into 8 parts so if you are amongst the 8, I shall give you." Ziyad ؓ says that it then occurred to him that he had asked for zakah even though he had sufficient wealth. The Hadith then continues to a point where Ziyad ؓ says that after Rasulullah ﷺ had completed salah, he approached Rasulullah ﷺ with the 2 letters saying, "O Rasulullah ﷺ! Pardon me of these 2." Rasulullah ﷺ asked, "What has happened to you?" He replied, "O Rasulullah ﷺ! I heard you say that there is no good for a Mu'min in being appointed as a leader and I am a Mu'min who believes in Allah and His Rasul. I also heard you say to the beggar that the person who begs from people despite possessing sufficient wealth, his begging shall earn him nothing besides a headache and stomach disease. I had asked from you despite having sufficient wealth." Rasulullah ﷺ said, "That being the case, you still have the option to either accept it or leave it." Ziyad ؓ said, "I would rather leave it." Rasulullah ﷺ then said to him, "Show me someone whom I may appoint as your leader." Ziyad ؓ pointed out one of the persons who had come with the delegation and Rasulullah ﷺ appointed him the leader. *(Bayhaqi as quoted in Al Bidayah wan Nihayah)*

Bujair bin Zuhair bin Abi Sulm ؓ Writes a Letter to his Brother Ka'b

Abdur Rahman bin Ka'b narrates that the 2 sons of Zuhair who were Bujair and Ka'b left on a journey and had reached a spring called Abraqal Azzaf. Bujair then said to Ka'b, "Stay here with the animals. I am going to see that person (Rasulullah ﷺ) and hear what he has to say." Ka'b stayed and Bujair left to meet Rasulullah ﷺ who presented Islam to him and he accepted. When the news reached Ka'b, he recited a few couplets:

"Will you not convey this message to Bujair woe be on another (Abu Bakr), to what has he led you?
He has led you to a way on which you will not find your parents neither will you find your brother Abu Bakr has made you drink from a terrible cup that slave has made you drink from it time and time again"

When Rasulullah ﷺ heard about these couplets, he permitted Ka'b's execution when he said, "Whoever finds Ka'b should kill him!" Bujair wrote to Ka'b informing him that Rasulullah ﷺ had ordered his execution. He also wrote, "Save yourself! However, I do not think that you will be able to escape." Bujair later wrote back to Ka'b saying, " Rasulullah ﷺ accepts the word of anyone who comes to him to testify that there is none worthy of worship but Allah and that Muhammad ﷺ is Allah's Rasul. You should therefore accept Islam and come here as soon as this letter reaches you." Ka'b accepted Islam and recited a poem in praise of Rasulullah ﷺ. He then came to Madinah and made his mount sit down at the door of the Masjid. He then entered the Masjid where he found Rasulullah ﷺ sitting in the middle of the Sahabah just as a table cloth is placed at the center with people sitting around it. The Sahabah crowded around Rasulullah ﷺ forming several rings. At times, he turned towards a group while addressing them and at other times he turned towards another group. Ka'b ؓ himself says, "I made my mount sat down at the door of the Masjid. I took a few steps forward and sat by him where it declared that I had accepted Islam when I said, 'I testify that there is none worthy of worship but Allah and that you are Allah's Rasul. I seek amnesty, O Rasulullah ﷺ!" Rasulullah ﷺ asked, "Who are you?" "I am Ka'b bin Zuhair." Rasulullah ﷺ

said, "Was it you who said….." He then turned to Abu Bakr ؓ and asked, "What was it that he said, O Abu Bakr?" Abu Bakr recited the couplet which meant, "Abu Bakr has made you drink from a terrible cup. That slave has made you drink from it time and time again." Ka'b ؓ interjected by saying, "I did not say it like this, O Rasulullah ﷺ." "Then how did you say it?" asked Rasulullah ﷺ. Ka'b said, "I said he altered a few words to compose a couplet which meant 'Abu Bakr has made you drink from a quenching cup. That trustworthy man has made you drink from it time and time again.'" Rasulullah ﷺ then said, "By Allah! He certainly is a trustworthy man." Ka'b ؓ then recited the entire poem he had composed, which will be quoted shortly. *(Hakim)*

Musa bin Aqba says that Ka'b bin Zuhair ؓ recited his poem "Banat Su'ad" to Rasulullah ﷺ in his Masjid in Madinah until he reached the couplets which meant:

.. Without doubt, Rasulullah ﷺ is a sword from which light is derived and a drawn rapier from amongst the swords Allah he was with some youths of the Quraish who had accepted Islam when one of them said (to Disbeliever), 'Move out of the way!'

Rasulullah ﷺ then signaled to the Sahabah with his sleeve for them to listen attentively. The narrator says that Bujair ؓ had written to his brother Ka'b to warn him and to invite him to accept Islam. He also wrote a few couplets in the letter:

"Who will convey the message to Ka'b? Is he inclined towards that which he wrongly criticized whereas it is most resolute.
Come to the One Allah and not towards Uzza nor Lat then you will attain salvation if you do this and will remain safe, you will then attain salvation on the day when none shall escape from the Fire except the pure-hearted Muslim.
The religion of (our father) Zuhair is nothing but falsehood and the religion of (our grandfather) Abu Sulma is forbidden to me" (Hakim, Haythami, Isaba, Al Bidayah wan Nihayah)

Khalid bin Walid ؓ Writes to the People of Persia

Abu Wa'il ؓ narrates *(Tabarani, Haythami, Hakim in Mustadark)* that Khalid bin Walid ؓ wrote the following letter to the Persian people, inviting them to Islam.
In the name of Allah The Most Kind The Most Merciful
From Khalid bin Walid
To Rustam, Mahran and the Persian leadership
Peace be on those who follow the guidance. We invite you to accept Islam. Should you refuse, you may pay the Jizya by hand as subjects. If you refuse even this, then I have people with me who love to be killed while fighting in the Path of Allah more than you Persians love wine.
Peace be on those who follow the guidance.

Khalid bin Walid ؓ Writes to the People of Mada'in

Sha'bi رحمة الله narrates that Banu Buqaila read to him the letter that Khalid bin Walid ؓ wrote to the people of Mada'in:
From Khalid bin Walid
To the Persian leadership
Peace be on those who follow the guidance.
All praises belong to Allah Who has fragmented your unity, taken away your kingdom and weakened your plans. Take note that whoever performs our salah, faces our Qibla and eats what we slaughter, he is a Muslim who shall enjoy the privileges we have and also bear the responsibilities we bear. After this I wish to add that when this letter reaches you, you should send securities to me to ratify our peace agreement and you may rest assured that I shall give you your protection. Otherwise, I swear

by the Being besides Whom there is no other deity that I shall dispatch against you people who love death as you love life. When the Persians in the Mada'in district read this letter, they were taken aback. This occurred in the year 12CE *(Ibn Jareer)*

Khalid bin Walid ﷺ Writes to Hurmuz

Imam Sha'bi رحمة الله says *(Ibn Jareer)* that Khalid bin Walid ﷺ wrote a letter to Hurmuz before he left with Uzadhiba, the father of Ziyadhiba, who was from Yamamah. In those days, Hurmuz was in charge of defending the Persian borders. The letter read: Accept Islam and you will remain safe. Otherwise you may subject yourself and your people to our protection and accept to pay the Jizya. If not, you have none but yourself to blame for I shall march with people who love death as much as you people love life. Another narration *(Ibn Jareer)* states that when Khalid bin Walid ﷺ conquered one of the 2 regions of Iraq's fertile plains, he summoned a person from the people of Hira. With this person he sent a letter to the Persians who were scattered in different groups in Mada'in and taking support from each other after the death of their leader Ardser. However, they had appointed Bahman Jadhway as their leader stationed in a place called Buharsir where he commanded the army's frontline; with Bahman Jadhway was Uzadhiba and several other generals. Khalid bin Walid ﷺ summoned another person from Saluba and sent 2 letters with the 2 envoys. One letter was addressed to the senior leadership while the other was addressed to the regular commanders. The one envoy was therefore from Hira while the other was a Nabti from the non-Arab settlers of Iraq. When Khalid ﷺ asked the envoy from Hira what his name was, the man said that it was Murra (meaning 'bitter'). Khalid ﷺ said to him, "Take this letter to the Persians. Perhaps Allah will make their lives bitter or they will accept Islam and turn in repentance to Allah." Khalid ﷺ asked the Nabti envoy what his name was. When the man said that it was Hizqil (means 'to destroy'). Khalid ﷺ told him to deliver the letter and prayed, "O Allah! Destroy them." Ibn Jareer says that the 2 letters contained the following:

In the name of Allah The Most Kind The Most Merciful
From Khalid bin Walid. To the Persian royal family
All praises belong to Allah Who has thrown your establishment in mayhem, Who has weakened your plans and fragmented your unity. It would have been worse for you if He had not done this. Enter our Deen and we shall leave you and your land and pass by to proceed to other people. If you do not willingly enter Islam, you will still be subject to our authority and forced to suffer defeat at the hands of people who love death like you love life.

In the name of Allah The Most Kind The Most Merciful
From Khalid bin Walid
To the Persian leaders
Accept Islam and you may live in peace. If not, you may submit to my protection and pay the Jizya. Otherwise I shall march to you with people who love death more than you people love to drink wine."

The Sahabah Give Da'wah in the Battlefield During the Time of Rasulullah ﷺ The Da'wah of Harith bin Muslim Tamemi ﷺ

Harith bin Muslim Tamemi ﷺ narrates that Rasulullah ﷺ once sent them on a military expedition. When they reached the place they intended to attack, he urged his horse and soared ahead of the others. However, the people of the town were weeping as they met them. Harith bin Muslim ﷺ said to them, "Say 'La Ilaha Illallah' and you will be saved." The people then said what they were told. When the other Sahabah arrived there, they rebuked Harith bin Muslim ﷺ and said, "You have deprived

us of the booty after it already become cold in our hands." When they returned to Madinah and mentioned the incident to Rasulullah ﷺ, he called Harith bin Muslim ﷺ and congratulated him for what he had done. Rasulullah ﷺ also told him that Allah had granted him tremendous rewards for everyone of the people of the town. One of the narrators named Abdur Rahman says that it was he who forgot the specific rewards that Rasulullah ﷺ mentioned. Rasulullah ﷺ then said to him, "I shall write an inheritance in your favor to all the Muslim leaders who come after me." Rasulullah ﷺ did so, sealed the letter and handed it over to him. Thereafter, Rasulullah ﷺ said to him, "When you have performed your Fajr salah, recite 7 times:

اللهُمَّ أَجِرْنِيْ مِنَ النَّار *"O Allah! Save me from the fire"*

If you die during that day, Allah will record your safety from the fire. Then when you have performed your Maghrib salah, again recite 7 times: اللهُمَّ أَجِرْنِيْ مِنَ النَّار
"O Allah! Save me from the fire"
If you die during that night, Allah will record your safety from the fire." Harith bin Muslim ﷺ says, "When Allah took Rasulullah ﷺ away, I went to Abu Bakr ﷺ who opened the seal, read the letter and gave me some wealth as Rasulullah ﷺ instructed. Thereafter, he sealed the letter. Later after the death of Abu Bakr ﷺ I went to Omar ﷺ, who did the same. Thereafter, I went to Uthman ﷺ when he was the Khalifa and he did exactly the same." Muslim bin Harith ﷺ says, "My father Harith bin Muslim passed away during the Khilafah of Uthman ﷺ and the letter stayed with us until Omar bin Abdul Aziz رحمة الله became the Khalifah. He wrote a letter to the governor of the region where we stayed instructing him to send Muslim the son of Harith bin Muslim ﷺ to him with the letter that Rasulullah ﷺ had written for his father. When I was sent to him, he read the letter, ordered that I be given some wealth and then sealed it." *(Kanzul Ummal, Muntakhab)*

The Da'wah of Ka'b bin Umair Ghifari ﷺ

Zuhri رحمة الله narrates that Rasulullah ﷺ sent Ka'b bin Umair Ghifari ﷺ with a group of 15 men. They rode to a place in Sham called Dhat Itla where they encountered a very large concentration of people. When they invited these people to Islam, they refused to accept and started firing arrows at them. Seeing this, the Sahabah started fighting them most fiercely but all of them were martyred except one man who was left wounded amongst the dead. When night arrived, he somehow managed to get himself to Rasulullah ﷺ. Rasulullah ﷺ was on the verge of sending a battalion after them when the news reached him that the people had moved to another place. *(Al Bidayah wan Nihayah, Ibn Sa'd in Tabaqat, Isaba)*

The Da'wah of Ibn Abil Awja ﷺ

Zuhri رحمة الله narrates that it was in Dhul Hijjah 7CE that Rasulullah ﷺ returned from performing the Umrah he had missed. He then sent Ibn Abil Awja Sulami ﷺ on a military expedition with 50 horsemen. However, an enemy spy warned his people and informed them about the Sahabah. The people therefore prepared a very large army. When Ibn Abil Awja arrived, they were already prepared for battle. When he saw them all there, he invited them to accept Islam but they started firing arrows at him without even listening. They said, "We have no need for what you are calling us to." They continued firing arrows for a long time and reinforcements started pouring in until the Sahabah were surrounded on all sides. The Sahabah fought very fiercely until most of them were martyred. Ibn Abil Awja ﷺ was wounded but managed to carry himself back to Madinah along with the other survivors. They returned on the first of Safar 8 CE. *(Bayhaqi in Al Bidayah wan Nihayah, Tabaqat)*

The Sahabah Give Da'wah in the Battlefield During the time of Abu Bakr ؓ: Abu Bakr ؓ Instructs his Commanders to Give Da'wah When he Dispatched Armies to Sham

Sa'eed bin Musaib رحمة الله narrates that when Abu Bakr ؓ sent armies to Sham, he appointed Yazid bin Abi Sufian ؓ, Amr bin Al Aas ؓ and Shurabil bin Hasana ؓ as commanders. When they were mounted, Abu Bakr ؓ walked with them up to Thaniyatul Wada to see them off. The commanders said, "O Khalifa of Rasulullah ﷺ! You are walking while we ride?" Abu Bakr ؓ said, "I am taking these steps with the intention of being rewarded for taking them in the Path of Allah." He then advised them saying, "I advise you to be ever-conscious of Allah. Wage war in the Path of Allah and fight all those who reject Allah. Indeed, Allah will assist Islam. Do not steal from the booty, do not deceive, do not be cowardly, do not spread corruption on earth and do not go against your orders. If Allah decrees that you meet the enemy who are disbelievers, invite them to accept one of 3 options. Should they accept any of the option, acknowledge it and refrain from harming them. Firstly invite them to accept Islam. If they accept, acknowledge it and refrain from harming them. Thereafter if they accept Islam invite them to move from their homes to the home of the Muhajir. If they are prepared to do this, inform them that they will enjoy the privileges that the Muhajir enjoy and shall have to bear the same responsibilities that the Muhajir bear. If after accepting Islam they prefer their own homes to that of the Muhajir, inform them that they will assume the status of the Muslims in the outlying areas. The injunctions that Allah has enjoined for all Muslims shall still apply to them but they shall receive no share of booty unless they participate in the battle. However, if they refuse to enter the fold of Islam then invite them to the 2nd option which is to pay the Jizya. If they accept, acknowledge it and refrain from harming them. If they refuse this, then the 3rd course of action is that you ask Allah for help and fight them if this is what Allah decrees. When you are fighting you should never chop down or burn any date palms nor destroy any animals or any fruit-bearing trees. Do not destroy any places of worship or kill any children, elderly people or women. You will also find people wh9 have secluded themselves in monasteries. Leave them to that which they have secluded themselves. You will also find people who have made nests for Saitan on their heads. When Allah decrees that you find these people, cut off their heads. *(Bayhaqi in Kanzul Ummal)*

Abu Bakr ؓ's Instructions to Khalid bin Walid ؓ When he Sent Him to Fight the Rejectors of Islam

Urwa ؓ narrates that when Abu Bakr ؓ sent Khalid bin Walid ؓ to fight those Arabs who had forsaken Islam, he instructed him to invite them back to Islam and to explain to them their privileges and responsibilities. Abu Bakr ؓ eagerly desired that they receive guidance and also instructed Khalid bin Walid ؓ that he should acknowledge their acceptance whether they are white or black. He said that this was because the only people to be fought were those who chose to disbelieve in Allah rather than believe in Him. Once a person accepted Islam and displays sincere faith, there was no way to harm him because Allah shall judge him. Those rejectors were to be fought who do not accept the Islam they are invited. *(Bayhaqi in Kanzul Ummal)*

Khalid bin Walid ؓ Gives Da'wah to the People of Hira

Salih bin Kaisan رحمة الله narrates that when Khalid bin Walid ؓ arrived in Hira, the nobles of Hira accompanied by Qabisa bin Ayas bin Hayya Tai left to meet him. Qabisa had been appointed governor of Hira by the Kisra after Nu'man bin Mundhir. Addressing Qabisa and the others, Khalid bin Walid ؓ said, "I invite you towards Allah and towards Islam. If you accept, you shall be part of the Muslim Ummah and shall enjoy the privileges that the Muslims enjoy and shall have to bear the same responsibilities that the Muslims bear. If you refuse, you will have to pay the Jizya. If you refuse even this, then bear in mind that I have come with people who are more greedy for death than you are for life. We shall then fight you until Allah decides the matter between us." Qabisa said to him, "We have no need to fight you. We shall remain as believers to our religion and pay you the Jizya." Khalid bin Walid ؓ then entered into an agreement with them to pay 70,000 Dirhams. *(Ibn Jareer, Tabari)*. Another narration states that Khalid bin Walid ؓ said to them, "I invite you to Islam and to testify that there is none worthy of worship but the One Allah and that Muhammad ﷺ is Allah's servant and Rasul. I call you to establish salah, to pay zakah, and to accept all the injunctions binding on the Muslims. In exchange you shall enjoy the privileges that the Muslims enjoy and shall have to bear the same responsibilities that the Muslims bear." Hani asked, "If I do not accept this, then what?" Khalid ؓ replied, "If you do not accept this, you shall have to pay the Jizya by hand." "And if we refuse to do this?" was the next question. Khalid ؓ replied, "If you refuse even this, such people shall crush you underfoot to whom death is more beloved than life is to you." Hani requested, "Allow us the night to think the matter over." Khalid ؓ granted the request. The next morning, Hani came back to Khalid ؓ and said, "We have decided to pay the Jizya. Let us now enter into an agreement." The narration continues. *(Bayhaqi)*. Another narration adds that when the 2 armies faced each other before the Battle of Yarmuk, Abu Ubaidah bin Jarrah ؓ and Yazid bin Abi Sufian ؓ together with Dirar bin Azur ؓ, Harith bin Hisham ؓ and Abu Jandal bin Suhail ؓ stepped forward and announced, "We want to meet your leader." When they were permitted to meet Tadaruk the brother of Heraclius, they found him sitting on a tent made of silk. The Sahabah said, "It is not permissible for us to enter this." Tadaruk then had a silken rug spread out for them but they refused to sit on it. He then sat where they chose to sit. They agreed to enter into a treaty and the Sahabah returned after inviting him to accept Islam. However, the treaty did not materialize and the battle was fought. *(Al Bidayah wan Nihayah)*

Khalid bin Walid ؓ Invited the Roman Commander Jarja to Islam and he Accepts

Waqidi reports that during the battle of Yarmuk, one of the most senior Roman commanders by the name of Jarja stepped forward from the line of soldiers and asked to meet Khalid bin Walid ؓ. Khalid ؓ went to meet him and drew so close that the necks of their horses met. The following conversation ensued:

Jarja: O Khalid! I want you to tell me something, but do speak the truth and do not lie because a free man never lies. Do not deceive me either because a respectable person never deceives someone who trusts him. Has Allah given your Nabi a sword from the heavens which he has given to you by virtue of which you defeat anyone against whom you draw it?

Khalid ؓ: No

Jarja: Then why are you called the sword of Allah ('Saifullah')?

Khalid ؓ: Allah sent His Nabi amongst us who preached to us. We expressed resentment and kept our distance from him. Even I was amongst those who treated him like a liar and disliked him.

Thereafter, Allah seized our hearts and guided us through him. We then pledged allegiance to him. He once said to me, 'You are a sword from the swords of Allah whom Allah has drawn against the disbelievers.' He then prayed to Allah to assist me. This is why I am called the sword of Allah. I am therefore amongst the strongest of Muslims against the disbelievers.

Jarja: O Khalid! Towards what do you call?

Khalid 🙠: We call people to testify that there is none worthy of worship but Allah and that Muhammad 🙢 is Allah's servant and Rasul. We also call them to accept everything that Rasulullah 🙢 has brought from Allah.

Jarja: What about those who do not accept this?

Khalid 🙠: They will have to pay the Jizya and we will protect them.

Jarja: What if they do not pay it?

Khalid 🙠: We then declare war against them and fight.

Jarja: What is the status of a person who accepts what you say and enters the fold of your religion?

Khalid 🙠: We all share the same status with respect to the injunctions that Allah has made binding on us regardless of whether we have a high social standing or not and regardless of whether we accepted Islam earlier or later.

Jarja: Will a person entering Islam today have the same reward as yourself?

Khalid 🙠: Certainly! In fact, his rewards shall be greater.

Jarja: How can such a person be rated equal to you when you have accepted Islam before him?

Khalid 🙠: We had no option but to accept Islam because our allegiance was pledged while our Nabi was alive and in our midst. Revelation from the heavens would come to him and he would recite the Qur'an to us and show us miracles. For anyone who saw what we saw and who heard what we heard there was no option but to accept Islam and to pledge allegiance to him. As for you people, you have not seen the miraculous events and signs of his prophethood that we saw and heard. Whoever of you will enter into Islam with sincerity shall be better than us.

Jarja: I swear by Allah that you have been honest with me and did not deceive me either.

Khalid 🙠: By Allah! I have certainly spoken the truth and Allah is witness to the fact that I have responded to your questions to the best of my ability.

Jarja then turned his shield around as an indication that he did not intend to fight and turned to Khalid 🙠 saying, "Teach me Islam." Khalid 🙠 took him to his tent, poured a waterbag of water over him to assist him to bath and then led him as he performed 2 Rakats salah. Thinking that the Muslims were planning something when Jarja left with Khalid 🙠, the Romans launched an offensive that caught the Muslims completely by surprise. Every Muslim regiment was rooted from their position besides the Muhamiya regiment led by Ikrama bin Abi Jahal 🙠 and Harith bin Hisham 🙠. The Romans were already in the midst of the Muslim camp when Khalid 🙠 mounted his horse with Jarja following closely. The Muslims called to each other and managed to regain their foothold. The Romans were then forced to return to their base. Khalid 🙠 then gradually advanced the Muslim army until they crossed swords with the enemy. Khalid 🙠 and Jamja continuously fought the Romans from noon until the sun was about to set. The fighting was so fierce that the Muslims performed the Zuhr and Asr salats with indications. Jarja was mortally injured in the battle and passed away the same day. The only salah he therefore performed for Allah were the 2 he performed with Khalid 🙠. May Allah shower His mercy on him. *(Al Bidayah wan Nihayah, Isaba)*. Another narration states

that Khalid bin Walid 🙠 once delivered a lecture to the Muslims and encouraged them to go to the non-Arab countries and leave the Arabian lands. He also told them, "You have not seen the many types of foods that are there. By Allah! Even if Jihad in the Path of Allah and calling people towards Islam were not obligatory for us and all we needed to do was earn a living, I would still propose that we fight for these fertile lands to gain control over it. We would then hand over hunger and hard living to those who are weighed down at home and not fighting as you are." *(Al Bidayah wan Nihayah, Ibn Jareer)*

The Sahabah Give Da'wah in the Battlefield During the Time of Omar 🙠 who Advised His Commanders to do so: Omar 🙠 Writes to Sa'd to Invite People to Islam for 3 Days

Yazid bin Abi Habib narrates that Omar bin Khattab 🙠 wrote to Sa'd bin Abi Waqqas 🙠 saying, "I have already written to you to tell you that you should invite people to Islam for 3 days. Whoever accepts what you say before you start fighting shall be one of the Muslims. He shall enjoy the privileges of the Muslims and shall receive a share in the booty. Whoever accepts Islam after the battle or after defeat; his wealth shall become part of the booty to be shared by the Muslims because they had already become its owners before he accepted Islam. This is my instruction and the reason writing this letter." *(Kanzul Ummal)*

Salman Farsi 🙠 Invites people to Islam for 3 Days at Qasrul Abiad

Abul Bakhtari narrates that when a Muslim army under the command of Salman Farsi 🙠 sieged a Persian fortresses, the soldiers said to him, "O Abu Abdullah! Shall we not attack them'?" Salman 🙠 said, "Let me first invite them to Islam as I have heard Rasulullah 🙢 do." Addressing the Persians, he then said, "I am a Persian like you and as you see, the Arabs obey me. If you accept Islam, you shall enjoy the privileges that we enjoy and shall have to bear the same responsibilities that we bear. However, should you refuse to accept anything but your own faith, we shall not fight you but you will have to pay the Jizya by hand as subjects submitting to Muslim authority." Salman 🙠 explained to them in Persian that they will then have no authority. Salman 🙠 then continued, "If you refuse even this, then we shall face you on the battlefield on equal terms." The Persians said, "We are not the type to accept Islam nor the type that will pay Jizya. We shall rather fight you." When the Muslim soldiers again requested permission to attack, Salman 🙠 refused until he had presented the same invitation for 3 days. It was only after this that he commanded the Muslims to attack, which they did and conquered the fortress. *(Abu Nu'aym, Ahmad, Hakim in Nasbur Ra'ya)*. Another narration states that Salman Farsi 🙠 was the commander of the Muslim army and had been appointed to invite the enemy to Islam. Atiya الله رحمة states that it was Salman 🙠 who was also appointed to invite the people of Bahursher to Islam and again given the task at Qasrul Abiad. All of these people he invited to Islam for 3 days. The Da'wah he presented is the same as mentioned in the Hadith above. *(Kanzul Ummal)*.

Nu'man bin Muqarrin 🙠 and his Companions Give Da'wah to Rustam During the Battle of Qadisiyya

Sa'd bin Abi Waqqas 🙠 sent a group of leading Sahabah to invite Rustam to Islam. The group included Nu'man bin Muqarrin, Furat bin Hayyan, Handhala bin Rabi Tamemi, Utarid bin Hajib, Ash'ath bin Qais, Mughiera bin Shu'ba and Amr bin Ma'dikarib 🙠. Rustam asked them why they had come, they replied, "We have come because Allah has promised us that we shall take over your lands, capture your women and children and take ownership of you wealth. We are convinced that this is going to happen." Rustam himself had seen in a dream that an angel descended from the heavens, placed a seal on the weapons of the Persians and handed them over to Rasulullah ﷺ. Rasulullah ﷺ handed them over to Omar ﷺ. *(Al Bidayah wan Nihayah)*

Mughiera bin Shu'ba ﷺ Gives Da'wah to Rustam

Saif narrates from his teachers that when the 2 armies (Muslim and Persian) faced each other, Rustam sent a message to Sa'd bin Abi Waqqas ﷺ requesting him to send someone intelligent with the knowledge to answer his questions. Sa'd ﷺ sent Mughiera bin Shu'ba ﷺ. When Mughiera ﷺ came to meet him, Rustam said to him, "You are our neighbors. We have always been good to you and have never caused you any harm. Why do you rather not return to your land and we will not prevent you from trading with in our land." Mughiera ﷺ said to him, "We have no desire for this world. Our concern and our sole objective is the hereafter. Allah has sent a Nabi to us and said to him, 'I shall give this group (Sahabah) control over those who do not adopt Islam. Thus shall I use them to exact revenge from those who reject Islam. I shall allow them to dominate as long as they adhere to Islam. It is the true Islam and whoever turns away from it shall be disgraced. On the other hand, whoever holds fast to it shall have great honor.'" Rustam asked, "What is this Islam'?" Mughiera ﷺ said, "Its pillars without which no part of it can be correct are testification that there is none worthy of worship but Allah, that Muhammad ﷺ is Allah ﷻ's Rasul and accepting everything that Rasulullah ﷺ has brought from Allah." Rsutam exclaimed, "How excellent! And what else?" Mughiera ﷺ said, "To remove people from being slaves of people and to take them towards being the slaves of Allah." Rustam remarked, "This is also excellent. What else?" Mughiera ﷺ added, "All of mankind are the children of Adam السلام عليه and have a single father and mother." Rustam said, "This is also excellent. Tell me. If we were to enter your religion, would you then leave our land?" "Certainly," replied Mughiera ﷺ, "By Allah! We shall not draw close to your land except for trade or some other necessity." Rustam said, "This is also excellent." The narrators says, "When Mughiera ﷺ left Rustam, he spoke to his commanders about Islam but they were unhappy and refused to accept Islam. May Allah destroy and disgrace them! In fact, Allah did just that."

Ribi bin Amir ﷺ Invites Rustam to Islam

The narrators state that at the request of Rustam, Sa'd sent another envoy who happened to be Ribi bin Amir ﷺ. When Ribi ﷺ arrived, the court of Rustam was decorated. There were cushions decorated with gold, rugs of silk, shiny emeralds, priceless pearls and other elaborate decorations. Rustam wore his crown and other expensive garments and accessories as he sat on a throne of gold. Wearing old clothing, Ribi ﷺ entered with his sword, his shield and undersized horse. He continued riding the horse even crushing on the edges of the rugs. He then dismounted and tied his horse on one of the couches. He then walked along with his weapons and armor still wearing his helmet. When the courtiers asked him to remove his weapons, he said. "I have not come with my own accord but have come on your request. Either leave me as I am or grant me leave," Rustam instructed them to grant him entry and he came with his spear, which tore most of the rug as he walked while leaning on it. The courtiers asked, "What brings you here?" Ribi ﷺ replied, "We have not come on our own accord but Allah has sent us to remove those whom He wills from the slavery of man to take them to the slavery of Allah, to remove them from the

narrowness of this world towards its vastness and from the oppression of other religions towards the justice of Islam. Giving us Islam, Allah has sent us to call His creation towards it. Whoever accepts it, we shall acknowledge it and leave him alone. As for those who refuse, we shall fight them forever until we reach Allah's promised place." They asked, "What is Allah's promised place?" He replied, "It is paradise, which shall be the lot of people who die fighting those who reject Islam. Victory shall be the lot of those who survive." Rustam asked, "I have heard what you have to say. Will you allow us grace so that you and us may look into the matter?" "Certainly," Ribi ﷺ responded, "How much time do you require? One day? 2 days?" "No," said Rustam, "We need time to write to our consultative assembly and our leaders." Ribi ﷺ said, "Rasulullah ﷺ has not set such a precedent that allows enemies more than 3 days interval at the time of battle. Look into the matter for your benefit and for the benefit of your people and then choose one of the 3 options before the expiry of the 3-days term." Rustam asked, "Are you the leader of your people?" "No," replied Ribi ﷺ, "but all Muslims are like a single body. The lowest of them may grant amnesty to an enemy which is binding on the highest of them." Rustam gathered the leaders of his people and asked. "Have you ever heard words more powerful yet as gentle as those of that man?" They said, "Allah forbid that you should have taken a liking to anything that he said and forsake your religion for that dog! Did you not see his clothing?" Rustam said to them, "Shame on you! Do not look at clothing but rather look at the caution, the speech, and the personality. The Arabs care little for clothing and food but are jealous about their lineage."

Hudhaifa bin Mihsin ﷺ and Mughiera bin Shu'ba ﷺ Present the Da'wah to Rustam on the 2ⁿᵈ and 3ʳᵈ Days

The next day, the Persians asked for another person and Sa'd ﷺ sent Hudhaifa bin Mihsin ﷺ who addressed them in the manner that Ribi ﷺ did. On the 3ʳᵈ day, Mughiera bin Shu'ba ﷺ was sent and he spoke to them in a very pleasant manner and in great detail. In their discussion, Rustam said to Mughiera ﷺ, "Your coming to our land is like a fly that saw some honey and announced, 'Whoever takes me to the honey shall receive 2 Dirhams.' However, when the fly fell into the honey, it started drowning and could not find any escape despite all its efforts. It then announced, 'Whoever removes me from the honey shall receive 4 Dirhams.' Your example is also like a weak fox that entered a vineyard through a hole in the wall. Seeing that the fox was very weak, the owner of the vineyard took pity on it and left it alone. However, when the fox became fat, it started causing great damage to the vineyard so that owner came with a stick and sought help from 2 of his slaves. When the fox tried to escape through the hole, it was unable to do so because it had grown fat and the owner of the vineyard hit it until it died. This is how you people will leave our land." Rustam then filled with rage and took an oath by the sun saying, "I shall kill you all tomorrow!" Mughiera bin Shu'ba ﷺ calmly said, "You will soon find out." Rustam then said to Mughiera ﷺ, "I have issued the command that each of you should receive a set of clothing and that your commander should receive 1,000 Dinars together with a set of clothing and a conveyance. You should then leave us." Mughiera ﷺ said, "Do you wish to do this after we have weakened your kingdom and diminished your respect? We have been in your kingdom for a while and shall take the Jizya from you, which you shall pay by hand as subjects submitting to our authority. Regardless of what you think, you will soon become our slaves. *(Al Bidayah wan Nihayah, Tabari)*

Sa'd ﷺ Sends a Group of Sahabah to Give Da'wah to the Persian Leader Before Engaging in Battle

Abu Wa'il ﷺ narrates, "Sa'd ﷺ marched with the Muslim army until they set up camp at a place called Qadisiyya. I cannot say precisely but we numbered no more than 7,000 or 8,000 while the disbelievers numbered 30,000." This is the figure according to this narration, However, according to a narration of Saif (Al Bidayah wan Nihayah), the disbeliever army numbered 80,000. Another narration places the figure of Rustam's army at 120,000 with another 80,000 reinforcements. In addition to this, Rustam had 33 elephants, led by the largest one which was a white elephant belonged to Sabur. All the other elephants obeyed this elephant. Like this narration, there are many other various figures. Because of their might, the Persians told the Sahabah, "You have no strength, no power, and no weapons to resist us. You should rather go back home." The Sahabah reiterated that they were not going back. The Persians also laughed at the arrows of the Sahabah and would say, "Dook! Dook!" By this they compared the arrows to spindles ("dook" is a Persian word refer to knitting needles), However, when the Sahahah refused to return, the Persians said, "Send one of your intellectuals to us to explain what brings you here." Mughiera bin Shu'ba ﷺ volunteered for the task. When he went, he sat on Rustam's throne, causing the courtiers to breathe out and shout. Mughiera ﷺ said to them, "This neither elevates my status nor reduces that of your leader." Rustam said, "Now tell me why you have come?" Mughiera ﷺ said, "We were a nation that was involved in evil and abnormal acts. Allah then sent a Nabi to us by means of which Allah guided us and provided sustenance for us. Amongst the foods Allah granted us were grains which grow in these parts. When we ate this and fed it to our families, they said, 'This is not sufficient. Take us to that land so that we may eat those grains." Rustam exclaimed, "We shall then kill you all!" Mughiera ﷺ said, "If you kill us, we shall enter paradise but if we kill (defeat) you, those who die will enter hell and those who survive will have to pay the Jizya." When Mughiera ﷺ spoke about paying the Jizya, the courtiers breathed out and shouted, "There can be no agreement between you and us!" Mughiera ﷺ asked, "Should we cross the river to come to you or will you cross the river to come to us'?" Rustam said, "We shall cross over." The Muslim army withdrew a short distance for the Persians to cross the river and attacked and defeated them. (Ibn Jareer in Al Bidayah wan Nihayah)

Mu'awiya bin Qurra ﷺ narrates that when the battle of Qadisiyya took place, Mughiera ﷺ was sent to meet the Persian leader. Mughiera ﷺ asked for 10 men who went with him. He straightened his clothes, took his shield and then left. When they reached, Mughiera ﷺ told his companions to put down a shield on which he sat. The big Persian commander said, "O Arabs! I know well what has brought you here. You people do not have sufficient food in your country to fill your bellies. We shall give all the food you need as we are fire-worshippers and do not like to fight you. You will only make our land impure." Mughiera ﷺ said to him, "By Allah! This is certainly not the reason that brought us. We were a nation that used to worship stones and idols. Whenever we used to make a stone round that looked better than another, we would discard the first one and adopted the next. We knew no deity until Allah sent to us a Rasul from amongst our own people. He called us to Islam and we followed him. We have not come for food but we have been commanded to fight those enemies of ours who reject Islam. We have not come for food but have come to kill your soldiers and capture your families. As for what you have mentioned about the scarcity of food in our land, I swear by my life that we certainly do not have enough to fill our bellies and sometimes we do not even find anything to drink for a long time. After coming to your lands, we have found an abundance of food and water. By Allah! Now we shall not leave here until this land belongs either to you or us." The Persian commander said in his language, "He has spoken the truth." He then said, "Your eye shall lose an eye tomorrow." As Allah wished Mughiera ﷺ lost an eye next day when a stray arrow struck him. (Hakim, Haythami)

Saif narrates that Sa'd ﷺ sent a group of Sahabah to the Persian leader to invite him to Islam before the battle. When they requested permission to see him, permission was granted and the people of the city came to have a look at their appearance. The Sahabah were wearing their shawls over their shoulders, carried their whips in their hands, were wearing sandals and their horses were extremely weak because of which they walked heavily on the ground. The people were surprised with their mysterious look when they saw them. They wondered how these people could defeat their larger and well-equipped armies. When the Sahabah were allowed to meet the Persian king Yazdajird, he made them sit in front of him. He was an arrogant man with little respect for others. He questioned them about the names of their garments, their shawls, their shoes and their whips. Each time they told him the name, he took an sign from them in his favor. However, Allah ensured that each sign backfired against him. He then asked them, "What has brought you to our lands? Have you become bold because our civil war has started?" Nu'man bin Muqarrin ﷺ said, "Allah has showered His mercy on us when He sent a Rasul to us who guided us towards good and commanded us with virtue. He defined evil for us and forbade us from it. He promised us the good of this world as well as the Hereafter if we accepted his call to good. Whenever he invited a tribe towards this, they divided into 2 groups, one that drew close to him and the other that distanced itself from him. It was only the few selected ones who drew close to him. He continued his preaching in this manner for as long as Allah wanted him to. Thereafter, Allah commanded him to handle those Arabs who opposed him and he started with them before proceeding to the non-Arabs. When he did this, they all joined him as 2 groups: those who were forced to join but were happy later that they had done so and those who did so happily and whose happiness then increased. We all realized that Islam he called us towards was far superior to the hostility and the narrow lives we had been leading. He then instructed us to start handling the nations around us and to invite them towards justice. We are therefore inviting you towards Islam which regards all good as good and all evil as evil. But if you refuse to accept Islam, there are 2 unpleasant options, the one is more demeaning than the other. One option is to pay the Jizya and if you refuse, then the other is war. On the other hand, if you accept Islam, we shall leave the Book of Allah behind with you. We shall give you help in it so that you may rule by its laws and we shall leave you to your affairs and your territories. If you wish to pay the Jizya, we shall accept it from you and give you protection. Otherwise if you refuse Islam and Jizya, we shall fight you."

Yazdajird said, "I do not know of any nation on earth that is more wretched than you people, fewer in number than you and experiencing as much internal strife as you people. We have already handed over to you the regions around you so that it may be sufficient for you from our side as you may be content with it and not need to come to our main lands. The Persians have never fought you so do not think that you can stand in their way. If your numbers have increased, let this never fool you about thinking that you can overpower us. If it is poverty that has called you here, we shall provide relief for you until you become prosperous. We shall also honor your leaders, provide clothing for you and appoint for you a king who will be kind towards you." The Sahabah remained silent until Mughiera bin Shu'ba ؓ stood and said, "O King! These are all leaders of the Arabs and their aristocrats. They are all respectable people and it is only respectable people who show consideration for respectable people and who honor respectable people. They only give importance to the rights of respectable people. They have not yet told you everything they were sent to tell you and have not replied to all of your questions. They have done well to do this and it is only people like them who can act this respectfully. You should rather be conversing with someone like me. I shall convey the message to you and they will testify to what I say." Mughiera bin Shu'ba ؓ continued, "By the way in which you have described us, it appears that you are unaware of our situation. Concerning the statement you made about our poor condition, it is true as there was none in a poorer condition than we had been. With regard to hunger, none suffered the hunger more than we suffered. Regarding the food for them, we used to even eat dung beetles, other insects, scorpions and snakes. As for our homes, it used to be the bare earth and our clothing consisted of only what we wove from the skins of camels and hairs of goats. Killing and oppressing each other was our way of life and there were even those amongst us who would bury his infant daughter alive because he disliked that she should share his food. Our condition in the past was exactly as you have described. Allah then sent to us a man whom we knew and we were aware of his lineage. We were well acquainted with his personality and his place of birth. His land was the best of our lands, his lineage the best of our lineages, his family the best of our families and his tribe the best of our tribes. Despite the terrible conditions prevailing then, he was also the best person amongst us, the most truthful and most forbearing. When he called us towards Islam, none of us accepted besides his childhood friend who became the Khalifa after him. When he spoke, we said something else and when he told us the truth, we regarded them as lies. However, his followers increased while ours decreased. Whatever he said became reality and Allah eventually inspired us to believe in him and to follow him. He then became our link with Allah. Whatever he told us was actually from Allah and whatever he commanded was actually Allah's commands. He told us, 'Your Rabb says, '1 am the One Allah Who has no partner. I have been existing when nothing else existed and everything besides My countenance shall eventually perish. I have created everything and everything shall return to me. My mercy has reached you and I have sent to you this man to guide you towards the path by which I shall save you from My punishment after you die and lead you to the home I have created, which is the Home of Peace (Paradise)." We testify that Rasulullah ﷺ certainly brought the truth from the True Allah. Allah also said, 'Whoever follows you in Islam shall enjoy the privileges you enjoy and shall bear the responsibilities you bear. As for those who refuse to accept, propose the option of Jizya to him and then protect him as you would protect your own lives. You should then fight those who refuse even this. 1 shall be the Judge between you. I shall enter into My Paradise those of you who are martyred and those of you who survive shall have My assistance with them against those who oppose you.'" Mughiera ؓ then issued the ultimatum to Yazdajird when he said, "You may choose to pay the Jizya if you wish, in which case you will live as subjects. You may also choose the sword if you wish. Otherwise, you are at liberty to save yourselves by accepting Islam." Yazdajird replied angrily by saying, "You dare face me with these proposals!" Mughiera ؓ said, "I address whoever is speaking to me. Had another person been speaking to me, I would have presented them to him." Yazdajird burst out saying, "Had it not been for the principle that envoys cannot be killed, I would have surely killed you for you have no status in my estimation." Yazdajird then said to his courtiers, "Bring me a basket of sand and place it on the head of the person of the highest birth amongst them. Then lead him to the outskirts of Mada'in."

Addressing the Sahabah, Yazdajird said "Go back to your leader and inform him that I shall send Rustam to him who will bury him along with his army in the trenches of Qadisiyyah. Those coming afterwards shall learn a lesson from what happened to him and to you people. I shall then send Rustam to your land and he shall torture you worse than Sabur (a Persian prince who treated Arabs harshly) did." Yazdajird then asked, "Which of you is of the highest birth?" After a brief silence, Asim bin Amr ؓ volunteered to take the sand without consulting the others and said, "I am of the highest birth amongst them all. Let me carry the sand." "Is that so?" asked Yazdajird. When the other Sahabah agreed, the basket of sand was placed on his neck. He carried it out of the palace and to the outskirts where he mounted his animal and loaded the basket on it. He then raced his mount to take it to Sa'd bin Abi Waqqas ؓ. He rode ahead of the other Sahabah and passed by the gates of Qudays (a palace in Qadisiyyah) calling, "Give the Amir glad tidings of victory! Inshallah, we shall certainly be victorious!" Asim ؓ then rode on until he placed the sand on Arabian soil. Returning to Sa'd ؓ, he informed him about what had happened. Sa'd ؓ said, "Glad tidings! By Allah! Allah has already given us the keys of their kingdom." The Muslims took a good sign from this that they would capture the lands of the Persians. *(Al Bidayah wan Nihayah, Ibn Jareer Tabari)*

Abdullah bin Mu'tam ؓ Gives Da'wah to the Banu Taghlib Tribe and Others During the Battle for Tikrit

Muhammad الله رحمة Talha رحمة الله and others narrate that during the battle for Tikrit, the Romans saw that every offensive they launched against the Muslims backfired on them and that they were defeated every time they clashed with the Muslims in battle. They therefore deserted their leaders and loaded their belongings on their boats to leave the area. When the spies from the Arab-Christian Taghlib, Iyad, and Namir tribes brought the news to the Muslim commander Abdullah bin Mu'tam ؓ, they requested that he enter into a peace treaty with these Arab tribes and added that these tribes were willing to accept Islam. Abdullah ؓ sent a message to them stating, "If you people are sincere, you should testify that there is none worthy of worship but Allah and that Muhammad ﷺ is Allah's Rasul. In addition to this, you should accept everything that Rasulullah ﷺ brought from Allah. You should then inform us of your plan of action." The messengers went with the message and returned with news that the people had accepted Islam. *(Ibn Jareer)*

Amr bin Al Aas ؓ Gives Da'wah During the Battle for Egypt

Khalid ؓ and Ubadah ؓ narrate that Amr bin Al Aas ؓ marched to Egypt after Omar ؓ had returned to Madinah from Sham. Zubair ؓ followed him with another battalion and the 2 joined up when Amr bin Al Aas ؓ reached a place called Ilyun. There they were met by the chief priest of Egypt Abu Maryam who was there with another high priest and the Egyptian army. Maqoqis, the king of Egypt had sent them to defend the country.

When Amr ﷺ arrived there, they immediately prepared to attack but Amr ﷺ sent a message telling them that they should not be quick and should first listen to their reason for coming, after which they could make a decision. The Egyptians were then called off and Amr ﷺ send a message stating, "I am coming forward to talk, so send Abu Maryam. The Egyptians accepted and each party guaranteed the safety of the other." Amr ﷺ said to the 2 men, "You 2 are senior priests of this country, so do listen. Allah has sent Muhammad ﷺ with the truth and commanded us to follow it. Muhammad ﷺ has conveyed this command to us together with every other command Allah has issued. Muhammad ﷺ then passed on. May Allah's choicest blessings and mercies be showered on him. However, he fulfilled his duty and left us on a clear path. Amongst his instructions to us was to wish people well and we therefore invite you to accept Islam. Whoever accepts shall be one of us and whoever refuses to accept shall be given the option of paying Jizya. We shall then do everything in our capacity to provide protection. Rasulullah ﷺ has informed us that we shall certainly conquer you people and advised us to be good to you to maintain the family ties that exist between us. If you accept this option of paying Jizya, you shall have in your favor another right of being family in addition to the right of protection (that we will be obliged to give you). Amongst the commands that our Amir had given are his words, 'Treat the Copts (Egyptians) well because Rasulullah ﷺ has advised that the Copts should be treated well by virtue of the fact that they are relatives and deserve protection as well.'" To this, the Egyptians said, "It is only the Ambiya ﷺ who would maintain such distant relations. Referring to Hajera, the wife of Ibrahim ﷺ, they said she was a celebrated and honorable lady who was the daughter of our king. She belonged to the House of Manf who was the ruling family. However, the House of Aynush Shams attacked them, killed many of them, seized the kingdom and the rest of them were forced into exile. She then became the wife of Ibrahim. His coming was most welcome and a happy event for us. Do leave us in peace until we return to you after consulting with the others. Amr bin Al Aas ﷺ said, "You will be unable to me. You therefore have 3 days to ponder over the matter and to consult with your people. Otherwise if you fail to return within 3 days, we shall have to attack you." When the 2 priests requested an extension of time, Amr ﷺ gave them an additional day. They then asked for more time and he added another day. They then returned to Maqoqis who seriously considered the alternatives. However, a person called Artabun (Roman general defeated by Amr) refused to submit and ordered an attack against the Muslims. The 2 priests said to the people, "We shall do our best to defend you without returning to the Muslims. However, there are still 4 days left in which we can hope for nothing but peace from them." The people of Farqab launched a surprise attack against Amr and Zubair ﷺ at night but Amr was prepared for the attack. He engaged the enemy and killed the people of Farqab along with those with them Artabun was also killed with them, after which the rest of them fled. Amr and Zubair ﷺ then left for Aynush Shams. (Ibn Jareer). Abu Haritha and Abu Uthman narrate that when Amr ﷺ set up camp at Aynush Shams, the Egyptian people said to their king, "What do you wish to do against people who have defeated Kisra and Caesar and occupied their lands? Enter into negotiations with them and draw up a treaty without yourself fighting them or leading us against them." This took place on the 4th day. The king refused and the Egyptians attacked the Muslims. The Muslims repulsed the attack and Zubair ﷺ managed to climb the wall of their stronghold. The Egyptians noticed, they opened the gates for

Amr ﷺ and came out to enter into negotiations. Amr ﷺ accepted their submission and Zubair ﷺ descended the wall. (Ibn Jareer)

The Sahabah Give Da'wah During a Battle Under the Leadership of Salama bin Qais Ash'jai ﷺ

Sulaiman bin Buraida narrates that whenever a Muslim regiment was gathered, the Ameerul Mu'mineen Omar ﷺ appointed someone with knowledge and sound judgment as their commander. Therefore, he once appointed Salama bin Qais Ash'jai ﷺ as the Amir of a particular regiment and addressed them saying, "March in the name of Allah and for the pleasure of Allah you should fight those who commit kufr. When you meet the enemy, invite them to accept one of 3 options. Firstly invite them to Islam. If they accept Islam and choose to remain in their hometowns, then they will have to pay zakah from their wealth and will have no share in the booty that the Muslims receive. On the other hand, if they choose to join you, they will enjoy the same privileges that you do and will have to bear the same responsibilities that you bear. Secondly if they refuse to accept Islam, call them to pay the Jizya. If they agree to pay the Jizya, then fight their enemies for them and do not place responsibilities on them that are beyond their capability. Thirdly if they refuse even this, fight them and Allah shall assist you against them. If they take refuge in a fortress and ask you to allow them to emerge on the conditions of Allah and His Rasul ﷺ, do not allow them to emerge on these conditions because you do not know what instructions Allah and His Rasul ﷺ will issue concerning them. If they ask to be allowed to emerge into the protection of Allah and His Rasul, do not allow them this, but rather allow them to emerge into your protection. If they fight you, ensure that you do not steal from the booty, do not deceive, do not mutilate and do not kill any child." Salama ﷺ says, "We marched and met the disbelieving enemy, we gave them the Da'wah. When they refused to accept Islam, we called them to pay the Jizya, which they refused. We fought them and Allah assisted us to defeat them. We killed their soldiers, captured their families, and collected their wealth as booty." (Ibn Jareer)

Abu Musa Ash'ari ﷺ Gives Da'wah to the People of Isfahan Before Engaging Them in Battle

Banu Umayya narrates that when Abu Musa Ash'ari ﷺ set up camp at Isfahan, he invited the people to accept Islam. When they refused to accept Islam, he proposed the Jizya and they opted to enter into negotiations with him. Whereas they opted for peace that night, the following morning they betrayed the Muslims and launched a surprise attack. It was very soon that Allah granted the Muslims victory over them. (Ibn Sa'd)

The Character and Actions of the Sahabah That Inspired People to Accept Islam: Amr bin Jamooh ﷺ Accepts Islam and the Role of His Son and Mu'adh bin Jabal ﷺ

Ibn Is'haq narrates that after some of the Ansar had pledged allegiance to Rasulullah ﷺ in Makkah, they came back to Madinah and Islam started spreading in Madinah. However, there were still those disbelievers amongst the Ansar who sticked to their religion. Amongst these was Amr bin Jamooh ﷺ, whose son Mu'adh ﷺ had also pledged allegiance to Rasulullah ﷺ at Aqaba. Amr bin Jamooh ﷺ was one of the leaders of the Banu Salma tribe and one of the most respected persons amongst them. As was the practice of the noble people of those times, Amr bin Jamooh ﷺ also kept a wooden idol in his house that he named Manal. He regarded it as his deity and always kept it clean. After accepting Islam, some of the youngsters of the Banu Salma tribe together with others who had pledged allegiance to Rasulullah ﷺ at Aqaba such as Mu'adh bin Jabal ؓ and Amr bin Jamooh ؓ's son Mu'adh ؓ used to take away the idol of Amr bin Jamooh ؓ at night and then throw it with head first into one of the pits they used as a rubbish dump. In the mornings, Amr bin Jamooh used to say, "Woe be to those who have manhandled our god last night!" He would then go looking for the idol. When he found it, he would wash it, clean it thoroughly and apply perfume to it. Then he would say, "I swear by Allah that if I found out who did this, I would certainly disgrace him." However, as soon as Amr bin Jamooh ؓ went to sleep, the youngsters again repeated their deed. When they had carried out their deed too often for him, he took the idol out from where they had thrown it, after cleaning it and applying perfume, he hung his sword around its neck. He then said to it, "By Allah! I have no idea who is doing this to you. However, if you have the courage, you should defend yourself for you now have this sword with you." When night fell and Amr bin Jamooh ؓ went to sleep, the youngsters again seized the idol and after removing the sword from its neck, they tied a dead dog to it and threw it into an unused well of the Abnu Salma that was full of rubbish. The following morning when Amr bin Jamooh ؓ did not find the idol in its place, he went out in search of it and found it lying on its head in the well with the dead dog tied to it. Seeing this, he realized the helplessness of the idol. After the Muslims of his tribe had spoken to him, he accepted Islam, becoming an excellent Muslim. May Allah shower His mercy on him. *(Abu Nu'aym in Dala'il)*. Another narration states that when a few member of the Banu Salma tribe accepted Islam, the wife and son of Amr bin Jamooh also accepted Islam. Amr bin Jamooh ؓ said to his wife, "Do not allow any of the children to go to your family until I investigate what they are doing." She said, "I shall do as you say, but will you not listen to what your son has heard from that person (Rasulullah ﷺ)?" Amr bin Jamooh ؓ said, "Perhaps he has become irreligious." His wife replied, "No, he has merely one of the people." Amr bin Jamooh ؓ sent for his son and said, "Tell me what you have heard from that person." His son recited:

بِسْمِ اللهِ الرَّحْمَنِ الرَّحِيمِ (1)

الْحَمْدُ لِلَّهِ رَبِّ الْعَالَمِينَ (2) الرَّحْمَنِ الرَّحِيمِ (3) مَالِكِ يَوْمِ الدِّينِ (4) إِيَّاكَ نَعْبُدُ وَإِيَّاكَ نَسْتَعِينُ (5) اهْدِنَا الصِّرَاطَ الْمُسْتَقِيمَ (6) صِرَاطَ الَّذِينَ أَنْعَمْتَ عَلَيْهِمْ غَيْرِ الْمَغْضُوبِ عَلَيْهِمْ وَلَا الضَّالِّينَ (7)

In the Name of Allah, the Most Beneficent, the Most Merciful. All the praises and thanks be to Allah, the Lord of the Alameen (mankind, jinns and all that exists). The Most Beneficent, the Most Merciful. The Only Owner of the Day of Recompense (the Day of Resurrection). You (Alone) we worship, and You (Alone) we ask for help (for each and everything). Guide us to the Straight Way. The Way of those on whom You have bestowed Your Grace, not (the way) of those who earned Your wrath, nor of those who went astray. (Al-Fatiha:1-7)

Amr bin Jamooh ؓ commented, "This is most excellent and beautiful! Is all his speech like this'?" His son said, "Even better than this, dear father. Do you wish to follow him'? Most of your people are already doing so." Amr bin Jamooh ؓ said, "I shall not do so until I have consulted with Manat and see what he says." When the disbelievers usually spoke to Manat, an old woman used to stand behind the idol and speak on its behalf. However, the woman was not there when Amr bin Jamooh ؓ approached the idol. He stood by the idol, praised it excessively and then said, "O Manat! You should know that you are being faced with a serious danger that you are unaware of. A man has arrived who forbids us from worshiping you and who instructs us

to get rid of you. I did not want to pledge allegiance to him until I had consulted with you." Amr ؓ spoke to the idol for long time but received no response. He then said, "You seem to be angry with me whereas I have done nothing offensive to you." He then stood up and broke the idol. *(Ibn Is'haq)*. Yet another narration adds that when Amr bin Jamooh ؓ accepted Islam and recognized the authority of Allah, he composed some couplets speaking about the helplessness of the idols that he had experienced. He also thanked Allah for saving him from the spiritual blindness and deviation he was trapped in. his couplets are translated as follows:

I repent to Allah for the wrongs I had committed in the past and I desire that Allah rescued me from the fire of Hell.
I praise Him for His bounties He Who is the Rabb of the Kabah and its covering. May He be glorified to the extent of the numbers of sinners and the extent of the raindrops falling from the skies. He guided me when I was in darkness when I was worshipping Manat and other stones alter my hairs had turned white because of old age.
He saved me from the blight of idol worship and its shame.
I was on the verge of being totally destroyed in darkness.
But He rescued me by His tremendous might
I therefore praise Him and thank Him as long as I live.
He Who is the Rabb of mankind and All Powerful over them when I say these words my only desire is to earn proximity to Allah in His home (Paradise)"

Condemning his idol, Amr bin Jamooh ؓ composed the following couplets, the meaning of which is:

"By Allah! Had you been a true god, you would never have been right down a well, bound tightly to a dog curses to the place where you have been thrown, lying there in disgrace despite being a god. We have now discovered your tremendous harmfulness. All praises belong to the Exalted Allah Who bestows favors The Giver, the Sustailler and the One Who rewards every good practice. It was He Who rescued me before I became a grave trapped in darkness." (Ibn Is'haq)

Abu Darda ؓ accepts Islam and role of Abdullah bin Rawaha ؓ

Waqidi says that it is commonly believed that Abu Darda ؓ was the last person from his family to accept Islam. He was extremely dedicated to the worship of his idol and kept it covered in a cloth. Abdullah bin Rawaha ؓ had been his bosom friend during the period of ignorance and now called him to accept Islam, but he constantly refused. One day, when Abdullah bin Rawaha ؓ noticed Abu Darda ؓ leaving the house, he entered the house and surprised Abu Darda ؓ's wife who was busy combing her hair. When he asked her where Abu Darda ؓ was, she replied, "Your brother has just left." With an axe in his hand, Abdullah bin Rawaha ؓ then entered the room where the idol stayed and smashed it to bits. As he did this, he took the name of each idol as he hymned the couplet:

"Behold! Everything that is worshipped besides Allah is a fake"

Abu Darda ؓ's wife had been hearing the noise of the axe and when Abdullah bin Rawaha ؓ emerged from the room, she burst out, "O son of Rawaha! You have ruined me!" He had just left the house when Abu Darda ؓ entered the house and found his wife sitting there crying out of fear for his reaction. When he asked her what was wrong, she said, "Your brother Abdullah bin Rawaha ؓ came here by surprise and did what you see." Abu Darda ؓ became very angry but then thought to himself that if his idol was of any good, it would have defended itself. He then went to Rasulullah ﷺ who was with Abdullah bin Rawaha ؓ and accepted Islam. *(Hakim in Mustadark)*

The Letter that Omar 🙐 Wrote to Amr bin Al Aas 🙐 Concerning Jizya and Prisoners of War

Ziyad bin Jaz Zubaidi narrates a lengthy report about what happened after the Muslims conquered Alexandria during the Khilafah of Omar 🙐. In this report he also mentions that they stopped at a place called Balhib where they waited for the letter of Omar 🙐 to reach them. When it arrived, Amr bin Al Aas 🙐 read the letter to the Muslims, which stated: Your letter has reached me with the news that the king of Alexandria has opted to pay the Jizya on condition that all the prisoners of his country are returned to him. By my life! The Jizya that we receive and that the Muslims after us shall receive is more beloved to me than the booty that is distributed and then finished: Suggest to the king of Alexandria that he should pay the Jizya on condition that the prisoners in your custody should be given the choice of either accepting Islam or remaining faithful to their religion. Whoever amongst them accepts Islam would become one of the Muslims and shall enjoy the privileges all Muslims enjoy together with bearing the responsibilities all Muslims bear. Those who choose the religion of their people shall have to pay the same amount of Jizya fixed for the people of his faith. For those prisoners who have dispersed into Arabia and reached places like Makkah, Madinah or Yemen, we shall be unable to return them to him and cannot enter into an agreement that we will be unable to fulfill.

What the Sahabah did During the Conquest of Alexandria

Ziyad bin Jaz states further, "Amr bin Al Aas 🙐 then sent a letter to the king of Alexandria, explaining to him the instructions that the Ameerul Mu'mineen had written to him. The king accepted the proposal and we then gathered all the prisoners with us. When all these Christian prisoners had gathered, we approached each one of them and allowed him to choose between Islam and Christianity. When any of them accepted Islam, we shouted 'Allahu Akbar' louder than we did when conquering any town and took him into our protection. If any of them chose Christianity, the Christians would make a noise and take him into their protection. We would then impose the Jizya on him. When this happened, we were so grieved that it appeared as if one of us had defected to them. This continued until all the prisoners had been given the choice. Amongst those who came to us was Abu Maryam whose name was Abdullah bin Abdur Rahman." Another narrator by the name of Qasim says that he met Abu Maryam when he was chief of the Banu Zubaid tribe. Ziyad bin Jaz continues saying, "When we approached Abu Maryam whose parents and brothers were all Christians and gave him the choice between Islam and Christianity, he opted to accept Islam. As we took him into our protection, his parents and brothers dashed across to pull him away from us and actually tore his clothing apart. However, he is now our chief as you can see." *(Ibn Jaeer)*

The incident of Ali 🙐's Armor and his Interaction With a Christian Who Then Accepted Islam

Sha'bi narrates that when the Ameerul Mu'minin Ali 🙐 once went to the marketplace, he found a Christian selling a coat of armor. Recognizing the coat of armor, Ali 🙐 said, "That armor belongs to me. Let us have the judge of the Muslims decide the matter between us." The presiding judge at that time was Qadhi

Shuray and Ali 🙐 asked him to rule in the matter. When Qadhi Shuray saw the Ameerul Mu'mineen Ali 🙐, he got up from his place and made the Ameerul Mu'mineen sit there. He then sat in front of the Ameerul Mu'mineen next to the Christian. Ali 🙐 said, "O Shuray! Had my adversary been a Muslim, I would have sat with him. However, I have heard Rasulullah ﷺ say about the non-Muslims living in a Muslim country, 'Do not shake hands with them, do not be first to greet them, do not visit them when they fall ill, do not perform their funeral prayers, make them use the narrow part of the pathway and keep them in a lowered position as Allah has kept them in a lowered position'. Do pass judgment between us, O Shuray." Qadhi Shuray asked, "What do you have to say, O Ameerul Mu'minin'?" Ali 🙐 declared, "This coat of armor belongs to me. I had lost it a long time ago." Qadhi Shuray then asked, "What have you to say, O Christian'?" The Christian pleaded, "No. The Ameerul Mu'minin is mistaken. The armor is mine." Qadhi Shuray ruled, "The armor cannot be taken from the Christian unless you have proof of your ownership, O Ameerul Mu'minin." Ali 🙐 submitted, "Shuray is right." The Christian then said, "As for me, I testify that it is certainly the judgment of the Ambiya ﷽ that the Ameerul Mu'mineen can come to a judge under his power who passes judgment against him. O Ameerul Mu'mineen! I swear by Allah that the armor belongs to you. As I walked behind you one day, the armor fell off your brown camel and I picked it Lip." He then declared:

اَشْهَدُ اَنْ لَا اِلَهَ اِلَّا اللهُ وَاَشْهَدُ اَنَّ مُحَمَّدًا وَرَسُوْلُ الله

"I testify that there is none worthy of worship but Allah and that Muhammad ﷺ is Allah's Rasul."

Ali 🙐 said to him, "Now that you have accepted Islam, you may have it." The man then loaded it on his horse. *(Tirmidhi, Hakim).* A narration of Hakim states that the armor of Ali 🙐 once fell off his camel and was found by a person who sold it. When the armor was found in the possession of a Jew, Ali 🙐 took the case to Qadhi Shuray. Ali 🙐's son Hasan 🙐 and his freed slave Qambar testified in favor of Ali 🙐. Qadhi Shuray said, "Bring me another witness in place of Hasan." "Do you not accept the testimony of Hasan'?" asked Ali 🙐. "No," replied Qadhi Shuray, "but I recall that you told me that it is not permissible for a son to testify in favor of his father." Yazid Tamemi reports a lengthy narration in which he states that Qadhi Shuray said to Ali 🙐, "We shall accept the testimony of your freed slave but not that of your son." Ali 🙐 said, "Good grief! Have you not heard Omar report that Rasulullah ﷺ said, 'Hasan and Husain shall be the leaders of the youth of paradise?'" Turning to the Jew, Ali 🙐 then said, "You may have the armor, O Jew!" The Jew said in astonishment, "The Ameerul Mu'mineen takes the case before the judge of the Muslims who passes judgment against him and he still accepts it! O Ameerul Mu'mineen! I swear by Allah that you have spoken the truth. The armor is yours. I picked it up when it fell off your camel." He then declared: اَشْهَدُ اَنْ لَا اِلَهَ اِلَّا اللهُ وَاَشْهَدُ اَنَّ مُحَمَّدًا وَرَسُوْلُ الله

"I testify that there is none worthy of worship but Allah and that Muhammad ﷺ is Allah's Rasul."

Ali 🙐 then gave him the armor as a gift along with 700 Dirhams. The man then faithfully stayed close to Ali 🙐 until he was martyred in the battle of Siffin. *(Hakim, Abu Nu'aym in Hila, Kanzul Ummal)*

The Chapter on the Bay'ah (Pledge of Allegiance)

This chapter highlights how the Sahabah pledged allegiance to Rasulullah ﷺ and to the Khulafa ؓ after Rasulullah ﷺ and the conditions on which they pledged their allegiance.

Pledging Allegiance to Islam: The Hadith of Jareer ؓ in this Regard

Jareer ؓ narrates, "The condition on which we (male Sahabah) pledged allegiance to Rasulullah ﷺ was similar to the conditions on which the females pledged allegiance. (ref. Mumtahina:12). Rasulullah ﷺ guaranteed that any of us would enter paradise if he died without committing any sins. If anyone did commit any sin before dying but served the due Shari'ah punishment, this would be a source of compensation for him. Whoever died after committing any sin but his crime had been kept secret, Allah will decide his case. Allah may then either forgive him or punish him." (Tabrani, Haythami, Kanzul Ummal)

The Pledge of Allegiance that Elders, Youngsters, Men and Women Took on the Day Makkah was Conquered

Aswad ؓ narrates he saw people pledging their allegiance to Rasulullah ﷺ on the day Makkah was conquered. Rasulullah ﷺ sat at a place called Qarn Musqila where people pledged their allegiance to Islam and to the Shahada. The narrator says that he asked his teacher Abdullah bin Uthman, "What is the Shahada?" He replied, "My teacher Muhammad bin Aswad bin Khalaf informed me that Rasulullah ﷺ required the Sahabah to pledge their allegiance to their belief in Allah and to their testimony that there is none worthy of worship but Allah and that Muhammad ﷺ is Allah's servant and Rasul. (Ahmad, Haythami). A narration of Bayhaqi adds that everyone from the youngsters to the elders as well as men and women all pledged their allegiance to Islam and to the Shahada at the hands of Rasulullah ﷺ. (Al Bidayah wan Nihayah, Tabrani, Kanzul Ummal)

Mujashi ؓ and His Brother Pledge Allegiance to Islam and Jihad

Mujashi bin Mas'ood ؓ narrates that he and his brother went to Rasulullah ﷺ and he said, "Accept our pledge of allegiance to Hijra." Rasulullah ﷺ said to them, "Hijra to Madinah has finished with those who have already made Hijra, compulsory migration to Madinah no longer exists." Mujashi ؓ asked what was it that he could pledge his allegiance to, Rasulullah ﷺ replied, "Pledge your allegiance to Islam and to Jihad." (Bukhari, Muslim)

Jareer bin Abdullah ؓ Pledges Allegiance to Islam

Ziyad bin Ilaqa narrates that when Mughiera bin Shu'ba ؓ passed away, he heard Jareer bin Abdullah ؓ address the people saying, "I advise you to fear the One Allah Who has no partner and to remain graceful and calm. With these hands of mine I pledged allegiance to Islam at the hands of Rasulullah ﷺ and he specified that always remain a well-wisher for every Muslim. I swear by the Rabb of the Kabah that I wish well for each one of you." He then sought forgiveness from Allah and descended from the pulpit. (Abu Awana, Bukhari). Bayhaqi and others have narrated from Ziyad bin Harith Sudai ؓ that he approached Rasulullah ﷺ and pledged allegiance to Islam. The rest of the Hadith has already been mentioned in the Chapter of Da'wah.

Pledging Allegiance to the Injunctions of Islam: Bashir bin Khasasiya ؓ Pledges Allegiance to Islam, Sadaqa, and Jihad

Bashir bin Khasasiya ؓ narrates that when he approached Rasulullah ﷺ to pledge his allegiance, he asked, "O Rasulullah ﷺ! To what should I pledge my allegiance?" Rasulullah ﷺ stretched out his hand and said, "Testify that there is none worthy of worship but Allah and that Muhammad ﷺ is Allah's servant and Rasul. Perform your 5 salats on their times, pay the obligatory zakah, fast during the month of Ramadhan, perform Hajj, and fight in the Path of Allah." Bashir ؓ said, "O Rasulullah ﷺ! I can carry out all of these besides 2 of them. The first is Zakah, as I have only 10 camels. My family needs the camel milk to live on and they are the only beasts we have. The second is fighting in Jihad because I am a timid person. Since people say that the one who flees from the battlefield returns with the wrath of Allah, I fear that when I go to the battle and flee for fear of my life, I shall return with the wrath of Allah." Rasulullah ﷺ then withdrew his hand and shaking his hand said, "O Bashir! By virtue of what deed will you enter paradise without zakah and Jihad?" Bashir then said, "O Rasulullah ﷺ! Extend your hand." When Rasulullah ﷺ did so, Bashir ؓ pledged his allegiance to all the actions. (Tabarani, Abu Nu'aym, Hakim, Bayhaqi, Kanzul Ummal)

Jareer bin Abdullah ؓ Pledges his Allegiance to Islam and Wishes well for Every Muslim

Jareer ؓ narrates that he pledged allegiance at the hand of Rasulullah ﷺ that he would establish salah, pay zakah and wish well for every Muslim. (Ahmad, Kanzul Ummal, Bukhari, Muslim, Tirmidhi, Targheeb wat Tarheeb). Another narration states from Jareer ؓ states that he said, "O Rasulullah ﷺ! Do state the conditions of the pledge for me as you are best aware of the conditions." Rasulullah ﷺ said, "I require you to pledge that you would worship none but the One Allah without ascribing any partners to Him, that you would establish salah, pay zakah, wish every Muslim well and absolve yourself from Shirk." (Ahmad, Nasai in Al Bidayah wan Nihayah, Kanzul Ummal). Another narration states that when Jareer ؓ came to Rasulullah ﷺ, Rasulullah ﷺ asked him to stretch out his hand to pledge his allegiance. Jareer ؓ asked, "On what should I pledge my allegiance?" Rasulullah ﷺ replied, "That you would surrender yourself to Allah and wish well for every Muslim." Jareer ؓ accepted the conditions. Since he was an intelligent man, he said, "O Rasulullah ﷺ! I shall abide by these conditions as far as I am able to do so." This concession was then allowed for everyone after him. (Tabrani in Kanzul Ummal)

Awf bin Malik ؓ and His Companions Pledge Their Allegiance to Islam and That They will not Beg from People

Awf bin Malik Ash'jai ؓ narrates that he was with 7, 8 or 9 persons in the company of Rasulullah ﷺ when he said, "Will you not pledge allegiance to the Rasul of Allah?" When Rasulullah ﷺ repeated this 3 times, they stretched out their hands and pledged their allegiance at the hands of Rasulullah ﷺ. They then asked, "O Rasulullah ﷺ! Now that we have pledged our allegiance, do inform us what the conditions of our pledge are." Rasulullah ﷺ replied, "You have pledged that you will worship Allah without ascribing any partners to Him, that you will perform the 5 salats..." Rasulullah ﷺ whispered another condition, which was, "...that you will not ask anything from people." Awf bin Malik ؓ says that he had seen people from this group who would not ask anyone to pass them their whip which had fallen from their hands as they rode their animals. (Royani, Ibn Jareer in Kanzul Ummal,

Muslim, Trimidhi, Nasai in Targheeb wat Tarheeb)

Thowban ❀ Pledges That He Would Not Ask Anyone for Anything

Abu Umamah ❀ narrates that Rasulullah ﷺ once asked, "Who would like to pledge their allegiance?" Thowban ❀ who was the slave of Rasulullah ﷺ said, "Do accept our pledge of allegiance, O Rasulullah ﷺ." Rasulullah ﷺ said, "Pledge that you would not ask anyone for anything." Thowban ❀ asked, "What will one receive for making this pledge?" Rasulullah ﷺ replied, "Paradise." Thowban then made this pledge with Rasulullah ﷺ. Abu Umamah ❀ says that he saw Thowban ❀ riding amongst a large crowd in Makkah and even when his whip sometimes fell on someone's shoulders and the person would attempt to give it back to him, he would not allow it and would dismount the animal to pick it up himself. *(Tabarani, Ahmed, Nasai)*. Other narrations *(Targheeb wat Tarheeb)* report that Abu Bakr ❀ would also not ask people to pass him his whip when it fell.

Abu Dhar ❀ Pledges Allegiance to 5 Factors

Abu Dhar ❀ narrates that he pledged allegiance at the hands of Rasulullah ﷺ 5 times, that Rasulullah ﷺ took promises from him 7 times and Rasulullah ﷺ made Allah witness over him 7 times that he would never fear the criticism of any critic concerning the commands of Allah. Abul Muthana reports from Abu Dhar ❀ that Rasulullah ﷺ once called him and asked, "Do you wish to pledge allegiance in exchange for paradise?" Abu Dhar ❀ complied and stretched out his hands. Rasulullah ﷺ said that he should never ask anything from anyone. When Abu Dhar ❀ agreed, Rasulullah ﷺ added, "Even if your whip falls from your hand you should not ask anyone to retrieve it but rather dismount and get it yourself." Another narration states that Rasulullah ﷺ said to Abu Dhar ❀ that after 6 days he should think of what would be said to him. On the 7th day, Rasulullah ﷺ told him, "I advise you to adopt Taqwa in privacy and in public. When you do a wrong, immediately carry out a good deed, never ask anyone for anything even if your whip falls from your hand and never accept any trust." *(Ahmad)*

Sahl bin Sa'd ❀ and Other Sahabah Pledge Their Allegiance to Islam

Sahl bin Sa'd ❀ said that he was with Abu Dhar, Ubadah bin Samit, Abu Sa'eed Khudri, Muhammad bin Maslama and a 6th Sahabi when they pledged that they would never be affected by the criticism of any critic when it concerned the commands of Allah. When the 6th person requested to be relieved of the pledge, Rasulullah ﷺ relieved him. *(Kanzul Ummal, Tabrani, Haythami)*. Ubadah bin Samit ❀ narrates that he was with a few leaders of Madinah who pledged their allegiance to Rasulullah ﷺ. He adds that they pledged that they would not ascribe partners to Allah, would not steal, would not fornicate, would not kill a soul whose killing Allah has prohibited unless it is with a warrant, would not plunder and would not be disobedient. They were promised paradise if they would abide by this and if they commit any of these sins, their decision would rest with Allah. *(Muslim)*. Ubadah bin Samit ❀ narrates that they were with Rasulullah ﷺ when he said, "Pledge allegiance at my hand that you will not ascribe any as partner to Allah, that you will not steal, and not fornicate. Whoever fulfils this pledge shall have his reward guaranteed by Allah and whoever commits any of these sins and Allah conceals them without subjecting to the Shari'a, then his matter rests with Allah Who may either punish or forgive him. *(Kanzul Ummal)*.

Ubadah bin Samit ❀ and Other Sahabah Pledged Their Allegiance to Rasulullah ﷺ at Aqaba

Ubadah bin Samit ❀ narrates that they were 11 people when the pledge of allegiance was taken for the first time at Aqaba. He says that because fighting in Jihad was not then compulsory, their pledge was the same that the women took. They pledged that they will not ascribe any partner to Allah, that they will not steal, that they will not fornicate, that they will not come forth with slander which they fabricate before their hands and legs by claiming that their child is another's, that they will not kill their children, and that they will not disobey Rasulullah ﷺ in any good deed that he commands. They were assured that whoever fulfils this pledge shall have his reward guaranteed by Allah and whoever commits any of these sins, his matter rests with Allah Who may, either punish him or forgive him. The same people returned to Makkah next year to again pledge their allegiance. *(Kanzul Ummal, Bukhari, Muslim in Al Bidayah wan Nihayah)*

Pledging Allegiance to Undertake the Hijra: Ya'la bin Munia ❀ Pledges Allegiance on Behalf of his Father

Ya'la bin Munia ❀ narrates that he approached Rasulullah ﷺ the day after Makkah was conquered and said, "O Rasulullah ﷺ! Allow my father to pledge that he will undertake the Hijra." Rasulullah ﷺ said, "I shall rather allow him to pledge his allegiance to Jihad because the compulsory Hijra to Madinah has been terminated on the day Makkah was conquered." The narration of Mujashi ❀ in this regard has already passed at the beginning of this chapter in which he asked Rasulullah ﷺ, "Accept our pledge of allegiance to Hijra." Rasulullah ﷺ said to them, "Hijra to Madinah has finished with those who have already made Hijra the compulsory migration to Madinah no longer exists." The Hadith of Jareer ❀ has also passed in which Rasulullah ﷺ told him to pledge that he would separate himself from Shirk. Rasulullah ﷺ told Jareer ❀ to pledge that he would wish well for every Mu'min and separate himself from the disbelievers. *(Bayhaqi)*

Sahabah Pledge Their Allegiance to Hijra During the Battle of Khandaq

Harith bin Ziyad Sa'idi ❀ narrates that he approached Rasulullah ﷺ during the battle of Khandaq while people were busy pledging their allegiance to Hijra at his hands. Thinking that everyone (residents and nonresidents of Madinah) was being called to take this pledge, Harith ❀ asked, "Will you accept this man's pledge to undertake the Hijra?" "Who is he?" asked Rasulullah ﷺ. Harith ❀ replied, "He is my cousin Howt bin Yazid or Yazid bin Howt according to another narration." Rasulullah ﷺ said, "The pledge to undertake Hijra cannot be taken from you (Ansar). People make Hijra to you while you need not make Hijra towards them. I swear by the Being in Whose control is my life! The person who loves the Ansar until he meets Allah, Allah will love him when He meets him. The person who hates the Ansar until he meets Allah, Allah will hate him when He meets him." *(Ahmad, Bukhari, Abu Nu'aym, Tabrani in Kanzul Ummal, Abu Dawood in Isaba, Haythami)*. Abu Usaid Sa'idi ❀ narrates that when the trench was being dug for the Battle of Khandaq, people came to Rasulullah ﷺ to pledge that they would undertake the Hijra. When Rasulullah ﷺ completed, he said, "O assembly of Ansar! The pledge to undertake Hijra cannot be taken from you, as people make Hijra towards you. The person who loves the Ansar until he meets Allah, Allah shall love him when He meets him. The person who hates the Ansar until he meets Allah, Allah shall hate him when

He meets him." *(Tabrani, Haythami)*

Pledging Allegiance to Assist Others: 70 Sahabah From the Ansar Pledge Their Assistance in the Valley of Aqaba

Jabir ؓ narrates that during the 10 years that Rasulullah ﷺ lived in Makkah after announcing his prophethood, he would visit people at the places where they stayed during the seasons of Hajj. This was at the market places of Ukaz and Majina. He would ask the people, "Who will give me asylum? Who will assist me so that I could propagate the message of my Rabb? Whoever does this shall receive paradise." However, he found none to grant him asylum and assistance. Instead of assisting him, matters reached such a low point that when a person from Yemen or from the Mudhar tribe left for Makkah, the people of his tribe and his relatives would say to him, "Beware that the man from the Quraish does not get you into trouble." People even pointed at Rasulullah ﷺ as he passed between their camps. Jabir ؓ continues, "This situation prevailed until Allah sent us (the Ansar) to him from Yathrib. We offered him asylum and believed in him. Whenever a person from us left for Makkah, he would believe in Rasulullah ﷺ, who would recite the Qur'an to him. He would then return to his family in Madinah and they would all accept Islam by virtue of his Islam. Eventually there was hardly a family from the Ansar that did not have a group of Muslims who made their Islam public." Jabir ؓ says further that they all then discussed with each other saying, "Until when will we leave Rasulullah ﷺ to call on people, to be kicked around in the mountains of Makkah and face the threats of others'?" Consequently, 70 men of the Ansar rode off and met Rasulullah ﷺ during the Hajj season. After agreeing to meet at the valley of Aqaba, they arrived there one-by-one until they were all present. They then asked, "O Rasulullah ﷺ! How much should we pledge allegiance at your hands?" Rasulullah ﷺ replied, "You should pledge that you would always listen and obey instructions whether your hearts are willing or not. You should also pledge that you would spend during times of hardship and ease and that you would command good and forbid evil. In addition to this, you should pledge that you would speak for (the pleasure of) Allah and will not fear the criticism of a critic when it concerns the commands of Allah. You should also pledge that you would assist me and when I come to you, you should protect me as you would protect your own lives, wives and children. If you comply, you shall have Paradise."

The Ansar then stood before Rasulullah ﷺ and As'ad bin Zurarah ؓ, who was among the youngest present there, took hold of Rasulullah ﷺ's hand. According to the narration of *Bayhaqi*, Jabir ؓ said that As'ad ؓ was the youngest after him. As'ad ؓ then said to them, "Take it easy, O people of Madinah! We have undertaken this journey only because we are convinced that he is the Nabi of Allah. Taking him away will signal the enmity of all the Arabs, the killing of the best of you and swords will then make pieces of you. If you people can endure this, then take Rasulullah ﷺ away and you will receive your reward from Allah. However, if you have some fears then leave him and make yourselves clear, this will be a better way of excusing yourselves before Allah." The others said, "Make way, O As'ad! By Allah! We shall never forsake this pledge of allegiance and no one can ever make us do so!" The Ansar then pledged their allegiance to Rasulullah ﷺ. Rasulullah ﷺ took promises from them and informed them of their responsibilities, in exchange for which they would attain Paradise. *(Ahmad, Al Bidayah wan Nihayah, Fathul Bari, Haythami)*

Ka'b bin Malik ؓ narrates that when they (the Ansar)

gathered in the valley of Aqaba, they waited for Rasulullah ﷺ until he arrived with Abbas bin Abdul Muttalib ؓ. Although Abbas ؓ was then still following the religion of his people, he wished to be present with his nephew and take assurances from the Ansar on his behalf. When Rasulullah ﷺ sat down, the first to speak was Abbas ؓ. He said, "O assembly of the Khazraj! As you well know, Muhammad is one of us and we have been shielding him against people who share our opinion about him who have not accepted Islam as we have not. He enjoys respect amongst his people and protection in his city. However, he has made up his mind to move to you and join forces with you. If you feel that you will be able to fulfill the claim you have made to him and that you will protect him from his enemies, then I leave you to your responsibility. On the other hand, if you feel that you may surrender him to his enemies and betray him after he has come to you, then leave him now, for he enjoys respect amongst his people and protection in his city." The Ansar said, "We have heard what you have to say." Addressing Rasulullah ﷺ, they said, "O Rasulullah ﷺ! Take from us whatever promises you need for yourself and for your Rabb." Rasulullah ﷺ addressed them, recited the Qur'an, gave Da'wah towards Allah and encouraged them to be steadfast in Islam. Rasulullah ﷺ then said, "I wish you to pledge that you will protect me just as you would protect you wives and children." Bara bin Ma'rur ؓ took hold of Rasulullah ﷺ's hand and said, "Certainly! I swear by the Being Who has sent you with the truth that we shall definitely protect you just as we protect our families. Do accept our pledge of allegiance. By Allah! We are the children of war and have inherited war from generation to generation." As Bara ؓ spoke, Abul Haytham bit Tayyihan ؓ interrupted by saying, "O Rasulullah ﷺ! We have a long-standing relationship with some people viz. the Jews. We shall now for your sake break this relationship. Could it be that we do this for you and then when Allah gives you victory, you would return to your people and leave us?" Rasulullah ﷺ smiled and said, "My blood is yours, my grave shall be with yours for I am from you and you are from me. I shall fight those whom you fight and make peace with those with whom you make peace."

The Ansar Select 12 Leaders

Ka'b ؓ narrates further that Rasulullah ﷺ said to them, "Send to me 12 leaders from among you who will head your people in all matters." The Ansar then selected 12 leaders who comprised of 9 from the Khazraj tribe and 3 from the Aws tribe. *(Al Bidayah wan Nihayah, Ahmad, Tabrani in Majma'uz Zawa'id, Haythami)*

Abul Haitham ؓ Pledges Allegiance and His Address to His People

Urwa ؓ narrates that amongst the first people to pledge allegiance to Rasulullah ﷺ was Abul Haitham bit Tayyihan ؓ. He said, "O Rasulullah ﷺ! There are pledges and treaties existing between us and others. Could it ever happen that you return to your people after we have broken these relations and fought against there people?" Rasulullah ﷺ smiled and said, "My blood is yours and my grave shall be where your graves lie." Pleased with this response from Rasulullah ﷺ, Abul Haitham ؓ turned to his people and said, "This is truly the Nabi of Allah and I testify to his truthfulness. Today he is in the sacred land and protection of Allah and in the midst of his tribe and family. You should take careful note of the fact that once you take him away with you, the Arabs shall attack you from a united platform. Therefore, if you are ready to fight in the Path of Allah and lose your wealth and children, you may call him to your land for he certainly is the

Nabi of Allah. On the other hand, if you fear that you will be unable to assist him, then say so now." Upon hearing this, the others said, "We accept whatever duties Allah and His Rasul ﷺ entrust us with. O Rasulullah ﷺ! We shall do with our lives as you request. O Abul Haitham ؓ! Leave us to pledge our allegiance to Rasulullah ﷺ." Abul Haitham ؓ said, "I shall be the first to pledge my allegiance." Thereafter, they all followed him. The Hadith continues further. *(Tabrani, Haythami)*

The Statement of Abbas bin Ubadah ؓ When the Bay'ah Took Place

Asim bin Omar bin Qatadah ؓ narrates that when the Ansar gathered to pledge their allegiance to Rasulullah ﷺ, Abbas bin Ubadah bin Nadhla ؓ who belonged to the Ba'lu Salim bin Awf tribe said, "O assembly of the Khazraj! Do you know on what conditions you are pledging allegiance to this man?" When they replied in the affirmative, he said, "You are pledging to wage war against every fair and dark skinned person! If you fear that you will surrender him to his enemies when your wealth starts getting destroyed and your leaders start getting killed, you better leave him now. By Allah! If you do that (desert him later), it would mean disgrace in this world as well as in the Hereafter. However, if you feel that you would be able to fulfill the claim you have made to him despite the destruction of your wealth and the killing of your leaders, you should take him with you. By Allah! This would mean the best for you in this world as well as in the Hereafter." The Ansar confirmed, "We are prepared to take him even though it means the destruction of our wealth and the deaths of our leaders. O Rasulullah ﷺ! What will we gain if we fulfill our pledge?" Rasulullah ﷺ replied by saying, "Paradise." They then asked Rasulullah ﷺ to stretch out his hand and when he did, they pledged their allegiance to him. *(Al Bidayah wan Nihayah)*. According to a narration reported by Abdullah bin Ka'b ؓ, Rasulullah ﷺ said to the Ansar after they had pledged their allegiance, "Leave for your camps." Abbas bin Ubadah ؓ then said, "O Rasulullah ﷺ! I swear by the Being Who has sent you with the truth that if you wish, we shall attack the people at Mina with our swords by tomorrow." Rasulullah ﷺ said, "You have not been commanded to do this. You may however leave for your camps. *(Al Bidayah wan Nihayah)*

Pledge Allegiance to Jihad

Anas ؓ narrates that when Rasulullah ﷺ went to the trench before the Battle of Ahzab early one morning, he found the Muhajir and Ansar digging in the cold because they had no slaves to do the work for them. When he saw the fatigue and hunger they were suffering, he said:

اَللّٰهُمَّ لَا عَيْشَ إِلَّا عَيْشُ الْاخِرَةِ فَاغْفِرْ الْأَنْصَارَ وَالْمُهَاج

"O Allah! There is no life but the life of the hereafter
Do forgive the Ansar and the Muhajirah (the Muhajir)"
In response to this, the Sahabah said: نَحْنُ الَّذِيْ بَايَعُوْا مُحَمَّدَا
"We are those who have pledged allegiance to Muhammad
عَلَى الْجِهَادِ مَا بَقِيْنَا أَبَدَا

Pledged to wage Jihad as long as we are alive" (Bukhari)

The Hadith of Mujashi ؓ has already discussed which states that when Mujashi ؓ asked what was it that he could pledge his allegiance to, Rasulullah ﷺ replied, "Pledge your allegiance to Islam and to Jihad." Similarly, the Hadith of Bashir bin Khasasiyah ؓ has also discussed in which Rasulullah ﷺ said, "O Bashir! By virtue of what deed will you enter Paradise without Zakah and Jihad?" Bashir then said, "O Rasulullah ﷺ! Extend your hand." When Rasulullah ﷺ did so, Bashir ؓ pledged his allegiance to all the actions. In the same regard, the Hadith of

Ya'la bin Muniah ؓ has passed in which he said, "O Rasulullah ﷺ! Allow my father to pledge that he will undertake the Hijra." Rasulullah ﷺ said, "I shall rather allow him to pledge his allegiance to Jihad."

Pledging to Die: Salama bin Akwa ؓ Pledges to Die for Islam

Salama bin Akwa ؓ narrates that after he pledged allegiance to Rasulullah ﷺ, he took shade beneath a tree. When there were fewer people, Rasulullah ﷺ said to him, "O lbn Akwa! Are you not going to pledge allegiance?" When he submitted that he had already pledged allegiance, Rasulullah ﷺ told him to do so again and he pledged allegiance for the 2nd time. The narrator asked Salama ؓ what it was that they pledged, he replied, "Death." *(Bukhari, Muslim, Tirmidhi, Nasai, Bayhaqi)*. Abdullah bin Zaid ؓ reports that during the Battle of Harra in 63CE, someone said to him that people were pledging to die at the hands of Ibn Handhala. Abdullah bin Zaid ؓ said, "None may pledge this after the demise of Rasulullah ﷺ." *(Bukhari, Muslim, Bayhaqi)*

Pledging to Listen and to Obey: The Statement of Ubadah bin Samit ؓ in this Regard

Ubaidullah bin Rafi ؓ narrates that when a few containers of wine arrived from somewhere, Ubadah bin Samit ؓ tore them open. He then said, "We pledged to Rasulullah ﷺ that we would always listen and obey instructions whether our hearts are willing or not. We also pledged that we would spend during times of hardship and ease and that we would command good and forbid evil. In addition to this, we pledged that we would speak for the pleasure of Allah and will not fear the criticism of a critic when it concerns the commands of Allah. We also pledged that we would assist Rasulullah ﷺ and that when he would come to Yathrib, we would protect him as we protect ourselves, our wives and our children. We were promised Paradise in exchange. This was the pledge of allegiance that we made with Rasulullah ﷺ." *(Bayhaqi)*. Ubadah ؓ also reported, "We pledged a wartime pledge at the hands of Rasulullah ﷺ that we will listen and obey instructions regardless of whether we were in difficulty or ease, whether we were willing or unwilling and even if others were given preference over us. We also pledged that we would not wrestle power from those in authority, that we would speak the truth wherever we are and that we would not fear the criticism of a critic when it concerns the commands of Allah." *(Al Bidayah wan Nihayah, Bukhari, Muslim in Targheeb wat Tarheed)*

Jareer bin Abdullah ؓ Pledges to Listen, to Obey and to Wish Well for All Muslims

Ibn Jareer narrates from Jareer ؓ that he pledged to listen, to obey and wish well for all Muslims. *Ibn Jareer* also reports another narration from Jareer ؓ in which he states that he approached Rasulullah ﷺ and said, "May I pledge at your hands that I shall listen and obey whether I am willing or unwilling?" Rasulullah ﷺ asked, "Do you have the ability to do this? Refrain from saying so and say rather that you will do so to the best of your ability." Jareer ؓ then added, "To the best of my ability." Rasulullah ﷺ accepted the pledge together with the pledge to wish well for all Muslims. *(Kanzul Ummal)*. *Abu Dawood* and *Nasai* narrate from Jareer ؓ that he pledged to listen, to obey and wish well for all Muslims. Therefore, whenever Jareer ؓ bought or sold anything, he would say to the opposite person, "The thing I have taken from you is more beloved to me than that which I have given to you, so decide whether you want to proceed with the transaction or not." *(Targheeb wat Tarheeb)*

Utba bin Abd ؓ Pledges Allegiance and Rasulullah ﷺ's Advice to Add the Words "to the Best of My Ability"

Abdullah bin Omar ؓ narrates that whenever the Sahabah pledged to listen and to obey at the hands of Rasulullah ﷺ, he told them to add the clause: "To the best of my ability." *(Bukhari, Nasai, Ibn Jareer in Kanzul Ummal).* Utba bin Abd ؓ narrates that he pledged allegiance to Rasulullah ﷺ 7 times. On 5 occasions he pledged obedience and on 2 he pledged his love. *(Baghwi, Kanzul Ummal).* Anas ؓ says, "With these very (his) hands did I pledged allegiance to Rasulullah ﷺ that I would listen and obey to the best of my ability." *(Kanzul Ummal)*

Women Pledged Their Allegiance: The Ansar Women Pledged Their Allegiance When Rasulullah ﷺ Arrived in Madinah

Ummu Atiya ؓ narrates that all the women of the Ansar gathered in a house when Rasulullah ﷺ arrived in Madinah. Rasulullah ﷺ sent Omar ؓ to them and standing at the door of the house, he greeted the women. After they had replied to his greeting he said, "I am the envoy of Rasulullah ﷺ to you." They responded by saying, "Welcome to Rasulullah ﷺ and to the envoy of Rasulullah ﷺ." He then asked them, "Do you pledge that you will not ascribe any partner to Allah, will not steal, will not fornicate, will not kill your children, will not come forth with slander which you fabricate before your hands and legs by claiming that another man's child is her husband's and that you will not disobey Rasulullah ﷺ in any good deed that he commands you to do?" When the women confirmed that they agreed to the terms, Omar ؓ stretched out his hand from outside the door and all the women stretched out their hands from inside without any of their hands touching Omar ؓ's. He then said, "O Allah! You be Witness." Omar ؓ then instructed the women to take even menstruating women and girls who have just come of age for the Eid salah though they would not join in the salah but would increase the numbers of the Muslims. He also forbade them from following funeral processions and informed them that the Jumu'ah salah was not compulsory for them. The narrator says that when he asked his teacher for the meaning of 'slander' and the phrase *'that they will not disobey you in any good'* *(Mumtahina: 60),* he replied that it referred to screaming and waling when a person died. *(Abu Dawud, Bukhari, Kanzul Ummal)*

Salmah bin Qais ؓ was one of Rasulullah ﷺ's maternal aunts. She belonged to the Banu Adi bin Najjar tribe and had performed salah facing both Qiblas behind Rasulullah ﷺ. She narrates that together with a few ladies from the Ansar, she approached Rasulullah ﷺ and pledged allegiance to him. Rasulullah ﷺ said that they should not ascribe any partner to Allah, not steal, not fornicate, not kill their children, not come forth with slander which they fabricate before their hands and legs by claiming that another man's child is their husbands' and .not disobey him (Rasulullah ﷺ) in any good deed that he commands them to do. Rasulullah ﷺ also added that they should not deceive their husbands. Salmah ؓ says that they then pledged allegiance to these factors and as they were returning, she asked one of the ladies to ask Rasulullah ﷺ what he meant when he said that they should not deceive their husbands. When the lady asked, Rasulullah ﷺ replied, "That the wife takes her husband's money and gives it to another person against the husband's wishes." *(Ahmad, Abu Ya'la, Tabrani, Haythami).*

Uqaila bint Atiq bin Harith ؓ narrates that she, her mother Qarira bint Harith Utwariyyah and other women from the Muhajir approached Rasulullah ﷺ to pledge their allegiance as he was pitching his tent at Abtah. Rasulullah ﷺ asked them to pledge that they would not ascribe partners to Allah together with all the other clauses mentioned in the verse of the Qur'an *(Mumtahina:60).* After accepting all the conditions, the ladies stretched out their hands to affirm the pledge. Rasulullah ﷺ said to them, "I cannot touch the hands of strange women." Rasulullah ﷺ then sought Allah's forgiveness for the ladies. This was their Bay'ah. *(Tabrani, Haythami).* Umayma bint Ruqaiqa ؓ narrates that she approached Rasulullah ﷺ together with a few other ladies to pledge their allegiance. They said, "O Rasulullah ﷺ! We pledge that we shall not ascribe any partner to Allah, not steal, not fornicate, not kill our children, not come forth with slander which we fabricate before our hands and legs by claiming that another man's child is our husbands' and that we shall not disobey you in any good deed that you command us to do." Rasulullah ﷺ added, "To the best of your ability and according to your capability." The ladies commented, "Allah and His Rasul are more merciful towards us than we are to ourselves. Come give us you hand, O Rasulullah ﷺ. Let us now pledge our allegiance to you." Rasulullah ﷺ said, "I cannot shake the hand of a woman. What I say to 100 women is the same as I say to one woman their pledge is confirmed by speech." *(Malik, Ibn Hibban, Tirmidhi in Isabah)*

Umaima bint Ruqaiqa ؓ Pledges Allegiance to Islam

Abdullah bin Amr ؓ narrates that Umayma bint Ruqaiqa ؓ appeared to pledge allegiance to Islam. Rasulullah ﷺ said to her, "I require you to pledge that you shall not ascribe any partner to Allah, not steal, not fornicate, not kill your child, not come forth with slander which you fabricate before your 2 hands and legs, not cry at the death of anyone and not to make a sight of yourself as women used to make sight of themselves during the period of ignorance." *(Tabrani, Nasai, Ibn Majah, Ahmad, Tirmidhi)*

Fatima bint Utba ؓ Pledges Allegiance

Aisha ؓ narrates that Fatima bint Utba bin Rabiah ؓ came to pledge her allegiance at the hand of Rasulullah ﷺ. Rasulullah ﷺ asked her to pledge that she would not ascribe partners to Allah together, will not fornicate, and added all the other clauses mentioned in the verse of the Qur'an *(ref. Mumtahina:60).* Out of modesty, Fatima bin Utba ؓ placed her hand on her head, an act that impressed Rasulullah ﷺ. Aisha ؓ then said to her, "Confirm this, O woman because I swear by Allah that all of us pledged this." She responded by saying, "In that case, I also accept." Rasulullah ﷺ accepted her pledge of allegiance to conform with the verse of the Qur'an. *(Ahmad, Bazzar in Majma'uz Zawa'id)*

Azza bint Khabil ؓ Pledges Allegiance to Rasulullah ﷺ

Azza bint Khabil ؓ approached Rasulullah ﷺ and pledged that she would not fornicate, would not steal, and would not bury her children alive neither in public nor in secrecy. Azza ؓ says, "I knew well what Rasulullah ﷺ meant by publicly burying children alive but I did not ask Rasulullah ﷺ what burying them alive in secrecy meant, neither did he inform me. However, it occurred to me that it refers to spoiling children. By Allah! I shall never spoil any child of mine." *(Tabrani, Haythami)*

Fatima bint Utba ؓ Pledges Allegiance With Her Sister Hind ؓ who was the Wife of Abu Sufyan ؓ

Fatima bint Utba bin Rabiah bin Abdish Shams ؓ narrates that Abu Hudhayfa bin Utba ؓ took her along with (her sister) Hind bint Utba ؓ to Rasulullah ﷺ so that they could pledge their allegiance to him. Rasulullah ﷺ took their promises and then asked Rasulullah ﷺ, "O my cousin! Have you noticed any of these evils or deficiencies in your people?" Abu Hudaifa ؓ said, "Be quiet and make your pledge! It is with these words and conditions that the pledge of allegiance is made. Hind then said, "I shall not pledge to abstain from stealing because I steal from my husband." Then both she and Rasulullah ﷺ held back until Rasulullah ﷺ sent someone to (her husband) Abu Sufyan ؓ to get him to permit her (to take from his possessions without asking permission). Abu Sufyan ؓ permitted her to take from the wet things like foodstuffs but did not permit her to take from the dry things like non-food items such as money and clothing or from luxuries. The 2 ladies then pledged allegiance to Rasulullah ﷺ and said to Rasulullah ﷺ, "There was not a tent that I hated more than your tent and I wished that Allah would destroy it and everything in it. However, I now wish more for your tent than any other that Allah should make it prosperous and full of blessings." Rasulullah ﷺ said, "This should be because I swear by Allah that none of you can have true faith until I am more beloved to him than even his children and parents." *(Hakim)*. Aisha ؓ narrates that when Hind bint Utba ؓ came to pledge allegiance to Rasulullah ﷺ, he looked at her hands and said, "Go and transform your hands by applying henna." After she had applied henna, she returned to Rasulullah ﷺ who said to her, "I ask you to pledge that you will not ascribe any partners to Allah, will not steal and will not commit adultery." She asked, "Does a free woman ever commit adultery?" Rasulullah ﷺ said, "And that you will not kill your children for fear of poverty." "You have not left us any child to kill," she mentioned referring to her children who were killed during fighting against the Muslims. She pledged allegiance and with reference to the 2 gold bangles she wore on her hand, she asked, "What do you say about these 2 bangles?" Rasulullah ﷺ replied, "These are 2 coals from the fire of Hell when zakah is not paid for them." *(Abu Ya'la, Haythami)*

Another famous narration *(Istaba)* states that when Rasulullah ﷺ said, "That you do not commit adultery", she said, "Does a free woman ever commit adultery?" and when Rasulullah ﷺ said, "And that you will not kill your children for fear of poverty", she said, "We grew them up as children and then you killed them when they were big." According to yet another narration *(Ibn Sa'd from Iman Sha'bi)*, when Rasulullah ﷺ said, "That you do not commit adultery", she said, "Does a free woman ever commit adultery?" and when Rasulullah ﷺ said, "And that you will not kill your children for fear of poverty", she said, "It is you who killed them". A similar narration quotes her as saying, "Have you left us any children after the battle of Badr?" Hind said to her husband Abu Sufyan ؓ, "I wish to pledge allegiance to Muhammad ﷺ." Abu Sufyan said, "But I have noticed that you have always been rejecting what he says." She replied, "By Allah! That it true. However, I swear by Allah that before this night I have never seen Allah being worshipped in this Masjid as He deserves to be worshipped. By Allah! The Muslims spent the entire night performing salah standing, bowing down and prostrating." Abu Sufyan ؓ said, "But you have done many things against Islam. Take someone from your people along with you," Hind went to Omar ؓ, who accompanied her and sought permission from Rasulullah ﷺ to allow her in. She entered the presence of Rasulullah ﷺ wearing a veil. Her Bay'ah followed. This narration of admission that she had wasted a great deal of Abu Sufyan ؓ's money, he said, "Whatever she has taken from my wealth is permissible and I have pardoned her." *(Ibn Mandah)*

Ibn Jareer has reported the same narration from Abdullah bin Abbas ؓ in great detail. This narrates, "I permit for you whatever wealth you have taken from me whether it is used up or

still existing." When Rasulullah ﷺ heard this, he recognized who she was. He then smiled and hold of Rasulullah ﷺ's hand and pleaded her case. When Rasulullah ﷺ asked her if she was indeed Hind, she said, "May Allah forgive what has happened in the past." Rasulullah ﷺ then turned away from her towards other women present and continuing with the formal pledge of allegiance, he said, "And will not commit adultery." Hind said, "Does a respectable woman ever commit adultery'?" Rasulullah ﷺ replied, "By Allah! A respectable woman never commits adultery." Rasulullah ﷺ was again interrupted by saying, "It was you who killed them during the Battle of Badr. However, you and they know more." Rasulullah ﷺ completed the Bay'ah by reciting the rest of the verse, "That they will not kill their children, that they will not come forth with slander which they fabricate before their hands and legs, and that they will not disobey their hands and legs, and that they will not disobey you O Rasulullah ﷺ in any good." The narrator says that here Rasulullah ﷺ forbade the women from crying when someone died because during the period of ignorance, during crying women used to tear their clothes, scratch their faces, pull their hair and pray for their own destruction and death. *(Tafseer Ibn Kathir)*. Usaid bin Abi Usaid Barrad narrates from one woman who pledged allegiance to Rasulullah ﷺ that amongst the things that Rasulullah ﷺ asked them to pledge was that they would not disobey him in any good, would not scratch their faces, would not mess up their hair, would not tear their collars and would not pray for destruction. *(Tafseer Ibn Kathir)*

Hasan, Husain, Abdullah bin Abbas, Abdullah bin Ja'far ؓ, Abdullah bin Zubair, and Abdullah bin Ja'far ؓ Pledge Allegiance

Abdullah bin Zubair ؓ and Abdullah bin Ja'far ؓ have stated that they went to pledge their allegiance to Rasulullah ﷺ when they were only 7 years of age. When Rasulullah ﷺ saw the 2 of them, he smiled, stretched out his hands and accepted their pledges. *(Tabrani, Haythami, Muntakhab)*. Hirmas bin Ziyad ؓ narrates that he was still a child when he stretched out his hands to pledge his allegiance to Rasulullah ﷺ but Rasulullah ﷺ did not accept the pledge from him. *(Nasai in Jam'ul Fawa'id)*

The Sahabah Pledge Their Allegiance at the Hands of the Khulafa: The Sahabah Pledge Their Allegiance at the Hand of Abu Bakr ؓ

Muntashir narrates from his father that when the Sahabah pledged their allegiance at the hands of Rasulullah ﷺ, he said that their pledges be solely for the pleasure of Allah and that they pledge to always obey the truth. This was after the revelation of the verse: إِنَّ الَّذِينَ يُبَايِعُونَكَ إِنَّمَا يُبَايِعُونَ اللَّهَ

Verily, those who give pledge to you (O Muhammad ﷺ) they are giving pledge to Allah. (Al-Fath:10)

When Abu Bakr ؓ took the pledge of allegiance from people, he said to them, "You are obliged to honor your pledge to me as long as I am obedient to Allah." Thereafter, the pledge of allegiance that Omar ؓ and those after him took from people was like the pledge that Rasulullah ﷺ took from people. *(Ibn Shahin in Istaba)*. Ibn Afif ؓ narrates that he saw Abu Bakr ؓ accepting the pledge of allegiance from people after the demise of Rasulullah ﷺ. When a group of Sahabah would gather before him, he would say to them, "Do you pledge at my hands that you would listen and obey Allah, His Book and then the Amir?" Only when they agreed to this, Abu Bakr ؓ accepted their pledges of allegiance. Ibn Afif ؓ says further, "It was when I came of age or some time afterwards that I used to stand by Abu Bakr ؓ and memorized the conditions he made with people during their pledge of allegiance. I then approached and started saying, 'I pledge at your hands that I will listen and obey Allah, His Book and then the Amir.' He then looked at me from top to bottom. I guessed that I must have impressed him. (He then accepted my pledge of allegiance) May Allah shower His mercy on him." *(Bayhaqi)*. Abu Safar ؓ narrates that whenever Abu Bakr ؓ sent an army to Sham, he would make them pledge that they would fight with spears if needed and remain steadfast if they encounter a plague. *(Kunzul Ummal)*

The Sahabah Pledge Their Allegiance at the Hand of Omar ؓ

Anas ؓ narrates, "I arrived in Madinah after Abu Bakr ؓ had passed away and Omar ؓ had assumed the post of Khalifah. I said to Omar ؓ, 'Raise your hand so that I may pledge at your hand what I pledged at the hand of your companion i.e. Abu Bakr ؓ; that I will always listen and obey instruction to the best of my ability." *(Ibn Sa'd, Ibn Abi Shaiba, Tayalisi in Kanzul Ummal)*. Umair bin Atiya Laithi ؓ narrates that he went to Omar ؓ and said, "O Ameerul Mu'mineen! Raise your hand - may Allah always keeps it high - so that I may pledge my allegiance at your hand in the manner shown by Allah and His Rasul." Omar ؓ smiled and raised his hand saying, "This pledge gives us some rights over you and gives you some rights over us." Abdullah bin Hakim ؓ says, "With these hands did I pledge to Omar ؓ that I would always listen and obey him." *(Ibn Sa'd in Kanzul Ummal)*.

Delegation from Hamra Pledge Allegiance at the Hand of Uthman ؓ

Saleem Abu Amir ؓ narrates that a delegation from Hamra came to Uthman ؓ and pledged that they would not ascribe anything as partner to Allah, would establish salah, pay zakah, fast during Ramadhan, and forsake the festivities of the fire-worshippers. Uthman ؓ accepted their pledge of allegiance after they had agreed to all these clauses. *(Ahmad in Kanzul Ummal)*

The Letter that Omar ؓ Wrote to Amr bin Al Aas ؓ: The Muslims Pledge Their Allegiance to the Khilafa of Uthman ؓ

Miswar bin Makhrama ؓ narrates that the group of 6 Sahabah that Omar ؓ had appointed to select Khalifa from amongst themselves had gathered and were consulting with each other when Abdur Rahman bin Auf ؓ said to them, "I do not want to compete with you to become the Khalifa. However, if you agree, I shall select one of you on your behalf. The others granted him this privilege, after which the attention of the people was focused on him without anyone paying any attention to the others. Everyone then turned to Abdur Rahman bin Auf ؓ and presented their opinions to him. Finally when the morning after the final night arrived, the people pledged their allegiance to Uthman ؓ. Miswar ؓ says, "Abdur Rahman bin Auf ؓ once came to me after some portion of the night had already passed and knocked at the door until I awoke. He then said to me, 'I see that you were sleeping peacefully. By Allah! I have hardly had any sleep the entire night. Go and call Zubair and Sa'd.' After I had called them and he had consulted with them, he called me and said, 'Call Ali.'

When I had called Ali ؓ, Abdur Rahman ؓ spoke to him in confidence until half the night had passed. When Ali ؓ left Abdur Rahman ؓ, he looked hopeful to become the Khalifa but Abdur Rahman ؓ looked fearful of something about appointing Ali. Abdur Rahman ؓ then asked me to call Uthman ؓ. When I called him, he spoke to him in private until the Mu'adhin separated them with the Fajr Adhan." Miswar ؓ narrates further that after the Fajr salah, the group of 6 Sahabah gathered around the pulpit. Abdur Rahman ؓ then sent for all the Muhajir and Ansar who were present and for the leaders of all the groups that had accompanied Um'ar on that year's Hajj. When everyone had gathered, Abdur Rahman ؓ recited the Shahada and then said, "O Ali! I have looked deeply at the opinions of the people and they all do not see anyone equal to Uthman ؓ. Please do not harbor anything in your heart." Abdur Rahman ؓ then hold Uthman ؓ's hand and said, "I pledge allegiance to you according to manner shown by Allah, His Rasul ﷺ and the 2 Khalifas after him." Abdur Rahman ؓ then pledged his allegiance to Uthman ؓ after which the people pledged; first the Muhajir, followed by the Ansar, the leaders of the armed forces, and then the Muslim public. *(Bukhari, Bayhaqi)*

Hardships for the Pleasure of Allah

This chapter highlights how Rasulullah ﷺ and the Sahabah endured hardships and difficulties, hunger, and thirst to propagate Islam and how they attached little importance to themselves when striving to elevate the word of Allah.

The Comments of Miqdad ؓ Concerning the Conditions Under Which Rasulullah ﷺ was Sent to Propagate Islam

Nufair narrates that they were once sitting with Miqdad bin Aswad ؓ when someone passed by and said, "Blessed are the eyes that saw Rasulullah ﷺ! By Allah! We dearly wish that we had seen what you saw and were present in the gatherings you were present in!" Nufair says that he had heard the man carefully and when Miqdad ؓ became angry, he was surprised because the man had good words to say. Turning to the man, Miqdad ؓ said, "What makes you people wish to be present at a time that Allah made you absent from without you knowing what would have become of you had you been present then? By Allah! There were many people who were present during the time of Rasulullah ﷺ but Allah had thrown then headlong into Hell because they did not accept him and refused to believe him. Will you people rather not thank Allah for being born as people who know only Allah ﷻ as your Rabb and believe in everything that Rasulullah ﷺ brought? You were fortunate that hardships had been borne by people other than yourselves. I swear by Allah, that Allah sent Rasulullah ﷺ as a Rasul during a time that was more difficult was prevalent than any other time in which Allah had sent Ambiya عليهم السلام. It was a time when the succession of Ambiya عليهم السلام had long been paused and when people were steeped in ignorance. People saw no religion better than idol-worship. Rasulullah ﷺ arrived with a criterion (the Qur'an) that differentiated between truth and falsehood and even divided father and son. The situation was so heartbreaking that a believing person whose heart was unlocked to be filled with Iman had to see his father or his son or his brother live as a disbeliever knowing well that whoever enters Hell shall be destroyed. He was therefore unable to experience any coolness (comfort) knowing that his close relative was destined for Hell. It is about this that Allah says in the Qur'an:

رَبَّنَا هَبْ لَنَا مِنْ أَزْوَاجِنَا وَذُرِّيَّاتِنَا قُرَّةَ أَعْيُنٍ

And those who say: "Our Lord! Bestow on us from our wives and our offspring who will be the comfort of our eyes." (Al-Furqan:74) (Abu Nu'aym in Hila, Tabrani, Haythami)

The Comments of Hudhaifa ؓ in this Regard

Muhammad bin Ka'b Qurazi narrates that a person from Kufa once asked Hudhaifa ؓ, "O Abu Abdullah! Did you people see Rasulullah ﷺ and associate with him?" "Yes, my dear nephew," replied Hudhaifa ؓ. The person then asked, "What was it that you people used to do?" Hudhaifa ؓ replied, "By Allah! We used to exert ourselves tremendously." The person then said, "By Allah! Had we been in the time of Rasulullah ﷺ, we would not have allowed him to walk on the earth but we would have carried him on our shoulders." Hudhaifa ؓ said, "My dear nephew! I swear by Allah that I have been with Rasulullah ﷺ during the battle of Khandaq..." He then proceeded to relate the extreme fear, hunger and cold that they had to endure. A narration of Muslim states that Hudhaifa ؓ said to the man. "Is that what you would have done? I have been with Rasulullah ﷺ on the night of the battle of Ahzab when there blew an extremely fierce and icy wind." He then proceeded to relate the entire

incident. The narration of *Hakim and Bayhaqi* states that Hudhaifa ؓ said to the man, "Do not wish for that." He mentioned details as will appear in the chapter discussing the fear that Rasulullah ﷺ and the Sahabah had to endure. *(Ibn Is'haq)*

Rasulullah ﷺ Endures Hardship and Difficulty When Giving Da'wah Towards Allah

Anas ؓ reports that Rasulullah ﷺ said, "I have been harassed for the sake of Allah like no other and I have been threatened for the sake of Allah like no other. 30 consecutive days and nights would pass without enough for me and Bilal to eat. All that we could get was so little that it could be hidden in the armpit of Bilal." *(Ahmad in Al Bidayah wan Nihayah, Tirmidhi, Ibn Hibban, Ibn Majah in Targheeb wat Tarheeb)*

Rasulullah ﷺ Talked to his Uncle When he Thought that he Would Reduce his Support

Aqil bin Abi Talib ؓ narrates that members of the Quraish approached Abu Talib and complained, "Your nephew Rasulullah ﷺ comes to us in our homes and gatherings and tells us things that upset us. So if you have the ability to stop him, please do so." Turning to his son, Abu Talib said, "O Aqil! Would you please look for your cousin and bring him to me." Aqil ؓ says, "I found Rasulullah ﷺ in one of Abu Talib's smaller rooms. As he walked with me, he looked for shade to walk but was unable to find any until he reached Abu Talib." Abu Talib said, "Dear nephew! By Allah! You know well that I am always willing to obey you. Your people have come with the complaint that you visit them in their homes and gatherings and tell them things that upset them. Do you not think that you should stop this?" Raising his eyes to the sky, Rasulullah ﷺ said, "I am unable to forsake the responsibility I have been sent to fulfill just as any of you are unable to control a spark of flame from the sun." Abu Talib said to the members of the Quraish still present there, "I swear by Allah that my nephew never lies. You may all return peacefully to your homes." *(Tabrani, Haythami, Bukhari). Bayhaqi* reports that Abu Talib called for Rasulullah ﷺ and told him that the people had come to him and told him many things about what Rasulullah ﷺ was doing. Addressing Rasulullah ﷺ, he said further, "Have mercy on me and on you and do not cast on me a burden that neither of us can bear. Stop telling the people things that they dislike." Hearing this, it crossed Rasulullah ﷺ's mind that his uncle had changed his opinions, that he would stop assisting him, that he would now hand him over to the people, and that he had lost courage in supporting him. Rasulullah ﷺ said, "O my uncle! Even if the sun were placed in my right hand and the moon in my left hand, I would not forsake this work of propagation until Allah makes Islam dominant or I am destroyed in the process." After he said this, his eyes were filled with tears and he began weeping. When Rasulullah ﷺ turned to leave and Abu Talib realized his firm resolve, he called out, "Dear nephew!" When Rasulullah ﷺ turned to him, Abu Talib said, "Continue with your message and do as you please because I swear by Allah that I shall never desert you." *(Al Bidayah wan Nihayah)*

Rasulullah ﷺ's Hardship After his Uncle's Death

Abdullah bin Ja'far ؓ narrates that when Abu Talib passed away, a fool from the Quraish approached Rasulullah ﷺ and threw sand at him. When Rasulullah ﷺ returned home, one of his daughters came to wipe the sand from his face and then began weeping. He said to her, "O beloved daughter! Do not weep for Allah shall protect your father." Amongst other things, he also said to her, "Until Abu Talib passed away, the Quraish dared not do anything unpleasant to me. Now they have started." *(Bayhaqi in Al Bidayah wan Nihayah)*. Abu Hurairah ؓ mentioned that when Abu Talib passed away, the Quraish started treating Rasulullah ﷺ very harshly. Rasulullah ﷺ then said, "O my uncle! I am very quickly feeling your loss." *(Abu Nu'aym in Hilya)*

Rasulullah ﷺ's Harassment From the Quraish and his Response

Harith bin Harith ؓ narrates that he once asked his father, "What is this gathering all about?" His father replied, 'These people have gathered around a nonreligious man from amongst them." Harith ؓ says that when they dismounted they saw that it was Rasulullah ﷺ there calling people towards the Oneness of Allah and towards Iman. However, they were rejecting what he was saying and harming him. The people eventually left him when half the day had passed. A lady whose neck was exposed then came to him with a dish full of water and a cloth. Taking water from the dish, Rasulullah ﷺ drank some and then made wudhu. He then raised his head and said, "Dear daughter! Wear a scarf around you neck and do not fear for your father." Harith says that when they asked who the lady was, people informed them that she was Zainab ؓ, the daughter of Rasulullah ﷺ. *(Tabrani, Haythami)*. Muneeb Azdi ؓ narrates that during the period of ignorance he saw Rasulullah ﷺ saying to the people. "O people! Say 'La Ilaha Illallah' and you will be successful." However, some people spat on his face, some threw sand at him and others swore him. This continued until midday when a girl would come to him with a dish of water. He then washed his face and hands and would say to her, "O beloved daughter! Do not fear that your father will ever be killed suddenly or humiliated." Muneeb ؓ says that when he asked some people who the girl was, they informed him that it was Rasulullah ﷺ's daughter Zainab ؓ. He also adds that she was a very pretty girl. *(Tabrani, Haythami)*. Urwa narrates that he once asked Abul Aas ؓ about the worst thing that the disbelievers did to Rasulullah ﷺ. He said, "When Rasulullah ﷺ was once performing salah in the Hatem of the Kabah, Uqba bin Abi Mu'eet came and placed a cloth around the neck of Rasulullah ﷺ. He then started throttling Rasulullah ﷺ very severely. Abu Bakr ؓ then arrived and grabbing Uqba by the shoulders, pushed him away from Rasulullah ﷺ. Abu Bakr ؓ then recited the following verse of the Qur'an:

أَتَقْتُلُونَ رَجُلًا أَنْ يَقُولَ رَبِّيَ اللَّهُ وَقَدْ جَاءَكُمْ بِالْبَيِّنَاتِ مِنْ رَبِّكُمْ

"Would you kill a man because he says: My Lord is Allah ﷻ and he has come to you with clear signs (proofs) from your Lord? (Ghafir:28)

Amr bin Al Aas ؓ narrates that he had never seen the Quraish try to assassinate Rasulullah ﷺ except on one occasion when a group of them were sitting together and discussing while Rasulullah ﷺ was performing salah near the Maqam of Ibrahim عليه السلام Uqba bin Abi Mu'eet then stood before Rasulullah ﷺ and wrapping his shawl around the Rasulullah ﷺ's neck, he pulled it so hard that Rasulullah ﷺ fell to his knees. The people started shouting and thought that Rasulullah ﷺ had been killed. Abu Bakr ؓ carne running and from the back he grabbed hold of Rasulullah ﷺ under his armpits. He then said, "Will you kill a man for saying, 'Allah is my Rabb'." When the people had left Rasulullah ﷺ, he stood up and continued performing salah. After completing his salah, he passed by the group of Quraish as they sat in the shade of the Kabah. He said to them, "O assembly of Quraish! I swear by the Being Who controls the life of Muhammad that I have come to you for killing the offenders." As he spoke, Rasulullah ﷺ passed his finger across his throat as an indication. Abu Jahal said to Rasulullah ﷺ, "You have never been one to make foolish statements." Rasulullah ﷺ said to him, "You are also amongst them those who will be killed." *(Kanzul Ummal, Abu Ya'la, Tabrani, Haythami)*. Urwa bin Zubair ؓ narrates that he once asked Abdullah bin Amr ؓ, "In venting their enmity, what was the worst that you saw the Quraish do to harm Rasulullah ﷺ?" Abdullah bin Amr ؓ said that he was once with a group of leaders from the Quraish who had gathered in the Hateem. They were saying to each other, "We have never had to tolerate so much as we have tolerated from this man (Rasulullah ﷺ)! He has made fools of our intelligent people, insulted our forefathers, found fault with our religion, disunited our people and abused our gods. We have tolerated him to a very great extent." As they were speaking words like this, Rasulullah ﷺ arrived and walked up to the Black Stone. He then passed by the gathering while performing Tawaf of the Kabah. As he passed by them, they poked fun at him with the things they said. Abdullah bin Amr ؓ says, "I noticed from the face of Rasulullah ﷺ that he felt offended. However, when he passed by them the second time, they again poked fun at him and I again noticed that he felt offended. He continued again without saying anything. However, when they repeated themselves the 3rd time, he said to them, 'Will you not listen, O assembly of Quraish? I swear by the Being Who controls the life of Muhammad that I have come to you for killing.' This statement took such a grip on their hearts that each one of them was stunned motionless. In fact, even the person who had been most harsh towards Rasulullah ﷺ just a moment before, humbly uttered the best words that he could muster when he said, 'O Abul Qasim! Do proceed in peace. By Allah! You have never been one to make foolish statements.' Rasulullah ﷺ then left them." Abdullah bin Amr ؓ says that he was again with them the following day when they gathered in the Hateem. They said to each other, "You have mentioned the hardships you have given him and the problems he has given us but when in reply he told you something you did not like, you left him alone without doing anything." Rasulullah ﷺ arrived as they were busy discussing and they all confronted him together. They surrounded him and, stating everything they had heard about what he said concerning their gods and religion, they asked him whether it was he who had leveled these insults. Rasulullah ﷺ replied, "It was certainly I who said this." Abdullah bin Amr ؓ continues, "I then saw one of them grab hold of Rasulullah ﷺ's collar. Abu Bakr ؓ stood up in defense of Rasulullah ﷺ and was in tears when he said, 'Will you kill a man for saying, 'Allah is my Rabb'?' They then left Rasulullah ﷺ alone. This was the worst that I had seen the Quraish behave against Rasulullah ﷺ. *(Ahmad, Haythami, Bayhaqi in Al Bidayah wan Nihayah)*. Some people once asked Asma bint Abi Bakr ؓ what was worst she had seen the disbelievers do to Rasulullah ﷺ. She replied by saying, "The disbelievers used to sit in the Masjidul Haram to discuss Rasulullah ﷺ and what he had to say about their gods. As they were doing this one day, Rasulullah ﷺ arrived and they all attacked him. The shouts reached my father Abu Bakr as the people called out, 'Help your friend!' As my father left us, I can still clearly remember that his hair had 4 locks and he was saying: أَتَقْتُلُونَ رَجُلًا أَنْ يَقُولَ رَبِّيَ اللَّهُ وَقَدْ جَاءَكُمْ بِالْبَيِّنَاتِ مِنْ رَبِّكُمْ

"Would you kill a man because he says: My Lord is Allah ﷻ and he has come to you with clear signs (proofs) from your Lord? (Ghafir:28) (Bukhari)

The mob then left Rasulullah ﷺ and turned on Abu Bakr ؓ. When he returned to us, he was beaten so badly that merely touching the locks of his hair would cause it to fall off. However, he was saying, 'You are most Blessed, O the Possessor of Majesty and Honor.'" *(Abu Ya'la, Haythami, Ibn Abdil Barr in Isti'ab, Abu Nu'aym in Hilya).* Anas bin Malik narrates that the disbelievers once beat Rasulullah up so badly that he fell unconscious. Abu Bakr then said, "Shame on you people! Will you kill a man for saying, 'Allah is my Rabb'?" When someone asked who he was, the others replied, "He is the madman Abu Bakr." *(Abu Ya'la)* Another narration *(Bazzar, Haythami, Hakim)* states that at this juncture, the people left Rasulullah and attacked Abu Bakr.

The Comment of Ali Concerning the Courage of Abu Bakr to Deliver a Sermon

While addressing the people, Ali once asked, "O people! Who is the most courageous person?" "You are, O Ameerul Mu'mineen," the people submitted. Ali then said, "Although I have defeated everyone who has confronted me, the most courageous person is Abu Bakr. We had constructed a shed for Rasulullah during the battle of Badr and then asked who would remain with Rasulullah so that the disbelievers do not attack him. By Allah! Whenever a Mushrik even drew close to us, Abu Bakr was there with his sword drawn near the head side of Rasulullah. He attacked anyone who dared to attack Rasulullah. He was certainly the bravest of people." Ali continues, "I have seen the Quraish grab hold of Rasulullah with one person treating him angrily and another shaking him while they said to him, 'Do you make all the gods into one?!' By Allah! None of us dared go close to Rasulullah for fear of beating besides Abu Bakr. He would hit one person, wrestle with another and shake someone else as he said, 'Shame on you people! Will you kill a man for saying, 'Allah is my Rabb'?'" Ali lifted the shawl he was wearing and wept until his beard became wet. He then said, "I ask you to swear by Allah whether the Mu'min *(ref. Ghafir: 28-45)* from the court of Fir'oun was better or Abu Bakr." When everyone remained silent, Ali said, "By Allah! A moment of the life of Abu Bakr is better than the earth full of people like the Mu'min from the court of Fir'oun. While the Mu'min from the court of Fir'oun concealed his Iman, Abu Bakr made his Iman public." *(Bazzar in Al Bidayah wan Nihayah, Haythami)*

Some Quraish Leaders Throw the Intestines of an Animal on Rasulullah and Abul Baktari Takes Revenge on his Behalf

Abdullah bin Mas'ood narrates that while Rasulullah was performing salah in the Masjidul Haram, 7 members of the Quraish were sitting in the Hatem. They were Abu Jahal bin Hisham, Shaiba bin Rabiah, Utba bin Rabiah, Uqba bin Abi Mu'eet, Umayyah bin Khalaf and another 2 persons. Whenever Rasulullah went into Sejdah (prostration), he lengthened his Sejdah. Abu Jahal asked the others which of them would volunteer to go to a certain tribe that had slaughtered some camels and bring back the intestines of a camel to throw on Rasulullah. The worst of them who was Uqba bin Abi Mu'eet brought it and threw it on the shoulders of Rasulullah while he was in Sejdah. Abdullah bin Mas'ood says that he stood there watching but was unable to say anything because there was no one there to protect him if the mob would attack him. As he was leaving, the daughter of Rasulullah; Fatima heard about the incident and came there. After she had removed the filth from 'Rasulullah's shoulders, she turned to the members of the Quraish present there and admonished them. None of them were able to give her a reply. Rasulullah then lifted his head as he normally lifted it after completing the Sejdah and when he had

finished his salah, he prayed, "O Allah! You deal with the Quraish; deal with Utba, Uqba, Abu Jahal and Shaiba." Rasulullah made this Du'a 3 times and then left the Masjid. Wearing his whip as a belt, Abul Baktari met Rasulullah. Noticing the disturbed look on Rasulullah's face, he asked, "What is the matter?" Rasulullah said, "Please leave me to myself." Abul Baktari insisted, "Allah knows that I shall never leave you to yourself until you tell me what had happened. Have you been hurt?" When Rasulullah realized that Abul Baktari would not leave him alone, he informed him that the intestines of a camel were thrown on him by the instruction of Abu Jahal. Abul Baktari said, "Come to the Masjid." When Rasulullah and Abul Baktari entered the Masjid, Abul Baktari confronted Abu Jahal and asked, "O Abul Hakam! Is it you who instructed that the intestines of a camel should be thrown on Muhammad'?" When Abu Jahal admitted that he did, Ahul Baktari lifted his whip and hit Abu Jahal on the head. As the people started fighting with each other, Abu Jahal shouted, "Shame on you people! Muhammad wants us to be at loggerheads while he and his companions remain safe." *(Bazzar, Tabrani, Abu Nu'aym in Dala'il).* Bukhari, Muslim, Tirmidhi and others have also reported the incident or Abul Baktari in brief. *Bukhari* states that after they had thrown the intestines on Rasulullah, the disbelievers started laughing so much that they actually fell on top of each other. The narration of *Ahmad* quotes from Abdullah bin Mas'ood that he saw all 7 of these disbelievers killed during the Battle of Badr. *(Al Bidayah wan Nihayah)*

Hamza is Outraged When Abu Jahal Harasses Rasulullah

Yaqub bin Utba narrates that Abu Jahal once approached Rasulullah at Safa and caused him great harm. During those days, Hamza was a keen hunter and was out hunting that day. His wife had seen what Abu Jahal did and when Hamza returned, she said to him, "O Abu Omarah! If only you had seen what that man (Abu Jahal) had done to your nephew!" Hamza was furious and without even entering his home, he proceeded as he was. With his bow still hanging from his shoulders, he entered the Masjidul Haram where he found Abu Jahal sitting in a gathering of the Quraish. Without saying a word, he lifted his bow above Abu Jahal's head and wounded him. When some others members of the Quraish stood up to restrain Hamza, he said, "My religion is the same as that of Muhammad. I testify that he is the Rasul of Allah. I swear by Allah that I shall never budge from this. You may try to stop me if you are true in your religion!" When Hamza accepted Islam, Rasulullah and the Muslims were strengthened and they became more steadfast in their affairs. The Quraish became frightened because they knew that Hamza would be there to protect Rasulullah. *(Tabrani, Haythami).* Muhammad bin Ka'b Qurazi narrates that once when Hamza was returning from doing some archery, a woman met him and told him that his nephew (Rasulullah) had suffered terribly at the hands or Abu Jahal who had sworn at him, hurt him and done many terrible things to him. Hamza asked, "Did anyone see him doing this?" When she informed him that many people had witnessed the incident, he proceeded to a gathering near Safa and Marwa. There he found the gathering still present with Abu Jahal sitting amongst them. Leaning on his bow, Hamza told the people what he had shot with his bow and other things he had done. He then took hold of the bow with both hands and struck Abu Jahal so hard on the middle of his head that the bow broke. He then said, "Take that with a bow. Next time it will be a sword. I testify that he (Muhammad) is the Rasul of Allah who had brought the truth from Allah." The people said, "O Abu Omarah! He insults our gods and although you are better than him, we would never tolerate that even from you. However, O Abu Omarah, you have never been an unpleasant person." *(Tabarani, Haythami, Hakim in Mutadark)*

Abu Jahal Resolves to Harm Rasulullah ﷺ and Allah Humiliates Him

Abbas ؓ narrates that he was once in the Masjidul Haram when Abu Jahal arrived and said, "I have vowed for Allah ﷻ that if I see Muhammad in Sejdah, I will tramp on his neck." Abbas ؓ says, "When I informed Rasulullah ﷺ about this, Rasulullah ﷺ left angrily for the Masjidul Haram and was in such a hurry to get there that instead of using the door, he scaled the wall. I said, 'This is bound to be a horrible day.' I tied my lower garment tightly and followed Rasulullah ﷺ." When Rasulullah ﷺ entered the Masjidul Haram, he recited:

اقْرَأْ بِاسْمِ رَبِّكَ الَّذِي خَلَقَ (1) خَلَقَ الْإِنْسَانَ مِنْ عَلَقٍ (2)

Read! In the Name of your Lord, Who has created (all that exists), has created man from a clot (a piece of thick coagulated blood). (Al-'Alaq:1-2)

Rasulullah ﷺ continued reciting the Surah until he reached the verses referring to Abu Jahal, which read:

كَلَّا إِنَّ الْإِنْسَانَ لَيَطْغَى (6) أَنْ رَآهُ اسْتَغْنَى (7)

Nay! Verily, man (like Abu Jahal) does transgress all bounds (in disbelief and evil deed). Because he considers himself self-sufficient. (Al-'Alaq:6-7)

When someone informed Abu Jahal that Rasulullah ﷺ had arrived, he said, "Do you not see what I see? By Allah! The horizons have been shut before me!" Rasulullah ﷺ went into Sejdah when he had completed reciting the Surah. *(Bayhaqi in Al Bidayah wan Nihayah, Tabrani in Kabir and Awsat, Haythami in Mustadak)*

Tulaib bin Umair ؓ Avenges the Harm that Abu Jahal Caused to Rasulullah ﷺ

Bara bint Abi Tajra narrates that Abu Jahal and few others once approached Rasulullah ﷺ and cause him much harm. Tulaib bin Umair went to Abu Jahal and gave him a blow that wounded his head. When the other disbelievers grabbed hold of Tulaib, Abu Lahab stood up to defend him. When news of the accident reached Arwa ؓ (Tulaib's mother), she exclaimed, "Verily, the best day of Tulaib's life is the day he assisted his cousin (Rasulullah ﷺ)." When Abu Lahab was told that his sister Arwa ؓ had accepted Islam, he came to admonish her. She said, "You should also stand in defense of your nephew because if he dominates, you shall have some choice and if he does not, you will be excused because he is your nephew." Abu Lahab said, "Do we have strength to fight against all the Arabs? Yet he has introduced a religion." *(Ibn Sa'd in Isaba)*

Rasulullah ﷺ Curses Utaiba bin Abi Lahab Because of His Hurt and He is Eventually Killed

Qatada narrates that Rasulullah ﷺ's daughter Ummu Kulsum ؓ was married to Utaiba the son of Abu Lahab. At the same time, Rasulullah ﷺ's other daughter Ruqayya ؓ was married to Abu Lahab's other son Utba. However, she had not yet started living with her husband when Rasulullah ﷺ announced his Nabuwat. Allah then revealed the Surah:

تَبَّتْ يَدَا أَبِي لَهَبٍ وَتَبَّ (1) مَا أَغْنَى عَنْهُ مَالُهُ وَمَا كَسَبَ (2) سَيَصْلَى نَارًا ذَاتَ لَهَبٍ (3) وَامْرَأَتُهُ حَمَّالَةَ الْحَطَبِ (4) فِي جِيدِهَا حَبْلٌ مِنْ مَسَدٍ (5)

Perish the 2 hands of Abu Lahab (an uncle of the Prophet), and perish he! His wealth and his children (etc.) will not benefit him! He will be burnt in a Fire of blazing flames! And his wife too, who carries wood (thorns of Sadan which she used to put on the way of the Prophet (Rasulullah ﷺ), or use to slander him). In her neck is a twisted rope of Masad (palm fibre). (Al Masad:1-5)

Abu Lahab then said to his sons Utba and Utayba, "I shall have nothing to do with you 2 if you do not divorce the daughters of Muhammad ﷺ." Their mother was the daughter of Harb bin Umayyah and she is referred to in the above Surah as "That woman who carries firewood". She said, "My beloved sons! Divorce them for they have forsaken their religion." The sons therefore divorced their wives. After Utaiba divorced, he went to Rasulullah ﷺ and said, "I reject your religion and have divorced your daughter so that you never come to me and I never have to come to you." He then assaulted Rasulullah ﷺ and even tore his upper garment. This occurred when he was bound to leave for Sham on business. Rasulullah ﷺ said, "I pray that Allah unleashes one of his dogs on you." Utaiba then left with a group of traders from the Quraish. When they pitched camp at a place called Zarqa one night, a lion circled their camp. Utaiba said, "May my mother be destroyed! By Allah this lion is certainly going to eat me as Muhammad had mentioned. Ibn Abi Kabsha (Rasulullah ﷺ) has killed me while he is in Makkah and I am in Sham." Ignoring the others, the lion attacked Utaiba and killed him with a single bite. Narrating from Hisham bin Urwa and his father, Zuhair bin Ala states that after circling them that night, the lion left. The traders then slept, placing Utaiba between them all. However, the animal jumped over all of them and bit Utaiba's head off. *(Tabrani, Haythami).*

Rasulullah ﷺ Suffers at the Hands of his 2 Neighbors Abu Lahab and Uqba bin Abi Mu'eet

Rabiah bin Ubaid Dili ؓ once said to the people around him, "I hear you people talking a lot about the difficulties that the Quraish gave Rasulullah ﷺ. I have seen much of this harassment. The house of Rasulullah ﷺ was between those of Abu Lahab and Uqba bin Abi Mu'eet. When Rasulullah ﷺ would return home, he used to find intestines of animals, blood and filth hanging on his door. Removing these with the end of his bow, Rasulullah ﷺ would say, "O Quraish! These are terrible neighbors indeed! *(Bukhari, Muslim).*

Rasulullah ﷺ Endured Pain in Taif

Urwa ؓ narrates from Aisha ؓ the wife of Rasulullah ﷺ that she once asked, "Have you experienced a day more difficult than the day the battle of Uhud was fought?" Rasulullah ﷺ replied, "Although I have experienced tremendous hardship from your people, the worst occurred on the day of Aqaba (Taif) when I presented my case to their chief Ibn Abd Yalil bin Abd Kulal asking him to accept Islam and grant me asylum. However, he refused to accept. I then walked away in great distress and my depression decreased only when I reached Qarn Thalib. When I lifted my head, I saw a cloud shading me. When I looked closer, I noticed Jibra'el عليه السلام in the cloud, he called me saying, 'Your Rabb has certainly heard what your people have said to you and how they responded to you. Allah has sent the angel in charge of the mountains to you so that you may command him as you like.' The angel in charge of the mountains then greeted me and said, 'O Muhammad ﷺ! What Jibra'el عليه السلام said is true. What do you wish? Do you want me to make the 2 mountains meet and crush the people between them?'" Rasulullah ﷺ's reply to him was, "I rather wish that Allah creates people from their progeny who will worship only the One Allah without ascribing any partners to Him." *(Bukhari, Muslim, Nasai)*

Ibn Sihab narrates that after Abu Talib passed away, Rasulullah ﷺ went to Taif hoping that the people there would grant him asylum. There he met 3 leaders of the Thaqif clan who were all brothers. Their names were Abd Yalil, Habib, and Mas'ood who were all the sons of Amr. Rasulullah ﷺ presented his case to them and told them about the disrespectful treatment he received from his people. However, their response was most terrible. *(Fat'hul Bari).* Urwa bin Zubair ؓ narrates that after Abu Talib passed away, the harassment that Rasulullah ﷺ experienced increased tremendously. He then went to the Thaqif tribe in Ta'if, hoping that they would grant him asylum and assist him. There he met 3 chiefs of the Thaqif clan. They were all brothers whose names were Abd Yalil bin Amr, Habib bin Amr, and Mas'ood bin Amr. Rasulullah ﷺ presented his case to them and told them about the torment and disrespectful treatment he received from his people. However, one of them said, "If Allah has sent you with anything at all, I shall steal the covering of the Kabah!" The other said, "By Allah! I shall never speak a word to you again after this! If you are really a Nabi, you are too honorable to speak to me." The 3rd one said, "Was Allah unable to find anyone besides you to make a Nabi?" When news of what the chiefs said to Rasulullah ﷺ spread throughout the town, the people gathered to poke fun at Rasulullah ﷺ. They sat in rows on either side of the road and took stones in their hands. Rasulullah ﷺ was unable to even lift a foot or put it down without them throwing a stone at him. They continued poking fun at him and mocking him. After Rasulullah ﷺ had passed through their rows, he proceeded to one of their vineyards with blood flowing down from his feet. There he took shade beneath some vines and sat down on the ground in great distress and pain. Blood was still running down his feet. In the vineyard, Rasulullah ﷺ saw Utba bin Rabia and Shaiba bin Rabia. However, even though he was suffering tremendous pain and difficulty, he did not want to approach them because he knew the enmity they had for Allah and His Rasul ﷺ. They then sent some grapes to Rasulullah ﷺ with their slave Addas who was a Christian from Nineveh. Addas brought the grapes and placed it in front of Rasulullah ﷺ. When Rasulullah ﷺ recited "In the name of Allah before eating", Addas was amazed. Rasulullah ﷺ asked, "Where are you from, O Addas?" When he informed Rasulullah ﷺ that he was from Nineveh, Rasulullah ﷺ said, "You are from the town of the pious man Yunus bin Matta ﷺ." Addas asked, "How do you know about Yunus bin Matta ﷺ?" Rasulullah ﷺ then informed him what he knew about Yunus ﷺ. It was the nature of Rasulullah ﷺ that he never treated anyone to be inferior to himself and even though Addas was a slave, he conveyed the message of Allah to him. When Addas asked to know more about Yunus ﷺ and told him what had been revealed to him, Addas prostrated to Rasulullah ﷺ. He then started kissing the feet of Rasulullah ﷺ although blood was flowing from them. Utba and his brother Shaiba kept silent when they saw what their slave was doing and when he returned to them, they asked him, "What is the matter with you that you were prostrating before Muhammad and kissing his feet? We have never seen you do this for anyone else." Addas explained, "That is a pious man. The things he told me reminded me of a Nabi that Allah had sent to us by the name of Yunus bin Mata ﷺ. He also told me that he is Allah's Rasul." Utba and Shaiba laughed and said, "Let him not take you away from Christianity because he is a man who deceives." Rasulullah ﷺ then returned to Makkah. *(Abu Nu'aym in Dala'il)*

Another narration states that the people of Ta'if sat in 2 rows along the road of Rasulullah ﷺ and when he passed, he could not even lift a foot or put it down without them throwing stones at him. Because of this, he was covered in blood and by the time he had passed through them, blood flowed down from his feet. A narration of Ibn Is'haq states that after Rasulullah ﷺ had lost all hope of any good coming from them, he stood up and among other things, he said to them, "Although you have done to me what you did, at least do me the favor of not mentioning any of this to my people." Rasulullah ﷺ did not want his people to know about what had happened to him because it would make them confident against him. However they would not do this and the gangsters and slaves amongst them attacked Rasulullah ﷺ. They swore and shouted at him until a large mob gathered against Rasulullah ﷺ and forced him to seek shelter in an orchard belonging to Utba bin Rabiah and Shaiba bin Rabiah, who happened to be there. The gangsters who were chasing him then returned and Rasulullah ﷺ took shade under some grape vines where he sat as Utba and Shaiba looked on. They had already witnessed the treatment he had received from the Ta'if gangsters. The narrator says that among the reports he received was that Rasulullah ﷺ met a woman from the Banu Jamh tribe and said to her, "Your in-laws certainly gave me great difficulty!"

The Du'a Rasulullah ﷺ Made After Leaving Ta'if

Once Rasulullah ﷺ felt that he was safe from the Ta'if mob, he made the following Du'a:

اَللَّهُمَّ اِلَيْكَ اَشْكُوْا ضُعْفَ قُوَّتِي وَقِلَّةَ حِيْلَتِي وَهَوَانِي عَلَى النَّاسِ يَا اَرْحَمَ الرَّحِمِيْنَ اَنْتَ رَبُّ الْمُسْتَضْعَفِيْنَ وَاَنْتَ رَبِّي اِلَى مَنْ تَكِلُنِيْ؟ اِلَى عَدُوٍّ يَّتَجَهَّمُنِي اَمْ اِلَى قَرِيْبٍ مَّلَّكْتَهُ اَمْرِيْ اِنْ لَمْ يَكُنْ بِكَ غَضَبٌ فَلَا اُبَالِي وَلٰكِنَّ عَافِيَتَكَ هِيَ اَوْسَعُ لِيْ اَعُوْذُ بِنُوْرِ وَجْهِكَ الَّذِيْ اَشْرَقَتْ لَهُ الظُّلُمَاتُ وَصَلَحَ عَلَيْهِ اَمْرُ الدُّنْيَا وَالْاٰخِرَةِ اَنْ يَّنْزِلَ بِيْ غَضَبُكَ اَوْ يَحِلَّ بِيْ سَخَطُكَ لَكَ الْعُتْبٰى حَتّٰي تَرْضٰي وَلَاحَوْلَ وَلَا قُوَّةَ اِلَّا بِاللهِ

"O Allah! Only to you do I communicate my weakness, my lack of ingenuity and lack of importance among people. O the most Merciful of those who show mercy, You are certainly the Rabb of the weak and You are my Rabb. To whom shall you hand me over? To an enemy who will treat me harshly or to a near one to whom You shall give control over me? If You are not angry with me, I care for nothing. All I require is that Your protection should be vast enough for me. In the light of Your Countenance by which multitudes of darkness are turned to light and by which the affairs of this world and the Hereafter are remedied, I seek protection from being afflicted by Your wrath and displeasure. The causes of Your displeasure should be removed until You are pleased. There is no power and no might but with Allah."

Addas Who was a Christian Accepts Islam and Testifies that Rasulullah ﷺ is Certainly the Rasul of Allah

When Utba and Shaiba, the 2 sons of Rabiah saw what had happened to Rasulullah ﷺ, their kinship with Rasulullah ﷺ moved them and they said to their Christian slave Addas, "Take a stalk of this grape vine, put it in a plate and take it to that man. Tell him that he should eat it." Addas did as he was told. He took the grapes, placed it in front of Rasulullah ﷺ and told him to eat. When Rasulullah ﷺ put his hand in the plate, he recited "In the name of Allah". Addas looked into Rasulullah ﷺ's face and said, "By Allah! The people of this area do not say such words." Rasulullah ﷺ asked, "From the people of which area do you belong O Addas? What is your religion?" Addas replied, "I am a Christian from the people of Nineveh." Rasulullah ﷺ commented, "You are from the town of the pious man Yunus bin Matta ﷺ." "How do you know about Yunus bin Matta ﷺ?" asked Addas.

"He is my brother. He was a Nabi and I am a Nabi." Addas then bowed in front of Rasulullah ﷺ and kissed his head, hands and feet. One of Rabia's sons said to the other, "He has caused problems for you with your slave." When Addas returned to them, they said to him, "Shame on you, O Addas! What made you that you kissed the head, hands and feet of that man?" Addas replied, "O my master! There is no person on this earth better than that man. He told me things that only a Nabi could know." They said to him, "Shame on you, O Addas! Let him never shift you from your religion because your religion is better than his." *(Al Bidayah wan Nihayah).* Another narration states that Addas said to Rasulullah ﷺ, "I testify that you are the servant and messenger of Allah." *(Istaba).* Aisha ﷺ narrates that her father Abu Bakr ﷺ once said, "If only you had seen Rasulullah ﷺ and me as we climbed up to the cave of Thowr enroute to Madinah! The feet of Rasulullah ﷺ were dripping with blood while I had said, "Rasulullah ﷺ was never used to walking barefoot." *(Ibn Mardway in Kanzul Ummal)*

The Hardship Rasulullah ﷺ Bore During the Battle of Uhud

Anas ﷺ narrates that the canine teeth of Rasulullah ﷺ were broken during the battle of Uhud and he was severely injured on the head. Wiping the blood from his face, he said, "How can a nation be successful when they have injured his head and broken his teeth when he calls them to Allah?!" It was on this occasion that Allah revealed the verse:

لَيْسَ لَكَ مِنَ الْأَمْرِ شَيْءٌ أَوْ يَتُوبَ عَلَيْهِمْ أَوْ يُعَذِّبَهُمْ فَإِنَّهُمْ ظَالِمُونَ (128)

Not for you (O Muhammad ﷺ but for Allah) is the decision; whether He turns in mercy to (pardons) them or punishes them; verily, they are the Zalimun (polytheists, disobedient, and wrong-doers, etc.). (Al-Imran:128) (Bukhari, Muslim, Tirmidhi in Jam'ul Fawa'id)

Abu Sa'eed Khudri ﷺ narrates that when Rasulullah ﷺ sustained an injury to his face during the battle of Uhud, Malik bin Sinan ﷺ turned to him, wiped the wound and then swallowed the blood. Rasulullah ﷺ then said, "Whoever wishes to see someone whose blood is mixed with mine, should look at Malik bin Sinan." *(Tabrani in Jam'ul Fawa'id).* Aisha ﷺ narrates that whenever Abu Bakr ﷺ spoke about the battle of Uhud, he would say, "Every credit for that day goes to Talha." He then continued to explain, "I was the first person to return to the fight after the Muslims were surprised by the enemy attack and I saw someone very fiercely defending Rasulullah ﷺ. I said to myself 'I hope that it would be Talha!' Since I had missed that rewards of defending Rasulullah ﷺ, I wanted him to be a man from my people so that we may have the honor and Talha was from my people. Between the disbelievers and myself there was another person whom I did not recognize. While I was closer to Rasulullah ﷺ, he was running much faster than I could. He turned out to be Abu Ubaidah bin Jarrah. When we reached Rasulullah ﷺ, his canine tooth was already broken and his face was injured when 2 links of his helmet pierced his cheeks. Rasulullah ﷺ said, 'See to your companion!' Rasulullah ﷺ was referring to Talha ﷺ who had become weak due to loss of blood. However, seeing the condition of Rasulullah ﷺ we failed to comply with the instruction and I went to Rasulullah ﷺ to remove the links from his face. Abu Ubaidah ﷺ pleaded to me, 'By the right that I have as your Muslim brother, do leave it to me.' So I left it for him. Because of the pain that it would have caused Rasulullah ﷺ, Abu Ubaidah ﷺ disliked pulling the links out with his hand so he bit hard onto it and pulled out one of the links. However, one of his front teeth fell out in the process. When I motioned to do as he

did, he again pleaded, 'By the right that I have, do leave it to me.' He then repeated what he had done the first time and another front tooth fell out with the link. Abu Ubaidah ﷺ was one of the best looking person without front teeth. After treating Rasulullah ﷺ, we went to Talha ﷺ who had fallen into a ditch. He had suffered 70 odd wounds inflicted by spears, arrows and swords. We then nursed him." *(Tayalist in Al Bidayah wan Nihayah, Shasi, Bazzar, Tabrani, Ibn Hibban, Dar Qutni in Afrad, Abu Nu'aym in Ma'rifa, Kanzul Ummal).*

The Sahaba Endure Hardships and Difficulties When Giving Da'wah Towards Allah: Abu Bakr ﷺ insists on Preaching Islam Openly and is Grievously Hurt After Delivering a Sermon

Aisha ﷺ narrates that on one occasion when 83 companions of got together, Abu Bakr ﷺ asked Rasulullah ﷺ for permission to preach Islam openly. Rasulullah ﷺ said, "O Abu Bakr! We are too few." However, Abu Bakr ﷺ continued insisting until Rasulullah ﷺ gave the permission. The Muslims then scattered in different areas of the Masjidul Haram, each one taking a place amongst his tribesmen. Abu Bakr ﷺ then stood up to deliver a sermon as Rasulullah ﷺ remained seated. This was the very first public sermon dedicated to inviting people towards Allah and His Rasul ﷺ. The disbelievers then attacked Abu Bakr ﷺ and the Muslims wherever they were in the Masjidul Haram and they were beaten very severely. Abu Bakr ﷺ was crushed and beaten most savagely. The wretched Utba bin Rabia started hitting Abu Bakr ﷺ with his shoes that had a sole stuck onto another making them thick and hard. He hit Abu Bakr ﷺ very much and also jumped on his stomach so that the soles actually twisted and the nose of Abu Bakr ﷺ could not be differentiated from his face. The Banu Taym tribe (Abu Bakr ﷺ belonged) came running and pushed the disbelievers away from Abu Bakr ﷺ. They then carried him in a sheet and took him home. By then they were convinced that he would die. The Banu Taym then returned to the Masjidul Haram and announced, "By Allah! We shall definitely kill Utba bin Rabia if Abu Bakr ﷺ dies!" Then they returned to Abu Bakr ﷺ with his father Abu Quhafa and they started talking to Abu Bakr ﷺ to get him to respond. Abu Bakr ﷺ finally spoke after the day had passed and asked, "How is Rasulullah ﷺ?" His people rebuked and criticized him. They then stood up to leave and said to his mother Ummul Khair, "Take care of him and give him something to eat or drink." When his mother was alone with him, she insisted that he eat, but he kept asking, "How is Rasulullah ﷺ?" She said, "I swear by Allah that I have no knowledge about your friend." He said, "Go and ask Ummu Jamil bint Khattab about Rasulullah ﷺ." His mother left to meet Ummu Jamil and asked her, "Abu Bakr ﷺ wants to know from you about Muhammad bin Abdullah." Ummu Jamil responded by saying, "I neither know Abu Bakr nor Muhammad bin Abdullah. However, if you like, I shall go with you to see your son." Ummul Khair agreed and Ummu Jamil accompanied her sit) and extremely ill. Coming closer, Ummu Jamil cried, "By Allah! Those who did this to you must be people of Kufr and sin! I hope that Allah takes revenge from them on your behalf." Abu Bakr ﷺ then asked, "How is Rasulullah ﷺ?" Ummu Jamil said, "Your mother is listening." He said, "You have nothing to fear from her." She then replied, "Rasulullah ﷺ is safe and sound." "Where is he?" Abu Bakr ﷺ asked further. Ummu Jamil said, "He is in the house of Arqam." Abu Bakr ﷺ vowed, "I swear by Allah that I shall neither eat nor drink until I go to Rasulullah ﷺ." The 2 ladies then waited for a time (late at night) when the movement of people had calmed down and people were resting. Giving him support, they then took him to Rasulullah ﷺ.

When he saw Abu Bakr ♦, Rasulullah ﷺ hugged him and kissed him. The other Muslims also hugged him and seeing his battered condition Rasulullah ﷺ took great pity on him. Abu Bakr ♦ said, "May my parents be sacrificed for you, O Rasulullah ﷺ! There is nothing wrong with me except for what that wretch did to my face. This is my mother who has been exceptionally good to me. You are a most blessed person so invite her towards Allah and pray for her. Perhaps Allah shall use you to save her from the Fire of Hell." Rasulullah ﷺ then made Du'a for her and invited her to believe in Allah. She then accepted Islam. For a month, the Muslims who numbered 39 individuals stayed with Rasulullah ﷺ in that house. Hamza bin Abdul Muttalib ♦ (the uncle of Rasulullah ﷺ) accepted Islam on the day that Abu Bakr ♦ was beaten up.

Rasulullah ﷺ Prays for Omar and He Accepts Islam

Rasulullah ﷺ made Du'a for (Allah to guide) Omar ♦ or Abu Jahal bin Hisham. The Du'a was made on a Wednesday and Omar ♦ accepted Islam on Thursday. When Omar ♦ accepted Islam, the Muslims shouted "Allahu Akbar" so loudly that their shout was heard in the upper parts of Makkah. The father of Arqam who was a blind man and a nonbeliever came out of his house saying, "O Allah! Forgive my child Arqam for he has rejected our religion." After accepting Islam Omar ♦ said to Rasulullah ﷺ, "Why should we keep our religion secret when we are on the truth while the false religion of the disbeliever is made public?" Rasulullah ﷺ replied, "We are too few and you have just seen the beating we received." Omar ♦ said, "I swear by the Being that has sent you with the truth that I shall make my Iman known to all the gatherings of nonbelievers which I had been part of before." Omar ♦ then performed Tawaf around the Kabah and passed by the leaders of the Quraish as they watched. Abu Jahal bin Hisham said, "Someone mentioned that you have forsaken your religion?" Omar ♦ declared: وَاَشْهَدُ اَنْ مُحَمَّدًا عَبْدُهُ وَرَسُوْلُهُ

"I testify that there is none worthy of worship but the One Allah Who has no partner and that Muhammad ﷺ is Allah's servant and Rasul."

When the disbelievers got up to assault him, Omar ♦ attacked Utba bin Rabia and after overpowering him bended over him and continued beating him up and poking his fingers in his eyes until Utba screamed. Fearing that Omar ♦ would make their leader blind, the others retreated. Omar ♦ stood up and left Utba once the others had moved away. In the same way, whenever any group approached him to assault, he would grab hold of their leader, would beat him up and threaten to blind him until the others gave up. He then proceeded to all the gatherings he used to frequent as a disbeliever and proclaimed the message of Iman there. After showing his dominance over the disbelievers, Omar ♦ went to Rasulullah ﷺ and said, "May my parents be sacrificed for you! By Allah! You now have no fear. Without any fear or anxiety, I have proclaimed the message of Iman in every gathering I used to frequent as a disbeliever." With Omar ♦ in front of him, Rasulullah ﷺ went with Hamza to the Masjidul Haram where they performed Tawaf of the Kabah and then performed the Zuhr salah without any fear. Thereafter, Rasulullah ﷺ returned to house of Arqam ♦ with the company of Omar ♦. Omar ♦ later left by himself and then Rasulullah ﷺ also left. The most correct opinion is that Omar ♦ accepted Islam only after some Sahabah had migrated to Abyssinia, which was 6 years after Rasulullah ﷺ announced his Prophethood. *(Al Bidayah wan Nihayah, Isaba)*

Abu Bakr ♦ Leaves for Abyssinia When the Muslims Face Intense Harassment and Meets Ibnud Daghina

Aisha ♦ says, "I never knew my parents to be supporter of any religion besides the Deen of Islam. Not a day passed when Rasulullah ﷺ did not visit us every morning and night. When the Muslims were being harassed greatly, my father Abu Bakr decided to migrate to Abyssinia. When he reached a place called Barkul Ghimad, Ibnud Daghina who was the leader of the Qara tribe met him and asked, 'Where are you going, O Abu Bakr?' Abu Bakr ♦ replied, 'My people have exiled me and I intend to travel and worship my Rabb.'" Aisha ♦ narrates further that Ibnud Daghina said, "O Abu Bakr!' A person like you cannot leave and cannot be made to leave. You give people what they cannot find, you maintain family ties, you carry the burdens of others, you entertain guests and you assist in all good avenues. I shall grant you protection; go and worship your Rabb in your town." Ibnud Daghina then returned with Abu Bakr ♦ and he went around to all the leaders of the Quraish telling them, "A person like Abu Bakr ♦ cannot leave and cannot be made to leave. How can you exile a person who gives people what they cannot find, who maintains family ties, who carries the burdens of others, who entertains guests and who assists in all good avenues." The Quraish did not oppose the amnesty that Ibnud Daghina had granted but said to him, "Tell Abu Bakr that he should worship his Rabb in his house, perform his salah there and recite as much of the Qur'an he wishes. However, he should not annoy us by doing this in public because we fear that he would then mislead our women and children." Ibnud Daghina conveyed this message to Abu Bakr ♦. Abu Bakr ♦ then stayed like this. He worshipped Allah in his house, did not perform salah in public and did not recite Qur'an in any house but his own. It then occurred to him that he should construct a Masjid in the courtyard of his house. Here he used to perform salah and recite the Qur'an. The women and children of the disbelievers crowded around to look at him for they were overwhelmed by him. He was a man who wept easily and could not control his eyes when he recited the Qur'an. This development alarmed the leaders of the Quraish and they send for Ibnud Daghina. When Ibnud Daghina met them, they said to him, "We sanctioned the amnesty that you granted to Abu Bakr on condition that he worships his Rabb within the boundary of his house. He has now overstepped the bounds by building a Masjid in the courtyard of his house where he openly performs salah and recites the Qur'an. We greatly fear that he shall mislead our women and children. You better stop him. If he confines the worship of his Rabb to his house, he may do so. However, if he is adamant to do so publicly, ask him to absolve you of your amnesty because we would hate to break our promise to you. We cannot under any circumstances allow Abu Bakr to make things public." Aisha ♦ narrates further that when Ibnud Daghina came to Abu Bakr ♦, he said, "You know well the conditions of the agreement I made with you. You may either confine yourself to these conditions or absolve me of the amnesty I have granted because I would not like to hear the Arabs say that I had broken an agreement I had made with someone." Abu Bakr ♦ said, "I absolve you of the amnesty you have granted and I am pleased with the protection of Allah." The details of the Hadith shall be mentioned in the discussion of Hijrah. *(Bukhari)*

A similar narration of *Ibn Is'haq* states that after leaving Makkah with the intention of migrating, Abu Bakr ♦ was 1 or 2 days journey away when Ibnud (clans of the Qara tribe). When he asked Abu Bakr where he was going, Abu Bakr ♦ replied, "My people have exiled me after harassing me and making things difficult for me." Ibnud Daghina said, "Why should they do this? By Allah! You are the pride of the family, you assist in all good causes, you are always doing good and you give people what they cannot find. Return to Makkah for you are under my protection." Abu Bakr ؓ therefore returned with lbnud Daghina and when they entered Makkah, lbnud Daghina stood beside Abu Bakr ؓ and announced, "O Quraish! I have taken the son of Abu Quhafa into my protection so everyone should treat him well." The people therefore stopped harassing Abu Bakr ؓ. The concluding part of this narration states that lbnud Daghina said, "O Abu Bakr! I did not grant you amnesty so that you may annoy your people. They dislike the place you have adopted in your courtyard and it annoys them. Go into your house and do as you please." Abu Bakr ؓ said, "Should I rather absolve you of your protection and content myself with the protection of Allah?" Ibnud Daghina said, "Do absolve me of the protection I have granted you." When Abu Bakr ؓ absolved Ibnud Daghina, he stood up and announced, "O assembly of the Quraish! The son of Abu Quhafa has absolved me of the protection I have granted him. You may do as you please with him." *(Al Bidayah wan Nihayah)*

Another narration of *Ibn Is'haq* states that after Abu Bakr ؓ gave up the protection that Ibnud Daghina had given him, one of the foolish people from the Quraish who passed him on the way to the Kabah threw some sand on his head. When Walid bin Mughiera or Aas bin Wa'il passed by, Abu Bakr ؓ said to him, "Did you not see what that fool did?" The reply was, "You have done this to yourself." Abu Bakr ؓ then said, "O my Rabb! How tolerant are You! O my Rabb! How tolerant are You! O my Rabb! How tolerant are You! *(Al Bidayah wan Nihayah)*. The narration reported by Asma ؓ has already passed which states, "The shouts reached my father Abu Bakr ؓ as the people called out, 'Help your friend!'. As my father left us, I can still clearly remember that his hair had 4 locks and he was saying:

أَتَقْتُلُونَ رَجُلًا أَنْ يَقُولَ رَبِّيَ اللَّهُ وَقَدْ جَاءَكُمْ بِالْبَيِّنَاتِ مِنْ رَبِّكُمْ

"Would you kill a man because he says: My Lord is Allah, and he has come to you with clear signs (proofs) from your Lord? (Ghafir:28)

The mob left Rasulullah ﷺ and turned on Abu Bakr. When he returned to us, (he was beaten so badly) merely touching the locks of his hair would cause it to fall off. He was saying, 'You are most Blessed, O the Possessor of Majesty and Honor.'"

Omar ؓ Endures Hardships and Difficulties

Abdullah bin Omar ؓ narrates, "When my father Omar ؓ accepted Islam, he asked, 'Which person of the Quraish is the best informant?' When he was told that it was Jamil bin Ma'mar Jumhi, he went to him early in the morning. I followed my father to see what he was doing. Although I was then still a child, I understood everything I saw. When he arrived, Omar ؓ said, 'O Jamil! Do you know that I have accepted Islam and entered into the religion of Muhammad ﷺ?' By Allah! Jamil gave no response and left, pulling his shawl along with him. Omar ؓ followed him and I followed my father." Abdullah bin Omar ؓ narrates further that Jamil arrived at the door of the Masjidul Haram as the people were sitting in their gatherings around the Kabah. He then screamed at the top of his voice, "O assembly of the Quraish! The son of Khattab has become different!" Standing behind him, Omar ؓ said, "He is lying! The fact is that I have accepted Islam and I testify that there is none worthy of worship but Allah and that Muhammad ﷺ is Allah's Rasul." The people then attacked Omar ؓ and they continued fighting him until the sun stood above their heads (midday). Omar ؓ then sat down with exhaustion and the people stood over him. He said, "Do as you please. I swear by Allah that we now number 300 strong and we shall either leave Makkah for you, or you leave it for us." As they were talking, an old man from the Quraish arrived wearing clothes made in Yemen with a striped upper garment. He asked, "What is the matter with you people?" When they told him that Omar ؓ had accepted Islam, he said, "Then stop this. Do you think that the Banu Adi tribe to which he belongs will hand their man over to you just like that? Leave the man alone." Abdullah bin Omar ؓ says, "By Allah! The people then disappeared quickly as if a sheet had been lifted from Omar ؓ. After migrating to Madinah, I once asked my father, 'Dear father! Who was that old man who drove those people away from you in Makkah when they were fighting with you on the day you accepted Islam?' He replied, 'Dear son, that man was Aas bin Wa'il Sahmi.'" *(Ibn Is'haq in Al Bidayah wan Nihayah)*. Another narration quotes Abdullah bin Omar ؓ who says, "As Omar ؓ was sitting at home in fear, As bin Wa'il Sahmi arrived wearing clothing made in Yemen with an upper garment threaded with silk. He belonged to the Banu Sahm tribe who were our allies during the period of ignorance. He asked, 'What is the matter?' Omar ؓ replied, 'Your people want to kill me because I have accepted Islam.' As bin Wa'il said, 'They can do nothing to you for you are in my protection.' I felt safe when he said this. He then left and met with so many people that they filled the valley. When he asked them where they were headed, they replied, 'We want that son of Khattab who has forsaken his religion.' As bin Wa'il said, 'You can do him nothing.' The people dispersed." *(Bukhari)*

Uthman ؓ Endures Hardships and Difficulties

Muhammad bin Ibrahim Taymi narrates that when Uthman bin Affan ؓ accepted Islam, his uncle Hakam bin Abil As bin Umayyah securely bound him in ropes. He then said to Uthman ؓ, "Have you turned away from the faith of your forefathers and turned to a new religion?" I swear by Allah that I shall never release you until you forsake the religion you follow." Uthman ؓ replied, "I swear by Allah ﷻ that I shall never leave it." When Hakam saw how steadfast Uthman ؓ was in his religion, he released him. *(Ibn Sa'd)*

Talha ؓ Endures Hardships and Difficulties

Mas'ood bin Khirash ؓ narrates, "While we were walking between Safa and Marwa, we saw a large group of people following a young man whose arm was in a hanger around his neck. When I asked who the man was, I was told that he was Talha bin Ubaidullah ؓ who had accepted Islam. Behind him was a woman who looked furious and was swearing him. When I asked who the woman was, I was informed that she was his mother Sa'ba bint Khadrami." *(Bukhari)*. Ibrahim bin Muhammad bin Talha narrates that Talha bin Ubaidullah ؓ once told him, "I once visited the fair in Busra in Sham when I heard a monk announce from his monastery, 'Ask the people in this fair if anyone of them is from the Haram.' I said, 'Yes! I am.' He asked, 'Has Ahmad made his appearance yet?' 'Who is Ahmad?' I asked. He replied, 'He is the son of Abdullah and the grandson of Abdul Muttalib.' This is the month when he will make his appearance and he is the last of all the Ambiya. His origin will be from the Haram and the place to which he will migrate will be a place with date orchards and land that is rocky and salty. Beware that others do not beat you to go to him." Talha ؓ says further, "His words affected my heart and I rushed back to Makkah. When I arrived and asked people if anything had developed recently, they replied, 'Yes. Muhammad the son of Abdullah (also known as Al Amin 'the trustworthy') claims that he is a Rasul and the son of Abu Quhafa (Abu Bakr ◈) is following him.' I then went to Abu Bakr ◈ and asked, 'Do you follow this man?' Abu Bakr ◈ replied, 'Yes. Go meet him and follow him because he certainly calls towards the truth.'" When Talha ◈ informed Abu Bakr ◈ about what the monk had said, Abu Bakr took Talha ◈ to Rasulullah ﷺ and he accepted Islam. Rasulullah ﷺ was pleased to hear what the monk had to say. After Abu Bakr ◈ and Talha ◈ had accepted Islam, Naufal bin Khuwaylid bin Adawiyya who was known as the "Lion of the Quraish" captured them both and tied them up with the same rope. Even the Banu Tauym tribe (Abu Bakr ◈ belonged) could not rescue them. Because the 2 were tied together, Abu Bakr ◈ and Talha ◈ were named "The 2 Companions". The narration of *Bayhaqi* states that Rasulullah ﷺ then made the following Du'a: "O Allah! Save us from the evil of Ibn Adawia." *(Hakim in Mustadrak, Al Bidayah wan Nihayah)*

Zubair bin Awam ◈ Endures Hardships and Difficulties

Abul Aswad narrates that Zubair bin Awam ◈ accepted Islam when he was only 8 years of age and migrated to Madinah when he was 18 years old. The uncle of Zubair ◈ used to hang him up in a straw mat and used a fire to make smoke from the bottom. He would then say, "Return to disbelief!" Zubair ◈ used to say, "I shall never be a disbeliever again!" *(Abu Nu'aym in Hilya, Tabraani, Haythami, Hakim in Mustadrak)*. Hafs bin Khalid narrates that an old man from Mosul came to them and said that he had accompanied Zubair bin Awam ◈ on a journey. He said, "We were in a dry land when Zubair ◈ required a bath. He therefore told me to arrange for some privacy, which I did. As he was bathing, my gaze accidentally fell on his body and I noticed his entire body marked by sword wounds. I said, 'By Allah! The scars I have seen on you I have never seen on anyone else.' He asked, 'Did you see them?' 'Yes,' I replied. He responded by saying, 'Every wound of these was sustained with Rasulullah ﷺ in the Path of Allah." *(Abu Nu'aym, Tabrani, Hakim in Mustadrak, Muntakhab, Haythami)*. Ali bin Zaid narrates that someone who saw Zubair ◈ informed him that there were scars resembling eyes on his chest which were made by arrows and spears. *(Abu Nu'aym in Hilya)*.

The Mu'addhin Bilal bin Rabah ◈ Endures Hardships and Difficulties: The First Person to Make his Islam Public with Rasulullah ﷺ

Abdullah bin Mas'ood ◈ narrates that 7 persons were the first to make their conversion to Islam public. These were Rasulullah ﷺ, Abu Bakr ◈, Ammar ◈, his mother Sumayya, Suhaib ◈, Bilal ◈ and Miqdad ◈. While Allah protected Rasulullah ﷺ through his uncle and Abu Bakr ◈ through his tribe, the others were captured by the disbelievers and made to wear coats of steel armor and left to swelter in the sun. Each one of them besides Bilal ◈ was compelled to do as the disbelievers wanted. For the pleasure of Allah, he thought nothing of himself. Since the people regarded him as an inferior being, they used to capture him and hand him over to youngsters who would pull him through the streets of Makkah. He kept saying, "Ahad! Ahad! (Allah is One!)" *(Ahmad, Ibn Majah in Al Bidayah wan Nihayah, Hakim, Abu Nu'aym in Hilya, Kanzul Ummal, Isti'ab)*.

The Hardships Bilal ◈ Endured for the Sake of Allah

A narration of Mujahid states that the other Muslims were made to wear coats of steel armor and then left to bake in the sun.

Therefore they suffered terribly from the combined heat of the sun and the burning armor. When night fell, Abu Jahal would come to them with his spear and start insulting and threatening them. *(Abu Nu'aym in Hilya)*. Another narration of Mujahid states that the disbelievers used to lead Bilal ◈ through the 2 mountains of Makkah with a rope around his neck. *(Ibn Sa'd)*. Urwa bin Zubair ◈ narrates that Bilal ◈ was a slave of a lady from the Banu Jumh tribe. The disbelievers used to torture him on the burning sands of Makkah, making him lie flat on the hot sand and place a heavy rock on his chest so that he should commit shirk. However, he would continuously say, "Ahad! Ahad!" When Waraqa bin Naufal, the cousin of Khadija ◈ would pass by as Bilal ◈ was being tortured, he would say, "Ahad, Ahad, O Bilal (Allah is certainly One). Addressing the disbelievers, he would say By Allah! If you kill this man, I shall definitely make his grave a place of attracting Allah's blessings and mercy." *(Isabah)*. Urwa ◈ narrates that when Waraqa bin Naufal used to pass by Bilal ◈ as he was being tortured and calling out "Ahad" ("Allah is One"), he would say, "Allah is One, O Bilal." Waraqa bin Naufal would then turn to Umayyah bin Khalaf who was responsible for torturing Bilal ◈ and say, "I swear by Allah that if you kill this man, I shall definitely make his grave a place of attracting Allah's blessings and mercy." Eventually, when Abu Bakr ◈ passed by one day as the disbelievers were torturing Bilal ◈, he said to Umayyah, "Do you not fear Allah for what you are doing to this poor man? Until when will you continue?" Umayyah said, "It is you who had landed him into this trouble. You may rescue him from this treatment you are witnessing." Abu Bakr ◈ said, "I am prepared to do so. I have an Abyssinian slave who is stronger than him and more steadfast on your religion. I shall give him to you in exchange for this man." Umayyah accepted the proposal, Abu Bakr said, "You have a deal." Abu Bakr ◈ gave Umayyah the slave and after taking possession of Bilal ◈, set him free. Before migrating to Madinah, Abu Bakr ◈ set free 7 slaves besides Bilal for the pleasure of Allah ﷻ. *(Abu Nu'aym in Hilya)*

A narration of *Ibn Is'haq* states that when the afternoon heat grew intense, Umayyah would take Bilal ◈ outside and throw him down on the burning sands of Makkah. He would then command others to place a heavy rock on the chest of Bilal ◈ and say to him, "You shall be left like this until you die or reject Muhammad and worship Lat and Uzza!" Despite his extreme suffering, Bilal ◈ would continuously say, "Ahad! Ahad!" Speaking about the torture that Bilal ◈ and the others suffered and about how Abu Bakr ◈ freed them because of which Abu Bakr received the title of "Atiq" from Rasulullah ﷺ, meaning "The one freed from Hell" Ammar bin Yasir ◈ used to recite some couplets which mean:

"On behalf of Bilal ◈ and his companions, may Allah abundantly reward Atiq and humiliate Fakih (uncle of Abu Jahal) and Abu Jahal. I shall never forget the night when the 2 of them resolved to hurt Bilal without having a concern for doing the evil that intelligent men.
They tortured him only because of his belief in the Oneness of the Rabb of all creation and because of his statement 'I testify that Allah is my Rabb and my heart is content with this.' 'If they kill me, let them kill me but I shall never associate partners with Ar Rahman because of fear for death' 0 the Rabb of Ibrahim, Yunus, Musa and Isa, rescue me and do not let me be tested by those from the family of Ghalib who continue plunging into deviation who are neither righteous not just" *(Abu Nu'aym in Hilya)*

Rasulullah ﷺ Gives Glad Tidings of Paradise to Ammar and his Family When he Sees Them Being Tortured

Jabir narrates that when Rasulullah ﷺ once passed by Ammar and his family (his parents) as they were being tortured by the disbelievers, he said, "O family of Yasir! Hear the glad tidings that your promised abode shall be Paradise." *(Tabrani, Hakim, Bayhaqi, Ibn Asakir, Haythami).* Uthman narrates that he was once walking with in Bat'ha a rocky area of Makkah when they saw Ammar and his parents being tortured in the sun to make them forsake Islam. Ammar 's father Yasir cried, "O Rasulullah ﷺ! This has been happening forever." Rasulullah ﷺ said, "Be patient, O family of Yasir. O Allah! Forgive the family of Yasir, which You have most certainly already done." *(Hakim, Ibn Asakir, Ahmad, Bayhaqi, Baghawi, Uqaili, Ibn Mandah, Anu Nu'aym, Kanzul Ummal, Ibn Sa'd in Tabaqat)*

Sumayya, the Mother of Ammar ﷺ Becomes the First Martyr in Islam

Abdullah bin Ja'far narrates that when Rasulullah ﷺ once passed by Ammar and his family (his parents) as they were being tortured by the disbelievers, he said, "Be patient, O family of Yasir. Be patient, O family of Yasir for your promised abode is Paradise." *(Hakim Qazwini, Ibn Kalbi).* Kalbi states that Abdullah bin Yasir was being tortured with his brother Ammar and his parents. She was martyred when Abu Jahal pierced his spear into the most private part of her body. Yasir was martyred during the torture and his son Abdullah fell dead when an arrow was fired at him. *(Isabah).* Mujahid stated, "The first martyr was the mother of Ammar who was martyred during the early days of Islam when Abu Jahal pierced his spear into the most private part of her body." *(Al Bidayah wan Nihayah)*

Ammar ﷺ is Tortured Until he is Forced to Utter Words of Kufr While his Heart was Content with Iman

Abu Ubaidah bin Muhammad bin Ammar narrates that the disbelievers captured Ammar and tortured him so brutally that to save his life he was eventually forced to blaspheme against Rasulullah ﷺ and praise the gods of the disbelievers. When he came to Rasulullah ﷺ, Rasulullah ﷺ asked him what happened. He replied, "Happenings have been foul indeed, O Rasulullah ﷺ. The disbelievers continued torturing me so much that I was forced to blaspheme against you and praise their gods. "How is the condition of your heart?" asked Rasulullah ﷺ. Ammar replied, "I find that my heart is content with Iman." Rasulullah ﷺ said, "If the disbelievers repeat their torture, you may repeat what you said to save your life." *(Abu Nu'aym in Hilya, Ibn Sa'd in Tabaqat).* Muhammad bin Ammar narrates that Rasulullah ﷺ met Ammar as he was weeping. Wiping the tears from his face, Rasulullah ﷺ said, "The Disbeliever captured you and immersed you in water so many times that you were forced to say certain things (words of disbelief). Should they do so again, you may say it to them again." Amirul Mu'minin bin Maymon narrates that Rasulullah ﷺ was passing by as the disbelievers used open fire to burn Ammar. Passing his hand over the head of Ammar, Rasulullah ﷺ said, "O fire! Become cool and comfortable for Ammar as you were for Ibrahim." Rasulullah ﷺ informed Ammar that he would not die from the torture but a group of rebels would martyr him. *(Ibn Sa'd in Tabaqat)*

Khabbab bin Arat ﷺ and Omar ﷺ Endure Difficulties and Hardships

Imam Sha'bi narrates that when Khabbab bin Arat ﷺ once came to the gathering of Omar bin Khattab ﷺ, Omar ﷺ made him sit on his own cushion. Omar ﷺ then said, "Besides one man, there is none on the surface of this earth who deserves to occupy this place more than you." "Who is this man, O Amirul Mu'minin'?" asked Khabbab. Omar ﷺ replied, "He is Bilal ﷺ." Khabbab ﷺ said, "He is really not more deserving than me because there were people amongst the disbelievers whom Allah used to protect him while there was none to protect me. I had seen myself on a day when they captured me, lit a fire and then put me to roast in it. A man then placed his foot on my chest and there was only my back to extinguish the fire." Khabbab ﷺ then exposed his back which seemed to be affected by leprosy. *(Ibn Sa'd in Tabaqat, Kanzul Ummal).*

The Torture that Khabbab ﷺ Suffered

Imam Sha'bi narrates that when Omar ﷺ asked Khabbab ﷺ about the tortures he suffered at the hands of the disbelievers, he said, "O Amirul Mu'minin! Take a look at my back." Omar ﷺ says, "I have never before seen anything like it." Khabbab ﷺ then related, "They made a fire for me and after throwing me in there was nothing but the fat on my back to extinguish it." *(Abu Nu'aym in Hilya).* Abu Laila Kindi narrates that when Khabbab ﷺ came to Omar ﷺ, Omar ﷺ told the people to allow him to come to the front and said, "Besides Ammar bin Yasir, there is none on the surface of this earth who deserves to occupy this place more than you." It was on that occasion that Khabbab ﷺ showed Omar ﷺ the scars on his back that were made by the torture that disbelievers put him through. *(Abu Nu'yum, Ibn Sa'd, Ibn Shaiba in Kanzul Ummal).*

Khabbab ﷺ says, "I was a blacksmith and As bin Wa'il owed me some money. When I approached him to settle the debt, he said, 'By Allah! I shall never pay you until you reject Muhammad!' I responded by saying, 'Never! I swear by Allah that I shall never reject Muhammad ﷺ even after you die and be resurrected!' He said, "Then come to me after I die and resurrect. There I shall have plenty of wealth and children and I shall then pay you. ", It was then that Allah revealed the following verses of the Qur'an:

أَفَرَأَيْتَ الَّذِي كَفَرَ بِآيَاتِنَا وَقَالَ لَأُوتَيَنَّ مَالًا وَوَلَدًا (77) أَطَّلَعَ الْغَيْبَ أَمِ اتَّخَذَ عِنْدَ الرَّحْمَنِ عَهْدًا (78) كَلَّا سَنَكْتُبُ مَا يَقُولُ وَنَمُدُّ لَهُ مِنَ الْعَذَابِ مَدًّا (79) وَنَرِثُهُ مَا يَقُولُ وَيَأْتِينَا فَرْدًا (80)

Have you seen him who disbelieved in Our Ayat (this Qur'an and Muhammad ﷺ) and (yet) says: "I shall certainly be given wealth and children (if I will be alive (again))," Has he known the unseen or has he taken a covenant from the Most Beneficent (Allah)? Nay! We shall record what he says, and We shall increase his torment (in the Hell); and We shall inherit from him (at his death) all that he talks of (i.e. wealth and children which We have bestowed upon him in this world), and he shall come to Us alone. (Maryam:77-80) (Ahmad in Al Bidayah wan Nihayah, Ibn Sa'd in Tabaqat).

Khabbab ﷺ narrates that he once approached Rasulullah ﷺ as he lay in the shade of the Kabah using a shawl as a pillow. It was a time when the Muslims were suffering terrible torture at the hands of the disbelievers. Khabbab ﷺ asked Rasulullah ﷺ, "Will you not pray to Allah to stop the hardships?" Rasulullah ﷺ sat up straight and his face was red as he said, "Before you there were people whose flesh and tissues were scraped to the bone with iron combs. However, even this did not make them turn away from their religion. Allah will bring this Islam to a completion until a time comes when a lone rider will travel from Sa'a to Hadramaut fearing nothing but Allah and wolves attacking his goats. However, you people want to rush it."

(Bukhari, Abu Dawud, Nasai, Hakim in Mustadrak).

Abu Dhar 🙵 Dispatches his Brother When he Hears About the Prophethood of Rasulullah 🙵

Abdullah bin Abbas 🙵 narrates that when Abu Dhar 🙵 heard that Rasulullah 🙵 was sent as a Rasul, he said to his brother, "Ride to that valley of Makkah and find out for me about the man who claims that he is a Rasul and that revelation comes to him from the heavens. Hear what he has to say and then report back to me." His brother arrived in Makkah, heard what Rasulullah 🙵 said and then reported back to Abu Dhar 🙵 saying, "I saw him teaching excellent character and reciting words that are not poetry." Abu Dhar 🙵 said, "Your report has not informed me what I needed to know."

Abu Dhar 🙵 Arrives in Makkah, Accepts Islam and is then Suffers for the Sake of Allah

Abu Dhar 🙵 took some provisions and a filled waterbag along with him and rode off to Makkah. When he entered the Masjidul Haram, he searched for Rasulullah 🙵 but did not recognize him. He did not want to ask anyone about Rasulullah 🙵 either and when night fell, he lay down to sleep. Ali 🙵 saw him and realized that he was a stranger. Ali 🙵 offered to be his host for the night and Abu Dhar then went with Ali. Neither person asked the other any questions until morning. Abu Dhar 🙵 took his waterbag and provisions along with him to the Masjidul Haram and spent the day there. However, when evening arrived, he had not yet seen Rasulullah 🙵. He had returned to the place where he intended to lie down when Ali 🙵 passed by and said, "Has the man not yet found his destination?" Ali 🙵 then helped him up and took him home without any of them exchanging questions. When things turned out the same on the 3ʳᵈ day and Abu Dhar 🙵 again stayed with Ali 🙵, Ali 🙵 asked, "Will you not tell me what brings you here?" Abu Dhar replied, "I shall inform you if you give me your word that you would give me proper direction." When Ali 🙵 agreed, Abu Dhar 🙵 informed him. Ali 🙵 said, "It is true that he is the Rasul of Allah. Follow me closely tomorrow morning. If I see anything that may jeopardize your safety, I shall stop pretending my need to relieve myself but you should proceed. When I continue walking, you should follow me once more and enter the place I enter. Abu Dhar 🙵 did this and followed in the footsteps of Ali 🙵 until Ali 🙵 came to Rasulullah 🙵 and Abu Dhar 🙵 entered with him. Abu Dhar 🙵 listened to Rasulullah 🙵 and accepted Islam on the spot. Rasulullah 🙵 said to him, "Return to your people and convey the message to them until I send further instructions." Abu Dhar 🙵 said, "I swear by the Being Who controls my life that I shall shout it now aloud amongst them all!" He then proceeded to the Masjidul Haram where he called out at the top of his voice:

اَشْهَدُ اَنْ لَّا اِلٰهَ اِلَّا اللهُ وَاَشْهَدُ اَنَّ مُحَمَّدًا رَّسُوْلُ الله

"I testify that there is none worthy of worship but Allah and that Muhammad 🙵 is Allah's Rasul."

The disbelievers then beat him to the ground. Abbas 🙵 arrived and threw himself over Abu Dhar 🙵 to shield him saying, "Fools! Don't you realize that he belongs to the Ghifar tribe and that your traders have to pass them on the route they use to Sham?!" In this way, Abbas 🙵 saved him. The following day, Abu Dhar 🙵 repeated himself. The disbelievers again assaulted him and Abbas 🙵 had to throw himself over him to save him. (*Bukhari*). Another narration of *Bukhari* states that Abu Dhar 🙵 announced, *"O assembly of Quraish! I testify that there is none worthy of worship but Allah and that Muhammad 🙵 is Allah's servant and Rasul."* The disbelievers shouted, "Get that person who changed!" They then beat him up with the intention of killing him when Abbas 🙵 arrived and threw himself over him. Turning to the people, Abbas 🙵 said, "Fools! You wish to kill a man from the Ghifar when your trade route goes by them and you have to pass by them?!" The people then left Abu Dhar 🙵. Abu Dhar 🙵 narrates further, "The following day I returned and repeated what I had said the previous day. The people again called out, 'Grab that person who changed!' and they did what they had done the previous day. Abbas 🙵 found me there and threw himself over me and again told the people what he had told them the previous day." (*Bukhari*)

Abu Dhar 🙵 is the First Person to Greet Rasulullah 🙵 with the Greeting of Islam

Imam Muslim describes Abu Dhar 🙵's entry into Islam quite differently. He reports from Abu Dhar 🙵 that after his brother returned from Makkah, he said to Abu Dhar 🙵, "I went to Makkah and saw the man whom the people call a changed person. He looks very much like you." Abu Dhar 🙵 says, "When I arrived in Makkah, I saw a person taking his name and asked, 'Where is the changed person?' The man raised his voice above mine and shouted, 'Here is the changed person! Here is the changed person!' The people then started stoning me until I looked like a red idol. The disbelievers used to put blood of sacrifice on the idol during the period of ignorance. I then hid between the Kabah and its covering, where I remained hidden for approximately 15 days and nights without food or drink. All I had to drink was Zamzam water. I then met Rasulullah 🙵 and Abu Bakr 🙵 when they entered the Masjidul Haram one day. By Allah! I was the first person to greet Rasulullah 🙵 with the greeting of Islam when I said:

السَّلامُ عليك يا رسوْلَ الله َ *'Peace be on you, O Rasulullah 🙵.'*

Rasulullah 🙵 replied by saying: وَعليك السَّلامُ وَرحمة الله

'Peace be on you too as well as Allah's mercy.' Rasulullah 🙵 then asked, 'Who are you?' I replied, 'I am a man from the Banu Ghifar tribe.' His companion Abu Bakr 🙵 said, 'O Rasulullah 🙵! Allow me to entertain him for the night.' He then took me home in the lower part of Makkah and brought for me a few handfuls of raisins. Afterwards, I went to my brother and informed him that I had accepted Islam. He said, 'I shall follow your Islam.' We then went to our mother, who also said, 'I shall follow your Islam.' Thereafter, when I invited my people to accept Islam, a few of them did follow me."

The Courage of Abu Dhar 🙵 When he Announced his Conversion to Islam and was Made to Suffer for it

Abu Dhar 🙵 stated that he stayed a while in Makkah with Rasulullah 🙵 who taught him about Islam. He also learnt a part of the Qur'an. He then said, "O Rasulullah 🙵! I wish to declare my Islam in public." Rasulullah 🙵 said, "I fear that you may be killed." Abu Dhar 🙵 insisted, "I have to do it even if I am killed." When Rasulullah 🙵 remained silent, Abu Dhar 🙵 proceeded. The members of the Quraish were sitting in various groups in the Masjidul Haram and talking when Abu Dhar 🙵 announced:

اَشْهَدُ اَنْ لَّا اِلٰهَ اِلَّا اللهُ وَاَشْهَدُ اَنَّ مُحَمَّدًا رَّسُوْلُهُ

"I testify that there is none worthy of worship but Allah 🙵 and that Muhammad 🙵 is Allah's Rasul."

In his own words, Abu Dhar 🙵 narrates, "The groups then broke up and the people beat me up until they left me like a red idol thinking that they had killed me. When I regained consciousness, I went to Rasulullah 🙵 and when he saw my condition, he said, 'Did I not forbid you?' I replied, 'O Rasulullah

! It was a need in my heart that I had to fulfill.' I then remained with Rasulullah ﷺ. One day, Rasulullah ﷺ said to me, 'Go back to your people and come to me when you hear that I am victorious.'" *(Tabrani, Abu Nu'aym in Hilya)*. Another narration quotes that Abu Dhar said, "When I came to Makkah, all the people of the valley turned on me with lumps of earth and bones until I fell unconscious. When I eventually stood up, I looked like a red idol." *(Abu Nu'aym in Hilya, Hakim)*.

Omar ﷺ hits Sa'eed ﷺ and His Wife Fatima ﷺ and then Accepts Islam by Virtue of the Du'a of Rasulullah ﷺ

Qais narrates that in the Masjid of Kufa he heard Sa'eed bin Zaid bin Amr bin Nufail ﷺ say, "By Allah! I saw the time when Omar ﷺ would tie me up in ropes because I had accepted Islam." He then continued to relate the complete account. *(Bukhari)* Another narration states that he said, "If only you had seen me bound in ropes by Omar ﷺ when he was not yet a Muslim because I had accepted Islam." *(Bukhari)*. Anas ﷺ narrates that Omar ﷺ once left home with his sword hanging from his neck when a person from the Banu Zuhra tribe asked him where he was going. He replied, "I intend to kill Muhammad." The man asked, "How will you remain safe from the Banu Hashim and Banu Zuhra tribes who will kill you if you kill him." Omar ﷺ said, "It appears to me that you have also become a changed person and forsaken the religion you had been following." The man said, "Should I not inform you of something even more astonishing?" "What is it?" asked Omar ﷺ. The man replied, "Your sister and brother-in-law have both become changed persons and forsaken the religion that you follow." Omar ﷺ walked away in a rage and when he came to them, someone from amongst the Muhajir called Khabbab ﷺ was with them. When Khabbab ﷺ heard Omar ﷺ approaching, he hid somewhere in the house. When Omar ﷺ arrived, he asked, "What was the whispering I heard?" They had been busy reciting Surah Ta-Ha, but they replied, "It was nothing but something we were discussing." Omar ﷺ said, "It appears that you 2 have become changed persons." His brother-in-law said, "O Omar! What if the truth lies in a religion other than yours?" Omar ﷺ jumped at him and crushed him most violently. When his sister intervened to push him away from her husband, he slapped her so hard that her face started to bleed. She became furious and said, "O Omar! What if the truth lies in a religion other than yours? I testify that there is none worthy of worship but Allah and that Muhammad ﷺ is Allah's Rasul!" Omar ﷺ gave up and said, "Give me that book you have with you so that I may read it." Omar ﷺ was literate. However, his sister said, "You are impure and only pure people may touch it. First take a bath or wash yourself." After washing himself, Omar ﷺ took the book and started reciting Surah Ta-Ha up to the verse: (14) إِنَّنِي أَنَا اللَّهُ لَا إِلَهَ إِلَّا أَنَا فَاعْبُدْنِي وَأَقِمِ الصَّلَاةَ لِذِكْرِي

"Verily! I am Allah! La ilaha illa Ana (none has the right to be worshipped but I), so worship Me, and establish Salat for My Remembrance. (Ta-Ha:14)

Omar ﷺ then said, "Take me to Muhammad ﷺ." When Khabbab ﷺ heard this, he came out from hiding inside the house and said, "Glad tidings for you, O Omar! I have strong hope that the Du'a Rasulullah ﷺ made on Wednesday night was accepted in your favor when he said, 'O Allah! Strengthen Islam with either Omar bin Khattab or Abu Jahal bin Hisham.'" Rasulullah ﷺ was then in a house at the foot of Safa and Omar ﷺ went to the house. At the door of the house were Hamza, Talha and several other Sahabah. When Hamza ﷺ noticed that they were frightened of Omar ﷺ's coming, he said, "Yes, it is Omar. If Allah intends

good for him, he will accept Islam and follow Rasulullah ﷺ. On the other hand, if Allah intends otherwise, it will be easy for us to kill him." At that moment, Rasulullah ﷺ was inside the house and revelation was descending on him. Rasulullah ﷺ then came out of the house and grabbing hold of Omar ﷺ's collar and sword handle, said to him, "When will you stop, O Omar! Are you waiting for Allah to send the humiliation and punishment that he sent to Waled bin Mughiera? O Allah! Here is Omar bin Khattab. O Allah! Strengthen Islam with Omar bin Khattab." Omar ﷺ then said, "I testify that you are the Rasul of Allah." After he had accepted Islam, he told Rasulullah ﷺ to come out of the house and to perform salah openly in the Masjidul Haram. *(Ibn Sa'd, Ibn Is'haq in Al Bidayah wan Nihayah)*

Thowban ﷺ narrates that Rasulullah ﷺ prayed, "O Allah! Strengthen Islam with Omar bin Khattab." Early one night, Omar ﷺ had heard his sister recite: (1) اقْرَأْ بِاسْمِ رَبِّكَ الَّذِي خَلَقَ
Read! In the Name of your Lord, Who has created (all that exists), (Al-'Alaq:1)
He then beat her up so badly that he thought he had killed her. When he awoke before dawn the next morning, he heard her voice again reciting: (1) اقْرَأْ بِاسْمِ رَبِّكَ الَّذِي خَلَقَ
Read! In the Name of your Lord, Who has created (all that exists), (Al-'Alaq:1)
He then said, "I swear by Allah that this is neither poetry nor meaningless whispers." He therefore went to Rasulullah ﷺ and found Bilal ﷺ at the door. When he knocked at the door, Bilal ﷺ asked who he was. When he said that he was Omar bin Khattab ﷺ, Bilal ﷺ told him to wait until he sought permission from Rasulullah ﷺ for him to enter. Bilal ﷺ then said to Rasulullah ﷺ, "Omar bin Khattab is at the door." Rasulullah ﷺ said, "If Allah intends good for Omar, he will enter into Islam." Rasulullah ﷺ permitted Bilal ﷺ to open the door and then grabbed hold of Omar ﷺ's collar and shook him saying, "What do you want? Why have you come?" Omar ﷺ replied, "Present to me what you call people towards." Rasulullah ﷺ said, "You should testify that there is none worthy of worship but the One Allah Who has no partner and that Muhammad is Allah's servant and Rasul." Omar ﷺ accepted Islam on the spot and then told Rasulullah ﷺ to come out of the house and to perform salah openly in the Masjidul Haram. *(Tabrani, Haythami)*.

Omar ﷺ's slave Aslam narrates that Omar ﷺ once asked him, "Do you wish to know about the days when I first accepted Islam?" When Aslam asked to be informed, Omar ﷺ said, "I used to be one of Rasulullah ﷺ's strongest opponents. It was during an extremely hot day in one of the alleys of Makkah when someone saw me and asked where I was going. When I informed him that I was going after Rasulullah ﷺ, he said, 'O son of Khattab! You are saying this when this Islam has entered your very household!' 'What are you saying?' I asked. He explained, 'Even your sister has accepted Islam.' In a rage, I returned and knocked at her door. It was the practice of Rasulullah ﷺ to connect people without any wealth to others who were able to spend on them. There were therefore 2 Sahabah who were bonded in this manner to my sister's husband. When I knocked at the door and was asked to identify myself, I said, 'Omar bin Khattab.' They (the 2 Sahabah with my brother-in-law) had been busy reading a manuscript they had with them and when they heard my voice, they hid somewhere inside the house, forgetting to take the manuscript with them. When my sister opened the door, I shouted, 'O enemy of yourself! Have you become a changed person?' I then lifted something in my hand and hit her on the head. She wept and said, 'O son of Khattab! Do what you like for I have already accepted Islam.' She went in and I took a seat. It was then that I noticed the manuscript by the door. 'What is that manuscript over there?' I asked. My sister replied, 'Keep away from it, O son of Khattab because you do not take the ceremonial bath or clean yourself thoroughly. Only pure people may touch it.' However, I insisted until she gave it to me." The rest of the narration continues. *(Bazzar, Haythami)*

Uthman bin Madh'un ☆ Endures Hardships and Difficulties

Omar ☆ narrates that Uthman bin Madh'un ☆ noticed that while he could walk around in safety under the protection of Walid bin Mughiera ☆, the other Sahabah were suffering great torment. He then said to himself, "There must be a great deficiency in my judgment because my days and nights are spend in safety under the protection of a disbeliever while my companions and members of my religion are suffering torture and hardships." He then went to Walid bin Mughiera ☆ and said to him, "O Abu Abdish Shams!' You have certainly fulfilled your duty, but I wish to absolve you of the protection you have granted me." Walid asked, "Why is it, O nephew? Has one of my people perhaps harmed you?" "No," replied Uthman bin Madh'un ☆, "I prefer rather the protection of Allah and do not want to seek protection from anyone besides Him." Walid ☆ said, "Let us proceed to the Masjidul Haram to announce that I have been absolved of my protection just as I had announced the granting of my protection in the first place." The 2 men proceeded to the Masjidul Haram where Walid announced to the people, "Uthman here has come to absolve me of the protection I had been giving him." Uthman bin Madh'un ☆ then addressed the people saying, "What he says is true. He has been true to his word and an honorable guardian. However, because I prefer not to seek protection from anyone other than Allah, I have absolved him of his protection." Uthman bin Madh'un ☆ was returning when he noticed the famous poet Labid bin Rabiah bin Malik bin Kilab Qaisi reciting poetry to a gathering of the Quraish. Uthman bin Madh'un ☆ sat with them as Labid was reciting a couplet which meant, "Behold! Everything other than Allah has no substance." Uthman bin Madh'un ☆ congratulated him by saying, "That's true." Labid then recited another couplet which meant, "And every bounty must definitely come to an end." To this, Uthman bin Madh'un ☆ commented, "You are mistaken because the bounties of Paradise will never come to an end." Labeed said, "O assembly of Quraish! A person in your company is usually never offended to my poetry before. Since when has this started amongst you'?" Someone in the gathering said, "This person is one of many fools like him who have forsaken our religion. Think nothing of what he says." Uthman bin Madh'un ☆ replied to the man and their dispute became so intense that the man stood up and slapped Uthman bin Madh'un ☆ so hard that his eye was blackened. Watching what had happened from close by, Walid bin Mughiera ☆ said, "Dear nephew! By Allah! Your eye would not have received what it had if you still been in my protection. You were enjoying a secure protection." Uthman bin Madh'un ☆ replied by saying, "True! However, dear Abu Abdish Shams, my good eye is very much in need of what its sister eye received for the sake of Allah. I am now in the protection of One Who is much more honorable and more powerful than you." Concerning what happened to his eye, Uthman bin Madh'un ☆ used to say a few couplets which mean:

"So what if my eye suffered for the pleasure of my Rabb at the hands of an irreligious and misguided person?
Ar Rahman has already granted His rewards in exchange and whoever pleases Ar Rahman is certainly most fortunate

without doubt, even though you call me one who is misguided, astray and a fool, I shall still adhere to the Deen of Muhammad ﷺ.
In this I seek only the pleasure of Allah and our Islam is undoubtedly the truth even though this displeases those who oppress us and who overstep the limits"

Ali bin Abi Talib ☆ composed the following couplets concerning the blackened eye of Uthman bin Madh'un:

"In thinking of times of danger, have you become grieved and weep like a distressed person?
Or do you weep in thinking of foolish people who harshly oppress those who invite towards Islam
These people shall never desist from immoral behavior as long as they remain healthy while deception is way with them and they cannot be trusted
Have you not seen that Allah has reduced the good in them and that we are upset about what happened to Uthman bin Madh'un ☆
When they fearlessly slapped him over the eye persistently taunting and hitting without abate although he did not die instantly, Allah shall certainly punish them measure for measure, they shall be punished without any reduction"
(Abu Nu'aym in Hilya)

A narration of *Ibn Is'haq* states that Walid invited Uthman bin Madh'un ☆ to return to his protection, but Uthman bin Madh'un ☆ refused. *(Al Bidayah wan Nihayah, Haythami)*

Mus'ab bin Umair ☆ Endures Difficulties and Hardships

Muhammad Abdari narrated from his father that Mus'ab bin Umair ☆ was an extremely handsome youth of Makkah whose hair was exceptionally well groomed. His parents loved him dearly. His mother was a very rich and wealthy woman who clothed him in the best and most beautiful clothing. He wore the best perfume in Makkah and shoes made in Hadhramaut (considered the best). When speaking of Mus'ab ☆, Rasulullah ﷺ would say, "I have never seen anyone in Makkah with better hair, finer clothes and enjoying as many bounties as Mus'ab bin Umair." When Mus'ab ☆ heard that Rasulullah ﷺ was inviting people to Islam in the house of Arqam bin Abi Arqam, he went to the house where he accepted Islam and believed in Rasulullah ﷺ. After leaving the house, he kept his conversion a secret for fear of his mother and family. He frequently visited Rasulullah ﷺ in secret but Uthman bin Talha once saw him performing salah and informed his mother and family about it. They therefore captured him and kept him jailed until he finally managed to migrate to Abyssinia with the first group of Muslims immigrants. He later returned to Makkah with the other Muslims but his condition had changed because he lived a difficult life. His mother then stopped rebuking him. *(Ibn Sa'd)*

Abdullah bin Hudhafa ☆ Suffers at the Hands of the Roman Emperor and Omar ☆ Kisses his Head

Abu Rafi narrates that Omar ☆ once dispatched and army to fight the Romans. This army had a Sahabi by the name of Abdullah bin Hudhafa ☆. However, he was taken prisoner and brought before the Roman Emperor. When the soldiers informed the emperor that Abdullah ☆ was one of the companions of Rasulullah ﷺ, the tyrant said, "I shall share my kingdom and my authority with you if you become a Christian." Abdullah ☆ replied, "If you offer me your kingdom coupled with the kingdom of all the Arabs in exchange for leaving Islam of Muhammad ﷺ for a duration equal to the blinking of an eye, still I would not do so." The emperor said, "I shall then have you killed." "Do as you please," said Abdullah ﷺ. The emperor commanded his men to tie Abdullah ﷺ to a cross and then instructed his archers to shoot their arrows close to his hands and then close to his legs without killing/hurting him as the emperor continued telling him to forsake Islam. However, Abdullah ﷺ kept refusing. The emperor then had him untied and commanded his men to fill a big container with water and bring it to a boiling point. 2 Muslim prisoners were then brought and one of them was thrown into the container. After showing him this, the emperor again asked Abdullah ﷺ to become a Christian, but he again refused. The emperor then gave orders that Abdullah ﷺ should be thrown into the container. As Abdullah ﷺ was being led to the container, he began weeping. When the emperor was informed about this, he thought that Abdullah ﷺ was frightened, so he called him back. Again he asked Abdullah to become a Christian, but the offer was again refused. The emperor then asked, "Then what made you weep?" Abdullah ﷺ replied, "I wept when I thought to myself that once I am thrown into the fire, I will be killed instantly. I wish that I had as many lives as the hairs on my body so that each one could be offered for the pleasure of Allah." The tyrant said, "Would you kiss my head in exchange for your freedom?" Abdullah ﷺ asked, "In exchange for all the prisoners?" The emperor agreed, "In exchange for all the prisoners." Abdullah ﷺ said to himself, "Although he is an enemy of Allah, I don't mind kissing his head in exchange for my freedom as well as the freedom of all the Muslim prisoners." Abdullah ﷺ therefore drew closer and kissed his head, after which all the prisoners were handed over to him. Abdullah ﷺ then brought them all back to Omar ﷺ. Omar ﷺ was informed about the events, he said, "It is compulsory for every Muslim to kiss the head of Abdullah bin Hudhafa ﷺ and I shall be the first." Omar ﷺ then stood up and kissed his head so that Abdullah should forget the unpleasant experience of kissing the emperor's head." *(Bayhaqi, Ibn Asakir in Kanzul Ummal, Istaba)*

The Torture the Sahabah suffered at the Hands of the Disbelievers

Sa'eed bin Jubair narrates that he once asked Abdullah bin Abbas ﷺ, "Was the torture that the disbelievers put the Sahabah through so severe that they would have been excused if they had to forsake Islam?" Abdullah bin Abbas ﷺ replied, 'Certainly. By Allah! The disbelievers would beat one of the Muslims up and keep him so hungry and thirsty that he would be unable to even sit up because of his intense suffering. He was eventually forced to do whatever evil they asked him to do. They would torture him so much that he would even agree with them if they told him that Lat and Uzza were deities apart from Allah. In fact, the torture was so harsh that if a beetle was passing and they asked, 'Is this beetle your deity apart from Allah?' he would say. 'Yes.' They were forced to say this to save their lives because the torture was too much to bear." *(Ibn Is'haq in Al Bidayah wan Nihayah)*.

The Condition of Rasulullah ﷺ and the Sahabah after Migrating to Madinah

Ubay bin Ka'b ﷺ says that once Rasulullah ﷺ and the Sahabah arrived in Madinah and were hosted by the Ansar, the Arabs started fighting them from a united platform. They were then forced to carry their weapons day and night. They would say to each other, "Will the time ever come when we can spend the night in peace without having to fear anything besides Allah'?" On this occasion Allah revealed the following verse of the Qur'an:

وَعَدَ اللَّهُ الَّذِينَ آمَنُوا مِنكُمْ وَعَمِلُوا الصَّالِحَاتِ لَيَسْتَخْلِفَنَّهُمْ فِي الْأَرْضِ كَمَا اسْتَخْلَفَ الَّذِينَ

مِن قَبْلِهِمْ وَلَيُمَكِّنَنَّ لَهُمْ دِينَهُمُ الَّذِي ارْتَضَى لَهُمْ وَلَيُبَدِّلَنَّهُم مِّن بَعْدِ خَوْفِهِمْ أَمْنًا يَعْبُدُونَنِي لَا يُشْرِكُونَ بِي شَيْئًا وَمَن كَفَرَ بَعْدَ ذَٰلِكَ فَأُولَٰئِكَ هُمُ الْفَاسِقُونَ (55)

Allah has promised those among you who believe, and do righteous good deeds, that He will certainly grant them succession to (the present rulers) in the earth, as He granted it to those before them, and that He will grant them the authority to practice their religion, that which He has chosen for them (i.e. Islam). And He will surely give them in exchange a safe security after their fear (provided) they (believers) worship Me and do not associate anything (in worship) with Me. But whoever disbelieved after this, they are the Fasiqoon (rebellious, disobedient to Allah). (An-Nur:55) (Ibn Mundhir, Tabrani, Hakim, Ibn Mardway, Bayhaqi, Kanzul Ummal)

Another narration quotes from Ubay bin Ka'b ﷺ that the above verse of the Qur'an was revealed when the Arabs started fighting the Muslims from a united platform once Rasulullah ﷺ and the Sahabah migrated to Madinah and were accommodated by the Ansar. *(Tabrani, Haythami)*.

The Difficulties that Rasulullah ﷺ and the Sahabah Suffered During the Dhatur Riqa Expedition

Abu Musa Ash'ari ﷺ narrates that during one of expeditions they fought with Rasulullah ﷺ and transport was so scarce that 6 people had to take turns riding a camel. He says further that because of walking barefoot on rocky land, their feet were cut and not only were his feet cut, his nails actually fell off. They then had to tie bandages on their feet and it was because of tying these bandages that the expedition was known as Dhatur Riqa ('An expedition of Bandages). *(Ibn Asakir, Abu Ya'la in Kanzul Ummal)*. Another narration from Abu Burda ﷺ states that after narrating the incident, Abu Musa Ash'ari ﷺ said, "I would not have liked to mention this incident." He said this because he disliked that his good deeds should be made known. He would also say, "Allah shall reward this.' *(Abu Nu'aym in Hilya)*.

Enduring Hunger When Inviting People Towards Allah and Rasul ﷺ: Rasulullah ﷺ Suffers Extreme Hunger

Nu'man bin Bashir ﷺ once said, "Do you not enjoy as much food and drink as you like? I have seen your Nabi ﷺ during times when he could not even find poor quality dates to fill his belly. *(Muslim, Tirmidhi)*. In another narration, Nu'man ﷺ narrates that when the Muslims received large amounts of wealth as booty during the Khilafa of Omar ﷺ, Omar ﷺ said to the people, "I have seen Rasulullah ﷺ restless the entire day because he could not even find poor quality dates to fill his stomach." *(Muslim in Targheeb wat Tarheeb, Ahmad, Ibn Sa'd, Ibn Majah, Abu Awana in Kanzul Ummal)*.

A Hungry Person will not Encounter Meticulous Reckoning

Abu Hurairah ﷺ narrates that when he once visited Rasulullah ﷺ, Rasulullah ﷺ was performing salah in a sitting position. He asked, "O Rasulullah ﷺ! What has happened to you that I see you performing salah in a sitting position?" Rasulullah ﷺ replied, "Hunger, O Abu Hurairah." Abu Hurairah ﷺ burst out in tears. Rasulullah ﷺ comforted him by saying, "Do not weep, O Abu Hurairah. Verily the hungry person will not encounter meticulous reckoning on the Day of Judgment if he hopes for reward by enduring the hunger with patience in this world." *(Abu Nu'aym in Hilya, Ibn Asakir, Ibn Najjar in Kanzul Ummal)*.

No Lantern or Fire is Lit in the House of Rasulullah ﷺ

Aisha ﷺ narrates that the family of Abu Bakr ﷺ once sent

the leg of a goat to them. She then held it as Rasulullah ﷺ cut it or it was she who cut it as Rasulullah ﷺ held it. The narrator states that whenever Aisha ؓ narrated this she would add that this was done without using a lantern. *(Ahmad)* Another narration adds that the narrator asked Aisha ؓ, "O Ummul Mu'mineen! Was this done in the light of a lantern?" She replied, "If we had oil to light a lantern, we would have rather ate the oil." *(Tabrani in Targheeb wat Tarheeb, Jareer in Kanzul Ummal)*. Abu Hurairah ؓ says, "Many moons (months) would pass by the wives of Rasulullah ﷺ without any of them being able to light a lantern or make a fire to cook. If they ever got any oil then instead of using it to light a lantern, they would rub it on their bodies and if they ever got any fat, they would eat it." *(Abu Ya'la in Targheeb wat Tarheeb, Haythami)*. Abu Hurairah ؓ says, "The new moon would pass by the family of Rasulullah ﷺ, followed by another new moon (2 months would pass) and still a fire would not be lit in their rooms to bake bread or to cook any food." People asked, "O Abu Hurairah! What was it that they used to live on?" He replied, "2 black things, dates and water. They had Ansar neighbors. May Allah reward them with the best rewards, who owned milk-giving animals and would send them some milk." *(Ahmad, Bazzar, Haythami)*. Urwa ؓ narrates that Aisha ؓ used to say, "Dear nephew! I swear by Allah that we the wives of Rasulullah ﷺ used to look at one new moon go by followed by another and yet another without a fire being lit in the rooms of Rasulullah ﷺ during this period of 2 months with the new moons." Urwa ؓ asked, "Dear aunt! What was it that you lived on?" She replied. "2 black things, dates and water. The only exceptions were the times when the Ansar neighbors of Rasulullah ﷺ who possessed milk-giving animals would send some milk to him, which he would give us to drink." *(Bukhari, Muslim in Targheeb wat Tarheeb, Ibn Jareer, Ahmad, Bazzar in Majma'uz Zawa'id)*. Aisha ؓ narrates that they would spend periods of 40 days without a fire or anything else being lit in the house of Rasulullah ﷺ. The narrator asked, "What was it that you lived on?" She replied, "2 black things, dates and water whenever we could find some." *(Ibn Jareer in Kanzul Ummal)*. Masrooq narrates that he once visited Aisha ؓ and she invited him to share a meal. She then said to him, "Whenever I eat to my fill I cannot fight the urge to cry." "Why is that?" asked Masrooq. Aisha ؓ replied, "Because I think of the condition in which Rasulullah ﷺ left this world. By Allah! There was never a day when Rasulullah ﷺ twice ate his fill with bread or meat." *(Tirmidhi in Targheeb wat Tarheeb)*. Another narration states that Aisha ؓ said, "From the time Rasulullah ﷺ arrived in Madinah until the time he passed away, he was never able to eat barley bread to his fill for 3 consecutive days." Yet another narration from Aisha ؓ states that until Rasulullah ﷺ passed away, the family of Rasulullah ﷺ were never able to fill themselves with bread made of wheat flour for 2 consecutive days. A 3rd narration from the same source quotes the following words of Aisha ؓ: "When Rasulullah ﷺ passed away, he could not fill himself with even the 2 black things, dates and water." *(Ibn Jareer in Kanzul Ummal)*. A narration of *Bayhaqi* states that Aisha ؓ said, "Rasulullah ﷺ never filled himself for 3 consecutive days though we would do so if we pleased because he always preferred others above himself and would give others rather than eat himself." *(Targheeb wat Tarheeb)*.

The Difficult Life of Rasulullah ﷺ

Hasan ؓ says, "Rasulullah ﷺ used to assist people personally and even patch his clothing with pieces of leather. Until his demise, he could never eat both lunch and dinner for 3

consecutive days." *(Ibn Abu Dunya)*. Anas ؓ says that until he passed away, Rasulullah ﷺ never ate on a table and never ate bread made from finely ground flour. Another narration states that Rasulullah ﷺ never even saw a roasted goat - a specially prepared delicacy during those times. *(Bukhari)*. Abdullah bin Abbas ؓ narrates that many consecutive nights would pass by Rasulullah ﷺ when his family would be hungry without anything to eat for dinner. The bread they ate most often was made from barley. *(Tirmidhi)*. Abu Hurairah ؓ once passed by some people who were busy eating a roasted goat. When they invited him to eat, he refused saying, "Rasulullah ﷺ left this world without being able to eat his fill of even barley bread." *(Bukhari, Tirmidhi)*. Anas ؓ narrates that when Fatima ؓ once gave Rasulullah ﷺ piece of barley bread to eat, he said, "This is the first food your father has eaten in 3 days." A narration of *Tabrani* adds that asked, "What is this?" Fatima ؓ said, "I baked a loaf of bread and could not allow myself to eat it until I brought you this piece." Rasulullah ﷺ then told her what is mentioned above. *(Ahmad, Haythami)*. Abu Hurairah ؓ narrates that when some hot food was brought to Rasulullah ﷺ, he ate it and then said, "All praise be to Allah ﷻ. I have not eaten hot food for such a long time." *(Ibn Majah, Bayhaqi)*. Sahl bin Sa'd ؓ says, "From the time Allah instructed Rasulullah ﷺ to announce his prophethood until his demise, Rasulullah ﷺ did not even see fine white flour." When someone asked Sahl ؓ whether there were sifts during the time of Rasulullah ﷺ, he replied, "From the time Allah instructed Rasulullah ﷺ to announce his prophethood until his demise, Rasulullah ﷺ did not even see a sift." Someone asked, "Then how were you able to eat unsifted barley?" He replied, "After grinding the barley, we used to blow on it and whatever could fly away, would fly. The rest we used to make dough." *(Bukhari)*. Aisha ؓ has mentioned that neither a little nor a large amount of barley bread would ever remain behind on the tablecloth of Rasulullah ﷺ. Another narration states that there was never even a small remainder of food on the tablecloth of Rasulullah ﷺ when it was lifted. *(Tabrani, Haythami)*.

Rasulullah ﷺ and the Sahabah Tie Stones to Their Stomachs to Suppress their Hunger

Abu Talha ؓ narrates that the Sahabah once complained of hunger to Rasulullah ﷺ and showed him their stomachs that had stones tied to them. Rasulullah ﷺ then showed them his stomach to which 2 stones were tied. *(Tirmidhi)*. A Sahabi by the name of Ibn Bujair ؓ states that when Rasulullah ﷺ suffered severe hunger one day, he tied a stone to his stomach and said, "Behold! Many are those who eat well and enjoy many bounties in this world, but will be hungry and naked on the Day of Judgment. Behold! Many are those who appear to be generous to themselves by doing things they desire but are actually humiliating themselves because their desires lead them to Hell. Behold! Many are those who appear to be humiliating themselves by suppressing their desires to abide by Allah's commands but are actually being generous to themselves because they are heading for Paradise." *(Ibn Abi Dunya, Khateeb, Ibn Mandah)*.

The Statement of Aisha ؓ Concerning Overeating

Aisha ؓ once said, "The first calamity to occur with this Ummah after the demise of its Nabi ﷺ is overeating because when a nation fills their bellies too much, their bodies become fat, their hearts become weak and their physical desires get out of control." *(Bukhari, Ibn Abi Dunya)*.

Rasulullah ﷺ, Abu Bakr ◉ and Omar ◉ Suffer Extreme Hunger and Meet with Abu Ayub ◉

Abdullah bin Abbas ◉ narrates that when the afternoon heat was at its peak, Abu Bakr ◉ left for the Masjid. Hearing him, Omar ◉ asked, "O Abu Bakr! What has made you leave your house at this hour? Abu Bakr ◉ replied, "It is the extreme pain of hunger that has made me leave home." Omar ◉ said, "By Allah! It is nothing else that has made me leave my home also." As they spoke, Rasulullah ﷺ arrived there and asked, "What has made you 2 leave your homes at this hour'?" "It is the extreme pain of hunger that has made us leave home." Rasulullah ﷺ said, "I swear by the Being Who controls my life! It is nothing else that has made me leave my home." The 3 then went to the door of Abu Ayub ◉ who always used to keep some food or milk aside for Rasulullah ﷺ. However, Rasulullah ﷺ had been late that day and did not arrive at the usual time to receive the food. So Abu Ayub ◉ fed the food to his family and had left to work in his orchard. When they arrived at the door, the wife of Abu Ayub ◉ came and said, "Welcome to the Nabi of Allah and to those with him." When Rasulullah ﷺ asked her where Abu Ayub ◉ was, Abu Ayub ◉ happened to overhear this as he was working in his orchard and came running. Abu Ayub ◉ said, "Welcome to the Nabi ﷺ of Allah ﷻ and to those with him. O Nabi ﷺ of Allah! This is not the time you usually come." "That is true," replied Rasulullah ﷺ. Abu Ayub ◉ then left to cut off a branch of a date palm which contained a variety of ripe dates, juicy dates, and dry dates. Rasulullah ﷺ asked him, "Why have you done this? Why did you not rather select a few ripe dates from the branch'?" Abu Ayub ◉ replied, "O Rasulullah ﷺ! I wanted you to eat from the variety of ripe, juicy and dry dates. Say what you may. I am now going to slaughter an animal to eat with this." Rasulullah ﷺ said, "If you are slaughtering something, do not slaughter a milk-giving animal." Abu Ayub ◉ then slaughtered a young goat and said to his wife, "Make some dough for us and bake some bread as you know better how to bake." Abu Ayub ◉ then cooked half of the goat and roasted the other half. When the food was prepared and placed in front of Rasulullah ﷺ and his companions, Rasulullah ﷺ took a piece of meat and placing it in a piece of bread, said, "O Abu Ayub ◉! Send this to Fatima ◉ because she has not had anything like it for many days." Abu Ayub ◉ took it to Fatima ◉. After they had all eaten to their fill, Rasulullah ﷺ's eyes filled with tears as he said, "Bread, meat, ripe dates, juicy dates, and dry dates. I swear by the Being Who controls my life! These are the bounties about which you will be questioned on the Day of Judgment." Seeing that this statement had a profound effect on his companions, Rasulullah ﷺ added, "When you receive something like this and start eating, recite: بسم الله

'In the name of Allah' and once you have eaten to your fill, recite:

أَحَمْدُ لِلّٰهِ الَّذِيْ هواسبعنا و انعم علينا فافضل

'All praise is due to Allah Who has filled our bellies, showered His bounties on us and granted us plenty.'

Rasulullah ﷺ further told them that reciting this Du'a shall compensate for the food and one will not be questioned about it on the Day of Judgment. When they got up to leave, Rasulullah ﷺ told Abu Ayub ◉ to see him the following day because whenever someone did him a good thing, he liked to repay it. However, Abu Ayub ◉ did not hear what Rasulullah ﷺ said so Omar ◉ told him, "Rasulullah ﷺ commands you to see him tomorrow." When Abu Ayub ◉ met Rasulullah ﷺ the following day, Rasulullah ﷺ gave him a slave woman he possessed and said, "O Abu Ayub ◉! I request you to treat her well because we have only seen good in her since she has been with us." After leaving Rasulullah ﷺ, Abu Ayub ◉ said to himself, "I see no better way of complying with the request of Rasulullah ﷺ other than setting her free." He therefore set her free. *(Tabrani, Ibn Hibban).* Abdullah bin Abbas ◉ reports that he once heard Omar ◉ narrate that Rasulullah ﷺ left home one afternoon and found Abu Bakr ◉ in the Masjid. "What brings you here at this hour?" asked Rasulullah ﷺ. Abu Bakr ◉ replied, "The same thing that brought you here, O Rasulullah ﷺ!" When Omar ◉ arrived there, Rasulullah ﷺ asked, "What brings you here at this hour?" Omar ◉ replied, "The same thing that brought the 2 of you here." Rasulullah ﷺ then started talking to them. He then said, "Do you 2 have the strength to walk to an orchard where we shall find food, drink and shade?" Rasulullah ﷺ then took them to the house of Abul Haytham bin Taihan ◉ who was from the Ansar. A lengthy Hadith follows. *(Bazzar, Abu Ya'la, Uqaili, Ibn Mardaway, Bayhaqi, Muslim, Malik).* Imam Mundhiri *(Targheeb wat Tarheeb)* says that this incident probably occurred once with Abu Ayub ◉ and once with Abul Haytham ◉.

Fatima ◉ and Ali ◉ Suffer Extreme Hunger

Fatima ◉ narrates that when Rasulullah ﷺ once came to visit her, he asked, "Where are my 2 sons'?" He was referring to his grandsons Hasan ◉ and Husain ◉. Fatima ◉ replied, "This morning there was nothing to even taste in our house so Ali told me that he would take them out with him because they would only cry with me and I will have nothing to give them. He then went to a certain Jewish man to find some work." Rasulullah ﷺ left to meet Ali ◉ and found the 2 boys playing in a pond with some dates in front of them. Rasulullah ﷺ said, "O Ali! Should you not take my boys home before the heat gets intense'?" Ali ◉ replied, "We had nothing to eat this morning. Why don't you sit awhile until I gather some dates for Fatima ◉." Rasulullah ﷺ sat down until Ali ◉ had gathered some dates, placed them in a bag and left. Rasulullah ﷺ carried one of the boys and Ali ◉ carried the other until they brought them home. *(Tabrani, Haythami).* *Ata* narrates that he was told that Ali ◉ said, "Many days passed by when neither us nor Rasulullah ﷺ had anything to eat. I left home one day and found a coin of Dinar lying on the road. For a moment, I thought to myself whether I should pick it up or not. Because of the hardship we were suffering, I risked to pick it up and took it to a shop, where I bought some flour. Taking the flour to Fatima ◉, I told her to make dough and bake some bread. She made the dough with lot of hardship as she could not even stand up straight and in her bent over position her forelock kept hitting against the dish. After she had made the bread, I went to Rasulullah ﷺ and informed him about what had happened. Rasulullah ﷺ said, 'Eat the bread because it is a provision that Allah has provided for you from unseen sources.'" *(Kanzul Ummal, Abu Dawud).* *Muhammad bin Ka'b Qurazi* narrates that Ali ◉ said, "I have seen the time when I was with Rasulullah ﷺ and had a stone tied to my stomach because of hunger whereas the zakah I now pay equals 40,000 Dinars." Another narration states that he said, "…whereas the zakah I pay nowadays is 40,000." *(Ahmad, Haythami).*

Rasulullah ﷺ Encourages Ummu Sulaim ◉ to Endure her Hunger with Patience

Umme Sulaim ◉ narrates that once Rasulullah ﷺ said to her, "Be patient for I swear by Allah that the family of Muhammad ﷺ has had nothing to eat for 7 days and no fire has been lit under their pots for 3 days. By Allah! If I pray to Allah to turn the mountains of Tihama into gold, he would certainly do it." *(Tabrani).*

The Hunger Endured by Sa'd bin Abi Waqqas ﷺ and he was the First Arab to Fire an Arrow in the Path of Allah

Sa'd ؓ say, "Together with Rasulullah ﷺ, we used to experience harsh and difficult lives in Makkah. Whenever difficulties came, we accepted it, prepared for it, and exercised patience. I saw a time when we were with Rasulullah ﷺ in Makkah and I went out one night to pass urine. As I passed urine, I heard something making a sound as my urine fell on it. When I saw that it was a piece of camel leather, I picked it up, washed it and then toasted it. Thereafter, I placed it between 2 stones and grinded it. I then swallowed the powder and drank water over it. This gave me strength for 3 days." *(Abu Nu'aym in Hilya)*. Sa'd ؓ says, "I was the first Arab to fire an arrow in the Path of Allah. When we used to fight battles with Rasulullah ﷺ, the only food we had were the leaves of the acacia arid lotus trees. In fact, when any of us relieved himself, his droppings resembled those of a goat because it was not at all sticky." *(Bukhari, Muslim)*.

The Hunger Endured by Miqdad bin Aswad and his 2 Companions

Miqdad bin Aswad ؓ narrates, "Myself and 2 others were once suffering such great hunger that we were on the verge of losing our hearing and sight. We presented our situations to the other Sahabah but none could host us because they were all in difficulty. Finally, Rasulullah ﷺ took us home where his wives shared 3 goats which they milked. Rasulullah ﷺ distributed the milk amongst us and we kept a portion aside for him. Whenever Rasulullah ﷺ entered the house, he greeted with a voice that was audible to someone who was awake but would not disturb a sleeping person. Saitan whispered to me to drink the milk that was the share of Rasulullah ﷺ for he only needed to go to the Ansar who would give him something. This Satanic thought hunted my mind until I drank it up. After drinking it, I blamed myself saying, 'What have you done? When Muhammad ﷺ comes and does not find his drink, he will curse you and you will be destroyed.' While my 2 companions had drunk their share and fallen asleep, I could not sleep. I was wearing a shawl which was so small that when I covered my head, my feet would be exposed and when I covered my feet, my head would be exposed. Rasulullah ﷺ then entered as he usually did and performed salah for a while. He then looked for his drink and when he found nothing, he raised his hands in prayer. I said to myself, 'He will now curse me and I will be destroyed!' However, Rasulullah ﷺ prayed, 'O Allah! Feed the one who feeds me and give drink to the one who gives me something to drink.' Taking my shawl along, I took a knife and went towards the goats. Checking all of them for the fattest one to slaughter for Rasulullah ﷺ, I found to my surprise that the udders of each of them was full of milk whereas they have just been emptied earlier. I then took the utensil belonging to the wives of Rasulullah ﷺ which they used for the milk and then drew from the goats. I then milked the goats and so much milk came out that foam began to rise to the top. I took the milk to Rasulullah ﷺ and he drank. He then passed it to me and I drank. I passed it back to him and after he drank, he again passed it to me. I drank the milk and then burst out laughing so much that I fell to the ground. He said to me, 'Is this one of your tricks, Miqdad?' When I informed him about what had happened, he said, 'The milk appearing in the udders is only by the mercy of Allah. If you would kindly awaken your 2 companions so that they may also have some.' I said, 'I swear by the Being Who sent you with the truth! After you have drunk and then given me the left-over milk to drink, I care not who receives it or not.'" Another narration states that Miqdad ؓ said, "When we arrived in Madinah, Rasulullah ﷺ grouped us in groups of 10, each group attached to a household of the Ansar. I happened to be in the group of 10 that included Rasulullah ﷺ. We had only one goat, the milk from which we shared between ourselves." *(Abu Nu'aym in Hilya)*.

The Hunger Endured by Abu Hurairah ﷺ and he Ties Stones to His Stomach Because of Hunger

Mujahid narrates that Abu Hurairah ؓ used to say, "By Allah! I used to press my stomach on the ground to suppress my hunger and also tie stones to my stomach for this reason. One day, I sat by the road side which the Sahabah frequented. When Abu Bakr ؓ passed by, I asked him about a verse of the Qur'an only with the hope that he would ask me to follow him home. However, he did not do this. When Omar ؓ passed by, I asked him about a verse of the Qur'an again only with the hope that he would ask me to follow him home. However, he also did not do so. When Abul Qasim ﷺ passed, he immediately recognized the look on my face and what I needed. He said, 'O Abu Hurairah!' 'I am at your service, O Rasulullah ﷺ!' I exclaimed. He asked me to accompany him home and when he entered the house. I asked permission to enter, which was granted. I noticed a cup of milk and Rasulullah ﷺ asked his wife, "From where did you get this milk?' The reply came that a certain person or family had sent it. Rasulullah ﷺ then said, 'O Abu Hurairah!' 'I am at your service, O Rasulullah ﷺ!' I responded. He said, 'Go and call the men of Suffa for me.' The men of Suffa were the guests of the Muslims who had neither any families nor wealth. Whenever Rasulullah ﷺ received any gift, he took some of it and sent the rest to them. On the other hand, whenever Rasulullah ﷺ received any Sadaqa, he gave everything to them without taking anything for himself. This depressed me because I thought that I would at least have a sip of the milk which would give me strength for the rest of the day and night. I also thought that since I was to invite them, I would have to serve them once they arrived. What would then be left for me? However, obedience to Allah and His Rasul ﷺ is compulsory and I left to call them. When they all arrived, they requested permission to enter. When Rasulullah ﷺ permitted them to enter, they took their seats. Rasulullah ﷺ then said, 'O Abu Hurairah, take the cup and serve.' I therefore took the cup and served it to them. Each person took the cup and drank to his fill before returning it. Eventually, I reached the last person and then came to Rasulullah ﷺ. There was some milk left over when Rasulullah ﷺ took the cup in his hand and lifted his head to look at me. He smiled and said, 'O Abu Hurairah! It's just you and I left.' 'That's right, O Rasulullah ﷺ!' I replied. He then told me to sit down and drink, which I did. He then asked me to drink more which I did. He then continued to ask me to drink more until I submitted, 'I swear by the Being Who has sent you with the truth! I have no space for more.' Rasulullah ﷺ then told me to hand the cup over to him and when I handed it over, he drank what was left." *(Ahmad, Bukhari, Tirmidhi, Hakim)*

The Extreme Hunger that Abu Hurairah ﷺ Suffered

Abu Hurairah ؓ says, "I had not eaten for 3 days and as I was proceeding towards the Suffa, a raised platform in the Masjid, I started to fall down. Seeing this, 2 children said, 'Abu Hurairah has gone mad.' I called out to them, 'It is you who are mad!' As I reached the Suffa, I saw that 2 dishes of Tharid (broken bread with meat) were brought to Rasulullah ﷺ and he had invited the men of Suffa to eat with him. As they ate, I hoped that Rasulullah ﷺ would invite me as well. When they stood up after eating, all that was left in the dish was a little on the sides. Rasulullah ﷺ gathered the leftovers together into a morsel and carrying it in his fingers said, 'Eat in the name of Allah.' I swear by the Being Who controls my life that I continued eating until I was full." *(Ibn Hibban)*. Ibn Sireen narrates that they were with Abu Hurairah who was wearing 2 reddish colored cloths made in Kattan. Wiping his nose with one of them, he said, "Wow! Abu Hurairah is wiping his nose with a cloth from Kattan whereas there was a time when I saw myself fall down unconscious in front of Rasulullah ﷺ's pulpit and the room of Aisha ﷺ. Someone would then come and place his foot on my neck thinking that I was insane whereas I was suffering from extreme hunger." *(Bukhari, Tirmidhi)*. Another narration adds that Abu Hurairah ﷺ said, "I had seen the time when I was the servant of the son of Affan and the daughter of Ghazwan. My payment was my food and a turn to ride the animal when traveling. When they rode, I would drive the animal from the behind and when they dismounted, I would take care of their needs. The daughter of Ghazwan once said to me, 'You should come barefoot to the animal and mount it while it is standing because we cannot wait for you while you wear your shoes and then you get to the animal and then wait for it to sit down for you.' Now that Allah has brought the daughter of Ghazwan into my marriage, I jokingly told her, 'You should come barefoot to the animal and mount it while it is standing.'" Yet another narration from *Salim bin Hayan* quotes from his father that Abu Hurairah ﷺ said, "I was brought up as an orphan, migrated as a poor and worked for Bujra the daughter of Ghazwan for a wage that was only food for my stomach and a turn to ride the animal when traveling. I used to serve them when they were not traveling and pulled the animals along when they rode. Allah has now given her to me in marriage. All praise be to Allah Who has made Islam a means by which the affairs of people are stabilized and Who has made Abu Hurairah ﷺ a leader of Islam." *(Abu Nu'aym in Hilya)*. Abdullah bin Shaqiq narrates that he stayed in the company of Abu Hurairah ﷺ for a year in Madinah. One day, they were near the room of Aisha ﷺ, when Abu Hurairah ﷺ said to him, "I saw the time when we had nothing to wear besides coarse cloths and days would pass when we would not have anything to eat that could keep our backs straight. Eventually, we had to tie stones to our stomachs and then wrap our clothes around so that we could keep our backs straight. *(Ahmad, Haythami)*. Another narration quotes that Abu Hurairah ﷺ said, "All the food we had to eat with Rasulullah ﷺ was dates and water. By Allah! We never used to see wheat and did not even know what it was. The only clothing we wore during the time of Rasulullah ﷺ were the untidy and hot woolen shawls that Bedouins wore."*(Ahmad, Haythami, Bazzar)*

The Hunger Endured by Asma bint Abu Bakr ﷺ

Asma ﷺ the daughter of Abu Bakr ﷺ says, "I was once in the Banu Nadhir district where Rasulullah ﷺ had allocated land to Abu Salma and my husband Zubair ﷺ. Zubair ﷺ had left with Rasulullah ﷺ on a journey. Our neighbor was a Jew who has slaughtered a goat and cooked it. When I smelt the aroma, I experienced a desire like I never felt before. At that time, I was expecting my daughter Khadija and could not bear the desire. I then went to the Jewish woman to ask for some fire with the hope that she would give me some to eat because I really had no need for the fire. When I smelt the aroma from inside the house and saw the food, my desire grew even more intense and extinguished the fire she had given me. I then returned a 2nd time to ask for fire and again a 3rd time. When she did not give me anything, I eventually sat down to cry and prayed to Allah. When the Jewish lady's husband returned, he asked her, 'Has anyone been to you?' 'Yes,' she replied,' an Arab lady came to ask for

some fire.' He said, 'I shall never eat the food until you send some to her.' A plate of food was then sent to me. There was nothing on earth that I enjoyed more than that meal." *(Tabrani in Isaba, Haythami)*

The Extreme Hunger and Cold that the Sahabah Suffered During the Battle of Khandaq

The son of a Sahabi called Abu Jihad ﷺ once told him, "Dear father! You have seen Rasulullah ﷺ and enjoyed his company." The son then went on to describe the many deeds that he would have carried out had he seen Rasulullah ﷺ. His father said, "Fear Allah and continue doing what is correct. I swear by the Being Who controls my life that we experienced a time with Rasulullah ﷺ during the battle of Khandaq when Rasulullah ﷺ announced, 'The person who will go and gather intelligence about the enemy, Allah shall make him my companion on the Day of Judgment.' No one stood up to volunteer because of the intense hunger and cold that we were suffering. Eventually when no one responded, Rasulullah ﷺ announced the 3rd time, 'O Hudhaifa come forward for the task.'" *(Abu Nu'aym in Isaba)* The detailed hadith of Hudhaifa ﷺ will InsAllah be quoted in the chapter discussing the extreme cold the Sahabah had to endure. Abdullah bin Mas'ood ﷺ narrates that when Rasulullah ﷺ once saw from their faces the extreme hunger that his companions were suffering, he said, "Hear the glad tidings that the time will soon come when each of you shall have a dish of Tharid to eat every morning and evening." They asked, "O Rasulullah ﷺ! Will we be better off then?" "No," replied Rasulullah ﷺ, "you are better off today than during that time." *(Bazzar)*. Muhammad bin Sireen says, "3 consecutive days would pass by a companion of Rasulullah ﷺ without him having anything to eat. He would then toast a piece of leather and eat it. If he found nothing, he would tie a stone to his stomach to keep his back straight." *(Ibn Abi Dunya)*.

Some Sahabah Collapse in Salah Because of Extreme Hunger and Weakness

Fudhala bin Ubaid ﷺ narrates that when Rasulullah ﷺ used to lead the salah, many men used to collapse in the salah because of starvation. They were the men of Suffa. Seeing them some Bedouins would comment that they were insane. After completing the salah, Rasulullah ﷺ would turn to them and say, "If you knew what Allah has for you as reward for your suffering, you would wish that your hunger and poverty should increase." *(Tirmidhi, Ibn Hibban)*.

The Sahabah Eat Leaves in the Path of Allah and How They Suffered Extreme Hunger

Anas ﷺ narrates that 7 Sahabah used to survive by sucking on to one date and eating fallen leaves until their mouths would be filled with sores. *(Tabrani, Haythami)*. Abu Hurairah ﷺ says that they were 7 Sahabah who were suffering from intense hunger when Rasulullah ﷺ gave him 7 dates, one for each of them. *(Ibn Majah)*. Abu Hurairah ﷺ narrates that severe hunger caused him to leave his house one day and headed for the Masjid. There he met a group of Sahabah who asked him what it was that made him leave home at that hour. When he informed them that it was hunger that made him leave the house, they said, "By Allah! It is nothing but hunger that has also made us also leave our homes." They stood up and went to Rasulullah ﷺ who asked them, "What brings you here at this hour?" They replied, "O Rasulullah ﷺ! Severe hunger brings us here." Rasulullah ﷺ then sent for a plate that contained some dates and gave each person 2 dates. He then said to them, "Eat these 2 dates and drink some water. It will suffice for you for the day." Abu Hurairah ؓ says that he ate one date and kept the other in his lower garment. Rasulullah ﷺ asked, "O Abu Hurairah! Why have you kept that date away?" Abu Hurairah ؓ replied, "I have kept it for my mother." "Eat it," said Rasulullah ﷺ, "I shall give you 2 dates for her as well." Rasulullah ﷺ then gave him another 2 dates. (Ibn Sa'd). Anas ؓ narrates that when Rasulullah ﷺ went to the trench before the battle of Ahzab early one morning, he found the Muhajirins and Ansar digging in the cold because they had no slaves to do the work for them. When he saw the fatigue and hunger they were suffering, he said:

"O Allah! There is no life but the life of the Hereafter
Do forgive the Ansar and the immigrants"

In response to this, the Sahabah said:

نَحْنُ الَّذِيْ بَايَعُوْا مُحَمَّدَا   عَلَى الجِهَادِ مَا بَقِيْنَا أَبَدَا

"We are those who have pledged allegiance to Muhammad
ﷺ pledged to wage Jihad as long as we are alive"

Another narration from Anas ؓ states that as the immigrants and Ansar dug the trench around Madinah and carried the sand on their backs, they sang: نَحْنُ الَّذِيْ بَايَعُوْا مُحَمَّدَا   عَلَى الجِهَادِ مَا بَقِيْنَا أَبَدَا

"We are those who have pledged allegiance to Muhammad
ﷺ pledged to wage Jihad as long as we are alive"

In response to this, Rasulullah ﷺ would say:

"O Allah! There is no real good but the good of the hereafter. Do bless the Ansar and the immigrants."

Anas ؓ narrates further that even when 2 handfuls of barley was brought, it was cooked with decaying fat and served to people who were extremely hungry and ate it even though it would not go down easily and had an unpleasant odor. (Bukhari). Jabir ؓ says, "As we were digging the trench for the battle of Khandaq, a very hard and large boulder got in our way. We went to Rasulullah ﷺ and said, 'This large boulder in the trench has come in the way. Rasulullah ﷺ said, 'I shall come down to see.' As Rasulullah ﷺ stood up, we noticed that he had a stone tied to his stomach and we had not tasted any food for 3 days." The Hadith continues in detail. (Bukhari). Abdullah bin Abbas ؓ narrates that Rasulullah ﷺ and the Sahabah dug the trench while they had stones tied to their stomachs because of hunger. (Tabrani) The details of the above 2 narrations shall be mentioned in the chapter discussing the assistance that the Sahabah received from unseen sources. Another narration (Ibn Abi Duniya) states that the Sahabah numbered 800 when they were digging the trench. Amir ؓ said, "Rasulullah ﷺ once sent us on a military expedition with only a bag of dates as provisions. The commander would initially distribute handfuls of it amongst us until he could give us only one each." His son asked, "What use you have for one date?" Amir ؓ said, "Do not say that, dear son. We realized the value of the one date when we did not even have one date." (Abu Nu'aym in Hilya, Ahmad, Bazzar, Tabrani)

Abu Ubaidah ؓ and His Companions Experience Severe Hunger on a Journey

Jabir ؓ says, "Rasulullah ﷺ appointed Abu Ubaidah ؓ as our commander and sent us to intercept a caravan of the Quraish. Unable to find anything else, we took a bag of dates with us for our provisions. From there, Abu Ubaidah ؓ used to give us each a single date." The narrator asked Jabir ؓ, "What would you do with just a single date?" He replied, "We would suck on it as a child suckles and then drink water. This would meet our requirements for the day until the night. We also used our staffs to bring leaves down from the trees, which we soaked in water to

eat." The Hadith continues. (Bayhaqi). A narration of Malik, Bukhari, Muslim and others state that the Sahabah numbered 300 on the expedition while a narration of Tabrani places the figure above 600. (Haythami) A narration of Imam Malik states that a student. of Jabir ؓ asked him, "Of what use was the one date?" He replied, "When all the dates were finished, we missed even that one date."

The Hunger Rasulullah ﷺ and the Sahabah Suffered During the Tihama Expedition

Abu Khunais Ghifari ؓ narrates that he accompanied Rasulullah ﷺ on the Tihama expedition. When they reached Usfan, the Sahabah approached Rasulullah ﷺ and said, "O Rasulullah ﷺ! We are suffering extreme hunger. Permit us to eat one of the riding animals." Rasulullah ﷺ granted the permission. When Omar was informed about this, he came to Rasulullah ﷺ and said, "O Nabi of Allah ﷺ! What have you done? If you have instructed the people to slaughter their riding animals, what will they ride?" "What do you suggest, O son of Khattab?" asked Rasulullah ﷺ. Omar ؓ replied, "I suggest that you instruct them to bring all their leftover provisions which you should gather together and place in a dish. You should then pray to Allah for them." Rasulullah ﷺ then gave the order to collect all their leftover provisions in a dish, after which he made Du'a. Thereafter, he told them all to bring their bags and each person's bag was filled. (Bazzar, Tabrani). Omar ؓ narrates that they were with Rasulullah ﷺ on an expedition when they said, "O Rasulullah ﷺ! The enemy is here. They have eaten well while our people are hungry." The Ansar offered, "Should we not slaughter our camels and feed the people?" Rasulullah ﷺ said, "Whoever has any leftover food should bring it here." While some people brought a Mudd, others brought a Saa. Some brought more while others brought less. The sum of all the food the people brought was 20-odd Saa. Rasulullah ﷺ sat aside and prayed to Allah to bless the food. He said, "Take but do not loot." The Muslims then started taking, someone in his basket and another in his bag. Everyone filled their bags and people even tied knots in the sleeves and filled them with sleeves which were made very wide in those days. When everyone had finished taking, the food was still the same as it had been at the beginning. Rasulullah ﷺ then said, "I testify that there is none worthy of worship but Allah and that I am Allah's Rasul. Whoever says this with sincerity, Allah will save him from the heat of Hell." (Abu Ya'la, Haythami).

The Lady who Fed Some of the Sahabah Every Friday

Sahl bin Sa'd ؓ says, "There was a woman from amongst our tribe who used to grow beetroot in her garden. Every Friday she would remove the beetroot, place it in a pot together with a handful of barley which she would grind. The beetroot then served the purpose of meat. After the Jumu'ah salah, we used to go to her and greet her. She would then serve the dish to us. We looked forward to Fridays because of this meal." The meal was no fat and not sticky and the Sahabah would be very happy on Fridays because of this food. (Bukhari).

The Sahabah eat Locusts and Never Ate Bread Made of Wheat During the Period of Ignorance

Abdullah bin Abi Awfa ؓ narrates that they fought 7 battles with Rasulullah ﷺ in which they ate locusts. (Ibn Sa'd, Abu Nu'aym in Hilya). Abu Barza ؓ narrates, "During an expedition, we confronted some disbelievers and managed to chase them away from their place where they had ovens in the ground to bake bread with wheat flour. We ate bread there. During the period of ignorance we used to hear that eating wheat bread made a person fat. So each of us started looking at his sides after eating the bread to see whether he had grown fat.' *(Tabrani, Haythami).* Another narration states, "We were with Rasulullah ﷺ during the battle of Khaibar when we chased off the enemy from the bread they made from fine wheat flour they left the bread behind." *(Tabrani).* Abu Hurairah ؓ says, "After winning the Battle of Khaibar, we passed by some Jews who were baking bread made of wheat flour in ovens made in the ground. We chased them off and shared the bread. I received a piece of it, part of which was burnt. Because I had heard that eating this bread made one fat, after eating it, I looked at my sides to see whether I had become any fatter." *(Abu Nu'aym in Hilya)*

The Sahabah Suffered Intense Thirst During the Tabuk Expedition

Abdullah bin Abbas ؓ narrates that Omar ؓ was once asked to give an account of "The Hour of Difficulty" (the Tabuk expedition). Omar ؓ said, "When we left for Tabuk, the heat was intense and when we stopped over at a place, we were so thirsty that we thought our necks would fall off and we would die. In fact, when any of us went out in search of his mount, he really thought that he would die by the time he returned. The situation was so severe that when one of us slaughtered a camel, he would extract the liquids from its intestines to drink and then rub the remainder on his stomach so that the coolness could penetrate his stomach." Abu Bakr ؓ then said, 'O Rasulullah ﷺ! Allah is always good to you so make Du'a to Allah on our behalf.' 'Do you really want me to do so?' asked Rasulullah ﷺ. 'Please do,' Abu Bakr ؓ pleaded. Rasulullah ﷺ then raised his hands to the heavens to make Du'a and had not yet dropped his hands when clouds started gathering in the sky. First a drizzle fell and then the rains came pouring down. The Sahabah filled whatever containers they had and when we left the place, we discovered that the rain had no fallen further than the area where the army was camped." *(Ibn Wahab as quoted in Al Bidayah wan Nihayah, Ibn Sa'd, Bazzar, Tabrani).*

Harith, Ikrama and Ayash ؓ suffer Extreme Thirst During the Yarmuk Battle

Habib bin Abi Thabit ؓ narrates that Harith bin Hisham, Ikrama bin Abi Jahal and Ayash bin Rabi'ah ؓ were all fatally wounded during the battle of Yarmuk. When Harith bin Hisham ؓ asked for some water and was about to drink it, Ikrama looked at him. Harith ؓ said, "Give the water to Ikrama." When Ikrama ؓ took the water, Ayash ؓ looked at him. Ikrama ؓ therefore asked that the water be given to Ayash ؓ. However, before the water could reach Ayash ؓ, he had already passed away. By the time the water reached the others, they had also passed away. *(Aby Nu'aym, Ibn Asakir in Kanzul Ummal, Hakim in Mustadark, Ibn Sa'd in Istiab).*

Abu Amr Ansari ؓ Endures Severe Thirst in the Path of Allah

Muhammad bin Hanafia ؓ says, "Abu Amr Ansari ؓ had participated in the battles of Badr, Uhud, and the pledge at Aqaba. I once saw him fasting on the battlefield, restless because of severe thirst. He asked his slave to pass him his shield and when the slave did so, he fired an arrow which did not go far because he had grown weak with thirst. When he had fired 3 arrows, he said that he had heard say, 'Whoever fires an arrow in the Path of Allah, the arrow shall be a source of light for him on the Day of Judgment whether it reaches its target or not.' Abu Amr ؓ was martyred before sunset of that day." *(Tabrani, Hakim).*

The Sahabah Dig the Trench in Extreme Cold

Abu Raihana ؓ who was with Rasulullah ﷺ in a battle narrates, "We took shelter near a hill one night when the cold was so severe that some men dug holes in the ground, got in and covered holes with their shields. When Rasulullah ﷺ noticed this, he announced, 'Who will stand guard over us tonight? I shall make such a Du'a for him, the virtues of which he will certainly receive.' A man from the Ansar stood up and volunteered. When Rasulullah ﷺ asked who he was, he gave his name. Rasulullah ﷺ asked him to come closer and when he did, Rasulullah ﷺ held a part of his clothing and started making Du'a for him. When I heard the Du'a, I also volunteered. Rasulullah ﷺ asked me who I was and I informed him that I was Abu Raihana. Rasulullah ﷺ then made a Du'a for me that was shorter than the one he made for the other person. Rasulullah ﷺ said, 'The fire of Hell has been forbidden for the eye that stands guard in the Path of Allah." *(Ahmad, Nasai and Tabrani in Isaba, Haylhami, Bayhaqi).*

Lack of Clothing When Inviting People Towards Allah: The Burial of Hamza ؓ

Khabbab bin Arat ؓ narrates, "I saw the burial of Hamza ؓ when we could find nothing to shroud his body besides a single shawl. However, the shawl was so small that when we covered his feet. his head would be exposed and when we covered his face, his feet would be exposed. We eventually covered his head and put some Idhkhir grass over his feet." *(Tabrani)*

The Incident of Shurabil bin Hasana ؓ with Rasulullah ﷺ

Shafa bint Abdullah ؓ narrates that she once went to Rasulullah ﷺ to ask for some charity. However, he had nothing to give her, Rasulullah ﷺ excused himself. Because she knew him well, she started to tell him off. When the time for salah arrived, she left and went to her daughter who was married to Shurabil bin Hasana ؓ. When she found Shurabil ؓ at home, she asked, "Salah has started and you are still at home?" She then started to rebuke him. He said, "Dear aunt! Do not scold me because I have only one cloth to wear and Rasulullah ﷺ has borrowed it. She then said, "May my parents be sacrificed! I had been telling Rasulullah ﷺ off for the past day for not giving me anything whereas I was unaware that his condition is so bad that he has to borrow clothes from others." Shurabil ؓ said, "That too is only an upper garment that we had to patch up." *(Tabrani, Bayhaqi in Targheeb wal Tarheeb, Ibn Asaakir in Kanzul Ummal)*

Abu Bakr ؓ Suffers from a Lack of Clothing and Jibra'el عليه السلام Gives Him Glad Tidings

Abdullah bin Omar ؓ says that Rasulullah ﷺ was once sitting with Abu Bakr ؓ, who was wearing a robe on which he used thorns as buttons at the chest. At that moment, Jibra'el عليه السلام descended from the heavens and after conveying Allah's greetings to Rasulullah ﷺ, he asked, "Why do I see Abu Bakr ؓ wearing a robe that he buttons at the chest with thorns?" Rasulullah ﷺ replied, "O Jibra'el عليه السلام! He had spent all his wealth on me before the conquest of Makkah and has nothing left for himself." Jibra'el عليه السلام said to Rasulullah ﷺ, "Convey Allah's greetings to him and tell him that his Rabb asks, 'Are you pleased with Me in this state of poverty or not pleased'?" Rasulullah ﷺ turned to Abu Bakr ؓ and said, "O Abu Bakr! Jibra'el عليه السلام is here. He conveys to you the greetings from Allah Who asks, 'Are you pleased with Me in this state of poverty or not pleased?'" Abu Bakr ؓ started to cry and said, "Can I ever be displeased with my Rabb? I am pleased with my Rabb!" I am pleased with my Rabb!" *(Abu Nu'aym in Hilya, Kanzul Ummal)*

Ali ﷺ and Fatima ﷺ Suffer From a Lack of Clothing

Ali ﷺ narrates that when he married Fatima ﷺ, all they had was a bedding of sheepskin that they slept on by night and on which they served food to their camel during the day. They had no servant. *(Kanzul Ummal).*

The Sahabah have Only Coarse Woolen Clothing to Wear and ate Constantly Only Dates and Water

Abu Burda says that his father Abu Musa Ash'ari ﷺ once said to him, "If you had seen us during the time of Rasulullah ﷺ when we would be caught in the rain, you would have thought that we smelt just like sheep because our clothes were made from sheepskin." *(Abu Dawud, Tirmidhi, Ibn Majah).* Another narration *(Ibn Sa'd)* from *Abu Burda* states that his father Abu Musa Ash'ari ﷺ said to him, "Dear son! If you had to see us during the time of Rasulullah ﷺ when we were caught in the rain, you would have found us smelling like sheep because of our woolen clothing. Yet another narration adds that Abu Musa Ash'ari ﷺ said, "Our clothes were made of sheepskin while our food was the 2 black things, dates and water." *(Tabrani, Haythami, Abu Dawud).*

The Men of Suffa Suffer From a Lack of Clothing

Abu Hurairah ﷺ says, "I saw 70 men of Suffa, none of whom possessed a large shawl. They either wore a lower garment only or a small sheet that they tied around their necks. Whereas the garment of some reached halfway past their calves, there were those whose garments just reached their ankles. However, they would hold the garment together because they did not like their private parts to be exposed." *(Bukhari, Abu Nu'aym).* Wathila bin Asqa ﷺ says, "I was one of the men of Suffa. None of us had a complete set of clothing and because our bodies were exposed, our perspiration would form lines of dirt and dust on our bodies.'" *(Abu Nu'aym).* Someone came to Aisha ﷺ while she had a slave woman with her who was wearing a shirt worth 5 Dirhams. Aisha ﷺ said to the person, "Lift your gaze and look at this slave woman of mine. Look at her! She is not happy to wear this shirt in the house whereas during the time of Rasulullah ﷺ I had a shirt just like it and every woman in Madinah would borrow it when she was being beautified for marriage." *(Bukhari).*

The Sahabah Suffer Extreme Fear, Hunger and Cold During the Battle of Ahzab

Abdul Aziz ﷺ who was the nephew of Hudhaifa ﷺ narrates that when Hudhaifa ﷺ had mentioned the battles that the Sahabah fought by the side of Rasulullah ﷺ, the people sitting in the gathering wished various brave deeds they would have done had they been present then. Hudhaifa ﷺ said to them, "Do not wish for that. I have seen the time one night during the battle of Ahzab when we were sitting in rows with the army of Abu Sufian above us outside Madinah and the Jews of the Banu Quraiza beneath us inside Madinah as we feared that they would attack our families. We had never before experienced a night that was darker than that night nor a night in which the wind blew more fiercely. The wind made sounds resembling thunder and the darkness was so intense that we could not even see our fingers. The hypocrites started asking Rasulullah ﷺ for permission to return home with the excuse that their houses were exposed to attack but actually they were not. Rasulullah ﷺ permitted everyone of them to return. As Rasulullah ﷺ granted them permission, they silently left and we were left with approximately 300. Rasulullah ﷺ approached each man until he

came to me. I had no protection against the enemy and all the protection I had against the cold was my wife's woolen shawl that barely covered my knees. I was sitting on my knees when Rasulullah ﷺ came to me and asked who I was. When I informed him that I was Hudhaifa, he called me saying, 'O Hudhaifa!' Reluctant to stand up, I lowered down to the ground as I replied, 'Yes, O Rasulullah ﷺ!' When I stood up, Rasulullah ﷺ said, 'Something has happened amongst the enemy. I want you to bring me some information from them.' Although I was the most frightened at the time and feeling the coldest, I left. Rasulullah ﷺ then prayed, 'O Allah! Protect him from the front, from the back, from the right, from the left, from above and from beneath.'" Hudhaifa ﷺ says, "I swear by Allah that after this Du'a every bit of fear and cold in me then left and I experienced none of it. As I left, Rasulullah ﷺ instructed, 'O Hudhaifa! Do not do anything amongst them until you return.' When I drew close to the enemy army, noticed the light of a fire that they had lit. There I saw a large dark-skinned man warming his hands at the fire and rubbing them on his sides as he said, 'Let us leave! Let us leave!' I had not known Abu Sufian before this. I removed an arrow with a white feather from my quiver and placed it on my bow to fire at him in the light when I recalled the instruction of Rasulullah ﷺ: 'Do not do anything amongst them until you return.' I then restrained myself and put the arrow back into the quiver. I then gathered my courage and proceeded amongst the army. The closest people to me were the Banu Amir tribe who were announcing, 'O family of Amir! Leave! Leave! You cannot stay here!' The wind was raging within their ranks without blowing even a hand's span outside their quarters. By Allah! I could hear the sounds of rocks smashing against their carriages and beddings as the wind threw them up. I then left to return to Rasulullah ﷺ. When I had reached halfway or close to halfway, I met approximately 20 horsemen all wearing turbans. They said to me, 'Inform your leader that Allah has acted on his behalf.' When I returned to Rasulullah ﷺ, I found him performing salah wrapped in a small shawl. By Allah! The cold returned to me as soon as I returned and I started shivering. While performing salah, Rasulullah ﷺ signaled me with his hand. When I drew closer to him, he put the edge of the shawl on me. It was the practice of Rasulullah ﷺ to perform salah whenever anything worried him. I then informed Rasulullah ﷺ about what had happened and told him the enemy was leaving when I left them. Then that Allah revealed the following verses of the Qur'an:

يَا أَيُّهَا الَّذِينَ آمَنُوا اذْكُرُوا نِعْمَةَ اللَّهِ عَلَيْكُمْ إِذْ جَاءَتْكُمْ جُنُودٌ فَأَرْسَلْنَا عَلَيْهِمْ رِيحًا وَجُنُودًا لَمْ تَرَوْهَا وَكَانَ اللَّهُ بِمَا تَعْمَلُونَ بَصِيرًا (9)

وَرَدَّ اللَّهُ الَّذِينَ كَفَرُوا بِغَيْظِهِمْ لَمْ يَنَالُوا خَيْرًا وَكَفَى اللَّهُ الْمُؤْمِنِينَ الْقِتَالَ وَكَانَ اللَّهُ قَوِيًّا عَزِيزًا (25)

O you who believe! Remember Allah's favor to you, when there came against you hosts, and We sent against them a wind and forces that you saw not (i.e. troops of angels during the battle of Al-Ahzab (the Confederates)). And Allah is ever All-Seer of what you do. And Allah drove back those who disbelieved in their rage, they gained no advantage (booty, etc.). Allah sufficed for the believers in the fighting (by sending against the disbelievers a severe wind and troops of angels). And Allah is Ever All-Strong, All-Mighty. (Al-Ahzab:9, 25) (Hakim, Bayhaqi, Abu Dawud, Ibn Asakir in Kanzul Ummal)

Yazid Taymi narrates that they were with Hudhaifa ﷺ when someone asked him, "Had I met Rasulullah ﷺ, I would have fought fiercely and sacrificed my life." Hudhaifa ﷺ said, "Would you really have? I saw a time when we were with

Rasulullah ﷺ during the battle of Ahzab. It was en extremely violent night with icy wind. Rasulullah ﷺ then announced, 'The person who will go and gather intelligence about the enemy, Allah shall make him my companion on the Day of Judgment.'" The rest of the Hadith is similar to the narration of Abdul Aziz quoted above. This narration however, quotes that Hudhaifa ؓ said, "When I returned to Rasulullah ﷺ, the cold struck me as soon as I arrived and I shivered. When I informed Rasulullah ﷺ about events, he covered me with the extra part of the shawl while he was performing salah. I then slept until dawn. When dawn arrived, Rasulullah ﷺ said, 'Wake up, O sleepy head." *(Muslim)*. Another narration states that Rasulullah ﷺ announced, "Who will go and see what the enemy is doing and return with the news?" Rasulullah ﷺ then said that the person will return and added, "I shall make Du'a to Allah that he should be my companion in Paradise." However, no one stood up because of the intense fear, hunger and cold that everyone was suffering. *(Ibn Is'haq)*.

The Incident of 2 Men From the Banu Abdul Ash'hal Tribe During the Battle of Uhud

Abu Sa'ib ؓ narrates that a man from the Banu Abdul Ash'hal tribe reported, "My brother and I participated in the Battle of Uhud and we both returned wounded. When Rasulullah ﷺ's caller announced that we should march in pursuit of the enemy, I said to my brother or he said to me, 'Can we miss this opportunity to march with Rasulullah ﷺ?' By Allah! Although we had no transport to ride and were both heavily wounded, we went with Rasulullah ﷺ. Since my wounds were less serious than my brother's, I carried him when he could not manage and he walked at other times. In this manner, we eventually reached the place where the other Muslims were." *(Ibn Is'haq in Al Bidayah wan Nihayah)*. Another narration states that it was Abdullah bin Sahl ؓ and his brother Rafi bin Sahl ؓ who proceeded to Hamra'ul Asad in a wounded condition and without transport as the one carried the other. *(Ibn Sa'd)*

The Story of Amr bin Jamuh ؓ and his Martyrdom During the Battle of Uhud

Several elders of the Banu Salma tribe have reported that Amr bin Jamuh ؓ was badly crippled while his 4 sons were like lions and participated in every battle by the side Rasulullah ﷺ. When the battle of Uhud took place, his sons tried to prevent him

from participating saying, "Allah has excused you." He then approached Rasulullah ﷺ saying, "My sons want to stop me from leaving with you to participate in this battle. By Allah! I wish to walk in Paradise with my paralysis." Rasulullah ﷺ said to him, "Allah has excused you. Jihad is not compulsory for you." Rasulullah ﷺ then said to his sons, "You need not prevent him from participating because Allah may perhaps grant him the high rank of martyrdom." Amr bin Jamuh ؓ then left with Rasulullah ﷺ and was martyred during the battle of Uhud. *(Ibn Is'haq in Al Bidayah wan Nihayah)*. Abu Qatadah ؓ who participated in the battle of Uhud says that Amr bin Jamuh ؓ who was crippled once approached Rasulullah ﷺ and said, "O Rasulullah ﷺ! If I fight in the Path of Allah and am killed, will I walk with a healthy leg in Paradise?" "Certainly,' replied Rasulullah ﷺ. Subsequently, the disbeliever martyred Amr bin Jamuh ؓ, his nephew and their slave during the battle of Uhud. When Rasulullah ﷺ passed by the corpse of Amr bin Jamuh ؓ, he said, "I can see him walking in Paradise with a healthy leg." Rasulullah ﷺ then instructed that Amr bin Jamuh ؓ, his nephew and slave should be buried in one grave. *(Ahmad, Haythami, Bayhaqi)*

The Story of Rafi bin Khadij ؓ

Yahya bin Abdul Hamid narrates from his grandfather that an arrow struck Rafi bin Khadij ؓ during either the battle of Uhud or the battle of Hunain. He then went to Rasulullah ﷺ and asked him to remove the arrow. Rasulullah ﷺ said, "O Rafi! If you want, I could remove the shaft together with arrowhead. Otherwise, I could remove only the shaft without arrowhead and testify on the Day of Judgment that you are a martyr." Rafi ؓ said, "O Rasulullah ﷺ! Remove the shaft without the arrowhead and testify for me on the Day of Judgment that I am a martyr." Rasulullah ﷺ did this. Rafi ؓ lived until the period when Mu'awiya was Khalifa, when the wound reopened and he passed away after Asr. Such is the report according to this narration. However, the correct version of the story according to *Al Bidayah wan Nihayah* is that Rafi bin Khadij ؓ passed away after the Khilafa of Mu'awiya ؓ. *Isabah* states that a period elapsed between the time his wound reopened and the time that he passed away. *(Bayhaqi, Tabrani in Isaba)* Several such Ahadeeth shall be quoted in the chapter discussing patience.

The Chapter Concerning Hijra (Migration)

This chapter highlights how the Sahabah left their loved homelands, an act that is extremely difficult for a person. They also left with the intention of never returning until their deaths. This chapter also highlights the fact that doing this was more beloved to them than the world and all its pleasures and that they gave preference to Islam above ordinary pleasures and were not concerned when these pleasures were lost. It emphasizes how the Sahabah traveled from place to place to protect Islam from evil, as if they were specially created for the Hereafter.

The Hijrah of Rasulullah ﷺ and Abu Bakr ؓ

Urwa ؓ narrates that after the Hajj season, Rasulullah ﷺ was in Makkah during the remaining days of Dhul Hijjah, Muharram and Safar. The disbelievers then gathered to conspire against him, thinking that he would soon be leaving Makkah since they knew that Allah had created a place of safety and protection for him in Madinah. They had also found out that the Ansar had accepted Islam and the immigrants were going to them. The disbelievers planned to capture Rasulullah ﷺ and assassinate him, imprison him, exile him or keep him tied up. Allah informed Rasulullah ﷺ about their plot and revealed the following verse:

وَإِذْ يَمْكُرُ بِكَ الَّذِينَ كَفَرُوا لِيُثْبِتُوكَ أَوْ يَقْتُلُوكَ أَوْ يُخْرِجُوكَ وَيَمْكُرُونَ وَيَمْكُرُ اللَّهُ وَاللَّهُ خَيْرُ الْمَاكِرِينَ (30)

And (remember) when the disbelievers plotted against you (O Muhammad ﷺ) to imprison you, or to kill you, or to get you out (from your home, i.e. Makkah); they were plotting and Allah too was planning, and Allah is the Best of the planners. (Al-Anfal:30)
The day when Rasulullah ﷺ went to the house of Abu Bakr ؓ, Nabi ﷺ was informed that the disbelievers planned to assassinate him as he slept that night.

Rasulullah ﷺ Leaves Makkah with Abu Bakr ؓ and They Hide in the Cave of Thowr

Under the veil of the night, Rasulullah ﷺ and Abu Bakr ؓ left for the cave in the Thowr Mountain, which is mentioned in the Qur'an. *(At-Tauba: 40)*. Ali bin Abi Talib ؓ slept on Rasulullah ﷺ's bed so that Rasulullah ﷺ could hide from disbelieving spies who would think that Rasulullah ﷺ is asleep in the house. The disbelievers spend the night walking around and discussing how they would leap on to the person sleeping and tie him up. They continued in this manner until dawn broke and they saw Ali ؓ stand up from Rasulullah ﷺ's bed. When they asked Ali ؓ where Rasulullah ﷺ was, he said that he did not know. They then realized that Rasulullah ﷺ had left Makkah. The disbelievers then took to their mounts and started searching for Rasulullah ﷺ. They also sent messages to the people at the various oases, instructing them to capture Rasulullah ﷺ and promising them large rewards. They reached the cave of Thowr where Rasulullah ﷺ and Abu Bakr ؓ hid and had even climbed on top of the cave where the entrance was. Rasulullah ﷺ heard their voices and Abu Bakr ؓ became worried and frightened. Rasulullah ﷺ then said to him لَا تَحْزَنْ إِنَّ اللَّهَ مَعَنَا

"... Be not sad (or afraid), surely Allah is with us...." (At-Tauba:40)
Rasulullah ﷺ then made Du'a to Allah and Allah sent peace and tranquility to them as referred to in the following verse:

فَأَنْزَلَ اللَّهُ سَكِينَتَهُ عَلَيْهِ وَأَيَّدَهُ بِجُنُودٍ لَمْ تَرَوْهَا وَجَعَلَ كَلِمَةَ الَّذِينَ كَفَرُوا السُّفْلَى وَكَلِمَةُ اللَّهِ هِيَ الْعُلْيَا وَاللَّهُ عَزِيزٌ حَكِيمٌ (40)

... Then Allah sent down His Sakinah (calmness, tranquility, peace, etc.) upon him, and strengthened him with forces (angels) which you saw not, and made the word of those who disbelieved the lowermost, while it was the Word of Allah that became the uppermost, and Allah is All-Mighty, All-Wise. (At-Tauba:40)

Abu Bakr ؓ had several milk-giving goats that were brought to him and also taken to his family in Makkah. He also had an honest and trustworthy slave by the name of Amir bin Fuhaira ؓ who was a very good Muslim. Abu Bakr ؓ sent him to hire a guide to take them to Madinah and Amir ؓ hired a man called Ibnul Ayqadh. He belonged to the Banu Abd bin Adi tribe who were allies of the Banu Sahm branch of the Banu Aas bin Wa'il tribe that belonged to the Quraish. This guide from the Banu Adi tribe was a disbeliever then and it was his occupation to guide people on the journeys. During those nights when they hid the cave, the 2 of them (Amir ؓ and the guide) hid the camels of Rasulullah ﷺ and Abu Bakr ؓ while Abdullah ؓ the son of Abu Bakr ؓ would come to them every evening and relate to them the events taking place in Makkah. Every night, Amir ؓ would bring them some goats, which they would milk and slaughter one to eat. Early in the mornings, he would take the goats away to the grazing fields that the people used for their goats and no one realized what was happening. This continued until the talk of Rasulullah ﷺ and Abu Bakr ؓ died down and they learnt that things were quiet. Their 2 companions arrived with the camels and they left. They had already been in the cave for 2 days and 2 nights. They took Amir bin Fuhaira ؓ with them, who drove the camels, served them and assisted them. Abu Bakr ؓ would let him ride the camel behind him in turns. Besides Amir ؓ and the guide from the Banu Adi, no one else joined Rasulullah ﷺ and Abu Bakr ؓ. *(Tabrani, Haythami).*

The Preparations of Abu Bakr ؓ for the Hijra

Aisha ؓ narrates, "Rasulullah ﷺ never failed to visit Abu Bakr ؓ during one of the ends of the day. He either visited during the mornings or during the evenings. This was his practice until the day arrived when Allah permitted him to migrate and to leave Makkah in the midst of all the people. That day, Rasulullah ﷺ came to our house at midday which was a time that he usually never visited. When Abu Bakr ؓ saw him come, he said, 'Rasulullah ﷺ will come during this hour only if something important has cropped up.' When Rasulullah ﷺ arrived, Abu Bakr ؓ moved back on his bed to make way for him and Rasulullah ﷺ sat down. There was nobody with Abu Bakr ؓ besides myself and my sister Asma bint Abu Bakr ؓ. Rasulullah ﷺ said, 'Send everyone else away from you.' Abu Bakr ؓ replied, 'It is only my 2 daughters. May my parents be sacrificed for you, there is no harm in them being here.'" Aisha ؓ continues further, "Rasulullah ﷺ then said, 'Allah has permitted me to migrate and to leave Makkah.' Abu Bakr ؓ asked, 'May I accompany you?' Rasulullah ﷺ replied, 'You may accompany me.' I swear by Allah that before then I had never known anyone to cry out of joy until I saw Abu Bakr ؓ cry that day. Abu Bakr ؓ then said, 'O Nabi of Allah! I have kept those 2 camels ready for this purpose.' He then hired Abdullah bin Uraiqid as a guide to show them the way. He was a disbeliever from the Banu Du'il bin Bakr tribe whose mother belonged to the Banu Sahm bin Amr tribe. They gave him their 2 camels and he kept them and grazed them until the appointed day." *(Ibn Is'haq).* Aisha ؓ states that when Abu Bakr ؓ asked Rasulullah ﷺ whether he could accompany him and Rasulullah ﷺ agreed, Abu Bakr ؓ said, "1 have 2 camels that I have fed for the past 6 months for this purpose. Take anyone of the 2." Rasulullah ﷺ said, "I shall rather buy it."

Rasulullah ﷺ then bought the camel from Abu Bakr ؓ and they both left. They then stayed in the cave. *(Baghawi in Kanzul Ummal).* Asma ؓ who was the daughter of Abu Bakr ؓ narrates that that when they were staying in Makkah, Rasulullah ﷺ usually visited them twice each day. However, one day he arrived in the afternoon. She said to Abu Bakr ؓ, "Father, here comes Rasulullah ﷺ. May my parents be sacrificed! It must be something important that has brought him at this hour." Rasulullah ﷺ came and said, "Do you know that Allah has permitted me to leave Makkah?" Abu Bakr ؓ asked, "May I accompany you, O Rasulullah ﷺ?" "Certainly," replied Rasulullah ﷺ. Abu Bakr ؓ said, "I have 2 camels that I have been keeping for a long time in anticipation for this day. You may take one." Rasulullah ﷺ said, "Only at a price, Abu Bakr." Abu Bakr ؓ replied, "May my parents be sacrificed for you! You may have it at a price if you so wish." Asma ؓ continues, "We then prepared the food for their journey. I cut my belt and used part of it to fasten their provisions." Rasulullah ﷺ.and Abu Bakr ؓ then left and stayed in a cave in the Thowr Mountain. When they arrived at the cave, Abu Bakr ؓ entered first and placed his finger in every hole, fearing that there may be an insect there which would harm Rasulullah ﷺ. When the Quraish found out that they were gone, they set out in search of them and fixed a reward of 100 camels for anyone who captured Rasulullah ﷺ. They searched the mountains of Makkah and eventually reached the mountain where Rasulullah ﷺ and Abu Bakr ؓ were hiding. Referring to a person who was facing the cave, Abu Bakr ؓ said, "O Rasulullah ﷺ! He will surely see us." "Never," replied Rasulullah ﷺ, "because the angels are hiding us with their wings." Still facing the cave, the man then sat down to pass urine. Rasulullah ﷺ said, "Had he seen us, he would never have done that." They stayed 3 nights in the cave and every evening Amir bin Fuhaira ؓ would bring the goats of Abu Bakr ؓ to them. At night, he would take them back and by the morning they would be grazing with the shepherds in the grazing lands. Amir ؓ used to return the goats in the evening with the other shepherds, but would walk very slowly so that he would be left behind and then take the goats to Abu Bakr ؓ once the night became dark. Abdullah ؓ the son of Abu Bakr ؓ used to spend the day in Makkah finding out the news and then inform Rasulullah ﷺ and Abu Bakr ؓ when he met them at night. He then left them late at night and was in Makkah by the dawn.

Rasulullah ﷺ Leaves the Cave and Heads for Madinah

Rasulullah ﷺ and Abu Bakr ؓ left the cave after 3 days and took a route along the coast. Abu Bakr ؓ traveled in front of Rasulullah ﷺ but whenever he felt any danger from the rear, he traveled at the back. The entire journey passed in this manner. Abu Bakr ؓ was a well known man. Therefore, whenever someone met him, they would ask who was with him. He would reply, "He is a guide who is showing me the way." By saying this, he meant that Rasulullah ﷺ was guiding him in Islam but the person thought that Rasulullah ﷺ was someone showing him the road. When they reached the settlement of Qudaid which lay on their route, someone told the Banu Mudlaj tribe who lived there, "I have seen 2 riders near the coast. I think that they are the men from the Quraish whom you are searching for." Suraqa bin Malik said to the person, "Those are 2 men whom we have sent out to do some work for the people." Suraqa knew that the riders were Rasulullah ﷺ and Abu Bakr ؓ, but said this so that he could have them to himself and earn the reward. Suraqa then called for his slave woman and whispered to her to get his horse. He then set out on the trail of Rasulullah ﷺ and Abu Bakr ؓ. *(Tabrani,*

Haythami) The story of Suraqa will be related later.

Abu Bakr ؓ Fears for Rasulullah ﷺ When They Leave the Cave and Omar ؓ Praises Abu Bakr ؓ

Ibn Sirin narrates that during the Khilafa of Omar ؓ, some Sahabah's sacrifices were mentioned and it appeared as if the people regarded Omar ؓ to be better than Abu Bakr ؓ. When Omar ؓ heard about this, he said, "I swear by Allah ﷻ that a single night of Abu Bakr ؓ is better than the entire family of Omar ؓ and single day of Abu Bakr ؓ is better than the entire family of Omar ؓ. When Rasulullah ﷺ left for the cave that night, Abu Bakr ؓ was with him. At times he walked ahead of Rasulullah ﷺ and at other times he walked at the back. When Rasulullah ﷺ noticed this, he asked, 'O Abu Bakr! Why do you walk sometimes ahead of me and sometimes at the back?' He said, 'When I think that there may be someone searching for you, I walk at the back but I then walk ahead when I think that someone may be lying in ambush.' Rasulullah ﷺ said, 'O Abu Bakr! If anything has to happen, do you prefer that it happens to you rather than me?' 'Certainly! I swear to this by the Being Who has sent you with the truth!' replied Abu Bakr ؓ. When they reached the cave, Abu Bakr ؓ said, 'O Rasulullah ﷺ! You stay here until I have cleaned the cave for you.' He then entered the cave and cleaned it. When he came out and remembered that he had not cleaned the holes, he said, 'O Rasulullah ﷺ! You stay here until I have cleaned it.' He entered the cave and cleaned out the holes. He then told Rasulullah ﷺ to enter and Rasulullah ﷺ did. I swear by the Being Who controls my life! That single night is better than the entire family of Omar!" *(Bayhaqi in Al Bidayah wan Nihayah, Hakim in Kanzul Ummal).*

Abu Bakr ؓ Fears for Rasulullah ﷺ When They were in the Cave

Hasan Basri narrates that that when Rasulullah ﷺ and Abu Bakr ؓ went to the cave, the Quraish came to search for Rasulullah ﷺ. However, when they saw that a spider had made a web on the entrance, they concluded that no one could have entered the cave. Rasulullah ﷺ was busy performing salah and Abu Bakr ؓ was keeping watch when Abu Bakr ؓ said, "Here comes your people in search for you. By Allah! I have no concern for myself but I fear that I should not see anything unpleasant happen to you." Rasulullah ﷺ comforted him saying, "O Abu Bakr! Do not fear for Allah ﷻ is with us." *(Abu Bakr Qadhi).* Anas ؓ narrates that Abu Bakr ؓ told him, "When we were in the cave I said to Rasulullah ﷺ, 'If anyone has to look to his feet, he would certainly spot us beneath his feet.' Rasulullah ﷺ said, 'O Abu Bakr! What do you think of the 2 who have Allah as the 3rd?'" *(Ahmad, Bukhari, Muslim, Tirmidhi).*

Abu Bakr ؓ's Hijra with Rasulullah ﷺ and Their Encounter with Suraqa bin Malik

Bara bin Azib narrates that Abu Bakr ؓ once bought a saddle from his father Azib for 13 Dirhams. Abu Bakr ؓ then asked Azib ؓ to tell his son Bara ؓ to help him carry it to his house. Azib replied, "I shall not. Tell him, until you relate to us your experience when Rasulullah ﷺ left Makkah with you." Abu Bakr ؓ related, "We left the cave early at night and traveled quickly during the day and in the afternoon when the heat became intense. I then strained my eyes to see whether I could see any shade to take shelter. When I spotted a large boulder, I hurried to it and found that it still offered some shade. I then leveled the ground for Rasulullah ﷺ and spread out a coat for him. I then requested him to lie down and he did. Thereafter, I went to see whether I could spot anyone who was searching for us." Abu Bakr ؓ related further, "When I saw a shepherd and asked him who he worked for, he mentioned the name of a man from the Quraish whom I knew, 'Do any of the goats have milk?' I asked. 'Yes,' he replied. 'Will you milk some for me?' I enquired. When he agreed, he held the animal still as I had asked. I then asked him to wipe off the sand from the udders which he did with his hands and I then asked him to dust his hands off. I had a container with me that had a cloth tied to the mouth. After he had milked a bit of milk for me, I threw water onto a cup so that its bottom got cold and the milk as well. I then went to Rasulullah ﷺ and found him awake. I said, 'Drink, O Rasulullah ﷺ! He then drank so much that I became very pleased. 'Is it not the time to leave?' I said. We then left. Although people were searching for us, no one caught up with us besides Suraqa bin Malik bin Ju'shum, who did so on his horse. Seeing him approach, I said, "O Rasulullah ﷺ! Here comes someone in search of us. He has caught up with us.' Rasulullah ﷺ said, 'Do not grieve because Allah is with us.' When Suraqa drew close and was only the distance of 1 or 2 spear lengths away from us, I cried and said, 'O Rasulullah ﷺ! He has caught up with us!' Rasulullah ﷺ asked, 'What makes you weep?' I replied, 'I swear by Allah that it is not for my own safety that I weep but I am crying for your safety.' Rasulullah ﷺ then made Du'a saying, 'O Allah! Deal with him on our behalf as You please.' Suraqa's horse suddenly sank into the ground up to its belly although the ground was hard. Suraqa got off the horse and said, 'O Muhammad ﷺ! I know that you have done this. Please pray to Allah to save me from this trouble and I swear by Allah that I shall throw every other tracker I meet off your trail. Take an arrow from my quiver here and when you pass by a certain place where you will see my camels and goats, show this arrow to the shepherds and take whatever you need.' Rasulullah ﷺ said, 'I have no need for that.' Rasulullah ﷺ then made Du'a to Allah and Suraqa was freed. He then returned to his people. Rasulullah ﷺ and I continued until we reached Madinah where the people came to welcome him. They climbed the roofs on either side of the road as servants and children ran on the road saying, 'Allahu Akbar! Rasulullah ﷺ had arrived! Muhammad ﷺ has come!' When the people started quarrelling about who would be his host, Rasulullah ﷺ said, 'I shall stay the night with the Banu Najjar tribe who are the maternal relatives of Abdul Muttalib so that I may honor them.' The following morning, Rasulullah ﷺ stayed where he was commanded to stay by Allah." *(Ahmad, Bukhari, Muslim, Ibn Khuzaima, Kanzul Ummal).*

Rasulullah ﷺ Arrives in Madinah, Stays in Quba and the Joy of the People of Madinah

Urwa bin Zubair ؓ narrates that Zubair ؓ who was with a caravan of Muslim traders met as they were returning from Sham. He gave white clothing wear to both Rasulullah ﷺ and Abu Bakr ؓ. When the Muslims in Madinah heard that Rasulullah ﷺ had left from Makkah, they left for Hara every morning to wait for him until the extreme afternoon heat made them return home. After waiting for a long time one day, they returned and took shelter in their homes. It was then that a Jew who had climbed on top of a Jewish fortress saw if something happened, spotted Rasulullah ﷺ and his companions all dressed in white. As they arrived, the mirage on the horizon started to recede. The Jew could not help calling out at the top of his voice, "O Arabs! Here comes the chief you have been waiting for!" The Muslims rushed for their weapons to receive Rasulullah ﷺ with ceremony and met Rasulullah ﷺ at Hara. Rasulullah ﷺ led them to the right of Hara where they stopped in the neighborhood of

the Banu Amr bin Awf tribe. This happened on the 2nd of Rabi'ul Awwal. Abu Bakr ؓ remained standing while Rasulullah ﷺ sat down quietly. Those Ansar who had never before seen Rasulullah ﷺ started greeting Abu Bakr thinking that he was Rasulullah ﷺ. It was only when the sun got directly on Rasulullah ﷺ and Abu Bakr ؓ started shading him with his shawl that the people realized who Rasulullah ﷺ was. Rasulullah ﷺ stayed with the Banu Amr bin Awf tribe for more the 10 nights where he laid the foundation for the Masjid that Allah refers to in the Qur'an when He says: لَمَسْجِدٌ أُسِّسَ عَلَى التَّقْوَى

" ... *The Masjid that was established on Taqwa ... " (At-Tauba:108)*

Rasulullah ﷺ performed salah there and then mounted his camel. The people walked with him until the camel sat at the location of Rasulullah ﷺ's Masjid (Masjidun Nabawi). It was there that the Muslim males had been performing their salah at the time. It was a piece of land where dates were dried and it belonged to two orphaned children called Sahl and Suhail who were under the guardianship of As'ad bin Zurara ؓ. When the camel sat there, Rasulullah ﷺ said, "InsAllah, this shall be the place where we shall stay." Rasulullah ﷺ then called for the 2 orphans to buy the land so that a Masjid could be built on it. They said, "Instead of selling the land, we would rather give it to you as a gift, O Rasulullah ﷺ!" Rasulullah ﷺ refused to accept it from them as a gift until they he was able to buy it from them. Rasulullah ﷺ then had the site fixed for a Masjid. Rasulullah ﷺ himself carried the unbaked bricks for the Masjid with the Sahabah. As he carried the bricks he sang:

هذا الْجَمَالُ لَاجمَالُ خَيْبَرْ هذا أَبَرُّ رَبَّنَا وَأَطْهَ

"Lifting these bricks is not like lifting the dates and grapes of Khaibar. O our Rabb! This is more virtuous and purer"

Another couplet Rasulullah ﷺ would recite was:

اللّهُمَّ إِنَّ الْأَجْرَ أَجْرُ لَاخِرَهُ   فَارْحَمِ الْأَنْصَا وَالْمُهَاجِرَهُ

"O Allah! The true rewards are those of the Hereafter. So do shower Your mercy on the Ansar and immigrants (Muhajir)"

The narrator says that Rasulullah ﷺ also recited the poem says, *"Besides these couplets, no Hadith has reached us in which Rasulullah ﷺ has recited a complete poem." (Bukhari)*

Anas bin Malik ؓ says, "I was one of the children running as the people said, 'Muhammad ﷺ has arrived!' I ran on but could not see anything. When the people again called, 'Muhammad ﷺ has arrived!' I ran again but still could not see anything. Rasulullah ﷺ and his companion Abu Bakr ؓ eventually arrived and sat down in an uninhabited area of Madinah. They then sent a Bedouin to announce to the Ansar that they had arrived. Consequently, approximately 500 Ansar came out to welcome them. When the Ansar came, they said, 'Come along. You are both safe and will be obeyed.' Rasulullah ﷺ and his companion walked amongst us and the people of Madinah all came out to welcome them. In fact, even the young girls stood above the houses looking at each other as they asked, 'Which of them is Rasulullah ﷺ? Which of them is Rasulullah ﷺ?' We had never seen a sight like this." Anas ؓ also said, "I have seen Rasulullah ﷺ the day he arrived in Madinah and the day he passed away and have never seen any days like them." *(Ahmad, Bayhaqi).* Aisha ؓ narrates that when Rasulullah ﷺ arrived in Madinah, the women and children sang: طَلَعَ الْبَدْرُ عَلَيْنَا   مِنْ ثَنِيَّةِ الْوَدَاع

وَجَبَ الشُّكْرُ عَلَيْنَ   مَادَعَا لِلّهِ دَاع

"The full moon has risen above us from the Valley of Wada Gratitude is incumbent on us as long as a caller calls to Allah" (Bayhaqi)

The Hijra of Omar ﷺ and Some Other Sahabah

Bara bin Azib ﷺ says, "The first Muslims from Makkah to migrate to us in Madinah were Mus'ab bin Umair ﷺ and Ibn Ummu Maktum ﷺ. The 2 of them started teaching us the Qur'an. Thereafter, Ammar ﷺ, Bilal ﷺ and Sa'd ﷺ migrated, followed by Omar ﷺ accompanied by 20 others. I have never seen the people of Madinah happier on any occasion than the occasion when they arrived. By the time they arrived, I had already learnt *Sura A'la* amongst other Mufassal Suras." *(Ibn Abi Shaiba in Kanzul Ummal)*. Another narration states that Bara bin Azib ﷺ said, "The first from amongst the immigrants to come to us was Mus'ab bin Umair ﷺ who belonged to the Banu Abdid Dar tribe. Ibn Ummu Maktum ﷺ came who was a blind man of the Banu Fihr tribe. Omar bin Khattab ﷺ arrived with 20 mounted men. When we asked him what had happened to Rasulullah ﷺ, he said that Rasulullah ﷺ was coming after him. Rasulullah ﷺ and Abu Bakr ﷺ arrived later. By the time Rasulullah ﷺ arrived, I had already learnt several Suras from the Mufassal Surahs." *(Ahmad, Bukhari, Muslim in Al Bidayah wan Nihayah)*.

The Hijra of Omar bin Khattab ﷺ and His 2 Companions

Omar ﷺ says, "When I decided to migrate to Madinah, Ayash bin Abi Rabi'ah, Hisham bin Aas and I arranged to meet at the valley of Tanadhib which was a place after Sarif at the oasis of the Banu Ghifar tribe. We agreed that if any of us was not there by dawn, it meant that he was stopped and the other 2 were to proceed. Consequently, Ayash and I were at Tanadhib by dawn and Hisham was prevented from coming. He was put in difficulty by the disbelievers and he left Islam. When we arrived in Madinah, we stayed with the Banu Amr bin Awf tribe at Quba. Ayash was the cousin and step brother of Abu Jahal bin Hisham and Harith bin Hisham. The 2 of them therefore came for him in Madinah to take him back to Makkah at a time when Rasulullah ﷺ was still in Makkah." The 2 of them spoke to Ayash and said, 'Your mother has taken a vow never to comb her hair and never to take shade from the sun until she sees you.' Ayash took pity on his mother. I said to him, 'Beware of them because I swear by Allah that all they want is to take you away from Islam. By Allah! When the lice start harassing your mother, she will start combing her hair and when the heat of Makkah becomes unbearable, she will have to take shade.' However, Ayash said, 'I shall fulfill the vow of my mother. In any case, I still have some wealth in Makkah that I need to collect.' I pleaded with him saying, By Allah! You know that I am one of the wealthiest people of the Quraish. You can have half of my wealth if you do not go with them.' In spite of this, he refused my offer and insisted on going with them. When I saw that he was adamant to go, I said to him, 'since you want to do as you want to do, at least take this camel of mine for she is of good breed and very obedient. Stay on her and if you doubt anything your people do, use her to escape and save yourself." Omar ﷺ narrates further, "Ayash then left with the 2 and on the road, Abu Jahal said to him, 'Dear brother! By Allah, this camel of mine has become very lazy. Will you not allow me to ride with you on that camel?' 'Certainly,' replied Ayash. He therefore made the camel sit down and the 2 others also made their camels sit so that Abu Jahal could change camels. When they were on the ground, the 2 men attacked Ayash and tied him up very securely. They then took him to Makkah and when they pressured him to forsake Islam, he gave up to the pressure. We believed that Allah would never accept the repentance of a person who forsakes Islam and this is what those who forsook Islam also thought. It was only when Rasulullah ﷺ arrived in Madinah that Allah revealed the following verses of the Qur'an:

قُلْ يَا عِبَادِيَ الَّذِينَ أَسْرَفُوا عَلَى أَنْفُسِهِمْ لَا تَقْنَطُوا مِنْ رَحْمَةِ اللَّهِ إِنَّ اللَّهَ يَغْفِرُ الذُّنُوبَ جَمِيعًا إِنَّهُ هُوَ الْغَفُورُ الرَّحِيمُ (53) وَأَنِيبُوا إِلَى رَبِّكُمْ وَأَسْلِمُوا لَهُ مِنْ قَبْلِ أَنْ يَأْتِيَكُمُ الْعَذَابُ ثُمَّ لَا تُنْصَرُونَ (54) وَاتَّبِعُوا أَحْسَنَ مَا أُنْزِلَ إِلَيْكُمْ مِنْ رَبِّكُمْ مِنْ قَبْلِ أَنْ يَأْتِيَكُمُ الْعَذَابُ بَغْتَةً وَأَنْتُمْ لَا تَشْعُرُونَ (55)

Say: "O Ibadee (My slaves) who have transgressed against themselves (by committing evil deeds and sins)! Despair not of the Mercy of Allah, verily Allah forgives all sins. Truly, He is Oft-Forgiving, Most Merciful. And turn in repentance and in obedience with true Faith to your Lord and submit to Him, (in Islam), before the torment comes upon you, then you will not be helped. (Az-ZOmar:53-55)

Omar ﷺ says that he wrote down these verses and sent them to Hisham bin Aas. Hisham says, "When the verses reached me, I started reading them at Dhu Tuw and looked at them from top to bottom but could not understand them. I then prayed to Allah to make me understand and Allah inspired my heart that they were revealed with reference to people like me and the belief we entertained that we will never be forgiven after forsaking Islam. I returned to my camel, sat on it and rode off until I met Rasulullah ﷺ in Madinah. *(Ibn Is'haq in Al Bidayah wan Nihayah, Isaba, Bazzar, Bayhaqi, Ibn Shihab in Majma'uz Zawa'id)*

Uthman ﷺ Migrates to Abyssinia and Becomes the First Person After Lut ﷺ to Migrate with his Family for the Pleasure of Allah

Qatada ﷺ says, "The first person to migrate with his family for the pleasure of Allah was Uthman bin Affan ﷺ. I heard Nadhar bin Anas ﷺ say that he heard Abu Hamza viz. Anas ﷺ say, 'Uthman ﷺ left for Abyssinia with his wife Ruqayya ﷺ who was the daughter of Rasulullah ﷺ. News about them was slow in reaching Rasulullah ﷺ until a woman from the Quraish came to him and said, 'O Muhammad ﷺ! I have seen your son-in-law with his wife.' 'How were they?' asked Rasulullah ﷺ. She said, 'I saw him mount his wife on a very weak donkey as he drove it along from the rear.' Rasulullah ﷺ commented, 'May Allah go with them. Uthman ﷺ is the first person to migrate with his family after Lut.'" *(Bayhaqi, Ibn Mubarak in Isaba)*. When Rasulullah ﷺ received no news of them, he went out of his house to wait for some news. Eventually a woman came to him and gave him news about them. *(Tabrani, Haythami)*.

The Hijra of Ali bin Abi Talib ﷺ

Ali ﷺ says, "When Rasulullah ﷺ left for the Hijra to Madinah, he told me to stay behind to return the trusts that people had left with him. It was because of this that people called him "Al Amin" ("The Trustworthy"). I stayed on for 3 days after Rasulullah ﷺ left and made myself seen without hiding from the people for even a single day. I then left Makkah and followed the road Rasulullah ﷺ took until I reached the neighborhood of the Banu Amr bin Awf tribe in Quba where Rasulullah ﷺ was staying. I stayed at the house of Kulthoom bin Hidm and Rasulullah ﷺ was also staying there." *(Ibn Sa'd, Kanzul Ummal)*.

Rasulullah ﷺ Permits the Sahabah to Migrate to Abyssinia

Muhammad bin Hatib ﷺ narrates that Rasulullah ﷺ once said, "I have seen in a dream a land of dates. You people should go there." Consequently, my father Hatib ﷺ and Ja'far ﷺ left for the sea and I was born on the very ship they took." *(Ahmad, Tabrani in Majma'uz Zawa'id)*. Ja'far ﷺ once asked, "O Rasulullah ﷺ! Permit me to go to a land where I will be able to worship Allah without having to fear anyone." When Rasulullah permitted him, he went to Najashi, the king of Abyssinia. The detailed Hadith will follow. *(Tabrani, Bazzar, Haythami).*

The Quraish send Amr bin Al Aas ﷺ to Najashi to Bring the Sahabah Back to Them

Ummu Salama ﷺ narrates that a time came when it became too difficult for the Sahabah to live in Makkah. They were being tortured and put through many difficulties. They realized that these great difficulties and tests were directed at them because of Islam and that Rasulullah ﷺ was unable to protect them. Under the protection of his tribe and his uncle, Rasulullah ﷺ was not suffering as they were. Rasulullah ﷺ therefore said to them, "The land of Abyssinia has a king who does not oppress anyone in his kingdom. Go to his country and stay there until Allah creates an escape for you from your suffering." Ummu Salama ﷺ says further, "We therefore left in several groups until a number of us had gathered there. We had settled in a nice place with good neighbors where we could peacefully practice Islam without fearing any oppression. However, when the Quraish saw that we had found a safe haven, they disliked it very much. They therefore decided to send a delegation to Najashi to have us removed from his country and returned to them. The persons they sent were Amr bin Al Aas and Abdullah bin Abi Rabi'ah. They also collected many gifts for Najashi and for his generals. There was not a person for whom they did not have a gift." Ummu Salama ﷺ narrates further that the Quraish briefed the 2 delegates saying, "Give every general his gift before you speak about the Muslims. Thereafter, give Najashi his gifts. If possible, try to have the Muslims handed over to you before you have to speak about them to Najashi." The 2 men left and gave every general his gift and spoke to them. They said, "We have come to your king concerning some fools from our people who have forsaken the religion of their people and have not even embraced your religion. Their people have sent us to negotiate with you so that the king should send them back to us. When we speak to the king we would appreciate it if you could advise him to do this." They all agreed to comply. They then went to Najashi and gave him his gifts. The gift Najashi loved most was the leather of Makkah. After giving him the gifts, they said to him, "O King! Some foolish people from our people have forsaken the religion of their people and have not even embraced your religion. They have fabricated a religion that is strange to us and have sought asylum in your country. Their tribes, parents, uncles and people have sent us to bring them back for they know them best. Because they are people who will not enter into your religion, you need not keep them here." Najashi became furious and said, "Never by the life of Allah! I shall never send them back to their people until I have called them, spoken to them, and looked into the matter. They are people who have sought asylum in my country and chosen to be my neighbors rather than that of others. If they are as you claim, I shall return them. However, if they are not like you say, I shall keep them here. I shall not come in between them and their people neither shall give their people the pleasure of having them back. Najashi then sent for the Muslims.

Sahabah meet Najashi and his Views on Isa ﷺ and Maryam ﷺ

When the Muslims came to Najashi, they greeted him with Salam without prostrating before him. Najashi said, "O people! Tell me why you have not greeted me by prostrating as the others from your people have greeted me when they arrived? Tell me also what you have to say about Isa ﷺ and what your religion is. Are you Christians?" When the Muslims replied in the negative, Najashi asked, "Are you then Jews?" "No," they replied. "Then what is your religion?" he asked. When they informed him that they followed Islam, he asked them what Islam is. They replied, "We worship Allah and do not ascribe any as partner to Him." Najashi asked further, "Who has brought this religion to you?" They replied, "A man from amongst our own people brought it to us. We knew him and his lineage very well. Allah sent him as a Rasul to us just as Allah sent many prophets before us. He instructed us to do good, to be charitable, to fulfill promises and to return trusts. He prohibited us from worshipping idols and rather worship the One Allah Who had no partner. We believed in him and recognized the word of Allah. We are convinced that whatever he taught is from Allah. When we did what he told us, our people became our enemies and they also became the enemies of the true Nabi ﷺ. They called him a liar and also wanted to kill him. They wanted us to worship idols and we therefore fled from them and came to you with our Islam and lives still intact." Najashi exclaimed, "By Allah! This is the same light that has come from Musa ﷺ." Ja'far ﷺ then said, "Regarding the greeting, Rasulullah ﷺ has informed us that the greeting of the people of Paradise is the Salam and he has commanded us to greet in this manner. It is with the same greeting we use between ourselves that we have greeted you. Regarding Isa ﷺ the son of Maryam ﷺ, he was the servant of Allah ﷺ, His Nabi, His word that he cast on Maryam ﷺ and the spirit that Allah created. He was the son of a chaste virgin." Najashi picked up a stick and said, "I swear by Allah that the son of Maryam ﷺ would not add even the weight of this stick to what you have mentioned." The Abyssinian leaders exclaimed, "By Allah! If the people of Abyssinia hear what you have said, they will certainly overthrow you." Najashi replied, "By Allah! I shall never say anything more about Isa ﷺ. When Allah returned my kingdom to me, He did not bother about what the people had to say, so why should I bother about what they say about Islam? Allah forbids that I should do such a thing!" *(Ibn Is'haq in Al Bidayah wan Nihayah).*

A lengthy narration also from Ummu Salama ﷺ the wife of Rasulullah ﷺ states that Najashi sent a message to the Sahabah to come to him. When the message reached them, they convened a gathering. They consulted with each other saying, "What will we say about Isa ﷺ when we go to Najashi?" The response was, "By Allah! We will say what we know and what Rasulullah ﷺ has instructed us regardless of what the consequences may be." Najashi had also called his priests, who were sitting around him with the pages of their scriptures opened when the Muslims arrived. Najashi asked, "What is this religion with which you have separated from your people and for which you will neither embrace my religion nor the religion of any other nation?" The spokesperson for the Muslims was Ja'far bin Abi Talib ﷺ. He responded by saying, "O King! We were a nation of ignorance. We worshipped idols, ate carrion, committed acts of immorality, severed family ties, behaved badly towards our neighbors, and the strong amongst us lived off the weak. We were in this pathetic condition when Allah sent a Rasul to us who was from among us. We were well aware of his lineage, his truthfulness, his honesty and his chaste behavior. He called us to believe in the Oneness of Allah, to worship Allah and to forsake the stones and idols that we and our forefathers worshipped other than Allah. He enjoined us to always speak the truth, to return trusts, to maintain family ties, to behave well with our neighbors and to abstain from unlawful things and from spilling people's blood. He had forbidden us from immoral behavior, from giving false evidence, from seizing the wealth of orphans and from slandering chaste women. He has also commanded us to worship Allah without ascribing any partners to Him and to establish salah and pay zakah." As Ja'far ؓ spelled out the injunctions of Islam, the other Muslims confirmed what he said until he said, "So we believed in him and followed whatever he brought to us. We worship the one Allah without ascribing any partners to him. We also regard as forbidden all those things that Allah had made Haram for us just as we regard permissible all those things that he had made Halal for us. However, our people became our enemies. They started torturing us and putting us through many difficulties because of Islam so that we should revert to worshipping idols instead of worshipping Allah. They want us to regard the many vices as lawful which we used to regard as lawful in the past. When their high handedness and oppression became too much for us and became an obstacle between us and Islam, we left for your country. O King! We preferred you over others and preferred to be your neighbors hoping that we will not be oppressed by you." Najashi asked, "Do you know anything that has been revealed from Allah?" "Yes indeed," replied Ja'far ؓ. Najashi requested, "Then recite it" Ja'far ؓ recited before him the opening verses of Surah Maryam. Najashi wept until his beard was soaked with tears. When the priests heard the recitation, they .also started to weep until their scriptures were soaked with tears. Najashi commented by saying, "I swear by Allah that this and the words that came to Musa عليه السلام emerge from the same lantern. Turning to the 2 delegates of the Quraish, Najashi said, "You may leave because I swear by Allah that I will never hand them over to you and will never consider doing so for even a moment."

Relating further, Ummu Salama ؓ says, "When the 2 delegates left Najashi, Amr bin Al Aas said, "I swear by Allah that tomorrow I shall definitely defame them so much in front of Najashi that they will be uprooted!" Abdullah bin Rabi'ah who was the softer of the 2 towards the Muslims said, "Do not do so. They are after all our relatives even though they have opposed us." Amr bin Al Aas then said, "By Allah! I shall then tell Najashi that they regard Isa bin Maryam to be a servant of Allah." The following day, they returned to the king and said, "O King! These people say awful things about Isa bin Maryam. Summon them and ask them what they have to say about him." When Najashi called them to question, the Muslims convened a meeting because nothing like this had happened before. They asked each other what their reply to Najashi would be when he asked about Isa. They resolved, "By Allah! We shall say what Allah ﷻ has said about him and what our Nabi ﷺ has brought regardless of what the consequences are." When they went to Najashi and he asked them what they had to say about Isa عليه السلام, Ja'far ؓ replied, "We say what our Nabi ﷺ has brought to us about him that he was the servant of Allah, His Nabi, the spirit that Allah created and His word that he cast on the chaste virgin Maryam ؓ. Najashi slapped his hands on the ground and picked up a little stick. He then said, "By Allah! Even Isa bin Maryam will not add to what you said more than the extent of this little stick." When Najashi said this, all the priests gathered around exhaled in anger. Najashi said to them, "This is the truth, even though you may exhale. Turning to the Muslims, he said, "Go. You are safe in my land and whoever swears at you shall be penalized." He said, "Whoever swears at you shall be penalized. Whoever swears at you shall be penalized. Even in exchange for a mountain of gold, I would not want to harm anyone of you."

Addressing his courtiers, Najashi then said, "Return the gifts to the 2 of them for I have no need for it. By Allah! When Allah restored to me my kingdom, He took no bribes. Why should I then accept any bribes? When Allah did not bother about what the people had to say about me, why should I bother about what

they say about Allah?" Ummu Salama ؓ narrates further, "The 2 delegates of the Quraish therefore had to return in humiliation with their gifts thrown back at them. We then stayed in a nice place with excellent neighbors. By Allah! Najashi remained as he was until he was suddenly attacked by people who wanted to take his kingdom. By Allah! I do not know a time when we were more grieved than we were on that occasion because we feared that if Najashi was defeated, another person would not accord us our rights as Najashi had done. Najashi marched against the enemy. Between him and the enemy was the River Nile which Najashi crossed with his army and engaged the enemy in battle. The Sahabah said, 'Who will go to witness the battle and report back to us?' Zubair bin Awam ؓ who was one of the youngest persons there volunteered. Everyone agreed that he was best suited for the task and they blew up a water bag filled with air, which they tied to his chest. He swam across to the bank where the battle was raging and then walked the rest of the way until he reached the armies." Narrating further, Ummu Salama ؓ says, "We all made Du'a to Allah for Najashi's victory over his enemy and for the stability of his kingdom. We were making Du'a and waiting for the result of the battle when Zubair ؓ suddenly came running. He was waving a cloth saying, 'Glad tidings for you. Najashi has been victorious. Allah has destroyed his enemy and restored stability to his kingdom.' By Allah! We never knew joy like the joy we experienced on that occasion. Najashi returned after Allah had annihilated his enemy, stabilized his kingdom and restored his control over the land of Abyssinia. We remained with him in the best of places until we returned to Rasulullah ﷺ while he was still in Makkah." *(Ahmad, Haythami, Abu Nu'aym in Hilya, Bayhaqi in Siyar).*

Abdullah bin Mas'ood ؓ narrates that Rasulullah ﷺ sent approximately 80 of them to Najashi. Amongst them were Abdullah bin Mas'ood ؓ, Ja'far ؓ, Abdullah bin Ufuta ؓ, Uthman bin Madh'un ؓ and Abu Musa Ash'ari ؓ. When they went to Najashi in Abyssinia, the Quraish sent Amr bin Al Aas and Omarah bin Walid with gifts for Najashi. When they arrived, the 2 of them prostrated before Najashi and then quickly sat on his right and left hand sides. Then they said to Najashi, "Turning away from us and our religion, some of our cousins have come to settle in your country." "Where are they?" asked Najashi. The 2 replied, "They are here in your country. Why do you not send for them?" When Najashi sent for the Muslims, Ja'far ؓ said, "I shall be your spokesman today." The Muslims followed him and when he entered the court of the king, Ja'far ؓ greeted Najashi with Salam but did not prostrate before him. The courtiers asked, "What is wrong with you that you did not prostrate before the king?" Ja'far replied, "We prostrate only before Allah." Najashi asked, "What is this all about?" Ja'far ؓ explained, "Allah has sent a Rasul to us who has commanded us not to prostrate before anyone but Allah. He has also commanded us to perform salah and to pay zakah." Amr bin Al Aas said to Najashi, "They differ with you concerning Isa bin Maryam." When Najashi asked them what they had to say about Isa عليه السلام and his mother, Ja'far ؓ responded by saying, "We say what Allah says, that Isa عليه السلام was the word of Allah and the spirit He created and cast on to the chaste virgin whom no man had touched and who had not lost her virginity by any child before the birth of Isa." Picking up a little stick from the ground, Najashi said, "O assembly of Abyssinians, priests and monks! These people have not added even the extent of this stick to what we have to say. Turning to the Muslims, he said, "Welcome to you and to the man from whom you have come. I testify that he is certainly the Rasul of Allah and the one whose mention we find in the Injeel (Bible).

He is undoubtedly the Rasul about whose coming Isa ﷺ gave glad tidings. I swear by Allah ﷻ that had I not been occupied with ruling my kingdom, I would have surely gone to him and been the one who carries his shoes." Najashi then ordered that the gifts sent by the Quraish should be returned. Abdullah bin Mas'ood ؓ quickly returned afterwards and participated in the Battle of Badr. *(Ahmad, Ibn Hajar in Fat'hul Bari, Haythami)*

Abu Musa Ash'ari ؓ narrates that Rasulullah ﷺ instructed them to leave for Abyssinia with Ja'far bin Abi Talib ؓ. When the news reached the Quraish that they had settled there, they sent Amr bin Al Aas and Omarah bin Walid to have the Muslims send back. The rest of the narration is similar to that quoted above from Abdullah bin Mas'ood ؓ. However, this narration adds that Najashi said, "Had I not been occupied with ruling my kingdom, I would have definitely gone to him and kissed his feet." He then told the Muslims that they were free to stay wherever they liked and even gave them food and clothing. *(Tabrani, Haythami, Bayhaqi, Abu Nu'aym)*. Ja'far bin Abi Talib ؓ says that the Quraish sent Amr bin Al Aas and Omarah bin Walid to Najashi with gifts from Abu Sufian. When the Muslims were already staying by Najashi in Abyssinia, the 2 men said to Najashi, "Some foolish and low class people from our community have come to your country. Do hand them over to us." Najashi said, "I shall not do so until I have heard them." He then sent for the Muslims and when they arrived, he asked, "What are these men (Amr and Omarah) saying?" The Muslims replied, "These people worship idols while we believe and accept the Rasul whom Allah has sent to us." Najashi asked the 2, "Are they your slaves?" When they replied in the negative, Najashi asked, "Are they then indebted to you?" When they replied in the negative, Najashi said, "Then leave them alone." The Muslims then left Najashi's court. Amr bin Al Aas then said to Najashi, "Their beliefs concerning Isa ﷺ is different from that which you believe." Najashi remarked, "If they say anything about Isa that is different from what I say, I shall not allow them to stay for a moment in my country." Najashi again sent for the Muslims. This 2nd summoning was more difficult for them than the first. When Najashi asked them about what Rasulullah ﷺ said concerning Isa ﷺ, they replied, "He believes that Isa ﷺ is the spirit that Allah created and His word that He cast on to the chaste virgin." Najashi then sent for certain priests and monks. When several of them appeared before him, he asked them, "What do you say about Isa bin Maryam?" "You know better than us," they submitted, "What do you say?" Picking up something small from the ground, Najashi said, "Isa ﷺ did not say any more than what these people say even to the extent of this little thing." Najashi asked the Muslims, "Has anyone harmed you?" "Yes," they replied. Najashi had a public crier announce that whoever harms the Muslims shall have to pay a penalty of 4 Dirhams. "Is this enough?" he asked the Muslims. When the Muslims said that it was not enough, Najashi had the amount doubled.

The Sahabah Leave for Madinah, Najashi Accepts Islam and Rasulullah ﷺ Prays for his Forgiveness

Ja'far ؓ narrates further that when Rasulullah ﷺ migrated to Madinah and was dominant, the Muslims approached Najashi and said, "Rasulullah ﷺ has become dominant, has migrated to Madinah and had killed those whom we used to complain to him about. We now intend to go to him. Do grant us leave." Najashi gave them his blessings and even provided transport and provisions for the journey. He then said to them, "Inform your leader about how I have treated you. My heir here shall go with you. I testify that there is none worthy of worship but Allah and

that he is Allah's messenger. Ask him to seek forgiveness for me." Ja'far ؓ says, "We left and when we reached Madinah, Rasulullah ﷺ met me and hugged me. He then said, 'I do not know whether I am happier without conquest at Khaibar or with the arrival of Ja'far.'" The arrival of Ja'far ؓ coincided with the Muslims' victory at Khaibar. When Rasulullah ﷺ sat down, Najashi's envoy said, "Ask Ja'far how our leader treated him." Ja'far ؓ said, "Why of course!" He then explained the excellent treatment that Najashi gave them and that he had even provided transport and provisions for their journey. Ja'far ؓ also said, "Najashi has testified that there is none worthy of worship but Allah and that you are Allah's Rasul. He also told me to ask you to seek forgiveness on his behalf." Rasulullah ﷺ stood up, made wudhu and then said thrice, "O Allah! Forgive Najashi." All the Muslims said "Aamin" to this Du'a. Ja'far ؓ then said to the envoy, "Go and tell your leader what you have seen Rasulullah ﷺ do." *(Ibn Asakir, Haythami)*.

The Virtues of Those Sahabah who Migrated to Abyssinia and Then to Madinah

Ummu Abdullah bint Abi Hathma ؓ says, "By Allah! We were preparing to leave for Abyssinia when my husband Amir had to leave for something we needed. In the meantime, Omar ؓ who was still a disbeliever came to me. We had been suffering difficulties and cruel treatment at his hand. He said, 'O Ummu Abdullah! Are you leaving?' 'We certainly are!' I replied, 'By Allah! We are going to a land from the lands of Allah because you people have harassed us and acted cruelly towards us until Allah has made an escape for us.' Omar ؓ said, 'May Allah go with you.' I saw such gentleness in him that I had never seen before. He then left and he seemed to be truly grieved by our departure. When Amir returned after fulfilling the task, I said to him, 'O Abu Abdullah! If only you had seen Omar ؓ just now. He was extremely gentle and actually grieved by our departure.' He asked, 'Are you hopeful that he will accept Islam?' 'I certainly do,' I replied. Because Amir had lost hope of Omar ؓ accepting Islam after seeing his harshness and opposition against Islam, he commented, 'The man you saw (Omar ؓ) shall never accept Islam until the donkey of Khattab accepts Islam!'" *(Ibn Is'haq, Haythami, Hakim)* The name of Ummu Abdullah ؓ was Layla. *(Isaba)*. Khalid bin Sa'eed bin Al Aas ؓ and his brother Amr ؓ were amongst those who migrated to Abyssinia. He narrates that it was a year after the battle of Badr that they returned from Abyssinia and Rasulullah ﷺ met them when they arrived. Because they were sad that they were unable to participate in the Battle of Badr, Rasulullah ﷺ said to them, "Why should you be sad? Whereas other people have undertaken only one Hijra, you have undertaken 2. You made Hijra when you went to the king of Abyssinia and after returning from him, you made Hijra to me." *(Ibn Mandah, Ibn Asakir in Kanzul Ummal)*.

Abu Musa Ash'ari ؓ narrates that they lived in Yemen and when they heard that Rasulullah ﷺ had migrated to Madinah, his brothers and he migrated to Rasulullah ﷺ. He was the youngest of them and the others were Abu Burda ؓ and Abu Ruhm ؓ The narrator is unsure whether Abu Musa Ash'ari said that they were accompanied by a 50 odd people, by 53 people or by 52 people from their tribe. He says that they boarded a ship but the ship took them to Abyssinia where they met Ja'far ؓ and stayed there for a while. They all then left together for Madinah and met Rasulullah ﷺ when he had conquered Khaibar. Many people used to tell those Sahabah who had been on the ship, "We beat you to the Hijra." Asma bint Umays ؓ was also amongst those who had been on the ship and had migrated to Abyssinia. One day she was visiting Ummul Mu'mineen Hafsa when Omar came there. When he saw Asma there with his daughter Hafsa, he asked, "Who is this?" When his daughter informed him that the lady was Asma bint Umays, Omar asked, "Is she the one who has been to Abyssinia and at sea?" As soon as Asma confirmed that it was her, he said, "We beat you to the Hijra. We have more right to Rasulullah ." Asma became furious and said, "Never! By Allah! You people were with Rasulullah who fed your hungry amongst you and advised the ignorant amongst us while we were in a land where the people were far from Islam and hated it. All this we did for the pleasure of Allah and His Rasul . I swear that I shall neither take food or drink until I tell Rasulullah what you said and ask him about it. I swear that I shall neither lie to him nor distort or add to what you have said." She then went to Rasulullah and informed him about what Omar had said. "What did you then tell him?" asked Rasulullah . After she had informed about her reply to Omar, Rasulullah said, "He does not have a greater right to me than you. He and his companions have only one Hijra to their credit while you and the people on the ship have 2 Hijra to your credit."

Asma says, "I saw Abu Musa Ash'ari and the other people on the ship came to me in groups to ask about this statement of Rasulullah . Nothing in the world made them happier and they regarded nothing to be greater than this statement that Rasulullah had made in their favor." She also mentioned, "I saw Abu Musa listening to this Hadith from me over and over again." Abu Musa Ash'ari narrates that Rasulullah said, "I recognize the voices of the Ash'arin travelers (the tribes of Abu Musa Ash'ari) when they enter by night and by their melodious voices I can locate their camps at night even though I had never seen their camps by day." Amongst them was a person called Hakim who was extremely brave and would say to the enemy who intend to flee, "My companions ask you to wait for them so do not leave without a fight". He would say to the Muslim cavalry, "My companions from the infantry ask you to wait for them so do not begin the fight without us." *(Bukhari, Muslim)*. Asma bint Umays narrates that she asked, "O Rasulullah ! Some people are boasting to us and saying that we are not amongst the first immigrants." Rasulullah said, "You have 2 Hijra to your credit. You migrated to Abyssinia and migrated afterwards." *(Ibn Sa'd in Fathul Bari, Ibn Shaibah in Kanzul Ummal)*

Abu Salama and Ummu Salama Migrate to Madinah

Ummu Salama says, "When my husband Abu Salama decided to migrate to Madinah, he tied a carriage for me on his camel and put me on it. He then put our son Salama bin Abi Salama on my lap and led the camel away with me. When some men from the Banu Mughiera tribe saw him, they stood before him and said, 'While you may have authority over yourself, you may go where you like but why should we allow you to go away with that woman from our tribe?' They then snatched away the reins of the camel and took me away from my husband. When this happened, the Banu Asad tribe to which Abu Salma belonged became angry and said, 'We swear by Allah that we shall never leave our son with his mother since you have snatched her away from our tribesman.' The people of the 2 tribes then started pulling my son Salama until they dislocated his arm. The Banu Asad then left with him while the Banu Mughiera kept me with them. My husband Abu Salama proceeded to Madinah. I was thus separated from my husband and son. Every morning, I would go out to Abtah where I would sit and cry continuously until the evening. This continued for a year or close to a year.

Eventually, one of my cousins also from the Banu Mughiera tribe passed by and seeing my condition, he took pity on me. He said to the Banu Mughiera tribesmen, 'Will you not allow this poor woman to leave? You have already separated her from her husband and son.' My tribesmen then permitted me to join my husband and when this happened, the Banu Asad returned my son to me. I fastened my carriage to my camel and taking my son in my lap, I prepared to leave to my husband in Madinah without anyone to accompany me. When I reached Tanim. I met Uthman bin Talha bin Abi Talha who belonged to the Abd Daar tribe. He asked, 'Where are you heading, O daughter of Abu Umayyah?' 'I am off to meet my husband in Madinah,' I replied. "Is there nobody with you?' he queried. I replied, 'None besides Allah and this little son of mine.' He said, 'By Allah! You cannot be left alone.' He then took hold of the reins of my camel and led my camel with great speed. By Allah! I have never been with any Arab man more dignified than him. Whenever we reached a stop, he made the camel sit and then moved away. After I had dismounted, he would take the camel away, remove the carriage and tie the camel to a tree. He then went to some tree and lay down beneath it. Whenever the time came to leave, he would get up, fasten the carriage on the camel and bring it to me. He then moved away and told me to mount it. After I had mounted and settled on the camel, he would return to take hold of the reins and lead the camel away until we reached the next stop. This procedure continued until he brought me to Madinah. When we reached the locality of the Banu Amr bin Awf in Quba where Abu Salama had taken up residence, he said, 'Your husband is in that locality so go there with the blessings of Allah.' He then returned to Makkah." Ummu Salama used to say, "I do not know of any Muslim family who experienced the hardships that the family of Abu Salama experienced and I have never seen a traveling companion as dignified as Uthman bin Talha. The same Uthman bin Talha bin Abi Talha Abdari accepted Islam after the Treaty of Hudaibiyah was signed and migrated together with Khalid bin Walid." *(Ibn Is'haq in Al Bidayah wan Nihayah)*

Suhaib bin Sinan Leaves Makkah to Migrate and Encounters Some Youngsters of the Quraish

Suhaib narrates that Rasulullah said, "I have been shown the place to which you people will migrate. It is a salty land that lies between 2 rocky plains. It is either Hajar or Yathrib." In the company of Abu Bakr, Rasulullah then left for Madinah. I had intended to leave with him, but some youngsters from the Quraish stopped me. When I spent the night standing without being able to sit, the youngsters said, 'Allah has alleviated your concerns about him by giving a stomach ailment.' They then fell soundly asleep. However, there was nothing wrong with me so I left. After I had left, some of them came after me to bring me back. I said to them, 'Will you leave me if I give you several awqiya of gold? Are you prepared to fulfill such an undertaking?' When they agreed, I followed them back to Makkah where I said to them, 'Dig under the threshold of that door. There are many awqiya of gold lies buried there and then go to a certain woman and take the 2 sets of clothing she has of mine.' I then left and arrived in Quba before Rasulullah moved from there. Rasulullah saw me, he said, 'O Abu Yahya! Your transaction has been profitable.' I submitted, 'O Rasulullah ! No one could have come to you before me with the news. It is none but Jibrail who has informed you." *(Bayhaqi in Al Bidayah wan Nihayah, Tabrani, Haythami, Abu Nu'aym in Hilya)*.

Suhaib ؆ Arrives in Quba Where Rasulullah ﷺ Gives Him the Glad Tidings of a Qur'anic Verse that Allah had Revealed About Him

Sa'eed bin Musaib ؆ narrates that when Suhaib ؆ left to migrate to Rasulullah ﷺ, a group of disbelievers from the Quraish pursued him. Suhaib ؆ dismounted and emptied his quiver saying, "O assembly of Quraish! You know well that I am the best archer of you all. I swear by Allah that none of you shall get close to me until I have fired every arrow in my quiver at you. I shall fight you with my sword as long as it is in my hand. You may therefore decide what you want to do. On the other hand, if you agree, I can direct you to my wealth in Makkah, if you leave me alone." When the men agreed, the deal was made and he gave them the directions. It was with regard to this event that Allah ؆ revealed to Rasulullah ﷺ the following verse of the Qur'an:

(٢٠٧) وَمِنَ النَّاسِ مَنْ يَشْرِي نَفْسَهُ ابْتِغَاءَ مَرْضَاةِ اللهِ وَاللهُ رَؤُوفٌ بِالْعِبَادِ

And of mankind is he who would sell himself, seeking the Pleasure of Allah. And Allah is full of Kindness to (His) slaves. (Al-Baqara:207)

When Rasulullah ﷺ saw Suhaib ؆, he said, "Your transaction has been profitable, O Abu Yahya! Your transaction has been profitable, O Abu Yahya!" Rasulullah ﷺ then recited the above verse to him. *(Abu Nu'aym, Ibn Sa'd in Kanzul Ummal, Ibn Birr in Isti'ab)*. Ikrama narrates that when Suhaib ؆ left to migrate to Madinah, some people of Makkah pursued him. Suhaib ؆ emptied his quiver and found 40 arrows. He then said to them, "None of you shall come close to me without me placing an arrow into everyone of you. Thereafter, I shall use my sword and you know well that I am a man of great strength and courage. However, Abdullah bin Omar ؆ has left 2 slave women behind in Makkah whom you can have if you let me go." *(Hakim in Mustadrak)*. Anas ؆ narrated similar report with the addition that it was on that occasion that Allah revealed the following verse:

(٢٠٧) وَمِنَ النَّاسِ مَنْ يَشْرِي نَفْسَهُ ابْتِغَاءَ مَرْضَاةِ اللهِ وَاللهُ رَؤُوفٌ بِالْعِبَادِ

And of mankind is he who would sell himself, seeking the Pleasure of Allah. And Allah is full of Kindness to (His) slaves. (Al-Baqara:207)

When Rasulullah ﷺ saw Suhaib ؆, he said, "Your transaction has been profitable, O Abu Yahya!" Rasulullah ﷺ recited the above verse to him. *(Hakim in Istaba, Ibn Sa'd)*. Suhaib ؆ narrates that when he decided to migrate from Makkah to Rasulullah ﷺ, the Quraish said to him, "O Suhaib! When you came to us, you had no wealth. You are now leaving as a wealthy man. By Allah! We can never allow this!" Suhaib ؆ proposed to them, "Will you let me go if I give you all my wealth?" When they agreed, he gave his wealth to them and they let him go. By the time Suhaib ؆ reached Madinah, Rasulullah ﷺ was already aware of the incident and said, "You've earned a grand profit, O Suhaib! You've earned a grand profit, O Suhaib!"*(Ibn Mardaway, Ibn Sa'd in Tabaqat)*.

The Hijra of Abdullah bin Omar ؆

Muhammad bin Zaid narrates that whenever Abdullah bin Omar ؆ passed by his house in Makkah from which he migrated; he would close his eyes and would not even look at it or stop there. *(Abu Nu'aym in Hilya)* Another narration *(Bayhaqi in Istaba)* states that whenever Abdullah bin Omar ؆ spoke about Rasulullah ﷺ, he would cry and whenever he passed his house in Makkah, he would close his eyes.

The Hijra of Abdullah bin Jahash ؆

Abdullah bin Abbas ؆ narrates that Abdullah bin Jahash ؆ (actually his brother Abd bin Jahash ؆, as it will clarify from the next Hadith) was the last person to migrate to Madinah and had become blind. When he decided to migrate, his wife who was the daughter of Abu Sufian bin Harb bin Umayya disliked it. She advised him to rather migrate to someone else other than Rasulullah ﷺ. Disregarding her advice, he took his family and wealth and secretly left the Quraish and came to Rasulullah ﷺ in Madinah. His brother-in-law Abu Sufian became very angry and immediately sold his house in Makkah. Afterwards leather was kept in the house to cure causing it to stink. When Abu Jahal bin Hisham, Utba bin Rabiah, Shaiba bin Rabiah, Abbas bin Abdil Muttalib and Huwaitib bin Abdil Uzza passed by the house, Utba's eyes flowed with tears as he recited the following:

"Despite how long it remains intact, every house shall one day face ruin and desertion"

Abu Jahal then turned to Abbas ؆ and said, "You people (the family of Rasulullah ﷺ) have caused these problems for us." When Rasulullah ﷺ conquered Makkah and entered, Abu Ahmad (Abd bin Jahash) stood up to ask for his house. On the instruction of Rasulullah ﷺ, Uthman ؆ stood up and took Abu Ahmad aside. After speaking to him, Abu Ahmad stopped asking for his house. Abdullah bin Abbas ؆ says that as Rasulullah ﷺ was sitting, Abu Ahmad ؆ recited the following couplets which mean:

"How beloved a valley is Makkah where I can walk without guide. Iin Makkah my visitors are many and it is there where my pegs are securely fixed." (Tabrani, Haythami)

Ibn Is'haq narrates that after Abu Salama ؆, the first person from the immigrants to arrive in Madinah was Amir bin Rabiah and Abdullah bin Jahash ؆. Abdullah bin Jahash ؆ arrived with his family and his brother Abd (who was known as) Abu Ahmad ؆. Abu Ahmad ؆ was a blind man who could walk in the upper and lower parts of Makkah without a guide. He was also a poet. His wife was Faria the daughter of Abu Sufian bin Harb ؆ and his mother was Umaima ؆ the daughter of Abdul Muttalib bin Hashim. The family home of the Jahash family was therefore locked because they had all migrated. Whenever Utba would pass by the house, he would recite some couplets as quoted in the previous Ahadeeth. *(Ibn Is'haq in Al-Bidayah wan Nihayah)*. It is clear that the Hadith of Abdullah bin Abbas ؆ refers to Abd bin Jahash ؆ because it was he who was blind and not his brother Abdullah bin Jahash ؆. Referring to the Hijra of his family, Abu Ahmad bin Jahash ؆ recited the following couplets:

"When (my wife) Ummu Ahmad saw me leaving in the protection of the One I fear without having seen Him
She said, 'If you have to migrate somewhere then take us somewhere else far from Yathrib'
I said to her, 'Yathrib is no bad place and a servant must do what Ar Rahman wants' My attention is towards Allah and His Rasul ﷺ and whoever focuses his attention to Allah ؆ someday will never be deprived. How many were the bosom friends and well-wishers that we left behind.
And how many were those well-wishers who cried while the criers thought that being distant from our land brought our destruction We think that the rewards for good deeds is something to look forward to. I called the Banu Ghanam towards the protection of their lives and towards the truth when the clear path became apparent to people
Allah be praised because they all accepted when the caller called them towards the truth and towards success and they marched in battle. Some of our companions veered away from guidance they aligned themselves and gathered to take up weapons against us.
We are like 2 armies, the one being guided to the truth and rightly guided while the other is being punished. They

transgressed and entertained false hopes for Iblees misled them from the truth, because of which they were at a loss and deprived. We had turned to the words of the Nabi Muhammad ﷺ So the allies of the truth from amongst us and pure and have been purified by the ties we have with our near relatives we seek to be close. Were it not for these ties of kinship, there would be no closeness to them

After us, which nephew will feel safe from you and which brother-in-law will you consider after me. On the day when people and their words will be separated you will come to know which of us had been adopting the truth.

The Hijra of Dhamra bin Abil Ees / Dhamra bin Ees ﷺ

Sa'eed bin Jubair ﷺ narrates that many poor Muslims in Makkah thought that they were exempted from making Hijra when the following verses of the Qur'an were revealed:

لَا يَسْتَوِي الْقَاعِدُونَ مِنَ الْمُؤْمِنِينَ غَيْرُ أُولِي الضَّرَرِ وَالْمُجَاهِدُونَ فِي سَبِيلِ اللَّهِ بِأَمْوَالِهِمْ وَأَنْفُسِهِمْ فَضَّلَ اللَّهُ الْمُجَاهِدِينَ بِأَمْوَالِهِمْ وَأَنْفُسِهِمْ عَلَى الْقَاعِدِينَ دَرَجَةً وَكُلًّا وَعَدَ اللَّهُ الْحُسْنَى وَفَضَّلَ اللَّهُ الْمُجَاهِدِينَ عَلَى الْقَاعِدِينَ أَجْرًا عَظِيمًا (95) دَرَجَاتٍ مِنْهُ وَمَغْفِرَةً وَرَحْمَةً وَكَانَ اللَّهُ غَفُورًا رَحِيمًا (96)

Not equal are those of the believers who sit (at home), except those who are disabled (by injury or are blind or lame, etc.), and those who strive hard and fight in the Cause of Allah ﷺ with their wealth and their lives. Allah ﷺ has preferred in grades those who strive hard and fight with their wealth and their lives above those who sit (at home). Unto each, Allah has promised good (Paradise), but Allah has preferred those who strive hard and fight, above those who sit (at home) by a huge reward; degrees of (higher) grades from Him, and Forgiveness and Mercy. And Allah is Ever Oft-Forgiving, Most Merciful. (An-Nisa':95-96). However, they realized that the compulsion still stood when the following verse was then revealed:

إِنَّ الَّذِينَ تَوَفَّاهُمُ الْمَلَائِكَةُ ظَالِمِي أَنْفُسِهِمْ قَالُوا فِيمَ كُنْتُمْ قَالُوا كُنَّا مُسْتَضْعَفِينَ فِي الْأَرْضِ قَالُوا أَلَمْ تَكُنْ أَرْضُ اللَّهِ وَاسِعَةً فَتُهَاجِرُوا فِيهَا فَأُولَئِكَ مَأْوَاهُمْ جَهَنَّمُ وَسَاءَتْ مَصِيرًا (97)

Verily! As for those whom the angels take (in death) while they are wronging themselves (as they stayed among the disbelievers even though emigration was obligatory for them), angels say (to them): "In what (condition) were you?" They reply: "We were weak and oppressed on earth." They (angels) say: "Was not the earth of Allah spacious enough for you to emigrate therein?" Such men will find their abode in Hell - What an evil destination! (An-Nisa':97)

The Muslims then said, "This verse is certainly sounds a fearful warning." Allah then revealed the following verses which exempted those Muslims with physical disabilities:

إِلَّا الْمُسْتَضْعَفِينَ مِنَ الرِّجَالِ وَالنِّسَاءِ وَالْوِلْدَانِ لَا يَسْتَطِيعُونَ حِيلَةً وَلَا يَهْتَدُونَ سَبِيلًا (98) فَأُولَئِكَ عَسَى اللَّهُ أَنْ يَعْفُوَ عَنْهُمْ وَكَانَ اللَّهُ عَفُوًّا غَفُورًا (99) وَمَنْ يُهَاجِرْ فِي سَبِيلِ اللَّهِ يَجِدْ فِي الْأَرْضِ مُرَاغَمًا كَثِيرًا وَسَعَةً

Except the weak ones among men, women and children who cannot devise a plan, nor are they able to direct their way. For these there is hope that Allah will forgive them, and Allah is Ever Oft-Pardoning, Oft-Forgiving. He who emigrates (from his home) in the Cause of Allah, will find on earth many dwelling places and plenty to live by. (An-Nisa':98-100)

After this verse was revealed, Dhamra bin Ees ﷺ who was a wealthy blind man from the Banu Laith tribe said, "Although I am blind, I am still able to devise a plan to make Hijra as I have wealth and slaves." He gave instructions that he should be put on to his mount. He was very ill and when he was put on to his

conveyance, he traveled very slowly. He passes away when he reached Tanim and is buried by the Masjid at Tanim. With special reference to him, this verse of the Qur'an was revealed:

وَمَنْ يُهَاجِرْ فِي سَبِيلِ اللَّهِ يَجِدْ فِي الْأَرْضِ مُرَاغَمًا كَثِيرًا وَسَعَةً وَمَنْ يَخْرُجْ مِنْ بَيْتِهِ مُهَاجِرًا إِلَى اللَّهِ وَرَسُولِهِ ثُمَّ يُدْرِكْهُ الْمَوْتُ فَقَدْ وَقَعَ أَجْرُهُ عَلَى اللَّهِ وَكَانَ اللَّهُ غَفُورًا رَحِيمًا (100)

He who emigrates (from home) in the Cause of Allah, will find on earth many dwelling places and plenty to live by. And whosoever leaves his home as an emigrant unto Allah and His Messenger, and death overtakes him, his reward is then surely incumbent upon Allah. And Allah is Ever Oft-Forgiving, Most Merciful. (An-Nisa':100) (Firiabi, Ibn Mandah, abi Hatim in Isaba)

Abdullah bin Abbas ﷺ narrates that when Dhamra bin Jundub ﷺ left his house to make Hijra, he told his family members, "Put me on my mount. Remove me from the land of the disbelievers and take me to Rasulullah ﷺ." However, he passed away en route before reaching Rasulullah ﷺ. It was then that the following verse of the Qur'an was revealed:

وَمَنْ يُهَاجِرْ فِي سَبِيلِ اللَّهِ يَجِدْ فِي الْأَرْضِ مُرَاغَمًا كَثِيرًا وَسَعَةً وَمَنْ يَخْرُجْ مِنْ بَيْتِهِ مُهَاجِرًا إِلَى اللَّهِ وَرَسُولِهِ ثُمَّ يُدْرِكْهُ الْمَوْتُ فَقَدْ وَقَعَ أَجْرُهُ عَلَى اللَّهِ وَكَانَ اللَّهُ غَفُورًا رَحِيمًا (100)

He who emigrates (from his home) in the Cause of Allah, will find on earth many dwelling places and plenty to live by. And whosoever leaves his home as an emigrant unto Allah and His Messenger, and death overtakes him, his reward is then surely incumbent upon Allah. And Allah is Ever Oft-Forgiving, Most Merciful. (An-Nisa':100) (Abu Ya'la, Haythami)

The Hijra of Wathila bin Asqa ﷺ

Wathila bin Asqa ﷺ narrates that he left home with the intention of accepting Islam and came to Rasulullah ﷺ. Since Rasulullah ﷺ was leading the salah at the time, he joined the rows at back and performed salah with the Sahabah. After completing the salah, Rasulullah ﷺ went to Wathila ﷺ at the back and asked him what it was that he wanted. When he replied that he intended to accept Islam, Rasulullah ﷺ said, "That is best for you." Rasulullah ﷺ asked him whether he intends to make Hijra. When he replied in the affirmative, Rasulullah ﷺ asked, "Will it be a Hijra Badi or a Hijra Bati?" "Which is better?" asked Wathila ﷺ. "The Hijra Bati," replied Rasulullah ﷺ. Rasulullah ﷺ explained, "The Hijra Bati is that you live with Rasulullah ﷺ in Madinah while the Hijra Badi is that you return to your locality. You will be required to obey my commands and the commands of Allah during the conditions of ease and adversity, whether you are willing or not and even though others are given preference over you." After Wathila had agreed, Rasulullah ﷺ stretched out his hand. Wathila ﷺ stretched out his hand to pledge allegiance. Rasulullah ﷺ saw that Wathila ﷺ was not going to make any exceptions to the pledge, Rasulullah ﷺ prompted him to add, "As far as I am able." Wathila ﷺ added, "As far as I am able." Rasulullah ﷺ took his hand so that he could pledge his allegiance. *(Ibn Jabeer in Kanzul Ummal).*

The Hijra of the Banu Sulaim Tribe

Salama bin Akwa ﷺ narrates that when the Banu Sulaim tribe was affected by an epidemic, Rasulullah ﷺ advised them to live outside the town. They said, "We dislike to turn back on our heels and return to the outskirts." Rasulullah ﷺ said to them, "You shall be our country people and we shall be your city people. We shall respond if you call for us and you would respond when we call for you. You will be regarded as immigrants wherever you are." *(Abu Nu'aym in Kanzul Ummal)*

The Hijra of Junadah bin Abi Umayya ◈

Junadah bin Abi Umayya Azdi ◈ narrates that there was a difference of opinion amongst them when they made Hijra during the time of Rasulullah ﷺ. While some Sahabah maintained that making Hijra had come to an end, others were of the opinion that it did not. Junadah ◈ says that he then asked Rasulullah ﷺ about this and Rasulullah ﷺ said, "Hijra shall not come to an end as long as Jihad is waged against the disbeliever." *(Abu Nu'aym in Kanzul Ummal).* Abdullah bin Sa'di ◈ narrates, "I was the youngest amongst a delegation of 7 or 8 people from the Banu Sa'd bin Bakr tribe. When the delegation met Rasulullah ﷺ, they all had their needs fulfilled, leaving me behind to look after the animals. I later approached Rasulullah ﷺ and said, 'O Rasulullah ﷺ! Do address my need as well.' When Rasulullah ﷺ asked me what my need was, I posed the question to which I needed a reply, 'People are saying that making Hijra has come to an end.' Rasulullah ﷺ replied, 'Your need is the best or he said, your need is better than theirs. Hijra shall not come to an end as long as Jihad is waged against the disbeliever." *(Ibn Manda, Ibn Asakir in Kanzul Ummal, Ibn Hibban, Nasa'ee in Isaba).*

Safwan bin Umayya ◈ and Others Concerning Hijra

Abdullah bin Abbas ◈ narrates that while Safwan bin Umayya ◈ was in the upper part of Makkah, he was told that the person who did not undertake Hijra has no Islam. He therefore said, "I shall never go home until I have first been to Madinah." When he arrived in Madinah, he stayed with Abbas bin Abdil Muttalib ◈ and then went to see Rasulullah ﷺ. When Rasulullah ﷺ asked him what had brought him, he informed Rasulullah ﷺ that he was told that the person who did not undertake the Hijra had no Islam. Rasulullah ﷺ said, "O Abu Wahab! Return to the rocky plains of Makkah and stay in your homes. Hijra has come to an end after the conquest of Makkah. All that is left is Jihad and the intention of waging Jihad. You should therefore respond when you are called for Jihad." *(Ibn Asakir in Kanzul Ummal, Abu Hatim, Ibn Hibban, Nasai in Istaba).* Another narration states that someone said to Safwan bin Umayya ◈ that the person who did not perform the Hijra is destroyed. Safwan ◈ took an oath that he would never wash his hair until he went to Rasulullah ﷺ. He then took to his mount and rode off to Madinah. Finding Rasulullah ﷺ at the door of the Masjid, he asked, "O Rasulullah ﷺ! I have been told that the person who does not make Hijra is destroyed. I have therefore taken a vow never to wash my hair until I have come to you to ask about it." Rasulullah ﷺ replied, "When Safwan heard about Islam, his heart was content to accept it as his Islam. Compulsory Hijra to Madinah has come to an end after the conquest of Makkah. However, there still remains Jihad and the intention of waging Jihad. You should therefore respond when you are called for Jihad." *(Abdul Razzaq in Kanzul Ummal)*

Salih bin Bashir bin Fudaik narrates that his grandfather Fudaik ◈ once approached Rasulullah ﷺ and asked, "O Rasulullah ﷺ! Some people say that the person who does not migrate is destroyed." Rasulullah ﷺ replied, "O Fudaik! Establish salah, pay zakah, migrate away from evil and live wherever you want in the land of your people, you will still be regarded as one who has migrated." *(Baghawi, Ibn Mandah, Abu Nu'aym in Kanzul Ummal).* Ata bin Abi Rabah narrates that he visited Aisha ◈ in the company of Ubaid bin Umair Laithi ◈. When they asked her about Hijra, she replied, "There is no compulsory Hijra nowadays. In the past a person used to flee with his Islam towards Allah and His Rasul ﷺ, fearing that he would be severely tortured and forced to forsake Islam. Allah has made Islam dominant today and a person can worship his Rabb wherever he pleases. Yet, there still remains Jihad and the intention to wage Jihad." *(Bukhari, Bayhaqi).*

The Hijra of Rasulullah ﷺ's Family and the Family of Abu Bakr ◈

Aisha ◈ narrates, "When Rasulullah ﷺ made Hijra, he left us and his daughters behind in Makkah. When he had settled, he sent Zaid bin Haritha ◈ and his slave Abu Rafi ◈ to take us. He gave them 2 camels and 500 Dirhams which he had taken from my father Abu Bakr ◈. With this he wanted to purchase as many camels as he required. Abu Bakr ◈ sent Abdullah bin Uraiqidh ◈ with the 2 men along with 2 or 3 camels. He also wrote a letter to my brother Abdullah bin Abu Bakr ◈, instructing him to mount my mother Ummu Roman ◈, myself and my sister Asma ◈ the wife of Zubair ◈ on the camels. The 3 men left together and when they reached Qudaid, Zaid ◈ used the 500 Dirhams to purchase 3 camels. They happened to meet Talha bin Ubaidullah ◈ who intended to make Hijra and left Makkah with him. Zaid ◈ and Abu Rafi ◈ took along with them Rasulullah ﷺ's 2 daughters Fatima ◈ and Ummu Kulthum ◈ together with Rasulullah ﷺ's wife Sauda bint Zam'ah ◈. Zaid ◈ also took on his camel his wife Ummu Ayman ◈ and his son Usama ◈. When we reached Baida, my camel ran off as I sat in the carriage together with my mother Ummu Ruman ◈. My mother started shouting, "Oh my beloved daughter! Oh the new bride!" Aisha ◈ was by then already married to Rasulullah ﷺ. Our camel was eventually caught after it had already crossed the valley of Harsha. Allah ﷻ had kept us safe. When we reached Madinah, I stayed with the family of Abu Bakr ◈ while the family of Rasulullah ﷺ stayed with him. Rasulullah ﷺ was building his Masjid and several rooms around the Masjid that he intended to be the living quarters for his wives. We stayed like this for a while." The rest of the Hadith concerns the details of the marriage of Aisha ◈. *(Ibn Abdil Birr in Istiab, Haythami in Majma'uz Zawa'id).* Aisha ◈ quotes, "As we were making Hijra, we were passing by a difficult/dangerous valley when the camel I was on suddenly ran off very furiously. By Allah! I shall never forget the words of my mother as she screamed, 'Oh my little bride!' The camel continued running. When I heard someone shout, 'Throw down its reins,' I threw it down and the camel stood still in a shock as if someone was holding it up." *(Haythami, Tabrani, Hakim in Mustadrak).*

The Hijra of Rasulullah ﷺ's Daughter Zainab ◈ and the Words of Rasulullah ﷺ Concerning the Hardships she Encountered en Route

Rasulullah ﷺ's daughter Zainab ◈ says, "As I was preparing the provisions for my journey (Hijra), Hind bint Utba met me. She said, 'O daughter of Muhammad ﷺ! Do you think that the news has not reached me that you wish to meet with your father?' 'I have no such intention,' I replied. She said, 'Dear cousin! Do not do this. If you need any goods for your journey or any money to help you reach your father, I have what you need. You should therefore not keep secrets from me because the disputes between men should not creep between us women.'" Zainab ◈ narrates further when she says, "By Allah! I certainly think that she meant what she said but I was scared for her and denied that I intended to migrate." *Ibn Is'haq* further narrates that Zainab ◈ continued her preparations and when it was completed, her husband's brother Kinana bin Rabi brought her a camel which she mounted. He took his bow and quiver along with him. He took her out of Makkah during the day and led the camel as she sat in her carriage. When some men of the Quraish started talking about this, they set out after her and eventually caught up with her at

Dhu Tuwa. The first to catch up with her was Habbar bin Aswad Fihri. As she sat in her carriage, he frightened the camel with his spear until it threw her off. According to what people say, she was expecting at the time. Kinana sat on his knees, emptied his quiver and said, "By Allah! I shall place an arrow into anyone who even draws close to me." The men drew back from him. Just then, Abu Sufian arrived with a group of senior members of the Quraish. He called out to Kinana saying, "Dear man! Hold back your arrows until we have a chance to speak to you." Kinana held back and Abu Sufian came forward until he stood before Kinana. He said, "You have made a great mistake. You have taken the lady openly in full view of everyone when you know the hardships and difficulties we have experienced at the hand of her father Muhammad ﷺ. If you take her away from our midst so openly and in full view of the people, it would be an embarrassment to us and people would regard this to be a sign of our weakness. I swear by my life that we have no need to keep her away from her father and have no revenge to take from her. You should take her back now and secretly take her away to be reunited with her father only once people have calmed down and the word spreads that we have made her return to Makkah." Kinana then did this. *(Ibn Is'haq in Al Bidayah wan Nihayah).*

Urwa bin Zubair ؓ narrates that as someone was leaving Makkah with Zainab ؓ the daughter of Rasulullah ﷺ, they were intercepted by 2 men from the Quraish who fought him and after gaining the upper hand, pushed her down. She fell on to a rock and miscarried, causing her to bleed a lot. They then took her to Abu Sufian, who handed her over to some women from the Banu Hashim who had come to him. It was only after this that she eventually managed to make Hijra, However, the injury persisted until she finally passed away on account of the injury. People therefore considered her to be a martyr. *(Tabrani, Haythami).*

Another narration from Aisha ؓ states that after Rasulullah ﷺ had left Makkah, his daughter Zainab ؓ also left with Kinana or his brother. The disbelievers left in search of her and it was Habbar bin Aswad who caught up with her. He continued sticking his spear into her camel until it dropped her down, causing her miscarriage. She bore the injury with patience and the Banu Hashim and Banu Umayya tribes disputed about who will care for her. The Banu Umayya claimed to have a greater right to her because she was married to their cousin Abul Aas. However, she ended up in the care of Hind bint Utba bin Rabiah who used to say to Zaynab ؓ, "This is all because of your father." Rasulullah ﷺ one day said to Zaid bin Haritha ؓ, "Will you not go and bring Zainab?" "Certainly, O Rasulullah ﷺ!" replied Zaid. Rasulullah ﷺ said, "Take my ring and give it to her." Zaid ؓ carefully used various means to reach Zainab ؓ and eventually met a shepherd. He asked the shepherd, "For whom are you grazing?" When the shepherd informed him that he was grazing for Abul Aas (the husband of Zainab ؓ), Zaid ؓ asked to whom the goats belonged. "To Zainab the daughter of Muhammad ﷺ," was the reply. Zaid ؓ walked awhile with the shepherd and after gaining his confidence said to him, "May I give you something to give to her without informing anyone?" When the shepherd agreed, Zaid ؓ gave him the ring. Zainab ؓ recognized the ring and asked the shepherd, "Who gave this to you?" "Some man," he replied. "Where did you leave this man?" she enquired further. When he described the place to her, she remained silent and went there once night had fallen. When she met Zaid ؓ, he told her to sit in front of him on the camel. She refused, telling him to sit in the front. He mounted the camel and she mounted behind him (the laws of Hijab were not revealed at that time). They eventually arrived in Madinah. Rasulullah ﷺ

used to say about Zainab ؓ, "This is the best of my daughters who has suffered for my sake." When this Hadith reached *Ali bin Husain*, he approached Urwa and said, "What is this Hadith I hear you are reporting in which the status of Fatima ؓ is being reduced?" Urwa said, "I swear by Allah that I would not want to reduce the status of Fatima ؓ in exchange for everything between the east and the west. I shall not be reporting this Hadith again." *(Tabrani, Bazzar, Haythami).*

The Hijra of Durra bint Abi Lahab ؓ

Abdullah bin Omar ؓ, Abu Hurairah ؓ and Ammar bin Yasir ؓ all report that when Durra ؓ the daughter of Abu Lahab made Hijra, she stayed at the residence of Rafi bin Mu'alla Zuraqi ؓ. While sitting with her, some women from the Banu Zuraiq tribe asked her whether she was the daughter of the person about whom Allah says:

$$\text{تَبَّتْ يَدَا أَبِي لَهَبٍ وَتَبَّ (1) مَا أَغْنَى عَنْهُ مَالُهُ وَمَا كَسَبَ (2)}$$

Perish the two hands of Abu Lahab (an uncle of the Prophet), and perish him! His wealth and his children (etc.) will not benefit him! (Al-Masad:1,2)

They then said, "Your will therefore be of no use to you." Durra ؓ then went to Rasulullah ﷺ to complain about what the women had said. Rasulullah ﷺ consoled her and asked her to be seated. After leading the Zuhr salah, Rasulullah ﷺ sat on the pulpit for a while and said, "O people! What is it that I should be harmed through my family? I swear by Allah that on the Day of Judgment, I shall even intercede on behalf of the Haa, Hakam, Suda and Sahlab tribes. Therefore I shall surely intercede on behalf of my family also." *(Tabrani, Haythami).* Also related to this chapter concerning the Hijra of women are the narrations that have passed about the Hijra of Ummu Salama ؓ, mentioned under the subheading "Abu Salama ؓ and Ummu Salama ؓ migrate to Madinah". Also, relevant is the Hijra of Asma bint Umays ؓ and Ummu Abdullah Laila bint Abi Hathma ؓ, both of which are mentioned under the heading " Jafar bin Abi Talib ؓ and other Sahabah migrate to Abyssinia and then to Madinah."

The Hijra of Abdullah bin Abbas and other Children

Abdullah bin Abbas ؓ says, "We reached Rasulullah ﷺ 5 years after he had made Hijra and were with the Quraish when they marched during the year in which the battle of Ahzab was fought. I was with my brother Fadl and our slave Abu Rafi was with us. When we reached a place called Arj, we lost our way and instead of taking the Rakuba road, we took the Jathjatha road. We eventually arrived in the locality of the Banu Amr bin Awf in Quba from where we entered Madinah. We found Rasulullah ﷺ in the trench that was dug around Madinah. I was then 8 years old while my brother was 13." *(Tabrani, Haythami).*

The Chapter on Nusrah (Assistance) in the propagation of Islam

This chapter highlights how rendering assistance to the cause of Islam and the straight path was more beloved to the Sahabah than everything else and how they engaged themselves for this more than they engaged themselves for worldly honor. It also brings to light how they sacrificed their pleasures for it, doing it for Allah ﷻ's pleasure and in compliance with the commands of Rasulullah ﷺ. May Allah ﷻ shower His mercy, blessings and peace on him, his family and all his companions.

The Beginning of the Nusrah that the Ansar Rendered: Ahadith of Aisha ؓ

Aisha ؓ says, "Every year Rasulullah ﷺ used to present his case to the various Arab tribes, asking them to grant him asylum with their people so that he could propagate Allah's word and message. He promised them Jannah in return for their assistance. However, no Arab tribe accepted his offer until the time came when Allah ﷻ decided that Islam should become dominant, that his Nabi ﷺ should receive assistance and that His promises should be fulfilled. It was then that Allah pulled forward the tribe of the Ansar. They accepted the offer of Rasulullah ﷺ and thus Allah created a place to which Rasulullah ﷺ could migrate." *(Tabrani in Awsat, Haythami).*

A Hadith of Omar ؓ in this Regard

Omar ؓ says, "When Rasulullah ﷺ stayed in Makkah, he went to every Arab tribe and presented his case to them during the Hajj season. However, he could find none to respond to him until Allah brought this tribe of the Ansar because of the good fortune that Allah had decreed for them and the honor He wished to bestow on them. They therefore granted him a sanctuary and assisted him. Allah rewards them with abundant good on behalf of His Nabi ﷺ. *(Bazzar in Kanzul Ummal).* Another narration adds that Omar ؓ said, "By Allah! We failed to fulfill the pledge we made with the Ansar when we said to them that while we remain the leaders, they shall be the high officials. If I live to the end of the year, every governor of mine shall be from the Ansar." *(Jam'ul Fawa'id, Majma'uz Zawa'id).*

A Hadith of Jabir ؓ in this Regard

Jabir bin Abdullah ؓ says, "Rasulullah ﷺ presented his case to the people as they stayed at their camps during the Hajj season. He would say, 'Who will take me to his people because the Quraish are preventing me from propagating the word of Allah?' Eventually a man from Hamdan came to Rasulullah ﷺ. When Rasulullah ﷺ asked him where he came from and he said that he was from Hamdan, Rasulullah ﷺ asked further, 'Do your people have military might?' 'They do,' he replied. However, when the man feared that his people may not honor his word to Rasulullah ﷺ and came back to Rasulullah ﷺ and said, 'I shall first go to my people and inform them. Thereafter, I shall come back to you.' Rasulullah ﷺ agreed and the man left. A delegation from the Ansar then approached Rasulullah ﷺ in the month of Rajab." *(Ahmad, Haythami, Fat'hul Bari).* In the chapter entitled "Pledging Allegiance to Assist Others", the narration has passed in which Jabir ؓ narrates that during the 10 years that Rasulullah ﷺ lived in Makkah after announcing his prophethood, he would visit people at the places where they stayed during the seasons of Hajj. This was at the marketplaces of Ukaz and Majina. He would ask the people, "Who will give me asylum? Who will assist me so that I could propagate the message of my Rabb?

Whoever does this shall receive Jannah." However, he found none to grant him asylum and assistance. However, instead of assisting him, matters reached such a point that when a person from Yemen or from the Mudhar tribe left for Makkah, the people of his tribe and his relatives would say to him, "Beware that the man from the Quraish does not get you into trouble." People even pointed at Rasulullah ﷺ as he passed between their camps. Jabir ؓ continues, "This situation prevailed until Allah sent us (the Ansar) to him from Yathrib. We offered him asylum and believed him. Whenever a person from us left for Makkah, he would believe in Rasulullah ﷺ, who would recite the Qur'an to him. He would then return to his family in Madinah and they would all accept Islam by virtue of his Islam. Eventually there was hardly any family from the Ansar that did not have a group of Muslims who made their Islam public." Jabir ؓ says that they all discussed each other saying, "Until when will we leave Rasulullah ﷺ to call on people, to be kicked about in the mountains of Makkah and face threats of others?" 70 men of the Ansar rode off and met Rasulullah ﷺ during the Hajj season. After agreeing to meet at the valley of Aqaba, they arrived there one-by-one until they were all present. They then asked, "O Rasulullah ﷺ! To what should we pledge allegiance at your hands?" The narration continues further. *(Hakim in Mustadrak)*

A Hadith of Urwa ؓ in this Regard

Urwa ؓ narrates that when one of the Hajj seasons arrived, a group of individuals from the Ansar left for Hajj. Amongst them from the Banu Mazin bin Najjar tribe was Mu'adh bin Afra ؓ and As'ad bin Zurara ؓ. From the Banu Zuraiq tribe was Rafi bin Malik ؓ and Dhakwan bin Abdil Qais ؓ, from the Banu Abdil Ash'hal tribe was Abul Haytham bit Taihan ؓ and from the Banu Amr bin Awf was Uwaim bin Sa'ida ؓ. Rasulullah ﷺ approached them and informed them that Allah had chosen him for prophethood and great honor. Rasulullah ﷺ also recited the Qur'an to them. They were silent when they listened to Rasulullah ﷺ and their hearts were satisfied with his Da'wah. By the appearance of Rasulullah ﷺ and by the Da'wah he gave, the Ansar recognized in him what they had been hearing the Ahlul Kitab say about him. They therefore accepted what he said, believed in him and became the vehicles of good. They said to Rasulullah ﷺ, "You know about the bloodshed that takes place between the Aws and Khazraj tribes. We like Allah has guided your effort and we are prepared to make every effort for Allah and for you. We would also advise you to do as you have, but for now you should wait here in Makkah with your trust in Allah until we return to our people to inform them about you and invite them towards Allah and towards His Rasul ﷺ. Perhaps Allah shall reconcile between us and reunite us. At present, we are far from each other and harbor enmity for each other. Therefore, if you were to come to us right now while we have not yet reconciled, we shall be unable to unite around you. However, we promise to meet you in the forthcoming Hajj season." Rasulullah ﷺ was happy with what they said and they returned to their people. They started giving Da'wah to the people in secret and informing them about Rasulullah ﷺ. They also informed the people about the message Allah had sent with Rasulullah ﷺ and to which he called with the Qur'an. Eventually, there was hardly a home amongst the households of the Ansar that did not have some Muslims. *(Tabrani, Haythami)* The rest of the hadith is similar to that quoted earlier under the subheading "The Da'wah that Mus'ab bin Umair Rasulullah ﷺ gave" This appears under the heading "The Da'wah that the Sahabah gave to individuals".

A few Couplets Composed by Sirmah bin Qais ﷺ in this Regard

Yahya bin Sa'eed narrates from an old lady from the Ansar that she used to see Abdullah bin Abbas ﷺ frequently visit Sirma bin Qais ﷺ to learn the following couplets which mean:

"He stayed with the Quraish for a few years more than 10 advising people with the hope of meeting a suitable friend offering himself to the people coming for Hajj without seeing anyone to offer asylum nor anyone offering an invitation when he came to us (Ansar) and settled.

He became happy and pleased in Taiba (Madinah) he then had no fear of a distant tyrant oppressively taking something away nor any fear of people revolting for him we spent most of our wealth as well as our lives in battles and in comforting (the immigrants) we were enemies of all those who were his enemies even though they had been the best of our friends (all this because). We were convinced that there is nothing (worthy of worship) but Allah that the Book of Allah is our guide" (Hakim in Mustadrak)

The bond of Brotherhood between the Muhajirins and the Ansar

Anas ﷺ narrates that when Abdur Rahman bin Auf ﷺ arrived in Madinah, Rasulullah ﷺ established a bond of brotherhood between him and Sa'd bin Rabee Ansari ﷺ. Sa'd said to Abdur Rahman ﷺ, "Dear brother! I am the wealthiest person in Madinah and you may have half of my wealth. I also have 2 wives. You may choose the one you like best and I shall divorce her." Abdur Rahman ﷺ replied, "May Allah bless you in your family and wealth. Just show me the way to the marketplace." When Sa'd ﷺ showed Abdur Rahman ﷺ where the marketplace was, Abdur Rahman ﷺ started buying and selling until he had made a profit. He returned with some cheese and butter. He continued like this for a while until one day he appeared with the color of saffron on his clothes. "What is this all about?" asked Rasulullah ﷺ. "I have married," he replied. "What dowry did you give your wife?" Rasulullah ﷺ asked further. Abdur Rahman ﷺ replied, "The weight of a date stone in gold." Rasulullah ﷺ then advised, "Host a Walima even if you have to feed a goat." Referring to the blessings that Allah had granted him in business, Abdur Rahman ﷺ used to say, "Even if I were to pick up a stone, I could hope to receive gold or silver in exchange." *(Ahmad in Al Bidayah wan Nihayah, Bukhari, Muslim in Isaba, Ibn Sa'd in Tabaqat)*

The Muhajir and Ansar Inherit From Each Other

Abdullah bin Abbas ﷺ narrates that when the immigrants first arrived in Madinah, an immigrant would inherit from his Ansar brother because of the bonds of brotherhood that Rasulullah ﷺ created between them. In fact, even the relatives of the Ansar would not inherit from their families as the immigrant would. However, this practice was cancelled when Allah revealed the following verse of the Qur'an: وَلِكُلٍّ جَعَلْنَا مَوَالِيَ

And to everyone (man and woman,) We have appointed heirs. (An-Nisa:33) (Bukhari)

While this narration states that the above verse cancelled the inheritance of a partner (the Muhajir whom Rasulullah ﷺ appointed as a brother to an Ansari), the next narration makes it clear that the verse which cancelled the practice was:

وَأُولُو الْأَرْحَامِ بَعْضُهُمْ أَوْلَى بِبَعْضٍ فِي كِتَابِ اللَّهِ إِنَّ اللَّهَ بِكُلِّ شَيْءٍ عَلِيمٌ (75)

But kindred by blood are nearer to one another regarding inheritance in the decree ordained by Allah. Verily, Allah is the All-Knower of everything. (Al-Anfal:75)

Hafidh Ibn Hajar states that this narration is more reliable.

However, he also points out that this practice could have been cancelled twice. It is possible that in the early stages, the only form of inheritance was between those whom Rasulullah ﷺ appointed as brothers, without any inheritance being fixed for relatives. However, relatives were also given a share of inheritance together with the confederates when Allah revealed the verse: وَلِكُلٍّ جَعَلْنَا مَوَالِيَ

And to everyone (man and woman,) We have appointed heirs. (An-Nisa:33)

This is the interpretation of the narration reported by Abdullah bin Abbas ﷺ. However, inheritance was left exclusively for relatives and the inheritance of partners was completely cancelled by the following verse of Al-Ahzab:

وَأُولُو الْأَرْحَامِ بَعْضُهُمْ أَوْلَى بِبَعْضٍ فِي كِتَابِ اللَّهِ مِنَ الْمُؤْمِنِينَ وَالْمُهَاجِرِينَ إِلَّا أَنْ تَفْعَلُوا إِلَى أَوْلِيَائِكُمْ مَعْرُوفًا كَانَ ذَلِكَ فِي الْكِتَابِ مَسْطُورًا (6)

And blood relations among each other have closer personal ties in the Decree of Allah (regarding inheritance) than (the brotherhood of) the believers and the Muhajiroon (emigrants from Makkah, etc.), except that you do kindness to those brothers (when the Prophet SAW joined them in brotherhood ties). This has been written in the (Allah's Book of Divine) Decrees (Al-Lauh Al-Mahfooz). (Al-Ahzab:6)

After this verse was revealed, all that the partners could have from the inheritance of the Ansar was what the Ansar gave them as goodwill to assist them. By this interpretation, all the Ahadeeth have their explanation. *(Fat'hul Bari).* A large group of Tabi'een have narrated that when Rasulullah ﷺ arrived in Madinah, he forged ties of brotherhood between the immigrants themselves and between the immigrant and the Ansar so that they may care for each other. They used to inherit from each other and numbered 70 individuals from amongst the immigrants and the Ansar. Some say that they numbered a 100. Nevertheless, they stopped inheriting from each other on the basis of this brotherhood when Allah revealed the verse:

وَأُولُو الْأَرْحَامِ بَعْضُهُمْ أَوْلَى بِبَعْضٍ فِي كِتَابِ اللَّهِ مِنَ

And blood relations among each other have closer personal ties in the Decree of Allah... (Al-Ahzab:6) (Ibn Sa'd in Fat'hul Bari).

The Financial Assistance that the Ansar gave to the Muhajirins Sharing Dates and an Ansari Refuses to be Paid Back

Abu Hurairah ﷺ narrates that the Ansar once said to Rasulullah ﷺ, "Share out our date plantations between us and our (Muhajir) brothers." Rasulullah ﷺ said, "No. Instead of giving up ownership of the land, will you rather forgive us (Muhajir) of working on the plantations and share the dates with us?" The Ansar replied, "We hear and we obey." Abdur Rahman bin Zaid bin Aslam narrates that Rasulullah ﷺ said to the Ansar, "Your (Muhajir) brothers have left behind their wealth and their families to come to you." The Ansar said, "Distribute our land and plantations between us and them." Rasulullah ﷺ said, "Why not do something else?" "What else, O Rasulullah ﷺ?" they asked. Rasulullah ﷺ replied, "Since the Muhajir do not know how to work on the plantations, will you rather not do the work for them and share the dates with them?" "We shall indeed," replied the Ansar. *(Bukhari in Al Bidayah wan Nihayah).* Anas ﷺ narrates that the Muhajirins said, "O Rasulullah ﷺ! We have never seen people better than those to whom we have come (the Ansar). They are prepared to assist even though they have little and when they have plenty, they spend most generously. They do all the work on the plantations for us and share the dates with us. They do so much for us that we actually fear that they should not take all the rewards." Rasulullah ﷺ said, "This will not happen as long as you keep praising them and making du'a for them." *(Ahmad in Al Bidayah wan Nihayah, Ibn Kathir, Ibn Jareer, Hakim, Bayhaqi in Kanzul Ummal)*

Jabir ﷺ narrates that whenever the Ansar harvested their crops, they would divide the crop into 2 parts, the one part being smaller than the other. They would then place branches with the smaller portion to make it look bigger than the other portion. Thereafter, they gave the Muhajirs the choice between the 2 portions. The Muhajirs would choose the larger portion - the portion without the branches, thinking that they were leaving the larger portion for the Ansar. The Ansar would then take the smaller portion for themselves. This practice continued until Khaibar was conquered. When Khaibar was conquered, Rasulullah ﷺ said to the Ansar, "You have fulfilled your duty towards us. Now, if you please, you may hand over your shares of plantations in Khaibar to the Muhajirs and have your date crops in Madinah all for yourselves without sharing it with the Muhajirs, who will now receive from Khaibar." The Ansar accepted the proposal and said, "You have placed several responsibilities on us while you have taken the responsibly that in exchange for this, we shall have Jannah. We have now fulfilled what you had asked of us and require your condition to be met." Rasulullah ﷺ said, "You have it." *(Bazzar, Haythami).* Anas ﷺ narrates that Rasulullah ﷺ once called for the Ansar to distribute the land of Bahrain amongst them. However, they refused to have any of it unless the Muhajirs also received an equal amount of land. Rasulullah ﷺ then said to them, "In that case, we cannot distribute the land." Rasulullah ﷺ then added, "You Ansar should exercise patience until you meet me on the Day of Judgment because after my death others will be given preference over you." *(Bukhari).*

How the Ansar Severed the Ties They had During the Period of Ignorance to Strengthen the Ties of Islam

Jabir bin Abdullah ﷺ narrates that Rasulullah ﷺ said, "Who is a there to see Ka'b bin Ashraf because he has caused great harm to (Islam) Allah and to His Rasul ﷺ?" Muhammad bin Maslama stood up and said, "Do you want me to kill him?" "Yes," replied Rasulullah ﷺ. Muhammad bin Maslama then said, "Do permit me to say something to him as well." Rasulullah ﷺ granted him permission. Taking some companions along with him, Muhammad bin Maslama ﷺ went to Ka'b bin Ashraf and said, "That man (Rasulullah ﷺ) had asked us for charity and had exhausted us with requests. We have therefore come to you for a loan." Ka'b said, "By Allah! He will again exhaust you out afterwards." Muhammad bin Maslama ﷺ said, "We have started following him and do not like to leave him until we see what happens to him in the end. We want you to lend us a Wasaq or 2 of grain." Ka'b replied, "Fine, but I need collateral first." Muhammad bin Maslama ﷺ and the other Sahabah asked, "What collateral do you want?" Ka'b said, "Give me your women as collateral." They responded by saying, "How can we give you our women as collateral when you are the most handsome of the Arabs?" Ka'b said, "Then give me your children." They said, "How can we give our children as collateral when people will taunt by saying that these are the children who were given as collateral for a mere one or 2 Wasaq of grain? This would be too embarrassing for us. We shall rather give you our weapons as collateral." When Ka'b agreed, they arranged to meet at night. Muhammad bin Maslama ﷺ arrived at night with Abu Na'ilah ﷺ who was Ka'b's foster brother by virtue of being suckled by the same woman. Ka'b called them to a fortress and came down to meet them. Ka'b's wife asked, "Where are you going at this

hour?" He replied, "It is only Muhammad bin Maslama and my brother Abu Na'ilah." According to another narration, she said, "I hear a sound resembling the dripping of blood." Ka'b reassured her saying, "It is only my brother Muhammad bin Maslama and my foster brother Abu Na'ila. A brave person responds even if he is called to a confrontation at night." Muhammad bin Maslama ﷺ brought another 2 or 3 men with him and said to them, "When he arrives, I shall hold his hair to smell it and you shall also ask me to smell. When you see that I have a good hold of his head, you should attack him," Ka'b arrived wearing a belt fitted with jewels and gave off the fragrance of perfume. Muhammad bin Maslama ﷺ exclaimed, "To this day have I never smelt anything so good!" Ka'b said, "I have the most fragranced Arab women and the most beautiful ones." Muhammad bin Maslama ﷺ said, "Do allow me to smell your head." "Certainly," Ka'b said gladly. Muhammad bin Maslama ﷺ smelt Ka'b's head and allowed his companions to do so as well. Thereafter, Muhammad bin Maslama ﷺ asked, "Will you permit me a second time?" When Ka'b allowed him, Muhammad bin Maslama ﷺ took firm hold of Ka'b's head and said to the others, "Get him!" They then killed him and reported back to Rasulullah ﷺ. According to a narration of Urwa ﷺ, Rasulullah ﷺ praised Allah ﷺ when they reported back to him. A narration of *Ibn Sa'd* states that after killing Ka'b when Muhammad bin Maslama ﷺ and his companions reached Baqee Gharqad (the graveyard), they shouted "Allahu Akbar!" Rasulullah ﷺ was busy performing salah that night and when he heard them shout "Allahu Akbar!", he also shouted "Allahu Akbar!" because he guessed that they had already killed Ka'b. When they came to him, Rasulullah ﷺ commented, "You have the faces of successful people." "Your face is too, O Rasulullah ﷺ," they responded. They threw Ka'b's head before Rasulullah ﷺ and he praised Allah for Ka'b's death.

A narration of Ikrama states that after Ka'b's death, the Jews became terrified and came to Rasulullah ﷺ. They said, "Our leader was killed by deception." Rasulullah ﷺ reminded them of Ka'b's treacherous ways and about how he instigated against Islam and harmed the Muslims. *Ibn Sa'd* adds that after this, the Jews became scared and kept silent. *(Bukhari in Fat'hul Bari).* *Ibn Is'haq* narrates that Rasulullah ﷺ once announced, "Who will see to Ibn Ashraf for me?" Muhammad bin Maslama ﷺ said, "I shall see to him for you, O Rasulullah ﷺ. I shall kill him." Rasulullah ﷺ said, "Do so if you can." Muhammad bin Maslama ﷺ spent the next 3 days without eating or drinking anything besides what was needed to preserve his life. Rasulullah ﷺ was informed about this, he called Muhammad bin Maslama ﷺ and asked him why he had stopped eating and drinking. He replied, "I have promised you something that I am unsure whether I will be able to fulfill." Rasulullah ﷺ said to him, "All you have to do is to try." Another narration of *Ibn Is'haq* from Abdullah bin Abbas ﷺ states that Rasulullah ﷺ walked with Muhammad bin Maslama ﷺ and his companions up to Baqee Gharqad and pointed them in the direction saying, "Proceed with the name of Allah. O Allah! Assist them." *(Al Bidayah wan Nihayah, Fat'hul Bari)*

Abu Rafi Salam bin Abul Huqaiq is Killed

Abdullah bin Ka'b bin Malik ﷺ says that amongst the many advantages that Allah had granted Rasulullah ﷺ to facilitate the effective propagation of Islam was that the 2 Ansar tribes of the Khazraj and Aws were always competing to serve Rasulullah ﷺ just as 2 wrestlers compete. Whenever the Aws did something to benefit Rasulullah ﷺ, the Khazraj would say, "By Allah! By doing this you shall not surpass our standing with Rasulullah ﷺ." They would then stop at nothing to match the deed. Similarly, whenever the Khazraj did something to win Rasulullah ﷺ's favor, the Aws would say the same thing. Therefore, when the Aws managed to kill Ka'b bin Ashraf for his hostilities towards Rasulullah ﷺ, the Khazraj said, "By Allah! You people shall never surpass us by doing this." They then discussed who was as hostile towards Rasulullah ﷺ as Ka'b bin Ashraf was. They arrived at the conclusion that such a person was Ibn Abul Huqaiq who lived in Khaibar. They therefore sought permission from Rasulullah ﷺ to kill him and when permission was granted, 5 men from the Banu Salama family of the Khazraj left. They were Abdullah bin Ateek ﷺ, Mas'ood bin Sinan ﷺ, Abdullah bin Unais ﷺ, Abu Qatadah Harith bin Rib'ee ﷺ and Khuza'ee bin Aswad ﷺ who was their ally from the Bani Aslam family. When they left, Rasulullah ﷺ appointed Abdullah bin Ateek ﷺ as their Amir and forbade them from killing any women and children. When the Sahabah reached Khaibar, they went to the house of Ibn Abul Huqaiq at night. Every room in the house was locked from outside so that none could come out. Ibn Abul Huqaiq had an upstairs room connected with a ladder made of date fibers. The Sahabah climbed the ladder and standing at his door, they sought permission to enter. When Ibn Abul Huqaiq's wife came out to ask who they were, they said that they were Arabs looking for grain supplies. She pointed them to Ibn Abul Huqaiq and they entered the room. The Sahabah narrate, "When we entered the room, we locked the door behind us fearing that nothing should become an obstacle between us and him. His wife started screaming to alert him about our arrival and we rushed to him showing off our swords as he lay on the bed. By Allah! It was only the whiteness of his body that led us to him in the darkness of the night. He appeared to be in a white Coptic cloth thrown on the bed. When his wife gave us away, one of our men lifted his sword over her but immediately retrained himself when he remembered the instructions of Rasulullah ﷺ. Had it not been for this we would have killed her that night. When we attacked him with out swords and Abdullah bin Unais ﷺ pushed his sword into Ibn Abul Huqaiq's belly with such force that the sword went right through him as he pleaded, "Enough! Enough!" We then left the room. Abdullah bin Atik ﷺ was poor sighted and fell from a step, injuring his leg very badly. We carried him until we reached one of the water inlets of a Jewish fortress. We crawled in as the Jews lit fires and vigorously searched for us everywhere. When they eventually lost hope of finding us, they returned to Ibn Abul Huqaiq and surrounded him as he was dying. We asked ourselves, 'How would we get to know whether the enemy of Allah has died?' One of us volunteered to go and find out. He proceeded and walked amongst the Jews." The Sahabi who went says, "I found his wife and several Jewish men around Ibn Abul Huqaiq. His wife carried a lantern in her hand and was speaking to the others as she looked at her husband's face. She was saying, 'I swear by Allah that I heard the voice of Ibn Atik but I then disagreed with myself and said, 'How can Ibn Atik be in this place?!' She then looked properly at the face of Ibn Abul Huqaiq and said, 'By the lord of the Jews! He is dead!' Nothing pleased me more than hearing this." The Sahabi reported back to his companions and carrying Abdullah bin Atik ﷺ, they returned to Rasulullah ﷺ and informed him of the death of Allah's enemy. They then started disputing about who had killed him, each one of them claiming to have done it. Rasulullah ﷺ asked them to give him their swords and after inspecting them, said about the sword of Abdullah bin Unais ﷺ, "This one had killed him for I see traces of food on it." *(Ibn Is'h'aq in At Bidayah wan Nihayah and the Seerah of Ibn Hisham).*

Bara ﷺ narrates that Rasulullah ﷺ sent some men from the Ansar to kill Abu Rafi. Rasulullah ﷺ appointed Abdullah bin Atik ﷺ as their Amir. Abu Rafi used to harm Rasulullah ﷺ greatly and assist others against him. He was staying in a fortress somewhere in Hijaz (Khaibar). When the Sahabah drew close to the fortress, the sun had already set and the people had already returned home with their animals. Abdullah bin Atik ﷺ said to the others, "Sit here. I shall go and devise a plan with the gatekeeper to enter the gate." When he approached the gate of the fortress, he covered himself with his clothes so that he resembled a person answering the call of nature. By then all the people had already entered. The gatekeeper then shouted to him, "O servant of Allah! If you wish to enter, please do so because I want to lock the gates." Abdullah ﷺ narrates further. He says, "So I entered and hid myself away. Eventually, when everyone had entered, the gatekeeper locked the gates and hung the keys on a nail. I went to the keys, took them and opened the gates. Stories used to be recited every night to Abu Rafi who was in the upper story of his home. When the storytellers had left, I climbed the ladder to his room. As I opened each door, I locked it behind me saying to myself that if the people find out about me, they will only reach me after I had killed Abu Rafi. When I reached him, he was in a dark room with his wife and I had no idea where he was in the room. I said, 'Abu Rafi!' When he replied, 'Who is it?' I charged in the direction of the voice and struck him with my sword. However, because I was afraid, my strike did not kill him. When he started screaming, I left the room and waited awhile. I then entered and asked, "What is all this uproar, O Abu Rafi?' He said; 'Woe to your mother! Someone in the room has just struck me with a sword.' I then struck him again but rather than killing him, I only succeeded in wounding him. I then pushed the blade of my sword into his belly until it reached his back and I was convinced that I had killed him. I then started opening door after door until I reached the ladder. As I climbed down, I reached a place where I placed my foot down thinking that I had reached the ground, but I fell in the moonlit night. My shinbone broke and I carried on walking after bandaging it with my turban. I then sat at the gate telling myself that I shall not leave until I am certain that I had killed him. When the cock crowed, an announcer stood on the wall and announced, 'Abu Rafi the trader of Hijaz has died.' I walked back to my companions and said, 'Success! Allah has killed Abu Rafi. When I got back to Rasulullah ﷺ and informed him about the events, he asked me to stretch out my leg. When I did so, he passed his and over my leg and it was cured so well that it felt as if nothing was ever wrong with it." *(Bukhari).* Another narration states that when Abdullah bin Atik ﷺ and the others came back to Rasulullah ﷺ, he was on the pulpit and seeing them approaching, he said, "The faces of success!" They replied, "It is your face that is successful, O Rasulullah ﷺ!" He then asked, "Have you killed him?" When they replied in the affirmative, Rasulullah ﷺ asked to see the sword. Rasulullah ﷺ then drew the sword from its sheath and after inspecting it he said, "Yes! Here are traces of food on the blade." *(Bukhari, Al Budayah wan Nihayah).*

Ibn Shaiba is Killed

The daughter of Muhaisa ﷺ narrates from her father that when Rasulullah ﷺ once permitted the Sahabah to kill any Jew they could, Muhaisa ﷺ attacked and killed a Jewish trader called Ibn Shaiba who interacted and traded with the Muslims. When Muhaisa ﷺ did this, his elder brother Huwaisa ﷺ who was not yet a Muslim started hitting Muhaisa ﷺ saying, "You enemy of Allah! You have killed him whereas I can swear by Allah that most of the fat in your stomach has come from his wealth."

Muhaisa ☺ replied, "I swear by Allah that had Rasulullah ﷺ commanded me to kill you, I would have killed you." This was the beginning of Huwaisa's conversion to Islam. Surprised by this statement of his brother, Huwaisa ☺ asked, "Had Muhammad ﷺ commanded you to kill me, you would have done it?" Muhaisa ☺ replied, "By Allah! I certainly would." Huwaisa ☺ then commented, "By Allah! The religion that has taken you to this must certainly be amazing." (Abu Nu'aym in Kanzul Ummal). Another narration quotes that Muhaisa ☺ said, "That personality has commanded me to kill Ibn Shaiba for whom I shall even kill you if he so commands me." This narration also adds that Huwaisa ☺ then accepted Islam. (Ibn Is'haq, Abu Dawud).

The Ansar in the Battles Against the Banu Qaynuqa, Banu Nadhir and Banu Quraiza Tribes

Abdullah bin Abbas ☺ narrates that after Rasulullah ﷺ had defeated the Quraish in the Battle of Badr, he gathered the Jews of Madinah in the marketplace of the Banu Qaynuqa tribe. He then said to them, "O Jews! Accept Islam before you suffer the same fate as the Quraish suffered in the Battle of Badr." The Jews said, "The Quraish does not know how to fight. If you were to fight against us, you would learn that we are real men." It was then that Allah revealed the following verse of the Qur'an:

قُلْ لِلَّذِينَ كَفَرُوا سَتُغْلَبُونَ وَتُحْشَرُونَ إِلَى جَهَنَّمَ وَبِئْسَ الْمِهَادُ (12) قَدْ كَانَ لَكُمْ آيَةٌ فِي فِئَتَيْنِ الْتَقَتَا فِئَةٌ تُقَاتِلُ فِي سَبِيلِ اللَّهِ وَأُخْرَى كَافِرَةٌ يَرَوْنَهُمْ مِثْلَيْهِمْ رَأْيَ الْعَيْنِ وَاللَّهُ يُؤَيِّدُ بِنَصْرِهِ مَنْ يَشَاءُ إِنَّ فِي ذَلِكَ لَعِبْرَةً لِأُولِي الْأَبْصَارِ (13)

Say (O Muhammad ﷺ) to those who disbelieve: "You will be defeated and gathered together to Hell and worst indeed is that place to rest." There has already been a sign for you (O Jews) in the two armies that met (in combat i.e. the battle of Badr): One was fighting in the Cause of Allah, and as for the other (they) were disbelievers. They (the believers) saw them (the disbelievers) with their own eyes twice their number (although they were thrice their number). And Allah supports with His Victory whom He pleases. Verily, in this is a lesson for those who understand. (Al-Imran:12-13) (Ibn Is'haq in Fathul Bari)

Another narration states that the Jews said to Rasulullah ﷺ, "O Muhammad ﷺ! Do not pride yourself on the fact that you have killed some people of the Quraish who were unseasoned in the art of warfare and did not know how to fight. Should you fight against us, you would soon learn that we are real men and that you have not met us in battle." (Abu Dawud). Imam Zuhri رحمة الله narrates that after the disbelievers were defeated at Badr, the Muslims said to their Jewish acquaintances, "Accept Islam before Allah makes you suffer a day like the day of Badr." Malik bin Saif commented, "Are you deceived by that fact that you have defeated a group of people from the Quraish who have no knowledge of warfare? If we resolve to put all our forces against you, you would have no power to fight us." Ubadah bin Samit ☺ then said, "O Rasulullah ﷺ! I have many Jewish friends who are powerful men with plenty weapons and great influence. However, I release myself from their friendship to adopt the friendship of Allah and His Rasul ﷺ. I shall have no protecting friend besides Allah and His Rasul." To this, (the hypocrite) Abdullah bin Ubay commented, "On the contrary, I shall not release myself from the friendship of the Jews for I am a person who needs them." Addressing Abdullah bin Ubay, Rasulullah ﷺ said, "O Abu Hubab! You have opted for the friendship of the Jews in defiance of what Ubadah bin Samit has said. You may have their friendship for he does not." Abdullah bin Ubay said, "In that case, I am contented with this state of affairs." It was then that Allah revealed the following verses of the Qur'an:

يَا أَيُّهَا الَّذِينَ آمَنُوا لَا تَتَّخِذُوا الْيَهُودَ وَالنَّصَارَى أَوْلِيَاءَ بَعْضُهُمْ أَوْلِيَاءُ بَعْضٍ وَمَنْ يَتَوَلَّهُمْ مِنْكُمْ فَإِنَّهُ مِنْهُمْ إِنَّ اللَّهَ لَا يَهْدِي الْقَوْمَ الظَّالِمِينَ (51) .... وَاللَّهُ يَعْصِمُكَ مِنَ النَّاسِ

O you who believe! Take not the Jews and the Christians as Auliya (friends, protectors, helpers, etc.), they are but Auliya to one another. And if any amongst you takes them as Auliya, then surely he is one of them. Verily, Allah guides not those people who are the Zalimoon (polytheists and wrongdoers and unjust)...Allah will protect you from the people. (Al-Ma'idah:51...67) (Ibn Jareer)

Another narration states that when the Jewish Banu Qaynuqa tribe started hostilities against Rasulullah ﷺ, Abdullah bin Ubay bin Salul sided with them and stood in their defense. Ubadah bin Samit who was also an ally of the Banu Qaynuqa just like Abdullah bin Ubay was, went to Rasulullah ﷺ and made it clear that he was forsaking them in favor of Rasulullah ﷺ and releasing himself from the alliance he had previously forged with them so that he could adopt complete allegiance to Allah and His Rasul ﷺ. He said, "O Rasulullah ﷺ! I choose to adopt the friendship of Allah, His Rasul ﷺ and the Mu'minin while I release myself from the alliance and friendship of those disbeliever." It was with reference to Ubadah ☺ and Abdullah bin Ubay that the following verses of Al-Ma'idah were revealed:

يَا أَيُّهَا الَّذِينَ آمَنُوا لَا تَتَّخِذُوا الْيَهُودَ وَالنَّصَارَى أَوْلِيَاءَ بَعْضُهُمْ أَوْلِيَاءُ بَعْضٍ وَمَنْ يَتَوَلَّهُمْ مِنْكُمْ فَإِنَّهُ مِنْهُمْ إِنَّ اللَّهَ لَا يَهْدِي الْقَوْمَ الظَّالِمِينَ (51) .... وَمَنْ يَتَوَلَّ اللَّهَ وَرَسُولَهُ وَالَّذِينَ آمَنُوا فَإِنَّ حِزْبَ اللَّهِ هُمُ الْغَالِبُونَ (56)

O you who believe! Take not the Jews and the Christians as Auliya (friends, protectors, helpers, etc.), they are but Auliya to one another (and cannot be your friends) ... And whosoever takes Allah, His Messenger, and those who have believed, as Protectors, then the party of Allah will be the victorious. (Al-Ma'idh:51...56) (Ibn Is'haq in Al Bidayah wan Nihayah).

The Episode of the Banu Nadhir Tribe

A Sahabi narrates that before the battle of Badr, the disbeliever of the Quraish wrote to the hypocrite Abdullah bin Ubay and others like him who worshipped idols. In their correspondence, they intimidated them for granting shelter to Rasulullah ﷺ and the Sahabah and threatened to attack them with a combined force of all the Arabs. Abdullah bin Ubay and the others therefore resolved to fight the Muslims. Rasulullah ﷺ then approached them and said, "No one has planned against you as the Quraish have done. All they intend doing is to sow discord amongst you because the members of your own families are Muslims." They realized that Rasulullah ﷺ was right and dispersed giving up the idea of fighting the Muslims. After the battle of Badr, the disbeliever of the Quraish wrote to the Jews telling them that the Jews were well fortified and well armed and could therefore fight the Muslims. In their letter, they also threatened the Jews with aggression if the Jews refused to fight the Muslims. The Jews of the Banu Nadhir tribe therefore resolved to betray the trust of the Muslims. They sent a message to Rasulullah ﷺ saying, "Come to us with 2 of your companions and 3 of our scholars will meet you. If they accept Islam and follow you, we shall all follow suit." As Rasulullah ﷺ prepared to meet them, the 3 Jews hid daggers in their covers. However, before Rasulullah ﷺ met with them, a Jewish woman from the Banu Nadhir whose brother had accepted Islam and was living amongst the Ansar sent a message to her brother informing him about the scheme of the Banu Nadhir. Rasulullah ﷺ then returned and marched with a battalion against them early in the morning. The Muslims laid siege to their fortress that day and the following day Rasulullah ﷺ marched on to the fortress of the Banu Quraiza. Rasulullah ﷺ also laid siege to their fortress and they entered into a treaty with him. Rasulullah ﷺ then returned to the Banu Nadhir and when they refused to enter into a treaty, he fought them until they finally surrendered on condition that they go into exile and be allowed to take with them anything besides weapons that could be loaded on their camels. They then loaded their camels to the extent that they even loaded the doors of their houses. They therefore demolished their homes with their own hands and loaded on their camels the scraps of wood that suited them. This expulsion was the first exile to Sham. *(Ibn Mardaway, Fat'hul Bari, Abu Dawud, Abdur Razzaq, Ibn Mundhir, Bayhaqi in Badlul Majhud, Durrul Manthur)*

Abdullah bin Abbas ﷺ narrates that Rasulullah ﷺ maintained the siege of the Banu Nadhir until they could not hold out any longer and were forced to give in to all his demands. They eventually agreed that their lives would be spared and that they would be expelled from their home to settle in Adhra'at in Sham (a place close to Amman and Balqa). Rasulullah ﷺ allowed them a camel and a water bag between every 3 persons. *(Bayhaqi)*. Rasulullah ﷺ sent Muhammad bin Maslama ﷺ to the Banu Nadhir with instructions to allow them 3 days to leave. *(Bayhaqi)*. The message that Rasulullah ﷺ sent with Muhammad bin Maslama ﷺ read, "Leave my land and never live with me as long as you intend to be treacherous. I am giving you 10 days to leave." *(Ibn Sa'd in Fat'hul Bari)*.

The Episode of the Banu Quraiza Tribe

Aisha ﷺ says, "I came out of the house during the battle of Khandaq and was following the people when I heard footsteps on the ground behind me. It was Sa'd bin Mu'adh and his nephew Harith bin Aws ﷺ carrying a shield. I immediately sat down on the ground and Sa'd passed by wearing a coat of steel armor. Because of his extraordinary height, part of his body was exposed and I feared for those parts that an enemy should not strike him there. Sa'd ﷺ was one of the largest and tallest of people and was reciting the following couplets as he passed:
"Wait awhile until Hamal reaches the battle how beautiful is death when its term arrives"

I then stood up and entered an orchard where I found a group of Muslims sitting. Amongst them was Omar ﷺ and a person wearing a helmet. When he saw me, Omar ﷺ said, 'What brings you here? By Allah! You are certainly a brave woman. Do you not fear that a calamity may befall us or that we are defeated?' He continued warning me until I wished that the earth should open up at that moment so that I could enter it. The other person then lifted his helmet and I saw that he was Talha bin Ubaidullah ﷺ. He said, 'Shame on you Omar. You have been overdoing things since today. Where else can we run to except to Allah?' A man from the Quraish called Ibn Arqa shot an arrow at Sa'd bin Mu'adh ﷺ and said, 'Take that for my name is Ibn Arqa!' The arrow struck an artery in his arm and cut it wide open. Sa'd ﷺ had been an ally of the Banu Quraiza during the period of ignorance and prayed to Allah saying, 'O Allah! Do not let me die until I have had the pleasure of seeing what is to become of the Banu Quraiza'. His artery then stopped bleeding. Allah then sent a cyclonic wind against the disbelievers, thereby alleviating the Mu'minin of having to fight. Allah is Most Powerful and Mighty." Aisha ﷺ continues narrating. She says that since the disbelievers were forced to retreat, Abu Sufian and those with him returned to Tihama while Uyaina bin Badr and his people returned to Najd. The Banu Quraiza returned and locked themselves up in their fortresses. Meanwhile, Rasulullah ﷺ

returned to Madinah and had a tent pitched for Sa'd ﷺ in the Masjid. Jibra'el then arrived and had sand on his front teeth indicating that he was still engaged in battle. He asked Rasulullah ﷺ, "Have you already put down your weapons? By Allah, the angels have not yet put down their weapons. You should now fight the Banu Quraiza." Rasulullah ﷺ therefore wore his armor and had an announcement made that the Sahabah should march for battle. As they passed by the Banu Ghanam tribe who lived in the neighborhood of the Masjid, Rasulullah ﷺ asked them if anyone had passed by them. They told him that Dihya Kalbi ﷺ had passed by. The beard, age and face of Jibra'el resembled that of Dihya Kalbi ﷺ as Jibra'el عليه السلام appeared in the semblance of Dihya ﷺ. It was therefore Jibra'el عليه السلام whom the Banu Ghanam tribesmen had seen passing. When Rasulullah ﷺ arrived at the fortresses of the Banu Quraiza, he laid siege to them for 25 nights. When the Banu Quraiza could no longer bear the siege and their suffering grew intense, they were asked to surrender to the decision of Rasulullah ﷺ. When they consulted with Abu Lubaba ﷺ, he indicated to them that they would be killed. They then asked to surrender to the decision of Sa'd bin Mu'adh ﷺ. Rasulullah ﷺ allowed them to do so and Sa'd bin Mu'adh ﷺ was brought on a donkey fitted with a carriage made from he bark of a date palm. He was lifted on to the donkey and his people surrounded him. Interceding on behalf of the Banu Quraiza, the people said to Sa'd ﷺ, "O Abu Amr! They are your allies, your friends, they are of assistance during times of need and people whom you know." However, Sa'd ﷺ gave no reply and did not even pay any attention to them. Eventually, when he drew close to the settlement of the Banu Quraiza, Sa'd ﷺ turned to his people and said, "The time has come for me not to be concerned about the criticism of critics when it concerns Allah." Aisha ﷺ narrates further from Abu Sa'eed Khudri that when Sa'd ﷺ arrived, Rasulullah ﷺ said to the Sahabah, "Stand up for your leader and help him to dismount." Omar ﷺ remarked, "Our leader is Allah." Rasulullah ﷺ repeated, "Help him down." After the Sahabah had helped Sa'd ﷺ down, Rasulullah ﷺ said to him, "Decide their fate." Sa'd ﷺ said, "I have decided that all their warriors should be executed, that their families should be taken captive and that their wealth be distributed as booty." Rasulullah ﷺ commented, "You have decided their fate according to the decision of Allah and His Rasul ﷺ." Sa'd ﷺ then made the following Du'a, "O Allah! If you have reserved any battle for your Nabi ﷺ against the Quraish, then preserve me for it. However, if You have terminated all battles between him and them, then take me to You." Although his wound had already healed by then and the only sign of it was a mark resembling an earring, it opened up again. He then had to return to the tent that Rasulullah ﷺ had pitched for him in the Masjid. Aisha ﷺ narrates further, "Rasulullah ﷺ, Abu Bakr ﷺ and Omar ﷺ went to visit him. I swear by the Being in Whose control is the life of Muhammad ﷺ! As I sat in my room, when Sa'd ﷺ passed away after a few days, I could recognize the crying of Omar ﷺ from that of Abu Bakr ﷺ. The Sahabah were just as Allah ﷻ described them in the Qur'an when He says: رُحَمَاءُ بَيْنَهُمْ

"Merciful amongst themselves" (Al-Fatah:29)
Alqama narrates that he then asked Aisha ﷺ, "Dear mother! What did Rasulullah ﷺ then do?" Aisha ﷺ replied, "Although Rasulullah ﷺ would not cry often upon the death of anyone, when he was really grieved, he would hold his beard." *(Ahmad, Ibn Sa'd, Haythami, Abu Nu'aym)*. Aisha ﷺ also narrates that when Sa'd bin Mu'adh ﷺ passed away, Rasulullah ﷺ held his beard when his grief grew intense. She says further, "I could also recognize the crying of my father Abu Bakr ﷺ from that of Omar

." *(Ibn Jareer in Kanzul Ummal).* Another narration states that when Rasulullah ﷺ returned from the burial of Sa'd bin Mu'adh *,* his tears flowed on to his beard. *(Tabrani, Haythani).*

The Ansar Prided Themselves on Their Accomplishments in Islam

Anas * says that on one occasion the Aws and Khazraj tribes boasted to each other. The Aws said, "Amongst us was the person whom the angels bathed after his martyrdom.' He was Handhala bin Rahib *. Also amongst us was the person for whom the throne of Allah shook when he passed away. He was Sa'd bin Mu'adh * Amongst us was also the person who was protected by a swarm of wasps when the disbelievers intended to mutilate his body. He was Asim bin Thabit bin Abil Aflah *. We also had in our ranks the person whose testimony was allowed by Rasulullah ﷺ in place of the testimony of 2 people. He was Khuzayma bin Thabit *. May Allah ﷺ be pleased with all of them." In response to this, the members of the Khazraj said, "We have 4 persons who memorized the entire Qur'an during the lifetime of Rasulullah ﷺ. There were none besides them who achieved this honor. They were Zaid bin Thabit *, Ubay bin Ka'b *, Mu'adh bin Jabal * and Abu Zaid *. May Allah be pleased with all of them." *(Abu Ya'la, Bazzar, Tabrani, Haythami Abu Awana and Ibn Asakir in Muntakhab)*

The Ansar Sacrifice Worldly Pleasures and Tts Temporary Possessions in Exchange for the Pleasure of Allah and His Rasul ﷺ

Abdullah bin Rabah * says, "Abu Hurairah * and I were part of many delegations that came to Mu'awiya * during Ramadhan. We used to prepare food for each other and Abu Hurairah * very often invited us to his camp for meals. I once told myself that I should also invite everyone to my camp for meals. I therefore had meals prepared and when I met Abu Hurairah * for the Isha salah, I said to him, 'O Abu Hurairah *! Meals will be served at my place tonight.' He commented, 'You have beaten me to it.' 'I certainly have,' I replied. When the people were with me after I had called them, Abu Hurairah * said, 'O gathering of Ansar! Should I not inform you about an incident about your people?'" Abu Hurairah * then continued to relate the incident of the conquest of Makkah. He said that when Rasulullah ﷺ entered Makkah, he appointed Zubair * to take charge of one of the sides of the army. He then appointed Khalid bin Walid * to take charge of the other side of the army while Abu Ubaidah * was put in charge of those Muslims who had no armor. As Rasulullah ﷺ remained with his contingent, the rest marched through the centre of the valley. The Quraish gathered the worthless people of their society and said, "We will send this lot against the Muslims. If they achieve any success, we shall join them. If they are defeated, we shall have to give in to the demands of Rasulullah ﷺ."

Abu Hurairah * narrates further that when Rasulullah ﷺ lifted his gazes, he saw him and called for him. Abu Hurairah * replied, "I am at your service, O Rasulullah ﷺ!" Rasulullah ﷺ said, "Call the Ansar for me and ensure that none but them come." Abu Hurairah * called for them and they arrived. When they had gathered around Rasulullah ﷺ, he said to them, "Do you see the worthless people of the Quraish and those with them?" Passing his one hand over the other, Rasulullah ﷺ then said, "Mow them down and then meet me at Safa." Abu Hurairah * says, "We then proceeded. We were in a position of killing as many of the Quraish as we pleased, while none of them were in a position to offer any resistance." Abu Sufian * then said, "O Rasulullah ﷺ! You have permitted the extermination of all the Quraish. There shall be none of the Quraish left after today." Rasulullah ﷺ said, "Whoever locks his door shall be safe and whoever enters the house of Abu Sufian shall be safe." The people then locked their houses. Rasulullah ﷺ then went to the Kabah and starting from the Black Stone, he performed Tawaf. As he performed Tawaf, Rasulullah ﷺ passed an idol standing next to the Kabah, which people used to worship. He was holding a bow on one end and poked the eye of the idol as he recited the following verse of the Qur'an:

وَقُلْ جَاءَ الْحَقُّ وَزَهَقَ الْبَاطِلُ إِنَّ الْبَاطِلَ كَانَ زَهُوقًا (81)

And say: "Truth has come and falsehood has vanished. Surely falsehood is ever bound to vanish." (Al-Isra':81)

Rasulullah ﷺ then went to Mount Safa and climbed it until he could see the Kabah. He then raised his hands and engaged in Dhikr and Du'a for some time. Standing below him, the Ansar said to each other, "It seems like the love for his city and pity for his people has overtaken Rasulullah ﷺ." Abu Hurairah * says further, "Revelation then started to descend on Rasulullah ﷺ and when this happened it was no secret to any of us and no one would look at Rasulullah ﷺ until it was finished." Once the revelation had stopped, Rasulullah ﷺ lifted his gazes and said, "O assembly of Ansar! Was it you who said, 'It seems like the love for his city and pity for his people has overtaken Rasulullah ﷺ?' When the Ansar admitted that they had made the statement, Rasulullah ﷺ said, "What will my name then be?' I am certainly the servant of Allah and His Rasul. I have made Hijra towards Allah and towards you people. My life shall be with you and my death as well." The Ansar then came weeping to Rasulullah ﷺ saying, "By Allah! We only said what we did so that Allah and His Rasul ﷺ should remain exclusively ours as we feared that you should not leave us to settle in Makkah." Rasulullah ﷺ said, "Verily Allah and His Rasul ﷺ believe you and accept your excuse believing that you said it out of extreme love." *(Ahmad, Muslim, Nasai in Al Bidayah wan Nihayah, Ibn Abi Shaiba in Kanzul Ummal).*

The Story of the Ansar During the Battle of Hunain and the Statement of Rasulullah ﷺ About Them

Anas * narrates that when the battle of Hunain took place, the Hawazin, Ghitfan and other tribes came to the battlefield with their stock animals as well as their families indicating that they intended to fight until the end. Rasulullah ﷺ arrived with 10,000 Sahabah and many others who had been granted amnesty when Makkah was conquered. However, when the Muslim army was caught by surprise, the Muslims fled the battlefield and Rasulullah ﷺ was left all alone. Rasulullah ﷺ then made 2 distinct announcements. Turning to his right, Rasulullah ﷺ said, "O Assembly of Ansar!" The Ansar responded by saying, "We are at your service, O Rasulullah ﷺ! Accept the glad tidings that we are with you." He then turned to his left and announced, "O Assembly of Ansar!" The Ansar again responded by saying, "We are at your service, O Rasulullah ﷺ! Accept the glad tidings that we are with you." Rasulullah ﷺ then dismounted his white mule saying, "I am the servant of Allah and His Rasul." The disbelievers were later defeated and Rasulullah ﷺ received a vast amount of booty. Rasulullah ﷺ distributed the booty amongst the Muhajir and those who had been granted amnesty. The Ansar received nothing. Some people of the Ansar then commented, "We are called when times are difficult, but the booty is given to others." When this statement reached Rasulullah ﷺ, he gathered the Ansar in a tent and asked, "O Assembly of Ansar! What is this that has reached me?" When they remained silent, Rasulullah ﷺ said, "O assembly of Ansar! Does it not please you that while people return home with worldly articles, you would be returning with the Rasul ﷺ of Allah, who you shall keep in your homes?" The Ansar replied, "It certainly does please us." Rasulullah ﷺ added, "If everyone walks another valley and the Ansar walk another valley, I shall walk the valley of the Ansar." A narrator by the name of Hisham says that he then asked Anas ؓ, "O Abu Hamza! Were you present here?" Anas ؓ replied, "How could I absent myself?" *(Bukhari in Al Bidayah wan Nihayah, Abi Asakir in Kanzul Ummal)*

Abu Sa'eed Khudri ؓ narrates that when Rasulullah ﷺ received the booty from the Battle of Hunain, he distributed it amongst the members of the Quraish whose hearts he wanted to win over and amongst the Arabs who asked for a share. When the Ansar neither received a small or large part of it, they were so hurt that one of them said, "By Allah! Rasulullah ﷺ has rejoined with his people." Sa'd bin Ubadah ؓ went to Rasulullah ﷺ and said, "O Rasulullah ﷺ! This tribe of Ansar feels hurt about you." "Why is that?" asked Rasulullah ﷺ. Sa'd ؓ replied, "Because of the way in which you distributed the booty amongst your people and the other Arabs without giving them anything." Rasulullah ﷺ asked, "What are your feelings, O Sa'd?" Sa'd ؓ replied, "I am but one of my people and I feel the same way." Rasulullah ﷺ said, "Gather your people (the Ansar) in this enclosure and call me once they have gathered." Sa'd ؓ went out and shouted for them. Once he had gathered them in the enclosure, some Muhajir also arrived and Sa'd ؓ permitted them to enter. When some other Muhajir came, he sent them away. When every member of the Ansar had arrived, Sa'd ؓ went to Rasulullah ﷺ and said, "O Rasulullah ﷺ! The Ansar tribes have all gathered in the place where you instructed me to gather them." Rasulullah ﷺ then went there and stood up to deliver a sermon. After praising Allah, Rasulullah ﷺ said, "O Assembly of Ansar! When I came to you, were you not all astray, after which Allah guided you? Were you not poverty stricken after which Allah enriched you? Were you not enemies after which Allah bonded your hearts?" "Certainly," they replied. Rasulullah ﷺ then said, "O Assembly of Ansar! Why do you not respond?" They submitted, "What can we say, O Rasulullah ﷺ? What response should we make? The favor is from Allah and His Rasul ﷺ." Rasulullah ﷺ said, "By Allah! You would be speaking the truth and you would be believed in if you were to say to me, 'You came to us as an outcast and we granted you shelter. You came to us as a destitute person and we granted you financial assistance. You came to us as in fear and we granted you security. You came to us without any helpers and we granted you the assistance you needed.'" The Ansar repeated, "The favor is from Allah and His Rasul ﷺ." Rasulullah ﷺ then comforted them by saying, "O Assembly of Ansar! Do you feel hurt because I have given some short-lived things of this world to some new Muslims whose hearts I intend winning over whereas I have left you to the bounty of Islam that Allah has granted you? O Assembly of Ansar! Does it not please you to know that while other people return home with goats and camels, you will return home with the Rasul of Allah? I swear by the Being Who controls my life that if everyone walks a valley and the Ansar walk another valley, I shall walk the valley of the Ansar. Had it not been for the great virtue of Hijra, I would have been a man from the Ansar. O Allah! Shower Your mercy on the Ansar, on the children of the Ansar and the grandchildren of the Ansar." The Ansar then wept until their beards were soaked and they said, "We are pleased with Allah as our Rabb and with the distribution of Rasulullah ﷺ." Rasulullah ﷺ then returned to his tent and the Ansar dispersed. *(Bukhari, Ibn Is'haq in Al Bidayah wan Nihayah; Haythami, Ibn Abi Shaiba in Kanzul Ummal).*

Sa'ib bin Yazid ؓ narrates that as a gesture of goodwill, Rasulullah ﷺ distributed the booty received from the Hawazin in the Battle of Hunain amongst the Quraish and others. This made the Ansar upset. When Rasulullah ﷺ heard about this, he went to the Ansar where they were staying and said, "Whoever is amongst the Ansar from other tribes should go to his tent." Thereafter, Rasulullah ﷺ recited the Shahada, praised Allah and said, "O Assembly of Ansar! I have heard about your feelings concerning the booty that I preferred to give others to win over their hearts so that they should participate in Jihad after this day after Allah has entered Islam deep into their hearts. O Assembly of Ansar! Has Allah not favored you by granting you Iman, by granting you special virtue and by granting you the best of names, namely the Ansar (helpers) of Islam of Allah and the Ansar (helpers) of Allah's Rasul ﷺ? Had it not been for the great virtue of Hijra, I would have been a man from the Ansar. If everyone walks a valley and the Ansar walk another valley, I shall walk the valley of the Ansar. Does it not please you to know that while other people return home with goats, animals, and camels, you should return home with the Rasul of Allah Rasulullah ﷺ?" When the Ansar heard this, they exclaimed, "This pleases us." Rasulullah ﷺ then said, "Respond to what I have said." They said, "O Rasulullah ﷺ! You found us in darkness and through you Allah removed us from the darkness taking us into light. You found us on the crumbling edge of Jahannam and through you Allah saved us. You found us astray and through you Allah guided us. We are pleased with Allah as our Rabb, with Islam as our Deen, and with Muhammad ﷺ as our Nabi. O Rasulullah ﷺ! With an open heart we say that you may do as you please." Rasulullah ﷺ said, "By Allah! Had you responded by saying something else, I would have said that you have spoken the truth. You could have said to me, 'Did you not come to us as an outcast and we granted you shelter? Were people not calling you a liar when we believed you? Did we not accept what people were rejecting from you?' You would be true had you said this." The Ansar said, "On the contrary, the favor is from Allah and His Rasul ﷺ. It is the favor and grace of Allah's Rasul ﷺ that is upon us and on others." The Ansar started crying lot and Rasulullah ﷺ wept with them. *(Tabrani, Haythami)*

Anas bin Malik ؓ narrates that when Allah grave the wealth of the Hawazin tribe as booty to Rasulullah ﷺ, he started giving as much as 100 camels to some people. It was then that some people from the Ansar commented, "May Allah forgive Rasulullah ﷺ. He is giving the Quraish and leaving us out whereas it is our swords that are dripping with blood of the Hawazin." When Rasulullah ﷺ was informed about what they said, he called for the Ansar and gathered them in a leather tent. He did not call anyone besides them. When they had gathered, Rasulullah ﷺ stood up and said, "What is it that has reached me about you?" Some Ansar of understanding replied, "O Rasulullah ﷺ! Our seniors have said nothing but it was some youngsters who said, 'May Allah forgive Rasulullah ﷺ. He is giving the Quraish and leaving us out whereas it is our swords that are dripping with blood of the Hawazin'" Rasulullah ﷺ said, "I have only given to some people who have newly accepted Islam to win them over. Does it not please you to know that while other people return home with wealth, you will return home with the Rasul of Allah? I swear by Allah that what you return with is much better than what they return with." When the Ansar submitted that they were pleased with this, Rasulullah ﷺ said to them, "You people will soon find that others will be given great preference over you. Exercise patience until you meet Allah and His Rasul ﷺ. I shall be waiting for you at my pond of Kowthar." Anas ؓ says that it so happened that the Ansar were unable to exercise the necessary patience. (Bukhari). Another narration from Anas ☺ states that Rasulullah ﷺ said to the Ansar, "You are like under clothing to me while others are like outer garments. Does it not please you to know that while other people return home with goats and camels, you will return home with the Rasul of Allah?" "Most certainly!" they replied. Rasulullah ﷺ added, "The Ansar are like an abdomen to me and a place where special clothing is kept (very close to me). If everyone walks a valley and the Ansar walk another valley, I shall walk the valley of the Ansar and had it not been for the great virtue of Hijra, I would have been from the Ansar." (Ahmad in Al Bidayah wan Nihayah)

The Qualities of the Ansar

Anas ☺ narrates that when some wealth came to Rasulullah ﷺ from Bahrain whilst the Muhajir and Ansar heard about it from each other; they came to Rasulullah ﷺ early in the morning. The rest of the Hadith is lengthy, but in it Rasulullah ﷺ mentioned to the Ansar, "As far as I know, you people turn out in large numbers when situations are hazardous and turn out in small numbers when the occasion arrives for receiving something you are always there to assist others and care little about receiving things for yourselves." (Askari in Kanzul Ummal). Anas ☺ narrates that Rasulullah ﷺ once said to Abu Talha ☺, "Convey my Salam to your people (the Ansar) and inform them that as far as I know, they are extremely chaste and patient people." (Bazzar, Haythami). Anas ☺ states that when Abu Talha ☺ visited Rasulullah ﷺ during the illness in which Rasulullah ﷺ passed away, Rasulullah ﷺ said to him, "Convey my Salam to your people (the Ansar) for they are extremely chaste and patient people." (Abu Nu'aym in Kanzul Ummal, Hakim).

Rasulullah ﷺ's Statement When Sa'd bin Mu'adh ☺ Passed Away

Abdullah bin Shaddad ☺ narrates that Rasulullah ﷺ visited Sa'd bin Mu'adh ☺ as he was on his deathbed. Rasulullah ﷺ said, "O chief of his people! May Allah reward you well. You have fulfilled the pledge you made to Allah and Allah shall certainly fulfill His pledge to you." (Ibn Sa'd). Aisha ☺ narrates that Rasulullah ﷺ said, "No harm can come to a woman whether she stays between 2 homes of the Ansar or between her own parents." (Ahmad, Bazzar, Haythami)

The Hospitality of the Ansar and the Story of Usaid bin Hudhair ☺

Anas ☺ narrates that Usaid bin Hudhair ☺ once came to Rasulullah ﷺ who had just finished distributing food. Usaid bin Hudhair ☺ mentioned to Rasulullah ﷺ that a family of the Ansar from the Banu Zafar tribe were very needy. He also added that most of the members of that family were women. Rasulullah ﷺ said to him, "O Usaid! You left us without saying anything until everything has left our hands. However, if you hear that we receive anything, do remind me of that family." A while later, some barley and dates came to Rasulullah ﷺ from Khaibar. Rasulullah ﷺ then distributed it amongst the Muslims and especially gave a large amount to the Ansar and to that particular family. Expressing his gratitude, Usaid bin Hudhair ☺ said, "May Allah grant you the most sublime rewards, O Nabi of Allah." Rasulullah ﷺ said, "In fact, may Allah grant the most sublime rewards to you, O assembly of Ansar. As far as I know, you have always been most chaste and most patient. However, after I die, you shall soon see that others will be given preference over you in leadership and in distribution of wealth. I urge you to be patient until you meet me at the pond of Kowthar." (Ibn Adi, Bayhaqi, Ibn Asakir in Kanzul Ummal; Hakim in Mustadrak,

Haythami). Usaid bin Hudhair ☺ narrates that that 2 families approached him requesting that he ask Rasulullah ﷺ to include them in the distribution of food or to give them something from it. The one family was from the Banu Zafar tribe while the other was from the Banu Mu'awiya tribe. When he spoke to Rasulullah ﷺ, Rasulullah ﷺ said to him, "Certainly. I shall grant each of them a portion. When Allah gives us again, we shall give them." Usaid ☺ said, "May Allah grant you the best rewards, O Rasulullah ﷺ." Rasulullah ﷺ said, "In fact, may Allah grant the best rewards to you Ansar. As far as I know, you have always been most chaste and most patient. However, after I die, you shall see that others will be given preference over you."

Usaid ☺ says, "When Omar bin Khattab ☺ became the Khalifa and was distributing some clothing amongst the people, he sent me a set of clothing, which I regarded to be very little. As I was performing salah, I noticed a youngster from the Quraish wearing the same set of clothing which was so big for him that he was dragging along. I then recalled the words of Rasulullah ﷺ: 'After I die, you shall see that others will be given preference over you'. I then said, 'Allah and His Rasul ﷺ have spoken the truth.' When someone informed Omar ☺ about this, he came to me as I was still performing salah. He asked me to continue my salah and when I had finished, he asked, 'What is it that you said?' After informing him, he said, 'I had given that set of clothing to a Sahabi who had participated in the battle of Badr, the battle of Uhud and the pledge of Aqaba. The youngster from the Quraish who you saw went to him, bought it from him and then wore it. Did you think that giving preference to others over the Ansar would occur during my time?' I conceded, 'I swear by Allah that I do not think that it would occur during your rein as Khalifa.'" (Ahmad, Haythami)

The Story of Muhammad bin Maslama ☺ and Omar ☺

Muhammad bin Maslama ☺ narrates that as he was going to the Masjid, he noticed a man from the Quraish wearing a set of good clothing. When he asked the man who gave him the clothing, the man replied, "The Amirul Mu'minin." After he had passed by Muhammad bin Maslama ☺ noticed another man from the Quraish wearing a set of good clothing. When he asked the man who gave him the clothing, the man also replied that the Amirul Mu'minin had given it to him. When Muhammad bin Maslama ☺ entered the Masjid, he exclaimed in a loud voice, "Allahu Akbar! Allah ﷻ and His Rasul have spoken the truth! Allahu Akbar! Allah and His Rasul ﷺ have spoken the truth!" When Omar ☺ heard this, he sent someone to call him. Muhammad bin Maslama ☺ told the man that he first had to perform 2 Rakahs of salah. Omar ☺ sent the messenger again with the message that he insists that Muhammad bin Maslama ☺ should go to him. However, Muhammad bin Maslama ☺ was adamant that he would not go to Omar ☺ until he had performed 2 Rakahs of salah. He therefore started his salah. Omar ☺ then came himself and sat beside Muhammad bin Maslama ☺. When he had completed his salah, Omar ☺ asked, "Do tell me why you raised your voice calling the Takbeer in the place where Rasulullah ﷺ performed salah. And why did you say, 'Allah and His Rasul have spoken the truth'." Muhammad bin Maslama ☺ replied, "O Amirul Mu'minin! I was proceeding to the Masjid when I noticed a certain man from the Quraish wearing a set of good clothing. When I asked him who gave him the clothing, the man replied that the Amirul Mu'minin had given it to him. After he had passed by I noticed another man from the Quraish wearing a set of good clothing. When I asked the man who gave him the clothing, the man also replied that the Amirul Mu'minin had given it to him. After he had passed by I noticed a man from the Ansar wearing a set of clothing that was less expensive than the 2 others. When I asked him who give him the clothing, he informed me that the Amirul Mu'minin had given it to him. Although Rasulullah ﷺ had stated: 'After I die, you shall see that others will be given preference over you', I do not want it to happen at your hands, O Amirul Mu'minin." Omar ؓ then started to weep and said, "I seek forgiveness from Allah ﷻ! I shall never do it again," Thereafter, Omar ؓ was never seen giving preference to a person from the Quraish over a person from the Ansar. *(Ibn Asakir in Kanzul Ummal)*

Rasulullah ﷺ Honors Sa'd bin Ubadah ؓ

Zaid bin Thabit ؓ narrates that Sa'd bin Ubadah once visited Rasulullah ﷺ with his son. When he greeted with Salam, Rasulullah ﷺ said, "Here and here." Rasulullah ﷺ then made Sa'd ؓ sit on his right and said, "Welcome to the Ansar. Welcome to the Ansar." Out of respect for Rasulullah ﷺ Sa'd ؓ then made his son stand in front of Rasulullah ﷺ. Rasulullah ﷺ told the youth to sit and when he did, Rasulullah ﷺ asked him to sit closer to him. The youth came closer and started kissing the hands and feet of Rasulullah ﷺ. Rasulullah ﷺ said, "I am from the Ansar and from the children of the Ansar." Sa'd ؓ remarked, "May Allah honor you as you have honored us." Rasulullah ﷺ said, "Verily Allah has honored you before I could honor you. However, after I die, you shall soon see that others will be given preference over you. I urge you to be patient until you meet me at the pond of Kowthar." *(Ibn Asakir, Bukhari in Kanzul Ummal; Basai, Dar Qutni, Ali bin Madeni in Mizan)*

Jareer ؓ Serves Anas ؓ

Anas ؓ narrates that Jareer ؓ served him greatly as they traveled together on a journey. Jareer ؓ said, "I have seen the Ansar do great services to Rasulullah ﷺ and I therefore serve every person from the Ansar whom I see." *(Baghawi, Bayhaqi, Ibn Asakir in Kanzul Ummal)*.

Abu Ayub Ansari ؓ Stays with Abdullah bin Abbas ؓ who Places Himself at his Service

Habib bin Abi Thabit narrates that Abu Ayub Ansari ؓ once went to Mu'awiya ؓ to complain about a debt he had asking Mu'awiya ؓ for financial assistance. However, Abu Ayub Ansari ؓ did not receive the desired response, but rather received a response that was unpleasant. He then said, "I have heard Rasulullah ﷺ say, 'After I die, you shall see that others will be given preference over you (Ansar)'." Mu'awiya ؓ said, "What else did Rasulullah ﷺ say to you?" Abu Ayub ؓ replied that Rasulullah ﷺ advised them to exercise patience. Mu'awiya ؓ then said, "Then be patient." Abu Ayub ؓ remarked, "I swear by Allah that I shall never again ask you for anything!" Abu Ayub ؓ then went to Basra where he stayed with Abdullah bin Abbas ؓ. Abdullah bin Abbas ؓ emptied his home for Abu Ayub ؓ and said, "I shall do for you as you had done for Rasulullah ﷺ." He then instructed his family to leave the house, which they did. Thereafter, he said to Abu Ayub ؓ, "You may use anything in the house." In addition, he left with him 40,000 Dirhams and 20 slaves." *(Royani, Ibn Asakir in Kazmul Ummal)*. Another narration adds that Abu Ayub ؓ then went to Abdullah bin Abbas ؓ in Basra, who had been appointed as its governor by Ali ؓ. Abdullah bin Abbas ؓ said, "O Abu Ayub! I wish to leave this house for you just as you left your house for Rasulullah ﷺ." He then instructed his family to leave, which they did. Thereafter, he gave everything in the house to Abu Ayub. When Abu Ayub ؓ was leaving the place, Abdullah bin Abbas ؓ asked him, "How much do you need?" Abu Ayub ؓ told him that he required the amount that he usually received as a grant and 8 slaves to work in his fields. His grant was 4,000 Dirhams, so Abdullah bin Abbas ؓ gave him 5 times the amount, which was a sum of 20,000 Dirhams and 40 slaves. *(Tabrani in Majma'uz Zawa'id, Haythami, Hakim)*

Abdullah bin Abbas ؓ Goes Out of His way to Have the Needs of the Ansar Fulfilled

Hassan bin Thabit ؓ narrates that there was a group of the Ansar who needed to place a request before the Amirul Mu'minin who was either Omar ؓ or Uthman ؓ. They proceeded with Abdullah bin Abbas ؓ and a group of other Sahabah. Abdullah bin Abbas ؓ and the other Sahabah all spoke to the Amirul Mu'minin and mentioned the virtues of the Ansar. However, the Amirul Mu'minin had to make an excuse. The need of the Ansar was an urgent one and the Sahabah repeated the request several times. However, they all eventually accepted the excuse and just stood there. Not Abdullah bin Abbas ؓ. He persisted and said, "Never! By Allah! I shall never accept the excuse because then the Ansar will have no status. They assisted Rasulullah ﷺ and granted him protection." He then continued recounting the virtues of the Ansar and referring to Hassan bin Thabit ؓ, he added, "Here stands the poet of Rasulullah ﷺ, who used to compose poems in defense of Rasulullah ﷺ whenever the disbelievers composed poems against Rasulullah ﷺ." In this manner, Abdullah bin Abbas ؓ continued presenting convincing arguments and replied to all objections until the Amirul Mu'minin had no option but to accede to the request. Hassan ؓ continues to narrate, "We then left after Allah had fulfilled our need through the speech of Abdullah bin Abbas ؓ. I then took hold of his hand, praising him and making Du'a for him. In the Masjid we passed the group of Sahabah who were with us and who were unable to achieve what Abdullah bin Abbas ؓ had achieved. When they came within earshot, I said to them, 'Abdullah bin Abbas ؓ has proved to be closer to us than you.' 'He certainly has,' they replied. I then said to Abdullah bin Abbas ؓ, 'By Allah! This is the filtration of prophethood and the legacy of Nabi Ahmad ﷺ of which you are most worthy.' I then recited the following couplets in praise of him which mean:
"When he (Abdullah bin Abbas ؓ) speaks, he leaves nothing for another to speak because in his concise speech that contains nothing superfluous his speech is so convincing and comforting for the soul that it leaves nothing for a needy person to add (Abdullah). You have reached towering heights without difficulty and have reached the apex without being wretched or weak" (Hakim)

Another narration states that Hassan ؓ said to the other Sahabah, "By Allah! Abdullah bin Abbas is worthier than you (of being sympathetic towards us for this is the filtration of prophethood and the legacy of Nabi Ahmad ﷺ. It is his lineage and excellent character that guides him." The others said, "Do be brief and give us a poem, O Hassan." "What they say is true," Abdullah bin Abbas ؓ agreed. Hasaan ؓ then recited a poem in praise of Abdullah bin Abbas ؓ which means:
"When Ibn Abbas ؓ shows you his face you will see virtue and grace in every gathering"
He then recited the couplets mentioned above, adding the following couplet to it:
"You have been created as an ally of affection and benevolence and as an orator without being neither inefficient nor incompetent"

The Amirul Mu'minin said, "In using the word 'inefficient', Hassan ⌘ was referring to none but me. Allah shall decide between him and me." *(Tabrani in Majma'uz Zawa'id).*

The Du'a that Rasulullah ⌘ Made for the Ansar and the Statement Abu Bakr ⌘ Made About Them in his Sermon

Anas bin Malik ⌘ narrates that when it became difficult for the Ansar to continuously use camels to draw and carry water, they gathered before Rasulullah ⌘ to request that a flowing river be made for them. Rasulullah ⌘ said, "A warm welcome to the Ansar! A warm welcome to the Ansar! A warm welcome to the Ansar! I shall grant you anything that you ask from me today and anything I ask Allah for you will be granted." The Ansar said to each other, "Make the most of the situation and ask him to pray for our forgiveness." They then asked, "O Rasulullah ⌘! Pray to Allah for our forgiveness." Rasulullah ⌘ then made Du'a saying, "O Allah! Forgive the Ansar, the children of the Ansar and the grandchildren of the Ansar." Another narration states that Rasulullah ⌘ also asked Allah ⌘ to forgive the spouses of the Ansar. *(Ahmad, Haythami).* Another narration states that Rasulullah ⌘ said, "O Allah! Forgive the Ansar, the children of the Ansar, the grandchildren of the Ansar and their neighbors." *(Bazzar, Tabrani, Haythami).* Another report mentions that Rasulullah ⌘ said, "O Allah! Forgive the Ansar, the children of the Ansar and the friends of the Ansar." *(Tabrani, Haythami).* Uthman ⌘ narrates that he heard Rasulullah ⌘ say, "Iman belongs to Yemen and in the progeny of Qahtan, an ancient king to whose progeny belongs all the people of Yemen as well as the Ansar. Hard-heartedness is to be found amongst the progeny of Adnan whereas in the Himyar tribe is the commander and leader of the Arabs. While the Madh'hij tribe is the chief and defense of the Arabs and the Azd tribe is their shoulders and head bearing the weight of important matters, the Hamdan tribe is their crest and their summit. O Allah! Give honor to the Ansar through whom Allah established Islam; who gave me shelter, who assisted me and who gave me their fearless support. They are my companions in this world, shall be my party in the Akhirah and the first of my Ummah to enter Jannah." *(Bazzar, Haythami).* Uthman bin Muhammad Zubairi narrates that in one of his sermons; Abu Bakr ⌘ related the relationship between the Muhajir and the Ansar to the poem that states:

"May Allah reward Ja'far (the Ansar) on our behalf who
helped us when our shoes made us slip and fall in the Path
of those who wished to trample us.
They refused to become frustrated with us (through times)
that even our mothers would become frustrated with us, were
our mothers to suffer what they (the Ansar) suffered because
of us" *(Ibn Abi Dunya in Ashraf, Kanzul Ummal)*

Others are Given Preference Over the Ansar in the Matter of Khilafa: What Rasulullah ⌘ Said About the Quraish

Humaid bin Abdur Rahman Himiari narrates that when Rasulullah ⌘ passed away, Abu Bakr ⌘ was at one end of Madinah where he lived. When he arrived, he opened the face of Rasulullah ⌘ and said, "May my parents be sacrificed for you! You are so pure in life and death. I swear by the Rabb of the Kaba that Muhammad ⌘ has indeed passed away." When he heard that the Ansar had gathered to discuss the Khilafa, Abu Bakr ⌘ followed by Omar ⌘ went to the Ansar. In his talk to the Ansar, Abu Bakr ⌘ did not omit to mention any verse of the Qur'an or statement of Rasulullah ⌘ concerning the virtues of the Ansar. He also said, "I am also aware that Rasulullah ⌘ said, 'If everyone

walks a valley and the Ansar walk another valley, I shall walk the valley of the Ansar.' O Sa'd! Because you were sitting there, you know that Rasulullah ⌘ said, 'The Quraish are the successors of this matter (Khilafa). Righteous people will follow the righteous of the Quraish while sinful will follow the sinful of the Quraish." Sa'd confirmed this when he said to Abu Bakr ⌘, "You have spoken the truth. We shall be administrative people while you are the leaders." *(Ahmad, Ibn Jareerin Kanzul Ummal, Haythami)*

The Incident that Occurred in the Hall of the Banu Sa'ida Tribe

Abu Sa'eed Khudri ⌘ narrates that after Rasulullah ⌘ passed away, several speakers from the Ansar delivered lectures in the orchard of the Sanu Sa'ida tribe where the Muhajir and the Ansar had gathered to discuss the Khilafah. One of them said, "O assembly of. Muhajir! Whenever Rasulullah ⌘ appointed one of you to a post, he would also put one of us with him. We therefore feel that 2 persons should take this post, one from us and one from you." The other speakers from the Ansar followed suit until Zaid bin Thabit stood up and said. "Since Rasulullah ⌘ was from amongst the Muhajir, the leader should be from the Muhajir. We shall be his Ansar (helpers) just as we were the Ansar (helpers) of Rasulullah ⌘." Abu Bakr ⌘ then stood up and said, "O Assembly of Ansar! May Allah reward you all tremendously. May Allah keep this speaker of yours steadfast. By Allah! Should you do other than what Zaid ⌘ has mentioned, we would not reconcile with you." Zaid bin Thabit ⌘ then took hold of the hand of Abu Bakr ⌘ and said, "This is the man. Pledge your allegiance to him." *(Tayalisi, Ibn Sa'd, Ibn Abi Shaiba, Bayhaqi in Kanzul Ummal; Haythami, Tabrani, Ahmad).*

Qasim bin Muhammad narrates that when Rasulullah ⌘ passed away, the Ansar gathered around Sa'd bin Ubadah ⌘. Abu Bakr ⌘, Omar ⌘ and Abu Ubaidah bin Jarrah ⌘ also arrived there. Hubab bin Mundhir ⌘ who had participated in the battle of Badr stood up and said, "One leader from you (Muhajir) and one from us (Ansar). O honored group of Muhajirs! I swear by Allah that we do not have grudge against you for this position but we fear that such a person may become the leader whose fathers or brothers we (Ansar) may have killed when fighting for Islam. He should then not wish to take revenge against us." Omar ⌘ said, "If it ever happens, you should rather die fighting him if you are able to." Abu Bakr ⌘ then started to speak. He said, "We shall be the leaders while you be the administrative people. This matter will be shared equally between us just as the leaf of a date palm divides at the centre." The first person to pledge his allegiance was Bashir bin Sa'd also known as Abu Nu'man ⌘. After everyone had united under the leadership of Abu Bakr ⌘, an occasion arrived when he had to distribute some wealth amongst the people. He sent Zaid bin Thabit ⌘ to an old lady from the Sanu Adi bin Najar tribe with her share of the wealth. When she asked what it was, Zaid ⌘ told her that it was her share of the wealth that Abu Bakr ⌘ had given to her. She remarked, "Do you wish to bribe me away from my Islam'?" "Certainly not," replied Zaid ⌘. She then asked, "Do you fear that I shall leave Islam I follow?" "Definitely not," responded Zaid ⌘. She then said, "I swear by Allah that I shall never accept anything from him in future." When Zaid ⌘ returned and informed Abu Bakr ⌘ about what the old lady had expressed, Abu Bakr ⌘ said, "We shall also not take back anything that we have given her." *(Ibn Sa'd, Ibn Jareer in Kanzul Ummal).*

The Chapter Concerning Jihad (Striving in the Path of Allah)

This chapter highlights how Rasulullah ﷺ and the Sahabah struggled in the Path of Allah and how they went out to give Da'wah towards Allah and towards His Rasul ﷺ regardless of whether their circumstances were favorable or unfavorable, or whether they had a choice or not. The chapter makes clear how they prepared during times of difficulty and ease, hot or cold.

Rasulullah ﷺ Encourages Striving in the Path of Allah and Spending one's Wealth for This Cause

Abu Ayub Ansari (Tabrani, Haythami) ؓ narrates that they were all in Madinah when Rasulullah ﷺ said, "I have been informed that the trade caravan of Abu Sufian is arriving from Sham with plenty of wealth. Do you want to march to the caravan so that Allah should perhaps give you plenty of booty'?" When the Sahabah agreed, Rasulullah ﷺ marched out of Madinah with them. After marching a day or two, Rasulullah ﷺ said to the Sahabah, "The Quraish have received intelligence about us and have prepared an army to fight us, so what do you say about fighting them?" The Sahabah said, "By Allah! We do not have the strength to fight them because we intended to take on only the caravan." Rasulullah ﷺ repeated, "What do you say about fighting them?" When the Sahabah gave the same response, Miqdad bin Aswad ؓ stood up and said, "Then, O Rasulullah ﷺ if we have to fight them, we shall not say to you what the people of Musa عليه السلام said to him when they said:

فَاذْهَبْ أَنْتَ وَرَبُّكَ فَقَاتِلَا إِنَّا هَاهُنَا قَاعِدُونَ (24)

They said: "O Musa! We shall never enter it as long as they are there. So go you and your Lord and fight you two, we are sitting right here." (Al-Ma'idah:24)

Abu Ayub ؓ says, "We Ansar wished that we had said what Miqdad ؓ had said. This would have been more beloved to us than having an abundance of wealth." It was then that Allah revealed the following verse of the Qur'an:

كَمَا أَخْرَجَكَ رَبُّكَ مِنْ بَيْتِكَ بِالْحَقِّ وَإِنَّ فَرِيقًا مِنَ الْمُؤْمِنِينَ لَكَارِهُونَ (5)

As your Lord caused you (O Muhammad ﷺ) to go out from your home with the truth, and verily, a party among the believers disliked it. (Al-Anfal:5) (Ibn Abi Hatim, Ibn Mardaway in Al Bidayah wan Nihayah, Majma'uz Zawa'id, Haythami). Anas ؓ narrates that when Rasulullah ﷺ consulted with the Sahabah to march to Badr, Abu Bakr ؓ gave his opinion in favor of marching. Rasulullah ﷺ again asked for opinions and Omar ؓ gave his. When Rasulullah ﷺ again asked for opinions, someone from the Ansar said, "O assembly of Ansar! It is your opinion that Rasulullah ﷺ wants." A person from the Ansar then said, "In that case, O Rasulullah ﷺ if we have to fight them, we shall not say to you what the Bani Isra'el said to Musa عليه السلام when they told him, 'You and your Rabb both go ahead and fight. We shall remain sitting here.' In fact, we swear by the Being Who sent you with the truth that we shall follow you even if you travel to the distant city of Barkul Ghimad in Yemen." *(Ahmad, Al Bidayah wan Nihayah, Thulathi).* Another narration from Anas ؓ states that when Rasulullah ﷺ heard about the arrival of the caravan of Abu Sufian, he consulted with the Sahabah. When Abu Bakr ؓ voiced his opinion to march, Rasulullah ﷺ turned away from him. Thereafter, when Omar ؓ voiced his opinion, Rasulullah ﷺ turned away from him as well. Sa'd bin Ubadah ؓ (from the Ansar) then said, "It is our opinion that Rasulullah ﷺ wants." Addressing Rasulullah ﷺ, he then said, "I swear by the Being Who controls my life! If you command us to ride our animals into the sea, we shall readily do so and if you command us to travel to the distant city of Barkul Ghimad in Yemen, we shall certainly do so." It was only then that Rasulullah ﷺ gave the command for the Sahabah to march. *(Ahmad, Al Bidayah wan Nihayah, Ibn Asakir in Kanzul Ummal).* Alqama bin Waqqas Laythi ؓ narrates that after leaving for Badr, when he reached a place called Rowha, Rasulullah ﷺ addressed the Sahabah asking, "What is your opinion?" Abu Bakr ؓ responded by mentioning the news that had reached them about the extensive battle preparations that disbelievers had made. When Rasulullah ﷺ again asked for opinions, Omar responded as Abu Bakr ؓ had done. When Rasulullah ﷺ again asked for opinions, Sa'd bin Mu'adh (from the Ansar) said, "O Rasulullah ﷺ! It seems like it is our opinion that you are asking for. I swear by the Being Who has honored you and revealed the Qur'an to you that although I have never traveled the road and have no knowledge about it, we shall definitely travel with you even if you were to travel up to Barkul Ghimad which lies in Yemen. We shall also not be like those people who said to Musa عليه السلام, 'You and your Rabb both go ahead and fight. We shall remain sitting here.' We shall rather say, 'You and your Rabb both go ahead and fight. We shall be there right behind you.' You had possibly left for a purpose after which Allah intended you to do something else. Look into the matter that Allah intends you to do and then do it. You may join ties with whoever you please, severe ties with whoever you please, initiate hostilities towards whoever you please, enter into peace treaties with whoever you please, and take as much of our wealth as you please." It was with reference to this statement of Sa'd ؓ that Allah revealed the following verse of the Qur'an:

كَمَا أَخْرَجَكَ رَبُّكَ مِنْ بَيْتِكَ بِالْحَقِّ وَإِنَّ فَرِيقًا مِنَ الْمُؤْمِنِينَ لَكَارِهُونَ (5)

As your Lord caused you (Muhammad) to go out from your home with the truth, and verily, a party among the believers disliked it. (Al-Anfal:5) (Ibn Mardaway in Al Bidayah wan Nihayah)

Sa'd ؓ also said to Rasulullah ﷺ, "Take as much of our wealth as you please and leave as much as you please but what you take from us is more beloved to us than what you leave. Our wills are submissive to the commands you give us. I swear by Allah that even if you continue traveling until you reach Barkul Ghamdan, we shall travel with you." *(Umawi in Maghazi, Al Bidayah wan Nihayah).* Ibn Is'haq has narrated that Sa'd bin Mu'adh ؓ said, "It appears as if it is our opinion that you want, O Rasulullah ﷺ." When Rasulullah ﷺ confirmed that it was the case, Sa'd ؓ said, "We have believed in you, accepted you and testified that whatever you have brought to us is the truth. We have pledged to you that we will always listen to and obey you. O Rasulullah ﷺ, you may proceed to do as you please for we are with you. I swear by the Being Who has sent you with the truth that even if you take us to the sea and dive inside, we shall dive with you without any of us staying behind. We do not mind if you lead us in battle against the enemy because we are decided in battle and fearless when we encounter the enemy. Allah shall show you actions from us that will bring you great pleasure. Proceed with the blessings of Allah." Rasulullah ﷺ was pleased with these words of Sa'd ؓ and was re-energized. He said, "March and hear the glad tidings that Allah had promised me that one of the 2 groups - either capture the caravan or defeat the Quraish army. By Allah! It is as if I can actually see the places where the disbelievers will fall dead." *(Al Bidayah wan Nihayah)*

Rasulullah ﷺ Gives Encouragement Before a Battle and the Statement of Umair bin Hamam ؓ

Anas ؓ says, "Rasulullah ﷺ sent Basbas ؓ to spy on what

the caravan of Abu Sufian was doing. When he reported back to Rasulullah ﷺ, there was none with him in the room besides myself." The narrator says that Anas ؓ also mentioned the names of some wives of Rasulullah ﷺ who were in the room but he (the narrator) does not remember who they were. After Basbas ؓ had informed Rasulullah ﷺ about the news, Rasulullah ﷺ left the house and announced, "We are leaving in pursuit of the caravan. Whoever has his mount present should ride with us." When some Sahabah requested permission to fetch their animals that were in the upper part of Madinah, Rasulullah ﷺ said, "No. Only those whose mounts are present may ride." Rasulullah ﷺ and the Sahabah then rode off and arrived at Badr before the disbelievers. When the disbelievers arrived, Rasulullah ﷺ said to the Sahabah, "None of you should do anything until I act." When the disbelievers came close, Rasulullah ﷺ said, "Stand up and advance to a Jannah that is as wide as the heavens and the earth!" Umair bin Hamam ؓ from the Ansar asked. "O Rasulullah ﷺ! A Jannah that is as wide as the heavens and the earth?" "Certainly," confirmed Rasulullah ﷺ. Umair ؓ exclaimed, "Wow!" When Rasulullah ﷺ asked him why he said this, Umair ؓ replied, "O Rasulullah ﷺ! By Allah! There is no reason other than that I should be among its inhabitants." Rasulullah ﷺ assured him, "You are certainly from amongst its inhabitants." Umair ؓ took out some dates from his quiver and started eating. He said, "If I live until I have eaten these dates, it would take too much time." He threw the dates he had left and jumped into the thick of battle until he was martyred. May Allah shower His mercy on him. *(Ahmad, Muslim in Al Bidayah wan Nihayah, Bayhaqi, Hakim)*

Ibn Is'haq narrates that Rasulullah ﷺ went to the Sahabah to give them encouragement saying, "I swear by the Being Who controls the life of Muhammad! Allah shall enter into Jannah every man who fights the disbelievers today and is martyred while he is patient, hoping for rewards from Allah, advancing against the enemy and not fleeing from the battlefield." Umair bin Hamam ؓ who belonged to the Banu Salama tribe was eating some dates he had with him. When he heard what Rasulullah ﷺ said, he exclaimed, "Wow!" All that stands between me and my entry into Jannah is the disbelievers killing me." He threw down the dates in his hand, grabbed his sword and fought until killed. *Ibn Jareer* has mentioned that when he was martyred, Umair ؓ was reciting the following couplets:

"I am running to Allah without any (physical) provisions besides Taqwa, deeds for the Hereafter and steadfastness in Jihad for the sake Allah. Certainly, all provisions shall come to an end besides those of Taqwa, righteousness and correct guidance" (Al Bidayah wan Nihayah)

The Expedition to Tabuk and the Wealth that the Sahabah Spent on This Occasion

Abdullah bin Abbas ؓ says that he came to Rasulullah 6 months after Rasulullah ﷺ returned from Ta'if. Allah had then commanded Rasulullah ﷺ to march to Tabuk, which Allah refers to as "the hour of hardship" in the Qur'an. This took place when the heat was intense, when hypocrisy was widespread and the men of Suffa were plenty. Suffa was a platform in the Masjid where the very poor Muslims gathered. The Sadaqa that came to Rasulullah ﷺ for distribution and the Sadaqa of the Muslims went to them. Whenever there was a military expedition, a Muslim would take one or more of them, feed him well, equip him for battle and they would fight with the other Muslims. In this way, the Muslims anticipated more reward for spending on them. Rasulullah ﷺ instructed the Muslims to spend in the Path of Allah with the intention of gaining rewards. They therefore spent most generously with the expectation of reward. However, there were others (the hypocrites) who did not spend with the intention of gaining rewards from Allah. They spent for show and to conceal their true identities. While transport was provided for many poor people, many were left without transport. The person who donated the most on that day was Abdur Rahman bin Auf ؓ, who gave 200 Awqia of silver (8,000 Dirhams). Omar ؓ gave 100 Awqia of silver (equal to 4,000 Dirhams) while Asim Ansari ؓ gave 90 Wasaq of dates. Omar ؓ said, "O Rasulullah ﷺ! I think that Abdur Rahman ؓ has committed a sin because he has not left anything for his family." Rasulullah ﷺ then asked Abdur Rahman ؓ if he had left anything behind for his family. He replied, "Yes, what I have left is more than what I have spent and better." When Rasulullah ﷺ asked him how much he had left for them, he replied, "The sustenance and good that Allah and His Rasul ﷺ have promised." A Sahabi from the Ansar by the name of Abu Aqil ؓ brought a mere Saa of dates, which was his donation. When the hypocrites saw the donations, they started mocking. If someone donated a large sum, they would say that he was a show-off and when another donated a small amount of dates, which was all he could afford, they would say, "He is more in need of what he has brought." When Abu Aqil ؓ brought his Saa of dates, he said, "I spent the entire night pulling a rope to draw water from a well in exchange for 2 Saa of dates. By Allah! I have nothing besides this." In an effort to excuse his small contribution and feeling embarrassed about it, he concluded by saying, "I have brought one Saa and left the other for my family." The hypocrites commented, "He needs the Saa more than anyone else." The hypocrites continued in this manner as the wealthy and the poor amongst them waited to receive a share of the donations.

When the time drew close for Rasulullah ﷺ to leave, the hypocrites came in large numbers to seek exemption. They complained about the intense heat and also said that if they had to embark on the expedition, they would face many tests. They even went to the extent of taking oaths to justify their lies. Not knowing what their hearts concealed, Rasulullah ﷺ exempted them. It was a group from amongst them who built the Masjid of hypocrisy in expectation of the arrival of the evil-doer Abu Amir, Kinana bin Abd Yalil, and Alqama bin Ulatha Amiri. Abu Amir had aligned himself with the Roman emperor Heraclius with whom he plotted to attack the Muslims. The 'Masjid' was built as a meeting place for him. It was with reference to them that Sura At-Taubab was revealed part by part. Abdullah bin Abbas ؓ continues to narrate that it was also in Sura At-Taubab that a verse was revealed which does not exempt anyone from marching in Jihad. The sincere Muslims who were loyal to Allah and His Rasul ﷺ but were weak, unwell or poor and complained to Rasulullah ﷺ when the following verse of the Qur'an was revealed: اِنْفِرُوا خِفَافًا وَّثِقَالًا

March forth (in the path of Allah), whether you are light (being healthy, young and wealthy) or heavy (being ill, old and poor). ...(At-Taubab:41)

They said, "There is now no exemption from this to miss the expedition." At that stage, many of the signs of the hypocrites were still concealed and only became apparent afterwards. Many of them stayed behind the expedition without any physical ailment because they had no conviction in Allah. The Surah At-Taubab was revealed to Rasulullah ﷺ with much clarification and detail, informing him about the people who had joined him. When he reached Tabuk, Rasulullah ﷺ dispatched Alqama bin Mujazar ؓ to Palestine and Khalid bin Walid ؓ to Dowmatul Jandal. Rasulullah ﷺ said to Khalid, "Move quickly for you may find the ruler of Dowmatul Jandal out hunting and will be able to capture him." Khalid ؓ found the ruler out hunting and captured him. In the meantime, the hypocrites in Madinah were anxious to hear bad news about the Muslims. Consequently, when they heard that the Muslims were suffering great hardships and difficulties, they rejoiced and said, "We expected this and therefore steered clear from it." On the other hand, when they heard that the Muslims were safe and sound, they grew very depressed. Every enemy of the hypocrites in Madinah could clearly see the enmity towards the Muslims among the hypocrites. Every Bedouin and non-Bedouin hypocrite was engaging in some secret act, which was eventually exposed. Every unwilling Muslim was anxiously waiting for Allah to reveal verses of the Qur'an that would excuse them. As Surah At-Taubab was being revealed bit by bit, the Muslims started entertaining all types of thoughts about themselves. Until the entire Surah was revealed, they feared that some punishment would be cited about every major and minor sin that they ever committed. Once the revelation was complete, the position of every person became clear. It was clear who was rightly guided and who was drifting astray. *(Ibn Asakir in Kanzul Ummal)*

The Response of Rasulullah ﷺ When Jadd bin Qais Sought Exemption from the Expedition and the Verses of Qur'an Revealed

Abdullah bin Abu Bakr bin Hazam ؓ narrates that whenever Rasulullah ﷺ intended to leave on a military expedition, he made it seem as if he was going in another direction. However, when he intended to leave for Tabuk, he made it clear to the people and announced that he intended to fight the Romans. This happened at a time when people were experiencing difficulty, when the heat was intense, the land was drought-stricken and the crops were ripe and ready for harvesting. The people therefore preferred to stay behind to look after their crops and sit in the shade. They were very reluctant to separate from their comforts. As Rasulullah ﷺ was busy with preparations one day, he asked Jadd bin Qais (one of the hypocrite), "O Jadd! Are you ready to fight the Romans?" Jadd replied, "O Rasulullah ﷺ! Excuse me (from the expedition) and do not expose me to temptation. My people know well that there is none as obsessed with women as I am. I therefore fear that I may be cast into temptation when I see the Roman women. Do exempt me, O Rasulullah ﷺ." Rasulullah ﷺ turned away from him saying, "I exempt you." Then Allah ﷻ revealed this verse: وَمِنْهُمْ مَنْ يَقُولُ ائْذَنْ لِي وَلَا تَفْتِنِّي أَلَا فِي الْفِتْنَةِ سَقَطُوا

Among them (the hypocrites) is he who says, "Excuse me (from fighting) and do not expose me to temptation (I will be unable to control me when I see the enemy women)." Behold! In temptation did he (already) fall (by being reluctant to fight)..!(At-Taubab:49). This verse tells us that staying behind from the expedition and have greater concern for himself than for Rasulullah ﷺ is a worse crime than his falling for the Roman women. Jadd had therefore already fallen for temptation before even leaving on the expedition. Referring to all those after Jadd as well, the verse goes on to state: وَإِنَّ جَهَنَّمَ لَمُحِيطَةٌ بِالْكَافِرِينَ (49)

...And verily, Hell is surrounding the disbelievers. (At-Taubab:49). When one of the hypocrites said to the others, "Do not march in the heat," Allah revealed the following verse:

قُلْ نَارُ جَهَنَّمَ أَشَدُّ حَرًّا لَوْ كَانُوا يَفْقَهُونَ (81)

... Say, "The fire of Hell is more intense in heat;" if only they could understood! (At-Taubab:81)

Rasulullah ﷺ then intensified his preparations for the journey and gave the Muslims encouragement to fight in Jihad. He gave special encouragement to the wealthy Muslims to spend their wealth and to provide transport for the pleasure of Allah. Many wealthy Sahabah provided transport only with the intention of earning reward from Allah. In this regard Uthman ؓ spent most generously and none was able to match his spending. He provided 200 camels. *(Bayhaqi, Ibn Is'haq, Ibn Asakir, Al Bidayah wan Nihayah).* Abdullah bin Abbas ؓ narrates that as Rasulullah ﷺ was preparing for the Tabuk expedition, he asked Jadd bin Qais, "What do you say about fighting the Romans?" He said, "O Rasulullah ﷺ! I am a man who is obsessed by women. When I see the Roman women, I shall be cast into temptation. Will you permit me to stay behind and not expose me to temptation?" Then Allah revealed the verse:

وَمِنْهُمْ مَنْ يَقُولُ ائْذَنْ لِي وَلَا تَفْتِنِّي أَلَا فِي الْفِتْنَةِ سَقَطُوا

Among them (the hypocrites) is he who says, "Excuse me (from fighting) and do not expose me to temptation (I will be unable to control me when I see the enemy women)." Behold! In temptation did he (already) fall (by being reluctant to fight)..!(At-Taubab:49)

Rasulullah ﷺ Dispatches the Sahabah to Makkah and to Various Tribes to Recruit People for Jihad

Ibn Asakir narrates that Rasulullah ﷺ sent Sahabah to several tribes and to Makkah to recruit people to fight their enemies. Rasulullah ﷺ sent Buraida bin Husaib ؓ to the Banu Aslam tribe with instructions to proceed to a place called Fura. Rasulullah ﷺ sent Abu Ruhm Ghifari ؓ to his people with instructions to gather them all in their territory. Abu Waqid Laythi ؓ went to his people and Abu Ja'd Dhamri ؓ went to his people who were on the coast. Rasulullah ﷺ also dispatched Rafi bin Makith and Jund bin Makith ؓ to the Juhaia tribe, Nu'aym bin Mas'ood ؓ to the Ash'ja tribe and several Sahabah to the Bau Ka'b bin Amr tribe. Amongst these Sahabah was Budai bin Waraqa ؓ, Amr bin Salim ؓ and Bishr bin Sufian ؓ. Amongst the many Sahabah Rasulullah ﷺ sent Abbas bin Mirdas ؓ to the Banu Sulaim tribe.

The Sahabah Spend Generously for the Expedition to Tabuk

Rasulullah ﷺ gave the Sahabah plenty of encouragement to fight in Jihad and asked them to spend for the pleasure of Allah. The Sahabah therefore donated most generously. The first to spend so generously was Abu Bakr ؓ who donated, everything he owned, equaling 4,000 Dirhams. Rasulullah ﷺ asked him, "Have you left anything for your family?" he replied, "I have left Allah and His Rasul for them." Omar ؓ then arrived with half of his belongings. When Rasulullah ﷺ asked him if he had left anything for his family, he replied, "Yes, I have left half of what I have brought." Another narration states that he had left as much as he had brought. When Omar ؓ heard about what Abu Bakr ؓ had brought he said, "He has beaten me each time we have competed to do good." Abbas bin Abdil Muttalib ؓ, Talha bin Ubaidullah ؓ, Sa'd bin Ubadah ؓ and Muhammad bin Maslama ؓ all donated large sums. Abdur Rahman bin Auf ؓ donated 200 Awqiya of silver (equal to 8,000 Dirhams) while Asim bin Adi ؓ contributed 90 Wasaq of dates. Uthman bin Affan ؓ equipped a 1/3rd of the army and provided everything for a 1/3rd of the army, he became the person who spent the most. In fact, he gave so much that it is said that he left them without any needs. The Sahabah report that Rasulullah ﷺ then said, "Nothing that Uthman ؓ does after this can cause him any harm."

With great enthusiasm, the wealthy Sahabah spent in this good cause anticipating the rewards from Allah. Those Sahabah who were less wealthy assisted those who were poorer than them. They would even bring their camels to one or two persons, asking them to ride in turns. Some people would even bring some money and give it to someone leaving on the expedition. In fact, even the ladies assisted those in every way they could. Ummu Sinan Aslamia 🙏 says that she saw a cloth spread out in front of Aisha 🙏 in her room, which was filled with bangles, bracelets, anklets, earrings, rings and other jewellery that the women had sent to assist the Muslim army in its preparations. The Muslims were suffering poverty at that time and because it was a time when the fruit crops were ripe. Some people therefore preferred to stay at home and disliked leaving. Rasulullah 🌼 hastened and intensified preparations and made the army camp at Thaniatul Wada just outside Madinah. The army was so large that their names could not be contained in one register. Few were those who intended to absent themselves for they knew that their absence would be unknown only until Allah reveals some revelation to Rasulullah 🌼 at time when they would suffer much embarrassment. When Rasulullah 🌼 was ready to leave, he appointed Siba bin Urfuta Ghifari 🙏 as his deputy in Madinah. According to others, Rasulullah 🌼 appointed Muhammad bin Maslama 🙏. Rasulullah 🌼 instructed the Sahabah saying, "Take many pairs of shoes along because as long as a person is wearing shoes, he is like one who is riding." As Rasulullah 🌼 traveled, Ibn Ubay and other hypocrites drew back saying, "Muhammad wants to fight the Romans despite his difficult condition coupled with the extreme heat and the long journey towards an army he has no power to combat. Does he think that fighting the Romans is child's play?" The hypocrites with Ibn Ubay expressed the same opinions. To make people panic about the safety of Rasulullah 🌼 and the Sahabah, he also added, "By Allah! It is as if I can see the companions of Muhammad 🌼 tied up in ropes tomorrow." When Rasulullah 🌼 left from Thaniatul Wada for Tabuk, he had flown the large and small flags. He handed over the biggest flag to Abu Bakr 🙏, another large flag to Zubair 🙏, the flag of the Aws tribe to Usaid bin Hudhair 🙏 and the flag of the Khazraj tribe to either Abu Dujana 🙏 or to Hubab bin Mundhir 🙏. There were 30,000 people with Rasulullah 🌼 including 10,000 horsemen. Rasulullah 🌼 instructed every tribe of the Ansar to carry its own large and small flags. The other Arab tribes carried their large and small flags. *(Ibn Asakir)*. Rasulullah 🌼 was careful to dispatch the army of Usama bin Zaid 🙏 even on his deathbed, after which Abu Bakr 🙏 gave the same importance when he became the Khalifa.

Rasulullah 🌼 Dispatches the Army of Usama 🙏 With Senior Sahabah and Rejects the Argument About the Appointment of Usama 🙏

Usama bin Zaid 🙏 narrates that Rasulullah 🌼 gave him instructions to attack the inhabitants of Ubna in Palestine at dawn and to destroy their town to the ground. Rasulullah 🌼 then said to him, "Proceed in the name of Allah." Usama 🙏 then left flying the flag that Rasulullah 🌼 gave him and handed it over to Buraida bin Husaib 🙏 from the Banu Aslam tribe, who then carried it to the house of Usama 🙏. On the instruction of Rasulullah 🌼, the army of Usama 🙏 camped at a place called Jurf, which is today called Siqaya Sulaiman close to Madinah. The soldiers then started to leave. Whoever had fulfilled his necessities would leave for his camp and whoever did not, would engage in completing it. Everyone of the earliest Muhajir were part of this expedition including Omar 🙏, Abu Ubaidah 🙏, Sa'd bin Abi Waqqas 🙏, Abu A'war Sa'eed bin Zaid bin Amr bin Nufail 🙏 and several others. Amongst the Ansar who were part of the army were Qatada bin Nu'man 🙏 and Salama bin Aslam bin Harish 🙏. Many of the Muhajir, Aiash bin Abi Rabiah 🙏

being the most vocal of them, remarked, "This youth has been appointed as Amir of the earliest Muhajir!" This talk then became widespread. When Omar 🙏 heard some of the talk, he disproved what the speaker said and then reported it to Rasulullah 🌼. Rasulullah 🌼 became very angry and although he had a bandage tied to his head because of his illness and was covered in a shawl, he left his room and ascended the pulpit. After praising Allah, he said, "O people! What is this talk of yours that has reached me concerning the appointment of Usama as Amir? By Allah! If you object to my appointing him as Amir, you must have objected to my appointing his father Zaid bin Haritha 🙏 before him. I swear by Allah that just as he was fit for leadership, his son after him is also fit for it. Just as his father was the most beloved person to me, he is the most beloved to me. Both are the most suitable people for any good. Accept my decision to treat Usama well for he is the best amongst you." Rasulullah 🌼 descended from the pulpit and went to his room. This took place on saturday 10th Rabiul Awal.

The Muslims who were due to leave in the army of Usama 🙏 came to bid farewell to Rasulullah 🌼. Amongst them was Omar 🙏. As they came, Rasulullah 🌼 kept saying, "Dispatch the army of Usama." Usama 🙏's mother Ummu Ayman 🙏 came to Rasulullah 🌼 and said, "O Rasulullah 🌼! Do leave Usama to stay at the camp in Jurf until you are well. If you send him like this, he will not be able to even help himself because of his concern for you." However, Rasulullah 🌼 repeated, "Dispatch the army of Usama." The Muslims therefore returned to the camp and spent saturday night there. On sunday morning, Usama 🙏 came to Madinah to see Rasulullah 🌼. Rasulullah 🌼 was extremely ill and unconscious. This was the day in which Rasulullah 🌼 was given medicine. With tears in his eyes, Usama 🙏 entered the room of Rasulullah 🌼 where Abbas 🙏 and the wives of Rasulullah 🌼 sat around him. Usama 🙏 bent down to kiss Rasulullah 🌼. Rasulullah 🌼 was unable to speak and lifted his hands towards the sky and then placed them on Usama 🙏. Usama 🙏 says that he knew that Rasulullah 🌼 was making du'a for him. Usama 🙏 then returned to the camp. On monday, Rasulullah 🌼 was well and Usama 🙏 came to meet him early in the morning. Rasulullah 🌼 said to him, "Travel with the blessing of Allah." When Usama 🙏 bade farewell to Rasulullah 🌼, he was looking well. Rasulullah 🌼's wives were even combing each others' hair out of happiness at the recovery of Rasulullah 🌼. Abu Bakr 🙏 came to Rasulullah 🌼 and said, "O Rasulullah 🌼! With the grace of Allah, you look well this morning. Today is my day with my wife Bint Kharija 🙏. Permit me to go to her." When Rasulullah 🌼 permitted him, he left for the Sunh district in the upper part of Madinah. In the meanwhile, Usama 🙏 went to the army's camp and called for the others to join up with the army. When he reached the camp, he descended and commanded the men to leave. Then the sun was already high.

Rasulullah 🌼 Passes Away and the Sahabah Return to Madinah

As Usama 🙏 was preparing to leave from Jurf, a messenger came to him from Ummu Ayman 🙏 who was his mother. The messenger informed him that Rasulullah 🌼 was in the throes of death. Usama 🙏 returned to Madinah together with Omar 🙏 and Abu Ubaidah 🙏. When they arrived, Rasulullah 🌼 was in the last few moments. Rasulullah 🌼 passed away close to midday on Monday 12th Rabiul Awal. Muslims camping at Jurf returned to Madinah. Buraida bin Husaib 🙏 came with the flag of Usama 🙏 still flying and stuck it in the ground at the door of Rasulullah 🌼's room. After Abu Bakr 🙏 became the Khalifa, he instructed Buraida 🙏 to take the flag to the house of Usama 🙏 and not to remove it from the staff until Usama ﷺ had led the Muslims in battle. Buraida ﷺ says, "I took the flag to the house of Usama ﷺ, after which I took it to Sham with Usama ﷺ. I returned it to the house of Usama ﷺ where it was flying until he passed away."

Abu Bakr ﷺ Insists on Dispatching the Army of Usama ﷺ in Compliance with the Orders of Rasulullah ﷺ

When the news of Rasulullah ﷺ's demise reached the other Arabs, many of them renounced Islam. Abu Bakr ﷺ then said to Usama ﷺ, "Proceed as Rasulullah ﷺ had commanded you to go." Consequently, the army started to march and camped where they were previously camped. Buraida ﷺ also took the flag to the previous camp. This decision to dispatch the army did not appeal to the senior Sahabah. Consequently, Omar ﷺ; Uthman ﷺ, Abu Ubaidah ﷺ, Sa'd bin Abi Waqqas ﷺ and Sa'eed bin Zaid ﷺ approached Abu Bakr ﷺ. They said, "O successor of Rasulullah ﷺ! Everywhere the Arabs are rebelling against you and you will not be able to do anything by separating this large army from yourself. Rather use them to combat those who have forsaken Islam. Another concern we have is that we fear that Madinah may be attacked while there are only women and children here. Why do you not postpone the dispatching of this army against the Romans until stability returns and those who have forsaken Islam have either returned to Islam or are destroyed by the sword. You are then at liberty to dispatch Usama ﷺ. We are confident that the Romans will not be marching against us yet." After listening to everything they had to say, Abu Bakr ﷺ asked, "Does anyone have anything else to add?" They replied, "No, you have heard everything we have to say." Abu Bakr ﷺ then said, "I swear by the Being Who controls my life! I shall dispatch this army even if I knew that wild animals would eat me in Madinah without them here to defend me. This has to be the first task I shall undertake as Khalifa. How can I not do it when revelation had been descending on Rasulullah ﷺ from the heavens as he kept saying, 'Dispatch the army of Usama.' Of course, there is one thing that I need to speak to Usama ﷺ about. It is that Omar ﷺ stays behind with us in Madinah because we cannot do without him. By Allah! I have no idea whether Usama will do so or not. I swear by Allah that if he refuses I shall not compel him to concede." The Sahabah then realized that Abu Bakr ﷺ was determined to send the army of Usama ﷺ. Abu Bakr ﷺ then went to see Usama ﷺ at his house and spoke to him about leaving Omar ﷺ behind. When Usama ﷺ agreed, Abu Bakr ﷺ said to him, "Are you giving permission with a happy heart?" "I certainly am," replied Usama ﷺ. Abu Bakr ﷺ then left the house and instructed someone to announce, "I strongly emphasize that no one who had marched with Usama ﷺ during the lifetime of Rasulullah ﷺ should remain behind. If anyone is brought to me who had stayed behind, I shall make him join the army on foot." Abu Bakr ﷺ then sent for those Muhajir who objected to the appointment of Usama ﷺ as Amir. He was strict with them and took an undertaking from them that they will march with Usama ﷺ. Consequently, no one stayed behind. Abu Bakr ﷺ then left to see Usama ﷺ and the Muslims off. When they left from Jurf, they numbered 3,000 men and had 1,000 horses. As they rode off, Abu Bakr ﷺ walked by the side of Usama ﷺ for a while and said to him, "I entrust in Allah your Islam, your belongings, and the result of your actions. Rasulullah ﷺ has already briefed you, so fulfill the instructions of Rasulullah ﷺ. I shall neither command nor prevent you from proceeding for I am merely executing the instruction that Rasulullah ﷺ issued." Usama ﷺ set off quickly and passed through peaceful areas where the people had not forsaken Islam, such as the areas of the Juhaina clan and other

tribes belonging to the Quda'ah tribe. When he reached Wadi Qura, Usama ﷺ sent a spy ahead from the Banu Udhra tribe, whose name was Huraith. Taking to his mount, he rode ahead of Usama ﷺ until he reached Ubna their intended destination. He surveyed the area and searched for the best route for the army to take. He then returned quickly and rejoined Usama ﷺ at a place that lay a distance of 2 night's journey from Ubna. He informed Usama ﷺ that the people were unaware of the Muslim army and had not even started their own army. Usama ﷺ then ordered the Muslim army to move quickly and attack the enemy before they had a chance to prepare their forces. *(Ibn Asakir in Mukhtasar in Ibn Asakir, Kanzul Ummal, Fat'hul Bari)*

Usama ﷺ Seeks Permission to Return to Madinah but Abu Bakr ﷺ Refuses Permission

Hasan bin Abil Hasan narrates that before he passed away, Rasulullah ﷺ formed an army comprising of the people of Madinah and surrounding areas. Included in this army was Omar ﷺ. Rasulullah ﷺ appointed Usama bin Zaid ﷺ as the Amir of this army. The last man of the army had not yet passed by the trench when Rasulullah ﷺ passed away. Usama ﷺ halted the army and said to Omar ﷺ, "Request the Khalifa of Rasulullah ﷺ to permit me to return the army to Madinah for I have with me the noblest and leading Sahabah and I fear that the disbelievers may attack the Khalifa and the families of Rasulullah ﷺ and the Muslims." Some of the Ansar said to Omar ﷺ that if Abu Bakr ﷺ is determined to dispatch the army, he should convey the message from them that an Amir who is older than Usama ﷺ should be appointed. Upon the instruction of Usama ﷺ, Omar ﷺ proceeded to Abu Bakr ﷺ and informed him about what Usama ﷺ had said. Abu Bakr ﷺ said, "I would not reverse a decision that Rasulullah ﷺ made even if wild dogs and wolves were to snatch away my body." Omar ﷺ then said, "The Ansar have requested me to convey the message that they want you to appoint an Amir over them who is elder than Usama ﷺ." Abu Bakr ﷺ had been sitting, but when he heard this, he jumped up and grabbed hold of the beard of Omar ﷺ. He then said, "May your mother lose you, O son of Khattab! You are asking me to relieve him of a post to which Rasulullah ﷺ appointed him?!" Omar ﷺ returned and the people asked him what had happened, he said, "March on. May your mothers lose you because of what I have suffered today at the hands of the Khalifa of Rasulullah ﷺ on your account."

Abu Bakr ﷺ Sees the Army of Usama ﷺ Off

Abu Bakr ﷺ then proceeded to see the army off and to give them encouragement. Abu Bakr ﷺ walked as Usama ﷺ rode while Abdur Rahman bin Auf ﷺ led Abu Bakr ﷺ's animal. Usama ﷺ said, "O Khalifa of! Either you ride or I dismount." Abu Bakr ﷺ replied, "By Allah! You should not dismount. By Allah! I shall not ride. What harm is there if I make my feet dusty for a while in the Path of Allah? Every step taken by the person leaving in Jihad earns the reward of 700 good deeds, has his ranks raised by 700 stages and erases 700 sins from his account." He was about to leave, Abu Bakr ﷺ asked, "If you feel that you could help me by leaving Omar bin Khattab ﷺ with me, could you please do so." Usama ﷺ granted permission. *(Ibn Asakir in Mukhtasar Ibn Asakir, Kanzul Ummal, Al Bidayah wan Nihayah)*

Abu Bakr ﷺ Rejects the Request of the Muhajir and Ansar to Hold Back the Army of Usama ﷺ

Urwa ﷺ narrates that after the Sahabah had pledged their allegiance to Abu Bakr ﷺ and were satisfied, Abu Bakr ﷺ said to Usama, "Proceed as Rasulullah ﷺ had commanded you." Several individuals from the Muhajir and the Ansar discussed the matter with Abu Bakr ﷺ. They said to him, "Hold back Usama ﷺ and his army because we fear that the other Arabs may attack us when they hear about the demise of Rasulullah ﷺ." Being more resolute and knowledgeable about the situation, Abu Bakr ﷺ said, "How can I hold back an army that Rasulullah ﷺ had dispatched? I would then be doing something very bold! I swear by the Being Who controls my life that I would prefer having all the Arabs attack me rather than restraining an army that Rasulullah ﷺ had dispatched! O Usama! Proceed with your army as Rasulullah ﷺ had commanded you and fight in the area of Palestine where Rasulullah ﷺ had commanded. Fight the people of Mu'ta for Allah shall be sufficient for those whom you are leaving behind in Madinah. However, if you would, could you please permit Omar ﷺ to remain behind. I need his counsel and his assistance for he has excellent opinions and is a great well-wisher to the cause of Islam. Usama permitted Omar ﷺ to remain behind. Most of the Arab tribes had by then renounced Islam. They included most of the tribes in the east as well as the Ghitfan tribe, the Banu Asad tribe and most of the Ash'ja tribe. The Banu Tay tribe though held on to their religion. Most of the Sahabah were of the opinion that the army of Usama ﷺ should be held back and rather used against the Ghitfan and other tribes who had renounced Islam. Refusing to withhold the army of Usama ﷺ, Abu Bakr ﷺ said, "You know well that from the period of Rasulullah ﷺ it had been our practice to consult with each other concerning matters about which no practice of Rasulullah ﷺ was found and about which no verse of the Qur'an was revealed. You have expressed your opinions and I shall now express mine. If it is correct, you should practice accordingly for Allah shall never make you all united on anything that it misguided. I swear by the Being Who controls my life that I do not see anything better than fighting those who refuse to give me even a piece of rope that Rasulullah ﷺ used to take from them as zakah." The Muslims approved of the opinion of Abu Bakr ﷺ and agreed that it was better than theirs. Abu Bakr ﷺ then dispatched Usama bin Zaid ﷺ in the direction that Rasulullah ﷺ had commanded. Usama gathered a large booty in the battle and Allah returned him and his army safely. When Usama ﷺ had left, Abu Bakr ﷺ took an army of Muhajir and Ansar to fight those who left Islam but when they heard of his army approaching, the Bedouins fled with their families. When the Muslims received intelligence about the Bedouins fleeing with families, they said to Abu Bakr ﷺ, "Return to Madinah to our families and women and appoint an Amir in your place from amongst your companions, handing over your command to him." They kept insisting until Abu Bakr ﷺ eventually decided to return. He appointed Khalid bin Walid ﷺ as commander of the army with instructions that any of them was at liberty to return to Madinah as soon as the people returned to Islam and paid their zakah. Abu Bakr ﷺ then returned to Madinah. *(Ibn Asakir in Mukhtasar Ibn Asakir, Kanzul Ummal)*

Urwa ﷺ narrates that when the pledge of allegiance was taken on the hand of Abu Bakr ﷺ, the Ansar became united in the matter of Khilafa about which they had differed. Abu Bakr ﷺ dispatched the army of Usama ﷺ and many Arab tribes renounced Islam. While in some cases, complete tribes renounced Islam, it was only individuals in other tribes who renounced Islam. Hypocrisy started to surface and Judaism and Christianity began raising their heads. Because they had just lost their Nabi ﷺ and because they were so few compared to the other enemy, the Muslims appeared to be like wet sheep on a cold night. It was then that people said to Abu Bakr ﷺ, "The army of Usama ﷺ is the most distinguished of the Muslims and as you

see, the Arabs are refusing to follow you. It is therefore not the appropriate time to split up the ranks of the Muslims by dispatching the army. Abu Bakr ﷺ responded by saying, "I swear by the Being Who controls the life of Abu Bakr! I shall ensure that the army of Usama ﷺ is sent according to the instruction of Rasulullah ﷺ even though I know that wild animals will attack me as I remain all alone in Madinah and steal away my body. I shall dispatch the army even though there is none left in any of the towns besides myself." *(Al Bidayah wan Nihayah)*. Aisha ﷺ says, "After Rasulullah ﷺ passed away, all the Arab tribes renounced Islam and hypocrisy reared its ugly head. By Allah! Such conditions faced my father Abu Bakr ﷺ that would crush a mighty mountain. The Sahabah of Rasulullah ﷺ appeared to be wet sheep on a rainy night in a forest infected with wild animals. By Allah! Whenever the Sahabah disputed any matter, my father would eliminate its harm, take control of the reins and pass decisive judgment." *(Tabrani, Haythami)*. Abu Hurairah ﷺ says, "I swear by the Being besides Whom none other is worthy of worship that none would have been worshipping Allah had Abu Bakr ﷺ not been appointed as Khalifa." He then repeated this a 2nd and a 3rd time. When someone asked him to stop repeating himself, Abu Hurairah ﷺ added, "Rasulullah ﷺ dispatched an army of 700 of Quraish and total army was 3,000 under the command of Usama bin Zaid ﷺ. However, when they had just reached Dhi Khushub when Rasulullah ﷺ passed away and the Arab tribes around Madinah renounced Islam. It was then that the Sahabah of Rasulullah ﷺ came to Abu Bakr ﷺ and said, 'O Abu Bakr! Recall the army. How can they be heading to Rome when the Arabs around Madinah are renouncing Islam?!' Abu Bakr ﷺ replied, 'I swear by the Being besides Whom there is none worthy of worship! Even though wild dogs should drag the legs of the wives of Rasulullah ﷺ as there is none in Madinah to defend them, I shall never recall an army that Rasulullah ﷺ had dispatched nor untie a flag that Rasulullah ﷺ had tied.'" Usama ﷺ left with the army and they passed by a tribe that was thinking to renounce Islam, the people of the tribe said, "If the Muslims are not still powerful, an army like this would never have left them. We shall leave them until they meet the Roman army then we shall see their strength." The Muslim army engaged the Romans in combat and defeated them, returned safe and sound. Those who were thinking to renounce Islam remained as Muslims. *(Bayhaqi in Al Bidayah wan Nihayah, Ibn Asakir in Mukhtasar)*.

Abu Bakr ﷺ Addresses Omar ﷺ Before he Passes Away

Saif narrates that after Khalid bin Walid ﷺ had left for Sham, Abu Bakr ﷺ fell ill. Due to this illness he passed away a few months later. Abu Bakr ﷺ was close to death and had appointed Omar ﷺ as the next Khalifa when Muthanna arrived from Sham and informed Abu Bakr ﷺ about events there. Abu Bakr ﷺ sent for Omar ﷺ and when he arrived, Abu Bakr ﷺ said, "O Omar! Listen carefully to what I say and carry it out. I expect that I shall die today (monday). If I die now, you should prepare people to leave with Muthanna for Sham before the evening and if I die later, you should prepare people to leave with Muthanna before dawn. Regardless of the magnitude of any hurdle, never let it prevent you from the matters of Islam and the commands of your Rabb. You have seen how I acted when Rasulullah ﷺ passed away although it was a time when the creation was afflicted with a calamity like no other. By Allah! Had I postponed the command of Allah and His Rasul ﷺ, Allah would not have assisted us and would have punished us. The whole Madinah would have been engulfed in flames." *(Ibn Jareer)*

Abu Bakr ؓ Consults With the Muhajir and the Ansar About Waging Jihad and Delivers a Sermon Against the People Refuted Islam and Refused to Pay Zakah.

Abdullah bin Omar ؓ narrates that when Rasulullah ﷺ passed away, hypocrisy raised its ugly head in Madinah. At the same time, many Arab tribes left the fold of Islam while the non-Arab nations began issuing threats. They posed a danger to Muslim security and gathered at Nahawind, where they made statements to the effect that the person who had been a cause for the domination of the Arabs had passed away. Abu Bakr ؓ assembled the Muhajir and the Ansar and said to them, "The Arabs refuse to pay the zakah for their goats and camels and have turned away from their religion. On the other front, the non-Arabs have gathered at Nahawind to fight you from a united platform, arrogantly thinking that the person who had been the cause for your domination has passed away. Do give me your opinions, for I am merely a man from amongst you who is most heavily burdened with this load." After they had their heads bowed for long while, it was Omar ؓ who spoke first. He submitted, "O successor of Rasulullah ﷺ! By Allah! I am of the opinion that you content yourself with accepting only salah from them and waive the zakah because they have only recently accepted lslam after the Period of Ignorance and Islam has not yet prepared them fully. Perhaps Allah shall take them back towards good or if Allah grants further strength to Islam and they still refuse to yield, we shall be able to wage war against them. The Muhajir and Ansar who are left do not have the might to take on the Arabs and the non-Arabs all at once." When Abu Bakr ؓ turned to Uthman ؓ, he offered a similar opinion. Thereafter, Ali ؓ and the rest of the Muhajir echoed the same view. When Abu Bakr ؓ turned to the Ansar, they also agreed. When Abu Bakr ؓ realized that they all felt the same way, he mounted the pulpit and after praising Allah, he said, "When Allah ﷻ sent Muhammad ﷺ the truth was undermined and without support. Islam was a stranger and an outcast, hanging only by a thread. Although its supporters were few, Allah assembled them through Muhammad ﷺ and formed them into the best of nations destined to survive. I swear by Allah that I shall remain devoted to the laws of Allah and continue fighting in Jihad until Allah fulfils His promise to us. Those of us who are killed shall be martyrs bound for Jannah while those who survive shall remain as Allah's deputies on His earth and successors of His bondsmen. Allah has spoken the truth and there can be no going back on His word. Allah has declared:

وَعَدَ اللَّهُ الَّذِينَ آمَنُوا مِنكُمْ وَعَمِلُوا الصَّالِحَاتِ لَيَسْتَخْلِفَنَّهُمْ فِي الْأَرْضِ كَمَا اسْتَخْلَفَ الَّذِينَ مِن قَبْلِهِمْ وَلَيُمَكِّنَنَّ لَهُمْ دِينَهُمُ الَّذِي ارْتَضَىٰ لَهُمْ وَلَيُبَدِّلَنَّهُم مِّن بَعْدِ خَوْفِهِمْ أَمْنًا يَعْبُدُونَنِي لَا يُشْرِكُونَ بِي شَيْئًا وَمَن كَفَرَ بَعْدَ ذَٰلِكَ فَأُولَٰئِكَ هُمُ الْفَاسِقُونَ (55)

Allah has promised those among you who believe, and do righteous good deeds, that He will certainly grant them succession to (the present rulers) in the earth, as He granted it to those before them, and that He will grant them the authority to practice their religion, that which He has chosen for them (i.e. Islam). And He will surely give them in exchange a safe security after their fear (provided) they (believers) worship Me and do not associate anything (in worship) with Me. But whoever disbelieved after this, they are Fasiqoon (disobedient to Allah). (An-Nur:55)

I swear by Allah that if the Arabs refusing to pay zakah and refuse to pay me even a string which they used to pay to Rasulullah ﷺ as zakah and then confront me together with the trees, the rocks, all of Jinn and all of mankind, I shall fight them until my soul meets with Allah! Allah has never separated salah

and zakah and then combined them again. How is it then possible for me to acknowledge their salah and ignore zakah?." Omar ؓ shouted, "Allahu Akbar!" and said, "By Allah! After Allah had fixed the resolve in the heart of Abu Bakr ؓ to wage Jihad against those who refused to pay zakah, I also realized that this was right." *(Khatib in Kanzul Ummal).* Salih bin Kaisan رحمة الله narrates that when people started leaving the fold of Islam after the demise of Rasulullah ﷺ, Abu Bakr ؓ stood up to address the Muslims. After praising Allah, he added, "All praises are due to Allah who guides, suffices, and Who gives as He makes others independent of the creation. When Allah sent Muhammad ﷺ, he was treated as a fugitive while true Islam was treated as a stranger and an outcast. It hung by a thread and was already around for a very long time. So its supporters had gone astray and Allah was displeased with the Ahlul Kitab. He gave them no good because of any good in them nor did He avert evil from them because of evil was dominant in them. They had distorted their scriptures and introduced in it things that did not belong there. On the other hand, the illiterate Arabs had no relationship with Allah. Neither did they worship Him nor were they praying to Him. They lived the hardest lives, their religion was most deviated and they lived in a most hostile land. Although Rasulullah ﷺ had only a few companions, Allah assembled them around him through his blessings and formed them into the best of nations. Allah ﷻ assisted them by those who followed them and made them dominate others until Allah finally took His Nabi ﷺ away. Saitan then climbed back on to the Arabs to assume the position he had been enjoying formally when Allah removed him from there. He has now taken them by the hand and intends to destroy them." Abu Bakr then recited this verse of the Qur'an:

وَمَا مُحَمَّدٌ إِلَّا رَسُولٌ قَدْ خَلَتْ مِن قَبْلِهِ الرُّسُلُ أَفَإِن مَّاتَ أَوْ قُتِلَ انقَلَبْتُمْ عَلَىٰ أَعْقَابِكُمْ وَمَن يَنقَلِبْ عَلَىٰ عَقِبَيْهِ فَلَن يَضُرَّ اللَّهَ شَيْئًا وَسَيَجْزِي اللَّهُ الشَّاكِرِينَ (144)

Muhammad ﷺ is no more than a Messenger, and Messengers have passed away before him. If he dies or is killed, will you then turn back on your heels (as disbelievers)? And he who turns back on his heels, not the least harm will he do to Allah, and Allah will give reward to those who are grateful. (Al-'Imran:144)

The Arabs around you are refusing to pay the zakah due for their goats and camels. Although they have only now reverted to their former religions, their inclination to do so was never more than it is today. On the other hand, your resolve in Islam is no stronger today than it had been the day you lost the blessing of your Nabi ﷺ. Rasulullah ﷺ had handed you over into the custody of the very first Being Who had always been sufficient for you; the very Being Who had found Rasulullah ﷺ without a Shari'a and then granted him one and Who had found him without wealth and then made him wealthy. It was He Who saved you people when you were about to collapse of a face over the fire of Jahannam. I swear by Allah that I shall never avoid fighting for a single command of Allah until Allah fulfils His promise to us. Those of us who are killed shall be martyrs bound for Jannah while those who survive shall remain as Allah's deputies and successors on His earth. Allah has spoken the truth and there can be no going back on His word when He declares:

وَعَدَ اللَّهُ الَّذِينَ آمَنُوا مِنكُمْ وَعَمِلُوا الصَّالِحَاتِ لَيَسْتَخْلِفَنَّهُمْ فِي الْأَرْضِ كَمَا اسْتَخْلَفَ الَّذِينَ مِن قَبْلِهِمْ وَلَيُمَكِّنَنَّ لَهُمْ دِينَهُمُ الَّذِي ارْتَضَىٰ لَهُمْ وَلَيُبَدِّلَنَّهُم مِّن بَعْدِ خَوْفِهِمْ أَمْنًا يَعْبُدُونَنِي لَا يُشْرِكُونَ بِي شَيْئًا وَمَن كَفَرَ بَعْدَ ذَٰلِكَ فَأُولَٰئِكَ هُمُ الْفَاسِقُونَ (55)

Allah has promised those among you who believe, and do righteous good deeds, that He will certainly grant them succession to (the present rulers) in the earth, as He granted it to those before them, and that He will grant them the authority to practice their religion, that which He has chosen for them (i.e. Islam). And He will surely give them in exchange a safe security after their fear (provided) they (believers) worship Me and do not associate anything (in worship) with Me. But whoever disbelieved after this, they are Fasiqoon (disobedient to Allah). (An-Nur:55). Abu Bakr ؓ stepped down from the pulpit. *(Ibn Asakir, Ibn Kathir, Kanzul Ummal, Al Bidayah wan Nihayah).*

Abu Bakr ؓ Censures Those Who Were Hesitant and Wanted to Delay Jihad

Omar ؓ narrates that when the Arab tribes renounced Islam, the Muhajir together with himself arrived at a common conclusion. They said to Abu Bakr ؓ, "O successor of Rasulullah ﷺ! Leave the people continue to perform salah without paying zakah because they will soon accept the obligation of zakah once true Iman enters their hearts." Abu Bakr ؓ responded by saying, "I swear by the Being Who controls my life! I prefer falling headlong from the sky rather than neglecting to fight for something that Rasulullah ﷺ fought for." Abu Bakr ؓ then fought those who refused to pay zakah until they all returned to the fold of Islam. Omar ؓ says, "I swear by the Being Who controls my life that single day of Abu Bakr ؓ is better than the life's deeds of the family of Omar." *(Adani in Kanzul Ummal).* Omar ؓ narrates that when Rasulullah ﷺ passed away, many Arab tribes left the fold of Islam when they said that they would perform salah without paying zakah. He narrates further that he then approached Abu Bakr ؓ and said, "O Khalifa of Rasulullah ﷺ! Be sympathetic towards the people and show mercy towards them for they are like wild animals." Abu Bakr ؓ said, "Whereas I was hopeful of your help, you have come to inform me that you will not render any assistance. While you had been powerful during the period of ignorance, have you become weak in Islam? Why should I sympathize with them using composed verse or pretend magic? Unbelievable! Rasulullah ﷺ has passed away and revelation has stopped. I swear by Allah that I shall fight them as long as my hand can hold a sword and if they refuse to pay even a string that is due from them as zakah." Omar ؓ says, "I found Abu Bakr to be more competent and resolute than myself. He trained the people in many matters which made many of my tasks easy when I was appointed Khalifa." *(Isma'ili in Kanzul Ummal).*

Dabba bin Mihsin Anzi narrates that that he once asked Omar bin Khattab ؓ, "Are you better than Abu Bakr ؓ?" Omar ؓ began to weep and said, "A single night of Abu Bakr ؓ and a single day of his is better than the life's deeds of Omar ؓ and the entire family of Omar ؓ. Should I not inform you of that night and that day of Abu Bakr ؓ?" When Dabba asked to be informed, Omar ؓ said, "The night was the night when Rasulullah ﷺ left the people of Makkah. He left at night and Abu Bakr ؓ followed him." He then proceeded to narrate the incident as reported in the chapter concerning Hijra. Omar ؓ then continued, "The day of his was when Rasulullah ﷺ had passed away and many Arab tribes abandoned Islam. While some of them said that they would perform salah without paying zakah, others said that they would neither perform salah nor pay zakah. I then approached him with the sincere intention of offering good counsel. I said to him, 'O Khalifa of Rasulullah ﷺ! Be compassionate towards the people...'" The rest of the Hadith is similar to the one quoted above. *(Dinowri in Majalasah, Abul Hasan in Fawa'id, Bayhaqi in Dala'il and La'lakai, Kanzul Ummal).* Abu Hurairah ؓ narrates that after Rasulullah ﷺ had passed away and Abu Bakr ؓ succeeded him, many Arab tribes abandoned Islam. It was then that Omar ؓ approached Abu Bakr ؓ

and said, "O Abu Bakr ؓ! How can we fight these people when Rasulullah ﷺ said, 'I have been commanded to fight people until they declare 'La Ilaha IllAllah'. When someone declares 'La Ilaha IlIallah', his property and life is safe from me except by the right of Allah. A warrant by which his property or life may be taken as a penalty. Then Allah shall reckon with him." Abu Bakr ؓ responded by saying, "I swear by Allah that I shall definitely fight anyone who differentiates between salah and zakah for zakah is a right of wealth just as salah is a right due from the body. By Allah! If they refuse to pay to me as a part of zakah a string that they were paying to Rasulullah ﷺ, I shall certainly fight them for it!" Omar ؓ says, "I swear by Allah that Abu Bakr ؓ said this as he had assurance from Allah that he ought to wage Jihad. I was therefore convinced that this was the right thing to do." *(Bukhari, Muslim, Abu Dawood, Tirmidhi, Nasa'ee, Ibn Hibban and Bayhaqi, in Kanzul Ummal).* Abu Bakr ؓ ensures that armies are dispatched in the Path of Allah. He encourages the Muslims to march in Jihad and consults with the Sahabah about fighting the Romans.

Abu Bakr ؓ Encourages the Muslims to Fight in Jihad in his Sermon

Qasim bin Mahmood رحمة الله reports that Abu Bakr ؓ once stood up to deliver a sermon. After praising Allah and sending salutations to Rasulullah ﷺ, he said, "Everything has principles which shall meet the requirements of the one who sticks to them. Whoever does something solely for Allah; Allah shall see to his needs. You should ensure that you work hard and exercise moderation, for it is moderation that will take you to your destination. Listen attentively! There is no Islam in one who has no Iman, there is no reward for the one who does not expect any and no deed for one who has no intention. Listen carefully! There are rewards promised in the Book of Allah for those engaged in Jihad in the Path of Allah that it is only appropriate for a Muslim to wish that they are reserved for Him. This is the trade that Allah has pointed towards *(ref. As-Saff:10),* which shall provide release from humiliation and secure honor in both worlds." *(Ibn Asakir in Mukhtasar, Kanzul Ummal, Ibn Jareer Tabari)*

The Letter of Abu Bakr ؓ to Khalid bin Walid ؓ and Other Sahabah Concerning Jihad in the Path of Allah

Ibn Is'haq bin Yasar narrates from Khalid bin Walid ؓ that they were still on the battlefield of Yamamah after the battle when Abu Bakr ؓ wrote a letter to Khalid ؓ. The letter read:
From Abdullah, Abu Bakr the Khalifa of Rasulullah ﷺ
To Khalid bin Walid, the Muhajir and Ansar with him as well as all those who follow them in good faith
Peace be on you all
Before you all, I praise Allah besides Whom there is none worthy of worship.
All praises belong to Allah Who has fulfilled His promise, assisted His servant, granted honor to His friends, disgraced His enemies and defeated the coalition of forces by Himself. The very Allah besides Whom there is no deity has declared:

وَعَدَ اللّٰهُ الَّذِينَ آمَنُوا مِنْكُمْ وَعَمِلُوا الصَّالِحَاتِ لَيَسْتَخْلِفَنَّهُمْ فِي الْأَرْضِ كَمَا اسْتَخْلَفَ الَّذِينَ مِنْ قَبْلِهِمْ وَلَيُمَكِّنَنَّ لَهُمْ دِينَهُمُ الَّذِي ارْتَضَى لَهُمْ وَلَيُبَدِّلَنَّهُمْ مِنْ بَعْدِ خَوْفِهِمْ أَمْنًا يَعْبُدُونَنِي لَا يُشْرِكُونَ بِي شَيْئًا وَمَنْ كَفَرَ بَعْدَ ذَٰلِكَ فَأُولَٰئِكَ هُمُ الْفَاسِقُونَ (55)

Allah has promised those among you who believe, and do righteous good deeds, that He will certainly grant them succession to (the present rulers) in the earth, as He granted it to those before them, and that He will grant them the authority to practice their religion, that which He has chosen for them (i.e. Islam). And He will surely give them in exchange a safe security after their fear (provided) they (believers) worship Me and do not associate anything (in worship) with Me. But whoever disbelieved after this, they are Fasiqoon (disobedient to Allah). (An-Nur:55)

This is a promise from Allah which cannot be left unfulfilled and statement that cannot be doubted. Allah has made Jihad obligatory on the Mu'minin. He declares:

كُتِبَ عَلَيْكُمُ الْقِتَالُ وَهُوَ كُرْهٌ لَكُمْ وَعَسَى أَنْ تَكْرَهُوا شَيْئًا وَهُوَ خَيْرٌ لَكُمْ وَعَسَى أَنْ تُحِبُّوا شَيْئًا وَهُوَ شَرٌّ لَكُمْ وَاللَّهُ يَعْلَمُ وَأَنْتُمْ لَا تَعْلَمُونَ (216)

Jihad (holy fighting in Allah's Cause) is ordained for you (Muslims) though you dislike it, and it may be that you dislike a thing which is good for you and that you like a thing which is bad for you. Allah knows but you do not know. (Al-Baqara:216)

You should therefore adopt those avenues by which the promises of Allah to you will be fulfilled and continue obeying Him in everything He has made obligatory on you even though the effort may seem tremendous, the hardship may be intense, the journey may be distant and you may suffer loss to your wealth or health. All of these are insignificant before the great rewards of Allah. So fight in the way of Allah, may Allah have mercy on you. انْفِرُوا خِفَافًا وَثِقَالًا وَجَاهِدُوا بِأَمْوَالِكُمْ وَأَنْفُسِكُمْ فِي سَبِيلِ اللَّهِ

March forth, whether you are light (being healthy, young and wealthy) or heavy (being ill, old and poor), strive hard with your wealth and your lives in the Cause of Allah. This is better for you, if you but knew. (At-Tauba:41). I have commanded Khalid bin Walid to march to Iraq and stay there until I issue further instructions. You should all proceed with him without hesitation as this is a path in which Allah has multiplied the rewards for those whose intentions are good and who are enthusiastic about good things. When you reach Iraq, stay here until my instructions reach you. May Allah take care of mine and your concern of this world and the hereafter. Peace be on you with the mercy and blessings of Allah. *(Bayhaqi in Sunan)*

Abu Bakr Consults with the Senior Sahabah Concerning a Military Offensive Against the Romans and Delivers a Speech

Abdullah bin Abi Awfa narrates that when Abu Bakr intended to launch a military offensive against the Romans, he first called for Ali, Omar, Uthman, Abdur Rahman bin Auf, Sa'd bin Abi Waqqas, Sa'eed bin Zaid, Abu Ubaidah bin Jarrah and other senior Sahabah from amongst the Muhajir and Ansar. He called both those who participated in the battle of Badr and those who did not. Amongst them was Abdullah bin Abi Awfa, who narrates further that when they all arrived, Abu Bakr addressed them saying, "Verily the bounties of Allah on His servants cannot be counted and all our deeds can never compensate for these. All praises belong to Allah who has united you, reconciled you, guided you to Islam, and distanced Saitan from you. Saitan now has no hope of you committing shirk or of you taking a deity other than Allah. The Arabs are the children of a single father and mother." Abu Bakr continued, "I have decided that the Muslims should march in Jihad against the Romans in Sham so that Allah may strengthen the Muslims and elevate the Kalima. Together with this, the Muslims shall have a tremendous share because whoever is killed shall die as a martyr and the rewards with Allah are best for the righteous. Whoever survives shall survive to defend Islam and will deserve great rewards due to those who wage Jihad. This is merely my opinion. Anyone of you is at liberty to advise me."

The Speech of Omar in Support of the Opinion of Abu Bakr to March in Jihad

Omar then stood up and said, "All praises are due to Allah Who blesses those of His servants with good whom He pleases. by Allah! When we competed for good, you always beat us to it. This is the bounty of Allah whom Allah grants to whoever He wills. Allah is the One Who possesses the greatest bounties. As a matter of fact, I had intended to approach you concerning the very matter you have raised. However, it was destined that you should be the first to mention it. Your opinion is most accurate. May Allah always guide you to what is correct. Dispatch troops of cavalry one after the other and troops of infantry one after the other. Armies should march in succession and Allah shall assist Islam, grant honor and strength to Islam and the Muslims."

The Opinion of Abdur Rahman bin Auf on the Battle Strategy

Thereafter, Abdur Rahman bin Auf stood up and said, "O Khalifa of Rasulullah! They are Romans and the progeny of Romans. They are extremely powerful and as solid as a pillar. I do not think that you should launch a full front attack but you should rather dispatch cavalry battalions to start clashes along their borders and then return to you. When this is done several times, the Romans will suffer many losses and our battalions will capture many outlying areas. By then the Romans will also grow weary. Thereafter, you should send a message to the various areas of Yemen and to the furthest members of the Rabiah and Mudhar tribes so that they may all gather around you. You may then lead an attack by yourself or appoint another leader while you attend to affairs from Madinah." After this address, Abdur Rahman bin Auf remained silent, as did the others present.

Uthman Supports the Opinion of Abu Bakr and the Other Sahabah and Echo the Same Opinion

Abu Bakr then asked the others what their opinions were. A response came from Uthman who said, "O Khalifa of Rasulullah! I believe that you are truly a well-wisher of everyone who follows this Islam and are concerned about them. Therefore, whenever you have an opinion that you think is in the best interests of the masses, do feel free to carry it out for you can never be slandered for it." In response to this, Talha, Zubair, Sa'd, Abu Ubaidah, Sa'eed bin Zaid and all the other Muhajir and Ansar present there said, "Uthman has spoken the truth. Do feel free to carry out what you feel for we shall never oppose you or slander you." They made other similar statements as well. Although Ali was also present, he remained silent all the time..

Ali Gives Glad tidings to Abu Bakr, who is Pleased by This and Delivers a Lecture to motivate the Sahabah to March in Jihad

Addressing Ali, Abu Bakr said, "What is your opinion, O Abul Hasan?" Ali said, "I feel that you march against them yourself or you send others against them, you will have Allah's assistance, InsAllah." Abu Bakr said, "May Allah always give you good news! How do you know this?" Ali replied, "I have heard Rasulullah say that this Islam will always dominate those who oppose it until Islam and its supporters are victorious." Abu Bakr exclaimed, "Subhanallah! What a beautiful Hadith! You have made me very happy with this. May Allah always keep you happy." Abu Bakr stood up to address the people. After praising Allah and sending salutations to Rasulullah, he said, "O people! Allah has blessed you with Islam and honored you with the institution of Jihad. Through this Islam Allah has elevated your status over the people of other religions. Therefore, O servants of Allah, prepare to fight the Romans in Sham. I shall appoint commanders over you and make flags for you. Obey your Rabb, do not disobey your commanders and make good your intentions and your provisions for food and drink for Allah is with those who have Taqwa and who do things well."

An Exchange of Words Between Omar ☙ and Amr bin Sa'eed ☙ and Khalid bin Sa'eed ☙ Advises His Brother to Assist Abu Bakr ☙

After listening to the address of Abu Bakr ☙, the Sahabah were silent without any of them offering any response. Omar ☙ then said, "O assembly of Muslims! What is the matter with you that you do not respond to the Khalifa of Rasulullah ﷺ when he is calling you towards that which will give life to you? Had the gains been near at hand and the journey an easy one, you would have certainly jumped to it." *(Ref At-Tauba:42).* In response to this, Amr bin Sa'eed ☙ stood up and responded, "O son of Khattab! Are you comparing us to the example of the hypocrites? What prevented you from taking the initiative to do that which you accused us of not doing?" Omar ☙ replied, "Abu Bakr ☙ knows well that I will surely respond if he calls me and fight if he asks me to." Arm bin Sa'eed ☙ rejoined, "If we fight, it will not be for you because we fight only for Allah." Omar ☙ then said, "May Allah guide you! You have spoken well." Abu Bakr ☙ then said to Amr bin Sa'eed ☙, "Please be seated. May Allah shower His mercy on you. In saying what you heard him say, Omar ☙ did not intend to hurt or to insult any Muslim. All he intended by what he said was to encourage those who were hesitant to fight in Jihad." Thereafter, Khalid bin Sa'eed ☙ the brother of Amr bin Sa'eed ☙ stood up and said, "The Khalifa of Rasulullah ﷺ is right. Please be seated, dear brother." When Amr bin Sa'eed ☙ sat down, Khalid ☙ continued, "All praises belong to Allah besides Whom none is worthy of worship. Who has sent Muhammad ﷺ with guidance and the true Islam to make it dominate over all other religions even though the disbelievers dislike it. All praises are due to Allah Who fulfils His promises, Who makes them come to realization and Who destroys His enemies. We neither oppose you nor have any opposition amongst ourselves. You are a well-wishing and concerned leader and we are prepared to march whenever you command and prepared to obey you whenever you issue an order." Abu Bakr ☙ was extremely pleased by this speech and said, "May Allah reward you well, my brother and friend! You had accepted Islam willingly, migrated with the hope of reward when you escaped from the disbeliever with your Islam so that Allah and His Rasul ﷺ may be pleased and so that the Kalima may be elevated. You are one of the commanders of the people, so prepare to march. May Allah shower His mercy on you." Abu Bakr ☙ descended from the pulpit. Khalid bin Sa'eed ☙ then left to make the necessary preparations. In the meantime, Abu Bakr ☙ instructed Bilal ☙ to make the following announcement: "O people! March in Jihad against the Romans in Sham!" There were no doubts amongst the people that Khalid bin Sa'eed ☙ was their commander. He was the first to reach the army camp, after which people started arriving there in tens, twenties, thirties, forties, fifties and hundreds. Eventually, a very large army had gathered. Accompanied by several leading Sahabah, Abu Bakr ☙ proceeded to the camp one day. Although he saw an impressive number of men, he did not think that the number was adequate to fight the Romans. Turning to his companions, he asked, "What would you say if I send this number of men to Sham?" Omar ☙ replied, "I do not think that this number is sufficient for the large Roman army." Turning to the others, Abu Bakr ☙ asked, "What do you men think?" they replied, "We second the opinion of Omar ☙." Abu Bakr ☙ then said, "Should I rather not write to the people of Yemen, calling them to Jihad and encouraging them with the rewards for Jihad?" All his companions shared his opinion and said, "That is an excellent idea! Go ahead." Abu Bakr ☙ wrote the letter.

The letter of Abu Bakr ☙ to the People of Yemen Calling Them to Fight in Jihad

In the name of Allah the Most Kind the Most Merciful
From the Khalifa of Rasulullah ﷺ to every Muslim and Mu'min of Yemen to whom this letter is read.
Peace be to you.
Before you all, I praise Allah besides Whom there is none worthy of worship. Verily Allah has made Jihad obligatory for the Mu'minin and has commanded them to proceed in the Path of Allah when light or heavy and exert themselves with their wealth and lives in Allah's way. Jihad is a greatly emphasized obligation and its rewards with Allah are tremendous. We have prepared the Muslims to march in Jihad against the Roman in Sham. They have prepared to it with noble intentions and with great hopes of being rewarded. Therefore, O servants of Allah, you should also prepare to that towards which they have prepared, ensuring that your intentions are good. You are assured one of 2 excellent virtues; either martyrdom or victory and booty. Remember that Allah is not pleased with only words from His servants that are not accompanied by actions. Furthermore, Jihad against the enemies of Islam shall continue until they accept Islam and accept the injunctions of the Qur'an. May Allah preserve your Islam for you, guide your hearts, purify your deeds and bless you with the rewards of those who wage Jihad and who are steadfast." Abu Bakr ☙ sent this letter with Anas bin Malik ☙. *(Asakir in Mukhtasar, Kanzul Umma).*

The Lecture of Abu Bakr ☙ When the Muslim Army Left for Sham

Abdur Rahman bin Jubair رحمة الله, narrates that when Abu Bakr ☙ was seeing the army off to Sham, he stood up amongst them. He praised Allah, instructed them to march to Sham and gave them the glad tidings that Allah would grant them victory to the extent that they would even build Masjid there. He said, "You should never think that you are going there for sport. Sham is a land of plenty that has plenty of food for you so beware of developing pride for I swear by the Rabb of the Kabah that pride and showing off will certainly come to you. I advise you with 10 things, so always keep them in mind. Never kill a helpless old man..." The Hadith continues. *(Ibn Asakir in Kanzul Ummal)*

Omar Bin Khattab ☙ Encourages Jihad in the Path of Allah and Consults with the Sahabah in Matters Arising Before Him

Qasim bin Muhammad narrates that Muthanna bin Haritha ☙ once addressed the people saying, "O people! You should never regard marching against the Persians as something difficult. We have already captured their fertile grounds and the best half of Iraq. We already have half of their kingdom and have caused them tremendous losses. Our people are bold against them and InsAllah we shall soon also have their remaining lands." Omar ☙ then stood up and said, "The region of Hijaz is not your original homeland. You only stay where you can find some vegetation and it is only by that the people of Hijaz manage to survive. Where are those Muhajir who were leaping towards the promises of Allah? March to the lands that Allah has promised in His Book that He would make you inherit. Allah declared: لِيُظْهِرَهُ عَلَى الدِّينِ كُلِّهِ
that He may make it (Islam) superior over all religions. (Al-

Fath:28. Allah shall therefore make His Islam dominate, give honor to those who assist His Islam and make its supporters the inheritors of the territories of all nations. Where are the righteous servants of Allah then?" The first to respond was Abu Ubaid bin Mas'ood ☺, followed by either Sa'd bin Ubaid or Saleet bin Qais ☺. When the party gathered, Omar ☺ was told to appoint someone from the senior Muhajir and Ansar as their commander. However, Omar ☺ said, "By Allah! I shall not do this. Allah only gives status on account of your eagerness and enthusiasm to fight the enemy. Therefore, should you get smaller and dislike meeting the enemy, then the most deserving of leadership will be he who was the first to come forward and respond to the call. By Allah! I shall appoint as commander only he who was the first to respond." Omar ☺ then summoned Abu Ubaid, Saleet and Sa'd ☺, and said to Saeet and Sa'd ☺, "If you 2 had beaten him, I would have appointed you as commander and you would have deserved it because you are Muslims longer." Omar ☺ then appointed Abu Ubaid ☺ as commander of the army and said to him, "Listen to the Sahabah of Rasulullah ﷺ and consult with them. Never do anything hastily until you have verified the facts. This is warfare and only that person succeeds in it who is calm and who knows when to attack and when not to attack." *(Ibn Jareer Tabari).* Sha'bi رحمة when Omar ☺ was told to appoint a Sahabi as commander, he said, "The virtue of the Sahabah is on account of them being the first to volunteer and being present when others refused to present themselves. However, when they express reluctance and others do what they had been doing, then those who are prepared to march when heavy or light become more deserving. By Allah! I shall only appoint as their commander the one who had been first to respond." Omar ☺ appointed Abu Ubaid ☺ as the commander and advised him concerning the army. *(Ibn Jareer Tabari).*

Omar ☺ Consults with the Sahabah Concerning a Military Offensive Against the Persians

Omar bin Abdul Aziz says that when the news of the martyrdom of Abu Ubaid bin Mas'ood ☺ reached Omar ☺ and he learnt that the Persians aligned behind someone from the family of the Kisra, he had an announcement of Jihad made amongst the Muhajir and the Ansar and instructed them to meet at a place called Sirar. Omar ☺ left for Sirar and sent Talha bin Ubaidullah ☺ ahead to a place called Ahwas. He then appointed Abdur Rahman bin Auf ☺ as commander of the army's right side, Zubair bin Awam ☺ as commander of the left side and appointed Ali ☺ as his deputy in Madinah. When Omar ☺ consulted with the Sahabah, they all shared the opinion that he should march against the Persians. However, Omar ☺ did not consult with them before reaching Sirar and before Talha ☺ had returned from Ahwas. When Omar ☺ consulted with the eminent Sahabah, Talha ☺ also expressed the same opinion as the others to march against the Persians but Abdur Rahman bin Auf ☺ was against the idea. Abdur Rahman bin Auf ☺ said, "After the demise of Rasulullah ﷺ, I have never before this day and shall never afterwards say that I shall sacrifice my parents for anyone. Now I say that may my parents be sacrificed for you O Amirul Mu'minin! Leave this matter to me. You remain in Madinah and send out an army. I have noticed that the decree of Allah has always been in favor of your armies. The defeat of your army is not as demoralizing as your defeat. I fear that if you are martyred or defeated in battle, the Muslims will be so demoralized that they will never again cry out 'Allahu Akbar' or recite *'La Ilaha IllAllah'*." Omar ☺ accepted this opinion and was looking for a commander and they were still busy consulting when a letter

arrived from Sa'd ☺ who had been employed to collect zakah of the people of Najd. Omar ☺ asked those with him to suggest who should command the army, Abdur Rahman bin Auf ☺ said, "You have just found him." "Who is he?" asked Omar ☺. Abdur Rahman ☺ replied, "He is the clawed and valiant lion Sa'd bin Malik ☺." The other members agreed. *(Ibn Jareer Tabari).*

Uthman ☺ Encourages People Towards Jihad

Abu Salih who was the freed slave of Uthman ☺ narrates that he hard Uthman ☺ saying from the pulpit, "O people! I had kept secret from you a Hadith that I had heard from Rasulullah ﷺ fearing that you would disperse from around me and proceed in Jihad. I then decided to mention it to you so that each person may decide to do as he pleases. I have heard Rasulullah ﷺ say, 'A single day spent guarding the borders of the Muslim state for the pleasure of Allah is better than 1,000 other days spent at other places'." *(Ahmad).* Mus'ab bin Thabit bin Abdullah bin Zubair ☺ narrates that Uthman ☺ mentioned the following in a sermon from the pulpit: "I intent narrating to you a Hadith that I had heard from Rasulullah ﷺ. All that prevented me from narrating it to you previously was to keep you behind with me here in Madinah to tend to the affairs of the capital city. I heard Rasulullah ﷺ say, 'A single day spent guarding the borders of the Muslim state for the pleasure of Allah is better than 1,000 other days spent in salah coupled with days spent fasting'." *(Ahmad).*

Ali ☺ Encourages People Towards Jihad

Zaid bin Wahab narrates that Ali ☺ once stood up to address the people. He said, "All praises belong to Allah Who when He crushes something, none can mend it and when He wants something to remain intact, and none can smash it. If Allah wills, no 2 persons would have a quarrel and the Ummah would never dispute any of His laws. If He wills, no underling would reject the virtue of his superiors. Fate has drawn us and others to this place. Allah sees and hears us and if He wills, He could hasten our punishment. Allah controls change and has the power to expose the oppressor and make it known where the truth lies. Allah made this world a place of actions and has made the Hereafter a place to live forever.

$$\text{لِيَجْزِيَ الَّذِينَ أَسَاءُوا بِمَا عَمِلُوا وَيَجْزِيَ الَّذِينَ أَحْسَنُوا بِالْحُسْنَى (31)}$$

He may requite those who do evil with that which they have done (i.e. punish them in Hell), and reward those who do good, with what is best (i.e. Paradise). (An-Najm:31). Listen attentively! Tomorrow you will face enemy so spend a long time in salah tonight, recite Qur'an abundantly and beg Allah ﷻ for assistance and steadfastness. Fight them with determination, caution and remain firm." Ali ☺ left. *(Tabari)*

Ali ☺ Encourages the Muslims During the Battle of Siffin

Abu Amra Ansari narrates that when giving courage to the Muslims during the battle of Siffin, Ali ☺ said, "Allah has shown you a trade which will save you from a painful punishment and take you closer to all goodness *(ref. As-Saff:10-13)*; the trade is Iman in Allah and His Rasul ﷺ and Jihad in the Path of Allah. Allah has determined that the rewards for this shall be forgiveness from Allah and wonderful mansions in the eternal Jannah. Allah has informed you that He loves those who fight the enemies of Islam in His path standing in rows in front of the enemy with dedication and unity as if they are a building. You should straighten your rows like a solid building. Those wearing armor should be in front and those without armor should fall behind. Persevere with firmness." *(Tabari)*

Ali ❀ Encourages the Muslims to Fight the Khawarij

Abul Wadak Hamdani narrates that when Ali ❀ camped at a place called Nukhaila close to Kufa and had lost hope in the Khawarij, he stood up to address the people. After praising Allah, he said, "He who discards Jihad and compromises the laws of Allah, borders with destruction unless Allah rescues him by His grace. Fear Allah and fight those who oppose Allah, who attempt to extinguish the light of Allah, who is in error, deviant, oppressive and sinful. They are not proficient in reciting the Qur'an, no understanding of Islam, no knowledge of interpreting the Qur'an and are not even long in Islam that they could be worthy of Khilafa. By Allah! If they become your rulers, they will rule you in the way that Kisra and Heraclius ruled. Prepare well for your march against your enemies from the West. I have sent a message to your brothers from Basra to come to assist you. We shall all march together against the Khawarij as soon as they arrive. There is no power or might but with Allah." *(Tabari)*

Ali ❀ speaks on the Reluctance of the Muslims to March in Jihad

Zaid bin Wahab narrates that in his first address to the Muslims after the battle Nahrwan, Ali ❀ said, "O people! Prepare to march against the enemy in a Jihad that will draw you close to Allah and secure a great status for you near Him. They are people who are confused about the truth, know nothing about the Qur'an, are far from Islam, are confused in rebellion and have fallen headlong into the abyss of deviation. Prepare to use in battle against them with whatever forces of strength (weapons) you can muster, as well as trained horses. Trust in Allah for Allah suffices as Defender and Allah suffices as Helper." When the people failed to march and to prepare, Ali ❀ left them alone for a few days. Eventually, when he lost hope that they would prepare, he summoned their leaders and influential people. When Ali ❀ asked them for their opinions and about what it was that caused them to put off, some of them complained of illness while others excused themselves on account of some pressing circumstances. Only a few of them were willing. Ali ❀ then stood up to deliver a lecture. He said, "O servants of Allah! What is the matter with you that you cling to the ground when you are commanded to march? Do you prefer the life of this world to that of the Hereafter? Do you prefer humiliation and dishonor over respect? Each time I call you to wage Jihad, your eyes start to turn like a person close to death. It then seems as if your hearts have lost their senses, leaving you without any understanding and as if your eyes have been blinded so that you see nothing. By Allah! When there is comfort and luxury, you are like the lions of the Shira forest but when you are called towards battle, you become clever foxes. I have permanently lost confidence in you people. You are not the type of horsemen with whom an attack can be launched neither people of nobility with whom refuge can be sought. I swear by Allah that you people are the worst and most incompetent in battle. The plots of the enemy are sure to succeed against you whereas your strategies would be useless against them. Your limbs are being severed and you cannot defend each other. Your enemies are not asleep whereas you are oblivious. A fighter is vigilant, and intelligent whereas one who bows to a truce becomes humiliated. Those who fight amongst themselves are soon defeated and defeated people are suppressed and looted. You should now understand that I have rights over you just as you have rights over me. Your rights over me are that I should be your well-wisher as long as I am with you, that I should increase your shares of booty, that I should educate you so that you do not remain ignorant and that I should teach you etiquette and manners so that you are able to learn. My rights that

are due from you are that you fulfill your pledge of loyalty to me and that you remain my well-wishers in my presence as well as in my absence. You ought to respond to me when I summon you and obey me when I issue an order. If Allah intends good for you, you would forsake that which displeases me and return to that which pleases me. By doing this, you will receive what you want and achieve what you aspire for." *(Tabari)*.

Howsab Himiari calls Ali in the Battle of Siffin and received Reply

Abdul Wahid Damishqi narrates that during the battle of Siffin, Howsab Himiari called to Ali ❀ saying, "O son of Abu Talib! Leave us alone for the sake of yours and our blood! We shall leave Iraq for you and you leave Sham for us. Thus the blood of Muslims will be spared." Ali ❀ replied by saying, "Unbelievable, O son of Umm Zulaym! I swear by Allah that I would do this if I knew that I am permitted to compromise Islam of Allah. In fact, this would cause me less trouble. When Allah is disobeyed and the people of the Qur'an have the might to take a stand and wage Jihad until Allah's commands dominate, Allah does not like them to remain silent and to compromise the Deen." *(Ibn Abdil Birr in Isti'ab, Abu Nu'aym In Hilya)*

Sa'd bin Abi Waqqas ❀ Encourages the Muslims to Wage Jihad During the Battle of Qadisiya

Muhammad, Talha and *Ziyad* ❀ all narrate that during the battle of Qadisiya, Sa'd bin Abi Waqqas ❀ stood up to address the Muslims. After praising Allah, he said "Allah is definitely True. He has no partner in His kingdom and never goes back on His word. Allah The Majestic declares:

وَلَقَدْ كَتَبْنَا فِي الزَّبُورِ مِنْ بَعْدِ الذِّكْرِ أَنَّ الْأَرْضَ يَرِثُهَا عِبَادِيَ الصَّالِحُونَ (105)

And indeed We have written in Zaboor (Psalms) (i.e. all the revealed Holy Books the Taurat (Torah), the Injeel (Gospel), the Qur'an) after (We have already written in) Al-Lauh Al-Mahfooz (the Book, that is in the heaven with Allah), that My righteous slaves shall inherit the land (i.e. the land of Paradise). (Al-Ambiya:105)

This earth is your legacy and the promise of your Rabb. For the past 3 years, Allah has given you use of this land. You are feeding others from it and yourselves eating from it. To this day, you have killed its people in the wars that took place, collected their wealth and taken prisoners from amongst them. In the previous battles, those before you have caused much harm to them. Now their army has come to you (the army of Yazdgird with approximately 200,000). You are amongst the pride of the Arabs, their nobles, the cream of every tribe, and the most honorable of those you have left behind you. If you are detached from the world and hopeful of the Hereafter, Allah shall grant you both worlds. This battle cannot take you any closer to your deaths. If you lose courage, become cowardly and weak, your strength will leave and you will be destroying your Hereafter."

The Speech of Asim bin Amr ❀ During the Battle of Qadisiya

Asim bin Amr ❀ stood up and said, "Allah has subjected the people of this land of Iraq to you for the past 3 years and the harm you have done to them in weakening their military strength is more than the harm they have caused to you. You are now in a position of superiority and Allah shall remain with you on condition that you are steadfast and use your swords and spears properly. You will have possession of their wealth, their women, their children and their country. On the other hand, if you weaken and become cowardly - may Allah protect you from this - their large army shall not leave a single survivor from amongst you for fear that you would return to destroy them. Fear Allah! Fear Allah and remember the previous battles in which Allah had blessed you. Do you not look back to the land of Arabia behind you that is barren without any vegetation? It had neither any shade nor offers any sanctuary where refuge can be taken and a defense organized. Make the Hereafter your objective." *(Tabari).*

The Fervor of the Sahabah to go to Jihad for the Pleasure of Allah

Abu Umamah ❀ narrates that he got ready to join Rasulullah ﷺ when Rasulullah ﷺ intended to leave for the battle of Badr. His uncle Abu Burda bin Niyar ❀ advised him to rather stay behind with his mother. To this, Abu Umamah ❀ said, "Why do you rather not stay behind with your sister (my mother)?" When this was mentioned to Rasulullah ﷺ, he instructed Abu Umamah ❀ to remain with his mother while Abu Burda ❀ left with Rasulullah ﷺ. When Rasulullah ﷺ returned, Abu Umamah ❀'s mother had just passed away and Rasulullah ﷺ led the Janazah (funeral) prayer. *(Abu Nu'aym in Hilya).*

The Enthusiasm of Omar ❀ for Jihad and his Statement that Jihad is Better than Hajj

Omar ❀ is reported to have said, "I would have preferred to meet Allah had it not been for 3 things; for walking in the Path of Allah, for placing my head on the sand in prostration before Allah and for sitting in the company of people who choose their words just as the best dates are selected." *(Ahmad in Zuhd, Sa'eed bin Mansoor, Ibn Abu Shaiba in Kanzul Ummal).* Omar ❀ said to the people, "Ensure that you perform Hajj for it is a virtuous deed that Allah has commanded. However, Jihad is even more virtuous." *(Ibn Abu Shaiba in Kanzul Ummal)*

The Enthusiasm of Abdullah bin Omar ❀ for Jihad

Abdullah bin Omar ❀ once said, "When I was brought before Rasulullah ﷺ to participate in the Battle of Badr, Rasulullah ﷺ thought that I was too young and did not accept me. I had never experienced no night like that night. Because Rasulullah ﷺ did not accept me to fight in Jihad, I did not sleep a moment, was overcome with grief and wept continuously. When I was brought before him the following year and Rasulullah ﷺ accepted me, I praised Allah for it." Someone then asked him, "O Abu Abdur Rahman! Did you people turn back on the day the 2 armies met during the battle of Uhud?" "Yes," replied Abdullah bin Omar ❀, "but Allah forgave all of us, and all thanks are due to Him." *(Ibn Asakir in Muntakhab Kanz).*

Omar ❀ with the Person who Intended to Proceed in Jihad

Anas ❀ narrates that a man came to Omar ❀ and requested, "O Amirul Mu'minin! Please provide me with transport because I want to proceed in Jihad." Omar ❀ then told someone to take the man to the public treasury so that he could take whatever he required form there. When the man entered the treasury and found gold and silver, he asked, "What is all this? I need none of this. All I require are provisions for a journey and transport." The people took the man back to Omar ❀ and informed him about what he had said. Omar ❀ issued instructions that the man should be provided with provisions and transport. When these were brought, Omar ❀ himself tied the saddle to the animal. After mounting the animals, the man raised his hands praised Allah for the treatment he received and for what Omar ❀ had given him. Omar ❀ was walking behind him with the hope that the man would make du'a for him. Praising Allah, the man said, "O Allah! Grant Omar ❀ the best of rewards." *(Hannad in Kanzul Ummal).*

The Statement of Omar ❀ About the Virtue of the Person Who Marches Out and Stands Guard in the Path of Allah

Artat bin Mundhir narrates that Omar ❀ once asked those sitting in his company, "Which person deserves the greatest rewards?" The people started making mention of salah and fasting and mentioning the names of people who are best after the Amirul Mu'minin. Thereafter, Omar ❀ said, "Shall I not inform you of those whose rewards are greater than those you have mentioned and who is even better than the Amirul Mu'minin?" When the people asked to be informed, Omar ❀ replied, "A small unimportant man in Sham leading his horse by its reins as he walks while guarding the capital city of the Muslims in Sham. He neither knows whether a wild animal may attack him, whether a poisonous reptile may bite him or whether an enemy may overpower him. That is the person whose rewards are greater than all those you have mentioned and who is even better than the Amirul Mu'minin." *(Ibn Asakir in Kanzul Ummal)*

Omar ❀ and Abu Bakr ❀ Concerning the Departure of Mu'adh ❀

Ka'b bin Malik ❀ narrates that Omar ❀ used to say, "The departure of Mu'adh bin Jabal ❀ to Sham was an event that presented difficulty to Madinah and its people with regard to questions of Islamic jurisprudence and the religious rulings (Fatawa) that Mu'adh ❀ issued. I had spoken to Abu Bakr ❀ about keeping Mua'dh ❀ behind in Madinah because the people needed him but Abu Bakr ❀ refused this request saying, 'I cannot stop a man who wants to go somewhere in search of martyrdom.' I responded by saying, 'By Allah! When a person is serving important interests of his town's people, he will be blessed with the status of a martyr even as he lies on his bed in his own home.'" Ka'b bin Malik ❀ says that Mu'adh bin Jabal ❀ used to give Fatawa during the time of Rasulullah ﷺ as well as during the time that Abu Bakr ❀ was Khalifa. *(Ibn Sa'd in Kanzul Ummal).*

Omar ❀ Gives Preference to Those Who Were the First to Migrate Over the Popular Leaders of People

Naufal bin Amarah narrates that Harith bin Hisham and Suhail bin Amr ❀ came and sat with Omar ❀ in a manner that he was between the 2 of them. Thereafter, the first among those to migrate to Madinah started arriving. As each one of them arrived, Omar ❀ said, "Move aside, O Suhail! Move aside, O Harith!" In this manner, Omar ❀ moved the 2 of them further from him. As the Ansar started coming to Omar ❀, he moved the 2 men further in a like manner until they were behind everyone. When the 2 men left the presence of Omar ❀, Harith bin Hisham ❀ said to Suhail bin Amr ❀, "Did you see how we were treated?" Suhail ❀ replied, "Dear man! We should not blame Omar ❀, but should blame ourselves. When those people were invited to accept Islam, they were quick to do so while we delayed." When the Muhajir and Ansar had left Omar ❀, the 2 men approached him and said, "O Amirul Mu'minin! We noticed what you did today and realize that is was due to our own shortcomings. However, is there any way in which we could gain the status we have not been able to achieve?" Omar ❀ said to them, "I know of no other way but in that direction." He then pointed towards the Roman borders where the Muslims were waging Jihad against the Romans. The 2 men then left for Sham, where they both passed away. *(Ibn Asakir in Kanzul Ummal, Ibn Abdil Birr in Isti'aab).*

The Statement of Suhail bin Amr ❀ to the Leaders Over Whom Omar ❀ had Given Preference to the Early Muhajir

Hasan رحمة الله narrates that several persons came to the door of Omar ﷺ. Amongst them were Suhail bin Amr ﷺ, Abu Sufian bin Harb ﷺ and other prominent leaders of the Quraish. Omar ﷺ's doorkeeper came out and allowed inside those Sahabah who participated in the battle of Badr such as Suhaib ﷺ, Bilal ﷺ and Ammar ﷺ. Hasan رحمة الله says, "I swear by Allah that Omar ﷺ had participated in the battle of Badr. He loved those who participated in the battle of Badr and always advised others to show preference to them. Abu Sufian ﷺ said, "I have never seen a day like today! He allows these slaves to enter without paying any attention to us sitting there." Hasan رحمة الله narrates further by saying, "Suhail bin Amr ﷺ responded to him. What an excellent and intelligent man he was! He said, 'O people! By Allah! I see the expressions on your faces. If you are angry, be angry with yourselves. You were also invited to accept Islam when these people were invited. They were quick to respond while you delayed. Listen well! I swear by Allah that the virtue of accepting Islam early by which they have excelled ahead of you is a greater loss to you than their beating you to this door of the Amirul Mu'minin for which you are competing.'" Suhail bin Amr ﷺ continued, "As you see, these men have beaten you and I swear by Allah that you have no way of reaching the status that they have to beat you. You should look towards waging Jihad and hold tightly to it. Perhaps Allah shall bless you with the honor of waging sincere Jihad and martyrdom." Suhail bin Amr ﷺ stood up, dusted his clothing and proceeded to Sham. Hasan رحمة الله added, "Suhail bin Amr ﷺ had spoken the truth. Allah has not made the person who is quick like the one who delays and cannot share the same status." (Hakim in Isti'aab, Haythami, Bukhari).

Suhail bin Amr ﷺ Marches in Jihad and Remains in the Path of Allah Until his Death

Abu Sa'eed bin Fudala ﷺ was a Sahabi who narrated, "Suhail bin Amr ﷺ and I went together to Sham. I heard him say, 'I heard Rasulullah ﷺ say, 'A moment spent standing in the Path of Allah is better than a lifetime of deeds one of you can do while with his family.' I shall guard the borders of the Islamic state until I die and shall never return to Makkah.'" Abu Sa'eed ﷺ says that Suhail bin Amr ﷺ then remained in Sham until he passed away in the plague of Amwas. (Ibn Sa'd in Isaba, Hakim).

Harith bin Hisham ﷺ Leaves for Jihad Despite the Misery of the People of Makkah

Abu Naufal bin Abi Aqrab narrates that when Harith bin Hisham ﷺ left Makkah, the people of Makkah became extremely sad and besides suckling infants, everyone left to see him off. When he reached an elevated spot of Bat'ha or somewhere close to it, he stopped and the people around him also stopped. They were all weeping. Seeing the sorrow of the people, he said, "O people! I swear by Allah that I am not leaving because I love myself more than you nor because I prefer another city to yours. However, when Islam came, there were many men of the Quraish who left Makkah and left in Jihad for the sake of Islam even though they were not from amongst the prominent people of the Quraish nor from its nobility. By Allah! Our condition at present is that even if the mountains of Makkah were solid gold and we spent all of it in the Path of Allah, we would never equal a day of theirs. By Allah! Although they have surpassed us in this world, we hope that we shall be on par in the Hereafter. Every person who carries out any deed should fear Allah." He then left for Sham together with all those who followed him and was later martyred. May Allah shower His mercy on him. (Isti'ab, Hakim).

The Fervor of Khalid bin Walid ﷺ for Jihad and Desire for Martyr

Ziyad who was a freed slave of the family of Khalid bin Walid ﷺ narrates that on his deathbed, Khalid bin Waled ﷺ said, "There is no night on earth more beloved to me than a night out on a military expedition with the Muhajir which is so cold that water turns to ice and we are to attack the enemy the following dawn. You people should steadfastly cling to Jihad." (Ibn Sa'd in Istaba). Khalid bin Walid ﷺ has also mentioned, "The night in which my newly-wed bride whom I love dearly is brought to my house or from whom I am given the news of a son to be born is not dearer to me then that night out on a military expedition with the Muhajir which is so cold that water turns to ice and we are to attack the enemy the following dawn." (Abu Ya'la in Majma'uz Zawa'id). Another narration states that Khalid bin Walid ﷺ said, "Involvement in Jihad in the Path of Allah prevented me from learning much of the Qur'an." (Abu Ya'la, Haythami). Khalid bin Walid ﷺ said, "Involvement in Jihad has preoccupied me from learning much about the Qur'an." (Abu Ya'la in Isaba). Abu Wa'il narrates that when Khalid bin Walid ﷺ was about to pass away, he said, "I searched for martyrdom wherever I anticipated it to be but I was destined to die on my bed. After my recitation of 'La Ilaha IllAllah', there is no deed I have more hope in than the night I spent wearing my helmet as the rain poured all the time until dawn. We launched a surprise attack on the enemy positions. When I die, I want you to gather my weapons and my horse and donate it as equipment in the Path of Allah." After Khalid bin Walid ﷺ had passed away, Omar ﷺ came for the funeral prayer and said, "There is no harm if the family of Walid ﷺ shed their tears as long as they do not tear their clothes and cry loudly." (Ibn Mubarak in Kitabul Jihad, Tabrani, Haythami).

The Enthusiasm of Bilal ﷺ to Proceed in the Path of Allah

The fathers of Abdullah bin Muhammad, Omar bin Hafs and Ammar bin Hafs all narrate from their fathers that Bilal ﷺ once approached Abu Bakr ﷺ saying, "O Khalifa of Rasulullah ﷺ! I have heard Rasulullah ﷺ say that the best deed of the Mu'minin is Jihad in the Path of Allah. I have therefore decided to guard the borders for the pleasure of Allah until I die." Abu Bakr ﷺ responded by saying, "O Bilal! I plead to you in the name of Allah and for the sake of my honor and the rights I have not to leave me. My age has advanced, my strength has weakened and my death is near." Bilal ﷺ therefore stayed with Abu Bakr ﷺ. After Abu Bakr ﷺ had passed away, Omar ﷺ gave Bilal ﷺ a similar reply when he requested to proceed in Jihad. However, Bilal ﷺ refused to accept the reply. Omar ﷺ then asked, "Who then will call out the Adhan?" Bilal ﷺ replied, "Leave it to Sa'd ﷺ, for he also called out the Adhan in Quba during the time of Rasulullah ﷺ." Omar ﷺ then appointed Sa'd ﷺ to call out the Adhan and decided that his progeny after him should call out the Adhan. (Tabrani, Haythami, Ibn Sa'd). Muhammad bin Ibrahim Taymi narrates that after the demise of Rasulullah ﷺ, Bilal ﷺ called out the Adhan before Rasulullah ﷺ was buried. The people in the Masjid started to weep non stop when he called out the words: اَشْهَدُ اَنْ مُحَمَّدًا رَّسُوْلُ الله

"I testify that Muhammad ﷺ is the Rasul of Allah."

After Rasulullah ﷺ was buried and Abu Bakr ﷺ asked Bilal ﷺ to call out the Adhan, Bilal ﷺ said, "If you had freed me so that I should always remain with you, then it is alright that I shall do so. However, if you freed me for Allah then leave me to the One for Whom you had freed me." When Abu Bakr ﷺ made it clear that he had freed Bilal ﷺ solely for the pleasure of Allah, Bilal ﷺ said, "I therefore prefer not to call out the Adhan for anyone else after the demise of Rasulullah ﷺ." Abu Bakr ؓ acknowledged this by saying, "The choice is yours." Bilal ؓ then remained in Madinah until an army was leaving for Sham. He then joined them to Sham. Sa'eed bin Musaib رحمة الله narrates that when Abu Bakr ؓ once ascended the pulpit on the day of Jumu'ah, Bilal ؓ called for him. "At your service," replied Abu Bakr ؓ. Bilal ؓ asked, "Did you free me for the pleasure of Allah or for yourself?" "Only for Allah's pleasure," was the reply. "Then, permit me to wage Jihad in the Path of Allah." continued Bilal ؓ, with the permission of Abu Bakr ؓ, Bilal ؓ left for Sham where he passed away. (Ibn Sa'd, Abu Nu'aym in Hilya).

Miqdad ؓ Refuses to Miss a Jihad Expedition Because of the Qur'anic Verse Exhorting Jihad

Abu Yazid Makki narrates that Miqdad ؓ and Abu Ayub ؓ used to say, "We have been commanded to proceed in Jihad in all conditions." This was their explaanation of the اِنْفِرُوا خِفَافًا وَثِقَالًا

March forth (in the path of Allah), whether you are light (being healthy, young and wealthy) or heavy (being ill, old and poor), (At-Tauba:41) (Abu Nu'aym in Hilya).

Abu Rashid Habrani رحمة الله narrates that he once happened to meet Miqdad bin Aswad ؓ who was part of Rasulullah ﷺ's cavalry. He was sitting on the box of a currency exchanger and because his body was sizeable and had on extra weight in his old age, part of his body hung over the box. This was in Hims and Miqdad ؓ was intending to march in Jihad. Abu Rashid said to him, "Allah has excused you from Jihad because of your condition." Miqdad ؓ replied, "The verse of Surah At-Taubah has come to us in which Allah says: اِنْفِرُوا خِفَافًا وَثِقَالًا

March forth (in the path of Allah), whether you are light (healthy, young and wealthy) or heavy (ill, old and poor), (At-Tauba:41) (Abu Nu'aym in Hilya, Tabrani, Haythami, Ibn Sa'd, Hakim). Jubair bin Nufair رحمة الله narrates that they were sitting in the company of Miqdad bin Aswad ؓ in Damascus. Miqdad ؓ was sitting on a box which had no space left on it because his weight had become uncontrollable. Someone said to him, "You should sit out the year without fighting in Jihad because of your ill health." He replied by saying, "The verse of Surah At-Taubah has come to us." He was referring to Surah Taubah. He continued, "Allah says: اِنْفِرُوا خِفَافًا وَثِقَالًا

March forth (in the path of Allah), whether you are light (healthy, young and wealthy) or heavy (ill, old and poor), (At-Tauba:41). I find myself to be light and therefore have no excuse to remain behind." (Bayhaqi).

The Incident of Abu Talha ؓ in this Regard

Anas ؓ narrates that Abu Talha ؓ was reciting sure At-Taubah when he came to verse: اِنْفِرُوا خِفَافًا وَثِقَالًا

March forth (in the path of Allah), whether you are light (being healthy, young and wealthy) or heavy (being ill, old and poor), (At-Tauba:41). He said, "I have no doubts that our Rabb intends to encourage us to proceed in Jihad whether we are young or old. O my sons. Prepare my provisions for the journey. Prepare my provisions for the journey." His sons said to him, "May Allah has mercy on you! You fought with Rasulullah ﷺ until he passed away. Thereafter, you fought with Abu Bakr ؓ until he passed away and then with Omar ؓ until he passed away. Now let us fight on your behalf." "Never!" exclaimed Abu Talha ؓ, "Just prepare my provisions." He then joined the naval expedition and passed away while at sea. It was only after 7 days that an island could be found on which to bury him. When he was buried there,

his body had not even started to decay. (Isti'ab, lbn Sa'd, Bayhaqi and Hakim, Abu Ya'la in Majma'uz Zawa'id).

The Incident of Abu Ayub ؓ in this Regard

Muhammad bin Sirin رحمة الله has mentioned that Abu Ayub Ansari ؓ was present at the battle of Badr with Rasulullah ﷺ. Thereafter, apart from one year, he never missed a single military expedition. He sat out that year because a youngster had been appointed as commander of the army. However, after that year, he was always regretful and would repeat 3 times, "I care not who is appointed as commander over me." He fell ill while with an army under the command of Yazid bin Mu'awiya ؓ. When he came to see Abu Ayub ؓ, Yazid ؓ asked, "Is there anything you need?" Abu Ayub ؓ replied, "When I die, I want you to place my body on an animal and take me as far as you can into the land of the enemy. Eventually, when you are unable to take me any further, you may bury me." Consequently, after Abu Ayub ؓ passed away, Yazid ؓ had his body placed on an animal and took him as far as he could into enemy territory. When he could no longer take him along, he buried him and then left the area. Abu Ayub ؓ used to recite the verse: اِنْفِرُوا خِفَافًا وَثِقَالًا

March forth (in the path of Allah), whether you are light (healthy, young and wealthy) or heavy (ill, old and poor), (At-Tauba:41)

Thereafter, he would say, "I always find myself to be either light or heavy and never being excused from marching in Jihad." (Hakim, Ibn Sa'd in Isaba). Abu Dhabian narrates from his teachers from Abu Ayub Ansari ؓ that he fell ill as he was on a military expedition during the rule of Mu'awiya ؓ. When his illness worsened, he said to his companions, "Load me on an animal after I die and bury me beneath your feet when you stand in your rows in front of the enemy. They did as he requested. The narration still continues further. (Isti'ab). Abu Dhabian also narrates that when Abu Ayub ؓ was on a military campaign under the command of Yazid bin Mu'awiya ؓ, he said, "Take me to enemy territory after I die and bury me beneath you feet wherever you clash with the enemy." Thereafter he said, "The person who dies without ascribing partners to Allah shall enter Jannah." (Ahmad in Al Bidayah wan Nihayah, Ibn Sa'd).

Abu Khaithama ؓ Forsakes the Luxuries of this World and Proceeds in the Path of Allah

Ibn Is'haq رحمة الله narrates that it was a few days after Rasulullah ﷺ had already left for Tabuk that Abu Khaithama ؓ returned home on an extremely hot day. He found his 2 wives beneath their shelters in his orchard. Each one of them had sprinkled water on their shelters and kept cold water for him together with food they had prepared. When he entered the orchard and stood at the door of a shelter, he saw his wives and what they had done for him. He then said, "Rasulullah ﷺ is boiling in the sun, hot winds and heat while Abu Khaithama ؓ is enjoying cool shade, prepared meals and beautiful wives as he remains with his wealth. This is not fair! I swear by Allah that I shall not enter the shelter of any of you before meeting with Rasulullah ﷺ. Prepare my journey's provisions." They prepared the provisions and brought his camel. He saddled the camel and left in search of Rasulullah ﷺ until he finally caught up when Rasulullah ﷺ had set up camp in Tabuk. Abu Khaithama ؓ met with Umair bin Wahab Jamahi ؓ on the road who was also looking for Rasulullah ﷺ. The 2 rode together until they came close to Tabuk. Abu Khaithama ؓ then said to Umair ؓ, "Since I am at fault for not joining the army earlier and have to meet

Rasulullah ﷺ as soon as possible, why do you not ride behind me for you have no hurry so that I may reach Rasulullah ﷺ first." Umair ؓ complied and when Abu Khaithama ؓ drew close to Rasulullah ﷺ in Tabuk, the Sahabah said, "Here comes a rider on the road." Rasulullah ﷺ said, "Let it be Abu Khaithama ؓ." The Sahabah then said, "O Rasulullah ﷺ! By Allah! It really is Abu Khaithama ؓ!" When Abu Khaithama ؓ had made his camel sit down, he approached Rasulullah ﷺ. After he had greeted Rasulullah ﷺ, Rasulullah ﷺ said to him, "Shame on you, O Abu Khaithama ؓ!" After Abu Khaithama ؓ had explained the incident to Rasulullah ﷺ, Rasulullah ﷺ commended him and prayed for him. *(Al Bidayah wan Nihayah).* Sa'd bin Khaithama ؓ says, "I was unable to march with Rasulullah ﷺ. When I entered my orchard, I saw a shelter sprinkled with water and my wife. I then said, 'This is not fair! Rasulullah ﷺ is suffering in hot winds and heat while I am enjoying shade and luxury.' I then went to load my camel and took along some dates as my provisions. My wife called out, 'Where are you heading, O Abu Khaithama ؓ?' 'I am going to Rasulullah ﷺ,' I replied." Narrating further, Abu Khaithama ؓ says, "I then left to find Rasulullah ﷺ. On the road Umair bin Wahab ؓ met me. I said to him, 'You are a brave man and have nothing to fear being alone. I know where Rasulullah ﷺ is and I am at fault for not joining the army sooner. Do ride behind me so that I may meet Rasulullah ﷺ alone.' Umair ؓ did as I asked and as I set sight on the Muslim army, they also spotted me. Rasulullah ﷺ said, 'Let it be Abu Khaithama ؓ.' I approached Rasulullah ﷺ and said, 'I had almost destroyed myself, O Rasulullah ﷺ!' After narrating my story to him, Rasulullah ﷺ had good words to say and made Du'a for me." *(Tabrani in Majma'uz Zawa'id, Haythami).*

The Incident of Abu Layla and Abdullah bin Mugaffal ؓ

Ibn Is'haq says that the report reached him that Ibn Yamin Nasri ؓ once met Abu Layla ؓ and Abdullah bin Mugaffal ؓ, both of whom were weeping. Ibn Yamin ؓ asked, "What makes you 2 weep?" They replied, "We approached Rasulullah ﷺ to provide transport for us so that we could proceed in Jihad but we found nothing with him that we could use as transport. We also have nothing which could enable us to leave for Jihad with Rasulullah ﷺ. Ibn Yamin then gave them his camel and some dates for the journey's provision. The 2 then left with Rasulullah ﷺ. A narration of Yunus bin Bukair also from *Ibn Is'haq* adds that another Sahabi by the name of Ulba bin Zaid ؓ who also did not have the means to proceed in Jihad left at night and engaged in salah for a considerable portion of the night. He started weeping and said, "O Allah! You have issued the command to wage Jihad and encouraged it. However, You have not given me the means with which to do it and have also not given to Your Rasulullah ﷺ the means to provide transport for me. Now I wish to distribute to all the Muslims as Sadaqa the rewards for me forgiving every injustice that has been done to me in my wealth, my body and my honor." He came out in the morning with the other Muslims, Rasulullah ﷺ asked, "Where is the person who gave Sadaqa last night?" When no one replied, Rasulullah ﷺ repeated, "Where is the person who gave Sadaqa? Let him stand up." Ulba ؓ stood up and related his story. Rasulullah ﷺ commended him saying, "Hear the good news! I swear by the Being Who controls my life that your Sadaqa has been recorded as an accepted act of zakah." *(Al Bidayah wan Nihayah, Isaba)*

The story of Ulba bin Zaid ؓ

Abu Abs bin Jabar narrates about a companion of Rasulullah ﷺ Ulba bin Zaid bin Haritha ؓ. When the Sahabah were encouraged to spend in Sadaqa, each one of them brought whatever he could afford and whatever he had. Ulba said, "O Allah! I have nothing to spend in Sadaqa. O Allah! I spend the rewards for me forgiving every insult to my honor caused by any of Your creation." The next morning Rasulullah ﷺ appointed someone to announce, "Where is the person who donated his honor as Sadaqa last night?" Ulba ؓ stood up, Rasulullah ﷺ said, "Your Sadaqa has been accepted." *(Ibn Manda, Bazzar, Ibn Abi Dunya, Ibn Shahin, Ibn Najjar in Kanzul Ummal).*

Censuring Those Who Delayed Marching in the Path of Allah

Abdullah bin Abbas ؓ narrates that when Rasulullah ﷺ dispatched an army to Mu'ta, he appointed Zaid bin Haritha ؓ as the commander. Rasulullah ﷺ added that if Zaid ؓ is martyred, Ja'far ؓ was to take command and if he were martyred, Ibn Rawaha ؓ was to take command. If Ibn Rawaha ؓ delayed in leaving and performed the Jumu'ah salah behind Rasulullah ﷺ. When Rasulullah ﷺ saw him, he asked, "What has delayed you?" Ibn Rawaha ؓ replied, "Performing the Jumu'ah salah with you." Rasulullah ﷺ told him, "A single morning or evening in the Path of Allah is better than the entire world and its contents." *(Ahmad in Al Bidayah wan Nihayah, Ibn Abi Shaiba in Kanzul Ummal).* Abdullah bin Abbas ؓ narrates that on the Jumu'ah day when Rasulullah ﷺ dispatched Abdullah bin Rawaha ؓ with an army, Ibn Rawaha ؓ let the others proceed ahead and said to them, "I shall remain behind to perform the Jumu'ah salah with Rasulullah ﷺ. I shall catch up with you." Rasulullah ﷺ saw him after the salah and asked, "What prevented you from leaving with your companions in the morning?" Ibn Rawaha ؓ replied, "I wanted to perform the Jumu'ah salah with you and catch them up later." Rasulullah ﷺ said, "Even if you spent everything on earth you would be unable to gain the rewards of their morning." *(Tirmidhi in Al Bidayah wan Nihayah)*

Rasulullah ﷺ Rebukes One of the Sahabah Who Delayed Marching in the Path of Allah

Mu'adh bin Anas ؓ narrates that Rasulullah ﷺ once commanded some Sahabah to march on a military expedition. One of them said to his wife, "I shall stay behind to perform salah with Rasulullah ﷺ. Thereafter, I can make salam with him and bid him farewell. He would then make a Du'a for me that would reach the Day of Judgment and benefit me there." After Rasulullah ﷺ had completed the salah, the man came forward to greet him. Rasulullah ﷺ asked, "Do you know how far ahead your companions have gone?" "Yes," replied the Sahabi, "They are ahead of me by half a day." Rasulullah ﷺ said, "I swear by the Being Who controls my life! They have excelled you in virtue by a measure that is greater than the distance between the east and the west." *(Ahmad, Haythami).*

Rasulullah ﷺ Commands a Battalion to Leave by Night

Abu Hurairah ؓ narrates that Rasulullah ﷺ once asked a battalion to leave. They asked, "O Rasulullah ﷺ! Should we leave tonight or wait until the morning?" Rasulullah ﷺ said, "Would you not like to spend the night in a garden from amongst the magnificent gardens of Jannah?" *(Bayhaqi, Tabrani, Haythami).*

Omar ؓ Censures Mu'adh bin Jabal ؓ for Delaying his Departure

Abu Zur'ah bin Amr bin Jareer narrates that Omar ؓ once dispatched an army that included Mu'adh bin Jabal ؓ. After the army had left, Omar ؓ saw Mu'adh ؓ and asked, "What has kept you back?" Mu'adh ؓ replied, "I wanted to leave after performing the Jumu'ah salah." Omar ؓ scolded him by saying,

"Have you not heard Rasulullah ﷺ say, 'A single morning or evening in the Path of Allah is better than the entire world and its contents'?" *(Ibn Rahway, Bayhaqi in Kanzul Ummal).*

Censuring Those who Delayed Marching in the Path of Allah Because of Negligence : The Story of K'ab bin Malik ﷺ

Ka'b bin Malik ﷺ says, "Besides the military expedition to Tabuk, I did not miss a single military expedition in which Rasulullah ﷺ participated. I also missed the battle of Badr, but no one was reprimanded for missing that expedition because Rasulullah ﷺ had only intended to intercept a caravan of the Quraish, after which Allah brought the Muslims and their enemy together without any pre-arrangement. I was present on the night that the pledge of Aqaba took place with Rasulullah ﷺ. This was the night that we pledged our allegiance to Islam. I would not like to exchange that night for being at the battle of Badr even though the battle of Badr is more popularly spoken about amongst people. This is my story: I was never more healthier or more financially prosperous than the time when I missed the Tabuk expedition with Rasulullah ﷺ. I had never before owned 2 animals as I had at the time of the expedition. Until this expedition took place, it was always the practice of Rasulullah ﷺ to conceal the destination and make it seem that he was heading in a different direction. When Rasulullah ﷺ intended to march on this expedition, the heat was extreme, the journey was long and across barren land and the enemy were large in number. Rasulullah ﷺ therefore disclosed the matter to the Muslims so that they could make proper preparations for the expedition. He informed the Muslims exactly where he intended to march this time. The Muslims marching with Rasulullah ﷺ were so many that a single register could not contain their names. In fact, anyone who intended absenting himself knew that his absence would not be noted unless Allah sent revelation about it. Rasulullah ﷺ left on this expedition at a time when the date crop and the shade were most appealing because the dates were ripe for picking and the intense heat drew everyone towards the shade. However, the Muslims started their preparations along with Rasulullah ﷺ. Each morning I left to start my preparations with the other Muslims but returned home every time without doing anything, telling myself that I have the means to prepare and can even do so at short notice. This thinking continued until others had prepared in earnest and the morning arrived when Rasulullah ﷺ marched with the Muslims. By then I had still not yet made any preparations but told myself that I would get ready in a day or two and then catch up with them. After they had left, I started the morning with the intention of making preparations, but returned home without accomplishing anything. The next morning was the same and again I returned home without accomplishing anything. This continued happening to me and the Muslims marched very fast until every chance to catch up with the expedition was lost. I had a firm decision to ride out to meet them and wish that I had. However, I was never been able to do so. When I walked amongst the people after Rasulullah ﷺ had left, it saddened me greatly to see only people whose hearts were tainted by hypocrisy or ailing people whom Allah ﷻ had excused to stay behind. Rasulullah ﷺ made no mention of me until the Muslims had reached Tabuk. As he was sitting amongst the others at Tabuk, he asked, 'What has happened to Ka'b?' Someone from the Banu Salma tribe commented, 'O Rasulullah ﷺ! His fine clothing (wealth) has obstructed him.' Mu'adh bin Jabal ﷺ interjected by saying, 'You have made a terrible statement! O Rasulullah ﷺ! I swear by Allah that we only know him to be an excellent person.' Rasulullah ﷺ remained silent."

Ka'b bin Malik ﷺ continues to narrate, "When the news reached me that Rasulullah ﷺ was returning, I became worried and started thinking of false excuses. I asked myself what I could do to avert the anger of Rasulullah ﷺ and I also sought advice from every wise person of my family. When the news arrived that Rasulullah ﷺ was about to arrive, all false excuses vanished from my mind and I knew that I could never come out of the situation with anything connected to lies. I therefore decided to tell Rasulullah ﷺ the truth. Rasulullah ﷺ arrived and according to his normal practice after returning from a journey, he proceeded to the Masjid where he performed 2 Rakahs of salah. He then sat to meet with people. As Rasulullah ﷺ did this, those who stayed behind started approaching him and presented their excuses. They numbered 80 odd men and even took oaths before Rasulullah ﷺ to substantiate their excuses. Rasulullah ﷺ accepted their excuses at face value, renewed their pledges of allegiance and sought Allah's forgiveness on their behalf. He then handed over the inner details of their affairs to Allah. When I approached Rasulullah ﷺ and greeted him with Salam, he smiled as an angry person and said, 'Do come forward.' I walked to him and sat in front of him. He asked, 'What kept you behind? Had you not already purchased your conveyance?' I responded by saying, 'That's true. By Allah! Had I been sitting before someone other than you from amongst worldly men, I would have certainly escaped your anger by making some excuse because I have been given the ability to present convincing arguments. However, I swear by Allah that if I lie to you today and manage to secure your pleasure, the time will soon come when Allah shall make you angry with me. On the other hand, if I tell you the truth and you become angry with me, I have strong hopes of Allah's forgiveness. I swear by Allah that I really had no excuse. By Allah! I was never more healthier or more financially prosperous than the time when I missed the expedition.' Rasulullah ﷺ said, 'At least this man had spoken the truth. You may leave and wait until Allah decides your matter.' As I stood up, some men from the Banu Salma tribe to which I belonged also stood up and followed me. They said to me, 'By Allah! We have never known you to commit a sin before this! Could you not make an excuse like the others who stayed behind had made excuses? The forgiveness that Rasulullah ﷺ would have sought on your behalf should have then sufficient for our sin.' They kept scolding me in this manner so much that I actually made up my mind to return to Rasulullah ﷺ and deny whatever I had told him. I then asked them, 'Has anyone else experienced the same treatment as I have?' They replied, 'Yes. Two others said similar to what you did and received the same reply you received.' 'Who are they?' I asked. 'Murarah bin Rabi Amri and Hilal bin Umaia Waqifi,' came the reply. The 2 men they named were 2 righteous men who had participated in the battle of Badr and who made excellent examples to follow. I left on my way when they mentioned those 2 names to me.

Rasulullah ﷺ subsequently prevented people from speaking only to the 3 of us as opposed to the others who had missed the expedition. People avoided us and ignored us so much so that even the earth seemed like a different place to me. It was not the same place used to be for me. We remained in this condition for 50 days. My 2 companions became helpless and. confined themselves to their homes, weeping excessively. Since I was the youngest and most daring of us, I used to go out and join the Muslims for salah. I even walked about in the marketplace but no one spoke to me. When Rasulullah ﷺ sat in gatherings after salah, I would approach him and greet him with Salam. I would then ask myself whether his lips moved in reply to my Salam or not. I also performed salah close to Rasulullah ﷺ and steal a glance at him. I noticed that whenever I was engaged in salah, he looked at me and would avert his glance as soon as I turned towards him. The time eventually arrived when the attitude of the people became too much to bear, I walked to the orchard of Abu Qatadah and scaled the wall. He was my cousin and my best friend. I swear by Allah that he did not even reply to my Salam when I greeted him. I protested by saying, 'O Abu Qatadah! I ask you in the name of Allah to tell me whether I have love for Allah and His Rasul ﷺ?' When he gave no reply, I repeated the question and again asked in the name of Allah. He remained silent. Yet again, I repeated myself and took the name of Allah. All he said was, 'Allah and Rasulullah ﷺ know best.' My eyes filled with tears and I turned around to again scale the wall."

Continuing with the story, Ka'b ؓ says, "As I was walking in the marketplace one day, I heard the voice of a farmer from the farmers of Sham who had come to Madinah to sell his grains. He was announcing, 'Who will show me where is Ka'b bin Malik?' As the people pointed him in my direction, he handed over to me a letter from the king of Ghassan wrapped in a silken cloth. The letter read: 'The news has reached me that your master is being harsh towards you. Allah has not made you a low and ruined person. Join forces with us and we shall honor you.' After reading the letter, I said to myself, 'This is part of the test.' I then went to an oven where I burnt the letter. When 40 of the 50 days have passed, a messenger of Rasulullah ﷺ suddenly came to me with the message that I need to separate from my wife. 'Should I divorce her?' I asked. 'No,' he replied, 'Just be separated from her and do not go near her.' The same message was sent to my 2 companions. I then said to my wife, 'Go to your family and stay with them until Allah decides this matter.' The wife of Hilal bin Umayya ؓ approached Rasulullah ﷺ and pleaded, 'O Rasulullah ﷺ! Hilal bin Umayya is an extremely old and helpless man who has no servant. Would you object if I serve him?' 'No,' replied Rasulullah ﷺ, 'Just ensure that he has no intimate relations with you.' She commented, 'By Allah! He has no inclination to do anything. By Allah! He has wept continuously since this affair started and continues to do so.'" Ka'b ؓ continues, "Some of my family members advised me to also request that my wife stays to serve me as Hilal bin Umayya ؓ had requested permission. I told them that I would never seek such permission from Rasulullah ﷺ for I do not know what reply Rasulullah ﷺ would give me as a young man who can care for himself. I then remained in this condition without my wife for 10 days until full 50 nights had passed since Rasulullah ﷺ banned others from speaking to us. After performing the Fajr salah on the morning of the 50th night, I was still on the roof of my house and sitting there in the condition that Allah describes in the Qur'an in Surah At-Tauba:118; the earth had narrowed for me despite its vastness. I could find no place to hide myself and my own soul had narrowed for me. I had become frustrated with myself. It was then that I heard the voice of a caller who had climbed to the top of Mount Sala. He announced at the top of his voice, 'Rejoice, 'O Ka'b!' I fell prostrate in Sejdah for I knew that relief had arrived.

After performing the Fajr salah, Rasulullah ﷺ had announced to the people that Allah had accepted our repentance. Many people came to congratulate us and went to congratulate my 2 companions. As Zubair bin Awam ؓ urged his horse to reach me, a man from the Banu Aslam tribe Hamza bin Amr Aslami ؓ rushed to climb the hill and his voice was faster than the horse. When the person whose voice I had heard came to me, I took off the 2 sheets of cloth I was wearing and gave them to him as thanks for the good news he had given me. I swear by

Allah that I had no other clothes besides this at the time. I therefore borrowed some clothes and went to Rasulullah ﷺ. Droves of people came to congratulate me on my repentance saying, 'Congratulations! Allah has accepted your repentance.' When I eventually reached the Masjid, Rasulullah ﷺ was sitting there surrounded by people. It was Talha bin Ubaidullah ؓ who stood up and rushed towards me to shake my hands and to congratulate me. By Allah! No other person from amongst the Muhajir stood up to receive me. I shall never forget this gesture of Talha ؓ. I then greeted Rasulullah ﷺ. With his face beaming with delight, Rasulullah ﷺ said, 'Rejoice about the best day that has passed you since the day you were born. I asked, 'Is this from your side, O Rasulullah ﷺ or from Allah?' Rasulullah ﷺ replied, 'It is from Allah's side.' Whenever Rasulullah ﷺ was happy, his face would shine and appear to be a portion of the moon. We would therefore always recognize when he was happy. When I sat in front of Rasulullah ﷺ, I said, 'O Rasulullah ﷺ! As part of my Taubah, I wish to give all my wealth as Sadaqa for the pleasure of Allah and His Rasul ﷺ.' Rasulullah ﷺ advised, 'It would be best if you keep some of your wealth for yourself.' 'I shall then keep my allotted piece of land in Khaibar,' I said. I added, 'O Rasulullah ﷺ! Allah has saved me because of the truth I spoke and as part of my repentance; I shall speak only the truth as long as I live.' By Allah! I do not know of any Muslim whom Allah had given a better reward than Allah had given me from the time I spoke the truth to Rasulullah ﷺ. From the time I mentioned this to Rasulullah ﷺ; I have not spoken any lies up to this day and hope that Allah protects me from it as long as I remain alive. Allah has revealed the following verse to :

لَقَدْ تَابَ اللَّهُ عَلَى النَّبِيِّ وَالْمُهَاجِرِينَ وَالْأَنْصَارِ الَّذِينَ اتَّبَعُوهُ فِي سَاعَةِ الْعُسْرَةِ مِنْ بَعْدِ مَا كَادَ يَزِيغُ قُلُوبُ فَرِيقٍ مِنْهُمْ ثُمَّ تَابَ عَلَيْهِمْ إِنَّهُ بِهِمْ رَءُوفٌ رَحِيمٌ (117) وَعَلَى الثَّلَاثَةِ الَّذِينَ خُلِّفُوا حَتَّى إِذَا ضَاقَتْ عَلَيْهِمُ الْأَرْضُ بِمَا رَحُبَتْ وَضَاقَتْ عَلَيْهِمْ أَنْفُسُهُمْ وَظَنُّوا أَنْ لَا مَلْجَأَ مِنَ اللَّهِ إِلَّا إِلَيْهِ ثُمَّ تَابَ عَلَيْهِمْ لِيَتُوبُوا إِنَّ اللَّهَ هُوَ التَّوَّابُ الرَّحِيمُ (118) يَا أَيُّهَا الَّذِينَ آمَنُوا اتَّقُوا اللَّهَ وَكُونُوا مَعَ الصَّادِقِينَ (119)

Allah has forgiven the Prophet ﷺ, the Muhajiroon (Muslim emigrants who left their homes and came to Al-Madinah) and the Ansar (Muslims of Al-Madinah) who followed him (Muhammad ﷺ) in the time of distress (Tabook expedition, etc.), after the hearts of a party of them had nearly deviated (from the Right Path), but He accepted their repentance. Certainly, He is unto them full of Kindness, Most Merciful. And (He did forgive also) the three (who did not join the Tabook expedition (whom the Prophet ﷺ)) left (i.e. he did not give his judgment in their case, and their case was suspended for Allah's Decision) till for them the earth, vast as it is, was straitened and their ownselves were straitened to them, and they perceived that there is no fleeing from Allah, and no refuge but with Him. Then, He accepted their repentance, that they might repent (unto Him). Verily, Allah is the One Who accepts repentance, Most Merciful. O you who believe! Be afraid of Allah, and be with those who are true (in words and deeds). (At-Tauba:117-119). I swear by Allah that after guiding me to Islam, Allah has not granted me a greater blessing than making me speak the truth to Rasulullah ﷺ rather than lying, thereby causing me to be destroyed like those who had lied. When Allah sent revelation, he used the worst of terms for those who had lied than for anyone else. Allah states:

سَيَحْلِفُونَ بِاللَّهِ لَكُمْ إِذَا انْقَلَبْتُمْ إِلَيْهِمْ لِتُعْرِضُوا عَنْهُمْ فَأَعْرِضُوا عَنْهُمْ إِنَّهُمْ رِجْسٌ وَمَأْوَاهُمْ جَهَنَّمُ جَزَاءً بِمَا كَانُوا يَكْسِبُونَ (95) يَحْلِفُونَ لَكُمْ لِتَرْضَوْا عَنْهُمْ فَإِنْ تَرْضَوْا عَنْهُمْ فَإِنَّ اللَّهَ لَا يَرْضَى عَنِ الْقَوْمِ الْفَاسِقِينَ (96)

They (Hypocrites) will swear by Allah to you (Muslims) when you return to them, that you may turn away from them. So turn away from them. Surely, they are Rijsun (i.e. Najasun (impure) because of their evil deeds), and Hell is their dwelling place, - a recompense for that which they used to earn. They (the hypocrites) swear to you (Muslims) that you may be pleased with them, but if you are pleased with them, certainly Allah is not pleased with the people who are Al-Fasiqoon (rebellious, disobedient to Allah). (At-Tauba:95-96)

The matter of the 3 of us was postponed until after the matter of those whose excuses Rasulullah ﷺ accepted. When they swore oaths before Rasulullah ﷺ, he renewed their pledges of allegiance and sought Allah's forgiveness for them. Rasulullah ﷺ then postponed our matter until Allah had passed judgment. It is with reference to this that Allah says: وَعَلَى الثَّلَاثَةِ الَّذِينَ خُلِّفُوا

And Allah (has also turned in mercy towards) the 3 whose matter was postponed... (At-Tauba:118). In this verse, Allah is not referring to our staying behind from the expedition but to the postponement of our case after deciding the case of the others who had sworn oaths before Rasulullah ﷺ and who had made excuses that Rasulullah ﷺ accepted. *(Bukhari, Muslim, Ibn Is'haq, Ahmad in Al Bidayah wan Nihayah, Abu Dawud, Nasai, Tirmidhi in Targheeb wat Tarheeb, Bayhaqi).*

A Warning to Those who Forsake Jihad to Remain with Their Families and Wealth

Abu Imran ﷺ narrates that they were in Constantinople with Uqba bin Amir ﷺ as the commander of the Egyptian forces and Fudhala bin Ubaid ﷺ as commander of the forces from Sham. When an extremely large Roman army marched from Constantinople, the Muslims formed their rows to face them. One of the Muslims assaulted the Roman army so hard that he penetrated their ranks and then returned to his own ranks. The other Muslims shouted at him saying, "SubhanAllah! He is throwing himself into destruction by his own hands." It was then that Abu Ayub Ansari ﷺ a Sahabi of Rasulullah ﷺ stood up and said, "O people! You people are interpreting this verse in this manner whereas it was actually revealed with reference to us the Ansar community. When Allah gave strength to Islam and there were many people to assist its cause, we said to each other without the knowledge of Rasulullah ﷺ, 'Our fields have been destroyed out of neglect. We should therefore stay in Madinah to repair the damage done. In response to what we had intended, Allah revealed the verse: وَأَنْفِقُوا فِي سَبِيلِ اللَّهِ وَلَا تُلْقُوا بِأَيْدِيكُمْ إِلَى التَّهْلُكَةِ وَأَحْسِنُوا إِنَّ اللَّهَ يُحِبُّ الْمُحْسِنِينَ

(195). *And spend in the Cause of Allah (i.e. Jihad of all kinds, etc.) and do not throw yourselves into destruction (by not spending your wealth in the Cause of Allah), and do good. Truly, Allah loves Al-Muhsinoon (the good-doers). (Al-Baqara:195)* The destruction referred to is our staying behind in Madinah to tend to our fields, as we had intended to do." Abu Ayub Ansari ﷺ thereafter instructed the others to fight and remained fighting in the Path of Allah until Allah took him away. *(Bayhaqi)*

In another narration, *Abu Imran* narrates that when they were attacking the city of Constantinople under the leadership of Abdur Rahman bin Khalid bin Walid ﷺ, the Romans had their backs against the walls of the city. As one of the Muslim soldiers courageously attacked the enemy, the others shouted, "Stop! Stop! La Ilaha IllAllah! He is throwing himself into destruction by his own hand." Abu Ayub Ansari ﷺ then said, "That verse was revealed with reference to us the Ansar community. When Allah's assistance came to His Nabi ﷺ and Islam became

dominant, we said, 'Let us stay in our fields and look after them.' Allah then revealed the verse: وَأَنْفِقُوا فِي سَبِيلِ اللَّهِ وَلَا تُلْقُوا بِأَيْدِيكُمْ إِلَى التَّهْلُكَةِ وَأَحْسِنُوا إِنَّ اللَّهَ يُحِبُّ الْمُحْسِنِينَ

(195). *Spend in the Path of Allah and do not throw (lead yourselves) into destruction by (the doing of) your own hands. (Al-Baqara:195).* The destruction by our own hands refers to staying behind in our fields and looking after them while neglecting Jihad." *Abu Imran* says that Abu Ayub ﷺ continued fighting in the Path of Allah until he was eventually buried in Constantinople. *(Bayhaqi)*

Abu Irnran narrates that someone from amongst the Muhajir attacked the ranks of the enemy soldiers at Constantinople and actually penetrated them. To this, some people commented, "He is throwing himself into destruction by his own hand!" In the army was Abu Ayub Ansari ﷺ who then said, "We know this verse best for it was revealed with reference to us. We remained in the company of Rasulullah ﷺ, fought many battles with him and were there to assist him. However, when Islam spread and became dominant, we the Ansar community gathered together for the love of Islam and said, 'Allah has honored us with the companionship of Rasulullah ﷺ and gave us the ability to assist him until Islam has spread and its supporters have multiplied greatly. We had given preference to Islam over our families, our wealth and our children and now that the wars have stopped, we should return to our families and children and look after them. With reference to this, the verse was revealed: وَأَنْفِقُوا فِي سَبِيلِ اللَّهِ وَلَا تُلْقُوا بِأَيْدِيكُمْ إِلَى التَّهْلُكَةِ وَأَحْسِنُوا إِنَّ اللَّهَ يُحِبُّ الْمُحْسِنِينَ

(195). *And spend in the Cause of Allah (i.e. Jihad of all kinds, etc.) and do not throw yourselves into destruction (by not spending your wealth in the Cause of Allah), and do good. Truly, Allah loves Al-Muhsinoon (the good-doers). (Al-Baqara:195)*

The destruction referred to is staying with our families and properties and neglecting Jihad." *(Abu Dawud, Tirmidhi, Nasai, Abd bin Humayd, Ibn Abi Hatim, Ibn Jareer, Ibn Mardway, Abu Ya'la in Musnad, Ibn Hibban, Hakim in Mustadrak)*

Warnings to Those who Forsake Jihad Because of Their Preoccupation with Farming

Yazid bin Abi Habib narrates that the news reached Omar ﷺ that Abdullah bin Harr Anasi ﷺ had started farming on his land in Sham. Omar ﷺ therefore took the land away from him and gave it to someone else saying, "You have taken the disgrace and humiliation from the necks of these prominent people and placed it on your neck." *(Ibn Aa'idh in Maghazi, Isaba).*

Abdullah bin Amr bin Al Aas ﷺ rebukes Man who Neglected Jihad

Yahya bin Abi Amr Shaibani narrates that a group of people from Yemen once passed by Abdullah bin Amr bin Al Aas ﷺ. They asked him, "What is your comment about a person who accepts Islam in a most beautiful fashion, then undertakes Hijra in a most perfect manner and also wages Jihad most superbly. However, he then returns to his parents in Yemen to serve them and to care for them." Abdullah bin Amr bin Al Aas ﷺ asked them, "What is your comment on such as person?" They replied, "In our opinion, he has turned back on his heels." Abdullah bin Amr bin Al Aas ﷺ corrected them saying, "In fact, this person shall be in Jannah. Let me tell you of someone who has turned back on his heels. He is a man who accepts Islam in a most beautiful fashion, then undertakes Hijra in a most perfect manner and also wages Jihad most superbly. However, he then goes to the land of a non-Muslim farmer in Sham and takes over the land together with the Jizya that was being paid and the monthly quota of produce which is given to the Muslim state. Thereafter, he develops the land and forsakes Jihad. This man is one who has turned back on his heels." *(Abu Nu'aym in Hilya)*

Moving Urgently in the Path of Allah to Uproot Strife: The Expedition of Muraysi

Jabir bin Abdullah 🙵 narrates that the Sahabah were once on an expedition when someone from the Muhajir punched another Sahabi from the Ansar on the back. When the Ansari called the other Ansar for help, the Muhajir called for the other Muhajir to help him as well. When Rasulullah 🙵 heard this, he exclaimed, "What are these calls of the period of ignorance?" When the Sahabah informed Rasulullah 🙵 that a Muhajir had punched an Ansari, Rasulullah 🙵 said, "Forget these talks for they are foul-smelling." When Abdullah bin Ubay (the leader of the Munafiqin) heard about this, he commented" "Are the Muhajir doing this? By Allah! If we return to Madinah, the honorable ones among us (the people of Madinah) shall certainly exile the humiliated ones (the Muhajir)." When the news of this statement reached Rasulullah 🙵, Omar 🙵 stood up and said, "O Rasulullah 🙵! Permit me to cut off the neck of that Munafiq!" Rasulullah 🙵 replied, "Leave him. We do not want people to say that Muhammad 🙵 kills his companions." Whereas the Ansar were in the majority when the Muhajir arrived in Madinah, the Muhajir later outnumbered them. *(Bukhari, Muslim, Ahmad and Bayhaqi)*. Urwa bin Zubair 🙵 and Amr bin Thabit Ansari 🙵 narrates that Rasulullah 🙵 was on the expedition of Muraise when he demolished the idol Manat that stood between Qafa Mushallal and the coast. Rasulullah 🙵 had dispatched Khalid bin Walid 🙵 to destroy the idol. It was during the same expedition that 2 men started fighting with each other. One belonged to the Muhajir while the other belonged to the Bahz tribe who were allies of the Ansar. The man from the Muhajir had floored the man from the Bahz tribe and was on top of him when the man from the Bahz cried out, "O assembly of Ansar!" When some members of the Ansar came to his assistance, the Muhajir called to the Muhajir for help. A few Muhajir responded. When a fight was about to break out between the group of the Ansar and the group of the Muhajir, they were stopped. When this occurred, every Munafiq and those with the disease of hypocrisy in their hearts went to Abdullah bin Ubay bin Salul (the leader of the Munafiqin) saying, "We used to entertain hopes in you previously and you always used to defend us. However, you can no longer cause any harm nor any benefit. These Jalabib have assisted each other against us." They referred to the new Muhajir as Jalabib. Allah's enemy Abdullah bin Ubay responded by saying, "By Allah! If we return to Madinah; the honorable ones among us (the people of Madinah) shall certainly exile the humiliated ones (the Muhajir)." Another Munafiq by the name of Malik bin Dukhshun commented, "Did I not tell you people not to spend on those who are with Rasulullah 🙵 until they disperse." When Omar 🙵 heard about this, he went to Rasulullah 🙵 and said, "O Rasulullah 🙵! Permit me to cut off the neck of that man who is causing disagreement," Here Omar 🙵 was referring to Abdullah bin Ubay. Rasulullah 🙵 said to Omar 🙵, "Will you really kill him if I give the command?" "Certainly," replied Omar 🙵, "I swear by Allah that I shall cut off his neck as soon as you issue the command to kill him." Rasulullah 🙵 then told Omar to be seated. Usaid bin Hudhair 🙵 who belonged to the Banu Abdul Ash'hal family of the Ansar then approached Rasulullah 🙵 and said, "O Rasulullah 🙵! Permit me to cut off the neck of that man who is causing disagreement." Rasulullah 🙵 said to Usaid

🙵, "Will you really kill him if I give the command?" "Certainly," replied Usaid 🙵, "I swear by Allah that I shall strike my sword beneath his earlobes as soon as you issue the command to kill him." Rasulullah 🙵 then told him to be seated. Rasulullah 🙵 then instructed the Sahabah to announce that the army would be leaving. Rasulullah 🙵 left with the Sahabah during the afternoon and traveled the entire day and night until the following afternoon. Rasulullah 🙵 then set up camp and again left with the Sahabah in the afternoon as he did previously until after the 3rd day of traveling they reached Qafa Mushallal in the morning. When Rasulullah 🙵 reached Madinah, he sent for Omar 🙵 and said to him, "O Omar! Would you have killed him if I issued the command?" When Omar 🙵 replied in the affirmative, Rasulullah 🙵 said, "Had you killed him on that day, many of the Ansar would have felt insulted because the battle had just taken place in which the Ansar were in a weaker position. However, if I issue the command today, even they would be prepared to execute him. Had you killed him then, people would have said that I attack my own companions, take them out of their homes in Jihad and then kill them after having them bound."

It was with reference to this incident that Allah revealed this:

هُمُ الَّذِينَ يَقُولُونَ لَا تُنْفِقُوا عَلَى مَنْ عِنْدَ رَسُولِ اللَّهِ حَتَّى يَنْفَضُّوا وَلِلَّهِ خَزَائِنُ السَّمَاوَاتِ وَالْأَرْضِ وَلَكِنَّ الْمُنَافِقِينَ لَا يَفْقَهُونَ (7) يَقُولُونَ لَئِنْ رَجَعْنَا إِلَى الْمَدِينَةِ لَيُخْرِجَنَّ الْأَعَزُّ مِنْهَا الْأَذَلَّ وَلِلَّهِ الْعِزَّةُ وَلِرَسُولِهِ وَلِلْمُؤْمِنِينَ وَلَكِنَّ الْمُنَافِقِينَ لَا يَعْلَمُونَ (8)

They (hypocrites) are the ones who say: "Spend not on those who are with Allah's Messenger, until they desert him." And to Allah belong the treasures of the heavens and the earth, but the hypocrites comprehend not. They (hypocrites) say: "If we return to Al-Madinah, indeed the more honorable (Abdullah bin Ubai bin Salul, the chief of hypocrites at Al-Madinah) will expel from there the meaner (i.e. Allah's Messenger 🙵)." But honor, power and glory belong to Allah, His Messenger (Muhammad 🙵), and to the believers, but the hypocrites know not. (Al-Munafiqun:7-8) *(Ibn Abi Hatim, Ibn Kathir, Ibn Hajar in Fat'hul Bari)*

Ibn Is'haq has also reported the narration with the addition that Rasulullah 🙵 traveled with the Sahabah the entire day until the evening and throughout the night until the morning. They also traveled the following day until the sun hurt them. Rasulullah 🙵 set up camp and because of exhaustion they all fell sleep as soon as they touched the ground. Rasulullah 🙵 did this so that the Sahabah do not have the opportunity to discuss what had been said the previous day by Abdullah bin Ubay.

Rebuke One who had not Completed 40 Days in the Path of Allah

Zaid bin Abi Habib narrates that when a man once came to Omar 🙵. Omar 🙵 asked, "Where have you been?" "I have been guarding the borders," the man replied. Omar 🙵 asked further, "How many days did you spend on guard?" "30 days," was the reply. Omar 🙵 commented, "Why did you rather not complete 40 days?" *(Al Bidayah wan Nihayah)*

Spending 3 Periods of 40 Days in the Path of Allah: The Incident of a Woman and the Decision of Omar 🙵

Ibn Juraij narrates that someone whom he regards to be a truthful person informed him that as Omar 🙵 was patrolling the streets of Madinah, he overheard a woman saying:

فَلَوْ لَا حِذَارُ اللَّهِ لَا شَيْءَ مِثْلُهُ لَزُعْزِعَ مِنْ هَذَا السَّرِيرِ جَوَانِبُهُ

"The night is long and its ends have become dark I am unable to sleep because I have no beloved to fondle were it not for fear of Allah, which is something without a match every end of this bed would be shaken furiously."

When Omar ؓ asked her what the matter was, she replied, "My husband has been away for several months and I have great desire for him." Omar ؓ asked, "Have you no evil intentions?" "Allah forbid!" she exclaimed. Omar ؓ then said to her, "Control yourself for I shall sent a message to him." When Omar ؓ had done this, he went to his daughter Hafsa ؓ and asked, "I wish to ask you something that worries me, so do remove my worries from me. Tell me after how long a period does a woman start desiring for her husband?" Hafsa ؓ cast down her gazes out of modesty. Omar ؓ said, "Verily Allah does not shy away from the truth." She then motioned with her hands to indicate 3 months, otherwise 4. Omar ؓ then wrote to the governors of all the regions that no army was to be kept away from home for more than 4 months. *(Abdul Razzaq in Kanzul Ummal).* Abdullah bin Omar ؓ narrates that Omar ؓ left the house at night. He happened to overhear a woman recite the following:

"The night is long and its ends have become dark I am unable to sleep because I have no beloved to touch"

Omar ؓ asked his daughter Hafsa ؓ, "What is the maximum period that a woman can do without her husband?" She replied, "4 to 6 months." Omar ؓ said, "I shall then not keep an army away from home for mere than this period." *(Bayhaqi).*

The Keenness of the Sahaba to Encounter Dust in the Path of Allah: Rasulullah ﷺ Rebukes Those Who Disliked Experiencing Dust While Out in the Path of Allah

Rabi bin Zaid ؓ narrates that Rasulullah ﷺ was once in the center of the road, he noticed a youngster from the Quraish walking off the road. Rasulullah ﷺ took the youngster's name and asked whether it was he, the Sahabah confirmed that it was. Rasulullah ﷺ asked the Sahabah to call him. When he arrived, Rasulullah ﷺ asked him, "Why are you walking off the road?" "I dislike the dust," he replied. Rasulullah ﷺ said, "Do not walk off the road because I swear by the Being Who controls my life that this dust is a fragrance from Jannah." *(Tabrani, Haythami)*

The Incident of Jabir bin Abdullah ؓ in this Regard

Abul Musabbih Muqrai narrates that they were once traveling in the Roman territories as a group under the command of Malik bin Abdullah Khath'ami ؓ. Malik ؓ passed by Jabir bin Abdullah ؓ who was leading his mule along. Malik ؓ said to Jabir ؓ, "O Abu Abdullah! Ride because Allah has provided you with a conveyance." Jabir ؓ replied, "I have kept my animal in a good condition and require nothing from my people. However, I am walking because I have heard Rasulullah ﷺ say that Allah has forbidden Jahannam for the person whose feet become dusty in the Path of Allah." Malik ؓ then proceeded further until he was just within earshot of Jabir ؓ, he then shouted at the top of his voice, "O Abu Abdullah! Ride because Allah has provided you with a conveyance." Jabir ؓ understood what Malik ؓ wanted that everyone should hear his reply so he called out, "I have kept my animal in a good condition and require nothing from my people. However, I am walking because I have heard Rasulullah ﷺ say that Allah has forbidden Jahannam for the person whose feet become dusty in the Path of Allah." Abul Musabbih says, "At that instant all the people jumped off their animals and I have never seen so many people walking as I saw that day." *(Ibn Hibban, Abu Ya'la).* Abu Ya'la says that Jabir ؓ said, "I heard Rasulullah ﷺ says, 'When the feet of a servant of Allah gets dusty in the Path of Allah, Allah forbids Jahannam from them'." Then Malik ؓ and the other people dismounted form their animals and more people were not see walking as on that day. *(Targheeb wat Tarheeb, Haythami, Isaba, Bayhaqi).*

Serving others while out in the Path of Allah: Those who were not Fasting serve the Fasting ones in the Path of Allah

Anas ؓ narrates that on a certain expedition with Rasulullah ﷺ, some of them were fasting while others were not. When they stopped to set up camp, the heat was extreme and those with the most shade were those with shawls who used their shawls to shade themselves. Others used their hands to shield themselves from the blazing sun. Those who were fasting fell to the ground while those who were not fasting stood up to pitch the tents and water the animals. Rasulullah ﷺ commented, "Today those who are not fasting have taken all the rewards." *(Muslim).* A narration of *Bukhari* states that those with the most shade with Rasulullah ﷺ were those who used their shawls to shade themselves. Whereas the fasting ones could do nothing, those who were not fasting sent the animals for watering, exerted them to serve and did other boring tasks. Rasulullah ﷺ commented, "Today those who are no fasting have taken all the rewards." *(Bukhari).*

The Sahabah Serve a Man Absorbed in Reciting the Qur'an and Performing Salah

Abu Qilaba ؓ narrates that after returning from a journey, the Sahabah were full of praise for one of their companions. They said, "We have not seen anyone like him. Whenever we traveled, he was busy reciting the Qur'an and whenever we set up camp, he was engaged in salah." Rasulullah ﷺ asked, "Who did his everyday jobs for him?" Rasulullah ﷺ asked, "Who used to feed his animal?" When the others replied that they had been doing this, Rasulullah ﷺ said, "Then all of you are better than him because you have gained all his rewards by serving him." *(Abu Dawud in Marasel, Targheeb wat Tarheeb)*

The Freed Slave of Rasulullah ﷺ Called Safina ؓ Carries the Goods of the Sahabah

Sa'eed bin Jumhan narrates that he once asked Safina ؓ about his name. He replied, "It was Rasulullah ﷺ who gave me the name Safina (ship)." "But why did Rasulullah ﷺ call you Safina ؓ?" Sa'eed asked. Safina ؓ replied, "Rasulullah ﷺ once left on a journey with his Sahabah. When their goods became too heavy for them, Rasulullah ﷺ said to me, 'Spread out your shawl'. When I spread it out, Rasulullah ﷺ tied up all the goods in it and placed it on me, saying, 'Carry this as you are Safina (ship).' Had Rasulullah ﷺ loaded the load of not only 1 or 2 but 5 camels, it would not have been heavy for me." *(Abu Nu'aym in Hilya).*

The Incidents of Ahmar ؓ the Freed Slave of Ummu Salma ؓ and Mujahid with Abdullah bin Omar ؓ

Ahmar ؓ who was the freed slave of Ummu Salma ؓ narrates that they were traveling with Rasulullah ﷺ on an expedition when they passed by a stream. As Ahmar ؓ started transporting people across the stream, Rasulullah ﷺ commented, "You are certainly a Safina (a ship) today." *(Hasan bin Sufian, Ibn Mandah, Malini and Abu Nu'aym in Muntakhab).* Mujahid رحمة الله, narrates, "I used to accompany Abdullah bin Omar ؓ on his journeys. Whenever I would mount my animal, he would come and hold and whenever I got on to the animal, he would put my clothes right. Once he came to me to do give me the same service, I expressed my annoyance. He then said, 'O Mujahid! You have a very clear personality.'" *(Abu Nu'aym in Hilya).*

Rasulullah ﷺ and the Sahabah Fast During Extreme Heat While Out in the Path of Allah

Abu Darda ؓ says, "I saw us on some journeys with Rasulullah ﷺ during such extreme heat that people would place their hands over their heads because of the severity of the heat. None would be fasting then besides Rasulullah ﷺ himself and Abdullah bin Rawaha ﷺ." *(Muslim)* Another narration states that this was during the month of Ramadhan. Abu Sa'eed Khudri ﷺ says, "We went on expeditions with Rasulullah ﷺ during the month of Ramadhan. Whilst some of us fasted, others did not. Neither would the fasting ones get upset with the non-fasting ones, nor would the non-fasting ones get upset with the fasting ones. Each one thought that if someone had the strength, he would fast and that was best for him. Conversely if someone felt weak, he would not fast and that was best for him." *(Muslim)*.

Abdullah bin Makhrama ﷺ Fasts During the Battle of Yamamah

Abdullah bin Omar ﷺ narrates that during the battle of Yamamah he approached Abdullah bin Makhrama ﷺ, who was lying on the ground. When Abdullah bin Omar ﷺ stopped by him, Abdullah bin Makhrama ﷺ asked him whether the time had come to break the fast. When Abdullah bin Omar ﷺ replied that the time had already come, Abdullah bin Makhrama ﷺ said, "Fill some water in that wooden shield so that I may break my fast with it." Abdullah bin Omar ﷺ went to a pond which was overflowing with water and used his leather shield to scoop up water to fill the wooden shield. Abdullah bin Omar ﷺ returned to Abdullah bin Makhrama ﷺ, he found that he had already passed away. *(Isti'ab, Ibn Abi Shaiba, Bukhari, Ibn Mubarak in Jihad)*.

The Fast of Awf bin Abi Haya and the Statement of Omar ﷺ

Mudrik bin Awf Ahmis states that he was once with Omar ﷺ when a messenger from Nu'man bin Mugan'in ﷺ arrived. When Omar ﷺ asked him about the condition of the people, he mentioned those Muslims who had been martyred. He mentioned the names of the martyrs and added that there were many whom he did not recognize. Omar ﷺ commented, "But Allah knows them all." Some people then said that there was a person who had sold his soul. They were referring to Awf bin Abi Haya Ahmisi, also known as Abu Shubail. Mudrik bin Awf interjected by saying, "O Amirul Mu'minin! These people are of the opinion that that uncle of mine threw himself into destruction." Omar ﷺ replied, "They are wrong. In fact, he bought the Hereafter in exchange for this world." Awf had been fasting on the day that he was wounded. He was still alive when he was removed from the battlefield and refused to drink any water until he eventually passed away in the state of fasting. *(Ibn Abi Shaibah in Isaba)*.

The Fast of Abu Amr Ansari ﷺ

In the chapter entitled "Enduring thirst when inviting people towards Allah and His Rasul ﷺ", it has already been narrated from Muhammad bin Hanafiya ﷺ who says, "Abu Amr Ansari ﷺ had participated in the battles of Badr, Uhud and the pledge at Aqaba. I once saw him fasting on the battlefield, restless because of severe thirst. He asked his slave to pass to him his shield and when the slave did so, he fired an arrow which did not go far because he had grown weak with thirst. When he had fired 3 arrows, he said that he had heard Rasulullah ﷺ say, 'Whoever fires an arrow in the Path of Allah, the arrow shall be a source of light for him on the Day of Judgment whether it reaches its target or not.' Abu Amr ﷺ was martyred before sunset of that day.

The Salah of Rasulullah ﷺ on the Night Before the Battle of Badr

Ali ﷺ says, "There was not a single horseman amongst us during the battle of Badr besides Miqdad ﷺ. I noticed that each one of us was asleep the night before the battle besides Rasulullah ﷺ. He was performing salah under a tree and weeping until dawn broke." *(Ibn Khuzaima in Targheeb wat Tarheeb)*.

Rasulullah ﷺ Performs Salah in Usfan

Abdullah bin Abbas ﷺ narrates that they were with Rasulullah ﷺ at a place called Usfan when the disbeliever's army under the command of Khalid bin Walid ﷺ confronted them. The disbeliever's army was positioned between the Muslims and the Qibla. When Rasulullah ﷺ led the Sahabah in the Zuhr salah, the disbelievers said, "If only we had taken advantage of the state of unawareness that they were in during their salah and attacked them!" However, they consoled themselves by saying, "A salah is approaching (the Asr salah) that is more beloved to them than their children and even their own selves." However, between the Zuhr and Asr salah, Jibra'el السلام عليه came with the revelation of the following verses of the Qur'an describing the Salatul Khowf: وَإِذَا كُنْتَ فِيهِمْ فَأَقَمْتَ لَهُمُ الصَّلَاةَ *When you (O Muhammad ﷺ) are among them and lead them in salah... (An-Nisa':102) (Ahmad)*. A narration of Muslim from Jabir ﷺ states that the disbelievers said, "There shall soon come a salah which is more beloved to them than even their own children." *(Al Bidayah wan Nihayah)*.

The Salah of Abbad bin Bishr ﷺ in the Path of Allah

Jabir ﷺ narrates that they were accompanying Rasulullah ﷺ to a place called Nakhl during the expedition of Dhatur Riqa. It so happened that one of the Muslims killed or captured the wife of one of the disbelievers. The woman's husband had been away and only returned after Rasulullah ﷺ had left. When he was informed about what had happened, he took an oath that he would never rest until he spilt the blood of the companions of Rasulullah ﷺ. He therefore set off to follow the tracks of Rasulullah ﷺ. When Rasulullah ﷺ set up camp, he asked, "Who shall stand guard over us tonight?" A volunteer from amongst the Muhajir and another from amongst the Ansar stood up and said, "We shall do so, O Rasulullah ﷺ!" Rasulullah ﷺ gave them instructions to stand guard at the mouth of the valley. The 2 volunteers were Ammar bin Yasir ﷺ and Abbad bin Bishr ﷺ. When the 2 men reached the mouth of the valley, Abbad ﷺ (Ansari) said to Ammar ﷺ (Muhajir), "For which part of the night would you like me to relieve you as we take turns to keep watch? Will it be the first part of the night or the second?" The Muhajir replied, "Relieve me for the first part of the night." The Muhajir then lay down to sleep as the Ansari stood up to perform salah. Subsequently, the man who swore to spill the blood of the Muslims arrived there and when he saw the shadow of a person, he took the Ansari to be a spy and immediately fired an arrow which struck the Ansari. The Ansari removed the arrow from his body, threw it aside and continued standing in salah. The disbeliever fired another arrow which also struck the Ansari. The Ansari also removed this arrow from his body, threw it aside and continued standing in salah. When the disbeliever fired a 3rd arrow which also struck the Ansari, the Ansari removed the arrow from his body, threw it aside and then completed his Ruku, Sejdah, and his salah. He then awoke his companion saying, "Sit up because I am injured." The Muhajir jumped up and when the disbeliever saw the 2 of them, he realized that they had been alerted and he fled. When the Muhajir saw the blood on the Ansari, he exclaimed, "SubhanAllah! Why did you not wake me up when he shot at you the first time?" the Ansari replied, "I had started reciting a Surah and did not like to cut it short before completing it. However, when the firing persisted, I went into Ruku and completed my salah and informed you. I swear by Allah that had it not been for fear of risking the mouth of the pass that Rasulullah ﷺ had instructed me to guard, I would have given my life rather than cut the Surah short." *(Ibn Is'haq, Abu Dawud in Al Bidayah wan Nihayah, Ibn Hibban in Sahih, Hakim in Mustadrak, Bayhaqi in Sunan, Bukhari (Ta'leeqan) quoted in Nasbur Ra'ya).* While Ammar ؓ went to sleep, Abbad ؓ stood in salah. The narration also adds that Abbad ؓ said, "I was reciting Surah Kahaf in my salah and did not like to cut it short."

The Salah of Abdullah bin Unais ؓ in the Path of Allah

Abdullah bin Unais ؓ narrates that Rasulullah ﷺ called him and said, "I have intelligence that Khalid bin Sufian bin Nubay of the Banu Hudhail tribe had prepared a force to attack me. He is now at Urna. Go there and kill him." Abdullah bin Unays ؓ asked, "O Rasulullah ﷺ! Describe him to me so that I may recognize him." Rasulullah ﷺ said, "When you see him, you will find him shivering." Abdullah bin Unais ؓ relates that he left with his sword hanging around his neck and proceeded until he found him at Urna with his wives. The time for Asr had already arrived and Khalid was looking for a place to settle his wives. Abdullah bin Unais ؓ says, "When I saw him, I recognized the shivering that Rasulullah ﷺ described and I advanced towards him. Fearing that nothing should prove an obstacle to prevent me from my salah as I attempted to kill him, I performed my salah as I walked towards him. I performed Ruku and Sejdah by making gestures with my head. When I reached him, he asked, 'Who is this man?' I replied, 'I am an Arab who has heard about you and about your preparing forces against that person (Rasulullah ﷺ). I have come to you in this regard." He said, 'Yes, I am busy.'" Continuing further, Abdullah bin Unais ؓ says, "I then traveled with him for awhile until I found an opportunity. I then attacked him with my sword and killed him. I then left, leaving his wives falling over him. When I came to Rasulullah ﷺ and he saw me, he said, 'A look of success.' 'I have killed him,' I said. 'True,' was the reply. Rasulullah ﷺ then stood up with me, took me in his room and gave me a staff saying, 'Keep this staff with you, O Abdullah bin Unays.' When I left with the staff and came to the people, they asked, 'What is this staff?' I replied, 'Rasulullah ﷺ gave it to me with instructions to keep it with me.' When they told me to return to Rasulullah ﷺ to ask him about it, I complied. When I got to Rasulullah ﷺ, I asked, 'O Rasulullah ﷺ! Why have you given me this staff?' Rasulullah ﷺ replied, 'It is a token between you and me on the Day of Judgment because on that day there shall be few people carrying staffs of their good deeds.'" Abdullah bin Unais ؓ tied the staff to his sword and it remained with him throughout his life. When he passed away, he instructed that it should be included in his burial clothes and buried with him. *(Ahmad in Al Bidayah wan Nihayah)*

Performing Salah at Night While Out in the Path of Allah

Urwa ؓ narrates that when the 2 armies confronted each other for the battle of Yarmuk, Qubqular a Roman commander dispatched an Arab to spy on the Muslims. The last portion of the narration states that after the spy returned, Qubqular asked him what he had noticed. The spy replied, "They Muslims are engaged in worship by night and seasoned horsemen by day." *(Tabari).* In a lengthy narration of *Abu Is'haq*, it is mentioned that Heraclius the Roman Emperor asked his generals, "What is the matter? Why are you being defeated by the Muslims?" An old man from amongst his senior officers replied, "Because the Muslims stand in worship during the night and fast during the day." *(Ahmad bin Marwan Maliki, Ibn Asakir from Ibn Is'haq).* More Ahadeeth on this subject will be discussed in the chapter dealing with the reasons for which divine assistance came. In the

chapter titled "Women pledged their allegiance", the narration has passed which states that the wife Abu Sufian ؓ Hind ؓ said to her husband, "I wish to pledge allegiance to Muhammad ﷺ." Abu Sufian ؓ said, "But I have noticed that you have always been rejecting what he says." She replied, "By Allah! That it true. I swear by Allah that before this night I have never seen Allah being worshipped in this Masjid as He deserves to be worshipped. By Allah! The Muslims spent the entire night performing salah standing, bowing down and prostrating."

The Dhikr of the Sahabah the Night They Conquered Makkah

Sa'eed bin Musaib رحمة الله narrates that on the night after the Muslims entered Makkah as conquerors, they continuously recited "Allahu Akbar", "La Ilaha IllAllah" and performed Tawaf of the Kabah until dawn broke. Abu Sufian ؓ then said to his wife Hind ؓ, "Do you not see that all this is from Allah?" "Yes," she replied, "this certainly is from Allah." The next morning Abu Sufian went early to Rasulullah ﷺ. Rasulullah ﷺ said, "Last night you said to Hind, 'Do you not see that all this is from Allah? And she replied, 'Yes, this certainly is from Allah.'" Abu Sufian ؓ exclaimed, "I testify that you are certainly the servant and Rasul of Allah! I swear by the Being in Whose name I take oaths that no one but Hind heard this statement of mine." *(Bayhaqi in Al Bidayah wan Nihayah, Ibn Asakir in Kanzul Ummal).*

The Dhikr of the Sahabah as They Stood Over a Valley During the Battle of Khaibar

Abu Musa Ash'ari ؓ narrates that when Rasulullah ﷺ left on a military expedition to Khaibar, the Sahabah had reached a valley when they raised their voices reciting, "Allahu Akbar! La Ilaha IllAllah!" Rasulullah ﷺ said to them, "Have mercy on yourselves and do not exert yourselves for you are not calling someone who is deaf or absent. You are calling One Who is All-Hearing, Who is close and Who is always with you." Abu Musa Ash'ari ؓ narrates that he was behind the animal of Rasulullah ﷺ when Rasulullah ﷺ overheard him say, "*La Howla wa La Quwwata Illa Billah* (There is no power or might except with Allah)." Rasulullah ﷺ then said, "O Abdullah bin Qais!" Abu Musa Ash'ari ؓ replied, "I am at your service, O Rasulullah ﷺ!" Rasulullah ﷺ told him, "Should I not inform you of words that are from the treasures of Jannah?" Abu Musa Ash'ari ؓ said, "Please do, O Rasulullah ﷺ! May my parents be sacrificed for you." Rasulullah ﷺ enlightened him by saying, "(The words are) *La Howla wa La Quwwata Illa Billah* (There is no power or might except with Allah)." *(Bukhari, Al Bidayah wan Nihayah)*

The Sahabah Recite Takbir and Tasbih When Ascending and Descending Inclines

Jabir ؓ narrates that when the Sahabah ascended an incline, they recited Takbir and whenever they descended from an incline, they recited Tasbih. *(Bukhari, Nasai in Yawm wal Layla)*

The Statement of Abdullah bin Omar ؓ That the People Embarking on Military Expeditions are of 2 Types

Abdullah bin Omar ؓ said, "On an expedition, people are of 2 types. One type is those who go out and abundantly engage in the Dhikr of Allah together with maintaining the awareness of Allah. They stay away from evil on their journey, assist their companions physically and financially and spend the best of their wealth. They are more keen on the wealth they spend in the Path of Allah than the wealth they use to benefit their worldly lives. When they are in war situations, they feel ashamed that Allah should discover any doubts in their hearts' or that He should find them failing to assist the Muslims. Even if they are in a position of misusing the booty, they cleanse their hearts and deeds from any such activity. Saitan is therefore unable to involve them in sin or to whisper evil into their hearts. It is through such people that Allah strengthens and gives honor to Islam and defeats His enemies. As for the second type, they go out without engaging in abundant Dhikr and without being conscious of Allah. They do not abstain from evil and are reluctant to spend their wealth. They regard whatever they spend as a tax and this is what Saitan tells them. In the battle situation they remain with those rights at the back and those who render absolutely no help. They stick to the tops of mountains watching what the others are doing and speak the worst of lies when Allah grants victory by boasting about feats they did not achieve. Should they have the opportunity to misuse the spoils of war, they boldly do so with the booty of Allah, as Saitan tells them that these are merely spoils of war and they therefore have a right to do as they please with it. When conditions are favorable, they boast and when they encounter any obstacle, Saitan misleads them to place their needs before people. They shall have no share of the rewards of the Mu'minin. They shall have to show their bodies with the bodies of the Mu'minin and that they traveled with the Mu'minin. Their intentions and deeds vary and Allah shall judge them on the Day of Judgment." *(Ibn Asakir in Kanzul Ummal).*

The Du'a of Rasulullah ﷺ as he Left Makkah for the Hijra

Muhammad bin Is'haq says that when Rasulullah ﷺ left Makkah to make Hijra to Madinah for the pleasure of Allah, he said, "All praises belong to Allah Who has created me when I had been nothing. O Allah! Assist me against the fears of this world, the evils of the times and the calamities of the nights and days. O Allah! Be my companion on my journey, be my deputy amongst my family and grant me blessings in that which You provide for me. Make me humble before You, keep me steadfast on good character, make me beloved to You and never hand me over to people. O Rabb of the weak ones, you are my Rabb. I seek refuge in Your generous approval by which the skies and the earth are illuminated, by which darkness is dispersed, and by which the affairs of the past people were set right. I seek Your protection from attracting Your wrath on me and having Your anger descend on me. I seek Your protection from losing Your bounties, from Your sudden punishment, from losing Your safety and from all causes of Your wrath. Securing Your pleasure is better than all the deeds I can do. There is no power or might except with You." *(Abu Nu'aym in Al Bidayah wan Nihayah)*

The Du'a Rasulullah ﷺ When he Saw Khaibar

The grandfather of Abu Marwan Aslami narrates that they accompanied Rasulullah ﷺ to Khaibar. When they got close to Khaibar and could see it, Rasulullah ﷺ instructed the Sahabah to stop. When they came to a halt, Rasulullah ﷺ prayed, "O Allah, the Rabb of the 7 skies and whatever they shade! O Rabb of the 7 earths and whatever they bear! O Rabb of the Saiatin and whoever they mislead! O Rabb of the winds and whatever they carry! We beg of you the best of this town, the best of its inhabitants and the best of whatever it contains. We seek Your protection from the evil of this town, the evil of its inhabitants and the evil of whatever it contains." Rasulullah ﷺ then said to the Sahabah, "Proceed in the name of Allah!" *(Bayhaqi, Ibn Is'haq in Al Bidayah wan Nihayah, Tabrani, Haythami).* A narration of *Tabrani* states that Rasulullah ﷺ used to make this Du'a each time he entered a town.

The Du'a Rasulullah ﷺ Made on the Occasion of the Battle of Badr

Omar ﷺ narrates that on the day of the battle of Badr, Rasulullah ﷺ looked at his Sahabah who numbered just over 300. He then looked at the disbelievers who numbered over 1,000. Wearing only an upper and lower garment, Rasulullah ﷺ then turned towards the Qibla and prayed, "O Allah! Fulfill Your promise to me. O Allah! If this group of Muslims is destroyed, You will never again be worshipped on earth." Rasulullah ﷺ continued seeking Allah's help and praying to Him until his upper garment fell off. Abu Bakr ﷺ came to put the garment on again and then held on to Rasulullah ﷺ from behind saying, "O Rasulullah ﷺ! What you have so persistently asked from your Rabb is sufficient for He will certainly fulfill the promise He made to you." It was then that Allah revealed the verse:

إِذْ تَسْتَغِيثُونَ رَبَّكُمْ فَاسْتَجَابَ لَكُمْ أَنِّي مُمِدُّكُمْ بِأَلْفٍ مِنَ الْمَلَائِكَةِ مُرْدِفِينَ (9)

(Remember) when you (O Muhammad ﷺ) sought help of your Lord and He answered you: "I will help you with a thousand of the angels each behind the other (following one another) in succession." (Al-Anfal:9) (Ahmad, Muslim, Abu Dawud, Tirmidhi, Ibn Jareer in Al Bidayah wan Nihayah, Ibn Abi Shaiba, Abu Awana, Ibn Hibban, Abu Nu'aym, Ibn Mundhir, Ibn Abi Hatim, Abu Shaikh, Ibn Mardway, Bayhaqi, in Kanzui Ummal)

Abdullah bin Amr bin Al Aas ﷺ narrates that Rasulullah ﷺ left for Badr with 315 men. When they reached Badr, Rasulullah ﷺ prayed, "O Allah! They (my Sahabah) are barefoot, so do grant them transport. O Allah! They are poorly clothed, so do clothe them. O Allah! They are hungry, so do fill their bellies." When Allah granted them victory in the battle of Badr and they returned, there was not a single one of them who did not possess 1 or 2 camels. They also had clothing to wear and had eaten to their fill. *(Abu Dawud in Jam'ul Fawa'id, Bayhaqi, Ibn Sa'd).* Abdullah bin Mas'ood ﷺ says that he had never heard a Du'a more persistent than the Du'a Rasulullah ﷺ made on the occasion of the battle of Badr. He prayed, "O Allah! I am pleading You in the name of Your promise and pledge. O Allah! If this group is destroyed, You will not be worshipped." Rasulullah ﷺ turned around, his face appeared to be a part of the moon as he said, "It is as if I can see the places where the dead disbelievers will lie by tonight." *(Nasai in Ai Bidayah wan Nihayah, Tabrani, Haythami)*

The Du'a Rasulullah ﷺ Made on the Occasions of the Battle of Uhud and the Battle of Khandaq

Anas ﷺ narrates that on the day that the battle of Uhud was fought, Rasulullah ﷺ repetitively said, "O Allah! Do assist us. If You choose not to assist us none would worship You on earth." *(Ahmad, Muslim in Al Bidayah wan Nihayah).* Abu Sa'eed Khudri ﷺ narrates that on the occasion of the battle of Khandaq, the Sahabah asked Rasulullah ﷺ, "O Rasulullah ﷺ! Is there any Du'a that we could make on this occasion because our hearts have reached our throats." Rasulullah ﷺ replied, "Yes," and then recited the following Du'a: اللَّهُمَّ اسْتُرْ عَوْرَاتِنَا وَآمِنْ رُوْعَاتِنَا

"O Allah! Conceal our faults and calm our fears."

Abu Sa'eed Khudri ﷺ completes the narration by saying, "When we started reciting the du'a, Allah heavily damaged the faces of His enemies (defeated them) by sending a powerful wind against them." *(Ahmad, Ibn Hatim).* Jabir ﷺ narrates that Rasulullah ﷺ once went to Masjid Ahzab and placed his shawl aside. He then stood up and stretched his hands out to curse the disbeliever's army. On this occasion, he did not perform any salah. Rasulullah ﷺ then went there again, again cursed them and this time performed 2 Rakahs salah. *(Muslim, Ahmad).* A narration of *Bukhari and Muslim* state that Rasulullah ﷺ cursed the gathering of disbeliever forces when they attacked Madinah by saying, "O Allah Who has revealed the Qur'an, Who is quick in reckoning and Who will defeat the mass of troops! O Allah! Defeat them and shake (destabilize) them." Rasulullah ﷺ prayed, "O Allah! Defeat them and assist us against them." Another narration of *Bukhari* related by Abu Hurairah ﷺ mentions that the Du'a Rasulullah ﷺ made was: "There is none worthy of worship but the One Allah Who has given honor to His army, assisted His servant and defeated the coalition of forces all by Himself. There is nothing after Him." *(Al Bidayah wan Nihayah)*

The Du'a Rasulullah ﷺ made during the Battle of Badr

Ali ﷺ says, "After fighting for a while during the battle of Badr, I rushed to see how Rasulullah ﷺ was keeping. When I arrived there, Rasulullah ﷺ was in Sejdah praying, 'Ya Hayyu! Ya Qayyum! Ya Hayyu! Ya Qayyum! ('O The Living, The Controller! O The Living, The Controller!')' Rasulullah ﷺ said nothing more. I then returned to the fight and when I got back to Rasulullah ﷺ, he was still in Sejdah repeating the same words. Rasulullah ﷺ continued in this manner until Allah gave him victory." *(Bayhaqi, Nasai in Al Yown wal Layla, Al Bidayah wan Nihayah, Bazzar, Abu Ya'la, Firyabi, Hakim, Kanzul Ummal).*

The Du'a Rasulullah ﷺ Made on the Night Before the Battle of Badr

Ali ﷺ narrates that on the night before the battle of Badr, Rasulullah ﷺ spent the night in salah praying, "O Allah! If this group is destroyed, You will never again be worshipped on earth." That night, some rain fell causing the firm ground where the disbelievers stood to become muddy and the soft ground where the Muslims stood to become firm. *(Ibn Mardway, Sa'eed bin Jubair in Kanzul Ummal).* Another narration from Ali ﷺ states that although Rasulullah ﷺ was a Musafir (traveler), he had spent the entire night in Ibadah till the morning that the battle of Badr was fought. *(Abu Ya'la, Ibn Hibban in Kanzul Ummal).*

The Du'a of Rasulullah ﷺ After the Battle of Uhud

Rifah Zuraqi ﷺ narrates that when the disbelievers had returned after the battle of Uhud, Rasulullah ﷺ said, "Stand straight so that I may praise my Rabb ﷻ." When the Sahabah had arranged themselves into rows behind Rasulullah ﷺ, he said, "O Allah! Every type of praise belongs to You. O Allah! There is none to restrain what You give in abundance and none to give anything that You restrain. None can guide the one whom You cause to deviate and none can deviate the one whom You guide. None can give what You hold back and none can hold back what You give. None can bring close that which You make distant and none can make distant that which You bring close. O Allah! Grant us in abundance Your blessings, Your mercy, Your grace and Your sustenance. O Allah! I ask from You Your everlasting bounties that never change and are never lost. O Allah! I beg You for bounties on that day of poverty (Judgment) and for safety on the day of fear. O Allah! I seek Your protection from the evil of that which You have given us and from the evil of that which You have held back from us. O Allah! Make Iman beloved to us and beautify it in our hearts. Make kufr, sin and disobedience distasteful to us and make us amongst the rightly guided ones. O Allah! Grant us death as Muslims, keep us living as Muslims and allow us to meet up with the righteous ones in the Hereafter without suffering any humiliation and without having to endure any trials. O Allah! Destroy the disbeliever who call Your messengers liars and who prevent others from Your path. Set on them Your punishment and chastisement. O Allah! O the True Deity! Destroy also those disbelievers to whom You have given

scriptures." *(Ahmad, Nasai in Al Yowm wal Laylah, Al Bidayah wan Nihayah, Bukhari, Tabrani, Baghawi, Bawardi, Abu Nu'aym in Hilya, Hakim, Bayhaqi in Kanzul Ummal, Dhahabi, Haythami).* The Du'a that Rasulullah ﷺ made after giving Da'wah to the people of Ta'if has already been related in the chapter entitled: "Rasulullah ﷺ endures hardship and difficulty when giving Da'wah towards Allah."

Being Particular About Ta'lim (Learning and Teaching) When in Jihad in the Path of Allah

The statement of Abdullah bin Abbas ﷺ concerning the verse "It is not for the Mu'minin to proceed in Jihad all together..." Abdullah bin Abbas ﷺ says, "Allah has stated:

يَا أَيُّهَا الَّذِينَ آمَنُوا خُذُوا حِذْرَكُمْ فَانْفِرُوا ثُبَاتٍ أَوِ انْفِرُوا جَمِيعًا (71)

O you who believe! Take your precautions, and either go forth (on an expedition) in parties, or go forth all together. (An-Nisa':71)

انْفِرُوا خِفَافًا وَثِقَالًا وَجَاهِدُوا بِأَمْوَالِكُمْ وَأَنْفُسِكُمْ فِي سَبِيلِ اللَّهِ ذَلِكُمْ خَيْرٌ لَكُمْ إِنْ كُنْتُمْ تَعْلَمُونَ (41)

March forth (in the Path of Allah) whether you are light (being healthy, young and wealthy) or heavy (being ill, old and poor), strive hard with your wealth and your lives in the Cause of Allah. This is better for you, if you but knew. (At-Tauba:41)

إِلَّا تَنْفِرُوا يُعَذِّبْكُمْ عَذَابًا أَلِيمًا وَيَسْتَبْدِلْ قَوْمًا غَيْرَكُمْ وَلَا تَضُرُّوهُ شَيْئًا وَاللَّهُ عَلَى كُلِّ شَيْءٍ قَدِيرٌ (39)

If you march not forth, He will punish you with a painful torment and will replace you by another people, and you cannot harm Him at all, and Allah is Able to do all things. (At-Tauba:39). However, these verses were later abrogated when Allah ﷻ revealed the verse:

وَمَا كَانَ الْمُؤْمِنُونَ لِيَنْفِرُوا كَافَّةً فَلَوْلَا نَفَرَ مِنْ كُلِّ فِرْقَةٍ مِنْهُمْ طَائِفَةٌ لِيَتَفَقَّهُوا فِي الدِّينِ وَلِيُنْذِرُوا قَوْمَهُمْ إِذَا رَجَعُوا إِلَيْهِمْ لَعَلَّهُمْ يَحْذَرُونَ (122)

And it is not (proper) for the believers to go out to fight (Jihad) all together. Of every troop of them, a party only should go forth, that they (who are left behind) may get instructions in (Islamic) religion, and that they may warn their people when they return to them, so that they may beware (of evil). (At-Tauba:122)

It was the practice that while a party of Muslims would march with Rasulullah ﷺ another party would remain behind. Those that remained behind with Rasulullah ﷺ would attain a deep understanding of Islam so that they may warn their people who had been engaged in Jihad when they return to them from the expeditions. In this manner, they were aware of what Allah revealed in the Qur'an, about their obligations and about the limits that Allah had set." *(Bayhaqi).*

Omar ﷺ's Letter to his Commanders on the Understanding of Deen

Ahwas bin Hakim bin Umair Absi narrates that Omar ﷺ wrote the following in a letter addressed to the commanders of the various Muslims armies, "Endeavor to attain a deep understanding of Islam because no person can be excused for pursuing falsehood thinking that it is the truth. Similarly, no one can be excused for forsaking the truth in the belief that it is falsehood." *(Adam bin Abi Ayas in Kanzul Ummal).*

Sahabah sit in Gatherings (to Learn and Teach) while on Journey

Hitan bin Abdullah Raqashi narrates that they were once part of an army under the command of Abu Musa Ash'ari ﷺ. They were traveling along the banks of the Tigris river when the time for salah arrived. After someone had called out the Adhan for the Zuhr salah, the people started making wudhu and Abu Musa Ash'ari ﷺ also made wudhu. He then led them in salah, after which they all sat in groups. When the time for the Asr salah arrived, someone called out the Adhan for Asr and the people again stood up to make wudhu. Abu Musa Ash'ari ﷺ then instructed the Mu'adhin to announce, "Take note that none should make wudhu besides those whose wudhu had broken." Abu Musa Ash'ari said, "It seems imminent that knowledge shall disappear and ignorance will prosper so much that because of ignorance, a man will use his sword to kill his own mother." *(Abdur Razaq in Kanzul Ummal, Tanawi in Sharhu Ma'anil Athar)*

Spending of Some Sahabah in the Path of Allah

Abu Mas'ood Ansari ﷺ narrates that a man came with a reined camel and said, "I am donating this camel in the Path of Allah." Rasulullah ﷺ said, "You shall have 700 camels in exchange for it on the Day of Judgment. Each one of those will also have reins." *(Muslim, Nasai in Jam'ul Fawa'id). Abdullah bin Samit* narrates, "I was with Abu Dhar ﷺ when he received his allowance from the state treasury. Abu Dhar ﷺ had his slave girl with him, who started paying off all his expenses with the money. Only 7 Dirhams were left which he instructed her to convert into change. I said to him, 'Would not it be better if you kept it back for a need that may arise or for a guest that may come to you?' He replied, 'My beloved friend Rasulullah ﷺ advised me saying, 'Any gold or silver that is tied up in a bag to set aside for the future is live coal for its owner until he spends it in the Path of Allah.''' *Ahmad and Tabrani* states that Rasulullah ﷺ said, "When a person ties gold or silver in a bag and does not spend it in the Path of Allah, it will be live embers on the Day of Judgment which will be used to brand him." *(Ahmad in Targheeb wat Tarheeb).* Qais bin Sala Ansari ﷺ narrates that his brothers laid a complaint against him before Rasulullah ﷺ when they alleged that he wasted his wealth and gave out plenty. Qais ﷺ said, "O Rasulullah ﷺ! I take only my share of the dates and spend it in the Path of Allah and on those in my company." Rasulullah ﷺ placed his hand on the chest of Qais ﷺ and thrice said, "Spend and Allah will spend on you." Qais ﷺ says, "I always had transport when I went out in the Path of Allah and today I am the wealthiest person in my family because of the blessings of spending in the Path of Allah." *(Tabrani in Awsat, Targheeb wat Tarheeb, Ibn Mandah in Isaha).*

The Rewards of Spending in the Path of Allah

Mu'adh bin Jabal ﷺ narrates that Rasulullah ﷺ said, "Glad tidings for the person who abundantly engages in the Dhikr of Allah while out in Jihad in the Path of Allah because for every word he shall receive the rewards of 70,000 good deeds. The reward for each one of these good deeds shall be multiplied 10 times together with the extra that he will receive which is with Allah." Someone asked, "O Rasulullah ﷺ! And what about spending in the Path of Allah?" Rasulullah ﷺ replied, "Spending is rewarded likewise." One of the narrators by the name of *Abdur Rahman* says that he then asked Mu'adh ﷺ, "But the reward of spending in the Path of Allah is multiplied 700 times." Mu'adh ﷺ commented, "Your understanding is deficient. That reward multiplied 700 times is for people who spend on others in the Path of Allah while they are themselves with their families at home and not out on an expedition. However, when they march out themselves and then spend, Allah keeps aside for them such things from the treasures of His mercy that far exceeds the knowledge of man and his ability to describe it. Such people are the party of Allah and the party of Allah is always victorious." *(Tabrani, Hythami).* Ali ﷺ, Abu Darda ﷺ, Abu Hurairah ﷺ, Abu Umama ﷺ, Abdullah bin Amr bin Al Aas ﷺ, Jabir ﷺ and

Imran bin Husain ﷺ all narrate that Rasulullah ﷺ stated, "The person who spends funds in the Path of Allah while he remains at home shall be rewarded with 700 Dirhams for every Dirham that he spends. On the other hand, the person who himself marches out in the Path of Allah and then spends for Allah's pleasure shall be rewarded with 700,000 Dirhams for every Dirham that he spends." Rasulullah ﷺ recited this verse: وَاللَّهُ يُضَاعِفُ لِمَنْ يَشَاءُ *And Allah gives manifold increase (rewards) to whom He wills. (Al-Baqara:261) (Qazweeni in Jam'ul Fawa'id).* In the chapter "Rasulullah ﷺ encourages striving in the Path of Allah and spending one's wealth for this cause", it was narrated how much was spent by Sahabah such as Abu Bakr ﷺ, Omar ﷺ, Uthman ﷺ, Talha ﷺ, Abdur Rahman bin Auf ﷺ, Abbas ﷺ, Sa'd bin Ubadah ﷺ, Muhammad bin Maslama ﷺ and Asim bin Adi ﷺ.

Proceeding in Jihad in the Path of Allah with a Sincere Intention

Abu Hurairah ﷺ narrates that someone asked, "O Rasulullah ﷺ! Tell me about a person who intends to wage Jihad and also has the intention of earning some worldly profits." Rasulullah ﷺ replied, "He shall not be rewarded." Regarding this as a very serious matter, the Sahabah said to the person, "Please repeat what you have asked Rasulullah ﷺ. Perhaps you did not explain yourself to him properly." The man asked for the second time, "O Rasulullah ﷺ! Tell me about a person who proceeds in Jihad with the intention of earning some worldly profits?" Rasulullah ﷺ repeated, "He shall not be rewarded." Again regarding this as a very serious matter, the Sahabah instructed the person to again repeat the question. The man asked for the 3rd time, "O Rasulullah ﷺ! Tell me about a person who proceeds in Jihad with the intention of earning some worldly profits?" Rasulullah ﷺ again repeated, "He shall not be rewarded." *(Abu Dawud, Ibn Hibban, Hakim in Targheeb wat Tarheeb).* Abu Umamah ﷺ narrates that a man approached Rasulullah ﷺ with the query, "Tell me about a person who wages Jihad in search of fame and fortune. What is there for him?" "There shall be nothing for him," replied Rasulullah ﷺ. When the man repeated his question 3 times, Rasulullah ﷺ replied each time, "There shall be nothing for him." Rasulullah ﷺ added, "Allah accepts only those actions that are carried out solely for Him, through which His pleasure is sought." *(Abu Dawud and Nasai in Targheeb waf Tarheeb).*

The Story of Quzman

Asim bin Amr bin Qatadah ﷺ narrates that a man lived amongst them whose identity no one really knew. He was only known as Quzman. Whenever his name was mentioned, Rasulullah ﷺ used to say, "He is from the inmates of Jahannam." He fought very fiercely during the battle of Uhud and single-handedly killed 7 to 8 disbelievers. He was a true warrior. However, he was eventually injured by a nasty wound. When he was carried to the Banu Zafar district, many Muslims said to him, "You fought with great courage today, O Quzman! Glad tidings to you!" He said, "Glad tidings for what? By Allah! I fought only for the good name of my people. Had it not been for this, I would never have fought." When his wound became too much for him to bear, he took an arrow from his quiver and used it to commit suicide. *(Ibn Is'haq in Al Bidayah wan Nihayah).*

The Story of Usairam

It is reported that Abu Hurairah ﷺ used to often ask the people around him, "Tell me about the person who entered Jannah without every performing a single salah?" When the people were unable to identify the person, they asked Abu Hurairah ﷺ about him. Abu Hurairah ﷺ would then say, "He was

Usairam from the Banu Abdul Ash'hal tribe whose real name was Amr bin Thabit bin Qais." One of the narrators, Husain says that when he asked Mahmood bin Labid about the story of Usairam &, he narrated, "He always refused to accept Islam when his people invited him. On the day that the battle of Uhud was fought, it suddenly occurred to him to accept Islam and he did so. He then took his sword and proceeded until he entered the side of the enemy. There he fought until a wound crippled him. As some people from the Banu Abdul Ash'hal tribe were searching the battlefield for their dead, they suddenly saw Usairam and exclaimed, "By Allah! This is Usairam! What has brought him here? We had left him behind in Madinah for he refused to accept the Kalimah." They therefore questioned him, "What has brought you here, O Amr? Was it the fondness of your people or your devotion to Islam?" He replied, "It was my devotion to Islam. I believed in Allah and His Rasul &, accepted Islam, took my sword and marched with Rasulullah &. I then fought until I was injured." It was not long after this that he passed away in their hands. When the incident was mentioned to Rasulullah &, he said, "He is certainly from amongst the people of Jannah." *(Ibn Is'haq in Al Bidayah wan Nihayah, Isaba, Abu Nu'aym in Ma'rifa, Kanzul Ummal, Ahmad in Majma'uz Zawa'id).* Abu Hurairah & narrates that because Amr bin Uqaish & had given out a loan on interest during the period of ignorance, he disliked accepting Islam until he had received the payment. When the battle of Uhud took place, he asked, "Where are my cousins?" When he was informed that they were at Uhud, he exclaimed, "At Uhud!" He then donned his helmet, mounted his horse and rode towards them. Seeing him arrive, the Muslims called out, "Go away, O Amr!" He responded by saying, "I have already accepted Iman." He then fought fiercely until he was wounded and carried off to his family as a wounded man. Sa'd bin Mu'adh & then arrived there and asked his sister to ask Amr & whether he fought because of his friendship with his people or because he felt for Allah and His Rasul &. Amr & replied, "Because I felt for Allah and His Rasul &." He then passed away and entered Jannah even though he had never had the opportunity to perform a single salah for Allah. *(Abu Dawud, Hakim in Isaba, Bayhaqi).*

The Story of a Bedouin

Shaddad ibnul Haad narrates that a Bedouin once came to Rasulullah &, accepted Iman and became a devoted follower of Rasulullah &. He made Hijra and stay with Rasulullah & in Madinah. After the battle of Khaibar, much booty came to Rasulullah & and he distributed it amongst the Muslim soldiers. Rasulullah & specified a share for that particular Bedouin Sahabi and handed it over to his friends to give it to him since he was busy grazing the animals. When they came to give his share of the booty to him, the Sahabi asked, "What is this?" "It is your share of the booty that Rasulullah & has specified for you," they replied. He said, "I did not follow him for this. Instead, I followed him so that I may die and enter Jannah when an arrow strikes me here." He then pointed towards his throat. Rasulullah & said, "If you are true, Allah will make it come true." The Sahabah engaged in battle against the enemy and after fighting and being martyred, the Sahabi was brought to Rasulullah &. He had been struck by an arrow at exactly the same spot he had pointed towards. Rasulullah & asked, "Is it he?" When the Sahabah confirmed that it was him, Rasulullah & said, "He was true to Allah and Allah made his intention come true." Rasulullah & then shrouded the Sahabi in a coat that belonged to Rasulullah &, after which he placed the corpse before him and led the Janaza salah. While making du'a for the Sahabi, the following words of

Rasulullah & were heard: "O Allah! Here lies Your servant who migrated in Your path. He was killed as a martyr and I am his witness." *(Bayhaqi, Nasai in Al Bidayah wan Nihayah, Hakim).*

The Story of a Black Sahabi

Anas & narrates that a man came to Rasulullah & saying, "O Rasulullah &! I am a man with a black skin, an ugly face and without any wealth. Will I enter Jannah if I fight those people (the disbeliever army)?" "Certainly," replied Rasulullah &. The man then advanced and fought until he was martyred. When Rasulullah & came by his corpse, Rasulullah & said, "Allah has beautified your face, made you fragrant and increased your wealth." Addressing the Sahabah, Rasulullah & then said, "I have seen his 2 wives from the wide-eyed damsels of Jannah pulling at his coat, disputing with each other about who will enter between his skin and his coat." *(Bayhaqi in Al Bidayah wan Nihayah, Hakim in Targheeb wat Tarheeb).*

The Story of Amr bin Al Aas &

Amr bin Al Aas & narrates that Rasulullah & once sent a message to him stating, "Get your clothes and weapons on and come to me." When he got to Rasulullah &, Rasulullah & said, "I wish to send you out in command of an army. Allah will keep you safe and grant you much booty. I shall also grant you a fine portion of the booty." Amr bin Al Aas & said, "O Rasulullah &! I did not accept Islam for wealth but accepted Islam for the love of Islam." Rasulullah & said, "O Amr! Good wealth is a fine thing for a good man." *(Ahmad in Isaba).* According to another narration, Amr bin Al Aas & also said, "I accepted Islam for the love of Islam and to be with the Rasul of Allah." Rasulullah & said, "Indeed, but good wealth is a fine thing for a good man." *(Tabrani in Awsat and Kabeer, Majma'uz Zawa'id).*

The Statements of Omar & Concerning Martyrs

Abul Bakhtari Ta'ee narrates that many people in Kufa gathered with Abul Mukhtar the father of Mukhtar bin Abu Ubaid at the bridge of Abu Ubaid. This was the place where Abu Ubaid Thaqafi was martyred along with his entire battalion in the year 13 AH. All were martyred except for 2 or 3 men who used their swords to attack the enemy lines with such force that they opened up a path for themselves through which to escape. They eventually reached Madinah. As the 3 were sitting one day and discussing about the others who were killed in the battle, Omar & came to them and asked, "Tell me what you have been discussing about them?" They replied, "We were seeking forgiveness on their behalf and making Du'a for them." Omar & threatened, "You will have to tell me what you were saying about them otherwise you will receive harsh treatment from me." They said, "We were saying that they are martyrs." Omar & then said, "I swear by the Being besides Whom there is no deity, Who has sent Muhammad & with the truth and without Whose command Judgment will never take place! No living being knows what a dead person will receive by Allah except for the Nabi of Allah because Allah has forgiven all his past and future errors. I swear by the Being besides Whom there is no deity, Who has sent Muhammad & with the truth and guidance and without Whose command Judgment will never take place! There are people who fight to show off, others who fight for their tribal passion, those who fight to attain worldly gain and those who fight for wealth. All those who fight will receive from Allah only that which was in their hearts." *(Kanzul Ummal).* Malik bin Aws bin Hadathan & narrates that they were busy discussing an army that was martyred during the Khilafa of Omar & when one of them commented, "They were the workers of Allah out in the Path of Allah so their rewards will be with Allah." Another person observed, "Allah will resurrect them on the Day of Judgment according to the intentions they died with." To this, Omar ؓ remarked, "Correct. I swear by the Being Who controls my life that Allah will certainly resurrect them according to the intentions they died with. There are people who fight for show and boasting while others fight with the intention of gaining things of this world. There are also those whom the battle takes by surprise and they have no option but to fight. Then there are those who fight with firmness and with hope of rewards from Allah. These are the true martyrs. In fact, even I have no idea of what will happen to me in the Hereafter or of what will happen to you. All I do know is that the occupant of this grave (Rasulullah ﷺ) has all his past and future errors forgiven." *(Tammam)*. *Masruq* narrates that when mention was made of some martyrs in front of Omar ؓ, he addressed the people saying, "Whom do you regard to be martyrs?" The people replied, "O Amirul Mu'minin! Martyrs are those who are killed in these battles." When he received this reply, Omar ؓ said, "In that case, martyrs will be plenty. Let me enlighten you on the subject. Bravery and cowardliness are natural traits amongst people which Allah places wherever He wills. The truly brave person is therefore is the one who fights with dedication without caring whether he returns to his family or not. The coward is the one who flees from the battlefield on account of his wife. The true martyr is he who gives his life with the hope of earning rewards from Allah. The true Muhajir is he who leaves the acts that Allah forbids and the true Muslim is he from whose tongue and hands other Muslims are safe." *(Ibn Abi Shaiba in Kanzul Ummal)*.

The Story of Abdullah bin Zubair ؓ and His Mother ؓ

Dimam narrates that Abdullah bin Zubair ؓ sent a message to his mother Asma ؓ saying, "People have deserted me while my enemies are calling for a truce." Her reply was, "If you are out to revive the Book of Allah and the Sunnah of Allah's Nabi ﷺ, then die on the truth. However, if you are out in search of worldly gain, then there is no good in you whether you are alive or dead." *(Nu'aym bin Hammad in Fitan, Kanzul Ummal)*.

Abu Musa Ash'ari ؓ rebukes one who did not follow Instructions

Abu Malik Ash'ari ؓ narrates, "Rasulullah ﷺ sent us on an expedition and appointed Sa'd bin Abi Waqqas ؓ as our commander. We set out and set up camp. When a man stood up to saddle his horse, I asked him where he was off to. He replied, 'I am off to get food.' I said, 'Do not do anything until we ask our Amir.' We went to Abu Musa Ash'ari ؓ who was in command of our battalion and spoke to him. He said, 'It seems as if you want to return to you family.' When the man denied it, Abu Musa Ash'ari ؓ cautioned him, 'Watch what you say.' 'No, I do not wish to return home,' repeated the man. Abu Musa Ash'ari ؓ said, 'You may proceed on the Path of virtue.' The man left and returned late night. Abu Musa Ash'ari ؓ asked, 'Did you perhaps go to your family?' The man denied it, Abu Musa Ash'ari ؓ cautioned, 'Watch what you say.' The man admitted that he did. Abu Musa Ash'ari ؓ said, 'You went to your family in fire, sat there in fire and returned in fire. Start to do good so that your sin be annulled." *(Ibn Asakir in Kanzul Ummal)*

Rasulullah ﷺ Criticizes Separating in Valleys and Sealing Roads

Abu Tha'laba Khushani ؓ narrates that when the Muslims camped at a valley, they separated and dispersed. Rasulullah ﷺ said, "Your separating in valleys is from Saitan." Thereafter,

whenever they set up camp, they would stay together. *(Abu Dawud and Nasai in Targheeb wat Tarheeb)* Another narration *(Bayhaqi, Ibn Asakir in Kanzul Ummal)* adds that the Sahabah stayed so close together thereafter that if a sheet was thrown over them, it would cover them all. Mu'adh Juhani ؓ narrates that he was on a certain expedition with Rasulullah ﷺ when the Muslims were separated as they made the camp small so that it was difficult for others to find space and crowded the road so that no one could pass. Rasulullah ﷺ then sent someone to announce, "There is no rewards for Jihad for the person who makes the camp small or seals a road." *(Bayhaqi, Abu Dawud in Mishkat)*.

Anas bin Abi Marthad Ghanawi ؓ Stands Guard

Sahl bin Handhaliya ؓ narrates that they marched with Rasulullah ﷺ for the battle of Hunain and were marching with great speed until the afternoon. Sahl ؓ narrates further that he had completed the Zuhr salah with Rasulullah ﷺ when a horseman came to Rasulullah ﷺ saying, "O Rasulullah ﷺ! I rode ahead of you and got to the top of a certain mountain where I chanced to see the Hawazin tribe on the watering their camels of their fathers along with their women, their animals and goats. They have all gathered at Hunain. Rasulullah ﷺ smiled and said, "InsAllah that will all be booty for the Muslims tomorrow." Rasulullah ﷺ then announced, "Who will stand guard over us tonight?" Anas bin Abi Marthad Ghanawi ؓ said, "I will, O Rasulullah ﷺ!" Rasulullah ﷺ then instructed him to get mounted. When he mounted his horse and came to Rasulullah ﷺ, Rasulullah ﷺ briefed him by saying, "Go to that narrow valley in front and get to the top of it. Be vigilant as you stand guard there and let not the enemy deceitfully get to you tonight." The next morning, Rasulullah ﷺ went to the place where they performed salah and performed 2 Rakahs salah. He then asked, "Do you people know anything about your rider?" "No," replied the Sahabah, "We know nothing of him." The Iqamah was then called out and as Rasulullah ﷺ led the salah, he kept glancing towards the narrow valley. When Rasulullah ﷺ completed the salah and had made the Salam, he said, "Listen to the glad tidings that your rider has arrived." When the Sahabah looked between the trees of the narrow valley, they saw him come. He stopped before Rasulullah ﷺ, greeted with salam and said, "I went up to the highest point of the narrow valley as Rasulullah ﷺ had instructed me. In the morning I studied both walls of the narrow valley but saw no one." Rasulullah ﷺ asked, "Did you dismount during the night?" "No," replied Anas bin Abi Marthad ؓ, "except for salah and to relieve myself." Rasulullah ﷺ said, "You have made it (Jannah) compulsory for yourself. Your rewards are so great that it matters not if you do no Nafl deeds after this." *(Abu Dawud, Bayhaqi, Abu Nu'aym in Muntakhab)*.

Another Sahabi Stands Guard

Abu Atia ؓ reports that Rasulullah ﷺ was once sitting when he was informed that a man had passed away. Rasulullah ﷺ asked, "Has any of you seen him do any good deed?" "Yes," replied another Sahabi, "I once stood guard with him in the Path of Allah." Rasulullah ﷺ and those with him stood up and Rasulullah ﷺ led the Janaza salah (funeral prayer) for the deceased. When the Sahabi was placed in the grave, Rasulullah ﷺ threw some sand with his hands and then said, "Although your companions think that you are amongst the inmates of Jahannam, I testify that you are from amongst the inhabitants of Jannah." Addressing Omar bin Khattab ؓ, Rasulullah ﷺ then said, "Do not ask about the evil actions of people, but rather enquire about their good deeds which are acts of Islam." *(Tabrani, Haythami)*.

Abu Atia ◈ narrates that when a person passed away during the time of Rasulullah ◈, some of the Sahabah said, "O Rasulullah ◈! Do not lead the Janaza salah for him." Rasulullah ◈ then asked, "Has anyone seen him do any good deed." The Hadith continues further. *(Ibn Asakir in Kanzul Ummal)*. Abu Aa'idh ◈ states that Rasulullah ◈ left for the Janaza of a Sahabi. When the deceased was placed before Rasulullah ◈, Omar bin Khattab ◈ said, "Do not lead the Janaza salah for him, O Rasulullah ◈, because he was a sinful man." Rasulullah ◈ turned to the other Sahabah and asked, "Has anyone seen him do any good deed." The Hadith continues like above. *(Bayhaqi in Mishkat)*

Abu Rayhana ◈, Ammar ◈ and Abbad ◈ Stand Guard

The Hadith of Abu Rayhana ◈ has passed in the chapter entitled "Enduring extreme cold when inviting people towards Allah ◈." In the narration, he states, "Rasulullah ◈ announced, 'Who will stand guard over us tonight? I shall make such a Du'a for him, the virtues of which he will certainly receive.' A man from the Ansar stood up and volunteered. Rasulullah ◈ asked who he was, he gave his name. Rasulullah ◈ asked him to come closer and when he did, Rasulullah ◈ held a part of his clothing and started making Du'a for him. When I heard the Du'a, I also volunteered. Rasulullah ◈ asked me who I was and I informed him that I was Abu Rayhana. Rasulullah ◈ made a Du'a for me that was shorter than the one he made for the other person. Rasulullah ◈ said, 'The fire of Jahannam has been forbidden for the eye that stands guard in the Path of Allah.'" *(Ahmad, Nasai, Tabrani, Bayhaqi)*. In the chapter entitled "Performing salah while out in the Path of Allah", the narration is reported by Jabir in which it is mentioned that Rasulullah ◈ asked, "Who shall stand guard over us tonight?" A volunteer from amongst the Muhajir and another from amongst the Ansar stood up and said, "We shall do so, O Rasulullah ◈!" Rasulullah ◈ gave them instructions to stand guard at the mouth of the valley. The 2 volunteers were Ammar bin Yasir ◈ and Abbad bin Bishr ◈. The Hadith continues further as already narrated. *(Ibn Is'haq)*.

The Story of Ubay bin Ka'b ◈ and His Du'a to Endure Fever

Abu Sa'eed Khudri ◈ narrates that Rasulullah ◈ said, "Whenever a Mu'min is hurt on his body, Allah uses it as a means to annul some of his sins." Ubay bin Ka'b ◈ then prayed, "O Allah! I beg You to allow a fever to inflict the body of Ubay bin Ka'b ◈ until the day he meets you until I die. However, it should not prevent him from salah, fasting, Hajj, Urnrah or Jihad in Your path." A fever then overcame him where he stood and did not leave him until he passed away. Even while suffering the fever, he was always present for salah, observed his fasts, performed Hajj and Umrah and participated in military expeditions. *(Ibn Asakir)*. Abu Sa'eed Khudri ◈ narrates that a person came to Rasulullah ◈ and asked, "Tell me what we receive in exchange for these illnesses that keep afflicting us?" Rasulullah ◈ replied, "They annul sins." Ubay ◈ asked, "Even if it is something mild?" Rasulullah ◈ said, "Even if it be a prick of a thorn or something milder." Then Ubay ◈ prayed to Allah that fever should never leave him until his death but should not prevent him from Hajj, Umrah, Jihad in the Path of Allah or salah in congregation. Whenever someone touched him, the heat of the fever could be felt. This continued until the day he passed away. *(Ibn Asakir, Ahmad, Abu Ya'la in Kanzul Ummal, Isaba, Ibn Abi Dunya, Ibn Hibban, Tabrani, Abu Nu'aym in Hilya)*.

The Injuries that Rasulullah ◈ Suffered

Jundub bin Sufian ◈ reports that as Rasulullah ◈ was

walking, his foot struck a stone and he fell. This caused his finger to start bleeding. Rasulullah ◈ then said:

You are merely a finger that is bleeding
But whatever you suffer is in the Path of Allah

The Hadith of Anas ◈ has already passed in the chapter entitled "Rasulullah ◈ endures hardship and difficulty when giving Da'wah towards Allah." There he narrates that the canine teeth of Rasulullah ◈ were broken during the battle of Uhud and he was also severely injured on the head. The Hadith is narrated by *Bukhari, Muslim* and others.

The Injuries Sustained by Talha bin Ubaidullah ◈ and Abdur Rahman bin Auf ◈

The Hadith has also passed in which Aisha ◈ narrates that whenever Abu Bakr ◈ spoke about the battle of Uhud, he would say, "Every credit for that day goes to Talha." Later on in the narration, Abu Bakr ◈ says further, "When we reached Rasulullah ◈, his canine tooth was already broken and his face was injured when 2 links of his helmet pierced his cheeks. Rasulullah ◈ said, 'See to your companion!' Rasulullah ◈ was referring to Talha who had become weak due to loss of blood. Later on in the Hadith, Abu Bakr ◈ continues, "After tending to Rasulullah ◈, we went to Talha who had fallen into a ditch. He had suffered 70 odd wounds inflicted by spears, arrows and swords. We nursed him." *(Tayalisi in al Bidayah wan Nihayah)*. Ibrahim bin Sa'd says that the report reached him that during the battle of Uhud, Abdur Rahman bin Auf ◈ sustained 21 wounds. A leg injury caused him to limp. *(Abu Nu'aym in Muntakhab)*

The Injury of Anas bin Nadhr ◈

Anas bin Malik ◈ says that his paternal uncle, Anas bin Nadhar bitterly regretted his inability to participate in the battle of Badr. He addressed Rasulullah ◈ saying, "I was unable to participate in the first opportunity to fight the disbelievers. If Allah affords Muslim the opportunity to fight them, I shall show my bravery and Allah will see what I can do." Consequently, he participated in the battle of Uhud. When the Muslims suffered a reversal in the battle, he supplicated to Allah saying, "O Allah! I apologize for what they (the Mu'minin) have done and I forgive myself from what they (the disbeliever) have done." Saying this, he advanced into the enemy lines. He passed by Sa'd bin Mu'adh ◈ and said, "O Sa'd! I swear by the Rabb of my father Nadhar that I can smell the fragrance of Jannah coming from the direction of Uhud." Sa'd ◈ later said, "O Rasulullah ◈! I would never have been able to do what he did." Anas bin Malik ◈ reports that there were more than 80 sword, spear and arrow wounds on his body. When his corpse was found, it was badly mutilated and it was only his sister who could recognize his body and by his fingertips. Anas bin Malik ◈ says that they all believed that it was with reference to people like his uncle that Allah revealed the verse: مِنَ الْمُؤْمِنِينَ رِجَالٌ صَدَقُوا مَا عَاهَدُوا اللَّهَ عَلَيْهِ فَمِنْهُمْ مَنْ قَضَى نَحْبَهُ وَمِنْهُمْ مَنْ يَنْتَظِرُ وَمَا بَدَّلُوا تَبْدِيلًا (23) *Among the believers are men who have been true to their covenant with Allah (i.e. they have gone out for Jihad (holy fighting), and showed not their backs to the disbelievers), of them some have fulfilled their obligations (i.e. have been martyred), and some of them are still waiting, but they have never changed (i.e. they never proved treacherous to their covenant which they concluded with Allah) in the least. (Al-Ahzab:23) (Bukhari, Muslim, Nasai in Targheeb wat Tarheeb, Ahmad, Tirmidhi)*. Anas bin Malik ◈ narrates, "My paternal uncle after whom I was named did not participate in the battle of Badr at the side of Rasulullah ◈. This was difficult for him to come to terms with and he would say, 'I missed the first battle that Rasulullah ﷺ fought. If Allah affords me the opportunity to participate in another battle with Rasulullah ﷺ, Allah shall certainly see what I can do.' He was afraid to say more than this. He then participated in the Battle of Uhud with Rasulullah ﷺ. There he passed by Sa'd bin Mu'adh ﷺ and said to him, 'Where are you off to, O Abu Amr? How wonderful is the fragrance of Jannah that I smell coming from behind Mount Uhud!' He then fought until he was martyred. Over eighty sword, spear and arrow wounds were found on his body. His sister and my paternal aunt Rubai bint Nadhar said that she recognized his body only by his fingertips. It was then that Allah revealed the following verse of the Qur'an: مِنَ الْمُؤْمِنِينَ رِجَالٌ صَدَقُوا مَا عَاهَدُوا اللَّهَ عَلَيْهِ فَمِنْهُمْ مَنْ قَضَى نَحْبَهُ وَمِنْهُمْ مَنْ يَنْتَظِرُ وَمَا بَدَّلُوا تَبْدِيلًا (23) *Among the believers are men who have been true to their covenant with Allah (i.e. they have gone out for Jihad (holy fighting), and showed not their backs to the disbelievers), of them some have fulfilled their obligations (i.e. have been martyred), and some of them are still waiting, but they have never changed (i.e. they never proved treacherous to their covenant which they concluded with Allah) in the least. (Al-Ahzab:23).* The Sahabah were of the opinion that this verse was revealed with reference to people like him." *(Ahmad, Tirmidhi, Nasai in Al Bidayah wan Nihayah, Tayalisi, Ibn Sa'd, Ibn Abi Shaiba, Harith, Ibn Jareer, Ibn Mundhir, Ibn Abi Hatim and Ibn Mardway in Kanzul Ummal, Abu Nu'aym in Hilya, Bayhaqi).*

The Wounds Sustained by Ja'far bin Abu Talib ﷺ

Abdullah bin Omar ﷺ narrates, "Rasulullah ﷺ appointed Zaid bin Haritha ﷺ as commander of the expedition to Mu'ta. Rasulullah ﷺ then added, 'If Zaid is killed, Ja'far should take command and if Ja'far is killed, then Abdullah bin Rawaha should take command.' I was with the Muslim army in this battle and when we searched for Ja'far bin Abu Talib, we found him already dead. We counted over 90 sword and arrow wounds on his body." Another narration adds that not a single wound was on the back of his body indicating that he advanced all the time and never turned his back to the enemy. *(Bukhari in Al Bidayah wan Nihayah, Tabrani in Isaba, Abu Nu'aym in Hilya, Ibn Sa'd).*

The Wounds Sustained by Sa'd bin Mu'adh ﷺ

Amr bin Shurabil ﷺ reports that when Sa'd bin Mu'adh was struck with an arrow during the battle of Khandaq, his blood spilled on Rasulullah ﷺ. Abu Bakr ﷺ arrived and seeing the condition of Sa'd ﷺ said, "Oh, my back has been broken!" This was an expression of shock. After Rasulullah ﷺ bade him to be silent, Omar ﷺ arrived and exclaimed, "Inna Lillahi wa inna Ilayhi Raji'oon!" *(Ibn Abi Shaiba in Kanzul Ummal).*

The Eye of Abu Sufian ﷺ is Injured During the Battle at Ta'if

Sa'eed bin Ubaid Thaqafi ﷺ reports, "During the battle at Ta'if, I spotted Abu Sufian ﷺ sitting and eating on the wall of Abu Ya'la. I shot an arrow at him, which struck his eye. He went to Rasulullah ﷺ and said, 'This eye of mine has been injured in the Path of Allah." Rasulullah ﷺ said to him, 'If you wish, I could pray to Allah to return the eye. If you wish otherwise, you could have Jannah in return for your injury.' Abu Sufian ﷺ replied, 'Let it be Jannah instead.'" *(Ibn Akasir in Kanzul Ummal)*

The Wounds Sustained to the Eyes of Qatadah bin Nu'man ﷺ and Kifa'ah bin Rafi ﷺ During the Battle of Badr

Qatadah bin Nu'man ﷺ narrates that when his eye was injured during the battle of Badr, his eyeball hung on his cheek and the Sahabah wanted to cut it off. The rest of the Hadith will be quoted in the chapter concerning the manner in which the Sahabah received assistance. *(Baghawi, Abu Ya'la).* Rifa'h bin Rafi ﷺ says, "The disbelievers amassed around Umayyah bin Khalaf during the battle of Badr as we approached him. When I noticed that a portion of his amour was broken below his armpit, I struck the area with my sword. I was struck by an arrow during the battle of Badr because of which my eye was ruptured. Rasulullah ﷺ applied some of his saliva to the eye and prayed for me. I then felt absolutely no pain." *(Bazzar, Tabrani, Haythami).*

The Incident of Rafi bin Khadij ﷺ and 2 Other Sahabah From the Banu Abdul Ash'hal Tribe

The incident reported by *Yahya bin Abdul Hamid* has passed in which he narrates from his grandfather that an arrow struck Rafi bin Khadij ﷺ in the chest during either the battle of Uhud or the battle of Hunain. He then went to Rasulullah ﷺ and asked him to remove the arrow. In the same chapter entitled "Enduring injuries and illness when inviting people towards Allah" another narration from Abu Sa'ib ﷺ states that a man from the Banu Abdul Ash'hal tribe reported, "My brother and I participated in the battle of Uhud and we both returned wounded. When Rasulullah ﷺ's caller announced that we should march in pursuit of the enemy, I said to my brother or he said to me, 'Can we miss this opportunity to march with Rasulullah ﷺ?' By Allah! Although we had no transport to ride and we were both heavily wounded, we went with Rasulullah ﷺ. Since my wounds were less serious than my brother's, I carried him when he could not manage and he walked at other times. In this manner, we eventually reached the place where the other Muslims were."

The Wounds Sustained by Bara bin Malik ﷺ and Now He Lost the Flesh on His Bones

Anas ﷺ reports that during the battle against Musailama Kadhab, Bara threw himself on to the people in the orchard and the defenders of Musailama locked themselves in an orchard. Bara ﷺ scaled the wall of the orchard to get in and he then fought them single-handedly until he was able to open the gate of the orchard. Bara ﷺ sustained over 80 arrow and sword wounds and had to be carried away to the camp for treatment. Khalid ﷺ stayed with him and nursed him for a month. *(Khalifa and Baqi bin Makhlad in Isaba).* Is'haq bin Abdullah bin Abu Talha ﷺ narrates that Anas ﷺ and his brother were fighting at an enemy fortress in Hariq, a place in Iraq. The disbeliever were throwing hooks fixed to heated chains and when it caught hold of someone, they would pull him up to them in the fortress. They managed to get hold of Anas ﷺ in this manner and were pulling him in. However, Bara ﷺ advanced, kept watch at the wall for an opportunity and then grabbed at the chain. He kept holding on to the burning hot chain until the rope gave way. When he then looked at his hand, the bone was visible because all the flesh on it had burnt away. In this way, Allah had saved Anas bin Malik ﷺ. *(Tabrani in Isaba).* The hooks caught Anas bin Malik ﷺ and the disbeliever started pulling at him until he was lifted off the ground. While his brother Bara ﷺ was fighting the enemy, he was told to catch hold of his brother. He came running, jumped on to the wall and grabbed the chain as it kept turning. He kept tugging the chain from the disbeliever with his hands burning until the rope finally gave way. Then when he looked at his hands and saw that the bone was visible because all the flesh on it had burnt away. *(Tabrani in Majma'uz Zawa'id).*

Rasulullah ﷺ Wishes to be Killed in the Path of Allah

Abu Hurairah ؓ reports that he heard Rasulullah ﷺ say, "I swear by the Being Who controls my life! I would not have missed a single expedition in the Path of Allah if it were not for many men who would dislike staying behind me and for whom I am unable to provide transport. I swear by the Being Who controls my life! I wish that I was killed in the Path of Allah and then given life again, then again killed and again given life, again killed and given life once more and then killed." (Bukhari). Abu Hurairah ؓ narrates that Rasulullah ﷺ said, "Allah stands security for the person who goes out in the Path of Allah. Allah says for the person who leaves home for no other reason but to strive in My path with belief in Me and belief in My Ambiya, I stand guarantee to either enter him into Jannah if he is martyred or if he survives to return him to his family together with great rewards or a share of the booty. I swear by the Being Who controls the life of Muhammad ﷺ! Every wound sustained in the Path of Allah shall appear on the Day of Judgment as fresh as it was the day it took place. The color shall be that of blood, the smell will be the fragrance of musk. I swear by the Being Who controls the life of Muhammad ﷺ! Had it not been for the difficulty it would cause to the Muslims, I would not have missed a single expedition marching in the Path of Allah. Neither can I provide nor do they have the necessary means of transport to proceed in the Path of Allah and without transport they will find it distressing to stay behind me. I swear by the Being Who controls the life of Muhammad ﷺ! I wish that I was killed in the Path of Allah and given life again, killed and given life, killed and given life again." (Muslim, Ahmad, Nasai in Kanzul Ummal)

Omar ؓ Wishes for Martyrdom

Qais bin Abi Hazim narrates that Omar ؓ once delivered a sermon in which he said, "There is a palace in the everlasting Jannah that has 500 doors. At each door there are 5,000 wide-eyed damsels. None but a Nabi can enter it." He then turned to the grave of Rasulullah ﷺ and said, "All the best to you, O occupant of this grave." Thereafter, he continued, "Or a Siddiq may enter it." He then turned to the grave of Abu Bakr ؓ and said, "All the best to you, O Abu Bakr." Then he continued saying, "Or a martyr may enter it." He then turned to himself saying, "How will you ever attain martyrdom, O Omar?" He then added, "The same Allah Who took me out of Makkah to migrate to Madinah has the power to pull martyrdom to me." (Tabrani, Ibn Asakir in Kanzul Ummal) Abdullah bin Mas'ood ؓ says, "Allah gave martyrdom to him at the hands of the worst of creation who was a slave of Mughiera ؓ. (Tabrani, Haythami in Majma'uz Zawa'id). Aslam narrates that Omar ؓ used to make the following Du'a, "O Allah! Bless me with martyrdom in Your path and make my death in the city of Your Rasul." (Bukhari). Hafsa ؓ states that Omar ؓ prayed, "O Allah! Let me be killed in Your path and have my death in the city of your Nabi ﷺ." Hafsa ؓ asked him how this was possible, he replied, "Allah shall make it happen when He wills." (Isma'eli in Fat'hul Bari).

Abdullah bin Jahash ؓ Wishes for Martyrdom

Sa'd bin Abi Waqqas ؓ says that on the day when the battle of Uhud was to take place, Abdullah bin Jahash ؓ said to him, "Will you not make Du'a to Allah'?" The 2 men then stepped aside and Sa'd ؓ prayed, "O my Rabb! When we meet the enemy, let me clash with an excellent fighter and fierce warrior. Let me engage him in fierce combat and let him also fight aggressively. Thereafter, allow me to gain the upper hand over him, kill him and have his possessions as booty." Abdullah bin Jahash ؓ said "Amin" to the Du'a. Thereafter, Abdullah bin Jahash ؓ prayed, "O Allah! Allow me to meet in combat a man who is a fierce warrior and an excellent fighter. Let me fight him for You and let him also fight back. Let him then kill me and sever my nose and my ears and then when I meet You tomorrow, You may ask, 'Who has severed your nose and ears'?' I may then reply, 'It was done for Your pleasure and the pleasure of Your Rasul ﷺ.' You may then confirm by saying, 'You have spoken the truth.'" Narrating the account Sa'd ؓ said, "O my son! The Du'a of Abdullah bin Jahash ؓ was better than mine. By the end of the day, I saw his nose and ears strung in a thread." (Tabrani, Haythami, Baghawi in Isaba, Ibn Wahab in Isti'ab, Bayhaqi, Abu Nu'aym in Hilya). Sa'eed bin Musaib رحمة الله narrates that Abdullah bin Jahash ؓ said, "O Allah! I beg You that I should meet an enemy tomorrow who should kill me, tear my belly open and then sever my pose and my ears. You should then ask me on the Day of Judgment why this has happened so that I may reply, 'It was for You.'" Sa'eed bin Musaib رحمة الله says, "I have strong hope that as Allah fulfilled the first part of his appeal, Allah will fulfill the last part." (Hakim, Ibn Shahin, Ibn Mubarak in Jihad, Isaba, Abu Nu'aym in Hilya, Ibn Sa'd).

Bara bin Malik ؓ Hopes for Martyrdom

Anas ؓ reports that Rasulullah ﷺ said, "There are many people wearing 2 old pieces of cloth and who are not given any attention but Allah will certainly fulfill their vows if they make any. Amongst them in Bara bin Malik ؓ." When the battle for Tustar was raging and the Muslims were suffering a reverse, they said, "O Bara! Make a vow to your Rabb so that we could win the battle." He then prayed, "O Allah! I swear in Your name that You should give us the shoulders of the enemy in our hands and allow me to meet with Your Nabi ﷺ." He was then martyred. (Abu Nu'aym in Kanzul Ummal, Tirmidhi in Isaba). Anas ؓ narrates that Rasulullah ﷺ said, "There are many weak people whom others regard as weak and who wear 2 old pieces of cloth. However, Allah will certainly fulfill their vows if they make any in His name. Amongst them in Bara bin Malik." Bara ؓ once clashed with a disbelieving army who had inflicted heavy casualties to the Muslims. The Muslims therefore called to him saying, "O Bara! Rasulullah ﷺ had mentioned that Allah ﷻ would certainly fulfill the vows you make. Therefore make a vow to your Rabb." Bara ؓ then said, "O my Rabb! I make a vow in Your name that You should give us their shoulders." Allah then gave the Muslims victory. Thereafter the Muslims clashed with an enemy at the bridge of the town Sus where the disbelievers again inflicted heavy casualties to the Muslims. Again the Muslims called to Bara ؓ to make a vow to Allah. Consequently, Bara ؓ prayed, O Allah! I make a vow in Your name that You should give us the shoulders of the enemy in our hands and allow me to meet with Your Nabi ﷺ." The Muslims were then given victory and Bara was martyred. (Hakim, Abu Nu'aym in Hilya)

Humama ؓ Hopes for Martyrdom

Humaid bin Abdur Rahman Himyari narrates that a Sahabi by the name of Humama ؓ once fought a battle in Isfahan during the Khilafah of Omar ؓ when he prayed thus, "O Allah! Humama claims that he loves to meet You. O Allah, if he is true, grant him the resolve to search for martyrdom and if he is false, then give him death in Your path even though he dislikes it." The remainder of the Hadith states that he was finally martyred and that Abu Musa Ash'ari ؓ also testified that he was a true martyr. (Abu Dawud, Musaddad, Harith Abi Shaibah, Ibn Mubarak in Isaba). A narration of Imam Ahmad adds that Humama ؓ also said, "Give Humama death in Your path even though he dislikes it. O Allah! Let Humama ؓ not return home from this journey. He passed away on the journey. Affan once said that Humama ؓ was afflicted with a stomach disease because of which he passed away in Isfahan. After his death, Abu Musa Ash'ari ؓ said, "O people! By Allah as far as we have heard from our Nabi ﷺ and as far as our knowledge reaches, Humama ؓ passed away as a martyr." *(Ahmad, Haythami, Abu Nu'aym in Muntakhab).*

Nu'man bin Muqarrin ؓ Hopes for Martyrdom

Ma'qal bin Yasar ؓ reports that Omar ؓ once consulted with the Hurmuzan, a Persian leader who accepted Islam after being defeated by the Muslims. Omar ؓ asked, "What are your opinions? Should we start with Faris, Azerbaijan or Isfahan?" Hurmuzan replied, "Faris and Azerbaijan are wings while Isfahan is the head. If you cut one wing, the other wing will take over but if you cut the head, both wings will become useless. Start with the head." Omar ؓ then entered the Masjid where he found Nu'man bin Muqarrin ؓ performing salah. Omar ؓ sat beside Nu'man and when he had completed his salah, Omar ؓ said, "I wish to appoint you as commander." Nu'man ؓ said, "Not as a collector but as a warrior." "As a warrior indeed," confirmed Omar ؓ. Omar ؓ then sent him to Isfahan. In the remainder of the Hadith, it is reported that Mughiera ؓ said to Nu'man ؓ, "May Allah have mercy on you! Launch the attack because we are being pressed as the arrows of the enemy are coming fast and furious." Nu'man ؓ replied, "You are undoubtedly a man of many virtues. However, I have fought with Rasulullah ﷺ and whenever he did not launch an attack at the beginning of the day, he would postpone it for the time when the sun had passed the meridian, when the wind started to blow and Allah's help would descend." Thereafter, Nu'man ؓ said, "I shall wave my flag thrice. When I wave it the first time, every man should attend to the call of nature and then perform wudhu. When I wave it the 2nd time, every man should check his weapons and shoe straps and fix them. Then when I wave it for the 3rd time, you should attack and should not turn your attention to each other. If Nu'man is killed, none should turn their attention to him as I will make a Du'a to Allah which I stress that every person says Amin. He made the Du'a saying: O Allah! Grant Nu'man martyrdom with your help to the Muslims and make them victorious."

Nu'man ؓ then waved his flag the first time, followed by the second and then the third. He then wore his armor and launched the attack. He was the first to fall in battle. Ma'qal ؓ reports, "I went up to Nu'man ؓ but then recalled his instruction. I therefore marked the spot and proceeded. Whenever we killed an enemy soldier, his companions immediately became unmindful of us. The Persian leader Dhul Hajibain fell from his mule, causing his abdomen to cut open. Allah then granted us victory. I then went to Nu'man ؓ with a container of water. As I washed the sand from his face, he asked who I was. When I informed him that I was Ma'qal bin Yasar, he asked, 'What has happened to the Muslims?' 'Allah has given them victory,' I replied. He then said, 'All praise to Allah! Write to Omar ؓ informing him of this.' It was then that his soul departed." *(Tabari).* Jubair ؓ has narrated the battle of Nahawind in detail. In his narration he quotes the following words of Nu'man ؓ, "Whenever Rasulullah ﷺ fought a battle and did not launch an attack at the beginning of the day, he did not rush until the time of Zuhr salah had arrived, the winds started to blow and the battle could take place in a pleasant manner. It was this practice of Rasulullah ﷺ that prevented me from attacking. He then prayed: O Allah! Bring comfort to my eyes today by granting such a victory to the Muslims that gives honor to Islam and disgrace to the disbeliever. Thereafter, grant me death as a martyr." He then addressed the Muslims saying, 'Say 'Amin', may Allah bless you." The others then said "Amin" and started to weep. *(Tabari, Tabrani, Haythami, Hakim).*

The Incident of Khaithama ؓ and His Son During the Battle of Badr

Sulaiman bin Bilal narrates that as Rasulullah ﷺ was leaving for the battle of Badr, Sa'd bin Khaithama ؓ and his father Khaitama ؓ both decided to leave with Rasulullah ﷺ. When Rasulullah ﷺ heard about this, he instructed that only one of them should leave and to decide who it would be so that they draw lots. It was then that Khaitama ؓ said to his son Sa'd ؓ, "One of us will have to remain behind. Why don't you stay with the women?" Sa'd ؓ replied, "Had it not been to attain Jannah, I would have certainly given you preference to have it your way. However, I really do aspire for martyrdom on this trip." When they drew lots, Sa'd ؓ's name was drawn. He therefore left for Badr with Rasulullah ﷺ where he was martyred by Amr bin Abd Wadd. *(Hakim, Ibn Mubarak in Isaba).*

The Martyrdom of Ubaidah bin Harith ؓ

Muhammad bin Ali bin Husain narrates that when Utba called for challengers during the battle of Badr, Ali bin Abi Talib ؓ stood up to challenge Walid bin Utba. The 2 were young and of equal body type. By turning the palm of his hand and placing it on the ground, the narrator indicated that Ali ؓ floored Walid and killed him. Thereafter, Shaiba bin Rabiah stood up and Hamza ؓ got up to accept the challenge. These 2 men were also of equal body type. Raising his hands higher, the narrator indicated in a like manner that Hamza ؓ killed Shaiba. Thereafter, when Utba stood up, Ubaidah bin Harith ؓ got up to accept his challenge. The narrator pointed to 2 pillars and added that the 2 men were like those pillars. When the 2 men exchanged blows, the blow of Ubaidah ؓ left Utba's left arm hanging. However, Utba got close and struck at Ubaidah ؓ's leg with his sword, severing his calf. Ali ؓ and Hamza ؓ then returned and settled Utba's affair. They then carried Ubaidah away to Rasulullah ﷺ beneath a canopy. When they made him over to Rasulullah ﷺ, the Nabi of Allah made him lie down. Rasulullah ﷺ took his head on his lap and started to wipe the dust from his face when Ubaidah said, "O Rasulullah ﷺ! Had Abu Talib seen me now, he would be convinced that his words are more applicable to me than him when he said with regards to protecting Rasulullah ﷺ:

وَنُسْلِمُهُ حَتَّى نُصَرَّعَ حَوْلَهُ وَنَذْهَلَ عَنْ أَبْنَائِنَا وَالْحَلَائِل

We shall protect him until we are wounded and fall dead around him being totally oblivious of our own children and wives"

Ubaida ؓ then asked, "Am I not a martyr?" "Certainly," replied Rasulullah ﷺ, "and I am witness to the fact." He then passed away. Rasulullah ﷺ buried him in a valley called Safra and he went into the grave to lay the body. Rasulullah ﷺ had never before that entered the grave of any person. *(Ibn Asakir in Kanzul Ummal).* Zuhri narrates that when Ubaidah ؓ and Utba exchanged blows, the blow of each one injured the other. Returning to the battlefield, Ali ؓ and Hamza ؓ approached Utba and killed him. They then carried their companion away. When they came to Rasulullah ﷺ, Ubaidah ؓ's leg was severed and his arteries were bleeding profusely. When the 2 men brought Ubaidah ؓ to Rasulullah ﷺ, he asked, "Am I not a martyr, O Rasulullah ﷺ?" "Certainly," came the reply. Ubaidah ؓ then said, "Had Abu Talib been alive, he would be convinced that his words are more applicable to me than him when he said:

وَنُسْلِمُهُ حَتَّى نُصَرَّعَ حَوْلَهُ وَنَذْهَلَ عَنْ أَبْنَائِنَا وَالْحَلَائِل

We shall protect him until we are wounded and fall dead around him being totally oblivious of our own children and wives"

During the Battle of Uhud

Abdullah bin Omar narrates that on the day that the battle of Uhud was fought, Omar said to his brother, "Take my armor, dear brother." His brother replied, "I desire martyrdom just as you do." They both therefore left the armor. *(Tabrani, Haythami, Abu Nu'aym in Hilya).*

Ali Resolves to Fight to Death

Sa'eed bin Mansoor reports that Ali said, "Once the people had left Rasulullah during the battle of Uhud, I looked through all the dead and did not see Rasulullah there. I then said to myself, 'By Allah! It is impossible for Rasulullah to flee and I do not see him amongst the dead. I think that Allah has become angry with us because of what we did and had lifted his Nabi. It is best for me to fight until I am killed.' I broke the sheath of my sword and attacked the disbelievers. They gave way, I suddenly saw Rasulullah in their midst." *(Abu Ya'la, Ibn Abi Asim, Sa'eed in Mansur in Kanzul Ummal, Haythami).*

The Incident of Anas bin Nadhar

Qasim bin Abdur Rahman bin Rafi who belonged to the Banu Adi bin Najjar tribe narrates that Anas bin Nadhar the uncle of Anas bin Malik came across some men from the Muhajir and the Ansar during the battle of Uhud who had lost all morale to fight. Amongst them was Omar bin Khattab and Talha bin Ubaidullah. Anas bin Nadhar asked, "What makes you sit here?" "Rasulullah has been martyred," they replied. He said to them, "What is the use of living after him? Stand up and die for that which Rasulullah died for!" He faced the enemy and fought until killed. *(Ibn Is'haq in Al Bidayah wan Nihayah)*

The Incident of Thabit bin Dabdaba

Abdullah bin Ammar Khatmi reports that Thabit bin Dahdaha came before the Muslims during the battle of Uhud when they were all scattered and without morale. He shouted, "O assembly of Ansar! Come to me! Come to me! I am Thabit bin Dahdaha! If Muhammad has been killed, remember that Allah is living and never dies. Fight for Islam, Allah shall give you victory and shall assist you." A group of the Ansar jumped towards him and Thabit started attacking the disbeliever with the Muslims by his side. A fully armed and powerful battalion stood before them comprising of leading commanders such as Khalid bin Walid, Amr bin Al Aas, Ikrama bin Abu Jahal and Darar bin Khattab. A fierce fight started and Khalid bin Walid attacked a spear at Thabit, which went through his body. He then fell as a martyr. All the Ansar with him also fell as martyrs. They are supposed to be the last Muslims to fall (during that battle). *(Waqidi in Isti'ab).*

The Incident of a Muhajir and an Ansari

Abu Najih reports that during the battle of Uhud, a Muhajir passed by an Ansari lying in a pool of blood. The Muhajir said to the Ansari, "Do you know that Muhammad has been martyred?" The Ansari responded by saying, "If Muhammad has been martyred, then his duty is complete because he has already delivered the message. You people should continue fighting for Islam." It was then that Allah revealed:

وَمَا مُحَمَّدٌ إِلَّا رَسُولٌ قَدْ خَلَتْ مِنْ قَبْلِهِ الرُّسُلُ أَفَإِنْ مَاتَ أَوْ قُتِلَ انْقَلَبْتُمْ عَلَى أَعْقَابِكُمْ وَمَنْ يَنْقَلِبْ عَلَى عَقِبَيْهِ فَلَنْ يَضُرَّ اللَّهَ شَيْئًا وَسَيَجْزِي اللَّهُ الشَّاكِرِينَ (144)

Muhammad is no more than a Messenger, indeed Messengers have passed away before him. If he dies or is killed, will you then turn back on your heels (as disbelievers)? And he who turns back on his heels, not the least harm will he do to Allah, and Allah will give reward to those who are grateful. (Al-Imran:144) (Bayhaqi in Dala'ilun Nubuwwah, Al Bidayah wan Nihayah)

The Incident of Sa'd bin Rabi

Zaid bin Thanbit narrates, "During the battle of Uhud, Rasulullah sent me to look for Sa'd bin Rabi. Rasulullah instructed, 'If you see him, convey my Salam to him and tell him that Rasulullah asks how he is keeping.' I searched for him amongst the dead and found him in his dying moments with 70 wounds inflicted by swords, spears and arrows. I informed him that Rasulullah had sent Salam and wished to know how he was feeling. He said, 'Salam to Rasulullah and to you. Tell Rasulullah that I can smell the fragrance of Jannah and tell my Ansar brothers that they will have no excuse to offer before Allah if the disbeliever reach him while they have the power to wink an eye.' He then passed away. May Allah shower His mercy on him." *(Hakim).* Another narration reported by Abdur Rahman bin Abu Sasa states that Rasulullah said, "Who will see what has happened to Sa'd bin Rabi for me?" The rest of the Hadith is similar to the one above. It states also that Sa'd said, "Inform Rasulullah that I am amongst the dead. Also convey my Salam to him and tell him that Sa'd says, 'May Allah rewards you with the best rewards on our behalf and on behalf of the entire Ummah." *(Hakim, Ibn Is'haq, Al Bidayah wan Nihayah, Malik).*

The Incident of 7 Ansars Martyred During the Battle of Uhud

Anas reports that when the disbelievers surrounded Rasulullah during the battle of Uhud, Rasulullah was with 7 men from the Ansar and one from the Quraish. Rasulullah said, "Who will repulse them from us and be my companion in Jannah?" An Ansari stepped forward and fought until he was martyred. When the disbelievers again surrounded Rasulullah, he again announced, "Who will repulse them from us and be my companion in Jannah?" Another Ansari went forward and fought until he was also martyred. Rasulullah and the others were repeatedly surrounded and repulsed by each one of the 7 Ansar until eventually all 7 had been martyred. Rasulullah then said, "We have not been fair to our companions by leaving them to fight single-handedly." *(Ahmad, Muslim).* Another narration from Jabir states that after being overwhelmed during the battle of Uhud, the Muslims dispersed from around Rasulullah and the only people with him were 11 men from the Ansar and Talha bin Ubaidullah. Rasulullah had begun climbing the mountain when the disbelievers caught up with him. Rasulullah then asked, "Is there anyone to repulse them?" "I am here, O Rasulullah!" responded Talha. "Stay where you are, O Talha," Rasulullah instructed. One of the Ansar then said, "I shall, O Rasulullah!" As the Ansari fought in their defense, Rasulullah and the others with him continued climbing. The Ansari was eventually martyred and the disbelievers were again catching up with Rasulullah.

Rasulullah again asked, "Is there none to repulse them?" When Talha again volunteered for the task, Rasulullah gave him the same instruction as before. One of the Ansar said, "Then I shall, O Rasulullah!" As the Ansari fought in their defense, the others continued climbing. This Ansari was also martyred and the disbelievers again started catching up with Rasulullah. Rasulullah then repeated his request as before and every time an Ansari was martyred defending them to which Talha repeatedly volunteered himself. Rasulullah ﷺ however, kept holding him back, to which an Ansari volunteered himself and received permission to fight. Each one then fought as the others had fought until none but Talha ؓ was left with Rasulullah ﷺ. However, the disbelievers again surrounded Rasulullah ﷺ. When Rasulullah ﷺ announced, "Is there anyone to repulse them?" Talha ؓ replied, "I shall". Talha ؓ then fought as much as all the previous Sahabah combined. When his finger tips became severely injured, he exclaimed, "Hass!"(An Arabic expression means "Oh Dear!") Rasulullah ﷺ said to him, "Had you exclaimed Bismillah, the angels would have lifted you to the heavens in full view of the people and enter you into the skies." Rasulullah ﷺ then climbed to the top of the mountain where he joined the other Sahabah who had regrouped there. *(Bayhaqi in Al Bidayah wan Nihayah).*

The Martyrdom of Yaman and Thabit bin Qais ؓ

Mahmood bin Labid says that when Rasulullah ﷺ marched to Uhud, Yaman bin Jabir ؓ, the father of Hudhaifa ؓ and Thabit bin Qais ؓ were taken to a fortress together with the women and children since they were very old men. The one said to the other, "Shame on you! What are we waiting for? By Allah! What is left of any of our lives is equivalent to the amount of thirst a donkey can bear (of all animals, donkey is least capable of enduring thirst). We shall have to die either today or tomorrow. Why don't we take our swords and join Rasulullah ﷺ?" The 2 men then joined the Muslim army without the knowledge of anyone. While Thabit bin Qais ؓ was killed by the disbelievers, the father of Hudhaifa ؓ was killed by the swords of the Muslims who did not recognize him. Hudhaifa ؓ shouted, "My father! My father!" but the Muslims who had killed him truthfully said, "We swear by Allah that we did not recognize him." Hudhaifa ؓ acknowledged what they said by saying, "May Allah forgive you for He is the Most Merciful of those who show mercy." When Rasulullah ﷺ wanted to pay the blood money, Hudhaifa ؓ forgave it. This increased the status of Hudhaifa ؓ in the eyes of Rasulullah ﷺ. *(Hakim).* Another narration adds that the 2 men also said, "We shall then join up with Rasulullah ﷺ. Perhaps Allah shall bless us with martyrdom as we fight by the side of Rasulullah ﷺ." They then took their swords and joined up with the Muslim army without the knowledge of anyone. The concluding portion of this narration states that this forgiving of the blood money considerably increased the status of Hudhaifa ؓ in the eyes of Rasulullah ﷺ. *(Abu Nu'aym in Muntakhab).*

Asim, Khubaib and Their Companions are Martyred During the Battle of Raji

Abu Hurairah ؓ narrates that Rasulullah ﷺ once sent an expedition on a spying duty under the command of Asim bin Thabit ؓ who was the maternal grandfather of Asim bin Omar bin Khattab ؓ. The expedition proceeded and was at a place between Usfan and Makkah when their presence was reported to a clan from the Hudhail tribe known as the Banu Lihyan. With close to 100 archers, the people of this tribe set out after the Sahabah and traced their tracks until they arrived at a place where the Sahabah had set up camp earlier. There they found some date stones from the provisions that the Sahabah had brought from Madinah. Seeing this, they said, "These are dates from Yathrib." They then continued tracing the tracks until they eventually caught up with the Sahabah. Asim ؓ and his companions took shelter on a hillock as the Banu Lihyan surrounded them. The Banu Lihyan called out, "We make a promise that we shall not kill any of you if you surrender to us."

Asim ؓ said, "As for myself, I shall never surrender into the custody of a Kafir." He then prayed, "O Allah! Inform Your Nabi ﷺ about us." The Sahabah then fought the Banu Lihyan, who martyred Asim ؓ and another 7 Sahabah with arrows. The only ones who survived were Khubaib, Zaid and another Sahabi. When the Banu Lihyan again offered their promise, these Sahabah agreed to it and came down from the hillock. However, no sooner did the Banu Lihyan have control over them then they removed the strings from their bows and used it to tie the Sahabah up. To this, the 3rd Sahabi said, "This is the first breach of your promise." He then refused to accompany them. Despite their efforts to pull and drag him, he would not budge. They eventually killed him.

They then took Khubaib ؓ and Zaid ؓ away and sold them in Makkah. The sons of Harith bin Amir bin Naufal bought Khubaib ؓ because he had killed their father Harith bin Amir in the battle of Badr. He lived as a prisoner with them until they eventually decided to kill him. Khubaib ؓ asked one of the ladies of the household for a razor to shave with and she lent it to him. Narrating the incident later she says, "I was unmindful of one of my little children who went towards him. When the child came to him, he put the child on his lap. When I saw this, I became terribly alarmed for he was holding the razor in his hand. I thought that he would use the razor to kill the child.. Sensing fear, he said, "Are you afraid that I will kill this child? By the will of Allah, I shall never do such a thing." The lady narrates further, "I have never seen a prisoner better than Khubaib ؓ. I saw him eating a bunch of grapes at a time when there was no fruit in Makkah and he was bound in chains. It was nothing short of unseen sustenance that Allah had provided for him." When Khubaib ؓ was led outside the area of the Haram to be executed, he requested to be left to perform 2 Rakahs of salah. After performing the salah, he turned to the people and said, "I would have lengthened the salah if it were not for you thinking that I am doing so because I am afraid to die." Khubaib ؓ was the first to start the practice of performing 2 Rakahs salah at the time of execution. He then said, "O Allah! Do not leave any of them alive." He recited some couplets:

When I am killed as a Muslim, I care not on which side I fall.
This is all for Allah and if He wills, He could bless the severed limbs of my body.

Thereafter, Uqba bin Harith martyred him. Because Asim ؓ had killed one of the leaders of the Quraish during the battle of Badr, the Quraish sent some people to bring a portion of his body to them which they may recognize as his. However, Allah sent a swarm of wasps to his body and they protected him from the people whom the Quraish had sent. They were therefore unable to get anything from the body. *(Bukhari, Bayhaqi, Abdur Razzaq in Isti'ab, Abu Nu'aym in Hilya).* Asim bin Amr bin Qatadah reports that after the battle of Uhud, a delegation from the Adhal and Qara tribes came to Rasulullah ﷺ and said, "O Rasulullah ﷺ! Islam has come to us so send with us a group of your Sahabah to make us understand Islam, to teach us the Qur'an, and to educate us about the Shari'ah of Islam." Rasulullah ﷺ therefore sent with them 6 Sahabah, whose names have been recorded. These Sahabah proceeded with these people until they reached Raji, which was a well of the Hudhail tribe situated at one end of Hijaz where the Hada region starts. There the people accompanying the Sahabah betrayed them and solicited help from the Hudhail tribe. Unaware of what was happening, the Sahabah were in their camp when they were suddenly surrounded by many men waving their swords. When the Sahabah grabbed their swords to fight them, the men said, "We swear by Allah that we do not wish to kill you. All we want is to get some money from the people of Makkah in exchange for you. We give you assurance in the name of Allah that we shall not kill you." However, Marthad ◉, Khalid bin Bukair ◉ and Asim ◉ said, "By Allah! We shall never ever accept promise or pledge from a disbeliever."

The Couplets that Asim ◉ Recited and His Body is Protected From the Disbelievers

Asim ◉ then recited some couplets which meant:

"Far from being a sick man, I am a powerful archer and my bow has a sturdy string Arrows with long and wide shafts glide over it. Death is true whereas life is a fake. Whatever Allah has destined will certainly happen to a man and man will have to return to Him. May my mother forsake me if I do not fight you"

Asim ◉ also said the following:

I am Abu Suleiman with arrow made by (the expert arrow-maker) Muq'ad and with a bow that is like a kindled fire
I feel no fear when a warrior comes storming on a speedy camel and my shield is made from the hide of a bull with little hair. (To top it all) I am a firm believer in everything revealed to Muhammad ﷺ He is also reported to have said:
I am Abu Suleiman and warriors like me are excellent archers I am also from a tribe that is a most honorable one

Asim ◉ then fought the disbelievers until he and his 2 companions were martyred. After killing Asim ◉, the Hudhail intended to severe his head to sell it to Sulafa bint Sa'd bin Shuhaid. When her son was killed in the battle of Uhud, she made a vow that if she ever got the head of Asim ◉, she would drink wine from his skull. However, a swarm of wasps protected his body. When the disbelievers were prevented from getting to it, they said, "Leave him until the evening when the wasps would leave. We can then have him." Allah then sent heavy rains flowing down the valley, which carried his body away. Asim ◉ had made a promise to Allah that because the disbelievers were impure, none of them should ever touch him and he would not touch any of them either. When the news of the wasps protecting the body of Asim ◉ reached Omar ◉, he said, "Allah protects the Mu'min servant. Asim ◉ vowed that no disbeliever should touch him and that he would not touch any disbeliever during his lifetime, so Allah prevented it from happening after his death just as Allah prevented it during his lifetime."

The story of Zaid bin Dathana ◉ and His Statement About His Love for Rasulullah ﷺ

The 3 Sahabah in the group of Khubaib ◉, Zaid bin Dathana ◉ and Abdullah bin Tariq ◉ chose the easier option and chose to remain alive. They therefore surrendered and were taken prisoner. The disbelievers took them to Makkah to sell them. When they reached a place called Zahran, Abdullah bin Tariq ◉ slipped his hands from the bonds and grabbed a sword. The disbelievers stepped away from him and started throwing rocks at him until they eventually martyred him. His grave is in Zahran. This left Khubaib ◉ and Zaid bin Dathana ◉, they were taken to Makkah and exchanged for 2 prisoners from the Hudhail who had been in Makkah. While Hujair bin Abi Ihab Tamimi bought Khubaib ◉, Safwan bin Umaiah bought Zaid bin Dathana ◉ to execute him for the death of his father. Safwan sent Zaid bin Dathana ◉ outside the Haram to Tan'im with his slave Nistas so that he could be executed. Amongst the group that gathered there was Abu Sufian bin Harb. When Zaid bin Dathana ◉ was brought for execution, Abu Sufian said to him, "O Zaid! I ask you to swear by Allah whether you wish that Muhammad was here with us in your place to have his head severed while you could be with your family." Zaid ◉ replied, "I swear by Allah that I would not even like a thorn to prick Muhammad ﷺ where he is while I am sitting with my family." Abu Sufian said, "I have never seen people love anyone as much as the companions of loved Muhammad ﷺ." Nistas then executed Zaid ◉.

The Story of Khubaib ◉ in Makkah and His Salah at the Time of Death

Ibn Is'haq narrates the story of Khubaib bin Adi ◉ from Abdullah bin Najih who was informed by Mariya, the freed slave of Hujair bin Ihab. After accepting Islam, she narrated, "Khubaib ◉ was held prisoner in my home. I once saw him eating from a bunch of grapes the size of a human head at a time when there was not a grape to be eaten in all of Allah's land." *Ibn Is'haq* narrates further from Asim bin Omar bin Qatadah and Abdullah bin Najih that she said, "When the time for his execution drew near, he asked me to send him a razor so that he may clean himself before his death. I gave the razor to a little boy from the family and told him to give it to the man in the house. By Allah! I had just sent the boy with the razor to him when I exclaimed, 'What have I done! By Allah! That man will have his revenge by killing the boy and have a life in exchange for his own!' However, when the boy handed the razor over to Khubaib ◉, he took it and said, 'By your life! Did your mother not fear any treachery from me when she sent you with this razor?' He then sent the boy off." Ibn Hisham says that it is commonly believed that the boy was the son of Maria. *Ibn Is'haq* narrates further from Asim that the disbelievers took Khubaib ◉ out of the Haram to Tan'im where they intended to crucify him. He then requested, "If you permit, could I please perform 2 Rakahs salah." "Go ahead," they agreed, "Perform your salah." Khubaib ◉ then performed 2 complete and perfect Rakahs of salah. Thereafter, he turned to the people and said, "By Allah! Due to the fact that you would say I lengthened the salah for fear of death, I would have performed a longer salah." It was Khubaib ◉ who was the first to initiate the practice of Muslims to perform 2 Rakahs salah at the time of execution. The disbelievers lifted him up and they tied him on the wooden structure, he prayed, "O Allah! We have conveyed the message of Your Rasul ﷺ. Do inform him tomorrow of what has happened to us." He added, "O Allah! Count each one of these disbelievers, kill each one of them and leave not one of them alive." He was then martyred.

Mu'awiya bin Abu Sufian ◉ used to say, "I was also present on that day with my father Abu Sufian and others. I saw my father throw me down on the ground out of fear for the curse of Khubaib ◉. He did this because people used to say that if a person lies on his back when he is cursed, the curse would miss him. The *Maghazi* of Musa bin Uqba narrates that Khubaib ◉ and Zaid bin Dathana ◉ were both martyred on the same day and on that day Rasulullah ﷺ was saying, "Salams to you 2 as well. The Quraish have martyred Khubaib." It is also narrated that when the disbelievers crucified Zaid bin Dathana ◉, they first speared him to make him forsake Islam. However, this only increased his Iman and faith in Islam. Mosa bin Uqba narrates that Khubaib ◉ was lifted to the wooden frame, the disbelievers asked him to swear by Allah whether he preferred to have Rasulullah ﷺ in exchange for his own freedom. Khubaib ◉ replied, "Never! I swear by the Exalted Allah that I would not even accept a thorn pricking the foot of Rasulullah ﷺ as ransom for my life." The disbelievers laughed at this. *Ibn Is'haq* reported. *(Ibn Is'haq in Al Bidayah wan Nihayah)*

The Statement of Khubaib 🙏 Concerning His Love for Rasulullah 🙏 and the Couplets He Recited before His Execution

A lengthy narration of Urwa bin Zubair 🙏 states that the children of the disbelievers killed at Badr executed Khubaib 🙏. While he was tied to the cross they were using their weapons on him, they asked him in a loud voice to swear whether he preferred Rasulullah 🙏 to be in his place. He responded by saying, "I swear by the Magnificent Allah that I would not even accept a thorn pricking the foot of Rasulullah 🙏 as ransom for my life." The disbelievers laughed at this. When he was lifted on to the cross, Khubaib 🙏 recited some couplets which meant:

"The groups have amassed around me and have also gathered their tribes and have collected a large gathering. They have also gathered their women and children as I have been brought to a large trunk of a palm tree (to be crucified). To Allah do I plead my case of estrangement and my grief and the place these groups have prepared for my death. O Master of the glorious Throne! Grant me fortitude against what they intend to do to me. They have cut through my flesh and my hopes have be exposed. This is all for Allah and if He wills, He could bless the severed limbs of my body by my life! When I am killed as a Muslim I care not in what condition will my resting place be for Allah" (Tabrani, Haythami)

Another narration adds the following line after the first couplet:
"They all express their hatred for me and make every effort to oppose me because I am in fetters and in a place of destruction"
The following lines are then added after the fifth couplet:
"They have given me a choice between kufr and death whereas death is better. My eyes are tearing but not out of any fear I have no fear for death because I have to die. I have fear only for the leaping flames of the raging fire By Allah! When I die as a Muslim, I care not on which side I shall fall for the sake of Allah. I shall express no fear to my enemy because my return shall be to Allah"
(Ibn Is'haq in Al Bidayah wan Nihayah)

The Story of the Sahabah at Bir Ma'oona

Several men of knowledge including Mughiera bin Abdur Rahman and Abdullah bin Abu Bakr bin Muhammad bin Arm bin Hazam narrate that the expert spear-thrower Abu Bara Amir bin Malik bin Ja'far once came to Madinah to meet Rasulullah 🙏. Rasulullah 🙏 presented Islam to him and invited him to accept. However, he neither accepted Islam nor avoided it. Instead he said, "O Muhammad 🙏! If you send some of your companions to the people of Najd to call them towards Islam, I strongly feel that they would accept." Rasulullah 🙏 replied, "I fear harm coming to them from the people of Najd." Abu Bara reassured Rasulullah 🙏 by saying, "I stand surety for their safety. Do send them to invite people towards Islam." Rasulullah 🙏 then sent Mundhir bin Amr 🙏 who was called "Al Mu'niq Liyamut" (one who is eager to die) together with 70 Sahabah who were amongst the best of the Muslims. They included Harith bin Sima 🙏, Haram bin Milhan 🙏 of the Banu Adibin Najjar, Urwa bin Asma bin Silt Sulami 🙏, Nafi bin Budail bin Warqa Khuzai 🙏 and Amir bin Fuhaira 🙏 who was the freed slave of Abu Bakr 🙏. The group traveled until they reached Bir Ma'oona, which was a well located between the lands of the Banu Amir tribe and the rocky plain of the Banu Sulaim tribe. When they set up camp there, Haram bin Milhan 🙏 sent the letter of Rasulullah 🙏 to Amir bin Tufail. When the messenger arrived, Amir did not even look at the letter before attacking the messenger and killing him. He then solicited help from the Banu Amir tribe but they declined to respond to his call. They made it clear that they would never betray Abu Bara who had entered into a treaty with them. Amir then sought help from Usaia, Ri'al and Dhakwan clans who belonged to the Banu Sulaim tribe. They responded to his call and left with him. They amassed around the Sahabah and surrounded their camp. When the Sahabah saw the enemy they grabbed their swords and fought until all of them were martyred. May Allah shower His mercies on them. The only survivor was Ka'b bin Zaid 🙏 from the Banu Dinar bin Najjar tribe. There was still life in him when the attackers left and he was removed from amongst the dead. He still lived until he was martyred during the battle of Khandaq.

Amr bin Umaiah Dhamri 🙏 and an Ansari from the Banu Amr bin Auf tribe were busy grazing the animals and were unaware of the attack on the other Sahabah. All that made them aware was carrion-eating birds hovering above the camp. They said, "By Allah! Something must have happened for these birds to be here." The 2 men then went to investigate and found the Muslims lying in pools of blood. The horsemen who had attacked the Sahabah were still there. The Ansari asked Amr bin Umaiah 🙏, "What do you suggest?" "I suggest that we go and inform Rasulullah 🙏 about what had happened," he replied. The Ansari then said, "To save my life I would not like to leave a place where someone like Mundhir bin Amr 🙏 has been martyred. I would also not like to just inform others about people who have been martyred. I prefer to be amongst them." He fought until he was martyred. Amr bin Umaiah 🙏 was taken prisoner but later released by Amir bin Tufail when he informed them that he belonged to the Mudhar tribe. Amir 🙏 cut off Amr's forelocks and gave him freedom because his mother was required to free a slave, so he freed Amr 🙏 on her behalf. *(Ibn Is'haq in Al Bidayah wan Nihayah, Tabrani, Haythami).*

The Last Words of Haram 🙏 Because of Which His Killer Accepted Islam during the Battle of Mu'ta

Anas 🙏 narrates that Rasulullah 🙏 once dispatched Haram 🙏 the brother of Ummu Sulaim 🙏 together with 70 riders on an expedition. The leader of the disbelievers in the region where the expedition went was Amir bin Tufail. He had given Rasulullah 🙏 a choice between 3 options when he said, "Either (1) you have the villagers for yourself and leave the city dwellers to me or (2) you appoint me as your successor or (3) I shall fight you with the support of thousands of men from the Ghitfan tribe." However, Amir was afflicted with a plague in the home of a certain woman. He said, "It is a sore like that which afflicts camels and in the house of some woman." He regarded it below his dignity to die in the house of some simple woman with whom he stayed during his travels. Bring me my horse." He then died on the back of his horse. Haram 🙏 the brother of Ummu Sulaim 🙏 a crippled Sahabi and another Sahabi from some tribe left to deliver the letter. Haram 🙏 said to the other two, "Stay close until I return to you. If they grant me safety, you join me, and if they kill me, you can go back to your companions." Haram 🙏 the approached the disbelievers and said, "Will you grant me safety so that I may deliver the message of Rasulullah 🙏?" As he was busy talking to them, they motioned to a man to come up to Haram 🙏 from the back and stabbed him with a spear. One of the narrators by the name of Hammam says that he was stabbed with a spear that pierced right through his body. He then exclaimed, "Allahu Akbar! By the Rabb of the Kaba, I am successful!" The Sahabah" who were with Haram 🙏 joined with the others but they were all martyred except for the crippled Sahabi who had been on top of a hillock. It was with reference to these martyred Sahabah that

Allah revealed the following verse of the Qur'an: *"We have met our Rabb Who is happy with us and has made us happy."* For 30 mornings afterwards, Rasulullah ﷺ cursed the Ri'al, Dhakwan, Banu Lihyan and Usaia tribes who opposed Allah and His Rasul ﷺ. *(Bukhari).* Another narration of *Bukhari* states that when Haram ؓ the uncle of Anas ؓ was stabbed with a spear on the expedition to Bir Ma'oona, he wiped his blood on his face and was heard saying, "By the Rabb of the Kabah, I am successful!" A narration reported by Waqidi says that the person who martyred Haram ؓ was Jabbar bin Salma Kilabi. When he stabbed Haram ؓ with a spear, Haram ؓ cried out, "By the Rabb of the Kabah, I am successful!" Afterwards when Jabbar asked about the meaning of the statement "I am successful", the people told him that Haram ؓ was referring to his successful entry into Jannah. He then said, "By Allah! He has spoken the truth." Jabbar then accepted Islam. *(Al Bidayah wan Nihayah)*

Abdullah bin Rawaha ؓ Weeps Upon Leaving and His Poem Asking For Martyrdom During the Battle of Mu'ta

Urwa bin Zubair ؓ reports that Rasulullah ﷺ sent an expedition to Mu'ta in Jumadal Ula 8AH. Rasulullah ﷺ appointed Zaid bin Haritha ؓ as commander of the expedition. Rasulullah ﷺ then added, "If Zaid is killed, Ja'far bin Abi Talib should take command and if Ja'far is killed, then Abdullah bin Rawaha should take command." The Sahabah prepared their provisions for the journey and then got ready to leave. They were 3,000 in number. When they started leaving, the people came to bid farewell to the commanders that Rasulullah ﷺ appointed. As Abdullah bin Rawaha ؓ was being greeted along with the others, he started weeping. When the people asked him what it was that made him weep, he said, "I swear by Allah that it is neither love for this world nor my attachment to you that makes me weep. However, I have heard Rasulullah ﷺ recite a verse for the Qur'an that speaks of the fire of Jahannam: وَإِن مِّنكُمْ إِلَّا وَارِدُهَا ۚ كَانَ عَلَىٰ رَبِّكَ حَتْمًا مَّقْضِيًّا (71) *There is not one of you but will pass over it (Hell); this is with your Lord; a Decree which must be accomplished. (Maryam:71).* I have no idea how am I to return after this crossing." The other Muslims said to him, "May Allah be your companion. May He remove your worries and return you to us hail and healthy." Abdullah bin Rawaha ؓ recited the following:

"I implore Ar Rahman for forgiveness and the strike of a wide sword that causes foaming blood to spurt forth. Or (I implore Allah for) the fatal strike of a blood-thirsty enemy's spear that pierces through my intestines and liver and when people pass by my grave, it will be said, 'May Allah care for this warrior' who has already been cared for"

As the army were preparing to leave, Abdullah bin Rawaha went to greet Rasulullah ﷺ. He recited the following couplets:

"May Allah preserve all the good He has granted you as He did for Musa, and may He assist you as others were assisted I see you ever increasing in good and Allah knows that my sight is excellent. You are the Rasul and whoever is deprived of your munificence and your attention truly is ill-fated"

The army left. Rasulullah ﷺ left to bid farewell to them and he turned back to return to Madinah, Abdullah bin Rawaha ؓ said:

"May peace remain with the great man whom I have greeted amongst the date palms, who is the best of those who bid farewell and the best of friends"

Abdullah bin Rawaha ؓ encourages Sahabah towards Martyrdom

The expedition marched until they set up camp at a place called Ma'an which was located in Sham. There they received intelligence that Heraclius had arrived in Ma'ab in the district of Balqa with 100,000 Roman soldiers. In addition to this, he had been reinforced by another 100,000 soldiers from the Lakhm, Judham, Qayn, Bahra and Bali tribes. Commanding the reinforcements was a man named Malik bin Zafila who belonged to the Irasha clan, an offshoot of the Bali tribe. When this news reached the Muslims, they stayed in Ma'an for 2 nights, discussing their situation. They said, "We should send a message to Rasulullah ﷺ informing him about the numbers of the enemy. He will either send reinforcements to us or issue further instructions for us to follow." Then Abdullah bin Rawaha ؓ boosted the courage of the Muslim by saying, "O people! By Allah! The thing that you seem to dislike is the very thing for which you have left, martyrdom. We have never fought with reliance in our numbers and our strength. We have always fought on the strength of Islam that Allah had blessed us with. March ahead! You will have either one of 2 excellent things, victory or martyrdom." The others echoed, "By Allah! Ibn Rawaha has spoken the truth!" The Sahabah then proceeded to the border of Balqa, where the coalition of Heraclius's Roman army and the Arab forces met them at one of the villages of Balqa called Masharif. As the enemy forces drew closer, the Muslims regrouped at a village called Mu'ta. It was there that the armies clashed. The Muslims arranged their army by appointing a Sahabi from the Banu Udhra tribe called Qutba bin Qatadah as commander of the right side and a Sahabi from the Ansar called Abaia bin Malik as commander of the left side. Thus they met the enemy and started fighting. Zaid bin Haritha ؓ fought with the flag of Rasulullah ﷺ until he was martyred by a spear. Ja'far ؓ grabbed hold of the flag and fought until he was also martyred. He was the first Muslim in the history of Islam who disabled his animal to dispel thoughts of fleeing from the battlefield. *(Ibn Is'haq in Al Bidayah wan Nihayah).* Urwa ؓ states that after the martyrdom of Zaid ؓ, Ja'far ؓ grabbed hold of the flag and fought with it until when the battle became inclined, he dismounted his red horse and restricted it. He fought until he was also martyred. He was the first Muslim in the history of Islam to disable his animal. *(Tabrani, Haythami, Abu Nu'aym in Hilya)*

The Couplets That Abdullah bin Rawaha ؓ Recited During Journey

Zaid bin Arqam ؓ says, "I was an orphan in the care of Abdullah bin Rawaha ؓ. He took me along on the journey to Mu'ta and seated me behind him on his bag. He was traveling one night when I heard him recite the following couplets:

'(O my camel) When you take me closer, carrying my carriage along for 4 days after leaving Hisa. May you then have comfort and not any more hardship for I shall not be returning to my wife and family (because I shall become a martyr, you will have no more work to do).

The Muslims shall return and leave me there in the land of Sham where my final stay will be my close relatives who are close to Allah will take you back. Whereas (by my death) my relationship with them shall cease at this stage I neither have concern for date palms that grow by themselves nor for those that need to be watered'

Zaid bin Arqam ؓ continues to narrate, "When I heard these couplets from him, I began to weep. He struck me with his whip and said, 'You little imp! Why should it be a. bother for you if Allah blesses me with martyrdom and you can ride back to Madinah on my camel?" *(Ibn Is'haq in Al Bidayah wan Nihayah, Abu Nu'aym in Hilya, Tabrani in Majma'uz Zawa'id)*

The Couplets that Abdullah bin Rawaha ؓ recited during the Battle

Abbad bin Abdullah bin Zubair ؓ narrates from his foster father from the Banu Murrah clan that Abdullah bin Rawaha ؓ grabbed hold of the flag after Ja'far bin Abi Talib ؓ was martyred. He took it forward riding on his horse. Because his heart seemed reluctant to dismount to engage the enemy, he said to himself:

"O my heart! 1 command you in the name of Allah to dismount. You will have to dismount either willingly or unwillingly (especially) if the enemy gather and shout out in loud voices (as they attack). Why do 1 see you displaying an aversion for Jannah for a long time you have enjoyed a good life. You are merely like a drop in a waterbag (will come to an end very soon)"

Abdullah bin Rawaha ؓ also recited the following couplets: *"O my heart! If you are not killed, you will still have to die some day. This is the pronounced decree of death that you will have to enter you have been granted whatever you desire. Now if you do what those 2 (Zaid and Ja'far ؓ) have done, you will have been rightly guided"*

He then dismounted his horse. As he did so, his cousin came to him with a piece of meat saying, "Strengthen yourself with this because you have experienced much hunger the last few days." Abdullah bin Rawaha took the meat and had taken just one bite from it when he heard an uproar at one end of the battlefield. He said to himself, "The Muslims are giving their lives. And you are still engrossed in worldly affairs?" Throwing the meat from his hand, he grabbed his sword and went forward, fighting until he was martyred. *(Ibn Is'haq in Al Bidayah wan Nihayah, Abu Nu'aym in Hilya, Tabrani, Haythami).*

Ja'far ؓ disables his Horse and recites Couplets as he Fights

Abbad bin Abdullah bin Zubair ؓ narrates that his foster father from the Banu Murrah who participated in the battle of Mu'ta said, "By Allah! It is as if I can still see Ja'far ؓ dismounting his red horse and then constrained it. He then fought the enemy until he was martyred. As he fought, he was reciting the following couplets which meant:

'O how delightful is Jannah and drawing close to it with its pure and cool waters. Their punishment has drawn close to the Romans who are non-believers without any mutual relations. When I meet them on the battlefield, I shall have to strike at them with my sword'." *(Ibn Is'haq, Al Bidayah wan Nihayah, Abu Nu'aym in Hilya, Abu Dawood in Isaba).*

Zaid bin Khattab ؓ and Other Sahabah Encourage the Muslims to be Steadfast and to Seek Martyrdom During the Battle of Yamamah

Abdur Rahman ؓ who was the son of Zaid bin Khattab ؓ narrates that his father Zaid bin Khattab ؓ carried the flag of the Muslims during the Battle of Yamamah. The Muslims were on the verge of being defeated when their enemy the Hanifa tribe overwhelmed the Muslim infantry. Zaid bin Khattab ؓ then said to the Muslims, "Do not return to the camp for the infantry has been defeated." Shouting at the top of his voice, he then said, "O Allah! I beg Your pardon on behalf of my companions who have fled and I clear myself from the evil that Musailama and Muhakkam bin Tufail, the commander of Musailama's army have caused." He then firmly grabbed hold of the flag and advanced with it in the midst of the enemy, where he fought courageously with his sword until he was martyred. May Allah shower His mercies on him. When the flag fell from his hand, it was taken up by Salim the freed slave of Abu Hudhaifa ؓ. The Muslims said to him, "We fear that the enemy would attack us from your side."

He replied, "I shall fight any attacks they launch form my side." Zaid bin Khattab ؓ was martyred in 12 AH. *(Hakim, Ibn Sa'd).*

Thabit ؓ and Salim ؓ Dig Holes During a Battle to Keep Them From Fleeing and to Ensure That They are Martyred

The daughter of Thabit bin Qais bin Shammas ؓ narrates that Abu Bakr ؓ requested the Muslim to fight against those who forsook Islam from Yamamah and the followers of Musailama. Thabit bin Qais bin Shammas ؓ was amongst those who marched. The Muslim army clashed with Musailama and the Banu Hanifa tribe, the Muslims were defeated in 3 battles. Thabit bin Qais bin Shammas ؓ and Salim the freed slave of Abu Hudhaifa ؓ said, "This was not how we fought during the time of Rasulullah ﷺ." They then dug a foxhole for themselves, got in and fought until they were both martyred. *(Tabrani, Haythami, Ibn Abdul Birr in Isti'ab, Baghawi in Isabah).* Muhammad bin Thabit bin Qais bin Shammas ؓ narrates that the Muslims were initially defeated during the Battle of Yamamah, Salim the freed slave of Abu Hudhaifa ؓ said, "This was not how we fought during the time of Rasulullah ﷺ." He dug a foxhole for himself and stood in it. Carrying the flag of the Muhajir with him, he fought until he was martyred. May Allah ﷻ shower His mercy on him. This occurred during the battle of Yamamah during the Khilafah of Abu Bakr ؓ in 12 AH. *(Ibn Sa'd)*

The Call Abbad bin Bishr ؓ Made to the Ansar Before He Was Martyred

Abu Sa'eed Khudri ؓ reports that Abbad bin Bishr ؓ said to him, "O Abu Sa'eed! Last night I saw in a dream that the sky opened up for me and then shut behind me after 1 had entered. InsAllah, this indicates martyrdom." Abu Sa'eed Khudri ؓ says, "I told him that he had seen an excellent dream. During the Battle of Yamamah, I then saw him calling to the Ansar, 'Break the cover of your swords and separate from the others. Let us (Ansars) separate from the other soldiers so that we may show our courage and encourage the others thereby!' 400 soldiers only from the Ansar gathered aside. Abbad bin Bishr ؓ, Abu Dujanah ؓ and Bara bin Malik ؓ led them to the orchard where the enemy had fortified themselves and fought very hard. Abbad bin Bishr ؓ was martyred. May Allah shower His mercies on him. I saw so many wounds on his face that I could recognize him only by signs on his body." *(Ibn Sa'd).*

The Call Abu Aqil ؓ Made to the Ansar Before he was Martyred

Ja'far bin Abdullah bin Aslam Hamdani ؓ narrates that the first casualty during the battle of Yamamah was Abu Aqil Unaifi ؓ. An arrow struck him between his shoulder and heart. The arrow bent and therefore did not kill him. When the arrow was removed, the left side of his body became paralyzed because of the injury. This occurred during the early part of the day and he was taken to the camp. When the fighting grew intense, the Muslims were being defeated and driven back behind their camp. As Abu Aqil ؓ lay in a weak condition because of his wound, he hear Ma'n bin Adi ؓ calling to Ansar, "Trust in Allah! Trust in Allah and attack the enemy once again." Ma'n ؓ was walking quickly ahead of the others. This was during the time when the Ansar were shouting, "Let us Ansar separate! Let us Ansar separate!" One by one, the Ansar started separating from the others and grouped together to launch an attack that encouraged others. Abdullah bin Omar ؓ says, "Abu Aqil ؓ jumped up to join his people (Ansars). I said to him, 'What are you doing, Abu Aqil? You are in no condition to fight.' He replied, 'A caller has announced my name.' 'He has called for the Ansar and is not referring to the injured,' I explained. He replied, 'I am from the Ansar and 1 shall respond even though I have to crawl.'"

Abdullah bin Omar ؓ narrates further that Abu Aqil ؓ then fastened his back and took a naked sword in his right hand. He then started calling, "O Ansar! Attack the enemy once more like the battle of Hunain." The Ansar then regrouped and spearheaded an extremely fierce attack on the enemy, forcing them to retreat to an orchard. The Muslims and the enemy met at close quarters and crossed swords with each other. Abdullah bin Omar ؓ says that he saw the injured arm of Abu Aqil ؓ severed from the shoulder and lying on the ground. Abu Aqil ؓ sustained 14 wounds, each of which were fatal by themselves. Musailama was killed and when Abdullah bin Omar ؓ reached Abu Aqil ؓ, he was lying on the ground breathing his last. When Abdullah bin Omar ؓ called Abu Aqil ؓ's name, he responded by mumbled in a faint voice, "At your service! Who has won the battle?" Abdullah bin Omar ؓ informed him, "Glad tidings that we have been victorious!" Raising his voice, Abdullah bin Omar ؓ added, "The enemy of Allah had been killed!" Abu Aqil ؓ pointed his finger towards the heavens, praised Allah and then passed away. May Allah shower His mercy on him. Abdullah bin Omar ؓ says that after returning, he informed his father Omar ؓ about the events that transpired, to which Omar ؓ commented, "May Allah shower His mercy on him. He continued asking for martyrdom and searching for it. He was amongst the best of Rasulullah ﷺ's companions and was one of the early Muslims." (Ibn Sa'd)

The Martyrdom of Thabit bin Qais ؓ

Anas ؓ says that when the Muslim army suffered defeat initially during the battle of Yamamah, he saw Thabit bin Qais applying perfume in preparation for entering the battlefield. Anas ؓ said to him, "O uncle! Do you not see what is happening to the Muslim that they are busy retreating?" He replied, "This is not how we used to fight during the time of Rasulullah ﷺ! Terrible is the habit that you people have made the enemy accustomed to by being repeatedly defeated! O Allah! I pardon myself from what these people (the Muslims) have done by fleeing and from what those people (the enemy) have done." He fought until he was killed. (Tabrani in Isaba, Haythami, Hakim). When the Muslims were being defeated during the Battle of Yamamah, Thabit ؓ said, "Shame on those people (the enemy) and whatever they worship and shame on these people (the Muslim) for what they have done!" He killed a man standing on an inclination of a wall of the orchard that they were using as a fortress. Thabit ؓ was then martyred. (Ibn Sa'd in Fat'hul Bari, Bayhaqi).

Ikrama bin Abu Jahal ؓ is Martyred Together with 400 Muslims During the Battle of Yarmuk

Thabit Bunani ؓ narrates that during the battle of Yarmuk, Ikrama bin Abu Jahal ؓ dismounted from his animal and was walking when Khalid bin Walid ؓ said to him, "Do not do that for your death will be a hard blow to the Muslims." Ikrama bin Abu Jahal ؓ replied, "Leave me alone, O Khalid. You were one of the early ones with Rasulullah ﷺ while my father and I were amongst his bitter opponents." He then continued on foot until he was martyred.(Ya'qub bin Abu Sufian and Ibn Asakir in Kanzul Ummal, Bayhaqi). Abu Uthman Ghassani narrates from his father that during the battle of Yarmuk, Ikrama bin Abu Jahal ؓ said, "I fought several battles against Rasulullah ﷺ. Should I now flee from you people today?!" He then announced, "Who will pledge to fight to their deaths?" His uncle Harith bin Hisham ؓ, Dirar bin Azwar ؓ and 400 other prominent Muslims and horsemen took the pledge at his hand. They then fought in front

of Khalid ؓ's tent until their wounds made them out of action. A large number of them were martyred. Amongst those martyred was Dirar bin Azwar ؓ. (Saif bin Omar in Al Bidayah wan Nihayah). While most of the 400 men were martyred, some of them survived. Amongst them was Dirar bin Azwar ؓ. The next morning, Ikrama bin Abu Jahal ؓ and his son Amr were brought to Khalid bin Walid ؓ in badly wounded conditions. Khalid placed the head of Ikrama bin Abu Jabal ؓ on his thigh and that of his son Amr on his calf. He started wiping their faces and putting drops of water into their throats saying, "The son of Hantama (Omar ؓ) said that we would not be martyred but Allah has blessed us with martyrs."

The Enthusiasm of Ammar bin Yasir ؓ to Fight in the Path of Allah

Abul Bakhtari and Maisara narrates that Ammar bin Yasir ؓ was fighting in the battle of Siffin but was not being martyred. He then approached Ali ؓ and said, "O Amirul Mu'minin! This is that very day about which Rasulullah ﷺ said that I would be martyred. How come I am still alive?." Ali ؓ replied, "Do not worry about that." This occurred 3 times until Ammar ؓ was given some milk. He drank it and said, "Indeed, Rasulullah ﷺ said that milk will be the last drink that I shall drink in this world." He then stood up and fought until he was martyred. (Tabrani, Abu Ya'la, Haythami). Abu Sinan Duwali ؓ who was a Sahabi reports that he saw Ammar bin Yasir ؓ was calling his slave to bring him something to drink. The slave brought a cup of milk, which Ammar ؓ drank. He said, "Rasulullah ﷺ has spoken the truth. Today I shall meet my beloved friends, Muhammad ﷺ and his companions." The rest of the Hadith follows. (Tabrani, Haythami). Ibrahim bin Abdur Rahman bin Auf ؓ narrates that during the battle of Siffin, where Ammar bin Yasir ؓ was martyred, he heard Ammar ؓ call out, "I am to meet Al Jabbar (Allah) and marry the damsels of Jannah! Today I shall meet my beloved friend Muhammad ﷺ and his companions as Rasulullah ﷺ informed me that the last provision of my worldly life shall be the curds of milk." (Tabrani, Haythami, Imam Ahmad).

The Martyrdom of Bara bin Malik ؓ in Persia

Anas ؓ narrates, "I came to my brother Bara bin Malik ؓ while he was singing something. I said, 'Allah has given you something (the Qur'an) that is better than the poems you sing.' He replied, 'Do you fear that I shall die on my bed? Never! I swear by Allah that He will never deprive me of martyrdom. I have already killed 100 disbelievers apart from those whom I killed with the help of others.'" (Baghawi in Isaba, Haythami, Hakim, Abu Nu'aym in Hilya). When the Muslims retreated during the battle of Aqaba in Persia, Bara bin Malik ؓ stood up and mounted his horse as another person guided it from behind. He said to his companions, "Terrible is the habit that you people have made the enemy accustomed by being repeatedly defeated!" He then led the attack against the enemy and Allah gave victory to the Muslims. On that day Bara ؓ was martyred. (Hakim).

The Thoughts of Omar ؓ When Uthman bin Madh'un ؓ Passed Away Without Being Martyred

Ubaidullah bin Abdullah bin Utba ؓ says that the news reached him that Omar bin Khattab ؓ said, "When Uthman bin Madh'un ؓ died naturally without being martyred, his status appeared in my eyes. I said to myself, 'Look at this man who was extremely absent from the world and then passed away without being martyred!' Uthman ؓ stayed in this position in my estimation until Rasulullah ﷺ passed away. I then said, 'Shame on me! Even the best of people pass away naturally.' When Abu

Bakr passed away naturally, I said, 'Shame on me! Even the best of us pass away naturally.' The status of Uthman bin Madh'un was then restored to the position it previously enjoyed in my sight." *(Ibn Sa'd, Abu Ubaid in Gharib, Muntakhab).*

The Bravery of Abu Bakr Siddiq

Ali asked, "O people! Who is the bravest person?" "You are, O Amirul Mu'minin," the people submitted. Ali then said, " I have defeated everyone who has confronted me, I want you people to tell me who is the bravest person." "Who then?" the people said, "Who is the bravest person?" Ali replied, "He was Abu Bakr. We had constructed a shed for Rasulullah during the battle of Badr and then asked who would remain with Rasulullah so that the disbelievers do not attack him. Abu Bakr volunteered for the task when all others were unable to do. By Allah! When a disbeliever drew close to us, Abu Bakr was there with his sword drawn near the head side of Rasulullah. He attacked anyone who dared to attack Rasulullah. He was certainly the bravest of people." *(Bazzar in Majma'uz Zawa'id).*

The Bravery of Omar bin Khattab

Ali bin Abi Talib says, "I know of no person who did not make Hijra secretly except for Omar bin Khattab. When he decided to make Hijra, he hung his sword from his neck, carried his bow on his shoulder and took a few arrows in his hand. He then proceeded to the Kabah where the leaders of the Quraish were sitting in their gatherings. He went around the Kabah 7 times and then performed 2 Rakahs salah by the Maqam Ibrahim. Thereafter, he approached each gathering separately, saying, "May your faces be disfigured! Whoever wants his mother to mourn him, his children to become orphans and his wife to become a widow should meet me behind this valley to try and stop my Hijra." None dared follow him out. *(Ibn Asakir in Muntakhab Kanzul Ummal).*

The Bravery of Ali bin Abi Talib : The poem of Ali After the Battle of Uhud

Jabir narrates that after the battle of Uhud, Ali came home to Fatima and said the following couplets which meant:
"O Fatima! Take this flawless sword from me. I am neither shaken (with fear} nor a worthless man, by my life! I have exerted myself to assist Muhammad and for the pleasure of my Rabb Who has complete knowledge about His bondsmen"

Rasulullah then said, "If you think that you fought well, so have Sahal bin Hunaif and Ibn Simma." Rasulullah also mentioned the name of a third Sahabi whose name a narrator called Mu'ala had forgotten. Jibra'el commented, "O Muhammad! I swear by your father that this is certainly an occasion of grief." Rasulullah said, "O Jibra'el! Ali is from me." To this, Jibra'el said, "And I am from the 2 of you." *(Bazzar, Haythami).* Abdullah bin Abbas narrates that after the battle of Uhud, Ali came home to Fatima and said, "O Fatima! Take this flawless sword from me." Rasulullah then said, "If you think that you fought well, so have Sahal bin Hunaif and Abu Dujana Simak bin Harasha." *(Tabrani, Haythami).*

Ali Kills Amr bin Abd Wadd

Ubaidullah bin Ka'b bin Malik says that during the battle of Khandaq, Amr bin Abd Wadd donned himself identifiable so that his presence should be noticed by also bringing a flag in his hand. As he stood with his horse, Ali asked, "O Amr! Did you make a pledge to the Quraish in Allah's name that if anyone called you to accept 2 matters, you would surely accept one of them?" "I certainly have," replied Amr. Ali continued, "I call you towards Allah, His Rasul and towards Islam." "I have no need for that!" Amr replied angrily. "Then," said Ali, "I challenge you to dismount and fight on the battlefield." Amr responded by saying, "Why, O nephew? By Allah, I would not like to kill you." Ali angered Amr by smiling broadly, "I swear by Allah that I like to kill you." Amr stormed forward. Both men dismounted their animal, circled the battlefield and started a furious duel. Ali killed Amr. *(lbn Jareer in Kanzul Ummal)*

The Couplets Ali Recited When he Killed Amr bin Abd Wadd

A narration of *Ibn Is'haq* states that Amr bin Abd Wadd was covered in armor when he stepped forward and called, "Who will fight me?" Ali bin Abi Talib stood up and said, "I shall accept the challenge, O Nabi of Allah." Rasulullah said, "That is Amr. Be seated." Amr then called out again saying, "Is there nobody to fight me?" He then started making fun of the Muslims by saying, "Where is that Jannah of yours about which you claim that anyone killed from you will enter? Can you not send even one man to fight me?" Ali again stood up and volunteered for the task. However, Rasulullah again asked him to seat. When Amr pronounced his challenge for the 3rd time and also recited some poetry (to ridicule the Muslims), Ali got up and said, "O Rasulullah! I shall do it." "But that is Amr," cautioned Rasulullah. Ali replied, "I am prepared to fight even though it is Amr." With the permission of Rasulullah, Ali walked towards Amr with the following couplets on his lips:
"Do not be hasty because coming your way is a respondent to your challenge who is not at all helpless. He comes with true resolve and foresight for it is truth that brings salvation to every successful person. I have great hope of setting on you. Women who cry over the bodies of the dead using such a powerful strike of the sword that will be spoken about in all battles"

"Who are you?" Amr asked. "I am Ali," came the reply. The son of Abd Manaf?" asked Amr. Ali replied, "I am Ali the son of Abu Talib." Amr said, "Dear nephew! Have you any uncles who are elder than you, rather send them to fight me for I do not like to spill your blood." Ali remarked, "However, I swear by Allah that I would love to spill your blood." Amr flew into. a rage at this. He dismounted from his animal and drew his sword which appeared to be a spark of fire. He then stormed angrily at Ali, who faced him with his leather shield. Amr struck the shield with such force that the sword cut right through it and injured Ali's head. Ali then struck an artery of Amr's shoulder so forcefully that Amr fell to the ground. Dust then began to fly and when Rasulullah heard "Allahu Akbar", the Sahabah knew that Ali had killed Amr. Ali then recited the following couplets:
"Will a band of horsemen launch a surprise attack against me? O my companions, retreat and leave them to me. Today my anger prevents me from fleeing from the battlefield as did the unmistaken strike of a sword to my head"
He concluded with a few verses that meant: *"By his foolish judgment, he worshipped stones while by my correct judgment, I worship the Rabb of Muhammad When I returned, I left him lying on the ground like a fallen trunk of a palm lying somewhere between sand dunes and higher ground I preserved my dignity by not taking his clothes but had I been the one to fall, he would have snatched away all my clothing. O coalition of forces! Never think that Allah will stop assisting His Deen and His Nabi"*

Ali ﷺ went to Rasulullah ﷺ, whose face was shinning. Omar bin Khattab ﷺ asked him, "Why did you not take his armor? No Arab has armor better than his." Ali ﷺ replied, "When I struck him with my sword, he used it to shield himself because of which his private parts became exposed, so I felt too shy for this cousin to take off his armor." *(Bayhaqi in Al Bidayah wan Nihayah).*

Ali ﷺ Kills Marhab During the Battle of Khaibar

Salama bin Akwa ﷺ narrates a lengthy Hadith in which he mentions of the Sahabah returning from fighting the Banu Fazara. They had hardly stayed in Madinah for 3 days when they had to march to Khaibar. Salama ﷺ says that his uncle Amir ﷺ also left with the army as he recited the following couplets which meant:

"By Allah! Were it not for You (O Allah) we would not have received guidance nor would we have given charity or performed salah. We can never be independent of Your grace. So do send tranquility to us and make our feet firm when we clash (with the enemy)"

Rasulullah ﷺ asked, "Who is saying that?" When the Sahabah informed Rasulullah ﷺ that it was Amir ﷺ, he said, "May your Rabb forgive you." Salama ﷺ says, "Whenever Rasulullah ﷺ said this to anyone, they were always martyred." Riding his camel, Omar ﷺ commented, "O Rasulullah ﷺ! You should have allowed us to benefit more from Amir." When the Sahabah reached Khaibar, one of the bravest Jewish warriors Marhab came out waving his sword and reciting the following:

"All of Khaibar knows that I am Marhab a well-armed and experienced hero (who thrives) When the leaping flames of war arrive"

Amir ﷺ Met Marhab's Challengea Duel as he Recited the Following:

"All of Khaibar knows that I am Amir a well-armed hero who throws himself in the thick of battle"

The 2 men exchanged blows with their swords. When Marhab's sword got stuck in Amir ﷺ's shield, he attacked Marhab from beneath but his sword accidentally severed an artery in his own arm. This caused death to Amir ﷺ. Salama ﷺ says that as he was passing by a group of Sahabah", he overheard them say, "All Amir's deeds have been wasted because he killed himself." Salama ﷺ then went weeping to Rasulullah ﷺ who asked him what the matter was. Salama ﷺ replied, "They are saying that all the deeds of Amir are wasted." "Who is saying this?" asked Rasulullah ﷺ. "A group of your Sahabah," came the reply. Rasulullah ﷺ then said, "They are wrong. In fact, his reward will be double." Rasulullah ﷺ then sent for Ali ﷺ, who was experiencing some pain in his eyes. "Tomorrow," declared Rasulullah ﷺ, "I shall give this flag to someone who loves Allah and His Rasul." Salama says that it was he who led Ali ﷺ to Rasulullah ﷺ. Rasulullah ﷺ then applied some of his saliva to Ali ﷺ's eyes, which cured them instantly. He then handed the flag over to Ali ﷺ. When the battle started, Marhab then again came forward to issue a challenge as he said:

"All of Khaibar knows that I am Marhab a well-armed and experienced hero (who thrives) When the leaping flames of war arrive"

Ali ﷺ stepped forward to accept his challenge as he said:

"I am the one whose mother calls a lion like the lion of a terrifying jungle. I give the enemy his full measure just like an open scale"

Ali ﷺ then swung his sword to deliver a blow that separated Marhab's head. This led to the conquest of Khaibar. *(Muslim, Bayhaqi in Al Bidayah wan Nihayah, Imam Ahmad).* Abu Rafi

who was the freed slave of Rasulullah ﷺ narrates that they marched with Ali ﷺ to Khaibar, where Rasulullah ﷺ sent him ahead with the flag. When Ali ﷺ approached one of the fortresses, the people inside came out to fight him. One of the Jews struck Ali ﷺ's shield, causing it to fall from his hand. Ali ﷺ then ripped off one of the doors of the fortress and used it as a shield. He kept fighting with it in his hand until Allah gave victory to the Muslims. He then threw it away. Abu Rafi says, "I saw myself with a group of 7 others of which I was the 8th. We tried to turn that door over, we did not succeed." Jabir ﷺ reports that during the battle of Khaibar, Ali ﷺ lifted up the door of a fortress, which the Muslims used to climb over the walls. This led to their victory. When the people tried to lift the door afterwards, 40 of them were unable to do so. *(Bayhaqi, Hakim)* Another narration states that 70 men had to exert themselves before they were able to put the door back on its place. *(Al Bidayah wan Nihayah).* Jabir bin Samura ﷺ states that during the battle of Khaibar, Ali ﷺ lifted up the door of a fortress, which the Muslims used to climb over the walls. This led to their victory. When the people tried to lift the door afterwards, it took 40 of them to do so. *(Ibn Abi Shaiba in Muntakhab Kanzul Ummal).*

The Bravery of Talha bin Ubaidullah ﷺ

Talha ﷺ reports that during the battle of Uhud, he recited the following couplets which meant:.

"We are the protectors of the Ghalib and Malik tribes fighting in defense of our blessed Rasulullah ﷺ Striking people with our swords on the battlefield for him as we strike the hump of a large-humped camel (when cleaning it after slaughtering)."

As the Muslims were leaving Uhud, Rasulullah ﷺ told the famous poet Hassan ﷺ to say something in praise of Talha ﷺ. He obliged by saying the following couplets which meant:

"On the day of the valley (the battle of Uhud), Talha assisted Muhammad ﷺ during a time of extreme hardships and difficulties with his bare hands he shielded (Rasulullah ﷺ) from the arrows and placed his hand beneath the swords (to shield Rasulullah ﷺ) because of which it was paralyzed. After Muhammad ﷺ, he led all the others he erected the mill of Islam until it could function by itself"

Abu Bakr ﷺ then recited the following which meant:

"Talha defended the Nabi of guidance as the cavalry chased him when they eventually caught up, he defended all of Deen he patiently bore the injuries when his comrades had left. At that time, people were either rightly guided or misguided O Talha bin Ubaidillah! Incumbent for you is the gardens of Jannah and marriage to its beautiful wide eyed damsels"

Omar ﷺ said the following couplet in praise of Talha ﷺ:

"He defended the Nabi of guidance with his drawn sword at a time when everyone had fled and dispersed"

Rasulullah ﷺ then commented, "What you have said is true, O Omar." *(Ibn Asakir in Muntakhab Kanzul Ummal, Ibn Hibban in Lisan)* The manner in which Talha ﷺ fought during the battle of Uhud has already been narrated in the chapter "Rasulullah ﷺ endures hardship and difficulty when giving Da'wah towards Allah" under the subheading "The hardship Rasulullah ﷺ bore during the battle of Uhud".

Zubair bin Awwam ﷺ Emerges with a Drawn Sword in Makkah Before the Hijra

Sa'eed bin Musaib ﷺ says that the first person to draw a sword for the pleasure of Allah ﷺ was Zubair bin Awwam. He was in Makkah one day when he heard that Rasulullah ﷺ was assassinated. He immediately left home with a drawn sword when he came face-to-face with Rasulullah ﷺ. Rasulullah ﷺ enquired, "What is the matter, Zubair?" "I heard that you had been assassinated," he replied. "What were you intending to do in that case?" Rasulullah ﷺ asked. "By Allah!" replied Zubair ﷺ, "I intended to undertake all the people of Makkah." Rasulullah ﷺ then prayed for him. It is with reference to this that Asadi said the following poem which meant:

"That was the first sword drawn for the pleasure of Allah. The sword of the beloved leader Zubair ﷺ in the defense of Deen, it happened by the grace of his courage. It occasionally happens that one who hears a lot musters many forms of courage" (Ibn Asakir)

Urwa ﷺ narrates that after accepting Islam, Zubair bin Awwam ﷺ once heard a whisper from Saitan stating that Rasulullah ﷺ had been captured. Although he was only a boy of 12 years, he drew his sword and searched the gullies of Makkah. At that time, Rasulullah ﷺ was in the upper area of Makkah when Zubair ﷺ met him with sword in hand. Rasulullah ﷺ enquired, "What is the matter?" "I heard that you had been captured," he replied. "What were you intending to do in that case?" Rasulullah ﷺ asked. Zubair ﷺ replied, "I had intended to use this sword on whoever it was who captured you." Rasulullah ﷺ then prayed for Zubair ﷺ and for his sword and told him that he could leave. His was the first sword drawn in the Path of Allah. *(Ibn Asakir, Abu Nu'aym in Hilya, Mutnkhab Kanzul Ummal, Isaba, Dala'il).*

Zubair ﷺ Kills Talha Abdari During the Battle of Uhud

Ibn Is'haq narrates that Talha bin Abu Talha Abdari bore the flag of the disbelievers during the battle of Uhud. When he called for someone to challenge him to a duel, the Muslims hesitated. The only person to accept the challenge was Zubair bin Awwam ﷺ. Zubair ﷺ jumped on to Talha's own camel, threw him off and killed him with his own sword. In praise of him, Rasulullah ﷺ said, "Every Nabi has a devoted friend in Jannah and mine shall be Zubair." Rasulullah ﷺ also said, "Had Zubair not accepted the challenge, I would have done so myself after seeing the hesitance of the others." *(Yunus in Al Bidayah wan Nihayah)*

Zubair ﷺ Kills Naufal Makhzumi and Another Person

Ibn Is'haq narrates that during the battle of Khandaq, Naufal bin Abdullah bin Mughiera Makhzumi stepped ahead of the ranks of the disbelievers and issued a challenge for someone to fight him. Zubair bin Awwam ﷺ responded and struck Naufal so forcefully with his sword that Naufal's body was split into 2 and Zubair ﷺ's sword was dented. Zubair ﷺ then returned reciting the following couplets which meant:

"I am man who defends himself and also defends The chosen and unlettered Nabi" (Yunus in Al Bidayah wan Nihayah).

Asma bint Abu Bakr ﷺ narrates that a fully-armed man from the disbelievers advanced from the ranks of the enemy and climbed on top of a high place. He then announced, "Who will come out for a challenge?" Rasulullah ﷺ asked one of the Sahabah." "Will you take him on?" "If it pleases you, O Rasulullah ﷺ," the man replied. When Zubair ﷺ started peering to look, Rasulullah ﷺ noticed him and said, "Stand up, O son of Safiya!" Zubair ﷺ then walked up to the man until he stood level to him. The 2 men started exchanging blows with their swords, after which one of them grabbed the other in a bear hug. They both then started rolling down. Rasulullah ﷺ commented, "Whichever of them first falls into the ditch will be killed." Rasulullah ﷺ and the Sahabah started making Du'a. It was the Kafir who landed first in the ditch. As soon as this happened,

Zubair ﷺ fell on to the Kafir's chest and killed him. *(Ibn Jareer in Kanzul Ummal)*

Zubair ﷺ Fights During the Battles of Khandaq and Yarmuk

Abdullah bin Zubair ﷺ says, "During the battle of Khandaq, myself and Omar bin Abu Salama were stationed with the women and children in a fortress because we were both very young. He would bend over for me to get on to his back so that I could watch the battle. I watched my father Zubair ﷺ sometimes fighting here, sometimes there and tackling anyone who confronted him. When he came to us in the fortress that evening, I said to him, 'Dear father, I watched you today and saw what you were doing.' 'Did you really see me?' he asked. 'I sure did,' I replied. He then said, 'May my parents be sacrificed for you." *(Bayhaqi in Al Bidayah wan Nihayah).* Urwa ﷺ says that during the battle of Yarmuk, the Sahabah said to Zubair ﷺ, "Will you not lead an attack so that we may join you?" Zubair ﷺ said to them, "If I lead the attack, you will fail in your word to fight with me." "We will not," they assured him. Zubair ﷺ then attacked the enemy so fiercely that he penetrated past their ranks without the support of anyone else. However, as he returned, the enemy grabbed the reins of his horse and inflicted 2 wounds on his shoulder on either side which he sustained during the battle of Badr. Urwa ﷺ says that the wounds were so deep that as a child he used to playfully put his finger into those wounds. On that day Zubair was with his son Abdullah who was only 10 years of age. Zubair ﷺ put Abdullah ﷺ on a horse and left him in the care of one of the men. *(Bukhari).* When the Sahabah approached Zubair ﷺ with the same request a second time, he complied and did as he had done the first time. *(Al Bidayah wan Nihayah).*

Sa'd ﷺ is the First Person to Fire an Arrow in the Path of Allah

Zuhri reports that Rasulullah ﷺ once sent an expedition to a place called Rabigh that was situated on one end of Hijaz. Sa'd bin Abi Waqqas ﷺ was also part of this expedition. When the disbelievers attacked the Muslims, Sa'd ﷺ defended them with his arrows and was the first person to fire an arrow in the Path of Allah. This was the first battle fought for Islam. Concerning his archery, Sa'd bin Abi Waqqas ﷺ recited the following couplets:

"Behold! Has the news reached Rasulullah ﷺ yet that I have defended my companions with my arrowheads? Using them, I made the enemy flee over every type of ground, hard and soft. No archer fighting the enemy can be counted who has fired an arrow before me, O Rasulullah ﷺ"
(Ibn Asakir in Kanzul Ummal)

Sa'd bin Abi Waqqas ﷺ Kills 3 People with a Single Arrow During the Battle of Uhud

Ibn Shihab narrates that Sa'd bin Abi Waqqas ﷺ killed 3 people with a single arrow during the battle of Uhud. When the disbelievers first shot the arrow at the Muslims, Sa'd ﷺ shot it back at them killing one of them. When the disbelievers again fired the same arrow back, Sa'd ﷺ shot it back at them a 2nd time, killing another man. When the arrow came back, Sa'd ﷺ fired it back at them a 3rd time, taking the life of yet another disbeliever. Everyone was astonished by what Sa'd ﷺ had done. He said to them, "The arrow was handed to me by none other than Nabi ﷺ." Rasulullah ﷺ said to him, "May my parents be sacrificed for you. *(Ibn Asakir in Kanzul Ummal).* Abdullah bin Mas'ood ﷺ says that during the battle of Badr, Sa'd bin Abi Waqqas ﷺ fought with Rasulullah ﷺ in the roles of both cavalry and infantry. Although Sa'd ﷺ was part of the infantry, he fought as efficiently as a cavalryman. *(Bazzar, Haythami).*

The Bravery of Hamza bin Abdil Muttalib ﷺ During the Battle of Badr and the Statement of Umaiah bin Khalaf in this Regard

Harith Taymi narrates that during the battle of Badr, Hamza bin Abdil Muttalib ﷺ distinguished himself by wearing ostrich feathers. One disbeliever asked, "Who is the man who marks himself with ostrich feathers?" "He is Hamza bin Abdil Muttalib," came the reply. The man said, "It was he who carried out all those major offensives against us." *(Tabrani, Haythami).* Abdur Rahman ﷺ says that Umaiah bin Khalaf once asked him, "O Abdul Ila! Who was the man who marked his chest with ostrich feathers during the battle of Badr?" "He was the uncle of Rasulullah ﷺ. He was Hamza bin Abdil Muttalib," replied Abdur Rahman ﷺ. Umaiah commented, "It was he who carried out all those major offensives against us." *(Bazzar, Haythami).*

Rasulullah ﷺ weeps Bitterly as he sees the Dead Body of Hamza ﷺ

Jabir bin Abdullah ﷺ narrates that as they were returning from the battlefield of Uhud, Rasulullah ﷺ could not find Hamza. Someone said, "I saw him by that tree as he was saying, 'I am the lion of Allah and the lion of His Rasul ﷺ. O Allah! I pardon myself from what those people (Abu Sufian and the others) have done and I seek pardon from what these people (the Muslims) have done by causing their own defeat." Rasulullah ﷺ went in that direction and started crying when he caught sight of Hamza ﷺ's forehead. However, when Rasulullah ﷺ saw how the body of Hamza ﷺ was mutilated, he wept uncontrollably. Rasulullah ﷺ then asked, "Is there no burial shroud?" One of the Ansar stood up and threw a cloth over the body. Thereafter, Rasulullah ﷺ said, "In the sight of Allah, Hamza shall be the leader of all martyrs on the Day of Judgment." *(Hakim).*

The Martyrdom and Mutilation of Hamza ﷺ

Ja'far bin Amr bin Umaiah Dhamri says that it was during the Khilafa of Mu'awiya ﷺ when he and Abdullah bin Adi bin Khiyar went out. He then goes on to report a lengthy narration in which he states that when the 2 of them sat before Wahshi ﷺ, they asked, "We have come here so that you may relate to us how you managed to martyr Hamza ﷺ." He responded by saying, "I shall relate the incident to you as I had related it to Rasulullah ﷺ when he asked me about it. I had been a slave of Jubair bin Mut'im, whose uncle Tu'ayma bin Adi was killed in the battle of Badr. When the Quraish marched to Uhud, Jubair said to me, 'You will be a free man if you manage to kill Hamza the uncle of Rasulullah ﷺ to compensate for the death of my uncle.' I was an Abyssinian man who could throw the spear with the accuracy of the Abyssinians. I seldom ever missed a target. I therefore marched with the others and when we engaged the Muslims in battle, I set out to locate Hamza ﷺ. I searched for him until I eventually saw him at one end of the army. With his muscular body covered in dust, he looked like a brown camel, smashing people with his sword so fiercely that nothing could stand before him. By Allah! I prepared well for him and hid myself behind a tree or a rock until he drew close to me. However, Siba bin Abdul Uzza beat me to him. When Hamza ﷺ saw Siba, he called to him, "Come to me, O son of a circumcised woman!" Hamza ﷺ then struck Siba so forcefully that his head fell off as if by mistake. I then shook my spear until I was satisfied that it would hit the target and then let it fly. The spear struck him beneath the navel and penetrated his body until it emerged from between his legs. He started to come to me, but fell unconscious. I then left him like that until he passed away. I later returned, took my spear and returned to the camp. I then sat there because I had no need for anything else. I had killed Hamza ﷺ only to secure my

freedom. I then returned to Makkah and was set free. I remained there until Rasulullah ﷺ conquered Makkah, after which I escaped to Ta'if. I stayed there until the time when a delegation from Ta'if went to Rasulullah ﷺ to accept Islam. All avenues were then shut for me and I thought, 'Should I go to Sham, to Yemen or someplace else?' By Allah! I was still absorbed in these thoughts, when someone said to me, 'Shame on you! Do you still not know that Muhammad never kills anyone who enters Islam and recites the Shahada of truth.' I then set out until I reached Rasulullah ﷺ in Madinah. Rasulullah ﷺ had no idea of my arrival and nothing warned him of my presence besides me standing over his head reciting the Shahada of truth. When he saw me, Rasulullah ﷺ asked, 'Are you Wahshi?' 'Yes, O Rasulullah ﷺ,' I replied. He then said to me, 'Sit down and tell me how you managed to kill Hamza ﷺ.' I then related the incident to Rasulullah ﷺ as I have related it to you. Once I had completed the narration, Rasulullah ﷺ said to me, 'Hide your face from me so that I do not have to see you. Do not let me see you because it reminds me of my uncle's death.' I would then avoid the places where Rasulullah ﷺ was so that he would not have to look at me. I continued doing this until Allah took the life of Rasulullah ﷺ.

When the Muslims marched to fight the great "liar Musailama from Yamamah, I marched with them. I took along with me the same spear I had used to martyr Hamza ﷺ. The battle then began. Although I never knew him from before, I recognized Musailama standing with sword in hand. As I prepared to kill him, someone from the Ansar was also preparing to kill him from another direction. I then shook my spear until I was satisfied that it would hit the target and let it fly. As the spear struck him, the Ansari attacked him and struck him with his sword. Only your Rabb knows which of us had killed him. If I had killed him, then I had martyred the best of people after Rasulullah ﷺ (Hamza ﷺ), I had killed the worst of people (Musailama)." *(Ibn Is'haq in Al Bidayah wan Nihayah). Bukhari* narrated by Ja'far bin Amr adds that when the armies formed their rows for the battle, Siba stepped forward and said, "Is there anyone to fight me?" Hamza bin Abdil Muttalib ﷺ accepted the challenge and said, "O Siba! O son of Ummu Anmar the circumcised woman! Do you oppose Allah and His Rasul ﷺ?" He attacked Siba and finished him so clearly as if it was a past day.

Abbas ﷺ snatches Handhala ﷺ from the Hands of the Disbelievers

Jabir ﷺ narrates that during the battle of Ta'if, Rasulullah ﷺ sent Handhala bin Rabi ﷺ to the people of Ta'if. However, when Handhala ﷺ had spoken to them, they captured him and were taking him up to their fortress when Rasulullah ﷺ called out, "Who will take care of them and rescue Handhala ﷺ? Such a person will receive the reward of this entire expedition." It was only Abbas ﷺ who rose to the occasion. He intercepted the enemy as they were taking Handhala ﷺ into the fortress. Abbas ﷺ was a powerful man and he wrestled Handhala from them until he was able to snatch him away from their hands. Rasulullah ﷺ prayed for him all the time and he brought Handhala ﷺ to Rasulullah ﷺ despite the rocks that the people in the fortress rained down on him. *(Ibn Asakir in Kanzul Ummal).*

The Bravery of Mu'adh bin Amr bin Jamooh ﷺ and Mu'adh bin Afra ﷺ on How They Killed Abu Jahal During the Battle of Badr

Abdur Rahman bin Auf ﷺ says, "As I stood in line during the battle of Badr, I looked to my right and left and saw 2 boys from the Ansar who were very young in age. I was hoping that I had rather been between 2 stronger men, when one of them pushed me saying, 'Dear uncle! Do you know who Abu Jahal is?'

'Certainly,' I replied, 'What have you to do with him?' He replied, 'I have been told that he abuses Rasulullah ﷺ. I swear by the Being Who controls my life that if I see him, I shall not leave him until the first of us dies.' I was very impressed with this. The other boy pushed me and we had a similar conversation. No sooner did I spot Abu Jahal doing his rounds amongst his people, when I said to the boys, 'Look over there! There is the man you were asking me about.' The 2 rushed towards him with their swords and struck him until they had killed him. They went to Rasulullah ﷺ and reported it to him. Rasulullah ﷺ asked which of them killed Abu Jahal, they both claimed to have done so. 'Have you wiped your swords yet?' Rasulullah ﷺ asked. 'No,' they replied. Rasulullah ﷺ examined their swords and said, 'You have both killed him.' Rasulullah ﷺ decided to award Abu Jahal's possessions to Mu'adh bin Amr bin Jamooh ﷺ. The other youngster was Mu'adh bin Afra ﷺ. *(Bukhari, Muslim, Hakim, Bayhaqi)*. Another narration from *Bukhari* quotes that Abdur Rahman bin Auf ﷺ said, "I was standing in the rows during the battle of Badr and happened to look to my right and my left when I noticed 2 youngsters on either side. I began to feel unsafe in my position when one of them addressed me in a manner that the other should be unaware of. He requested, 'Dear uncle! Do show me who Abu Jahal is?' 'Dear nephew,' I asked, 'What will you do about him?' He responded by saying, 'I have taken a pledge with Allah that as soon as I see him, I will either kill him or I shall be killed in the attempt.' Thereafter, the second youngster also had a similar conversation with me that the first was unaware of. Impressed by their courage, I then did not want to be between any other men other than them. When I pointed Abu Jahal out to them, they attacked him like 2 falcons and struck him with their swords. They were the 2 sons of Afra: Mu'adh and Mu'awadh. Mu'adh bin Amr bin Jamooh ﷺ was most probably with them. Abdullah bin Abbas ﷺ and Abdullah bin Abu Bakr ﷺ both narrate from Mu'adhbin Arm bin Jamooh ﷺ of the Banu Salma tribe that he said, "During the battle of Badr, Abu Jahal seemed to be in a dense forest because he was surrounded by soldiers on all sides. The people therefore said that it was impossible for anyone to reach him. No sooner had I heard this, then I resolved to get to him and went in his direction. I attacked him as soon as I got the opportunity and struck him with my sword causing his foot to fly off from halfway down his calf. By Allah! The only comparison I can draw of his foot flying off is like a date stone flies off a grindstone when it is thrown against it. Abu jahal's son Ikrama then struck me on the shoulder. The blow severed my arm and it hung by its skin to my side. The battle occupied me from feeling the pain and I fought most of the day with the arm trailing behind me. However, when it became too cumbersome, I placed my foot on the hanging arm and pulled hard until the skin gave way and I could cast the arm aside. *(Ibn Is'haq in Al Bidayah wan Nihayah)*.

The Bravery of Abu Dujana Simak bin Harasha ﷺ from the Ansar

Abu Dujana ﷺ Takes a Sword From Rasulullah ﷺ and Fulfils Its Rights During the Battle of Uhud

Anas ﷺ reports that Rasulullah ﷺ took hold of a sword during the battle of Uhud and announced, "Who will take this sword from me?" When several Sahabah took the sword to have a look at it, Rasulullah ﷺ said, "I am not giving it for looking. Who will take this sword and fulfill it rights." This made everyone hesitate and it was Abu Dujana Simak bin Harasha ﷺ who said, "I shall take it and fulfill its rights." He then used it to efficiently kill the disbelievers. *(Ahmad, Muslims in Al Bidayah wan Nihayah, Ibn Sa'd)*. Zubair bin Awwam ﷺ narrates that

Rasulullah ﷺ took hold of a sword during the battle of Uhud and announced, "Who will take this sword and fulfill its rights." It was Abu Dujana Simak bin Harasha ﷺ who said, "O Rasulullah ﷺ! I shall take it and fulfill its rights, but what are its rights?" Rasulullah ﷺ then handed the sword over to him and he left. Zubair ﷺ says that he followed Abu Dujana ﷺ and saw that he destroyed everything he used the sword on. He eventually came across some disbelieving women at the foot of the mountain. Amongst them was Hind who was reciting the following couplets to incite the disbelievers:

"We are the daughters of prominent people who walk on exquisite cushions. We wear musk on our heads and are ready to embrace Islam when you arrive. We shall however protect from you if you flee the battlefield separate in a manner after which there shall be no reconciliation"

When Abu Dujana ﷺ intended to attack her because she was an active participant in the battle, she started calling for help in the battlefield. However, no one came to her assistance. He then left her. Zubair ﷺ said to him, "I have been extremely impressed by everything I have seen you do besides the fact that you did not kill that woman." Abu Dujana said, "When no one responded to her call for help, I did not want the sword of Rasulullah ﷺ to strike a helpless woman." *(Bazzar, Haythami)*. Zubair ﷺ narrates, "During the battle of Uhud, Rasulullah ﷺ took hold of a sword and announced, 'Who will take this sword with its rights.' I said, 'I shall, O Rasulullah ﷺ!' Rasulullah ﷺ ignored me and again announced, 'Who will take this sword with its rights.' Abu Dujana Simak bin Harasha ﷺ then responded by saying, 'I shall take it with its rights, O Rasulullah ﷺ! What are its rights?' Rasulullah ﷺ replied, 'Its rights are that you do not use it to kill any Muslim and do not flee the battlefield with it.' Rasulullah ﷺ then handed the sword over to him. Whenever he intended to fight, he would make himself noticeable by wearing a red handkerchief. I said to myself, 'I shall watch him closely today to see what he does.' I saw that he destroyed everything he used the sword on..." The rest of the Hadith is similar to the one quoted above. *(Hakim)*. Zubair bin Awwam ﷺ is reported to have said, "I was disappointed when I asked Rasulullah ﷺ for the sword and he refused to give it to me, giving it to Abu Dujana ﷺ instead. I said to myself, 'I am the son of his aunt Safiya and from the Quraish. However, when I stood up and asked for the sword before Abu Dujana ﷺ, Rasulullah ﷺ gave it to him instead of myself! By Allah! I shall certainly watch him to see how he performs.' I then started following him. When he took out his red handkerchief and tied it around his head, the Ansar said, 'Abu Dujana ﷺ has taken out his handkerchief of death.' This they always said whenever he wore his handkerchief. He then left with the following couplets on his lips which meant:

'It was with me that my good friend took an undertaking as we stood at the foot of a mountain among the date palms. (The undertaking was) That throughout my life I should never stand in the rear end of the battlefield. I shall now be using the sword of Allah and His Rasul (to fight the enemy)'"

Zubair ﷺ continues to narrate, "Abu Dujana ﷺ killed every enemy soldier who confronted him. One of the disbelievers was such that after searching for the wounded Muslims, he did not leave any of them alive. When this disbeliever drew close to Abu Dujana ﷺ I prayed to Allah to let them confront each other. The 2 men then clashed and exchanged blows with their swords. When the disbeliever struck at Abu Dujana ﷺ with his sword, Abu Dujana ﷺ defended himself with his shield, which trapped the sword. Abu Dujana then killed the disbeliever with a single blow. I also saw him raise the sword over the head of Hind bint

Utba and then turning the sword away from her. I said, 'Allah and His Rasul ﷺ know best who most deserves to be killed by this sword.'" (Ibn Hisham in Al Bidayah wan Nihayah). Musa bin Uqba narrates that when Rasulullah ﷺ offered the sword to the Sahabah, Omar ؓ first asked for it. When Rasulullah ﷺ ignored him, Zubair bin Awwam ؓ asked for it. Rasulullah ﷺ ignored him as well. The 2 felt very disappointed about it. When Rasulullah ﷺ offered it for the 3rd time, Abu Dujana ؓ asked to have it. Rasulullah ﷺ gave it to him and he truly fulfilled the rights of that sword. Ka'b bin Malik ؓ says, "I was also part of that battle with the Muslims. However, what I saw the disbelievers injuring the bodies of the Muslims made me stand still in my tracks. When I walked ahead, I saw a fully-armed disbeliever passing by the Muslims saying, 'Herd together to be slaughtered as goats herd together!' I then noticed that a Muslim wearing a helmet was waiting for the approach of this disbeliever. I went ahead until I stood behind him. I then visually assessed the strength of the Muslim and the disbeliever, arriving at the conclusion that the disbeliever was better armed and better prepared for battle. I then waited until the 2 men clashed. The Muslim struck the disbeliever so powerfully that after the sword struck the artery of his shoulder, it penetrated through his body and emerged from his back. His body was therefore cut into 2. The Muslim then removed his helmet and said, 'How was that, Ka'b? I am Abu Dujana.'" (Al Bidayah wan Nihayah).

The Bravery of Qatadah bin Nu'man ؓ

Qatadah bin Nu'man ؓ Uses His Face to Shield Rasulullah ﷺ From Arrows During the Battle of Uhud

Qatadah bin Nu'man ؓ narrates, "Rasulullah ﷺ was given a bow as a gift, which he gave to me during the battle of Uhud. I used it to fire arrows in front of Rasulullah ﷺ until the string broke. I then remained standing where I was, shielding the face of Rasulullah ﷺ with my own. Whenever an arrow headed for the face of Rasulullah ﷺ, I turned my head to protect the face of Rasulullah ﷺ for I had no bow to use. The last of the arrows to come was one that caused my eyeball to fall into my hand. I rushed to Rasulullah ﷺ with the eyeball in my hand and when he saw me, tears rolled from his eyes. He then said, 'O Allah! Qatadah shielded Your Nabi ﷺ with his face so make this injured eye the better of his 2 eyes and the one with sharper vision. After Rasulullah ﷺ placed the eyeball back into its place, the eye did turn out to be the better one and the one with sharper vision. (Tabrani, Haythami). Qatadah ؓ narrates, "During the battle of Uhud, I was standing in front of Rasulullah ﷺ, shielding Rasulullah ﷺ's face with my own. Also during the battle of Uhud, Abu Dujana Simak bin Harasha was behind Rasulullah ﷺ, shielding Rasulullah ﷺ's back with his back until his back was full of arrows." (Tabrani, Haythami).

The Bravery of Salama bin Akwa ؓ During the Fight at Dhu Qarad

Salama bin Akwa ؓ narrates, "It was during the period when the peace treaty of Hudaibiya was being followed and after that we returned to Madinah with Rasulullah ﷺ. Rasulullah ﷺ's helper Rabah ؓ and I then took the camels of Rasulullah ﷺ to graze and water and I also took the horse of Talha bin Ubaidullah ؓ to water and graze with the camels. It was during the last part of night that Abdur Rahman bin Uyayna (with a band of disbelievers) launched an attack and killed the shepherd tending to Rasulullah ﷺ's camels. He and those with him then started taking the camels away when I said to Rabah ؓ, 'Take this horse back to Talha ؓ and inform Rasulullah ﷺ that his camels are being stolen.' I then stood on the top a hill facing towards Madinah and thrice shouted, 'Ya Sabaha!' This was a call for help when under attack from an enemy. I then chased after them with my sword and arrows. I started shooting arrows at them and injuring their animals every time I came by an outcrop of trees. Whenever any rider turned on me, I sat by the roots of a tree and shot an arrow. In this manner, I managed to injure the horse of every rider that approached me. As I fired the arrows, I was chanting the following couplet which meant:

'I am the son of Akwa and today is the day of (destroying) the wretches'

When I on foot caught up with one of them as he rode, I let an arrow fly. As the arrow struck his leg, I was so close that I could almost strike his shoulder when 1 said:

'Take that! For 1 am the son of Akwa and today is the day of (destroying) the wretches'

Whenever I found some trees, I would assault them with my arrows and when a valley narrowed, I would climb to the top and throw stones at them. This is how I kept pursuing them and reciting my couplets until I had recaptured and put behind me every camel of Rasulullah ﷺ. I then continued shooting arrows at them until, in all effort to lighten themselves, they had thrown off more than 30 spears and more than 30 shawls. Whenever they threw anything down, I placed a stone on it and placed it on the road that Rasulullah ﷺ would be taking. By mid-morning, Uyayna bin Badr Fazari arrived to reinforce them at a narrow valley. I then climbed to the top of the hill and was high above them. Uyayna asked them, 'Who is this person I see chasing you?' They replied, 'He has given us a difficult time. He has been chasing us from daybreak until now and had taken everything we had and left it behind him.' Uyayna said, 'If he had known that a search party was coming up after him, he would certainly have left you. A few of you will have to get him.' Then 4 of them stood up and climbed the hill. As soon as they came within earshot, I called out, 'Do you know who I am?' 'Who are you?' they enquired. I responded by saying, 'I am the son of Akwa. I swear by the Being Who has honored Muhammad ﷺ that none of you can ever catch me if you chase me whereas you would never escape me if I chase you.' One of them commented, '1 think so too.' I kept my position there until I saw Rasulullah ﷺ's riders weaving between the trees. In the lead was Akhram Asadi ؓ and close on his heels was Abu Qatada who was Rasulullah ﷺ's special rider. Behind him was Miqdad bin Aswad Kindi ؓ. The disbelievers took flight and I descended from the hill. I grabbed hold of the reins of Akhram ؓ's horse and said, 'Beware of them for I fear that they would cut you to pieces. Wait until Rasulullah ﷺ and his companions arrive.' He said, 'O Salama! If you believe in Allah and the Last Day and know that Jannah and Jahannam are true, you would not stand between me and martyrdom.' I then let go his horse's reins and he caught up with Abdur Rahman bin Uyayna. Abdur Rahman turned to fight him and the 2 exchanged blows with their spears. As Akhram ؓ hamstrung Abdur Rahman's horse, Abdur Rahman stabbed Akhram ؓ and martyred him. Abdur Rahman then got on to Akhram ؓ's horse just as Abu Qatadah ؓ confronted him. When the 2 started their duel using spears, Abdur Rahman hamstrung Abu Qatadah's horse and Abu Qatadah ؓ killed Abdur Rahman. Abu Qatadah ؓ then took Akhram's horse." Salama bin Akwa ؓ continues, "I then started running after the bandits until we had gone so far that I could not see the dust of the Sahabah. Just before sunset, they entered a valley where there was a watering place called Dhu Qarad. They had intended to drink some water there but when they saw me in hot pursuit, they abandoned the idea and climbed up the ridge of Dhu Bir. As the sun set, I caught up with one of them and while shooting an arrow at him, I said:

'Take that! For I am the son of Akwa and today is the day of (destroying) the wretches'

When the arrow struck him, he moaned, 'If only the mother of Akwa had lost him early in the morning!' 'Is that so, O enemy of himself?'. I shouted, He was the same person whom I had shot early that morning. I then fired another arrow at him. Both arrows were now stuck to him. They left behind 2 horses and I brought them down to Rasulullah ﷺ who was at the watering place from which I had chased the bandits off, namely Dhu Qarad. Rasulullah ﷺ was there with 500 men. Bilal ؓ had slaughtered one of the camels I had left behind and was busy roasting for Rasulullah ﷺ parts of its liver and hump. I said, 'O Rasulullah ﷺ! Allow me to choose 100 of your companions so that I may capture those disbeliever at night. I shall not leave any of them to tell the tale. 'Would you really be able to do so, Salama?' asked Rasulullah ﷺ. 'Certainly, I swear by the Being Who had honored you!' Rasulullah ﷺ then smiled so broadly that I could see his molar teeth in the light of the fire. He then said, 'By now they would already be entertained in Banu Ghitfan territory.' A man from the Banu Ghitfan later informed us that some people from the Ghitfan tribe passed by him and he slaughtered a camel for them. However, they were still busy skinning the animal when they saw a dust trail. They then left the camel as it were and fled for their lives. The next morning, Rasulullah ﷺ announced, 'Our best cavalryman is Abu Qatadah and our best infantryman is Salama.' Rasulullah ﷺ then gave me the share of a cavalryman as well as the share of an infantryman. As we returned to Madinah, Rasulullah ﷺ seated me behind him on his camel Adhba. Eventually all that was left of the journey equaled the distance traveled between sunrise and mid-morning. Amongst us was a person from the Ansari who was not defeated in a road race. He started to announce, 'Is there anyone to race? Will anyone race me to Madinah?" He repeated himself several times as I was seated behind Rasulullah ﷺ. I said to him, 'Don't you respect any honorable person or fear any respectable person?' The Ansari said, 'I care for none after Rasulullah ﷺ.' Thereupon, I said, 'O Rasulullah ﷺ! May my parents be sacrificed for you! Permit me to race him.' Rasulullah ﷺ replied, 'If you wish.' I said to the man, 'I am on my way.' He jumped off his camel. I doubled up my legs and also jumped from the camel. We then started the race. I initially held myself back for one or two hills so that he could run ahead and then I ran faster until I caught up with him and hit my hands between his shoulders. I said something like, 'By Allah! I have beaten you.' He laughed and said, 'I think so too.' We then reached Madinah." A narration of Muslim adds that Salama ؓ said, "I then beat him to Madinah. We had not even stayed 3 days in Madinah when we marched for Khaibar." *(Ahmad in Al Bidayah wan Nihayah)*

The Bravery of Abu Hadrad Aslami ؓ

Abu Hadrad ؓ says, "I married a woman from my tribe and agreed to give her a dowry of 200 Dirhams. I then approached Rasulullah ﷺ for some financial assistance for my marriage. 'How much did you agree to pay her as dowry?' asked Rasulullah ﷺ. '200 Dirhams,' I replied. 'SubhanAllah!' exclaimed Rasulullah ﷺ thinking it to be too much for someone like myself, 'Had you married any lady from the town, you would not have had to pay so much, they demand higher because she is from your tribe. I swear by Allah that I have nothing to assist you with.' I then stayed like that for a few days when a man from the Jusham bin Mu'awiya tribe arrived with a large group from the Jusham tribe and others and camped at a place called Ghaba close to Madinah.

His name was either Rifa'ah bin Qais or Qais bin Rifa'ah and he was a prominent person amongst the Jusham tribe. His intention was to rally the Qais tribe to fight against Rasulullah ﷺ. Rasulullah ﷺ then summoned me and 2 other Muslims and instructed us saying, 'Go to this man and gather any information you can.' Rasulullah ﷺ then gave us a weak and old camel. When even one of us mounted her, she was unable to stand because of her weakness. It was only with the assistance of several men supporting her from behind that she was able to stand. Rasulullah ﷺ said, 'You will reach there on her.'

With the blessing of Rasulullah ﷺ's Du'a, Allah gave her the strength and we rode her. We left with our weapons which included arrows and swords and reached their camp as the sun was setting. As I hid in a corner, I instructed my 2 companions to hide in another corner of the camp. I said to them, 'When you hear me shout 'Allahu Akbar' as I attack them, you 2 should also shout 'Allahu Akbar' and attack with me.' By Allah! We sat waiting for an opportunity to attack when they became unmindful. The night covered us until there was only darkness. There was a shepherd of theirs who had gone out to graze the flocks and had not yet returned. They feared for his life and their leader Rifa'ah bin Qais stood up and hung his sword around his neck. He said, 'By Allah! I shall find out for sure what has happened to our shepherd. Some harm must have come to him.' A group of his men said, 'Do not go. We shall do it for you.' However, he instructed, 'No! I shall go alone.' 'Let us accompany you,' they appealed. 'No!' he insisted, 'None of you should follow me.' He then left and passed by me. I had him perfectly in my sights, I fired an arrow that penetrated his heart. By Allah! He made no sound. I jumped at him and severed his head. I attacked one end of the camp, calling '*Allahu Akbar!*' My 2 companions also sprung to the attack shouting '*Allahu Akbar!*' Whoever was there only thought of getting to safety as they called out, 'Save yourselves! Save yourselves!' They made a dash for it, taking with them only their wives and children and the lightest of their possessions. We managed to take a great number of camels and goats, which we brought to Rasulullah ﷺ. I took Rifa'ah's head along with me. Rasulullah ﷺ gave me 13 camels from the booty, which I could use for the dowry and to get my wife home." *(Ibn Is'haq in Al Bidayah wan Nihayah, Imam Ahmad, Isabah)*

Khalid bin Walid ؓ Breaks 9 Swords During the Battle of Mu'ta

Khalid bin Walid ؓ says, "9 swords broke in my hand during the battle of Mu'ta. It was only a Yemeni sword that remained in my hand." *(Bukhari in Isti'ab, Hakim, Ibn Sa'd).*

Khalid ؓ Kills Hurmuz

Aws bin Haritha bin Lam ؓ narrates, "There was none who hated the Muslim Arabs more than Hurmuz. After we had finished fighting Musailama and his people, we marched towards Basra. We clashed with Hurmuz with an extremely large army at a place called Kadhima. Khalid ؓ stepped forward and challenged Hurmuz to a duel. Hurmuz accepted the challenge and Khalid ؓ killed him. When Khalid ؓ wrote to Abu Bakr ؓ about this, Abu Bakr ؓ awarded Hurmuz's belongings to Khalid bin Walid ؓ. Hurmuz's crown was valued at 100,000 Dirhams because the Persians always gave their leaders crowns valued at 100,000 Dirhams." *(Hakim)*

Khalid bin Walid ؓ Weeps as he Passes Away on His Bed

Abu Zinad narrates that when Khalid bin Walid ؓ was about to pass away, he started weeping. He named the various battles he had participated and said, "There is not an area on my body equal to a hand's span that does not have wound inflicted on it either by a sword, a spear or an arrow. Here I am dying a natural death on my bed like a camel dies. May the eyes of cowards never have any sleep." *(Waqidi in Al Bidayah wan Nihayah)*

The Bravery of Bara bin Malik ﷺ

Anas ﷺ reports that during the battle of Yamamah, Khalid bin Walid ﷺ said to Bara bin Malik ﷺ, "Stand up, O Bara!" When Bara bin Malik ﷺ mounted his horse, he praised Allah ﷺ and said, "O people of Madinah! There should be no Madinah for you today because you should prepare yourselves to die in Jihad and not return to Madinah. All that should .remain for you should be the One Allah ﷺ and Jannah." He then led the attack with the others and the people of Yamamah were defeated. Bara bin Malik ﷺ encountered the enemy leader Mukakkam Yamamah and floored him with a blow from his sword. He then took Muhakkam's sword and struck him so forcefully that the sword broke. *(Saraj in Tarikh)*. Bara bin Malik ﷺ said, "On the day that we fought Musailama, I encountered a man who was called the donkey of Yamamah. He was a large and powerfully built man who carried a white sword. When I struck his legs, they came off as if by mistake and he fell on his back. I then covered my sword, attacked him with it until it broke." *(Baghawi in Isaba)*

Bara bin Malik ﷺ scales a Wall and Fights the Enemy all by Himself

Ibn Is'haq narrates that the Muslims drove back the disbelievers during the battle of Yamamah until they were forced to take refuge in an orchard. Musailama the enemy of Allah was with them. Bara bin Malik ﷺ then said, "O Muslims! Throw me on to them." He was then lifted up and when he was level with the top of the wall, he threw himself upon the enemy and fought them until he was able to open the gate for the Muslims. The Muslims then stormed the orchard and Allah had Musailama killed. *(Isti'ab)*. *Muhammad bin Sirin* reports that during the battle of Yamamah, the Muslims reached the orchard where the disbelievers were hiding and found the gate locked. Bara bin Malik ﷺ sat on a shield and said to the others, "Lift me up with your spears and throw me on them." They lifted the shield with their spears and threw him over the wall. When the Muslims joined up with him after he had opened the gate for them, they found that he had already killed 10 disbelievers. *(Bayhaqi)*. *Muhammad bin Sirin* narrates that Omar ﷺ decreed that Bara bin Malik ﷺ should not be appointed as the commander of any expedition because this would spell destruction as he cared not for his life and would lead to others to places where the risk may be too much for them. *(Ibn Sa'd in Muntakhab)*.

The Bravery of Abu Mihjin Thaqafi ﷺ in Fierce Fighting During the Battle of Qadisiya That Made People Think He was an Angel

Ibn Sirin reports that Abu Mihjin Thaqafi ﷺ was always being lashed for drinking wine. Eventually, when his drinking became too much, he was jailed and kept in fetters. When he saw the Muslims fighting the Battle of Qadisiya, it appeared to him that the disbelievers were causing great harm to the Muslims. He therefore sent a message through the slave girl or the wife of the Muslim commander Sa'd bin Abi Waqqas ﷺ saying, "Abu Mihjin says that if you set him free, give him a horse and weapons, he will be the first to return to you after the battle if he is not martyred." He then recited the following couplets:

"It is enough to make me grieve that a horse is carrying
spears to the fight while I am left in fetters in the jailhouse.
When I stand up, my shackles restrain me all avenues to
martyrdom have been closed to me as the caller (to Jihad)

makes me deaf'

When the girl passed the message on to Sa'd ﷺ's wife, she had his fetters removed, gave him a horse that was at home and some weapons. He then urged the horse on until he reached the Muslim army. He killed every disbelieving soldier he met and broke the man's back. When he saw this, Sa'd ﷺ was astonished and asked, "Who is that horseman?" It was not long thereafter that Allah had the enemy defeated. Abu Mihjin ﷺ then returned, gave the weapons back and secured his legs to the fetters as they had been. When Sa'd ﷺ returned, his wife or slave girl asked, "How was the battle?" Informing them of the battle, Sa'd ﷺ replied, "We were being defeated until Allah sent a rider on a black and white horse. Had I not left Abu Mihjin ﷺ here in fetters, I would have thought that certain features of the man were that of Abu Mihjin ﷺ." The lady then said, "By Allah! That was Abu Mihjin ﷺ!" She then narrated the story to Sa'd ﷺ. Sa'd ﷺ called for Abu Mihjin ﷺ, removed his fetters and said, "I swear by Allah that I shall never again have you lashed for drinking wine." Abu Mihjin then said, "And I swear by Allah that I shall never drink it again. I had been repeatedly drinking because of the lashings that you were giving me." He then never drank wine ever again. *(Abdul Razzaq in Isti'ab, Isaba)*. Another lengthy narration from Muhammad bin Sa'd states that after joining the Muslim army, every side that Abu Mihjin ﷺ attacked was defeated by the permission of Allah. The Muslims stared, "He must be an angel!" As Sa'd ﷺ watched, he observed, "The horse's leap is that of my horse Balqa and the man's style is that of Abu Mihjin. However, Abu Mihjin ﷺ is in prison." When the enemy was defeated, Abu Mihjin returned secured his feet back in the fetters. When the daughter of Hasfa informed Sa'd ﷺ about what had happened with Abu Mihjin ﷺ, Sa'd ﷺ said, "I swear by Allah that I shall never again penalize the person whom Allah has granted honor to the Muslims." When Sa'd ﷺ had set him free, Abu Mihjin ﷺ said, "I always continued drinking when 1 was being punished because 1 would then be cleansed from the sin. Now that you have decided not to punish me, I swear by Allah that 1 shall never drink wine ever again." *(Abu Ahmad, Hakim, Ibn Abi Shaiba, Ibn Abdul Barr in Isti'ab)*. *Saif* narrates that Abu Mihjin ﷺ fought extremely well and shouted "Allahu Akbar" each time he attacked. No enemy could stand before him as he massacred them. Although the Muslims were unable to recognize him, they marveled at his performance. *(Isabah)*

The Bravery of Ammar bin Yasir ﷺ as He Lends Courage to the Muslims and Fights Bravely During the Battle of Yamamah

Abdullah bin Omar ﷺ reports that during the battle of Yamamah, he saw Ammar bin Yasir ﷺ standing on a boulder and shouting, "O Assembly of Muslims! Are you running away from Jannah? I am Ammar bin Yasir! Are you running away from Jannah? I am Ammar bin Yasir! Come to me!" Abdullah bin Omar ﷺ says that he saw Ammar bin Yasir ﷺ fighting fiercely though his ear was cut and it hung loose. *(Hakim, Ibn Sa'd)*.

His Desire for Jannah as he Fought

Abu Abdur Rahman Sulami ﷺ says that he participated in the battle of Siffin by the side of Ali ﷺ. They had appointed 2 men to guard Ali ﷺ, who kept launching attacks whenever he could catch the opposition. Ali ﷺ would then not return from the attack until his sword was well colored with blood. He would then say, "Do excuse me for returning but I swear by Allah that I do not return until my sword has been dented." Abu Abdur Rahman Sulami ﷺ narrates further that he saw Ammar bin Yasir ﷺ and Hashim bin Utba ﷺ as Ali ﷺ was fighting between 2 rows of the enemy. Looking at Ali ☀, Ammar ☀ said, "O Hashim! By Allah, this man's commands are being violated and his army is being deserted. O Hashim! Jannah lies beneath flashing swords. Today I shall meet those I love, Muhammad ﷺ and his group. O Hashim! You are one-eyed and one-eyed people are no good if they do not swamp the battlefield." With this provocation from Ammar ☀, Hashim ☀ waved the flag and said the following:

"This one-eyed man has spent his life in search of a home for his family until he has become tired. He will now fight until he defeats the opposition or is defeated"

He then went into one of the valleys of Siffin to fight. Abu Abdur Rahman Sulami ☀ says, "I then saw the Sahabah of Rasulullah ﷺ follow Ammar ☀ as if he were their flag. (*Hakim*).

Abu Abdur Rahman Sulami ☀ says, "I noticed that during the battle of Siffin, whenever Ammar ☀ went into any of the valleys of Siffin, all the Sahabah Rasulullah ﷺ who were there followed him. I also saw him approach Hashim bin Utba ☀ who bore the flag of Ali ☀'s army. He said, 'O Hashim! Advance! Jannah lies beneath the shadow of swords and death lies at the points of spears. The doors of Jannah have been wide open and the damsels of Jannah have been beautified. Today I shall meet those I love, Muhammad ﷺ and his group. He launched an attack with Hashim ☀ and they were both martyred. At that moment, Ali ☀ and his army launched an attack on the people of Sham as if they were all one man. It seemed as if the 2 men - Ammar ☀ and Hashim ☀ were their banner." (*Ibn Jareer in Al Bidayah wan Nihayah, Tabrani, Abu Ya'la, Imam Ahmad, Haythami*).

The Bravery of Amr bin Ma'dikarib Zubaidi ☀ as His-Exemplary Fighting During the Battle of Yarmuk

Malik bin Abdullah Khath'ami ☀ says, "I have not seen anyone step forward to challenge an opponent in the Battle of Yarmuk who was better than a certain Muslim. When a powerfully built Kafir came to meet his challenge, he killed him. When another came forward, he also killed him. When the disbeliever were defeated and fled, he chased and proceeded to his huge tent. There he called for a large utensil of food and invited all those around him to eat. 'Who is this?' I asked. 'He is Amr bin Ma'dikarib,' came the reply. (*Ibn Aa'idh in Maghazi*).

He Fights Single-Handedly During the Battle of Qadisiya

Qais bin Abi Hazim ☀ reports that he was present during the battle of Qadisiya with Sa'd ☀ commanding the Muslim army. Amr bin Ma'dikarib ☀ passed through the rows saying, "O assembly of Muhajir! Be fierce lions and launch such an attack that will prompt the enemy cavalry to throw their spears because riders soon lose hope after throwing their spears." Just then, one of the Persian commanders shot an arrow at Amr ☀, which struck the edge of his bow. Amr ☀ attacked the man so forcefully with his spear that the man's back was broken. He then dismounted and took the man's possessions. (*Ibn Abi Shaibah, Ibn Aa'idh, Ibn Sakan, Saif bin Amr, Tabrani*). Ibn Asakir has narrated a longer version of the story. At the end of his narration, it is stated that when an arrow struck the front of Amr ☀'s saddle, he attacked the man who fired it and lifted him up like a little girl is lifted up. He then placed him between the rows of the Muslims and the disbeliever and cut off his head while telling the others, "Do it this way." *Waqidi* had narrated from *Isa bin Khayyat* that during the battle of Qadisiya, Amr bin Ma'dikarib ☀ attacked the disbelievers all by himself and fought with his sword until the other Muslims could join him. When the Muslims saw that the disbelievers had surrounded Amr ☀ who was still wielding his sword, they drove the disbelievers away from him. *Tabrani*

narrated from Muhammad bin Salam Jumhi ☀ that Omar wrote to Sa'd ☀ saying, "I shall reinforce you with 2,000 men. They are Amr bin Ma'dikarib and Tulaiha bin Khuwailid ☀." Abu Salih bin Wajih ☀ says, "The Battle of Nahawind took place during the year 21 AH and the Muslims were defeated when Nu'man bin Muqarrin ☀ was martyred. Amr bin Ma'dikarib ☀ then resumed the fight on that day until he had transformed the defeat into victory. However, an injury injured him and he passed away in the village of Rowdha." (*Dowlabi in Isaba*).

The Bravery of Abdullah bin Zubair ☀ as His Fight Against Hajjaj and Subsequent Martyrdom

Urwa bin Zubair ☀ reports that after Mu'awiya ☀ passed away, it became very difficult for Abdullah bin Zubair ☀ to be subservient to Mu'awiya ☀'s son Yazid. When Abdullah bin Zubair ☀ once insulted Yazid in public, Yazid vowed that if Abdullah bin Zubair ☀ was not brought before him wearing a yoke around his neck, he would send an army to get him. The people said to Abdullah bin Zubair ☀, "Should we not make for you a yoke out of silver which you could wear under your clothing so that his vow could be fulfilled? It is best that you make peace with him." Abdullah bin Zubair ☀ exclaimed, "May Allah ﷻ never fulfill his vow!" He recited the following couplet:

"I shall never soften to his demands that oppose the truth until rock is softened for the molars to chew"

He then declared, "By Allah! The strike of a sword in honor is better than the lash of a whip in disgrace." Thereafter, he started calling for support and proclaimed his opposition to Yazid bin Mu'awiya. Yazid then dispatched an army from Sham under the command of Muslim bin Uqba Murri with explicit instructions to fight the people of Madinah and then march to Makkah. When Muslim entered Madinah, the Sahabah who were left there were already gone. Muslim humiliated the people of Madinah and went on a killing spree. He then left Madinah and was on the way to Makkah when he died. However, he had already appointed Husain bin Numair Kindi as his successor and said to him, "O bearer of the donkey's carriage! Beware of the plotting of the Quraish. First wage war against them and then kill them selectively." Husain then proceeded to Makkah and when he reached there, he fought Abdullah bin Zubair ☀ for a few days. Later on the narration states that when the news reached Husain bin Numair that Yazid had passed away, he fled. When Yazid bin Mu'awiya had passed away, Marwan bin Hakam campaigned for support. Further on, the narration states that after Marwan died, Abdul Malik called people to pledge their allegiance to him. The people of Sham responded to him and he delivered a sermon in which e said, "Who will kill Abdullah bin Zubair ☀?" When Hajjaj volunteered, Abdul Malik silenced him. However, after being silenced for a second time, he again volunteered saying, "I shall do it, O Amirul Mu'minin because I saw in a dream that I had snatched his cloak away from him and wore it." Abdul Malik then appointed Hajjaj as commander and dispatched him with an army. He started the war against Abdullah bin Zubair ☀ as soon as he reached Makkah. Addressing the people of Makkah, Abdullah bin Zubair ☀ said, "Guard the 2 mountains because you will always remain in good condition and dominant as long as they do not climb the mountains. Hajjaj and his men managed to climb Mount Abu Qubais, where they set up a catapult. They relentlessly rained down rocks on Abdullah bin Zubair ☀ and his men who were stationed in the Masjidul Haram.

On the morning of the day in which Abdullah bin Zubair ☀ was martyred, he went to his mother Asma, the daughter of Abu

Bakr ﷺ. Although she was then 100 years old, not a single tooth had fallen out nor had she lost her eyesight. She asked her son, "O Abdullah! What has happened to your battle?" He informed her of the extent to which the enemy had advanced and then laughed as he said, "There is peace in death." She said, "Dear son! I hope that you do not wish death to me because I do not want to die until I see one of 2 results. Either you become the ruler and give pleasure to my eyes or you are martyred and I may expect rewards from Allah by exercising patience." As he bade farewell to her, she said, "Dear son! Ensure that you never compromise on any aspect of Islam for fear of being killed." Abdullah bin Zubair ﷺ then proceeded to the Masjidul Haram where they had placed 2 thresholds across the Hajar Aswad (Black Stone) to protect it from the catapult. As Abdullah bin Zubair ﷺ was sitting near the Hajar Aswad, someone came to him and asked, "Should we not open the door of the Kabah for you so that you go inside and be saved from them?" Abdullah bin Zubair ﷺ looked at the person and said, "You may protect your brother from everything except his death. Has the Kabah have any sanctity that this place does not have? If the enemy does not respect the Masjid itself, they will not respect the Kabah either. I swear by Allah that they would kill you even if you were clinging on to the shroud of the Kabah." Someone then suggested, "Should you not discuss making peace with them?" He replied, "Is this the time for making peace? I swear by Allah that even if they find you inside the Kabah, they would slaughter you all." He then recited the following couplets which meant:

"I shall not sell my life for something that is flawed nor shall I climb a ladder for fear of death. I aspire for an arrow that strikes and cannot be shifted. How can one who desires death have any other aspiration?"

Abdullah bin Zubair ﷺ then addressed the family of his father Zubair ﷺ saying, "Each one of you should look after his sword as he looks after his face. He should ensure that it does not break otherwise he will have to defend himself with his hands as if he were a woman. By Allah! I have always been in the front line of every battle and I have never felt the pain of any wound unless I applied medicine to it." As they were talking, some people suddenly entered through the door of Banu Jumh. Amongst them was black man. "Who are they?" asked Abdullah bin Zubair ﷺ. When he was informed that they were people from Hims, he attacked them carrying 2 swords. The first person he met was the black man, whom he attacked with his sword and severed his leg. The man shouted in pain and said, "O son of an adulteress!" Abdullah bin Zubair ﷺ responded by saying, "Get lost, O son of Ham! Was Asma ever an adulteress?!" Abdullah bin Zubair then removed them all from the Masjid and returned. Just then another group of people barged through the Banu Salam door. When Abdullah bin Zubair ﷺ asked who they were, he was informed that they were people from Jordan. He then attacked them as he recited the following couplets which meant:

"I do not trust an attack that comes in floods the dust of which does not settle until the night"

After he had removed them also from the Masjid, another group of people rushed in through the Banu Makhzum door. This time, Abdullah bin Zubair ﷺ attacked them reciting the following couplet which meant:

"Had my opponent been a single person, I would have been more than able to settle with him"

There were many supporters of Abdullah bin Zubair ﷺ on the roof of the Masjid who were throwing bricks on the invaders. However, as Abdullah bin Zubair ﷺ attacked the enemy, a brick struck the centre of his head, causing a terrible wound. He paused for a while as he said:

"Our wounds do not bleed on to our heels. On the contrary, our blood drops on to our feet (rather than having wounds on the back of our bodies as cowards have, our wounds are on the front parts of our bodies instead)"

He then fell to the ground. His 2 slaves bend over him saying:

"The slave protects his master as well as himself"

However, the enemy soon closed in on him and cut off his head. *(Tabrani, Haythami, Ibn Abdil Birr in Isti'ab, Abu Nu'aym in Hilya, Hakim in Mustadrak)*

Is'haq bin Abi Is'haq says, "I was present when Abdullah bin Zubair ﷺ was martyred in the Masjidul Haram. The armies continued entering through the doors of the Masjid and each time one entered, he drove them back single-handedly. As he was doing this, one of the rocks of the Masjid fell on his head and floored him. He was then reciting the following couplet:

"O (beloved mother) Asma! Don't weep for me if I am killed for my ancestry and Deen are still intact so is my sword that my right hand is too weak to hold" *(Abu Nu'aym, Tabrani*

Admonition to Those Who Flee the Battlefield in the Path of Allah: The Sahabah Admonish Salama bin Hisham ﷺ

Ummu Salama ﷺ once asked the wife of Salama bin Hisham bin Mughiera ﷺ, "Why do I not see your husband Salama attend the salah with Rasulullah ﷺ and the Muslims?" She replied, "By Allah! He is unable to leave the house because whenever he does so, people shout at him saying, 'Deserter! Did you flee in the Path of Allah?!' This reached the extent that he now sits at home and is unable to leave." He had participated in the battle of Mu'ta with Khalid bin Walid ﷺ. *(Hakim confirmed by Dhahabi, Ibn Is'haq, Al Bidayah wan Nihayah).*

A Man Admonishes Abu Hurairah ﷺ

Abu Hurairah ﷺ says, "There was a problem between my cousin and myself. However, I had no reply to give him when he provoked me by saying, 'Were you not one of those who fled during the battle of Mu'ta?" *(Hakim).*

Abdullah bin Omar ﷺ and His Companions Regret and Grieve After Retreating During the Battle of Mu'ta

Abdullah bin Omar ﷺ says, "I was part of an expedition that Rasulullah ﷺ dispatched. I was amongst some of them who had retreated. As we were returning to Madinah, we said, 'What shall we do? We had fled the battlefield and are returning with the wrath of Allah. Perhaps we should return to Madinah and spend the night before approaching Rasulullah ﷺ.' However, we then said, 'Let us rather present ourselves before Rasulullah ﷺ immediately upon returning. If we can be forgiven, it is fine, otherwise we shall have to leave Madinah.' We then went to Rasulullah ﷺ before the Fajr salah. When he emerged from his room, he asked, 'Who are you?' We replied, 'We are those who have fled.' 'No,' Rasulullah ﷺ assured them, 'You are those who have returned to your base only to seek reinforcements and then to return to the fight again. I am your base and the base for all Muslims. *(ref. Al-Anfal:16)* We then came forward and kissed Rasulullah ﷺ's hand." *(Ahmad).* In another narration, Abdullah bin Omar ﷺ says, "Rasulullah ﷺ once dispatched us on an expedition. When we met the enemy and were defeated in the very first attack, some of us returned to Madinah at night and hid away. We then decided to approach Rasulullah ﷺ and plead our case to him. We then left and when we met him, we said, 'O Rasulullah ﷺ! We are those who have fled.' Rasulullah ﷺ responded by saying, 'You are rather those who shall attack a second time and I am your base to whom you have returned for reinforcements before returning to the battle.'" The narration of Aswad quotes that Rasulullah ﷺ added, "I am also the base for every Muslim." *(Ahmad in Al Bidayah wan Nihayah).* A similar narration of Abdullah bin Omar ؓ reads, "We then said, 'O Rasulullah ﷺ! We are those who have fled.' He said, 'You are only those who shall return to the fight after returning to base.' We said, 'O Rasulullah ﷺ! Because of embarrassment, we had intended not to enter Madinah, but to undertake a sea voyage to a foreign land.' Rasulullah ﷺ reassured us saying, 'Do no such thing for I am the base of every Muslim.'" *(Bayhaqi, Abu Dawud, Tirmidhi, Ibn Majah, Ahmad, Ibn Sa'd).*

The Anxiety of the Muhajir and the Ansar When They Fled During the Battle for the Bridge and the Statement of Omar ؓ

Aisha ؓ reports that as Abdullah bin Zaid ؓ was passing the door of her room, she heard Omar ؓ call out, "Let us hear the news, O Abdullah bin Zaid!" Omar ؓ was inside the Masjid. When Abdullah bin Zaid ؓ entered the Masjid, Omar repeated, "What news do you have, O Abdullah bin Zaid?" Abdullah bin Zaid ؓ said, "I am bringing you the news, O Amirul Mu'minin." When he came before Omar ؓ, Abdullah bin Zaid ؓ informed him about what had transpired. Aisha ؓ says that she had never heard a more and accurate account of any incident given by someone who had been present there. When the defeated Muslim army returned and Omar ؓ noticed the anxiety of the Muhajir and the Ansar because they had fled the battlefield, he said, "Do not worry, O assembly of Muslims! I am your base to which you have withdrawn to refill your strength before returning to battle."

The Anxiety of Mu'adh Qari ؓ When he Fled During the Battle for the Bridge and the Statement of Omar ؓ

Muhammad bin Abdur Rahman bin Husain and others report that Mu'adh Qari ؓ from the Banu Najjar tribe was amongst those who was present and had fled during the battle for the Bridge of Abu Ubaid. He always wept whenever he recited the following verse of the Qur'an: وَمَنْ يُوَلِّهِمْ يَوْمَئِذٍ دُبُرَهُ إِلَّا مُتَحَرِّفًا لِقِتَالٍ أَوْ مُتَحَيِّزًا إِلَى فِئَةٍ فَقَدْ بَاءَ بِغَضَبٍ مِنَ اللَّهِ وَمَأْوَاهُ جَهَنَّمُ وَبِئْسَ الْمَصِيرُ (16)

And whoever turns his back to them on such a day - unless it be a stratagem of war, or to retreat to a troop (of his own), - he indeed has drawn upon himself wrath from Allah. And his abode is Hell, and worst indeed is that destination! (Al-Anfal:16)

Omar ؓ would then say to him, "Do not weep, O Mu'adh. I am your base to whom you have retreated to regroup and have reinforcements before launching another attack." *(Ibn Jareer).*

Sa'd bin Ubaid Qari ؓ Returns to the Land of the Battle From Which he Fled to Redeem Himself

Abdur Rahman bin Abu Laila ؓ says that Sa'd bin Ubaid ؓ was a companion of Rasulullah ﷺ who was with the army that was defeated on the day that Abu Ubaid ؓ was martyred at the bridge. He received the title of Qari, a title that no other companion of Rasulullah ﷺ received. Omar ؓ once said to him, "Do you wish to go to Sham where the Muslims are in a weak position and the enemy is becoming bold against them. Perhaps you will be able to cleanse the mistake of your fleeing." Sa'd ؓ replied, "No. I shall go only to the land from which I fled and fight only that enemy who forced me to do what I did." He then went to Qadisiya where he was martyred. *(Ibn Sa'd).*

Rasulullah ﷺ Gives his Weapons to Usama or to Ali ؓ

Jabala bin Haritha ؓ narrates that whenever Rasulullah ﷺ was not participating in a battle, he would give his weapons to Usama ؓ or to Ali ؓ. *(Tabrani, Ahmad, Haythami).*

An Ansari Gives Everything he Has Prepared to Another Person When he fell Ill

Anas ؓ reports that a youngster from the Banu Aslam tribe said, "O Rasulullah ﷺ! I wish to proceed in Jihad but do not have any wealth with which to make the necessary preparations," Rasulullah ﷺ sent him to a certain Ansari saying, "He had made the necessary preparations for Jihad but had fallen ill. Tell him that Rasulullah ﷺ has sent Salam to him and ask him to give you whatever he had prepared." The youngster went to the Ansari and conveyed the message to him. The Ansari then said to his wife, "Give him everything you have prepared for me without holding anything back. By Allah! Allah will never bless anything that you hold back from him." *(Abu Dawud, Muslim, Bayhaqi).*

Referring a Person Going out in the Path of Allah to Someone who can Assist Him

Abu Mas'ood Ansari ؓ narrates that a man came to Rasulullah ﷺ and said, "Please provide transport for me because my animal has died." "I have nothing for you," Rasulullah ﷺ replied. Another Sahabi said, "O Rasulullah ﷺ! I can refer him to someone who can provide transport for him." Rasulullah ﷺ said, "The one who points others towards good shall have the reward of the one who actually carries it out." *(Muslim, Bayhaqi).*

Rasulullah ﷺ Encourages the Sahabah to Assist Those Proceeding in the Path of Allah

Jabir bin Abdullah ؓ reports that when Rasulullah ﷺ was once embarking on an expedition, he said, "O assembly of Muhajir and Ansar! There are many of your brothers who have neither wealth nor families, who can assist them?. Therefore each of you should attach 2 or 3 of them to himself." Jabir ؓ says further, "As a result, each one of us who had an animal would share a turn to ride the animal just as the others without animals shared their turns. I attached 2 or 3 men to myself and my turn to ride was just like the turns that they had." *(Bayhaqi, Hakim).*

An Ansari Sahabi Assists Wathila bin Asqa ؓ

Wathila bin Asqa ؓ narrates, "After Rasulullah ﷺ had announced the pending march to Tabuk, I just went to my family and had returned when the first group of Sahabah had already left. I then started going around Madinah announcing, 'Who will provide transport for a man in exchange for his share of booty?' An old man from the Ansar responded by saying, 'We shall take his share of the booty on condition that he rides in turns with us and eats with us.' When I agreed, he asked me, 'Let's proceed with the blessings of Allah.' I then traveled with the man who was the best of traveling companions. When Allah granted us the booty, I received a few young camels as my share and led them away to my companion. Emerging from his tent, he sat on one of the saddle bags of his camel and said, 'Take them backwards.' After I had done so, he said, 'Now take them forward.' After doing this he commented, 'These are fine camels you have here.' I said, 'This is the booty that I had set for you.' 'Keep your camels, dear nephew,' he said, 'I had intended to have something else.'" *Bayhaqi* says that what the Ansari meant to say was: "By doing what I did, I had never intended to take compensation from you. All that I want is to share in your rewards."

The Statement of Abdullah bin Mas'ood ؓ

Abdullah bin Mas'ood ؓ said, "Providing a rope to someone

proceeding in the Path of Allah is more beloved to me than performing Hajj after Hajj." *(Tabrani, Haythami).*

The Story of a Man and Auf bin Malik ؓ

Auf bin Malik ؓ says, "When Rasulullah ﷺ sent me on a military expedition, a man came up to me and said, 'I shall go with you on condition that you grant me a share of booty.' He then added, 'I swear by Allah that I do not even know whether there shall be any booty at all. You will be unable to stipulate a specific share for me.' I fixed a payment of 3 Dinars for him. We then left on the expedition. and happened to receive some booty. When I asked Rasulullah ﷺ about the situation, Rasulullah ﷺ said, 'I see nothing in this world and in the Hereafter for him besides the 3 Dinars that he has taken.'" *(Tabrani, Haythami).*

The Story of a Man with Ya'la bin Munya ؓ

Abdullah bin Daylami narrates that Ya'la bin Munya ؓ said, "I was an old man with no servant when Rasulullah ﷺ announced that an expedition would leave. I therefore looked for someone to hire and specified that he would receive a full share from the booty. I finally found someone. When the time was close for our departure, he came to me and said, 'I have no idea whether there shall be any booty and I cannot say what my share will be. Why don't you rather specify a fixed amount that I would receive whether there is any booty or not.' I therefore fixed an amount of 3 Dinars. When my share of the booty came to me, I intended to give him his complete share but then remembered the 3 Dinars. For this reason, I approached Rasulullah ﷺ and narrated the account to him. Rasulullah ﷺ said, 'I see nothing in this world and in the Hereafter for him as reward for this expedition besides the 3 Dinars that he has specified.'" *(Bayhaqi)*

Those who Proceed in the Path of Allah Using the wealth of Others: Maymuna bint Sa'd ؓ Asks Rasulullah ﷺ About This

Maymuna bint Sa'd ؓ reports that she once asked" "O Rasulullah ﷺ! Inform us about a person who cannot proceed in the Path of Allah but sponsors the means by which Jihad can be carried out. Will this person receive the reward or the person who actually goes out?" Rasulullah ﷺ replied, "He shall receive the reward for his wealth while the one who goes out shall be rewarded for the intention he makes." *(Tabrani, Haythami)*

The Story of Ali ؓ and Another Man

Ali bin Abi Rabi'ah ؓ said that a man came to Ali bin Abi Talib ؓ with his son whom he intended to send on an expedition in his place. Ali ؓ said to him, "I prefer the judgment of an adult to the fighting of a youngster." *(Bayhaqi in Kanzul Ummal)*

Omar ؓ Admonishes a Youngster who Begged From People so That he Could Proceed in the Path of Allah

Nafi narrates that a robust and healthy youngster entered the Masjid. He held a large arrow in his hand and announced, "Who will assist me to proceed in the Path of Allah?" Omar ؓ sent for him and he was brought, Omar ؓ announced, "Who will hire this man from me to work his fields?" One of the Ansar said, "I shall hire him, O Amirul Mu'minin. What do you ask as his monthly salary?" When the Ansari specified an amount, Omar ؓ handed the youngster over to him. The youngster worked in the fields for several months when Omar ؓ asked the Ansari, "How is our laborer?" "He is a fine man, O Amirul Mu'minin," replied the Ansari. Omar ؓ instructed the Ansari to bring the youngster along together with his salaries that he had collected. The Ansari brought the youngster together with a bag of Dirhams. Omar ؓ

said to the youngster, "Take this. If you wish, you may proceed now in the Path of Allah and if you wish, you may sit at home." *(Bayhaqi in Kamul Ummal).*

The Sahabah Seek Loans From Rasulullah ﷺ

Abdullah bin Mas'ood ؓ narrates that someone asked, "Have you heard Rasulullah ﷺ say anything about horses?" "Yes," he replied, "I have heard Rasulullah ﷺ say, 'Virtue has been secured to the forelocks of horses until the Day of Judgment. Buy with trust in Allah and take loans with trust in Allah' When someone asked Rasulullah ﷺ how could a person buy with trust in Allah and take loans with. trust in Allah, Rasulullah ﷺ replied, 'Tell the borrower to give you the loan until you are able to pay him back when the spoils of war are distributed and tell the seller to sell to you now until you are able to pay him when Allah grants victory in battle and you are able to pay from the share you receive of the booty. You will always remain in good standing as long as your Jihad remains fresh, as long as you fight with enthusiasm. Towards the end of time there shall be people who will have doubts about Jihad. You should continue waging Jihad during their time and fighting because Jihad will be fresh during those times as well. Allah's assistance and booty will be found as well.'" *(Abu Ya'la, Haythami).*

Encouraging people to proceed in the Path of Allah and seeing them off: Rasulullah ﷺ Walks with the Mujahidin and Advises Them

Abdullah bin Abbas ؓ reports that Rasulullah ﷺ walked with them up to Baqi Gharqad when he sent them off on an expedition. He said to them, "Proceed in the name of Allah. O Allah! Assist them." *(Hakim).* Abdullah bin Yazid ؓ was invited for a meal, he said to the people that when Rasulullah ﷺ bade farewell to an army, he prayed, "In Allah's care do I hand over your Islam, your trusts and the results of your deeds." *(Hakim).*

Abu Bakr ؓ Sees the Army of Usama ؓ Off

In a narration discussing the dispatching of Usama ؓ's army, Hasan ؓ narrates that Abu Bakr ؓ left his home to meet the army. As he saw them off, Abu Bakr ؓ was walking while Usama ؓ rode his animal. In the meantime, Abdur Rahman bin Auf ؓ was leading Abu Bakr ؓ's animal along. Usama ؓ said, "O Khalifah of Rasulullah ﷺ! Either you ride or I shall dismount." Abu Bakr ؓ instructed, 'By Allah! Neither should you dismount nor shall I ride! What harm can there be if my feet get dusty for a while in the Path of Allah? A person proceeding in the Path of Allah receives the reward of 700 good deeds for every step he takes. In addition to this, his status is elevated by 700 degrees and 700 of his sins are forgiven." After Abu Bakr ؓ had seen them off, and was returning, he requested, "If you deem it appropriate to assist me with leaving Omar ؓ behind with me in Madinah, please do so." Usama ؓ then allowed Omar ؓ to stay back. *(Ibn Asakir in Kanzul Ummal).* Yahya bin Sa'eed reports that when Abu Bakr dispatched several armies to Sham, he walked with Yazid bin Abu Sufian ؓ who was in command of one of the 4 armies. Yazid said to Abu Bakr ؓ, "Either you ride or I shall dismount" Abu Bakr ؓ instructed, "By Allah! Neither will you dismount nor shall I ride! I hope to be rewarded for these steps in the Path of Allah." *(Malik, Bayhaqi in Kanzul Ummal).* Jabir Ru'ayni ؓ narrates that as Abu Bakr ؓ was walking as he saw an army off. He then said to them, "All praises are for Allah Who has allowed our feet to accumulate dust in His path." Someone asked, "How have our feet become dusty in the Path of Allah when we are merely seeing them off?" Abu Bakr ؓ replied, "Because we have helped them prepare, have seen them off and are making Du'a for them, we shall therefore also share in the rewards of going out in the Path of Allah." *(Bayhaqi, Ibn Abi Shayba in Kanzul Ummal).*

Abdullah bin Omar ؓ sees off People going in the Path of Allah

Mujahid reports that as he was proceeding in the Path of Allah, Abdullah bin Omar ؓ came to see them off. As Abdullah bin Omar ؓ was about to part from them, he said, "I have nothing to give you, but I have heard Rasulullah ﷺ say that whenever something is handed over in Allah's care, Allah protects it. I therefore hand over in Allah's care, your Islam, your trusts and the results of your deeds." *(Bayhaqi).*

Welcoming those returning from the Path of Allah: The People Came Outside Madinah When the Sahabah Returned From Tabuk

Sa'ib bin Yazid ؓ says, "The people of Madinah came to welcome Rasulullah ﷺ when he returned from the expedition to Tabuk. I also met him along with other children at Thaniyatul Wada." *(Abu Dawud).* Sa'ib bin Yazid ؓ also reports, "When Rasulullah ﷺ returned from the expedition to Tabuk, the people came out of Madinah to Thaniyatul Wada to welcome him. Still as a boy then, I also accompanied the others." *(Bayhaqi).*

Rasulullah ﷺ Travels to Badr and Makkah During Ramadhan

Omar ؓ says that it was during Ramadhan that they marched with Rasulullah ﷺ for the battle of Badr and for the conquest of Makkah. *(Tirmidhi in Fat'hul Bari).* Another narration quotes that Omar ؓ said, "We marched on 2 military expeditions with Rasulullah ﷺ during Ramadhan; the battle of Badr and the conquest of Makkah. On both occasions, we did not fast." *(Ibn Sa'd, Ahmad in Kanzul Ummal).* Abdullah bin Abbas ؓ says, "313 Muslims participated in the battle of Badr. Amongst these, 76 were from the Muhajir. It was on Friday the 17th of Ramadhan that the disbelievers were defeated in the battle of Badr." *(Ahmad in Al Bidayah wan Nihayah).* Another narration from Abdullah bin Abbas ؓ states that the Sahabah participating in the battle of Badr numbered just more than 310. The narration also adds, "The Ansar numbered 236 and it was Ali ؓ who carried the flag of the Muhajir." *(Bazzar, Tabrani, Haythami).* Yet another from Abdullah bin Abbas ؓ states, "When Rasulullah ﷺ left for the journey, he appointed Abu Ruhm Kulthum bin Husain bin Utba bin Khalaf Ghifari ؓ as his deputy in Madinah. It was on the 10th of Ramadhan that he left. Rasulullah ﷺ fasted and so did the Sahabah with him. However, when they reached Kudaid, an oasis located between Usfan and Amaj, Rasulullah ﷺ terminated his fast. Rasulullah ﷺ then proceeded until he set up camp at Marruz Zahran along with 10,000 Sahabah with him." *(Ibn Is'haq, Bukhari in Al Bidayah wan Nihayah, Tabrani, Haythami).* Abdullah bin Abbas ؓ has also narrated that Rasulullah ﷺ proceeded in Ramadhan to conquer Makkah and fasted until he reached Kudaid. *(Abdur Razzaq, Ibn Abi Sahiba).* When Rasulullah ﷺ left to conquer Makkah during Ramadhan, he was fasting until the road passed by Qudaid at midday. The Sahabah were thirsty and were in search of water. They had started becoming uneasy when Rasulullah ﷺ asked for a cup of water. He took it in his hand so that everyone could clearly see it. He drank the water and the Sahabah followed suit. *(Abdur Razzaq in Kanzul Ummal, Bukhari, Muslim, Nasai in Jam'ul Fawa'id).*

Recording the Names of People Proceeding in the Path of Allah

Abdullah bin Abbas ؓ narrates that Rasulullah ﷺ once said, "No strange (non-Mahram) man should ever be alone with a strange (non-Mahram) woman and no woman can travel without a Mahram." A Sahabi stood up and said that his name had been written for a particular military expedition while his wife had left to perform Hajj. He inquired whether he should continue with the expedition or join his wife for Hajj. Rasulullah ﷺ instructed him to perform Hajj with his wife instead. *(Bukhari).*

Rasulullah ﷺ Performs Salah Upon his Return

Ka'b ؓ narrates that whenever Rasulullah ﷺ returned from a journey during the morning, he would first enter the Masjid and perform 2 Rakahs salah before being seated. *(Bukhari).* Another narration from Jabir ؓ states that he accompanied Rasulullah ﷺ on a journey and when they returned, Rasulullah ﷺ said to him, "Enter the Masjid and perform 2 Rakahs salah." *(Bukhari).*

Slaughtering an Animal Upon Returning to Feed People

Jabir ؓ has also narrated that when Rasulullah ﷺ once returned to Madinah, he slaughtered a cow or a camel. Another narration quotes that Jabir ؓ said, "Rasulullah ﷺ purchased a camel from me for 2 Awqiya and a Dirham or for 2 Dirhams. When he reached Sirar, Rasulullah ﷺ had a cow slaughtered and the Sahabah ate from it. Thereafter when he reached Madinah, Rasulullah ﷺ instructed me to first go the Masjid to perform 2 Rakahs salah. Rasulullah ﷺ then weighed out the price for my camel and paid me." *(Bukhari).*

Women proceed in the Path of Allah: Aisha ؓ Participated in the Banu Mustaliq Expedition

Aisha ؓ says, "Whenever Rasulullah ﷺ embarked on an expedition, he would draw lots between his wives and whoever's name was drawn would accompany him. When the Banu Mustaliq expedition was to take place, Rasulullah ﷺ again drew lots as he usually did. This time my name emerged as the one to accompany him. Rasulullah ﷺ therefore took me along. During those times women ate just enough to sustain themselves. The fat on their bodies was therefore less and they were lighter in weight. For this reason I would sit in my carriage when it was loaded on my camel. The men who fastened the carriage to the camel for me would lift the carriage from the bottom, lift me up and place the carriage on to the camel. They would then secure it with ropes, take the camel by the head and lead it along. After the journey was done, Rasulullah ﷺ left for Madinah and we were close to Madinah when we set up camp and spent part of the night there. When the announcer announced that it was time to depart, everyone got ready to move. Wearing a necklace of mine that was decorated with onyx from the Yemeni tribe of Dhifar, I went out of the camp to relieve myself. When I had completed, the necklace had slipped from my neck without me knowing it. It was only after returning to my carriage that I looked for my neck and could not find it. The people had already started leaving when I returned to the place I had been. There I looked for it until I eventually found it. The men who usually tied my carriage had by then already tied it to the camel. Thinking that I was inside, they did what they always did and took the carriage away. Without even once suspecting that I was not inside, they picked up the carriage and loaded it on to the camel. They then took the camel by the head and led it away. When I eventually returned to the camp, there was not a soul in sight. Everyone had left. I then spread out my shawl at the place where I had been and lay down. I knew that once my absence would be detected, people would return to where I was to search for me. By Allah! I was still lying there when Safwan bin Mu'attal Sulami ؓ passed by. He had fallen behind the expedition for some reason and had not spent the night in the camp. Seeing my silhouette, he came closer until he stopped by me. He had seen me before we were instructed to don the Hijab and when he saw that it was I lying there, he exclaimed in astonishment, 'Inna Lillahi wa Inna Ilaihi Raji'un! The wife of Rasulullah ﷺ!' I was properly wrapped up in my clothing when he said, 'May Allah have mercy on you. How did you get left behind?' I did not speak a word to him. He brought his camel next to me and said, 'Mount the camel and stay behind me.' I mounted the camel and he led it quickly along by its head, in search of the rest. By Allah! Neither did we catch up with the others until the morning, nor did they notice my absence. The army had set up camp and were resting when Safwan ﷺ was seen leading me on the camel. It was then that the slanderers said what they did about me being an adulteress, causing much uproar amongst the army. I swear by Allah that I was then still in the dark concerning what was happening.

After we had returned to Madinah, no news had still reached me about the slander when I happened to fall terribly ill. In the meantime, the news had reached Rasulullah ﷺ and my parents, none of whom breathed a word to me. All that I noticed was a lack in the affection that Rasulullah ﷺ usually showed towards me. Whereas he expressed tremendous love and affection towards me whenever I fell ill, he did not do so this time. This greatly disappointed me. When he came to me as my mother was nursing me, he asked, 'How are you feeling?' That was all he said. I eventually grew upset with his apparent unconcern and asked, 'O Rasulullah ﷺ! Permit me to move to my mother's place for she has been nursing me all along. When Rasulullah ﷺ indicated that it was not a problem, I moved to my mother's place. I was then still completely in the dark about what had been happening until I had started to recover from my illness after 20 odd days. We Arabs were not accustomed to building toilets inside our houses like the non-Arabs do. We disliked this and regarded it as something deplorable. We used to go outside Madinah to relieve ourselves and every night us women would go there together. I had gone out to relieve myself one day in the company of Ummu Mistah who was the daughter of Abu Ruhm bin Abdul Muttalib. By Allah! We were still walking when she tripped over her shawl and exclaimed, 'May Mistah be destroyed!' 'By Allah!' I criticized, 'What a terrible thing to say about a man from amongst the Muhajir who has participated in the battle of Badr!' She then asked, 'Has the news not yet reached you, O daughter of Abu Bakr?' 'What news?' I enquired. She then informed me about what the slanderers were saying. 'Has all this really been happening?' I asked in disbelief. 'Yes,' she replied, 'I swear by Allah that it certainly has.' By Allah! After hearing all of this I was unable to even relieve myself properly and returned. I then wept continuously until I actually thought that my liver would burst. I said to my mother, 'May Allah forgive you! The people have been saying what they have said and you didn't even mention a word to me!' My mother responded by saying, 'Take it easy, dear daughter! When a beautiful woman has a husband who loves her greatly and has co-wives as well, it does happen that the wives and other people pick on her.'

Unknown to me, Rasulullah ﷺ had already delivered a sermon to the people. After praising Allah, he said, 'O people! What is the matter with some of you who cause me hurt with regards to my family by saying things that are not true? I swear by Allah that I see only good in my wives. They are also making allegations about a man (Safwan bin Mu'attal ﷺ) about whom I also swear that I know only as a good man. He never enters any of my rooms without me with him.' Most of the slander was publicized by the Munafiq Abdullah bin Ubay bin Salul along with some men from the Khazraj tribe. Also involved were Mistah ﷺ and Hamna bint Jahash ﷺ. Hamna bint Jahash ﷺ was involved because her sister Zainab ﷺ bint Jahash was a wife of Rasulullah ﷺ and from all the other wives of Rasulullah ﷺ, she was the only one who was of any competition to me. Since Allah protected Zainab ﷺ because of her piety, she had only good words to say and did not slander me; On the other hand, Hamna ﷺ passed around plenty of slander for the sake of her sister. In this manner, she defamed only herself. After Rasulullah ﷺ had delivered the sermon, Usaid bin Hudhair ﷺ of the Aws tribe said, 'O Rasulullah ﷺ! Had the slanderers been from the Aws tribe, we would have dealt with them on your behalf. If they are from our brothers of the Khazraj tribe, we shall do as you command. By Allah! They ought to be executed!' It was then that Sa'd bin Ubadah ﷺ stood up. Although he was always regarded as a good man, he said angrily to Usaid ﷺ, 'By Allah! You are lying! They shall not be executed! I swear by Allah that you say this only because you know that they are from the Khazraj. You would never have said it had you known that they were from your tribe!' Usaid bin Hudhair ﷺ replied, 'By Allah! It is you who are lying! You must be a Munafiq since you are defending the Munafiqin!' The Sahabah belonging to the Aws and the Khazraj tribes stood up to confront each other until a fight almost erupted between the 2 tribes. Rasulullah ﷺ descended from the pulpit and came to me. After some time revelation had stopped coming to him, he called for Ali bin Abi Talib ﷺ and Usama bin Zaid ﷺ to consult with them about separating from his wife (myself). Usama ﷺ had only good to say and added, 'O Rasulullah ﷺ! We only know your family to be good. The news is a blatant lie.' On the other hand, Ali ﷺ only said, 'O Rasulullah ﷺ! Women are plenty and you are able to get others in their place. Ask the girl (Barirah ﷺ) for she will give you the truth.' Rasulullah ﷺ summoned Barirah ﷺ, Ali ﷺ rapped her quite harshly and said, 'Be truthful to Rasulullah ﷺ!' Barirah ﷺ said, 'By Allah! I know of nothing but good in Aisha ﷺ. I can find no fault in her besides the fact that after I have pressed the dough and instructed her to look after it, she falls asleep and along comes the goat to eat it up.'" Continuing the story further, Aisha ﷺ says, "Rasulullah ﷺ then came to me when I was staying with my parents. A woman from the Ansar was with me at the time and she wept with me as I wept. Rasulullah ﷺ sat down and after praising Allah, he said, 'O Aisha! The talk of people has already reached your ears. Do fear Allah. If you have come close to what the people are saying, repent to Allah for He accepts the repentance of His servants.' By Allah! As soon as Rasulullah ﷺ said this, my tears immediately stopped and I could not even feel them. I waited for my parents to reply to Rasulullah ﷺ, but they said nothing. By Allah! I never regarded myself so distinguished that verses of the Qur'an should be revealed about me to clear my name, which would be recited forever and read in salah. However, all I wished for was that Rasulullah ﷺ should see a dream in which Allah would deny the allegations on my behalf, for Allah knew that I was innocent. All that I expected was that Allah would inform Rasulullah ﷺ accordingly. In no way did I regard myself worthy of having verses of the Qur'an revealed about me. Nevertheless, when I noticed that my parents were not going to say anything in my defense, I said to them, 'Are you 2 not going to reply to Rasulullah ﷺ?' 'By Allah!' they replied, 'We do not know what to say.' By Allah! I do not know of any family that had so much difficulty come upon them as had come to the family of Abu Bakr ﷺ during that period. When my parents said nothing, tears welled in my eyes and I burst out crying. I then snapped, 'By Allah! I shall never repent to Allah for what they say I did! By

Allah! Should I admit to what they say when Allah knows well that I am innocent of it, I shall only be admitting to something I have never done. On the other hand, if I deny it, they will never believe me.' I then searched for the name of Ya'qub عليه السلام but could not remember it. Nonetheless, I said that I would say exactly what the father of Yusuf عليه السلام said:

فَصَبْرٌ جَمِيلٌ وَاللَّهُ الْمُسْتَعَانُ عَلَى مَا تَصِفُونَ (18)

So (for me) patience is most fitting. And it is Allah (Alone) Whose help can be sought against that which you assert." ' (Al-Yusuf:18)

Rasulullah ﷺ was still sitting where he was. When revelation started descending on him and he started passing out as he did when revelation descended. A shawl was placed over Rasulullah ﷺ and. a leather pillow was placed beneath his head. By Allah! When I saw this happen, I neither felt any fear nor was I worried in the least because I knew that I was innocent and that Allah would never be unjust towards me. Not so for my parents. I swear by the Being Who controls the life of Aisha that as long as the condition did not leave Rasulullah ﷺ, I thought that the 2 of them would die out of fear that Allah would prove the slander of the people to be true. Rasulullah ﷺ sat up after the condition had passed and although it was a cold day, drops of perspiration decorated his face like pearls. As he wiped the perspiration from his face, he said, 'Good news, O Aisha! Allah has confirmed your innocence.' 'All praise be to Allah!' I exclaimed. Rasulullah ﷺ then went out to the people and delivered a sermon. He recited to them the verses of the Qur'an that Allah had revealed in this regard and instructed that Mistah bin Uthatha, Hassan bin Thabit رضي الله عنهم and Hamna bint Jahash رضي الله عنها be lashed according to the prescribed penalty because of the part they played in spreading the accusation of immoral behavior. *(Ibn Is'haq, Bukhari, Muslim, Al Bidayah wan Nihawah).*

Another detailed narration quoted that Aisha رضي الله عنها added, "After the verses of my innocence were revealed, my mother said to me, 'Stand up and go to Rasulullah ﷺ to thank him.' I said, 'I swear by Allah ﷻ that I shall not go to him and shall thank none but Allah for it was Allah Who confirmed my innocence.' Allah ﷻ revealed 10 verses beginning with: ......إِنَّ الَّذِينَ جَاءُوا بِالْإِفْكِ عُصْبَةٌ مِّنكُمْ

Verily! Those who brought forth the slander (against Aisha رضي الله عنها the wife of the Prophet ﷺ) are a group among you.... (An-Noor:11)

My father Abu Bakr رضي الله عنه used to support Mistah رضي الله عنه because he was related to us and because he was very poor. However, after the verses attesting to my innocence were revealed, Abu Bakr رضي الله عنه said, 'I swear by Allah that I shall never support him because of what he said about Aisha!' It was then that Allah revealed the verse:

وَلَا يَأْتَلِ أُولُو الْفَضْلِ مِنكُمْ وَالسَّعَةِ أَن يُؤْتُوا أُولِي الْقُرْبَىٰ وَالْمَسَاكِينَ وَالْمُهَاجِرِينَ فِي سَبِيلِ اللَّهِ وَلْيَعْفُوا وَلْيَصْفَحُوا أَلَا تُحِبُّونَ أَن يَغْفِرَ اللَّهُ لَكُمْ وَاللَّهُ غَفُورٌ رَّحِيمٌ (22)

And let not those among you who are blessed with graces and wealth swear not to give (any sort of help) to their kinsmen, Al-Masakeen (the poor), and those who left their homes for Allah's Cause. Let them pardon and forgive. Do you not love that Allah should forgive you? And Allah is Oft-Forgiving, Most Merciful. (An-Noor:22)

After revelation of this verse, Abu Bakr رضي الله عنه said, 'By Allah! Of course I would like Allah to forgive me.' He then continued giving Mistah رضي الله عنه the allowance he had been giving him and said, 'I swear by Allah that I shall never stop giving it to him ever.'" *(Ahmad in Ibn Kathir, Tabrani in Majma'uz Zawa'id).*

A Woman From the Banu Ghifar Tribe Accompanies Rasulullah ﷺ on a Military Expedition

A lady from the Banu Ghifar tribe narrates, "Together with a few women from the Banu Ghifar, I approached Rasulullah ﷺ and requested, 'O Rasulullah ﷺ! We want to accompany you on the expedition ahead to Khaibar so that we may nurse the wounded and assist the Muslims in any way we can.' Rasulullah ﷺ replied, 'You are welcome with the blessings of Allah.' We then went with Rasulullah ﷺ. Since I was a very young girl, Rasulullah ﷺ put me to sit behind him on the bag of his camel. When Rasulullah ﷺ dismounted from the camel the next morning, I also dismounted from the bag and was surprised to find blood on it. It was the first time that I had menstruated so I was terribly embarrassed and clung on to the camel. Gauging what had happened to me, Rasulullah ﷺ said, 'What's the matter? Perhaps you menstruated?' When I replied in the affirmative, Rasulullah ﷺ said, 'Get yourself organized and then get a utensil of water. Add salt to the water and then wash off the part of the bag that had blood on it. You may then return to your seat.'" She continues the story by saying, "After Allah had given us victory at Khaibar, and Rasulullah ﷺ gave us (women) a small share of the spoils. Rasulullah ﷺ took this necklace you see on my neck and gave it to me. Rasulullah ﷺ personally hung it on my neck and I have sworn by Allah that it would never leave my neck." The necklace remained on her neck until she passed away, when she requested that it be buried with her. Whenever she took a bath after menstruating, she always added salt to the water and made a request that salt be added to the water used to bathe her dead body. *(Ibn Is'haq, Ahmad, Abu Dawud, Waqidi in Ai Bidayah wan Nihayah).*

The Story of a Woman who Left in the Path of Allah and Her Goat

Humaid bin Hilal narrates that a man from the Banu Tufawa tribe often passed by and would narrate Ahadeeth to their tribe. He once narrated, "I arrived in Madinah with one of our caravans. After selling our goods, I told myself that I should meet with Rasulullah ﷺ and inform the others at home about him. When I came to him, Rasulullah ﷺ pointed out a house to me and said, 'A woman who lived in that house went out on an expedition with the army and left behind 12 goats and her needle with which she used to knit. When she lost one of her goats and her needle, she prayed, 'O my Rabb! You have undertaken to protect those who go out in Your path in every way. I have lost one of my goats and my needle. I ask You in Your name for my goat and my needle.' Rasulullah ﷺ described to me the determined manner in which she prayed to Allah. Next morning she had her goat and another just like it as well as her needle with another needle just like it. There she comes. There she is. You may ask her if you like.' 'No,' 1 replied, 'I believe what you say.'" *(Ahmad, Haythami).*

Ummu Haram bint Milhan رضي الله عنها, the Aunt of Anas رضي الله عنه Goes Out in the Path of Allah

Anas رضي الله عنه narrates that Rasulullah ﷺ once visited Ummu Haram bint Milhan رضي الله عنها, where he lay down to sleep. He then woke up smiling. When she asked him why he smiled, Rasulullah ﷺ replied, "I saw in a dream some people from my Ummah who were navigating the green seas in the Path of Allah looking as if they were kings on their thrones Ummu Haram رضي الله عنها said, "O Rasulullah ﷺ! Pray to Allah that I should be amongst them." Rasulullah ﷺ prayed, "O Allah! Make her from amongst them." Rasulullah ﷺ then again fell asleep and again woke up smiling. When she again asked him the reason for the smiling, he gave her the same reply. She again asked him to pray that she should be amongst them, he said, "You are with the first group and not with the second." Anas ﷺ says that Ummu Haram ﷺ married Ubadah bin Samit and joined the naval expedition with Bint Qaradha the wife of Mu'awiya ﷺ. Upon return she was riding an animal when it bolted. This caused her to fall and she passed away. *(Bukhari)*.

The services of women in Jihad: Women March with Rasulullah ﷺ to Tend to the Ill and Wounded

Ummu Sulaim ﷺ narrates that several women from the Ansar proceeded on military expeditions with Rasulullah ﷺ, where they would provide water for the ill and treat the wounded. *(Tabrani, Haythami)*. Anas ﷺ narrates that Ummu Sulaim ﷺ and other women of the Ansar would march with Rasulullah ﷺ on military expeditions. Their function was to provide water and tend to the wounded. *(Muslim, Tirmidhi)*.

The Services of Rubai Bint Mu'awidh ﷺ, Ummu Atia ﷺ and Laila Ghifaria ﷺ in Jihad

Rubai Bint Mu'awidh ﷺ reports that when they (women) were with Rasulullah ﷺ on military expeditions, they would provide water for the soldiers, treat the wounded and retrieve the bodies of the dead. *(Bukhari)*. Bukhar quotes that she said, "We would proceed on military expeditions with Rasulullah ﷺ where we would fetch water for the people, serve them and return the dead and wounded to Madinah when the battlefield was close to Madinah. *(Ahmad in Muntaqa)*. Ummu Atia ﷺ from the Ansar says, "I accompanied the army of Rasulullah ﷺ on 7 military expeditions. I would stay behind in their camp preparing food for them, nursing their wounded and tending to those with various diseases." *(Ahmad, Muslim, Ibn Majah in Muntaqa)*. Laila Ghifaria ﷺ narrates, "I used to proceed on military expeditions with Rasulullah ﷺ to nurse the wounded." *(Tabrani, Haythami)*.

The Services of Aisha ﷺ, Ummu Sulaim ﷺ and Ummu Salit ﷺ During the Battle of Uhud

Anas ﷺ says, "When the Muslims suffered some defeat during the Battle of Uhud and were unable to stay with Rasulullah ﷺ, I saw Aisha ﷺ the daughter of Abu Bakr ﷺ and Ummu Sulaim ﷺ with their shawls folded high to allow free movement. I could see their ankle bracelets as they ran with water bags." The 2 of them were carrying water bags on their backs, emptying the water into the mouths of the wounded and then returning to refill them. They then again returned to empty the water into the mouths of the injured. *(Bukhari, Muslim, Bayhaqi)*. Tha'laba bin Abu Malik ﷺ narrates that Omar ﷺ was distributing some cloth amongst the women of Madinah. When a single good cloth was still left, some people with him said, "O Amirul Mu'minin! Give it to the granddaughter of Rasulullah ﷺ married to you." They were referring to Ummu Kulthum ﷺ, the daughter of Ali ﷺ and Fatima ﷺ. Omar ﷺ said, "Ummu Salit ﷺ is more deserving." Ummu Salit ﷺ was a woman from the Ansar who had pledged allegiance to Rasulullah ﷺ. Omar said, "Because she sewed water bags for us during the battle of Uhud." *(Bukhari, Abu Nu'aym, Abu Ubaid in Kanzul Ummal)*

Women Proceed for the Battle of Khaibar to Render Services

The grandmother of Hashraj bin Ziyad ﷺ narrates that women also accompanied Rasulullah ﷺ for the battle of Khaibar. In her narration she mentions that Rasulullah ﷺ asked them the reason for going, they replied, "We are going out to weave ropes from animal hair to assist in the Path of Allah. We shall also nurse the wounded, retrieve arrows and give the soldiers barley to drink." *(Abu Dawud)*. Zuhri narrates that women participated in the battles with Rasulullah ﷺ by providing water and nursing the wounded. *(Abdur Razzaq in Fat'hul Bari)*

Ummu Ammara ﷺ Fights in the Battle of Uhud

Sa'eed bin Abu Zaid Ansari ﷺ narrates from Ummu Sa'd bint Sa'd bin Rabi ﷺ that she used to go to her maternal aunt Ummu Ammara ﷺ and ask her to relate her story. Ummu Ammara ﷺ would say, "It was at the beginning of the day that I ventured out with a bag of water to see what was happening to the Muslims. When I reached Rasulullah ﷺ, he was with his companions and the Muslims were enjoying victory and steadfastness. When the Muslims later started losing the battle, I drew close to Rasulullah ﷺ and openly started fighting. As I fended off the disbelievers from Rasulullah ﷺ, 1 also fired some arrows with a bow until I sustained many injuries." Ummu Sa'd ﷺ says that she noticed a very deep wound on the shoulder of Ummu Ammara ﷺ and asked her who had afflicted it. She replied, "It was Ibn Qami' Ahmad. May Allah disgrace him! The Sahabah had withdrawn from Rasulullah ﷺ, he came shouting, 'Show me where is Muhammad! I cannot be safe if he is safe!' Myself, Mus'ab bin Umair ﷺ and a few others who had remained with Rasulullah ﷺ also confronted him. It was then that he afflicted this wound to me. Although I struck several blows at him with my sword, the enemy of Allah was wearing 2 coats of armor." *(Ibn Hisham in Al Bidayah wan Nihayah, Waqidi in Isabah)*. Omarah bint Ghaziah narrates that during the battle of Uhud, Ummu Ammara ﷺ killed a disbelieving horseman. Omar ﷺ said, "I heard say, 'Whether it was to the right or to the left, in whichever direction I turned I saw her (Ummu Ammara ﷺ) fighting in my defense.'" *(Waqidi in Isaba)*. Hamza bin Sa'eed ﷺ narrates that some woolen shawls were once brought to Omar ﷺ. Amongst them was a very large one of excellent quality. Some people indicated that it was of great value and should be sent to Safia bint Ubaid who was recently married to Omar ﷺ's son Abdullah ﷺ. Omar ﷺ said, "I shall send it to someone who is more deserving to it, namely Ummu Ammara Nusaiba bint Ka'b ﷺ about whom I heard Rasulullah ﷺ say, 'Whether it was to the right or to the left, in whichever direction I turned I saw her fighting in my defense.'" *(Ibn Sa'd, Waqidi, JKanzul Ummal)*

Safia ﷺ Fights During the Battle of Uhud and the Battle of Khandaq

Hisham narrates from his father that when the Muslims were being defeated during the battle of Uhud, Safia ﷺ arrived with a spear in her hand to hit the retreating Muslims in the face and send them back to the battlefield. Rasulullah ﷺ said to her son Zubair ﷺ, "O Zubair! Look after the lady (your mother)." *(Ibn Sa'd in Isabah)*. Abbad narrates that during the battle of Khandaq, Safia bint Abdul Muttalib ﷺ was in a fortress called Fari, which belonged to Hassan bin Thabit ﷺ. She narrates, "Hassan was with us (women and children) in the fortress when a Jew passed by and started circling the fortress. The Jewish Banu Quraizah tribe had declared war on Rasulullah ﷺ and had severed the ties they had with him. There was none to defend us from the Jews since Rasulullah ﷺ and the Muslims were at the necks of the enemy and were unable to turn their attention towards us. When the intruder came towards us, I said, 'O Hassan! As you can see, this Jew is circling the fortress. By Allah! I fear that he will inform the Jews behind us about our secrets while Rasulullah ﷺ and his companions are occupied elsewhere. Go down and kill him.' Hassan ﷺ replied, 'May Allah forgive you, O

Daughter of Abdul Muttalib. You know well that I am unable to do that.' When he said this to me and I saw that I could expect no support from him, I took a tent peg and came down from the fortress. I struck the Jew until he died. I returned to the fortress and said, 'O Hassan! Go and take his possessions. The thing that prevented me from taking them was that he is a man.' Hassan said, 'I have no need for this, O daughter of Abdul Muttalib.'" *(Ibn Is'haq in Al Bidayah wan Nihayah, Bayhaqi, Kanzul Ummal, Majma'uz Zawa'id)*

Ummu Sulaim takes up a Dagger to fight in the Battle of Hunain

During the Battle of Hunain, Abu Talha came laughing to Rasulullah. He said, "O Rasulullah! Have you seen my wife Ummu Sulaim with a dagger in her hand?" Rasulullah asked, "O Ummu Sulaim! What do you intend doing with that?" She replied, "My intention is to stab any disbeliever who comes close to me." *(Ibn Abi Shaiba in Kanzul Ummal, Ibn Sa'd in Isaba).* Anas reports that during the battle of Hunain, Ummu Sulaim took a dagger and kept it with her. Abu Talha saw her with it, he said to Rasulullah, "Look at Ummu Sulaim with a dagger!" "What is this dagger for?" Rasulullah asked her. She replied, "I am keeping it to tear the belly of any disbeliever who approaches me." This made Rasulullah smile. *(Muslim).*

Asma bint Yazid kills 9 Enemies during the Battle of Yarmuk

Muhajir narrates that Asma bint Yazid bin Sakan was the cousin of Mu'adh bin Jabal. Using a tent peg, she killed 9 Romans during the battle of Yarmuk. *(Tabrani, Haythami).*

Rasulullah refuses permission to Ummu Kabsha on Jihad

Ummu Kabsha belonged to the Banu Qudha a clan of the Udhra tribe. When she once requested permission from Rasulullah to participate in a particular expedition, Rasulullah refused. She said, "O Rasulullah! I do not wish to fight. All I intend doing is to nurse the wounded and sick and to give water to the ill." Rasulullah replied, "Had I not feared that this would become a regular practice and that people would say, 'But she went out (why can't I)', I would have granted you permission. You should rather stay at home." *(Tabrani, Haythami).*

The Reward For Obedience to One's Husband and Fulfilling His Rights Equals That of Jihad

Abdullah bin Abbas narrates that a woman once came to Rasulullah and said, "O Rasulullah! I have been sent to represent all the women before you. Allah has made Jihad compulsory on the men. They are rewarded when they suffer any injuries and if they are martyred, they remain alive by their Rabb and are sustained. On the other hand, all we women do is to serve the men. What rewards will we then receive?" Rasulullah replied, "Make it clear to every woman you meet that the reward for obedience to the husband and for fulfilling his rights equals this (reward for Jihad). There are few of you who do this." *(Bazzar). Tabrani* reported that a woman came to Rasulullah

and asked, "I have been sent to you as an envoy from the other women. Every woman who knows about my coming here and every woman who does not know about it have wished me to come. Allah is the Rabb of men and women alike and he is also the Rabb of women. Similarly, you are Allah's Rasul to men and women. Allah has made Jihad compulsory on the men. They receive the booty when they do well and are victorious and if they are martyred, they remain alive by their Rabb and are sustained. Which good deed of a woman can equal these deeds of men?" Rasulullah replied, "Obedience to their husbands and recognizing the rights they owe. There are few of you who actually do this." *(Tabrani in Targheeb wat Tarheeb)*

A Child Fights and is Injured in the Battle of Uhud

Sha'bi narrates that when the battle of Uhud was to take place, a woman gave her son a sword. Because he was unable to carry it, she tied it securely to his arm using leather straps. She then took him to Rasulullah saying, "O Rasulullah! This son of mine shall fight for you." As the battle progressed Rasulullah said to the boy, "Dear son! Attack here" and "Dear son! Attack there." The boy was later wounded and fell to the ground. When he was brought to Rasulullah, Rasulullah said, "Dear son! You must be terrified?" "No, O Rasulullah," he replied, "Not at all." *(Ibn Abi Shayba in Kanzul Ummal).*

Umair bin Abi Waqqas Weeps and is Granted Permission

Sa'd bin Abi Waqqas narrates that Rasulullah sent Umair bin Abi Waqqas back as they were proceeding to Badr because Rasulullah thought that he was too young. However, when Umair started weeping out of disappointment, Rasulullah granted him permission. Sa'd bin Abi Waqqas says, "I then tied a knot on the belt that held his sword because it was too large for him. I also participated in the battle of Badr at a time when there was only a single hair on my face that I could hold in my fingers because my beard had just started growing." *(Ibn Asakir in Kanzul Ummal, Hakim, Baghawi).*

Umair bin Abi Waqqas is Martyred

Sa'd bin Abi Waqqas says, "Before we presented ourselves to Rasulullah for the battle of Badr, I noticed my brother Umair bin Abi Waqqas hiding from Rasulullah. 'What is the matter, dear brother?' I asked. 'I fear that Rasulullah would see me and send me back to Madinah thinking that I a too young whereas I would love to march so that Allah should bless me with martyrdom.' When he was presented to Rasulullah, Rasulullah asked him to return. However, when he started weeping, Rasulullah permitted him. I then tied knots to the belt that held his sword because of his small size. He was later martyred at the tender age of 16." *(Ibn Sa'd in Isaba, Bazzar, Haythami).*

The Chapter Concerning the Unity

This chapter highlights how the Sahabah attached great importance to unity in word and in deed and how they abstained from disagreement and dispute in matters that had consequences on Da'wah to Allah and His Rasul ﷺ and matters of Jihad.

The Statement of Abu Bakr ؓ Concerning Disagreement

Ibn Is'haq reports the historic sermon that Abu Bakr ؓ delivered in the orchard of the Banu Sa'idah. Abu Bakr ؓ said, "It is not permissible for the Muslim to have 2 leaders. As soon as this happens, disagreement springs up in all their affairs and all the commands issued. Their unity is then fragmented and they start to fight amongst themselves. At this point, the Sunnah is forsaken, Bid'ah raises its ugly head and anarchy intensifies. No one can then set matters right." *(Bayhaqi)*.

The Statement of Omar ؓ Concerning Disagreement

In the narration discussing the scenario before the pledge of allegiance was taken at the hand of Abu Bakr ؓ, Salim bin Ubaid states that someone from the Ansar said, "Who do we not appoint a leader from amongst us (Ansar) and another from amongst you (Muhajirin)." Omar ؓ responded to this by saying, "2 swords in one sheath!? They will never fit." *(Bayhaqi)*.

The Sermon of Abdullah bin Mas'ood ؓ in Which he Warned About the Dangers of Disagreement

Abdullah bin Mas'ood ؓ once said, "O people! You should hold fast to obedience to your leader and preserving your unity because unity is the rope of that Allah has commanded you to hold fast. What you dislike in staying united is much better than what you like in being divided. In everything that Allah has created, He has also predetermined its end. Islam is thriving right now and the time will soon come when it will also draw near to its end. It will then flourish and weaken until the Day of Qiyamah. The sign of this is extreme poverty. Poverty will be so great that a poor man will not find anyone to give him anything and even a rich man will not regard what he has to be sufficient for him. In fact, a person will place his need before his blood brother and cousin, but none will give him anything. The situation will be so bad that a beggar will beg from Friday to Friday without anyone putting anything in his hand. When matters reach this ebb, a splitting sound will emerge from the earth, which will lead the people of every area to think that it is coming from the ground beneath them. There will then be silence for as long as Allah wills, after which the earth will stir and start to vomit out all her prized possessions." When someone asked Abdullah bin Mas'ood ؓ what the prized possessions of the earth are, he replied, "Pillars of gold and silver. From that day onwards, none shall benefit form gold and silver until the Day of Judgment." *(Tabrani, Haythami)*. Abdullah bin Mas'ood ؓ said, "Family ties will be severed to the extent that the rich will only fear poverty and the poor will have none to show compassion towards him. In fact, even if a person has to place his need before his own brother or cousin, none would show a bit of sympathy to give him a thing." *(Abu Nu'aym in his Hilya)*.

The Statement of Abu Dhar ؓ Concerning Disagreement

A man related that they once took some things for Abu Dhar ؓ. However, when they reached Rabdha (place where he lived) and asked for him, he was not available. Someone told them that Abu Dhar ؓ had requested the Amirul Mu'minin to perform Hajj and had received permission. The men then left for Mina where they found him. They were once sitting in his company when someone informed him that the Amirul Mu'minin Uthman ؓ had performed 4 Rakahs salah in Mina. This upset Abu Dhar ؓ greatly and he had strong words to say. He also said, "When I performed salah behind Rasulullah ﷺ in Mina, he performed only 2 Rakahs salah. I then performed salah behind Abu Bakr ؓ and Omar ؓ both of whom also performed 2 Rakahs." Despite saying this Abu Dhar ؓ then stood up when the salah was performed and performed 4 Rakahs salah behind Uthman ؓ. Someone said to him, "You have just criticized the Amirul Mu'minin but you now do the same thing he did?" Abu Dhar ؓ replied, "Causing disagreement by opposing the Amirul Mu'minin is even worse. I have heard Rasulullah ﷺ say'. 'There shall be kings after me. Never disgrace them because whoever ventures to do so will have taken off the rope of Islam from his neck and cast it away. The repentance of such a person will never be accepted until he fills the void he has created by repairing the damage he has done to Islam, which he will be unable to do and he then returns to the ranks of those who honor the king.' Rasulullah ﷺ asked us not to allow the kings to overpower us with regards to 3 factors although we should honor them, this should prevent us: (1) that we enjoin people to do good, (2) that we prevent them from evil and (3) that we teach them the Sunnah." *(Ahmad, Haythami)*

The Statement of Abdullah bin Mas'ood ؓ

Qatadah narrates that Rasulullah ﷺ, Abu Bakr ؓ and Omar ؓ all performed 2 Rakahs Fardh salah in Makkah and in Mina. Uthman ؓ also used to do this during the initial years of his Khilafa. He then started performing 4 Rakahs. When this news reached Abdullah bin Mas'ood ؓ, he recited "*Inna Lillahi wa Inna Ilaihi Raji'un*" but when the salah was performed, he stood up and performed 4 Rakahs salah behind Uthman ؓ. Someone said to him, "You have just recited '*Inna Lillahi wa Inna Ilaihi Raji'un*' but you have performed 4 Rakahs salah?" Abdullah bin Mas'ood ؓ replied, "Causing disagreement by opposing Amirul Mu'minin is even worse." *(Abdur Razzaq in Kanzul Ummal)*.

The Statement of Ali ؓ Concerning Disagreement, Bid'ah, Unity and Disunity

Ali ؓ once said to the people, "Continue doing as you have been doing during the terms of the previous Khalifah because I hate disunity. Either people remain an undivided nation or I die without seeing any disunity as my companions Abu Bakr ؓ, Omar ؓ and Uthman ؓ had passed away." *Ibn Sirin* was of the opinion that most of the narrations that some people of extreme viewpoints narrated from Ali ؓ were false as they fabricated narrations to cause more disunity. *(Bukhari, Abu Ubaid in Kanzul Ummal, Isfahani in Hujjah, Muntakhab)*. *Salim bin Qais Amiri* narrates that Ibnul Kawwa once asked Ali ؓ about the Sunnah, Bid'ah, unity and disunity. Ali ؓ replied, "O Ibnul Kawwa! Just as you have memorized the question, so too should you remember the reply. The Sunnah is the way of Rasulullah ﷺ while Bid'ah is everything that contradicts it. By Allah, unity is the consensus of the people of truth even though they may be few while disunity is the consensus of the people of falsehood even though they may be many." *(Asaki in Kazul Ummal)*.

The Demise of Rasulullah ﷺ and the Sermon of Abu Bakr ؓ as Khalifa

Urwa bin Zubair ؓ says that after hearing about the demise of Rasulullah ﷺ, Abu Bakr ؓ came on his animal from the Sunh district of Madinah. He then dismounted at the door of the

Masjid. He was filled with sorrow and grief as he sought permission to enter the room of his daughter Aisha ﷺ. When she gave permission, he entered the room where Rasulullah ﷺ had passed away on the bed. Sitting around Rasulullah ﷺ were his wives who veiled their faces and concealed themselves from Abu Bakr ﷺ. Of course, there was no need for Aisha ﷺ to do so. Abu Bakr opened the face of Rasulullah ﷺ and then knelt on his knees to kiss Rasulullah ﷺ. He wept as he said, "What the son of Khattab says is not true. I swear by the Being Who controls my life that Rasulullah ﷺ has certainly passed away. May Allah's mercy be showered on you, O Rasulullah ﷺ! You are so pure in life and in death!" Abu Bakr ﷺ then covered the face of Rasulullah ﷺ and hastened to the Masjid, skipping over the shoulders of people sitting there until he reached the pulpit. When he saw Abu Bakr ﷺ approach, even Omar ﷺ sat down. Standing at the side of the pulpit, Abu Bakr ﷺ called the people and they all sat down and kept silent. He recited the Shahada as he knew it and said, "Allah had given the news of the demise of His Nabi ﷺ when he was still alive amongst you. He has also given you the news of your own deaths. Death is a reality and there will come a time when none but Allah will be alive. Allah has declared:

وَمَا مُحَمَّدٌ إِلَّا رَسُولٌ قَدْ خَلَتْ مِنْ قَبْلِهِ الرُّسُلُ أَفَإِنْ مَاتَ أَوْ قُتِلَ انْقَلَبْتُمْ عَلَى أَعْقَابِكُمْ وَمَنْ يَنْقَلِبْ عَلَى عَقِبَيْهِ فَلَنْ يَضُرَّ اللَّهَ شَيْئًا وَسَيَجْزِي اللَّهُ الشَّاكِرِينَ (144)

'Muhammad ﷺ is no more than a Messenger, and indeed (many) Messengers have passed away before him. If he dies or is killed, will you then turn back on your heels (as disbelievers)? And he who turns back on his heels, not the least harm will he do to Allah, and Allah will give reward to those who are grateful. (Al-Imran:144)

Omar ﷺ exclaimed, "Is this verse in the Qur'an? By Allah, to this day, I had never known that it was ever revealed. I had completely forgotten about it!" Abu Bakr ﷺ continued, "Allah has also mentioned the following about Muhammad ﷺ:

إِنَّكَ مَيِّتٌ وَإِنَّهُمْ مَيِّتُونَ (30)

Verily, you (O Rasulullah ﷺ) will die, and verily they (too) will die!.'' (Az-ZOmar:30)

Allah has also mentioned:

كُلُّ شَيْءٍ هَالِكٌ إِلَّا وَجْهَهُ لَهُ الْحُكْمُ وَإِلَيْهِ تُرْجَعُونَ (88)

'Everything will perish save His Face, His is the Decision, and to Him you (all) shall be returned.' (Al-Qasas:88)

Allah also says: كُلُّ مَنْ عَلَيْهَا فَانٍ (26) وَيَبْقَى وَجْهُ رَبِّكَ ذُو الْجَلَالِ وَالْإِكْرَامِ (27)

Whatsoever is on it (the earth) will perish. And the Face of your Lord full of Majesty and Honor will remain forever. (Ar-Rahman:26-27)

Allah says in another verse:

كُلُّ نَفْسٍ ذَائِقَةُ الْمَوْتِ وَإِنَّمَا تُوَفَّوْنَ أُجُورَكُمْ يَوْمَ الْقِيَامَةِ

Everyone shall taste death. And only on the Day of Resurrection shall you be paid your wages in full. (Al-Imran:185)

Abu Bakr ﷺ continued, "Allah had given a lifetime to Rasulullah ﷺ and kept him alive until he established Islam, made the commands of Allah explicit, passed on the message of Allah and exerted himself in the Path of Allah. In this condition, Allah then took him away after he had left you on a path. Now whoever dies will die after being exposed to the clear proofs of Iman and the great cure to kufr, which is the Qur'an. Therefore, whoever took Allah as his Rabb should know that Allah is Alive and shall never die. On the other hand, whoever worshipped Muhammad ﷺ and took him as a god should know that their god is no more. Fear Allah, O people! Hold fast to your Islam and rely on your Rabb because Islam has been established and the word of Allah is complete. Allah will assist whoever assists Islam and it is Allah Who will strengthen Islam. Indeed, the Book of Allah that is amongst you is a light and a source of healing. It is through this Book that Allah had guided Muhammad ﷺ and it contains the details of the things that Allah has made Halal and what He has made Haram. By Allah! We have no concern for any of Allah's creation that wishes to attack us because the swords of Allah are drawn and we shall never put them down. We shall continue fighting those who oppose us just as we did with Rasulullah ﷺ. Whoever oppresses shall be oppressing only himself." The Muhajirin left together with Abu Bakr to attend the burial of Rasulullah ﷺ. *(Bayhaqi in Al Bidayah wan Nihayah).*

The Sermon of Omar ﷺ When Most of the Sahabah Pledge Their Allegiance to Abu Bakr ﷺ

Anas ﷺ reports that he heard the closing sermon of Omar ﷺ as he sat on the pulpit the day after Rasulullah ﷺ passed away. Abu Bakr ﷺ sat in silence without saying a word. Omar ﷺ said, "I wished that Rasulullah ﷺ would remain alive until we had all passed away, so that he would be the last of us alive. However, we have nothing to fear because even though Muhammad ﷺ has passed away, Allah has left in our midst a light (the Qur'an) by which we are guided and which has also guided Muhammad ﷺ. Abu Bakr ﷺ is the close companion of Rasulullah ﷺ. He was the second of the 2 (in the cave with Rasulullah ﷺ during the Hijra) and he is the most worthy of administering the affairs of the Muslims. You should stand up and pledge your allegiance to him." Although a large group had already pledged their allegiance to Abu Bakr ﷺ in the orchard of the Banu Sa'ida, the general pledge of all the Muslims took place in the Masjid. *(Bukhari)* Imam Zuhri narrates from Anas ﷺ that on that day Omar ﷺ kept insisting that Abu Bakr ﷺ mount the pulpit until he was forced to do so. The general public pledged their allegiance.

The Sahabah Pledge Their Allegiance to Abu Bakr ﷺ in the Orchard

Imam Zuhri narrates from Anas ﷺ that the day after the Sahabah had pledged their allegiance to Abu Bakr ﷺ in the orchard, Abu Bakr ﷺ sat on the pulpit in the Masjid as Omar stood by. Speaking before Abu Bakr ﷺ, Omar ﷺ duly praised Allah and then said, "O people! What I told you yesterday that Rasulullah ﷺ had not passed away was incorrect. Neither have I found this in the Book of Allah nor has Rasulullah ﷺ instructed me to say it. However, I always thought that Rasulullah ﷺ would be the last of us and found it difficult to accept that he had left the world before us. Nevertheless, Allah has left with you His Book by which He guided Rasulullah ﷺ. If you hold fast to it, Allah shall guide you to that which He has guided Rasulullah ﷺ. Allah has also united you under the leadership of the best amongst you, namely the close companion of Rasulullah ﷺ who was 'the second of the two when they were in the cave'. So stand up and pledged your allegiance to Abu Bakr ﷺ." The general public then pledged their allegiance to Abu Bakr ﷺ after some had already pledged their allegiance in the orchard. Abu Bakr ﷺ then addressed the people. After duly praising Allah, he said, "O people! Although I have been appointed as your leader, I am by no means the best of you. Should I do what is right, do assist me and should I do wrong, do correct me. To be truthful is a great trust while lying is a terrible misuse of trust. The weak amongst you are powerful in my eyes and I shall see that I remove the causes for his complaint. On the other hand, the powerful ones amongst you are weak in my eyes and I shall endeavor to take from them the dues they owe to others, InsAllah. Whenever a nation forsakes Jihad, Allah humiliates them and whenever immoral behavior becomes widespread amongst them, Allah surrounds them with calamities. Obey me as long as I obey Allah and His Rasul. However, should I ever disobey Allah and His Rasul ﷺ, you are not obliged to obey me at all. You may now stand up for your salah. May Allah shower His mercies on you all." *(Ibn Is'haq in Al Bidayah wan Nihayah).*

The Khilafa of Abu Bakr ؓ and the Lecture that Omar ؓ Delivered Concerning What Happened in the Orchard of the Banu Sa'ida

Abdullah bin Abbas ؓ says that he used to teach the Qur'an to Abdur Rahman bin Auf ؓ and he was waiting for Abdur Rahman bin Auf ؓ one day in Mina during the final Hajj that Omar bin Khattab ؓ performed. When Abdur Rahman bin Auf ؓ returned to the place where they were staying, he informed Abdullah bin Abbas ؓ that a man had approached Omar ؓ and told him about someone else who had said, "When Omar ؓ passes away, I shall pledge my allegiance to a certain man (Talha bin Ubaidullah ؓ) because the pledge of allegiance taken to Abu Bakr ؓ was a very sudden thing and came to a completion (I shall also do so all of a sudden and he will automatically become the Khalifa)." Omar ؓ said, "InsAllah I shall deliver a lecture to the people tonight to warn them about this group that wishes to snatch away the Khilafah." However, Abdur Rahman bin Auf ؓ said, "Do not do that, O Amirul Mu'minin because Hajj brings together even the riff-raff and people of low understanding. When you stand up to address the people, it is these types of people who will dominate the gathering and when you speak, they will exaggerate your words without understanding them and give them interpretations they were never intended to mean. Wait until you reach Madinah because it is the place of Hijra and the Sunnah. There you should gather the learned scholars and prominent people and address them at ease. They will understand you and interpret your words as you intend them." Omar ؓ then said, "If I reach Madinah, I shall definitely address the people about this at the first opportunity."

Abdullah bin Abbas ؓ relates further, "When we returned to Madinah on a Friday during the end of Dhul Hijjah, I hastened to the Masjid at midday without bothering about the intense heat. There I saw that Sa'eed bin Zaid ؓ had preceded me and was sitting on the right hand side of the pulpit. I sat in front of him with my knees touching his. It was not long before Omar ؓ arrived. I said, 'This afternoon he will say such things on this pulpit that were never said before.' Sa'eed bin Zaid ؓ refuted what I said by saying, 'It is unlikely that he will say anything that no other has mentioned before.' Omar ؓ sat down and after the Mu'adhin had finished, he stood up. After duly praising Allah, he said, 'O people! What I wish to say today has been predestined for me to say for I know not whether death may be waiting before me. Therefore, whoever understands what I say and remembers it should take it as far as his conveyance can carry him. However, I do not give permission for anyone who does not understand it well to go and lie about me.'" Omar ؓ continued, "Allah had sent Muhammad ﷺ with the truth and revealed a Book to him. Amongst the verses revealed to him were the verses of Rajm, stoning to death of a married person found guilty of adultery. We read the verse, memorized it and understood it. Rasulullah ﷺ therefore had people stoned and we did so after him. I fear that as lengthy periods of time pass by you, people would begin to say, 'We do not find the verse of Rajm in the Qur'an.' They will therefore go astray by forsaking a compulsory injunction that Allah has detailed. Rajm is therefore established

in the Book of Allah to be enforced on married males and females when either proven guilty beyond doubt, when pregnancy takes place or when the person confesses. Take note that we also used to read, 'Do not turn away from your forefathers by associating yourselves with others because turning away from them is extreme ingratitude.' Just as it was with the verse of Rajm, the words of this verse were abrogated without the injunction being cancelled. Listen well! Verily Rasulullah ﷺ said, 'Never be excessive in praising me as people were excessive in praising Isa the son of Maryam ﵎. I am only a servant of Allah, so refer to me as Allah's servant and His Rasul ﷺ.' The news has also reached me that one of you has said, 'When Omar ؓ passes away, I shall pledge my allegiance to so-and so.' No person should ever be fooled into saying that the pledge of allegiance taken to Abu Bakr ؓ was a very sudden thing and came to a completion. Although it did happen very quickly, Allah had saved the entire Ummah from any evil that would have been the result of it being delayed. In addition to this, you have no one today of the caliber of Abu Bakr ؓ for whom people would sacrifice their very lives.

What happened on the day that Rasulullah ﷺ passed away was that Ali ؓ, Zubair ؓ and those with them stayed behind in the house of Fatima ؓ the daughter of Rasulullah ﷺ. On the other hand, everyone of the Ansar stayed behind in the orchard of the Banu Sa'ida while the Muhajirin gathered around Abu Bakr ؓ. I said, 'O Abu Bakr ؓ! Let us go to our Ansar brothers.' As we walked towards them, we met 2 righteous men: Uwaim Ansari ؓ and Ma'n ؓ who informed us about what the Ansar were doing. They asked, 'Where are you off to, O assembly of Muhajirin?' 'We are off to see our brothers from the Ansar,' we replied. 'No!' they said, 'There is no need for you to do that. Why don't you Muhajirin rather discuss your own affairs.' I said, 'By Allah! We shall definitely go to them.' We then went to the orchard of the Banu Sa'ida where we found the Ansar gathered together.' In their midst we saw someone wrapped in a blanket. 'Who is that?' I asked. 'Sa'd bin Ubada,' they replied. I asked further, 'What is wrong with him?' 'He is ill,' came the reply. After we were seated, one of the Ansar stood up to give a lecture. After duly praising Allah, he said, 'We are the Ansar (helpers) of Allah's Islam and the army of Islam. You, O assembly of Muhajirin, are the group of our Nabi ﷺ and one of you has mentioned things that give us the impression that you wish to ignore us and keep the Khilafa away from us. When he was silent, I intended to say something that I had prepared. It was an impressive speech that I intended saying before Abu Bakr ؓ in which my usual harshness was well concealed. However, Abu Bakr ؓ bade me to be quiet and I did not wish to oppose him since he was more knowledgeable and more composed than me, so I remained seated. By Allah! When he spoke, Abu Bakr ؓ did not omit to say anything that impressed me from what I had prepared. Until he had completed, he either said exactly what I wanted to say or better than that. He said, 'You (Ansar) are most worthy of whatever good you have already mentioned. The Arabs associate leadership only with the Quraish tribe because their lineage and their city is the best. I have selected 2 persons for you. You may pledge your allegiance to whichever one of them you choose.' Abu Bakr ؓ then took hold of my hand and the hand of Abu Ubaidah bin Jarrah ؓ. Besides this, there was nothing of his speech that I disliked. By Allah! I would prefer being led to be executed for committing no crime rather than being the leader of a community that includes Abu Bakr ؓ. This is what I felt at that time and I do not know whether this opinion would change at the time of my death.

Someone from the Ansar then said, 'I have the perfect solution and the best medicine for this. O assembly of Quraish! Let there be an Amir from amongst us and another from amongst you.' Order was then lost and voices started being raised. This reached such a point that we feared serious disagreement. I then said, 'Stretch out your hand, O Abu Bakr!' When he stretched out his hand, I pledged my allegiance to him and all the Muhajirin followed suit. The Ansar then also pledged their allegiance to him. In the furor we happened to bump Sa'd bin Ubadah ؓ over. When someone said, 'You have killed Sa'd,' I replied, 'Allah has killed Sa'd.' By Allah! From all matters that we have jointly participated in, there was no matter more timely done than the pledge of allegiance taken at the hand of Abu Bakr ؓ. We acted quickly because we feared that if we left the Ansar without any pledge of allegiance being taken, they would take the pledge of allegiance by themselves at the hands of someone else. We would then either be forced to pledge our allegiance as they had done against our wishes or we would have to oppose them, the obvious result of which would have been anarchy and disorder. The root is that whoever pledges his allegiance to another without consulting the Muslims has not pledged any allegiance and neither has the other person any authority as a leader. In fact, it is feared that they would both be killed. A narration of *Zuhri* from Urwa ؓ states that the 2 men who met Abu Bakr ؓ and Omar ؓ were Uwaim bin Sa'ida ؓ and Ma'n bin Adi ؓ. A narration of Sa'eed bin Musaib clarifies that the Sahab who said, "I have the perfect solution and the best medicine for this" was Huba bin Mundhir ؓ. *(Ahmad, Malik in Al Bidayah wan Nihayah, Bukhari, Abu Ubaid in Ghara'ib, Bayhaqi, Ibn Abi Shayba in Kanzui Ummal).*

The Narration of Abdullah bin Abbas ؓ Concerning the Talk of Khilafa That Took Place in the Orchard of the Banu Sa'ida

Omar ؓ narrates that what actually happened after Rasulullah ﷺ passed away was that someone came and informed them that the Ansar had gathered with Sa'd bin Ubadah ؓ in the orchard of the Banu Sa'ida where they intended taking the pledge of allegiance. Omar ؓ, Abu Bakr ؓ, and Abu Ubaidah bin Jarrah ؓ stood up in alarm and hastened towards the Ansar fearing that they may introduce something strange into Islam. They happened to meet 2 truthful men on their way, Uwaim bin Sa'ida ؓ and Ma'n bin Adi ؓ. When the 2 men asked where the others were off to, the others replied, "We are off to see your people (the Ansar) concerning what we have heard about their activities.' The 2 men said, "You may return because you can never be opposed and nothing can be done without your approval." Omar ؓ says, "We refused to listen to them and continued. In the meantime, I was preparing a speech to' say to them. When we eventually reached them, we found them all around Sa'd bin Ubadah ؓ who was lying on a bed due to illness." When the Muhajirin arrived, the Ansar addressed them saying, "O assembly of the Quraish! Let there be an Amir from amongst us and another from amongst you." Hubab bin Mundhir ؓ added, "I have the perfect solution and the best medicine for this. By Allah! If you agree, we could make this as pleasant as a young camel." "Take it easy," said Abu Bakr ؓ. As he started talking, he first bade Omar ؓ to be silent. Thereafter, he praised Allah and said, "O assembly of Ansar! I swear by Allah that we do not deny your virtues. We neither deny the high status that you have reached in Islam nor the rights that we owe you. However, even you acknowledge that no other tribe enjoys the status that the Quraish enjoys amongst all the Arabs. You also know well that the Arabs will unite only under the leadership of

one of them. While we from the Quraish shall be the leaders, you (Ansar) shall be our ministers. Fear Allah! Do not cause divisions in Islam and do not be the first to introduce something strange into Islam. I have selected 2 men referring to Omar ؓ and Abu Ubaidah bin Jarrah ؓ. Whichever of them you choose to pledge your allegiance, you may be rest assured that he is dependable." Omar ؓ says, "By Allah! There was nothing that I wanted said which Abu Bakr ؓ did not say except this part where he named me as a potential candidate. I swear by Allah that I would prefer being killed, then brought back to life and then being killed again for no crime on my part rather than being appointed leader of a community that includes Abu Bakr ؓ." Omar ؓ then addressed the gathering saying, "O assembly of Ansar! O assembly of Muslims! Indeed the person most worthy of leadership after Rasulullah ﷺ is 'the second of the 2 when they were in the cave'. He is Abu Bakr ؓ who was clearly the very first to enter Islam." Omar ؓ then grabbed the hand of Abu Bakr ؓ but before he could pledge his allegiance to Abu Bakr ؓ, an Ansari beat him to it. All the other people followed suit and no attention was given to Sa'd bin Ubadah ؓ. *(Ibn Abi Shayba in Kanzul Ummal).*

The Narration of Ibn Sirin Concerning What Happened in the Hall of the Banu Sa'ida

Ibn Sirin رحمة الله narrates from a man from the Banu Zuraiq tribe that on that fateful day when Rasulullah ﷺ passed away, Abu Bakr ؓ and Omar ؓ went to the Ansar. Abu Bakr ؓ said, "O assembly of Ansar! We certainly do not deny the rights owed to you. No Mu'min can deny these rights. By Allah! You have always shared in any good that came to us. However, the Arabs will never accept and shall never be happy with any leader that does not belong to the Quraish. This is because from all Arabs the Quraish are the most eloquent of people, have the best lineage, have the best city and feed the most people. So come to Omar and pledge your allegiance to him." "No!" replied the Ansar. "Why not?" asked Omar ؓ. The Ansar replied, "Because we fear that he will give others preference over us." Omar ؓ said, "Never! I shall never do this as long as I live. Rather pledge your allegiance to Abu Bakr ؓ." Abu Bakr ؓ said to Omar ؓ, "You are stronger than me." "But you are more virtuous than me," responded Omar ؓ. Omar ؓ repeated this 3 times. On the 3rd time, Omar ؓ added, "Together with your virtue, you shall have my strength with you." Addressing the people, he then said, "Pledge your allegiance to Abu Bakr ؓ." As people were pledging their allegiance to Abu Bakr ؓ, some people approached Abu Ubaidah bin Jarrah ؓ (to pledge allegiance to him). Abu Ubaidah ؓ said to them, "How can you come to me when you have amongst you 'the second of the two'?" *(Ibn Abi Shayba in Kanzul Ummah).*

A Narration of Ibn Asakir and the Statement of Abu Ubaidah bin Jarrah ؓ Concerning the Khilafa of Abu Bakr ؓ

Muslim narrates that Abu Bakr ؓ sent a message to Abu Ubaidah bin Jarrah ؓ saying, "Come forward so that I may make you the Khalifa because I have heard Rasulullah ﷺ say that every nation has an Amin, someone most trustworthy and that you are the Amin of this Ummah." Abu Ubaidah bin Jarrah ؓ replied, "I can never step ahead of a person (yourself) whom Rasulullah ﷺ had instructed to lead us in salah." *(Ibn Asakir in Kanzul Ummal, Hakim, Ibn Asakir, Ibn Shahin in Kanzul Ummal).*

A Hadith of Ahmad and the Statements of Abu Ubaidah bin Jarrah ؓ and Uthman ؓ Concerning the Khilafa of Abu Bakr ؓ

Abul Bakhtari narrates that Omar ؓ said to Abu Ubaidah

bin Jarrah, "Stretch out your hand so that I may pledge my allegiance to you because I have heard Rasulullah say that you are the Amin of this Ummah." Abu Ubaidah bin Jarrah replied, "I am not likely to step head of a person whom Rasulullah had commanded to lead us in salah and who then led us in salah until Rasulullah passed away." *(Ahmad, Haythami)*. Abu Ubaidah said, "Since accepting Islam I have never seen you do something so ridiculous! How can you pledge allegiance to me when you have amongst you As Siddiq who is 'the second of the two'?" *(Ibn Sa'd)*. Uthman bin Affan said, "Abu Bakr is the most worthy of it (Khilafa) as he was 'the 2nd of the 2' and close companion of Rasulullah." *(Kanzul Ummal)*

Abu Bakr declines to accept the Post of Khalifa and the Statements of Ali and Zubair he is Most Worthy of the Position

Sa'd bin Ibrahim bin Abdur Rahman bin Auf narrates that Abdur Rahman bin Auf was with Omar when Muhammad bin Masalama broke the sword of Zubair. Abu Bakr then stood up to address the people and excused himself from accepting the post as Khalifa. He said, "I swear by Allah that there was not a single day or night in which I desired leadership. Neither was I inclined towards leadership nor have I ever prayed to Allah for it in secret or in public. However, I accepted the post because I feared great anarchy amongst the Muslims without a leader. I derive no peace in leadership. I have been burdened with a formidable task that I have no power to do without the strength provided by Allah. I still wish that someone more powerful than me was in my position today." Although the Muhajirin accepted what Abu Bakr had to say, Ali and Zubair said, "The only grievance we have is that we were excluded from the consultations. However, we are also of the opinion that Abu Bakr is most worthy of the post after Rasulullah. He was the companion of Rasulullah in the cave and the '2nd of the 2'. We definitely acknowledge his status and his seniority. Rasulullah instructed him to lead the Muslims in salah while Rasulullah was alive." *(Hakim, Bayhaqi)*.

The Narration of Ibn Asakir Concerning the Difference of Opinion Between Ali and Abu Sufian

Suwaid bin Ghafala narrates that Abu Sufian once came to Ali and Abbas and said, "O Ali and Abbas! What is wrong that leadership is with the clan of the Quraish that is the lowest in rank and the fewest in number? By Allah! If you wish, I could fill Madinah with cavalry and infantry to oppose Abu Bakr." Ali replied, "No, by Allah! I have no desire for you to fill Madinah with cavalry and infantry. Had we not believed that Abu Bakr was worthy of the post, we would have never left it to him. O Abu Sufian! The Mu'minin are people who wish well for each other. They love each other though their homes and bodies may be far apart. On the other hand, it is the hypocrite who endeavors to deceive each other." *(Ibn Asakir in Kanzul Ummal)*. Another narration adds about the hypocrite, "Even though their homes and bodies are close by, they are people who deceive each other. We have pledged our allegiance to Abu Bakr and he is most worthy of the post." *(Kanzul Ummal)*

A Narration of Abdur Razzaq and Hakim Concerning What Happened Between Ali and Abu Sufian

Ibn Abjar reports that after the pledge of allegiance was taken at the hand of Abu Bakr, Abu Sufian went to Ali and said, "The smallest clan of the Quraish has overpowered you with regards to leadership! Listen well! If you wish, I could fill

Madinah with cavalry and infantry to oppose Abu Bakr." Ali said to him, "Even if you remain the enemy of Islam and the Muslims forever, it will not affect Islam and its people in the least. In our opinion, Abu Bakr is most worthy of the position." *(Ibn Mubarak in Isti'ab)*. Murra bin Tayib narrates that Abu Sufian bin Harb approached Ali to say, "How is it that leadership has gone to that clan of the Quraish who are the smallest in number and the lowest in rank referring to the clan of Abu Bakr. By Allah! If you wish, I could fill Madinah with cavalry and infantry to oppose Abu Bakr." Ali responded, "For as long as you wish to bear enmity for Islam and its people, Abu Sufian, you will not be able to harm them in the least. We have found Abu Bakr to be worthy of the post." *(Hakim)*.

The Differences Between Omar and Khalid bin Sa'eed Concerning the Khilafa of Abu Bakr

Sakhar who was Rasulullah's bodyguard. Rasulullah used bodyguards for a while, but then stopped using them when Allah revealed verse 67 of Sura Al-Ma'idah where Allah says, *"Allah shall protect you from the people"* narrates that Khalid bin Sa'eed bin Aas was in Yemen when Rasulullah passed away. He arrived in Madinah a month after Rasulullah's demise wearing a silken cover. When he met Omar and Ali, Omar called out to the people, "Tear up his cover! How can he wear silk when he is a Muslim man in times of peace?" After the people had torn his cover up, Khalid bin Sa'eed said, "O Abu Hasan (Ali)! O family of Abd Manaf! Have you been overpowered in leadership?" Ali said to him, "Do you view this as a power struggle or Khilafa?" Khalid bin Sa'eed said, "O family of Abd Manaf! No person better than you should overpower you in this matter. How could you allow Abu Bakr do so when he does not belong to the family of Abd Manaf?" Omar said to Khalid, "'May Allah smash your mouth! If any liar contemplates on what you have mentioned, he will do harm only to himself." *(Tabari, Saif and Ibn Asakir in Kanzul Ummal)*

A Narration of Ummu Khalid Concerning What Happened Between Abu Bakr and Khalid bin Sa'eed

Ummu Khalid who was the daughter of Khalid bin Sa'eed narrates that her father returned from Yemen only after the Muslims had already pledged their allegiance to Abu Bakr. Addressing Ali and Uthman, he said, "Do you people who are from the family of Abd Manaf accept that a person who does not belong to your clan should be appointed as your leader?" When Omar reported this to Abu Bakr, Abu Bakr ignored it while it remained in the heart of Omar. Khalid bin Sa'eed continued staying in Madinah for 3 months without pledging his allegiance to Abu Bakr. When Abu Bakr once passed by the house of Khalid bin Sa'eed one afternoon, Abu Bakr greeted him. Khalid said, "Do you want me to pledge my allegiance to you?" Abu Bakr replied, "All I want you to do is to enter into the agreement that all the Muslims have entered into." Khalid then said, "Let us make an appointment for tonight when I shall pledge my allegiance to you." Khalid arrived when Abu Bakr was seated on the pulpit and pledged his allegiance. Abu Bakr always had a good opinion of Khalid bin Sa'eed and respected him. When Abu Bakr once dispatched an army to Sham, he appointed Khalid as the commander (and gave him the flag). When Khalid took the flag home, Omar said to Abu Bakr, "How can you give command to Khalid when he had made those statements in the past?" Omar insisted so much that Abu Bakr eventually sent Abu Arwa Dowsi to Khalid with the message, "The

Khalifa of Rasulullah ﷺ requests you to return the flag to us." Khalid ؓ took out the flag and handed it over. He then said, "By Allah! Just as the appointment to command did not please me, the dismissal does not grieve me. The one to be blamed is someone other than the Khalifa (i.e. Omar ؓ)." Ummu Khalid narrated, "It was not long that Abu Bakr ؓ came to apologize to my father and took a promise from him not to every speak ill of Omar ؓ. By Allah! My father then always prayed for Omar until he passed away." *(Ibn Sa'd).*

Abu Bakr ؓ Marches for Jihad by Himself and the Statement of Ali ؓ in this Regard

Aisha ؓ narrates that Abu Bakr ؓ once drew his sword and rode his animal towards Dhu Qassah. Ali ؓ took hold of the animal's reins and said, "Where are you off to, O Khalifa of Rasulullah ﷺ? Today I shall say to you what Rasulullah ﷺ said to you during the battle of Uhud; 'Sheath your sword and do not cause me grief by getting yourself injured or martyred'. I swear by Allah that if we suffer any grief through you (coming to harm), Islam shall never regain its form." Abu Bakr ؓ then returned and dispatched an army instead. *(Saji in Kanzul Ummal, Dar Qutni in Al Bidayah wan Nihayah)*

The Lecture of Abu Bakr ؓ Concerning the Khilafa and his Statement That He Never Desired It For a Single Day or Night

Abu Bakr ؓ once said, "O people! You may think that I assumed the post as Khalifa because I had aspirations for it and because I desired to gain superiority over you. This is not true! I swear by the Being Who controls my life that I have never assumed the post because of any, aspirations and neither to attain superiority over you people or over any Muslim. I have never desired the position for a single night or day and I have never prayed to Allah for it either secretly- or in public. However, I have been burdened with this extremely formidable task which I have no strength to carry out without the assistance of Allah. I do wish that it be handed over to any other companion of Rasulullah ﷺ provided that he exercises justice. I am therefore returning the portfolio to you and acknowledge no pledge of allegiance from you. You may hand the post over to whoever you please for I am just an ordinary man amongst you." *(Abu Nu'aym in Fadha'ilus Sahabah, Kanzul Ummal)*

The response of the Sahabah to Abu Bakr ؓ and their statement confirming that he was the best amongst them

Isa bin Atia reports that the day after the Sahabah had pledged their allegiance to Abu Bakr ؓ, he stood up to deliver a lecture. He said, "O people! I am canceling your decision (to appoint me as Khalifa) for I am not the best of you. You should therefore pledge your allegiance to the person who is best amongst you." The Sahabah stood up and replied, "O Khalifa of Rasulullah ﷺ! We swear by Allah that you are the best amongst us." Abu Bakr ؓ said, "O people! There are people who entered into Islam willingly and those who entered unwillingly. They are how all in Allah's protection and His neighbors. If it is possible that Allah does not find you guilty of wronging anyone in His protection, then make sure that you do so. I also have a Saitan with me -so when you see me angry, stay away from me so that I may not harm even your hair or your skin. O people! Keep watch over the income of your slaves because flesh nourished with Haram cannot enter Jannah. Hear this well! Inspect me with your eyes and assist me when I do good. However should I deviate, then do correct me. Obey me as long as I obey Allah and disobey me if I disobey Allah." *(Tabrani in Kanzul Ummal, Haythami)*

Ali ؓ replied to Abu Bakr ؓ Emphasizing Never to Accept his Relinquishing the Khilafa nor would They Ask Him to Relinquish

Abul Jahaf narrates that for 3 days after people pledged their allegiance to Abu Bakr ؓ, he kept his door locked and on each day he would come out to say to the people, "O people! I have cancelled the pledge of allegiance that you have given me. You may pledge your allegiance to whoever you please." Each time he said this, Ali bin Abi Talib ؓ responded by saying, "Neither will we accept your relinquishing the Khilafa nor will we ever ask you to relinquish it. When Rasulullah ﷺ had placed you ahead, who can ever pull you back?" *(Usari in Kanzul Ummal).* Zaid bin Ali narrated from his seniors that on three occasions, Abu Bakr ؓ announced from the pulpit, "Is there anyone who is displeased with me being the Khalifa so that I may relinquish the post?" Each time it was Ali bin Abi Talib ؓ who replied, "Neither will we accept relinquishing the Khilafa nor will we ever ask you to relinquish it. Rasulullah ﷺ had placed you ahead, who can ever pull you back?" *(Ibn Najjar in Kanzul Ummal)*

Accepting Leadership for the Welfare of Islam: What Happened Between Abu Bakr ؓ and Ibn Abu Rafi ؓ

Rafi ibn Abu Rafi ؓ narrated, "After the people had appointed Abu Bakr ؓ as Khalifa, I said (to myself), 'This is the very man who told me never to assume leadership over even 2 persons (contrary to his own advice, he has now become the leader of all the Muslims).' I then left (home) and rode to Madinah. I then confronted Abu Bakr ؓ and said, 'O Abu Bakr! Do you recognize me?' 'I certainly do,' he replied. I asked further, 'Do you remember something that you once told me that I should not assume leadership over even 2 persons? You have assumed leadership over the entire Ummah.' He replied, 'When Rasulullah ﷺ left this world, the people were still new in Islam. Although I disliked it, I assumed the post because I feared that (without leadership) they would revert to kufr and dispute with each other. In addition, my companions also kept insisting.' Abu Bakr ؓ then continued giving me his reasons until my heart was content (that he assumed the post solely for the welfare of Islam)." *(Ibn Rahway, Adani, Baghawi, Ibn Khuzaima in Kanzul Ummal).*

Abu Bakr ؓ says to Omar ؓ, "It was You Who Forced me to Assume This Post"

A man from the family of Rabia says that that news reached him that Abu Bakr ؓ sat at home in grief after he was appointed as Khalifa. When Omar ؓ came to the house, Abu Bakr ؓ scolded him saying, "It was you who forced me to assume this post." When Abu Bakr ؓ complained to Omar ؓ that he found passing judgment a worrisome task, Omar ؓ said, "Don't you know that Rasulullah ﷺ said, 'When a leader applies himself and passes a ruling, he will receive twice the reward if he is correct. On the other hand, if he errs in his ruling after applying himself, he will still receive a single reward.'" This statement seemed to ease matters for Abu Bakr ؓ. *(Ibn Rahway, Khaythama in Fadh'ailus Sahabah, Kanzul Ummal).*

Abu Bakr ؓ's Last Words to Abdur Rahman bin Auf ؓ

Abdur Rahman bin Auf ؓ narrates that Abu Bakr ؓ said the following to him on his deathbed, "I have no regrets about anything that I have done except for 3 things that I wish I had never done. There are also 3 things I have never done that I wish I had. There are 3 other things that I wished I had enquired from Rasulullah ﷺ." Amongst the things that this narration contains is that Abu Bakr ؓ said, "I wish that on the day that we were selecting the Khalifa in the orchard of Banu Sa'jda, I had forced the post on to one of 2 persons, either Abu Ubaidah bin Jarrah or Omar. One of them would then have been the Amir while I could have served as his minister." It is also mentioned that he said, "I wish that at the time I had dispatched Khalid bin Walid to Sham, I had dispatched Omar to Iraq. In that way, I would have spread my right and left arms out in the Path of Allah. As for the three things that I wished I had enquired from Rasulullah ﷺ, I wish that I had asked him to identify those amongst whom Khilafa would be so that none would contest it from those who deserve it. I wish that I had asked Rasulullah ﷺ whether the Ansar would have any part in the Khilafa." *(Abu Ubaid, Uqaili, Tabrani, Ibn Asakir, Sa'eed bin Mansoor in Kanzul Ummal, Haythami).*

Abu Bakr ؓ Consults with Other Sahabah on His Deathbed Concerning His Successor

Abu Salama bin Abdur Rahman and others narrate that when Abu Bakr ؓ grew extremely ill and was close to death, he called for Abdur Rahman bin Auf ؓ and said, "Tell me about Omar bin Khattab ؓ." Abdur Rahman ؓ replied, "You are asking me about someone whom you know better than me." Abu Bakr ؓ said, "I still want you to tell me." Abdur Rahman ؓ then said, "He is the best of all those whom you see fit as your successor." Abu Bakr ؓ then summoned Uthman bin Affan ؓ and asked him, "Tell me about Omar bin Khattab ؓ." "You know him the best from all of us," responded Uthman ؓ. "Despite this, O Abu Abdullah." Uthman ؓ then said, "I swear by Allah that as far as I know, his inner self is even better than his (exemplary) outer appearance and there is none like him amongst us." Abu Bakr ؓ commented, "May Allah shower His mercy on you. By Allah! Should I leave him (as my successor), I would not be doing you any wrong." Abu Bakr ؓ then also consulted with Sa'eed bin Zaid Abu A'war ؓ, Usaid bin Hudhair ؓ and several other Sahabah from amongst the Muhajirin and the Ansar. Usaid ؓ had the - following to say, "By Allah! I rate him the best after you. He is pleased with that which pleases Allah and angry with that which angers Allah. His inner self is even better than his (excellent) outer appearance and there is none as capable for the post of Khilafa as he is." When some other Sahabah heard that Abdur Rahman bin Auf ؓ and Uthman ؓ had seen Abu Bakr ؓ privately, they went to Abu Bakr ؓ and one of them said, "What would you reply to your Rabb if He asked you about appointing Omar ؓ as your successor when you have already seen his harshness?" Abu Bakr ؓ asked someone to help him sit up and then said, "Do you wish to make me fear Allah?! Ruined is the person who carries injustice as his provision to the Hereafter! I would tell my Rabb that I have appointed the best of Your creation as my successor. Convey what I have told you to everyone else." Abu Bakr ؓ then lay down, called for Uthman bin Affan ؓ and told him to write the following:

The Letter of Abu Bakr ؓ Detailing the Appointment of Omar ؓ as his Successor, his Advice to Him and to the Public

"In the name of Allah the Most Kind, the Most Merciful. The following is the arrangement made by Abu Bakr bin Abu Quhafa during his last moments in the world, as he prepares to leave it and during the first moments of his life in the Hereafter as he prepares to enter it. This is a point where even Kuffar accept Iman, wrong-doers become convinced and liars speak the truth. I have appointed Omar bin Khattab as my successor over you. You should listen to him and obey his commands. In doing this I have not forfeited any good owing to Allah, His Rasul, Islam, myself nor owing to you people in any way. If he exercises justice, then this is exactly what I had expected from

him. On the other hand, if he has changed, then every man is accountable (to Allah) for the wrong he does. I have only intended good and have no knowledge of the unseen. (Allah declares:). Shortly after death the oppressors (wrongdoers) will come to know to which place they will return (jahannam). Peace be to you all together with the mercy of Allah. "

According to the orders of Abu Bakr ؓ, Uthman ؓ then sealed the letter. Some narrators state that Abu Bakr ؓ had only dictated the beginning of the letter and had not yet made mention of Omar ؓ when he fell unconscious. Although he had not named anyone, Uthman ؓ wrote the words: "I have appointed Omar bin Khattab ؓ as my successor over you." When Abu Bakr ؓ regained consciousness, he asked Uthman ؓ to read what he had written. When Uthman ؓ read the part about Omar ؓ, Abu Bakr ؓ exclaimed, "Allahu Akbar! I see that you feared people would fall into dispute concerning the Khilafa if my soul had left during my state of unconsciousness. May Allah reward you with the most excellent rewards on behalf of Islam and the people of Islam. I swear by Allah that you are also worthy of Khilafah." In compliance with the orders of Abu Bakr ؓ, Uthman ؓ then went out with the sealed letter. With him was Omar ؓ and Usaid bin Sa'eed Quradhi ؓ. Addressing the people, Uthman ؓ said, "Will you pledge your allegiance to the person mentioned in this letter?" All the people agreed. One of them even said, "We know who he is. He is Omar." Ibn Sa'd says that it was Ali ؓ who said this. All the people confirmed their approval and pledged their allegiance (to Omar). Abu Bakr ؓ then called Omar ؓ in private and gave him advice. When Omar ؓ had left, Abu Bakr ؓ raised his hands and prayed, "O Allah! I have done this only for their welfare and because I feared anarchy. You know best what I have done and I have truly applied my mind to the decision. I have appointed as their leader the one who is the best amongst them, who is the most capable and who has the greatest desire for their welfare. O Allah! The death that You have decreed for me has already arrived, so do succeed me amongst them because they are Your servants and their forelocks are in Your hands. Make their leader righteous for them and make him amongst the Khulafa Rashidin who follows the way of the Nabi of mercy ﷺ and the way of the pious ones after him. Make his subjects righteous for him." *(Ibn Sa'd in Kanzul Ummal)*

Hasan narrates that when Abu Bakr ؓ fell ill and was certain that he would soon leave the world, he gathered the people and said, "You can all see my condition. I am quite certain that I am soon to die. Allah has freed you from your obligation towards the allegiance you have pledged to me. Allah has undone the hold I have over you and returned your self-determination to you. You may now appoint whoever you please as your leader. If you appoint someone during my lifetime, it will be more conducive to your unity after my death." The people then left Abu Bakr ؓ alone and left (to consult with each other) but were unable to reach any decision. They then returned to Abu Bakr ؓ and said, "O Khalifa of Rasulullah ﷺ! You choose someone on our behalf." "You people may perhaps disagree with my decision," remarked Abu Bakr ؓ. When they assured him that they would not, Abu Bakr ؓ reaffirmed their resolution by saying, "Will you promise in Allah's name that you would be happy with my decision?" "We certainly will," they confirmed. Abu Bakr ؓ then said, "Then allow me some time to see what is in the best interests of Allah, Islam and His servants." Abu Bakr ؓ later sent for Uthman ؓ and said, "Recommend someone to me. By Allah! In my opinion, you are certainly most worthy of the post yourself." When Uthman ؓ recommended Omar ؓ, Abu Bakr ؓ instructed him to write the letter of appointment.

When Uthman ﷺ reached the point where the name of the successor was to be written, Abu Bakr ﷺ passed out. When he regained consciousness, he told Uthman ﷺ to write the name of Omar ﷺ. *(Ibn Asakir, Saif).*

Abu Bakr ﷺ replied to Talha on the Appointment of Omar ﷺ

Uthman bin Ubaidullah bin Abdullah bin Omar ﷺ narrates that when Abu Bakr ﷺ was about to pass away, he asked Uthman bin Affan ﷺ and dictated his last testament to him. However, he passed out before he could name his successor. Uthman ﷺ then himself named Omar bin Khattab ﷺ. When Abu Bakr ﷺ regained consciousness, he asked Uthman ﷺ whether he had written anyone's name. Uthman ﷺ replied, "I feared that you would not regain consciousness and that the people would then fall into dispute. I therefore wrote the name of Omar bin Khattab." Abu Bakr ﷺ said, "May Allah shower His mercies on you. Had you written your name instead, you are certainly worthy of the post." Talha bin Ubaidullah ﷺ then entered and said, "I have been sent to represent those behind me. They are saying that knowing the harshness of Omar during your lifetime, how will he be after your death when you hand over our affairs to him? Allah will certainly question you about this, so think well what reply you shall give." Abu Bakr ﷺ asked someone to help him sit up and said, "Do you wish to make me fear Allah?! Ruined is the person who employs guesswork in deciding, who should take charge of your affairs! If my Rabb questions me, I shall say, 'I have appointed the best of Your creation as my successor'. Convey what I have told you (to all those who have sent you)." *(La'alkala'i).*

The Narration of Ummul Mu'minin Aisha ﷺ in this Regard

Aisha ﷺ narrates that when her father Abu Bakr ﷺ was on his deathbed, he appointed Omar ﷺ as his successor. Ali ﷺ and Talha ﷺ then came to Abu Bakr ﷺ and asked him who he had appointed as his successor. When Abu Bakr ﷺ informed them that he had appointed Omar ﷺ, they said, "What reply will you give to your Rabb?" Abu Bakr ﷺ replied, "Do you wish to make me fear Allah? I know Allah and Omar ﷺ better then the 2 of you. I shall say to Allah that I have appointed over them the best of His creation as my successor." *(Ibn Sa'd in Kanzul Ummal, Bayhaqi, Ibn Jareer).*

The Narration of Zaid bin Haritb ﷺ

Zaid bin Harith ﷺ reports that when Abu Bakr ﷺ was on his deathbed, he sent for Omar ﷺ to appoint him as his successor. Some people commented, "You wish to appoint Omar ﷺ as your successor when he is harsh and ill-tempered? When he becomes our leader, he will be even more harsh and ill-tempered. What reply will you give to your Rabb when you meet Him after appointing Omar ﷺ as your successor over us?" Abu Bakr ﷺ replied, "Do you wish to make me fear Allah?! I shall say, 'O Allah! I have appointed the best of Your creation as my successor over the people'." *(Ibn Abi Shaiba in Kanzul Ummal).*

The Assassination of Omar ﷺ and His Selection of 6 Persons to Decide who Should be Khalifa

Abdullah bin Omar ﷺ narrates that when Abu Lu'lu'a attacked Omar ﷺ, he stabbed him twice with his spear. Then Omar ﷺ thought that he had perhaps wronged the people in a manner that he was unaware of. He therefore sent for Abdullah bin Abbas ﷺ, whom he was very fond of. Omar always kept Abdullah bin Abbas ﷺ in close confidence and would listen to what he had to say. Omar ﷺ said to Abdullah bin Abbas ﷺ, "I

wish to know whether this attack was a conspiracy of the general public." When Abdullah bin Abbas ﷺ went out to investigate, he found that every group of people that he passed was weeping bitterly. He therefore returned to Omar ﷺ and reported, "O Amirul Mu'minin! I saw every group of people that I passed weeping as if they had lost their first child."

"Who was responsible for the attack?" asked Omar ﷺ. Abdullah bin Abbas ﷺ replied, "It was the fire-worshipper Abu Lu'lu'a who was the slave of Mughiera bin Shu'ba." The signs of happiness were then visible on the face of Omar ﷺ as he said, "All praises are due to Allah Who has not made my assassin a reciter of *'La Ilaha IllAllah'* who could debate with me. Remember that I had prevented you people from bringing any foreign non-Muslim slaves here but you did not obey my instruction. Call my brothers here." When he was asked who his brothers were, Omar ﷺ named Uthman ﷺ, Ali ﷺ, Talha ﷺ, Zubair ﷺ, Abdur Rahman bin Auf ﷺ and Sa'd bin Abi Waqqas ﷺ. When these Sahabah were sent for, Omar ﷺ rested his head in the lap of his son Abdullah ﷺ, who informed him when the men had arrived. Omar ﷺ then said to them, "When I pondered deeply about the affairs of the Muslims, I found that you 6 men are the leaders of the people and the most influential. Leadership can only be amongst you and the affairs of the people will always be properly managed as long as you people remain straight. Should there arise any disputes, it would be amongst you first." Abdullah bin Omar ﷺ related further, "When I heard my father mention disputes and division, I knew that this would soon take place even though he used the words 'Should there arise'. This is because he seldom mentioned something that I did not see happen. He then started bleeding profusely and I noticed the 6 men enter into such urgent discussions that I feared they would already pledge their allegiance to one of them. I then said, 'The Amirul Mu'minin is still alive! There can never be 2 Khalifas staring at the faces of each other.'" Omar ﷺ asked them to help him up, which they did. He then said, "You people should discuss for 3 days, during which period Suhaib ﷺ should lead people in salah. "With whom should we consult?" they asked. Omar ﷺ replied, "You should consult with the Muhajirin, the Ansar and the commander of every army present here." Omar ﷺ asked for some milk to drink but when he drank it, the milk emerged from his 2 wounds. When this happened, Omar ﷺ realized that his death was imminent. He then said, "If I possessed the entire world, I would offer it as ransom to be saved from the terror of what is to come after death. However, with the grace of Allah, I foresee only good."

Abdullah bin Abbas commented, "May Allah reward you with the best of Islam and the Muslims through you when they were living in fear in Makkah? It was a tremendous reinforcement when you accepted Islam, because of which Islam, Rasulullah ﷺ and his Sahabah could come out in the open. When you migrated to Madinah, your migration was a great victory and since those very early days you did not miss a single military expedition that Rasulullah ﷺ fought against the disbeliever. Rasulullah ﷺ was pleased with you when he left the world, after which you advised his successor according to the pattern shown by Rasulullah ﷺ. Using those who accepted, you struck those who were averse until people entered into Islam willingly and unwillingly. The Khalifa of Rasulullah ﷺ was also happy with you when he left this world. You then assumed the role of Khalifa in the best manner that any person could do. Using you, Allah has populated many cities, brought plenty of wealth to the Muslims and destroyed many enemies. Allah has used you to bring abundance into every home in terms of Islam and in terms of their sustenance. Allah has now brought your life to an end with the great status of martyrdom. How fortunate are you not?"

Omar ؓ then said, "By Allah! The one whom you manage to deceive is truly deceived. O Abdullah! Will you testify on my behalf in front of Allah on the Day of Judgment?" "I certainly would," Abdullah bin Abbas ؓ assured him. Omar ؓ then praised Allah for having the cousin of Rasulullah ﷺ as a witness in his favor and asked his son Abdullah bin Omar ؓ to place his cheek on the ground. When Abdullah bin Omar ؓ placed his father's cheek on his lap instead, Omar insisted that his cheek be placed directly on the ground. Abdullah bin Omar ؓ then left his father's beard and cheek, allowing it to touch the ground. Addressing himself, Omar ؓ said, "O Omar! Your mother and you would be destroyed if Allah does not forgive you." He then passed away. May Allah shower His mercy on him. After Omar ؓ had passed away, the 6 appointed Sahabah summoned Abdullah bin Omar ؓ. However, he responded by saying that he would not come to them until they carried out the instruction of Omar ؓ to consult with the Muhajirin, the Ansar and the commanders of the armies present in Madinah. When someone mentioned to Hasan Basri رحمة الله the actions of Omar ؓ before his demise and his fear of Allah, Hasan رحمة الله commented, "Such is a true Mu'min. He carries out good deeds in the proper manner together with having fear for Allah. On the other hand, the Munafiq combines evil deeds with the false hope of being forgiven. I swear by Allah that in times past and present I have never seen a servant of Allah who excels in doing good deeds without excelling in his fear of Allah. In times past and present I have not seen any person excel in evil deeds without excelling in the false hope of being forgiven." *(Tabrani, Haythami)*

The Narration of Ibn Sa'd Concerning the Debts of Omar ؓ, his Burial with his 2 Companions and his Appointment of 6 Men to Decide Which One of Them Would be the Khalifa

In his narration concerning the assassination of Omar ؓ, *Amr bin Maymun* also says that Omar ؓ told his son Abdullah ؓ to check on his debts and add them up. When Abdullah bin Omar ؓ informed his father that the debts amounted to 86,000, Omar ؓ instructed, "If the amount can be paid from the wealth of Omar's family, then pay it from there on my behalf. If this is not possible, ask my tribe the Banu Adi bin Ka'b to settle the debt. If their wealth is also not sufficient, then ask the Quraish. However, you should not ask from anyone else besides them and do your best to settle my debts. I also want you to go to the mother of the Mu'minin Aisha ؓ. Greet her with Salam and say to her that Omar bin Khattab ؓ requests permission to be buried beside his 2 companions (Rasulullah ﷺ and Abu Bakr ؓ). However, do not say that the Amirul Mu'minin requests for permission because I am not the Amirul Mu'minin any more." When Abdullah bin Omar ؓ went to Aisha ؓ, he found her sitting and weeping. He greeted her and then addressed her saying, "Omar bin Khattab ؓ requests permission to be buried beside his 2 companions." Aisha ؓ replied, "By Allah! Although I had originally reserved the place for myself, I shall today give him preference over myself." When Abdullah bin Omar ؓ came back to his father, Omar ؓ asked, "What news do you have?" Abdullah bin Omar ؓ informed Omar ؓ that Aisha ؓ had granted the permission. Omar ؓ commented, "There was nothing more important to me than this. When I die, I want you to carry me on my bed and when you arrive at the door of Aisha ؓ seek permission again saying, 'Omar bin Khattab ؓ requests permission to enter.' If she permits my entry, then take me in, otherwise take me to the graveyard of all the Muslims." When the body of Omar ؓ was

taken for burial, it appeared that Muslims had never experienced such tragedy. Upon arrival at the door of Aisha ؓ, Abdullah bin Omar ؓ greeted her with Salam and said, "Omar bin Khattab ؓ requests permission to enter." Aisha ؓ granted permission and Omar ؓ was honored to be buried alongside Rasulullah ﷺ and Abu Bakr ؓ. May Allah shower His mercies on him.

When Omar ؓ was about to pass away, the people told him to appoint a successor. He said, "I find none more worthy of leadership than the 6 men with whom Rasulullah ﷺ was pleased when he passed away. Whoever they appoint shall be the Khalifa after me." Omar ؓ then named Uthman ؓ, Ali ؓ, Talha ؓ, Zubair ؓ, Abdur Rahman bin Auf ؓ and Sa'd bin Abi Waqqas ؓ. He then added, "If Sa'd becomes the Khalifa, that will be fine. Otherwise, whichever of them becomes the Khalifa should request his assistance because I had not dismissed him from his post as governor of Kufa because of any inability or treachery on his part." Omar ؓ then detailed the role of his son Abdullah ؓ as someone with whom the 6 could consult, emphasizing that he should not be allowed to assume the post as Khalifa. When the 6 Sahabah got together after. the demise of Omar ؓ, Abdur Rahman bin Auf ؓ proposed that 3 of them forfeit their entitlement to the other 3. Zubair ؓ handed his over to Ali ؓ. Talha ؓ gave his to Uthman ؓ and Sa'd ؓ gave his to Abdur Rahman bin Auf ؓ. The 3 remaining nominees consulted with each other when the decision was left to them entirely. Abdur Rahman bin Auf ؓ then said to the other 2 (Uthman ؓ and Ali ؓ), "Which of you wishes to free himself from making the decision and hand over the decision to me. I pledge to Allah that I shall not be negligent in selecting the one from amongst you who is the best and shall be best for the people." When the 2 Sahabah agreed, Abdur Rahman ؓ spoke to Ali ؓ in confidence saying, "You are the close relative of Rasulullah ﷺ and amongst the earliest Muslims. I ask you to tell me in Allah's name whether you would exercise justice if you were appointed Khalifa and that if I appointed Uthman ؓ as Khalifa, you would listen to him and obey him." When Ali ؓ attested that he would do so, Abdur Rahman bin Auf ؓ said the same thing in confidence to Uthman ؓ. Uthman ؓ agreed to do as asked, Abdur Rahman bin Auf ؓ asked Uthman ؓ to stretch out his hand. Uthman ؓ did so, Abdur Rahman ؓ pledged his allegiance to Uthman ؓ and was followed by Ali ؓ and the general public. *(Ibn Sa'd, Abu Ubaid, Ibn Abi Shaiba, Bukhari and Nasai)*

The Narration of Ibn Abi Shaiba and Ibn Sa'd in this Regard

Amr bin Maymun reports that when Omar ؓ was on his death bed, he called for Uthman ؓ, Ali ؓ, Talha ؓ, Zubair ؓ, Abdur Rahman bin Auf ؓ and Sa'd bin Abi Waqqas ؓ. When they came, Omar ؓ then addressed only Ali ؓ and Uthman ؓ. He said to Ali ؓ, "O Ali! These people recognize your kinship to Rasulullah ﷺ that you are his cousin and son-in-law and the tremendous knowledge and insight that Allah has granted you because of which they may select you to be the Khalifa. If you are nominated to be the Khalifa, you should fear Allah and never lift your tribe the Banu Hashim on to the necks of people." Omar ؓ then addressed Uthman ؓ saying, "O Uthman! These people know well that you were the son-in-law of Rasulullah ﷺ and they recognize your age and your respectability. If you are nominated to be the Khalifa, you should fear Allah and never lift your tribe on to the necks of people." Omar ؓ then asked the people to summon Suhaib ؓ. When he arrived, Omar ؓ said to him, "Lead the people in salah for 3 days during which period this group will gather in a room to discuss which of them should be the Khalifa. When they agree on one person, any person who opposes them should be executed." *(Ibn Abi Shaiba, Ibn Sa'd)*. Abu Ja'far reports that Omar ☙ said the following to the 6 members of the consultative assembly: "Consult with each other about who should be appointed as Khalifa. If your votes are tied at 2, 2 and 2 with each pair nominating a different person of 3 candidates, then repeat the consultation. However, if the votes are 4 to 2, accept the opinion of the majority." *(Ibn Sa'd)* A narration from *Aslam* quotes that Omar ☙ said, "If the opinions are tied at 3 to 3, adopt the side of Abdur Rahman ☙. Thereafter, you should listen to and obey the new Khalifa." Another narration from Anas ☙ states that a short while before Omar ☙ passed away; he sent for Abu Talha ☙ and said, "O Abu Talha! Be the 5th of a group of your people from the Ansar to be with the consultative assembly. I suppose that they will gather in a house belonging to one of them, so I want you and your group to stand at the door of that house. You should not allow anyone to enter with them and you should not allow the third day to pass by without them having appointed one of them as Khalifa." Omar ☙ then prayed, "O Allah! You are my successor over them." *(Kanzul Ummal)*.

The Lecture that Abu Bakr ☙ Gave on Who is Most Worthy of Assuming the Office of Khilafah

Asim narrates that during his final illness, Abu Bakr ☙ had the people gathered together and then had some men carry him to the pulpit. This was the last lecture that he ever delivered. After praising Allah, he said: "O people! Beware of this world and never place your trust in it for it is extremely deceptive. Rather give preference to the Hereafter over the world and inculcate great love for it. The love for anyone of the 2 develops hatred for the other. It is by this matter of Khilafa that all our affairs are governed and its end will be set right only by those factors that set right its initiation. Therefore, the only person worthy of assuming this office is the one who is most powerful amongst you, who can exercise the greatest control over his desires, who is most strict when the occasion demands severity and most compassionate when the occasion demands leniency. He should be one who is most willing to act on the opinions of people with knowledge and insight and does not occupy himself in useless efforts. He does not grieve over matters that do not present them to him, is not shy to learn and is not alarmed by emergencies. He is careful about managing finances and will neither misuse any funds nor fail in his duty towards it in a fit of anger or enmity. He is prepared for things to come and his preparation consists of fear for Allah and obedience to Him. Such a person is none other than Omar bin Khattab. "After saying this, Abu Bakr ☙ descended from the pulpit. *(Ibn Asakir in Kanzul Ummal)*.

The Qualities of a Khalifa as Described by Omar ☙

Abdullah bin Abbas ☙ says, "I served Omar ☙ in a manner that no other member of his family served him. I was also very informal with him in a manner that no member of his household was. He would sit with me and show me a lot of respect. We were sitting alone in his house one day when he lifted such a sigh that made me think he was about to die. I asked, 'Some grave matter of concern, O Amirul Mu'minin?' He replied, 'Some grave concern indeed.' 'What is it?' I asked. He then asked me to come closer to him. When I did so, he said, 'I can find no one worthy of this post of Khilafa.' I then named certain individuals and asked him what he thought of them. These happened to be the 6 men whom he chose as the consultative assembly. Omar ☙ said something about each one of these men and then said, 'No person is suitable for the post of Khilafa except someone who is strong without being harsh, who is lenient without being weak, who is generous without being extravagant and who is cautious about monetary affairs without being miserly."' *(Ibn Sa'd)*. Another narration also from Abdullah bin Abbas ☙ states, "I was sitting with Omar ☙ one day when he lifted such a sigh that I thought his ribs would crack. I said to him, 'O Amirul Mu'minin! It can only be a grave worry that would cause you to sigh like that.' He agreed by saying, 'It is indeed something grave. I do not know to whom I should hand the post of Khilafa over to.' He then turned to me and said, 'Perhaps you deem your companion Ali ☙ to be worthy of the post?' 'I certainly do,' I replied, 'he was one of the first Muslims and he possesses great qualities.' Omar ☙ commented, 'He is indeed as you say, but he is a man who enjoys jest and humor."' The narration then continues up to the point where Omar ☙ says, "No person is suitable for the post of Khilafa except someone who is strong without being harsh, who is lenient without being weak, who is generous without being extravagant, and who is cautious about monetary affairs without being miserly." Abdullah bin Abbas ☙ used to say, "These traits were combined in no other person besides Omar ☙." *(Abu Ubaid in Ghara'ib and Khatib in Ruwatul Malik)*.

Abdullah bin Abbas ☙ mentioned, "I used to serve Omar ☙ and always stood in fear of him. I went to his house one day as he sat there all alone. He heaved such a heavy sigh that I thought he was about to die. He raised his head to the sky and again breathed a heavy sigh. I then pulled up the courage and said to myself,' By Allah! I am certainly going to ask him about this.' I then said to him, 'By Allah! It must have been a grave concern that has made you sigh like this O Amirul Mu'minin.'He replied, 'By Allah! The concern is grave indeed! I cannot find anyone suitable to fill this post of Khilafa. Perhaps you feel that your companion Ali ☙ is worthy of the post.' I responded by saying, 'O Amirul Mu'minin! Is he not worthy of the post since he had made Hijra? Is he not worthy of the post because of his close companionship with Rasulullah ☙? Is he not worthy of the post because of his family ties with Rasulullah ☙?' Omar ☙ commented, 'He is indeed as you say, but he is a man who enjoys jest and humor."' The narration continues up to the point where Omar ☙ says, "No person can bear the post of Khilafa except someone who is strong without being harsh, who is lenient without being weak, who is generous without being extravagant, and who is cautious about monetary affairs without being miserly." Abdullah bin Abbas ☙ adds that Omar ☙ said, "None can shoulder this post of Khilafa besides a person who does not compromise on principles, who does not behave to show off and who does not give in to vain desires. None can shoulder this responsibility from Allah besides someone who never utters any word that forces him to contradict his resolve and who judges with fairness even against his own people." *(Ibn Asakir in Kanzul Ummal)*. Omar ☙ once said, "It is improper for anyone to assume his post of Khilafa except someone who possesses 4 qualities. Someone who is lenient without being weak, who is strong without being harsh, who is cautious about monetary affairs without being miserly, and who is generous without being extravagant. If anyone of these qualities is missing, the other 3 will become useless." *(Abdur Razzaq)* Another narration quotes Omar ☙ as saying, "None can shoulder this responsibility from Allah besides a person who does not compromise on principles, who does not behave to show off, who does not give in to vain desires, who is not concerned with developing his standing and who never conceals the truth even when angry." *(Abdur Razzaq, Ibn Asakir, in Kanzul Ummal)*. *Sufian bin Abi Awja* narrates that Omar bin Khattab ☙ once said, "By Allah! I know not whether I am a Khalifa or a king. If I am a king, then the matter is serious indeed." Someone from the audience said, "O Amirul Mu'minin! There is a distinct difference between the 2. A Khalifa only takes something rightfully and then uses it rightfully. By the grace of Allah, you are exactly like this. On the other hand, a king oppresses people by seizing things from some and then giving them to others." Omar ؓ remained silent. *(Ibn Sa'd).*

Salman ؓ reports that Omar ؓ once asked them, "Am I a king or a Khalifa?" Salman ؓ replied, "If you had ever unlawfully taken even a Dirham or less from the property of the Muslims and then used it illegally, you would be a king and not a Khalifa." Omar ؓ then began to weep bitterly. *(Ibn Sa'd in Muntakhab Kanzul Ummal).* A man from the Banu Asad tribe narrates that he was present when Omar ؓ once addressed his companions. Amongst them was Talha ؓ, Salman ؓ, Zubair ؓ and Ka'b ؓ. He said to them, "I want to ask you something. However, you should beware not to lie to me because you would then destroy me as well as yourselves. I ask you to tell me in the name of Allah whether I am a Khalifa or a king." Talha ؓ and Zubair ؓ said, "You are asking us something that we have no knowledge of. We are unable to distinguish a Khalifa from a king." Salman ؓ then testified with full conviction that Omar ؓ was a Khalifa and not a king. Omar responded by saying, "You have a right to comment because you had been frequenting the company of Rasulullah ﷺ." Salman ؓ then qualified his statement by saying, "I say this because you exercise justice amongst your subjects, you distribute between them with fairness, you treat them with the compassion that a man treats his own family and you pass judgment according to the Book of Allah." Ka'b ؓ then said, "I was under the impression that none in this gathering besides me could differentiate between a king and a Khalifa. However, it is evident that Allah has filled Salman ؓ with wisdom and knowledge." Ka'b ؓ then addressed Omar ؓ saying, "I testify that you are definitely a Khalifa and not a king." Omar ؓ then asked, "How is this?" Ka'b ؓ who had been scholar of the previous scriptures replied, "I have found mention of you in Allah's scriptures." "Was mention made of me by my name?" enquired Omar ؓ. "No," replied Ka'b ؓ, "but I have found mention of you by your qualities. I have found the following, 'Nubuwa and then Khilafa and mercy on the pattern of Nubuwa. Thereafter again Khilafa and mercy on the pattern of Nubuwa, followed by kingship with a bit of oppression'." *(Nu'aym bin Hammad in Fitan, Kanzul Ummal).*

Leniency and Firmness of a Khalifa

Sa'eed bin Musaib ؓ reports that when Omar ؓ was appointed as Khalifa, he delivered a lecture to the people from the pulpit of Rasulullah ﷺ. After praising Allah, he said: "O people! I know well the feelings of you people that I am too harsh and stern. However, I was like that because I had been with Rasulullah ﷺ as his servant and attendant and Rasulullah ﷺ was as Allah describes him in the Qur'an: "extremely forgiving and merciful towards the Mu'minin". I was therefore like a drawn sword for him unless he chose to sheath me or prevent me from doing something, in which case I would desist. Otherwise, I would be stern with people in place of the leniency that Rasulullah ﷺ showed. This was my behavior alongside Rasulullah ﷺ until Allah took him from this world in a condition that he was pleased with me. I thank Allah tremendously for that extremely good fortune. I then adopted the same attitude with the Khalifa of Rasulullah ﷺ Abu Bakr ؓ. You people know well his decency, his humility and his leniency. I was also at his service like a sword in his defense, combining my sternness with his leniency. If he took the initiative in any matter before I could, I

would restrain myself. Otherwise, I would forge ahead. This was my behavior alongside him until Allah took him from this world in a condition that he was pleased with me. I thank Allah tremendously for that extremely good fortune. Now that the Khilafa has been handed over to me, I know well that some of you would say, 'He was stern with us when someone else was the Khalifa, what will now happen once he is himself the Khalifa?' You people have no need to ask anyone about me because you know me and have had experiences with me. You know as much about the practices of your Nabi ﷺ as I do. I have asked Rasulullah ﷺ everything that I needed to ask and I now have no regrets about not asking him anything that I had wanted to ask. Now that I am Khalifa, you should understand well that the sternness you have been seeing in me shall be multiplied against an oppressor and a criminal. It will be employed to take back from the strong ones what they had taken from the weak. Despite all of this sternness, I shall still place my cheek on the ground for people who abstain from immoral behavior and evil and who are obedient. If there ever arises any differences between myself and any of you concerning any matter of judgment, I shall not refuse to walk with him to a third party whom you choose, who will look into the matter causing the conflict. So fear Allah, O servants of Allah and assist me against yourselves by restraining yourselves from carrying rumors and also assist me against myself by enjoining what is good and forbidding me from evil and presenting me with good counsel in the task that Allah has appointed me to." *(Hakim, Lalkala'l in Kanzul Ummal)*

Muhammad bin Zaid ؓ reports that Ali ؓ, Uthman ؓ, Zubair ؓ, Talha ؓ, Abdur Rahman bin Auf ؓ and Sa'd ؓ once got together. Because Abdur Rahman bin Auf ؓ was the most at ease with Omar ؓ, the others said to him, "O Abdur Rahman! Why don't you speak to the Amirul Mu'minin on behalf of all the people and tell him that it often happens that a person in need approaches him for his need but then returns without having his need fulfilled because his fear for the Amirul Mu'minin prevents him from presenting his case." Abdur Rahman bin Auf ؓ then went to Omar ؓ and addressed him saying, "O Ameirul Mu'minin! Do be more lenient towards the people because it often happens that a person in need approaches you for his need but then returns without having his need fulfilled because his fear for you prevents him from presenting his case." Omar ؓ said, "O Abdur Rahman! I want you to swear in the name of Allah whether or not it was Ali ؓ, Uthman ؓ, Talha ؓ, Zubayr ؓ and Sa'd ؓ who asked you to speak to me." Abdur Rahman bin Auf ؓ replied, "I swear by Allah that it was certainly them." Omar ؓ then said, "O Abdur Rahman! I swear by Allah that I had been so lenient with the people that I began to fear the wrath of Allah because of my leniency. Thereafter, I was so stern with the people that I began to fear the wrath of Allah because of my sternness. What course is there now available for me?" Abdur Rahman bin Auf ؓ stood up weeping and dragged along his shawl as he said, "O dear! What will happen to the people after you are gone! O dear! What will happen to the people after you are gone!" *(Ibn Sa'd, Ibn Asakir).* Sha'bi narrates that Omar ؓ once said, "I swear by Allah that for the sake of Allah my heart had become so soft that it was softer than butter and at times it had become so hard for Allah's sake that it was harder than a stone." *(Abu Nu'aym in Hilya).* Abdullah bin Abbas ؓ narrates that when Omar ؓ became the Khalifa, someone said to him, "Some people had made an effort to ensure that this post should be turned away from you." When Omar ؓ asked the reason for this, the person replied, "They felt that you were too harsh." To this, Omar ؓ commented, "All praise be to Allah Who has filled my heart with mercy for them and filled their hearts with fear for me." *(Mutakhab Kanzul Ummal)*.

Detaining People by Whom Divisions will be Caused in the Ummah

Sha'bi narrates that when Omar ؓ passed away, certain members of the Quraish had already become irritated by him. They were people whom Omar ؓ had detained in Madinah and did not permit them to leave the city. However, Omar ؓ still continued showering favors on them. Omar ؓ used to say, "What I fear most for this Ummah is that you should disperse into the various cities and neglect the seat of Khilafa." Besides the few individuals from the Muhajirin whom Omar ؓ had confined to Madinah, Omar ؓ did not impose the restriction to other people of Makkah. Whenever one of these Muhajirin who had been confined to Madinah would seek permission to fight in a battle, Omar ؓ said to him, "Your expeditions with Rasulullah ﷺ had been sufficient to enter you to Jannah. Better for you than fighting in battles today is for you not to see the world and for the world not to see you." Omar ؓ wanted these Sahabah to remain in Madinah so that Muslims from other parts would come to Madinah to benefit from them. In this manner, Muslims would preserve their attachment with the seat of Khilafa, thereby strengthening their unity. When Uthman ؓ became the Khalifa, he allowed them to go free and they dispersed in the various cities. Large numbers of people then started affiliating with them and staying where they stayed. Two of the narrators named Muhammad and Talha commented, "This was the first weakness that entered Islam and was certainly the first tragedy to befall the Ummah because instead of developing their affiliation with the seat of Khilafa, it caused Muslims to rather develop local ties, thus weakening the capital city." *(Saif and Ibn Asakir in Kanzul Ummal, Tabari).* Qais bin Abi Hazim reports that when Zubair ؓ sought permission from Omar ؓ to march for a battle, Omar ؓ said to him, "You should rather remain seated in your house because you have already fought by the side of Rasulullah ﷺ." Zubair ؓ repeated the request and it was on the 3rd or 4th occasion that Omar ؓ said, "Rather remain seated at home because I swear by Allah that if you and your companions leave the borders of Madinah, you may start rebellion against the companions of Muhammad ﷺ." *(Hakim confirmed by Dhahabi)*

Rasulullah ﷺ Consults with the Sahabah Concerning the Caravan of Abu Sufian and Concerning the Prisoners Taken at Badr

Anas ؓ states that when Rasulullah ﷺ heard about the arrival of the caravan of Abu Sufian, he consulted with the Sahabah. When Abu Bakr ؓ voiced his opinion to march, Rasulullah ﷺ turned away from him. Thereafter, when Omar ؓ voiced his opinion, Rasulullah ﷺ turned away from him as well. Sa'd bin Ubadah ؓ from the Ansar then said, "It is our opinion that Rasulullah ﷺ wants..." The complete narration has passed at the beginning of "The chapter concerning Jihad." In his narration describing the battle of Badr, Omar ؓ says that when Rasulullah ﷺ consulted with Abu Bakr ؓ, Omar ؓ and Ali ؓ about what to do with the prisoners of war captured at Badr, Abu Bakr ؓ said, "O Rasulullah ﷺ! These people are our cousins, our relatives and our brothers. My opinion is that we take ransoms from them, which would assist us against the Kuffar. Perhaps Allah would guide them and they would eventually become our allies." Rasulullah ﷺ then asked Omar ؓ what his opinion was. He replied, "I swear by Allah that I do not share the opinion of Abu Bakr ؓ. I strongly feel that you should hand so-and-so (a relative of Omar ؓ) over to me for execution, that you hand Aqil over to Ali for execution, and that you hand over to Hamza his brother

(Abbas ؓ) so that he could execute him. In this manner, Allah would know that we have no inclination towards the disbeliever in our hearts because these men are their leaders and the most influential people they have." Omar ؓ relates further, "Rasulullah ﷺ opted for the opinion of Abu Bakr ؓ and chose not to accept what I proposed. He therefore took ransom from the prisoners. The next day I found Rasulullah ﷺ and Abu Bakr ؓ weeping. 'O Rasulullah ﷺ!' I asked, 'Do inform me what makes you and your companion weep like this so that I may also weep with you if I am able to. If I am unable to weep, I shall pretend to do so to sympathize with your weeping.'" Rasulullah ﷺ replied by saying, "I am weeping because of the opinion that your companions presented to me to accept ransom from the prisoners. I had been shown their punishment from as close as that tree (referring to a tree nearby). Allah has also revealed a verse of the Qur'an stating:

مَا كَانَ لِنَبِيٍّ أَنْ يَكُونَ لَهُ أَسْرَى حَتَّى يُثْخِنَ فِي الْأَرْضِ تُرِيدُونَ عَرَضَ الدُّنْيَا وَاللَّهُ يُرِيدُ الْآخِرَةَ وَاللَّهُ عَزِيزٌ حَكِيمٌ (67)

It is not for a Prophet that he should have prisoners of war (and free them with ransom) until he had made a great slaughter (among his enemies) in the land. You desire the good of this world (i.e. the money of ransom for freeing the captives), but Allah desires (for you) the Hereafter. And Allah is All-Mighty, All-Wise. (Al-Anfal:67). (Ahmad, Muslim, Abu Dawood, Tirmidhi, Ibn Abi Shaiba, Abu Awanah, Ibn Jareer, Ibn Mundhir, Ibn Abi Hatim, Ibn Hibban, Abu Shaikh, Ibn Mardway, Abu Nu'aym and Bayhaqi in Kanzul Ummal)

The Narration of Anas ؓ About the Consultation Regarding the Prisoners of Badr

Anas ؓ narrates that when Rasulullah ﷺ consulted with the Sahabah about what needs to be done with the prisoners captured during the battle of Badr, he said, "Allah has now granted you control over them." Omar ؓ then said, "Execute them all O Rasulullah ﷺ!" However, Rasulullah ﷺ ignored his remark and said, "O people! Allah had now granted you control over them whereas they had been your brothers just yesterday." When Omar ؓ repeated his remark, Rasulullah ﷺ again ignored it. When Rasulullah ﷺ once again repeated what he had said, Abu Bakr ؓ said, "O Rasulullah ﷺ! I feel that we should forgive them and take ransoms from them." The worry on the face of Rasulullah ﷺ then disappeared and he subsequently forgave them and took the ransom. Allah then revealed the following verse of the Qur'an:

لَوْلَا كِتَابٌ مِنَ اللَّهِ سَبَقَ لَمَسَّكُمْ فِيمَا أَخَذْتُمْ عَذَابٌ عَظِيمٌ (68)

Were it not a previous ordainment from Allah, a severe torment would have touched you for what you took. (Al-Anfal:68) (Ahmad in Nasbur Ra'ya, Haythami)

The Narration of Ibn Mas'ood ؓ in this Regard

Abdullah bin Mas'ood ؓ reports that after the battle of Badr, Rasulullah ﷺ said, "What is your opinion concerning these prisoners?" Abu Bakr ؓ responded by saying, "O Rasulullah ﷺ! They are your people and your family. Allow them to live and grant them break. Perhaps Allah shall forgive them." Omar ؓ said, "O Rasulullah ﷺ! They exiled you and called you a liar. Bring them closer so that I may execute them all." Abdullah bin Rawaha ؓ spoke. He said, "O Rasulullah ﷺ! Look for a valley that had plenty of firewood. Put them all there and then set it alight upon them." Rasulullah ﷺ entered his room without passing any decision. In the meanwhile some people said that Rasulullah ﷺ would adopt the opinion of Abu Bakr ؓ. Others felt that he would accept the opinion of Omar ؓ, while another group felt that it would accept the opinion of Abdullah bin Rawaha ﷺ. When Rasulullah ﷺ emerged, he said, "Verily Allah has softened the hearts of some men so much that they have become softer than milk. Allah has also hardened the hearts of other men so much that their hearts have become harder than stones. Your likeness, O Abu Bakr, is like that of Ibrahim عليه السلام who prayed: (36) فَمَنْ تَبِعَنِي فَإِنَّهُ مِنِّي وَمَنْ عَصَانِي فَإِنَّكَ غَفُورٌ رَحِيمٌ

But whoso follows me, he verily is of me. And whoso disobeys me, - still You are indeed Oft-Forgiving, Most Merciful. (Ibrahim:36)

Your likeness, O Abu Bakr, is also like that of Isa عليه السلام who will pray: (118) إِنْ تُعَذِّبْهُمْ فَإِنَّهُمْ عِبَادُكَ وَإِنْ تَغْفِرْ لَهُمْ فَإِنَّكَ أَنْتَ الْعَزِيزُ الْحَكِيمُ

"If You punish them, they are Your slaves, and if You forgive them, verily You, only You are the All-Mighty, the All-Wise." (Al-Ma'idah:118)

Your likeness, O Omar, is like that of Nuh عليه السلام who prayed:

رَبِّ لَا تَذَرْ عَلَى الْأَرْضِ مِنَ الْكَافِرِينَ دَيَّارًا (26)

My Lord! Leave not one of the disbelievers (alive) on earth.' (Nuh:26)

Your likeness, O Omar, is also like that of Musa عليه السلام who prayed:

رَبَّنَا اطْمِسْ عَلَى أَمْوَالِهِمْ وَاشْدُدْ عَلَى قُلُوبِهِمْ فَلَا يُؤْمِنُوا حَتَّى يَرَوُا الْعَذَابَ الْأَلِيمَ (88)

Our Lord! Destroy their wealth, and harden their hearts, so that they will not believe until they see the painful torment. (Yunus:88)

Because you people are poverty-stricken, no prisoner shall be freed without either ransom or execution."

Narrating further, Abdullah bin Mas'ood ﷺ says, "I then said, 'O Rasulullah ﷺ! Do exclude Sahl bin Baida from this because I have heard him accept Islam.' Rasulullah ﷺ then remained silent and there was not a day that I saw myself more fearful than that day when I thought that a rock from the sky would soon fall on me. Rasulullah ﷺ then said, 'Sahl bin Baida is excluded.' It was after this incident that Allah revealed the verses: مَا كَانَ لِنَبِيٍّ أَنْ يَكُونَ لَهُ أَسْرَى حَتَّى يُثْخِنَ فِي الْأَرْضِ تُرِيدُونَ عَرَضَ الدُّنْيَا وَاللَّهُ يُرِيدُ الْآخِرَةَ وَاللَّهُ عَزِيزٌ حَكِيمٌ (67) لَوْلَا كِتَابٌ مِنَ اللَّهِ سَبَقَ لَمَسَّكُمْ فِيمَا أَخَذْتُمْ عَذَابٌ عَظِيمٌ (68)

It is not for a Prophet that he should have prisoners of war (free them with ransom) until he had made a great slaughter (among his enemies) in the land. You desire the good of this world (i.e. the money of ransom for freeing the captives), but Allah desires (for you) the Hereafter. And Allah is All-Mighty, All-Wise. Were it not a previous ordainment from Allah, a severe torment would have touched you for what you took. (Al-Anfal:67-68) (Ahmad, Tirmidhi, Hakim, Ibn Mardway in Al Bidayah wan Nihayah).

Rasulullah ﷺ Consults with Sa'd bin Ubadah ﷺ and Sa'd bin Mu'adh ﷺ Concerning the Produce of Madinah

Zuhri narrates that when the Muslims were suffering extreme hardship during the battle of Ahzab, Rasulullah ﷺ sent for Uyayna bin Hisn and Harith bin Auf Murri who were the 2 leaders of the Banu Ghitfan tribes. He offered them a 3rd of the produce of Madinah on condition that they withdraw their men from fighting the Muslims. The treaty was being concluded between Rasulullah ﷺ and the 2 leaders and they were already in the process of writing the document. Verbal discussions were still underway and the treaty was not yet concluded. The witnesses had also not yet been called. However, when Rasulullah ﷺ intended to conclude the agreement, he first summoned the 2 Sa'ds (Sa'd bin Mu'adh ﷺ and Sa'd bin Ubadah ﷺ). He presented the situation to them and asked them for their opinions. The 2 men asked, "O Rasulullah ﷺ! Is this something

that you are doing because you wish to do it, or something that Allah has commanded you to do, in which case we have no option but to carry it out? Or is it something that you are doing for our benefit?" Rasulullah ﷺ replied, "I am doing this only for your benefit because I see that the Arabs are attacking you from a united platform and are ravaging you from all sides. By engaging in this treaty, I wish to weaken their strength somewhat." Sa'd bin Mu'adh ﷺ then said, "O Rasulullah ﷺ! These people and us had been ascribing partners to Allah and worshipping idols. Neither did we worship Allah nor did we recognize who He was. During those times these people had never entertained hopes of eating a single date from Madinah unless it was offered to them as a token of hospitality or they bought it. How can we now give them any portion of our wealth once Allah has honored us with Islam, guided us to it, and accorded us tremendous respect because of it? By Allah! We have no need for this treaty. By Allah! All that we are willing to give them are the strokes of our swords until the time arrives when Allah passes judgment between us and them." Rasulullah ﷺ said, "You know best what you want." Sa'd bin Mu'adh ﷺ took hold of the script and erased whatever was written on it. He said, "They may now do their best to try to harm us!" *(Ibn Is'haq in Al Bidayah wan Nihayah)*

The Narration of Abu Hurairah ﷺ Concerning this Consultation

Abu Hurairah ﷺ narrates that Harith once approached Rasulullah ﷺ and said, "If you do not give us half the produce of Madinah, we shall fill her with cavalry and infantry." Rasulullah ﷺ replied by saying, "Wait until I consult with the Sa'ds (referring to Sa'd bin Mu'adh ﷺ and Sa'd bin Ubadah ﷺ)." When Rasulullah ﷺ consulted with them, they said, "By Allah! Even during the period of ignorance we never gave in to such humiliation, why should we do so now when Allah has blessed us with Islam." Rasulullah ﷺ then got back to Harith and informed him accordingly. Harith responded with anger, "You have betrayed me, O Muhammad!" *(Bazzar)*. Abu Hurairah ﷺ also reports that Harith from the Banu Ghitfan tribe once approached Rasulullah ﷺ with the demand, "Give us half the produce of Madinah." Rasulullah ﷺ replied, "Not until I have consulted with the Sa'ds." Rasulullah ﷺ then sent for Sa'd bin Mu'adh ﷺ, Sa'd bin Ubadah ﷺ, Sa'd bin Rabi ﷺ, Sa'd bin Khaithama ﷺ and Sa'd bin Mas'ood ﷺ. Rasulullah ﷺ then addressed them saying, "I know that the Arabs are attacking you from a united platform. However, Harith has come with a request that they be given half the produce of Madinah in exchange of making peace with you. If you wish, you may give him half of this year's crop and then see what you decide for the forthcoming years." They responded by saying, "If it is revelation from the heavens, then we are prepared to accept the command of Allah and if it is your wish and what you desire, then we are prepared to support your wishes. However, if you are doing this out of compassion for us, then by Allah, there was a time when they and us were on an equal footing. They were then unable to take a single date from us unless it was bought or given as a token of hospitality." Rasulullah ﷺ then said to them, "It is as you say, I am doing this out of compassion for you." Rasulullah ﷺ then addressed Harith and those with him and said, "You have heard what they have to say." Harith and the others looked angrily, "You have betrayed us, O Muhammad!"*(Tabrani, Haythami)*. *Musaddad* reports from Omar ﷺ that he would also be present when Rasulullah ﷺ would spend nights discussing the affairs of the Muslims with Abu Bakr ﷺ. *(Kanzul Ummal)*.

Abu Bakr ؓ Consults with Men of Knowledge and Insight who Constituted the Consultative Assembly During his Period and the Period of Omar ؓ

Qasim narrates that whenever a matter arose and Abu Bakr ؓ needed to consult with men of knowledge and wisdom, he would summon certain men from the Muhajirin and the Ansar. They included Omar ؓ, Uthman ؓ, Ali ؓ, Abdur Rahman bin Auf ؓ, Mu'adh bin Jabal ؓ, Ubay bin Ka'b ؓ and Zaid bin Thabit ؓ. These men used to issue Fatawa during his period and people would go to them for rulings. The period of Abu Bakr ؓ passed like this, and when Omar ؓ became the Khalifa afterwards, he also used to summon these men. When Omar ؓ was the Khalifa, the task of issuing Fatawa was entrusted to Uthman ؓ, Ubay ؓ and Zaid ؓ. *(Ibn Sa'd in Kanzul Ummal).*

The Incident Between Abu Bakr ؓ and Omar ؓ Concerning the Demarcation of Land for Certain Sahabah

Ubaida reports that Uyayna bin Hisn and Aqra bin Haris once approached Abu Bakr ؓ saying, "O successor of Rasulullah ﷺ! There is a barren piece of land in our area that bears no grass and is useless. If you see it fit, do make it over to us so that we may work on it and cultivate it." Abu Bakr ؓ decided to make it over to them and had the title deed written in their favor. He appointed Omar ؓ as witness to the deed, but because Omar ؓ was not present there, the 2 men had to take the deed to him so that he may be witness to it When Omar ؓ heard what the deed contained, he took it from the 2 men, spat on it and thereby erased what was written on it. The 2 men were infuriated and addressed him with harsh words. Omar ؓ said, "Rasulullah ﷺ used to appease you by granting you properties at a time when Islam was weak. Allah has now strengthened Islam and there is no need to appease you, so you may go and do whatever you can against me. May Allah offer you no protection even if you ask for it!" The 2 men stormed back to Abu Bakr ؓ in a fury and said, "By Allah! We do not know whether you are the Khalifa or Omar ؓ!" Abu Bakr ؓ replied, "He could have been the Khalifa if he chose to." Omar ؓ arrived in a rage and when he stood before Abu Bakr ؓ, he asked, "Tell me about this land that you handed over to these 2 men. Does it belong to you or is it the public property of the Muslims?" Abu Bakr ؓ replied, "It is the public property of the Muslims." "Why did you give it to these 2 men rather than anyone else from amongst the Muslims?" Omar ؓ demanded to know. Abu Bakr ؓ replied, "I had consulted with these people around me and they indicated that I do so." Omar ؓ said, "Although you consulted with those around. As it is not possible to seek the opinion of every person in every matter, Abu Bakr ؓ did not reply to Omar ؓ and said, "I did tell you that you are more capable of Khilafa than me, but you overpowered me and forced me to assume the task. *(Ibn Abi Shaiba, Bukhari in Tarikh, Ibn Asakir, Bayhaqi, Ya'qub bin Sufian in Kanzul Ummal, Isabah, Abdur Razzaq in Kanzul Ummal)*

The Question of the Kharaj from Bahrain

Atia bin Bilal and Sahm bin Minjab narrate that Aqra and Zabarqan approached Abu Bakr ؓ and said, "Hand over to us the Kharaj from Bahrain and we shall give you the guarantee that no one from our tribe will ever leave Islam." Abu Bakr ؓ agreed to the request and wrote a declaration to the effect. Amongst the witnesses appointed was Omar ؓ. Since the agreement was facilitated by Talha bin Ubaidullah ؓ, it was he who brought the written agreement to Omar ؓ. Omar ؓ looked at it, he refused to be a witness and said, "There is no need to honor people anymore!" He erased the content and tore it up. Talha ؓ became

very angry and returned to Abu Bakr ؓ saying, "Are you the Amir or Omar ؓ?" Abu Bakr ؓ replied, "He is the Amir although it is me who has to be obeyed." Hearing this, Talha ؓ was silent because his remark was such that it would have led to disunity, the reply of Abu Bakr ؓ was one that engendered unity. *(Saif and Ibn Asakir in Muntakhab Kanzul Ummal)*

Consultation with the Sahabah in Battle

Abdullah bin Amr ؓ reports that Abu Bakr ؓ once wrote to Amr bin Al Aas ؓ saying, "Rasulullah ﷺ used to consult in matters of war, so ensure that you do the same." *(Tabrani, Haythami, Bazzar, Uqayli in Kanzul Ummal).* A narration of Abdullah bin Abi Awfa ؓ has already passed discussing the consultation of Abu Bakr ؓ with men of knowledge before engaging the Romans in battle.

Omar ؓ informs his Consultative Assembly about his Proposal to the Daughter of Ali ؓ

Abu Ja'far narrates that Omar ؓ requested Ali ؓ for his daughter. Ummu Kulthum's hand in marriage. Ali ؓ said, "I had intended to marry all my daughters only to the sons of Ja'far." To this, Omar ؓ said, "O Ali! Marry her to me because I swear by Allah that there is no other person on earth who anticipates as much as I do by treating her well (this he explains later)." Ali ؓ then agreed to let Omar ؓ marry his daughter. Omar ؓ then approached the gathering of Muhajirin who always sat in the Masjid between the grave of Rasulullah ﷺ and the pulpit. They included Ali ؓ, Uthman ؓ, Zubair ؓ, Talha ؓ and Abdur Rahman bin Auf ؓ. Whenever any matter presented itself to him from far off places, Omar ؓ would always inform the members of this gathering and then seek their opinions about the matter. This time he came to them and said, "Congratulate me on my new marriage!" They all congratulated him and then asked, "Who did you marry, O Amirul Mu'minin?" "The daughter of Ali bin Abi Talib ؓ," he replied. He then started to explain, "Indeed Rasulullah ﷺ said, 'Every connection and relation shall be severed on the day of Judgment except my connections and my relations.' I had been a companion of Rasulullah ﷺ and now I wish to become his relative as well." *(Ibn Sa'd, Sa'eed bin Mansoor, Ibn Rahway in Kanzul Ummal, Hakim).*

Omar ؓ and Uthman ؓ Consult with Abdullah bin Abbas ؓ and the Good Comments that Omar ؓ and Sa'd ؓ Made About Him

Ata bin Yasar reports that Omar ؓ and Uthman ؓ used to call for Abdullah bin Abbas ؓ and consult with him along with those Sahabah who participated in the battle of Badr (the senior Sahabah). During the periods of Omar ؓ and Uthman ؓ, Abdullah bin Abbas ؓ used to issue Fatawa (rulings) and did so until he passed away. *Ya'qub bin Zaid* narrates that Omar bin Khattab ؓ used to consult with Abdullah bin Abbas ؓ about every matter of importance and would say to him, "Dive into the matter, dear diver because he was capable of reaching the essence of the problem at hand." Sa'd bin Abi Waqqas ؓ said, "I have not seen any person as quick-witted, as intelligent, as knowledgeable and as tolerant as Abdullah bin Abbas ؓ. I have seen Omar ؓ summon him to solve intricate problems and say, 'An intricate problem has presented itself to you.' Omar ؓ would then do only what Abdullah bin Abbas ؓ proposed even though he was surrounded by Muhajirin and Ansar who had participated in the battle of Badr." *(Ibn Sa'd). Ibn Shihab* reports that whenever an intricate problem presented itself before Omar ؓ, he would summon some young men to consult and choose to act according to the sharpness of their intellect. *(Bayhaqi, Ibn*

Sam'ani). Another narration states that Omar bin Khattab ﷺ would engage in so much consultation that he would even consult women when the need arose. In fact, there were several occasions when he liked the opinions that they expressed and acted on it. *(Bayhaqi, Ibn Sirin in Kanzul Ummal).*

A Remarkable Lecture of Omar ﷺ Concerning Consultation

Muhammad, Talha and Ziyad all report that Omar ﷺ once left Madinah and dismounted at an oasis called Sirar 3 miles from Madinah where he instructed that the army comes to a halt. The soldiers did not know whether he intended to camp there or proceed further. Whenever the Muslims intended to know something from Omar ﷺ, they always sent either Uthman ﷺ or Abdur Rahman bin Auf ﷺ. In fact, during the period of Omar ﷺ's Khilafa, Uthman ﷺ was known as "Radif'. According to the Arabs, a "Radif' is a person who is regarded as the leader's second-incommand and the term is meant for the one whom the people popularly see as the leader's successor. Whenever these 2 men were unable to extract from Omar ﷺ the information the people required, they would then send Abbas ﷺ. Uthman ﷺ then asked Omar ﷺ, "Has any intelligence reached you? What do you intend to do?" Omar ﷺ then announced that the people should gather as they do for salah and when they had assembled around him, he informed them of the latest intelligence. He then waited for their response. Majority of the people echoed that Omar ﷺ should march ahead with them in tow. Omar ﷺ commended this opinion for he did not like to disregard their opinion. He chose to rather discourage them in a kind manner. He therefore said, "Prepare yourself and prepare others. I shall continue with you unless I receive an opinion that is more appropriate." Omar ﷺ then sent for men of insight and the cream of Rasulullah ﷺ's companions and the most prominent Arab leaders gathered together. Omar ﷺ said to them, "I feel that I should proceed with the army, but I wish you to give me your opinion on the matter." The men gathered for discussion and unanimously agreed that another companion of Rasulullah ﷺ should be sent as commander of the army while Omar ﷺ stayed behind in Madinah to dispatch reinforcements. They felt that if victory is achieved, the result would be what everyone desired and if not, another commander and another army could always be sent. They said, the disbeliever would be further enraged, the Muslims would guard against making mistakes and Allah's assistance would arrive according to His promise. Omar ﷺ then again announced that the people should gather as they do for salah and they did. Omar ﷺ also sent for Ali ﷺ whom he had appointed as his deputy in Madinah and for Talha ﷺ whom he had sent ahead with the scouting party. At the same time, he also sent for Zubair ﷺ and Abdur Rahman bin Auf ﷺ, whom he had appointed as commanders of the 2 sides of the army. When everyone was present, Omar then stood amongst the people and said: "Verily Allah has gathered the Muslims around Islam, has created love between their hearts and made them brothers in Islam. The Muslims are therefore like a single body in their relationship with each other. No part is free from pain when another part is suffering. It is therefore incumbent on the Muslims that their matters be decided by mutual consultation between their men of insight, the consultative assembly. The masses need to follow the one who is their leader and are also bound by the decision of the consultative assembly. The people will have to adopt the course that these men plan. In fact, even the Amir is bound by the decision that the consultative assembly makes. People are also bound to follow the battle strategies that these men outline and approve of. O people! I was also a man like the rest of you

marching in Jihad until the men of knowledge and insight amongst you stopped me from proceeding ahead. I am now also of the opinion that I should rather stay behind in Madinah and send someone else as commander of the army. I have already presented this matter to all whom I have sent ahead and all who have been left behind." Although Omar ﷺ has appointed Ali ﷺ as his deputy in Madinah and had made Talha ﷺ the commander of the scouting group that had already reached a place called Ahwas, he ensured that even they were present to make the decision. *(Ibn Jareer).* Omar bin Abdul Aziz الله رحمة narrates that when Omar ﷺ was informed about the martyrdom of Abu Ubaidah bin Mas'ood and that the Persians had rallied around a common leader from the house of the Kisra, he summoned the Muhajirin and the Ansar and marched until they reached a place called Sirar. The rest of the narration is similar to the one mentioned above. *(Ibn Jareer).*

The Letter that Omar ﷺ Wrote to Sa'd ﷺ

Muhammad bin Sallam Baykindi narrates that during the period of ignorance; Amr bin Ma'diakrib ﷺ had achieved many feats. He became a Muslim after arriving with a delegation to meet Rasulullah ﷺ. Omar bin Khattab ﷺ sent him to Sa'd bin Abi Waqqas ﷺ who was commanding the Muslim army in Qadisiya, where his military genius was being put to the test. Omar ﷺ wrote to Sa'd ﷺ saying, "I am reinforcing you with 2,000 men. They are Amr bin Ma'diakrib ﷺ and Tulaiha bin Khuwailid ﷺ. Consult with them in military matters but do not appoint them to posts of command because their intimidating courage would place the lives of others at risk. *(Tabrani, Haythami).*

The First Commander Appointed in Islam

Sa'd bin Abi Waqqas ﷺ narrates, "When Rasulullah ﷺ arrived in Madinah, the Juhaina tribe approached him with the request, 'Now that you have arrived in our midst, do make a treaty with us so that we may bring our people to you.' After Rasulullah ﷺ had made the treaty with them, they accepted Islam. Rasulullah ﷺ dispatched us during the month of Rajab with instructions to attack the Banu Kinana tribe, who lived close to where the Juhaina tribe lived. We were not even 100 men when we attacked them, whereas they were greater in number. We sought assistance from the Juhaina tribe, they refused to render any help saying, 'Why are you fighting during a sacred month.' We told them that we were only fighting people who had exiled us from Makkah during a sacred month. Arabs considered the months of Dhul Qa'dah, Dhul Hijjah, Muharram and Rajab as sacred months in which fighting was forbidden. We then asked each other what to do. While some of us felt that we should report the matter to Rasulullah ﷺ, others were of the opinion that we should remain where we were. Me and a few others opted to attack a caravan of the Quraish. In those days, the practice was that whoever took anything as booty from the enemy, the possessions became his own property. So while we proceeded to attack the caravan, our companions went back to Rasulullah ﷺ and reported the incident. Rasulullah ﷺ's face became red with anger and he stood up saying, 'You left me as a united group and return separated! It was this very disunity that destroyed the nations before you. I shall now appoint as your commander a man who may not be the best of you but who is certainly the most enduring through hunger and thirst.' Rasulullah ﷺ appointed Abdullah bin Jahash Asadi ﷺ as our commander, who was the first commander appointed in Islam." *(Ahmad, Ibn Abi Shaiba in Kanzul Ummal, Baghawi in Isabah, Bayhaqi in Dala'il, Al Bidayah wan Nihayah, Haythami).*

Appointing an Amir over 10 Persons

Shihab Ambari narrates, "I was the first to set alight the gates of Tustar when Ash'ari ؓ was struck down by an arrow. When the city was conquered, Ash'ari ؓ appointed me as Amir over 10 members of my tribe." *(Ibn Abi Shaiba in Isabah)*

Appointing an Amir for a Journey

Omar ؓ once said, "When there are 3 people traveling, they should appoint one of them as Amir. This appointment has been commanded by Rasulullah ﷺ." *(Bazzar, Ibn Khuzaima, Dar Qutni, Hakim in Kanzul Ummal).*

Who Qualifies to be an Amir? Those who Know Most Qur'an Qualify to be Amir

Abu Hurairah ؓ narrates that Rasulullah ﷺ once dispatched an exceptionally large expedition. Rasulullah ﷺ made each one of them recite whatever portion of the Qur'an he knew. When Rasulullah ﷺ came to a man who was one of the youngest and asked him what portion of the Qur'an he knew, he named several Surahs that he knew including Surah Baqara. "Do you know Surah Baqara?" Rasulullah ﷺ enquired. When the man replied in the affirmative, Rasulullah ﷺ said, "Go ahead! You are now their Amir." One of the prominent persons amongst them said, "The only thing that prevented me from learning Surah Baqara was the fear that I would be unable to recite it in Tahajjud salah." Rasulullah ﷺ said, "Learn the Qur'an and recite it because the example of a person who learns the Qur'an and recites it is like a bag full of musk, from which fragrance originates and spreads in every direction. On the other hand, the example of a person who learns the Qur'an and then sleeps with it in his heart is like a bag of musk, the mouth of which has been sealed." *(Tirmidhi, Ibn Majah, Ibn Hibban in Targheeb wat Tarheeb).*

The Narration of Uthman ؓ About Those Knowing the Most Qur'an to be the Most Qualified for the Post of Amir

Uthman ؓ narrates that Rasulullah ﷺ once dispatched an expedition towards Yemen and appointed as their Amir someone who was the youngest amongst them. However, a few days had passed and they had not yet left. Rasulullah ﷺ met one of the men and addressing him by his name asked, "What is the matter? Why have you not yet left?" He replied, "O Rasulullah ﷺ! Our Amir has a problem with his leg." Rasulullah ﷺ then went to the man and 7 times recited:

بِسْمِ اللہ و با اللہ اعوذ با اللہ وقدر ته من ش ما فیها

"I commence in the name of Allah, I seek refuge in Allah, in the power of the bad in all things in it.'

Thereafter, Rasulullah ﷺ blew on him and he was cured. An elderly person belonging to the expedition said, "O Rasulullah ﷺ! How can you appoint him as our Amir when he is the youngest of us all?" When Rasulullah ﷺ mentioned the man's knowledge of the Qur'an, the elderly person said, "O Rasulullah ﷺ! I would have certainly learnt the Qur'an had I not feared that I would be satisfied and not recite it in the Tahajjud salah." Rasulullah ﷺ then mentioned, "The example of the Qur'an is like a bag that you fill with musk. Such is the example of the Qur'an when the Qur'an is in your heart and you recite it." *(Tabrani, Haythami).*

Abu Bakr ؓ Refuses to Give Authority / Leadership to the Veterans of Badr and the Statement of Omar ؓ in this Regard

Abu Bakr bin Muhammad Ansari reports that it was once said to Abu Bakr ؓ, "O successor of Rasulullah ﷺ! Why do you not give command to the veterans of Badr?" Abu Bakr ؓ replied, "I certainly acknowledge their high status, but I do not give them command because I do not like to spoil them with this world." *(Abu Nu'aym in Hilya, Ibn Asakir in Kanzul Ummal). Imran bin Abdullah* reports that Ubay bin Ka'b ؓ once asked Omar ؓ, "What is it that you do not give me command?" Omar ؓ replied, "I do not like to spoil your Islam." *(Ibn Sa'd).*

The Letter of Omar ؓ Concerning the Appointment of Commanders and His description of an Amir

Haritha bin Mudarrib narrates that Omar ؓ wrote the letter to them: I have sent Ammar bin Yasir ؓ as your Amir and Abdullah bin Mas'ood ؓ as your teacher and minister. They are both amongst the chosen companions of Rasulullah ﷺ and veterans of Badr. Learn from them and follow their example. By sending Abdullah ؓ to you, I have actually sacrificed my own need for him. I have also sent Uthman bin Hunaif ؓ to survey the rural areas of Iraq. I have fixed that their wages should be a goat every day. Half the goat and its entrails should be given to Ammar ؓ because as the Amir, he would naturally have guests to feed and the other half should be shared between the other 3 men (i.e. Abdullah bin Mas'ood ؓ, Uthman bin Hunaif ؓ, Hudhaifa bin Yaman ؓ, who was sent as an assistant surveyor)." *(Ibn Sa'd, Hakim and Sa'eed bin Mansoor in Kanzul Ummal, Tabrani, Bayhaqi).* Sha'bi narrates that Omar ؓ once asked, "Tell me who I should appoint to take charge of a public matter that is of great concern to me?" The name of Abdur Rahman bin Auf ؓ was suggested, Omar ؓ noted that he was not up to the task. When another name was suggested, Omar ؓ said, "I have no need for him." Omar ؓ was asked who it was that he required, he replied, "Someone who will be like one of the people when he becomes the Amir because of his humility and when he is not the Amir, he appears to be the Amir because of his high sense of responsibility." The people with Omar ؓ said, "We know of none suitable besides Rabi bin Ziyad Harithi." "That is true," confirmed Omar ؓ. *(Abu Ahmad Hakim in Kuna, Kanzul Ummal).*

Who Will be Successful as an Amir

Abu Wa'il Shaqiq bin Salama reports that Omar ؓ once appointed Bishr bin Asim ؓ to collect the Zakah of the Hawazin tribe. However, when Bishr ؓ failed to do so, Omar ؓ met him and asked, "What has kept you back? Is it not necessary to listen to me and to obey me?" "Of course," replied Bishr ؓ, "but I have heard Rasulullah ﷺ say, 'Whoever is appointed to carry out a public task shall be brought forward on the Day of Judgment and made to stand on the bridge across Jahannam. If he carried out the task well, he will be saved, but if he did not fulfill the responsibility, the bridge will shatter and he will fall for 70 years into Jahannam.'" Omar ؓ left in a very distressed and worried state. Abu Dharr ؓ then met him and asked, "Why do I see you so distressed and worried?" Omar ؓ replied, "Why should I not be distressed and worried when I have heard Bishr bin Asim say, "I have heard Rasulullah ﷺ say, 'Whoever is appointed to carry out a public task shall be brought forward on the Day of Judgment and made to stand on the bridge across Jahannam. If he carried out the task well, he will be saved, but if he did not fulfill the responsibility, the bridge will shatter and he will fall for 70 years into Jahannam.'" Abu Dhar ؓ asked, "Did you not hear Rasulullah ﷺ say this?" When Omar ؓ said that he had not, Abu Dhar ؓ said, "I testify that I had certainly heard Rasulullah ﷺ state, "Whoever is appointed to carry out any public task shall be brought forward on the Day of Judgment and made to stand on the bridge across Jahannam. If he carried out the task well, he will be saved, but if he did not fulfill the responsibility, the bridge will shatter and he will fall for 70 years into Jahannam, and Jahannam is extremely black and dark.' Now which of these 2 narrations creates more fear in your heart?" Omar ؓ replied, "They have both created great fear in my heart. Who will then be able to accept the responsibility and do justice to it?" Abu Dhar ؓ replied, "The person whose nose Allah intends to cut and whose cheek Allah wishes to bring to the ground whom Allah wishes to disgrace. However, we know only good of your Khilafa. Then again, it is possible that if you hand over the post to someone who does not exercise justice, you will also not be saved from the sin of his injustice." *(Tabrani in Targheeb wat Tarheeb, Haythami, Abdur Razzaq, Abu Nu'aym, Abu Sa'eed Naqqash, Baghawi, Dar Qutni in Kanzul Ummal, Ibn Abi Shaiba, Ibn Mandah in Isabah).*

Miqdad bin Aswad ؓ Refuses to be an Amir and the Statement of Anas ؓ in this Regard

Anas ؓ reports that Rasulullah ﷺ once appointed Miqdad bin Aswad ؓ as Amir of a troop of cavalrymen. When he returned from the expedition, Rasulullah ﷺ asked him what he thought about being an Amir. He replied, "I was helped to sit and to stand by the men who gave me great honor to the extent that I feel as if I am no longer myself and my humility has been diminished." Rasulullah ﷺ commented, "Leadership is like that and it does that to a person." Miqdad ؓ then said, "I swear by the Being Who has sent you with the truth that I shall never again assume any post of leadership." Thereafter, Miqdad ؓ would even decline when people asked him to lead them in salah. *(Bazzar, Haythami).* Anas ؓ quotes that Miqdad ؓ said, "I was helped on to my conveyance and helped to dismount until I felt as if I was superior to the others." Rasulullah ﷺ then told him, "Such is leadership. You may therefore either accept it or reject it." Miqdad ؓ hen swore, "I swear by the Being Who has sent you with the truth that I shall never again assume command of even 2 persons." *(Abu Nu'aym in Hilya).*

The Narration of Tabrani About the Incident of Miqdad ؓ

Miqdad bin Aswad ؓ says, "Rasulullah ﷺ sent me on an expedition. When we returned, he asked me, 'How do you find yourself?' I replied, 'I gradually started to think that the others were my servants. I swear by Allah that after this I shall never again take command of even 2 persons." *(Tabrani, Haythami).* It is reported that Rasulullah ﷺ once appointed someone to lead an expedition. When the man had completed his duties and returned, Rasulullah ﷺ asked him, "How was it to be the Amir?" The man replied, "Although I behaved like one of them, they all mounted when I did and dismounted when I did." Rasulullah ﷺ commented, "Leaders stand at the door of oppression and are prone to oppress except for those whom Allah saves from committing oppression." The man then said, "I swear by Allah that I shall never again accept command from you or from anybody else." Rasulullah ﷺ smiled broadly until even his back teeth were visible. *(Tabrani, Haythami)*

The Advice Abu Bakr ؓ Gave to Rafi Taa'i About Being an Amir

Rafi Taa'i ؓ narrates that he accompanied Abu Bakr ؓ on an expedition and when they were returning, he asked Abu Bakr ؓ for some advice. Abu Bakr ؓ said, "Establish the Fardh salah at its fixed hours, pay the Zakah due on your wealth with the pleasure of your heart, fast during the month of Ramadhan and perform pilgrimage to the House of Allah (Hajj). Remember well that Hijra in Islam is an excellent virtue, and to make Jihad in Hijra is very good. Also remember that you should never become an Amir. This post of leadership that appears to be so pleasurable today will soon become so widespread that people who are not fit for it will have it. The person who becomes an Amir shall be amongst those to experience the longest reckoning on the Day of Judgment and also the harshest of punishment for failing in his duties. On the other hand, the person who does not become an Amir will be amongst those to experience the shortest reckoning and the lightest of punishment. This is because leaders are most prone to oppress the Mu'minin and whoever oppresses the Mu'minin has breached his pledge with Allah since the Mu'minin are Allah's neighbors and His slaves. By Allah! If even the goat or camel of your neighbor has to come to do some harm, you would spend the night with swollen veins in anger repeatedly saying, 'My neighbor's goat!' or 'My neighbor's camel!' Allah has a greater right to get angry for the sake of His neighbors." *(Ibn Mubarak in Zuhd, Kanzul Ummal).*

The Incident that Occurred Between Abu Bakr ؓ and Rafi ؓ Concerning Leadership

Rafi ؓ narrates that Rasulullah ﷺ dispatched Amr bin Al Aas ؓ as commander of the army that marched to the battle of Dhatus Salasil. Together with him in the army Rasulullah ﷺ also sent Abu Bakr ؓ, Omar ؓ and other leading Sahabah. The army proceeded until they set up camp at the 2 mountains of the Tay tribe. When Omar ؓ suggested that they find a guide to show them the road, the others said that the only guide can be Rafi bin Amr because he had been a 'Rabil'. The narrator of the Hadith says that he asked his teacher Tariq what a 'Rabil' was and he was informed that a 'Rabil' was a robber who single-handedly tackles a group of people and robs them all. Rafi ؓ narrates further, "When we had completed the expedition and returned to the place from where we had left, I had already judged Abu Bakr ؓ to be an excellent man, so I approached him and said, 'O man of Halal! From amongst all your companions, I have judged you to be the best, so tell me something that will make me part of your people and just like you if I remember it.' Abu Bakr ؓ said, 'Can you remember your 5 fingers?' When I replied in the affirmative he said, 'Testify that there is none worthy of worship but Allah the One Who has no partner, that Muhammad ﷺ is the Rasul of Allah, establish salah, pay Zakah if you have wealth, perform the pilgrimage to the Kabah and fast during Ramadhan. Can you remember this?' 'Of course,' I replied. He then added, 'And there is also something else, that you should never become the Amir of even 2 persons.' I said, 'Can anyone be given command other than you veterans of Badr?' He' replied, 'This post will soon spread until it reaches you and even people whose status is inferior to yours.' Abu Bakr ؓ then continued, 'Verily when Allah sent His messenger, people started entering the fold of Islam. Amongst them were those whom Allah had guided and who gladly entered Islam. Others were those whom the sword had compelled to accept Islam. All these people have sought Allah's protection and are Allah's neighbors in his custody. When a man becomes the Amir and the people under his command oppress each other, Allah will take revenge from him if he does not give back to the oppressed what the oppressors had taken from them. This is just like the case when your neighbor's goat is taken away and you spend the entire day with swollen veins out of feeling for your neighbor. In the same way, Allah also lends his support to His neighbors.'" Rafi ؓ reports further, "It was a year later that Abu Bakr ؓ was made the Khalifa. I then rode off to meet him. I introduced myself as Rafi and reminded him where I had been his guide. When he confirmed that he remembered who I was, I said, 'You used to prevent me from becoming an Amir and now you have mounted a much greater task as the Amir of the entire Ummah of Muhammad ﷺ.' He replied, 'Indeed, because the one who does not enforce the Book of Allah amongst the people shall earn the curse of Allah." *(Tabrani, Haythami).*

The Sahabah Prefer Fighting Rather Than Taking Command

Sa'eed bin Amr bin Sa'eed bin Al Aas ؓ narrates that his uncles Khalid bin Sa'eed bin Al Aas ؓ, Aban bin Sa'eed bin Al Aas and Amr bin Sa'eed bin Al Aas ؓ all returned to Madinah from their posts as governors of various districts when they heard about the demise of Rasulullah ﷺ. Abu Bakr ؓ said to them, "None are more qualified to be governors than those whom Rasulullah ﷺ himself appointed and you should therefore return to your posts)." However, they replied, "We shall not command for anyone." They then returned to Sham where all of them were martyred." *(Hakim, Abu Nu'aym, Ibn Asakir in Kanzul Ummal).*

The Incident that Occurred Between Omar ؓ and Aban bin Sa'eed ؓ Concerning an Appointment to Command and Omar ؓ Dispatches Ala bin Hadhrami ؓ to Bahrain

Abdur Rahman bin Sa'eed bin Yarboo narrates that when Aban bin Sa'eed ؓ returned to Madinah, Omar ؓ said to him, "You have no right to come here and leave your post without the permission of your leader, especially under the present circumstances when people are revolting and the enemy is ready to pounce on us. It however seems that you have no fear." Aban ؓ replied, "I swear by Allah that I shall never accept command from anyone after Rasulullah ﷺ. If I were to accept command from anyone after Rasulullah ﷺ, I would accept a post from Abu Bakr ؓ because of his virtue and his early entry into Islam. However, I would still not want to accept any post of command from anyone after Rasulullah ﷺ." When Abu Bakr ؓ consulted with the Sahabah about whom to send to Bahrain, Uthman ؓ said, "Send the person whom Rasulullah ﷺ had sent to the people of Bahrain, the one who made them Muslims and subservient. Someone whom they will recognize, who recognizes them and who knows their land." Uthman ؓ was referring to Ala bin Hadhrami ؓ. Omar ؓ refused to accept the proposal and said, "Force Aban bin Sa'eed bin Al Aas ؓ to return because he is a man who has been there several times." Abu Bakr ؓ refused to force him saying, "I shall not do it. I cannot force a person who says that he will not accept a post of command from anyone after Rasulullah ﷺ." Abu Bakr ؓ confirmed that Ala bin Hadhrami ؓ would be sent to Bahrain. *(Ibn Sa'd in Kanzul Ummal).*

Abu Hurairah ؓ Refuses to Accept an Appointment as Amir

Abu Hurairah ؓ reports that Omar ؓ summoned him to accept a post as governor, but he refused to accept the post. Omar ؓ said, "You dislike an appointment to a post when someone better than you actually asked for it." Abu Hurairah ؓ asked who it was that asked for a post, Omar ؓ replied, "Yusuf bin Ya'qub عليهما السلام." Abu Hurairah ؓ then said, "Yusuf السلام was the Nabi of Allah and the son of a Nabi, while I am merely Abu Hurairah ؓ the son of Umaima. I fear 3 and 2 things equaling 5." "Why don't you just say '5 things'?" enquired Omar ؓ. Abu Hurairah ؓ replied, "I fear that I should say anything without knowledge, pass wrong judgment as a governor, because of which I would have my back lashed, have my wealth taken away and my reputation insulted." *(Abu Nu'aym in Hilya, Isabah, Ibn Sa'd).*

Abdullah bin Omar ؓ Refuses to be Appointed as Judge

Abdullah bin Mowhab reports that Uthman ؓ once said to Abdullah bin Omar ؓ, "Go and pass judgment between the people." Abdullah bin Omar ؓ requested, "Will you not excuse me, O Amirul Mu'minin?" Uthman ؓ emphatically said, "Never! I have sworn that you must be the judge." "Do not be hasty," Abdullah bin Omar ؓ spoke, "have you heard Rasulullah ﷺ say, 'The person who seeks protection from Allah has sought a great source of protection.'" When Uthman ؓ confirmed that he had heard the Hadith, Abdullah bin Omar ؓ said, "I then seek Allah's protection from being a judge." Uthman ؓ then asked, "What prevents you when your father was a judge?" Abdullah bin Omar ؓ replied, "I have heard Rasulullah ﷺ say, 'The person who is a judge and passes judgment in ignorance shall be one of the inmates of Jahannam. As for the one who is a knowledgeable judge and passes correct and just judgment, he will plead before Allah on the Day of Judgment for an acquittal that he should neither receive any rewards nor any sin.' What have I to hope for after this?" *(Tabrani in Kabir and Awsat, Bazaar, Ahmad, Haythami).* Ahmad adds that Uthman ؓ excused Abdullah bin Omar ؓ and told him not to inform anyone else about it otherwise none would be prepared. to act as judge and society would suffer. Abdullah bin Omar ؓ narrates that Uthman ؓ wanted him to act as judge, but he refused saying, "I have heard Rasulullah ﷺ say, 'Judges are of 3 types; one will attain salvation while 2 will end up in Jahannam. Those who pass judgment unjustly or by the dictates of their desires shall be destroyed while the one who passes judgment with the truth will attain salvation." *(Tabrani in Kabir and Awsat, Haythami, Abu Ya'la)*

The Incident Between Abdullah bin Omar ؓ and Ummul Mu'minin Hafsa ؓ Concerning Dowmatul Jandal

Abdullah bin Omar ؓ narrates, "It was on the day that Ali ؓ *(Haythami)* and Mu'awiya ؓ gathered at Dowmatul Jandal to reconcile their differences that my sister Ummul Mu'minin Hafsa ؓ said to me, 'It is really not nice that you refrain from participating in a reconciliation that Allah has brought about between the Ummah of Muhammad ﷺ since you are the brother-in-law of Rasulullah ﷺ and the son of Omar bin Khattab ؓ." That day, Mu'awiya ؓ arrived on a huge Bactrian camel and announced, "Who is desirous of Khilafa? Who is willing to risk his neck for it?" Abdullah bin Omar ؓ says, "Never before had my heart ever aspired for worldly things and I almost said, 'That person desires the Khilafa who had hit your neck and the neck of your father to accept Islam until he made you enter its fold!' However, I thought of Jannah and its bounties and refrained from saying it." *(Tabrani in Kabir, Haythami, Ibn Sa'd).* A narration of *Abu Husain* states that Mu'awiya ؓ said, "Who is more worthy than us of this post of Khilafa?" Abdullah bin Omar ؓ said, "I wanted to say, 'More worthy than you is the one who hit your neck and your father's neck to bring you into Islam.' However, I then thought about the bounties of Jannah and feared that I would be spoiling them by saying this." *(Ibn Sa'd).* Imam Zuhri states that when Hasan bin Ali ؓ and Mu'awiya ؓ got together, Mu'awiya ؓ announced, "Who is most worthy of the post of Khilafa than me?" Abdullah bin Omar ؓ said, "I wanted to say, 'More worthy than you is the one who hit your and your father's necks because of your Kufr.' I feared that if I said this, thoughts would be entertained about me that are not true and people would think that I desired to be the Khalifa which was not true."

Imran bin Husain ؓ Refuses to be an Amir

Abdullah bin Samit ؓ reports that when Ziyad wanted to dispatch Imran bin Husain ؓ as governor of Khurasan, he refused to accept the post. His friends asked, "Are you forsaking the opportunity to be governor of Khurasan?" He replied, "It does not please me at all that I should suffer the heat of Khurasan doing the hard work of governing while Ziyad and his followers enjoy its coolness by using the income from the region. I fear that if I am ever facing the enemy in battle and then a letter would come to me from Ziyad, which if I obey will result in my destruction and if I ignore it, will result in my execution at the hands of Ziyad." Ziyad then appointed Hakam bin Amr Ghifari as governor of Khurasan and Hakam accepted the post. Imran then asked someone to summon Hakam to him. A messenger went to Hakam and when he arrived, Imran said. to him, "Did you hear Rasulullah say that no person should be obeyed when the obedience to the person involves disobedience to Allah?" When Hakam confirmed that he had heard this from Rasulullah, Irnran exclaimed, "Alhamdu Lillah!" or "Allahu Akbar!" Another narration from Hasan states that when Ziyad appointed Hakam Ghifari as commander of the army, Imran bin Husain went to see him. Imran met him in public and asked, "Do you know why I have come to you?" When Hakam asked why he had come, Imran said, "Do you remember what Rasulullah said to the person whose Amir told him to throw himself into the fire and he was then stopped and prevented by others from doing what he was commanded. When the incident was reported to Rasulullah, he said to the person, 'Had he fallen into the fire, both of them would have entered Jahannam. There is no obedience to anyone when it involves disobeying Allah." Hakam confirmed that he remembered the Hadith. Imran then aid, "I only wished to remind you of this Hadith. *(Ahmad, Haythami, Tabrani).*

Respecting the Khalifas and Amirs and Obeying Their Commands: The Incident Between Khalid and Ammar during an Expedition

Abdullah bin Abbas narrates that Rasulullah once dispatched Khalid bin Walid bin Mughiera Makhzumi on expedition. With him was Ammar bin Yasir. The expedition left and finally drew close to the people whom they intended to ambush early in the morning. They set up camp there late at night. However, someone warned the people about the presence of the Sahabah and they all fled to a place of safety. One of the men amongst them who had accepted Islam together with his family stayed behind. He instructed his family to load their goods and then told them to wait until he returned. He then proceeded to meet Ammar and said, "O Abu Yaqdhan! My family and I have accepted Islam. Will this help me if I stay behind in the town because all my people had fled .when they heard about your arrival?" Ammar said to him, "You may stay behind, for you are safe." The man and his family then went back. When Khalid launched the attack the next morning, he found that the people had all fled. He then captured the man and his family. Ammar said, "You can do nothing to a man who has accepted Islam." Khalid said, "What have you to do with this? When I am the Amir, how could you grant a person amnesty without my permission?" Ammar replied, "I can indeed grant amnesty without your permission even though you are the Amir. This man has accepted Iman and if he wished to, he could have left with the others. Because he has Iman, I instructed him to stay behind." The 2 Sahabah then argued until they started abusing each other. When they returned to Madinah, they both went to Rasulullah and Ammar told him about the man and what he had done. Rasulullah then authorized the amnesty that Ammar had granted but at the same time also forbade people from granting amnesty to others without the permission of the Amir. The 2

Sahabah then again started arguing in the presence of Rasulullah. To this, Khalid remarked, "O Rasulullah! This slave is insulting me in your presence! I swear by Allah that had you not been here, he would have never used such terms for me." Rasulullah said, "O Khalid! Do not harass Ammar because Allah dislikes anyone who dislikes Ammar and Allah curses anyone who curses Ammar." Ammar the stood up and left. Khalid followed him, grabbed hold of his clothing and continuously made attempts to please Ammar until Ammar was pleased with him. It was then that Allah revealed the verse:

أَطِيعُوا اللَّهَ وَأَطِيعُوا الرَّسُولَ وَأُولِي الْأَمْرِ مِنْكُمْ فَإِنْ تَنَازَعْتُمْ فِي شَيْءٍ فَرُدُّوهُ إِلَى اللَّهِ وَالرَّسُولِ إِنْ كُنْتُمْ تُؤْمِنُونَ بِاللَّهِ وَالْيَوْمِ الْآخِرِ ذَلِكَ خَيْرٌ وَأَحْسَنُ تَأْوِيلًا (59)

Obey Allah and obey the Messenger (Muhammad ﷺ), and those of you (Muslims) who are in authority. (And) if you differ in anything amongst yourselves, refer it to Allah and His Messenger (ﷺ), if you believe in Allah and in the Last Day. That is better and more suitable for final determination. (An-Nisa':59) (Ibn Jareer, Ibn Asakir in Kanzul Ummal, Abu Ya'la, Ibn Asakir, Nasai, Tabraani, Hakim, Ibn Abi Shaiba, Ahmad, Haythami).

The Incident that Occurred between Auf bin Malik and Khalid bin Walid

Auf bin Malik Ashja'e reports that he was amongst those Muslims who marched with Zaid bin Haritha for the battle of Mu'ta. His companion was a man who had come with reinforcements from Yemen. He had nothing but his sword with him. When one of the Muslims slaughtered a camel, the man from Yemen asked him for a piece of the leather, which he gladly gave. The man made the piece of leather into a shield for himself and we then proceeded. When we faced the large Roman army there was a man amongst them riding a red horse. His saddle and his weapons were gold plated and he attacked the Muslims very fiercely. The man from Yemen waited for him behind a boulder and when the Roman passed by, the Yemeni restricted his horse. As the Roman fell, the Yemeni attacked and killed him. He then took possession of the Roman's belongings. After Allah had granted victory to the Muslims, Khalid bin Walid who was made the commander after the other commanders had been martyred, sent for the Yemeni and took away the belongings he had taken from the Roman. Auf bin Malik approached Khalid bin Walid and said, "O Khalid! Don't you know that Rasulullah has decreed that the one who kills an enemy soldier should take all his possessions?" Khalid replied, "Certainly, but I think that these possessions are too much." Auf objected by saying, "You must return it to him otherwise I shall definitely expose you before Rasulullah." Khalid still refused to return it. Auf narrated further that when they both got to Rasulullah, he related to Rasulullah the entire story of the Yemeni and how Khalid had treated him. Rasulullah asked Khalid the reason for his action, he replied, "O Rasulullah! I thought that the possessions were too much." Rasulullah then instructed Khalid to return the goods to the Yemeni. At this, Auf commented, "So there! Did I not tell you that I would do this complain about you to Rasulullah and have you punished?" "What was that all about?" Rasulullah enquired. Auf informed Rasulullah about his threat to Khalid, Rasulullah became very angry and said, "Do not return the goods Khalid! Will you people not leave my commanders alone for my sake and will you not show them respect?! You people under their command receive the benefit of the good they command while they suffer for their improper commands." *(Ahmad, Muslim, Abu Dawood in Al Bidayah wan Nihayah, Bayhaqi).*

The Incident Between Omar ✿ and Sa'd bin Abi Waqqas ✿ Concerning Respect for a Leader

Rashid bin Sa'd reports that some wealth came to Omar ✿ and he was distributing it amongst the people when they started crowding around him. Sa'd bin Abi Waqqas ✿ arrived and forced his way through the crowd until he reached Omar ✿. Omar ✿ lifted up his whip and said, "You came here as if you have no fear for Allah's commander on earth! I wish to teach you that Allah's commander on earth also has no fear for you.**" (Ibn Sa'd).**

The Incident Between Omar ✿ and Amr bin Al Aas ✿

Abdullah bin Yazid narrates that Rasulullah ﷺ once dispatched Amr bin Al Aas ✿ as commander of a military expedition that included Abu Bakr and Omar ✿. When they reached the place where the battle was to be fought, Amr bin Al Aas ✿ issued the command that no fires were to be lit. This angered Omar ✿ and he was about to object when Abu Bakr ✿ stopped him and said to him, "Rasulullah ﷺ has made him your commander because of his knowledge of warfare." Omar ✿ calmed down. *(Bayhaqi, Hakim).*

The Narration of Ayad bin Ghanam ✿ on the Respect for the Amir

Jubair bin Nufair ✿ reports that Ayadh bin Ghanam Ash'ari ✿ severely punished the governor of Dara when the Muslims conquered the place. Hisham bin Hakim ✿ came to him and harshly reprimanded him for this act. After a few days, Hisham ✿ came back to Ayadh ✿ with apology and said, "Do you not know that Rasulullah ﷺ said, 'The people who will be most severely punished on the Day of Judgment will be those who punished people most severely in this world'?" Ayadh ✿ responded by saying, "O Hisham! We have heard what you heard, we have seen what you have seen and we have been in the company of Rasulullah ﷺ just as you have been. O Hisham! Did you not hear Rasulullah ﷺ say, 'Whoever wishes to advise their leader should never address it to him in public. He should rather take him by the hand and address him in private. If the leader accepts it, he accepts it. Otherwise, the advisor has discharged the obligation and the right he owes to his leader.' However, O Hisham, you have been very bold against Allah's commander. Do you not fear that Allah's commander would have you killed and you would be known as one whom the commander had executed?" *(Hakim, Bayhaqi in Majma'uz Zawa'id, Haythami)*

The Statement of Hudhaifa ✿ Concerning Drawing Weapons Against the Amir

Zaid bin Wahab reports that during the time of Hudhaifa ✿, some people complained to him about the Amir. A man then entered the large Jami Masjid and weaved his way through the people until he reached Hudhaifa ✿. He stood by the head of Hudhaifa ✿ and said, "O companion of Rasulullah ﷺ! Will you not enjoin good and forbid evil?" Knowing what the man meant that Hudhaifa ✿ ought to oppose the Amir, Hudhaifa looked up and said to him, "Undoubtedly, enjoining good and forbidding evil is an excellent deed. Drawing weapons against your Amir is certainly not a Sunnah practice." *(Bazzar, Haythami).*

A Narration of Abu Bakrah ✿ Concerning Respect for an Amir

Ziyad bin Kusaib Adawi reports that Abdullah bin Amir ✿ used to deliver lectures to the people while wearing fine clothing and with well groomed hair. After leading the salah one day and entering his room, Mirdas Abu Bilal commented, "Would you look at the people's Ameer and leader! He wears fine clothes and adopts the appearance of the sinners!" Abu Bakrah ✿ was sitting next to the pulpit. When he heard this, he told his son Usaili to call Abu Bilal. When Abu Bilal arrived, Abu Bakrah ✿ said to him, "I have heard the comment you have just made about the Amir. I have heard Rasulullah ﷺ say, 'Allah will honor the person who honors His Amir and will disgrace the person who disgraces Allah's Amir." *(Bayhaqi).*

The Amir is Obeyed Only When he Instructs What is Right

Ali bin Abi Talib ✿ reports that Rasulullah ﷺ once appointed a Sahabi from the Ansar as commander of an expedition. Rasulullah ﷺ dispatched the expedition with instructions to listen to and to obey their commander. However, the others happened to aggravate their commander in some way and he ordered them to gather firewood. They did as they were ordered, he instructed them to light a fire. After they had lit the fire, he said to them, "Did Rasulullah ﷺ not instruct you listen to me and to obey me?" When they acknowledged the instruction, he said, "Then enter this fire." The men started looking at each other saying, "It was the fire of Jahannam that we were escaping from when we went to Rasulullah ﷺ." The commander's anger abated and the fire died off. The men returned and reported the incident to Rasulullah ﷺ, he said, "Had they entered it, they would have never emerged from it because after death they would have entered the fire of Jahannam. Obedience is only in matters of good." *(Bukhari, Muslim, Al Bidayah wan Nihayah, Kanzul Ummal, Isabah)*

The Narration of Abdullah bin Omar ✿ on Respecting the Amir

Abdullah bin Omar ✿ narrates that Rasulullah ﷺ was once with a group of the Sahabah when he turned to them and said, "Do you not know that I am verily the Rasul of Allah sent to you?" The Sahabah replied, "But of course. We testify that you are certainly the Rasul of Allah." Rasulullah ﷺ then asked them, "Do you not know that whoever obeys me obeys Allah and obedience to me is part of obedience to Allah?" The Sahabah responded by saying, "But of course. We testify that whoever obeys you obeys Allah and obedience to you is part of obedience to Allah." Rasulullah ﷺ went on to say, "For you to obey me is part of obedience to Allah and for you to obey your leaders is part of obedience to me. In fact, even if they perform salah sitting down, you should also perform salah sitting down." *(Abu Ya'la, Ibn Asakir, in Kanzul Ummal).*

The Advice Rasulullah ﷺ Gave to Abu Dhar ✿ Concerning Showing Respect to the Amir

Asma bint Yazid ✿ reports that Abu Dhrr Ghifari ✿ used to serve Rasulullah ﷺ and would return to the Masjid after he had completed. The Masjid was his home where he used to lie down to sleep. Rasulullah ﷺ happened to enter the Masjid one night where he found Abu Dhar ✿ sleeping on the ground. Rasulullah ﷺ poked him gently with his foot until Abu Dhar ✿ sat upright. Rasulullah ﷺ then said to him, "Did I not see you sleeping in the Masjid?" "Where should I sleep?" asked Abu Dhar ✿, "I have no home besides this." Rasulullah ﷺ then sat with him and said, "What will you do when the people expel you from the Masjid?" Abu Dhar ✿ replied, "I shall then go to Sham, which is the place of migration of the previous Ambiya السلام عليهم, the place where mankind will be resurrected and the land of many Ambiya السلام عليهم. I shall then become one of its people." Rasulullah ﷺ asked further, "What will you then do if they exile you from Sham?" "I shall then return to Madinah, which will be my home and place of residence." Rasulullah ﷺ again enquired, "And what if they exile you from here for the second time?" Abu Dhar ✿ resolved, "I shall then take up my sword and fight until I die." Rasulullah ﷺ smiled at him and placed his hand on him saying, "Should I rather guide you to something that is better than that?" Abu Dhar ؓ exclaimed, "Why not, O Rasulullah ﷺ? May my parents be sacrificed for you!" Rasulullah ﷺ said, "Follow them wherever they lead you and go along to wherever they drive you until you eventually meet me in that condition." *(Ibn Jareer in Kanzul Ummal, Ahmad, Haythami).*

Another narration from Abu Dhar ؓ states that Rasulullah ﷺ asked, "What will you then do when you are removed from Madinah?" Abu Dhar ؓ replied, "I shall take my sword and strike anyone who wants to remove me. Rasulullah ﷺ then placed his hand on the shoulder of Abu Dhar ؓ and said, "Overlook what they do O Abu Dhar. You should rather follow them wherever they lead you and go along to wherever they drive you even though you have to adopt this attitude even with an Abyssinian slave." Abu Dhar ؓ says, "When I settled in Rabdha on the instruction of Amirul Mu'minin Uthman ؓ, it once occurred that the Iqamah for salah was already called out and an Abyssinian man who had been appointed to collect Zakah went forward to lead the salah. However, when he saw me, he started going back and putting me forward. I said to him, 'Stay where you are, for I am obeying the command of Rasulullah ﷺ." *(Ibn Jareer).* Another narration states that when Abu Dhar ؓ went to Rabdha, he once found an Abyssinian slave of Uthman ؓ there. The man called out the Adhan and the Iqamah and then asked Abu Dhar ؓ to go forward to lead the salah. Abu Dhar ؓ said, "No. Rasulullah ﷺ instructed me to listen and to obey even an Abyssinian slave." The slave then went forward and Abu Dhar ؓ performed salah behind him. *(Abdur Razzaq in Kanzul Ummal).* Omar ؓ said, "Listen and obey your Amir even though the person appointed as your Amir is an Abyssinian slave with mutilated limbs. Exercise patience if he harms you and if he gives you an instruction, carry it out. Also exercise patience if he deprives you and even if he oppresses you. However, if he ever intends to diminish your Islam, then tell him, 'You may have my blood but not my Islam!' Also ensure that you never separate from the Jama'ah."*(Ibn Abi Shaiba, Ibn Jareer, Bayhaqi, Nu'aym bin Hammad in Kanzul Ummal).*

The Narration of Omar ؓ Concerning Showing Respect for the Amir and His Incident with Alqama in this Regard

Hasan narrates that Alqama bin Alatha once met Omar ؓ late at night. Because Omar ؓ resembled Khalid bin Walid ؓ, Alqama mistook him as Khalid ؓ and said, "O Khalid! Omar ؓ has dismissed you from your post as commanding officer! It is all because of his narrow sightedness. In fact, my cousin and I were about to ask him for something but we shall now never ask him anything because he has dismissed you." Omar ؓ said to him, "Is there anything else you wish to say?" Alqama continued, "Nevertheless, our leaders are people who have a right over us that we have to obey them in all conditions. We shall have our rewards with Allah when we fulfill the rights we owe to them." The next morning, Omar ؓ asked Khalid bin Walid ؓ, "What has Alqama said to you since last night?" Khalid ؓ replied, "By Allah! He has not said anything to me!" Omar ؓ said, "And you are even swearing in Allah's name about it." The narration of Abu Nadhra adds that Alqama then said to Khalid ؓ, "Be quiet, O Khalid do not deny it." Another narration from Saif bin Amr also narrating from Hasan concludes with the words of Omar ؓ who said, "You are both speaking the truth." The narration of Zubair bin Bakkar states that Omar ؓ then granted Alqama what he wanted and thus satisfied his need. During the night

conversation when Omar ؓ asked Alqama what he had to say, Alqama replied, "All I can advocate is that we listen and obey." Omar ؓ later said to Alqama that if everyone else shared his attitude, it would be more precious to him than all the wealth in the world. *(Ya'qub bin Sufian, Zubair bin Bakkar in Isabah).*

An Incident of a Leper Concerning Respect for the Amir

Ibn Abi Mulaika says that Omar ؓ passed by a lady suffering from leprosy as she was busy performing Tawaf. He said to her, "O servant of Allah! Do not cause difficulty to the people because they are afraid to perform Tawaf with you here. It would be best for you to remain at home." She then remained at home and stopped going to the Masjidul Haram. Later a man passing by her said to her, "The person who had prevented you has passed away. You may now come out." She responded by saying, "It is not befitting of me to obey him while he was alive and then disobey him after his death." *(Malik in Kanzul Ummal).*

The Consequences of Disobeying the Amir

Shamar narrates from a man who had been the chief of an area during the Khilafah of Ali ؓ that Ali ؓ once issued an order to them and then asked, "Will you do as you have been ordered?" When they said that they would not, Ali ؓ said, "I swear by Allah that you must do as you have been commanded otherwise the Jews and the Christians will definitely mount you necks." *(Ibn Abi Shaiba in Kanzul Ummal).*

The Incident Between Amr bin Al Aas ؓ, Abu Ubaidah and Omar ؓ

Urwa bin Zubair ؓ narrates that Rasulullah ﷺ once sent Amr bin Al Aas ؓ as Amir on a military expedition to the rural towns of Sham where the battle of Dhatus Salasil was fought. The towns were those of the Banu Bali tribe, the Banu Abdullah tribe, and the Banu Quda'ah tribe next to them. It was from the Banu Bali tribe that the maternal uncles of As bin Wa'il hailed (Aas bin Wa'il was the father of Amr bin Al Aas ؓ). When Amr bin Al Aas ؓ arrived at the place, he was anxious of the large numbers of the enemy and sent a message to Rasulullah ﷺ asking for reinforcements. Rasulullah ﷺ prepared the early Muhajirin for the task and amongst the most senior Muhajirin who got ready for the task were Abu Bakr and Omar ؓ. Rasulullah ﷺ appointed Abu Ubaidah bin Jarrah ؓ as their Amir and when they met Amr bin Al Aas ؓ, he said to them, "I am your Amir now for I had sent the message to Rasulullah ﷺ asking for you to come here as reinforcements. However, the group of Muhajirin said, "You may be the Amir of your army, but our Amir is Abu Ubaidah ؓ." Amr bin Al Aas ؓ reiterated what he said by saying, "You are only the reinforcements that I had requested." Abu Ubaidah ؓ was a man of excellent character and very soft-hearted. When he saw what was happening, he said, "You ought to know O Amr that the parting instruction Rasulullah ﷺ gave to me was, 'When you reach your companion, co-operate with him.' I shall obey you even if you wish to disobey me." Abu Ubaidah ؓ handed over the command to Amr ؓ. *(Bayhaqi in Ai Bidayah wan Nihayah Kanzu Ummal, Ibn Asakir)*

Another narration from *Zuhri* states that Rasulullah ﷺ dispatched 2 expeditions against the Banu Kalb tribe, the Ghassan tribe and other disbelieving tribes located in the rural towns of Sham. Rasulullah ﷺ appointed Abu Ubaidah bin Jarrah ؓ as Amir of one expedition and Amr bin Al Aas ؓ as Amir of the other. Marching in the army of Abu Ubaidah ؓ was Abu Bakr and Omar ؓ. When the 2 armies were about to leave, Rasulullah ﷺ called for Abu Ubaidah ؓ and Amr ؓ and said to them, "Never oppose each other." When the 2 armies had left

Madinah) Abu Ubaidah 🙵 took Amr 🙵 aside and said to him, "Rasulullah 🙵 had emphatically advised us never to oppose each other. It is either you who will obey me or I that will obey you." Amr 🙵 replied, "I would rather want that you obey me." Abu Ubaidah 🙵 then accepted to be under the command of Amr 🙵, who became the commander of both armies. Omar 🙵 became angry at this arrangement and said to Abu Ubaidah 🙵, "You have chosen to be under the command of Nabigha's son and have made him your Amir, the Amir of Abu Bakr 🙵 and our Amir?!" What sort of idea is this?" Abu Ubaidah 🙵 pacified Omar 🙵 by saying, "Dear brother! Rasulullah 🙵 emphatically advised me and Amr 🙵 never to oppose each other. I therefore feared that if I do not obey him, I would be disobeying Rasulullah 🙵. In this way, many people would be the cause of spoiling my relationship with Rasulullah 🙵. I swear by Allah that I shall now obey him until we return." When they returned from the expedition, Omar 🙵 complained about this to Rasulullah 🙵. Rasulullah 🙵 said, "After this, I shall appoint only someone from yourselves (senior Muhajirin) as your Ameer." *(lbn Asakir in Kanzul Ummal).*

The Statement of Omar 🙵 Regarding the Rights That Subjects Owe to Their Amir

Salama bin Shihab Abdi reports that Omar 🙵 once said, "O citizens! We the leaders have a right that you owe to us. It is that you always wish well for us even in our absence and that you assist us in all good works. Take note that there is nothing more beloved to Allah and which has a more widespread benefit than the tolerance and compassion of an Amir towards his subjects. On the contrary, there is nothing more disliked by Allah than the foolishness of an Amir and his harshness." *(Hannad in Kanzul Ummal, Tabari).* Another narration from *Abdullah bin Akim* states that Omar 🙵 said, "There is no tolerance more loved by Allah than the tolerance and compassion of an Amir towards his subjects. There is also no foolishness that is more disliked by Allah than the foolishness and harshness of an Amir. Those who overlook things that happen to him will receive health and safety and those who exercise justice between people even when it concerns himself shall be granted success in his affairs. Suffering disgrace when being obedient is closer to goodness than winning honor through sin." *(Hannad in Kanzul Ummal, Tabari).*

The Narration of Anas 🙵 Regarding the Prohibition From Speaking of the Amir

Anas 🙵 narrates, "The senior companions of Rasulullah 🙵 used to prevent us from misdeeds. They would say, 'Never speak ill of your leaders, never betray them and never disobey them. Fear Allah and exercise patience because the event (Day of Judgment/death) is close by." *(Ibn Jareer in Kanzul Ummal).*

Abdullah bin Omar 🙵 Tells Urwa 🙵 That They Used to Consider an Act of Hypocrisy Regarding Refraining From Speaking the Truth Before Leaders

Urwa 🙵 narrates that he once approached Abdullah bin Omar bin Khattab 🙵 and said, "O Abu Abdur Rahman! Sometimes we sit with these leaders of ours and we confirm what they say even though we know that it is not true. Even when they make unjust decisions, we still support them and make it seem credible to them. What do you think about this?" Abdullah bin Omar 🙵 said, "Dear nephew! During the time we were with Rasulullah 🙵 we regarded this to be an act of hypocrisy but I do not know what you regard it to be." *(Bayhaqi).* Another narration from the father of Asim bin Muhammad states that someone once said to Abdullah bin Omar 🙵, "When we are with our leaders,

we say things that are quite the opposite of what we say when we leave them." Abdullah bin Omar 🙵 commented, "We used to regard this as an act of hypocrisy." *(Bayhaqi in Targheeb wat Tarheeb).* *Bukhari* has reported a similar narration from Muhammad bin Zaid but adds that Abdullah bin Omar 🙵 said, "During the time of Rasulullah 🙵, we regarded this to be an act of hypocrisy." *Mujahid* reports that when a man came to Abdullah bin Omar 🙵, the latter asked him, "How is the relationship between you people and Abu Unays the Amir?" The man replied, "Our relationship is that when we meet with him, we tell him what he likes to hear and sing a different tune when we go away from him." Abdullah bin Omar 🙵 commented, "When we were with Rasulullah 🙵, this is the thing we regarded as hypocrisy." *(Ibn Asakir in Kanzul Ummal).* *Sha'bi* reports that they once said to Abdullah bin Omar 🙵, "When we enter the courts of our leaders, we say the things they like to hear but then say the opposite when we leave their presence." Abdullah bin Omar 🙵 said, "During the time of Rasulullah 🙵, we used to regard this as an act of hypocrisy." *(Abu Nu'aym in Hilya).*

The Narration of Alqama bin Waqqas Concerning the Prohibition of Laughing and Jesting in the Presence of the Amir

Alqama bin Waqqas narrates that there was a useless man who used to enter the courts of the governors and make them laugh. Alqama's grandfather said to the man, "Shame on you! Why do you enter the courts of these people and make them laugh?! I have heard from Bilal bin Harith 🙵 who was a companion of Rasulullah 🙵 that Rasulullah 🙵 said, 'A servant of Allah may utter a word that pleases Allah without him realizing its true potential and because of it, Allah becomes pleased with him until the day he meets Allah. On the contrary, a servant of Allah may utter a word that displeases Allah without him realizing its true potential and because of it, Allah becomes displeased with him until the day he meets Allah.'" *(Bayhaqi).* Another narration from *Alqama* states that Bilal bin Harith Muzani said to him, "I see that you enter the courts of these governors and overwhelm them. Do check what you are saying to them because I have heard Rasulullah 🙵 say, "A servant of Allah may utter a word..." The rest of the narration is like the one mentioned above.

The Statement of Hudhaifa That the Doors of the Rulers are Dens of Evil

Hudhaifa 🙵 once said, "Beware of the dens of evil!" "What are the dens of evil, O Abu Abdullah?" Someone enquired from him. He replied, "The doors of the rulers. A person enters the court of a ruler and then confirms the lies he speaks and praises him for qualities he does not possess." *(Abu Nu'aym in Hilya).*

The Advice Abbas 🙵 Gave his Son in this Regard

Abdullah bin Abbas 🙵 narrates that his father Abbas 🙵 once said to him, "Dear son! I notice that the Amirul Mu'minin calls for you, allows you to be close to him and even consults with you together with the Sahabah of Rasulullah 🙵. Now remember these 3 things that I am telling you. Fear Allah and never let him encounter any lies from you, i.e, never tell him a lie. You should also never disclose any of his secrets and never backbite about anyone in his presence." One of the narrators by the name of Amir says that he said to Abdullah bin Abbas 🙵, "Each one of these advices are better than 1,000. Abdullah bin Abbas 🙵 in turn said, "Each one of them is better than 10,000." *(Abu Nu'aym in Hilya, Tabrani, Haythami).* *Sha'bi* reports that Abbas 🙵 once said to his son Abdullah 🙵, "I notice that the great man (referring to Omar ◉) allows you to sit close to him and includes you amongst people with whom you do not belong (the veterans of Badr). You should therefore remember 3 things that I shall tell you. Never let him encounter any lies from you, i.e, never tell him a lie, never disclose any of his secrets and never backbite about anyone in his presence." *(Bayhaqi).*

The Incident Between Ubay ◉ and Omar and His Statement That There is no Good in an Amir in Whose Presence the Truth Cannot be Spoken

Hasan ◉ narrates that Omar ◉ once refused to accept a verse of the Qur'an from Ubay ◉ saying that it is either not in the Qur'an or not as Ubay ◉ said it appeared. Ubay ◉ said, "I had heard it from Rasulullah ﷺ at a time when you were preoccupied with trade in Baqi." Omar ◉ then said, "You have spoken the truth. I knew that the verse is in the Qur'an but I refused to accept it because I only wanted to test whether there are people amongst you who would speak the truth before the Amir. There is no good in an Amir in whose presence the truth cannot be spoken and who does not speak the truth." *(Ibn Rahway in Kanzul Ummal).* Abu Mijlaz reports that Omar ◉ accused Ubay ◉ of lying when he recited the verse *(Al-Ma'idah:107):* مِنَ الَّذِينَ اسْتَحَقَّ عَلَيْهِمُ الْأَوْلَيَانِ

...nearest in kin from amongst those who claim a lawful right.... Ubay ◉ retorted by saying, "Your lie is worse!" Someone reprimanded Ubay ◉ by saying, "Are you calling the Amirul Mu'minin a liar?" Ubay ◉ replied, "I have more respect for the rights of the Amirul Mu'minin than you have. I have falsified him only to confirm the truth of Allah's Book and I can never confirm what the Amirul Mu'minin says when it entails falsifying the Book of Allah." Omar then said, "He has spoken the truth." *(Abd bin Humaid, Ibn Jareer, Ibn Adi in Kanzul Ummal).*

Bashir bin Sa'd says to Omar ◉: "If you do That, We will Set You Straight as an Arrow is Straightened"

Nu'man bin Bashir ◉ reports that in a gathering of Muhajirin and Ansar, Omar ◉ once asked, "What will you people do if I were permissive in certain matters?" When everyone remained silent, Omar ◉ repeated the question for a 2nd and then a 3rd time. Bashir bin Sa'd then responded by saying, "If you do that, we will set you straight as an arrow is straightened." Omar ◉ commented, "You are then certainly the ones capable of being with me! You are then certainly the ones!" *(In Asakir, Abu Dar Harawi in Majami, Kanzul Ummal).*

The Incident of Omar and Muhammad bin Maslama ◉ in this Regard

Musa bin Abu Isa narrates that when Omar bin Khattab ◉ went to the pond of the Banu Haritha, he met Muhammad bin Maslama there. Omar ◉ asked him, "What do you think of me?" Muhammad bin Maslama ◉ replied, "I swear by Allah that in my opinion you are as I like to see you and as anyone who likes good likes to see you. I see that you are careful in collecting wealth, are also abstinent from it and distribute it justly. If however, you stray, we shall straighten you just as arrows are straightened with weights." Omar ◉ then said, "Excellent! You say, 'If however, you stray, we shall straighten you just as arrows are straightened with weights'. All praise belongs to Allah Who has placed me amongst people who will rectify me when I stray." *(Ibn Mubarak in Muntakhab Kanzul Ummal).*

Mu'awiya ◉ Tells Someone who Objected to His Words, "This Man has Given me Life, may Allah Give Him Life"

Abu Qabil narrates that Mu'awiya ◉ once ascended the pulpit on the day of Jumu'ah and said in his lecture, "The wealth is all ours and the spoils of war are all ours. We shall give it to whom we will and refuse whoever we will." Since no one responded to this statement, Mu'awiya ◉ repeated it the following Jumu'ah. When no one objected this time as well, he again repeated it on the third Jumu'ah. On that occasion, a man in the Masjid stood up and said, "Never! The wealth is ours and the spoils of war are ours. If anyone poses an obstacle between us and it, we shall have him dealt with by Allah or by our swords." After Mu'awiya ◉ descended from the pulpit, he sent for the man, who was allowed in his court. "He is destroyed!" the people commented. However, when the people entered the court of Mu'awiya ◉, they found the man sitting with Mu'awiya ◉ on his bed. Mu'awiya ◉ then said to the people, "This man has given me life, may Allah give him life. I have heard Rasulullah ﷺ say, 'Soon after me there shall come rulers who will say wrong things and no one would object to them. They will fall over each other in Jahannam just as monkeys jumping from a tree fall over each other.' When no one objected to what I said on the first Jumu'ah, I feared that would be amongst these rulers. When no one objected on the second Jumu'ah, I said to myself that I must be from amongst them. When I spoke on the 3rd Jumu'ah, this man objected. He has given me life, may Allah give him life." *(Tabrani in Kabir and Awsat, Abu Ya'la, Haythami)*

The Incident of Abu Ubaidah ◉ and Khalid bin Walid ◉

Khalid bin Hakim bin Hizam reports that when Abu Ubaidah ◉ was governor of Sham, he punished some local disbelivers for not paying the Jizya *(Bawardi).* Khalid bin Walid ◉ stood up and spoke to him about the error of his act. The people said, "You have made the Amir angry." Khalid bin Walid ◉ said, "I had never intended to make him angry but heard Rasulullah ﷺ say that the people who will be most severely punished on the Day of Judgment will be those who punished people most severely in this world *(Ibn Abi Asim, Baghawi, Ahmad, Bukhari in Tarikh, Bawardi, Tabrani in Isabah, Haytham)*

The Narration of Hasan ◉ in this Regard

Hasan ◉ reports that when Ziyad dispatched Hakam bin Amr Ghifari ◉ as governor of Khurasan, the Muslims there managed to win a large amount of booty. Ziyad then wrote to Hakam ◉ saying, "The Amirul Mu'minin Mu'awiya ◉ has written to say that all the gold and silver should be reserved for him and should therefore not be distributed amongst the Muslims." Hakam ◉ wrote back to Ziyad saying, "You have written to me about the letter of the Amirul Mu'minin. However, I have received the book of Allah before the letter of the Amirul Mu'minin. I shall therefore not obey his command which contradicts that of the Qur'an. I swear by Allah that even if the skies and earth have to close up on a person, Allah will create an escape for him between them and give him peace if he is one who fears Allah." Hakam ◉ then had an announcer announce to the people that they should present themselves for the booty by the morning. He then distributed the booty including the gold and silver amongst the people. When he did this, Mu'awiya ◉ sent some people to arrest Hakam ◉ and place him in chains. Hakam ◉ passed away in these chains and was buried in Khurasan. He said, "I shall contest my case against Mu'awiya in the court of Allah." *(Hakim).* Another narration adds that after Hakam ◉ had distributed the booty amongst the people, he prayed, "O Allah! If

You have any good for me with You, then raise me to You." He then passed away in the town of Maru in Khurasan. *(Isti'ab)* *Isabah* states that it was actually when Hakam received the letter of Ziyad noting his displeasure, he prayed to Allah for a swift death, after which he passed away.

The Way that Imran bin Husain Dealt with the Zakah Money

Ata reports that Ziyad or his son once sent Imran bin Husain to collect Zakah. When Imran returned, he brought nothing. "Where is the money?" asked Ziyad (or his son). "Did you send me to bring back any money?" Imran asked, "I collected it as we used to do during the time of Rasulullah and used it in the avenues we used it during the time of Rasulullah. I distributed it amongst the needy of the area. *(Hakim confirmed by Dhahabi)*.

Omar Enquires from Delegations About the Qualities of Their Governors

Aswad bin Yazid narrates that whenever a delegation came to Omar, he would ask them about their governor. He would ask, "Does he visit the ill? Does he respond to the pleas of slaves? How does he treat those who stand at his door to have a need fulfilled?" If the delegates had to give a negative answer to any of the questions, Omar would dismiss the governor. *(Bayhaqi in Kanzul Ummal, Tabari)*. *Ibrahim* reports that when Omar appointed a governor to an area and a delegation had to come to him from the same area, he would ask them, "How is your governor? Does he visit the slaves? Does he follow funeral processions? How is his door, is he accessible? Is it welcoming?" If the people replied that the governor's door was welcoming and that he visited the slaves, Omar would leave the man in his post. Otherwise, he would send a messenger to dismiss him. *(Hannad in Kanzul Ummal)*.

The Conditions Omar Made with His Governors

Asim bin Abi Nujud states that whenever Omar dispatched governors, he would. make the conditions with them that they should never ride Turkish horses, should not eat refined white flour, should not wear fine clothing, and should not lock their doors to those who were in need. He made it clear to them that if they were ever to do any of this, they would be liable for punishment. It was only after making these conditions that he saw them off and walked a distance with them. When he was about to return, he would further tell them, "I am not sending you to give you sovereignty over the blood of people, over their skins, over their honor, and over their wealth. I am sending you to ensure that the people establish salah, to distribute the spoils of war amongst them, and to judge between them with justice. If you encounter any difficulties, do refer it to me. Beware that you never hit an Arab for this would humiliate them. Never prevent them from returning to their homelands because this would place them in great difficulty and never level false accusations against them because you would then be depriving them of their rights. Also ensure that you keep the words of the Qur'an separate from the Ahadeeth and from commentaries so that these will not confuse as part of the Qur'an." *(Bayhaqi in Kanzul Ummal)*. Another similar narration states that Omar said, "Keep the Qur'an separate and report fewer narrations from Rasulullah. I shall also join you in doing this." Omar would also enforce the necessary punishment on his governors when they deserved it and whenever a complaint was brought to him about any governor, he would gather the complainant and the governor in one place. Thereafter, if the complaint was proven to be valid and the governor needed to be taken to task, Omar would take him

to task. *(Tabari)*. Abu Khuzaima bin Thabit reports that Omar appointed someone as governor, he would make a group of the Ansar and some others witness to the appointment and say to the new governor, "I am not sending you to give you sovereignty over the blood of people..." The rest of the narration is similar to the one quoted earlier. *(Ibn Abi Shaiba in Kanzul Ummal)*.

The Statement of Omar Concerning the Duties of an Amir

Abdur Rahman bin Sabit reports that Omar once sent for Sa'eed bin Amir Jumhi and said to him, "We wish to appoint you in command of this regiment whom you should lead into enemy territory to wage war with them." Sa'eed said, "O Omar! Please do not try me." Omar resolved "I shall never leave you. You people have cast this responsibility of Khilafa on my neck and now you wish to leave me all alone! I am sending you with a group of people from whom you are not the best. I am not sending you to whip them or to humiliate them but only to lead them in Jihad against their enemies and to distribute their booty amongst them." *(Ibn Abi Shaiba in Kanzul Ummal)*.

The Statement of Abu Musa Ash'ari in this Regard

Abu Musa Ash'ari once addressed the people saying, "The Amirul Mu'minin Omar bin Khattab has sent me here to teach you the Book of your Rabb, the Sunnah of your Nabi and to administrate over municipal affairs." *(Ibn Asakir, Abu Nu'aym in Hilya, Kanzul Ummal, Haythami)*.

An Incident Between Omar and Amr bin Al Aas Regarding Rulers who Live Lives Above the Standards of the Common People and Who Veil Themsehres From People in Need

Abu Salih Ghifari narrates that Amr bin Al Aas while in Egypt once wrote to Omar stating: "We have reserved a house for you here next to the Jami Masjid." Omar wrote back saying, "Why should a man living in Hijaz have a house in Egypt?" Omar ordered that the area be converted into a market for the Muslims. *(Ibn Abdul Hakim in Kanzul Ummal)*

Omar Writes to Amr bin Al Aas to Demolish a Pulpit

Tamim Jayshani reports that Omar wrote the following letter to Amr bin Al Aas: "The news has reached me that you have had a pulpit made by which you climb high above the people's necks when delivering a sermon. Is it not sufficient for you to remain standing with the Muslims beneath your heels. I command you in the name of Allah that you should demolish it." *(Ibn Abdul Hakim in Kanzul Ummal)*.

The Letter of Omar to Utba bin Farqad About not Raising his Standards Above that of the Public

Abu Uthman reports that Omar wrote a letter to them when they were in Azerbaijan. He wrote: "O Utba bin Farqad! Your position and wealth has not been the fruits of your efforts, nor the fruits of your father's or mother's efforts. Feed the people in their homes with that which you feed yourself in your home. Guard yourself against indulging in luxuries, from imitating the appearance of the disbeliever and from wearing silk clothing.' *(Muslim in Targheeb wat Tarheeb)*.

Omar Takes the Amir of Hims to Task for Constructing a Lofty Residence

Urwa bin Ruwaim narrates that Omar was inquiring about the condition of the people during the Hajj when some people from Hims passed by him. "How is your Amir?" asked Omar. They replied, "He is the best of Amirs except for the fact that he had built a lofty residence in which he lives. Omar ৬ then wrote a letter, which he sent with a messenger with instructions to bum the building down. When the messenger reached Hims, he gathered firewood and set fire to the door. When the Amir was informed about it, he said, "Leave him alone because he has been sent by the Amirul Mu'minin." The messenger then handed the letter over to the Amir. After reading the letter the Amir did not even put the letter down when he rode off to Omar ৬. When Omar ৬ saw him arrive, he told the Amir to meet him at Hara where the Zakah camels were kept. When he met him there, Omar ৬ asked him to remove his clothes and then gave him a garment of camel hide to wear. Omar ৬ instructed him to fetch water from the well to give the camels to drink. The man continued going in and out of the well until he was exhausted. Omar ৬ then asked him, "How much longer will you be in this world?" "For only a short while," came the reply. Omar ৬ said, "Is it for this short while that you have built the mansion and adopted a standard of living that exceeds those of the poor, the widows and orphans? Go back to your post and never repeat yourself." *(Ibn Asakir in Kanzul Ummal).*

Omar ৬ Takes Sa'd ৬ to Task for Building a Mansion

Attab bin Rifa'ah narrates that Omar ৬ once received the news that Sa'd ৬ had built a mansion and had a door put on it, saying that the noise from the marketplace has now been cut off form entering the mansion. Omar ৬ then dispatched Muhammad bin Maslama ৬ whom he always sent when he needed a task done exactly as he wanted. The instructions he gave Muhammad bin Maslama ৬ was to bring Sa'd to him and to bum down the door. When Muhammad bin Maslama ৬ arrived in Kufa, someone came to Sa'd ৬ and informed him about the arrival and when the features of Muhammad bin Maslama ৬ were described to Sa'd ৬, he recognized him. Sa'd ৬ then went to meet Muhammad bin Maslama ৬, who said to him, "The news has reached the Amirul Mu'minin that you commented about the noise being cut off." When Sa'd ৬ swore that he never made such a statement, Muhammad bin Maslama ৬ said, "We shall do as we have been commanded while you will have to convey what you will convey to the Amirul Mu'minin." When Sa'd ৬ offered to provide Muhammad bin Maslama ৬ with provisions for the journey, he refused to take any and rode off until he reached Madinah. When Omar ৬ saw him, he said, 'If I did not have a good opinion of you, I would have thought that, you did not fulfill the task." Muhammad bin Maslama ৬ informed Omar ৬ that he had hurried back and assured Omar ৬, "I have fulfilled the task. However, Sa'd ৬ excuses himself and swears that he had never made the statement." Omar ৬ asked, "Did he give you any provisions for the journey?" Muhammad bin Maslama ৬ replied, "No, but what prevented you from giving the provisions?" Omar ৬ said, "I disliked giving you any provisions because although you would have had ease, I would have had to suffer for it in the Hereafter since hunger is killing the people around me in Madinah. Have you not heard Rasulullah ৠ say that a Mu'min should not fill his belly while his neighbor goes hungry?" *(Ibn Mubarak, Ibn Rahway and Musaddad in Kanzul Ummal, Isabah, Haythami).* Another narration from Abu Bakrah ৬ and Abu Hurairah ৬ states that the news that reached Omar ৬ stated that Sa'd ৬ kept aloof from the people and locked them out of his house. Omar ৬ then dispatched Ammar bin Yasir ৬ with instructions to go to Sa'd ৬ and if he found the door locked, he was to burn it down. *(Tabrani, Haythami).*

The Incident Between Omar ৬ and a Group of Sahabah in Sham

Abu Darda ৬ once sought permission from Omar ৬ to go to Sham. Omar ৬ told him that he would be allowed to go there only on condition that he became a governor of one of the areas. When Abu Darda ৬ refused to be a governor, Omar ৬ refused to grant the permission. Abu Darda ৬ then said, "I shall go there to teach people the Sunnah of their Nabi ৠ and lead them in salah." Omar ৬ then granted him permission. Omar ৬ later visited Sham and when he drew close to where the Sahabah were staying, he stopped until evening fell. When the night cast its veil over him, he called to his slave saying, "O Yarfa! Let us go to Yazid bin Abi Sufian ৬. You will see that he has story-tellers with him, lanterns will be burning and rugs of silk and velvet will be spread out, which have been taken from the booty belonging to the Muslims. You will greet him and he will reply, after which you will ask permission to enter and he will not grant permission until he enquires who you are." The 2 men proceeded until they reached the door of Yazid bin Abi Sufian ৬. Omar ৬ greeted by saying, "As Salamu Alaykum!" to which Yazid ৬ replied, "Wa Alaykumus Salam." When Omar ৬ asked whether he could enter, Yazid ৬ first asked, "Who are you?" To this Yarfa replied, "This is the one who is about to spoil your fun. This is the Amirul Mu'minin." Omar ৬ then opened the door and found story-tellers there, lanterns burning, and rugs of silk and velvet. Omar ৬ urgently instructed Yarfa to shut the door and struck Yazid ৬ with his whip right between the ears. Omar ৬ then folded up all the goods and placed it at the centre of the room. He then issued the command that no one should move until he returned. Omar ৬ and Yarfa then left Yazid ৬. Omar ৬ said; "O Yarfa! Come with me to Amr bin Al Aas ৬. You will see that he has story-tellers with him, lanterns will be burning and rugs of velvet will be spread out, which have been taken from the booty belonging to the Muslims. You will greet him and he will reply, after which you will ask permission to enter and he will not grant permission until he enquires who you are." The 2 men proceeded until they reached the door of Amr bin Al Aas ৬. Omar ৬ greeted by saying, "As Salamu Alaykum!" to which Amr replied, "Wa Alaykumus Salam." When Omar ৬ asked whether he could enter, Amr ৬ first asked, "Who are you?" To this Yarfa replied, "This is the one who is about to spoil your fun. This is the Amirul Mu'minin." Omar ৬ then opened the door and found storytellers there, lanterns burning and rugs of velvet. Omar urgently instructed Yarfa to shut the door and struck Amr with his whip right between the ears. Omar ৬ then folded up all the goods and placed it at the centre of the room. He then issued the command that no one should move until he returned.

After leaving Amr bin Al Aas ৬, Omar ৬ said, "O Yarfa! Let us go to Abu Musa Ash'ari ৬. You will see that he has story-tellers with him, lanterns will be burning and rugs of wool will be spread out, which have been taken from the booty belonging to the Muslims. You will greet him and he will reply, after which you will ask permission to enter and he will not grant permission until he enquires who you are." The 2 men proceeded until they reached the door of Abu Musa Ash'ari ৬. Omar ৬ greeted by saying, "As Salamu Alaykum!" to which Abu Musa ৬ replied, "Wa Alaykumus Salam." When Omar ৬ asked whether he could enter, Abu Musa ৬ first asked, "Who are you?" To this Yarfa replied, "This is the one who is about to spoil your fun. This is the Amirul Mu'minin." Omar ৬ then opened the door and found story-tellers there, lanterns burning and rugs of wool spread out. Omar ৬ struck Abu Musa ৬ with his whip right between the ears and then said, "You too, O Abu Musa ৬, have you also changed since leaving Madinah?" Abu Musa Ash'ari ৬ said, "O

Amirul Mu'minin! This is what I have which is less than the others. You have already seen what my companions are doing whereas I had also received what they have received but have not gone to the extent they have." Omar asked, "Then what is all this about?" Abu Musa Ash'ari replied, "The people of the city believe that this is the only way by which to rule." Omar then folded up all the goods and placed it at the centre of the room. He then issued the command that no one should move until he returned.

When the 2 had left Abu Musa Ash'ari, Omar said, "O Yarfa! Come with me to my brother Abu Darda. You will see that he has no story-tellers with him, no lanterns will be burning and his door will be unlocked. You will greet him and he will reply, after which you will ask permission to enter and he wilt' grant you permission without enquiring who you are." The 2 men proceeded until they reached the door of Abu Darda. Omar greeted by saying, "As Salamu Alaykum!" to which Abu Darda replied, "Wa Alaykumus Salam." When Omar asked whether he could enter, Abu Darda granted permission. As Omar pushed open the door, he found that it had no lock. The 2 men entered the dark room and Omar had to feel his way around until he found Abu Darda. When Omar felt the pillow of Abu Darda, he found that it was made from the blanket used on animals. When he felt the ground, there was only sand and when he felt the clothing of Abu Darda, he discovered that it was a flimsy shawl. Abu Darda asked, "Who is this? Is it the Amirul Mu'minin?" When Omar confirmed that he was the Amirul Mu'minin, Abu Darda said, "You are late. We had been waiting for you all year." Omar said, "May Allah have mercy on you. Have I not granted you sufficient wealth? Have I not given you plenty?" Abu Darda said, "O Omar! Do you not remember a Hadith that Rasulullah mentioned to us?" "Which Hadith?" asked Omar. Abu Darda replied, "The Hadith in which Rasulullah said, 'The limit of a person's possessions in this world should be like the provisions of a traveler.'" "Oh yes, I have heard the Hadith" confirmed Omar. Abu Darda then asked, "Now what have we done after Rasulullah, O Omar?" The 2 Sahabah then continued reminding each other of the words of Rasulullah with tears in their eyes until morning arrived. (Ibn Asakir, Yashkari in Kanzul Ummal).

The Incident of Abu Bakr and Omar Enquiring about the Condition of the Citizens

Abu Salih Ghifari narrates that there was an extremely old blind lady living on the outskirts of Madinah whom Omar used to regularly visit at night. He would go there to fetch water for her from the well and do other chores for her. However, whenever he got to her, he would find that someone else had beaten him there and had already seen to her needs. He went to her many times only to find that he was not the first to get there. One day, he sat in wait for the person who always beat him and found that the person was Abu Bakr. Abu Bakr would serve the old lady even though he was the Khalifa. Omar exclaimed, "By my life! It could only be you!" (Khateeb in Kanzul Ummal). Awza'e reports that Talha once spotted Omar coming out of his house late at night. Omar entered a house and then another house. The following morning, Talha went to the house, where he found an old woman who was blind and crippled. Talha asked her, "Why does that man come to you?" She then informed Talha that Omar had been frequently coming to her for many years to see to her needs and remove all the filth from her house. Talha then said to himself, "Shame on you, O Talha! Were you searching for faults in Omar?!" (Abu Nu'aym in Hilya).

The Statement of Omar Regarding Passing Judgment by What is Apparent

Abdullah bin Utba bin Mas'ood says that he heard Omar say, "People would be taken to task by means of revelation during the time of Rasulullah when Allah would send revelation to disclose the secrets of some people. However, revelation has been terminated and now we are able to take you people to task by your apparent actions. Therefore, we will trust and bring close to us only those people whose apparent actions appear good to us because we have no knowledge of his inner self. Allah is the One Who will take him to task for his inner condition. On the other hand, we cannot trust and cannot believe those whose apparent actions appear evil to us even though he may claim that his inner condition is good." (Abdur Razzaq in Kanzul Ummal, Bayhaqi, Bukhari). Hasan states that in the first lecture that Omar delivered after becoming the Khalifa, he first praised Allah and then said: "Now that 1 have become Khalifa, I am being tested through you people and you will be tested through me. I have been made the Khalifa after my 2 companions (Rasulullah and Abu Bakr). We shall deal directly with those in our presence and to deal with those who are not in our presence, we shall appoint over them people who are capable and trustworthy. We shall treat well those people who do good and punish those who do evil. May Allah forgive you and me." (Ibn Sa'd, Bayhaqi in Kanzul Ummal).

The statement of Omar Regarding Inspecting the Performance of Those Appointed to Posts

Tawos narrates that Omar asked the people, "Tell me whether I would be discharging my responsibility if I appoint over you a person who is the best of you in my knowledge and I command him to be just?" "Most certainly," came the reply. Omar said, "No I would still not have discharged my responsibility, unless I inspect whether or not he is doing what I have commanded him." (Bayhaqi, Ibn Asakir in Kanzul Ummal)

The Statement of Abdullah bin Ka'b bin Malik Regarding Continuously Dispatching Troops

Abdullah bin Ka'b bin Malik Ansari stated that a regiment of the Ansar were posted to Persian territory with their Amir. Although Omar would continuously dispatch troops every year to relieve others, he happened to be preoccupied with other tasks and failed to relieve the particular regiment. When their term expired, the troops posted at that border of the regiment of Ansar who returned. Omar became very angry and threatened action against them because he had not yet sent anyone in their place. They all happened to be Sahabah of Rasulullah and they said, "O Omar! You were too preoccupied to worry about us and failed to implement the command of Rasulullah to continuously dispatch troops." (Abu Dawud in Kanzul Ummal).

The Incident Between Omar and Abu Ubaid During the Plague of Amwas

Abu Musa narrates that as soon as the Amirul Mu'minin Omar heard about the plague that was affecting the people in Sham, he wrote this letter to Abu Ubaidah bin Jarrah: "I require you to fulfill a need I have and I cannot do so without you having it fulfilled. If this letter of mine reaches you at night, I forcefully command you not to let the morning arrive without you riding off to me in Madinah. If this letter of mine reaches you in the morning, I forcefully command you not to let the evening arrive without you riding off to me." After reading the letter, Abu Ubaidah remarked, "I know well what need has presented itself to the Amirul Mu'minin. He wishes to preserve someone who cannot remain living i.e., he wants me to escape the plague by returning to Madinah." Abu Ubaidah ؓ then wrote back to Omar ؓ saying: "I am part of a Muslim army. I am not prepared to leave them to save my own life. I am well aware of the need that has presented itself to you. You wish to preserve someone who cannot remain living. When this letter of mine reaches you, do pardon me of your command and permit me to remain here." When Omar ؓ read this letter, his eyes welled with tears and he began to weep. The people with him asked, "O Amirul Mu'minin! Has Abu Ubaidah ؓ passed away?" "No," replied, Omar ؓ, "but it is as if he already has." Omar ؓ then wrote back to Abu Ubaidah ؓ saying: "Indeed the entire land of Jordan has been affected by the epidemic whereas the region of Jabiya is free from it. You should therefore take the Muhajirin there." When Abu Ubaidah ؓ had read the letter, he said, "We shall certainly listen to and obey this command of the Amirul Mu'minin." Abu Musa ؓ reports further, "Abu Ubaidah ؓ then ordered me to mount my animal and to keep the people in their living quarters. In the meantime, my wife also got affected by the plague. When I reported this to Abu Ubaidah ؓ, he personally proceeded to confine the people to their quarters, after which he was also afflicted and passed away. The plague then came to an end." Abul Muwajjih says, "It is believed mal Abu Ubaidah ؓ was part of an army of 36,000 people. Everyone of them save 6,000 died." *(Ibn Asakir in Kanzul Ummal)*. Another narration states that when he read the letter from Omar ؓ, Abu Ubaidah ؓ said, "May Allah forgive the Amirul Mu'minin. He wishes to preserve the lives of people who cannot remain living forever." Abu Ubaidah ؓ then wrote back to Omar ؓ saying, "Verily, I am with an army from amongst the armies of the Muslims whom I am not prepared to leave to save my own life from that which had afflicted them." *(Hakim confirmed by Dhahabi)*. Abu Ubaidah ؓ wrote to Omar ؓ saying: "O Amirul Mu'minin! I knew well your need from me. However, I am part of a Muslim army that I do not wish to leave to save my own life. I have no desire to leave them until Allah passes His decree concerning me and concerning them. O Amirul Mu'minin! Do release me from your command to return to Madinah and leave me with my army." *(Ibn Is'haq in Al Bidayah wan Nihayah, Tabari)*.

The Hadith of Abu Usaid ؓ Regarding Compassion of the Amir

Abu Ja'far reports that Abu Usaid ؓ once brought to Rasulullah ﷺ some captives from Bahrain. Looking at a woman from amongst them weeping, Rasulullah ﷺ asked, "What is the matter?" She replied, "He has sold my son." "Have you sold her son?" Rasulullah ﷺ asked. "Yes," replied Abu Usaid ؓ. "To which tribe?" Rasulullah ﷺ asked further. Abu Usaid ؓ replied, "To the Banu Abs tribe." Rasulullah ﷺ then instructed Abu Usaid ؓ saying, "Ride to them and bring him back yourself." *(Ibn Abi Shayba in Kanzul Ummal)*.

The Lecture of Omar ؓ in this Regard

Buraida ؓ narrates that he was sitting with Omar ؓ one day when he heard a scream. Omar ؓ instructed his slave Yarfa to see where the noise was coming from. After checking, Yarfa reported, "The mother of a girl from the Quraish is being sold as a slave, because of which the child is screaming." Omar ؓ then instructed him to summon the Muhajirin and the Ansar. After a short while, the room and the entire house was filled. After praising Allah, Omar ؓ then said: "Do you people know whether the severing of family ties was amongst the teachings that Rasulullah ﷺ brought?" When they replied in the negative, Omar ؓ

continued, "Because it has started to spread rapidly amongst you." He then recited the following verse of the Qur'an:

فَهَلْ عَسَيْتُمْ إِنْ تَوَلَّيْتُمْ أَنْ تُفْسِدُوا فِي الْأَرْضِ وَتُقَطِّعُوا أَرْحَامَكُمْ (22)

Would you then, if you were given the authority, do mischief in the land, and sever your ties of kinship? (Muhammad:22)

Omar ؓ continued, "What form of severing family ties is worse than selling the mother of a girl from amongst you when Allah has given you abundance?" The Sahabah said, "Do as you see fit." Omar ؓ then wrote to all the regions of the Islamic empire instructing that the mother of no free woman should be sold as a slave because it involves severing family ties which is not permissible.*(Ibn Munthir, Hakim, Bayhaqi in Kanzul Ummal)*

A Hadith of Abu Uthman Nahdi in this Regard

Abu Uthman Nahdi reports that after Omar ؓ had appointed a man from the Banu Asad tribe as governor, the man came to him to collect the certificate of appointment. In the meantime, one of Omar ؓ's children was brought to him and he started kissing the child. The man from the Banu Asad tribe asked, "Do you kiss children, O Amirul Mu'minin? By Allah! I have never kissed a child to this day." Omar ؓ then said, "In that case, I swear by Allah that you will be even less compassionate towards people. Give the certificate of appointment back. You should never act as governor for me ever again." Omar ؓ then cancelled his appointment. *(Bayhaqi, Hannaad in Kanzul Ummal)*. A narration of *Muhammad bin Salam* states that Omar ؓ said to the man, "What crime I did that mercy has been extracted from your heart? Allah has mercy only on those servants of His who show mercy." Omar ؓ then removed him from the post and said, "If you have no mercy for your own children, how will you have mercy on the masses?" *(Daynowri in Kanzul Ummal)*.

The Incident of the Makhzumiya Woman and the Lecture Rasulullah ﷺ Gave

Urwa ؓ narrates that at the time of Rasulullah ﷺ a woman stole during the conquest of Makkah. The members of her Banu Makhzum tribe hurried to Usama bin Zaid ؓ to ask him to intercede on her behalf before Rasulullah ﷺ so that her hand should not be cut off." When Usama ؓ spoke about it to Rasulullah ﷺ, Rasulullah ﷺ's face turned red with anger and he said, "Are you talking to me about waiving a penalty that Allah has imposed?" Usama ؓ shy away and said, "Seek Allah's forgiveness for me, O Rasulullah ﷺ!" That evening, Rasulullah ﷺ stood up to deliver a lecture. After duly praising Allah, he said: "The nations before you were destroyed because whenever a noble person amongst them stole, they let it go. However, when a weak person from a family holding no status stole, they imposed the penalty on him. I swear by the Being Who controls my life that even if Fatima ؓ the daughter of Muhammad ﷺ would has stolen; I would cut off her hand." Rasulullah ﷺ then issued the necessary instructions and the woman's hand was cut off. She then repented sincerely to Allah and even got married. Aisha ؓ says, "Thereafter, she used to come to me and I would present her needs to Rasulullah ﷺ." *(Bukhari, Muslim in Al Bidayah wan Nihayah, Targheeb waf Tarheeb)*.

The Narration of Abu Qatadah ؓ in this Regard

Abu Qatadah ؓ reports, "After we had left with Rasulullah ﷺ for the Battle of Hunain and met with the enemy, we suffered a temporary defeat. When I saw a man from the disbeliever overpowering one of the Muslims, I used my sword to strike his vein on the shoulder from behind. My blow cut through his armor and he turned to me. He then grabbed hold of me and started squeezing me so hard that I could get the smell of death. Fortunately, because he had lost a lot of blood, death overcame him and he let me go. I then met Omar ؓ and asked, 'What has happened to the people, why did the Muslims suddenly flee?' He replied, 'It was the command of Allah.' However, the Muslims then regrouped and fought back to defeat the disbeliever. When the Muslims returned from the battlefield, Rasulullah ﷺ sat down and said, 'Whoever killed someone and has a witness to testify shall have the possessions of the dead man.' I stood up and asked, 'Who will testify for me?' When I received no response, I sat down again. When Rasulullah ﷺ repeated the announcement, I again stood up and asked, 'Who will testify for me?' When I again received no response, I sat down. Rasulullah ﷺ repeated the announcement and again I stood up and asked, 'Who will testify for me?' When I received no response this time, I sat down yet again. When Rasulullah ﷺ again repeated the announcement, I stood up. Rasulullah ﷺ asked, 'What is the matter, O Abu Qatadah?' After I had informed him of the incident, someone said, 'He had spoken the truth and the dead man's possessions are with me. O Rasulullah ﷺ! Satisfy him on my behalf; give him something else so that I may keep the possessions.' Abu Bakr ؓ then said, 'Never! By Allah! In that case, whenever one of the lions of Allah fight for Allah and His Rasul should he give you what is taken from the enemy?' Rasulullah ﷺ confirmed what was said by saying, 'He is right. Hand over the possessions.' The man handed me the possessions and with it I bought an orchard in the Banu Salma district. This was the first time that I had received any wealth as a Muslim."

The Incident of Abdullah bin Abu Hadrad ؓ with a Jew

Abdullah bin Abu Hadrad Aslami ؓ narrates that he owed 4 Dirhams to a Jewish man, who then complained about him to Rasulullah ﷺ saying, "O Muhammad ﷺ! That man owes me 4 Dirhams but he keeps overpowering me by refusing to pay whenever I ask him. Rasulullah ﷺ said to Abdullah bin Abu Hadrad ؓ, "Pay this man his dues." Abdullah bin Abu Hadrad ؓ replied, "I swear by the Being Who has sent you with the truth that I cannot pay him." "Pay this man his dues," Rasulullah ﷺ repeated. Abdullah bin Abu Hadrad ؓ pleaded, "I swear by the Being Who controls my life that I am unable to pay him. I have already informed him that you would soon send us to Khaibar from where I hope to return with some spoils of war that you would give us. I would then be able to pay him back." However, Rasulullah ﷺ again instructed, "Pay the man his dues." It was the habit of Rasulullah ﷺ that he never repeated anything after the 3rd time saying something 3 times meant that it was final. Abdullah bin Abu Hadrad ؓ then proceeded to the marketplace. He was wearing a turban on his head and a shawl as his lower garment. He removed the turban from his head and used it as a lower garment. He then removed the shawl and said to the Jew, "Buy this shawl from me." The Jew bought it from him for 4 Dirhams. An old woman then passed by and asked, "What is the matter, O companion of Rasulullah ﷺ?" When Abdullah bin Abu Hadrad ؓ related the incident to her, she took off a shawl she was wearing and threw it over him saying, "Take this shawl." *(Ibn Asakir in Kanzul Ummal, Ahmad in Isabah).*

The Incident of 2 Men From the Ansar in this Regard

Ummu Salama ؓ reports that 2 men from the Ansar brought to Rasulullah ﷺ their dispute concerning some inheritance for which they could produce no evidence or any witnesses. Rasulullah ﷺ said to them, "You are bringing your dispute to me when I can pass judgment only by my estimation in matters concerning which no revelation has come to me. Therefore, if I decide in the favor of someone because of his stronger case, thereby severing any right of his brother, he should not accept it. In that case, I would be allocating for him a part of Jahannam. On the Day of Judgment he will come with it as a yoke around his neck." The 2 men started weeping and each one of them said, "O Rasulullah ﷺ! I hand over my right to him." Rasulullah ﷺ said, "Since you want it that way, go and ponder about the right, divide it between yourselves and draw lots to decide who should have which share. Each of you should permit his share for the other so that none stands responsible for taking the right of the other." *(Ibn Abi Shaiba, Abu Sa'eed Naqqash in Kanzul Ummal)*

An Incident of a Bedouin in this Regard

Abu Sa'eed ؓ reports that a Bedouin once came to Rasulullah ﷺ to demand payment of a debt Rasulullah ﷺ owed to him. He behaved very harshly with Rasulullah ﷺ saying, "I shall continue cursing you until you pay the debt!" The companions of Rasulullah ﷺ admonished the man saying, "Shame on you! Do you know with whom you are talking?!" The man said, "I am only asking for my right." Rasulullah ﷺ said to them, "Why are you not defending the one who has a right?" Rasulullah ﷺ then sent for Khowla bint Qais ؓ and asked her, "Borrow me some dates if you have any and I shall pay you back when I receive some dates." She said, "Most certainly! May my parents be sacrificed for you, O Rasulullah ﷺ!" She then borrowed the dates to Rasulullah ﷺ, with which he paid the Bedouin off together with something extra: The man then said, "You have given me full payment, may Allah give you in full." Rasulullah ﷺ then said, "They are the best of people who support those with a right. There is no good in a nation whose weak people cannot claim their right without hesitation." *(Ibn Majah, Bazzar, Tabarani in Targheeb wat Tarheeb).*

The Narration of Khowla bint Qais ؓ in this Regard

Khowla bint Qais ؓ who was the wife of Hamza bin Abdul Muttalib ؓ narrates, "Rasulullah ﷺ owed a Wasaq (~25kg) of dates to a man from the Banu Sa'ida tribe. When the man came to claim repayment, Rasulullah ﷺ instructed someone from the Ansar to pay it. When the Ansari paid the man in dates which were of an inferior quality, he refused to accept it. The Ansari said, "Are you refusing Rasulullah ﷺ?" The man said, "Yes. Who is more worthy of exercising justice than Rasulullah ﷺ?" Rasulullah ﷺ's eyes filled with tears as he said, "He is right. Who is more worthy of exercising justice than me? May Allah not bless a nation whose weak ones cannot claim their rights from their powerful ones and cannot demand them either." Rasulullah ﷺ then said, "O Khowla! Count and settle his debt because when a creditor is satisfied when he leaves his debtor, all creatures on earth and fish in the oceans pray for the debtor. However, when a debtor delays in paying when he has the means to pay, Allah records a sin in his records for every day and night that passes without him paying. *(Tabrani, Ahmad in Targheeb wat Tarheeb).*

The Narration of Abdullah bin Amr ؓ Regarding Justice

Abdullah bin Amr bin Al Aas ؓ reports that Abu Bakr ؓ stood up one Friday and announced, "Bring the Zakah camels tomorrow morning so that we may distribute them. Remember that none should come to see us without permission." A woman said to her husband, "Take this rein to be given with the camels to the poor. Perhaps Allah shall make it a means of providing a camel for us." The man arrived at a time when Abu Bakr ؓ and

Omar ♦ were with the camels and entered the enclosure with them. Abu Bakr ♦ turned around and asked, "Who allowed you to come here?" Abu Bakr ♦ then took the rein from the man and hit him with it. After he had completed distributing the camels Abu Bakr ♦ summoned the man and handing him the rein, said, "Take your revenge." Omar ♦ quickly intervened and said, "By Allah! He should not take revenge from you. You should not make this a custom that people should take revenge from an Amir who needs to teach a lesson to people." Abu Bakr ♦ said, "Then who will defend me in Allah's court on the Day of Judgment?" Omar ♦ replied, "Compensate him somehow." Abu Bakr ♦ then instructed his slave to give the man a riding camel together with its carriage and blanket. In addition to this, he also gave him 5 Dinars of gold coins. In this manner, Abu Bakr ♦ secured the man's pardon. *(Bayhaqi in Kanzul Ummal).*

The Incident of Omar ♦ and Ubay bin Ka'b ♦ Regarding Justice

Sha'bi reports that a dispute arose between Omar ♦ and Ubay bin Ka'b ♦. Omar ♦ said, "Appoint someone to decide the matter between us." They then agreed to appoint Zaid bin Thabit ♦ to settle the matter between them. When the 2 men came to Zaid ♦, he made place at the head side of his bedding saying, "Sit here, O Amirul Mu'minin." Omar ♦ said, "That is the first wrong you have committed in your decision-making procedure. I shall rather sit with my contestant." The 2 men then sat in front of Zaid ♦. Ubay ♦ made his claim and Omar ♦ refuted it. Zaid ♦ then said to Ubay ♦, "Pardon the Amirul Mu'minin from taking an oath, which is the next step of the procedure since no witnesses were presented. I would not have asked for this concession for anyone else besides the Amirul Mu'minin." However, Omar ♦ still took the oath and then said, "Zaid ♦ will be unable to judge unless he treats Omar ♦ as a man from the ranks of the common Muslims." *(Ibn Asakir, Sa'eed bin Mansoor, Bayhaqi).* Ibn Asakir states that Omar ♦ and Ubay bin Ka'b ♦ disputed about the harvesting of a date crop. With tears in his eyes, Ubay bin Ka'b ♦ said, "Is this how it will be under your rule, O Omar?" Omar ♦ said, "Then appoint someone to decide between us." When Ubay ♦ suggested the name of Zaid bin Thabit ♦, Omar ♦ accepted and the 2 of them went to him. The rest of the narration is like the one above. *(Kanzul Ummal).*

The Dispute Between Omar ♦ and Abbas ♦ Concerning the Expansion of the Masjidun Nabawi

Zaid bin Aslam reports that Abbas ♦ had a house next to the Masjid of Madinah. Omar ♦ asked Abbas ♦ to sell the house to him because he intended adding it to the Masjid. However, Abbas ♦ refused to sell it. When Omar ♦ requested him to give it as a gift, Abbas ♦ refused this as well. Omar ♦ said, "You have no option but to accept one of the 2 proposals." When Abbas ♦ still refused, Omar ♦ told him to appoint someone to decide the matter between them. Abbas ♦ appointed Ubay ♦ and the 2 men took their case to him. After hearing the case, Ubay ♦ said to Omar ♦, "I do not see anyway in which you can remove him from his house without his consent." Omar ♦ asked, "Tell me whether you found this judgment in the Book of Allah or in a Hadith of Rasulullah ♣?" "It is in a Hadith of Rasulullah ♣," replied Ubay ♦. When Omar ♦ asked for proof, Ubay ♦ said, "I have heard Rasulullah ♣ say that while Sulaiman ﷺ the son of Dawood ﷺ was constructing Baytul Maqdas, he found the walls destroyed every morning after he had them built. Allah then sent revelation telling him that he would be unable to build anything on the land of another person without the person's consent."

A Narration of Sa'eed bin Musaib Concerning Expansion of the Masjidun Nabawi

Sa'eed bin Musaiib narrates that Omar ♦ once intended to take the house of Abbas ♦ to include it in the Masjid. However, Abbas ♦ refused to hand the house over. When Omar ♦ resolved that he would certainly have possession of the house, Abbas proposed that they appoint Ubay bin Ka'b ♦ to pass judgment between them. Omar ♦ agreed and they both approached Ubay ♦. After they had related the matter to him, Ubay ♦ said, "Allah sent revelation to Sulaiman bin Dawood ﷺ instructing him to construct the Baytul Maqdas. The land belonged to a man whom Sulaiman ﷺ approached to buy it from him. However, when Sulaiman ﷺ handed over the money to the man, he asked, 'Is this price that you are paying better or is that which you are taking from me better?' Sulaiman ﷺ replied, 'Certainly that which I am taking from you is better.' 'In that case,' said the man, 'I shall not accept it.' Sulaiman ﷺ then gave the man a higher price. The man then did the same thing 2 or 3 times until Sulaiman ﷺ made a condition with him, 'I am buying this land from you at the price you fix: You may therefore not ask me which of the 2 is better.' Sulaiman ﷺ took the purchased land from him at the price he fixed, which happened to be 12,000 Qintar of gold (one Qintar equals 4,000 gold coins). Sulaiman ﷺ then felt that the amount was too big to give the man. Allah then sent revelation to him saying, 'If you are paying him from something that is your own, then you know best what you have to do. However, if you are paying him from what We have provided for you, then give him whatever he is pleased with.' Sulaiman then paid the amount." Ubay ♦ continued, "I feel that Abbas has a greater right to his house, which cannot be taken from him until he is pleased." Abbas ♦ then said, "Since you have made the decision in my favor, I wish to make it Sadaqa for the Muslims." *(Abdur Razzaq in Kanzul Ummal, Ibn Sa'd, Ibn Asakir, Bayhaqi).*

The Incident of Abdur Rahman bin Omar bin Khattab ♦ and Abu Saru'ah ♦

Abdullah bin Omar ♦ reports that his brother Abdur Rahman and Abu Saru'ah both drank some wine while they were in Egypt during the Khilafa of Omar ♦. They were both intoxicated and next morning they approached Amr bin Al Aas ♦ who was the Amir of Egypt. They said to him, "Purify us by imposing the penalty because we had both become intoxicated with what we drank." Abdullah bin Omar ♦ says, "When my brother mentioned to me that he had become intoxicated, I said to him, 'Come into the house and I will purify you.' I did not know then that he had already been to Arm bin Al Aas ♦. When my brother told me that he had already informed the Amir of Egypt, I said, 'Your head will not be shaved in front of all the people today. Go into the house and I will myself shave your head.' The practice of governors in those days was that they shaved the heads of criminals together with imposing the penalty. The 2 men then entered the house. I shaved my brother's head with my own hand and then Amr ♦ had them lashed." Abdullah bin Omar ♦ continues, "When Omar ♦ heard about this, he wrote to Amr ♦ with instructions to send Abdur Rahman to him on a carriage. Arm ♦ complied and when Abdur Rahman reached his father Omar ♦, Omar ♦ lashed him and punished him further because of his relationship with him. Omar ♦ then let him go and he lived hail and healthily for a month after which his predestination caught up with him and he passed away. People commonly believe that he died because of the lashing he received from Omar ♦, it is evident that he did not die because of this lashing." *(Abdur Razzaq, Bayhaqi in Muntakhab Kanzul Ummal, Ibn Sa'd)*

The Incident of Omar ؓ and a Woman Whose Husband was Missing

Hasan narrates that Omar ؓ once sent for a woman whose husband had gone missing. Omar ؓ objected to the fact that people used to frequently visit her. When she was summoned, it was said to her, "Respond to the call of Omar." She regretted, "Alas! I am destroyed! What does Omar want with me?!" She was pregnant and as she was still on her way, she became so frightened that labor pains struck. She entered a house where the child was born. However, the child screamed only twice and then it died. When Omar ؓ consulted with the Sahabah, he felt responsible for the death of the child who was born prematurely because the mother's fear for him, some of them told him that nothing was due from him because he was after all the ruler and therefore had a right to reprimand people and summon them when they do wrong. Ali ؓ remained silent. Omar ؓ turned to Ali ؓ and asked him what his opinion was. He said, "If they are speaking their opinions without proof, then their opinions are wrong. If however, they are speaking from their desires, then they have not advised you well. I think that you are responsible for paying the Diyah (blood money) because it was you who frightened her. She miscarriaged the child because of you." Ali ؓ instructed that payment of the blood money should be divided amongst the Quraish, meaning that the money would be taken from the entire Quraish tribe because the death was a mistake not intentional. *(Abdur Razzaq, Bayhaqi in Kanzul Ummal)*

The Practice of Omar ؓ During the Hajj Season to Ensure Justice Between the People

Ata reports that Omar ؓ used to command all his governors to meet with him during the Hajj season. When they gathered before him, he would say to the masses, "O people! I have not appointed my governors over you to take your skins, your wealth, and your honor. I have appointed them to prevent oppression between you and to distribute the spoils of war amongst you. Therefore, if anything has been done to any of you, he should stand up and report it." On one occasion no one stood up but one man. He said, "O Amirul Mu'minin! That governor of yours had whipped me 100 lashes." Omar ؓ turned to the governor and said, "Why did you lash him?" He then instructed the man to take his revenge. Amr bin Al Aas ؓ then stood up and said, "O Amirul Mu'minin! If you do this, you will have plenty of complaints coming to you and this practice of people taking revenge from their governors would become routine amongst those after you and every Amir will not be able to continue the practice." Omar ؓ said, "How can I not have revenge taken from my governors when I had seen Rasulullah ﷺ have people take revenge from himself." Amr bin Al Aas ؓ said, "Then do permit us to satisfy the man." When Omar ؓ granted them the permission, they compensated the man by giving him 2 Dinars for every lash, equaling the sum of 200 Dinars. *(Ibn Sa'd, Ibn Rahway in Muntakhab Kanzul Ummal).*

The Incident of Amr bin Al Aas ؓ and an Egyptian

Anas ؓ narrates that an Egyptian man once came to Omar bin Khattab ؓ and said, "O Amirul Mu'minin! I have come to seek refuge with you from oppression." Omar ؓ replied, "You have sought refuge with one who will certainly grant it." The man said, "I had a race with the son of Amr bin Al Aas ؓ and I beat him. He then started whipping as he said, 'I am the son of honorable men!'" Omar ؓ then wrote to Amr bin Al Aas ؓ instructing him to come to Madinah with his son. When they arrived, Omar ؓ called for the Egyptian and when he came said,

"Take this whip and hit." As the Egyptian whipped the son of Amr bin Al Aas ؓ, Omar ؓ said, "Whip the son of disgraceful people!" Anas ؓ says, "By Allah! The man whipped well just as we liked him to do and then stopped whipping just when we felt that he should stop." Omar ؓ then said to the Egyptian, "Now put a lash across Amr's head." Omar ؓ wanted to caution Amr ؓ for not teaching his son well enough. The Egyptian said, "O Amirul Mu'minin! It was his son who hit me and I have already had my revenge." Omar ؓ then said to Amr bin Al Aas ؓ, "Since when have you been enslaving people when their mothers had given them birth as free people?" Amr bin Al Aas ؓ pleaded, "O Amirul Mu'minin! I did not know about this, neither did the man complain to me otherwise I would have dealt with my son." *(Ibn Abdul Hakam in Muntakhab Kanzul Ummal).*

Omar ؓ Takes the Governor of Bahrain to Task

Yazid bin Abu Mansur narrates that it was brought to the attention of Omar ؓ that the governor of Bahrain whose name was Thnul Jarud or Ibn Abu Jarud executed a man called Adiryas. When Adiryas was brought before the governor, the evidence against him was a letter allegedly written by him and addressed to the enemy, stating that he intended to defect to their ranks. As he was being executed, he called out, "Save me, O Omar! Save me, O Omar!" Omar ؓ wrote a letter to the governor, ordering him to come to him in Madinah. When he arrived, Omar ؓ sat in wait for him with a spear in his hand. As he entered the room, Omar ؓ lifted the governor's beard with the spear and said, "I am at you service, O Adiryas! I am at your service, O Adiryas!" Jarud started pleading, "O Amirul Mu'minin! He wrote about confidential information of the Muslims and had intended to defect." Omar ؓ said, "You killed him because of his intentions! Which of us does not make intentions to do evil? Had it not been for the fear that it would become routine, I would have killed you for killing him.

The Hadith of Zaid bin Wahab in this Regard

Zaid bin Wahab narrates that Omar ؓ once emerged from his home with his fingers in his ears and saying, "If only I could have been at your service! If only I could have been at your service!". When the people asked what the matter was, Omar ؓ informed them that a messenger had come to him from one of his governors stating that a river presented an obstacle to the progress of their army and they could not find a boat to cross over. The Amir of the army instructed the others to find a man who knew how to gauge the depth of a river. They brought an old man who pleaded to the Amir saying, "I fear the cold." Although it was winter, the Amir forced him to go into the river and it was no long before the cold overcame him and the last thing he shouted before he drowned was, "Help me, O Omar!" Omar ؓ wrote to the Amir to come to Madinah and when he arrived, Omar ؓ ignored him for a few days. Omar ؓ usually did this when he was angry with someone. Omar ؓ then asked him, "What wrong was done by the man you killed?" The Amir said, "O Amirul Mu'minin! I never intended to kill him. Because we could find nothing with which to cross over, we only wanted to ascertain the depth of the water." He then went on to enumerate the many territories they had conquered. However, Omar ؓ said, "A single Muslim is more valuable to me than all your achievements. Had I not feared that it would become a common practice, I would have executed you. Pay the Diyah to his family and go somewhere where I would not see you again.' *(Bayhaqi in Kanzul Ummal)*

The Incident of Abu Musa Ash'ari 🙵 and Another Man and the Letter Omar 🙵 Wrote

Jareer narrates that a man who was with Abu Musa Ash'ari 🙵 in a battle managed to gain a large booty. Abu Musa Ash'ari 🙵 gave the man some share of the booty, it was not the complete share. The man refused to accept anything less than his complete share. Abu Musa Ash'ari 🙵 gave the man 20 lashes and shaved off his hair. The man collected his hair and went to Omar 🙵. He took out the hair from his pocket and thrust it on Omar's chest. "What is the matter?" asked Omar 🙵. The man explained the incident to Omar 🙵, the Khalifa wrote a letter to Abu Musa Ash'ari 🙵. Greeting Abu Musa 🙵, Omar 🙵 wrote the name of the man who had informed him of the incident and wrote the details of what he heard. He wrote: "I order you in the name of Allah that if you had carried out the act in public, you should sit in public and allow him to have his revenge from you. If you had done in private, you should sit in private and allow him to have his revenge." This letter reached Abu Musa 🙵, he sat down for the man to take revenge, but the man said, "I have forgiven him for the pleasure of Allah." *(Bayhaqi in Kanzul Ummal)*

The Incident of Fayruz Daylami 🙵 and a Youngster From the Quraish

Hirmazi reports that Omar 🙵 wrote this letter to Fayruz Daylami 🙵: "The news has reached me that you are much occupied with eating refined bread with honey. When this letter of mine reaches you, come to me in the name of Allah and fight in the way of Allah." When Fayruz Daylami 🙵 arrived in Madinah, he sought permission to see Omar 🙵 and permission was granted. Just then, as he was about to enter, a youngster from the Quraish also rushed in and pushed Fayruz 🙵. Fayruz 🙵 lifted his hand and slapped the Quraishi on the nose. The Quraishi entered the presence of Omar 🙵 with a bleeding nose and Omar 🙵 asked him, "Who did this to you?" "Fayruz," came the reply. Fayruz 🙵 was still standing at the door and then entered after Omar 🙵 gave him permission to do so. Omar 🙵 then asked, "What is this, O Fayruz?" he replied, "O Amirul Mu'minin! It was just recently that we had been kings. You had written to me (to come here) but did not write to him. You had also permitted me to enter and did not permit him. However, he wanted to enter before me with the permission I had been granted. I then did what he has informed you about." Omar 🙵 said, "Retribution!" "Does it have to be?" asked Fayruz 🙵. "It will have to be," Omar 🙵 confirmed. Fayruz 🙵 then knelt on his knees and the youngster stood ready to have his revenge. Omar 🙵 interrupted by saying, "Hold it boy until I inform you about what I heard say one morning. He said, 'Last night Aswad Anasi the great liar (claimed to be a Nabi) was killed. It was the pious servant Fayruz Daylami who killed him.' Can you see yourself taking revenge from him after hearing this from Rasulullah 🕮?" The youngster said, "I have forgiven him after you have informed me about this statement of Rasulullah 🕮." Fayruz 🙵 asked Omar 🙵, "Tell me whether my admission to guilt and his pardoning me without pressure would save me from punishment in the Hereafter?" "Certainly," replied Omar 🙵. "In that case," said Fayruz 🙵, "I make you the witness that I am giving my sword, my horse and 30,000 of my wealth to this youngster as a gift." Omar 🙵 said to the youngster, "Your pardon is rewarded by Allah in the Hereafter, O brother of the Quraish and you have also received plenty of wealth in this world." *(Ibn Asakir in Kanzul Ummal)*

The Incident of a Slave Woman and the Justice of Omar 🙵

Abdullah bin Abbas 🙵 reports that a slave woman once came to Omar 🙵 and said, "My master has accused me of fornication and made me sit on a fire until my private organ was burnt." Omar 🙵 asked her, "Did anyone witness you commit the act?" When she replied in the negative, he asked further, "Did you make any confession before him?" When she again said that she did not, Omar 🙵 exclaimed, "I shall deal with him." When Omar 🙵 saw the man, he asked, "Do you punish with punishment that is reserved for Allah with fire?!" The man pleaded, "O Amirul Mu'minein! I was suspicious of her." "Did you see her commit the act?" Omar 🙵 demanded to know. "No," came the reply. Omar 🙵 enquired further, "Did she then confess to you that she committed the act?" Again he said, "No." Omar 🙵 then exclaimed, "I swear by the Being Who controls my life that I would have taken retribution from you had I not heard Rasulullah 🕮 say, 'Retribution cannot be taken from a master for anything he does to his slave and also not from a father for anything he does to his child.' Omar 🙵 had the man lashed 100 times and then said to the woman, "You may go because you are now freed for the pleasure of Allah. You are now the freed slave of Allah and His Rasul. I testify that I have heard Rasulullah 🕮 say, 'The person who is burnt by fire or disfigured by it is a free person and is the freed slave of Allah and His Rasul 🕮." *(Tabrani in Awsat, Ibn Asakir, Bayhaqi in Kanzul Ummal).*

The Incident Between a Farmer and Ubadah bin Samit 🙵 and the justice of Omar 🙵 in the Matter

Makhul narrates that Ubadah bin Samit 🙵 once called a non-Arab Christian farm laborer to hold his animal next to Baytul Maqdas. When the laborer refused, Ubadah 🙵 hit him so hard that his head was cut. The laborer sought help from Omar bin Khattab 🙵, who then asked Ubadah 🙵, "What made you do that to him?" Ubadah 🙵 replied, "O Amirul Mu'minin! He refused to hold my animal when I asked him to do so, so I hit him because I am a short-tempered man." Omar 🙵 instructed Ubadah 🙵 to sit down so that the laborer could have his revenge. Just then, Zaid bin Thabit 🙵 interrupted by saying, "O Amirul Mu'minin! Will you allow your slave to take revenge from your brother?" Omar 🙵 left out the retribution and determined that Ubadah 🙵 should compensate the laborer in money. *(Bayhaqi in Kanzul Ummal)*

The Incident of Awf' bin Malik Ashja'e 🙵 with a Jew and the Justice of Omar 🙵 in This Matter

Suwaid bin Ghafala 🙵 reports that when Omar 🙵 once arrived in Sham, a man belonging to the Ahlul Kitab said to him, "O Amirul Mu'minin! A man from amongst the Mu'minin did this to me." The man's head was cut and he had been beaten. Omar 🙵 became extremely angry and then said to Suhaib 🙵, "Go and investigate who is responsible for this and then bring the culprit to me." Suhaib 🙵 proceeded and discovered that the person responsible was Awf bin Malik Ashja'e 🙵. Suhaib 🙵 said to Awf bin Malik 🙵, "The Amirul Mu'minin is extremely angry with you. Bring along Mu'adh bin Jabal 🙵 to speak to him because I fear that he will be very hasty in deciding your matter." After Omar 🙵 had completed his salah, he called for Suhaib 🙵 and asked him whether he had brought the person. "Yes," replied Suhaib 🙵. In the meanwhile, Awf bin Malik 🙵 had already approached Mu'adh 🙵 and narrated the incident to him. Mu'adh 🙵 then stood up and said, "O Amirul Mu'minin! The man is Awf bin Malik 🙵. Please give him a hearing and do not be hasty with him." Turning to Awf bin Malik 🙵 Omar 🙵 asked, "What has happened between you and this person?" Awf bin Malik 🙵 said, "O Amirul Mu'minin! I saw this man pushing along the donkey of a Muslim woman. He then poked the donkey so that it should throw her off, but it did not. He then pushed the donkey and it dropped her. Thereafter, he fell on to her and raped her. Unable to bear this, I then hit him." Omar ﷺ said, "Bring the woman to me so that she may confirm what you said." When Awf bin Malik ﷺ went to her, her father and her husband said, "What do you want with our woman? You have already disgraced us by relating the story." However, the woman said, "By Allah! I shall definitely go with him!" Her father and husband then said, "We shall rather go and relate the incident on your behalf." The 2 men then went to Omar ﷺ and related the story just as Awf bin Malik ﷺ had. Omar ﷺ then had the Jew crucified and said to the Jewish population, "This type of behavior was not amongst the clauses of our treaty with you." He then said, "O people! Fear Allah with regard to those under the guardianship of Muhammad ﷺ. However, there shall be no guardianship for those of them who do this (rape Muslim women)." Suwaid Says That the Jew Was the First Person he had seen Crucified in Islam. (Abu Ubaid, Bayhaqi, Ibn Asakir in Kanzul Ummal, Tabrani Haythami)

The incident of Bakr bin Shaddah ﷺ with a Jew and the Justice of Omar ﷺ

Abdul Malik bin Ya'la Laythi narrates that Bakr bin Shaddah Laythi ﷺ used to serve Rasulullah ﷺ when he was a child. After he came of age, he approached Rasulullah ﷺ saying, "O Rasulullah ﷺ! I used to go into the homes of your wives, but I have now reached the age of a man. Rasulullah ﷺ then prayed for him saying, "O Allah! Make his speech always truthful and grant him success." It happened during the Khilafa of Omar ﷺ that a Jew was found murdered. Omar ﷺ regarded this to be a very serious matter and was very troubled. He mounted the pulpit and said, "Will people be suddenly killed during the period in which Allah has made me the Khalifa? In the name of Allah do I request anyone with any knowledge of the murder to inform me likewise." Bakr bin Shaddah ﷺ then stood up and said, "It was I who did it." Omar ﷺ exclaimed, "Allahu Akbar! You are confessing to the murder! Explain your excuse." "Certainly," said Bakr bin Shaddah ﷺ, "When a certain Muslim left to fight in Jihad, he appointed me to the task of caring for his family. I came one day and found this Jew in the Muslim's house saying:

"Islam has deceived Ash'ath (the Muslim out in Jihad) so much that I have spent the entire night alone with his wife. I spent the night on her breasts while she spent the night on bare-backed and lean camel. It appears that at the place where her thighs meet are waves crashing on to waves"

Omar ﷺ believed Bakr bin Shaddah ﷺ because of the prayer of Rasulullah ﷺ and acquitted him for the murder. (Ibn Mandah, Abu Nu'aym in Kanzul Ummal, Ibn Abi Shaiba in Isabah).

The Letter that Omar ﷺ Wrote to Abu Ubaidah ﷺ Concerning the Murder of a Jew

Qasim bin Abi Bazza reports that a Muslim once killed a Dhimmi in Sham. The case was brought before Abu Ubaidah bin Jarrah ﷺ, who then wrote to Omar ﷺ. Omar ﷺ wrote back with the instruction that if killing Dhimmis is a habitual practice of the Muslim, he should be executed. However, if he did it in a fit of rage, he should pay a penalty of 4,000 Dirhams. (Abdur Razzaq, Bayhaqi in Kanzul Ummal).

Omar ﷺ Writes to the Commander of an Army Forbidding the Killing of Disbelievers (who Surrender)

It is reported that Omar ﷺ once wrote this letter to one of the army commanders he had dispatched: "The news has reached me that some of your men seek out the strongly built disbelieving soldiers and even if they flee to the mountains where they feel safe, your men tell them 'Matras' (a Persian word meaning 'Have no fear', used to assure the person that he would not be harmed). Thereafter, when they have the man in custody after he had given himself up upon the assurance of safety, they kill him. I swear by the Being Who controls my life! If the news reaches me that any of you does this, I shall have him executed. (Malik). Another narration from Abu Salama states that Omar ﷺ said, "I swear by the Being Who controls my life! If any of you points your finger towards the sky for any disbeliever assuring him safety and then kills him when he surrenders himself, I shall have him executed." (Ibn Sa'd and Lalka'i in Kanzul Ummal).

The Incident of Hurmuzan and Omar ﷺ

Anas ﷺ says, "When we laid siege to the city of Tustar, their leader Hurmuzan eventually surrendered on the verdict of Omar ﷺ. I then brought him to Omar ﷺ. When we arrived, Omar ﷺ told Hurmuzan to speak. Hurmuzan asked, 'Should I speak like a dead man or like a living person?' Omar ﷺ replied, 'You may speak, 'La Ba's' (without fear).' Hurmuzan then said, 'O Arabs! As long as Allah had left you and us to ourselves, we used to enslave you, kill you and seize your wealth. However, since Allah has been with you, we have no strength against you.' 'What have you to say?' Omar ﷺ asked me. I said, 'O Amirul Mu'minin! I have left behind me a large enemy force who have tremendous strength. If you kill him, his people will lose hope in living and their strength will be even greater so do not kill him.' Omar ﷺ said, 'Can I allow the murderer of great people like Bara bin Malik (the brother of Anas ﷺ) and Hajza bin Thowr ﷺ to remain alive?' When I feared that Omar ﷺ was going to kill Hurmuzan, I said, 'You have no right to kill someone to whom you have said, 'You may speak 'La Ba's' (because this is an assurance of amnesty).' Omar ﷺ asked, 'Did you receive a bribe or anything else from him?' I replied, 'I swear by Allah that I neither received a bribe nor anything else from him.' Omar ﷺ then warned, 'You will have to bring forth someone besides yourself to testify that the words 'La Ba's' is an assurance of amnesty otherwise I shall punish you first.' I left and found Zubair bin Awwam ﷺ, who testified on my behalf. Omar ﷺ restrained himself from killing Hurmuzan. Hurmuzan then accepted Islam and Omar ﷺ fixed an allowance for him from the public treasury." (Bayhaqi, Imam Shafi in Kanzul Ummal, Bayhaqi in Al Bidayah wan Nihayah)

Omar ﷺ fixes Allowance from the State Treasury for an Old Dhimmi

Abdullah bin Abi Hadrad Aslami ﷺ narrates that when they arrived with Omar ﷺ in Jabiya, they came across an old Dhimmi man begging for food. When Omar ﷺ enquired about the man, he was informed that the man was a Dhimmi who had grown very old and weak and even had a family to support. Omar ﷺ then pardoned him of paying the Jizya he was obliged to pay and said, "You have made him pay the Jizya and when he eventually became weak, you left him to beg for food?" Omar then fixed an allowance of 10 Dirhams for the man from the state treasury. (Ibn Asakir, Waqidi). Omar ﷺ once passed by an old Dhimmi begging at the doors of the Masajid. Omar ﷺ said, "We have not treated you fairly. We had been taking Jizya from you when you were young and now that you are old, we have not cared for you." Omar ﷺ then had an allowance given to him from the public treasury that was adequate for him. (Abu Ubaid, Ibn Zanjway, Uqaili in Kanzul Ummal).

The Incident of Omar ؓ and a Dhimmi

Yazid bin Abi Malik reports that Omar ؓ was with the Muslims of Jabiya when a Dhimmi reported to him that people had ransacked his vineyard. Omar ؓ went to investigate and even found one of the Sahabah carrying a shield full of grapes. "You also?" stared Omar ؓ. The Sahabi said, "O Amirul Mu'minin! We are starving." Omar ؓ then left him and gave instructions that the owner of the vineyard should be paid from the state treasury for his grapes. *(Abu Ubaid in Kanzul Ummal).*

Omar ؓ Passes Judgment in Favor of a Jew Against a Muslim

Sa'eed bin Musaib narrates that a Muslim and Jew once brought their dispute to Omar ؓ. Omar ؓ saw that the Jew was right, he passed judgment in his favor. The Jew said to him, "By Allah! You have judged by the truth!" Omar ؓ blew him with a whip and asked, "How do you know?" The Jew replied, "By Allah! We read in the Torah that whenever a judge resolves to pass judgment by the truth, there is an angel by his right and another by his left who continue guiding him aright and inspiring him. When he forsakes to judge by the truth, they ascend to the heavens and leave him." *(Malik in Targheeb wat Tarheeb)*

The Incident of Omar ؓ and Salama

Iyas bin Salama narrates from his father Salama, "Omar ؓ once passed through the marketplace with a whip in his hand. He lightly struck me with the whip which hit the edge of my clothes as he said, 'Move from the path.' The following day when he met me, he asked, 'O Salam! Do you intend to perform Hajj?' When I replied in the affirmative, he led me by my hand to his house and gave me 600 Dirhams. He then said, 'Use this to help you in your Hajj and you should know that it is in compensation for the lash that I gave you.' I said, "O Amirul Mu'nunin! I do not even remember it.' He said, 'And I have never forgotten it." *(Tabrani)*

The Justice of Uthman ؓ: Dealing with His Slave

Abul Furat narrates that Uthman ؓ said to his slave, "I once twisted your ears and I want you to take retribution. The slave hold of his ears, Uthman ؓ asked to twist harder, "How lovely is retribution in this world without any in the Hereafter."*(Samman in Muwafaqa, Riyadhun Nadhrah by Tabari)*

His Justice with a Bird

Nafi bin Abdul Harith narrates, "Omar ؓ once arrived in Makkah where he went to the Darun Nadwa on a Friday. He intended to reach the Masjid earlier in this way. He hung his shawl on a peg in a room and a pigeon came to sit on it. When Omar ؓ chased the pigeon away, a snake attacked it and killed it. After he had led the Jumu'ah salah, Uthman bin Affan ؓ and I came to him. He said, 'Do pass a verdict concerning something that I had done today. I had entered this room with the intention of reaching the Masjid earlier and hung my shawl on this peg. A pigeon perched on top of it, I feared that it would mess the shawl with its droppings and I therefore chased it off. It then perched on another peg where a snake attacked and killed it. It now occurs to me that it was I who had chased it away from a place of safety to one of danger, I had been the cause of its death.' I said to Uthman ؓ, 'What do you think about having the Amirul Mu'minin pay with a white goat 3 years of age?' Uthman ؓ said, 'I also feel that way.' Omar ؓ then had it paid." *(Iman Shafi'ee in Musnad).*

The Justice of Ali ؓ: Distribution of the Booty Won at Isfahan

Kulaib narrates that the booty won at Isfahan came to Ali ؓ, he divided it into 7 shares. He found in it a loaf of bread and even divided that into 7 parts, placing a piece of it on everyone of the 7 portions. He summoned the commanders of the 7 parts of the army and had them draw lots to decide which of them will be given their share first. *(Bayhaqi in Kanzul Ummal, Ibn Abdul Birr in Isti'ab).*

The Incident of an Arab Woman and Her Freed Slave

The grandfather of Isa bin Abdullah Hashimi narrates that 2 women came to ask from Ali ؓ. The one was an Arab and the other was her freed slave. Ali ؓ instructed that each of them be given a bag of grain and 40 Dirhams. The freed slave took what she was given and left. The Arab woman said, "O Amirul Mu'minin! You have given me as much as you have given her whereas I am an Arab and she is a freed slave?" Ali ؓ replied, "I have studied the Book of Allah and have not found in it anything denoting that the progeny of Isma'el ﷺ (Arabs) should be given preference over the progeny of Is'haq ﷺ." *(Bayhaqi).*

An Incident that took Place Between Ali ؓ and Ja'da bin Hubaira ؓ

Ali bin Rabi'ah reports that Ja'da bin Hubaira once said to Ali ؓ, "O Amirul Mu'minin! 2 people will come to you to judge their dispute. The one is more beloved to you than your own self or he said, "more beloved to you than your family and your wealth" while the other would readily slaughter you if he got the chance. You should therefore pass judgment in favor of the first rather than the second." Ali ؓ lightly hit him on the chest and said, "If this passing judgment was to please myself, I would have certainly done this. However, this is something that is done to please Allah and I shall therefore pass judgment according to the truth." *(Ibn Asakir in Kanzul Ummal).*

The Narration of Asbagh bin Nabata in this Regard

Asbagh bin Nabata narrates that he once accompanied Ali ؓ to the marketplace. When Ali ؓ noticed that the traders had trespassed their boundaries, he asked, "What is this?" When the people confirmed that the traders had indeed trespassed their boundaries, Ali ؓ said, "They have no right to do that. The Muslim marketplace is like the place where they perform salah. Whoever arrives first at a place, it is his for the day unless he chooses to forfeit it." *(Abu Ubaid in Amwal, Kanzul Ummal).* The incident of Ali ؓ and a Jew has already passed in the chapter dealing with incidents about the character and actions of the Sahabah that inspired people to accept Islam.

The Justice of Abdullah bin Rawaha ؓ With the People of Khaibar

In a lengthy narration concerning the disbeliever in the battle of Khaibar, Abdullah bin Omar ؓ says that Abdullah bin Rawaha ؓ used to go to Khaibar every year to estimate their crop output and would then make them pay half the amount according to the agreement they made with Rasulullah ﷺ. The Jews complained to Rasulullah ﷺ about the harshness of his estimations and even tried to bribe him. He however said to them, "O enemies of Allah! Do you wish to feed me of food what is forbidden? By Allah, I have come to you from someone whom I love most of all people while I hate each of you people more than apes and pigs. However, my hatred for you and my love for him will not prompt me from being unjust towards you." The Jews then said, "It is because of such justice that the skies and the earth remain in existence." *(Bayhaqi in Al Bidayah wan Nihayah)*

The Justice of Miqdad bin Aswad ؓ: Narration of Haritb and Statement of Miqdad ؓ, "I shall die while Islam is Dominant"

Harith bin Suwaid narrates that Miqdad bin Aswad ؓ was

once part of a military expedition that was surrounded by the enemy. The Amir of the army gave explicit instructions that no one should take their animals for grazing. However, the news did not reach one of the men and he grazed his animal. The Amir therefore beat him for it. The men then returned saying, "Never before have I been treated as I have been treated today." Miqdad ❁ happened to pass by and asked the man what the matter was. When the man related the incident, Miqdad ❁ hung his sword around his neck and proceeded with the man to the Amir. Miqdad ❁ said to Amir, "Allow him to take retribution from you." When the Amir allowed the man to do so, the man forgave him. Miqdad ❁ then went back saying, "InshaAllah I shall die while Islam is dominant, when the weak are able to restore the wrong that the powerful do to them." *(Abu Nu'aym in Hilya).*

The Narration of Dahhak on the fear That Abu Bakr ❁ Had for Allah

Dahhak reports that Abu Bakr Siddiq ❁ once saw a bird perched on a tree and said, "How fortunate you are, O bird! By Allah! I wish I had been like you. You perch on trees, eat fruit and then fly off without fear of any reckoning or punishment. By Allah! I wish that I was a shrub on the roadside that a passing camel takes into its mouth, chews and then swallows to eventually emerge as dung. I wish I had never been a human with worries of reckoning and punishment." *(Ibn Abi Shaiba, Hannad, Bayhaqi).* Another narration also from *Dahhak bin Muzahim* states that Abu Bakr ❁ was once looking at a sparrow when he said, "How fortunate are you, O sparrow. You eat from the fruit, fly amongst the trees and have no worries of reckoning or punishment. By Allah! I wish that I had been a sheep that some family feeds and when I eventually become as big and fat as I possibly can be, they slaughter me. Thereafter, they roast a part of me, dry parts of me and then eat me. They then dispose of me as waste in the toilet. I wish that I was never created as a human being." *(Ibn Fathaway in Wajal).* Yet another narration quotes that Abu Bakr ❁ said, "I wish that I had been a hair on the body of a Mu'min." *(Ahmad in Zuhd, Muntakhab Kanzul Ummal).*

A Narration of Dahhak About the Fear that Omar ❁ had for Allah

Dahhak narrates that Omar ❁ once said, "I wish that I had been the sheep of a family who feeds me up as much as they please. When I then become as fat as I can be, some of their loved ones pay them a visit and they roast a part of me, dry a part of me and then eat me. They then eventually dispose of me as waste. If only I had never been a human being." *(Hannad, Abu Nu'aym in Hilya, Bayhaqi).*

A Narration of Ibn Asakir and Abu Nu'aym About the Fear that Omar ❁ had for Allah

Amir bin Rabia reports that he once saw Omar ❁ pick up a twig from the ground and say, "I wish that I had been this twig. I wish that I had never been created. I wish that I had been nothing. I wish that my mother had never given birth to me. I wish that I had been something gone and forgotten." *(Ibn Mubarak, Ibn Sa'd, Ibn Abi Shayba, Musaddad, Ibn Asakir).* Omar ❁ said, "If a caller from the heavens had to announce, 'O people! Each one of you shall enter Jannah besides one person' I would fear that the one person may be me. On the other hand, if the announcer had to announce, 'O people! Each one of you shall enter Jahannam besides one person' I would wish that the one person should be me." *(Abu Nu'aym in Hilya).*

The Incident between Omar ❁ and Abu Musa Ash'ari ❁

Abdullah bin Omar ❁ narrates that Omar ❁ once met Abu Musa Ash'ari and asked him, "O Abu Musa! Will it please you to have for yourself the rewards for all the good deeds you carried out during the time of Rasulullah ﷺ and that when it concerns the deeds you did after the demise of Rasulullah ﷺ, especially during your term as Amir you should emerge with a clean sheet i.e. your good deeds should be cancelled out with your evil acts and your evil acts with your good deeds so that you neither have rewards for your good deeds nor punishment for your evil acts?" Abu Musa Ash'ari ❁ replied, "No, O Amirul Mu'minin! By Allah, when I arrived in Basra, rudeness was widespread amongst its people. I then taught them the Qur'an and the Sunnah and fought with them in the Path of Allah. I now aspire to reap the benefits of this." Omar ❁ said, "I wish to emerge with a clean sheet, having my good deeds cancelled with my evils acts and my evil acts cancelled with my good deeds. All that I require to have for myself are the good deeds that I carried out during the time of Rasulullah ﷺ." *(Ibn Asakir in Muntakhab Kanzul Ummal).*

The Narration of Abdullah bin Abbas ❁ Concerning the Fear Omar ❁ had for Allah

Abdullah bin Abbas ❁ says, "After Omar ❁ was stabbed, I went to him and said, 'Glad tidings to you, O Amirul Mu'minin because it was through you that Allah has populated cities, repulsed hypocrisy and made sustenance widespread.' Omar ❁ asked, 'Are you praising me for my leadership, O son of Abbas?' 'For other reasons as well,' I replied. He then said, 'I swear by the Being Who controls my life that I wish to emerge from it just as I had entered into it without any rewards and without any sin." *(Abu Nu'aym in Hilya, Tabrani, Abu Ya'la in Majma'uz Zawa'id, Ibn Sa'd).* Another narration states that Abdullah bin Abbas ❁ said to Omar ❁, "Accept the glad tidings of Jannah for you have been in the company of Rasulullah ﷺ for a very long time. Thereafter, when you became the Amir of the Mu'minin, you lent tremendous strength to them and fulfilled the trust placed on your shoulders." Omar ❁ responded by saying, "As for the glad tidings of Jannah that you have given me, I swear by the Being besides Whom there is none worthy of worship that if I owned the world and all its contents, I would have offered it as ransom to be saved from the frightening scene that lies ahead of me. As for what you have said about my leadership over the Mu'minin, I swear by Allah that I wish it were a clean sheet without any rewards in my favor nor any punishment. As for what you have mentioned about my companionship with Rasulullah ﷺ, this is something precious, for which I can expect great rewards." *(Ibn Sa'd).* Abdullah bin Ubaid bin Umair narrates that a lengthy narration in which he states that Omar ❁ asked those around him to help him sit up. When they did this, he asked Abdullah bin Abbas ❁ to repeat what he had said. When Abdullah bin Abbas ❁ repeated his words, Omar ❁ asked, "Will you testify to this before Allah on the day you meet Him?" "Certainly," replied Abdullah bin Abbas ❁. Omar ❁ then became very happy and was pleased. *(Ibn Sa'd).*

The Narration of Abdullah bin Omar ❁ and Miswar Concerning the Fear Omar ❁ had for Allah

Abdullah bin Omar ❁ says, "Omar ❁'s head was on my lap when he was suffering the illness that eventually claimed his life. 'Put my head on the ground,' he said to me. I said, 'What difference would it make if it is on my lap or on the ground?' However, he again ordered me to place it on the ground and I complied. He then said, 'My mother and I are destroyed if my Rabb does not have mercy on me!'" When Omar ❁ was stabbed, Miswar said, "If I possessed enough gold to fill the earth, I would have given it to ransom myself from the punishment of Allah before I can even see it." *(Abu Nu'aym in Hilya).*

The Narration of Sa'eb bin Yazid ﷺ About Fear of Criticism

Saa'eb bin Yazid ﷺ narrates that someone once asked Omar ﷺ, "Is it better for me not to fear anybody's criticism in matters pertaining to Allah or to rather look into myself for reformation?" Omar ﷺ replied, "Those who have been entrusted with overseeing the affairs of the people should not fear anybody's criticism in matters he has to do for Allah. As for the person who is not charged with any public duty, he should look to his own reformation and advice the one who is entrusted to oversee public affairs." *(Bayhaqi in Kanzul Ummal).*

The Advice that Abu Bakr ﷺ Gave to Omar ﷺ When he Intended to Appoint Him as his Successor

Aghar from the Banu Malik tribe reports that when Abu Bakr ﷺ decided to appoint Omar ﷺ as his successor, he sends for him. When Omar ﷺ came, Abu Bakr ﷺ said to him, "I am summoning you to a duty that .exhausts the person it is entrusted to O Omar! Fear Allah by obeying Him and obey Him by fearing Him because the one who fears Allah is safe from fears and protected from all harm. You should also understand that whatever you do in this position will be presented before Allah for reckoning. None is worthy of this post except the one who fulfills it rights. None of the hopes of a person is realized when he commands people to do what is right while he engages in wrong and who enjoins good while doing evil. All this person's deeds will soon be wasted and will not benefit him in the Hereafter. If you are appointed as the Amir of the people, you should do your best to keep your ends dry of their blood, your stomach empty of their wealth and your tongue free of their honor. There is no power to do good except from Allah." *(Tabrani, Haythami, Hafidh Mundhiri in Targheeb wat Tarheeb).*

The Advice Abu Bakr ﷺ gave on his Deathbed about the Appointment of Omar ﷺ as Successor and his Advice to Omar ﷺ

Salim bin Abdullah bin Omar ﷺ narrates that when death carne to Abu Bakr, he gave these parting advices:

بِسْمِ اللَّهِ الرَّحْمَنِ الرَّحِيمِ

This is a parting request from Abu Bakr ﷺ that he is making during his final moments in this world as he is leaving it and during his initial moments in the Hereafter as he enters it. This is a time when a disbeliever accepts Iman, a sinner develops fear for Allah and even a liar speaks the truth. I have appointed Omar bin Khattab ﷺ as my successor. If he exercises justice, then this has always been my expectation of him. However, if he changes and oppresses, then my intentions have only been good and I have no knowledge of the unseen.

وَسَيَعْلَمُ الَّذِينَ ظَلَمُوا أَيَّ مُنْقَلَبٍ يَنْقَلِبُونَ (227)

And those who do wrong will come to know by what overturning they will be overturned. (Ash-Shu'ara:227).

Abu Bakr ﷺ then sent for Omar. When he arrived, Abu Bakr ﷺ called him in and said, "O Omar! There are those who hate you as well as those who love you. It is however, a very old practice for people to hate good and to love evil." Omar ﷺ interjected, "I have no need for Khilafah." "But the Khilafah has a need for you," added Abu Bakr ﷺ. Abu Bakr ﷺ then continued, "You have seen Rasulullah ﷺ and spent time in his company. You have also seen how he gave preference to us over himself. In fact, we used to actually give his family what was left over from that which came to us from him, he gave us before even giving his family. Then you have also seen me and spent time in my company. I have only been following in the footsteps of the one who passed before me. By Allah! I am not sleeping and dreaming this nor am I in doubt about what I am seeing. I shall also not turn off the course I am taking. O Omar! Take note that Allah has a right during the night that He does not accept during the day a right that He does not accept during the night. The scales of those with heavy scales on the Day of Judgment have only become heavy because they have always followed the truth. It is also the right of the scales to weigh heavily when they contain nothing but the truth. On the other hand, the scales of those with light scales on the Day of Judgment have only become light because they have always followed falsehood. It is also the right of the scales to be light when they contain nothing but falsehood. The first thing that I wish to warn you about is your own self. I also wish to warn you about the people because their eyes are always envious and their desires have swollen. However, when they are disgraced because of these evil characters, they become alarmed, so beware of becoming a cause of this. They will remain in awe of you as long as you fear Allah. This is my parting advice. I now wish you peace." *(Ibn Asakir in Kanzul Ummal).*

The Narration of Abdur Rahman bin Sabit and Others About the Advice That Abu Bakr ﷺ Gave to Omar ﷺ Before his Death

Abdur Rahman bin Sabit, Zaid bin Zubaid bin Harith and Mujahid all report that when death approached Abu Bakr ﷺ, he summoned Omar ﷺ and said, "Fear Allah, O Omar! Take note that Allah has some acts owing to Him during the night that He does not accept during the day and some acts owing to Him during the day that He does not accept during the night. Also note that Allah does not accept Nafl acts until the Fara'idh are fulfilled. The scales of those with heavy scales on the Day of Judgment have only become heavy because they have always followed the truth in this world and have had high regard for it. It is also the right of a scale in which the truth is placed tomorrow that it should weigh heavily. On the other hand, the scales of those with light scales on the Day of Judgment have only become light because they have always followed falsehood in this world and have made light of it. It is also the right of a scale in which falsehood is placed tomorrow that it should weigh lightly. Where Allah has made mention of the people of Jannah, He has mentioned the best of their deeds and overlooked their sins. Whenever I think of them, I say, 'I fear that I may never join them.' Wherever Allah has also made mention of the people of Jahannam, He has mentioned them by the worst of their actions and rejected their good deeds. Whenever I think of them, I say, 'I fear that I may be from amongst them.' Allah has mentioned verses of mercy and verses of punishment so that Allah's servant should become hopeful of Allah's mercy and fearful of His punishment. Never entertain false hopes in Allah by continuing with sin in the hope that you would be forgiven but also never lose hope in Allah's mercy. Never throw yourself into destruction by the doings of your own hands. If you remember this advice of mine, there will never be an unseen thing more beloved to you than death, which will certainly come to you. However, if you put it to waste, there will never be an unseen thing more hated to you than death, which you will never be able to escape." *(Ibn Mubarak, Ibn Abi Shaiba, Hannad, Ibn Jareer, Abu Nu'aym in Hilya, Muntakhab Kanzul Ummal).*

The Advice Abu Bakr ﷺ Gave to Amr bin Al Aas ﷺ When he Appointed Him Commander of the Armies Proceeding to Sham

Abdullah bin Abu Bakr bin Muhammad bin Amr bin Hazm

narrates that Abu Bakr ؓ had resolved to combine the armies marching to Sham. The first of the commanders to march was Amr bin Al Aas ؓ. Abu Bakr ؓ had instructed him to pass Eela en route to Palestine. His army numbered 3,000 and consisted of many Muhajirin and Ansar. When seeing them off, Abu Bakr ؓ walked by the side of Amr ؓ's animal and advised him saying, "O Amr! Fear Allah in private and in public and feel shamed before Him because He sees you and the actions you do. As you can see, I have put you ahead of people who are your seniors and who are more valuable to Islam and the Muslims than you are. You should therefore act for the Hereafter and do everything to please Allah. Be a father towards the people and never disclose their secrets. Suffice yourself with their apparent condition and apply yourself to your task. Be steadfast when you meet the enemy in battle and never show cowardice. Give importance to eradicating misuse of the booty and punish people for it. Keep your talk brief when you address your people and as long as you keep yourself straight, your subordinates will also remain straight." *(Ibn Sa'd in Kanzul Ummal, Ibn Asakir)*

The Advice of Abu Bakr ؓ to Amr bin Al Aas ؓ and to Walid bin Uqaba ؓ

Qasim bin Muhammad narrates that Abu Bakr ؓ once wrote a letter to Amr bin Al Aas ؓ and to Walid bin Uqaba ؓ, both of whom were appointed to collect half the Zakah of the Quda'ah tribe. When he dispatched them to collect the Zakah, Abu Bakr ؓ saw them off and gave both of them the same advice. He said, "Fear Allah in private and in public because whoever fears Allah, Allah will create for him an exit from every difficulty and provide for him from sources he does not expect. Whoever fears Allah, Allah will annul his sins and grant him an immense reward. This is because Taqwa is the best thing about which Allah's servants encourage each other. You are in a path from amongst the paths of Allah. You have no scope of compromising, dropping measures and being negligent concerning those matters that ensure the stability of Islam and the best interests of your duty. You should therefore never weaken and never be careless." *(Ibn Jareer, Tabari, Ibn Asakir).*

The Letter Abu Bakr ؓ Wrote to Amr bin Al Aas ؓ Concerning Khalid bin Walid ؓ

Muttalib bin Sa'ib bin Abu Wada'ah ؓ narrates that Abu Bakr ؓ wrote this letter to Amr bin Al Aas ؓ: "I have written to Khalid bin Waleed ؓ to march upwards as to reinforce you. when he comes to you, you should behave well with him and never assert your authority over him. You should never make any decisions without him because I have placed you ahead of him and others by making you the Amir. Consult with the others and never oppose their views." *(Ibn Sa'd in Kanzul Ummal).*

The Narration of Ibn Sa'd About the Advice Abu Bakr ؓ Gave to Amr bin Al Aas ؓ

Abdul Hamid bin Ja'far narrates from his father that Abu Bakr ؓ said to Amr bin Al Aas ؓ, "I have appointed you as Amir of all the people you pass, the Baliy tribe, the Udhra tribe, the remaining branches of the Quda'ah tribe and all the other remnants of Arab tribes. Encourage them to wage Jihad in the Path of Allah and motivate them for this. Provide transport and provisions for those of them who follow you and foster a bond between them. Treat every tribe according to their status and keep quarters separate from other tribes." *(Ibn Sa'd in Kanzul Ummal, Ibn Asakir)*

The Advice Abu Bakr ؓ Gave to Shurabil bin Hasana ؓ

Muhammad bin Ibrahim bin Harith Taymi ؓ reports that when Abu Bakr ؓ relieved Khalid bin Sa'eed ؓ of his duties, he gave this advice to Shurabil bin Hasana ؓ, who was also one of the Muslim governors: "Give due regard to Khalid bin Sa'eed ؓ and acknowledge the rights he has over you just as you would like him to acknowledge the rights you have over him had he been the governor over you. You know well the status he has in Islam and that at the time when Rasulullah ﷺ passed away, he had been a governor for Rasulullah ﷺ. Although I had planned to reinstate him as governor, I later decided to relieve him of the post. Perhaps this will be better for his Islam because I do not envy the governorship of any person. When I gave him the choice of choosing a commander from all the army commanders, he chose you over even his own cousin. If you are ever faced with a matter that requires the advice of a pious and well-wishing person, let the first person you consult be Abu Ubaidah bin Jarrah ؓ. Thereafter, consult Mu'adh bin Jabal ؓ and the third should be Khalid bin Sa'eed ؓ. In these men you will certainly find excellent counsel and good results. Beware of ever implementing your opinion without taking theirs and of concealing any intelligence from them." *(Ibn Sa'd in Kanzul Ummal).*

The Advice Abu Bakr ؓ Gave to Yazid bin Abu Sufian ؓ

Harith bin Fadhl reports that when Abu Bakr ؓ gave the flag to Yazid bin Abu Sufian ؓ and appointed him commander of the army. He said to him, "O Yazid! You are a youthful person who is well thought of on account of an act that you have been observed doing in private. I have decided to put you to a test and to take you away from your family, so carefully watch yourself and how you exercise your authority. I shall also be informed about you. Should you do well, I shall promote you and should you botch-up; I will have to dismiss you. I am now appointing you to the post of Khalid bin Sa'eed." Abu Bakr ؓ then briefed Yazid bin Abu Sufian ؓ about the responsibility ahead. He said, "I advise you to treat Abu Ubaidah bin Jarrah ؓ well. You well recognize his status in Islam and that Rasulullah ﷺ said, 'Every Ummah has a trustworthy person and the trustworthy person of this Ummah is Abu Ubaidah bin Jarrah ؓ.' You should therefore acknowledge his virtue and his being one of the earliest Muslims. You should also show due regard to Mu'adh bin Jabal ؓ. You know well the battles he fought with Rasulullah ﷺ and that Rasulullah ﷺ said, 'On the Day of Judgment Mu'adh ؓ would come ahead of the Ulema holding a distinguished position.' You should therefore never make a decision without the 2 of them for they will never fail to give you good advice." Yazid ؓ asked, "O Khalifa of Rasulullah ﷺ! Do advise the 2 of them about their behavior with me as you have advised me about them." Abu Bakr ؓ said, "I shall not fail to advise them about their behavior towards you." Yazid ؓ then gave the following Du'a, "May Allah shower His mercy on you and may Allah grant you the best rewards on behalf of Islam." *(Ibn Sa'd in Kanzul Ummal).* Yazid bin Abu Sufian ؓ narrates that Abu Bakr ؓ called him and said, "O Yazid! The worst that I fear from you is that you might give preference to your relatives when appointing people to posts of leadership. Rasulullah ﷺ said, 'Whoever is given charge over the affairs of the Muslims and then wrongfully appoints someone to any post over the people merely because of his love for the person, Allah's curse will be on him and Allah will neither accept any of his Fardh or Nawafil until Allah enters him into Jahannam. Whoever gives wealth of his brother to another person because of his love for him, Allah's curse will be on him or Allah's protection will take leave from him." *(Ahmad, Hakim,*

Mansoor bin Shu'ba Baghdadi in Arba'een, Kanzul Ummal, Haythami).

The Advice Omar ﷺ Gave to his Successor

Omar ﷺ once said, "My parting advice to my successor is that he recognizes the rights of the early Muhajirin and upholds their honor and respect I also advise him to give recognition to those Ansar who do good and to overlook those who do wrong because the Ansar are the ones who adopted Madinah as their home before the Muhajirin and had adopted Iman. I also advise him to treat well the people of the other cities because they are the assistants of Islam, an invaluable source of income for the Muslim state and a source of fury for the enemy. He should take from them only their excess wealth and only with their consent. I also advise him to treat the Bedouins well because they are the native Arabs and the foundation of Islam. He should take only from their young animals, which should then be given back to the poor amongst them. I also advise him to honor the treaty of those in the custody of Allah and His Rasul ﷺ i.e. the Dhimmis. He should fight those who threaten them and should not charge them with more than they can bear." *(Ibn Abi Shaiba, Abu Ubaid in Amwal, Abu Ya'la, Nasai, Ibn Hibban, Bayhaqi, in Muntakhab Kanzul Ummal).* Qasim bin Muhammad narrates that Omar ﷺ once said, "My successor should know that many close and distant people will want to take the Khilafah away from him. Even I have to exert myself to fight people off. Had I known of anyone who will make a more powerful Khalifa than myself, I would prefer him to be the Khalifa and that I should be executed rather than be appointed to the post." *(Ibn Sa'd, Ibn Asakir in Kanzul Ummal).*

The Advice that Omar ﷺ Gave to Abu Ubaidah bin Jarrah ﷺ

Salih bin Kaisan narrates that the first letter that Omar ﷺ wrote after becoming the Khalifa was to Abu Ubaidah bin Jarrah ﷺ to give him command over the army of Khalid bin Walid ﷺ. He wrote: I advise you to fear Allah Who will remain forever and besides Whom all will come to an end. It is He Who has guided us after being astray and Who has removed us from darkness and brought us into the light. I have appointed you as commander of the army of Ibn Walid, so fulfill the task that is binding on you. Never send the Muslims to their destruction with the hope of winning booty. Never let them camp at a place until you have had it examined for them and until you know its approaches. Whenever you dispatch any group, send them as a complete unit and guard against ever sending them to their destruction. Allah has put you to test through me and put me to test through you, so lower your gaze to the world and detach your heart from it. Beware that the world should ever destroy you as it destroyed those before you, whose places of destruction you have already witnessed." *(Ibn Jareer).*

Omar ﷺ's Advice to Sa'd bin Abi Waqqas ﷺ

Muhammad and Talha narrate that Omar ﷺ once sent for Sa'd bin Abi Waqqas ﷺ. When he arrived, Omar ﷺ appointed him commander of the military offensive in Iraq. Omar ﷺ then advised him saying, "O Sa'd! Sa'd of the Banu Wuhaib tribe! Let the fact never deceive you that you are called the maternal uncle of Rasulullah ﷺ and that you have had the opportunity of being in his company. Allah never erases evil with evil but erases evil with good. Allah has no relation with anyone besides the relation of obedience to Him. All of mankind whether they are respectable or not are equal in the sight of Allah. Allah is their Rabb and they are all His servants. They attain superiority over

each other only by their abstinence and they attain what is with Him only by obeying Him. Consider everything you saw Rasulullah ﷺ do from the time he announced his prophethood until the time he left us. Hold fast to this because this is the actual objective. This is my advice to you. Should you ignore it and turn away from it, your deeds would be destroyed and you would be amongst the losers." Thereafter, when Sa'd bin Abi Waqqas ﷺ was about to leave, Omar again called for him and said, "Since I have appointed you to command the offensive in Iraq, remember my advice. You are going towards an extremely difficult and unpleasant task from which nothing but treading the Path of the truth will deliver you. Make yourself and those with you accustomed to do good and seek Allah's assistance through this good. Remember that every good habit requires preparation. The preparation for good deeds is patience and this patience involves enduring every condition that comes to you. By this, you will attain the fear of Allah. You should know that the fear for Allah is found in 2 things, in obeying Allah and in abstaining from disobedience to Him. Those who obey Him obey Him because of their disgust for this world and their love for the Hereafter, while those who disobey Him disobey Him because of their love for this world and their disgust for the Hereafter. You should also know that hearts have certain realities that Allah has created most wonderfully. The one is hidden while the other is apparent. As for apparent one, it is when those who praise a good act and those who condemn it are viewed in the same light, when a good deed is done solely for Allah regardless of whether people praise or condemn it. As for the hidden reality, it is recognized when wisdom from the heart surfaces on a person's tongue and when the people love him. You should not abstain from earning the love of people because even the Ambiya ﷺ asked Allah for the love of the people. Whenever Allah loves a person, Allah makes him loved by others and whenever Allah dislikes someone, He makes him disliked by others as well. You can therefore assess your position in Allah's sight by your position in the eyes of those people who are always with you." *(Ibn Jareer).*

The Advice that Omar ﷺ Gave to Utba bin Ghazwan ﷺ

Abdul Malik bin Umair narrates that when Omar ﷺ dispatched Utba bin Ghazwan ﷺ to Basra, he said to him, "O Utba! I have appointed you as governor of India (Basra is connected to Indian subcontinent through Persian Gulf), which is amongst the strongholds of the enemy. I have great hope that Allah will suffice for you against those around you and will assist you against them. I have already written to Ala bin Hadhrami ﷺ to reinforce you with Arjafa bin Harthama who is a fierce fighter against the enemy and a great strategist against them. When he comes to you, you should consult with him and keep him close to you. Call people towards Allah and welcome those who respond. As for those who refuse to accept Islam, they will have to pay the Jizya in humiliation and live under Muslims rule. Otherwise if these 2 options are refused, it will have to be the sword without any sympathy. Fear Allah in the post that you have been appointed to and beware that your internal desire should ever pull you towards pride because this will ruin your Hereafter. You had been a companion of Rasulullah ﷺ and through him you had attained honor after being disgraced. Through him did you attain strength after weakness so much so that you have become an Amir in a position of great authority and a ruler whose commands are obeyed. People listen when you speak and your commands are obeyed. What a great bounty this is on condition that it does not make you think that your status is higher than it is and that it does not make you display arrogance over those of lower ranks. Guard against this bounty just as you would guard against sin. This post is one of the 2 things (besides sin) that I fear most for you, that they should gradually deceive you and then drop you so hard that they eventually lead you into Jahannam. I seek Allah's protection for you and for myself against this. People rush towards doing the work of Allah when the world is lifted for them and when they stand to receive worldly gain by it and they then make it their objective. You should therefore have the intention of pleasing only Allah and not to acquire worldly gains. You should also always beware of the place where oppressors will fall (Jahannam)." *(Ibn Jareer, Ali bin Muhammad Mada'ini in Al Bidayah wan Nihayah).*

The Advice that Omar ؓ Gave to Ala bin Hadhrami ؓ

Sha'bi reports that Omar ؓ once wrote this letter to Ala bin Hadhrami ؓ who was in Bahrain: "Proceed to Utba bin Ghazwan ؓ because I have appointed you to his post. Remember that you are going to someone from the very first Muhajirin for whom Allah has already decreed Jannah. I am not dismissing him because he has not been chaste, strong and a good fighter. I am dismissing him only because I feel that you would be of more use to the Muslims of that region. You should therefore respect his status. I had already appointed someone else to this post before you, but he passed away before he could reach there. Therefore, if Allah wishes that you take charge there, you will become the governor. However, if Allah wills that Utba remains the governor, then all creation and decisions are the rights of Allah the Rabb of the universe. Remember that every decision that Allah makes is protected by Him and will certainly come to pass. You should therefore concern yourself only with the purpose for which you were created and Allah will take care of the rest. Apply yourself to this task and forsake everything else because this world is destined to come to an end while the Hereafter is eternal. You should therefore never allow yourself to be preoccupied with something the good of which will soon end rather than something the evil of which is everlasting. Hasten towards the pleasure of Allah and get away from His displeasure. For those whom He wishes, Allah combines high merit in their leadership as well as in their knowledge. We beg Allah to grant you and us assistance to do good and protection from His punishment." *(Ibn Sa'd).*

The Advice that Omar ؓ Gave to Abu Musa Ash'ari ؓ

Dabba bin Mihsin narrates that Omar ؓ wrote this letter to Abu Musa Ash'ari ؓ: "People usually develop a dislike for their rulers. I therefore seek Allah's protection that this should even happen to me or to you. Ensure that you enforce the penalties of the Shari'a even though it be only for a while during the day if not more often. If you are faced with 2 decisions, the one being for Allah and the other for worldly gain, then give preference for the one that is for Allah because this world will come to an end while the Hereafter is everlasting. Install fear into criminals and keep them separate so that they never have the opportunity to conspire together. Visit the sick Muslims, attend their funerals, keep your door open and do the work of the Muslims yourself because you are after all a man from amongst them. The only difference is that Allah has placed a heavier burden on you. The news has reached me that you and your family have adopted a trend in your clothing, your food and your conveyance that the average Muslims cannot afford. O servant of Allah! Beware that you should become like a beast that passes by an abundant valley and then has no other objective but getting fat, whereas it is getting fat that will kill it. Remember that when a governor

becomes corrupt, his subordinates become corrupt and the most wretched of all people is the person who is the cause of his subordinates becoming corrupt." *(Daynurwi in Kanzul Ummal, Ibn Abi Shaiba, Abu Nu'aym in Hilya).*

Dahhak Reports that Omar ؓ Wrote the Following Letter to Abu Musa Ash'ari ؓ:

"Strength in leadership is attained when leaders refrain from postponing today's tasks for tomorrow. When you do this, the tasks accumulate to the extent that you do not know which one to begin with. They are all eventually destroyed. When you are faced with 2 matters, the one being for this world and the other for the Hereafter, opt for the one that is for the Hereafter rather than the one that is for this world because this world will come to an end while the Hereafter is eternal. Always remain afraid of Allah and study the Book of Allah because it is the fountainhead of knowledge and springtime of the hearts as it revives the heart and is a balm for it." *(Ibn Abi Shaiba).*

The Parting Advices of Uthman Dhun Nurain ؓ

Ala bin Fadhl narrated from his mother that after Uthman ؓ was martyred, the people searched for his wealth and found a locked box. When they opened the box, they found in it a paper on which this was written: "This is the parting advice of Uthman. I begin with the name of Allah the Most Kind the Most Merciful. Uthman bin Affan testifies that there is none worthy of worship but the One Allah Who has no partner and that Muhammad ﷺ was Allah's servant and Rasul. He also testifies that Jannah is real, Jahannam is real and that Allah shall resurrect those in the graves on a day about which there is no doubt. Indeed, Allah never breaks a promise. Upon this did I live, upon this did I die and with this will I be resurrected, InsAllah."

A narration of Nizamul Mulk states that the following couplets were written on the reverse side of this paper which means:

"Independence makes one so content that his status soars even though it suppresses him to the extent that poverty threatens though you should be patient when it strikes, remember that difficulty. Never Comes without ease following on its heels. Whoever does not compare times cannot understand grief the promises of time are to be found in the changing of the days" (Fadha'ili Razi)

The Incident Between Ali ؓ and Uthman ؓ on the Day his House was Under Siege

Shaddad bin Aws ؓ narrates that when the siege of Uthman ؓ's house became too difficult, he peeped out to see the people and said, "O servants of Allah!" Shaddad ؓ says that he then saw Ali bin Abi Talib ؓ outside his house wearing the turban of Rasulullah ﷺ and his sword around his neck. In front of him was Hasan ؓ, Abdullah bin Omar ؓ and a group of the Muhajirin and Ansar. They launched an assault on the rebels surrounding the house and dispersed them all. They then entered the house where Ali ؓ said to Uthman ؓ, "As Salamu Alayka, O Amirul Mu'minin! Verily Rasulullah ﷺ did not attain this dominance until he struck those who turned away with those who came forward. By Allah! I believe that these people want nothing but to kill you, so issue the command for us to fight them. Uthman ؓ said, "In the name of Allah do I implore a person who acknowledges the right he owes to Allah and the right he owes to me that he should not spill even a cupping-glass of blood because of me and that he should not even spill his own blood because of me." When Ali ؓ repeated his request, Uthman ؓ gave the same reply. Ali ؓ then left the house saying, "O Allah! You know well that we have tried our level best." He then entered the Masjid, where it was time to perform salah. "O Abul Hasan!" the people said to him, "Go forward and lead the salah." Ali ☙ replied, "I shall not lead you in salah when your Imam is under siege. I shall rather perform salah by myself." He then performed the salah by himself and then went to his house. His son met him and said, "Dear father! I swear by Allah that the rebels have barged into the house." Ali ☙ sighed, "Inna Lillahi wa Inna Ilayhi Raji'un! By Allah! They will certainly martyr him." Some people asked, "O Abul Hasan! Where will Uthman ☙ be when they martyr him?" He replied, "In Jannah. I swear by Allah that he will enjoy an extremely close position to Allah." Then they asked, "And where will the murderers be, O Abu Hasan?" Ali ☙ trice repeated, "By Allah! They will be in Hell." (Abu Ahmad in Riyadun Nudhra fi Munaqibil Ashara).

The Narration of Abu Salama bin Abdur Rahman ☙ in this Regard

Abu Salama bin Abdur Rahman reports that Abu Qatadah ☙ and another person went to Uthman ☙ while his house was under siege. They requested permission to proceed for Hajj and he granted them permission. They then asked, "With whom should we affiliate if these rebels gain the upper hand?" Uthman ☙ replied, "Stick with the majority." They then asked, "But what if these rebels who gain the upper hand form the majority? Who then should we affiliate with?" Uthman ☙ repeated, "Stick with the majority wherever they may be." The narrators says, "We were leaving when we met Hasan bin Ali ☙ at the door as he was going to Uthman ☙. We returned with him to hear what he had to say. He greeted Uthman ☙ and then said, 'O Amirul Mu'minin! Command us to do as you wish.' Uthman ☙ replied, 'Dear nephew! Go and sit in your home until Allah brings His decision to pass.' When he left, we left with him but then met Ibn Omar ☙ at the door as he was going to Uthman ☙. We returned with him to hear what he had to say. He greeted Uthman ☙ and then said, 'O Amirul Mu'minin! I had been in the company of Rasulullah ☙ and I listened and obeyed. Thereafter, I had been in the company of Abu Bakr ☙ and I listened and obeyed. After that, I had been in the company of Omar ☙ and I also listened and obeyed, dutifully acknowledging his rights as my father and as the Khalifa. I am now present to obey you, O Amirul Mu'minin. Command us to do as you wish.' Uthman ☙ twice repeated, 'May Allah reward you with the best rewards', O family of Omar ☙.' He then added, 'However, I do not need blood to be spilt.'" (Abu Ahmad in Riyadun Nudhra fi Munaqibil Ashara).

The Narration of Abu Hurairah ☙ in this Regard

Abu Hurairah ☙ says, "I was under siege with Uthman ☙ in his house when one of our men was struck by an arrow. I said, 'O Amirul Mu'minin! Now that one of our men has been killed, it is alright for us to fight back.' He replied, 'O Abu Hurairah! I strictly command you to throw down your sword. It is my life that is wanted and is prepared to save the Mu'minin by giving my own life.' I then threw away my sword and do not know where it is to this day." (Abu Omar in Kanzul Ummal).

The Advice that Ali bin Abi Talib ☙ Gave to his Governors

Muhajir Amiri narrates that in the letter of appointment that Ali bin Abi Talib ☙ wrote to some governors of certain towns, he wrote: "Never be away from the public for an extended period of time because when governors are away from the public, it frustrates the people and reduces his knowledge of their affairs. In fact, by being away and not interacting with the people, the governors will have no knowledge about that which they had

been absent from. As a result of this, small things and people will seem big to them while big things and people will seem small to them. In a like manner; they will see evil as being good, good as evil and confuse the truth with falsehood. A governor is after all a human and had no idea about what people hide from him and their mere speech bears no indications by which the truth can be decoded from falsehood. A governor should therefore guard against interferences in people's rights by reducing his absence and he should make himself accessible so that he can remain in touch with affairs and will not be misled into abusing the rights of people. You are either one of 2 persons. You may be a person who has a generous nature and who always gives where is its right. In that case, why should you remain aloof from people, thereby refraining from giving them what is right and from displaying your generous disposition? On the other hand, you may be a miserly person. In that case, people will very soon stay away from you and stop asking from you when they give up hope of receiving anything. Most of the needs people will ask from you require no effort on your part because it will either be a complaint of injustice or an appeal for justice and in this case you have nothing to fear and therefore have no need to keep aloof from them. Reap full benefit from what I have described. I shall suffice with these few words which will InsAllah benefit and guide you." (Dinowri, Ibn Asakir in Muntakhab Kanzul Ummal).

Another of his Letters to His Governors

Mada'ini reports that Ali ☙ wrote this letter to his governors: "Slow down and imagine that you have reached your death and your actions have been presented before you in a place where a person is deceived by the world will lament, where the one who wasted his life will wish he had repented and where the oppressor would wish to return to the world to redress the wrong he did."(Dinowri, Ibn Asakir in Muntakhab Kanzul Ummal).

His Advice to the Governor of Ukbara

A man from the Thaqif tribe narrates that Ali ☙ once appointed him as governor of Ukbara. While the local people of the area were with him, Ali ☙ advised him saying, "The people of rural Iraq are deceitful people so beware that they never deceive you. Also ensure that you take all that is due from them." He then told the man to see him that evening and when he did, Ali ☙ said, "I had mentioned to you what I did so that those people should hear it. Never tie anyone of them for a Dirham and never punish them by letting them stand in the sun. You should also never take from them a goat or a cow. We have been commanded only to take from them what is extra so it is not difficult for them to give. Do you know what is extra? It is obedience." (Ibn Zanjway in Kanzul Ummal). Ali ☙ said, "Never sell off their grains, their summer and winter clothing or their animals of labor. Never make any of them stand in the sun as punishment to receive a Dirham." The man said, "In that case, O Amirul Mu'minin, I shall return to you as I have left without receiving anything from them." Ali ☙ said, "Even if you have to return as you have left because we have been commanded to take from them only what is more than their needs." (Bayhaqi).

The Advice that Sa'eed bin Amir Gave to Amirul Mu'minin Omar ☙

Makhul ☙ states a Sahabi of Rasulullah ☙ by the name of Sa'eed bin Amir bin Judhaim Jumhi ☙ once told Omar ☙ that he wished to offer some advice. "Certainly! Go ahead," Omar ☙ told him. Sa'eed ☙ then said, "I advise you to fear Allah when dealing with the people. Never let your words and deeds contradict each other because the best of words are those that are confirmed by actions. Never pass 2 conflicting judgments for one matter, for then conflicts will arise and you will turn away from the truth. If you accept the position that is backed by evidence, you will be successful; Allah will assist you and reform your citizens for you. Devote your attention and your judgments for those Muslims over whom Allah has made you the ruler, whether they are far away or close by. Like for them what you would like for yourself and for your family and dislike for them what you would dislike for yourself and for your family. Dive deep to extract the truth and never fear the condemnation of anyone who condemns what you have done for Allah." Omar ؓ asked, "Who can possibly do this?" Sa'eed ؓ replied, "Someone like yourself whom Allah has given charge over the Ummah of Muhammad ﷺ and who will not allow anyone to come between himself and Allah." *(Ibn Sa'd, Ibn Asakir in Kanzul Ummal)*

The Narration of Abdullah bin Buraida ؓ in this Regard

Abdullah bin Buraida narrates that Omar ؓ once gathered the people upon the arrival of a delegation. He then said to Azina bin Arqam, "Look out for the Sahabah of Rasulullah ﷺ and allow them in first. You may then allow the groups after them to come in. when the people gathered and formed rows before Omar ؓ, he looked at them all. When his gaze fell on a hefty man wearing a decorative shawl, he motioned him to come forward. When the man came forward, Omar ؓ thrice said to him, "Say something." However, each one of the 3 times the man said, "No, you say something." Omar ؓ said, "Shame on you! Stand up." The man stood up and left. When Omar ؓ again looked at the people, he noticed an Ash'ari. The man was fair in complexion, slender, short and relaxed. When Omar ؓ motioned to him, he came forward. "Say something," Omar ؓ said. "You rather say something," the man responded. Omar ؓ again asked him to say something, the man said, "O Amirul Mu'minin! You start a conversation and we will talk." Omar ؓ said, "Shame on you! Stand up. A sheep herder like me can never be of any use to you?" The man stood up and left. Omar ؓ again looked at the people, his eyes fell on a man who was also fair in complexion and thin. Omar ؓ motioned to him and he also came forward. When Omar ؓ asked him to say something, he jumped to the occasion. He praised Allah, spoke about Allah and then said, "You have been given charge of this Ummah, so fear Allah with regard to the position you have been given over the Ummah and your citizens. Fear Allah especially with regard to your personal self because you will be taken to task and questioned. You are in a position of trust and are responsible to fulfill what you have been entrusted with. You will be rewarded only according to what you do." Omar ؓ said, "Since I became the Khalifa no one besides you has ever spoken so frankly to me. Who are you?" "I am Rabi bin Ziyad," he replied. "The brother of Muhajir bin Ziyad?" Omar ؓ asked. 'Yes," came the reply. Omar ؓ prepared some troops. He appointed the Ash'ari as commander and said to him, "Watch Rabi bin Ziyad. If he proves true to his word, he will be of great help in your task. You may then also appoint him to a post of leadership. You should inspect him every 10 days and write to me about his conduct as a leader in so much detail that I can feel as if I had appointed him." Omar ؓ added, "Rasulullah ﷺ once advised us, 'What I fear most for you after me is the hypocrite with the tongue of a knowledgeable person.'" *(Ibn Rahway, Harith, Musaddad, Abu Ya'la in Kanzul Ummal).*

The Letter that Abu Ubaidah ؓ and Mu'adh ؓ Wrote to Omar ؓ and his Response

Muhammad bin Suqa reports that he once went to Nu'aym bin Abu Hind who took out a paper on which this was written: "From Abu Ubaidah bin Jarrah and Mu'adh bin Jabal to Omar bin Khattab. سَلَامٌ عَلَيْكَ

We have observed that you are always concerned about your self reformation. You have now been given charge of this Ummah, Arabs and non-Arabs alike. You have before you people who are noble and ignoble as well as people who are enemies and those who are friends. Each of them should have their share of justice. O Omar! You should therefore watch how you deal with all of them. We caution you about a day when faces will be cast down, hearts will dry up with fear and all evidence will hold no weight against the evidence of the Sovereign Whose supremacy overpowers all of them. All of creation will stand before Him in humility, hoping for His mercy and fearing His punishment. We have been informed of a Hadith stating that towards the end of time the condition of this Ummah will retrogress to the extent that on the surface people will be friends but are actually enemies on the inside. We seek refuge in Allah that this letter of ours should be interpreted to mean what our hearts never intended to mean. We write this only to give you good advice. وَالسَّلَامُ عَلَيْكَ

Omar ؓ Wrote the Following Letter Back to the Two:

From Omar bin Khattab to Abu Ubaidah and Mu'adh. سَلَامٌ عَلَيْكُمَا Your letter has reached me in which you state that you 2 have observed that I have always been concerned about my self reformation. You mentioned, 'You have now been given charge of this Ummah, Arabs and non-Arabs alike. You have before you people who are noble and ignoble as well as people who are enemies and those who are friends. Each of them should have their share of justice.' You have also stated, 'O Omar! You should therefore watch how you deal with all of them.' However, Omar ؓ has neither the power nor the strength to do any of this without the help of Allah. You have also cautioned me about something that all the nations before us were cautioned about. Since ancient times have the days and nights been interchanging with the deaths of people continuing. This system draws closer those who are far, makes every new thing old, brings every promise to pass and will continue until people have reached their places in Jannah or Jahannam. You have also warned me saying that towards the end of time the condition of this Ummah will degrade to the extent that on the surface people will be friends but are actually enemies on the inside. However, the 2 of you are not like this, neither is this that period of time. That will be a period when people will have great motivation and also great fear. However, their motivation to meet each other will be solely to improve their lot in this world. You have also written to seek refuge in Allah that your letter should be interpreted to mean what your hearts never intended to mean. You say that you had written the letter only to give me good advice. You are both true and should never stop writing to me because I cannot do without the two of you. وَالسَّلَامُ عَلَيْكُمَا

(Abu Nu'aym in Hilya, Ibn Abi Shaiba, Hannad in Kanzul Ummal, Tabrani).

The Advice of Abu Ubaidah bin Jarrah ؓ to the Muslims at the Time of His Death in Jordan

Sa'eed bin Musaib says that when Abu Ubaidah bin Jarrah ؓ was afflicted by the plague in Jordan, he summoned all the Muslims with him and said, "I am about to give you some advices which will keep you on the Path of righteousness if you accept them. Establish salah, fast during the month of Ramadhan, pay Zakah, perform Hajj, perform Umrah, encourage each other to do good, wish well for your leaders, never deceive them and never let the world preoccupy you from preparing for the Hereafter. Even if a person is given a life of 1,000 years, he will have no option but to head towards the death that you see. Allah has decreed death for the children of Adam ﷺ and they will all have to die. The wisest of them is he who is most obedient to his Rabb and who works most of the day for his return to Allah.

وَالسَّلَامُ عَلَيْكُمْ وَرَحْمَةُ اللهِ *Lead the salah, O Mu'adh bin Jabal."*

When Abu Ubaidah bin Jarrah ؓ passed away, Mu'adh bin Jabal ؓ addressed the people saying, "O people! Repent to Allah for your sins because when a servant meets Allah after having repented for his sins, Allah has to forgive him. Whoever has debts should settle them because a person will be detained because of his debts and will not be allowed to move on the Day of Judgment until he settles them by paying with his good deeds. Whoever has broken ties with his brother should meet him and reconcile with him for it behaves not a Muslim to severe ties with his brother for more than 3 days. O Muslims! You have been given the shocking news of the death of a great man. I do not think that I have seen any servant of Allah with a more righteous heart than his, who was further from evil than he, who had more love for the masses than he and who was more well wishing than he had been. You should therefore pray to Allah to shower His mercy on him and present yourselves for his Janaza salah." (*Riyadun Nudhra fi Munaqibil Ashara by Muhib Tabari*).

The Life of Abu Bakr Siddiq ؓ: Before Becoming the Khalifa and Afterwards

Ibn Said has combined Ahadeeth reported by Abdullah bin Omar ؓ, Aisha ؓ, Sa'eed bin Musaib and others to relate that people pledged their allegiance to Abu Bakr ؓ on the day that Rasulullah ﷺ passed away, which was Monday 12th Rabiul Awwal 11 AH. He was then living in the area of Sunh with his wife Habiba bint Kharija bin Zaid bin Abu Zuhair ؓ who belonged to the Harith bin Khazraj tribe. He lived in a tent woven from animal hairs and did not add to this until he moved to his house in Madinah. He continued living here in Sunh for 6 months after becoming the Khalifa and would walk in the mornings to Madinah. He sometimes also rode to Madinah on his horse and he wore only a loin cloth and a shawl that was dyed a reddish color. He would come to Madinah to lead the people in salah and return to his family in Sunh after performing the Isha salah. Whenever he came, he would lead the people in salah but when he could not make it, Omar ؓ would lead the salah. On Fridays he used to remain at home during the morning to apply henna to his head and beard and then arrive in Madinah at the time of the Jumu'ah salah when he would lead the people in salah. He was a businessman by trade and would proceed to the marketplace every morning to buy and sell. He also had a flock of goats that would come to him in the evenings. He sometimes took them out himself for grazing and sometimes had someone else graze them. He used to milk goats for the people of his locality so when he became the Khalifa, a little girl said, "Now there will be none to milk our animals." When he heard her saying this, Abu Bakr ؓ said, "Why not! I swear by my life that I shall definitely still milk for you. I hope that what I have entered into will never change the personality I always had." He then continued milking for the people and would sometimes say to the little girl of the locality, "Dear girl! Would you like me to make the milk foamy or without foam?" At times she-would ask for foamy milk while at times she asked for it to have no foam. He then did exactly as she asked. In this way, he stayed in Sunh for 6 months, after which he moved into Madinah. When he started living there, he thought about his post and said, "By Allah! The affairs of the people can

never be set right if I am to continue with my trade. Their affairs can be rectified only if I free myself from trade and look into their matters. My family still needs their necessities." He then left trade and drew from the public treasury only what he required for himself and his family for each day and what he needed for performing Hajj and Umrah. Those in charge of the public treasury fixed an amount of 6,000 Dirhams per annum for him.

When he was on his deathbed, Abu Bakr ؓ said, "Return to the public treasury whatever of its money we have in out possession because I do not wish to derive any benefit from it." He also instructed that a certain piece of land he owned should be given to the Muslims for the public treasury in lieu of the money he had been using from there. After he passed away, the land, a milk-giving camel, a slave who sharpened swords and a shawl valued at 5 Dirhams were all handed over to Omar ؓ. Omar ؓ said, "Abu Bakr ؓ has set a difficult example for his successors to follow." In the year 11 AH, Abu Bakr ؓ appointed Omar ؓ as the Amir of Hajj and performed Umrah in Rajab of the year 12 AH. Abu Bakr ؓ arrived in Makkah at midmorning and when he went to his residence, his father Abu Quhafa ؓ was sitting at the door talking to some youngsters. When someone said to him that his son had arrived, Abu Quhafa ؓ quickly started to stand up. Abu Bakr ؓ hurried to seat his camel and jumped off while it was still standing as he said, "Do not stand, dear father!" He then met his father, hugged him and kissed him between his eyes. The old man then burst out crying out of joy at his son's arrival. The governor of Makkah Attab bin Usaid ؓ, Suhail bin Amr ؓ, Ikrama bin Abu Jahal ؓ and Harith bin Hisham ؓ all came to greet Abu Bakr ؓ saying, "As Salamu Alaykum, O Khalifa of Rasulullah ﷺ!" When they all shook his hands and when they spoke of Rasulullah ﷺ, Abu Bakr ؓ started weeping. When they all greeted Abu Quhafa ؓ, he said, "O Atiq (a title of Abu Bakr ؓ)! These are all leaders, so do treat them well." Abu Bakr ؓ said, "Dear father! There is no power to do good and no strength to abstain from evil except with the help of Allah. I have been charged with an extremely great task which I have no power to fulfill without the assistance of Allah." He then entered the house, took a bath and then emerged. When his companions started following him, he bade them to disperse telling them, "Walk calmly, there is no need to stay behind me." People started meeting him and walking with him. As they sympathized with him over the demise of Rasulullah ﷺ, he wept bitterly. When he reached the Kabah, he threw his upper garment under his right shoulder so that it is exposed, kissed the Black Stone and then completed 7 circles around the Kabah. Thereafter, he performed 2 Rakahs salah and returned to the house. Abu Bakr ؓ came out again at the time Zuhr and again performed Tawaf. He then sat close to Darun Nadwa and said, "Is there anyone who wishes to lodge a complaint of injustice or who wants to demand a right?" However, no one came forward and they all praised their governor. He then performed the Asr salah and remained sitting for the people to greet him. Thereafter, he left for Madinah. When Hajj arrived in 12 AH, Abu Bakr ؓ led the people in Hajj. He performed the Ifrad Hajj (donned the Ihram only for Hajj and not for Umrah) and appointed Uthman bin Affan ؓ as his deputy in Madinah. (*Ibn Sa'd, Ibn Kathir*).

The Incident of Umair bin Sa'd Ansari ؓ When Omar ؓ Appointed Him as Governor of Hims

Antara narrates from Umair bin Sa'd Ansari ؓ that Omar ؓ send him to be the governor of Hims but after a year had still not received any news from him. Omar ؓ then said to his scribe, "Write a letter to Umair. By Allah! I feel that he has betrayed us!" This was then sent to Umair : "Come here as soon as this letter reaches you. When you look at this letter, you should immediately come with all the booty of the Muslims that you have collected." Umair then took his leather bag, put his journey's provisions and a dish into it and hung his water bag onto it. He also took his spear with him and left Hims on foot. When he arrived in Madinah, he was pale, his face was covered in dust and his hair was very long. He went to Omar and greeted him saying, "Peace be on you, a Amirul Mu'minin together with Allah's mercy and His blessings." "What is wrong with you?" asked Omar . Umair responded by saying, "What do you see wrong in me? Do you not see that I am in good health, with pure blood and that I am dragging the world along with its horns?" Thinking that he had brought much wealth along, Omar asked, "What do you have with you?" Umair replied, "I have my bag with me in which I have my provisions. I have my dish in which I eat and wash my hair and clothes in. I also have my water bag in which I carry the water for my wudhu and for drinking. Then I have my spear from which I take support and use to fight off any enemy that confronts me. By Allah! The world is dependent only on these possessions of mine and they are enough for all my needs." Omar then asked, "Have you come walking?" When Umair replied in the affirmative, Omar said, "Was there no one who could lend you their animal to ride?" Umair replied, "Neither did they offer nor did I ask." "What terrible Muslims you have come from!" Omar exclaimed. Umair cautioned, "Fear Allah, O Omar! Allah has prohibited us from backbiting and I have seen them perform their Fajr salah. Those who perform their Fajr salah are in the custody of Allah and none should harm them in any way, physically or verbally." Omar then asked him, "Where did I send you? *(Tabrani reports that he asked, "Where is that for which I had sent you?")* what have you done there?" "What are you asking?" queried Umair . "SubhanAllah!" gasped Omar . Umair then explained, "Were it not for the fear that it would depress you, I would not have informed you. However, you sent me and I reached the place, I then gathered all the pious people from amongst them and charged them with collecting the booty of the Muslims. When they had done so, I spent it all in the appropriate avenues. Had there been a share for you in it, I would have surely brought it to you." "Then you have brought back nothing?" asked Omar . "Nothing at all," came the reply. Omar then issued the command for Umair 's term as governor to be renewed. However, Umair submitted, "This (as a governor) is something that I can neither do for you nor for anyone else after you. By Allah! I have not been saved from the evils of governorship. I once said to a Christian woman, 'May Allah humiliate you!' This is the evil that you have exposed me to, O Omar . The worst of my days were those in which I stayed behind in this world without dying earlier with you, O Omar. Umair then asked to leave and Omar granted it. He then returned to his home, which lay a few miles outside Madinah.

After Umair had left, Omar said, "I still think that he has betrayed us and he has brought back much wealth and kept it at his house." Omar then gave 100 Dinars (gold coins) to a man called Harith and sent him with the instructions, "Go to Umair as if you are a guest. If you see signs of a good life, return to me immediately. However, if you see him in extreme poverty, give him these 100 Dinars. When Harith arrived at the house, he found Umair sitting against a wall and removing lice from his upper garment. Harith greeted Umair who said to him, "Why not dismount, may Allah have mercy on you." Harith dismounted and Umair asked him, "Where are you coming from?" When Harith replied that he was coming from Madinah, Umair asked, "How was the Amirul Mu'minin when you left?" "He was fine," replied Harith. "And how were the Muslims?" was the next question. "They were also fine," Harith replied. "Does the Amirul Mu'minin enforce the penal code?" asked Umair . "Oh yes," responded Harith, "he even lashed his son who had done wrong, because of which he died." This was not so because he died of natural causes a month after the lashing. Umair prayed, "O Allah! Assist Omar because as far as I know, he has great love for You." Harith then stayed there for 3 days. The family had nothing to eat besides a loaf of barley bread, which they fed to Harith while they stayed hungry. Eventually, when the hunger was too much for them to bear, Umair said to Harith, "Your presence has caused us hunger, so if you can, would you please go somewhere else?" Harith then took out 100 Dinars and handed it to Umair saying, "The Amirul Mu'minin has sent this for you, so use it." Umair exhaled deeply and said, "I have no need for this. Take it back." His wife then came and said, "Use it if you need it, otherwise spent it where it should be spent." Umair said, "By Allah! I have nothing to spend it on." His wife then tore off the bottom part of her scarf and gave it to him. He put the money in the piece of cloth and then went out to spend the money on the children of the martyrs and the poor. He returned. Harith thought that Umair would give him also something, but all that Umair said was, "Convey my Salams to the Amirul Mu'minin."

When Harith returned, Omar asked, "What did you see?" "O Amirul Mu'minin!" Harith replied, "I see an extremely difficult life." "What did he do with the Dinars?" Omar enquired. "I do not know," submitted Harith. Omar then wrote to Umair with instructions to come to him without even putting the letter down. When Umair arrived and went to see Omar , the Amirul Mu'minin asked, "What did you do with the Dinars?" Umair replied, "I did what I had to do with it. Why should you ask about it?" Omar demanded, "I command you in the name of Allah to tell me what you did with it!" Umair then responded by saying, "I sent it ahead (to the Hereafter) for myself." "May Allah shower His mercy on you!" exclaimed Omar . Omar then issued instructions for Umair to be given 2 Wasaqs of grain and 2 sets of clothing. Umair said, "I have no need for the food because I have at home 2 Saa of barley and Allah will provide more when I have eaten that." He therefore did not take the food. With regard to the clothing he said, "A certain person's mother has no clothes. I shall give it to her." He then took it and returned home. It not long afterwards that he passed away. May Allah shower His mercies on him. When Omar received the news, he was distressed and prayed to Allah to shower His mercy on Umair . Omar walked to Baqi Gharqad, the graveyard of Madinah and was accompanied by many others walking with him. Omar said to those with him,"Express your wishes." Someone said, "O Amirul Mu'minin! I wish that I had plenty of wealth so that I could buy and set free so many slaves." Another person said, "O Amirul Mu'minin! I wish that I had a lot of wealth to spend in the Path of Allah." Someone else said, "O Amirul Mu'minin! I wish that I had a lot of strength so that I may draw buckets of water to give the people performing Hajj." Omar expressed his wish when he said, "I wish that I had a person like Umair bin Sa'd to assist me in administering the affairs of the Muslims." *(Abu Nu'aym in Hilya, Tabrani, Haythami, Ibn Asakir in Kanzul Ummal).*

The Incident of Sa'eed bin Amir bin Hudhaim Jumhi ﷺ: His Behavior as the Governor of Hims

Khalid bin Ma'dan narrates that Omar ﷺ appointed Sa'eed bin Amir bin Judhaim ﷺ as their governor in Hims. When Omar ﷺ visited Hims, he asked, "O people of Hims! How have you found your governor?" The people then started complaining about him. Hims was termed 'small Kufa' because of the complaints they always had against their governors (the people of Kufa are noted for this). The people said, "We have 4 complaints against him. He does not come out to us until nearly half the day has passed." "That is a serious complaint," remarked Omar ﷺ, "What else?" They continued, "He does not see anyone at night." "Another serious complaint," Omar ﷺ commented, "What else?" They said, "There is a day in every month when he does not come out at all." Omar ﷺ said, "That is also serious. What else?" They concluded by saying, "At times he suffers bouts of unconsciousness and appears to be dead." Omar ﷺ then brought the people of Hims and Sa'eed ﷺ together and prayed, "O Allah! Do not allow my opinion of him to fail." He then asked the people to lodge their complaints. They said, -"He does not come out to us until nearly half the day has passed." Sa'eed ﷺ exclaimed, "By Allah! I do not want to speak about this but the fact of the matter is that I do not have a servant. I therefore massage the dough myself, wait for it to rise and then bake my bread. Thereafter, I perform wudhu and go out." Omar ﷺ again asked, "What is your complaint?" The people said, "He does not see anyone at night." "What have you to say about this?" Omar ﷺ asked. Sa'eed ﷺ replied, "I would also not like to mention this but I reserve the day for the people and the night for Allah." "What is your next complaint?" Omar ﷺ asked them. They said, "There is a day in every month when he does not come out at all." "What have you to say about this?" Omar ﷺ asked. Sa'eed ﷺ replied, "Because I have no servant, I have to wash my clothes myself and have nothing else to change into. I therefore wash my clothes and then wait for them to dry. Because they are thick, they become firm and I have to rub them before they soften up. This takes the entire day and I am then only able to see the people by the evening." Omar ﷺ again asked, "What is your complaint?" The people said, "At times he suffers bouts of unconsciousness and appears to be dead." "What have you to say about this?" Omar ﷺ asked him. Sa'eed ﷺ replied, "I was present in Makkah when Khubaib Ansari ﷺ was martyred. The Quraish had cut his flesh in pieces and when they crucified him, they asked, 'Do you wish that Muhammad ﷺ was here with us in your place?' He replied, 'I swear by Allah that I would not even like a thorn to prick Muhammad ﷺ where he is while I am sitting with my family.' He then called out, 'O Muhammad ﷺ!' Whenever I recall that day and the fact that I did nothing to help him and that I was a disbeliever who did not believe in Allah, I think that Allah will never forgive me for that sin. It is then that I fall unconscious." Omar ﷺ then exclaimed, "All praise is due to Allah Who has not made my instinct fail."

Omar ﷺ then sent 1,000 Dinars for Sa'eed ﷺ saying, "Use it for yourself." His wife exclaimed, "All praise is due to Allah Who has made us independent of your work!" He said, "Do you not want something better than this? That we give this to whoever will bring it back to us at a time that we will need it even more desperately on the Day of Judgment." When she happily agreed, Sa'eed ﷺ called someone from his family whom he trusted and placed the Dinars into several bags. He then instructed the man to take one bag to a certain widow, another to a certain orphan, another to a certain poor person and another to a certain distressed person. This was done until there remained only a few Dinars. He then gave this to his wife and said, "Spend this." He continued the activities of the governorship. She said, "Will you not get us a servant then? What has happened to the wealth?" Sa'eed ﷺ replied, "It will come to you at a time when you need it most (in the Hereafter)." *(Abu Nu'aym in Hilya).*

The Incident of Abu Hurairah ﷺ

Tha'laba bin Abu Malik Qurazi says, "It was during the period that Abu Hurairah ﷺ was the governor of Madinah for Marwan and that he came to the marketplace carrying a bundle of wood. He joked, 'Widen the road for the Amir, O Ibn Abu Malik!' 'But the road is wide enough for you,' I joked. He the said, 'Widen the road for the Amir with the bundle on his head.'" *(Abu Nu'aym in Hilya).*

The Chapter About How the Sahabah Spent in the Path of Allah

This chapter highlights how Rasulullah ﷺ and the Sahabah spent their wealth and everything that Allah granted them in the Path of Allah and in avenues where Allah's pleasure is found. The chapter also highlights how they loved this more than spending on themselves and how they preferred others above themselves even though they suffered poverty.

The Narration of Jareer ◈ Regarding the Encouragement that Rasulullah ﷺ Gave to Spend in the Path of Allah

Jareer reports that they were once with Rasulullah ﷺ one morning when some people belonging to the Mudar tribe arrived. They were barefoot and practically naked. All they had were striped shawls or cloaks and their swords hanging from their necks. The expression on Rasulullah ﷺ's face actually changed when he saw their poverty. He then went into his room and when he emerged, he gave instructions to Bilal ◈, who duly called out the Adhan and then the Iqama. After Rasulullah ﷺ led the salah, he addressed the people with the following verses of the Qur'an:

يَا أَيُّهَا النَّاسُ اتَّقُوا رَبَّكُمُ الَّذِي خَلَقَكُمْ مِنْ نَفْسٍ وَاحِدَةٍ وَخَلَقَ مِنْهَا زَوْجَهَا وَبَثَّ مِنْهُمَا رِجَالًا كَثِيرًا وَنِسَاءً وَاتَّقُوا اللَّهَ الَّذِي تَسَاءَلُونَ بِهِ وَالْأَرْحَامَ إِنَّ اللَّهَ كَانَ عَلَيْكُمْ رَقِيبًا (1)

O mankind! Be dutiful to your Lord, Who created you from a single person (Adam), and from him (Adam) He created his wife (Hawwa), and from them both He created many men and women and fear Allah through Whom you demand your mutual (rights), and (do not cut the relations of) the wombs (kinship). Surely, Allah is Ever an All-Watcher over you. (An-Nisa':1)

اتَّقُوا اللَّهَ وَلْتَنْظُرْ نَفْسٌ مَا قَدَّمَتْ لِغَدٍ

Fear Allah and keep your duty to Him. And let every person look to what (good deeds) he has sent forth for tomorrow (to be rewarded on the Day of Qiyamah). (Al-Hashr:18)

Rasulullah ﷺ then continued to say, "A man should therefore contribute something from his Dinars, from his Dirhams, from his clothing, from his Saa of barley, from his Saa of dates. Rasulullah ﷺ continued until he said, "Even if it be a piece of a date. Everyone ought to give something regardless of how little it is." An Ansari Sahabi then brought a bag of food, that was so full that he could not even carry it. Jabir ◈ says, "The others soon followed suit until I saw 2 heaps of food and clothing and I saw the face of Rasulullah ﷺ sparkle as if it were a piece of gold& Rasulullah ﷺ then said, 'Whoever starts a good practice in Islam will receive the reward for it along with the rewards of all those who do the same after him without any of their rewards being diminished in the least. On the contrary, whoever starts an evil practice in Islam will be burdened with the sin of it in addition to the sins of' all those who do the same after him without the burden of any of their sins being lightened in the least!

A Narration from Jabir ◈ in this Regard

Jabir ◈ narrates that it was a Wednesday when Rasulullah ﷺ visited the Banu Amr bin Auf tribe. The Hadith continues to the point where Rasulullah ﷺ said, "O assembly of Ansar!" The Ansar responded by saying, "We are at your service, O Rasulullah ﷺ!" Rasulullah ﷺ addressed them saying, "During the Period of Ignorance when you were not worshipping Allah, you used bear the burdens of others, engage your wealth in good deeds and care for travelers. Now that Allah has blessed you with Islam and His Nabi, you are suddenly locking away your wealth whereas you should be spending even more now. There are

rewards for whatever man eats from your property and there are also rewards for whatever birds eat." The Ansar then went to their orchards and each one of them made 30 doors leading into their orchards. *(Hakim in Targheeb wat Tarheeb).*

The Sermon of Rasulullah ﷺ Concerning the Virtues of Generosity and the Abomination of Miserliness

Anas ◈ narrates that in the first sermon that Rasulullah ﷺ delivered, he praised Allah and then said, "O people! Verily Allah has chosen Islam to be your religion so enhance your relationship with Islam by generosity and good character. Take note that generosity is a tree in Jannah that has its branches in this world. Therefore, whoever is generous continues attaching himself to one of its branches until it eventually transports him to Jannah. Behold! Miserliness is a tree of Jahannam that has its branches in this world. Therefore, whoever is miserly attaches himself to its branches until it eventually plummets him into Jahannam. Be generous for Allah's sake! Be generous for Allah's sake!" *(Ibn Asakir in Kanzul Ummal).*

The Fervor that Rasulullah ﷺ and the Sahabah had to spend in the Path of Allah: The Hadith of Omar ◈ in this Regard

Omar ◈ narrates that a man came to ask Rasulullah ﷺ to give him something. Rasulullah ﷺ said, "I have nothing to give you, but you may give something on my name and I shall settle the payment as soon as something comes my way." Omar ◈ said, "O Rasulullah ﷺ! You had given him something, so why incur a debt when Allah has not charged you with what you cannot bear." Rasulullah ﷺ disliked the statement of Omar ◈, but an Ansari said, "O Rasulullah ﷺ! Continue spending without fearing any decrease from the Rabb of the Throne." The statement of the Ansari made Rasulullah ﷺ smile and he said, "That is exactly what I have been asked to do." *(Tirmidhi in Al Bidayah wan Nihayah, Bazzar, Ibn Jareer, Khara'iti in Makarimul Akhlaq, Sa'eed bin Mansoor in Kanzul Ummal, Haythami)*

A Narration from Jabir ◈ in this Regard

Jabir ◈ reports that someone came to ask Rasulullah ﷺ for something and he gave it to him. Thereafter, another person came to ask for something and because Rasulullah ﷺ had nothing to give him, Rasulullah ﷺ promised to give him something. Omar ◈ then stood up and out of pity for Rasulullah ﷺ, he said, "O Rasulullah ﷺ! Someone asked you for something, you gave it to him. Then someone else asked you for something and you gave him as well. Thereafter, another person came to ask from you and you promised to give him something. Then when another person came to ask from you, you again made a promise to give. Why do you burden yourself when you do not have anything to give?" Rasulullah ﷺ seemed to dislike this statement of Omar ◈, but just then Abdullah bin Hudhafa Sahmi ◈ stood up and said, "O Rasulullah ﷺ! Continue spending without fearing any decrease from the Rabb of the Throne." Rasulullah ﷺ said, "That is exactly what I have commanded to do." *(Ibn Jareer in Kanzul Ummal)*

The Narration of Ibn Mas'ood ◈ about Rasulullah ﷺ's Instruction to Bilal ◈ to Spend

Abdullah bin Mas'ood ◈ reports that Rasulullah ﷺ once went to Bilal ◈ at a time when he had a few heaps of dates before him. "What is this, Bilal?" asked Rasulullah ﷺ. He Bilal ◈ replied, "I have kept this in preparation for the guests you receive." Rasulullah ﷺ said, "O Bilal! Do you not fear that the smoke of Jahannam may reach you? That you will have to account for this if you die without spending it on others? O Bilal!

Continue pending without fearing any decrease from the Rabb of the Throne. *(Bazzar, Tabrani, Abu Nu'aym in Hilya, Abu Ya'la in Targheeb wat Tarheeb).*

The Narration of Anas Concerning what Transpired Between Rasulullah and His Servant

Anas reports that Rasulullah was once given 3 birds as a gift, he gave one to his servant to eat. The following day, she came with the same bird to him. Rasulullah said, "Did I not tell you not to leave anything for the next day because Allah provides sustenance for each coming day." *(Abu Ya'la, Haythami)*

A Narration of Ali About what Transpired Between Omar and the People with Regards to Excess Wealth

Ali reports that Omar once said to the people, "We have some excess funds, what should we do with it?" The people replied, "O Amirul Mu'minin! Since we have kept you too busy to attend to your family and your business, you may have it for yourself." Omar then asked Ali, "What do you have to say?" Ali replied, "The people have already given you their opinion." However, when Omar insisted, Ali said, "Why should you change your conviction into assumption, when you are certain that the wealth cannot be yours, why change this on the assumption that the people are right?" Omar said, "You will have to prove what you are saying." "Certainly," responded Ali, "By Allah, I can certainly prove myself. Do you recall the time when Rasulullah sent you to collect Zakah? Remember when you approached Abbas bin Abdil Muttalib and he refused to pay his Zakah to you because there had been a problem between you and him? You then told me to accompany you to Rasulullah to inform him about what Abbas did. We then went to Rasulullah but returned because we discovered that he was feeling very cheerless. We then went back to him the following morning and when we found him in a cheerful mood, I informed him about what Abbas had done. He then said to you, 'Do you not realize that a person's paternal uncle is like his father?' We then mentioned to Rasulullah that we had found him to be cheerless on the first day but again happy on the second. He said to us, "When you came on the first day, I still had with me 2 Dinars of Sadaqa funds left over and it was this that caused me to in that mood, because I was worried that I should not die with it in my possession. When you came on the second day, I had already spent it and that had put me in the good mood that you saw." Omar then said, "You are right. I am grateful to you for the first thing you told me about changing conviction to assumption and for the second thing of reminding me of the incident." *(Ahmad, Abu Ya'la, Dowraqi, Bayhaqi, Abu Dawud in Kanzul Ummal, Abu Nu'aym in Hilya, Haythami).*

The Incident Between Omar and Ali Concerning the Distribution of Some Wealth

Talha bin Obaidullah reports that some wealth once came to Omar and he duly distributed it amongst the people. When some of it was left over, he consulted with the people about what to do with it. They said, "You should keep it for any needs that may arise." Ali who was also present there, remained silent without expressing any opinion. Omar asked him, "What is the matter, O Abul Hasan? Why are you not saying anything?" "The people have already spoken," replied Ali. When Omar insisted that Ali voice his opinion, Ali said, "Allah has already distributed this wealth by detailing the recipients in the Qur'an. The remaining amount should also be distributed likewise." Ali then proceeded to mention the incident when

wealth arrived from Bahrain and Rasulullah had not yet distributed all of it when nightfall prevented him from completing. Rasulullah then performed all his salahs as he stayed in the Masjid without returning home and the concern to complete the task was clearly noticeable on his face until everything had been distributed. Omar then instructed Ali to complete the distribution, which he did. Talha says that his share from this amounted to 800 Dirhams. *(Bazzar, Haythami).*

The Narration of Ummu Salama about the Spending of Rasulullah

Ummu Salama narrates, "Rasulullah once came to me with great concern on his face. Fearing that he was in pain, I asked, 'O Rasulullah! What is the matter that I see you so concerned?' He replied, 'It is on account of 7 Dinars that were brought to us yesterday. It is already evening and it is still lying on the edge of our bedding.'" Rasulullah said, "It was brought to us and we have not yet spent it i.e., not yet given it to the needy." *(Ahmad, Abu Ya'la, Haythami).*

The narration of Sahl bin Sa'd in this Regard

Sahl bin Sa'd reports that Rasulullah had 7 Dinars with him, which he left in the custody of Aisha. When Rasulullah fell ill, he said, "O Aisha! Send the gold (the Dinars) to Ali." He then fell unconscious and Aisha became preoccupied with tending to him. Rasulullah then repeated the instruction several times but each time he fell unconscious and Aisha was again preoccupied with nursing him. Rasulullah eventually sent for Ali, who then gave the Dinars to the poor as Sadaqa. On Tuesday evening when Rasulullah started suffering the pain of death, Aisha sent her lantern to a lady who was her neighbor with the message, "Please fill some oil in our lantern for us because Rasulullah is already suffering the pain of death." *(Tabrani in Kabir, Ibn Hibban in Targheeb wat Tarheeb).* Another narration quotes that Aisha said, "During his illness, Rasulullah instructed me to give in Sadaqa some gold that we had. When he regained consciousness, Rasulullah asked, 'What did you do?' I replied, 'Seeing the seriousness of your condition, I became preoccupied with nursing you and was therefore unable to fulfill your request.'" Rasulullah then asked her to bring it to him and she did so. A narrator named Abu Hazim was uncertain whether there were 7 or 9 Dinars. When Aisha brought it, Rasulullah said, "What would Muhammad think if he had to meet Allah while this is with him? These Dinars would have left nothing of Muhammad's trust in Allah should it remain with him when he meets his Rabb." *(Ahmad, Haythami, Bayhaqi).*

The Narration of Ubaidullah bin Abbas Concerning Spending Wealth

Ubaidullah bin Abbas reports that Abu Dhar said to him, "Dear nephew! Rasulullah was holding my hand when he said, 'O Abu Dhar! If I possessed gold and silver equal to Mount Uhud to spend in the Path of Allah, I would not like to die with even a Qirat (1/20th of a Dinar) still in my possession.' I said, 'O Rasulullah! You mean a Qintar (a large amount equal to 4,000 Dinars)?' Rasulullah said, 'O Abu Dhar! You are referring to a large sum while I am referring to a small amount. I desire the hereafter while you desire this world. It is a Qirat that I mean.' He repeated this to me 3 times." *(Bazzar, Haythami, Tabrani)*

The Incident of Abu Dhar and Ka'b in Presence of Uthman

Abu Dhar narrates that he once went to Uthman bin Affan. When Uthman allowed him in, he entered with a staff in his hand. Addressing Ka'b Ahbar, Uthman ؓ asked, "O Ka'b! What is your opinion of Abdur Rahman bin Auf ؓ who had left behind plenty of wealth when passed away?" Ka'b ؓ replied, "There shall be no reckoning in that as long as he had fulfilled the rights owed to Allah." Abu Dhar ؓ struck Ka'b ؓ with his staff and said, "Even if I possessed gold equal to this Mount Uhud to spend in Sadaqa and it is all accepted by Allah, I would still not like to die with even 6 Awqiya still in my possession.'" Abu Dhar ؓ then thrice asked, "O Uthman! I ask you to say in the name of Allah whether you had heard this from Rasulullah ﷺ" Uthman ؓ confirmed that he had heard It. *(Ahmad, Haythami, Abu Ya'la).* A detailed narration of Ghazwan bin Abu Hatim states that Uthman ؓ asked Ka'b, "O Abu Is'haq! Do you think that a person will be required to account for his wealth when he has paid the Zakah due on it?" "No," replied Ka'b. Abu Dhar ؓ then stood up and struck Ka'b on the head saying, 'O son of a Jewess! Do you think that after paying the Zakah there are no other rights due from a person's wealth when Allah has stated:

وَيُؤْثِرُونَ عَلَى أَنْفُسِهِمْ وَلَوْ كَانَ بِهِمْ خَصَاصَةٌ

....And (they) give them (emigrants) preference over themselves, even though they were in need of that... (Al-Hasr:9)
Allah has also mentioned: (8) وَيُطْعِمُونَ الطَّعَامَ عَلَى حُبِّهِ مِسْكِينًا وَيَتِيمًا وَأَسِيرًا
And they give food, inspite of their love for it (or for the love of Him), to Miskin (poor), the orphan, and the captive. (Ad-Dahr:8)
Allah also says: (25) وَالَّذِينَ فِي أَمْوَالِهِمْ حَقٌّ مَعْلُومٌ (24) لِلسَّائِلِ وَالْمَحْرُومِ
And those in whose wealth there is a recognized right. For the beggar who asks, and for the unlucky who has lost his means of living has been straitened). (Al-Ma'arij:24-25)
Abu Dhar ؓ then continued quoting several similar verses from the Qur'an. *(Bayhaqi in Kanzul Ummal).*

The Statement of Omar ؓ Concerning How Abu Bakr ؓ was Always in the Lead When it Came to Spending in Charity

Omar ؓ says, "Rasulullah ﷺ once instructed us to spend in charity at a time when I happened to have a considerable sum of wealth with me. I therefore said to myself, 'If there be any day when I shall beat Abu Bakr ؓ at spending in the Path of Allah, it shall be this day.' I then brought half of all my wealth. Rasulullah ﷺ asked, 'What have you left for your family'? 'I have left something for them,' I responded. Rasulullah ﷺ repeated, 'What have you left for them'? I said, 'I have left with them as much as I have brought.' Abu Bakr ؓ then arrived with everything that he possessed. When Rasulullah ﷺ asked him what he had left for his family, he replied, 'I have left the pleasure of Allah and His Rasul ﷺ for them.' Then I declared that I will never be able to beat him at anything afterwards. *(Abu Dawud, Tirmidhi, Darmi, Hakim, Bayhaqi, Abu Nu'aym in his Hilya, Muntakhab Kanzul Ummal).*

The Incident of Uthman ؓ and Another Man in this Regard

Hasan narrates that a man once said to Uthman ؓ, "You wealthy people have far superseded us (poor) on doing good because you are able to give Sadaqa, free slaves, perform Hajj and spend in the Path of Allah." Uthman ؓ asked, "Do you envy us?" "We certainly do," the man responded. Uthman ؓ then said, "I swear by Allah that a single Dirham that a person donates while he is in financial difficulty is better than 10,000 Dirhams given when there is still so much more left." *(Bayhaqi in Shu'abul Iman).*

The Incident of Ali ؓ and a Beggar

Ubaidullah bin Muhammad bin Aisha narrates that when a beggar came to the Amirul Mu'minin Ali ؓ, he said to his son

Hasan ؓ or Husain ؓ, "Go to your mother and tell her to give one of the 6 Dirhams that I had left with her." His son went and later returned with the message that she said, "You have left the 6 Dirhams to purchase flour." Ali ؓ said, "The Iman of a person cannot be true until he has more trust in that which is in Allah's hands than that which is in his hands." He then sent a message to her to send all 6 Dirhams. When she did so, he gave it all to the beggar. Ali ؓ had not yet even changed his posture when a man arrived selling a camel. "How much for the camel'?" Ali ؓ asked. "140 Dirhams," the man replied. Ali ؓ told the man to tie the camel by him with the understanding that he would pay for it after a while. The man tied the camel there and then left. Another man then passed by and asked who the camel belonged to. When Ali ؓ informed him that the camel was his, the man asked him whether he would sell it. "Certainly," replied Ali ؓ. "How much'?" he asked. "For 200 Dirhams," was the reply. The man agreed to buy it, handed over the 200 Dirhams and then took the Camel. Ali ؓ then paid 140 Dirhams to the man whom he had promised to pay and then returned with the 60 Dirhams to his wife Fatima ؓ. Seeing the money she asked, "What is this?" Ali replied, "This is what Allah has promised us on the lips of His Nabi ﷺ: مَنْ جَاءَ بِالْحَسَنَةِ فَلَهُ عَشْرُ أَمْثَالِهَا *Whoever brings a good deed (Islamic Monotheism and deeds of obedience to Allah and His Messenger ﷺ) shall have ten times the like thereof to his credit (Al-Anam:160) (Askari in Kanzul Ummal)*

A Sahabi Gives a Larger Camel as Zakah

Ubay ؓ narrates, "Rasulullah ﷺ once sent me to collect Zakah. I passed by a man and when he gathered all his wealth together, I calculated that all that was due from him was a one-year old male camel. I therefore said to him, 'Give me a one-year old male camel because that is all that is due from you.' He said, 'But such a camel neither gives milk nor can it be used for transport or loading. Why don't you rather take this young, large and fat she-camel' I said to him, 'I cannot accept anything that I was not instructed to take. However, Rasulullah ﷺ is not far from you, so if you wish you may make the same offer to him. If he accepts the offer, I shall accept and if he rejects, I shall do the same.' The man agreed to do so and left with me, taking along the camel that he had offered to give. When we came to Rasulullah ﷺ, the man said, 'O Nabi of Allah! Your messenger came to me to take the Zakah due on my wealth. By Allah! Never before has the Rasul of Allah or any messenger ever come to collect my Zakah. I gathered together all my wealth for him, he calculated that all that was due from me was a one-year old male camel, whereas such an animal neither gives milk nor can it be used for transport or loading. However, when I offered him to rather take this large and young she-camel, he refused take it. Here is she now. I have brought her to you, O Rasulullah ﷺ.' Rasulullah ﷺ said to him, 'Although all that was due from you was the one-year old camel, if you wish to give something extra, Allah will reward you for it and we shall accept it from you.' 'Here is she now, O Rasulullah ﷺ,' the man said, 'I have brought her to you, so do take her.' Rasulullah ﷺ instructed someone to take the camel and prayed for the man's wealth to be blessed. *(Ahmad, Abu Dawud, Abu Ya'la, Ibn Khuzaimah in Kanzul Ummal).*

The Generosity of Aisha ؓ and her sister Asma ؓ

Abdullah bin Zubair ؓ says, "I have never seen women as generous as Aisha ؓ and her sister Asma ؓ. Their forms of generosity were however different. As for Aisha ؓ, she would collect things and then distribute them when she had collected a considerable amount. As for Asma ♦, she would never keep with her anything for the next day." *(Bukhari in Adabul Mufrid).*

An Incident Concerning the Generosity of Mu'adh ♦

Abdul Rahman bin Ka'b bin Malik narrates that Mu'adh bin Jabal ♦ was an extremely generous, youthful and handsome man who was amongst the most righteous persons of his tribe. He never kept anything back and would continue taking loans to assist others until all his wealth was tied up in debt. He then approached Rasulullah ﷺ to request his creditors to write off the debts, but when Rasulullah ﷺ did so, they all refused. If there was anyone through whose intercession they would have written off any other person's debt, it would have been through the intercession of Rasulullah ﷺ. Rasulullah ﷺ then sold all of Mu'adh ♦'s possessions to repay his debts until he was left with absolutely nothing. During the year that Makkah was conquered, Rasulullah ﷺ dispatched Mu'adh ♦ as governor of a region of Yemen so that he may have the opportunity of recovering his losses. Mu'adh ♦ then stayed in Yemen as the governor and was the first person to ever use Allah's wealth (Zakah funds) to trade with. There he earned a considerable amount of wealth and it was during this period that Rasulullah ﷺ passed away.

When Mu'adh ♦ returned to Madinah, Omar ♦ said to Abu Bakr ♦, "Send for Mu'adh ♦ and take away the wealth he has except for that amount which he requires to survive." Abu Bakr ♦ said, "Unless he gives it of his own accord, I cannot take anything away from him because Rasulullah ﷺ had sent him to recover his losses." When Abu Bakr ♦ refused to submit to his request, Omar ♦ himself went to Mu'adh ♦ and informed him of his intentions. Mu'adh ♦ responded by saying, "Since Rasulullah ﷺ had sent me so that I may recover my losses, I do not have to do this." (Since Mu'adh ♦ had paid back the capital he took from the Zakah funds, he felt entitled to the profits he earned. Omar ♦ was of the opinion that although Mu'adh ♦ could use what he needed, the excess was to be returned to the public whose money was a means to the profits). When Mu'adh ♦ met Omar ♦ some time later, he said, "I have obeyed you and have done as you instructed me. I saw in a dream that I was surrounded by water and was in danger of drowning when you rescued me, O Omar." Mu'adh ♦ then went to Abu Bakr ♦ and related the incident to him. He disclosed all his assets and swore that he would not hide anything even disclosing the whip that he owned. Abu Bakr ♦ said, "By Allah! I shall take none of this from you. You may have it all as a gift." Omar ♦ said, "Now this is good for you and permissible." Mu'adh ♦ thereafter left for Sham. *(Abdul Razzaq, Ibn Rahway in Kanzul Ummal).* Another narration from the son of Ka'b bin Malik ♦ states that Mu'adh bin Jabal ♦ was an extremely youthful, handsome and generous man who was amongst the most righteous persons of his tribe. He gave away everything that he was asked for until all his wealth was tied up in debt. The rest is same as quoted above. *(Abu Nu'aym in Hilya, Ahdur Rzzaq, Hakim confirmed by Dhahabi).*

The Narration of Jabir ♦ Concerning the Generosity of Mu'adh bin Jabal ♦

Jabbir ♦ reports that Mu'adh bin Jabal ♦ was amongst the most handsome of people, amongst those with the best character and the most open-handed. However, to assist others he accumulated a large debt and when his creditors started pushing him to pay; he hid away from them in his house for several days. The creditors eventually sought Rasulullah ﷺ's assistance. When Rasulullah ﷺ sent for Mu'adh, he came with the creditors in trail. They pleaded, "O Rasulullah ﷺ! Please claim our dues from

him." Rasulullah ﷺ said, "Allah will shower His mercy on the person who is charitable towards him and who writes off the debt." Consequently, some of them wrote off their debts while others refused. They still insisted, "O Rasulullah ﷺ! Do reclaim our rights from him." Rasulullah ﷺ said, "O Mu'adh! Be patient with them and settle their debts even though you have to lose all your wealth." Rasulullah ﷺ then took away everything that Mu'adh possessed and handed it over to the creditors. When they distributed it amongst themselves, only 5/7th of the dues were settled. They then said, "O Rasulullah ﷺ! Sell him as a slave to settle the debts." Rasulullah ﷺ refused saying, "Leave him alone. You cannot lodge any claims against him now." Mu'adh ♦ then went to live with the Banu Salama tribe where someone said to him, "O Abu Abdur Rahman! Why do you not ask Rasulullah ﷺ for something now that you have become so poor." Mu'adh ♦ however refused to ask from Rasulullah ﷺ and stayed there a few days more until Rasulullah ﷺ sent for him. Rasulullah ﷺ dispatched him to Yemen to act as governor and said to him, "Perhaps Allah shall redeem your losses and payoff your debt for you." Mu'adh ♦ then proceeded to Yemen where he stayed until the demise of Rasulullah ﷺ. It was in the year that Abu Bakr ♦ appointed Omar ♦ as the Amir of Hajj that Mu'adh ♦ also happened to be in Makkah for Hajj. Mu'adh ♦ and Omar ♦ therefore met on the 8th of Dhul Hijjah and they both embraced each other and consoled each other about the loss of Rasulullah ﷺ. As they then sat down on the ground and started talking, Omar ♦ noticed that Mu'adh ♦ had several slaves. *(Hakim, Ibn Sa'd)* The rest of the narration is the same as the one reported by Abdullah bin Mas'ood ♦ which will be quoted next.

The Narration of Abdullah bin Mas'ood ♦ Concerning the Generosity of Mu'adh ♦

Abdullah bin Mas'ood ♦ reports that after the demise of Rasulullah ﷺ, the people appointed Abu Bakr ♦ as his successor. Rasulullah ﷺ had appointed Mu'adh ♦ as governor of Yemen and it was in the year that Abu Bakr ♦ had appointed Omar ♦ as the Amir of Hajj that Omar ♦ met Mu'adh ♦ in Makkah. Noticing several slaves with Mu'adh ♦, Omar ♦ asked, "Who are these people'?" Mu'adh ♦ replied, "The people of Yemen gave these as a gift to me while the others are for Abu Bakr ♦." Omar ♦ said, "I think that you should rather give them all to Abu Bakr ♦." When the 2 men met again the following day, Mu'adh ♦ said, "O Ibn Khattab! When you saw me last night I was heading for the fire of Jahannam, but you grabbed hold of my waist to save me by advising me to give all the slaves to Abu Bakr ♦. I now feel that I should do as you say." Mu'adh ♦ then brought all the slaves to Abu Bakr ♦ saying, "These have been given as gifts to me, while the others are yours." Abu Bakr ♦ said, "We have authorized your gifts for you and you may have them for yourself." Mu'adh ♦ then proceeded to perform his salah and the slaves all performed salah behind him. He then asked them, "For whom are you performing salah'?" "For Allah," they replied. Mu'adh ♦ said, "Then you are all for Allah." Saying this, he set them all free. *(Hakim confirmed by Dhahabi).*

Omar ♦ Donates his Land in Khaibar

Abdullah bin Omar ♦ narrates that Omar ♦ received a piece of land in Khaibar. He then approached Rasulullah ﷺ saying, "I have received a piece of land in Khaibar. Never before have I received any property more excellent than this. What do you advise me to do with it'?" Rasulullah ﷺ replied, "If you wish, you could make the property an endowment and donate the proceeds in charity." Omar ♦ therefore made the land an endowment on the condition that it should never be sold, never be given away as a gift, never be inherited and that its proceeds be given to the poor, to his relatives, to free slaves, in the Path of Allah, and to guests. He also specified that the caretaker of the land may take from the proceeds what is normally paid and what is required to feed his guests. He however had no permission to amass wealth from it. *(Sihah Sitta in Nasbur Ra'yah).*

Omar ☸ Frees a Slave Woman Whom he had Obtained From Abu Musa Ash'ari ☸

Omar ☸ once wrote to Abu Musa Ash'ari ☸ to buy for him a slave woman from Jalola, a place en route to Khurasan that the Muslims had conquered. Abu Musa Ash'ari ☸ did as requested and sent the woman to Omar ☸. Omar ☸ then called for her one day and said, "Allah says in the Qur'an: لَنْ تَنَالُوا الْبِرَّ حَتَّى تُنْفِقُوا مِمَّا تُحِبُّونَ

By no means shall you attain Al-Birr (piety, righteousness, etc., it means here Allah's Reward, i.e. Paradise), unless you spend (in Allah's Cause) of that which you love. (Al-Imran:92)
Omar ☸ then set her free. *(Abel bin Humaid, Ibn Jareer and Ibn Mundhir in Kanzul Ummal).*

The Incident of Abdullah bin Omar ☸ and a Slave Woman

Nafi narrates that Abdullah bin Omar ☸ owned a slave woman. When his love for her became intense, he freed her and married her to one of his freed slaves. She later bore a son. *Nafi* reports further that he saw Abdullah bin Omar ☸ pick up the little boy and kiss him. Referring to the slave woman he freed, he said, "What a beautiful fragrance coming from her!" *(Ibn Sa'd).*

The incident of Abdullah bin Omar ☸ when he heard a verse of the Qur'an

Abdullah bin Omar ☸ says, "I brought to mind everything that Allah had given me when I heard the verse:

لَنْ تَنَالُوا الْبِرَّ حَتَّى تُنْفِقُوا مِمَّا تُحِبُّونَ

By no means shall you attain Al-Birr (piety, righteousness, etc., it means here Allah's Reward, i.e. Paradise), unless you spend (in Allah's Cause) of that which you love. (Al-Imran:92)

However, I could think of no possession more beloved to me than Marjana, my Roman slave woman. I then said, 'She is free for the pleasure of Allah.' If I were to ever go back on something that I had allocated to Allah, I would have certainly married her." *(Bazzar, Haythami).* Another narration adds that Abdullah bin Omar ☸ got her married to Nafi and she thus gave birth to his child. *(Hakim, Abu Nu'aym in Hilya)*

The Narration of Nafi on Spending of Abdullah bin Omar ☸

Nafi narrates, "Whenever the love of Abdullah bin Omar ☸ for any of his possessions became intense, he offered it to his Rabb by giving away as Sadaqa. His slaves knew this well and they would sometimes exert themselves in good deeds and attach themselves to the Masjid. When he saw this excellent behavior, Abdullah bin Omar ☸ would then set them free. His companions said to him, 'O Abu Abdur Rahman! By Allah! They are only deceiving you.' He would reply to this by saying, 'We fall for the deceit of anyone who deceives us with acts pleasing to Allah.'" *Nafi* continues, "I can recall one evening when Abdullah bin Omar ☸ was riding an excellent camel for which he had paid a large sum. When he became extremely impressed with the way it carried itself, he made it sit down and then dismounted. He then said, 'O Nafi! First remove its reins and saddle and then put a blanket on it, mark it and include it amongst the sacrificial animals." *(Abu Nu'aym in Hilya).* Another narration also from

Nafi states that once while Abdullah bin Omar ☸ was riding a camel, he was very impressed by its ride. He then said, "lkh! lkh! (words said to get a camel to sit down)" When the camel sat down, he said, "O Nafi! Remove its saddle." *Nafi* says, "I thought that this was because he needed to use the saddle for something or because he had some doubts about the camel. When I removed the saddle, he said to me, 'Look and see whether another camel can be bought with the goods this camel carries?' Because he intended to slaughter the camel for the pleasure of Allah and because he liked it, he needed another for his journey. I said, 'I can tell you in the name of Allah that if you so wish, you can easily purchase another with the price of this if you sell it.' Abdullah bin Omar ☸ then put a blanket on the camel's back, put a garland around its neck to mark it and then included it amongst the sacrificial animals. Whenever any of his possessions caught his liking, he always sent it ahead to the Hereafter. Another narration quoted *Nafi* as saying, "Whenever any of his possessions caught his liking, Abdullah bin Omar ☸ would remove it from his possessions and give it away for the pleasure of Allah. He would sometimes give in Sadaqa as much as 30,000 Dirhams in a single sitting. Ibn Amir twice gave him 30,000 Dirhams and he said to me, 'O Nafi! I fear that the Dirhams of Ibn Amir should not put me to trial. Go! You are free.' Abdullah bin Omar ☸ would sometimes not eat meat for an entire month unless he was on a journey or it was the month of Ramadhan.' *Nafi* said, "He would sometimes not even taste meat for an entire month." *(Abu Nu'aym in Hilya, Tabrani in Majma'uz Zawa'id, Ibn Sa'd).*

The Incident of Abdullah bin Omar ☸ when he Stayed over in Juhfa

Sa'eed bin Abu Hilal reports that Abdullah bin Omar ☸ was once ill when he stayed over at Juhfa. When he expressed the desire to eat fish, the people searched for fish but could find only one fish. His wife Safiya bint Abu Ubaid prepared it for him and then gave it to him. A poor person then arrived and stood there. Abdullah bin Omar ☸ told him to have the fish. "SubhanAllah!" exclaimed his family, "We have tired ourselves to prepare this fish and we have our provisions to give the poor man." He replied, "Abdullah likes the fish and it should therefore be given to the poor person." *(Abu Nu'aym in Hilya).* His wife said, "We shall give him a Dirham which will be more useful for him than the fish, while you will be able to fulfill your desire to eat it." Abdullah bin Omar ☸ said, "My desire is what I want you to do." *(Abu Nu'aym in Hilya, Ibn Sa'd)*

Abu Talha ☸ Donates the Orchard of Bir Ha

Anas ☸ narrates that Abu Talha ☸ was the wealthiest of all the Ansar in terms of the date plantations he owned. However, what he loved most of all his possession was the orchard of Bir Ha. It was situated opposite the Masjid and even Rasulullah ﷺ used to go there to drink from its pure and excellent water. However, Abu Talha ☸ went to Rasulullah ﷺ as soon as the verse was revealed in which Allah states:

لَنْ تَنَالُوا الْبِرَّ حَتَّى تُنْفِقُوا مِمَّا تُحِبُّونَ

By no means shall you attain Al-Birr (piety, righteousness, etc., it means here Allah's Reward, i.e. Paradise), unless you spend (in Allah's Cause) of that which you love. (Al-Imran:92)

He said to Rasulullah ﷺ, "O Rasulullah ﷺ! Indeed, Allah stated: 'You shall never reach righteousness until you spend of that which you love.' Bir Ha is certainly the possession that I love most, so it is now Sadaqa for the pleasure of Allah. I aspire for the good of this and that Allah will keep it as a treasure for me in the Hereafter. O Rasulullah ﷺ! Utilize it as Allah shows you." Rasulullah ﷺ said, "Wow! This is an excellent investment! This is an excellent investment!" *(Bukhari, Muslim in Targheeb wat Tarheeb).* Another narration of *Bukhari* adds that Rasulullah ﷺ said, "I have heard what you have to say, but think that you should rather divide it amongst your relatives." Abu Talha ﷺ then said, "I shall definitely do so, O Rasulullah ﷺ! He then divided it amongst his relatives and his nephews.

Zaid bin Haritha ﷺ Gives His Horse Away as Sadaqa

Muhammad bin Munkadir narrates that Zaid bin Haritha ﷺ brought along his horse called "Shibla" when the following verse of the Qur'an was revealed: لَنْ تَنَالُوا الْبِرَّ حَتَّى تُنْفِقُوا مِمَّا تُحِبُّونَ

By no means shall you attain Al-Birr (piety, righteousness, etc., it means here Allah's Reward, i.e. Paradise), unless you spend (in Allah's Cause) of that which you love. (Al-Imran:92)

This horse was the most prized of all his possessions. He said to Rasulullah ﷺ, "This is Sadaqa." Rasulullah ﷺ took it from him and handed it over to Zaid ﷺ's son Usama ﷺ. Noticing the expression of unhappiness on Zaid ﷺ's face, Rasulullah ﷺ said, "Allah has certainly accepted it from you." *(Sa'eed bin Mansoor, Abd bin Humayd, Ibn Mundhir, Ibn Abi Hatim, Ibn Jareer, Abdur Razzaq Durrul Manthoor)*

The Statement of Abu Dhar ﷺ That There are 3 Partners in One's Wealth

Abu Dhar ﷺ stated, "There are 3 partners in one's wealth. The first is predestination that will not consult with you as it takes your valuable and useless wealth either by destruction or by death of animals. The 2nd is the heir who is waiting for you to put your head down in the grave so that he my drag everything away while looking down on you. You are the 3rd partner. So do your best never to be the most helpless of the 3 partners. Verily Allah says: لَنْ تَنَالُوا الْبِرَّ حَتَّى تُنْفِقُوا مِمَّا تُحِبُّونَ

By no means shall you attain Al-Birr (piety, righteousness, etc., it means here Allah's Reward, i.e. Paradise), unless you spend (in Allah's Cause) of that which you love. (Al-Imran:92)

Take note that this camel is the most beloved of my possessions, so I wish to send it ahead for myself to the Hereafter." *(Abu Nu'aym in Hilya).*

The Incident of Rasulullah ﷺ on Sending in Charity While in Need

Sahl bin Sa'd ﷺ narrates that a woman once brought a shawl to Rasulullah ﷺ. It was woven with a woven edge as well. She said, "O Rasulullah ﷺ! I have come to give you this to wear." Rasulullah ﷺ really needed a shawl and he took it from her and wore it immediately. When one of the Sahabah saw him wearing it, he commented, "What a beautiful shawl is this, O Rasulullah ﷺ! Will you not give it to me to wear?" "Certainly," said Rasulullah ﷺ. After Rasulullah ﷺ had left, the other Sahabah reprimanded the man saying, "You had done a terrible thing by asking for the shawl when you saw that Rasulullah ﷺ accepted it because he really needed it. You know well that Rasulullah ﷺ never refuses anything he is asked for." The man replied, "By Allah! The only thing that prompted me to ask for it was that I hoped for its blessings after Rasulullah ﷺ had worn it. I hope to be buried with it as my shroud." *(Ibn Jareer).* Another narration from Sahl bin Sa'd ﷺ states that a striped set of clothing with white edging was knitted for Rasulullah ﷺ out of black wool. Rasulullah ﷺ was wearing it when he went to meet the Sahabah. Striking his hand on his thigh, he said, "Do you not think that these clothes look good?" A Bedouin said, "May my parents be

sacrificed for you, O Rasulullah ﷺ! Will you not give it to me?" Because it was the habit of Rasulullah ﷺ never to refuse anything he was asked for, he agreed and gave the clothes to the man. He sent for his old set of clothes and wore it. Rasulullah ﷺ later had another set of similar clothes knitted for him but it was still being made when he passed away. *(Ibn Jareer in Kanzul Ummal).*

The Incident of Abu Aqil ﷺ

Abu Aqil ﷺ narrates that to earn 2 Saa of dates he spent an entire night drawing water from a well with a rope tied to his back. He took one Saa to his family for their use and the other he reserved to attain proximity to Allah. When he brought it to Rasulullah ﷺ and informed him how he had earned it. Rasulullah ﷺ instructed him to add it to the Sadaqa that had been collected. Mocking Abu Aqil ﷺ, the hypocrites commented, "Of what use is it to this man to contribute a mere Saa of dates when he needs it more?" It was then that Allah revealed the verse:

الَّذِينَ يَلْمِزُونَ الْمُطَّوِّعِينَ مِنَ الْمُؤْمِنِينَ فِي الصَّدَقَاتِ وَالَّذِينَ لَا يَجِدُونَ إِلَّا جُهْدَهُمْ فَيَسْخَرُونَ مِنْهُمْ سَخِرَ اللَّهُ مِنْهُمْ وَلَهُمْ عَذَابٌ أَلِيمٌ (79)

Those who defame such of the believers who give charity (in Allah's Cause) voluntarily, and those who could not find to give charity (in Allah's Cause) except what is available to them, so they mock at them (believers), Allah will throw back their mockery on them, and they shall have a painful torment. (At-Tauba:79) (Tabrani, Haythami)

Abu Salama and Abu Hurairah ﷺ narrate that Rasulullah ﷺ once called the Sahabah for contributions because he intended to dispatch a military expedition. Abdur Rahman bin Auf ﷺ said, "O Rasulullah ﷺ! I have 4,000 Dirhams. I shall lend 2,000 to my Rabb and leave 2,000 for my family." Rasulullah ﷺ said, "May Allah bless what you gave and may Allah also bless what you keep behind." A Sahabi from the Ansar spent the entire night laboring to earn 2 Saa of dates. He then said, "O Rasulullah ﷺ! I have earned 2 Saa of dates. One for my Rabb and the other for my family." The hypocrites then started to mock as they said, "Those who contribute like Abdur Rahman bin Auf ﷺ should do so to boast while Allah and His Rasul ﷺ have no need for the meager Saa of the other."

It was then that Allah revealed the verse:

الَّذِينَ يَلْمِزُونَ الْمُطَّوِّعِينَ مِنَ الْمُؤْمِنِينَ فِي الصَّدَقَاتِ وَالَّذِينَ لَا يَجِدُونَ إِلَّا جُهْدَهُمْ فَيَسْخَرُونَ مِنْهُمْ سَخِرَ اللَّهُ مِنْهُمْ وَلَهُمْ عَذَابٌ أَلِيمٌ (79)

Those who defame such of the believers who give charity (in Allah's Cause) voluntarily, and those who could not find to give charity (in Allah's Cause) except what is available to them, so they mock at them (believers), Allah will throw back their mockery on them, and they shall have a painful torment. (At-Tauba:79) (Bazzar, Haythami)

The Incident of Abdullah bin Zaid ﷺ

Abdullah bin Zaid bin Abdi Rabbihi ﷺ was the Sahabi who was shown the Adhan in his dream. He once approached Rasulullah ﷺ saying, "O Rasulullah ﷺ! This orchard of mine is for Sadaqa. I am handing it over to Allah and His Rasul to spend it as they please." His parents then came to Rasulullah ﷺ and said, "Our livelihood depended on that orchard." Rasulullah ﷺ handed it over to them and after a while they passed away. Thereafter, their son inherited it. *(Hakim, Dhahabi)*

The Incident of a Man From the Ansar

Abu Hurairah ﷺ narrates that a man came to Rasulullah ﷺ complaining of severe hunger. Rasulullah ﷺ then sent a message to one of his wives to send some food but received the reply, "I swear by the Being Who has sent you with the truth that I have nothing but water with me." He then sent the same message to another wife and received the same reply. When the message was sent to each of his wives, each one of them replied saying, "I swear by the Being Who has sent you with the truth that I have nothing but water with me." Rasulullah ﷺ then announced, "Who will host this man tonight and Allah will shower His mercy on him." A man from the Ansar volunteered and took the man home, where he said to his wife, "Do you have any food?" She replied, "There is nothing besides the children's food." He said, "Pacify them with something and then put them to sleep when they want their supper. When our guest arrives, put out the lantern and pretend that we are eating." Another narration states that he said, "When he starts to eat, stand up to set the lantern right and while doing so put it off." They all then sat down and the guest ate while the couple went to sleep hungry. When he went to Rasulullah ﷺ the next morning, Rasulullah ﷺ said, "Allah was impressed by what you 2 did last night." Another narration adds that it was then that Allah revealed the verse: وَيُؤْثِرُونَ عَلَى أَنْفُسِهِمْ وَلَوْ كَانَ بِهِمْ خَصَاصَةٌ *They give them (emigrants) preference over themselves, even though they were in need of that.* (Al-Hashar:9) *(Muslim in Targheeb wat Tarheeb, Bukhari, Nasai, Tabrani in Fat'hul Bari)*

The Incident of the 7 Houses

Abdullah bin Omar ؓ reports that a goat's head passed between 7 houses because the people of each home preferred others above themselves. Although each household needed it, it eventually returned to the house from which it originally left. *(Ibn Jareer in Kanzul Ummal).*

Abu Dahda ؓ Sells His Orchard for a Date Palm in Paradise

Anas ؓ reports that a man came to Rasulullah ﷺ saying, "O Rasulullah ﷺ! A particular man has a date palm with which I need to set right a wall of mine. Please tell him to give it to me so that I may fix my wall." Rasulullah ﷺ said to the man, "Give it to him in exchange for a date palm in Jannah." The man however refused to do so. Abu Dahda ؓ then arrived and said to the man, "Sell me your date palm in exchange for my orchard." The man readily agreed. Abu Dahda ؓ then came to Rasulullah ﷺ and said, "I have bought the date palm in exchange for my orchard. You may give it to the man because I am handing it over to you." Rasulullah ﷺ said, "There shall be so many laden and large date palms for Abu Dahda ؓ in Paradise!" Rasulullah ﷺ repeated this statement several times. Abu Dahda ؓ then went to his wife in the orchard and said, "O Ummu Dahda! You will have to leave this orchard because I have sold it in exchange for a date palm in Jannah." "An excellent transaction!" she exclaimed. *(Ahmad, Baghawi, Hakim in Isabah, Haythami, Tabrani).*

The Incident of Abu Dahda ؓ when he said, "I have Lent My Orchard to my Rabb"

Abdullah bin Mas'ood ؓ narrates that Abu Dahda ؓ approached Rasulullah ﷺ when Allah revealed the verse: مَنْ ذَا الَّذِي يُقْرِضُ اللَّهَ قَرْضًا حَسَنًا *Who is he that will lend to Allah a goodly loan.* (Al-Baqara:245) He said, "O Rasulullah ﷺ! Does Allah require a loan from us?" "Yes, O Abu Dahda," replied Rasulullah ﷺ. "Show me your hand," said Abu Dahda ؓ. When Rasulullah ﷺ gave him his hand, Abu Dahda ؓ said, "I have lent my orchard to my Rabb." His orchard contained 600 date palms. He then walked back to the orchard where his wife Ummu Dahda ؓ and his family were. He then shouted, "O Ummu Dahda!" "At your service!" she responded. He shouted back, "Leave orchard because I have lent it to my Rabb." *(Abu Ya'la, Tabrani, Haythami, Bazzar in Majma'uz Zawa'id, Ibn Mandah in Isabah, Ibn Abi Hatim in Ibn Kathir).* The statement of Abdur Rahman bin Auf ؓ has just passed in the previous few pages, where he said, "O Rasulullah ﷺ! I have 4,000 Dirhams. I shall lend 2,000 to my Rabb and leave 2,000 for my family."

Spending to Encourage People Towards Islam

Anas ؓ reports that whenever Rasulullah ﷺ was asked for anything to draw a person to Islam or to make him steadfast in it, he readily gave it. Therefore, when a person once came to him, gave instructions that the goats of Sadaqa that filled an entire valley should be given to him. The man returned to his tribe and said, "O my people! Accept Islam because Muhammad ﷺ gives without fearing poverty." Another narration states that even when a person came to Rasulullah ﷺ only to acquire worldly possessions, the evening would not come without Islam being more beloved and more honored in his sight than the world and all that it contains. *(Ahmad in Al Bidayah wan Nihayah, Muslim).*

A Narration of Zaid bin Thabit ؓ in this Regard

Zaid bin Thabit ؓ reports that an Arab once came to Rasulullah ﷺ to ask for a piece of land between 2 mountains. Rasulullah ﷺ had it given to him in writing after which he accepted Islam. The man returned to his tribe and said, "O my people! Accept Islam because I have come to you from a man who gives without fearing poverty." *(Tabrani, Haythami)*

The Cause of Safwan bin Umaiah ؓ Acepting Islam and His statement About Rasulullah ﷺ

The story of how Safwan bin Umaiah ؓ accepted Islam, it has already passed that as Rasulullah ﷺ was walking amongst the booty to have a look at it. Safwan ؓ was with him. Safwan then started looking at a valley filled with camels, goats and shepherds. Rasulullah ﷺ watched his long stares at the scene and said to him, "O Abu Wahab! Do you like this valley?" When he replied in the affirmative, Rasulullah ﷺ said to him, "It is all yours." Safwan ؓ accepted Islam on the spot and said, "It is only be the heart of a Nabi that can be so generous. I testify that there is none worthy of worship but Allah and Muhammad ﷺ is Allah's servant and Rasul." *(Waqidi, Ibn Asakir in Kanzul Ummal)*

The Spending of Abu Bakr ؓ on the Occasion of the Hijra and the Incident Between Abu Quhafa ؓ and Asma ؓ

Asma ؓ says, "When my father Abu Bakr ؓ left with Rasulullah ﷺ for Hijra, Abu Bakr ؓ took along all the money he had which amounted to 5,000-6,000 Dirhams. My grandfather Abu Quhafa ؓ who had lost his sight then came home. He said, 'By Allah! I expect that together with alarming you by his leaving, Abu Bakr ؓ has also alarmed you with his money by taking it all along with him.' I said, 'Not at all, dear grandfather. He has left plenty of money with us.' I then gathered some stones and placed them in the dish in which my father usually put his money. Thereafter, I covered it with a cloth and took his hand saying, 'Here, grandfather. Put your hand on this money.' He put his hand on it and thinking that it was Dirhams said, 'Then there is no problem. If he has left this money for you, he has done very well. There should be sufficient money here to see to your needs.' By Allah! My father had not left a thing for us but all that I wished to do by this was to put the old man's heart at rest." *(Ibn*

Is'haq in Al Bidayah wan Nihayah, Ahmad, Tabrani, Haythami). The narration has already passed in which it is stated that Abu Bakr ♦ spent all of his 4,000 Dirhams for the Tabuk expedition.

The Spending of Uthman bin Affan ♦ on the 'Expedition of Difficulty' and the Statement of Rasulullah ♦ About Him

Abdur Rahman bin Khabbab Sulami ♦ reports that Rasulullah ♦ once delivered a sermon in which he encouraged the Sahabah to spend on the 'expedition of difficulty' (the expedition to Tabuk). Uthman ♦ then said, "I shall provide 100 camels together with their saddle blankets and saddles." Rasulullah ♦ then stepped down a step of the pulpit and again encouraged the Sahabah. This time again Uthman ♦ stood up and said, "I shall provide another 100 camels together with their saddle blankets and saddles." Abdur Rahman ♦ says that he then saw Rasulullah ♦ shaking his hand as a person does when expressing wonder. A narrator by the name of Abdus Samad demonstrated this action by taking out his hand and shaking it. Rasulullah ♦ then said, 'After this, Uthman ♦ need not carry out any other optional deed." (Ahmad). Rasulullah ♦ gave encouragement 3 times and that Uthman ♦ took it upon himself to provide 300 camels together with their saddle blankets and saddles. Abdur Rahman says, "I was present there as Rasulullah ♦ stood on the pulpit saying, 'No sin can harm Uthman after this' or he said, 'No sin can harm Uthman after this day.'" (Bayhaqi in Al Bidayah wan Nihayah, Abu Nu'aym in Hilya)

The Narration of Abdur Rahman bin Samura ♦ About the Spending of Uthman ♦ on the 'Expedition of Difficulty'

Abdur Rahman bin Samura ♦ narrates that on the occasion when Rasulullah ♦ was preparing the 'Expedition of Difficulty', Uthman ♦ came with 1,000 Dinars and emptied them into Rasulullah ♦'s bag. As Rasulullah ♦ turned the coins over in his hands, he said, "No act that Uthman does after this day will cause him any harm." Rasulullah ♦ repeated this several times. (Hakim). Another narration from Abdullah bin Omar ♦ states that Rasulullah ♦ prayed, "O Allah! Do not forget this deed of Uthman." Rasulullah ♦ also added, "After this, Uthman ♦ need not carry out any other optional deed." (Abu Nu'aym in Hilya)

The Narration of Hudhaifa bin Yaman ♦ about the Spending of Uthman ♦ on the 'Expedition of Difficulty'

Hudhaifa bin Yaman ♦ narrates that Rasulullah ♦ sent someone to Uthman ♦ to request his assistance for the 'Expedition of Difficulty'. Uthman ♦ sent 10,000 Dinars, which were poured out in front of Rasulullah ♦. As Rasulullah ♦ turned the coins over in his hands, turning them from top to bottom, he said, "O Uthman, may Allah forgive you every sin that you committed secretly, every sin that you committed openly, every sin that you hid from others and every sin that you may commit until the Day of Judgment. Uthman need not worry to carry out any non-obligatory good deeds after this." (Ibn Abi Dar Qutni, Abu Nu'aym, Ibn Asakir in Munthakhab Kanzul Ummal).

The Narration of Abdur Rahman bin Auf ♦, Qatadah and Hasan in this Regard

Abdur Rahman bin Auf ♦ narrates that he was when Uthman ♦ handed over to Rasulullah ♦ what he needed to dispatch the 'Expedition of Difficulty.' On that day, he brought 700 Awqiya of gold. (Abu Ya'la, Tabrani, Haythami). Qatadah reports that Uthman ♦ donated 1,000 animals for the expedition to Tabuk. Amongst these were 50 horses as well. (Abu Nu'aym in Hilya). Hasan narrates that for the expedition to Tabuk, Uthman

donated 950 camels and 50 horses or 970 camels and 30 horses. (Ibn Asakir in Munthakhab Kanzul Ummal). The narration mentioned that Uthman ♦ provided a third of the army's needs during the expedition to Tabuk so that it was said that he saw to each and every need they expressed.

Abdur Rahman bin Auf ♦ donates 700 Camels Together with Their Carriages and Supplies

Anas ♦ narrates that while Aisha ♦ was in her room, she heard a lot of noise in Madinah. "What is that?" she enquired. The people informed her, "That is the caravan of Abdur Rahman bin Auf ♦ that had arrived from Sham carrying everything with it." Anas ♦ says that there were 700 camels in the caravan and that all of Madinah was echoing with the noise. Aisha ♦ said, "I have heard Rasulullah ♦ say that he saw Abdur Rahman bin Auf ♦ entering Jannah on his knees, exhausted after accounting for all his wealth." When these words reached Abdur Rahman bin Auf ♦, he said, "I shall do my best to enter Jannah standing upright." He donated all the camels in the Path of Allah together with their carriages and the supplies they carried. (Ahmad, Al Bidayah wan Nihayah, Abu Nu'aym in Hilya, Ibn Sa'd).

His spending for Allah during the Lifetime of Rasulullah ♦

Imam Zuhri reports that during the lifetime of Rasulullah ♦, Abdur Rahman bin Auf ♦ donated half his wealth in the Path of Allah, which amounted to 4,000 Dirhams. Thereafter, he also donated 40,000 Dirhams and then 40,000 Dinars. He also donated 500 horses in the Path of Allah and again 1,500 camels in the Path of Allah. Most of his fortune was earned through trade. (Abu Nu'aym in Hilya). Another narration from Imam Zuhri states that Abdur Rahman bin Auf ♦ donated 500 camels in the Path of Allah. (Al Bidayah wan Nihayah).

Narration of Zuhri about the spending of Abdur Rahman bin Auf ♦

Imam Zuhri reports that during the lifetime of Rasulullah ♦, Abdur Rahman bin Auf ♦ donated half his wealth in the Path of Allah. Thereafter, he donated 40,000 Dinars and also 500 horses in the Path of Allah and again another 500 camels. Most of his fortune was earned through trade. (Ibn Mubarak in Isabah). The narration has passed in which it is stated that Abdur Rahman bin Auf ♦ donated 200 Awqiya of silver for the expedition to Tabuk.

The Spending of Hakim bin Hizam ♦ on Those Proceeding in the Path of Allah

Abu Hizam says that they had never heard of anyone in Madinah who provided more transport for people proceeding in the Path of Allah than Hakim bin Hizam ♦. Two Bedouins once came to Madinah to ask for someone to provide them with transport to proceed in the Path of Allah. When they were directed to Hakim bin Hizam ♦, they approached him while he was with his family. When he asked them what they required and they duly informed him, he told them not to be hasty and to wait until he comes out to see them. When he came out, he was wearing clothing that was brought from Egypt. It resembled a spider's web and cost 4 Dirhams. He took his staff with him and his slaves also accompanied him. Each time he passed by a rubbish dump, he used the end of his staff to pick up any piece of cloth that could be used to patch up the satchels of the camels going out in the Path of Allah. He would then dust off the cloth and hand it over to his slave saying, "Keep this piece of cloth to mend the satchels." One of the Bedouins said to the other, "Oh dear! Save us from him! By Allah! All this man has with him are pieces of cloth from rubbish dumps." The other said, "Shame on you! Do not be hasty. Let us first wait and see." Hakim 🌸 then took them to the marketplace where he saw 2 large fat and pregnant camels. He purchased them along with their supplies and said to his slave, "Use the pieces of cloth to mend any of the satchels that need mending." Thereafter, he loaded on the camels some food, wheat and fat. Furthermore, he gave the 2 men money for their expenses and made over the camels to them. The one Bedouin then said to his companion, "By Allah! I have never seen a better collector of cloth pieces than this man!" *(Tabrani in Majma'uz Zawaa'id).*

He Donates his House in the Path of Allah for the Poor and for Slaves

Hakim bin Hizam 🌸 once sold a house to Mu'awiya 🌸 for 60,000 Dirhams. Some people said to him, "By Allah! Mu'awiya has deceived you by paying so little." Hakim 🌸 said, "By Allah! During the period of ignorance, I bought it for a mere bag of wine. I now make you all witness that I am giving the price away in the Path of Allah for the benefit of poor and for setting slaves free. Now which one of us has been deceived?" He sold the house for 100,000 Dirhams. *(Tabrani, Haythami)*

Abdullah bin Omar 🌸 Donates 100 Camels in the Path of Allah

Nafi reports that Abdullah bin Omar 🌸 once sold a property of his for 200 camels. He then donated 100 camels in the Path of Allah and made a condition with the riders that they were not to sell them before reaching Wadi Qura. *(Abu Nu'aym in Hilya)*

Omar 🌸, Asim bin Adi 🌸 and Others Spend in the Path of Allah

It has already passed in a previous chapter describing the encouragement Rasulullah 🌸 gave to the Sahabah to spend in the Path of Allah that Omar 🌸 gave 100 Awqiya of silver, equal to 4,000 Dirhams while Asim Ansari 🌸 gave 90 Wasaq of dates for the expedition to Tabuk. On the same occasion, Abbas bin Abdil Muttalib 🌸, Talha bin Ubaidullah 🌸, Sa'd bin Ubadah 🌸 and Muhammad bin Maslama 🌸 all donated large sums of money. A narration has also passed about a man bringing along a camel in the Path of Allah and how Qais bin Sala Ansari 🌸 spent in Jihad.

Zainab bint Jahash 🌸 Spends in the Path of Allah and What Other Women Contributed Towards the Expedition to Tabuk

Aisha 🌸 narrates that Rasulullah 🌸 once said to his wives, "The one to meet me first after death from all of you is the one with the longest arms." The wives then started measuring whose arms were the longest and then when they realized that the statement was metaphorical, it was Zainab bint Jahash 🌸 whose arms turned out to be the longest because she made things by hand and gave the proceeds in Sadaqa. Another narration quotes Aisha 🌸 as saying, "After the demise of Rasulullah 🌸, whenever we gathered in any of our houses, we used to measure our arms against the wall to see whose were the longest. We continued doing this until Zainab bint Jahash 🌸 passed away. She was a short woman whose arms were by no means the longest. It was then that we realized that Rasulullah 🌸 was referring to spending in Sadaqa when he mentioned long arms. Zainab bint Jahash 🌸 was skilful with her hands. She used to dye leather and stitch it and then donate the proceeds in the Path of Allah." *(Bukhari, Muslim in Isabah).* Another narration from Aisha 🌸 states that Zainab bint Jahash 🌸 used to weave cloth and give it to those proceeding in battle, who sewed it and used it in battle. *(Tabrani in Awsat, Haythami).* The narration has already passed in which it is stated to assist the Muslim army in its preparations for Tabuk, the women had sent their bangles, bracelets, anklets,

earrings, rings and other jewellery that filled a cloth spread out in front of Rasulullah 🌸.

The Incident of a Bedouin Lady and Omar 🌸 on Their Spending on the Poor and Those in Need

Umair bin Salama Duwali 🌸 narrates that Omar 🌸 was sleeping under a tree at midday when a Bedouin lady arrived in Madinah. She searched around for someone to assist her and eventually approached Omar 🌸 not knowing that he was the Amirul Mu'minin. She then said to him, "I am a poor woman with 2 children. The Amirul Mu'minin Omar bin Khattab 🌸 had sent Muhammad bin Maslama 🌸 to collect Zakah in our area but he did not give me anything. Perhaps you could intercede before him on our behalf. May Allah have mercy on you." Omar 🌸 shouted for his servant Yarfa to summon Muhammad bin Maslama 🌸. The lady said, "It may have been more helpful to me if you had taken me to him." Omar 🌸 put her heart at rest by saying, "InsAllah, he will soon fulfill your need." Yarfa went to Muhammad bin Maslaina 🌸 and told him to respond to the call of Omar 🌸. Muhammad bin Maslama 🌸 came to Omar 🌸 and said, "As Aalamu Alayka, O Amirul Mu'minin!" The lady felt embarrassed when she realized that it was the Amirul Mu'minin himself whom she was talking to. Omar 🌸 then said, "By Allah! I spare no pains to ensure that I select the best man for any task. What answer will you give when Allah asks you about this lady?" When he heard this, the eyes of Muhammad bin Maslama 🌸 filled with tears. Omar 🌸 then continued, "Allah had sent His Nabi 🌸 to us and we believed in him and followed him. He did as Allah commanded him and gave the Zakah funds to those poor people who deserved it. This he continued doing until Allah took him away. Thereafter, Allah appointed Abu Bakr 🌸 as his successor and he followed the Sunnah of Rasulullah 🌸 until Allah took him away as well. Allah then made me his successor and I have always done my best to select the very best of you to collect and distribute the Zakah funds. When I send you again, ensure that you give this lady her share for the year as well as her share for the previous year. In fact, I do not even know whether I would be sending you at all." Omar 🌸 sent for a camel for the lady and also gave her some flour and oil. He said to her, "Take this until you meet us at Khaibar because we intend coming there." She came to Omar 🌸 at Khaibar, he called her forward and gave her 2 more camels saying, "Take this, for it will suffice for your needs until Muhammad comes to you again. I have already instructed him to give you your dues for the year as well as for the previous year." *(Abu Ubaid in Amwal, Kanzul Ummal).*

The Incident of the Daughter of Khufaf bin Eema Ghifari 🌸 with Omar 🌸

Aslam says that he once left with Omar 🌸 to the marketplace where he met a young lady who said, "O Amirul Mu'minin! My husband has passed away and has left behind small children. By Allah! They do not even have anything to cook nor any plantation or any milk-giving animal. I fear that the drought may destroy them. I am the daughter of Khufaf bin Eema Ghifari 🌸 and my father was with Rasulullah 🌸 at Hudaibiyah." Omar 🌸 stood motionless awhile and then said, "Welcome to a close relative." He then went home where a fine pack camel was tied. He loaded the animal with 2 sacks filled with food placed between the 2 some money and clothing. Thereafter, he handed the reins of the camel to the lady saying, "Take this away. Allah shall provide for you before it is finished." When someone commented that Omar 🌸 had given her too much, Omar 🌸 said, "May your mother lose you! Her father was at Hudaibiyah with

Rasulullah ﷺ. By Allah! I saw her father and her brother lay siege to a fortress for a long time and then conquer it. We received large shares from the booty earned from it. She deserves the large amount that I gave her." *(Abu Ubaid in Amwal, Bukhari, Bayhaq in Kanzul Ummal)*

The Spending of Sa'eed bin Amir bin Judhaim Jumhi ﷻ as the Governor of Sham

Hassan bin Atia reports that when Omar ﷻ relieved Mu'awiya of his post as governor of Sham, he sent Sa'eed bin Amir bin Judhaim Jumhi ﷻ to replace him. He left with his young and beautiful wife from the Quraish but it was not long before they began suffering extreme poverty. When Omar ﷻ heard about this, he sent 1,000 Dinars for them. Sa'eed ﷻ took the money to his wife saying, "Omar ﷻ has sent for us all that you see." She said, "Why do you not buy us something with which to prepare some gravy and some flour. We can then store the rest." He then told her, "Should I rather not tell you of something better than that? Should we rather not give the money to someone who will invest it in business so that we may use the profits. He will then also be responsible for the money. When she agreed, he bought something with which to prepare gravy and some flour as well as 2 camels and 2 slaves. The slaves loaded on the camels all sorts of necessities and then distributed it all to the poor and needy. After a short while, his wife informed him that the food they had bought was finished. She said further, "Why do you not approach the man trading on our behalf and take some of the profits to buy some food." Sa'eed ﷻ remained silent. When she repeated herself, he again remained silent until she started rebuking him. He then stopped coming home during the day and would return only at nights. There was a person from her family who used to frequent the house with Sa'eed ﷻ. He said to Sa'eed's wife, "What are you doing? You are now really hurting him whereas he has given all the money away as Sadaqa." She started weeping bitterly in remorse about the money, Sa'eed ﷻ came to her one day and said, "Take it easy. I had some companions who have left me. Even in exchange for the world and all its contents, I would not like to leave the path they walk. If a single damsel of Jannah has to even peep into this world from the sky everything on earth would be illuminated and the radiance of her face would outshine the sun and the moon. The scarf that she is given to wear is more precious than the world and all that it contains. It is more appropriate that I leave you for them rather than leaving them for you." His wife accepted what had happened and was satisfied. *(Abu Nu'aym in Hilya).*

The Narration of Abdur Rahman bin Sabit ﷻ Concerning This

The narration of *Abdur Rahman bin Sabit Jumhi* states that whenever Sa'eed ﷻ received his salary, he bought what was necessary for his family and then gave the rest out in Sadaqa. When she asked him about the remainder of his salary, he told her that he had lent it out. Some people once approached him and said, "Verily your family has rights over you and your in-laws also have a right over you." He replied, "I have never given others preference the rights I owe to my family and in-laws. However, I shall also not seek the pleasure of people when I am searching for the large-eyed damsels of Jannah. If a single damsel of Jannah has to even peep into this world, on earth would be illuminated just as the sun the earth. I am also not prepared to be left behind first group to enter Jannah after I had heard Rasulullah ﷺ say, 'Allah will gather the people for reckoning when the Mu'minin will race towards Jannah as doves race. When they will be told to wait for the reckoning, they will

say, 'We have nothing to account for because we had been given nothing.' Their Rabb will say, 'My servants are right.' A gate of Jannah will then be opened for them and they will enter Jannah 70 years before anyone else.'" *(Abu Nu'aym in Hilya).* The narration passed in which Sa'eed ﷻ said to his wife, ""Do you not want something better than this? That we give this to whoever will bring it back to us at a time that we will need it even more desperately (on the Day of Judgment)." When she happily agreed, Sa'eed ﷻ called someone from his family whom he trusted and placed the Dinars into several bags. He then instructed the man to take one bag to a certain widow, another to a certain orphan, another to a certain poor person and another to a certain distressed person. This was done until there remained only a few Dinars. He gave this to his wife and said, "Spend this." He continued the activities of the governorship. She said, "Will you not get us a servant then? What has happened to the wealth?" Sa'eed ﷻ replied, "It will come to you at a time when you need it most (in the Hereafter)." *(Abu Nu'aym in Hilya).*

A Narration of Nafi About the Spending of Abdullah bin Omar ﷻ

Nafi reports, "When Abdullah bin Omar ﷻ once fell ill, a bunch of grapes was bought for him for one Dirham. When a poor person arrived there, Abdullah bin Omar ﷻ instructed that it be given to the person. Someone from the household then went to buy the bunch from the poor person for a Dirham because grapes were no longer available elsewhere and brought it back to Abdullah bin Omar ﷻ. The poor person returned to beg and again Abdullah bin Omar ﷻ instructed that it be given to the person. Again someone went to buy the bunch back from the poor person for a Dirham. When he brought it back to Abdullah bin Omar ﷻ, the poor person returned to beg and once again Abdullah bin Omar ﷻ instructed that it be given to him. This time also someone went to buy the bunch from the poor person for a Dirham and brought it back to Abdullah bin Omar ﷻ. When the poor person intended to return yet again, he was prevented from doing so. Had Abdullah bin Omar ﷻ known about this, he would not have even tasted the grapes." *(Abu Nu'aym in Hilya)*

Another Narration From Nafi in this Regard

Nafi says, "When Abdullah bin Omar ﷻ once fell ill, he desired to eat grapes. I bought a bunch of grapes for him for a Dirham and then placed it in his hand." The rest of the narration is the same as the one reported above. However, this narration concludes with the words, "The beggar continued returning and Abdullah bin Omar ﷻ kept instructing that the grapes be given to him until it was the third or fourth occasion when I eventually said to the beggar, 'Shame on you! Are you not embarrassed?!' I then bought the grapes back from him for a Dirham and brought it to Abdullah bin Omar ﷻ. This time, he managed to eat it." *(Abu Nu'aym in Hilya, Ibn Mubarak in Isaaba, Ibn Sa'd, Tabrani in Majma'uz Zawa'id, Haythami)*

The Spending of Uthman bin Abul Aas ﷻ

Abu Nadhra reports, "It was during the first 10 days of Dhul Hijjah that I visited Uthman bin Abul Aas ﷻ in a room that he reserved for conversing with visitors. When someone passed by with a sheep, Uthman bin Abul Aas ﷻ asked the man what he paid for the sheep. The man replied that he had paid 12 Dirhams for it. I then said to myself, 'If only I had 12 Dirhams, I could have also bought a sheep, slaughtered it and fed it to my family for the occasion of Eid that was forthcoming.' When I returned home, Uthman bin Abul Aas ﷻ had sent someone behind me with a bag containing 50 Dirhams. I had never before seen money that had as much blessings as those Dirhams. He gave them to me with the intention of being rewarded and at a time when I most needed it." *(Tabrani, Haythami)*.

The Spending of Aisha 🌸

Imam Malik reports that the report reached him, that a poor person once came to beg from Aisha 🌸 the wife of Rasulullah 🌸. She was fasting that day and had no food at home besides a piece of unleavened bread. When she instructed her servant to give it to the beggar, the servant pleaded, "You will then have nothing to terminate your fast with." However, Aisha 🌸 insisted that she give it to the beggar. The servant continues the story and says, "I then gave it to the beggar. That evening some family or some person who usually did not give us gifts, sent for us some cooked goat meat with many pieces of bread. Aisha 🌸 then called for me and said, 'Eat some of this. It is much better than that piece of bread that we gave away.'" *Imam Malik* reports that another narration also reached him about a poor person who asked Aisha 🌸 for some food at a time when she had a grape in front of. She then said to someone present there, "Take a grape and give it to him." Looking at the single grape, the person expressed surprise. Aisha 🌸 said to him, "You seem surprised. How many atoms' weights do you see in that grape?" Here she was referring to the verse of the Qur'an that states: *"Whoever (sincerely) does an atom's weight of good will see it (its consequences when he is rewarded for it)... ")* *(Mu'atta)*

The Incident of Haritha bin Nu'man 🌸 and the Statement of Rasulullah 🌸 concerning Giving the Poor with one's Own Hand

Uthman narrates that when Haritha bin Nu'man 🌸 lost his eyesight, he tied a string from the place where he performed salah to the door of his room. When a beggar came, he took something from his basket, hold on to the string to lead him to the door and then give the thing to the beggar. his family offered to do it for him, he said, "I heard Rasulullah 🌸 say that personally giving something to the poor saves one from a horrible death." *(Tabrani, Hasan bin Sufian in Isabah, Ibn Sa'd, Abu Nu'aym in Hilya)*.

The Virtue of Personally Giving a Beggar Something

Amr Laythi narrates that they were with Wathila bin Asqa 🌸 when a beggar came. Wathila 🌸 took a piece of bread, put a coin on it and then stood up to personally place it in the beggar's hand. Amr asked, "O Abu Asqa! Is there none from your family who can do this for you?" "Of course there is," he replied, "but the person who stands up to give something as Sadaqa to a poor person, a sin of his will be forgiven for every step he takes. When he then places the thing in the person's hand, 10 sins are forgiven for ever step." *(Ibn Asakir in Kanzul Ummal)*

The Incident of Abdullah bin Omar 🌸 in this Regard

Nafi says, "Abdullah bin Omar 🌸 used to gather all of his family to eat from one platter every night. It often happened that when he heard the plea of a poor person, he would take his share of meat and bread to the poor person. By the time he gave the food away and returned, others would have finished everything in the platter. If I found anything in the platter, he would find it; otherwise he would fast in the morning." *(Ibn Sa'd)*.

The Incident of a Bedouin with Rasulullah 🌸

Anas 🌸 reports that Rasulullah 🌸 entered the Masjid one day wearing a shawl from Najran that had thick edging. A Bedouin came from behind and pulled at a corner of the shawl so hard that the edging left marks on Rasulullah 🌸's neck. The Bedouin said, "O Muhammad! Give some of Allah's money that you have with you!" Rasulullah 🌸 turned around and smiled. He then said to the Sahabah, "Give him something." *(Ibn Jareer in Kanzul Ummal, Bukhari, Muslim in Al Bidayah wan Nihayah)*

Another Incident in this Regard

Abu Hurairah 🌸 says, "We used to sit with Rasulullah 🌸 in the Masjid in the mornings and when he stood up to leave, we would also stand and remain standing until he entered his room. On one occasion, Rasulullah 🌸 stood up to leave and had reached the centre of the Masjid when a Bedouin met him and said, "O Muhammad! Give me 2 camels to ride because you are neither giving them from your own wealth nor from the wealth of your father!" As he met Rasulullah 🌸, he pulled so hard on Rasulullah 🌸's shawl that it left a red streak across his neck. Rasulullah 🌸 then thrice repeated, "No. I seek Allah's forgiveness. Not until you allow me to take retribution for the injury you have caused me." Rasulullah 🌸 then forgave the man and called someone saying, "Give him 2 camels, one loaded with barley and the other loaded with dates." *(lbn Jareer in Kanzul Ummal, Ahmad, Bukhari, Muslim, Abu Dawood in Al Bidawyah wan Nihayah)*.

Narration of Nu'man bin Muqarrin 🌸 in this Regard

Nu'man bin Muqarrin 🌸 narrates that they were 400 people from the Muzaina tribe who came to Rasulullah 🌸. After Rasulullah 🌸 had taught them aspects of Islam and they were departing, some of them asked, "O Rasulullah 🌸! We have no food for the journey." Rasulullah 🌸 instructed Omar 🌸 to supply them some provisions, but he submitted, "O Rasulullah 🌸! I have nothing but some left-over dates which I do not think will be of any benefit to them." Rasulullah 🌸 said to him, "Go and give them some provisions." Omar 🌸 then took the people to an upstairs room where there were dates that resembled a little brown calf in color and height. Omar 🌸 told the people to help themselves and each of them took as much as they needed. Nu'man 🌸 says, "I was the last of the lot and when I looked at the dates, I could not see a single date missing from the original heap although 400 people had already taken from it." The dates did not diminish because of the blessings of complying with the order of Rasulullah 🌸. *(Ahmad, Haythami, Tabrani)*.

The Incident of Dhukain bin Sa'eed Khath'ami 🌸 in this Regard

Dhukain bin Sa'eed Khath'ami 🌸 reports that they were 440 people who approached Rasulullah 🌸 for food. Rasulullah 🌸 instructed Omar 🌸 to give them some food, but he submitted, "O Rasulullah 🌸! I have only that much which would suffice for my children and me during the 4 months of summer and it would not be enough for these people." Rasulullah 🌸 repeated the instruction and Omar 🌸 said, "I hear and obey you, O Rasulullah 🌸!" Omar 🌸 left with the people and took them to an upstairs room where he took out the key from his waist string and opened the door. In the room there was a heap of dates that resembled a baby camel that was sitting down. Omar 🌸 told the people to help themselves and each of them took as much as they needed. Dhukain 🌸 says, "I was the last of the lot and when I looked at the dates, it appeared as if we had not reduced the number of dates at all." *(Tabrani, Haythami, Abu Dawud)*.

Another Narration of Dhukain 🌸

Dhukain 🌸 says, "We were 400 people when we asked Rasulullah 🌸 for food." The narration is then that same as the above narration but with the difference that Omar 🌸 said to

Rasulullah ﷺ, "I have nothing besides a few Saa of dates that would suffice only for my children and me during the 4 months of summer." Abu Bakr ؓ said to him, "Listen and obey." Omar ؓ said, "I hear and I obey." *(Abu Nu'aym in Hilya)*

The Behavior of Abdullah bin Omar ؓ with Beggars

Aflah bin Kathir says, "Abdullah bin Omar ؓ never refused any beggar and even a leper with fingers dripping with blood could be seen eating with him from the same plate."

The Incident of Abu Bakr ؓ on Spending in Sadaqa

Hasan Basri reports that Abu Bakr ؓ once brought his Sadaqa to Rasulullah ﷺ. He secretly gave it to Rasulullah ﷺ saying, "O Rasulullah ﷺ! This is my sadaqa contribution and I shall give again for Allah whenever necessary." Thereafter, Omar ؓ arrived with his Sadaqa. He gave it openly to Rasulullah ﷺ and said, "O Rasulullah ﷺ! Here is my Sadaqa contribution and I shall have my reward with Allah." Rasulullah ﷺ said, "O Omar! You have strung your bow without a string. The difference in the Sadaqa of you 2 is just like the difference in your words." Although the Sadaqa of both men were accepted, the intention of Abu Bakr ؓ was the pleasure of Allah, whereas that of Omar ؓ was also to attain reward. Abu Bakr ؓ's intention was therefore superior. *(Abu Nu'aym in Hilya, Muntakhab Kanzul Ummal)*

Uthman ؓ Purchases the Well of Romah and Donates It to the Muslim public

Abdullah bin Omar ؓ narrates that Rasulullah ﷺ once announced, "Who will purchase the well of Romah for us and donate it as Sadaqa for the Muslim public? Allah will quench his thirst on the Day of Judgment." Uthman ؓ then bought it and donated it to the Muslim public. *(Ibn Adi, Ibn Asakir).*

The Narration of Ibn Asakir About the Incident

Bashir Aslami ؓ narrates that when the Muhajirin arrived in Madinah, the water did not agree with them. There was a well called Romah which was owned by a man from the Ghifar tribe but he sold a waterbag full of the water for a Mudd. Rasulullah ﷺ once said to him, "Sell me the well in exchange for a fountain in Jannah." However, he submitted, "O Rasulullah ﷺ! I have no source of income for my family and myself besides this well. I am therefore unable to sell it." When this news reached Uthman ؓ, he bought the well from the man for 35,000 Dirhams. He then approached Rasulullah ﷺ and said, "Rasulullah ﷺ"! If I buy the well, will you promise me the same fountain in Jannah that you had promised him?" "Certainly," replied Rasulullah ﷺ. Uthman ؓ then said, "I have already purchased it and I am donating it as Sadaqa for the Muslim public." *(Tabrani, Ibn Asakir in Muntakhab Kanzul Ummal)*

Talha ؓ Donates a 100,000 Dirhams in a Single Day

Su'da the wife of Talha ؓ reports that Talha ؓ gave away 100,000 Dirhams as Sadaqa on a single day and that he was delayed from going to the Masjid that day because she had to stitch 2 parts of his garment together. Although he gave so much in Sadaqa, he did not even possess an extra garment to wear. *(Abu Nu'aym in Hilya)*

The Sadaqa of Abdur Rahman bin Auf ؓ During the Lifetime of Rasulullah ﷺ

The narration has already passed in which it is mentioned that Abdur Rahman bin Auf ؓ donated half his wealth in the Path of Allah, which amounted to 4,000 Dirhams. Thereafter, he also donated 40,000 Dirhams and then 40,000 Dinars.

The Sadaqa of Abu Lubabah ؓ When Allah Accepted his Taubah

Sa'ib ؓ the son of Abu Lubabah ؓ reports from his father that when Allah forgave him, he approached Rasulullah ﷺ and said, "O Rasulullah ﷺ! I wish to leave the home amongst my people in which I committed the wrong and desire to give away all of my wealth as Sadaqa to Allah and His Rasul." Rasulullah ﷺ said, "O Abu Lubabah! It will suffice for you to give a third." Abu Lubabah ؓ gave away a 1/3ʳᵈ of wealth in Sadaqa. *(Hakim).*

Salman ؓ

Nu'man bin Humaid ؓ says, "I went with my uncle to visit Salman ؓ in Mada'in where he served as governor as he was making something with the leaves of a date palm. I heard him say "I buy the leaves for one Dirham and then sell them for 3 Dirhams after making something out of them. One Dirham I then use to buy more leaves, one Dirham I spend on my family and the other I give in Sadaqa. I shall not stop doing this even if Amirul Mu'minin Omar ؓ stops me." *(Ibn Sa'd).*

The Gift Uthman ؓ Gave to Rasulullah ﷺ During One of the Military Expeditions

Abu Mas'ood ؓ narrates, "We were with Rasulullah ﷺ on an expedition when we started experiencing extreme hardship. I could see the strains of hardship on the faces of the Muslims and I could also notice the happiness on the faces of the hypocrites who were happy to see the Muslims suffer. When Rasulullah ﷺ noticed this, he said, 'Allah shall provide sustenance before the sun sets.' Uthman ؓ knew that the words of Allah and His Rasul ﷺ were always true, so he bought 14 camels together with the loads of food they carried. He then sent 9 to Rasulullah ﷺ. When Rasulullah ﷺ saw them, he asked, 'What are these?' 'They are a gift to you from Uthman,' came the reply. The happiness on the face of Rasulullah ﷺ was then clearly noticeable, while the faces of the hypocrites displayed only unhappiness. I then saw Rasulullah ﷺ raise his hands so high to pray for Uthman ؓ that I could even the see the whiteness of his armpits. He made such Du'a for Uthman ؓ that I had never before or ever after heard him make for anyone else. He prayed to Allah to reward Uthman ؓ abundantly and to treat him graciously." *(Tabrani, Ibn Asakir in Muntakhab Kanzul Ummal, Haythami).*

The Statement of Abdullah bin Abbas ؓ Concerning the Virtues of Giving Gifts

Abdullah bin Abbas ؓ once stated, "For me to fulfill the necessities of a Muslim family for a month or for a week or for whatever period of time Allah pleases is more beloved to me than performing Hajj after Hajj. Buying a utensil for even a Daniq (1/6ᵗʰ of a Dirham) and giving it to my brother as a gift for the pleasure of Allah is more beloved to me than spending a Dinar in the Path of Allah." *(Abu Nu'aym in Hilya).*

The Statement of Ali ؓ About the Virtue of Feeding Others

Ali ؓ once mentioned, "To gather a few of my friends to share a Saa of food is more beloved to me than proceeding to the marketplace to purchase a slave and set him free." *(Bukhari in Adabul Mufrid, Ibnul Zanjway in Kanzul Ummal)*

The Narration of Jabir ؓ in this Regard

Abdul Wahid bin Ayman reports from his father that when some guests came to Jabir, he brought some bread and vinegar for them and said, "Eat this because I have heard Rasulullah ﷺ

say that vinegar is excellent gravy. Destroyed are those people who look down on what is offered to them and destroyed is the person who feels ashamed to offer his companions whatever is in his house." *(Bayhaqi in Shu'abul Iman, Kanzul Ummal, Ahmad, Tabrani in Awsat, Haythami)* Jabir ﷺ stated, "To look down on what is being served to him is sufficient to render a man sinful." *(Abu Ya'la, Haythami).*

The Narration of Anas ﷺ in this Regard

Humaid Taweel reports that when people came to visit Anas ﷺ. When he fell ill, he said to his slave, "Bring something for our guests though it be a piece of bread because I heard Rasulullah ﷺ say that good character is amongst the deeds that lead to Jannah." *(Tabrani in Targheeb wat Tarheeb, Haythami, Ibn Asakir).*

The Narration of Shaqiq bin Salama ﷺ in this Regard

Shaqiq bin Salama ﷺ reports that he once visited Salman Farsi with a friend. Salman ﷺ said to them, "Had Rasulullah ﷺ not forbidden us from imposing on ourselves, I would have certainly imposed on myself to entertain you." He tbrought for them some bread and salt because he had nothing else. Shaqiq ﷺ's friend said, "It would have been nice if there was some mint with the salt." Salman ﷺ pawned his jug to buy some mint and brought it. After the men had eaten, Shaqiq ﷺ's friend made a Du'a which meant, "All praise is for Allah Who has granted us contentment with the sustenance He has provided." Salman then remarked, "Had you been content with what Allah had provided for you, my jug would not have been pawned." Salman ﷺ also said, "Rasulullah ﷺ and Ali ﷺ had forbidden us from imposing on ourselves by providing for our guests what we do not have." *(Tabrani, Haythami)*

The Incident between Suhaib ﷺ and Omar ﷺ in this Regard

Hamza bin Suhaib reports that Suhaib ﷺ had the habit of feeding a lot of people. Omar ﷺ said to him, "O Suhaib! You feed too many people, which is extravagant behavior. To this, Suhaib ﷺ replied, "I have heard Rasulullah ﷺ say that the best of people are those who feed others and who reply to greetings. It is this that prompts me to feed people." *(Abu Nu'aym in Hilya)*

Rasulullah ﷺ Feeds People

Jabir ﷺ says, "I was once sitting at home when Rasulullah ﷺ passed by and motioned to me. I stood up and went to him. Taking me by the hand, Rasulullah ﷺ led me to the homes of one of his wives and he entered. He allowed me to enter and I entered the secluded area of the room where Rasulullah ﷺ asked, 'Is there anything for lunch?' 'Yes,' came the reply and we were served 3 pieces of bread that were placed in a container of a date palm. Rasulullah ﷺ placed a piece of bread before me, another before him and broke the third into two. Half he placed before himself and the other before me. He asked, 'Is there any gravy?' When he was informed that there was nothing besides some vinegar, he said, 'Bring it because it is an excellent gravy.'" *(Muslim, Abu Dawud, Tirmidhi, Nasai, Ibn Majah, Jam'ul Fawa'id).*

The Story of Uthman ﷺ in this Regard

Abdullah bin Salam ﷺ reports that Rasulullah ﷺ once saw Uthman ﷺ leading a camel laden with flour, butter and honey. Rasulullah ﷺ instructed Uthman ﷺ to make the camel sit down and when he did so, Rasulullah ﷺ asked for a stone pot. He put some flour, butter and honey in the pot and then had a fire made beneath it. When the food was cooked, Rasulullah ﷺ told the Sahabah to eat it and him also had some. He then said to them,

"This is what the Persians call 'Khabis'." *(Tabrani in Jam'ul Fawa'id, Haythami, Tabrani, Saghir, Awsat)*

The Narration of Abdullah bin Busr ﷺ in this Regard

Abdullah bin Busr ﷺ narrates that Rasulullah ﷺ had a large plate that had to be carried by 4 men. It was called "Gharra" and was brought out at midmorning after the Sahabah had performed their Duha (Chast) salah. Tharid (dish of gravy and meat mixed with bread) would be prepared in it and the Sahabah would gather around to eat. There were too many people, Rasulullah ﷺ would sit in a squat position. A Bedouin once asked, "What type of sitting position is this?" Rasulullah ﷺ said, "Allah has made me a generous slave and not an arrogant tyrant (this posture is one of humility)." Rasulullah ﷺ said to the Sahabah, "Eat from the sides and leave the center for last because it is where blessings descend." *(Abu Dawud in Mishkatul Masabih)*

An Incident of Abu Bakr ﷺ and His Guests

Abdur Rahman ﷺ the son of Abu Bakr ﷺ reports, "It was the practice of my father to engage in conversation with Rasulullah ﷺ at nights. Therefore, when we received some visitors one day, he was proceeding to see Rasulullah ﷺ as usual when he said to me, 'O Abdur Rahman! Take care of the visitors and feed them without waiting for me.' When evening arrived, I took their food to them but they refused to eat saying, 'We shall not eat until the man of the house eats with us.' I said to them, 'My father is a strict man and I fear that he may beat me if I have not fed you.' However, they still refused to eat. When my father arrived, the guests were his first concern and he asked the members of the household, 'Have you taken care of the guests?' 'We have not yet seen to them,' came the reply. 'Had I not instructed Abdur Rahman to see to them?' he asked. I had made myself scarce by then as he shouted, 'Abdur Rahman!' I remained in hiding and he again shouted, 'You scamp! In the name of Allah am I commanding you to come here if you can hear my voice!' Then I went to him and said, 'By Allah! It was no fault of mine. You can even ask your guests that I had brought them their food but they refused to eat until you arrive.' My father then said to them, 'Why will you people not accept the food we give you? I swear by Allah that I shall not eat anything tonight.' The guests responded by also swearing, By Allah! We shall also have none of it until you do.' Abu Bakr ﷺ then said, 'I have never known a night worse than this! Why will you not accept the food we give you? Nevertheless, the first oath I took not to eat was from Saitan. Bring the food.' When the food was brought, he recited Bismillah and ate. The guests then followed suit." The following morning, Abu Bakr ﷺ went to Rasulullah ﷺ and said, "O Rasulullah ﷺ! While my guests fulfilled their oath, I breached mine." He then proceeded to inform Rasulullah ﷺ about the incident. Rasulullah ﷺ said, "In fact, you are better at fulfilling oaths than them and a better person than they are." The narrator of the Hadith says, "No news has reached me about whether Abu Bakr ﷺ gave Kaffara for his oath or not." Abu Bakr ﷺ obviously did give Kaffara because according to the consensus of the Ulema, Kaffara is binding in such a situation.

Omar ﷺ Feeds People

Aslam reports, "I once informed Omar ﷺ that there was a blind camel amongst the pack animals. He said, 'Give it to some family who can derive some benefit from it.' 'But it is blind,' I submitted. He said, 'They can tie it to the others in the caravan and it will follow the rest.' I again asked, 'But how will it graze?' Omar ﷺ then asked, 'Is it from amongst the animals collected as

Jizya or from the animals collected as Zakah?' When I informed him that it was from amongst those collected as Jizya, he said, 'By Allah! You people intend to eat it because anyone may eat from such an animal, unlike the animals of Zakah.' I then said to him, 'I am not just saying this but it really has the markings of the Jizya animals on it.' Omar ؓ then issued the order that the camel should be slaughtered. He kept with him 9 plates and whenever some fruit or delicacy came to him, he would always place some of it on each plate and send then to the 9 wives of Rasulullah ﷺ. He would also ensure that he sent the plate of his daughter Hafsa ؓ last so that if there were any defects, it would be in her share and none could accuse him of nepotism. He then put some of the camel's meat into these plates and sent them to the wives of Rasulullah ﷺ. Thereafter, he gave instructions for the remaining meat to be cooked. When it was cooked, he invited the Muhajirin and the Ansar to share it." *(Malik in Jm'ul Fawa'id)*

The Practice of Talha ؓ and the Statement of Rasulullah ﷺ

Salama bin Akwa ؓ reports that when Talha bin Ubaidullah ؓ purchased a well at the foot of a mountain, he invited people for a meal. It was then that Rasulullah ﷺ said, "You, O Talha, are 'Fayyadh' an extremely generous person." *(Hasan bin Suniyan, Abu Nu'aym in Ma'rifa, Muntakhab Kanzul Ummal)*

Ja'far bin Abu Talib ؓ Feeds People

Abu Hurairah ؓ says, "The person who most benefited the poor was Ja'far bin Abu Talib ؓ. He would take us home and feed us with whatever he had in his house. In fact, when there was nothing he would break open the butter container so that we could lick whatever butter remained." *(Ibn Sa'd)*

The Incident of Suhaib ؓ with Rasulullah ﷺ

Suhaib ؓ says, "I prepared some food for Rasulullah ﷺ and went to invite him while he sat amongst a group of Sahabah. I stood in front of him and gestured to him to come to eat. He gestured back to ask whether the others could also join us. When I indicated that they could not, he remained silent. I remained standing where I was. When Rasulullah ﷺ again looked my way, I gestured yet again for him to come and eat. For the second time, Rasulullah ﷺ asked whether the others could join us and again I repeated that they could not. This happened 2 or 3 times until I agreed that they should also join us. Rasulullah ﷺ brought the others along and they all ate. Although it was only a little food that I had prepared for Rasulullah ﷺ, there was still food left over after all had eaten to their fill" *(Abu Nu'aym in Hilya)*

Abdullah bin Omar ؓ Feeds People

Muhammad bin Qais reports that Abdullah bin Omar ؓ never ate without a poor person to join him. This eventually injured his health because the poor people often finished the food, leaving him hungry. His wife made for him a drink from dates, which she would give him whenever he ate to replenish his strength. *Abu Bakr bin Hafs* reports that Abdullah bin Omar ؓ would eat when an orphan was present at his tablecloth. *(Abu Nu'aym in Hilya)*.

An Incident with an Orphan

Hasan reports that Abdullah bin Omar ؓ ate lunch or dinner (the Arabs never ate breakfast), he would invite an orphan from the vicinity. When he sat down to lunch one day, he sent for an orphan, but none could be found. After his lunch, he would drink some barley cereal. The orphan then arrived after the family had eaten the lunch and the cereal was still in Abdullah bin Omar ؓ's hand. He gave the cup to the orphan saying, "Take this. I do not think that you have lost out completely."

The narration of Maymoon bin Mahran about Abdullah bin Omar ؓ

Maymoon bin Mahran reports that some people approached the wife of Abdullah bin Omar ؓ concerning him. They said to her, "Have you no mercy for the old man? He is growing weaker by the day, why don't you feed him properly?" She responded by saying, "What am I to do? Whenever we prepare some food for him, he invites someone to eat it up." His wife then sent some food to the poor people who usually sat on the path that Abdullah bin Omar ؓ took from the Masjid. She then gave them instructions not to sit by the roadside as he passed. When Abdullah bin Omar ؓ returned home, he asked for certain poor people to be brought to eat with him because he did not find them by the roadside that day. However, when his wife had sent food to them, she had also given them instructions not to come when Abdullah bin Omar ؓ called for them. When they failed to turn up, Abdullah bin Omar ؓ said to his family, "Do you wish that I should not eat tonight?!" That night he did not have anything for dinner. *(Abu Nu'aym in Hilya, Ibn Sa'd)*

A Similar Incident When He was at Juhfa

Abu Ja'far Qari says, "My master Abdullah bin Ayash bin Abu Rabi'ah Makhzumi instructed me to proceed with Abdullah bin Omar ؓ on a journey to serve him. Abdullah bin Omar ؓ camped at an oasis, he would invite the local people to share his meals. His eldest sons would also share the meals. Because of the large number of people each person would have only 2 or 3 morsels to eat. When he arrived in Juhfa and the locals arrived to eat, a black boy who was scarcely dressed also came along. Abdullah bin Omar ؓ called him to eat, he said, 'I cannot find any place to sit.' The people were sitting close together so I saw Abdullah bin Omar ؓ move a bit from his place so that the boy sat against his chest." *(Abu Nu'aym in Hilya)*

The Practice of Abdullah bin Omar ؓ on His Journeys

Abu Ja'far Qari says, "I accompanied Abdullah bin Omar ؓ on a journey from Makkah to Madinah. Around his large dish containing Thareed (Dish of gravy and meat mixed with pieces of bread), his sons, his companions and everyone else who presented themselves there would eat. Because of the large crowd some would have to eat standing. He had a camel that carried 2 filled containers, one with Nabeedh (water in which dates are left overnight to lend its sweetness) and the other with plain water. Every person received a cup of barley cereal with the Nabeedh, which would satiate him completely." *(Ibn Sa'd)*

The Narration of Ma'n About Abdullah bin Omar ؓ

Ma'n reports that when Abdullah bin Omar ؓ's meals were prepared and a well-off man passed by, he would not invite him. However, his sons and nephews would invite such a person. On the other hand, if a poor person passed Abdullah bin Omar ؓ, he would invite the person while his sons and nephews would not. Concerning this, he would say, "They invite those who do not want the food and leave out those who want it." *(Ibn Sa'd)*

Abdullah bin Amr bin Al Aas ؓ Feeds People

Sulaiman bin Rabi'ah reports that he once performed Hajj during the Khilafah of Mu'awiya ؓ. With him was Muntasir bin Harith and a group of Qurra from Basra. They were determined not to return home until they had the opportunity to meet a distinguished companion of Rasulullah ﷺ who would relate some

Ahadeeth to them. They kept enquiring until they were informed that Abdullah bin Amr bin Al Aas ؓ was staying over in the lower part of Makkah. When they went to see him, they found a large array of 300 camels. 100 camels were riding camels, while the other 200 were laden with goods. Upon enquiry, they were informed that the contingent belonged to Abdullah bin Amr ؓ. In surprise, they asked, "Does all of this belong to him?! We were told that he is an extremely modest person so why does he need all of this?" They were then informed that everything was not for his personal use, but that the 100 riding camels were to transport his brothers while the goods on the 200 camel were for his guests and the people of the various towns he passed by on his travels. When the group expressed surprise, they were told, "Do not be so surprised! Abdullah bin Amr ؓ is a wealthy man who sees it as a right to others that he should have ample provisions to cater for the people who come to meet him." The group then asked where he could be found and they were told that he is in the Masjidul Haram. They searched for him, they found him sitting behind the Kabah. He was a short man with watery eyes whose shoes hung at his left side. He wore 2 sheets of cloth and a turban without a sewn upper garment. *(Abu Nu'aym in Hilya, Ibn Sa'd)*

Sa'd bin Ubadah ؓ feeds People and an Incident with Rasulullah ﷺ

Sa'd bin Ubadah ؓ narrates that he went to Rasulullah ﷺ with a large utensil full of camel's brains. Rasulullah ﷺ said, "O Abu Thabit! What is this'?" Sa'd ؓ replied, "I swear by Allah who sent you with the truth! I have slaughtered 40 camels and would like to feed you with these brains until you are full." Rasulullah ﷺ ate it and made Du'a. *(Ibn Asakir in Kanzul Ummal)*

Narration of Anas ؓ about the Du'a that Rasulullah ﷺ made for Sa'd ؓ

Anas ؓ narrates that Sa'd bin Ubadah ؓ once invited Rasulullah ﷺ for a meal. When Rasulullah ﷺ arrived at Sa'd ؓ's house, Sa'd ؓ brought some dates and bread, which Rasulullah ﷺ ate. He then brought a cup of milk which Rasulullah ﷺ drank. Rasulullah ﷺ then prayed, "May the righteous always eat your food, may fasting people end their fasts with you and may the angels always pray for your forgiveness. O Allah! Shower Your choicest mercies on the family of Sa'd bin Ubada." *(Ibn Asakir in Kanzul Ummal)*. Anas ؓ states that Sa'd ؓ served some sesame seeds and dates to Rasulullah ﷺ. *(Kanzul Ummal)*

Another Incident of His Hospitability

Urwa ؓ reports that he once saw Sa'd bin Ubadah ؓ announce from his house, "Whoever wishes to eat fat or meat should go to Sa'd bin Ubadah!" I then also saw his son doing the same after his father's death. He narrates further that after the death of the son he was once walking in the streets of Madinah when Abdullah bin Omar ؓ passed by him and as he was preceding to his property in the upper part of Madinah, Abdullah bin Omar ؓ said, "Dear youngster! Go and see whether there is anyone announcing from the house of Sa'd bin Ubada." When Urwa ؓ saw that there was no one announcing and reported back, Abdullah bin Omar ؓ said, "You are right none could be as generous as that father and son." *(Ibn Sa'd)*

Abu Shu'aib Ansari ؓ Feeds People and an Incident with Rasulullah ﷺ

Abu Mas'ood Ansari ؓ reports that there was a Sahabi from amongst the Ansar who was called Abu Shu'aib ؓ. He had a slave who was an expert in cooking meat. He once instructed his slave to prepare a meal so that he could invite Rasulullah ﷺ and four other people. He then invited Rasulullah ﷺ and four others. However, another person came along with them. When they arrived at the house Rasulullah ﷺ said to Abu Shu'aib, "You have invited 5 of us but this person has come along with us. You may permit him to join or leave him out." Abu Shu'aib ؓ said, "He is most welcome." *(Bukhari)*. Another narration states that when Abu Shu'aib ؓ once saw Rasulullah ﷺ, he noticed the sign of hunger on Rasulullah ﷺ's face. He then said to his slave, "How terrible! Cook some food for 5 people." *(Muslim)*.

A Tailor Invites Rasulullah ﷺ for a Meal That he Prepared

Anas ؓ narrates, "A tailor once invited Rasulullah ﷺ to share a meal that he had prepared. I accompanied Rasulullah ﷺ for the meal. He served barley bread to Rasulullah ﷺ and gravy made of pumpkin and strips of meat. I then saw Rasulullah ﷺ search for the pieces of pumpkin on the sides of the plate. Since that day, I had always loved pumpkin." *(Muslim, Bukhari)*

Jabir bin Abdullah ؓ Feeds People During the Battle of Khandaq

Jabir ؓ narrates, "As we were busy digging the trench for the battle of Khandaq, an extremely hard boulder became an obstacle. When the Sahabah reported to Rasulullah ﷺ that the boulder posed an obstacle in the digging, he said, 'I am coming down there.' Rasulullah ﷺ then stood up with a stone tied to his belly to suppress the hunger because we had already gone 3 days without even tasting any food. Rasulullah ﷺ then took up a pickaxe and with one strike, reduced it to a heap of dust. I then asked permission from Rasulullah ﷺ to go home and when I reached home I said to my wife, 'I have seen such hunger on Rasulullah ﷺ that I am unable to bear. Do you have anything to eat?' She replied, 'I have some barley and a kid goat.' I then slaughtered the kid as she ground the barley. We placed the meat in a pot to cook and when I went to call Rasulullah ﷺ, the dough had already risen and the pot was on the fire with the food almost cooked. I said, 'O Rasulullah ﷺ! I have a little food, so why don't you and one or two persons come?' When Rasulullah ﷺ asked me how much food there was, I informed him accordingly. He said, 'That is plenty and most excellent. Tell your wife not to take the pot off the fire and not to take the bread out of the oven until I arrive.' He then told the Sahabah to stand up to join in the meal and the Muhajirin, the Ansar and all with them stood up."

When Jabir ؓ came to his wife, he said, "Oh dear! Rasulullah ﷺ has come with the Muhajirin, the Ansar and everyone else!" She asked, "Did Rasulullah ﷺ ask you about this'?" Jabir ؓ confirmed that Rasulullah ﷺ had asked him and she was therefore content that Rasulullah ﷺ would make further arrangements. When the Sahabah reached the house, Rasulullah ﷺ said to them, "Enter the house, but do not crowd it." Rasulullah ﷺ then started breaking the bread into pieces, placed meat on them and served them to the Sahabah. Whenever Rasulullah ﷺ took anything from the pot or the oven, he covered them again. Rasulullah ﷺ continued breaking the bread and dishing out the food until everyone was full and there was still plenty leftovers. He then said to the lady, "Eat from this and give some to others because hunger had afflicted everyone." *(Bukhari)*. A more detailed narration states that when Rasulullah ﷺ found out about the amount of food, he addressed all the Muslims saying, "Come to Jabir's place." Jabir ؓ says, "Such extreme embarrassment overcame me that Allah alone knows. I said to myself, 'Rasulullah ﷺ is coming with such a large group whereas I have prepared only one Saa of barley and a kid goat!' When I came to my wife, I said, 'You are soon to be embarrassed! Rasulullah ﷺ is coming with everyone digging the trench!' 'Has Rasulullah ﷺ asked you how much food you have?' she asked. When I confirmed that he did, she assured me, 'Then Allah and His Rasul ﷺ know best what they intend.' A tremendous worry then disappeared from my mind." Rasulullah ﷺ then arrived and said to Jabir's wife, "Continue what you are doing but hand the meat over to me." Rasulullah ﷺ then broke the bread into the food and served the meat. As he did this, he kept covering the bread and the meat. In this manner, he continued serving food to the Sahabah until they were all full and both the pot and the oven were as full as they had ever been. Thereafter, Rasulullah ﷺ said to the lady, "Eat and give others." She continued eating and giving others from there the entire day. *(Bayhaqi in Dala'ilun Nubuwah)* Another narration *(Ibn Abi Shaiba in Al Bidayah wan Nihayah)* states that the Sahabah numbered 300 and another narration states 800 on that occasion. In another narration, Jabir ﷺ says, "Rasulullah ﷺ announced, 'O people digging the trench! Jabir ﷺ has prepared a meal, so all of you should come!' Rasulullah ﷺ then said to me, 'Do not take the pot off the fire and do not bake the bread until I arrive.' I arrived home as Rasulullah ﷺ led the others. When I got to my wife, I said, 'Oh dear! I did exactly as you said but things seem to have gone wrong.' When Rasulullah ﷺ arrived she gave him the dough and he mixed some of his blessed saliva in it and made Du'a for blessings. Rasulullah ﷺ said to me, 'Call another lady to bake with you and dish out from the pot without taking it off the fire.' Although the Sahabah present there numbered 1,000, I swear by Allah that they ate so much that they had to leave the food and go away. Even then the pot was still cooking with food as it had been and the oven was baking bread as it had been." *(Bukhari, Muslim).*

The Narration of Tabrani About Such an Incident

Jabir ﷺ says, "My mother cooked some food and asked me to invite Rasulullah ﷺ for a meal. I went to Rasulullah ﷺ and whispered to him, 'My mother has cooked something.' Rasulullah ﷺ then told the Sahabah to stand up and 50 of them came along. Sitting at the door, Rasulullah ﷺ told them to enter 10 at a time. They all ate to their fill and the food still remained as it had been." *(Tabrani, Haythami)*

Abu Talha ﷺ feeds people and an incident with Rasulullah ﷺ

Anas ﷺ says, "Abu Talha ﷺ once said to his wife (my mother) Ummu Sulaim ﷺ, 'I have heard Rasulullah ﷺ's voice go very weak and I know that it is because of extreme hunger. Do you have any food with you?' 'Yes,' she replied and then took out a few loafs of barley bread. She wrapped the bread with a part of her scarf, put it beneath my clothes and then wrapped the rest of the scarf around me. Thereafter she sent me off to Rasulullah ﷺ. I went with the bread and found Rasulullah ﷺ sitting in the Masjid with some people. When I stood by them, Rasulullah ﷺ asked, 'Has Abu Talha sent you?' 'Yes,' I replied. 'Is it for food?' Rasulullah ﷺ enquired further. When I again replied in the affirmative, Rasulullah ﷺ said to those with him, 'Stand up.' They then all accompanied Rasulullah ﷺ to the house. Rasulullah ﷺ walked to the house and I walked in front of them. When I reached Abu Talha ﷺ, I informed him about the situation and he said, 'O Ummu Sulaim! Rasulullah ﷺ is coming with many people and we have nothing to feed them.' She replied, 'Allah and His Rasul ﷺ know best, we have no cause of concern.'" Abu Talha ﷺ then went to receive Rasulullah ﷺ on the road and Rasulullah ﷺ walked with him until they both entered the house. Rasulullah ﷺ then said, "Bring whatever you have, O Ummu Sulaim." When she brought the bread, Rasulullah ﷺ instructed that it be broken into small pieces and that Ummu Sulaim ﷺ squeeze out from her container whatever butter was left to make some gravy. Rasulullah ﷺ then recited something on the food and said, "Allow 10 people in." When they were allowed in, they ate to their fill and then left. Rasulullah ﷺ asked for another 10 to be allowed in, who also ate to their fill before leaving. Rasulullah ﷺ again asked another 10 persons to come in and in this manner, everyone ate to their fill. In total, they numbered 70 or 80 men. *(Muslim, Bukhari, Ahmad, Abu Ya'la, Baghawi, Al Bidayah wan Nihayah)* Another narration states that there were approximately 100 men. *(Tabrani, Abu Ya'la, Haythami).*

Ash'ath bin Qais Kindi ﷺ Feeds People During his Walima Celebration

Qais bin Abu Hazim reports that after re-entering the fold of Islam after leaving it, Ash'ath ﷺ was brought as a prisoner to Abu Bakr ﷺ who was then the Khalifa. Because he had accepted Islam again, Abu Bakr ﷺ opened his shackles and married him to his sister. Ash'ath ﷺ then drew his sword and entered the camel market where he hamstrung every camel he saw. The people started shouting, "Ash'ath has become a Kafir!" When he completed what he was doing, he threw his sword aside and said, "By Allah! I have not become a Kafir. What happened was that a great man (Abu Bakr ﷺ) married his sister to me and had I been in my area, we would have celebrated a Walima unlike this. O people of Madinah! Slaughter and eat these camels. O owners of these camels! Come and collect the price of these camels from me." *(Tabrani in Isabah, Majma'uz Zawa'id, Haythami).*

Abu Barzah ﷺ Feeds People

Hasan bin Hakim reports from his mother that Abu Barzah ﷺ kept a large dish of Thareed ready every morning and evening for the widows, orphans and the poor. *(Ibn Sa'd)*

The Narration of Talha bin Amr ﷺ Entertaining People who Visited Madinah Tayyiba

Talha bin Amr ﷺ says, "Whenever a person came to meet Rasulullah ﷺ in Madinah, he stayed with someone he knew. If he did not know anyone, he stayed with the men of Suffa. I was amongst those who stayed on the Suffa ﷺ. I was coupled with another person and each day there came from Rasulullah ﷺ a Mudd of dates for every 2 persons. One day after Rasulullah ﷺ had completed the salah, one of us called out to him saying, 'O Rasulullah ﷺ! The dates have burnt our stomachs and our shawls are in tatters.' Rasulullah ﷺ turned towards the pulpit, mounted it and then praised Allah before recounting the difficulties that his people had given him. He said, 'There was a time when my companion and I passed more than 10 nights without anything to eat besides the fruit of acacia trees. We then came to our Ansar brothers after Hijra and because dates were their staple diet, they saw to our needs by giving us dates to eat. By Allah! If I could feed you bread and meat, I would have definitely done so. However, you would probably see a time soon when your clothes will be made of a fabric similar to that used to drape the Kabah and you will be served large dishes of food every morning and evening.'" *(Abu Nu'aym in Hilya, Tabrani, Bazzar, Haythami, Ibn Jareer in Kanzul Ummal, Ahmad, Hakim, Ibn Hibban in Isabah)*

The Narration of Fudalah Laythi ﷺ in this Regard

Fudalah Laythi ﷺ says, "Whenever a person came to meet Rasulullah ﷺ in Madinah, he stayed with someone he knew. If he did not know anyone, he stayed on the Suffa. Because I knew no one, I was amongst those who stayed on the Suffa. One Friday, someone called out saying, 'O Rasulullah ﷺ! The dates are burning our stomachs.' Rasulullah ﷺ said, 'A time will soon come when those of you living then will be served large platters of food every morning and evening and you will be clothed as the Kabah is draped with expensive fabric." *(Tabrani, Haythami)*

The Narration of Salama bin Akwa ؓ in this Regard

Salama bin Akwa ؓ narrates that after the salah; Rasulullah ﷺ would turn to the Sahabah and say to them. Each of you should take as many guests as he can host. Some would take home one person, others two and others three. Rasulullah ﷺ would then take those who remained. *(Bayhaqi in Kanzul Ummal)*

The Narration of Muhammad bin Sirin ؓ in this Regard

Muhammad bin Sirin reports that in the evenings Rasulullah ﷺ used to distribute the men of Suffa ؓ amongst the rest of the Sahabah. Some would take one person, others would take two, others three and in a like manner, some would even take 10 persons. Sa'd bin Ubadah ؓ would return to his family every night with 80 men of Suffa for supper. *(Abu Nu'aym in Hilya, Ibn Abi Dunya, Ibn Asakir in Muntakhab Kanzul Ummal)*

Rasulullah ﷺ Invites All the Men of Suffa

Abu Hurairah ؓ narrates, "Rasulullah ﷺ once called out, 'O Abu Hirr!' 'I am at your service, O Rasulullah ﷺ,' I responded. He said, 'Go to the men of Suffa and invite them all.' The men of Suffa were the guests of Islam who had neither any wealth nor family. Whenever Rasulullah ﷺ received any Sadaqa, he would send it all to them without taking any of it. However, whenever he would receive a gift, Rasulullah ﷺ would send for them. He would then partake of it and share it with them." *(Abu Nu'aym in Hilya, Bukhari, Muslim)*

The Narration of Abu Dhar ؓ Concerning the Manner in Which the Men of Suffa were Entertained

Abu Dhar ؓ says, "I was amongst the men of Suffa. Every evening we would go to Rasulullah ﷺ's door and he would instruct someone who would take one of us as his guest. There would always be 10 persons left over, sometimes more and sometimes less. They would then join Rasulullah ﷺ when his supper was brought. When we finished eating, Rasulullah ﷺ would say, 'You may sleep in the Masjid.' Rasulullah ﷺ once passed by me as I was asleep on my face lying on my belly. Rasulullah ﷺ pushed me with his foot and said, 'O Jundub! What is this manner of lying down?! This is how Saitan lies down.'" *(Abu Nu'aym in Hilya)*

The Narration of Ibn Qais ؓ in this Regard

Tugfa bin Qais ؓ narrates, "In compliance with the instruction of Rasulullah ﷺ, some Sahabah took one person from the men of the Sulfa as his guest while others took two and I was eventually left as one of four other men. Rasulullah ﷺ told us to proceed with him and we accompanied him to Aisha ؓ. When Rasulullah ﷺ asked her to give us something to eat and drink, she served some coarsely ground wheat cooked with meat. After we had eaten it, she served us a sweet dish made of dates, which was of brownish color. After we had eaten it, Rasulullah ﷺ asked Aisha ؓ for something to drink and she brought a small cup of milk from which we all drank. Rasulullah ﷺ then said, 'If you please, you may either spend the night here or proceed to the Masjid.' We told him that we would rather go to the Masjid. As I was lying in the Masjid on my stomach, someone started nudging me with his foot saying, 'This is a manner of lying down that Allah abhors.' When I looked up (to see who it was), I saw that it was Rasulullah ﷺ." *(Abu Nu'aym in Hilya).*

Entertaining Those who Intended Accepting Islam

Jahja Ghifari ؓ says, "I arrived in Madinah with a group from my tribe with the intention of accepting Islam. When we presented ourselves before Rasulullah ﷺ and greeted him, he said to the Sahabah, 'Each person should take the hand of the person sitting next to him and take the person home for meals.' When the Sahabah did as told, there was none left in the Masjid besides Rasulullah ﷺ and myself. No one approached me to take me for a meal because I was large in size and very tall. Rasulullah ﷺ took me home where he milked a goat for me. When he brought the milk to me, I drank it all up. Rasulullah ﷺ eventually milked 7 goats and I drank up all the milk. He then served a pot of food and I ate this as well. Ummu Ayman ؓ commented, 'May Allah starve the person who has starved Rasulullah ﷺ!' 'Be quiet, O Ummu Ayman!' said Rasulullah ﷺ, 'He has only eaten the sustenance destined for him. Allah shall provide our sustenance.'" Early next morning, Jahja Ghifari ؓ and his companions gathered and started discussing what food they had been served the previous night. He said, "7 goats were milked for me and I drank all the milk. A pot of gravy as then served and I ate it all as well." After they had all performed the Maghrib salah, Rasulullah ﷺ again announced, "Each person should take the hand of the person sitting next to him and take the person home for meals." Jahja ؓ narrates further, "When the Sahabah did as told, there was none left in the Masjid besides Rasulullah ﷺ and myself. No one approached me to take me for a meal because I was large in size and very tall. Rasulullah ﷺ took me home where he milked a goat for me. When he brought the milk to me, I drank it and was full. Ummu Ayman ؓ asked, 'O Rasulullah ﷺ! Is this not the same guest we had last night?' Rasulullah ﷺ replied, "He is the same man. Tonight he has eaten with the intestine of a Mu'min whereas before this he had been eating with the intestine of a Kafir. While a Kafir eats to fill 7 intestines, a Mu'min eats to fill only one.'" *(Tabrani, Abu Nu'aym in Kanzul Ummal, Ibn Abi Shaiba in Isabah, Bazzar, Abu Ya'la in Majma'uz Zawa'id, Haythami)*

Feeding the Men of Suffa During Ramadhan

Wathila bin Asqa ؓ says, "We were amongst the men of Suffa when Ramadhan arrived and we all fasted. Whenever the time came to end the fast, one of the Sahabah who had pledged allegiance to Rasulullah ﷺ would approach one of us and take him for meals. However, there arrived an evening when no one came to us. We then spent the morning hungry) Again the following evening, no one arrived to take us for meals so we approached Rasulullah ﷺ and informed him of the situation. Rasulullah ﷺ then sent a message to each of his wives to ask if they had any food with them. Every wife swore on oath that there was not even enough food in her home that evening to feed a single person. Rasulullah ﷺ then asked us to gather around and when we did so, he prayed to Allah saying, 'O Allah! I beg You for Your grace and mercy, for it is only in Your power and none other has control over it.' Rasulullah ﷺ had hardly completed when someone asked permission to enter. He brought a roasted goat and many loaves of bread. By the instruction of Rasulullah ﷺ, the food was placed before us and we all ate until we were full. Rasulullah ﷺ then said to us, 'We had asked Allah for His grace and His mercy. This food was from His grace and He has kept His mercy in store for us with Him for the Hereafter."' *(Bayhaqi in Al Bidayah wan Nihayah)*

The Narration of Abdur Rahman bin Abu Bakr

Abdur Rahman bin Abu Bakr reports, "Because the men of Suffa were poor people, Rasulullah once said to the Sahabah, 'Whoever has food for 2 persons should take 3 persons for meals and whoever has food for 4 should take 5 or 6 people.' While Rasulullah took 10 person home, my father Abu Bakr brought 3 people whereas my mother, my father and I were there." One of the narrators said, "I cannot remember whether he also said 'my mother, my father and I were there together with my wife and a servant who worked at both my father's house and mine.'" The food therefore had to suffice for 5 people at home in addition to the 3 guests). Abu Bakr ate with Rasulullah and stayed him until the Isha salah. He then returned to Rasulullah after the Isha salah and waited until Rasulullah had eaten. He only returned home after a considerable portion of the night had already passed thinking that his family would have already fed the guests. His wife said to him, "What has kept you from seeing to your guests?" "Have you not given them their supper yet?" he said in surprise. His wife replied, "They refuse to eat until you arrive. Despite our insistence, they refused to eat and had their way." Abdur Rahman hid himself away for fear of his father and Abu Bakr shouted at him, "You scamp!" After much scolding, Abu Bakr told the guests to eat but in anger swore that he would not touch the food. The guests then swore that they would not eat until he did. When his anger cooled, Abu Bakr then started eating with them. Abdur Rahman reports further. He says, "By Allah! Each time we took a morsel, more food appeared beneath it, making it more than it was. When everyone had eaten to their fill, there was more food than there had been initially. Abu Bakr saw that there was still food remaining and even more than there had been, he exclaimed addressing his wife, 'O daughter of the Banu Firas tribe! What is happening?!' She said, 'By the coolness of my eyes! It is 3 times more than it had been!' Abu Bakr then ate some more saying, 'That my oath had been from Saitan.' After eating another morsel, he took the rest to Rasulullah and the food stayed there until the morning. There had been a treaty between us Muslims and a tribe of Kuffar which had expired. Twelve of us had been appointed as commanders of an army marching against the tribe and each one commanded a large group of men. Only Allah knows how many men were under each person's command. Nevertheless, every person ate from the food. " The Muslims were divided into 12 groups. *(Bukhari, Muslim in Al Bidayah wan Nihayah)*

The Story of Qais bin Sa'd

Yahya bin Abdul Aziz narrates that Sa'd bin Ubadah would proceed in Jihad one year and his son Qais would proceed the following year. It was while Sa'd was once out on a military expedition that Rasulullah received a large group of guests. When Sa'd heard about this, he said, "If Qais is truly my son, he would say to my slave, 'O Nistas! Give me the keys to my father's storehouse so that I may take for Rasulullah what he needs to feed his guests.' Nistas will then say, 'First produce a letter from your father to authorize it.' Qais will then punch Nistas on the nose and take the keys from him to provide Rasulullah with whatever he needs." Matters transpired exactly as Sa'd had mentioned and Qais took for Rasulullah 100 Wasaq of provisions. *(Dar Qutni in Kitabul Askiya, Isabah)*

Feeding Bedouins During a Drought

Maymuna bint Harith one of Rasulullah's wives reports, "The Bedouins always came to Madinah and Rasulullah would instruct someone to take a Bedouin by the hand as his guest and serve him a meal. It was during a year of drought when a Bedouin came to Rasulullah one night. All Rasulullah had was a little food and some milk. The Bedouin ate everything without leaving anything for Rasulullah. Rasulullah brought Bedouin for a night or 2 and he always ate everything. I therefore said, 'May Allah not bless this Bedouin who eats the food of Rasulullah, leaving him without any.' Rasulullah then brought the Bedouin another night after the man had accepted Islam and he ate only a little. When I mentioned this to Rasulullah, he said, 'While a Kafir eats to fill 7 intestines, a Mu'min eats to fill only one.'" *(Tabrani, Haythami, Ahmad)*.

The Practice of Amirul Mu'minin Omar during the year of drought

Aslam reports that during the 'Year of Ashes (destruction)', Arabs from all over collected in Madinah. Omar appointed certain persons to go to these people and distribute food and gravy amongst them. These persons were Yazid bin Ukht Namir, Miswar bin Makhrama, Abdur Rahman bin Abdul Qari and Abdullah bin Utba bin Mas'ood. Each one of them was appointed to a particular sector of Madinah and they reported back to Omar every evening. The Bedouins were stationed from the beginning of Thaniatul Wada up to the Ra'ij mountain and the areas of the Banu Haritha, the Banu Abdil Ash'hal, the Banu Quraiza tribes. They even extended to the Baqe cemetery and some of them reached up close to the area of the Banu Salama tribe. They had virtually surrounded Madinah. One night after the people had their supper with Omar, he gave instructions that the people who eat with him should be counted. When they were counted the following night, they numbered 700. Omar then instructed that the families, the ill and the children who were unable to attend should also be counted. When they were counted, they were found to number 40,000. After a few nights, the numbers increased. When Omar had them counted, those eating with him numbered 10,000 and the rest numbered 50,000. This continued until Allah sent the rains.

Aslam narrates further, "After the rains had fallen, I saw Omar appoint a man from every area to send the Bedouin people back to their rural areas and to also provide them with transport and provisions to get back. In fact, I saw Omar personally engage in this exercise. Many deaths occurred amongst the people stricken by the drought and I estimate that $2/3^{rd}$ of them perished while only $1/3^{rd}$ remained alive. The people tending the large pots of Omar used to start preparing the Kurkur (dish prepared with coarsely ground grain) before dawn and continued well into the morning. They then served it to ill after which they added butter and prepared another dish. According to the instructions of Omar, olive oil used to be boiled in large amount to eliminate its inherent sharpness and heat. Bread was then broken into the oil to make a type of Thareed. By eating too much of oil, the Arabs generally suffered from fever because they were used to using butter instead of oil. During the Year of Ashes, Omar ate nothing from the homes of his children or his wives. He ate only what was prepared for the suffering people until Allah gave life back to the people by sending the rains." *(Ibn Sa'd)*

The Narration of Firas Daylami in this Regard

Firas Daylami reports that from the camels that Amr bin Al Aas sent from Egypt, Omar would have 20 slaughtered every day for his table to feed those who were stricken by the drought. *(Ibn Sa'd in Muntakhab Kanzul Ummal)*

The Story of Omar ﷺ With a Poor Family

Aslam reports that Omar ﷺ was going on his usual rounds one night when he came across a woman in a house surrounded by crying children. The woman had a pot of water boiling over the fire. Omar ﷺ went to the door asked, "O servant of Allah! Why are these children crying?" The woman replied, "Because they are hungry." Omar ﷺ asked further, "What is in the pot?" "Only water to soothe the children so that they may go to sleep in the belief that food is being prepared for them." Omar ﷺ wept and went straight to the public treasury where he took a sack and put in it some flour, fat, butter, dates, clothing and some money. When the sack was full, he said to Aslam, "Put this sack on my back, Aslam." "Please, O Amirul Mu'minin! Let me carry the sack," pleaded Aslam. Omar ﷺ remarked, "Never! I shall carry the sack because I will be questioned about these people in the Hereafter." Aslam most reluctantly placed the bag on Omar ﷺ's back, who carried it to the woman's home. Omar ﷺ put a little flour and some dates and fat in the pan and began to stir it. He also blew into the fire to kindle it. Aslam says, "I saw the smoke passing through his thick beard. When the food was ready, he himself served it to the family and they ate to their fill. He then left and knelt near the house in a humble position. I was too scared to say anything. He remained watching in this manner until the children were playing and laughing. He then stood up and said, 'Do you know why I sat there, Aslam?' When I admitted that I did not, he said, 'I had seen them weeping in distress and disliked to leave until I saw them laughing. I was satisfied when they started to laugh.'" *(Denowi, Ibn Shadhan, Ibn Asakir in Muntakhab Kanzul Ummal).* Aslam said, "I accompanied Omar ﷺ one night to Harrah and Aqim. When we came to Sarar, we noticed a fire burning. He said, 'O Aslam! There seems to be a caravan here that had to camp over because of nightfall. Let us go there.' When we arrived there, we found a woman with her children..." The rest of the narration is similar to the one above. *(Al Bidayah wan Nihayah, Imam Tabari).*

A Narration of Anas ﷺ on Sharing Food

Anas ﷺ reports that Ukaidir the ruler of Dowmatul Jandal once sent a bag full of sweetmeats as a gift to Rasulullah ﷺ. Rasulullah ﷺ had performed the salah, he passed by some people and started giving pieces of it to each one of them. Rasulullah ﷺ gave Jabir ﷺ a piece and then returned to give him another piece. Jabir ﷺ said, "But you have already given me a piece." Rasulullah ﷺ told him, "This is for the daughters of Abdullah, for your sisters." *(Ahmad in Jam'ul Fawa'id, Haythami)*

A Narration of Hasan ﷺ in this Regard

Hasan ﷺ reports, "Ukaidir who was the ruler of Dowmatul Jandal once sent a bag full of sweetmeats as a gift to Rasulullah ﷺ. By Allah?! Rasulullah ﷺ and his family were truly in need of it in those days because they had no food to eat. When Rasulullah ﷺ had performed the salah, he instructed someone to take the bag around to the Sahabah. Each of them would then put his hand in the bag and eat whatever he took out. When the bag came around to Khalid bin Walid ﷺ and he placed his hand in the bag, he said, 'O Rasulullah ﷺ! While the others have taken only once, I have had twice.' Rasulullah ﷺ said to him, 'Eat and give your family to eat some as well.'" *(Ibn Jareer in Kanzul Ummal)*

Rasulullah ﷺ Shares Some Dates with the Sahabah

Abu Hurairah ﷺ narrates, "Rasulullah ﷺ once distributed some dates amongst the Sahabah. He gave each person 7 dates. I also received 7 dates, one of them being without a seed. This was the best of the lot because it was firm and took long to chew." *(Bukhari).* Another narration from Anas ﷺ states that when some dates were once brought to Rasulullah ﷺ, he shared it with the Sahabah. Rasulullah ﷺ was sitting in a squat position and eating quickly because he was probably leaving to go somewhere.

The Letter Omar ﷺ Sent to Amr bin Al Aas ﷺ During the Year of Ashes and His Reply

Laith bin Sa'd reports that a severe drought afflicted the people of Madinah during the Khilafah of Omar ﷺ, in what was called the Year of Ashes. Omar ﷺ wrote the following letter to Amr bin Al Aas ﷺ in Egypt.

> From the servant of Allah the Amirul Mu'minin
> To the sinful son of Aas
> Salams to you. O Amr! I swear by my life that while you and those with you are eating to your fill you seem to have no concern for my companions and I who are on the verge of destruction. Do assist! Do assist!

Amr bin Al Aas ﷺ sent the following reply:

> To the servant of Allah Amirul Mu'minin
> From Amr bin Al Aas
> I am at your service! I am at your service! I have dispatched a train of camels, the first of which will be by you when the last will still be here with me. Peace be on you as well as Allah's mercy and blessings.

Omar ﷺ Distributes the Food that Amr bin Al Aas ﷺ Sent Amongst the Residents of Madinah

Amr bin Al Aas ﷺ then sent a train of camels so large that when the first camel reached Madinah, the last camel was still leaving Egypt. When the camels arrived, Omar ﷺ generously distributed it amongst the people. He gave every household in Madinah a camel with all the food it carried. He appointed Abdur Rahman bin Auf ﷺ, Zubair bin Awam ﷺ and Said bin Abi Waqqas ﷺ to distribute amongst the people. They then gave every household a camel with all the food it carried so that they may eat the food and slaughter the camel to eat the meat, use the fat for cooking, make shoes from the hide and use the satchels for the purpose they desired, such as making quilts, etc. As a result of this generosity, Allah extended further generosity to the people and sent abundant rains. The narration still continues, in which it is stated that to get the provisions to Makkah and Madinah, a canal was dug from the Nile to the Red Sea. *(Ibn Abdil Hakam).* A narration from *Aslam* also mentions the letter Omar ﷺ wrote to Amr bin Al Aas ﷺ. The narration also states that when the first camel reached Madinah, Omar ﷺ called for Zubair ﷺ and said to him, "Take the first camel to Najd and bring back to me as many families as you can. As for those whom you are unable to bring, you should issue instructions for each household to receive a camel together with all the provisions it carries. Then instruct them to wear 2 sheets, to slaughter the camel, to melt the fat for cooking, to dry the meat and to make shoes from the hide. Thereafter, they should take a part of the meat, a part of the fat and a handful of flour to cook a meal to eat. In this manner, they should keep eating until Allah makes further provisions available." When Zubair ﷺ excused himself from the task, Omar ﷺ said to him, "By Allah! You will never have another chance of gaining such immense rewards until you leave this world!" Omar ﷺ then called for another person who the narrator assumes was Talha ﷺ. However, when he also excused himself, Omar ﷺ sent for Abu Ubaidah bin Jarrah ﷺ, who left to fulfill the task. The narration continues further and states that Omar ﷺ gave Abu Ubaidah bin Jarrah ﷺ 1,000 Dinars, which the latter refused to accept. However, when Omar ﷺ insisted that he accept, he eventually did. *(lbn Khuzaima in Muntakhab Kanzul Ummal).*

Rasulullah ﷺ Gives Away his 2 Shawls to People

Jaz Sulami ﷺ reports that he brought to Rasulullah ﷺ a prisoner of war that his people had captured. When Jaz ﷺ accepted Islam and Rasulullah ﷺ intended giving him 2 shawls, Rasulullah ﷺ said to him, "Go to Aisha ﷺ and she will give you 2 of the shawls she has with her." He then went to Aisha ﷺ and said, "May Allah always keep you hail and healthy! Choose for me any 2 shawls from the ones you have with you because Rasulullah ﷺ has instructed that I have 2 of them." Aisha ﷺ placed each shawl on the end of a long Miswak taken from an acacia tree and handed them over saying, "Take this. Take this." The narrator says that Arab women did not expose themselves because of the laws of Hijab. *(Muntakhab Kanzul Ummal).*

The Incident of Omar ﷺ and the Grandsons of Rasulullah ﷺ

Ja'far bin Muhammad reports from his father that some clothing came to Omar ﷺ from Yemen; he distributed it amongst the people. As Omar ﷺ was sitting between the grave of Rasulullah ﷺ and the pulpit that evening, the people came wearing their new garments. They greeted Omar ﷺ and made Du'a for him. Hasan ﷺ and Husain ﷺ, the grandsons of Rasulullah ﷺ then came out of the house of their mother Fatima ﷺ without wearing any of the new garments. As they approached stepping over the shoulders of people, the face of Omar ﷺ dropped and he became very depressed. He said to the people around him, "By Allah! I am not at all pleased by the clothing I have given you to wear." "O Amirul Mu'minin!" they consoled him, "You have done an excellent thing by providing clothing for your subjects." Omar ﷺ explained, "I am depressed about those 2 youngsters stepping over the shoulders of the people. They have none of these garments on them because the garments were too large for them and they were too small to fit into them." Omar ﷺ then wrote to the governor of Yemen to speedily send 2 sets of clothing for Hasan ﷺ and Husain ﷺ. When the governor sent it, Omar ﷺ gave it to the 2 to wear. *(Ibn Sa'd in Kanzul Ummal).* In the chapter concerning honoring the Ansar, the incident has already passed about Usaid bin Hudhair ﷺ and Muhammad bin Maslama ﷺ with Omar ﷺ when he distributed clothing amongst the people. Also in this regard, the incident has passed about the new shawl that Omar ﷺ gave to Ummu Ammara ﷺ because she had been amongst the women who fought in the battle of Uhud.

The Practice of Amiml Mu'minin Omar ﷺ

Shafa bint Abdullah Adawiya ﷺ reports that Omar ﷺ once sent a message that she should come to see him the following morning. She says, "When I got there in the morning, I found Atika bint Usaid bin Abil Ees ﷺ at his door. We entered together and spoke for a while when Omar ﷺ sent for a shawl and gave it to her. He then sent for a shawl of inferior quality and gave that to me. I said, 'O Omar! I accepted Islam before her and I am also your cousin while she is not. Furthermore, you had sent for me while she came of her own accord, why did she then receive a better shawl?' He replied, 'I had originally kept that shawl for you but when the 2 of you came together, it occurred to me that she was more closely related to Rasulullah ﷺ than you are. I therefore gave preference, to the relatives of Rasulullah ﷺ over my own.'" *(Zubair bin Bakkar in Isabah)*

The Practice of Amirul Mu'minin Ali ﷺ

Asbagh bin Nubata reports that a man came to Ali ﷺ saying, "O Amirul Mu'minin! I have a need that I have already placed before Allah before coming to you. If you are able to fulfill it, I shall praise Allah and be thankful to you. If you are unable to fulfill it, I shall praise Allah and excuse you." Ali ﷺ said, "Write down your request on the ground because I do not like to see the humiliation of begging on your face." The man then wrote that he was a destitute. Ali ﷺ instructed that a set of clothing be brought to him and when it came, he gave it to the man. The man wore the clothes and the recited the following couplets in praise of Ali ﷺ, which mean:

"You have given me clothing, the beauty of which will soon fade while I shall give you the most excellent clothing of praise. Should you receive my good praise, you have received great honor. And you will want nothing else in return for what I have to say.
Praise revives the mention of a person. Just as the waters of the rain revive the plains and mountains. Never give up the good that Allah inspires you to do. Because every servant shall be rewarded for the deeds they do"

Ali ﷺ then sent for some gold coins and when 100 coins were brought to him, he gave it all to the man. To this, Asbagh remarked, "O Amirul Mu'minin! A set of clothing and 100 gold coins?!" Ali ﷺ replied, "Certainly! I have heard Rasulullah ﷺ say, 'Treat people according to their status' and this is the status of this man in my regard." *(Ibn Asakir, Abu Musa Madeni in Kitabu Istid'ail Libas, Kanzul Ummal).*

The Reward of Giving a Muslim Clothing to Wear

When a beggar once came to Abdullah bin Abbas ﷺ, he asked the man, "Do you testify that there is none worthy of worship but Allah and that Muhammad ﷺ is Allah's Rasul?" When the man replied in the affirmative, Abdullah bin Abbas ﷺ asked him further, "And do you fast during Ramadhan?" "Yes," was the reply. Abdullah bin Abbas ﷺ then said, "You have asked for something and it is our duty to assist you." He then gave the beggar a garment and said, "I have heard Rasulullah ﷺ say, 'When a Muslim gives a garment to another Muslim, he remains in Allah's protection as long as even a rag of the garment remains on the person." *(Tirmidhi in Jam'ul Fawa'id).*

The Practice of Qais bin Sa'd ﷺ in Feeding the Mujahidin

Jabir bin Abdullah ﷺ reports that Rasulullah ﷺ once dispatched an army under the command of Qais bin Sa'd bin Ubadah ﷺ. When the army suffered hunger, he slaughtered 9 riding animals (for them to eat). After the expedition returned and the incident was mentioned to Rasulullah ﷺ, he said, "Verily generosity is the hallmark of that family." *(Abu Bakr in Gailaniat, Ibn Asakir).* Another narration from Rafi bin Khudaij ﷺ states that Abu Ubaidah ﷺ and Omar ﷺ both approached Qais bin Sa'd ﷺ and implored him not to slaughter any more camels because it would deprive the army of their transport. However, he still went ahead to do so. When the news reached Rasulullah ﷺ, he said, "He is after all from the house of generosity." This occurred during the "Expedition of Leaves" when the Sahabah were forced to eat leaves because they had no food. *(Ibn Abi Dunya, Ibn Asakir in Kanzul Ummal)*

A Giant Fish Comes to the Shore for the Mujahidin

Jabir ﷺ narrates, "Qais bin Sa'd bin Ubadah ﷺ once passed by us during the time of Rasulullah ﷺ when we were suffering severe hunger. He slaughtered 7 camels for us and we continued on our expedition. When we set up camp along the shore, we found a giant fish lying here. We lived off it for 3 days and took along with us as much of its fat we could store in our water bags and satchels. We then traveled back until we came to Rasulullah ﷺ and informed him of what had transpired." The Sahabah who were part of the expedition said, "If we had assurance that the fish would not rot before we reached Rasulullah ﷺ, we would have loved to take some back for him." *(Tabrani, Haythami)*

The Incident between Omar ؓ and Bilal ؓ about feeding Mujahidin

Qais bin Abu Hazim reports that when Omar ؓ arrived in Sham and was with the commanders of the various armies, Bilal ؓ came calling, "Omar! Omar!" "Here I am!" responded Omar ؓ. Bilal ؓ said, "You are between these people and Allah whereas there is none between yourself and Allah. Look carefully at those before you, those on your right and those on your left. By Allah! These who have come to you eat only the meat of birds; they eat well whereas those under their command are ill fed." Omar ؓ replied, "You are right. I shall not stand up from here until each one of them guarantees me that he would provide every Muslim under his command 2 Mudd of barley and an appropriate measure of vinegar and olive oil." Commanders assured Omar ؓ saying, "We give you our guarantee that we will take this responsibility upon us, for Allah has granted us an abundance of wealth." "That is fine," Omar ؓ expressed in satisfaction. *(Abu Ubaid in Kanzul Ummal, Tabrani, Haythami)*

The Incident of Bilal ؓ and a Mushrik

Abdullah Howzini reports that he once met Bilal ؓ the Mu'adhin of Rasulullah ﷺ in Aleppo. When he asked Bilal ؓ to explain to him how Rasulullah ﷺ manages his finances, Bilal said, "From the time Rasulullah ﷺ announced his prophethood until the time of his demise, I had been the one to take charge of anything that he possessed. Whenever any Muslim came to him whom he regarded to be destitute, he gave me instructions to borrow some money to purchase some clothing or some food to give the person to wear or to eat. This continued until one of the disbelievers once came to me and said, 'O Bilal! I have plenty of wealth. You therefore need to borrow money from none besides me.' I then did as he said. One day after performing wudhu and standing up to call out the Adhan, the man arrived with a group of traders. When he saw me, he said, 'Hey Abyssinian!' When I replied, he treated me rudely and spoke very harshly. He then asked, 'What remains of the month?' 'Not much,' I replied. He continued, 'There are only four nights of the month left, after which I shall take you as a slave if you do not settle the debt. I have not given you the loans out of any regard for you or for your chief Rasulullah ﷺ. I gave you the loans so that you should become my slave and I could have you grazing goats as you had been doing previously.' My heart was left filled with every thought a person could possibly have. I then proceeded to call out the Adhan. After we had performed the Isha salah and Rasulullah ﷺ had returned to his home, I sought permission to see him. When he permitted me in, I said to him, 'May my parents be sacrificed for you, O Rasulullah ﷺ! The disbeliever I told you about from whom I was taking loans has told me much and demands repayment whereas neither you nor I have the means to settle the debt. He will certainly humiliate me if I am unable to pay. Do permit me to go into hiding to some tribe that has accepted Islam until Allah gives His Rasul ﷺ something to payoff my debt. I then left for home where I placed my sword, my bag, my spear and my shoes by my headside and faced towards the horizon from where the sun rises. Each time I fell

asleep, I awoke out of worry but when I realized that there was still night left, I slept again. Eventually the first pillar of dawn broke through the sky and I decided to leave. However, I suddenly heard someone calling, 'Bilal! Hurry, Rasulullah ﷺ is calling you.' Walked to Rasulullah ﷺ and found 4 loaded camels there. When I came to Rasulullah ﷺ and sought permission to enter, he said to me, 'Rejoice, for Allah has sent the means to settle your debt.' I praised Allah and Rasulullah ﷺ asked, 'Did you not pass by the 4 camels sitting there?' When I informed him that I did, Rasulullah ﷺ said, 'I hand them over to you together with their loads. Take them and settle your debts.' The camels were loaded with clothing and food that the chief of Fidak gave as a gift to Rasulullah ﷺ.

I did as Rasulullah ﷺ bade me and offloaded the camels. I then fed them and proceeded to call out the Adhan for the Fajr salah. After Rasulullah ﷺ had led the salah, I went to Baqe where I placed my fingers in my ears and called out, 'Whoever has a debt due from Rasulullah ﷺ should present themselves!' I then offered the goods to people, sold them and paid of the debts until there was no debt on earth due from Rasulullah ﷺ. I was even left with 2 or one and a half Awqiya. When I later left for the Masjid, most of the day had already passed and Rasulullah ﷺ was sitting there all by himself. When I greeted him with Salam, he asked, 'Have you fulfilled what you had to do?' I replied, 'Allah has settled every debt that was due from His Rasul ﷺ and nothing is outstanding'. He then asked me if anything was left over and I informed him that 2 Dinars were left. This was all that was left from the 2 or one and a half Awqiya since the balance was also used to pay creditors on the way back to Masjid. Rasulullah ﷺ then said, 'Do try to give me peace from that as well by giving it away because I cannot return to any of my wives until I have peace from it.' However, since no one deserving came to us, Rasulullah ﷺ spent the entire night in the Masjid. He then spent the second day in the Masjid as well. It was at end of the day when 2 riders eventually came. I approached them and gave them food and clothing. When Rasulullah ﷺ had led the Isha salah, he asked me, 'Have you fulfilled what you had to do?' I replied by saying, 'Allah has given you peace from it' Rasulullah ﷺ then exclaimed 'Allahu Akbar' and praised Allah because he feared that death should overcome him while he had wealth in his possession. I walked behind him as he greeted each one of his wives in turn and reached his place for the night." *(Bayhaqi in Al Bidayah wan Nihayah, Tabrani in Kanzul Ummal).*

The Manner in which Rasulullah ﷺ Distributed Wealth: The Narration of Ummul Mu'minin Ummu Salama ؓ

Ummu Salama ؓ narrates, "I know of the largest amount of wealth that came to Rasulullah ﷺ during his entire lifetime. It was during the early hours of the night when a bag came to Rasulullah ﷺ containing 800 Dirhams and a letter. Rasulullah ﷺ sent the bag to me because it was my turn to spend the night with him. He then returned after performing the Isha salah and started performing salah in the place he reserved for salah. I had already made the bed for us and was waiting for him. He however took very long time and left the room only to return again after a while. This continued until the Adhan was called out for the Fajr salah. He led the salah and then returned saying, 'Where is that bag? It troubled me the entire night.' He took the bag and then distributed everything it had. I then asked him, O Rasulullah ﷺ! You had behaved in a manner that is not your usual behavior. Why is this?' He replied by saying, 'Whenever I started my salah, I started thinking of the bag. I then had to leave to see it and then return to my salah." *(Tabrani, Haythami)*

Rasulullah ﷺ Distributes 80,000 Dirhams that Ala bin Hadhrami ؓ Had Sent

Abu Musa Ash'ari ؓ narrates that Ala bin Hadhrami ؓ once sent 80,000 dishams to Rasulullah ﷺ form Bahrain. Never before or afterwards had so much money been sent to Rasulullah ﷺ. According to the instruction of Rasulullah ﷺ, the money was spread out on a mat and the Adhan was called out. Bending over the money after the salah was over; Rasulullah ﷺ then started giving to the people as they came. That day there was no counting and no weighing. All Rasulullah ﷺ did was to give out handfuls. Abbas ؓ then arrived saying, "O Rasulullah ﷺ! I had to pay the ransom for myself and for my nephew Aqil after the battle of Badr because he did no have any money then. Do give me some of that money." "Take some," Rasulullah ﷺ said to him. Abbas ؓ then spread out the embroidered black shawl he was wearing and filled it. When he was ready to get up to leave, he was unable to carry it. He then looked up to Rasulullah ﷺ and said, "O Rasulullah ﷺ! Please lift this on to me." Rasulullah ﷺ smiled so widely that his teeth showed. He said, "Take only what you can carry." Abbas ؓ did as told and then left with the money he took. As he left, he said, "As for one of the things Allah has promised, He has certainly fulfilled. I do not know about the second promise." He then recited the verse:

يَا أَيُّهَا النَّبِيُّ قُلْ لِمَنْ فِي أَيْدِيكُمْ مِنَ الْأَسْرَىٰ إِنْ يَعْلَمِ اللَّهُ فِي قُلُوبِكُمْ خَيْرًا يُؤْتِكُمْ خَيْرًا مِمَّا أُخِذَ مِنْكُمْ وَيَغْفِرْ لَكُمْ

O Prophet ﷺ! Say to the captives that are in your hands: If Allah knows any good in your hearts, He will give you something better than what has been taken from you, and He will forgive you. (Al-Anfal:70)

He said further, "This money is better than that which was taken from me as ransom but I have no idea about the promise of forgiveness." *(Hakim confirmed by Dhahabi, lbn Sa'd)*

The Practice of Abu Bakr ؓ in Distributing Wealth and the Public Treasury During his Period as Khalifa

Sahl bin Abi Hathma and others report that Abu Bakr ؓ had the Baytul Maal (public treasury) in Sunh. It was known to all and no one guarded it. When people voiced the concern that it should be guarded, he said, 'None should fear about it." "Why not'?" they asked. "Because it has a lock on it," was the simple reply. Abu Bakr ؓ used to distribute everything the Baytul Maal so that nothing remained. Abu Bakr ؓ moved from Sunh to Madinah, he kept the Baytul Maal in the house he lived. Proceeds from the mines of the Qabiliya and Juhayna tribes came to him. The mine of the Banu Sulaim was also opened during his khilafa, so the Zakah came from there as well. Everything was kept in the Baytul Maal. Abu Bakr ؓ used to convert this into gold and silver nuggets and give every 100 people a specified amount which they shared between themselves. He was fair in his distribution and all received justly whether they were slaves or free people, men or women, young or old. He also used the money to purchase camels, horses and weapons for people proceeding in Jihad. During one of the years, he bought warm woolen shawls from the rural areas and distributed them amongst the widows of Madinah during winter. When Abu Bakr ؓ passed away, Omar ؓ called a few trustworthy person and they went into the Baytul Maal of Abu Bakr ؓ. Amongst others, they included Abdur Rahman bin Auf ؓ and Uthman bin Affan ؓ. When they opened the Baytul Maal, they neither found a Dinar nor a Dirham. All they found was a coarse cloth for storing money and when they shook it, all that emerged was a single Dirham. They all prayed for Abu Bakr ؓ. There was a man in Madinah who weighed Dinars and Dirhams even during the time of Rasulullah ﷺ. It was he who used to do the weighing for Abu Bakr ؓ. When he was asked what the value of the wealth was that came to Abu Bakr ؓ, he replied that it amounted to 200,000. *(Ibn Sa'd in Kanzul Ummal)*.

The Narration of Isma'el bin Muhammad and Others About the Fairness in the Manner that Abu Bakr ؓ Distributed Wealth

Isma'el bin Muhammad reports that whenever Abu Bakr ؓ distributed wealth amongst the people, he always gave equally. Omar ؓ once objected saying, "O Khalifa of Rasulullah ﷺ! How can you give the same to the veterans of Badr as you give to other people?" Abu Bakr ؓ replied, "The things of this world are merely a means of existence and the best of such means are those that are moderate and this applies equally to all people. The superiority of the veterans of Badr shall be seen in their rewards in the Hereafter. *(Ahmad in Kitabuz Zuhd)*. Another narration states that when it was mentioned to Abu Bakr ؓ that he ought to give preference to some people in the distribution of wealth, he said, "Their virtues shall be rewarded by Allah (in the Hereafter). With regard to their worldly existence, equality is best." *(Abu Ubaid in Kanzul Ummal)*. Yet another narration from Aslam states that when Abu Bakr ؓ became the Khalifa and distributed equally amongst the people, someone said to him, "O Khalifa of Rasulullah ﷺ! Why do you not give preference to the Muhajirin and the Ansar by giving them a larger share?" Abu Bakr ؓ replied, "Should I buy their virtues from them? With regard to people's existence in this world, equality is better than showing preference." A narration from Amr bin Abdullah states that after Abu Bakr ؓ distributed wealth for the first time, Omar ؓ said to him, "Why do you not show preference to the earliest Muhajirin and the earliest Muslims?" Abu Bakr ؓ responded by saying, "Should I buy from them the lead they have?" He then continued to exercise equality whenever he distributed. *(Bayhaqi)*.

The Incident of the wealth that arrived from Bahrain

About Omar ؓ, the freed slave of Ghafra reports that when Rasulullah ﷺ passed away, plenty of wealth arrived from Bahrain. Abu Bakr ؓ made an announcement saying, "Whoever Rasulullah ﷺ owed money to or whom Rasulullah ﷺ had promised some money should come and collect his dues." Jabir ؓ stood up and said, "Rasulullah ﷺ told me that when the wealth came from Bahrain, he would give me so much. He then indicated 3 handfuls." Abu Bakr ؓ told him to take from the money and when he took one handful, he had 500 Dirhams. Abu Bakr ؓ then gave instructions that he be given another 1,000 Dirhams to complete 3 handfuls. Thereafter, he distributed all the wealth by giving each person 10 Dirhams as he said, "This is the fulfillment of the promise that Rasulullah ﷺ made to the people." The following year even more money arrived and Abu Bakr ؓ gave the people 20 Dirhams each. When there was still some money remaining, he gave the slaves 5 Dirhams each. He addressed the people saying, "We have given something to these slaves of yours because they serve you and do your work for you." The people then requested, "Why do you not give more to the Muhajirin and the Ansar because they were the earliest Muslims and because Rasulullah ﷺ held them in high esteem." However, Abu Bakr ؓ said, "Their rewards are reserved with Allah in the Hereafter. In this world, equality is better than giving preference." This was his practice throughout the period of his Khilafa. *(Bayhaqi, Ibn Abi Shayba, Bazzar, Hasan bin Sufian in Kanzul Ummal)* The rest of the narration will be quoted in the narration of the next chapter. The narration has already passed about the equality that Ali ؓ exercised when he said to the Arab woman to whom he had given as much as he gave a slave woman, "I have studied the Book of Allah and have not found in it anything denoting that the progeny of Isma'el علیہ السلام (Arabs) should be given preference over the progeny of Is'haq علیہ السلام."

The Manner in which Omar ؓ Distributed Wealth and the Preference he Gave to People According to Their Precedence in Islam and Their Ties with Rasulullah ﷺ

Omar ؓ the freed slave of Ghafra reports the narration appearing above. The narration continues to state that after Abu Bakr ؓ passed away, Omar ؓ succeeded him. During the Khilafa of Omar ؓ, Allah granted the Muslims numerous conquests and even more wealth poured into Madinah. Omar ؓ said, "While Abu Bakr ؓ had his opinion about the distribution of this wealth, I have another opinion. I do not hold those who fought against Rasulullah ﷺ in the same esteem as those who fought alongside him." He therefore gave preference to the Muhajirin and the Ansar. He stipulated an allowance of 5,000 for the veterans of Badr and 4,000 for those who had accepted Islam before the veterans of Badr but had not participated in the battle of Badr. He stipulated an allowance of 12,000 for all the wives of Rasulullah ﷺ besides Safiya ؓ and Juwayriya ؓ, for whom he had stipulated 6,000. However, the 2 ladies refused to accept the amount. Omar ؓ explained that he was giving more to the others because they had made Hijra whereas the 2 of them had not. They argued, "You have not stipulated their share because of their Hijra. You have stipulated a share for them because of their relationship with Rasulullah ﷺ and we all share the same relationship." Omar ؓ thought the matter over and then stipulated an equal allowance of 12,000 for them all. Omar ؓ also stipulated an allowance of 12,000 for Abbas bin Abdil Muttalib ؓ because of his relationship with Rasulullah ﷺ. Furthermore, he stipulated 4,000 for Usama bin Zaid ؓ and 5,000 each for Hasan ؓ and Husain ؓ, an amount equal to that which their father (Ali ؓ) received because of their relationship (as grandsons) to Rasulullah ﷺ. When he stipulated for his son Abdullah ؓ 3,000, his son said, "Dear father! You have stipulated 4,000 for Usama ؓ and only 3,000 for me whereas his father had no more status than my father and he has no more status than I?" Omar ؓ replied, "His father was more beloved to Rasulullah ﷺ than your father and he was more beloved to Rasulullah ﷺ than you."

Omar ؓ also stipulated 2,000 for the sons of every veteran of Badr. When Omar the son of Abu Salama ؓ passed by, Omar ؓ instructed his servants to give him an additional 1,000. To this, Muhammad the son of Abdullah bin Jahash ؓ enquired, "Why are you giving him more than us when his father had no more status than our fathers'?" Omar ؓ replied, "I stipulated 2,000 for him because of his father Abu Salamah ؓ and then increased a further 1,000 because of his mother Ummu Salamah ؓ the wife of Rasulullah ﷺ. If you had a mother like Ummu Salamah ؓ, I would have also given you another 1,000." While Omar ؓ stipulated 800 for Uthman bin Ubaidullah the brother of Talha bin Ubaydullah ؓ, he stipulated 2,000 for Nadhar bin Anas ؓ. To this, Talha bin Ubaidullah ؓ remarked, "When someone like Uthman bin Ubaidullah comes to you, you stipulate 800 for him but when a youngster from the Ansar comes to you; you include him amongst those who receive 2,000?" Omar ؓ replied, "I met the father of that youngster on the battlefield of Uhud and he asked me about Rasulullah ﷺ. When I told him that I assumed that Rasulullah ﷺ had been martyred, he drew his sword, extended his wrist and said, 'If Rasulullah ﷺ is dead, then Allah is still alive and can never die. It is after all for Allah that we are fighting.' He then fought until he was martyred. On the other hand, this person Ubaidullah the father of Uthman was grazing goats at the time. Do you expect me to have the same regard for both persons?" Omar ؓ maintained this practice throughout his period of Khilafa. *(Bazzar in Majma'uz Zawa'id, Haythami)*

The Narration of Anas ؓ in this Regard

Anas bin Malik ؓ and Sa'eed bin Musaib both report that Omar ؓ stipulated 5,000 for the Muhajirin, 4,000 for the Ansar and also 4,000 for the sons of the Muhajirin who could not fight in the battle of Badr. Amongst these were Omar ؓ the son of Abu Salama bin Abdul Asad Makhzumi ؓ, Usama ؓ the son of Zaid ؓ, Muhammad ؓ the son of Abdullah bin Jahash Asadi ؓ and Abdullah ؓ the son of Omar ؓ. To this, Abdur Rahman bin Auf ؓ said that Abdullah bin Omar ؓ (the son of Omar ؓ) did not belong to this group because of his virtues. He then enumerated the virtues meaning that he should receive more than the others. Abdullah bin Omar ؓ said, "Give it to me if I have a right to it, otherwise do not." Omar ؓ said to Abdur Rahman bin Auf ؓ, "Include him amongst those who are to receive 5,000 and record me amongst those who to receive 4,000." "This is not at all what I meant." Abdullah bin Omar ؓ clarifies. Omar ؓ said, "By Allah! You and I cannot both be amongst those receiving 5,000." *(Bayhaqi, Ibn Abi Shaybah in Kanzul Ummal)*.

The Narration of Zaid bin Aslam in this Regard

Zaid bin Aslam narrates that when Omar ؓ was stipulating allowances, he stipulated 2,000 Dirhams for Abdullah, the son of Handhala ؓ. Talha ؓ brought his cousin along and Omar ؓ stipulated a lesser amount for him, Talha ؓ asked, "O Amirul Mu'minin! You have given more to that Ansari than to my cousin who is a Muhajir." "Yes," replied Omar ؓ, "because I saw his father Handhala ؓ during the battle of Uhud shielding himself with only his sword (he had no shield). He was moving it like a camel; he moved its tail in all directions. He did this to deflect enemy swords and arrows."*(Ibn Asakir in Kanzul Ummal)*

The Narration of Nashira bin Sumay Yazani in this Regard

Nashira bin Sumay Yazani reports that on the day Omar ؓ was in Jabia, he heard Omar ؓ delivering a lecture in which he said, "Allah has made me the administrator and distributor of this wealth. It is in fact Allah who distributes it by setting the guidelines. I begin distributing by giving to the wives of Rasulullah ﷺ and then those who hold high status." Omar ؓ had stipulated 10,000 for each of the wives of Rasulullah ﷺ besides Juwayriya ؓ, Safiya ؓ and Maymuna ؓ. However, when Aisha ؓ remarked that Rasulullah ﷺ used to treat them all with equality, Omar ؓ also did likewise and gave them an equal amount. Omar ؓ also said in his lecture, "I then start with my companions who are the very first Muhajirin because we were oppressively and forcefully banished from our homes. Thereafter, I give to the most noble amongst them." Omar ؓ therefore stipulated 5,000 for those Muhajirin who were veterans of Badr and 4,000 for the Ansar who were veterans of Badr. Those who fought at Uhud were given 3,000. Omar ؓ said further, "I readily give to those who readily made Hijra and delay giving those who delayed in making Hijra. You should blame nothing else but the sitting down of your riding animals. Do excuse me from dismissing Khalid bin Walid ؓ from his post. I had dismissed him because instead of reserving some money for the poor Muslims as I had instructed, he rather gave it to people who were powerful, noble and eloquent. I handed over command to Abu

Ubaidah." At this point, Abu Amr bin Hafs said, "By Allah! You shall never be excused, O Omar bin Khattab! You have dismissed a commander that Rasulullah ﷺ had appointed! You have sheathed a sword that Rasulullah ﷺ had drawn and lowered a flag that Rasulullah ﷺ had hoisted! You were only jealous of my cousin!" Omar ؓ responded by saying, "You are obviously a close relative of Khalid ؓ. You are young and are angry for the sake of your cousin." (Ahmad by Haythami, Bayhaqi).

Omar ؓ Files a register for the Allowances Issued: The Condition of Omar ؓ when Abu Musa Ash'ari ؓ brought lot of Wealth

Abu Hurairah ؓ says that he brought to Omar bin Khattab ؓ 800,000 Dirhams from Abu Musa Ash'ari ؓ. Omar ؓ asked, 'What have you come with?' 'I have come with 800,000 Dirhams,' replied Abu Hurairah ؓ. Omar ؓ asked further, 'Is it all lawful?' 'It certainly is,' was the reply. Omar ؓ stayed awake the entire night until the Adhan was called out for Fajr. His wife then asked, "Have you not slept last night?" He replied, "How could Omar bin Khattab sleep when so much wealth has come that has never come since the beginning of Islam? Omar has no assurance that he may die when all this wealth is still with him and he has not spent it where it ought to be spent." After leading the Fajr salah, a group of Sahabah gathered around Omar ؓ and he said, "Last night the people received so much money that they have never received since the beginning of Islam. I have an opinion but require your guidance. I feel that I should give it to the people by weight." The others disagreed saying, "Do not do that, O Amirul Mu'minin! People are continuously entering the fold of Islam and the wealth coming in is also increasing. It would therefore be difficult to keep track of who received what. Rather keep their records in a register and give them accordingly." Omar ؓ agreed and said, "Advise me about whom to start with." They said, "With yourself, O Amirul Mu'minin because you are the ruler." Others said, "Because the Amirul Mu'minin is most knowledgeable." Omar ؓ remarked, "No. I shall rather start with Rasulullah ﷺ and those who are closest to him." Omar ؓ had the register drawn up in this manner, starting with the Banu Hashim and the family of Abdul Muttalib. After giving them all, he gave the Banu Abd Shams and the Banu Naufal bin Abd Manaf. He gave the Banu Abd Shams because they were related to the mother of Hashim. (Ibn Sa'd, Bayhaqi in Kanzul Ummal).

The Register of Omar ؓ and His Giving First to the Relatives of Rasulullah ﷺ

Jubair bin Huwayrith ؓ reports that Omar ؓ consulted with the people concerning the filing of a register. Ali ؓ advised him to annually distribute the money collected without keeping back anything. Uthman bin Affan ؓ said, "I feel that plenty of wealth will be coming in, which will be enough to give everyone. If record is not kept of the people to know who had taken and who had not, the matter will get out of control." Thereafter, Waleed bin Hisham bin Mughiera said, "O Amirul Mu'minin! I have been to Sham where I saw the rulers keep registers and records of the soldiers in their armies. You should therefore also keep registers and records of the soldiers in the army." Omar ؓ accepted this proposal and called for Aqil bin Abi Talib ؓ, Makhrama bin Naufal ؓ and Jubair bin Mut'im ؓ, all of whom very well knew the lineage of the Quraish. Omar ؓ gave the 3 men instructions to make a record of all the people according to their status. When they started writing the record, they commenced with the Banu Hashim, the family of Rasulullah ﷺ. Thereafter, they recorded Abu Bakr ؓ and his tribe, followed by Omar ؓ and his tribe. They did this to correspond with the

sequence of the Khilafa. When Omar ؓ looked at the register, he said "By Allah! This is how I would have liked it to be. However, I want you to start with Rasulullah ﷺ followed by all his relatives according to their closeness in relationship to him. You should eventually place Omar wherever Allah has had him placed." (Ibn Sa'd, Tabari in Kanzul Ummal).

The Incident Between Omar ؓ and the Banu Adi Tribe concerning the Distribution of Wealth

Aslam reports that after Omar ؓ opposed the view to place him and his tribe after Abu Bakr ؓ and his tribe the Banu Adi (the tribe of Omar ؓ) came to him and said, "You are the successor of Rasulullah ﷺ." Omar ؓ corrected them saying, "Rather the successor of Abu Bakr ؓ, because Abu Bakr ؓ was the successor of Rasulullah ﷺ." They continued, "Whatever it may be. However, why do you rather not leave yourself where the 3 men have written it." Omar ؓ exclaimed, "Oh! Oh! Dear Banu Adi! Do you wish to get on my back and eat before other people, thereby destroying all my good deeds? I swear by Allah that I shall never do so, I shall start with relatives of Rasulullah ﷺ even though your names are written last. I have 2 companions who have walked a path and if I tread a different path, I shall not reach the destination. By Allah! We have no honor in this world and cannot expect any of Allah's rewards in the Hereafter for our deeds without Muhammad ﷺ. He is the source of our honor and his tribe is the most honorable of all Arabs. The next in kin to him are then most honorable and then those closest in kinship after them. The Arabs have honor only because of Rasulullah ﷺ. Perhaps the lineage of some of us meets us with his after many generations. Once the generations meet up, our lineage does not part from his until it reaches Adam عليه السلام after a few more generations. Despite all of this closeness to Rasulullah ﷺ, if the non-Arabs arrive on the day of Judgment with plenty of good deeds and we arrive with none, they will be closer to Rasulullah ﷺ than us. A person should therefore never look at his kinship and should carry out deeds for the rewards that Allah holds. Verily, the one whose actions keep him lagging behind cannot be hurried along by his lineage." (Ibn Sa'd, Tabari).

Omar ؓ Reverts to the Opinion of Abu Bakr ؓ and Ali ؓ Concerning the Distribution of Wealth

Omar bin Abdullah ؓ the freed slave of Ghafra reports that when Rasulullah ﷺ passed away, plenty of wealth arrived from Bahrain. He then narrated the entire narration as has appeared earlier. The narration also mentions that Omar ؓ once came out for the Jumu'ah salah and after praising Allah, he addressed the people saying, "The news has reached me that some of you have said that when Omar ؓ dies or they said when the Amirul Mu'minin dies, we will instantly pledge allegiance to a certain person just as people instantly pledged allegiance to Abu Bakr ؓ. There is no doubt that pledge of allegiance to Abu Bakr ؓ took place very suddenly, but where will we find another person like Abu Bakr ؓ to whom we would be prepared to fully submit ourselves as we did for Abu Bakr ؓ? Abu Bakr ؓ was of the opinion that the distribution of wealth should be with total equality whereas my opinion was that some people be given more. However, if I live this year, I shall switch to the opinion of Abu Bakr ؓ because his opinion is better then mine." The narration still continues further. (Bazzar, Haythami).

Omar ؓ Gives Abbas ؓ What Remained in the Baytul Maal

Hasan reports that once after Omar ؓ had distributed money amongst the people, there was still some left over in the Baytul

Maal. Abbas ؓ then said to Omar ؓ and the people there, "Tell me if the uncle of Musa اللهﷻ was living amongst you, would you honor him?" "Certainly," they all replied. He then said, "Then I am more deserving of the honor for I am the uncle of your Nabi ﷺ." After discussing with the others, Omar ؓ then gave the remaining amount to Abbas ؓ. *(Ibn Sa'd)*

The Narration of Aisha ؓ in this Regard

Aisha ؓ narrates that when a perfume holder once came to Omar ؓ, those around him looked at him to see whom he would give it to. He said, "Would you permit me to send this to Aisha ؓ because of the love that Rasulullah ﷺ had for her?" When they agreed, it was brought to Aisha ؓ. As she opened it, she was told that Omar ؓ had sent it for her. She remarked, "How many conquests have taken place at the hands of Omar after Rasulullah ﷺ!" She then prayed, "O Allah! Let me not live until the next gift of Omar ؓ comes in the coming year." *(Abu Ya'la, Haythami)*

The Narration of Anas ؓ in this Regard

Anas bin Malik ؓ says that Abu Bakr ؓ had appointed him to collect the Zakah. By the time he returned, Abu Bakr ؓ had already passed away. Omar ؓ then asked him, "O Anas! Have you brought us some animals?" When Anas ؓ replied that he had, Omar ؓ told him to hand over the animals and to keep the money for himself. "But the money is a large amount," said Anas ؓ. Omar ؓ insisted, "Take it even though it is so much." Anas ؓ says, "The money amounted to 4,000 and I therefore became the richest person in Madinah." *(Ibn Sa'd in Kanzul Ummal).*

Omar ؓ Gives a Gift to a Person Injured in the Path of Allah

Abdullah bin Ubaid bin Umair reports that while people were busy taking their gifts before Omar ؓ, he looked up and was surprised to see a man with a scar on his face. Upon enquiry, the man informed Omar ؓ that he had sustained the wound in a battle. Omar ؓ then gave instructions that the man be given 1,000 Dirhams. After the money was given, Omar ؓ turned the money over in his hands for a while and then said. "Give him another 1,000." Another 1,000 Dirhams were handed over. This occurred 4 times so that the amount totaled 4,000. Feeling embarrassed that he was being given so much, the man left. When Omar ؓ asked about him, the people informed him that they felt he had left out of the embarrassment of being given so much. Omar ؓ then said, "By Allah! Had he stayed, I would have continued giving him until there was not a single Dirham left. This is because the sword-wound he sustained in the Path of Allah had left a black scar on his face." *(Abu Nu'aym in Hilya).*

Ali bin Abi Talib ؓ Distributes Wealth

Ali ؓ distributed things amongst the people thrice in a year. When some wealth arrived from Isfahan, he announced, "Come early in the morning for the 4th round of gifts, for I am not your treasurer, I do not amass wealth for you." He then distributed everything, even the ropes that held the animals. While some people took them, others returned them. *(Abu Ubaid in Amwal, Kanzul Ummal)*

Omar ؓ Distributes All the Wealth and Rejects the Proposal of a Person who Advocated Keeping Reserves

Sa'eed narrates that Omar ؓ instructed the public treasurer Abdullah bin Arqam ؓ to distribute everything in the Baytul Maal every month. Thereafter, he issued instructions for everything to be distributed once a week. He eventually gave the instruction for the distribution to be on a daily basis. Someone

then said, "O Amirul Mu'minin! Why do you no keep something in reserve for an emergency or when other areas call for assistance?" Addressing the person, Omar ؓ said, "It is Saitan speaking on your lips. Allah has inspired me with the answer and protected me from the evil of the act. What I have prepared for such situations is exactly what Rasulullah ﷺ had prepared, and that is obedience to Allah and His Rasul ﷺ." *(Bayhaqi).*

The Narration of Abdullah bin Omar ؓ in this Regard

Abdullah bin Omar ؓ reports that some wealth once came to Omar ؓ from Iraq. He was about to distribute it when someone stood up to say, "O Amirul Mu'minin! Why do you rather not reserve this wealth to fend off an enemy that may suddenly attack or for another unforeseen emergency that may strike?" Omar ؓ admonished the person saying, "What is the mater with you?! May you be destroyed! It is Saitan speaking with your tongue. Allah has inspired me with the response and I swear by Allah that I shall never disobey Him today for the emergencies of tomorrow. I shall not do as you say but shall rather prepare for the Muslims that which Rasulullah ﷺ had prepared for them: obedience to Allah and Rasulullah ﷺ." *(Abu Nu'aym in Hilya).*

The Incident Between Omar ؓ and Abdur Rahman bin Auf ؓ

Salama bin Sa'eed reports that when some wealth once came to Omar ؓ, Abdur Rahman bin Auf ؓ approached him saying, "Why do you rather not keep this money in reserve in the Baytul Maal for any emergency that may arise or for anything else that may occur'?" Omar ؓ responded by saying, "These are words that only Saitan could mention. Allah has already inspired me with the response and saved me from its tribulation. Should I disobey Allah in a year for fear of something that may come during the next year? I have prepared Taqwa as a defense for the Muslims. Allah mentions:

وَمَنْ يَتَّقِ اللَّهَ يَجْعَلْ لَهُ مَخْرَجًا (2) وَيَرْزُقْهُ مِنْ حَيْثُ لَا يَحْتَسِبُ

.....*He (Allah) will make a way for him to get out (from every difficulty). And He will provide him from (sources) he never could imagine.... (At-Talaq:2-3)*
However, the words of Saitan will soon become a test for those coming after me." *(Ibn Asakir in Muntakhab Kanzul Ummal).*

The Letter Omar ؓ Wrote to Abu Musa Ash'ari ؓ

Hasan narrates that Omar ؓ wrote the following letter to Abu Musa Ash'ari ؓ: I wish that there comes a day in the year when here remains not a single Dirham in the Baytul Maal and it is empty of everything so that Allah may know that I have given every person his right. *(Ibn Sa'd, Ibn Asakir in Kanzul Ummal).*

The Letter of Omar ؓ to Hudhayfa ؓ

Hasan also reports that Omar ؓ wrote to Hudhayfa ؓ that he must give every person his dues and specified allowances. Hudhayfa ؓ wrote back saying that a large sum of money still remained after had done so. Omar ؓ replied with a letter stating, "These are the spoils of the people that neither belongs to Omar nor to his family. Distribute it amongst the people." *(Ibn Sa'd).*

Ali ؓ Distributes All the Wealth

Ali bin Rabi'ah Walibi reports that Ibn Nabbaj once came to Ali ؓ and said, "O Amirul Mu'minin! The Baytul Maal of the Muslims is full of gold and silver." Ali ؓ exclaimed, "Allahu Akbar!" and then stood up with the support of Ibn Nabbaj. Standing by the Baytul Mall, Ali ؓ recited the following couplet (which means):

"These are the fruits ready for picking and the best of it is still here (I have taken none of it). Whereas the picker usually has his hand to his mouth (ready to consume the fruit)"

He then continued, "O Ibn Nabbaj! Bring the people of Kufa here." When an announcement was made and the people arrived, Ali ﷺ distributed everything that lay in the Baytul Maal. As he distributed, he said, "O gold and O silver! Deceive someone else besides me." Addressing the people, he said, "Take! Take!" Eventually there was not a single Dinar or Dirham left. Ali then instructed Ibn Nabbaj to wash out the Baytul Maal and (after it was washed out) he performed 2 Rakahs salah in it. *(Abu Nu'aym in Hilya)*. Mujamma Taymi reports that Ali ﷺ used to sweep the Baytul Maal and perform salah in it. He made it a place for his salah in the hope that it would testify on his behalf on the day of Qiyamah. *(Isti'ab)*. Mu'adh bin Ala reports from his grandfather that he heard Ali ﷺ say, "I have received nothing from your spoils of war besides this date container that a chief of one of the rural towns gave me as a gift." He then went down to the Baytul Maal where he distributed everything it contained. He then recited the following couplet (which means):

"Successful is the one who has a little basket from which he eats once a day"

Antara Shaibani says that Ali ﷺ used to collect Jizya and Kharaj from every artisan. For this, he took something of their crafts. In fact, he even took from cloth makers some of their needles, knitting needles, cottons and thread. He then distributed this amongst the people. He would never leave anything for a night in the Baytul Maal without distributing it. The only time he would leave it for the morning was when he was too preoccupied with something else. He would always say, "O world! Go and deceive someone other than myself." He often recited the following couplet (which means):

"These are the fruits ready for picking and the best of it is ill here (I have taken none of it). Whereas the picker usually has his hand to his mouth (ready to consume the fruit)"

Abu Ubaid reports a narration from Antara which states that he once went to Ali ﷺ when (his slave) Qambar arrived and said, "O Amirul Mu'minin! You have left nothing after distribution whereas your family is also entitled to a share of the wealth. However, I have kept something aside." "What have you kept aside?" enquired Ali ﷺ. "Come and see for yourself," Qambar replied. He then took Ali ﷺ to the house where there was a large gold plated dish filled with dishes of gold and silver. When he saw this, Ali ﷺ exclaimed, "Shame on you! Do you wish to fill my house with a raging fire?!" He started weighing the dishes and giving a portion to the chiefs of every tribe. Thereafter, he said:

"These are the fruits ready for picking and the best of it is still here (1 have taken none of it). Whereas the picker usually has his hand to his mouth (ready to consume the fruit)"

Addressing the wealth, he added further, "Do not deceive me. Go and deceive someone e1se." *(Abu Nu'aym in Hilya in Muntakhab Kanzul Ummal, Ahmad in Zuhd and Musaddad)*.

The Opinion of Omar ﷺ About the Rights of the Muslims in Wealth

Aslam reports that he heard Omar ﷺ say, "Gather around to consult and ponder about who should be the recipients at this wealth. When the peop1e forming the consultative assembly had gathered, Omar ﷺ said to them, "I have instructed you to gather here to ponder about who should receive this wealth. I have studied a few verses of the Qur'an in which Allah says:

مَا أَفَاءَ اللَّهُ عَلَى رَسُولِهِ مِنْ أَهْلِ الْقُرَى فَلِلَّهِ وَلِلرَّسُولِ وَلِذِي الْقُرْبَى وَالْيَتَامَى وَالْمَسَاكِينِ وَابْنِ السَّبِيلِ كَيْ لَا يَكُونَ دُولَةً بَيْنَ الْأَغْنِيَاءِ مِنْكُمْ وَمَا آتَاكُمُ الرَّسُولُ فَخُذُوهُ وَمَا نَهَاكُمْ عَنْهُ فَانْتَهُوا وَاتَّقُوا اللَّهَ إِنَّ اللَّهَ شَدِيدُ الْعِقَابِ (7) لِلْفُقَرَاءِ الْمُهَاجِرِينَ الَّذِينَ أُخْرِجُوا مِنْ دِيَارِهِمْ وَأَمْوَالِهِمْ يَبْتَغُونَ فَضْلًا مِنَ اللَّهِ وَرِضْوَانًا وَيَنْصُرُونَ اللَّهَ وَرَسُولَهُ أُولَئِكَ هُمُ الصَّادِقُونَ (8)

What Allah gave as booty (Fai) to His Messenger (Muhammad SAW) from the people of the townships, - it is for Allah, His Messenger (Muhammad ﷺ), the kindred (of Messenger Muhammad ﷺ), the orphans, Al-Masakin (the poor), and the wayfarer, in order that it may not become a fortune used by the rich among you. And whatsoever the Messenger (Muhammad ﷺ) gives you, take it, and whatsoever he forbids you, abstain (from it), and fear Allah. Verily, Allah is Severe in punishment. (And there is also a share in this booty) for the poor emigrants, who were expelled from their homes and their property, seeking Bounties from Allah and to please Him. And helping Allah (i.e. helping His religion) and His Messenger (Muhammad ﷺ). Such are indeed the truthful (to what they say). (Al-Hasr:7-8)

وَالَّذِينَ تَبَوَّءُوا الدَّارَ وَالْإِيمَانَ مِنْ قَبْلِهِمْ يُحِبُّونَ مَنْ هَاجَرَ إِلَيْهِمْ وَلَا يَجِدُونَ فِي صُدُورِهِمْ حَاجَةً مِمَّا أُوتُوا وَيُؤْثِرُونَ عَلَى أَنْفُسِهِمْ وَلَوْ كَانَ بِهِمْ خَصَاصَةٌ وَمَنْ يُوقَ شُحَّ نَفْسِهِ فَأُولَئِكَ هُمُ الْمُفْلِحُونَ (9)

And those who, before them, had homes (in Al-Madinah) and had adopted the Faith, love those who emigrate to them, and have no jealousy in their breasts for that which they have been given (from the booty of Banee An-Nadeer), and give them (emigrants) preference over themselves, even though they were in need of that. And whosoever is saved from his own covetousness, such are they who will be the successful. (Al-Hasr:9)

Omar ﷺ said, "By Allah! This wealth is not only for these people. There are others also as mentioned in the forthcoming verse).

وَالَّذِينَ جَاءُوا مِنْ بَعْدِهِمْ يَقُولُونَ رَبَّنَا اغْفِرْ لَنَا وَلِإِخْوَانِنَا الَّذِينَ سَبَقُونَا بِالْإِيمَانِ وَلَا تَجْعَلْ فِي قُلُوبِنَا غِلًّا لِلَّذِينَ آمَنُوا رَبَّنَا إِنَّكَ رَءُوفٌ رَحِيمٌ (10)

And those who came after them say: "Our Lord! Forgive us and our brethren who have preceded us in Faith, and put not in our hearts any hatred against those who have believed. Our Lord! You are indeed full of kindness, Most Merciful. (Al-Hasr:10)

Omar ﷺ said, "By Allah! There is not a single Muslim who does not have a right to this wealth, whether it is given to him to not, even though he may be a shepherd in Adan." *(Bayhaqi)*.

The Narration of Malik bin Hadathan ﷺ

Narrating the same incident, Malik bin Aws bin Hadathan reports that Omar ﷺ also recited the following verses:

إِنَّمَا الصَّدَقَاتُ لِلْفُقَرَاءِ وَالْمَسَاكِينِ وَالْعَامِلِينَ عَلَيْهَا وَالْمُؤَلَّفَةِ قُلُوبُهُمْ وَفِي الرِّقَابِ وَالْغَارِمِينَ وَفِي سَبِيلِ اللَّهِ وَابْنِ السَّبِيلِ فَرِيضَةً مِنَ اللَّهِ وَاللَّهُ عَلِيمٌ حَكِيمٌ (60)

As-Sadaqat (here it means Zakat) are only for the Fuqara (poor), and Al-Masakin (the poor) and those employed to collect (the funds); and for to attract the hearts of those who have been inclined (towards Islam); and to free the captives; and for those in debt; and for Allah's Cause (i.e. for Mujahidoon - those fighting in the holy wars), and for the wayfarer (a traveler who is cut off from everything); a duty imposed by Allah. And Allah is All-Knower, All-Wise. (At-Tauba:60)

He then added, "Zakah is reserved for these people." Thereafter, he recited:

وَاعْلَمُوا أَنَّمَا غَنِمْتُمْ مِنْ شَيْءٍ فَأَنَّ لِلَّهِ خُمُسَهُ وَلِلرَّسُولِ وَلِذِي الْقُرْبَى وَالْيَتَامَى وَالْمَسَاكِينِ وَابْنِ السَّبِيلِ إِنْ كُنْتُمْ آمَنْتُمْ بِاللَّهِ وَمَا أَنْزَلْنَا عَلَى عَبْدِنَا يَوْمَ الْفُرْقَانِ يَوْمَ الْتَقَى الْجَمْعَانِ وَاللَّهُ

عَلَى كُلِّ شَيْءٍ قَدِيرٌ (41)

And know that whatever of war-booty that you may gain, verily one-fifth (1/5th) of it is assigned to Allah, and to the Messenger, and to the near relatives (of the Messenger (Muhammad ﷺ)), (and also) the orphans, Al-Masakin (the poor) and the wayfarer, if you have believed in Allah and in that which We sent down to Our slave (Muhammad ﷺ) on the Day of criterion (between right and wrong), the Day when the two forces met (the battle of Badr) - And Allah is Able to do all things. (Al-Anfal:41)

Omar ﷺ then said, "The spoils of war for these people." He then continued reciting:

مَا أَفَاءَ اللَّهُ عَلَى رَسُولِهِ مِنْ أَهْلِ الْقُرَى فَلِلَّهِ وَلِلرَّسُولِ وَلِذِي الْقُرْبَى وَالْيَتَامَى وَالْمَسَاكِينِ وَابْنِ السَّبِيلِ كَيْ لَا يَكُونَ دُولَةً بَيْنَ الْأَغْنِيَاءِ مِنْكُمْ وَمَا آتَاكُمُ الرَّسُولُ فَخُذُوهُ وَمَا نَهَاكُمْ عَنْهُ فَانْتَهُوا وَاتَّقُوا اللَّهَ إِنَّ اللَّهَ شَدِيدُ الْعِقَابِ (7) لِلْفُقَرَاءِ الْمُهَاجِرِينَ الَّذِينَ أُخْرِجُوا مِنْ دِيَارِهِمْ وَأَمْوَالِهِمْ يَبْتَغُونَ فَضْلًا مِنَ اللَّهِ وَرِضْوَانًا وَيَنْصُرُونَ اللَّهَ وَرَسُولَهُ أُولَئِكَ هُمُ الصَّادِقُونَ (8)

What Allah gave as booty (Fai) to His Messenger (Muhammad ﷺ) from the people of the townships, - it is for Allah, His Messenger (Muhammad ﷺ), the kindred (of Messenger Muhammad ﷺ), the orphans, Al-Masakin (the poor), and the wayfarer, in order that it may not become a fortune used by the rich among you. And whatsoever the Messenger (Muhammad ﷺ) gives you, take it, and whatsoever he forbids you, abstain (from it), and fear Allah. Verily, Allah is Severe in punishment. (And there is also a share in this booty) for the poor emigrants, who were expelled from their homes and their property, seeking Bounties from Allah and to please Him. And helping Allah (i.e. helping His religion) and His Messenger (Muhammad ﷺ). Such are indeed the truthful (to what they say). (Al-Hashr:7-8)

He added. "That refers to the Muhajirin." He then continued:

وَالَّذِينَ تَبَوَّءُوا الدَّارَ وَالْإِيمَانَ مِنْ قَبْلِهِمْ يُحِبُّونَ مَنْ هَاجَرَ إِلَيْهِمْ وَلَا يَجِدُونَ فِي صُدُورِهِمْ حَاجَةً مِمَّا أُوتُوا وَيُؤْثِرُونَ عَلَى أَنْفُسِهِمْ وَلَوْ كَانَ بِهِمْ خَصَاصَةٌ وَمَنْ يُوقَ شُحَّ نَفْسِهِ فَأُولَئِكَ هُمُ الْمُفْلِحُونَ (9)

And those who, before them, had homes (in Al-Madinah) and had adopted the Faith, love those who emigrate to them, and have no jealousy in their breasts for that which they have been given (from the booty of Banee An-Nadeer), and give them (emigrants) preference over themselves, even though they were in need of that. And whosoever is saved from his own covetousness, such are they who will be the successful. (Al-Hashr:9)

Omar ﷺ said. "That refers to the Ansar." Finally he recited:

وَالَّذِينَ جَاءُوا مِنْ بَعْدِهِمْ يَقُولُونَ رَبَّنَا اغْفِرْ لَنَا وَلِإِخْوَانِنَا الَّذِينَ سَبَقُونَا بِالْإِيمَانِ وَلَا تَجْعَلْ فِي قُلُوبِنَا غِلًّا لِلَّذِينَ آمَنُوا رَبَّنَا إِنَّكَ رَءُوفٌ رَحِيمٌ (10)

And those who came after them say: "Our Lord! Forgive us and our brethren who have preceded us in Faith, and put not in our hearts any hatred against those who have believed. Our Lord! You are indeed full of kindness, Most Merciful. (Al-Hashr:10)

He then said, "This verse encompasses all people. There is therefore no Muslim apart from your slaves who do not have a right to this wealth. If I live InsAllah, there shall not be a single Muslim who will receive his right even though he be a shepherd in the upper reaches of Himyar (in Yemen). His right will reach him without a drop of perspiration on his forehead (without any effort on his part)." (Bayhaqi, Ibn Jareer, Ibn Kathir).

Talha bin Ubaidullah ﷺ Distributes Wealth

Su'da ﷺ narrates, "I once went to my husband Talha bin Ubaidullah ﷺ and noticed that he was carrying a burden of grief. 'What is the matter?' I asked, 'Did we perhaps cause this grief to overcome you?' 'Not at all,' he replied, 'you are an excellent wife

to any Muslim man. The problem is that some wealth has accumulated by me and I do not know what to do with it.' I said, 'Why should this perturb you? Call up your family people and distribute amongst them.' He told his slave to call all of his family and he gave it all to them. I asked his treasurer how much was distributed and he informed me that it was 400,000." (Tabrani in Targheeb wat Tarheeb, Haythami, Ibn Sa'd, Abu Nu'aym)

The Narration of Hasan ﷺ in this Regard

Hasan reports that Talha ﷺ once sold a piece of land he owned for 700,000. Because the money stayed the night with him, he stayed awake the entire night out of fear that he should die without giving it away. He then distributed it all as soon as morning arrived. (Abu Nu'aym in Hilya, Ibn Sa'd).

Talha 'Fayyadh' (The very generous) ﷺ

Su'da ﷺ the wife of Talha ﷺ reports that she once came to Talha ﷺ and found him to be extremely distressed. She asked, "Why are you so distressed? Have we caused this grief to overcome you?" He replied, "By Allah! You have caused me no distress at all. You are a most excellent wife. It is some money that has been collected with me that I am concerned about." Su'da ﷺ reports, "I advised him to send for his family and his tribe and to distribute it amongst them. After he had done so, I asked the treasurer how much money there was. He informed me that it amounted to 400,000. His daily earnings amounted to 1,000 Wafi (approximately 1666 Dirhams) and he was given the title of Talha Fayyadh (The very generous)." (Hakim).

Zubair bin Awwam ﷺ Distributes Wealth

Sa'eed bin Abdul Aziz ﷺ reports that Zubair bin Awwam ﷺ had 1,000 slaves who worked and gave their earnings to him. He then distributed the money every night and had nothing left by the time he returned home. (Abu Nu'aym in Hilya). Mughith bin Sumay reports that although Zubair bin Awwam ﷺ had 1,000 slaves who worked and gave their earnings to him, not a single Dirham of these earnings entered his house, he gave everything away to the needy. (Bayhaqi, Ya'qub bin Sufiyan in Isabah).

The Incident Between Zubair ﷺ and his Son Abdullah ﷺ Concerning his Debts

Abdullah bin Zubair ﷺ says, "When my father Zubair ﷺ stood for the battle of Jamal, he called for me. As I stood by his side, he said, 'Dear son!' None but an oppressor or an oppressed person shall be killed today and I strongly feel that I shall be killed today as one oppressed. However, my greatest worry is my debts. Do you think that our debts will leave any of our money behind? Nevertheless, dear son, I want you to sell our properties to settle my debts.' He also made a bequest for a third to be given away and a third of that third was to be given to the grand children. In this regard, he said, 'A third of the third. He explained, if anything remains after settling the debts, a third of the third should go to your children.'" One of narrators by the name of Hisham says that some of the children of Abdullah bin Zubair ﷺ such as Khubaib and Abbad were the same age as some of Zubair ﷺ's sons. At that time; Zubair ﷺ had 9 sons and 9 daughters. Abdullah ﷺ narrates further, "Advising me about the debt, my father said, 'Dear son! If you are unable to settle something, seek help from my friend.' 'Who is your friend, O father?' I asked. 'Allah,' he replied. By Allah! Each time I encountered any difficulty concerning the debt, I said, 'O friend of Zubair! Settle his debt for him.' Allah would then settle the debt." Zubair ﷺ was martyred that day without leaving behind a single Dinar or Dirham. All that he left were a few properties, one of which was in Ghaba. He also left 11 houses in Madinah, 2 in Basra, one in Kufa and another in Egypt. The only reason that he had debts was because when people would bring their money to him for safekeeping, he would say to them, 'I cannot accept it as a trust but shall treat it as a loan because I fear that it should not be destroyed. If it is destroyed as a loan, I am liable to pay you back whereas I am not liable to do so if it is only a trust.' My father never was a governor nor did he ever accept appointment as a collector of zakah. All he did was to accompany Rasulullah ﷺ, Abu Bakr ﷺ, Omar ﷺ and Uthman ﷺ on the battlefields. When I calculated his debts, they totaled 2,200,000." Abdullah ﷺ narrates further, he says, "Hakim bin Hizam ﷺ once met him and asked, 'Dear nephew! How rich was the debt of my brother Zubair ﷺ?' I did not disclose the entire figure to him and replied, '100,000.' He then said, 'By Allah! I do not think that you have enough money for that.' I said, 'What would you say if it was 2,200,000?' He replied, 'I do think that you would ever be able to settle it. If you need any assistance, do not hesitate to ask me.'"

Zubair ﷺ had purchased the piece of land in Ghaba for 170,000. Abdullah ﷺ evaluated its value to be 1,600,000; he then divided it into 16 parts, each worth 100,000. He then made the announcement, "Whoever has a debt due from Zubair should meet us at Ghaba." Abdullah bin Ja'far ﷺ came up. He was owed a sum of 100,000. He said to Abdullah ﷺ, "If you please, I could write off the debt." "No," replied Abdullah ﷺ. "Otherwise," said Abdullah bin Ja'far ﷺ, "if you so wish, you could include me amongst those who are the last to be paid." When Abdullah ﷺ did not agree to this either, Abdullah bin Ja'far ﷺ asked to be given a piece of the land in settlement. Abdullah ﷺ then gave him a piece of the land saying, "You may have the land from this point to this point." Abdullah ﷺ then sold the other pieces of land and settled all the debts in full. At the end, there were only 4½ properties left from the 16. Abdullah ﷺ then approached Mu'awiya ﷺ who was then in the company of Amr bin Uthman ﷺ, Mundhir bin Zubair ﷺ and Ibn Zam'ah ﷺ. "How much did you evaluate the property at Ghaba to be?" When Abdullah ﷺ informed him that each portion was valued at 100,000, Mu'awiya ﷺ asked how many portions were still available. "4½," replied Abdullah ﷺ. "I shall take one portion for 100,000," said Mundhir bin Zubair ﷺ. "And I shall take another for 100,000," said Amr bin Uthman ﷺ. "I too shall take one for 100,000," said Ibn Zam'ah. Mu'awiya ﷺ then asked, "How many does that leave?" "1½ portions," replied Abdullah. "I shall take them for 150,000," said Mu'awiya ﷺ. Abdullah bin Ja'far ﷺ also sold his portion of land to Mu'awiya ﷺ for 600,000.

When Abdullah ﷺ had settled all the debts, the children of Zubair ﷺ asked for their inheritance to be distributed. However, Abdullah ﷺ refused and said, "By Allah! I shall not distribute anything amongst you until I make an announcement during 4 Hajj seasons calling all people who were owed any money by our father Zubair ﷺ." He then made the announcement during 4 consecutive years during the Hajj season. It was only after the 4th year that he finally distributed the inheritance amongst his brothers and sisters. Zubair ﷺ had 4 wives and he had also bequeathed a third of the estate. Despite this, each wife received an amount of 1,200,000. His entire estate amounted to 50,200,000. (Bukhari). Ibn Kathir has mentioned, "The total amount distributed between the heirs was 38,400,000. The total amount bequeathed to others totaled 19,200,000. The sum of 2 was therefore 57,600,000. The debts paid before this amounted to 2,200,000, making the sum total of entire estate 59,800,000. We have mentioned this only because of the objections that arise about the narration of Bukhari. It is therefore necessary that this matter be clarified." (Al Bidayah wan Nihayah).

Abdur Rahman bin Auf ﷺ Distributes Wealth

Ummu Bakr bint Miswar reports that Abdur Rahman bin Auf ﷺ once sold a property of his for 40,000. He then distributed it amongst the Banu Zuhrah tribe, the poor Muslims, the Muhajirin and the wives of Rasulullah ﷺ. When he sent some of the money to Aisha ﷺ, she asked who it was that sent it. When she was informed that Abdur Rahman bin Auf ﷺ had sent it and the entire incident was reported to her, she said, "Rasulullah ﷺ once said to his wives, 'After my demise, none but the truly steadfast ones will show compassion towards you.' May Allah allow Abdur Rahman bin Auf to drink from the fountain of Salsabil in Jannah." (Hakim, Dhahabi, Ibn Sa'd). Rasulullah ﷺ said, "After my demise, none but the truly righteous ones will show compassion towards you." Ja'far bin Burqan says, "The report reached me that Abdur Rahman bin Auf ﷺ freed 30 families of slaves. (Hakim, Abu Nu'aym in Hilya).

Abu Ubaidah bin Jarrah ﷺ, Mu'adh bin Jabal ﷺ and Hudhaifa ﷺ Distribute Wealth

Malik Dar ﷺ reports that Omar ﷺ once placed 400 Dinars in a bag and said to his slave, "Take this to Abu Ubaidah bin Jarrah and then busy yourself with something in the house for a while to see what he does with it." The slave took the bag and said to Abu Ubaidah ﷺ, "Amirul Mu'minin says that you should use this for your needs." Abu Ubaidah ﷺ prayed, "May Allah reward him and shower His mercy on him." He then called for his slave girl and instructed her to give 7 coins to a certain person, another 5 to another and another 5 to someone else. In this manner, he gave everything away. The slave then returned to Omar ﷺ and informed him about what had transpired. Omar ﷺ then had the same amount of money placed in a bag for Mu'adh bin Jabal ﷺ. Addressing his slave once more, Omar ﷺ said, "Take this to Mu'adh bin Jabal ﷺ and then busy yourself with something in the house for a while to see what he does with it." The slave took the bag and said to Mu'adh Jabal ﷺ, "Amirul Mu'minin says that you should use this for your needs." Mu'adh bin Jabal ﷺ prayed, "May Allah shower His mercy on him and reward him." He then called for his slave girl and instructed her to give an amount to a certain family, another amount to another and so forth until all the money was finished. When Mu'adh bin Jabal ﷺ's wife came to know about this, she came to him and said, "What about us? By Allah! We are also poor. Do give us some of it." By then all that was left in the bag was 2 Dinars, which he handed over to her. When the slave reported back to Omar ﷺ, he was very pleased and said, "They are all brothers of each other and therefore act alike." (Tabrani in Kabir, Targheeb wat Tarheeb, Haythami, Hafidh in Isabah, Abu Nu'aym in Hilya, Ibn Sa'd).

Aslam reports that Omar ﷺ once asked those around him to express their wishes. Someone said, "I wish that this room was filled with Dirhams that I could spend in the Path of Allah." When Omar ﷺ asked another person to express his wish, he said, "I wish that this room was filled with gold that I could spend in the Path of Allah." When Omar ﷺ repeated the request, another person said, "I wish that this room was filled with gems or something as valuable that I could spend in the Path of Allah." When Omar ﷺ once again asked them to express their wishes, they submitted, "What more can we wish for?" Omar then said, "Unlike you, I wish that this room was filled with men like Abu Ubaidah bin Jarrah, Mu'adh bin Jabal ﷺ and Hudhaifa bin

Yaman ؓ so that I could employ them in the service of Allah. Omar ؓ then sent some money to Hudhaifa ؓ and instructed the person taking it to see what he does with it. When the money came to him, Hudhaifa ؓ distributed it all to the poor. Omar ؓ then sent some money to Mu'adh bin Jabal ؓ and he also distributed it all. Thereafter, he sent some money to Abu Ubaidah bin Jarrah ؓ and again gave instructions to the person taking it that he should see what Abu Ubaidah ؓ does with the money. When he also gave all the money to the needy, Omar ؓ said to the people, "Did I not tell you that these are men of worth?"

Abdullah bin Omar ؓ Distributes Wealth

Maymun bin Mahran reports that Abdullah bin Omar ؓ once received 20,000 Dinars as he was sitting in a gathering. He distributed all of it before standing up from the gathering. Nafi narrates that when Mu'awiya ؓ sent 100,000 to Abdullah bin Omar ؓ, there was nothing left of it by the time the year came to an end (he spent all in the Path of Allah). (Abu Nu'aym in Hilya).

He Spends Thousands in Cash in a Single Day

Ayub bin Wa'il Rasibi reports that when he went to Madinah, a neighbor of Abdullah bin Omar ؓ told him, "Abdullah bin Omar ؓ once received a sum of 4,000 from Mu'awiya ؓ, 4,000 from another person, a further 2,000 from someone else as well as a shawl. He then came to the marketplace to buy some fodder for his animal for a Dirham. When he made the purchase on credit, I recalled the large amount of money that came to him and approached one of his slaves. I said to her, 'I wish to ask you something and want you to tell me the truth. Did Abu Abdur Rahman (Abdullah bin Omar ؓ) not receive 4,000 from Mu'awiya ؓ, 4,000 from another person, a further 2,000 from someone else as well as a shawl?' 'Yes, he did,' she replied. 'Then why did he just buy some fodder on credit for a Dirham?' I asked. She said, 'He had spent all of it in the Path of Allah before sleeping. He the put the shawl on his back and also gave that away before returning home.' I then made an announcement saying, 'O assembly of traders! Why are you toiling for this world when Abdullah bin Omar ؓ received 10.000 proper Dirhams last night and in the morning he is buying a Dirham's worth of fodder on credit?!" (Abu Nu'aym in Hilya).

Another Similar Incident About Him

Nafi reports that Abdullah bin Omar ؓ once received 20,000 as he sat in a gathering. Before getting up from the gathering, he had already given it all away together with some more that he added. He continued giving until everything he had was finished. A person came to him whom he usually gave but the money was already finished by then. Abdullah bin Omar ؓ took a loan from someone whom he had already given money to and gave it to the person who had come late. Maymun says, "I swear by Allah that the person who called Abdullah bin Omar a miser is definitely wrong. He was never miserly in worthy causes." Of course he never spent in unworthy causes and on himself. (Ibn Sa'd).

Ash'ath bin Qais ؓ Distributes Wealth

Abu Is'haq reports, "A man from the Kinda tribe owed me some money and left to see him before dawn to collect the money. I happened to be at the Masjid of Ash'ath bin Qais ؓ at the time of Fajr and performed the Fajr salah. After the Imam had made the Salam, Ash'ath bin Qais ؓ placed before every person a set of clothing, a pair of shoes and 500 Dirhams. I told the people that I was not from the locality but they still let me have it. When I asked what the gifts were for, the people informed me that

Ash'ath bin Qais ؓ had just returned from Makkah and was therefore giving gifts to the people. (Tabrani, Haythami)

Aisha ؓ Distributes Wealth

Ummu Durra says, "100,000 was once brought to Aisha ؓ and she distributed it all even though she was fasting. I said to her, 'Could you not use a Dirham from the money to buy some meat to break your fast?' Se replied, 'Had you reminded me about it, I would have done so.'" (Ibn Sa'd in Isabah)

Sauda bint Zam'ah ؓ Distributes Wealth

Muhammad bin Sirin reports that Omar ؓ once sent a bag full of Dirhams to Sauda ؓ, one of the wives of Rasulullah ﷺ. "What is this'?" she asked. When she was told that it was Dirhams, she remarked, "In a bag like dates?" She then distributed all the money amongst the poor. (Ibn Sa'd in Isabah).

Zainab bint Jahash ؓ Distributes Wealth

Barra bint Rafi narrates, "When some surplus wealth was being distributed, Omar ؓ sent to Zainab bint Jahash ؓ her share. When it was brought to her, she said, 'May Allah forgive Omar ؓ. My sisters besides me are better at distributing this than I am, take it to them rather.' When she was told that it was all hers, she exclaimed, 'SubhanAllah!' She then veiled herself and told the people bringing it to put it down and cover it with a cloth. Thereafter, she instructed me to put my hand beneath the cloth, to take a handful of coins and give it to the people of certain tribes, all of whom were her relatives and orphans. Eventually when there was only a little left beneath the cloth, I said to her, 'May Allah forgive you, O Ummul Mu'minin! By Allah! We also have a right to this.' 'You may have whatever is left beneath the cloth,' she said. We found 85 Dirhams there. She raised her hands to the sky and prayed, 'O Allah! Let not the surplus of Omar reach me after this year.' She passed away not long afterwards." (Ibn Sa'd).

Another Similar Incident About Her ؓ

Muhammad bin Ka'b narrates that the share of Zainab bint Jahash ؓ from the surplus wealth amounted to 12,000. She however, only took it once. After receiving it, she prayed, "O Allah! Do not let me have this wealth next year because it is a great tribulation." She then gave it all out to her family and to needy people. When this news reached Omar ؓ, he said, "She is a woman with whom Allah intends only good." He then went to her door and sent her salam saying, "The news has reached me about how you gave away all the money without keeping anything for yourself. I am therefore sending you another 1,000 to keep for yourself." However, Zainab ؓ did the same ring and gave all of it to others. (Ibn Sa'd in Isabah).

An Incident of a Woman and Omar ؓ When He Stipulates an Allowance for Every Muslim Baby

Abdullah bin Omar ؓ reports that when a trade caravan arrived in Madinah, they set up camp at the place where the Muslims performed the Eid salah. Omar ؓ asked Abdur Rahman bin Auf ؓ whether he was prepared to accompany him to guard the camp against theft that night. Abdur Rahman bin Auf agreed and the 2 men spent the night guarding the camp and performing salah in turn. Hearing the cry of a child, Omar ؓ went in the direction and said to the mother, "Fear Allah and treat your child well." He then returned to where he was. When he again heard the child cry, he went back to the mother and repeated what he had said earlier. He then returned to his place. When he again heard the child cry towards the end of the night, he returned to the mother and said, "Shame on you! You seem to be a terrible mother! It seems like your child has not be calmed the entire night." The mother responded by saying, "O servant of Allah! You have harassed me all night. I have been trying to pacify my child to wean him but he refuses to do so." "Why are you doing this?" enquired Omar ♦. "Because," the lady explained, "Omar only gives allowances to children who have been weaned." "How old is the child?" asked Omar ♦. When the woman informed him that the child was only a few months old, Omar ♦ said, "Please do not rush him." When Omar ♦ led the Fajr salah, the people could barely understand his recitation of the Qur'an because of his excessive weeping. After saying the Salam, he exclaimed, "Woe to Omar! How many Muslim children has he killed'?!" He then instructed someone to announce, "Take note! Do not rush your children into weaning because we have now fixed an allowance for every Muslim child born." He wrote to all the Muslim territories, notifying an allowance has been stipulated for every new born Muslim child. (Ibn Sa'd in Kanzul Ummal)

Omar ♦'s Handling of Public Funds and his Abstention From It

Omar ♦ once said, "I treat Allah's money (public funds) as if it is the wealth of orphans. I stay away from it as long as I am able to do without it and use it within reason only if I really have to. Another narration states that Omar ♦ once said, "I treat Allah's money like the wealth of orphans." He then recited the following verse of the Qur'an: وَمَنْ كَانَ غَنِيًّا فَلْيَسْتَعْفِفْ وَمَنْ كَانَ فَقِيرًا فَلْيَأْكُلْ بِالْمَعْرُوفِ ......whoever (whichever guardian) is rich, he should take no wages, but if he is poor, let him have for himself what is just and reasonable (according to his work).... (An-Nisa':6)

Urwa states that Omar ♦ once said, "It is permissible for me to take from this public money only as much as I spend from my earnings." (Ibn Sa'd in Muntakhab Kanzul Ummal).

The Incident Between Omar ♦ and the Public Treasurer

Imran narrates that whenever Omar ♦ needed money, he would approach the public treasurer and take a loan from him. There were times when Omar ♦ was unable to pay back on time and the treasurer would come to him to demand payment. He would press Omar ♦ and Omar ♦ would make the necessary arrangements for repayment. Omar ♦ would also pay him back from his share of the surplus wealth that he received. (Ibn Sa'd).

The Incident of Omar ♦ and Abdur Rahman bin Auf ♦

Ibrahim reports that Omar ♦ used to gage in trade when he was Khalifa. When he once prepared a caravan to send to Sham, he sent someone to arrange a loan of 4,000 Dirhams for him from Abdur Rahman bin Auf ♦. Abdur Rahman bin Auf ♦ sent a message back with the messenger that Omar ♦ should take the loan from the public treasury and pay it back later. When the message reached him, Omar ♦ felt it most difficult to do so. When Omar ♦ met Abdur Rahman bin Auf ♦, he asked him, "Are you the one who said that I should take the money from the public treasury? Had I died before the caravan returns, you would say, 'The Amirul Mu'minin had taken the money. Let us waive it.' I shall be taken to task for it on the Day of Judgment. I shall never do such a thing. I prefer to take the money from a man who is as greedy and stingy as you are to ensure that he takes it from my estate if I die." (Ibn Sa'd in Muntakhab Kanzul Ummal).

The Incident of Omar ♦ and the Honey From the Public Treasury

One of the sons of Bara bin Ma'rur reports that Omar ♦ once fell ill and honey was prescribed to treat him. At that time there was a vial of honey in the public treasury. Omar ♦ therefore came out and mounted the pulpit saying to the people, "I shall use the honey in the public treasury only if you people permit. Otherwise it will be Haram for me." The people gladly gave their permission. (Ibn Asakir in Muntakhab Kanzul Ummal).

The Incident Between Omar ♦ and His Daughter Hafsa ♦ Concerning Public Funds

Hasan narrates that some money once came to Omar ♦. When his daughter Hafsa ♦ heard about it, she approached him saying, "O Amirul Mu'minin! Relatives also have a right to that money because Allah has advised kind treatment of relatives." He responded by saying, "Dear daughter! My relatives have a right only in my personal wealth. As for this, it is the spoils of the Muslims. Do you wish to deceive your father? Please leave." She then left, dragging her dress along. (Ahmad in Zuhd, Muntakhab Kanzul Ummal).

The Incident of Omar ♦ and Abdullah bin Arqam ♦

Aslam reports that he once saw Abdullah bin Arqam ♦ go to Omar ♦ and say, "O Amirul Mu'minin! We have some jewels and silver utensils from Jalula. See if you have some free time some day to have a look and tell us what to do." Omar ♦ said to him, "Remind me one day if you see that I have some time." Abdullah bin Arqam ♦ therefore came to Omar ♦ one day and said, "I see that you have some time today." "I do," said Omar ♦, "Spread out the leather tablecloth and place the jewels and utensils on it." After Abdullah bin Arqam ♦ did as told, Omar ♦ came to tablecloth and as he stood there, he said, "O Allah! You have mentioned this when You say:

زُيِّنَ لِلنَّاسِ حُبُّ الشَّهَوَاتِ مِنَ النِّسَاءِ وَالْبَنِينَ وَالْقَنَاطِيرِ الْمُقَنْطَرَةِ مِنَ الذَّهَبِ وَالْفِضَّةِ وَالْخَيْلِ الْمُسَوَّمَةِ وَالْأَنْعَامِ وَالْحَرْثِ ذَلِكَ مَتَاعُ الْحَيَاةِ الدُّنْيَا وَاللَّهُ عِنْدَهُ حُسْنُ الْمَآبِ (14)

Beautified for men is the love of things they covet; women, children, much of gold and silver (wealth), branded beautiful horses, cattle and well-tilled land. This is the pleasure of the present worldly life; but Allah has the excellent return (Paradise with flowing rivers, etc.) with Him. (Al-Imran:14)

He said further, "O Allah! You have also mentioned:

لِكَيْ لَا تَأْسَوْا عَلَى مَا فَاتَكُمْ وَلَا تَفْرَحُوا بِمَا آتَاكُمْ

In order that you may not be sad over matters that you fail to get, nor rejoice because of that which has been given to you. (Al-Hadid:23)

We seem unable to avoid getting overjoyed by those things that have been beautified for us. O Allah! Grant us the ability to spend in the right avenues and protect us from its evil." Just then one of Omar ♦'s sons called Abdur Rahman bin Bahia, born to Omar ♦'s slave girl Bahia was brought to him. The child said, "Dear father! Do give me a ring." Omar ♦ said, "Go to your mother. She will give you some barley porridge to drink." The narrator says, "By Allah! Omar ♦ did not give his son anything from the wealth." (Ibn Abi Shaiha, Ahmad, Ibn Abi Dunya, Ibn Abi Hatim, Ibn Asakir in Muntakhab Kanzul Ummal).

The Incident of the Musk and Ambergris From Bahrain

Isma'el bin Muhammad bin Sa'd bin Abi Waqqas ♦ reports that when some musk and ambergris perfume came to Omar ♦ from Bahrain, he said, "I wish that I could find a woman who is good at weighing, to weigh this perfume for me so that I may distribute it amongst the people." His wife Aatika bint Zaiel bin Arm bin Nufail ♦ offered, "I am good a weighing. Bring it here and I will weigh it for you." However, Omar ♦ refused to give it to her. "Why not?" she enquired. Omar ؓ replied, "I fear that while weighing you may take some of it and do this (he then put his finger on his temples) and apply some on your neck. In this manner, you will be receiving a greater share than other Muslims." *(Ahmad in Zuhd, Muntakhab Kanzul Ummal).*

The Incident of Abdullah bin Omar ؓ with His Father Omar ؓ

Hasan narrates that Omar ؓ once saw a little girl dragging her feet as she walked because of weakness. "Who is this child?" he asked. "She is one of your daughters," replied his son Abdullah ؓ. "Which daughter of mine is she?" Omar ؓ enquires further. Abdullah ؓ explained, "She is my daughter." "What has made her reach the condition I see?" Omar ؓ asked. "Your practice," replied Abdullah ؓ, "because you do not spend on her." Omar ؓ exclaimed, "By Allah! My dear man, I do not intend fooling you about your children. You need to earn for your children. Do not expect me to provide for them from the Baytul Maal." *(Ibn Sa'd, Ibn Abi Shaibah, Ibn Asakir in Muntakhab Kanzul Ummal).*

The Narration of Asim the Son of Omar ؓ

Asim bin Omar ؓ, the son of Omar ؓ says, "When Omar ؓ got me married, he provided for me from the Baytul Maal for a month. He then sent his slave Yarfa to call me. When I went to him, he said, 'By Allah! Even before becoming the Khalifa I never regarded the money of the Baytul Maal to be permissible for me to use unless the cause was right. Now that I am the Khalifa, it is even more prohibited for me because it is now a trust in my care. I have used Allah's money (money from the Baytul Maal) to support you for a month and cannot do so any longer. I shall however, assist you with the produce from my orchard at Ghaba. Pick the fruit and sell it. Then take the money and go to a trader from your tribe and stand by his side. When he makes purchases, become his partner and use the proceeds of your business partnership to spend on your family." *(Ibn Sa'd, Abu Ubaid in Amwal, Muntakhan Kanzul Ummal).*

The Incident of Omar ؓ's Wife

Malik bin Aws bin Hadathan reports that when the envoy of the Roman Emperor came to Omar ؓ, Omar ؓ's wife borrowed a Dinar and bought some perfume. She put the perfume in a glass bottle and sent it with the envoy to the Emperor's wife. When the perfume reached the Roman Empress, she emptied out the perfume in another container and filled the glass bottle with gems. She then gave instructions to the envoy to take the bottle to the wife of Omar ؓ. When the bottle reached Omar ؓ's wife, she emptied the gems on her bed to have a look at them. Omar ؓ walked in and asked, "What is this'?" She related the incident to him, he took the gems and sold them. He gave his wife a Dinar from the money and deposited the rest in to the Baytul Maal. *(Denowri in Mujalaash, Muntakhab Kanzul Ummal).*

The Incident of Omar ؓ and His Son's Camel

Abdullah bin Omar ؓ says that he once purchased a camel and kept it in the grazing fields of the Baytul Maal. Once it grew fat, he brought it to the marketplace to sell. Omar ؓ came to the marketplace where he saw the fat camel. "Whose camel is this?" he asked. When he was informed that the camel belonged to his son Abdullah ؓ, he called out, "O Abdullah bin Omar! How excellent! The son of the Amirul Mu'minin!" Abdullah bin Omar ؓ came running and said, "What is the matter, O Amirul Mu'minin?" Omar ؓ asked, "What have you to say about this camel?" Abdullah ؓ explained, "I bought this camel and sent it

to the grazing fields of the Baytul Maal asking that profits from it which other Muslims seek." Omar ؓ marked, "When you sent it there, the shepherds must have said, 'Ensure that the camel of Amirul Mu'minin's son feeds well. Ensure that the camel of the Amirul Mu'minin's son has plenty to drink.' Thus your camel received special attention and became fat. O Abdullah bin Omar! You may have your capital back from the sale but return to the Baytul Maal whatever profits are earned." *(Sa'eed bin Mansrro, Ibn Abi Shaybah, Bayhaqi in Muntakhab Kanzul Ummal)*

Omar ؓ Rebukes His In-Laws for Asking From the Baytul Maal

Muhammad bin Sirin narrates that one of Omar ؓ's in-laws once approached him and suggested that something be given to him from the Baytul Maal. Omar ؓ rebuked him saying, "Do you want me to meet Allah as a dishonest despot?" Some time afterwards, Omar ؓ gave the man 10,000 Dirhams from his own money. *(Ibn Sa'd in Kanzul Ummal)*

The Incident of Amirul Mu'minin Ali ؓ in This Regard

Antara reports that he went to Ali bin Abi Talib ؓ in a suburb of Kufa called Khowrnaq. Ali ؓ was wearing a shawl and shivering from the cold. Antara said, "O Amirul Mu'minin! You are shivering from cold when Allah has allotted a share for you and your family from the wealth of the state?" Ali ؓ replied, "I swear by Allah that I do not wish to take anything from the wealth of the people. I have even brought this shawl from my house in Madinah." *(Abu Ubaid in Al Bidayah wan Nihayah, Abu Nu'aym in Hilya).*

Rasulullah ﷺ Refuses to Accept Wealth Given to him: The Incident of Rasulullah ﷺ with Jibra'el عليه السلام and Another Angel

Abdullah bin Abbas ؓ reports that Allah once sent to Rasulullah ﷺ and angel with Jibra'el عليه السلام. The angel said to Rasulullah ﷺ, "Allah has given you a choice to either be a Nabi who is a slave of Allah or a Nabi who is a king. Rasulullah ﷺ turned to Jibra'el عليه السلام to get his opinion. Jibra'el عليه السلام indicated to Rasulullah ﷺ that he should adopt humility. Rasulullah ﷺ then replied, "I would rather be a Nabi who is a slave." After that day (like a true slave) Rasulullah ﷺ never ate anything while reclining until the day he met Allah. *(Ya'qub bin Sufian and Bukhari in Tarikh, Al Budayah wan Nihayah).*

Another Incident with Jibra'el عليه السلام in this Regard

Abdullah bin Abbas ؓ narrates that Rasulullah ﷺ and Jibra'el عليه السلام were once together on Mount Safa when Rasulullah ﷺ said, "O Jibra'el! I swear by the Being Who has sent you with the truth that the family of Muhammad have neither had a mouthful of flour nor a handful of porridge this evening." Rasulullah ﷺ had barely completed his sentence when he was startled by a loud clamor from the sky. Rasulullah ﷺ asked, "Has Allah given the command for the Day of Judgment to take place?" "No," replied Jibra'el عليه السلام, "Allah has commanded Israfil عليه السلام to come to you when he heard what you said." Israfil عليه السلام then came to Rasulullah ﷺ and said, "Allah had heard what you said and has sent me with the keys to the treasures of the earth. Allah has instructed me to make you the offer that if you wanted, I could transform the mountains of Tihama into emeralds, pearl, gold and silver and make them travel with you wherever you go. If you so wish, you could either be a Nabi who is a king or a Nabi who is a slave." Jibra'el عليه السلام indicated to Rasulullah ﷺ that he should adopt humility, because of which Rasulullah ﷺ thrice repeated, "I would rather be a Nabi who is a slave." *(Tabrani, Bayhaqi in Targheeb waf Tarheeb, Tabrani in Awsat, Haythami).*

The Narration of Abu Umamah 🙏 About This

Abu Umamah 🙏 reports that Rasulullah 🙏 said, "My Rabb had offered to transform the rocky plains of Makkah into gold for me. I submitted, 'No, my Rabb. I would rather like to eat one day and be hungry the next day.' This Rasulullah 🙏 repeated 3 or more times. He then continued, 'So that I can be humble before You and remember You when I am hungry and thank and praise You when I have eaten." *(Tirmidhi in Targheeb wat Tarheeb).*

The Narration of Ali 🙏 About This

Ali 🙏 narrates that Rasulullah 🙏 once informed them that an angel came to him and said, "O Muhammad 🙏! Your Rabb sends salams to you and offers to turn the rocky plains of Makkah into gold for you if you would have it." However, Rasulullah 🙏 looked towards the sky and said, "No, O my Rabb! I prefer to rather have something to eat one day so that I may thank you and stay hungry the next day so that I may beg You." *(Askari in Kanzul Ummal).*

The Incident of the Money for a Dead Mushrik

Abdullah bin Abbas 🙏 reports that when a Mushrik was killed during the battle of Ahzab, the disbeliever sent a message to Rasulullah 🙏 that they would give him 12,000 if he sent them the body. Rasulullah 🙏 remarked, "There is neither any good in his body nor in the money." A narration of Ahmad states that Rasulullah 🙏 said to the Sahabah, "Hand the corpse over to them because both the corpse and the money are terrible." Rasulullah 🙏 then refused to accept any payment. *(Bayhaqi, Tirmidhi in Al Bidayah wan Nihayah).* Yet another narration states that a person named Naufal or Ibn Naufal died when he fell from his horse during the battle of Ahzab. Abu Sufian 🙏 who was not a Muslim then sent 100 camels to Rasulullah 🙏 as payment to have the body. Rasulullah 🙏 refused the money saying, 'Take the body because both the money and the corpse are despicable." *(Ibn Abi Shabah in Kanzul Ummal).*

The Clothing of Dhu Yazan

Urwa 🙏 narrates that Hakim bin Hizam 🙏 once went to Yemen where he bought a suit of clothing that belonged to the Yemeni ruler Dhu Yazan. When he brought it to Madinah, he presented it as a gift to Rasulullah 🙏. Rasulullah 🙏 however refused to accept it saying, "We do not accept gifts from disbeliever." Hakim 🙏 was not yet a Muslim then. When Hakim 🙏 went to sell it, Rasulullah 🙏 instructed someone to purchase it for him. After buying it, Rasulullah 🙏 put it on and entered the Masjid. Hakim 🙏 says, "I have never seen anyone look more outstanding in that clothing than Rasulullah 🙏. He was as striking as the full moon and when I saw him, I could not restrain myself from saying (these couplets which mean):

"How can rulers even think to issue commands after the emergence of the clear, bright and gleaming one (Rasulullah 🙏 because they are now all constrained to follow him). When honor is matched to his, he surpasses them because honor has been poured over him like water poured over a person from a large bucket"

When he heard these couplets, Rasulullah 🙏 smiled.
(Ibn Jareer in Kanzul Ummal, Tabrani in Majma'uz Zawa'id, Haythami)

Hakim bin Hizam 🙏 says that even during the period of ignorance, Rasulullah 🙏 was the person he liked most. After Rasulullah 🙏 announced his Prophethood and went to Madinah, Hakim 🙏 left for Yemen during the Hajj season. There he found a set of clothing that belonged to Dhu Yazan on sale for 50 Dirhams. He purchased it to give it as a gift to Rasulullah 🙏. When he brought it back to Madinah, he did his best to make Rasulullah 🙏 accept it, but Rasulullah 🙏 refused. One of the narrators by the name of Ubaidullah says that he thinks that Rasulullah 🙏 said, "We do not accept anything from the disbeliever. However, if you please, we could pay you for it." Hakim 🙏 then sold it to Rasulullah 🙏. Narrating further, Hakim 🙏 says, "I saw Rasulullah 🙏 wearing the clothes when he was on the pulpit. I have never seen anything as impressive as Rasulullah 🙏 wearing those clothing that day." Rasulullah 🙏 then gave the clothing to Usama bin Zaid and when I saw Usama 🙏 wearing it, I said, 'O Usama! Are you wearing the clothes of Dhu Yazan?' Usama replied, 'Yes! I am better than Dhu Yazan. My father is better than his father and my mother is better than his mother.' I then left for Makkah where the people were shocked to hear the statement of Osama 🙏. *(Hakim by Dhahabi).*

The Gift of a Horse and a Camel

Amir bin Tufail Amiri 🙏 reports that Amir bin Malik once gave Rasulullah 🙏 a horse as a gift with a letter stating, "A sore has emerged on my stomach, so please send me the cure you have." Rasulullah 🙏 refuse to accept gift but sent to him a container of honey, telling him to use it as medication. Another narration from Ka'b bin Malik 🙏 narrates that 'The Spear Juggler' (Amir bin Malik) once brought a gift for Rasulullah 🙏. Rasulullah 🙏 invited him to accept Islam but he refused. Rasulullah 🙏 therefore said, "I do not accept the gift of a Mushrik." *(Ibn Asakir in Kanzul Ummal).* Another narration from Ayadh bin Himar Mujashi 🙏 states that when he once presented to Rasulullah 🙏 a camel or something else as a gift, Rasulullah 🙏 asked him whether he was a Muslim. When he replied in the negative, Rasulullah 🙏 said, "I have been prohibited from accepting gifts from disbeliever." *(Abu Dawud, Tirmidhi, Ibn Jabeer, Bayhaqi in Kanzul Ummal).*

Abu Bakr 🙏 Refuses to Accept Wealth Given to Him

Hasan narrates that Abu Bakr 🙏 once addressed the people. After praising Allah, he said, "Verily the best of all intelligence is Taqwa." The narration continues to the point where it states that Abu Bakr 🙏 was proceeding to the marketplace early next morning when Omar 🙏 met him and asked, "Where are you off to?" When Abu Bakr 🙏 informed him that he was on his way to the marketplace, Omar 🙏 remarked, "You have been appointed to a post that will preoccupy you from any engagements at the marketplace." "SubhanAllah!" exclaimed Abu Bakr 🙏, "Will it preoccupy me from providing for my family?" Omar 🙏 replied, "We shall fix a reasonable allowance for you." Abu Bakr 🙏 remarked, "Woe to you, O Omar! I fear that it may not be permissible for me to take anything from that wealth." By consultation with the other Sahabah, an allowance was fixed for Abu Bakr 🙏. During his period of just over 2 years, Abu Bakr 🙏 used 8,000 Dirhams from the Baytul Maal. On his deathbed, he said, "I had mentioned to Omar 🙏 that I fear that it may not be permissible for me to take anything from that wealth but he overpowered me. Now that I am dying, I want you to take 8,000 Dirhams from my estate and deposit it in the Baytul Maal." When this money was brought to Omar 🙏, he said, "May Allah shower His mercy on Abu Bakr 🙏, He has certainly exhausted those to come after him. *(Bayhaqi)*

The Incident Between Abu Bakr 🙏 and Aisha 🙏

Abu Bakr bin Hafs bin Omar narrates that Aisha 🙏 came to her father Abu Bakr 🙏 when he was ill and about to breathe his last. She recited a couplet (which means):

"By your life! Prosperity is of no benefit to the youth when the pangs of death arrive and the chest has tightened"

Abu Bakr ؓ looked at her angrily and said, "O Ummul Mu'minin! Matters are not like that, but (Allah states):

وَجَاءَتْ سَكْرَةُ الْمَوْتِ بِالْحَقِّ ذَلِكَ مَا كُنْتَ مِنْهُ تَحِيدُ (19)

And the stupor of death will come in truth: "This is what you have been avoiding!" (Qaf:19)

He addressed her further saying, "I had given you an orchard as a gift, but am not satisfied with it. You should therefore return it to my estate." Aisha ؓ readily agreed and made it over. Abu Bakr ؓ then said, "Since my appointment as Khalifa, I have neither taken a Dinar or a Dirham of the Muslims. We have of course eaten from their coarse food to fill our bellies and worn their coarse cloth on our backs. Besides that we have none of their spoils apart from this Abyssinian slave, this camel for drawing water and this worn woolen shawl. When I die, I want you to send these items to Omar ؓ, thereby alleviating me from being responsible for them." After Abu Bakr ؓ passed away, Aisha ؓ did as her father had requested. When the messenger came to Omar ؓ to bring him the items, he wept so profusely that his tears fell on the ground. He said, "May Allah shower His mercy on Abu Bakr ؓ. He has certainly exhausted those to come after him. May Allah shower His mercy on Abu Bakr ؓ. He has certainly exhausted those to come after him." He then commanded his slave to receive all the items. Abdul Rahman bin Auf ؓ then remarked, "SubhanAllah! Are you snatching away from Abu Bakr ؓ's family their Abyssinian slave, their watering camel and their worn woolen shawl worth only 5 Dirhams?" "What do you advise'?" Omar ؓ asked. Abdur Rahman bin Auf ؓ advised Omar ؓ to give the items back to Abu Bakr ؓ's family. Omar ؓ however disagreed and said, "No! I swear by the Being Who has sent Muhammad ﷺ with the truth that this shall never happen during my term of Khilafa. Abu Bakr ؓ would not have escaped from his responsibility for them if I return them to his family and death is ever close by, what will I tell him when I meet him after death'?" *(Ibn Sa'd).*

Omar ؓ Refuses to Accept Wealth Given to Him

Ata bin Yasar reports that when Rasulullah ﷺ once sent a gift to Omar ؓ, he returned it. "Why have you returned it?" Rasulullah ﷺ asked. Omar ؓ replied, "O Rasulullah ﷺ! Did you not tell us that it is best not to take anything from anyone?" Rasulullah ﷺ replied, "That applies to asking. When you are given something without asking for it, it is a provision that Allah has sent for you." Omar ؓ then said, "I swear by the Being Who controls my life that I shall never ask anyone for anything and I shall accept anything that comes to me without asking." *(Malik, Bayhaqi in Targheeb waf Tarheeb).*

An Incident with Abu Musa Ash'ari ؓ

Abdullah bin Omar ؓ reports that Abu Musa Ash'ari ؓ sent a fine silken mat as a gift for Aatika bint Zaid bin Amr bin Nufail ؓ who was the wife of Omar ؓ. The narrator estimates that the mat was an arm's length long and a handspan wide. When Omar ؓ came to her and saw the mat, he asked, "Where did you get this from?" When she told him that Abu Musa Ash'ari ؓ had sent it as a gift for her, Omar ؓ grabbed the mat and struck her so hard over the head that her braids opened up. He then gave instructions that Abu Musa Ash'ari ؓ be brought to him in a hurry even it he got tired by running. Abu Musa Ash'ari ؓ was then brought very quickly and was made very tired in the rush.

As he came, he said, "Please do not be hasty with me, O Amirul Mu'minin!" Omar ؓ rebuked him saying, "What makes you send gifts to my wives?" He took hold of the mat and struck it across the Abu Musa ؓ's head saying, "Take this as we have no need for it." *(Ibn Sa'd, Ibn Asakir in Muntakhab Kanzul Ummal).*

The Sale of the Foot of the Muqattam Hill

Laith bin Sa'd narrates that Maqoqis, the once king of Egypt asked Amr bin Al Aas ؓ the governor of Egypt to sell to him the foot of the Muqattam hill for 70,000 Dinars. Surprised at the high offer, Amr bin Al Aas ؓ informed him that he will first have to write to Amirul Mu'minin Omar ؓ about it. After sending the letter, Omar ؓ replied saying, "Ask him why he wants to pay you so much when the land cannot be cultivated, no water can be extracted from it and it is of no benefit?" When Amr bin Al Aas ؓ asked Maqoqis about this, he replied that their scriptures informed them that a tree of Jannah grows at that place. Amr bin Al Aas ؓ then wrote back to Omar ؓ about this and received the reply stating, "As far as we are concerned, the tree of Jannah are reserved for the Mu'minin. You should bury the Muslims with you at that place and should not sell it to him." *(Ibn Abdul Hakam in Kanzul Ummal).*

Abu Ubaidah bin Jarrah ؓ Refuses to Accept Wealth Given to Him

Aslam reports that during the "Year of Ashes" when the lands of the Arabs were stricken by drought, Omar ؓ wrote a letter to Amr bin Al Aas ؓ. The narration then continues to a point where Omar ؓ sent for Abu Ubaidah bin Jarrah ؓ to appoint him to fulfill a certain task. Abu Ubaidahh ؓ left for the appointment and after returning, Omar ؓ sent him 1,000 Dinars. Abu Ubaidah ؓ said, "I did not do the work for your sake, O son of Khattab. I have done it for Allah and will therefore not take any remuneration." Omar ؓ responded by saying, "Rasulullah ﷺ gave us something for work that he appointed us to do and when we disliked accepting it, he told us not to refuse it. Therefore, my dear man, you should accept this and use it to assist you in the affairs of this world and for Islam." Only then did Abu Ubaidah ؓ accept the money. *(Bayhaqi in Muntakhab Kanzul Ummal)*

Sa'eed bin Amir ؓ Refuses to Accept Wealth Given to Him

Abdullah bin Ziyad narrates that Omar ؓ once gave Sa'eed bin Amir ؓ 1,000 Dinars. Sa'eed ؓ refused the money saying, "I have no need for it. Rather give it to someone else." Omar ؓ said, "Take it easy! Let me first tell you what Rasulullah ﷺ said. Thereafter you are at liberty to decide whether you want it or not. When Rasulullah ﷺ once gave me something and I said to him what you just said to me, he remarked, 'When someone is given something without him asking for it and without craving for it, then it is a provision from Allah that he should not refuse.'" "Did you hear this from Rasulullah ﷺ?" asked Sa'eed ؓ. When Omar ؓ confirmed that he did, Sa'eed ؓ accepted the money. *(Shashi, Ibn Asakir in Kanzul Ummal)*

The Narration of Hakim and Bayhaqi

Zaid bin Aslam reports that Omar ؓ once said to Sa'eed bin Amir bin Hudham ؓ who was a governor in Sham, "Why is it that the people of Sham love you so much?" Sa'eed ؓ replied, "It is because I am always concerned about their rights and sympathize with them." Omar ؓ then gave him 10,000 Dirhams. However, he refused it saying, "I have several slaves and horses and have sufficient wealth. I want my services to be a charity towards the Muslims." "Do not refuse this money," said Omar ؓ, "because Rasulullah ﷺ once gave me some money less than this amount of 10,000 and I also replied as you did. He then said to me, 'When Allah gives you some wealth without you asking for it and without you having a craving for it, then accept it because it is a provision that Allah is giving to you. (Hakim). Another narration from Aslam states that Omar ؓ once said to a man whom the people Sham dearly loved, "Why do the people of Sham like you so much?" He replied, "Because I lead them in Jihad and sympathize with them." Omar ؓ then offered him 10,000 Dirhams saying, "Use this to assist you in your affairs of this world and in your religious matters." However, he refused saying, "But I have sufficient wealth." The rest of the narration is like the one above. (Bayhaqi, Ibn Asakir in Kanzul Ummal)

Abdullah bin Sa'di ؓ Refuses to Accept Wealth Given to Him

Abdullah bin Sa'di ؓ narrates that he once approached Omar ؓ during the period of his Khilafah. Omar ؓ said to him, "I have been told that you have done many things for public welfare but whenever you are given some remuneration, you do not like to accept it. Is this true?" When Abdullah ؓ confirmed that it was, Omar ؓ enquired further, "Why do you do this?" He replied, "I have several horses and slaves and sufficient wealth. I want my services to be a charity for the Muslims." Omar ؓ advised him saying, "Do not do this. I also had the same intentions. Whenever Rasulullah ﷺ gave me anything, I would tell him to give it to someone more deserving. When he again gave me something on one occasion, I again told him to give it to someone more deserving. He then said, 'Take it and then either keep it for yourself or give it away as Sadaqa. Whenever any wealth comes to you without you asking for it or without you craving for it, then make sure that you accept it. However, if you had been craving for it, then do not follow your desire by accepting it'" (Ahmad, Humaidi, Ibn Abi Shaibah, Darmi, Muslim, Nasai in Kanzul Ummal). In another narration, Abdullah bin Sa'di ؓ says, "Omar ؓ once employed my services and after I had completed the task, he gave me the remuneration. I refused to accept it saying, 'I had done it for the pleasure of Allah and Allah will reward me for it.' However, Omar ؓ insisted, 'Please take it because I had also completed some work during the time of Rasulullah ﷺ and gave Rasulullah ﷺ the same reply that you did when he offered me remuneration. Rasulullah ﷺ said to me, 'Whenever I give you something without you asking me, then either keep it for yourself or give it away as Sadaqa.'" (Ibn Jareer in Kanzul Ummal)

Hakim bin Hizam ؓ Refuses to Accept Wealth Given to Him

Sa'eed bin Musaib reports that Rasulullah ﷺ gave Hakim bin Hizam ؓ something after the battle of Hunain but because he regarded it to be too little, Rasulullah ﷺ gave him some more. Hakim ؓ then asked, "O Rasulullah ﷺ! Which of the 2 amounts is better'?" Rasulullah ﷺ replied, "The first that you received without asking. Dear Hakim bin Hizam! This wealth is green and sweet. Whoever takes it with a generous heart to give others and to use it in good avenues; he will receive blessings in it. On the other hand, whoever takes it with greed and to use it in evil avenues; he will receive no blessings and will be like a person who keeps eating without being satisfied. The upper (giving) hand is better than the lower (receiving) hand." Hakim ؓ asked, "even though one asks from you, O Rasulullah ﷺ?" "Even from me," replied Rasulullah ﷺ. Hakim ؓ then swore, "I swear by the Being Who has sent you with the truth that I shall never accept anything from anyone after you." He then never accepted even his allowance from the Baytul Maal and anything else he was given until he passed away. Omar ؓ used to pray, "O Allah! I

call You to witness that I have called him to accept his share of this wealth but he refuses." Hakim ؓ said to him, "By Allah! I shall never accept anything from you or from anyone else." (Abdul Razzaq in Kanzul Ummal)

The Incident with Omar ؓ

Hakim bin Hizam ؓ narrates that he once asked Rasulullah ﷺ for something and Rasulullah ﷺ gave it to him. When he again asked, Rasulullah ﷺ gave him once more. When he asked for a 3rd time, Rasulullah ﷺ again complied. Rasulullah ﷺ then said to him, "Dear Hakim! This wealth is green and sweet." The narration then reads like the previous narration. The narration later states that even when Abu Bakr ؓ used to call Hakim ؓ to accept his money, he would refuse to accept any part of it. Thereafter, Omar ؓ used to call him to take his dues and he would refuse Omar ؓ as well. Omar ؓ then addressed the people saying, "O assembly of Muslims! I call you to be witness to the fact that I have offered Hakim ؓ his dues from the spoils that Allah has distributed but he refuses to accept it." After Rasulullah ﷺ passed away, Hakim ؓ did not accept anything from anyone until the day he passed away. (Bukhari and Muslim in Targheeb waf Tarheeb, Tirmidhi and Nasai). Another narration from Urwa ؓ states that Hakim ؓ did not accept anything from Abu Bakr ؓ until the Khalifa's death. Thereafter, he also refused to accept anything from Omar ؓ until the demise of the Amirul Mu'minin and also from Uthman ؓ and from Mu'awiya ؓ until the day he passed away. (Hakim)

Amir bin Rabi'ah ؓ Refuses Land

Aslam reports that when an Arab man came to stay with Amir bin Rabi'ah ؓ, he entertained his guest well and spoke to Rasulullah ﷺ about addressing the need of the man. The man later came to Amir ؓ after meeting Rasulullah ﷺ and said, "I have asked and received from Rasulullah ﷺ a valley in Arabia that is the best of all valleys. I now wish to allocate a portion of it for you and for your progeny after you." Amir ؓ replied, "I have no need for your land because today a Sura has been revealed that makes us oblivious of this world:

اقْتَرَبَ لِلنَّاسِ حِسَابُهُمْ وَهُمْ فِي غَفْلَةٍ مُعْرِضُونَ (1)

Draws near for mankind their reckoning, while they turn away in heedlessness. (Al-Ambiya:1) (Abu Nu'aym in Hilya)

Abu Dhar ؓ Refuses to Accept Wealth Given to Him

Abdullah bin Samit the nephew of Abu Dhar ؓ says that he once accompanied his uncle Abu Dhar ؓ to see Amirul Mu'minin Uthman ؓ. Abu Dhar ؓ requested, "Allow me go to and live in Rabdha." Uthman ؓ replied, "Go ahead. We shall give instructions for some of the zakah animals to go to you early in the mornings and in the evenings so that you may use their milk." "I have no need for it," said Abu Dhar ؓ, "because the little flock of Abu Dhar suffices for him." He then stood up and said, "While you people remain devoted to this world, do leave us to our Rabb and Islam." The estate of Abdur Rahman bin Auf ؓ was being distributed at that time when Ka'b a Jewish Rabbi who accepted Islam was with Uthman ؓ. Uthman ؓ asked Ka'b, "What is your opinion of a man who had collected all this wealth and used to contribute in Sadaqa in good causes and did various good works with it?" Ka'b replied, "I anticipate good for him." Abu Dhar ؓ became angry at this and raised his staff over Ka'b saying, "What do you know, O son of a Jewess? On the Day of Judgment the owner of this wealth will wish that scorpions should sting the most delicate part of his heart rather than having to account for all that wealth." *(Abu Nu'aym in Hilya)*. Another narration is that when a man approached Abu Dhar ؓ to offer him some money for his expenses, Abu Dhar ؓ said to him, "I already have some goats that I milk, some donkeys for transport, a freed slave to serve me and a shawl that is more than the clothing I require. I fear that I shall be required to account for anything over and above my needs." *(Ibn Abi Shaibah in Hilya)*

The Incident with Habib bin Maslama ؓ

Abu Bakr bin Munkadir narrates that Habib bin Maslama ؓ who was the Amir of Sham sent 300 Dinars for Abu Dhar ؓ with the message, "Use this for your needs." Abu Dhar ؓ said to the messenger, "Take this back. Could he not find someone else who is more deceived about Allah than we are? All we have and need is shade of a house in which we can take shelter, a small flock of goats who come to us in the evenings after grazing for our milk and meat and a freed slave who serves us for free. Despite this, I still fear owning anything extra." *(Abu Nu'aym in Hilya)*

The Incident with Uarith Qurashi ؓ

Muhammad bin Sirin narrates that Harith belonged to the Quraish tribe and lived in Sham. When the news reached him that Abu Dhar ؓ was living a life of poverty, he sent 300 Dinars to him. When the money reached him, Abu Dhar ؓ remarked, "Could he not find any servant of Allah lower in his eyes than me? I have heard Rasulullah ﷺ say, 'Whoever has 40 Dirhams and still asks from the people has begged is disliked by Allah.' Abu Dhar has 40 Dirhams, 40 goats and 2 servants." *(Tabrani, Haythami, Abu Nu'aym)*

Abu Rafi ؓ the Freed Slave of Rasulullah ﷺ Refuses to Accept Wealth Given to Him: The Incident with Rasulullah ﷺ

Abu Rafi the freed slave of Rasulullah ﷺ narrates that Rasulullah ﷺ once said to him, "O Abu Rafi! What will be your condition when you become a poor man?" He replied, "Should I then not send some money forward to the Hereafter by giving Sadaqa since I will have nothing to give when I become poor?" "Of course," replied Rasulullah ﷺ, "but how much do you have?" Abu Rafi ؓ replied, "I have 40,000 Dirhams and I wish to give them all for the pleasure of Allah." Rasulullah ﷺ advised, "No do not give it all away. Rather give only some away and keep some for yourself so that you may treat your son well." Abu Rafi ؓ enquired, "Do they (our children) have rights due from us as we have rights cue from them?" Rasulullah ﷺ replied, "Certainly! The right that a father owes his child is to teach him the Book of Allah, archery and swimming." A narration of Yazid adds, "and to leave lawful wealth for him as inheritance." "When will I become a poor man?" asked Abu Rafi ؓ. "After my demise," came the reply. Abu Sulaim says, "I saw Abu Rafi ؓ as a poor man sitting and saying, 'Who will be charitable towards old and blind man? Who will be charitable towards a man whom Rasulullah ﷺ had informed that he would become poor after Rasulullah ﷺ's demise? Who will be charitable because the highest hand is Allah's, the middle hand is that of the giver and the lowest hand is that of the beggar? Whoever begs unnecessarily will have an unsightly scar that will be seen on the Day of Judgment. It is not permissible for a person to accept charity when he is wealthy or when he is in perfect health.' I then saw a man give him 4 Dirhams. When he returned one Dirham, the man said, 'O servant of Allah! Please do not refuse my charity.' Abu Rafi ؓ explained, 'Rasulullah ﷺ had forbidden me from hoarding extra wealth.' I saw the time when he became so wealthy that I even saw the collectors of Ushr (a 10th of crop

given as zakah) come to him. He then used to say, 'If only Abu Rafi had died when he was a poor man!' In exchange for their freedom, he would take from his slaves only that amount that he paid for them." *(Abu Nu'aym in Hilya)*

Abdur Rahman ؓ the Son of Abu Bakr ؓ Refuses to Accept Wealth Given to Him

Abdul Aziz bin Abdur Rahman bin Auf ؓ narrates that Mu'awiya ؓ once sent 100,000 Dirhams to Abdur Rahman bin Abu Bakr after he refused to pledge allegiance to Yazid who was the son of Mu'awiya ؓ. Abdur Rahman ؓ refused to accept the money saying, "Should I sell Islam for my worldly gain?" He proceeded to Makkah where he passed away. *(Hakim, Isabah)*

Abdullah ؓ the Son of Omar ؓ refuses to Accept Wealth

Maymun reports that Mu'awiya ؓ thrust onto Arm bin Al Aas ؓ the responsibility of determining what the intentions of Abdullah bin Omar ؓ were, whether he would resort to a fight or not if Yazid were made the Khalifa? Amr bin Al Aas ؓ said to Abdullah bin Omar ؓ, "O Abu Abdur Rahman! What prevents you from proclaiming yourself Khalifa so that we may pledge our allegiance to you? You after all a companion of Rasulullah ﷺ, the son of an Amirul Mu'minin and most deserving of the post of Khilafa." Abdullah bin Omar ؓ asked, "Does everyone agree to what you are saying?" "O yes," replied Amr ؓ, "all except a small band of people." Abdullah bin Omar ؓ then said, "If everyone save 3 individuals from Hajar supported the idea, I still have no need for the post." Amr ؓ then concluded that Abdullah bin Omar ؓ would not resort to fighting for the Khilafa. Amr ؓ further enquired, "Would you be interested in pledging allegiance to a person whom almost everyone is willing to accept as Khalifa in exchange for so much of land and wealth that neither you nor your progeny will ever be in need of anything afterwards." Abdullah bin Omar ؓ said, "Shame on you! Leave me and never set foot here again! Woe to you! Islam is not based on your Dinars and Dirhams. I wish to leave this world with my hands clean from the wealth of this world." *(Ibn Sa'd)*. Another narration from Maymun bin Mahran states that Abdullah bin Omar ؓ once entered into a contract of Kitaba (that a slave can purchase freedom in exchange for an agreed sum of money) with his slave and fixed the installments of his payment. When the time arrives for the first installment, the slave came with the payment. When Abdullah bin Omar ؓ asked him how he had earned the money, the slave replied, "I worked for it and also begged from the people." Abdullah bin Omar ؓ said, "Do you wish to feed me with the dirt of people's money? You are free for the pleasure of Allah and you may have all the money you have brought." *(Abu Nu'aym in Hilya)*

Abdullah bin Ja'far ؓ Refuses to Accept Money Given to Him

Muhammad bin Sirin narrates that a chief of a rural area of Iraq once requested Abdullah bin Ja'far ؓ to ask Amirul Mu'minin Ali ؓ to address a need he had. Abdullah bin Ja'far ؓ therefore interceded on his behalf and Ali ؓ agreed to the request. The chief then sent 40,000 Dirhams to the Abdullah bin Ja'far ؓ with the message that it was from him. Abdullah bin Ja'far ؓ returned the money with the message, "We do not sell our good deeds." *(Ibn Abi Dunya, Khara'iti in Isabah)*

Abdullah bin Arqam ؓ Refuses to Accept Money Given to Him

Amr bin Dinar narrates that Uthman ؓ appointed Abdullah bin Arqam ؓ as treasurer of the Baytul Maal. When Uthman ؓ gave him 300,000 as remuneration, Abdullah bin Arqam ؓ refused to accept the money. The rest of the narration is the same, which states that when Uthman ؓ gave Abdullah bin Arqam ؓ 30,000 as remuneration, he refused to take the money saying, "I did it for the pleasure of Allah." *(Baghawi in Isabah)*

Amr bin Nu'man bin Muqarrin ؓ refuses to accept Money

Mu'awiya bin Qurra reports that he was once staying with Amr bin Nu'man bin Muqarrin ؓ. When Ramadhan arrived, someone came with a bag of Dirhams saying, "The Amir Mus'ab bin Zubair conveys his Salams and says that his gifts shall reach every Qari and you are one of them. Please use this money." Amr bin Nu'man ؓ said to the messenger, "Tell him that we swear by Allah that we do not recite the Qur'an with the intention of earning worldly profits." He returned the money. *(Ibn Abi Shaybah in Isabah)*

Aisha ؓ and Asma ؓ the 2 Daughters of Abu Bakr ؓ Refuse to Accept Money Given to Them

Abdullah bin Zubair ؓ reports that Qutaila bint Abdul Uzza bin Abd Sa'd from the Banu Malik bin Hisl tribe was still a Mushrik when she brought some gifts to her daughter Asma ؓ the daughter of Abu Bakr ؓ. The gifts included a type of badger which the Arabs ate, some bread and some butter. However, because her mother was not a Muslim, Asma ؓ refused to accept the gifts and even refused to allow her mother into her house. When her sister Aisha ؓ asked Rasulullah ﷺ about this, Allah revealed the verse:

لَا يَنْهَاكُمُ اللَّهُ عَنِ الَّذِينَ لَمْ يُقَاتِلُوكُمْ فِي الدِّينِ وَلَمْ يُخْرِجُوكُمْ مِنْ دِيَارِكُمْ أَنْ تَبَرُّوهُمْ وَتُقْسِطُوا إِلَيْهِمْ إِنَّ اللَّهَ يُحِبُّ الْمُقْسِطِينَ (8)

Allah does not forbid you to deal justly and kindly with those who fought not against you on account of religion and did not drive you out of your homes. Verily, Allah loves those who deal with equity. (Al-Mumtahanah:8)

Rasulullah ﷺ then instructed Asma ؓ to accept her mother's gift and to allow her into her home. *(Ahmad, Bazzar, Haythami)*

The Incident of Aisha ؓ and a Poor Lady

Aisha ؓ relates, "A poor lady once came to me with a gift. I however refused to accept it out of pity for her because she needed it more than I did. Rasulullah ﷺ then told me, "Why did you rather not accept her gift and give her something else in return? I think that you may have been looking down on her. Humble yourself, O Aisha because Allah loves the humble ones and detests the proud ones." *(Abu Nu'aym in Hilya)*

Abstention from Asking from People: The Incident of Abu Sa'eed Khudri ؓ and Rasulullah ﷺ

Abu Sa'eed Khudri ؓ reports, "My family was suffering from extreme poverty when my wife told me to approach Rasulullah ﷺ to ask for something. However, as I came to Rasulullah ﷺ, the first thing I heard him say was, 'Allah will make that person independent who asks Him for independence and will grant chastity to the one who asks Him for it. We shall however not keep back something that a person asks from us.' I then returned home without asking him. We then lived with the situation and continued making and effort for Islam, as a result of which the world later fell at our feet." *(Ibn Jareer)*. Abu Sa'eed Khudri ؓ once spent the morning with a stone tied to his belly to suppress his extreme hunger. It was then either his wife or his slave who told him to approach Rasulullah ﷺ and ask him for something because someone else had done so and Rasulullah ﷺ complied. Abu Sa'eed ؓ says, "When I came there, Rasulullah ﷺ

was addressing the people and I heard him say, 'Allah will grant chastity to the one who asks Him for it and will make that person independent who asks Him for independence. As for the one who asks from us, we shall either give him something or if we have nothing, we shall sympathize with him. Nevertheless, we prefer those who do not depend on us over those who ask from us.' I then returned without asking for anything. Allah then continued providing for us until a time came when the Ansar knew none wealthier than us." *(Ibn Jareer in Kanzul Ummal)*

The Incident of Abdur Rahman bin Auf ؓ and Rasulullah ﷺ

Abdur Rahman bin Auf ؓ says, "Rasulullah ﷺ once promised me some money. When the Banu Quraizah was conquered, I approached him to fulfill the promise. However, I then overheard him say, "Allah will make that person independent who asks Him for independence and will grant contentment to the one who is content.' I then said to myself, 'In that case, I shall not ask from Rasulullah ﷺ." *(Targheeb wat Tarheeb, Ibn Ma'een)*

The Incident of Thowban ؓ

Thowban ؓ reports that Rasulullah ﷺ once said, "Whoever guarantees me that he will not ask people for anything, I shall guarantee Jannah for him." Thowban ؓ responded by saying that he would be the person. Thereafter, true to his word, he did not ask anyone for anything. The narration of *Ibn Majah* states that Rasulullah ﷺ instructed Thowban ؓ not to ask from anyone. Consequently, even when Thowban ؓ's whip fell as he rode his animal, he would not tell anyone on the ground to hand it to him. He would rather dismount and pick it up himself. In the chapter concerning how the Sahabah pledged their allegiance to the injunctions of Islam, a narration of Abu Umamah ؓ appears about how Thowban ؓ pledged that he would not ask anyone for anything. Abu Umamah ؓ says that he saw Thowban ؓ riding amongst a large crowd in Makkah and even when his whip sometimes fell on someone's shoulders and the person would attempt to give it back to him, he would not allow it and would dismount the animal to pick it up himself. *(Tabrani in Kabir, Targheeb wat Tarheeb, Ahmad, Nasai)*

The Incident of Abu Bakr ؓ

Ibn Abi Mulaika reports that when the rein of his camel would sometimes fall from the hands of Abu Bakr ؓ, he would hit the front legs of the camel to make it sit down and then pick up the rein. People would say, "Why do you rather not tell us to get it for you?" He would then tell them, "Verily my beloved friend Rasulullah ﷺ instructed me never to ask people for anything." *(Ahmad in Kanzul Ummal)*

The Fear of Rasulullah ﷺ for Worldly Prosperity

Uqba bin Amir ؓ reports that 8 years after they had been martyred, Rasulullah ﷺ again performed the Janazah salah for the martyrs of Uhud. Rasulullah ﷺ seemed to be bidding farewell to all those alive and all those deceased. Thereafter, he mounted the pulpit and said, "I shall be going ahead before you to the Hereafter and shall be your witness. Our promised rendezvous shall be the fountain of Kowthar and I can actually see it as I stand here because Allah has allowed me to see it from here. I have no fear that you would revert to Shirk but I fear that you would vie with each other in acquiring the things of this world." Uqba says that this was the last time that he ever saw Rasulullah ﷺ. *(Bukhari)*. Uqba bin Amir ؓ also states that Rasulullah ﷺ once came out of his home and performed the Janazah salah for the martyrs of Uhud. The rest of the narration continues until the point where Rasulullah ﷺ said, "By Allah! I am looking at my fountain right now and I have been handed the keys to the treasures of the earth because of which the Muslims later conquered lands far and wide. I swear by Allah that it is not your reverting to Shirk after my demise that worries me but I fear that you would start competing with each other in acquiring the things of this world." *(Bukhari in Riqaq)*

The Statement of Rasulullah ﷺ When Abu Ubaidah ﷺ Brought the Wealth from Bahrain

Amr bin Al Auf Ansari ﷺ narrates that Rasulullah ﷺ sent Abu Ubaidah bin Jarrah ﷺ to collect the Jizya from Bahrain. When he returned and the Ansar heard about his arrival, they all presented themselves to perform the Fajr salah behind Rasulullah ﷺ. After performing the salah, Rasulullah ﷺ started walking away when they all came before him. When he saw them, Rasulullah ﷺ smiled and said, "I assume that you all heard about Abu Ubaidah returning from Bahrain with something?" "We certainly did, O Rasulullah ﷺ," they replied. Rasulullah ﷺ then said to them, "I have good news for you and you may also hope for some joy because you will all receive a portion of the wealth and much more in future. By Allah! It is not poverty that I fear for you. On the contrary, I fear that the world would be spread out before you as it was spread out to the people before you, after which you would .compete with each other in acquiring it just as they competed. It would then eventually destroy you as it destroyed them." *(Bukhari, Muslim in Targheeb wat Tarheeb)*

The Narration of Abu Dhar ﷺ in this Regard

Abu Dhar ﷺ narrates that while Rasulullah ﷺ was sitting, an uncultured Bedouin stood up and said, "O Rasulullah ﷺ! The drought has consumed us!" Rasulullah ﷺ responded by saying, "It is not that which I fear for you. I fear the time when worldly wealth will be poured on to you. Alas! If only my Ummah would not wear gold!" *(Ahmad, Bazzar in Targheeb wat Tarheeb)*

The Narration of Abu Sa'eed Khudri ﷺ in this Regard

Abu Sa'eed Khudri ﷺ reports that they were sitting around Rasulullah ﷺ when he was on the pulpit. He said to them, "Amongst the things that I fear for you is the splendor and wealth of the world that Allah will open up to you." *(Bukhari, Muslim in Targheeb wat Tarheeb)*

The Narration of Sa'd bin Abi Waqqas ﷺ in this Regard

Said bin Abi Waqqas ﷺ narrates that Rasulullah ﷺ said, "More than you being tested with difficulties, I fear more that you will be tested with prosperity. When you were tested with difficulties, you have exercised patience but the world is extremely sweet and full of growth, it cannot be said whether you would be able to resist its temptation." *(Abu Ya'la, Bazzar in Targheeb wat Tarheeb)*

The Narration of Auf bin Malik ﷺ in this Regard

Auf bin Malik ﷺ reports that Rasulullah ﷺ once stood up amongst the Sahabah and said, "It is poverty and hard-living that you fear or are you concerned about the world? Allah shall certainly grant you conquests over Rome and Persia and worldly wealth will be rained down on you. It will then be nothing but this which will divert you from the straight path." *(Tabrani in Targheeb wat Tarheeb)*

The Fear of Omar ﷺ and his Weeping Over Worldly Prosperity

Miswar bin Makhrama ﷺ narrates that when some of the booty won at the battle of Qadisiya was brought to Omar ﷺ, he was inspecting it when he began to weep. Abdur Rahman bin Auf ﷺ who was with him at the time said, "O Amirul Mu'minin! This is a day of joy and happiness because we won the battle. Why are you weeping?" Omar ﷺ replied, "It certainly is but whenever a nation is given such wealth, they get enmity and hatred along with it." *(Bayhaqi, Khara'iti in Kanzul Ummal)*

The Narration of Ibrahim bin Abdur Rahman bin Auf ﷺ

Ibrahim bin Abdur Rahman bin Auf ﷺ narrates that when the treasures of the Kisra, Persian Emperor were brought to Omar ﷺ, Abdullah bin Arqam Zuhri ﷺ asked, "Shall we deposit this in the Baytul Maal?" "No," replied Omar ﷺ, "We shall not deposit it in the Baytul Maal until we have distributed it." Omar ﷺ then started to weep. Abdur Rahman bin Auf ﷺ asked, "What makes you weep, O Amirul Mu'minin? Today is a day of gratitude and joy." Omar ﷺ replied, "Whenever Allah gives this to a nation, he casts enmity and hatred between them." *(Bayhaqi, Ibn Mubarak, Abdur Razzaq, Ibn Abi Shaibah in Kanzul Ummal, Ahmad in his Zuhd, Ibn Asakir)*

The Narration of Hasan Basri ﷺ About the Crown of the Kisra

Hasan reports that when the crown of the Kisra was before Omar ﷺ, he placed it before him together with other crown jewels. Amongst the people was Suraqa bin Malik bin Ju'shum ﷺ. Omar ﷺ threw to him the 2 bracelets of Kisra bin Hurmuz and he put them on, they reached up to his shoulders. Seeing the bracelets on Suraqa ﷺ's arms, Omar ﷺ exclaimed, "All praise is for Allah! The bracelets of Kisra bin Hurmuz on the arms of Suraqa bin Malik bin Ju'shum a Bedouin from the Banu Mudlaj tribe! O Allah! I know that Your Rasul ﷺ liked getting wealth only to spend it in Your path and on Your servants. However, You chose a better way and kept it away from him. O Allah! You know that Abu Bakr ﷺ also liked getting wealth only to spend it in Your path and on Your servants. However, You chose a better way and kept it away from him as well. Now this wealth has come during my term as Khalifa O Allah! I seek Your protection that this should be a trap from You for Omar." He then recited the following verse:

أَيَحْسَبُونَ أَنَّمَا نُمِدُّهُم بِهِ مِن مَّالٍ وَبَنِينَ (55) نُسَارِعُ لَهُمْ فِي الْخَيْرَاتِ بَل لَّا يَشْعُرُونَ (56)

Do they think that We enlarge them in wealth and children, We hasten unto them with good things (in this worldly life so that they will have no share of good things in the Hereafter)? Nay, but they perceive not. (Al-Mu'minun:55-56) (Bayhaqi, Abd bin Humayd, Ibn Mundhir, Ibn Asakir in Kanzul Ummal)

The Narration of Abu Sinan Duwali ﷺ

Abu Sinan Duwali reports that he once went to see Omar ﷺ at a time when a group of the earliest Muhajirin were with him. Omar ﷺ sent for a basket resembling a sack or a bag which was brought to him from a fortress in Iraq. The basket contained a ring which one of Omar ﷺ's sons snatched up and put in his mouth. Omar ﷺ took it out of the child's mouth and began to weep. One of the persons with him asked, "Why do you weep when Allah has granted you so many conquests, given you victory over your enemies and satisfied you?" Omar ﷺ replied, "I heard Rasulullah ﷺ say, 'Whenever worldly wealth is opened up to a nation, Allah casts enmity and hatred amongst them until the Day of Judgment. This is what frightens me." *(Ahmad, Bazzar, Abu Ya'la in Targneeb wat Tarheeb)*

Narration of Abdullah bin Omar ﷺ About the Crying of Omar ﷺ

Abdullah bin Omar ﷺ reports, "After leading the salah, Omar ﷺ would remain seated for awhile so that a person with any need may speak to him. He would stand up when there was none with any need. However, it once occurred that he led several salahs without sitting afterwards. I said to his slave, 'O Yarfa! Is the Amirul Mu'minin not well?' When he informed me that the Amirul Mu'minin was in good health, I sat down and Uthman bin Affan ﷺ also joined me. After a while Yarfa came out and said, 'Come, O son of Affan! Come, O son of Abbas!' When we entered the room, we found before Omar ﷺ several heaps of money with a shoulder blade on each heap. Shoulder blades were used as paper in those days. He said, 'Looking through all the people of Madinah, I found that the 2 of you had the biggest families. Therefore, take this money and distribute it. You should then bring back what is left over. While Uthman ﷺ took as much as he could, I knelt down and said, 'Will you give us more if it is less?' He replied, 'You are a chip off the old block just like your father! Was all of this not with Allah when Muhammad ﷺ and his companions were eating scraps of leather?' I replied, 'Most certainly! It was all with Allah while Muhammad ﷺ was alive. However, if these conquests took place at his hands, he would not have done as you are doing.' Omar ﷺ became angry at this and asked, 'What then would he have done?' 'He would have eaten from it and fed us as well,' I replied. Omar ﷺ then started weeping loudly until his ribs heaved. He said, 'I wish that I could escape from this Khilafah with a clean sheet, nothing in my favor and nothing against.'" *(Humaydi, Ibn Sa'd, Bazzar, Sa'eed bin Mansoor, Bayhaqi in Kanzul Ummal, Haythami).* Another narration from Abdullah bin Omar ﷺ states, "Omar once called for me and when I went to him, I found a leather tablecloth in front of him on which there was gold spread out. He said, 'Come and distribute this amongst your people. Allah knows best why he kept this away from His Nabi ﷺ and from Abu Bakr ﷺ and it has come to me. Is it good that I have been given or evil?' He burst out crying as he said, 'Not at all! I swear by the Being Who controls my life! It was not for any evil reason that Allah kept it away from His Nabi Rasul ﷺ and from Abu Bakr ﷺ and gave it to me for good reason (it is a test for me)." *(Abu Ubaid, Ibn Sa'd, Ibn Rahway, Shashi and Hasan in Kanzul Ummal)*

The Incident with Abdur Rahman bin Auf ﷺ

Abdur Rahman bin Auf ﷺ narrates that Omar ﷺ sent for him. When he reached the door, he heard Omar ﷺ crying loudly. He said, "*Inna Lillahi wa Inna Ilayhi Raji'oon!* A calamity must have struck Amirul Mu'minin!" He entered the room and held Omar ﷺ's shoulders saying, "No need to grieve. No need to grieve." Omar ﷺ remarked, "There is every need to grieve." He took Abdur Rahman bin Auf ﷺ by the hand and led him through the door. There lay several bags stacked one upon the other. Omar ﷺ said, "The family of Khattab now has no value in the sight of Allah. If Allah willed, He could have given this to my 2 predecessors: Rasulullah ﷺ and Abu Bakr ﷺ and I could have followed the practice they would have set in this regard." Abdur Rahman bin Auf ﷺ consoled Omar ﷺ by saying, "Sit down with us (the senior Sahabah) and we shall discuss the matter." They then determined that Rasulullah ﷺ's wives should receive 4,000 each while everyone else received 2,000 each. Eventually, all the money was distributed. *(Abu Ubaid, Adani in Kanzul Ummal)*

The Fear of Abdur Rahman bin Auf ﷺ and His Weeping over Worldly Prosperity

Ibrahim reports that some food was once served to Abdur Rahman bin Auf ﷺ after he had fasted. He said, "Mus'ab bin Umair ﷺ who was a better person than I was martyred and shrouded in a sheet so small that would leave his legs exposed when his head was covered, and his head exposed when his feet were covered. Hamza ﷺ who was also a better person than me, was also martyred. Thereafter, worldly wealth was spread out before us and we fear that our good deeds may have been rewarded in advance in this world rather than in the Hereafter." He then started weeping so much that he even left his food. *(Bukhari, Abu Nu'atm in Hilya)*

Another Incident About Abdur Rahman bin Auf ﷺ

Naufal bin Ayadh Hudhali says, "Abdur Rahman bin Auf ﷺ was our companion and an excellent one indeed. He took us home one day and when he entered he first took a bath before sitting down with us. A platter with bread and meat was then served to us. When the platter was put down, Abdur Rahman bin Auf ﷺ started to weep. 'What makes you weep, O Abu Muhammad?' we asked. He replied, 'Rasulullah ﷺ passed away without him or his family filling their bellies with even barley bread. I do not think that what we have been kept back to enjoy is better than what they had." *(Abu Nu'aym in Hilya, Tirmidhi, Siraj in Isabah)*

He asks Ummu Salama ﷺ About Worldly Prosperity and Her Reply

Abdur Rahman bin Auf ﷺ once went to Ummu Salama ﷺ and asked, "Dear mother! I fear that my wealth will destroy me because I am the wealthiest of the Quraish." She advised him saying, "Dear son! Then spend in charity because I have heard Rasulullah ﷺ say, 'Verily there are some of my companions who will never see me after I part from them.'" Abdur Rahman bin Auf ﷺ then left and happened to meet Omar ﷺ. When he informed Omar ﷺ about what Ummu Salama ﷺ had told him, Omar ﷺ went to her and asked, "I ask you in the name of Allah to tell me whether I am amongst them." She replied, "You are not. I shall henceforth not fulfill the request of anyone else who takes Allah's name and asks me to inform them if they are amongst those companions or not." *(Bazzar by Haythami)*

The Fear of Khabbab bin Arat ﷺ and is Weeping Over Worldly Prosperity

Yahya bin Ja'dah reports that some Sahabah once visited Khabbab ﷺ during his illness. They said, "Good news for you, O Abu Abdullah! You shall meet Muhammad ﷺ at the pond." He then pointed to the top and bottom storey of his house and said, "How is that possible with all this when Rasulullah ﷺ said, 'All that one of you requires are the provisions of a traveler'?" *(Abu Ya'la, Tabrani in Targheeb wat Tarheeb)*

The Incident When he Passed Away

Tariq bin Shihab reports that a group of Sahabah once visited Khabbab during his illness and said, "Good news for you, O Abu Abdullah! You shall be meeting your brothers tomorrow." Khabbab ﷺ then started weeping saying, "Remember that 1 am not afraid of death. However, I am crying because you have reminded me of a group of people and called them my brothers whereas they have passed on with all their rewards intact, all reserved for the Hereafter without receiving any part of it in this world. What I fear is that we may have already been given the rewards for the deeds you have mentioned in this world since we have lived on after them and received much wealth." *(Abu Nu'aym in Hilya, Ibn Sa'd).* Haritha bin Mudarrib reports that when they visited Khabbab ﷺ, he had already taken 7 brands with a hot iron on his stomach as treatment for his illness) He said, "Had Rasulullah ﷺ not stated that no person should ever wish for death, I would have certainly wished for it now." Someone said to him, "Why worry about your future'? Rather call to mind your companionship with Rasulullah ﷺ and that you will soon be going to him." Khabbab ؓ responded by saying, "I fear that what I have with me, may prevent me from meeting with him. I have 4,000 Dirhams here in my house." *(Abu Nu'aym in Hilya)*. Another similar narration adds that Khabbab ؓ said, "I saw a time when I was with Rasulullah ﷺ without a single Dirham to my name. I now have beside my room 40,000 Dirhams." When his burial shroud was brought and he saw it, he wept as he said, "On the other hand, no shroud could be found for Hamza ؓ besides a striped sheet so small that when his head was covered, his feet would be uncovered and when his feet were covered, his head would be uncovered. Eventually, his head was covered and his feet covered with Idhkhir grass." *(Abu Nu'aym in Hilya, Ibn Sa'd)*. Abu Wa'il Shaqiq bin Salama says that when they visited Khabbab bin Arat ؓ during his final illness, he said, "There is 80,000 Dirhams in that box. By Allah! Neither have I ever tied it up or refused it to any beggar, I never intended hoarding it, but it was too much to spend. "He then started weeping. When the others asked him what made him weep, he replied, "I am crying because my companions have passed on without the world decreasing any of their rewards because they passed away as poor people. On the other hand, we have lived on after them and received plenty wealth to the extent that we found no place for the wealth except in sand in buildings." *(Abu Nu'aym in Hilya)*. A narration of Abu Usama states that Khabbab ؓ expressed the wish that the world should have been something like dung. Yet another narration from Qais reports that Khabbab ؓ said, "A group of people have passed on before us who did not receive any worldly wealth. However, we lived on after them and received so much wealth that we could find nothing to spend it on besides on sand buildings. A Muslim can be rewarded for everything he spends on except for that which he spends on sand in unnecessary building." *(Abu Nu'aym in Hilya)*

The Narration of Bukhari About the Fear of Khabbab ؓ

Bukhari reports that Khabbab ؓ said, "We migrated with Rasulullah ﷺ with no motives besides attaining the pleasure of Allah. Our rewards are therefore forthcoming from Allah. From us there were those who passed on without enjoying any part of their rewards in this world. Amongst them was Mus'ab bin Umair who was martyred during the battle of Uhud. All that he left behind was a sheet so small that would leave his legs exposed when we covered his head, and his head exposed when we covered his feet. Rasulullah ﷺ then instructed us to cover his head to cover his feet with Idhkhir grass. Then there are those of us whose fruits have ripened and they are busy picking it, they are enjoying the rewards of their deeds already in this world." *(Bukhari, Ibn Sa'd, Ibn Abi Shaibah in Kanzul Ummal)*

The Fear of Salman Farsi ؓ and his weeping on Worldly Prosperity

A man from the Banu Abs tribe says, "I was once in the company of Salman Farsi ؓ when he spoke about the treasures of Kisra, the Persian Emperor that Allah caused to fall to the hands of the Muslims. He then said, 'That Allah Who gave all of this to you, Who gave you these victories and blessed you with what you have has kept it all away when Muhammad ﷺ was alive. In those times the Sahabah would start the mornings without a single Dinar, Dirham or even a Mudd of grain. Thereafter, O brother of the Banu Abs, we have this situation

when we have now plenty of wealth.' We were later passing by some silos where grain was being separated from the chaff. Salman ؓ then repeated, 'That Allah Who gave all of this to you, Who gave you these victories and blessed you with what you have has kept it all away when Muhammad ﷺ was alive. In those times the Sahabah would start the mornings without a single Dinar, Dirham or even a Mudd of grain. Thereafter, O brother of the Banu Abs, we have this situation'." *(Abu Nu'aym in Hilya)*. A man from the Banu Abs tribe says, "I was once traveling with Salman ؓ along the banks of the Tigris River when he said to me, 'O brother from the Banu Abs tribe! Dismount and drink.' After I had drunk, he asked, 'How much of the river has your drinking decreased from the Tigris?' 'It decreased practically nothing,' I responded. He commented, 'That is knowledge. People take from it and decrease none of it.' He then told me to mount the animal again and as we passed by some wheat and barley silos, he said, 'All of this has been opened up to us and kept back from Rasulullah ﷺ and his companions. Do you think that this is for our benefit or not?' 'I do not know?' I replied. 'Well I know the answer,' he continued, 'it is bad for us and good for them. Until the day he met Allah, Rasulullah ﷺ never filled his belly for 3 consecutive days." *(Tabrani, Haythami)*

Sa'd bin Abi Waqqas ؓ Visits Salman ؓ

Abu Sufian reports from his teachers that Sa'd bin Abi Waqqas ؓ visited Salman ؓ during his final illness. When Salman ؓ started to weep, Sa'd bin Abi Waqqas ؓ asked, "What makes you cry? You are off to meet your companions and shall join Rasulullah ﷺ at the pond. Rasulullah ﷺ was pleased with you when he passed away." Salman ؓ replied, "I am neither crying for fear of death nor for greed of this world. However, Rasulullah ﷺ once emphatically told us, 'Your means of living in this world should be only as much as the provisions a traveler takes on a journey.' Yet look at all these black snakes around me, these worldly possessions." The narrator says that all that he possessed were a jug for water, a utensil for washing clothes and similar such household necessities. Sa'd ؓ then said to him, "Give us some advices that we could hold onto after your demise." Salman ؓ said, "Remember your Rabb whenever you intend doing something, at the time of passing judgment and whenever you are distributing." *(Abu Nu'aym in Hilya, Targheeb waf Tarheeb, lbn Sa'd, lbnul A'rabi in Kanzul Ummal)*

A Narration of Hakim States That All Salman ؓ possessed at the Time was a Dish for Washing Clothes, a Plate and a Jug.

Anas ؓ narrates that when Salman fell ill. Sa'd ؓ visited him. When he saw Salman ؓ weeping, Sa'd ؓ asked, "What makes you cry, dear brother? Did you not spend time in the company of Rasulullah ﷺ?" Sa'd ؓ then continues to enumerate various accomplishments of Salman ؓ to give him encouragement. Salman replied, "I am not crying for anyone of 2 things. I am not crying for greed of this world nor for dislike of the Hereafter. I am crying because Rasulullah ﷺ gave me explicit instructions that I have transgressed." "What did he instruct you with?" asked Sa'd. Salman said, "The instructions of Rasulullah ﷺ were that only the provisions of a traveler are sufficient for us. I think that I have certainly transgressed the instruction. As for you, O Sa'd. My advice is that you fear Allah when you pass judgment, when you distribute and when you make any intentions." A narrator called Thabit says that he received the news that the estate that Salman ؓ left amounted to only 20 odd Dirhams and a little money for expenses. *(Ibn Majah in Targhrrb war Tarheeb)*

Why Salman was Concerned at the Time of Death?

Amir bin Abdullah narrates that when Salman "al Khayr" (title given to him by Rasulullah) was on his deathbed, the people noticed that he was somewhat uneasy. They asked, "O Ab'u Abdullah! What makes you so restless when you were amongst the earliest Muslims and when you accompanied Rasulullah in great battles and coveted conquests?" Salman replied, "What concerns me is that when he was parting from us, my beloved friend Rasulullah explicitly instructed that the mere provisions of a traveler should suffice for us. This is what makes me so uneasy," When all the possessions were evaluated, it amounted to only 15 Dirhams. *(Ibn Hibban in Targheeb wat Tarheeb)*. Although other narrations *(Ibn Asakir, Ibn Hibban in Kanzul Ummal, Abu Nu'aym in Hilya)* state that Salman's estate amounted to 15 Dinars, others are unanimous that they totaled less than 20 Dirhams (not Dinars). A narration from Ali bin Badhima *(Tabrani in Targheeb wat Tarheeb)* states that after all his assets were sold, they fetched a price of only 14 Dirhams.

The Fear of Abu Hashim bin Utba bin Kabi'ah Qurashi: The Incident with Mu'awiya at the Time of Death

Abu Wa'il narrates that Mu'awiya came to visit Abu Hashim bin Utba when he fell ill. Finding him in tears, Mu'awiya asked, "What makes you weep dear uncle? Are you suffering with pain or are you grieving over leaving this world?" "Not at all," he replied, "I am crying because Rasulullah had given us explicit advice that we failed to adhere to." "What was that advice?" enquired Mu'awiya. Abu Hashim replied, "I heard Rasulullah say, 'It is sufficient to possess a servant and a transport to use in the Path of Allah.' Today I find that I have accumulated plenty of wealth." After the demise of Abu Hashim bin Utba, all his assets were evaluated 30 Dirhams including a dish that he used for rubbing dough and for eating. *(Tirmidhi, Nasai, Ibn Majah, Ibn Hibban in Targheeb wat Tarheeb, Baghawi, Ibnus Sakan in Isabah, Hakim in Kanzul Ummal)*

Fear of Abu Ubaidah bin Jarah and his Weeping Over Worldly Prosperity

Abu Hasana Muslim bin Akias the freed slave of Abdullah bin Amir reports that when someone once went to Abu Ubaidah bin Jarah, he found him weeping. "What makes you weep, O Abu Ubaidah?" he asked. Abu Ubaidah replied, "I am weeping because Rasulullah once made mention of the conquests and spoils of war that Allah would grant the Muslims. He also made mention of conquering Sham and then said, 'O 'Abu Ubaidah! If your life is prolonged to see the times of these conquests, 3 servants will be enough for you; 'one servant to serve you, one to travel with you and another for your family to serve them. At that time, 3 animals will be enough for you; one to ride, one to transport your goods and another for your servant.' I see that my house is full of servants and that my stables are full of animals and horses. How will I meet Rasulullah after this? Rasulullah also said to us, 'The most beloved and closest of you to me is the one who meets me in the condition that he left me." *(Ahmad, Haythami, Ibn Asakir in Muntakhab Kanzul Ummal)*

The Abstinence of Rasulullah and the Sahabah and How They Left the World Without Bothering About It: The Narration of Omar about the Imprint of a Mat on Rasulullah's Side

Abdullah bin Abbas reports that Omar once told him about the time when he visited Rasulullah. Rasulullah was lying on a straw mat and when Omar sat down he noticed that Rasulullah because was not wearing an upper garment, the mat had made imprints on his side. Omar was also startled to see that all the room contained was a handful of barley close to a Saa in weight, some acacia leaves in one corner used for dying cloth and a piece of leather hanging. When tears started flowing from Omar's eyes, Rasulullah asked, "What makes you weep, O son of Khattab?" Omar replied, "O Nabi of Allah! Why should I not weep when the mat has left an imprint on your side and what I see here is the sum total of all your belongings? You are the Nabi of Allah and His chosen servant and this is all you have whereas the Emperors of Rome and Persia have all types of fruits and rivers and other luxuries!" Rasulullah consoled him saying, "O son of Khattab! Are you not satisfied that they should have the world while we have the Hereafter?" *(Ibn Majah)*. Omar states, "I once sought permission to see Rasulullah. When I entered an upper storey room he was occupying, Rasulullah was lying on a coarse cloth with part of his body in the sand. His pillow was filled with the bark of a date palm; hanging over his head was a piece of leather and in a corner of the room lay some acacia leaves. After greeting Rasulullah and sitting down, I asked, "You are the Nabi of Allah and His chosen servant lying on a little coarse cloth while the Emperors of Persia and Rome are sleeping on golden beds with bedding made of velvet and silk." Rasulullah replied, "Their luxuries have been brought to them in this world and will soon come to an end whereas our luxuries are postponed for the Hereafter and will never finish." *(Hakim, Ibn Hibban, Targheeb waf Tarheeb, Ahmad, Abu Ya'la, Haythami)*. Omar went to see Rasulullah. Rasulullah was lying down on a straw mat that had left an imprint on his side. Omar said, "O Rasulullah! Why do you not choose a softer bedding?" Rasulullah replied, "What interest I have in this world? My relationship with this world is merely like a traveler on a journey during summer. He stops to take shade beneath a tree for a short while and proceeds on his journey, leaving the tree behind." *(Ahmad, Ibn Hibban, Bayhaqi in Targheeb wat Tarheeb, Ibn Majah, Tirmidhi in Targheeb wat Tarheeb, Tabrani, Majma'uz Zawa'id)*.

The Bedding of Rasulullah

Aisha says, "A woman from the Ansar once visited me and noticed that the bedding of Rasulullah was merely a double-folded sheet. She then sent me a bedding that was filled with wool. When Rasulullah came to me, he asked, "What is this, O Aisha?" I then informed him that the Ansari lady had come and when she saw the bedding, she left and sent this bedding. Rasulullah said, "Return it, O Aisha. By Allah! If I wanted, Allah would make mountains of gold and silver travel with me." *(Bayhaqi in Targheeb wat Tarheeb)*

The Food and Clothing of Rasulullah

Anas reports that Rasulullah wore woolen clothing and patched shoes. He also said that Rasulullah ate Bashi and his clothing was made of coarse cloth. When someone asked Hasan what Bashi was, he replied that it was coarsely ground barley which Rasulullah only managed to swallow with a sip of water. *(Ibn Majah, Hakim in Targheeb wat Tarheeb)*

The Incident of Rasulullah and Ummu Ayman

Ummu Ayman narrates that she once sifted some flour and made bread for Rasulullah with the refined flour rather than with the coarse flour Rasulullah was used to. When she served it to Rasulullah, he asked, "What is this?" Ummu Ayman replied, "It is something we prepare in our country (Abyssinia) and I wished to make you some bread from it."

Rasulullah ﷺ said, "Put is back in the mill and massage it again so that it can be made into a coarse type of bread." (Ibn Majah, Ibn Abi Dunya in Targheeb wat Tarheeb)

A Narration of Salma ؓ

Salma ؓ the wife of Abu Rafi ؓ reports that Hasan bin Ali ؓ, Abdullah bin Ja'far ؓ and Abdullah bin Abbas ؓ came to her and said, "Make for us some food that Rasulullah ﷺ liked to eat." She said to them, "But you may not like it nowadays because you are used to better foods." However she stood up and ground some barley. She blew off the very rough chaff and made some bread. The gravy for the bread was olive oil and she sprinkled some chilies on it. She served saying, "This is what Rasulullah ﷺ liked." (Tabrani, Haythami, Targheeb wat Tarheeb)

The Narration of Abdullah bin Omar ؓ About the Abstinence of Rasulullah ﷺ

Abdullah bin Omar ؓ reports that they once accompanied Rasulullah ﷺ into an Ansari's orchard. Rasulullah ﷺ picked up some dates from the ground and ate them. "What is the matter, O son of Omar? Why are you not eating?" Abdullah bin Omar ؓ replied, "1 do not feel like eating." "Well, I certainly do," said Rasulullah ﷺ, "because it is now 4 day since I have had anything to eat. If I wished, I could have prayed to my Rabb to give what the Emperors of Rome and Persia have. O son of Omar! What will be your condition when you live on to be with people who will store a year's provisions and people's trust in Allah will be weak." Abdullah bin Omar ؓ says, "By Allah! We were still standing there when Allah revealed the verse:

وَكَأَيِّنْ مِنْ دَابَّةٍ لَا تَحْمِلُ رِزْقَهَا اللَّهُ يَرْزُقُهَا وَإِيَّاكُمْ وَهُوَ السَّمِيعُ الْعَلِيمُ (60)

And so many a moving (living) creature there is, that carries not its own provision! Allah provides for it and for you. And He is the All-Hearer, the All-Knower. (Al-Ankabut:60)

Rasulullah ﷺ then said, "Allah has neither commanded me to amass worldly possessions nor to follow my desires. Whoever amasses worldly wealth with the intention of using it in the remaining portion of his life should remember that life is in Allah's hands. Take note that I do not amass Dinars or Dirhams and I do not store provisions for tomorrow." (Ibn Hibban in Targheeb wat Tarheeb, Ibn Abu Hatim in Ibn Kathir)

The Narration of Ummul Mu'minin Aisha ؓ

Aisha ؓ narrates that when a cup containing milk and honey was given to Rasulullah ﷺ, he commented, "A combination of 2 drinks as well as 2 meals in one cup. I have no need for such a thing. Take note that I do not say that this is Haram but on the Day of Judgment I do not like my Rabb to question me about the extravagance of this world. I humble myself before Allah. Whoever humbles himself for Allah, Allah will elevate him and whoever behaves arrogantly, Allah will lower him. Allah will grant independence to the one who spends carefully and Allah will love the one who remembers death." (Tabrani in Aswat, Targheeb wat Targheeb, Haythami)

The Abstinence of Abu Bakr ؓ

Zaid bin Arqam ؓ narrates, "We were once with Abu Bakr ؓ when he asked for something to drink. When some water mixed with honey was brought and put in his hand, he started to cry and sobbed a lot. He wept so that we thought that something was seriously wrong with him. However, we did not ask him anything. When he stopped crying, we asked, 'O Khalifa of Rasulullah ﷺ! What made you weep so much?' He replied, 'I was

once with Rasulullah ﷺ when I saw him repel something from himself which I could not see. I asked, 'O Rasulullah ﷺ! What was it I saw you repel from yourself when I could see nothing?' He replied, 'The world came towards me and I repelled it as I said, 'Get away from me!' It then said, 'I know that you will never take me.' It was this that made it difficult for me to drink the honey water. I feared that I may oppose the way of Rasulullah ﷺ and that the world would get hold of me." (Bazzar, Haythami, Ibnul Mundhir in Targheeb wat Tarheeb, Ibn Abi Dunya). In another narration, Zaid bin Arqam ؓ reports that when Abu Bakr ؓ once asked for a drink, he was given a cup with honey mixed in water. As he took it to his mouth, he started weeping and this made everyone around him cry as well. When he stopped crying, the people around him were still in tears. The same thing happened a second time and this time he cried so much that the people could not even ask him anything. When he eventually wiped his face and stopped crying, the people asked him the reason for his crying. The rest of the narration is similar to the one above except that he also said, "It is the world, then said from Rasulullah ﷺ, 'Remember! I swear by Allah that you have slipped through my grasp, those after you will be unable to do so." (Abu Nu'aym in Hilya, Hakim, Bayhaqi in Kanzul Ummal)

Narration of Aisha ؓ Stating that Abu Bakr ؓ Left Nothing Behind

Aisha ؓ says, "Abu Bakr ؓ passed away without leaving behind a Dinar or a Dirham. Just before his demise, he took all his money and deposited it in the Baytul Maal." Another narration from Urwa ؓ states that when he was made Khalifa, Abu Bakr ؓ deposited every Dinar and Dirham he possessed into the Baytul Maal. He said, "I used to trade and seek my livelihood with this money. Now that I am the Khalifa, public affairs have preoccupied me from trade and earning a livelihood." (Ahmad in Zuhd, Kanzul Ummal)

The Incident Between Him and Omar ؓ

Ata bin Sa'ib narrates that the morning after Abu Bakr ؓ was appointed Khalifa, he had some shawls over his arm and was proceeding to the marketplace to do business as usual. "Where are you off to?" asked Omar ؓ. "I am off to the marketplace," replied Abu Bakr ؓ. Omar ؓ enquired further, "What will you be doing there now that you have been put in charge of the Muslims?" "How will I then feed my family?" asked Abu Bakr ؓ. Omar ؓ replied, "Let us go to Abu Ubaidah ؓ and he will fix an allowance for you from the Baytul Maal." The 2 men then proceeded to Abu Ubaidah ؓ who said, "I shall fix for you the average allowance of a Muhajir which is neither too much nor too little. You will also receive a set of clothing for summer and one for winter but when you have worn out a set of clothing, you will return it before taking another." They then determined that he would receive half a goat every day without the head and innards. (Ibn Sa'd in Kanzul Ummal)

The Narration of Humaid bin Hilal ؓ

Humaid bin Hilal reports that when Abu Bakr ؓ was appointed as Khalifa, some of the Sahabah suggested that he should receive an allowance from the Baytul Maa1. It was later agreed that he should receive 2 shawls and he wore them out, he could receive another 2 after returning the old ones. He would also receive an animal for traveling and as much for household expenses as he normally spent before becoming the Khalifa. Abu Bakr ؓ was happy with this. (Ibn Sa'd in Kanzul Ummal)

Some Sahabah Feel That Omar ﷺ Should Receive a Larger Allowance But He Rejects the Idea

Salim bin Abdullah reports that when Omar ﷺ became the Khalifa, he took the same allowance that was fixed for Abu Bakr ﷺ. Although he continued with it, it became difficult for him to fulfill his needs with it. When a group of the Muhajirin that included Uthman ﷺ, Talha ﷺ and Zubair ﷺ once convened, it was Zubair ﷺ who suggested Omar ﷺ be informed that his allowance should be increased. Ali ﷺ agreed saying, "That is exactly what I had wanted some time ago. Let us go." However, Uthman ﷺ cautioned, "This is Omar ﷺ we are talking about! Let us first ascertain what his reaction would be. Let us rather approach his daughter Hafsa ﷺ and ask her. We will also ask her to keep the matter a secret." They then went to Hafsa ﷺ and told her that she should inform Omar ﷺ about the suggestion coming from a group of people. They stressed that she should not mention their names unless Omar ﷺ accepted the proposal. They then left. When Hafsa ﷺ met Omar ﷺ to discuss the matter, she noticed the anger on his face. "Who are these people?" Omar ﷺ demanded to know. "I cannot tell you until I know your opinion," she replied. Omar ﷺ then said, "If I knew who they were, I would scar their faces. You are my only medium with them. I ask you to tell me in the name of Allah what was the best clothing that Rasulullah ﷺ wore in your house?" She replied, "Two reddish brown garments which he wore when receiving delegations and delivering sermons on Fridays." "And what was the best food Rasulullah ﷺ ate at house?" Omar ﷺ asked further. Hafsa ﷺ replied, "I once made bread from barley flour and when it was still hot, I poured over it some oil left at the bottom of our oil can. This made it moist and soft and Rasulullah ﷺ ate it with great relish." Omar ﷺ then asked, "And what bedding did Rasulullah ﷺ use with you that was most comfortable?" She replied, "It was made from a thick material which we four-folded in summer beneath us. During winter we double-folded it beneath us and used the other portion to cover ourselves." Omar ﷺ then said, "Dear Hafsa! Take this message from me to the group of Muhajirin that Rasulullah ﷺ had set a precedent in all matters. He had kept extravagance in its place without indulging in it and sufficed only with what was necessary. By Allah! I shall also keep extravagance in its place and suffice with bare necessities. The example of me and my 2 companions: Rasulullah ﷺ and Abu Bakr ﷺ are like 3 persons on a road. The 1st took along his provisions and reached his destination. The 2nd followed suit and also reached the destination. Now the 3rd is on the road. If he sticks to their way and is content with the provisions they took, he will meet them and be with them. However, if he takes a road other than the one they took, he will not be able to meet up with them." *(Tabrani, Ibn Asakir in Muntakhab Kanzul Ummal)*

The Narration of Hasan Basri ﷺ

Hasan Basri says that he once attended a gathering in the Jami Masjid of Basra where he found some Sahabah speaking about the abstinence of Abu Bakr ﷺ and Omar ﷺ. They were also discussing the personalities of the 2 man and the military conquests that Allah had give Islam under their leadership. Moving closer to the gathering, he found Ahnaf bin Qais Tamimi ﷺ sitting with them. Ahnaf ﷺ was saying, "Omar bin Khattab ﷺ dispatched us on a military expedition to Iraq and it was then that Allah allowed us to conquer Iraq and various Persian cities. There we took possession of white Persian and Khurasan cloth, which we took with us and started to wear. When we came to Omar ﷺ in Madinah, he turned his face away from us and did not

speak to us. This was a hard blow to the Sahabah. We then approached his son Abdullah bin Omar ﷺ who was sitting in the Masjid. When we complained to him about the cold treatment we received from the Amirul Mu'minin, he said, 'The Amirul Mu'minin ignored you because he saw you wearing clothing that he neither saw Rasulullah ﷺ nor his successor Abu Bakr ﷺ wearing.'" Ahnaf ﷺ continues, "We then returned to our homes, removed the clothing and wore the clothing that Omar ﷺ was used to seeing us wear. When we again went to meet him, Omar ﷺ stood up and greeted each one of us individually. He even embraced each of us as if he had never seen us before. When we brought the booty before him, he distributed it equally between us. Amongst the booty presented to him was a container with yellow and red sweetmeats. When he tasted it, he found it to be extremely delicious. He then turned to us and said, 'O assembly of Muhajirin and Ansar! I swear by Allah that it will be for food like this that a son will kill his father and a brother will kill his brother.' According to his instructions, the sweetmeats were distributed amongst the children of those Sahabah who were martyred during the time of Rasulullah ﷺ. Omar ﷺ got up and left with the Sahabah walking behind him."

Some of the Sahabah said, "O assembly of Muhajirin and Ansar! Just look at the abstinence of this man and his attire. We have had to endure plenty of embarrassment on account of him because since Allah has granted him victory over the domains of Rome and Persia and the far reaches of the East and West, many Arab and non-Arab delegations come to him and see him wearing the same robe with 12 patches. You people are the senior companions of Rasulullah ﷺ who are veterans of many great battles. You are also the early vanguards from the Muhajirin and Ansar. Therefore, O companions of Rasulullah ﷺ, why do you not ask him to change his robe for something softer that would make fear into someone looking on. He should also have an elaborate meal platter served to him every morning and another every evening from which he could eat and also feed the Muhajirin and Ansar with him." All of them unanimously agreed that only 2 persons could suggest this to Omar ﷺ. They were Ali bin Abi Talib ﷺ because he was the boldest before Omar ﷺ and also his father-in-law. The other was Omar ﷺ's daughter Hafsa ﷺ because she was the wife of Rasulullah ﷺ. Omar respected her because of her relationship with Rasulullah ﷺ. When they approached Ali ﷺ, he refused to do it and referred the people to the wives of Rasulullah ﷺ because they were after all the mothers of all Mu'minin and could address Omar ﷺ without fear.

They then asked Aisha ﷺ and Hafsa ﷺ at a time when the 2 happened to be together. When Aisha ﷺ agreed to ask Omar ﷺ, Hafsa ﷺ said, "I don't think that he will oblige. However, you will soon find out." When the 2 ladies went to Omar ﷺ, he welcomed them in. Aisha ﷺ said, "O Amirul Mu'minin! Will you permit us to say something?" "Go ahead and speak, O Ummul Mu'minin," replied Omar ﷺ. She said, "Rasulullah ﷺ has passed on to his way to Jannah and to Allah's pleasure without taking an portion of this world and without the world coming to him. Abu Bakr ﷺ passed on in a like manner in the footsteps of Rasulullah ﷺ after reviving his Sunnah, finishing off those who rejected Islam and giving thorough replies to those who walked the Path of falsehood. He exercised justice amongst the people, distributed wealth amongst them with equity and pleased the Rabb of creation. Allah then took him into His mercy and joined him with His Nabi ﷺ and those most high, the Ambiya in the high ranks of Jannah. Neither did he desire this world not did it come to him. Allah has now conquered the treasures of Roman and Persian Emperors at your hands and gave you their lands.

Their wealth has been carried to you and the ends of the East and West have fallen to your feet. We now anticipate even more from Allah to bolster Islam. Envoys from the various non-Arab tribes come to you and many Arab delegations also meet with you while you are wearing that robe that has 12 patches. Why do you not change your robe for something softer that would make fear into someone looking on and have a meal platter served to you every morning and another every evening from which you could eat and also feed the Muhajirin and Ansar with you?"

When he heard this, Omar ؓ started weeping profusely. He then asked, "I ask you to tell me in the name of Allah whether Rasulullah ﷺ ever filled himself with even barley bread for 10 nights or even 5 or 3 nights? Or did he ever eat both a morning and evening meal in a day until he met Allah?" Addressing Aisha ؓ, Omar ؓ continued, "Do you ever know of a time when food was served to Rasulullah ﷺ on a table that was even a handspan higher than the ground? Or was it that when he wanted food, it was placed on the ground and after eating, it was then taken away?" Both ladies replied, "We swear by Allah that this was the case." He then said, "The 2 of you are the wives of Rasulullah ﷺ and the mothers of the Mu'minin. You have rights over all the Mu'minin and especially over me. However, you have come to encourage me towards things of this world when I know that Rasulullah ﷺ wore a woolen robe so rough in texture that it actually scratched his skin. Do you know about this?" "We swear by Allah that we do!" they both admitted.

Omar ؓ continued, "Do you not know that Rasulullah ﷺ used to sleep on a single folded robe? And, O Aisha, did you not have a coarse sheet made of animal hairs that Rasulullah ﷺ used as a rug during the day and bedding during the nights? When we used to come to see him, we could always notice the imprints of the straw mat on his sides. O Hafsa! Remember that you told me that one night you double folded the bedding and finding it soft, Rasulullah ﷺ slept through the night and woke up only with Bilal's Adhan. He then said to you, 'O Hafsa! What have you done? You had double folded the bedding last night, causing sleep to carry me through to the morning. What need have I for this world? Why do you preoccupy me with soft beds?' O Hafsa! Don't you know that all Rasulullah ﷺ's earlier and later error had been forgiven? Yet he went hungry in the evenings, spent his sleeping hours in Sejdah and remained in Ruku, Sejdah, weeping and humbling himself before Allah throughout the hours of the day and night. This he did until the day Allah took him into the fold of His mercy and pleasure. Omar ؓ shall never eat good foods, and shall never wear fine clothing because he has a perfect example in his 2 companions: Rasulullah ﷺ and Abu Bakr ؓ. He shall also never eat 2 meals at the same time except for having salt and olive oil together. He shall eat meat only once a month just so that his month passes like the masses." The 2 ladies then left and informed the Sahabah about what had transpired. Omar ؓ remained like this until he eventually left to meet Allah." *(Ibn Asakir in Muntakhab Kanzul Ummal)*

His Abstinence in Eating

Ikrama bin Khalid narrates that Hafsa ؓ, Ibn Muti ؓ and Abdullah bin Omar ؓ once addressed Omar ؓ saying. "If you eat good food, it would give you more strength to establish the truth." Omar replied. "I know well that each of you wish me well, but I have left my two companions Rasulullah ﷺ and Abu Bakr ؓ on a certain route and if I leave that route, I shall not be able to meet them at the destination." *(Abdur Razzaq, Bayhaqi, Ibn Asakir in Muntakhab Kanzul Ummal)*. Abu Umamah bin Sahl bin Hunaif ؓ says that for a long period of time, Omar ؓ

took nothing from the Baytul Maal. He eventually reached a stage where he started suffering poverty because involvement in public matters gave him no time to engage in trade. He then sent for some of the Sahabah to consult with them. He addressed them saying, "My task has preoccupied me from earning, so what allowance do you see appropriate for me?" Uthman bin Affan ؓ replied, "So much that you are able to eat and feed others as well." Sa'eed bin Zaid bin Amr bin Nufail ؓ echoed the opinion. Omar ؓ then asked Ali ؓ, "What have you to say about it?" Ali ؓ replied, "So much that is sufficient for your morning and evening meals." Omar ؓ abided by this opinion. *(Ibn Sa'd in Muntakhab Kanzul Ummal)*. Qatadah ؓ reports that Omar ؓ used to say, "Had I so wished, I could be eating the best of foods wearing the finest of clothing. However, I prefer to rather her perpetuate my luxuries by reserving them for the hereafter." It has also been narrated that when Omar ؓ once arrived in Sham, food that he had never before set eyes upon was prepared for him. He asked, "While we eat this, what will the poor Muslims have who die without filling themselves with even barley bread?" Omar bin Walid replied, "They shall have Jannah." Tears then started to flow from the eyes of Omar ؓ as he said, "If this food is our share while they have made off with Jannah, then they have certainly excelled us with a tremendous virtue." *(Abi bin Humaid, Ibn Jareer in Muntakhab Kanzul Ummal)*

The Incident with His Son Abdullah ؓ and Daughter Hafsa ؓ

Abdullah bin Omar ؓ (the son of Omar ؓ) narrates that Omar ؓ once came to his house while he was eating. Omar ؓ made space for his father at the head of the table. When he sat down, Omar ؓ said, "Bismillah" and then put his hand to the food. He ate a morsel and then another. Thereafter, he commented, "I can taste the presence of something that is not the natural fat of meat, this meat has not been cooked in its own fat." Abdullah bin Omar ؓ submitted, "O Amirul Mu'minin! I went to the marketplace with 2 Dirhams to look for some fatty meat to buy but found that it was too expensive (more than 2 Dirhams). I then bought the meat of a thin animal for a Dirham and cooked it with some butter that I bought for another Dirham. I wanted each member of my family to have at least one bone to eat. Omar ؓ then said, "Whenever these 2 things (meat and butter) came to Rasulullah ﷺ, he only ate one of them and gave the other away as Sadaqa. I shall therefore not eat." Abdullah bin Omar ؓ said, "Please eat, O Amirul Mu'minin! Whenever the 2 again come in my possession at the same time, I shall also do the same." "I cannot," replied Omar ؓ. *(Ibn Majah in Kanzul Ummal)*. Abu Hazim reports that Omar ؓ once went to see his daughter Hafsa ؓ who served him some cold gravy and bread. She then poured some olive oil into it. "2 gravies in one!" remarked Omar ؓ, "I shall not eat this until the day I meet Allah." *(Ibn Sa'd)*

The Narrations of Anas ؓ and Sa'ib bin Yazid ؓ Concerning the Food of Omar ؓ

Anas ؓ says, "When he was Khalifa, I saw that when a Saa of dates was given to Omar ؓ, he would even eat the dates that were of an inferior quality." Sa'ib bin Yazid ؓ reports, "I often had dinner with Omar ؓ when he ate bread and dry meat. He would then wipe his hands on his feet saying, 'This is the napkin of Omar and his family.'" A narration of *Deenowri from Thabit* states that when Jarud once ate with Omar ؓ and had finished the meal, he asked one of the servants to get him a napkin to wipe his hands. Omar ؓ said, "Wipe your hands off on your sleeve because the meal was dry and your hands have hardly been soiled." *(Ibn Sa'd)*

Omar ﷺ Reminds People of a Verse of the Qur'an

Abdur Rahman bin Abu Laila reports that when some people from Iraq once came to Omar ﷺ, he noticed that they ate very little because they were used to good food and did not like his simple food. He then said to them, "O Iraqis! If I wanted, I could also have luxurious meals prepared for me as you have. However, we wish to rather continue our luxuries of this world by forsaking them here to find them in the Hereafter. Have you not heard that in the Hereafter Allah will say to some people:

أَذْهَبْتُمْ طَيِّبَاتِكُمْ فِي حَيَاتِكُمُ الدُّنْيَا

"You received your good things in the life of the world (and therefore have nothing for yourselves here). (Al-Ahqaf:20) (Abu Nu'aym in Hilya).

A companion of Habib bin Abi Thabit narrates that Omar ﷺ once met a group of Iraqis with whom was Jareer bin Abdullah ﷺ. When a platter of food prepared from bread and olive oil was served to them, they ate only very little because they did not like it. Omar ﷺ then said to them, "I have seen what you have done. What do you want? Do you want various types of sweets and foods served hot and cold according to your desire and then have to cram it all into your bellies?" *(Abu Nu'aym in Hilya, Muntakhab Kanzul Ummal).*

Humaid bin Hilal reports that Hafs bin Abul Aas often joined Omar ﷺ for meals but ate nothing. Omar ﷺ asked, "What prevents you from eating our food?" Hafs replied, "Your food is very coarse and thick. I prefer to eat the smooth variety of food that is prepared for me." Omar ﷺ told him, "Do you think that I cannot give instructions for all the hairs of a goat to be removed and then the meat roasted for me? Do you think that I cannot give instructions for flour to be sifted through a cloth and then prepared as refined bread? Do you think that I cannot give instructions for raisins to be put into a container and then soaked in water to produce a delicious drink that resemble the blood of a deer in color?" Hafs commented, "You seem to know all about living a good life." "Certainly," replied Omar ﷺ, "I swear by the Being Who controls my life! Had I not disliked that it should reduce my good deeds on the Day of Judgment, I would have joined you in your lives of luxury." *(Ibn Sa'd in Muntakhab Kanzul Ummal).* Salim bin Abdullah narrates that Omar ﷺ used to say, "By Allah! We have no concern for the luxuries of this world. We could easily give instructions for the hairs of a kid goat to be removed and then roasted. We could likewise give instructions for the best of wheat to be used for our bread and for raisins to be soaked overnight in a container to produce a sweet drink until it resembles the eyes of a partridge. We could then have all these things to eat and drink. However, we prefer to perpetuate our luxuries because we have heard Allah say to some people on the Day of Judgment: أَذْهَبْتُمْ طَيِّبَاتِكُمْ فِي حَيَاتِكُمُ الدُّنْيَا

"You received your good things in the life of the world (and therefore have nothing for yourselves here). (Al-Ahqaf:20) (Abu Nu'aym in Hilya)

The Incident with Abu Musa Ash'ari ﷺ

Abu Musa Ash'ari ﷺ narrates, "I came to Omar ﷺ with a delegation from Basra. Whenever we met him and ate with him, we noticed that every day he was served pieces of the same bread. At times, we would have something like butter, olive oil or milk with it. There were times when we would have boiled strips of dried meat as well. Although we sometimes ate fresh meat, those occasions were very rare. One day Omar ﷺ said to us, 'By Allah?! I have noticed how little you eat and that you seem to dislike my food. By Allah! Had I so wished, I could be

eating the best of foods and leading the wealthiest life. Take note that I am not unaware of delicacies like roasted breast and hump meats of a camel, refined bread and spicy relishes. However, I do not have them because I have heard Allah reprimanding a nation for something they had done when he says:

أَذْهَبْتُمْ طَيِّبَاتِكُمْ فِي حَيَاتِكُمُ الدُّنْيَا

"You received your good things in the life of the world (and therefore have nothing for yourselves here). (Al-Ahqaf:20)

Abu Musa Ash'ari ﷺ suggested to his companions that they speak to Amirul Mu'minin about allotting to them some food from the Baytul Maal. When they addressed him, Omar ﷺ said, "O assembly of governors! Are you not satisfied with that with which I satisfy myself?" They submitted, "O Amirul Mu'minin! Madinah is located in an area where living is hard. We do not think that your food is eaten when it is served to others. However, we live in a fertile land and when the food of our leaders is served, it is always well eaten, we therefore have to many people to feed." Omar ﷺ lowered his head for awhile and then raised it saying, "I shall allow you 2 goats and 2 bags of flour from the Baytul Maal every day. In the mornings, a goat and bag should be prepared. You should eat from it and feed those with you. You may also have a Halal drink prepared, from which you drink first and then give to those on your right and then those after them. You should proceed for your necessities. Later in the evenings, the other goat and bag should be prepared for you and your companions to eat from. Remember that you should also provide for the people at their homes and ensure that their families are well fed. If you do not provide enough for the people, their character will never improve and their hungry ones will not be satiated. I swear by Allah that despite this allowance I have allotted, I still believe that ruination will come quickly to a town from which 2 goats and 2 bags are taken every day." *(Ibn Mubarak, Ibn Sa'd in Muntakhab Kanzul Ummal).*

The Incident With Utba bin Farqad ﷺ

Utba bin Farqad reports, "I once brought to Omar ﷺ a few baskets full of sweetmeats. 'What is this?' he asked. I replied, 'Because you spend the beginning of the day fulfilling the needs of the people, I wanted you to have some food to return to so that you may refill your strength.' Omar ﷺ opened one of the baskets and asked, 'O Utba! Tell me in the name of Allah whether you have given every Muslim a basket like this.' 'O Amirul Mu'minin!' I replied, 'You would be unable to do that even if you spent all the money of the Qais tribe.' 'Then I have no need for this,' he said. Omar ﷺ then called for a plate of Tharid made from coarse bread and tough meat. He relished the meal as we ate together. I stretched my hand towards a piece of food that I thought was from the hump of the camel, only to discover that it was muscle tendons. I kept chewing on a piece of meat that I could not get down my throat and when I noticed that Omar ﷺ was not looking at me, I put it between the plate and the tablecloth. Omar ﷺ called for a large container of Nabidh (raisin/dates left overnight in water) that was so old that it had almost become vinegar. He told me to drink it but I could not get it down my throat. He then took it and drank. After drinking, he said, 'Listen O Utba! We slaughter a camel every day and give all the fat and the best meat to Muslims visitors from other places. As for the neck, it is reserved for the family of Omar ﷺ so that they may have the toughest meat. They drink this strong Nabidh to break up the tough meat to aid in digestion so that it causes us no harm.'" *(Hannad in Muntakhab Kanzul Ummal).*

His Fear when served water mixed with Honey

Hasan narrates that Omar ﷺ was thirsty when he once visited someone. When he asked the man for something to drink, some honey mixed in water was brought to him. "What is this?" asked Omar ﷺ. "Honey," came the reply. Omar ﷺ then said, "This should not be amongst the things about which I will be questioned on the Day of Judgment. I shall therefore not be having any." *(Ibn Sa'd, Ibn Asakir in Muntakhab Kanzul Ummal).* When Omar ﷺ once asked for a drink, he was served some water mixed with honey. He said, "This is most excellent, but I have heard Allah rebuke a nation for following the dictates of their desires. Allah says: أَذْهَبْتُمْ طَيِّبَاتِكُمْ فِي حَيَاتِكُمُ الدُّنْيَا *"You received your good things in the life of the world (and therefore have nothing for yourselves here). (Al-Ahqaf:20) (Razeen in Targheeb wat Tarheed)*

His Clothes, His Spending and Other Facets of His Biography

Urwa ﷺ says that Omar ﷺ arrived in Eela with a group of Muhajirin and Ansar. Because the journey was long and difficult, the seat of his upper garment had torn even though it was made from a thick material. He therefore gave it to a priest to have it washed and patched. The priest took the garment and had it patched. He also sewed another identical garment for Omar ﷺ. When he brought the garments back to Omar ﷺ that evening, Omar ﷺ asked, "What is this?" The priest replied, "This is your garment that I washed and patched. This, however, is a garment I wish to give you." Omar ﷺ looked at the new garment and felt it. He then wore his old garment and returned the other one to the priest, he then said, "This old garment better absorbs perspiration." *(Tabari, Ibn Mubarak in Muntakhab Kanzul Ummal).* Qatadah ﷺ reports that when he was Khalifa, Omar ﷺ wore a patched woolen robe that had some patches of leather. He used to walk through the marketplace with a whip on his shoulder to reprimand errant people. He passed by any thread or date stones lying around, he picked up and threw them in people's yards so that they may find use. *(Deenowri, Ibn Asakir).*

Hasan reports that when Omar ﷺ was Khalifa, he was once delivering a lecture wearing a lower garment that had 12 patches. *(Ahmad in Zuhd, Hannad, Ibn Jareer, Abu Nu'aym in Kanzul Ummal).* Anas ﷺ says, "When Omar ﷺ was the Amirul Mu'minin, I once saw that his garment had 3 patches between the shoulders, one overlapping on to the other." *(Malik in Targheeb wat Tarheeb).* Abdullah bin Omar ﷺ reports, "The food that Omar ﷺ took from the Baytul Maal was only what was absolutely necessary for his family and for himself. He also received a set of clothing for the summer. There were times when his lower garment would tear but he would keep patching it up without taking another until the time came for him to receive another. Whenever the Baytul Maal received more funds, I noticed that rather than having something better his clothing appeared worse than those he wore the previous year. When his daughter Hafsa ﷺ spoke to him about this, he replied, 'I receive my clothing from the money of the Muslims and this suffices for me.'" *(Ibn Sa'd in Muntakhab Kanzul Ummal).* Muhammad bin Ibrahim reports that the daily allowance Omar ﷺ received from the Baytul Maal for his and his family's needs was only 2 Dirhams. *(Ibn Sa'd in Muntakhab Kanzul Ummal)*

The Abstinence of Uthman bin Affan ﷺ: His Clothing, Food, and Sleeping on a Straw Mat in the Masjid

Abdul Malik bin Shaddad says that he once saw Uthman ﷺ on the pulpit on a Friday wearing a thick lower garment sewn in Aden that was worth no more than 4 or 5 Dirhams. His upper garment was made of a reddish brown Kufi material. *(Abu Nu'aym in Hilya).* When Hasan was asked about the people who slept in the Masjid in the afternoons, he replied, "During his period as Khalifa, I saw Uthman bin Affan ﷺ sleep in the Masjid in the afternoon. When he got up, the imprint of the straw mat was visible on his side. The people used to say, 'That is the Amirul Mu'minin! That is the Amirul Mu'minin!'" *(Abu Nu'aym in Hilya, Ahmad in Sifatus Safwa).* Shurabil bin Muslim says that although Uthman ﷺ used to feed people the luxurious meals of a ruler, he would eat simple vinegar and olive oil at home.

The Abstinence of Ali bin Abi Talib ﷺ, His food

A man from the Thaqif tribe says, "Ali ﷺ appointed me as governor of a place called Ukbara. It was a place in rural Iraq where no Muslims lived. Ali ﷺ told me to meet him the following day at the time of Zuhr. When I went to him, I found no doorman to prevent me from entering and saw him sitting down with a jug and a glass of water. When he asked for a bag to be brought to him, I thought, 'Perhaps he trusts me so much that he is going to give me a precious jewel'. I had no idea what was in the bag. It was sealed and when he broke the seal, I was surprised to find that there was barley flour inside. He took some out of the bag, put it in a cup and then poured water into it. He drank the mixture and also gave me drink. Unable to contain myself, I said, 'O Amirul Mu'minin! You are having this in Iraq, when Iraq has foods much better than this?' He replied, 'By Allah! I do not have these bags sealed because of stinginess. The reason for sealing them is that I buy exactly how much I need from Madinah and fear that it should not deplete by spilling because I would then have to cook something else from Iraq. This is my way of looking after it because I do like anything but pure foods to enter my belly.'" A'mash reports that although Ali ﷺ used to feed people well at lunches and dinners, he only ate food brought for him from Madinah. *(Abu Nu'aym in Hilya)*

His Statement When He was Served Some Faluda

Abdullah bin Sharik reports form his grandfather that some Faluda (sweet drink) was served to Ali ﷺ. Addressing the Faluda, Ali ﷺ said, "You have an excellent fragrance, a wonderful color and delicious taste. But I do not wish to get myself accustomed to something that I am not used to having." *(Abu Nu'aym in Hilya, Zawa'id, Muntakhab Kanzul Ummal)*

His Clothing

Zaid bin Wahab narrates that Ali ﷺ once came before them wearing a shawl and lower garment tied to his waist with a strip of cloth. When someone commented on this, Ali ﷺ said, "I am wearing this because it keeps pride away, it is convenient for performing salah and so that it may become a common practice amongst the Mu'minin." *(Ibn Mubarak, Muntakhab Kanzul Ummal).* It is reported that Ali ﷺ wore a lower garment made of coarse cloth. He once said, "I bought this garment for 5 Dirhams and will sell it to anyone who gives me a profit of one Dirham." *(Bayhaqi, Muntakhab Kanzul Ummal)*

He Sells his Sword to Buy a Garment

Mujammi bin Sam'an Taimi narrates that Ali ﷺ once took his sword to the marketplace and announced, "Who will buy this sword from me? I would never have sold it if I had 4 Dirhams to buy myself a lower garment." *(Ya'qoob bin Sufiyan in Al Bidayah wan Nihayah).* Salih bin Abil Aswad reports from someone else that he once saw Ali ﷺ riding a donkey with both his legs hanging on one side as he said, "It is I who holds the world in contempt." *(Baghawi in Al Bidayah wan Nihayah)*

His Statement About How Much of Public Funds are Permissible for the Khalifa

Abdullah bin Razin reports that they once went to meet Ali ؓ on the occasion of Eidul Adha. Ali ؓ served them a dish prepared with cubes of meat and fiber. We remarked, "May Allah always keep you well! It would have been better if you had fed us duel because Allah has given plenty." Ali ؓ replied, "O Ibn Razin! I heard Rasulullah ﷺ say, if it is no permissible for a Khalifa to take anything from Allah's money (public funds) besides 2 dishes. One for himself and his family and the other to place before people.'" *(Ahmad in Ai Bidayah wan Nihayah)*

The Abstinence of Abu Ubaidah bin Jarrah ؓ

Urwa ؓ reports that Omar ؓ once went to see Abu Ubaidah bin Jarrah ؓ, he found him lying down on a saddle blanket using the animal's bag as a pillow. Omar ؓ said, "Why have you not adopted those luxuries which your companions have adopted?" Abu Ubaidah ؓ replied, "O Amirul Mu'minin! This is sufficient to take me to the grave." In his narration, Ma'mar narrates that when Omar ؓ arrived in Sham, the common people as well as the leaders came to meet him. "Where is my brother?" Omar ؓ asked. "Who is he?" the people enquired. "Abu Ubaidah," Omar ؓ replied. The people said, "Here he comes." Abu Ubaidah ؓ came, Omar ؓ descended from his animal and embraced him. Omar ؓ went to Abu Ubaidah ؓ's house and saw nothing there but his sword, his shield, and his conveyance. The rest of the narration is same as above. *(Abu Nu'aym in Hilya, Ahmad in Sifatus Safwa, Ibn Mubarak in Isabah)*

The Abstinence of Mus'ab bin Umair ؓ

Ali ؓ says, "One winter morning I left home extremely hungry with the cold almost killing me. There was a piece of undyed leather at home which was still smelly. I cut it to put my head through and tied it to my chest to ward off the cold. By Allah, there was nothing at home that I could eat and had there been any food in Rasulullah ﷺ's house, some of it would have definitely reached me. As I was walking in one end of Madinah, I peeped through a hole in the wall of an orchard where I saw a Jew standing in his orchard. He said, 'What is the problem, O Bedouin? Are you prepared to earn a date for every bucket of water you draw from the well?' 'Certainly,' I replied, 'open the gate.' I entered the orchard after he opened the gate and started drawing water. He gave me a date for every bucket I drew until my hand was full of dates. I then said, 'That is enough for now.' I ate the dates and then put my mouth to a stream of water to drink. Thereafter, I arrived before Rasulullah ﷺ who was sitting in the Masjid with a group of Sahabah. It was then that Mus'ab bin Umair ؓ appeared wearing a patched shawl. Rasulullah ﷺ mentioned the wealth that Mus'ab used to have before becoming a Muslim and seeing his condition at the time, Rasulullah ﷺ's eyes filled with tears and he started weeping. Rasulullah ﷺ then said, 'What will be your condition when that time comes when one of you would be wearing an outfit in the mornings and then another in the evenings, and your homes will be adorned like the covering of the Kabah?' We replied, 'In that time, we shall be in a better position because we will have others to do the hard work for us while we free ourselves for Ibadah.' 'No,' said Rasulullah ﷺ, 'You are better off today than you would be during those days.'" *(Tirmidhi, Abu Ya'la, Ibn Rahway in Kanzul Ummal, Haythami)*

The Hardships Mus'ab Bin Umair ؓ Endured After Becoming a Muslim

Omar ؓ narrates that Rasulullah ﷺ once saw Mus'ab Bin Umair ؓ approach wrapped in a sheepskin. Rasulullah ﷺ remarked, "Look at that man whose heart Allah has illuminated. I saw him at a time when his parents would give him the best of foods and drinks. I also saw him wearing an outfit that was bought for 200 Dirhams. It was then the love for Allah and the love for Allah's Rasul that called him to the situation that you now see." *(Tabrani, Bayhaqi in Targheeb wat Tarheeb, Hasan bin Sufian Abu Abdur Rahman Sulami, Hakim in Kanzul Ummal, Abu Nu'aym in Hilya)*. Zubair ؓ reports that Rasulullah ﷺ was once sitting with a group of Sahabah in Quba when Mus'ab Bin Umair ؓ arrived wearing a shawl that could hardly cover his body. The Sahabah lowered their heads and when he reached them and greeted with Salam, they replied to his greeting. Rasulullah ﷺ had only good words to say about him and praised him. Thereafter, Rasulullah ﷺ said, "I had seen this man with his parents in Makkah when they showered their love and favors on him. There was not a youngster from all of the Quraish as fortunate as he was. He then left all of that wealth in search of Allah's pleasure and to assist Islam and Allah's Rasul ﷺ. Behold! In a short period of time, Allah shall grant you conquests over Persia and Rome. You will then have so much wealth that there will be those amongst you who will wear an outfit in the mornings and another in the evenings and a platter of food will be served to you in the mornings and again in the evenings." The Sahabah asked, "O Rasulullah ﷺ! Are we in a better position today or in those days?" Rasulullah ﷺ replied, "You are certainly better off today as you will be during those days. Take note! If you knew about this world what I know, you would never be at ease with it." *(Hakim)*. Another narration from Khabab ؓ states that all that Mus'ab Bin Umair ؓ left behind after his death was a sheet so small that when it was used as a burial shroud, it would leave his feet exposed when his head was covered and his head exposed when his feet were covered. Rasulullah ﷺ then instructed the Sahabah to cover his head with the sheet and his feet with Idhkhir grass. *(Isabah)*

The Abstinence of Uthman bin Madh'un ؓ

Ibn Shihab narrates that Uthman bin Madh'un ؓ once entered the Masjid wearing a striped shawl that he patched with a piece of leather because it tore. Seeing his pitiful condition Rasulullah ﷺ started weeping and the Sahabah also started weeping upon the crying of Rasulullah ﷺ. Rasulullah ﷺ then remarked, "What will be your condition at the time when one of you would wear an outfit in the morning and another in the evening. As one platter of food would be placed before him, another will be taken away and you will be decorating your homes as the Kabah is adorned." The Sahabah said, "We wish that such a time had already come so that we could enjoy ease and comfort." Rasulullah ﷺ said, "That time will certainly be coming. However, you are in a better position today that the people of those times." *(Abu Nu'aym in Hilya)*

His Demise

Abdullah bin Abbas ؓ reports that after Uthman bin Madh'un ؓ had passed away, Rasulullah ﷺ came to him and bent over him as if advising him. Rasulullah ﷺ then raised his head and signs of crying could be noticed from his eyes. Rasulullah ﷺ then bend over the corpse again and when he raised his head, he was weeping. Thereafter, Rasulullah ﷺ bent over him for the 3rd time and when he raised his head this time, he was sobbing profusely. The Sahabah understood that Uthman bin Madh'un ☺ had certainly passed away and they all started to weep. "Stop," said Rasulullah ☷, "This is from Saitan, so repent to Allah." Addressing Uthman bin Madh'un ☺, Rasulullah ☷ then said, "O Abu Sa'ib! Do not grieve, for you have left this world without taking anything of it with you." *(Tabrani, Haythami, Abu Nu'aym in Hilya, Ibn Abdul Birr in Isti'ab)*. Another narration states that Rasulullah ☷ said, "May Allah shower His mercy on you, O Uthman! Neither have you taken from this world nor has it taken from you." *(Abu Nu'aym in Hilya)*

The Abstinence of Salman Farsi ☺

Atia bin Amir says that he once saw Salman Farsi ☺ being forced to eat more. He said, "That is enough for me. That is enough for me as I heard Rasulullah ☷ say, 'Those who are most full in this world all be most hungry in the Hereafter. O Salman! This world is a prison for the Mu'min and paradise for the Kafir.**"** *(Abu Nu'aym in Hilya, Askari in Amthal, Kanzul Ummal)*

His Abstinence as Governor

Hasan reports that the allowance Salman Farsi ☺ received was 5,000 Dirhams and he was governor of approximately 30,000 Muslims. However, he still delivered lectures to the people wrapping a part of his robe over himself while spreading the other part on the ground to sit upon. He always spent the allowance on others whenever he received it and would live on the income he received from the baskets he weaved from the fibers of palm leaves. *(Abu Nu'aym in Hilya, Ibn Sa'd)*

The Incident between him and Hudhaifa ☺ on Building a Room

A'mash reports that he heard the incident from people that Hudhaifa ☺ once said to Salman Farsi ☺, "O Abu Abdullah! Should I not build a room for you?" Salman ☺ did not like this. Hudhaifa ☺ then added, "Hang on until I explain. I intend building you a room that when you lie down, your head touches one end and your feet the other. When you stand up, your head hits the roof." Salman ☺ commented, "It appears as if you live in my heart, you know exactly what I want." *(Abu Nu'aym in Hilya)*

Another Incident in this Regard

Malik bin Anas narrates that Salman Farsi ☺ had no room from which to administer public affairs. He would sit in the shade of a tree and move wherever the shadow moved. Someone one day offered, "Should I not build a room for you which you may have shade from the heat and have shelter from the cold?" When Salman ☺ agreed and the man was leaving, Salman ☺ called to him saying, "How will you build this room?" The man replied, "I shall build it so that your head touches the roof when you stand and your feet touch the wall when you lie down." "Exactly," replied Salman ☺. *(Ibn Sa'd)*

The Abstinence of Abu Dhar Gifari ☺ While Living in Rabdha

Abu Asma reports that he once visited Abu Dhar ☺ who was then staying in Rabdha. Abu Dhar ☺ at that time was with an unattractive black woman with disheveled hair, who wore no perfume at all. Abu Dhar ☺ said, "Will you not look at this little woman?! She is telling me to go to live in Iraq. However, I know well that when I go there, the people will bring to me all their worldly possessions whereas my good friend Rasulullah ☷ had informed me that before the bridge of Sirat is an extremely slippery path. We would be able to pass it more easily when our loads are light and compact than when we are burdened with heavy loads." *(Ahmad in Targheeb wat Tarheeb, Abu Nu'aym in Hilya, Ibn Sa'd)*. Abdullah bin Khirash reports that he once saw Abu Dhar ☺ sitting in the shade in Rabdha. He was sitting on a piece of coarse sack cloth with his wife who was a black woman. In pity someone said to him, "You have no surviving children." Abu Dhar ☺ replied, "All praises are for Allah Who has taken them from this temporary world and kept them as a treasure for us in the everlasting world." When someone then suggested that he get himself another wife, he said, "I prefer marrying a wife who is a cause for humility developing in me rather than one who is a cause of pride developing." "Why do you rather not use a mat that is softer than this one?" Abu Dhar ☺ responded by praying, "O Allah! Forgive me. Take from me as many bounties as You please." *(Abu Nu'aym in Hilya, Haythami)*

His Food

Ibrahim Taymi reports from his father that someone once suggested to Abu Dhar ☺ that he should become a land owner like some other person was doing. Abu Dhar ☺ replied, "Why should I become a rich man? Sufficient for me every day is my drink of water or milk and the Qafiz (a unit of weight that has varying specifications in the various Arab countries) of wheat in Fridays." Another narration states that Abu Dhar ☺ said, "During the time of Rasulullah ☷, I lived on a Saa and I shall never increase this until I meet Allah." *(Abu Nu'aym in Hilya)*

The Abstinence of Abu Darda ☺

Abu Darda ☺ says, "I had been a trader before Rasulullah ☷ announced his prophethood. After Rasulullah ☷ announced that he was a Rasul, I tried combining my trade with Ibada but was unable to do so. I therefore gave up trade and devoted my attention to Ibada." *(Tabrani, Haythami)*

The Reason for his Abstinence

A narration similar to the one above adds that Abu Darda ☺ said, "I swear by the Being Who controls the life of Abu Darda! Even today I would not like to have a shop at the door of the Masjid that without missing a single salah with Jama'ah, gives me a profit of 40 Dinars all of which I spend in the Path of Allah." "Why would you not like that, O Abu Darda?" someone asked. Abu Darda ☺ replied, "Because of the intensity of reckoning." *(Abu Nu'aym in Hilya, Ibn Asakir in Kanzul Ummal)*. Another narration states that Abu Darda ☺ said, "It gives me no pleasure to stand on the step of the Masjid, buying and selling to earn a profit of 300 Dinars without missing a single salah in the Masjid. I am not saying that Allah has not made trade permissible and has not made interest Haram, but I wish to be amongst those people whom neither trade nor commerce distracts from the Dhikr of Allah. *(Ref. Sura Noor)* *(Abu Nu'aym in Hilya)*. Khalid bin Hudair Aslami narrates, "I once met Abu Darda ☺ lying on a bedding made of leather or wool. He was covered with a woolen blanket and his shoes were even woolen. He happened to be ill that day and was perspiring profusely. I said, 'If you wished, you could cover your bedding with the thin cloth and yourself with the Saffron colored shawl that the Amirul Mu'minin had sent to you.' He replied, 'We have a permanent abode, the Hereafter towards which we are heading and for which we carry out our deeds. It is therefore best to give our wealth to the poor so that it may benefit us in the Hereafter.'"

Another narration from Hasan bin Atia states that Abu Darda ☺ had a few friends whom he would entertain as his guests and who entertained him. Because of a shortage of bedding some of them when they spent the night at his home slept on saddle blankets while others had to sleep on the garments they were wearing. When Abu Darda 🙵 went to them early the next morning, he sensed their feelings disappointment with his inadequate arrangements. He then said to them, "We have another abode, the Hereafter for which we carry out our deeds and for which we are making preparations." *(Abu Nu'aym in Hilya)*. Muhammad bin Ka'b reports that when some people stayed as guests with Abu Darda 🙵 on a very cold night, he sent hot food for them but did not send any blankets. One of them remarked, "He has sent food for us but it gives us no joy with this cold for we have nothing to keep us warm. I shall have to go to tell him about this." Although the others tried to dissuade him, he insisted on going. When he arrived at Abu Darda 🙵's door, he saw Abu Darda 🙵 sitting down with his wife whose clothing was not even worth mentioning because they were so inadequate for the cold. As he was returning, the man said, "I suppose that you will also be spending the night just as we will without anything to cover ourselves." Abu Darda 🙵 replied, "We have an abode that we will be going to. We have therefore sent our bedding and our blankets there by giving them away as Sadaqa. If I had anything with me, I would have definitely sent it for you. We have a steep valley ahead of us that is extremely difficult to climb. The one who travels light there shall be better off than the one who is heavily laden. Do you understand what I am telling you?" "I certainly do," the man replied. *(Sifatus Safawah)*

The Incident Between Him and Omar 🙵

The narration has already passed in the chapter entitled "Condemning Rulers who Live Lives Above the Standards of the Common People" that when Omar 🙵 pushed open the door of Abu Darda 🙵's home, he found that it had no lock. The 2 men entered the dark room and Omar 🙵 had to feel his way around until he found Abu Darda 🙵. When Omar 🙵 felt the pillow of Abu Darda 🙵, he found that it was made from the blanket used on animals. When he felt the ground, there was only sand and when he felt the clothing of Abu Darda 🙵, he discovered that it was a flimsy shawl. Abu Darda 🙵 asked, "Who is this? Is it the Amirul Mu'minin?" When Omar 🙵 confirmed that he was the Amirul Mu'minin, Abu Darda 🙵 said, "You are late. We had been waiting for you all year." Omar 🙵 said, "May Allah have mercy on you. Have I not granted you sufficient wealth? Have I not given you plenty?" Abu Darda 🙵 said, "O Omar! Do you not remember a Hadith that Rasulullah ﷺ mentioned to us?" "Which Hadith?" asked Omar 🙵. Abu Darda 🙵 replied, "The Hadith in which Rasulullah ﷺ said, 'The limit of a person's possessions in this world should be like the provisions of a traveler.'" "Oh yes I have heard the Hadith," confirmed Omar 🙵. Abu Darda 🙵 then asked, "Now what have we done after Rasulullah ﷺ, O Omar?" The 2 Sahabah then continued reminding each other of the words of Rasulullah ﷺ with tears in their eyes until morning arrived.

The Abstinence of Mu'adh bin Afra 🙵: The Incident with Omar 🙵 Concerning his Attire

Aflah the freed slave of Abu Ayub 🙵 narrates that Omar 🙵 used to have a set of exclusive clothing made for the veterans of Badr. When he sent such a set to Mu'adh bin Afra 🙵, Mu'adh told Aflah to sell it. When Aflah sold it for 1,500 Dirhams, Mu'adh 🙵 instructed him to purchase some slaves with the money. Afla managed to buy 5 slaves. Mu'adh 🙵 then said, "By Allah! Any man who prefers wearing 2 sheets of cloth to setting 5 slaves free is certainly most foolish." He then set all the slaves free. When Omar 🙵 heard that Mu'adh bin Afra 🙵 did not wear the clothing he sent to him, he had a crude set of clothing made for him that cost 100 Dirhams. When the messenger brought the clothing to him, Mu'adh 🙵 said, "I do not think that the Amirul Mu'minin had sent you to give that to me." When the messenger swore that he had been sent to him, Mu'adh 🙵 took the outfit and went to Omar 🙵. He then asked, "O Amirul Mu'minin! Have you sent this outfit for me?" Omar 🙵 replied, "Yes. We had sent to you an outfit that we had made for you and your brethren but subsequently heard that you did not wear it and therefore sent you this simple clothing." Mu'adh 🙵 said, "O Amirul Mu'minin! Even though I do not wear such clothing, I would still like to receive the best of that which you receive." Omar 🙵 then gave him the same type of good clothing as he had been giving before. *(Omar bin Shaba in Sifatus Safwa)*

The Abstinence of Jalaj Ghitfani 🙵 From Eating to His Fill After Accepting Islam

Jalaj 🙵 says, "Since the time I accepted Islam at the hands of Rasulullah ﷺ, I have never filed my belly. I eat only what is sufficient to sustain me." A narration of *Bayhaqi* states that he lived to a ripe old age of 120 years, 50 years during the period of ignorance and 70 years as a Muslim. *(Tabrani in Targheeb wat Tarheeb, Abul Abbas Sarraj in Tareekh, Khatib in Muttafaq, Isabah, Ibn Asakir in Kanzul Ummal)*

The Abstinence of Abdullah bin Omar 🙵

Hamza bin Abdullah bin Omar 🙵 says that whenever Abdullah bin Omar 🙵 had plenty of food, he would never eat to his fill after he had found someone to share it with him. Ibn Mutee once came to visit him. Seeing that Abdullah bin Omar 🙵's body had become very frail, he said to Abdullah bin Omar 🙵's wife Safia 🙵, "Do you not look after him? Why do you not prepare good food for him so that his body could return to him?" She replied, "That is exactly what we do. However, he leaves out no family person and no other person who comes to him without inviting them to eat with him, they then eat and he does not. You speak to him about it." Ibn Mutee then said to Abdullah bin Omar 🙵, "O Abu Abdur Rahman! Why do not eat so that your body could return to you?" Abdullah bin Omar 🙵 replied, "For the past 80 years I have never once eaten to my fill or he said, "I have only once eaten to my fill". Now you want me to fill my belly when all that remains of my life is like the thirst of a donkey, only a few moments?" *(Abu Nu'aym in Hilya)*. Omar bin Hamza bin Abdullah bin Omar 🙵 reports that he was once sitting with his father when a man passed by. Hamza asked, "Tell me what you were saying to my father Abdullah bin Omar 🙵 that day when I saw you speaking to him at Jurf." The man replied, "I said, 'O Abu Abdur Rahman! Your body has become frail, your age has advanced and those attending your gatherings neither acknowledge your rights nor your position because of which they exhaust you by keeping you engaged for extended periods of time. Why do you not instruct your wife to prepare some especially good food for you when you return home. Abdullah bin Omar 🙵 angrily replied, "Shame on you! By Allah! I have never eaten to my fill for not only 11 years, 12 years, 13 years or 14 years but for 80 years. I have not done so even once. Why should I do so now when all that remains of my life is like the thirst of a donkey, only a few moments?" *(Abu Nu'aym in Hilya)*

His Statement When He Was Presented With 'Jawarish'

Ubaidullah bin Adi who was a freed slave of Abdullah bin Omar 🙵 reports that he once returned from Iraq and went to Abdullah bin Omar 🙵. After greeting him, he said, "I have brought you a gift." "What is it?" asked Abdullah bin Omar 🙵. "Jawarish," was the reply. "What is Jawarish?" enquired

Abdullah bin Omar ﷺ. Ubaidullah explained, "It aids the digestion of food." Abdullah bin Omar ﷺ remarked, "What will I do with it when I have never filled my belly for the past 40 years?" (Abu Nu'aym in Hilya). Muhammad bin Sirin narrates that someone once said to Abdullah bin Omar ﷺ, "Should I prepare some Jawarish for you?" "What is this Jawarish?" enquired Abdullah bin Omar ﷺ. The man replied, "It is a preparation that aids digestion when you have eaten too much and feel bloated." Abdullah bin Omar said, "I have never eaten to my fill for the past 4 months. This is not because I cannot find any food to eat. However, I have lived with Rasulullah ﷺ and the Sahabah who would sometimes eat and stay hungry at other times." (Abu Nu'aym in Hilya, Ibn Sa'd)

His Abstinence After the Demise of Rasulullah ﷺ

Abdullah bin Omar ﷺ once said, "Since the time Rasulullah ﷺ was taken away, I have never laid a brick upon a brick, never built anything and never planted a single date palm." (Abu Nu'aym in Hilya, Ibn Sa'd)

The Narration of Jabir ﷺ and Suddi ﷺ

Jabir ﷺ says, "Besides Abdullah bin Omar ﷺ, there was none amongst us who received worldly wealth without the world turning towards him and he being inclined towards it." (Abu Sa'eed A'rabi). Suddi says, "I have seen a large group of Sahabah who felt that besides Abdullah bin Omar ﷺ, none of them remained in the same condition in which Rasulullah ﷺ left them." (Abul Abbas Saraj in Tarikh, Isabah)

The Abstinence of Hudaifa bin Yaman

Sa'idah bin Sa'd bin Hudaifa narrates that Hudaifh ﷺ used to say, "No day is more comforting and more pleasing to me than the day I return to my family to find that they have no food and are saying, 'We have been unable to get anything to eat.' This is because I have heard Rasulullah ﷺ say, 'More than the family of a sick person prevents him from harmful food, Allah prevents a Mu'min from the wealth of this world. Allah cares more to safeguard Mu'min from hardship than a father cares to safeguard his own son.'" Abu N'uaym in Hilya, Tabrani, Haythami)

Rebuking and Advising Caution to Those Who do not Abstain From Worldly Luxuries and Who Indulge Themselves

Aisha ﷺ says, "Rasulullah ﷺ once saw that I had eaten full meals twice during a single day and said, 'O Aisha! Are you not interested in any activity besides your stomach? Eating twice during one day is extravagance and Allah does not like the extravagant ones." (Bayhaqi in Targheeb wat Tarheeb)

The Parting Advice Rasulullah ﷺ Gave to Aisha ﷺ

Aisha ﷺ says, "I was sitting and weeping by the side of Rasulullah ﷺ at his deathbed when he said, 'What makes you weep? If you wish to meet with me in the Hereafter, you should suffice in this world with the mere provisions of a traveler and should never mix with the rich.'" (Ibnul A'rabi in Kanzul Ummal). Another narration states that Rasulullah ﷺ added, "Never replace your clothing until you have patched them and can wear them no more." (Tirmidhi, Hakim, Bayhaqi) A narration from Urwa ﷺ stares that Aisha ﷺ never got new clothing until she had patched her old clothing to the extent that some patches overlapped others. Mu'awiya ﷺ once sent her 80,000 Dirhams but by the evening there was not a single Dirham left with her, she spent it all on the poor. Her servant asked, "Why did you not use a Dirham from it to buy us some meat?" Aisha ﷺ said, "I would have done so had you reminded me about it." (Razin in Targheeb wat Tarheeb)

The Advice Rasulullah ﷺ Gave to Abu Juhaifa ﷺ

Abu Juhaifa ﷺ says that he once ate Tharid prepared with fatty meat because of which he was burping as he went to Rasulullah ﷺ. Rasulullah ﷺ said, "Please do not burp in front of us, O Abu Juhaifa. Remember that those who fill themselves most in this world shall suffer the most hunger on the Day of Judgment." Abu Juhaifa never ate to his fill until the day he left this world. Whenever he ate during the mornings, he would not eat in the evenings and whenever he ate in the evenings, he would not eat in the mornings. (Tabrani, Haythami, Ibn Abdul Birr in Isti'ab, Bazzar, Haythami, Abu Nu'aym in Hilya)

The Incident Between Rasulullah ﷺ and a Man with a Large Stomach

Ja'da ﷺ narrates that Rasulullah ﷺ once saw a man with a large stomach. Sticking his finger into the man's stomach, Rasulullah ﷺ said, "It would have been best for you if this food was in another poor person's stomach." Another narration states that a person once saw a dream about Rasulullah ﷺ. Rasulullah ﷺ sent for him and he hesitated to relate the dream to Rasulullah ﷺ. Because he was a man with a large belly, Rasulullah ﷺ stuck his finger in the man's belly saying, "It would have been best for you if this was in another place, in the belly of a poor man." (Tabrani, Haythami, Ahmad)

Omar ﷺ Rebukes Jabir ﷺ for Buying Meat for His Family

Yahya bin Sa'eed reports that Omar ﷺ once saw Jabir bin Abdullah with a man who was carrying some meat for him. Omar ﷺ said, "Does none of you ever desire to keep himself hungry for the sake of his neighbor or cousin? Where has the verse of the Qur'an left you in which Allah says:

أَذْهَبْتُمْ طَيِّبَاتِكُمْ فِي حَيَاتِكُمُ الدُّنْيَا

"You received your good things in the life of the world (and therefore have nothing for yourselves here). (Al-Ahqaf:20) (Malik in Targheeb wat Tarheeb)

Jabir ﷺ reports, "Omar bin Khattab ﷺ once met me after I had purchased some meat for a Dirham. 'What is this, O Jabir?' I replied, 'Because my family had a strong craving for meat, I bought them this meat for a Dirham.' Omar ﷺ then started repeating my words, 'My family had a strong craving' so much that I wished the Dirham had fallen away from me and that I had never met Omar ﷺ." (Bayhaqi in Targheeb wat Tarheeb, Ibn Jareer in Muntakha Kanzul Ummal). Abdullah bin Omar ﷺ narrates that Omar ﷺ once saw a Dirham in the hand of Jabir ﷺ. "What is that Dirham for?" asked Omar ﷺ. Jabir ﷺ replied, "I intend to use it to purchase some meat for my family since they were craving for some." Omar ﷺ remarked, "Will you always buy something merely because you crave for it? Where has the verse of Qur'an left you in which Allah says:

أَذْهَبْتُمْ طَيِّبَاتِكُمْ فِي حَيَاتِكُمُ الدُّنْيَا

"You received your good things in the life of the world (and therefore have nothing for yourselves here). (Al-Ahqaf:20) (Sa'eed bin Mansoor, Abd bin Humayd, Ibnul Mundhir, Hakim, Abu Dawood, Bayhaqi in Muntakhab Kanzul Ummal)

Omar ﷺ Rebuked his son Abdullah ﷺ When he Sees Meat with Him

Hasan ﷺ reports that Omar ﷺ once went to his son Abdullah ﷺ's house at a time when he was eating some meat. "Why are you eating this meat?" Abdullah ﷺ replied, "I was craving for some." Omar rebuked him saying, "Will you always buy something merely because you crave for it? It is enough to classify a person as extravagant for him to eat whatever he craves for." *(Abdur Razzaq, Ahmad in Zuhd, Askari in Mawa'idh, Ibn Asakir in Muntakhab Kanzul Ummal)*

The Advice Omar Gave to Yazid bin Abu Sufian

Sa'eed bin Jubair reports that the news reached Omar that Yazid bin Abu Sufian ate various types of meats. Omar then said to his slave Yarfa, "Let me know when his evening meal is served to him." When the meal was served to Yazid, Yarfa duly informed Omar. Omar went to Yazid, greeted with Salam and sought permission to enter. He entered when permission was granted and Yazid offered Omar his dinner. When Tharid and meat were served, Omar joined Yazid in the meal. When roasted meat was served, Yazid took some while Omar did not. Omar then exclaimed, "Allah! Are you eating a meal after a meal, O Yazid bin Abu Sufian? I swear by the Being Who controls the life of Omar! If you oppose the lifestyle of Rasulullah and the Sahabah, you will certainly be led off their path and not reach the highest place of Jannah." *(Ibn Mubarak in Muntakhab Kanzul Ummal)*

Omar Criticizes the World Before the Sahabah

Hasan reports that Omar once passed by a rubbish dump and stopped there. When his companions felt disgusted at the sight and stink, Omar said, "This is your world that you aspire for or he said, "This is your world that you rely upon"." *(Abu Nu'aym in Hilya)*

The Letter Omar Wrote to Abu Darda When he Built a Tall Building

Salma bin Kulthum reports that when Abu Darda built a tall building in Damascus, the news reached Omar in Madinah. Omar wrote to him saying: "O little builder, the son of the little builder's mother! Are the buildings of the Persians and Romans not sufficient for you that you had to go and build so many new buildings? O companions of Muhammad! You are an example to others, others will emulate your examples." *(Ibn Asakir)*. Another narration from Rashid bin Sa'd states that when the news reached Omar that Abu Darda had built porches at house entrances in Hims, he wrote to him saying: "O little builder! Were the worldly decorations built by the Romans and Persians not sufficient for you? How can you be doing this when Allah has commanded that these things be destroyed?" *(Ibn Asakir, Hannad, Bayhaqi in Kanzul Ummal)*

Another narration states that Omar added:

"Were the worldly decorations and renovations built by the Romans and Persians not sufficient for you? How can you be doing this when Allah has announced that these things should be destroyed? As soon as this letter reaches you, you should move from Hims to Damascus." Sufian says that this instruction was a form of punishment. *(Abu Nu'aym in Hilya)*

The Letter Omar Wrote to Amr bin Al Aas to Demolish the Double Storey Building of Kharija bin Hudhafa

Yazid bin Abu Habib reports that Kharija bin Hudhafa was the first person to build a double storey building in Egypt. When he received news of this, Omar wrote the following letter to Amr bin Al Aas (the governor of Egypt):
"Peace be on you.
The news has reached me that Kharija bin Hudhafa has built a

double storey building. By doing this Kharija will be spying on his neighbors. You should therefore demolish the house as soon as this letter reaches you, InshaAllah.
Peace be on you." *(Ibn Abdul Hakam in Kanzul Ummal)*

Ummu Talq and the Instruction of Omar

Abdullah Roomi narrates that he once entered the house of Ummu Talq. Noticing that the roof of her house was extremely low, he asked, "O Ummu Talq! Why is your roof so low?" "Dear son," she replied, "Omar bin Khattab issued instructions to all his governors saying, 'Do not construct tall buildings because your worst days will come when you construct tall buildings.'" *(Ibn Sa'd, Bukhari in Adab, Kanzul Ummal)*

The Letter Omar Wrote to Sa'd When he Sought Permission to Build a House

Sufian bin Uyayna reports that when Sa'd bin Abi Waqqas was governor of Kufa, he wrote to Omar, seeking permission to build himself a house. Omar wrote in reply, "Build only what is necessary to shield you from the sun and give you shelter from the rain because this world is only a place to make do with." Omar also wrote to Amr bin Al Aas the governor of Egypt saying, "Treat your subjects as you would like a governor to treat you." *(Ibn Abi Dunya, Deenowri in Muntakhab Kanzul Ummal)*

Omar Rebukes a Man Who Built with Baked Bricks

Sufyan reports that the news reached Omar that a man used baked bricks to build. Omar said, "I had no idea that there will be people like Fir'oun in this Ummah because it was Fir'oun who said: فَأَوْقِدْ لِي يَا هَامَانُ عَلَى الطِّينِ فَاجْعَلْ لِي صَرْحًا

...O Haman, to bake (bricks out of) clay, and set up for me a Sarhan (a lofty tower, or palace, etc.)...(Al-Qasas:38) *(Abu Nu'aym in Hilya)*

Abu Ayub Ansari Rebukes Abdullah bin Omar For Decorations on the Walls When His Son Got Married

Salim the son of Abdullah bin Omar says, "I got married during the lifetime of my father. Amongst the people that my father invited was Abu Ayub. The walls of my room were covered with green curtains as decorations. When Abu Ayub entered, he lowered his head to scrutinize the wall and discovered that they were indeed covered. He said, 'O Abdullah! You people cover your walls?' My father was embarrassed and said, 'Our women have overpowered us, O Abu Ayub.' Abu Ayub remarked, 'I feared that others may be overpowered by their women, but I never had the fear of you being overpowered by them. I shall neither enter your house nor eat your food.'" *(Ibn Asakir in Kanzul Ummal)*

The Parting Advice Abu Bakr Gave to Salman

Salman reports that he once went to Abu Bakr and asked for some advice. Abu Bakr said, "Fear Allah, O Salman! You should know that there will be many conquests. Your share from it should be only that food which you need for your stomach and that clothing which you need to cover yourself. You should know that whoever performs his 5 salahs is in the protection of Allah in the mornings and in the evenings. You should also never kill anyone in Allah's protection because you will then be breaching the security of Allah because of which Allah will throw you headlong into Jahannam." *(Ahmad in Zuhd, Ibn Sa'd in Kanzul Ummal)*. Hasan states that Salman Farsi visited Abu Bakr on his deathbed and asked, "Do give me some advice, O Khalifa of Rasulullah." Abu Bakr said, "Allah shall open up the world to you so none of you should ever take more than what he needs just to get along." *(Deenowri in Kanzul Ummal)*

The Parting Words Abu Bakr Spoke to Abdur Rahman bin Auf

Abdur Rahman bin Auf once visited Abu Bakr on his deathbed and greeted him with Salam. Abu Bakr said, "Although it has not yet arrived, I can see worldly wealth approaching. It will however arrive and you people will then have curtains of silk and cushions of velvet. You will then be so used to luxury that you will experience difficulty using the woolen beddings of Azerbaijan, feeling as if you are lying on the thorns of the Su'dan tree. By Allah! For one of you to be brought forward and executed is better for him than swimming in the intoxication of this world. *(Abu Nu'aym in Hilya, Tabrani in Muntakhab Kanzul Ummal)*

Amr bin Al Aas Rebukes His Companions About Their Lack of Abstinence and His Narration Concerning the Abstinence of Rasulullah

Ali bin Rabah narrates that he once heard Amr bin Al Aas say, "You people spend the morning and the evenings hankering after that which Rasulullah abstained from. You have started hankering after the world when Rasulullah stayed away from it. By Allah! Not a night passed Rasulullah in his entire life without his debts exceeding his dues." Some of the Sahabah then said, "We did see Rasulullah taking loans." *(Ahmad in Targheeb wat Tarheeb).* Another narration states that Amr bin Al Aas said, "Never did 3 days pass Rasulullah in his entire life without his debts exceeding his dues." *(Hakim, Ibn Hibban).* Yet another narration states that Amr bin Al Aas said, "How far are your lifestyles to that of your Nabi! Whereas he abstained from the world, you people are most desirous of it." *(Haythami, Ibn Asakir, Ibn Najjar in Kanzul Ummal)*

What Abdullah bin Omar said to His Son Who Asked Him for a New Garment

Maymun reports that when one of Abdullah bin Omar's sons asked him for new lower garment claiming that his was torn, Abdullah bin Omar said, "Cut your garment off from where it is torn and then wear the rest." When he noticed that the youngster did not like the response, he said, "Shame on you! Do not be one of those people who spend everything that Allah provides for them on their bellies on food and backs on clothing." *(Abu Nu'aym in Hilya)*

The Incident Between Abu Dhar and Abu Darda

Thabit reports that Abu Dhar once passed by Abu Darda who was busy building a house for himself. Abu Dhar remarked, "You are loading large boulders on people's necks." Abu Darda explained, "I am having a house built." When Abu Dhar repeated his remark, Abu Darda said, "Dear brother! It appears as if you are upset with me for this." Abu Dhar replied, "Had I passed you when you were tending to the faces of your family, it would have been more pleasing to me than what I am now seeing." *(Abu Nu'aym in Hilya)*

What Abu Bakr Said to His Daughter Aisha When He Saw Her Wearing New Clothes

Aisha says, "I once wore a new upper garment of mine and was taken aback by it as I looked at it. Abu Bakr said to me, 'What are you looking at? Allah is not looking at you with affection.' 'Why not?' I asked. He replied, 'Don't you know that when self-admiration enters a servant because of worldly beauty, Allah detests the person until the beauty is lost and the self-admiration with it.' I then took off the garment and gave it away as Sadaqa. Abu Bakr then said, 'That shall perhaps agreed for you.'" *(Abu Nu'aym in Hilya)*

The Incident of Abu Bakr and a Son of His Who was About to Pass Away

Habib bin Hamza says that when death came to one of Abu Bakr's sons, the youngster kept looking at the pillow. After he has passed away, the people informed Abu Bakr that they noticed his son looking towards the pillow. When the people lifted the corpse off the pillow, they noticed 5 or 6 Dinars beneath it. Abu Bakr hit one hand on to the other saying, "Inna Lillahi wa Inna Ilayhi Raji'oon! I do not think that your skin will be able to withstand the punishment for not spending in Sadaqa those Dinars." *(Abu Nu'aym in Hilya)*

What Ammar Said to Abdullah bin Mas'ood When He Called Him to See the House he Had Built

Abdullah bin Abu Hudhail reports that when Abdullah bin Mas'ood built his house, he said to Ammar, "Come and have a look at what I have built." Ammar went with him but when he saw the house, he said, "You have built a sturdy structure and have long hopes of living there for a long time yet your death is very near." *(Abu Nu'aym in Hilya)*

The Statement of Abu Sa'eed Khudri When Invited for a Walima

Ata narrates that he was once with Abu Sa'eed Khudri when he was invited for a Walima. When Abu Sa'eed Khudri saw a variety of dishes, he remarked, "Do you not know that if Rasulullah ate in the mornings, he would not have dinner and if he ate dinner, he would not have meals in the morning?" *(Abu Nu'aym in Hilya)*

The Chapter on how the Sahabah Relinquished their Carnal Desires

This chapter highlights how the Sahabah gave up the instinctive feelings they had for their parents, their children, their brothers, their spouses, their families, their wealth, their businesses and their homes so that they could cling to the love of Allah, the love of and the love of every Muslim attached to Allah and Rasulullah ﷺ. The chapter also highlights how honored every person who had been attached to Rasulullah ﷺ in any way.

Abu Ubaidah bin Jarrah ؓ Kills his Father during the Battle of Badr

Ibn Showdhab reports that the father of Abu Ubaidah ؓ kept confronting him during the battle of Badr as Abu Ubaidah ؓ continued avoiding him. However, when his father's confrontations became too persistent, Abu Ubaidah ؓ killed him. It was then that Allah revealed the following verse:

لَا تَجِدُ قَوْمًا يُؤْمِنُونَ بِاللَّهِ وَالْيَوْمِ الْآخِرِ يُوَادُّونَ مَنْ حَادَّ اللَّهَ وَرَسُولَهُ وَلَوْ كَانُوا آبَاءَهُمْ أَوْ أَبْنَاءَهُمْ أَوْ إِخْوَانَهُمْ أَوْ عَشِيرَتَهُمْ أُولَئِكَ كَتَبَ فِي قُلُوبِهِمُ الْإِيمَانَ وَأَيَّدَهُمْ بِرُوحٍ مِنْهُ وَيُدْخِلُهُمْ جَنَّاتٍ تَجْرِي مِنْ تَحْتِهَا الْأَنْهَارُ خَالِدِينَ فِيهَا رَضِيَ اللَّهُ عَنْهُمْ وَرَضُوا عَنْهُ أُولَئِكَ حِزْبُ اللَّهِ أَلَا إِنَّ حِزْبَ اللَّهِ هُمُ الْمُفْلِحُونَ (22)

You (O Muhammad ﷺ) will not find any people who believe in Allah and the Last Day, making friendship with those who oppose Allah and His Messenger (Muhammad ﷺ), even though they were their fathers, or their sons, or their brothers, or their kindred (people). For such He has written Faith in their hearts, and strengthened them with Rooh (proofs, light and true guidance) from Himself. And We will admit them to Gardens (Paradise) under which rivers flow, to dwell therein (forever). Allah is pleased with them, and they with Him. They are the Party of Allah. Verily, it is the Party of Allah that will be the successful. (Al-Mujadalah:22) (Abu Nu'aym in Hilya, Bayhaqi, Hakim, Tabrani in Isaah)

The Incident of 2 Sahabah With Their Fathers

Malik bin Umair ؓ who had seen the period of ignorance reports that a man came to Rasulullah ﷺ and said, "Amongst the enemy I encountered my father. When he uttered ugly words of blasphemy against you, I was unable to control myself and killed him with a thrust of my spear." Rasulullah ﷺ remained silent. Another man arrived and said, "When I confronted my father in battle, I left him, hoping that someone else should rather kill him." This time Rasulullah ﷺ again remained silent. *(Bayhaqi)*

The Son of Abdullah bin Ubay seeks Permission to execute his Father

Abu Hurairah ؓ narrates that Rasulullah ﷺ once passed by Abdullah bin Ubay who was sitting on the shade of a fortress. Abdullah bin Ubay passed a remark saying, "The son of Ibn Kabsha, name of either Rasulullah ﷺ's maternal grandfather or the title of his wet-nurse Halima family, has thrown dirt on our faces." Abdullah bin Ubay's son Abdullah ؓ then said, "O Rasulullah ﷺ! I swear by the Being Who has given you honor that if you wish, I shall bring my father's head to you after executing him." Rasulullah ﷺ replied, "No. You should rather continue treating your father well and being good to him." *(Bazzar, Haythami)*. Another narration from Abdullah ؓ the son of Abdullah bin Ubay says that when he requested permission from Rasulullah ﷺ to execute his father, Rasulullah ﷺ told him not to. *(Tabrani)*. Yet another narration from Asim bin Omar bin

Qatadah states that Abdullah ؓ the son of Abdullah bin Ubay bin Salul once came to Rasulullah ﷺ and said, "O Rasulullah ﷺ! The news has reached me that you intend having Abdullah bin Ubay executed because of what you have heard about him. If you are really going to do so, give me the instruction and I shall bring his head to you. By Allah! All of the Khazraj tribe know well that there is none amongst them who honors their father more than I do. I fear that if you give the instruction to another person and he kills my father, my inner-self will not allow me to see my father's executioner walk freely amongst the people. I may then kill him, as a result of which I shall enter Jahannam for killing a Mu'min for the life of a Kafir." Rasulullah ﷺ replied, "Instead of executing him, we shall rather be lenient with him and continue treating him well as long as he remains with us." *(Ibn Is'haq in Al Bidayah wan Nihayah)*. Usama bin Zaid ؓ narrates that when Rasulullah ﷺ returned from the military offensive against the Banu Mustaliq tribe, Abdullah ؓ the son of Abdullah bin Ubay stood up and drew his sword before his father saying, "I swear by Allah. That I shall not sheath my sword until you say, 'Muhammad ﷺ is honorable while we are low.'" Abdullah bin Ubay then said, "Shame on you! Muhammad ﷺ is honorable while we are low." When Rasulullah ﷺ was informed of this, he was pleased and approved of the act. *(Tabrani, Haythami)*. Urwa ؓ reports that Handhala ؓ the son of Abu Amir and Abdullah ؓ the son of Abdullah bin Ubay bin Salul both sought permission from Rasulullah ﷺ to execute their fathers but Rasulullah ﷺ refused. *(Ibn Shahin in Kanzul Ummal)*

The Incident Between Abu Bakr ؓ and His Son Abdur Rahman ؓ During the Battle of Badr

Abdur Rahman ؓ the son of Abu Bakr ؓ once said to his father, "When I saw you during the battle of Uhud, I avoided you." Abu Bakr ؓ responded by saying, "Had I seen you, I would not have avoided you but would have attacked you because you were opposing Islam." *(Ibn Abi Shaibah in Kanzul Ummal)*. Waqidi reports that as a Kafir Abdur Rahman ؓ the son of Abu Bakr ؓ called for a contestant to fight him. Abu Bakr ؓ stood up to the challenge, Rasulullah ﷺ said, "Do not go because we still have much to benefit from you." *(Hakim, Bayhaqi)*

The Incident Between Omar ؓ and Sa'eed bin Al Aas ؓ Concerning the Death of His Father

It is reported by Abu Ubaidah and other scholars proficient in the knowledge of the various battles Rasulullah ﷺ fought, state that Omar ؓ once passed by Sa'eed bin Al Aas ؓ. Omar ؓ asked, "It seems to me that you are upset with me because you think that I had killed your father. Had I killed him, I would not have made any excuses for it because I killed my own maternal uncle Aas bin Hisham bin Mughiera. Nevertheless, the truth is that when I passed by your father on the battlefield he was lying down wounded and hitting his head on the ground as a bull hits its horns on the ground. I then steered away from him and it was his cousin Ali who headed for him and killed him. *(Ibn Hisham in Al Bidayah wan Nihayah)*. Another narration adds that Sa'eed ؓ said, "Even if you killed him, it was you who was on the truth while he was on falsehood." This statement greatly pleased Omar ؓ. *(Isti'ab, Isabah)*

Abu Hudhaifa ؓ's Reaction When he Saw His Father's Body Being Dragged to the Well After the Battle of Badr

Aisha ؓ narrates that according to the instructions of Rasulullah ﷺ, the bodies of the disbeliever killed during the battle of Badr were dragged to a unused well and thrown into it.

Rasulullah ﷺ then stood beside the well and. said, "O people of this well! Have you found the promise of your Rabb (punishment) to be true? I have indeed found the promise of my Rabb (victory) to be true." The Sahabah asked, "O Rasulullah ﷺ! Are you addressing dead people?" Rasulullah ﷺ replied, "They now know well that the promise of their Rabb is true." Rasulullah ﷺ noticed an expression of gloom on the face of Abu Hudhaifa ؓ as he saw the body of his father Utba being dragged to the well. "O Abu Hudhaifa!" Rasulullah ﷺ called out, "It seems that you dislike what you are seeing?" Abu Hudhaifa ؓ replied, "O Rasulullah ﷺ! Because my father was a leader of his people, I hoped that his Rabb would guide him to Islam. However, it depressed me to see how he has fallen without becoming a Muslim." Rasulullah ﷺ then made good Du'as for Abu Hudhaifa ؓ. *(Ibn Jareer in Kanzul Ummal, Hakim, Ibn Is'haq in Al Bidayah wan Nihayah).* Another narration from Abu Zinad states that when Abu Hudhaifa ؓ fought in the battle of Badr, he called his father Utba to challenge him to a duel. This narration also quotes the couplets that his sister Hind bin Utba ؓ recited about the incident. *(Hakim, Bayhaqi)*

The Incident of Mus'ab bin Umair ؓ and His Brother Who Was Taken Captive During the Battle of Badr

Nubay bin Wahab ؓ from the Banu Abdud Dar tribe reports that when Rasulullah ﷺ arrived with the captives from the battle of Badr, they distributed them amongst the Sahabah saying, "I emphatically command you to treat them well." Amongst the prisoners was Abu Aziz bin Umair bin Hisham, the real brother of Mus'ab bin Umair ؓ. Abu Aziz ؓ says; "When I was captured by one of the Ansar, my brother Mus'ab bin Umair ؓ passed by. He said to the Ansari, 'Tie both his hands well because his mother is very wealthy and she will pay a large ransom for him.' I was with a group of Ansar when we returned from the battle. Whenever the morning and afternoon meals were served, they gave me the bread and ate dates only because of the instruction of Rasulullah ﷺ to treat prisoners well. Whenever any of them happened to receive any bread, he would ensure that he gave it to me. When I returned it to him out of embarrassment, he would give it back without even touching it." Abu Yasar ؓ was the Ansari who captured Abu Aziz ؓ. After Mus'ab bin Umair ؓ had told Abu Yasar ؓ what he did about tying both hands well, Abu Aziz ؓ said, "Dear brother! Is this the advice you give him about your own brother?" Mus'ab ؓ replied, "He (Abu Yasar ؓ) is my brother and not you." When Abu Aziz ؓ's mother enquired what the highest ransom was that anyone from the Quraish had paid, she was informed that it was 4,000 Dirhams. She sent 4,000 Dirhams and ransomed her son. *(Ibn Is'haq in Al Bidayah wan Nihayah).* Ayub bin Nu'man narrates that during the battle of Badr, Abu Aziz bin Umair, the real brother of Mus'ab bin Umair ؓ was captured by the Muslims. He was placed in the custody of Muhriz bin Nadhla. Mus'ab ؓ said to Muhriz ؓ, "Tie both his hands well because he has a very wealthy mother in Makkah who will pay a large ransom for him." Abu Aziz ؓ said, "Is that your advice concerning me, dear brother?" Mus'ab ؓ replied, "Muhriz is my brother and not you." Abu Aziz ؓ's mother then sent 4,000 Dirhams (as ransom for her son). *(Waqidi in Nasbur Ra'ya)*

The Incident Between Abu Sufian ؓ and His Daughter Ummul Mu'minin Ummu Habiba ؓ

Zuhri reports that Abu Sufian ؓ once came to Madinah before accepting Islam to meet Rasulullah ﷺ at a time when Rasulullah ﷺ had intended to go to war with the people of Makkah. Abu Sufian ؓ spoke to Rasulullah ﷺ about extending the treaty of Hudaibiyah which the people of Makkah had already breached but Rasulullah ﷺ refused to do so. He then left Rasulullah ﷺ and went to see his daughter Ummu Habiba ؓ, the wife of Rasulullah ﷺ. As he was going to sit on Rasulullah ﷺ's bedding, Ummu Habiba ؓ quickly rolled it up. "Dear daughter!" Abu Sufian exclaimed, "Am I not worthy of this bedding or is it not worthy of the likes of me?" Ummu Habiba ؓ replied, "This is Rasulullah ﷺ's bedding and you are unfit to sit on it because you are an impure disbeliever." Abu Sufian ؓ responded by saying, "Dear daughter! You have really changed for the worse since leaving us." *(Ibn Sa'd)* Another narration states that Ummu Habiba ؓ added, "I would not like you to sit on his bedding." *(Ibn Is'haq in Al Bidayah wan Nihayah)*

The Statement of Abdullah bin Mas'ood ؓ Concerning a Sparrow and Its Fledglings

Abul Ahwas narrates, "We once visited Abdullah bin Mas'ood ؓ as he was with his 3 sons, who appeared radiant like 3 gold coins. As we looked at the 3 boys, Abdullah bin Mas'ood ؓ understood our feelings and said, 'It seems like you envy me because of these boys?' We replied, 'It is because of such things that a person is truly the envy of all.' Abdullah bin Mas'ood ؓ then looked up to the low ceiling of his house where a sparrow had built a nest. He said, 'I prefer dusting off from my hands the sand from the graves of these boys rather than a single egg falling and breaking from that sparrow's nest." Another narration from Abu Uthman states that he used to sit in the company of Abdullah bin Mas'ood ؓ in Kufa. He further says that at that time, Abdullah bin Mas'ood ؓ was married to 2 beautiful women of high birth and had the most beautiful children from them. As he was sitting on a raised place, a sparrow started chirping from above and then emptied its belly on Abdullah bin Mas'ood ؓ. As he wiped the mess off, he said, "I prefer that the family of Abdullah die and I follow them in death rather than this sparrow dying." *(Abu Nu'aym in Hilya)*

The Statement of Omar ؓ About the Prisoners from Badr

The narration has already passed concerning the statement that Omar ؓ made about what should be done with the prisoners from the battle of Badr. He said, "I swear by Allah that I do not share the opinion of Abu Bakr. I strongly feel that you should hand so-and-so a relative of Omar ؓ over to me for execution, that you hand Aqil over to Ali for execution and that you hand over to Hamza his brother Abbas ؓ so that he could execute him. In this manner, Allah would know that we have no inclination towards the disbeliever in our hearts because these men are their leaders and the most influential people they have." Many incidents have also passed about how the Ansar severed the ties they had with people during the period of ignorance.

The Love that Sa'd bin Mu'adh ؓ had for Rasulullah ﷺ

Abdullah bin Abu Bakr ؓ narrates that during the battle of Badr Sa'd bin Mu'adh ؓ said, "O Nabi of Allah ﷺ! Should we not build you a structure for shade so that you could stay there and your conveyance could stay in readiness with you. We shall then fight the enemy and if Allah grants us honor and victory over them, it would be what we want. However, if the contrary occurs, you could mount your conveyance and join up with those who have remained behind in Madinah. Many people have remained behind who love you no less than we do and who would have never stayed behind had they known that we were going to fight a battle. Allah shall use them to protect you because they are your well wishers and will fight by your side."

Rasulullah ﷺ praised this gesture of Sa'd ؓ and prayed for him. The structure was erected for Rasulullah ﷺ. *(Ibn Is'haq in Al Bidayah wan Nihayah)*

The Incident of the Love a Sahabi Expressed for Rasulullah ﷺ and the Verse Revealed in this Regard

Aisha ؓ narrates that a man came to Rasulullah ﷺ and said, "O Rasulullah ﷺ! I love you more than my own self and more than my children. When I am in my house and think of you, I have no peace until I come to see you. Now that I think of my death and yours, I realize that you will be elevated amongst those occupying the highest positions in Jannah and I fear that I will never get to see you when I get to Jannah. Rasulullah ﷺ gave no reply until Jibra'el عليه السلام came with the revelation of the verse:

وَمَنْ يُطِعِ اللَّهَ وَالرَّسُولَ فَأُولَئِكَ مَعَ الَّذِينَ أَنْعَمَ اللَّهُ عَلَيْهِمْ مِنَ النَّبِيِّينَ وَالصِّدِّيقِينَ وَالشُّهَدَاءِ وَالصَّالِحِينَ وَحَسُنَ أُولَئِكَ رَفِيقًا (69)

And whoso obeys Allah and the Messenger (Muhammad ﷺ), then they will be in the company of those on whom Allah has bestowed His Grace, of the Prophets, the Siddiqoon (those followers of the Prophets who were first and foremost to believe in them, like Abu Bakr As-Siddiq ؓ), the martyrs, and the righteous. And how excellent these companions are! (An-Nisa':69) *(Tabrani, Haythami, Abu Nu'aym in Hilya)*

Another narration from Abdullah bin Abbas ؓ states that a man once approached Rasulullah ﷺ saying, "O Rasulullah ﷺ! I love you so much that whenever I think of you, I feel that I would die if I do not come to see you. It now occurs to me that I would be on a level lower than yours when I enter Jannah and will be unable to see you. This grieves me terribly and I therefore wish to be on the same level as you." Rasulullah ﷺ gave no reply until Allah revealed the verse:

وَمَنْ يُطِعِ اللَّهَ وَالرَّسُولَ فَأُولَئِكَ مَعَ الَّذِينَ أَنْعَمَ اللَّهُ عَلَيْهِمْ مِنَ النَّبِيِّينَ وَالصِّدِّيقِينَ وَالشُّهَدَاءِ وَالصَّالِحِينَ وَحَسُنَ أُولَئِكَ رَفِيقًا (69)

And whoso obeys Allah and the Messenger (Muhammad ﷺ), then they will be in the company of those on whom Allah has bestowed His Grace, of the Prophets, the Siddiqoon (those followers of the Prophets who were first and foremost to believe in them, like Abu Bakr As-Siddiq ؓ), the martyrs, and the righteous. And how excellent these companions are! (An-Nisa:69)

Rasulullah ﷺ then called for the Sahabi and recited the verse to him. *(Tabrani, Haythami)*

The Incident of the Sahabi Whose Preparation for the Day of Judgment was His Love for Allah and Rasulullah ﷺ

Anas ؓ narrates that a man once asked Rasulullah ﷺ when Day of Judgment will take place. "What have you prepared for the Day of Judgment?" asked Rasulullah ﷺ. The Sahabi replied, "Nothing besides the love for Allah and His Rasul ﷺ." Rasulullah ﷺ told him, "(On the Day of Judgment) You shall be with those whom you love." Anas ؓ says, "Nothing made us as happy as the statement of Rasulullah ﷺ: 'You shall be with those whom you love'. I love Rasulullah ﷺ, Abu Bakr ؓ and Omar ؓ. Because of this love I bear for them, I hope to be with them." *(Tabrani, Haythami)*. Another narration of *Bukhari* states that a man from the desert once came to Rasulullah ﷺ and asked, "When will the day of Judgment take place?" "What!" exclaimed Rasulullah ﷺ, "What preparations have you made for it?" The man replied, 'I have made no preparations for it apart from the fact that I love Allah and His Rasul ﷺ." Rasulullah ﷺ said, "You shall be with those whom you love." Anas ؓ asked, "Does this apply to us as well?" "Certainly," replied Rasulullah ﷺ. Anas ؓ

says, "That day we were extremely overjoyed." *(Bukhari)*. *Tirmidhi* quotes that Anas ؓ said, "While I have seen the companions of Rasulullah ﷺ rejoice about many things, I have never seen them rejoice more than the time when a man came and asked, "O Rasulullah ﷺ! A person loves another for doing a good deed that he is unable do. Will this benefit him?" Rasulullah ﷺ replied, "A man shall be in the Hereafter with those whom he loves."

The Statement of Rasulullah ﷺ: "You, O Abu Dhar, shall be with Those Whom You Love"

Abu Dhar ؓ narrates that he once said to Rasulullah ﷺ, "O Rasulullah ﷺ! What will be the outcome of a man who loves a group of people but is unable to carry out the deeds they carry out?" Rasulullah ﷺ replied, "You, O Abu Dhar, shall be with those whom you love." Abu Dhar ؓ then said, "I love Allah and His Rasul ﷺ." "You shall therefore be with those whom you love," Rasulullah ﷺ assured him. When Abu Dhar ؓ repeated his words, Rasulullah ﷺ repeated what he had said. *(Abu Dawud in Targheeb wat Tarheeb)*

The Incident of Ali ؓ with Rasulullah ﷺ When he was Experiencing Extreme Hunger

Abdullah bin Abbas ؓ reports that the news once reached Ali ؓ that Rasulullah ﷺ was experiencing severe hunger. Ali ؓ therefore left home to look for some work by which he could earn something to alleviate the plight of Rasulullah ﷺ. When he entered the orchard of a Jewish man, the man asked him to draw 17 buckets of water from the well for a price of one date for every bucket drawn. The Jew then allowed Ali to choose what type of dates he wanted and Ali ؓ chose 17 Ajwah dates. When Ali ؓ brought the dates, Rasulullah ﷺ asked, "Where did you get this from, Abu Hasan?" Ali ؓ replied, "O Nabi of Allah! When I heard about your hunger, I went out to look for a job to get you this food." "Was it the love of Allah and for His Rasul ﷺ that motivated you to do this?" Rasulullah ﷺ asked. "It certainly was," came the reply. Rasulullah ﷺ then said, "Whenever a servant of Allah loves Allah and His Rasul ﷺ, poverty comes to him faster than water flowing downstream. The person who loves Allah and His Rasul ﷺ should prepare a shield of patience and abstinence against troubles." *(Ibn Asakir in Kanzul Ummal)*

The Incident of Ka'b bin Ujra ؓ

Ka'b bin Ujra ؓ narrates that he once went to Rasulullah ﷺ and found that his face had become extremely pale. "May my parents be sacrificed for you! What is that matter that I see your face so pale?" he asked. Rasulullah ﷺ replied, "Nothing that can enter the belly of any living creature has entered my belly for 3 days." Ka'b ؓ left and found a Jewish man watering his camel. He watered the camel for the man with the understanding that he would earn a date for every bucket drawn. When he had collected several dates, he took them to Rasulullah ﷺ who asked where he got them. After Ka'b ؓ explained the incident, Rasulullah ﷺ asked, "Do you have love for me, Ka'b?" "May my father be sacrificed for you!" Ka'b ؓ responded, "Of course I do." Rasulullah ﷺ then told him, "Poverty runs to a person who loves me faster than water returning to its source. Also troubles certainly come your way, so prepare a shield of patience and abstinence for it." Rasulullah ﷺ later did not see Ka'b ؓ and asked the Sahabah where he was. When they informed Rasulullah ﷺ that he was ill, Rasulullah ﷺ walked to his house. When Rasulullah ﷺ entered the house, he said, "Good news for you, O Ka'b!" Ka'b ؓ's mother then said, "Glad tidings of Jannah for you, Ka'b!" "Who is this lady who swears in Allah's name?" asked Rasulullah ﷺ. "She is my mother, O Rasulullah ﷺ!" replied Ka'b ﷺ. Rasulullah ﷺ said, "How can you be sure, O Ummu Ka'b? Perhaps Ka'b spoke something useless and refused to give to a needy person something that he did not need?" *(Tabrani, Haythami, Targheeb wat Tarheeb, Ibn Asakir in Kanzul Ummal)*

The Love That Talha bin Bara ﷺ had for Rasulullah ﷺ

Husain bin Wahwa Ansari ﷺ reports that when Talha bin Bara ﷺ met Rasulullah ﷺ, he embraced Rasulullah ﷺ and kissed his feet. He said, "O Rasulullah ﷺ! Command me to do as you please, for I shall never disobey any instruction you give." This surprised Rasulullah ﷺ because Talha was still a young boy. "Then go and kill your father," Rasulullah ﷺ said. As he left with the resolve to kill his father, Rasulullah ﷺ called him back saying, "Come back! I have not been sent to severe family ties." It was not long afterwards that Talha ﷺ fell ill. It was an icy cold and overcast winter's day when Rasulullah ﷺ came to visit him. As he left, Rasulullah ﷺ said to the family, "I think that death is coming to Talha. Do inform me when he passes away so that I may be present and perform the Janazah salah for him. However, do hurry with the burial procedures." Rasulullah ﷺ had not yet reached the area of the Banu Salim bin Auf tribe when Talha ﷺ passed away. However, by then the night had already enveloped him. Amongst other things that Talha ﷺ told his family was, "Bury me and allow me to meet my Rabb but do not call Rasulullah ﷺ because I fear that the Jews may cause him some harm as he comes here." Rasulullah ﷺ was therefore informed about his death only in the morning. Rasulullah ﷺ came to his grave and stood there as the people stood on rows with him. He then raised his hands and prayed, "O Allah! You be smiling when you meet Talha and let him be smiling as well." *(Tabrani in Kanzul Ummal, Baghawi, Ibn Abi Thaythama, Ibn Abi Asim, Ibn Shahin, Ibn Sakan in Isabah, Haythami, Abu Dawud)*

Talha bin Miskin narrates that Talha bin Bara ﷺ came to Rasulullah ﷺ and said, "Stretch out your hand so that I may pledge my allegiance to you." "Even if I command you to sever ties with your parents?" Rasulullah ﷺ asked. "No," replied Talha ﷺ. Talha ﷺ again came to Rasulullah ﷺ asking him to stretch out his hand. "To what do you want to pledge allegiance?" asked Rasulullah ﷺ. "To Islam," replied Talha ﷺ. "Even if I command you to sever ties with your parents?" Rasulullah ﷺ asked. "No," replied Talha ﷺ. Talha ﷺ approached Rasulullah ﷺ for the 3rd time with the same request. He had only a mother and was most dutiful towards her. This time Rasulullah ﷺ said to him, "O Talha! Severing of family ties has no place in our religion. All I wished to do by asking you if you would severe ties with your parents was to ensure that there were no doubts in Islam." Talha ﷺ accepted Islam and was an excellent Muslim. When he fell ill one day, Rasulullah ﷺ visited him and found him unconscious. Rasulullah ﷺ said, "I do not think that Talha will survive the night. Do send for me as soon as he regains consciousness." When Talha ﷺ did regain consciousness late at night, he asked, "Has Rasulullah ﷺ not come to visit me?" When he was informed that Rasulullah ﷺ did come and told about what Rasulullah ﷺ said, Talha ﷺ said, "Do not send for him at this hour for he must not be stung by a reptile or suffer some other harm. However, after I die, do pass my Salams to him and request him to seek forgiveness on my behalf." After Rasulullah ﷺ had led the Fajr salah, he enquired about Talha ﷺ and was informed that he had passed away. Rasulullah ﷺ then raised his hands and prayed, "O Allah! You be smiling when you meet Talha and let him be smiling as well." *(Tabrani, Haythami, Ibnus Sakan in Isabah).*

The Love that Abdullah bin Hudhafa ﷺ had for Rasulullah ﷺ

Zuhri reports that someone once complained to Rasulullah ﷺ that Abdullah bin Hudhafa ﷺ joked a lot and spoke many useless things. Rasulullah ﷺ said, "Leave him alone because he has a heart that loves Allah and His Rasul ﷺ." *(Ibn Asakir in Muntakhab Kanzul Ummal)*

The Statement of Rasulullah ﷺ when the Corpse of Abdullah bin Dhul Bijadain ﷺ was Carried

Adra ﷺ narrates that he was guarding Rasulullah ﷺ one night when he heard someone reciting Qur'an in a loud voice. When Rasulullah ﷺ came out, he said "O Rasulullah ﷺ! That person is showing off." "That man," Rasulullah ﷺ explained, "is Abdullah bin Dhul Bijadain ﷺ." Abdullah bin Dhul Bijadain ﷺ passed away in Madinah and after burial preparations were made and the body was carried, Rasulullah ﷺ said, "Be gentle with him as Allah is gentle with him because he had great love for Allah and His Rasul." When Rasulullah ﷺ came to the grave which was being dug, he said, "Widen it for him as Allah's mercy has been widened for him." One of the Sahabah asked, "O Rasulullah ﷺ! You seem very depressed about his death?" Rasulullah ﷺ replied, "Because he loved Allah and his Rasul ﷺ." *(Ibn Majah, Baghawi, Ibn Mandal, Abu Ny'aym in Muntakhab Kanzul Ummal)*

The Incidents of Abdullah bin Omar ﷺ, Zaid bin Dathana ﷺ and Khubaib bin Adi ﷺ

Abdur Rahman bin Sa'd reports, "I was once with Abdullah bin Omar ﷺ when his leg cramped. 'What is wrong with your leg?' I asked. 'The muscles have cramped from here to here,' he replied. I said, 'Then take the name of the person most beloved to you so that Allah should cure it thereby.' He then took the name of Muhammad ﷺ and was able to stretch his leg." *(Ibn Sa'd)*. The incident has already passed reporting the time when Zaid bin Dathana ﷺ was brought for execution and Abu Sufian said to him, "O Zaid I ask you to swear by Allah whether you wish that Muhammad ﷺ was here with us in your place to have his head severed while you could be with your family." Zaid ﷺ replied, "I swear by Allah that I would not even like a thorn to prick it Muhammad ﷺ where he is while I am sitting with my family." Abu Sufian said, "I have never seen people love anyone as much as the companions of Muhammad ﷺ loved Muhammad ﷺ." The story of Khubaib ﷺ has also passed narrating the incident about the time when the disbeliever asked him to swear by Allah whether he preferred to have Rasulullah ﷺ in his place in exchange for his own freedom. Khubaib ﷺ replied, "Never! I swear by the Exalted Allah that I would not even accept a thorn pricking the foot of Rasulullah ﷺ as ransom for my life."

The Sahabah Prefer the Pleasure of Rasulullah ﷺ to Their Own

Abu Bakr ﷺ weeps when his father embraces Islam because of his keenness for Abu Talib to accept Islam. In the narration discussing how Abu Quhafah ﷺ the father of Abu Bakr ﷺ accepted Islam, Anas ﷺ reports that when Abu Quhafah ﷺ stretched out his hands to pledge allegiance to Rasulullah ﷺ, Abu Bakr ﷺ started to cry. "What makes you cry?" Rasulullah ﷺ asked. Abu Bakr ﷺ replied, "It would have been more pleasing for me to see the hand of your uncle Abu Talib in the place of my father's hand and him accepting Islam instead so that Allah could please you in that manner." *(Omar bin Shabba, Abu Ya'la, Abu Bishr Simway in Fawa'id, Hakim in Isabah)*. Abdullah bin Omar ﷺ narrates that on the day that Makkah was conquered; Abu Bakr ﷺ led his aged and blind father Abu Quhafah ﷺ to Rasulullah ﷺ to accept Islam. Rasulullah ﷺ said, ""Why did you not leave the old man in his house and let me go to him?" Abu Bakr 🙵 replied, "I wanted him to be rewarded for it. O Rasulullah 🙵! Had your uncle Abu Talib accepted Islam, it would have made me happier than my father's embracing Islam because your happiness is all I wish to see." Rasulullah 🙵 replied, "You are true in your words because this is really what you feel."*(Tabrani, Bazzar, Haythami)*

The Incident Between Omar 🙵 and Abbas 🙵

Abdullah bin Omar 🙵 narrates that amongst the captives of the battle of Badr was Abbas bin Abdul Muttalib 🙵. A man from the Ansar captured him and the other Ansar threatened to kill him. Because this news reached Rasulullah 🙵, he said, "I was unable to sleep last night because the Ansar have said that they would kill my uncle Abbas." "Should I go to the Ansar and fetch Abbas 🙵?" Omar 🙵 offered. When Rasulullah 🙵 bade him to do so, he went to them and said, "Release Abbas." "Never," responded the Ansar, "we swear by Allah that we shall never release him." "Even if it pleases Rasulullah 🙵?" asked Omar 🙵. The Ansar immediately agreed saying, "If it pleases Rasulullah 🙵, you may have him." Omar 🙵 took in his custody and when Abbas was with him, Omar 🙵 said to him, "Accept Islam, O Abbas. I swear by Allah that your accepting Islam would please me more than my father Khattab accepting Islam. This is only because I know that your accepting Islam would please Rasulullah 🙵." *(Ibn Mardway, Hakim in Al Bidayah wan Nihayah).* Abdullah bin Abbas 🙵 narrates that Omar 🙵 once said to Abbas 🙵, "Accept Islam, O Abbas. I swear by Allah that your accepting Islam would please me more than my father Khattab accepting Islam. I am saying this only because I know that Rasulullah 🙵 would like you to be amongst the early ones to accept Islam." *(Ibn Asakir in Kanzul Ummal)*

Sha'bi reports that when Abbas 🙵 was pressurizing Omar 🙵 for something, he said, "O Amirul Mu'minin! Tell me. How would you treat the uncle of Musa if he came to you as a Muslim?" "By Allah!" exclaimed Omar 🙵, "I would certainly treat him well." "Well," remarked Abbas 🙵, "I am the uncle of Muhammad the Nabi 🙵." Omar 🙵 then said, "What do you think, O Abu Fadhl, do you think that I have no regard for you? I swear by Allah that your father is more beloved to me than my own father." "Really, do you swear by Allah?" Abbas staggered. "Really," replied Omar 🙵, "and that is because I know that Rasulullah 🙵 liked your father more than my father. I shall give preference to what Rasulullah 🙵 liked over that which I like." *(Ibn Sa'd).* Muhammad bin Ali narrates that Abbas 🙵 once approached Omar 🙵 saying, "Rasulullah 🙵 had allocated the land of Bahrain for me." "Who else knows about this?" asked Omar 🙵. "Mughiera bin Shu'ba does," replied Abbas 🙵. Abbas brought Mughiera 🙵, who testified on his behalf. Omar 🙵 did not pass judgment in Abbas's favor, apparently not accepting his evidence. Abbas said some harsh words to Omar 🙵, upon which Omar said to Abbas 🙵's son, "O Abdullah! Take your father's hand. O Abul Fadhl (Abbas's title). I swear by Allah that I was happier by your accepting Islam than if my father Khattab had accepted Islam because this pleased Rasulullah 🙵." *(Ibn Sa'd)*

The Narration of Abu Sa'eed Khudri 🙵 About Those who Passed Away in Madinah

Abu Sa'eed Khudri 🙵 says, "When Rasulullah 🙵 just arrived in Madinah, it was our practice to inform him whenever a person was about to pass away. Rasulullah 🙵 would then present himself and seek forgiveness on behalf of the person. He and those with him would leave only after the person passed away and would

sometimes also remain until after the burial. This would often delay Rasulullah 🙵 because it kept him back. When we sensed this inconvenience to Rasulullah 🙵, some of us said to the others, 'By Allah! We ought to inform Rasulullah 🙵 only after a person passes away so that it would not be inconvenient for him nor keep him back.' This was then what we did. We informed Rasulullah 🙵 after the person's death and he would lead the Janaza salah and seek forgiveness for the person. There were times when he would leave after the salah while at other times; he would remain behind until after the burial. This practice continued for awhile, after which the people said, 'By Allah! We ought not to bother Rasulullah 🙵 and should rather carry the deceased to Rasulullah 🙵's house and then call for him to lead the salah near his house. This would be more convenient and easier for Rasulullah 🙵.' This was then what we used to do." Omar bin Muhammad says that it was from that time that the place was called "Mowda'ul Jana'iz" the place for biers, because it was to this place that the biers were carried. It was from those times to this day that the practice continued of people carrying the funeral biers to this place and performing the salah there. *(Ibn Sa'd)*

The Affection Omar 🙵 had for Rasulullah 🙵's Daughter Fatima 🙵 Because He Loved Her

Aslam narrates that Omar 🙵 once went to Fatima 🙵 the daughter of Rasulullah 🙵 and said, "O Fatima! I have never seen anyone that Rasulullah 🙵 loved more than you. By Allah! After your father, there is none dearer to me than yourself." *(Hakim in Kanzul Ummal)*

The Respect the Sahabah Showed by not Raising Their Gazes in Front of Rasulullah 🙵

Anas 🙵 reports that when Rasulullah 🙵 went to the Sahabah as they were sitting with Abu Bakr 🙵 and Omar 🙵, none of them besides Abu Bakr 🙵 and Omar 🙵 would lift his gaze. It was only the 2 of them who would look at him and he would look at them. They would smile with him and he would smile at them. This was because Abu Bakr 🙵 and Omar 🙵 were close enough to act informally with Rasulullah 🙵. *(Tirmidhi in Shifa)*

The Manner in Which the Sahabah Sat Around Rasulullah 🙵

Usama bin Sharik 🙵 says, "We were sitting around Rasulullah 🙵 as if there were birds perched on our backs with no one uttering a word. Some people then arrived and asked, 'Which of Allah bondsmen are most beloved to Him?' Rasulullah 🙵 replied, 'Those whose character is the best.'" *(Tabrani, Ibn Hibban in Targheeb wat Tarheeb)* Another narration states that Usama bin Sharik 🙵 said, "I once came to Rasulullah 🙵 while his companions sat around him so still as if there were birds perched on their backs." *(Tirmidhi in Tarjumanus Sunnah)*

The Fear that Bara bin Azib 🙵 Felt for Rasulullah 🙵

Bara bin Azib 🙵 says, "I once wanted to ask Rasulullah 🙵 about something but delayed asking for 2 years because of the fear I felt for him." *(Abu Ya'la in Tarjumanus Sunnah)*

The Sahabah Seek Blessings From the Water Left Over From Rasulullah 🙵's Wudhu and Saliva

Zuhri reports, "Someone whose dependability is not questionable mentioned to me that whenever Rasulullah 🙵 made wudhu or spat, the Sahabah would race to get his saliva and leftover wudhu water to rub it on their faces and bodies. "Why do you do this?" asked Rasulullah 🙵. "Because we seek blessings from it," came the reply. Rasulullah 🙵 then told them, "Whoever loves to be loved by Allah and by His Rasul should always speak the truth, return trusts and should never harm his neighbor." *(Bayhaqi in Kanzul Ummal)*

The Statement of Urwa bin Mas'ood ﷺ Concerning the Respect the Sahabah had for Rasulullah ﷺ

The narration of Miswar bin Makhrama ﷺ and Marwan concerning the Treaty of Hudaybiya as reported in *Bukhari* and other books has already passed. This narration states that as he was negotiating with Rasulullah ﷺ, Urwa ﷺ started observing the Sahabah very closely. He says, "By Allah! Even when Rasulullah ﷺ would spit, someone would catch it and rub it on his face and body. Whenever he issued any command the Sahabah would immediately carry it out and when he made wudhu, they get close to fighting with each other to get the water falling off his limbs. They always lower their voices when speaking to him and do not look him in the eye out of respect for him." Urwa then returned to his people and said to them, "O people! I have been to the royal courts of Caesars, Kisras and Najashi. I have never seen the followers of any ruler so devoted to him as the followers of Muhammad ﷺ are to him.

The Narration of Abdur Rahman bin Harith ﷺ Concerning the Sahabah, Seeking Blessings from the Leftover Wudhu Water and Saliva of Rasulullah ﷺ

Abu Qurad Sulami ﷺ says, "We were with Rasulullah ﷺ when he asked for water. When it was brought, Rasulullah ﷺ dipped his hand in the water and started wudhu. As the water dripped off his limbs, we drank it up. 'What makes you do this?' Rasulullah ﷺ asked. We replied, 'It is the love for Allah and His Rasul ﷺ that makes us do this.' Rasulullah ﷺ said, 'If you want Allah and His Rasul ﷺ to love you, you should return something placed in your trust, always speak the truth and behave politely to the neighbors in your vicinity.'" *(Tabrani, Haythami)*.

Abdullah bin Zubair ﷺ Drinks the Blood of Rasulullah ﷺ

Aamir the son of Abdullah bin Zubair ﷺ reports form his father that he once approached Rasulullah ﷺ as Rasulullah ﷺ was having his blood cupped. When the cupping was complete, Rasulullah ﷺ said, "O Abdullah! Take this blood and throw it where no one sees you." However, when Abdullah bin Zubair ﷺ left Rasulullah ﷺ, he took the blood and drank it up. After returning, Rasulullah ﷺ asked him what he had done with the blood and he replied, "I have placed it in a most hidden place where I am sure that no one would know about it. Did you perhaps drink it?" Rasulullah ﷺ enquired. When he admitted that he did, Rasulullah ﷺ said, "Why did you drink the blood? Destruction shall come to people from you and destruction shall come to you from people. Here Rasulullah ﷺ was referring to the strife that took place during the time of Marwan and Abdul Malik." Abu Musa reports from Abu Asim that according to popular opinion, the phenomenal strength that Abdullah bin Zubair had come from this blood. *(Abu Ya'la, Bayhaqi in Dala'il, Isabah, Hakim, Tabrani, Haythami, Ibn Asakir, Kanzul Ummal)*. Kaysan who was the freed slave of Abdullah bin Zubair ﷺ reports that when Salman ﷺ once came to Rasulullah ﷺ, he noticed Abdullah bin Zubair ﷺ drinking something from a plate he had with him. When Abdullah bin Zubair ﷺ came before Rasulullah ﷺ, Rasulullah ﷺ asked, "Are you finished'?" When Abdullah bin Zubair ﷺ replied that he had, Salman ﷺ asked, "What was that, O Rasulullah ﷺ?" Rasulullah ﷺ replied, "I gave him to throw away what was cleaned out from my cupping." Salman ﷺ said, "I swear by the Being Who has sent you with the truth! He just drank it." "Did you drink it?" enquired Rasulullah ﷺ. "Yes, I did," came the reply. "Why did you do it'?" Rasulullah ﷺ asked. "Because," explained Abdullah bin Zubair ﷺ, "I wished to have the blood of Allah's Rasul ﷺ in my belly." Rasulullah ﷺ pointed to Abdullah bin Zubair ﷺ's head and said, "Destruction shall come to people from you and destruction shall come to you from people. The Fire of Jahannam shall not touch you except to fulfill the promise of passing over the Bridge of Sirat that spans Jahannam." *(Abu Nu'aym in Hilya, Ibn Asakir in Kanzul Ummal)*

Safinah drinks Rasulullah ﷺ's Blood

Safinah ﷺ says, "Rasulullah ﷺ once had himself cupped and said to me, 'Take this blood and bury it out of the reach of animals, birds and people.' As I disappeared out of sight, I drank it up. When I later mentioned it to Rasulullah ﷺ, he merely laughed." *(Tabrani, Haythami)*

The Incident of Rasulullah ﷺ and Malik bin Sinan ﷺ During the Battle of Uhud

Abu Sa'eed Khudri ﷺ reports that his father Malik Bin Sinan ﷺ licked the blood off Rasulullah ﷺ's face and then swallowed it. This happened after Rasulullah ﷺ's face was injured during the Battle of Uhud. Someone asked, "Are you drinking blood?" "Yes," he confirmed, "but this is the blood of Rasulullah ﷺ that I am drinking." Rasulullah ﷺ then said, "Once my blood has mixed with his, the Fire of Jahannam shall never touch him." *(Tabrani in Awsat, Haythami)*

The Narration of Hakimah bint Umayma Concerning the Drinking of Rasulullah ﷺ's Urine

Hakimah bint Umayma narrates from her mother that Rasulullah ﷺ had a wooden cup in which he used to urinate. He kept this cup beneath his bed. When he looked for it one day and could not find it, he asked where it was. He was then informed that Surrah ﷺ the maidservant of Ummu Salama ﷺ who had come with her from Abyssinia had drunk it. Rasulullah ﷺ said, "She has erected a solid barrier against the Fire of Jahannam." *(Tabrani, Haythami)*

The Narration of Abu Ayub ﷺ Concerning the Respect he Showed to Rasulullah ﷺ

Abu Ayub ﷺ reports that Rasulullah ﷺ stayed at his house when Rasulullah ﷺ arrived in Madinah. While Rasulullah ﷺ stayed in the lower storey of the house, Abu Ayub ﷺ and his family stayed on the upper storey. That morning and evening, the thought plagued Abu Ayub ﷺ that he was on the top of the house while Rasulullah ﷺ was beneath him, and he was therefore an impediment between Rasulullah ﷺ and revelation from the heavens. Abu Ayub ﷺ also did not sleep that night fearing that he may cause some dust to fall on Rasulullah ﷺ or that his movements may disturb Rasulullah ﷺ. Early next morning, he went to Rasulullah ﷺ and said, "O Rasulullah ﷺ! My eyes and those of my wife Ummu Ayub were unable to close all night." "Why was that, O Abu Ayub?" enquired Rasulullah ﷺ. Abu Ayub ﷺ replied, "The thought occurred to me that since I am above and you below me, dust would fall on you if I moved and my movements would disturb you. I also feared that I was an impediment between you and revelation." Rasulullah ﷺ put him at ease saying, "Do not worry like that in future, O Abu Ayub. Should I not teach you some words that if you recite them 10 times in the mornings and 10 times in the evenings, you will be granted the reward of 10 good deeds, 10 sins will be erased from your record, you will be elevated 10 stages in Jannah and on the

Day of Judgment you will have the reward of setting 10 slaves free? You should recite *(Tabrani in Kanzul Ummal):*

لَا إِلَهَ إِلَّا اللهُ الْمَلِكُ وَلَهُ الْحَمْدُ لَا شَرِيكَ لَهُ

Abu Ayub ؓ says, "When Rasulullah ﷺ came to stay with me, I said, 'May my parents be sacrificed for you! I do not like it that I am above you while you are below me.' Rasulullah ﷺ said, 'It is more convenient for us to be below because we would be swamped with visitors.' One of our jugs happened to break and the water started to spill. Ummu Ayub and I stood with our blanket and used it to dry up the water fearing that the water should not drop on Rasulullah ﷺ, thereby inconveniencing him. We had nothing else to cover ourselves and therefore spent the night without anything to cover ourselves. We used to prepare meals and send to Rasulullah ﷺ and when he sent back what was extra, we specifically sought out the parts where his fingers touched and ate from there with the intention of attaining blessings. One night when Rasulullah ﷺ sent back his dinner in which we had put garlic or onions, we did not see any traces of his fingers touching the food. When I mentioned our practice to Rasulullah ﷺ, adding that he sent back the food without eating it, he said, 'I could get the smell of that tree (garlic or onion) and because I am a person who engages in close conversation with Allah and the angels, I did not like the smell to stay with me. However, you people are at liberty to eat it.'" *(Tabrani in Kanzul Ummal, Hakim)*. Another narration states that Abu Ayub ؓ said, "O Rasulullah ﷺ! It is not proper for me to be above you. You should therefore move to the upper storey." Rasulullah ﷺ then had his luggage moved, which was very little. *(Abu Nu'aym, Ibn Asakir in Kanzul Ummal, Ibn Abi Shayba, Ibn Abi Asim, Isabal)*

The Incident Between Omar ؓ and Abbas ؓ Concerning a Gutter

Abdullah bin Abbas ؓ narrates that there was gutter belonging to Abbas ؓ that was on the road Omar ؓ used to the Masjid. Omar ؓ left his house one Friday after dressing for the Jumu'ah salah. Because Abbas ؓ had 2 birds slaughtered, the blood of the birds was thrown into his gutter and when Omar ؓ passed by, the blood fall on his clothing. Omar ؓ gave instructions that the gutter should be removed and then returned home where he removed the clothes and changed into something else. He then went back and led the salah. Abbas ؓ then went up to Omar ؓ and said, "By Allah! The gutter was on the place where Rasulullah ﷺ had it placed." Omar ؓ responded by saying, "I command you in the name of Allah that even if you have to climb on my back, you should replace it in the place where Rasulullah ﷺ had it laid." Abbas ؓ did just that. *(Ibn Sa'd in Kanzul Ummal)*. Omar ؓ actually carried Abbas ؓ on his neck, with his legs over his shoulders. He then replaced the gutter where Rasulullah ﷺ had laid it. *(Ibn Sa'd, Haythami)*

Abdullah bin Omar ؓ and the Other Sahabah Honor the Pulpit of Rasulullah ﷺ

Ibrahim bin Abdur Rahman bin Abdul Qari says that he saw Abdullah bin Omar ؓ place his hand on the place where Rasulullah ﷺ sat on his pulpit and then put the hand on his face. Another narration from Yazid bin Abdullah bin Qusait states that when the Masjid Nabawi was empty he saw several Sahabah use their right hands to pick up some of the shiny and smooth sand from that side of the pulpit which adjoined Rasulullah ﷺ's grave. They then made Du'a facing the Qibla.

The Incident of Usaid bin Hudhair ؓ Regarding the Kissing the Body of Rasulullah ﷺ

Abu Laila ؓ says that Usaid bin Hudhair ؓ was a good man who was always smiling and cheerful. One day as he was busy speaking to some people in the presence of Rasulullah ﷺ and making them laugh, Rasulullah ﷺ poked his side. "You've hurt me," he complained. "Then take your revenge," replied Rasulullah ﷺ. Usaid ؓ remarked, "But you have a garment on while I do not." Rasulullah ﷺ raised his upper garment and Usaid ؓ immediately embraced Rasulullah ﷺ and started kissing his sides. He said, "May my parents be sacrificed for you, O Rasulullah ﷺ! This is all I wanted to do." *(Hakim, Ibn Asakir)*

Sawad bin Ghuzaya ؓ Kisses Rasulullah ﷺ's Belly

Habban bin Wasi reports from senior scholars from his tribe that Rasulullah ﷺ had the shaft of an arrow in his hand during the Battle of Badr as he was straightening the rows of the Sahabah. Sawad bin Ghuzaya ؓ who was an ally of the Banu Adi bin Najjar tribe was standing ahead of the row. As Rasulullah ﷺ passed by him, Rasulullah ﷺ nudged the shaft in his belly saying, "Get in line, O Sawad." Sawad ؓ said, "You have hurt me, O Rasulullah ﷺ! Allah has sent you with the truth and with justice, so allow me to have retribution." Rasulullah ﷺ uncovered his belly and said, "You may have your retribution." Sawad ؓ then embraced and started kissing Rasulullah ﷺ's belly. "What makes you do this, O Sawad?" asked Rasulullah ﷺ. You can see what developments are that a battle is looming, so I wish that my last meeting with you if I am killed should be with my skin touching yours." Rasulullah ﷺ then made Du'a for him. *(Ibn Is'haq in Al Bidayah wan Nihayah)*

The Incident of Another Sahabi who Kissed Rasulullah ﷺ's Belly

Hasan narrates that Rasulullah ﷺ was once carrying the branch of a date palm in his hand when he met a man who had dyed his clothing yellow. Nudging the man's belly with the branch, Rasulullah ﷺ said, "Remove that Waras (yellow herb grows in Yemen). Did I not forbid you (men) from wearing that?" Although the jab made a mark on his belly, no blood emerged. The Sahabi said, "O Rasulullah ﷺ! Retribution will have to be taken." The other Sahabah exclaimed, "You wish to take retribution from Rasulullah ﷺ?" He replied, "None has a skin better than mine." Rasulullah ﷺ then exposed his abdomen saying, "You may have your retribution." The Sahabi then started kissing the belly of Rasulullah ﷺ saying, "I forsake the retribution on condition that you intercede for me on the Day of Judgment." *(Abdul Razzaq in Kanzul Ummal)*

The Incident of Sawad bin Amr ؓ

Hasan narrates that Rasulullah ﷺ once saw that Sawad bin Amr was wearing Khaluq, perfume made up largely of saffron with yellow color. "Remove the Waras! Remove the Waras!" Rasulullah ﷺ exclaimed. Rasulullah ﷺ then poked Sawad in the belly with a twig or a Miswak. The poke shook his belly and left a mark. The rest of the narration is like the one quoted above. *(Ibn Sa'd)*. Another narration from Hasan states that a man called Sawada bin Amr used to apply so much of Khaluq fragrance that he actually resembled the branch of a date palm because of the yellow color. Whenever Rasulullah ﷺ saw him, Rasulullah ﷺ would shake the fragrance off his clothes. One day when he again appeared before Rasulullah ﷺ wearing the Khaluq, Rasulullah ﷺ lightly struck him with a twig that was in his hand. However, because the twig hurt him, Sawada ؓ said, "There will have to be retribution, O Rasulullah ﷺ!" Rasulullah ﷺ handed the twig over to him and started lifting the 2 upper garments he was wearing. The people reprimanded him and he also retrained himself until the garment was lifted to the area where he was injured. He threw down the twig, held on Rasulullah ﷺ and started kissing him, saying, Rasulullah ﷺ"! I forsake the retribution on condition that you intercede for me on the Day of Judgment."*(Abdur Razzaq in Kanzul Ummal, Baghawi in Isabah)*

Talha bin Bara ؓ Kisses Rasulullah ﷺ's Feet

The narration of Husain bin Wahwa has already passed describing how Talha bin Bara ؓ embraced Rasulullah ﷺ and kissed his feet when he met Rasulullah ﷺ. The incident will also be quoted ahead about how Abu Bakr kissed Rasulullah ﷺ's forehead when Rasulullah ﷺ passed away.

The Incident of a Lady From the Ansar When She Heard That Rasulullah ﷺ Had Been Martyred in the Battle of Uhud

Anas bin Malik ؓ reports that when the people of Madinah were being defeated during the Battle of Uhud, the people started saying that Rasulullah ﷺ had been martyred. The people of Madinah started weeping so much that the cries of women could be heard in the furthest reaches of Madinah. One of the women from the Ansar left Madinah wearing her veil and headed for the battlefield. The corpses of her father, her son, her husband and her brother were all brought to her. The narrator says that he is not certain which of them was brought first. When she passed by anyone of them and asked who he was, she was informed that he was her father, her brother, her husband or her son. Undaunted from her intent to find out about Rasulullah ﷺ, she asked each time, "How is Rasulullah ﷺ?" "There he is in front of you," the people told her. When she eventually reached Rasulullah ﷺ, she held on to the edge of his garment and said, "May my parents be sacrificed for you, O Rasulullah ﷺ! When you are safe, I have no concern for all those who have passed on." *(Tabrani, Haythami)*. Zubair ؓ says that on the day the Battle of Uhud was fought, none but he was with Rasulullah ﷺ near Madinah. None of the Sahabah remained behind in Madinah because all of them were on the battlefield. So many Muslims were martyred that someone even announced that Rasulullah ﷺ had been martyred. All the women started weeping. However, one of them said, "Do not be so hasty to cry until I go and see for myself." She then left Madinah on foot without any purpose besides her concern for Rasulullah ﷺ and to find out about his welfare. *(Bazzar, Haythami)*. Sa'd bin Abi Waqqas ؓ reports that Rasulullah ﷺ passed by a lady from the Banu Dinar tribe whose husband, brother, and father had been martyred while fighting by the side of Rasulullah ﷺ in the Battle of Uhud. When she was informed about one of their deaths, she kept asking, "How is Rasulullah ﷺ?" Addressing her by her family name, the Sahabah said, "He is well. By the grace of Allah, he is exactly as you would like him to be." "Show me where he is so that I may see him," she asked. She was shown where Rasulullah ﷺ was and when she saw him, she said, "After I see you O Rasulullah ﷺ, every calamity seems trivial." *(Ibn Is'haq in Al Bidayah wan Nihayah)*

The Behavior of Abu Talha ؓ During the Battle of Uhud Because of His Love for Rasulullah ﷺ

Anas ؓ narrates that Abu Talha was firing arrows in front of Rasulullah ﷺ during the Battle of Uhud. He was a proficient archer and was shielding Rasulullah ﷺ. Each time, he fired an arrow, Rasulullah ﷺ looked up to see where the arrow landed. At the same time, Abu Talha ؓ would raise his chest to shield Rasulullah ﷺ saying, "May my parents be sacrificed for you, O Rasulullah ﷺ! Do not get up for an arrow should strike you. My neck is there to be sacrificed rather than yours." Abu Talha ؓ was ready to have himself killed in the defense of Rasulullah ﷺ.

He therefore kept saying, "O Rasulullah ﷺ! I am a strong man, so send me to fulfill any of your needs and give me any command you wish." *(Ahmad in Al Bidayah wan Nihayah, Ibn Sa'd)*

The Bravery of Qatadah ؓ for the Love of Rasulullah ﷺ

Qatadah bin Nu'man ؓ narrates, "Rasulullah ﷺ was given a bow as a gift which he gave to me during the Battle of Uhud. I used it to fire arrows in front of Rasulullah ﷺ until the string broke. I then remained standing where I was shielding the face of Rasulullah ﷺ with my own. Whenever an arrow headed for the face of Rasulullah ﷺ, I turned my head to protect the face of Rasulullah ﷺ for I had no bow to use." The rest of the narration is the same as appears in the chapter entitled "The bravery of Qatadah bin Nu'man ؓ."

The Sahabah Weep at the Mention of Rasulullah ﷺ Separating From Them: The Weeping of Abu Bakr ؓ

Abu Sa'eed ؓ narrates, "Rasulullah ﷺ once came out to us from his room during the illness in which he passed away. He had a bandage wrapped around his head and he went towards the pulpit until he sat upright on it. We followed Rasulullah ﷺ towards the pulpit, where he said, 'I swear by the Being Who controls my life that at this moment I am standing upon my fountain Kowthar. When servant of Allah was given the choice between this world with its splendor and the Hereafter, he chose the Hereafter.' No one understood the message of this statement besides Abu Bakr ؓ. His eyes therefore filled with tears and he started weeping. He then exclaimed, 'May my parents be sacrificed for you, O Rasulullah ﷺ! In fact, may all our fathers, our mothers, ourselves and our wealth be sacrificed for you!' Rasulullah ﷺ then descended from the pulpit and has not stood there again to this day." *(Ibn Abi Shayba in Kanzul Ummal, Ibn Sa'd)*

The Weeping of Fatima ؓ

Abdullah bin Abbas ؓ reports that Rasulullah ﷺ sent for Fatima ؓ after Allah revealed the Surah An-Nasr:

إِذَا جَاءَ نَصْرُ اللَّهِ وَالْفَتْحُ (1)

When comes the Help of Allah (to you, O Muhammad (ﷺ) against your enemies) and the conquest (of Makkah). (An-Nasr:1)
He said to her, "This tells me of my pending death." When she started to weep, Rasulullah ﷺ consoled her by saying, "Do not weep because you shall be the first of my family to meet me." She then started to laugh. Seeing her do this, one of Rasulullah ﷺ's wives asked, "I saw you cry and then laugh?" Fatima ؓ explained, "Rasulullah ﷺ said to me, 'This tells me of my pending death.' When I started to weep, Rasulullah ﷺ then consoled me by saying, 'Do not weep because you shall be the first of my family to meet me.' It was then that I started to laugh." *(Tabrani, Haythami)*. Aisha ؓ narrates, "During his final illness, Rasulullah ﷺ once called for his daughter Fatima ؓ. When he whispered something to her, she wept. He then called her again and when he whispered something to her this time, she started laughing. When I asked her about this, she replied, 'When Rasulullah ﷺ informed me that his life would be taken during this illness, I started to weep but when he told me that I would be the first of my family to meet him, I started to laugh.'" *(Ibn Sa'd)*. In another narration, Ummu Salama ؓ states, "When I asked Fatima ؓ about her laughing and crying, she replied, 'Rasulullah ﷺ first informed me that he was going to pass away and then informed me that I would be the leader of the women of Jannah after Maryam the daughter of Imran. It was this that made me laugh.'" *(Ibn Sa'd)*. Ala ؓ reports that when Rasulullah ﷺ was

about to leave this world, Fatima ؓ started weeping. Rasulullah ﷺ said to her, "Do not weep, dear daughter. When I pass on, you should say, *'Inna Lillahi wa Inna Ilayhi Raji'oon'* as by reciting these words a person receives something in return for every calamity." "Even in return for losing you, O Rasulullah ﷺ!" asked Fatima ؓ. "Even in return for losing me," replied Rasulullah ﷺ. *(Ibn Sa'd)*

The Weeping of Mu'adh bin Jabal ؓ

Mu'adh bin Jabal ؓ narrates that when Rasulullah ﷺ sent him as governor to Yemen, Rasulullah ﷺ walked with him as he gave him advice. Mu'adh ؓ was riding his animal while Rasulullah ﷺ walked beside the animal. After giving him the necessary advice, said, "O Mu'adh! You shall probably not meet me after this year. You shall perhaps be passing by only this Masjid of mine and my grave." Mu'adh ؓ then started weeping profusely because of this separation from Rasulullah ﷺ. Rasulullah ﷺ then turned around and faced towards Madinah as he said, "The people closest to me are those with Taqwa regardless of who they are and where they may be." *(Ahmad).* Rasulullah ﷺ also said, "Do not weep, O Mu'adh because this weeping is from Saitan." *(Ahmad, Haythami)*

The Narration of Abdullah bin Abbas ؓ Regarding the Fear of Rasulullah ﷺ Passing Away

Abdullah bin Abbas ؓ reports that Rasulullah ﷺ was once informed that the Ansar men and women were crying in the Masjid. "What makes them cry?" Rasulullah ﷺ enquired. When he was informed that they were crying because they feared he was going to pass away, Rasulullah ﷺ left his room and went to sit on his pulpit. He was wrapped in a shawl with the ends thrown over his shoulders. He also wore a stained bandage on his head. After duly praising Allah, he said, "O people! People will multiply as the Ansar dwindle in numbers until they are only as much as salt in food. Whoever is given charge over their affairs should accept the good from their good people and excuse their evil ones." *(Bazzar, Haythami, Ibn Sa'd)*

The Statement of Ummul Fadhl ؓ at the Demise of Rasulullah ﷺ

Ummul Fadhl bint Harith ؓ says that when she came to Rasulullah ﷺ during his final illness, she started weeping. Rasulullah ﷺ lifted his head and asked, "What makes you weep?" She replied, "We fear for you that you will pass away and do not know how people will treat us after your demise." Rasulullah ﷺ replied, "You will be the ones in a weaker position after I leave." *(Ahmad, Haythami)*

The Instruction Rasulullah ﷺ Gave Prior to His Demise Concerning His Burial, Bathing, Janaza Salah and Other Matters

Abdullah bin Mas'ood ؓ says, "May my father and I be sacrificed for our beloved Nabi ﷺ who gave us the news of his demise 6 days in advance. When his end drew near, he gathered us in the room of our mother Aisha ؓ. His eyes welled with tears as he looked at us and said, 'Welcome to you all. May Allah give you long lives. May Allah protect you. May Allah safeguard you. May Allah assist you, May Allah elevate you. May Allah guide you. May Allah provide for you. May Allah steer you to what is right. May Allah keep you safe. May Allah accept you. I advise you to adopt Taqwa. I plead to Allah to care for you and make Him my successor over you. I am a dear warner to you not to exert your authority over Allah with regard to His servants and lands, for Allah has mentioned to me and to you:

تِلْكَ الدَّارُ الْآخِرَةُ نَجْعَلُهَا لِلَّذِينَ لَا يُرِيدُونَ عُلُوًّا فِي الْأَرْضِ وَلَا فَسَادًا وَالْعَاقِبَةُ لِلْمُتَّقِينَ (83)

That home of the Hereafter (i.e. Paradise), We shall assign to those who rebel not against the truth with pride and oppression in the land nor do mischief by committing crimes. And the good end is for the Muttaqoon (pious). (Al-Qasas:83)

Allah also says: أَلَيْسَ فِي جَهَنَّمَ مَثْوًى لِّلْمُتَكَبِّرِينَ (60)

Is there not in Hell an abode for the arrogant ones? (Az-ZOmar:60)

Rasulullah ﷺ then continued, 'The term is coming to an ends. The time has come to return to Allah, to the Sidratul Muntaha, to Jannatul Ma'wa, level of Jannah where the pious abide, to glasses filled to the brim and to the Highest Companion (Allah).'" "Who shall bathe you then, O Rasulullah ﷺ!" the Sahabah enquired. Rasulullah ﷺ replied, "The men of family who are closest in relation, together with those who are closest after them." "In what shall we shroud you?" they enquired further. Rasulullah ﷺ replied, "In the clothing I am wearing. Otherwise, if you wish, you may shroud me in a Yemeni shawl or in white Egyptian sheets." "Which of us should then lead the Janaza salah," was the next question. The Sahabah and Rasulullah ﷺ then burst out crying. Rasulullah ﷺ said, "Take it easy. May Allah forgive you all and grant you the best of rewards on behalf of His Nabi. After you have bathed me and placed me on my bed in a corner of my room that will be my grave, then leave me alone for a while because the first to perform the Janaza salah for me shall be my friend the angel Jibra'el ؑ. After him shall be Mika'il ؑ, followed by Israfil ؑ, then the angel of death with his army and then all the angels. May Allah shower His blessings on all of them. You should then enter in groups to perform the salah and to greet me. You should however not allow any wailing woman to come to me nor any woman who is screaming and raising her voice. The first to perform the salah should be the men of my family and then the rest of you afterwards. Accept my reply to your greetings of Salam and convey my greeting of Salam to all my brothers who are not present and to every person who enters the fold of Islam after my demise. I make you witness to the fact that I am conveying my Salam to him and to every other person following me in my Islam from this day until the Day of Judgment." The Sahabah then asked, "Which of us should place you in your grave, O Rasulullah ﷺ?" Rasulullah ﷺ replied, "The men of my family together with a large host of angels who will be able to see you without you being able to see them." *(Bazzar, Haythami, Tabrani, Abu Nu'aym in Hilya)*

The Demise of Rasulullah ﷺ and the Statements of Abu Bakr ؓ and Omar ؓ

Yazid bin Babnus says, "A friend and I once went to Aisha ؓ and sought permission to enter. She threw us some cushions and then concealed herself behind a screen before allowing us in. 'What do you have to say about Arak, O Ummul Mu'minin?' my friend asked. 'What is Arak?' she asked. When I struck my friend on the shoulder to bid him not to ask about it, Aisha ؓ said, 'Do not do that for you have hurt your brother.' She then proceeded to ask, 'What is Arak? Is it about menstruation that you wish to know about, whether a man can touch his wife when she is menstruating? You should practice what Allah has mentioned in the Qur'an about menstruating women. Rasulullah ﷺ used to embrace me and kiss my head with only a sheet between us when I was menstruating.'" Aisha ؓ then went on to say: "It was the practice of Rasulullah ﷺ to tell me something of benefit every time he passed by my door. However, one day he passed my door 2 or 3 times without saying anything. I then told my maidservant to place a pillow at the door and I tied a bandage around my head pretending to be ill to get Rasulullah ﷺ's attention. When Rasulullah ﷺ passed by and saw me lying there, he asked, 'Dear Aisha! What is the matter?' 'My head is paining,' I responded. 'I too have severe pain in my head,' he replied. He then left and it was not long when he came to me carrying a blanket with him. He entered my room and then sent a message to his other wives saying, 'I am ill and am unable to come to all of you, Do permit me to stay with Aisha.' With the permission of the others I then started to nurse Rasulullah ﷺ whereas I had never nursed anyone else before him.

Rasulullah ﷺ's head was on my shoulder one day when it turned towards me. I thought that Rasulullah ﷺ wanted to kiss me when a drop of cold saliva dropped from his mouth. When it fell on the back of my neck, my entire body started to shiver. Thinking that he had fallen unconscious, I covered him with a sheet. Omar ؓ and Mughiera bin Shu'ba ؓ then arrived and sought permission to enter. I gave them permission and then pulled over my veil. Omar ؓ looked at Rasulullah ﷺ and said, 'O dear! Rasulullah ﷺ is unconscious! What a deep coma he seems to be in.' The 2 men then stood up. When they were near the door, Mughiera ؓ said, 'O Omar! Rasulullah ﷺ has passed away.' 'Never!' exclaimed Omar, 'You are always making statements that cause trouble! Rasulullah ﷺ will never pass away until Allah has wiped out the hypocrites.'" Aisha ؓ continues, "My father Abu Bakr ؓ then arrived and I lifted my veil. He looked at Rasulullah ﷺ and exclaimed, 'Inna Lillahi wa Inna Raji'oon! Rasulullah ﷺ has passed away.' He went to Rasulullah ﷺ from the headside, bowed his head and kissed Rasulullah ﷺ's forehead. He then said, 'O dear Nabi ﷺ!' Thereafter, he raised his head and again lowered his mouth to kiss Rasulullah ﷺ's forehead, saying, 'O my chosen friend!' For the 3rd time he then raised his head and again lowered his mouth to kiss Rasulullah ﷺ's forehead, saying, 'O my bosom friend! Rasulullah ﷺ has passed away.'" Abu Bakr ؓ then went to the Masjid where Omar ؓ was busy lecturing the people saying, "Indeed Rasulullah ﷺ shall never pass away until Allah destroys the hypocrites.' Abu Bakr ؓ then addressed the people. After duly praising Allah, he said, "Allah says:

إِنَّكَ مَيِّتٌ وَإِنَّهُمْ مَيِّتُونَ (30)

Verily, you (O Muhammad ﷺ) will die and verily, they (too) will die. (Az-ZOmar:30)

Thereafter, he recited the verse:

وَمَا مُحَمَّدٌ إِلَّا رَسُولٌ قَدْ خَلَتْ مِنْ قَبْلِهِ الرُّسُلُ أَفَإِنْ مَاتَ أَوْ قُتِلَ انْقَلَبْتُمْ عَلَى أَعْقَابِكُمْ وَمَنْ يَنْقَلِبْ عَلَى عَقِبَيْهِ فَلَنْ يَضُرَّ اللَّهَ شَيْئًا وَسَيَجْزِي اللَّهُ الشَّاكِرِينَ (144)

Muhammad (ﷺ) is no more than a Messenger, and indeed (many) Messengers have passed away before him. If he dies or is killed, will you then turn back on your heels (as disbelievers)? And he who turns back on his heels, not the least harm will he do to Allah, and Allah will give reward to those who are grateful. (Al-Imran:144). He then proceeded to say, "Whoever worships Allah should know that Allah is Alive and shall never die. Whoever worshipped Muhammad should know that Muhammad ﷺ has passed away." Omar ؓ asked, "Are those verses really in the Qur'an? O people! This is Abu Bakr ؓ and he is the highest achiever amongst us. Pledge your allegiance to him." *(Ahmad in Al Bidayah wan Nihayah, Haythami, Abu Ya'la, Ibn Sa'd)*

The Narration of Ali ؓ Regarding the Burial of Rasulullah ﷺ

Ali bin Abi Talib ؓ narrates that when the family of Rasulullah ﷺ started the burial preparations for Rasulullah ﷺ, they locked the door and did not allow anyone in. While the Ansar shouted, "We are the maternal relatives of Rasulullah ﷺ

and have a high standing in Islam!" the Quraish shouted, "We are his paternal relatives!" Abu Bakr ؓ then shouted saying, "O assembly of Muslims! Every family has a greater right to the burial of their family members than others do. We therefore plead to you in the name of Allah not to enter because if you enter, you will be pushing back those who are entitled to enter. By Allah! None should enter besides those who are called." A narration of Ali bin Husain states that the Ansar shouted, "We have a right to arrange the burial because Rasulullah ﷺ is the son of our sister and because we have a high standing in Islam." When they lodged their request with Abu Bakr ؓ, he said, "A family has the greatest right to members of their family. You may put the request to Ali ؓ and Abbas ؓ because none may enter the room besides those whom they permit." *(Ibn Sa'd)*

The Narration of Abdullah bin Abbas ؓ in this Regard

Abdullah bin Abbas ؓ reports that Aisha ؓ and Hafsa ؓ were with Rasulullah ﷺ when his illness grew severe. When Rasulullah ﷺ saw Ali ؓ enter the room, he lifted his head and said, "Come closer. Come closer." Ali ؓ let Rasulullah ﷺ lean against him and remained with Rasulullah ﷺ until he passed away. When Rasulullah ﷺ passed away, Ali ؓ stood up and locked the door. Abbas ؓ and the members of the Banu Abdul Muttalib family came and stood guard at the door. Addressing Rasulullah ﷺ, Ali ؓ said, "May my parents be sacrificed for you! You were so pure in life and now so pure in death." There drifted from the body of Rasulullah ﷺ an extremely wonderful fragrance that people had never smelt before. Abbas ؓ then said to Ali, "What is happening here? Leave all that weeping like the women do. Pay attention to your leader Rasulullah ﷺ." Ali ؓ then asked for Fadhl bin Abbas to be brought to him to assist him. At this stage the Ansar requested, "We plead to you in the name of Allah and by the affinity we have with Rasulullah ﷺ that you allow one of us to be part of the burial preparations." Ali ؓ and those with him allowed in an Ansari called Aws bin Khowlay who carried a bucket of water in one hand. Before starting the bathing, they heard a voice in the house saying, "Do not remove Rasulullah ﷺ's clothing. Bathe him as he is in his clothing." Ali ؓ then washed Rasulullah ﷺ by placing his hand beneath the clothing as Fadhl ؓ held the clothing up and the Ansari brought the water. Ali ؓ wore a cloth over his hand as a glove as he placed his hand beneath the clothing. *(Tabrani. Haythami, Ibn Majah, lbn Sa'd)*

The Narration of Abdullah bin Abbas ؓ Regarding the Janaza Salah for Rasulullah ﷺ

Abdullah bin Abbas ؓ narrates that when Rasulullah ﷺ passed away, groups of men were let into the room and they performed the Janazah salah individually without anyone being the Imam. When all the men were finished, the women were let in to perform the Janaza salah, followed by the children and then the slaves. None of the groups were led by an Imam. *(Ibn Is'haq)*

The Narration of Sahl bin Sa'd ؓ

Sahl in Sa'd ؓ says that after Rasulullah ﷺ was shrouded in the burial shroud, he was placed on a bed, which was then placed in the corner of the grave. The people then entered the room in groups to perform the Janaza salah without anyone leading them in the salah. *(Waqidi).* Musa bin Muhammad bin Ibrahim says that he found a book in which his father had written that after Rasulullah ﷺ was shrouded in the burial shroud, he was placed on a bed. Abu Bakr ؓ and Omar ؓ then entered the room together with as many Muhajirin and Ansar as could fit in the room. The 2 men said: السلام عليك ايها النبى ورحمة الله وبركاته

"Peace be on you, O Nabi ﷺ together with the mercy of Allah and His blessings."

The other Muhajirin and Ansar also greeted Rasulullah ﷺ as Abu Bakr ؓ and Omar ؓ did. They then formed rows without any of them being the Imam. Standing in the first row in front of Rasulullah ﷺ, Abu Bakr ؓ and Omar ؓ said, "O Allah! We testify that Rasulullah ﷺ conveyed whatever was revealed to him. He was a well-wisher of the Ummah who strove in the Path of Allah until Allah gave honor to Islam. His words (Islam) was completed and belief was established in the One Allah Who has no partner. O Allah! Make us people who follow the guidance revealed to him and allow us to meet him again with him recognizing us and us recognizing him. He was indeed most forgiving and most merciful unto the Mu'minin. We seek no worldly recompense for believing in him and shall never sell our Iman in him for any price." The other Sahabah said, "Amin! Amin!" They left and another group entered. After all the men had completed, the women entered, followed by the children. *(Al Bidayah wan Nihayah, Ibn Sa'd)*

The Narration of Ali ؓ

Ali ؓ narrates that when Rasulullah ﷺ was placed on a bed, he said to the people, "None shall be the Imam to lead the Janaza salah because Rasulullah ﷺ is the Imam while alive and after his demise. The people then started entering the room in groups and performed the salah in rows without any of them being the Imam. They all said "Allahu Akbar" as Ali ؓ stood directly in front of Rasulullah ﷺ and said: السلام عليك ايها النبى ورحمة الله وبركاته
"Peace be on you, O Nabi ﷺ together with the mercy of Allah and His blessings."

He then continued, "O Allah! We testify that Rasulullah ﷺ conveyed whatever was revealed to him. He was a well-wisher of the Ummah who strove in the Path of Allah until Allah gave honor to Islam and His Words was completed. O Allah! Make us people who follow the guidance revealed to him, keep us steadfast and allow us to t him again" The other Sahabah said, "Amin!" After all the men had completed, the women did the same, followed by the children. *(Ibn Sa'd in Kanzul Ummal)*

Abu Bakr ؓ Weeps and the Lecture he Gave to the People When Rasulullah ﷺ Passed Away and the Weeping of Sahaba at Their Separation From Him

Anas ؓ reports that when Rasulullah ﷺ passed away, the Sahabah were all whispering to each other. Abu Bakr ؓ instructed his slave to listen to what they were saying and report back to him. The slave reported that he overheard the Sahabah saying that Rasulullah ﷺ had passed away. Abu Bakr ؓ then hurried as he said, "O dear! My back has been broken!" He was so overcome with grief that the Sahabah thought that he would not even make it to the Masjid, but he did. *(Ibn Khusru in Kanzul Ummal)*. Abdullah bin Abbas ؓ narrates that on the day Rasulullah ﷺ passed away, Abu Bakr Siddiq ؓ emerged from Rasulullah ﷺ's room as Omar ؓ was busy addressing the Sahabah. He told Omar ؓ to be seated and after duly praising Allah, he said, "Whoever worshipped Muhammad ﷺ should know that Muhammad ﷺ has passed away. On the other hand, whoever worships Allah should know that Allah is Alive and shall never die. Verily Allah states:

وَمَا مُحَمَّدٌ إِلَّا رَسُولٌ قَدْ خَلَتْ مِنْ قَبْلِهِ الرُّسُلُ أَفَإِنْ مَاتَ أَوْ قُتِلَ انْقَلَبْتُمْ عَلَى أَعْقَابِكُمْ وَمَنْ يَنْقَلِبْ عَلَى عَقِبَيْهِ فَلَنْ يَضُرَّ اللَّهَ شَيْئًا وَسَيَجْزِي اللَّهُ الشَّاكِرِينَ (144)

Muhammad (ﷺ) is no more than a Messenger, and indeed (many) Messengers have passed away before him. If he dies or is killed, will you then turn back on your heels (as disbelievers)? And he who turns back on his heels, not the least harm will he do to Allah, and Allah will give reward to those who are grateful. (Al-Imran:144)

Abdullah bin Abbas ؓ says, "By Allah! Because they were so overcome with grief, it was as if the people never knew that such a verse was ever revealed until Abu Bakr ؓ recited it. They all took it from Abu Bakr ؓ and every one of them was reciting it. Omar bin Khattab ؓ said, 'By Allah! No sooner did I hear Abu Bakr ؓ recite the verse when my legs collapsed beneath me and were unable to carry me. I then fell to the ground when I heard it for I was then convinced that Rasulullah ﷺ had definitely passed away." *(Abdur Razzaq, Ibn Sa'd, Ibn Abi Shayba, Ahmad, Bukhari, Ibn Hibban, Kanzul Ummal)*

The Grief of Uthman ؓ

Uthman bin Affan ؓ says, "When Rasulullah ﷺ passed away, the Sahabah were so grieved that some of them even started having false thoughts that Islam had come to an end. I was among those who were deeply grieved and was once sitting on one of the hills of Madinah when Omar ؓ passed by me without even noticing me that he had passed. People had already pledged their allegiance to Abu Bakr ؓ. Omar ؓ proceeded immediately to Abu Bakr ؓ and said, 'O Khalifa of Rasulullah ﷺ! I have some shocking news for you! When I passed by Uthman ؓ and greeted him, he did not reply." The test of the narration shall soon be quoted in the chapter concerning greeting. *(Ibn Sa'd)*

The Grief of Ali ؓ

Abdur Rahman bin Sa'eed bin Yarbo ؓ narrates that Ali bin Abi Talib ؓ one day had his face covered and was extremely grieved. "I notice that you are deeply grieved," enquired Abu Bakr ؓ. Ali ؓ replied, "Such grief has overcome me that has not befallen you." To this Abu Bakr ؓ said, "Look at what he is saying! I ask you in the name of Allah to tell me whether any other person is more grieved about the demise of Rasulullah ﷺ than I am?" *(Ibn Sa'd)*

The Weeping of Ummu Salama ؓ

Ummu Salama ؓ says, "When we, the wives of Rasulullah ﷺ gathered together and were weeping over the demise of Rasulullah ﷺ, we did not have a wink of sleep. The blessed body of Rasulullah ﷺ was still in our rooms and we consoled each other every time we saw him lying on the bed. When we suddenly heard the sounds of shovels digging Rasulullah ﷺ's grave just before dawn, we started crying out of grief and the people in the Masjid also started crying. This caused all of Madinah to shake. When Bilal ؓ called out the Fajr Adhan and look the name of Rasulullah ﷺ as he said ......), he burst out crying. This added to our grief and the people started going towards the grave. The door was however locked to them. O what a calamity it was! Every calamity that befell us afterwards was insignificant when we thought about the calamity of Rasulullah ﷺ's demise." *(Waqidi in Al Bidayah wan Nihayah)*

The Crying of the People of Madinah

Abu Dhu'aib Hudhali says, "When I arrived in Madinah, the wailing of the people of Madinah pulsed like the calls of 'Labbaik' as from people performing Hajj. 'What is the matter?'" I enquired. They then informed me that Rasulullah ﷺ had passed away." *(Ibn Mandah, Ibn Asakir in Kanzul Ummal, Ibn Is'haq)*

The Condition of the Sahabah in Makkah When They Heard About Rasulullah ﷺ's Demise

Ubaidullah bin Umair ؓ reports that when Rasulullah ﷺ passed away, the governor of Makkah was Attab bin Usaid ؓ. When the news of Rasulullah ﷺ's demise reached the people of Makkah, the people in the Masjid burst out crying. Attab ؓ left Makkah and went to one of the valleys of Makkah. Suhail bin Amr ؓ approached him and told him to address the people. "I cannot speak after the demise of Rasulullah ﷺ," replied Attab ؓ. Suhail ؓ said, "Then come with me and I shall do it for you." They left and when they came to the Masjidul Haram, Suhail ؓ stood up to address the people. After duly praising Allah, he delivered a lecture that was identical to the one that Abu Bakr ؓ gave the people in Madinah. When Suhail was a captive of the Battle of Badr, Rasulullah ﷺ said to Omar ؓ, "What makes you want to extract his front teeth? Leave him alone because Allah shall perhaps place him on a platform that would bring you great pleasure." The platform Rasulullah ﷺ referred to was this one by which the authority of Attab ؓ was consolidated over Makkah and neighboring areas. *(Saif, Ibn Asakir in Kanzul Ummal)*

The Condition of Fatima ؓ

Abu Ja'far says, "After the demise of Rasulullah ﷺ, I never saw Fatima ؓ laugh. All I saw was her mouth extend on one side (as she smiled)." *(Ibn Sa'd)*

What the Sahabah said When Rasulullah ﷺ Passed Away: The Statement of Abu Bakr: "Today we Have Lost Revelation"

Is'haq reports that when Rasulullah ﷺ passed away, Abu Bakr ؓ said, "Today we have lost revelation and speech from Allah." *(Dala'ilut Towheed, Kanzul Ummal)*

The Statement of Ummu Ayman ؓ on the Loss of Revelation

Anas ؓ reports that when Rasulullah ﷺ passed away, Ummu Ayman ؓ wept bitterly. When asked what made her weep so bitterly about the demise of Rasulullah ﷺ, she replied, "I always knew that Rasulullah ﷺ would soon pass away, but what makes me weep is that revelation has now been lifted from us." *(Ahmad)*. Anas ؓ also reports that after the demise of Rasulullah ﷺ, Abu Bakr ؓ once said to Omar ؓ, "Come with me to visit Ummu Ayman ؓ." When they came to her, she started weeping. They consoled her saying, "What makes you weep? What is with Allah is better for Rasulullah ﷺ." She replied, "By Allah! I am not weeping because I do not know that what Allah has with Him is better for Rasulullah ﷺ. I am weeping cause revelation from the heavens has been terminated." his statement made both men start weeping. *(Bayhaqi in Al Bidayah wan Nihayah, Ibn Abi Shayba, Muslim, Abu Ya'la, Abu Awana, Ibn Sa'd, Kanzul Ummal)*. Another narration states that when Rasulullah ﷺ passed way, Ummu Ayman ؓ wept bitterly. When asked what made her weep, she replied, "What makes me weep is that news form the heavens has now been terminated." *(Ibn Abi Shayba in Kanzul Ummal, Ibn Sa'd)*. A narration of Musa bin Uqba quotes Ummu Ayman ؓ as saying, "I am weeping because the news from the heavens used to come to us in large quantities and fresh from the heavens every day and night. This has now been terminated and lifted. It is only this that makes me weep." This statement greatly surprised the people. *(Al Bidayah wan Nihayah)*

The Statement of Ma'n bin Adi ؓ

Abdullah bin Omar ؓ reports that when Rasulullah ﷺ passed away, the people wept bitterly and said, "We wished that we would pass away before Rasulullah ﷺ for we fear that we will be facing great tribulations after him." To this, Ma'n bin Adi ؓ said, "on the contrary, I swear by Allah that rather than wishing to die before Rasulullah ﷺ, I wish to believe in him after his demise just as I did during his lifetime." *(Malik in Al Bidayah wan Nihayah, Ibn Abdil Birr in Isti'ab)*

The Statement of Fatima ؓ the Daughter of Rasulullah ﷺ

Anas ؓ reports that when Rasulullah ﷺ fell seriously ill, Fatima ؓ regretted, "O! The pain my father is suffering!" Rasulullah ﷺ then said to her, "Your father will suffer no pain after this day." After Rasulullah ﷺ passed away, she said, "O my dear father! His Rabb really accepted his supplication. O my dear father! Jannatul Firdous, highest level of Jannah has become his abode! O my dear father! Jibra'el ؑ has informed us of his demise." After Rasulullah ﷺ was buried, Fatima ؓ said, "O Anas! How did your hearts allow you to throw sand over Rasulullah ﷺ?" *(Bukhari)*. Another narration quotes that Fatima ؓ said, "O Anas! How did your hearts allow you to return after burying Rasulullah ﷺ in the sand?" Hammad says that whenever Thabit related this narration, he sobbed so much that his ribs dragged. *(Ahmad in Al Bidayah wan Nihayah, Ibn Asakir, Abu Ya'la, Kanzul Ummal, Ibn Sa'd)*

The Couplets of Safiya ؓ the Aunt of Rasulullah ﷺ

Urwa ؓ reports that Safiya bint Abdul Muttalib ؓ recited a few couplets in memory of Rasulullah ﷺ. The meaning of these couplets is:

'My heart grieve and I have spent the night like he who has lost everything. I have stayed awake all night like the one whose every possession has been looted. It is all because of my grief and remorse that I cannot sleep

If only I were given the cup of death to sip from when they said that there came to Rasulullah ﷺ. The destined moment of death when we came to the family of Muhammad ﷺ

The hairs on our neck turned white (with grief) when we saw his rooms had become deserted. After him there was none there to live the life of a stranger because of this, a deep grief has come to me mixing in my heart filling it with fear"

Safiya ؓ also recited the following couplets (which means):

"Do listen, O Rasulullah ﷺ! You had been the one to give us ease. You had been good to us and never harsh. Our Nabi ﷺ had always been good and forgiving towards us.

Today everyone who wishes to weep should respond by my life! It is not because of his death that I weep for my Nabi ﷺ. It is rather because of the hardships that are to come after him because of the loss of Muhammad Rasulullah ﷺ

And because of the love for him, my heart has been branded by a hot iron. O Fatima! May the Rabb of Muhammad ﷺ shower His special mercies on the body that had taken up residence in Yathrib

I am looking at Hasan ؓ whom you have left as an orphan making him cry and call out for his grandfather who has gone so far. I am ready to sacrifice for Rasulullah ﷺ my mother, my aunt my uncle, myself and all of my near and dear families

You had endured much and conveyed the message with truth. You had left the world with Islam firm, apparent and clear

Had the Rabb of the Throne kept you alive with us, we would have been most fortunate, but His decision is final

May peace and greetings from Allah be showered on you as you are entered happily into the everlasting gardens"
(Tabrani, Haythami)

Another narration from Muhammad bin Ali bin Husain

states that when Rasulullah ﷺ passed away, Safiya ◉ came out of her house with her shawl as she said couplets which meant:

"After you there shall be many distressing and difficult times the dangers of which would not be so much had you been there" (Tabrani, Haythami)

Ghunaim bin Qais reports that he heard his father say some couplets after the demise of Rasulullah ﷺ. They ere:

'Behold! I have been destroyed by the departure of Muhammad ﷺ. In his life did I find my rest and peace in which my nights were calm until the mornings" (Bukhari, Baghawi in Isabah, Bazzar, Haythami, Ibn Sa'd)

The Sahabah Weep as They Think of Rasulullah ﷺ: The Incident Between Omar ◉ and an Old Lady

Zaid bin Aslam narrates that Omar ◉ left the house one night to keep watch. When he saw a lantern burning, he went closer and found an old woman carding wool to be spun. She was reciting some couplets which meant:

"May the salutations of all righteous people be showered on Muhammad ﷺ

May the chosen best people send their salutations to you (O Rasulullah ﷺ)

You had been regularly crying (in Ibada) before dawn but death has many ways and if only I knew whether the Hereafter will join me with my beloved (Rasulullah ﷺ)"

Omar ◉ sat down and began weeping. He continued weeping until he was able to knock at her door. "Who is it?" she asked. When he replied that he was Omar bin Khattab ◉, she said, "What has Omar to do with me? What brings Omar at this hour?" Omar ◉ put her at ease saying, "Open the door. May Allah have mercy on you. You are in no trouble." When she opened the door, Omar ◉ entered and requested, "Please repeat to me the words you just said." She then repeated the couplets. When she reached the closing words, Omar ◉ asked, "Do include me with you." She then added, "And Omar, do forgive him, O Most Forgiving." Omar was happy and returned. *(Ibn Mubarak, Ibn Asakir in Muntakhab Kanzul Ummal)*

The Condition of Abdullah bin Omar ◉ and Anas ◉ When Mentioning Rasulullah ﷺ

Asim bin Muhammad reports that his father said, 'I have never seen Abdullah bin Omar ◉ mention Rasulullah ﷺ without his eyes quickly filling with tears and crying." *(Ibn Sa'd).* Muthanna bin Sa'eed Dari reports that he heard Anas ◉ say, "I see my beloved Rasulullah ﷺ) every night in a dream." He then started weeping. *(Ibn Sa'd)*

How the Sahabah Hit out Against Anyone who reviled Rasulullah ﷺ

Ka'b bin Alqama narrates that a Sahabi by the name of Gharfa bin Harith Kindi ◉ once heard a Christian insulting Rasulullah ﷺ. Gharfa ◉ hit the Christian and broke his nose. When the case was brought before Amr bin Al Aas ◉, he said to Gharfa ◉, "We have entered into a treaty with them." Ghalfa ◉ respond by saying, "Allah forbids that we ever enter into a treaty with them permitting them to insult Nabi ﷺ! Our treaty with them says that we will not interfere with their churches and will allow them to say there what they wish. It also says that we will not charge them to do more than they can manage and that we will fight in their defense if an enemy attacks them. It says further that we will permit them to enforce their own laws unless they opt to abide by ours, in which case we will pass judgment between them based on the laws of Allah and Rasulullah ﷺ. We will also not prevent them if they wish to remain aloof from us."

Amr bin Al Aas ◉ then said, "You are absolutely right." *(Ibn Mubarak in Isti'ab, Bukhari in Tarikh, Isabah).* Gharfa bin Harith ◉ was a Sahabi who fought with Ikrama bin Abu Jahal ◉ against the apostates in Yemen. He narrates that he once passed by a Christian in Egypt called Mundaqun. When Gharfa ◉ invited the man to accept Islam, the Christian started insulting Rasulullah ﷺ. When Ghalfa ◉ hit the Christian, the case was brought before Amr bin Al Aas ◉. Amr ◉ sent for Gharfa ◉ and said to him, "We have entered into a treaty with them." The rest of the narration is the same as the one quoted above. *(Tabrani, Haythami, Bayhaqi).* Another narration states that Gharfa bin Harith Kindi ◉ was a Sahabi who once passed by a man with whom the Muslims had entered into a peace treaty. When Gharfa ◉ invited the man to accept Islam, the man swore Rasulullah ﷺ because of which Gharfa ◉ killed him. Amr bin Al Aas ◉ said to him when the case was brought up, "These people were safe from us because of the treaty, how could you then kill him?" Gharfa ◉ replied, "We did not enter into any treaty with them that permits them to injure us with regard to Allah and His Rasul ﷺ." The rest of the narration is similar to the ones already quoted. *(Ibn Asakir)*

Rasulullah ﷺ's Instructions are Obeyed During the Expedition to Nakhla

Urwa bin Zubair ◉ narrates that Rasulullah ﷺ once dispatched Abdullah bin Jahash ◉ on an expedition to a place called Nakhla. Rasulullah ﷺ's instructions were, "Stay there until you are able to bring us intelligence about the Quraish." Rasulullah ﷺ did not instruct him to engage the enemy. This occurred during one of the sacred months. Before informing him where he was to go, Rasulullah ﷺ had a letter written for him, and briefed him saying, "Proceed with your companions and open the letter only after you have traveled for 2 days. Read the letter and then proceed where I have instructed you in the letter. You should also not force any of your companions to travel with you." After traveling for 2 days, Abdullah ◉ opened the letter, which read, "Proceed until you set up camp in Nakhla from where you should gather any intelligence that comes to you about the Quraish." After reading the letter, Abdullah ◉ said to his companions, "I hear and I obey. Whoever desired martyrdom, should proceed with me because I intend fulfilling the instructions of Rasulullah ﷺ. Those who do not wish to do this may return because Rasulullah ﷺ has forbidden me from forcing any of you." They all marched with him. When they reached a placed called Buhran, Sa'd bin Abi Waqqas ◉ and Utba bin Ghazwan ◉ lost the camel they had been sharing and had to fall behind to look for it. The rest of the group forged ahead until they set up camp in Nakhla. It was then that Amr bin Hadhrami, Hakam bin Kaisan, Uthman bin Abdullah and Mughiera bin Abdullah passed by them with merchandise of leather and raisins that they were bringing back from Ta'if. When this group of traders saw the Sahabah, it was Waqid bin Abdullah whom they saw staring at them. Because Waqid happened to have his hair shaved off, the traders reasoned, "They have come to perform Umrah and we therefore have nothing to fear from them." It happened to be the last day of Rajab so the Sahabah urgently convened saying to each other, "If we fight them today, we will be fighting them in a sacred month during which the Arabs regard fighting as forbidden and if we leave them, they will be entering the grounds of the Haram by nightfall, because of which they will be protected from us because no person can be attacked within the boundaries of the Haram." They therefore decided to attack. Waqid bin Abdullah Tamimi ◉ shot an arrow at Amr bin

Hadhrami and killed him. Uthman bin Abdullah and Hakam bin Kaisan were taken captive while Mughiera bin Abdullah ran away and escaped. The Sahabah led the caravan away and brought it to Rasulullah ﷺ. Rasulullah ﷺ said to them, "By Allah! I never instructed you to launch any attack during a sacred month." Rasulullah ﷺ then refrained from doing anything to the captives and the caravan and took nothing from it. After Rasulullah ﷺ had told them what he did, these Sahabah became demoralized and thought that they were destroyed. Their Muslim brothers rebuked them and when the news reached the Quraish, they began saying, "Muhammad has spilt blood during a sacred month. He has also seized property during a sacred month, captured people and violated the sanctity of the month." It was then that Allah revealed the following verse of the Qur'an:

يَسْأَلُونَكَ عَنِ الشَّهْرِ الْحَرَامِ قِتَالٍ فِيهِ قُلْ قِتَالٌ فِيهِ كَبِيرٌ وَصَدٌّ عَنْ سَبِيلِ اللَّهِ وَكُفْرٌ بِهِ وَالْمَسْجِدِ الْحَرَامِ وَإِخْرَاجُ أَهْلِهِ مِنْهُ أَكْبَرُ عِنْدَ اللَّهِ وَالْفِتْنَةُ أَكْبَرُ مِنَ الْقَتْلِ

They ask you concerning fighting in the Sacred Months (i.e. 1st, 7th, 11th and 12th months of the Islamic calendar). Say, "Fighting therein is a great (transgression) but a greater (transgression) with Allah is to prevent mankind from following the Way of Allah, to disbelieve in Him, to prevent access to Al-Masjid-al-Haram (at Makkah), and to drive out its inhabitants, and Al-Fitnah is worse than killing. And they will never cease fighting you until they turn you back from your religion (Islamic Monotheism) if they can. And whosoever of you turns back from his religion and dies as a disbeliever, then his deeds will be lost in this life and in the Hereafter, and they will be the dwellers of the Fire. They will abide therein forever." (Al-Baqara:217)

This verse made it clear that committing kufr is a greater sin than killing. When the verse was revealed, Rasulullah ﷺ took the caravan and ransomed the 2 captives. The Sahabah (who had marched to Nakhla) asked, "(O Rasulullah ﷺ) Do you think that we will be rewarded for the expedition?" Allah then revealed the following verse with special reference to them:

إِنَّ الَّذِينَ آمَنُوا وَالَّذِينَ هَاجَرُوا وَجَاهَدُوا فِي سَبِيلِ اللَّهِ أُولَٰئِكَ يَرْجُونَ رَحْمَةَ اللَّهِ وَاللَّهُ غَفُورٌ رَحِيمٌ (218)

Verily, those who have believed, and those who have emigrated (for Allah's Religion) and have striven hard in the Way of Allah, all these hope for Allah's Mercy. And Allah is Oft-Forgiving, Most-Merciful. (Al-Baqara:218)

The Sahabah who were part of the expedition numbered 8 with their commander Abdullah bin Jahash ؓ being the 9th. *(Bayhaqi, Abu Nu'aym, Tabari, Isabah).* Jundub bin Abdullah ؓ narrates that Rasulullah ﷺ once dispatched an expedition with Ubaidah bin Harith as the commander. However, when they were leaving, he was overcome by his love for Rasulullah ﷺ and started weeping. Rasulullah ﷺ then dispatched a Sahabi called Abdullah bin Jahash ؓ in his place. Rasulullah ﷺ had a letter written for him and instructed him read the letter only when he reached a certain place. He received instructions not to force anyone to march with him. When he reached the specified destination, he read the letter and recited, *"Inna Lillahi wa Inna Ilayhi Raji'oon."* He then said, "I hear and obey the orders of Allah and His Rasul ﷺ." While 2 of the Sahabah left the expedition, the others proceeded with him. When they met with Ibn Hadhrami, they killed him, not knowing whether it was still the month of Rajab or whether it was Jumadal Akhirah that had already started. When the disbeliever claimed that the Sahabah had killed him during a sacred month, Allah revealed the verse:

يَسْأَلُونَكَ عَنِ الشَّهْرِ الْحَرَامِ قِتَالٍ فِيهِ قُلْ قِتَالٌ فِيهِ كَبِيرٌ وَصَدٌّ عَنْ سَبِيلِ اللَّهِ وَكُفْرٌ بِهِ

وَالْمَسْجِدِ الْحَرَامِ وَإِخْرَاجُ أَهْلِهِ مِنْهُ أَكْبَرُ عِنْدَ اللَّهِ وَالْفِتْنَةُ أَكْبَرُ مِنَ الْقَتْلِ

They ask you concerning fighting in the Sacred Months (i.e. 1st, 7th, 11th and 12th months of the Islamic calendar). Say, "Fighting therein is a great (transgression) but a greater (transgression) with Allah is to prevent mankind from following the Way of Allah, to disbelieve in Him, to prevent access to Al-Masjid-al-Haram (at Makkah), and to drive out its inhabitants, and Al-Fitnah is worse than killing. And they will never cease fighting you until they turn you back from your religion (Islamic Monotheism) if they can. And whosoever of you turns back from his religion and dies as a disbeliever, then his deeds will be lost in this life and in the Hereafter, and they will be the dwellers of the Fire. They will abide therein forever." (Al-Baqara:217)

Some Muslims then enquired, "Although what they did may have been alright, they will receive no reward for it." It was then that Allah revealed the verse:

إِنَّ الَّذِينَ آمَنُوا وَالَّذِينَ هَاجَرُوا وَجَاهَدُوا فِي سَبِيلِ اللَّهِ أُولَٰئِكَ يَرْجُونَ رَحْمَةَ اللَّهِ وَاللَّهُ غَفُورٌ رَحِيمٌ (218)

Verily, those who have believed, and those who have emigrated (for Allah's Religion) and have striven hard in the Way of Allah, all these hope for Allah's Mercy. And Allah is Oft-Forgiving, Most-Merciful. (Al-Baqara:218) (Bayhaqi, Ibn Abi Hatim in Al Bidayah wan Nihayah)

Obeying the Instructions of Rasulullah ﷺ When Marching against the Banu Quraizah

Abdullah bin Omar ؓ reports that after the Battle of Ahzab, Rasulullah ﷺ issued instructions to the Sahabah saying, "None of you should perform Asr salah until he reaches the Banu Quraizah." When the time for Asr arrived while some Sahabah were still on the way, some of them said, "We should not perform Asr until we reach the Banu Quraizah." Others said, "We should perform our Salah here on the road. Rasulullah ﷺ never meant this that we should not perform the salah on the road. He meant that we should hurry." When this difference of opinion was reported to Rasulullah ﷺ, he did not rebuke either party. *(Bukhari, Muslim).* Ka'b bin Malik ؓ narrates that after the Battle of Ahzab, Rasulullah ﷺ returned home and wore his armor for a second time after taking it off and cleansed himself. A narration of Duhaim adds that Rasulullah ﷺ said, "Jibra'el عليه السلام descended from the heavens and said, 'Prepare your fighters for battle against the Banu Quraiza. Why do I see you removing your armor when we have not yet removed ours?" Rasulullah ﷺ jumped up with a fright and emphatically instructed the Sahabah not to perform their Asr salah until they reach the Banu Quraizah. The Sahabah then wore their armor and left. They had not yet reached the Banu Quraizah when the sun started to set. The Sahabah then started arguing. Some of them said, "Perform your salah because Rasulullah ﷺ never intended that you miss your salah." There were others who argued, "Rasulullah ﷺ issued emphatic orders that we should not perform our salah until we reach the Banu Quraizah. We shall not be sinful for fulfilling the implicit instruction of Rasulullah ﷺ." A group of Sahabah performed their salah en-route with perfect belief that they are doing what is right and with the hope of being rewarded. The other group performed their salah only when they set up camp in the area of the Banu Quraizah. They performed their salah after sunset with perfect belief that they are doing what is right and with the hope of being rewarded. Rasulullah ﷺ did not rebuke either party. *(Tabrani, Haythami, Bayhaqi in Al Bidayah wan Nihayah)*

Obeying the Instructions of Rasulullah ﷺ During the Battle of Hunain

Jabir ؓ narrates that during the Battle of Hunain when Rasulullah ﷺ saw the Sahabah dispersing when caught by surprise, he instructed Abbas ؓ to call for the Ansar and those who pledged allegiance beneath the tree at Hudaybiya. They all responded saying, "At your service! At your service!" In fact, even those who were unable to get their camels to turn towards the call because the camels were too frightened, threw on their armors, grabbed their swords and shields and hurried on foot towards the call. Soon 100 Sahabah had gathered around Rasulullah ﷺ, Then enemy attacked them and the fight started. While the first call had been for all the Ansar, a second was made for the Khazraj tribe in particular because they were firm in battle. Rasulullah ﷺ peered out to see his cavalry and when he saw that they were fighting in earnest, he said, "Now is the time to heat the pebbles." Jabir ؓ continues. He says, "By Allah! The Sahabah ؓ had hardly returned to the battle when the Kuffar were already defeated and prisoners were being marched to Rasulullah ﷺ. Allah killed those Kuffar who were to die and those destined to be defeated were defeated. Allah then gave all the wealth and children of the enemy to Rasulullah ﷺ as booty." *(Bayhaqi in Al Bidayah wan Nihayah).* Another narration from Abbas ؓ states that Rasulullah ﷺ instructed Abbas ؓ to call for the men of the acacia tree, those who pledged allegiance beneath the tree at Hudaybiya. Abbas ؓ says, "By Allah! When they heard my voice, they returned to Rasulullah ﷺ just as a cow returned to her calves when she senses that they are in danger. They were all calling out, *"Ya Labbaika! Ya Labbaika!* (At your service! At your service!)'" *(Muslim in Al Bidayah wan Nihayah, Ibn Sa'd)*

The Incident Between Abu Sufian ؓ and the Sahabah Concerning the Breach of the Treaty of Hudaybiya

Ikrama ؓ reports that after Rasulullah ﷺ had entered into the treaty with the people of Makkah, the Banu Khuza'ah tribe who had been Rasulullah ﷺ's allies during the period of ignorance, opted to align with the Muslims in the treaty. On the other hand, the Banu Bakr tribe aligned themselves with the Quraish. When hostilities erupted between the Banu Khuza'ah and the Banu Bakr tribes, the Quraish assisted the Banu Bakr with arms and food. The Banu Bakr then launched an offensive against the Banu Khuza'ah, overpowered them and killed many of them. The Quraish feared that they had breached the treaty and immediately said to Abu Sufian ؓ who was then their leader, "Go to Muhammad ﷺ and do your best to ensure that the treaty remains in place and that reconciliation takes place." Abu Sufian ؓ therefore left and arrived in Madinah. Rasulullah ﷺ said to the Sahabah, "Abu Sufian has come to you. He shall soon return happy but without achieving his objective." Abu Sufian ؓ went to Abu Bakr ؓ and said, "O Abu Bakr! Let the treaty remain in place and reconcile between the people." Abu Bakr ؓ replied, "The matter does not rest with me. It rests with Allah and His Rasul ﷺ." Abu Sufian ؓ then approached Omar ؓ with the same request he had placed before Abu Bakr ؓ. Omar ؓ said, "You have yourselves breached the treaty. May Allah now make any new treaty old and sever any treaty that is firm." Abu Sufian ؓ remarked, "To this day I have never seen anyone as antagonistic against his own people as you are." Abu Sufian ؓ then approached Fatima ؓ and said, "O Fatima! Do you wish to do something by which you will become the leader of the women of your tribe?" He then placed to her the same request he placed before Abu Bakr ؓ. She however made herself clear when she said, "The matter does not rest with me. It rests with Allah and

His Rasul ﷺ." Abu Sufian ؓ then approached Ali ؓ with the same request that he took to Abu Bakr ؓ. Ali ؓ said, "To this day I have never seen anyone as lost as you are. You are the leader of your people. You should go and keep the treaty intact by not allowing the people to breach it and reconcile between the people." Abu Sufian ؓ hit his one hand on the other and said, "I have already given some of the people protection from others." He then left and when he came to the people of Makkah, he informed them of what he had done. They said, "By Allah! To this day we have never seen an ambassador like you! By Allah! Neither have you come to us with news of a war so that we could take precautions nor have you brought news of a treaty so that we could feel safe." The rest of the narration has already been quoted in the chapter discussing the conquest of Makkah. *(Ibn Abi Shayba in Muntakhab Kanzul Ummal)*

How the Sahabah Treated the Captives of Badr

Abu Aziz bin Umair ؓ who was the real brother of Mus'ab bin Umair ؓ says, "I was amongst the prisoners captured by the Muslims during the Battle of Badr. Rasulullah ﷺ said to the Sahabah, "I emphatically command you to treat the prisoners well." I was with a group of Ansar and whenever the morning and afternoon meals were served; they ate dates only and gave me the wheat bread because of the instruction of Rasulullah ﷺ to treat us prisoners well." *(Tabrani in Kabeer and Sagheer, Haythami)*

The Incident of Abdullah bin Rawaha ؓ When he Hastened to Fulfill the Command of Rasulullah ﷺ

Abdur Rahman bin Abu Laila ؓ reports that Abdullah bin Rawaha ؓ once came to Rasulullah ﷺ at a time when Rasulullah ﷺ was delivering a sermon. "Do sit down," said Rasulullah ﷺ during the course of his sermon. Abdullah bin Rawaha ؓ immediately sat down where he was outside the Masjid and remained seated there until Rasulullah ﷺ had completed the sermon. When this was reported to Rasulullah ﷺ, he said to Abdullah bin Rawaha ؓ, "May Allah increase your desire to obey Allah and His Rasul ﷺ." *(Ibn Asakir in Kanzul Ummal, Bayhaqi, Isabah).* Aisha ؓ narrates that when Rasulullah ﷺ sat down on the pulpit one Friday, he said, "Do be seated." Abdullah bin Rawaha ؓ heard the instruction of Rasulullah ﷺ and sat down in the Banu Ghanam district. Someone reported to Rasulullah ﷺ, "O Rasulullah ﷺ! There is Ibn Rawaha who sat down where he was when he heard you tell the people to be seated." *(Ibn Asakir in Kanzul Ummal, Tabrani in Awsat, Haythami, Isabah)*

Abdullah bin Mas'ood ؓ Obeys the Command of Rasulullah ﷺ

Ata ؓ reports that Rasulullah ﷺ was once delivering a sermon when he told the people to be seated. Abdullah bin Mas'ood ؓ heard this instruction at the door and immediately sat down. Rasulullah ﷺ then said, "O Abdullah! You may come inside." *(Ibn Abi Shaybah in Kanzul Ummal).* Jabir ؓ reports that Rasulullah ﷺ had just stood up on the pulpit when he told the people to be seated. Abdullah bin Mas'ood ؓ heard this instruction and immediately sat down at the door of the Masjid. When Rasulullah ﷺ saw him, he said, "Come in, O Abdullah bin Mas'ood." *(Ibn Asakir in Kanzul Ummal)*

A Dome is Demolished Because Rasulullah ﷺ Disliked It

Anas ؓ narrates that they were once with Rasulullah ﷺ when he stepped out. Seeing a large dome, Rasulullah ﷺ asked, "What is this?" When the Sahabah informed him that it belonged to one of the Ansar, Rasulullah ﷺ remained silent but kept it in mind. When the owner of the dome one day came to greet Rasulullah ﷺ amongst other people, Rasulullah ﷺ turned away from him. When this occurred several times, the man realized that Rasulullah ﷺ was angry and ignoring him. The man, brought up the matter with his friends saying, "By Allah! Rasulullah ﷺ has behaved strangely today." The others then told him that Rasulullah ﷺ was angry with him because he had seen his dome. The Sahabi then went out and demolished the dome to the ground. On another day, Rasulullah ﷺ again went out but did not see the dome. When he asked the Sahabah what had happened to it, they replied, "When the owner informed us that you had ignored him and we told him what the reason was, he demolished it." Rasulullah ﷺ then remarked, "Take note! Every building is a curse for its owner except what is absolutely necessary." *(Abu Dawud)*. Ibn Majah states that when Rasulullah ﷺ did not see the dome and asked about it, he was informed that the owner had demolished it because he had heard that Rasulullah ﷺ was displeased. Rasulullah ﷺ then prayed, "May Allah shower His mercies on him. May Allah shower His mercies on him."

Burning a Red Shawl Because Rasulullah ﷺ Disliked It

Abdullah bin Amr bin Al Aas ﷺ narrates that he was once wearing a red shawl when he was walking with Rasulullah ﷺ in Aqaba Adhakhir, a valley between Makkah and Madinah. Turning to him, Rasulullah ﷺ asked, "What is this garment?" Realizing that Rasulullah ﷺ disliked it, Abdullah ﷺ went to his camp where the oven was being lit and threw the shawl into the oven. When he returned, Rasulullah ﷺ asked him what had happened to the shawl. "I threw it in the oven," Abdullah ﷺ replied Rasulullah ﷺ said, "You could have given it to one of the ladies of your household." *(Dowlabi in Kuna)*

Khuraim ﷺ Cuts His Long Hair and Lifts His Lower Garment

Sahl bin Hadhaliya Abshami ﷺ narrates that Rasulullah ﷺ once said to him, "Khuraim Asadi is an excellent man if it were not for his long hair and his garment hanging below his ankles." When this statement reached Khuraim ﷺ, he immediately cut his hair up to the middle of his ears and raised his lower garment up to the middle of his calves. *(Ahmad, Bukhari in Tarikh, Ibn Asakir in Kanzul Ummal)*

Kanani ﷺ Gets Off a Golden Throne in Obedience to the command of Rasulullah ﷺ

Juthama bin Musahiq bin Rabi bin Qais Kanani ﷺ was Omar ﷺ's envoy to Heraclius, the emperor of Rome. He says, "I once sat on a throne when visiting Heraclius not knowing what it was. When I discovered that is was made of gold, I immediately got off. Heraclius laughed and said to me, 'Why did you get off that throne that we have honored you with?' I replied, 'Because I heard Rasulullah ﷺ forbid us from using such things.'" *(Abu Nu'aym in Kanzul Ummal, Ibn Mandah in Isabah)*

The Narration of Rafi bin Khadij ﷺ

Rafi bin Khadij ﷺ says, "My uncle came home one day and said to me, 'Today Rasulullah ﷺ had forbidden us from something that has been very beneficial for you. However, obedience to Allah and His Rasulullah ﷺ is even more beneficial for you...'" The rest of the narration concerns hiring out property. *(Abdur Razzaq in Kanzul Ummal)*

The Incident of Muhammad bin Aslam ﷺ

Muhammad bin Aslam bin Bujra ﷺ belonged to the Banu Harith bin Khazraj tribe and was a very old man. He reports about himself that he would often come to Madinah from his village nearby and then return home after doing what he needed to do at the marketplace. It was only after taking off his shawl after returning home that he would remember that he had not performed 2 Rakahs salah in the Masjid of Rasulullah ﷺ. He would say, "By Allah! I have not performed 2 Rakahs salah in the Masjid of Rasulullah ﷺ as Rasulullah ﷺ told the inhabitants of the nearby villages, 'Whichever of you comes to this town Madinah should never return home until he has performed 2 Rakahs salah in this Masjid of mine.' He would put on his shawl on and return to Madinah to perform the 2 Rakahs salah in the Masjid of Rasulullah ﷺ. *(Hasan bin Sufian, Abu Nu'aym in his Ma'rfa, Kanzul Ummal, Tabrani, Ibn Mandah, Isaaba)*.

The Incident of Fata ﷺ a Lady From the Ansar

Mughiera bin Shu'ba ﷺ reports, "I once proposed for the hand of a lady from the Ansar. When I mentioned this to Rasulullah ﷺ, he asked, 'Did you see her?' When I informed him that I did not, he said, 'See her because it contributes towards love developing between the 2 of you.' I then went to her home and when I mentioned this to her parents, they just stared at each other. I then got up and left. The lady then sent for me and stood in the corner of her veiled room as she said, 'If Rasulullah ﷺ had commanded you to see me, then you may look, otherwise you have no permission to do so.' I then looked at her and we were later married. I have never married a woman whom I loved as much as her and whom I respected as much as her, although I have married 70 women." *(Sa'eed bin Mansoor, Ibn Najjar in Kanzul Ummal)*

Abu Dhar ﷺ fulfils the command of Rasulullah ﷺ

Ma'roor bin Suwaid reports that he once saw Abu Dhar ﷺ in Rabdha. Abu Dhar ﷺ was wearing a thick shawl and his slave was wearing exactly the same thing. Some people suggested to him, "O Abu Dhar! Why don't you take your slave's shawl and make up for yourself a complete set of clothing. You may then always give your slave something else to wear." Abu Dhar ﷺ explained, "I once used bad language for Bilal ﷺ and because his mother was not an Arab, I also teased him for it." When he complained about me to Rasulullah ﷺ, Rasulullah ﷺ said, 'O Abu Dhar! You are a man who still has ignorance left in you. They (slaves) are your brothers over whom Allah has given you some superiority. You should sell those of them who do not suit you and never punish the creation of Allah." *(Abu Dawud)*. Another narration states that Rasulullah ﷺ said to Abu Dhar ﷺ, "They are your brothers whom Allah has placed in your custody. When Allah has placed someone's brother in his custody, he should feed him what he eats, clothe him with what he wears and should not give him more work than he can bear. If he has to give him more work than he can manage, he the master should assist." *(Bukhari, Muslim, Tirmidhi in Targheeb wat Tarheeb, Bayhaqi, Ibn Sa'd)*

The Incident Between Omar ﷺ and Abdur Rahman bin Auf ﷺ

Abu Salama bin Abdur Rahman narrates that Abdur Rahman bin Auf ﷺ once complained to Rasulullah ﷺ that he was getting too much of lice and therefore requested permission to wear silk garments. Rasulullah ﷺ granted him permission. After the demise of Rasulullah ﷺ and Abu Bakr ﷺ, Omar ﷺ was the Khalifa when Abdur Rahman bin Auf ﷺ once came to him with his son Abu Salma. Because Abu Salama was wearing a silk garment, Omar ﷺ asked, "What is this?" and then promptly put his finger into the collar and tore the garment right to the bottom. Abdur

Rahman bin Auf 🌸 protested, "Don't you know that Rasulullah 🌺 allowed me to wear silk?" Omar 🌸 said, "He only permitted you because you complained of lice. It is however not permitted for others besides you." *(Ibn Sa'd)*. Abu Salama states that Abdur Rahman bin Auf 🌸 once went to Omar 🌸 with his son Muhammad who was wearing a silk garment. Omar 🌸 stood up, caught hold of the collar of the garment and tore it. "May Allah forgive you!" protested Abdur Rahman bin Auf 🌸, "You have frightened the boy and set his heart racing." Omar 🌸 asked, "Do you allow them to wear clothes of silk'?" "But I wear silk," explained Abdur Rahman bin Auf 🌸. "Are they at all like you (do they have the same complaint)?" Omar 🌸 challenged. *(Ibn Uyaynah in Jaami, Musaddad, Ibn Jareer in Kanzul Ummal)*

Tearing Garments of Khalid bin Walid 🌸 and Khalid bin Sa'eed 🌸

Ibn Sirin reports that Khalid bin Walid 🌸 once went to Omar 🌸 wearing a silk garment. "What is this, O Khalid'?" enquired Omar 🌸. "What is wrong with it, O Amirul Mu'minin'?" Khalid 🌸 asked, "Does lbn Auf not wear this'?" Omar 🌸 replied, "Are you at all like Ibn Auf 🌸 and do have the problem he has? In the name of Allah do I entreat every person in this room to grab hold of that part of the garment closest to him and to tear it until nothing is left of it." *(Ibn Asakir in Kanzul Ummal)*. The narration has already passed in the chapter entitled "The Sahabah place Abu Bakr 🌸 ahead for Khilafa" that Khalid bin Sa'eed bin Aas 🌸 was in Yemen when Rasulullah 🌺 passed away. He arrived Madinah a month after Rasulullah 🌺's demise wearing a cloak. When he met Omar 🌸 and Ali 🌸, Omar 🌸 called out to the people, "Tear up his cloak! How can he wear silk when he is a Muslim man in times of peace?" The people then tore his cloak up. *(Tabari, Saif, Ibn Asakir)*

Omar 🌸 Cuts Off Silk Buttons From a Garment

Abdah bin Abu Lubaba reports that he was informed that Omar 🌸 once passed a person in the Masjid. The man was performing salah and wearing a green garment that had buttons of silk. Standing by his side, Omar 🌸 said, "Lengthen your salah as much as you please but I shall remain here until you complete." When he saw that the man had turned towards him (after the salah), Omar 🌸 said, "Show me your garment." Omar 🌸 then took the garment and cut off all the silk buttons before giving it back to the man. *(Ibn Jareer in Kanzul Ummal)*

Ali 🌸 Pulls Off the Cloak of Sa'eed Qari to Tear It Up

Sa'eed bin Sufian Qari says, "When my brother passed away, he made a bequest that 100 Dinars should be donated in the Path of Allah. I therefore went to Uthman 🌸 to find out what to do wearing a cloak, the collar and hem of which was decorated with silk. When I got there, Uthman 🌸 had a man sitting with him. When the man saw me, he came up to me and started pulling at my cloak so that he could tear it up. Seeing this, Uthman 🌸 told him to leave me alone and he did. Uthman 🌸 then said, 'You people have been too quick to start wearing silk.' I then proceeded to ask Uthman 🌸, 'O Amirul Mu'minin! My brother has passed away and made a bequest that 100 Dinars should be donated in the Path of Allah. What do you instruct me to do?' 'Have you asked anyone else before coming to me?' enquired Uthman 🌸. When I replied that I did not, he said, 'Had you been to seek a ruling from anyone else before coming to me and if he had passed a ruling other than what I shall pass, I would have had you executed for asking an ignorant person. When Allah commanded us to accept Islam, we all did so and by Allah's grace are all Muslims. Allah then commanded us to make Hijra so we

made Hijra and are all Muhajirin and residents of Madinah. Allah then commanded Jihad and when you people waged Jihad, you became Mujahidin and residents of Sham. Spend the money on yourself, on your family and on the needy ones around your relatives and neighbors. If you take a Dirham and buy some meat for yourself and your family to eat when necessary, you will have the reward of 700 Dirhams recorded to your name.' I then left him. When I made enquiries about the man who was wrestling my cloak from me, I was informed that he was Ali Abi Talib 🌸. I then visited him at his home and asked him what he saw me do wrong. He replied, 'I heard Rasulullah 🌺 say, 'It will not be long before my Ummah legalizes for themselves fornication and silk.' This is the first time that I have seen silk being worn by any Muslim.' I then left him and proceeded to sell the cloak." *(Ibn Asakir in Kanzul Ummal)*

Omar 🌸 Lashes His Governor Qudama 🌸 Who was the Maternal Uncle of Hafsah 🌸

Abdullah bin Amir bin Rabe'ah narrates that Omar 🌸 appointed Qudama bin Madh'un 🌸 as governor of Bahrain. Qudama 🌸 also happened to be the maternal uncle of Omar 🌸's 2 children Hafsa 🌸 and Abdullah 🌸. It then occurred that Jarud 🌸 who was the leader of the Abd Qais tribe one day arrived from Bahrain and went to Omar 🌸. He said, "O Amirul Mu'minin! Qudama drank something and was intoxicated. Because I have seen something that deserves the penalty of Allah, it is my duty to report it to you." "Who is there to testify with you?" enquired Omar 🌸. When Jarud 🌸 replied that Abu Hurairah 🌸 was also a witness, Omar 🌸 sent for him. "What have you seen?" Omar 🌸 asked Abu Hurairah 🌸. Abu Hurairah 🌸 replied, "Although I did not actually see him drink anything, I did see him in a state of intoxication and vomiting." Omar 🌸 remarked, "You are very precise in your testimony." Omar 🌸 then wrote to Qudama 🌸 to come to him from Bahrain. When Qudama 🌸 arrived, Jarud 🌸 said, "Enforce Allah's penalty on him." "Are you a plaintiff or a witness?" Omar 🌸 asked. "I am a witness," Jarud 🌸 replied. "Then you have already rendered your affidavit." Omar 🌸 reminded him. Jarud kept quiet but returned to Omar 🌸 the next morning to demand that the penalty be enforced. Omar 🌸 said to him, "To me you seem to be a plaintiff and have but only one witness." "I am then telling you to enforce the penalty in the name of Allah!" Omar 🌸 cautioned him saying, "Do control your tongue before I have to punish you!" Jarud 🌸 commented, "O Omar! It is wrong for you to punish me when it is your cousin who has drunk wine." Abu Hurairah 🌸 then spoke saying, "O Amirul Mu'minin! If you doubt our testimony, send for the daughter of Walid and ask her. She is Qudama's wife." Omar 🌸 then sent for Hind bint Walid and asked her to testify in the name of Allah. When she testified against her husband, Omar 🌸 said to Qudama 🌸, "I will be having you lashed." "If I did drink you claim," Qudama 🌸 argued, "you have no right to have me lashed." "Why is that?" asked Omar 🌸. Qudama 🌸 replied, because Allah states:

لَيْسَ عَلَى الَّذِينَ آمَنُوا وَعَمِلُوا الصَّالِحَاتِ جُنَاحٌ فِيمَا طَعِمُوا إِذَا مَا اتَّقَوْا وَآمَنُوا وَعَمِلُوا الصَّالِحَاتِ ثُمَّ اتَّقَوْا وَآمَنُوا ثُمَّ اتَّقَوْا وَأَحْسَنُوا وَاللَّهُ يُحِبُّ الْمُحْسِنِينَ (93)

Those who believe and do righteous good deeds, there is no sin on them for what they ate (in the past), if they fear Allah (by keeping away from His forbidden things), and believe and do righteous good deeds, and again fear Allah and believe, and once again fear Allah and do good deeds with Ihsan (perfection). And Allah loves the good-doers. (Al-Ma'idah:93)

Omar 🌸 said to him, "You have misinterpreted the verse.

Had you adopted Taqwa, you would have refrained from that which Allah has forbidden." Omar ✿ then turned to the people and asked, "What do you say about having Qudama lashed?" The people replied, "We think that he should not be lashed as long as he is ill." Omar ✿ then let the matter rest until after a few days when he renewed his resolve to have Qudama ✿ lashed. Again he asked the people, "What do you say about having Qudama lashed?" The people replied, "We think that he should not be lashed as long as he is ill." This time, Omar ✿ said, "I prefer that he meets Allah beneath the lash rather than me meeting Allah with the responsibility of lashing him still on my shoulders. Bring me a strong whip." When the whip was brought, Omar ✿ gave the instruction and Qudama ✿ was lashed. Omar ✿ was then angry with Qudama ✿ and broke off ties with him. Omar ✿ and Qudama ✿ later both performed Hajj while Omar ✿ was still angry with Qudama ✿. They were both returning from the Hajj, Omar ✿ camped at a place called Suqia, where he fell asleep. When he awoke from his sleep, he said, "Bring Qudama to me quickly. By Allah! Someone came to me in my dream saying, 'Reconcile with Qudama ✿ because he is your brother.' Bring him to me quickly." The people went to Qudama ✿, he refused to go. Omar ✿ instructed them to bring him by force. When he arrived, Omar ✿ spoke to him and sought Allah's forgiveness for him. *(Abdur Razzaq, Abu Ali bin Sakan in Kanzul Ummal)*

Abdullah bin Mas'ood ✿ Rebukes Someone Laughing During a Funeral

Yazid bin Ubaidullah reports from some of his companions that Abdullah bin Mas'ood ✿ once saw a man laughing at a funeral. Abdullah bin Mas'ood ✿ said to him, "Are you laughing while you are at a funeral? By Allah! I shall never speak to you again." *(Bayhaqi in Kanzul Ummal)*

Abu Hudhaifa ✿ Fears Something he said During the Battle of Badr

Abdullah bin Abbas ✿ narrates that on the day the Battle of Badr was fought, Rasulullah ﷺ said to the Sahabah, "I know well that the men from the Banu Hashim were forced to march and have no desire to fight against us. Whoever confronts anyone from the Banu Hashim should not kill him. Whoever confronts Abul Bakhtari bin Hisham bin Harith bin Asad should not kill him and whoever of you confronts Abbas bin Abdul Muttalib the uncle of Rasulullah ﷺ should also not kill him because he had been forced to fight." Abu Hudhaifa bin Utba bin Rabe'ah ✿ said, "Should we kill our fathers, our sons and our brothers and leave Abbas? By Allah! If I happen to confront Abbas, I shall cut him to pieces with my sword." When this reached Rasulullah ﷺ, he asked Omar ✿, "O Abu Hafs!" Omar ✿ says, "By Allah! This was the first time that Rasulullah ﷺ ever called me by the title of Abu Hafs" "Will the face of Rasulullah ﷺ's uncle be smitten with a sword?" Omar ✿ burst out, "O Rasulullah ﷺ! Permit me to behead Abu Hudhaifa! By Allah! He has certainly turned hypocrite!" Abu Hudhaifa ✿ says, "I have never felt safe from those words I uttered that day. I am always fearful of their repercussions unless martyrdom washes its effects off." Abu Hudhaifa ✿ was martyred during the Battle of Yamamah. *(Ibn Is'haq in Al Bidayah wan Nihayah, Ibn Sa'd, Hakim)*

Abu Lubaba Fears That he Betrayed Rasulullah ﷺ and Repents

Ma'bad bin Ka'b reports that the Muslims laid siege to the Jewish Banu Quraizah tribe for 15 days until the siege became too much for them to bear and Allah cast fear into their hearts. Eventually their chief Ka'b bin Asad proposed to them that they either accept Iman, launch a surprise attack that Saturday or kill their women and children and then go out to fight so that they would have nothing to lose. However, they said, "We shall never accept Iman, never violate the sanctity of the Saturday and what life will there be for us without our women and children?" They then called for Abu Lubaba bin Mundhir ✿ who had been one of their allies during the period of ignorance. When they conferred with him about surrendering to the command of Rasulullah ﷺ, he passed his finger across his throat to indicate that they would all be killed. Thereafter, Abu Lubaba ✿ bitterly regretted what he did and headed for the Masjid of Rasulullah ﷺ where he tied himself to a pillar until Allah accepted his repentance. *(Ibn Is'haq in Fat'hul Bari)*. Another narration from Musa bin Uqba states that the Banu Quraizah asked, "O Abu Lubaba! What is your opinion? What would you instruct us to do because we have no strength to fight?" Abu Lubaba ✿ passed his finger across his throat to indicate to them that they were to be executed. However, when Abu Lubaba ✿ left them, he deeply regretted his action and felt that a great tribulation had befallen him. He said, "By Allah! I shall never be able to look Rasulullah ﷺ in the face until I repent to Allah so sincerely that He may tell others that it is from deep within me." He then returned to Madinah where he bound his hands to a pillar of the Masjid. It is believed that he kept himself bound for close to 20 days. When Rasulullah ﷺ did not see Abu Lubaba ✿ after the Jews had called on him, he asked, "Has Abu Lubaba not finished with his allies'?" When the incident was related to Rasulullah ﷺ, he said, "A great trial has certainly afflicted him after he left me. Had he come to me after making the mistake, I would have sought Allah's forgiveness for him. However, since he has already done what he did by tying himself to the pillar, I shall not move him from there until Allah decides the matter as He pleases." *(Al Bidayah wan Nihayah)*

The Fear of Thabit bin Qais ✿ and the Glad Tidings Rasulullah ﷺ Gave Him

Anas bin Malik ✿ narrates that when Rasulullah ﷺ did not see Thabit bin Qais ✿ for awhile, a Sahabi volunteered to make enquiries about him. When the Sahabi came to Thabit bin Qais ✿, he found him sitting in his house with head bent down. "What's the matter'!" he asked. "Bad," replied Thabit ✿, "because I raise my voice above that of Rasulullah ﷺ, all my deeds are destroyed and I am amongst the inmates of Jahannam." This he felt because of a verse of the Qur'an referring to people who deliberately raise their voices above that of Rasulullah ﷺ. The Sahabi then reported back to Rasulullah ﷺ. Musa bin Anas reports that the Sahabi returned a 2nd time to Thabit bin Qais ✿ with glad tidings from Rasulullah ﷺ. Rasulullah ﷺ instructed the Sahabi to inform Thabit ✿ that far from being an inmate of Jahannam, he will be amongst the inhabitants of Jannah. *(Bukhari)*. The daughter of Thabit bin Qais bin Shammas ✿ narrates from her father that he became extremely worried when he heard the verse: اِنَّ اللّٰهَ لَا يُحِبُّ كُلَّ مُخْتَالٍ فَخُورٍ (18)

.....Verily Allah likes not any arrogant boaster. (Luqman:18)

He then locked himself in his house and started to weep. When Rasulullah ﷺ was informed about this, Rasulullah ﷺ called for him and he explained to Rasulullah ﷺ what it was that worried him. He said, "I am a man who loves beauty and to be the leader of my people." Rasulullah ﷺ reassured him saying, "You are not amongst those arrogant and boastful people. Your life shall be good, your death shall be good and Allah shall enter you into Jannah." Thabit ✿ then did the same thing when Allah revealed the verse:

يَا أَيُّهَا الَّذِينَ آمَنُوا لَا تَرْفَعُوا أَصْوَاتَكُمْ فَوْقَ صَوْتِ النَّبِيِّ وَلَا تَجْهَرُوا لَهُ بِالْقَوْلِ كَجَهْرِ بَعْضِكُمْ

O you who believe! Raise not your voices above the voice of the Prophet (ﷺ), nor speak aloud to him in talk as you speak aloud to one another, lest your deeds may be rendered fruitless while you perceive not. (Al-Hujurat:2)

When Rasulullah ﷺ was informed about this, Rasulullah ﷺ again called for him and he explained to Rasulullah ﷺ what it was that worried him. He explained that he naturally had a loud voice and feared that his deeds should not be laid to waste. Rasulullah ﷺ again consoled him by saying, "In fact, you shall live a praiseworthy life, be killed as a martyr and Allah shall enter you into Jannah." *(Tabrani, Haythami, Hakim)*. Muhammad bin Thabit Ansari ؓ reports that Thabit bin Qais ؓ once said to Rasulullah ﷺ, "O Rasulullah ﷺ! I fear that I have been destroyed." When Rasulullah ﷺ asked him why he felt that way, he explained, "Whereas Allah has prohibited us from liking to be praised for what we do not do, I seem to enjoy praise. Furthermore, whereas Allah has prohibited us from pride, I find myself liking beauty and whereas Allah has prohibited us from raising our voices above yours, I am a person with a loud voice." Rasulullah ﷺ said, "O Thabit! Would you not like to live a praiseworthy life, to be killed as a martyr and to enter Jannah?" "Certainly, O Rasulullah ﷺ!" Thabit ؓ responded. It happened that Thabit ؓ lived a praiseworthy life and was killed as a martyr the day the Muslims fought Musailama Kadhab. *(Hakim)*

The Sahabah follow Rasulullah ﷺ in Salah

Aisha ؓ narrates that Rasulullah ﷺ had a mat that he made into a room at nights to perform salah during Ramadhan and which he spread out during the day to sit on. The Sahabah then started flocking to Rasulullah ﷺ and performing salah with him. When there were too many people, Rasulullah ﷺ turned to them and said, "O people! Adopt those actions that you are capable of carrying out with consistency because Allah never tires of giving rewards until you tire yourselves. Indeed the most beloved deeds to Allah are those that are consistent even though they may be little." Another narration adds that whenever the family and close ones of Muhammad ﷺ started anything, they did it with consistency. *(Bukhari, Muslim in Targheeb wat Tarheeb)*

The Sahabah Remove Their Rings Because Rasulullah ﷺ Did

Anas bin Malik ؓ reports that it was for only a single day that he saw Rasulullah ﷺ wearing a silver ring when the Sahabah started having rings made for themselves and wearing it. When Rasulullah ﷺ discarded his ring, the Sahabah did the same. *(Abu Dawud, Bukhari)*. Another narration from Abdullah bin Omar ؓ states that Rasulullah ﷺ wore a gold ring but then discarded it saying, "I shall never wear it again!" The Sahabah then discarded their rings. *(Bukhari, Muslim in Al Bidayah wan Nihayah)*

Uthman ؓ Emulates Rasulullah ﷺ

Salamah ؓ narrates that when the Quraish sent Kharijah bin Kurz to spy for them, he returned full of praise for the Muslims. The Quraish said to him, "You are a Bedouin. All they had to do to make your heart flutter with fear was to shake their weapons. You have no idea about what they said nor about what you are saying." They then sent Urwa bin Mas'ood ؓ. When Urwa ؓ came to the Muslim camp, he said "O Muhammad! What is this new development? You invite towards the Being of Allah and then defame various tribes some of whom you know and others you do not know, you come to your own people to severe family ties and to plunder their honor, their blood and their wealth?"

Rasulullah ﷺ replied, "I have come to my people only to foster family ties and to give them Islam and life better than their religion and their lives." Urwa ؓ then also returned full of praise. However, the suffering of the Muslims living under the disbeliever in Makkah grew more intense. Rasulullah ﷺ therefore called for Omar ؓ and said, "O Omar! Will you go to Makkah to convey my message to your Muslim brothers who are prisoners?" "I am unable to do so, O Rasulullah ﷺ," Omar ؓ said, "for I have no family in Makkah to offer me protection. There are others who have more family in Makkah than I have." Rasulullah ﷺ then summoned Uthman ؓ and sent him. Uthman ؓ proceeded on his conveyance and was intercepted by some disbelieving soldiers who mocked him and addressed him with insulting words. It was then Uthman ؓ's cousin Aban bin Sa'eed bin Al Aas ؓ who took Uthman ؓ in his custody and made him ride behind him on his saddle. Uthman ؓ went with him wearing his lower garment halfway up his calves. Aban asked, "Dear cousin! Why do I see you humble yourself so much? Lower your garment." Uthman ؓ replied, "Such is the garment of our leader." Uthman ؓ then proceeded to convey Rasulullah ﷺ's message to every Muslim prisoner in Makkah. It was while the Muslims were asleep during the afternoon in Hudaybiya that they heard Rasulullah ﷺ's announcer call out, "O people! Come pledge your allegiance! Come pledge your allegiance! The Ruhul Qudus Jibra'el has descended!" The Sahabah hastened to Rasulullah ﷺ who was beneath an acacia tree, where they pledged their allegiance to fight to the death. It is with reference to this that Allah says: لَقَدْ رَضِيَ اللَّهُ عَنِ الْمُؤْمِنِينَ إِذْ يُبَايِعُونَكَ تَحْتَ الشَّجَرَةِ

Indeed, Allah was pleased with the believers when they gave their Baia (pledge) to you (O Muhammad ﷺ) under the tree,..." (Al-Fatah:18)

Rasulullah ﷺ pledged allegiance on behalf of Uthman ؓ by placing his one hand over the other. The Sahabah said, "How fortunate for Abu Abdullah Uthman ؓ that he is able to perform Tawaf of the Kabah while we are here." Rasulullah ﷺ remarked, "Even if he had to remain there for years on end, he would not perform Tawaf until I have performed Tawaf." *(Ibn Abi Shaybah in Kanzul Ummal, Royani, Abu Ya'la, Ibn Asakir)*. Another narration states that Aban said, "Dear cousin! I see that you are humbling yourself. Why do you not let your garment fall below your ankles as your tribe does?" Uthman ؓ replied, "This is how our leader wear his lower garment, halfway up his calves." Aban then said, "Dear cousin! Perform Tawaf of the Kabah." Uthman ؓ plied, "We do nothing until our guide does it and then we follow in his footsteps." *(Ibn Sa'd)*

The Incident Between Abu Bakr ؓ, Omar ؓ and Zaid ؓ Concerning the Compilation of the Qur'an

Zaid bin Thabit ؓ reports that Abu Bakr ؓ once sent for him after the Battle of Yam'amah. Abu Bakr ؓ at the time was with Omar ؓ. Abu Bakr ؓ said to Zaid ؓ, "He (Omar ؓ) has come and said, 'Many Huffadh of the Qur'an have been martyred in this battle of Yamamah (700 out of 1400 were Huffadh) and I fear that if all the other battles also take a heavy toll on the Huffadh, the Qur'an should not leave us. I have therefore decided that you should compile the Qur'an into a single manuscript.' 'How can we attempt to do something that Rasulullah ﷺ never did?' I asked him. 'But it is an excellent thing,' he replied Omar ؓ then continued convincing me until Allah put my heart at ease about the matter just as his heart was at ease. I now share Omar's opinion on the matter." Zaid ؓ narrates further, "Omar ؓ was sitting there without saying a word. Abu Bakr ؓ then continued,

'You are young and intelligent and we have no accusations to 1evel against you. Furthermore, you used to write down the Qur'an during the time of Rasulullah ﷺ. You should therefore do the compilation.'" Zaid ؓ says, "By Allah had they charged me with moving a mountain, it would not have been more difficult than the instruction to collect the Qur'an into one manuscript. I said, 'How can you do something that Rasulullah ﷺ never did?' 'By Allah!' said Abu Bakr ؓ 'the act is an excellent one.' Abu Bakr ؓ then continued convincing me until Allah put my heart at ease about the matter just as the hearts of Abu Bakr ؓ and Omar ؓ were at ease. I then shared their opinion on the matter. I then launched an intensive search for parts of the Qur'an that had been preserved on paper, white stones, collar bones, palm leaves and the hearts of men. It was only with Khuzaima bin Thabit Ansari that I could find in writing the closing verses of Surah Bara'ah:

$$ لَقَدْ جَاءَكُمْ رَسُولٌ مِنْ أَنْفُسِكُمْ عَزِيزٌ عَلَيْهِ مَا عَنِتُّمْ حَرِيصٌ عَلَيْكُمْ بِالْمُؤْمِنِينَ رَءُوفٌ رَحِيمٌ (128) فَإِنْ تَوَلَّوْا فَقُلْ حَسْبِيَ اللَّهُ لَا إِلَهَ إِلَّا هُوَ عَلَيْهِ تَوَكَّلْتُ وَهُوَ رَبُّ الْعَرْشِ الْعَظِيمِ (129) $$

Verily, there has come unto you a Messenger (Muhammad ﷺ) from amongst yourselves (i.e. whom you know well). It grieves him that you should receive any injury or difficulty. He (Muhammad SAW) is anxious over you (to be rightly guided, to repent to Allah, and beg Him to pardon and forgive your sins, in order that you may enter Paradise and be saved from the punishment of the Hell-fire), for the believers (he SAW is) full of pity, kind, and merciful. But if they turn away, say (O Muhammad ﷺ): "Allah is sufficient for me. La ilaha illa Huwa (none has the right to be worshipped but He), in Him I put my trust and He is the Lord of the Mighty Throne." (At-Tauba:128-129). The manuscript of the complete collected Qur'an remained with Abu Bakr ؓ throughout his life until he passed away. It then remained with Omar ؓ throughout his life until he passed away. Thereafter, it remained with Hafsa ؓ the daughter of Omar ؓ. *(Tayalisi, Ibn Sa'd, Ahmad, Bukhari Tirmidhi, Nasa'ee, Ibn Hibban in Kanzul Ummal)*

Abu Bakr ؓ Dispatches the army of Usama bin Zaid ؓ

The statement of Abu Bakr ؓ has already passed in which he said, "I swear by the Being Who controls my life! I prefer falling from the sky rather than neglecting to fight for something for which Rasulullah ﷺ fought." Abu Bakr ؓ then waged Jihad against the Arabs who had renounced Islam and those who refused to pay zakah. *(Adani)*. Another narration states that Abu Bakr ؓ said, "By Allah! I shall certainly fight those who differentiate between salah and zakah by performing Salat while omitting zakah because zakah is a right due from wealth. By Allah! Should they refuse to give me as part of the zakah dues even a rope that they used to give to Rasulullah ﷺ, I shall fight them for it." *(Bukhari, Muslim, Ahmad)*. Another narration has also passed in which Abu Bakr ؓ said, "I swear by the Being besides Whom there is none worthy of worship! Even though wild dogs should drag the legs of the wives of Rasulullah ﷺ because there is none in Madinah to defend them, I shall never recall an army that Rasulullah ﷺ had dispatched nor untie a flag that Rasulullah ﷺ had tied," He then dispatched the army of Usama ؓ. *(Bayhaqi)*. Yet another narration states that Abu Bakr ؓ said, "I wear by the Being Who controls the life of Abu Bakr! Even if I knew that wild animals would tear at my body as a result, I would still dispatch the army of Usama according to the commands of Rasulullah ﷺ. I would do so even if 1 were to be the only person left behind in Madinah." *(Saif)*. Another narration from Urwa ؓ quotes that Abu Bakr ؓ said, "I have

dared to do something extremely dangerous! I swear by the Being Who controls my life! I prefer having all the Arabs turn against me rather than holding back an army that Rasulullah ﷺ had dispatched. O Usama! Proceed whence you have been commanded to march and then fight in the parts of Palestine and against the people at Mu'ta as Rasulullah ﷺ had commanded you. Remember that Allah is enough for those you are leaving behind." *(Ibn Asakir)*. Hasan reports that Abu Bakr ؓ caught hold of the beard of Omar ؓ as he said, "May your mother lose you, O son of Khattab! You are asking me to relieve Usama ؓ of a post to which Rasulullah ﷺ appointed him?!" This narration has already been quoted in detail.

The Incident Between Omar ؓ and His Daughter Hafsa ؓ Concerning Clothing and Food

Sa'd bin Abi Waqqas ؓ reports that Hafsa ؓ once said to her father Omar ؓ, "O Amirul Mu'minin! Why don't you wear clothing of a better quality than those you wear and eat food that is better than the food you eat? Allah has now made food abundant and increased our wealth." Omar ؓ replied, "I shall have you prove the point against yourself. Do you recall the hard life that Rasulullah ﷺ lived?" He then continued reminding her of Rasulullah ﷺ's hard life until he made her weep. He then said, "By Allah! Now that you have admitted to the hard lives that Rasulullah ﷺ and Abu Bakr ؓ led, I wish to share their hard lives with them as far as I am able to. In this way I shall perhaps be able to join them in their lives of ease and comfort in the Hereafter." *(Abu Nu'aym in Hilya, Ibn Sa'd)*. Many similar narrations have passed in detail in the chapter dealing with the abstinence of Omar ؓ.

The Incident of Omar ؓ When he was Presented with a New Garment

Abu Umamah ؓ reports that Omar ؓ was once sitting amongst some friends when a cotton garment was brought. He started wearing it and had hardly pulled it over his collarbones when he recited:

$$ أَحْمَدُ لِلَّهِ الَّذِي كَسَانِي مَا أُوَارِي بِهِ عَوْرَتِي وَأَتَجَمَّلُ بِهِ فِي حَيَاتِي $$

"All praise is for Allah Who has given me clothing to wear to cover my private areas and with which I can beautify myself during my lifetime."

He then turned to the people and said, "Do you know why I said these words?" They replied, "We will not know until you inform us." He explained, "I was once with Rasulullah ﷺ when he was brought a set of new clothing. He put it on and then said:

$$ أَحْمَدُ لِلَّهِ الَّذِي كَسَانِي مَا أُوَارِي بِهِ عَوْرَتِي وَأَتَجَمَّلُ بِهِ فِي حَيَاتِي $$

Thereafter, he added, 'I swear by the Being Who has sent me with the truth! When Allah gives a Muslim new clothing to wear and only for the pleasure of Allah he gives his old clothes to a poor Muslim to wear, he will be in the safety, protection and guardianship of Allah as long as the poor person has even a thread of it on his body either while alive or dead.'" Omar ؓ then stretched out his arms to see how much the garment overlapped his fingers. He then said to his son Abdullah ؓ, "Dear son! Do bring the knife." Abdullah ؓ stood up and brought the knife. Omar ؓ then stretched out the sleeves over his arms and cut off what he saw to overlap. Those around him asked, "O Amirul Mu'minin! Should we not bring a tailor to stitch the ends?" "No," replied Omar ؓ. Abu Umamah ؓ says that afterwards he saw the threads of the sleeves dangling randomly over Omar ؓ's fingers where he did not have it stitched. *(Hannad in Kanzul Ummal)*. Abdullah bin Omar ؓ reports, "My father Omar ؓ once wore a new upper garment and then asked me to bring a knife. He then said, 'Dear son! Stretch the sleeves of my garment and hold firmly onto where my fingers are. Then cut off whatever overlaps my fingers.' I then cut off the ends of both sleeves and because I could not cut straight with the knife, the openings of the sleeves were unequal in length. I therefore said to him, 'Dear father! Why don't I cut them equally with a scissor?' 'Leave it, son,' he replied, 'because I have seen Rasulullah ﷺ do exactly the same.' The garment then remained on him in this manner until it eventually wore out. I would often see the threads falling over his foot." *(Abu Nu'aym in Hilya)*

Statements of the Sahabah concerning Kissing the Black stone and touching the 2 Western Pillars of the Kabah

Aslam narrates that Omar ؓ once addressed the Hajar Aswad (black stone) saying, "Behold! I swear by Allah that I know well that you can neither cause benefit nor harm. Had I not seen Rasulullah ﷺ kiss you, I would never have kissed you." After kissing it, he said, "Why should we perform Ramal? It was something that we did to show the disbeliever that we have strength. Allah has subsequently destroyed them and we therefore have no need to continue it! However, because it was something that Rasulullah ﷺ did, we do not like to forsake it." *(Bukhari in Al Bidayah wan Nihayah)*. A Sahabi reports that he saw Rasulullah ﷺ standing by the Hajar Aswad and saying, "I know well that you are a stone that can neither cause benefit nor do harm." Rasulullah ﷺ then kissed it. Thereafter, when Abu Bakr ؓ performed Hajj, he also stood by the Hajar Aswad and said, "I know well that you are a stone that can neither cause benefit nor do harm. Had I not seen Rasulullah ﷺ kiss you, I would have not done so." *(Ibn Abi Shayba, Darr Qutni in Ilal, Kanzul Ummal)*. Ya'la bin Umaya ؓ says, "I was performing Tawaf with Uthman ؓ. After kissing the Hajar Aswad, I was walking next to the Kabah. When we passed by the western pillar called (Rukn Iraqi) that comes after the Hajar Aswad, I pulled at Uthman ؓ's hand to touch it. 'What is the matter?' he asked. 'Are you not going to touch the pillar?' I asked. 'Did you not perform Tawaf with Rasulullah ﷺ?' he enquired. When I replied that I did, he asked, 'Did you see Rasulullah ﷺ touch any of the 2 western pillars of the Kabah (Rukn Iraqi and Rukn Shami)?' 'No,' I replied. He then said, 'Do you then not have a perfect example in Rasulullah ﷺ?' 'Most certainly,' I replied. He then bade me, 'Then leave it out and proceed.'" *(Ahmad)*

The Incident Between Abdullah bin Abbas ؓ and a Bedouin

Bakr bin Abdullah narrates that a Bedouin once asked Abdullah bin Abbas ؓ, "Why is it that on the occasion of Hajj the family of Mu'awiya gives people water and honey to drink, the family of another give milk while you people give only *Nabidh* (water with dates or raisins are left for a while to make it tasty)? Is it because you people are stingy or because you are poor?" Abdullah bin Abbas ؓ replied by saying, "It is neither because we are stingy nor because we are poor. However, Rasulullah ﷺ once came to us with Usama bin Zaid ؓ sitting behind him on the animal. When he asked for something to drink and we gave him this Nabidh to drink, he drank it and said, 'You have it prepared well. This is what you should continue doing.'" *(Ahmad)*. Ja'far bin Tammam reports that a man once approached Abdullah bin Abbas ؓ and asked, "Tell me about this Nabidh from raisins that you give people to drink. Is it because of a Sunnah that you are following or do you find this more convenient for yourselves than giving milk and honey?" Abdullah bin Abbas ؓ replied, "Indeed Rasulullah ﷺ once came to Abbas ؓ who was busy giving the people Nabidh to drink.

When Rasulullah ﷺ asked for something to drink. Abbas ؓ called for a few cups of Nabidh and handed one over to Rasulullah ﷺ. After drinking, Rasulullah ﷺ remarked, 'You have it prepared well. This is what you should continue doing.' It therefore gives me no pleasure to be a means of giving people milk and honey in place of the statement Rasulullah ﷺ made when he said, 'You have it prepared well. This is what you should continue doing.'" *(Ibn Sa'd)*

Incidents About How Abdullah bin Omar ؓ Followed in the Footsteps of Rasulullah ﷺ

Ibn Sirin narrates, "I was once with Abdullah bin Omar ؓ in Arafat. When the people left, I left with him until we reached the Imam and performed the Zuhr and Asr salah behind him. My companions and I then stayed there with him until the Imam left for Muzdalifa after sunset. We left with Abdullah bin Omar ؓ and when we eventually reached a narrow place just before Ma'zamain, he made his animal sit. We also made our animals sit, thinking that he intended performing salah. He however told us that it was at this place that stopped to relieve himself and that he also wished to relieve himself there." *(Ahmad in Targheeb wat Tarheeb)*. Another narration states that Abdullah bin Omar ؓ used to go to a certain tree between Makkah and Madinah beneath which he would have his afternoon nap. He mentioned that he did so because Rasulullah ﷺ used to do that. *(Bazzar, Haythami in Targheeb wat Tarheeb)*. Nafi narrates that Abdullah bin Omar ؓ was extremely particular about following in the footsteps of Rasulullah ﷺ. He would therefore note every spot where Rasulullah ﷺ performed salah during journeys and was so particular about this that even if Rasulullah ﷺ ever dismounted beneath any tree, Abdullah bin Omar ؓ would care for the tree and pour water on its roots so that it should not dry up. *(Ibn Asakir in Kanzul Ummal)*. Mujahid says, "We once accompanied Abdullah bin Omar ؓ on a journey. When he passed by a certain place, he turned to the side of the road. When we asked him why he had done this, he replied, 'I saw Rasulullah ﷺ do that.'" *(Ahmad, Bazzar in Targheeb wat Tarheeb)*. Nafi reports that Abdullah bin Omar ؓ used to turn his animal's head while traveling the road to Makkah to turn the animal in different directions. Turning the animal, he would say, "I am doing this so that the footstep of my animal falls on the footstep of Rasulullah ﷺ's animal." *(Abu Nu'aym in Hilya)*. Nafi says, "If you had to see Abdullah bin Omar ؓ following in the footsteps of Rasulullah ﷺ, you would say that he is mad." *(Abu Nu'aym in Hilya, Hakim)*. Aisha ؓ says, "There was none who followed so meticulously the footsteps of Rasulullah ﷺ in all his stops (during his travels) as Abdullah bin Omar ؓ did." *(Ibn Sa'd)*. If anyone had to see Abdullah bin Omar ؓ follow in the footsteps of Rasulullah ﷺ, they would think that his mind was affected. Nafi says, "No camel that has lost her little one in a desert searches as thoroughly as Abdullah bin Omar ؓ does when searching for the footsteps of Rasulullah ﷺ." *(Abu Nu'aym in Hilya)*

Abdur Rahman bin Umayya bin Abdullah reports that he once asked Abdullah bin Omar ؓ, "We find the salah of fear and the salah of a resident in the Qur'an, but do not find the salah of a traveler?" Abdullah bin Omar ؓ replied, "Allah sent his Nabi ﷺ to guide us when we were the most unrefined people. We therefore do as Rasulullah ﷺ did." *(Abdur Razzaq)*. Umayya bin Abdullah bin Khalid bin Usaid reports that he once asked Abdullah bin Omar ؓ, "In the Qur'an we find mention of shortening the salah of fear but do not find the shortening of the traveler's salah'?" Abdullah bin Omar ؓ replied, "We found our Nabi ﷺ doing something and we did the same." *(Ibn Jareer)*.

Warid bin Abu Asim reports that he once met Abdullah bin Omar ❀ in Mina and asked him about the salah performed on a journey. When Abdullah bin Omar ❀ replied that it was only 2 rakahs, Warid asked, "What is your opinion now that we are here in Mina'?" This infuriated Abdullah bin Omar ❀ and he said, "Shame on you! Have you heard about Rasulullah ❀?" Warid replied, "Certainly, and I believe in him." Abdullah bin Omar ❀ then said, "Whenever Rasulullah ❀ went on a journey, he would perform 2 Rakahs salah. You may therefore perform 2 Rakahs or leave it out." *(Ibn Jareer)*. Yet another narration from Abu Muneed Jurashi states that someone once enquired from Abdullah bin Omar about the verse:

وَإِذَا ضَرَبْتُمْ فِي الْأَرْضِ فَلَيْسَ عَلَيْكُمْ جُنَاحٌ أَنْ تَقْصُرُوا مِنَ الصَّلَاةِ إِنْ خِفْتُمْ أَنْ يَفْتِنَكُمُ الَّذِينَ كَفَرُوا إِنَّ الْكَافِرِينَ كَانُوا لَكُمْ عَدُوًّا مُبِينًا (101)

And when you (Muslims) travel in the land, there is no sin on you if you shorten your Salat (prayer) if you fear that the disbelievers may attack you, verily, the disbelievers are ever unto you open enemies. (A-Nisa':101)

The person then asked, "Should we also shorten the salah when we are in safety and not in fear while traveling?" Abdullah bin Omar ❀ replied, "There was certainly an excellent example for you in Rasulullah ❀." *(Ibn Jareer in Kanzul Ummal)*. Zaid bin Aslam reports that he once saw Abdullah bin Omar ❀ perform salah with his buttons open. When he asked Abdullah bin Omar about it, he replied, "I have seen Rasulullah ❀ doing this." *(Ibn Khuzyayma, Bayhaqi in Targheeb wat Tarheeb)*

Mu'awiya bin Qurra ❀ Opens His Buttons to Emulate Rasulullah ❀

Qurra ❀ says, "I went to Rasulullah ❀ in the company of a group from the Banu Muzaina tribe and we pledged our allegiance to him. Rasulullah ❀'s buttons were open and I put my hand into the collar of his upper garment and felt the seal of prophethood." Urwa bin Abdullah bin Qushair says, "Whether summer or winter, I always saw Mu'awiya the son of Qurra ❀ and his son with their buttons open emulating Rasulullah ❀." *(Ibn Majah, Ibn Hibban in Targheeb wat Tarheeb, Baghawi, Ibn Sakan in Isabah, Ibn Sa'd)*

A Group of Sahabah Argue About Their Relationship with Rasulullah ❀ and he Confirms what They Say

Ka'b bin Ujrah ❀ says, "We were all sitting before the room of Rasulullah ❀ in the Masjid. We were a group the Ansar and there was also a group from the Muhajirin and another from the Banu Hashim. We then started disputing about which of us were closer and more beloved to Rasulullah ❀. We said, 'It is us, the group of the Ansar. We believed in Rasulullah ❀, followed him, fought by his side and our army was always at the throats of the enemy. We are therefore closer and more beloved to Rasulullah ❀.' Our Muhajirin brothers then said, 'It is us migrated with Allah and Rasulullah ❀, separating from our tribes, families and wealth. In addition to this, we were also present where you were present and fought the battles you fought. We are therefore closer and more beloved to Rasulullah ❀.' Our brothers from the Banu Hashim then spoke, 'We are the family of Rasulullah ❀. We were also present where you were present and fought the battles you fought. We are therefore closer and more beloved to Rasulullah ❀.' Rasulullah ❀ then came out to us and facing towards us, he enquired, 'Were you discussing something?' When we repeated what we the Ansar had said, Rasulullah ❀ remarked, 'You are right. Who can deny you .this?' When we informed him about what our Muhajirin brothers had said, Rasulullah ❀ remarked, 'They are right. Who can deny them this?' When we then

informed him about what our brothers from the Banu Hashim had said, Rasulullah ❀ remarked, 'They are also right. Who can deny them this?' Rasulullah ❀ then said, 'Should I not pass a decision between you?' We all exclaimed, 'Please do! May all our fathers and mothers be sacrificed for you, O Rasulullah ❀!' Rasulullah ❀ said, 'As for you, O assembly of Ansar, I am your brother.' The Ansar rejoiced, 'Allahu Akbar! By the Rabb of the Kabah, we are pleased with this Rasulullah ❀ then said, 'As for you, O assembly O Muhajirin, I am one of you.' The Muhajirin rejoiced 'Allahu Akbar! By the Rabb of the Kabah, we are please with this!' Rasulullah ❀ continued, 'As for you, O Bam Hashim, you are from me and I am from you.' The Banu Hashim rejoiced, 'Allahu Akbar! By the Rabb of the Kabah, we are pleased with this!' We all then stood up and were all pleased and coveting our relationship with Rasulullah ❀." *(Tabrani, Haythami)*

Rasulullah ❀ Forbids Khalid ❀ From Hurting the Veterans of Badr and Forbids the People From Hurting Khalid ❀

Abdullah bin Abu Awfa ❀ narrates that Abdur Rahman bin Auf ❀ once complained to Rasulullah ❀ about Khalid bin Walid ❀. Rasulullah ❀ said, "O Khalid! Never hurt the veterans of Badr because you will never be able to match the deeds they carried out even though you spend as much as Mount Uhud in gold." Khalid ❀ responded by saying, "When people insult me, I respond to them in the same way." Rasulullah ❀ then said to the Sahabah, "Never hurt Khalid because he is a sword from amongst the swords of Allah that Allah rains down upon the Kuffar." *(Tabrani in Sagheer and Kabeer, Haythami, Bazzar, Ibn Asakir, Abu Ya'la in Kanzul Ummal, Ibn Abdul Birr in Isti'ab)*. Hasan reports that there once arose a dispute between Abdur Rahman bin Auf ❀ and Khalid bin Walid ❀. Khalid ❀ said to Abdur Rahman ❀, "Do not assert your superiority over me because you accepted Islam a day or 2 before me!" When the news of this reached Rasulullah ❀, he said, "Will you people not leave my companions alone for my sake! I swear by the Being Who controls my life that if any of you (non-veterans of Badr) have to spend the equivalent of Mount Uhud in gold, he will not even attain their reward of spending half a Mudd." Some time afterwards an argument sparked between Abdur Rahman bin Auf ❀ and Zubair ❀. Khalid bin Walid ❀ then approached Rasulullah ❀ and said, "O Nabi ❀! You forbade me from hurting Abdur Rahman but now Zubair is disputing with him." Rasulullah ❀ replied, "They are all veterans of Badr and because they are equal in rank, they have a right to dispute amongst each other." *(Ibn Asakir in Kanzul Ummal, Ahmad)*. Abu Hurairah ❀ narrates that there was a dispute between Abdur Rahman bin Auf ❀ and Khalid bin Walid ❀. Rasulullah ❀ commented, "Will you people not leave my companions alone for my sake! I swear by the Being Who controls my life that if any of you (non-veterans of Badr) have to spend the equivalent of Mount Uhud in gold, he will not even attain their reward for spending a Mudd or half of it." *(Bazzar, Haythami)*

Rasulullah ❀ says, "Allah has Selected My Companions From All in the Universe"

Jabir ❀ reports that Rasulullah ❀ said, "Allah has selected my companions from all in the universe apart from the prophets and messengers. He has then selected 4 of them for me viz. Abu Bakr, Omar, Uthman and Ali and made them my special companions. Of course, there is great good in everyone of my companions. Allah has also selected my Ummah over all other nations and then selected 4 generations from amongst my Ummah viz. the 1st (the period in which Rasulullah ❀ lived), the

2nd, the 3rd and the 4th generations." *(Bazzar, Haythami)*

The Advice Rasulullah ﷺ Gave Concerning the Muhajirin and the Ansar

Abdur Rahman bin Auf ؓ narrates that when Rasulullah ﷺ was on his deathbed, the Sahabah asked, "O Rasulullah ﷺ! Give us some advice." Rasulullah ﷺ said, "I advise you to be good towards those Muhajirin who were the earliest adherents to Islam and towards their children after them. If you fail to do this, neither your obligatory nor your optional deeds will be accepted." *(Tabrani, Haythami)*. Rasulullah ﷺ advised, "1 advise you to be good towards those Muhajirin who were the earliest adherents to Islam, towards their children after them and towards their children after them." *(Bazzar, Haythami)*. Zaid bin Sa'd reports from his father that when Rasulullah ﷺ was informed that he was soon to leave this world, he came out of his room wrapped in old clothing and sat on the pulpit. When the people and the business people heard about this, they all presented themselves in the Masjid. After praising Allah, Rasulullah ﷺ said, "O people! Keep me in mind when dealing with the Ansar because they are my belly in which I deposit my food and they are my treasure box, I place my total trust in them. You should therefore accept from those of them who do good and overlook those of them who do evil." *(Tabrani, Haythami)*

Rasulullah ﷺ Forbids People From Reviling the Sahabah

Anas ؓ reports that when mention was made of Malik bin Dukshun ؓ before Rasulullah ﷺ and some people started accusing him of being the head of the hypocrates, Rasulullah ﷺ said, "Do leave my companions alone for my sake and never revile them." *(Bazzar, Haythami)*. Abdullah bin Abbas ؓ narrates that Rasulullah ﷺ said, "Allah, the angels, and all of mankind curse the person who reviles my Sahabah." *(Tabrani, Haythami)*. Aisha ؓ reports that Rasulullah ﷺ said, "Never revile my Sahabah. May Allah curse the one who reviles my Sahabah." *(Tabrani, Haythami)*. Sa'eed bin Zaid bin Amr bin Nufail ؓ once said, "Are you people telling me to revile the Sahabah? May Allah rater shower His mercy on them and forgive them all." *(Tabrani in Awsat, Haythami)*

Abdullah bin Abbas ؓ Warns Those who Speak Ill of the Sahabah

Sa'eed bin Jubair reports that a man once asked Abdullah bin Abbas ؓ for some advice. Abdullah bin Abbas ؓ said, "I advise you to adopt Taqwa and to refrain from speaking ill of the Sahabah, because you have no idea about what has been destined for them." *(Tabrani in Awsat, Haythami)*

Rasulullah ﷺ's Advice Concerning the Members of his Household

Abdullah bin Omar ؓ narrates that the final words that Rasulullah ﷺ spoke were: "Be my successors over the members of my household, treat them well and care for them as I have been doing." *(Tabrani in Awsat, Haythami)*. Ummu Salama ؓ narrates that Rasulullah ﷺ's daughter Fatima ؓ once came to Rasulullah ﷺ carrying her sons Hasan ؓ and Husain ؓ on her hips. In her hand she was carrying a pot belonging to Hasan ؓ in which there was some hot food. When she put the pot down before Rasulullah ﷺ, he asked, "Where is Abul Hasan (Ali ؓ)?" When Fatima ؓ informed him that Ali ؓ was at home, Rasulullah ﷺ called him. Rasulullah ﷺ then sat down to eat with Ali, Fatima ؓ, Hasan ؓ and Husain ؓ. Ummu Salama ؓ continues, "However, Rasulullah ﷺ did not call me whereas whenever he ate food, he would always call for me if I was there. After eating, Rasulullah ﷺ covered them all in his shawl and said,

"O Allah! You be the enemy of those who are their enemies and You be the friend of those who are their friends." *(Abu Ya'la, Haythami)*. Abdullah bin Abbas ؓ narrates that Rasulullah ﷺ once said, "O progeny of Abdul Muttalib! I have asked Allah for 3 things for you. That He keeps steadfast those of you who are established on Islam, that He educates those of you who are ignorant and that He guides those of you who are misguided. I have also asked Allah to make you extremely generous and merciful. Even though a person may be engaged in Ibadah standing between the Hajar Aswod and Maqam Ibrahim and even though he performs salah and fasts, he will still enter Jahannam if he bears enmity for the members of Muhammad's household." *(Tabrani, Haythami)*. Uthman ؓ reports that Rasulullah ﷺ says. "Whoever does a good turn towards any member of Abdul Muttalib's progeny and is not rewarded in this world, it shall be my duty to repay him for it tomorrow on the Day of Judgment when he meets me." *(Tabrani in Awsat, Haythami)*

Omar ؓ is Overjoyed to be Related to Rasulullah ﷺ

Jabir ؓ narrates that on the occasion of Omar ؓ's marriage to the daughter of Ali ؓ, he heard Omar ؓ say to the people, "Will you not congratulate me? I have heard Rasulullah ﷺ say, 'On the Day of Judgment, all relations and family ties will be severed besides my relations and family ties.'" By marrying Ali ؓ's daughter, Omar ؓ therefore established a tie of kinship with Rasulullah ﷺ *(Tabrani in Awsat and Kabeer, Haythami)*

The Status of the Quraish

Muhammad bin Ibrahim Taymi reports that Qatadah bin Nu'man Dhafari ؓ once insulted the Quraish and appeared to use improper language. Rasulullah ﷺ said, "O Qatadah! Never speak ill of the Quraish because you will find amongst them such men whose actions and deeds make you light into insignificance and whom you will truly envy. Had I no fear of the Quraish becoming rebellious, I would have informed them of their high status in Allah's sight." *(Ahmad, Bazzar, Tabrani, Haythami)*. Ali ؓ reports that to the best of his knowledge, Rasulullah ﷺ stated, "Always put the Quraish forwards and never step ahead of them. Had I no fear of the Quraish becoming boastful, I would have informed them of their status in the sight of Allah." *(Tabrani, Haythami)*. Aisha ؓ reports that Rasulullah ﷺ once came to her and said, "Had I no fear of the Quraish becoming boastful, I would have informed them of their status in the sight of Allah." *(Ahmad, Haythami)*. Abu Hurairah ؓ narrates that Rasulullah ﷺ mentioned, "Look for trustworthiness amongst the Quraish because a trustworthy person from the Quraish is superior to a trustworthy person from another tribe and a powerful person from the Quraish in Islam and in leadership is twice as superior as a strong person from another tribe." *(Tabrani, Abu Ya'la, Haythami)*

Rifa'ah bin Rafi ؓ reports that Rasulullah ﷺ once instructed Omar ؓ, "Gather my people." Omar ؓ gathered them at Rasulullah ﷺ's room and then went in and asked, "O Rasulullah ﷺ! Should I get them to enter or shall you be going out to them?" Rasulullah ﷺ's reply was: "I shall rather go to them." When Rasulullah ﷺ went to them, he asked, "Is there anyone here who does not belong to you?" "Yes," they replied, "Amongst us are also our allies, the children of our sisters and our slaves." Rasulullah ﷺ said to them, "Our allies are part of us, the children of our sisters are part of us and our slaves are all part of us. Have you not heard that it is only those with Taqwa who are Allah's friends? If you are His friends, then it is excellent. Otherwise, you should give the matter deep thought. It should not be that other people arrive on the Day of Judgment with plenty of good deeds while you arrive there with sins, because of which I will have to turn away from you." Rasulullah ﷺ then raised his hands and said, "O people! The Quraish are trustworthy people. Allah will therefore grab by the nostrils the person who searches for their faults and throw him into the fire of Jahannam." Rasulullah ﷺ repeated this thrice. *(Bazzar, Ahmad, Tabrani, Haythami)*

Harboring Enmity for the Banu Hashim, the Ansar and for Arabs

Abdullah bin Abbas ؓ reports that Rasulullah ﷺ said, "Harboring enmity for the Banu Hashim and for the Ansar lead to Kufr and harboring enmity for Arabs is a sign of hypocrisy." *(Tabrani, Haythami)*

The Quraish shall be First to Meet Rasulullah ﷺ

Aisha ؓ says, "Rasulullah ﷺ once entered my room and said, 'O Aisha! Your people shall be first of my Ummah to meet me.' After Rasulullah ﷺ sat down, I asked, 'O Rasulullah ﷺ! May Allah sacrifice my life for you! You had entered saying something that gave me a fright.' 'What was that?' he asked. I explained, 'You said that my people shall be the first of the Ummah to meet with you.' 'That is what I said,' Rasulullah ﷺ confirmed. 'What will be the reason for that?' I enquired. Rasulullah ﷺ replied, 'Death shall harvest them and people will be jealous of them.' I then asked, 'What will be the condition of people afterwards?' 'They will be like young locusts, the strong of which will devour the weak. This will continue until Qiyamah eventually takes place over them.'" Another narration states that Rasulullah ﷺ said, "O Aisha! The first of people to be destroyed shall be your people." Aisha ؓ asked, "May Allah sacrifice my life for you! Will it be due to poisoning?" "No," replied Rasulullah ﷺ, "It will be their deaths that will come to this tribe of Quraish and people will be jealous of them. They will then be the first of people to be destroyed." Aisha ؓ enquired, "How long will life be after them?" Rasulullah ﷺ replied, "They are the backbone of people and people will be destroyed as soon as they are destroyed." *(Ahmad, Haythami, Tabrani in Awsat, Bazzar)*

Rasulullah ﷺ Gives Glad Tidings to Those to Come After Him

Omar ؓ narrates that he was once with Rasulullah ﷺ when Rasulullah ﷺ asked the Sahabah, "Tell me whose Iman is best from all those with Iman." The Sahabah replied, "It is the angels, O Rasulullah ﷺ. Rasulullah ﷺ replied, "They are on their place and it is expected of them to have strong Iman. What prevents them from this when Allah has accorded them the elevated status that He has? It is someone else." The Sahabah submitted, "O Rasulullah ﷺ! It must then be the Ambiya whom Allah has honored with His message and prophethood." Rasulullah ﷺ again said, "They are on their place and it is expected of them. What prevents them from this when Allah has accorded them the elevated status that He has? It is someone else." Thereafter, the Sahabah said, "O Rasulullah ﷺ! Then the martyrs who were martyred with the Ambiya ﷺ?" Yet again, Rasulullah ﷺ said, "They are on their place and it is expected of them. What prevents them from this when Allah has accorded them the elevated status that He has? It is someone else." "Then who?" the Sahabah begged to know. Rasulullah ﷺ explained, "People who are still in the backs of their forefathers. They will come after me and will believe in me without ever seeing me. They will believe what I say without seeing me and will practice on the teachings recorded on hanging pages of the Qur'an that they will find. These are the people whose Iman is best from all those who have Iman." *(Abu Ya'la, Haythami)*

Amr ؓ reports that Rasulullah ﷺ once asked, "Tell me which creation will hold the highest status in Allah's sight on the Day of Judgment." When the Sahabah submitted that it will be the angels, Rasulullah ﷺ commented, "What prevents them from this when they are so close to their Rabb? It is someone else." "Then it must be the Ambiya," the Sahabah said. Rasulullah ﷺ corrected them saying, "What prevents them from this when revelation descends on them? It is someone else." When the Sahabah begged to be informed, Rasulullah ﷺ said, "They are people who will come after you. They will believe in me without seeing me. All they will find will be hanging pages of the Qur'an in which they will believe. These are the people who will hold the highest status in Allah's sight on the Day of Judgment and whose Iman will be best in Allah's sight on the Day of Judgment." *(Bazzar)*. Abu Jumu'ah ؓ reports that they were once having a meal with Rasulullah ﷺ. Abu Ubaidah bin Jarrah ؓ was also present and it was he who asked, "O Rasulullah ﷺ! Is there anyone superior to us who have accepted Islam at your hand and waged Jihad by your side'?" Rasulullah ﷺ replied, "Yes. They are people who will come after me and will believe in me without seeing me." *(Ahmad, Abu Ya'la, Tabrani in Majma'uz Zawa'id)*. Abu Umama ؓ states that he heard Rasulullah ﷺ say, "Glad tiding for those who believe in me after seeing me and 7 times glad tidings for those who believe in me without seeing me." *(Ahmad, Tabrani in Majma'uz Zawa'id)*

Rasulullah ﷺ Wishes to See his Brothers

Abu Hurairah ؓ reports that Rasulullah ﷺ said. "There will be people coming after me who will wish that they could sacrifice their families and wealth just to see." *(Bazzar, Haythami)*. Anas ؓ narrates that Rasulullah ﷺ once said, "I wish that I could see my brothers who will believe in me without seeing me." *(Ahmad)* Another narration states that Rasulullah ﷺ said, "When will I meet my brothers?" "Are we not your brothers, O Rasulullah ﷺ?" asked the Sahabah. "You are my companions," replied Rasulullah ﷺ, "My brothers are those people who will believe in me even though they will not see me." *(Abu Ya'la, Haythami, Tabrani in Awsat, Bazzar in Majmu'az Zawa'id, Ibn Hajar)*

The Virtues of the Ummah of Rasulullah ﷺ

Ammar bin Yasir ؓ reports that Rasulullah ﷺ said, "The example of my Ummah is like the rain. It cannot be specified whether it is the first part that is better or the last part." *(Ahmad, Bazzar, Tabrani, Haythami)*. Abdullah bin Mas'ood ؓ narrates that Rasulullah ﷺ said, "Verily Allah has angels who travel extensively. They convey to me the greetings that my Ummah give me." Rasulullah ﷺ said, "My life is best for you because you talk to me, enquire about the injunctions of Islam and when revelation answers your questions, you are spoken to. My death shall be best for you because your actions will be presented to me. When I see good deeds, I shall praise Allah for it and when I see evil, I shall beg Allah to forgive you." *(Bazzar, Haythami)*.

Killing is the Punishment of this Ummah in this World

Abu Burdah ؓ says, "I was sitting with Ibn Ziyad and Abdullah bin Yazid ؓ as the heads of the Khawarij were brought. Whenever a head was passed, I said, 'He is headed towards Jahannam.' Abdullah ؓ said, 'Do not say that, dear nephew because I heard Rasulullah ﷺ say that the punishment of this Ummah shall be in this world (thus cleansing them for the Hereafter).'" *(Bayhaqi in Kanzul Ummal)*. Another narration quotes that Rasulullah ﷺ said, "Allah has made killing the punishment of this Ummah in this world." *(Abu Nu'aym in Hilya, Tabrani in Kabeer, Sagheer, Awsat, Haythami)*. In another narration, Abu Burdah ❁ says, "I left Ubaidullah bin Ziyad when I saw him giving extremely harsh punishment to the Khawarij. I then sat with one of the Sahabah who said, 'Rasulullah ❁ had mentioned that the punishment of this Ummah shall be administered by the sword.'" *(Tabrani, Haythami)*

Ahadeeth Warning Against Killing a Muslim

Abdullah bin Abbas ❁ narrates that a person was mysteriously killed during the time of Rasulullah ❁. Rasulullah ❁ mounted the pulpit and said, "O people! How can a person be killed under mysterious circumstances when I am still among you? If all the inhabitants of the heavens and the earth scheme to kill a single Muslim, Allah shall punish them all without restraint." *(Tabrani, Haythami)*. Abu Sa'eed ❁ narrates that when a person was killed during the time of Rasulullah ❁, he mounted the pulpit to address the people. Rasulullah ❁ thrice asked, "Does anyone know who killed the person among you?" When the Sahabah swore that they did not know, Rasulullah ❁ said, "I swear by the Being Who controls the life of Muhammad! If all the inhabitants of the heavens and the earth connive to kill a single Mu'min, Allah shall put them all in Jahannam. Whoever bears enmity for us; the members of my household, Allah shall fling him headlong into Jahannam." *(Bazzar, Haythami)*

Rasulullah ❁ rebukes Usama and Other Sahabah For Killing People who Recited the Shahada

Usama bin Zaid ❁ narrates, "Rasulullah ❁ sent us on a military expedition against a branch of the Juhaina tribe called the Banu Hurqa. We launched a surprise attack at dawn. Amongst them was a man who was the fiercest fighter when attacked and who would defend them as they retreated. One of the Ansar and myself managed to corner him and when we overpowered him, he recited, "La Ilaha IllAllah". While the Ansari backed off him, I proceeded to kill him. When the news reached Rasulullah ❁, he said, 'O Usama! Did you kill a man after he had recited *La Ilaha IllAllah*!' 'O Rasulullah ❁!' I argued, 'He said it only to save himself from being killed.' Rasulullah ❁ however continued repeating the statement until I wished that I had become a Muslim just that day so that I could be forgiven of the sin." *(Ahmad, Bukhari, Muslim)*. In another narration, Usama ❁ says, "When we returned to Rasulullah ❁ and informed him of the event, he said, 'O Usama! Who will defend you against *La Ilaha IllAllah*?' 'O Rasulullah ❁!' I explained, 'He said it only to protect himself from being killed.' Rasulullah ❁ repeated, 'O Usama! Who will defend you against 'La Ilaha IllAllah'?' I swear by the Being Who has sent him with the truth that Rasulullah ❁ kept repeating himself until I wished that my life as a Muslim before this had never been. I wished that I had accepted Islam only that day and that I had never killed him. I then said, 'I undertake a pledge with Allah that I shall never kill any person who professes 'La Ilaha IllAllah.' 'Even after me, O Usama?' Rasulullah ❁ queried. 'Even after you,' I affirmed." *(Ibn Is'haq in Al Bidayah wan Nihayah)*. Yet another narration quoted that Usama ❁ said, "Myself and one of the Ansar finally cornered Mirdas bin Nuhaik and when we drew our swords for him, he exclaimed: اَشْهَدُ اَنْ لاَ اِلَهَ اِلاَّ اللهُ
I testify that there is none worthy of worship but Allah'
However, we did not withdraw from him until we killed him. When we returned to Rasulullah ❁..." The rest of the narration is just like the one quoted above from Ibn Is'haq. *(Ibn Asakir)*. Another narration states that Rasulullah ❁ said, "He professed

La Ilaha IllAllah' and you still killed him?" Usama ❁ replied, "O Rasulullah ❁! He said it for fear of our weapons." Rasulullah ❁ asked, "Did you tear open his heart to know whether he said it for that reason or not? Who will defend you against *La Ilaha IllAllah'* on the Day of Judgment?" Usama ❁ says, "Rasulullah ❁ repeated the statement until I wished that I had become a Muslim just that day." *(Abu Dawud, Nasai, Tahawi, Abu Awanah, Ibn Hibban, Hakim in Kanzul Ummal, Bayhaqi)*

Rasulullah ❁ Rebukes Bakr bin Haritha ❁ as Well

Bakr bin Haritha ❁ narrates, "I was once part of an expedition that Rasulullah ❁ dispatched. When we clashed with the disbeliever, I attacked a man who sought protection from me by accepting Islam. I however killed him. When this was reported to Rasulullah ❁, he became very angry and distanced himself from me until Allah revealed the verse:

وَمَا كَانَ لِمُؤْمِنٍ أَنْ يَقْتُلَ مُؤْمِنًا إِلَّا خَطَأً.....

It is not for a believer to kill a believer except (that it be) by mistake... (An-Nisa':92)
(Because I had killed him in error) Rasulullah ❁ was then pleased with me and drew me closer." *(Duwali, Ibn Mandah, Abu Nu'aym in Kanzul Ummal)*

Rasulullah ❁ is Cold Towards Someone who Killed a Mu'min

Uqba bin Khalid Laythi ❁ reports that Rasulullah ❁ once dispatched an expedition that engaged the enemy in battle. When one of them started to flee, one of the Muslims pursued him with a drawn sword. As the man shouted, "I am a Muslim! I am a Muslim!" the Muslims paid no heed to his cry and killed him with a blow from his sword. When the news reached Rasulullah ❁, he used harsh words to condemn it. These words reached the man who killed and as Rasulullah ❁ was delivering a lecture, he stood up and said, "O Rasulullah ❁! I swear by Allah that he said it only to save himself from being killed." Rasulullah ❁ however ignored the man and those in his direction and continued with his lecture. The man repeated himself saying, "O Rasulullah ❁! He said it only to save himself from being killed." Rasulullah ❁ again ignored the man and those in his direction and continued with his lecture. When the man could bear it no more and repeated himself for a 3rd time, Rasulullah ❁ turned to him with anger apparent on his face. Rasulullah ❁ said, "Verily Allah has forbidden me from killing any Mu'min." This Rasulullah ❁ repeated thrice. *(Abu Ya'la, Haythami, Nasai, Baghawi, Ibn Hibban in Isabah, Khateeb in Muttafiq wal Muftariq, Kanzul Ummal, Bayhaqi, Ibn Sa'd)*

A Verse of the Qur'an is Revealed When Miqdad ❁ Kills a Man who Recited the Shahada

Abdullah bin Abbas ❁ reports that Rasulullah ❁ once dispatched an expedition which included Miqdad bin Aswad ❁. When the Sahabah found the tribe, they discovered that all the people had fled except for a single man with plenty of wealth who remained behind. The man professed: اَشْهَدُ اَنْ لاَ اِلَهَ اِلاَّ اللهُ
'I testify that there is none worthy of worship but Allah'
However, Miqdad ❁ still attacked and killed him. Another Sahabi said, "Have you killed someone who testifies that there is none worthy of worship but Allah? I shall definitely report this to Rasulullah ❁." When the Sahabah returned to Rasulullah ❁, they said, "O Rasulullah ❁! Miqdad ❁ killed a man who testified that there is none worthy of worship but Allah." Rasulullah ❁ then asked them to call for Miqdad ❁. When he arrived, Rasulullah ❁ asked, "O Miqdad! Did you kill a man who professed 'La Ilaha

IllAllah'? How will you fare tomorrow on the Day of Judgment against 'La Ilaha IllAllah'?" It was then that Allah revealed:

يَا أَيُّهَا الَّذِينَ آمَنُوا إِذَا ضَرَبْتُمْ فِي سَبِيلِ اللَّهِ فَتَبَيَّنُوا وَلَا تَقُولُوا لِمَنْ أَلْقَى إِلَيْكُمُ السَّلَامَ لَسْتَ مُؤْمِنًا تَبْتَغُونَ عَرَضَ الْحَيَاةِ الدُّنْيَا فَعِنْدَ اللَّهِ مَغَانِمُ كَثِيرَةٌ كَذَلِكَ كُنْتُم مِّن قَبْلُ

O you who believe! When you go (to fight) in the Cause of Allah, verify (the truth), and say not to anyone who greets you (by embracing Islam): "You are not a believer"; seeking the perishable goods of the worldly life. There are much more profits and booties with Allah. Even as he is now, so were you yourselves before till Allah conferred on you His Favors (i.e. guided you to Islam)... (An-Nisa':94)

Rasulullah ﷺ then said to Miqdad ◉, "A Muslim man was hiding his Iman while living with the Kuffar but when he got the opportunity to make it public, you went and killed him? In the same manner, you also had been hiding your Iman while living in Makkah previously." *(Bazzar, Haythami, Tabrani in Kabeer, Dar Qunti in Afrad)*

Muhallim bin Jathamah ◉ Kills Amir bin Athbat

Abdullah bin Abu Hadrad ◉ reports, "Rasulullah ﷺ sent us with a party of Muslims to Idham. Amongst us were Abu Qatadah Harith bin Rib'ee and Muhallim bin Jathamah bin Qais. We left Madinah and were in the heart of Idham when Amir bin Athbat Ashja'ee passed by us on his camel. He had a few goods with him and a bag or milk. When he greeted us with the greeting of Islam, we left him alone but Muhallim bin Jathamah attacked and killed him on account of a grudge he bore against him. He then seized his goods and bag. When we returned to Rasulullah ﷺ, we informed him about what had happened. It was then concerning us that Allah revealed the verse:

يَا أَيُّهَا الَّذِينَ آمَنُوا إِذَا ضَرَبْتُمْ فِي سَبِيلِ اللَّهِ فَتَبَيَّنُوا وَلَا تَقُولُوا لِمَنْ أَلْقَى إِلَيْكُمُ السَّلَامَ لَسْتَ مُؤْمِنًا تَبْتَغُونَ عَرَضَ الْحَيَاةِ الدُّنْيَا فَعِنْدَ اللَّهِ مَغَانِمُ كَثِيرَةٌ كَذَلِكَ كُنتُم مِّن قَبْلُ فَمَنَّ اللَّهُ عَلَيْكُمْ فَتَبَيَّنُوا إِنَّ اللَّهَ كَانَ بِمَا تَعْمَلُونَ خَبِيرًا (94)

O you who believe! When you go (to fight) in the Cause of Allah, verify (the truth), and say not to anyone who greets you (by embracing Islam): "You are not a believer"; seeking the perishable goods of the worldly life. There are much more profits and booties with Allah. Even as he is now, so were you yourselves before till Allah conferred on you His Favors (i.e. guided you to Islam), therefore, be cautious in discrimination. Allah is ever Well-Aware of what you do. (An-Nisa':94) (Ahmad, Ibn Is'haq in Al Bidayah wan Nihayah, Tabrani, Haythami, Bayhaqi, Ibn Sa'd)

Abdullah bin Omar ◉ reports that Rasulullah ﷺ once sent Muhallim bin Jathamah ◉ as part of an expedition. When Amir bin Athbat met them, he greeted them with the greeting of Islam. However, since they bore a grudge against him from the period of ignorance, Muhallim bin Jathamah ◉ shot an arrow that killed him. When the news reached Rasulullah ﷺ, Uyayna ◉ in defense of Amir and Aqra ◉ in defense if Muhallim ◉ started debating about the issue. Aqra ◉ said, "Set the precedent today by forgiving him and he will not do it in future." Uyayna ◉ said, "Never! By Allah! He should be executed so that his women should feel the grief that my women have felt for the death of Amir." Muhallim ◉ then arrived wearing 2 sheets and sat before Rasulullah ﷺ so that Rasulullah ﷺ may seek Allah's forgiveness for him. Rasulullah ﷺ said to him, "Allah has not forgiven you." He then stood up and left, wiping away the tears from his eyes. It was barely 7 days afterwards when he passed away. When the Sahabah buried him, the ground brought his body back to the surface. When the Sahabah reported this to Rasulullah ﷺ, he said,

"The earth accepts the bodies of people much worse than your companion. However, Allah intends to teach you people an important lesson to respect your sanctity, the sacredness of a Muslim's life." The Sahabah then threw the body into a valley between two mountains and covered it with rocks. It was then that Allah revealed the verse:

يَا أَيُّهَا الَّذِينَ آمَنُوا إِذَا ضَرَبْتُمْ فِي سَبِيلِ اللَّهِ فَتَبَيَّنُوا وَلَا تَقُولُوا لِمَنْ أَلْقَى إِلَيْكُمُ السَّلَامَ لَسْتَ مُؤْمِنًا تَبْتَغُونَ عَرَضَ الْحَيَاةِ الدُّنْيَا فَعِنْدَ اللَّهِ مَغَانِمُ كَثِيرَةٌ كَذَلِكَ كُنتُم مِّن قَبْلُ فَمَنَّ اللَّهُ عَلَيْكُمْ فَتَبَيَّنُوا إِنَّ اللَّهَ كَانَ بِمَا تَعْمَلُونَ خَبِيرًا (94)

O you who believe! When you go (to fight) in the Cause of Allah, verify (the truth), and say not to anyone who greets you (by embracing Islam): "You are not a believer"; seeking the perishable goods of the worldly life. There are much more profits and booties with Allah. Even as he is now, so were you yourselves before till Allah conferred on you His Favors (i.e. guided you to Islam), therefore, be cautious in discrimination. Allah is ever Well-Aware of what you do. (An-Nisa':94) (Ibn Jareer in Al Bidayah wan Nihayah)

The Earth Brings up the Body of a Man who Killed a Mu'min

Qabisah bin Dhuwaib ◉ narrates that a Sahabi once attacked a group of disbeliever who had already been defeated. He then overpowered one of the disbeliever who had given up and as he was about to raise his sword over the man, the disbeliever recited, "La Ilaha IllAllah". However, the Sahabi did not restrain himself and killed the man. He however felt extremely distressed about killing the man. When he related the incident to Rasulullah ﷺ, he said, "The man recited the Kalima only to protect himself." Rasulullah ﷺ rebuked him saying, "Did you tear open his heart to see his intention for reciting the Kalima? It is only by the tongue that a person can express the contents of the heart." It was not long thereafter that the Sahabi passed away. However, when he was buried, his body had surfaced by the morning. His family reported this to Rasulullah ﷺ, who instructed them to bury him again. When they buried him for the 2nd time, the body was again on the surface the following morning. This time when they reported it to Rasulullah ﷺ, he said, "The earth refuses to accept his body. You should therefore throw the body down a valley in the mountains." *(Abdur Razzaq, Ibn Asakir in Kanzul Ummal)*

The Incident of Khalid bin Walid ◉ and the Banu Jadhima Tribe

Abu Ja'far Muhammad bin Ali reports that when Makkah was conquered, Rasulullah ﷺ sent Khalid bin Walid ◉ to invite people to Islam and not to fight anyone. With him were several Arab tribes including the Banu Sulaim bin Mansoor and Banu Mudlaj bin Murrah tribes. When they came across the Banu Jadhima bin Amir bin Abd Manat bin Kinanah tribe and they spotted Khalid ◉, the immediately took up their weapons. Khalid ◉ said to them, "Put down your weapons because everyone has already accepted Islam since you cannot fight all the Arabs, you rather surrender. When the tribe laid down their weapons, they were all tied up with the order of Khalid ◉. Many of them were then put to the sword. When the news reached Rasulullah ﷺ, he raised his hands to the sky and said, "O Allah! I clear myself from what Khalid bin Walid has done." Rasulullah ﷺ then sent for Ali bin Abi Talib ◉ and instructed him saying, "O Ali! Go to those people and look into the matter, trampling the affairs of the period of ignorance underfoot." Ali ◉ then went to them with a large sum of money that Rasulullah ﷺ had given him. He then compensated the people for every life and item of property that they had lost, even to the extent of a container from which a dog drank. Eventually, when there was no life or article left to be compensated for, some money was still left over. Ali then asked the tribe's people after completing, "Is there any life or article that has not been compensated for?" When they declared that there was nothing, Ali said, "I am handing over to you this amount that has been left-over as a precaution from the side of Rasulullah for anything that has escaped either his or your attention. After doing this, he returned to report back to Rasulullah. Rasulullah commended him saying, "You did right and you did well." Rasulullah then stood up, faced towards the Qibla and raised both his hands so high that his armpits were visible. He then thrice repeated, "O Allah! I clear myself from what Khalid bin Walid has done." *(Ibn Is'haq)*

Abdullah bin Omar states that Rasulullah once dispatched Khalid bin Walid to the Banu Jadhima tribe. When he invited them towards Islam, they could not properly say that they had accepted Islam and rather said, "We have changed our religion! We have changed our religion!" Khalid then took them prisoner and handed one prisoner over to each member of his party. On one of the mornings, Khalid suddenly instructed every person to execute his prisoner. Abdullah bin Omar refused saying, "By Allah! I shall never execute my prisoner and neither shall any of my companions execute theirs!" When they returned to Rasulullah and informed him about what Khalid had done, Rasulullah raised his hands towards the sky and twice repeated, "O Allah! I clear myself from what Khalid bin Walid has done." *(Ahmad, Bukhari, Nasai, Abdur Razzaq). Ibn Is'haq* says that as far as he knows, it was because of this incident that there was a dispute between Khalid bin Walid and Abdur Rahman bin Auf. Abdur Rahman bin Auf said, "You have perpetrated an act of ignorance as a Muslim." Khalid responded by saying, "I had only avenged the murder of your father." "You are lying," Abdur Rahman interjected, "I had personally executed my father's murderer. You have only avenged the murder of your uncle Fakih bin Mughiera." The dispute then turned ugly and eventually reached the attention of Rasulullah. Rasulullah then said, "Take it easy, leave these matters aside Khalid! Leave my companion alone for my sake because I swear by Allah that if you possessed gold equivalent to Mount Uhud and spent it all in the Path of Allah, you would be unable to attain the reward equal to the reward that one of my companions who are veterans of Badr attain in a single morning or evening." *(Al Bidayah wan Nihayah)*

The Incident Between Rasulullah and Sakhar Ahmasi

Sakhar from the Ahmas tribe narrates that as soon as he heard that Rasulullah was fighting the Thaqif tribe, he led a party of horsemen to reinforce Rasulullah. He however discovered that Rasulullah had left without conquering the territory. He then took a vow never to leave the fortress until the enemy surrendered to the command of Rasulullah. True to his word, he did not leave them until they eventually submitted to the command of Rasulullah. Sakhar then wrote a letter to Rasulullah saying: "O Rasulullah! Verily the Banu Thaqif has surrendered to your command and I am escorting them with my cavalry." Rasulullah gathered Sahabah together with the announcement "As Salatu Jami'ah" and then prayed for the Ahmas tribe by repeating 10 times, "O Allah! Bless the Ahmas in their cavalry and infantry." When they arrived, Mughiera bin Shu'ba addressed Rasulullah saying, "O Rasulullah! Sakhar has captured my aunt whereas she has also entered the fold of Islam as the others have done." Rasulullah summoned Sakhar and said, "O Sakhar! When people accept Islam, they have safeguarded their blood and their wealth, so do hand over to

Mughiera his aunt." Sakhar handed her over and asked Rasulullah to make over to him the oasis of the Banu Sulaim who had renounced Islam and deserted the place. He said, "O Rasulullah! Hand the place over to me and my tribe to settle there." Rasulullah agreed and they settled there. The Banu Sulaim tribe accepted Islam again and approached Sakhar to hand the oasis back to them. When he refused to do so, they went to Rasulullah saying, "O Rasulullah! After we accepted Islam, we approached Sakhar to give us back our oasis, but he refused." Rasulullah then said to Sakhar, "O Sakhar! When people accept Islam, they have safeguarded their blood and their wealth, so do hand over their oasis back to the Banu Sulaim." Sakhar immediately complied and said, "Certainly, O Nabi of Allah." Rasulullah's face then turned red out of shyness because he had taken from Sakhar the lady as well as the oasis. *(Abu Dawood in Al Bidayah wan Nihayah, Ahmad, Darmi, Ibn Rahway, Bazzar, Ibn Abi Shayba, Tabrani in Nabur Ra'ya, Firyabi in Musnad, Baghawi, Ibn Shaheen in Isabah, Bayhaqi).*

Rasulullah Forbids Killing Anyone who Attests to the Oneness of Allah and the Prophethood of Rasulullah

Aws bin Aws Thaqafi reports that Rasulullah once approached them as they sat in a tent in the Masjid of Madinah. Someone then came to Rasulullah and whispered something to him that the others could not hear. Rasulullah said to him, "Go and tell them to execute him." Rasulullah then called the person back saying, "Did he perhaps not testify that there is none worthy of worship but Allah and that I am the Rasul of Allah?" When the man admitted that the person had done so, Rasulullah said, "Go and tell them that they should release him because I have been commanded to fight people only until they testify that there is none worthy of worship but Allah and that I am the Rasul of Allah. Once they say this, their blood and wealth is forbidden for me unless it needs to be taken for a right due to Allah. Their reckoning will then be Allah's responsibility." *(Ahmad, Darmi, Tahawi, Tayalisi).* Abdullah bin Adi Ansari narrates that Rasulullah was once sitting with some people when someone came and requested permission to speak to Rasulullah in private concerning a hypocrite who had been killed. Rasulullah however spoke to him loudly saying, "Did he not testify that there is none worthy of worship but Allah?" The man's response was, "Yes, but his testimony cannot be heeded." Rasulullah asked further, "Did he not testify that I am the Rasul of Allah?" Again the man replied by saying, "Yes, but his testimony cannot be heeded." Rasulullah then enquired, "Did he too perform salah?" "Yes," the man replied, "but his salah cannot be heeded." Rasulullah finally told him, "These are the people whom I have been prohibited from killing." *(Abdur Razzaq, Hasan bin Sufian in Kanzul Ummal)*

Uthman Prohibits Fighting When he was Besieged in His House

Aisha reports, "Rasulullah once said, 'Call one of my companions.' I asked, 'Abu Bakr?' 'No,' replied Rasulullah. 'Then Omar?' I asked. 'No,' Rasulullah again replied. 'then your cousin Ali?' I said. When Rasulullah again replied in the negative, I said, 'Then Uthman?' 'Yes,' Rasulullah replied. When Uthman arrived, Rasulullah took him aside and whispered something to him, which made Uthman's face grow pale. The day Uthman was besieged in his house by some Muslim rebels, we asked, 'O Amirul Muminin! Should we not fight them? He replied, 'No. Rasulullah undertook a pledge from me and I shall remain steadfast on it." *(Ahmad in Al Bidayah wan Nihayah, Ibn Sa'd)*

Uthman ؓ Narrates that Rasulullah ﷺ said, "A Person's Blood is Forbidden Unless For One of 3 Reasons"

Abdullah bin Omar ؓ narrates that when Uthman ؓ was besieged in his house; he looked out to the people the rebels and asked them, "For what reason do you want to kill me? I have heard Rasulullah ﷺ say, 'A person's blood is forbidden unless for one of 3 reasons; the married man who commits adultery shall be stoned to death, the one who intentionally murders shall be executed and the one who renounces Islam shall also be executed.' By Allah! I have never committed adultery, neither during the period of ignorance nor as a Muslim. I have also never murdered anyone because of which I should be executed and I have also never renounced Islam. I testify that there is none worthy of worship but Allah and that Muhammad ﷺ is the servant and Rasul of Allah." *(Ahmad, Nasai in Al Bidayah wan Nihayah).* Abu Umamah ؓ says, "I was with Uthman ؓ in his house when he was under siege. From the entrance we used, we could hear what the people were talking at the Salat. When Uthman ؓ entered through there one day, for some reason he came to us with his face pale. He said, "Those people have just threatened to kill me. We said to him, 'Allah shall suffice for you against them, O Amirul Muminin.' He continues, 'But why do they want to kill me when I have heard Rasulullah ﷺ say, 'A person's blood is forbidden unless foe one of 3 reasons; if a man renounces Islam, commits adultery after being married or murders another without a warrant.' By Allah! I have never committed adultery either during the period of ignorance or after Islam. Since Allah has guided me to Islam, I have never even wished for a replacement for Islam and I have never murdered anyone. Why do they want to kill me?'" *(Abu Dawud, Nasai, Ibn Majah, Tirmidhi in Al Bidayah wan Nihayah, Ibn Sa'd)*

The Letter Uthman ؓ Delivered to Those who Besieged Him

Abu Layla Kindi reports that he was present when Uthman ؓ was besieged in his house and peeped through a vent in the wall and said, "O people! Do not kill me and if I have sinned rather get me to repent. I swear by Allah that if you kill me, you Muslims shall never again be able perform salah together nor fight the enemy as a unified force. You will then be at big disputes until you become like this." He then interlaced his fingers. He then recited a verse of the Qur'an quoting the words of Shu'aib:

وَيَا قَوْمِ لَا يَجْرِمَنَّكُمْ شِقَاقِي أَنْ يُصِيبَكُمْ مِثْلُ مَا أَصَابَ قَوْمَ نُوحٍ أَوْ قَوْمَ هُودٍ أَوْ قَوْمَ صَالِحٍ وَمَا قَوْمُ لُوطٍ مِنْكُمْ بِبَعِيدٍ (89)

"And O my people! Let not my Shiqaq cause you to suffer the fate similar to that of the people of Nooh (Noah) or of Hood or of Salih (Saleh), and the people of Lout (Lot) are not far off from you!" (Hud:89)

Uthman ؓ sent for Abdullah bin Salam ؓ to ask him what his opinion was. Abdullah bin Salam ؓ replied, "Restraint!' Restrain your hand from the rebels because it lends more weight to your argument on the Day of Judgment." *(Ibn Sa'd)*

The Incident Between Mughiera ؓ and Uthman ؓ When he was Under Siege

Mughiera bin Shu'ba ؓ narrates that when Uthman ؓ was under siege, he approached him and said, "You are the leader of the masses and are in the mess you can see. I therefore have 3 proposals for you. You may choose any of them you like. You may go out and fight them for you have many supporters with great strength and you are on the truth while they are upon falsehood. Alternatively, you may open up a door from your house apart from the one where they are stationed from where you can mount your animal and go to Makkah. They shall never regard your blood as lawful for them to spill as long as you are there. Another option is that you go to Sham where the people of Sham are there for you as well as Mu'awiya ؓ." Uthman ؓ replied, "I cannot go out and fight them because I never want to be the first of the Ummah of Rasulullah ﷺ to shed the) blood of Muslims. Although they will never regard my blood to be lawful if I go to Makkah, I have heard Rasulullah ﷺ say, 'A man from the Quraish will go to Makkah and be a cause of spreading things that are not religious. He shall suffer the punishment of half the universe.' I never want that man to be me. I cannot also go to Sham although the people of Sham and Mua'wiya are there because I shall never leave the place of Hijra and the proximity of Rasulullah ﷺ" *(Ahmad in Al Bidayah wan Nihayah, Haythami)*

Uthman ؓ Forbids Some of the Sahabah From Fighting When he was Under Siege

Abu Hurairah ؓ reports that he entered Uthman ؓ's house when he was under siege and said, "O Amirul Mu'minin! It has now become permissible for you to fight these rebels." Uthman ؓ asked, "O Abu Hurairah! Would you like to kill all of mankind including myself?" "Certainly not," replied Abu Hurairah ؓ. Uthman ؓ then said, "By Allah! If you kill a single person it is tantamount to killing all of mankind." Abu Hurairah ؓ then returned without fighting. *(Ibn Sa'd in Muntakhab Kanzul Ummal).* Abdullah bin Zubair ؓ entered Uthman ؓ's house and said, "O Amirul Mu'minin! In your house you have such a group of people who will attract the help of Allah when fighting the rebels even though they may be few in number. Please issue the command so that we may fight." Uthman ؓ said, "I am pleading to every man in the name of Allah that he should not have his blood spilt for me and should not spill the blood of another for me." Another narration states that Abdullah bin Zubair ؓ said to Uthman ؓ, "Fight them because Allah has made it permissible for you to fight them." Uthman ؓ replied, "Never! I swear by Allah that I shall never fight them." *(Ibn Sa'd).* Abdullah bin Amir ؓ narrates that when he was under siege in his house, Uthman ؓ said, "The one most useful to me is he who restrains his hand and his weapon." *(Ibn Sa'd)*

Zaid bin Thabit ؓ approached Uthman ؓ and said, "The Ansars are at your door saying, 'If you permit, we shall be the helpers of the cause of Allah! If you permit, we shall be the helpers of the cause of Allah!'" Uthman ؓ refused their offer saying, "If they intend fighting, then I give no permission." *(Ibn Sa'd).* Ibn Sirin says, "With Uthman ؓ in the house were 700 men. Had he left them to fight, they would have crushed the rebels with the permission of Allah, completely removing them from the boundaries of Madinah. Amongst them was Abdullah bin Omar ؓ, Hasan bin Ali ؓ and Abdullah bin Zubair ؓ." *(Ibn Sa'd).* Abdullah bin Sa'idah ؓ reports that Sa'eed bin Al Aas ؓ came to Uthman ؓ and said, "O Amirul Mu'minin! For how long will you restrain our hands? These people have eaten at us. While some of them have fired arrows at us, others have thrown stones at us and some have even drawn their swords. Please give us the command to fight." Uthman ؓ replied, "I have no intention of fighting even though I know that I will be safe from them if I do so. I prefer to hand them over to Allah together with those who instigated them against me because we will all gather together before our Rabb. As for fighting them, I swear by Allah that I shall never issue the command." Sa'eed ؓ said, "By Allah! I shall never be asking anyone about you ever." He then left and fought until he sustained a fatal wound to his head. *(Ibn Sa'd)*

Sa'd bin Abi Waqqas ✿ Restrains Himself From Fighting

Amir the son of Sa'd bin Abi Waqqas ✿ approached his father and asked, "Dear father! People are fighting for the world and you are sitting here?" "Dear son," Sa'd ✿ replied, "Are you instructing me to become a leader of anarchy? By Allah! I shall never participate unless I am given a sword that when raised over a Mu'min, it misses him without injury and when raised over a Kafir, it kills him since this cannot be found, I cannot participate. I have heard Rasulullah ﷺ say, "Verily Allah loves the independent person who is not noticeable and possesses Taqwa." (Ahmad in Al Bidayah wan Nihayah, Abu Nu'aym in Hilya). Ibn Sirin narrates that someone once asked Sa'd bin Abi Waqqas ✿, "Why don't you take up arms because you are one of the consultative assembly and more deserving of the Khilafa than others?" Sa'd ✿ replied, "I shall never fight until you give me a sword that has 2 eyes, a tongue and 2 lips and which can differentiate between a Mu'min and a Kafir so that it kills only Kuffar and not Mu'minin. I used to wage Jihad at a time when I knew that it was really Jihad (the fighting taking place now is not against Kuffar and is waged with ulterior motives)." (Tabrani, Haythami, Abu Nu'aym in Hilya, Ibn Sa'd)

The Incident Between Sa'd ✿, Usama ✿ and Another Person About not Fighting

Ibrahim Taymi reports from his father that after eating a full meal, Usama bin Zaid ✿ said, "I shall never fight anyone who recites 'La Ilaha lllAllah'." Sa'd bin Malik bin Abi Waqqas ✿ then remarked, "By Allah! I shall also never fight a man who recites 'La Ilaha lllAllah'." Another man then said to the 2 of them, "Does Allah not say:

وَقَاتِلُوهُمْ حَتَّى لَا تَكُونَ فِتْنَةٌ وَيَكُونَ الدِّينُ كُلُّهُ لِلَّه

And fight them until there is no more Fitnah (disbelief and polytheism: i.e. worshipping others besides Allah) and the religion (worship) will all be for Allah Alone (in the whole of the world). (Al-Anfal:39)

The 2 Sahaba replied, "We fought until no corruption existed and until all religion was for Allah." (Ibn Sa'd in Ibn Kathir)

Abdullah bin Omar ✿ Restrains Himself From Fighting During the Troubled Times of Abdullah bin Zubair ✿

Nafi reports that 2 men approached Abdullah bin Omar ✿ during the period of Abdullah bin Zubair ✿ when fighting was raging. They asked, "People are dying while you are the son of Omar ✿ and a companion of Rasulullah ﷺ? What prevents you from going out and fight?" Abdullah bin Omar ✿ replied, "What prevents me is that Allah has made the blood of my brother Haram for me to spill." They argued, "Does Allah not say:

وَقَاتِلُوهُمْ حَتَّى لَا تَكُونَ فِتْنَةٌ وَيَكُونَ الدِّينُ كُلُّهُ لِلَّه

And fight them until there is no more Fitnah (disbelief and polytheism: i.e. worshipping others besides Allah) and the religion (worship) will all be for Allah Alone (in the whole of the world). (Al-Anfal:39)

Abdullah bin Omar ✿ replied, "We did fight until no corruption existed and until all religion was for Allah. However, you people are fighting so that corruption should appear and so that religion should be for others besides Allah. (Bukhari). Another narration states that a man approached Abdullah bin Omar ✿ and said, "O Abu Abdur Rahman! What makes you perform Hajj one year, Umrah the following year but leaving out waging Jihad in the Path of Allah whereas you know what encouragement Allah has given for it?" Abdullah bin Omar ✿ replied, "Dear nephew! Islam if founded on 5 pillars; Iman in Allah and His Rasul ﷺ, 5 salah, fasting in Ramadhan, paying zakah and performing Hajj." The person enquired further, "O Abu Abdur Rahman! Have you not heard that Allah says:

وَإِنْ طَائِفَتَانِ مِنَ الْمُؤْمِنِينَ اقْتَتَلُوا فَأَصْلِحُوا بَيْنَهُمَا فَإِنْ بَغَتْ إِحْدَاهُمَا عَلَى الْأُخْرَى فَقَاتِلُوا الَّتِي تَبْغِي حَتَّى تَفِيءَ إِلَى أَمْرِ اللَّه

And if two parties or groups among the believers fall to fighting, then make peace between them both, but if one of them rebels against the other, then fight you (all) against the one that which rebels till it complies with the Command of Allah... (Al-Hujurat:9)

وَقَاتِلُوهُمْ حَتَّى لَا تَكُونَ فِتْنَةٌ وَيَكُونَ الدِّينُ كُلُّهُ لِلَّه

And fight them until there is no more Fitnah (disbelief and polytheism: i.e. worshipping others besides Allah) and the religion (worship) will all be for Allah Alone (in the whole of the world)... (Al-Anfal:39)

Abdullah bin Omar ✿ replied, "We did that during the time of Rasulullah ﷺ when the supporters to Islam were few. Because of Islam, a person was put through trials either when the Kuffar killed him or tortured him. The people of Islam eventually increased in number and there no longer remained any corruption." The person then asked, "Then what is your opinion about Ali ✿ and Uthman ✿?" Abdullah bin Omar ✿ replied, "As for Uthman ✿, Allah has forgiven him whereas you people do not like him to be forgiven. As for Ali ✿, he was the cousin of Rasulullah ﷺ as well as his son-in-law." Pointing with his hand, Abdullah bin Omar ✿ then said, "That house you see was his." Yet another narration states that a person once asked Abdullah bin Omar ✿, "O Abu Abdur Rahman! Have you not heard Allah mention in the Qur'an:

وَإِنْ طَائِفَتَانِ مِنَ الْمُؤْمِنِينَ اقْتَتَلُوا فَأَصْلِحُوا بَيْنَهُمَا فَإِنْ بَغَتْ إِحْدَاهُمَا عَلَى الْأُخْرَى فَقَاتِلُوا الَّتِي تَبْغِي حَتَّى تَفِيءَ إِلَى أَمْرِ اللَّه

And if two parties or groups among the believers fall to fighting, then make peace between them both, but if one of them rebels against the other, then fight you (all) against the one that which rebels till it complies with the Command of Allah... (Al-Hujurat:9)

What prevents you from fighting as Allah has instructed in his Book?" Abdullah bin Omar ✿ replied, "Dear nephew! I prefer not to fight and be criticized for not practicing on this verse rather than being criticized for being guilty of perpetrating what Allah says in the verse:

وَمَنْ يَقْتُلْ مُؤْمِنًا مُتَعَمِّدًا فَجَزَاؤُهُ جَهَنَّمُ خَالِدًا فِيهَا وَغَضِبَ اللَّهُ عَلَيْهِ وَلَعَنَهُ وَأَعَدَّ لَهُ عَذَابًا عَظِيمًا (93)

And whoever kills a believer intentionally, his recompense is Hell to abide therein, and the Wrath and the Curse of Allah are upon him, and a great punishment is prepared for him. (An-Nisa':93) The man then argued, "But Allah also says:

وَقَاتِلُوهُمْ حَتَّى لَا تَكُونَ فِتْنَةٌ وَيَكُونَ الدِّينُ كُلُّهُ لِلَّه

And fight them until there is no more Fitnah (disbelief and polytheism: i.e. worshipping others besides Allah) and the religion (worship) will all be for Allah Alone (in the whole of the world).... (Al-Anfal:39)

To this, Abdullah bin Omar ✿ replied, "We did that during the time of Rasulullah ﷺ." The narration then proceeds like the one quoted above. (Bukhari, Abu Nu'aym in Hilya). Abdullah bin Omar ✿ also asked the man, "Do you know what is meant by 'corruption'? Muhammad ﷺ used to fight against the disbeliever and fighting them is fighting 'corruption'. It was nothing like how you fight nowadays for land. (Tafseer Ibn Kathir)

What Abdullah bin Omar ﷺ said to Abdullah bin Zubair ﷺ and Ibn Safwan ﷺ Concerning his Reluctance to Pledge Allegiance to Abdullah bin Zubair ﷺ

Abul Aliya Bara reports that Abdullah bin Zubair ﷺ and Abdullah bin Safwan ﷺ were one day sitting in the Hatem when Abdullah bin Omar ﷺ passed by while performing Tawaf. One of them said to the other, "Do you think that there is anyone alive who is better than that man'?" He then asked another man to call Abdullah bin Omar ﷺ when he had completed his Tawaf. When Abdullah bin Omar ﷺ completed his Tawaf and had performed the 2 Rakahs, the messenger that the 2 Sahabah had sent approached him saying, "Abdullah bin Zubair ﷺ and Abdullah bin Safwan ﷺ over there are calling for you." When Abdullah bin Omar ﷺ came to them, Abdullah bin Safwan ﷺ asked, "O Abu Abdur Rahman! What prevents you from pledging allegiance to the Amirul Mu'minin Abdullah bin Zubair ﷺ when the people of Makkah, Madinah, Yemen, Iraq and most of the people of Sham have already pledged their allegiance to him?" Abdullah bin Omar ﷺ replied, "By Allah! I shall never pledge my allegiance to you as long as the swords you hang over your necks are dripping with the blood of Muslims." *(Bayhaqi)*

Abdullah bin Omar ﷺ Refuses to Allow People to Pledge Their Allegiance to Him

Hasan says that when the Muslims were plunged in problems, they approached Abdullah bin Omar ﷺ and said, "You are a leader, the son of a leader and the people are happy with you. Why don't you come forward and allow people to pledge their allegiance to you'?" Abdullah bin Omar ﷺ replied, "Never! By Allah! As long as there is life in me, not even as much as a cupper's cupful of blood will be spilt for my sake." People later came and threatened him saying, "By Allah! If you do not come out to have the pledge of allegiance taken at your hand, you will be killed here on you bed." Undeterred by the threat Abdullah bin Omar ﷺ gave the same reply as he did the first time. Hasan continues, "By Allah! Until Abdullah bin Omar ﷺ passed away, the people were unable to attain their objectives through him." *(Abu Nu'aym in Hilya, Ibn Sa'd)*

The Statement of Abdullah bin Omar ﷺ on Unity and Disunity

Khalid bin Sumair narrates that some people once said to Abdullah bin Omar ﷺ, "Why don't you set matters right for the people by taking the reins of Khilafa because they are all happy with you." He said to them, "What if someone in the East opposes me?" They replied, "If anyone stands up in opposition, he will be killed because what is the death of one person for the sake of the Ummah's unity?" Abdullah bin Omar ﷺ then remarked, "By Allah ﷻ! If the entire Ummah of Muhammad ﷺ take hold of the shaft of a spear and I take hold of the head at the expense of a single person losing his life, I would not like it even if I were given the world and all its contents." *(Ibn Sa'd)*. Qatan reports that a man came to Abdullah bin Omar ﷺ and said, "No person has done worse for the Ummah of Muhammad ﷺ than you!" Abdullah bin Omar ﷺ responded by saying, "Why is that? By Allah! I have neither spilt their blood, divided their unity nor broken their strength." The man then proposed, "If you choose to become Khalifa no 2 persons would differ on the decision, everyone is pleased to have you as Khalifa." Abdullah bin Omar ﷺ replied, "I would never like the Khilafa to come to me when one man is saying 'no' and another 'why not'." *(Ibn Sa'd)*

Qasim bin Abdur Rahman reports that during the first period of strife when Ali and Mu'awiya were at war, the people once approached Abdullah bin Omar ﷺ saying, "Are you not going out to fight?" He replied, "I fought at a time when there were idols between the Hajar Aswad and the door of the Kabah until Allah wiped them out from the land of the Arabs. I do not like to fight people who recite 'La Ilaha IllAllah'." The people then accused him saying, "By Allah! That is not at all your view. All you want is for the Sahabah to kill each other off so that when none beside yourself is left, the people should say, 'Pledge allegiance to Abdullah bin Omar to lead the Mu'minin.'" Abdullah bin Omar ﷺ responded by saying, "I have no such inclinations within me. All I want is that when you say حي علي الصلوة ('Come to salah'), I want to respond and when you say حي علي الفلاح ('Come to success') I want to respond. Furthermore, when you divide, I do not wish to associate with you but when you unite, I shall never separate from you." *(Abu Nu'aym in Hilya)*. Nafi narrates that during the time when Abdullah bin Zubair ﷺ was struggling for the Khilafa and when the Khawarij and Khashabiyya sects were on the increase, someone said to Abdullah bin Omar ﷺ, "Why do you perform salah with those people and the others when they are killing each other yet you do not fight with either group?" Abdullah bin Omar ﷺ replied, "I respond to the one who says حي علي الصلوة ('Come to salah') and to the one who says حي علي الفلاح ('Come to success'). However, when someone says, 'Come to kill your brother Muslim and take his wealth', I respond with a definite 'No'." *(Ibn Sa'd)*

Hasan bin Ali ﷺ Dislikes Killing Mu'minin and Reconciles with Mu'awiya ﷺ

Abul Gharif says, "12,000 of us were part of the frontline forces of Hasan bin Ali ﷺ. Abu Umrata was our commander and in our eagerness to fight the forces from Sham, our swords were almost dripping with their blood. When the news reached us about the truce that Hasan bin Ali ﷺ and Mu'awiya ﷺ had made, it seemed as if our backs had been broken with the rage and frustration of it. When Hasan bin Ali ﷺ came to Kufa, one of our men called Abu Amir Sufian bin Layl stood up and said, 'As Salamu Alaykum, O humiliator of the Mu'minin!' 'Do not say that, O Abu Amir,' Hasan ﷺ said, 'I have not humiliated the Mu'minin but merely disliked killing them in pursuit of land." *(Hakim, Ibn Abdul Birr in Isti'ab, Khatib Baghdadi in Al Bidayah wan Nihayah)*. Sha'bi narrates that when Hasan bin Ali ﷺ and Mu'awiya ﷺ entered into a truce, Mu'awiya ﷺ said to Hasan ﷺ, "Stand up and address the people and inform them of your standpoint." Hasan ﷺ then stood up and addressed the people saying, "All praise is due to Allah Who has used our elders to guide our former ones and has now used us to save the blood of our latter ones. Behold! Indeed the most intelligent one is the one with the most Taqwa and the most helpless one is the sinner. The matter concerning which I had been disputing with Mu'awiya was either rightfully his or rightfully mine. I have however forsaken my right for the good of the Ummah of Muhammad ﷺ and to save their lives." He then turned to Mu'awlya ﷺ and addressed him with the verse: وَإِنْ أَدْرِي لَعَلَّهُ فِتْنَةٌ لَكُمْ وَمَتَاعٌ إِلَى حِينٍ (111)

And I know not, perhaps it may be a trial for you, and an enjoyment for a while. (Al-Anbiya:111)

After he descended, Amr ﷺ said to Mu'awiya ﷺ, "This is what you wanted." *(Ibn Abdul Birr in Isti'ab, Hakim, Bayhaqi)*

What Hasan ﷺ Said to Jubair bin Nufair Concerning the Khilafa

Jubair bin Nufair ﷺ narrates that he once said to Hasan bin Ali ﷺ, "The people say that you desire the Khilafa." Hasan ﷺ replied, "When I had all the Arab leaders in my hand and they were prepared to fight whom I wished to fight and make peace with whom I wanted to make peace, I forsook the post for the pleasure of Allah and to save the blood of the Ummah of Muhammad ﷺ. Would I now venture to snatch away the Khilafa with the displeasure of the people of Hijaz?" *(Hakim)*

Ayman Asadi ؓ Refuses to Fight with Marwan

Amir Sha'bi reports that when Marwan fought Dahhak bin Qais, he sent a message to Ayman bin Khuraim Asadi ؓ saying, "We would like you to fight by our side." However, Ayman ؓ sent a reply stating, "Verily my father and my uncle fought in Badr and they both took an undertaking from me never to fight anyone who recites 'La Ilaha IllAllah'. I shall fight alongside you only on condition that you bring me a certificate that guarantees me freedom from Jahannam." "Get lost!" Marwan said to Ayman ؓ before he started using bad language against the Sahabi. Ayman ؓ then recited some couplets (which mean):

"I cannot fight someone who performs salah for the sake of another king from the Quraysh
For me to fight another Muslims for no reason shall give me no benefit as long as I live while he has his kingdom and I am burdened with a sin
May Allah save me form such ignorance and foolishness"
(Abu Ya'la in Majma'uz Zawa'id, Tabrani, Bayhaqi)

What Hakam bin Amr ؓ said to Ali ؓ

A messenger from Ali ؓ once came to Hakam bin Amr ؓ with a message saying, "Verily you are most worthy of assisting me in this matter of Khilafa." Hakam ؓ's reply was, "I have heard my good friend who was your cousin ﷺ say that when matters are like this with Muslims fighting each other, it is best for you to take up a wooden sword. I have therefore already taken up a wooden sword." *(Tabrani, Haythami)*

Abdullah bin Abu Awfa ؓ Refuses to Fight for Yazid

Abu Ash'ath San'ani narrates, "Yazeed bin Mu'awiya sent me to Abdullah bin Abu Awfa ؓ. With him were many Sahabah when I asked, 'What would you command the people to do?' He replied, 'Abul Qasim ﷺ advised me that if I ever see such things happening (Muslims fighting Muslims), I should go to Mount Uhud, break my sword and remain seated in my house. 'What if someone barges into my house to kill me?' I asked. Rasulullah ﷺ replied, 'Then go to the inner room of your house and if they barge in there too, then sit on your knees preparing for death and say, 'Take my sins together with yours by killing me so that you may become one of the inmates of Jahannam. Such is the punishment for the oppressors.' I have already broken my sword and if anyone barges into my house, I shall enter the inner room. If they then enter the inner room, I shall sit on my knees and say to them what Rasulullah ﷺ told me to say.'" *(Bazzar, Haythami)*

Muhammad bin Maslamah ؓ Abides by the Advice of Rasulullah ﷺ

Muhammad bin Maslamah ؓ reports that Rasulullah ﷺ said, "When you see people fighting for worldly wealth, take your sword to the largest boulder in Harrah and strike it on the boulder until it breaks. Then remaining sitting in your home until the hand of a sinner reaches you to kill you or until death puts an end to you." Muhammad bin Maslamah ؓ then said, "I have already practiced on this command of Rasulullah ﷺ." *(Bazzar, Haythami)*. Muhammad bin Maslamah ؓ says, "Rasulullah ﷺ gave me a sword and said, 'O Muhammad bin Maslamah! Use this sword to wage Jihad in the Path of Allah until the time when you see 2 parties of the Muslims fighting each other. You should

then hit it against a rock until it breaks. You should remain sitting in your home until death puts an end to you or until the hand of a sinner reaches you to kill you.'" After the martyrdom of Uthman ؓ, when the affairs of people took the turn it did, Muhammad bin Maslamah ؓ went to a rock in his courtyard and struck his sword on it until it was broken. *(Ibn Sa'd).*

The Statement of Hudhaifa ؓ Concerning Fighting

Rib'ee reports that at the funeral of Hudhaifa, he overheard someone saying, "The person on this bier said, 'I have no doubts about what I heard Rasulullah ﷺ say. Therefore, if you people start fighting amongst yourselves, I shall enter my home and if anyone barges in, I shall tell him, 'You may kill me and take with you my sins coupled with your own." *(Ahmad, Haythami)*

The Incident Between Mua'wiya ؓ and Wa'il bin Hujar ؓ

Wa'il bin Hujar ؓ says, "When we heard about the appearance of Rasulullah ﷺ, I left with a delegation form my tribe when we reached Madinah, I met the companions of Rasulullah ﷺ before meeting him. They said, 'Rasulullah ﷺ had already given us the glad tidings of your arrival 3 days ago. He informed us that Wa'il bin Hujar would be coming to us.' Rasulullah ﷺ then met me, welcomed me and called me close to him. He spread out his shawl for me and made me sit on it. He then summoned the people and when they gathered, he mounted the pulpit, taking me along with him. As I sat just below him, he praised Allah and then said, 'O people! This is Wa'il bin Hujar who has come from a far off place. He has come from Hadhramout out of his free will and without any compulsion. He is from royal descent. May Allah bless you, O Wa'il bin Hujar and your children.' Rasulullah ﷺ dismounted. Rasulullah ﷺ then gave me a place to settle that was a bit far from Madinah and instructed Mu'awiya bin Abu Sufian to settle me there. He therefore left with me and when we were on the road, he said, 'O Wa'il! The hot sand is burning the soles of my feet, so please allow me to ride with you.' I replied, 'I am not selfish with this camel, but because you are not of royal birth, I would not like to spoil my name by riding the same animal with you.' Mu'awiya then requested, 'Then throw me your shoes so that I may have some protection from the sun.' I replied, 'I am not selfish with these shoes, but because you are not one who wears royal attire, I would not like to spoil my name with you.'" The narration continues to the point where it says that when Mu'awiya ؓ became Amirul Mu'minin, he dispatched an expedition a man from the Quraish called Busr bin Artat saying, "Since I have now annexed the entire region, I want you to leave with your army. When you leave the borders of Sham, draw your sword and kin anyone who refuses to pledge allegiance to me. Proceed in this manner to Madinah and even when you enter Madinah, I want you to kill anyone who refuses to pledge allegiance to me. And if you find Wa'il bin Hujar ؓ still alive, bring him to me. Busr did as commanded and finding Wa'il ؓ still alive, he brought him to Mu'awiya ؓ. Mu'awiya ؓ issued instructions that Wa'il ؓ be given royal welcome and after permitting him to his court, allowed him to sit on his throne. Mu'awiya ؓ then asked, "Is this throne of mine not better than your camel!'?" Wa'il ؓ replied, "O Amirul Mu'mineen! I was just newly out of ignorance and kufr at the time and that was the way we lived during the period of ignorance. Allah then brought Islam to us and Islam has concealed all that I did." Mu'awiya ؓ asked further, "Then what prevented you from assisting me when Uthman ؓ trusted you so much and even made you his son-in-law?" Wa'il ؓ replied, "Because you fought a man who was closer to Uthman ؓ than yourself. Mu'awiya ؓ remarked, "How can he be closer to Uthman ؓ than me when I am more closely related to Uthman ؓ?" Wa'il ؓ replied, "Rasulullah ﷺ forged a bond of brotherhood between Uthman ؓ and Ali ؓ and the bond is stronger than the bond of being a cousin as you are. I did not want to fight any of the Muhajirin." Mu'awiya ؓ asked, "Are we not Muhajirin as well?" Wa'il ؓ replied, "Did we not stay away from both groups? Another strong reason is that I was once with Rasulullah ﷺ with a large group when he looked towards the east He then looked back saying, 'Tribulations shall come to you like the many portions of a dark night They will be extremely difficult and unpleasant and will appear very fast' I was the only one who asked, 'O Rasulullah ﷺ! What will these tribulations be?' He replied, 'O Wa'il! When 2 swords cross in Islam, stay away from either one.'" Mu'awiya ؓ then said, "Have you now become a Shi'ee (supporter of Ali ؓ)?" "No," replied Wa'il ؓ, "I have only become a well-wisher of the Ummah." Mu'awiya ؓ said, "Had I heard this before, I would have never sent for you." Wa'il ؓ informed Mu'awiya ؓ, "Did you not see what Muhammad bin Maslama ؓ did when Uthman ؓ was martyred? He took his sword to a rock and hit it until it broke." Mu'awiya ؓ remarked, "They (Ansar) are after all people who have to be tolerated." Wa'il ؓ responded by saying, "What will you do about the statement of Rasulullah ﷺ 'Whoever loves the Ansar loves them because of his love for me and whoever hates the Ansar hates them because of his hatred for me.'"

Mu'aawiya ؓ's next statement was, "Choose whichever city you please to live in because you cannot return to Hadramout." Wa'il ؓ replied, "My tribesmen are in Sham while my family members are in Kufa." Mu'awiya ؓ commented, "A single member of you family is worth more than 10 tribesmen." Wa'il ؓ said, "After migrating I have never returned happily to Hadramout. It is also not appropriate for a Muhajir to return to the place he migrated from except with good reason." "What is your good reason'?" questioned Mu'awiya ؓ. Wa'il ؓ replied, "The statement of Rasulullah ﷺ concerning the tribulations. Because of your disputes, I have kept away from you but as soon as you unite, I shall come to you. This is the good reason." Mu'awiya ؓ offered, "I intend making you the governor of Kufa, so proceed there." "I cannot assume a post of governorship from anyone after Rasulullah ﷺ," Wa'il ؓ replied, "Did you not see that when Abu Bakr ؓ wanted to appoint me as governor, I refused'? When Omar ؓ wanted to appoint me as governor, I refused as well and even when Uthman ؓ wanted to appoint me as governor, I refused. Despite all of this, I never forsook the pledge of allegiance I took to any of them. The letter of Abu Bakr ؓ came to me when the people from my region had forsaken Islam and I stood up to fight in Jihad amongst them until Allah returned them all to the fold of Islam. This I did without having to fill the post of governorship." Mu'awiya ؓ sent for Abdur Rahman bin Ummul Hakam ؓ and said to him, "I have made you the governor of Kufa. Go there with Wa'il bin Hujar, honor him and fulfill his needs." Abdul' Rahman ؓ said, "O Amirul Mu'minin! Your opinion of me is not good. You have commanded me to honor someone whom I have seen being honored by Rasulullah ﷺ, Abu Bakr ؓ, Omar ؓ, Uthman ؓ and yourself." This statement made Mu'awiya very happy. Wa'il ؓ proceeded to Kufa with Abdur Rahman ؓ and it was not long that he passed away. *(Tabrani in Sagheer and Kabeer, Haythami)*

The Statement of Abu Barza Aslami ؓ About the Fight Between Marwan and Abdullah bin Zubair ؓ

Abul Minhal reports, "When Ibn Ziyad was expelled from Basra when Yazid passed away, Marwan seized power in Sham, Abdullah bin Zubair ؓ seized power in Makkah and a group calling themselves the 'Qurra' took control of Basra. My father was extremely grieved about the situation and said to me, 'May you have no father! Let us go to the companion of Rasulullah ﷺ Abu Barza Aslami ؓ.' I then accompanied him and when we entered the house, we found Abu Barza ؓ sitting in the shade of his balcony that was constructed from bamboo. It was an extremely hot day and we also sat down with him. My father started speaking about general matters until he finally got to ask, 'O Abu Barza! Do you not see what is happening? Do you not see what is happening?' The first thing that Abu Barza ؓ said was, 'I hope to be rewarded by Allah for becoming extremely angry with the tribes of the Quraish. O little Arab tribes! You know well the times when you were plunged in ignorance. Those were times when you were few in number, you were disgraced and astray. Allah then elevated you with Islam and with Muhammad ﷺ until you reached the heights you now enjoy. It is only the love of this world that has corrupted you. I swear by Allah that the one in Sham (Marwan) is fighting only for worldly gain. I swear by Allah that the one in Makkah (Ibn Zubair ؓ) is fighting only for worldly gain. I swear by Allah that those around you (in Basra) whom you call the Qurra are fighting only for worldly gain. I swear by Allah that those around you (in Basra) whom you call the Qurra are fighting only for worldly gain.' When Abu Barza ؓ had condemned everyone, my father asked, 'What would you then tell us to do in such situation?' Abu Barza ؓ replied, 'I see none better than the group who are attached to the ground.' He then pointed to the ground. He then continued, 'They are those whose bellies are empty of the wealth of others and whose backs are not burdened by the blood of others.'" *(Bayhaqi, Bukhari, Isma'eli, Ya'qub bin Sufian in Fat'hul Bari)*

The Statement of Hudhaifa ؓ Concerning Killing

Thamar bin Atiya reports that Hudhaifa ؓ once said to someone, "Will it please you to kill someone who is the worst of sinners?" When the man replied in the affirmative, Hudhaifah ؓ remarked, "In that case, you will be an even worse sinner than he." *(Abu Nu'aym in Hilya)*

Abstaining from Wasting the Life of a Muslim

Anas ؓ reports that Omar ؓ once asked him, "What do you do when you lay siege to any city'?" Anas ؓ replied, "We first make a strong shield from leather and send one of our men." "Now tell me," Omar ؓ continued, "What if rocks are thrown at him'?" "He will then be killed," replied Anas ؓ. Omar ؓ then said, "Never do that! I swear by the Being Who controls my life! It will never please me if you conquer a city of 4,000 warriors at the expense of wasting the life of single Muslim." *(Bayhaqi, Shafi'ee in Kanzul Ummal)*

Rescuing a Muslim From the Clutches of the Disbeliever

Omar ؓ once said, "More than having control over the entire Arabian peninsula, I prefer rescuing a single Muslim from the clutches of the Kuffar." *(Ibn Abi Shayba in Kanzul Ummal)*

Rasulullah ﷺ Forbids Frightening a Muslim

Abul Hasan ؓ was a Sahabi who participated in the pledge of Aqabah as well as in the Battle of Badr. He says, "We were sitting with Rasulullah ﷺ when a man stood up to leave forgetting his shoes behind. Another person took his shoes and put it beneath him. When the returned, he then asked the others where his shoes were, they replied that they had not seen it. After the Sahabi worriedly searched for his shoes, the other Sahabi who hid it away said, "Here are they." Rasulullah ﷺ then remarked, "How will you answer on the Day of Judgment for frightening a Mu'min'?" The Sahabah explained, "I only did it in jest." However, Rasulullah ﷺ repeated 2 or 3 times more, "How will you answer for frightening a Mu'min?" *(Tabrani in Targheeb wat Tarheeb, Haythami, Ibnus Sakan in Isabah)*. Amir bin Rabe'ah ؓ reports that a Sahabi once hid away the shoes of another Sahabi in jest. The matter was reported to Rasulullah ﷺ, he said, "Never frighten a Muslim because frightening a Muslim is a great injustice." *(Bazzar, Abush Sheikh, Ibn Hibban in Kitabut Towbigh, Targheeb wat Tarheeb, Haythami)*.

Other Narrations in this Regard

Nu'man bin Bashir ؓ narrates that they were once on a journey with Rasulullah ﷺ when one of them fell asleep on his animal. When another Sahabi removed an arrow from the sleeping man's quiver, he got up with a shock. Rasulullah ﷺ rebuked the Sahabi saying, "It is not at all permissible for anyone to frighten a Muslim." *(Tabrani in Kabir)*. Abdur Rahman bin Abu Layla reports that the Sahabah informed them that they were once traveling with Rasulullah ﷺ when one of them fell asleep. Another person went and grabbed the rope that the sleeping man was holding, causing him to get a fright. Rasulullah ﷺ rebuked the man saying, "It is not at all permissible for anyone to frighten a Muslim." *(Abu Dawud in Targheeb wat Tarheeb)*. Sulaiman bin Surad ؓ narrates that a Bedouin was once performing salah with Rasulullah ﷺ when someone took away the rope he had with him. After Rasulullah ﷺ has completed the salah with Salam, the Bedouin exclaimed, "My rope!" Some of the Sahabah involved in taking the rope away were busy laughing. Rasulullah ﷺ rebuked them saying, "Whoever believes in Allah and the Last Day should never frighten a Muslim." *(Tabrani, Haythami)*

Belittling and Looking Down at a Muslim: The Narrations of Aisha ؓ, Ata and Urwa ؓ about Usama bin Zaid ؓ

Aisha ؓ narrates that Usama bin Zaid ؓ once tripped and fell over a doorstep causing him to sustain a wound on his head. Rasulullah ﷺ said, "O Aisha! Wipe the blood off him." When Aisha ؓ felt repulsed to do it, Rasulullah ﷺ licked the blood off Usama ؓ's wound and then spat it out. He then said, "Had Usama been a girl, I would have adorned her with fine clothing and jewellery and got her married." *(Ibn Sa'd, Ibn Abi Shayba in Muntakhab Kanzul Ummal)*. Ata bin Yasar reports that as soon as he arrived in Madinah, Usama bin Zaid ؓ was afflicted with smallpox. He was still a little boy and mucus often ran from his nose to his mouth. This repulsed Aisha ؓ. Rasulullah ﷺ then entered the room, washed the boy's face and then kissed him. Aisha ؓ says, "By Allah! After seeing this, I shall never distance this boy from me." *(Waqidi, Ibn Asakir in Muntakhab Kanzul Ummal)*. Urwa ؓ narrates that Rasulullah ﷺ actually delayed leaving Arafah to proceed to Muzdalifa because he was waiting for Usama bin Zaid ؓ. When Usama bin Zaid ؓ who was a boy with a flat nose and a black skin arrived, the people of Yemen remarked, "Was it for someone like this that we were delayed?" Urwa says that it was because of this statement that the people of Yemen reverted to kufr." *Ibn Sa'd* says that he asked Yazid bin Ham'oon, "What did Urwa ؓ mean when he said that it was because of this that the people of Yemen reverted to kufr'?" He replied, "Their leaving the fold of Islam during the time of Abu Bakr ؓ was because they belittled the behavior of Rasulullah ﷺ (by waiting for Usama ؓ)." *(Ibn Sa'd)*. Urwa said, "After the demise of Rasulullah ﷺ, the people of Yemen reverted to kufr

because of their looking down at Usama bin Zaid ؓ." *(Ibn Asakir in Muntakhab Kanzul Ummal)*

The Statement of Omar ؓ in this Regard

Hasan reports that when a group of people once went to Abu Musa Ash'ari ؓ, he gave something to the Arabs amongst them while giving nothing to non-Arab slaves. Omar ؓ then wrote a letter to rebuke him saying, "Why did you not treat them equally? It is enough for a man to be regarded as an evil person when he looks own on his Muslim brother." *(Abu Ubaid in Kanzul Ummal, Ahmad in Zuhd)*

Making a Muslim Angry: The Incident Between Abu Bakr ؓ, Salman ؓ, Suhaib ؓ and Bilal ؓ with Regard to Abu Sufian ؓ

Aa'idh bin Omar narrates that Abu Sufian ؓ who was not yet a Muslim once approached a gathering that included Salman ؓ, Suhaib ؓ and Bilal ؓ. They passed a remark saying, "The swords of Allah had not yet taken the necks of Allah's enemies as they ought to have." Abu Bakr ؓ said to them, "Are you addressing those words to the elder of the Quraish and their leader?" When he then reported the matter to Rasulullah ﷺ, Rasulullah ﷺ said, "O Abu Bakr! You may have made them angry and if you did make them angry, you would have angered your Rabb as well" Abu Bakr ؓ then went back to them and asked, "Dear brothers! Have I made you angry?" They graciously replied, "Not at all. May Allah forgive you, dear brother." *(Muslim, Abu Nu'aym in Hilya, Ibn Abdul Birr in Isti'ab)*. Suhaib ؓ narrates that Abu Bakr ؓ was once passing by with a prisoner for whom he had sought amnesty from Rasulullah ﷺ. Suhaib ؓ who was sitting in the Masjid asked, "Who is this man with you?" Abu Bakr ؓ replied, "He is my disbelieving prisoner for whom I have sought amnesty from Rasulullah ﷺ." Suhaib ؓ commented, "His neck would have been a perfect place for a sword to strike." This infuriated Abu Bakr ؓ. Seeing Abu Bakr ؓ angry, Rasulullah ﷺ asked, "Why do I see you so angry?" Abu Bakr ؓ replied, "When I passed by Suhaib with this prisoner, he remarked, 'His neck would have been a perfect place for a sword to strike.'" "Have you not perhaps hurt him'?" Rasulullah ﷺ asked. When Abu Bakr ؓ swore by Allah that he had not, Rasulullah ﷺ said, "Had you hurt him, you would have hurt Allah and His Rasul as well." *(Ibn Asakir in Kanzul Ummal)*

Cursing a Muslim: The Narration of Omar ؓ Concerning Rasulullah ﷺ's Prohibition From Cursing Someone who Drank Wine

Omar ؓ narrates that during the time of Rasulullah ﷺ there was a man called Abdullah ؓ. He was nicknamed 'Himar' and used to make Rasulullah ﷺ laugh. Rasulullah ﷺ also had him lashed on one occasion for drinking wine. When he was again brought before Rasulullah ﷺ with guilty of drinking again, Rasulullah ﷺ issued the command for him to be lashed. Someone from the crowd remarked, "May Allah's curse be on him! How many times will he be brought?" Rasulullah ﷺ rebuked the person saying, "Do not curse him! By Allah! As far as I know, he loves Allah and His Rasul ﷺ." *(Bukhari, Ibn Jareer, Bayhaqi)*. Another narration states that a man nicknamed 'Himar' once gave Rasulullah ﷺ a container of butter and another of honey as a gift. When the owner of the butter and honey came to collect the payment and was not paid, he brought the man to Rasulullah ﷺ, saying, "O Rasulullah ﷺ! Please pay for the goods." All Rasulullah ﷺ did was to smile and then issue instructions for the man to be paid and he was. When he was brought one day to Rasulullah ﷺ on charges of drinking wine, someone from the crowd remarked..." The rest of the narration is same as quoted above. *(Abu Ya'la, Sa'eed bin Mansoor in Kanzul Ummal)*

The Narration of Zaid bin Aslam, Abu Hurairah ؓ and Salama bin Akwa ؓ in this Regard

Zaid bin Aslam narrates that Ibn Nu'man ؓ was once brought to Rasulullah ﷺ for drinking wine for which he was lashed. He was then brought 4 or 5 times again and lashed. Someone then remarked, "May Allah's curse be on him! How many times will he drink? How many times will he be lashed?" Rasulullah ﷺ rebuked the person saying, "Do not curse him because he is a man who loves Allah and His Rasul ﷺ." *(Abdur Razzaq in Kanzul Ummal, Ibn Sa'd)*. Abu Hurairah ؓ reports that when someone who had drunk wine was brought to Rasulullah ﷺ, the Sahabah hit him according to the instructions of Rasulullah ﷺ. While some of them hit him with their shoes, others hit him with their hands and others with their garments rolled up as lashes, Rasulullah ﷺ then told them to stop hitting him and to start rebuking him. They did so by telling him, "Are you not embarrassed in front of Rasulullah ﷺ by doing such things?" Rasulullah ﷺ then let him go. However, as he turned away, some people started cursing him and casting verbal abuse at him. When someone said, "O Allah! Humiliate him! O Allah! Curse him!" Rasulullah ﷺ interrupted by saying, "Do not say that! Do not assist Saitan against your brother. Rather say, 'O Allah! Forgive him. O Allah! Guide him,'" Another narration states that Rasulullah ﷺ said, "Do not say that! Do not assist Saitan. Rather say, 'May Allah have mercy on you.'" *(Ibn Jareer in Kanzul Ummal)*. Salamah bin Akwa ؓ says, "Whenever we saw a person cursing his brother Muslim, it was our belief that he had approached a door of the major sins, he had committed a major sin." *(Tabrani in Targheeb wat Tarheeb)*

Swearing a Muslim: A Narration of Aisha ؓ Concerning a Man who Swore His Slave

Aisha ؓ narrates that a man came and sat in front of Rasulullah ﷺ. He said, "I have many slaves who lie to me, cheat me, and disobey me. I retaliate when I swear and hit them. What is my position with them?" Rasulullah ﷺ replied, "On the Day of Judgment, their cheating, disobedience, and lies will be calculated together with the punishment you gave them. If your punishment is equal to their wrongs, the slate will be clean and you will neither have anything for you or against you. If your punishment exceeds their wrongs, they will be allowed to have revenge for the excess." The man stepped aside and started crying loudly. Rasulullah ﷺ said, "Did you not read Allah says:

وَنَضَعُ الْمَوَازِينَ الْقِسْطَ لِيَوْمِ الْقِيَامَةِ فَلَا تُظْلَمُ نَفْسٌ شَيْئًا وَإِنْ كَانَ مِثْقَالَ حَبَّةٍ مِنْ خَرْدَلٍ أَتَيْنَا بِهَا وَكَفَى بِنَا حَاسِبِينَ (47)

And We shall set up balances of justice on the Day of Resurrection, then none will be dealt with unjustly in anything. And if there be the weight of a mustard seed, We will bring it. And Sufficient are We as Reckoners. (Al-Anbiya:47). The man then said, "O Rasulullah ﷺ! I see nothing for them and myself better than being separated from each other. I make you witness that they are all free." *(Ahmad, Tirmidhi in Targheeb wat Tarheeb, Haythami)*

The Incident Between Rasulullah ﷺ and Abu Bakr ؓ When Someone was Swearing Him

Abu Hurairah ؓ narrates that someone started swearing Abu Bakr ؓ while Rasulullah ﷺ was also sitting there. Rasulullah ﷺ was impressed and kept smiling because Abu Bakr ؓ gave no reply. However, when the person's abuse became too much, Abu

Bakr ؓ replied to some of what he was saying. This angered Rasulullah ﷺ and he left. Abu Bakr ؓ then met Rasulullah ﷺ and asked, "O Rasulullah ﷺ! You were sitting there while he was swearing at me but when I replied to some of his abuse, you became angry and left?" Rasulullah ﷺ replied, "There was an angel with you who was responding on your behalf. However, when you started replying to some of his abuse, Saitan arrived and I could not sit with Saitan." Rasulullah ﷺ then added, "O Abu Bakr! 3 things are absolute facts. Whenever a person overlooks any injustice done to him, Allah lends him tremendous strength. Whenever a person opens the door of gifts with the intention of joining ties, Allah increases for him in abundance. Whenever a person opens the door of begging with the intention of amassing wealth, Allah speeds up the reduction of his wealth." *(Ahmad, Tabrani, Haythami)*

Omar ؓ Vows to Cut Off His Son's Tongue for Swearing Miqdad ؓ

When Abdullah ؓ the son of Omar ؓ once swore Miqdad ؓ, Omar ؓ said, "A vow is still binding on me if I do not cut off your tongue!" Even after others had spoken to Omar ؓ and pleaded with him to forgive his son, Omar ؓ said, "Leave me to cut off his tongue so that he may never again swear any companion of Rasulullah ﷺ." Bahia narrates that there once arose a dispute between Abdullah bin Omar ؓ and Miqdad ؓ. When Abdullah bin Omar ؓ swore Miqda ؓ, the latter complained to Abdullah ؓ's father Omar ؓ. Omar ؓ then vowed to cut off the tongue of his son. When Abdullah bin Omar ؓ feared that his father would fulfill the vow, he sent some people to intercede on his behalf. However, Omar ؓ said, "Leave me to cut off his tongue so that this becomes a precedent for others to emulate after me. Every person who then swears any of the companions of Rasulullah ﷺ will then have his tongue cut off." *(Ibn Asakir in Muntakhab Kanzul Ummal)*

Rasulullah ﷺ Admonishes a Sahabi for Speaking Ill of a Muslim

Anas ؓ reports that someone spoke ill of another in front of Rasulullah ﷺ. "Stand up and leave," said Rasulullah ﷺ, "for your Shahada is worthless." "O Rasulullah ﷺ! I shall never repeat myself," pleaded the Sahabi. Rasulullah ﷺ said, "You have mocked the Qur'an this morning. Whoever legalizes something that the Qur'an forbids cannot have Iman and this is what you appeared to have done by speaking ill of someone which the Qur'an forbids."*(Abu Nu'aym in Hilya, Kanzul Ummal)*.

The Incident Between Khalid ؓ and Sa'd ؓ

Tariq bin Shihab reports that there was once a dispute between Khalid ؓ and Sa'd ؓ. When someone started speaking ill of Khalid in front of Sa'd ؓ, he said, "Be quiet! Our dispute ended where it did and will not reach Islam, it should not affect our Islam by leading us to speak ill of each other." *(Abu Nu'aym in Hilya, Haythami)*

Rasulullah ﷺ Admonishes Those who Bckbite a Sahabi who was Pnished for Aultery

Abu Hurairah ؓ narrates that a Sahabi from the Banu Aslam tribe once approached Rasulullah ﷺ and 4 times on different occasions confessed that he had illegal intercourse with a woman. However, Rasulullah ﷺ ignored his confession each time. The narration then continues to the point where Rasulullah ﷺ finally gave the instruction for him to be stoned to death. After he was stoned, Rasulullah ﷺ overheard one of the Sahabah saying to another, "Look at this man! Whereas Allah had concealed him, he did not leave himself to be until he was stoned like a dog." Rasulullah ﷺ did not respond to the remark and walked on for a while. When they passed by the corpse of an ass whose one leg was raised in the air, Rasulullah ﷺ called for the 2 men. When they presented themselves, Rasulullah ﷺ said to them, "Dismount and eat from that corpse." Their response was, "O Nabi of Allah! May Allah forgive you! Who can eat from that?" Rasulullah ﷺ said, "What you just backbite about your brother is worse than eating that corpse. I swear by the Being Who controls my life that at this moment he is diving in the rivers of Jannah." *(Abdur Razzaq, Abu Dawud in Kanzul Ummal, Ibn Hibban in Saheeh, Targheeb wat Tarheeb, Bukhari in Adab, Hafidh from Ibn Hibban in Fat'hul Bari).* Ibnul Munkadir narrates that when Rasulullah ﷺ had a woman stoned, someone remarked, "All her deeds are destroyed!" To this, Rasulullah ﷺ responded by saying, "While the punishment absolved her of the sin, you will be taken to task for what you have said." *(Abdur Razzaq in Kanzul Ummal)*

The Narrations of Aisha ☺ and Zaid bin Aslam Concerning Safiya ☺ and Another Lady

Aisha ☺ narrates that she once said to Rasulullah ﷺ, "It will suffice you to know that Safiya is like that!" Narrators of the report say that Aisha ☺ was referring to the fact that Safiya ☺ was short. Rasulullah ﷺ then reprimanded Aisha ☺ saying, "Should the words you spoke be mixed with the ocean, it would surely spoil it." Aisha ☺ also reports that when she once imitated someone, Rasulullah ﷺ said that he would not like her to imitate someone in front of him even in exchange for an abundance of wealth. *(Abu Dawud, Tirmidhi, Bayhaqi).* A narration of *Abu Dawud* states that the camel of Safiya ☺ once fell ill. Because Zainab ☺ had extra riding camels, Rasulullah ﷺ asked her to give one to Safiya ☺. Zainab ☺ responded by saying, "Should I give my camel to that Jewess!" This angered Rasulullah ﷺ so much that he did not go to Zainab ☺ for the months of Dhul Hijjah, Muharram and a part of Safar. *(Targheeb wat Tarheeb)* Another narration *(Ibn Sa'd)* states that Rasulullah ﷺ kept away from her for the 2 months of Dhul Hijjah and Muharram or perhaps even 3 months. Zainab ☺ says that she had even lost hope of Rasulullah ﷺ ever returning to her. Aisha ☺ says, "I was once with Rasulullah ﷺ when I remarked that a certain woman wore a long hem. 'Spit out!' Rasulullah ﷺ exclaimed, 'Sit out!' When I spat, it was a piece of meat that came out." *(Ibn Abi Dunya in Targheeb wat Tarheeb).* Zaid bin Aslam reports that Rasulullah ﷺ's wives once gathered to see Rasulullah ﷺ during the illness in which he passed away. Safiya bint Huya ☺ said, "O Nabi of Allah ﷺ! By Allah! I wish that I should rather be suffering what you are suffering." Taking her words to be insincere, the other wives then started winking at each other. Seeing them do this, Rasulullah ﷺ told them all to rinse their mouths. When they enquired what it was they were required to rinse off, Rasulullah ﷺ replied, "Your winking at the expense of your companion. I swear by Allah that she is sincere in what she said." *(Ibn Sa'd in Isabah, Ibn Sa'd)*

Rasulullah ﷺ Rebukes Some Sahabah for Their Bckbiting

Abu Hurairah ☺ narrates that when a particular Sahabi once stood up and left, some of the Sahabah remarked, "What a feeble person he is, O Rasulullah ﷺ!" or they said, "What a weak person he is!". To this, Rasulullah ﷺ admonished, "You have backbitten your friend and eaten his flesh." A narration of *Tabrani* states that when a Sahabi got up to leave, the others noticed that he did so very feebly. "How very feeble is he!" they commented. Rasulullah ﷺ immediately said, "You have eaten your brother's

flesh and backbitten him." *(Targheeb wat Tarheeb, Haythami).* Mu'adh bin Jabal ☺ report to the above with the addition that the Sahabah who passed the remark enquired, "O Rasulullah ﷺ! We have stated only what is truly his nature." Rasulullah ﷺ explained, "That is still backbiting because he would not like to hear this. If you had mentioned what was not actually in him, you would be guilty of slandering him." *(Tabrani, Haythami).* Abdullah bin Amr ☺ reports that some of the Sahabah once passed a remark about a particular Sahabi saying, "He will never eat until he is fed and will not ride unless the animal is saddled for him, he is very lazy." "You have backbitten him," Rasulullah ﷺ scolded. "O Rasulullah ﷺ!" they submitted, "But we have only stated what is his nature." Rasulullah ﷺ replied, "It is enough to backbite that you merely mention a fault that your brother truly is within him." *(Isbani in Targheeb wat Tarheeb).* Abdullah bin Mas'ood ☺ narrates that they were once with Rasulullah ﷺ when a Sahabi got up to leave. After he had left, someone then spoke ill of him. "Repent," Rasulullah ﷺ instructed. "What should I repent for?" the person queried. Rasulullah ﷺ replied, "Because you have eaten your brother's flesh." *(Ibn Abi Shayba, Tabrani in Targheeb wat Tarheeb).* Rasulullah ﷺ said, "Pick your teeth". "What should I pick them for, O Rasulullah ﷺ?" the person queried, "I have not eaten any meat?" *(Majma'uz Zawa'id)*

The Incident of 2 Ladies who Ruined Their Fasts by Backbiting

Anas ☺ reports that Rasulullah ﷺ once instructed them to fast, making it clear that none was to end the fast until he permitted them. The Sahabah then observed the fast. By the evening, a man came and said, "O Rasulullah ﷺ! I have been fasting all day, so permit me to end the fast." Rasulullah ﷺ gave him permission. In this manner, people continued coming until a man came and said, "O Rasulullah ﷺ! 2 young ladies from your family have fasted all day and are too shy to come to you for permission to end the fast, so do grant them permission to terminate their fasts." Rasulullah ﷺ ignored the man. When the man repeated himself, Rasulullah ﷺ again ignored him. When he again repeated himself, Rasulullah ﷺ again ignored him. When he did so yet again, Rasulullah ﷺ still ignored him. Thereafter, Rasulullah ﷺ said, "The 2 of them definitely did not fast. How can a person fast when he has spent this day eating the flesh of people? Go and tell them that if they really have fasted, they should vomit." The man returned to them and when he informed them of Rasulullah ﷺ's instruction, they both vomited clots of blood. The man then reported back to Rasulullah ﷺ who said, "I swear by the Being Who controls my life that it had remained in their bellies, the Fire of Jahannam would have consumed both of them." *(Abu Dawud, Tayalisi, Ibn Abi Dunya, Bayhaqi, Ahmad).* When the man told one of the ladies to vomit, she vomited blood, puss and meat which half filled a cup. When he told the other lady to vomit, she vomited blood, puss and fresh meat which filled the cup. Rasulullah ﷺ said, "The 2 of them fasted from what Allah had made lawful for them food and drink but terminated their fasts with that which Allah had forbidden for them, backbiting. The one sat with the other and started eating the flesh of other people." *(Ahmad in Targheeb wat Tarheeb).*

The Incident of Abu Bakr ☺ and Omar ☺ with a Man Who Used to serve Them

Anas bin Malik ☺ reports that it was customary amongst the Arabs to serve each other during journeys. There was a man who used to serve Abu Bakr ☺ and Omar ☺ and it once occurred that the 2 of them slept away after charging the man to prepare their meal. He however also fell asleep. When the 2 awoke and the meal was not prepared, they remarked, "He is a real sleepy head." They then got him up and told him to go to Rasulullah ﷺ with the message, "Abu Bakr ؓ and Omar ؓ convey their salams to you and ask for some gravy." When the man brought the message, Rasulullah ﷺ said, "The 2 of them have already eaten the gravy." After informing them of Rasulullah ﷺ's statement, Abu Bakr ؓ and Omar ؓ came to Rasulullah ﷺ and said, "O Rasulullah ﷺ! What have we eaten as gravy'?" Rasulullah ﷺ replied, "The flesh of your brother. I swear by the Being Who controls my life that I can see his flesh between your teeth." The 2 men submitted, "Do seek Allah's forgiveness on our behalf, O Rasulullah ﷺ." Rasulullah ﷺ advised them saying, "Ask him to seek forgiveness for you." *(Hafidh Diya Maqdasi in Mukhtarah, Tafsir Ibn Kathir)*

Spying to Discover Faults in Muslims: Omar ؓ Turns a Blind Eye to People who were Drinking

Abdur Rahman bin Auf ؓ reports that one night he stood guard over Madinah with Omar ؓ. As they were walking along, they noticed a lantern in a house. They walked towards it and when they got close, they found the door ajar. It revealed some people talking in raised voices and making a noise. Taking hold of Abdur Rahman bin Auf ؓ's hand, Omar ؓ asked, "Do you know whose house is this'?" Abdur Rahman bin Auf ؓ replied, "This is the house of Rabe'ah bin Umayya bin Khalaf and the people here are drinking wine. What do you think we should do'?" Omar ؓ said, "We have perpetrated what Allah has prohibited when He says: وَلَا تَجَسَّسُوا ...*And do not spy... (Al-Hujurat:12)*

We have spied." Omar ؓ then went away and turned a blind eye to them. *(Abdur Razzaq, Abd bin Humaid, Ibn Mundhir, Sa'eed bin Mansoor in Kanzul Ummal)*

The Incident of Omar ؓ with an Individual and a Group of People

Sha'bi narrates that when Omar ؓ did not see one of his companions for some time, he told Abdur Rahman bin Auf ؓ to accompany him to the man's house to see what had happened to him. When they approached the house, they found the door open. The man was sitting there and his wife was busy pouring something in his cup and giving it to him. Omar ؓ said to Abdur Rahman bin Auf ؓ, "This is what had been keeping him away from us. Abdur Rahman ؓ asked, "How will you know what is in the cup? Omar ؓ said, "I fear that this may be spying." "But it is spying," Abdur Rahman ؓ confirmed. "What is the way to repent for this?" Omar ؓ asked. Abdur Rahman ؓ replied, "Do not inform him what has been learnt about his affairs and maintain only good thoughts about him." The 2 men then left. *(Ibn Mundhir, Sa'eed bin Mansoor in Kanzul Ummal).* Ta'oos reports that Omar ؓ left home one night to keep guard over some travelers who had set up camp on the outskirts of Madinah. It was late at night when he passed by a house where some people were drinking wine. Omar ؓ called out, "Is the command of Allah being disobeyed? Is the command of Allah being disobeyed?" One of them responded by saying, "Allah has prohibited you from this (spying)." Omar ؓ then went away and left them alone. *(Abdur Razzaq in Kanzul Ummal)*

Omar ؓ Scales the Wall of a Singer's House

Thowr Kindi narrates that Omar ؓ was patrolling Madinah one night when he heard a man singing in his house. Omar ؓ scaled the wall of the house and confronted the man saying, "O enemy of Allah! Do you think that Allah will conceal your wrongs when you disobey Him?" The man replied, "Do not be hasty, O Amirul Mu'minin! While I may have disobeyed Allah in

one respect, you have disobeyed on 3 counts. While Allah declares... وَلَا تَجَسَّسُوا
...*Do not spy.. (Hujurat:12)*, you have spied. While Allah says....' وَأْتُوا الْبُيُوتَ مِنْ أَبْوَابِهَا
...*so enter homes through their proper doors... (Al-Baqara:189)*, you have scaled the wall to get to me and have done so without permission whereas Allah states:

لَا تَدْخُلُوا بُيُوتًا غَيْرَ بُيُوتِكُمْ حَتَّى تَسْتَأْنِسُوا وَتُسَلِّمُوا عَلَى أَهْلِهَا ذَلِكُمْ خَيْرٌ لَكُمْ لَعَلَّكُمْ تَذَكَّرُونَ (27)

...*enter not houses other than your own, until you have asked permission and greeted those in them, that is better for you, in order that you may remember. (An-Nur:27)*

Omar ؓ submitted, "Will you employ the good in you if I overlook what you have been doing?" "Certainly," the man replied. Omar ؓ then pardoned the man, leaving the house and the man alone. *(Khara'iti in Kanzul Ummal)*

An Incident of Omar ؓ with an Old Man

Suddi reports that Abdullah bin Mas'ood ؓ was with Omar ؓ when he saw the light of a fire during the dead of night. Following the light, Omar ؓ entered a house lit by a lantern. There they discovered an old man sitting with some drink and a slave girl who was singing for him. The man perceived nothing until Omar ؓ confronted him. Omar ؓ exclaimed, "To this night, I have never seen a sight uglier than this old man waiting for his death in such sin!" The old man lifted his gaze and said, "Quite in order, O Amirul Mu'minin! But what you have done is even uglier. You have been spying when Allah has forbidden it and you have entered without permission." "You are right," Omar ؓ admitted. As he left biting his garment and weeping, he said, "Omar's mother may well have lost him if his Rabb does not forgive him. This old man thought that he was hiding himself from his family but will now continue sinning saying that Omar ؓ has already seen me what more have I to lose." The old man then stayed away from Omar ؓ's gatherings for a while. Omar ؓ was one day sitting in a gathering when the old man came unnoticeably and sat amongst the people at the back. Seeing him arrive, Omar ؓ sent someone to summon him. When the person told the old man that Omar ؓ was calling for him, the old man expected that Omar ؓ would now punish him for what he had seen him do. "Come closer to me," Omar ؓ bade the old man. Omar ؓ then kept calling him closer until he seated him right beside him. "Bring your ear closer to me," Omar ؓ told the old man. Omar ؓ then whispered in his ear saying, "Listen! I swear by the Being Who has sent Muhammad ﷺ as a Rasul with the truth that neither I nor Ibn Mas'ood who was with me has informed a soul about what we had seen you doing." The old man then said to Omar ؓ "O Amirul Mu'minin! Bring your ear closer to me". He then whispered in Omar ؓ's ear saying, "Listen! I swear by the Being Who has sent Muhammad ﷺ as a Rasul with the truth that up to the time that I have come to this gathering, I have never repeated myself." Omar ؓ then raised his voice saying, "Allahu Akbar!" and none present there had any idea why he had done so. *(Abu Shaikh in Kanzul Ummal)*

The Incident of Omar ؓ with Abu Mihjin Thaqafi ؓ

Abu Qilaba narrates that Omar ؓ was once informed that Abu Mihjin Thaqafi ؓ and some of his friends were drinking wine at his house. Omar ؓ left and entered the house, finding only one person with Abu Mihjin. Abu Mihjin ؓ said, "O Amirul Mu'minin! This is not at all permissible for you because Allah has forbidden you from spying." "What is he saying?" asked Omar ﷺ. Zaid bin Thabit ﷺ and Abdur Rahman bin Arqam ﷺ both agreed saying, "He is right, an Amirul Mu'minin! This falls into the category of spying." Omar ﷺ then left him alone. *(Tabrani in Kanzul Ummal)*

Concealing the Faults of Muslims: Omar ﷺ's Instructions to the Family of a Young Lady

Sha'bi reports that a man once came to Omar ﷺ saying, "I had a daughter whom I had buried alive during the period of ignorance. However, we then removed her from the ground before she died. Together with us, she then found the Period of Islam and accepted Islam. After accepting Islam, she became liable for capital punishment for violating the law of Allah. She then grabbed a dagger to kill herself but we managed to stop her after she had severed an artery. We then treated her and she has recovered. Subsequently, she has repented most sincerely. Now that she has received a proposal for marriage from a certain family, we have informed all about her past." Omar ﷺ said, "Do you wish to expose that which Allah has concealed? By Allah! If you ever again inform anyone about her past, I shall make you a lesson for all the people of the many cities to learn from. Marry her as you would marry any chaste Muslim woman." *(Hannas, Harith in Kanzul Ummal)*. Sha'bi narrates that a woman was once punishment for a crime of immorality. After her tribe had arrived as immigrants in Madinah, she repented very sincerely. When she received a proposal for marriage, her uncle did not approve of getting her married without first informing the people about her past. At the same time, he also disliked disclosing her secret. When he consulted Omar ﷺ about the matter, Omar ﷺ said, "Get her married as you would get any of your righteous girls married." *(Sa'eed bin Mansoor, Bayhaqi in Kanzul Ummal)*

The Incident of Omar ﷺ, a Little Child and 4 Women

Sha'bi also reports that a woman once came to Omar ﷺ saying, "O Amirul Mu'minin! I have found a child abandoned together with an Egyptian cloth bag containing 100 Dinars. I then took the child and hired a wet nurse for him. There are now 4 women who come to the child and kiss him. I do not know which of them may be his mother." Omar ﷺ then told her to inform him as soon as the women arrived again. When she did as told, Omar ﷺ came and asked one of the women, "Which of you is the child's mother?" She responded by saying, "O Omar! You have not done well and your approach is totally wrong. Do you wish to expose a woman whom Allah has concealed?" "You are right," Omar ﷺ admitted. He then said to the lady caring for the child, "Whenever these women come to you, you should not question them about anything and continue caring for the child." He then left. *(Bayhaqi in Kanzul Ummal)*

Anas ﷺ Instructs That a Lady Should not be Exposed

Salih bin Karz narrates, "I once brought before Hakam bin Ayub a slave girl of mine who had fornicated. I was sitting there when Anas bin Malik arrived and sat down as well. 'O Salih!' he asked, 'Who is this slave girl with you?' I replied, 'She is my slave girl who has fornicated and I wish to have her case brought before the governor so that she may be punished.' Anas ﷺ said, 'Do not do that. Rather take your slave girl back home. Fear Allah and conceal her folly.' When I refused to do as he said, he said, 'Do not go ahead and do as I say.' He then continued insisting until I eventually took her back." *(Abdur Razzaq in Kanzul Ummal)*

The Incident of Uqba bin Amir ﷺ's Scribe and a Group of People who had been Drinking

Dukhain Abul Haytham was a scribe for Uqba bin Amir ﷺ. He says, "I once said to Uqba ﷺ, 'We have a few neighbors who drink wine. I am going to call for the police to arrest them.' He advised, 'Do not do that. Advise and threaten them with arrest.' I replied, 'I have tried to stop them but they refuse to take heed. I will now have to call the police to arrest them.' Uqba ﷺ insisted, 'Shame on you! Do not do that because I heard Rasulullah ﷺ say, 'Whoever conceals a fault is like one who has brought back to life one who has been buried alive." *(Abu Dawud, Nasa'ee in Targheeb wat Tarheeb, Ibn Hibban, Mundhiri)*.

The Incident Between Abu Darda ﷺ and His Son Concerning the Criminals of Damascus

Bilal bin Sa'd Ash'ari narrates that Mu'awiya ﷺ once wrote to Abu Darda ﷺ to submit to him the names of all the criminals of Damascus. Abu Darda ﷺ said, "What have I to do with the criminals of Damascus? How am I to know who they are?" His son Bilal then offered to write their names and when he did, Abu Darda ﷺ said, "How do you know them? You would never know that they are criminals unless you are amongst them, so begin with your own name." He did not send the list. *(Bukhari in Adab)*

The Incident Between Jareer ﷺ and Omar ﷺ in this Regard

Sha'bi reports that Omar ﷺ was once in a room with Jareer bin Abdullah ﷺ and others when he smelt an odor from someone who had passed wind. Omar ﷺ said, "I command the person responsible for this odor to get up and perform wudhu." Jareer ﷺ then said, "O Amirul Mu'minin! Should everyone rather not perform wudhu so that the one person is not embarrassed?" Omar ﷺ praised him saying, "You were an excellent leader during the period of ignorance and now an excellent guide in Islam." *(Ibn Sa'd in Kanzul Ummal)*

Forgiving and Overlooking the Faults of a Muslim: The Letter of Hatib bin Abi Balt'ah ﷺ

Ali ﷺ narrates that Rasulullah ﷺ dispatched him, Zubair ﷺ and Miqdad ﷺ with instruction saying, "Ride until you reach Rawda Khakh, 12 miles from Madinah. There you will find a woman in her carriage with a note that you should take from her." The Sahabah raced their horses to the place where they saw the woman. When they asked here for the note, she denied having it in her possession. When they threatened to remove all her clothing if she did not surrender the note, she removed the note from the braid of her hair. When they brought the note to Rasulullah ﷺ, they discovered that it was from Hatib bin Abi Balt'ah ﷺ and it was addressed to the disbeliever of Makkah, passing on to them some information about the intentions of Rasulullah ﷺ. When Rasulullah ﷺ asked Hatib ﷺ what the matter was, Hatib ﷺ explained, "O Rasulullah ﷺ! Please do not be hasty. I am not one of the Quraish and was only living with them as an ally. Qurtubi mentions Hatib was from Yemen. The others who have migrated with you have relatives in. Makkah by virtue of whom their families and property are protected. Because I have no relatives there I wanted to do a favor for the Quraish so that they become indebted to me. In this way, they will see to the protection of my family. I did not do it out of apostasy nor because of being pleased with kufr after becoming a Muslim." After hearing the story, Rasulullah ﷺ said, "He has spoken the truth." Omar ﷺ then exclaimed, "O Rasulullah ﷺ! Permit me to behead this hypocrite." Rasulullah ﷺ said, "Hatib participated in the Battle of Badr and Allah has looked upon the veterans of

Badr saying, 'Do as you please because I have forgiven you'". It was with reference to this incident that Allah revealed:

يَا أَيُّهَا الَّذِينَ آمَنُوا لَا تَتَّخِذُوا عَدُوِّي وَعَدُوَّكُمْ أَوْلِيَاءَ تُلْقُونَ إِلَيْهِمْ بِالْمَوَدَّةِ وَقَدْ كَفَرُوا بِمَا جَاءَكُمْ مِنَ الْحَقِّ يُخْرِجُونَ الرَّسُولَ وَإِيَّاكُمْ أَنْ تُؤْمِنُوا بِاللَّهِ رَبِّكُمْ إِنْ كُنْتُمْ خَرَجْتُمْ جِهَادًا فِي سَبِيلِي وَابْتِغَاءَ مَرْضَاتِي تُسِرُّونَ إِلَيْهِمْ بِالْمَوَدَّةِ وَأَنَا أَعْلَمُ بِمَا أَخْفَيْتُمْ وَمَا أَعْلَنْتُمْ وَمَنْ يَفْعَلْهُ مِنْكُمْ فَقَدْ ضَلَّ سَوَاءَ السَّبِيلِ (1)

O you who believe! Take not My enemies and your enemies (i.e. disbelievers and polytheists, etc.) as friends, showing affection towards them, while they have disbelieved in what has come to you of the truth (i.e. Islamic Monotheism, this Qur'an, and Muhammad ﷺ), and have driven out the Messenger (Muhammad ﷺ) and yourselves (from your homeland) because you believe in Allah your Lord! If you have come forth to strive in My Cause and to seek My Good Pleasure, (then take not these disbelievers and polytheists, etc., as your friends). You show friendship to them in secret, while I am All-Aware of what you conceal and what you reveal. And whosoever of you (Muslims) does that, then indeed he has gone (far) astray, (away) from the Straight Path. (Al-Mumtahina:1) (Bukhari, Muslim, Abu Dawud, Tirmidhi, Nasa'ee in Al Bidayah wan Nihayah). Jabir ؓ adds that Hatib said, "Rasulullah ﷺ! I did not write the note because I am a hypocrite or because I wished to betray the messenger of Allah. I knew that Allah would grant victory to His Nabi and complete Islam irrespective of whether I wrote or not. I was always an alien in Makkah and my mother still lives there. So I wished that the people of Makkah become indebted to me and care for my mother on account of this." Omar ؓ exclaimed, "O Rasulullah ﷺ! Permit me to behead this hypocrite." Rasulullah ﷺ said, "Do you want to kill a veteran of Badr? Hatib participated in the Battle of Badr and Allah has looked upon the veterans of Badr saying, 'Do as you please.'" (Ahmad in Al Bidayah wan Nihayah, Haythami, Hakim in Kanzul Ummal, Abu Ya'la, Bazzar, Tabrani)

The Incident of Ali ؓ with a Thief

Abu Matar reports that he once saw a person being brought to Ali ؓ. The people accused him of stealing a camel. Ali ؓ said to him, "I do not think that he had stolen." "No," said the man, "I did steal" Ali ؓ then asked, "Perhaps you made a mistake, mistook someone else's camel as your own." However, the man confessed saying, "Not at all. I did steal" Ali ؓ then instructed his slave Qambar saying, "Take him and tie up his fingers. Then light a fire and summon the executioner to cut off his hand. Then wait for me to arrive." When Ali ؓ later arrived, he asked the man, "Did you steal?" This time his reply was, "No." Ali ؓ then let him go free. Some people asked, "O Amirul Mu'minin! Why did you let him go when he had already confessed before you?" Ali ؓ replied, "It was by his statement that I had apprehended him so I therefore let him go also because of his statement. When a person was brought to Rasulullah ﷺ for stealing, his hand was cut by the command of Rasulullah ﷺ. Rasulullah ﷺ then started to weep. When I asked him what made him weep, he replied, 'Why should I not weep when the hands of my Ummah are being cut?' Some people then asked, 'O Rasulullah ﷺ! Why did you then not pardon the man?' Rasulullah ﷺ replied, 'It is only an unfit ruler who would pardon a crime deserving corporal punishment. It is you people who should pardon each other for crimes committed against you rather than demand the punishment.'" (Abu Ya'la in Kanzul Ummal)

The Instruction of Abdullah bin Mas'ood ؓ Concerning a Drunk

Abu Majid Hanafi reports that a man once brought his drunken nephew to Abdullah bin Mas'ood ؓ saying, "I found him drunk." Abdullah bin Mas'ood ؓ said, "Shake him up and smell his mouth." When the people shook him up and smelt his mouth, they discovered that he smelt of wine. Abdullah bin Mas'ood ؓ then had him imprisoned. When the man was taken out of prison the following day, Abdullah bin Mas'ood ؓ issued instructions for the end of the whip to be hammered, flattened and softened so that it may not be too hard on the man. He then said to the flogger, "Do not lift your hand so high that your armpits show and give every limb its right." The man was wearing a cloak and trousers when he was being flogged. Abdullah bin Mas'ood ؓ had the man flogged lightly in this way and then set him free. Thereafter, Abdullah bin Mas'ood ؓ said with reference to the uncle, "By Allah! He is terrible guardian over an orphan! Neither did he train his ward well nor did he save him from disgrace. Allah is indeed Most Forgiving and loves forgiving people. It is improper for a governor not to enforce corporal punishment when the case is brought before him." He then started relating a Hadith, "The first Muslim whose hand was cut for theft was a man from the Ansar who was brought before Rasulullah ﷺ. This depressed so much that it appeared as if dust had been thrown over Rasulullah ﷺ's face. 'O Rasulullah ﷺ!' some people asked, 'It appears as if this is extremely hard for you?' Rasulullah ﷺ replied, 'What is there to prevent me from being depressed when you people are assisting Saitan against your brother by not forgiving him rather than demanding that he be punished. Allah is indeed Most Forgiving and loves to forgive. It is improper for a ruler not to enforce corporal punishment when the case is brought before him.' Rasulullah ﷺ then recited the verse:

وَلْيَعْفُوا وَلْيَصْفَحُوا أَلَا تُحِبُّونَ أَنْ يَغْفِرَ اللَّهُ لَكُمْ وَاللَّهُ غَفُورٌ رَحِيمٌ (22)

Let them pardon and forgive. Do you not love that Allah should forgive you? And Allah is Oft-Forgiving, Most Merciful. (An-Nur:22) (Abdur Razzaq, Ibn Abi Dunya, Ibn Abi Hatim, Tabrani, Hakim, Bayhaqi)

Amr bin Shu'aib narrates that the first instance of corporal punishment enforced in Islam was to a man who was brought to Rasulullah ﷺ. After the witnesses had testified against him, Rasulullah ﷺ gave the instruction for his hand to be cut. After the man's hand was amputated, Rasulullah ﷺ's face appeared as if dust had been thrown on it. The Sahabah asked, "O Rasulullah ﷺ! It appears as if the amputation of his hand had been hard for you?" 'What is there to prevent me from being depressed when you people are assisting Saitan against your brother?" "Why did you not release him then?" they asked. Rasulullah ﷺ said, "Why did you not do that before bringing him to me? When a ruler is presented with a case deserving of punishment, it is improper for him to ignore it when guilt is proven, the ruler cannot waive the punishment unless the aggrieved party pardons the criminal." (Abdur Razzaq in Kanzul Ummal)

The Incident of Abu Musa Ash'ari ؓ Flogging a Drunk and the Letter Omar ؓ wrote to Him

Abdullah bin Omar ؓ narrates that he was once with his father Omar ؓ for Hajj or Umrah when they spotted a rider arrive. "I think that he is looking for us," said Omar ؓ. When the man arrived, he started weeping. Omar ؓ consoled him saying, "What is the matter? If you are in debt, we shall assist you. If you are in fear, we shall grant you security; unless you have murdered someone and deserve to be executed. If you dislike living amongst certain people, we shall transfer you away from them." The man replied, "When living with the Banu Taym, I drank some wine. Abu Musa Ash'ari had me flogged, shaved off my hair, blackened my face and had me paraded through the streets announcing to the people, 'Do not associate with him and do not eat with him!' Three ideas then came to my mind. The first was to use my sword to kill Abu Musa, the second was to come to you so that you may transfer me to Sham where no one knows me, and the third was to join the enemy and to eat and drink with them." Omar ✿ then also started to weep saying, "Even if Omar ✿ were to have a staggering sum of wealth, it would give me no pleasure if you were to do these things. In fact, I had been one of the worst drunks during the Period of Ignorance. Drinking is not as serious a crime as adultery." Omar ✿ then wrote to Abu Musa Ash'ari ✿. After greeting and informing him that the particular person from the Banu Taym tribe had reported the incident to him, he wrote:

"I swear by Allah that if you ever repeat yourself, I shall ensure that I blacken your face and parade you through the streets. If you wish to know whether my words are true, go ahead and repeat what you did. Command the people to associate with the man and to eat with him. If he has repented, they should also accept his testimony."

Omar ✿ then gave the man transport together with 200 Dirhams. *(Bayhaqi in Kanzul Ummal).*

Interpreting the Actions of Muslims in a Favorable Manner: The Incident of Khalid bin Walid ✿ and Malik bin Nuwaira ✿

Abu Own and others reports that Khalid bin Walid ✿ once claimed that Malik bin Nuwaira ✿ had left the fold of Islam because of a statement he had been informed Malik ✿ made. However, Malik ✿ denied the allegation saying, "I am still firm on Islam and have not changed in the least." However, even though Abu Qatadah ✿ and Abdullah bin Omar ✿ testified in favor of Malik ✿, Khalid bin Walid ✿ brought Malik ✿ forward and commanded Dirar bin Azwar Asadi ✿ to execute Malik ✿, which he did. After the expiry of her Iddah, Khalid bin Walid ✿ then married Malik ✿'s wife Ummu Mutammim. When the news reached Omar ✿ that Khalid bin Walid ✿ had Malik ✿ executed and married his wife, Omar ✿ said to Abu Bakr ✿, "Khalid has committed adultery so have him stoned to death." However, Abu Bakr ✿ again said, "I cannot have him stoned because he had not done so intentionally but he had erred in his judgment." Omar ✿ insisted, "But you should have him executed because he had killed a Muslim." Abu Bakr ✿ said, "I cannot have him executed because he had not done so intentionally but he had erred in his judgment." "At least relieve him of his post," demanded Omar ✿. Abu Bakr responded by saying, "I shall never sheath a sword that Rasulullah ﷺ had drawn." *(Ibn Sa'd in Kanzul Ummal)*

Hating the Sin and not the Sinner: Abu Darda ✿ and Abdullah bin Mas'ood ✿ Forbid Swearing a Sinner

Abu Qilaba narrates that Abu Darda ✿ once passed by a person whom people were insulting for committing a sin." Abu Darda ✿ said to them, "If you people ever found him lying in a well, would you take him out of it?" When they replied that they certainly would, Abu Darda ✿ said, "Then do not insult your brother but rather thank Allah for safeguarding you from the sin." "Do you not hate him?" the people enquired. Abu Darda ✿ replied, "I only hate his evil act. When he forsakes it, he is again my brother." *(Ibn Asakir in Kanzul Ummal, Abu Nu'aym in Hilya).* Another narration states that Abdullah bin Mas'ood ✿ said, "When you see your brother commit a sin, do not assist Saitan against him by saying, 'O Allah! Humiliate him! O Allah! Curse him!' Rather ask Allah for safety from the sin. We the

companions of never said anything about a person until we knew in what condition he died. If he died in a good manner, we then knew for certain that he earned much good. On the other hand, if he died in a bad way, we feared for him." *(Abu Nu'aym in Hilya)*

Keeping the Heart Free From Ill-Feelings and Jealousy: The Incident of Abdullah bin Amr ✿ and a Sahabi Whom Rasulullah ﷺ had Given the Glad Tidings of Jannah

Anas ✿ reports that they were once sitting with Rasulullah ﷺ when he said, "A man from amongst the people of Jannah shall now appear before you." A man from the Ansar then arrived with his beard dripping water from his wudhu and hanging his shoes over his left hand. The next day Rasulullah ﷺ said the same thing and the same man again appeared as he did the first time. On the third day, Rasulullah ﷺ again repeated his words and the man appeared yet again in the same state as he did previously. After Rasulullah ﷺ had stood up and left, Abdullah bin Amr bin Al Aas ✿ followed the man saying to him, "I had an argument with my father and swore not to go home for 3 days. Do you think that you could accommodate me at your place until the period expires?" When the man agreed, Abdullah bin Amr ✿ stayed with him for 3 days. Abdullah bin Amr ✿ did not see the man perform any salah during the night. All he did was to engage in Dhikr and recite "Allahu Akbar" whenever he awoke at night and turned on another side. He then continued sleeping until the Fajr salah. "Apart from this," Abdullah bin Amr ✿ recalls, "I heard him speaking only good. After the 3 days had passed, I was on the verge of thinking that his deeds were not deserving of the tribute Rasulullah ﷺ paid to them, when I enquired, 'O servant of Allah! There was never any argument or severed tie between my father and 1. I wanted to stay with you because on 3 occasions I heard Rasulullah ﷺ say, 'A man from amongst the people of Jannah shall now appear before you.' On each of the 3 occasions, it was you who appeared. I therefore made up my mind to stay with you for 3 days to observe your actions so that I may follow suit. I have however not seen you do anything extraordinary. What is it that you do to deserve what Rasulullah ﷺ said?" "There is nothing besides what you have observed," the man replied. When Abdullah ✿ was leaving, the man called him back and said, "There is nothing besides what you have observed. Another thing is that I harbor absolutely no ill-feelings towards any Muslim and I do not begrudge anyone for any good that Allah has granted him." Abdullah ✿ confirmed, "It is this that has conveyed you to the status Rasulullah ﷺ gave you." *(Ahmad).* Another narration names the Sahabi as Sa'd ✿. The end of this narration states that Sa'd ✿ said, "There is nothing besides what you have observed, dear nephew. However, I never go to sleep with any ill-feelings for any Muslim." *(Abu Ya'la, Bazzar)* Yet another narration states that to this, Abdullah bin Amr ✿ remarked, "It is this that has conveyed you and it is something that we are incapable of doing." *(Nasa'ee, Bayhaqi, Isbahani in Targheeb wat Tarheeb, Haythami, Ahmad in Ibn Kathir).* Another narration names the Sahabi as Sa'd bin Abi Waqqas ✿ who said at the end, "There is nothing besides what you have observed, dear nephew. However, I do not harbor any ill-feelings for any Muslim and never speak any ill about them." To this, Abdullah bin Amr ✿ remarked, "It is this that has conveyed (glad tidings of Jannat) you and it is something that I am incapable of doing." *(Ibn Asakir in Kanzul Ummal)*

The Face of Abu Dujanah ✿ Shines During His Illness

Zaid bin Aslam ✿ reports that when people went to visit Abu Dujanah ✿ during his illness, his face was always shining and radiant. When he was asked the reason for his radiant face, he replied, "There are 2 deeds of mine that I have the most reliance on that they will be a source of my salvation and because of which my face is as you see. The 1st is that I never speak what is not necessary and the 2nd is that my heart is always clear towards all Muslims." *(Ibn Sa'd)*

Abdullah bin Abbas is Happy for the Happiness of the Muslims

Buraida Aslami narrates that when someone once insulted Abdullah bin Abbas, he responded by saying, "You are insulting me when I have 3 qualities in me. (1) Whenever I recite a verse of Allah's book, I wish that all of mankind also share the knowledge I have. (2) Whenever I hear of a Muslim ruler exercising justice amongst the people, I become extremely happy even though I may never have the opportunity of having a case judged by him. (3) Whenever I hear about rains falling upon any city of the Muslims, I become very happy for them even though I have no grazing animals in that area." *(Tabrani, Haythami, Bayhaqi in Isabah, Abu Nu'aym in Hilya)*

Rasulullah Behaves Cordially Towards a Man of Evil Disposition

Aisha reports that when a man asked permission to see Rasulullah, Rasulullah remarked, "He is the worst of his tribe." However, when he entered, Rasulullah received him most warmly and showed happiness to have him. After the man had left, another person arrived and asked permission to see Rasulullah. This time, Rasulullah remarked, "He is the best of his tribe." When this man entered, Rasulullah did not receive him as warmly as he did the first person and did not appear as happy as he did with the first. After he had left, Aisha asked, "O Rasulullah! When the 1st person arrived, you said what you did and then proceeded to receive him warmly and express happiness at his visit. You then said what you did about the 2nd person but did not receive him as you did the first person." Rasulullah replied, "Amongst the worst of people are those from whose abuse people have to guard themselves." *(Ahmad, Haythami, Bukhari in Adab)*

Safwan bin Assal narrates that they were once on a journey with Rasulullah when a man arrived. Seeing him arrive, Rasulullah commented, "He is the worst of his tribe and a terrible person." However, when he arrived, Rasulullah allowed him to sit close to him. After he has left, the Sahabah asked, "O Rasulullah! When you saw him, you said that he is the worst of his tribe and a terrible person. However, when he arrived, you allowed him to sit close to you?" Rasulullah replied, "He is a hypocrite and because of his hypocrisy I treat him cordially so that he may not spoil my name before others." *(Abu Nu'aym in Hilya)*. Buraida reports that they were once with Rasulullah when a man from the Quraish arrived. Rasulullah allowed him to sit close by and treated him like a close acquaintance. After the man had left, Rasulullah asked, "O Buraida! Do you know that man?" "Yes," replied Buraida, "He is the noblest and wealthiest of the Quraish." Rasulullah repeated the question thrice and Buraida repeated his reply each time until he eventually submitted, "O Rasulullah! I have informed you as much as I know about him. You however know better." Rasulullah then said, "He is amongst those for whose good deeds Allah shall not even erect a scale on the Day of Judgment because he has none." *(Tabrani in Awsat, Haythami)*.

The Statement of Abu Darda Concerning the Cordial Treatment of the Sahabah

Abu Darda once stated, "While we may be smiling in the faces of certain people, our hearts are actually cursing them." *(Abu Nu'aym in Hilya, Ibn Abi Dunya)*. Another narration adds that Abu Darda said, "We also laugh with them." *(Dinowri in Fat'hul Bari, Ibn Asakir in Kanzul Ummal)*

Making a Muslim Happy: Abu Bakr Regrets His Exchange of Words with Omar and Seeks Forgiveness

Abu Darda narrates that they were once sitting with Rasulullah when Abu Bakr came in a hurry holding the edge of his clothing and without realizing it because of which his knees were exposed. Rasulullah commented, "Look! Your friend has had an argument." After greeting with Salam, Abu Bakr said, "I had an argument with Omar Ibn Khattab and in the heat of the discussion I told him something. I then regretted the words and asked him to forgive me. However, he refused to do so and I have therefore come to you." Rasulullah thrice repeated, "May Allah forgive you, O Abu Bakr." Omar later regretted not forgiving Abu Bakr and went to his house. When he asked if Abu Bakr was at home, he was informed that Abu Bakr was not there. He then went to Rasulullah and greeted with Salam. However, Rasulullah's face was red with anger so much that Abu Bakr became alarmed. Kneeling down before Rasulullah, Abu Bakr pleaded, "O Rasulullah! I swear by Allah that it was I who was at fault." After Abu Bakr had repeated this twice, Rasulullah said, "When Allah sent me as a Nabi to you people, you all said that I was lying except for Abu Bakr who said, 'He is speaking the truth.' He supported me with his health and wealth, so will you people not leave my companion alone for my sake?" This Rasulullah repeated twice, after which no one hurt Abu Bakr ever again. *(Bukhari in Sifatus Safwa)*

Abdullah bin Omar narrates that Abu Bakr once used insulting words for Omar but then said, "Please forgive me, dear brother." However, Omar was extremely angry and refused to forgive him. Despite the fact that Abu Bakr repeated his request several times, Omar's anger did not abate. The incident was then reported to Rasulullah and when the Sahabah came to Rasulullah and sat before him, he said, "Your brother asked you to forgive him but you failed to do so." Omar replied, "I swear by the Being Who has sent you with truth! There was not a time that he asked me to forgive him when I did not do so privately. After you there is none of creation whom I like more than him." Abu Bakr added, "And I swear by the Being Who has sent you with the truth that after yourself there is none of creation whom I like more than him." Rasulullah remarked, "Do not hurt me concerning this companion of mine because when Allah sent me with guidance and the truth, you people said I am lying while Abu Bakr said, 'You are speaking the truth.' Had Allah not named him my companion in the Qur'an, I would have surely made him my 'Khalil', special friend. He is after all my brother in Islam. Take note! Seal off all accesses leading from some houses directly to the Masjid except the access leading from the house of Abu Bakr bin Abu Quhafa." *(Tabrani, Haythami)*

Ummu Habiba Forgives Aisha and Ummu Salama at the Time of Her Death

Aisha says, "Ummu Habiba the wife of Rasulullah called for me as she lay on her deathbed. She said, 'There had been incidents between us as occurs between co-wives. May Allah forgive me and you for all such incidents that occurred between us.' I replied by saying, 'May Allah forgive you all of that, overlook it and save you from the punishment of it all.' She said, 'You have made me happy. May Allah keep you happy.' She sent for Ummu Salama and said the same to her." *(Ibn Sa'd)*

Abu Bakr Goes to Fatima to Make Her Happy

Sha'bi narrates that when Fatima fell ill just before her demise, Abu Bakr went to request permission to address her. Her husband Ali said, "O Fatima! Abu Bakr wants permission to speak to you." "Do you want me to permit him?" she asked. When Ali replied in the affirmative, she granted permission. Abu Bakr then started saying things that would please her. He said, "By Allah! I forsook my home, wealth, family and tribe only for the pleasure of Allah, for the pleasure of His Rasul and for your pleasure, the household of Rasulullah." He then continued saying things to make her happy until she was pleased. *(Bayhaqi, Ibn Sa'd)*

Omar Asks Forgiveness From a Man Whom he Disliked

Sha'bi narrates that Omar once mentioned that he disliked a particular person. People then started asking him why Omar disliked him. Eventually, when too many people came to his house, he approached Omar and asked, "O Omar! Have I caused a rift in Islam amongst the Muslims?" When Omar replied that he did not, the man asked, "Have I then committed any crime?" When Omar again replied that he did not, the man further asked, "Have I started some new innovation in Islam?" "No," came the reply. The man then said, "For what reason do you then dislike me? Allah has mentioned:

وَالَّذِينَ يُؤْذُونَ الْمُؤْمِنِينَ وَالْمُؤْمِنَاتِ بِغَيْرِ مَا اكْتَسَبُوا فَقَدِ احْتَمَلُوا بُهْتَانًا وَإِثْمًا مُّبِينًا (58)

And those who annoy believing men and women undeservedly, bear on themselves the crime of slander and plain sin. (Al-Ahzab:58)

You have harmed me greatly by making the statement. May Allah not forgive you." Omar then said, "He is right. By Allah! neither has he caused any rift nor has he perpetrated any of the other wrongs. Do forgive me for that." Omar then continued pleading with the man to forgive him until he eventually did. *(Ibnul Mundhir in Kanzul Ummal)*

Abdullah bin Amr Seeks Pardon From Hasan bin Ali

Raja bin Rabe'ah narrates that he was once sitting in the Masjid of Rasulullah in Madinah. In the gathering with him were the likes of Abu Sa'eed and Abdullah bin Amr. When Hasan bin Ali passed by and greeted them with Salam, they all replied with the exception of Abdullah bin Amr, who remained silent. Abdullah bin Amr then watched Hasan leave and then replied: وَعَلَيْكَ السَّلَامُ وَرَحْمَةُ اللهِ

He then said further, "Of all the inhabitants of the earth, that man is most beloved to the inhabitants of the heavens. By Allah! I have not spoken to him since the days of the Battle of Siffin." Abu Sa'eed said, "Why do you then not go to him and present your excuse." Abdullah bin Amr agreed and when they went to Hasan's house, Abu Sa'eed asked permission to enter. He then entered and requested permission for Abdullah bin Amr to enter. When they had entered, Abu Sa'eed said to Abdullah bin Amr, "Tell us what you just said when Hasan passed by." "Of course," replied Abdullah bin Amr, "I had told you that of all the inhabitants of the earth, this man is most beloved to the inhabitants of the heavens." Hasan then said, "If you knew that I am the most beloved person on earth to the inhabitants of the heavens, why did you fight us and strengthen the ranks of the others during the Battle of Siffin?" Abdullah submitted, "I swear by Allah that I neither strengthened their ranks nor exerted

a sword with them. I just happened to be with my father." Hasan asked, "Did you not know that the creation cannot be obeyed when it entails disobeying the Creator?" "I did indeed," Abdullah explained, "but when I used to observe unbroken fasts during the time of Rasulullah, my father complained to Rasulullah. He said, 'O Rasulullah! Abdullah bin Amr fasts all day and engages in Ibadah all night.' Rasulullah then said, 'Fast on some days and do not fast on others. Observe Ibadah and sleep as well because I perform salah and sleep and I also fast at times and do not fast on other days.' Rasulullah then added, 'O Abdullah! Obey your father.' When my father left to fight in the Battle of Siffin, I had to leave with him." *(Bazzar, Haythami)*

Abdullah bin Amr Seeks Pardon From Husain bin Ali

Raja bin Rabe'ah narrates that he was once sitting in the Masjid of Rasulullah when Husain bin Ali passed by and greeted them with Salam. While they all replied Abdullah bin Amr, who remained silent. After the others became silent, Abdullah bin Amr replied: وَعَلَيْكَ السَّلَامُ وَرَحْمَةُ اللهِ وَبَرَكَاتُهُ

He then turned to the people saying, "Should I not inform you who of the inhabitant of the earth is most beloved to the inhabitants of the heavens?" When the people begged to know, he said, "It is that man whose back is now towards you. By Allah! Neither have I spoken a word to him nor has he spoken a word to me since the days of the Battle of Siffin. By Allah! For him to be on friendly terms with me is more beloved to me than a heap of wealth the size of Mount Uhud." Abu Sa'eed said, "Why do you then not go and present your excuse to him." Abdullah bin Amr agreed and the 2 arranged to go together the next morning. Raja says that he accompanied them the following morning. They went to Husain's house, Abu Sa'eed asked permission to enter. When Husain gave permission, he then entered with Raja and requested permission for Abdullah bin Amr to enter. When Husain refused, Abu Sa'eed kept insisting until Husain granted permission and Abdullah entered. When Abu Sa'eed saw Abdullah enter, he moved off his place to allow Abdullah to sit there but Husain pulled him back. Abdullah did not sit and when he saw this, Husain let go of Abu Sa'eed who then made place for Abdullah. Abdullah then proceeded to sit between the 2 men. Abu Sa'eed then explained the situation of Husain who asked, "It that so, O Ibn Amr? Do you now really believe that I am the most beloved person on earth to the inhabitants of the heavens?" "Indeed," replied Abdullah bin Amr, "I swear by the Rabb of the Kabah that you certainly are the most beloved inhabitant of earth to those of the heavens." "Then what made you fight my father and I during the Battle of Siffin when I can swear by Allah that my father was an even better person than I?" Abdullah submitted, "That is correct, my father complained about me to Rasulullah saying, 'Abdullah fasts all day and engages in Ibadah all night' Rasulullah then said, 'Observe Ibadah and sleep as well, fast on some days and do not fast on others and obey your father Amr.' When the Battle of Siffin took place, my father forced me in Allah's name to participate. I swear by Allah that I have neither strengthened their ranks, never exerted a sword for them, never threw a spear for them nor shot an arrow." Husain asked, "Did you not know that the creation cannot be obeyed when it entails disobeying the Creator?" "I did indeed," Abdullah replied. Husain accepted the explanation of Abdullah bin Amr. *(Tabrani in Awsat, Haythami).*

Fulfilling the Need of a Muslim

Ali said, "I cannot say which of the 2 favors of Allah to

me are greater. Whether it is a man coming to me with the sincere belief that I am able to fulfill his need or whether it is the favor of Allah fulfilling his need or at least alleviating some of it at my hand. Fulfilling the need of a Muslim I love more than the earth full of gold and silver." *(Nirsi in Kanzul Ummal)*

Fulfilling the Needs of a Muslim: Omar ؓ Stands Still for an Old Lady who Stopped Him

Ibn Yazid narrates that a lady called Khowla ؓ once met Omar ؓ as she was traveling with some people. When she bade Omar ؓ to stop, he obliged, came close to her and lowered his head to listen to her. He also placed his hand on her shoulders and stood there listening to her until she had stated her needs and had left. Someone asked, "O Amirul Mu'minin! You kept senior men of the Quraish waiting for that old lady?" "Shame on you!" Omar ؓ scolded, "Do you have any idea who that lady is?" When the man submitted that he did not, Omar ؓ said, "That is the woman whose complaint Allah heard from above the 7 heavens. That is Khowla bint Tha'laba. By Allah! Had she not turned away and left me until nightfall, I would have never turned away from her without hearing out her needs." *(Ibn Abi Hatim, Darmi, Bayhaqi)*. Thumama ibn Hazan ؓ reports that a lady once met Omar ؓ as he was riding his donkey. "Stop, O Omar!" she demanded. When Omar ؓ stopped, she addressed him most harshly. Someone then commented, "O Amirul Mu'minin! To this day have I not seen anything like this." Omar ؓ responded by saying, "Why should I not listen to her when Allah personally listened to her and revealed:

قَدْ سَمِعَ اللَّهُ قَوْلَ الَّتِي تُجَادِلُكَ فِي زَوْجِهَا وَتَشْتَكِي إِلَى اللَّهِ

Indeed Allah has heard the statement of her (Khaulah bint Thalabah) that disputes with you (O Muhammad ﷺ) concerning her husband (Aus bin As-Samit), and complains to Allah. (Al-Mujadala:1) (Bukhari in Tarikh, Ibn Mardway in Kanzul Ummal)

Abdullah bin Abbas ؓ leaves his I'tikaf to fulfill a Need of a Muslim

Abdullah bin Abbas ؓ was once observing I'tikaf in the Masjid of Rasulullah ﷺ when a man came to him. After the man had greeted with Salam and sat down, Abdullah bin Abbas ؓ said, "It seems that you are extremely concerned about something?" "That is true, O cousin of Rasulullah ﷺ!" the man replied, "I am indebted to someone and I swear by the. honor of the occupant of this grave of Rasulullah ﷺ that I am unable to settle it." "Should I speak to him on your behalf?" Abdullah bin Abbas ؓ offered. "If you please," the man replied. Abdullah bin Abbas ؓ then put on his shoes and left the Masjid. The man called out, "Have you forgotten what you were engaged in your I'tikaf?" "No," Abdullah bin Abbas ؓ replied, "It is something that I heard from the occupant of this grave and it was not a long time ago." His eyes then filled with tears as he continued, "I heard him say, 'Whoever walks to fulfill the need of a Muslim and applies himself in this regard, it will be better for him than 10 years of I'tikaf. As for the one who spends a single day in I'tikaf for the pleasure of Allah, Allah will place between him and the fire of Jahannam 3 trenches larger than the distance between the heavens and the earth." *(Tabrani, Bayhaqi, Hakim in Targheeb wat Tarheeb)*

Rasulullah ﷺ Often Visited the Ansar

Abdullah bin Qais ؓ narrated that Rasulullah ﷺ visited the Ansar very often, both on an individual basis and on a collective basis. When he visited someone on an individual basis, he would go to the person's house and when he visited them on a collective basis, he would go to the Masjid to meet them there. *(Ahmad, Haythami)*. Anas ؓ reports that Rasulullah ﷺ visited a home of the Ansar, where he had something to eat. As he was leaving, he had water sprinkled on a certain spot in the house where a mat was spread out for him. Rasulullah ﷺ then performed salah on the mat and made Du'a for the people of the household.

The Sahabah Visit Each Other

Anas ؓ reports that Rasulullah ﷺ used to forge a bond of brotherhood between every 2 Sahabah. The bond became so strong that the night would seem extremely long for each one of the 2 until he had met his brother. They would show great love and affection to each other when they did meet and would ask each other what he had done since they last met. As for the others between whom no bonds were formed, not even 3 days would pass any of them without him getting to know what had happened to his brother. *(Abu Ya'la, Haythami)*. Own narrates that when the companions of Abdullah bin Mas'ood ؓ came to see him, he said, "Do you people sit in each other's company?" "That we do not omit," they replied. "Do you still visit each other?" he enquired further. "Certainly, O Abu Abdur Rahman," they replied, "When one of us does not see his brother, he would go walking to the end of Kufa to meet him." Abdullah bin Mas'ood ؓ then remarked, "You people will certainly remain in good stead as long as you keep doing this." *(Tabrani in Targheeb wat Tarheeb)*. Ummu Darda ؓ says that Salman ؓ once came walking all the way from Mada'in to visit them (her husband Abu Darda ؓ) in Sham. He was then wearing a short shawl that just covered his knees. *(Bukhari in Adab)*

Rasulullah ﷺ Behaves Hospitably Towards Abdullah bin Omar ؓ

Abdullah bin Omar ؓ narrates, "When I once visited Rasulullah ﷺ, he threw to me a pillow stuffed with bark. However, I did not sit on it out of respect and it lay there between him and I." *(Ahmad, Haythami)*

Abu Bakr ؓ Behaves Hospitably Towards the Daughter of Sa'd bin Rabi ؓ

Ummu Sa'd ؓ who was the daughter of Sa'd bin Rabi ؓ reports that she once went to see Abu Bakr ؓ for some need because he was Khalifa. He spread out for her a sheet, on which she sat. Omar ؓ then entered and asked about her. Abu Bakr ؓ replied, "She is the daughter of someone who was greater than you and I." "Who is he, O Khalifa of Rasulullah ﷺ?" Omar ؓ asked. Abu Bakr ؓ replied, "He was a man who passed away during the time of Rasulullah ﷺ. He has already prepared his abode in Jannah while you are I are still alive not knowing what our plight will be." *(Tabrani in Isabah, Haythami, Hakim)*

Omar ؓ and Salman ؓ Behave Hospitably Towards Each Other

Anas bin Malik ؓ reports that Salman Farsi ؓ once came of visit Omar ؓ who was reclining on a cushion. Omar ؓ threw the cushion to Salman ؓ, the latter remarked, "Allah and His Rasul ﷺ have spoken the truth." "Narrate to us the Hadith, O Abu Abdullah," Omar ؓ asked. Salman ؓ replied, "I once went to visit Rasulullah ﷺ as he was reclining on a cushion. He then threw it to me and said to me, 'O Salman. When a Muslim goes to visit his brother Muslim and the host throws him a cushion to use as a gesture of hospitality, Allah forgives his sins." *(Hakim)*. Anas ؓ narrates that Salman Farsi ؓ came of visit Omar ؓ who was reclining on a cushion. Omar ؓ threw the cushion to Salman ؓ and said, "O Salman. When a Muslim goes to visit his brother

Muslim and the host throws him a cushion to use as a gesture of hospitality, Allah forgives his sins." *(Tabrani, Haythami)*. Anas ؓ reports that Omar ؓ went to visit Salman Farsi, Salman ؓ threw a cushion to Omar ؓ, who asked, "What is this, O Abu Abdullah," Salman ؓ replied, "I heard Rasulullah ﷺ say, 'When a Muslim goes to visit another Muslim and the host throws him a cushion to use as a gesture of hospitality and honor, Allah forgives his sins." *(Tabrani in Sagheer)*.

Abdullah bin Harith ؓ shows Hospitality to Ibrahim bin Nashit

Ibrahim bin Nashit reports that when he once visited Abdullah bin Harith bin Jaz Zubaidi ؓ, the latter threw to him a cushion that he had been sitting on. He also said, "Whoever is not hospitable towards his visitor has no ties with either Ahmad ﷺ or Ibrahim عليه السلام." *(Tabrani)*

Being hospitable towards a prominent person: Abu Usaid Sa'idi ؓ Entertains Rasulullah ﷺ

Sahl bin Sa'd ؓ narrates that Abu Usaid Sa'idi invited Rasulullah ﷺ for his wedding (Walima). His wife who was the new bride was actually serving the guests on that day. She said, "Do you know what I soaked for Rasulullah ﷺ? I soaked for him a few dates in a little earthen or stone container overnight so that he may enjoy a sweet drink next day." *(Bukhari in Adab)*.

The Statement of Ibn Jaz Zubaidi ؓ Concerning Hospitality Towards Guests

When 2 persons went to visit Abdullah bin Harith bin Jaz Zubaidi ؓ, he removed from beneath him a cushion that he had been sitting on and threw it to them. They said, "We do not need this because we have only come to hear something of benefit to us." Abdullah bin Harith ؓ then said, "Whoever is not hospitable towards his visitor has no ties with either Muhammad ﷺ or Ibrahim عليه السلام. Glad tidings for the one who spends the day holding the reins of his horse in the Path of Allah, ending his fast with only a piece of bread and some cold water. Destruction for those who are served a variety of foods and who serve them all saying, 'Take this away, servant! Bring that, servant!' While doing these, they fail to think of Allah." *(Ibn Jareer in Kanzul Ummal)*.

Rasulullah ﷺ Throws His Shawl for Jareer bin Abdullah ؓ to Sit On

Jareer bin Abdullah Bajali ؓ reports that he once went to see Rasulullah ﷺ in his room at a time when there was a large crowd present. As Jareer ؓ stood at the door, Rasulullah ﷺ looked to his right and his left but could not find any place for Jareer ؓ to sit. Rasulullah ﷺ then took his shawl, folded it and threw it to Jareer ؓ saying, "Sit on this." When Jareer ؓ caught the shawl, he held it against him, kissed it and then returned it to Rasulullah ﷺ saying. "O Rasulullah ﷺ! May Allah honor you as you have honored me." Rasulullah ﷺ said, "When a prominent person of a tribe comes to you, you should honor him."*(Tabrani in Saghir, Awsat, Haythami)*. Abu Hurairah ؓ narrates that when Jareer bin Abdullah ؓ once came to Rasulullah ﷺ's room, it was full of people and he could find nowhere to sit. Rasulullah ﷺ then threw to him his spare lower garment or shawl, saying to him, "Sit on this." Jareer ؓ caught the shawl, he kissed it, held it against him and then returned it to Rasulullah ﷺ saying, "O Rasulullah ﷺ! May Allah honor you as you have honored me." Rasulullah ﷺ said, "When a prominent person of a tribe comes to you, you should honor him." *(Tabrani in Awsat, Bazzar, Haythami)*

Rasulullah ﷺ Makes Uyanah bin Hisn ؓ Sit on Soft Fabric

Abdullah bin Abbas ؓ reports that Uyaynah bin Hisn ؓ once came to Rasulullah ﷺ whilst Abu Bakr ؓ and Omar ؓ were sitting there on the bare ground. Rasulullah ﷺ then had a soft fabric brought for Uyaynah ؓ and made him sit on it. Rasulullah ﷺ then said, "When a prominent person of a tribe comes to you, you should honor him." *(Tabrani, Haythami)*

Rasulullah ﷺ Gives a Cushion to Adi bin Hatim ؓ

Adi bin Hatim ؓ narrates that when he came to Rasulullah ﷺ, Rasulullah ﷺ gave him a cushion to sit on but he preferred to rather sit on the bare ground. Adi ؓ then said, "I testify that you neither seek superiority on earth nor any corruption." He then accepted Islam. The Sahabah commented, "O Nabi ﷺ! We have seen you do something today that we have not seen you do for anyone else." Rasulullah ﷺ replied, "When a prominent person of a tribe comes to you, you should honor him." *(Askari, Ibn Asakir in Kanzul Ummal)*

Rasulullah ﷺ Honors Abu Rashid ؓ

Abu Rashid bin Abdur Rahman ؓ says, "I went to Rasulullah ﷺ with 100 men from my tribe. When we drew close to Rasulullah ﷺ, we stopped and the others said to me, 'You go ahead, O Abu Mu'awiya. If you see what you like, come back to us and we shall all go to him. On the other hand, if you do not like what you see, come back to us and we shall all turn back.' Although I was the youngest of us all, I went to Rasulullah ﷺ and said, 'A very good morning to you, O Muhammad ﷺ.', 'That is not the greeting Muslims use amongst themselves,' Rasulullah ﷺ said. 'What is it then, O Rasulullah ﷺ?' I enquired. Rasulullah ﷺ replied, 'When you meet any Muslims, you should say:

اَلسَّلاَمُ عَلَيْكُمْ وَرَحْمَةُ اللهِ

I therefore said وَالسَّلاَمُ عَلَيْكُمْ وَرَحْمَةُ اللهِ وَرَحْمَةُ اللهِ وبركاته Rasulullah ﷺ replied by saying: وَعَلَيْكَ السَّلاَمُ ورحمة الله وبركاته Thereafter, Rasulullah ﷺ asked, 'What is your name and who are you?' When I informed Rasulullah ﷺ that my name was Abu Mu'awiya bin Abdul Lat wal Uzza, he remarked, 'You are rather Abu Rashid bin Abdullah.' Rasulullah ﷺ honored me and allowed me to sit beside him. He gave me his shawl and his shoes and staff. I accepted Islam. Some of those sitting with Rasulullah ﷺ said, 'O Rasulullah ﷺ! We see that you are showing great honor to this man?' Rasulullah ﷺ replied, 'He is a prominent person of his tribe and when a prominent person of any tribe comes to you, you should honor him.'" *(Duwali in Kuna, Ibn Mandah, Ibn Sakan in Isabah, Uqayli in Muntakhab Kanzul Ummal)*

Winning over the hearts of certain leaders: Rasulullah ﷺ Endearing the Leader of a Tribe

Abu Dhar ؓ narrates that Rasulullah ﷺ once asked him what he thought of Ju'ail ؓ. "I see him as just another poor man like many others," Abu Dhar ؓ replied. When Rasulullah ﷺ asked him what he thought of another man, Abu Dhar ؓ replied, "He is a great leader amongst the leaders of people." Rasulullah ﷺ then remarked, "But Ju'ail is better than the world full of that man." Abu Dhar ؓ then enquired, "O Rasulullah ﷺ! Why do you then treat him as well as you do when he is that bad a person?" Rasulullah ﷺ replied, "He is the leader of a tribe and I am merely winning them over attracting them towards Islam." *(Abu Nu'aym in Hilya, Kanzul Ummal, Ruyani in Musnad, Ibn Abdul Hakam in Futuh Misr, Ibn Hibban, Bukhari in Adab)*. Another narration states that someone said to Rasulullah ﷺ, "O Rasulullah ﷺ! You have given Uyaynah bin Hisn ؓ and Aqra bin Habis ؓ 100 camels each while you have left Ju'ail ؓ out. Rasulullah ﷺ responded by saying, "I swear by the Being Who controls my life! Ju'ayl bin Suraqa is better than the earth full of the likes of Uyaynah and Aqra. I am however doing this in an effort towards winning over the hearts of Uyaynah and Aqra. As for Ju'ail, I entrust him to his Iman, he needs nothing material to strengthen his Iman." *(Ibn Is'haq in Isabah, Abu Nu'aym in Hilya)*

The Parting Advice of Rasulullah ﷺ Concerning the Members of His Household

Yazid bin Hayyan says, "Husain bin Sabura, Amr bin Muslim and I once went to Zaid bin Arqam ؓ. When we sat down with him, Husain asked, 'You have seen some tremendous times, O Zaid. You saw Rasulullah ﷺ, you heard him speak, you fought battles by his side and you performed salah behind him. You have certainly seen some tremendous times. O Zaid, do tell us something that you heard from Rasulullah ﷺ.' Zaid ؓ said, 'Dear nephew! By Allah! I am now very old. The time I spent with Rasulullah ﷺ is now far past and I have forgotten some of the things that I remembered from him. You should therefore take note of what I narrate and do not force me to narrate that which I do not do so myself. Rasulullah ﷺ once stood up to deliver sermon at a pond between Makkah and Madinah called Khum. After praising Allah, giving advice and reminding us of some things, he said: 'O people! Take note that I am also a human and the messenger angel of death from my Rabb shall soon come and I shall have to respond. I am however leaving behind me 2 weighty things. The first is the Book of Allah that contains guidance and light. You should therefore grab Allah's Book and hold fast to it.' Rasulullah ﷺ encouraged the people to Allah's Book and added, 'The 2nd thing is the members of my household. I urge you to remember Allah when dealing with the members of my household. I urge you to remember Allah when dealing with the members of my household.' Husain then enquired, 'Who exactly are the members of Rasulullah ﷺ's household? Are his wives not members of his household?' Zaid ؓ replied, 'Rasulullah ﷺ's wives are members of his household, the actual members of his household are those to whom giving Zakah is forbidden after the demise of Rasulullah ﷺ.' When Husain asked for further elaboration, Zaid ؓ explained, 'They are the family of Ali ؓ, the family of Aqil ؓ, the family of Ja'far ؓ and the family of Abbas ؓ.' Husain enquired further, 'Is zakah forbidden for all of these people?' 'Yes,' was the reply." *(Muslim in Riyadhus Salihin, Ibn Jareer in Muntakhab Kanzul Ummal).* Abdullah bin Omar ؓ narrates that Abu Bakr ؓ said, "Consider Muhammad ﷺ when dealing with the members of his household." *(Bukhari in Muntakhab Kanzul Ummal)*

Rasulullah ﷺ Honors His Uncle Abbas ؓ

Ummul Mu'minin Aisha ؓ narrates that Rasulullah ﷺ was once sitting with his companions with Abu Bakr ؓ and Omar ؓ on his sides. When Abbas ؓ arrived, Abu Bakr ؓ made way for him and he sat down between Rasulullah ﷺ and Abu Bakr ؓ. Rasulullah ﷺ then said to Abu Bakr ؓ, "It is only people of virtue who acknowledge the virtue of other people of virtue." When Abbas started speaking to Rasulullah ﷺ, Rasulullah ﷺ's voice became extremely soft. Abu Bakr ؓ then said to Omar ؓ, "I am worried that some illness has suddenly afflicted Rasulullah ﷺ causing him to lose his voice." Abbas ؓ did not leave Rasulullah ﷺ until he had his needs met. When he left, Abu Bakr ؓ asked, "O Rasulullah ﷺ! Were you just now afflicted by some illness?" When Rasulullah ﷺ replied that nothing like that had happened, Abu Bakr ؓ queried, "But I noticed that your voice had become extremely soft." Rasulullah ﷺ explained, "When Abbas ؓ arrived, Jibra'el ؑ instructed me to lower my voice as you people have been commanded to lower your voices before me." *(Ibn Asakir in Kanzul Ummal).* Abdullah bin Abbas ؓ reports that Abu Bakr ؓ had a reserved sitting place near Rasulullah ﷺ which he would forsake for none other than Abbas ؓ Rasulullah ﷺ was very much impressed by his gesture. When Abbas ؓ arrived one day, Abu Bakr ؓ moved from his place. "What is the matter?" Rasulullah ﷺ asked Abu Bakr ؓ. "Your uncle has just arrived," replied Abu Bakr ؓ. Rasulullah ﷺ then saw Abbas ؓ arrive and smiled at Abu Bakr ؓ saying, "This is Abbas coming with white clothing. His progeny after him shall soon be wearing black clothing and 12 of them shall be kings." When Abbas ؓ arrived, he asked, "O Rasulullah ﷺ! Did you say something to Abu Bakr?" "I only told him what is good," Rasulullah ﷺ remarked. Abbas ؓ commented, "That is true. May my parents be sacrificed for you! You only speak what is good." Rasulullah ﷺ then said, "I said to him, 'This is Abbas coming with white clothing. His progeny after him shall soon be wearing black clothing and 12 of them shall be kings.'" *(Tabrani, Haythami, Ibn Asakir in Muntakhab Kanzul Ummal)*

Abu Bakr ؓ vacates His Place for Abbas ؓ

Ja'far bin Muhammad narrates from his great grandfather that Abu Bakr ؓ always sat on the right of Rasulullah ﷺ while Omar ؓ sat on left. Uthman ؓ sat in front of Rasulullah ﷺ for he used to write any confidential matters for Rasulullah ﷺ. When Abbas ؓ came along, Abu Bakr ؓ would move from his place and Abbas ؓ would sit there. *(Ibn Asakir in Kanzul Ummal).*

Rasulullah ﷺ Encourages People to have Love for Abbas ؓ

Muttalib bin Rabe'ah reports that Abbas ؓ once came to Rasulullah ﷺ in a rage. "What is the matter?" Rasulullah ﷺ enquired. "O Rasulullah ﷺ!" Abbas ؓ asked, "What is the problem between the Banu Hashim (us) and the Quraish?" Rasulullah ﷺ enquired further, "What has happened between yourself and the Quraish?" Abbas ؓ replied, "While the Quraish meet each other with smiling faces, they meet us with different faces." Rasulullah ﷺ then grew so angry that the vein between his eyes swelled. When his anger had cooled, Rasulullah ﷺ said, "I swear by the Being Who controls the life of Muhammad! Iman has not entered the heart of any person until he loves the Banu Hashim for the sake of Allah and His Rasul ﷺ." Rasulullah ﷺ then said further, "What is the matter with some people that they hurt me by hurting Abbas? A man's paternal uncle is just like his father." *(Hakim).* Abbas bin Abdul Muttalib ؓ reports that he once said to Rasulullah ﷺ, "O Rasulullah ﷺ! While the Quraish meet each other with open and smiling faces, whereas when they meet us, they do so with strange faces." Rasulullah ﷺ then grew extremely angry and he said, "I swear by the Being Who controls the life of Muhammad! Iman has not entered the heart of any person until he loves you (the Banu Hashim) for the sake of Allah and His Rasul ﷺ." *(Hakim).* Ismah narrates that when Abbas bin Abdul Muttalib ؓ entered the Masjid one day, he noticed resentment on the faces of some people. He then went to Rasulullah ﷺ's room and said, "O Rasulullah ﷺ! Why is it that I notice resentment on the faces of people when I enter the Masjid?" Rasulullah ﷺ then went to Masjid and said, "O people! You can never have Iman and cannot be called Mu'minin until you have love for Abbas." *(Tabrani, Haythami)*

The Incident between Omar ؓ and Abbas ؓ and the Du'a Rasulullah ﷺ Made for Omar ؓ Because of His Honoring Abbas ؓ

Abdullah bin Mas'ood ؓ narrates that Rasulullah ﷺ once sent Omar ؓ to collect zakah. The first person Omar ؓ met was

Abbas bin Abdul Muttalib ﷺ. "Bring along the zakah for your wealth, O Abu Fadhl," Omar ﷺ called out. Abbas ﷺ then burst out in a barrage of insults against Omar ﷺ to which Omar ﷺ replied, "By Allah! Remember that had it not been for fear of Allah your relationship with Rasulullah ﷺ, I would have given you a befitting reply for what you have said." The 2 then separated and took different paths. Omar ﷺ then met Ali bin Abi Talib ﷺ and related the incident to him. Ali ﷺ took Omar ﷺ by the hand and led him to Rasulullah ﷺ. "O Rasulullah ﷺ!" Omar ﷺ began, "When you sent me to collect zakah, the first person I met was your uncle Abbas ﷺ. 'Bring along the zakah for your wealth, O Abu Fadhl,' I called out. He burst out in a barrage of insults against me, to which I replied, 'By Allah! Remember that had it not been for fear of Allah your relationship with Rasulullah ﷺ, I would have given you a befitting reply for what you have said.'" Rasulullah ﷺ endorsed the behavior of Omar ﷺ saying, "May Allah honor you as you have honored him. Remember that the paternal uncle of a man is just like his father. Do not talk to Abbas ﷺ about zakah because I have taken 2 years zakah from him in advance." (Ibn Asakir in Muntakhab Kanzul Ummal)

Abbas ﷺ Slaps a Man who Insulted his Father

Abdullah bin Abbas ﷺ narrates that when someone spoke about the father of Abbas ﷺ and insulted him, Abbas ﷺ slapped the man. Some people gathered around and swore, "By Allah! We shall slap Abbas just as he slapped this man." When this news reached Rasulullah ﷺ, he stood up to address the people. "Which person is most honored by Allah?" Rasulullah ﷺ asked. "You, O Rasulullah ﷺ!" the people replied. Rasulullah ﷺ continued, "Abbas is from me and I am from him. Never insult the dead, thereby hurting the living." (Hakim). Another narration states that the people added, "O Rasulullah ﷺ! We seek Allah's protection from your anger! Do seek forgiveness from Allah on our behalf." Rasulullah ﷺ complied. (Ibn Asakir in Muntakhab Kanzul Ummal, Ibn Sa'd)

Abu Bakr ﷺ and Omar ﷺ Honor Abbas ﷺ During Their Terms as Khalifa

Ibn Shihab reports that during their terms as Khalifa, whenever Abu Bakr ﷺ or Omar ﷺ met Abbas ﷺ while they were riding, they would dismount the animal let Abbas ﷺ mount it and lead the animal while walking until Abbas ﷺ reached his place. Then they would leave. (Ibn Asakir in Kanzul Ummal).

Uthman ﷺ Lashes a Man Who Ridiculed Abbas ﷺ

Qasim bin Muhammad reports that amongst the rulings that Uthman ﷺ initiated and which was approved of by the Sahabah was having a man lashed for ridiculing Abbas bin Abdul Muttalib ﷺ in an argument. When someone raised an objection, Uthman ﷺ said, "When Rasulullah ﷺ honored his uncle, how can I allow people to ridicule him? Whoever allows such behavior will be opposing Rasulullah ﷺ." This ruling was then sanctioned by the Sahabah. (Ibn Asakir in Muntakhab Kanzul Ummal)

Abu Bakr ﷺ Honors Ali ﷺ and Vacates His Place for Him

Anas ﷺ narrates that Rasulullah ﷺ was once sitting in the Masjid with the Sahabah around him. Ali ﷺ then arrived, greeted with Salam and then stood there to look for a place to sit. Rasulullah ﷺ looked at the faces of the Sahabah to see which of them would make place for him. Abu Bakr ﷺ, who was sitting on Rasulullah ﷺ's right shifted from his place and said, "Come here, O Abul Hasan." Ali ﷺ then sat between Rasulullah ﷺ and Abu Bakr ﷺ. The Sahabah could actually see the happiness on the face of Rasulullah ﷺ as he said to Abu Bakr ﷺ, "O Abu Bakr! It is only the people of virtue who recognize others of virtue." (Ibnul A'rabi in Al Bidayah wan Nihayah).

A Group of the Ansar Address Ali ﷺ as "O Moulana"

Rabah bin Harith reports that a group of the Ansar once came to Ali ﷺ in Rahbah, a place in Kufa and greeted him with the words, "As Salamu Alayka, O Moulana, (O our master)!" Ali ﷺ asked, "How can I be your Moula (master) when you are Arabs and therefore cannot be slaves?" They replied, "On the day Rasulullah ﷺ delivered a lecture at the pond of Khum, we heard him say, 'For those to whom I am their Moula (master), then he (Ali ﷺ) is also their Moula.'" Rabah says that he followed the group after they had left and enquired who they were. I was informed that they were a group of the Ansar and amongst them was Abu Ayub Ansari ﷺ as well. (Ahmad, Tabrani, Haythami).

Rasulullah ﷺ says, "For Those to Whom I am Their Friend, then Ali Should also be Their Friend"

Buraida ﷺ reports, "Rasulullah ﷺ once dispatched us on an expedition to which he appointed Ali ﷺ as commander. After we returned, Rasulullah ﷺ asked us how we found our commander. It was either I or someone else who complained about him. While I was one who usually looked down, when I did lift my gaze, I saw that Rasulullah ﷺ's face had turned red with anger. He said, 'For those to whom I am their friend, then Ali should also be their friend.' I then submitted, 'I shall never hurt you again concerning Ali ﷺ." (Bazzar, Haythami).

Rasulullah ﷺ says, "Whoever Hurts Ali has Hurt Me"

Amr bin Shaas Aslami ﷺ who was with Rasulullah ﷺ at Hudaibiya says, "I was with the group of horsemen under the command of Ali ﷺ whom Rasulullah ﷺ had dispatched to Yemen. When Ali ﷺ behaved harshly with me, I harbored my anger within my heart. When we returned to Madinah, I complained about him in various gatherings and to whoever I met. One day, I went to the Masjid where Rasulullah ﷺ was sitting. When Rasulullah ﷺ saw me, he continued looking me in the eye until I sat down before him. As I sat down, he said, 'Take note, O Amr! You have hurt me deeply.' "Inna Lillahi wa Inna Ilayhi Raji'oon!' I exclaimed, 'I seek protection from Allah and in Islam from hurting the Rasul of Allah ﷺ!' Rasulullah ﷺ said, 'Whoever hurts Ali has hurt me." (Ibn Is'haq, Ahmad in Al Bidayah wan Nihayah, Tabrani, Bazzar in Majma'uz Zawa'id)

Sa'd ﷺ Seeks Protection From the Anger of Rasulullah ﷺ When he Insulted Ali ﷺ

Sa'd bin Abi Waqqas ﷺ says, "I was sitting in the Masjid with 2 other persons when we insulted Ali ﷺ. When Rasulullah ﷺ arrived, we could see the anger on his face, so we sought protection in Allah from his anger. Rasulullah ﷺ said, 'What have you got against me? Whoever hurts Ali has hurt me.'" (Abu Ya'la in Al Bidayah wan Nihayah, Haythami)

Omar ﷺ Reproaches Someone who Insulted Ali ﷺ

Urwa ﷺ narrates that someone insulted Ali ﷺ in the presence of Omar ﷺ. Omar ﷺ said, "Do you know that occupant of this grave? He is Muhammad ﷺ, the son of Abdullah, who was the son of Abdul Muttalib. Ali ﷺ is the son of Abu Talib who was the son of Abdul Muttalib. You should therefore only speak good of Ali ﷺ because if you hurt Ali ﷺ, you will be hurting the one in this grave." (Ibn Asakir in Muntakhab Kanzul Ummal)

Sa'd ﷺ says, "I Shall Never Revile Him Even if a Saw is Placed on My Head"

Abu Bakr bin Khalid bin Urfuta narrates that he once went to Sa'd bin Malik ﷺ and asked, "The news has reached me that in Kufa you people are being forced to revile Ali ﷺ. Have you ever reviled him?" Sa'd ﷺ replied, "Allah forbid! I swear by the Being Who controls the life of Sa'd that I have heard Rasulullah ﷺ say such things about Ali ﷺ that I would never revile him even if a saw is placed on my head." *(Abu Ya'la, Haythami)*

Sa'd ﷺ Forbids Mu'awiya ﷺ From Insulting Ali ﷺ

Sa'd bin Abi Waqqas ﷺ narrates that Mu'awiya bin Abu Sufian ﷺ once instructed him saying, "What prevents you from reviling Abu Turab (Ali ﷺ)?" Sa'd ﷺ replied, "If I had to my credit even one of the 3 virtues that Rasulullah ﷺ mentioned for Ali" I would prefer this to having red camels. I cannot revile him as long as I remember these. When Rasulullah ﷺ appointed Ali ﷺ as his deputy in Madinah when leaving for one of the battles, Ali ﷺ asked, 'O Rasulullah ﷺ! Are you leaving me behind with the women and children?' I then heard Rasulullah ﷺ say, 'Would you not like your relationship with me to be like the relationship between Haroon عليه السلام and Musa ﷺ. Of course, there shall be no Nabi after me.' I also heard Rasulullah ﷺ say during the Battle of Khaibar, 'I shall give the flag to someone who loves Allah and His Rasul ﷺ and whom Allah and His Rasul ﷺ also love.' I also hoped to get it but Rasulullah ﷺ then asked for Ali ﷺ to be summoned. When brought before Rasulullah ﷺ, he was suffering from pain in his eyes. Rasulullah ﷺ put some of his blessed saliva into Ali ﷺ's eyes and cured them and handed the flag over to him. Allah then granted the conquest at his hand. Furthermore, it was Ali ﷺ, Fatima ﷺ, Hasan ﷺ, and Husain ﷺ whom Rasulullah ﷺ called for when Allah revealed the verse:

فَقُلْ تَعَالَوْا نَدْعُ أَبْنَاءَنَا وَأَبْنَاءَكُمْ وَنِسَاءَنَا وَنِسَاءَكُمْ وَأَنْفُسَنَا وَأَنْفُسَكُمْ

...say: (O Muhammad ﷺ) "Come, let us call our sons and your sons, our women and your women, ourselves and yourselves... (Al-Imran:61). Thereafter, Rasulullah ﷺ said, "O Allah! This is my family." *(Ahmad, Muslim, Tirmidhi)*

Abu Nujaih narrates that when Mu'awiya ﷺ performed Hajj, he took hold of the hand of Sa'd bin Abi Waqqas ﷺ and said, "O Abu Is'haq! We are people whom all these battles have distanced from the Hajj to the extent that we have almost forgotten some of its Sunnah practices. You perform the Tawaf and we will follow you." After the Tawaf was complete, Mu'awiya ﷺ took Sa'd ﷺ into Darun Nadwa where he seated him upon his chair. He then spoke of Ali bin Abi Talib ﷺ and spoke ill of him. Sa'd ﷺ said, "You brought me into your room, seated me on your chair and then start to speak ill of Ali ﷺ?! By Allah! More than everything upon which the sun rises, I love to have even one of the 3 virtues he had. More than everything upon which the sun rises, I love to have for myself what Rasulullah ﷺ said to him when he left for the expedition to Tabuk. On that occasion, Rasulullah ﷺ said to Ali ﷺ, 'Would you not like your relationship with me to be like the relationship between Harun عليه السلام and Musa عليه السلام. Of course, there shall be no Nabi after me.' More than everything upon which the sun rises, I love to have for myself what Rasulullah ﷺ said about him during the Battle of Khaibar. On that occasion, Rasulullah ﷺ said to Ali Rasulullah ﷺ, 'I shall give the flag to someone who loves Allah and his Rasul ﷺ and whom Allah and His Rasul ﷺ also love. Allah shall grant the conquest at his hand and he is never one who flees from the battlefield.' More than everything upon which the sun rises, I love to have for myself the virtue of being the son-in-law of Rasulullah ﷺ by marrying his

daughter and having from her the children that he did. I shall never enter any room with you." Sa'd ﷺ shook off his shawl and left. *(Abu Zur'ah Dimishki in Al Bidayah wan Nihayah)*

Ummu Salama ﷺ Rebukes Someone who Reviled Ali ﷺ

Abu Abdullah Jadali reports, "I once went to Ummu Salama ﷺ, who asked, 'Do people amongst you revile Rasulullah ﷺ?' 'Allah forbid!' I exclaimed. I may also have made statements like 'SubhanAllah!' or something similar. She then said, 'I have heard Rasulullah ﷺ say, 'Whoever reviles Ali has reviled me." *(Ahmad, Haythami)*. Abu Abdullah Jadali reports that Ummu Salama ﷺ once asked him, "Do people amongst you revile Rasulullah ﷺ?" "How can Rasulullah ﷺ be reviled?" he asked. She replied, "Is Ali ﷺ and those he loves not reviled whereas Rasulullah ﷺ loved him?" *(Tabrani, Abu Ya'la, Haythami, Ibn Abi Shayba in Muntakhab Kanzul Ummal)*

The Statement of Ali ﷺ Concerning his Lineage and Deen

Abu Sadiq reports that Ali ﷺ once said to him, "My lineage is the same as that of Rasulullah ﷺ and Islam is also the same as that of Rasulullah ﷺ. Therefore, whoever reviles me actually reviles Rasulullah ﷺ." *(Khateeb in Muttafiq, Ibn Asakir in Muntakhab Kanzul Ummal)*

Abu Bakr ﷺ Honors Hasan ﷺ

Abdur Rahman bin Isbahani narrates that Abu Bakr ﷺ was sitting on the pulpit of Rasulullah ﷺ when Hasan bin Ali ﷺ who was still a child came there and said, "Do dismount my grandfather's place!" Abu Bakr ﷺ said, "You are right. This place is your grandfather's." Abu Bakr ﷺ then put Hasan ﷺ on his lap and started to weep thinking of Rasulullah ﷺ. Ali ﷺ excused himself saying, "By Allah! This was not by my instruction." "That's true," Abu Bakr ﷺ agreed, "I had no doubts about it." *(Abu Nu'aym, Jabiri in Juz)*. Urwa ﷺ narrates that Abu Bakr ﷺ was once delivering a sermon when Hasan ﷺ who was still a child arrived and also mounted the pulpit saying, "Do dismount my grandfather's pulpit!" Ali ﷺ then said, "This was done without my consultation." *(Ibn Sa'd in Kanzul Ummal)*

Omar ﷺ Honors Husain ﷺ

Urwa ﷺ narrates that Omar ﷺ was once delivering a sermon when Husain ﷺ who was still a child stood up and said, "Do dismount my grandfather's pulpit!" Omar ﷺ said, "It is indeed the pulpit of your grandfather and not that of mine. Who instructed you to do this?" Ali ﷺ then stood up and said, "No one instructed him to do it! Take note, you rascal! I shall definitely punish you for this." Omar ﷺ interceded by saying, "Do not punish my nephew for he has spoken the truth. By Allah! It is certainly his grandfather's pulpit." *(Ibn Asakir in Kanzul Ummal)*. Husain ﷺ narrates, "I once climbed the pulpit on which Omar ﷺ was and said, 'Do dismount my grandfather's pulpit and mount your father's pulpit!' 'My father does not have a pulpit,' he replied and he then made me sit with him. After dismounting and proceeding home, he asked, 'Dear child! Who taught you to do this?' When I assured him that no one did, he said, 'Dear son! It would be nice if you visited us frequently.' I therefore went to him one day but found him alone with Mu'awiya ﷺ while his son Abdullah ﷺ was standing at the door and did not have permission to enter. I therefore returned home. When Omar ﷺ met me afterwards, he asked, 'Dear son! Why is it that you have not visited us?' I replied, 'I had come when you were alone with Mu'awiya ﷺ. However, when I saw that your son Abdullah had to return without receiving permission to enter, I also returned.'

He said, 'You are more deserving of permission than my son Abdullah. Allah has crowned our heads because of your family of Rasulullah ﷺ.' He then placed his hand on my head." *(Ibn Sa'd, Ibn Rahway, Khateeb, Kanzul Ummal, Isabah)*

Abu Bakr ؓ Honors Hasan ؓ

Uqba bin Harith narrates that it was after the demise of Rasulullah ﷺ that he left the Masjid with Abu Bakr ؓ after performing the Asr salah. Ali ؓ was walking on the right of Abu Bakr ؓ when they passed by Ali ؓ's son Hasan ؓ playing with some other boys. Abu Bakr ؓ put the boy on his shoulders as he said a couplet which meant:

"May my father be sacrificed! This boy is the image of Nabi ﷺ and in no way resembled his father"
Ali ؓ laughed at this. *(Ibn Sa'd, Ahmad, Bukhari, Nasa'ee, Hakim in Kanzul Ummal)*

Abu Hurairah ؓ Kisses Hasan ؓ's Stomach

Umair bin Is'haq reports that he saw Abu Hurairah ؓ meet Hasan bin Ali ؓ and say, "Show me that part of your stomach where I saw Rasulullah ﷺ kiss." When Hasan ؓ did so, Abu Hurairah ؓ also kissed the spot. Another narration states that Abu Hurairah ؓ kissed his navel. *(Ahmad)*. When Hasan ؓ uncovered his belly, Abu Hurairah ؓ placed his hand on Hasan ؓ's navel. *(Tabrani, Haythami, Ibn Najjar, Kanzul Ummal)*

Abu Hurairah ؓ Uses the Words "My Guide" When Addressing Hasan ؓ

Maqbari reports that they were once with Abu Hurairah ؓ when Hasan bin Ali ؓ arrived and greeted them with Salam. The people returned the greeting but Abu Hurairah ؓ was unaware of what happened until somebody said to him, "That was Hasan bin Ali who greeted with Salam." Abu Hurairah ؓ then went to meet Hasan ؓ and said, "Salams to you too, O my leader." When someone asked Abu Hurairah ؓ why he had addressed Hasan as "my leader", Abu Hurairah ؓ replied, "I testify that I heard Rasulullah ﷺ say, 'He is a leader.'" *(Tabrani, Haythami, Abu Ya'la, Ibn Asakir, Kanzul Ummal)*

The Incident Between Abu Hurairah ؓ and Marwan Concerning Having Love for Hasan ؓ and Husain ؓ

Marwan once visited Abu Hurairah ؓ during the illness that claimed his life. Marwan said, "Since we have been living with you, nothing has angered us more than your love for Hasan and Husain." Abu Hurairah ؓ pulled himself together and sat up saying, "I testify that we were once traveling with Rasulullah ﷺ when he heard Hasan ؓ and Husain ؓ crying. They were with their mother Fatima ؓ at the time. Rasulullah ﷺ hurried to them and I heard him ask, 'What is the matter with my children?' When their mother informed Rasulullah ﷺ that they were suffering of thirst, Rasulullah ﷺ grabbed at his water bag to see if it had water but it did not have any. Water was extremely scarce those days and the people were searching for some. 'Does anyone have any water?' Rasulullah ﷺ announced. Every person then grabbed for his water bag to look for water but no one had a drop with them. 'Give one of them to me,' Rasulullah ﷺ asked. When Fatima ؓ gave one of them from beneath the carriage, I could see her forearms as she did so. Rasulullah ﷺ took the child and pressed him to his chest but the child continued screaming without stopping. Rasulullah ﷺ then took out his tongue and the child started sucking on it until he was pacified. I did not hear him cry afterwards. In the meantime, the other boy was still crying as he had been without stopping. 'Pass me the other one,' Rasulullah ﷺ

asked. When the other child was passed to Rasulullah ﷺ, he did the same and they were both quiet. I did not hear either of them make a sound again. Rasulullah ﷺ then called out, 'Let us move on!' Because we were traveling with women, we (men) moved from side to side and I was only able to meet up with Rasulullah ﷺ later along the road. How can I not love those 2 when I have seen Rasulullah ﷺ do that?" *(Tabrani, Haythami)*

Honoring Ulema, Elders and men of virtue: Abdullah bin Abbas ؓ and Zaid bin Thabit ؓ Honor Each Other

Ammar bin Abu Ammar reports that when Zaid bin Thabit ؓ was once about to mount his animal, Abdullah bin Abbas ؓ held the stirrup so that he may place his foot in it. "Go away, O cousin of Rasulullah ﷺ we should be serving you and not you us," Zaid ؓ bade Abdullah bin Abbas ؓ. However, Abdullah bin Abbas ؓ said, "This is how we have been commanded to honor our Ulema and elders." Zaid ؓ then said, "Show me your hand." When Abdullah bin Abbas ؓ did so, Zaid ؓ kissed the hand saying, "This is how we have been commanded to honor the family of our Nabi ﷺ." *(Ibn Asakir in Kanzul Ummal)*

Sha'bi reports that as Zaid bin Thabit ؓ was about to mount his animal one day, Abdullah bin Abbas ؓ caught hold of the stirrup. "Go away, O cousin of Rasulullah ﷺ," Zaid ؓ bade Abdullah bin Abbas ؓ. However, Abdullah bin Abbas ؓ said, "This is how we honor our Ulema and elders." *(Ya'qub bin Sufian in Isabah, Tabrani, Haythami, Ibn Sa'd, Hakim in Isabah)* Another narration states when Abdullah bin Abbas ؓ held the stirrup of Zaid bin Thabit ؓ's animal, he said, "We have been commanded to hold on to the stirrup of our teachers and our seniors." *(Ibn Najjar in Kanzul Ummal)*

Rasulullah ﷺ Honors Abu Ubaidah ؓ

Abu Umama ؓ narrates that a drink was once served when Rasulullah ﷺ was in the company of some Sahabah such as Abu Bakr ؓ, Omar ؓ and Abu Ubaidah bin Jarrah ؓ. When Rasulullah ﷺ passed the cup to Abu Ubaidah ؓ, he submitted, "You are more deserving of having it first, O Nabi of Allah." When Rasulullah ﷺ insisted that he take it, Abu Ubaidah ؓ took it but before drinking, he said, "You take it, O Nabi of Allah." Rasulullah ﷺ then said, "Please drink because blessings lie with our elders. That person has no relationship with us who does not have mercy on our youngsters and does not respect our elders." *(Tabrani, Haythami)*.

Rasulullah ﷺ Instructs that the Eldest Should be First to Speak

Rafi bin Khadij ؓ and Sahl bin Abi Hathma ؓ both reports that Abdullah bin Sahl ؓ and Muhayisa bin Mas'ood ؓ were separated from each other amongst the date palms of Khaibar when Abdullah bin Sahl ؓ was murdered. Abdur Rahman bin Sahl ؓ, Muhayisa bin Mas'ood ؓ and Huwayisa bin Mas'ood ؓ then went to Rasulullah ﷺ to discuss the matter with him. Abdur Rahman ؓ started speaking but because he was the youngest of the 3, Rasulullah ﷺ said that the eldest should speak first. After they had informed Rasulullah ﷺ about what had happened to their companion, Rasulullah ﷺ said, "Will you not have a right to the blood money by the oaths of 50 members of your tribe?" "O Rasulullah ﷺ!" they questioned, "But it was a case that we did not witness." Rasulullah ﷺ then said, "Then the Jews of Khaibar will be pardoned by the oaths of 50 of them." "O Rasulullah ﷺ!" the men argued, "But they are Kuffar and cannot be trusted." To settle the affair Rasulullah ﷺ then paid the blood money from his side. *(Bukhari)*

Rasulullah ﷺ Honors Wa'il bin Hujar ؓ

Wa'il bin Hujar ؓ says, "In Hadramaut we heard about the appearance of Rasulullah ﷺ at a time when we were in control of a large kingdom where people obeyed us. I then forsook everything and left with enthusiasm for Allah and His Rasul ﷺ. When I came to Rasulullah ﷺ, he had already given the people the news of my arrival. When I came to him and greeted with Salam, he replied to my greeting and spread out his shawl for me to sit on. He then mounted the pulpit and made me sit with him. Thereafter, Rasulullah ﷺ raised his hands, praised Allah, invoked Allah's mercy on the Ambiya عليهم السلام and gathered the people. He then said to them, 'O people! This is Wa'il bin Hujar who has come from far off, from Hadramaut. He has come of his own will, without compulsion and with enthusiasm for Allah, His Rasul ﷺ and Islam.' 'That is true,' I affirmed." *(Bazzar, Haythami)*. Wa'il bin Hujar ؓ says that when he came to Rasulullah ﷺ, Rasulullah ﷺ announced, "This is Wa'il bin Hujar who has come willingly without any displeasure. He has come to you for the love of Allah and His Rasul ﷺ." Rasulullah ﷺ then spread out his shawl for Wa'il ؓ to sit on. Rasulullah ﷺ made Wa'il ؓ to sit beside him and brought him very close. Thereafter, Rasulullah ﷺ mounted the pulpit and addressed the people saying, "Be kind to him because he has only just left his royal background." Wa'il ؓ said, "My family has taken away from me everything that I had." Rasulullah ﷺ consoled him saying, "I shall give you all that they have taken and double of that as well." The Hadith continues further. *(Tabrani, Haythami)*

Rasulullah ﷺ Honors Sa'd bin Mu'adh ؓ on his Deathbed

Abdullah bin Abbas ؓ narrates that when Sa'd bin Mu'adh ؓ's arm started bleeding profusely from a wound, Rasulullah ﷺ stood by him and embraced him even as the blood splashed over Rasulullah ﷺ's face and beard. The more someone tried to shield Rasulullah ﷺ form the blood, the closer Rasulullah ﷺ drew to Sa'd ؓ until he eventually passed away. *(Ibn Sa'd)*. One of the Ansar narrates that after Sa'd bin Mu'adh ؓ had passed judgment for the Banu Quraiza tribe and had returned to Madinah, his wound ruptured. When the news reached Rasulullah ﷺ, he went to Sa'd ؓ and placed his head in his lap. Sa'd ؓ was fair in complexion and large in stature so when he was covered in a white sheet, his feet were exposed when his face was covered. Rasulullah ﷺ then prayed, "O Allah! Sa'd strove in Your path, believed in Your Rasul and fulfilled his duties, so accept his soul in the best way that You accept any soul." Hearing the prayer of Rasulullah ﷺ, Sa'd ؓ opened his eyes and said, "*As Salamu Alayka*, O Rasulullah ﷺ! Take note that I testify that you are certainly Allah's Rasul." Seeing that Rasulullah ﷺ was holding Sa'd's head in his lap, Sa'd ؓ's family grew concerned. When Rasulullah ﷺ was informed of the concern of Sa'd ؓ's family, he said, "Angels as many as you people are in his house sought permission from Allah to be present for Sa'd's death." Sa'd ؓ's mother was weeping as she recited a couplet which meant:

> "Oh the mother of Sa'd is destroyed. He was a man who
> meticulously applied himself"

Someone rebuked her saying, "Are you reciting poetry for Sa'd?" Rasulullah ﷺ intervened saying, "Leave her alone because it is poets other than her who speak lie, she is true because her son was exactly as she says." *(Ibn Sa'd)*

Omar ؓ Honors a Sahabi Called Mu'aiqit ؓ

Kharija bin Zaid narrates that supper was once served to Omar ؓ when he was dining with some people. Omar ؓ then left the house to call Mu'aiqit bin Abu Fatima ؓ, who was a Sahabi who had migrated to Abyssinia. Omar ؓ said to him, "Come closer and sit down. By Allah! Had it been someone else suffering what you are suffering (leprosy), he would not have sat closer than a spear's length to me." When Omar bin Khattab ؓ once invited some people for a meal, they felt scared but accepted. Eating with them was Mu'aiqit ؓ, a Sahabi suffering from leprosy, Omar ؓ said to him, "Eat from that which is in front of you and what is nearest to you. Had it been anyone other than you, he would have never shared a plate with me but would have been a spear's length away from me." *(Ibn Sa'd)*

Omar ؓ Honors Amr bin Tufail ؓ

Abdul Wahid bin Aun Dowsi narrates that Tufail bin Amr ؓ returned from the region of his Dows tribe to Rasulullah ﷺ and remained with Rasulullah ﷺ in Madinah until Rasulullah ﷺ passed away. When some Arabs left the fold of Islam, Tufail ؓ left for the Battle of Yamama with his son Amr bin Tufail ؓ. While Tufail ؓ was martyred in the battle, his son Amr ؓ was severely injured and his hand was cut off. He was once with Omar ؓ when some food was served. When Amr bin Tufail ؓ stepped aside, Omar ؓ asked, "What is wrong? Are you stepping aside because of your injured hand which you feel embarrassed to put into a plate with someone else?" When Amr ؓ admitted that this was the reason, Omar ؓ said, "You should not do this! By Allah! I shall not even taste the food until you have put your hand into it. I swear by Allah that there is no person besides you who has a part of himself already in Jannah." Amr ؓ later left with the Muslims for the Battle of Yarmuk where he was martyred. *(Ibn Sa'd in Kanzul Ummal)*

Omar ؓ Writes to Abu Musa Ash'ari ؓ About Giving Precedence to People of Virtue

Hasan reports that Omar ؓ once wrote to Abu Musa Ash'ari ؓ saying, "The news has reached me that you allow a large group of people in all at once. When this letter of mine reaches you, I want you to begin with the people of virtue, status and personality. It is only after they have taken their places that you should permit the others in." *(Denowri in Kanzul Ummal)*

Giving Leadership to Seniors: The Advice Qais bin Asim ؓ Gave to His Sons

On his deathbed, Qais bin Asim ؓ gave the following advice to his sons: "Fear Allah and give leadership to the seniors because when people hand over leadership to their seniors, they follow the ways of their forefathers. However, when they hand leadership over to those who are youngest, their status falls in the estimation of their generations. Tend to the earning and investing of your wealth because it lends added honor to the honorable and makes them independent of the mean ones. Keep away from asking from people because this is the worst earning for a man. Do not weep when I die because no one wept when Rasulullah ﷺ passed away. Furthermore, when I die I want you to bury me in a place which the Banu Bakr bin Wa'il tribe has no knowledge of because during the period of ignorance I used to ambush them and they should not do anything nasty with my grave." *(Bukhari in Adab, Ahmad in Isabah, Ibn Sa'd)*

Honoring people despite differences in opinion and deed: The Instruction Ali ؓ Gave the People During the Battle of Jamal

Yahya bin Sa'eed narrates from his uncle who says, "When we participated in the Battle of Jamal, Ali ؓ formed our rows before engaging in battle and announced, 'No one should be the first to shoot an arrow, or to attack with a spear or to strike with a sword. Do not initiate the hostilities and speak kindly to them because they are also Muslims.' I think that he also said, 'Whoever is successful on this occasion will be successful on the Day of Judgment.' We then stood like this until the day had progressed considerably and the people of the other army started shouting to each other, 'O the avengers of Uthman, prepare yourselves!' Ali ؓ then called for Muhammad bin Hanafiya who was standing before us and bearing the flag. He asked, 'O Ibn Hanafiya! What are they saying?' Muhammad bin Hanafiya ؓ approached us and said, 'O Amirul Mu'minin! They are shouting, 'O the avengers of Uthman!" Ali ؓ then raised his hands and prayed, 'O Allah! Let the murderers of Uthman fall flat on their faces." (Bayhaqi). Muhammad bin Omar bin Ali bin Abi Talib reports that Ali ؓ did not engage the opposite army in battle until he had called them to forsake the weapons for 3 days. On the 3rd day, Hasan ؓ, Husain ؓ and Abdullah bin Ja'fa came to him and said, "These people have inflicted many casualties on us." "Dear nephew!" Ali ؓ said, "I am not at all in the dark concerning what is happening to the people." He then asked them to pour out some water for him and when they did, he made wudhu and performed 2 Rakahs of salah. After completing, he raised his hands and made Du'a to Allah. He then addressed the people saying, "If you are victorious over them, you should not chase after those who flee and should not kill any of the wounded. Take only those weapons of war that are brought to the battlefield and everything else that remains like clothing and other personal possessions shall remain the property of the heirs of those killed." Imam Bayhaqi says that the more authentic version of the narration states that Ali ؓ did not take any booty nor any of the possessions of those killed. (Bayhaqi). Ali bin Husain reports that when he once went to Marwan bin Hakam, the latter said to him, "I have never seen anyone so noble in victory as your grand father Ali ؓ. We had only just started fleeing from the battlefield of the Battle of Jamal after being defeated by him when one of his announcers called out, "Do not kill anyone fleeing nor any of the wounded." (Bayhaqi)

The Statement of Ali ؓ Concerning the People who Fought Him in the Battle of Jamal

Abd Khair reports that when Ali ؓ was questioned about those who fought him in the Battle of Jamal, he said, "They were simply our brothers whom we fought because they rebelled against us. However, they have since repented and we have pardoned them." Muhammad bin Omar bin Ali bin Abi Talib reports that on the day the Battle of Jamal was fought, Ali ؓ said, "We shall be gracious to them because they testify that there is none worthy of worship but Allah and we shall allow sons to be the heirs of their father's by not taking any of their possessions for ourselves." (Bayhaqi). Abul Bakhtari narrates that Ali ؓ was asked whether the people who fought him in the Battle of Jamal were disbeliever. He replied, "It is from Shirk that we fled." "Were they hypocrite?" he was asked. Ali ؓ replied, "Hypocrites very seldom think of Allah whereas these did so very often." "What were they?" came the question. Ali ؓ explained, "They were our brothers who rebelled against us." (Bayhaqi).

Ali ؓ Welcomes the Son of Talha ؓ and His Statements Concerning Talha ؓ and Zubair ؓ

Abu Habiba the freed slave of Talha ؓ says that it was after the Battle of Jamal that he once went to Ali in the company of Imran the son of Talha ؓ. Talha and Zubair both fought against Ali in the Battle of Jamal. Ali ؓ welcomed him most warmly and called him close. He then said, "I wish that Allah would

make your father and me amongst those about whom He says:

وَنَزَعْنَا مَا فِي صُدُورِهِم مِّنْ غِلٍّ إِخْوَانًا عَلَى سُرُرٍ مُّتَقَابِلِينَ (47)

And We shall remove from their breasts any sense of injury (that they may have), (So they will be like) brothers facing each other on thrones. (Al-Hijr:47)

Addressing Imran in the most appealing terms, Ali ؓ then asked him about all the wives and children of Talha ؓ by name. He further said, "We have taken possession of your lands these past few years only for fear that others may seize them." Addressing one of his men, Ali ؓ instructed, "Take him to Ibn Qardha and tell him to hand over to this man the revenue due to him for all these years together with his land." There were 2 men sitting in the corner, one of whom was Harith A'war. They remarked, "Allah is more just than that! How is it that they had been fighting us and still be our brothers in Jannah?" Ali ؓ said, "Get up you 2 and get away to the furthest of Allah's lands. Who else can the verse be referring to if it does not refer to Talha and me? Ali ؓ then addressed Talha ؓ's son saying, my dear brother's son! Come to me whenever you need something." (Bayhaqi, Ibn Sa'd). A narration of Rib'ee bin Hirash adds that when the 2 men passed their comment, Ali ؓ screamed so loud that the scream could have brought a palace tumbling down. He said, "Who will such people be if they are not Talha and I?" Ibrahim reports that when Ibn Jurmuz, the person who martyred Zubair ؓ sought permission to see Ali ؓ, the Khalifa was very unwilling to see him. "Is this how you treat those who fought hard for you?" Ali ؓ replied, "Take sand in your mouth! I have every hope that Talha, Zubair and I shall be amongst those about whom Allah says: وَنَزَعْنَا مَا فِي صُدُورِهِم مِّنْ غِلٍّ إِخْوَانًا عَلَى سُرُرٍ مُّتَقَابِلِينَ (47)

And We shall remove from their breasts any sense of injury (that they may have), (So they will be like) brothers facing each other on thrones. (Al-Hijr:47) (Ibn Sa'd)

Ammar ؓ Rebukes Those who Spoke Ill of Aisha ؓ

Amr bin Ghalib reports that when Ammar bin Yasir ؓ (Ibn Sa'd) overheard someone speak ill of Ummul Mu'minin Aisha ؓ, he said, "Be quiet! May you remain deprived of good and sworn at! I testify that she shall definitely be the wife of Rasulullah ﷺ in Jannah." (Ibn Asakir in Kanzul Ummal, Ibn Sa'd) Another narration adds that Ammar ؓ said to the man, "Get away! May you be deprived of all good! Are you insulting the beloved of Rasulullah ﷺ?" (Tirmidhi in Isabah). Ammar ؓ once said, "Our mother Aisha ؓ had her own opinion. We know for sure that she is the wife of Rasulullah ﷺ in this world as well as in the Hereafter, but Allah used her to test whether it was He (Allah) Whom we obeyed or her." (Ibn Asakir, Abu Ya'la in Kanzul Ummal). Abu Wa'il ؓ narrates that when Ali ؓ sent Ammar bin Yasir ؓ and Hasan bin Ali ؓ to Kufa to rally people to fight, Ammar ؓ addressed the people saying, "I know well that she (Aisha ؓ) is the wife of Rasulullah ﷺ in this world as well as the next, but Allah is using her to test if it is He (Allah) Whom we obey or her." (Bayhaqi, Bukhari)

Following the elders despite believing differently: Abdullah bin Mas'ood ؓ Instructs that Omar ؓ be Followed

Zaid bin Wahab reports, "I once went to Abdullah bin Mas'ood ؓ to teach me a particular verse of the Qur'an. When he taught it to me in a certain way, I informed him that Omar ؓ had taught it to me in a manner quite different to the way in which he taught it. He then started to weep so much that I saw his tears amongst the pebbles on the ground. He then said, 'Read it as Omar ؓ had read it because I swear by Allah that his recitation was clearer than that of the people of Sailahin, a place near Baghdad. Omar ؓ was a secure fortress of Islam. Islam would enter by him but never leave from him. When he was martyred, the fortress was holed and Islam has come out of the fortress without entering into it." *(Ibn Sa'd)*

Getting annoyed for the sake of one's elders: Omar ؓ is Annoyed by a Man who Insulted Abu Darda ؓ

Shuraih bin Ubaid reports that a man once said to Abu Darda ؓ, "What is the matter with you learned men? You are more cowardly than us, most miserly when asked for something and have the largest morsels when you eat!" Abu Darda ؓ ignored the man without replying. When the news reached Omar ؓ, he asked Abu Darda ؓ about it. Abu Darda ؓ said, "I seek Allah's forgiveness. Should we take them to task for everything we hear them say?" Omar ؓ then went to the man who made the remark to Abu Darda ؓ. Omar ؓ grabbed him, throttled him and brought him before Rasulullah ﷺ, where the man pleaded, "We were only talking and joking." It was then Allah revealed: If you have to ask them they will (brush it off and falsely) say,

وَلَئِن سَأَلْتَهُمْ لَيَقُولُنَّ إِنَّمَا كُنَّا نَخُوضُ وَنَلْعَبُ

If you ask them (about this), they declare: "We were only talking idly and joking." (At-Tauba:65) (Abu Nu'aym in Hilya)

Omar ؓ Rebukes and Warns a Person who Regarded Him to be Superior to Abu Bakr ؓ

Jubair bin Nufair reports that a group of people once came to Omar ؓ and said, "O Amirul Mu'minin! We swear by Allah that we have never seen anyone more just, more outspoken of the truth, and more sterner against the hypocrites than yourself. You are certainly the best of people after Rasulullah ﷺ." Awf bin Malik remarked, "You are wrong! By Allah! We have seen someone better than him after Rasulullah ﷺ." "Who is that O Awf?" Omar ؓ asked. When Awf ؓ replied that the person was Abu Bakr ؓ, Omar ؓ confirmed, "Awf is telling the truth while you people are false. I swear by Allah that Abu Bakr ؓ was purer than musk while I am in need of more guidance than our family's camel." *(Abu Nu'aym in Fada'ilus Sahabah, Muntakhab Kanzul Ummal).* Hasan reports that Omar ؓ had appointed informants amongst the masses who once informed him that a group of people had gathered and claimed that Omar ؓ was better then Abu Bakr ؓ. Omar ؓ became very angry and sent for these people. When they were brought; Omar ؓ addressed them saying, "O you most wretched of people! You most wretched of your tribes! You corrupters of a secure fortress!" Surprised, they enquired, "O Amirul Mu'minin! Why are you telling us this? What have we done?" After repeating himself 3 times, Omar ؓ then said, "Why have you created a division between Abu Bakr Siddiq ؓ and myself? I swear by the Being Who controls my life that I wish I could reach even that position of Jannah from where I can see Abu Bakr ؓ at the furthest point of my sight." *(Asad bin Musa).* Omar ؓ said, "Abu Bakr ؓ is the best of this Ummah after its Nabi ﷺ. Whoever claims otherwise after this declaration of mine is a slanderer and shall be punished as slanderers are punished." *(La'alka'i).* Ziyad bin Ilaqah states that Omar ؓ overheard someone saying about him, "This man is the best of this Ummah after its Nabi ﷺ." Omar ؓ started hitting the man with his whip saying, "This wretch is lying! Abu Bakr ؓ is definitely better than me, my father, yourself and your father!" *(Khaithama in Muntakhab Kanzul Ummal)*

Ali ؓ Rebukes a Person who Regarded Him to be Superior to Abu Bakr ؓ

Abu Zinad narrates that someone once asked Ali ؓ, "O Amirul Mu'minin! What is the matter with the Muhajirin and Ansar? They regard Abu Bakr ؓ as being superior to you whereas your virtues are more; you had accepted Islam before him and have excelled him." Ali ؓ asked, "If you belong to the Quraish tribe, I assume that you must be from the Aa'ida family." When the man confirmed that he was, Ali ؓ said, "Had a Mu'min not been in the protection of Allah, I would have certainly had you executed. If you were to survive, I would then chastise you in a manner that you would be unable to escape. Shame on you! Abu Bakr ؓ excelled me especially in 4 matters. (1) He was appointed to the position of being Imam before me when Rasulullah ﷺ put him forward as Imam. (2) He made Hijra before me, (3) he beat me to the cave, he was with Rasulullah ﷺ during the Hijra and (4) he also proclaimed his Islam before me. Shame on you! Whereas Allah has condemned mankind for not assisting Rasulullah ﷺ, Allah praised Abu Bakr ؓ when He says:

إِلَّا تَنصُرُوهُ فَقَدْ نَصَرَهُ اللَّهُ إِذْ أَخْرَجَهُ الَّذِينَ كَفَرُوا ثَانِيَ اثْنَيْنِ إِذْ هُمَا فِي الْغَارِ إِذْ يَقُولُ لِصَاحِبِهِ لَا تَحْزَنْ إِنَّ اللَّهَ مَعَنَا فَأَنزَلَ اللَّهُ سَكِينَتَهُ عَلَيْهِ وَأَيَّدَهُ بِجُنُودٍ لَّمْ تَرَوْهَا وَجَعَلَ كَلِمَةَ الَّذِينَ كَفَرُوا السُّفْلَى وَكَلِمَةُ اللَّهِ هِيَ الْعُلْيَا وَاللَّهُ عَزِيزٌ حَكِيمٌ (40)

If you help him (Muhammad ﷺ) not (it does not matter), for Allah did indeed help him when the disbelievers drove him out, the second of two, when they (Muhammad ﷺ and Abu Bakr ؓ) were in the cave, and he (ﷺ) said to his companion (Abu Bakr ؓ): "Be not sad (or afraid), surely Allah is with us." Then Allah sent down His Sakeenah (calmness, tranquility, peace, etc.) upon him, and strengthened him with forces (angels) which you saw not, and made the word of those who disbelieved the lowermost, while it was the Word of Allah that became the uppermost, and Allah is All-Mighty, All-Wise. (At-Tauba:40) (Khaithama, Ibn Asakir in Muntakhab Kanzul Ummal, Ishari in Muntakhab Kanzul Ummal)

The Incident Between Abu Bakr ؓ, Mughiera ؓ and Another Man

Mughiera bin Shu'ba ؓ narrates, "I was with Abu Bakr ؓ when a horse was brought to him. When a man from the Ansar asked for the horse to be given to him, Abu Bakr ؓ said, 'Rather than giving it to you, I prefer giving it to one of the youngsters who will be able to ride it despite his lack of experience.' The man became angry and blurted out, 'By Allah! I am a better horseman than both you and your father!' When he used these words to the Khalifa of Rasulullah ﷺ, I became angry and grabbing him by the head, I threw him down on his nose. His nose bled so much that it appeared as if a large water bag had burst open. The Ansar decided that they would have retribution from me, the news reached Abu Bakr ؓ. He rebuked saying, 'Do people think that I will allow them to have their retribution from Mughiera bin Shu'ba? I would prefer exiling them from their homes rather than them having retribution from someone who prevents Allah's servants from evil.'" *(Tabrani, Haythami)*

Omar ؓ Hits 2 Men for Their Insolence Towards Abdullah bin Mas'ood ؓ

Abu Wa'il narrates that when Abdullah bin Mas'ood ؓ once saw a man's garment hanging below his ankles, he told him to lift it up. The man retorted, "What about you, O Abdullah bin Mas'ood? You also lift up your garment higher." Abdullah bin Mas'ood ؓ replied, "I am not like you. My calves are extremely thin and I lead people in salah, therefore if I lift my garment too high, people would be repulsed." When news of this incident reached Omar ؓ, he hit the man saying, "Do you backchat Ibn

Mas'ood ?" *(Ibn Asakir in Kanzul Ummal).* Ala reports from his teachers that Omar was once standing by the home of Abdullah bin Mas'ood in Madinah, watching it being built when a man from the Quraish remarked, "O Amirul Mu'minin! Let someone else like the owner does this work for you." Omar grabbed hold of a brick and hurled it at the man saying, "Do you wish to make me dislike Ibn Mas'ood?" *(Ya'qub bin Sufiyan, Ibn Asakir in Kanzul Ummal)*

Omar Hits a Man for the Sake of Ummu Salama

Abu Wa'il narrates that because Ummu Salama owed something to a certain man, the man took an oath against her. For this, Omar had the man lashed 30 stripes, causing his skin to be cut and to become swollen. *(Abu Ubaid in Ghareeb, Sufiyan bin Uyaunah, La'alka'I in Muntakhab Kanzul Ummal)*

Ali Expresses the Intention to Execute Ibn Saba for Regarding Him to be Superior to Abu Bakr and Omar

Ummu Musa reports that when the news reached Ali that Ibn Saba claimed that he (Ali) was superior to Abu Bakr and Omar, Ali expressed the wish to have Ibn Saba executed. Someone remarked, "Will you execute a man for merely showing respect to you and for regarding you to be an esteemed person?" Ali then said, "Alright then, he need not be executed. However, he should never be allowed to live in the town where I reside." *(Abu Nu'aym in Hilya).* lbrahim reports that the news once reached Ali that Abdullah bin Aswad degraded the status of Abu Bakr and Omar. Ali asked for a sword with the intention of executing him. However, when someone spoke him out of it, he said, "Then he should never stay in a town where I reside." Abdullah was therefore exiled to Sham. *(Ishari, La'alka'I in Muntakhab Kanzul Ummal)*

Ali Rebukes a Man for Regarding Him to be Superior to Abu Bakr and Omar

Kathir narrates that a man once came to Ali saying, "You are the best of people." "Have you seen Rasulullah?" Ali enquired. When the man replied that he had not, Ali asked further, "Have you then seen Abu Bakr?" "No," came the reply. Ali then said, "Take note of this! Had you mentioned that you had seen, I would have had you executed and had you mentioned that you had seen Abu Bakr and Omar, I would have had you lashed for slander." *(Ishari).* Alqama reports that Ali once delivered a lecture to them. After duly praising Allah, he said, "The news has reached me that some people regard me to be superior to Abu Bakr and Omar. Had I warned against this previously, I would have certainly given punishment for it. However, I dislike making punishment for something I have not warned against. After this proclamation of mine if anyone says anything like this, he will be regarded as a slanderer and shall so be punished as one. The best of all people after Rasulullah is Abu Bakr and then Omar. When they had departed we started many new things concerning which Allah shall decide as He pleases (whether they were correct or not)." *(Ibn Asim, Ibn Shahin, La'alka'i, Isbahani, Ibn Asakir)*

A Historic Lecture of Ali Concerning the Superiority of Abu Bakr and Omar

Suwaid bin Ghafla narrates that he once passed by a group of people who were degrading the status of Abu Bakr and Omar. When he reported this to Ali, he said, "May Allah curse those who harbor anything besides good towards the 2 illustrious men. They were the brothers and extremely close

companions of Rasulullah." Ali then mounted the pulpit and delivered an eloquent lecture in .which he said: "What is the matter with some people who speak about the 2 leaders of the Quraish and the 2 fathers of the Muslims in a manner that I would never. I absolve myself from what they say and shall punish for it. I swear by the Being Who splits the seed and Who creates the soul that it is only the Allah-fearing Mu'min who loves these 2 men and only the sinful outcast who dislikes them. They were both true and loyal companions of Rasulullah who enjoined good, forbade evil, punished criminals and never trespassed the ways of Rasulullah in any matter. Rasulullah never valued any opinion as he did theirs and did not love anyone as he loved them. Rasulullah passed through this world well pleased with them and the people were also just as pleased. Abu Bakr was appointed by Rasulullah to lead the salah and when Rasulullah passed away, the Muslims entrusted the task of leading the salah with him and also handed over their zakah to him because these 2 (salah and zakah) are always coupled, mentioned together in the Qur'an. I was the first from amongst the progeny of Abdul Muttalib to nominate him as Khalifa. He however did not like to assume the post and wanted one of us to rather fill the post for him. By Allah! He was the best of those left after Rasulullah, the most compassionate of them, the kindest, the wisest in his piety and the first to accept Islam. Rasulullah likened him to Mika'el in his kindness and mercy and to Ibrahim in his forgiving nature and reputation. He walked the Path of Rasulullah until he passed away. May Allah shower His mercy on him."

Ali continued, "With consultation from the people, Abu Bakr appointed Omar bin Khattab as his successor. While some people disapproved and others approved, I was amongst those who approved. By Allah! Before he left this world, Omar won the approval of all those who had disapproved of his appointment. He managed affairs in the manner that Rasulullah and his companion (Abu Bakr) managed affairs and he followed in their footsteps just as a horse follows in the footsteps of its mother. By Allah! He was the best of all those who remained after Abu Bakr. He was compassionate and merciful and helped the oppressed against the oppressor. Allah brought the truth on his tongue to the extent that we actually thought that an angel spoke with his tongue. Allah strengthened Islam by his entering its fold and his migration was a bolster for Islam. While Allah filled the hearts of the Mu'minin with love for him, Allah also filled the hearts of the hypocrites with fear for him. Rasulullah likened him to Jibra'el in his sternness and austerity towards enemies and to Nuh in his admonishment and frustration towards the Kuffar. Which of you can compare to the 2 of them? Their heights cannot be reached without having love for them and following in their footsteps. Whoever loves them loves me. On the other hand, whoever dislikes them dislikes me and I am absolved of such a person. Had I warned against reviling the 2 of them previously, I would have certainly given the most severe punishment for it. Now after this proclamation of mine if anyone says anything like this, he will be punished as a slanderer is punished. Take note! The best person of this Ummah after its Nabi is Abu Bakr and then Omar. Allah knows best where the best person is after them. I have now made myself clear and seek Allah's pardon for myself and on your behalf." *(Khaithama, La'alka'i, Abu Hasan Baghdadi, Shirazi, Ibn Mandah, Ibn Asakir in Muntakhab Kanzul Ummal).*

The Incident Between Ali and Another Person on Uthman

Abu Is'haq reports that a man once came to Ali and said,

"Uthman (🙵) is in Jahannam." "What makes you say this?" Ali 🙵 enquired. The man replied, "Because he had started many new practices." "Tell me," Ali 🙵 said to the man, "If you had a daughter, would you marry her without consultation?" When the man said that he would not, Ali 🙵 continued, "Do you think that there could be an opinion better than the opinion Rasulullah 🙲 had concerning the marriage of his 2 daughters? Now tell me this about Rasulullah 🙲. Whenever he intended to do something, would he or would he not ask Allah for the best course to take?" The man replied, "Of course. Rasulullah 🙲 would certainly ask Allah for the best course to take.' Questioning the man further, Ali 🙵 said, "Would Allah then choose the best course for Rasulullah 🙲 or not?" "Indeed," the man responded, "Allah would definitely choose the best course for Rasulullah 🙲." Ali 🙵 said, "Now tell me this about Rasulullah 🙲. Did Allah not select Uthman 🙵 to marry the 2 daughters of Rasulullah 🙲? I have thought about having you executed but Allah has decided otherwise. Remember this! I swear by Allah that should you ever say anything else other than what I have explained to you, I shall have you executed." *(Ibn Asakir in Muntakhab Kanzul Ummal)*

The Statement of Abdullah bin Omar 🙵 About Someone who Complained About Uthman 🙵

Salim reports that his father once met one of the Sahabah who had a problem with his speech and could therefore not express himself clearly. When he complained about Uthman 🙵, Abdullah bin Omar 🙵 said, "By Allah! I do not know what you are saying. Nevertheless, O assembly of Muhammad 🙲's companions, you all know well that during the time of Rasulullah 🙲, we would always be saying, 'Abu Bakr, Omar and Uthman', their names were always taken together because all respected them most highly. However, now that wealth has become a priority, it is only when he gives someone a share that the person is pleased with him." *(Abu Nu'aym in Hilya)*

The Du'a of Sa'd 🙵 is Accepted Against Someone who Reviled Ali 🙵, Talha 🙵 and Zubair 🙵

Amir bin Sa'd narrates that Sa'd 🙵 was once walking somewhere when he overheard a person speaking ill of Ali 🙵, Talha 🙵 and Zubair 🙵. Sa'd 🙵 said, "You are reviling people who have received tremendous tributes from Allah. By Allah! If you do not stop from reviling them, I shall curse you." The man mocked, "He threatens me as if he were a prophet!" Sa'd 🙵 then prayed, "O Allah! If he is reviling people who have received tributes from You, then teach him his lesson this very day!" A Bactrian camel then came running and the people gave her way until she trampled the man and killed him." Amir says that he then saw the people walking behind. Sa'd 🙵 said in surprise, "O Abu Is'haq! Allah accepted your Du'a. *(Tabrani, Haythami).* Mus'ab bin Sa'd narrates that when someone reviled Ali 🙵, Sa'd bin Malik 🙵 (Sa'd bin Abi Waqqas 🙵) cursed him. A camel then ran forward and killed the man. Sa'd 🙵 then set a slave free and swore never to curse anyone again. *(Hakim).* Qais bin Abu Hazim reports that he was once walking about the marketplace in Madinah when he reached a place called Ahjaruz Zait. There he saw some people gathered around a horseman who had mounted an animal and was reviling Ali bin Abi Talib 🙵. The people were just standing there without saying or doing anything when Sa'd bin Malik 🙵 arrived, Stopping there, Sa'd 🙵 asked, "What is happening here?" When the people informed him that the man was busy reviling Ali 🙵, Sa'd 🙵 went forward and the people gave him way until he stood by the man. He then said, "What is this? For what reason, are you reviling Ali bin Abi Talib 🙵? Was he

not the first to accept Islam? Was he not the first to perform salah with Rasulullah 🙲? Was he not the most sober of people? Was he not the most knowledgeable of people?" He mentioned the virtues of Ali 🙵 until he said, "Was he not the son-in-law of Rasulullah 🙲? Was he not Rasulullah 🙲's flag-bearer in his battles?" Sa'd 🙵 then faced the Qibla, raised his hands and prayed, "O Allah! This man is reviling one of Your friends. Let this gathering not disperse without showing them Your power." Qais says, "By Allah! We had not yet dispersed when the animal started sinking in the ground and it threw him off. He landed head first on the stones, causing him to die as his head burst open." *(Hakim confirmed by Dhahabi, Abu Nu'aym in Dala'il).*

Sa'eed bin Zaid 🙵 is Annoyed by a Man who Swore Ali 🙵

Rabah bin Harith reports that Mughiera 🙵 was sitting in the largest Masjid with the people of Kufa on his right and his left when someone called Sa'eed bin Zaid 🙵 arrived. Mughiera 🙵 welcomed him and made him sit near his feet on the same platform. A man from Kufa then arrived and facing Mughiera 🙵, he started swearing. "Who is he swearing at, O Mughiera?" asked Sa'eed 🙵. Mughiera 🙵 replied, "He is swearing Ali bin Abi Talib 🙵." "O Mughiera bin Shu'ba! O Mughiera bin Shu'ba! O Mughiera bin Shu'ba!" Sa'eed 🙵 repeated, "Am I not hearing a companion of Rasulullah 🙲 being sworn at in your presence without you repulsing it or even doing anything to change the situation?! I testify to what my ears heard Rasulullah 🙲 say and what my heart memorized from him. I shall never report from him anything false that he will question me about when I meet him. I have heard him say, 'Abu Bakr shall be in Jannah, Omar shall be in Jannah, Uthman shall be in Jannah, Ali shall be in Jannah, Talha shall be in Jannah, Zubair shall be in Jannah, Abdur Rahman bin Auf shall be in Jannah and Said bin Malik shall be in Jannah.' The ninth person to accept Islam shall also be in Jannah and if I wished to, I would also take his name."

The people in the Masjid then started to make a noise asked him in the name of Allah to tell them who the 9th person to accept Islam was. Sa'eed 🙵 said, "You have asked me in the name of Allah and Allah is Great. I can therefore not refuse. I was the 9th person to accept Islam and Rasulullah 🙲 was the 10th (of the 10 Muslims we were at the time)." Sa'eed 🙵 then took an oath as he said, "When a man's face get dusty as he stands by Rasulullah 🙲 in a battle, this deed of his is better than every deed that any of you could do if he were given the lifespan of Nuh عليه السلام." *(Abu Nu'aym in Hilya).* Abdullah bin Dhalim Mazini narrates, "When Mu'awiya 🙵 left Kufa, he appointed Mughiera bin Shu'ba 🙵 as its governor. Mughiera 🙵 then appointed orators to revile Ali 🙵. I was sitting next to Sa'eed bin Zaid 🙵 when he became extremely angry at this. He then stood up and taking me by the hand said, 'Look at that man who oppresses himself. He is ordering the reviling of someone who is a dweller of Jannah. I am prepared to testify that 9 people shall definitely enter Jannah, amongst them is Ali 🙵 and I would not be sinful for testifying myself to the 10th one as well." *(Abu Nu'aym in Hilya, Ahmad, Abu Nu'aym in Ma'rifa, Ibn Asakir in Muntakhab Kanzul Ummal)*

Weeping over the deaths of elders: Suhaib 🙵 Weeps Upon the Death of Omar 🙵 and the Statement of Hafsa on This Occasion

Ibn Sirin reports that when a drink was brought to Omar 🙵 after he has been stabbed, the drink came out from his wounds as he drank. At this, Suhaib 🙵 cried out, "O poor Omar! O my dear brother! Who is there for us after him?" Omar 🙵 said, "Take it easy, dear brother. Don't you know that the person over whom people cry loudly will be punished?" Narrating from his father,

Abu Burda narrates that when Omar ؓ was stabbed, Suhaib ؓ arrived weeping in a loud voice. "Is it over me that you weep?" Omar ؓ enquired. When Suhaib ؓ replied that it was, Omar ؓ said, "Don't you know that Rasulullah ﷺ said, 'The person over whom people cry loudly shall be punished'?" Miqdam bin Ma'dikarib ؓ narrates that when Omar ؓ was wounded, his daughter Hafsa ؓ entered the room saying, "O companion of Rasulullah ﷺ! O father-in-law of Rasulullah ﷺ! O Amirul Mu'minin!" Omar ؓ said to his son, "O Abdullah ؓ! Help me to sit up because I cannot tolerate what I am hearing." When Abdullah bin Omar ؓ supported Omar ؓ against his chest, Omar ؓ said to Hafsa ؓ, "By the rights that I have over you, I prohibit you from crying over me after this. I have of course no control over your eyes for you are allowed to weep as much as you please. Whenever a deceased person is praised for what was not in him, the angels record this against him." (Ibn Sa'd)

Sa'eed bin Zaid ؓ and Abdullah bin Mas'ood ؓ Weep at the Death of Omar ؓ

Abdul Malik bin Zaid narrates from his father that as he was weeping, someone once asked Sa'eed bin Zaid ؓ, "What makes you weep, O Abu A'war?" Sa'eed ؓ replied, "I am weeping over the fate of Islam. It has sustained a void at the death of Omar ؓ that shall never be filled until the Day of Judgment." Abu Wa'il reports, "Abdullah bin Mas'ood ؓ once came to us and was given the news of Omar ؓ's death. I have never seen him weep more than that day and never saw him more depressed. He then said, 'By Allah! I would have even loved a dog if I knew that Omar ؓ loved it. By Allah! I am certain that even the thorny trees are distressed by the death of Omar ؓ.'" (Ibn Sa'd)

Omar ؓ Weeps Over the Death of Nu'man bin Muqarrin ؓ

Abu Uthman says, "When the news of Nu'man bin Muqarrin ؓ's death reached Omar ؓ, I saw him place his hands on his head and start to weep." (Ibn Abi Dunya in Kanzul Ummal)

Thumama ؓ, Zaid ؓ, Abu Hurairah ؓ and Abu Humaid ؓ Weep at the Death of Uthman ؓ

Abul Ash'ath San'ani says, "The governor of San'a was a Sahabi called Thumama bin Adi ؓ. When he heard the death of Uthman ؓ, he wept and said, 'Khilafa on the pattern of prophethood has been snatched away and it shall now be kingship and tyranny. Whoever has power over something will now devour it.'" (Abu Nu'aym in Muntakhab Kanzul Ummal). Zaid bin Ali narrates that Zaid bin Thabit ؓ wept over Uthman ؓ the day he was martyred in his home. Abu Salih reports, "Abu Hurairah ؓ wept when someone mentioned what had happened to Uthman ؓ. It is as if I can actually hear him say, 'Ah! Ah!' as he wept uncontrolled." Yahya bin Sa'eed reports that when Uthman ؓ was martyred, Abu Humaid Sa'idi ؓ, a veteran of the Battle of Badr vowed never to carry out certain actions and never to laugh until the day he meets Allah. (Ibn Sa'd).

The Statements of Abu Sa'eed Khudri ؓ, Ubay ؓ and Anas ؓ about the Changes Within Themselves After the Demise of Rasulullah ﷺ

Abu Sa'eed Khudri ؓ once said, "We had hardly left from burying Rasulullah ﷺ when we found a change within our hearts" (Bazzar, Haythami). Ubay bin Ka'b ؓ said, "When with Rasulullah ﷺ, we were united but no sooner did he leave us and we divided left and right." Another narration states that he said, "We all looked in the same direction when we were with Rasulullah ﷺ but when he passed away, we started looking this

way and that." (Abu Nu'aym in Hilya). Anas bin Malik ؓ said, "The day Rasulullah ﷺ passed away, everything in Madinah became dark. We had hardly finished burying Rasulullah ﷺ when we felt a change within our hearts." (Ibn Sa'd). In a narration discussing the Hijra of Rasulullah ﷺ, Anas ؓ says, "I saw Rasulullah ﷺ the day he came to us in Madinah. I have never seen a day better and brighter than the day Rasulullah ﷺ entered Madinah. I also saw him the day he passed away and have never seen a day worse or darker than that day." (Ibn Sa'd)

The Statement of Abu Talha ؓ the Day Omar ؓ Passed Away

Anas ؓ reports that when the consultative assembly appointed by Omar ؓ before his death assembled, Abu Talha ؓ saw what they were doing each one wishing the Khilafa for the next and said, "More than my fear that you should all be aspiring for the Khilafa is my fear that you should all want to pass it on another. Every Muslim home has suffered a deficiency in its religious and worldly affairs by the death of Omar ؓ." (Ibn Sa'd)

Rasulullah ﷺ Honors the Poor Muslims

Sa'd bin Abi Waqqas ؓ narrates that they were 6 Muslims with Rasulullah ﷺ when the disbelievers said to Rasulullah ﷺ, "Drive these people away from you." They then went on to belittle these Sahabah indicating that they as wealthy people could not sit with these poor men. The Sahabah included Sa'd bin Abi Waqqas ؓ, Abdullah bin Mas'ood ؓ, a Sahabi form the Banu Hudhail tribe, Bilal ؓ and 2 other Sahabah whose names the narrator had forgotten. When Rasulullah ﷺ started to consider the request, Allah revealed the verse:

وَلَا تَطْرُدِ الَّذِينَ يَدْعُونَ رَبَّهُمْ بِالْغَدَاةِ وَالْعَشِيِّ يُرِيدُونَ وَجْهَهُ

And turn not away those who invoke their Lord, morning and afternoon seeking His pleasure... (Al-An'am:52) (Abu Nu'aym in Hilya, Hakim)

Abdullah bin Mas'ood ؓ reports that a group of the Quraish once passed by Rasulullah ﷺ when he was in the company of some poor Muslims such as Suhaib ؓ, Bilal ؓ, Khabbab ؓ and Ammar ؓ. The disbelievers said, "O Muhammad! Are you content with the likes of these men from your people? Should we become followers of these people? Are these the people upon whom Allah has bestowed His favors? Drive them away from you for perhaps we may fellow you if you do so." It was then that Allah revealed the verse:

وَأَنْذِرْ بِهِ الَّذِينَ يَخَافُونَ أَنْ يُحْشَرُوا إِلَى رَبِّهِمْ لَيْسَ لَهُمْ مِنْ دُونِهِ وَلِيٌّ وَلَا شَفِيعٌ لَعَلَّهُمْ يَتَّقُونَ (51) وَلَا تَطْرُدِ الَّذِينَ يَدْعُونَ رَبَّهُمْ بِالْغَدَاةِ وَالْعَشِيِّ يُرِيدُونَ وَجْهَهُ مَا عَلَيْكَ مِنْ حِسَابِهِمْ مِنْ شَيْءٍ وَمَا مِنْ حِسَابِكَ عَلَيْهِمْ مِنْ شَيْءٍ فَتَطْرُدَهُمْ فَتَكُونَ مِنَ الظَّالِمِينَ (52)

And warn therewith (the Qur'an) those who fear that they will be gathered before their Lord, when there will be neither a protector nor an intercessor for them besides Him, so that they may fear Allah and keep their duty to Him (by abstaining from committing sins and by doing all kinds of good deeds which He has ordained). And turn not away those who invoke their Lord, morning and afternoon seeking His Face. You are accountable for them in nothing, and they are accountable for you in nothing, that you may turn them away, and thus become of the Zalimoon (unjust). (Al-An'am:51-52) (Abu Nu'aym in Hilya)

Rasulullah ﷺ Honors Ibn Umm Maktum ؓ After Being Scolded

Discussing the verse عَبَسَ وَتَوَلَّى (Abasa:1), Anas ؓ says that Ibn Umm Maktum ؓ who was blind once came to Rasulullah ﷺ while Rasulullah ﷺ was speaking to Ubay bin Khalaf who was one of the leaders of the Quraish and Rasulullah ﷺ was inviting

him to Islam. When Rasulullah ﷺ ignored Ibn Umm Maktum ؓ thinking that he could always see him later, Allah revealed the verses: عَبَسَ وَتَوَلَّى (1) أَنْ جَاءَهُ الْأَعْمَى (2)
(The Prophet ﷺ) frowned and turned away, because there came to him the blind man (i.e. Abdullah bin Umm-Maktum, who came to the Prophet (Peace be upon him) while he was preaching to one or some of the Quraish chiefs). (Abasa:1-2)
After this, Rasulullah ﷺ always honored Ibn Umm Maktum ؓ. *(Abu Ya'la)*

Aisha ؓ reports that the Surah....(80) was revealed with reference to the blind Sahabi Ibn Umm Maktum ؓ who once came to Rasulullah ﷺ saying, "Guide me." Because Rasulullah ﷺ was busy giving Da'wah to one of the leaders of the disbeliever, he ignored Ibn Umm Maktum ؓ. Devoting his attention to the disbeliever instead, Rasulullah ﷺ asked him, "Do you see anything wrong in what I have told you?" The man admitted that he saw nothing wrong with it. It was on this occasion that Allah revealed the Surah: بَسَ وَتَوَلَّى (1) أَنْ جَاءَهُ الْأَعْمَى (2)
(The Prophet ﷺ) frowned and turned away, because there came to him the blind man (i.e. Abdullah bin Umm-Maktum, who came to the Prophet (Peace be upon him) while he was preaching to one or some of the Quraish chiefs). (Abasa:1-2)
(Abu Ya'la, Ibn Jareer, Tirmidhi in Tafseer Ibn Kathir)

Allah Instructs Rasulullah ﷺ to Remain in the Company of the Poor Muslims

Khabbab bin Arat ؓ narrates that Rasulullah ﷺ was once in the company of some poor Muslims, amongst whom were Ammar ؓ, Suhaib ؓ, Bilal ؓ and Khabbab bin Arat ؓ. Just then Aqra bin Habis Tamimi and Uyayna bin Hisn Fazari arrived. The 2 of them held these Sahabah in low esteem and took Rasulullah ﷺ aside saying, "We feel embarrassed that the Arab delegations will be coming to see you and will see us sitting with these slaves. Therefore, when we come to you, you should get them to leave." When Rasulullah ﷺ agreed to do so, the 2 men asked to have it in writing. Rasulullah ﷺ then sent for a paper and called Ali ؓ to write. The poor Sahabah were still sitting there in a comer when Jibra'el عليه السلام descended with the verses:

وَلَا تَطْرُدِ الَّذِينَ يَدْعُونَ رَبَّهُمْ بِالْغَدَاةِ وَالْعَشِيِّ يُرِيدُونَ وَجْهَهُ مَا عَلَيْكَ مِنْ حِسَابِهِمْ مِنْ شَيْءٍ وَمَا مِنْ حِسَابِكَ عَلَيْهِمْ مِنْ شَيْءٍ فَتَطْرُدَهُمْ فَتَكُونَ مِنَ الظَّالِمِينَ (52) وَكَذَلِكَ فَتَنَّا بَعْضَهُمْ بِبَعْضٍ لِيَقُولُوا أَهَؤُلَاءِ مَنَّ اللَّهُ عَلَيْهِمْ مِنْ بَيْنِنَا أَلَيْسَ اللَّهُ بِأَعْلَمَ بِالشَّاكِرِينَ (53) وَإِذَا جَاءَكَ الَّذِينَ يُؤْمِنُونَ بِآيَاتِنَا فَقُلْ سَلَامٌ عَلَيْكُمْ كَتَبَ رَبُّكُمْ عَلَى نَفْسِهِ الرَّحْمَةَ أَنَّهُ مَنْ عَمِلَ مِنْكُمْ سُوءًا بِجَهَالَةٍ ثُمَّ تَابَ مِنْ بَعْدِهِ وَأَصْلَحَ فَأَنَّهُ غَفُورٌ رَحِيمٌ (54)

And turn not away those who invoke their Lord, morning and afternoon seeking His Face. You are accountable for them in nothing, and they are accountable for you in nothing, that you may turn them away, and thus become of the Zalimoon (unjust). Thus We have tried some of them with others, that they might say: "Is it these (poor believers) that Allah has favored from amongst us?" Does not Allah know best those who are grateful? When those who believe in Our Ayat (proofs, evidences, verses, lessons, signs, revelations, etc.) come to you, say: "Salamu Alaikum" (peace be on you); your Lord has written Mercy for Himself, so that, if any of you does evil in ignorance, and thereafter repents and does righteous good deeds (by obeying Allah), then surely, He is Oft-Forgiving, Most Merciful. (Al-An'am:52-54)

Khabbab ؓ related further, he says, "Rasulullah ﷺ then threw the paper away and called for us. When we came to him, he said – 'Peace be upon you'. We then drew so close to him that

our knees touched his. It was the practice of Rasulullah ﷺ when he sat with us to stand up and go when he needed to leave. However, Allah then revealed the verse:

وَاصْبِرْ نَفْسَكَ مَعَ الَّذِينَ يَدْعُونَ رَبَّهُمْ بِالْغَدَاةِ وَالْعَشِيِّ يُرِيدُونَ وَجْهَهُ وَلَا تَعْدُ عَيْنَاكَ عَنْهُمْ

And keep yourself (O Muhammad ﷺ) patiently with those who call on their Lord (i.e. your companions who remember their Lord with glorification, praising in prayers, etc., and other righteous deeds, etc.) morning and afternoon, seeking His Face, and let not your eyes overlook them... (Al-Kahaf:28)

Whenever we sat with Rasulullah ﷺ and it reached the hour when he would usually get up to leave, we would stand up and leave him. Had we not done this, he would restrain himself as long as we did not stand." *(Abu Nu'aym in Hilya, Ibn Majah in Al Bidayah wan Nihayah, Ibn Abi Shayba in Kanzul Ummal)*

Salman ؓ narrates that there came to Rasulullah ﷺ some new Muslims whose hearts Rasulullah ﷺ was still winning over to Islam. Amongst them was Uyayna bin Hisn and Aqra bin Habis. They said, "O Rasulullah ﷺ! Why don't you sit at the front of the Masjid and keep away from these people and the odor of their cloaks." They were referring to the likes of Abu Dhar ؓ, Salman ؓ and other poor Muslims who wore woolen cloaks because they could not afford finer material and therefore perspired with the thick wool. "If you do this," they continued, "we could sit with you, discuss with you and learn from you." It was then that Allah revealed the verses:

وَاتْلُ مَا أُوحِيَ إِلَيْكَ مِنْ كِتَابِ رَبِّكَ لَا مُبَدِّلَ لِكَلِمَاتِهِ وَلَنْ تَجِدَ مِنْ دُونِهِ مُلْتَحَدًا (27) وَاصْبِرْ نَفْسَكَ مَعَ الَّذِينَ يَدْعُونَ رَبَّهُمْ بِالْغَدَاةِ وَالْعَشِيِّ يُرِيدُونَ وَجْهَهُ وَلَا تَعْدُ عَيْنَاكَ عَنْهُمْ تُرِيدُ زِينَةَ الْحَيَاةِ الدُّنْيَا وَلَا تُطِعْ مَنْ أَغْفَلْنَا قَلْبَهُ عَنْ ذِكْرِنَا وَاتَّبَعَ هَوَاهُ وَكَانَ أَمْرُهُ فُرُطًا (28)

And recite what has been revealed to you (O Muhammad ﷺ) of the Book (the Qur'an) of your Lord (recite it, understand and follow its teachings and act on its orders and preach it to men). None can change His Words, and none will you find as a refuge other than Him. And keep yourself (O Muhammad ﷺ) patiently with those who call on their Lord (your companions who remember their Lord with glorification, praising in prayers, etc., and other righteous deeds) morning and afternoon, seeking His Face, and let not your eyes overlook them, desiring the pomp and glitter of the life of the world; and obey not him whose heart We have made heedless of Our Remembrance, one who follows his own lusts and whose affair (deeds) has been lost. (Kahaf:27-28)

These verses threaten people with the fire of Jahannam. Rasulullah ﷺ then stood up to look for the poor Muslims and found them engaged in Dhikr at the back of the Masjid. Rasulullah ﷺ said, "All praises belong to Allah Who has commanded me before my death to restrain myself in the company of a certain group from my Ummah. With you people shall I live and amongst you shall I die." *(Abu Nu'aym in Hilya)*

The Incident Between Ibn Matatiya and Mu'adh ؓ and the Lecture that Rasulullah ﷺ Delivered in this Regard

Abu Salama bin Abdur Rahman reports that Qais bin Matatiya once came to a gathering that included Salman Farsi ؓ, Suhaib Rumi ؓ and Bilal Habshi ؓ. He remarked, "Here in the gathering are the Aws and the Khazraj tribes who have stood up to assist that man (Rasulullah ﷺ), this I can understand because they are Arab and people of standing. However, what is the matter with these other people - these poor non-Arabs who have no social standing? Of what use are they?" Mu'adh ؓ stood up and grabbing Ibn Matatiya by the collar, brought him to Rasulullah ﷺ. Mu'adh ؓ reported the statement, Rasulullah ﷺ stood up in anger and pulling his shawl along, he entered the

Masjid. The announcement "Gather for salah was made to assemble the people and after duly praising Allah, Rasulullah ﷺ said, "O people! Verily your Rabb is but One Rabb, your father (Adam ﷺ) is but one father and Islam is but Islam. Take note that Arabic is neither your father nor your mother. It is merely a language and whoever speaks Arabic is Arab." Still holding on to the collar of Ibn Matatiya, Mu'adh ﷺ asked, "O Rasulullah ﷺ! What is your instruction concerning this hypocrite?" "Leave him to the Fire of Jahannam!" replied Rasulullah ﷺ. Ibn Matatiya was therefore amongst those who left the fold of Islam and was killed in this condition. *(Ibn Asakir in Kanzul Ummal)*

Honoring Parents: What Rasulullah ﷺ Said to a Man Who Asked About Fulfilling His Debt of Gratitude to His Mother

Buraida ﷺ narrates that a man once came to Rasulullah ﷺ and asked, "O Rasulullah ﷺ! I have carried my mother a distance of 2 Farsak (6 miles) on my neck over sands so scorching that a piece of meat would cook on it. Have I fulfilled the debt of gratitude I owe her?" Rasulullah ﷺ replied, "It may perhaps have paid off a single labor pain." *(Tabrani in Sagir, Haythami)*

The Advice Rasulullah ﷺ Gave a Man Concerning His Father

Aisha ﷺ narrates that someone came to Rasulullah ﷺ with an old man. "Who is he?" Rasulullah ﷺ asked. When he informed Rasulullah ﷺ that the old man was his father, Rasulullah ﷺ said, "Never walk in front of him, never sit down before him, never call him by his name and never make him the target of abuse by swearing at another person's father, thereby inciting him to swear one's own father." *(Tabrani in Awsat, Haythami)*.

The Advice Abu Hurairah ﷺ Gave Abu Ghassan on His Father

Abu Ghassan Dhabi says, "I was walking with my father on rocky ground in Madinah when Abu Hurairah ﷺ met me and asked me, 'Who is this?' When I informed him that it was my father, he said, 'Never walk in front of your father but walk either behind him or by his side. You should also never allow anyone to come between yourself and your father. Never walk upon your father's roof when there are no railings, for it will frighten him to think that you may fall and never eat a bone of meat that your father had his sights on, for he may be desiring to have it." *(Tabrani in Awsar, Haythami)*

Rasulullah ﷺ Commands a Person to Care for His Parents When he Came to Fight in Jihad

Abdullah bin Amr bin Al Aas ﷺ narrates that a man once came to Rasulullah ﷺ seeking permission to fight in Jihad. Rasulullah ﷺ asked, "Are your parents alive?" When the man replied in the affirmative, Rasulullah ﷺ said, "Then your Jihad is to be with them." *(Bukhari, Muslim, Abu Dawud, Tirmidhi, Nasa'ee)*. Another narration *(Muslim)* states that a man came to Rasulullah ﷺ saying, "I pledge at your hand my allegiance to migrate and to wage Jihad seeking rewards from Allah." "Are any of your parents alive?" Rasulullah ﷺ enquired. "Yes," the man replied, "In fact, they are both living." "Do you want rewards from Allah?" Rasulullah ﷺ asked. "Yes," the man replied. Rasulullah ﷺ then told him, "Then return to your parents and be good to them." Yet another narration *(Abu Dawud)* quotes that the man said, "While I have come to you to make a pledge to migrate, I have left my parents in tears." Rasulullah ﷺ said to him, "Return to them and make them laugh just as you have made them weep." Abu Sa'eed Khudri ﷺ reports that when a man from Yemen migrated to Rasulullah ﷺ in Madinah, Rasulullah ﷺ asked him, "Do you still have any family in Yemen?" "I have my

parents," he replied. "Did they permit you to come here?" Rasulullah ﷺ enquired further. "No," was the reply. Rasulullah ﷺ then said, "Return to them and seek their permission. You may proceed in Jihad only if they permit you, otherwise remain behind and be good to them." *(Abu Dawud)*. Anas ﷺ narrates that a man once said to Rasulullah ﷺ, "While I desire to march in Jihad, I do not have the means." Rasulullah ﷺ asked, "Are any of your parents still alive?" The man replied that his mother was still living. "Then," said Rasulullah ﷺ, "Meet Allah while involved in serving her. If you do this, you will be rewarded like one who has performed Hajj, Umrah and waged Jihad." *(Abu Ya'la, Tabrani in Targheeb wat Tarheeb)*

Rasulullah ﷺ Stops Abu Hurairah ﷺ From Prticipating in the Battle of Khaibar Because of His Mother

Abu Umama ﷺ narrates that once Rasulullah ﷺ announced, "Prepare to march on the town with oppressive inhabitants because if Allah wills, He will allow you to conquer it." Rasulullah ﷺ was referring to the Jewish town of Khaibar. Rasulullah ﷺ added, "No one with stubborn or frail animals should march with us." Abu Hurairah ﷺ then went to his mother and said, "Prepare my journey's provisions because Rasulullah ﷺ has just given the instruction to fight in Jihad." His mother said, "You are leaving when you know that I am unable to enter without you by my side?" "But I cannot stay behind Rasulullah ﷺ," Abu Hurairah ﷺ explained. His mother then indicated towards her breasts and pleaded with him to listen to her on account of the milk that she fed him. He however remained adamant. She then secretly went to Rasulullah ﷺ and stated her case before him. Rasulullah ﷺ reassured her saying, "You may go. Your case will be attended to without you having to come." When Abu Hurairah ﷺ came to Rasulullah ﷺ, Rasulullah ﷺ turned away from him. Abu Hurairah ﷺ said, "O Rasulullah ﷺ! Your turning away from me must be on account of some news that had reached you about me." Rasulullah ﷺ said, "You are the one whose mother had to indicate towards her breasts and plead with you to listen to her on account of the milk that she fed you but you still would not agree! Do you people think that you are not in the Path of Allah when you are with one or both of your parents? You are definitely in the Path of Allah when you treat them well and fulfill their rights." Abu Hurairah ﷺ then remained with his mother and was unable to fight any battles for 2 years until his mother passed away. The narration still continues further. *(Tabrani, Haythami)*

Rasulullah ﷺ Commands Some Sahabah to Forsake Jihad to Care for Their Parents

Abdullah bin Abbas ﷺ narrates that Rasulullah ﷺ was in Siqaia when a woman came to him with her son. She said, "This son of mine wants to march in Jihad but I am refusing to allow him." Rasulullah ﷺ said to the son, "Remain with your mother until she permits you or until death claims her life because this will earn you greater rewards." *(Tabrani)*. Another narration states that a man came with his mother to Rasulullah ﷺ. While he wanted to proceed in Jihad, she was reluctant to the idea. Rasulullah ﷺ advised him saying, "Stay glued to your mother and your reward with her shall be the same as what you would receive in Jihad." *(Tabrani, Haythami)*. Talha bin Mu'awiya Sulami ﷺ reports that he once approached Rasulullah ﷺ saying, "O Rasulullah ﷺ! I wish to wage Jihad in the Path of Allah." "Is your mother alive?" Rasulullah ﷺ enquired. When informed that she was, Rasulullah ﷺ said, "Stay glued to her feet because Jannah lies there." *(Tabrani, Haythami)*. Jahima ﷺ reports that when he approached Rasulullah ﷺ to seek advice about proceeding in Jihad, Rasulullah ﷺ asked him whether his parents were alive. When he informed Rasulullah ﷺ that they were, Rasulullah ﷺ said, "Stay glued to them because Jannah lies beneath their feet." *(Tabrani, Haythami).* Jahima ؓ says, "I went to Rasulullah ﷺ and said, 'O Rasulullah ﷺ! I intend fighting in Jihad and have come to consult with you.' 'Do you have a mother?' Rasulullah ﷺ asked. When I told him that I did, he said, 'Stay glued to her because Jannah lies beneath her feet.' When I repeated myself to Rasulullah ﷺ a 2ⁿᵈ and a 3ʳᵈ time on various occasions, his reply was always the same." *(Ibn Sa'd).* Nu'aym the freed slave of Ummu Salama ؓ reports that when Abdullah bin Omar ؓ left for Hajj and was somewhere between Makkah and Madinah, he recognized a particular tree and sat down beneath it. He then said, "I saw Rasulullah ﷺ beneath this tree when a young man from this valley came and stood by him. He said, 'O Rasulullah ﷺ! I have come to wage Jihad with you in the Path of Allah thereby seeking Allah's pleasure and the home of the Hereafter.' Rasulullah ﷺ asked him, 'Are both your parents alive?' 'Yes,' was his reply. Rasulullah ﷺ said, 'Then return and be good towards them.' The man then returned where he came from." *(Abu Ya'la, Haythami)*

The Incident Between Ali ؓ and His 2 Sons When Omar ؓ Proposed for His Daughter

Hasan ؓ narrates that when Omar ؓ proposed for Ummu Kulthum, her father Ali ؓ said, "She is still too young for marriage." Omar ؓ said, "I have heard Rasulullah ﷺ say, 'Every kinship by blood or marriage shall be severed on the Day of Judgment except for all my kinship by blood or marriage.' I therefore wish to establish a kinship with Rasulullah ﷺ by marrying your daughter." Ali ؓ said to his sons Hasan ؓ and Husain ؓ, "Get your uncle married to your sister." They remarked, "She is a woman of individuality and will choose for herself." This remark made Ali ؓ furious and when he stood up, Hasan ؓ grabbed hold of his father's clothes saying, "Dear father! I cannot bear you being detached from us, do forgive us!" "Then get him married," Ali ؓ said. *(Bayhaqi in Kanzul Ummal)*

Usama ؓ Feeds the Sap of a Date Palm to His Mother

Muhammad bin Sirin reports that the price of a date palm reached 1,000 Dirhams during the Khilafa of Uthman bin Affan ؓ. Usama ؓ bored to the centre of a date palm and extracted the sap, which he gave his mother to eat. People asked him, "What makes you do this when you know that a date palm can fetch a price of 1,000 Dirhams?" He replied, "My mother asked for it and if I can get it, I always give her anything she asks."*(Ibn Sa'd)*

Showing mercy to children and treating them with equality: Rasulullah ﷺ Descends the Pulpit for Husain ؓ

Abdullah bin Amr ؓ narrates that he once saw Rasulullah ﷺ delivering a sermon from the pulpit when Husain ؓ came out dragging a cloth around his neck. He then tripped and fell down on his face. Rasulullah ﷺ got off the pulpit to get to him but seeing what he intended; the Sahabah picked up the child and took him to Rasulullah ﷺ. Rasulullah ﷺ took the child and carried him saying, "May Allah destroy Saitan! Children are surely a trial. By Allah! In the eagerness of helping the child I had no idea that I had descended from the pulpit until the child was brought to me." *(Tabrani, Haythami)*

Hasan ؓ and Husain ؓ Climb on Rasulullah ﷺ's Shoulders During Salah and He Prolongs the Sejdah Because of It

Abu Sa'eed ؓ narrates that Hasan ؓ came to Rasulullah ﷺ while he was in Sejdah and climbed on his back. Rasulullah ﷺ held him and stood up. Rasulullah ﷺ proceeded into Ruku, the child then stood on his back. When he got up, Rasulullah ﷺ then left the boy and he went away. *(Bazzar, Haythami).* Zubair ؓ narrates that he once saw Hasan bin Ali ؓ climb on to Rasulullah ﷺ's back when he was in Sejdah. Rasulullah ﷺ did not make the boy get off and remained in Sejdah until the child himself decided to get down. Rasulullah ﷺ sometimes parted his legs so that boy could go in from one side and out the other side. *(Tabrani, Haythami).* Bahia narrates that he asked Abdullah bin Zubair ؓ who it was that most closely resembled Rasulullah ﷺ. He replied, "Hasan bin Ali ؓ most closely resembled Rasulullah ﷺ and he was the most beloved to Rasulullah ﷺ. While Rasulullah ﷺ was performing salah, he would come and sit on Rasulullah ﷺ's back. Rasulullah ﷺ would not move from his position until Hasan ؓ got off. He would go beneath Rasulullah ﷺ's abdomen and Rasulullah ﷺ would separate his legs for the boy to go out again." *(Bazzar, Haythami).* Abdullah bin Mas'ood ؓ reports that at times when Rasulullah ﷺ was in Sejdah, Hasan ؓ and Husain ؓ would climb on his back. When the Sahabah ventured to stop them from them doing so, Rasulullah ﷺ would indicate to them to leave the boys alone. After completing the salah, Rasulullah ﷺ would place them on his lap and say, "Whoever loves me should love these 2." *(Abu Ya'la, Bazzar in Majma'uz Zawa'id, Tabrani).* Anas ؓ narrates that when Rasulullah ﷺ was in Sejdah, Hasan ؓ and Husain ؓ would come and climb on his back. Rasulullah ﷺ would prolong the Sejdah. When asked why the Sejdah was prolonged, Rasulullah ﷺ would reply, "When my 2 grandchildren mounted my back, I did not like to get up to quickly." *(Abu Ya'la, Haythami).*

Rasulullah ﷺ Performs Salah with Umamah ؓ on His Shoulders

Abu Qatadah ؓ reports that Rasulullah ﷺ once came out of his room with his grand-daughter Umamah bint Abil Aas ؓ on his shoulders. He then proceeded to perform salah. He put her down whenever he went into Ruku and then picked her up again whenever he stood up from Sejdah. *(Bukhari, Ibn Sa'd)*

Rasulullah ﷺ Carries Hasan ؓ and Husain ؓ on His Shoulders and His Statement about Them

Abu Hurairah ؓ narrates that Rasulullah ﷺ once came out to them with Hasan ؓ on one shoulder and Husain ؓ on the other. He was kissing the one and the other in turn when someone asked, "O Rasulullah ﷺ! You seem to love them very much?" Rasulullah ﷺ said, "Whoever loves them loves me and whoever hates them hates me." *(Ahmad, Haythami, Bazzar, Ibn Majah)*

Rasulullah ﷺ Sucks the Tongue of Hasan ؓ

Mu'awiya ؓ said, "I have seen Rasulullah ﷺ suck his tongue, the tongue of Hasan bin Ali and the tongue or lips that Rasulullah ﷺ sucked can never suffer any punishment." *(Ahmad, Haythami).*

The Incident Between Rasulullah ﷺ and Aqra ؓ When Rasulullah ﷺ Kissed Hasan ؓ

Sa'ib bin Yazid ؓ narrates that Rasulullah ﷺ once kissed Hasan ؓ, Aqra bin Habis ؓ said, "Although I have 10 children of my own, I have never kissed one of them;" To this Rasulullah ﷺ remarked, "Allah does not show mercy to those who do not show mercy towards people." *(Tabrani, Haythami, Bukhari)*

Rasulullah ﷺ's Statement Concerning Children and His Visit to His Son Ibrahim ؓ

Aswad bin Khalaf reports that Rasulullah picked up Hasan, kissed him and turned to the Sahabah, saying, "It is because of his child that a man becomes miserly towards others, does foolish things and becomes cowardly fearing for the welfare of his child if anything happens to him." *(Bazzar, Haythami)*. Anas says, "Rasulullah was most compassionate towards his family. He had a son Ibrahim who was being suckled by the wife of a blacksmith at one end of Madinah. We would go to see the child at times when the house was filled with smoke from the burning of Idhkhir grass in the furnace. Rasulullah would kiss the child and smell him." *(Bukhari in Adab, Ibn Sa'd)*

Rasulullah gives Glad Tidings to those who are Compassionate towards Their Children and Who Strive to Treat Them Equally

Anas reports that a woman once came to Aisha with her 2 little daughters. When Aisha gave her 3 dates, the woman gave one to each child and was about to put the 3rd one into her mouth when the girls looked at her with craving for her date. The mother then broke the date into 2 parts, gave half to each girl and then left. When Rasulullah arrived and Aisha narrated to him what the woman had done, he said, "Because of her deed, she shall surely enter Jannah." *(Bazzar, Haythami)*. Hasan bin Ali reports that a woman once came to Rasulullah to beg for food with her 2 sons. Rasulullah gave her 3 dates, one for each of them. The woman gave one to each child and they both ate theirs. They then started looking at their mother, who then broke her date into 2 parts, giving half to each of them. To this, Rasulullah commented, "Allah shall be merciful towards her as she has been merciful towards her sons. *(Tabrani in Sagheer and Kabeer, Haythami)*. Abu Hurairah narrates that a man came to Rasulullah with his child. When the man hugged the child, Rasulullah asked, "Are you merciful towards him?" When the man replied that he was, Rasulullah said, "Allah is more merciful towards you than you are towards your child because He is the Most merciful of those who show mercy." *(Bukhari)*. Anas narrates that a man was sitting with Rasulullah when his son arrived. The man kissed the boy and seated him on his lap. When his daughter came, he merely seated her in front of him. To this, Rasulullah reprimanded, "Why have you not treated them equally?" *(Bazzar, Haythami)*.

Honoring one's neighbor: The Rights of Neighbors According to the Ahadeeth

Mu'awiya bin Hayda reports that he once asked Rasulullah what the rights of his neighbors were. Rasulullah replied, "You should visit him when he falls ill, attend his funeral when he passes away, give him a loan if he asks for one and conceal his poverty and help him in a way that no one else comes to know. You should also congratulate him if some good comes his way and sympathize with him when a calamity befalls him. Furthermore, you should not raise your building higher than his so as to obstruct the ventilation of his house and also not distress him by the aroma of your pot when he has no food unless you intend dishing out some of the food for him." *(Tabrani, Haythami)* Another narration adds, "You should provide clothing for him if he has none." *(Bayhaqi in Kanzul Ummal)*

The Incident of Muhammad bin Abdullah bin Salam and His Troublesome Neighbor

Muhammad bin Abdullah bin Salam says that he once complained to Rasulullah that his neighbor was causing him much trouble. Rasulullah encouraged him to exercise patience. When he again returned with the same complaint, Rasulullah gave him the same advice. When he lodged the same complaint for the 3rd time, Rasulullah said, "Take all your belongings out on the street and whenever anyone asks you what the matter is, tell him that your neighbor is giving you trouble. He will then receive the curses of the people. Whoever believes in Allah and the Last Day should honor his neighbor. Whoever believes in Allah and the Last Day should honor his guest. Whoever believes in Allah and the Last Day should either speak what is good or remain silent." *(Abu Nu'aym in Ma'rifa, Kanzul Ummal)*

Rasulullah Forbids a Person From Accompanying Him in Battle Because he Had Caused Harm to His Neighbor

Abdullah bin Omar reports that as Rasulullah was once leaving for a battle, he announced, "None who has caused harm to his neighbor should accompany us today." Someone asked, "I urinated at the base of my neighbor's wall." "You will not join us today," Rasulullah instructed. *(Tabrani in Awsat, Haythami)*

The Amplified Severity of Committing Adultery With One's Neighbor's wife and of Stealing From Him

Miqdad bin Aswad narrates that Rasulullah once asked the Sahabah, "What do you think of adultery?" They replied, "It is Haram. Allah and His Rasul have forbidden it and it will remain Haram until the Day of Judgment." Rasulullah then said to them, "The sin of committing adultery with 10 women is less severe than that of committing adultery with the neighbor's wife." Rasulullah then asked, "What do you think of stealing?" They replied, "Allah and His Rasul have forbidden it and it is haram." Rasulullah then said to them, "The sin of stealing from 10 homes is less severe than that of stealing from the neighbor's house." *(Ahmad, Tabrani in Khabeer and Awsat, Haythami)*

The Narration of Abu Dhar Stating That Allah Loves 3 Persons and Hates 3 Persons

Mutarrif bin Abdullah says, "I had always been hearing a Hadith narrated by Abu Dhar and desired to meet him to hear the Hadith directly from him. Therefore, when I eventually met Abu Dhar one day, I said to him, 'O Abu Dhar! I have been hearing a Hadith that you narrate and have always wished to meet you.' He exclaimed, 'May Allah bless your father! You have now met me, so tell me which Hadith it is.' I replied, 'The Hadith I heard was that Rasulullah once told you that Allah loves 3 persons and hates 3 persons.' Abu Dhar remarked, 'It never even occurs to me to lie about what Rasulullah said.' I asked, 'Who then are the 3 persons whom Allah loves?' He replied, 'The man who strives in the Path of Allah with steadfastness, expecting rewards only from Allah and then fights until he is martyred. You find mention of him in Allah's Book that is with you.' He then recited the verse:

إِنَّ اللَّهَ يُحِبُّ الَّذِينَ يُقَاتِلُونَ فِي سَبِيلِهِ صَفًّا كَأَنَّهُم بُنْيَانٌ مَّرْصُوصٌ (4)

Verily, Allah loves those who fight in His Cause in rows (ranks) as if they were a solid structure. (As-Safff:4)

I asked further, 'Who else?' he replied, 'The man whose evil neighbor gives him plenty of trouble but he exercises patience until Allah suffices for him by either life by changing the behavior of the neighbor or death by taking either one of them from this world.'" The Hadith still continues further. *(Ahmad, Tabrani, Haythami)*. Qasim narrates that Abu Bakr once passed by his son Abdur Rahman who was busy arguing with his neighbor. Abu Bakr said to him, "Do not argue with your neighbor because while other people with whom you argue will go away, your neighbor will always remain where he is and you will have to contend with him every day." *(Ibn Mubarak, Abu Ubaid in Gjareeb, Khaa'iti, Abdur Razzaq in Kanzul Ummal)*

Honoring a righteous travel companion: Rasulullah ﷺ Advises 2 Sahabah to Honor Rabah bin Rabi ؓ

Rabah bin Rabi ؓ narrates, "We were on a military expedition with Rasulullah ﷺ who had given every 3 of us a camel to ride. In the desert, 2 persons would ride while the 3rd drove the camel on form behind. However, in the mountains, all would dismount. Rasulullah ﷺ once passed by us while I happened to be walking and asked, 'I see you walking, O Rabah?' I replied, 'I have just dismounted, while my 2 companions have started to ride.' Rasulullah ﷺ then passed by my 2 companions and made the camel sit down. The 2 of them dismounted and when I passed by, they said, 'Mount the camel, sit at the front and remain there until we return to Madinah. We shall take turns to ride with you.' When I asked them why they insisted on this arrangement, they replied, 'Rasulullah ﷺ told us that we have a righteous travel companion whom we should treat well." *(Tabrani in Kanzul Ummal)*

Treating People According to Their Status: The Action of Aisha ؓ

Amr bin Mikhraq reports that when a man of prominent appearance passed by Aisha ؓ as she was having a meal, she invited him to share the meal with her and he sat down to eat. When another man passed by, she merely gave him a piece of bread. When someone asked her the reason for this, she replied, "Rasulullah ﷺ instructed us to treat people according to their status." *(Khatib in Muttafaq, Kanzul Ummal)*. Another narration states that when a beggar came to beg from Aisha ؓ, she had a piece of bread given to him. When a man of prominence then arrived, she allowed him to sit down and share the food she was eating. When someone asked her the reason for this, she replied, "Rasulullah ﷺ instructed us to treat people according to their status." *(Abu Dawud, Ibn Khuzaima, Bazzar, Abu Ya'la, Abu Nu'aym in Mustakhraj, Bayhaqi in Adab, Askari in Amthal)*. Yet another narration states that Aisha ؓ was once on a journey when she had a supper prepared for some people of the Quraish. When a wealthy man of prominence arrived there, she had him invited. He dismounted, partook of the meal and then left. When a beggar then arrived, she had a piece of bread given to him. Someone asked, "You instructed us to invite the rich man but had a piece of bread given to the beggar?" Aisha ؓ replied, "It would have been inappropriate for us to treat the rich man in any manner other than the manner in which we did. When the beggar asked for something, I had someone give him something that would please him. "Rasulullah ﷺ instructed us to treat people according to their status." *(Abu Nu'aym in Hilya, Zubaidi in Ihya)*. The narration has already passed in which Ali ؓ gave a man a set of clothing and 100 gold coins and said, "I have heard Rasulullah ﷺ say, 'Treat people according to their status' and this is the status of this man in my regard." *(Ibn Asakir, Abu Musa Madeni in Kitabu Istid'ail Libas, Kanzul Ummal)*

Greeting a Muslim: The Incident of Abu Bakr ؓ

Aghar ؓ from the Muzaina tribe says, "Rasulullah ﷺ once gave instructions for me to have a Jarib (unit measure) of dates that was with one of the Ansar. However, when the Ansari delayed, I spoke to Rasulullah ﷺ about it. Rasulullah ﷺ then instructed Abu Bakr ؓ to accompany me the next morning to get the dates. Abu Bakr ؓ promised to meet me at the Masjid after performing the Fajr salah. I found him where we had arranged to meet and we left. Whenever Abu Bakr ؓ saw anyone from far, he greeted him with Salam. He then said, 'Do you not see the tremendous virtue that others are gaining over you by beating you to greeting. Never let anyone beat you to making Salam.' Thereafter, whenever we saw anyone approach from a distance, we would greet him before he could greet us." *(Tabrani in Khabeer and Awsat, Targheeb wat Tarheeb, Bukhari in Adab, Ibn Jareer, Abu Nu'aym and Khara'iti in Kanzul Ummal)*. Zuhra bin Khamisa ؓ narrates, "I was once riding behind Abu Bakr ؓ on the same animal. Whenever we passed by any people and greeted them with Salam, their reply was longer than our greeting. Abu Bakr ؓ remarked, 'People have been overpowering us today.'" Another narration quotes him as saying, "People have surpassed us in great good today." *(Ibn Abi Shayba)*. Omar ؓ reports, "I was once riding behind Abu Bakr ؓ on the same animal. Whenever he passed by any people and greeted them with the words *'As Salamu Alaykum'*, they replied by saying, *'As Salamu Alaykum wa Rahmatullah wa Barakatuh'*. Abu Bakr ؓ remarked, "People have surpassed us tremendously today.'" *(Bukhari in Adab, Kanzul Ummal)*

The aAvice of Abu Umama ؓ in this Regard and the Behavior of the Sahabah

Abu Umama ؓ was once giving a lecture when he said, "Hold fast to patience because in markets that you like and those that you do not because patience is a most excellent quality. This world has certainly attracted you. It is dragging its skirt before you and has put on its dressing and adornments for you. On the other hand, the companions of Muhammad ﷺ! were so eager to earn the rewards of the Hereafter that they used to sit in their yards saying, 'We sit to greet with Salam and to be greeted.'" *(Ibn Asakir in Kanzul Ummal)*. Anas ؓ once said, "When we were with Rasulullah ﷺ and a tree came between us causing us to separate, we would greet each other with Salam as soon as we rejoined." *(Tabrani in Targheeb wat Tarheeb, Bukhari in Adab)*

The Incident of Abdullah bin Omar ؓ with Tufail ؓ

Tufail bin Ubay bin Ka'b narrates, "I used to accompany Abdullah bin Omar ؓ to the marketplace every morning. When we went there, he would not pass by any hawker, trader, poor person or any other person without greeting them with Salam. When I went to him one day and he requested me to follow him to the marketplace, I asked, 'What do you do at the marketplace when you do not make any purchases, do not enquire about any product, do not ask prices and do not even participate in the gatherings at the market? Why do we not rather sit here and talk.' Abdullah ؓ said, 'Dear chubby (Tufail was overweight and the term was one of kind word)! We go there for the sake of Salam, so that we may greet whoever we meet with Salam.'" *(Abu Nu'aym in Hilya, Jam'ul Fawa'id, Bukhari in Adab)*

The Practice of Abu Umamah ؓ

Abu Umama Bahili ؓ used to greet everyone he met with Salam. There was none who ever beat him to making Salam except a Jew who once hid behind a pillar and then surprised him by coming out to greet him. "Shame on you, a Jew!" Abu Umama ؓ cried out, "What made you do this?" The Jew replied, "I noticed that you are a man who greets very often so I knew that there must be great virtue in it. I therefore wished to have the virtue." Abu Umama ؓ then said to him, "I have heard Rasulullah ﷺ say, 'Verily Allah has made the Salam a greeting for the Muslims of my Ummah and a security for the Kuffar living under our Muslim rule." *(Tabrani, Haythami)*. Muhammad bin Ziyad reports, "I was holding the hand of Abu Umama ؓ as he proceeded to his house. He did not pass by any Muslim, Christian, youngster or adult without saying 'Salamun Alaykum', 'Salamun Alaykum'. When he reached the door of his house, he turned to us and said, 'a son of my brother! Our Nabi ﷺ commanded us to make Salam common amongst ourselves." *(Abu Nu'aym in Hilya).* Bashir bin Yasar says, "None could ever beat Abdullah bin Omar ﷺ to making Salam." *(Bukhari in Adab)*

Replying to a Greeting: The incident of Rasulullah ﷺ with Some of the Sahabah

Salman ﷺ reports that someone once came to Rasulullah ﷺ and greeted with the words: السَّلَامُ عَلَيْكَ يَا رَسُوْلَ اللهِ
Rasulullah ﷺ replied with the words:

وَعَلَيْكَ السَّلَامُ وَرَحْمَةُ اللهِ وبركاته

Thereafter, another Sahabi. arrived and greeted with the words:
السَّلَامُ عَلَيْكَ يَا رَسُوْلَ اللهِ وَ رَحْمَةُ اللهِ
Rasulullah ﷺ replied with the words:وَعَلَيْكَ السَّلَامُ وَرَحْمَةُ اللهِ وبركاته
Thereafter, a 3rd Sahabi arrived and greeted with the words:
السَّلَامُ عَلَيْكَ يَا رَسُوْلَ اللهِ وَ رَحْمَةُ اللهِ وبركاته
This time Rasulullah ﷺ only said, وعليك
The Sahabi asked, "O Rasulullah ﷺ! When those 2 came, you greeted them with words better than the words you used for me. Rasulullah ﷺ replied, "You had left nothing for me (to add because you used the full greeting). Allah says:

وَإِذَا حُيِّيْتُمْ بِتَحِيَّةٍ فَحَيُّوا بِأَحْسَنَ مِنْهَا أَوْ رُدُّوْهَا

When you are greeted with a greeting, greet in return with what is better than it, or (at least) return it equally. (An-Nisa:86)
I therefore returned your greeting (since there was no better reply)." *(Tabrani, Haythami)*

The Incident of Aisha ﷺ with Rasulullah ﷺ and Jibra'el ﷺ

Aisha ﷺ reports that Rasulullah ﷺ once said to her, "O Aisha! Jibra'el ﷺ is here and he conveys Salams to you." Aisha ﷺ replied by saying, وَعَلَيْكَ السَّلَامُ وَرَحْمَةُ اللهِ وبركاته
She was about to add to these words when Rasulullah ﷺ said, "The Salam ends at that." Jibra'el ﷺ then said, "May the mercy and blessings of Allah be on you, O Ahlul Bayt, members of Rasulullah ﷺ's household." *(Tabrani in Awsat, Haythami)*

The Incident of Rasulullah ﷺ with Sa'd bin Ubadah ﷺ

Anas ﷺ and other Sahabah narrate that when Rasulullah ﷺ once requested permission to enter the home of Sa'd bin Ubadah ﷺ, Rasulullah ﷺ greeted with the words: السَّلَامُ عَلَيْكُمْ و رَحْمَةُ اللهِ
Although Sa'd ﷺ replied by saying, وَعَلَيْكَ السَّلَامُ وَرَحْمَةُ اللهِ
he did so in a voice that was not audible to Rasulullah ﷺ. Rasulullah ﷺ greeted 3 times and each time, Sa'd ﷺ replied in a voice that was inaudible to Rasulullah ﷺ. When Rasulullah ﷺ turned to leave thinking that no one was at home, Sa'd ﷺ ran after him saying, "May my parents be sacrificed for you, O Rasulullah ﷺ! Every greeting of yours fell on my ears and I had replied each time in a voice that you could not hear. I did that because I wanted to get more of your Salams and blessings, because Salam is a Du'a for peace and blessings." He then took Rasulullah ﷺ into his house and served some olive oil, which Rasulullah ﷺ ate. After eating, Rasulullah ﷺ made the Du'a:
أَكَلَ طَعَامَكُمُ الْأَبْرَارُ وَصَلَّتْ عَلَيْكُمُ الْمَلَائِكَةُ وَأَفْطَرَ عِنْدَكُمُ الصَّائِمُوْنَ
"May the pious eat your food, may the angels pray for you and may fasting people end their fasts with you." (Ahmad, Abu Dawud)
Anas ﷺ narrates that Rasulullah ﷺ used to visit the Ansar and when he came to the locality of the Ansar, 'the children of the Ansar would gather around him. He would then make Du'a for them, pass his hand over their heads and greet them with Salam. When Rasulullah ﷺ arrived at the door of Sa'd bin Ubadah ﷺ's house, he greeted with the words: السَّلَامُ عَلَيْكُمْ و رَحْمَةُ اللهِ Although Sa'd ﷺ replied, he did so in a voice that was not audible to Rasulullah ﷺ. Rasulullah ﷺ greeted 3 times and it was his practice never to greet more than 3 times when seeking permission to enter. He would usually enter when granted permission or leave if no one replied after 3 Salams. Rasulullah ﷺ therefore turned to leave thinking that no one was at home, when Sa'd ﷺ came running after him. The rest of the narration is the same as the one above. *(Bazzar, Haythami)*

The Incident of Omar ﷺ with Uthman ﷺ

Muhammad bin Jubair reports that Omar ﷺ once passed by Uthman ﷺ and greeted him. Uthman ﷺ however did not reply to the greeting. Omar ﷺ proceeded immediately to Abu Bakr ﷺ and complained to him about this. When Abu Bakr ﷺ asked Uthman ﷺ why he did not reply to the greeting, Uthman ﷺ explained, "By Allah! I did not even hear him because I was so deep in thought." "What was it that you were deliberating upon?" enquired Abu Bakr ﷺ. Uthman ﷺ replied, "About opposing Saitan. He was plaguing my mind with thoughts that I do not even wish to express for all the wealth of the world. When he cast these thoughts in my heart, I said to myself, 'If only I had asked Rasulullah ﷺ about how we could save ourselves from these thoughts of Saitan!'" Abu Bakr ﷺ then said, "I expressed the very concern and question to Rasulullah ﷺ saying, 'How can we save ourselves from the thoughts that Saitan casts within us?' Rasulullah ﷺ replied, 'The very same thing that I told my uncle Abu Talib to say on his deathbed will save you if you say the same words. He however, did not say them." *(Abu Ya'la in Kanzul Ummal).* "O Khalifa of Rasulullah ﷺ! I have some shocking news for you! When I passed by Uthman ﷺ and greeted him, he did not even reply."

In a more lengthy narration, Uthman ﷺ says, "When Omar ﷺ went to Abu Bakr ﷺ, he said, 'O Khalifa of Rasulullah ﷺ! I have some shocking news for you! When I passed by Uthman ﷺ and greeted him, he did not even reply.' Taking Omar ﷺ by the hand, Abu Bakr ﷺ came to me and asked, 'O Uthman! Your brother Omar ﷺ has come to me saying that when he passed you and greeted you, you did not reply. What is the reason for this?' 'But I did no such thing, O Khalifa of Rasulullah ﷺ!' I defended. 'You certainly did,' Omar ﷺ asserted, 'By Allah! This pride is an old tradition of you Banu Umayya!' 'By Allah!' I protested, 'I have no idea that you even passed by me or that you greeted me with Salam.' Abu Bakr ﷺ then bore me out saying, 'You have spoken the truth. It appears to me that something on your mind had distracted you from realizing what had happened.' 'That is indeed so,' I confirmed. When Abu Bakr ﷺ asked me what it was, I replied, 'Rasulullah ﷺ passed away without me asking him what it was in which the salvation of this Ummah depend. I was occupied in this thought, startled at my negligence at this.' Abu Bakr ﷺ said, 'I have asked Rasulullah ﷺ about this and he informed me what it is.' 'What is it?' I begged to know. He replied, I posed the question to him, saying, 'O Rasulullah ﷺ! In what does the salvation of this Ummah lay?' Rasulullah ﷺ replied, 'Whoever accepts from me the words that I offered to my uncle but which he refused, those words shall be his salvation.' The words that Rasulullah ﷺ offered to his uncle was to testify that there is none worthy of worship but Allah and that Muhammad ﷺ is the Rasul sent by Allah i.e. the Kalima *'La Ilaha IllAllah Muhammadur Rasulullah ﷺ.'"* *(Ibn Sa'd)*

The Incident of Sa'd bin Abi Waqqas ﷺ and Uthman ﷺ

Sa'd bin Abi Waqqas ﷺ says, "I once passed by Uthman bin Affan ﷺ in the Masjid and greeted him. Although he could see me clearly, he still did not reply to my greeting. I then approached Amirul Mu'minin Omar bin Khattab ﷺ and twice asked, 'Has anything new developed in Islam?' 'What has happened?' he asked. 'Nothing much,' I replied, 'except the fact that when I passed by Uthman ﷺ in the Masjid and greeted him, he did not reply even though he could clearly see me.' Omar ﷺ then sent for Uthman ﷺ and asked, 'What prevented you from replying to your brother's Salam?' When Uthman ﷺ denied doing such a thing and I insisted that he did, he swore that he did not while I swore that he did. When the thought struck him, Uthman ﷺ exclaimed, 'I seek Allah's forgiveness and return to Him! When you passed by me just now, I was occupied in thinking about something that Rasulullah ﷺ once said. By Allah! Whenever I remember these words, my eyes and heart are engulfed by a veil.'" Uthman ﷺ then said, "Let me tell you what it was. Rasulullah ﷺ was about to mention to us how to begin a Du'a when a Bedouin arrived and distracted him so much that he then got up without completing what he was going to tell us. I then followed Rasulullah ﷺ and when I feared that he would enter his room before I reached him, I stamped my feet hard on the ground as I walked. Turning towards me, Rasulullah ﷺ asked, 'Who is that? Is that Abu Is'haq?' 'Yes, it is I, O Rasulullah ﷺ,' I replied. 'What is it then?' he asked. I said, 'Nothing much except that you were about to mention to us how to begin a Du'a when that Bedouin arrived and distracted you.' 'O yes,' Rasulullah ﷺ said, 'it is the Du'a of the man of the fish, Yunus السلام when he was in the belly of the fish, the words are:

لَا إِلَهَ إِلَّا أَنْتَ سُبْحَانَكَ إِنِّي كُنْتُ مِنَ الظَّالِمِينَ

'There is no Ilah but You (O Allah). You are Pure. I have certainly been from among the wrongdoers.'

Whenever a Muslim makes Du'a to Allah with these words, Allah will certainly accept his Du'a.'" *(Ahmad, Haythami, Tirmidhi, Abu Ya'la, Tabrani, Kanzul Ummal)*

Conveying Salams: The Incident of Salman ﷺ with Ash'ath bin Qais ﷺ and Jareer bin Abdullah ﷺ

Abul Bakhtari narrates that Ash'ath bin Qais ﷺ and Jareer bin Abdullah Bajali ﷺ once went to see Salman Farsi ﷺ. When they came to him in a fortress in a corner of Mada'in, they greeted him with the words السَّلَامُ عَلَيْكَ and حياك الله ("May Allah keep you alive"). They then asked, "Are you Salman Farsi?" When he replied that he was, they asked further, "Are you the companion of Rasulullah ﷺ?" "I am not sure," he replied. This put them in doubt and they said, "Perhaps you are not the person we want." Salman ﷺ put them at ease saying, "I am the person you want. I have seen Rasulullah ﷺ and have been in his company. He then said out of humility as for the companions of Rasulullah ﷺ, they are those who have entered Jannah with him and I am not sure whether I shall be amongst them. What do you 2 want?" The 2 Sahabah explained, "We have come to you from one of your brothers in Sham." "Who is he?" Salman ﷺ enquired. When they informed him that it was Abu Darda ﷺ, Salman ﷺ asked, "Then where is my gift that he has sent with you?" "He has not sent any gift with us," they asserted. Salman ﷺ warned them saying, "Fear Allah and hand over the trust that has been given to you! None has come to me from him without a gift for me." The 2 reasoned with him saying, "Please do not file a case against us for this. We have much wealth with us and you may choose whatever you want from it." "But I do not want your wealth," Salman ﷺ said, "All I want is the gift that he has sent

with you." "By Allah!" they swore, "He has sent us with nothing but these words: 'Amongst you is a certain man. Whenever Rasulullah ﷺ was alone with him, Rasulullah ﷺ wanted no one else. You go to him, do convey my Salams to him.'" Salman ﷺ said, "This was the only gift that I wanted from you. What gift can be better than Salam, which is a blessed and pure greeting from Allah?" *(Tabrani, Haythami, Abu Nu'aym in Hilya)*

Shaking hands and embracing: Narrations of Jundub ﷺ, Abu Dhar ﷺ and Abu Hurairah ﷺ Concerning the Practice of Rasulullah ﷺ with Regard to Shaking Hands

Jundub ﷺ says, "When meeting his companions, Rasulullah ﷺ never shook their hands until he had first greeted them with Salam." *(Tabrani, Haythami)*. Someone once asked Abu Dhar ﷺ, "I want to ask you about a Hadith of Rasulullah ﷺ." Abu Dhar ﷺ said, "I shall then narrate it to you unless it is a secret." The person then asked, "Was Rasulullah ﷺ in the habit of shaking your hands when you met him?" Abu Dhar ﷺ replied, "There was never a time that I met him without him shaking my hand." *(Ahmad, Ruyani in Kanzul ummal)*. Abu Hurairah ﷺ narrates that when Rasulullah ﷺ met Hudhaifa bin Yaman ﷺ and was going to shake his hand, Hudhaifa ﷺ turned away saying, "I am in a state of impurity." Rasulullah ﷺ said to him, "When a Muslim meets his brother Muslim and shakes his hand; their sins are shed off just as leaves are shed off a tree." *(Bazzar, Haythami)*

Narrations of Anas ﷺ and Aisha on the Practice of Rasulullah with Regard to Embracing and His Prohibition From Bowing

Anas ﷺ reports that the Sahabah once asked, "O Rasulullah ﷺ! Can we bow to each other when greeting?" "No," came the reply. They then asked, "Can we then embrace each other?" When Rasulullah ﷺ again said "No", they asked, "Can we then shake each other's hands?" This time, Rasulullah ﷺ's reply was "Yes". *(Dar Qunti, Ibn Abi Shayba in Kanzul Ummal)*. Anas ﷺ narrates that someone once asked, "O Rasulullah ﷺ! When any of us meets his brother or his friend, can he bow to him?" "No," replied Rasulullah ﷺ. "Can he embrace him and kiss him?" the Sahabi asked further. Again, Rasulullah ﷺ said" "No." He then asked, "Can he then take his hand and shake it?" "This he may do," replied Rasulullah ﷺ. *(Tirmidhi)*. When the Sahabi asked, "Can he then embrace him and kiss him?" Rasulullah ﷺ said, "No, unless he has returned from a journey." *(Razin in Jam'ul Fawa'id)*. Aisha ﷺ narrates, "Rasulullah ﷺ was in my house when Zaid bin Haritha ﷺ arrived in Madinah. When Zaid came to meet Rasulullah ﷺ and knocked at the door; Rasulullah ﷺ stood up in great excitement, dragging his clothing along with him but without wearing anything over his upper body. By Allah! I have never before or ever after seen Rasulullah ﷺ like this. Rasulullah ﷺ embraced Zaid ﷺ and kissed him." *(Tirmidhi)*.

The Practice of the Sahabah with Regard to Shaking Hands and Embracing

Anas ﷺ says, "It was the practice of the Sahabah to shake hands when meeting each other and embracing when returning from a journey." *(Tabrani in Awsat, Haythami)*. Hasan narrates that when Omar ﷺ thought of one of his companions during the night, he would sigh, "Oh how long is the night!" Then after performing the Fajr salah, he would hurry to the person and embrace him as soon as he met him. *(Muhamili in Kanzul Ummal)*. Urwa ﷺ reports that when Omar ﷺ arrived in Sham, the common people as well as the leaders came to meet him. "Where is my brother?" Omar ﷺ asked. "Who is he?" the people enquired. "Abu Ubaidah," replied Omar ﷺ. The people said,

"Here he comes." When Abu Ubaidah ؓ came, Omar ؓ descended from his animal and embraced him. The narration continues and will soon be quoted. *(Abu Nu'aym in Hilya)*

Kissing the hand, foot and head of a Muslim: Rasulullah ﷺ Kisses Ja'far bin Abu Talib ؓ

Sha'bi reports that Ja'far bin Abu Talib ؓ met Rasulullah ﷺ as he was returning from Khaibar. Rasulullah ﷺ embraced him and kissed him between the eyes saying, "I don't know whether it is the arrival of Ja'far or the conquest of Khaibar that makes me happier." Another narration states that Rasulullah ﷺ pulled Ja'far ؓ towards him and embraced him. *(Ibn Sa'd)*

The Sahabah Kiss the Hands and Feet of Rasulullah ﷺ

Abdur Rahman bin Razin reports that Salama bin Akwa ؓ said, "It is with these hands of mine that I pledged allegiance to Rasulullah ﷺ." Abdur Rahman says further that when they then kissed Salama ؓ's hands, he did not stop them. *(Tabrani in Awsat, Haythami)*. Abdullah bin Omar ؓ reports that he kissed Rasulullah ﷺ's hands. *(Abu Ya'la, Haythami, Abu Dawud)* Omar ؓ also reports that he kissed Rasulullah ﷺ's hands. *(Jam'ul Fawa'id)*. Ka'b bin Malik ؓ narrates that when the verses of the Qur'an were revealed to confirm his forgiveness for failing to participate in the expedition to Tabuk, he went to Rasulullah ﷺ and kissed his hands. *(Tabrani, Haythami, Abu Bakr bin Muqri)*. Zari bin Amir ؓ reports that when they arrived in Madinah and Rasulullah ﷺ was pointed out to them, they started kissing his hands and feet. *(Bukhari in Adab)*. Mazidah Abdi ؓ reports that Ashaj ؓ walked up to Rasulullah ﷺ and started kissing his hands. Rasulullah ﷺ said to him, "Remember! You have 2 qualities that Allah and His Rasul ﷺ love." He asked, "Are these natural qualities within me or have they been developed afterwards?" "No," replied Rasulullah ﷺ, "They have been naturally installed within you." Ashaj ؓ then said, "All praise is for Allah Who has installed within me such qualities that Allah and His Rasul ﷺ love." *(Bukhari in Adab)*

Omar ؓ Kisses the Head of Abu Bakr ؓ and Abu Ubaidah ؓ Kisses the Hand of Omar ؓ

Abu Raja Utaridi says, "When I arrived in Madinah, I beheld a gathering at the center of which a man was kissing the head of another man saying, 'We would have been destroyed had it not been for you.' When I enquired who the man kissing was, I was informed that he was Omar bin Khattab ؓ who was kissing the head of Abu Bakr ؓ for fighting the renegades who had refused to pay zakah." Abu Bakr ؓ was the only one who saw the need for this when all the other Sahabah did not see its necessity. *(Ibn Asakir in Muntakhab Kanzul Ummal)*. Tamim bin Salama reports that when Omar ؓ arrived in Sham, Abu Ubaidah bin Jarrah ؓ welcomed him, shook his hand and kissed it. The 2 men then sat by themselves and wept. Tamim always maintained that kissing the hand of pious people is Sunnah. *(Abdur Razzaq, Khara'iti in Makarimul Akhlaq, Bayhaqi, Ibn Asakir in Kanzul Ummal)*

Kissing the Hand of Wathila bin Asqa ؓ to Attain Blessings of the Pledge of Allegiance It Took with Rasulullah ﷺ

Yahya bin Harith Dhimari says, "When I met Wathila bin Asqa ؓ, I asked, 'Was it with these hands that you pledged allegiance to Rasulullah ﷺ?' When he confirmed that it was, I said, 'Bring them here so that I may kiss them.' He then gave me his hand and I kissed it." *(Tabrani, Haythami)*. Yunus bin Maisara narrates that they once went to visit an ailing Yazid bin Aswad when Wathila bin Asqa ؓ also arrived there. When he

saw him, Yazid stretched out his hand and took the hand of Wathila ؓ. He then passed Wathila's hand over his face and chest because it was with that hand that Wathila ؓ had pledged allegiance to Rasulullah ﷺ. Wathila ؓ asked, "O Yazid! How are your expectations of your Rabb?" "Good," replied Yazid. Wathila ؓ said, "Glad tidings for you! I have heard Rasulullah ﷺ say, 'Allah says, 'I treat my slaves according to their expectations of Me. If their expectations are good, I treat them well and if it is bad, I shall treat them badly.'" *(Abu Nu'aym in Hilya)*

Kissing the Hands of Salama bin Akwa ؓ, Anas ؓ and Abbas ؓ

Abdur Rahman bin Razin says, "As we were passing Rabdha, Salama bin Akwa ؓ was pointed out to us. I approached him and when we greeted him, he showed us his hands saying, 'It is with these hands that I pledged allegiance to Rasulullah ﷺ.' The palm he extended was as large as the front leg of a camel. We then stood up and started kissing his hand." *(Bukhari in Adabul Mufrid, Ibn Sa'd)*. Abu Jad'an narrates that Thabit once asked Anas ؓ, "Did you ever touch Nabi ﷺ with your hand?" When Anas ؓ said that he did, Thabit kissed his hand. *(Bukhari in Adab)*. Suhaib ؓ says that he saw Ali ؓ kiss the hand and feet of Abbas ؓ. *(Bukhari in Adab)*

Rasulullah ﷺ Welcomes Fatima ؓ and She Welcomes Him

Aisha ؓ narrates that she had not seen anyone who resembled Rasulullah ﷺ more in his speech and gestures than his daughter Fatima ؓ. Whenever Rasulullah ﷺ saw her arrive; he would welcome her, stand up, and kiss her. He would then take her by her hand and take her with him to sit where he had been sitting. In a like manner, whenever he went to her, she would also welcome him, stand up, and kiss him. When she came to see him during his final illness, he welcomed her, and kissed her. He then whispered something to her and she started weeping. Thereafter, he again whispered something to her and she started to laugh. Aisha ؓ narrates further, "I then said to some other women, 'I had always believed that this lady was superior to other women, but it appears that she is just like other women because while weeping, she suddenly started to laugh.' When I asked her what it was that Rasulullah ﷺ said to her, she replied, 'If I told you I would then be disclosing a secret.' However, after Rasulullah ﷺ passed away, she said, 'I started to weep when Rasulullah ﷺ whispered to me that he was going to pass away. I then became happy when he informed me that I would be the first of his family to meet him.'" *(Bukhari in Adab)*

The Sahabah Stand up for Rasulullah ﷺ

Hilal رحمة الله narrates from Abu Hurairah ؓ that when Rasulullah ﷺ left their gathering, they stood up for him and would not sit until he entered his room. *(Bazzar in Majmu'uz Zawa'id)*.

Rasulullah ﷺ Prohibits the Sahabah From Sanding Up For Him

Abu Umamah ؓ says, "When Rasulullah ﷺ once came out to us taking support from his staff, we stood up for him. He then said, "Do not stand up as the non-Arabs stand up in honor of each other." *(Ibn Jareer in Kanzul Ummal, Abu Dawud in Jam'ul Fawa'id)*. Ubadah bin Samit ؓ narrates that when Rasulullah ﷺ once came out to them, Abu Bakr ؓ (may Allah shower His mercy upon him) said, "Stand up and seek help from Rasulullah ﷺ in your case against the hypocrite." However, Rasulullah ﷺ said, "None should stand! Allah is the only One for Whom people ought to stand up." *(Ahmad, Haythami)*

The Practice of the Sahabah in this Regard

Anas ؓ says, "There was none whom the Sahabah loved to see more than Rasulullah ﷺ. Despite this, they would not stand up for him when they saw him because they knew that he disliked it." *(Bukhari in Adab, Tirmidhi, Ahmad, Abu Dawud).* Nafi reports from Abdullah bin Omar ؓ that Rasulullah ﷺ forbade a person from making another stand up from his place and then sitting in the same place. Therefore, whenever someone stood up from his place for Abdullah bin Omar ؓ, he would not sit there. *(Bukhari in Adab, Ibn Sa'd).* Abu Khalid Walibi says that when Ali ؓ once came out to them, they stood waiting for him to go ahead. Ali ؓ reprimanded them saying, "Why do I see you people standing with your chests out like soldiers?" *(Ibn Sa'd).* Abu Mijlaz reports that when Mu'awiya ؓ once came out while Abdullah bin Amir ؓ and Abdullah bin Zubair ؓ were seated. Abdullah bin Amir ؓ stood up while Abdullah bin Zubair ؓ who was the larger of the 2 remained sitting. Mu'awiya ؓ remarked, "I have heard Rasulullah ﷺ say that the person who likes Allah's servants to stand up for him should prepare for himself a house in Jahannam." *(Bukhari in Adab)*

Rasulullah ﷺ Shifts for a Person who Entered the Masjid

Wathila bin Khattab Qurashi ؓ reports that a person once entered the Masjid when Rasulullah ﷺ was there by himself. Rasulullah ﷺ shifted from his place for the man. When someone commented that there was enough space for the man and Rasulullah ﷺ did not need to move, Rasulullah ﷺ said, "It is the right of a Mu'min that his brother should shift from his place when he sees him arrive." *(Bayhaqi, Ibn Asakir in Kanzul Ummal).* Wathila bin Asqa ؓ narrates that Rasulullah ﷺ was all alone in the Masjid when a man entered. When Rasulullah ﷺ shifted for the man, someone asked, "O Rasulullah ﷺ! But there is plenty of space for him to sit. Why did you need to move?" Rasulullah ﷺ replied, "It is the right of a Muslim." *(Tabrani, Haythami).* Abu Bakr ؓ moved from his place for Ali bin Abi Talib ؓ saying, "Come here, O Abul Hasan." Ali ؓ then sat between Rasulullah ﷺ and Abu Bakr ؓ.

Honoring the Person Sitting with one Statements of the Sahabah in this Regard

Kathir bin Murra says, "I entered the Masjid on a Friday where I found Awf bin Malik Ashja'ee ؓ sitting in a gathering with his legs stretched out before him. He saw me arrive, he folded his legs in and said, "Do you know why I had stretched out my legs? I did it so that some pious person should come and sit here." *(Bukhari in Adab).* Muhammad bin Abbad bin Ja'far narrates that Abdullah bin Abbas ؓ said, "The person I have the most respect is the one with whom I am sitting." Ibn Abi Mulaika reports that Abdullah bin Abbas ؓ said, "The person I have the most respect for is the one with whom I am sitting, though he steps over people's shoulders to sit with me." *(Bukhari in Adab).*

The Hospitality of a Muslim: The Incident of Ali ؓ with 2 Men

Abu Ja'far narrates that when 2 men went to see Ali ؓ, he threw a cushion to each of them. While the one man sat on the cushion, the other sat on the ground. Addressing the man sitting on the ground, Ali ؓ said, "Get up and sit on the cushion because it is only a donkey who refuses hospitality." *(Ibn Abi Shayba, Abdur Razzaq in Kanzul Ummal)*

Concealing the secret of a Muslim: Abu Bakr ؓ Conceals Rasulullah ﷺ's Secret Concerning Marrying Hafsa ؓ

Omar ؓ narrates, "My daughter Hafsa ؓ was widowed when her husband Khunais bin Hudhafa Sahmi ؓ passed away in Madinah. He was a companion of Rasulullah ﷺ who participated in the Battle of Badr. When I met Abu Bakr ؓ, I said, 'If you agree, I would like to get you married to Hafsa ؓ the daughter of Omar.' He however gave me no reply. It was only a few days later that Rasulullah ﷺ proposed for her and I married her to Rasulullah ﷺ. Abu Bakr ؓ met me thereafter and said, 'You may have been angry with me when you proposed that I marry Hafsa ؓ and I gave no reply?' When I confirmed that I was, he explained, 'The only thing that prevented me from giving you a reply was that I had heard Rasulullah ﷺ make mention of proposing for her and I did not wish to reveal Rasulullah ﷺ's secret. Had he not married her, I certainly would have." *(Abu Nu'aym in Hilya, Ahmad, Ibn Sa'd, Bukhari, Nasa'ee, Bayhaqi, Abu Ya'la, Ibn Hibban in Muntakhab Kanzul Ummal)*

Anas ؓ Conceals Rasulullah ﷺ's Secret

Anas ؓ relates, "I was in Rasulullah ﷺ's service one day and when I had completed, I thought to myself that since Nabi ﷺ is having his rest, I may as well leave. I then saw some children playing and stood there watching them play. Rasulullah ﷺ then came where the children were, greeted them and then called for me. He then sent me on a task that remains in my mouth (because it was a secret. By the time I eventually reported back to Rasulullah ﷺ after completing the task, I was late in returning to my mother. "What kept you up?" she enquired. When I informed her that Rasulullah ﷺ had sent me on a task and she asked what it was, I replied, 'It is Rasulullah ﷺ's secret.' She then said, 'Then conceal the secret of Rasulullah ﷺ.' I have therefore not informed a soul about the task. Then addressing his student Thabit Banani, Anas ؓ said, If there was anyone I would tell, it would be you." *(Bukhari in Adab, Muslim in Jam'ul Fawa'id)*

Honoring Orphans: The Advice Rasulullah ﷺ Gave to Soften a Hard Heart

Abu Hurairah ؓ reports that when a man once complained to Rasulullah ﷺ about his hard heart, Rasulullah ﷺ said, "Pass your hand over the head of an orphan and feed a poor person." *(Ahmad, Haythami).* Abu Darda ؓ narrates that when a man once complained to Rasulullah ﷺ about his hard heart, Rasulullah ﷺ asked, "Do you want your heart to be softened and your needs to be fulfilled? Have mercy on the orphan, pass your hand over his head and feed him from your food. Your heart will then be softened and your needs will be fulfilled." *(Tabrani, Haythami)*

Honoring the friends of one's father: The Incident of Bashir bin Aqraba ؓ with Rasulullah ﷺ

Bashir bin Aqraba Juhani ؓ relates, "On the day the Battle of Uhud was fought, I asked Rasulullah ﷺ, 'What has happened to my father?' Rasulullah ﷺ replied, 'He has been martyred. May Allah shower His mercy on him.' When I started to weep, Rasulullah ﷺ picked me up, passed his hand over my head and put me with him on his animal saying, 'Will you not like me to be your father and Aisha ؓ to be your mother?'" *(Bazzar, Haythami, Bukhari in Tarikh, Isabah, Ibn Mandah and Ibn Asakir in Muntakhab Kanzul Ummal)*

Abdullah bin Omar ؓ Honors a Bedouin Whose Father was a Friend of Omar ؓ

Abdullah bin Omar ؓ had a donkey that he took along with him when traveling to Makkah. He would use the donkey to rest on when the camels grew tired. He also had with him a turban that he tied on his head on the journey. As he was riding the donkey one day, a Bedouin happened to pass by. "Are you not so-and-so?" Abdullah bin Omar ؓ asked. When the man confirmed that he was the person, Abdullah bin Omar ؓ gave him the donkey saying, "Ride this away." He also handed him the turban saying, "Tie this to your head." One of his companions remarked, "May Allah forgive you! You have given him the donkey you rest upon and the turban you tie on your head" Abdullah bin Omar ؓ replied, "I have heard Rasulullah ﷺ say, 'Indeed the best act of virtue is for a man to maintain good ties with those who were close to his father after his father's death.' This man's father was a close friend of my father Omar ؓ." (Abu Dawud, Tirmidhi, Muslim in Jam'ul Fawa'id). Someone asked Abdullah bin Omar ؓ, "Would giving him 2 Dirhams not suffice?" Abdullah bin Omar ؓ replied, "Nabi ﷺ said, 'Care for your father's associates and do not severe ties with them, otherwise Allah shall extinguish your noor." (Bukhari in Adab)

Treating Parents Well After Their Demise

Abu Usaid Sa'idi ؓ narrates that someone once asked, "Rasulullah ﷺ! Is there any good treatment that I may give to my parents after their demise?" Rasulullah ﷺ replied, "Certainly. Make Du'a for them, seek Allah's forgiveness for them, fulfill their promises, maintain the ties you have through them and honor their friends. (Abu Dawud)

Accepting the invitation of a Muslim: The Incident of Abu Ayub Ansari ؓ and Other Soldiers at Sea

Ziyad bin An'am Afriqi reports that they were once at sea as soldiers during the Khilafa of Mu'awiya ؓ when their vessel joined up with that of Abu Ayub Ansari ؓ. When their lunch was served, they invited Abu Ayub ؓ, who said, "You are inviting me when I am fasting. It is however imperative for me to accept your invitation because I heard Rasulullah ﷺ say, '6 rights are incumbent for a Muslim to fulfill towards his fellow Muslim brother. Should he neglect one of them, he has neglected a compulsory right due to his brother. These are: (1) He should greet him when he meets him, (2) he should accept his invitation, (3) he should respond to his sneeze by saying 'Yarhamu KaAllah', (4) he should visit him when he falls ill, (5) he should attend his funeral, and (6) he should give him good advice when he asks for it.'" The narration continues further. (Bukhari in Adab)

Some Statements of the Sahabah in this Regard

Humaid bin Nu'aym narrates that when Omar bin Khattab ؓ and Uthman bin Affan ؓ were once invited to a meal, they both accepted the invitation. As they were leaving, Omar ؓ said to Uthman ؓ, "Although I attended the meal, I wish that I had not." "Why is that?" Uthman ؓ asked. Omar ؓ replied, "I fear that it was hosted for show." (Ibn Mubarak, Ahmad in Zuhd, Kanzul Ummal). When he was the Amirul Mu'minin, Uthman ؓ was invited when Mughiera bin Shu'ba ؓ got married. When Uthman ؓ arrived, he said, "Although I am fasting, I wished to accept the invitation and to pray for blessings." (Ahmad in Zuhd, Kanzul Ummal). Salman Farsi ؓ said, "When your friend, neighbor or relative who works for the state gives you a gift or invites you for a meal, you should accept even though you doubt the legality of his earnings. If the earnings are actually illegal, this is something you will attain without any effort while the sin of the unlawful earnings will be his." (Abdur Razzaq in Kanzul Ummal)

Removing an Obstacle From the Path of a Muslim: The Incident of Ma'qal Muzani ؓ and Mu'awiya bin Qurra ؓ

Mu'awiya bin Qurra ؓ says, "I was once with Ma'qal Muzani ؓ when he removed an obstacle from the road. When I later saw something else on the road, I beat him to removing it. 'What made you do that, O son of my brother?' he enquired. I replied, 'I did something that I had seen you do.' He then remarked, 'You have done well, O son of my brother! I have heard Rasulullah ﷺ say, 'Whoever removes an obstacle from the Path of the Muslims shall have the rewards of a good deed recorded in his favor and whoever has even a single good deed accepted by Allah shall enter Jannah." (Bukhari in Adab)

Responding to a sneeze: The Guidance Rasulullah ﷺ Gave Responding to a Sneeze

Abdullah bin Omar ؓ narrates that they were once sitting with Rasulullah ﷺ when he sneezed. When the Sahabah responded by saying: يرحمك الله 'Yar-Hamu KaAllah', Rasulullah ﷺ said: يَهْدِيْكُمُ اللهُ وَيُصْلِحُ بَالِكُمْ "May Allah guide you and set all your affairs right." (Tabrani, Haythami). Aisha ؓ reports that someone once sneezed in the presence of Rasulullah ﷺ and then asked, "What should I say, O Rasulullah ﷺ?" Rasulullah ﷺ answered, "Say الحمد لله 'Alhamdu Lillah'." The other Sahabah then asked, "What should we then say in response, O Rasulullah ﷺ?" "You should say يرحمك الله 'Yar-hamu KaAllah'," Rasulullah ﷺ replied. The man then enquired further, "How should I then respond to them, O Rasulullah ﷺ? Rasulullah ﷺ then told him that he should say: يَهْدِيْكُمُ اللهُ وَيُصْلِحُ بَالِكُمْ "May Allah guide you and set all your affairs right." (Ahmad, Abu Ya'la, Haythami, Ibn Jareer, Bayhaqi in Kanzul Ummal)

Abdullah bin Mas'ood ؓ says, "Rasulullah ﷺ taught us to respond whenever someone sneezed." (Tabrani, Haythami)

Abdullah bin Mas'ood ؓ also mentioned, "Rasulullah ﷺ taught us that whenever anyone sneezed, he should say: الْحَمْدُ لِلَّهِ رَبِّ الْعَالَمِينَ 'Alhamdu Lillahi Rabbi l Aalamin'. When he says this, those with him should say, يرحمك الله 'Yar-Hamu KaAllah'. When they then say this, he (the one who sneezed) should reply by saying: يَغْفِرُ اللهُ لِي ولكم 'Yagh Firullahu Li wa Lakum'." (Tabrani, Haythami). Ummu Salama ؓ reports that a person once sneezed next to Rasulullah ﷺ's room and then said, الحمد لله 'Alhamdu Lillah'. To this, Rasulullah ﷺ said, يرحمك الله. 'Yar-Hamu KaAllah'". Thereafter, another person also sneezed next to Rasulullah ﷺ's room. This person said, الحمد لله كثيرا طيبا مباركا فيه 'Alhamdu Lillah Kathiran Tayyiban Mubarakan Fee'". To this, Rasulullah ﷺ responded by saying, "This man has superseded the other by 19 stages." (Ibn Jareer in Kanzul Ummal)

Rasulullah ﷺ Prohibits Replying to the Sneeze of Someone who does not Say "الحمد لله 'Alhamdu Lillah'"

Anas ؓ reports that when 2 persons sneezed in the presence of Rasulullah ﷺ, he replied to the one and not to the other. When he was asked about this, he replied, "Whereas the one said 'الحمد لله 'Alhamdu Lillah', the other did not." (Bukhari, Muslim, Abu Dawud, Tirmidhi in Jam'ul Fawa'id). Abu Hurairah ؓ narrates that 2 persons once sneezed in front of Rasulullah ﷺ, the one person belonging to a nobler social class than the other. When the nobler person sneezed, he failed to say "الحمد لله 'Alhamdu Lillah'", because of which Rasulullah ﷺ did not reply to his sneeze. When the other person sneezed, he said " الحمد

لله'Alhamdu Lillah'" and Rasulullah ﷺ therefore replied to his sneeze. The nobleman then asked, "You did not reply when I sneezed before you, but replied when he sneezed?" Rasulullah ﷺ replied, "He thought of Allah when he sneezed so I thought of him. On the other hand, you forgot Allah so I forgot you." *(Ahmad, Tabrani, Haythami, Bukhari in Adab, Bayhaqi, Ibn Shaheen, Ibn Najjar in Kanzul Ummal)*

The Incident of Abu Musa Ash'ari ﷺ with His Son and Wife

Abu Burda ﷺ narrates, "I once went to my father Abu Musa ﷺ when he was at the home of Ummu Fadhl bin Abbas ﷺ. When I happened to sneeze, he did not reply to my sneeze but when she sneezed, he replied to her sneeze. I informed my mother about this and when he came to her, she took him to task saying, 'When my son sneezed, you did not reply to his sneeze but when that lady sneezed, you replied to her sneeze?!' Abu Musa ﷺ replied, 'I have heard Rasulullah ﷺ say, 'When any of you sneezes and then says لله 'Alhamdu Lillah', you should reply to his sneeze. You should however not reply to his sneeze, when he does not say الحمد لله 'Alhamdu Lillah'.' Therefore, when my son sneezed and did not say الحمد لله 'Alhamdu Lillah', I did not reply to his sneeze. On the other hand, when the lady sneezed, she said الحمد لله 'Alhamdu Lillah' and replied to her sneeze.' 'You have done well,' my mother nodded in approval.

The Practices of Abdullah bin Omar ﷺ and Abdullah bin Abbas ﷺ in this Regard

Makhul Azdi reports that he was once with Abdullah bin Omar ﷺ in the Masjid when someone sneezed in the corner of the Masjid. To this, Abdullah bin Omar ﷺ said, يرحمك الله 'Yar-Hamu KaAllah' to you if you have said الحمد لله 'Alhamdu Lillah'." *(Bukhari in Adab).* Nafi narrates that whenever anyone replied to the sneeze of Abdullah bin Omar ﷺ by saying يرحمك الله 'Yar-Hamu KaAllah", he would say: يَرْحَمُنَا اللهُ وَإِيَّاكُمْ وَغَفَرَلَنَا وَلَكُمْ "May Allah shower us and you with His mercy and may He forgive us and you." *(Bayhaqi in Kanzul Ummal, Bukhari in Adab).* Nafi also reports that when a man once sneezed in front of Abdullah bin Omar ﷺ and said الحمد لله 'Alhamdu Lillah', Abdullah bin Omar ﷺ remarked, "You have acted in a very miserly fashion! Why did you not also sent salutations on Rasulullah ﷺ by reciting Durud when you said الحمد لله 'Alhamdu Lillah?" *(Bayhaqi).* Dahhak bin Qais Yashkari says, "When a man once sneezed in front of Abdullah bin Omar ﷺ and said الحمد لله 'Alhamdu Lillah', Abdullah bin Omar ﷺ remarked, 'Why did you not complete it by sending salutations to Rasulullah ﷺ by reciting Durud and Salam?" *(Kanzul Ummal).* Abu Jamara narrates that he once heard Abdullah bin Abbas ﷺ reply to someone's sneeze by saying: أَفَانَا اللهُ وَإِيَّاكُمْ مِنَ النَّارِ يَرْحَمُكُمُ اللهُ "May Allah save you and us from the Fire. May Allah shower His mercy on you." *(Bukhari in Adab)*

Visiting the ill and what to say to them: Rasulullah ﷺ Visits Zaid bin Arqam ﷺ and Sa'd bin Abi Waqqas ﷺ

Zaid bin Arqam ﷺ says, "Rasulullah ﷺ once visited me when I was suffering from an eye infection." *(Jam'ul Fawa'id).* Sa'd bin Abi Waqqas ﷺ says, "During the year in which the farewell Hajj was performed, Rasulullah ﷺ visited me when I fell extremely ill. I then said to him, 'My illness has become extremely severe and I being a wealthy man have none besides my daughter to inherit from me. Since 1/3 will be sufficient for her, May I then donate 2/3 of my wealth towards Sadaqa?' 'No,' replied Rasulullah ﷺ. 'May I then donate 1/2?' I asked. When Rasulullah ﷺ again replied in the negative, I asked, 'Then how much?' Rasulullah ﷺ replied, '1/3. And 1/3 is also plenty. It is better for you to leave your heirs wealthy than to leave them destitute and stretching their arms out to people. Whenever you spend anything for the pleasure of Allah, you will be rewarded for it, even for that morsel of food which you place in your wife's mouth.' I then said, 'O Rasulullah ﷺ! Will I be left behind with my companions to die here in Makkah while they return to Madinah?' Rasulullah ﷺ said, 'You will not be left behind. Every good deed you do will increase your status and your honor and while many nations will be greatly benefited by you, there will be the enemies of the Muslims who will suffer at your hands.' Rasulullah ﷺ then prayed, "O Allah! Allow the Hijra of my companions to be completed and never let them turn back on their heels. This Du'a I am making especially for Sa'd bin Khowla (Sa'd bin Abi Waqqas ﷺ).' Rasulullah ﷺ felt pity for me that I should die in Makkah." *(Bukhari, Muslim)*

Rasulullah ﷺ Visits Jabir ﷺ

Jabir bin Abdullah ﷺ says, "When I once fell ill, Rasulullah ﷺ came with Abu Bakr ﷺ to visit me. They both arrived on foot but found me unconscious. Rasulullah ﷺ then performed wudhu and sprinkled the wudhu water on me. I then recovered consciousness and when I saw Rasulullah ﷺ there, I asked, 'O Rasulullah ﷺ! What should I do with my wealth? How should I wrap up my estate?' Rasulullah ﷺ gave no reply until the verses of inheritance were revealed." *(Bukhari in Saheeh and Adab)*

Rasulullah ﷺ Visits Sa'd bin Ubadah ﷺ

Usama bin Zaid ﷺ reports that Rasulullah ﷺ once mounted a donkey saddled with a carriage that was covered in shawl made in Fidak. Rasulullah ﷺ then mounted Usama ﷺ behind him and rode off to visit Sa'd bin Ubadah ﷺ. Rasulullah ﷺ then rode by a gathering in which Abdullah bin Ubay bin Salul was present. Since this was before the Battle of Badr, Abdullah bin Ubay had not yet expressed his false conversion to Islam. The gathering included mostly of Muslims, disbeliever, idol-worshippers and Jews. Amongst them was also Abdullah bin Rawaha ﷺ. When the dust kicked up by the animal engulfed the gathering, Abdullah bin Ubay covered his nose with his shawl saying, "Do not kick dust on us!" Rasulullah ﷺ then greeted, stopped and dismounted. He invited them towards Allah and also recited the Qur'an to them. Abdullah bin Ubay responded by sneering, "Dear man! If what you say is the truth, there can be nothing better than it. Do not disturb us with it in our gatherings. Rather return to your home and address those of us who come to you." Abdullah bin Rawaha ﷺ then said, "Do carryon, O Rasulullah ﷺ! Continue coming to us in our gatherings because we enjoy it." The Muslims, disbeliever and Jews then started hurling abuse at each other until matters reached such a head that they almost came to blows. Rasulullah ﷺ continued calming them until they all fell still. Rasulullah ﷺ mounted his animal and when he entered the home of Sa'd bin Ubadah ﷺ, he asked, "O Sa'd! Did you hear what Abu Hubab just said?" Here Rasulullah ﷺ was referring to Abdullah bin Ubay. Sa'd ﷺ said, "Forgive him, O Rasulullah ﷺ and overlook what he said. Allah has given you the status and honor. He has granted you honor whereas just before you arrived, the people of this city had unanimously decided to crown him and to make him their chief. This was put off by the truth that Allah sent with you and this has stuck in his throat. It is because of this jealousy for you that he is doing what you see." *(Bukhari)*

Rasulullah ﷺ Visits a Bedouin

Abdullah bin Abbas ؓ reports that Rasulullah ﷺ once visited a villager. Whenever Rasulullah ﷺ visited a sick person, he would say: لَابَأَسَ طَهُوْرٌ إِنْ شَاءَ اللهُ

"Do not worry; this is a means of cleansing sins if Allah wills"

Rasulullah ﷺ therefore said this to the villager, who in turn said, "A means of cleansing sins?! Never! This fever has attacked an old man very viciously and will leave him only when he reaches the grave." Rasulullah ﷺ said, "It will then be as you say." (The man then died of the condition). *(Bukhari)*

Abu Bakr ؓ and Bilal ؓ Fall Ill Upon Arrival in Madinah

Aisha ؓ reports that when Rasulullah ﷺ arrived in Madinah, both Abu Bakr ؓ and Bilal ؓ suffered extreme fever. She went to them both and asked, "Dear father! How are you? O Bilal! How are you?" When Abu Bakr ؓ's fever rose, he recited some couplets which meant:

"Every person is given greetings of good morning to you
whereas death is closer than the straps of his shoe"

Whenever Bilal ؓ's fever came down, he would think of Makkah and say the following couplet which meant:

"If only I knew whether a single night I could pass in a
valley (in Makkah) surrounded by Idhkhir and Jalil grass
If only the waters of Majinna (place near Makkah) I could
one day attain or would I ever see Shaama and Tufail
(2 mountains near Makkah) ever again"

Aisha ؓ says that when she reported the condition to Rasulullah ﷺ, he made the following Du'a: "O Allah! Make Madinah even more beloved to us than Makkah. O Allah! Make Madinah a place of good health, bless us in its Mudd and Saa and transfer its epidemic to Juhfa." *(Bukhari)*

A Collection of Good Traits in Abu Bakr Siddiq ؓ

Abu Hurairah ؓ reports that Rasulullah ﷺ once asked which of them had started the day by fasting. When Abu Bakr ؓ replied that he had, Rasulullah ﷺ asked which of them had visited a sick person that day. When Abu Bakr ؓ again replied that he had done so, Rasulullah ﷺ asked which of them had followed a funeral procession that day. Again it was Abu Bakr ؓ who replied that he had done so. Rasulullah ﷺ then asked who had fed a poor person that day. This time again it was Abu Bakr ؓ who replied that he had done so. Rasulullah ﷺ then said that the person who carries out all these deeds on one day will certainly enter Jannah. *(Bukhari in Adab)*

Abu Musa Ash'ari ؓ Visits Hasan bin Ali ؓ

Abdullah bin Nafi narrates that when Abu Musa Ash'ari ؓ once visited an ailing Hasan bin Ali ؓ, Ali ؓ said, "Take note that when a Muslim visits his ailing Muslim brother in the morning, 70,000 angels visit with him, all the time praying for his forgiveness until the evening. In addition to this, a garden is prepared for him in Jannah. When a Muslim visits his ailing Muslim brother in the evening, 70,000 angels accompany him, praying for his forgiveness until the following morning and in addition to this, a garden is prepared for him in Jannah." *(Ibn Jareer, Bayhaqi in Kanzul Ummal, Abu Dawud).* Another narration states that when Abu Musa Ash'ari ؓ visited Hasan ؓ, Ali ؓ asked, "Have you come to visit him because he is ill or for another reason?" When Abu Musa ؓ confirmed that it was because he was ill, Ali ؓ said, "Take note that when a Muslim visits his ailing Muslim brother..." The rest of the narration is as it appears above. *(Ahmad).* Abu Fakhita narrates that when Abu Musa Ash'ari ؓ visited Hasan ؓ, Ali ؓ came in and asked, "Have you come to visit him because he is ill or for another reason?" "O Amirul Mu'minin!" Abu Musa Ash'ari ؓ replied, "It is not for another reason. I have come to visit him because he is ill." Ali ؓ then said, "I have heard Rasulullah ﷺ say, 'When a Muslim visits his ailing Muslim brother, 70,000 angels pray from the morning until the evening for Allah's mercy to be showered on him. Also a 'Kharif is prepared for him in Jannah." When the narrators asked him what a 'Kharif was, Ali ؓ relied that it was a stream by which date palms are irrigated. *(Ahmad)*

Amr bin Huraith ؓ Visits Hasan bin Ali ؓ

Abdullah bin Yasar reports that when Amr bin Huraith ؓ visited an ailing Hasan bin Ali ؓ, Ali ؓ asked, "You are visiting my son Hasan ؓ when your heart harbors an opinion that opposes mine." Amr ؓ replied, "You are not my Rabb to turn my heart in the direction you desire, it is Allah Who has placed in my heart an opinion that opposes yours." Ali ؓ then said, "Remember that this difference of opinion does not prevent us from telling you what would benefit you. I have heard Rasulullah ﷺ say, 'When a Muslim visits his ailing Muslim brother, Allah deputes 70,000 angels to pray for Allah's mercy to be showered on him from whichever hour of the morning it may be until the evening or whichever hour of the evening it may be until the morning." *(Ahmad, Haythami, Bazzar)*

What Salman ؓ Said to a Sick Man in Kinda

Sa'eed reports that he was once with Salman ؓ when he visited a sick man in the Kinda district of Kufa. When he entered the house, Salman ؓ said to him, "Glad tidings to you because Allah has made the illness of a Mu'min a means for him to attain Allah's forgiveness and pleasure. As for the illness of a sinner, it is like a camel whose owner had tied it up and then released it without knowing why it was tied up nor why it was released." *(Bukhari in Adab).* Sa'eed bin Wahab reports that he once accompanied Salman ؓ on a visit to a sick friend of his from the Kinda tribe. When they entered the house, Salman ؓ said to the man, "Allah sometimes tries His Mu'min servant with illness and then cures him, thereby making the illness a means of forgiveness for his past and a means of attaining His pleasure in future. At the same time, Allah Whose name is so exalted, also tries His sinful servant with illness and then cures him. In this case however, he is merely like a camel whose owner had tied him up and then released him. When they tie him up, he has no idea why he is being tied up and when they release him, he has no idea why he is being released." *(Abu Nu'aym in Hilya)*

What Abdullah bin Omar ؓ Said to a Sick Person and what Abdullah bin Mas'ood ؓ said to Someone who was with a Sick Person

Nafi reports that whenever Abdullah bin Omar ؓ came to a sick person, he would ask how the person was and whenever he left, he would say, "May Allah give you the best." He would say nothing more than this. *(Bukhari in Adab).* Abdullah bin Abu Hudhail reports that Abdullah bin Mas'ood ؓ once visited a sick person along with several other men. There happened to be a lady in the house and when one of the men started looking at her, Abdullah bin Mas'ood ؓ remarked, "It would be better for you if your eye had to burst!" *(Bukhari in Adab)*

What Rasulullah ﷺ Would Say to a Sick Person and Do For Him

Abdullah bin Abbas ؓ reports that when Rasulullah ﷺ

visited a sick person, he would sit by the person's head and recite the following Du'a 7 times:

أَسْأَلُ اللهَ الْعَظِيْمَ رَبَّ الْعَرْشِ الْعَظِيْمِ أَنْ يَّشْفِيَكَ

"I implore the Majestic Allah, Rabb of the Majestic Throne to cure you"
Thereafter, the person would be cured if it was not yet the time for his death. *(Bukhari in Adab)*

Ali ؓ narrates that whenever Rasulullah ﷺ visited a sick person, he would say:

أَذْهِبِ الْبَاسَ رَبَّ النَّاسِ وَاشْفِ أَنْتَ الشَّافِي لَاشَافِي إِلَّا أَنْتَ

"O Rabb of mankind, remove the difficulty. You grant a cure for only You can cure. There is none who can cure but You." *(Ibn Abi Shayba, Ahmad, Tirmidhi, Dowraqi)*
Another narration adds the words: لَاشِفَاءَ إِلَّاشِفَاؤُكَ شِفَاءً لَايُغَادِرُ سَقَمًا
"There is no cure like Your cure. Grant a cure that does not leave out any illness." *(Ibn Jareer in Kanzul Ummal)*

Ali ؓ also reports that whenever Rasulullah ﷺ visited a sick person, he would place his right hand on the person's right cheek and say:

لَابَاسَ أَذْهِبِ الْبَاسَ رَبَّ النَّاسِ اِشْفِ أَنْتَ الشَّافِي لَايَكْشِفُ الضُّرَّ إِلَّا أَنْتَ

"O Rabb of mankind, remove the difficulty. You grant a cure for only You can cure. There is none but You who can remove ailments." *(Ibn Mardway, Abu Ali Haddad in Mu'jam)*
Anas ؓ narrates that when Rasulullah ﷺ visited a sick person, he would say:

أَذْهِبِ الْبَاسَ رَبَّ النَّاسِ وَاشْفِ أَنْتَ الشَّافِي لَاشَافِي إِلَّا أَنْتَ شِفَاءً لَايُغَادِرُ سَقَمًا

"O Rabb of mankind, remove the difficulty. You grant a cure for only You can cure. There is none who can cure but You. Grant a cure that does not leave out any illness." *(Ibn Abi Shayba in Kanzul Ummal)*
Aisha ؓ reports that when Rasulullah ﷺ visited a sick person, he would place his hand on the part of the person's body that was in pain and then say *(Abu Ya'la, Haythami)*: بِسْمِ اللهِ لَابَاسَ

Salman ؓ says that Rasulullah ﷺ one visited him when he was ill. As Rasulullah ﷺ prepared to leave, he addressed Salman ؓ saying: كَشَفَ اللهُ ضُرَّكَ وَغَفَرَ ذَنْبَكَ وَعَافَاكَ فِيْ دِيْنِكَ وَجَسَدِكَ إِلَى أَجَلِكَ
"May Allah alleviate your difficulty, forgive your sins and grant you well being in Islam and your body until the day you die." *(Tabrani in Kabeer, Haythami)*
Aisha ؓ reports that whenever Rasulullah ﷺ went to see a sick person or whenever a sick person was brought to him, he would say:

أَذْهِبِ الْبَاسَ رَبَّ النَّاسِ اشْفِ وَأَنْتَ الشَّافِي لَاشِفَاءَ إِلَّا شِفَاؤُكَ شِفَاءً لَايُغَادِرُ سَقَمًا

"O Rabb of mankind, remove the difficulty. You grant a cure for only You can cure. There is no cure like Your cure. Grant a cure that does not leave out any illness." *(Bukhari)*
Aisha ؓ also says that Rasulullah ﷺ used these words when making Du'a for Allah's protection. She further narrates that when Rasulullah ﷺ's illness became severe when he was on his death-bed, she took his hand and passed it over his body while reciting these same words to secure Allah's protection. Rasulullah ﷺ then pulled his hand away and said: اَللّٰهُمَّ اغْفِرْلِيْ وَالْحِقْنِيْ بِالرَّفِيْقِ
"O Allah, forgive me and let me meet the (Highest) Friend (Allah)" These were the last words that Aisha ؓ heard Rasulullah ﷺ say. *(Ibn Sa'd)*

The Narration of Anas ؓ About Rasulullah ﷺ Greeting Thrice

Anas ؓ reports that Rasulullah ﷺ greeted with Salam to seek permission to enter a home, he did thrice and when he spoke anything of great importance, he would repeat it thrice. *(Bukhari)*

The Incident of Rasulullah ﷺ with Sa'd bin Ubadah ؓ

Qais bin Sa'd ؓ narrates, 'Rasulullah ﷺ once visited us at our home and greeted with the words: السَّلَامُ عَلَيْكُمْ وَ رَحْمَةُ اللهِ Although my father Sa'd bin Ubadah ؓ replied by saying,

وَعَلَيْكَ السَّلَامُ وَ رَحْمَةُ اللهِ

he did so in a voice that was not audible to Rasulullah ﷺ. 'Are you not going to allow Rasulullah ﷺ in?' I asked. My father replied, 'Allow Rasulullah ﷺ to make Salam to us many times so that it may be a prayer for us.' When Rasulullah ﷺ again greeted with the words: السَّلَامُ عَلَيْكُمْ وَ رَحْمَةُ اللهِ my father again replied in a voice that was inaudible to Rasulullah ﷺ. Thereafter, Rasulullah ﷺ repeated the greeting and then turned to leave thinking that no one was at home. My father ran after him saying, 'I heard you each time you greeted and I had replied in a voice that you could not hear so that I could get more of your Salams because Salam is a Du'a for peace and blessings.' Rasulullah ﷺ then accompanied my father home where he had some water brought for Rasulullah ﷺ. After Rasulullah ﷺ had taken a bath, Sa'd gave him a shawl to wear that was dyed in saffron or in Waras, a fragrant grass. Rasulullah ﷺ then raised his hands and made Du'a saying, 'O Allah! Shower Your special mercy and compassion on the family of Sa'd.' Rasulullah ﷺ then shared the food. When Rasulullah ﷺ intended to leave, Sa'd gave him a donkey that was prepared with a fine shawl draped over it. 'O Qais,' Sa'd called out, 'Go with Rasulullah ﷺ.' I then accompanied Rasulullah ﷺ. When Rasulullah ﷺ indicated me to ride with him, I declined the offer out of respect for him. Rasulullah ﷺ then said, 'You may either ride with me or go back.' I therefore went back." *(Abu Dawud in Jam'ul Fawa'id)*

The Incident of a Man who Sought Permission to Enter Without First Greeting

Rib'ee bin Hirash ؓ narrates from a man from the Banu Amir tribe who once came to Rasulullah ﷺ and asked, "May I come in?" Rasulullah ﷺ said to a slave girl, "Go outside and tell him that he should say, السَّلَامُ عَلَيْكَ *As Salamu Alaikum*. May I come in?' he has certainly not done well in his asking permission to enter." The man however overheard this before the girl could see him and said, "السَّلَامُ عَلَيْكُمْ *As Salamu Alaikum*. May I come in?" Rasulullah ﷺ responded by saying, "وَعَلَيْكَ *Wa Alaik*. You may now come in." The Hadith continues further. *(Bukhari in Adab, Abu Dawud in Jam'ul Fawa'id)*

Omar ؓ, Abu Hurairah ؓ and Ali ؓ Seek Permission to See Rasulullah ﷺ

Abdullah bin Abbas ؓ reports that Omar ؓ once came to see Rasulullah ﷺ in his upper storey room saying," السَّلَامُ عَلَيْكَ *As Salamu Alaika* O Rasulullah ﷺ! السَّلَامُ عَلَيْكُمْ *As Salamu Alaikum*. May Omar come in?" *(Ahmad, Haythami)*. Another narration *(Abu Dawud, Nasa'ee, Khateeb, Tirmidhi in Kanzul Ummal)* from Omar ؓ states that he said: السَّلَامُ عَلَيْكَ أَيُّهَا النَّبِيُّ وَرَحْمَةُ اللهِ وَبَرَكَاتُهُ. He then continued saying, "السَّلَامُ عَلَيْكُمْ *As Salamu Alaikum*. Can Omar come in?" Omar ؓ says that Rasulullah ﷺ granted him permission to enter after he had asked thrice. Abu Hurairah ؓ narrates that they once came to Rasulullah ﷺ after he had sent for them, they first sought permission to enter. *(Abu Ya'la, Haythami)*. Safinah ؓ narrates that he was with Rasulullah ﷺ when Ali ؓ arrived wanting to enter the room. As he knocked the door very lightly, Rasulullah ﷺ instructed for the door to be opened for him. *(Tabrani, Haythami)*

Rasulullah ﷺ Forbids Sa'd bin Ubadah ؓ From Seeking Permission to Enter While Standing Directly in Front of the Door

Sa'd bin Ubadah ؓ reports that he once sought permission to enter while standing directly in front of the door. Rasulullah ﷺ advised him saying, "Never seek permission to enter while standing directly in front of the door." Sa'd bin Ubadah ؓ says, "I once came to Rasulullah ﷺ while he was in his room. I then sought permission to enter while standing directly in front of the door. Rasulullah ﷺ then gestured to me to move to the side. I then did so and again. I sought permission to enter and after granted permission, Rasulullah ﷺ said, "Seeking permission to enter is done only for the purpose of safeguarding the sight from seeing what one ought not to see. This objective will therefore be defeated if one stands directly in front of the door in a manner that one can see inside the house." *(Tabrani, Haythami)*

Rasulullah ﷺ Rebukes a Man who Looked Inside His Room

Anas bin Malik ؓ reports, "A man was once peeping inside one of Rasulullah ﷺ's rooms. When seeing him Rasulullah ﷺ stood up and headed towards him with an arrowhead in his hand. I can still picture Rasulullah ﷺ appearing as if he was looking for an opportunity to thrust the arrowhead at the man." *(Bukhari)*. Sahl bin Sa'd Sa'idi ؓ narrates that a man was once peeping through a hole in the door of Rasulullah ﷺ's room while Rasulullah ﷺ was scratching his head with a comb. When Rasulullah ﷺ saw him, Rasulullah ﷺ said, "Had I known that you had been looking at me, I would thrust this comb into your eyes. Seeking permission to enter is done only for the purpose of safeguarding the sight from seeing what one ought not to see. This objective will therefore be defeated by peeping into a person's room)." *(Bukhari)*

The Incident of Abu Musa Ash'ari ؓ When Omar ؓ Did Not Grant Him Permission to Enter After Thrice Seeking Permission

Abu Sa'eed Khudri ؓ reports, "I was once sitting in a gathering of the Ansar when Abu Musa ؓ came looking extremely flustered. He explained, 'I thrice sought permission to see Omar ؓ without being granted permission. When I therefore left, he called for me and asked me what prevented me from entering. I said, 'When I received no reply after thrice seeking permission, I left because Rasulullah ﷺ said, 'When any of you receives no reply afer thrice seeking permission, he should leave.' Omar ؓ then demanded, 'By Allah! You will have to produce a witness to this. Did any of you hear this from Rasulullah ﷺ?'" Ubay bin Ka'b ؓ said, "By Allah! Because we have all heard it, it shall be the youngest amongst us who will go with you to attest to this Hadith." Abu Sa'eed Khudri ؓ continues, "Since I was the youngest, I went with him and informed Omar ؓ that Nabi ﷺ had stated these words." *(Bukhari)* Another narration *(Bukhari)* adds that Omar ؓ then said, "This instruction of Rasulullah ﷺ was unknown to me. Trade in the marketplace had distracted me from spending more time with Rasulullah ﷺ to learn more."

Abu Musa Ash'ari ؓ says, "It once occurred that I thrice sought permission to see Omar ؓ without being granted permission. When I therefore left, he called me back and asked, 'O servant of Allah! Were you so much in a hurry that you could not stand waiting at my door? Remember that in a like manner, people will also be too much in hurry to remain standing at your door.' I replied, 'But I went away only because you did not grant me permission to enter after I had thrice asked permission to enter.' He then asked, 'Did you or did you not hear this from Rasulullah ﷺ? If you do not produce a witness to this, I shall make you an example for others to learn from.' 'I then left and

approached a group of Ansar sitting in the Masjid. I asked them about this Hadith, they asked, 'Can anyone have any doubts about this?' I then informed them about what Omar ؓ had demanded. To this, they said, 'By Allah! Because we have all heard it, it shall be the youngest amongst us who will go with you to attest to this Hadith.' Abu Sa'eed Khudri ؓ or Abu Mas'ood then accompanied me to Omar ؓ and said to him, 'We once went with Rasulullah ﷺ to see Sa'd bin Ubadah ؓ. When we reached the house, Rasulullah ﷺ greeted but received no reply. He then greeted a second and a third time again without any reply. Rasulullah ﷺ then returned saying, 'We have fulfilled our duty.' Sa'd then came running behind and caught up with Rasulullah ﷺ saying, 'O Rasulullah ﷺ! I swear by the Being Who has sent you with the truth that I heard you each time you greeted and I had replied in a voice that you could not hear because I wished to get more of your Salams (Du'as for peace) for myself and my family.'" Omar ؓ was satisfied with this testimony to which Abu Musa ؓ asked, "By Allah! I have been totally trustworthy in my narration of the Ahadeeth of Rasulullah ﷺ." "Indeed," confirmed Omar ؓ, "I did not think that you would be untruthful, I only wished to have the matter confirmed." *(Bukhari in Adab)*.

Some Incidents of the Sahabah concerning seeking Permission

Amir bin Abdullah reports that a slave girl of his once accompanied the daughter of Zubair ؓ to see Omar ؓ. "May I come in?" she asked at the door. When Omar ؓ refused permission, she went back. Omar ؓ then sent someone after her with the message that she ought to say, "السَّلَامُ عَلَيْكَم As Salamu Alaykum. May I come in?" *(Bayhaqi in Kanzul Ummal)*. Aslam reports, "Omar ؓ's instructions to me were, 'O Aslam! Stand guard at my door but never accept anything from anyone.' When he one day saw me wearing new clothing, he enquired where I had gotten it from. 'Your son Ubaidullah bin Omar ؓ gave it to me,' I replied. To this, he said, 'You may take from Ubaidullah but from no one else.' Standing at the door one day, Zubair ؓ came and asked permission to enter. When I told him that the Amirul Mu'minin was busy at that moment, he lifted his hand and hit me so hard behind my head that I let out a scream. I then went in to Omar ؓ who asked me what the matter was. I informed him that Zubair ؓ had hit me and narrated the entire episode to him. 'By Allah!' Omar ؓ exclaimed, 'I shall see to Zubair. Send him in.' When I let Zubair ؓ in, Omar ؓ asked, 'Why did you hit the slave?' Zubair ؓ replied by saying, 'He was going to prevent us from seeing you.' 'Has he ever before refused you permission to enter my door?' Omar ؓ enquired. When Zubair ؓ replied in the negative, Omar ؓ said, 'Then when he tells you to be patient because the Amirul Mu'minin is busy at the moment, then do so and excuse me. By Allah! When an animal is mauled by one, all the other animals eat him up if you start hitting him, so will others.'" *(Ibn Sa'd in Kanzul Ummal)*

Zaid bin Thabit ؓ reports that Omar ؓ once sought permission to see him at a time when his head happened to be in the hands of his slave girl who was busy combing his hair. He granted Omar ؓ permission to enter and then quickly pulled his head away from her. Omar ؓ said, "Leave her to comb your hair." Zaid ؓ said, "O Amirul Mu'minin! Had you sent for me, I would have come to you." Omar ؓ's reply was, "It was I who is in need and I shall therefore have to come to you." *(Bukhari in Adab)*. Another narration states that when some people requested permission to see Abdullah bin Mas'ood ؓ after the Fajr salah, he allowed them in. He then veiled his wife with a shawl saying, "I did not want to keep you waiting any longer by taking more time in sending her out." *(Tabrani, Haythami)*. Musa bin Talha says, "I once went with my father to my mother. When he entered the room and I followed him in, he struck me so forcefully on the chest that I fell on my buttocks. He then said, 'Do you enter without permission?!" *(Bukhari in Adab, Hafidh in Fat'hul Bari).* Muslim bin Nadhir narrates that a man was already peeping in the house when he asked Hudhaifa permission to enter. Hudhaifa remarked, "Well ! Your eyes have already entered and all that remains now is your buttocks!" The man then asked, "Should I seek permission to enter even from my mother?" Hudhaifa replied, "If you do not, you would see something that you would not at all like to see." *(Bukhari in Adab).* Suwaid Abdi says, "We sat at the door of Abdullah bin Omar waiting for permission to enter. He delayed permission, I went up to the door of one of his rooms and peeped inside. He noticed this and when he did grant us permission to enter and we were seated, he asked, 'Which of you was peeping into my room just now?' When I admitted that it was I, he asked, 'For what reason did you deem it acceptable to peep into my room?' 'When you delayed in calling us,' I explained, 'I happened to look in without the express intention of doing so.' The others questioned him several things, after which I asked, 'O Abu Abdur Rahman! What do you say about Jihad?' He replied, "Whoever wages Jihad does so for his own benefit." *(Ahmad, Haythami).*

Loving a Muslim for the Pleasure of Allah: Rasulullah ﷺ Asks About the Strongest Link of Islam

Bara bin Aazib reports that they were once sitting with Rasulullah ﷺ when Rasulullah ﷺ posed the question, "Which is the strongest link of Islam?" When the Sahabah replied that it was salah, Rasulullah ﷺ remarked, "Salah is most excellent, but it is not this." "Then the fasts of Ramadhan," said the Sahabah. "They are most excellent," replied Rasulullah ﷺ, "but it is not this." Jihad was the next choice of the Sahabah. However, Rasulullah ﷺ responded by saying, "Jihad is most excellent, but it is not this. Indeed the strongest link of Iman is to love for Allah and to hate for Allah." *(Ahmad).* Another narration from Abu Dhar states that Rasulullah ﷺ once came to the Sahabah and asked, "Do you know which deeds Allah loves most?" Whereas someone mentioned that they were salah and zakah, another stated that it must be Jihad. Rasulullah ﷺ however stated, "Verily the deed that Allah loves most is to love for Allah and to hate for Allah." *(Ahmad, Abu Dawud in Majma'uz Zawa'id)*

Rasulullah ﷺ has Love for People of Taqwa and for Ammar ؓ and Abdullah bin Mas'ood ؓ

Aisha says, "Rasulullah ﷺ loved people who possessed Taqwa." *(Abu Ya'la, Haythami).* Uthman bin Abil Aas says, "There were 2 men whom Rasulullah ﷺ liked very much until the day he passed away. They were Abdullah bin Mas'ood and Ammar bin Yasir." *(Ibn Asakir).* Hasan narrates that Rasulullah ﷺ dispatched expeditions of Sahabah under the command of Amr bin Al Aas. Someone said to him, "Rasulullah ﷺ used to appoint you as commander, kept you close to him and liked you very much." Amr bin Al Aas remarked, "Although Rasulullah ﷺ used to appoint me as commander, I do not know whether it was because he was merely pacifying my heart or because he really liked me. I can show you 2 men whom Rasulullah ﷺ liked very much until the day he passed away. They were Abdullah bin Mas'ood and Ammar bin Yasir." *(Ibn Asakir in Muntakhab Kanzul Ummal).* The people remarked, "By Allah! Ammar was the very man whom you people killed during the Battle of Siffin!" "True," Amr bin Al Aas admitted, "By Allah! We were responsible for killing him." *(Ibn Sa'd)*

Ali ؓ and Abbas ؓ ask Rasulullah ﷺ which of his Family he like Most

Usama bin Zaid narrates, "I was once sitting at Rasulullah ﷺ's door when Ali and Abbas arrived to see Rasulullah ﷺ. 'O Usama!' they called out, 'Do request permission from Rasulullah ﷺ to see us.' I said, 'O Rasulullah ﷺ! Ali and Abbas are requesting permission to see you.' 'Do you know what brings them?' Rasulullah ﷺ asked. When I replied that I did not know, Rasulullah ﷺ said, 'But I know. Let them in.' The 2 men then entered and asked, 'O Rasulullah ﷺ! We have come to ask you which of your family members you like best. 'My daughter Fatima,' was the reply. 'But we are not asking you about your immediate family," they pleaded. Rasulullah ﷺ therefore said, 'Then the one I like most is the one on whom Allah had bestowed His grace and on whom I had bestowed my grace, Usama bin Zaid.' 'Who then after him?" they enquired further. Rasulullah ﷺ replied, 'Then it is Ali bin Abi Talib.' 'O Rasulullah ﷺ!' Abbas exclaimed, 'You have placed me, your uncle in the last position.' To this Rasulullah ﷺ remarked, 'Ali beat you to making Hijra.'" *(Tayalisi, Tirmidhi, Royani, Baghawi, Tabrani, Hakim in Muntakhab Kanzul Ummal)*

Rasulullah ﷺ's Love for Aisha ؓ and Abu Bakr ؓ

Amr bin Al Aas reports that Rasulullah ﷺ was once asked, "O Rasulullah ﷺ! Whom do you love most?" "Aisha," came the reply. "And from amongst the men?" the question came. Rasulullah ﷺ said, "Abu Bakr." "Whom then?" was the next question. "Then it is Abu Ubaidah," said Rasulullah ﷺ. *(Ibn Asakir in Muntakhab Kanzul Ummal).* Amr narrates that he once asked, "O Rasulullah ﷺ! Which person do you love most?" When Rasulullah ﷺ replied that it was Aisha that he loved most. Amr said, "I am asking about men." "Her father Abu Bakr," was the reply. *(Ibn Sa'd)*

Rasulullah ﷺ Tells the Sahabah to Inform the Person They Liked Solely for the Pleasure of Allah That They Liked Him

Anas narrates that a Sahabi was once sitting with Rasulullah ﷺ when another passed by. "O Rasulullah ﷺ!" the Sahabi said, "I really like that man." "Have you informed him about it?" Rasulullah ﷺ enquired. When the Sahabi replied that he had not, Rasulullah ﷺ told him to do so. The Sahabi then met the man and said to him, "I like you for the pleasure of Allah." The other responded by saying: أَحَبَّكَ الَّذِي أَحْبَبْتَنِي له
"May the One (Allah) for Whose pleasure you like me, also like you." (Abu Dawud in Jam'ul Fawa'id, Ibn Asakir, Ibn Najjar, Abu Nu'aym)

Abdullah bin Omar says, "I was once sitting with Rasulullah ﷺ when a man arrived. He greeted Rasulullah ﷺ and then left. I then said to Rasulullah ﷺ, 'O Rasulullah ﷺ! I really like that man.' 'Have you informed him about it?' Rasulullah ﷺ enquired. When I replied that I had not, Rasulullah ﷺ said,' 'Then inform your brother about it.' I then went up to him, greeted him and holding his shoulder, I said, 'By Allah! I like you only for the pleasure of Allah.' He responded by echoing, 'I too like you for the pleasure of Allah.' I then said, 'Had Rasulullah ﷺ not instructed me to do this, I would never have done so." *(Tabrani in Kabeer and Awsat, Haythami)*

Miscellaneous Incidents of Sahabah on their Love for Each other

Abdullah bin Sarjas reports that he once said to Rasulullah ﷺ, "O Rasulullah ﷺ! I really like Abu Dhar." "Have you informed him?" Rasulullah ﷺ enquired. When Abdullah replied that he had not, Rasulullah ﷺ told him to do so. He then met Abu Dhar ؓ and said to him, "I like you for the pleasure of Allah." Abu Dhar ؓ responded by saying:

أَحَبَّكَ الَّذِي أَحْبَبْتَنِي لَه

"May the One (Allah) for Whose pleasure you like me, also like you." When Abdullah ؓ reported back to Rasulullah ﷺ, Rasulullah ﷺ said, "Remember that even in mentioning, this has tremendous rewards." *(Tabrani, Haythami)*. Mujahid narrates that when a man passed by him, Abdullah bin Abbas remarked, "That man likes me a lot." "How do you know that, O Ibn Abbas?" the people enquired. Abdullah bin Abbas replied, "Because I like him very much." *(Abu Ya'la, Haythami)*. Mujahid also reports that a Sahabi once held him by his shoulders from the back and said, "You should know that I like you a lot." To this, Mujahid replied: أَحَبَّكَ الَّذِي أَحْبَبْتَنِي لَه

"May the One (Allah) for Whose pleasure you like me, also like you." The Sahabi continued, "Rasulullah ﷺ said, 'When someone likes another person, he should inform him about it.' Had Rasulullah ﷺ not said this, I would have never informed you." He then proceeded to propose a marriage to Mujahid saying, "I have a daughter. I wish you would marry. She is blessed with the most excellent qualities but I have to make matters plain to you and inform you that She is blind in one eye." *(Bukhari in Adab)*. Mujahid reports that Abdullah bin Omar ؓ once said, "Love for Allah's pleasure, hate for Allah's pleasure, make friends for Allah's pleasure and make enemies for Allah's pleasure because it is only by this that a person attains Wilaya, friendship with Allah. Even though a person may perform salah in abundance and fast very often, he will never taste true Iman until he does this. It is sad to note that bonds between people are now being forged only for worldly motives." *(Tabrani, Haythami)*

Severing Ties with a Muslim: The Incident of Aisha ؓ and Abdullah bin Zubair ؓ

Auf who was the son of Aisha ؓ's uterine brother Tufail reports that Aisha ؓ was once informed that when she gave away or sold something, her nephew Abdullah bin Zubair ؓ remarked, "By Allah! Aisha ؓ will have to stop being so open-handed or I shall have to restrict her allowance." "Did he really say this?" Aisha ؓ enquired. When the people confirmed that he did, Aisha ؓ took an oath saying, "It is to Allah that I vow never to speak to Ibn Zubair ever again!" When the separation became too long for Abdullah bin Zubair ؓ, he sent people to intercede on his behalf, but Aisha ؓ said, "By Allah! I shall never accept the intercession of anyone on his behalf and I shall never break my vow." When it became too much for Abdullah bin Zubair ؓ to bear, he spoke to Miswar bin Makhrama ؓ and Abdur Rahman bin Aswad bin Abd Yaghuth ؓ who both belonged to the Banu Zuhra tribe. He pleaded with them saying, "I beg you in the name of Allah to get me into the house of Aisha ؓ because it is not permissible for her to take a vow to severe ties with me. Consequently, Miswar ؓ and Abdur Rahman ؓ hid Abdullah bin Zubair ؓ in their shawls and sought permission to enter from Aisha ؓ saying: السَّلَامُ عَلَيْكَ أَيُّهَا النَّبِيُّ وَرَحْمَةُ اللهِ وَبَرَكَاتُهُ "May we come in." When Aisha ؓ gave them permission to enter, they asked, "Can we all come in?" "Of course," replied Aisha ؓ not knowing that Abdullah bin Zubair was with them, "you may all come in." as soon as they entered, Abdullah bin Zubair rushed behind the veil and embracing Aisha ؓ, he started weeping and pleading with her in the name of Allah. Miswar and Abdur Rahman ؓ also pleaded with her in the name of Allah that she should speak to Abdullah bin Zubair ؓ and accept his apology. They also said to her, "As you know, Rasulullah ﷺ forbade severing of ties and that it is not permissible for a

Muslim to severe ties with a Muslim brother for more than 3 days." When they took pains to remind her and were persistent, she started to weep as she addressed the 2 men saying, "I have taken and oath and an oath is a serious matter." They however continued convincing her until she started speaking to Abdullah bin Zubair. As expiation for her broken vow, she then freed 40 slaves and whenever she thought about the vow, she wept so much that her tears would wet her scarf. *(Bukhari in Adab)*

Urwa bin Zubair narrates that after Rasulullah and her father Abu Bakr ؓ, Aisha ؓ loved Abdullah bin Zubair ؓ the most and he always treated her most kindly. Whenever she received anything, she would never keep it with her and always gave it away in charity. Concerning this, Abdullah bin Zubair once remarked, "Her hands ought to be held back." When she heard about this remark, Aisha ؓ said, "Should my hands be held back?! It is to Allah that I vow never to speak to Ibn Zubair ever again!" Even though men of the Quraish and particularly the maternal uncles of Rasulullah ﷺ interceded on his behalf, Aisha ؓ refused to break her vow. It was some members of the Banu Zuhra family (Rasulullah ﷺ's mother's family) including Miswar bin Makhrama and Abdur Rahman bin Aswad bin Abd Yaghuth ؓ who one day said to Abdullah bin Zubair, "After we have secured permission to enter, you should rush behind the veil and plead with Aisha ؓ." Abdullah bin Zubair did as they suggested and he then sent to Aisha ؓ 10 slaves to set free as expiation for breaking the oath. She however continued freeing slave after slave until she had eventually set free 40 slaves. She then said, "I wish that I had specified an act to carry out when I took the oath e.g. saying that I would set 2 slaves free if I spoke to him so that I would now be finished and at ease, knowing for certain that I had fulfilled my duty." *(Bukhari)*

Reconciling between people: Rasulullah ﷺ Resolves the Dispute Between the People of Quba

Sahl bin Sa'd ؓ narrates that the people of Quba once fell into such a dispute that they started throwing stones at each other. When he heard about the matter, Rasulullah ﷺ said to the Sahabah, "Come. Let us go and settle the affair." *(Bukhari)*. Another narration states that when some people from the Banu Amr bin Auf tribe fell into a dispute, Rasulullah ﷺ took some of the Sahabah along with him and went to settle the dispute. The Hadith continues further. *(Bukhari)*

Rasulullah ﷺ Settles a Dispute When he Went to Visit Abdullah bin Ubay

Anas ؓ reports that a request was once made to Rasulullah ﷺ to visit Abdullah bin Ubay, the leader of the hypocrites. Rasulullah ﷺ therefore proceeded on his donkey while the Muslims walked along with him on the rocky ground. When Rasulullah ﷺ reached him, Abdullah bin Ubay exclaimed, "Get away from me because the stench of your donkey disgusts me!" One of the Ansar responded to this by remarking, "By Allah! The donkey of Rasulullah ﷺ smells better than you!" When a person from Abdullah bin Ubay's tribe became angry on his behalf, the 2 men started insulting each other. Eventually the men from both sides grew angry and they started fighting with sticks, fists and shoes. Anas ؓ says that they had been informed that it was with reference to this incident that Allah revealed the verse:

وَإِنْ طَائِفَتَانِ مِنَ الْمُؤْمِنِينَ اقْتَتَلُوا فَأَصْلِحُوا بَيْنَهُمَا فَإِنْ بَغَتْ إِحْدَاهُمَا عَلَى الْأُخْرَى فَقَاتِلُوا الَّتِي تَبْغِي حَتَّى تَفِيءَ إِلَى أَمْرِ اللهِ

If two parties or groups among the believers fall to fighting, then make peace between them both... (Al-Hujurat:9) *(Bukhari)*

The Hadith of Usama ﷺ from *Bukhari* has already been quoted in the chapter concerning visiting the ill. The narration mentions that the Muslims, disbeliever and Jews then started hurling abuse at each other until matters reached such a head that they almost came to blows. All the time, Rasulullah ﷺ continued calming them until they all fell still.

Rasulullah ﷺ Reconciles Between the Aws and the Khazraj Tribes

Anas ﷺ says that the Aws and the Khazraj tribes were 2 tribes of the Ansar between whom was enmity during the period of ignorance. When Rasulullah ﷺ came to them, all enmity disappeared and Allah created great love between their hearts. However, it once occurred that when they were once sitting in a gathering, someone from the Aws recited a couplet that ridiculed the Khazraj. In response, someone from Khazraj then recited a couplet that ridiculed the Aws. In this manner, the 2 continued reciting poetry mocking the other until some of them sprang up to attack others. They then grabbed hold of their weapons and were prepared to fight each other. When the news reached Rasulullah ﷺ, he had already received revelation to the effect. He hurried to them so quickly that his lower garment lifted and even his shins became exposed. When he saw them, Rasulullah ﷺ called them:

يَا أَيُّهَا الَّذِينَ آمَنُوا اتَّقُوا اللَّهَ حَقَّ تُقَاتِهِ وَلَا تَمُوتُنَّ إِلَّا وَأَنْتُمْ مُسْلِمُونَ (102) وَاعْتَصِمُوا بِحَبْلِ اللَّهِ جَمِيعًا وَلَا تَفَرَّقُوا وَاذْكُرُوا نِعْمَةَ اللَّهِ عَلَيْكُمْ إِذْ كُنْتُمْ أَعْدَاءً فَأَلَّفَ بَيْنَ قُلُوبِكُمْ فَأَصْبَحْتُمْ بِنِعْمَتِهِ إِخْوَانًا وَكُنْتُمْ عَلَى شَفَا حُفْرَةٍ مِنَ النَّارِ فَأَنْقَذَكُمْ مِنْهَا كَذَلِكَ يُبَيِّنُ اللَّهُ لَكُمْ آيَاتِهِ لَعَلَّكُمْ تَهْتَدُونَ (103)

O you who believe! Fear Allah (by doing all that He has ordered and by abstaining from all that He has forbidden) as He should be feared. (Obey Him, be thankful to Him, and remember Him always), and die not except in a state of Islam (as Muslims) with complete submission to Allah. And hold fast, all of you together, to the Rope of Allah (i.e. this Qur'an), and be not divided among yourselves, and remember Allah's Favor on you, for you were enemies one to another but He joined your hearts together, so that, by His Grace, you became brethren (in Islamic Faith), and you were on the brink of a pit of Fire, and He saved you from it. Thus Allah makes His Ayat (proofs, evidences, verses, lessons, signs, revelations, etc.,) clear to you, that you may be guided. (Al-Imran:102-103). The Ansar then immediately threw down their weapons and embraced each other. *(Tabrani, Haythami)*

The Parting Words of Abdullah bin Amr ﷺ About a Man to Whom He Had Promised to Marry His Daughter

Harun bin Rabab reports that Abdullah bin Amr ﷺ was on his deathbed, he instructed the people to look for a certain man saying, "I had mentioned to him something of a promise concerning my daughter that I would marry her to him. As I would not like to meet Allah with one of the 3 traits of a hypocrite- breaking of promises, I make all of you witness that I am marrying her off to him." *(Ibn Asakir in Kanzul Ummal).*

Abstaining from Harboring Ill Thoughts against a Fellow Muslim: The Incident of 2 Sahabah who took their case Before Rasulullah ﷺ

Anas ﷺ narrates that a man once passed by a gathering during the time of Rasulullah ﷺ and greeted them. After they had greeted him and he had passed by, one of them remarked, "I do not like him at all!" The others rebuked him saying, "Be quiet! By Allah! We are certainly going to inform him about this!" They then sent someone to inform the person about what had been said. After the messenger had informed the Sahabi, the Sahabi went to Rasulullah ﷺ and informed him about what had happened and about what the person had said. "O Rasulullah ﷺ!" the Sahabi said, "Send for him and ask him why he dislikes me so." Rasulullah ﷺ sent for the man and asked, "Why do you dislike him?" The other responded by saying, "O Rasulullah ﷺ! I am his neighbor and know him well. I have never seen him perform any Nafl salah besides the salah that the pious and the sinful ones all perform, the Fardh salah." The Sahabi defended himself by saying, "O Rasulullah ﷺ! Ask him whether I have ever made an improper wudhu for my salah or every delayed it until after its time had expired?" The other replied in the negative but then continued, "O Rasulullah ﷺ! I am his neighbor and know him well. I have never seen him feed a single poor person besides giving the zakah that the pious and the sinful ones all give." The other said in defense, "O Rasulullah ﷺ! Ask him whether he has ever seen me refuse anyone asking for charity?" Again the man was forced to say no, but spoke further saying, "O Rasulullah ﷺ! I am his neighbor and know him well. I have never seen him observe any Nafl fasts besides the fasts of the month in which the pious and the sinful ones all observe, the Fardh fasts during Ramadhan." the Sahabi said, "O Rasulullah ﷺ! Ask him whether he has ever seen me miss a single fast when I was not ill or not in a journey?" When the neighbor was forced to say no, Rasulullah ﷺ said to him, "It seems to me like he is a better man than you." *(Ibn Asakir in Kanzul Ummal).*

Incident between Rasulullah ﷺ and a man from Banu Laith Tribe

Ubadah bin Samit ﷺ narrates that a man from the Banu Laith tribe thrice asked Rasulullah ﷺ permission to recite a poem. Upon the 4th request Rasulullah ﷺ granted permission and he recited a poem in praise of Rasulullah ﷺ. Rasulullah ﷺ then said appreciatively, "If any poet had spoken well, it must surely be you." *(Tabrani, Haythami)*

Usama bin Zaid ﷺ Praises Khallad bin Sa'ib ﷺ

Khallad bin Sa'ib ﷺ narrates that he once visited Usama bin Zaid ﷺ, who praised him on his face. Usama ﷺ then said, "The only thing that made me praise you on your face is the fact that Rasulullah ﷺ said, 'When a Mu'min is praised on his face, the Iman in his heart grows far from becoming proud, he develops conviction in his good deeds when people show their appreciation for it.'" *(Tabrani, Haythami)*

What Rasulullah ﷺ said to a Person who overstated his Words of Praise

The father of Mutarrif says, "I accompanied the delegation from the Banu Amir tribe that went to Rasulullah ﷺ. 'You are our leader,' we said. 'Allah is the leader,' Rasulullah ﷺ responded. We then said, 'You are the highest of us in status and the most generous.' Rasulullah ﷺ said, 'These common words you may say, but rather state even less than this as Saitan should never gain control over you and urge you to transgress the limits of praise.'" *(Abu Dawud)*. Rasulullah ﷺ also added, "I do not want you to place me on a pedestal higher than that upon which Allah has placed me. I am Muhammad the son of Allah's servant and am myself the servant of Allah and His Rasul." *(Razin in Jam'ul Fawa'id)*. Anas ﷺ reports that someone addressed Rasulullah ﷺ saying, "O the best of us and the son of the best of us! Our leader and the son of our leader!" Rasulullah ﷺ corrected him saying, "Say only that which I tell you to say and never allow Saitan to mislead you into transgressing the limits of praise. Place me only upon that pedestal upon which Allah has placed me and no higher. I am the servant of Allah and His Rasul." *(Ibn Najjar in Kanzul Ummal, Ahmad in Al Bidayah wan Nihayah)*

What Rasulullah ﷺ Said to a Man Who Praised Another in His Face and Rasulullah ﷺ's Guidance in this Regard

Abu Bakra ؓ reports that when a man once praised another in front of Rasulullah ﷺ, Rasulullah ﷺ remarked, "Shame on you! You have cut off your companion's neck! You have cut off your companion's neck!" Rasulullah repeated this thrice and then added, "When any of you wishes to praise his brother for something he has certain knowledge of, he should say, 'I think that he is like this' because only Allah knows him for sure and a person cannot declare the righteousness of another before Allah. If he therefore knows a person to be such, he should merely state, 'I believe that he is like that.'" *(Bukhari, Muslim, Abu Dawud in Jam'ul Fawa'id).* Abu Musa Ash'ari ؓ narrates that Rasulullah ﷺ heard a person overstating his praise for another. Rasulullah ﷺ remarked, "You have broken the man's back (by exaggerating your praise for him)." *(Bukhari, Ibn Jareer in Kanzul Ummal).*

The Incident of Mihjin Aslami ؓ

Raja says, "I once accompanied Mihjin ؓ to the Masjid of Basra. There we found Buraida Aslami ؓ sitting at one of the doors while a man called Sabka was inside the Masjid performing a lengthy salah. Buraida ؓ was a man who liked making jokes and as Mihjin ؓ approached wearing his shawl, Buraida ؓ quipped, 'a Mihjin! Can you perform salah as Sabka does?' Mihjin ؓ did not reply and went back. He then said, 'Rasulullah ﷺ once led me by my hand and when we had climbed Mount Uhud, he looked over Madinah and said, 'Woe be the time when the inhabitants of the city will have to forsake it at a time when it will be most populous! When Dajjal will approach Madinah, he will find an angel at everyone of its gates and will be unable to enter it.' Rasulullah ﷺ then climbed down and when we reached the Masjid, Rasulullah ﷺ saw a man performing salah, absorbed in Ruku and Sejdah. 'Who is that?' Rasulullah ﷺ asked me. I then started heaping praises upon the man as I informed Rasulullah ﷺ who he was. Rasulullah ﷺ then bade me, 'Stop! Let him not hear you for you will then be destroying him.' Rasulullah ﷺ then continued walking and when he reached his room, he dusted off his hands and thrice repeated, 'The best deed of Islam is that which is easiest. The best deed of Islam is that which is easiest.'" *(Bukhari in Adab)*

Another narration from Raja also states that when he started heaping praises upon the man as he informed Rasulullah ﷺ who the man was, Rasulullah ﷺ bade him, "Stop! Let him not hear you for you will then be destroying him.' Rasulullah ﷺ then continued walking and when he reached his room, he let go of Mihjin ؓ's hand and said, "The best deed of Islam is that which is easiest. The best deed of Islam is that which is easiest. The best deed of Islam is that which is easiest." *(Ahmad).* After informing Rasulullah ﷺ who the man was, Mihjin ؓ continued to add that of all the people of Madinah, the man was the best or was the one who performed the most salah. To this Rasulullah ﷺ twice or thrice remarked, "Let him not hear you for you will then be destroying him." Rasulullah ﷺ added, "You are a nation for whom Allah wants ease." *(Ahmad in Kanzul Ummal)*

Praising a Muslim Angers Omar ؓ

Ibrahim Taymi reports from his father that they were once sitting with Omar ؓ when a man came to him and greeted with Salam. Another person then started heaping praises on the man in front of him. To this, Omar ؓ said, "You have slaughtered him. May Allah slaughter you! How can you praise a man Islam on his face?!" *(Ibn Abi Shayba, Bukhari in Adab, Kanzul Ummal).* Hasan narrates that when someone once praised Omar ؓ, Omar ؓ exclaimed, "You are destroying me as well as yourself." *(Ibn*

Abi Dunya in Samt, Kanzul Ummal)

The Incident of Omar ؓ and Jarud ؓ

Hasan reports that Omar ؓ was once sitting in the company of others with a whip in his hand when Jarud ؓ arrived. Someone commented, "Here is the leader of the Rabe'ah tribe!" This remark was heard by Omar ؓ, the people around him and by Jarud ؓ himself. When Jarud ؓ came close to Omar ؓ, the Khalifa struck him with the whip. "What has happened between us, O Amirul Mu'minin?" asked a startled Jarud. "What has happened between us?!" Omar ؓ echoed, "You had definitely heard the comment." Jarud ؓ replied, "I heard it, so what about it?" Omar ؓ explained, "I feared that some of it may penetrate your heart creating some pride in you and I wished to remove the effect from you." *(Ibn Abi Dunya in Samt, Kanzul Ummal)*

Miqdad ؓ Throws Sand in the Faces of People Who Praised Him

Hammam bin Harith reports that when someone started praising Uthman ؓ, Miqdad ؓ who was a large man, went towards the man and kneeling down, he started throwing pebbles in the man's face. "What is the matter?" Uthman ؓ asked. Miqdad ؓ replied, "Rasulullah ﷺ said, 'When you see the people who heap praises for ulterior motives, then throw sand in their faces." *(Muslim, Abu Dawud).* When someone started heaping praises on one of the Khalifas, Miqdad ؓ started throwing sand on the man's face saying, "Rasulullah ﷺ has commanded us to throw sand into the faces of those who heap praises for ulterior motives." *(Muslim, Tirmidhi, Bukhari in Adab)*

The Statement and Practice of Abdullah bin Omar ؓ in this Regard

Ata bin Abi Rabah narrates that when someone started heaping praises on another person in the presence of Abdullah bin Omar ؓ, Abdullah bin Omar ؓ started throwing sand at the man's mouth saying, "Rasulullah ﷺ said, 'When you see the people who heap praises (for ulterior motives), then throw sand in their faces." *(Bukhari in Adab).* Ata bin Abi Rabah narrates that when someone started heaping praises on Abdullah bin Omar ؓ, Abdullah bin Omar ؓ started throwing sand at the man's mouth saying, "I heard Rasulullah ﷺ say, 'When you see the people who heap praises, then thro sand in their faces." *(Ahmad, Tabrani, Haythami).* Nafi and other reports that a. person once addressed Abdullah bin Omar ؓ saying, "O the best of people!" or he said, "O the son of the best of people!" Abdullah bin Omar ؓ responded by saying, "I am neither the best of people nor the son of the best of people. I am merely a servant from amongst the servants of Allah who aspires for His mercy and fears (His punishment). By Allah! You people keep at a man (keep heaping praise on him) until you eventually destroy him by creating pride and vanity in him." *(Abu Nu'aym in Hilya).* Tariq bin Shihab reports that Abdullah bin Omar ؓ said, "A man may leave home with Islam intact and then return without any trace of it. This because he would approach a man who can neither harm nor benefit himself nor another and then swear in the name of Allah that he is so-and-so, heap praises on him. He then returns without having his need fulfilled because the man gave him nothing or nothing that would last but after incurring the wrath of Allah." *(Tabrani, Haythami)*

Fostering and Severing Family Ties: The Incident of Rasulullah ﷺ and Abu Talib

Abdullah bin Abbas ؓ reports that (before Rasulullah ﷺ proclaimed his prophethood) the Quraish suffered severe drought. Conditions were so hard that they were forced to eat even dried bones. During those times, there were none in better stead than Rasulullah ﷺ and his uncle Abbas bin Abdil Muttalib ؓ. Rasulullah ﷺ therefore said to Abbas ؓ, "Dear uncle! Your brother Abu Talib has many children and because the Quraish has been afflicted with the condition as you know, let us go to him and take some of his children in our care." The 2 then went to Abu Talib and said, "O Abu Talib! Your people have been afflicted with the drought and we know that you are one of them suffering as much as the rest. We have come to take some of your children in our care." Abu Talib replied, "Do as you please but please leave Aqil for me. Rasulullah ﷺ then took Ali ؓ in his care while Abbas ؓ took Ja'far ؓ in his care. The 2 then stayed with their custodians until they became independent. In fact, Sulaiman bin Dawud states that Ja'far ؓ remained with Abbas ؓ until the time he migrated to Abyssinia. *(Bazzar, Haythami)*

The Incident of Rasulullah ﷺ with Juwiriyya ؓ and Fatima ؓ

Jabir ؓ reports that when Juwairiyya ؓ informed Rasulullah ﷺ that she intended setting free one of her slaves, Rasulullah ﷺ advised her saying, "Rather give the slave to your uncle who lives amongst the Bedouins so that the slave may graze the animals for him. This will earn you a greater reward." *(Bazzar, Haythami)*. Abu Sa'eed Khudri ؓ narrates that when Allah revealed the verse: وَآتِ ذَا الْقُرْبَىٰ حَقَّهُ

And give to the kinsman his due... (Al-Isra:26), Rasulullah ﷺ said to Fatima ؓ, "O Fatima! You may have my land in Fidak." *(Hakim in Tarikh, Kanzul Ummal)*

Rasulullah ﷺ's Advice to the Person Who Complained About the Ill Treatment He Received From his Relatives

Abu Hurairah ؓ reports that a man once came to Rasulullah ﷺ complaining, "I have relatives who sever ties with me when I foster them, who behave ill towards me when I am good to them and who behave foolishly with me when I behave tolerantly with them." Rasulullah ﷺ's advice to him was, "If you are as you claim, then it is as if you are filing their mouth with burning ashes, they are harming themselves by behaving as they do. As long as you behave as you are doing, there shall remain with you an assistant (angel) from Allah." *(Muslim, Bukhari in Adab)*. Abdullah bin Amr ؓ narrates that a man came to Rasulullah ﷺ saying, "O Rasulullah ﷺ! I have relatives who severe ties with me when I attempt to foster them, who oppress me when I forgive them and who are bad to me when I am good to them. Should I do to them as they do to me?" Rasulullah ﷺ's response was, "In that case, you would all be partners in evil. You should rather adopt the better stance and continue bonding ties because as long as you behave as you are doing, there shall remain with you an assistant (angel) from Allah." *(Ahmad, Haythami)*

Incident of Abu Hurairah ؓ with a Man Who Severed Family Ties

Abu Ayub Sulaiman who was the freed slave of Uthman bin Affan ؓ says, "Abu Hurairah ؓ once came to us on the night between Thursday and Friday and said, '1 am stating with great emphasis that anyone who severs family ties should leave this gathering." No one left until he had repeated the announcement 3 times. A youngster then stood up and went to an aunt of his with whom he had severed ties for two years. Surprised, she asked, "Dear nephew! What brings you here?" When he informed her about what Abu Hurairah ؓ had mentioned, she said, "Go back to him and ask him why he had stated what he did." When the young man made the enquiry, Abu Hurairah ؓ said, "I have heard Rasulullah ﷺ say, 'The deeds of mankind are presented to Allah on every night between Thursday and Friday and while the deeds of all are accepted, the deeds of the one who severs family ties are not accepted." *(Bukhari in Adab)*

Abdullah bin Mas'ood ؓ Requests People who Severe Family Ties to Leave When he Intended Making Du'a

A'mash narrates that Abdullah bin Mas'ood ؓ was sitting in a gathering after the Fajr salah when he said, "In the name of Allah do I ask those who severe family ties to leave us because we intend making Du'a to our Rabb and the doors of the heavens are locked to those who sever family ties." *(Tabrani. Haythami)*.

This chapter highlights the character and traits of Rasulullah ﷺ and the Sahabah and how they interacted with each other.

The Statements of Aisha ؓ About the Character of Rasulullah ﷺ

Sa'd bin Hisham reports that he once asked Ummul Mu'mineen Aisha ؓ, "Tell me about the character of Rasulullah ﷺ." "Have you not read the Qur'an?" she asked. "Of course, I have," he replied. Aisha ؓ then said, "Rasulullah ﷺ's character was the Qur'an, every noble character trait mentioned in the Qur'an was to be found in the life of Rasulullah ﷺ." (Muslim, Ahmad in Al Bidayah wan Nihayah). Qatadah ؓ said, "Indeed the Qur'an brought every noble trait of good character." (Ibn Sa'd, Abu Nu'aym in Dala'il). Abu Darda ؓ reports that when he asked Aisha ؓ about the character of Rasulullah ﷺ, she relied, "His character was the Qur'an. He was pleased with what Allah is pleased and disliked what Allah dislikes." (Ya'qub bin Sufian) Zaid bin Babnus states that Aisha ؓ gave a similar reply when they asked her about the character of Rasulullah ﷺ. This narration however states that Aisha ؓ asked, "Have you read Surah Mu'minun?" She told them to read from the beginning of the Surah Al-Muminun and 10 verses thereafter. Thereafter she said, "Such was the character of Rasulullah ﷺ." (Bayhaqi, Nasa'ee in Al Bidayah wan Nihayah). Urwa ؓ reports that Aisha ؓ stated, "There was none with better character than Rasulullah ﷺ. When any of his companions or family called for him, he always responded by saying, 'At your service.' For this reason Allah revealed the verse: (4) وَإِنَّكَ لَعَلَى خُلُقٍ عَظِيمٍ

And verily, you (O Muhammad ﷺ) are on an exalted standard of character. (Qalam:4) (Abu Nu'aym in Dala'il).

Qais bin Wahab reports from a man from the Banu Surat tribe that he asked Aisha ؓ, "Tell me about the character of Rasulullah ﷺ." Aisha ؓ replied, "Have you not read the Qur'an where Allah says:…..?" She continued, "Rasulullah ﷺ was with his companions when I and Hafsa ؓ prepared some food for him. She beat me to sending the food, I asked my slave girl to overturn the platter. Hafsa ؓ was serving the food to Rasulullah ﷺ, the slave girl overturned it and the food was scattered. Rasulullah ﷺ gathered the food that had fallen on the ground and the Sahabah ate it. When I sent my platter, Rasulullah ﷺ handed it over to Hafsa ؓ saying, 'Take this platter in place of yours and eat whatever is in it' I did not notice even a hint of displeasure on the face of Rasulullah ﷺ." (Ibn Abi Shayba in Kanzul Ummal)

The Statement of Zaid bin Thabit ؓ in this Regard

Kharija bin Zaid narrates that a group of people once came to his father Zaid bin Thabit ؓ with the request, "Tell us something about the character of Rasulullah ﷺ." Zaid bin Thabit ؓ said, "I was Rasulullah ﷺ's neighbor. When revelation would come to him, he would send for me and I would come to him to write it down. Whenever we spoke of worldly matters, he also spoke about it, whenever we spoke of the Hereafter, he also spoke about it and whenever we spoke of food, he also spoke of the same (he was never aloof from us). I am narrating all this to you on behalf of Rasulullah ﷺ." (Abu Nu'aym in Dala'il, Tirmidhi, Bayhaqi in Al Bidayah wan Nihayah, Tabrani in Majma'uz Zawa'id, Ibn Abu Dawud in Masahif, Abu Ya'la, Ruyani, Ibn Asakir in Muntakhab Kanzul Ummal, Ibn Sa'd)

A Narration of Safiya ؓ

Safiya bint Huyay ؓ, Rasulullah ﷺ's wife says, "I have never seen anyone with better character than Rasulullah ﷺ. I was riding on the back of his camel with him as we returned from Khaibar. It was at night and as I began to fall asleep, my head hit the back of the carriage. Rasulullah ﷺ touched me gently as he said, 'Take it easy, dear lady. Take it easy, O daughter of Huyay, this is not the place to sleep.' When we reached a place called Shaba, he said to me, 'Do excuse me for what I had to do with your people, the Jews of Khaibar.' He then explained me what they had said and done to him because of which he was forced to act against them." (Tabrani, Abu Ya'la, Haythami)

Narrations of Anas ؓ in this Regard

Anas ؓ says, "Rasulullah ﷺ was one of the most compassionate people. I swear by Allah that he never refused even a slave or a child who brought water to him on a freezing morning to wash with it and then give it back to them for blessings. Despite the intense cold, he would wash his face and arms with the water. Whenever anyone came to him with a request, he would listen attentively to the person and not move away until the person moved away. Whenever anyone took him by the hand, he would give his hand and not pull it away until the person himself let go." (Abu Nu'aym in Dala'il). Anas bin Malik ؓ says, "After Rasulullah ﷺ performed the Fajr salah, the slaves of Madinah would come to him with their utensils of water. Rasulullah ﷺ would then dip his hands into every utensil brought so that the people may have the blessings of his blessed limbs. At times, people would come to him on an extremely cold morning! but he would still dip his hands into the water." (Muslim). Anas ؓ also reports, "Whenever Rasulullah ﷺ shook hands with anyone or whenever anyone shook his hands, he would never pull his hand away until the person pulled his own hand away first. He would also not turn away from a person he was facing when speaking until the person himself turned away first. He was also never to be seen stretching out his feet towards a person sitting before him." (Yaq'oob bin Sufiyan, Tirmidhi, Ibn Majah, Al Bidayah wan Nihayah, Ibn Sa'd). Anas ؓ narrates, "I have never seen Rasulullah ﷺ move his head away from anyone whispering into his ear until the person himself moved away. I have also never seen Rasulullah ﷺ pull his hand away from anyone holding his hand until the person himself let go of Rasulullah ﷺ's hand." (Abu Dawud in Al Bidayah wan Nihayah)

Narrations of Abu Hurairah ؓ and Anas ؓ Concerning Rasulullah ﷺ's Shaking Hands with the Sahabah

Abu Hurairah ؓ says, "Whenever anyone took Rasulullah ﷺ's hand to shake it, he never pulled it away until the person himself let go. Rasulullah ﷺ's feet were also never to be seen stretched out towards a person sitting in front of him. When someone shook his hand, Rasulullah ﷺ always turned his full attention towards the person and would not turn away until the person had finished what he had to say." (Bazzar, Tabrani, Haythami). Anas ؓ says, "Even if it were a child from amongst the common children of Madinah who took Rasulullah ﷺ by the hand, he would not pull his hand away from hers so that she could take him wherever she wanted to." (Ahmad, Ibn Majah) Another narration states that even the slave girls of Madinah could take Rasulullah ﷺ by the hand and take him wherever she needed him to go." (Ahmad, Bukhari in Adab, Al Bidayah wan Nihayah). Anas ؓ reports that a lady who was mentally disturbed once came to Rasulullah ﷺ and said, "O Rasulullah ﷺ! I need you to do something for me." Addressing her by her title, Rasulullah ﷺ said, "Choose any of the streets to explain it to me so that I may address you problem, Rasulullah ﷺ chose to speak to her privately in a place where people could see them so that no suspicions would be aroused. Rasulullah ﷺ stepped aside with her in one of the streets where she explained her problem." *(Muslim, Abu Nu'aym in Dala'il)*. Maslamah ؓ says, "Once I returned from a journey, Rasulullah ﷺ took me by the hand and did not leave it until I let go of his hand." *(Tabrani, Haythami)*.

Rasulullah ﷺ Always Chose the Easier of 2 Options and only Took Revenge for the sake of Allah

Aisha ؓ says, "Whenever Rasulullah ﷺ was faced with 2 options, he always chose the easier of the 2 so that it would be easy for the Ummah to emulate on condition that it did not involve sin. If it involved sin, he was then the most abstinent of people. He also never took revenge for personal reasons. He had people punished only when anything forbidden by Allah was violated, in which case he had the punishment carried out for the sake of Allah." *(Malik, Abu Dawud, Nasa'ee, Ahmad in Kanzul Ummal, Abu Nu'aym in Dala'il)*. Aisha ؓ says, "Rasulullah ﷺ never hit any servant or woman. In fact, he never hit anything unless he was fighting in Jihad in the Path of Allah. Whenever faced with 2 options, he always chose the easier of the 2 on condition that it did not involve sin. If it involved sin, he was then the most abstinent of people. He also never took revenge for anything done against him. He had people punished only when anything forbidden by Allah was violated, in which case he had the punishment carried out for the sake of Allah." *(Ahmad in Al Bidayah wan Nihayah, Muslim, Abu Nu'aym in Dala'il, Abdur Razzaq, Abd bin Humaid, Hakim in Kanzul Ummal)*. Aisha ؓ says, "I never saw Rasulullah ﷺ take revenge for any injustice done to himself. He had people punished only when anything forbidden by Allah was violated, then he was amongst the most enraged of people. Whenever faced with 2 options, he always chose the easier of the 2 on condition that it did not involve sin." *(Tirmidhi in Shama'il, Abu Ya'la, Hakim in Kanzul Ummal)*

Rasulullah ﷺ was Never Rude, Noisy, Vulgar or One Who Cursed

Abu Abdullah Jadali says that Aisha ؓ was questioned about the character of Rasulullah ﷺ, he heard her reply, "Rasulullah ﷺ was never rude and offensive and never even pretended to be so. He was never noisy in the marketplaces and never fought evil with evil. He always forgave and overlooked." *(Abu Dawud, Tayalisi, Tirmidhi in Al Bidayah wan Nihayah, Ibn Sa'd, Ahmad, Hakim in Kanzul Ummal)*. Salih narrates about Rasulullah ﷺ, Abu Hurairah ؓ said, "When he turned towards someone, he turned completely and when he turned away from someone, he turned completely. May my parents be sacrificed for him! Rasulullah ﷺ was never rude and offensive and never even pretended to be so. He was never noisy in the marketplace." Abu Hurairah ؓ added, "Never have I seen any like him before and never after." *(Ya'qoob bin Sufiyan)*. Anas ؓ says, "Rasulullah ﷺ was never offensive, never cursed people and never rude. The most he would tell someone when scolding him was, "What is the matter with him? May sand fall on his forehead!" *(Ahmad, Bukhari)*. Abdullah bin Amr ؓ reports, "Rasulullah ﷺ was never rude and offensive and never even pretended to be so. He always said, 'The best of you is the one with the best character." *(Bukhari, Muslim in Al Bidayah wan Nihayah)*

Rasulullah ﷺ's Sterling Character with His Servant Anas ؓ

Anas ؓ narrates, "When Rasulullah ﷺ arrived in Madinah, Abu Talha ؓ led me by my hand to Rasulullah ﷺ and said, 'O Rasulullah ﷺ! Anas ؓ is an intelligent lad. Do let him serve you.' I therefore remained Rasulullah ﷺ's servant at home and on journey. I swear by Allah that for anything I did, he never said, 'Why did you do that in that way?' and when I failed to do something, he never once asked, 'Why did you not do that like this?'" *(Muslim)*. Anas ؓ reports, "Rasulullah ﷺ had the very best of character. He sent me to do something one day to which I exclaimed, 'By Allah! I shall never do it!' In my heart, I had resolved that I would definitely carry out his instructions. After leaving, I passed by some children playing in the marketplace. As I stood there watching them, Rasulullah ﷺ suddenly grabbed hold of my neck from behind. As I looked at him, he was laughing as he said, 'Dear little Anas! Have you been to where I sent you?' 'Yes,' I replied, 'I am presently on my way there, O Rasulullah ﷺ.'" Anas ؓ reports further. He says, "By Allah! Although I was in Rasulullah ﷺ's service for 9 years, he never said to anything I did, 'Why did you do that?' and when I failed to do something, he never once asked, 'Why did you not do that?'" Another narration states that Anas ؓ said, "I served Rasulullah ﷺ for 10 years. I swear by Allah that he never once told me 'Oof!', similar to "Oh no!" or any other expression of displeasure. Not once did he ever ask me, 'Why did you do that?' or 'Why did you not do that?'" *(Muslim, Bukhari)*. Anas ؓ narrates, "Although I served Rasulullah ﷺ for 10 years, he never once scolded me for something that I had delayed in carrying out or that I had bungled. If any member of his household scolded me, he would tell them, 'Leave him alone. When something had been destined to happen, it will happen." *(Ahmad in Al Bidayah wan Nihayah, Ibn Sa'd)*. Anas ؓ says, "When Rasulullah ﷺ arrived in Madinah, I was a boy of 8. My mother took me to Rasulullah ﷺ saying, 'O Rasulullah ﷺ! Except for me, all the men and women of the Ansar have given you a gift. I have nothing to offer you as a gift save for this son of mine. Please accept him from me to serve you as you see fit.' Please accept him from me to serve you as you see fit.' I served Rasulullah ﷺ for 10 years, during which time he never once hit me, never insulted me and never even frowned at me." *(Ibn Asakir in Kanzul Ummal)*

The Statement of Abdullah bin Omar ؓ Regarding Uthman ؓ and Abu Ubaidah ؓ

Abdullah bin Omar ؓ says, "There are 3 men from the Quraish who are the most handsome, have the best character and have the most firm sense of modesty. When they speak to you, then can never be lying and when you speak to them, they will never regard you as a liar. They are Abu Bakr Siddiq ؓ, Uthman bi Affan ؓ and Abu Ubaidah bin Jarrah ؓ." *(Abu Nu'aym in Hilya)*. Abdullah bin Omar ؓ said, "There are 3 men from the Quraish who are the most handsome, have the best character and have the strongest sense of modesty. They are Abu Bakr ؓ, Uthman ؓ and Abu Ubaidah ؓ." *(Tabrani in Isabah)*

Rasulullah ﷺ testifies to the Excellent Character of Abu Ubaidah ؓ

Hasan reports that Rasulullah ﷺ once said, "If I chose to do so, I could take each of my companions to task for aspects of their character except for Abu Ubaidah bin Jarrah ؓ." *(Ya'qub bin Sufian in Isabah, Hakim)*

Rasulullah ﷺ says the Character of Uthman ؓ is Closest to His

Abdur Rahman bin Uthman Quraishi ؓ that Rasulullah ﷺ visited his daughter as she was washing the head of her husband Uthman ؓ. Rasulullah ﷺ said, "Beloved daughter! Treat Uthman ؓ well because from all my companions, his character is closest to my own." *(Tabrani, Haythami)*. Abu Hurairah ؓ reports that he went to Ruqayya ؓ who was the daughter of Rasulullah ﷺ and the wife of Uthman ؓ. She had a comb in her hand and she said, "Rasulullah ﷺ just left after I had combed his hair. 'How do you find Uthman ﷺ?' he asked. I replied that he was an excellent person, Rasulullah ﷺ said, 'Look after him well because from all my companions, his character is closest to my own." (Tabrani, Haythami, Hakim, Ibn Asakir in Muntakhab Hanzul Ummal)

Rasulullah ﷺ's Comments About the Character of Ja'far ﷺ, Zaid ﷺ, Ali ﷺ and Abdullah bin Ja'far ﷺ

Abdullah ﷺ who was the son of Rasulullah ﷺ's freed slave Aslam ﷺ reports that Rasulullah ﷺ once said to Ja'far ﷺ, "You resemble me both in looks and in personality."(Ahmad, Haythami). Ali ﷺ narrates, "Ja'far ﷺ, Zaid ﷺ and I once came to Rasulullah ﷺ. Rasulullah ﷺ said to Zaid ﷺ, 'You are our brother and friend.' Zaid skipped with joy. Rasulullah ﷺ then said to Ja'far ﷺ, 'You resemble me both in looks and in personality.' Ja'far ﷺ then skipped about even more than Zaid ﷺ. Thereafter, Rasulullah ﷺ said to me. 'You are from me and I from you.' I therefore skipped about more than Zaid ﷺ and Ja'far ﷺ." (Ibn Abi Shayba, Abu Ya'la, Bayhaqi in Muntakhab Kanzul Ummal). Usamah bin Zaid ﷺ reports that Rasulullah ﷺ said to Ja'far ﷺ, "Your personality is like mine and your physical appearance also resembles my own. You are from me. And you, O Ali. You are also from me and the father of my grandsons." (Tabrani, Haythami). Abdullah ﷺ the son of Ja'far ﷺ said, "I heard from Rasulullah ﷺ such words that I would not trade even for red camels. I heard Rasulullah ﷺ say, 'Ja'far most resembles my looks and my personality. As for you, O Abdullah! From all of Allah's creation, you most resemble your father, Ja'far ﷺ" (Uqayli, Ibn asakir in Muntakhab Kanzul Ummal)

The Excellent Character of Omar ﷺ

Bahriyya reports, "When my uncle Khidash ﷺ saw Rasulullah ﷺ eating from a particular plate, he asked Rasulullah ﷺ to give it to him. The plate then remained with us afterwards. Whenever Omar ﷺ used to ask for it to be taken out, we would fill it with Zamzam water and give it to him. He would then drink from it and pour it over his head and face. However, it once occurred that a thief did us a grave injustice when he stole the plate along with other possessions of ours. Omar ﷺ then came to us one day after the theft and asked us to take the plate out. 'O Amirul Mu'minin!' we submitted, 'It was stolen along with some other goods of ours.' Omar ﷺ exclaimed, 'A pretty clever thief to steal Rasulullah ﷺ's plate!' By Allah! Omar ﷺ neither swore the thief nor cursed him." (Ibn Sa'd, Bushran in Amali, Muntakhan Kanzul Ummal). Abdullah bin Abbas ﷺ narrates that when Uyaynah bin Hisn bin Hudhaifa bin Badr ﷺ arrived in Madinah, he stayed with his nephew Hurr bin Qais ﷺ who happened to be amongst those that Omar ﷺ kept close to him. It was only the learned ones whom Omar ﷺ kept in his company and with whom he consulted, regardless of whether they were young or old. Uyayna ﷺ said to his nephew, "Dear nephew! Since you have some status in the eyes of the Ameer, please secure permission for me to see him." When Omar ﷺ granted permission, Uyayna ﷺ called out, "Hey son of Khattab! By Allah! Neither do you give us much nor do you rule us with justice!" This outburst made Omar ﷺ so angry that he was close to assaulting Uyayna ﷺ. Hurr ﷺ then intervened saying, "O Amirul Mu'mineen! Allah had mentioned to His Nabi ﷺ:

خُذِ الْعَفْوَ وَأْمُرْ بِالْعُرْفِ وَأَعْرِضْ عَنِ الْجَاهِلِينَ (199)

Show forgiveness, enjoin what is good, and turn away from the foolish (i.e. don't punish them). (Al-A'raf:199)

This man is certainly from amongst the ignorant ones." The narrator says, "By Allah! When this verse was recited to him, Omar ﷺ did not do a thing. It was his noble trait to immediately forsake anything for the instruction of the Qur'an." (Bukhari, Ibn Mundhir, Ibn Abi Hatim, Ibn Mardawy, Bayhaqi, Muntakhan Kanzul Ummal). Abdullah bin Omar ﷺ says, "I have never seen a time when Omar ﷺ became angry and was not discouraged from taking action against the perpetrator by the mention of Allah, mention of fear for Allah or by someone reciting a verse of the Qur'an to him." (Ibn Sa'd). Bilal ﷺ once asked Aslam, "How do you find Omar ﷺ?" Aslam replied, "He is an excellent man. Matters are grave when he becomes angry." Bilal ﷺ advised him saying, "If you are with him at a time when he becomes angry, just recite the Qur'an until his anger vanishes." Malik Daar, one of Omar ﷺ's slaves says, "Omar ﷺ once shouted at me and was about to strike me with his whip when I said, 'I urge you to remember Allah!' He threw down his whip saying, 'You reminded me of a Great Being.'" (Muntakhab Kanzul Ummal)

The Excellent Character of Mus'ab ﷺ and Abdullah bin Mas'ood ﷺ

Aamir bin Rabe'ah ﷺ says, "Mus'ab bin Umair ﷺ was a friend of mine from the time he accepted Islam up to the time that he was martyred at Uhud. May Allah shower His mercy on him. He accompanied us on both migrations to Abyssinia and was my traveling companion. I must say that I have never seen a person with better character than him nor one who had fewer differences with people than he." (Ibn Sa'd). Habba bin Juwayn reports that they were with Ali ﷺ when they started to mention some of the statements of Abdullah bin Mas'ood ﷺ. Praising him, someone said to Ali ﷺ, "O Amirul Mu'minin! We have never seen a man with better character, nor anyone who teaches as compassionately, nor anyone who is better company nor anyone more pious than Abdullah bin Mas'ood ﷺ." Ali ﷺ asked, "I ask you to say in the name of Allah whether this is the truth in your hearts." When they expressed that it was, Ali ﷺ remarked, "O Allah! I make You the Witness that my opinion of Abdullah bin Mas'ood ﷺ is as these people have expressed or even better." In praise for Abdullah bin Mas'ood ﷺ, the person even added, "He reads the Qur'an, regarding what it makes lawful as lawful and what it forbids as forbidden. He has a deep understanding of Islam and has immense knowledge of the Sunnah." (Ibn Sa'd)

The Character of Abdullah bin Omar ﷺ and Mu'adh bin Jabal ﷺ

Salim says, "Abdullah bin Omar ﷺ never cursed a single slave save for one whom he then set free as compensation." Zuhri says that as he was about to curse a slave, Abdullah bin Omar ﷺ said, "O Allah! May Your cur..." He then did not complete the word curse and said, "That is a word that I hate to mention." (Abu Nu'aym in Hilya). The chapter entitled "The fervor that Rasulullah ﷺ and the Sahabah had to Spend in the Path of Allah," in which Jabir ﷺ says, "Mu'adh bin Jabal ﷺ was amongst the most handsome of people, amongst those with the best character and the most open-handed."

Rasulullah ﷺ's Tolerance with the Person Who Criticized the Manner in Which He Distributed the Booty of the Battle of Hunain

Abdullah bin Mas'ood ﷺ reports, "After the Battle of Hunain Rasulullah ﷺ gave extra booty to some people. He gave Aqra bin Habis ﷺ and Uyaynah bin Hisn ﷺ 100 camels each and gave a lot to certain other people as well. Someone remarked, 'Allah's pleasure was certainly not intended in this distribution.' I said, 'I am definitely going to report this to Rasulullah ﷺ!' When I reported it to Rasulullah ﷺ, he said, 'May Allah shower His mercy on Musa عليه السلام. Greater abuse than this was hurled at him but he exercised patience.'" Another narration states: "Someone said, 'By Allah! There is no justice in this distribution and Allah's pleasure was certainly not intended.' I said, 'I am definitely going to report this to Rasulullah ﷺ!' When I reported it to Rasulullah ﷺ, he said, 'Who will exercise justice when Allah and Rasul ﷺ do not? May Allah shower His mercy on Musa ﷺ. Greater abuse than this was hurled at him but he exercised patience." *(Bukhari)*

Rasulullah ﷺ is Tolerant Towards Dhu Khuwaisara

Abu Sa'eed Khudri ﷺ narrates that when they were with Rasulullah ﷺ while he was distributing the spoils of war, Dhu Khuwaysara who belonged to the Banu Tamim tribe came to him. Dhu Khuwaisara said, "O Rasulullah ﷺ! Be just!" Rasulullah ﷺ said, "Shame on you! Who will be just if I am not? May I be a failure and at a loss if I do not exercise justice! Who can possibly be just if I am not!" Omar bin Khattab ﷺ then asked, "O Rasulullah ﷺ! Permit me to behead him!" "Leave him," Rasulullah ﷺ replied, "because he has some friends before whose salah you would look down on your own salah and before whose fasts you would look down on your own fasts. Although they recite the Qur'an, it does not pass even their collarbones. They pass through Islam just as an arrow passes through prey and you find no trace of it on the arrow's head when you examine it closely. Even when you examine the thread that fixes the head to the shaft, you find no trace of the prey. Similarly, you find no trace of it even after examining the shaft and the feathers of the arrow through the arrow passed through the gut and blood of the prey. The outstanding feature of these people will be a dark-skinned man whose one arm will be hanging loose and will appear like a woman's breast or like a loose piece of flesh. They will make their appearance at a time when there will be disunity amongst the people." Abu Sa'eed Khudri ﷺ says further, "I testify that I had certainly heard these words from Rasulullah ﷺ and I also testify that I was with Ali bin Abi Talib ﷺ when he fought against these people. Upon the instruction of Ali ﷺ, a search was carried out for this man. When he was brought, I saw him to be exactly as Rasulullah ﷺ had described him." *(Bukhari, Muslim in Al Bidayah wan Nihayah)*

Rasulullah ﷺ is Tolerant with Omar ﷺ at the Death of Abdullah bin Ubay

Abdullah bin Omar ﷺ says that when Abdullah bin Ubay dies, his son approached Rasulullah ﷺ with the request. "Give me your upper garment so that I may shroud my father in it. I also want you to lead the funeral prayer for my father and to seek Allah's forgiveness for him." Rasulullah ﷺ gave him the garment and told him, "Let me know when I should lead the prayer." When the son called for Rasulullah and he was about to go, Omar ﷺ pulled Rasulullah ﷺ back saying, "Did Allah not forbid you from praying for the hypocrite?" Rasulullah ﷺ replied, "I have 2 choices because Allah says: اسْتَغْفِرْ لَهُمْ أَوْ لَا تَسْتَغْفِرْ لَهُمْ

Whether you (O Muhammad ﷺ) ask forgiveness for them (hypocrites) or ask not forgiveness for them... (At-Tauba:80)
Rasulullah ﷺ then proceeded to lead the salah, after which Allah revealed the verse: وَلَا تُصَلِّ عَلَى أَحَدٍ مِنْهُمْ مَاتَ أَبَدًا

And never (O Muhammad ﷺ) pray (funeral prayer) for any of them (hypocrites) who dies... (At-Tauba:84) (Bukhari, Muslim)

Omar ﷺ says, "When Abdullah bin Ubay died, Rasulullah ﷺ was called for the Janaza salah and he proceeded. When Rasulullah ﷺ stood before the corpse with the intention of leading the salah, I turned around and stood in front of him saying, 'O Rasulullah ﷺ! Will you perform the salah for the

enemy of Allah, Abdullah bin Ubay, the one who made all those blasphemous statements?' I then went on to recount the things he had said. Rasulullah ﷺ continued smiling and it was only when I had gone too far that he said, 'Do move away from me, O Omar as I have been given a choice and have made mine. I was told: اسْتَغْفِرْ لَهُمْ أَوْ لَا تَسْتَغْفِرْ لَهُمْ إِنْ تَسْتَغْفِرْ لَهُمْ سَبْعِينَ مَرَّةً فَلَنْ يَغْفِرَ اللَّهُ لَهُمْ بِأَنَّهُمْ كَفَرُوا بِاللَّهِ وَرَسُولِهِ وَاللَّهُ لَا يَهْدِي الْقَوْمَ الْفَاسِقِينَ (80)

Whether you (O Muhammad ﷺ) ask forgiveness for them (hypocrites) or ask not forgiveness for them ... (and even) if you ask seventy times for their forgiveness ... Allah will not forgive them, because they have disbelieved in Allah and His Messenger (Muhammad ﷺ). And Allah guides not those people who are Fasiqoon (rebellious, disobedient to Allah) (At-Tauba:80)

If I knew that he would be forgiven if I sought forgiveness for more than 70 times, I would certainly exceed 70.' Rasulullah ﷺ then proceeded to lead the salah and stood by the grave until the funeral was over. I was greatly perplexed by my boldness before Rasulullah ﷺ for Allah and His Rasul ﷺ know best what is right and what is not. By Allah! It was hardly much longer afterwards that Allah revealed the following 2 verses: وَلَا تُصَلِّ عَلَى أَحَدٍ مِنْهُمْ مَاتَ أَبَدًا وَلَا تَقُمْ عَلَى قَبْرِهِ إِنَّهُمْ كَفَرُوا بِاللَّهِ وَرَسُولِهِ وَمَاتُوا وَهُمْ فَاسِقُونَ (84) وَلَا تُعْجِبْكَ أَمْوَالُهُمْ وَأَوْلَادُهُمْ إِنَّمَا يُرِيدُ اللَّهُ أَنْ يُعَذِّبَهُمْ بِهَا فِي الدُّنْيَا وَتَزْهَقَ أَنْفُسُهُمْ وَهُمْ كَافِرُونَ (85)

And never (O Muhammad ﷺ) pray (funeral prayer) for any of them (hypocrites) who dies, nor stand at his grave. Certainly they disbelieved in Allah and His Messenger, and died while they were Fasiqoon (rebellious, - disobedient to Allah and His Messenger ﷺ). And let not their wealth or their children amaze you. Allah's Plan is to punish them with these things in this world, and that their souls shall depart (die) while they are disbelievers. (At-Tauba:84-85)

After this and up to the day he passed away, Rasulullah ﷺ never led the Janaza salah of any hypocrite and never stood by any of their graves." *(Ahmad, Tirmidhi, Bukhari)*. Jabir ﷺ reports that when Abdullah bin Ubay died, his son came to Rasulullah ﷺ saying, "O Rasulullah ﷺ! If you do not attend my father's funeral, people will always be insulting us." When Rasulullah ﷺ arrived at the funeral, he found that the body had already been placed into the grave. Rasulullah ﷺ said, "Why did you not call me before you lowered him in the grave?" The body was then taken out and Rasulullah ﷺ blew on it from head to foot and also shrouded it with his own garment primarily because Abdullah bin Ubay gave his garment to Rasulullah ﷺ's uncle Abbas ﷺ after the Battle of Badr. *(Ahmad, Nasa'ee)*. Another narration states that Rasulullah ﷺ came to the funeral Abdullah bin Ubay after he had been lowered into his grave. By the command of Rasulullah ﷺ, the body was then taken out and placing the body on his knees, Rasulullah ﷺ blew on the body and shrouded it with his own garment. *(Bukhari in Tafseer Ibn Kathir)*

Rasulullah ﷺ shows Tolerance towards the Jew who Cast a Spell Over Him

Zaid bin Arqam ﷺ says that because a Jew had cast a spell over Rasulullah ﷺ, Rasulullah ﷺ was ill for several days. Jibra'el ﷺ then came to Rasulullah ﷺ saying. "One of the Jews has cast a spell over you. He has tied few knots and placed them in a certain well. Send someone to fetch it." Rasulullah ﷺ sent Ali ﷺ who removed it from the well and brought it to Rasulullah ﷺ. When Rasulullah ﷺ untied the knots, it appeared as if he had been freed from bondage. Until his death, Rasulullah ﷺ never even mentioned this to the Jew and no anger could even be noticed on Rasulullah ﷺ's face. (Ahmad, Nasa'ee). Aisha ؓ narrates that a spell was cast on Rasulullah ﷺ because of which he would think that he had been to his wives when in reality he had not. One of the narrators called Sufian says that this is the worst effect of witchcraft. Rasulullah ﷺ one day said to Aisha ؓ, "O Aisha! Allah has given a reply to the question I posed to Him. Two angels in the form of men came to me. The one sat by my head and the other by my feet. The one by my head asked, 'What is the matter with this person?' 'He has been affected by witchcraft,' replied the other. 'Who is responsible for the witchcraft?' the first one asked further. 'Labid bin A'sam,' came the reply. Labid was a hypocrite belonging to the Banu Zuraiq tribe and was an ally to the Jews. The angel enquired further, 'Upon what did he carry it out?' 'Upon a comb and the hairs it had removed,' the other replied. 'Where is it now?' was the next question. The reply was, 'In the male leaf-like organ of a palm beneath a rock in the Dharwan well!.'" Rasulullah ﷺ then went to the well and had the thing removed. Rasulullah ﷺ also said, "This was the very well I was shown with water appearing like that used to wash a henna-filled container and the palms of which appeared to be the heads of the Sayatin." Aisha ؓ asked, "Why did you not publicize the event?" Rasulullah ﷺ replied, "Allah had cured me from it and I do not wish to start a scandal against someone." (Bukhari). Aisha ؓ also said, "It was for 6 months that Rasulullah ﷺ would think that he had been to his wives when in reality he had not. 2 angels came to him..." The rest of the Hadith is like above. (Muslim, Ahmad in Tafsir Ibn Kathir).

Rasulullah ﷺ Shows Tolerance Towards the Jewish Woman who Served Him Poisoned Meat

Anas ؓ reports that a Jewish woman once gave Rasulullah ﷺ a poisoned goat meat which he ate. When the woman was later brought before Rasulullah ﷺ when he discovered what she had done, he questioned her about it. "I wanted to kill you," she admitted. Rasulullah ﷺ responded by saying, "Allah would never give the power to kill me." "Are you not going to have her executed?" the Sahabah asked. "No," replied Rasulullah ﷺ. Anas ؓ says, "I could always notice the effect of the poison on the back tissue of Rasulullah ﷺ's tongue." (Bukhari, Muslim). Abu Hurairah ؓ narrates that a Jewish woman once presented some goat meat to Rasulullah ﷺ which was poisoned. "Hang on," Rasulullah ﷺ cautioned the Sahabah, "this is poisoned." Rasulullah ﷺ then questioned the woman, "What made you do this?" Her response was, "I wanted to know that if you really are a Rasul, Allah would inform you about it and if you are not, people could get rid of you." Rasulullah ﷺ did not take any action against her. (Bayhaqi, Abu Dawud, Ahmad, Bukhari). Abdullah bin Abbas ؓ adds that whenever Rasulullah ﷺ felt the effect of the poison, he would have his blood cupped. When he was on a journey and about to enter the state of Ihram on one occasion, he sensed its effect and had cupping done. (Ahmad)

Jabir ؓ reports that a Jewish woman from Khaibar once poisoned some roasted goat meat and presented it to Rasulullah ﷺ. Rasulullah ﷺ took a foreleg of the goat and started eating it while a group of Sahabah also joined him. Rasulullah ﷺ then said, "Take your hands off the food!" Rasulullah ﷺ then sent for the woman and when she arrived, her asked, "Did you poison this meat?" "Who told you about it?" she asked. Rasulullah ﷺ replied, "This foreleg here in my hand informed me." When she admitted that she did poison the meat, Rasulullah ﷺ asked her why she did it. She replied, "I said to myself that it would do you no harm if you really are a Rasul and if you not, we would get rid of you." Rasulullah ﷺ forgave her and did not punish her. However, some

of the Sahabah who had eaten from the meat passed away and because he had also eaten from it, Rasulullah ﷺ had blood cupped from his shoulder. Abu Hind ؓ who was a freed slave of the Ansar Banu Bayadha tribe did the cupping using a horn and a blade. Another narration from Abu Salama ؓ states that Bishr bin Bara bin Ma'roor ؓ passed away from the poisoning. The narration further states that because of this death Rasulullah ﷺ then had the woman executed. (Abu Dawud). Marwan bin Uthman bin Abu Sa'eed bin Mu'alla ؓ narrates that when Rasulullah ﷺ was on his deathbed, the sister of Bishr bin Bara bin Ma'roor came to visit him. Rasulullah ﷺ said to her, "O Ummu Bishr! I could now feel my arteries shredding because of what I ate with your brother in Khaibar." Because of this Muslims believe that together with the mantle of prophethood, Allah also blessed Rasulullah ﷺ with the mantle of martyrdom. (Ibn Is'haq in Al Bidayah wan Nihayah)

Rasulullah ﷺ Expressed Tolerance Towards a Man Who Wished to Assassinate Him

Ja'da bin Khalid bin Simmah Jushami ؓ narrates that Rasulullah ﷺ once saw a man with a large belly and pointed towards the man's belly. Ja'da ؓ heard Rasulullah ﷺ say, "It would have been better for you if that had been somewhere else if you had spent on those without food rather than feeding yourself." A man was brought and Rasulullah ﷺ was informed that the man had intended to assassinate Rasulullah ﷺ. "There is nothing to be feared," Rasulullah ﷺ said, "Had you tried it, Allah would have never given you power over me." (Ahmad, Tabrani)

Rasulullah ﷺ Behaves Tolerantly Towards a Party of the Quraish Who Planned an Ambush

Anas ؓ narrates that during the time when the treaty of Hudaibiyya was being concluded, 80 armed men from Makkah approached from Mount Tan'im with the express purpose of ambushing Rasulullah ﷺ and the Sahabah. However, they were captured when Rasulullah ﷺ made a Du'a to Allah. Rasulullah ﷺ then forgave them, after which Allah revealed the verse:

وَهُوَ الَّذِي كَفَّ أَيْدِيَهُمْ عَنْكُمْ وَأَيْدِيَكُمْ عَنْهُمْ بِبَطْنِ مَكَّةَ مِنْ بَعْدِ أَنْ أَظْفَرَكُمْ عَلَيْهِمْ وَكَانَ اللَّهُ بِمَا تَعْمَلُونَ بَصِيرًا (24)

And He it is Who has withheld their hands from you and your hands from them in the midst of Makkah, after He had made you victors over them. And Allah is Ever the All-Seer of what you do. (Al-Fath:24) (Ahmad, Muslim, Abu Dawud, Tirmidhi, Nasa'ee)

In a lengthy narration, Abdullah bin Mughattal ؓ say, "As we remained there, 30 armed men left Makkah and attacked us by surprise. Rasulullah ﷺ ever prayed to Allah and Allah made them all deaf. As they stood dumb, we then got up and captured them. Rasulullah ﷺ then asked them, "Have you men come under the protection of any treaty or has anyone granted you any amnesty?" When they replied in the negative, Rasulullah ﷺ let them go. It was then that Allah revealed the verse:

وَهُوَ الَّذِي كَفَّ أَيْدِيَهُمْ عَنْكُمْ وَأَيْدِيَكُمْ عَنْهُمْ بِبَطْنِ مَكَّةَ مِنْ بَعْدِ أَنْ أَظْفَرَكُمْ عَلَيْهِمْ وَكَانَ اللَّهُ بِمَا تَعْمَلُونَ بَصِيرًا (24)

And He it is Who has withheld their hands from you and your hands from them in the midst of Makkah, after He had made you victors over them. And Allah is Ever the All-Seer of what you do. (Al-Fath:24) (Ahmad, Nasa'ee in Tafsir Ibn Kathir)

Rasulullah ﷺ's Tolerance with the Daus Tribe

Abu Hurairah ؓ reports that Tufail bin Amr ؓ once came to Rasulullah ﷺ and said, 'The Daus tribe are disobedient and refuse to accept Islam. Please curse them." Rasulullah ﷺ then turned to face the Qibla and raised his hands to pray to which the Sahabah remarked, "Those people will certainly be destroyed." Rasulullah ﷺ then prayed, "O Allah! Guide the Daus tribe and bring them to us as Muslims. O Allah! Guide the Daus tribe and bring them. O Allah! Guide the Daus tribe and bring them." *(Bukhari)*

The Tolerance of the Sahabah

Abu Za'ra ؓ reports that Ali bin Abu Talib ؓ used to say, "My pure wives, pious progeny and myself have been the most tolerant people in youth and the most learned as adults. It is us that Allah uses to eradicate dishonesty, to shatter the teeth of extreme dogs, to deliver you from your tyrants, to remove the shackles from your necks, to start off things and to terminate them." *(Abdul Ghani bin Sa'eed in Idahul Askal, Mutakhab Kanzul Ummal)*. Sa'd bin Abi Waqqas ؓ also said, "I have not seen any person as quick-witted, as intelligent, as knowledgeable, and as tolerant as Abdullah bin Abbas ؓ."

Compassion and mercy: Rasulullah ﷺ shortens the Salah because of a Child's Cries and an Incident of his Compassionate Nature

Anas ؓ reports that Rasulullah ﷺ once said, "I sometimes start the salah with the intention of lengthening it when I hear the cries of a child and then shorten the salah because I know that the crying would pain the mother." *(Bukhari, Muslim in Safwatus Safwa)*. Anas ؓ narrates that a man once asked Rasulullah ﷺ, "Where is my father who died as a disbeliever'?" "In the fire of Jahannam," came the reply. When Rasulullah ﷺ saw the grief on the man's face, he consoled him by saying, "Both my father as well as yours are in the fire." *(Muslim in Safawatus Safwa)*

The Incident of Rasulullah ﷺ and a Bedouin who Addressed Him Very Harshly

Abu Hurairah ؓ narrates that a Bedouin once came to Rasulullah ﷺ to seek assistance in paying some blood money. After giving him a good amount, Rasulullah ﷺ asked "Have I done you justice?" "Not at all," the man replied, "You have not done me any good." This angered some Muslims so much that they wanted to get up and hit the man. Rasulullah ﷺ however motioned to them to restrain themselves. When Rasulullah ﷺ later stood up and went to his room, he called the Bedouin to his room saying, 'You came to us asking for something and we gave it to you. You then made the remark that you did." Rasulullah ﷺ then gave him some more and asked "Have I done you justice?" This time the Bedouin said, "You have indeed. May Allah reward you amply on behalf of all my family and relatives." Rasulullah ﷺ then said to him, "You came to us asking for something and we gave it to you. You then made the remark that you did, thus causing hurt to the hearts of my companions. Now when you leave, tell them what you have just said before me so that the hurt may leave their hearts." The man agreed and when he again arrived in the gathering, Rasulullah ﷺ said, "Your friend here came to us asking for something and we gave it to him. He then made the remark that he did. We then called for him and again gave him something. He now believes that he is satisfied. Is that not true, dear Bedouin?" the Bedouin replied. "It certainly is. May Allah reward you amply on behalf of all my family and relatives." Thereafter, Rasulullah ﷺ said, "Indeed the example of this Bedouin and myself is like a person who had a camel. When the camel bolted from him and the people ran after it, all that they achieved was to make it run further away. The owner of the camel then said. "Leave me to my camel because I am more compassionate towards it and know it better. He then headed for

the camel taking along with him some dates that had fallen to the ground. He called for the camel and it responded and came to him. He comfortably tied his carriage to it. Had I done as you wanted when he made the remark he did, he would certainly have been doomed for Jahannam." *(Bazzar in Tafsir Ibn Kathir, Ibn Hibban in Saheeh, Abush Shaikh and Ibn Jowzi in Wafa, Khafaji)*

The Compassion of the Sahabah

Asma'ee reports that when Omar ؓ became the Amirul Mu'minin, the people requested Abdur Rahman bin Auf ؓ to speak to Omar ؓ to be gentle with the people because even young damsels in their secluded quarters were overawed by him. When Abdur Rahman bin Auf ؓ had spoken to Omar ؓ, he said, "That is the way I see appropriate to treat the people. By Allah! If the people knew the gentleness, the mercy and the compassion I have for them, they would actually take the clothes off my back." *(Deenowri in Muntakhab Kanzul Ummal)*

The Statement of Abu Sa'eed Khudri ؓ Concerning the Modesty of Rasulullah ﷺ

Abu Sa'eed Khudri ؓ says, "Rasulullah ﷺ was more modest than a virgin in her own secluded quarters." Another narration adds that whenever Rasulullah ﷺ disliked something, it would be noticed on his face. *(Bukhari, Muslim in Al Bidayah wan Nihayah, Tirmidhi in Shama'il, Ibn Sa'd, Tabrani in Majma'uz Zawa'id)*. Anas ؓ reports that Rasulullah ﷺ said, "Modesty is goodness through and through." *(Bazzar, Haythami)*

Rasulullah ﷺ Dislikes Telling People What Would Displease Them

Anas ؓ narrates that Rasulullah ﷺ was once dispersed when he saw some Sufra, a fragrance usually worn by women that stains the clothing yellow on a person. After the person had left, Rasulullah ﷺ said to the other Sahabah do you people not instruct him to wash the Sufrah off?" Anas ؓ says, "It was never the habit of Rasulullah ﷺ to tell a person on his face something that would displease him." *(Ahmad, Nasa'ee in Yowm wal Layl, Abu Dawud)*. Aisha ؓ says, "Whenever the news reached Rasulullah ﷺ that someone had said something, he would never say, 'What is the matter with that person to say... ?' He would rather say, 'What is the matter with some people who say... ?'

The Statement of Aisha ؓ Concerning His Modesty With His Wives

Aisha ؓ said, "I have never seen the private parts of Rasulullah ﷺ." *(Tirmidhi in Shama'il)*

Rasulullah ﷺ's Statement About the Modesty of Uthman ؓ

Sa'eed bin Al Aas ؓ narrates that Rasulullah ﷺ's wife Aisha ؓ and Uthman ؓ both reported to him that Abu Bakr ؓ once sought permission to see Rasulullah ﷺ who was lying down on his bed wearing a shawl belonging to Aisha ؓ. Remaining as he was, Rasulullah ﷺ permitted Abu Bakr ؓ in and he left after completing the work he had with Rasulullah ﷺ. Rasulullah ﷺ was still in the same condition when Omar ؓ then asked permission to enter. Rasulullah ﷺ allowed him in and after completing his work with Rasulullah ﷺ, Omar ؓ also left. However, when Uthman ؓ sought permission to enter, Rasulullah ﷺ sat up and urgently asked Aisha ؓ to ensure that her clothes were covering her properly. After Uthman ؓ had completed the work he had with Rasulullah ﷺ, he then also left. Aisha ؓ then asked, "O Rasulullah ﷺ! Why is it that you became more anxious at the arrival of Uthman ؓ than you did at the arrival of both Abu Bakr ؓ and Omar ؓ?" Rasulullah ﷺ replied, "Uthman ؓ is extremely shy and I feared that if I let him under the condition that prevailed, he would have been unable to fulfill the need he had come for." Many narrators reports that Rasulullah ﷺ also said to Aisha ﷺ, "Why should I not be shy in front of that person in front of whom even the angels are shy?" (Ahmad, Muslim, Abu Yal'la, Hasan bin Urfa). Abdullah bin Omar ﷺ reports that Rasulullah ﷺ was once sitting with Aisha ﷺ behind when Abu Bakr ﷺ sought permission to enter and then entered after permission was granted. Thereafter, Omar ﷺ sought permission to enter and he also entered. Next came Sa'd bin Malik ﷺ who entered seeking permission to do so. Rasulullah ﷺ was busy talking to the others with his knees exposed when Uthman bin Affan ﷺ sought permission to enter. Rasulullah ﷺ then immediately covered his knees and told Aisha ﷺ to move away. After speaking some time, the men left. Aisha ﷺ asked, "O Nabi of Allah ﷺ! When my father and his companions entered, you did not place your clothes over your knees neither did you ask me to move away from you, why did you do so when Uthman ﷺ came in?." Rasulullah ﷺ replied, "Why should I not be shy in front of that person in front of whom even the angels are shy? I swear by the Being Who controls my life that the angels are shy for Uthman bin Affan ﷺ just as you are shy before Allah and His Rasul ﷺ. Had he entered when you were to me, he would neither speak nor raise his head until he left." (Tabrani in Al Bidayah wan Nihayah, Abu Ya'la in Majma'uz Zawa'id, Haythami)

A Narration of Hasan Concerning the Modesty of Uthman ﷺ and Abu Bakr ﷺ

Speaking about the extreme modesty of Uthman ﷺ, Hasan says, "Even though he was in a room behind a locked door, he would not remove his clothing to pour water over himself when taking a bath. His modesty would prevent him from standing straight up when bathing. He would do so while sitting." (Ahmad, Haythami, Abu Nu'aym in Hilya). Aisha ﷺ narrates that Abu Bakr ﷺ said, "Be modest in front of Allah. I cover my head out of modesty before Allah even when I enter the toilet." (Sufian in Kanzul Ummal)

The Modesty of Uthman bin Madh'un ﷺ

Sa'd bin Mas'ood ﷺ and Omarah bin Ghurab Yahsubi ﷺ both narrate that Uthman bin Madh'un ﷺ once came to Rasulullah ﷺ saying, "O Rasulullah ﷺ! I do not like my wife to see my private parts." "Why is that so?' asked Rasulullah ﷺ. Uthman bin Madh'un ﷺ replied, "Because I feel shy and I dislike it." Rasulullah ﷺ said to him, "Allah has made her your garment and made you hers. At times my wives see my private parts and I see theirs. "You do that, O Rasulullah ﷺ!" Uthman bin Madh'un ﷺ asked in surprise. When Rasulullah ﷺ confirmed that this was indeed so, Uthman bin Madh'un ﷺ said, "Who can there be after you for me to follow?" After he had left, Rasulullah ﷺ said, "Verily Ibn Madh'un ﷺ is extremely shy and one who always keeps his private area concealed." (Ibn Sa'd)

The modesty of Abu Musa Ash'ari ﷺ

Abu Mijlaz reports that Abu Musa Ash'ari ﷺ said, "I bath in a dark room and do not stand up straight until I have picked up my clothes. This I do out of shyness for my Rabb." (Abu Nu'aym in Hilya, Ibn Sa'd). Abu Qatadah ﷺ states that when Abu Musa Ash'ari ﷺ took a bath, he would do so in a dark room sitting down and bend over when getting his clothing without standing up straight. (Ibn Sa'd). Anas ﷺ says that Abu Musa Ash'ari ﷺ always wore some clothing when sleeping for fear of his private area becoming exposed. (Ibn Sa'd). Ubadah bin Nusai reports that Abu Musa Ash'ari ﷺ once saw some people standing in water without their lower garments. To this, he exclaimed, "I prefer to die and be raised again and again to die and be raised again rather than doing what these people are doing." (Ibn Sa'd)

The Modesty of Ashaj Abdul Qais ﷺ

Ashaj Abdul Qais ﷺ reports that Rasulullah ﷺ said to him, "You have 2 qualities that Allah loves." When he asked what they were, Rasulullah ﷺ said, "Tolerance and modesty." Ashaj ﷺ asked further, "Are these natural qualities within me or have they been developed afterwards?" "No," replied Rasulullah ﷺ, "They have been naturally installed within you." Ashaj ﷺ said, "All praise is for Allah Who has installed within me such qualities that He loves." (Ibn Abi Shayba, Abu Nu'aym in Kanzul Ummal)

The Humility of Rasulullah ﷺ: The Incident of Rasulullah ﷺ With Jibra'el عليه السلام and Another Angel

Abu Hurairah ﷺ reports that Jibra'el عليه السلام was once sitting with Rasulullah ﷺ when he looked towards the sky. An angel suddenly descended to which Jibra'el عليه السلام said, "Since he has been created, this angel has never descended until this moment." When the angel came down, he said, "O Muhammad ﷺ! Your Rabb has sent me to you. Allah asks whether 'Is it a Nabi who is a king that I should make you or a Rasul that is a slave of Allah?'" Advising Rasulullah ﷺ, Jibra'el عليه السلام said, "Adopt humility before your Rabb, O Muhammad ﷺ!" Rasulullah ﷺ then replied, "I would rather be a Rasul who is a slave." (Ahmad, Bazzar, Abu Ya'la, Haythami). Aisha ﷺ adds at the end. "After this, Rasulullah ﷺ never ate in a reclining position and would say, 'I eat as a slave eats and sit as a slave sits." A similar narration from Abdullah bin Abbas ﷺ has already passed.

A Narration of Abu Umama Bahili ﷺ

Abu Ghalib says that he asked Abu Umama ﷺ to narrate a Hadith that he had heard Rasulullah ﷺ. Abu Umama ﷺ replied, "Everything that Rasulullah ﷺ said was according to the Qur'an. He made Dhikr in abundance, kept his lectures brief, lengthened his salah and was never too stuck up, or proud to go with a poor or unimportant person to personally see his needs." (Tabrani, Haythami, Bayhaqi, Nasa'ee, Al Bidayah wan Nihayah).

A Narration of Anas ﷺ

Anas ﷺ says, "Rasulullah ﷺ made Dhikr in abundance, never engaged in arguments, rode a camel, wore woolen clothing and accepted the invitations of slaves. If only you saw him, you would realize the extent of his humility on the day the Battle of Khaibar was fought, he rode a donkey with reins made from the bark of a date palm." (Tayalisi). Rasulullah ﷺ also visited the ill and attended funerals. (Tirmidhi, Ibn Sa'd)

The Narrations of Abu Musa Ash'ari ﷺ, Abdullah bin Abbas ﷺ and Anas ﷺ in this Regard

Abu Musa Ash'ari ﷺ says, "Rasulullah ﷺ used to ride a donkey, wear woolen clothes, hold down a goat and milk it and personally serve guests." (Bayhaqi in Al Bidayah wan Nihayah, Tabrani, Haythami). Abdullah bin Abbas ﷺ says, "Rasulullah ﷺ would sit on the floor, eat on the floor, hold down a goat himself while milking it and even accept the invitation of a slave to share barley bread." Another narration states that even in the middle of the night Rasulullah ﷺ would accept the invitation to eat barley bread extended by a person from the upper part of Madinah." (Tabrani, Haythami). Anas ﷺ reports that Rasulullah ﷺ would accept an invitation even if it were to eat barley bread and foul-smelling fat. Rasulullah ﷺ also had a suit of armor that he pawned to a Jew and until the day he passed away, he did not have enough money to recover the armor from the man. *(Tirmidhi in Shama'il)*

A Narration of Omar bin Khattab

Omar says that a man called for Rasulullah 3 times, Rasulullah replied with "Labbaik", 'At your service' each time. *(Abu Ya'la, Haythami, Abu Nu'aym in Hilya, Kanzul Ummal)*

The incident of Rasulullah with a woman

Abu Umama narrates that during the time of Rasulullah there was an immoral woman who used to flirt with the men. She once passed by Rasulullah when he was busy eating Thareed. She shouted out, "Look at this man, sitting like a slave and eating like a slave!" Rasulullah remarked, "Which slave can be more devoted in his servitude to Allah than I?" She then said further, "He eats without giving me anything to eat." "Do eat," Rasulullah said. "Give me with your hand," she demanded. When Rasulullah gave her, she made a further demand saying, "Give me from what is in your mouth." When Rasulullah complied and she ate the food, its blessings were so profound that the woman was overcome with modesty and she never flirted with a man for the rest of her life. *(Tabrani, Haythami)*

The Incident of Rasulullah with one who was Shaking before Him

Jareer reports that when a man once came before Rasulullah, he started to shiver. Rasulullah put him at ease saying, "Take it easy. I am not a king but merely the son of a woman from the Quraish who used to eat dried meat." *(Tabrani, Haythami)*. *(Bayhaqi in Al Bidayah wan Nihayah)* from Abdullah bin Mas'ood states that it was on the day the Muslims conquered Makkah that a man started shivering while talking to Rasulullah. The rest of the narration is like the one above. Amir bin Rabe'ah says, "I was proceeding with Rasulullah to the Masjid when one of his shoe straps broke. I immediately got hold of the shoe to fix it when Rasulullah took it from my hand saying, "You are giving me preferential treatment and I dislike being given preferential treatment." *(Bazzar, Haythami)*

Rasulullah Dislikes Being Treated Differently From his Companions

Abdullah bin Jubair Khuza'e narrates that Rasulullah was walking with his companions when someone shaded him with a sheet. When he saw the shadow, Rasulullah looked up and saw the sheet that was shading him. "What is this?" Rasulullah exclaimed as he took hold of the sheet and put it down. He then said, "I am merely a human being like you and therefore do not need preferential treatment." *(Tabrani, Haythami)*. Abdullah bin Abbas reports that Abbas said, "I once said to myself, 'I wonder how long Rasulullah will still remain amongst us. To ascertain this I then proceeded to ask, 'O Rasulullah! Why do you not have a platform constructed for you?' Rasulullah replied, 'I prefer to remain amongst you like one of you with people trampling my heels and pulling at my shawl until the time when Allah finally gives me comfort and takes me away from the people.'" *(Bazzar, Haythami)*. In another narration from Ikrama, Abbas says, "I shall definitely find out how long Rasulullah will still be staying amongst us. I then asked, 'O Rasulullah! I see that the people and the dust they kick up is causing you harm. Why do you not have a platform built for you from which you may address them? Rasulullah replied, 'I prefer to remain amongst you...' The reply is the same as above. Abbas says further, "I then knew that Rasulullah

would be with us for only a very short while." *(Darmi in Jam'ul Fawa'id, Ibn Sa'd)*

Narrations of Aisha Concerning what Rasulullah did at Home

Aswad reports that he once asked Aisha, "What would Rasulullah do when he entered the house?" Aisha replied, "He would engage himself in some domestic chores and would leave to perform salah when the time for salah arrived." *(Ahmad, Bukhari, Ibn Sa'd)*. Urwa narrates that someone once asked Aisha, "Would Rasulullah carry out domestic chores at home?" "Certainly," she replied, "He would mend his shoes and stitch his clothes just as any of you do at home." *(Bayhaqi)*. Amrah reports that she once asked Aisha, "What would Rasulullah do at home?" Aisha replied, "Rasulullah was a human and would remove lice from his clothing, milk his goat and take care of himself." *(Bayhaqi, Tirmidhi in Shama'il, Al Bidayah wan Nihayah)*

Narrtions of Abdullah bin Abbas and Jabir Concerning the Humility of Rasulullah

Abdullah bin Abbas reports that Rasulullah never assigned to anyone the duty of making arrangements for his wudhu and also the duty of handing out the charity he gave. He would personally attend to these duties. *(Qazwini in Jam'ul Fawa'id)*. Jabir says, "When Rasulullah came to visit me, he was neither riding a mule nor a horse." *(Bukhari in Safwatus Safwah)*. Anas says, "Rasulullah performed Hajj on an old carriage atop his camel covered with a sheet that was worth 4 Dirhams. Even then he prayed, 'O Allah! Make this a Hajj devoid of pretension and boastfulness.'" *(Tirmidhi in Shama'il)*

The Humility of Rasulullah when he Victoriously Entered Makkah

Anas reports that when Rasulullah entered Makkah upon the conquest of Makkah and the people were crowding to have a look at him, he placed his head against his carriage out of humility. *(Abu Ya'la, Haythami)*. Anas says that when Rasulullah entered Makkah on the day Makkah was conquered, he had his chin on his carriage out of humility. *(Bayhaqi)*. Rasulullah reached Dhu Tuwa, he stood on his carriage. He wore his reddish, striped Yemeni shawl around his head with its end hanging over his face. When Rasulullah saw the great victory that Allah had blessed him with, he lowered his head so much in humility to Allah that his beard touched the centre of the carriage. *(Ibn Is'haq in Al Bidayah wan Nihayah)*

Rasulullah Stops Abu Hurairah from Carrying His Goods and from Kissing His Bands when Selling

Abu Hurairah reports, "I once entered the marketplace with Rasulullah. Rasulullah sat with some cloth merchants and bought a trouser for 4 Dirhams. The cloth merchants had with them a person would took measurements. Addressing this person, Rasulullah said, 'Let the benefit be for the buyer when taking measurements, give rather more than less.' Rasulullah then took the trousers and when I attempted to carry them for him, he said, 'The owner of an item has a greater right to carrying it unless he is too weak or unable to do so. In that case, his Muslim brother may lend him a hand.' I then said, 'O Rasulullah! Do you wear trousers?' He replied, 'Certainly. I wear them when on journey, when at home, during the night and during the day. I have been commanded to keep my private areas concealed and I find nothing more concealing than trousers.'" *(Tabrani in Awsat, Abu Ya'la, Ahmad in Nasimur Riyadh)*. Another narration adds that Rasulullah said, "Let the benefit be for the buyer when taking measurements." To this, the person taking measurements said, "I have never heard these words from any person before this." Abu Hurairah ﷺ said to him, "It is sufficient evidence of your ignorance and foolishness in Islam that you do not recognize your Nabi ﷺ!" The man threw aside his scale and leapt up to grab the hand of Rasulullah ﷺ in an effort to kiss it. Rasulullah ﷺ pulled his hand away from the man saying, "What is this?! It is only the non-Arabs who do this with their kings. I am not a king but a man from amongst you." The man took the measurements and let the benefit go to Rasulullah ﷺ. Rasulullah ﷺ took the cloth. The rest of the narration is like mentioned above. (Majma'uz Zawa'id, Tabrani, Abu Ya'la, Haythami)

The Humility of the Sahabah: Omar ﷺ Rides a Camel on his Journey to Sham

Aslam reports that when Omar ﷺ arrived in Sham riding a camel, the people started talking amongst themselves that he should have rather chosen a good horse for the journey. To this, Omar ﷺ remarked, "Their gazes are on the conveyances of people (the Kuffar) who have no portion in the Hereafter. They had rather look to the conveyances used by Rasulullah ﷺ and the Muslims."(Ibn Asakir, Ibn Mubarak, Muntakhab Kanzul Ummal)

Omar ﷺ Teaches Women to Make Flour

Hisham narrates that he once saw Omar ﷺ pass by a woman who was busy making Asida, a paste made from flour and clarified butter. "That is not how Asida is made," said Omar ﷺ. He then took a wooden spoon and showed her how to make it saying, 'This is how it is done." (Ibn Sa'd). Hisham bin Khalid says that he heard Omar bin Khattab ﷺ say as he taught some women to make Asida, "You should never add the flour until the water is hot. When the water gets hot, you should then add the flour gradually as you stir with a spoon because it will then mix well without forming lumps." (Muntakhab Kanzul Ummal)

Omar ﷺ goes barefoot to the Masjid and ridicules himself in his Sermon

Zirr says that he saw Omar ﷺ proceed barefoot for the Eid salah. (Muntakhab Kanzul Ummal). Omar Makhzumi reports that Omar bin Khattab ﷺ made an announcement for the people to gather in the Masjid. The people got together and Omar ﷺ mounted the pulpit. Praising Allah and sending salutations on Rasulullah ﷺ, he said. "O people! I have seen the time when I used to graze animals for my maternal aunts from the Banu Makhzum tribe. As wages they would then give me a handful of dates and raisins. I would then spend the entire day doing this and what days they were?!" When Omar ﷺ descended from the pulpit, Abdur Rahman bin Auf ﷺ said, "O Amirul Mu'minin! All you have done is ridicule yourself." "Shame on you, O Ibn Auf!" Omar ﷺ exclaimed, "When I was alone by myself, the thought came to mind that since I am the Amirul Mu'minin, there must be none better than me. By doing what I did I wanted to teach myself who I really was." (Deenowri in Muntakhab Kanzul Ummal). Omar ﷺ added, "O people! I have seen the time when I had no source of livelihood apart from a few handfuls of raisins that my aunts from the Banu Makhzum tribe would give me for bringing water for them." This narration ends with the words, "I found some pride in myself and wished to humble myself by telling the people what I did." (Ibn Sa'd)

Omar ﷺ Rides Behind a Young Boy on a Donkey

Hasan reports that Omar bin Khattab ﷺ once left home on an extremely hot day with a shawl thrown over his head. When a young boy passed by riding a donkey, Omar ﷺ asked, "Dear boy! Please give me a ride with you on the donkey." The boy immediately jumped off donkey saying, "You may get on, O Amirul Mu'minin!" "No," said Omar ﷺ, "you ride and I will ride behind you. You want me to have a comfortable place to ride when you are on a hard place (this cannot be)!" Omar ﷺ then rode behind the boy. When they entered Madinah, the people stared at them because Omar ﷺ was still riding behind the boy. (Deenowri in Muntakhab Kanzul Ummal)

Omar ﷺ Walks with a Boy to Protect Him from Other Boys

Sinan bin Salama Hudhali says, "I once went out with some other boys to pick up dates that had fallen to the ground. Omar ﷺ suddenly appeared with a lash in his hand when the boys saw him, they dispersed amongst the date palms. I stood where I was with the dates I had picked up collected in my lower garment. 'O Amirul Mu'minin,' I said, 'these are the dates that the wind has blown off.' He looked at what was in my garment but did not hit me. I said, 'O Amirul Mu'minin! The boys are now ahead of me and they take away all that I have.' 'Never,' Omar ﷺ assured me, 'Walk ahead.' He then accompanied me to my home." (Ibn Sa'd)

Omar ﷺ and Uthman ﷺ allow people to ride with them on Their Animals

The grandfather of Malik say that he saw Omar ﷺ and Uthman ﷺ when they arrived from Makkah and camped at a place called Mu'arras (Dhul Hulaifa). When the party rode again to enter Madinah, everyone of them took a youngster to ride with him. In this manner, they entered Madinah. Even Omar ﷺ and Uthman ﷺ had someone riding with them. One of the narrator's students asked, "Did they do this because of humility?" The reply was, "Certainly. In addition to this, they also wished to benefit others so that the person need not walk and did not want to be like other rulers who feel it below their dignity to allow an ordinary person to ride with them." The narrator then proceeded to criticize the new trend of rulers to make youngsters walk behind them as they rode. (Bayhaqi in Kanzul Ummal)

The Humility of Uthman ﷺ

Maymun bin Mahran reports from a man from Hamdan that he saw Uthman ﷺ riding a mule with his slave Na'il riding behind him on the same animal. This was during the time that Uthman ﷺ was Khalifa. (Abu Nu'aym in Hilya). Abdullah Rumi says that Uthman ﷺ fetched the water he needed to perform wudhu during the night. When someone suggested that he get one of the servants to do it for him, he refused saying, "The night is theirs to have a rest." (Ibn Sa'd, Ahmad in Zuhd, Ibn Asakir in Kanzul Ummal). The grandmother of Zubair bin Abdullah was a servant of Uthman ﷺ. She says, "Uthman ﷺ never awakened any members of the household at night when he awoke for Tahajjud. The only time he would ask any of them to get him water for wudhu was if he found them awake. He fasted continually." (Ibn Mubarak in Zuhd, Isabah). Hasan says, "I saw Uthman ﷺ sleeping in the Masjid covered in a shawl. He was the Amirul Mu'mmin, yet no one was around him." (Abu Nu'aym in Hilya)

The Humility of Abu Bakr ﷺ

Unaysa says, "The little girls of the locality would take their goats to Abu Bakr ﷺ for milking. Not only would he do it for them but he would also ask, 'Would you like me to milk for you like Ibn Afra (someone from Ansar) does?'" (Ibn Sa'd in Muntakhab Kanzul Ummal). The narrations of Aisha ﷺ, Abdullah bin Omar ﷺ and Ibn Musayab have already passed in the chapter entitled "The Lives of the Khulafa and Leaders". It is stated there that Abu Bakr ؓ was a businessman by trade and would proceed to the marketplace every morning to buy and sell. He also had a flock of goats that would come to him in the evenings. He sometimes took them out himself for grazing and sometimes someone else grazes them. He used to milk goats for the people of his locality so when he became the Khalifa, a little girl said, "Now there will be none to milk our animals." When he heard her saying this, Abu Bakr ؓ said, "Why not! I swear by my life that I shall definitely still milk for you. I hope that what I have entered into will never change the personality I always had." He then continued milking for the people and would sometimes say to the little girl of the locality, "Dear girl! Would you like me to make the milk foamy or without foam?" At times she would ask for foamy milk while at times she asked for it to have no foam. He then did exactly as she asked.

Episodes of the Humility of Amirul Mu'minin Ali ؓ

The blanket merchant Salih reports from his grandfather who says, "I saw Amirul Mu'minin Ali ؓ purchase dates for a Dirham and then carry them in his bag. When I or another man offered to carry it for him, he refused the offer saying, 'The father of a family has a greater right to carry their goods.'" (*Bukhari in Adab, Ibn Asakir in Muntakhab Kanzul Ummal, Abul Qasim Baghawi in Al Bidayah wan Nihayah*). Zadhan reports that even as Amirul Mu'minin, Ali ؓ used to walk alone in the marketplace where he would guide lost people, announce lost items and assist the weak. When passing by traders and grocers, he would open the Qur'an and recite to them:

تِلْكَ الدَّارُ الْآخِرَةُ نَجْعَلُهَا لِلَّذِينَ لَا يُرِيدُونَ عُلُوًّا فِي الْأَرْضِ وَلَا فَسَادًا

That home of the Hereafter (i.e. Paradise), We shall assign to those who rebel not against the truth with pride and oppression in the land... (Al-Qasas:83)

He would then say, "This verse was revealed with reference to rulers and people with authority over others who despite their positions, they exercise Justice and are humble." (*Ibn Asakir in Muntakhab Kanzul Ummal, Abul Qasim Baghawi in Al Bidayah wan Nihayah*). Jurmuz narrates that he saw Ali ؓ emerge from his house wearing 2 reddish cloths made in Qatar, a lower garment that reached halfway up his calves and wrapped in a shawl of about the same size. He also carried a lash and walked with it in the marketplace, instructing people to be wary of Allah and to trade in an amicable manner. He would also say, "Weigh and measure in full and do not blow into the meat (to make it appear large)." (*Ibn Sa'd, Ibn Abdul Birr in Isti'ab*). Abu Matar says, "I was once leaving the Masjid when suddenly heard someone behind me shouting, 'Lift your lower garment because it shows greater wariness of your Rabb and also keeps the garment cleaner. You should also trim your hair if you are a Muslim.' I then noticed that it was Ali ؓ holding a lash in his hand. He then went to the camel market where he said to the traders, 'Never take oaths when selling because although oaths sell goods, they destroy blessings.' When he went to a date seller, he found a servant weeping. When Ali ؓ asked her what the problem was, she informed him that her master refused to accept the dates that the date seller had sold to her for a Dirham. Addressing the seller, Ali ؓ instructed, 'Take back the dates and return her Dirham because she has no choice in the matter.' When it appeared as if the man would refuse, I said, 'Do you not know who this is?' He admitted that he did not. I then told him, 'He is Amirul Mu'minin Ali ؓ.' The man then readily poured out the dates into his own and returned the Dirham. Then he said, 'I want

you to be pleased with me, O Amirul Mu'minin.' Ali ؓ replied, 'I shall be immensely pleased with you if you give people their dues in full.' As he then passed by the other date sellers, Ali ؓ said, 'Feed the poor and your earnings will increase.' Ali ؓ proceeded further to the fish sellers, whom he instructed with the words, 'Never sell in our markets fish that are found floating in the water after dying.' Thereafter, Ali ؓ arrived at the cloth market where all the cloth merchants were found. Addressing one of them, he said, 'Dear old man! Give me a good deal on an upper garment for 3 Dirhams.' When the man recognized him, Ali ؓ did not buy from him but went to another merchant. However, when he also recognized Ali ؓ, the Amirul Mu'minin did not buy from him either. Ali ؓ then purchased a garment from a youngster who did not know him for 3 Dirhams. When he wore it, the sleeves reached up to his wrists while the rest of it reached his ankles. When the owner of the store arrived, someone told him that his son had sold a garment to the Amirul Mu'minin for 3 Dirhams. Reprimanding the boy, he said, 'Why did you rather not take 2 Dirhams?' He then took one Dirham and went to Ali ؓ saying, 'Please accept this Dirham.' 'What for?' Ali ؓ enquired. 'My son sold you the garment for 3 Dirhams when it costs only 2 Dirhams.' Ali ؓ refused to accept it saying, 'He sold it with my happiness and I bought it with his happiness.'" (*Ibn Raahway, Ahmad in Zuhd, Abd bin Humaid, Abu Ya'la, Bayhaqi, Ibn Asakir in Muntakhab Kanzul Ummal*)

The Humility of Fatima ؓ and Ummu Salama ؓ

Ata reports that when Rasulullah ﷺ's daughter Fatima ؓ pressed dough, her braid would hit against the bowl. (*Abu Nu'aym in Hilya*). Referring to Ummu Salamah ؓ Mutallib bin Abdullah says, "It was in the evening that the Arab widow came as the bride of the best of all Muslims, Rasulullah ﷺ and later that night she was grinding flour." (*Ibn Sa'd*)

Episodes of the Humility of Salman Farsi ؓ

Salama Ajali says, "One of my cousins from the countryside whose name was Qudama came to me with the request, 'I wish to meet Salman Farsi ؓ and greet him. We left to see him and found him in Mada'in in command of an army of 20,000 men. When we reached him, he was sitting on a platform, weaving baskets out of palm leaves. We greeted him and I said, 'O Abu Abdullah! This is my cousin visiting me from the countryside. He wishes to greet you.' Salman ؓ replied to the greeting:

وَعَلَيْهِ السَّلَام وَرَحْمَةُ اللهِ

I then continue to say, 'He also claims that he has a liking for you.' To this, Salman ؓ made the Du'a: أَحَبَّهُ اللهُ *'May Allah love him.'"* (*Abu Nu'aym in Hilya*)

Harith bin Umaira reports, "I once went to Salman ؓ and found him in his tannery scraping off some hide with his hands. When I greeted him with Salam, he said, 'Remain where you are until I come out.' 'By Allah!' I said, 'I do not think that you know who I am.' 'I certainly do.' he responded, 'My soul knew yours before I came to know you because all souls were a collective army before coming to this world. Those that acquainted themselves for the pleasure of Allah become friends and those who acquainted themselves for another besides Allah will have enmity between themselves.'" (*Ibn Asakir in Muntakhab Kanzul Ummal, Abu Nu'aym in Hilya*). Abu Qilaba narrates that someone once came to Salman ؓ as he was busy making dough. "What is this?" the man said in surprise. Salman ؓ replied, "I had already sent the servant out on a task and disliked giving him 2 jobs so I decided to do this myself. The person then conveyed to Salman ؓ greetings from another person. "When did you arrive?" Salman ؓ enquired from the man. When the man explained when he came, Salman ؓ said, "Remember well that had you not conveyed the greetings, it would remain an unfulfilled trust." *(Abu nu'aym in Hilya, Ibn Sa'd, Ahmad in Safwatus Safwa)*. Amr the son of Abu Quna Kindi says that his father once offered his sister in marriage to Salman ؓ. However, Salman ؓ refused the offer and instead married a freed slave woman named Buqayra who once belonged to Abu Quna. When the news reached Abu Quna that there had been an argument between Hudhaifa ؓ and Salman ؓ, he went to Salman ؓ but was told that Salman ؓ was in his field. There Abu Quna found Salman ؓ with a basket full of greens. He had put his staff through the handle of the basket and carried it over his shoulder. As they walked to Salman ؓ's house, Salman ؓ entered the house and said, "*As Salamu Alaykum*." He then allowed Abu Quna in. A bedding was spread out with a few bricks at the head side as pillows. There were also a few odds and ends lying about. Salman ؓ said to Abu Quna, "You may sit on the bedding that your slave had prepared for herself." *(Abu Nu'aym in Hilya)*. Maymun bin Mahran reports that a man from the Abdul Qais tribe once saw Salman ؓ riding a donkey as commander of an army. He wore trousers, the legs of which waved about in the wind. "Here comes the commander!" the soldiers called out in scorn. Salman ؓ said, "Good and bad will be known only after today in the Hereafter." *(Abu Nu'aym in Hilya)*. A man from the Abdul Qais tribe says, "I was with Salman ؓ when he was commanding an army. As he passed by 2 youngsters from the army, they laughed as they remarked, 'This is your commander!' 'O Abu Abdullah!' I protested, 'Do you not see what they are saying?' 'Leave them alone,' he bade me, 'Good and bad are to be seen after today in the Hereafter. If you are able to live off the earth, do so rather than being commander over even 2 persons. Beware of the curse of the oppressed and those left with no options because there is no barrier to their curses, Allah accepts it immediately.'" When Salman ؓ was the governor of Mada'in, he would go out to the people wearing his simple lower garment and shawl. When they saw him, the people would say, "Gurg Amad! Gurg Amad!" "What are they saying?" Salman ؓ asked. "They are comparing you to a toy of theirs," the people replied. To this, Salman ؓ remarked, "It does not matter what they say. Good will be seen only after this day in the Hereafter."

Huraim reports, "I once saw Salman ؓ riding a donkey that was unsaddled. He was wearing a garment made in Sumbulan which was short for him and was narrow at the bottom. He was a long-legged and hairy man and the garment reached only up to his knees. When I saw some youngsters poking his donkey from the back, I rebuked them saying, 'Will you not get away from your Amir?!' To this, Salman said. 'Leave them alone because good and evil will only be seen after this day." *(Ibn Sa'd)*. Thabit reports that Salman ؓ was the governor of Mada'in when a man arrived from Sham carrying figs. Because Salman ؓ was wearing his simple lower garment and shawl, the man not recognizing Salman ؓ and thinking him to be a common laborer called him saying, "Come and carry this!" Salman ؓ obliged and when the people saw him and recognized who he was, they exclaimed, "This is the governor!" When the man pleaded that he did not recognize Salman ؓ and wished to take the load back, Salman ؓ said to him, "Leave it until I reach your destination." Another narration states that Salman ؓ added, "I had already formulated an intention to please Allah by this service and I am therefore unable to put this down until I reach your house." *(Ibn Sa'd)*. Abdullah bin Buraida ؓ narrates that Salman ؓ used to make things with his hands and earned some money by selling

them, he would purchase some meat or fish. He would then invite some lepers to share the meal with him. *(Abu Nu'aym in Hilya)*

The Humility of Hudhaifa bin an Yaman ؓ

Muhammad bin Sirin reports that whenever Omar bin Khattab ؓ appointed a governor, he would write in the letter of appointment the following instruction to the people of the area, "You should listen to him and obey him as long as he exercises justice." However, when Omar ؓ appointed Hudhaifa ؓ as governor of Mada'in, he wrote the following in his letter of appointment: "Listen to him, obey him and give him whatever he asks you for." Hudhaifa ؓ then left Omar ؓ with a donkey fitted with a carriage to carry his goods. When Hudhaifa ؓ arrived in Mada'in and was received the people of the area and the local farmers, he was sitting on the carriage with a piece of bread and a bone with some meat in his hand. After reading out to them the letter of appointment, the people submitted, "You may ask us whatever you want." Hudhaifa ؓ said, "All I ask for is some food to eat and fodder for this donkey as long as I am with you." After staying there for some time, Omar ؓ sent for him to return. Upon receiving the news that Hudhaifa ؓ was approaching Madinah, Omar ؓ hid himself beside the road at a place where he would not be seen. When he saw Hudhaifa ؓ return in exactly the same condition he had left in, Omar ؓ came out of his hiding place and embraced Hudhaifa ؓ saying, "You are my brother and I am yours." *(Ibn Sa'd in Kanzul Ummal)*. Ibn Sirin narrates, "When Hudhaifa ؓ arrived in Mada'in, he arrived riding atop a carriage mounted on his donkey. He was eating a piece of bread with a bone with some meat." A narration of Talha bin Musarrif adds that at the time, Hudhaifa ؓ's legs were hanging on the side of the donkey. *(Abu Nu'aym in Hilya)*

The Humility of Jareer bin Abdullah ؓ and Abdullah bin Salam ؓ

Sulaym bin Abu Hudhail says, "I mended clothes by the door of Jareer bin Abdullah ؓ. Whenever he came out of his house and mounted his mule, he would take his slave along with him on the animal." *(Tabrani, Haythami)*. Abdullah bin Salam ؓ was once passing through the marketplace carrying a bundle of wood when someone said to him, "What makes you do this when Allah has freed you from it, you can always get someone else to do it for you'?" Abdullah bin Salam ؓ replied, "I wish to ward off pride because I have heard Rasulullah ﷺ say, 'The person in whose heart is an iota of pride will not enter Jannah." *(Tabrani, Isfahani in Targheeb wat Tarheeb)*

Ali ؓ says, "3 Factors form the Core of Humility"

Ali ؓ once said, "Three factors form the core of humility. These are: (1) That one is first to greet whoever one meets, (2) that one is content with an inferior position in a gathering rather than one of superiority and (3) that one dislikes showoff and boastfulness." *(Asakari in Kanzul Ummal)*

The Humor of Rasulullah ﷺ Despite Always Speaking the Truth

Abu Hurairah ؓ reports that the Sahabah once asked, "O Rasulullah ﷺ! You manage to joke with us'?" Rasulullah ﷺ replied, "However, I speak only the truth when I joke." *(Tirmidhi in Shama'il, Bukhari in Adab)*

Rasulullah ﷺ's Jokes with his Wife ؓ

A man once asked Abdullah bin Abbas ؓ whether Rasulullah ﷺ used to joke. When Abdullah bin Abbas ؓ replied that Rasulullah ﷺ used to joke, the man enquired about the nature of Rasulullah ﷺ's jokes. Abdullah bin Abbas ؓ replied,

"Rasulullah ﷺ once gave one of his wives a large shawl to wear saying, 'Wear it, thank Allah and drag it along like a bride's train." *(Ibn Asakir in Kanzul Ummal)*

Rasulullah ﷺ Jokes with Abu Umair ؓ

Anas ؓ says, "Rasulullah ﷺ had the best of character. I had a brother called Abu Umair who was just weaned off milk. Whenever Rasulullah ﷺ came and saw him, Rasulullah ﷺ would ask, "O Abu Umair! How is Nughair (from the word "Nughar", which was the little bird the boy played with)?' This was the little red-beaked bird that Abu Umair played with. At times, the time of salah would arrive while Rasulullah ﷺ was at our house. He would then have the mat he sat on spread out, swept and water sprinkled over it. Rasulullah ﷺ would then stand up in salah and we would stand behind him as he led the salah. The mat was made of palm leaves." *(Ahmad in Al Bidayah wan Nihayah)*. In another narration, Anas ؓ states, "Rasulullah ﷺ would associate with us so much that he would even ask my little brother, 'O Abu Umair! How is Nughair?" *(Bukhari in Adab, Tirmidhi)*. Anas ؓ narrates that Rasulullah ﷺ once visited Abu Talha ؓ (Anas ؓ's step-father) when he noticed that Abu Talha ؓ's son Abu Umair was looking depressed. Rasulullah ﷺ usually joked with him whenever he met him and asked, "Why is Abu Umair looking so sad?" When Rasulullah ﷺ was informed that the little bird with which the child played had died, Rasulullah ﷺ affectionately asked, "O Abu Umair! How is Nughair?" *(Ibn Sa'd)*

Rasulullah ﷺ Jokes with Someone

Anas ؓ reports that a man once came to Rasulullah ﷺ to ask for transport. Rasulullah ﷺ said to him, "We shall give you the child of a camel to ride." "O Rasulullah ﷺ!" the man said in surprise, "What will I do with the child of a camel, it is too small to ride?" Rasulullah ﷺ replied, "Is every camel not the child of another?" *(Ahmad, Abu Dawud, Tirmidhi in Al Bidayah wan Nihayah, Bukhari in Adab, Ibn Sa'd)*

Rasulullah ﷺ Jokes with Anas ؓ

Anas ؓ reports that Rasulullah ﷺ once jokingly called Anas ؓ saying, "O two-eared one!" *(Abu Dawud in Al Bidayah wan Nihayah, Tirmidhi in Shama'il, Abu Nu'aym, Ibn Asakir in Muntakhab Kanzul Ummal)*

Rasulullah ﷺ Jokes with Zahir ؓ

Anas ؓ reports that a man from the countryside called Zahir ؓ used to give Rasulullah ﷺ things from the countryside and when he left, Rasulullah ﷺ would give him things from the city. Rasulullah used to say, "Zahir is our countryside and we are his city." Although he was not a good looking person, Rasulullah ﷺ liked him a lot. As he was busy selling his wares in the marketplace one day, Rasulullah ﷺ grabbed him from the back and covered his eyes so that he could not see. "Release me!" Zahir ؓ shouted, but when he turned and recognized Rasulullah ﷺ, he started pressing his back closer to Rasulullah ﷺ's chest. "Who will buy this slave?" Rasulullah ﷺ announced. "O Rasulullah ﷺ!" Zahir ؓ said, "By Allah! If you sell me, you will run at a loss." "Not at all," Rasulullah ﷺ corrected, "You are not a loss in the sight of Allah. In Allah's sight, you are expensive." *(Ahmad, Tirmidhi in Shama'il, Ibn Hibban in Al Bidayah wan Nihayah, Abu Ya'la, Bazzar, Tabrani, Haythami)*

Rasulullah ﷺ Jokes with Aisha ؓ and his Other Wives ؓ

Nu'man bin Bashir ؓ narrates that when Abu Bakr ؓ was once about to ask permission to enter Rasulullah ﷺ's room, he heard his daughter Aisha ؓ raising her voice at Rasulullah ﷺ. When he entered, Abu Bakr ؓ grabbed her to give her a slap saying, "Are you raising your voice above that of Allah's Rasul ﷺ?!" However, Rasulullah ﷺ stopped him from taking action and Abu Bakr ؓ left in anger. After Abu Bakr ؓ had left, Rasulullah ﷺ said to Aisha ؓ, "Now what do you think of me after I rescued you from that man?" It was a few days later that Abu Bakr ؓ again sought permission to see Rasulullah ﷺ. This time he found that the couple had reconciled and said to them, "Now enter me into your peace as you had entered me into your war." "We certainly will," Rasulullah ﷺ said, "We certainly will." *(Abu Dawud in Al Bidayah wan Nihayah)*. Aisha ؓ reports, "I once accompanied Rasulullah ﷺ on one of his journeys when I was still a slim girl who had not put on much weight. Rasulullah ﷺ instructed the others to go ahead and when they did, he said to me, "Come! Let's have a race." I then beat him in the race. Rasulullah ﷺ let the matter rest until the time came when I had put on weight and forgotten about the incident. When I then accompanied him on a journey, he again instructed the others to proceed ahead. When they did so, he said to me, "Come! Let's have a race." This time he beat and he laughed as he said, "This is for that." *(Ahmad in Safwatus Safwa)*. Anas bin Malik ؓ narrates that Rasulullah ﷺ was once on a journey with his wives riding in front of him. Addressing the person who was reciting some poems to drive the camels faster, Rasulullah ﷺ said, "O Anjasha! Shame on you! Take it easy with the crystals, the women. Do not drive the camels too fast." *(Ahmad, Bukhari, Muslim in Al Bidayah wan Nihayah)*. In another narration, Anas ؓ says that Ummu Sulaim ؓ was with the wives of Rasulullah ﷺ on a journey when Rasulullah ﷺ came to them. Noticing that the camels were being driven too fast, Rasulullah ﷺ said to the person driving them along, "O Anjasha! Move easily with the crystals." Abu Qilaba says, "Rasulullah ﷺ made a statement that if any of you made, it would be held against him; the statement was, "Go easy with the crystals." *(Bukhari in Adab)*

Rasulullah ﷺ Jokes with an Old Woman

Hasan reports that an old woman once came to Rasulullah ﷺ with the request, "O Rasulullah ﷺ! Pray to Allah to enter me into Jannah." Addressing her by her title, Rasulullah ﷺ said, "Old women will not enter Jannah." When the lady was turning away in tears, Rasulullah ﷺ sent someone to give her the message that she would not enter Jannah as an old woman because Allah says:

إِنَّا أَنْشَأْنَاهُنَّ إِنْشَاءً (35) فَجَعَلْنَاهُنَّ أَبْكَارًا (36)

Verily, We have created them (maidens) of special creation. 36. And made them virgins. (Al-Waqia:35-36)

Awf bin Malik Ashja'e ؓ Jokes with Rasulullah ﷺ

Awf bin Malik Ashja'e ؓ reports, "I went to Rasulullah ﷺ during the expedition to Tabuk while he was in a very small leather tent. I greeted Rasulullah ﷺ with Salam and he replied, I asked, 'May I enter?' When Rasulullah ﷺ permitted me to enter, I asked, 'All of me, O Rasulullah ﷺ?' Rasulullah ﷺ replied, 'All of you.' I then entered." Walid bin Uthman bin Abu Aliya explains that Awf bin Malik ؓ joked "All of me" because the tent was very small. *(Abu Dawud in Al Bidayah wan Nihayah)*

Aisha ؓ and Abu Sufian ؓ Joke with Rasulullah ﷺ

Ibn Abu Mulaika ؓ narrates that when Aisha ؓ only cracked a few jokes with Rasulullah ﷺ, her mother said, "O Rasulullah ﷺ! Many of our tribe's jokes come from the Kinana tribe." "In fact," Rasulullah ﷺ remarked, "this tribe is the subject of many of our jokes." *(Bukhari in Adab).* Abul Haitham reports from someone that he heard Abu Sufian bin Harb ﷺ joking with Rasulullah ﷺ in the house of his daughter Ummu Habiba ﷺ who was one of Rasulullah ﷺ's wives. Abu Sufian ﷺ said, "By Allah! As soon as I left you alone (stopped fighting you), all the Arabs also left you, otherwise the horned ones and hornless ones would all still be fighting because of you." Rasulullah ﷺ smiled as he said, "You and what you say, O Abu Handhala." *(Zubair in Bakkar, Ibn Asakir in Kanzul Ummal)*

The Sahabah Throw Melons at Each Other and the Statement of Ibn Sirin About Their Humor

Bakr bin Abdullah says, "Although the Sahabah of Rasulullah ﷺ used to throw melons at each other, they were still the most resolute men when matters were serious." *(Bukhari in Adab).* Qurra narrates that he said to Ibn Sirin, "Did the Sahabah joke and play?" Ibn Sirin replied, "They were just like other people. Abdullah bin Omar ﷺ used to say the following in jest:

"He is so miserly that loves to drink wine from the money of his companions and dislikes to part with his own money" *(Majma'uz Zawa'id)*

Nu'aiman ﷺ Plays a Trick on Suwaibit ﷺ

Ummu Salamah ﷺ narrates that Abu Bakr ﷺ went on a trade journey to Busra. Accompanying him were Nu'aiman ﷺ and Suwaibit bin Harmala ﷺ, both of them were veterans of the Battle of Badr. Suwaibit ﷺ was in charge of the goods, Nu'aiman ﷺ asked him for something to eat. Suwaibit ﷺ refused saying that they would have to wait for Abu Bakr ﷺ. Nu'aiman ﷺ who was a joker and full of tricks, went to the people of the locality with his camel in trail. "Who will buy from me an intelligent Arab slave?" he announced. When some people agreed to the sale, Nu'aiman ﷺ warned, "He is a good talker and may claim to be a free person. If you intend letting him go on this pretext of his, let it be and do not complicate matters for me and do not make the purchase." "No!" the people insisted, "We shall buy him from you in exchange for 10 young camels." Nu'aiman ﷺ returned, leading the camels and the buyers along with him. He said to them, "There he is. Grab him!" Suwaibit ﷺ pleaded, "He is lying! I am a free man." "He has already told us about you," the people said as they threw a rope around his neck and took him away. When Abu Bakr ﷺ returned and was informed about what had happened, he went to the people with his companions, returned the 10 camels to them and got Suwaibit ﷺ back. Rasulullah ﷺ was informed about the incident and it kept him and the Sahabah laughing for an entire year. *(Ahmad, Abu Dawud, Tayalisi, Rooyani, Isabah, Ibn Abdul Birr in Isti'ab)*

Nu'aiman ﷺ Plays a Trick on a Bedouin

Rabe'ah bin Uthman ﷺ narrates that a Bedouin once came to see Rasulullah ﷺ and put his camel to sit in the courtyard of the Masjid. Some of the Sahabah then suggested to Nu'aiman bin Amr Ansari ﷺ who was referred to as An-Nu'aiman, "We have a strong desire to eat some meat so why don't you slaughter that camel for us to eat. Rasulullah ﷺ will then recompense the owner for it." Nu'aiman ﷺ went ahead to slaughter it and when the Bedouin came out of the Masjid and saw his camel slaughtered, he screamed, "Oh dear! My camel has been slaughtered, O Muhammad!" Rasulullah ﷺ came out and asked, "Who did that?" When the Sahabah informed him that it was Nu'aiman ﷺ, Rasulullah ﷺ searched him. After making queries about his whereabouts, Rasulullah ﷺ finally found him in the house of Subagha bint Zubair bin Abdul Muttalib ﷺ. He was hiding in a

hole and covered himself with palm leaves bark. Pointing his finger towards the hole, someone shouted as he said, "I have not seen him, O Rasulullah ﷺ!" When Rasulullah ﷺ got Nu'aiman ﷺ out of the hole, his face was messed with the palm bark that had fallen onto it. "What made you do that?" Rasulullah ﷺ asked him. "O Rasulullah ﷺ!" Nu'aiman ﷺ submitted, "The same people who led you to me were the ones who instructed me to do it." Rasulullah ﷺ then smiled as he started wiping Nu'aiman ﷺ's face. Thereafter, Rasulullah ﷺ recompensed the Bedouin for his camel. *(Ibn Abdul Birr in Ist'iab, Zubair bin Bakkar in Isabah)*

Nu'aiman ﷺ Plays a Trick on Makhrama bin Naufal ﷺ

Abdullah bin Mus'ab ﷺ narrates that Makhrama bin Naufal bin Uhaib Zuhri ﷺ was an extremely old blind man in Madinah who had already reached the age of 115. One day he stood in the Masjid ready to urinate when the people started shouting at him. It was then that Nu'aiman bin Amr bin Rifa'ah bin Harith bin Sawad Najari ﷺ came to him and led him to the corner of the Masjid saying, "Sit here." There he made him sit and urinate. As Makhrama urinated, the people started to scream at him. When he had finished, Makhrama ﷺ asked, "Shame on you people! Who was it that brought me here'?" When he was informed that it was Nu'aiman, Makhrama ﷺ cursed him saying. "Take note! I swear by Allah that if I ever get the upper hand over him, I will hit him most severely with this staff of mine." After some time, Makhrama ﷺ had forgotten about the incident when Nu'aiman ﷺ came to him. At the time, Uthman ﷺ was performing salah in the corner of the Masjid and it was his habit not to ever pay attention to anything else whilst performing salah. Nu'aiman ﷺ asked Makhrama ﷺ, "Are you still after Nu'aiman?" "O yes," Makhrama ﷺ said, "Where is he? Lead me to him." Nu'aiman ﷺ then led Makhrama ﷺ to Uthman ﷺ saying, "Here he is. Grab him!" Makhrama ﷺ then took his staff into both hands and hit Uthman ﷺ so hard that his head was severely injured. Someone then told Makhrama ﷺ, "It was the Amirul Mu'minin that you hit!" When Makhrama ﷺ's tribe the Banu Zuhra heard about the incident, they got together to punish Nu'aiman ﷺ but Uthman ﷺ said, "May Allah's mercy be far from him. Leave Nu'aiman ﷺ alone because he is a veteran of Badr." *(Isti'ab, Isabah)*

Statements of the Sahabah About the Generosity of Rasulullah ﷺ

Abdullah bin Abbas ﷺ says, "Rasulullah ﷺ was the most generous of people. He was even more generous on Ramadhan when he met Jibra'el ﷺ every night and revised the Qur'an with him. Rasulullah ﷺ was even more generous than the blowing wind that benefits all and sundry." *(Bukhari, Muslim in Safwatus Safwa, Ibn Sa'd).* Jabir ﷺ says, "Rasulullah ﷺ never said 'No' to anything asked of him." *(Bukhari, Muslim in Al Bidayah wan Nihayah).* In a lengthy Hadith from Abdullah bin Abu Bakr, Abu Sa'eed ﷺ says, "Rasulullah ﷺ never refused thing asked of him." *(Ahmad, Haythami).* Ali ﷺ also says, "When asked to do something, Rasulullah ﷺ always said 'yes' when he intended doing it and would remain silent when he did not intend doing it when it was not to the benefit of the person asking. He never said 'No' to anything asked of him." *(Tabrani in Awsat, Haythami)*

Rasulullah ﷺ's Generosity Towards Rubayi bint Mu'awwidh and to Ummu Sumbula ﷺ

Rubayi bint Mu'awwidh bin Afra ﷺ says, "My father Mu'awwidh bin Afra ﷺ sent me to Rasulullah ﷺ with a Saa of fresh dates topped with slices of newly grown cucumbers because Rasulullah ﷺ loved cucumbers. Rasulullah ﷺ had then just received some jewels from Bahrain so he scooped up a handful of the jewels and gave them to me." Another narration states that Rasulullah ﷺ filled her hand with either jewels or gold. *(Tabrani, Haythami)* Rasulullah ﷺ told her, "Adorn yourself with these." *(Ahmad, Haythami, Tirmidhi in Al Bidayah wan Nihayah).* Ummu Sumbula ؓ narrates that she once presented a gift to Rasulullah ﷺ, his wives refused to accept it, saying, "We cannot accept this." They took it when Rasulullah ﷺ instructed them to do so. Rasulullah ﷺ then allotted to her a piece of land between 2 mountains. It was this piece of land that Abdullah bin Jahash ؓ bought from Hasan bin Ali ؓ. *(Tabrani, Haythami).* Other incidents about the generosity of Rasulullah ﷺ are in the chapters concerning spending of wealth in the Path of Allah.

The Generosity of the Sahabah

Abdullah bin Omar ؓ reports that a woman once came to Rasulullah ﷺ saying, "I want to give this garment to the most generous of all Arabs." Pointing to Sa'eed bin Al Aas ؓ who was standing there, Rasulullah ﷺ said, "Give it to this young man." It is for this reason that such garments are referred to as Sa'ediya. *(Zubair bin Bakkar, Ibn Asakir in Muntakhab Kanzul Ummal).*

Preferring Others Above Oneself

Abdullah bin Omar ؓ says, "There passed a time when we had so much concern for each other that none of us (Sahabah) thought himself more worthy of a Dinar or a Dirham than his fellow Muslim brother. Unfortunately, we are now in a time when Dinars and Dirhams are more beloved to us than our fellow Muslim brothers." *(Tabrani, Haythami).* Several incidents have passed in the chapter dealing with spending on others despite being in need and other stories about the Ansar. There, incidents were mentioned how they gave others despite their intense thirst and need for clothing and other necessities.

Patience and perseverance: Eercising Patience in Illness

Abu Sa'eed Khudri ؓ reports that he once visited Rasulullah ﷺ when Rasulullah ﷺ was suffering extreme fever and was covered in a blanket. Placing his hand on the blanket, Abu Sa'eed ؓ said, "What a high fever you have, O Rasulullah ﷺ!" Rasulullah ﷺ remarked, "Thus are difficulties intensified for us and likewise are the rewards multiplied." "O Rasulullah ﷺ!" Abu Sa'eed ؓ asked, "Who are the people who suffer the most difficulties?" "The Ambiya ﷺ," came the reply. "Who next?" Abu Sa'eed ؓ asked further. Rasulullah ﷺ replied, "The Ulema." When Abu Sa'eed ؓ asked who was next, Rasulullah ﷺ informed him, "The pious people. Some of them are so troubled by lice that they are killed and others are so impoverished that they own only the garment they wear. Despite all of this, they are as pleased with difficulties as any of you are pleased with bounties." *(Ibn Majah, Ibn Abi Dunya, Hakim in Targheeb wat Tarheeb, Bayhaqi in Kanzul Ummal, Abu Nu'aym in Hilya).* Abu Ubaidah bin Hudhaifa ؓ reports from his aunt Fatima ؓ that she was with a few women who visited Rasulullah ﷺ when he was suffering high fever. Because of the intensity of the fever, Rasulullah ﷺ had a water bag hung overhead from a branch and lay beneath it so that drops of water fell on to his head. "O Rasulullah ﷺ!" she said, "Why don't you pray to Allah to cure you?" Rasulullah ﷺ replied, "Those who suffer the most difficulties are the Ambiya ﷺ, then those closest to them, then those closest to them and then those closest to them." *(Bayhaqi in Kanzul Ummal, Ahmad, Tabrani in Majma'uz Zawa'id).* Aisha ؓ narrates that when Rasulullah ﷺ was once overcome with pain, he was in great suffering and turned from side to side on his bed. Aisha ؓ asked, "Would you not be angry with any of us if we

had to do this?" Rasulullah ﷺ replied, "Difficulties will continue harassing a Mu'min but whenever he is pricked by a thorn or suffers any other pain, a sin is forgiven and a stage (in the Hereafter) is elevated." *(Ibn Sa'd, Hakim, Bayhaqi in Kanzul Ummal, Ahmad, Haythami)*

The People of Quba and the Ansar Patiently Bear Fever

Jabir narrates that fever (in the human form Allah had granted it) once sought permission to see Rasulullah ﷺ. "Who is it?" Rasulullah ﷺ asked. "Ummu Mildam," was the reply. Rasulullah ﷺ instructed it to go to the people of Quba and when it did only Allah knows how many people were afflicted. When the people of Quba came to complain about it to Rasulullah ﷺ, he asked, "You have a choice. If you wish, I shall pray to Allah to remove it from you or if you prefer, it could remain amongst you and thereby be a means of purification for you from sin." "Can you really do this?" they asked. When Rasulullah ﷺ conformed that he could, they bade him to let it stay. *(Ahmad in Targheeb wat Tarheeb, Abu Ya'la, Ibn Hibban).* Salman ؓ narrates that when fever once sought permission to see Rasulullah ﷺ, he asked who it was. It replied, "I am fever. I peel at flesh and suck blood." "Go to the people of Quba," Rasulullah ﷺ instructed. It then proceeded there and after a while the people of Quba came to Rasulullah ﷺ with pale faces. When they complained about the fever to Rasulullah ﷺ, he asked them, "You have a choice. If you wish, I shall pray to Allah and He will remove it from you or if you prefer, you could leave it to remain amongst you and thereby be a means of removing all the sins you may have left." Their reply was, "Why should we not want our sins forgiven? Leave it, O Rasulullah ﷺ!" *(Tabrani, Haythami, Bayhaqi in Al Bidayah wan Nihayah).* Abu Hurairah ؓ narrates that fever once came to Rasulullah ﷺ with the request, "O Rasulullah ﷺ! Sent me to those people or those of your companions who are most beloved to you." "Go to the Ansar," Rasulullah ﷺ said. It then went to them and floored them. The Ansar then came to Rasulullah ﷺ pleading, "O Rasulullah ﷺ! Fever has afflicted us, so do pray to Allah to cure us." Rasulullah ﷺ prayed and they were cured. A woman then ran behind Rasulullah ﷺ saying, "O Rasulullah ﷺ! Pray for me as well because I am from the Ansar. Pray for me as you have prayed for them." Rasulullah ﷺ replied, "What do you prefer? Would you rather have me pray for you and that you be cured or would you rather exercise patience and remain with the illness in which case it will be incumbent for you to enter Jannah?" She submitted 3 times, "No! I swear by Allah O Rasulullah ﷺ that I would rather exercise patience." She added, "By Allah! I shall never jeopardize His Jannah for anything." *(Bayhaqi in Al Bidayah wan Nihayah, Bukhari in Adab)*

One of the Sahabah Patiently Bears with his Fever

Aisha ؓ narrates that Rasulullah ﷺ once did not notice someone who regularly attended his gatherings. When Rasulullah ﷺ asked what the matter was that the person was not to be seen, the Sahabah informed Rasulullah ﷺ that the man had been struck down by a tense fever. "Let us go and visit him," Rasulullah ﷺ said to them. When Rasulullah ﷺ entered the room, the young man started to cry. "Do not cry," Rasulullah ﷺ consoled him, "because Jibra'el ﷺ has just informed me that fever is my Ummah's share of Jahannam if they suffer it in this world, they will not be subjected to Jahannam in the hereafter, InsAllah." *(Tabrani, Haythami)*

The Patience of Abu Bakr ؓ and Abu Darda ؓ

Abu Safar reports that when some people came to visit Abu

Bakr ؓ during his illness, they said, "O Khalifa of Rasulullah ﷺ! Should we not get a physician to see you?" "He has already been to see me," Abu Bakr ؓ informed them. "And what did he say to you?" they asked. Referring to Allah Abu Bakr ؓ replied, "He said, 'I do as I please'." *(Ibn Sa'd, Ibn Abi Shaybah, Ahmad in Zuhd, Abu Nu'aym in Hilya, Kanzul Ummal).* Mu'awiya bin Qurra ؓ narrates that when Abu Darda ؓ fell ill, his friends came to visit him. "What is the problem?" they asked. "My sins," he replied. "What do you wish for?" they enquired. "I wish for Jannah," was his reply. "Should we get a physician for you?" they asked. Abu Darda ؓ replied, "It is Allah Who has made me lay here with this illness." *(Abu Nu'aym in Hilya, Ibn Sa'd)*

The Patience Mu'adh ؓ and his Family exercised during Plague

Abdur Rahman bin Ghanam reports that when the plague struck Sham, Amr bin Al Aas ؓ announced, "This plague is a punishment, so flee from it to the valleys and gullies." When news of this statement reached Shurabil bin Hasana ؓ, he became incensed and said, "Amr bin Al Aas is wrong! I was a companion of Rasulullah ﷺ at a time when Amr was more astray than the camel his family owns. This plague is the Du'a of your Nabi ﷺ, the mercy of your Rabb and the way in which many pious people lost their lives in the past." When this news reached Mu'adh ؓ, he prayed. "O Allah! Grant the family of Mu'adh their share in full" His 2 daughters then passed away in the plague and his son Abdur Rahman was also afflicted. Advising his son, Mu'adh ؓ recited the verse: ٱلْحَقُّ مِنْ رَّبِّكَ فَلَا تَكُونَنَّ مِنَ الْمُمْتَرِينَ

(147) *(This is) the truth from your Lord. So be you not one of those who doubt. (Al-Baqara:147)*

To this, his son replied with the following verse of the Qur'an: سَتَجِدُنِي إِنْ شَاءَ اللّٰهُ مِنَ الصَّابِرِينَ (102)

Insha Allah (if Allah will), you shall find me of As-Sabirin (the patient ones, etc.)." (As-Saffat:102)

The plague then struck Mu'adh ؓ himself and it showed up first on the back of his hand. "This," Mu'adh ؓ said, "is more beloved to me than red camels." When he saw a man weeping beside him, he asked, "What makes you weep?" The man replied, "I am crying over the knowledge I used to gain from you which I shall no longer be gaining after your demise." "Do not cry," Mu'adh ؓ consoled him, "because although Ibrahim عليه السلام was in a place where there was no knowledge to be learnt, Allah gave him the knowledge. After I die, seek knowledge from 4 men: Abdullah bin Mas'ood ؓ, Abdullah bin Salam ؓ, Salman ؓ and Abu Darda ؓ." *(Ibn Khuzaima, Ibn Asakir in Kanzul Ummal, Ahmad, Bazzar in Mazma'uz Zawa'id).* Another narration states that Mu'adh ؓ, Abu Ubaidah bin Jarrah ؓ, Shurabil bin Hasana ؓ and Abu Malik Ash'ari ؓ were all struck by the plague on the same day. Mu'adh ؓ said, "This is the mercy of your Rabb, the Du'a of your Nabi ﷺ and the manner in which the lives of the pious ones before you were taken. O Allah! Grant the family of Mu'adh their full share of this mercy." The night was yet to over when his only son Abdur Rahman was struck by the plague. Abdur Rahman was the most beloved person to Mu'adh ؓ and it was with his name that Mu'adh ؓ received his title of Abu Abdur Rahman. Returning from the Masjid, Mu'adh ؓ found his son restless and asked, "O Abdur Rahman! How are you?" In reply, his son said, "Beloved father, "The truth is from your Rabb so never be among those who doubt." Mu'adh ؓ said to him, "If Allah wills, you will soon find me to be among the patient ones." Abdur Rahman passed away that night and Mu'adh ؓ buried him the following morning. Mu'adh ؓ was also afflicted with the plague and when the pangs of death struck him, they struck more

severely than they did any other person. Each time he regained consciousness from his coma; he opened his eyes and said, "O Rabb! You may strangle as often as you please because I swear by Your honor that You know how much my heart loves You." *(Abu Nu'aym in Hilya, Hakim, Ahmad, Haythami)*

Abu Ubaidah bin Jarrah ؓ and Other Muslims Persevere Through the Plague

Shahr bin Howshab reports from a man from his tribe called Raba that when the plague started to spread, Abu Ubaidah bin Jarrah ؓ addressed the people saying, "O people! This plague is the mercy of your Rabb, the Du'a of your Nabi ﷺ and the manner in which the lives of the pious ones before you were taken. Abu Ubaidah prays that Allah grant him his full share of it." Abu Ubaidah ؓ was then struck with the plague and passed away. Mu'adh bin Jabal ؓ was then appointed commander over the troops and he later addressed the people saying, "O people! This plague is the mercy of your Rabb, the Du'a of your Nabi ﷺ and the manner in which the lives of the pious ones before you were taken. Mu'adh prays that Allah grant his family their full share of it." His son Abdur Rahman was then struck by the plague and passed away. Mu'adh ؓ then prayed to Allah that the plague strike him and it did with the first signs appearing on his palm. The narrator says, "I saw Mu'adh ؓ looking at his palm and then turning it around saying, 'I swear by Allah that I would not like to exchange you for anything in this world.'" After Mu'adb ؓ passed away, Amr bin Al Aas ؓ was appointed commander. When he stood up to address the people, he said, "O people! When this plague strikes, it spreads like wildfire so seek shelter from it in the mountains." To this, Abu Wathila Hudhali ؓ remarked, "You are wrong! By Allah! I was in the company of Rasulullah ﷺ when you were worse than this donkey of mine!'! Amr ؓ's response was, "By Allah! I shall not reply to what you are saying but I swear by Allah that we shall not be staying on here." The narrator continues, "Amr ؓ then left, the people scattered and Allah removed the plague from them. When the opinion of Amr bin Al Aas ؓ reached (Amirul Mu'minin) Omar bin Khattab ؓ, he said "I swear by Allah that he did not condemn it." *(Ibn Is'haq in Al Bidayah wan Nihayah)*

The Statement of Mu'adh ؓ Concerning the Plague of Amwas

Abu Qilaba narrates that when the plague struck Sham, Amr bin Al Aas ؓ said, "This is a plague that has come so flee from it to the mountains and gullies." When this statement reached Mu'adh ؓ, far from confirming it, he said, "Not at all! It is martyrdom, a mercy and the Du'a of your Nabi ﷺ." Abu Qilaba narrates further, "While I knew that it was a form of martyrdom and a mercy, I did not know how it was the Du'a of Rasulullah ﷺ until I was informed that while performing salah one night, Rasulullah ﷺ thrice made Du'a saying, 'Then let it be fever or a plague.' The following morning, one of his family members asked, 'O Rasulullah ﷺ! I overheard you making a Du'a last night.' 'You heard it?' Rasulullah ﷺ asked. 'I certainly did,' came the reply. Rasulullah ﷺ then explained, 'I asked my Rabb not to let my Ummah perish through drought and this Du'a was accepted. I prayed to Allah never to allow an enemy to overpower them and annihilate them, this was granted. I prayed to Him never to let my Ummah break into groups, waging wars against each other. This Du'a was refused. It was then I thrice said, 'Then let it be fever or a plague'." *(Ahmad, Haythami)*

Abu Ubaidah bin Jarrah ؓ's Joy at the Plague

Urwa bin Zubair ؓ reports that Abu Ubaidah bin Jarr'ah ؓ

and his family were unaffected by the plague of Amwas when he prayed to Allah saying, "O Allah! Grant the family of Abu Ubaidah ☙ their share." When a sore erupted on his little finger, Abu Ubaidah started looking at thinking that it was a sign of the plague but he was assured that it meant nothing. He then said, "I wish that Allah blesses it because when he blesses something little, it becomes a lot. (Ibn Asakir). Harith bin Abu Umaira Harithi narrates that Mu'adh bin Jabal ☙ sent him to ask Abu Ubaidah ☙ how he was when the plague struck him. Abu Ubaidah ☙ showed Harith a sore at had erupted on his palm. It looked serious to Harith and gave him a fright. Abu Ubaidah ☙ swore in the name of Allah that he would not want to trade it even for red camels. (Ibn Asakir in Muntakhab Kanzul Ummal)

Patiently bearing loss of sight: Zaid bin Arqam ☙ Exercises Patience When he Loses His Sight

Zaid bin Arqam ☙ says, "When I developed a cataract, Nabi ☙ came to visit me. He asked, 'O Zaid! What would you do if you lost your eye?' 'I shall exercise patience and look forward to the rewards from Allah,' I replied. Rasulullah ☙ then said, 'If after losing your eye you exercise patience and anticipate the rewards, your reward will be Jannah.'" (Bukhari in Adab). Anas ☙ narrates that he accompanied Rasulullah ☙ to visit Zaid bin Arqam ☙ when he was suffering from an eye ailment. Rasulullah ☙ said to him, "O Zaid! If you lose your eye and exercise patience and anticipate the rewards, you will meet Allah without a single sin against your name." (Ahmad, Haythami). Zaid bin Arqam ☙ narrates that Rasulullah ☙ once visited him when he was ill. Rasulullah ☙ said, "No harm will come to you from this illness but what will you do if you reach old age after my demise and then lose your eyesight?" Zaid ☙ replied, "I shall then exercise patience and anticipate the rewards." "In that case," Rasulullah ☙ remarked, "you shall enter Jannah without reckoning." Zaid ☙ later did go blind after Rasulullah ☙'s demise. (Abu Ya'la, Ibn Asakir, Bayhaqi in Kanzul Ummal). After the demise of Rasulullah ☙, Zaid ☙ did go blind but Allah restored his eyesight before he passed away, May Allah shower his mercies on him. (Tabrani, Haythami)

A Sahabi Exercises Patience Upon the Loss of his Eyesight

Qasim bin Muhammad narrates that some people visited a Sahabi who had lost his eyesight, he said, "I wanted my sight to see Rasulullah ☙. Rasulullah ☙ has passed away, it would not please me to use them to see a gazelle from the gazelles of Tabala, a place in Yemen." (Bukhari in Adab, Ibn Sa'd)

Rasulullah ☙'s Patience Upon the Demise of is Son Ibrahim ☙

Anas ☙ says, "I saw Rasulullah ☙'s son Ibrahim ☙ surrendering his soul in front of Rasulullah ☙. With his eyes filled with tears, Rasulullah ☙ said, 'Although the eyes weep and the heart grieves, we shall say only that which pleases Allah. O Ibrahim! I swear by Allah that we are deeply saddened by your demise.'" (Ibn Sa'd). Makhul narrates that Rasulullah ☙ was leaning on Abdur Rahman bin Auf ☙ as he entered the room where his son Ibrahim was surrendering his soul. When the boy passed away, Rasulullah ☙'s eyes filled with tears. Abdur Rahman bin Auf ☙ said, "O Rasulullah ☙! Is this not what you forbade people from doing? When the Muslims see you weep, they will also weep." When his tears stopped, Rasulullah ☙ said, "This tears is because of mercy, soft-heartedness and whoever is not merciful will not have mercy shown to him. What we have been forbidding people from doing is from wailing and from praising attributes of a deceased person that he never possessed.

Had it not been for Allah's promise to gather people together for reckoning, for the fact that death is a well traveled path and for the fact that the last of us will meet with the first of us, we would have felt grief more severe than this. Because of our sorrow over his death our eyes weep and our hearts grieve but we shall never say anything that will anger our Rabb. The balance of his suckling will be done in Jannah." (Ibn Sa'd)

Rasulullah ☙'s Patience Upon the Death of his Grandson

Usama bin Zaid ☙ narrates that they were with Rasulullah ☙ one day when one of his daughters sent for him with the message that her son was dying. Rasulullah ☙ instructed someone saying, "Go and inform her that to Allah belongs all that He takes and all that He gives and He has decreed a fixed term for everything. Instruct her to exercise patience and to look forward to the rewards from Allah for her patience." The messenger returned to Rasulullah ☙ saying, "She is begging you to come in the name of Allah." Rasulullah ☙ got up to leave and a few of the Sahabah went with him. Amongst them were Sa'd bin Ubadah ☙, Mu'adh bin Jabal ☙, Ubay bin Ka'b ☙ and Zaid bin Thabit ☙. Usama ☙ says, "I also accompanied them and when the child was given to Rasulullah ☙, he was quivering in the throes of death making a sound as if the soul was in an old water bag. As Rasulullah ☙'s eyes welled with tears, Sa'd ☙ asked, 'What is this tear, O Rasulullah ☙!' Rasulullah ☙ replied, 'This is the mercy that Allah has placed in the hearts of His servants and it is only upon His merciful servants that Allah showers His mercy.'" (Tayalisi, Ahmad, Abu Dawud, Tirmidhi, Ibn Majah, Abu Awana, Ibn Hibban in Kanzul Ummal)

Rasulullah ☙'s Patience on the Martyrdom of his Uncle Hamza ☙

Abu Hurairah ☙ reports that as Rasulullah ☙ stood by the body of Hamza bin Abdul Muttalib ☙ when he was martyred, the sight was more painful than anything he had ever witnessed because the body had been savagely mutilated. Rasulullah ☙ said words similar in effect to: "May Allah shower His mercy on you. As far as I know, you were one who maintained family ties and always did good works. By Allah! If it were not for the added grief it would cause your family, I would prefer to leave you in this condition so that Allah may resurrect you from the bellies of wild animals that will eat your corpse." Rasulullah ☙ then added, "Take note! I swear by Allah that to avenge you, I shall have 70 of the Kuffar mutilated as they have done to you." It was then that Jibra'el arrived with the following verse:

وَإِنْ عَاقَبْتُمْ فَعَاقِبُوا بِمِثْلِ مَا عُوقِبْتُم بِهِ وَلَئِن صَبَرْتُمْ لَهُوَ خَيْرٌ لِّلصَّابِرِينَ (126)

And if you punish (your enemy, O you believers in the Oneness of Allah), then punish them with the like of that with which you were afflicted. But if you endure patiently, verily, it is better for As-Sabirin (the patient ones, etc.). (An-Nahl:126)

Rasulullah ☙ then paid the compensation for not fulfilling the oath and restrained himself from taking action. (Bazzar, Tabrani, Haythami, Hakim). Abdullah bin Abbas ☙ narrates that when Rasulullah ☙ saw what was done to his uncle Hamza ☙, he remarked, "If it were not for the grief it would cause to our women, I would not bury him and would leave him in this condition that Allah would resurrect him from the bellies of wild animals and birds of prey." When the sight grieved him too deeply, Rasulullah ☙ said, "If I get the upper hand over them (disbeliever), I shall mutilate 30 of them." It was then that Allah revealed the verse:

وَإِنْ عَاقَبْتُمْ فَعَاقِبُوا بِمِثْلِ مَا عُوقِبْتُم بِهِ وَلَئِن صَبَرْتُمْ لَهُوَ خَيْرٌ لِّلصَّابِرِينَ (126) وَاصْبِرْ وَمَا صَبْرُكَ إِلَّا بِاللهِ وَلَا تَحْزَنْ عَلَيْهِمْ وَلَا تَكُ فِي ضَيْقٍ مِّمَّا يَمْكُرُونَ (127)

And if you punish (your enemy, O you believers in the Oneness of Allah), then punish them with the like of that with which you were afflicted. But if you endure patiently, verily, it is better for As-Sabirin (the patient ones, etc.). And endure you patiently (O Muhammad ﷺ), your patience is not but from Allah. And grieve not over them (polytheists and pagans, etc.), and be not distressed because of what they plot. (An-Nahl:126-127)

Rasulullah ﷺ then gave instructions for the body of Hamza ﷺ to be turned towards the Qibla and performed the Janaza salah with 9 Takbirs. All the other martyrs were then brought to Rasulullah ﷺ. Each time a martyr was brought, he was placed beside Hamza ﷺ and Rasulullah ﷺ would perform the Janaza salah for the martyr and Hamza ﷺ. In this manner, Rasulullah ﷺ performed the Janaza salah 72 times for Hamza ﷺ. Rasulullah ﷺ stood by the Sahabah until the martyrs were buried. After the above verse was revealed, Rasulullah ﷺ forgave the disbeliever and forsook the idea of mutilation. *(Tabrani, Haythami)*

Rasulullah ﷺ's Grief Upon the Demise of Zaid bin Haritha ﷺ

Usama bin Zaid ﷺ says, "When my father Zaid bin Haritha ﷺ was martyred, I went to see Rasulullah ﷺ. When he saw me, Rasulullah ﷺ started weeping. When I again went to him the next day, he said, 'Even today I felt the grief I feel when I saw you yesterday.'" *(Ibn Abi Shaybah, Ibn Mani, Bazzar, Bawardi, Dar Qutni in Afrad, Sa'eed bin Mansur in Muntakhab Kamzul Ummal).* Khalid bin Shmair ﷺ reports that when Zaid bin Haritha ﷺ was martyred and Rasulullah ﷺ went to the Sahabah, Zaid ﷺ's daughter burst out crying in front of Rasulullah ﷺ. Rasulullah ﷺ then started weeping profusely, Sa'd bin Ubadah ﷺ asked, "What is this, O Rasulullah ﷺ?" "This," replied Rasulullah ﷺ, "is the longing a friend has for his friend." *(Ibn Sa'd)*

Rasulullah ﷺ's Grief Upon the Demise of Uthman bin Madh'un ﷺ

Aisha ﷺ reports that when Rasulullah ﷺ kissed Uthman bin Madh'un ﷺ after his demise, his eyes were flowing with tears. *(Tirmidhi in Isabah).* Aisha ﷺ says, "I saw Rasulullah ﷺ's tears flowing on the cheek of Uthman bin Madh'un ﷺ" *(Ibn Sa'd)*

Ummu Haritha ﷺ Exercises Patience Upon the Demise of her Son

Anas ﷺ reports that Haritha bin Suraqa ﷺ was killed during the Battle of Badr. Although he was a non-combatant, he was killed by a stray arrow. His mother came there asking, "O Rasulullah ﷺ! Tell me what has become of Haritha. If he is in Jannah, I shall exercise patience. If not, I shall show Allah what I will do." She was referring to wailing, which had not yet been forbidden at the time. "Shame on you!" Rasulullah ﷺ exclaimed, "Are you mad? There are 8 levels of Jannah and your son had reached Firdous which is the highest of them all." *(Bukhari, Muslim in Al Bidayah wan Nihayah).* Another narration *(Bayhaqi, Ibn Abi Shaybah in Kanzul Ummal, Hakim, Ibn Sa'd)* states that she said, "I shall exercise patience if he is Jannah. If not, I shall exert myself in crying." "O Ummu Haritha!" Rasulullah ﷺ consoled her, "There are many levels of Jannah and your son had reached Firdous which is the highest of them all." Yet another narration states that Rasulullah ﷺ said, "O Ummu Haritha! There is not only one Jannah. There are many levels of Jannah and he is in Firdous which is the highest of them all." She then said, "I shall then exercise patience." *(Tabrani in Kanzul Ummal).* Anas ﷺ states that Ummu Haritha ﷺ said, "O Rasulullah ﷺ! If he is in Jannah, I shall not weep and will not be grieved. However, if he is in Jahannam, I shall continue weeping as long as I live." "O Ummu Harith!" Rasulullah ﷺ consoled her. "There is not only one Jannah. There are many levels of Jannah

and Harith is in Firdous which is the highest of them all." She then returned laughing as she said, "Well done, Harith! Well done!" *(Ibn Najjar in Kanzul Ummal)*

Ummu Khallad ﷺ Exercises Patience Upon the Demise of her Son

Muhammad bin Thabit bin Qais bin Shammas ﷺ narrates that when the Muslims fought the Banu Quraiza tribe, a man from the Ansar called Khallad ﷺ was martyred. Someone went to inform her that he had been martyred, she went to receive his body while wearing her veil. Someone said, "Khallad has been killed and you are wearing a veil?!" She replied, "I may have lost Khallad but I have not lost my modesty." When Rasulullah was informed of this, he said. "Take note that Khallad ﷺ shall receive the rewards of 2 martyrs." Someone asked the reason, Rasulullah ﷺ replied, "Because he was killed by the Ahlul Kitab." *(Ibn Sa'd, Abu Nu'aym in Kanzul Ummal, Abu Ya'la in Isabah)*

Abu Talha ﷺ and Ummu Sulaim ﷺ Exercise Patience Upon the Demise of Their Son

Anas ﷺ reports that his mother Ummu Sulaim ﷺ once came to his father Abu Anas saying, "Today I have come with news that you will dislike." His response was: "You are always coming with news from that Bedouin that I dislike." She said, "He is a Bedouin whom Allah has selected and made a Nabi." "What is the news you have brought?" he asked. "Wine has been forbidden," she replied. To this he said, "Then this is where we separate." He then died as a disbeliever. When Abu Talha ﷺ approached Ummu Sulaim ﷺ with a marriage proposal, she said, "I cannot marry you when you are a disbeliever." "No," exclaimed Abu Talha ﷺ. "By Allah! That is not your motive." "Then what is my motive?" asked Ummu Sulaim ﷺ. "Your motive is gold and silver." he replied. "In that case," retorted Ummu Sulaim ﷺ, "I make you and the Nabi of Allah ﷺ witness to the fact that if you accept Islam, I shall be content with you giving me only your acceptance of Islam as dowry. I want nothing else." "Who will stand guarantee for me to this agreement?" Abu Talha ﷺ asked. Ummu Sulaim ﷺ then said, "O Anas! Get up and go with your uncle." Anas ﷺ got up and with Abu Talha ﷺ's hand on his shoulder, they proceeded. When they got close to where Rasulullah ﷺ was and he heard their voices, he remarked. "Here is Abu Talha with the radiance of Islam sparkling between his eyes." Abu Talha ﷺ greeted Rasulullah ﷺ and then professed: اَشْهَدُ اَنْ لاَ اِلَهَ اِلاَّ اللهُ وَاَشْهَدُ اَنَّ مُحَمَّدًا عَبْدُهُ وَرَسُوْلُهُ
I testify that there is none worthy of worship but Allah and that Muhammad ﷺ is the Rasul of Allah

Rasulullah ﷺ then married him to Ummu Sulaim ﷺ on the condition of his accepting Islam. Abu Talha ﷺ later fathered a son who was the apple of his father's eye. However, when the child started to walk, Allah decided to take the child away. Still unaware that the child had passed away, Abu Talha ﷺ came to Ummu Sulaim ﷺ asking, "How is my son, O Ummu Sulaim?" "Better than he had been (because death has relieved him of his illness)," she replied. She then said further, "Why don't you have your supper because it is already late." After serving him his supper, she asked, "O Abu Talha! When a trust is given to some people for safekeeping and the owners of the trust send a message after some time that they require it back, can those who have it in trust refuse to return it?" "Not at all" replied Abu Talha ﷺ. Ummu Sulaim ﷺ then said, "Your son has left this world." "Where is now?" Abu Talha ﷺ asked. When she informed that the child was in the inner room, Abu Talha ﷺ went there, opened the face and recited: اِنَّا لِلّهِ وَاِنَّا اِلَيْهِ رَاجِعُوْنَ
"To Allah we belong and to Him shall we return"

He then went to inform Rasulullah ﷺ about the statement of Ummu Sulaim ﷺ, to which Rasulullah ﷺ said, "I swear by the Being Who has sent me with the truth that because of her patience at the demise of her child, Allah has already placed another son in her womb." After Ummu Sulaim ﷺ had delivered the child, Rasulullah ﷺ said, "O Anas! Go and tell your mother that after cutting the umbilical cord, she should not feed anything to the baby without first sending for me." Anas says, "She then gave the baby in my arms and I took it to Rasulullah ﷺ. When I placed the baby before Rasulullah ﷺ, he asked for 3 Ajwa dates. When I brought them, he removed the stones, chewed on them and then opened the child's mouth to place it inside. The child immediately started turning it about in his mouth, to which Rasulullah ﷺ remarked, 'The Ansar certainly love dates.' Thereafter, Rasulullah ﷺ said to me, 'Go and tell your mother, 'May Allah bless you in this child and make him obedient and pious." (Bazzar, Haythami, Ibn Sa'd). Anas ﷺ narrates that Abu Talha ﷺ's son was ill and passed away one day when he was out. When he returned, Abu Talha ﷺ asked, "How is my son?" Ummu Sulaim ﷺ replied, "He is calmer than he had been." She then served him supper and after he had completed, the couple engaged in sexual relations. It was only afterwards that she told him to bury the child. The next morning when Abu Talha ﷺ informed Rasulullah ﷺ about what had happened, Rasulullah ﷺ asked, "Did you have relations with your wife last night?" After receiving a positive reply, Rasulullah ﷺ prayed, "O Allah! Bless them." Ummu Sulaym ﷺ then gave birth to a son. Abu Talha ﷺ then instructed Anas ﷺ to carefully take this child to Rasulullah ﷺ. Ummu Sulaim ﷺ also sent some dates with the baby and when Rasulullah ﷺ took the child, he asked, "Has something come with him?" When the Sahabah informed him that some dates had also come, Rasulullah ﷺ asked for them. After chewing them, Rasulullah ﷺ took it from his mouth, placed it in the child's mouth and rubbed it on the child's palate called Tahnik. Rasulullah ﷺ then named the child Abdullah. (Bukhari). Rasulullah ﷺ said, "Allah shall bless them in their night." Sufian reports that a man from the Ansar mentioned, "I saw 9 of Ummu Sulaim ﷺ and Abu Talha ﷺ's children all of whom were proficient scholars of the Qur'an." (Bukhari)

Abu Bakr ﷺ was patience on the death of his Son Abdullah ﷺ

Qasim bin Muhammad narrates that Abdullah ﷺ the son of Abu Bakr ﷺ was struck by an arrow in the battle for Ta'if. After healing his wound reopened 40 days after the demise of Rasulullah ﷺ, causing him to pass away. When he went to his daughter Aisha ﷺ, Abu Bakr ﷺ said, "Dear daughter! By Allah! It seems as if a goat was pulled by the ear and removed from our house." She said, "All praise belongs to Allah who has strengthened your heart and kept you firm on what is right." After leaving, he again came to her saying, "Dear daughter! Are you not afraid that Abdullah may have been buried while he was still alive?" Aisha ﷺ declared, "Dear father! إِنَّا لِلَّهِ وَإِنَّا إِلَيْهِ رَاجِعُوْنَ
To Allah we belong and to Him shall we return."

Abu Bakr ﷺ then said, "I seek protection from Allah the All Hearing and All Knowing from the accursed Saitan! Dear daughter! Each and every person has influences. One comes from an angel and the other from Saitan." When a delegation from the Thaqif tribe of Ta'if came to Abu Bakr ﷺ, he still had with him the arrow that killed his son. Taking it out, he asked them, "Does any of you recognize this arrow?" Sa'd bin Ubaid ﷺ of the Banu Ajlan tribe replied, "It is I who made that arrow, who attached its feathers and head and who shot it." Abu Bakr ﷺ said, "It was this arrow that killed my son Abdullah. All praise belongs to that

Allah Who honored him with martyrdom at your hand and Who did not disgrace you with death as a Kafir at his hand. Allah is the greatest Protector." (Hakim). Bayhaqi states that Abu Bakr ﷺ said, "The good that Allah grants is indeed vast to both of you."

The Patience of Uthman ﷺ and Abu Dhar ﷺ

Amr bin Sa'eed ﷺ narrates that whenever a child was born to Uthman ﷺ, he would ask for the child while it was still wrapped after birth. He would then smell the child. When asked why he did this, Uthman ﷺ replied, "I like to do this because should anything happen to the child, there would be love for the child in my heart, I would then be rewarded for the greater patience I would need to exercise." (Ibn Sa'd in Kanzul Ummal). Someone once said to Abu Dhar ﷺ, "None of your children seem to stay alive?" Abu Dhar ﷺ replied, "All praise belongs to Allah Who takes them away from this temporary world and stores them as a treasure for me in the eternal abode of the Hereafter." (Abu Nu'aym in Kanzul Ummal)

The Patience of Omar ﷺ Upon the Demise of his Brother Zaid ﷺ

Omar bin Abdur Rahman bin Zaid bin Khattab narrates that when a calamity befell Omar ﷺ would console himself saying, "When I was struck with the calamity of the death of my brother Zaid bin Khattab, I managed to exercise patience. Why should I not do so now?" Omar ﷺ saw the person who killed his brother Zaid ﷺ, he said to him, "It is pity that you killed my brother. I think of him every time the wind blows." (Hakim, Bayhaqi)

The Patience of Safiya ﷺ Upon the Death of her Brother Hamza ﷺ

Abdullah bin Abbas ﷺ reports that when Hamza ﷺ was martyred, his sister Safiya ﷺ, unaware of what had happened, came looking for him. When she met her nephew Ali ﷺ and her son Zubair ﷺ, Ali ﷺ said to Zubair, "Tell your mother that her brother has been martyred." "No," replied Zubair ﷺ, "You go ahead and tell "your aunt." "How is Hamza'?" Safiya ﷺ asked. The 2 men made it seem her that they knew nothing. She then approached her nephew Rasulullah ﷺ who said, "I fear for her sanity if she knew the truth." Rasulullah ﷺ placed his hand on her chest and made Du'a. Then when he informed her, she wept as she said: إِنَّا لِلَّهِ وَإِنَّا إِلَيْهِ رَاجِعُوْنَ
"To Allah we belong and to Him shall we return."
Rasulullah ﷺ then stood by the mutilated body and said, "If it were not for the grief it would cause to our women, I would not bury him and would leave him in this condition so that Allah would resurrect him from the bellies of wild animals and birds of prey." Thereafter Rasulullah ﷺ gave instructions for all the martyrs to be brought forward and he started performing the Janaza salah for them. 9 bodies were brought and laid beside that of Hamza ﷺ. Rasulullah ﷺ performed the salah with 7 Takbirs. The bodies were then taken away while that of Hamza ﷺ was left. Thereafter, another 9 bodies were brought and Rasulullah ﷺ performed the Janaza salah for them with 7 Takbirs. These bodies were then carried away while that of Hamza ﷺ was left behind. Yet again, another 9 bodies were brought and Rasulullah ﷺ performed the Janaza salah for them also with 7 Takbirs. These bodies were then carried away while that of Hamza ﷺ was left behind. This continued until Rasulullah ﷺ had performed the Janaza salah for them all. (Hakim, Ibn Abi Shaybah, Tabrani in Muntakhab Kanzul Ummal, Bazzar in Majma'uz Zawa'id)

Zubair bin Awam ﷺ narrates, "A woman came running during the Battle of Uhud and would have seen the dead bodies when Rasulullah ﷺ called out, 'Stop the woman! Stop the woman!' Rasulullah disliked that women should see the bodies.

When I guessed that she was my mother Safiya, I ran to her and reached her before she could reach the dead. She was a strong woman and struck me in the chest saying, 'Get away from me. The ground does not belong to you!' I said, 'Rasulullah ﷺ has emphatically prohibited you from going there.' She then halted in her tracks and took out 2 sheets saying, 'I have brought these 2 sheets for my brother Hamza ﷺ. The news of his death has already reached me and I want you to bury him in these.' We then took the sheets to enshroud Hamza ﷺ in but found next to him someone from the Ansar who was also killed and mutilated as Hamza ﷺ was. Because we felt difficult to enshroud Hamza ﷺ in 2 sheets while the Ansari had one, we decided that one sheet would be used for Hamza ﷺ and the other for the Ansari. After measuring the 2 sheets, we found the one to be larger than the other. To decide who would have which sheet, we then drew lots between the 2 and enshrouded each one in the sheet that fell to his lot." (Bazzar, Ahmad, Abu Ya'la, Haythami). Discussing the martyrdom of Hamza ﷺ, it is reported that when Safiya bint Abdul Muttalib ﷺ came to see her brother, Zubair ﷺ met her saying, "Dear mother! It is the instruction of Rasulullah ﷺ that you return." She said, "Why should I? I have already heard that my brother's body has been mutilated. This has taken place for the sake of Allah and we are pleased with Allah's decree. I shall definitely exercise patience and look forward to the rewards from Allah." When Zubair ﷺ reported her words to Rasulullah ﷺ, Rasulullah ﷺ said, "Let her go." She then went to the body of Hamza ﷺ and prayed for his forgiveness. Rasulullah ﷺ then gave instructions for him to be buried. (Ibn Is'haq in Isabah)

The Patience of Ummu Salamah ﷺ on the Death of her Husband

Ummu Salamah ﷺ says, "My husband Abu Salama ﷺ once came to me from Rasulullah ﷺ saying, 'I have heard from Rasulullah ﷺ something that gives me great pleasure. Rasulullah ﷺ said that whenever a Muslim is afflicted with any calamity, he will be rewarded and granted something better in return if he recites: إِنَّا لِلَّهِ وَإِنَّا إِلَيْهِ رَاجِعُوْنَ

'To Allah we belong and to Him shall we return'
followed by the Du'a: أَللّهُمَّ اجُرْنِيْ فِيْ مُصِيْبَتِيْ وَاخْلُفْ لِيْ خَيْرًا مِّنْهَا
'O Allah! Reward me in my calamity and replace me with something better'
I learnt the Du'a from him and when Abu Salama ﷺ passed away, I recited: إِنَّا لِلَّهِ وَإِنَّا إِلَيْهِ رَاجِعُوْنَ
'To Allah we belong and to Him shall we return.'
اللّهُمَّ اجُرْنِيْ فِيْ مُصِيْبَتِيْ وَاخْلُفْ لِيْ خَيْرًا مِّنْهَا
'O Allah! Reward me in my calamity and replace me with something better' I then thought to myself, 'Where will I get someone better than Abu Salama ﷺ?' However, after completing my Iddah, I was one day dying a piece of leather when Rasulullah ﷺ sought permission to see me. After washing the Qaridh leaves used for dying from my hands, I permitted him in and placed for him a leather cushion stuffed with the bark of a palm. Rasulullah ﷺ sat on it and then proposed for my hand in marriage. After Rasulullah ﷺ had spoken, I said, 'O Rasulullah ﷺ! I have no reason for not wanting to marry you. I am a woman who is very possessive and I fear that you may see something in me because of my possessiveness that would cause Allah to punish me. In addition to this, I am not young anymore and I have children. Rasulullah ﷺ replied, 'As for your possessiveness, Allah will soon dispel it. As for your age, I am affected by advanced age just as you are. As for your children, they shall be my children as well.' I then accepted, saying, 'I shall then hand myself over to the Rasul of Allah ﷺ.' Allah really did replace

Abu Salama ﷺ for me with someone better, with Rasulullah ﷺ." (Ahmad, Nasa'ee, Ibn Majah, Tirmidhi in Al Bidayah wan Nihayah, Ibn Sa'd)

The Patience Usaid bin Hudhair ﷺ after his Wife's Death

Aisha ﷺ says that they were returning from Hajj or Umrah and were welcomed at Dhul Hulaifa where the children of the Ansar normally met their families. When the people met Usaid bin Hudhair ﷺ and gave him the news of his wife's death, he covered his face and started to weep. "May Allah forgive you," Aisha ﷺ said to him, "You are a companion of Rasulullah ﷺ and are one of the first people to enter the fold of Islam. Why would you be weeping over a woman?" Usaid ﷺ uncovered his face and said, "You are right. I swear by my life that after the death of Sa'd bin Mu'adh ﷺ" I have no right to weep over anyone else especially after what Rasulullah ﷺ said about him." "What did Rasulullah ﷺ say about him?" Aisha ﷺ asked. Usaid ﷺ then informed her that Rasulullah ﷺ said, "The Throne of Allah actually shook at the death of Sa'd bin Mu'adh." Aisha ﷺ says, "At that time, Usaid bin Hudhair ﷺ was walking between Rasulullah ﷺ and I." (Ibn Abi Shaybah, Ahmad, Shashi, Ibn Asakir in Kanzul Ummal, Ibn Sa'd, Hakim). Another narration states that Usaid bin Hudhair ﷺ said, "Have I no right to weep when I heard Rasulullah ﷺ say, 'The pillars of the Arsh shook with the death of Sa'd bin Mua'dh.'" (Abu Nu'aym in Kanzul Ummal). Another narration states that he said, "Why should I not weep when I heard Rasulullah ﷺ say..." The rest of the narration is the same as the one above. (Tabrani in Majma'uz Zawa'id)

The Patience of Abdullah bin Mas'ood ﷺ Upon the Death of his Brother Utba ﷺ

Awn reports that Abdullah bin Mas'ood ﷺ heard about the death of his brother Utba ﷺ, he started to weep. When asked what made him weep, he replied, "He was my real brother and my companion with Rasulullah ﷺ. Despite this, I would not have liked to die before him because for him to pass away and for me to anticipate the rewards for my patience at losing him is dearer to me than for me to pass away and for him to anticipate the rewards for his patience at losing me." (Abu Nu'aym in Hilya). Khaithama ﷺ narrates that Abdullah bin Mas'ood ﷺ received the news of the death of his brother Utba ﷺ, his eyes filled with tears as he said, "This weeping is because of the mercy that Allah has placed in the heart that man has no control of." (Ibn Sa'd)

The Patience of Abu Ahmad bin Jahash ﷺ Upon the Death of his Sister Zainab bint Jahash ﷺ

Abdullah bin Abu Salit ﷺ narrates, "I saw Abu Ahmad bin Jahash ﷺ carrying the funeral bier of his sister Zainab bint Jahash ﷺ. He was blind and in tears. As the people started crowding about the bier, I heard Omar ﷺ say, 'O Abu Ahmad ﷺ! Move away from the bier so the people will not hurt you.' Abu Ahmad ﷺ replied, 'O Omar! It is from her that I received every good. This carrying her bier cools the heat of the grief I am feeling.' 'Hold tight,' Omar ﷺ said, 'Hold on tight.'" (Ibn Sa'd).

The Patience of the Muslims Upon the Death of Omar ﷺ

Ahnaf bin Qais ﷺ says, "I once heard Omar ﷺ say, 'The Quraish are leaders and when any of them enter a door, an entire group of people enter with them.' I however did not fully understand what he meant until he was stabbed. On his deathbed, he instructed Suhaib ﷺ to lead the salah for 3 days and also gave instructions for food to be served to the people until his successor was appointed. When the people returned from the funeral, the food was served and the tablecloths laid out. However, because of their grief, the people refrained from eating. Abbas bin Abdul Muttalib ؓ then said, 'O people! We ate and drank after the demise of Rasulullah ﷺ and we also ate and drank after the demise of Abu Bakr ؓ. Now it is also necessary for us to eat this food." He stretched out his hand and ate. The people followed suit. I then understood what Omar ؓ said about the Quraish being leaders." *(Ibn Sa'd in Kanzul Ummal, Tabrani, Haythami)*

Abu Bakr ؓ and Ali ؓ Advise People to Exercise Patience Upon the Deaths of Close Relatives

Abu Uyayna ؓ reports that when Abu Bakr ؓ consoled a person, he said, "There is no calamity when there is patience and no benefit when there is impatience. What precedes death is simple while that which follows it is difficult. If you think of the loss of Rasulullah ﷺ, your tragedy will seem light and Allah will inflate your reward." *(Ibn Abi Khaithama, Dinowi, Ibn Asakir in Kanzul Ummal)*. Sufian reports that when consoling Ash'ath bin Qais ؓ upon the death of his son, Ali ؓ said, "It is the right of your family relationship that you should grieve but if you exercise patience, Allah shall replace the loss of your son. If you are patient, fate will take its course and you will be rewarded. However, if you are irritated, fate will still take its course and you will be sinful." *(Ibn Asakir in Kanzul Ummal)*

An Ansari Woman Perseveres with her Epilepsy

Abdullah bin Abbas ؓ narrates that Rasulullah ﷺ was once in Makkah when a woman from the Ansar came to him saying, "O Rasulullah ﷺ! There is this evil spirit that overpowers me, please cure me." Rasulullah ﷺ said to her, "If you persevere with this problem, you will appear on the Day of Qiyamah without any sins and will have no reckoning to give." She replied, "I swear by the Being Who has sent you with the truth, I prefer to persevere until I meet Allah." She then added, "However, I fear that the evil spirit would strip me naked." Rasulullah ﷺ then prayed for her and whenever she feared that the spirit was approaching, she would cling on to the shroud of the Kabah and say to it, "Get away!" It would then leave her. *(Bazzar)*. Ata ؓ reports that Abdullah bin Abbas ؓ once said to him, "Should I not show you a woman who shall be amongst the inhabitants of Jannah?" "Please do," Ata ؓ responded. Abdullah bin Abbas ؓ then said, "There was this black woman who once approached Rasulullah ﷺ with the request, 'Please pray for me because I suffer from epilepsy and in the fit my clothing opens up and my body becomes exposed.' Rasulullah ﷺ said to her, 'If you want, you can persevere and earn yourself Jannah, otherwise I can pray to Allah to cure you.' 'Not at all,' she replied, 'I shall rather persevere (and be assured of Jannah), but do pray to Allah that my body does not become exposed.' Rasulullah ﷺ then made Du'a for her. *(Ahmad, Bukhari, Muslim)* Another narration adds that Ata ؓ then saw the lady holding on to the shroud of the Kabah. She was called Ummu Zufar ؓ and she was a tall black woman. *(Bukhari in Al Bidayah wan Nihayah)*

The Incident of a Man with a Woman who had been a Prostitute During the Period of Ignorance

Abdullah bin Mughaffal ؓ narrates that a woman who had been a prostitute during the period of ignorance once passed by a man who stretched out his hand towards her. "Stop!" she cautioned, "Allah has obliterated Shirk and brought Islam, I am therefore no longer a prostitute." He then left her and turned away. However, as he continued looking at her, he struck his face on a wall and was injured. He then went to Rasulullah ﷺ and

reported the incident to him. Rasulullah ﷺ said, "You are a person for whom Allah intends good. When Allah had good intentions for a person, He hastens the punishment for his sins in this world so that he suffers no punishment in the Hereafter. On the other hand, when Allah does not intend good for a person, He holds back the punishment in this world until the person receives his punishment in full on the Day of Judgment when the punishment will be much worse." *(Bayhaqi in Kanzul Ummal)*

The Statement of Omar ؓ that Everything Which Affects a Mu'min is a Calamity if he does not Like It

Abdullah bin Khalifa narrates that he was with Omar ؓ when the strap of his sandal broke. Omar ؓ recited:

إِنَّا لِلَّهِ وَإِنَّا إِلَيْهِ رَاجِعُوْنَ

"To Allah we belong and to Him shall we return"
Thereafter (to explain why he said this), Omar ؓ said, "Everything that is unpleasant to you is regarded as a calamity." *(Ibn Sa'd, Ibn Abi Shaybah, Abd bin Humaid, Ibn Mundhir, Bayhaqi)*

Sa'eed bin Musaiib narrates that when the front portion of Omar ؓ's shoe broke, he exclaimed: إِنَّا لِلَّهِ وَإِنَّا إِلَيْهِ رَاجِعُوْنَ
"To Allah we belong and to Him shall we return"
"O Amirul Mu'minin!" the people enquired, "You are reciting

إِنَّا لِلَّهِ وَإِنَّا إِلَيْهِ رَاجِعُوْنَ

for a mere front portion of a shoe?" Omar ؓ replied, "When anything that he finds unpleasant happens to a Mu'min, it is regarded as a calamity." *(Marwazi in Kanzul Ummal)*

Omar ؓ Commands Abu Ubaidah ؓ to Persevere Against the Enemy and the Perseverance of Uthman ؓ Until he was Martyred

Aslam reports that Abu Ubaidah ؓ once wrote to Omar bin Khattab ؓ informing him that the Romans were launching a massive military offensive and also stating the grave dangers the Muslim army faced. In his reply after duly praising Allah, Omar ؓ wrote, "Whenever any difficulty afflicts a Mu'min, Allah creates ease afterwards and no difficulty can overpower 2 eases (ref. Qur'an). Allah states in His book:

يَا أَيُّهَا الَّذِينَ آمَنُوا اصْبِرُوا وَصَابِرُوا وَرَابِطُوا وَاتَّقُوا اللَّهَ لَعَلَّكُمْ تُفْلِحُونَ (200)

O you who believe! Endure and be more patient (than your enemy), and guard your territory by stationing army units permanently at the places from where the enemy can attack you, and fear Allah, so that you may be successful. (Al-Imran:200) *(Malik, Ibn Abi Shaybah, Ibn Abi Dunya, Ibn Jareer, Hakim, Bayhaqi in Kanzul Ummal)*. Abdur Rahman bin Mahdi says that Uthman ؓ possessed 2 virtues that neither Abu Bakr ؓ nor Omar ؓ had. One was his perseverance until it led to his martyrdom and the other was that he united the Muslims on one standard version of the Qur'an. *(Abu Nu'aym in Hilya)*

Gratitude: Rasulullah ﷺ Prolongs his Sejdah in Gratitude to Allah

Abdur Rahman bin Auf ؓ reports, "Rasulullah ﷺ once left the Masjid and headed for his room on the upper storey. After entering, he faced towards the Qibla and fell into Sejdah. He prolonged his Sejdah so much that I thought his soul had been taken. I therefore went close to him and sat down. Raising his head from the ground, he asked, 'Who is there?' When I told him that I was Abdur Rahman, he asked further, 'What is the matter?' 'O Rasulullah ﷺ!' I explained, 'You Sejdah was so long that I feared Allah may have taken your soul in it.' Rasulullah ﷺ said, 'Jibra'el ؑ just came to me saying that Allah says, 'Whoever invokes My mercy on you (recites Durud), I shall shower My mercies on him and whoever invoked peace on you (sends

Salams), I shall bless him with peace.' I therefore made Sejdah to Allah in gratitude.'" *(Ahmad, Haythami)*. Mu'adh bin Jabal ؓ says, "I once approached O Rasulullah ﷺ and found him standing and performing salah. He continued standing until dawn broke and made such a long Sejdah that I thought his life had been taken. Afterwards he asked, 'Do you know what that (long Sejdah) was for?' 'Allah and His Rasul ﷺ know best,' I submitted. After repeating the question three or four times, Rasulullah ﷺ explained, 'I performed as much salah as my Rabb had ordained for me when my Rabb appeared and addressed me. At the end of the conversation, he asked me, 'What shall I do with your Ummah?' 'O my Rabb,' I declared, 'you know best what You shall do with them.' After repeating the question three or four times, Allah again asked, 'What shall I do with your Ummah?' When I again submitted that He knew best, Allah said, 'I shall never make you grieve over your Ummah.' I then fell into Sejdah because my Rabb is appreciative and loves those who show gratitude.'" *(Tabrani, Haythami)*

Abdur Rahman Abu Bakr ؓ narrates that when he once went to visit Rasulullah ﷺ, Rasulullah ﷺ was busy receiving revelation. When the revelation stopped. Rasulullah ﷺ asked Aisha ؓ to pass him his shawl. He then left the house and entered the Masjid where he found some people besides whom there was no one else there. Rasulullah ﷺ sat on one side until the person addressing them had completed his talk. Thereafter, Rasulullah ﷺ recited Surah Tanzil Sejdah (Surah) and made such a long Sejdah that people living as far as 2 miles away arrived there as people started telling each other about the Sejdah. Aisha ؓ sent a message to her family telling them to come because she was seeing Rasulullah ﷺ do something she had never seen him do before. After Rasulullah ﷺ had lifted his head (from Sejdah), Abu Bakr ؓ asked, "O Rasulullah ﷺ! You prolonged your Sejdah so much?" Rasulullah ﷺ replied, "I prostrated to my Rabb out of gratitude for the Ummah He has granted me. There shall be 70,000 of them who shall enter Jannah without reckoning." Abu Bakr ؓ said, "O Rasulullah ﷺ! You have an Ummah that is large and extremely pure. You should have asked for more for them." This he repeated two or three times when Omar ؓ added, "May my parents be sacrificed for you, O Rasulullah ﷺ! You have asked a great gift for your Ummah." *(Tabrani, Haythami)*

The Gratitude Rasulullah ﷺ Showed When he saw a Man Suffering From a Terminal Disease

Abdullah bin Omar ؓ narrates that when Rasulullah ﷺ once passed by a man suffering from a terminal disease, he dismounted from his animal and made Sejdah. When Abu Bakr ؓ passed by the man, he also dismounted and made Sejdah and Omar ؓ followed suit when he passed by. *(Tabrani, Haythami)*

Rasulullah ﷺ Thanks Allah for Returning His Family Members Safely From an Expedition

Ali ؓ reports that Rasulullah ﷺ dispatched an expedition comprising of his family members, he prayed, "O Allah! If You return them to me safely, I owe it to You to thank You as You ought to be thanked." It was not long afterwards that they came back safely and Rasulullah ﷺ said, "All praise belongs to Allah for all the bounties of Allah." "O Rasulullah ﷺ!" Ali ؓ asked, "Did you not say that if Allah returned them safely, you owed it to Him to thank Him as He ought to be thanked?" "Did I not just do that?" Rasulullah ﷺ replied. *(Bayhaqi in Kanzul Ummal)*

The Gratitude of a Man to Whom Rasulullah ﷺ Gave a Single Date

Anas ؓ reports that when a beggar once came to Rasulullah ﷺ, he gave instructions for a date to be given to the man. The beggar however thinking it to be too little, threw it away. Another beggar then arrived and again Rasulullah ﷺ gave instructions for a date to be given to him. The man exclaimed in joy, "Subhanallah! A date from Rasulullah ﷺ!" Rasulullah ﷺ then said to one of the servants, "Go to Ummu Salamah and instruct her to give this man the 40 Dirhams she has with her." Hasan narrates that when a beggar once came to Rasulullah ﷺ and he gave him a date, the beggar exclaimed in scorn, "SubhanAllah! A Nabi from the Ambiya giving a mere date as Sadaqah!" Rasulullah ﷺ said to him, "Don't you know that there are multitudes of atoms in that?" Thereafter, another man came to beg. Rasulullah ﷺ gave him a date as well, he exclaimed in joy, "A date from a Nabi from the Ambiya! I shall never part with this date as long as I live and shall always anticipate its blessings." Rasulullah ﷺ asked people to be good to the man and he soon became a wealthy man. *(Bayhaqi in Kanzul Ummal)*.

The Gratitude Omar ؓ Showed to Allah for Elevating his Status and his Words Concerning Patience and Gratitude

Sulayman bin Yasir narrates that when Omar ؓ once passed by a place called Dajnan, he said, "I once saw myself grazing animals in this place for my father Khattab. By Allah! As far as 1 know, he was a stern and harsh man. By the grace of Allah I then became the guide of the Ummah of Muhammad ﷺ." He then recited the following couplets (which mean):

"There is nothing in the things you see besides superficial enjoyment while wealth and children are temporary, all that shall remain is Allah" He spurred his camel on saying, "Howb!"*(Ibn Sa'd, Ibn Asakir in Muntakhab Kanzul Ummal)*. Omar ؓ once said, "When 1 come to the conveyance of gratitude and the conveyance of patience, 1 care not which of the two 1 ride." *(Ibn Asakir in Muntakhab Kanzul Ummal)*

The Statement of Omar ؓ Concerning a Leper and Another Man

Ikrama ؓ reports that Omar ؓ once passed by a leper who was also blind, deaf and dumb. Addressing the people with him, Omar ؓ asked, "Do you see any of Allah's bounties in this man?" When the people replied that they saw none, Omar ؓ said, "Why not? Do you not see that he is able to urinate with ease without the urine holding back or coming out with difficulty? This is and extremely great bounty from Allah." *(And bin Humaid in Kanzul Ummal)*. Ibrahim reports that Omar ؓ heard a man say, "O Allah! I wish to spend my wealth and my life in Your path." To this, Omar ؓ said, "Why doesn't any of you remain silent, exercising patience when in difficulty and expressing gratitude when enjoying prosperity?"*(Abu Nu'aym in Hilya, Kanzul Ummal)*

What Omar ؓ said to a Man who Greeted Him, His Letter to Abu Musa Ash'ari ؓ and His Statement about People who are Grateful

Anas ؓ reports that after a man greeted Omar ؓ and he had replied to the greeting, Omar ؓ asked him, "How are you?" "I only have the praises of Allah to sing before you," the man replied. "That is exactly what I wanted from you," said Omar ؓ? *(Malik, Ibn Mubarak, Bayhaqi in Kanzul Ummal)*. Hasan Basri narrates that Omar ؓ wrote the following letter to Abu Musa Ash'ari ؓ: "Be content with the sustenance Allah provides for you in this world because Allah gives more sustenance to some of His servants and less to others to test all of them. He tests those whom He has given plenty to see whether they are grateful. His gratitude to Allah fulfils the duty he owes to Allah for the sustenance and bounties Allah has blessed him with." *(Ibn Abi Hatim in Kanzul Ummal)*. Omar ؓ once said, "The grateful ones always received more from Allah so seek more from Allah. This is because Allah says: لَئِنْ شَكَرْتُمْ لَأَزِيدَنَّكُمْ

...If you give thanks (by accepting Faith and worshipping none but Allah), I will give you more (of My Blessings)... (Ibrahim:7) (Dinowri in Kanzul Ummal)

Uthman ؓ Shows Gratitude for not Encountering Some People who were Involved in Evil

Sulaiman bin Musa narrates that Uthman bin Affan ؓ was once called to deal with some people who were involved in some evil activity. When Uthman ؓ went to them, he found that they had dispersed even though the effects of their evil were still visible. Uthman ؓ praised Allah for not encountering them and as a token of gratitude, he freed a slave. *(Abu Nu'aym in Hilya)*

The Statement of Ali ؓ Concerning Bounties and Gratitude

Ali ؓ once said, "Every bounty should be followed by gratitude and gratitude is followed by an increase (in the bounty). Gratitude and an increase in bounties are directly proportional to each other. Therefore, Allah will never stop increasing the bounties on His servant until the servant stops being grateful in which case they stop." *(Bayhaqi)*. Muhammad bin Ka'b Qurazi narrates that Ali bin Abi Talib ؓ once said, "It never occurs that Allah opens the door of gratitude and closes the door of increasing bounties. It also never occurs that Allah opens the door of Du'a and closes the door of acceptance. Similarly, it never occurs that Allah opens the door of Tauba and closes the door of forgiveness. I shall recite this from Allah's Book. Allah says: ادْعُونِي أَسْتَجِبْ لَكُمْ

Invoke Me, (i.e. believe in My Oneness (Islamic Monotheism)) (and ask Me for anything) I will respond (Ghafir:60)

Allah also says: لَئِنْ شَكَرْتُمْ لَأَزِيدَنَّكُمْ

...If you give thanks (by accepting Faith and worshipping none but Allah), I will give you more (of My Blessings)... (Ibrahim:7)

Allah says further: فَاذْكُرُونِي أَذْكُرْكُمْ

Therefore remember Me (by praying, glorifying, etc.). I will remember you... (Al-Baqara:152)

Allah also says:

وَمَنْ يَعْمَلْ سُوءًا أَوْ يَظْلِمْ نَفْسَهُ ثُمَّ يَسْتَغْفِرِ اللَّهَ يَجِدِ اللَّهَ غَفُورًا رَحِيمًا (110)

And whoever does evil or wrongs himself but afterwards seeks Allah's Forgiveness, he will find Allah Oft-Forgiving, Most Merciful. (Nisa:110) (Ibn Majah, Askari in Kanzul Ummal)

The Statements of Abu Darda ؓ, Aisha ؓ and Asma ؓ Concerning Gratitude

Abu Darda ؓ said, "When a night or a day passes without people seeing me suffer any difficulty, I see this as an extremely great bounty from Allah." Another narration quotes him as saying, "The person who sees Allah's bounties only in food and drink has a limited understanding and has his punishment ever present." *(Ibn Asakir in Kanzul Ummal, Abu Nu'aym in Hilya)*. Aisha ؓ once said, "Gratitude is binding on the person who drinks even plain water that enters his body without difficulty and then exits without difficulty." *(Ibn Abi Dunya in Kanzul Ummal)*. When her son Abdullah bin Zubair ؓ was martyred, Asma bint Abu Bakr ؓ happened to lose something that Rasulullah ﷺ gave her and which she kept in a bag. When she finally found it after some searching, she fell into Sejdah in gratitude to Allah. *(Tabrani, Haythami)*

The Fervor of Rasulullah ﷺ

Abdullah bin Mas'ood ؓ narrates that when the Muslims went for the Battle of Badr, every 3 of them had to share a camel to ride in turns because of a shortage of transport. Abu Lubaba ؓ and Ali ؓ shared a camel with Rasulullah ﷺ and when it was Rasulullah ﷺ's turn to walk, they both offered to walk instead. Rasulullah ﷺ refused saying, "Neither are you two stronger than I nor am I less in need of rewards than you." *(Nasa'ee in Al Bidayah wan Nihayah, Bazzar in Majmu'az Zawa'id)*

The Sahabah Exert Themselves to Stand in Salah to Earn Rewards

Muttalib bin Abu Wada'ah ؓ reports that when Rasulullah ﷺ once saw a person performing salah while sitting down, he said, "The salah of a sitting person is half in reward of the salah of a standing person." Thereafter the Sahabah exerted themselves greatly to perform salah while standing despite suffering extreme hunger and weakness at times. *(Tabrani, Haythami)*. Anas ؓ reports that when Rasulullah ﷺ arrived in Madinah, he was suffering with high fever and the other Muslims were also suffering of the same. When Rasulullah ﷺ entered the Masjid one day and found the people sitting and performing salah because of their illness, he said, "The salah of a sitting person is half in reward of the salah of a standing person." *(Ahmad in Fat'hul Bari)*. Abdullah bin Amr bin Al Aas ؓ narrates that when Rasulullah ﷺ and his companions from Makkah arrived in Madinah, they were so afflicted by the fever in Madinah that they became extremely ill. They were able to perform salah only while sitting down. Allah cured Rasulullah ﷺ from the condition. Rasulullah ﷺ left his room one day and found the Sahabah sitting and performing salah, he said, "Take note that the salah of a sitting person is half in reward of the salah of a standing person." The Sahabah exerted themselves greatly to perform salah while standing despite their extreme weakness and illness solely for additional rewards. *(Ibn Is'haq in Al Bidayah wan Nihayah)*

The Incident of Kaba'ah bin Ka'b ؓ with Rasulullah ﷺ

Raba'ah bin Ka'b ؓ says, "I was Rasulullah ﷺ's servant and served him all day until he performed the Isha salah. I would then sit by his door when he entered his room saying to myself, 'Perhaps Rasulullah ﷺ will need something.' I would then remain sitting there hearing Rasulullah ﷺ say, 'SubhanAllahi wa Bihamdihi,' until I would get tired or until my eyes overwhelmed me and I would fall asleep right there. Seeing my fervor to serve him and feeling that he owed something to me, Rasulullah ﷺ one day asked me, 'O Raba'ah bin Ka'b! Ask from me and I shall give you.' 'O Rasulullah ﷺ!' I submitted, 'Allow me to think about it and then I shall inform you.' I then addressed myself saying, 'The things of this world are temporary and will soon come to an end. In any case, I have my preordained sustenance in this world which is sufficient for me and will come to me, it is therefore futile to ask Rasulullah ﷺ for some worldly thing. I shall therefore ask Rasulullah ﷺ for something of benefit for my life in the Hereafter because he enjoys an exalted status with Allah.' I then approached Rasulullah ﷺ and he asked, 'What have you decided, O Rabee'ah?' 'I have made a decision, O Rasulullah ﷺ,' I said, 'My request to you is to intercede on my behalf that Allah frees me from Jahannam.' Rasulullah ﷺ asked, 'Who told you to say this, O Rabee'ah?' I explained to him saying, 'O Rasulullah ﷺ! I swear by the Being Who has sent you with the truth that no one told me what to say. You asked me to ask from you and because you enjoy a high status in Allah's sight, I though the matter over. Realizing that the things of this world are temporary and will soon come to an end and that I have my preordained sustenance in this world which will come to me I decided to ask you for something of benefit for my life in the Hereafter.' Rasulullah ﷺ remained silent for a long while after which he said, 'I shall do that but do assist me against your carnal wish by making Sejdah in abundance.'" *(Ahmad in Al Bidayah wan Nihayah, Tabrani, Muslim, Abu Dawud).* Rabee'ah ؓ says, "I used to spend the night in the service of Rasulullah ﷺ bringing him his water for wudhu and seeing to his other needs. When he asked me to make a request, I said, 'I request your company in Jannah.' 'Anything else?' he asked. When I insisted that this was all, he said, 'Then assist me against your carnal wish by making Sejdah in abundance." *(Muslim in Targheeb wat Tarheeb)*

Abdul Jabbar bin Harith ؓ seeks Rewards for his Companionship with Rasulullah ﷺ

Abdul Jabbar bin Harith bin Malik Hadasi Manari ؓ narrates, "I was part of a delegation to Rasulullah ﷺ from the land of Sarat. When I came to Rasulullah ﷺ, I greeted him with the traditional Arab greeting saying, 'May you have a good morning!' Rasulullah ﷺ said, 'Allah has given Muhammad ﷺ and his Ummah another greeting. They greet each other with the words of Salam.' I then said: اللسلام عليك يا رسول الله
Rasulullah ﷺ replied by saying, وعَلَيْك السَّلَامُ
When he asked what my name was, I informed him that I was Jabbar bin Harith. I then accepted Islam and pledge my allegiance to Rasulullah ﷺ. After I had pledge my allegiance someone said to Rasulullah ﷺ, 'This Manari is one of the accomplished horsemen of his tribe.' Rasulullah ﷺ gave me a horse and I remained fighting by his side. Rasulullah ﷺ one day missed the neighing of the horse he had given me, he asked, 'Why do I not hear the neighing of the Hadasi's horse?' 'O Rasulullah ﷺ!' I explained, 'I was told that its neighing was disturbing you so I had it castrated to make it quiet.' Then Rasulullah ﷺ forbade castrating horses. Someone suggested me to request Rasulullah ﷺ for a note of guaranteeing for something as my cousin Tamim Dari ؓ had done. 'Did he ask for something of this world or for something of the Hereafter?' I asked. When I was told that it was for something of this world, I said, 'It was from this world that I have turned away. I shall rather ask Rasulullah ﷺ to assist me tomorrow when I appear before Allah." *(Ibn Mandah, Ibn Asakir in Muntakhab Kanzul Ummal)*

The Statement of Rasulullah ﷺ concerning Amr bin Taghlib ؓ and Amr ؓ's response

Amr bin Taghlib ؓ reports that when Rasulullah ﷺ gave something to some people and not to others, it appeared as if they were upset. Rasulullah ﷺ then said, "I give to some people only for fear of their impatience and agitation. Then there are those whom I hand over to the goodness and independence Allah has placed in their hearts. Amongst these people is Amr bin Taghlib." Amr bin Taghlib ؓ said, "I would not trade these words of Rasulullah ﷺ even for red camels." *(Bukhari in Al Bidayah wan Nihayah, Ibn Abdul Birr in Isti'ab)*

The Incident of Ali ؓ and Omar ؓ with a Man who Performed Tawaf with his Mother

Amr bin Hammad reports that Ali ؓ and Omar ؓ were leaving from performing Tawaf when they saw a Bedouin carrying his mother on his back reciting the following couplets which mean:

"1 am her conveyance that never bolts and when other conveyances become crazed, I shall not. She did more when she carried me and suckled me"

He then called out, لبيك اللهم لبيك

Addressing Omar ؓ, Ali ؓ said, "O Abu Hafs! Let us go back to perform Tawaf so that the mercy descending (on the Bedouin) may encompass us as well." They then started performing Tawaf as the Bedouin repeated:

"1 am her conveyance that never bolts and when other conveyances become crazed, I shall not. She did more when she carried me and suckled me"
(At your service, O Allah, I am at your service)" لبيك اللهم لبيك
At the same time, Ali ؓ reciting the following couplets (which mean):
"Allah is Most Appreciative if you care for your mother. He shall then grant you in abundance for your little effort."
(Bayhaqi in Kanzul Ummal)

Abdullah bin Omar ؓ looks Forward to the Rewards for his Stolen Camel and for Freeing Its Shepherd and Marries to Earn Rewards

Maymun bin Mahran reports that people from Harura who were associated with Najda, one of the leaders of the Khawarij once passed by a camel belonging to Abdullah bin Omar ؓ and took it along with them. The shepherd went to Abdullah bin Omar ؓ saying, "O Abu Abdur Rahman! Look forward to the rewards for your camel." "What has happened to her?" asked Abdullah ؓ. The shepherd replied, "The people from Harura who are associated with Najda passed by and took her along with them." "But how," Abdullah ؓ asked, "did they take the camel away and leave you alone?" "They took me along as well but I managed to escape from them," the shepherd replied. Abdullah ؓ asked him further, "What made you leave them and come to me when you would no longer be a slave if you escaped?" "Because I love you more than them," the man replied. Abdullah ؓ then enquired, "Will you swear by the Being besides Whom there is no god that you love me more than them?" When the shepherd swore on oath, Abdullah ؓ said, "Then I look forward to the reward for freeing you together with that of the came!" By so saying, he set the slave free. It was a while later when someone came to Abdullah bin Omar ؓ saying, "Do you still want that camel of yours." The person even took the name of the camel and continued, "She is there being sold in the marketplace." "Give me my shawl," Abdullah ؓ said and he stood up as he placed the shawl over his shoulders. He then sat down again and removed the shawl saying, "I had been looking forward to the rewards for losing her and will therefore not go out and get her back." *(Abu Nu'aym in Hilya, Siraj in Tarikh, Abu Nu'aym in Isabah).* Amr bin Dinar narrates that when Abdullah bin Omar ؓ made up his mind not to marry, his sister Hafsa ؓ said to him, "Get married because if your children pass away, you will be rewarded for your patience and if they live, they will make Du'a for you." *(Ibn Sa'd)*

The Words of Ammar ؓ on the Way to the Battle of Siffin

Abdur Rahman bin Abza ؓ reports that en route to Siffin when he was on the bank of the Euphrates River, Ammar bin Yasir ؓ said, "O Allah! If I knew that you would be pleased with me for throwing myself off a mountain and rolling down as I fall, I would certainly do so. O Allah! If I knew that you would be pleased with me for kindling a large fire and throwing myself into it, I would certainly do so. O Allah! If I knew that you would be pleased with me for throwing myself into the water and drowning, I would certainly do so. O Allah! I am fighting to please You and I am certain that you will never make me unsuccessful as long as I do things to please You." *(Ibn Sa'd, Abu Nu'aym in Hilya)*

The Statement of Abdullah bin Amr Concerning his Actions After the Demise of Rasulullah

Abdullah bin Arm bin Al Aas once said, "For me to do a good deed today is more beloved to me than 2 liked deeds done during the time of Rasulullah because when we were with Rasulullah, our only concern was the Hereafter and not this world. Today, however, the world has fallen for us." *(Abu Nu'aym in Hilya, Tabrani, Haythami)*

The Exertion of Our Guide Rasulullah

Alqama narrates that he asked Aisha, "Was Rasulullah in the habit of specially setting aside certain days for worship?" "Not at all," Aisha replied, "His deeds were perpetual, but which of you is capable of doing what Rasulullah did?" *(Bukhari, Muslim in Safwatus Safwa)*. Mughiera bin Shu'ba reports that Rasulullah stood in salah until his feet cut open." Someone asked, "Did Allah not forgive all your past and future errors?" he replied, "Should I then not be a grateful servant?" *(Bukhari, Muslim in Al Bidayah wan Nihayah, Ibn Sa'd)*

The Exertion of Uthman and Abdullah bin Zubair

Zubair bin Abdullah reports from his grandmother whose name was Zuhaima that Uthman fasted perpetually and stood in salah throughout the night save for a portion at the beginning of the night when he slept. *(Abu Nu'aym in Hilya, Muntakhab Kanzul Ummal)*. Mujahid narrates that the level of worship Abdullah bin Zubair reached was unmatched. When a flood prevented people from performing Tawaf, Abdullah bin Zubair performed several circuits swimming. *(Ibn Asakir in Muntakhab Kanzul Ummal)*. Qatan bin Abdullah narrates that Abdullah bin Zubair would fast for 7 days continuously to the extent that his intestines dried up. Hisham bin Urwa states that Abdullah bin Zubair would fast for 7 days continuously and it was only when he became extremely old that he reduced it to 3 days. *(Ibn Jareer in Muntakhab Kanzul Ummal)*

Statements of Anas and Ali Concerning the Bravery of Rasulullah

Anas says, "Rasulullah was the most handsome of people, the most generous and the bravest. When a frightening sound scared the people of Madinah one night, they ventured towards the sound. However, Rasulullah beat them to it and was already returning from the place when he met them. He was riding Abu Talha's bare-backed horse with a sword dangling from his neck. He assured the people saying, "There is nothing to be alarmed about. There is nothing to be alarmed about." Although the horse was known to be a lazy one, Rasulullah commented, "He was like an ocean, moving speedily and fluidly. This happened by the blessings of Rasulullah." *(Bukhari, Muslim)*. Another narration states that when an alarm was raised in Madinah, Rasulullah borrowed Abu Talha's horse whose name was Mandub. Rasulullah mounted the horse and after investigating he reassured the people saying, "We have seen nothing alarming but have found this horse to be like an ocean." Anas also said, "Whenever the battle grew furious, we always sought refuge with Rasulullah." *(Muslim)*. Ali says, "During the Battle of Badr, we sought refuge from the disbeliever by the side of Rasulullah because he was the most furious of fighters." *(Ahmad, Bayhaqi in Al Bidayah wan Nihayah)*

Rasulullah's Bravery During the Battle of Hunain and the Statement of Bara in this Regard

Abu Is'haq reports that a man from the Qais tribe once asked Bara bin Azib, "Did you people desert Rasulullah during the Battle of Hunain?" *Abu Is'haq* then heard Bara reply, "However, Rasulullah did not desert. The Hawazin tribe was first rate archers. When we attacked them, they were defeated but when we occupied ourselves with collecting the booty, they intercepted us with a flood of arrows. I saw Rasulullah still on his white mule with Abu Sufian holding its reins. Rasulullah was saying أَنَا النَّبِيُّ لَا كَذِبْ *I am a Nabi without a lie'.*"

Rasulullah said: أَنَا النَّبِيُّ لَا كَذِبْ، أَنَا ابْنُ الْمُطَّلِبْ
"I am a Nabi without a lie. I am the son of Abdul Muttalib"
Yet another narration states that Rasulullah then dismounted the mule. *(Bukhari, Muslim, Nasa'ee)*

Bara also narrates, "Rasulullah then descended from his mule and prayed for assistance saying:
أَنَا النَّبِيُّ لَا كَذِبْ، أَنَا ابْنُ الْمُطَّلِبْ، اللَّهُمَّ نَزِّلْ نَصْرَتَك
"I am a Nabi without a lie. I am the son of Abdul Muttalib. O Allah! Send down Your assistance"
Bara says further, "When the battle grew furious, we took refuge with Rasulullah and it was only the bravest ones who could fight by his side." *(Al Bidayah wan Nihayah)*. In the chapter concerning the bravery of the Sahabah in Jihad, the incidents have already passed about the bravery of Abu Bakr, Omar, Ali, Talha, Zubair, Sa'd, Hamza, Abbas, Mu'adh, Ibn Omar, Mu'adh bin Afra, Abu Dujana, Qatadah, Salama bin Akwa, Abu Hadrad, Khalid bin Walid, Bara bin Malik, Abu Mihjin, Ammar bin Yasir, Amr bin Ma'dikarib and Abdullah bin Zubair.

The Piety and Thoroughness of our Guide Rasulullah

Abdullah bin Amr bin Al Aas reports that one night Rasulullah found a date lying by his side and ate it. When he was unable to sleep that night, one of his wives asked, "O Rasulullah! You stayed awake all night?" Rasulullah replied, "I ate a date that I found at my side and because we had the Sadaqa dates with us, I feared that this could be one of those." *(Ahmad in Al Bidayah wan Nihayah)*

The Piety and Thoroughness of Abu Bakr

Muhammad bin Sirin says that besides Abu Bakr, he knows of no one who forcibly vomited out the food he had just eaten. Once after eating some food he had been served, someone informed him that the food had been provided by Ibn Nu'aiman. Abu Bakr exclaimed, "Were you feeding me the charm fares of Ibn Nu'ayman?!" He then forced himself to vomit. *(Ahmad in Zuhd)*. Abdur Rahman bin Abu Layla reports that Ibn Nu'ayman was an extremely handsome Sahabi. During the period of ignorance, some people once came to him asking if he knew anything that would help cure a woman who always miscarries. "Oh yes, 1 do," he replied. When they asked him what it was, he recited to them an incantation (which means):

"O disobedient womb! Be still and stop spoiling blood
You are depriving her of bearing many children
If only these many children were in the disobedient womb
Because then she would bear them and recover"

In exchange for this, the people gave him a goat and some butter after he had already become a Muslim. He then brought some of the meat to Abu Bakr, who ate. However, after being informed of the incident Abu Bakr stood up and forced himself to vomit. He then re reprimanded. "Why do you people bring me food without informing me where it has come from?!" *(Baghawi in Muntakhab Kanzul Ummal)*. Zaid bin Arqam reports that Abu Bakr had a slave who earned an income for him. When the slave brought some food one night and Abu Bakr ﷺ ate a morsel, the slave asked, "What has happened to you that you have not questioned me tonight about the source of the food when you usually do so every night?" Abu Bakr ﷺ replied, "It was extreme hunger that made me do it. Where did you get it from?" The slave explained, "During the period of ignorance, I passed by some people and to assist them out of some difficulty, I recited some charm for them. They had promised to pay me and it was only today that I happened to pass by them as they were celebrating a wedding. They then gave me this food." "You would have killed me!" Abu Bakr ﷺ exclaimed as he thrust his fingers in his mouth to vomit out the food. However, the food would not come out because he had eaten it when he was very hungry. When someone suggested that it would come out only with water, Abu Bakr ﷺ asked for a bowl of water and he continued vomiting out the water until the food also came out. "May Allah have mercy on you," someone remarked, "All this trouble merely for that morsel?" Abu Bakr ﷺ said, "I would have taken it out even if it cost me my life because I heard Rasulullah ﷺ say, 'The fire of Jahannam is most deserving of a body nourished by that which is unlawful.' I therefore feared that any part of my body should receive nourishment from that morsel." *(Abu Nu'aym in Hilya, Bukhari in Afrad, Safwatus Safwa, Hasan bin Sufian, Dinowri in Mujalasa, Muntakhab Kanzul Ummal)*

The Piety and Thoroughness of Omar ﷺ and Ali ﷺ

Zaid bin Aslam reports that Omar ﷺ drank some milk and finding the taste surprising, he asked the person who brought it, "Where did you get this milk from?" The person explained, "We were passing by a watering place where some zakah camels were being watered. The herders milked the camels for us and I put some in this water bag of mine from which you just drank." Omar ﷺ thrust his fingers into his throat and vomited the milk out. *(Malik, Bayhaqi in Muntakhab Kanzul Ummal)*. Miswar bin Makhrama ﷺ says, "We stuck close to Omar ﷺ to learn piety and thoroughness from him." *(Ibn Sa'd)*. Sha'bi narrates that Ali ﷺ was once out in Kufa when he stopped by a house and asked for water. When a little girl came out with a jug and a napkin, Ali ﷺ asked, "Dear girl! Whose house is this?" When she informed him the person's name and that he was a coin evaluator, Ali ﷺ said, "I have heard Rasulullah ﷺ say that one should never drink from the well of a coin evaluator and never take shade under anything belonging to a tax collector." *(Ibn Asakir in Kanzul Ummal)*

The Piety and Carefulness of Mu'adh ﷺ and Abdullah bin Abbas ﷺ

Yahya bin Sa'eed narrates that Mu'adh bin Jabal ﷺ had 2 wives. He was so particular about treating them equally that when it was the turn of the one to be with him, he would not even make wudhu in the house of the other. It so happened that both of them passed away on the same day from the plague that struck in Sham. Because the people were extremely busy that day, both ladies had to be buried in one grave. Mu'adh ﷺ still careful about being just between them then drew lots to decide which of the 2 would be placed first in the grave. Another narration states that Mu'adh ﷺ had 2 wives and would not even drink water from the house of one of them if it was the turn of the other to be with him. *(Abu Nu'aym in Hilya)*. Tawus says, "I testify that I heard Abdullah bin Abbas ﷺ say, 'I testify that I heard Omar ﷺ recite the Talbiya.' We were standing on Arafat when a man asked, 'Tell me when Omar ﷺ left Arafat.' Abdullah bin Abbas ﷺ, because of his cautiousness replied, 'I do not know.' The people were very surprised by this cautiousness of Abdullah bin Abbas ﷺ. *(Ibn Sa'd in Muntakhab Kanzul Ummal)*

The Tawakkul of Muhammad Rasulullah ﷺ: The Incident of a Bedouin who wanted to Kill Rasulullah ﷺ as he slept under a Tree

Jabir ﷺ narrates that he accompanied Rasulullah ﷺ on an expedition to Najd. On the way back, it was the time for their siesta when they came to a valley filled with thorny trees. As the Sahabah dispersed to take shade beneath the trees, Rasulullah ﷺ also found some shade beneath a tree and hung his sword on it. Jabir narrates further, "We had slept only a short while when Rasulullah ﷺ called for us. When we responded to his call, we found a Bedouin sitting with him. Rasulullah ﷺ said, 'This person drew my sword while I was asleep. When I awoke, it was already drawn and in his hand as he said, 'Who will save you from me?' 'Allah!' I replied. When he again asked, 'Who will save you from me?' I again replied, "Allah!' He then covered the sword and sat down. Rasulullah ﷺ did not punish the man despite what he had done. *(Bukhari, Muslim)*. Jabir ﷺ narrates that Rasulullah ﷺ had been fighting the Muharib and Ghatfan tribes in Nakhla in Najd. It was at a time when the enemy found the Muslims in negligence when a man from them named Ghowrath bin Harith approached Rasulullah ﷺ with a sword. Standing over Rasulullah ﷺ's head, he asked, "Who will save you from me?" "Allah!" Rasulullah ﷺ replied. The sword fell from the man's hand and Rasulullah ﷺ took hold of it saying, "Now who will save you from me?" Rasulullah ﷺ asked. Ghowrath begged, "Do be a good captor." "Do you testify that there is one worthy of worship but Allah?" Rasulullah ﷺ asked. "No," Ghowrath replied, "But I pledge that I shall never fight against you and neither join forces with anyone who fights against you." Rasulullah ﷺ let him go. He returned to his comrades, he said to them, "I have come to you from the best of people." The narration then continues to explain the Salatul Khowf. *(Bayhaqi in Al Bidayah wan Nihayah)*

The Tawakkul of Amirul Mu'minin Ali ﷺ

Yahya bin Murra narrates, "When Ali ﷺ used to go to the Masjid at night to perform Nafl salah, we would also go with to guard him. After completing his salah, he would ask us, 'What are you sitting here for?' When we informed him that we were there to guard him, he asked, 'Is it against the inhabitants of the heavens that you are guarding me or against the inhabitants of the earth?' 'Only from the inhabitants of the earth,' we submitted. He then said, 'Nothing happens on earth until it is decided in the heavens. There are 2 angels assigned to every person who protect and guard him. However, when a predestined matter arrives, they leave him to it. I have a fortified shield from Allah which will leave me only when death arrives. No person can taste the sweetness of Iman until he is convinced that whatever difficulty afflicts him would never have passed him by and whatever good passes him by would never have come to him in the first place.'" *(Abu Dawud, Ibn Asakir)*. Qatadah ﷺ reports that Ali ﷺ was extremely restless throughout the last night he spent in this world. This made his family very concerned and after secretly convening, they arrived at a decision and asked him in the name of Allah not to leave the house. He said to them, "2 angels are assigned to each and every person to protect him from that which is not destined for him and this happens as long as what is predestined does not come to him. However, when something predestined comes his way, the two angels leave him to it." Ali ﷺ then proceeded to the Masjid and he was assassinated. *(Abu Dawud, Ibn Asakir)*. Abu Mijlaz narrates that a man from the Murad tribe came to see Ali ﷺ when he was busy performing salah in the Masjid. After Ali ﷺ completed the salah, the man said to him, "Appoint some guards because the people of the Murad tribe are planning to assassinate you." He said to them, "2 angels are assigned to each and every person to protect him from that which is not destined for him. When something predestined comes his way, the 2 angels leave him to it. One's appointed term is a fortified shield because nothing can violate it." *(Ibn Sa'd, Ibn Asakir in Kanzul Ummal).* Yahya bin Kathir reports that people offered to guard Ali ؓ, he said, "A person's appointed term guards him." *(Abu Nu'aym in Hilya).* Muhammad Baqir reports that 2 men presented their dispute to Ali ؓ for judgment. When he sat at the base of a wall, one of the men cautioned, "O Amirul Mu'minin! That wall is going to fall." Ali ؓ reassured him saying, "Continue. Allah suffices as a protector." Ali ؓ passed judgment and up, the wall fell down. *(Abu Nu'aym in Dala'il)*

The Tawakkul of Abdullah bin Mas'ood ؓ

Abu Dhabiya reports that when Abdullah bin Mas'ood ؓ was on his deathbed, Uthman bin Affan ؓ visited him. "What is the problem?" Uthman ؓ asked. "My problem is my sins," Abdullah bin Mas'ood ؓ replied. Uthman ؓ asked further, "What do you wish for?" Abdullah bin Mas'ood ؓ replied, "For the mercy of my Rabb." Uthman ؓ then asked, "Should I not have a physician see you?" Referring to the fact that Allah is the greatest of curers, Abdullah bin Mas'ood ؓ said, "It was the physician (Allah) Who gave me the illness." Uthman ؓ further asked, "Should I then not have an allowance fixed." "I have no need for an allowance," Abdullah bin Mas'ood ؓ assured him. "But it would belong to your daughters after your demise," Uthman ؓ explained. "Do you fear that my daughters would suffer poverty after my death?" Abdullah bin Mas'ood ؓ asked in surprise. He then continued, "I have instructed my daughters to recite Sura Waqi'a every night because I have heard Rasulullah say that poverty shall never ever afflict the person who recites Sura Waqi'a every night." *(Ibn Asakir in Tafsir Ibn Kathir)*

The Statements of Omar ؓ, Abu Dhar ؓ, Ali ؓ and Abdullah bin Mas'ood ؓ About Being Content with Allah's Decision

Omar ؓ once said, "I care not how my morning goes, whether it be in a manner that I like or in a manner that I dislike because I know not whether goodness is in what I like or in what I dislike." *(Ibn Mubarak, Ibn Abi Dunya in Faraj, Asaki in Mawa'idh, Kanzul Ummal).* Hasan reports that someone once said to Ali ؓ, "Abu Dhar ؓ says that he prefers poverty to riches and illness to good health." Ali ؓ remarked, "May Allah have mercy on Abu Dhar ؓ. My opinion is that the person who relies on Allah's good choice for him will never wish to be in a condition other than that which Allah has chosen for him. This is the highest level of contentment with the decision of Allah." *(Ibn Asakir in Kanzul Ummal).* It was \Ali ؓ who said, "Whoever is happy with what Allah decides will have Allah's decision pass over him together with being rewarded. Whoever is unhappy with what Allah decides will still have Allah's decision pass over him but his deeds will be laid to waste." *(Ibn Asakir in Kanzul Ummal).* Abdullah bin Mas'ood ؓ said, "On the Day of Judgment, each and every person will wish that in this world he had only that much of food which he could subsist on. The conditions a person experiences each morning and evening in this world will be detrimental to him only if his heart is filled with anger and discontentment. It is better for any on you to bite on a coal and bum himself rather than say anything that Allah had decreed, 'If only that had not happened.'" *(Abu Nu'aym in Hilya)*

Taqwa: Ali ؓ Addresses the People in a Graveyard and His Statement Concerning Taqwa

Kumail bin Ziyad says that he was with Ali ؓ when they reached a graveyard. Turning towards the graves, Ali ؓ said, "O inhabitants of the grave! O inhabitants of the place of decay! O inhabitants of the place of loneliness! What news have you! The news from us is that your wealth has already been distributed, your children have become orphans and your wives have remarried. What news have you?" Ali ؓ turned and said, "O Kumail! Had they been permitted to respond, they would have told us that the best provision is Taqwa." He started weeping as he continued, "O Kumail! The grave is a box containing one's actions and it is only at the time of death that one finds out about it." *(Dinowri, Ibn Asakir in Kanzul Ummal).* Qais bin Abu Hazim reports that Ali ؓ said, "Give more importance to have your deeds accepted than to Taqwa because while a deed with Taqwa can never be undermined, how can one that is accepted ever be undermined?" *(Abu Nu'aym in Hilya, Ibn Asakir).* Ali ؓ said, "When a deed with Taqwa can not be determined, how can one that is accepted ever be undermined or undermined?" *(Abu Nu'aym in Hilya, Ibn Abi Dunya in Kanzul Ummal)*

The Statements of Abdullah bin Mas'ood ؓ, Abu Darda ؓ and Ubay bin Ka'b ؓ Concerning Taqwa

Abdullah bin Mas'ood ؓ said, "The knowledge that Allah has accepted even a single deed of mine is more beloved to me than the earth full of gold." *(Ya'qub bin Sufian, Ibn Asakir in Kanzul Ummal).* Abu Darda ؓ said, "How grand is the sleep of the intelligent ones who prepare for the Hereafter and their days without fasting! How won't they object to the waking nights and fasts of the foolish ones who have no concern for the Hereafter. An atom's weight of good that a person with Taqwa and conviction carries out is greater, more rewarding and more likely to be accepted than a mountain's weight of worship carried out by the negligent ones." *(Abu Nu'aym in Hilya).* Abu Darda ؓ also said, "For me to know with certainty that Allah has accepted even one salah of mine is more beloved to me than the entire world and its contents as Allah says: إِنَّمَا يَتَقَبَّلُ اللَّهُ مِنَ الْمُتَّقِينَ (27) *Verily, Allah accepts only from those who are Al-Muttaqoon (the pious). (Al-Ma'ida:27) (Ibn Abi Hatim in Tafsir Ibn Kathir)*

Ubay bin Ka'b ؓ said, "Whenever a person leaves out something for the pleasure of Allah, Allah grants him something much better from sources he does not expect. However, when someone is careless and takes things without knowledge of the legality of sources, Allah afflicts him with difficulties from sources he does not expect." *(Ibn Asakir in Kanzul Ummal)*

Fear of Allah: The Fear of our Guide Muhammad Rasulullah ﷺ

Abdullah bin Abbas ؓ reports that Abu Bakr ؓ once remarked, "O Rasulullah ﷺ! I see that your hair is getting white'?" Rasulullah ﷺ replied, "Sura Hood, Waqi'a, Mursalat, Amma Yatasa'alun and Idhash Shamsu Kuwwirat have given me these white hairs." Another narration states that when Omar ؓ commented that Rasulullah ﷺ was getting white hairs very early, Rasulullah ﷺ said, "Sura Hood and its companions, namely *Waqi'ah, Amma Yatasa'alun and Idhash Shamsu Kuwwirat* have given me these white hairs." *(Bayhaqi in Al Bidayah wan Nihayah).* Abu Sa'eed Khudri ؓ narrates that Rasulullah ﷺ said, "How can I possibly enjoy life when the one with the horn (the angel Israfel عليه السلام) already has it between his lips with his head bent forward and straining his ears in anticipation of the command (to blow the horn to announce the Day of Qiyamah)." "O Rasulullah ﷺ!" the Sahabah asked, "What should we say'?" Rasulullah ﷺ replied, "You should recite:

حَسْبُنَا اللهُ وَنِعْمَ الْوَكِيْلُ، عَلَى اللهِ تَوَكَّلْنَا

'Allah is Sufficient for us and He is the best of all Guardians. It is solely in Allah that we trust'.
(Ahmad, Tirmidhi in Al Bidayah wan Nihayah)

Abdullah bin Omar ؓ narrates that Rasulullah ﷺ fell unconscious when he heard someone recite the verse:

إِنَّ لَدَيْنَا أَنكَالًا وَجَحِيمًا (12)

Verily, with Us are fetters (to bind them), and a raging fire. (Al-Muzammil:12) (Ibn Najjar in Kanzul Ummal)

A Fear of a Young Ansari

Sahl bin Sa'd ؓ narrates that when the fear for Allah gripped a young Ansari, he wept so much every time he heard mention of Jahannam that this kept him indoors. When this was mentioned to Rasulullah ﷺ, he went to the house. As Rasulullah ﷺ entered, he embraced the Ansari, who then expired in Rasulullah ﷺ's arms. Rasulullah ﷺ then said, "Enshroud your companion because fear has ruptured his liver." *(Hakim, Bayhaqi in Targheeb wat Tarheeb).* Hudhaifa ؓ has reported a similar narration with the addition that when the youngster saw Rasulullah ﷺ, he stood up, embraced Rasulullah ﷺ and then fell down dead. Rasulullah ﷺ then said, "Enshroud your companion because fear for Jahannam has ruptured his liver. I swear by the Being Who controls my life that Allah has saved him from it. Whoever aspires for something shall seek it and whoever fears something shall run away from it." *(Ibn Abi Dunya, Ibn Qudama in Kanzul Ummal).* Abdullah bin Abbas ؓ narrates that after it was revealed to Rasulullah ﷺ, he one day recited to the Sahabah the verse: يَا أَيُّهَا الَّذِينَ آمَنُوا قُوا أَنفُسَكُمْ وَأَهْلِيكُمْ نَارًا وَقُودُهَا النَّاسُ وَالْحِجَارَةُ

O you who believe! Ward off from yourselves and your families a Fire (Hell) whose fuel is men and stones... (At-Tahrim:6)

A young Sahabi then fell unconscious. When Rasulullah ﷺ placed his hand on the Sahabi's heart, it was racing. Rasulullah ﷺ said to him, "Dear boy! Recite *'La Ilaha Illallah'.*" When he recited it, Rasulullah ﷺ gave him the glad tidings of Jannah. The other Sahabah then asked, "Does this apply to all of us or is it exclusively for him." Rasulullah ﷺ replied, "Have you not read the verse: ذَلِكَ لِمَنْ خَافَ مَقَامِي وَخَافَ وَعِيدِ (14)

This (promise) is for him who fears standing before Me (on the Day of Resurrection or fears My Punishment) and also fears My Threat. (Ibrahim:14) (Hakim in Targheeb wat Tarheeb)

The statements of Omar ؓ and Abu Bakr ؓ on the Fear and Hope

Sa'eed bin Musaib reports that when Omar ؓ once fell ill, Rasulullah ﷺ went to visit him. "How are you feeling, O Omar?" Rasulullah ﷺ asked. "I have hope in Allah's mercy as well as fear for Allah's punishment." Rasulullah ﷺ then said, "Whenever fear and hope are coupled in the heart of a Mu'min, Allah grants him his hope and saves him from his fear." *(Bayhaqi in Kanzul Ummal).* Hasan narrates that Abu Bakr ؓ once said, "Do you not see that Allah mentions the verses of ease together with those of hardship and the verses of difficulty together with those of ease so that a Mu'min may be hopeful in Allah's mercy as well as fearful for Allah's punishment? In this manner, he will never have such hopes in Allah that are unfounded and will also not throw himself into destruction." *(Abush Shaikh in Kanzul Ummal).* Other incidents concerning the fear that Abu Bakr ؓ and Omar ؓ had for Allah have passed in the chapter entitled "The Fear that the Khulafa had for Allah".

The Statements that Uthman ؓ, Abu Ubaidah bin Jarrah ؓ and Imran bin Husain ؓ Made About Fear

Abdullah bin Rumi reports that news reached him that

Uthman ؓ said, "If I were between Jannah and Jahannam, not knowing into which of the 2 I will be ordered to go, I would prefer to be turned into ashes before knowing towards which of them I would be heading." *(Abu Nu'aym in Hilya, Ahmad in Zuhd, Muntakhab Kanzul Ummal).* Qatadah narrates that Abu Ubaidah bin Jarrah ؓ said, "1 wish that I was a sheep whom my owners would slaughter and eat my flesh and my gravy." Qatadah narrates that Imran bin Husain ؓ said, "1 wish that I were sand on the top of a hill that the wind would blow away on a windy day." *(Ibn Asakir in Muntakhab Kanzul Ummal, Ibn Sa'd).* Qatadah narrates that Imran bin Husain ؓ said, "1 wish that I were sand that the wind would blow away." *(Ibn Sa'd)*

The Fear of Abdullah bin Mas'ood ؓ

Amir bin Masruq narrates that someone once mentioned in the presence of Abdullah bin Mas'ood ؓ, "I do not want to be amongst the 'As'habul Yamin' but wish to be amongst the 'Muqarrabin *(ref. Sura Waqi'a)'.*" To this, Abdullah bin Mas'ood ؓ remarked, however, you have here a person (myself) who wishes to be not even be resurrected after dying, let alone wanting to be amongst a certain group." Another narration from Hasan states that Abdullah bin Mas'ood ؓ said, "If I were placed between Jannah and Jahannam and then told, 'Choose between either entering one of these or becoming dust', I would rather be turned to dust." *(Abu Nu'aym in Hilya)*

The Fear of Abu Dhar ؓ, Abu Darda ؓ and Abdullah bin Omar ؓ

Abu Dhar ؓ said, "By Allah! If you people knew what I know, you will neither make advances to your wives nor find rest on your beds. By Allah! I wish that the day Allah created me, He should have created me as a tree that is felled and whose fruit is eaten." *(Abu Nu'aym in Hilya).* Hizam bin Hakim reports that Abu Darda once stated, "If you people knew what you will see after death, you would neither derive pleasure out of eating nor out of drinking. You would then not go into your homes for shade but would rather go out onto the plains beating your chests and weeping over your condition. I wish that I were a tree that would be felled and then its fruit eaten." *(Abu Nu'aym in Hilya).* Abu Darda ؓ also mentioned, "1 wish that I were a sheep belonging to some people who have visitors passing by. They will then pass a knife over my jugular veins, eat me and feed others." *(Abu Nu'aym in Hilya).* Abdullah bin Omar ؓ once said, "I wish that I was this pillar. *(Ibn Sa'd)*

The Fear of Mu'adh ؓ and Abdullah bin Omar ؓ

Tawus reports, "When Mu'adh bin Jabal ؓ came to our land, our scholars said to him, 'If you just give the word, we shall take these rocks and trees and build a Masjid for you.' Mu'adh ؓ replied, 'I fear that I may be made to carry it on my back on the Day of Qiyamah.' *(Abu Nu'aym in Hilya).* Nafi says, "When Abdullah bin Omar ؓ entered the Kabah, I heard him say the following when he was in Sejdah: 'O Allah! You know that it is only my fear for You that prevents me from opposing the Quraish for their position in this world." *(Abu Nu'aym in Hilya).* Abu Hazim narrates that when Abdullah bin Omar ؓ passed by a man from Iraq who had fallen down unconscious, he asked, "What is the matter with him?" The people said, "This happens to him every time the Qur'an is recited to him." Abdullah bin Omar ؓ remarked, "Although we also fear Allah, we never fall down." *(Abu Nu'aym in Hilya)*

The Fear of Shaddad bin Aws Ansari ؓ

It is reported that whenever Shaddad bin Aws Ansari ؓ lay

on the bed, he would turn from side to side without being able to fall asleep. He would then say, "O Allah! The fire of Jahannam has dispelled my sleep." Thereafter, he would stand up and perform salah until the morning. *(Abu Nu'aym in Hilya)*

The Fear of Ummul Mu'mineen Aisha ؓ

Amr bin Salama ؓ narrates that Aisha ؓ said, "By Allah! I wish that I were a tree. By Allah! I wish that I were sand. By Allah! I wish that Allah had not created me at all." When Abdullah bin Abbas ؓ came to Aisha ؓ before her death, he praised her saying, "Glad tidings for you, O wife of Rasulullah ﷺ. Rasulullah ﷺ never married a virgin besides you and your innocence was proclaimed from the heavens. It was then that Abdullah bin Zubair ؓ entered from the opposite side. Aisha ؓ said to him, "Abdullah bin Omar ؓ is heaping praises on me when I do not wish to hear anyone praise me today. I only wish that I had been completely forgotten." *(Ibn Sa'd)*

The Weeping of our guide Muhammad Rasulullah ﷺ

Abdullah bin Mas'ood ؓ reports, "Rasulullah ﷺ once said to me, 'Recite the Qur'an to me.' I replied, 'How can I recite to you when it was to you that the Qur'an was revealed?' Rasulullah ﷺ said, 'I would like to hear the Qur'an recited by someone else.' I then recited Surah Nisa until I reached the verse:

فَكَيْفَ إِذَا جِئْنَا مِنْ كُلِّ أُمَّةٍ بِشَهِيدٍ وَجِئْنَا بِكَ عَلَى هَؤُلَاءِ شَهِيدًا (41)

How (will it be) then, when We bring from each nation a witness and We bring you (O Muhammad ﷺ) as a witness against these people? (An-Nisa':41)

Rasulullah ﷺ then said, 'That's enough.' When I then looked up, I saw that tears were flowing from his eyes." *(Bukhari in Al Bidayah wan Nihayah)*

The Men of Suffa Weep When a Verse is Revealed

Abu Hurairah ؓ narrates that the men of Suffa wept excessively when Allah revealed the verse:

أَفَمِنْ هَذَا الْحَدِيثِ تَعْجَبُونَ (59) وَتَضْحَكُونَ وَلَا تَبْكُونَ (60)

Do you then wonder at this recital (the Qur'an)? And you laugh at it and weep not. (An-Najm:59-60)

They wept so much that tears flowed on their cheeks. Hearing them, Rasulullah ﷺ also started weeping and seeing him weep, the other Sahabah also wept. Rasulullah ﷺ then said, "The person who weeps out of fear for Allah shall never enter Jahannam and the person who sins persistently shall never enter Jannah. If you never sin, Allah shall create a nation that does sin and He will then forgive them when they repent sincerely because He loves to forgive." *(Bayhaqi in Targheeb wat Tarheeb)*

An Abyssinian Weeps in Front of Rasulullah ﷺ When he Recited a Verse of the Qur'an

Anas ؓ narrates that Rasulullah ﷺ once recited the verse:

وَقُودُهَا النَّاسُ وَالْحِجَارَةُ

...(The fire of Jahannam) the fuel of which is people and stones... (At-Tahrim:6)

Rasulullah ﷺ then said, "The Fire of Jahannam was strengthened for 1,000 years until it became red. It was then strengthened for another 1,000 years until it became white. Thereafter, it was again strengthened for 1,000 years until it became black. It is now pitched black and dark and its flames cannot be extinguished." In front of Rasulullah ﷺ was an Abyssinian man who then started to weep very loudly. Jibra'el علیه السلام then descended and asked Rasulullah ﷺ, "Who is this man weeping in front of you?" Rasulullah ﷺ informed Jibra'el علیه السلام that

the man was from Abyssinia and also praised the man. Jibra'el علیه السلام then told Rasulullah ﷺ that Allah said, "I swear by My honor, by My power and by My Highness over My throne that whenever the eye of My servant weeps in this world out of fear for Me, I shall definitely increase his laughter in Jannah." *(Bayhaqi, Isfahani in Targheeb wat Tarheeb)*

The Weeping of Abu Bakr ؓ and Omar ؓ

Qais bin Abu Hazim ؓ says, "I once went to see Rasulullah ﷺ and found that Abu Bakr ؓ had already taken his place and he had become the Khalifa. In his address to the people Abu Bakr ؓ praised Allah tremendously and wept excessively." *(Abdur Razzaq in Muntakhab Kanzul Ummal)*. Hasan bin Muhammad bin Ali bin Abi Talib ؓ states that during the Friday sermon, Omar ؓ used to recite the Sura Takwir until he reached the verse: عَلِمَتْ نَفْسٌ مَا أَحْضَرَتْ (14)

(Then) every person will know what (actions) he has brought (of good and evil). (At-Takwir:14)

At this point, his voice would stop because of his excessive weeping. *(Shafi'ee)*

Hasan narrates that Omar ؓ once recited the verse:

إِنَّ عَذَابَ رَبِّكَ لَوَاقِعٌ (7) مَا لَهُ مِنْ دَافِعٍ (8)

Verily, the Torment of your Lord will surely come to pass. There is none that can avert it. (At-Tur:7-8)

After reciting it, his voice ballooned because of the emotion. This caused him to fall ill and because of it, people were visiting him for 20 days. *(Abu Ubaid)*. Ubaid bin Umair ؓ reports that Omar ؓ led them in the Fajr salah and started reciting Sura Yusuf. However, he started weeping and had to stop when he reached the verse: وَابْيَضَّتْ عَيْنَاهُ مِنَ الْحُزْنِ فَهُوَ كَظِيمٌ (84)

(Refering to Ya'qub) he lost his sight because of the sorrow that he was suppressing. (Yusuf:84)

Omar ؓ then went into Ruku. *(Abu Ubaid in Muntakhab Kanzul Ummal)*

Abdullah bin Shaddad bin Haad narrates that even while standing in the last rows of the congregation, he could hear the sobbing of Omar ؓ during the Fajr salah. Omar ؓ was reciting Sura Yusuf and because of his excessive weeping, he had to stop when he reached the verse: إِنَّمَا أَشْكُو بَثِّي وَحُزْنِي إِلَى اللهِ

I only complain of my grief and sorrow to Allah. (Yusuf:86)
(Abdur Razzaq, Sa'eed bin Mansur, Ibn Sa'd, Ibn Abi Shaybah, Bayhaqi in Muntakhab Kanzul Ummal)

Hisham bin Hasan narrates that Omar ؓ would sometimes recite a verse of the Qur'an that would choke him with emotion. He would then weep so much that he would fall down. Because of weakness, he would then have to stay indoors and people would visit him thinking him to be ill. *(Abu Nu'aym in Hilya)*

The Weeping of Uthman ؓ

Hani who was the freed slave of Uthman bin Affan ؓ says that whenever Uthman ؓ stopped at a graveyard, he would weep so much that his beard would get wet. Someone once asked him, "You do not weep when you think of Jannah and Jahannam but weep when you think of the grave?" He replied, "I have heard Rasulullah ﷺ say, 'The grave is the first stage from amongst the many stages of the Hereafter. If one is successful there, the later stages are easier. However, if one is unsuccessful there, the later stages will be extremely difficult.'" Uthman ؓ also added, "I have also heard Rasulullah ﷺ say that he had never seen a sight more frightening than that of the grave." In his narration, Hani adds that he heard Uthman ؓ recite the following couplet by a grave (which means):

"If you are saved from this (the punishment in the grave), then you are saved from something enormous. If not, then I do not think that you will be saved (from future torment)" (Tirmidhi in Targheeb wat Tarheeb, Abu Nu'aym in Hilya)

The Weeping of Mu'adh

Abdullah bin Omar narrates that Omar once passed by Mu'adh bin Jabal who was weeping. "What makes you weep?" Omar asked. Mu'adh replied, "A Hadith that I heard from Rasulullah which states that, 'The amount of showiness is equal to Shirk and the most beloved to Allah are those with Taqwa who are anonymous. They are those who will not be missed if they are not there and will not be recognized when they are present. They are the torchbearers of guidance and the beacons of knowledge." (Hakim, Abu Nu'aym in Hilya)

The Weeping of Abdullah bin Omar

Abdullah bin Omar was once reciting the Sura Mutaffifin. However, he started weeping when he reached the verse:

يَوْمَ يَقُومُ النَّاسُ لِرَبِّ الْعَالَمِينَ (6)

The day when (all) mankind will stand before the Lord of the 'Alamin (mankind, jinn and all that exist)? (Al-Mutaffifin:6)

He wept so much that he fell down and was unable to recite further. (Abu Nu'aym in Hilya, Ahmad in Safwatus Safwa). Nafi reports that there was not a single occasion when Abdullah bin Omar did not weep when reciting the following verses:

وَإِنْ تُبْدُوا مَا فِي أَنْفُسِكُمْ أَوْ تُخْفُوهُ يُحَاسِبْكُمْ بِهِ اللَّهُ فَيَغْفِرُ لِمَنْ يَشَاءُ وَيُعَذِّبُ مَنْ يَشَاءُ وَاللَّهُ عَلَى كُلِّ شَيْءٍ قَدِيرٌ (284)

…whether you disclose what is in your ownselves or conceal it, Allah will call you to account for it. Then He forgives whom He wills and punishes whom He wills. And Allah is Able to do all things. (Al-Baqara:284). He would then say, "Verily, this accountability is a grave matter." (Abu Nu'aym in Hilya, Ahmad in Safwatus Safwa). Nafi also reports that Abdullah bin Omar would cry uncontrollably whenever he recited the verse:

أَلَمْ يَأْنِ لِلَّذِينَ آمَنُوا أَنْ تَخْشَعَ قُلُوبُهُمْ لِذِكْرِ اللَّهِ

Has not the time come for the hearts of those who believe (in the Oneness of Allah - Islamic Monotheism) to be affected by Allah's Reminder (this Qur'an)… (Al-Hadid:16) (Abu Nu'aym in Hilya, Abul Abbas in Tarikh, Isabah)

Yusuf bin Mahak says, "I walked with Abdullah bin Omar to Ubaid bin Umair who was busy lecturing to some of his companions. When I again looked at Abdullah bin Omar after he had been listening awhile, I saw that tears were flowing from his eyes." (Ibn Sa'd, Abu Nu'aym in Hilya)

Ubaid bin Umair once recited the verse:

فَكَيْفَ إِذَا جِئْنَا مِنْ كُلِّ أُمَّةٍ بِشَهِيدٍ وَجِئْنَا بِكَ عَلَى هَؤُلَاءِ شَهِيدًا (41)

How (will it be) then, when We bring from each nation a witness and We bring you (O Muhammad) as a witness against these people? (An-Nisa':41)

Upon hearing this verse Abdullah bin Omar started weeping so profusely that his beard and collar became wet with tears. Abdullah says, "The man sitting beside Abdullah bin Omar said to me, 'I actually considered getting up and telling Ubaid bin Umair to curtail his talk because of the difficulty he was causing the elderly man like Abdullah bin Omar ." (Ibn Sa'd)

The Weeping of Abdullah bin Abbas and Ubadah bin Samit

Abdullah bin Abu Mulaika says, "I accompanied Abdullah bin Abbas from Makkah to Madinah and wherever he set up camp, he stood in salah for half the night." When Ayub asked him what Abdullah bin Abbas 's recitation of the Qur'an was like, he replied, "He once cried painfully as he continuously recited the following verse with slow intonation:

وَجَاءَتْ سَكْرَةُ الْمَوْتِ بِالْحَقِّ ذَلِكَ مَا كُنْتَ مِنْهُ تَحِيدُ (19)

And the stupor of death will come in truth: "This is what you have been avoiding!" (Qaf:19) (Abu Nu'aym in Hilya)

Abu Raja says, "The lines on the face of Abdullah bin Abbas where his tears ran resembled 2 old shoe straps." (Abu Nu'aym in Hilya). Uthman bin Abu Sauda says that he once saw Ubadah bin Samit on the wall of the Masjid that Allah showed Rasulullah a vantage point that overlooked a valley of Jahannam. His chest was upon the wall and he was weeping. "O Abu Walid!" Uthman asked, "What makes you weep so?" Ubadah replied, "Rasulullah informed us that it was in this place that he saw Jahannam." (Abu Nu'aym in Hilya)

The Weeping of Abdullah bin Amr and Abu Hurairah

Ya'la bin Ata reports from his mother who made kohl for Abdullah bin Amr that he wept excessively. In fact, he would lock his door and weep so much that he developed a condition that caused his eyes to emit a white fluid all the time. Ya'la says that it was for this reason that his mother prepared the kohl for Abdullah bin Amr . (Abu Nu'aym in Hilya). Muslim bin Bishr reports that when Abu Hurairah was weeping during his illness before his death, someone asked him what it was that made him weep. He replied, "Take note that it is not for this world of yours that I weep. I am weeping. because of the long journey ahead and the deficiency of my provisions. I have climbed a rise that leads down either to Jannah or to Jahannam and I do not know which of the 2 I shall be heading."(Ibn Sa'd, Abu Nu'aym in Hilya)

Contemplation and meditation: The Meditation of Abu Raihana

Dhamra bin Habib reports from a freed slave of the Sahabi Abu Rayhana that when Abu Rayhana once returned from a military expedition, he ate supper, made wudhu and then stood to perform salah at the place where he performed salah. He started reciting a Surah of the Qur'an and stood rooted to the spot until the Mu'adhin called out the Adhan for the Fajr salah. "O Abu Rayhana!" his wife said, "You have just marched on an expedition that was extremely exhausting. You returned and engrossed yourself in salah without a thought for me. Is there no share for us in your time?" Abu Rayhana replied, "By Allah! Of course there is a share for you in my time, if I had only thought of you." "Then what was it that preoccupied you from thinking of me?" she asked. He replied, "Deep meditation about the descriptions Allah has given about Jannah and its pleasures had engrossed my mind until I heard the Muadhin." (Ibn Mubarak in Zuhd, Isabah)

The Meditation of Abu Dhar

Muhammad bin Wasi narrates that a man rode from Basra to see Ummu Dhar after the demise of her husband Abu Dhar to ask her about the Ibada of Abu Dhar . When he arrived, he said to her, "I have come to you so that you may inform me about the Ibada of Abu Dhar ." She said, "He would spend the entire day only meditating in solitude." (Abu Nu'aym in Hilya)

The Meditation of Abu Darda

Aun bin Abdullah bin Utba reports that he once asked Ummu Darda about the best deed of her husband Abu Darda.

She replied, "Meditation and heeding to lessons." Another narration states that when she was asked about the deed that Abu Darda ﷺ did most frequently, she replied, "Heeding to lessons." Yet another narration states that her reply was, "Meditation." *(Abu Nu'aym in Hilya, Ahmad in Saftawus Safwa).* Abu Darda ﷺ once said, "Meditation for a moment is better than standing in salah an entire night." *(Abu Nu'aym in Hilya, Ahmad, Ibn Sa'd).* Abu Darda ﷺ also said, "Amongst people there are those who are the keys to good and the locks of evil. They shall have great rewards. There are then also those who are the keys to evil and locks of good. They will be terribly punished. Meditation for a moment is better than standing in salah an entire night." *(Ibn Asakir in Kanzul Ummal).* Habeeb bin Abdullah narrates that a man intending to march in jihad came to Abu Darda ﷺ for advice. Abu Darda ﷺ said, "Think of Allah in prosperity and He will think of you when you are in difficulty. When you admire something of this world, think about what it is to become old and then turned to dust." Salim bin Abil Ja'd reports that 2 bulls once passed by Abu Darda ﷺ as they were being worked. When one of them stopped as the other continued, Abu Darda ﷺ said, "There is certainly a great lesson in this while the one will be whipped for stopping, the other will be saved from the whipping." *(Abu Nu'aym in Hilya, Ahmad in Safwatus Safwa)*

The Statements of Abu Bakr ﷺ and Omar ﷺ About Taking Stock

One of Abu Bakr ﷺ's freed slaves reports that Abu Bakr ﷺ once said, "Whoever angers his carnal wish for the sake of Allah will be saved from Allah's anger." *(Ibn Abi Dunya in Muhasabatun Nafs, Kanzul Ummal).* Thabit bin Hajjaj narrates that Omar ﷺ once said, "Weigh yourselves up before you are weighed and assess yourselves before you are assessed because reckoning with yourself in this world is easier than the reckoning you will face tomorrow in the Hereafter. You should adorn yourselves with good deeds before the Day of Judgment about which Allah says: يَوْمَئِذٍ تُعْرَضُونَ لَا تَخْفَى مِنْكُمْ خَافِيَةٌ (18)

That Day shall you be brought to Judgment, not a secret of you will be hidden. (Al-Haqah:18) (Abu Nu'aym in Hilya)

Anas ﷺ reports, "I was one day with Omar bin Khattab ﷺ when he went into an orchard. There was a wall between us and he was standing in the middle of the orchard when I heard him say to himself, 'O Amirul Mu'minin! By Allah! You should fear Allah or He will definitely punish you." *(Mali, Ibn Sa'd, Ibn Abi Dunya in Mahasabatun Nafs, Abu Ny'aym in M'arifa, Ibn Asakir in Muntakhab Kanzul Ummal)*

The Silence and guarding the Tongue of Our Guide Rasulullah ﷺ

In a lengthy narration, Simak says that he once asked Jabir bin Samura ﷺ, "Did you associate often with Nabi ﷺ?" Jabir replied, "Yes. He was a person who often remained silent." *(Ahmad, Tabrani, Haythami).* Abu Malik Ashja'e ﷺ reports that his father said, "We were little boys when we used to sit in the company of Rasulullah ﷺ and have never seen anyone remain silent as much as Rasulullah ﷺ did. Whenever his companions would talk too much, he merely smiled." *(Tabrani, Haythami).* Ubadah bin Samit ﷺ narrates that Rasulullah ﷺ was once out with his companions. As he rode, one of them stepped out ahead of him. Mu'adh bin Jabal ﷺ said, "O Rasulullah ﷺ! I pray that Allah takes our lives before yours. May Allah never show us the day of your demise, but should we see it, what deeds should we carry out after you? May my parents be sacrificed for you, O Rasulullah ﷺ! Should it be Jihad in the Path of Allah?" Rasulullah ﷺ replied, "Jihad in the Path of Allah is an excellent

deed, but people have become accustomed to it. What you should be doing is something that exercises greater restraint on the carnal wish." "Then fasting and Sadaqah?" Mu'adh ﷺ asked. "Fasting and Sadaqah are excellent deeds," Rasulullah ﷺ commented, "but people have become accustomed to it. What you should be doing is something that exercises greater restraint on the carnal wish." Mu'adh ﷺ then went on to mention every type of good deed, but each time Rasulullah ﷺ's reply was. "But people have become accustomed to it. What you should be doing is something that exercises greater restraint on the carnal wish." Mu'adh ﷺ eventually asked. "If people have become accustomed to these deeds, what is that thing that exercises greater restraint on the carnal wish?" Pointing to his mouth, Rasulullah ﷺ said, "Remaining silent at all times save when speaking what is good." "Will we be taken to task for what our tongues speak?" Mu'adh ﷺ asked in surprise. Striking his hand on Mu'adh ﷺ's thigh, Rasulullah ﷺ said something like, "Your mother ought to have lost you!" He then added. "It is because of what the tongue speaks that people will be thrown headlong into Jahannam. Whoever believes in Allah and the Last Day should speak only what is good or remain silent about evil. Speak what is good and you will reap the rewards. Remain silent about evil and you will be safe." *(Tabrani, Haythami)*

Rasulullah ﷺ says about a Martyr, "He may have Mentioned Something that was Futile"

Abu Hurairah ﷺ narrates that when someone was martyred, a lady was weeping over him saying, "Oh dear martyr!" Addressing her, Rasulullah ﷺ said, "Stop saying that. How do you know that he is a martyr and is guaranteed immediate access into Jannah? He may have mentioned something that was futile or was miserly with something that would not have cost him anything." *(Abu Ya'la, Haythami).* Anas ﷺ states that when one of the Sahabah was martyred during the Battle of Uhud, a rock was found tied to his belly which he had tied because of hunger. Wiping the dust off his face, his mother said, "Glad tidings for you, O beloved son of Jannah." Addressing her, Rasulullah ﷺ said, "How do you know that he is a martyr and is guaranteed immediate access into Jannah? He may have said something that was futile or refused something that would not have harmed him." *(Tabrani, Haythami, Tirmidhi, Mishkat)*

The Silence of Ammar ﷺ, Mu'adh ﷺ and Statement of Abu Bakr ﷺ

Khalid bin Numair says, "Ammar bin Yasir ﷺ often remained silent for prolonged periods of time and always seemed depressed. When he did speak, he was mostly seeking Allah's protection from trials." *(Abu Nu'aym in Hilya).* Abu Idris Khowlani says, "I once entered the Masjid of Damascus when my eyes caught sight of a man with sparkling front teeth. He was a very quiet man and whenever the people with him disagreed on some issue, they referred it to him and readily accepted his verdict. I enquired who he was, I was informed that he was Mu'adh bin Jabal ﷺ." *(Hakim).* Aslam narrates that Omar ﷺ found Abu Bakr ﷺ pulling his tongue, he asked, "What are you doing, O Khalifa of Rasulullah ﷺ?" Abu Bakr ﷺ replied, "There is not a part of the body that does not complain of the sharpness of the tongue." *(Abu Ya'la, Haythami, Abu Nu'aym in Hilya).*

Abdullah bin Mas'ood ﷺ and Abdullah bin Abbas ﷺ Rebuke Their Tongues

Abu Wa'il narrates that when Abdullah bin Mas'ood ﷺ climbed Mount Safa, he caught hold of his tongue saying, "O tongue! Speak what is good and reap the rewards. Shun speaking evil and you will remain safe before having to regret." He narrated, "I have heard Rasulullah ﷺ say, 'Most of man's sins stem from the tongue." (Tabrani, Haythami). Sa'eed Jariri reports, "I once saw Abdullah bin Abbas ؓ holding the point of his tongue as he said, 'Shame on you! Speak what is good and reap the rewards. Shun speaking evil and you will remain safe.' Someone asked, 'O Ibn Abbas ؓ! Why do I see you holding your tongue and saying that?' Abdullah bin Abbas ؓ replied, "I heard that on the Day of Judgment a person will be angrier with his tongue than anything else." (Abu Nu'aym in Hilya).

The Silence of Shaddad bin Aws ؓ After he Pledged Allegiance at the Hand of Rasulullah ﷺ

Thabit Bunani narrates that Shaddad bin Aws ؓ once said to one of his companions, "Lay the tablecloth so that we may dig in to it!" Another of his companions said in surprise, "I have never heard you speak like that since I have come to know you." Shaddad ؓ said, "Since I separated from Rasulullah ﷺ, every statement I have made was a harnessed one, said with much thought. By Allah! Another like this shall never again escape." (Abu Nu'aym in Hilya). Sulaiman bin Musa reports that Shaddad bin Aws ؓ once said, "Lay the tablecloth so that we may play with it." The people with him immediately picked at his words saying, "Look at Abu Ya'la (Shaddad ؓ's title)! What a statement has come from him!" Shaddad ؓ then said, "Dear son of my brother! Since the time I pledged allegiance at Rasulullah ﷺ's hand, every statement I have made had been a harnessed one, except for this one. Come, forget this and let me tell you something better for you to note. It is this Du'a, 'O Allah! We seek steadfastness in our affairs and the resolve to do good. We ask You for the ability to be grateful for Your bounties and for the ability to worship You in a most beautiful manner. We ask You for a pure heart and a truthful tongue. We beseech You for the good You are aware of and for protection from the evil You know about.' Learn this from me and forget the other words I said without thinking." (Abu Nu'aym in Hilya). Shaddad ؓ added, "Do not learn these words from me, but rather learn what I shall narrate to you that I heard Rasulullah ﷺ say, 'When people started hoarding treasures of gold and silver, fill your treasures with the words: 'O Allah! We seek steadfastness. Our affairs and the resolve is to do good.'" Shaddad ؓ added, "O Allah I seek forgiveness from You from the sins You know I have committed. You are the One who knows well all that is hidden." (Abu Nu'aym in Hilya, Ahmad in Tafsir Ibn Kathir)

The Statement of Abdullah bin Mas'ood ؓ about the Dangers of the Tongue

Isa bin Uqba narrates that Abdullah bin Mas'ood ؓ once said, "I swear by the Being besides Whom there is none worthy of worship that nothing on earth is more deserving of a long prison sentence than the tongue." (Abu Nu'aym in Hilya, Tabrani, Haythami). Abdullah bin Mas'ood ؓ once said, "Beware of futile speech. All you need to say it that which would get your needs fulfilled." (Tabrani, Haythami) Another narration states that Abdullah bin Mas'ood ؓ said, "The people guilty of the most sins on the Day of Judgment shall be those who most engaged in idle talk." (Tabrani, Haythami)

Ali ؓ and Abu Darda ؓ Encourage Silence

Ali ؓ said, "The tongue is the basis of the body's well-being. When the tongue is upright, the other limbs are all upright. However, as soon as the tongue is out of control no other limb stays under control." Another narration states that he once said,

"Keep a low profile and you will not be talked about thus saving you from pride. Remain silent and you will remain safe." Another narration states that he said, "Silence invites towards Jannah." It was Ali ؓ who mentioned the following couplets which mean:

"Never disclose your secrets except to yourself because there is an advisor to every advisor and I have also seen many misguided men who do not leave upright men unscathed (by their insults)" (Ibn Abi Dunya in Samt, Kanzul Ummal)

Abu Darda ؓ once said, "Learn to remain silent just as you learn to speak because silence is a great source of self-control. You ought to be more interested in listening than speaking and should never speak about things that do not concern you. You should also not laugh when there is nothing to laugh about or go somewhere you do not have to go." (Ibn Asakir in Kanzul Ummal). Abu Darda ؓ said, "There is no limb of a Mu'min that Allah loves more than his tongue because it is means of this that he will enter Jannah. At the same time, there is no limb of a Kafir that Allah hates more than his tongue because it is by means of this that he will enter Jahannam." (Abu Nu'aym in Hilya)

The Statements of Abdullah bin Omar ؓ and Anas ؓ About Guarding the Tongue

Abdullah bin Omar ؓ said, 'The limb that a person needs to purify most is his tongue.' (Abu Nu'aym in Hilya). Anas ؓ said, "A person can never have Taqwa until he controls his tongue." (Ibn Sa'd)

The Sahabah Describe the Speech of Rasulullah ﷺ

Aisha ؓ says, "Rasulullah ﷺ's speech was so clear that if anyone wished to count the words, they could have easily done so." She also mentioned, "Shall I not surprise you? A certain person actually came and spoke to Rasulullah ﷺ beside my room so loudly that I could hear him talk as I was busy with my salah. He then left before I could complete my salah. Had I been able to find him before that, I would have certainly given him a piece of my mind." She added. "Rasulullah ﷺ never spoke continuously and quickly as you people do." (Bukhari, Ahmad, Muslim, Abu Dawud). Aisha ؓ says, "Rasulullah ﷺ's speech was so clear that everyone could understand it. He would never speak continuously and quickly." (Ahmad, Abu Dawud). It was Jabir ؓ or Abdullah bin Omar ؓ who said, "Rasulullah ﷺ's speech was crisp, with every letter distinctly pronounced." (Abu Ya'la). Anas ؓ reports, "When Rasulullah ﷺ spoke anything of marked importance, he would repeat it thrice and whenever he approached a gathering, he would greet thrice." (Bukhari). Thumama bin Anas ؓ narrates that whenever Anas ؓ spoke something of importance, he repeated himself thrice and would say that when Rasulullah ﷺ greeted with Salam to seek permission to enter a home, he did so thrice: 1st seeking permission to enter, then 2nd time when entering, and finally a 3rd time when leaving and when he spoke something of great importance, he would repeat it thrice. (Ahmad) Anas also reported that when Rasulullah ﷺ spoke, he would repeat himself thrice so that people could understand what he was saying." (Tirmidhi). Abu Hurairah ؓ narrates that Rasulullah ﷺ once said, "I have been sent with concise yet comprehensive speech and have been assisted with fear. When I was sleeping once, the keys to the treasures of the heavens and the earth were brought to me and placed in my hand." (Ahmad, Bukhari). Abdullah bin Salam ؓ reports, "When Rasulullah ﷺ sat down to talk, he would often look towards the sky hoping for revelation." (Ibn Is'haq, Abu Dawud in Adab, Al Bidayah wan Nihayah)

Amr bin Al Aas ❀ regrets the Many Questions he Posed to Rasulullah ﷺ

Amr bin Al Aas ❀ says. "Even when speaking to the worst of people, Rasulullah ﷺ would turn his full attention to the person so that they would feel special and their hearts would be won over. When speaking to me, Rasulullah ﷺ also turned his full attention towards me until I eventually felt that I was the best of all the Sahabah. 'O Rasulullah ﷺ!' I once asked, 'Am I better or Abu Bakr ❀?' 'Abu Bakr,' came the reply. 'O Rasulullah ﷺ!' I asked further, 'Am I better or Omar ❀?' When Rasulullah ﷺ replied that Omar ❀ was better, I pursued the enquiry saying, 'O Rasulullah ﷺ! Am I better or Uthman ❀?' 'Uthman ❀,' he replied. After asking Rasulullah ﷺ and after he had been truthful to me, I wished that I had never asked him these questions." *(Tirmidhi in Shama'il, Tabrani, Haythami)*

The Smiling and Laughing of Rasulullah ﷺ

Aisha ❀ says, "I have never seen Rasulullah ﷺ laugh so much in a manner that I could see his bottom of the tongue. All he did was smile." *(Bukhari, Muslim)*. Abdullah bin Harith bin Jaz ❀ says, "I have never seen anyone smile as much as Rasulullah ﷺ." In another narration, he says, "Rasulullah ﷺ never laughed but only smiled." *(Tirmidhi)*. Simak bin Harb reports that he once asked Jabir bin Samura ❀, "Were you frequently in the company of Rasulullah ﷺ?" Jabir replied, "Yes, I was often in his company. He never stood up from his place of performing the Fajr salah until the sun rose. He would then get up while the Sahabah were sometimes discussing events that occurred during the period of ignorance. As they laughed, Rasulullah ﷺ would merely smile." *(Muslim)*. In another narration, Simak bin Harb reports that he once asked Jabir bin Samura ❀, "Were you frequently in the company of Rasulullah ﷺ?" Jabir ❀ replied, "Yes. He often remained silent and would laugh very little. The Sahabah would often recite poetry to him and when he said something that made them laugh, he would merely smile." *(Tayalisi in Al Bidayah wan Nihayah, Ibn Sa'd)*. Husain bin Yazid Kalbi ❀ says, "I have never seen Rasulullah ﷺ laugh. He would only smile. There were also times when he would have to tie a rock to his belly because of extreme hunger." *(Abu Nu'aym, Ibn Asakir in Kanzul Ummal, Ibn Qani in Isabah)*

Amra questions Aisha ❀ about Rasulullah ﷺ's Domestic Life

Amra reports that she asked Aisha ❀ about Rasulullah ﷺ's behavior when he was with his wives. Aisha ❀ replied, "He was like any other man except that he was the noblest of them all and the most compassionate. He laughed and smiled very often." *(Khara'iti, Hakim in Al Bidayah wan Nihayah, Ibn Sa'd)*

Rasulullah ﷺ's Laughing

Jabir ❀ says, "When revelation would come to Rasulullah ﷺ or when he was delivering a lecture, he would appear like a person warning his people of an approaching punishment. When this was not happening, you would see that he had the most smiley face. He was the most cheerful of people and the most handsome of all men." *(Bazzar, Haythami)*. Abu Umama ❀ says, "Rasulullah ﷺ was one of the most cheerful of people and the one with the best personality." *(Tabrani, Haythami)*.

Rasulullah ﷺ Laughs During the Battle of Khandaq

Amir bin Sa'd reports that Sa'd ❀ said to him, "I saw Rasulullah ﷺ smile so broadly during the Battle of Khandaq that his molar teeth actually became visible." When Amir asked what the reason for Rasulullah ﷺ's laughter was, Sa'd ❀ explained that a man from the enemy was waving his shield to and from to protect his forehead thereby teasing the Muslim archers to get him. Being a crack archer, Sa'd ❀ took out an arrow, placed it on the bow and waited for the chance. As soon as the man raised his head, Sa'd ❀ shot the arrow which struck the man squarely on the forehead. The man fell to the ground while his leg remained extended into the air. Rasulullah ﷺ then smiled to broadly that his molars became visible. "What made Rasulullah ﷺ laugh so?" someone asked. The narrator replied, "It was the shrewdness with which Sa'd dealt with the man." *(Tirmidhi in Shama'il)*

Rasulullah ﷺ Laughs at What a Poor Man did During Ramadhan

Abu Hurairah ❀ reports that a man came to Rasulullah ﷺ saying, "I am destroyed! I have engaged in sexual relations with my wife during Ramadhan." "Then free a slave," Rasulullah ﷺ advised. When he declared that he was unable to afford it, Rasulullah ﷺ advised, "Then fast for 2 consecutive months." When he said that he would be unable to do that as well, Rasulullah ﷺ said, "Then feed 60 poor people." "I cannot afford that either," the man said. Someone later presented a basket of dates to Rasulullah ﷺ, he summoned the man and instructed him to give the dates away as Sadaqah. "Should I give it to someone more in need than I? By Allah! There is no family between the rocky plains of Madinah more in need of it than my family." Rasulullah ﷺ smiled so widely that his molars became visible as he said, "Then let it be spent on your family." *(Bukhari)*.

The Narrations of Abu Dhar ❀ and Abdullah bin Mas'ood ❀

Abu Dhar ❀ narrates that Rasulullah ﷺ once said, "I know the first person to enter Jannah and the last to emerge from Jahannam. A man will be summoned on the Day of Judgment and his minor sins will be presented before him while his major sins will be concealed. Given the precise dates and times, he will be asked whether he committed certain evil acts. Unable to deny anything, he will admit to it all, fearing the major sins still to be accounted for. It will then be said, 'Grant him a good deed in place of every sin he committed.' He will then quickly say, "But I have committed other sins that I do not see here."' Abu Dhar says, "I then saw Rasulullah ﷺ smile so widely that his molars were visible." *(Tirmidhi in Shama'il)*. Abdullah bin Mas'ood ❀ reports that Rasulullah ﷺ said, "I know who the last person to emerge from Jahannam will be. He will come out of Jahannam crawling, unable to stand up straight because of the intensity of the punishment and will be told to enter Jannah. As he starts proceeding towards Jannah, he will see that other people have already occupied its levels. He will then return to Allah saying, "O my Rabb! People have occupied the various levels leaving no place for me." He will then be asked, "Do you remember the times you had in the world?" "I certainly do," he will reply. "Then wish for all you would like to have," he will be told. After wishing for everything he can think of, he will be told, "You shall have everything you have wished for together with 10 times more of what the world had to offer." He will say in disbelief, "Are You joking with me when You are the King of the worlds?" Abdullah bin Mas'ood ❀ says, "I saw Rasulullah ﷺ smile so widely that his molars were visible." *(Tirmidhi in Shama'il)*

The Dignified Behavior of Rasulullah ﷺ

Kharija bin Zaid ❀ says, "Rasulullah ﷺ was the most dignified person in his gatherings and as he sat, none of his limbs extended towards the people." *(Qadhi Ayadh in Shifa, Abu Dawud in Marasil, Sharhush Shifa)*

The Dignified Behavior of Mu'adh bin Jabal

Shahr bin Howshab says that when the Sahabah spoke in the presence of Mu'adh bin Jabal, they kept looking at him out of fear for him. Abu Muslim Khowlani narrates, "I once entered the Masjid of Hims where I came across close to 30 middle-aged Sahabah of Rasulullah. Amongst them was a young man with kohl around his eyes and sparkling front teeth. He spoke not a word and remained silent. When the others disagreed about anything, they turned to him and asked him. When I asked the person beside me who the man was, he informed me that he was Mu'adh bin Jabal. I liked him and remained with the group until they dispersed." Abu Muslim narrates, "I once entered the Masjid with some Sahabah during the early years of Omar's Khilafa. There were more of them present that day than any other and the gathering I sat in included over 30 Sahabah, all narrating Ahadeeth from Rasulullah. Sitting in the gathering was a young man who was brown in complexion, who spoke extremely well and who was good looking. He was the youngest of the group, they referred to him whenever they doubted anyone's narration. He would correctly narrate the Hadith they doubted to them. Unless they asked him, he did not narrate anything else to them. 'Who are you, O servant of Allah?' I asked him. 'I am Mu'adh bin Jabal,' came the reply." *(Abu Nu'aym in Hilya)*

Suppressing One's Anger

Abu Barza narrates, "When a man spoke harshly to Abu Bakr, I said, 'Should I not execute him?' Abu Bakr rebuked me saying, 'Such punishment is not warranted for anyone speaking harshly to anyone after Rasulullah.'" *(Tayalisi, Ahmad, Humaidi, Abu Dawud, Tirmidhi, Abu Ya'la, Sa'eed bin Mansur in Kanzul Ummal)*. Omar once said, "No person cannot sip any milk or honey that is better than a sip of his anger." *(Ahmad in Zuhd, Kanzul Ummal)*

The Possessiveness of Ubay bin Ka'b

Ubay bin Ka'b narrates that a man reported to Rasulullah that a certain person frequently went to see his father's wife with apparently sinister intentions. Ubay bin Ka'b exclaimed, "Had it been me, I would have killed him." Rasulullah laughed as he said, "How possessive are you, O Ubay! However, I am more possessive than you and Allah is more possessive than I." *(Ibn Asakir in Muntakhab Kanzul Ummal)*

The Possessiveness of Sa'd bin Ubadah

Mughiera narrates that Sa'd bin Ubadah once said, "If I find any man with my wife, I would strike him with the sharp edge of my sword." When this was reported to Rasulullah, he said, "Are you surprised with Sa'd's possessiveness? By Allah! I am more possessive than him and Allah is more possessive than I. It is because of Allah's possessiveness that He has forbidden all types of indecency, be it apparent or hidden. There is also none who loves to be absolved of blame more than Allah and it is because of this that He has sent warners and givers of glad tidings, the Ambiya so that people cannot say that they did not know. There is also none who loves praise more than Allah and it is because of this that He created jannah." *(Bukhari, Muslim)*. Abu Hurairah reports that Sa'd bin Ubadah once asked, "If I find a man with my wife, am I not allowed to touch him until I present 4 witnesses'?" "That's right," Rasulullah replied. Sa'd then said, "That cannot be! I swear by the Being Who has sent you with the truth that before that I would speed up his journey with my sword." "Listen to what your leader has to say," Rasulullah said to the Sahabah, "He is extremely

possessive, but I am more possessive than him and Allah is more possessive than I." *(Muslim in Mishkatul Masabih)*. Abdullah bin Abbas adds that the Sahabah said, "O Rasulullah! Do not rebuke him because he is an extremely possessive person. By Allah! He has only married virgins and because of his possessiveness, none of us has ever dared to marry any woman he has divorced." Sa'd said, "O Rasulullah! I know that the injunction of presenting 4 witnesses to prove adultery is true and is from Allah but I find it strange that when I find a man rubbing his thighs against those of an immoral woman, I am unable to move him until I bring 4 witnesses. By Allah! By the time I come with them, he would have fulfilled his desire and left." *(Abu Ya'la, Ahmad, Haythami)*

The Possessiveness of Aisha

Aisha reports that when Rasulullah left her one night, she became extremely jealous. Rasulullah then returned to see what she was doing and commented, "What is the matter, O Aisha'? Have you been overcome with possessiveness'?" Aisha replied, "Why should someone like myself not be possessive over someone like yourself'?" "Your Saitan must have come to you," Rasulullah remarked. "O Rasulullah!" Aisha asked, "Is there a Saitan with me'?" "Certainly," Rasulullah replied. "And with you, O Rasulullah'?" Aisha enquired. "Yes," Rasulullah replied, "but Allah has assisted me and he has become a Muslim and therefore does not influence me to do evil." *(Muslim in Miskatul Masabih)*. Aisha narrates, "When Rasulullah married Ummu Salamah, I became extremely depressed because people always told us about her beauty. When I managed to secretly steal a glance at her, I found her to be much more beautiful than people had described. I then mentioned this to Hafsa. Aisha and Hafsa were extremely close. She said, 'By Allah! This is only because of your extreme possessiveness. She cannot be as beautiful as you people say.' When Hafsa also managed to steal a glance at her, she said, 'I have seen her and I swear by Allah that she is not as beautiful as you say. She is not close to what you have described, although I do admit that she is pretty.'" Aisha says further, "I went to see her again and I swear by my life that she was just as Hafsa had mentioned. Because of my extreme possessiveness that I found her to be more beautiful than she actually was." *(Ibn Sa'd)*

Ali Rebukes People Deprived of Any Possessiveness

Ali once addressed the people saying, "The news has reached me that your women crowd the marketplaces with Kuffar men. Have you people no sense of possessiveness? There can be no good in a person who is deprived of all possessiveness." Another narration states that Ali said, "There are 2 types of possessiveness. The first is commendable and a means by which a person keeps his family in check. The other is the type that leads a person to Jahannam." *(Rustah in Kanzul Ummal)*

Rasulullah Narrates the Incident of People of the Past who were Tortured for Enjoining What is Good and Forbidding What is Evil

Abdullah bin Mas'ood narrates that Rasulullah came indoors one day and said, "O Ibn Mas'ood!" "At your service, O Rasulullah!" Abdullah bin Mas'ood repeated thrice. Rasulullah then asked, "Do you know who are the best of people?" "Allah and His Rasul know best," Abdullah bin Mas'ood submitted. Rasulullah said, "Indeed the best of people are those who do the best deeds when they have acquired a deep understanding of Islam." "O Ibn Mas'ood!" Rasulullah said again. "At your service, O Rasulullah!" Abdullah bin

Mas'ood ﷺ replied. "Do you know who are the most learned people?" Again Abdullah bin Mas'ood ﷺ submitted, "Allah and His Rasul ﷺ know best." Rasulullah ﷺ explained, "Indeed the most learned of people are those with the deepest insight into the truth when people are in disagreement even though they fall short in deeds and are dragging themselves along on their buttocks. Those before me were divided into 72 groups, amongst which all besides 3 were destroyed. One of these groups opposed the kings and fought them for the sake of their Islam which was the Islam of Isa bin Maryam (عليه السلام). They were captured and killed when their bodies were cut up with saws. Another group amongst them neither had the power to fight the kings nor to live amongst the masses and invite them to Allah and to the Islam of Isa bin Maryam (عليه السلام). They therefore dispersed in the land and adopted monasticism. It is with regard to these people that Allah says:

وَرَهْبَانِيَّةً ابْتَدَعُوهَا مَا كَتَبْنَاهَا عَلَيْهِمْ إِلَّا ابْتِغَاءَ رِضْوَانِ اللَّهِ فَمَا رَعَوْهَا حَقَّ رِعَايَتِهَا فَآتَيْنَا الَّذِينَ آمَنُوا مِنْهُمْ أَجْرَهُمْ وَكَثِيرٌ مِنْهُمْ فَاسِقُونَ (27)

Then, We sent after them, Our Messengers, and We sent Isa (Jesus) son of Maryam (Mary), and gave him the Injeel (Gospel). And We ordained in the hearts of those who followed him, compassion and mercy. But the Monasticism which they invented for themselves, We did not prescribe for them, but (they sought it) only to please Allah therewith, but that they did not observe it with the right observance. So We gave those among them who believed, their (due) reward, but many of them are Fasiqoon (rebellious, disobedient to Allah). (Al-Hadid:27)

Rasulullah ﷺ then added, "Those of them who believe in me and follow me have observed its demands as it ought to be observed. As for those who do not follow me, they shall be destroyed." Another narration states that Rasulullah ﷺ said, "A group from them remained with the kings and tyrants to invite them towards the Islam of Isa (عليه السلام). However, they were captured and killed after being cut into pieces with saws and then burnt. They were steadfast until they met Allah." The rest of the narration is the same as the one above. *(Tabrani, Haythami)*

Rasulullah ﷺ Warns Those who do not Enjoin What is Good and do not Forbid What is Evil

Mu'adh bin Jabal ﷺ narrates that Rasulullah ﷺ said, "You people shall remain on the clear Path of your Rabb as long as 2 intoxicants do not become manifest amongst you; the intoxicant of ignorance and the intoxicant of love for this world. You may be enjoining what is good, forbidding what is evil and waging Jihad in the Path of Allah, as soon as the intoxicant of love for this world manifests itself amongst you, you will stop enjoining what is good, forbidding what is evil and waging Jihad in the Path of Allah. Those who speak by the Qur'an and the Sunnah during such times will be like the very first to accept Islam from the Muhajirin and the Ansar." *(Bazzar, Haythami)*

The Rank on the Day of Judgment of Those who Enjoin What is Good and Forbid What is Evil

Yazid Raqashi reports from Anas ﷺ that Rasulullah ﷺ said, "Should I not inform you about a group of people who although not belonging to the Ambiya (عليهم السلام) and the Shuhada (martyrs), will be the envy of the Ambiya (عليهم السلام) and Shuhada on the Day of Judgment because of their closeness to Allah. They will be recognized by the pulpits of light upon which they will be seated." "Who are they, O Rasulullah ﷺ?" the Sahabah begged to know. Rasulullah ﷺ replied, "They are those who travel the world advising people so that Allah's servants become beloved to Him and He becomes beloved to them." Anas ﷺ asked, "I can understand how they can make Allah beloved to His servants, but how do they make Allah's servants beloved to Him?" Rasulullah ﷺ explained, "They enjoin them to do what Allah likes and forbid them from doing what Allah dislikes. When the people follow this advice of theirs, they become beloved to Allah." *(Bayhaqi, Naqash in Mu'jim, Ibn Najjar in Kanzul Ummal)*

When will this Ummah Forsake Enjoining What is Good and Forbidding What is Evil?

Hudhaifa ﷺ narrates that he once asked Nabi ﷺ, "O Rasulullah ﷺ! When will people forsake enjoining what is good and forbidding what is evil, whilst these 2 deeds are the chief actions of righteous people?" Rasulullah ﷺ replied, "When that which afflicted the Bani Isra'el afflicts you as well." "O Rasulullah ﷺ! What was it that afflicted the Bani Isra'el?" Hudhaifa ﷺ asked. Rasulullah ﷺ replied, "When for worldly gain the good amongst you become lenient towards the sinners, when the knowledge of Islam goes to the worst amongst you and when leadership goes to the youngsters. When this happens, you will suffer adversities that will keep coming your way and towards which you will keep going." *(Tabrani, Haythami, Ibn Asakir, Ibn Najjar, Ibn Abi Dunya in Kanzul Ummal)*

Abu Bakr ﷺ Explains the verse: "Take Care of Your Own Selves"

Qais bin Abu Hazim narrates that when Abu Bakr ﷺ had become Khalifa, he mounted the pulpit and after duly praising Allah, he said, "O people! You recite the verse:

يَا أَيُّهَا الَّذِينَ آمَنُوا عَلَيْكُمْ أَنْفُسَكُمْ لَا يَضُرُّكُمْ مَنْ ضَلَّ إِذَا اهْتَدَيْتُمْ

O you who believe! Take care of your ownselves, (do righteous deeds, fear Allah much (abstain from all kinds of sins and evil deeds which He has forbidden) and love Allah much (perform all kinds of good deeds which He has ordained)). If you follow the right guidance and enjoin what is right (Islamic Monotheism and all that Islam orders one to do) and forbid what is wrong (polytheism, disbelief and all that Islam has forbidden) no hurt can come to you from those who are in error... (Al-Ma'ida:105)

However, you people have been misinterpreting the verse. I have heard Rasulullah ﷺ say, 'Whenever people see evil and fail to change it, the time is close when Allah shall engulf them all in great punishment: the evil-doers for the evil and the others for failing to prevent them.'" *(Ibn Abi Shaybah, Ahmad, Abd bin Humaid, Adani, Ibn Munee, Abu Dawud, Tirmidhi, Nasa'ee, Ibn Majah, Abu Ya'la, Dar Qutni in Ilal, Abu Nu'aym in Ma'rifa, Bayhaqi, Sa'eed bin Mansur)*. Abdullah bin Abbas ﷺ narrates that on the day he was named Khalifa, Abu Bakr ﷺ sat on Rasulullah ﷺ's pulpit. After duly praising Allah and sending salutations to Rasulullah ﷺ, he stretched out his hands and placed them on the spot of the pulpit where Rasulullah ﷺ used to sit. He then said, "As he was sitting on this very same spot, I heard my beloved friend Rasulullah ﷺ explain the meaning of the verse:

يَا أَيُّهَا الَّذِينَ آمَنُوا عَلَيْكُمْ أَنْفُسَكُمْ لَا يَضُرُّكُمْ مَنْ ضَلَّ إِذَا اهْتَدَيْتُمْ

O you who believe! Take care of your ownselves, (do righteous deeds, fear Allah much (abstain from all kinds of sins and evil deeds which He has forbidden) and love Allah much (perform all kinds of good deeds which He has ordained)). If you follow the right guidance and enjoin what is right (Islamic Monotheism and all that Islam orders one to do) and forbid what is wrong (polytheism, disbelief and all that Islam has forbidden) no hurt can come to you from those who are in error... (Al-Ma'ida:105)

In his explanation to us, Rasulullah ﷺ said, 'Yes. When evil is committed in a community and they are being corrupted with vices without them making an attempt to change matters or to even oppose it, it becomes binding on Allah to engulf them all in great punishment. Thereafter even their Du'as will not be accepted.'" Abu Bakr ◈ then placed his fingers into his ears saying, "May both these ears become deaf if I had not heard this from my beloved friend Rasulullah ◈." *(Ibn Mardway in Kanzul Ummal).* Abu Bakr ◈ said, "When people commit evil in the midst of others who are more powerful than them but who do not prevent them, Allah shall engulf them all in a great calamity that will not be alleviated." *(Bayhaqi in Kanzul Ummal)*

Omar ◈ and Uthman ◈ Instruct People to Enjoin What is Good and Forbid What is Evil

Omar ◈ once said, "When you people see a fool dishonoring people, what prevents you from opposing him?" When the people admitted that they feared abuse from the person, Omar ◈ said, "In that case, you will be unable to be witnesses for the Ambiya علیهم السلام on the Day of Judgment." *(Ibn Abi Shaybah, Abu Ubaid in Ghareeb, Ibn Abi Dunya in Samt, Kanzul Ummal).* Uthman ◈ said, "Enjoin what is good and forbid what is evil before the worst amongst you are given authority over you. When the best of you make Du'a against them, that Du'a will not be accepted." *(Ibn Abi Shaybah in Kanzul Ummal)*

Ali ◈ Encourages People to Enjoin Good and Warns Them Against Giving up Forbidding Evil

Ali ◈ once said, "You people must enjoin what is good, forbid what is evil and defend Islam, otherwise Allah shall place in authority over you such people who will punish you, after which Allah will punish them as well." Another narration states that Ali ◈ said, "You people must enjoin what is good and forbid what is evil otherwise Allah shall place the worst amongst you in authority over you and then when even the best of you make Du'a, their Du'as will not be accepted." *(Ibn Abi Shaybah).* In one of his sermons, Ali ◈ said, "O people! Those who were destroyed before you were destroyed because when they committed sin, their Rabbis and religious scholars did not prohibit them. Each time they transgressed all limits of sin and their Rabbis and religious scholars did not prevent them, punishment overtook them. You should therefore enjoin what is good and forbid what is evil before you suffer a like fate. Remember that enjoining what is good and forbidding what is evil can neither deprive you of your sustenance nor hasten your death." *(Ibn Abi Hatim in Kanzul Ummal).* Ali ◈ once said, "Jihad is of 3 categories; Jihad with the hand, Jihad with the tongue and Jihad with the heart. The first of these to disappear will be the Jihad of the hand, followed by Jihad of the tongue, and then Jihad of the heart. Eventually when the heart fails to recognize what is good and does not reject evil; it will be turned completely upside down." *(Masadad, Bayhaqi).* Ali ◈ once said, "The first Jihad to disappear will be the Jihad of your hands, followed by Jihad of your tongue and then Jihad of your heart. The heart that fails to recognize what is good and does not reject evil will be turned completely upside down just as a water bag is turned upside down to empty out everything inside." *(Ibn Abi Shaybah, Abu Nu'aym in Nusr fi Hujjah, Kanzul Ummal)*

The Statements of Abdullah bin Mas'ood ◈ Concerning Enjoining what is Good and Forbidding what is Evil

When Idris bin Urub Shaibani once came to Abdullah bin Mas'ood ◈ and said, "Destroyed is the person who does not enjoin good and forbid evil." Abdullah bin Mas'ood ◈ responded by saying, "That stage comes afterwards. In fact, the person whose heart does not recognize good and does not reject evil is

already destroyed." *(Tabrani, Haythami, Abu Nu'aym in Hilya, Ibn Abi Shaybah and Nu'aym in Fitan, Kanzul Ummal).* Abdullah bin Mas'ood ◈ once said, "People are of 3 types. There is no good in anyone who does not fall into one of these 3 categories. The 1st is the person who sees a group fighting in the Path of Allah and then he fights using his own wealth. The 2nd is the person who wages Jihad with his tongue in the defense of Islam and enjoins good and forbids evil. The 3rd is the man who recognizes the truth with his heart." *(Tabrani, Haythami).* Abdullah bin Mas'ood ◈ said, "Wage Jihad against the hypocrites with your tongues and if you can do nothing else besides frown at them to express your displeasure with them, then go ahead and frown at them." *(Ibn Asakir in Kanzul Ummal, Tabrani, Haythami).* Abdullah bin Mas'ood ◈ also said, "When you see an evil and are unable to change it, it will suffice for Allah to know that you hate it within your heart." Another narration quotes that he said, "When a person witnesses an evil being perpetrated in his presence and he dislikes it, he is like one who had not witnessed it at all. However, when a person approves of an evil that is carried out in his absence, he is like one who has witnessed it. *(Ibn Abi Shaybah and Nu'aym in Kanzul Ummal).* It was also Abdullah bin Mas'ood ◈ who said, "Many evils will take place in the future. Those who approve of them are like those witnessing them even though they may not be present. On the other hand, those who actually witness them but despise them are like those who have not witnessed it at all." *(Nu'aym and Ibn Najjar in Kanzul Ummal).* In another narration, Abdullah bin Mas'ood ◈ said, "The righteous ones shall leave this world first, leaving behind only doubtful people who will be unable to recognize good or reject evil." *(Abu Nu'aym in Hilya)*

The Statements of Hudhaifa ◈ Concerning Enjoining What is good and Forbidding What is Evil

Abur Ruqad says, "I was a youngster when I went out with my master one day. We were somehow led to a gathering addressed by Hudhaifa ◈ who was saying, "In a single sitting, I hear some of you 4 times making a statement that if spoken during the time of Rasulullah ◈ would render a person a hypocrite. You people must enjoin good, forbid evil and encourage each other to do good otherwise Allah shall uproot you people with punishment. Alternatively, Allah shall grant the worst of you authority over you, after which the Du'as of even the best of you will not be answered." *(Abu Nu'aym in Hilya, Kanzul Ummal).* Hudhaifa ◈ once said, "Allah's curse is on those who are not amongst us. By Allah! You people must enjoin good and forbid evil otherwise there shall be fighting amongst you and the evil ones will overpower the righteous ones. They shall then kill them all until there is none left alive to enjoin good and forbid evil. Thereafter, Allah will be so annoyed with you that he will not even accept your Du'as." *(Abu Nu'aym in Hilya).* In another narration, Hudhaifa ◈ says, "There shall certainly come a time when the best of people will be deemed to be those who do not enjoin good and do not forbid evil." *(Abu Nu'aym in Hilya, Ibn Abi Shaybah, Ibn Abi Dunya, Kanzul Ummal)*

The Statements of Adi ◈ and Abu Darda ◈

Adi bin Hatim ◈ once said, "The good you do today was considered an evil in times gone by and the evil of today will be considered something good in times to come. You will always remain on the right as long as you do not regard good as evil and evil as good and as long as your scholars continue speaking the truth without demeaning it." *(Ibn Asakir in Kanzul Ummal).* Abu Darda ◈ once said, "I enjoin on you to do something that I do not do in the hope that Allah will grant me the reward for it." *(Ibn Asakir in Kanzul Ummal, Abu Nu'aym in Hilya)*

Omar ❧ Forbids his Family From Something he Forbade the People From Doing and His Comment About Hisham bin Hakim ❧

Abdullah bin Omar ❧ says that Omar ❧ intended forbidding the people from anything, he first approached his family saying, "Should I come to know of any of you perpetrating what I am forbidding the people from, I shall assign double the punishment to him." *(Ibn Sa'd, Ibn Asakir in Kanzul Ummal)*. Ibn Shihab reports that Hisham bin Hakim bin Hizam ❧ and few men with him together engaged in enjoining good and forbidding evil. Omar ❧ used to say, "Evil shall not take place as long as Hisham and I are alive." *(Malik, Ibn Sa'd in Kanzul Ummal)*

The Advice Umair bin Habib ❧ Gave His Son

Abu Ja'far Khatmi reports that his grandfather Umair bin Habib bin Khumasha ❧ was a Sahabi who had been in the company of Rasulullah ﷺ since the time he came of age. He advised his son saying, "Dear son! Beware of the company of the foolish ones because keeping their company is a disease. The person who tolerates the foolish ones without responding to their foolish statements shall remain happy while the one who responds to them has regrets. Whoever cannot tolerate the little bother he gets from such people shall soon have to tolerate a whole lot more. The person who intends enjoining good and forbidding evil will have to get the habit of exercising patience in the face of harm and will have to be convinced about the rewards from Allah. Verily the person who is convinced about the rewards from Allah shall never be harmed by the touch of harm." *(Tabrani, Haythami, Abu Nu'aym in Kitabuz Zuhd, Isabah)*

Abu Bakra ❧ Fears Living in a Time When There is no Enjoining Good and Forbidding Evil

Abdul Aziz bin Abu Bakra narrates that Abu Bakra ❧ married a woman from the Banu Ghudana who later passed away. As he carried her to the graveyard, her brothers prevented him from leading the Janaza salah. He said to them, "Do not stand in my way because I am more worthy of leading the salah than you are." "The companion of Rasulullah ﷺ is right," they finally agreed. After he had performed the salah and was going to enter the grave, some people pushed him so hard that he fell down and collapsed. When he was taken home, all 20 of his sons and daughters started screaming. Abdul Aziz says that he was one of the youngest children. When Abu Bakra ❧ regained consciousness, he said, "Do not scream and cry over me because I would not like the death of anyone more than that of Abu Bakra." When then children had settled, they asked, "Why is that, dear father?" Abu Bakra ❧ replied, "I fear living in a time when I will be unable to enjoin good and forbid evil. There shall be no good in such a time." *(Tabrani, Haythami)*

Anas ❧ and Abdullah bin Omar ❧ Shun Preventing Hajjaj From Evil Out of Fear for Being Harmed

Ali bin Zaid reports that he was once with Hajjaj in a castle as Hajjaj was busy interrogating people about their links with Ibnul Ash'ath. Anas ❧ arrived there and when he drew close, Hajjaj called out to him, "Come here, you evil, you rebel! You are sometimes siding with Ali bin Abi Talib, sometimes with Ibn Zubair and sometimes with Ibnul Ash'ath. I swear by the Being Who controls my life! I shall peel you just as glue is peeled off and skin you just as a lid is skinned!" Anas ❧ remarked, "Who is the Amir referring to? May Allah rectify him." "It is you I am

referring to," Hajjaj snapped, "May Allah make you deaf!" Anas ❧ simply recited, "*Inna Lillahi wa Inna Ilayhi Raji'un*" and left. He said, "Had I not thought of my children and feared what Hajjaj would do to them, I would have told him such things on the spot for which he would have no reply."*(Tabrani, Haythami)*. Abdullah bin Omar ❧ said, "I heard Hajjaj say something in his lecture that I did not like. I intended objecting it, I recalled the words of Rasulullah ﷺ who said, 'It is not appropriate for a Mu'min to humiliate himself.' I asked Rasulullah ﷺ how it was possible for a Mu'min to humiliate himself. Rasulullah ﷺ replied, 'When he instigates such difficult conditions to come to himself that he is unable to bear.'" *(Bazzar, Tabrani, Haythami)*.

The Statement of Omar ❧ Concerning Keeping to Oneself

Omar ❧ once said, "In keeping to oneself, one finds an escape from mixing with bad company." *(Ibn Abi Shaybah, Ahmad in Zuhd, Ibn Abi Dunya in Azlah)* In another narration, Omar ❧ stated, "Take your full share of keeping to yourself." *(Ahmad, Ibn Hibban in Rowdah, Askari in Mawa'idh, Kanzul Ummal, Ibn Mubarak in Raqa'iq, Fat'hul Bari)*. Mu'afa bin Imran reports that Omar ❧ once passed by some people who were following a man who had been arrested for committing a crime. Omar ❧ said, "There is no welcome for faces that are seen only on occasions of evil." *(Dinowri in Kanzul Ummal)*

The Statement of Abdullah bin Mas'ood ❧ About Keeping to Oneself and His Advice to His Son and to Another Person

Adasa Ta'i reports, "I was in Sarif when Abdullah bin Mas'ood ❧ arrived there and my family sent me to him with a few things as gifts. It so happened that a few of our slaves who tended to the camels brought a bird from a place to which it took 4 days to travel. When they sent the bird to Abdullah ❧, he asked from where it had been brought. I replied, 'A few of our slaves who tend to the camels brought the bird from a place which lies 4 days away.' He then remarked, 'I wish that I was at that place where I need not speak to anyone about anything and no one would speak to me either until the day I meet Allah." *(Tabrani, Haythami, Ibn Asakir in Kanzul Ummal)*. Qasim narrates that a man came to Abdullah bin Mas'ood ❧ asking for advice. Abdullah bin Mas'ood ❧ advised, "Let your home accommodate you, stay indoors, restrain your tongue and weep at the though of your sins." *(Abu Nu'aym in Hilya)*. Isma'eel bin Abu Khalid narrates that Abdullah bin Mas'ood ❧ gave 3 advices to his son Abu Ubaidah, when he said, "Dear son! I advise you to adopt Taqwa, to have your house accommodate you, stay indoors and to weep over your sins." *(Tabrani, Haythami)*.

Hudhaifa ❧, Abdullah bin Abbas ❧, Abu Jahm ❧ and Abu Darda ❧ all Encourage Keeping to Oneself

Hudhaifa ❧ once said, "I wish I had someone to manage my finances so that I could lock my door and neither have anyone come to meet me nor go out to meet anyone until the day I meet Allah." *(Hakim in Kazul Ummal, Abu Nu'aym in Hilya)*. Abdullah bin Abbas ❧ said, "Had it not been for the evil whisperings of Saitan, I would go to a place where I have no friends so that I could spend my time in solitude. It is only people who corrupt people." *(Ibn Abi Dunya in Kanzul Ummal)*. Yahya bin Sa'eed says that Abu Jahm bin Harith bin Simma ❧ was a person who did not associate with his fellow Ansar. When this solitude was mentioned to him, he remarked, "People are worse than solitude." *(Ibn Abi Dunya in Kanzul Ummal)*. Abu Darda ❧ said, "The best monastery for a Muslim is his home where he is able to keep his carnal wish, his eyes and his private organs under control. Beware of the gatherings in the marketplaces because they involve a person in negligence and futile activities." *(Ibn Asakir in Kanzul Ummal)*

The Solitude of Mu'adh bin Jabal

Abdullah bin Amr passed by Mu'adh bin Jabal who was standing by his door and pointing with his fingers as if speaking to himself. "What is the matter, O Abu Abdur Rahman?" Abdullah bin Amr asked, "Why are talking to yourself?" Mu'adh replied, "What else can I do? That enemy of Allah, Saitan is trying to divert me from what I heard Rasulullah say. Saitan says, 'Why do you distress yourself by remaining at home all the time? Why do you not join the gatherings of people? I heard Rasulullah say that the person who goes out in the Path of Allah is in the custody of Allah, the person who visits the ill is in the custody of Allah, the person who goes morning or evening to the Masjid is in the custody of Allah, the person who goes out to assist the just Muslim ruler is in the custody of Allah and the person who stays at home without backbiting about anyone is in the custody of Allah.' This enemy of Allah wishes to take me out of my house to sit in various gatherings of people."*(Tabrani, Bazzar, Ahmad, Haythami)*

Omar Encourages Contentment

Abdullah bin Ubaid narrates that when Omar once saw Ahnaf wearing a new upper garment, he asked, "O Ahnaf! What did you pay for this garment'?" "I bought it for 12 Dirhams," Ahnaf replied. "Shame on you!" Omar exclaimed, "Couldn't you buy one for 6 Dirhams and use the balance in something, some good cause that you know of?" *(Ibn Mubarak in Kanzul Ummal). Hasan Basri* reports that in a letter to Abu Musa Ash'ari , Omar wrote, "Be content with whatever sustenance you receive in this world because the simple fact is that Ar Rahman gives some people more sustenance than others. In fact, each person is tested in this manner. Allah tests those whom He gives in abundance to see whether they are grateful. Their gratitude to Allah is expressed by their fulfilling the binding duties connected to the wealth Allah has blessed them with." *(Ibn Abi Hatim in Kanzul Ummal)*

The Contentment of Ali and the Advice that he and Sa'd gave in this Regard

Abu Ja'far narrates that Ali once ate some dry dates, drank some water and then placed his hand on his belly saying, "May Allah distance from His mercy the person whose stomach gets him admitted into Jahannam." He recited a couplet:

"Whenever you give your stomach and genitals whatever they ask for. They will both attain only the heights of regret"
(Askari in Kanzul Ummal)

Sha'bi narrates that Ali bin Abi Talib once said, "O son of Adam! Never bring the worry of the approaching day before the worry of the present day, by worrying about what you are to eat the following day because if you are not destined to die tomorrow, your sustenance win definitely be coming to you. You should also remember that when you accumulate wealth that is more than your basic necessities, you are actually acting as treasurer for someone else who will soon be taking possession of it." *(Dinowri in Kanzul Ummal).* Sa'd bin Abi Waqqas advised, "Dear son! When you seek to be independent, do so with contentment because when a person is not content, his wealth will never make him independent because he will never have enough."*(Ibn Asakir in Kanzul Ummal)*

Rasulullah 's Marriage to Khadija

It was Jabir bin Samura or another Sahabi who reported that as a youngster before announcing his prophethood, Nabi grazed goats but later gave it up when he and a partner of his started a rental business with camels. They once rented some camels to the sister of Khadija and when the journey had been completed, she still owed them some money. When Rasulullah 's partner started going to her to collect the money, he asked Rasulullah to accompany him. "You go ahead," Rasulullah would tell him, "because I feel too shy." When the partner one day went to her, she asked, "Where is Muhammad?" the partner explained that whenever he asked Rasulullah to accompany him, Rasulullah would say that he is too shy. She remarked, "I have never seen a man more modest than he, chaste than him..." She then continued to enumerate the excellent qualities of Rasulullah , causing her sister Khadija to fall in love with Rasulullah . Khadija communicated a message to Rasulullah saying, "Go to my father and propose for my hand in marriage." Rasulullah communicated a message back saying, "Your father is a very wealthy man and will not accept a proposal from a poor man such as I am." She however persisted saying, "Go meet him and speak to him. I shall arrange matters further. Go see him when he is drunk." Rasulullah did as she directed and when he approached her father, the father got him married. The following morning when her father attended a gathering, someone remarked, "You have done well to get Muhammad married to your daughter." "I did such a thing?" he asked in surprise. When the people confirmed that he did, he got up and went to Khadija. "The people tell me that I got Muhammad married to you," he said. "Indeed," she replied, "you need never regret your decision because Muhammad is ..." she then started enumerating the great virtues of Rasulullah so much that he was happy with the marriage. Khadija later sent 2 Awqiya of silver or gold to Rasulullah telling him to use it to purchase a set of clothing to give her as a gift as well as a sheep and some other items with which to host a meal. Rasulullah did as she told." *(Tabrani, Bazzar, Haythami)* Another narration substitutes the words "Go see him when he is drunk" with the words "Go see him (my father) without pressure on either party". The narration states that Khadija told Rasulullah to buy the clothing and give it as a gift to her father. *(Bazzar).* Abdullah bin Abbas reports that Rasulullah once mentioned how the father of Khadija was reluctant to marry her to Rasulullah . She however prepared a meal and invited her father along with several members of the Quraish who ate and drank until they were drunk. It was then that she said to him, "Muhammad bin Abdullah has proposed to marry me. Do marry me to him." When he got her married, she applied Khaluq, a type of fragrance to him and gave him a set of clothing to wear, in keeping with the custom of their forefathers. When he became sober and noticed the Khaluq and clothing, he exclaimed, "What has happened to me? What is this?" When Khadija informed him that he had married her to Muhammad bin Abdullah, he cried out, "Did I get Abu Talib's married'?! By my life! This can never be!" "Have you no shame'?" Khadija remarked, "Do you wish to make yourself look like a fool in front of the Quraish who will inform the people that you were drunk?" She then continued convincing him until he was happy with the marriage. *(Ahmad, Tabrani, Haythami)*

Nafisah reports, "Khadija bint Khuwailid was an extremely wise, strong and noble woman. She was all of this together with the honor and good that Allah had in store for her. During her time, she was noted as a woman of highest birth who was the most respected and also the wealthiest amongst the Quraish. Every man of her people desired to marry her if he got the opportunity to do so. In fact, many had asked for her hand in marriage and had spent large sums of money in their quest. When Muhammad ﷺ one day returned with her caravan from a journey to Sham, Khadija ☺ sent me to him to extract some information. 'O Muhammad ﷺ!' I said, 'What prevents you from getting married?' 'I have no money at hand with which to marry,' he replied. I went further and asked, 'What if your expenses were taken care of and you were asked to marry a beautiful, wealthy and respectable woman who was perfectly suited to you'? Would you accept the offer?' 'Who is she'?' he enquired. When I told him that she was Khadija ☺, he remarked, 'How is it possible for me when she is so wealthy and I a so poor'?' 'That is my responsibility,' I assured him. 'Then I am prepared,' he confirmed. When I reported back to her, she sent him a message informing him exactly when to arrive for the ceremony. She then sent for her uncle Amr bin Asad to get her married. Just after Amr had arrived, Rasulullah ﷺ also arrived with several of his uncles and it was one of them who conducted the marriage ceremony. Amr bin Asad remarked, 'He is a partner that can never be turned down.' At the time of this marriage, Rasulullah ﷺ was 25 years old while Khadija ☺ was 40. She was born 15 years before the year of the elephant." *(Ibn Sa'd)*

Rasulullah ﷺ's Marriage to Aisha ☺ and Sauda ☺

Aisha ☺ reports that when Khadija ☺ passed away, Rasulullah ﷺ was still living in Makkah. It was then that Khowla bint Hakim bin Awqa ☺ the wife of Uthman bin Madh'un ☺ suggested, "O Rasulullah ﷺ! Are you not interested in getting married'?" "To whom'?" Rasulullah ﷺ asked. She replied, "A virgin if you wish or a previously married woman if you wish." "Who is the virgin'?" Rasulullah ﷺ asked. Khowlah ☺ replied, "She is the daughter of the person you like best, Aisha ☺ the daughter of Abu Bakr ☺." "And who is the previously married woman'?" Rasulullah ﷺ asked. "She is Saudah bint Zam'ah ☺," came the reply, "she has believed in you as Allah's Rasul ﷺ and follows you in Islam." Rasulullah ﷺ then said to her, "Go and mention my name to them." Khowla ☺ went to Abu Bakr ☺'s house where she found Ummu Ruman ☺ who was the mother of Aisha ☺. "O Ummu Ruman," she said, "What tremendous goodness and blessings is Allah about to shower on your family! Rasulullah ﷺ has sent me to propose for Aisha's hand in marriage." Ummu Ruman ☺ said, "I would love it, but let us wait for Abu Bakr ☺ who is soon to arrive." When he came, Khowla ☺ said to him, "What tremendous goodness and blessings is Allah about to shower on your family! Rasulullah ﷺ has sent me to propose for Aisha's hand in marriage." Abu Bakr ☺ asked, "Is she suitable for him'? She is the daughter of his brother." Khowla ☺ reported back to Rasulullah ﷺ the doubt that Abu Bakr ☺ expressed. Rasulullah ﷺ said, "Go back and tell him that he is my brother in Islam and that I am his brother in Islam, not by blood. His daughter is therefore suitable for me." When she conveyed the message to Abu Bakr ☺, he said, "Call Rasulullah ﷺ here." Rasulullah ﷺ then came and Abu Bakr ☺ got Aisha ☺ married to him. Another narration states at the end that Rasulullah ﷺ told Khowla ☺, "Go back and tell him that I am his brother in Islam, not by blood and that he is my brother in Islam. His daughter is therefore suitable for me." When Khowla ☺ returned with the message, Abu Bakr ☺ told her to wait and then left the house. Ummu Ruman ☺ says that Mut'im bin Adi had requested the hand of Aisha ☺ for his son Jubayr and Abu Bakr ☺ had promised it to him. Because Abu Bakr ☺ never broke a promise, he went to see Mut'im. At that time Mut'im was with his wife who was the mother of the boy in question (Jubair). She however spoke to Abu Bakr ☺ in such harsh terms that the desire to fulfill his promise to Mut'im was forced out of Abu Bakr ☺'s heart. Abu Bakr ☺ asked Mut'im, "What have you to say about my daughter'? Are you still interested in getting your son married to her'?" Mut'im however turned to his wife saying, "What have you to say'?" She turned to Abu Bakr ☺ and said, "It seems that if we marry the boy to her, you will make him irreligious and enter him into the religion you follow." Abu Bakr ☺ again turned to Mut'im and asked, "What have you to say?" Mut'im replied, "You have heard what she has to say, I stand by that." Abu Bakr ☺ then left them. Allah had removed from his heart the worry for the promise he had made. He then said to Khowla ☺, "Call Rasulullah ﷺ here." She called Rasulullah ﷺ and when he arrived, Abu Bakr ☺ got Aisha ☺ married to him. Aisha ☺ was then 6 years old.

Khowla ☺ then left them and went to Sauda bint Zam'ah ☺. She said to Sauda ☺, "What tremendous goodness and blessings is Allah about to shower on you!" "What is it?" Sauda ☺ asked. "Rasulullah ﷺ has sent me to propose for your hand in marriage." "I would love to marry him. Go and tell my father about it." Her father was an extremely old man who was unable to even perform Hajj. Khowla ☺ went to him and greeted him with the greeting of the period of ignorance. "Who is there?" he asked. "Khowla bint Hakim," she replied. When he asked her why she had come, she replied, "Muhammad ﷺ bin Abdullah has sent me to propose for Sauda's hand in marriage." "What has she to say?" the old man asked. "She would very much like to marry him," Khowla ☺ replied. The old man then asked her to call for Rasulullah ﷺ and when he arrived, he married her to Rasulullah ﷺ. When Sauda ☺'s brother Abd bin Zam'ah returned from Hajj, he started throwing sand on his head out of sorrow. However, after he had accepted Islam, he remarked, "By my life! I was a real fool the day I threw sand on my head because Rasulullah ﷺ married Sauda bint Zam'ah." Aisha ☺ relates further, "When we arrived in Madinah, we stayed in Sunh with the Banu Harith bin Khazraj tribe. When Rasulullah ﷺ came to our house one day, my mother came to me as I was swinging on a swing suspended between 2 palm branches. She took me off the swing and neatened my hair which was very short. She then wiped my face with some water and led me to the door. I was out of breath by then and stood there until my breathing had returned to normal. My mother then took me into the room where Rasulullah ﷺ was sitting on a seat with several men and women of the Ansar. My mother closed the door behind me and said, 'This is now your family. May Allah bless you with them and bless them with you." All the men and women then stood up and left. It was then in our house that the marriage was completed. Neither was any camel nor any goat slaughtered for my marriage until Sa'd bin Ubadah sent a platter of food which he usually sent to Rasulullah ﷺ whenever he was with any of his wives. I was then 7 years old however, several more authentic narrations confirm that Aisha ☺ was then 9 years old." *(Ahmad, Haythami)*

Rasulullah ﷺ's Marriage to Hafsa the Daughter of Omar ☺

Abdullah bin Omar ☺ narrates that Hafsa ☺ became a widow when her husband Khunais bin Hudhafa Sahmi ☺ who was a veteran of the Battle of Badr, passed away in Madinah. When this happened, Omar ☺ met Uthman ☺ and asked, "If you agree, I can get you married to my daughter Hafsa." "I shall think about it," Uthman ☺ replied. After a few days, Uthman ☺ said to Omar ☺, "I have decided not to marry." Omar ☺ himself narrates further. He says, "I then approached Abu Bakr ﷺ saying, 'If you agree, I can get you married to my daughter Hafsa.' He however remained silent. This made me angrier than I had been with Uthman ﷺ but it was only a few days later that Rasulullah ﷺ proposed for her hand in marriage. After I had married her to Rasulullah ﷺ, Abu Bakr ﷺ met me and said, 'You were perhaps very angry with me when I failed to give you a reply the day you proposed that I marry Hafsa?' 'I certainly was,' I replied. He then explained, 'The only thing that prevented me from getting back to you was that I knew Rasulullah ﷺ had spoken about proposing for her and I could not reveal Rasulullah ﷺ's secret. I would have accepted the proposal had Rasulullah ﷺ left her.'" (Bukhari, Nasa'ee in Jam'ul Fawa'id). When Omar ﷺ complained to Rasulullah ﷺ about Uthman ﷺ not accepting the proposal, Rasulullah ﷺ remarked, "Hafsa shall be married to someone better than Uthman ﷺ and Uthman ﷺ shall be married to someone better than Hafsa." Rasulullah ﷺ later got Uthman ﷺ married to his daughter and himself married Hafsa ﷺ. (Ahmad, Bayhaqi, Abu Ya'la, Ibn Hibban in Muntakhab Kanzul Ummal)

Rasulullah ﷺ's Marriage to Ummu Salamah bint Abu Umayyah ﷺ

Ummu Salamah ﷺ reports that when her Iddah had expired, Abu Bakr ﷺ proposed for her hand in marriage but she did not marry him. When Rasulullah ﷺ sent someone to extend his proposal of marriage, she said, "Do inform Rasulullah ﷺ that I am a woman who is extremely possessive, that I have children, and that none of my guardians are present." When the message reached him, Rasulullah ﷺ said, "Tell her, 'As for your statement that you are extremely possessive, I shall pray to Allah to dispel it. As for your statement that you have children, they shall be well taken care of and as for your statement that you have no guardians present, none of them who are either present or absent shall object to this." When the message reached her, Ummu Salamah ﷺ instructed her son Omar ﷺ saying, "Get up and get Rasulullah ﷺ married." He then got Rasulullah ﷺ married to his mother. (Nasa'ee in Isabah, Jam'ul Fawa'id). When Ummu Salamah ﷺ arrived in Madinah and told the people that she was the daughter of Abu Umayyah bin Mughiera, they refused to believe her. When some of them were leaving for Hajj, they asked her if she wanted to write to her family in Makkah. She sent a letter with them by which they managed to confirm who she was and when they returned, they believed her. This then increased her status amongst them. After she had given birth to her daughter Zainab, signaling the expiry of her Iddah, Rasulullah ﷺ proposed for her hand in marriage. She said, "Can a woman such as I be married? I am unable to bear children because of my age, am extremely possessive and have children of my own." Rasulullah ﷺ replied, "I am elder than you, Allah shall remove your extreme possessiveness and your children shall be the responsibility of Allah and His Rasul ﷺ." Rasulullah ﷺ then married her and whenever he came to her, he would affectionately ask, "Where is Zainab?" This continued until one day Ammar bin Yasir ﷺ took the child away saying, "Her presence is preventing Rasulullah ﷺ from his needs with his new bride." During that period, Ummu Salamah ﷺ was still breast feeding the child. When Rasulullah ﷺ came later and asked "Where is Zainab?", Qarina bint Abu Umayyah ﷺ, Ummu Salama ﷺ's sister who happened to be there, informed him that Ammar ﷺ had taken her away so that Rasulullah ﷺ could have some privacy. Rasulullah ﷺ then told Ummu Salamah ﷺ that he would see her that night. Ummu Salamah ﷺ then put down her leather spread beneath her grindstone for the dirt to fall upon and took out some barley grains from her earthen pot. After grinding the barley, she then mixed the barley with some fat to make a type of porridge for Rasulullah ﷺ to eat. After Rasulullah ﷺ had spent the night with her, he said, "You deserve the respect of your family. If you wish, I could spend 7 nights with you, but then I would have to do the same for all my other wives." (Ibn Asakir in Kanzul Ummal, Nasa'ee in Isabah)

Rasulullah ﷺ's Marriage to Ummu Habibah ﷺ the Daughter of Abu Sufian ﷺ

Isma'el bin Amr reports that Ummu Habiba bint Abu Sufian ﷺ said, "What I remember well about the time I was in Abyssinia was the arrival of the messenger of the king Najashi. She was a lady called Abraha and was in charge of the king's clothing and oils. She sought permission to enter and when I allowed her in, she said, 'The king says, 'Rasulullah ﷺ has written to me to get you married to him.' I replied by saying, 'You have given me most excellent news, I accept.' She then said, 'The king asks you to appoint someone to hand you over in marriage.' I sent for Khalid bin Sa'eed bin Al Aas and appointed him for the task. Thereafter, out of joy for the news she had brought me, I gave Abraha 2 silver bangles, 2 silver anklets and every silver toe ring I was wearing." That evening, Najashi invited Ja'far bin Abi Talib and all the other Muslims who were there. Najashi then delivered a lecture saying, "All praise is due to Allah The Supreme King, The Most Pure, The Giver of Peace, The Mighty and Most Powerful. I testify that there is none worthy of worship but Allah and that Muhammad ﷺ is His Rasul, and the one about whose arrival Isa bin Maryam ﷺ had given the glad tidings. I wish to tell you that Rasulullah ﷺ has asked me to marry him to Ummu Habiba the daughter of Abu Sufian. I have complied with his wish and am giving her a dowry of 400 gold coins." He then poured out the coins in front of the people. Thereafter, Khalid bin Sa'eed ﷺ spoke. He said, "All praise belongs to Allah. It is He that I praise and from Him do I seek forgiveness. I testify that there is none worthy of worship but Allah and that Muhammad ﷺ is the servant and Rasul of Allah whom Allah has sent with guidance and the true Islam that shall overcome all other religions even though the disbeliever detest it. I wish to say that I also comply with the wish of Rasulullah ﷺ and hand over Ummu Habiba bint Abu Sufian ﷺ to him in marriage. May Allah bless Rasulullah ﷺ." Najashi then handed over the coins to Khalid ﷺ, who accepted it on behalf of Ummu Habibah ﷺ. When the Muslims then started to leave, Najashi said to them, "Do remain seated. It has been the practice of the Ambiya ﷺ host a meal on the occasion of a marriage. He then sent for the food and the Muslims ate before leaving. (Zubair bin Bakkar in Al Bidayah wan Nihayah)

Isma'el bin Amr bin Sa'eed bin Al Aas reports that Ummu Habiba bint Abu Sufian ﷺ said, "I saw my husband Ubaidulla bin Jahash in a dream looking most horrible and ugly. I awoke with a fright and said, 'By Allah! His condition must have changed.' That morning he surprised me by saying, 'O Ummu Habiba! I have thought about religion and see no religion better than Christianity. I had been a Christian before entering the religion of Muhammad. I have now reverted to Christianity.' 'By Allah!' I exclaimed, 'There is no good for you in this.' When I informed him about my dream, he simply ignored it and then got hooked on wine until he died." Continuing her narration, Ummu Habibah ﷺ says, "I then saw someone in a dream addressing me with the title of 'Ummul Mu'minin'. I awoke with a start and interpreted the dream to mean that Rasulullah ﷺ would soon marry me. As soon as my Iddah had expired, I well recall when the messenger of Najashi came to me..." The rest of the narration is like the one above. The narration adds at the end that Ummu Habibah 🕮 said, "After the Muslims had eaten and left and the money came to me, I sent for Abraha 🕮 who had brought me the good news. I said to her, 'I gave you what I did that day only because I had no money then. Here are 50 gold coins. Please take it and use it for yourself.' She produced a box containing everything I had given her. Returning it to me, she said, 'The king made me promise that I shall not take anything from you as long as I am in charge of his clothing and oils. I am also a follower of Islam of Rasulullah 🕮 and have submitted to Allah. The king has already instructed his wives to send to you all the perfumes they have in their possession.' The next morning, she brought me plenty of fragrances such as Ood, Waras, Amber and Zabad. I brought back all of this to Rasulullah 🕮 and although he saw it with me and saw me wearing it, he never objected. Abraha 🕮 then said to me, 'My only request to you is that you convey my Salams to Rasulullah 🕮 and that you inform him that I have become a follower of Islam. She treated me very kindly and even helped me prepare for the journey. When she came to me, she would say, 'Do not forget my request.' When I got to Rasulullah 🕮 and informed him about the proposal and the behavior of Abraha 🕮, he merely smiled and when I conveyed her Salams to him, he replied by saying: وَعَلَيْكِ السَّلَامُ وَرَحْمَةُ اللهِ وَبَرَكَاتُهُ *'May Allah's peace, mercy and blessings be on her.'* (Hakim, Ibn Sa'd)

Rasulullah 🕮's Marriage to Zainab bint Jahash 🕮

Anas 🕮 reports that when the Iddah of Zainab bint Jahash 🕮 had expired, Rasulullah 🕮 told Zaid 🕮 to ask her if she would marry him. When Zaid 🕮 saw her as she was kneading dough, her status soared so much in his heart because Rasulullah 🕮 wanted to marry her and that he was unable to even look at her. He therefore turned on his heels and facing his back to her, he said, "O Zainab! Glad tidings to you! Rasulullah 🕮 has sent me to propose for your hand in marriage." Zainab 🕮 replied by saying, "I am unable to do anything until I consult with my Rabb." She then stood at the place where she performed her salah and engaged in salah. It was then that Allah revealed some verses of the Qur'an in which Allah says, "We married her, Zainab to you O Rasulullah 🕮... " (*ref. Ahzab:37*). Because Allah had conducted the marriage, Rasulullah 🕮 then went to Zainab 🕮 without asking permission. Anas 🕮 says further, "I was also there when Rasulullah 🕮 went to Zainab 🕮 and fed us bread and meat to celebrate the occasion. While some people ate and left, others remained behind in the room to talk after eating. Rasulullah 🕮 left the room and I followed him. He then visited the rooms of all his wives to greet them and they all asked him how he found his new bride. I cannot remember if it was I or someone else who informed Rasulullah 🕮 that the guests had all left, upon which he went back to Zainab 🕮's room. As I was about to enter with Rasulullah 🕮, he drew a curtain between himself and I because the verses of Hijab had just been revealed. Also revealed was the verse teaching etiquette to the people, which states:

يَا أَيُّهَا الَّذِينَ آمَنُوا لَا تَدْخُلُوا بُيُوتَ النَّبِيِّ إِلَّا أَنْ يُؤْذَنَ لَكُمْ إِلَى طَعَامٍ غَيْرَ نَاظِرِينَ إِنَاهُ وَلَكِنْ إِذَا دُعِيتُمْ فَادْخُلُوا فَإِذَا طَعِمْتُمْ فَانْتَشِرُوا وَلَا مُسْتَأْنِسِينَ لِحَدِيثٍ إِنَّ ذَلِكُمْ كَانَ يُؤْذِي النَّبِيَّ فَيَسْتَحْيِي مِنْكُمْ وَاللَّهُ لَا يَسْتَحْيِي مِنَ الْحَقِّ وَإِذَا سَأَلْتُمُوهُنَّ مَتَاعًا فَاسْأَلُوهُنَّ مِنْ وَرَاءِ حِجَابٍ ذَلِكُمْ أَطْهَرُ لِقُلُوبِكُمْ وَقُلُوبِهِنَّ وَمَا كَانَ لَكُمْ أَنْ تُؤْذُوا رَسُولَ اللَّهِ وَلَا أَنْ تَنْكِحُوا أَزْوَاجَهُ مِنْ بَعْدِهِ أَبَدًا إِنَّ ذَلِكُمْ كَانَ عِنْدَ اللَّهِ عَظِيمًا (53)

O you who believe! Enter not the Prophets houses, except when leave is given to you for a meal, (and then) not (as early as) to wait for its preparation. But when you are invited, enter, and

when you have taken your meal, disperse, without sitting for a talk. Verily, such (behavior) annoys the Prophet, and he is shy of (asking) you), but Allah is not shy of the truth. And when you ask (his wives) for anything you want, ask them from behind a screen, that is purer for your hearts and for their hearts. And it is not (right) for you that you should annoy Allah's Messenger, nor that you should ever marry his wives after him (his death). Verily! With Allah that shall be an enormity. (Al-Ahzab:53) (Ahmad, Muslim, Nasa'ee)

In another narration, Anas 🕮 states, "To celebrate his marriage to Zainab bint Jahash 🕮, Rasulullah 🕮 hosted a meal of bread and meat. I was sent to invite the people to the meal and as they arrived, they ate and then left. When I could find no one more to invite, I submitted, 'O Nabi of Allah 🕮! I cannot find anyone else to invite.' Rasulullah 🕮 then gave the instruction for the food to be taken away but there were still 3 people who stayed behind to talk. Rasulullah 🕮 therefore left the room and went to the room of Aisha 🕮. When he greeted her with the words: السَّلَامُ عَلَيْكُمْ أَهْلَ الْبَيْتِ وَرَحْمَةُ اللهِ وَبَرَكَاتُهُ she replied by saying: وَعَلَيْكَ السَّلَامُ وَرَحْمَةُ اللهِ وَبَرَكَاتُهُ She then asked, 'How did you find your wife? May Allah bless you.' Rasulullah 🕮 then went to each of his wives' rooms in turn. As he was greeting them as he greeted Aisha 🕮, they said to him what Aisha 🕮 had said. When Rasulullah 🕮 returned to the room of Zainab, he found the 3 men still sitting there and talking. Because Rasulullah 🕮 was extremely bashful, rather than telling them to leave he again walked off towards the room of Aisha 🕮. I cannot recall whether it was someone else or I who informed him that the men had left. He then returned and his one foot was still on the threshold and the other outside when he dropped the curtain between himself and I and the verse of Hijab was revealed." *(Bukhari)*. Anas 🕮 also reports that after Rasulullah 🕮 had completed his marriage to one of his wives, Ummu Sulaim 🕮, Anas's mother cooked some Hais (dish prepared with dates, butter, flour), placed it in a dish and instructed Anas 🕮 saying, "Take this to Rasulullah 🕮 and inform him that it is a little something from us." This occurred during times when the Sahabah were suffering great poverty and hardship. When Anas 🕮 took it to Rasulullah 🕮, he said, "O Rasulullah 🕮! Ummu Sulaim 🕮 has sent this to you. She conveys Salams to you with the message that this is a little something from us." Rasulullah 🕮 looked at the food and instructed Anas 🕮 to place it in the corner of the room. Thereafter, he named a large number of people and told Anas 🕮 to invite them all. In addition to those people, Rasulullah 🕮 also told Anas 🕮 to invite every other Muslim he met. Anas 🕮 proceeded to invite the named persons as well as everyone else he met. When he returned, the room, the platform and the courtyard was full of people. When one of the narrators asked Anas 🕮 how many people there were, he said that they were approximately 300. Rasulullah 🕮 then asked Anas 🕮 to bring the food and when he did, Rasulullah 🕮 placed his hand on it, made Du'a and said a few other things. Thereafter, Rasulullah 🕮 said, "Let them sit in circles of 10, recite 'Bismillah' and then every person should eat what is in front of him." The people then started by reciting 'Bismillah' and ate in turns until all of them had eaten to their fill. Anas 🕮 says, "Rasulullah 🕮 then told me to pick up the dish and when I did so and looked at it, I could not tell whether it was more when I put it down or when I picked it up." However, some of the men remained sitting and talking in Rasulullah 🕮's room while Rasulullah 🕮's wife had to sit with her face turned towards the wall. When they prolonged their discussion, it became very inconvenient for Rasulullah 🕮 but he was an extremely bashful person and could not tell them to leave.

Had they known about the inconvenience they were causing, it would have been difficult for them to continue sitting. Rasulullah ﷺ got up and went to greet all his other wives. When the men saw him return, it occurred to them that they were causing him inconvenience. They hastened to the door and left. Rasulullah ﷺ entered the room and drew the curtain closed, leaving Anas ؓ in the courtyard. In the little while that Rasulullah ﷺ was in the room, Allah revealed some verses of the Qur'an and as he emerged from the room, he was reciting the verses:

يَا أَيُّهَا الَّذِينَ آمَنُوا لَا تَدْخُلُوا بُيُوتَ النَّبِيِّ إِلَّا أَنْ يُؤْذَنَ لَكُمْ إِلَى طَعَامٍ غَيْرَ نَاظِرِينَ إِنَاهُ وَلَكِنْ إِذَا دُعِيتُمْ فَادْخُلُوا فَإِذَا طَعِمْتُمْ فَانْتَشِرُوا وَلَا مُسْتَأْنِسِينَ لِحَدِيثٍ إِنَّ ذَلِكُمْ كَانَ يُؤْذِي النَّبِيَّ فَيَسْتَحْيِي مِنْكُمْ وَاللَّهُ لَا يَسْتَحْيِي مِنَ الْحَقِّ وَإِذَا سَأَلْتُمُوهُنَّ مَتَاعًا فَاسْأَلُوهُنَّ مِنْ وَرَاءِ حِجَابٍ ذَلِكُمْ أَطْهَرُ لِقُلُوبِكُمْ وَقُلُوبِهِنَّ وَمَا كَانَ لَكُمْ أَنْ تُؤْذُوا رَسُولَ اللَّهِ وَلَا أَنْ تَنْكِحُوا أَزْوَاجَهُ مِنْ بَعْدِهِ أَبَدًا إِنَّ ذَلِكُمْ كَانَ عِنْدَ اللَّهِ عَظِيمًا (53) إِنْ تُبْدُوا شَيْئًا أَوْ تُخْفُوهُ فَإِنَّ اللَّهَ كَانَ بِكُلِّ شَيْءٍ عَلِيمًا (54)

O you who believe! Enter not the Prophets houses, except when leave is given to you for a meal, (and then) not (as early as) to wait for its preparation. But when you are invited, enter, and when you have taken your meal, disperse, without sitting for a talk. Verily, such (behavior) annoys the Prophet, and he is shy of (asking) you (to go), but Allah is not shy of (telling you) the truth. And when you ask (his wives) for anything you want, ask them from behind a screen that is purer for your hearts and for their hearts. And it is not (right) for you that you should annoy Allah's Messenger, nor that you should ever marry his wives after him (his death). Verily! With Allah that shall be an enormity. Whether you reveal anything or conceal it, verily, Allah is Ever All-Knower of everything. (Ahzab:53-54)

Anas ؓ says, "Rasulullah ﷺ recited these verses to me before anyone else, making me the first person to have the honor of hearing them." *(Ibn Abi Hatim, Muslim, Nasa'ee, Tirmidhi, Bukhari, Ibn Jareer in At Bidayah wan Nihayah, Ibn Sa'd)*

Rasulullah ﷺ's Marriage to Safiya bint Huyay bin Akhtab ؓ

Anas ؓ reports that when the prisoners captured after the Battle of Khaibar were mustered together, Dihia ؓ approached Rasulullah ﷺ with a request. "O Rasulullah ﷺ!" he said, "Give me a slave woman from the captives." "Go and take one," Rasulullah ﷺ said. Dihia ؓ proceeded to take Safiya bint Huyay. Someone then came to Rasulullah ﷺ saying, "O Nabi of Allah ﷺ! You have given to Dihia Safiya bint Huyay who is the leader of the Banu Quraiza and Banu Nadhir tribes! She is suitable only for you." Rasulullah ﷺ then sent for her and when he saw her, he instructed Dihia to take another woman. Rasulullah ﷺ then set her free and married her. *(Abu Dawud, Bukhari, Muslim)*. Anas ؓ narrates that they marched to Khaibar and after conquering the fortress there, Rasulullah ﷺ was informed about Safiya bint Huyay bin Akhtab. She was an extremely beautiful lady whose husband had been killed while she was still a new bride. Rasulullah ﷺ chose to marry her and after leaving Khaibar it was only when they reached the boundary of Sahba that she stopped menstruating. It was therefore only there that Rasulullah ﷺ was able to complete the marriage. Rasulullah ﷺ then had some Hais, dish prepared with dates, butter, flour prepared and served on a leather tablecloth. Anas ؓ was then instructed to invite whoever was in the area to partake of the food. This was the Walima meal for Rasulullah ﷺ's marriage to Safiya bint Huyay ؓ. Anas ؓ reports that on the way back to Madinah, he saw Rasulullah ﷺ use a shawl to make a screen for her behind him. He would then kneel beside his camel and place his knee upright for her to step on as she mounted the camel. *(Bukhari)*

Anas ؓ states, "Rasulullah ﷺ camped at a place between Khaibar and Madinah for 3 days. It was here that he completed his marriage to Safiya ؓ, after which I invited the Muslims present there to a Walima meal that featured neither bread nor meat. All that it consisted of was Rasulullah ﷺ's instruction to Bilal ؓ to spread out a leather tablecloth. He then scattered some dates, cheese and butter onto it which the people ate. Some of the Muslims asked, 'Is she one of the Ummahatul Mu'minin, wives of Rasulullah ﷺ or his slave woman?' Others replied, 'If Rasulullah ﷺ veils her, she is one of the Ummahatul Mu'minin, otherwise she is his slave woman.' When the army started to leave, Rasulullah ﷺ spread something behind him for her to sit on and then pulled a veil over." *(Bukhari in Al Bidayah wan Nihayah)*. Jabir ؓ reports, "When Safiya bint Huyay bin Akhtab ؓ entered Rasulullah ﷺ's tent as his wife, many people including myself presented ourselves there to have a share of the Walima food. When he emerged from the tent, Rasulullah ﷺ said, 'Leave your mother (my wife) alone', they all therefore left. When we gathered at the time of Isha, Rasulullah ﷺ came out to us carrying in the edge of his shawl close to one and a half Mudd (unit of weight) of Ajwah dates. Handing them over to us Rasulullah ﷺ said, 'Eat from the Walima of your mother." *(Ahmad, Haythami, Ibn Sa'd)*. Abdullah bin Omar ؓ narrates that because there were bluish marks around the eyes of Safiya bint Huyay ؓ, Rasulullah ﷺ asked her the reason for it. She replied, "When I told my husband that in a dream I had seen the moon falling in my lap, he slapped me saying, 'Do you desire the king of Yathrib (Madinah)?'" Safiya bint Huyay ؓ narrates, "There was no one more loathsome in my eyes than Rasulullah ﷺ who had killed both my father and husband. However, this feeling disappeared from my heart when Rasulullah ﷺ repeatedly clarified his position to me by telling me that my father had been responsible for instigating the Arabs against him and for numerous other felonies." *(Tabrani, Haythami)*. Abu Hurairah ؓ narrates that when Rasulullah ﷺ entered his tent with Safiya ؓ, Abu Ayub ؓ spent the night guarding the entrance. When he saw Rasulullah ﷺ the next morning, he was still carrying his sword and exclaimed, "Allahu Akbar! O Rasulullah ﷺ! Because she was only recently married and you had her father, brother and husband killed, I did not trust her with you. It is for this reason that I have stood guard here all night." Rasulullah ﷺ laughed and praised Abu Ayub ؓ. *(Hakim, Ibn Asakir in Kanzul Ummal)*. Abu Ayub ؓ added, "Had she made any movement to harm you, I would have been close by to defend you." *(Ibn Sa'd)*. Ata bin Yasir narrates that when Safiya bint Huyay ؓ arrived in Madinah, she stayed in a house belonging to Haritha bin Nu'man ؓ. The women of the Ansar heard about her, they came to see her celebrated beauty. Wearing her veil, Aisha ؓ also went to see her and as she was leaving, Rasulullah ﷺ followed her out and asked, "What have you seen, O Aisha?" "I have seen only a Jewess!" Aisha ؓ replied. "Do not say that," Rasulullah ﷺ warned, "She has accepted Islam and is an excellent Muslim." *(Ibn Sa'd)*. Sa'eed bin Musaib narrates that when Safiya bint Huyay ؓ arrived in Madinah, she was wearing gold earrings in the shape of palm leaves. She gave these as a gift to Rasulullah ﷺ's daughter Fatima ؓ and some other ladies who were with her. *(Isabah)*

Rasulullah ﷺ's Marriage to Juwayriya Bint Harith Khuza'ee ؓ

Aisha ؓ narrates that when the captives of the Banu Mustaliq tribe were distributed amongst the Muslim army, Juwayriya bint Harith ؓ happened to fall in the lot of Thabit bin Qais bin Shammas ؓ or one of his nephews. Rather than being a conventional slave, Juwayriya ؓ entered into a contract of Kitaba between a slave and master in which slave gradually pay the master certain sum of money to secure freedom from him. She was an extremely beautiful woman who attracted anyone who saw her. Aisha ؓ says, "She once came to Rasulullah ﷺ to seek assistance with paying off her Kitaba. By Allah! I disliked her as soon as I saw her standing at the door of my room because I knew that Rasulullah ﷺ would see in her what I saw. When she entered the room, she said, 'O Rasulullah ﷺ! I am Juwayriya the daughter of Harith bin Abu Dirar, the leader of his tribe. As you know, a calamity has befallen me when I was captured and taken as a slave. I fell to the lot of Thabit bin Qais bin Shammas and entered into a contract of Kitaba with him. I have now come to seek your assistance to pay off the Kitaba.'" "Do you not want something better?" Rasulullah ﷺ asked. "What is that, O Rasulullah ﷺ?" she asked. Rasulullah ﷺ said, "I should payoff your Kitaba and then marry you." "Certainly, O Rasulullah ﷺ!" she replied, "I am most willing." When the news reached the Sahabah that Rasulullah ﷺ had married Juwayriya ؓ, they said, "The tribe of Juwayriya ؓ are now the in-laws of Rasulullah ﷺ so free those of them whom you own as your slaves." Aisha ؓ says, "As a result of Rasulullah ﷺ's marriage to Juwayriya ؓ, 100 families of the Banu Mustaliq tribe were set free. I do not know of any woman who was a greater blessing for her tribe than Juwayriya ؓ." *(Ibn Is'haq in Al Bidayah wan Nihayah, Ibn Sa'd)*. Urwa ؓ reports that Juwayriya bint Harith ؓ said, "3 days before the arrival of Rasulullah I dreamt that the moon came from Yathrib and fell into my lap. I did not tell anyone until Rasulullah ﷺ actually arrived. When we were taken captive, the dream gave me hope that Rasulullah ﷺ will set me free and marry me. By Allah! I never spoke to Rasulullah ﷺ about freeing my people until the Muslims freed them by themselves. I found out about it when one of my cousins informed me. I then praised Allah for it." *(Waqidi in Al Bidayah wan Nihayah, Hakim)*

Rasulullah ﷺ's Marriage to Maymuna bint Harith Hilaliya ؓ

Ibn Shihab narrates that it was the year after signing the Treaty of Hudaybiya that Rasulullah ﷺ left to perform Umra. This occurred 7 years after the Hijra during the month of Dhul Qa'dah, which was the same month in which the disbeliever had prevented Rasulullah ﷺ from entering the Masjidul Haram (the previous year). When he reached a place called Ya'jij, Rasulullah ﷺ sent Ja'far bin Abu Talib ؓ to propose on his behalf for the hand of Maymuna bint Harith bin Hazan Amiriya ؓ in marriage. Maymuna ؓ handed over her affairs to Abbas bin Abdul Muttalib ؓ who was married to her sister Ummu Fadhl ؓ. Abbas ؓ then handed her over in marriage to Rasulullah ﷺ. Rasulullah ﷺ stayed over in Sarif for a while until Maymuna ؓ arrived there and the marriage was completed. Allah had decreed that Maymuna ؓ should pass away at the same place where her marriage to Rasulullah ﷺ was completed. *(Hakim)*. After marrying Maymuna bint Harith ؓ, Rasulullah ﷺ stayed in Makkah for 3 days. On the 3rd day, Huwaitib bin Abdul Uzza came to Rasulullah ﷺ with a few men of the Quraish and said, "Your stay has expired, so leave us." Rasulullah ﷺ said to them, "What harm will it do to you if you leave me to complete my marriage in your midst, after which I shall host a meal which you all can attend?" "We have no need for you food," they snapped, "do leave us." Rasulullah ﷺ therefore left Madinah with Maymuna ؓ and completed his marriage at Sarif. *(Hakim)*

Rasulullah ﷺ Marries his Daughter Fatima ؓ to Ali bin Abi Talib ؓ

Ali ؓ narrates, "When a marriage proposal for Fatima ؓ

was sent to Rasulullah ﷺ, a slave of mine asked. 'Do you know that a marriage proposal for Fatima ؓ has been sent to Rasulullah ﷺ?' When I declared that I did not know, she said, 'Well! She has already received a proposal. What stops you from approaching Rasulullah ﷺ and requesting him to marry her to you?' 'Do I have anything with which to many her?' I said. She said, You only have to approach Rasulullah ﷺ and he will marry her to you.' By Allah! She then continued giving me hope until I went to see Rasulullah ﷺ. However, when I sat before Rasulullah ﷺ, I was unable to utter a word out of respect and fear for him. Rasulullah ﷺ asked, 'What brings you here? Is there something you need?' When I remained silent, Rasulullah ﷺ said, 'Have you perhaps come to propose for Fatima?' 'Yes,' I managed to reply. 'Have you got anything to give as dowry?' Rasulullah ﷺ asked. 'By Allah!' I replied, 'I have nothing.' 'What has happened to the suit of armor I gave you?' he asked. I swear by the Being Who controls the life of Ali ؓ that the armor was the type made by the Hatma bin Muharib tribe was barely worth 400 Dirhams. When I informed Rasulullah ﷺ that I still had it with me, he said, 'Then I have handed her over in marriage to you so send it to her as dowry.' This was therefore the dowry of Fatima ؓ the daughter of Rasulullah ﷺ." *(Bayhaqi in Daia'il, Al Bidayah wan Nihayah, Dowlabi in Dhurriya Tahira, Kanzul Ummal)*. Buraida ؓ narrates that a group of the Ansar once suggested to Ali ؓ that he propose for Fatima ؓ's hand in marriage. When he approached Rasulullah ﷺ, Rasulullah ﷺ asked, "What does the son of Abu Talib need?" "O Rasulullah ﷺ!" Ali ؓ replied, "I wish to propose for the hand of Fatima the daughter of Rasulullah ﷺ." All Rasulullah ﷺ said was, "*Marhaban wa Ahlan.*" Ali ؓ then left and met with the group of Ansar who had been waiting for him. When they asked him what had happened, he replied, "All I know is that Rasulullah ﷺ said, '*Marhaban wa Ahlan.*'" They said, "Even one of 2 things Rasulullah ﷺ gave you are sufficient. He gave you both Ahl (family) as well as Marhab (comfortable home)." After handing Fatima ؓ over in marriage, Rasulullah ﷺ said, "O Ali! It is necessary for a Walima to be hosted after completion." Sa'd ؓ offered a sheep he owned for the meat and the Ansar collected a few Saa of wheat for the bread. When the night of the consummation arrived, Rasulullah ﷺ gave the instructions to do nothing until he arrived. When Rasulullah ﷺ got there, asked for water, performed wudhu and sprinkled some water on to Ali ؓ saying:

اَللّٰهُمَّ بَارِكْ فِيْهِمَا وَبَارِكْ لِهِلَامَا فِي بِنَائِهِمَا

"*O Allah! Bless the 2 of them and bless them in their consummation.*" *(Tabrani in Majma'uz Zawa'id)*
Another narration similar to the above, states that the Du'a Rasulullah ﷺ made was: اَللّٰهُمَّ بَارِكْ فِيْهِمَا وَبَارِكْ لَهُمَا فِيْ شِبْلَيْهِمَا

"*O Allah! Bless the two of them and bless them in their 2 lion like sons.*" *(Bazzar, Haythami)*
A 3rd narration quotes the Du'a of Rasulullah ﷺ as:

اَللّٰهُمَّ بَارِكْ فِيْهِمَا وَبَارِكْ عَلَيْهِمَا وَبَارِكْ لَهُمَا فِي بِنَائِهِمَا وَبَارِكْ فِيْ نَسْلِهِمَا

"*O Allah! Bless the 2 of them, shower Your blessings on them, bless them in their consummation and bless them in their progeny.*" *(Ruyani and Ibn Asakir in Kanzul Ummal, Nasa'ee in Al Bidayah wan Nihayah)*
Another narration states that Rasulullah added:

وَبَارِكْ لَهُمَا فِيْ شَمْلِهِمَا

"*. . . and bless their communion.*" *(Al Bidayah wan Nihayah, Ibn Sa'd)*

Asma bint Umays ؓ narrates that after Fatima ؓ was married to Ali ؓ, all that they saw in her house was a straw mat spread out on the ground, a pillow stuffed with the bark of a palm tree, an earthen jug and an earthen mug. On the night of the marriage Rasulullah ﷺ sent a message saying, "Do nothing" or "Do not get close to your wife until I come." When Rasulullah ﷺ arrived, he asked, "Is my brother here?" When Rasulullah ﷺ forged bonds of brotherhood between the Sahabah, he forged his brotherhood with Ali ؓ. Ummu Ayman ؓ, a pious woman who was an Abyssinian and the mother of Usama bin Zaid asked in surprise, "O Rasulullah ﷺ! He is your brother and you have married your daughter to him?" Rasulullah ﷺ replied, "This marriage can take place despite this type of brotherhood, O Ummu Ayman." Rasulullah ﷺ then sent for a container of water, uttered some words and then passed his hands over the chest and face of Ali ؓ. He then called Fatima ؓ who stood by him shivering in her shawl out of modesty. Rasulullah ﷺ sprinkled some of the water on her and also uttered some words. He then said to her, "I have not failed you in my duty to get you married to the family member I love most." Asma ؓ narrates further. She says, "Rasulullah ﷺ then noticed a figure behind the curtain or behind the door and asked, 'Who is that?' 'Asma,' I replied. 'Asma bint Umais?' Rasulullah ﷺ asked. 'Yes, O Rasulullah ﷺ,' I confirmed. He then asked, 'Have you come to be of service to Rasulullah ﷺ and his family?' 'Yes,' I replied, 'because a young girl must have a family woman with her on her first night to take care of anything she might need.' Rasulullah ﷺ then made such a wonderful Du'a for me that it is the one deed that I have most hope in to deliver me to salvation in the Hereafter. Rasulullah ﷺ then said to Ali ؓ, 'Look after you wife' and as he left, he continued making Du'a for them until he disappeared in his rooms." *(Tabrani, Haythami)*. In another narration, Asma bint Umais ؓ says, "I was present the night Rasulullah ﷺ's daughter Fatima ؓ became a new bride. That morning, Rasulullah ﷺ arrived and knocked at the door. When Ummu Ayman ؓ got up and opened the door, Rasulullah ﷺ asked, 'O Ummu Ayman! Call my brother for me.' She said, 'He is your brother and you got him married to your daughter?' 'O Ummu Ayman!' Rasulullah ﷺ continued, 'Do call him for me.' When the other women heard Rasulullah ﷺ's voice, they dispersed and he took a seat in the corner. Ali ؓ then arrived and after making Du'a for him, Rasulullah ﷺ sprinkled some water on him as well. Thereafter, Rasulullah ﷺ sent for Fatima ؓ. She arrived all covered in perspiration and taking short steps out of her extreme modesty. 'Relax,' Rasulullah ﷺ reassured her, 'I have married you to the family member I love the most.'" The rest of the narration is like the one quoted above. *(Tabrani in Majma'uz Zawa'id)*. Ali ؓ narrates that when Rasulullah ﷺ got him married to Fatima ؓ, Rasulullah ﷺ sent for some water and then gargled with it. Rasulullah ﷺ then took Ali ؓ into the room where he sprinkled the water on his chest and between his shoulders and then sought Allah's protection for him by reciting Surah Ikhlas and the Mu'awadhatain *(Surah Falaq and Surah Nas)*. *(Ibn Asakir in Kanzul Ummal)*

Alba bin Ahmar reports from Ali ؓ that when he proposed for Rasulullah ﷺ's daughter Fatima ؓ, he sold a suit of armor he owned as well as some of his other possessions for a sum of 480 Dirhams. Rasulullah ﷺ instructed him to use 2/3rd for perfume and the remaining 1/3rd for clothing. Rasulullah ﷺ then gargled in a utensil of water and told the couple to bath with it. Rasulullah ﷺ also instructed Fatima ؓ not to feed any of her children before he got to the child, but she started feeding Husain ؓ before Rasulullah ﷺ could arrive. As for Hasan ؓ, Rasulullah ﷺ put some unknown thing in his mouth because of which he was more knowledgeable than his brother. *(Abu Ya'la, Sa'eed bin Mansoor in Kanzul Ummal, Ibn Sa'd)*. Jabir ؓ narrates, "We attended the marriage of Ali ؓ and Fatima ؓ and have not witnessed a better marriage. The matting on which we sat was stuffed with the bark of a date palm and we were served raisins and dates to eat. Her bedding on her first night was a sheepskin." *(Bazzar, Haythami)*. Ali ؓ reports that when Fatima ؓ got married, Rasulullah ﷺ gave her a blanket, a water bag and a leather pillow stuffed with Idhkhir grass. *(Bayhaqi in Dala'il, Kanzul Ummal)*. Abdullah bin Amr ؓ reports that when Rasulullah ﷺ sent Fatima ؓ to her husband Ali ؓ, Rasulullah ﷺ gave her a blanket, a water bag and a leather pillow stuffed with the bark of a date palm and Idhkhir grass. The couple slept on half of the blanket and used the other half to cover themselves. *(Tabrani, Haythami)*

The Marriage of Kabe'ah Aslami ؓ

Rabe'ah ؓ says, "I was Rasulullah ﷺ's servant. One day he asked, 'O Rabe'ah! Are you not interested in getting married?' I replied, 'I have no intention of marrying. While I have nothing with which to support a wife, I also do not want anything to preoccupy me from serving you.' When Rasulullah ﷺ turned away from me, I said to myself, 'By Allah! Rasulullah ﷺ definitely knows better than me what is best for me in this world and in the Hereafter. By Allah! Should he ever again ask me whether I am interested in getting married, I shall reply, 'Certainly, O Rasulullah ﷺ! Instruct me as you please.' When Rasulullah ﷺ did ask me whether I was interested in getting married, I replied, 'Certainly, O Rasulullah ﷺ! Instruct me as you please.' Rasulullah ﷺ then instructed me to go to a particular tribe of the Ansar who did not frequently meet with Rasulullah ﷺ. He told me to tell them that he had sent me to them with instructions to get me married to a certain girl from amongst them. I therefore went to them and informed them that Rasulullah ﷺ had sent me with instructions that they get me married. 'Welcome to Rasulullah ﷺ and the messenger of Rasulullah ﷺ!' they cried out, 'By Allah! The messenger of Rasulullah ﷺ shall never return without having his need fulfilled. They then got me married and treated me exceptionally well without even asking for a witness. I returned depressed to Rasulullah ﷺ; saying, 'O Rasulullah ﷺ! I have been to people who are extremely generous. They got me married and treated me exceptionally well without even asking for a witness. However, I have no dowry to give. Rasulullah ﷺ then called for Buraida Aslami ؓ, the leader of my tribe and instructed him to collect some gold for me equivalent to the weight of a date stone. When I took possession of what the people collected for me, I brought it to Rasulullah ﷺ who said, 'Take this to them and tell them this is her dowry.' When I did so and told them that this was her dowry, they accepted it with great happiness and said, 'This is excellent and so much!' When I again returned depressed to Rasulullah ﷺ, he asked, 'Why so gloomy, O Rabe'ah?' 'O Rasulullah ﷺ!' I began, 'I have never met people as wonderful as them. They were happy with what I gave them and treated me extremely well. They even told me that the dowry was excellent and so much.' However, I have nothing with which to host a Walima. 'O Buraida!' Rasulullah ﷺ called out, 'Collect money for a goat for him.' After the people of my tribe had collected enough to buy a large and fat sheep, Rasulullah ﷺ instructed me to go to Aisha ؓ and tell her to give me the basket containing the grains. I did as I was ordered and she said, 'Here is the basket containing 7 Saa of barley. By Allah! By Allah! We have no other food besides this. You may have it.' I took the basket to Rasulullah ﷺ and informed him about what Aisha ؓ had said. Rasulullah said, 'Take this to your in-laws and tell them to bake this barley into bread and to cook the sheep.' When I took it to them, they said, 'While we can take care of the bread for you, you will have to see to the sheep for us.' Some men of the Aslam tribe and I took the sheep, slaughtered it, skinned it and then cooked it. We had bread and meat with us and I hosted the Walima. I invited Rasulullah ﷺ.

Thereafter, Rasulullah ﷺ gave me a piece of land and gave a piece to Abu Bakr ؓ as well. The world had finally come to me. It however occurred that Abu Bakr ؓ and I fell into a dispute regarding a date palm which I claimed was on my property and he claimed was on his. When an argument followed, Abu Bakr ؓ told me something that I disliked. He however regretted what he did and said to me, 'O Rabe'ah! Please repeat the words to me so that justice is done.' 'I shall never do so,' I replied. He said, 'If you do not repeat the words, I shall complain about you to Rasulullah ﷺ.' When I adamantly refused, he forsook the land issue and went to Rasulullah ﷺ. I went behind him. Some men of the Aslam tribe came and said, 'May Allah have mercy on Abu Bakr ؓ! What will he complain to Rasulullah ﷺ about when it was he who said those words?' 'Do you people know who that is?' I asked. 'That is Abu Bakr Siddiq!' I emphasized, 'He was the 2nd of the 2 in the cave and the oldest Muslim. Beware that he should not turn and see you assisting me against him and then become angry. When he then goes to Rasulullah ﷺ, Rasulullah ﷺ should not become angry because of his anger and then Allah should not become angry because the 2 of them are angry. If that happens, Rabe'ah shall be doomed.' 'What do you want us to do?' they asked. I then told them to return. As Abu Bakr ؓ proceeded to Rasulullah ﷺ and I followed him by myself. After he had narrated the incident as it had occurred, Rasulullah ﷺ looked up to me and said, 'O Rabe'ah! What is the problem between you and Siddiq?' I explained the situation to Rasulullah ﷺ adding that when he told me something I disliked, he said, 'Please repeat the words to me so that justice is done.' I then refused to do so. Rasulullah ﷺ said, 'That was right. You should not repeat the words. However, you could have at least said, 'May Allah forgive you, O Abu Bakr." Abu Bakr ؓ then turned around weeping. *(Ahmad, Tabrani, Haythami, Abu Ya'la in Al Bidayah wan Nihayah, Hakim in Kanzul Ummal, Ibn Sa'd)*

The Marriage of Julaibib ؓ

Abu Barza ؓ reports that Julaibib ؓ was a man who frequently visited women and joked with them. Abu Barza ؓ himself instructed his wife never to allow Julaibib ؓ to see her and threatened to do many things if she ever did so. It was a practice amongst the Ansar never to get any of their widows married until they were sure that Rasulullah ﷺ was not interested in marrying her. Rasulullah ﷺ once said to one of the Ansar, "Will you allow me to marry your daughter?" "Of course," the man obliged, "it will be a great honor and pleasure." "I do not wish to marry her to myself but to someone else," Rasulullah ﷺ pointed out. "Then for whom?" the Ansari asked. "For Julaibib," Rasulullah ﷺ replied. The Ansars said, "I shall consult with her mother." He then asked his wife, "Rasulullah ﷺ has proposed for your daughter." "Of course," she agreed, "it will be a great pleasure." "However," the Ansari explained, "he is not proposing for himself, but on behalf of Julaibib." The lady burst out, "To Julaibib! Never! To Julaibib! Never! I swear by life that we shall never marry him to our daughter!" As the Ansari was about to get up to inform Rasulullah ﷺ about what the mother said when the daughter asked, "Who was it that brought to you a proposal for me?" When the mother informed her that it was Rasulullah ﷺ who brought the proposal, the girl asked, "Are you then rejecting the command of Rasulullah ﷺ? Hand me over in marriage to him for he shall never destroy me since the marriage is with

Rasulullah ﷺ's approval." Her father then went to Rasulullah ﷺ and reported the incident to him, saying, "My daughter places her affairs in your hands. You may marry her to whomever you please." Rasulullah ﷺ then proceeded to get her married to Julaibib ﷺ. It then occurred that Rasulullah ﷺ once went out to a battle. After Allah had given Rasulullah ﷺ a large booty, he asked, "Is someone missing?" When the Sahabah said that they found no one missing, Rasulullah ﷺ said, "But I notice that Julaibib ؓ is missing. Look for him." When the Sahabah went out in search of him, they found him beside the bodies of 7 men of the enemy whom he had killed before the enemy managed to kill him. They then reported back saying, "O Rasulullah ﷺ! He is there beside the bodies of 7 men of the enemy whom he had killed before the enemy managed to kill him." Rasulullah ﷺ went to the body of Julaibib ؓ and said, "He killed 7 before they managed to kill him. He is from me and I am from him." Rasulullah ﷺ repeated this 2 or 3 times and took him in his arms. A grave was then dug for him and there was no bier besides the arms of Rasulullah ﷺ. Rasulullah ﷺ himself laid the body in the grave. The Hadith does not state whether the body was bathed or not. When Thabit noted that there was no widow from the Ansar who was more charitable than the widow of Julaibib ؓ, Is'haq bin Abdullah bin Abu Talha said to him, "Do you know what Du'a Rasulullah ﷺ made for her? He said, 'O Allah! Pour down good on her in abundance and never give her a life of hardship.' For this reason there was not a widow amongst the Ansar more charitable than her." *(Ahmad, Haythami)*

The Marriage of Salman Farsi ؓ

Salman Farsi ؓ reports that he once married a woman from the Kinda tribe and completed the marriage in her house. On the night of the marriage, his friends walked with him to her house and when they reached it, he said to them, "You may return now. May Allah reward you." He did not allow them to enter the house as foolish people generally do. When he looked at the house which had been decorated with drapes on all sides, he remarked, "Is your house feverish because of which you had to bandage it or has the Kabah been moved to the Kinda tribe?" The people replied, "Neither is the house feverish nor has the Kabah been moved to the Kinda tribe." Salman ؓ then refused to enter the house until all drapes were removed except for the drape covering the entrance. When Salman ؓ finally entered the house, he saw a large amount of goods there. "Whose goods are these?" he asked. "Yours and your wife's," the people replied. Salman ؓ said, "This does not conform with the advice my beloved friend Rasulullah ﷺ gave me. My beloved friend ﷺ advised me to have only that much of worldly goods that a traveler has as provisions." When he saw a few female servants, he asked, "Whose servants are these?" When he was informed that the servants also belonged to him and his wife, he said, "This also does not conform with the advice my beloved friend Rasulullah ﷺ gave me. He advised me to keep only those female servants whom I can marry or who I can get married to others. If I do keep them and they fornicate because they have none to satisfy their needs, their sins will be on me without any reduction to the sin they will be guilty of."

Salman ؓ then turned to the women around his wife and said, "Will you ladies leave me to be alone with my wife?" They readily agreed and left. Salman ؓ then went to the door, shut it and drew the drape over it. Thereafter, he sat with his wife, held her forelock and made Du'a for blessings. He then asked her, "Will you obey any instructions I give you?" Her reply was, "You are sitting in the position of a person who has to be obeyed." He continued to say, "My beloved friend Rasulullah ﷺ advised me that when I meet with my wife for the first time, I should meet with her in the obedience of Allah. "He then got up and proceeded to the place of salah with her following him. After performing salah for some time, they left the place of salah and he then fulfilled with her the need a man has with his wife. Early next morning his friends came to him asking, "How did you find your wife?" When he ignored them, they repeated the question. Again he ignored them but again they repeated themselves. When they repeated the question a 3rd time, he ignored them yet again but then finally said, "Allah has made drapes, curtains and doors to conceal what lies behind them. It is sufficient to ask about things that are apparent but one should never ask about things that are hidden. I heard Rasulullah ﷺ say that those people who narrate such private things are like donkeys having intercourse on the street." (Abu Nu'aym in Hilya). Abdullah bin Abbas ﷺ states that when Salman ﷺ returned after a long absence, Omar ﷺ met him and remarked, "You are a most beloved servant of Allah." Salman ﷺ said, "Then get me married to one of your daughters." Omar ﷺ remained silent. Salman ﷺ further said, "You consider me a beloved servant of Allah but are not happy to have me as your son-in-law?" The next morning, some of Omar ﷺ's family members approached Salman ﷺ. "Do you people need something?" he asked. When they admitted that they did, he said, "What is it? It shall gladly be fulfilled." They said, "We request that you abandon the matter i.e. your proposal to Omar ﷺ." "By Allah!" Salman ﷺ emphasized, "You should remember well that I did not make the proposal because of his being the Khalifa and ruler. The truth is that I thought to myself that because he is a pious man, perhaps Allah will produce pious offspring from his progeny and mine." Salman ﷺ then got married to a woman from the Kinda tribe. The rest of the narration is like above. (Abu Nu'aym in Hilya, Haythami)

The Marriage of Abu Darda ﷺ

Thabit Bunani reports that Abu Darda ﷺ once went with Salman Farsi ﷺ to extend a proposal on his behalf for a woman of the Banu Laith tribe. Abu Darda ﷺ went in to see the family and told them in detail that Salman ﷺ was one of the early Muslims and also recounted his acceptance of Islam. He then proceeded to mention to them that Salman ﷺ wished to marry a particular girl of their family. Their reply was, "While we do not wish to get Salman ﷺ married to our daughter, we wouldn't mind getting you married to her." They then handed her over in marriage to him and he left. When he met Salman ﷺ, Abu Darda ﷺ said, "Something has happened that I am too embarrassed to tell you about." "What is it?" Salman ﷺ asked. When Abu Darda ﷺ related the incident to him, Salman ﷺ said, "I should be the one embarrassed since I proposed for a woman whom Allah had destined for you." (Abu Nu'aym in Hilya, Tabrani, Haythami)

Abu Darda ﷺ Gets his Daughter Darda Married to One of the Poor and Simple Muslim

Thabit Bunani narrates that when Yazid bin Mu'awiya sent to Abu Darda ﷺ a proposal for his daughter Darda, he rejected the proposal. One of Yazid's companions said, "May Allah mend your affairs. Will you allow me to marry her?" The man persisted, "Then allow me? Allah will mend your affairs." "Alright," Yazid said. The man proceeded to propose and Abu Darda ﷺ got him married to his daughter. The news spread that while Abu Darda ﷺ rejected Yazid's proposal, he accepted the proposal of a poor and simple Muslim and then married his daughter to him. Abu Darda ﷺ's comment was, "I did it in the best interests of Darda. What do you think would be her condition when in Yazid's wealthy household she has castrated slaves standing over her all the time and when her eyes are dazzled when she sees the wealthy house? Where will Islam be when she is obsessed with worldly wealth?" (Abu Nu'aym in Hilya, Imam Ahmad in Safwatus Safwah)

Ali ﷺ Married his Daughter Ummu Kulthum to Omar bin Khattab ﷺ

Abu Ja'far reports that Omar ﷺ once sent a proposal to Ali ﷺ for his daughter Ummu Kulthum's hand in marriage. When Ali ﷺ sent a message stating that she was still too young, someone told Omar ﷺ that the statement meant that Ali was refusing. When Omar ﷺ explained to Ali ﷺ his reason for wanting to marry her, Ali ﷺ agreed to get her married to him and said, "Consider the marriage done so I am sending her to you and she is your wife if you are pleased with her." Ali ﷺ then sent her to Omar ﷺ, who knowing that she was his wife ventured to lift the garment from her legs. Not realizing that the marriage was already concluded, she however exclaimed, "Leave it! Had you not been the Amirul Mu'mineen, I would have slapped you across the face!" (Abdur Razzaq, Sa'eed bin Mansur in Kanzul Ummal, Ibn Omar Maqdasi in Isabah). Muhammad narrates that when Omar ﷺ proposed to Ali ﷺ for his daughter Ummu Kulthum's hand in marriage, Ali ﷺ said, "I am reserving my daughters for the sons of my brother Ja'far." Omar ﷺ pleaded, "Please marry her to me because I swear by Allah that no man on earth will ensure that she is honored as I will." Ali ﷺ agreed and married her to Omar ﷺ. Omar ﷺ then went to the Muhajirin and said, "Congratulate me on my new marriage!" They all congratulated him and then asked, "Who did you marry, O Amirul Mu'minin?" "The daughter of Ali bin Abi Talib," he replied. He then started to explain, "Indeed Rasulullah ﷺ said, 'Every connection and relation shall be severed on the day of Judgment except my connections and my relations.' I had been a father-in-law of Rasulullah ﷺ and now I wish this as well to become his relative by marrying his grand-daughter." Another narration from Ata Khurasani states that Omar ﷺ gave her a dowry of 40,000 Dirhams. (Ibn Sa'd on Isabah)

Adi bin Hatim ﷺ Marries his Daughter to Amr bin Huraith ﷺ

Sha'bi narrates that Amr bin Huraith ﷺ once proposed for the daughter of Adi bin Hatim ﷺ. Adi ﷺ said, "I shall marry her to you only if you fulfill my condition." "What is it?" Amr asked. Adi explained, "There was indeed a sterling example for you in Rasulullah ﷺ. I therefore instruct you to pay the dowry Rasulullah ﷺ gave for Aisha ﷺ, which is a sum of 480 Dirhams." Another narration states that Amr bin Huraith ﷺ sent a proposal for the daughter of Adi bin Hatim ﷺ with an appended message to Adi ﷺ stating, "Let me know what you decide about me." Adi ﷺ sent a message stating, "I have decided that you should pay a dowry of 480 Dirhams, which is the Sunnah of Rasulullah ﷺ." (Ibn Asakir in Kanzul Ummal)

The Marriages of Bilal ﷺ and his Brother

Sha'bi narrates that when Bilal ﷺ and his brother extended marriage proposals to family from Yemen, Bilal ﷺ said, "I am Bilal and this is my brother. We were both slaves from Abyssinia. When we were misguided, Allah guided us and when we were slaves, Allah set us free. If you marry us to your daughters, then all praise is due to Allah, we shall be grateful and if you refuse, we will not mind because Allah is still the Greatest and He will open other avenues for us. The family agreed and got them married. Maymun reports that one of Bilal ﷺ's brothers claimed that he was of Arab descent and considered himself an Arab. When he once proposed for an Arab woman, the family said, "We will marry you only if Bilal is present." Bilal presented himself and after reciting the words of the Khutba, he said, "I am Bilal bin Rabah and this is my brother. He is a poor man and with religious practices. You may get him married if you please and if you chose to refuse, you are at liberty to do so." The family said, "We shall certainly marry anyone who is a brother of yours." They got him married. *(Ibn Sa'd)*

Condemning Those Whose Marriages Resemble the Disbeliever

Urwa bin Ruwaim reports that Abdullah bin Qurt Thumali who was a companion of Rasulullah was appointed governor by Omar. He was patrolling the streets of Hims one night when he passed by a bride in front of whom people were lighting several fires. Abdullah started hitting the people with his whip until they all dispersed. The next morning he sat on his pulpit and after duly praising Allah, he said, "When Abu Jandala married Umamah, he prepared some handfuls of food as a Walima for his marriage to her. May Allah shower His compassion on Abu Jandala and may He shower His special mercies on Umamah. May Allah curse your wedding of last night! The people were lighting fires and imitating the Kuffar whereas Allah has extinguished their light!" *(Abu Shaykh in Kitabun Nikah, Isabah)*

The Dowry of Rasulullah

Aisha reports that that the dowry Rasulullah gave her was 12 Awqiya and a Nash, which totaled an amount of 500 Dirhams. She then went on to specify that an Awqiya amounted to 40 Dirhams and a Nash amounted to 20 Dirhams. *(Ibn Sa'd)*

Omar Forbids Exorbitant Dowries and a Woman's Objection

Masruq narrates that Omar once the pulpit and said, "I do not know who increased above 400 Dirhams because the dowry Rasulullah and the Sahabah gave was always 400 Dirhams or less. Had larger dowries been an act of Taqwa or honor, people would have never beat Rasulullah and the Sahabah to it." After Omar got off from the pulpit, a woman from the Quraish objected. "O Amirul Mu'minin!" she said, "Are you forbidding the people from paying dowries in excess of 400 Dirhams?" When Omar confirmed it, she said, "Have you then not heard Allah say in the Qur'an: وَآتَيْتُمْ إِحْدَاهُنَّ قِنْطَارًا

...and you have given one of them (your wives) a Qintar (of gold i.e. a great amount as Mahr)... (An-Nisa:20)

Omar then said, "Allah forgive me! Everyone has more understanding than Omar." He then returned to the pulpit and said, "O people! I had forbidden you from paying dowries in excess of 400 Dirhams, the prohibition no longer stands. Therefore whoever wishes to give whatever he pleases from his wealth, he may do so." *(Sa'eed bin Mansur, Abu Ya'la, Muhami in Kanzul Ummal, Haythami, Ibn Sa'd)*. Sha'bi reports that Omar bin Khattab once delivered a sermon. After duly praising Allah, he said, "Take note that you people should not make your dowries exorbitant. If the news ever reaches me that any of you has paid more that what Rasulullah paid or what was paid to him as dowry for his daughters, I shall deposit the excess into the public treasury." After Omar got off from the pulpit, a woman from the Quraish objected. "O Amirul Mu'minin!" she said, "Is the Book of Allah more worthy of following or your words'?" "The Book of Allah of course." Omar replied, "what do you mean by this'?" She explained, "You just forbade the people from paying dowries in excess of 400 Dirhams whereas Allah says in

His Book: وَآتَيْتُمْ إِحْدَاهُنَّ قِنْطَارًا فَلَا تَأْخُذُوا مِنْهُ شَيْئًا

...and you have given one of them (your wives) a Qintar (of gold i.e. a great amount as Mahr) take not the least bit of it back... (An-Nisa:20)

Omar 2 or 3 times repeated, "Everyone has more understanding than Omar." He then returned to the pulpit and said, "O people! I had forbidden you from paying dowries in excess of 400 Dirhams, the prohibition no longer stands. A man is at liberty to give whatever he pleases from his wealth." *(Sa'eed bin Mansur, Bayhaqi)*. Omar once said. "Had exorbitant dowries been source of status and elevation in the Hereafter, the daughters and wives of Rasulullah would have been more deserving of it." *(Abu Omar bin Fadal in Amali, Kanzul Ummal)*

The Practices of Omar, Uthman, Abdullah bin Omar and Hasan bin Ali in the Matter of Dowry

Ibn Sirin reports that Omar allowed dowries of 2,000 Dirhams while Uthman allowed dowries of 4,000. *(Ibn Abi Shaybah in Kanzul Ummal)*. Nafi reports that Abdullah bin Omar married Safiya for a dowry of 400 Dirhams. She however returned it saying that it was insufficient. He then added another 200 Dirhams without Omar knowing about it. *(Ibn Abi Shaybah in Kanzul Ummal)*. Ibn Sirin narrates that when Hasan bin Ali married a woman, he sent 100 slave women to her, each one of them carrying 1,000 Dirhams. *(Tabrani, Haythami)*

The Relationship Between Aisha and Sauda

Aisha reports, "I once brought Rasulullah some Harirah that I had cooked. Sauda was sitting between Rasulullah and I, so I told her to have some as well. When she refused, I said, 'If you do not eat, I shall smear it on your face.' She however still refused so I put my hand in the Harirah and plastered it on her face. Rasulullah laughed as he put his hand in it saying, 'Now you smear her face.' Sauda then smeared it on my face and again Rasulullah laughed. Just then Omar passed by calling out for someone called Abdullah. Thinking that he would soon enter, Rasulullah said, 'Get up and wash your faces!' Thereafter, I always stood in fear of Omar because of the respect Rasulullah had for him." Another narration adds that Abu Bakr said, "Rasulullah lowered his knee for Sauda to step on so that she could get even with me. She then took some Harirah from the dish and spread it on my face as Rasulullah laughed." *(Abu Ya'la, Haythami, Ibn Asakir in Muntakhab Kanzul Ummal, Ibn Najjar in Kanzul Ummal)*

The Relationship Between Aisha and Hafsa with Sauda Yamaniya

Razinah was a freed slave of Rasulullah reports that Sauda Yamaniya once visited Aisha at a time when Hafsa was with her. Sauda arrived looking eye-catching and well-dressed with a Yemeni shawl and matching scarf. She also wore 2 spots of aloe and saffron on their places near her eyes which resembled 2 pimples. A narrator called Ulaila says that she found women beautifying themselves with aloe and saffron. Hafsa said to Aisha, "O Ummul Mu'mineen! Rasulullah is due to arrive when this woman is shiny here between us." "Fear Allah, O Hafsa!" Aisha warned. However, Hafsa said, "I am going to ruin her adornment for her." Sauda who was hard of hearing asked, "What are you 2 saying?" "O Sauda!" Hafsa said, "The one-eyed (Dajjal) has appeared!" "Really!?" Sauda cried out. She was extremely shocked and started to shiver. "Where shall I hide?" she asked. "You will have to go to the tent," Hafsa told her. The tent was made of palm leaves and was a hiding place for the people. It was however filled with dirt and spider webs. Sauda went to hide there as Rasulullah arrived. Seeing the 2 women laughing so much that they were unable to talk, Rasulullah asked, "What is all the laughter about?" Rasulullah repeated the question thrice before they pointed towards the tent. Rasulullah went to the tent where he found Sauda shivering with fear. "What is the matter, O Sauda?" Rasulullah asked. "O Rasulullah !" she said, "The one-eyed one has appeared." "He has not appeared," Rasulullah clarified, "but he is still to appear. He has not appeared but is still to appear." Rasulullah then helped her out and dusted the dirt and spider webs off her. *(Abu Ya'la)*. Hafsa said to Aisha , "Rasulullah is coming to see us and we are looking so disheveled while she is shiny between us." *(Tabrani, Haythami)*

Rasulullah 's Relationship with Aisha

Aisha narrates, "Rasulullah was sitting down when he heard the people and children making a lot of noise. When he looked out, he saw some Abyssinians dancing with the people around them. 'O Aisha!' Rasulullah called out, 'Come and have a look.' Placing my cheek against his shoulder, I started looking from between his shoulders and head. 'O Aisha,' Rasulullah kept saying as I kept looking for a long time, 'have you not had your fill?' To assess my status with Rasulullah , I kept saying that, I had not. 1 saw Rasulullah taking support on one leg and then the other as he grew tired of standing so long. When Omar appeared, the people and children all dispersed and Rasulullah remarked, 'I see the human and jinn devils all flee from Omar .'" The narration still continues further. *(Ibn Abi and Ibn Asakir in Muntakhab Kanzul Ummal)*. In another narration, Aisha says, "By Allah! I saw Rasulullah standing at the door of my room as some Abyssinians amused the people with their spears in the courtyard of the Masjid. Rasulullah screened me with his shawl as I watched their deeds from between his ear and shoulder. Rasulullah then remained standing because of me until I grew tired and turned away. You can well imagine how eager a young girl as I am for amusement and for how long I stood watching." *(Bukhari, Muslim in Mishkatul Masabih)*

The Relationship Between Rasulullah 🌙 and his Wives and Between the Wives Themselves

Aisha reports, "Rasulullah used to spend time at Zainab bint Jahash 's place drinking honey. Hafsa and I therefore collaborated and that whichever of us Rasulullah came to would tell him, 'I get the smell of Maghafir, odorous resin of a particular type of palm tree called Urfat palm. Have you eaten Maghafir suggesting that the bees that made the honey ate Maghafir.' Consequently, when Rasulullah came to one of us, she said the piece. Rasulullah replied, 'Not at all. But I did have honey by Zainab bint Jahash. I shall however never do so again.' It was then that Allah revealed the verses:

يَا أَيُّهَا النَّبِيُّ لِمَ تُحَرِّمُ مَا أَحَلَّ اللَّهُ لَكَ تَبْتَغِي مَرْضَاةَ أَزْوَاجِكَ وَاللَّهُ غَفُورٌ رَحِيمٌ (1) قَدْ فَرَضَ اللَّهُ لَكُمْ تَحِلَّةَ أَيْمَانِكُمْ وَاللَّهُ مَوْلَاكُمْ وَهُوَ الْعَلِيمُ الْحَكِيمُ (2) وَإِذْ أَسَرَّ النَّبِيُّ إِلَى بَعْضِ أَزْوَاجِهِ حَدِيثًا فَلَمَّا نَبَّأَتْ بِهِ وَأَظْهَرَهُ اللَّهُ عَلَيْهِ عَرَّفَ بَعْضَهُ وَأَعْرَضَ عَنْ بَعْضٍ فَلَمَّا نَبَّأَهَا بِهِ قَالَتْ مَنْ أَنْبَأَكَ هَذَا قَالَ نَبَّأَنِيَ الْعَلِيمُ الْخَبِيرُ (3) إِنْ تَتُوبَا إِلَى اللَّهِ فَقَدْ صَغَتْ قُلُوبُكُمَا

O Prophet! Why do you ban (for yourself) that which Allah has made lawful to you, seeking to please your wives? And Allah is Oft-Forgiving, Most Merciful. Allah has already ordained for you (O men), the dissolution of your oaths. And Allah is your Maula (Lord, or Master, or Protector, etc.) and He is the All-

Knower, the All-Wise. And (remember) when the Prophet (🌙) disclosed a matter in confidence to one of his wives (Hafsah), so when she told it (to another i.e. Aisha), and Allah made it known to him, he informed part thereof and left a part. Then when he told her (Hafsa) thereof, she said: "Who told you this?" He said: "The All-Knower, the All-Aware (Allah) has told me". If you two (wives of the Prophet 🌙, namely Aisha and Hafsa) turn in repentance to Allah, (it will be better for you), your hearts are indeed so inclined (to oppose what the Prophet 🌙 likes) (At-Tahrim:1-4)

Hisham says that the words "When the Nabi 🌙 whispered something to one of his wives" refer to the statement Rasulullah 🌙 made to one of his wives when he said, "I shall never do so again (drink honey) and this is a vow. However, you should not inform anyone about this." *(Bukhari, Muslim)*. Aisha says, "Rasulullah 🌙 loved sweet things and honey. After performing the Asr salah, it was his practice to visit all his wives and get close to one of them. When he once went to Hafsa the daughter of Omar , he stayed longer than he usually stayed. Overcome with greed, I made enquiries about this and was informed that a woman from her family had given her a container of honey, which she mixed into a drink and gave Rasulullah 🌙. 'By Allah!' I resolved, 'I am definitely going to make some scheme.' I then said to Sauda bint Zam'ah , 'Rasulullah 🌙 will soon be coming to you. When he gets close to you, ask him whether he ate Maghafir. When he tells you that he has not eaten any, ask him what it is then that you can smell. He will then tell you that Hafsa gave him a drink of honey, to which you should say, 'The bee must have sucked nectar from the Urfut palm, the palm containing Maghafir.' I will also say the same thing and you O Safiya should also do likewise." Sauda later reported to Aisha , "By Allah! Because of my fear for you, I almost called out what you told while Rasulullah 🌙 was still standing at the door. Controlling myself when he drew closer, I said, 'O Rasulullah 🌙! Have you eaten Maghafir?' 'No,' he replied. 'Then what is that I smell on you?' I asked. He replied, 'Hafsa gave me a drink of honey.' I then said, 'The bee must have sucked nectar from the Urfut palm.'" When Rasulullah 🌙 went to Aisha , she also said the same thing and Safiya also followed suit. When Rasulullah 🌙 again went to Hafsa and she offered him some honey to drink, he declined saying, "I do not need any." "By Allah!" Sauda said to Aisha , "We have stopped Rasulullah 🌙 from honey." "Be quiet" Aisha told her. *(Bukhari, Muslim in Tafsir Ibn Kathir, Abu Dawud in Jam'ul Fawa'id, Ibn Sa'd)*

The Incident of Rasulullah 🌙 When he Intended Divorcing his Wives

Abdullah bin Abbas reports, "I had always been eager to ask Omar about the 2 wives of Rasulullah 🌙 concerning whom Allah says in the Qur'an: إِنْ تَتُوبَا إِلَى اللَّهِ فَقَدْ صَغَتْ قُلُوبُكُمَا

If you two (wives of the Prophet 🌙, namely Aisha and Hafsa) turn in repentance to Allah, (it will be better for you), your hearts are indeed so inclined (to oppose what the Prophet 🌙 likes) (At-Tahrim:4)

This thought lingered on until the time when Omar performed Hajj and I performed Hajj with him. We were still traveling when Omar went off the road to answer the call of nature. I also turned off taking a jug of water along with me. After he had completed, Omar came to me and I started pouring water into his hands as he made wudhu. 'O Amirul Mu'minin!' I said, 'Who were the 2 wives of Rasulullah 🌙 concerning whom Allah says:

إِنْ تَتُوبَا إِلَى اللَّهِ فَقَدْ صَغَتْ قُلُوبُكُمَا

If you two (wives of the Prophet ﷺ, namely Aisha and Hafsa ؓ) turn in repentance to Allah, (it will be better for you), your hearts are indeed so inclined (to oppose what the Prophet ﷺ likes) (At-Tahrim:4)

Omar ؓ said, "I am surprised at you, O Ibn Abbas! That despite your vast knowledge, you are still unaware of this incident." Zuhri comments that although Omar ؓ was surprised at the question, he still proceeded to relate it in detail without concealing anything. "They were Hafsa and Aisha," Omar ؓ began. He then started narrating the incident. He said, "We members of the Quraish always had the upper hand over our wives. When we arrived in Madinah, we encountered the Ansar whose women had the upper hand over them. Our women then started learning from their women. My house was located in the vicinity of Banu Umayya bin Zaid, which was in the upper reaches of Madinah. When I became angry with my wife one day and told her something, she surprised me by back chatting. When I objected to her back chatting, she said, 'What are you objecting about my back chatting when I can swear by Allah that the wives of Rasulullah ﷺ backchat to him? In fact some of them when angry shun him morning to evening.' I then left the house and went to my daughter Hafsa. 'Do you backchat Rasulullah ﷺ?' When she replied in the affirmative, I asked further, 'Does any of you when angry shun Rasulullah ﷺ morning to evening?' When she again replied in the affirmative, I said, 'Whichever of you does that is at a loss and destroyed! Do any of you not fear that Allah would be angry with her because His Rasul ﷺ is angry with her? She will then most certainly be destroyed. You should never backchat Rasulullah ﷺ and never ask for him for anything. Rather ask from me whatever you please and never be deceived by the fact that your companion Aisha ؓ is prettier than you and more beloved to Rasulullah ﷺ, do not emulate everything she does.' I had a friend from amongst the Ansar who took turns with me in attending Rasulullah ﷺ's gatherings. He would go one day and me the next so that he brought me the news of revelation one day and I brought it to him the next day. It was during the time when there was a lot of talk about the Ghassan tribe preparing themselves to attack us when my friend came to me at night. Knocking at my door, he called for me until I came out. 'Something serious has taken place," he said. 'What is it?' I asked, 'Have the Ghassan tribe came?' 'No,' he replied, 'it is more serious than that and with longer lasting implications. Rasulullah ﷺ has divorced his wives!' 'Hafsa is at a loss and destroyed!' I cried, 'I had a feeling that this would happen.' After performing the Fajr salah, I dressed and went down to Madinah where I went to see Hafsa. She was in tears. 'Has Rasulullah ﷺ divorced you?' I queried. 'I do not know,' she replied, 'but he is now there in the upper story room.' I went to Rasulullah ﷺ's Abyssinian slave and asked him to seek permission from Rasulullah ﷺ for me to enter. The slave went in and then emerged saying, 'I mentioned your name to him but Rasulullah ﷺ merely remained silent.' I then left and went towards the pulpit where I saw a group sitting, some of them in tears. I sat for awhile, but then my anxiety got the better of me and I went back to the slave saying, 'Seek permission for Omar.' Again the slave went in and then emerged saying, 'I mentioned your name to him but Rasulullah ﷺ merely remained silent.' I again left to sit near the pulpit but again my anxiety got the better of me and I returned to request the slave to seek permission for me to enter. Yet again the slave went in and emerged saying, 'I mentioned your name to him but he merely remained silent.' As I turned to leave, the slave suddenly called for me saying. 'You may enter; for Rasulullah ﷺ has granted you permission.'

When I entered, I found Rasulullah ﷺ reclining against a straw mat that had left imprints on his side. 'Have you divorced your wives, O Rasulullah ﷺ?' I asked. Raising his head, he replied, 'No.' 'Allahu Akbar!' I cried out. I then said, 'O Rasulullah ﷺ! You have seen that we the members of the Quraish always had the upper hand over our wives. When we arrived in Madinah, we encountered the Ansar whose women had the upper hand over them. Our women then started learning from their women. When I became angry with my wife one day and told her something, she surprised me by back chatting. When I objected to her back chatting, she said, 'What are you objecting about my back chatting when I can swear by Allah that the wives of Rasulullah ﷺ backchat to him? In fact some of them when angry shun him morning to evening. I said, 'Whichever of them does that is at a loss and destroyed! Does any of them not fear that Allah would be angry with her because His Rasul ﷺ is angry with her? She will then most certainly be destroyed.' This made Rasulullah ﷺ smile. 'O Rasulullah ﷺ!' I continued, 'I then went to Hafsa and told her, 'Never be deceived by the fact that your companion Aisha ؓ is prettier than you and more beloved to Rasulullah ﷺ.' Rasulullah ﷺ smiled again. Then I asked, 'Should I continue with this light-hearted talk?' 'By all means,' Rasulullah ﷺ said. I then sat down and I swear by Allah that when I looked about the room, all I saw was 3 pieces of undyed leather. 'O Rasulullah ﷺ!' I said, 'Pray to Allah to grant an abundance of wealth to your Ummah. Allah has given abundance to the Romans and Persians even though they do not worship Him so He will readily give us as well.' Rasulullah ﷺ then sat up straight and said, 'Are you also in doubt, O son of Khattab? They are people whose rewards for their good deeds have been brought forward to this world without any share left for the Hereafter.' I then quickly said, 'Do seek forgiveness for me, O Rasulullah ﷺ.' Because he was so angry with them at the time, Rasulullah ﷺ had vowed not to go to his wives for an entire month until Allah directed him otherwise." *(Ahmad, Bukhari, Muslim, Tirmidhi, Nasa'ee)*. Abdullah bin Abbas ؓ reports that Omar ؓ said, "When Rasulullah ﷺ separated from his wives, I entered the Masjid where I saw the people fondling pebbles, they said, 'Rasulullah ﷺ has divorced his wives!' This took place before the injunction of Hijab was ordained. I said to myself, 'I am going to find out properly what is happening, whether Rasulullah ﷺ had divorced them or not.'" The Hadith continues to mention how Omar ﷺ went to both Hafsa ؓ as well as Aisha ؓ to admonish them. Thereafter, the narration quotes Omar ؓ who says, "When I then went to Rasulullah ﷺ, I found him on the doorstep of the room on the upper storey. I called out saying, 'O Rabah! Secure permission for me to see Rasulullah ﷺ... '" The rest of the narration is like the one above until the part where Omar ؓ said, "O Rasulullah ﷺ! Do not let the matter of your wives disturb you. If you have divorced them, then Allah is with you as well as His angels, Jibreel ؑ, Mikal ؑ, myself, Abu Bakr ؓ and all the Mu'minin. I praise Allah for the fact that whenever I spoke, I had firm hope that Allah would confirm what I said. It was therefore with reference to this that Allah revealed the following verse:

إِنْ تَتُوبَا إِلَى اللَّهِ فَقَدْ صَغَتْ قُلُوبُكُمَا وَإِنْ تَظَاهَرَا عَلَيْهِ فَإِنَّ اللَّهَ هُوَ مَوْلَاهُ وَجِبْرِيلُ وَصَالِحُ الْمُؤْمِنِينَ وَالْمَلَائِكَةُ بَعْدَ ذَلِكَ ظَهِيرٌ (4) عَسَى رَبُّهُ إِنْ طَلَّقَكُنَّ أَنْ يُبْدِلَهُ أَزْوَاجًا خَيْرًا مِنْكُنَّ مُسْلِمَاتٍ مُؤْمِنَاتٍ قَانِتَاتٍ تَائِبَاتٍ عَابِدَاتٍ سَائِحَاتٍ ثَيِّبَاتٍ وَأَبْكَارًا (5)

If you two (wives of the Prophet ﷺ, namely Aisha and Hafsa ؓ) turn in repentance to Allah, (it will be better for you), your hearts are indeed so inclined (to oppose what the Prophet ﷺ likes), but if you help one another against him (Muhammad ﷺ), then verily, Allah is his Maula (Lord, or Master, or Protector, etc.), and

Jibrael (Gabriel), and the righteous among the believers, and furthermore, the angels are his helpers. It may be if he divorced you (all) that his Lord will give him instead of you, wives better than you, Muslims (who submit to Allah), believers, obedient to Allah, turning to Allah in repentance, worshipping Allah sincerely, fasting or emigrants (for Allah's sake), previously married and virgins. (At-Tahrim:4-5)

'Have you divorced them?' I asked. 'No,' Rasulullah ﷺ replied. I then stood at the door of the Masjid and called out in my loudest voice, "Rasulullah ﷺ's wives have not been divorced!" It was with reference to this that Allah revealed the verse:

وَإِذَا جَاءَهُمْ أَمْرٌ مِّنَ الْأَمْنِ أَوِ الْخَوْفِ أَذَاعُوا بِهِ وَلَوْ رَدُّوهُ إِلَى الرَّسُولِ وَإِلَى أُولِي الْأَمْرِ مِنْهُمْ لَعَلِمَهُ الَّذِينَ يَسْتَنبِطُونَهُ مِنْهُمْ

When there comes to them some matter touching (public) safety or fear, they make it known (among the people), if only they had referred it to the Messenger or to those charged with authority among them, the proper investigators would have understood it from them (directly). (An-Nisa:83)

Omar ﷺ continues, "It was I who researched this matter." *(Muslim in Tafsir Ibn Kathir, Abdur Razzaq, Ibn Sa'd, Ibn Hibban, Bayhaqi, Ibn Jareer, Ibn Mundhir, Ibn Mardway, Kanzul Ummal)*

Jabir ﷺ reports that Rasulullah ﷺ was sitting in his house while the Sahabah were sitting by his door. When Abu Bakr ﷺ arrived and sought permission to enter, Rasulullah ﷺ did not grant him permission. Omar ﷺ then arrived and Rasulullah ﷺ did not grant him permission to enter either. Rasulullah ﷺ later granted permission to both Abu Bakr ﷺ and Omar ﷺ and they both entered the room where Rasulullah ﷺ was sitting in silence with his wives around him. Omar ﷺ said to himself, "I am going to say something to make Rasulullah ﷺ laugh." He then proceeded to say, "O Rasulullah ﷺ! If only you had seen my wife, the daughter of Zaid just now when I slapped her across the neck when she asked me for an increase in her allowance!" Rasulullah ﷺ smiled so broadly that his molars became visible. He said, "Here are my wives around me also asking me for an increase in their allowances." Abu Bakr ﷺ then stood up to hit his daughter Aisha ﷺ and Omar ﷺ also got up to hit his daughter Hafsa ﷺ. Both men were rebuking their daughters saying, "How can you ask Rasulullah ﷺ for something he does not have?!" Rasulullah ﷺ however stopped the 2 men and the women said, "By Allah! After this, we shall never again ask Rasulullah ﷺ for something he does not have." It was on this occasion that Allah revealed the verse offering a choice to Rasulullah ﷺ's wives. Rasulullah ﷺ first approached Aisha ﷺ saying, "I am about to present to you an offer that I do not want you to be hasty in deciding until you have consulted with your parents." "What is it?" she asked. Rasulullah ﷺ then recited for her the verse:

يَا أَيُّهَا النَّبِيُّ قُل لِّأَزْوَاجِكَ إِن كُنتُنَّ تُرِدْنَ الْحَيَاةَ الدُّنْيَا وَزِينَتَهَا فَتَعَالَيْنَ أُمَتِّعْكُنَّ وَأُسَرِّحْكُنَّ سَرَاحًا جَمِيلًا (28) وَإِن كُنتُنَّ تُرِدْنَ اللَّهَ وَرَسُولَهُ وَالدَّارَ الْآخِرَةَ فَإِنَّ اللَّهَ أَعَدَّ لِلْمُحْسِنَاتِ مِنكُنَّ أَجْرًا عَظِيمًا (29)

O Prophet (Muhammad ﷺ)! Say to your wives: If you desire the life of this world, and its glitter, Then come! I will make a provision for you and set you free in a handsome manner (divorce). But if you desire Allah and His Messenger, and the home of the Hereafter, then verily, Allah has prepared for Al-Muhsinat (good-doers) amongst you an enormous reward. (Al-Ahzab:28-29)

Aisha ﷺ immediately said, "Should I consult my parents about having you?! I definitely choose Allah and His Rasul ﷺ. Please do not inform any of your other wives what I have

decided." Rasulullah ﷺ told her, "Allah has sent me to make matters easy for people and not to make them difficult. Therefore, if any of them asks me about your decision, I will certainly inform her." *(Ahmad, Muslim, Nasa'ee)*. Abdullah bin Abbas ﷺ reports that Aisha ﷺ said, "When the verses giving us the choice were revealed, Rasulullah ﷺ began with me before any of his other wives. He said, 'I am about to present to you a choice about which you are in no hurry to decide until you have consulted with your parents.' Rasulullah ﷺ said this despite knowing well that my parents would never tell me to separate from Rasulullah ﷺ. Rasulullah ﷺ then continued, 'Allah says:

يَا أَيُّهَا النَّبِيُّ قُل لِّأَزْوَاجِكَ إِن كُنتُنَّ تُرِدْنَ الْحَيَاةَ الدُّنْيَا وَزِينَتَهَا فَتَعَالَيْنَ أُمَتِّعْكُنَّ وَأُسَرِّحْكُنَّ سَرَاحًا جَمِيلًا (28) وَإِن كُنتُنَّ تُرِدْنَ اللَّهَ وَرَسُولَهُ وَالدَّارَ الْآخِرَةَ فَإِنَّ اللَّهَ أَعَدَّ لِلْمُحْسِنَاتِ مِنكُنَّ أَجْرًا عَظِيمًا (29)

O Prophet (Muhammad ﷺ)! Say to your wives: If you desire the life of this world, and its glitter, Then come! I will make a provision for you and set you free in a handsome manner (divorce). But if you desire Allah and His Messenger, and the home of the Hereafter, then verily, Allah has prepared for Al-Muhsinat (good-doers) amongst you an enormous reward. (Al-Ahzab:28-29)

Aisha ﷺ says, "I immediately said, "Is there anything to consult my parents about? I certainly want Allah, His Rasul ﷺ and the home of the Hereafter.'" Rasulullah ﷺ then presented the choice to all his wives and the reply each of them gave was similar to that of Aisha ﷺ. *(Ibn Abi Hatim, Bukhari, Muslim)*. Another narration quotes that Aisha ﷺ said, "When Rasulullah ﷺ gave us a choice and we chose to remain with him, he did not count this choice as a divorce against us." *(Bukhari, Muslim, Ahmad in Tafsir Ibn Kathir)*

Rasulullah ﷺ's Relationship with Aisha ﷺ and Maymuna ﷺ

Aisha ﷺ reports that Rasulullah ﷺ once said to her, "I know exactly when you are happy with me and when you are angry." When she asked Rasulullah ﷺ how he knew that, he replied, "When you are happy with me, you say, 'No, by the Rabb of Muhammad ﷺ!' and when you are angry with me, you say, 'No, by the Rabb of Ibrahim عليه السلام.'" "That's true," Aisha ﷺ said, "but it is only your name that I leave out while the love for you in my heart remains just as strong." *(Bukhari, Muslim in Mishkatul Masabih)*. Aisha ﷺ narrates, "I was once on a journey with Rasulullah ﷺ when I ran a race with him and beat him. After I had put on some weight, I again ran a race with him, but this time he beat me. He then said, 'This is in lieu of the last race.'" *(Abu Dawud in Mishkatul Masabih)*. Abdullah bin Abbas ﷺ relates, "As a young boy I was once the guest of my maternal aunt Maymuna ﷺ on a night when she was not performing salah. She brought one shawl and then another, which she lay it down by the head-side of the bedding. She then lay down, pulled the shawl over her and made a bed for me beside her. I shared her pillow with her. Rasulullah ﷺ arrived after performing the Isha salah and when he reached the bed, he took the shawl lying by the head-side of the bed and tied it as a lower garment. Thereafter, he removed the 2 he was wearing, hung them up and got in to the bed with his wife. Towards the final hours of the night, he got up and took a water bag that was hanging there. He opened it and started making wudhu. I was about to get up to pour the water for him when it occurred to me that I would not like him to know that I had been awake. He then came to the bed, got dressed in his 2 garments and removed the shawl. He stood at the place where he performed salah and started performing salah. I got up, made wudhu and stood on his left. Rasulullah ﷺ held me from his back and made me stand on his right. With me following him, he then proceeded to perform 13 Rakahs of salah. Rasulullah ﷺ then sat down and as I sat beside him, his cheek leaned towards mine as he fell asleep and I could hear him breathing like a sleeping person. Bilal ؓ then arrived and called out, 'Salah, O Rasulullah ﷺ.' Rasulullah ﷺ then stood up in the place where he performed salah and started performing 2 Rakahs salah as Bilal ؓ started calling out the Iqamah." *(Ibn Najjar in Kanzul Ummal)*

Rasulullah ﷺ's Kind Treatment of an Old Woman

Aisha ؓ reports that when an old woman once came to Rasulullah ﷺ, he asked her who she was. When she informed him that her name was Jathama Muzaniya. Rasulullah ﷺ said, "You are now Hasana Muzaniya." He then proceeded to ask her how they were, how their life was, and how they had been since he last met them. "May my parents be sacrificed for you, O Rasulullah ﷺ!" she said, "We have been well." After she had left, Aisha ؓ asked, "O Rasulullah ﷺ! You gave such an excellent reception to the old lady?" "Dear Aisha," Rasulullah ﷺ explained, "She used to visit us when Khadija ؓ was alive. Maintaining old acquaintances is a part of Iman." *(Bayhaqi, Ibn Najjar)*. Aisha ؓ says, "When a particular old woman used to visit Nabi ﷺ, he became very happy and would honor her greatly. 'May my parents be sacrificed for you!' I said, 'You treat this woman better than you treat anyone else.' Rasulullah ﷺ explained, 'She used to visit us when Khadija ؓ was alive. Do you not know that honoring bonds of affection is a part of Iman?'" Abu Tufail ؓ relates, "I saw Rasulullah ﷺ distributing meat in Jirrana when I was a young boy who could carry only the limb of a camel. When a particular lady came to him, he spread out his shawl for her to sit. I asked someone who she was, I was informed that she was the woman who suckled him as a baby." *(Bukhari in Adab)*

Rasulullah ﷺ's Relationship with an Abyssinian Slave and with Abdullah bin Mas'ood ؓ

Omar ؓ reports that when he once went to see Rasulullah ﷺ. Rasulullah ﷺ's short Abyssinian slave was busy rubbing his back. "O Rasulullah ﷺ!" Omar ؓ asked, "Did you hurt yourself?" Rasulullah ﷺ replied, "The camel dropped me down last night." *(Tabrani, Bazzar in Kanzul Ummal)*. Qasim bin Abdur Rahman reports that Abdullah bin Mas'ood ؓ used to put on Rasulullah ﷺ's shoes for him. He would then walk ahead with Rasulullah ﷺ's staff in his hand. When Rasulullah ﷺ reached the gathering, Abdullah bin Mas'ood ؓ would remove Rasulullah ﷺ's shoes, place it under his arms and hand the staff over. As soon as Rasulullah ﷺ decided to get up, Abdullah bin Mas'ood ؓ would give him his shoes and again walk ahead with the staff until he entered the room before Rasulullah ﷺ. Another narration state that Abdullah bin Mas'ood ؓ used to screen Rasulullah ﷺ when he bathed, would wake him up when he slept, and would walk about with him when there was no one else. *(Ibn Sa'd)*

Rasulullah ﷺ's Relationship with Anas ؓ

Anas ؓ says, "When Rasulullah ﷺ arrived in Madinah, I was a young boy of 10 and when he passed away, I was only 20. It was my mother and aunts who encouraged me to serve Rasulullah ﷺ. *(Ibn Abi Shaybah, Abu Nu'aym)*. Thumama narrates that when someone asked Anas ؓ whether he was present during the Battle of Badr, he replied, "Shame on you! How could I ever absent myself?" Muhammad bin Abdullah Ansari reports that Anas ؓ accompanied Rasulullah ﷺ to Badr to serve him while he was still a young boy. *(Ibn Sa'd, Ibn Asakir in Muntakhab Kanzul Ummal)*

The Services that the Ansar Youth and the Sahabah Rendered to Rasulullah ﷺ

Anas ؓ narrates that there were 20 youngsters from the Ansar who always stuck close to Rasulullah ﷺ. Rasulullah ﷺ would always dispatch them whenever he needed something done. *(Bazzar, Haythami)*. Abdur Rahman bin Auf ؓ reports that there were always 4 or 5 Sahabah who never parted from Rasulullah ﷺ when on journey or from Rasulullah ﷺ's door when at home. *(Bazzar, Haythami)*. Abu Sa'eed Khudri ؓ relates, "We used to take turns to be at Rasulullah ﷺ's service so that we could fulfill any need he had or he could dispatch us for any task. Eventually, the people anticipating rewards for this service increased and there were plenty of people taking turns. As we were one day discussing Dajjal, Rasulullah ﷺ came out to ask, 'What are these whispered discussions all about? Have I not forbidden you from whispered discussion?'" *(Bazzar, Haythami)*. Assim bin Sufian says that it was either Abu Darda ؓ or Abu Dhar ؓ whom he heard say, "I once sought permission from Rasulullah ﷺ to spend the night at his door so that he could awaken me for any need he may have. Rasulullah ﷺ granted permission and I spent the night there." *(Bazzar, Haythami)*. Hudhaifa reports, "I once performed salah with Rasulullah ﷺ during the month of Ramadhan. He got up to take a bath and I screened him. When some water was left over in the container, he said, 'If you wish, you may use it to bath, or you may add some more water to it.' 'O Rasulullah ﷺ!' I replied, 'This left-over water of yours is more beloved to me than anything more I may add.' I started to bath, Rasulullah ﷺ screened me. 'You need not screen me,' I said. He replied, 'Why not? I must screen you just as you screened me.'" *(Ibn Asakir in Muntakhab Kanzul Ummal)*.

Rasulullah ﷺ's Relationship with his Son Ibrahim and Other Children of his Family

Anas ؓ says, "I have never seen anyone more compassionate towards his family than Rasulullah ﷺ. His son Ibrahim was given to a woman in the upper reaches of Madinah for suckling. With us in his company, Rasulullah ﷺ used to go to the house, which would be filled with smoke because the nursing mother's husband was a blacksmith. Rasulullah ﷺ would always pick up the child and kiss him before leaving." Amr ؓ reports that when Ibrahim passed away, Rasulullah ﷺ said, "Ibrahim was my son and has passed away while still suckling. Verily he shall have 2 nursing mothers in Jannah who will complete his period of suckling." *(Muslim, Ahmad in Al Bidayah wan Nihayah)*. Abdullah bin Harith ؓ narrates that Rasulullah ﷺ used to place Abdullah, Ubaidulla and Kathir, all the children of Abbas ؓ in a line and would then promise a prize to whichever of them beat the others to him. They would then race towards him and jump on to his back and chest as he hugged and kissed them. *(Ahmad, Haythami)*. Abdullah bin Ja'far ؓ reports, "Whenever Rasulullah ﷺ returned from a journey, the children of his family were brought to receive him. When he once returned from a journey, I was brought first to him so he placed me in front of him on the animal. Thereafter, one of Fatima ؓ's children either Hasan or Husain was brought to him and he placed him behind him. When we entered Madinah, we were therefore 3 people on the animal." *(Ibn Asakir, Muslim)*. Abdullah bin Ja'far ؓ also narrates, "Rasulullah ﷺ once passed by me as I was playing with some children. He then picked me up together with one of Abbas's children and placed us on his animal. We were therefore 3 on the animal." *(Ibn Asakir)*. In another narration, Abdullah bin Ja'far ؓ says, "You should have seen the time when we were children and I would be playing with Ubaidulla and Quthm, both the sons of

Abbas ✿. Passing by, Rasulullah ✿ would say, 'Pick that child up and give him to me.' I was then passed to him and he would then put me in front of him. Thereafter, Rasulullah ✿ would say, 'Pick that child up and give him to me.' He would then put the other child behind him. Although Abbas ✿ liked Ubaidulla more than Quthm, Rasulullah ✿ would not be embarrassed in front of his uncle Abbas to take Quthm on the animal and leave Ubaidulla. Rasulullah ✿ would then pass his hand over my head thrice and say each time, 'O Allah! You be Ja'far's successor for his children.'" *(Ibn Asakir in Muntakhab Kanzul Ummal)*. Omar bin Khattab ✿ says, "When I saw Hasan and Husain riding on Rasulullah ✿'s shoulders, I remarked, 'What a fine horse you 2 are riding!' Rasulullah ✿ then said, 'And what fine horsemen are they!?'" *(Abu Ya'la in Kanzul Ummal, Majmu'az Zawa'id, Bazzar, Ibn Sahahin in Kanzul Ummal)*. Abdullah bin Abbas ✿ narrates that Rasulullah ✿ came out of the house carrying Hasan ✿ on his shoulders when someone commented, "Dear child! What a fine conveyance you have!" To this Rasulullah ✿ said, "And he is a mighty fine rider too." *(Ibn Asakir in Kanzul Ummal)*. Bara bin Azib ✿ reports that Rasulullah ✿ was once performing salah when Hasan ✿ and Husain ✿ or one of them arrived and climbed upon his back. When Rasulullah ✿ got up, he held the child or the 2 children with his hand and after completing the salah said, "What an excellent mount you had mounted." *(Tabrani, Haythami)*. Jabir ✿ says that he once went to Rasulullah ✿ as he was on all 4 with Hasan ✿ and Husain ✿ on his back. Rasulullah ✿ said, "You 2 have an excellent camel and are both excellent loads." *(Tabrani, Haythami)*

The Incident of Rasulullah ✿ with Hasan ✿ and Husain ✿ When They got Lost

Salman ✿ reports that it was midday when they were sitting around Rasulullah ✿. Ummu Ayman ✿ arrived saying, "O Rasulullah ✿! Hasan ✿ and Husain ✿ are lost!" Rasulullah ✿ said to the Sahabah, "Get up and look for my sons!" Every person went in the direction he was facing and Salman ✿ went in the direction Rasulullah ✿ went. Rasulullah ✿ kept searching until he was at the foot of a mountain when he saw the 2 boys clinging on to each other. In front of them was a snake standing on its tail with flames flashing from its mouth. Allah had perhaps sent it to ensure that the boys ventured no further. As Rasulullah ✿ rushed towards it, it turned to look at him and then slid away into a hole. Rasulullah ✿ then went to the boys and as he separated them, he wiped their faces saying, "May my parents be sacrificed for you! How honorable you 2 are in the sight of Allah!" When he then carried one of them on his right shoulder and the other on his left shoulder, Salman ✿ remarked, "Glad tidings to you 2. What an excellent mount you have!" To this, Rasulullah ✿ said, "What excellent riders are they and their father is even better than them." *(Tabrani. Haythami, Ya'la bin Murra in Kanzul Ummal)*. Jabir ✿ says, "We were with Rasulullah ✿ when we were invited for a meal. When we came across Husain ✿ playing with other children in the street, Rasulullah ✿ ran ahead of the others and stretched out his hands to grab the boy. Husain ✿ started running to and fro as Rasulullah ✿ made him laugh in front of everyone there. Rasulullah ✿ then stretched out his arms and held the boy with one hand on his chin and the other between his head and ears. Thereafter, Rasulullah ✿ hugged and kissed him saying, 'Husain is from me and I am from him. May Allah love those who love him. Hasan ✿ and Husain ✿ are 2 distinguished grandsons from amongst grandsons.'" *(Tabrani in Kanzul Ummal)*

Rasulullah ✿ tells Uthman bin Madh'un ✿ to Treat his Wife Better

Ibn Is'haq Sabi'ee reports that the wife of Uthman bin Madh'un ✿ once came to the wives of Rasulullah ✿ dressed in unattractive and old clothes. When they asked her what the problem was, she informed them that her husband stood in salah all night and fasted all day and therefore had no time for her, because of which she felt no need to look attractive. When Rasulullah ✿ was informed of what she said, he met Uthman bin Madh'un ✿, rebuked him and said, "Don't you have an excellent example in me?" Uthman bin Madh'un ✿ replied, "Certainly. May my parents be sacrificed for you!" Thereafter, his wife was always looking attractive and wearing enchanting scents. On his deathbed, his wife recited some couplets which meant:

"Dear eyes! Be generous with your tears and never let them stop over the demise of Uthman bin Madh'un over a man who spent the entire night pleasing his Creator over the loss of someone who will be buried. Glad tidings of Jannah to him! Baqee and its Gharqad trees are graced to be his home and after being troubled (by having Kuffar buried there), the ground shall be illuminated
All that the heart shall inherit will be grief that knows no end until death comes, my tear ducts shall never dry."
(Abu Nu'aym in Hilya, Ibn Sa'd)

Another narration names the wife of Uthman bin Madh'un ✿ as Khowla bint Hakim ✿ and that it was Aisha ✿ whom she visited. The narration also states that Rasulullah ✿ said to Uthman bin Madh'un ✿, "O Uthman! Monasticism has not been ordained for us. Am I not a perfect example for you? By Allah! It is I who fears Allah most and who is most mindful of the limits He has set." *(Abdur Razzaq in Kanzul Ummal)*

Rasulullah ✿ Tells Abdullah bin Amr bin Al Aas ✿ to Treat His Wife Better

Abdullah bin Amr bin Al Aas ✿ reports, "My father got me married to a woman from the Quraish. However, when she first came to me, I paid no attention to her because of my overriding enthusiasm for acts of Ibada such as salah and fasting. My father Amr bin Al Aas ✿ once came to his daughter-in-law (my wife) and asked, 'How do you find your husband?' She replied, 'He is the best of husbands but has not yet ventured to expose any part of my body and has not even come near our bed.' My father then came to me and rebuked me most severely. Biting into me with his tongue, he said, 'I got you married to an honorable lady of the Quraish and you have left her hanging in suspension?!' After detailing more of the things I was doing, he then went to complain about me to Rasulullah ✿. Rasulullah ✿ sent for me and when I arrived, he verified, 'Do you fast every day?' 'Yes,' I replied. He then asked further, 'And do you stand in salah all night?' When I again I replied in the affirmative, Rasulullah ✿ said, 'But while I fast regularly, there are also days when I do not fast. While I perform salah at night, I also sleep and I also touch my wives. Whoever turns away from my way of life cannot be my follower.' Rasulullah ✿ then proceeded to say, 'Complete a recitation of the Qur'an once a month.' 'But I can do more than that,' I said. 'Then complete it once every 10 days,' Rasulullah ✿ permitted. When I insisted that I could do more than that as well, Rasulullah ✿ told me that I could then complete a recitation in 3 days. Thereafter, Rasulullah ✿ said, 'Fast only 3 days a month.' When I informed Rasulullah ✿ that I was capable of much more, he continued increasing the number of days until he finally said, 'Then fast one day and skip the next. This is the best type of fast and was the manner in which my brother Dawud ✿ used to fast.'" In his narration, Husain states that Rasulullah ✿ added,

"Every keen worshipper has a period of great enthusiasm but every such period comes with a waning phase. When this phase comes, the person either resorts to the Sunnah or towards Bid'ah. Whoever during this phase resorts towards the Sunnah has been rightly guided and whoever turns towards Bid'ah has been destroyed." Mujahid says that when Abdullah bin Amr bin Al Aas ؓ grew old and weak, he would fast several days in a row and then skip several days to regain his strength. When reciting the Qur'an he would also sometimes recite more and sometimes less. Nevertheless, he would ensure that he completed a recitation within a period of either 7 days or 3 days. Thereafter when he grew even weaker, he would say, "Had I accepted the concession Rasulullah ﷺ offered me, I would have liked it more than what extra Ibada he had to send my way because of my insistence. However, I shall now not reduce it because I would not like to do anything other than what I was doing at the time I separated from Rasulullah ﷺ when he passed away." (Abu Nu'aym in Hilya, Bukhari in Safwatus Safwa)

The Incident Between Salman ؓ and Abu Darda ؓ in this Regard

Abu Juhaifa ؓ reports that Rasulullah ﷺ had made a bond of brotherhood between Salman ؓ and Abu Darda ؓ. When Salman ؓ once came to visit Abu Darda ؓ, he found his wife Ummu Darda ؓ in a disheveled condition. When he enquired what the matter was, she replied, "Your brother Abu Darda ؓ has no need for this world." Abu Darda ؓ then arrived and when he got a meal prepared for Salman ؓ, he said, "You eat because I am fasting." Salman ؓ refused saying, "I shall not eat until you eat." Abu Darda ؓ was then forced to terminate the fast and join in the meal. That night when Abu Darda ؓ started to perform salah, Salman ؓ instructed him to sleep. Abu Darda ؓ slept awhile and was again about to get up when Salman ؓ again told him to go back to sleep. It was only when the night was drawing to an end that Salman ؓ said to Abu Darda ؓ, "You may now get up." The 2 men then performed Tahajjud salah. Salman ؓ then advised Abu Darda ؓ saying, "You have rights owing to your Rabb as well as rights owing to your body and rights owing to your wife. You should therefore give every recipient their due rights." When Abu Darda ؓ reported the matter to Rasulullah ﷺ, Rasulullah ﷺ said, "Salman is right." (Bukhari, Abu Nu'aym in Hilya, Kanzul Ummal, Tirmidhi, Bazzar, Ibn Khuzaima, Dar Qutni, Tabrani, Ibn Hibban in Fat'hul Bari, Ibn Sa'd)

Zubair bin Awwam ؓ's Possessiveness Over his Wife Asma ؓ

Asma ؓ the daughter of Abu Bakr ؓ relates, "When Zubair ؓ married me, he possessed neither any property, money, slaves nor anything else apart from his horse. I used to feed his horse for him, tend to it and care for it. I also used to crush the date stones to feed his camel that drew water from the well and fed it myself. In addition to this, I would give it water to drink, sew the water bags that the camel used to draw water and knead dough. However, because I was not good at making the bread, my Ansar neighbors would do it for me. They were extremely sincere and true friends. I used to carry the date stones on my head from the property Rasulullah ﷺ gave to Zubair ؓ, which lay 2/3rd of a Farsakh (~ 2 miles) from Madinah. As I was coming one day with the date stones on my head, I met with Rasulullah ﷺ and some Sahabah. Rasulullah ﷺ called for me as he instructed his camel to sit so that I may ride on it behind him. I was however too shy to travel with men and also thought of Zubair ؓ's possessiveness. He was one of the most possessive people to be found. When Rasulullah ﷺ realized that I was too shy, he carried on. When I met Zubair ؓ, I said to him, 'Rasulullah ﷺ and a few

Sahabah met me while I was carrying the date stones on my head. When he made his camel sit down for me to ride on, I felt too shy and also thought of your possessiveness.' He said, 'By Allah! Your carrying the date stones is more difficult for me to bear than your riding with Rasulullah ﷺ.' This continued until my father Abu Bakr ؓ sent me a servant who relieved me of tending to the horse and it seemed like he had set me free." (Ibn Sa'd). Asma ؓ the daughter of Abu Bakr ؓ was married to Zubair bin Awwam ؓ. She complained to her father about her husband's strict nature, Abu Bakr ؓ said, "Dear daughter! Be patient as when a woman has a pious husband and she does not remarry after he dies, Allah will reunite them in Jannah." (Ibn Sa'd)

The Incident of a Woman who complained to Omar ؓ about her Husband

Kahmas Hilali reports that they were once sitting with Omar ؓ when a lady arrived. She sat down and said, "O Amirul Mu'minin! While the evil nature of my husband has increased, his good nature has dwindled." "Who is your husband?" Omar ؓ asked. When she informed him that her husband was a man called Abu Salama, Omar ؓ said, "He was a companion of Rasulullah ﷺ and is a righteous man." He then asked the men around him, "Is he not so?" "O Amirul Mu'minin!" they replied, "We know him to be just as you say." Omar then instructed someone sitting there to call for the husband. When her husband was sent for, the lady got up and sat behind Omar ؓ. It was not long before the 2 men arrived together and the husband sat in front of Omar ؓ. "What has this woman sitting behind me have to say?" Omar ؓ asked. "Who is she, O Amirul Mu'minin?" the man asked. "She is your wife," Omar ؓ replied. "And what has she to say?" he asked. Omar ؓ replied, "She claims that while your evil nature has increased, your good nature has dwindled." The husband said, "A terrible thing she has said, O Amirul Mu'minin! She is amongst the most righteous women of her tribe. In addition to this, she also has the most clothing and the most comfortable home. However, her husband is an old man." Addressing the wife, Omar ؓ asked, "And what have you to say?" "He has spoken the truth," she replied. Omar ؓ got up with his whip and struck her with it saying, "O enemy of yourself! You have eaten his wealth and finished his youth and then go even further to make false allegations against him!" "O Amirul Mu'minin!" she pleaded, "Do not be hasty. I swear by Allah that I shall never sit in this position as complainant against my husband ever again." Omar ؓ then instructed that she be given 3 garments and said, "Take this in lieu of what I have done to you when I hit you. However, I am warning you never to complain about this old man again." The narrator says, "I remember the incident so clearly that it is as if I can actually see her standing up with those garments." Omar ؓ then turned to her husband and said, "Let not what you have seen me do to her ever provoke you to treat her badly." The husband promised that he would not and they both left. Omar ؓ then said, "I have heard Rasulullah ﷺ say, 'The best period of my Ummah is that in which I am the first period, followed by the second period and then the third. Thereafter, such people shall come who will take oaths before testifying and who will testify before being asked to do so. There will also be people whose marketplaces will be very noisy." (Tayalisi, Bukhari in Tarikh, Hakim in Kuna, Kanzul Ummal, Abu Bakr bin Abu Asim in Isabah)

The Incident of Another Woman and her Husband with Omar ؓ

Sha'bi narrates that a woman once came to Omar ؓ saying, "I have come to complain to you about a man who is the best of all men apart from a man whose deeds are superior or whose deeds match his. He stands in salah all night until dawn and fasts all day until evening." She was then overcome with shyness and said, "Excuse me, O Amirul Mu'minin." "May Allah reward you tremendously," Omar ؓ said, "You have certainly praised him well. You are excused." When she left, Ka'b bin Sur remarked, "O Amirul Mu'minin! She has certainly been eloquent in her complaint to you." "What was her complaint?" Omar ؓ asked. "Her husband," Ka'b replied. Omar ؓ then sent for the couple and when they arrived, said to Ka'b, "Now you pass judgment between them." Ka'b said, "How can I pass judgment when you are present?" Omar ؓ insisted saying, "It was you who understood what I did not" Ka'b then said, "Allah has mentioned:

فَانْكِحُوا مَا طَابَ لَكُمْ مِنَ النِّسَاءِ مَثْنَى وَثُلَاثَ وَرُبَاعَ

...then marry (other) women of your choice, two or three, or four... (An-Nisa:3)

You should therefore fast for 3 days and then not fast the next day which you will spend with your wife. You may also spend 3 nights in salah and then a night you're your wife." Omar ؓ remarked, "This decision I find more amazing than your first statement" Omar ؓ then appointed him as judge of Basra. *(Ibn Sa'd)*. Another narration states that Omar ؓ said to the lady, "Be honest with me and do not shy away from the truth." She then said, "O Amirul Mu'minin! I am a woman who desires what all women desire." *(Yashkari)*. Qatadah narrates that a woman once said to Omar ؓ, "My husband stands in salah all night and fasts all day." Omar ؓ said to her, "Are you instructing me to stop him from performing salah at night and from fasting during the day?" She then went away, but returned some time later with the same complaint. Omar ؓ again repeated what he had said the first time. Ka'b bin Sur pointed out, "O Amirul Mu'minin! She has a right." "What is her right?" Omar ؓ asked. Ka'b replied, "Allah has permitted 4 wives for him, so count her as one of 4. She is entitled to one night in every 4 nights and one day in every 4 days." Omar ؓ asked the husband and instructed him to spend one of every 4 nights with her and to skip a fast in every 4 fasts. *(Abdur Razzaq in Kanzul Ummal, Ibn Abi Shaybah in Isabah)*

The Incident of Abu Gharza ؓ and his Wife with Omar ؓ

Abu Gharza ؓ once led Ibn Arqam by the hand to his wife and asked her, "Do you hate me." "Yes I do," she replied. "What made you do this?" Ibn Arqam ؓ asked. Abu Gharza ؓ explained, "People have been saying too many things about me." When Ibn Arqam ؓ reported the matter to Omar ؓ, the Amirul Mu'minin called for Abu Gharza ؓ and asked, "What made you do that?" Again Abu Gharza ؓ replied, "People have been saying too many things about me." Omar ؓ then sent for the wife. She arrived with the shrewd aunt of hers who told her, "When he questions you about your abrupt statement, say, 'Because he made me say it on oath, I did not like to tell a lie.'" When she came before him, Omar ؓ asked, "What made you say what you did?" She replied, "Because he made me say it on oath, I did not like to tell a lie." Omar ؓ said, "Why not? One of you ought to lie and say something nice because every home is not built on love. Many homes are built on polite interaction stalking from social status and Islam." *(Ibn Jareer in Kanzul Ummal)*

The Incident of Aatika ؓ the Daughter of Zaid bin Amr ؓ

Abu Salama bin Abdur Rahman bin Auf ؓ narrates that Aatika ؓ the daughter of Zaid bin Amr bin Nufail ؓ was married to Abdullah ؓ the son of Abu Bakr ؓ. He loved her very much and even gave her an orchard on condition that she does not remarry after his death. He was struck by an arrow during the battle at Ta'if and it was 40 days after the demise of Rasulullah ﷺ that the wound ruptured and he passed away. In his memory, Aatika ؓ recited the following couplets which meant:

"I swear that my eye shall always remain hot with tears over you and that my skin shall always be covered in dust because I shall never adorn myself for anyone else. This I shall do forever, as long as the doves of the dense forest fuss and as long as the night issues forth the bright morning"

When Omar ؓ proposed for her afterwards, she informed him that Abdullah ؓ had given her an orchard with the condition that she should not remarry after him. Omar ؓ advised her to acquire a verdict from someone. She then enquired from Ali bin Abi Talib ؓ whose verdict was that she was free to remarry after returning the orchard to the family of Abdullah ؓ. Omar ؓ then married her and invited a few Sahabah for the Walima meal. Amongst the guests was Ali ؓ, who was the person with whom Abdullah ؓ had made a bond of brotherhood. "Permit me to have a word with her (your new bride)," Ali ؓ asked Omar ؓ. With Omar ؓ's permission, Ali ؓ said, "O Aatika!

'I swear that my eye shall always remain hot with tears over you and that my skin shall always be covered in dust'"

Hearing this Aatika ؓ started weeping very loudly. Omar ؓ said to Ali ؓ, "May Allah forgive you! Do not upset my wife's mood for me." *(Waki in Kanzul Ummal, Ibn Sa'd in Isabah)*

The Incident of Abdullah bin Abbas ؓ with his Wife and What His Aunt Maymuna ؓ Said to Him

Nadba the freed slave of Maymuna ؓ reports that her mistress Maymuna ؓ once sent her to Abdullah bin Abbas ؓ. When she entered the house, she found that there were 2 beds. When she returned to Maymuna ؓ, she said, "It appears to me that Ibn Abbas ؓ has separated from his wife." Maymuna ؓ then sent for Ibn Abbas ؓ's wife who was the daughter of Sarj Kindi. When she asked her about it, the wife replied, "There is nothing between us. I am only menstruating." Maymuna ؓ sent a message to Abdullah bin Abbas ؓ reprimanding him, "Are you averse to the Sunnah of Rasulullah ﷺ!? Rasulullah ﷺ used to touch his wives while they were menstruating and wearing a cloth that reached up to the knees or halfway down the thighs." *(Abdur Razzaq in Kanzul Ummal)*

The Incident of Abdullah bin Abbas ؓ and a Cousin of his with a Slave Woman

Ikrama says that he is not sure whether it was Abdullah bin Abbas ؓ who invited his cousin for a meal or whether it was his cousin who invited him. Nevertheless, while a slave woman was working in front of them as they were eating, one of them called her an adulteress. "Stop that!" Abdullah bin Abbas ؓ cautioned, "Even though you will not be lashed for that slander in this world, you will certainly be punished in the Hereafter." The cousin said, "But what if she is as I have said?" Abdullah bin Abbas ؓ replied, "Verily Allah does not like people who are rude and who adopt offensive language, it is inappropriate for you to make such a statement." *(Bukhari in Adab)*

The Incident of a Slave Woman with the Wife of Amr bin Al Aas ؓ

Abu Imran of Palestine reports that while the wife of Amr bin Al Aas ؓ was busy cleaning his hair of lice, she called for her slave woman. When the slave delayed in arriving, Amr ؓ's wife called her an adulteress. "Have you seen her commit adultery?" Amr ؓ asked. When his wife replied that she had not, Amr ؓ said, "By Allah! On the Day of Judgment, you will certainly be lashed 80 times as punishment for slander." His wife then spoke to the slave and asked her for forgiveness. When the slave forgave her, Amr remarked, "She has no option but to forgive you because she is in your control. You had rather set her free." "Will that compensate for it?" his wife asked. "Perhaps," Amr ⬥ replied. *(Ibn Asakir in Kanzul Ummal)*

Some Incidents About the Mutual Relations Between the Sahabah

Abul Mutawakkil narrates that Abu Hurairah ⬥ had a Negro slave who had caused grief to the entire household because of something she had done. Raising his whip over her one day, Abu Hurairah ⬥ said, "Had it not been for Qisas (the Day of Judgment), I would have beat you unconscious. However, I shall sell you to someone who pays your price in full. Go (free)! You are Allah's." *(Abu Nu'aym in Hilya)*. Abdullah bin Qais or Ibn Abul Qais says that he was with the delegation of Abu Ubaidah bin Jarrah ⬥ that received Omar ⬥ when he arrived in Sham. As Omar ⬥ was traveling, he was met by some entertainers from Adhri'at who were carrying their swords to entertain Omar ⬥ as he entered their town. "Hold on!" Omar ⬥ said, "Stop them and send them back." "O Amirul Mu'minin!" Abu Ubaidah ⬥ said, "This is the custom of the non-Arabs. If you stop them, they will think that you wish to annul the pact with them that you wish to prevent them from freely practicing their customs." Omar ⬥ said, "Then leave them. Omar ⬥ and his family are all under the command of Abu Ubaida." *(Abu Nu'aym in Hilya, Kanzul Ummal)*. Abdullah bin Omar ⬥ reports that when Omar ⬥ and Zubair ⬥ once had a race, Zubair ⬥ beat Omar ⬥ and cried out, "I beat you! By the Rabb of the Kabah!" When they raced a second time, Omar ⬥ beat Zubair ⬥. Omar ⬥ then called out, "I beat you! By the Rabb of the Kabah!" *(Muhamili in Kanzul Ummal)*. Saleem bin Handhala reports, "We once went to Ubay bin Ka'b ⬥ to listen to Ahadeeth from him. When he had completed, he stood up and we also stood up and walked with him. Omar ⬥ then met him and said, "Don't you think that this walking with people following you is a danger (source of pride) for the one being followed and a source of dishonor for the ones following?" *(Ibn Abi Shaybah, Khatib in Jami, Kanzul Ummal)*. Abul Bakhtari narrates that a man once came to Salman ⬥ and said, "How pleasant was the behavior of people today! I had been traveling and I swear by Allah that every person I stayed with seemed to be the son of my own father. Each one of them treated me exceptionally well and was extremely kind towards me." Salman ⬥ said, "My dear brother's son! That is a sign of Iman being fresh and superb. Don't you see that when an animal is just loaded, it carries the load quickly because it is fresh but when the journey is prolonged, it walks in a spread out motion?" Therefore when Iman is continually refreshed, it is capable of doing much. *(Abu Nu'aym in Hilya)*

Haya bint Abu Haya reports, "It was midday when a man came to my house. 'What is it you want, O servant of Allah?' I asked. He explained, 'My friend and I have been searching for our camel and while he is still out looking, I have come here to take some shade and to have something to drink.' I got up and gave him some yogurt to drink. I then looked at him closely and asked, 'Who are you, O servant of Allah?' When he told me that his name was Abu Bakr, I asked, 'The same Abu Bakr who was the companion of Rasulullah ﷺ and about whom I heard so much?' 'Yes,' he replied. I then started mentioning to him the battles that my tribe had fought with the Banu Khath'am and all the fights we Arabs had been having with each other during the period of ignorance. I then spoke of the love that Allah had created between us because of Islam and asked, 'O servant of Allah! Until when will this status quo of mutual love last?' 'As long as the leaders are upright,' he replied. 'Who are the leaders?' I enquired. He said, 'Do you not see that every tribe has a leader whom they follow and whom they obey? It shall last as long as these people remain upright." *(Musaddad, Ibn Muni, Darmi in Kanzul Ummal)*. Harith bin Mu'awiya narrates that when he came to Omar ⬥, Omar ⬥ asked, "In what condition did you leave the people of Sham?" After he had informed Omar ⬥ about the condition of the people there, Omar ⬥ praised Allah and said, "Are you people perhaps socializing with the disbeliever?" When Harith assured Omar ⬥ that they were not, Omar ⬥ said, "When you start socializing with them, you will start eating and drinking with them and your situation will remain good only when you do not do that." *(Ya'qub bin Sufian, Bayhaqi, Ibn Asakir in Kanzul Ummal)*. Ayadh narrates that Omar ⬥ once instructed Abu Musa Ash'ari ⬥ to present to him all his earnings and expenditure as governor on a single piece of leather. Abu Musa Ash'ari ⬥ had a Christian accounts keeper and when he presented it, Omar ⬥ was impressed and said, "He has an excellent memory. Will you read out a letter that has come from Sham in the Masjid?" "He will be unable to do so," Abu Musa Ash'ari ⬥ said. "Why not?" Omar ⬥ asked, "Is he impure?" "No," Abu Musa Ash'ari ⬥ replied, "he is a Christian," Omar ⬥ then reprimanded Abu Musa Ash'ari ⬥ and hit him on the thigh saying, "Dismiss him!" He recited the verse:

يَا أَيُّهَا الَّذِينَ آمَنُوا لَا تَتَّخِذُوا الْيَهُودَ وَالنَّصَارَى أَوْلِيَاءَ بَعْضُهُمْ أَوْلِيَاءُ بَعْضٍ وَمَن يَتَوَلَّهُم مِّنكُمْ فَإِنَّهُ مِنْهُمْ إِنَّ اللَّهَ لَا يَهْدِي الْقَوْمَ الظَّالِمِينَ (51)

O you who believe! Take not the Jews and the Christians as Auliya (friends, protectors, helpers, etc.), they are but Auliya to one another. And if any amongst you takes them as Auliya, then surely he is one of them. Verily, Allah guides not those people who are the Zalimoon (polytheists and wrongdoers and unjust). (Al-Ma'ida:51) (Ibn Abi Hatim in Tafsir Ibn Kathir)

Practices of Rasulullah ﷺ and the Sahabah with Food and Drink

Abu Hurairah ⬥ narrates, "Rasulullah ﷺ never found fault with food ever. If he liked it, he ate and if he did not, he would leave it without comment." *(Bukhari, Muslim in Al Bidayah wan Nihayah)*. Ali ⬥ reports that the portion Rasulullah ﷺ liked most of a goat was the foreleg. *(Ibn Asakir in Kanzul Ummal)*. Abdullah bin Mas'ood ⬥ says, "Rasulullah ﷺ liked the foreleg of an animal. When the foreleg was once poisoned, everyone suspected that it was the Jews who poisoned it." *(Tirmidhi in Shama'il)*. Jabir ⬥ narrates that when Rasulullah ﷺ came to visit them in their house, they slaughtered a goat in his honor. Rasulullah ﷺ said, "It seems like they knew we like meat." There is a more detailed story attached to this incident. *(Tirmidhi in Shama'il)*. Anas ⬥ says, "Rasulullah ﷺ loved bottle yogurt so when some food was served, I started searching for it in the plate and placing them in front of him because I knew that he loved it." *(Tirmidhi in Shama'il)*. Anas ⬥ also narrates that whenever Rasulullah ﷺ ate food, he licked his 3 fingers with which he ate. *(Tirmidhi in Shama'il)*. Abdullah bin Abbas ⬥ says, "Rasulullah ﷺ was so humble that he ate on the floor, tied the feet of goats when they were to be milked and even accepted the invitation of slaves to eat plain barley bread." *(Ibn Najjar in Kanzul Ummal)*. Yahya bin Abu Kathir reports that a plate of Tharid came to Rasulullah ﷺ every day from Sa'd bin Ubadah ⬥. It went with him to the house of whichever wife he was with. *(Ibn Asakir in Kanzul Ummal)*. Anas ⬥ reports that when some goat's milk was milked for Rasulullah ﷺ, he drank it and then gargled his mouth saying, "It has some stickiness which needs to be rinsed out to preserve oral hygiene." *(Ibn Jareer in Kanzul Ummal)*. Abu Bakr reports that Rasulullah ﷺ once stopped over at a certain place, a woman sent her son with a goat to Rasulullah ﷺ. Rasulullah ﷺ milked the goat and told the boy to take it to his mother. After she had drunk to her fill, the boy brought another goat. After milking it, Rasulullah ﷺ gave the milk to Abu Bakr ﷺ. When the boy brought a third goat, Rasulullah ﷺ milked it and only this time did he drink. *(Abu Ya'la in Kanzul Ummal)*. Rasulullah ﷺ used to keep his right hand free for acts such as eating, drinking and making wudhu. His left hand he would keep free for acts such as Istinja, cleaning his nose and other such acts. *(Sa'eed bin Mansoor in Kanzul Ummal)*. Ja'far bin Abdullah says, "Hakam ﷺ once saw me eating from various parts of the plate, he said, 'Dear boy! Do not eat like that as Saitan eats. When Rasulullah ﷺ ate, his fingers would not stray from his hands, they stayed in front of him." *(Abu Nu'aym in Kanzul Ummal, Isabah)*

Rasulullah ﷺ Teaches the Sahabah the Etiquette of Eating and to Recite Bismillah at the Beginning

Omar bin Abu Salama ﷺ reports, "I was once eating with Rasulullah ﷺ when I started taking meat from all over the plate. Rasulullah ﷺ said to me, 'Eat from that which is in front of you." *(Ibn Najjar in Kanzul Ummal)*. Ummaya bin Makhshi ﷺ reports that Rasulullah ﷺ once saw a man eating without first reciting Bismillah. When there was only a single morsel left, he lifted it to his mouth and before eating it, he recited: بِسْمِ اللهِ أَوَّلَهُ وَآخِرَهُ Rasulullah ﷺ then laughed and said, "By Allah! Saitan continued eating with you until you took Allah's name. He then vomited out everything that was in his belly." Another narration states that Rasulullah ﷺ said, "... until when you took Allah's name, he forcefully vomited out everything in his belly." *(Ahmad, Abu Dawud, Nasa'ee, Ibn Qani, Tabrani, Hakim, Kanzul Ummal)*. Hudhaifa ﷺ narrates that they were once with Rasulullah ﷺ when a platter of food was brought and placed before them. When Rasulullah ﷺ held back his hand, the Sahabah did the same because they never ate until Rasulullah ﷺ did. A Bedouin then came appearing as if he was being pushed along. As he was about to grab at the platter to eat from the food, Rasulullah ﷺ caught hold of his hand. Just then, a little girl came also appearing as if she was being pushed along. When she also attempted to get her hand into the food, Rasulullah ﷺ grabbed her hand as well. Rasulullah ﷺ then said, "Verily people's food becomes lawful for Saitan when they do not take Allah's name. When Saitan saw that we were holding our hands back, he brought the girl so that the food could become lawful for him when she eats without saying Bismillah. I however, grabbed her hand. He had also brought the Bedouin to make the food lawful for himself, but I had grabbed his hand as well. I swear by the Being besides Whom there is none worthy of worship! His hand is now in my hands together with the hands of the 2 of them." *(Nasa'ee in Kanzul Ummal)*. Aisha ﷺ narrates *(Ibn Najjar in Kanzul Ummal)* that Rasulullah ﷺ was eating with 6 others when a Bedouin came and ate all the food in 2 morsels. Rasulullah ﷺ remarked, "Had he recited Bismillah, the food would have sufficed for them all. When you eat, you should take the name of Allah and if he forgets, he should recite: بِسْمِ اللهِ أَوَّلَهُ وَآخِرَهُ

Rasulullah ﷺ is Entertained by the Sahabah

Abdullah bin Busr ﷺ relates, "Nabi ﷺ once stopped over by my father who served him a meal of Sawee (type of porridge from barley) and Hais (sweet prepared with dates, butter and flour). After Rasulullah ﷺ had eaten, my father brought something to drink. After drinking, Rasulullah ﷺ passed the cup on to the person on his right. When eating dates, Rasulullah ﷺ

threw the stones like this." Abdullah bin Busr ﷺ then pointed with his finger towards his back to indicate that Rasulullah ﷺ threw the stones behind him. Narrating further, he says that when Rasulullah ﷺ got on his mule, his father held the reins and said, "Do make Du'a for us, O Rasulullah ﷺ!" Rasulullah ﷺ then made the following Du'a: اللَّهُمَّ بَارِكْ لَهُمْ فِيمَا رَزَقْتَهُمْ وَاغْفِرْ لَهُمْ وَارْحَمْهُمْ *"O Allah! Bless them in the sustenance You give them, forgive them and have mercy on them." (Ibn Abi Shaybah, Abu Nu'aym)*

In another narration, Abdullah bin Busr ﷺ says, "When my father once asked my mother to prepare some food for Rasulullah ﷺ, she prepared some Tharid. My father then proceeded to invite Rasulullah ﷺ for the meal and when he arrived, Rasulullah ﷺ placed his hand on the top of the dish saying to the Sahabah, 'Dish out taking the name of Allah.' They then dished out from the sides. After everyone had eaten, Rasulullah ﷺ made the following Du'a: اللَّهُمَّ اغْفِرْ لَهُمْ وَارْحَمْهُمْ وَبَارِكْ لَهُمْ فِيمَا رَزَقْتَهُمْ *"O Allah! Forgive them, have mercy on them and bless them in the sustenance You give them." (Hakim in Kanzul Ummal)*

The Practices of Ali ﷺ and Omar ﷺ with Food and Drink

Ibn A'bad reports that Ali ﷺ once asked, "O Ibn A'bad! Do you know what is the right of food?" "What is the right of food?" Ibn A'bad asked. Ali ﷺ replied, "That you recite:
بِسْمِ اللهِ اللَّهُمَّ بَارِكْ لَنَا فِيمَا رَزَقْتَنَا
'I begin with the name of Allah. O Allah! Bless us in the sustenance You give us'"
Thereafter, Ali ﷺ asked, "And do you know how to express gratitude after you have finished?" "How do you express gratitude?" Ibn A'bad asked. Ali replied, "By saying:
الْحَمْدُ لِلهِ الَّذِي أَطْعَمَنَا وَسَقَانَا
'All praise is for Allah Who has given us food and drink." (Ibn Abi Shaybah, Ibn Abi Dunya in D'ua, Abu Nu'aym in Hilya, Bayhaqi in Kanzul Ummal)

Omar ﷺ once said, "Beware of excessive eating and drinking because it harms the body, is the cause of many diseases and leads to lethargy in salah. Rather be moderate in your eating and drinking because it is healthier for the body and further from extravagance. Allah detests the obese scholar who makes eating a priority and a person shall never be destroyed until he gives precedence to his desires over Islam." *(Abu Nu'aym in Kanzul Ummal)*. Abu Mah'dhura ﷺ reports that he was once sitting with Omar ﷺ when Safwan bin Umayyah ﷺ brought a platter of food and placed it in front of Omar ﷺ. Omar ﷺ summoned some poor people and slaves in the vicinity and they all shared the food with him. Thereafter, Omar ﷺ remarked, "May Allah curse the people who are reluctant to their slaves eating with them." To this, Safwan ﷺ said, "We are not reluctant to them eating with us. We eat by ourselves only because we do not find sufficient good food to feed both us and them." *(Ibn Asakir in Kanzul Ummal)*

The Practices of Abdullah bin Omar ﷺ and Abdullah bin Abbas ﷺ with Food and Drink

Malik bin Anas reports that when Abdullah bin Omar ﷺ stopped over in Juhfa, Ibn Amir bin Kuraiz instructed his baker to take food to Abdullah bin Omar ﷺ. When he brought one plate of food, Abdullah bin Omar ﷺ told him to put it down. When the baker returned with an other plate of food and was going to take the first plate away, Abdullah bin Omar ﷺ asked, "What are you doing?" "I am taking the plate away," the baker replied. "No," said Abdullah bin Omar ﷺ, "just pour the food into this other food." Later every time a different dish was served, Abdullah bin Omar ﷺ made the man pour it into the other food. When the baker returned to Ibn Amir, he remarked, "That man must be an uncultured Bedouin!" Ibn Amir corrected the baker saying, "That man is your leader. He is Ibn Omar ." *(Abu Nu'aym in Hilya).* Ja'far narrates that Abdullah bin Abbas always ate the seeds of the pomegranate, someone asked, "O Ibn Abbas! Why do you do that?" He explained, "I have heard that every pomegranate on earth grows from a seed from amongst the seeds from Jannah. This seed is perhaps the one." *(Abu Nu'aym in Hilya)*

The Practices of Salman , Abu Hurairah and Ali with Food and Drink

Salim says, "I was with Zaid bin Sowhan when Salman Farsi passed by us after purchasing a Wasaq of grain. 'O Abu Abdullah!' Zaid called out, 'You are buying so much when you are the companion of Rasulullah ?' Salman replied, 'The soul is at ease when it has secured its sustenance. It can then free itself for Ibada and Waswas (the devil that whispers evil into the heart) loses hope in adversely influencing it.'" *(Abu Nu'aym in Hilya).* Abu Uthman Nahdi narrates that Salman Farsi said, "I love to eat from the efforts of my own hands. *(Abu Nu'aym in Hilya).* Abu Hurairah said, "I had 15 dates so I broke my fast with 5, ate Sehri with 5 and kept the other 5 to break my fast with." *(Abu Nu'aym in Hilya).* Muslim who was the freed slave of Ali bin Abi Talib says, "When Ali once asked for a drink, I brought him a cup of water and blew into it. He refused to drink it and returned it to me saying, 'You drink it." *(Ibn Sa'd)*

The Practices of Rasulullah and the Sahabah Regard to Clothing

Abdur Rahman bin Abu Layla says that he was once with Omar when he said, "I saw Rasulullah wearing a narrow-sleeved cloak made in Sham." *(Ibn Sa'd in Kanzul Ummal).* Jundub bin Makith says, "Rasulullah wore s best clothing whenever he received a delegation and would instruct the senior Sahabah to do the same. On the day a delegation arrived from Kinda tribe, I saw Rasulullah wearing clothing made in Yemen and both Abu Bakr and Omar were wearing the same." *(Ibn Sa'd).* Salamah bin Akwa says that Uthman 's loincloth always reached halfway up his calves and he would say, "Such was the garment of my beloved Nabi ." *(Ibn Abi Shaybah, Tirmidhi in Shama'il, Kanzul Ummal).* Ash'ath bin Sulaim reports from his aunt that her uncle said, "I was walking in Madinah one day when someone behind me said, 'Lift up your loincloth because it keeps it cleaner and makes it last longer.' When I turned around, I saw that it was Rasulullah . 'O Rasulullah !' I said, 'It is but a simple black and white striped shawl.' Rasulullah replied, 'Don't you have an example in me?' When I looked at him, I saw that Rasulullah 's garment reached halfway up his calves." *(Tirmidhi in Shama'il)*

The Sahabah Describe the Attire of Rasulullah

Abu Burdah narrates that Aisha once took out and showed them a patched shawl and a loincloth made of coarse cloth. She said, "It was in these 2 garments that the soul of Rasulullah was taken away." *(Tirmidhi in Shama'il).* Ummu Salamah says, "The garment Rasulullah loved most was his Qamees (long, loose upper garment)." *(Tirmidhi in Shama'il).* Asma bint Yazid reports that the sleeve of Rasulullah 's Qamees reached his wrists. Jabir narrates that Rasulullah was wearing a black turban when he entered Makkah the day he conquered. Amr bin Huraith reports that Rasulullah delivered a sermon wearing a black turban. Abdullah bin Abbas says that during his illness Rasulullah delivered a sermon while wearing an oily bandage. Nafi reports from Abdullah bin

Omar that Rasulullah tied his turban, he would let the tails hang between shoulders. Abdullah bin Omar tied his turban in the same way and a narrator Abdullah said that he saw Qasim bin Muhammad and Salim do the same. *(Tirmidhi in Shama'il)*

Rasulullah 's Bedding

When Aisha was once asked about Rasulullah 's bedding, she replied, "It was made of leather and stuffed with the bark of a date palm." *(Bukhari, Muslim, Ibn Sa'd).* Aisha relates, "A lady from the Ansar once visited me and saw that Rasulullah 's bedding comprised of cloak that was double-folded. She then left and later sent bedding stuffed with wool. When Rasulullah came to me, he asked, 'What is this, O Aisha?' I then informed him about the lady from the Ansar who had seen his bedding and then sent this. Rasulullah told me to return it. Because I liked to have it in my room, I did not return it until Rasulullah repeated the instruction 3 times. He finally said, 'Return it, O Aisha. I swear by Allah that if I willed, Allah would have made mountains of gold and silver travel with me wherever I went." *(Hasan bin Arafa, Ibn Sa'd).* Muhammad narrates that he once asked Aisha , "What was Rasulullah 's bedding like in your home?" She replied, "It was made of leather and stuffed with the bark of a date palm." When he then posed the same question to Hafsa , she replied, "Rasulullah used to sleep on a coarse sheet that we double-folded. One night I thought that it would be more comfortable if I 4-folded it so I did that. The next morning, Rasulullah asked, 'What did you spread down for me last night?' 'It was the same bedding,' I explained, 'all that I did was to 4-fold it so that it would be more comfortable for you.' Rasulullah said, 'Leave it as it was as its softness prevented me from performing salah last night." *(Tirmidhi in Shama'il, Al Bidayah wan Nihayah, Ibn Sa'd)*

What Rasulullah Recited When Wearing New Clothing

Omar reports that he saw Rasulullah send for some new clothing. When it reached his collar-bone as he was putting it on, he recited: اَلْحَمْدُ لِلَّهِ الَّذِي كَسَانِي مَاأُوَارِي بِهِ عَوْرَتِيْ وَأَتَجَمَّلُ بِهِ فِيْ حَيَاتِيْ
"All praise is for Allah Who has given me clothing to conceal my private areas and with which I can look beautiful in this life." Rasulullah said, "I swear by the Being Who controls my life! When a Muslim wears new clothing, recites these words and then purely for Allah's pleasure gives the old clothes that he is removing to a poor person, he will remain in the care, the security and the protection of Allah as long as there remains even a single thread of the garment left on the poor person. This applies whether he is alive or dead." *(Ibn Mubarak, Tabrani, Hakim, Bayhaqi in Kanzul Ummal)*

Rasulullah Praises the Trousers

Ali reports that he was sitting with Rasulullah near the graveyard of Baqi on a rainy day when a woman passed by on her donkey carrying a heavy load. As she passed through a slope in the ground, she fell off the donkey. Rasulullah turned his face away so as not to see her body as it became exposed because of the fall. When someone informed Rasulullah that the lady was wearing trousers because of which her body did not become exposed, Rasulullah said, "O Allah! Forgive all the women of my Ummah who wear trousers." Addressing the Sahabah, Rasulullah then said, "O people! Always wear trousers because it is amongst the most concealing of clothing. Ensure that you protect your women with it whenever you go out." *(Bazzar, Uqayli, Ibn Adi in Kanzul Ummal, Ibn Jowzi in Mowdu'at)*

The Incident of Rasulullah ﷺ with Dihya and Usama ؓ

Dihya bin Khalifa Kalbi ؓ reports that Rasulullah ﷺ once sent him as envoy to Heraclius, the Byzantine Emperor. Upon his return, Rasulullah ﷺ gave Dihya ؓ a delicate white Egyptian cloth saying, "Use a part of it to make a Qamis for you and give your wife the other portion to use as a scarf." As Dihya ؓ was leaving, Rasulullah ﷺ called him back saying, "Tell her to wear something underneath the scarf so that it is not revealing." (Ibn Mandah, Ibn Asakir in Kanzul Ummal). Usama bin Zaid ؓ relates, "Rasulullah ﷺ gave me some of the thick but delicate white Egyptian cloth that he had given Dihya ؓ. Later I gave it to my wife to make something out of it to wear. Rasulullah ﷺ later asked me, 'What is the matter? Why are you not wearing the white Egyptian cloth?' When I informed Rasulullah ﷺ that I had given it to my wife to wear,' he said, 'Tell her to wear something underneath because I fear that it would reveal the shape of her bones." (Ibn Abi Shaybah, Ibn Sa'd, Ahmad, Ruyani, Barodi, Tabrani, Bayhaqi, Sa'eed bin Mansur in Kanzul Ummal)

The Incident of Aisha ؓ and her Father When she Wore Clothing that Appealed to Her

Aisha ؓ reports that when she once wore some clothing, she kept looking down at it as she walked about in the room, turning about as she did so. Her father Abu Bakr ؓ then entered and said to her, "Don't you know that Allah is presently not looking at you with affection." (Ibn Mubarak, Abu Nu'aym in Hilya). In another narration, Aisha ؓ says, "I once wore a new upper garment of mine and was very taken aback by it as I looked at it. Abu Bakr ؓ said to me, 'What are you looking at? Allah is not looking at you with affection.' 'Why not?' I asked. He replied, 'Don't you know that when self-praise enters a servant because of worldly beauty, Allah detests the person until the beauty is lost and the self-praise with it.' I then took off the garment and gave it away as Sadaqa. Abu Bakr ؓ then said, 'That shall perhaps atone for you.'" (Abu Nu'aym in Hilya, Kanzul Ummal)

The Practices of Omar ؓ and Anas ؓ with Regard to Clothing

Abdul Aziz bin Abu Jamila Ansari reports that the sleeves of Omar ؓ's Qamis never extended past his wrists. (Ibn Sa'd). Badil bin Maysara reports that Omar ؓ went for the Jumu'ah salah wearing a cloak made in Sumbulan. Apologizing to the people for coming late, he said, "It was this cloak that delayed me." He pulled his sleeves forward and as he let go of them, they returned to the ends of his fingers. (Ibn Sa'd). Hisham bin Khalid reports that he saw Omar ؓ tie his loincloth above his navel. Amir bin Ubaidah Bahili narrates that he asked Anas ؓ about Khazz, a material in which there is a small element of silk, Anas ؓ replied, "I wish that Allah had never created it. Apart from Omar ؓ and his son, all the Sahabah wore it." Anas ؓ disliked it because it was a fabric worn by rich non-Muslims. (Muntakhab Kanzul Ummal). Masruq narrates that Omar ؓ came out to them wearing cotton clothing. The people stared at him, he recited a couplet:

'The beauty of everything you see will never last. Allah will last when all wealth and children will be destroyed" He remarked, "By Allah! Compared to the Hereafter, this world is just a leap of a rabbit." (Hanad, Ibn Abi Dunya in Kanzul Ummal)

The Practices of Uthman ؓ with Regard to Clothing

Abu Abdullah who was the freed slave of Shaddad bin Had says, "It was on a Friday that I once saw Uthman bin Affan ؓ standing on the pulpit wearing a shawl made in Kufa and a coarse loincloth made in Aden that was worth a mere 4 or 5 Dirhams. He was a thin, handsome man with a long beard." (Hakim, Tabrani, Haythami). Musa bin Talha says, "Uthman ؓ used to lean on a staff as he came to the Masjid on Fridays. He was one of the most handsome men wearing his cream-colored loincloth and shawl as he came to the pulpit and sat on it." (Tabrani, Haythami). Sulaim Abu Amir says, "I saw Uthman bin Affan ؓ wearing a Yemeni shawl worth 100 Dirhams." (Ibn Sa'd). Muhammad bin Rabe'ah bin Harith says, "The Sahabah used to spend generously on such clothing for their wives that was both beautiful as well as concealing. I once saw Uthman ؓ wearing a shawl edged with silk that was worth 200 Dirhams. He said, 'This belongs to my wife Na'ila. I had given it to her to wear and am wearing it now only to make her happy." (Ibn Sa'd)

The Practices of Ali ؓ with Regard to Clothing

Zaid bin Wahab narrates that a delegation from Basrah once came to see Ali ؓ. Amongst them was a man belonging to the Khawarij whose name was Ja'd bin Na'ja. When he started criticizing Ali ؓ's clothing, Ali ؓ said, "What problem have you got with my clothing when it is far away from pride and a most appropriate example for the people to follow." (Abu Nu'aym in Hilya). Amr bin Qais reports that when someone asked Ali ؓ why he patched his Qamis, he replied, "The heart humbles with it and the Mu'min is able to follow the example." (Hanad in Muntakhab Kanzul Ummal, Ibn Sa'd). Ata Abu Muhammad says, "I once saw Ali ؓ wearing an unwashed Qamis made of extremely coarse cloth." (Ibn Abi Shaybah, Hanad). Abdullah bin Abu Hudhail reports, "I once saw on Ali bin Abi Talib ؓ a Qamis made in Ray which was such that when he stretched out his arms, the sleeves reached the ends of his fingers and when he retracted them, they reached close to halfway up his forearms." (Hanad, Ibn Asakir in Muntakhab Kanzul Ummal). Whenever Ali ؓ wore a Qamis, he would pull the sleeve until it reached his fingers. He would then cut off what was extra extending further than the fingers saying, "The sleeves should never extend further than the hands." (Ibn Uyaynah in Jami, Asaki in Mawa'idh, Sa'eed bin Mansur, Bayhaqi, Ibn Asakir in Kanzul Ummal). Abu Sa'eed Azdi who was one of the Imams of the Azd tribe reports that he once saw Ali ؓ come to the marketplace and say, "Who has a good Qamis for 3 Dirhams?" When one of the traders said that he had one, Ali ؓ went to him and liked the Qamis very much. "This must be worth more than 3 Dirhams!" Ali ؓ remarked thinking that the man was reducing the price because Ali ؓ was the Amirul Mu'minin. "Not at all," the man replied, "that is really the price." Abu Sa'eed says that he then saw Ali ؓ untie a knot in his clothing containing some Dirhams and giving it to the trader. Ali ؓ then wore the Qamis, which happened extend past the ends of his fingers. By his instruction, the excess that extended past his fingers was then cut off. (Abu Nu'aym in Hilya). A freed slave of Abu Udhain reports that he once saw Ali ؓ come out of his house and approach cloth merchant saying, "Do you have a Qamis made in Sumbulan?" The man took out one and when Ali ؓ wore it, it reached halfway down his calves. Looking down to his right and left, Ali ؓ remarked, "I have not seen a better fit. How much is this?" "4 Dirhams, O Amirul Mu'minin," the man replied. Ali ؓ then untied the money from his loincloth, handed it over to the man and then left. (Ahmad in Zuhd, Al Bidayah wan Nihayah)

The Practices of Abdur Rahman bin Auf ؓ, Abdullah bin Omar ؓ and Abdullah bin Abbas ؓ with Regard to Clothing

Sa'd bin Ibrahim says, "I saw Abdur Rahman bin Auf ؓ

wearing a shawl or a suit of clothing worth 400 or 500 Dirhams." (Ibn Sa'd). Qur'ah relates that when he saw Abdullah bin Omar wearing coarse and stiff clothing, he approached him saying, "O Abu Abdur Rahman! I have brought you soft clothing made in Khurasan and it would give me great pleasure to see you wearing them because your clothing is extremely coarse and stiff." "Show it to me so that I may see it for myself," Abdullah bin Omar said. Feeling it with his hand, Abdullah bin Omar asked, "Is this silk?" "No, it is cotton," Qur'ah assured him. Abdullah bin Omar however said, "I fear wearing this because I fear becoming a boastful snob. Verily Allah detests the boastful snob." (Abu Nu'aym in Hilya). Abdullah bin Hubaish relates that he saw Abdullah bin Omar wearing 2 cloths made by the Ma'afir, a tribe in Yemen which reached halfway down his calves. (Abu Nu'aym in Hilya, Ibn Sa'd). Waqdan reports that he once heard a person asking Abdullah bin Omar, "What clothing should I wear?" Abdullah bin Omar replied, "Clothing that will neither cause foolish people to ridicule you nor cause intelligent people to criticize you for being extravagant." "What type of clothing is that?" the man asked. "What costs between 5 and 10 Dirhams," came the reply. (Abu Nu'aym in Hilya). Abu Is'haq reports that he saw Abdullah bin Omar wear his loincloth halfway down his calves. In another narration, he mentions that he saw several Sahabah, such as Usama bin Zaid, Zaid bin Arqam, Bara bin Azib and Abdullah bin Omar all wearing their loincloths halfway down their calves. (Abu Nu'aym in Hilya). Uthman bin Abu Sulaiman reports that Abdullah bin Abbas once purchased and wore a garment worth 1,000 Dirhams.

The Practices of Aisha and Asma with Regard to Clothing

Kathir bin Ubaid says that once he went to Ummul Mu'mineen Aisha, she told him to wait until she completed stitching her old garment. As he waited, he remarked, "O Ummul Mu'mineen! If I went out and informed the people about this, they would regard it as miserliness from your side thinking that you are too miserly to buy new clothes." Aisha said, "Do as you see fit. The person who does not wear old clothes does not deserve new clothes and may not have them in the Hereafter." (Bukhari in Adab). Abu Sa'eed reports that when someone entered Aisha's room as she was stitching her old garment, he remarked, "O Ummul Mu'mineen! Has Allah not granted an abundance of wealth to buy new clothing rather than patch old clothing?" Aisha replied, "Leave us alone! The person who does not wear old clothes does not deserve new clothes." (Ibn Sa'd). When Mundhir bin Zubair arrived from Iraq, his mother Asma bint Abu Bakr had already become blind. He sent for her delicate and beautiful garments made in Marw and Quw and when she felt it, she exclaimed, "Alas! Send this clothing back to him." Mundhir felt hurt and said, "Dear mother! The garments are not transparent." She replied, "Even though they are not transparent, they are revealing." When he bought for her common garments made in Marw and Quw, she accepted saying, "These types of garments you should give me to wear." (Ibn Sa'd)

The Practice of Omar with Clothing

Anas reports that a woman once came to Omar saying, "O Amirul Mu'minin! My upper garment is all tattered." "Have I not given you anything to wear?" Omar asked. "You have given me," she replied, "but it is torned." Omar immediately sent for a beautiful upper garment and some thread to be given to her. He then said to her, "Wear that old clothing when you are making bread and cooking and then wear this new garment once you have finished. Those who do not wear old clothing do not deserve new clothes." (Bayhaqi in Kanzul Ummal). Kharasha bin Hurr reports that he was once looking at Omar as a youngster passed by, wearing his loincloth below his ankles and dragging it along as he walked. Omar called for him and asked, "Are you menstruating?" "What! O Amirul Mu'minin!" asked the youngster in surprise "Do men also menstruate?" Omar replied, "Then what is the matter with you hanging your garment below your ankles?" Omar then sent for a knife, gathered the end of the loincloth and cut off whatever hung beneath the ankles." Kharasha says, "It is as if I can still see the threads hanging over his heels." (Sufian bin Uyayna in Jami, Kanzul Ummal). Abu Uthman Nahdi reports that they were in Azerbaijan under the command of Utba bin Farqad when a letter from Omar arrived. The letter read: "Ensure that you wear your loincloths, shawls and shoes and throwaway your socks and trousers. Make sure that you adopt the attire of your forefather Isma'el and stay away from lives of luxury and the attire of the non-Arabs. Remain in the sun because it is the bath of the Arab. Dress simply like Ma'd bin Adnan, live tough lives, wear old clothes, mount your animals without stirrups, do target practice and jump directly onto your horses from the ground. Remember that Rasulullah forbade men from wearing silk unless it be only this much. Rasulullah then indicated with his middle finger." (Abu Dhar Harawi in Jami, Bayhaqi in Kanzul Ummal)

The Homes of Rasulullah 's Wives

Mu'adh bin Muhammad Ansari says that they were sitting in a gathering between the pulpit and the grave of Rasulullah. In the gathering was Imran bin Abu Anas and Ata Khurasani was saying, "I saw that the rooms of Rasulullah 's wives were made from the trunks of palm trees and their doors were simply veils made from black animal hairs. I was also present when the letter of the king Walid bin Abdil Malik was read out, giving instructions for the rooms of Rasulullah 's wives to be avoided within the Masjid. I have never seen more people weeping than I did that day. On that day, I heard Sa'eed bin Musayib say, 'By Allah! I wish that they would leave the rooms as they are so that future generations of Madinah's people and people coming from other lands could see with how little Rasulullah sufficed in his life. This would cause people to abstain from amassing wealth and from boasting about worldly commodities." Mu'adh relates that Ata Khurasani had completed narration, Imran bin Abu Anas said, "There were 4 rooms made from unbaked bricks with courtyards of palm trunks while the other 5 were made of plastered palm trunks with no courtyards at all. Their doors were simple veils made from black animal hair. I measured the veils, I found that they were 3 arm's lengths in height and more than an arm's length in width. Regarding weeping you mentioned, I can recall myself sitting in a gathering with a group of the Sahabah's children. Amongst them was Abu Salama bin Abdur Rahman, Abu Umama bin Sahl bin Hunaif and Kharija bin Zaid. They wept so much that their beards were wet. Abu Umama said, 'If they had preserved the rooms without demolishing them so that by seeing them people would reduce their building endeavors and see what Allah preferred for His Nabi even though He possessed the keys to the treasures of the world." (Ibn Sa'd).

The chapter Concerning the Belief of Sahabah on Unseen

This chapter highlights how the Sahabah believed in the unseen and how for the news Nabi ﷺ gave them, they forsook temporary pleasures, human evidence, transitory opinions and worldly experiences. It was as if they were actually witnessing the unseen and rejecting what they witnessed.

The Magnificence of Iman

Rasulullah ﷺ gives the glad tidings of Jannah for the person who testifies with conviction that there is none worthy of worship but Allah. Abu Hurairah ؓ narrates, "We were a group of Sahabah including Abu Bakr ؓ and Omar ؓ sitting around Rasulullah ﷺ, when he got up to leave. Because Rasulullah ﷺ delayed in returning to us, we feared that he may have come to some harm in our absence. This alarmed us and we quickly got up. I was the first to be alarmed and in my search for Rasulullah ﷺ, I reached an orchard belonging to the Banu Najjar tribe of the Ansar. I circled the orchard looking for a gate, but could not find any. I then came across a stream running into the orchard from a well outside. I therefore squeezed through and found Rasulullah ﷺ there. 'Abu Hurairah?' Rasulullah ﷺ asked. 'Yes, O Rasulullah ﷺ,' I replied. 'What is the matter?' he asked. I explained, 'You were with us when you left. When you delayed in returning to us, we feared that you may have come to some harm in our absence. This alarmed us and I was the first to be alarmed. When I reached this orchard, I squeezed through as a fox would do and entered. The others are all behind me.' Handing me his shoes, Rasulullah ﷺ said, 'O Abu Hurairah! Take these shoes of mine and give the glad tidings of Jannah to every person you meet outside this orchard who testifies with conviction of the heart that there is none worthy of worship but Allah.' The first person I met was Omar ؓ. 'What are these shoes, O Abu Hurairah?' he asked. These are Rasulullah ﷺ's shoes. He has sent me to give the glad tidings of Jannah to every person I meet who testifies with conviction of the heart that there is none worthy of worship but Allah.' Omar ؓ struck me so hard on the chest that I fell down on my buttocks. He instructed me to return and I returned to Rasulullah ﷺ seeking help in tears. Omar ؓ was almost upon me as he came in my footsteps. 'What has happened to you, O Abu Hurairah?' Rasulullah ﷺ asked. I related the incident to him saying, 'I met Omar ؓ and when I told him the message you had sent me with, he struck me so hard on the chest that I fell down on my buttocks. He told me to return.' 'O Omar!' Rasulullah ﷺ said, 'What made you do that?' Omar ؓ said, 'May my parents be sacrificed for you, O Rasulullah ﷺ! Did you send Abu Hurairah ؓ with your shoes to give the glad tidings of Jannah to every person he meets who testifies with conviction of the heart that there is none worthy of worship but Allah?' 'I certainly did,' Rasulullah ﷺ replied. 'Do not do that,' Omar ؓ pleaded, 'because I fear that people would pin all their hopes in this and stop doing good deeds. Rather leave them to continue doing good deeds.' Rasulullah ﷺ said, 'Leave them.'" *(Muslim in Jam'ul Fawa'id).*

Rasulullah ﷺ gives the Glad Tidings of Jannah for the Person who dies Without Committing Shirk

Abu Dhar ؓ narrates, "When I came outdoors one night, I happened to see Rasulullah ﷺ walking all alone. Thinking to myself that perhaps Rasulullah ﷺ did not like anyone to be walking with him, I started walking where the moonlight was not shining so that he may not notice me. Rasulullah ﷺ however turned around and when he saw me, he asked, 'Who is there?' I replied by saying, 'It is Abu Dhar'. May Allah sacrifice me for you!' 'Come here, O Abu Dhar,' Rasulullah ﷺ called out. After walking with him for a while, Rasulullah ﷺ said, 'Verily those with plenty of wealth will have the least rewards on the Day of Judgment except for the person whom Allah gives wealth in abundance and he distributes it to his right, his left, in front of him and behind him, using it all in good causes.' I then walked on a while longer with Rasulullah ﷺ when he said, 'Sit down here.' It was an open plain surrounded by stones where he made me sit. He then said to me, 'Remain here until I return.' Rasulullah ﷺ then walked away into the rocky plain until he disappeared from my view. He was away for a long time until I eventually heard him say as he returned, 'Even though he commits adultery or steals?' When he returned, I could not wait to ask, 'May Allah sacrifice me for you, O Nabi of Allah ﷺ! With whom were you talking amongst the rocks? I heard no one reply to you.' Rasulullah ﷺ replied, 'That was Jibra'el عليه السلام who came to me when I was amongst the rocks. He said, 'Give your Ummah the good news that whoever of them dies without committing Shirk shall enter Jannah.' 'O Jibra'el!' I asked, 'Even though he commits adultery or steals?' 'Yes,' he replied. 'Even though he commits adultery or steals, O Rasulullah ﷺ?' I echoed. 'Yes,' Rasulullah ﷺ replied. I repeated, 'Even though he commits adultery or steals?' 'Certainly,' Rasulullah ﷺ replied, 'even though he drinks wine." *(Bukhari, Muslim in Jam'ul Fawa'id).* After Abu Dhar ؓ repeated the question for the 4th time, Rasulullah ﷺ said, "Even though Abu Dhar's nose is rubbed in dust i.e. this shall be the case even though Abu Dhar may not agree." *(Tirmidhi)*

The Incident of the Bedouin with Great Understanding

Anas ؓ reports that an old Bedouin called Alqama bin Ulatha ؓ once came to Rasulullah ﷺ and said, "O Rasulullah ﷺ! I am an old man who is unable to learn the Qur'an. However, I do testify that there is none worthy of worship but Allah and I testify that Muhammad ﷺ is the servant and Rasul of Allah. In this I have firm conviction." When the old man had left, Rasulullah ﷺ remarked, "That man has great understanding." It has also been reported that Rasulullah ﷺ said, "That companion of yours has great understanding." *(Ibn Asakir in Kanzul Ummal, Kara'iti in Makarimul Akhlaq, Dar Qutni in Afrad, Isabah).*

The Narration of Uthman ؓ Stating that Jahannam is Forbidden to the one Who Recites the Shahadah

Uthman ؓ narrates that he heard Rasulullah ﷺ say, "I know a statement which if a person says sincerely from his heart, he will become forbidden to the fire of Jahannam." To this, Omar ؓ said, "Should I not tell you what it is? It is the statement of sincerity upon which Allah has made Muhammad ﷺ and his Sahabah steadfast. It is the statement of Taqwa that the Nabi of Allah ﷺ had encouraged his uncle Abu Talib to recite at the time of his death. It is to testify that there is none worthy of worship but Allah." *(Ahmad in Majma'uz Zawa'id, Abu Ya'la, Ibn Khuzaima, Ibn Hibban, Bayhaqi in Kanzul Ummal)*

Rasulullah ﷺ gives the Glad Tidings of Forgiveness to the Sahabah who Recited the Shahada with him in a Particular Gathering

Ya'la bin Shaddad reports that Ubadah bin Samit ؓ was also present and confirming Abu Sbaddad ؓ when he said, "We were with Rasulullah ﷺ when he asked, 'Is there any stranger amongst you?' Rasulullah ﷺ was referring to the presence of any Jews or Christians. When we assured Rasulullah ﷺ that there was none, he had the door closed and said, 'Raise your hands and say: *La*

Ilaha IllAllah'. We raised our hands with Rasulullah ﷺ, after which Rasulullah ﷺ put his hands down saying, "All praise is for Allah. O Allah! You sent me with this Kalima, instructed me with believing in it and promised me Jannah. Verily, You never break Your promises." *(Ahmad, Tabrani, Bazzar, Haythami)*

Rasulullah ﷺ gives Glad Tidings to the Sahabah in Kudaid

Rufa'ah Juhani ؓ reports that they were once returning with Rasulullah ﷺ to Madinah when we arrived in Kudaid. When some people started seeking permission from Rasulullah ﷺ to return to their families, Rasulullah ﷺ granted permission. Rasulullah ﷺ then stood up and after duly praising Allah, he said, "What is the matter with some men who feel that the side of the tree near Rasulullah ﷺ is more repulsive to them than the other side?" When Rasulullah ﷺ said this, there was not a person who was not in tears. Someone then remarked, "Whoever seeks leave after this must be a fool!" Rasulullah ﷺ then praised Allah, said many good things and then added, "I testify before Allah that when a person testifies with sincerity of heart that there is none worthy of worship but Allah, that I am the Rasul of Allah ﷺ and he then proceeds to walk on the right, he will certainly walk the path to Jannah as soon as he dies. My Rabb has promised me that He will admit 70,000 members of my Ummah into Jannah without reckoning or punishment. However, I strongly believe that even before they enter, you people as well your righteous forefathers, spouses and progeny will have already occupied your abodes in Jannah." *(Ahmad, Ibn Majah, Haythami)*. Abu Bakr ؓ who said, "Whoever seeks leave after this must be a fool!" *(Darmi, Ibn Khuzaima, Ibn Hibban, Tabrani in Kanzul Ummal)*

The Shahada Atones for a False Oath

Anas ؓ narrates that when Rasulullah ﷺ charged a particular person for doing something, the man denied it saying, "No. I swear by the Being besides Whom there is none worthy of worship that I did not do it." Rasulullah ﷺ was however certain that the man had done it, so after repeating himself several times, Rasulullah ﷺ said, "Atone for this by attesting that there is none worthy of worship but Allah." *(Bazzar)*. Rasulullah ﷺ said, "Atone for your lie by confirming that there is none worthy of worship but Allah." *(Abu Ya'la, Bazzar, Haythami, Ibn Hajar)*. Abdullah ؓ reports that Rasulullah ﷺ said, "When a man took a false oath using the words 'I swear by the Being besides Whom there is none worthy of worship', Allah forgave him (because he recited the words of the Kalima)." *(Tabrani, Haythami)*

People who Recited the Shahada will Leave Jahannam

Abu Musa Ash'ari ؓ narrates that Rasulullah ﷺ said, "When the people of Jahannam will get together, amongst them will also be those who faced the Qibla (Muslims). The Kuffar will then say to the Muslims, 'Were you people not Muslims?' When the Muslims reply in the affirmative, the Kuffar will ridicule, 'Then of what use was your Islam when you have ended up with us here in the fire?' The Muslims will reply, 'We were detained because of the sins that we committed.' When Allah hears what the Kuffar have to say, He will issue orders that all those who faced the Qibla should be removed from Jahannam. When the Kuffar remaining behind in Jahannam see this, they will mourn, 'If only we had been Muslims so that we could leave just as they have left.'" Rasulullah ﷺ then recited:

الر تِلْكَ آيَاتُ الْكِتَابِ وَقُرْآنٍ مُبِينٍ (1) رُبَمَا يَوَدُّ الَّذِينَ كَفَرُوا لَوْ كَانُوا مُسْلِمِينَ (2)

Alif-Lam-Ra. (These letters are one of the miracles of the Qur'an, and none but Allah (Alone) knows their meanings).These

are the Verses of the Book, and a plain Qur'an. Perhaps (often) will those who disbelieve wish that they were Muslims (those who have submitted themselves to Allah's Will in Islam Islamic Monotheism, this will be on the Day of Resurrection when they will see the disbelievers going to Hell and the Muslims going to Paradise). (Al-Hijr:1-2) (Tabrani, Ibn Abi Hatim)

Anas ؓ narrates that Rasulullah ﷺ said, "When some believers in the Kalima 'La Ilaha IllAllah' will enter Jahannam because of their sins, the worshippers of (the idols Lat and Uzza will ridicule them saying, 'Of what use was your recitation of 'La Ilaha IllAllah' when you are with us in Jahannam.' Allah will then get angry for their part. He will remove the Muslims from Jahannam and put them in the river of life where their burns will be healed just as the moon recovers from its eclipse. They will then enter Jannah where they will be called 'the people from Jahannam'." *(Tabrani in Tafsir Ibn Kathir).* Tabrani reports that because of the blackness on their faces, they will be called 'the people from Jahannam'. They will then plead to Allah saying, "O Rabb! Remove this name from us." Allah will command them to bath in a river in Jannah, after which the name will be removed from them because the blackness will be removed.

A Group of Mu'mineen that will be Saved from Jahannam

Hudhaifa ؓ narrates that Rasulullah ﷺ said, "Islam shall fade away just as decorative work fades from a garment People will have no idea what fasting, Sadaqa or sacrifice are. Then such a night will pass over the Qur'an after which not a single verse of the Qur'an will be found on earth, the angels will remove every Qur'an from earth. There shall then remain only a few pockets of people amongst whom an old man and an old lady will say, 'Because we found our forefathers reciting this Kalima 'La Ilaha IllAllah', we also recite it'" To this, one of the narrators called Sila asked, "Of what use will the Kalima 'La Ilaha IllAllah' be to them when they will have no idea what fasting, Sadaqa or sacrifice are?" When Hudhaifa ؓ ignored the question, Sila repeated it thrice. Each time, Hudhaifa ignored the question until on the third occasion; he turned to Sila and said, "O Sila! It will save them from Jahannam! It will save them from Jahannam! It will save them from Jahannam!" *(Hakim)*

The Statements of Ali ؓ, Abu Darda ؓ and Abdullah bin Mas'ood ؓ Concerning the Shahada and Those Reciting It

Ali ؓ once said, "The people with the clearest record with Allah and who know Him best are those who have the most love for and who most honor the sanctity of the believers in 'La Ilaha IllAllah'." *(Abu Nu'aym in Hilya, Kanzul Ummal).* Salim bin Abul Ja'd reports that someone once informed Abu Darda ؓ that Abu Sa'd bin Munabbih had set 100 slaves free. Abu Darda ؓ remarked, "Setting 100 slaves free from the wealth of a single person is a great deed. If you please, I can inform you of something better than that. It is Iman that is attached to the heart day and night and keeping your tongue moist with the Dhikr of Allah." *(Abu Nu'aym in Hilya, Ibn Abi Dunya in Targheeb wat Tarheeb).* Abdullah bin Mas'ood ؓ said, "Verily Allah has distributed good character amongst you just as He has distributed your sustenance. Allah has given wealth to those whom He loves as well as those whom He does not love. But He gives Iman only to those whom He loves. So it is only when Allah loves someone that He gives him Iman. The person who is too miserly to spend in Sadaqa, too scared to fight the enemy in Jihad and cannot exert himself in Ibadah at nights should recite 'La Ilaha Illallah', 'Allahu Akbar', 'Al Hamdu Lillah' and 'Subhanallah' plenty." *(Tabrani, Haythami, Mudhiri in Targheeb waf Tarheeb)*

The Eagerness of Abdullah bin Rawaha ﷺ to Participate in the Gatherings of Iman

Anas bin Malik ﷺ narrates that whenever Abdullah bin Rawaha ﷺ met one of the Sahabah, he says to him, "Come! Let us believe in our Rabb for a moment, let us refresh our Iman by talking about Allah for a while." When he said this to someone one day, the man became angry and reported it to Rasulullah ﷺ saying. "O Rasulullah ﷺ! Look at Ibn Rawaha. He prefers your Iman to the Iman of a moment." Nabi ﷺ replied, "May Allah forgive Ibn Rawaha. He loves the gatherings about which lie angels boast." *(Ahmad in Targheeb wat Tarheeb, Hafidh in Al Bidayah wan Nihayah)*. Ata bin Yasir narrates that Abdullah bin Rawaha ﷺ said to one of his companions, "Come here so that we may believe for a while." "Are we not already believers?" the other asked. "Certainly," Abdullah bin Rawaha ﷺ replied, "but let us talk about Allah so that our Iman can be increased." *(Bayhaqi)*. Shuraih bin Abdullah reports that Abdullah bin Rawaha ﷺ would grab hold of the hand of one of the Sahabah and say, "Stand with me so that we may believe for a while by sitting in a gathering of Dhikr." *(Hafidh Abul Qasim Lalka'ee)*. Abu Darda ﷺ says, "Abdullah bin Rawaha ﷺ caught hold of my hand saying, 'Come! Let us believe for a moment because the heart overturns faster than a pot boiling at its pitch." *(Tayalisi)*. Abu Darda ﷺ says, "When Abdullah bin Rawaha ﷺ would meet me, he would say, 'O Uwaimir! Sit down so that we may discuss Iman for a while.' We would then sit down and discuss, after which he would say. 'This is a gathering of Iman. The example of Iman is like that of your Qamis. When you have taken it off, you will again be putting it on and when you have put it on, you will again be taking it off. The heart overturns faster than a pot boiling at its pitch." *(Ibn Asakir in Kanzul Ummal)*

The Eagerness of Omar ﷺ and Mu'adh ﷺ to Participate in the Gatherings of Iman

Abu Dhar ﷺ reports that Omar ﷺ would grab the hands of 1 or 2 Sahabah and say, "Stand with me so that we may renew our Iman." They would talk about Allah. *(Ibn Abi Shaybah, Laika'ee in Sunnah, Kanzul Ummal)*. Aswad bin Hilal reports that they were walking with Mu'adh bin Jabal ﷺ when he said to them, "Sit with us so that we may believe." *(Abu Nu'aym in Hilya)*

Renewing Iman

Abu Hurairah ﷺ reports that Rasulullah ﷺ said, "Renew your Iman." "O Rasulullah ﷺ!" someone asked, "How can we renew Iman?" Rasulullah ﷺ replied, "Abundantly recite *'La Ilaha IllAllah'*."*(Ahmad, Tabrani, Mundhiri in Targheeb wat Tarheeb)*

Rejecting Experience and Eye-Witness Accounts: The Incident of a Man with Diarrhea

Abu Sa'eed Khudri ﷺ narrates that a man came to Rasulullah ﷺ saying, "My brother is suffering from diarrhea." "Give him honey to drink," Rasulullah ﷺ said. The man went, gave honey to his brother and returned saying, "O Rasulullah ﷺ! I gave him honey but it only made his diarrhea worse." "Go and give him honey to drink." Rasulullah ﷺ repeated. The man went, again gave his brother honey and returned yet again saying, "His diarrhea is now even worse." Rasulullah ﷺ said, "Allah speaks the truth and it is your brother's belly that is lying. Go and give him honey." When the man gave honey to his brother, he was fully cured.*(Bukhari, Muslim in Tafsir Ibn Kathir)*

The Incident of Abdullah bin Mas'ood ﷺ and his Wife

Zainab ﷺ who was the wife of Abdullah bin Mas'ood ﷺ says, "Whenever my husband Abdullah came home after relieving himself, he would clear his throat at the door and spit so that he does not enter upon us unexpectedly while we are in a condition that he would find unpleasant. He happened to return one day while I had with me an old lady who was busy reciting some charms to cure me from erysipelas (severe bacterial skin rash with fever and vomiting). When he cleared his throat, I quickly hid her beneath the bed. He then came in and sat next to me. Noticing a thread around my neck, he asked, 'What is this thread for?' I replied, 'A charm has been read on it for me.' He held it, cut it and then said, 'The family of Abdullah has no need for Shirk. I have heard Rasulullah ﷺ say that charms, talismans and amulets amount to Shirk when people believe that they possess the inherent quality of healing.'" Zainab ﷺ continues, "I then said to him, 'Why do you say that when it is true that I often experience pain in my eye and whenever I go to a particular Jewish lady who recites charms on it, the pain subsides?' He replied, 'That is because Saitan pokes your eye and when the charms are read on it, he stops poking at it. All you need to do is to recite what Rasulullah ﷺ used to recite which is: أَذْهِبِ البَّاسَ رَبَّ النَّاس وَاشْفِ أَنْتَ الشَّافِي لاَشِفَاءَ إِلاَّ شِفَاؤُكَ شِفَاءً لاَيُغَادِرُ سَقَمَا

"O Lord of mankind, remove the difficulty. You grant a cure for there is none who can cure besides You. There is also no cure like Your cure. Grant a cure that does not leave out any illness." *(Ahmad in Tafsir Ibn Kathir)*

The Incident of Abdullah bin Rawaha ﷺ and his Wife

Ikrama reports that Abdullah bin Rawaha ﷺ was once lying beside his wife when he got up and went to have intercourse with one of his slave women in another part of the house. His wife was alarmed when she did not see him lying where he had been so she immediately got up and left the room. When she saw him on the slave woman, she returned to her room, took a knife and went back. Abdullah bin Rawaha ﷺ had just finished and had stood up when he met her carrying the knife. "What is the matter?" he asked. "What is the matter indeed!" she replied, "Had I found you where I had seen you just now, I would have plunged this knife between your shoulders!" "And just where did you see me'!" he asked. "I saw you upon the slave," she replied. "It could not have been me that you saw." he said. He continued, "Rasulullah ﷺ has prohibited anyone from reciting the Qur'an when one is impure as I should be if I had intercourse, yet I can recite for you." "Then recite," she challenged. He recited the following couplets:

"Rasulullah ﷺ came to us reciting the Book that shines forth like the rising dawn. He brought guidance after darkness and our hearts are convinced that whatever he says must happen while he spends the night separated from his bed (engaged in Ibada) the disbeliever lie heavily on their beds"

Thinking that these were verses of the Qur'an his wife said, "I believe in the Book of Allah and reject what the eyes have seen." Abdullah ﷺ went to Rasulullah ﷺ the next morning and informed him about what transpired, Rasulullah ﷺ smiled so broadly that his molars were visible. *(Dar Qutni in Ta'liqul Mughni)*

The Incident of Omar ﷺ and Rasulullah ﷺ at Hudaibiya

Habib bin Abu Thabit narrates that when he went to pose some questions to Abu Wa'il ﷺ, the Sahabi related to them that when they were fighting at Siffin, someone asked, "Have you not seen those who are called towards the Book of Allah to settle their disputes?" "Yes, we have," replied Ali bin Abi Talib ﷺ. It was then that Sahl bin Hunaif ﷺ said, "You have only yourselves to blame! I have seen us at Hudaibiya when Nabi ﷺ entered into a peace treaty with the disbelievers. Had we deemed fighting to be the solution, we would have fought but it was in the best interest to enter into the treaty." He then continued to narrate that at the time Omar ؓ asked, "Are we not on the truth and the disbelievers on falsehood? Will not our martyrs go to Jannah while their dead will go to Jahannam?" "Certainly," Rasulullah ﷺ replied. "Then why should we compromise our Deen?" Omar ؓ asked, "Why should we return when Allah has not yet decided between us and the disbelievers?" Rasulullah ﷺ reassured him saying, "O son of Khattab! I am the Rasul of Allah and Allah shall never ever lead me to destruction." Omar ؓ was still upset when he went away. He proceeded straight to Abu Bakr ؓ and asked, "O Abu Bakr! Are we not on the truth and the Mushrikin on falsehood?" "O son of Khattab!" Abu Bakr ؓ said, "He is the Rasul of Allah ﷺ and Allah shall never ever lead him to destruction." It was after this that Allah revealed Surah Fatah. (Bukhari, Muslim). Another narration states that Sahl bin Hunaif ؓ said, "O people! You have only your own opinions to blame! I have seen myself on the day of Abu Jandal when Rasulullah ﷺ was forced to hand him over to the disbelievers according to the demands of the treaty. Had I the ability to reverse this decision of Rasulullah ﷺ, I would have certainly done so but no one's Iman would allow him to oppose a decision coming from Rasulullah ﷺ. Yet another narration adds that when Surah Fatah was revealed, Rasulullah ﷺ sent for Omar ؓ and recited it to hum. (Nasa'ee in Tafsir Ibn Kathir). In the chapter concerning Da'wah towards Allah and His Rasul ﷺ (chapter #1) and under the discussion of the treaty of Hudaibiya, the narration of Miswar bin Makhram has already been quoted. The narration states that Abu Jandal ؓ addressed the Muslims saying, "O gathering of Muslim! Why should I be returned to the disbelievers when I have come as a Muslim? Have you not seen how I have suffered?" Abu Jandal ؓ had endured severe torture at the hands of the disbelievers.

Omar ؓ then approached Rasulullah ﷺ and said, "Are you not the true Nabi of Allah?" "I am indeed," replied Rasulullah ﷺ. Omar ؓ asked further, "Are we not on the truth and our enemies on falsehood?" "Certainly," said Rasulullah ﷺ. "Then," asked Omar ؓ, "Why do we have to submit?" Rasulullah ﷺ said to him, "I am certainly the Rasul of Allah. I cannot disobey Him and He is my Helper." Omar ؓ asked, "Did you not tell us that we shall arrive at the Kabah and perform Tawaf around it?" Rasulullah ﷺ replied, "Indeed I did but did I tell you that it would be this year?" "No," said Omar ؓ. "Then you shall certainly arrive there and perform Tawaf around it," Rasulullah ﷺ assured him. Omar ؓ approached Abu Bakr ؓ and asked him, "Is he not the true Nabi of Allah?" "He is indeed," replied Abu Bakr ؓ. Omar ؓ asked further, "Are we not on the truth and our enemies on falsehood?" "Certainly," said Abu Bakr ؓ. "Then," asked Omar ؓ, "Why do we have to submit?" Abu Bakr ؓ said to him, "O person! He is certainly the Rasul of Allah. He cannot disobey Allah and Allah is his Helper." Omar ؓ asked, "Did Rasulullah ﷺ not tell us that we shall arrive at the Kabah and perform Tawaf around it?" Abu Bakr ؓ replied, "He did indeed, but did he tell you that it would be this year?" "No," said Omar ؓ. " You shall arrive there and perform Tawaf around it," Abu Bakr ؓ assured him. After narrating this, Omar ؓ says that he later carried out numerous good deeds to make amends for this behavior.

The Happiness of Rasulullah ﷺ when Revelation on Forgiveness and Victory arrived as they were returning From Hudaibiya

Anas ؓ narrates that as Rasulullah ﷺ was returning from Hudaibiya, Allah revealed the verse: وَمَا لِيَغْفِرَ لَكَ اللَّهُ مَا تَقَدَّمَ مِنْ ذَنْبِكَ تَأَخَّرَ *That Allah may forgive you your sins of the past and the future...* (Al-Fatah:2)

Rasulullah ﷺ then said, "Such a verse was revealed to me tonight that I love more than everything on earth." When Rasulullah ﷺ recited the verse to the Sahabah, they said, "Congratulations to you, O Nabi of Allah ﷺ. Allah has made it clear how He will be treating you, but what about us?" It was then that the following verse was revealed:

لِيُدْخِلَ الْمُؤْمِنِينَ وَالْمُؤْمِنَاتِ جَنَّاتٍ تَجْرِي مِنْ تَحْتِهَا الْأَنْهَارُ خَالِدِينَ فِيهَا وَيُكَفِّرَ عَنْهُمْ سَيِّئَاتِهِمْ وَكَانَ ذَلِكَ عِنْدَ اللَّهِ فَوْزًا عَظِيمًا (5)

That He may admit the believing men and the believing women to Gardens under which rivers flow (i.e. Paradise), to abide therein forever, and to expiate from them their sins, and that is with Allah, a supreme success. (Al-Fatah:5) (Ahmad, Bukhari, Muslim, Tafsir Ibn Kathir)

Anas ؓ reports that after Rasulullah ﷺ had been prevented from performing Umra, he was returning from Hudaibiya when the following verse was revealed: إِنَّا فَتَحْنَا لَكَ فَتْحًا مُبِينًا (1) *Verily, We have given you (O Muhammad ﷺ) a manifest victory.* (Al-Fatah:1)

When Rasulullah ﷺ and the Sahabah slaughtered their sacrificial animals at Hudaibiya, they were filled with grief and sorrow. Rasulullah ﷺ then said, "Such a verse was revealed to me that I love more than the entire world." He recited to them the verse:

إِنَّا فَتَحْنَا لَكَ فَتْحًا مُبِينًا (1) لِيَغْفِرَ لَكَ اللَّهُ مَا تَقَدَّمَ مِنْ ذَنْبِكَ وَمَا تَأَخَّرَ وَيُتِمَّ نِعْمَتَهُ عَلَيْكَ وَيَهْدِيَكَ صِرَاطًا مُسْتَقِيمًا (2) وَيَنْصُرَكَ اللَّهُ نَصْرًا عَزِيزًا (3) *Verily, We have given you (O Muhammad SAW) a manifest victory. That Allah may forgive you your sins of the past and the future, and complete His Favor on you, and guide you on the Straight Path; and that Allah may help you with strong help.* (Al-Fatah:1- 3)

When Rasulullah ﷺ recited the verse to the Sahabah, they said, "Congratulations to you, O Nabi of Allah ﷺ ..." The rest if the narration is the same as the one above. (Ibn Jareer). Mujammi bin Jariya Ansari ؓ who was one of those Sahabah who were proficient in the knowledge of the Qur'an reports that he was also present at Hudaibiya. After they had left, they saw people racing their camels. "What is the matter with them?" they asked each other. When they were informed that revelation had come to Rasulullah ﷺ, they all rushed to Rasulullah ﷺ, who was sitting on his camel at a place called Kura'ul Ghamim. When the Sahabah had gathered around, Rasulullah ﷺ recited: إِنَّا فَتَحْنَا لَكَ فَتْحًا مُبِينًا (1) *Verily, We have given you (O Muhammad ﷺ) a manifest victory.* (Al-Fatah:1). Someone asked, "O Rasulullah ﷺ! Is this a victory?" "Yes," Rasulullah ﷺ replied, "I swear by the Being Who controls the life of Muhammad that this is certainly a victory." The Hadith continues further. (Ahmad, Abu Dawud in Tafsir Ibn Kathir). Bara ؓ once said, "You people regard the conquest of Makkah as the 'victory' referred to in the first verse of Sura Fatah. Although that certainly was a great victory, we the Sahabah regard the 'victory' to be the pledge of Ridwan taken at Hudaibiya." The narration still continues further. (Bukhari in Tafsir Ibn Kathir). Jabir ؓ says, "We regard the 'victory' to be nothing other than the treaty of Hudaibiya." (Ibn Jareer)

The Incident of the River Nile During the Khilafa of Omar ؓ

Qais bin Hajjaj reports from his teacher that after Egypt was conquered by the Muslims, the people approached the governor Amr bin Al Aas ؓ when the month of Bu'na, a month in

Egyptian calendar started. "O governor!" they said, "There is a ritual we carry out for our Nile without which it will not flow." "What is the ritual?" Amr ◌ enquired. They then explained, "After 12 days of this month have passed, we look for a virgin living with her parents. After satisfying her parents with a vast sum of money, we adorn her with the best of jewels and clothing and then throw her into the Nile." "This cannot happen in Islam," Amr ◌ told them, "Islam wipes out all rituals that takes place before it." It so happened that the Nile did not flow and although the people stayed in Egypt all through the month of Bu'na, they eventually decided to leave Egypt. Amr ◌ wrote a letter to Omar ◌ and informed him about the situation. Omar ◌ wrote back to Amr ◌ saying, "Your course of action was correct. I have enclosed a note with this letter that you should throw into the Nile..." The narration continues in the chapter discussing unseen assistance from Allah. The narration states that the note was thrown into the Nile and on the next morning which was a Saturday, the people found that the Nile was flowing 16 arm's length high in a single night. Thus Allah cut out the Egyptian ritual to this day. (Lalka'ee in Sunnah, Tafsir Ibn Kathir)

Ala bin Hadhrami ◌ Leads the Muslim Army into the Ocean

Sahm bin Minjab reports, "We were on a military expedition with Ala bin Hadhrami ◌ when we approached the island of Darain. The ocean however posed an obstacle for us to land on the island. Ala ◌ then prayed to Allah saying, 'O Alim! O Halim! O Aliy! O Adhim! Verily Your servants are in Your path fighting Your enemies. O Allah! Create for us a way to reach them.' He then led us into the water and as deep as we went, the water did not even reach our saddle-cloths. In this manner, we reached the enemy." (Abu Nu'aym in Hilya). Another narration from Abu Hurairah ◌ adds that when Ibn Muka'bir the Persian Emperor's governor saw the Muslims traveling through the water), he said, "No! By Allah! We can never fight such people!" He then boarded his ship and returned to Persia. (Abu Nu'aym in Hilya, Tabrani, Ibn Abi Dunya, Bayhaqi). Sahm bin Minjab, Abu Hurairah ◌ and Anas ◌, said similar narrations, will soon appear in the chapter detailing the control that Allah gave Muslims over the oceans. There the narration will appear showing how Sa'd bin Abi Waqqas crossed the Tigris river during the Battle of Qadisiya. The narration cites the announcement Hujr bin Adi ◌ that when he said, "What prevents you from crossing over these few droplets viz. the Tigris." He recited the following verse: وَمَا كَانَ لِنَفْسٍ أَنْ تَمُوتَ إِلَّا بِإِذْنِ اللَّهِ كِتَابًا مُؤَجَّلًا And no person can ever die except by Allah's permission and at an appointed term... (Al-Imran:145). He then plunged his horse into the river and the other followed. When the enemy saw them, they took to their heels shouting, "Demons! Demons!"

Tamim Dari ◌ drives a Fire Away

Mu'awiya bin Harmal reports a narration that mentions a fire emerging from Harra, a rocky terrain near Madinah. Omar ◌ then came to Tamim Dari ◌ saying, "Go and see to that fire!" "Who am I and what am I" Tamim ◌ said. Omar ◌ however insisted until Tamim ◌ went with him. The narrator reports that he followed them as they proceeded to the fire where Tamim ◌ rounded up the fire with his bare hands until it returned into the gap it had come out from, with Tamim ◌ behind it. Omar ◌ said, "The one who has witnessed this can never be like the one who has not because it serves to boost one's Iman." (Abu Nu'aym in Dala'il). Bayhaqi and Baghawi reported similar narration.

What Rasulullah ﷺ Saw When he Struck a Boulder During Preparations for the Battle of Khandaq and the Glad Tidings he Gave the Sahabah

When Rasulullah ﷺ gave the command for the trench to be dug, a large boulder presented an obstacle to the digging. Rasulullah ﷺ took up spade, placed his shawl beside the trench and recited: وَتَمَّتْ كَلِمَةُ رَبِّكَ صِدْقًا وَعَدْلًا لَا مُبَدِّلَ لِكَلِمَاتِهِ وَهُوَ السَّمِيعُ الْعَلِيمُ

(115) And the Word of your Lord has been fulfilled in truth and in justice. None can change His Words. And He is the All-Hearer, the All-Knower. Al-An'am:115)

When Rasulullah ﷺ struck it, a spark flashed and a 3rd of the boulder crumbled as Salman Farsi ◌ watched. When Rasulullah ﷺ struck it a 2nd time, he again recited the verse:

وَتَمَّتْ كَلِمَةُ رَبِّكَ صِدْقًا وَعَدْلًا لَا مُبَدِّلَ لِكَلِمَاتِهِ وَهُوَ السَّمِيعُ الْعَلِيمُ (115)

And the Word of your Lord has been fulfilled in truth and in justice. None can change His Words. And He is the All-Hearer, the All-Knower. Al-An'am:115)

Again a spark flashed and another 3rd of the boulder crumbled. Salman ◌ witnessed this. Rasulullah ﷺ then struck it a 3rd time as he recited: وَتَمَّتْ كَلِمَةُ رَبِّكَ صِدْقًا وَعَدْلًا لَا مُبَدِّلَ لِكَلِمَاتِهِ وَهُوَ السَّمِيعُ الْعَلِيمُ

(115) And the Word of your Lord has been fulfilled in truth and in justice. None can change His Words. And He is the All-Hearer, the All-Knower. Al-An'am:115)

This time, the last 3rd of the boulder crumbled. Rasulullah ﷺ then got out from the trench, took his shawl and sat down. "O Rasulullah ﷺ!" Salman ◌ said, "I was watching as you struck the boulder and noticed that every time you struck it, a brilliant spark flashed." "O Sulaiman!" Rasulullah ﷺ said, "Did you also see that'?" "I swear by the Being Who has sent you with the truth that I definitely did," Salman ◌ replied. Rasulullah ﷺ then explained, "When I struck it the first time, the cities of the Persian Emperor, their surroundings and numerous other cities were shown to me so vividly that I could see their every detail" The Sahabah who were present there said, "O Rasulullah ﷺ! Pray to Allah that He allows us to conquer those places, to have their progeny as our booty and to raze the place down with our hands." Rasulullah ﷺ made the Du'a and then continued, "When I struck it the second time, the cities of the Roman Emperor and their surroundings were shown to me so vividly that I could see their every detail" "O Rasulullah ﷺ!" the Sahabah asked, "Pray to Allah that He allows us to conquer those places, to have their progeny as our booty and to raze the place down with our hands." Rasulullah ﷺ again complied. Thereafter, Rasulullah ﷺ continued, "When I struck it the third time, the cities of Abyssinia and the cities in their surroundings were shown to me so vividly that I could see their every detail. You should however leave the Abyssinians alone as long as they leave you alone and also leave the Turks alone as long as they leave you alone." (Nasa'ee in Al Bidayah wan Nihayah, Abu Dawud). Amr bin Auf Muzani reports a similar narration. This narration states that when Nabi ﷺ arrived, he took a spade from Salman ◌. He then struck the boulder so hard that the boulder was crushed and a spark so bright flashed that it lit up everything between the 2 mountains of Madinah. It actually appeared as if it was a lantern in the middle of a dark night. Rasulullah ﷺ cried out "Allahu Akbar" as people cry out when they attain victory over an enemy. The Sahabah echoes the cry of Rasulullah ﷺ. When Rasulullah ﷺ struck the boulder a second time, the same thing happened and on the 3rd strike again. When Salman ◌ and the other Sahabah spoke about this to Rasulullah ﷺ, they asked him what the meaning of the light was. Rasulullah ﷺ explained, "On the first occasion, the palaces of

Hira and the cities of the Persian Emperor were lit up for me, appearing shining like the canines of a hound. Jibra'el ﷺ then informed me that my Ummah shall conquer these places. On the second occasion, the red palaces of Rome were lit up for me appearing like the canines of a hound. Jibra'el then informed me that my Ummah shall conquer these places as well. Eventually, on the third occasion, the palaces of San'a were lit up for me, appearing like the canines of a hound. Jibra'el ﷺ again informed me that my Ummah shall conquer these places. You should therefore rejoice about this." The Sahabah became very happy and Said, "Al Hamdu Lillah! The promise is true indeed." When the disbelieving armies arrived, the Mu'minin said:

هَذَا مَا وَعَدَنَا اللَّهُ وَرَسُولُهُ وَصَدَقَ اللَّهُ وَرَسُولُهُ وَمَا زَادَهُمْ إِلَّا إِيمَانًا وَتَسْلِيمًا (22)

This is what Allah and His Messenger (Muhammad ﷺ) had promised us, and Allah and His Messenger (Muhammad ﷺ) had spoken the truth, and it only added to their faith and to their submissiveness (to Allah). (Al-Ahzab:22)

The hypocrites quipped, "He tells you that from Yathrib he can see the palaces of Hira, Mada'in and the Persian Emperor and that you people will be conquering these places when you are digging a trench and are unable to even contest the enemy on the battlefield." With reference to this that Allah revealed the verse:

وَإِذْ يَقُولُ الْمُنَافِقُونَ وَالَّذِينَ فِي قُلُوبِهِمْ مَرَضٌ مَا وَعَدَنَا اللَّهُ وَرَسُولُهُ إِلَّا غُرُورًا (12)

And when the hypocrites and those in whose hearts is a disease (of doubts) said: "Allah and His Messenger (SAW) promised us nothing but delusions!" (Al-Ahzab:12) (Ibn Jareer in Al Bidayah wan Nihayah). A narration from Abdullah bin Abbas ﷺ will soon appear in the chapter discussing the unseen assistance from Allah with regard to the blessings in food. The narration states that when called for the boulder Rasulullah ﷺ said, "Let me be the first to strike it." Rasulullah ﷺ recited "Bismillah" and struck the boulder, causing a 3rd of it to be crushed. He exclaimed. "Allahu Akbar! The palaces of Rome, by the Rabb of the Kabah!" Rasulullah ﷺ struck the boulder a 2nd time and another portion was crushed. This time he cried out, "*Allahu Akbar!* The palaces of Persia, by the Rabb of the Kabah!" The hypocrites said, "We are busy digging a trench to save our lives and he is promising the palaces of Rome and Persia?!"*(Tabrani, Haythami)*

Khalid ﷺ drinks Poison and the Statement of a Christian About the Sahabah

Also coming shortly in the chapter discussing the unseen assistance from Allah is the incident of poison having no effect on Khalid bin Walid ﷺ and his statement that no soul can die until its time is up." Also to appear are the words of the Christian, Amr who said, "O assembly of Arabs! I swear by Allah that you will always have sovereignty over any region you want as long as there is a single member of this generation of Sahabah with you." Addressing the people of Hira, he also said, "To this day, I have never seen anything as viable as this."

Statements of the Sahabah Attesting that Large Numbers does not Bring Assistance

Soon to appear in the chapter discussing the sources of assistance is the statement of Thabit bin Aqram ﷺ who said, "O Abu Hurairah! Do you perhaps see a large concentration of forces?" "O yes," replied Abu Hurairah ﷺ. Thabit ﷺ then said, "You did not witness the Battle of Badr with us for then you would have seen that it was not large numbers that assisted us." There it will also be narrated that when someone remarked. "The Romans are so many while the Muslims so few!" Khalid bin Walid ﷺ responded by saying. "The Romans are so few while

the Muslims so many! Armies are increased only by Allah's assistance and reduced only by Allah withdrawing His assistance, and not by their numbers. By Allah! I wish that my horse Ashqar was well and that the enemy was doubled in number." Also to appear there is the letter Abu Bakr ﷺ wrote to Amr bin Al Aas ﷺ in which he said, "You letter has just reached me detailing the massive build-up of Roman forces. Verily it was neither with large numbers nor with large armies that Allah assisted us during the time of His Nabi ﷺ. When we were with Rasulullah ﷺ, we sometimes fought battles with only 2 horses and at times we even had to take turns riding our camels. When we fought the Battle of Uhud with Rasulullah ﷺ, we had only one horse which Rasulullah ﷺ rode. It was Allah Who backed us and assisted us against those who opposed us."

The narration has already passed discussing how Abu Bakr ﷺ dispatched the army of Usama ﷺ. This was during a time when the Arabs were revolting on all fronts, when apart from a few tribes all the Arab tribes started turning away from Islam, when hypocrisy started surfacing and the Jews and Christians started rearing their ugly heads. At the time, the Muslims were like a lone goat caught in a stormy night because they were still reeling from the loss of their Nabi ﷺ and their numbers were very few compared to the large number of the enemy. However, when the Sahabah proposed to Abu Bakr ﷺ that he delay the departure of the army of Usama ﷺ, he said, "How can I hold back an army that Rasulullah ﷺ had dispatched? I would then be doing something very bold! I swear by the Being Who controls my life that I would prefer having all the Arabs attack me rather than restraining an army that Rasulullah ﷺ had dispatched! O Usama! Proceed with your army whence Rasulullah ﷺ had commanded you and fight in the area of Palestine where Rasulullah ﷺ had commanded. Fight the people of Mu'ta for Allah shall be sufficient for those whom you are leaving behind (in Madinah)." The narration has also passed discussing the Battle of Mu'ta when Abdullah bin Rawaha ﷺ addressed the Muslims as the enemy amassed a force of 200,000 troops. He said to them, "O people! By Allah! The thing that you seem to dislike is the very thing for which you have left; martyrdom. We have never fought with reliance in our numbers and our strength. We have always fought on the strength of this Deen that Allah had blessed us with. March ahead! You will have either one of two excellent things, victory or martyrdom." The others echoed, "By Allah! Ibn Rawaha has spoken the truth!" There are so many more such incidents of the Sahabah scattered throughout this book and many other books discussing Hadith, battles and biographies of Rasulullah ﷺ. We shall not lengthen this book with mentioning them all and repeating them.

Rasulullah ﷺ asks Harith Bin Malik ﷺ How he felt and His reply

Anas ﷺ reports that Rasulullah ﷺ entered the Masjid one day where he found Harith bin Malik ﷺ asleep. Pushing him with his foot, Rasulullah ﷺ said, "Raise your head." As he raised his head, Harith ﷺ exclaimed, "May my parents be sacrificed for you, O Rasulullah ﷺ!" "How do you feel this morning, O Harith bin Malik?" Rasulullah ﷺ asked. Harith ﷺ replied, "I feel like a true Mu'min this morning, O Rasulullah ﷺ." Rasulullah ﷺ said, "Every fact requires substantiation, so how do you substantiate your statement?" Harith ﷺ replied, "I have turned my eyes away from this world, I keep myself thirsty during the days because I am fasting and I stay awake in Ibadah during the nights. In addition to that, it is as if I can actually see the Arsh of my Rabb and as if I can actually see the people of Jannah visiting each other and the people of Jahannam barking at each other."

Rasulullah ﷺ remarked, "You are a man whose heart Allah has illuminated. You have understood the reality of Iman so now remain steadfast." *(Ibn Asakir)*. Haritha bin Nu'man ؓ states that Rasulullah ﷺ said to him, "You have seen the reality of Iman, so remain steadfast. He is a man in whose heart Allah has illuminated Iman." "O Rasulullah ﷺ!" Haritha ؓ then asked, "Pray to Allah that I become a martyr." Rasulullah ﷺ then made the Du'a for him. One day the announcement was made, "O horsemen of Allah! Mount your horses and ride out in Jihad." Haritha ؓ was the first to take to his horse and also became the first to be martyred? *(Asaki in Muntakhab Kanzul Ummal)*. Anas ؓ narrates that Rasulullah ﷺ was walking somewhere when he met a young man from the Ansar. "How do you feel this morning, O Harith?" Rasulullah ﷺ asked. He replied, "This morning I feel like a true believer in Allah." "Consider well what you say," Rasulullah ﷺ advised, "because every statement requires substantiation." He replied, "O Rasulullah ﷺ! I have turned my eyes away from this world..." The rest of the Hadith is similar as quoted above. *(Ibn Najjar in Muntakhab Kanzul Ummal)*. Rasulullah ﷺ said, "Every statement requires substantiation, so how do you substantiate your Iman?" *(Ibn Mubarak in Zuhd, Hafidh in Isabah, Abdur Razzaq, Tabrani, Ibn Mandah, Bayhaqi, Bazzar, Haythami)*

Rasulullah ﷺ asks Mu'adh ؓ How he Felt and His Reply

Anas bin Malik ؓ narrates that when Mu'adh bin Jabal ؓ arrived one day, Rasulullah ﷺ asked him. "How do you feel this morning, O Mu'adh?" Mu'adh ؓ replied, "I feel like a true believer in Allah." "Every statement requires substantiation," Rasulullah ﷺ told him, "so how do you substantiate your statement?" "O Nabi of Allah ﷺ!" Mu'adh ؓ explained, "Every morning I feel that I will not see the evening and every evening I feel that I will never see the morning. Every time I take a step, I feel like I shall not follow it up with another and it is as if I can actually see every nation kneeling on the Day of Judgment, being called to their records of deeds with their Ambiya and the idols they worshipped. As if I can actually see the punishment of the people of Jahannam and the rewards of the people of Jannah." Rasulullah ﷺ commended him saying, "You have understood the reality of Iman so now remain steadfast." *(Abu Nu'aym in Hilya)*

Rasulullah ﷺ Asks Suwaid bin Hiaritha ؓ and his Companions

In the chapter discussing giving Da'wah towards Allah and His Rasul ﷺ, the narration of Suwaid bin Harith ؓ has passed. In the narration he states that he was one of 7 people who met Rasulullah ﷺ as a delegation. When they arrived in his presence and spoke to him, he was impressed by their gestures and appearance. Rasulullah ﷺ asked, "What are you?" They replied, "Mu'minin." Rasulullah ﷺ said, "Every statement has a reality to substantiate it. What is the reality of your Iman?" They replied, "15 attributes prove the existence of our Iman. 5 are those that your messengers have commanded us to believe in, 5 are those that your messengers have commanded us to carry out and 5 are those that we have adopted from the period of ignorance and are still practicing until now unless you dislike them in which case we are prepared to forsake them..." The narration mentions belief in Allah, His angels, His Books, His prophets, predestination - whether good or bad, Islam and in good character.

The Incident of a Munafiq who Approached Rasulullah ﷺ to Seek Forgiveness on His Behalf

Abdullah bin Omar ؓ narrates that they were sitting with Rasulullah ﷺ when Harmala bin Zaid Ansari ؓ of the Banu Haritha tribe came and sat in front of Rasulullah ﷺ. Pointing to his tongue, he said "O Rasulullah ﷺ! Iman is here." He then pointed to his chest saying, "But in here is only hypocrisy. This heart remembers Allah very little." Rasulullah ﷺ remained silent, but Harmala ؓ repeated himself. Rasulullah ﷺ then held the tip of Harmala ؓ's tongue and prayed. "O Allah! Grant him a truthful tongue, a grateful heart, love for me, love for those who love me and point him in the right direction." Harmala ؓ then said, "O Rasulullah ﷺ! I have many brothers who are Munafiqin and I had been their leader. Should I not point them out to you?" Rasulullah ﷺ replied, "If they come to us as you have come, we shall seek forgiveness on their behalf as we have done for you. It is best that Allah deals with those of them who are stubborn in their ways." *(Abu Nu'aym, Kanzul Ummal, Tabrani, Ibn Mandah)*

A Sahabi Recites Surah Ikhlas in Abundance

Aisha ؓ narrates that a Sahabi whom Rasulullah ﷺ dispatched as commander of an expedition used to lead his companions in salah but would always conclude the Rakah by reciting Surah Ikhlas. When they returned and reported this to Rasulullah ﷺ, he told them to ask him why he did this. When they asked him, he replied, "I recite it so often because it discusses the attributes of Ar Rahman. I love to recite it." Rasulullah ﷺ then told the Sahabah, "Inform him that Allah loves him as well." *(Bayhaqi in Asma was Sifat, Bukhari, Muslim)*

Rasulullah ﷺ confirms what a Jewish Scholar said about Allah

Abdullah bin Mas'ood ؓ reports that a Jewish scholar once came to Rasulullah ﷺ using the address of "O Muhammad" or "O Rasulullah ﷺ", he said, "Verily Allah shall place the heavens on one finger, the worlds on another finger, the mountains and trees on another finger, water and clay on another finger and the rest of creation on another finger. He will then shake them saying, 'I am the King.'" In confirmation of the scholar's statement, Rasulullah ﷺ smiled so broadly that his molars became visible. He then recited the verse: وَمَا قَدَرُوا اللَّهَ حَقَّ قَدْرِهِ وَالْأَرْضُ جَمِيعًا قَبْضَتُهُ يَوْمَ الْقِيَامَةِ وَالسَّمَاوَاتُ مَطْوِيَّاتٌ بِيَمِينِهِ سُبْحَانَهُ وَتَعَالَى عَمَّا يُشْرِكُونَ (67)

They made not a just estimate of Allah such as is due to Him. And on the Day of Resurrection the whole of the earth will be grasped by His Hand and the heavens will be rolled up in His Right Hand. Glorified is He, and High is He above all that they associate as partners with Him! (Az-ZOmar:67) *(Bayhaqi in Asma was Sifat, Bukhari, Muslim)*

The Narrations of Anas ؓ and Abu Dhar ؓ About How Allah will Resurrect People

Anas bin Malik ؓ narrates that someone once asked Rasulullah ﷺ, "How will the Kafir be resurrected on his face *(Ref. Israel:97, Furqan:34)* on the Day of Judgment?" Rasulullah ﷺ replied, "Indeed the One who makes him walk with his legs can certainly make him walk on his face on the Day of Judgment." *(Bayhaqi in Asma was Sifat, Bukhari, Muslim, Ahmad, Nasa'ee, Ibn Abi Hatim, Hakim, Kanzul Ummal)*. Hudhaifa bin Usaid reports that Abu Dhar ؓ once said, "O tribe of Ghifar! Talk to each other without taking oaths because the truthful one to whom the truth was always brought (viz. Rasulullah ﷺ) told me that people will be resurrected in 3 groups on the Day of Judgment. One group will be riding, eating and well dressed. Another will be walking and running, while the third will be dragged by the angels on their faces and driven towards Jahannam." Someone from the audience said, "Two of the groups we are aware of, but what about those who will be walking and running?" Abu Darr ؓ replied, "Allah shall send a calamity on all riding animals causing them all to die so that there shall be not a single one left. A person will want to give away his magnificent orchard in exchange for an old camel with a carriage. He will be unable to do this because no animal will be available." (Ahmad in Tafsir Ibn Kathir, Hakim)

Rasulullah ﷺ Instructs the Sahabah to say مَا شَاءَ اللهُ وَحْدَهُ لَاشَرِيكَ لَهُ

Tufail bin Abdullah ؓ who was Aisha ؓ's half brother relates that he once saw a group of Christians in a dream. He said to them, "You people are excellent people, had it not been for your belief that Masih (Isa) ؑ is Allah's son." They responded by saying, "And you people are excellent people had it not been for your saying: مَا شَاءَ اللهُ وشاء محمد ('What Allah and Muhammad ﷺ wills')," Thereafter he met a group of Jews and said to them, "You people are excellent people had it not been for your belief that Uzair is Allah's son." They also responded by saying, "And you people are excellent people had it not been for your saying, مَا شَاءَ اللهُ وشاء محمد ('What Allah and Muhammad ﷺ wills')." Tufail then went to Rasulullah ﷺ and related the dream to him, "Did you relate this to anyone else afterwards?" Rasulullah asked. When he declared that he did, Rasulullah ﷺ praised Allah and then addressed the Sahabah saying, "The dream that your brother has seen has already reached you. You should therefore not say those words but should rather say: مَا شَاءَ اللهُ وَحْدَهُ لَاشَرِيكَ لَهُ

('What the One Allah Who has no partner wills')." (Bayhaqi in Asma was Sifat)

Hudhaifa ؓ narrates that one of the Muslims saw in a dream that he met a man from the Ahlul Kitab who said to him, "You people are excellent people had it not been for your committing Shirk by saying' مَا شَاءَ اللهُ ومحمد ('What Allah and Muhammad ﷺ wills')." When he reported the dream to Rasulullah ﷺ, Rasulullah ﷺ said, "I had always disliked you saying this. You should rather say, 'What Allah wills'. Thereafter, you may add what someone else wills." (Bayhaqi in Asma was Sifat). Abdullah bin Abbas ؓ narrates that when a man came to discuss something with Rasulullah ﷺ, the man said, "What Allah wills and what you will." Rasulullah ﷺ rebuked him saying, "Are you equating me with Allah!? It is only what the One Allah wills (that will happen)." (Bayhaqi in Asma was Sifat)

A Jew Questions Rasulullah ﷺ About Act of Will

Imam Awza'i reports that a Jew once approached Rasulullah ﷺ asking about will. Rasulullah ﷺ replied, "Everything occurs by the will of Allah." "What if I decide to stand up?" the man asked. "Then it is by Allah's will that you will stand," Rasulullah ﷺ replied. The man asked further, "And if I decide to sit?" "Then it is by Allah's will that you will sit," Rasulullah replied. Again the Jew asked, "And what if I decide to cut down this date palm?" Again Rasulullah ﷺ replied, "Then it is by Allah's will that you will cut it" "And if I then decide to leave it alone?" he asked. "Then," Rasulullah ﷺ replied, "It is by Allah's will that you will leave it." Jibra'el ؑ then came and said to Rasulullah ﷺ, "You have been inspired to present the correct facts just as Ibrahim ؑ was inspired." It is same meaning that Allah says in the Qur'an:

مَا قَطَعْتُمْ مِنْ لِينَةٍ أَوْ تَرَكْتُمُوهَا قَائِمَةً عَلَى أُصُولِهَا فَبِإِذْنِ اللهِ وَلِيُخْزِيَ الْفَاسِقِينَ (5)

What you (O Muslims) cut down of the palm-trees (of the enemy), or you left them standing on their stems, it was by Leave of Allah, and in order that He might disgrace the Fasiqoon (rebellious, disobedient to Allah). (Al-Hashar:5) (Bayhaqi in Asma was Sifat)

Rasulullah ﷺ and the Sahabah Oversleep by the Will of Allah

Abdullah bin Mas'ood ؓ reports that when Rasulullah ﷺ was returning with the Sahabah from Hudaybiya, he set up camp at a particular place in the last portion of the night. "Who will stand guard over us'?" Rasulullah ﷺ asked. "I will," Abdullah bin Mas'ood ؓ said, "I will." "You?" Rasulullah ﷺ said, "You? You will fall asleep" Rasulullah ﷺ repeated this twice or thrice but eventually appointed Abdullah bin Mas'ood for the task. He then stood guard as the others slept. As dawn was beginning to rise, Rasulullah ﷺ's words held true and Abdullah bin Mas'ood ؓ fell asleep. None of the Sahabah woke up until the sun started beating down on their backs. Rasulullah ﷺ stood up and did as he usually did. He then led the Fajr salah, after which he said, "Had Allah willed, you would have not slept through Fajr. However, Allah willed that this should be a lesson for those after you who would now know what to do in such a situation if they oversleep through the time of salah or forget to perform their salah." (Bayhaqi in Asma was Sifat). Abu Qatadah ؓ reports that Rasulullah ﷺ said, "Verily Allah seizes your souls when He wills as you sleep and releases them when He wills." The Sahabah proceeded to relieve them and perform wudhu. By the time they had finished, the sun was already white. Rasulullah ﷺ then stood up and led them in salah. (Bayhaqi in Asma was Sifat, Bukhari)

A Jew Questions Omar ؓ About the Verse "Jannah has the Vastness of the Heavens and the Earth"

Tariq bin Shihab narrates that a Jew asked Omar ؓ, "Tell me where is Jahannam when Allah says: وَجَنَّةٍ عَرْضُهَا السَّمَوَاتُ وَالْأَرْضُ

…and for Paradise as wide as the heavens and the earth… (Al-Imran:133)
Addressing the Sahabah present there, Omar ؓ said, "Give him an answer." When no one could give a reply, Omar ؓ said, "Tell me where the day goes when the night appears and fills the earth?" "It is where Allah wills," the man replied. "Then," said Omar ؓ, "Jahannam is also where Allah wills." The Jew then remarked, "1 swear by the Being Who controls my life that what you have mentioned is exactly what appears in Allah's revealed Book: the Torah." (Abd bin Humaid, Ibn Jareer, Ibn Mundhir, Ibn Khusu in Kanzul Ummal)

Ali ؓ Debates with a Man About Act of Will

Muhammad narrates that Ali ؓ was once introduced to a man debating the issue of will. "O servant of Allah!" Ali ؓ said, "Has Allah created you as He willed or as you will?" "As He willed," the man replied. "Does He make you ill when He wills or when you will?" "When He wills," the man admitted. Ali ؓ asked him, "Does He then cure you when He wills or when you will?" The man replied, "When He wills." "Does Allah take you where He wills or where you will?" "Where He wills," came the reply. "By Allah!" Ali ؓ said, "Had you replied differently, I would have used my sword to severe the part of your body that hosts your eyes." (Ibn Abi Hatim in Tafsir Ibn Kathir)

Rasulullah ﷺ tells the Sahabah What Hypocrisy is Not

Anas ؓ narrates that the Sahabah said, "O Rasulullah ﷺ! We experience a wonderful frame of mind when we are with you, but no sooner we leave your company, our frame of mind changes, we therefore fear being hypocrites." "How is your relationship with your Rabb?" Rasulullah ﷺ asked. "Allah is our Rabb in private and in public," they replied. "Then," replied Rasulullah ﷺ, "that is not hypocrisy." (Bazzar in Tafsir Ibn Kathir)

Rasulullah ﷺ with a Bedouin Asking About Reckoning

Abu Hurairah ؓ reports that a Bedouin once approached Rasulullah ﷺ with a question. "O Rasulullah ﷺ!" he asked, "Who will ask the creation to render their accounts on the Day of Judgment?" "Allah," Rasulullah ﷺ replied.' "By the Rabb of the Kabah!" the Bedouin cried out, "We are then saved." "What do you mean, O Bedouin?" Rasulullah asked. The Bedouin explained, "When someone magnanimous is in authority, He always forgives." *(Ibn Najjar in Kanzul Ummal)*

The Incident of Mu'adh ؓ when Omar ؓ Sent him to Collect Zakah

Sa'eed bin Musaib narrates that Omar ؓ once sent Mu'adh ؓ to collect zakah from the Banu Kilab tribe. Mu'adh ؓ distributed everything amongst the poor people of the tribe until nothing was left. All he returned with was the sack he had left with, carrying it around his neck. His wife asked, "Where is the gift that collectors usually bring back for their families?" Mu'adh ؓ replied, "I had an inspector with me and therefore could not bring anything back." She exclaimed, "You were trusted by Rasulullah ﷺ and Abu Bakr ؓ but Omar ؓ sent an inspector with you?" She made a furor about it amongst the women of her tribe as she complained about Omar ؓ. The news reached Omar ؓ, he sent for Mu'adh ؓ and asked, "Did I send an inspector with you?" Mu'adh ؓ replied, "I had no other excuse but this to give my wife." Omar ؓ laughed and gave Mu'adh ؓ something saying, "Give her this to make her happy." *Ibn Jareer* mentioned that Mu'adh ؓ was referring Allah when he mentioned inspector. *(Abdur Razzaq, Muhamili in Amali, Kazul Ummal)*

The Narration of Aisha ؓ Concerning the Lady who Debated

Aisha ؓ said, "All praise belongs to Allah Who hears everything. The Mujadalah (the lady who debated) came to speak with Rasulullah ﷺ and although I was in the corner of the room, I heard nothing. Allah then revealed the verse:

قَدْ سَمِعَ اللَّهُ قَوْلَ الَّتِي تُجَادِلُكَ فِي زَوْجِهَا وَتَشْتَكِي إِلَى اللَّهِ وَاللَّهُ يَسْمَعُ تَحَاوُرَكُمَا إِنَّ اللَّهَ سَمِيعٌ بَصِيرٌ (1)

Indeed Allah has heard the statement of her (Khaulah bint Thalabah) that disputes with you (O Muhammad ﷺ) concerning her husband (Aus bin As-Samit), and complains to Allah. And Allah hears the argument between you both. Verily, Allah is All-Hearer, All-Seer. (Al-Mujadalah:1) (Ahmad, Bukhari in Tafsir Ibn Kathir)

Aisha ؓ said, "Blessed is that Allah Whose hearing captures everything. As I was listening to Khowla bint Tha'laba complain to Rasulullah ﷺ about her husband, there were words that I could not hear. 'O Rasulullah ﷺ!' she said, 'He has consumed my wealth, finished my youth and my womb has even borne him children. Eventually, when I have grown old and I can no longer bear children, he has practiced Zihar (form of divorce during the time) with me.' She then prayed, 'O Allah! To You do I place my complaint.' She had not yet stood up when Jibra'el عليه السلام arrived with the verse:

قَدْ سَمِعَ اللَّهُ قَوْلَ الَّتِي تُجَادِلُكَ فِي زَوْجِهَا وَتَشْتَكِي إِلَى اللَّهِ وَاللَّهُ يَسْمَعُ تَحَاوُرَكُمَا إِنَّ اللَّهَ سَمِيعٌ بَصِيرٌ (1)

Indeed Allah has heard the statement of her (Khaulah bint Thalabah) that disputes with you (O Muhammad ﷺ) concerning her husband (Aus bin As-Samit), and complains to Allah. And Allah hears the argument between you both. Verily, Allah is All-Hearer, All-Seer. (Al-Mujadalah:1) (Mujadalah:1)

Her husband was Aws bin Samit ؓ." *(Ibn Abi Hatim in Tafsir Ibn Kathir, Bayhaqi in Asma was Sifat)*

The Statements of Abu Bakr ؓ Concerning Belief in Allah

Abdullah bin Omar ؓ reports that when Rasulullah ﷺ passed away, Abu Bakr ؓ addressed the people saying, "O people! If Muhammad ﷺ was your deity whom you worshipped, then you should know that he has passed away. However, if your deity was the One in the heavens, then you should remember that He will never die." He then recited the verse:

وَمَا مُحَمَّدٌ إِلَّا رَسُولٌ قَدْ خَلَتْ مِنْ قَبْلِهِ الرُّسُلُ أَفَإِنْ مَاتَ أَوْ قُتِلَ انْقَلَبْتُمْ عَلَى أَعْقَابِكُمْ وَمَنْ يَنْقَلِبْ عَلَى عَقِبَيْهِ فَلَنْ يَضُرَّ اللَّهَ شَيْئًا وَسَيَجْزِي اللَّهُ الشَّاكِرِينَ (144)

Muhammad (ﷺ) is no more than a Messenger, and indeed (many) Messengers have passed away before him. If he dies or is killed, will you then turn back on your heels (as disbelievers)? And he who turns back on his heels, not the least harm will he do to Allah, and Allah will give reward to those who are grateful. (Al-Imran:144) (Bukhari in Tarikh, Uthman Darmi in Radd alal Jahamiya, Isfahani in Hujja, Ibn Kathir in Kanzul Ummal)

The sermon that Abu Bakr ؓ delivered has already been quoted in the chapter discussing how the Sahabah rallied around Abu Bakr ؓ. Abu Bakr ؓ said, "Allah had given a lifetime to Rasulullah ﷺ and kept him alive until he established the Deen of Allah, made the commands of Allah explicit, passed on the message of Allah and exerted himself in the Path of Allah. In this condition, Allah then took him away after he had left you on a path. Now whoever dies will die after being exposed to the clear proofs of Iman and the great cure to kufr, which is the Qur'an. Therefore, whoever took Allah as his Rabb should know that Allah is Alive and shall never die. On the other hand, whoever worshipped Muhammad ﷺ and took him as a god should know that their god is no more. Fear Allah, O people! Hold fast to your Deen and rely on your Rabb because the Deen of Allah has been established and the word of Allah is complete. Allah will assist whoever assists the Deen of Allah and it is Allah Who will strengthen His Deen. Indeed, the Book of Allah that is amongst you is a light and a source of healing. It is through this Book that Allah had guided Muhammad ﷺ and it contains the details of the things that Allah has made Halal and what He has made Haram. By Allah! We have no concern for any of Allah's creation that wishes to attack us because the swords of Allah are drawn and we shall never put them down. We shall continue fighting those who oppose us just as we did with Rasulullah ﷺ."

The Statement of Aisha ؓ when a woman passed away in Sejdah

Alqoma narrates from his mother that a woman once entered the room of Aisha ؓ to visit the tomb of Rasulullah ﷺ. She was perfectly healthy when she started performing salah near the grave of Rasulullah ﷺ but she passed away without lifting her head from Sejdah. To this, Aisha ؓ said, "All praise to Allah who gives life and death! There is certainly a lesson in this for me with regard to the death of my brother Abdur Rahman bin Abu Bakr ؓ." Abdur Rahman bin Abu Bakr ؓ had been sleeping one afternoon in the place where he always slept and when some people went to wake him up, they found that he had passed away. This caused Aisha ؓ to doubt whether something foul had been done or whether the people had been too hasty to declare him dead and had buried him alive. Aisha ؓ took a lesson from the sudden death of this woman and the doubts she had surrounding the death of her brother vanished from her heart. *(Hakim)*

Belief in the Angels: The Statement of Ali ؓ Concerning the Turbulence of the Water and Wind When Nation of Nuh عليه السلام and the Nation 'Ad were Destroyed

Ali ؓ once said, "Every drop of water passes through a

measure in the hand of an angel, referring to the *Khazzan* whom Allah has appointed to the task. However, on the day of Nuh علیه السلام when his nation was punished, Allah commanded the water directly without commanding the *Khazzan*. The water therefore went out of the *Khazzan's* control and burst forth. It is for this reason that Allah says: إِنَّا لَمَّا طَغَى الْمَاءُ *Verily! When the water rose beyond its limits (Noah's Flood)... (Al-Haqa:11)*

Similarly, Every gust of wind passes through a measure in the hand of an angel whom Allah has appointed to the task. However, on the day of 'Ad when they were punished, Allah commanded the wind directly without commanding the *Khazzan*. The wind therefore went out of his control. Allah refers to this when He says: بِرِيحٍ صَرْصَرٍ عَاتِيَةٍ (6)

...(for Ad) they were destroyed by a furious violent wind. (Al-Haqa:6) (Ibn Jareer in Kanzul Ummal)

Salman ؓ says at the time of his death, "I have a few visitors who have entered"

Buqaira ؓ who was the wife of Salman ؓ says, "When Salman ؓ was on his deathbed, he called for me to his upper story room that had 4 doors. He said, 'O Buqaira! Open all the doors because I shall have a few visitors today and I know not from which of these doors they will enter. He then asked for some musk and said, 'Dilute it in small container.' When I did this, he said. 'Sprinkle it all around my bed and then go and wait downstairs. When you come to look soon, you shall see something on my bed.' I did as he asked and when I came to see, I saw him lying on his bed with his soul having already departed. He appeared as if he was sleeping." *(Ibn Sa'd)*. Sha'bi reports that when Salman ؓ was on his deathbed, he called for his wife and said, "Bring me the bag I asked you to keep away." When she brought the bag of musk, he asked for a cup of water. He then put some musk into the water and dissolved it by hand. He said, "Sprinkle this around me because such creations of Allah (angels) are coming to me who can smell fragrances but do not eat food. You may then lock the doors behind you and go downstairs." His wife did as he asked and sat for only a short while when she heard a faint sound. When she went upstairs, Salman ؓ had already passed away. *Ata bin Sa'ib* states that Salman ؓ said, "Because tonight some angels will be coming to me who can smell fragrances but do not eat food." *(Ibn Sa'd)*

Belief in Predestination: Rasulullah ﷺ's Words to Aisha ؓ at the Funeral of a Child from the Ansar

Aisha ؓ reports that when Rasulullah ﷺ was called to the funeral of a child from the Ansar, she remarked, "O Rasulullah ﷺ! Glad tiding for him! A sparrow from amongst the sparrows of Jannah! Neither did he do any evil, nor did he reach the age to do any." Rasulullah ﷺ said, "It is not like that, O Aisha! Verily Allah has created Jannah and some people whom He has destined shall be its inhabitants even while they are in the backs of their fathers. Allah has created Jahannam and some people whom He has destined shall be its inhabitants even while they are in the backs of their fathers." *(Muslim in Tafsir Ibn Kathir)*

Ubadah bin Samit ؓ Enjoins his Son to Believe in the Predestination of Good and Evil

Walid bin Ubadah narrates, "I went to see my father Ubadah bin Samit ؓ. He was so ill that I anticipated he would soon pass away. 'Dear father,' I said, 'Do take the pains of advising me.' 'Help me to sit,' he said. We helped him to sit, he said, 'Dear son! You shall never taste Iman and shall never reach the true reality of knowledge about Allah until you believe in the predestination of all good and evil.' 'Dear father!' I asked, 'How shall I know what predestination is good and what is evil?' He replied, 'You should know that whatever fortune or ill-fortune passes you by was never intended to strike you and whatever strikes you was never intended to pass you by. Dear son! I have heard Rasulullah ﷺ say that the first thing that Allah created was the pen. He instructed it to start writing and from that time onwards, it started writing everything that is to happen until the Day of Judgment. Dear son! If you die without subscribing to this belief, you shall be entering Jahannam." *(Ahmad, Tirmidhi in Tasfir Ibn Kathir)*

A Sahabi Weeps on his Deathbed because he knew not What Allah had Destined for Him

Abu Nadhra narrates that a companion of Rasulullah ﷺ known as Abu Abdullah ؓ was weeping when his companions came to visit him. "Why are you weeping?" they asked, "Did Rasulullah ﷺ not say to you, 'Trim your moustache and then remain like this until you meet me', you will be in the company of Rasulullah ﷺ in the Hereafter." "Rasulullah ﷺ did say this," he confirmed, "however, I have also heard Rasulullah ﷺ say, 'Allah grabbed a handful of souls with his right hand and said, 'These are for that Jannah and I care not any more.' Allah grabbed another handful of souls with his other hand and said, 'These are for that Jahannam and I care not any more.' I am weeping because I know not in which handful I was." *(Ahmad, Haythami)*

Mua'dh ؓ Weeps on his Deathbed Because he knew not What Allah had Destined for Him

When death came to Mua'dh bin Jabal ؓ, he started weeping. "What makes you weep?" someone asked. Mua'dh ؓ replied, "By Allah! It is neither fear for death nor an unsettled debt that makes me weep. I heard Rasulullah ﷺ say, 'There were only 2 handfuls of souls that Allah took. While one handful will go to Jahannam, the other will go to Jannah.' I am weeping as I know not in which handful I shall be." *(Tabrani, Haythami)*

What Abdullah bin Abbas ؓ said out People who Contested Belief in Predestination

Muhammad bin Ubaid Makki reports that someone once said to Abdullah bin Abbas ؓ, "A man who denies predestination has come to us." Abdullah bin Abbas ؓ had gone blind by then, so he told the people to lead him to the person. "What will you do with the man?" the people asked. He replied, "I swear by the Being Who controls my life that if I get my hands on him, I will bite his nose until I sever it from his face and should his neck fall in my hands, I shall break it. This is because I heard Rasulullah ﷺ say, 'It is as if I can actually see the Mushrik women of the Banu Fihr shaking their buttocks as they circle the Khazraj. This denying predestination is the first Shirk to take place amongst this Ummah. I swear by the Being Who controls my life that this evil belief will lead them to deny that Allah predestines good just as they will deny that He predestines evil." *(Ahmad)*. Ata bin Abu Rabah relates, "I came to Abdullah bin Abbas ؓ at a time when he was drawing water from the Zamzam well and the bottom of his clothing had already become wet. 'People have started objecting to predestination,' I said. 'Are they really doing that?' he asked. When I confirmed that they were indeed, he said, 'By Allah! It was with reference to them alone that the verse was revealed: ذُوقُوا مَسَّ سَقَرَ (48) إِنَّا كُلَّ شَيْءٍ خَلَقْنَاهُ بِقَدَرٍ (49)

...(it will be said to them): "Taste you the touch of Hell!" Verily, We have created all things with Qadar (Divine Preordainments

of all things before their creation, as written in the Book of Decrees Al-Lauh Al-Mahfooz). (Al-Qamar:48-49)

Such people are the worst of this Ummah! You should neither visit their ill nor perform the Janaza salah for their dead. If I should ever see any of them, I shall pierce his eye with these very fingers of mine." *(Ibn Abi Hatim in Tafsir Ibn Kathir).* Abdullah bin Abbas ؓ once said, "I wish that there was a person who denied predestination with me so that I could trample his head." "Why would you do that?" someone asked. He replied, "Because Allah has created the Lowhul Mahfoodh from a pearl. Its 2 covers are made of rubies, its pen and wiring are of celestial light and its width spans the distance between the heavens and the earth. Every day Allah glances at it 360 times and with every glance He creates, gives life, gives death, gives honor, gives disgrace and does as He pleases." *(Abu Nu'aym in Hilya)*

Abdullah bin Omar ؓ Severs Relations with a Friend who Objected to Predestination

Nafi reports that Abdullah bin Omar ؓ had a friend in Sham with whom he corresponded regularly. Abdullah bin Omar ؓ wrote to him one day saying, "The news has reached me that you have raised some objections to the belief in predestination. I warn you never to write to me again because I have heard Rasulullah ﷺ say, 'There shall be people in my Ummah who will deny predestination.'" *(Ahmad, Abu Dawud in Tafsir Ibn Kahir)*

The Statement of Ali ؓ Concerning Predestination and Those who Object to It

Nazzal bin Sabra narrates that someone once said to Ali ؓ, "O Amirul Mu'minin! There are people here who believe that Allah does not know about something until it actually takes place." "Their mothers ought to have lost them!" Ali ؓ exclaimed, "From where did they deduce this?" The person replied, "It is their interpretation of the verse:

وَلَنَبْلُوَنَّكُمْ حَتَّى نَعْلَمَ الْمُجَاهِدِينَ مِنْكُمْ وَالصَّابِرِينَ وَنَبْلُوَ أَخْبَارَكُمْ (31)

And surely, We shall try you till We test those who strive hard (for the Cause of Allah) and the patient ones, and We shall test your facts (i.e. the one who is a liar, and the one who is truthful). (Muhammad: 31)

Ali ؓ said, "Those without knowledge are destroyed." He then mounted the pulpit, duly praised Allah and said, "O people! Acquire knowledge, practice it and teach it. Whoever finds it difficult to understand any part of the Qur'an should ask me. The news has reached me that some people believe that Allah does not know about something until it actually takes place. They say this because of the misunderstanding they have about the verse:

وَلَنَبْلُوَنَّكُمْ حَتَّى نَعْلَمَ الْمُجَاهِدِينَ مِنْكُمْ

And surely, We shall try you till We test those who strive hard (for the Cause of Allah)... (Muhammad:31)

The words "until we come to know" mean "until we see whether those upon whom striving for Deen and steadfastness have been enjoined actually strive and actually remain steadfast through the hardships that have been destined for them." *(Ibn Abdul Birr in Ilm, Kanzul Ummal).* In chapter on Tawakkul, the narration has passed in which Ali ؓ said, "Nothing happens on earth until it is decided in the heavens. There are 2 angels assigned to every person who protect and guard him. However, when a predestined matter arrives, they leave him to it. I therefore have a fortified shield from Allah which will leave me only when death arrives. No person can taste the sweetness of Iman until he is convinced that whatever difficulty afflicts him would never have passed him by and whatever good passes him

by would never have come to him in the first place."

The Couplets Omar ؓ would Recite on the Pulpit Concerning Predestination

Abdullah bin Mas'ood ؓ reports that very often when delivering a sermon on the pulpit, Omar ؓ would recite the following couplets which mean:

"Go easy on yourself because the destinies of all matters are in Allah's hand
Those that He has thwarted can never come to you just as those that He has commanded can never be let down"
(Bayhaqi in Asma was Sifat)

Belief in the signs of Judgment: The Words of Rasulullah ﷺ When Allah Revealed the verse "When the Trumpet is Blown"

Abdullah bin Abbas ؓ says that when the verse: فَإِذَا نُقِرَ فِي النَّاقُورِ (8)

Then, when the trumpet is sounded (to signal the arrival of Judgment)... (Al-Muddathir:8)

was revealed, Rasulullah ﷺ said, "How can I live in luxury when the blower of the horn already has the horn in his mouth and is waiting with his forehead bowed for the command to blow." The Sahabah then asked, "What Du'a should we make?" Rasulullah ﷺ then told them to recite: حَسْبُنَا اللهِ وَنِعْمَ الْوَكِيلُ، عَلَى اللهِ تَوَكَّلْنَا

"Allah is Sufficient for us and He is the Best of Guardians. In Allah do we trust." *(Ibn Abi Shaibah, Tabrani, Ibn Mardway in Kanzul Ummal).* Another narration states that when the Sahabah heard this from Rasulullah ﷺ, they were troubled and asked, "O Rasulullah ﷺ! What should we do." Rasulullah ﷺ then told them to recite: حَسْبُنَا اللهِ وَنِعْمَ الْوَكِيلُ

"Allah is Sufficient for us and He is the Best of Guardians." *(Bawardi in Kanzul Ummal)*

The Fear of Sauda Yamaniya ؓ for the Appearance of Dajjal

In the chapter discussing the relationships of women in which Hafsa ؓ said to Sauda Yamaniya ؓ, "The one-eyed Dajjal has appeared!" "Really!?" Sauda ؓ cried out. She was extremely shocked and started to shiver. "Where shall I hide?" she asked. "You will have to go to the tent," Hafsa ؓ told her. The tent was made of palm leaves and was a hiding place for the people. It was however filled with dirt and spider webs. Sauda ؓ went to hide there as Rasulullah ﷺ arrived. Seeing the 2 women laughing so much that they were unable to talk, Rasulullah ﷺ asked, "What is all the laughter about?" Rasulullah ﷺ had to repeat the question thrice before they pointed towards the tent. Rasulullah ﷺ went to the tent where he found Sauda ؓ shivering with fear. "What is the matter, O Sauda?" Rasulullah ﷺ asked. "O Rasulullah ﷺ!" she said, "The one-eyed one has appeared." "He has not appeared," Rasulullah ﷺ clarified, "but he is still to appear. He has not appeared but is still to appear." Rasulullah ﷺ helped her out and dusted the dirt and spider webs off her.

The Statements of Abu Bakr ؓ and Abdullah bin Abbas ؓ Concerning Dajjal

Sa'eed bin Musaib narrates that Abu Bakr ؓ once asked, "Is there a place in Iraq called Khurasan?" When he was informed that there was, he said, "Verily Dajjal will emerge from there." *(Ibn Abi Shaybah).* Abu Bakr Siddiq ؓ stated that Dajjal would be from the Jews of a place called Marw. *(Nu'aym bin Hammad in Kanzul Ummal).* Abdullah bin Abu Mulaika ؓ narrates, "When I went to Abdullah bin Abbas ؓ early one morning, he said, 'I have not had a wink of sleep all night' 'Why is that?' I asked. He replied, 'The tailed star has appeared and I now fear that the smoke shall appear, which is a sign of Judgment. It is for this reason that I have not slept all night.'" *(Ibn Jareer in Tafsir Ibn Kathir)* Another similar narration states that Abdullah bin Abbas ﷺ said, "I now fear that Dajjal shall appear." *(Hakim)*

The Words of Abu Bakr Siddiq ﷺ on his Deathbed

Ubadah bin Nasi reports that when death came to Abu Bakr ﷺ, he said to his daughter Aisha ﷺ, "Wash these 2 garments of mine and bury me in them because in the grave your father shall be one of 2 types of men; either one who will be dressed in the best of clothing or one whose garments will be most brutally torn off." *(Ahmad in Zuhd, Muntakhab Kanzul Ummal)*. Aisha ﷺ reports that when Abu Bakr ﷺ was about to pass away, she recited a couplet which means:

"By your life! An abundance of wealth are useless to a youth when his breath heaves one day and his chest tightens as he dies"

"Do not say that, dear daughter," Abu Bakr ﷺ said, "Rather say:

وَجَاءَتْ سَكْرَةُ الْمَوْتِ بِالْحَقِّ ذَلِكَ مَا كُنْتَ مِنْهُ تَحِيدُ (19)

And the stupor of death will come in truth: "This (death) is what you have been avoiding!" (Qaf:19)

He then continued, "Take these 2 garments of mine, wash them and bury me in them. The living needs new clothing more than the dead because the clothing of the dead is intended to be destroyed." *(Ahmad, Ibn Sa'd, Dagholi)*. Aisha ﷺ narrates that when Abu Bakr ﷺ became extremely ill, she started weeping and when he fell unconscious, she recited a couplet:

"When tears are forever veiled, they must burst forth (at some time)"

Abu Bakr ﷺ regained consciousness and said; Do not say that, dear daughter. Rather say:

وَجَاءَتْ سَكْرَةُ الْمَوْتِ بِالْحَقِّ ذَلِكَ مَا كُنْتَ مِنْهُ تَحِيدُ (19)

And the stupor of death will come in truth: "This (death) is what you have been avoiding!" (Qaf:19)

He then asked, "On what day did Rasulullah ﷺ pass away?" "On a Monday," Aisha ﷺ replied. "And what is today?" he asked further. When she informed him that it was a Monday, he said, "I hope in Allah that he will take my soul between now and tonight." He then passed away on Monday night, the night between Monday and Tuesday. Thereafter, Abu Bakr ﷺ asked, "In how many sheets was Rasulullah ﷺ shrouded." Aisha ﷺ replied, "We shrouded him in 3 new white sheets made in *Sahool* that neither included a Qamis nor a turban." He then said, "Wash this cloth of mine that has traces of Saffron and add 2 new sheets with it to complete a shroud of 3." "But it is old," Aisha ﷺ noted. Abu Bakr ﷺ however said, "The living needs new clothing more than the dead because the clothing of the dead are intended to be destroyed." *(Abu Ya'la, Abu Nu'aym, Dagholi, Bayhaqi in Muntakhab Kanzul Ummal)*. Another narration states that he said, "... because it (clothing of the dead) will only be given over to body fluids and decay." *(Ibn Sa'd)*

The Words of Omar ﷺ on his Deathbed

Yahya bin Abu Rashid Nasri narrates that when death approached Omar bin Khattab ﷺ, he said to his son, "Dear son! When death is approaching, turn me on my right side; place your knees against my back, your right hand on my forehead and your left hand beneath my chin. Then when I pass away, close my eyes and shroud me in a shroud of average quality because if there is good in store for me with Allah, He will exchange it for something much better. However, if things are otherwise, He will quickly remove it. You should also give me an average grave

because if there is good in store for me with Allah, He will extend it for me as far as the eyes can see. However, if things are otherwise, He will narrow it so much that my ribs will interlock. Do not take any women along with you for my funeral and do not explain any virtues that were never mine because Allah knows me best. When you are carrying me to the grave then walk swiftly because if there is good in store for me with Allah, you are taking me to something much better. However, if things are otherwise, then you will need to quickly throw off our shoulders a most terrible thing that you are carrying." *(Ibn Sa'd, Ibn Abi Dunya in Qubur, Mutakhab Kanzul Ummal)*. In the chapter discussing the fear that the Khulafa had for Allah, the narration has already passed in which Omar ﷺ said when he was about to die, "I swear by the Being besides Whom there is none worthy of worship that if I owned the world and all its contents, I would have offered it as ransom to be saved from the frightening scene that lies ahead of me." The narration has also passed there in which Omar ﷺ instructed his son Abdullah bin Omar ﷺ to place his head on the ground. When Abdullah moved his head from his lap to the ground, Omar ﷺ said, "My mother and I are destroyed if my Rabb does not have mercy on me!"

The Weeping of Uthman ﷺ Whenever Stood by a Grave

In chapter on the weeping of the Sahabah, the narration stating that whenever Uthman ﷺ stopped at a graveyard, he would weep so much that his beard would get wet. Someone once asked him, "You do not weep when you think of Jannah and Jahannam but weep when you think of the grave?" He replied, "I have heard Rasulullah ﷺ say, 'The grave is the first stage from amongst the many stages of the Hereafter. If one is successful there, the later stages are easier. However, if one is unsuccessful there, the later stages will be extremely difficult'" Uthman ﷺ also added, "I have also heard Rasulullah ﷺ say that he had never seen a sight more frightening than that of the grave."

The Words of Hudhaifa ﷺ on his Deathbed

Khalid bin Rabee narrates that when his tribe and the Ansar heard that Hudhaifa ﷺ was gravely ill, they went to him sometime during the middle of the night or at dawn. "What time is it?" he asked them. When they informed him that it was sometime during the middle of the night or dawn, he remarked, "I seek Allah's protection from the morning of Jahannam." He then asked, "Have you brought something to enshroud me with?" When they told him that they had, he said, "Do not use an expensive shroud because if there is good in store for me by Allah, it will be exchanged for something much better. However, if things are otherwise, it will be quickly removed." *(Bukhari in Adab, Abu Nu'aym in Hilya, Abu Wa'il in Mustadrak, Hakim)*. Sila bin Zufar narrates, "Hudhaifa ﷺ sent Abu Mas'ood ﷺ and me to purchase a burial shroud for him, we bought a striped and decorated sheet for him for 300 Dirhams. 'Show me what you have bought for me,' Hudhaifa ﷺ asked. When we showed it to him, he remarked, 'This shroud is not for me. All I need are 2 plain white sheets without a Qamis because it will be only a short while before it is exchanged for something either much better or worse.' We then proceeded to purchase 2 plain white sheets for him." *(Abu Nu'aym in Hilya)*. Hudhaifa ﷺ said to them, "What will you do with that? If your companion (myself) is a righteous person, Allah will exchange it for something else much better and if your companion is otherwise, it will be thrown from one end of the grave to the other until the Day of Judgment." *(Abu Nu'aym in Hilya)*. He said, "...if your companion is otherwise, Allah will smite his face with it on Day of Judgment." *(Hakim)*

The Words of Abu Musa at the Approach of Death

Dahhak bin Abdur Rahman reports that when death drew close to Abu Musa Ash'ari, he called his attendants and instructed them, "Go and dig me a wide and deep grave." They complied and returned saying, "We have dug your grave wide and deep." Abu Mosa then said, "By Allah! The grave is one of 2 places. It may either be broadened so much that each corner is 40 arm's length wide. Then a door to Jannah will be opened for me so that I can look at my wives and my palaces and every other token of hospitality that Allah has prepared for me. I will then know my way to that home better than I know my home in this world today. Thereafter the breeze and comforts of Jannah shall reach me until the Day of Judgment. However, if things are otherwise - may Allah protect us from it - my grave shall narrow around me until it is narrower than the end of a spear where it meets the head. Then a door to Jahannam will be opened for me from which I can look at my chains, yokes and fellow inmates. I will then know my way to that home better than I know my home in this world today. Thereafter the smoke and fire of Jahannam shall reach me until the day I am resurrected."

Usaid bin Hudhair Longs to be in One of 3 Conditions

Aisha narrates that Usaid bin Hudhair was the best of people. He would say, "I have no doubts about being amongst the inhabitants of Jannah if I could remain in 1 of 3 conditions. (1) The condition when I am reciting Qur'an or listening to it being recited, (2) the condition when I am listening to Rasulullah's sermon and (3) the condition when I am present at a funeral. At every funeral I have been, I have thought about nothing other than what will be of the deceased or where it is heading." (Abu Nu'aym, Bayhaqi, Ibn Asakir in Muntakhab Kanzul Ummal).

Belief in the Hereafter: Rasulullah's Description of Jannah

Abu Hurairah narrates that the Sahabah once said, "O Rasulullah! Whenever we see you, our hearts are softened and we think only of the Hereafter. However, when we separate from you, the world appeals to us and we start smelling (enjoying) our wives and children." Rasulullah consoled them saying, "Should you remain at all times in the state you are when with me, the angels will actually shake your hands with theirs and visit you in your homes, this is however impossible. If you do not sin, Allah will replace you with a nation that does sin merely so that He may forgive them when they repent because He loves to forgive." The Sahabah asked further, "O Rasulullah! Tell us about Jannah and its buildings." Rasulullah described, "One brick of the buildings will be gold and the next silver with cement made of fragrant musk. The pebbles will be pearls and rubies while the grass will be saffron. Whoever enters Jannah shall only enjoy luxuries and never experience any difficulty. He will live forever without ever dying. Neither will his clothing fade nor will his youth ever fade. There are 3 persons whose Du'as are never rejected; the just ruler, the fasting person until he terminates fast and oppressed person. Their Du'a is lifted above the clouds where the doors of the heavens are opened and Allah says, 'I swear by My honor that I shall definitely assist you even though it may be after some time." (Ahmad in Tafsir Ibn Kathir)

The Incident of Fatima When she Went to Her Father for Something of Benefit in This World and Returned with Something of Benefit in the Hereafter

Suwaid bin Ghafala narrates that when Ali was suffering extreme hunger one day, he suggested his wife Fatima to approach her father Rasulullah for some food. When she went to Rasulullah, Ummu Ayman happened to be there. Hearing Fatima knocked on the door, Rasulullah said, "That is the knock of Fatima. She has come at a time that we are not accustomed to having her come to us." "O Rasulullah!" Fatima said, "The food of the angels is to recite 'La Ilaha IllAllah', 'SubhanAllah' and 'Al Hamdu Lillah'. What is our food?" Rasulullah replied, "I swear by the Being Who has sent me with the truth! For the last 30 days, no fire to cook has been lit in the house of the family of Muhammad. However, a few goats have come to us. If you please, I shall have 5 given to you. Alternatively, if you so please, I shall teach you 5 words of supplication that Jibra'el has taught me." Fatima immediately said, "Do rather teach me the 5 words that Jibra'el has taught you." Rasulullah then told her to say the following words: يَا أَوَّلَ الأَوَّلِيْنَ وَيَا اَخِرَ لاخِرِيْنَ وَيَا ذَالْقُوَّةِ الْمَتِيْنَ وَيَا رَاحِمَ الْمَسَاكِيْنَ وَيَا أَرْاحِمِيْنَ

Fatima then left and when she came back to Ali, he asked, "What happened?" She replied, "While I left you to get something of benefit in this world, I returned with something of benefit in the Hereafter." "This is the best of all your days," Ali remarked. (Abu Shaikh in Kanzul Ummal)

The Statement of Abu Musa Ash'ari Concerning the Reason for People Being Unaware of the Hereafter

Anas bin Malik reports that they were on a journey with Abu Musa Ash'ari when he heard people talking and having eloquent discussions. "O Anas," he said, "what benefit is there for me in that. Come, let us engage in the Dhikr of our Rabb because it seems like those people can even skin a person with their tongues." He then asked, "O Anas! What has made the people delay in matters of the Hereafter and what has made them unaware of it?" "Their desires and Saitan," Anas replied. "No, by Allah!" Abu Musa said, "It is because the world is before them and the Hereafter is still to come. Had they witnessed the Hereafter, they would never turn away from it and never incline towards the world." (Abu Nu'aym in Hilya)

Belief in the what is to happen on the Day of Judgment: Rasulullah's Desire for his Ummah to Comprise of Half the People of Jannah

Imran bin Husain narrates that Rasulullah was on a journey when the verse was revealed:

يَا أَيُّهَا النَّاسُ اتَّقُوْا رَبَّكُمْ إِنَّ زَلْزَلَةَ السَّاعَةِ شَيْءٌ عَظِيْمٌ (1) يَوْمَ تَرَوْنَهَا تَذْهَلُ كُلُّ مُرْضِعَةٍ عَمَّا أَرْضَعَتْ وَتَضَعُ كُلُّ ذَاتِ حَمْلٍ حَمْلَهَا وَتَرَى النَّاسَ سُكَارَى وَمَا هُمْ بِسُكَارَى وَلَكِنَّ عَذَابَ الله شَدِيْدٌ (2)

O mankind! Fear your Lord and be dutiful to Him! Verily, the earthquake of the Hour (of Judgment) is a terrible thing. The Day you shall see it, every nursing mother will forget her nursling, and every pregnant one will drop her load, and you shall see mankind as in a drunken state, yet they will not be drunken, but severe will be the Torment of Allah. (Al-Hajj:1-2)

Rasulullah then asked the Sahabah, "Do you know what day is that?" "Allah and His Rasul know best," the Sahabah submitted. Rasulullah then explained, "That will be the day when Allah shall say to Adam, 'Dispatch the people of Jahannam.' 'O my Rabb!' Adam will say, 'Who are those to be dispatched to Jahannam?' Allah will reply, '(From every 1,000) 999 shall go to Jahannam and one will go to Jannah.'" This made the Sahabah weep. Rasulullah then said to them, "Adopt moderation and continue treading the straight path. Remember that before the coming of every Nabi is a period of ignorance.

The quota for Jahannam will first be completed from these people. Otherwise if they are not sufficient, it will be completed from the hypocrites. Your example and that of other nations is like a little lump on the foreleg of an animal or like a mole on the side of a camel. I however have great hope that you people (members of my Ummah) will comprise 1/4th of the people of Jannah." "Allahu Akbar!" the Sahabah exclaimed. Rasulullah ﷺ then added, "In fact, I have great hope that you people will comprise 1/3rd of the people of Jannah." Again the Sahabah exclaimed, "Allahu Akbar!" Thereafter, Rasulullah ﷺ said, "I also have great hope that you people will comprise 1/2 the people of Jannah." This time again the Sahabah cried out, "Allahu Akbar!" The narrator says that he is not sure whether or not Rasulullah ﷺ later said that he had hopes of them being as much as 2/3 of the people of Jannah. (Tirmidhi, Ahmad, Ibn Abi Hatim). A narration from Abu Sa'eed Khudri ؓ also discussing the explanation of the above verse states that Nabi ﷺ said, "On the Day of Judgment, Allah will call for Adam الﻌﻠﻴﻪ. He will respond by saying, 'At your service, Our Rabb! It is an honor to serve you.' A voice will then tell him, 'Allah commands you to remove from your progeny those to be dispatched to Jahannam.' 'O my Rabb!' Adam الﻌﻠﻴﻪ will say, 'Who are those to be dispatched to Jahannam?' Allah will reply, '(From every 1,000) 999 shall go to Jahannam and one will go to Jannah.' It is on this occasion that expected mothers will abort their fetuses and youngsters will turn white. وَتَرَى النَّاسَ سُكَارَى وَمَا هُمْ بِسُكَارَى وَلَكِنَّ عَذَابَ اللَّهِ شَدِيدٌ (2)

...and you shall see mankind as in a drunken state, yet they will not be drunken, but severe will be the Torment of Allah. (Hajj:2)

This had a great impact on the Sahabah and their faces actually turned pale. Rasulullah ﷺ then said, "(From every 1,000) 999 will be from the Ya'juj Ma'juj and only one shall be from amongst you. Compared to the rest of people, you resemble only a single black hair on the side of a white bull or only a single white hair on the side of a black bull. I have great hope that you people (members of my Ummah) will comprise a quarter of the people of Jannah." The Sahabah, exclaimed, "Allahu Akbar!" Rasulullah ﷺ then added, "In fact, I have great hope that you people will comprise a 1/3 of the people of Jannah." Again the Sahabah exclaimed, "Allahu Akbar!" Thereafter, Rasulullah ﷺ said, "I also have great hope that you people will comprise 1/2 the people of Jannah." This time again the Sahabah cried out, "Allahu Akbar!" (Bukhari, Muslim, Nasa'ee in Tafsir Ibn Kathir). Another narration states that what Rasulullah ﷺ said about 999 going to Jahannam, the impact was heavy on the Sahabah and they became very grieved and worried.

Zubair ؓ asks Rasulullah ﷺ About Conditions in the Hereafter

Abdullah bin Zubair ؓ reports that when the verse:

ثُمَّ إِنَّكُمْ يَوْمَ الْقِيَامَةِ عِندَ رَبِّكُمْ تَخْتَصِمُونَ (31)

Then, on the Day of Resurrection, you will be disputing (against each other) before your Lord. (Az-ZOmar:31)

was revealed, Zubair ؓ asked, "O Rasulullah ﷺ! Will cases be repeatedly brought against us?" When Rasulullah ﷺ replied in the affirmative, Zubair ؓ remarked, "In that case, the matter will be a serious one indeed." (Ibn Abi Hatim)

Another narration adds the verse: ثُمَّ لَتُسْأَلُنَّ يَوْمَئِذٍ عَنِ النَّعِيمِ (8)

Then on that day (of Judgment) you shall be asked about the delights (you indulged in, in this world). (At-Takathur:8)

was revealed, Zubair ؓ asked, "O Rasulullah ﷺ! What types of bounties will we questioned about when all that we have are the 2 black things; dates and water?" (Ahmad, Tirmidhi, Ibn Majah) Yet another narration states that when the verse:

إِنَّكَ مَيِّتٌ وَإِنَّهُم مَّيِّتُونَ (30) ثُمَّ إِنَّكُمْ يَوْمَ الْقِيَامَةِ عِندَ رَبِّكُمْ تَخْتَصِمُونَ (31)

Verily you (O Rasulullah ﷺ) will die, and verily they (too) will die. Then, on the Day of Resurrection, you will be disputing (against each other) before your Lord. (Az-ZOmar:30-31)

was revealed, Zubair ؓ asked, "O Rasulullah ﷺ! Together with having to account for specific sins, will cases be repeatedly brought against us regarding the dealings we have between each other?" "Certainly," Rasulullah ﷺ replied, "cases will be brought until everyone to whom a right is due receives his right." "By Allah!" Zubair ؓ remarked, "In that case, the matter will be a serious indeed." (Ahmad, Tirmidhi in Tafsir Ibn Kathir, Hakim)

Abdullah bin Rawaha ؓ Weeps at the Thought of a Verse Concerning Jahannam

Qais bin Abu Hazim reports that Abdullah bin Rawaha ؓ was lying down in his wife's lap when he started to weep. His wife also started to weep. "What makes you weep?" he asked. "Seeing you weep has made me weep also," she replied. He said, "I thought of the verse: وَإِن مِّنكُمْ إِلَّا وَارِدُهَا كَانَ عَلَى رَبِّكَ حَتْمًا مَّقْضِيًّا (71)

There is not one of you but will pass over it (Hell); this is with your Lord; a Decree which must be accomplished. (Maryam:71)

I am weeping because I know not whether I shall be rescued from it or not." A narration states that Abdullah bin Rawaha ؓ was ill at the time. (Abdul Razzaq in Tafsir Ibn Kathir)

Ubadah ؓ asks his Family and Neighbors to Take Retribution From Him When Death Approached

Ubadah bin Muhammad bin Ubadah bin Samit narrates that when death approached Ubadah bin Samit ؓ, he requested that his slaves, servants, neighbors and everyone associated with him should be gathered. When they had all gathered, he said, "I expect that this will be my last day in this world and my first night in the Hereafter. I know not whether my hands or tongue may have caused you any harm which - I swear by the Being Who controls my life - will be a cause for retribution to be taken from me on the Day of Judgment. It is with great emphasis that I stress to each one of you in whose heart is something about this that he must take retribution from me before my soul departs." Because Ubadah ؓ had never spoken ill even to his servants, everyone said, "You were a father and a mentor to us, we therefore have no grievance against you." Ubadah ؓ then asked, "Do you then forgive anything of the sort that may have happened?" When they said that they did, Ubadah ؓ said, "O Allah! You be witness!" He then continued, "Since there is nothing of the sort, then remember this parting advice of mine. It is with great emphasis that I stress to each one of you not to weep for me. When my soul departs, each of you should perform wudhu properly, go to the Masjid, perform salah and then seek Allah's forgiveness for Ubadah and his soul because Allah says: وَاسْتَعِينُوا بِالصَّبْرِ وَالصَّلَاةِ

......And seek help in patience and As-Salat. (Al-Baqara:45, 153)

You should hasten with my corpse to the grave without following me with any fire and without placing a purple cloth beneath me." (Bayhaqi, Ibn Asakir in Kanzul Ummal)

Omar ؓ's Fear for Reckoning on the Day of Judgment

In chapter on cautiousness in spending, the narration has already passed in which Omar ؓ asked Abdur Rahman bin Auf ؓ for a loan of 4,000 Dirhams. Abdur Rahman bin Auf ؓ sent a message back with the messenger that Omar ؓ should take the loan from the public treasury and pay it back later. When the message reached him, Omar ؓ felt it most difficult to do so.

When Omar ؓ met Abdur Rahman bin Auf ؓ, he asked him, "Are you the one who said that I should take the money from the public treasury? Should I die before the caravan returns, you would say, 'The Amirul Mu'minin had taken the money. Let us waive it.' I shall be taken to task for it on the Day of Judgment."

The Weeping of Abu Hurairah ؓ and Mu'awiya ؓ When They Heard a Hadith About the Hereafter

In chapter on being influenced by the knowledge of Allah and of Rasulullah ﷺ, it will be narrated in which Abu Hurairah ؓ gave heavy sigh and collapsed upon his face when he mentioned in the Hadith concerning Allah's taking accountability from a man knowledge about the Qur'an, a wealthy person and a martyred in the Path of Allah. It will InshaAllah be narrated that how Mu'awiya ؓ wept so much when he heard this Hadith that the people thought he would die.

Belief in intercession: Rasulullah ﷺ says, "My Intercession shall be for Those Members of my Ummah who Never Commit Shirk"

Auf bin Malik ؓ reports, "We were with Rasulullah ﷺ when we set up camp towards the end of the night. Laying down our heads by the foot of our carriages, we all went to sleep. I awoke sometime during the night and was alarmed when I did not see Rasulullah ﷺ by his carriage. I then started to search for Rasulullah ﷺ, I found Abu Musa Ash'ari ؓ and Mu'adh bin Jabal ؓ, also alarmed by the same thing that alarmed me. As we stood in that condition, we heard a sound from the top of the valley that resembled the sound of a grindstone grinding. We headed in that direction, we found Rasulullah ﷺ and we then informed him what our concern was. Rasulullah ﷺ explained, 'An angel came to me from my Rabb giving me a choice between intercession and having 1/2 my Ummah admitted into Jannah. I chose intercession because in this way there was hope of even more being admitted into Jannah.' 'O Nabi of Allah ﷺ!' I pleaded, 'I ask you in the name of Allah and in consideration of our relationship with you to include us amongst those you will be interceding for.' 'You people shall certainly be amongst those I will be interceding for,' Rasulullah ﷺ confirmed. We then accompanied Rasulullah ﷺ back to the camp where we found all the others also alarmed by Rasulullah ﷺ's absence. Rasulullah ﷺ then explained to them saying, 'An angel came to me from my Rabb giving me a choice between intercession and having 1/2 my Ummah admitted into Jannah. I chose intercession.' 'O Nabi of Allah ﷺ!' they pleaded, 'We ask you in the name of Allah and in consideration of our relationship with you to include us amongst those you will be interceding for.' When they had all gathered around Rasulullah ﷺ, he said, 'I make everyone present here witness to the fact that my intercession shall be for those members of my Ummah who never commit Shirk.'" (Baghawi, Ibn Asakir in Kanzul Ummal)

The Du'a Rasulullah ﷺ will Make for his Ummah Before Allah shall be his Intercession on Their Behalf

Abdur Rahman bin Abu Aqil ؓ reports, "I went to Rasulullah ﷺ with a delegation from the Thaqif tribe. We made our animals sit at the door, there was not a person we hated more than the man we had come to see. By the time we left, there was no one more loved to us than the man we had been to see. One of us said, 'O Rasulullah ﷺ! Why don't you ask Allah for a kingdom like the kingdom of Sulaiman عليه السلام?' Rasulullah ﷺ laughed and said, 'Your companion here (myself) shall perhaps receive something better from Allah than the kingdom of Sulaiman عليه السلام. Allah has granted every Nabi عليه السلام that He sent a special prayer that is sure to be accepted. There were those who used the prayer

for this world while others used it to curse their nations when they disobeyed them. It was because of it that these nations were destroyed. Allah granted me one such prayer that I have kept in store with my Rabb and shall use it to intercede for my Ummah on the Day of Judgment." (Baghawi, Ibn Mandah, Ibn Asakir in Kanzul Ummal, Bukhari, Harith bin Abu Usanah in Isabah)

Rasulullah ﷺ says, "I am an excellent man for the Sinners of my Ummah"

Ummu Salama ؓ narrates that Rasulullah ﷺ once said, "I am an excellent man for the sinners of my Ummah." "O Rasulullah ﷺ!" a man from the Muzaina tribe asked, "If you are such for the sinful ones, then what about the righteous ones?" Rasulullah ﷺ replied, "While the righteous ones of my Ummah shall enter Jannah because of their good deeds, the sinners shall await my intercession. My intercession shall be available to every member of my Ummah, it will not be for a person who diminishes the rank of my Sahabah." (Shirazi in Alqab, Ibn Najjar in Kanzul Ummal)

The Verse of the Qur'an that Kindles Most Hope According to Ali ؓ

Ali bin Abi Talib ؓ narrates that Rasulullah ﷺ once said, "I shall continue interceding on behalf of my Ummah until my Rabb asks, 'Are you now satisfied, O Muhammad?' I shall then say, 'Yes. I am satisfied.' Turning to the people, Ali ؓ said, 'O people of Iraq! Don't you people believe that the verse of the Qur'an that kindles the most hope is the verse:

قُلْ يَا عِبَادِيَ الَّذِينَ أَسْرَفُوا عَلَى أَنْفُسِهِمْ لَا تَقْنَطُوا مِنْ رَحْمَةِ اللَّهِ إِنَّ اللَّهَ يَغْفِرُ الذُّنُوبَ جَمِيعًا إِنَّهُ هُوَ الْغَفُورُ الرَّحِيمُ (53)

Say: O Ibadee (My slaves) who have transgressed against themselves (by committing evil deeds and sins)! Despair not of the Mercy of Allah, verily Allah forgives all sins. Truly, He is Oft-Forgiving, Most Merciful. (Az-ZOmar:53)

When the people admitted that they believed so, Ali ؓ said, "However, we who are members of Rasulullah ﷺ's family believe that the verse of the Qur'an that kindles the hope is the verse:

وَلَسَوْفَ يُعْطِيكَ رَبُّكَ فَتَرْضَى (5) *And verily, your Lord will give you (all good) so that you will be well-pleased. (Ad-Duha:5).*

What Allah will grant Rasulullah ﷺ shall be the privilege of intercession." (Ibn Mardway in Kanzul Ummal)

The Statement of Buraida ؓ in Front of Mu'awiya ؓ Concerning Intercession

Ibn Buraida narrates that his father Buraida ؓ went to Mu'awiya ؓ where a man was busy talking in praise of Mu'awiya ؓ. "Will you permit me to speak, O Mu'awiya," Buraida ؓ asked. Thinking that he will also speak as the previous person was doing, Mu'awiya ؓ granted him permission. Buraida ؓ said, "I heard Rasulullah ﷺ say, 'On the Day of Judgment I expect to intercede on behalf of as many people as there are trees and stones on earth.' You, O Mu'awiya should pin your hopes in this because you will need it while Ali ؓ need not pin his hopes as he will enter Jannah without it." (Ahmad in Tafsir Ibn Kathis)

The Reply Jabir ؓ Gave a Person who Denied Intercession

Talq bin Habib says, "I was a person who strongly denied intercession until I met Jabir ؓ. After I recited to him all the verses of the Qur'an I could recite that spoke of the people of Jahannam remaining there forever, he said, 'O Talq! Do you think that you have more knowledge of the Qur'an and the Sunnah than I? The verses you have recited refer to those who belong in Jahannam. They are the disbelievers. However, those for whom intercession will take place are people (Mu'minin) who have sinned, who will be punished for their sins and then be removed from Jahannam.' He then held both his ears and said, 'May these become deaf if I have not heard Rasulullah ﷺ say that they will leave Jahannam after having entered it because of Rasulullah ﷺ's intercession. We also recite the Qur'an as you recite." (Ibn Mardway). Yazid Faqir reports, "I was once sitting with Jabir bin Abdullah ﷺ as he was busy narrating Ahadeeth. When he narrated that some people would leave Jahannam, I became very angry because during those days I was one who rejected such a belief. I therefore said, 'I am not as astonished with common people making such statements as I am astonished with you companions of Rasulullah ﷺ! You believe that people will leave the fire of Jahannam when Allah says:

يُرِيدُونَ أَنْ يَخْرُجُوا مِنَ النَّارِ وَمَا هُم بِخَارِجِينَ مِنْهَا وَلَهُمْ عَذَابٌ مُقِيمٌ (37)

They will long to get out of the Fire, but never will they get out from there, and theirs will be a lasting torment. (Al-Ma'idah:37)
His companions started rebuking me, but he was the most tolerant of them all. 'Leave the man alone!' he said. He then explained, 'That verse refers to the Kuffar.' He then recited the verse: إِنَّ الَّذِينَ كَفَرُوا لَوْ أَنَّ لَهُم مَّا فِي الْأَرْضِ جَمِيعًا وَمِثْلَهُ مَعَهُ لِيَفْتَدُوا بِهِ مِنْ عَذَابِ يَوْمِ الْقِيَامَةِ مَا تُقُبِّلَ مِنْهُمْ وَلَهُمْ عَذَابٌ أَلِيمٌ (36) يُرِيدُونَ أَنْ يَخْرُجُوا مِنَ النَّارِ وَمَا هُم بِخَارِجِينَ مِنْهَا وَلَهُمْ عَذَابٌ مُقِيمٌ (37) *Verily, those who disbelieve, if they had all that is in the earth, and as much again therewith to ransom themselves thereby from the torment on the Day of Resurrection, it would never be accepted of them, and theirs would be a painful torment. They will long to get out of the Fire, but never will they get out from there, and theirs will be a lasting torment. (Al-Ma'idah:36-37).*
He then asked, 'Do you recite the Qur'an?' 'I certainly do,' I replied, 'in fact, I have memorized it.' He then said, 'Does Allah not say: وَمِنَ اللَّيْلِ فَتَهَجَّدْ بِهِ نَافِلَةً لَّكَ عَسَى أَن يَبْعَثَكَ رَبُّكَ مَقَامًا مَّحْمُودًا (79)
And in some parts of the night (also) offer the Salat (prayer) with it (i.e. recite the Qur'an in the prayer), as an additional prayer (Tahajjud optional prayer Nawafil) for you (O Muhammad ﷺ). It may be that your Lord will raise you to Maqaman Mahmooda (a station of praise and glory, i.e. the honor of intercession on the Day of Resurrection!). (Al-Isra:79). That Maqam Mahmood is the position of intercession. Allah will detain some people in Jahannam for a while because of their sins without speaking to them. When Allah wills, He will remove them from Jahannam.'" Yazid says, "After this, I never repeated mistake of denying this belief." (lbn Abi Hatim in Kanzul Ummal)

The Sahabah Picture the Scene of Jannah in a Gathering with Rasulullah ﷺ as if They can Actually see it Before Their Eyes

Handhala Katib Usaidi ﷺ who was one of Rasulullah ﷺ's scribes narrates, "We were with Rasulullah ﷺ when we spoke of Jannah and Jahannam with so much conviction that it seemed to appear before our very eyes. I then went to my wife and children with whom I started laughing and playing. However, when I thought of the state of mind I had been in with Rasulullah ﷺ, I left the house. I then met Abu Bakr ﷺ, to whom 1 said, "O Abu Bakr! I have become a Munafiq.' 'Why do you say that?' he asked. I explained, 'When we are with Nabi ﷺ and he speaks to us about Jannah and Jahannam, it seems as if it is before our very eyes. When we leave his presence and become engrossed with our wives, children and occupations, we forget.' Abu Bakr ﷺ remarked, 'But we do the same.' I approached Rasulullah ﷺ and mentioned this to him. Rasulullah ﷺ said, 'O Handhala! If you

can be with your families as you are when you are with me, the angels will actually shake hands with you on your beds and on the street. O Handhala! There are times for this and times for that." (Hasan bin Sufian, Abu Nu'aym in Kanzul Ummal)

Rasulullah ﷺ Tells the Sahabah About the Last Day

Abdullah bin Mas'ood ﷺ narrates that one night they spent a long time speaking to Rasulullah ﷺ. When they went to him early the following morning, Rasulullah ﷺ said, "I was shown the Ambiya عليهم السلام and their Ummahs (nations). As the Ambiya عليهم السلام passed by me, I would see a Nabi with a group of followers, another with 3 persons and another with no followers at all" At this juncture Qatadah recited the verse: (78) أَلَيْسَ مِنكُمْ رَجُلٌ رَّشِيدٌ
…Is there not among you a single right-minded man? (Hud:78)
Rasulullah ﷺ continued, "Eventually Musa bin Imran عليه السلام passed by me with a large group of the Bani Isra'el. I asked, 'O Rabb! Who is this?' 'This,' I was told, 'is your brother Musa and those of the Bani Isra'el who followed him,' I then asked, 'Dear Rabb! And where is my Ummah?' 'Look to your right amongst the hills,' Allah said. When I looked, I saw the faces of scores of people,' 'Are you satisfied?' Allah asked. 'I am satisfied, my Rabb,' I replied. Allah then said, 'Now look to the horizon on your left.' When I looked, I again saw the faces of scores of people.' 'Are you satisfied?' Allah asked again and again I replied by saying, 'I am satisfied, my Rabb.' Allah then said further, 'Verily with these there are also 70,000 who will enter Jannah without reckoning.'" At that moment, Ukasha bin Mihsin ﷺ who was a veteran of the Battle of Badr said, "O Nabi of Allah ﷺ! Pray to Allah to include me amongst them." "O Allah!" Rasulullah ﷺ prayed, "Include him amongst them." Another man then stood up with the request, "O Nabi of Allah ﷺ! Pray to Allah to include me amongst them as well" Rasulullah ﷺ however, said, "Ukasha has beat you to it." Rasulullah ﷺ then said, "May my parents be sacrificed for you! If you are able to include yourselves amongst the 70,000, you should certainly do so. Otherwise, you must include yourselves amid the men amongst the hills or amongst the men on the horizon because I have seen a great many whose conditions were unlike these. I however have great hope that you people (members of my Ummah) will comprise a 1/3rd. Rasulullah ﷺ then added, "In fact, I have great hope that you people will comprise 1/2 of the people of Jannah." Again the Sahabah exclaimed, "Allahu Akbar!" Thereafter, Rasulullah ﷺ recited the verses: (40) ثُلَّةٌ مِّنَ الْأَوَّلِينَ (39) وَثُلَّةٌ مِّنَ الْآخِرِينَ
A multitude of those (on the Right Hand) will be from the first generation (who embraced Islam). And a multitude of those (on the Right Hand) will be from the later times (generations). (Al-Waqi'a:39-40)
The Sahabah later started discussing amongst themselves about who the 70,000 would be, some opined, "They must be those who were born to Muslims and then never committed Shirk." When this reached Rasulullah ﷺ, he clarified saying, "They will be those who never brand themselves with something hot as a form of treatment, who never use charms, never divine with birds and who have trust only in their Rabb." (Ibn Abi Hatim, Ibn Jareer in Tafsir Ibn Kathir, Muntadrak, Hakim)

A Bedouin Asks Rasulullah ﷺ About a Tree in Jannah

Sulaim bin Amir reports that the Sahabah always used to say, "Verily Allah gave us tremendous benefit from the Bedouins and their questions." A Bedouin came one day and said, "O Rasulullah ﷺ! Allah has mentioned a tree in Jannah that is harmful to its owner." "What tree is that?" Rasulullah ﷺ asked,

"It is the lotus tree that has thorns which can hurt a person." Rasulullah ﷺ replied, "Does Allah not say: (28) فِي سِدْرٍ مَخْضُودٍ *(They will be) among thornless lote-trees. (Al-Waqi'a:28)*

Allah will remove the thorns from the trees and replace each of them with a fruit. The tree will actually grow fruit and each fruit will have 72 different flavors, with no 2 flavors being alike." *(Ibn Najjar).* Utba bin Abdus Sulami ﷺ reports that he was sitting with Rasulullah ﷺ when a Bedouin arrived and said, "O Rasulullah ﷺ! I hear you speak about a tree in Jannah that has more thorns than any other tree I know, the acacia tree." Rasulullah ﷺ replied, "Allah will remove the thorns from the trees and replace each of them with a fruit resembling the testes of a large goat. Each fruit will have 72 different flavors with no 2 flavors being alike." *(Ibn Abu Dawud in Kanzul Ummal)*

A Bedouin asks Rasulullah ﷺ About the Fruit of Jannah

Utba bin Abdus Sulami ﷺ reports that a Bedouin once came to Rasulullah ﷺ to enquire about the pond (Kowthar) and to speak about Jannah. He asked, "Are there fruits there?" "Of course," Rasulullah ﷺ replied, "And there is also a tree there called Tuba." The narrator says that Rasulullah ﷺ then mentioned a few other things that he cannot recall. However, the Bedouin then asked, "Which tree in our region resembles the trees of Jannah?" Rasulullah ﷺ replied, "There is nothing there resembling the trees in your region, but have you been to Sham?" When the Bedouin said that he had not, Rasulullah said, "There is a tree in Sham that bears a resemblance. The tree is the walnut tree, which grows on a single trunk with the upper branches spreading out." The Bedouin asked further, What is the size of its clusters?" Rasulullah ﷺ replied, "The distance a spotted crow flies in a month." "And what is the size of its roots?" he asked. Rasulullah ﷺ said, "Should one of your young camels start traveling, it will be unable to cover the distance of its roots even after its ribs break because of old age." The Bedouin asked further, "Are there grapes in Jannah?" "There are," Rasulullah ﷺ replied. "Then," the Bedouin 'asked, "What is the size of a grape?" "Has your father slaughtered a large goat?" Rasulullah ﷺ asked. When he replied in the affirmative, Rasulullah ﷺ asked further, "And then did he skin the goat and give your mother the skin saying, 'Make this into a bucket for us?'" "Oh yes," the Bedouin replied. Each grape will be the size of such a bucket. The Bedouin then asked, "Then will such a grape be able to fill my family and me?" "Certainly," Rasulullah ﷺ replied, "and it will also fill most of your tribe." *(Ahmad in Tafsir Ibn Kathir)*

An Abyssinian Man Dies in Rasulullah ﷺ's Gathering after Hearing the Description of Jannah

Abdullah bin Omar ﷺ narrates that an Abyssinian man once came to Rasulullah ﷺ. "Ask what you wish," Rasulullah ﷺ said to him. The man said, "O Rasulullah ﷺ! You people have been favored above us in terms of looks, complexion and now Prophethood. Tell me. If I believe in all that you believe in and do as you do, will I be with you in Jannah?" "Of course," Rasulullah ﷺ replied. Rasulullah ﷺ then added, "In fact, I swear by the Being Who controls my life that the brilliant complexion of a black person will be seen in Jannah from a distance of 1,000 years, Whoever recites 'La Ilaha IllAllah' has entered into a pledge with Allah and whoever recites *'SubhanAllah wa Bihamdihi'* shall earn the reward of 124,000 good deeds." The man asked further, "How will we be destroyed after this, O Rasulullah ﷺ?" Rasulullah ﷺ said, "A person will come on the Day of Judgment with so many good deeds that they will be even

too heavy for a mountain to bear. Thereafter, Allah's bounties to the person will be brought to be paid for by the good deeds and if it were not for Allah's mercy enshrouding the person, the bounties would surely exhaust all the deeds. Thereafter Allah revealed the verses:

هَلْ أَتَى عَلَى الْإِنْسَانِ حِينٌ مِنَ الدَّهْرِ لَمْ يَكُنْ شَيْئًا مَذْكُورًا (1)..........

وَإِذَا رَأَيْتَ ثَمَّ رَأَيْتَ نَعِيمًا وَمُلْكًا كَبِيرًا (20)

Has there not been over man a period of time, when he was nothing to be mentioned?.......And when you look there (in Paradise), you will see a delight (that cannot be imagined), and a great dominion. (Ad-Dahr:1-20)

The Abyssinian then asked, "Will my eyes be able to see whatever your eyes will see in Jannah?" "Most assuredly," Rasulullah ﷺ replied. The man then started weeping until he passed away. Abdullah bin Omar ﷺ says, "I saw Rasulullah ﷺ personally lowering the man's body into the grave." *(Tabrani in Tafsir Ibn Kathir).* Abdullah bin Wahab reports from Ibn Zaid ﷺ that an Abyssinian man was with Rasulullah ﷺ when Allah revealed the Surah: هَلْ أَتَى عَلَى الْإِنْسَانِ حِينٌ مِنَ الدَّهْرِ لَمْ يَكُنْ شَيْئًا مَذْكُورًا (1) *Has there not been over man a period of time, when he was nothing to be mentioned? (Ad-Dahr:1)*

Rasulullah ﷺ recited the Surah to the Sahabah and when he reached the verses describing Jannah, he gave a deep sigh and passed away. Rasulullah ﷺ remarked, "It was the longing for Jannah that took out the soul of your brother." *(Tafsir Ibn Kathir)*

Ali ﷺ gives Omar ﷺ the Glad Tidings of Jannah on His Deathbed

Abu Matar reports that he heard Ali ﷺ say, "When Omar ﷺ was stabbed by Abu Lu'lu, I went to him and found him weeping. 'What makes you weep, O Amirul Mu'minin?' I asked. He replied, 'It is the news from the heavens that makes me weep. I know not whether I shall be taken to Jannah or to Jahannam.' I then said to him, 'Rejoice with the glad tidings of Jannah because more times than I can count I have heard Rasulullah ﷺ say, 'The 2 leaders of the middle-aged people of Jannah shall be Abu Bakr and Omar. What excellent men are they both?!' Omar ﷺ asked, 'Will you testify to my entering Jannah, O Ali?' I said, 'I certainly will. O Hasan! You also be witness for your father that Rasulullah ﷺ said, 'Verily Omar shall be amongst the inhabitants of Jannah.'" *(Ibn Asakir in Muntakhab Kanzul Ummal)*

Omar ﷺ Weeps at the Mention of Jannah

In chapter on the abstinence of Omar ﷺ, it states theat narration when served a good meal, Omar ﷺ said, "While we eat this, what will the poor Muslims have who die without filling themselves with even barley bread?" Omar bin Walid replied, "They shall have Jannah." Tears started to flow from the eyes of Omar ﷺ as he said, "If this food is our share while they have made off with Jannah, they have excelled us with a lot of virtue."

Sa'd bin Abi Waqqas ﷺ is Hopeful of Jannah on his Deathbed

Mus'ab bin Sa'd, the son of Sa'd bin Abi Waqqas ﷺ relates, "My father's head was in my lap as he was about to die. He saw my eyes filling with tears, he asked, 'What makes you weep, dear son?' I replied, 'Your position and condition I see you in.' 'Don't cry for me,' he said, 'Allah will never punish me and I shall be amongst the inhabitants of Jannah as Rasulullah ﷺ stated. As long as Mu'minin do things to please Allah, Allah will reward them. As for the Kuffar, their good deeds done for Allah will serve to lighten their punishment. When their good deeds are finished, it will be said, 'Everyone who did anything should claim the reward of their deeds from those they did it for.'" *(Ibn Sa'd)*

Ann bin Al Aas ﷺ Fears the Life After Death at the Time of Death

Ibn Shamasa Mahri reports that they went to see Amr bin Al Aas ﷺ when he was on his deathbed. Turning his face towards the wall, he wept for a long while his son recounted to him the glad tidings that Rasulullah ﷺ had given him. He kept weeping all the while with his face towards the wall until he finally turned his face towards the people and said, "Verily the best deed that I have to my account is my recitation of the Shahada *'La ilaha IllAllah Muhammadur Rasulullah ﷺ'*. I have however passed through 3 stages. The first stage I found myself in was the time when there was none I hated more than Rasulullah ﷺ. At that time there was nothing I would have liked more than to grab hold of him and kill him. Had I died during that period, I would have surely been from amongst the inmates of Jahannam. Allah then placed Islam in my heart and I approached Rasulullah ﷺ to pledge my allegiance to him saying, 'Do give me your right hand so that I may pledge allegiance to you, O Rasulullah ﷺ.' However, when he gave me his hand, I withdrew mine. 'What is the matter, O Amr?' he asked. 'I wish to make a condition,' I replied. 'What is the condition?' he queried. I said, 'The condition is that I should be forgiven.' Rasulullah ﷺ explained, 'O Amr! Don't you know that Islam wipes out everything every sin that took place before it, that Hijra wipes out everything that took place before it and that Hajj wipes out everything that took place before it?'" Amr bin Al Aas ﷺ continued, "At that time I saw myself in a state that none was more beloved to me nor more respected in my sight than Rasulullah ﷺ. If I was asked to describe Rasulullah ﷺ, I would be unable to do so because I was never able to look at him directly out of respect for him. Had I died during that stage of my life, I would have expected to be amongst the inhabitants of Jannah. Thereafter came the 3rd stage when we became governors and I know not what is my condition after this. When I die, let not any wailing woman or fire accompany my bier. Throw the sand into a heap when you bury me and when you have completed the burial, I want you to stand by my graveside for as long as it takes to slaughter a camel and distribute its meat. In this way, I will have company for awhile until I can prepare the answers I will have to give to the messengers from my Rabb." *(Ibn Sa'd, Muslim)*

Abdur Rahman bin Shamasa narrates that when death approached Amr bin Al Aas ﷺ, he started to weep. His son Abdullah ﷺ asked, "What makes you weep? Is it for fear of death?" "Not at all," Amr ﷺ replied, "By Allah! It is for what is to happen after death." His son said, "But you have lived in a most excellent period." He then started reminding his father about his association with Rasulullah ﷺ and about his conquests in Sham. Amr ﷺ said, "You have omitted to mention the best of all; the Shahada 'La Ilaha IllAllah'..." The narration continues briefly like the one above. The narration however ends with Amr ﷺ saying, "When I die, no woman should wail over me, neither should any such person follow me who praises me or carries a fire. Tie my loincloth firmly because I shall be in a struggle when the angels wrestle my soul from me, in which condition my body should not become exposed. Heap the sand upon my grave because my right side is by no means more deserving of sand than the left. You should also not place any wood or stones in my grave." *(Ahmad in Al Bidayah wan Nihayah)*. Another narration adds that afterwards Amr ﷺ again turned his face to the wall and said, "O Allah! You issued commands but we disobeyed. You forbade us but we did not abstain. We now need nothing else but Your forgiveness." Yet another narration adds Amr then placed his hand around his neck like a yoke, raised his head to the sky and said, "O Allah! I am not powerful enough to take revenge and not innocent enough to offer excuses. I do not deny any of my sins but am seeking pardon. There is none worthy of worship but You." He continued repeating this until he passed away. May Allah be pleased with him. *(Muslim)*. Amr ﷺ also said the following after advising his son: "O Allah! You issued commands that we did not fulfill and You forbade us from things but we destroyed ourselves by doing them. I am not innocent enough to offer excuses and not powerful enough to take revenge. There is none worthy of worship but You." He continued repeating this until he passed away. *(Ibn Sa'd)*

The Previously Quoted Statements of the Sahabah Concerning Belief in Jannah and Jahannam

In the chapter discussing the assistance rendered to Rasulullah ﷺ, the words of the Ansar have been quoted when Khaibar was conquered; Rasulullah ﷺ said to the Ansar, "You have fulfilled your duty towards us. Now, if You please, you may hand over your shares of plantations in Khaibar to the Muhajirin and have your date crops in Madinah all for yourselves without sharing it with the Muhajirin, who will now receive from Khaibar." The Ansar accepted the proposal and said. "You have placed several responsibilities on us while you have taken the responsibly that in exchange for this we shall have Jannah. We have now fulfilled what you had asked of us and require your condition to be met." Rasulullah ﷺ said, "You have it." In the chapter discussing Jihad, the words of Umair bin Humam ﷺ have passed. When Rasulullah ﷺ encouraged them on to fight during the Battle of Badr, he exclaimed, "Wow! All that stands between me and my entry into Jannah is the disbelievers killing me." He then threw down the dates in his hand, grabbed his sword and fought until he was killed. Another narration states that when he exclaimed. "Wow!" Rasulullah ﷺ asked him why he said this. He replied, "O Rasulullah ﷺ! By Allah! There is no reason other than that I should be among its inhabitants." Rasulullah ﷺ assured him, "You are certainly from amongst its inhabitants.' Umair ﷺ took out some dates from his quiver and started eating them. However, he then said, "If I live until I have eaten these dates, it would take too much time." He then threw down the dates he had left and jumped into the thick of battle until he was martyred. May Allah shower His mercy on him. In the chapter discussing injuries sustained in Jihad, the words of Anas bin Nadhr ﷺ have passed when he said. "How wonderful is the fragrance of Jannah that I smell coming from behind Mount Uhud!" He then fought until he was martyred. In the chapter discussing the desire the Sahabah had for fighting in the Path of Allah, the words of Sa'd bin Khaithama ﷺ have passed who said, "Had it not been to Jannah, I would have certainly given you (O father) preference to have it your way. However, I really do aspire for martyrdom on this trip." This he said after his father stated that only one of them will be able to participate in the expedition to Badr. The words of Sa'd bin Rabi ﷺ have also passed who said during the Battle of Uhud, "Salams to Rasulullah ﷺ and to you. Tell Rasulullah ﷺ that I can smell the fragrance of Jannah." This he said to Zaid bin Thabit ﷺ who brought him the message that Rasulullah ﷺ had sent Salams for him and wished to know how he was feeling. Also quoted were the words of Haram bin Milhan ﷺ in the chapter discussing the battle at Bir Ma'oona. When he was martyred, he cried out, "By the Rabb of the Kabah, I am successful!" he was referring to his successful entry into Jannah. In the chapter discussing the valor of Ammar ﷺ, his words are quoted as follows: "O Hashim! Advance! Jannah lies beneath the shadow of swords and death lies at the points of spears. The doors of Jannah have been flung wide open and the damsels of Jannah have been beautified. Today I shall meet those I love, Muhammad ﷺ and his group. He then launched an attack with Hashim ؓ and they were both martyred. Again in the chapter are his words when he said. "O Assembly of Muslims! Are you running away from Jannah? I am Ammar bin Yasir! Are you running away from Jannah? I am Ammar bin Yasir! Come to me!"

In the chapter discussing refusal to be an Ameer, the words of Abdullah bin Omar ؓ are quoted when he said. "Never before had my heart ever aspired for worldly things and I almost said, 'That person (myself) desires the Khilafa who had hit your neck and the neck of your father to accept Islam until he made you two enter its fold!' However, I thought of Jannah and its bounties and refrained from saying it." This he said when Mu'awiya ؓ announced, "Who is desirous of the Khilafa?" The words of Sa'eed bin Amir ؓ has also passed. When after spending in Sadaqa, he was told that his wife and in-laws also have a right, he said, "Just as I would not give preference to anything else over their rights, I would also not forsake my desire for the wide-eyed damsels of Jannah in exchange for pleasing some people. Should a damsel of Jannah peep into this world, the world will be illuminated just as the sun illuminates it." Another narration states that he once told his wife, "Take it easy. I had some companions who have recently left me. Even in exchange for the world and all its contents, 1 would not like to leave the path they walk. If a single damsel of Jannah has to even peep into this world from the sky, everything on earth would be illuminated and the radiance of her face would outshine the sun and the moon. The scarf that she is given to wear is more precious than the world and all that it contains. It is therefore more appropriate that I leave you for them rather than leaving them for you." His wife then accepted what had happened and was satisfied. Also quoted in the chapter discussing perseverance through illness are the words of a woman from the Ansar who thrice repeated, "No! By Allah! I would rather exercise patience, O Rasulullah ﷺ instead of jeopardizing my entry into Jannah." This she said when Rasulullah ﷺ said to her, "Which would you prefer; that I pray to Allah to cure you of your fever or that you exercise patience and be assured of Jannah'?" Also quoted were the words of Abu Darda ؓ when he said, "I wish for Jannah" when his friends asked him what he wished for. Also quoted in the chapter discussing patience upon the death of children were the words of Ummu Haritha ؓ upon the martyrdom of her son. She said, "O Rasulullah ﷺ! Tell me what has become of Haritha. If he is in Jannah, I shall exercise patience. If not, I shall show Allah what I will do." She was referring to wailing, which had not yet been forbidden at the time. Another narration states that she said, "O Rasulullah ﷺ! If he is in Jannah, I shall not weep and will not be grieved. However, if he is in Jahannam, I shall continue weeping as long as I live." "O Ummu Harith!" Rasulullah ﷺ consoled her, "There is not only one Jannah. There are many levels of Jannah and Harith is in Firdous which is the highest of them all." She returned laughing as she said, "Well done, Harith! Well done!"

Aisha ؓ Weeps at the Thought of Jahannam and the Words of Rasulullah ﷺ

Aisha ؓ narrates that she once started to weep at the thought of Jahannam. "What is the matter, O Aisha'?" Rasulullah ﷺ asked. She replied. "I thought of Jahannam and started to weep. Will you think of your family on the Day of Judgment?" Rasulullah ﷺ said, "There are 3 places where none shall think of another. (1) At the scales until a person knows whether his scale of good deeds is heavy or light. (2) When the books of actions will be handed out until a person will call out of jubilation 'Come and see my book!' or until he knows whether his book will be given in his right hand (a sign of success) or in his left hand from behind his back (a sign of failure). (3) At the bridge of Sirat when it is spanned across Jahannam. There shall be hooks on either side and plenty of thorns. Allah shall detain whoever He wills until they find out whether they have attained salvation or not." (Hakim, Dhahabi)

An Old Man and a Youngster died at the mention of Jahannam

When Rasulullah ﷺ recited to them the verse:

يَا أَيُّهَا الَّذِينَ آمَنُوا قُوا أَنْفُسَكُمْ وَأَهْلِيكُمْ نَارًا وَقُودُهَا النَّاسُ وَالْحِجَارَةُ

O you who believe! Ward off from yourselves and your families a Fire (Hell) whose fuel is men and stones... (At-Tahrim:6)

"O Rasulullah ﷺ!" an old man asked, "Are the stones of jahannam like the stones of this world?" Rasulullah ﷺ replied, "I swear by the Being Who controls my life that a single boulder of Jahannam is larger than all the mountains of this world." The old man then fell unconscious. Placing his hand on the old man's heart, Rasulullah ﷺ discovered that he was still alive. Rasulullah ﷺ therefore said, "Respected old man! Say 'La llaha IllAllah'." When the old man recited the Kalima, Rasulullah ﷺ gave him the glad tidings of Jannah. The Sahabah remarked, "Is this tiding of Jannah only for him?" Rasulullah ﷺ replied, "Yes, because Allah says: ذَلِكَ لِمَنْ خَافَ مَقَامِي وَخَافَ وَعِيدِ (14)

....This is for him who fears standing before Me (on the Day of Resurrection or fears My Punishment) and also fears My Threat. (Ibrahim:14) (Ibn Abi Hatim in Tafsir Ibn Kathir)

In the chapter discussing the fear the Sahabah had for Allah, a similar incident as occurred to the old man is reported about a youngster. It is also related there that when the fear for Allah gripped a young Ansari, he wept so much every time he heard mention of Jahannam that this kept him indoors. When this was mentioned to Rasulullah ﷺ, he went to the house. As Rasulullah ﷺ entered, he embraced the Ansari, who expired in Rasulullah ﷺ's arms. Rasulullah ﷺ then said, "Enshroud your companion because fear of Jahannam has ruptured his liver." (Hakim)

The Previously Quoted Statements of the Sahabah Concerning Fear for Jahannam

The restlessness of Shaddad bin Aws ؓ in his bed has already been quoted with his words. "O Allah! The fire of Jahannam has dispelled my sleep." Thereafter, he would stand up and perform salah until the morning. Several incidents have also reported in the chapter discussing the weeping of the Sahabah. In the chapter discussing the Battle of Mu'ta, the weeping of Abdullah bin Rawaha ؓ has been reported together with his words: "I swear by Allah that it is neither love for this world nor my attachment to you that makes me weep. However, I have heard Rasulullah ﷺ recite a verse for the Qur'an that speaks of the fire of Jahannam: وَإِنْ مِنْكُمْ إِلَّا وَارِدُهَا كَانَ عَلَى رَبِّكَ حَتْمًا مَقْضِيًّا (71)

There is not one of you but will pass over it (Hell); this is with your Lord; a Decree which must be accomplished. (Maryam:71) I have no idea how am I to return after this crossing."

The Conviction of Abu Bakr ؓ in the Battle Between the Romans and the Persians as Promised by Allah

Nayyar bin Mukram Aslami ؓ reports that the Persians were prevailing over the Romans at the time when Allah revealed:

الم (1) غُلِبَتِ الرُّومُ (2) فِي أَدْنَى الْأَرْضِ وَهُمْ مِنْ بَعْدِ غَلَبِهِمْ سَيَغْلِبُونَ (3) فِي بِضْعِ سِنِينَ

Alif-Lam-Mim. (These letters are one of the miracles of the Qur'an, and none but Allah (Alone) knows their meanings). The Romans have been defeated. In the nearer land (Sham, Iraq, Jordan, and Palestine), and they, after their defeat, will be victorious. Within three to nine years... (Ar-Rum:1-4)

The Muslims liked the Romans to be victorious because they were people with a divine scripture just like the Muslims. It is for this reason that Allah says:

وَيَوْمَئِذٍ يَفْرَحُ الْمُؤْمِنُونَ (4) بِنَصْرِ اللَّهِ يَنْصُرُ مَنْ يَشَاءُ وَهُوَ الْعَزِيزُ الرَّحِيمُ (5)

And on that Day, the believers (i.e. Muslims) will rejoice (at the victory given by Allah to the Romans against the Persians), With the help of Allah, He helps whom He wills, and He is the All-Mighty, the Most Merciful.. (Ar-Rum:4-5)

On the other hand, the Quraish liked the Persians to be victorious because neither of them had a divine scripture nor believed in resurrection. When Allah revealed these verses, Abu Bakr ؓ went out of his house shouting:

الم (1) غُلِبَتِ الرُّومُ (2) فِي أَدْنَى الْأَرْضِ وَهُمْ مِنْ بَعْدِ غَلَبِهِمْ سَيَغْلِبُونَ (3) فِي بِضْعِ سِنِينَ

Alif-Lam-Mim. (These letters are one of the miracles of the Qur'an, and none but Allah (Alone) knows their meanings). The Romans have been defeated. In the nearer land (Sham, Iraq, Jordan, and Palestine), and they, after their defeat, will be victorious. Within three to nine years... (Ar-Rum:1-4)

Some members of the Quraish then said to him, "This will decide the affair between us and you, it will prove whether your religion is true or not. Since your guide assumes that Rome will defeat Persia in a few years time, let us place a bet on it. Abu Bakr ؓ agreed because betting had not yet been forbidden at the time. Abu Bakr ؓ and the disbelievers therefore took a bet and agreed on the sum. They then said to Abu Bakr, "How would you specify 'a few' which can be anything between 3 to 9 years? Specify a time in between so that we may have a time frame between us when we will determine who has won and who has lost. The time period they then set was 6 years. When 6 years passed without the Romans attaining victory, the disbelievers took the payment from Abu Bakr ؓ. However, it was when the 7th year entered that the Romans defeated the Persians. Some Muslims therefore criticized Abu Bakr ؓ for stipulating 6 years because Allah had only mentioned "a few years" without specifying. Seeing that the Qur'anic prediction was true, many people accepted Islam.

Bara ؓ narrates that when the verses:

الم (1) غُلِبَتِ الرُّومُ (2) فِي أَدْنَى الْأَرْضِ وَهُمْ مِنْ بَعْدِ غَلَبِهِمْ سَيَغْلِبُونَ (3)

Alif-Lam-Meem. (These letters are one of the miracles of the Qur'an, and none but Allah (Alone) knows their meanings). The Romans have been defeated. In the nearer land (Sham, Iraq, Jordan, and Palestine), and they, after their defeat, will be victorious. (Ar-Rum:1-3)

were revealed, the disbelievers said to Abu Bakr ؓ, "Don't you see what your master believes? He assumes that Rome will defeat Persia." Abu Bakr ؓ replied, "My master is true." They challenged Abu Bakr ؓ to a bet and specified a time period. When the time expired before Rome could defeat Persia and the news reached Rasulullah ﷺ, he was displeased and asked Abu Bakr, "What made you do this?" Abu Bakr ؓ replied, "To prove the reality of Allah and His Rasul ﷺ." Rasulullah ﷺ advised him saying, "Now approach them to increase the bet and set the time for 'بضع' (a period between 3 and 9 years)." Abu Bakr ؓ then approached the disbelievers saying, "Would you like to renew the bet? The renewal is a better deal." They agreed. It was before the expiry of the specified years that Rome defeated Persia, set up a stronghold in Mada'in and built the city of Romiya. After

collecting the payment, Abu Bakr ؓ came to Rasulullah ﷺ with it saying, "This is unlawful, what should I do with it." Rasulullah ﷺ told him to give it away as Sadaqa. *(Ibn Abi Hatim, Ahmad, Tirmidhi, Nasa'ee, Ibn Jareer in Tafsir Ibn Kathir)*

The Conviction of Ka'b bin Adi ؓ About the Domination of Islam

Ka'b bin Adi ؓ says, "I came with a delegation from Hira to Nabi ﷺ. When Rasulullah ﷺ presented Islam to us, we accepted and then returned to Hira. It was not long thereafter that the news of Rasulullah ﷺ's demise reached us. My companions started having doubts and said, 'Had he been a true Nabi, he would not have died.' I said to them, 'But the Ambiya ﷺ before him all passed away as well.' I therefore remained steadfast and left for Madinah. On the way I happened to pass by a monk without whom we usually made no decisions. I said to him, 'Tell me about the purpose I am heading for because some uncertainty has cropped up in my heart. 'Bring something with your name,' he said. I then brought an anklebone because an anklebone is also called Ka'b in Arabic. He took out some hairs and told me to throw the anklebone into them. When I did so, I saw Rasulullah ﷺ as I had seen him and saw his demise taking place at the exact time he passed away. My sights on my Iman were therefore bolstered and I continued to Madinah. Upon arrival in Madinah I went to see Abu Bakr ؓ and after reporting everything to him, I stayed on with him. He dispatched me to Maqoqis, the king of Alexandria and when I returned after he had passed away, Omar ؓ sent me back. I therefore returned to Maqoqis with Omar ؓ's letter of appointment. This was after the Battle of Yarmuk about which I had no idea. Maqoqis said to me, 'Do you know that the Romans fought a battle with the Arabs and defeated them?' 'That is not possible,' I said. 'Why not?' he asked. I said, 'Allah promised His Nabi ﷺ that He would make his Deen dominate over all religions. Allah never breaks a promise.' Maqoqis said, 'By Allah! The Arabs massacred the Romans just as the nation of 'Ad was massacred. Your Nabi ﷺ had spoken the truth.' Maqoqis asked me about all the prominent Sahabah and sent gifts for them. I said to him, 'Abbas ؓ who is the uncle of Rasulullah ﷺ is still alive. You should maintain good relations with him.'" Ka'b ؓ continues, "I had been Omar ؓ's business partner and when he formed a registry to distribute allowances, he included me amongst his tribe the Banu Adi bin Ka'b." *(Baghawi, Ibn Shahin, Abu Nu'aym, Ibn Sakan, Ibn Yunus in Isabah)*

The Statements of Abu Bakr ؓ, Omar ؓ and Sa'd ؓ About Conviction in the Allah's Promise to Assist the Mu'minin

In the chapter discussing the Jihad against the deserters, the following words of Abu Bakr ؓ are quoted: He said, "I swear by Allah that I shall remain devoted to the laws of Allah and continue fighting in Jihad until Allah fulfils His promise to us. Those of us who are killed shall be martyrs bound for Jannah while those who survive shall remain as Allah's deputies on His earth and successors of His bondsmen. Allah has spoken the truth and there can be no going back on His word. Allah has declared:

وَعَدَ اللَّهُ الَّذِينَ آمَنُوا مِنْكُمْ وَعَمِلُوا الصَّالِحَاتِ لَيَسْتَخْلِفَنَّهُمْ فِي الْأَرْضِ كَمَا اسْتَخْلَفَ الَّذِينَ مِنْ قَبْلِهِمْ وَلَيُمَكِّنَنَّ لَهُمْ دِينَهُمُ الَّذِي ارْتَضَى لَهُمْ وَلَيُبَدِّلَنَّهُمْ مِنْ بَعْدِ خَوْفِهِمْ أَمْنًا يَعْبُدُونَنِي لَا يُشْرِكُونَ بِي شَيْئًا وَمَنْ كَفَرَ بَعْدَ ذَلِكَ فَأُولَئِكَ هُمُ الْفَاسِقُونَ (55)

Allah has promised those among you who believe, and do righteous good deeds, that He will certainly grant them succession to (the present rulers) in the earth, as He granted it to those before them, and that He will grant them the authority to practice their religion, that which He has chosen for them (i.e. Islam). And He will surely give them in exchange a safe security after their fear (provided) they (believers) worship Me and do not associate anything (in worship) with Me. But whoever disbelieved after this, they are the Fasiqoon (rebellious, disobedient to Allah). (An-Nur:55)

The wards of Omar ؓ have also passed when he encouraged the Muslims to wage Jihad saying, "Where are those Muhajirin who were always leaping towards the promises of Allah? March to the lands that Allah has promised in His Book that He would make you inherit. Allah has declared: لِيُظْهِرَهُ عَلَى الدِّينِ كُلِّهِ

...to make it (Islam) superior over all other religions... (At-Tauba:33, Al-Fath:28 and As-Saff:9)

Also quoted are the wards of Sa'd bin Abi Waqqas ؓ when he encouraged the Muslims to wage Jihad saying, "Allah is definitely True. He has no partner in His kingdom and never goes back on His ward. Allah the Majestic declares:

وَلَقَدْ كَتَبْنَا فِي الزَّبُورِ مِنْ بَعْدِ الذِّكْرِ أَنَّ الْأَرْضَ يَرِثُهَا عِبَادِيَ الصَّالِحُونَ (105)

And indeed We have written in Zaboor (Psalms) (i.e. all the revealed Holy Books the Taurat (Torah), the Injeel (Gospel), the Qur'an) after (We have already written in) Al-Lauh Al-Mahfooz (the Book, that is in the heaven with Allah), that My righteous slaves shall inherit the land (i.e. the land of Paradise). (Al-Anbiya:105)

This earth is your legacy and the promise of your Rabb. For the past 3 years, Allah has give you use of this land. You are feeding others from it and yourselves eating from it. To this day, you have killed its people in the wars that took place, collected their wealth and taken prisoners from amongst them. In the previous battles, those before you have caused much harm to them. Now their army has came to you (the army of Yazdgird, numbering approximately 200,000). You are amongst the pride of the Arabs, their nobles, the cream of every tribe and the most honorable of those you have left behind you. If you are detached from the world and aspirant to the Hereafter, Allah shall grant you bath worlds. This battle cannot take you any closer to your deaths because death is predestined. However, if you lose courage, become cowardly and weak, your strength will leave you and you will be destroying your Hereafter."

Khuzaima bin Thabit Confirms the Words of Rasulullah ﷺ in a Dispute with a Bedouin

Omara bin Khuzaima bin Thabit narrates from his uncle who was a Sahabi that Rasulullah ﷺ once purchased a horse from a Bedouin. Rasulullah ﷺ asked the Bedouin to follow him home so that he could give him the money. The Bedouin however fell behind because Rasulullah ﷺ walked very briskly. Not knowing that Rasulullah ﷺ had already purchased the horse, 2 men entered into negotiations with the Bedouin to buy the horse. When one of them offered him a price higher than that which Rasulullah ﷺ agreed to pay, the Bedouin called to Rasulullah ﷺ saying, "If you wish to buy the horse, buy it now. Otherwise, I am going to sell it" Rasulullah ﷺ stood still when he heard this and, returning to the Bedouin, he said, "Did I not already buy it from you?" The Bedouin denied it saying, "No! I swear by Allah that I did not sell it to you!" "But I did buy it from you," Rasulullah ﷺ insisted. As the 2 contested the issue, people started gathering around them. The Bedouin finally said, "Then present a witness to attest that you did buy it from me." Every Muslim who came by reprimanded the Bedouin saying, "Shame on you! Rasulullah ﷺ speaks nothing but the truth!" In the meantime, Khuzaima bin Thahit had also come along and heard the exchange of words between Rasulullah ﷺ and the Bedouin. When the Bedouin demanded a witness from Rasulullah ﷺ, Khuzaima said, "I testify

that you sold it to Rasulullah ﷺ." Turning to Khuzaima, Rasulullah ﷺ asked, "On what basis do you testify'?" Khuzaima replied, "On the basis that I believe in you, O Rasulullah ﷺ!" Thereafter, Rasulullah ﷺ regarded the testimony of Khuzaima as equal to the testimony of 2 men. *(Ibn Sa'd, Abu Dawud).* Another narration states that Rasulullah ﷺ asked, "O Khuzaima! On what basis do you testify when you were not with us?" "O Rasulullah ﷺ!" he replied, "When I believe the news you give from the heavens, how can I not believe what you say?" Rasulullah ﷺ then always considered the testimony of Khuzaima to be equal to the testimony of 2 men. Another narration states that Khuzaima ؓ said, "I am convinced that you speak only the truth and we have believed you in matters of our Deen that are much more important" Rasulullah ﷺ then permitted his testimony. *(Ibn Sa'd)*

Abu Bakr ؓ Verifies Rasulullah ﷺ's Account of His Night Journey to the Heavens

Aisha ؓ narrates that after Rasulullah ﷺ was taken on the historic night journey to Masjidul Aqsa and then to the heavens, he narrated it to the people the following morning. On that occasion by disbelieving it, some people who had previously professed Iman left the fold of Islam. The people then rushed to Abu Bakr ؓ saying, "What have you now to say about your friend who claims that he was taken on a night journey to Baytul Maqdas?" "Did he say that?" asked Abu Bakr ؓ. "Yes, he did," they confirmed. Abu Bakr ؓ then said, "If he said it, then he is speaking the truth." The people exclaimed, "Do you believe that he could have gone to Baytul Maqdas at night and then returned before dawn?" "Of course," Abu Bakr ؓ said, "In fact, I believe him regarding matters that seem much more unbelievable than that I believe in the news from the heavens that he brings day and night." It was because of this that Abu Bakr ؓ received the title of Siddiq. *(Bayhaqi in Tafsir Ibn Kathir).* Another narration states that on this occasion, some people who had previously professed Iman left the fold of Islam, while others believed without question. The incident was in essence a great test for the people. *(Abu Nu'aym in Muntakhab Kanzul Ummal).* Yet another narration states that after hearing Rasulullah ﷺ's account, they went to Abu Bakr ؓ saying, "What have you now to say about your friend who says that he traveled a distance of a month's journey last night and returned before dawn?" "Did he say that?" asked Abu Bakr ؓ. The rest of the narration is the same as above. *(Ibn Abi Hatim in Tafsir Ibn Kathir)*

Omar ؓ's Conviction in the Words of Rasulullah ﷺ Concerning the Extinction of Species

Jabir bin Abdullah ؓ reports that during the year in which Omar ؓ became the Khalifa, the number of locusts declined drastically. When Omar ؓ made enquiries and received no response, he sent riders to many areas including Sham and Iraq to enquire whether locusts had been seen or not. A rider eventually retuned from Yemen with a handful of locusts that he placed before Omar ؓ. When he saw them, Omar ؓ thrice exclaimed, "Allahu Akbar!" He said, "I heard Rasulullah ﷺ say, 'Allah has created 1,000 species; 600 in the oceans and 400 on land. The first of these to become extinct is the species of locusts. As soon as they become extinct, the others will follow like the beads of a necklace when the string is cut." *(Abu Ya'la in Tafsir Ibn Kathir)*

Ali ؓ's conviction in the words of Rasulullah ﷺ on Assassination

Fudhala bin Abu Fudhala Ansami relates, "I accompanied my father Abu Fudhala ؓ to Yamba to visit Ali ؓ who had become extremely ill there. My father who was also a veteran of the Battle of Badr said to him, 'What keeps you camping at this place? If you die here, there are none here but the Bedouins of the Banu Juhaina tribe. Persevere until you reach Madinah and should you die there, your companions will be nearby and they will perform the Janaza salah for you.' Ali ♦ however said, 'I shall not die from this illness because Rasulullah ﷺ emphatically told me that I shall not die until I become the Khalifa and then his beard becomes dyed with the blood of his forehead.'" *(Ahmad in Zawa'id, Ibn Abi Shaybah, Bazzar, Harith, Abu Nu'aym, Bayhaqi in Dala'il, Ibn Asakir in Muntakhab Kanzul Ummal).* Ali ♦ narrates that Abdullah bin Salam ♦ one day came to him as he placed his foot in the stirrup of his animal, ready to ride off. "Where do you intend going?" Abdullah bin Salam ♦ asked. When Ali ♦ informed him that he was headed for Iraq, Abdullah bin Salam ♦ remarked, "Remember that if you go there, it will be the sharp edge of a sword that is sure to strike you." Ali ♦ says, "I swear by Allah that I had heard this from Rasulullah ﷺ even before he (Abdullah bin Salam ♦) said it." *(Humaidi, Bazzar, Abu Ya'la, Ibn Hibban, Hakim, Muntakhab Kanzul Ummal).* Mu'awiya bin Jareer narrates that Ali ♦ was once inspecting the cavalry when Ibn Muljim passed by. When Ali ♦ asked him his name, he gave a name other than that of his father. "You are lying," Ali ♦ told him. When he eventually gave his father's name, Ali ♦ said, "Now you have spoken the truth. Turning to the others, Ali ♦ said Rasulullah ﷺ informed me that my assassin will be a man from amongst the Jews and this man is from them. Let him go." *(Ibn Adi, Ibn Asakir in Muntakhab Kanzul Ummal)*

Ubaida narrates that whenever Ali ♦ saw Ibn Muljim, he would recite the following couplet which means:

"While I wish him life, he wishes to kill me. Bring me an excuse from a friend from the Murad clan" *(Abdur Razzaq, Ibn Sa'd, Wakee in Muntakhab Kanzul Ummal)*

Abu Tufail narrates that he was with Ali bin Abi Talib ♦ when Abdur Rahman bin Muljim came. After issuing instructions for his allowance to be given to him, Ali ♦ pointed towards his beard and said, "None can stop this wretch from dying, from the top with the blood of my forehead." Ali ♦ then recited the following couplets which mean:

"Bolster your heart for death because death shall come your way and never fear being murdered when murder arrives at your valley"
(Ibn Sa'd, Abu Nu'aym in Muntakhab Kanzul Ummal)

Ammar ♦'s Conviction in the Words of Rasulullah ﷺ on his Death

Ummu Ammar ♦ who brought Ammar ♦ up reports that when Ammar ♦ became very ill one day, he said, "I am not going to die from this illness because my beloved friend Rasulullah ﷺ informed me that I will be killed in a battle between 2 warring armies of Mu'minin." *(Ibn Asakir in Muntakhab Kanzul Ummal).* Already quoted in the chapter discussing the enthusiasm of the Sahabah to die in the Path of Allah are his words when he said, "I am to meet Al Jabbar (Allah) and marry the damsels of Jannah! Today I shall meet my beloved friends, Muhammad ﷺ and his companions because Rasulullah ﷺ informed me that the last provision of my worldly life shall be the curds of milk." Also in the same chapter the narration has passed stating that Ammar bin Yasir ♦ was fighting in the Battle of Siffin but was not martyred. He approached Ali ♦ and said, "O Amirul Mu'minin! This is that very day about which Rasulullah ﷺ said that I would be martyred. How come I am still alive?.." Ali ♦ replied, "Do not worry about that." This occurred 3 times until Ammar ♦ was given some milk. He drank it and

said, "Indeed, Rasulullah ﷺ said that this milk will be the last drink that I shall drink in this world." He then stood up and fought until he was martyred. Khalid bin Walid ♦ reports from the daughter of Hisham bin Walid bin Mughiera who nursed Ammar ♦ that Mu'awiya ♦ once visited Ammar ♦ when he was ill. When he left, Mu'awiya ♦ said, "O Allah! Do not let his death be on our hands because I have heard Rasulullah ﷺ say that it will be a rebellious group that will kill Ammar."*(Abu Ya'la, Ibn Asakir in Muntakhab Kanzul Ummal)*

Abu Dhar ♦'s Conviction in the Words of Rasulullah ﷺ Concerning his Death

Ibrahim bin Ashtar narrates from his father that when death approached Abu Dhar ♦, his wife started to weep. "What makes you weep?" he asked. "I am weeping," she said, "because I do not have the strength to bury you or a cloth large enough to shroud you." "Do not weep," he consoled her, "because I was part of a group of persons to whom Rasulullah ﷺ said, 'One of you shall certainly die in a wilderness in the presence of a party of Mu'minin.' Since every person from that group has passed away in a city amongst large numbers of people, it will definitely be I who will die in a wilderness. By Allah! Neither am I lying nor did Rasulullah ﷺ tell me a lie. Go watch the road." She said, "But the people performing Hajj have long stopped traveling and the road is closed." She however still ran to a hillock, stood upon it and looked to the road. When she saw no one, she then returned to nurse Abu Dhar ♦. Thereafter, she would again run to the hillock. As she was busy doing this, she suddenly noticed some travelers whose animals were carrying them along swiftly, appearing like vultures perched on their carriages. When she waved to them with her sheet, they turned towards her. As they reached her and asked her what the matter was, she replied, "There is a man from amongst the Muslims who is about to pass away. Will you please shroud him and bury him?" "Who is this man?" they enquired. As soon as she informed them that he was Abu Dhar ♦, they all exclaimed, "May our parents be sacrificed for him!" They then whipped their animals and raced towards him. When they reached him, Abu Dhar ♦ said, "Congratulations to you because Rasulullah had referred to you as Mu'minin!" He then related the Hadith to them and said, "I have heard Rasulullah ﷺ say that when 2 or 3 children of a couple pass away and they exercise patience and anticipate rewards from Allah, they will not even see Jahannam. Do listen well. Had I a sheet large enough to be my burial shroud, I would have not wanted to be shrouded in anything else but that which is my own. Similarly, if my wife had a sheet large enough to be my burial shroud, I would not have wanted to be shrouded in anything else but that which is hers. However, we have nothing of the sort, so we appeal to one of you to give something. I however plead to you in the name of Allah and Islam that no such person should provide the shroud who has been a governor, a chief, a leader or an envoy." Every member of the group had assumed one of these posts at some stage besides a young man from the Ansar, who said, "I shall provide the shroud because I have not assumed any of the positions you have mentioned. I shall shroud you in the shawl I am wearing and 2 more sheets in my bag that my mother had woven for me." Abu Dhar ♦ said, "You should then be the one to shroud me." The young Ansari then shrouded Abu Dhar ♦ in the presence of the group. Amongst the group was Hujr bin Adbar and Malik Ashtar and all of them hailed from Yemen. *(Ibn Sa'd).* Abdullah bin Mas'ood ♦ narrates that Uthman ♦ had sent Abu Dhar ♦ to a place called Rahdha, where his death came to him. At the time, there was none with him besides his wife and slave. His parting instructions to them was, "Bathe me, shroud me and then place me in the centre of the road. Then say to the first passing caravan, 'This is Abu Dhar ؓ a companion of Rasulullah ﷺ. Do assist us in burying him.'" When he passed away, the 2 did as he instructed and placed him in the centre if the road. It was Abdullah bin Mas'ood ؓ with a group of people from Iraq who happened to pass by on their way to performing Umra. It was the sight of a corpse on the road that startled the party just as their camels were about to trample upon it. Abu Dhar ؓ's slave approached them saying, "This is Abu Dhar ؓ, a companion of Rasulullah ﷺ. Do assist us in burying him." Abdullah bin Mas'ood ؓ burst out crying loudly as he said, "Rasulullah ﷺ spoke the truth when he said to Abu Dhar ؓ, 'You walk by yourself, will die by yourself and will be resurrected by yourself.'" He dismounted with his companions and they buried Abu Dhar ؓ. Abdullah bin Mas'ood ؓ informed the people about Abu Dhar ؓ and what Rasulullah ﷺ mentioned to him on the journey to Tabuk. *(Ibn Sa'd)*

Khuraim bin Aws ؓ's Conviction in the Words of Rasulullah ﷺ Concerning Shaima bint Buqaila

Khuraim bin Aws ؓ relates, "I migrated to Rasulullah ﷺ and met him upon his return from Tabuk, when I accepted Islam. I heard Rasulullah ﷺ say, 'I have been shown the city of Hira together with Shaima bint Buqaila from the Azd tribe riding a white mule and wearing a black scarf.' 'O Rasulullah ﷺ!' I said, 'When we conquer Hira and find her as you have described, may I have her as my slave?' 'She is yours,' Rasulullah ﷺ replied. After the demise of Rasulullah ﷺ when people started leaving the fold of Islam, no one from my tribe the Banu Tay left Islam. We then marched to Hira with Khalid bin Walid ؓ and the first sight that met us as we entered the city was Shaima bint Buqaila just as Rasulullah ﷺ had described her. She was riding a white mule and wearing a black scarf. I immediately seized her saying, 'She is the one whom Rasulullah ﷺ described to me.' When Khalid bin Walid ؓ asked me for witnesses, Muhammad bin Maslama ؓ and Muhammad bin Bashir ؓ both from the Ansar stood witness for me. He then made her over to me. When he came to make a treaty with the Muslims, Shaima's brother Abdul Masih bin Buqaila offered to buy her from me. 'I shall accept nothing less than 1,000 for her,' I told him. He readily gave me 10,000 Dirhams and I handed her over to him. When the other Muslims told me that he would have easily paid me 100,000 had I asked for it because he was extremely wealthy, I submitted, 'I never knew that there existed a number greater than 10,000.'" *(Abu Nu'aym in Dala'il, Tabrani in Isabah, Bukhari, Ibn Mandah)*

Mugheira bin Shu'ba ؓ is Convinced by the Words of Rasulullah ﷺ Promising Assistance and Victory

Jubair bin Haya reports, "When the Kafir leader Bandarfan sent a message that the Muslims send someone to him for negotiations, Mugheira bin Shu'ba ؓ was selected for the task. I can actually picture him with his long hair and one eye. Mugheira ؓ proceeded to see the leader and when he returned, we asked him what he said. He said, 'I praised Allah and then said, 'We lived in a most remote place, were the hungriest of people, the most ill-fortuned of them and furthest from prosperity until Allah sent a Nabi to us. He promised us assistance (Allah's) in this world and Jannah in the Hereafter. We have then continued to know only victory and assistance from our Rabb every since Rasulullah ﷺ came to us. We have now come to you where we see a vast kingdom and prosperous lives. By Allah! After seeing all of this, we shall now never return to our ill-fortuned times. We shall now either take control over everything in your hands or be killed in your land." *(Abu Nu'aym in Dala'il)*. Jubair bin Haya also narrates a lengthy Hadith in which an army under the command of Nu'man bin Muqarrin ؓ was sent to the people of Ahwaz. When they requested for someone to be sent to them, Mugheira bin Shu'ba ؓ was sent. When the interpreter asked, "What kind of people are you?" Mugheira ؓ replied, "We are Arabs who had suffered immense misfortune and hardship for a very long time. Out of hunger, we were forced to suck on leather and date stones. Our clothing was made of animal's hair and wool and we worshipped trees and rocks. Suffering in this condition, the Rabb of the heavens and the earth sent to us a Nabi from our own people, whose parents we knew well. Rasulullah ﷺ instructed us to fight you people until you either worship the One Allah or pay the Jizya. Rasulullah ﷺ conveyed the message of our Rabb that any of us who die while fighting shall go to Jannah where he will enjoy bounties that have never been seen before. As for those of us who survive, they will have you people as saves." *(Bayhaqi in Asma was Sifat, Bukhari, Abu Nu'aym in Dala'il)*

The Conviction of Abu Darda ؓ in the words Rasulullah ﷺ Taught Him for Protection

Talq narrates that a man once came to Abu Darda ؓ saying, "O Abu Darda! Your house has burnt down!" "It could not have burnt," Abu Darda ؓ said. Another person then came with the same news and again Abu Darda ؓ adamantly said, "It could not have burnt." Eventually a 3rd person came to him saying, "O Abu Darda! A fire raged through your street but went off as soon as it reached your house." Abu Darda ؓ said, "I knew that Allah would never do that, never allow my house to burn down." "O Abu Darda!" the people said, "We do not know which of your words are more astonishing; whether it is 'It could not have burnt' or 'I knew that Allah would never do that'." Abu Darda ؓ then explained, "That is because of some words that I heard from Rasulullah ﷺ. Whoever recites them in the morning will not suffer any calamity until the evening. The words are:

اللهم انت ربي لااله الا انت عليك توكلت و انت رب العرش الكريم ما شاء الله كان وما لم يشا لايكون ولا حول ولا قوة الا بالله العلي العظيم اعلم ان الله علي كل شيء قدير و ان الله قد احاط بكل شيء علما اللهم اني اعوذ بك من شر نفسي ومن شركل د ابة انت اخذ بناصيتها ان ربي علي صراط مستقيم

"O Allah! You are my Rabb. There is none worthy of worship but You. In You do I place my trust and You are the Rabb of the Glorious Throne. Whatever Allah wills shall happen and what He does not will can never happen. There is no power or might but with the High and Majestic Allah. I know that Allah has power over all things and that He has knowledge of all things. O Allah! I seek Your protection from the evil in me and from the evil of every creature over which You have control. My Rabb is (One Who guides people) on the straight path." (Bayhaqi in Asma was Sifat)

Statements of the Sahabah that have been Quoted Previously Concerning Conviction in the Words of Rasulullah ﷺ

In the chapter of Da'wah, the words of Adi ؓ have been quoted who said, "I swear by the Being in whose control is my life, the third prophesy shall also come true because Rasulullah ﷺ said it." Also quoted were the words Hisham bin Al Aas ؓ and other Sahabah who said to Jabala bin Ayham, "By Allah! We shall soon be taking from you this place where you sit and we shall also be taking the kingdom of your high emperor Heraclius, Insha Allah! Our prophet Muhammad ﷺ has informed us of this."

In the chapter discussing the importance Abu Bakr 🙲 gave to dispatching armies to Sham were the words of Ali 🙲 to Abu Bakr 🙲. He said, "I feel that whether you march against them yourself or whether you send others against them, you will have Allah's assistance, InshaAllah." Abu Bakr 🙲 said, "May Allah always give you good news! How do you know this?" Ali 🙲 replied, "I have heard Rasulullah 🙲 say that this Deen will always dominate those who oppose it until the Deen and its adherents are victorious." Abu Bakr 🙲 exclaimed, "SubhanAllah! What a beautiful Hadith! You have made me very happy with this. May Allah always keep you happy." Soon to be narrated in the chapter discussing the unseen assistance that Allah gave the Muslims shall be the narration in which Abdullah bin Omar 🙲 grabbed hold of a lion's ear, pinched it and removed it from the road saying, "Rasulullah 🙲 has not spoken an untruth about you. I heard Rasulullah 🙲 say, 'Only that which man fears shall gain the upper hand over him. If man fears only Allah, nothing but Allah will have the upper hand over him.'"

The Conviction of Abu Bakr 🙲 in the Recompense for Actions

Abu Asma narrates that Abu Bakr 🙲 was once having lunch with Rasulullah 🙲 when the verse was revealed:

فَمَنْ يَعْمَلْ مِثْقَالَ ذَرَّةٍ خَيْرًا يَرَهُ (7) وَمَنْ يَعْمَلْ مِثْقَالَ ذَرَّةٍ شَرًّا يَرَهُ (8)

So whosoever does good equal to the weight of an atom (or a small ant), shall see it. And whosoever does evil equal to the weight of an atom (or a small ant), shall see it. (Az-Zilzal:7-8)
Abu Bakr 🙲 stopped eating and said, "O Rasulullah 🙲! Will we be punished for each and every evil that we perpetrate?" Rasulullah 🙲 replied, "Everything that happens to you in this world which you dislike is retribution for your sins, while the rewards for good deeds will be given to those who deserve them in the Hereafter." *(Ibn Abi Shaybah, Ibn Rahway, Abd bin Humaid, Hakim).* Another narration states that Rasulullah 🙲 replied, "O Abu Bakr! Do you see everything that happens which you dislike? Well, these are from the punishment for the weight of sins while the rewards for the weight of good deeds will be kept in store for you and be given in full on the Day of Judgment. Confirmation for this appears in Allah's Book where He says:

وَمَا أَصَابَكُمْ مِنْ مُصِيبَةٍ فَبِمَا كَسَبَتْ أَيْدِيكُمْ وَيَعْفُو عَنْ كَثِيرٍ (30)

And whatever of misfortune befalls you, it is because of what your hands have earned. And He pardons much. (Ash-Shura:30) *(Ibn Mardway in Kanzul Ummal)*
Abu Bakr 🙲 reports that he was with Rasulullah 🙲 when this was revealed: مَنْ يَعْمَلْ سُوءًا يُجْزَ بِهِ وَلَا يَجِدْ لَهُ مِنْ دُونِ اللَّهِ وَلِيًّا وَلَا نَصِيرًا (123)
...whosoever works evil, will have the recompense thereof, and he will not find any protector or helper besides Allah. (An-Nisa:123)
Rasulullah 🙲 then said, "O Abu Bakr! Should I not recite to you a verse that was just revealed to me?" When Abu Bakr 🙲 asked to hear it, Rasulullah 🙲 recited it for him. Abu Bakr 🙲 says, "All I know is that it seemed my back was about to break, causing me to yawn. 'What is the matter with you, O Abu Bakr?' Rasulullah 🙲 asked. I said, 'O Rasulullah 🙲! Which of us do not sin? Will we be punished for everything we do wrong?' Rasulullah 🙲 replied, 'As for you and the Mu'minin, you will suffer retribution for your sins in this world so that you have no sins to your account when you meet Allah. However, the Kuffar shall have their accounts accrued until they are punished for it on the Day of Judgment." *(Abd bin Humaid, Tirmidhi, Ibn Mundhir).* Abu Bakr 🙲 once asked, "O Rasulullah 🙲! When we will be punished for every sin, who can keep himself good as said in this verse:

...مَنْ يَعْمَلْ سُوءًا يُجْزَ بِهِ *...whosoever works evil, will have the recompense thereof... (An-Nisa:123).* Rasulullah 🙲 said, "May Allah forgive you, O Abu Bakr! Do you not fall ill? Do you not get tired? Do you never feel depressed? Do you never suffer hardship? Do calamities never befall you?" "These things happen," Abu Bakr 🙲 replied. Rasulullah 🙲 said, "This is retribution for sins in this world. *(Ahmad, Ibn Mundhir, Abu Ya'la, Ibn Hibban, Hakim, Bayhaqi in Kanzul Ummal)*

The Conviction of Omar bin Khattab 🙲 in the Reward for Actions

Muhammad bin Muntashir narrates that a man once came to Omar 🙲 saying, "I know which is the harshest verse in Allah's Book." Because referring to a verse of the Qur'an as being harsh is disrespectful, Omar 🙲 got down and struck the man with his lash saying, "Have you studied the verse so deeply that you know all about it?" The man then went away. The following morning Omar 🙲 said to the man, "Which verse were you referring to yesterday?" The man said that it was the verse: مَنْ يَعْمَلْ سُوءًا يُجْزَ بِهِ

...whosoever works evil, will have the recompense thereof... (An-Nisa:123)

He then said, "This means that since everyone of us commits sins, we will be punished for it." Omar 🙲 said, "When this verse was revealed, neither did we enjoy food nor drink until Allah relieved us by revealing the verse:

وَمَنْ يَعْمَلْ سُوءًا أَوْ يَظْلِمْ نَفْسَهُ ثُمَّ يَسْتَغْفِرِ اللَّهَ يَجِدِ اللَّهَ غَفُورًا رَحِيمًا (110)

And whoever does evil or wrongs himself but afterwards seeks Allah's Forgiveness, he will find Allah Oft-Forgiving, Most Merciful. (An-Nisa:110) (Ibn Rahway in Kanzul Ummal)

The Conviction of Amr bin Samura 🙲 and Imran bin Husain 🙲

Tha'laba 🙲 narrates that Amr bin Samura bin Habib bin Abdus Shams 🙲 once came to Rasulullah 🙲 and said, "O Rasulullah 🙲! I have stolen a camel from a certain tribe, so please do cleanse me." When Rasulullah 🙲 sent a message to the people of the tribe, they confirmed that one of their camels was missing. Rasulullah 🙲 then gave instructions for his hand to be amputated, upon which he said to his hand, "All praise belongs to Allah Who has cleansed me of you who wanted to admit my entire body into Jahannam." *(Ibn Majah in Tafsir Ibn Kathir).* Hasan narrates that some friends went to visit Imran bin Husain 🙲 when he was suffering from a disease. One of them said, "We are extremely distressed by what we see of your ailing body." "Do not be distressed by what you see," he said, "What you see is because of my sins and those that Allah has forgiven without punishing me are even more." He then recited the verse:

وَمَا أَصَابَكُمْ مِنْ مُصِيبَةٍ فَبِمَا كَسَبَتْ أَيْدِيكُمْ وَيَعْفُو عَنْ كَثِيرٍ (30)

And whatever of misfortune befalls you, it is because of what your hands have earned. And He pardons much. (Ash-Shura:30) (Ibn Abi Hatim in Tafsir Ibn Kathir)

The Belief of Abu Bakr 🙲 and Another Sahabi Concerning Recompense

The narration has already been quoted that when death came to one of Abu Bakr 🙲's sons, the youngster kept looking at the pillow. After he has passed away, the people informed Abu Bakr 🙲 that they noticed his son looking towards the pillow. When they lifted the corpse off the pillow, they noticed 5 or 6 Dinars beneath it. Abu Bakr 🙲 hit one hand on to the other saying, "Inna Lillahi wa Inna Ilayhi Raji'un! I do not think that your skin will be able to withstand the punishment for not spending in Sadaqa those Dinars." *(Ahmad, Abu Nu'aym in Kanzul Ummal).* Also previously quoted in the chapter discussing swearing at a Muslim are the words of Rasulullah ﷺ to a man who came to enquire about his slaves. Rasulullah ﷺ said, "On Day of Judgment, their cheating, disobedience and lies will be calculated together with the punishment you gave them. If your punishment is equal to their wrongs, the slate ill be clean and you will neither have anything for you or against you. If your punishment exceeds their wrongs, they will be allowed to have revenge for the excess." The man stepped aside and started crying loudly. Rasulullah ﷺ said, "Did you not read in the Qur'an that Allah says:

وَنَضَعُ الْمَوَازِينَ الْقِسْطَ لِيَوْمِ الْقِيَامَةِ فَلَا تُظْلَمُ نَفْسٌ شَيْئًا وَإِنْ كَانَ مِثْقَالَ حَبَّةٍ مِنْ خَرْدَلٍ أَتَيْنَا بِهَا وَكَفَى بِنَا حَاسِبِينَ (47)

And We shall set up balances of justice on the Day of Resurrection, then none will be dealt with unjustly in anything. And if there be the weight of a mustard seed, We will bring it. And Sufficient are We as Reckoners. (Al-Anbiya:47)

The man then said, "O Rasulullah ﷺ! I see nothing for them and myself better than being separated from each other. I make you witness that they are all free." *(Tirmidhi)*

The Sahabah Abide by the Verse "Whether you Make Known What is in Your Hearts or Hide it..."

Abu Hurairah ؓ narrates that the Sahabah felt a hard blow when Allah revealed the verse:

لِلَّهِ مَا فِي السَّمَاوَاتِ وَمَا فِي الْأَرْضِ وَإِنْ تُبْدُوا مَا فِي أَنْفُسِكُمْ أَوْ تُخْفُوهُ يُحَاسِبْكُمْ بِهِ اللَّهُ فَيَغْفِرُ لِمَنْ يَشَاءُ وَيُعَذِّبُ مَنْ يَشَاءُ وَاللَّهُ عَلَى كُلِّ شَيْءٍ قَدِيرٌ (284)

To Allah belongs all that is in the heavens and all that is on the earth, and whether you disclose what is in your ownselves or conceal it, Allah will call you to account for it. Then He forgives whom He wills and punishes whom He wills. And Allah is Able to do all things. (Al-Baqara:284)

They approached Rasulullah ﷺ, knelt down and said, "O Rasulullah ﷺ! We have been instructed to do something that is beyond our capabilities." Rasulullah ﷺ said, "Do you wish to say what the people given the 2 previous books before you said when they stated, 'We hear and we disobey!' Rather say, "We hear and we obey. We ask Your forgiveness, O our Rabb. To You is our return." When the Sahabah started to say the same words and their tongues used to it, Allah sent the followed verses:

آمَنَ الرَّسُولُ بِمَا أُنْزِلَ إِلَيْهِ مِنْ رَبِّهِ وَالْمُؤْمِنُونَ كُلٌّ آمَنَ بِاللَّهِ وَمَلَائِكَتِهِ وَكُتُبِهِ وَرُسُلِهِ لَا نُفَرِّقُ بَيْنَ أَحَدٍ مِنْ رُسُلِهِ وَقَالُوا سَمِعْنَا وَأَطَعْنَا غُفْرَانَكَ رَبَّنَا وَإِلَيْكَ الْمَصِيرُ (285)

The Messenger (Muhammad ﷺ) believes in what has been sent down to him from his Lord, and (so do) the believers. Each one believes in Allah, His Angels, His Books, and His Messengers. They say, "We make no distinction between one another of His Messengers" - and they say, "We hear, and we obey. (We seek) Your Forgiveness, our Lord, and to You is the return (of all)." (Al-Baqara:285)

When this happened, Allah abrogated the initial decree by revealing:

لَا يُكَلِّفُ اللَّهُ نَفْسًا إِلَّا وُسْعَهَا لَهَا مَا كَسَبَتْ وَعَلَيْهَا مَا اكْتَسَبَتْ رَبَّنَا لَا تُؤَاخِذْنَا إِنْ نَسِينَا أَوْ أَخْطَأْنَا رَبَّنَا وَلَا تَحْمِلْ عَلَيْنَا إِصْرًا كَمَا حَمَلْتَهُ عَلَى الَّذِينَ مِنْ قَبْلِنَا رَبَّنَا وَلَا تُحَمِّلْنَا مَا لَا طَاقَةَ لَنَا بِهِ وَاعْفُ عَنَّا وَاغْفِرْ لَنَا وَارْحَمْنَا أَنْتَ مَوْلَانَا فَانْصُرْنَا عَلَى الْقَوْمِ الْكَافِرِينَ (286)

Allah burdens not a person beyond his scope. He gets reward for that (good) which he has earned, and he is punished for that (evil) which he has earned. "Our Lord! Punish us not if we forget or fall into error, our Lord! Lay not on us a burden like that which You did lay on those before us (Jews and Christians); our Lord! Put not on us a burden greater than we have strength to

bear. Pardon us and grant us Forgiveness. Have mercy on us. You are our Maula (Patron, Supporter and Protector, etc.) and give us victory over the disbelieving people." (Al-Baqara:286)* *(Ahmad, Muslim)*

Mujahid says that he once approached Abdullah bin Abbas ؓ and said, "I was with Abdullah bin Omar ؓ when he recited a verse and started weeping." "What is the verse?" Abdullah bin Abbas ؓ enquired. Mujahid replied that it was the verse:

وَإِنْ تُبْدُوا مَا فِي أَنْفُسِكُمْ أَوْ تُخْفُوهُ يُحَاسِبْكُمْ بِهِ اللَّهُ فَيَغْفِرُ لِمَنْ يَشَاءُ وَيُعَذِّبُ مَنْ يَشَاءُ وَاللَّهُ عَلَى كُلِّ شَيْءٍ قَدِيرٌ (284)

To Allah belongs all that is in the heavens and all that is on the earth, and whether you disclose what is in your ownselves or conceal it, Allah will call you to account for it. Then He forgives whom He wills and punishes whom He wills. And Allah is Able to do all things. (Al-Baqara:284)

Abdullah bin Abbas ؓ explained, "When this verse was revealed, it filled the Sahabah with worry and extreme anxiety. 'O Rasulullah ﷺ!' they said, 'We are destroyed! While we may be taken to task for what we say and do, our hearts are beyond our control, we cannot control our thoughts.' Rasulullah ﷺ said, 'Say, 'We hear and we obey'.' When they said 'We hear and we obey', the decree was abrogated by the verse:

آمَنَ الرَّسُولُ بِمَا أُنْزِلَ إِلَيْهِ مِنْ رَبِّهِ وَالْمُؤْمِنُونَ كُلٌّ آمَنَ بِاللَّهِ وَمَلَائِكَتِهِ وَكُتُبِهِ وَرُسُلِهِ لَا نُفَرِّقُ بَيْنَ أَحَدٍ مِنْ رُسُلِهِ وَقَالُوا سَمِعْنَا وَأَطَعْنَا غُفْرَانَكَ رَبَّنَا وَإِلَيْكَ الْمَصِيرُ (285) لَا يُكَلِّفُ اللَّهُ نَفْسًا إِلَّا وُسْعَهَا لَهَا مَا كَسَبَتْ وَعَلَيْهَا مَا اكْتَسَبَتْ

The Messenger (Muhammad ﷺ) believes in what has been sent down to him from his Lord, and (so do) the believers. Each one believes in Allah, His Angels, His Books, and His Messengers. They say, "We make no distinction between one another of His Messengers" - and they say, "We hear, and we obey. (We seek) Your Forgiveness, our Lord, and to You is the return (of all)." Allah burdens not a person beyond his scope. He gets reward for that (good) which he has earned, and he is punished for that (evil) which he has earned... (Al-Baqara:285-286)

People are therefore excused for their thoughts and will be taken to task only for what they actually do." *(Ahmad).* A brief narration states that Rasulullah ﷺ advised the Sahabah to say, "We hear, we obey and we accept". Allah then entrenched Iman into their hearts. *(Ahmad, Muslim, Ibn Jareer, Tafsir Ibn Kathir)*

The Response of the Sahabah to the Verse "Those who do not Mix Their Iman with Wrong-Doing"

Abdullah bin Mas'ood ؓ narrates that it was a hard blow to the Sahabah when Allah revealed the verse: وَلَمْ يَلْبِسُوا إِيمَانَهُمْ بِظُلْمٍ

...those who believe (in the Oneness of Allah and worship none but Him Alone) and confuse not their belief with Zulm (wrong i.e. by worshipping others besides Allah)...(Al-An'am:82)

They asked Rasulullah ﷺ, "Which of us does not commit Dhulm (wrongs)?" Rasulullah ﷺ clarified the matter saying, "It is not as you think. Dhulm in this context does not refer to mere wrong-doing. Luqman said to his son:(13) يَا بُنَيَّ لَا تُشْرِكْ بِاللَّهِ إِنَّ الشِّرْكَ لَظُلْمٌ عَظِيمٌ

O my son! Join not in worship others with Allah. Verily! Joining others in worship with Allah is a great Zoolm (wrong) indeed. (Luqman:13). (The word Dhulm in the verse therefore refers to Shirk and not just any sin). (Ibn Abi Hatim, Bukhari)

Another narration states that when the verse: وَلَمْ يَلْبِسُوا إِيمَانَهُمْ بِظُلْمٍ

...those who believe (in the Oneness of Allah and worship none but Him Alone) and confuse not their belief with Zulm (wrong i.e. by worshipping others besides Allah)...(Al-An'am:82)

was revealed, Rasulullah ﷺ said, "I was told by Allah that I am amongst such people." *(Ibn Mardway in Tafsir Ibn Kathir)*

The Response of the Ladies of the Sahabah When Allah Revealed the verse: "They Should Wear Their Scarves Over Their Chests"

Safiya bint Shaiba ؓ reports that they were once with Aisha ؓ discussing the women of the Quraish and their virtues. Aisha ؓ remarked, "No doubt the women of the Quraish have great virtues, but I swear by Allah that I have not seen women better than the women of the Ansar. They were the strongest believers in the Qur'an and in revelation. When Allah revealed the verse of Surah Nur: وَلْيَضْرِبْنَ بِخُمُرِهِنَّ عَلَى جُيُوبِهِنَّ

... and to draw their veils over their hearts... (An-Nur:31)

Their men went to the them to recite the verse to them. Every man recited the verse to his wife, his daughter, his sister and to every Mahram of his. Everyone of these women took their decorated shawls and wrapped it around themselves because of their strong faith in what Allah has revealed in this Book. The next morning they all performed salah behind Rasulullah ﷺ with their shawls wrapped and protruding above their heads because of its large size and looking as if there were crows perched on their heads." *(Ibn Abi Hatim, Abu Dawud, Tafsir Ibn Kathir)*

The Incident of an Old Man who had Committed Many Sins and the Incident of Abu Farwa ؓ

Makhul narrates that an extremely old man whose eyebrows had actually fallen over his eyes once came and said, "O Rasulullah ﷺ! There is a man who had been treacherous and sinful. There was not a passion (right or wrong) that he did not grab at with his right hand and should his sins be distributed amongst the inhabitants of the earth, they would all be destroyed. Is there any repentance for him?" "Have you accepted Islam?" Rasulullah ﷺ asked. The old man said, "I testify that there is none worthy of worship but Allah and I testify that Muhammad ﷺ is the servant and Rasul of Allah." Rasulullah ﷺ then said, "As long as you remain like this as a Muslim, Allah shall forgive all your treachery and sins and convert all your evils into good deeds." "O Rasulullah ﷺ!" The man said, "All my treachery and sins?" "Yes," Rasulullah ﷺ assured him, "all you treachery and sins." The man then left reciting "Allahu Akbar" and "La Ilaha IllAllah Muhammadur Rasulullah." *(Ibn Abi Hatim)*. Abu Farwa ؓ narrates that a man once came to Rasulullah ﷺ saying, "O Rasulullah ﷺ! Tell me about a man who had committed every type of sin and has not left any passion unfulfilled. Can he repent?" "Have you accepted Islam?" Rasulullah ﷺ asked. When the confirmed that he did, Rasulullah ﷺ said, "Do good deeds and abstain from evil. Allah will then convert them all your past sins into good deeds." The man said, "Even all my treachery and sins?" "Certainly," Rasulullah ﷺ assured him. The man then continued calling out "Allahu Akbar" until he disappeared from sight. *(Tabrani in Tafsir Ibn Kathir)*

The Incident of a Sinful Woman and Abu Hurairah ؓ

Abu Hurairah ؓ relates, "A woman once came to me and asked, 'Is there any repentance for me when I have committed adultery, given birth to a child and then killed it?' 'Not at all!' I cried out, 'Neither can you expect and goodness or honor.' She then got up and left with deep remorse. After performing the Fajr salah behind Rasulullah ﷺ, I related to him what the lady had said and what reply I gave her. Rasulullah ﷺ said, 'Your reply was a terrible one indeed! Do you not recite the verse:

وَالَّذِينَ لَا يَدْعُونَ مَعَ اللَّهِ إِلَهًا آخَرَ وَلَا يَقْتُلُونَ النَّفْسَ الَّتِي حَرَّمَ اللَّهُ إِلَّا بِالْحَقِّ وَلَا يَزْنُونَ وَمَنْ

يَفْعَلْ ذَلِكَ يَلْقَ أَثَامًا (68) يُضَاعَفْ لَهُ الْعَذَابُ يَوْمَ الْقِيَامَةِ وَيَخْلُدْ فِيهِ مُهَانًا (69) إِلَّا مَنْ تَابَ وَآمَنَ وَعَمِلَ عَمَلًا صَالِحًا فَأُولَئِكَ يُبَدِّلُ اللَّهُ سَيِّئَاتِهِمْ حَسَنَاتٍ وَكَانَ اللَّهُ غَفُورًا رَحِيمًا (70)

And those who invoke not any other ilah (god) along with Allah, nor kill such life as Allah has forbidden, except for just cause, nor commit illegal sexual intercourse and whoever does this shall receive the punishment. The torment will be doubled to him on the Day of Resurrection, and he will abide therein in disgrace; Except those who repent and believe (in Islam), and do righteous deeds, for those, Allah will change their sins into good deeds, and Allah is Oft-Forgiving, Most Merciful. (Al-Furqan:68-70). When I then recited these verses to the woman, she fell down in Sajdah saying, "All raise belongs to Allah Who has created an escape for me." *(Ibn Abi Hatim)*. Another narration states that she cried out, "O dear! Has this beauty been created for Jahannam?" The same narration further says that after leaving Rasulullah ﷺ, Abu Hurairah ؓ searched for the woman throughout the neighborhood of Madinah but was unable to find her. It was only when she came to him the following night that he was able to inform her about what Rasulullah ﷺ said. She then fell down in Sejdah saying, "All praise belongs to Allah Who has created an escape for me and had allowed me repentance from my actions." She then set free a slave woman she owned together with the slave's child and proceeded to repent sincerely to Allah. *(Ibn Jareer in Tafsir Ibn Kathir)*

The Response of Rasulullah ﷺ's Poets When Allah Revealed the verse: "Only Deviant People Follow the Poets"

Abul Hasan the freed slave of Tamim Dari ؓ narrates that when the verse: وَالشُّعَرَاءُ يَتَّبِعُهُمُ الْغَاوُونَ (224)

As for the poets, the erring follow the., (Ash-Shu'ara:224) was revealed, Hassan bin Thabit ؓ, Abdullah bin Rawaha ؓ and Ka'b bin Malik ؓ all came weeping to Rasulullah ﷺ. They said, "Allah knew well that we are all poets when He revealed this verse (the verse therefore refers to us)." Rasulullah ﷺ then recited the verse: إِلَّا الَّذِينَ آمَنُوا وَعَمِلُوا الصَّالِحَاتِ

Except those who have Iman, who do good acts...

"That is you," Rasulullah ﷺ said. وَذَكَرُوا اللَّهَ كَثِيرًا

...who remember Allah abundantly...

"That is also you," Rasulullah ﷺ said. وَانْتَصَرُوا مِنْ بَعْدِ مَا ظُلِمُوا

...and vindicate themselves after they have been wronged (by replying back in poetry to the unjust poetry (which the pagan poets utter against the Muslims))...(Shu'ara:227)

"And that is also you," Rasulullah ﷺ said (you men are therefore excluded from the deviant poets). *(Ibn Is'haq, Ibn Abi Hatim, Ibn Jareer in Tafsir Ibn Kathir, Hakim)*

Longing to Meet Allah and Dislike to Meet Him

Ata bin Sa'ib narrates that the first time he saw Abdur Rahman bin Abu Laila ؓ was when he saw an old man with white hair and a white beard following a funeral procession on his donkey. He was narrating from someone else that Rasulullah ﷺ said, "Whoever loves Allah, Allah loves to meet him and whoever dislikes meeting Allah, Allah dislikes meeting him." When the people present there started to weep, he asked, "What makes you all weep?" They replied, "We dislike death." "That is not what is meant," he explained, "what is meant is that when a person is about to die, he will like to meet Allah when (angels) give the good news: فَأَمَّا إِنْ كَانَ مِنَ الْمُقَرَّبِينَ (88) فَرَوْحٌ وَرَيْحَانٌ وَجَنَّةُ نَعِيمٍ

Then, if he (the dying person) be of the Muqarraboon (those brought near to Allah), (There is for him) rest and provision, and a Garden of delights (Paradise). (Al-Waqi'a:88-89)

At the same time, Allah loves to meet him even more. On the other hand, he dislikes meeting Allah and Allah dislikes meeting him even more when he is told:

وَأَمَّا إِنْ كَانَ مِنَ الْمُكَذِّبِينَ الضَّالِّينَ (92) فَنُزُلٌ مِنْ حَمِيمٍ (93) وَتَصْلِيَةُ جَحِيمٍ (94)

But if he (dying person) be of the denying (of the Resurrection), the erring (away from the Right Path of Islamic Monotheism), Then for him is entertainment with boiling water. And burning in Hell-fire. (Al-Waqi'a:92-94) (Ahmad in Tafsir Ibn Kathir)

Abu Bakr ؓ Weeps When Allah Reveals the Verse: "When the Earth shall Quake most Violently"

Abdullah bin Amr bin Al Aas ؓ narrates that Abu Bakr Siddiq ؓ was sitting somewhere and started weeping excessively when Allah revealed the verse: (1) إِذَا زُلْزِلَتِ الْأَرْضُ زِلْزَالَهَا

When the earth is shaken with its (final) earthquake. (Az-Zilzal:1)

"What makes you weep so, O Abu Bakr?" Rasulullah ﷺ asked. "It is this Surah that makes me weep," Abu Bakr ؓ replied. Rasulullah then said, "If you people were such that you neither erred nor sinned so that Allah could forgive you, Allah would create a nation that errs and sins just so that He could forgive them." *(Ibn Jareer in Tafsir Ibn Kathir)*

Rasulullah ﷺ informs Omar ؓ on What Would Happen in the Grave

Omar ؓ reports that Rasulullah ﷺ once said to him, "O Omar! What would be your condition when you are in a piece of ground measuring 4 arm's lengths by 2 arm's lengths and when you see Munkar and Nakir?" "O Rasulullah ﷺ!" Omar ؓ asked, "What is Munkar and Nakir?" Rasulullah ﷺ replied, "They are the 2 examiners in the grave. They will dig the grave open with their canines and approach treading on their extremely long hairs. Their voices will be like devastating thunderclaps and their eyes like blinding lightning. They will both be carrying hammers so large that all the people of Mina are unable to even lift, yet for them it will be as easy as carrying this staff." Rasulullah ﷺ shook a little staff in his hand. They will then examine you. Should you fail to answer or delay, they will strike you with their hammers and reduce you to dust." Omar ؓ asked, "O Rasulullah ﷺ! Will I be in the condition I am in now of control of my senses?" Rasulullah ﷺ replied in the affirmative, Omar ؓ said, "In that case, I shall be able to handle them." *(Abu Dawud in Ba'th, Abu Shaikh in Sunnah, Hakim in Kuna, Bayhaqi in Kitabu Adhabil Qabr, Isfahani in Hujja, Kanzul Ummal, Sa'eed bin Mansur)*

Another narration adds that Rasulullah ﷺ then said to Omar ؓ, "I swear by the Being Who has sent me with the truth that Jibra'el has just informed me that when the two of them come to you and pose the questions, you will say to them, 'Allah is my Rabb, who is Yours? Muhammad ﷺ is my Nabi, who is yours? Islam is my Deen, what is yours?' They will then both exclaim, 'How strange! We do not know whether we have been sent to you to question or whether you have been sent to question us!'" *(Abdul Wahid Maqdasi in At-Tabsir, Riyadhun Nudhra)*

The Statement of Omar ؓ on the Strength of Uthman ؓ's Iman

Abul Bahriya Kindi narrates that Omar ؓ once came out of his home and found a gathering in which Uthman bin Affan ؓ was present. Referring to Uthman ؓ, he said to the people, "You have amongst you a man whose Iman is such that if it is distributed amongst an entire army, it would suffice for them all." *(Ibn Askar in Muntakhab Kanzul Ummal)*

Words of the Sahabah that have Already been Quoted About the Strength of Iman

When someone once asked Abdullah bin Omar ؓ if the Sahabah ever laughed, he replied, "Yes. However, the Iman in their hearts still remained firmer than mountains." Already quoted in the chapter discussing how the Sahabah bore hardships, is the statement of Ammar ؓ who said, "I find that my heart is content with Iman." This he said after the Mushrikin forced him to praise their gods and Rasulullah ﷺ asked him, "How is the condition of your hearts?" *(Abu Nu'aym in Hilya, Ibn Sa'd, Ibn Jareer, Bayhaqi in Tafsir Ibn Kathir)*. In the chapter discussing the appointment of a Khalifa, the words of Abu Bakr ؓ have passed, who said, "Are you scaring me with my Rabb? My prayer is, 'O Allah! I have appointed the best of them to be my successor.'" In another narration he said, "I know Allah and Omar better than you." Also passed were the words of Omar ؓ when he decided to distribute all the funds in the state treasury and someone advised him to keep some behind in case an enemy attacks or for any other emergency. He said, "It is Saitan speaking with your tongue. Allah has inspired me with the response and I swear by Allah that I shall never disobey Him today for the emergencies of tomorrow. I shall not (do as you say) but shall rather prepare for the Muslims that which Rasulullah ﷺ had prepared for them the obedience to Allah and Rasulullah ﷺ." He also said, "I swear by Allah that I shall never disobey Him for the emergencies of tomorrow." Yet another narration quotes him as follows: "I have prepared Taqwa as a defense for the Muslims. Allah mentions:

وَمَنْ يَتَّقِ اللَّهَ يَجْعَلْ لَهُ مَخْرَجًا (2) وَيَرْزُقْهُ مِنْ حَيْثُ لَا يَحْتَسِبُ

....He (Allah) will make a way for him to get out (from every difficulty). And He will provide him from (sources) he never could imagine.... (At-Talaq:2-3)

In the chapter discussing the fervor of the Sahabah to spend in the Path of Allah, the words of Ali ؓ are quoted thus: "The Iman of a person cannot be true until he has more trust in that which is in Allah's hands than that which is in his hands." This he said when he wanted to spend on a beggar and Fatima ؓ said, "You had left the 6 Dirhams to purchase flour." Also quoted were the word of Amir bin Rabe'ah ؓ who said, "I have no need for your land because today a Surah has been revealed that makes us oblivious of this world: (1) اقْتَرَبَ لِلنَّاسِ حِسَابُهُمْ وَهُمْ فِي غَفْلَةٍ مُعْرِضُونَ

Draws near for mankind their reckoning, while they turn away in heedlessness. (Al-Anbiya:1)

The words of Aisha ؓ have also quoted when she said, "Usaid bin Hudhair ؓ was amongst the best of people. He would always say, 'I have no doubts about being amongst the inhabitants of Jannah if I could remain in 1 of 3 conditions. (1) The condition when I am reciting Qur'an or listening to it being recited, (2) the condition when I am listening to Rasulullah ﷺ's sermon and (3) the condition when I present at a funeral. At every funeral I have been, I have thought about nothing other than what will become of the deceased or where it is heading.'" *(Hakim)*

The chapter Concerning the Sahabah Getting Together for Salah

This chapter highlights how Nabi ﷺ and the Sahabah gathered together in the Masjid for salah, how great was their fervor for this, how they encouraged others to do the same and how they understood that as they proceeded from salah to salah, they were required to allow their lives to progress from one command of Allah to another. It also highlights how they forsook their occupations to do the acts Allah had commanded, which contributed to the strength of their Iman and the features of their Iman. The chapter also tells us how they spread their knowledge together with the deeds linked to knowledge, how they added life to Dhikr and made Du'a with all its requirements for acceptance. They therefore never turned their attention towards the apparent means and took no benefit except fron1 the Creator of these means and the One Who controls them.

The Encouragement Nabi ﷺ gave for Salah: The Narrations of Uthman ؓ and Salman ؓ

Harith who was the freed slave of Uthman ؓ narrates that they were once sitting with Uthman ؓ when the Mu'adhin arrived to call out the Adhan. Uthman ؓ asked for a utensil which the narrator estimates contained approximately a Mudd of water. After performing wudhu, he said, "I saw Rasulullah ﷺ performing wudhu just as I have performed it and then say, 'Whoever performs a wudhu like this and then stands up to perform the Zuhr salah, all his sins between the Fajr salah and Zuhr salah are forgiven. When he performs the Asr salah, all his sins between the Zuhr salah and Asr salah are forgiven. Thereafter, when he performs the Maghrib salah, all his sins between the Asr salah and Maghrib salah are forgiven. Similarly, when he performs the Isha salah, all his sins between the Maghrib salah and Isha salah are also forgiven. He may then pass the night in sin, but if he wakes up, performs wudhu and then the Fajr salah, all his sins between the Isha salah and Fajr salah are forgiven. These salats are the good that wipe out sins *(ref. Surah Hud:114).*'" The people then asked, "O Uthman! If these are the good deeds, what then are the 'lasting good deeds' *(ref. Surah Kahaf:46)*!?" Uthman ؓ replied, "That is to recite 'La Ilaha IIlallah', لا إلَهَ إلاَّ الله 'SubhanAllah', سُبْحَانَ الله 'Al Hamdu Lillah', وَالْحَمْدُ لِلّهِ 'Allahu Akbar' and الله أَكْبَر 'La Howla wa La Quwata Illa Billah'." ولاحول ولا قوة الا بِاللّهِ *(Ahmad, Abu Ya'la, Bazzar in Targheeb wat Tarheeb, Haythami).* Abu Uthman reports that he was once with Salman beneath a tree when Salman ؓ caught hold of a dry branch and shook it until its leaves all fell off. "O Abu Uthman!" he said, "Will you not ask me why I did that?" "Why did you do that?' Abu Uthman ؓ asked. Salman ؓ replied, "This is exactly what Rasulullah ﷺ did when I was once standing with him beneath a tree. He took hold of a dry branch and shook it until its leaves all fell off. 'O Salman!' he said, 'Will you not ask me why I did that?' 'Why did you do that?' I asked. Rasulullah ﷺ explained, 'When a Muslim performs wudhu properly and performs his 5 salats, his sins fall off him just as these leaves have fallen.' Rasulullah ﷺ then recited the verse: وَأَقِمِ الصَّلاَةَ طَرَفَيِ النَّهَارِ وَزُلَفًا مِنَ اللَّيْلِ إِنَّ الْحَسَنَاتِ يُذْهِبْنَ السَّيِّئَاتِ ذَلِكَ ذِكْرَى لِلذَّاكِرِينَ (114) *And perform As-Salat), at the two ends of the day and in some hours of the night (i.e. the five compulsory Salat (prayers)). Verily, the good deeds remove the evil deeds (i.e. small sins). That is a reminder (an advice) for the mindful (those who accept advice). (Hud:114) (Ahmad, Nasa'ee, Tabrani in Targheeb wat Tarheeb)*

The incident of 2 brothers who passed away, one as a Martyr and the other some time later

Amir the son of Sa'd bin Abi Waqqas narrates that he heard his father and other Sahabah narrate that 2 brothers lived during the time of Rasulullah ﷺ. The one who was the better of the 2 died a martyr while other lived some after him before also passing away 40 days later *(Tabrani in Awsat).* When someone mentioned to Rasulullah ﷺ that the one was a better person who carried out more good deeds, Rasulullah ﷺ asked, "Was he not performing salah?" When the Sahabah confirmed that the person was performing salah, Rasulullah ﷺ remarked, "You have no idea where his salats after the demise of his brother may have taken him." It was on this occasion that Rasulullah ﷺ said, "The example of salah is like a deep and pure river running by the door of a person. When he bathes in it 5 times a day, do you think that any dirt can remain on his body?" *(Ahmad, Haythami, Malik, Nasa'ee, Ibn Khuzaima, Targheeb wat Tarheeb).* Abu Hurairah ؓ narrates that 2 men from the Baliy branch of the Qudha tribe accepted Islam at the hands of Rasulullah ﷺ. While the one was martyred, the other lived another year after which he passed away naturally. It was Talha bin Ubaidulla who saw in a dream that the one who passed away later entered Jannah before the martyr. Surprised at this, he or someone else reported it to Rasulullah ﷺ the next morning. Rasulullah ﷺ explained, "Did he not fast a Ramadhan after the other and perform 6,000 odd more Rakats of salah in the year afterwards?" *(Ahmad in Targheeb wat Tarheeb)* Another narration adds that the difference in their stages was as large as the distance between the heavens and the earth. *(Ibn Majah, Ibn Hibban)*

Rasulullah ﷺ tells a Sahabi that his Salah is Compensation for Sin

Ali ؓ narrates that they were once with Rasulullah ﷺ in the Masjid when a man stood up and said, "O Rasulullah ﷺ! I have committed a sin." Rasulullah ﷺ ignored him and after the salah was complete, the man again stood up and repeated himself. Rasulullah ﷺ asked him, "Did you not perform the salah with us after making a proper wudhu?" When the man replied that he had, Rasulullah ﷺ said, "That is then compensation for your sin." *(Tabrani, Haythami)*

Rasulullah ﷺ's reply to a Man who asked on the Best of all Deeds

Abdullah bin Amr ؓ narrates that a man once asked Rasulullah ﷺ what the best of all deeds was. "Salah," Rasulullah ﷺ replied. "What then?" the man asked. Again Rasulullah ﷺ said that it was salah. For the 3rd time the man repeated the question and again Rasulullah ﷺ told him that it was salah. When he repeated the question too often, Rasulullah ﷺ said, "Jihad in the Path of Allah." "But I have parents," the man said. "Then," Rasulullah ﷺ said, "I instruct you to treat your parents well." Thereafter the man said, "I swear by the Being Who has sent you as a Nabi with the truth that I shall fight in Jihad and leave them." To this, Rasulullah ﷺ said, "You know best that they have someone else to serve them while you are away." *(Ahmad, Haythami, Ibn Hibban in Targheeb wat Tarheeb)*

Rasulullah ﷺ Tells a Man who has Fulfilled the Pillars of Islam that he is From Amongst the Siddiqin and the Martyrs

Amr bin Murra Juhani narrates that a man once said, "O Rasulullah ﷺ! Tell me in which category of people I will belong if I testify that there is none worthy of worship but Allah, that you are the Rasul of Allah and if I perform my 5 salats, pay my zakah, fast in Ramadhan and perform Nafl salah during Ramadhan?" Rasulullah ﷺ replied, "You shall be amongst the Siddiqin and the martyrs." *(Ibn Khuzaima, Ibn Hibban in Targheeb wat Tarheeb)*

Rasulullah ﷺ Emphasizes the Salah Even on his Deathbed

Anas ؓ says, "What Rasulullah ﷺ emphasized most on his deathbed was, 'Take good care of your salah and your slaves.' In fact, he was saying these words even when his soul had reached his throat and he was unable to say them clearly." *(Bayhaqi, Nasa'ee, Ibn Majah)*. Another narration states that what Rasulullah ﷺ emphasized most on his deathbed was, "Take good care of your Salah and your slaves" until his breath was caught in his chest and he was unable to bring the words to his tongue." *(Ahmad)*. Ali ؓ relates, "Rasulullah ﷺ instructed me to bring him a slate to write down something that his Ummah should never forget after his demise. Fearing that he would pass away before I could bring it, I said, "Tell it to me and I shall memorize it well." He said, "I wish to emphasize that my Ummah take good care of their salah, zakah and their slaves." *(Ahmad in Al Bidayah wan Nihayah)*. Another similar narration adds that Ali ؓ said, "Rasulullah ﷺ then emphasized the performing of salah, the paying of zakah and kind treatment of slaves until his soul departed. It was also right up to the departure of his soul that he also emphasized the reciting of the Shahada that there is none worthy of worship but Allah and that Muhammad ﷺ is the servant and Rasul of Allah. He mentioned that the fire of Jahannam is forbidden for the person who testifies to these 2 beliefs (contained in the Shahada)." *(Ibn Sa'd)*. Yet another narration from Ali ؓ states that the last words of Rasulullah ﷺ were, "Guard your Salah! Guard your Salah! Fear Allah with regard to your slaves." *(Ahmad, Bukhari in Adab, Abu Dawud, Ibn Majah, Ibn Jareer, Abu Ya'la, Bayhaqi in Kanzul Ummal)*

The Statements of Abu Bakr ؓ and Omar ؓ Concerning salah

Abu Bakr ؓ said, "It is by salah that a person secures Allah's protection on earth." *(Hakim)*. Abu Malih reports that he heard Omar ؓ say from the pulpit "There can be no Islam in the person who does not perform salah." *(Ibn Sa'd in Kanzul Ummal)*

The Statements of Zaid ؓ, Hudhaifa ؓ, Abdullah bin Omar ؓ and Abdullah bin Amr ؓ Concerning Salah

Zaid bin Thabit ؓ said, "When a man performs Nafl salah at home, it is a source of light for the house. As a person stands in salah, his sins stand suspended above his head and they are erased each time he prostrates." *(Abdur Razzaq)*. Hudhaifa ؓ said, "When a person performs wudhu properly and then stands for salah, Allah turns towards him and converses with him. Allah then does not turn away from him until the person himself turns away or turns towards the right or left." *(Abdur Razzaq)*. Abdullah bin Omar ؓ said, "Salah is an extremely virtuous deed and I care not who joins me in it." *(Abdur Razzaq in Kanzul Ummal)*. Abdullah bin Amr ؓ said, "Whenever a Muslim goes to an elevated location or to a Masjid built of stone and performs salah there, the ground says; 'Salah has been performed for Allah on his ground. O person! I shall testify on your behalf the day you meet Allah. *(Ibn Asakir)*. Abdullah bin Amr ؓ narrates that when a sore developed on Adam's neck, he performed salah. This made the sore fall to his chest. He again performed salah, the sore dropped to his hip and then to his ankle when he performed salah again. After performing salah again, the sore moved to his toe and then finally left his body when he performed salah again.

(Abdur Razzaq in Kanzul Ummal)

Some Statements of Abdullah bin Mas'ood ؓ, Salman ؓ and Abu Musa Ash'ari ؓ Concerning Salah

Abdullah bin Mas'ood ؓ said, "You are knocking at the King's (Allah's) door as long as you are performing salah and the door of the King opens to whoever knocks." *(Abu Nu'aym in Hilya)*. Another narration states that he said, "Stack your needs on the Fard salats." Abdullah bin Mas'ood ؓ also said, "The salats compensate for all sins committed between them as long as major sins are avoided."*(Abdur Razzaq)*. He also said, "Salah compensates for the sins committed after them. Adam ؑ once developed a sore on his toe that went up to his foot and then further to his knee. Thereafter, it traveled further to the base of his hips and then to the base of his neck. He then performed salah, causing it to fall to his shoulders. When he again performed salah, the sore dropped to his hip and then to his knee when he performed salah yet again. After performing salah again, the sore moved to his foot and then finally left his body when he performed salah once more." *(Ibn Asakir in Kanzul Ummal)*. Salman Farsi ؓ said, "When a person stands up to perform salah, his sins are raised above his head and by the time he completes his salah, they fall away from him just as the fronds of a palm fall to the right and left." *(Abdur Razzaq)*. Another narration states that Salman ؓ once said, "As a person stands in salah, his sins are all gathered above his head. They then fall off each time he prostrates just as leaves fall off a tree." *(Ibn Zanjway)*.

Tariq bin Shihab narrates that he once spent the night with Salman ؓ to observe how he exerted himself in Ibada. Salman ؓ however woke up only in the last portion of the night to perform Tahajjud and Tariq therefore did not see what he had expected (he expected that Salman would spend the entire night in Ibada). When this was mentioned to Salman ؓ, he remarked, "Guard the five Fard salats well because they compensate for all one's sins as long as major sins were not perpetrated which are forgiven only after Tauba. At night people are divided into 3 categories. There are those who have good to their credit and no sin to their loss. Then there are those who have no good to their credit and only sin to their loss. Finally, there are those who have neither good to their credit nor sin to their loss. The person who exploits the negligence of the people and the darkness of the night to stand in salah until the morning is the one with good to his credit and no sin to his loss. As for the person who exploits the negligence of the people and the darkness of the night to immerse his head in sin is the one with no good to his credit but only sin to his loss. Then there is the person who goes to sleep immediately after performing his Isha salah without getting up to perform the Tahajjud salah. This is the person with neither good to his credit nor sin to his loss. Beware of exerting yourself so much in Ibada that you are unable to cope and continue. Ensure that you always adopt moderation and constancy." *(Abdur Razzaq in Kanzul Ummal, Tabrani in Kabir, Haythami)*. Abu Musa Ash'ari ؓ said, "By committing sins we are constantly burning ourselves up but when we perform the Fard salah, our sins are compensated for. When we again burn ourselves up, the salah we perform again compensates for the sins committed before it." *(Abdur Razzaq in Kanzul Ummal)*.

Rasulullah ﷺ says that the Coolness of his Eyes is in Salah and the Remark of Jibra'el ؑ

Anas bin Malik ؓ narrates that Rasulullah ﷺ once said, "Perfume and women have been made beloved to and the coolness of my eyes (my source of comfort and joy) has been kept in salah." *(Ahmad, Nas'ee)*. Abdullah bin Abbas 🕮 narrates that Jibra'el الخطة once said to Rasulullah 🕮, "Salah has been made beloved to you, so take from it as much as you please." *(Ahmad in Al Bidayah wan Nihayah, Tabrani in Kabir, Haythami)*

Rasulullah 🕮 says, "My Passion is for Standing in Salah at Night"

Abdullah bin Abbas 🕮 narrates Nabi 🕮 was once sitting with the Sahabah around him when he said, "Allah has given every Nabi 🕮 a desire for something and my desire is for standing in Tahajjud salah at night. Therefore, when I stand up for salah at night, none of you should ever follow me. Allah has also created a means of income for every Nabi 🕮 and my source of income is the Khums (1/5th of the spoils of war). When I pass away, it will go to the leaders of the Muslims after me." *(Tabrani, Haythami)*.

Statement of the Sahabah on Rasulullah 🕮's Salah at Night

Anas 🕮 narrates that Rasulullah 🕮 used to stand so long in Tahajjud salah that his feet would swell. Another narration states that his calves would swell. Someone asked him. "Has Allah not forgiven all your past and future mistakes, then why do you exert yourself so?" Rasulullah 🕮 replied. "Should I then not be a grateful servant?" *(Abu Dawud in Kanzul Ummal, Abu Ya'la, Bazzar, Tabrani, Haythami)*. Abu Hurairah 🕮 also narrates that Rasulullah 🕮 used to stand so long in Tahajjud salah that his feet would swell. *(Bazzar, Haythami, Tabrani)*. Abdullah bin Mas'ood 🕮 also reports that Rasulullah 🕮 used to stand so long in Tahajjud salah at night that his feet would swell. The rest of the narration is as quoted above. *(Tabrani in Saghir and Awsat)*. Nu'man bin Bashir 🕮 narrates that Rasulullah 🕮 used to stand so long in Tahajjud salah that his feet would cut after becoming extremely chapped. The rest of the narration is as quoted above. *(Tabrani in Awsat, Majma'uz Zawa'id)*. Aisha 🕮 says, "Rasulullah 🕮 used to stand so long in Tahajjud salah at night that his feet would rupture. I said to him, 'O Rasulullah 🕮! Why do you do this when Allah has forgiven all your past and future mistakes?' He replied, 'Should I then not be a grateful servant?'"*(Bukhari, Muslim)* The same has been reported from Mughiera 🕮 *(Riyadh)* and Abu Hurairah 🕮. *(Ibn Najjar)*. Anas 🕮 says, "Rasulullah 🕮 used to exert himself much in Ibada that he became like an old water bag. 'O Rasulullah 🕮!' the Sahabah said, 'What makes you do this? Has Allah not forgiven all your past and future mistakes?' He replied. 'Of course! Should I then not be a grateful servant?'" *(Ibn Najjar in Kanzul Ummal)*. Humaid narrates that when Anas bin Malik 🕮 was once questioned about the salah Rasulullah 🕮 performed at night, he replied. "The times we wanted to see Rasulullah 🕮 performing salah at night, we would see him and the times we wanted to see him asleep, we also saw him (he would spend part of the night in salah and also sleep). There were times when he fasted so often during the month that we would think he will now not stop fasting. There were also times when he would not fast for so long that we would think he would not fast at all that month."*(Bukhari, Muslim)*

Abdullah bin Mas'ood 🕮 relates, "I followed Rasulullah 🕮 in salah one night and he remained standing so long that I contemplated doing something terrible." "What was it that you contemplated?" the people asked. Abdullah bin Mas'ood 🕮 replied, "I actually contemplated sitting down and leaving." *(Bukhari, Muslim in Safwatus Safwa)*. Abu Dhar 🕮 narrates that Rasulullah 🕮 once stood the entire night until dawn in salah reciting the verse:

إِنْ تُعَذِّبْهُمْ فَإِنَّهُمْ عِبَادُكَ وَإِنْ تَغْفِرْ لَهُمْ فَإِنَّكَ أَنْتَ الْعَزِيزُ الْحَكِيمُ (118)

If You punish them, they are Your slaves, and if You forgive them, verily You, only You are the All-Mighty, the All-Wise. (Al-Ma'ida:118) (Ahmad in Al Bidayah wan Nihayah)

Anas 🕮 narrates that Rasulullah 🕮 was injured one day. The following morning, someone remarked, "O Rasulullah 🕮! The effect of the injury is still clearly noticeable on you." Rasulullah 🕮 said, "Despite that, I recited 7 lengthy Surahs last night." *(Abu Ya'la, Haythami)*.

The Incident of Hudhaifa 🕮 with Rasulullah 🕮

Hudhaifa 🕮 says, "I performed salah behind Rasulullah 🕮 one night and when he commenced with Surah Baqarah, I said to myself that he would proceed into Ruku after completing 100 verses. When he carried on after 100, I told myself that he would complete the Surah in 2 Rakats. However, when he still continued, I anticipated that he would complete the Surah and then proceed into Ruku. After completing Surah Baqarah Rasulullah 🕮 however then started reciting Surah Nisa and after completing it, he commenced Surah Al Imran. Rasulullah 🕮 recited slowly. Whenever he recited a verse mentioning Tasbih, he recited Tasbih, when he passed a verse speaking of asking from Allah, he asked from Allah and when he passed a verse speaking of seeking Allah's protection, he sought Allah's protection. Thereafter, Rasulullah 🕮 proceeded into Ruku, in which he recited,

'Subhana Rabbiyal Adheem'. سبحان ربي العظيم

The time he took for Ruku was almost as long as the time he spent standing. Thereafter, he said, سمع الله لمن حمده

'Sami lahu Liman Hamidah' and stood up from Ruku. The time he remained standing was almost as long as the time he spent in Ruku, after which he proceeded into Sejdah.

In Sejdah, he recited, سبحان ربي الاعلى

'Subhana Rabbiyal A'la' and the time he took in Sejdah was almost as long as the time he spent standing." *(Muslim in Safwatus Safwa)*. Hudhaifa 🕮 relates, "I once came to Rasulullah 🕮 as he was busy performing salah and I joined him in salah at the back without him knowing. When he started Surah Baqarah, I thought that he would soon proceed into Ruku, but he continued reciting even after completing the Surah. Rasulullah 🕮 went on to perform 4 Rakats with him, Ruku being as long as the standing posture. When I mentioned this to Rasulullah 🕮, he said, 'Why did you not let me know that you were behind me?' I said, 'I swear by the Being Who has sent you as a Nabi 🕮 with the truth that even now I can feel the strain in my back.' Rasulullah 🕮 remarked, 'Had I known that you were behind me, I would have shortened the salah.'" *(Tabrani, Haythami)*.

The Narration of Aisha 🕮 Concerning Rasulullah 🕮's Recitation of Qur'an in Salah

When it was reported to Aisha 🕮 that some people completed a recitation of the Qur'an once or twice in a single night, she remarked, "Although those people have recited the Qur'an, they have actually not done so. I used to stand in salah with Rasulullah 🕮 the entire night and he would recite only Surah Baqarah, Surah Al Imran and Surah Nisa. Whenever he passed a verse containing a warning, he would pray to Allah and seek protection. Whenever he passed a verse giving glad tidings, he would pray to Allah and look forward to it." *(Ahmad, Haythami)*

Rasulullah 🕮 Issues the Command During his Illness that Abu Bakr 🕮 Should Lead the People in Salah

Aswad reports that they were once with Aisha 🕮 when they spoke about the importance of salah and constancy in performing it. Aisha ☙ then said, "When Rasulullah ﷺ was suffering the illness that claimed his life, the time for salah arrived and Bilal ☙ called out the Adhan. 'Tell Abu Bakr to lead the people in salah,' Rasulullah ﷺ instructed. One of Rasulullah ﷺ's wives remarked, 'Abu Bakr is a soft man who will be unable lead the salah when he stands in your place.' Rasulullah ﷺ however repeated the instruction, but again met with the same response. When this happened a 3rd time, Rasulullah ﷺ said, 'You women are just like the women around Yusuf ﷺ. Tell Abu Bakr to lead the people in salah.' Abu Bakr ☙ then stepped forward to lead the salah and, feeling a bit better, Rasulullah ﷺ came out of his room with the support of 2 men. I can still picture his feet leaving lines on the ground as he was dragging them, too weak to lift them because of the severity of his illness. Seeing Rasulullah ﷺ arrive, Abu Bakr ☙ decided to step back, but Rasulullah ﷺ indicated to him to remain where he was. Rasulullah ﷺ was then brought to sit beside Abu Bakr." Another narration states that Aisha ☙ said, "I continuously repeated myself to Rasulullah ﷺ trying to convince him not to appoint Abu Bakr ☙ to lead the salah only because I feared that the people would regard him as a foreboding that Rasulullah ﷺ is going to pass away. I knew well that anyone who stood in Rasulullah ﷺ's place would be regarded by the people as a foreboding and I wished that Rasulullah ﷺ would divert this from my father Abu Bakr ☙ to someone else." (Bukhari)

Yet another narration from Aisha ☙ states that she said, "O Rasulullah ﷺ! Abu Bakr ☙ is extremely soft-hearted and cannot control his tears when he recites the Qur'an. Why don't you command someone else to lead the salah in your place?" Aisha ☙ says, "By Allah! The only thing that made me say this was my dislike that people should regard the first person to stand in Rasulullah ﷺ's place as a bad omen. I therefore repeated myself to Rasulullah ﷺ 2 or 3 times, but he insisted saying, 'Abu Bakr should lead the people in salah. You women are just like the women around Yusuf ﷺ.'" (Muslim in Al Bidayah wan Nihayah). Ubaidulla bin Abdullah narrates that he once went to Aisha ☙ with the request, "Will you not tell me about the final illness of Rasulullah ﷺ?" "Certainly," she obliged, "When Rasulullah ﷺ illness became severe, he asked, 'Have the people performed their salah'? 'No,' we replied, 'they are waiting for you, O Rasulullah ﷺ.' He then asked us to pour water for him in a basin and when we did so, he took a bath. However, as he tried to stand up, he fell unconscious. When he recovered, he again asked, 'Have the people performed their salah'? 'No.' we replied, 'they are waiting for you, O Rasulullah ﷺ. 'He again asked us to pour water for him in a basin and when we did so, he took another bath. As he tried to stand up, he again fell unconscious. After recovering, Rasulullah ﷺ asked yet again whether the people had performed their salah'? 'No,' we replied, 'they are still waiting for you. O Rasulullah ﷺ. 'He then asked us to pour water for him in a basin and when we did so, he took a bath. However, as he tried to stand up, he fell unconscious. When he recovered, he asked once more, 'Have the people performed their salah'? 'No,' we replied, 'they are waiting for you, O Rasulullah ﷺ. 'The people were patiently seated in the Masjid awaiting Rasulullah ﷺ's arrival for the Isha salah. Rasulullah ﷺ then sent a message to Abu Bakr ☙ to lead the salah. Abu Bakr ☙ was a soft person so he said to Omar ☙, 'You lead the salah, O Omar ☙!' Omar ☙ however said, 'You are more worthy of the privilege.' Abu Bakr ☙ then led the salah during those days." The narration goes on to speak about how Rasulullah ﷺ came out of his room afterwards, as mentioned in the narration above. (Ahmad in Al Bidayah wan Nihayah, Bayhaqi, Ibn Abi Shayba in Kanzul Ummal, Ibn Sa'd)

The Happiness of the Muslims When They saw Rasulullah ﷺ Looking at Them as Abu Bakr ☙ Led the Salah

Anas ☙ relates, "Abu Bakr ☙ used to lead the people in salah during Rasulullah ﷺ's final illness. It was on Monday and the Sahabah were standing in their rows in salah when Rasulullah ﷺ opened the curtain leading to his room and looked at us. As he stood there, his face was as radiant as a page of the Qur'an and he smiled in happiness to see them fulfilling Allah's command as a united Ummah. We were on the verge of breaking our salah out of our sheer joy at seeing Rasulullah ﷺ. Thinking that Rasulullah ﷺ was coming out for salah, Abu Bakr ☙ stepped back into the first row but Rasulullah ﷺ indicated to us that we should complete the salah. Rasulullah ﷺ then dropped the curtain. It was on that very day that Rasulullah ﷺ passed away." (Bukhari). In another narration, Anas ☙ says, "Rasulullah ﷺ did not come out of his room for 3 days. On Monday when the Iqama was called out and Abu Bakr ☙ stepped forward to lead the salah, Rasulullah ﷺ gave the instruction for the curtain between his room and the Masjid to be lifted. When the curtain was lifted and Rasulullah ﷺ's face became visible to us, there was nothing that pleased us so much as to look at his face. Rasulullah ﷺ indicated to Abu Bakr ☙ to step forward to lead the salah and the curtain was then dropped. Until he passed away that day, Rasulullah ﷺ was unable to this again." (Bukhari, Muslim in Al Bidayah wan Nihayah, Abu Ya'la, Ibn Asakir, Ibn Khuzaima, Ahmad in Kanzul Ummal, Majma'uz Zawa'id, Bayhaqi, Ibn Sa'd)

Omar ☙ is Roused From his Coma with the Announcement of Salah

Miswar bin Makhrama ☙ reports, "I went to see Omar ☙ when he was covered in a sheet and still in a coma after he had been attacked. 'How is he?' I asked. 'Just as you see him, he has not yet roused from his coma,' the others replied. I then said, 'Rouse him with salah because there is nothing as effective in rousing him as salah.' The others then called out, 'Salah, O Amirul Mu'minin!' 'What!' Omar ☙ said with a start, 'By Allah! I will then have to perform it. There is no part in Islam for the person who does not perform his salah.' He then performed his salah even though blood was flowing from his wound." (Tabrani, Haythami). Another narration from Miswar ☙ states that after Omar ☙ was stabbed, he fell into a coma. Someone said, "If he is still alive, you will not be able to rouse him with anything more effective in jolting him than with salah." Someone then said, "Salah, O Amirul Mu'minin! The time for salah has already set in!" Omar ☙ regained consciousness and said, "What! Salah!? By Allah! I will then have to perform it. There is no part in Islam for the person who does not perform his salah." (Ibn Sa'd)

Uthman ☙ Spends the Whole Night Reciting the Entire Qur'an in a Single Rakah Salah

Muhammad bin Miskin narrates that when the rebels surrounded the house of Uthman ☙, his wife said to them, "You wish to assassinate him?! Whether you kill him or leave him, he spends the whole night reciting the entire Qur'an in a single Rakah of salah." (Tabrani, Haythami, Abu Nu'aym in Hilya). Another narration states that when the rebels assassinated Uthman bin Affan ☙, his wife said, "You have killed him when he was a man who spent the whole night reciting the entire Qur'an in a single Rakah of salah!" (Abu Nu'aym in Hilya). Uthman bin Abdur Rahman Taymi reports that his father said, "I once told myself that I would ensure that I was the only one to stand in Ibada by the Maqam Ibrahim one night. Therefore, after performing the Isha salah, I had the Maqam to myself as I stood there. As I was standing there, someone placed their hand on my shoulder. It was Uthman bin Affan ﷺ. He started with Ummul Qur'an (Surah Fatiha) and continued reciting until he had completed the entire Qur'an. Thereafter, he performed Ruku and Sejdah, completed the second Rakah and then took his shoes and left. I cannot however recall whether he had performed any other salah before that or not." *(Abu Nu'aym in Hilya)*. Uthman bin Abdur Rahman Taymi relates, "I saw Uthman ﷺ step forward to the Maqam Ibrahim one night where he recited the entire Qur'an in a single Rakah before leaving." *(Ibn Mubarak in Zuhd, Ibn Sa'd, Ibn Abi Shaybah, Ibn Munee, Yahawi, Dar Qutni, Bayhaqi in Muntakhab Kanzul Ummal)*. Ata bin Abi Rabah reports that after leading the people in salah, Uthman ﷺ would stand behind the Maqam Ibrahim where he would recite the entire Qur'an in a single Rakah of his Witr salah. Muhammad bin Sirin would stand in salah all night in which he would complete the entire Qur'an in a single Rakah. *(Ibn Sa'd in Muntakhab Kanzul Ummal)*

Abdullah bin Abbas ﷺ Refuses to Forego Standing in Salah for Treating his Blindness

Musaib bin Rafi narrates that when Abdullah bin Abbas ﷺ became blind, a man came to him saying, "If you are able to restrain yourself from standing and performing salah for 7 days, I shall be able to treat you and InshaAllah cure you. You may however perform salah while lying down and making gestures." Abdullah bin Abbas ﷺ sent for opinions from various Sahabah of Rasulullah ﷺ including Aisha ﷺ and Abu Hurairah ﷺ. The message from all of them was: "What will you do with your salah if you happen to die during the 7 days?" Abdullah bin Abbas ﷺ therefore abandoned the treatment. *(Hakim)*. Another narration states that when Abdullah bin Abbas ﷺ lost his eyesight, someone offered to treat him on condition that he does not perform salah for few days. Abdullah bin Abbas ﷺ said, "Never, I cannot forsake salah. Rasulullah ﷺ said that the person who does not perform salah will meet Allah in a condition at Allah will be angry with him." *(Bazzar, Tabrani, Haythami)*. Ali bin Abu Jamila reports that Abdullah bin Abbas ﷺ made Sejdah 1,000 times every day. *(Tabrani, Haythami)*

The Fervor Abdullah bin Mas'ood ﷺ had for Salah

Abdullah bin Mas'ood ﷺ would not do optional fast very often because he would say, "I become too weak to perform salah when I fast and I love salah more than fasting." When he did observe (optional) fasts, he fast only 3 days a month. *(Tabrani, Haythami)*. It was only the midmorning (Duha) salah that he was not very regular with. Abdur Rahman bin Yazid narrates that when Abdullah bin Mas'ood ﷺ was questioned about why he did not fast very often, he replied, "I become too weak to perform salah when I fast and I love salah more than fasting." *(Ibn Jareer in Kanzul Ummal)*. Abdur Rahman bin Yazid says, "I have not seen a Faqeeh who has deep knowledge of Shari'ah who fasted less (optional) than Abdullah bin Mas'ood ﷺ. When someone asked him why he did not fast optional, he replied, "I have given preference to salah over fasts because I become too weak to perform salah when I fast." *(Ibn Sa'd)*

The Zeal Salim ﷺ the Freed Slave of Abu Hudhaifa ﷺ had for Salah

Aisha ﷺ reports, "I was late in coming to Rasulullah ﷺ one night after Isha. When I came to him and he asked where I had been, I replied, 'We were listening to one of your Sahabah reciting the Qur'an in the Masjid. I have never heard a voice like his nor such recitation from any of your other Sahabah.' Rasulullah ﷺ got up and I got up with him as he listened attentively to the man. He turned to me saying, 'That is Salim ﷺ the freed slave of Abu Hudhaifa ﷺ. All praise belongs to Allah Who has made such people amongst my Ummah!'" *(Hakim)*

The Fervor Abu Musa Ash'ari ﷺ and Abu Hurairah ﷺ had for Salah

Masruq reports, "We were with Abu Musa Ash'ari ﷺ on a journey when the night gave us sanctuary in a plantation. When we set up camp there, Abu Musa ﷺ stood up in a part of the night to perform salah." Masruq then went on to describe the beautiful voice of Abu Musa ﷺ and his melodious recitation of the Qur'an. Whenever he passed a verse invoking a supplication, he made the supplication and then prayed, "O Allah! You are the giver of peace and You love peace. You are the giver of safety and You love the Mu'min. You are the giver of protection and You love those who give protection. You are the truthful and You love the truthful ones." *(Abu Nu'aym in Hilya)*. Abu Uthman Nahdi says, "I was the guest of Abu Hurairah ﷺ for 7 days. His servant, his wife and he would take turns to each spend 3rd of the night in Ibada." *(Abu Nu'aym in Hilya)*

The Fervor Abu Talha Ansari ﷺ and Another Sahabi had for Salah

Abdullah bin Abu Bakr ﷺ narrates that Abu Talha Ansari ﷺ was once performing salah in his orchard when a little bird flew by and, unable to find an opening through the thick growth, it started to flap about. The sight captivated Abu Talha ﷺ's attention and his eyes followed the bird for an instant. When he refocused his attention to his salah, he had forgotten how many Rakats he had performed. He said, "A great test has afflicted me in this property of mine." He then went to Rasulullah ﷺ and recounting the loss he suffered in his salah, he said, "O Rasulullah ﷺ! I give over this orchard in Sadaqa. Dispose of it as you please." *(Malik in Targheeb wat Tarheeb)*. Abdullah bin Abu Bakr ﷺ also narrates that an Ansari ﷺ was once performing salah in his orchard in the vicinity of Quf; which was one of the valleys of Madinah. The season for dates was at its peak with the branches of the date palms hanging low with the weight of the dates. When his glance happened to fall on the laden palms, the sight of the dates captivated his attention and when he turned his attention back to his salah, he had forgotten how many Rakats he had performed. "A great test has afflicted me in this property of mine." he sighed. He went to Uthman bin Affan ﷺ who was the Khalifa and related the incident to him, saying. "I am donating it as Sadaqa, so use it for some good cause." Uthman ﷺ sold the orchard for 50,000 Dirhams, because of which the property was then named the 'Khamsin' ('the fifty'). *(Malik in Awjaz)*

The Fervor Abdullah bin Zubair ﷺ and Adi bin Hatim ﷺ for Salah

Asma ﷺ reports that her son Abdullah bin Zubair ﷺ passed the nights in salah and the days fasting. He was therefore called the pigeon of the Masjid because he was always there. *(Abu Nu'aym in Hilya)*. Adi bin Hatim ﷺ says. "When the time for any salah arrives, I have prepared for it and am brimming with fervor for it." *(Ibn Asakir in Kanzul Ummal, Ibn Mubarak in Isabah)*

The Narration of Abu Hurairah ﷺ and Talq bin Ali ﷺ Concerning the Construction of Masjidun Nabawi

Abu Hurairah ﷺ reports, "Rasulullah ﷺ was with us as we carried the bricks to the construction site of the Masjid Nabawi. This incident took place after the Battle of Khaibar when the Masjid was rebuilt. When I met Rasulullah ﷺ carrying a brick lengthways across his abdomen. I felt that this would be difficult for him. I therefore said, 'Give it to me, O Rasulullah ﷺ!' Rasulullah ﷺ said, 'Take another, O Abu Hurairah! There is no life other the life of the Hereafter.'" *(Ahmad, Haythami)*. Talq bin Ali ؓ says, "When I assisted in the construction of the Masjid together with Rasulullah ﷺ, he said to the others, 'Let this Yamami (Talq ؓ) handle the mortar because he mixes it best and has the strongest shoulders." *(Ahmad, Tabrani, Haythami)*. Talq bin Ali ؓ relates, "I came to Rasulullah ﷺ at the time when his Sahabah were busy constructing the Masjid. It appeared to me that Rasulullah ﷺ was not too pleased with the manner in which the work was being done, so I took a spade and started mixing the mortar. Rasulullah ﷺ seemed to like the manner in which I handled the spade and the work I was doing, so he said to the others. "Leave the Hanafi to the mortar because he is most proficient with it.'" *(Ahmad, Haythami)*

The Effort that the Wife of Abdullah bin Abu Awfa ؓ put into the Construction of the Masjidun Nabawi

Abdullah bin Abu Awfa ؓ narrates that when his wife passed away, he said to the people, "Carry her bier with great fervor because she and her slaves would carry rocks for the construction of the Masjidun Nabawi that was founded on Taqwa during the night while we would manage carrying only 2 rocks at a time during the day." *(Bazzar, Haythami)*

Rasulullah ﷺ's desire to have Masjid like the Shelter of Musa ﷺ

Ubadah bin Samit ؓ narrates that the Ansar once said to him, "For how long will Rasulullah ﷺ perform salah beneath a roof made of these palm branches?" They then collected many gold coins which they presented to Rasulullah ﷺ saying, "We wish to renovate and beautify this Masjid." Rasulullah ﷺ however replied, "I do not wish to turn from the example of my brother Musa ﷺ who had a shelter made of palm branches. The ceiling of the Masjid should remain like the shelter of Musa ﷺ." *(Tabrani, Haythami)*. Another narration states that the Ansar once collected a sum of money which they presented to Rasulullah ﷺ saying, "O Rasulullah ﷺ! Rebuild this Masjid and beautify it. How long will we perform salah beneath these branches?" Rasulullah ﷺ replied, "I do not wish to turn from the example of my brother Musa ﷺ. The ceiling of this Masjid should remain like the shelter of Musa ﷺ." *(Bayhaqi in Dala'il)*

Describing the Shelter of Musa ﷺ, Hasan Explains that When Musa ﷺ Merely Lifted his Hand, it Would Reach the Top. (Bayhaqi)

Ibn Shihab reports, "The pillars of the Masjidun Nabawi during the time of Rasulullah ﷺ were trunks of palm trees while the roof was made of palm branches and leaves without any plaster. The Masjid would therefore be full of mud whenever it rained. The Masjid was in effect just like a shade." *(Bayhaqi)*

Rasulullah ﷺ Prostrates in Mud in the Masjid

In chapter discussing Laylatul Qadr, *Imam Bukhari* reports a narration from Abu Sa'eed Khudri ؓ that states: "Rasulullah ﷺ said, 'In a vision informing me when Laylatul Qadr will be, I saw myself prostrating in mud. Therefore, all those who had been observing I'tiqaf with Rasulullah ﷺ should come back.' We then returned although we saw not a trace of clouds in the sky. A cloud however appeared and when it rained, the water flowed through the roof, which was made of palm branches. When salah started, I saw Rasulullah ﷺ prostrate in mud. Traces of the mud were later visible on his forehead." *(Wafa'ul Wafa)*

Rasulullah ﷺ refuses to build Masjid Like the Buildings in Sham

Khalid bin Ma'dan narrates that Abdullah bin Rawaha ؓ and Abu Darda ؓ were once measuring the Masjid with a stick. Coming out of his room, Rasulullah ﷺ asked, "What are you 2 doing?" They replied, "We wish to construct the Masjid of Rasulullah ﷺ like the buildings of Sham are built. The expenses shall be borne by the Ansar." "Bring me that stick," Rasulullah ﷺ instructed. He then took the stick from them and walked away with it. When he reached his door, Rasulullah ﷺ threw the stick away and said, "Never! The Masjid should never be built like that! It should be made of grass, sticks and roof like the shelter of Musa ﷺ. Death is much nearer at hand." When someone asked what the shelter of Musa ﷺ was like, Rasulullah ﷺ replied, "When he stood up, his head touched the roof." *(Ibn Zabala in Wafa'ul Wafa)*

The Masjid is extended during the periods of Omar ؓ and Uthman ؓ

Nafi narrates, "Omar ؓ extended the Masjid from the pillars to the Maqsura, the room built for the Imam. He said, 'Had I not heard Rasulullah ﷺ say, 'We ought to extend our Masjid', I would never have extended it." *(Ahmad)*. Nafi reports from Abdullah bin Omar ؓ that during the time of Rasulullah ﷺ, the Masjid was built with unbaked bricks, the roof was made of palm branches and the pillars were palm trunks. While Abu Bakr made no extensions to the Masjid, Omar ؓ did. He however built the Masjid as it was during the time of Rasulullah ﷺ using unbaked bricks, palm branches and replacing the pillars of palm trunks. Uthman ؓ changed the building and made a large extension. He used decorative stones and plaster for the walls with decorative stones for the pillars and teakwood for the roof. *(Bukhari, Abu Dawud)*. Atiya narrates that Abdullah bin Omar ؓ said, "During the time of Rasulullah ﷺ, the pillars of the Masjid consisted of palm trunks with the top shaded with palm branches. When this deteriorated during the Khilafa Abu Bakr ؓ, he rebuilt it also using palm trunks branches. When it again deteriorated during the Khalifa of Uthman ؓ, he had it rebuilt with baked bricks and it has remained standing to this day." *(Abu Dawud)*. Mahmud bin Labid reports that when Uthman ؓ expressed the intention to rebuild the Masjid, people disliked the idea because they wanted him to leave it as it was. He however said, "I heard Rasulullah ﷺ say that whoever builds a Masjid for the pleasure of Allah, Allah will build him one just like it in Jannah." *(Muslim)*.

Muttalib bin Abdullah bin Ibn Hantab narrates that when Uthman ؓ became the Khalifa in the year 24 AH, the people requested him to extend the Masjid, complaining that it was too congested on Fridays, because of which they were forced to perform salah on the adjoining ground. Uthman ؓ then consulted with the senior Sahabah and they unanimously decided that the building be demolished and extended. After leading the Zuhr salah, Uthman ؓ mounted the pulpit and after praising Allah, he said, "O people! I have decided to demolish the Masjid of Rasulullah ﷺ and to extend it. I testify that I have heard Rasulullah say, 'Whoever builds a Masjid for Allah, Allah shall build him a home in Jannah.' I have also a precedent and leader who has passed before me and paved the way for me. He was Omar bin Khattab ؓ who also extended and rebuilt the Masjid. In addition to this, I have consulted with the senior Sahabah of Rasulullah ﷺ, who are unanimous that the Masjid be demolished, rebuilt and extended." The people liked the idea and made Du'a for him. The following morning, Uthman ؓ summoned the builders and he participated in the construction even though he was person who always fasted by day and performed salah during the night. In fact, he was a person who seldom left the Masjid. His instructions were that filtered plaster be made in

Batn Nakhl. Construction work commenced in the month of Rabi'ul Awwal in the year 29 AH and was completed when the new year entered with the arrival of the crescent of Muharram of the year 30 AH. The construction took 10 months. *(Muslim in Wafa'ul Wafa)*

Rasulullah ﷺ Demarcates a Location in Madinah for a Masjid for the Juhaina Tribe

Jabir bin Usama Juhani ؓ says, "Once I run into Rasulullah ﷺ and some of his companions in the market, I asked them where Rasulullah ﷺ was going. They replied, 'He is going to demarcate a Masjid for your people.' By the time I got there, Rasulullah ﷺ had demarcated an area and stuck a stick into the ground to fix the direction of the Qibla." *(Tabrani in Awsat and Kabir, Haythami, Abu Nu'aym in Hilya, Kanzul Ummal, Bawardi)*

The Letter of Omar ؓ to the Governors of the Various Districts Concerning the Construction of Masajid

Uthman bin Ata narrates that Omar ؓ started conquering cities, he wrote to Abu Musa Ash'ari ؓ who was the governor of Basra. He instructed him to build a large and central Masjid for salah to take place in congregation and also several small Masajid for the various tribes in their localities. The people were all together in the central Masjid on Fridays to perform the Jumu'ah salah. He wrote a letter with the same instructions to Sa'd bin Abi Waqqas ؓ who was the governor of Kufa and to Amr bin Al Aas ؓ who was the governor of Egypt. He wrote to the commanders of the various armies not to base themselves in rural areas but to set up bases in the cities and to build only one Masjid and not several Masajid for every tribe as was being done in Basra, Kufa and Egypt. The people abided strictly by this instruction of Omar ؓ. *(Ibn Asakir in Kanzul Ummal)*

Rasulullah ﷺ's Instruction for Places of Salah to be Made Inside Houses and That They be Kept Clean

Urwa bin Zubair ؓ reports that one of the Sahabah said, "Rasulullah ﷺ used to instruct us to make places of salah within our homes, to build them well and to keep them clean." *(Ahmad, Haythami)*. Aisha ؓ reports that Rasulullah ﷺ gave instructions for places of salah to be made within homes and that they be kept clean and fragranced. *(Abu Dawud, Tirmidhi, Ibn Majah in Mishkatul Masabih)*

Rasulullah ﷺ sees a Woman in Jannah who Used to Keep Masjid Clean

Abdullah bin Abbas ؓ narrates that a woman who used to remove dirt from the Masjid passed away, the Sahabah did not inform Rasulullah ﷺ about her funeral and they proceeded to bury her. When he found out, Rasulullah ﷺ said to them, "You must inform me when any of you passes away." Rasulullah ﷺ performed the Janaza salah and then said, "I saw her in Jannah picking up dirt from the Masjid." *(Tabrani, Haythami)*.

Omar ؓ Burns Incense in the Masjidun Nabawi

Abdullah bin Omar ؓ reports that Omar ؓ used to burn incense in the Masjid of Rasulullah ﷺ every Friday. *(Abu Ya'la, Haythami)*

The Incident of an Ansari who walked to the Masjid from his Distant Home

Ubay bin Ka'b ؓ says, "There was a person who in my knowledge lived furthest from the Masjid. He however never missed a single salah. Someone once suggested to him, "Why do you not buy a donkey that you could ride in the dark and through the blistering sands'?" The man replied, Let alone doing that, I would not even be happy with a house right next to the Masjid because I want my walking to the Masjid and my retuning to my family to be recorded for me in my record of good deeds." Rasulullah ﷺ remarked, "Allah has accumulated it all for you." *(Ahmad, Muslim, Darmi, Abu Awana, Ibn Khuzaima, Ibn Hibban)*. In another narration, Ubay bin Ka'b ؓ says, "There was a person from the Ansar whose house was the furthest from the Masjid in Madinah. He never missed a single salah with Rasulullah ﷺ. Taking pity on him, I suggested, 'Why do you not buy a donkey that could protect you from the blistering sands and creatures on the ground'? The man replied, 'Listen well! By Allah! Let alone doing that, I would not even be happy with a house right next to that of Muhammad ﷺ.' This statement weighed heavily on me and I reported it to Rasulullah ﷺ. When Rasulullah ﷺ summoned the man and questioned him, he repeated himself, explaining that he hoped for rewards in every step. Rasulullah ﷺ said, "You shall have what you hope for.'" *(Tayalisi, Ibn Majah, Muslim)*. Rasulullah ﷺ also said, "His stages in Jannah are elevated with every step that he takes." *(Humaidi, Abu Dawud in Kanzul Ummal)*

Rasulullah ﷺ Shortens his Steps to the Masjid

Zaid bin Thabit ؓ narrates that when he used to walk with Rasulullah ﷺ when they went for salah, Rasulullah ﷺ took short steps. "Do you know why I shorten my steps?" Rasulullah ﷺ asked. "Allah and His Rasul ﷺ know best," Zaid ؓ replied. Rasulullah ﷺ explained, "A person remains in salah receives the rewards of salah as long as he is engaged in the effort of salah, doing anything contributing towards salah." *(Tabrani)* Another narration states that Rasulullah ﷺ's explanation was: "I am doing this only so that my steps in the effort of going for salah are increased." *(Tabrani, Haythami)*

Anas bin Malik ؓ Shortens his Steps When Walking to the Masjid

Thabit ؓ says, "I was once walking with Anas bin Malik ؓ in Zawiya, a district of Basra when he heard the Adhan. He then started to shorten his steps until he entered the Masjid. 'O Thabit!' he asked, 'Do you know why I have walked with you in this manner?' 'Allah and His Rasul ﷺ know best,' I replied. He said, 'So that my steps in the effort of salah are increased.'" *(Tabrani in Kabir, Haythami)*

Abdullah bin Mas'ood ؓ Hurries for Salah

Abdullah bin Mas'ood ؓ once left home for the Masjid. When he started to hurry, someone asked, "Why are you doing this when you prevent others from it?" Abdullah bin Mas'ood ؓ replied, "I wish to attain the frontier of salah, which is the first Takbir." *(Tabrani)*. Salama bin Kuhail narrates that when someone objected to Abdullah bin Mas'ood ؓ hurrying for salah, he replied, "Of the things that you hurry towards, is salah not the most deserving of them all?" *(Tabrani, Haythami)*

Rasulullah ﷺ Prohibits Running for Salah

Abu Qatadah narrates that as they were once performing salah behind Rasulullah ﷺ, he heard some uproar from the people at the back. After completing salah, Rasulullah ﷺ asked what the matter was. When the Sahabah informed him that it was them running for the salah. Rasulullah ﷺ said, "Do not do that. You should not hurry and then perform the Rakats you manage to join and complete afterwards the ones you could not join." *(Tabrani, Haythami)*

The Sahabah Condemn a Bedouin who Urinated in the Masjid and the Stance Rasulullah ﷺ Took in the Matter

Anas ؓ narrates that they were once in a Masjid with Rasulullah ﷺ when a Bedouin stood in the Masjid and started urinating there. "Stop! Stop!" the Sahabah shouted. Rasulullah ﷺ said to them, "Do not stop him from urinating. Leave him alone!" The Sahabah then allowed him to finish urinating. Rasulullah ﷺ then called him and said, "These Masajid are not intended for the purpose of urinating and any other filth. They are there for the remembrance of Allah, for salah and for the recitation of the Qur'an." Rasulullah ﷺ instructed someone to bring a bucket of water, which was poured over the impure area. *(Muslim, Tahawi)*

The Incident of Rasulullah ﷺ with Some Sahabah who were Sitting in the Masjid to Engage in Dhikr

Abu Sa'eed Khudri ؓ narrates that Mu'awiya ؓ once approached a group of people in the Masjid. "What makes you people sit here?" he asked. "We are sitting here to make the Dhikr of Allah," they replied. Mu'awiya ؓ asked further, "Do you swear by Allah that there is no other reason for your sitting here?" When they confirmed that there was no other motive, Mu'awiya ؓ said, "I have not asked you to swear by Allah because I am suspicious that you may lie to me. There is none who despite being as close to Rasulullah ﷺ as I was, narrated fewer Ahadeeth than I have out of cautiousness, I narrate very few Ahadeeth. I shall now narrate one to you people. Rasulullah ﷺ once came out of his room where he found a group of his Sahabah sitting in the Masjid. 'What makes you people sit here?' Rasulullah ﷺ asked. They said, 'We are sitting here to engage in the Dhikr of Allah and to praise Him for guiding us to Islam and for blessing us with the bounty of Islam.' Rasulullah ﷺ asked further, 'Do you swear by Allah that there is no other reason for your sitting here?' 'We swear by Allah that there is no other reason for us sitting here?' they replied. Rasulullah ﷺ said to them, 'I have not asked you to swear by Allah because I am suspicious that you may lie to me. Jibra'el عليه السلام has come to inform me that Allah is boasting about you before the angels.'" *(Muslim in Riyadhus Salihin, Tirmidhi, Nasa'ee, Jam'ul Fawa'id)*

The Incident of Rasulullah ﷺ with 3 Persons and the Incident When he sat with Those Busy with the Qur'an

Abu Waqid Harith bin Auf ؓ narrates that they were once sitting with Rasulullah ﷺ when 3 persons arrived. Two of them came towards Rasulullah ﷺ, the other turned and left. From the 2 that came to Rasulullah ﷺ, one saw a space in the gathering and occupied it while the other sat behind the people. When Rasulullah ﷺ had finished, he said, "Should I not tell you about 3 persons? As for one of them, he sought a place with Allah and Allah granted it to him. The 2nd was shy, so Allah treated him accordingly without depriving him of His mercy. The 3rd turned away from Allah, so Allah turned away from him." *(Bukhari, Muslim in Riyadhus Salihin, Malik, Tirmidhi in Jam'ul Fawa'id).* Abul Qamra ؓ relates, "We were sitting in several gatherings in Rasulullah ﷺ's Masjid, discussing Ahadeeth when Rasulullah ﷺ came out from one of his rooms. Looking at the various gatherings, Rasulullah ﷺ sat down with those busy with learning and teaching Qur'an. He said, 'I have been commanded to sit with this gathering.'" *(Ibn Mandah in Isabah, Ibn Abdul Birr in Isti'ab, Abu Amr Dani in Tabaqatul Qur'an, Kanzul Ummal)*

The Statement of Ali Concerning the Qurra of the Qur'an

Kulaib bin Shihab narrates that Ali ؓ once heard a lot of sound from the Masjid as people were busy reciting the Qur'an and teaching others to do so. He remarked, "Glad tidings for these people! These are the people whom Rasulullah ﷺ loved the most." *(Tabrani in Awsat, Majma'uz Zawa'id, Haythami, Ibn Munee in Kanzul Ummal).* Kulaib narrates that Ali ؓ was once in the Masjid of Kufa when he heard a lot of sound. "Who is that?" he asked. When he was informed that the sound was coming from some people who were busy reciting or learning the Qur'an, he commented, "Take note that it was such people whom Rasulullah ﷺ loved most." *(Bazzar in Majma'uz Zawa'id)*

The Incident of Abu Hurairah ؓ with the People in the Market Place

Hasan reports that Abu Hurairah ؓ once passed through the market place of Madinah when he stood there and called out, "O traders! What makes you so helpless?" "What are you talking about, O Abu Hurairah ؓ?" they asked. He said, "There you have the inheritance of Rasulullah ﷺ being distributed whereas you people are still here! Are you not going to claim your shares?" "Where is it?" they all asked. "In the Masjid," he replied. They rushed to the Masjid as Abu Hurairah ؓ remained there waiting for them. When they returned and he noted sadness on their faces, he asked, "What is the matter?" "O Abu Hurairah ؓ!" they replied, "We went to the Masjid but found nothing being distributed." Abu Hurairah ؓ asked, "Did you see absolutely no one there?" "O yes we did," they replied, "We saw some people performing salah, others reciting the Qur'an, and others discussing what was Halal and what was Haram." Abu Hurairah ؓ remarked, "Shame on you! That is the inheritance of Rasulullah ﷺ." *(Tabrani in Awsat, Targheeb wat Tarheeb)*

Omar ؓ Praises the Gatherings in the Masjid

Ibn Mu'awia Kindi reports that when he once went to see Omar ؓ in Sham, Omar ؓ asked him about the condition of the people and said further, "Does it not happen that when a man enters the Masjid like escaped camel and then sits with a group only if they belong to his tribe or if they are people whom he knows?" "Not at all," Ibn Mu'awia, replied, "In fact, there are several gatherings in our Masjid in which the people participate to learn and to rehearse good to each other." To this Omar ؓ remarked, "You people will always remain in good condition as long as you remain like this." *(Marwazi, Ibn Abi Shaybah in Kanzul Ummal)*

Rasulullah ﷺ walks from Masjid with the Sahabah to Speak to Jews

Abu Hurairah ؓ narrates that they were sitting in the Masjid one day when Rasulullah ﷺ came out of his room and said, "Let us go to the Jews." When he reached them, Rasulullah ﷺ said, "Accept Islam and you will live in peace. "But you have already conveyed this message to us," they replied. "But that is still what I want that you people accept Islam. So I repeat, do accept Islam and you will live in peace." Again the Jews responded by saying, "But you have already conveyed this message to us." "But that is still what I want," Rasulullah ﷺ reiterated. When Rasulullah ﷺ repeated himself for the 3rd time and they again refused to accept, he added, "You ought to know that the earth belongs to Allah and His Rasul ﷺ. I now wish to expel you from this land. Whoever wishes to sell any of his belongings may do so, otherwise you should bear in mind that the earth belongs to Allah and His Rasul ﷺ." *(Bukhari, Muslim, Abu Dawud in Jam'ul Fawa'id)*

Rasulullah ﷺ has Sa'd bin Mu'adh ؓ Placed in the Masjid When the Latter was Injured During the Battle of Khandaq

Aisha ؓ narrates that Sa'd bin Mu'adh ؓ was injured during the Battle of Khandaq when a person by the name of Hibban bin

Ariqa shot an arrow that struck Sa'd ❀'s artery. Rasulullah ❀ had a tent pitched for Sa'd bin Mu'adh ❀ in the Masjid so that he could be close by to visit him. When Nabi ❀ returned from the Battle of Khandaq, he removed his armor and took a bath. It was then that Jibra'el ☁ came to Rasulullah ❀, wiping dust off his head. "By Allah!" Jibra'el ☁ said, "You have already removed your armor whereas we the angels have not yet removed ours. March to them." "Where should we march?" Rasulullah ❀ asked. Jibra'el pointed towards the Banu Quraiza tribe. Rasulullah ❀ then marched with the Sahabah to the Banu Quraiza and after a siege; they surrendered themselves with the agreement that Rasulullah ❀ decides their fate. Rasulullah ❀ however handed over to Sa'd ❀ the decision to decide what to do with them. Sa'd ❀ pronounced his decision stating, "I pronounce that all their able-bodied fighters be executed, that their women and children be taken as slaves and that their wealth be distributed as booty." A narrator by the name of Hisham reports from his father who reports from Aisha ❀ that Sa'd ❀ prayed, "O Allah! You know well that I do not love to fight anyone more than the people who rejected your Rasul ❀ and expelled him. O Allah! I have a feeling that You have ended the fighting between them and us but if there are any more wars to take place between us and the Quraish, do allow me to live on to fight them for your pleasure. However, if You have ended the fighting between us and the Quraish, then allow this wound to open so that I may die because of it." The wound then erupted close to his chest and a group of people from the Banu Ghifar who were in the Masjid were not alerted except by the blood that came running towards them. "O people of the tent!" they called out, "What is this we see coming from your direction?" They then discovered that it was the bleeding wound of Sa'd's wound, from which he passed away. *(Bukhari, Muslim, Jam'ul Fawa'id)*

The Men of Suffa, Abu Dhar ❀ and other Sahabah sleep in the Masjid

Yazid bin Abdullah bin Qusait ❀ says that the men of the Suffa were men during the time of Rasulullah ❀ who had no homes. They slept and took shelter in the Masjid for they had no other shelter. Rasulullah ❀ would call them at night when he ate supper and after distributing them amongst the Sahabah, there would still be a group of them who ate with Rasulullah ❀. This took place until Allah made them independent. *(Ibn Sa'd)*. Asma bint Yazid ❀ narrates that Abu Dhar ❀ used to be in the service of Rasulullah ❀ and whenever he had finished, he took shelter in the Masjid, which was his home where he lay down to rest. When Rasulullah ❀ entered the Masjid one night, he found Abu Dhar ❀ lying on the ground. When Rasulullah ❀ nudged him with his foot, Abu Dhar ❀ sat up straight. "Did I see you sleeping?" Rasulullah ❀ asked. "O Rasulullah ❀!" Abu Dhar ❀ said, "Where can I sleep? Which other home do I have?" The rest of the Hadith has been reported in the chapter dealing with the Khilafa. *(Ahmad, Tabrani, Haythami)*. Abu Dhar ❀ himself reports that after serving Rasulullah, he used to lie down in the Masjid. *(Tabrani)*. Several incidents describing how the Sahabah slept in the Masjid has passed in the chapter discussing hospitality towards guests. When Hasan ❀ was asked about people taking their rest in the Masjid, he replied, "I have seen Uthman bin Affan ❀ taking his rest in the Masjid during the period when he was Khalifa." *(Bayhaqi, Ibn Asakir in Kanzul Ummal)*. Abdullah bin Omar ❀ said, "When we were still youngsters during the time of Rasulullah ❀, we used to spend the night at the Masjid." He also said, "After gathering for the Jumu'ah salah, we would return to the Masjid to have our rest."

(Ibn Abi Shaybah in Kanzul Ummal). Omar ❀ once said, "When any of you has been sitting too long in the Masjid, there is no harm in him lying down on his side because this is the most appropriate manner to prevent his sitting from tiring him." *(Ibn Sa'd)*. Khalid bin Abu Is'haq narrates that he once asked Abdullah bin Abbas ❀ about sleeping in the Masjid. Abdullah bin Abbas ❀ replied, "There is no harm in it if you are sleeping to gain strength for performing salah or Tawaf." *(Abdur Razzaq in Kanzul Ummal)*

Rasulullah ❀ Hastens to the Masjid When the Wind Blows Fiercely and During an Eclipse

Jabir ❀ says, "Whenever the wind blew fiercely at night, Rasulullah ❀ hastened towards the Masjid and would main there until the wind subsided. He would also hasten the place of salah whenever the sun or the moon eclipse." *(Ibn Abi Dunya in Kanzul Ummal)*. Ata reports that a Sahabi by the name of Ya'la bin Umaya ❀ used to sit for even a moment in the Masjid with the intention of performing I'tiqaf. *(Abu Nu'aym in Hilya)*

Rasulullah ❀ Makes a Delegation from the Thaqif Stay in the Masjid

Atiya bin Sufian bin Abdullah ❀ narrates, "When a delegation from the Thaqif came to Rasulullah ❀ one Ramadhan, Rasulullah ❀ pitched a tent for them in the Masjid. When they accepted Islam, they started to fast with Rasulullah ❀." *(Tabrani, Haythami)*. Uthman bin Abil Aas ❀ narrates that when the Thaqif delegation came to Rasulullah ❀, he accommodated them in the Masjid so that it would soften their hearts. The rest of the narration has already passed in the chapter concerning Da'wah towards Allah and His Rasul ❀.

What the Sahabah did in the Masjid Apart from Ibadah and Dhikr

Abdullah bin Zubair ❀ says, "We once ate roasted meat with Rasulullah ❀ in the Masjid. When the Iqama was called out for salah, all we did was wipe our hands with some pebbles." *(Tabrani, Haythami)*. Abdullah bin Omar ❀ reports that the Masjidul Fadikh got its name from the fact that it was in this Masjid that some Fadikh (sweet drink with crushed dates) was served to Rasulullah ❀ and 'he drank it" *(Ahmad)* Another narration states that Rasulullah ❀ was in the Masjidul Fadikh when he was brought a jug of Fadikh made from half-ripe dates. Because Rasulullah ❀ drank the Fadikh there, the Masjid was named Masjidul Fadikh." *(Abu Ya'la, Haythami)*. In the chapter discussing spending of wealth, narrations have already been quoted stating that food and wealth were distributed in the Masjid. Narrations have also passed mentioning that the people pledged allegiance to Uthman ❀ and Abu Bakr ❀ in the Masjid. The incident describing the Da'wah given to Dimam ❀ in the Masjid has also passed, which also states that it was in the Masjid that he accepted Islam. The chapter discussing Da'wah towards Allah and His Rasul ❀ also states the narration in which Ka'b bin Zuhair ❀ accepted Islam and then recited a famous poem in the Masjid. The chapter discussing unity also contains a Hadith in which it is stated that the consultative assembly also gathered in the Masjid. Another narration in the chapter of spending makes it evident that it was in the Masjid that the Sahabah sat with Rasulullah ❀ in the mornings. The chapter discussing how the Sahabah feared having too much of wealth also states that Omar ❀ used to sit in the Masjid after salah to tend to the needs of people. It is also established that it was also in the Masjid that Abu Bakr ❀ and the other Sahabah sat and wept when Rasulullah ❀ passed away. This was quoted in the love that he Sahabah had for Rasulullah ❀.

Rasulullah ﷺ Disapproves of Interlacing the Fingers when in the Masjid

A freed slave of Abu Sa'eed Khudri ؓ says that he was with Abu Sa'eed Khudri ؓ and Rasulullah ﷺ when they entered the Masjid. There they saw a person sitting in the Idtiba posture with his fingers interlaced. When Rasulullah ﷺ gestured to him not to do what he was doing, he failed to understand the gesture. Rasulullah ﷺ turned to Abu Sa'eed Khudri ؓ and said, "When you are in the Masjid, he should never interlace his fingers because interlacing the fingers is prompted by Saitan. As long as you remains in the Masjid, he remains in salah and continues receiving rewards of salah until he leaves.' *(Ahmad, Haythami)*

Rasulullah ﷺ Disapproves of a Person Entering the Masjid After Eating Garlic or Onions

Abu Bakr ؓ narrates that after Rasulullah ﷺ conquered Khaibar, the Sahabah became obsessed with garlic and started eating it often. It was then that Rasulullah ﷺ said, "The person who eats this strong vegetable should never come near our Masaajid." *(Tabrani, Haythami)*. In his Jumu'ah lecture, Omar bin Khattab ؓ once said, "The next thing, O people, is that there are 2 plants you people eat from, which I regard as being too strong; namely onions and garlic. I have noticed that whenever Rasulullah ﷺ smelt these on a person in the Masjid, he would give instructions that the person be removed from the Masjid and taken to Baqee. Therefore, whoever wishes to eat them should first kill the odor by cooking them." *(Muslim, Nasa'ee, Ibn Majah in Targheeb wat Tarheeb)*

Rasulullah ﷺ Disapproves of Spitting in the Masjid

Abdullah bin Omar ؓ narrates that as Rasulullah ﷺ was once delivering a lecture, he noticed some spitting on the wall in the direction of the Qibla. Rasulullah ﷺ became very angry with the people and then scraped it off. He then sent for some saffron, which he applied to the area and then said, "Allah is in front of a person's face when he performs salah, so he should never spit in front of him." *(Bukhari, Muslim, Abu Dawud)*. A narration from Abu Sa'eed Khudri states that Rasulullah ﷺ then turned to the people in anger saying, "Does someone amongst you like to spit in the face of a person facing him? When any of you is performing salah, His Rabb is in front of him and an angel is on his right. He should therefore never spit in front of him nor on his right." *(Ibn Khuzaima in Targheeb wat Tarheeb)*. Yet another narration from Abu Hurairah ؓ states that Rasulullah ﷺ said, "Verily the Masjid shrinks with spitting just as a piece of flesh or skin shrinks with fire." *(Abdur Razzaq in Kanzul Ummal)*

Rasulullah ﷺ and the Sahabah Disapprove of Drawing a Sword in the Masjid

Jabir ؓ reports that Banna Juhani ؓ informed him that Rasulullah ﷺ once saw or passed by some people who were exchanging naked swords amongst themselves in the Masjid. Rasulullah ﷺ remarked, "Allah curses the people who do this. Have I not forbidden you from this? When a person draws his sword and then intends giving it to another, he should wrap it before handing it over." *(Baghawi, Ibnus Sakan, Tabrani in Kanzul Ummal)*. Sulaiman bin Musa narrates that when Jabir ؓ was asked about drawing swords in the Masjid, he said, "We have always disapproved of it. In fact, when a person was giving an arrow away as Sadaqa in the Masjid, Rasulullah ﷺ instructed him not to pass through the Masjid with arrows unless he held their heads firmly." *(Abdur Razzaq in Kanzul Ummal)*. Muhammad bin Abdullah narrates that they were in the Masjid with Abu Sa'eed Khudri ؓ when a person turned an arrow around. Abu Sa'eed Khudri said, "Does he not know that Rasulullah ﷺ forbade the turning around of weapons in the Masjid?" *(Tabrani, Haythami)*

Rasulullah ﷺ and his Sahabah Disapprove of Announcing Lost Items in the Masjid

Buraida ؓ narrates that a man once made an announcement in the Masjid saying, "Who has called for the owner of a red camel that he has found?" Rasulullah ﷺ remarked. "May you not find it! The Masaajid were built for their specific purposes and not for announcing lost items." *(Muslim, Nasa'ee, Ibn Majah in Targheeb wat Tarheeb)*. When Abdullah bin Mas'ood ؓ heard a person announcing a lost item in the Masjid, he told him to be silent and reprimanded him. "We have been forbidden from doing this," he added. *(Tabrani in Targheeb wat Tarheeb)*. Ibn Sirin reports that when Ubay bin Ka'b ؓ heard a person asking after his lost item in the Masjid, he became angry and rebuked the man. "O Abul Mundhir!" the man said, "You were never one to be so harsh." Ubay ؓ replied, "We have been commanded to do this, to rebuke people who announce lost items in the Masjid." *(Abdur Razzaq in Kanzul Ummal)*

Omar ؓ Disapproves of Raising the Voice, Making a Noise and Reciting Poetry in the Masjid

Sa'ib bin Yazid ؓ narrates that he was once sleeping in the Masjid when someone threw a pebble at him. When he looked up, he saw that it was Omar ؓ. Omar ؓ said to him, "Go and bring those 2 men to me." When Sa'ib ؓ brought them, Omar ؓ asked them who they were. "We are from Ta'if." they replied. Omar ؓ then said, "Had you been from this town (Madinah), I would have certainly punished you. How can you raise your voices in the Masjid of Rasulullah ﷺ?" *(Bukhari, Bayhaqi)*. Sa'eed bin Ibrahim reports from his father that when Omar ؓ heard someone speaking in the Masjid, he asked, "Do you know where you are? Do you know where you are?" Omar ؓ dislikes hearing people speak loudly in the Masjid. *(Ibrahim bin Sa'd, Ibn Mubarak in Kanzul Ummal)*. Abdullah bin Omar ؓ narrates that whenever Omar ؓ went to the Masjid, he announced in the Masjid, "Do refrain from making a noise." Another narration states that Omar ؓ would announce at the top of his voice. "Refrain from noise in the Masjid!" *(Abdur Razzaq, Ibn Abi Shaybah, Bayhaqi)*. It is reported that Omar ؓ forbade noise in the Masjid saying, "Voices should never be raised in our Masaajid." *(Abdur Razzaq, Ibn Abi Shaybah in Kanzul Ummal)*. Salim narrates that Omar ؓ had a platform built next to the Masjid, which he called Butaiha. He would then say, "Whoever wishes to make a noise, to recite a poem or to raise his voice should go to the platform." *(Malik, Bayhaqi in Kanzul Ummal)*. Tariq bin Shihab narrates that a person in the masjid was brought before Omar ؓ for some crime. Omar ؓ gave instructions that the man be taken out of the Masjid before being given a beating. *(Abdur Razzaq in Kanzul Ummal)*

Abdullah bin Mas'ood ؓ Disapproves of Reclining Against the Wall of the Masjid in the Direction of the Qibla

Between the Adhan and Iqama of Fajr, Abdullah bin Mas'ood ؓ saw some people reclining against the wall of the Masjid in the direction of the Qibla. He said to them, "Do not be an obstacle between the angels and their salah." *(Tabrani, Haythami)*

Habis Ta'ee ❀ Disapproves of People Performing Salah at the Front of the Masjid Before Dawn

Abdullah bin Amir Alhani narrates that a Sahabi by the name of Habis bin Sa'd Ta'ee ❀ once entered the Masjid before dawn and saw some people performing salah at the front of the Masjid. "By the Rabb of the Kabah!" He exclaimed, "They are showing off! Scare them off because whoever will scare them off has obeyed Allah and His Rasul ❀." Some people then approached them and saw them off. Habis ❀ said, "Verily the angels perform salah at the front of the Masjid before dawn." *(Ahmad, Tabrani, Haythami, Ibn Asakir, Abu Nu'aym in Kanzul Ummal, Ibn Sa'd)*

Abdullah bin Mas'ood ❀ Disapproves of Performing Salah Behind Every Pillar in the Masjid

Murra Hamdani says, "I told myself that I would perform 2 Rakats salah behind every pillar of the Masjid in Kufa. As I was busy performing salah, Abdullah bin Mas'ood ❀ appeared there and as I was about to inform him about my resolve, someone else beat me to it. Abdullah bin Mas'ood ❀ then said, "If he knew that Allah is at the closest pillar, he would not pass it without completing all the salats he had undertaken to perform because the reward is the same at all the pillars." *(Tabrani, Haythami)*

Rasulullah ❀ Rejects the Proposals to Ring a Bell or to Blow a Trumpet to Announce the Salah

Abu Umair bin Anas narrates from his uncles who belonged to the Ansar that when Rasulullah ❀ became concerned about how to gather the people for salah, someone suggested that a flag should be flown when the time for salah arrived and when they saw it, people would inform each other. When this idea did not appeal to Rasulullah ❀, someone else suggested the trumpet. This also held little appeal for Rasulullah ❀ and he dismissed the idea saying, "It is a practice of the Jews." When someone else suggested ringing a bell, Rasulullah ❀ also dismissed it saying. "It is the practice of the Christians." Abdullah bin Zaid ❀ left with the concern of Rasulullah ❀ foremost in his mind and he was shown the Adhan in his dream. The Hadith still continues further. *(Abu Dawud).* Abu Sheikh narrates that Abdullah bin Zaid ❀ said, "Announcing the salah was a great concern for Rasulullah ❀ during the early days. Whenever the time for salah arrived, he would have a person climb high and wave his hands. Whoever saw the man came for salah and whoever did not see him did not know about the salah. This made Rasulullah ❀ very worried. 'Rasulullah ❀!' someone said, 'Why don't you have a bell rung.' 'No,' Rasulullah ❀ replied, 'That is the practice of the Christians.' Others suggested, 'Then why don't you have a trumpet blown?' 'No,' Rasulullah ❀ replied, 'That is the practice of the Jews.' I then returned home, overcome with the worry that I saw Rasulullah ❀ so troubled. It was just before dawn when sleep eventually overcame me and as I lay there halfway between awareness and sleep, I saw a man wearing 2 green garments. He stood on the roof of the Masjid, placed his fingers in his ears and called out the Adhan." *(Abush Sheigh in Kanzul Ummah).* Anas ❀ states that when the time for salah arrived during the early period of Rasulullah ❀, someone would run through the streets calling out, "Salah! Salah!" This was difficult for the people and some of them suggested ringing a bell..." The Hadith continues further. *(Abush Sheikh in Kanzul Ummal)*

Before the Directive to Call Out the Adhan, the Call "As Salatu Jami'ah" was Made During the Time of Rasulullah ❀

Nafi bin Jubair, Urwa bin Zaid bin Aslam and Sa'eed bin Musayib all relate that before receiving the directive to call out the Adhan, Nabi ❀'s caller would call out, "As Salatu jami'ah". This was how the people gathered for salah and it was only once the Qibla was changed to the Kabah that the command for Adhan was given. Since one of Rasulullah ❀'s greatest worries was how to inform people about the times of salah, the Sahabah suggested some methods of getting the people together for salah. While some of them suggested the trumpet, others suggested the bell. The Hadith continues further to the point where it states that when the Adhan was being called out to call people for salah, the announcement of "As Salatu jami'ah" was made only when important matters arose so that the people could present themselves and be informed. In this manner they were informed about conquests or about commands that they were to fulfill. At such times, "As Salatu jami'ah" was called out to gather the people even though it was not the time for salah. *(Ibn Sa'd)*

Sa'd Qaradh ❀ Calls Out the Adhan for Rasulullah ❀ at Quba

Sa'd Qaradh ❀ reports that whenever Rasulullah ❀ arrived in Quba, Bilal ❀ would call out the Adhan to inform the people that Rasulullah ❀ had arrived so that they could gather before him. However, when Rasulullah ❀ arrived one day without Bilal ❀, the non-Muslim slaves started looking at each other. Sa'd Qaradh ❀ immediately climbed up a date palm and called out the Adhan. "What made you call out the Adhan, O Sa'd?" Rasulullah ❀ asked. Sa'd ❀ replied, "May my parents be sacrificed for you! I saw you with only a handful of people and did not see Bilal ❀ with you. I then noticed the slaves looking at each other and at you, I feared that they would harm you, so I called out the Adhan so that other Muslims would come quickly." "You did the right thing, O Sa'd," Rasulullah ❀ said. "Whenever you see Bilal not with me, you should call out the Adhan." Sa'd called out Adhan thrice during Rasulullah ❀'s Lifetime. *(Tabrani, Haythami)*

Statements of the Sahabah Concerning the Adhan and the People who Call Out the Adhan

Sa'd bin Abi Waqqas ❀ said, "The share of rewards of those who call out the Adhan on the Day of Judgment will be like the share of those who wage Jihad. During the time between the Adhan and the Iqama, the Mu'adhin is like the martyr tossing and turning in his blood in the Path of Allah. Abdullah bin Mas'ood ❀ said, "If I were a Mu'adhin, I care not whether I perform Hajj or Umra or wage Jihad." Omar bin Khattab ❀ said, "If I were a Mu'adhin, my affairs would have been perfected and I care not whether I woke up for Nafl salah during the night or whether I fasted (optional) during the day because I heard Rasulullah ❀ pray, 'O Allah! Forgive those who call out the Adhan. O Allah! Forgive those who call out the Adhan.' 'O Rasulullah ❀!' I said. 'But why do you emphasize calling out the Adhan so much when you have left us in a condition that we would draw swords to call out the Adhan?' Rasulullah ❀ replied, "That is not the case, O Omar because there will soon come a time when people will leave the Adhan to the weak ones amongst them. The flesh that is forbidden for Jahannam is the flesh of those who call out the Adhan." Aisha ❀ mentioned that it is the Mu'adhin whom to Allah refers in the verse:

وَمَنْ أَحْسَنُ قَوْلًا مِّمَّن دَعَا إِلَى اللَّهِ وَعَمِلَ صَالِحًا وَقَالَ إِنَّنِي مِنَ الْمُسْلِمِينَ (33)

And who is better in speech than he who (says: "My Lord is Allah (believes in His Oneness)," and then stands straight (acts upon His Order), and) invites (men) to Allah's (Islamic Monotheism), and does righteous deeds, and says: "I am one of the Muslims." (Fussilat:33)

She says further, "The Mu'adhin calls towards Allah when he says, حي علي الصلوة
'Come to salah', he performs a righteous deed when he performs the salah, and he is certainly amongst the Muslims when he says, لا اله الا الله
(There is none worthy of worship but Allah)." (Bayhaqi in Shu'sbul Imam, Kanzul Ummal, Adbushah Shaikh, Rasafi in Kitabul Adhan)

Omar ؓ once said, "Had I been a Mu'adhin, I care not if I neither perform Hajj or Umrah except for the Fard Hajj. Had the angels descended on earth, none would be able to beat them to calling out the Adhan, they would allow no one else to do it because they know its tremendous virtue." (Ibnuz Zanjway in Kanzul Ummal). Qais bin Abu Hazim narrates that when they went to Omar ؓ, he asked, "Who calls out the Adhan amongst you people?" They informed him that it was their slaves who did it, Omar ؓ said, "That is a grave deficiency in you. Had I the choice of being a Mu'adhin instead of the Khalifa, I would have chosen to be a Mu'adhin." (Abdur Razzaq, Ibn Abi Shaybah, Bayhaqi in Kanzul Ummal). Ali ؓ said, "I regret not requesting Rasulullah ﷺ to assign the duty of calling out the Adhan to my sons Hasan and Husain." (Tabrani, Haythami). Abdullah bin Mas'ood ؓ said, "I do not approve of you appointing blind people to call out the Adhan because they are unable to determine correct times of salah and I also do not approve of you appointing learned scholars of the Qur'an to call out the Adhan because this would affect their teaching." (Tabrani, Haythami)

Abdullah bin Omar ؓ's Words to a Man who Adopted a Singing Tone When Calling Out the Adhan and Took Payment for It

Yahya Bakka narrates that a man once said to Abdullah bin Omar ؓ, "I love you for the sake of Allah." Abdullah bin Omar ؓ responded by saying, "But I detest you for the sake of Allah." When the man asked why this was, Abdullah bin Omar ؓ replied, "Because you adopt a singing tone when calling out the Adhan and you take payment for it." (Tabrani, Haythami).

Rasulullah ﷺ and Abu Bakr ؓ Instruct that Jihad be Waged Against Tribes Amongst Whom the Adhan is not Called Out

When Rasulullah ﷺ dispatched Khalid bin Sa'eed bin Al Aas ؓ to Yemen, he gave him instructions to take as prisoners the inhabitants of all the towns he passed in which the Adhan was not called out. Therefore, when Khalid ؓ passed by the Banu Zubaid tribe and did not hear them call out the Adhan, he took them all as prisoners. However, when Amr bin Ma'dikarib ؓ spoke to him about them, Khalid ؓ released them into his custody. (Ibn Asakir in Kanzul Ummal). Talha bin Abdullah bin Abdur Rahman bin Abu Bakr ؓ reports that when Abu Bakr ؓ dispatched his armies against the deserters, he instructed the commanders saying, "When you hear the Adhan in a town that you surround, take no action until you question them about their grievances. If you do not hear the Adhan, you should launch your attack, fight them, burn their property and be exhausted in inflicting casualties so that they see that the demise of your Nabi ﷺ has brought no weakness in you." (Bayhaqi). Zuhri narrates that when Abu Bakr ؓ dispatched his armies against the deserters, he instructed them saying, "Monitor them overnight and take no action if you hear the Adhan because the Adhan is a sign of Iman." (Abdur Razzaq in Kanzul Ummal)

Rasulullah ﷺ's Directive on Waiting for Salah

Ali ؓ narrates that when the time for salah arrived and Rasulullah ﷺ saw that the people were few in number, he remained sitting and did not lead the salah. He would then lead the salah only when he saw a substantial gathering. (Abu Dawud in Kanzul Ummal). Abdullah bin Abu Awfa ؓ reports that Rasulullah ﷺ would wait until he heard the sounds of people's shoes. (Ibn Abi Shaybah in Kanzul Ummal)

The Sahabah Wait for Salah Until Half the Night had Passed

Omar ؓ reports that Rasulullah ﷺ was busy dispatching an army until half the night had already passed or was about to. He then came out for salah and said to those waiting, "While other people have performed their salah and left, you people are still waiting for salah. Take note that you have remained in salah, kept earning its rewards as long as you have been waiting for it." (Ibn Abi Shaybah, Ibn Jareer in Kanzul Ummal)

Rasulullah ﷺ's Words to Those who Waited for the Next Salah After Maghrib and After Zuhr

Abdullah bin Amr ؓ narrates that after Rasulullah ﷺ had performed the Maghrib salah, some people left while others remained seated. Rasulullah ﷺ then went to those still sitting and said. "Your Rabb has opened a door to the heavens and is boasting before the angels saying. 'My servants have completed a Fard and are now waiting for the next.'" (Ibn Jareer in Kanzul Ummal, Ibn Majah in Targheeb wat Tarheeb). Abu Umama Thaqafi ؓ reports that after leading the Zuhr salah, Mu'awiya ؓ told the people to remain where they were until he returned. He then left and put on his shawl. After leading the Asr salah, he said. "Should I not inform you of something that Rasulullah ﷺ did?" When the people asked, Mu'awiya ؓ said, "The Sahabah once performed the Zuhr salah behind Rasulullah ﷺ and remained sitting. When Rasulullah ﷺ came out again for the Asr salah, he asked. 'Have you people not left after the last salah' 'No.' came the reply. Rasulullah ﷺ then said, 'If only you could have seen your Rabb open a door from the heavens to show you to the angels and boast about you sitting in wait for salah.'" (Tabrani in Majma'uz Zawa'id)

Rasulullah ﷺ's Address to Those who Waited Until Midnight for the Isha Salah

Anas ؓ narrates that Rasulullah ﷺ once delayed the Isha a salah until midnight. After leading the salah, he turned to face the Sahabah saying. "Whereas other people have already performed their salah and gone to sleep, you people have remained in salah for as long as you have been waiting for it." (Bukhari). Abu Hurairah ؓ reports that Rasul ﷺ said, "A person is in salah for as long as it is salah that keeps him waiting and all the while the angels keep praying, 'O Allah! Forgive him. O Allah! Shower Your mercy on him.' This continues for as long as he does not stand up from his place of salah or does not break his wudhu." (Bukhari). Another narration states that a person remains in salah for as long as he remains on his place of salah or as long as he does not break his wudhu. (Muslim, Abu Dawud) Yet another narration states that a person remains in salah for as long as he remains on his place of salah, waiting for the next salah. And all this while the angels keep praying, 'O Allah! Forgive him. O Allah! Shower Your mercy on him.' This continues for as long as he does not leave or does not break his wudhu." "How will his wudhu break?" one of the narrators asked. Abu Hurairah ؓ replied, "When he passes wind either audibly or silently." (Muslim, Abu Dawud in Targheeb wat Tarheeb)

Rasulullah ﷺ Encourages Waiting for Salah

Jabir bin Abdullah ؓ reports that Rasulullah ﷺ said. "Shall I not point you towards something that wipes out sins and is expiation for misdeeds?" "Why not, O Rasulullah ﷺ?" the Sahabah said. Rasulullah ﷺ said, "Making a proper wudhu in adverse conditions, taking many steps towards the Masjid and waiting for one salah after another. This will earn the reward of guarding the borders." *(Ibn Hibban in Targheeb wat Tarheeb)*

Abu Hurairah ﷺ's Interpretation of Guarding the Borders During the Time of Rasulullah ﷺ

Dawud bin Salih narrates that Abu Salama once asked him if he knew why Allah revealed the verse: اصْبِرُوا وَصَابِرُوا وَرَابِطُوا

...endure and be more patient (than your enemy), and guard your territory... (Al-Imran:200)
When Dawud admitted that he did not know, Abu Salama said, "I heard Abu Hurairah ﷺ say that during the time of Rasulullah ﷺ there was no war because of which the borders had to be guarded, but waiting for one salah after another was their form of guarding the borders." *(Hakim in Targheeb wat Tarheeb)*

The Statement of Anas ﷺ Concerning the Verse "Their Sides Part from Their Beds"

Anas ﷺ said that it is waiting for the Isha salah that is referred to in the verse: تَتَجَافَى جُنُوبُهُمْ عَنِ الْمَضَاجِعِ
Their sides forsake their beds... (As-Sajdah:16) (Tirmidhi in Targheeb wat Tarheeb)

The Importance Rasulullah ﷺ Showed to Salah in Congregation and his Unwillingness to Allow a Blind Man to Forego It

Amr bin Ummu Maktum ﷺ once said, "O Rasulullah ﷺ! I am a blind man who lives far from the Masjid. While I have a guide, he is a person with whom I cannot get along. Are you able to grant me permission to perform salah at home?" "Can you hear the Adhan'?" Rasulullah ﷺ asked. When Amr said that he could, Rasulullah ﷺ said, "I am then unable to grant you permission." *(Ahmad, Abu Dawud, Ibn Majah, Ibn Khuzaima, Hakim).* Another narration states that Rasulullah ﷺ once came to the Masjid and found only a few people there. He then said, "I have a good mind to appoint an Imam to lead the people in salah and to then go out and burn down the house of every person I find who does not come for salah." Ibn Ummu Maktum ﷺ then said, "O Rasulullah ﷺ! There are many palms and trees between my house and the Masjid and I cannot find a guide at all times. Is it possible for me to perform salah at home'?" Rasulullah ﷺ asked, "Can you hear the Iqama?" When he replied that he could, Rasulullah ﷺ said, "Then you should come to the Masjid for salah." *(Ahmad in Targheeb wat Tarheeb)*

The Statements of Abdullah bin Mas'ood ﷺ and Mu'adh bin Jabal ﷺ About Salah in Congregation

Abdullah bin Mas'ood ﷺ once said, "Whoever wishes to meet Allah tomorrow as a Muslim should regularly perform these Fard salats in the place where the Adhan is called out because Allah has selected for His Nabi ﷺ certain practices that give guidance and amongst these practices are the salats in congregation. Should you ever perform your salah at your homes as those staying behind at home do, you will be forsaking the Sunnah of your Nabi ﷺ and as soon as you do this, you will go astray. Whenever a person purifies himself properly and then heads for one of the Masjid, Allah records for him the reward of a good deed for every step he takes, Allah elevates his rank by a stage and erases a sin from his record. I saw a time when none of us would dare miss a salah in congregation except for an open

hypocrite. In fact, a man who was very ill would be brought with the support of 2 men and placed in the row." Another narration states that Abdullah bin Mas'ood ﷺ said, "I saw a time when none of us would dare miss a salah in congregation except for a person whom everyone recognized as a hypocrite or a very sick person. If a sick man was capable of walking with the support of 2 men, he would come for the salah." Abdullah bin Mas'ood ﷺ also added, "Verily our Nabi ﷺ has taught us certain practices that give guidance and amongst these practices is to perform salah in the Masjid where Adhan was called out." *(Muslim, Abu Dawud, Nasa'ee, Ibn Majah in Targheeb wat Tarheeb, Abdur Razzaq, Diya in Mukhtara, Kanzul Ummal).* Abdullah bin Mas'ood ﷺ added. "And now I cannot find who does not have a place of salah inside his house where he performs salah. If you perform salah in your homes and forsake the Masjid, you will be forsaking the Sunnah of your Nabi ﷺ." *(Tayalisi).* Mu'adh bin Jabal ﷺ said, "Whoever would like to go peacefully to Allah should perform these 5 Fard salats at a place where the Adhan is called out because these are amongst the practices that give guidance and what your Nabi ﷺ practically showed you. You should never say that you have reserved a place in your house where you perform salah because if you do that you will be forsaking the Sunnah of your Nabi ﷺ and as soon as you forsake his Sunnah, you will go astray." *(Abu Nu'aym in Hilya)*

The Sahabah's Suspicion About the Person who did not Perform the Fajr and Isha Salats in Congregation

Abdullah bin Omar ﷺ says, "When we did not see a person for the Fajr and Isha salats, we became suspicious of him (because it is the Munafiqin who do not perform these salats)." *(Tabrani, Ibn Khuzaima in Targheeb wat Tarheeb, Sa'eed bin Mansoor, Kanzul Ummal, Bazzar in Majma'uz Zawa'id)*

Omar ﷺ's Statement about a Person who Missed the Fajr Salah in Congregation Because he had Stayed Awake at Night in Ibada

Abu Bakr bin Sulaiman bin Abu Hathma narrates that Omar ﷺ once did not see Sulaiman bin Abu Hathma ﷺ for the Fajr salah. Omar was on his way to the marketplace that morning and because Sulaiman ﷺ's house happened to be between the Masjid and the marketplace, Omar passed by Sulaiman ﷺ's mother Shifa ﷺ. "I did not see Sulaiman for the Fajr salah," Omar ﷺ said. She explained, "He spent the night in salah and sleep overpowered him." To this, Omar ﷺ remarked. "I prefer attending the Fajr salah in congregation to standing in salah all night." *(Malik in Targheeb wat Tarheeb).* Ibn Abu Mulaika ﷺ narrates that Shifa ﷺ who belonged to the Banu Adi bin Ka'b tribe once came to Omar ﷺ during Ramadhan. Enquiring about her husband, Omar ﷺ asked. "Why did I not see Abu Hathma for the Fajr salah?" "O Amirul Mu'minin!" she explained, "He exerted himself in Ibada throughout the night and was too tired to go out to perform the Fajr salah. So he performed salah at home and slept." Omar ﷺ remarked, "By Allah! Had he been present for the Fajr salah, it would have been more beloved to me than his exertion throughout the night." Shifa bint Abdullah ﷺ says, "Omar ﷺ once came to my house where he found 2 men (my husband and son) fast asleep. 'What is the matter with these 2 that they were not present with us for salah'?' he asked. 'O Amirul Mu'minin!' I explained, 'They fell asleep after performing their Fajr salah at home.' To this Omar ﷺ remarked, 'I prefer performing Fajr salah in congregation to performing optional salah throughout the night and until dawn." *(Abdur Razzaq in Kanzul Ummal)*

The Statement of Abu Darda 🕮 Concerning Salah in Congregation and the Action Abdullah bin Omar 🕮 Took When he Missed Isha Salah in Congregation

Ummu Darda 🕮 says that when her husband Abu Darda 🕮 once came home angry, she asked him what the matter was. He replied, "By Allah! I know nothing else about the affairs of Muhammad 🕮 except that the Muslims performed salah only in congregation and now people are starting to do otherwise." *(Bukhari)*. Nafi narrates that when Abdullah bin Omar 🕮 missed the Isha salah in congregation, he would remain in Ibadah for the rest of the night. *(Abu Nu'aym in Hilya)* Another narration states that whenever Abdullah bin Omar 🕮 missed any salah in congregation, he would remain engaged in salah until the next salah. *(Bayhaqi in Isabah)*

Harith bin Hassan 🕮 Leaves Home for the Fajr Salah the Night he got Married and the Taunting he Received

Ambasah bin Azhar narrates that it was customary for a newly married man to remain indoors for a few days after getting married and not to leave for the Fajr salah. When a Sahabi by the name of Harith bin Hassan 🕮 was married, he was leaving for Fajr when someone taunted, "You are leaving when you have just married this night?" Harith 🕮 said, "By Allah! The woman who prevents me from performing the Fajr salah in congregation is a terrible woman indeed." *(Tabrani in Majma'uz Zawa'id)*

The Importance Rasulullah 🕮 Attached to Straightening the Rows of the Sahabah in Salah

Barra bin Aazib 🕮 narrates that Rasulullah 🕮 used to go to the ends of the rows and straighten the chests and shoulders of the people saying, "Do not be in disarray otherwise your hearts will be in disarray, you will be disunited. Verily Allah bestows His special mercy on the people standing in the first row and the angels pray for their forgiveness. *(Ibn Khuzaima in Targheeb wat Tarheeb)*. Bara bin Aazib 🕮 says, "Rasulullah 🕮 used to weave between the rows from one end to the other, touching our chests and shoulders when straightening the rows and saying, 'Do not stand in disarray." *(Abu Dawud in Targheeb wat Tarheeb)*. Jabir bin Samura 🕮 narrates that Rasulullah 🕮 once came out to them and said, "Will you not form your rows as the angels form theirs in front of their Rabb?" When the Sahabah enquired how it was that the angels formed their rows. Rasulullah 🕮 replied, "They first complete the front rows and stand close to each other." *(Muslim, Abu Dawud, Nasa'ee, Ibn Majah in Targheeb war Tarheeb)*. Jabir bin Samura 🕮 also narrates that they were once performing salah with Rasulullah 🕮 when he motioned them to sit down. When they sat down, Rasulullah 🕮 said, "What prevents you from forming your rows as the angels form theirs?" The rest of the narration is similar to the one above. *(Abu Dawud, Ibn Majah in Kanzul Ummal)*. Nu'man bin Bashir 🕮 says, "Rasulullah 🕮 used to straighten our rows as meticulously as he would straighten an arrow. This he did until we had understood him perfectly. On one occasion when Rasulullah 🕮 came out for salah, he stood there and was about to say 'Allahu Akbar' when he noticed someone's chest standing out from the row. He then said. 'O servants of Allah! You will have to straighten your rows otherwise Allah will cast disunity between you." *(Malik, Muslim, Abu Dawud, Tirmidhi, Ibn Majah, Nasa'ee)*. Nu'man 🕮 also added, "I saw a man touching his shoulders with those of the person beside him, touching his knees with those of the other man and also touching his ankles with those of the other man." *(Abu Dawud in Targheeb wat Tarheeb)*

Omar 🕮, Uthman 🕮 and Ali 🕮 Instruct the Straightening of Rows Before the Takbir

Nafi narrates that Omar 🕮 used to instruct the people to straighten their rows and it was only when they reported to him that the rows were straightened did he call out the Takbir to start the salah. *(Malik, Abdur Razzaq, Bayhaqi)*. Abu Uthman Nahdi 🕮 reports that Uthman 🕮 used to instruct the people to straighten their rows and would actually call people by their names to tell them to move forward. He also said, "When people keep staying back. Allah will eventually keep them back." *(Abdur Razzaq)*. Abu Uthman 🕮 also reports that he noticed that whenever Omar 🕮 stepped forward to lead the salah, he would look at the shoulders and feet of the followers to see if they were in line." *(Abdur Razzaq in Kanzul Ummal)*. Abu Nadhar narrates that when salah was about to begin, Omar bin Khattab 🕮 would tell people to straighten their rows and would take people's names as he told them to either move forward or backward. He would also add, "Keep your rows straight because Allah wishes you to adopt the method of the angels (when they form their rows)." He would then recited the verse: وَإِنَّا لَنَحْنُ الصَّافُّونَ (165) وَإِنَّا لَنَحْنُ الْمُسَبِّحُونَ (166)

Verily, we (angels), we stand in rows for the prayers (as you Muslims stand in rows for your prayers); Verily, we, (angels), we are they who glorify (Allah's Praises i.e. perform prayers). (As-Safat:165-166) (Abd bin Humaid, Ibn Jareer, Ibn Abi Hatim in Kanzul Ummal)

Malik says, "I was with Uthman bin Affan 🕮 when the people stood up for salah. I was busy requesting him to grant me an allowance and continued doing so as he straightened some pebbles with his shoe. Eventually some men whom he had appointed to straighten the rows reported to him that the rows had been straightened. He then told me to stand straight in one of the rows and called out the Takbir." *(Abdur Razzaq, Bayhaqi in Kanzul Ummal)*. Ali 🕮 used to say to the people standing in rows for salah, "Stand straight and your hearts will be straight, stand close to each other and you will have compassion for each other." *(Ibn Abi Shaybah in Kanzul Ummal)*

The Statement of Abdullah bin Mas'ood 🕮 Concerning the Straightening of Rows

Abdullah bin Mas'ood 🕮 said, "I saw a time when salah would not begin until we had completed the rows of salah." *(Ahmad, Haythami)*. Abdullah bin Mas'ood 🕮 also said, "Verily Allah bestows His special mercy on the people who advance through the rows to the first row of salah and the angels pray for their forgiveness." *(Tabrani, Haythami)*

Statements of Rasulullah 🕮 and Abdullah bin Abbas 🕮 Concerning the First Row

Abdul Aziz bin Rufay reports, "It was during the Khilafa of Abdullah bin Zubair 🕮 that Amir bin Mas'ood Qurashi 🕮 was trying to get ahead of me to the first row at the Maqam Ibrahim in Makkah. 'Is there much good mentioned about the first row?' I asked. 'By Allah! There certainly is,' he replied, 'Rasulullah 🕮 said that if people realized the value of the first row, the only way in which the rows would be formed would be by drawing lots." *(Tabrani, Haythami)*. Abdullah bin Abbas 🕮 said, "Ensure that you always stand in the first row and ensure that it is on the right of the first row. You should also refrain from forming rows between pillars." *(Tabrani, Haythami)*

Rasulullah 🕮 Instructs that the Muhajirin and Ansar should Occupy the First Row

Qais bin Ubadah says, "I was present in Madinah when the

people stood up for salah. I then forged ahead and stood in the first row. Omar ✿ arrived and made his way through the rows to get to the front to lead the salah. With him was a tanned man with a thin beard. Looking at the faces of the people there, his eyes fell on me and he pushed me aside to stand in my place. This hurt me very deeply. However, when the salah was over, he turned to me and said. 'Let not what had happened upset you or cause you grief because I am sure that it hurt you. However, I have heard Rasulullah ✿ say that none save the Muhajirin and Ansar should occupy the first row.' When I asked the people who the man was, they informed me that he was Ubay bin Ka'b ✿." (Hakim in Mustadrak). In another narration, Qais says, "As I was performing salah in the first row of the Masjid of Madinah, someone came from behind, pulled me back and stood in my place. After the salah was over, he turned to me and realized that he was Ubay bin Ka'b ✿. He then said to me. "May Allah never make you upset, dear youngster. This was something that Rasulullah ✿ enjoined upon us..." The narration then continues like the one above. (Abu Nu'aym in Hilya)

Rasulullah ✿'s Involvement with the Needs of the People After the Iqama has been Called Out

Usama bin Umair ✿ says. "People would have already stood up for salah when a person would stand between Rasulullah ✿ and the Qibla, presenting his need to Rasulullah ✿. He would remain standing there and talking with Rasulullah ✿ for such a long time that I sometimes saw some people nodding off to sleep because of the long while Rasulullah ✿ had to remain standing there." (Abdur Razzaq in Kanzul Ummal Abush Sheikh). Anas ✿ narrates that the people would be ready to perform the Isha salah when Rasulullah ✿ needed to speak to a person. A few of the Sahabah would actually fall asleep during the wait and would then wake up when the salah began. (Ibn Asakir in Kanzul Ummal). Urwa ✿ narrates that people would discuss their needs with Rasulullah ✿ after the Mu'adhin had called out the Iqama and the people had already hushed. Rasulullah ✿ would then see that the need was fulfilled. Anas ✿ mentions that Rasulullah ✿ had a staff on which he would lean when the dialogue became too long. (Abush Sheikh in Adan, Kanzul Ummal). Anas ✿ says, "Rasulullah ✿ was the most compassionate of people and whenever someone came to him with a request, he would promise it to him if he did not have then and then give it to him when he had it. People had already stood up for salah one day when a Bedouin arrived and, grabbing on to Rasulullah ✿'s clothing he demanded, 'A small portion of what I need is still due and I fear that I may forget about it so I want it now)' Rasulullah ✿ stood up with him and only returned to lead the salah after he had finished with the man." (Bukhari in Adab)

Omar ✿ and Uthman ✿'s Involvement with such Matters

Abu Uthman Nahdi says, "Salah would be about to start when a person would come before Omar ✿ to discuss something. In fact, some of us would actually sit down because we would be standing so long." (Abdur Rabi Zahrani in Kanzul Ummal). Musa bin Talha says, "As he sat on the pulpit and the Mu'adhin was busy calling out the Iqama. I heard Uthman bin Affan ✿ asking people about their conditions and market prices." (Ibn Hibban in Kanzul Ummal, Ibn Sa'd). The narration has passed in the chapter discussing the straightening of rows in which Malik says, "I was with Uthman bin Affan ✿ when the people stood up for salah. I was busy requesting him to grant me an allowance and continued doing so as he straightened some pebbles with his shoe..."

The Statement of Abu Sufian ✿ Concerning the Discipline of the Sahabah When he saw Them Performing Salah

Detailed narrations have already appeared in the chapter discussing the treaty of Hudaybiya and the conquest of Madinah in which it is stated that Rasulullah ✿ said to Abu Sufian ✿, "O Abu Sufian! Accept Islam and live in peace." After Abu Sufian ✿ accepted Islam, he proceeded with Abbas to his camp. The next morning when the Sahabah rushed to perform wudhu, Abu Sufian ✿ asked, "What is the matter with the people, O Abul Fadhl? Have they received an order?" "No," replied Abbas ✿, "they are preparing for salah." Abu Sufian ✿ then performed wudhu on the instructions of Abbas ✿, who then took him to Rasulullah ✿. Rasulullah ✿ started the salah and when he called out the Takbir, the Sahabah followed suit. They all then made Ruku when Rasulullah ✿ made Ruku and got up again when Rasulullah ✿ got up. To this, Abu Sufian ✿ remarked, "To this day have I never seen such discipline from a nation who have been gathered together from such varying backgrounds! Neither are the nobles of Persia nor the long-established Romans as well disciplined as this!" Addressing Abbas ✿, he said further, "O Abul Fadhl! Your nephew has certainly founded a great kingdom." "It is not a kingdom," Abbas ✿ replied, "This is Nubuwah." (Ibn Abi Shaybah in Kanzul Ummal). Another narration from Maymuna ✿ quoted in the chapter discussing the conquest of Makkah states that when Rasulullah ✿ got up to perform wudhu, the Muslims would compete to get the wudhu water and rub it on their faces. To this, Abu Sufian ✿ remarked, "O Abul Fadhl! Your nephew has certainly founded a great kingdom." "It is not a kingdom," Abbas ✿ replied, "This is Nubuwah and it is this that the people are so zealous about." (Tabrani, Haythami). Urwa ✿ states that when Abu Sufian ✿ awoke the morning after he had spent the night with Abbas ✿, he saw the Sahabah eagerly preparing for salah and scattering about to purify themselves. Abu Sufian ✿ became alarmed at this sight and asked Abbas ✿ what the matter was. Abbas ✿ replied, "They have heard the Adhan and are now scattering about to prepare for salah." When salah started and Abu Sufian ✿ saw the Sahabah bow and prostrate when Rasulullah ✿ did so, he remarked, "O Abbas! Do they do everything he instructs them to do." "Certainly," Abbas ✿ replied, "they would obey Rasulullah ✿ even if he were to command them to forsake their food and drink." (Al Bidayah wan Nihayah)

The Sahabah Perform salah Behind Abu Bakr ✿ Upon the Instruction of Rasulullah ✿

In the chapter discussing the enthusiasm Rasulullah ✿ had for salah, a narration from Aisha ✿ has already passed stating that when he was critically ill, Rasulullah sent a message to Abu Bakr to lead the salah. Abu Bakr ✿ was a soft person so he said to Omar ✿, "You lead the salah, O Omar!" Omar ✿ however said, "You are more worthy of the privilege." Abu Bakr ✿ then led the salah during those days. A narration of Bukhari also quoted in the chapter states that Rasulullah ✿ said, "Tell Abu Bakr to lead the people in salah," Rasulullah ✿ instructed. One of Rasulullah ✿'s wives remarked, "Abu Bakr is a soft man who will be unable lead the salah when he stands in your place." Rasulullah ✿ however repeated the instruction, but again met with the same response. When this happened a third time, Rasulullah ✿ said, "You women are just like the women around Yusuf ✿. Tell Abu Bakr to lead the people in salah." Abdullah bin Zam'ah ✿ reports, "A few Muslims and I happened to be with Rasulullah ✿ when his illness had become critical. When Bilal ✿ called out the Adhan, Rasulullah ✿ said, 'Appoint someone to lead the salah.' I left and found Omar ؓ amongst the people. Abu Bakr ؓ was not there. I therefore told Omar ؓ to lead the salah. Omar ؓ then stood up and when he said 'Allahu Akbar' Rasulullah ﷺ heard his voice because his voice was very loud. Rasulullah ﷺ then asked, 'Then where is Abu Bakr? Neither Allah nor the Muslims can accept this! Neither Allah nor the Muslims can accept this!' Rasulullah ﷺ then sent for Abu Bakr ؓ and when he arrived, Omar had already completed the salah. Abu Bakr ؓ then lead the people in salah. Omar ؓ then said to me, 'O dear! What have you done, O Ibn Zam'ah? I swear by Allah that when you told me to lead the salah, I thought that it was an instruction from Rasulullah ﷺ. Had I known better, I would have never led the salah.' I explained, 'By Allah! Rasulullah ﷺ certainly did not instruct me to appoint you, but when I did not see Abu Bakr ؓ and only saw you, I regarded you as being most worthy of leading the salah.'" *(Ahmad, Abu Dawud in Al Bidayah wan Nihayah, Hakim)*

Another narration states that when Rasulullah ﷺ heard Omar ؓ's voice, he came out and with his head out of the room, he said angrily, "No! No! None but the son of Abu Quhafa i.e. Abu Bakr ؓ should lead the salah." *(Abu Dawud in Al Bidayah wan Nihayah)*. In the chapter discussing how the Sahabah elected Abu Bakr ؓ to the post of Khilafa under the heading "The Sahabah place Abu Bakr ؓ ahead for Khilafa, are pleased to select him and condemn anyone who desires to divide their unity" and the subheading "A Hadith of Ahmad and the statements of Abu Ubaidah bin Jarrah ؓ and Uthman ؓ concerning the Khilafa of Abu Bakr ؓ", a narration has passed in which Abu Ubaidah bin Jarrah ؓ said, "I am not likely to step head of a person whom Rasulullah ﷺ had commanded to lead us in salah and who then led us in salah until Rasulullah ﷺ passed away." Also quoted in the same chapter under the subheading "Abu Bakr ؓ declines to accept the post of Khalifa and the statements of Ali ؓ and Zubair ؓ he is most worthy of the position" is the statement that Ali ؓ and Zubair ؓ made when they said, "However, we are also of the opinion that Abu Bakr ؓ is most worthy of the post after Rasulullah ﷺ. He was the companion of Rasulullah ﷺ in the cave and the 'second of the two'. We definitely acknowledge his status and his seniority. After all, Rasulullah ﷺ did instruct him to lead the Muslims in salah while Rasulullah ﷺ was alive."

The Statements of Omar ؓ and Ali ؓ Concerning Abu Bakr ؓ Leading the Salah

Abdullah bin Mas'ood ؓ narrates that when Rasulullah ﷺ passed away, the Ansar said, "There should be an Amir from us and one from you, Muhajirin." Omar ؓ went to them and said, "Did you not know that Rasulullah ﷺ had placed Abu Bakr ؓ to lead the salah?" The Ansar said, "Allah forbid that we should ever place ourselves ahead of Abu Bakr ؓ!" *(Nasa'ee in Jam'ul Fawa'id)*. Ali ؓ said, "Rasulullah ﷺ certainly instructed Abu Bakr ؓ to lead salah when I was present, available not ill. To take charge of our matters of this world as Khalifa we are pleased to have the person whom Nabi ﷺ selected to take charge of our matters of Deen, our salah." *(Muntakhab Kanzul Ummal)*

The Statement of Salman Farsi ؓ Concerning the Arab Leadership

Abu Laila Kindi reports that Salman Farsi ؓ once arrived with a group of 12 or 13 riders from amongst the companions of Rasulullah ﷺ. When the time for salah arrived, the others addressed Salman ؓ saying, "Go forward to lead the salah, O Abu Abdullah." Salman ؓ declined saying, "We, non-Arabs cannot lead you Arabs in salah nor marry your women because it is through you that Allah has guided us." One of the men from

the group then went ahead and performed 4 Rakats salah. After he had completed, Salman ؓ said, "Why did we need to perform 4 Rakats salah when half of it (2 Rakats) would have sufficed. Since we are on a journey, we are most in need of concessions." *(Abu Nu'aym in Hilya, Tabrani, Abu Ya'la, Haythami)*

The Sahabah Follow Slaves in Salah

Abu Sa'eed was a slave of the Banu Usaid tribe. He prepared a meal one day and invited Abu Dhar ؓ, Hudhaifa ؓ and Abdullah bin Mas'ood ؓ. When the time arrived for salah, Abu Dhar ؓ stepped forward to lead the salah when Hudhaifa ؓ said to him, "Step back because the owner of the house is entitled to leading the salah." "Is that so, O Ibn Mas'ood?" Abu Dhar ؓ asked. When Abdullah bin Mas'ood ؓ confirmed what Hudhaifa ؓ said, Abu Dhar ؓ stepped back. Abu Sa'eed says, "They then put me forward (to lead the salah) whereas I was just a slave. Nevertheless, I led them in the salah." *(Abdur Razzaq in Kanzul Ummal)*. Nafi reports, "People had stood up for salah in a Masjid in a district of Madinah where Abdullah bin Omar ؓ had a property. The Imam of the Masjid was a slave and when Abdullah bin Omar ؓ came for the salah, the Imam requested him to lead the salah. Abdullah bin Omar ؓ declined saying, 'You have a greater right to lead the salah in your Masjid.' The Imam then proceeded to lead the salah." *(Abdur Razzaq in Kanzul Ummal)*. Abdullah bin Handhala ؓ narrates, "We were in the house of Qais bin Sa'd bin Ubadah ؓ with a group of Sahabah when we told him to lead the salah, 'I cannot do so (in presence of men better than I),' he submitted. I said, 'Rasulullah ﷺ said that a man has a greater right to the front of his bed, to the front of his animal and to lead the salah in his house.' He asked one of his slaves who went forward and led the salah." *(Bazzar, Tabrani, Haythami)*

Abdullah bin Mas'ood ؓ Performs Salah Behind Abu Musa Ash'ari ؓ in His House

Alqama narrates that Abdullah bin Mas'ood ؓ once visited Abu Musa Ash'ari ؓ at his house. When the time for salah arrived, Abu Musa ؓ said to Abdullah bin Mas'ood ؓ, "Go forward to lead the salah, O Abu Abdur Rahman because you are elder and more knowledgeable than I." Abdullah bin Mas'ood ؓ replied, "You rather go forward because I have come your house and your Masjid. You therefore have a greater right." Abu Musa ؓ then stepped forward and removed his shoes and led the salah. After he had completed, Abdullah bin Mas'ood ؓ asked, "What was your reason for removing your shoes? Are you on the Wadi Muqaddas (where Musa ؑ was when he had to remove his shoes)?" *(Ahmad, Haythami)*. Abdullah bin Mas'ood ؓ said to Abu Musa Ash'ari ؓ, "O Abu Musa! You know well that the Sunnah practice is for the owner of the house to go forward (to lead the salah)." However, Abu Musa Ash'ari ؓ refused to do so until one of their slaves went forward. *(Tabrani, Haythami)*

Furat bin Hayyan ؓ Performs Salah in his Masjid Behind Handhala bin Rabi ؓ on the Instruction of Rasulullah ﷺ

Qais bin Zuhair ؓ says, "I once walked with Handhala bin Rabi ؓ to the Masjid of Furat bin Hayyan ؓ. When the time for salah arrived, Furat ؓ told Handhala ؓ to go forward (to lead the salah). Handhala ؓ refused saying, "I cannot lead you in salah when you are elder than me and have migrated before me. In addition to this, it is your Masjid." Furat ؓ however said, "I have heard Rasulullah ﷺ say something about you because of which I can never lead you in salah." "So were you also present during the Battle of Ta'if when Rasulullah ﷺ sent me as a spy?"

Handhala 🙵 asked. When Furat 🙵 confirmed that he was present, Handhala 🙵 stepped forward and led the salah. When the salah was over, Furat 🙵 turned to the people and said, "O tribe of Ijal! I have made him lead the salah because Rasulullah ﷺ once sent him to Ta'if as a spy and when he reported back, Rasulullah ﷺ said to him, 'Your information is correct. You may return to your camp because you have been awake all night.' As he turned and left, Rasulullah ﷺ said to us, 'Always follow him and the likes of him.'" *(Tabrani, Haythami, Abu Ya'la, Baghawi, Ibn Asakir in Kanzul Ummal)*

The Amir of Makkah Appoints Ibn Abza as His Deputy to Lead the Salah to the Approval of Omar 🙵

Abdur Rahman bin Abu Laila 🙵 narrates that when he once accompanied Omar 🙵 to Makkah, they were received by the Nafi bin Alqama 🙵 who was the Amir of Makkah. "Who have you appointed as your deputy over the people?" Omar 🙵 asked. "Abdur Rahman bin Abza 🙵," came the reply. Omar 🙵 said, "You chose a man from amongst the slaves over members of the Quraish and the Sahabah of Rasulullah ﷺ?" "That I have done," Nafi 🙵 replied, "Because I found him to be the most proficient reciter of the Qur'an and because Makkah is a place where people from all parts gather, I wanted them to listen to Allah's Book from a person who recited well." "Your judgment is excellent," Omar 🙵 commended, "Abdur Rahman bin Abza 🙵 is certainly amongst the people whom Allah has elevated through the Qur'an." *(Abu Ya'la in Muntakhab Kanzul Ummal)*

Miswar 🙵 Pulls Back an Imam Whose Recitation was not Clear and Omar 🙵 Sanctions His Act

Ubaid bin Umair 🙵 said that it was during the Hajj season when a large gathering of people amassed around a spring in Makkah. When the time for salah arrived, a person who was not Arabic speaking and who belonged to the family of Abu Sa'ib Makhzumi 🙵 stepped forward to lead the salah. Miswar bin Makhrama 🙵 pulled the man back and put another man forward. When the news reached Omar 🙵, he said nothing to Miswar until Miswar arrived in Madinah. It was only when Miswar 🙵 came to Madinah that Omar 🙵 questioned him about it. "Give me a chance, O Amirul Mu'minin!" Miswar 🙵 entreated. He then explained, "The man was not Arabic-speaking whose recitation was unclear and because it was during Hajj, I feared that some people who were there for Hajj would hear his recitation and adopt its non-Arabic mode of recitation." "Was that the express reason for what you did?" Omar asked. When Miswar 🙵 confirmed that it was, Omar 🙵 said, "You did the right thing." *(Abdur Razzaq, Bayhaqi in Kanzul Ummal)*

Talha 🙵 Asks a Congregation he had Led in Salah Whether They were Pleased With His Salah

Talha bin Ubaidullah 🙵 once led some people in salah. When he turned to them after completing the salah, he said, "I had forgotten to consult with you before going ahead and leading the salah. Are you pleased with my salah?" "Of course," the congregation replied, "who will be displeased with it, a selected companion of Rasulullah ﷺ." Talha 🙵 then said, "I have heard Rasulullah ﷺ say that when a person leads others in salah and they are displeased with him, the salah does not even pass his ears let alone reach the heavens." *(Tabrani, Haythami)*

Anas 🙵's Differences with Omar bin Abdul Aziz and Abu Ayub 🙵's Differences with Marwan Concerning Salah

Omar bin Abdul Aziz once asked Anas 🙵 why he did not perform salah behind him before he became the Khalifa. Omar bin Abdul Aziz used to prolong the salah until the time expired, just as the Umayyad rulers used to do. This was why Anas 🙵 refused to follow him in salah. When Omar bin Abdul Aziz became the Khalifa, he stopped doing this. Anas 🙵 replied, "I had seen Rasulullah ﷺ perform salah and I shall perform salah with you only when your salah is consistent with Rasulullah ﷺ's. When your salah differs from Rasulullah ﷺ's salah, I shall perform salah by myself and then return to my family." *(Ahmad, Haythami)*. Marwan bin Hakam asked Abu Ayub 🙵 why he did not perform salah behind him. Abu Ayub 🙵 replied, "I have seen Rasulullah ﷺ perform salah in a certain manner and will follow you only when your salah conforms to his salah. However, when your salah differs from Rasulullah ﷺ's salah, I shall perform salah by myself and then return to my family." *(Tabrani, Haythami)*

The Statements of Abu Hurairah 🙵, Anas 🙵 and Adi 🙵 About the Salah of the Sahabah Behind Rasulullah ﷺ

Abu Jabir Walidi says, "I once asked Abu Hurairah 🙵 after he had led the salah, 'Was the salah of Rasulullah ﷺ like this?' 'What did you not like about the way I performed salah?' he asked. 'There is nothing I do not like but I only wanted to know,' I replied. He said, 'Yes, it was like this, only shorter.' His Qiam was as long as it takes a Mu'adhin to descend from the Minaret and reach the row of salah." Another narration states that Abu Jabir added, "I once saw Abu Hurairah 🙵 performing a very short salah." *(Ahmad, Abu Ya'la, Haythami)*. Anas 🙵 once said, "The salah we performed with Rasulullah ﷺ was such that you people will criticize if anyone had to perform the same because of its brevity." *(Ahmad, Haythami)*. Adi bin Hatim 🙵 once attended a gathering and when the time for salah arrived, the Imam went forward and led the salah. Because he prolonged the sitting posture, Adi 🙵 said after the salah was completed, "The person leading the salah should complete the Ruku and Sejdah properly but not prolong the Qiam and sitting postures because behind him are young children, old people, sick people, travelers and people with urgent needs." When the time arrived for the next salah, Adi 🙵 went forward and while completing the Ruku and Sejdah properly, he made the salah brief. After completing the salah, he turned to the people and said, "That was how we performed salah behind Rasulullah ﷺ." *(Tabrani, Ahmad, Haythami)*

Rasulullah ﷺ Weeps in Salah

Aisha 🙵 says, "After spending the night, Rasulullah ﷺ would be summoned to salah by Bilal 🙵 calling out the Adhan. He would then get up and take a bath. I would then see the water dripping on his cheek and beard as he left for salah, after which I would hear him weep in salah." *(Abu Ya'la, Haythami)*. Ubaid bin Umair 🙵 once asked Aisha 🙵, "Tell me what the most remarkable incident that you saw with Rasulullah ﷺ." Aisha 🙵 was silent for awhile and then she said, "One night Rasulullah ﷺ said to me, 'Do excuse me to worship my Rabb tonight.' 'By Allah!' I replied, 'While I love to be near you, I also love anything that pleases you.' Rasulullah ﷺ then stood up, performed wudhu and started performing salah. He wept so much as he was sitting that his lap became wet with tears. He then continued weeping until his beard was soaked. He had then eventually wept so much more that the ground around him became soaked. When Bilal 🙵 came to inform him that the time for salah had arrived, he saw Rasulullah ﷺ weeping and asked, 'O Rasulullah ﷺ! Why do you weep so much when Allah has forgiven all your previous and future errors?' Rasulullah ﷺ

replied, 'Should I then not be a grateful slave? A tremendous verse has been revealed to me tonight. Woe be to the person who recites it without pondering over it: The verse is:

إِنَّ فِي خَلْقِ السَّمَاوَاتِ وَالْأَرْضِ وَاخْتِلَافِ اللَّيْلِ وَالنَّهَارِ لَآيَاتٍ لِأُولِي الْأَلْبَابِ (190) الَّذِينَ يَذْكُرُونَ اللَّهَ قِيَامًا وَقُعُودًا وَعَلَى جُنُوبِهِمْ وَيَتَفَكَّرُونَ فِي خَلْقِ السَّمَاوَاتِ وَالْأَرْضِ رَبَّنَا مَا خَلَقْتَ هَذَا بَاطِلًا سُبْحَانَكَ فَقِنَا عَذَابَ النَّارِ (191)

Verily! In the creation of the heavens and the earth, and in the alternation of night and day, there are indeed signs for men of understanding. Those who remember Allah (always, and in prayers) standing, sitting, and lying down on their sides, and think deeply about the creation of the heavens and the earth, (saying): "Our Lord! You have not created (all) this without purpose, glory to You! (Exalted be You above all that they associate with You as partners). Give us salvation from the torment of the Fire. (Al-Imran:190-191) (Ibn Hibban in Targheeb wat Tarheeb)

Mutarraf reports from his father ؓ who says, "I saw Rasulullah ﷺ performing salah while there came from his chest a sound resembling the sound of a grindstone because of his weeping." *(Abu Dawud)* Another narration states that the sound from Rasulullah ﷺ's chest resembled the sound of a boiling pot. *(Nasa'ee in Targheeb wat Tarheeb)*

Omar ؓ Weeps in Salah

Abdullah bin Shaddad bin Al Had says, "I was standing in one of the last rows during the Fajr salah and I could hear Omar ؓ cry aloud as he recited Surah Yusuf and reached the verse:

إِنَّمَا أَشْكُو بَثِّي وَحُزْنِي إِلَى اللَّهِ

I only complain of my grief and sorrow to Allah, and I know from Allah that which you know not. (Yusuf:86) (Abdur Razzaq, Sa'eed bin Mansur, Ibn Abi Shaybah, Ibn Sa'd, Bayhaqi in Muntakhab Kanzul Ummal). Abdullah bin Omar ؓ says, "During salah behind Omar ؓ, I could hear his weeping from 3 rows back." *(Abu Nu'aym in Hilya)*

The Devotion of Abu Bakr ؓ and Abdullah bin Zubair ؓ in Salah

Sahl bin Sa'd ؓ says that Abu Bakr ؓ could not be distracted when performing salah. *(Ahmad in Zuhd, Muntakhab Kanzul Ummal).* Mujahid says, "Abdullah bin Zubair ؓ would stand still like a stick in salah, which was exactly as Abu Bakr ؓ used to do. That is what devotion in salah means." *(Muntakhab Kanzul Ummal).* Mujahid says, "Abdullah bin Zubair ؓ would stand still like a stick in salah. It is said that this was due to his devotion in salah." *(Abu Nu'aym in Hilya, Isabah).* Ibnul Munkadir says, "Had you seen Abdullah bin Zubair ؓ performing salah, you would surely say that he is a branch of a tree that the wind laps over. In fact, missiles fired would be falling all about around him as he performed salah but he would pay no attention to them." Another narration from Ata states that when Abdullah bin Zubair ؓ performed salah, he was like a cane fixed in the ground. *(Abu Nu'aym in Hilya, Tabrani, Haythami)*

The Devotion of Abdullah bin Omar ؓ and Abdullah bin Mas'ood ؓ in Salah

Zaid bin Abdullah Shaibani says, "Abdullah bin Omar ؓ walked so slowly for salah that if an ant were walking beside him, you would say that he will not beat the ant." *(Ibn Sa'd).* Wasi bin Hibban says, "Abdullah bin Omar ؓ liked everything of his to face the Qibla when he performed salah and would even face his thumbs towards the Qibla." *(Ibn Sa'd).* Tawus says, "I have never seen anyone perform salah like Abdullah bin Omar

ؓ. He was so particular about facing the Qibla that even his face, palms and feet faced Qibla." *(Abu Nu'aym in Hilya).* Abu Burda narrates, "I once performed salah next to Abdullah bin Omar ؓ. When he was in Sejdah, I heard him say, 'O Allah! Make yourself the most beloved entity to me and the one I fear most.' I also heard him recite in salah: رَبِّ بِمَا أَنْعَمْتَ عَلَيَّ فَلَنْ أَكُونَ ظَهِيرًا لِلْمُجْرِمِينَ (17)

My Lord! For that with which You have favored me, I will never more be a helper for the Mujrimoon (criminals, disobedient to Allah, polytheists, sinners, etc.)! (Al-Qasas:17)

He also said, "Whenever I perform salah, I hope that it will be a means of atonement for my sins." *(Abu Nu'aym in Hilya).* A'mash stated that whenever Abdullah bin Mas'ood ؓ performed salah, he was so still that he appeared to be a discarded piece of cloth. *(Tabrani, Haythami)*

Abu Bakr ؓ Reprimands his Wife Ummu Ruman ؓ for Leaning in Her Salah

Umme Ruman ؓ says, "When Abu Bakr ؓ once saw me leaning while performing salah, he reprimanded me so sternly that I almost terminated my salah. He then said, 'I heard Rasulullah ﷺ say. 'When any of you stand in salah, his limbs should be at ease and he should never lean to any side as the Jews do. Being at ease during salah serves to complete the salah.'" *(Ibn Adi, Abu Nu'aym in Hilya, Kanzul Ummal)*

Aisha ؓ's Narration of the Sunnah Salats of Rasulullah ﷺ

Abdullah bin Shaqiq reports that he once enquired from Aisha ؓ about the optional salats that Rasulullah ﷺ performed. She replied, "Rasulullah ﷺ would perform 4 Rakats at home before the Zuhr salah. He would leave for the Masjid to lead the people in salah. He would return to my room and perform 2 Rakats. After leading the people in Maghrib salah, he would return to my room and perform 2 Rakats. He would lead the people in Isha and then return to perform 2 Rakats in my room. At night, he would perform 9 Rakats salah including the Witr. At times he would perform salah for long time standing while at other times; he would perform salah for a long time sitting. When performing salah standing, he would perform Ruku and Sejdah from a standing position and when performing salah sitting, he would perform Ruku and Sejdah from a sitting position. When dawn broke, he would perform 2 Rakats before leaving for the Masjid to lead the people in the Fajr salah." *(Muslim in Safwatus Safwa, Abu Dawud, Tirmidhi in Jam'ul Fawa'id)*

The Extreme Importance Rasulullah ﷺ gave to the 2 Rakats Before the Fajr Salah

Aisha ؓ says, "Rasulullah ﷺ did not attach as much importance to any optional salats as much as he attached to the 2 Rakats of Fajr." *(Bukhari, Muslim)* In another narration, Aisha ؓ states, "I have not seen Rasulullah ﷺ so eager to do any good deed as much as he was to perform the 2 Rakats before Fajr. In fact he was not even that eager for booty." *(Ibn Khuzaima in Targheeb wat Tarheeb).* Aisha ؓ also mentioned that Rasulullah ﷺ would never omit the 4 Rakats before Zuhr salah and the 2 Rakats before Fajr. *(Bukhari).* Bilal ؓ reports that he once went to inform Rasulullah ﷺ that the time for Fajr had arrived. Aisha ؓ occupied Bilal ؓ by asking him about something until the sky had started to get very bright. Bilal ؓ then started to call Rasulullah ﷺ several times, but Rasulullah ﷺ did not come out. After a while, Rasulullah ﷺ came out and after leading the salah. Bilal ؓ informed him that Aisha ؓ had occupied him by asking him about something and that despite him calling Rasulullah ﷺ had delayed in coming out. Rasulullah ﷺ said, "I was delayed because I had been performing the 2 Rakats of Fajr." "O Rasulullah ﷺ!" Bilal asked, "Why did you not leave it out because the sky had already become very bright?" Rasulullah ﷺ replied, "Even if the sky had become brighter than that, I would have still performed it and performed it well and properly." (Abu Dawud, Nawawi in Riyadhur Salihin)

The Extreme Importance Rasulullah ﷺ gave to the 4 Rakats Before the Fardh of Zuhr Salah

Qabus reports that his father once sent someone to ask Aisha ﷺ which salah apart from the Fara'idh, Rasulullah ﷺ most loved to perform with consistency. Aisha ﷺ replied, "It was the 4 Rakats before Zuhr in which Rasulullah ﷺ prolonged the Qiyam and meticulously performed the Ruku and Sejdah." (Ibn Majah in Targheeb wat Tarheeb). Abdullah bin Sa'ib ﷺ narrates that Rasulullah ﷺ used to perform 4 Rakats salah after the sun had crossed the meridian but before the Fardh of Zuhr. To this Rasulullah ﷺ would say, "This is the hour when the doors to the skies are opened and I would love to have my good deeds ascend through them." (Ahmad, Tirmidhi in Targheeb wat Tarheeb). Ali ﷺ reports that Rasulullah ﷺ used to perform 4 Rakats before the Fardh of Zuhr and 2 Rakats after. (Tirmidhi). Aisha ﷺ narrates that if Rasulullah ﷺ was unable to perform the 4 Rakats before the Fardh of Zuhr, he would perform them afterwards. (Tirmidhi). Abu Ayub ﷺ says that from the time Rasulullah ﷺ started staying with him, he noticed that Rasulullah ﷺ regularly performed 4 Rakats before Zuhr and said, "The doors of the skies are opened when the sun crosses the meridian and no door closes until the Zuhr salah has been performed. I therefore love to have a good deed of mine raised during this time." (Tabrani in Targheeb wat Tarheeb, Kanzul Ummal)

Rasulullah ﷺ's Salah Before Asr and after Maghrib

Ali ﷺ said, "Before the Asr salah Rasulullah ﷺ would perform 4 Rakats salah, separating them with Salam to the high-ranking angels and the Muslims and Mu'minin who follow them." (Tirmidhi) Another narration from Ali ﷺ states that Rasulullah ﷺ performed 2 Rakats before Asr. (Abu Dawud in Riyadhur Saliheen, Abu Ya'la, Tabrani, Majma'uz Zawa'id). Abdullah bin Abbas ﷺ narrates that after the Maghrib salah Rasulullah ﷺ used to perform 2 Rakats salah in which he prolonged the recitation of the Qur'an so long that the people in the Masjid had already dispersed by the time he completed. (Tabrani, Haythami)

The Importance Omar ﷺ Gave to the Sunnah Salats Before the Fajr and Zuhr Salats

Sa'eed bin Musayib narrates that Omar ﷺ said about the 2 Rakats before Fajr, "They are more beloved to me than red camels." (Ibn Abi Shaybah in Kanzul Ummal). Abdur Rahman bin Abdullah reports that he once went to Omar bin Khattab when the latter was performing salah before Zuhr. "What salah is this?" Abdur Rahman asked. Omar ﷺ replied, "It is counted from amongst the salah of the night i.e. it carries the reward of the Tahajjud salah." (Ibn Jareer). Abdullah bin Utba says, "I performed 4 Rakats salah with Omar ﷺ in his house before the Zuhr salah." (Ibn Abi Shay bah in Kanzul Ummal)

The Importance Ali ﷺ and Abdullah bin Mas'ood ﷺ gave to the Sunnah Salats Before the Zuhr Salah

Hudhaifa bin Usaid reports that he noticed Ali bin Abi Talib ﷺ performing 4 long Rakats of salah after the sun has crossed its meridian and asked about it. Ali ﷺ replied, "I saw Rasulullah ﷺ performing this salah..." The rest of the Hadith is similar to the narration of Abu Ayub ﷺ quoted above. (Ibn Abi Shaybah in Kanzul Ummal). Abdullah bin Yazid says, "Someone closest to Abdullah bin Mas'ood ﷺ informed me that after the sun had crossed its meridian, Abdullah bin Mas'ood ﷺ would stand up and perform 4 Rakats salah in which he would recite 2 Surah from the Mi'een, Surahs that have more than 100 verses. Thereafter, when the Mu'adhin called out the Adhan, he would dress fully and then leave for the Masjid for the salah." (Tabrani, Haythami). Aswad, Murra and Masruq all narrate that Abdullah bin Mas'ood ﷺ said, "No salah of the day equals the salah of the night except for the 4 Rakats before Zuhr. The virtue of this salah ever the other optional salats of the day is like the virtue of the congregational salah over the salah performed individually. (Tarbani, Haythami). Abdullah bin Mas'ood ﷺ said, "No salah of the day equals the salah of the night except for the 4 Rakats before Zuhr because they have always been regarded as being on par with the Tahajjud salah." (Ibn Jareer in Kanzul Ummal).

The Importance Bara ﷺ and Abdullah bin Omar ﷺ gave to the Sunnah Salats Before the Zuhr salah

It is reported that both Bara ﷺ and Abdullah bin Omar ﷺ performed the 4 Rakats of Sunnah salah. (Ibn Jareer in Kanzul Ummal). It is also narrated that whenever the sun passes its meridian, Abdullah bin Omar ﷺ would proceed to the Masjid where he would perform 12 Rakats salah before the Fardh of Zuhr. Only then would he sit down. (Ibn Jareer in Kanzul Ummal). Nafi narrates that Abdullah bin Omar ﷺ would perform 8 Rakats salah before the Zuhr salah and then 4 Rakats afterwards. (Ibn Jareer in Kanzul Ummal)

The importance Ali ﷺ gave to the Sunnah Salah Before the Asr Salah and the Importance Ali ﷺ and Abdullah bin Omar ﷺ Attached to the Sunnah Salats Between the Maghrib and Isha Salats

Ali ﷺ said, "Rasulullah ﷺ emphatically advised me never to forsake 3 acts throughout my life. One of them is to perform 4 Rakats before Asr. I shall never leave them out for as long as I live." (Ibn Najjar in Kanzul Ummal). Abu Fakhta narrates that Ali ﷺ mentioned that the salats between the Maghrib and Isha salats are called Salatul Ghafla ('salah of neglectful'), he added; "Now you people have fallen into neglectful because you neglect these salats." (Ibn Abi Shaybah in Kanzul Ummal). Abdullah bin Omar ﷺ said, "The person who performs 4 Rakats salah after Maghrib is like the person fighting battle after battle in the Path of Allah." (Ibn Zanjway in Kanzul Ummal)

A Narration of Aisha ﷺ Concerning the Importance that Rasulullah ﷺ attached to Qiyamul Layl

Abdullah bin Abul Qais narrates that Aisha ﷺ said, "Never omit the Qiyamul Layl because Rasulullah ﷺ never left it out. Even when he was ill or very tired, he would perform it sitting down rather that leaving it out." (Abu Dawud, Ibn Khuzaima in Targheeb wat Tarheeb)

The Narration of Jabir ﷺ About the Tahajjud Salah Being Compulsory Before Concession was granted

Jabir ﷺ says, "Qiyamul Layl became compulsory for us with the revelation of the verse: يَا أَيُّهَا الْمُزَّمِّلُ (1) قُمِ اللَّيْلَ إِلَّا قَلِيلًا (2)

O you wrapped in garments (i.e. Prophet Muhammad ﷺ)! Stand (to pray) all night, except a little. (Al-Muzammil:1-2)

We therefore stood so long in salah that our feet would swell. Allah then revealed the verses granting concession when He said:

عَلِمَ أَنْ سَيَكُونُ مِنْكُمْ مَرْضَى وَآخَرُونَ يَضْرِبُونَ فِي الْأَرْضِ يَبْتَغُونَ مِنْ فَضْلِ اللَّهِ وَآخَرُونَ يُقَاتِلُونَ فِي سَبِيلِ اللَّهِ فَاقْرَءُوا مَا تَيَسَّرَ مِنْهُ وَأَقِيمُوا الصَّلَاةَ وَآتُوا الزَّكَاةَ وَأَقْرِضُوا اللَّهَ قَرْضًا حَسَنًا وَمَا تُقَدِّمُوا لِأَنْفُسِكُمْ مِنْ خَيْرٍ تَجِدُوهُ عِنْدَ اللَّهِ هُوَ خَيْرًا وَأَعْظَمَ أَجْرًا وَاسْتَغْفِرُوا اللَّهَ إِنَّ اللَّهَ غَفُورٌ رَحِيمٌ (20)

... He (Allah) knows that you are unable to pray the whole night, so He has turned to you (in mercy). So, recite you of the Qur'an as much as may be easy for you. He knows that there will be some among you sick, others traveling through the land, seeking of Allah's Bounty; yet others fighting in Allah's Cause. So recite as much of the Qur'an as may be easy (for you), and perform As-Salat (Iqamat-as-Salat) and give Zakat, and lend to Allah a goodly loan, and whatever good you send before you for yourselves, (i.e. Nawafil non-obligatory acts of worship: prayers, charity, fasting, Hajj and Umrah, etc.), you will certainly find it with Allah, better and greater in reward. And seek Forgiveness of Allah. Verily, Allah is Oft-Forgiving, Most-Merciful. (Al-Muzammil:20) (Bazzar, Haythami).

Sa'eed bin Hisham asks Aisha About Rasulullah ﷺ's Witr Salah

Sa'eed bin Hisham divorced his wife and then journeyed to Madinah to sell the property he had there. He intended to invest the money from the sale in horses and weapons to use in the Jihad against the Romans until he died. On the way, he met a group of people from his tribe who narrated to him that when 6 persons of his tribe also wanted to do the same thing during the time of Rasulullah ﷺ. Rasulullah ﷺ forbade them saying, "Do you not have an example in me?" Sa'eed then took his wife back in marriage and made the group witness to this. He later returned to his people and informed them that he had been to Abdullah bin Abbas ؓ to ask about Rasulullah ﷺ's Witr salah. Abdullah bin Abbas ؓ said, "Should I not tell you which person has more knowledge than anyone else about the Rasulullah ﷺ's Witr?" When Sa'eed asked to know, Abbas ؓ said, "Go to Aisha ؓ and ask her. Thereafter, I want you to return and inform me what she told you." Sa'eed narrates further, "I then approached Hakim bin Afla ؓ to request him to accompany me to Aisha ؓ. He said, 'I shall not go near her because when I forbade her from speaking out against the 2 factions (the group of Ali ؓ and that of Mu'awiya ؓ), she still did so.' However, when I begged him in the name of Allah, he accompanied me. When we went to her house, she recognized Hakim ؓ and asked, 'Is that Hakim?' When he confirmed that it was he, she asked, 'Who is that with you?' 'He is Sa'eed bin Hisham,' Hakim replied. 'Which Hisham?' she enquired further. 'The son of Amir,' came the reply. Aisha ؓ then made Du'a for Amir ؓ's forgiveness and remarked, 'What an excellent man Amir was!' 'O Ummul Mu'mineen!' I asked, 'Do tell me about Rasulullah ﷺ's character'. 'Do you recite the Qur'an?' Aisha ؓ asked. When I confirmed that I did, she said, 'Well, the character of Rasulullah ﷺ was the Qur'an.' I then started to get up but it occurred to me to ask about Rasulullah ﷺ's salah at night. I therefore asked, 'O Ummul Mu'minin! Do inform me about the salah of Rasulullah ﷺ at night.' 'Do you recite the Surah of the Qur'an (Surah Muzammil)?' When I told her that I did, she said, 'Allah had made Qiyamul Layl compulsory at the beginning of the Surah, because of which Rasulullah ﷺ and the Sahabah stood for such long periods at night that their feet would become swollen. Allah held the end of the Surah back in the

heavens for 12 months, after which he revealed the concession. Therefore, Qiyamul Layl became optional after it had been compulsory.'" Sa'eed continues, "I was again about to leave when it occurred to me to ask about the Witr salah. Therefore, I said, 'O Ummul Mu'mineen! Do inform me about Rasulullah ﷺ's Witr salah. She replied, 'We would keep Rasulullah ﷺ's Miswak and wudhu water ready and when Allah wished him to awake, he would get up, brush his teeth with the Miswak and then perform wudhu. Rasulullah ﷺ would then perform 8 Rakats salah without sitting in between for the final sitting preceding the Salam except in the 8th Rakah. He would engage in Dhikr of Allah and making Du'a to Him while he sat, after which he get up for the 9th Rakah without making Salam. He would then perform the 9th Rakah and then sit down. As he sat, he would again engage in Dhikr and Du'a before making Salam audibly. After the Salam, he would perform 2 Rakats salah in a sitting posture. That, dear son, was 11 Rakats. However, as Rasulullah ﷺ grew older and heavier, he would make the 7th Rakah the Witr and then perform the other 2 Rakats. That, dear son, was 9 Rakats. Whenever Rasulullah ﷺ performed a salah, he liked to be consistent with it and if sleep, pain or illness ever prevented him from Qiyamul Layl, he would perform 12 Rakats the next day. I do not know of Rasulullah ﷺ completing the entire Qur'an in one the night until dawn and I am unaware of him fasting an entire month except for the month of Ramadhan.' I returned to Abdullah bin Abbas ؓ and when I informed him about what Aisha ؓ had told me, he said, 'She is right. If I have gone to her, I would have reported the narration directly from her.'" *(Ahmad, Muslim in Tafsir Ibn Kathir)*

The Narration of Abdullah bin Abbas ؓ Concerning the Witr of the Sahabah After Surah Muzammil was Revealed

Abdullah bin Abbas ؓ reports, "When the beginning of Surah Muzammil was revealed, the Sahabah stood in salah as long as they did during Ramadhan. A year had passed between the revelation of the first part of the Surah and the last part." *(Ibn Abi Shaybah in Kanzul Ummal)*

The Tahajjud salah of Abu Bakr ؓ and Omar ؓ

Yahya bin Sa'eed narrates that Abu Bakr ؓ used to perform his Witr salah at the beginning of the night and when he stood for Tahajjud salah, he would perform it in units of 2 Rakats. *(Ibn Abi Shaybah in Kanzul Ummal)*. Aslam says, " Omar bin Khattab ؓ used to perform salah for a long while at night and when half the night had passed, he would awaken his family for salah, saying, 'Salah!' He would then recite the verse:

وَأْمُرْ أَهْلَكَ بِالصَّلَاةِ وَاصْطَبِرْ عَلَيْهَا لَا نَسْأَلُكَ رِزْقًا نَحْنُ نَرْزُقُكَ وَالْعَاقِبَةُ لِلتَّقْوَى (132)

And enjoin As-Salat (the prayer) on your family, and be patient in offering them (i.e. the Salat (prayers)). We ask not of you a provision (i.e. to give us something: money, etc.); We provide for you. And the good end (i.e. Paradise) is for the Muttaqoon (pious) (TaHa:132) (Malik, Bayhaqi in Muntakhab Kanzul Ummal). Hasan narrates that when Uthman bin Abul Aas ؓ married one of Omar ؓ's widows, he said, "By Allah! I did not marry her simply for wealth or children. I however wanted her to inform me about Omar ؓ's nights (in Ibadah)." When he asked her how it was that Omar would perform salah at night, she explained, "After performing the Isha salah, he would instruct us to place a dish of water at his headside and to keep it covered. When he then woke up at night, he would dip his hand into the water, wipe his face and hands and then engage in Dhikr for a while. He would doze off and it would occur several times that he would awaken, engage in Dhikr and doze off until the time for him to get up for the Tahajjud salah arrived." One of the narrators called) Ibn Buraida asked Hasan, "Who narrated this to you?" Hasan replied that it was the daughter of Uthman bin Abul Aas ◆, Ibn Buraida conformed that she was a reliable source. *(Tabrani, Haythami)*. Sa'eed bin Musayib reports that Omar ◆ loved to perform salah in the middle of the night. *(Ibn Sa'd)*

The Tahajjud of Abdullah bin Omar ◆

Nafi narrates that Abdullah bin Omar ◆ used to perform salah for a long while at night and then ask, "Nafi! Has the last portion of the night arrived?" If Nafi replied in the negative, Abdullah bin Omar ◆ would continue performing salah. He would then ask later on, "Nafi! Has the last portion of the night arrived?" When Nafi would eventually reply that the time had arrived, Abdullah bin Omar ◆ would sit down and engage in Istighfar and Du'a until dawn broke. *(Abu Nu'aym in Hilya, Isabah, Tabrani)*. Muhammad says, "Abdullah bin Omar ◆ would start performing salah whenever he awoke during the night." Abu Ghalib says, "Abdullah bin Omar ◆ used to stay with us in Makkah and always performed the Tahajjud salah. One night just before dawn he said to me, 'O Abu Ghalib! Why don't you get up and perform salah, even if you recite only a third of the Qur'an?' I said, 'But how will I recite a 3rd of the Qur'an when dawn is so close by?' He replied, 'Verily Sura Ikhlas is equal to a 3rd of the Qur'an.'" *(Abu Nu'aym in Hilya)*

The Tahajjud salah of Abdullah bin Mas'ood ◆ and Salman ◆

Alqama bin Qais relates, "I once spent the night with Abdullah bin Mas'ood ◆. He got up during the early part of the night and started performing salah. He recited as an Imam in the local Masjid would recite, steadily and without adopting a singing tune. He recited audibly enough for the people around him to hear and he would not repeat his voice. Eventually when only that part of the night was left equal to the time it takes between the Maghrib Adhan and the end of the Maghrib salah, he would perform his Witr salah." *(Tabrani, Haythami)*. Tariq bin Shihab reports that he once spends a night with Salman ◆ to see how he exerted himself in Ibadah at night. When Salman ◆ got up to perform salah during the last portion of the night, Tariq did not get to see what he expected. When he mentioned this to Salman ◆, the Sahabi explained, "Guard your 5 Fardh salats closely because they atone for the sins you commit, except for the major sins. After people have performed the Isha salah, they are divided into 3 groups. One of the groups has nothing for them but plenty against them. The other group has something for them but nothing against them, while the last group has neither anything for them nor against. The person with nothing for him but plenty against him is the one who takes advantage of the darkness of the night and unawareness of people to outdo himself in sinning, because of which he has plenty of sin to his loss and no good to his name. The person with something for him and nothing against him is the one who also takes advantage of the darkness of the night and unawareness of people, but uses it to engage in salah. For this reason that he has much to his credit but nothing to his detriment. As for the person with neither anything for him nor against, he is the one who goes to bed immediately after performing the Isha salah. He will therefore have no sin to his account, nor any good. Beware of being hasty and always adopt moderation and constancy." *(Tabrani, Haythami)*

The Narrations of Ummu Hani ◆ and Aisha ◆ Concerning the Salatud Duha that Rasulullah ﷺ Performed

Ummu Hani ◆ whose was the daughter of Abu Talib, reports that when Makkah was conquered, she went to see Rasulullah ﷺ. When she got to him, Rasulullah ﷺ was busy taking a bath. After completing the bath, Rasulullah ﷺ performed 8 Rakats salah, which is referred to as Salatud Duha, the midmorning salah. *(Bukhari, Muslim in Riyadh)*. Aisha ◆ says, "While Rasulullah ﷺ usually performed 4 Rakats of Salatud Duha, he also sometimes increased the number of Rakats." *(Muslim in Riyadh)*

Narrations of Anas ◆ and Abdullah bin Abu Awfa ◆ Concerning the Salatud Duha that Rasulullah ﷺ Performed

Anas ◆ narrates, "I saw Rasulullah ﷺ perform 6 Rakats of Salatud Duha and I have never forsaken them thereafter." *(Tabrani, Haythami)*. Another narration from Ummu Hani ◆ states that when Rasulullah ﷺ went to her house the day Makkah was conquered; he performed 6 Rakats Salatud Duha. *(Tabrani in Awsat and Kabir, Haythami)*. When Abdullah bin Abu Awfa ◆ performed only 2 Rakats Salatud Duha, his wife asked, "You have performed only 2 Rakats?" He replied, "Rasulullah ﷺ also performed 2 Rakats of this salah when he was given the good news of a victory and also when the head of Abu Jahal was brought to him." *(Bazzar, Tabrani, Haythami, Ibn Majah)*

The Narration of Abdullah bin Abbas ◆ From Ummu Hani ◆ Concerning the Salatud Duha that Rasulullah ﷺ Performed

Abdullah bin Abbas ◆ once said, "There is a verse of the Qur'an that I used to recite without understanding what it referred to. The verse is: بِالْعَشِيِّ وَالْإِشْرَاقِ (18)

... in the Ashi (i.e. after the mid-day till sunset) and Ishraq (i.e. after the sunrise till mid-day)... (Sad:18)

This was until Ummu Hani ◆ narrated to me that Rasulullah ﷺ once came to her and asked for a dish of water to make wudhu. She said, 'I could still see traces of dough in the dish because I had just used it for making dough. Rasulullah ﷺ made wudhu and performed the Salatud Duha saying, 'O Ummu Hani! This is the 'Ishraq' salah ('the daybreak salah,).'" *(Tabrani, Haythami)*

Rasulullah ﷺ Encourages the Performing of Salatud Duha and Explains its Virtues

Abu Hurairah ◆ reports that when Rasulullah ﷺ once dispatched an army, they returned very quickly with a large booty. Someone remarked, "O Rasulullah ﷺ! I have never before seen an army returning so quickly with such a large booty." Rasulullah ﷺ said, "Shall I not inform you of an army that returns even quicker with an even larger booty'? It is the person who performs wudhu properly, proceeds to the Masjid to perform the Fajr salah and then follows this up with performing the Salatud Duha. Such a person returns quicker with a larger booty." *(Abu Ya'la, Bazzar, Ibn Hibban, Tirmidhi in Targheeb wat Tarheeb)*

Ali ◆, Abdullah bin Abbas ◆ and Sa'd bin Abi Waqqas ◆ Perform Salatud Duha

Ata Abu Muhammad says that he saw Ali ◆ performing the Salatud Duha in the Masjid. *(Tabrani in Kanzul Ummal)*. Ikrama reports that Abdullah bin Abbas ◆ would perform the Salatud Duha once every 10 days. *(Ibn Jareer in Kanzul Ummal)*. The daughter of Sa'd bin Abi Waqqas ◆, Aisha narrates that her father Sa'd ◆ used to perform 8 Rakats of Salatud Duha. *(Ibn Jareer in Kanzul Ummal)*

The Importance Attached to the Nawafil Between Zuhr and Asr

Sha'bi reports that Abdullah bin Mas'ood ◆ did not perform the Salatud Duha, he performed Nawafil salats between Zuhr and Asr together with the long shift he took at night. *(Tabrani on Kabir, Haythami)*. *Nafi* narrates that Abdullah bin Omar ؓ engaged in salah between Zuhr and Asr. *(Abu Nu'aym in Hilya)*

The Salah Rasulullah ﷺ Performs Between Maghrib and Isha and the Salah of Ammar ؓ

Hudhaifa ؓ says, "I went to Rasulullah ﷺ and performed the Maghrib salah with him. Rasulullah ﷺ continued performing salah until Isha. *(Nasa'ee in Targheeb wat Tarheeb)*. Muhammad bin Ammar bin Yasir reports that he saw his father Ammar bin Yasir ؓ perform 6 Rakats salah after the Maghrib salah. Ammar ؓ said, "I saw my beloved friend Rasulullah ﷺ perform 6 Rakats salah after the Maghrib salah. Rasulullah ﷺ said, 'Whoever performs 6 Rakats salah after the Maghrib salah will have all his sins forgiven even though they may be as much as the foam on the oceans.'" *(Tabrani in Thalatha, Tabrani, Mundhiri)*

The Salah of Abdullah bin Mas'ood ؓ and Abdullah bin Abbas ؓ Between Maghrib and Isha

Abdur Rahman bin Yazid says, "There was a time when I would always find Abdullah bin Mas'ood ؓ engaged in salah. The time was between Maghrib and Isha. I once said to him, 'Whenever I come to you during this time, I always find you engaged in salah. Why is this?' He replied, 'This is a time of negligence when people are generally negligent of Allah.'" *(Tabrani, Haythami)*. Aswad bin Yazid reports that Abdullah bin Mas'ood ؓ said, "How excellent is the time of negligence i.e. the time between Maghrib and Isha." *(Tabrani, Haythami)*. Abdullah bin Abbas ؓ said, "Verily the angels surround the people who perform salah between Maghrib and Isha, which is the Salatul Awabin." *(Ibn Zanjway in Kanzul Ummal)*

Giving Importance to Salah When Entering and Leaving the House

Abdur Rahman bin Abu Laila ؓ narrates that when someone married the widow of Abdullah bin Rawaha ؓ and asked her about some special deed that he carried out, she replied, "He would perform 2 Rakats salah whenever he left the house and whenever he entered." *(Ibn Mubarak in Isabah)*

Rasulullah ﷺ Encourages the Tarawih Salah

Abu Hurairah ؓ says, "Rasulullah ﷺ encouraged standing in Tarawih salah during Ramadhan without forcefully commanding it so that it should not be regarded as Fardh. He would say. 'Whoever stands in (Tarawih) salah during Ramadhan with Iman and hope in being rewarded shall have all his previous sins forgiven.'" *(Muslim in Riyadh)* Another narration adds that Abu Hurairah ؓ also said, "After Rasulullah ﷺ passed away, matters remained the same during the Khilafa of Abu Bakr ؓ and during the beginning of Omar ؓ's Khilafa." *(Bukhari, Muslim, Abu Dawud, Tirmidhi, Nasa'ee, Ibn Majah in Kanzul Ummal)*

Ubay bin Ka'b ؓ Leads the People in Tarawih and the Tarawih Salah During the Time of Rasulullah ﷺ and the Time of Omar ؓ

Abu Hurairah ؓ reports that it was during Ramadhan that Rasulullah ﷺ once saw some Sahabah performing salah in congregation in the corner of the Masjid. "Who are they?" Rasulullah ﷺ asked. Someone said, "They are people who do not know the entire Qur'an by memory and are following Ubay bin Ka'b ؓ as he leads them in salah." Rasulullah ﷺ remarked. "What they are doing is correct and an excellent deed." *(Abu Dawud in Jam'ul Fawa'id)*. Abdur Rahman bin Abdul Qari says, "I entered the Masjid with Omar bin Khattab ؓ one night in

Ramadhan where we found people in various groups. Everywhere there were individual people performing salah, each with a group following them. Omar ؓ remarked, 'It would be much better if all these people were collected behind one Qari.' Therefore, according to his resolve, Omar ؓ got everyone to perform salah collectively behind Ubay bin Ka'b ؓ. When I again entered the Masjid with Omar ؓ another night, the people were all performing the Tarawih salah behind their Qari (Ubay ؓ). To this, Omar ؓ remarked, 'This is an excellent innovation! However, the part of the night in which you are asleep (the latter part) is much better than the part in which you stand in salah.' This Omar ؓ said because the people used to perform the Tarawih salah during the early part of the night." *(Malik, Bukhari, Ibn Khuzaima in Kanzul Ummal and Jam'ul Fawa'id)*. Naufal bin Iyas Hudhali says, "In Ramadhan during the Khilafa of Omar bin Khattab ؓ, we used to stand in various groups everywhere in the Masjid while performing the Tarawih salah because people would be inclined to follow the person whom they felt had the best voice. To this Omar ؓ remarked, 'In my opinion, people have made the Qur'an a song. By Allah! I shall definitely change this if I have the ability.' Barely 3 days had passed when Omar ؓ instructed Ubay bin Ka'b ؓ to lead the people in salah. Then standing in last of the rows, Omar ؓ said, 'If this is regarded to be an innovation, it is truly an excellent innovation.'" *(Ibn Sa'd)*

Omar ؓ has the Masjid lit up for the Tarawih Salah to be Performed and the Du'a Ali ؓ made for him on this Occasion

Abu Is'haq Hamdani reports that Ali ؓ once entered the Masjid on the first night of Ramadhan to find lanterns burning and the Book of Allah being recited. To this he said (to Omar ؓ), "O Ibn Khattab! May Allah illuminate your grave as you have illuminated the Masajid of Allah with the Qur'an." *(Ibn Shahin in Kanzul Ummal, Khatib in Amalin, Ibn Asakir in Muntakhab Kanzul Ummal)*

Ubay ؓ, Tamim Dari ؓ and Sulaiman bin Abu Hathma ؓ Lead the People in Tarawih.

Urwa ؓ reports that when Omar ؓ had all the people perform the Tarawih salah of Ramadhan collectively, he gathered the men behind Ubay bin Ka'b ؓ and the women behind Sulaiman bin Abu Hathma ؓ. *(Firyabi, Bayhaqi in Kanzul Ummal)*. Omar bin Abdullah Ansi reports that it was Ubay bin Ka'b ؓ and Tamim Dari ؓ who stood in the place of Rasulullah ﷺ to lead the men in Tarawih salah inside the Masjid while Sulaiman bin Abu Hathma ؓ led the women in Tarawih salah in the courtyard of the Masjid. This was during the Khilafa of Omar ؓ. However, when Uthman bin Affan ؓ became the Khalifa, he had both men and women follow one Qari, who happened to be Sulaiman bin Abu Hathma ؓ. Uthman ؓ would instruct the women to stay back and they were only allowed to leave the Masjid after the men had all left. *(Ibn Sa'd)*. Arjafa says, "Ali bin Abi Talib ؓ used to instruct the people to perform the Tarawih salah of Ramadhan and would appoint an Imam for the men and another for the women. I was the Imam of the women." *(Bayhaqi in Kanzul Ummal)*

Ubay bin Ka'b ؓ Leads Women of his Household in Tarawih Salah

Jabir ؓ reports, "Ubay bin Ka'b ؓ came to Rasulullah ﷺ one night of Ramadhan saying, 'O Rasulullah ﷺ! I have done something tonight and wish to know if it was correct. ' 'What is it, O Ubay?' Rasulullah ﷺ enquired. Ubay ؓ explained, 'The women of my household said to me, 'Since we cannot recite the entire Qur'an from memory, we shall follow you in salah.' I therefore led them in 8 Rakats of salah and then performed the Witr.' Rasulullah ﷺ approved and did not condemn what Ubay ؓ did. The act is therefore established as a Sunnah because of Rasulullah ﷺ's approval." *(Abu Ya'la, Tabrani, Haythami)*

Salatut Tauba

Burayda ؓ narrates that Rasulullah ﷺ asked Bilal ؓ one morning, "O Bilal! How did you beat me to Jannah? When I entered Jannah last night, I heard your footsteps ahead of me." Bilal ؓ said, "O Rasulullah ﷺ! Whenever I commit a sin, I perform 2 Rakats Salatut Tauba and whenever my wudhu breaks, I make wudhu immediately and then perform 2 Rakats Tahiyyatul wudhu." *(Ibn Khuzaima in Targheeb wat Tarheeb)*

Salatul Hajah: Anas ؓ Performs Salah at the Time of Need and his Need is Fulfilled

Thumama bin Abdullah narrates that during the summer months, the caretaker of Anas ؓ's orchard came to him complaining about the drought. Anas ؓ sent for some water, made wudhu and started performing salah. He then asked the man to see if he could see anything (any clouds). When the man reported that he saw nothing, Anas ؓ returned indoors and again performed salah. It was after the third or 4th time of asking the man to look that the man reported back to say that he saw a cloud the size of a bird's wing. Anas ؓ then continued performing salah and making Du'a until the caretaker came to him and said, "The sky had become overcast and rain has fallen." Anas said to him, "Take the horse that Bishr bin Shighaf had sent and see up to where the rain had reached." When the man went to have a look, he discovered that the rain had not fallen further than the Musayirin and Ghadban areas i.e. it had fallen precisely on the land belonging to Anas ؓ." *(Ibn Sa'd)*

Rasulullah ﷺ Performs Salah for Ali ؓ to be Cured and he is Cured

Ali ؓ relates, "I was once suffering intense pain, so I went to Rasulullah ﷺ. He put me where he was standing, covered me with the end of his shawl and started performing salah. He then said, "You will be alright now, O son of Abu Talib? There is nothing to worry about. Whenever I ask anything from Allah, I always ask the same for you. Allah has granted me everything I have asked, but I have been informed that there shall be no Nabi

after me.' When I then stood up, it seemed as if I had never had any pain at all." *(Ibn Abi Asim, Ibn Jareer, Tabrani in Awsat, Ibn Shahin in Sunnah, Muntakhab Kanzul Ummal)*

The Du'a of a Sahabi Abu Mu'liq ؓ is Answered When a Robber Wanted to Kill Him

Anas ؓ narrates that there was a companion of Rasulullah ﷺ called Abu Mu'liq ؓ. He was a trader who traded both his own goods as well as those of others. He was a person who was always engaged in Ibadah and was extremely abstinent. He was out on business one day when an armed robber confronted him. "Put down your goods." the robber demanded, "because I am going to kill you." "You may have all the goods," Abu Mu'liq ؓ told him, "It is only your life that I want," the robber barked. "Then permit me to perform salah," Abu Mu'liq ؓ requested. The robber laughed, "You may perform as much salah as you please." Abu Mu'liq ؓ made wudhu and started performing salah. On he made this dual:

يَاوَدُوْدُ يَاذَاا الْعَرْشِ الْمَجِيْدِ! يَافَعَّالاً لِمَا يُرِيْدُ! أَسْئَلُكَ بِعِزَّتِكَ الَّتِي لاتُرَامُ وَمُلْكِكَ الَّذِيْ لاَيُضَامُ وَبِنُوْرِكَ الَّذِي مَلأَ أَرْكَانَ عَرْشِكَ أَنْ تَكْفِيْنِي شَرَّ هَذَا اللِّصِّ، يَامُغِيْثُ أَغِثْنِي

"O The Most Loving! O Master of the Glorious Throne! O the One Who does as He pleases! By Your Honor that none can hope to have, by Your kingdom that none can harm and by Your light that fills the foundations of Your throne do I implore You to protect me from the evil of this robber. O Helper, do help me."

When he had made this Du'a thrice, a rider suddenly appeared with a spear held high above his head. The rider thrust the spear at the robber and killed him. He then went up to the trader and asked, "Who are you?" Abu Mu'liq ؓ replied, "I am the one whom Allah has rescued through you." The rider then explained, "I am an angel of the 4th heaven. When you first made the Du'a, I heard the doors of the heavens rattle. When you made the Du'a the 2nd time, I heard the inhabitants of the heavens cry out. When you again made the Du'a for the 3rd time and it was announced that this was the Du'a of a person in distress. I sought permission from Allah to grant me the ability of killing the robber. You ought to know that good news that whoever makes wudhu, performs 4 Rakats salah and then makes that Du'a, his Du'a will be answered whether he is in distress or not." *(Ibn Abi Dunya in Mujabad Da'wah, Isabah).*

The Chapter is about Knowledge and the Zeal of the Sahabah

This chapter highlights the tremendous fervor that Nabi ﷺ and the Sahabah had for divine knowledge and how they encouraged it. It further discusses how they taught and learnt knowledge pertaining to Iman and good deeds and also how they preoccupied themselves with it whether they were on journey or at home, undergoing hardship or enjoying prosperity. Also highlighted is how they dedicated themselves to teaching guests who arrived in Madinah Munawwara. The chapter illustrates how they blended the dissemination of divine knowledge with Jihad and earning a living. In addition to this, it describes how they dispatched individuals to cities to disseminate divine knowledge and how they gave importance to inculcating within themselves qualities that promote the absorption of this knowledge.

Rasulullah ﷺ welcomes Safwan bin Assal ﷺ who came to seek Knowledge

Safwan bin Assal Muradi ﷺ says, "I once came to Rasulullah ﷺ in the Masjid as he was reclining on his red shawl. 'O Rasulullah ﷺ!' I said, 'I have come to seek knowledge.' Rasulullah ﷺ exclaimed, 'Welcome to the seeker of knowledge! Verily out of the love for what the person seeking knowledge is out to seek, the angels encircle him with their wings and then mount each other until they reach the sky above the earth.'" *(Ahmad, Tabrani, Ibn Hibban, Hakim in Targheeb wat Tarheeb)*

Rasulullah ﷺ's words to Qabisa ﷺ When he came to seek Knowledge

Qabisa bin Mukhariq ﷺ says, "When I once went to Rasulullah ﷺ, he asked me what brought me there. I replied, 'I have grown old and my bones have weakened. I have come to you to teach me something by which Allah will grant me great benefit.' Rasulullah ﷺ said, 'Every stone, tree and mound of sand that you passed on your way here prayed for your forgiveness. O Qabisa! You will be saved from blindness, leprosy and paralysis if after performing your Fajr salah, you recite 3 times the Du'a, ...O Qabisa! You should also recite the Du'a:

$$\text{اللَّهُمَّ إِنِّي أَسْأَلُكَ مِمَّا عِنْدَكَ وَأَفِضْ عَلَيَّ مِنْ فَضْلِكَ وَانْشُرْ عَلَيَّ مِنْ رَحْمَتِكَ وَأَنْزِلْ عَلَيَّ مِنْ بَرَكَتِكَ}$$

'O Allah! I implore You for that which is with You. Pour Your grace upon me, shower Your mercy upon me and send Your blessing to me'"*(Ahmad in Jam'ul Fawa'id, Mundhiri, Haythami)*

Rasulullah ﷺ Tells 2 Sahabah that Seeking Knowledge atones for Sins

Sakhbara ﷺ narrates that 2 men were passing by when Rasulullah ﷺ was busy giving a talk. Rasulullah ﷺ said to them, "Sit down because you 2 are upon great goodness." When Rasulullah ﷺ completed and got up, the Sahabah dispersed. The 2 men got up and asked, "O Rasulullah ﷺ! Youmentioned that the 2 of us were upon great goodness. Is this for us exclusively or for the general public as well?" Rasulullah ﷺ replied, "Whenever a servant of Allah seeks knowledge, it atones for all his past sins."*(Tirmidhi, Tabrani in Targheeb wat Tarheeb)*

The Superiority of an Alim Over an Ordinary Worshipper in the Words of Rasulullah ﷺ

Abu Umama Bahili ﷺ says that someone once spoke to Rasulullah ﷺ about 2 men, one being an Alim and the other an ordinary worshipper. Rasulullah ﷺ remarked, "The superiority of an Alim over an ordinary worshipper is like my superiority over the lowest amongst you." Rasulullah ﷺ then proceeded to say, "Verily Allah showers His mercy on the person who teaches people to do good. In addition to this, the angels, the inhabitants of the heavens and even the ants in their ant-hills and the fish in the oceans pray for his forgiveness." *(Tirmidhi).* Another narration does not mention the incident of the 2 men but continues to state that Rasulullah ﷺ said, "The superiority of an Alim over an ordinary worshipper is like my superiority over the lowest amongst you." Thereafter, Rasulullah ﷺ recited the verse:

$$\text{إِنَّمَا يَخْشَى اللَّهَ مِنْ عِبَادِهِ الْعُلَمَاءُ}$$

...It is only those who have knowledge among His slaves that fear Allah... (Fatir:28)
The rest of this ends just like the one quoted above. *(Darmi).* Hasan narrates that Rasulullah ﷺ was once questioned about 2 men who were from amongst the Bani Isra'el. While one was an Alim who performed only the compulsory salats and then sat to teach the people good, the other fasted throughout the day and performed salah all night. The Sahabah wanted to know which of the 2 were better. Rasulullah ﷺ's reply was: "The superiority of the Alim who performed only the compulsory salats and then sat to teach the people good over the one who fasted throughout the day and performed salah all night is like my superiority over the lowest amongst you." *(Darmi in Mishkatul Masabih)*

The Encouragement Rasulullah ﷺ gave for Seeking Knowledge

Uqba bin Amir ﷺ says that they were on the Suffa platform when Rasulullah ﷺ came out of his room and said, "Which of you every day would like to go to the marketplaces of Buthan or Aqiq and return with 2 excellent camels with large humps without committing any sin or severing any family ties?" "O Rasulullah ﷺ!" the Sahabah said, "Each one of us would love to do that." Rasulullah ﷺ then said, "If you go to the Masjid and teach or learn 2 verses of the Qur'an, it will be better for you than the 2 camels. Similarly, 3 verses are better than 3 camels, 4 verses better than 4 camels and any number of verses better than an equal number of camels." *(Muslim in Mishkatul Masabih, Abu Nu'aym in Hilya)*

Rasulullah ﷺ's Words to a Working Man who Complained of his Brother who was Busy Acquiring Knowledge

Anas ﷺ reports that during the time of Rasulullah ﷺ there were 2 brothers, one of whom worked while the other was always with Rasulullah ﷺ to learn from him. When the working brother complained about his brother to Rasulullah ﷺ that he did not work, Rasulullah ﷺ said to him, "It is perhaps because of him that you are granted sustenance." *(Tirmidhi in Jam'ul Fawa'id, Ibn Abdul Birr in Jami Bayanil Ilm, Hakim in Mustadrak)*

Ali ﷺ Encourages Acquiring Knowledge and the Narration of Kumail from Him

Abu Tufail narrates that Ali ﷺ used to say, "Indeed the people closest to the Ambiya are those who practice most on what they brought." He would then recite the verse:

$$\text{إِنَّ أَوْلَى النَّاسِ بِإِبْرَاهِيمَ لَلَّذِينَ اتَّبَعُوهُ وَهَذَا النَّبِيُّ وَالَّذِينَ آمَنُوا}$$

Verily, among mankind who has the best claim to Ibrahim (Abraham) are those who followed him, and this Prophet (Muhammad ﷺ) and those who have believed (Muslims).... (Al-Imran:68). He would then explain, "The verse (the words 'this Nabi and those who have Iman') refers to Muhammad ﷺ and those who follow him. You people should therefore never change because those close to Muhammad ﷺ are those who obey Allah. On the other hand, the enemies of Muhammad ﷺ are those who disobey Allah even though they may be close relatives of Muhammad ﷺ." *(Lalkala'ee in Kanzul Ummal).* Kumail bin Ziyad narrates, "Ali bin Abi Talib ؓ once caught hold of my hand and took me into the desert. When we were in the desert, he sat down, sighed and said, 'O Kumail bin Ziyad! Hearts are like containers and the best of hearts are those that take heed the most. Remember well what I have to say to you. People fall into 3 categories. There is the Alim who is attached to Allah, the learner who is on the Path of salvation and a mean uncultured type of person who follows every noisemaker, who sways with the wind, who has gained nothing from the light from divine knowledge and who has not even taken support from a strong pillar. Knowledge is better than wealth because while knowledge guards you, you have to guard wealth and while knowledge increases with spending by practicing on it and teaching it, wealth decreases with spending. Love for knowledge is a loan that will be repaid by Allah. Knowledge earns authority for the Alim in this life and loving memories after his death while the achievements of wealth disappear once the wealth is no more. Even though they are alive, the treasurers of wealth are really dead while the Ulema live on throughout the annals of time. While the Ulema after death may not be visible to the eye, their honor and love still lives on in the hearts of people."

"Ah!" Ali ؓ sighed. Pointing to his chest, he said, "Verily in here is such knowledge that I wish I could find a bearer for it. However, all I can find are quick-witted people who cannot be trusted. They use the instruments of Deen for worldly purposes by employing Qur'anic arguments against the Qur'an and the bounties of Allah against His servants. The only other type of person I find is one who follows people of the truth but has no insight into inspiring it. He therefore falls into doubt with the first doubt that presents itself, because of which he does not know where he stands. The other type of person I find is one immersed in carnal pleasures, who is a devout follower of passions. The other type I find is the one who is obsessed with wealth and amassing wealth. In fact, the last 2 types are not even callers to the Deen and the most fitting description of them is to liken them to grazing animals. So knowledge dies with the death of people capable of bearing it. At the same time, the earth is never empty of people who stand up for Allah using His contentions so that everything that Allah has proved and made clear to people should never be lost to mankind. Such people are however exceptionally few in number but most valued by Allah. It is by them that Allah refutes criticism against His arguments until they pass on and cultivate their knowledge and expertise to others like them. Their profound knowledge swiftly guides to them perceive the reality of all matters, making it easy for them to understand details that are beyond those who live in wealth and luxury. They are comfortable with matters that perplex and frighten ignorant people. While their bodies are in contact with the world, their souls are attached to a greater scene - the Hereafter. Such people are Allah's deputies in the lands and the callers to His Deen. Ah! Ah! How I long to meet them! I seek Allah's forgiveness for me and for you. You may now leave if you please." *(Abu Nu'aym in Hilya, Ibn Ambari in Masahif, Murhabi in Ilm, Nasr in Hujja, Ibn Asakir in Kanzul Ummal, Ibn Abdul Birr in his Jami Bayanil Ilm)*

The Encouragement Mu'adh bin Jabal ؓ Gave Towards Knowledge

Mu'adh bin Jabal ؓ said, "Acquire divine knowledge because learning it is fear of Allah, going out in search of it is

Ibada, rehearsing it is Tasbih, discussing it is Jihad, teaching it to those who do not know is Sadaqah and spending it on those worthy of receiving it promotes nearness to Allah. This is so because knowledge highlights what is Halal and what is Haram, it is a beacon for people on the road to Jannah, it is a companion in loneliness, a friend in the wilderness, a partner to talk to in solitude and a guide in prosperity and in adversity. Knowledge is also a weapon against the enemy and makes one shine out when amongst friends. Allah elevates nations by virtue of this knowledge, making them leaders in virtue so that people follow in their footsteps, emulate their actions and always adopt their opinions. In addition to this, the angels are eager to be with them and rub their wings against them. Everything on land and water seek forgiveness for them, even the fish and other creatures in the oceans and the wild and tame animals on land. This is all because divine knowledge brings life to hearts that have died after suffering from ignorance; it is a lantern of the eyes against darkness and by virtue of this knowledge, a person reaches the ranks of the chosen ones of Allah and elevated stages in this world as well as in the Hereafter. Thinking deeply about such knowledge equals fasting while learning and teaching it equals standing in salah. It is because of this knowledge that family ties are maintained and the lawful is distinguished from the unlawful. This knowledge is the leader of deeds and all deeds follow from it. It is only the fortunate who is inspired with it, while those deprived of it are most unfortunate." *(Abu Nu'aym in Hilya, Ibn Abdul Birr in Jami Bayanil Ilm, Rargheeb wat Tarheeb)*

The Encouragement of Abdullah bin Mas'ood ؓ Towards Knowledge

Haroon bin Rabab narrates that Abdullah bin Mas'ood ؓ said, "Start your mornings as either an Alim or one busy acquiring the knowledge of Deen but do not be something other than these 2 because anyone other than these is an ignorant person. Verily, out of their happiness for what he is doing, the angels spread out their wings for a person who ventures out in the morning to seek knowledge." *(Ibn Abdul Birr in Jami Bayanil Ilm).* Zaid reports that Abdullah bin Mas'ood ؓ once said, "Start your mornings as either an Alim or one busy acquiring the knowledge of Deen but do not be one who knows nothing and follows blindly." *(Ibn Abdul Birr in Jami Bayanil Ilm).* Abdullah bin Mas'ood ؓ once addressed the people saying, "O people! Ensure that you acquire the knowledge of Deen before it is taken away from this world. The manner by which it will be taken away is the departure of its bearer. Ensure that you acquire the knowledge of Deen because none of you knows just when you will need it. Ensure that you acquire the knowledge of Deen but beware of hair-splitting and excessiveness. You should also ensure that you follow traditions because there will soon appear people who will recite the Qur'an but then cast it behind their backs. *(Tabrani, Haythami, Abdur Razzaq in Jami, Ibn Abdul Birr).* Abul Ahwas narrates that Abdullah bin Mas'ood ؓ said, "No person is born an Alim. Knowledge is gained only through studies." *(Ibn Abdul Birr in Jami Bayanil Ilm).* Abdullah bin Mas'ood ؓ also said, "Start your mornings as either an Alim or one busy acquiring the knowledge of Deen but do not be something other than these 2. It you are unable to do this, then at least have love for the Ulema and never look down on them." *(Tabrani, Haythami)*

The Encouragement Abu Darda ؓ Gave Towards Knowledge

Hasan narrates that Abu Darda ؓ once said, "Either be an Alim, a student acquiring the knowledge of Deen, one who loves such people or one who follows them. However, never be the 5th person otherwise you will be destroyed." Humaid says that when he asked Hasan who the 5th person was, he replied, "He is the one who innovates acts of Bid'ah." *(Ibn Abdul Birr in Jami Bayanil Ilm)*. Dahhak narrates that Abu Darda ؓ once addressed the people saying, "O people of Damascus! You people are our brothers in Deen, our neighbors in nationality and our allies against the enemy. However, what prevents you from being friendly with me when it is others and not you who are paying my expenses. Why is it that I see your learned ones leaving while the ignorant ones fail to learn? Why do I see you people hankering after that sustenance which is being taken care of on your behalf while you neglect that which you have been commanded to do? Remember that there were people who constructed sturdy buildings, who amassed an abundance of wealth and who entertained distant hopes. However, their buildings became their graves, their hopes proved to be deceptive and all they amassed was destroyed. Remember that you must learn and teach others because the reward of the student and the teacher is alike and had it not been for these 2, there would be no good in the rest of people." *(Abu Nu'aym in Hilya)*

Hassan reports that Abu Darda ؓ addressed the people of Damascus saying, "Are you people content to just filling yourselves with bread made of wheat flour year in and year out without speaking of Allah in your gatherings? Why is it that your Ulema are leaving and your ignorant ones are not learning? If your Ulema had the desire, their numbers could increase and if your ignorant ones look for knowledge, they will certainly find it. Do what will benefit you rather than that which will harm you. I swear by the Being Who controls my life that every nation that was destroyed, was destroyed only because they followed the dictates of their passions and regarded themselves as spiritually pure." *(Abu Nu'aym in Hilya)*. Qurra narrates that Abu Darda ؓ once said, "Acquire knowledge before it is taken away because its disappearance will be affected by the demise of the Ulema. There are only 2 categories of men; the Alim and the student. There is no good in those who do not fall into these categories." *(Abu Nu'aym in Hilya)*. Abdur Rahman bin Mas'ood Farazi reports that Abu Darda ؓ once said, "Whenever anyone proceeds to the Masjid to learn or to teach anything virtuous, he receives the reward of a Mujahid who returns with booty." *(Ibn Abdul Birr in Jami Bayanil Ilm)*. Ibn Abu Hudhail narrates that Abu Darda ؓ said, "A person is lacking in intelligence and good judgment if he thinks that spending mornings and evenings in learning and imparting knowledge is not Jihad." *(Ibn Abdul Birr in Jami Bayanil Ilm)*. Raja bin Hayat reports that Abu Darda ؓ said, "Knowledge is derived from studies." *(Ibn Abdul Birr in Jami Bayanil Ilm)*

The encouragement Abu Dhar ؓ and Abu Hurairah ؓ gave Towards Knowledge

Abu Dhar ؓ and Abu Hurairah ؓ both said, "Learning even a single chapter of knowledge is more beloved to me than 1,000 Rakats of Nafl salah." They narrate that Rasulullah ﷺ said, "If death comes to someone studying the knowledge of Deen when he is still studying, he dies as a martyr." *(Bazzar, Tabrani in Targheeb wat Tarheeb)*. They also stated, "Learning even a single chapter of knowledge is more beloved to me than 1,000 Rakats of Nafl salah, regardless of whether the knowledge is practiced upon or not." *(Ibn Abdul Birr in Jami Bayanil Ilm)*

The Encouragement of Abdullah bin Abbas ؓ Towards Knowledge

Ali Azdi reports that when he once asked Abdullah bin

Abbas ؓ about Jihad, the Sahabi replied by saying, "Should I not tell you about something that is better than Jihad? It is that you go to the Masjid and teach the Qur'an, Fiqh or the Sunnah." *(Ibn Zanjway in Kanzul Ummal)*. Ali Azdi reports that he once asked Abdullah bin Abbas ؓ about Jihad. Abdullah bin Abbas ؓ replied by saying, "Should I not tell you about something that is better than Jihad? It is that you build a Masjid and then teach the Qur'an, the Sunnah of Rasulullah ﷺ and Deeni Fiqh." *(Ibn Abdul Birr in Jami Bayanil Ilm)*. Abdullah bin Abbas ؓ said, "Everything seeks forgiveness for the one who teaches people what is good, even the fish in the oceans." *(Ibn Abdul Birr in Jami Bayanil Ilm)*

The Encouragement Safwan bin Assal ؓ gave Towards Knowledge

Zirr bin Hubaish reports that when he went to Safwan bin Assal ؓ one morning, Safwan ؓ asked, "What brings you here this morning, O Zirr?" "I have come in search of knowledge," Zirr replied. Safwan ؓ remarked, "Begin your mornings as either an Alim or a student of Deen, but never as anyone else." *(Tabrani in Awsat, Haythami)*. Safwan bin Assal ؓ said, "Whoever leaves home in search of knowledge should know that the angels spread out their wings for the student and the Alim of Deen." *(Tabrani in Kabir, Haythami)*

The Statement Mu'adh ؓ Made on his Deathbed About his Fervor for Knowledge

When he was on his deathbed, Mu'adh bin Jabal ؓ asked the people to see whether dawn had broken. When they reported that it had not yet come, he again sent them to see. After this happened several times, they reported to him that dawn had broken. To this, he said, "I seek Allah's protection from the night followed by a morning that takes one to Jahannam. I welcome death with open arms. It is that long absent visitor and a friend in need. O Allah! While I had always been afraid of You, today I long to meet You. O Allah! You know well that I never loved this world or to live long here to dig canals or to plant trees. I loved it only for the thirst in the extreme afternoon heat when fasting, for enduring times of hardship and to sit on my knees when associating with the Ulema in gatherings of knowledge." *(Abu Nu'aym in Hilya, Ibn Abdul Birr in Jami Bayanil Ilm)*

The Fervor that Abu Darda ؓ had for Knowledge

Abu Darda ؓ once said, "Had it not been for 3 things, I would have loved to be no longer in this world. When asked what the 3 things were, Abu Darda ؓ said, " (1) Placing my head on the ground before my Creator in Sejdah during the hours of day and night so that it is sent ahead as rewards for my true life in the Hereafter. (2) Enduring thirst during hot afternoons while fasting and (3) sitting with people who choose their speech as carefully as you choose your fruit." The narration continues further.

The Fervor that Abdullah bin Abbas ؓ had for Acquiring Knowledge

Abdullah bin Abbas ؓ says, "When Rasulullah ﷺ passed away, I said to an Ansari friend of mine, 'The Sahabah are plenty in number. Come, let us learn from them.' 'I am astonished at you, O Ibn Abbas!' he said, 'Do you think that people will need you to learn from when so many of Rasulullah ﷺ's senior Sahabah are amongst them?' I left that as it were and proceeded to learn from the companions of Rasulullah ﷺ. I heard that a Hadith was narrated by someone, I would go to his door and if he was having his rest, I would roll up my shawl there and use it as a pillow. As I waited there, the wind would blow sand on me and when the man came out, he would ask, 'What brings you here, O cousin of Rasulullah ﷺ? Why did you not send for me and I would have come to you?' I would then say to him, 'No. It is I who should be coming to you.' I would ask him about the Hadith. My Ansari friend happened to live to the time when he saw people gathering around me to learn and would say, 'He has been a much smarter youngster than 1.'" (Hakim in Mustadrak confirmed by Dhahabi, Darmi and Harith in Masanid, Isabah, Tabrani, Haythami, Ibn Abdul Birr in Jami, Ibn Sa'd). Abdullah bin Abbas ﷺ says, 'When various cities were being conquered by the Muslims and people started focusing their attention towards the things of this world, I started focusing my attention on Omar ﷺ."Because of this most of the Ahadeeth narrated by Abdullah bin Abbas ﷺ are from Omar ﷺ. (Bazzar, Haythami)

Abu Hurairah ﷺ's Fervor for Knowledge

Abu Hurairah ﷺ narrates, "Rasulullah ﷺ once said to me. 'Are you not going to ask me for a share of the booty as your companions are asking me?' I replied, 'All I ask of you is to teach me that which Allah has taught you.' I then spread out the striped shawl I was wearing between us. In fact, I can even picture seeing the lice crawling on it. Rasulullah ﷺ then narrated Ahadeeth to me and when I had heard everything, he told me to pick up the shawl and wear it which I did. Thereafter, I have never forgotten even a single letter of what Rasulullah ﷺ had narrated to me." (Abu Nu'aym in Hilya). Abu Hurairah ﷺ once said, "People say that Abu Hurairah narrates plenty of Ahadeeth! It is with Allah that we have an appointment and He will judge. People ask why the Muhajirin and Ansar do not narrate as many Ahadeeth as Abu Hurairah ﷺ! While trade in the marketplaces occupied my Muhajirin brothers and commitments to their properties occupied my Ansar brothers, I was a poor man who stuck close to Rasulullah ﷺ so that my belly could be filled. I would therefore be present with Rasulullah ﷺ when they were not. I also remembered much when they had forgotten. Rasulullah ﷺ one day said, 'If any of you spreads out a cloth until I finish speaking and then holds it close to his chest, he will never forget anything that I say.' I therefore spread out my striped shawl because I had nothing else to spread out. After Rasulullah ﷺ had finished speaking, I put it to my chest. I swear by the Being Who sent Rasulullah ﷺ with the truth that from that day to this, I have never forgotten anything Rasulullah ﷺ said. By Allah! Had it not been for two verses of the Qur'an, I would never have narrated anything to you people. The verses are:

إِنَّ الَّذِينَ يَكْتُمُونَ مَا أَنْزَلْنَا مِنَ الْبَيِّنَاتِ وَالْهُدَى مِنْ بَعْدِ مَا بَيَّنَّاهُ لِلنَّاسِ فِي الْكِتَابِ أُولَئِكَ يَلْعَنُهُمُ اللَّهُ وَيَلْعَنُهُمُ اللَّاعِنُونَ (159) إِلَّا الَّذِينَ تَابُوا وَأَصْلَحُوا وَبَيَّنُوا فَأُولَئِكَ أَتُوبُ عَلَيْهِمْ وَأَنَا التَّوَّابُ الرَّحِيمُ (160)

Verily, those who conceal the clear proofs, evidences and the guidance, which We have sent down, after We have made it clear for the people in the Book, they are the ones cursed by Allah and cursed by the cursers. Except those who repent and do righteous deeds, and openly declare (truth which they concealed). These, I will accept their repentance. And I am the One Who accepts repentance, the Most Merciful. (Al-Baqara:159-160) (Bukhari)

Abu Hurairah ﷺ once said, "People complain that Abu Hurairah narrates too many Ahadeeth. I was a person who stuck with Rasulullah ﷺ to have my belly filled because it was a time when I was unable to eat coarse bread, wear silk or have slaves in attendance. Because of extreme hunger, I would press my stomach against stones so that the coolness of the stones would alleviate the burn of the hunger. I would ask a person to recite a verse of the Qur'an for me although I knew it so that as we

engaged in discussion, he may offer to take me home for meals. The person who treated the poor best was Ja'far bin Abi Talib ﷺ. He would take us home and feed us everything he had in his house. He would take out a honey or butter container that was empty, wipe out whatever remained stuck to the sides and bottom and give this to us to suck." (Bukhari in Targheeb wat Tarheeb)

Rasulullah ﷺ's concern on the True Meaning of Knowledge

Abu Musa Ash'ari ﷺ narrates that Rasulullah ﷺ said, "The example of the guidance and knowledge that Allah has sent me with is like a soaking rain that falls on a particular piece of ground. While a part of the ground is fertile and absorbs the water to grow grass and an abundance of vegetation, another portion of the ground is hard and holds the water. However, Allah still allows it to benefit people because they drink from it, give their animals to drink from it and also irrigate their fields with it. The rain also falls on another portion of the ground that consists of a rocky terrain which neither holds the water nor grows any grass. Such is the example of a person who has a deep understanding of the Deen of Allah. That which Allah has sent me with benefits him, because of which he becomes knowledgeable and teaches others as well. It is also the example of the person who pays no heed to it and refuses to accept it." (Bukhari, Muslim in Miskatul Masabih). Abdullah bin Mas'ood ﷺ narrates that Rasulullah ﷺ said, "Every Nabi ﷺ that Allah has sent before had close friends and companions who adopted his ways and obeyed his instructions. However, there came after them generations who did not practice what they preached and who did what they were not instructed to do. Whoever resists them physically is a Mu'min, whoever resists them verbally is also a Mu'min and whoever resists them by heart by disapproving of what they do is also a Mu'min. After these 3 categories of people there remains none with even a mustard seed of Iman." (Muslim in Mishkatul Masabih). Abdullah bin Amr ﷺ reports that Rasulullah ﷺ said, "Knowledge is of 3 types; explicit verses of the Qur'an, concrete Ahadeeth with authenticity that is beyond doubt and injunctions of the same standing: Ijma and Qiyas that is beyond doubt. Everything apart from this is extra, it is not compulsory to learn." (Abu Dawud and Ibn Majah in Mishkatul Masabih, Ibn Abdul Birr in Jami). Amr bin Auf ﷺ reports that Rasulullah ﷺ said, "I have left with you 2 factors that you will never go astray as long as you hold fast to them. They are the Book of Allah and the Sunnah of your Nabi ﷺ." (Ibn Abdul Birr in Jami Bayanil Ilm). Abu Hurairah ﷺ reports that Rasulullah ﷺ once entered the Masjid where he found the people gathered around a man. "What is happening?" Rasulullah ﷺ asked. "O Rasulullah ﷺ!" the Sahabah replied, "He is an Allama." "What is an Allama?" Rasulullah ﷺ enquired. The Sahabah said, "Someone who knows Arabic better than anyone else and also has the most knowledge of poetry and the differences between the Arabs." Rasulullah ﷺ remarked, "That is knowledge that does not benefit a person and no harm will be done to remain ignorant of it." (Ibn Abdul Birr in Jami Bayanil Ilm)

The Statements of Abdullah bin Omar ﷺ and Abdullah bin Abbas ﷺ Concerning the Real Meaning of Knowledge

Abdullah bin Omar ﷺ once said, "Knowledge is in 3 things; the talking book (the Qur'an), the perpetual Sunnah and to say 'I do not know' (when one does not know something)." (Ibn Abdul Birr in Jami Bayanil Ilm). Abdullah bin Abbas ﷺ said, "Knowledge is really in the Book of Allah and the Sunnah of Rasulullah. Based on personal opinion, if anyone says anything other than this, I cannot say whether he will find it included amongst his good deeds or amongst his sins." *(Ibn Abdul Birr in Jami Bayanil Ilm)*. Mujahid says, "Abdullah bin Abbas ؓ was once performing salah while Ata, Tawus and Ikrama and I, all his students, were sitting together. A man arrived and asked, 'Is there a Mufti amongst you?' 'Ask your question,' I said. He said, 'Every time I urinate, a dense liquid follows the urine out.' 'Is it the type of liquid from which a child is born?' we asked. When he replied in the affirmative, we ruled that he should take a bath each time it happened. The man then turned away saying, 'Inna Lillahi wa Inna Ilayhi Raji'un'. Abdullah bin Abbas ؓ hastened with his salah and as soon as he made the Salam, he said, 'Ikrama! Go bring that man back.' When Ikrama brought him back, Abdullah bin Abbas ؓ turned to us saying, 'Tell me whether the verdict you gave this man was sourced from the Book of Allah?' 'No,' we admitted. 'Then was it sourced from the Sunnah of Rasulullah ﷺ?' he asked further. When we again conceded that it was not, he asked, 'Then was it from the Sahabah of Rasulullah ﷺ?' Again we said no. 'Then from who did you learn it?' he asked. 'We derived it from our own judgment,' we replied. He remarked, 'For this reason that Rasulullah ﷺ said, 'A single jurist is more difficult for Saitan to contend with than 1,000 ignorant worshippers.' He then turned to the man and asked, 'Tell me. Do you feel any lust in your heart when this happens to you?' 'No, I do not,' the man replied. Abdullah bin Abbas ؓ asked further, 'Then do you feel any weakness in your body after it emerges?' When the man again replied negatively, Abdullah bin Abbas ؓ said, 'This happens because of coldness in the body, so wudhu would suffice for you, there is no need to bath." *(Ibn Asakir in Kanzul Ummal)*

Reprimanding those who Occupy Themselves with Learning that are Contrary to that Which Rasulullah ﷺ Taught

Amr bin Yahya bin Ja'da ؓ narrates that when someone brought to Rasulullah ﷺ a scripture written on the shoulder blade of an animal, Rasulullah ﷺ remarked, "It is enough for a person to have himself classified as a fool or a person gone astray just to turn his attention away from what his Nabi ﷺ, has brought and to focus it on what another Nabi ﷺ, had brought, or to turn his attention to a scripture other than his own." It was then that Allah revealed the verse: أَوَلَمْ يَكْفِهِمْ أَنَّا أَنْزَلْنَا عَلَيْكَ الْكِتَابَ يُتْلَى عَلَيْهِمْ
Is it not sufficient for them that We have sent down to you (O Rasulullah ﷺ) the Book (the Qur'an) which is recited to them? (Al-Ankabut:51) (Ibn Abdul Birr in Jami Bayanil Ilm)

Omar ؓ Rebukes a Man who Wrote the Scripture of Daniyal and his Incident with Rasulullah ﷺ

Khalid bin Urfuta narrates that he was with Omar ؓ when a man from the Abdul Qais tribe was brought. The man lived in a place called Soos where Daniyal ؑ is believed to be buried. When Omar ؓ asked him whether he was a particular person from the Abd tribe, the man replied that he was. Omar ؓ then struck him with a staff that he had with him. "O Amirul Mu'minin!" the man cried, "What have I done?" Omar ؓ told him to sit down and when he did, Omar recited the following: الر تِلْكَ آيَاتُ الْكِتَابِ الْمُبِينِ (1) إِنَّا أَنْزَلْنَاهُ قُرْآنًا عَرَبِيًّا لَعَلَّكُمْ تَعْقِلُونَ (2) نَحْنُ نَقُصُّ عَلَيْكَ أَحْسَنَ الْقَصَصِ بِمَا أَوْحَيْنَا إِلَيْكَ هَذَا الْقُرْآنَ وَإِنْ كُنْتَ مِنْ قَبْلِهِ لَمِنَ الْغَافِلِينَ (3)
Alif-Lam-Ra. (These letters are one of the miracles of the Qur'an, and none but Allah (Alone) knows their meanings).These are the Verses of the Clear Book (the Qur'an that makes clear the legal and illegal things, legal laws, a guidance and a blessing). Verily, We have sent it down as an Arabic Qur'an in order that you may understand. We relate unto you (Muhammad SAW) the best of stories through Our Revelations unto you, of

this Qur'an. And before this (i.e. before the coming of Divine Inspiration to you), you were among those who knew nothing about it (the Qur'an). (Yusuf:1-3)*

Omar ؓ recited the verses 3 times and hit the man 3 times. Again the man asked, "What have I done, O Amirul Mu'minin?" Omar ؓ said, "You are the person who wrote the scriptures of Daniyal ؑ." "I am prepared to do whatever you instruct me," the man said. Omar ؓ then said to him, "Go and erase it by pouring hot water over it and the wiping with white wool. I neither want you to read it or to give it to anyone else to read. If the news reaches me that you had read it or had given it to someone else to read, I shall punish you very severely." Omar ؓ then told the man to sit down, and when he sat in front of Omar ؓ, the Amirul Mu'minin narrated, "I once copied a scripture from the Ahlul Kitab on a piece of leather. When Rasulullah ﷺ asked me what it was I had in my hand, I said, 'O Rasulullah ﷺ! It is a scripture that I copied to supplement the knowledge we have.' Rasulullah ﷺ then became so angry that his cheeks flamed red. By the instruction of Rasulullah ﷺ the announcement 'As Saiatu Jami'ah' was made to gather the people to which the Ansar said, 'Take your weapons! Take your weapons! Your Nabi ﷺ has been angered.' The people then amassed around Rasulullah ﷺ's pulpit. Rasulullah ﷺ said, 'O people! I have been granted speech that is comprehensive, conclusive, yet very concise. I have also brought to you a creed that it exceptionally pure. Therefore, you need never be confused and never allow yourselves to be deceived by the confused ones (the Ahlul Kitab).'" Omar ؓ continues, "I then stood up and said, 'I am satisfied with Allah as my Rabb, with Islam as my religion and with you as my Nabi.' Rasulullah ﷺ then descended from the pulpit." *(Abu Ya'la, Haythami, Ibnul Mundhir, Ibn Abi Hatim, Uqayli, Nasr Maqdasi, Sa'eed bin Mansur, Abdur Razzaq in Kanzul Ummal)*

Jabir ؓ narrates that Omar bin Khattab ؓ once brought to Rasulullah ﷺ a scripture that he got from some people of the Ahlul Kitab. "O Rasulullah ﷺ!" he said, "I just got an excellent scripture from some people of the Ahlul Kitab." Rasulullah ﷺ became angry and said, "Are you people in doubt, O son of Khattab? I swear by the Being Who controls my life! What I have brought to you is clear and pure. You therefore have no need to ask them. The danger is that they might tell you some truth that you may reject or tell that you may believe. I swear by the Being Who controls my life that even if Musa ؑ was alive, he would have no option but to follow me." *(Ibn Abdul Birr in Jami, Ahmad, Abu Ya'la, Bazzar, Haythami)*. Abdullah bin Thabit ؓ narrates that Omar bin Khattab ؓ once came to Rasulullah ﷺ and said, "I was passing by a friend from the (Jewish) Banu Quraiza tribe, so he wrote down for me some quotations from the Torah. Should I read them to you." When Rasulullah ﷺ's face started reddening (with anger), Abdullah bin Thabit ؓ said to Omar ؓ, "Can you not see Rasulullah's face?" Omar immediately exclaimed, "I am satisfied with Allah as my Rabb, with Islam as my religion and with Muhammad ﷺ as my Nabi." Rasulullah ﷺ's anger then subsided and he said, "I swear by the Being Who controls the life of Muhammad! If Musa ؑ had to be amongst you and you leave me to follow him. you would certainly go astray. You are meant to be my Ummah and I am meant to be your Nabi." *(Ahmad, Tabrani, Haythami)*

Omar ؓ Rebukes a Man who Told Him that he Found a Scripture with Wonderful Content

Maymun bin Mahran narrates that a man came to Omar ؓ saying, "O Amirul Mu'minin! When we conquered Mada'in, I found a scripture with wonderful content." "Is the content consistent with the Book of Allah?" Omar ❀ asked. When the man said that it was not, Omar ❀ sent for his whip, lashed the man and recited the verse:

الر تِلْكَ آيَاتُ الْكِتَابِ الْمُبِينِ (1) إِنَّا أَنْزَلْنَاهُ قُرْآنًا عَرَبِيًّا لَعَلَّكُمْ تَعْقِلُونَ (2) نَحْنُ نَقُصُّ عَلَيْكَ أَحْسَنَ الْقَصَصِ بِمَا أَوْحَيْنَا إِلَيْكَ هَذَا الْقُرْآنَ وَإِنْ كُنْتَ مِنْ قَبْلِهِ لَمِنَ الْغَافِلِينَ (3)

Alif-Lam-Ra. (These letters are one of the miracles of the Qur'an, and none but Allah (Alone) knows their meanings).These are the Verses of the Clear Book (the Qur'an that makes clear the legal and illegal things, legal laws, a guidance and a blessing). Verily, We have sent it down as an Arabic Qur'an in order that you may understand. We relate unto you (Muhammad SAW) the best of stories through Our Revelations unto you, of this Qur'an. And before this (i.e. before the coming of Divine Inspiration to you), you were among those who knew nothing about it (the Qur'an). (Yusuf:1-3)

He then said, "Those before you (the Jews and Christians) were destroyed only because they forsook the Torah and Injeel and turned to the books of their scholars and priests. These 2 scriptures then eventually disappeared along with the knowledge they contained." *(Nasr Maqdasi in Kanzul Ummal)*

Abdullah bin Mas'ood ❀ and Abdullah bin Abbas ❀ Condemn Questioning the Ahlul Kitab

Huraith bin Zuhair reports that Abdullah bin Mas'ood ❀ said, "Never question the Ahlul Kitab about anything because since they are misguided, they cannot guide you. The danger is that they might tell you some truth that you may reject or tell you some false that you may believe." *(Ibn Abdul Birr in Jami, Abdul Razzaq)*. Abdullah bin Mas'ood ❀ also said, "If you have to ask them (the Ahlul Kitab), then consider what they say. If it coincides with the teachings of Allah's Book, you may accept it, but you must reject it if it does not." *(Ibn Abdul Birr in Jami, Tabrani, Haythami)*. Abdullah bin Abbas ❀ said, "How can you people ask the Ahlul Kitab about anything when you have with you the Book that Allah has revealed to His Nabi ❀, which happens to be the latest scripture from your Rabb? It is new and has not been interpolated. Has Allah not informed you in His Book that they (the Ahlul Kitab) had altered Allah's scriptures (the Torah and Injeel) with their own hands and said that it was from Allah? This was done only to earn some meager worldly profits. Does the knowledge that has come to you not prevent you from asking them? By Allah! I have never seen any of them asking you about what Allah has revealed!" *(Ibn Abdul Birr in Jami)*. Abdullah ❀ said, "You ask the Ahlul Kitab about their scriptures when you have Allah's Book which is the latest of Allah's scriptures? It is new, has not been interpolated and you areable to read it." *(Ibn Abi Shaybah in Jami of Ibn Abdul Birr)*

Abu Hurairah ❀ and Mu'awiya ❀ are Affected by a Hadith of Rasulullah ❀

Shufai Asbahi narrates, "Upon entering Madinah one day, I saw many people gathered around a particular man. When I asked who the man was, I was informed that he was Abu Hurairah ❀. I then went close and sat down in front of him as he narrated Ahadeeth. After he had completed and was alone, I asked, 'I ask you in the name of the rights I have upon you in that I am a Muslim, a traveler and a student to narrate to me a Hadith that you heard from Rasulullah ❀ and that you understood well' He said, 'By all means. I shall narrate to you a Hadith that Rasulullah ❀ narrated to me and which I understand well' He then sighed so deeply that he was close to falling unconscious. We waited a while until he regained his composure and said, 'I

shall relate to you a Hadith that Rasulullah ❀ narrated to me in this very house when there was none here besides him and I. Abu Hurairah ❀ then again sighed so deeply that he was close to falling unconscious. When he regained his composure, he wiped his face and said, 'I shall relate to you a Hadith that Rasulullah ❀ narrated to me in this very house when there was none here besides him and I. Abu Hurairah ❀ then again sighed so deeply that he actually fell on his face. I held him up for a long while and when he regained consciousness, he said, 'Rasulullah ❀ narrated to me that on the Day of Judgment, every nation will be on its knees when Allah will descend to pass judgment between the people. The first to be summoned for reckoning will be the person who memorized the Qur'an, the person who was martyred in the Path of Allah and the man with plenty of wealth. Addressing the Qari, Allah will say, 'Did I not teach you that which I revealed to my messenger?' 'Indeed you did, O my Rabb!' he will respond. Allah will ask him further, 'And what did you do with that which I taught you?' He will reply, 'I recited it day and night.' 'You are lying,' Allah will declare. The angels will reiterate saying, 'You are lying.' Allah will then add, 'Yom only motive was that people should call you a Qari, which they have already done.' Next, the wealthy man will be summoned. Allah will ask him, 'Did I not grant you plenty so that you never depended on anyone else?' 'Indeed you have, my Rabb!' he will admit. 'Then what did you do with that which I gave you?' Allah will ask. He man will say, 'I used to maintain family ties and give charity.' 'You are lying,' Allah will declare. 'You are lying,' the angels will reiterate. Allah will then say, 'Your only motive was that people should call you a generous person, which they have already done.' Next to be summoned will be the one who was martyred in the Path of Allah. Allah will ask him, 'For what objective were you killed?' His reply will be, 'because we were commanded to fight in Jihad, I fought until I was killed.' 'You are lying,' Allah will declare. 'You are lying,' the angels will reiterate. Allah will then say, 'Your only motive was that people should call you a brave person, which they have already done.' Rasulullah ❀ then hit his hands on my knees and said, 'O Abu Hurairah! These 3 will be the first of Allah's creation with whom the fire of Jahannam will be fuelled on the Day of Judgment.'" After hearing this Hadith from Abu Hurairah ❀ Shufai then went to Mu'awiya ❀ and narrated the Hadith to him. Ala bin Hakim says that Shufai was the person who tended to Mu'awiya ❀'s swords. He reports, "When this Hadith from Abu Hurairah ❀ was narrated to Mu'awiya ❀, Mu'awiya ❀ remarked, 'If this is what will happen to these 3, what about the rest of mankind?' He then wept so much that we thought he would expire. We said, 'This man has certainly brought a calamity upon us by upsetting the Khalifa in this manner!' When Mu'awiya ❀ regained his calmness, he wiped his face and said, 'Allah and His Rasul ❀ have spoken the truth when they say:

مَنْ كَانَ يُرِيدُ الْحَيَاةَ الدُّنْيَا وَزِينَتَهَا نُوَفِّ إِلَيْهِمْ أَعْمَالَهُمْ فِيهَا وَهُمْ فِيهَا لَا يُبْخَسُونَ (15) أُولَئِكَ الَّذِينَ لَيْسَ لَهُمْ فِي الْآخِرَةِ إِلَّا النَّارُ وَحَبِطَ مَا صَنَعُوا فِيهَا وَبَاطِلٌ مَا كَانُوا يَعْمَلُونَ (16)

Whosoever desires the life of the world and its glitter; to them We shall pay in full (wages of) their deeds therein, and they will have no diminution therein. They are those for whom there is nothing in the Hereafter but Fire; and vain are the deeds they did therein. And of no effect is that which they used to do. (Hud:15-16) (Tirmidhi, Ibn Khuzaima, Ibn Hibban in Targheeb wat Tarheeb). Abu Salama bin Abdur Rahman bin Auf ❀ reports that when Abdullah bin Omar ❀ and Abdullah bin Amr bin Al Aas ❀ met at Marwa, they were discussing Ahadeeth. When Abdullah bin Amr ❀ left, Abdullah bin Omar ❀ remained there weeping.

"What makes you weep so much, O Abu Abdur Rahman?" someone asked. Abdullah bin Omar ؓ replied, "Abdullah bin Amr ؓ says that he heard Rasulullah ﷺ say, 'Allah will throw a person headlong into the Jahannam if he has pride equal to even a mustard seed in his heart.'"*(Targheeb wat Tarheeb)*

Abdullah bin Rawaha ؓ and Hassan ؓ Weep When Allah Revealed the verse: "Only Deviant People Follow the Poets"

Abul Hasan the freed slave of the Banu Naufal tribe reports that Abdullah bin Rawaha ؓ and Hassan bin Thabit ؓ both acclaimed poets came weeping to Rasulullah ﷺ when Allah revealed Surah Shu'ara. Rasulullah ﷺ recited to them the verses:

وَالشُّعَرَاءُ يَتَّبِعُهُمُ الْغَاوُونَ (224) أَلَمْ تَرَ أَنَّهُمْ فِي كُلِّ وَادٍ يَهِيمُونَ (225) وَأَنَّهُمْ يَقُولُونَ مَا لَا يَفْعَلُونَ (226) إِلَّا الَّذِينَ آمَنُوا وَعَمِلُوا الصَّالِحَاتِ وَذَكَرُوا اللَّهَ كَثِيرًا وَانْتَصَرُوا مِنْ بَعْدِ مَا ظُلِمُوا

As for the poets, the erring follow them, See you not that they speak about every subject (praising others right or wrong) in their poetry? And that they say what they do not do. Except those who believe (in the Oneness of Allah Islamic Monotheism), and do righteous deeds, and remember Allah much, and reply back (in poetry) to the unjust poetry (which the pagan poets utter against the Muslims)... (Ash-Shu'ara:224-227)

When Rasulullah ﷺ recited the verse "Except those who have Iman, who do good acts", he said, "That refers to you." Thereafter, when he recited "who remember Allah abundantly", he again said, "That refers to you". Again, when reciting the verse "and those who avenge themselves after being oppressed", he said, at refers to you." *(Hakim)*

The People of Yemen Weep When They Hear the Qur'an During the Khilafa of Abu Bakr ؓ

Abu Salih narrates that some people from Yemen came to Madinah during the Khilafa of Abu Bakr ؓ and heard the Qur'an, they started weeping excessively. Abu Bakr ؓ remarked in humility, "That is how we used to be, but hearts started to harden." Abu Nu'aym explains the term "hearts started to harden" means that their hearts strengthened and became content with the recognition of Allah. *(Abu Nu'aym in Hilya, Kanzul Ummal)*

A Warning to the Alim who does not Teach Others and to Ignorant Person who does not Learn

Abzah Abu Abdur Rahman ؓ reports that Rasulullah ﷺ once praised certain groups of the Muslims in his sermon. Thereafter, Rasulullah ﷺ said, "What is the matter with certain tribes who neither make their neighboring tribes understand Deen, nor do they teach it to them, explain it to them, enjoin them to do good or forbid them from evil? What also is the matter with other tribes who neither learn from their neighbors nor make an attempt to understand the Deen or to be conversant with it? Take note that people will have to teach Deen to their neighbors, explain it to them, enjoin them to do good and forbid them from evil. At the same time, others will have to learn Deen from their neighbors and make an attempt to understand it; otherwise they will all be punished very soon in this very world." Rasulullah ﷺ then descended from the pulpit and entered his room. "Who do you think Rasulullah ﷺ was referring to?" some people asked. "We think that he must have been referring to the Ash'ar tribe who have a good understanding of Deen while their neighbors are uncultured Bedouins living at an oasis. When the news reached the people of the Ash'ar tribe, they came to Rasulullah ﷺ and said, "O Rasulullah ﷺ! Why is it that when you praised some people, you criticized us? What have we done?" Rasulullah ﷺ replied, "That people will have to teach Deen to their neighbors, explain it to them, enjoin them to do good and forbid them from evil. At the same time, others will have to learn Deen from their neighbors and make an attempt to understand it, otherwise they will all be punished very soon in this very world." "O Rasulullah ﷺ!" they pleaded, "Will we be held responsible for the wrongs of others?" When Rasulullah ﷺ repeated his words, they again asked, "O Rasulullah ﷺ! Will we be held responsible for the wrongs of others?" This time again, Rasulullah ﷺ repeated what he had said. They then requested Rasulullah ﷺ for a year's grace to educate their neighbors and to give them a sound understanding of Deen. Rasulullah ﷺ granted them the grace. Rasulullah ﷺ then recited the verse:

لُعِنَ الَّذِينَ كَفَرُوا مِنْ بَنِي إِسْرَائِيلَ عَلَى لِسَانِ دَاوُودَ وَعِيسَى ابْنِ مَرْيَمَ ذَلِكَ بِمَا عَصَوْا وَكَانُوا يَعْتَدُونَ (78) كَانُوا لَا يَتَنَاهَوْنَ عَنْ مُنْكَرٍ فَعَلُوهُ لَبِئْسَ مَا كَانُوا يَفْعَلُونَ (79)

Those among the Children of Israel who disbelieved were cursed by the tongue of Dawood (David) and Iesa (Jesus), son of Maryam (Mary). That was because they disobeyed (Allah and the Messengers) and were ever transgressing beyond bounds. They used not to forbid one another from the Munkar (wrong, , sins, polytheism, disbelief, etc.) which they committed. Vile indeed was what they used to do. (Al-Ma'ida:78-79) (Ibn Rahway, Bukhari in Wahdan, Ibnus Sakan, Ibn Mandah, Tabrani, Abu Nu'aym, Ibn Asakir, Bawardi and lbn Mardway in Kanzul Ummal)

The words of Mu'adh ؓ to a man who was weeping by his bedside before his death

Abdullah bin Salama narrates that a man came to the bedside of Mu'adh bin Jabal ؓ and started to weep. "What makes you weep?" Mu'adh ؓ asked. The man replied, "By Allah! I am neither crying because of the ties of kinship we have nor because of the material gains I used to get from you. What makes me weep is the fear that the knowledge I used to collect from you will soon come to an end." Mu'adh ؓ consoled him saying, "Do not cry because whoever strives to acquire knowledge and Iman, Allah will grant them to him just as He granted Ibrahim عليه السلام during times when there was no knowledge and Iman." *(Abu Nu'aym in Hilya)*. Harith bin Umaira reports that when Mu'adh bin Jabal ؓ was about to pass away, the people around him started to cry. "What makes you people cry?" he asked. They replied, "We are crying because of the knowledge that will stop coming to us when you pass away." Mu'adh ؓ said, "Verily knowledge and Iman shall remain as they are until the Day of Judgment. Whoever searches for them shall find them in the Qur'an and the Sunnah. While you ought to judge every piece of information by the standards of the Qur'an, never judge the Qur'an by the standards of any piece of information. Seek knowledge from Omar ؓ, Uthman ؓ and Ali ؓ and if you do not meet them, seek knowledge from 4 men; from Uwaymir ؓ (Abu Darda ؓ), Abdullah bin Mas'ood ؓ, Salman ؓ and from Abdullah bin Salam ؓ, who had been a Jew before becoming a Muslim. In fact, I heard Rasulullah ﷺ say that Abdullah bin Salam ؓ will be the 10th of 10 people to enter Jannah without reckoning. You must however ensure that you beware of the mistakes of an Alim. You should accept the truth from whoever brings it to you and reject falsehood from whoever brings it to you, regardless of who the person may be." *(Ibn Asakir and Saif in Kanzul Ummal)*. Yazid bin Umaira narrates, "During the illness that claimed his life, Mu'adh bin Jabal ؓ would often fall unconscious and then regain consciousness. When he once fell unconscious for a long time, we feared that he had passed away. When he regained consciousness, I was standing in front of him crying. 'What makes you cry?' he asked. I replied by saying, 'By

Allah! It is not because of the worldly benefits I received from you that I am weeping and also not because of our kinship. What makes me weep is the departure of the knowledge of Deen and knowledge of Islamic law that I had been acquiring from you.' His response was, 'Do not weep because knowledge and Iman shall remain as they are and whoever seeks them shall surely find them. Seek them as Ibrahim ﷺ sought them. When he had not acquired them fully, he asked Allah saying:

وَقَالَ إِنِّي ذَاهِبٌ إِلَى رَبِّي سَيَهْدِينِ (99) *And he said (after his rescue from the fire): "Verily, I am going to my Lord. He will guide me!" (As-Saffat:99)*. After I die, seek knowledge from 4 persons. If you cannot find what you seek with anyone of them, then ask the people for the best amongst them. The 4 men are Abdullah bin Mas'ood ﷺ, Abdullah bin Salam ﷺ, Salman ﷺ and Uwaymir Abu Dard ﷺa. You should also beware of the blunders of the wise and the verdict of a hypocrite.' 'How will I identify the blunder of a wise man?' I asked. He explained, 'It is misguided speech that Saitan casts on the tongue of a man which he utters without thinking. It sometimes also occurs that a hypocrite speaks what is true. You should therefore absorb sound knowledge from wherever it comes to you because there is light in the truth. Matters that are dubious should however be avoided.'" *(Hakim)*. Amr bin Maymun narrates, "We were in Yemen when Mu'adh bin Jabal ﷺ came there and addressed us saying, 'O people of Yemen! Accept Islam and live in peace. I am the envoy of Rasulullah ﷺ to you.' Since then, I took a liking to him and never parted from him until he passed away. When he was leaving the world and I started to weep, he asked, 'What makes you cry?' I replied, 'I am weeping because of the knowledge that will be leaving with you.' He consoled me saying, 'Verily knowledge and Iman shall remain until the Day of Judgment...'" The rest of the narration is similar to the ones above. *(Ibn Asakir in Kanzul Ummal)*

The Statements of Abdullah bin Omar ﷺ, Jundub bin Abdullah ﷺ and Ali ﷺ About Learning Iman, Knowledge and Practice All at the Same Time

Abdullah bin Omar ﷺ said, "During the greater portion of my life I have seen that a man from the Sahabah learns Iman before the Qur'an. Whenever a Surah was revealed to Muhammad ﷺ, the man would learn what was proclaimed lawful and unlawful and where it was appropriate to stop just as you people learn the words of the Qur'an itself. I now see people learning the Qur'an before Iman and while they have read from Surah Fatiha up to the end of the Qur'an, they have no idea about what the Qur'an instructs and what it prohibits. They also do not know where it is appropriate to stop and scatter the verses about like unwanted dates." *(Tabrani, Haythami)*. Jundub bin Abdullah ﷺ said, "We were youngsters almost coming of age when we learnt Iman before the Qur'an with Rasulullah ﷺ. When we then learnt the Qur'an, our Iman grew even stronger." *(Ibn Majah)*. Ali ﷺ once said, "Whenever a Surah, a verse or a few verses were revealed during the time of Rasulullah ﷺ, it would serve to strengthen the Iman and submission of the Mu'minin and if it contained a prohibition, they would immediately abstain." *(Askari and Ibn Mardway in Kanzul Ummal)*

How the Sahabah would not Learn Another Verse of the Qur'an Until They had Learnt How to Practice on the Previous Verse

Abu Abdur Rahman Sulami says, "The Sahabi who taught us mentioned that when they learnt 10 verses from Rasulullah ﷺ, they would not proceed to another 10 verses until they had learnt everything about the previous 10 verses and how to practice on them. He would also say, 'Our knowledge consisted of both theory and practice.'" *(Ahmad, Haythami)*. The Sahabi also said, "We used to learn the Qur'an as well as how to practice on it. Some people will come who will inherit the Qur'an after us who will drink up the Qur'an like water without it passing by their collarbones. In fact, it will not even pass here." He then placed his hand on his throat. *(Ibn Sa'd)*. Abdullah bin Mas'ood ﷺ said, "Whenever we learnt 10 verses of the Qur'an from Rasulullah ﷺ, we would not proceed to learn the next 10 verses until we had learnt whatever was in them." When someone asked narrator Sharik whether this referred to practicing the 10 verses first, he replied in the affirmative. *(Ibn Asakir in Kanzul Ummal)*

The Words of Salman ﷺ to a Man From the Banu Abs Tribe to Acquire Islamic knowledge

Hafs bin Omar Sa'di narrates from his uncle that Salman ﷺ once said to Hudhaifa ﷺ, "O member of the Banu Abs! While knowledge is abundant, life is short. You should therefore acquire only that much of Islamic knowledge that you need and leave out that which does not concern you." *(Abu Nu'aym in Hilya)*. Abul Bakhtari reports that a man from the Banu Abs tribe was once in the company of Salman ﷺ when he took a sip of water from the Tigris River. "Drink again," Salman ﷺ bade the man. When the man declared that he was full, Salman asked, "Do you think that your sip decreased much from the river?" The man said, "How can the sip I took decrease anything from it?" Salman ﷺ then remarked, "In the same manner, knowledge never decreases. You should therefore glean as much knowledge as would benefit you." *(Abu Nu'aym in Hilya)*

The Words of Abdullah bin Omar ﷺ to a Man who Wrote to Ask Him About Knowledge

Abu Qaila reports that when a man wrote to ask Abdullah bin Omar ﷺ about knowledge, the Sahabi wrote back saying, "You have written to me asking about knowledge. Knowledge is something much greater than I can write back to you about. However the advice I will offer is if it is possible for you to accomplish, you must make an effort to meet Allah in a manner that you have held your tongue from dishonoring a Muslim, you do not have the burden of any Muslim's blood on your back, your belly is empty of the wealth of the Muslims and you have remained united with them." *(Ibn Asakir in Kanzul Ummal)*

Rasulullah ﷺ Teaches the Deen to Abu Rifa'ah ﷺ

Abu Rifa'ah ﷺ narrates, "I came to Rasulullah ﷺ at a time when he was busy delivering a sermon. 'O Rasulullah ﷺ!' I said, 'A stranger has come to enquire about his Deen as he knows not what his Deen is.' Leaving the sermon aside, Rasulullah ﷺ turned and came to me. His chair, the legs of which I think were of iron, was brought. Rasulullah ﷺ sat on it and started teaching me that which Allah had taught him. He returned to his sermon and completed what remained of it." *(Muslim, Bukhari in Adab, Nasa'ee in Zinah, Tabrani and Abu Nu'aym in Kanzul Ummal)*

Rasulullah ﷺ Teaches Deen to a Bedouin, to Farwah bin Musaik ﷺ and to a Delegation From Bahra

Jareer ﷺ reports that a Bedouin once came to Rasulullah ﷺ saying, "Teach me Islam." Rasulullah ﷺ explained, "Islam is that you testify that there is none worthy of worship but Allah and that Muhammad ﷺ is the servant and Rasul of Allah, that you establish salah, pay zakah, fast during Ramadhan, perform Hajj of the Kabah, love for people what you love for yourself and dislike for people what you dislike for yourself." *(Ibn Jareer in Kanzul Ummal)*. Muhammad bin Omara bin Khuzaima bin Thabit says, "Farwah bin Musaik Muradi ؓ forsook the royalty of Kindah and arrived with a delegation to follow Rasulullah ﷺ. He stayed with Sa'd bin Ubadah ؓ where he learnt the Qur'an, the Fara'idh of Islam and the Shari'ah." The narration continues further. *(Ibn Sa'd)*. Duba'ah bint Zubair bin Abdul Muttalib ؓ reports that a delegation from Bahra in Yemen once came to Madinah. They were 13 men and when they arrived, they led their animals to the door of Miqdad bin Amr ؓ in the district of the Banu Jadila tribe. Miqdad ؓ met them, extended a warm welcome to them and hosted them in a room of his house. They came before Rasulullah ﷺ, they all accepted Islam. They stayed several days and learnt about the Fara'idh of Islam. They later returned to Rasulullah ﷺ to bid him farewell, Rasulullah ﷺ had gifts for them, after which they left for their homes. *(Ibn Sa'd)*

Abu Bakr ؓ and Omar ؓ Teach Deen

Ibn Sirin reports that when teaching Islam to the people, Abu Bakr ؓ and Omar ؓ would say, "Worship Allah without ascribing any partners to Him. Establish on time the salah that Allah has made obligatory for you because any deficiency in this spells certain destruction. Pay zakah with a cheerful heart, fast during Ramadhan and listen to and obey your leaders." *(Abdur Razzaq, Ibn Abi Shaybah, Ibn Jareer, Rustah in Iman, Kanzul Ummal)*. Hasan narrates that a Bedouin once came to Omar ؓ saying, "O Amirul Mu'minin! Teach me the Deen." Omar ؓ said, "The Deen of Islam is to testify that there is none worthy of worship but Allah and that Muhammad ﷺ is the Rasul of Allah, to establish salah, to pay zakah, to perform Hajj of the Kabah and to fast during Ramadhan. You should also look only at the apparent actions of people and beware not to probe their private lives. Furthermore, beware not to do anything that will be a cause of embarrassment if people found out and when you meet Allah, tell Him that Omar instructed you to do these things." *(Bayhaqi, Isfahani in Hujjah)*. Another narration states that Omar ؓ added, "O servant of Allah! Hold fast to this and when you meet Allah, then tell Him whatever comes to mind." *(Ibn Adi, Bayhaqi in Kanzul Ummal)*. Hasan narrates that a man approached Omar ؓ saying, "O Amirul Mu'minin! I am a man from the countryside and have many duties to tend to. Do advise me to do something that I can trust in to convey me to Jannah." Omar ؓ said to him, "Give me your hand and understand me well" When the man gave him his hand, Omar ؓ said, "You should worship Allah without ascribing partners to him, establish salah, pay the obligatory zakah, perform Hajj, perform Umrah and obey your leaders. You should also look only at the apparent actions of people and beware not to probe their private lives. Do every such deed that will not embarrass you when the news of it spreads amongst people and stay away from every such act that will be a cause of embarrassment and disgrace when the news reaches others." "O Amirul Mu'minin!" the man said, "I shall practice on this advice and when I meet my Rabb, I shall say, 'It was Omar bin Khattab who told me to do this.'" To this, Omar ؓ remarked, "Hold fast to this and when you meet your Rabb, you may tell Him whatever you like." *(Ibn Asakir in Kanzul Ummal)*

Rasulullah ﷺ Teaches the Sahabah How to Perform Salah

Abu Malik Ashja'ee reports from his father ؓ that salah was the first thing Rasulullah taught anyone who accepted Islam. *(Tabrani, Bazzar, Haythami)*. Hakam bin Umair ؓ reports that Rasulullah ﷺ taught them thus: "When you stand up for salah, say 'Allahu Akbar' and raise your hands without passing your ears. Then recite: سُبْحَانَكَ اللّٰهُمَّ وَبِحَمْدِكَ وَتَبَارَكَ اسْمُكَ وَتَعَالٰى جَدُّكَ وَلَاإِلٰهَ غَيْرُكَ *'You are Pure, O Allah and we praise You, Blessed is Your name, Lofty is Your honor and there is none worthy of worship but You.'" (Abu Nu'aym in Kanzul Ummal)*

Rasulullah ﷺ, Abu Bakr ؓ, Omar ؓ and Abdullah bin Mas'ood ؓ Teach the Tashahhud

Abdullah bin Omar ؓ says, "Abu Bakr ؓ used to teach us the Tashahhud from the pulpit just as little children are taught at school." *(Musaddad, Tahawi in Kanzul Ummal)*. Abdullah bin Abbas ؓ says *(Dar Qutni in Kanzul Ummal)*, "Omar bin Khattab ؓ once took hold of my hand and taught me the Tashahud, informing me that Rasulullah ﷺ has also taken him by the hand and taught him the Tashahud, which is:

التَّحِيَّاتُ اللهِ، الصَّلَوَاتُ، الطَّيِّبَاتُ الْمُبَارَكَاتُ اللهِ

Abdur Rahman bin Abd Qari narrates that he heard Omar bin Khattab ؓ teaching the Tashahud to the people from the pulpit. He was telling the people to recite. The narration still continues further. *(Malik, Shafi'ee, Tahawi, Abdur Razzaq)*. Abdullah bin Abbas ؓ says, "Rasulullah ﷺ used to teach us the Tashahud just as he taught us a Surah of the Qur'an." *(Ibn Abi Shaybah)*. Abdullah bin Mas'ood ؓ said, "Rasulullah ﷺ taught me the Tashahud with my hand in his just as he would teach me a Surah of the Qur'an." The narration then proceeds to cite the words of the Tashahud. *(Ibn Abi Shaybah)*. Abdullah bin Mas'ood ؓ also mentioned, "Rasulullah ﷺ used to teach us the beginnings of the Surahs and the Qur'an, as well as the Khutbahs for salah and for other occasions such as the Khutbah for marriage." The narration then continues to discuss the Tashahud. *(Askari in Amthal)*. Aswad reports, "Abdullah bin Mas'ood ؓ used to teach us the Tashahud just as he would teach us a Surah of the Qur'an. In fact, he would even correct the simple errors we made in the Alif and Waw." *(Ibn Najjar in Kanzul Ummal)*

Hudhaifa ؓ Teaches Salah to a Man who could not Perform Well

Zaid bin Wahab reports thatHudhaifa ؓ once entered the Masjid, he noticed a man was performing salah without carrying out the Ruku and Sajdah properly. When the man had completed, Hudhaifa ؓ said to him, "For how long have you been performing salah like this?" When the man informed that he had been performing salah in that manner for the past 40 years, Hudhaifa ؓ said, "You have performed no salah for the last 40 years. Had you died while performing salah like this, you would not have died on the creed in which Allah created Muhammad ﷺ." As Hudhaifa ؓ proceeded to teach the man how to perform salah, he said, "Even though a man makes his salah brief, he must carry out the Ruku and Sejdah properly." *(Abdur Razzaq, Ibn Abi Shayba, Bukhari, and Nasa'ee in Kanzul Ummal)*

Rasulullah ﷺ Teaches Adhkar and Du'as to Ali ؓ

Ali bin Abi Talib ؓ narrates that Rasulullah ﷺ once said to him, "Should I give you 5,000 goats or teach you 5 phrases that contain the welfare of your Deen and your worldly life?" "O Rasulullah ﷺ!" Ali ؓ replied, "While 5,000 goats are plenty, I prefer that you teach me the 5 phrases." Rasulullah ﷺ then told Ali ؓ to recite the following: اللّٰهُمَّ اغْفِرْ لِي ذَنْبِي وَوَسِّعْ لِي خُلُقِي وَطَيِّبْ لِي كَسْبِي وَقَنِّعْنِي بِمَا رَزَقْتَنِي وَلَا تَذْهَبْ قَلْبِي إِلٰى شَيْءٍ صَرَفْتَهُ عَنِّي *"O Allah! Forgive my sins, make my character accommodating, make my earnings lawful, make me content with what You provide for me and never allow my heart to hanker after something that You have not decreed for me." (Ibn Najjar in Kanzul Ummal)*

Ali ؓ Teaches Adhkar and Du'as to Abdullah bin Ja'far ؓ

Abdullah bin Ja'far ؓ used to teach his daughters certain words of Du'a and instructed them to always recite them. He mentioned that it was Ali ؓ who taught these to him and informed him that Rasulullah ﷺ used to recite them whenever he faced a difficulty or was worried about something. The words were: لَا إِلٰهَ إِلَّا اللهُ الْحَلِيْمُ الْكَرِيْمُ، سُبْحَانَهُ تَبَارَكَ اللهُ رَبُّ الْعَالَمِيْنَ وَرَبُّ الْعَرْشِ الْعَظِيْمِ وَالْحَمْدُ للهِ رَبِّ الْعَالَمِيْنَ *There is none worthy of worship but Allah The Most Tolerant and Magnanimous. Pure is He the Most Blessed Allah Who is the Rabb of the universe and the Rabb of the Glorious Throne. All praise belongs to Allah the Rabb of the universe."* (Nasa'ee, Abu Nu'aym in Kanzul Ummal)

Abdullah bin Ja'far ؓ says, "Ali ؓ once said to me, 'Dear nephew! I shall teach you some words that I heard from Rasulullah ﷺ. Whoever recites them at the time of his death shall certainly enter Jannah. They are to recite 3 times: لَا إِلٰهَ إِلَّا اللهُ الْحَلِيْمُ الْكَرِيْمُ *'There is none worthy of worship but Allah The Most Tolerant and Magnanimous'*
To recite 3 times: الْحَمْدُ للهِ رَبِّ الْعَالَمِيْنَ
'All praise belongs to Allah the Rabb of the universe'
To recite 3 times: تَبَارَكَ الَّذِيْ بِيَدِهِ الْمُلْكُ يُحْيِيْ وَ يُمِيْتُ وَهُوَ عَلٰى كُلِّ شَيْءٍ قَدِيْرٌ *'Blessed is the Being in whose hand is all kingdom, who gives life and death and Who has power over all things'* (Khara'iti in Makarimul Akhlaq, Kanzul Ummal)

Rasulullah ﷺ Teaches Adhkar and Du'as to Some Sahabah

Sa'd bin Junada ؓ says, "I was one of the first persons from the people of Ta'if to meet Rasulullah ﷺ to accept Islam. I left early in the morning from Sarat in the upper reaches of Ta'if and reached Mina at the time of Asr. I then climbed a mountain and descended to Makkah where I accepted Islam. Rasulullah ﷺ then taught me the words: سُبْحَانَ اللهِ وَالْحَمْدُ للهِ وَلَا إِلٰهَ إِلَّا اللهُ وَاللهُ أَكْبَرُ Rasulullah ﷺ then said, "These words are the Baqiyatus Salihat (everlasting good deeds) (ref. Kahaf:46 and Maryam:76) (Tabrani in Tafsir Ibn Kathir)

Ubay bin Ka'b ؓ narrates that Rasulullah ﷺ taught them to recite the following Du'a every morning: أَصْبَحْنَا عَلٰى فِطْرَةِ الْإِسْلَامِ وَكَلِمَةِ الْإِخْلَاصِ وَسُنَّةِ نَبِيِّنَا مُحَمَّدٍ صَلَّى اللهُ عَلَيْهِ وَسَلَّمَ وَمِلَّةِ إِبْرَاهِيْمَ حَنِيْفًا وَّمَا كَانَ مِنَ الْمُشْرِكِيْنَ
"We begin the morning on the natural way of Islam, the Kalima of sincerity, the Sunnah of our Nabi Muhammad ﷺ and on the creed of Ibrahim who was never a Mushrik."
Rasulullah ﷺ also taught them to recite the same Du'a in the evenings." (Abdullah bin Ahmad in Zawa'id, Kanzul Ummal)

Sa'd ؓ reports that Rasulullah ﷺ taught them the following Du'a just as a teacher would teach children to write: اللّٰهُمَّ إِنِّيْ أَعُوْذُبِكَ مِنَ الْبُخْلِ وَأَعُوْذُبِكَ مِنَ الْجُبْنِ وَأَعُوْذُبِكَ مِنْ أَنْ أُرَدَّ إِلٰى أَرْذَلِ الْعُمُرِ وَأَعُوْذُبِكَ مِنْ فِتْنَةِ الدُّنْيَا وَعَذَابِ الْقَبْرِ
"O Allah! I beseech You to protect me from miserliness, from cowardice, from being returned to an age of infirmity (senility), from the tribulations of this world and from punishment in the grave." (Ibn Jareer in Kanzul Ummal)

Naufal ؓ narrates, "Rasulullah ﷺ taught us the following Du'a to be recited when a person passes away: اللّٰهُمَّ اغْفِرْ لِإِخْوَانِنَا وَأَصْلِحْ ذَاتَ بَيْنِنَا وَأَلِّفْ بَيْنَ قُلُوْبِنَا اللّٰهُمَّ هٰذَا عَبْدُكَ فُلَانُ ابْنُ فُلَانٍ وَلَا نَعْلَمُ إِلَّا خَيْرًا وَأَنْتَ أَعْلَمُ بِهِ مِنَّا فَاغْفِرْ لَنَا وَلَه
'O Allah! Forgive our brothers, unite us and create love between us. O Allah! We know only good of this servant of Yours (take his name) but You know him better than us. Do forgive us and him.'
I was the youngest of the Sahabah at the time and I asked, 'And what if I do not know anything good about him?' Rasulullah ﷺ

replied, 'Say only that which you are certain of." (Abu Nu'aym in Kanzul Ummal). Ubadah bin Samit ؓ narrates that when Ramadhan arrived, Rasulullah ﷺ would teach them the following Du'a: اللّٰهُمَّ سَلِّمْنِيْ لِرَمَضَانَ وَسَلِّمْ رَمَضَانَ لِيْ وَسَلِّمْهُ لِيْ مُتَقَبَّلًا
"O Allah! Keep me safe and well for Ramadhan, keep Ramadhan safe and well for me and accept it (fasting and Ibadah) from me." (Tabrani in Du'a, Daylami in Kanzul Ummal)

Ali ؓ Teaches People How to Send Salutations to Rasulullah ﷺ

Salama Kindi narrates that Ali ؓ taught the people to send salutations to Rasulullah ﷺ with the following words: دَاحِيَ الْمَدْحُوَّاتِ وَبَارِئَ الْمَسْمُوْكَاتِ وَجَبَّارَ الْقُلُوْبِ عَلٰى فِطْرَتِهَا شَقِيّهَا وَسَعِيْدِهَا اجْعَلْ شَرَائِفَ صَلَوَاتِكَ وَنَوَاحِيَ بَرَكَاتِكَ وَرَأفَةَ تَحَنُّنِكَ عَلٰى مُحَمَّدٍ عَبْدِكَ وَرَسُوْلِكَ الْخَاتِمِ لِمَا سَبَقَ وَالْفَاتِحِ لِمَا اغْلَقَ وَالْمُعْلِنِ الْحَقَّ بِالْحَقِّ وَالدَّامِغِ لِجَيْشَاتِ الْأَبَاطِيْلِ كَمَا حُمِّلَ فَاضْطَلَعَ بِأَمْرِكَ بِطَاعَتِكَ مُسْتَوْفِزًا فِيْ مَرْضَاتِكَ غَيْرَ نِكِلٍ عَنْ قَدَمٍ وَّلَامُؤَنٍ فِيْ عَزْمٍ وَاعِيَالِوَحْيِكَ حَافِظًا لِعَهْدِكَ مَاضِيًا عَلٰى نَفَاذِ أَمْرِكَ حَتّٰى أَوْرٰى قَبَسًالِقَابِسٍ بَعْدَ خَوْضَاتِ الْفِتَنِ وَالاثْمِ وَأَبْهَجَ مُوْضِحَاتِ الْأَعْلَامِ وَمُنِيْرَاتِ الْإِسْلَامِ وَنَائِرَاتِ الْأَحْكَامِ فَهُوَأَمِيْنُكَ الْمَأمُوْنُ وَخَازِنُ عِلْمِكَ الْمَخْزُوْنِ وَشَهِيْدُكَ يَوْمَ الدِّيْنِ وَبَعِيْثُكَ نِعْمَةً وَرَسُوْلُكَ بِالْحَقِّ رَحْمَةً اللّٰهُمَّ افْسَحْ لَه مُفْسَحًا فِيْ عَدْنِكَ وَاجْزِهِ مُضَاعَفَاتِ الْخَيْرِ مِنْ فَضْلِكَ مُهَنَّآتٍ غَيْرَ مُكَدَّرَاتٍ مِنْ فَوْزِ ثَوَابِكَ الْمَعْلُوْلِ وَجَزِيْلِ عَطَائِكَ الْمَخْزُوْنِ اللّٰهُمَّ أَعْلِ عَلٰى بِنَاءِ النَّاسِ بِنَاءَه وَأَكْرِمْ مَثْوَاهُ لَدَيْكَ وَنُزُلَه وَأَتْمِمْ لَه نُوْرَه وَاجْزِهِ مِنِ ابْتِعَاثِكَ لَه مَقْبُوْلَ الشَّهَادَةِ وَمَرْضِيَّ الْمَقَالَةِ ذَامَنْطِقٍ عَدْلٍ وَكَلَامٍ فَصْلٍ وَحُجَّةٍ وَبُرْهَانٍ عَظِيْمٍ
"O Allah The One Who has spread out the earth and created the heavens. O The One Who has authority over the nature of hearts, they be good or evil. Bestow Your most selected mercies, Your every increasing blessings and the kindest of Your compassion on Muhammad ﷺ who is Your servant and Rasul, who is the seal of the prophets before him, the key to the locked treasures of wisdom and Your graces, the one who used the truth to make the truth evident and who repelled the armies of falsehood. As was entrusted to him, he fulfilled Your commands with the valor of his obedience to You and was always prepared to please you without shuffling his feet about and without weakness in his resolve. He called towards Your revelation, fulfilled his pledge to You and constantly strove to enact Your commands until the fire of Islam had been strengthened for anyone wishing to take a spark from it. It is by him that hearts were guided after being immersed in evil and vice. It was him who made manifest the clear signs and distinct features of Islam and its unmistakable injunctions. He is the one whom You trust and with whom You have placed Your trust. He is the treasurer to Your knowledge and the one in whom You have vested Your knowledge. He shall be Your witness on the Day of Judgment and it is he whom You have sent with Your bounties. He is after all, Your true Rasul. O Allah! Expand Your eternal Jannah for him and from Your ever-increasing grace, do reward him with the purest of rewards that are given time and time again and grant him from Your abundant bounties that are safely treasured. O Allah! Raise his house above all others, grant him the best hospitality with You and grant him the most complete light. When You raise him (on the Day of Judgment), do also grant him the privilege of having his testimony accepted by Yourself and let his words be pleasing to You, just, decisive and a clear and triumphant proof against the Kuffar." (Tabrani in Awsat, Abu Nu'aym in Awali of Sa'eed bin Mansur, Kanzul Ummal, Tafsir Ibn Kathir)

Teaching Guests who came to Madinah: Rasulullah ﷺ asks the Sahabah to Teach the Delegation from the Abdul Qais Tribe

Shihab bin Abbad reports that he heard a Sahabi who had

been part of the Abdul Qais delegation say, "When we came to Rasulullah ﷺ, the Muslims were extremely happy with our arrival and they made ample way for us to sit when we reached their gathering. Rasulullah ﷺ welcomed us and as he looked at us, he asked who our leader was. When we all indicated that he was Mundhir bin A'idh, Rasulullah ﷺ remarked, 'Is he the Ashaj (the one with the scar on his face)?' This was the first time that this name was used for him on account of an injury to his face caused by the hoof of a donkey. 'That is him, O Rasulullah ﷺ!' we confirmed. Mundhir ؓ had stayed behind the rest of the delegation when they went before Rasulullah ﷺ to tie their animals and secure their belongings. He then took out his bag, removed his traveling clothes and wore his best clothes. When he made his way to Rasulullah ﷺ, Rasulullah ﷺ was reclining with his legs stretched out. As he approached the gathering, the people made way for him, saying, 'Sit here, O Ashaj.' Rasulullah ﷺ was now sitting up, holding his legs up. Rasulullah ﷺ said, 'Sit here, O Ashaj.' He sat on Rasulullah ﷺ's right hand side and, sitting up straight, Rasulullah ﷺ welcomed him and treated him warmly. Rasulullah ﷺ then asked him about his land, taking the names of various places in the territory of Hajar, such as Safa and Mushaqar. 'May my parents be sacrificed for you, O Rasulullah ﷺ!' Mundhir ؓ said in astonishment, 'You know the names of our towns better than us.' Rasulullah ﷺ said, 'I have traveled extensively through your land.' Rasulullah ﷺ then turned to the Ansar saying, 'O assembly of Ansar! Treat your brothers well because together with being Muslims like you, they also resemble you most closely in hair and complexion. Like you they have accepted Islam willingly and have neither been forced to accept nor was there any need to attack and fight them for refusing to accept.' The Ansar then hosted the delegation. Some time later, Rasulullah ﷺ asked the delegation, 'How did you find the hospitality that your brothers gave you?' They replied, 'They are the best of brothers. They gave us soft beds to sleep in; superb food to eat and they spent their days and nights teaching us the Book of our Rabb and the Sunnah of our Nabi ﷺ.' This impressed Rasulullah ﷺ and made him very happy. Rasulullah ﷺ then turned to each one of us to assess what we had learnt and what we had been taught. While some of us had learnt the Tashahud, some had learnt Surah Fatiha, others had learnt a Surah, others 2 Surahs and there were also others who had learnt 1 or 2 Sunnah practices." The narration continues further in great detail. (Ahmad, Haythami, Mundhiri in Targheeb wat Tarheeb)

Abu Sa'eed Khudri ؓ reports, "We were sitting with Rasulullah ﷺ when he said, 'A delegation from the Abdul Qais have come.' We could see no one, but after a short while, we saw that they had arrived. After they had greeted Rasulullah ﷺ, he said to them, 'Have you any dates or any provisions left over?' When they said that they had, Rasulullah ﷺ had leather spread laid out. They then poured out the dates they had left over and Rasulullah ﷺ gathered the Sahabah around. Rasulullah ﷺ then said to them, 'This date is called Barni.' He then proceeded to name all the different varieties of dates and the delegation confirmed all the names as correct. Thereafter Rasulullah ﷺ gave instructions for every man of the delegation to be hosted by one of the Muslims, who would teach him the Qur'an and salah. They stayed a week after which Rasulullah ﷺ summoned them and assessed that they had not yet learnt well enough and had not yet developed a keen understanding of Islam. Rasulullah ﷺ then handed them over to another group of Muslims, with whom they stayed for another week When Rasulullah ﷺ again summoned them and assessed them, he discovered that they had learnt well and developed a sound understanding. 'O Rasulullah ﷺ!' they

submitted, 'Allah has taught us tremendous good and granted us understanding. However, we are now yearning for home.' Rasulullah ﷺ permitted them to return home. Theysaid, 'Why don't we ask Rasulullah ﷺ about the drinks that we consume in our land?'......The Hadith proceeds to cite the prohibition of consuming drinks fermented in pumpkin shells, hollowed wood and dyed containers. (Abdur Razzaq in Kanzul Ummal)

Rasulullah ﷺ Teaches the Injunctions of Deen While Traveling for the Farewell Hajj

Jabir ؓ narrates that after living in Madinah for 9 years, Rasulullah ﷺ did not perform Hajj until the announcement was made one day that Rasulullah ﷺ would be performing Hajj that year. A great multitude of people then arrived in Madinah with the intention of following Rasulullah ﷺ and doing what he did. There were still 5 days left of Dhul Qa'dah when Rasulullah ﷺ left Madinah with the Sahabah. It was when they reached Dhul Hulaifa that Muhammad bin Abu Bakr ؓ was born to Asma bint Umais. She sent a message to ask Rasulullah ﷺ what she needed to do, Rasulullah ﷺ replied saying, "Take a bath, use a cloth to hold the blood and enter into Ihram." Rasulullah ﷺ then proceeded further and it was when his camel took him to Baida that he called out the Talbiya of Towheed saying:

لَبَّيْكَ اللّٰهُمَّ لَبَّيْكَ لَبَّيْكَ لَاشَرِيْكَ لَبَّيْكَ إِنَّ الْحَمْدَ وَالنِّعْمَةَ لَكَ وَالْمُلْكَ لَاشَرِيْكَ لَكَ

The Sahabah also recited the Talbiya and although Rasulullah ﷺ heard some of them add phrases like ذا المعارج ("Dhal Ma'arij"), he did not rebuke them. Jabir ؓ says, "The people in front of Rasulullah ﷺ reached as far as I could see. They were on foot and on animals. Behind Rasulullah ﷺ were just as many people, and there were also that many on his right and his left. Rasulullah ﷺ was in our midst and he was well aware of the meanings of the Qur'anic verses that came to him. We did exactly what we saw Rasulullah ﷺ doing." (Ahmad in Al Bidayah wan Nihayah). The aspects of Deen that Rasulullah ﷺ taught the Sahabah on this journey and in the sermons he delivered during the Hajj will be quoted in the chapter on Hajj.

The Incident of How Jabir Ghadiri ؓ Acquired Knowledge During Rasulullah ﷺ's Journey

Jabir bin Azraq Ghadiri ؓ says, "I was riding my animal and carrying my provisions when I came to Rasulullah ﷺ. I rode with him until we reached a waypoint. Rasulullah ﷺ dismounted and entered a leather tent, the door of which was guarded by more than 30 men armed with whips. As I drew closer, one of them started pushing me away. I said, 'If you push me, I shall push you and if you hit me, I shall hit you.' 'You must be the worst of all men!' he remarked. 'By Allah!' I retorted, 'You are worse than me.' 'How is that?' he asked. I have come form the far ends of Yemen to listen to Rasulullah ﷺ so that I may report back to my people at home, yet you are pushing me away.' 'You are right,' the man submitted, 'I swear by Allah that I am worse than you.' Rasulullah ﷺ rode on and it was from the Jamarah Aqabah in Mina that people started crowding around him in great numbers to ask him questions. However, because of their large numbers, none of them could get close to him. A man who had trimmed and not shaven off his hair came to Rasulullah ﷺ saying, 'O Rasulullah ﷺ! Do pray that Allah showers His mercy on me.' Rasulullah ﷺ said, 'May Allah shower His mercy on those who shave off their hair.' Again the man pleaded, 'Do pray that Allah showers His mercy on me.' Rasulullah ﷺ repeated, 'May Allah shower His mercy on those who shave off their hair.' The man again appealed, 'Do pray that Allah showers His mercy on me', Rasulullah ﷺ said, 'May Allah shower His mercy on those who shave off their hair.' Rasulullah ﷺ repeated 3 times, the man went to have his hair shaved off. Later, I only saw men with shaved heads." *(Abu Nu'aym in Kanzul Ummal, Ibn Mandah in Isabah)*

Ibn Jareer's Interpretation of the Verse "It is not for the Mu'minin to Proceed in Jihad All Together"

Ibn Jareer has cited numerous interpretations of the verse:

وَمَا كَانَ الْمُؤْمِنُونَ لِيَنفِرُوا كَافَّةً فَلَوْلَا نَفَرَ مِن كُلِّ فِرْقَةٍ مِّنْهُمْ طَائِفَةٌ لِّيَتَفَقَّهُوا فِي الدِّينِ وَلِيُنذِرُوا قَوْمَهُمْ إِذَا رَجَعُوا إِلَيْهِمْ لَعَلَّهُمْ يَحْذَرُونَ (122)

And it is not (proper) for the believers to go out to fight (Jihad) all together. Of every troop of them, a party only should go forth, that they (who are left behind) may get instructions in (Islamic) religion, and that they may warn their people when they return to them, so that they may beware (of evil). (At-Tauba:122)

After citing them, he states: "With regard to the phrase "to attain a deep understanding of Deen so that they may warn their people when they return to them so that they may beware" the most correct interpretation is that of those scholars who say that the deep understanding of Deen is attained by the group proceeding out in Jihad because they witness first-hand the help that Allah renders to the people of the Deen and to the companions of Rasulullah ﷺ against the enemies and Kuffar. It is by this first-hand observation that they can make people understand the truth of Islam and that it will prevail over all other religions. At the same time, when they return home, they may warn their own people against doing anything that will attract Allah's punishment as they had witnessed it afflict the disbelievers whom they had conquered. Thus their people will beware not to transgress Allah's commands. The verse tells us that when these people warn their people about what they have seen, their people would take heed and their Iman in Allah and His Rasul ﷺ would increase out of fear that they should not be afflicted by the punishment that afflicted the people they have been informed about." *(Ibn Jareer)*

The statement of Abu Sa'eed Khudri ؓ About How the Sahabah Combined Fighting Battles with Acquiring Knowledge

Abu Sa'eed Khudri ؓ says, "When we marched to battles, we would leave behind one or two men to listen to Ahadeeth from Rasulullah ﷺ and when we returned from the battle, they would narrate to us all that Rasulullah ﷺ said. Therefore, when we narrate these Ahadeeth, we can say that Rasulullah ﷺ said it." *(Ibn Abi Khaithama, Ibn Asakir in Kanzul Ummal)*

The Narration of Anas ؓ about How the Sahabah Combined Earning with Acquiring Knowledge

Thabit Bunani reports that Anas bin Malik ؓ mentioned 70 men from the Ansar who would go to a specific place in Madinah as soon as night fell. They would then spend the night there learning and teaching the Qur'an. When morning arrived, whoever amongst them still had some strength would gather firewood and fetch drinking water. Those who had some money would then slaughter a goat, prepare the meat and hang it at Rasulullah ﷺ's rooms. Anas ؓ continues, "When Khubaib ؓ was martyred in Makkah, Rasulullah ﷺ dispatched these 70 Sahabah on an expedition. Amongst the group was my uncle Haram bin Milhan ؓ. When they approached a clan belonging to the Banu Sulaim tribe who seemed hostile, Haram ؓ addressed the leader of the clan saying, 'May I inform your people that we have no intention of attacking them so that they may leave us alone.' The leader agreed but it was when Haram ؓ was addressing the people that someone thrust a spear at him that penetrated right through his body. When Haram felt the spear strike his belly, he exclaimed, 'Allahu Akbar! I swear by the Rabb of the Kabah that I am successful!' The people of the clan then attacked the other Sahabah and did not spare anyone to tell the tale. I have never seen Rasulullah so pained about any expedition than he was at this. In fact, every time Rasulullah ﷺ performed the Fajr salah, I would see him raise his hands to curse the people of the clan." *(Abu Nu'aym in Hilya)*. Thabit narrates that Anas ؓ said, "A group of people once approached Rasulullah ﷺ with the request, 'Send some people with us to teach us the Qur'an and the Sunnah.' Rasulullah ﷺ sent a group of Ansar with them who were referred to as the Qurra. Amongst the Qurra was my uncle Haram ؓ. These were a group of Sahabah who were proficient in the Qur'an and who spent the nights learning and teaching the Qur'an. During the day they would fetch water to place in the Masjid and also gather firewood to sell. The profits of their sales were then employed to purchase food for the men of Suffa and other poor people. When Rasulullah ﷺ sent them, they were attacked and martyred before they could even reach their destination. Their final Du'a was, 'O Allah! Convey the message to Your Nabi ﷺ on our behalf that we have already met with You, that we are pleased with You and that You are pleased with us.' It was from the back that a man thrust a spear right through the body of my uncle Haram ؓ. When this happened, Haram ؓ exclaimed, 'I swear by the Rabb of the Kabah that I am successful!' Rasulullah ﷺ in Madinah informed the Sahabah about the situation saying, 'Your brothers have been martyred and have prayed, 'O Allah! Convey the message to Your Nabi ﷺ on our behalf that we have already met with You, that we are pleased with You and that You are pleased with us.'" *(Ibn Sa'd)*

Omar ؓ and his Ansari Neighbor Take Turns to Learn

Abdullah bin Abbas ؓ reports that Omar ؓ said, "I had an Ansari neighbor from the upper reaches of Madinah who belonged to the Banu Umayya bin Zaid tribe. He took turns with me in attending Rasulullah ﷺ's gatherings. He would go one day and me the next so that he brought me the news of revelation and other matters the day he went and I brought it to him the day I went. It was on the day when it was his turn that he came knocking hard on my door, calling, 'Is Omar here!' I was alarmed and came out immediately. 'Something serious has taken place,' he said... When I went to see Hafsa, she was in tears. 'Has Rasulullah ﷺ divorced you?' I queried. 'I do not know,' she replied; I then went to Rasulullah ﷺ and was still standing when I asked, 'Have you divorced your wives?'. When Rasulullah ﷺ declared that he had not, I cried out 'Allahu Akbar!'" *(Bukhari)*

Bara ؓ says that All of Them could not Hear Ahadeeth From Rasulullah ﷺ

Bara ؓ says, "All of us (Sahabah) were unable to devote all our time to listen to Ahadeeth from Rasulullah ﷺ because we had properties and occupations that kept us busy. However, during those days, no one spoke lies and those who were with Rasulullah ﷺ would convey the Ahadeeth to those who were absent." *(Hakim)*. Bara ؓ said. "We did not hear every Hadith directly from Rasulullah ﷺ but our companions would narrate them to us when we were unable to be with Rasulullah ﷺ because we were grazing the camels." *(Hakim in Ma'rifa Uloomil Hadith), Ahmad, Haythami, Abu Nu'aym in Kanzul Ummal)*

Talha ؓ says that it was During the Ends of the Day that They went to Rasulullah ﷺ

Abu Anas Malik bin Abu Amir Asbahi says that he was with Talha bin Ubaidullah ؓ when a man came to him saying, "O

Abu Muhammad! By Allah! We do not know whether Abu Hurairah ﷺ knows more about Rasulullah ﷺ than the rest of you Sahabah! He seems to be making stories about Rasulullah ﷺ that you others do not mention." Talha ﷺ replied, "By Allah! We have no doubts about the fact that he has heard from Rasulullah ﷺ what we have not heard and knows what we do not know. Because we were independent people with houses and families, we would go to Rasulullah ﷺ at the 2 ends of the day, after which we would return home. On the other hand, Abu Hurairah ﷺ was a poor man with neither wealth, family or children. He was always with Rasulullah ﷺ and went wherever Rasulullah ﷺ went. We have no doubts about the fact that he knows what we do not know and has heard from Rasulullah ﷺ what we have not heard. None of us have ever accused him of attributing to Rasulullah ﷺ statements that he never made." *(Hakim)*

Learning the Deen Before earning a Living

Omar ﷺ said, "None may trade in our marketplace unless he had developed an understanding of Deen so he can trade in a manner that complies with the Shari'ah." *(Tirmidhi in Kanzul Ummal)*

Ali ﷺ's Interpretation of the Verse: "Save Yourselves and Your Families From the Fire"

Allah says in the Qur'an: اقُوا اَنْفُسَكُمْ وَاَهْلِيكُمْ نَارًا

"... Ward off yourselves and your families against a Fire (Hell)..." (At-Tahrim:6)

On the above verse, Ali ﷺ said, "Educate yourselves and your families in all that is good." *(Hakim in Targheeb wat Tarheeb).* Ali ﷺ's interpretation as, *"Teach them (your families) and educate them in good manners." (Tabari in Tafsir).*

Rasulullah ﷺ Instructs People to Teach and Educate Their Families

Malik bin Huwairith ﷺ reports, "We were a few youngsters of similar ages when we came to Rasulullah ﷺ and stayed with him for 20 days. When Rasulullah ﷺ sensed that we were yearning for home, he asked us about our families and we told him about them. Rasulullah ﷺ was extremely compassionate and merciful so he said to us, 'You may return home. You should however teach your families the Deen you have learnt, instruct them to fulfill the requisites of Deen and perform your salah as you have seen me performing salah. When the time for salah arrives, one of you should call out the Adhan and the eldest amongst you should lead the salah" *(Bukhari in Adab)*

Rasulullah ﷺ Instructs Zaid ﷺ to Learn the Jewish Language

Zaid bin Thabit ﷺ says, "When Rasulullah ﷺ just arrived in Madinah and I was brought before him, the people said, 'O Rasulullah ﷺ! This boy from the Banu Najjar tribe has already learnt 17 of the Surahs that have been revealed to you.' When I then recited to Rasulullah ﷺ, he was very impressed and said, 'O Zaid! Would you learn how to write the Jewish language because I swear by Allah, I do not trust them to write for me.' I started learning the language and it was barely half a month later that I had mastered it. I was therefore Rasulullah's scribe when he wrote to the Jews and I would read to him the letters they wrote to me." *(Abu Ya'la, Ibn Asakir).* In another narration, Zaid ﷺ says, "Rasulullah ﷺ once asked me, 'Do you know the Syrian language well because letters written in that language come to me?' When I declared that I did not, Rasulullah ﷺ requested me to learn it. I then learnt the language in 17 days." *(Abu Ya'la, Ibn Asakir, Ibn Abi Dawud).* Rasulullah ﷺ once said to Zaid ﷺ, "Certain letters come to me that I would not like just anyone to read for me. Would it be possible for you to learn to write in the Hebrew or Syrian language?" Zaid ﷺ complied and learnt it in 17 days. *(Ibn Abi Dawud, Ibn Asakir in Mumtakhab Kanzul Ummal)*

Abdullah bin Zubair ﷺ Understands the Language of His Slaves

Omar bin Qais says, "Although Abdullah bin Zubair ﷺ had 100 slaves, all of whom spoke a different language, he was capable of speaking to each of them in his own language. Whenever I saw him engaged in any worldly affair, I would say, 'Here is a man who does not think of Allah for the blinking of an eye.' Then when I would see him engaged in any matter of the Hereafter, I would say, 'Here is a man who does not think of this world for the blinking of an eye.'" *(Hakim, Abu Nu'aym in Hilya).*

Omar ﷺ Instructs the Study of Astronomy and Genealogy

Omar ﷺ said, "Study as much astronomy as will assist you to navigate over land and sea during the darkness. Thereafter you should stop." *(Ibn Abdul Birr in Ilm).* Another narration states that Omar ﷺ said, "Study as much astronomy as will assist you in navigation and study as much genealogy as will assist you in maintaining good family ties." *(Hannad in Kanzul Ummal)*

Ali ﷺ Instructs Abul Aswad Duwali to Write the Fatha, Dhamma and Kasra into the Qur'anic Text

Sa'sa'a bin Sowhan narrates that a Bedouin once came to Ali ﷺ and asked, "O Amirul Mu'minin! How do you recite the verse:........'Only those who take steps shall eat it (the filth of Jahannam)'? By Allah! Every one of us takes steps!" Ali ﷺ smiled and recited the verse thus: لَا يَأْكُلُهُ إِلَّا الْخَاطِئُونَ (37)

None will eat except the Khatioon (sinners, disbelievers, polytheists, etc.). (Al-Haqqa:37)

The Bedouin said, "You have spoken the truth, O Amirul Mu'minin. It is not like Allah to just leave His servant in Jahannam." Ali ﷺ turned to Abul Aswad Duwali and said, "All types of non-Arabs are entering into the fold of Islam, so include something in the Qur'anic script by which they may receive guidance to recite properly." Then the Fatha, Dhamma and Kasra were written. *(Bayhaqi, Ibn Asakir, Ibn Najjar in Kanzul Ummal)*

For a Leader to Appoint Someone to Teach the People

Urwa ﷺ reports that Rasulullah ﷺ left for Hunain, he appointed Mu'aadh bin Jabal ﷺ over the Makkans with instructions to teach the Qur'an to the people and to create an understanding of Deen. Rasulullah ﷺ left for Madinah, he appointed Mu'aadh ﷺ over the Makkans *(Hakim).* Mujahid narrates that Rasulullah ﷺ appointed Mu'adh ﷺ over the Makkans when he left for Hunain so that he should create an understanding of Deen and teach them the Qur'an. *(Ibn Sa'd)*

Omar ﷺ confines Zaid bin Thabit ﷺ in Madinah to teach the People

Qasim narrates that whenever Omar ﷺ left on a journey, he would leave Zaid bin Thabit ﷺ as his deputy in Madinah. Whereas Omar ﷺ used to dispatch men to various cities for teaching, he would send Zaid bin Thabit ﷺ only for the most vital tasks but would otherwise keep him in Madinah. When requests were made by the people of the various Islamic territories to send specific people and Zaid ﷺ was asked for by name, Omar ﷺ would say, "Zaid's status in my estimation has not fallen at all. I keep him back only because the people of Madinah need Zaid in the matters they encounter and cannot get from anyone else what they get from him." *(Ibn Sa'd).* Salim bin

Abdullah says, "We were with Abdullah bin Omar ؓ the day Zaid bin Thabit ؓ passed away. 'A great Alim has passed away today,' I remarked. 'May Allah shower His mercy on him today,' Abdullah bin Omar ؓ commented, 'He was certainly a great Alim and academic during the Khilafa of Omar ؓ. While Omar ؓ dispatched many people to the various cities and forbade them from passing verdicts by their own judgment, Zaid ؓ used to sit in Madinah and pass verdicts for the people of Madinah and those coming from outside.'" *(Ibn Sa'd)*

Zaid bin Thabit ؓ Teaches People During the Khilafa of Uthman ؓ and the Statement of Omar ؓ about Mu'adh ؓ's Leaving for Sham

Abu Abdul Rahman Sulami reports that he used to recite the Qur'an to Uthman ؓ. However, Uthman ؓ once told him, "If you continue to do this, you will be distracting me from tending to public matters. You had rather go to Zaid bin Thabit ؓ because he has more time for this. Recite to him because his and my recitation is the same, without any differences whatsoever." *(Ibn Ambari in Muntakhab Kanzul Ummal)*. Ka'b bin Malik ؓ narrates that Omar ؓ used to say, "The departure of Mu'adh bin Jabal ؓ to Sham was an event that presented much difficulty to Madinah and its people with regard to questions of Islamic jurisprudence and the religious rulings (Fatawa) that Mu'adh ؓ issued. I had spoken to Abu Bakr ؓ about keeping Mua'dh ؓ behind in Madinah because the people needed him but Abu Bakr ؓ refused this request saying, 'I cannot stop a man who wants to go somewhere in search of martyrdom.' I responded by saying, 'By Allah! When a person is serving important interests of his people, he will be blessed with the status of a martyr even as he lies on bed in his own home.'"

Sending Sahabah to various lands for teaching: Rasulullah ﷺ sends a Group of Sahabah to Educate the Udhal and Qara Tribes

Asim bin Omar bin Qatadah narrates that delegates from the Udhal and Qara tribes, both branches of the Jadila clan, came to Rasulullah ﷺ after the battle of Uhud. They requested Rasulullah ﷺ saying, "Islam has come to our land, so please send some of your companions with us to teach us the Qur'an and assist us in understanding Islam." Rasulullah ﷺ then sent 6 Sahabah, the Amir of whom was Marthad bin Abu Marthad ؓ, who was a close friend of Hamzah bin Abdul Muttalib ؓ. The Hadith then continues to speak about the battle of Raji. *(Hakim)*

Rasulullah ﷺ Sends Ali ؓ and Abu Ubaidah bin Jarrah ؓ to Yemen

Ali ؓ narrates, "Some people from Yemen once came to Rasulullah ﷺ saying, 'Please send to us someone who will help us develop an understanding of the Deen, who will teach us the Sunnah and judge between us by the Book of Allah.' Rasulullah ﷺ said, 'O Ali! Go to the people of Yemen, develop an understanding of Deen amongst them, teach them the Sunnah and judge between them by the Book of Allah.' I responded by saying, 'But the people of Yemen are foolish who will bring me cases about which I will have no knowledge.' Rasulullah ﷺ placed his hand on my chest and reassured me saying, 'Go. Allah shall guide your heart and make your tongue firm.' By the blessings of this Du'a until this day, I have never doubted my judgment I have passed between 2 persons." *(Ibn Jareer in Muntakhab Kanzul Ummal)*. Anas ؓ narrates that some people from Yemen approached Rasulullah ﷺ with the request, "Send with us someone who will teach us the Qur'an." Rasulullah ﷺ took hold of the hand of Abu Ubaidah ؓ and sent him saying, "This is the most trustworthy person of my Ummah." *(Hakim)*.

The people of Yemen requested Rasulullah ﷺ for someone who would teach them the Sunnah and Islam. *(Ibn Sa'd)*

Rasulullah ﷺ Sends Amr bin Hazam ؓ, Abu Musa Ash'ari ؓ and Mu'adh bin Jabal ؓ to Yemen

Abu Bakr bin Muhammad bin Amr bin Hazam said. "Here with us is the letter of appointment that Rasulullah ﷺ had written for Amr bin Hazam ؓ when Rasulullah ﷺ sent him to Yemen to educate the people in Islam, to teach them the Sunnah and to collect their zakah. The letter was an undertaking from Amr bin Hazam ؓ and a briefing. The letter stated:
*"In the name of Allah, the Most Kind, the Most Merciful
This is a letter from Allah and His Rasul ﷺ.*

يَا أَيُّهَا الَّذِينَ آمَنُوا أَوْفُوا بِالْعُقُودِ

O you who believe! Fulfill (your) obligations... (Al-Ma'ida:1)

This is an undertaking that Rasulullah ﷺ is making with Amr bin Hazam when dispatching him to Yemen. His instructions are to have Taqwa in all matters because verily Allah loves those who have Taqwa and those who do good." *(Ibn Abi Hatim in Tafsir Ibn Kathir)*. Abu Musa Ash'ari ؓ reports that Rasulullah ﷺ send him and Mu'adh bin Jabal ؓ to Yemen with instructions to teach the Qur'an to the people. *(Abu Nu'aym in Hilya)*

Rasulullah ﷺ sends Ammar ؓ to a Clan of the Qais Tribe

Ammar bin Yasir ؓ relates, "Rasulullah ﷺ sent me to a clan belonging to the Qais tribe to teach them the Shari'ah of Islam. I found them to be like wild camels, with their gazes always aspiring for more and with no other interests besides their goats and camels. I therefore returned to Rasulullah ﷺ, who asked, 'O Ammar! What happened?' When I related to Rasulullah ﷺ what the people were like and how indifferent they were, Rasulullah ﷺ said, 'O Ammar! Should I not inform you of people even stranger than these? They are people who know what these people are ignorant of and are still indifferent towards it as these people are.'" *(Bazzar, Tabrani in Kabir, Targheeb wat Tarheeb)*

Omar ؓ Dispatches Ammar ؓ and Abdullah bin Mas'ood ؓ to Kufa and Sends Imran ؓ to Basra

Haritha bin Mudarib narrates that he read the letter Omar ؓ wrote to the people of Kufa. The letter read:
> *"I have sent Ammar ؓ as your governor and Abdullah bin Mas'ood ؓ as your teacher and advisor. These two are from amongst the choicest companions of Rasulullah ﷺ, so listen to them and follow them. Take note that I have given precedence to you people over myself by sending Abdullah bin Mas'ood ؓ to you (because I require him here in Madinah)." (Ibn Sa'd)*

Abul Aswad Duwali says, "When I arrived in Basra, Imran bin Husain ؓ was there. Omar bin Khattab ؓ had sent him there to create an understanding of Deen amongst people." *(Ibn Sa'd)*

Omar ؓ dispatches Mu'adh bin Jabal ؓ and Abu Darda ؓ to Sham

Muhammad bin Ka'b Qurazi ؓ reports that only 5 persons from amongst the Ansar had memorized the entire Qur'an during the lifetime of Rasulullah ﷺ. These were Mu'adh bin Jabal ؓ, Ubadah bin Samit ؓ, Ubay bin Ka'b ؓ, Abu Ayub ؓ and Abu Darda ؓ. It was during the Khilafa of Omar ؓ that Yazid bin Abu Sufian ؓ wrote to Omar ؓ with the request. "The population of Sham is great. The cities are overflowing with people who have accepted Islam and are in dire need of people to teach them the Qur'an and to create an understanding of Deen amongst them. O Amirul Mu'minin! Do assist me by sending men who will teach them." Omar ؓ then sent for the 5 Ansar mentioned and said to them. "Your brothers in Sham have pleaded to me to send to them people who will be able to teach them the Qur'an and create and understanding of Deen amongst the people. Please assist me with 3 of you. May Allah shower His Mercy on you! You may draw lots if you please, or if there are any volunteers amongst you, they may leave immediately." "There is no need to draw lots." they submitted. "While this man Abu Ayub ؓ is too old, this man Ubay bin Ka'b ؓ is ill." It was therefore Mu'adh bin Jabal ؓ, Ubadah bin Samit ؓ and Abu Darda ؓ who went. Omar ؓ's instructions to them were, "Start with Hims because there is a variety of people there and there you will find such people who learn very quickly. When you identify such people, direct the others towards them to learn. When you are eventually satisfied with the people there, one of you may remain behind while the second proceeds to Damascus and the third to Palestine." The 3 Sahabah therefore proceeded to Hims, where they stayed until they were satisfied with the learning of the people. Ubadah ؓ stayed there while Abu Darda ؓ proceeded to Damascus and Mu'adh ؓ to Palestine. Mu'adh ؓ stayed in Palestine until he passed away there in the plague of Amwas. Ubadah bin Samit ؓ left for Palestine and passed away there. As for Abu Darda ؓ, he lived in Damascus until his death. *(Ibn Sa'd, Hakim in Kanzul Ummal, Bukhari in Tarikh Sagheer)*

Undertaking Journeys in Search of Knowledge

Jabir ؓ travels to Sham and to Egypt to hear 2 Ahadeeth of Rasulullah ﷺ Abdullah bin Muhammad bin Aqil reports that he once heard Jabir ؓ, say, "The news once reached me that there was a man who had heard a particular Hadith from Rasulullah ﷺ. I purchased a camel, tied a carriage to it and rode for a month until I reached Sham. When I discovered that the man was Abdullah bin Unais ؓ, I went to his house and said to his usher, 'Tell him that Jabir is at the door.' 'The son of Abdullah?' he enquired. When I replied in the affirmative, Abdullah bin Unais ؓ rushed out, tripping over his clothes in the rush. He hugged me and I hugged him, after which I asked, 'A Hadith narrated by you has reached me concerning retribution. I have come to you as I feared that either you or I would die before I had the opportunity of hearing it directly from you." Abdullah bin Unais ؓ said, "I heard Rasulullah ﷺ say, "On the Day of Judgment Allah shall resurrect people naked, uncircumcised and empty-handed.' Someone asked one of the narrators what was meant by empty-handed, he replied that people will have nothing of their worldly possessions with them. In a voice that those far off can hear just as well as those nearby, Allah will make an announcement stating, 'I am the One Who pays back in full and I am the Master! It is not proper for any person destined for Jahannam to enter Jahannam while a person in Jannah owes him some right that I have not claimed for him. It is not proper for any person destined for Jannah to enter Jannah while a person in Jahannam owes him some right that I have not claimed for him, even though it may be retribution for a single slap.' We asked. 'How will this retribution be done when people will be naked, uncircumcised and empty-handed?' Rasulullah replied, 'It will be done with good and bad deeds. People will pay for their injustices by giving their good deeds to the wronged party and when their good deeds are exhausted, they will be burdened with the sins of the wronged party.'" *(Ahmad, Tabrani, Haythami, Bukhari in Adab, Abu Ya'la in Fat'hul Bari, Ibn Abdul Birr in Jami, Hakim)*

Jabir ؓ says, "I used to hear Hadith from Rasulullah ﷺ concerning retribution which was being narrated by someone in Egypt. I therefore purchased a camel and traveled until I reached Egypt. I then headed for the door of the man..." The Hadith is then similar to the one above. *(Tabrani in Masnadush Shami'een and Tammam in Fawa'id, Fat'hul Bari)*. Maslama bin Mukhallad ؓ narrates, "It was during the period that I was governor of Egypt that my escort once came to me saying, 'There is a Bedouin at the door riding a camel who is requesting to see you.' 'Who are you?' I asked. 'I am Jabir bin Abdullah of the Ansar,' he replied. Looking at him from the upper storey, I said, 'I can come down to you or, if you prefer, you may come up here.' He said, 'Neither should you come down, nor shall I be coming up. I have heard that you narrate a particular Hadith from Rasulullah ﷺ about concealing the faults of a Mu'min. I have come to listen to it.' I said, 'I have heard Rasulullah ﷺ say that the person who conceals a fault of a Mu'min is like one who has given life to a girl who has been buried alive.' He then whipped his camel to lead it back home." *(Tabrani in Awsat, Haythami)*. Munib narrates that the news once reached a particular Sahabi that another Sahabi was narrating a Hadith stating that when a Muslim conceals the faults of his fellow Muslim brother in this world, Allah shall conceal his faults on the Day of Judgment. He traveled to Egypt to ask the Sahabi about the Hadith. The other Sahabi confirmed saying, "Yes, I have heard Rasulullah ﷺ say that when a Muslim conceals the faults of fellow Muslim in this world, Allah shall conceal his faults on the Day of Judgment." The first Sahabi then said, "I too have heard this Hadith from Rasulullah ﷺ." *(Ahmad, Haythami)*

Abu Ayub Ansari ؓ Travels to Egypt to Hear a Hadith from Uqba bin Amir ؓ

Ibn Juraij narrates that Abu Ayub Ansari ؓ traveled all the way to Egypt to see Uqba bin Amir ؓ. When he arrived there, he said, "I wish to ask you about a Hadith that besides you and me, no other companion of Rasulullah ﷺ survives who had heard it. What did you hear Rasulullah ﷺ say about concealing the faults of a Muslim?" Uqba replied, "I have heard Rasulullah ﷺ say, 'Whoever conceals the fault of a Mu'min in this world, Allah shall conceal his faults on the Day of Judgment.'" Abu Ayub ؓ returned to Madinah and narrated the Hadith before even getting off from his conveyance. *(Ahmad, Ibn Abdul Birr in Tsti'ab)*

Uqba bin Amir ؓ Travels to See Maslama bin Mukhallad ؓ and another Sahabi Travels to see Fudhala bin Ubaid ؓ

Makhul narrates that when Uqba bin Amir ؓ went to see Maslama bin Mukhallad ؓ, an argument ensued between the usher and Uqba ؓ. Hearing the voice of Uqba ؓ, Maslama ؓ permitted him entry. When he entered Uqba ؓ said, "I have not come merely to visit you, but have come for an urgent need. Do you remember the day when Rasulullah ﷺ said, 'If a person conceals a sin that he knows his brother committed" Allah will conceal his sins on the Day of Judgment'?" When Maslama ؓ confirmed that he did remember, Uqba ؓ said, "That is why I have come." *(Tabrani in Kabir and Awsat, Haythami)*. Abdullah bin Buraida narrates that a Sahabi once traveled all the way to Egypt to see Fudhala bin Ubaid ؓ about a Hadith. *(Abu Dawud in Fat'hul Bari)* Another similar narration adds the Sahabi came to Fudhala ؓ at a time when he was feeding his camel. When Fudhala ؓ welcomed the Sahabi, he said, "I have not come on a mere visit. Both you and I have heard a particular Hadith from Rasulullah ﷺ and I have come in the hope that you still remember it." "What is the Hadith'?" Fudhala ؓ asked. The narration continues further. *(Darmi)*

Ubaidullah bin Adi ؓ Travels to see Ali ؓ and the Statement of Abdullah bin Mas'ood ؓ about Traveling in Search of Knowledge

Ubaidullah bin Adi ؓ says, "When I heard that Ali ؓ knew a particular Hadith, I feared that if he passed away. I would be unable to hear it from anyone else. I therefore embarked on my journey until I reached him in Iraq." (Khateeb in Fat'hul Bari, Ibn Asakir in Kanzul Ummal). Another narration adds that Ubaidullah bin Adi ؓ said, "When I asked Ali ؓ about the Hadith, he narrated it to me but then made me promise that I would never report it to anyone else. I wish that he had not done that so that I could have narrated it to you people." (Ibn Asakir in Kanzul Ummal). Abdullah bin Mas'ood ؓ said, "If I knew of anyone who has more knowledge of Allah's Book than I, I would definitely travel to him." (Bukhari). Abdullah bin Mas'ood ؓ said, "If a camel could take me to a person who has more knowledge of what has been revealed to Muhammad ﷺ than I have, I shall certainly go to him to increase the knowledge I have." (Ibn Asakir).

Rasulullah ﷺ Sends Abu Tha'laba ؓ to Learn from Abu Ubaidah bin Jarrah ؓ and Praises Him

Abu Tha'iaba ؓ says. "I once went to Rasulullah ﷺ with the request to refer me to someone who could teach well. Rasulullah ﷺ then referred to Abu Ubaidah bin Jarrah ؓ, saying, 'I am referring you to someone who will give you excellent education and teach you exceptional manners." (Ibn Asakir in Kanzul Ummal). Another narration states that Abu Tha'laba ؓ added, "When I came to Abu Ubaidah bin Jarrah ؓ, he was busy talking with Bashir bin Sa'd Abu Nu'man ؓ. Seeing me approach, they fell silent. 'O Abu Ubaidah!' I said, 'By Allah! This is not how Rasulullah ﷺ addressed me; he did not fall silent when I came.' He said, 'Sit down so that' we may narrate a Hadith to you. Rasulullah ﷺ said, 'While you now have a Nabi in your midst, there shall soon come Khilafa on the pattern of Nabuwat, to be followed by monarchy and tyranny." (Tabrani, Haythami).

Rasulullah ﷺ Makes it Clear that Seeking Knowledge From Unworthy People is Amongst the Signs of Judgment

Anas ؓ narrates. "I once asked Rasulullah when the time will come when people will stop enjoining good and forbidding evil. Rasulullah ﷺ replied. 'When that appears amongst you as appeared amongst the Bani Isra'el before you.' 'O Rasulullah ﷺ!' we submitted, 'And what was that?' Rasulullah ﷺ replied, 'When the best amongst you start to compromise principles, when the sinners amongst you start being shameless, when kingship falls to the lot of your youngsters and when the knowledge of Deen is carried by the wretches amongst you." (Ibn Asakir and Ibn Najjar in Kanzul Ummal, Ibn Abdul Birr in Jami). Abu Umayya Jumhi ؓ reports that when they once asked Rasulullah ﷺ about the signs of Judgment, Rasulullah ﷺ said, "Amongst the signs of Judgment is that knowledge will be sought from juniors." (Ibn Andul Birr in Jami, Tabrani, Haythami)

Statements of Omar ؓ and Abdullah bin Mas'ood ؓ Concerning Acquiring Knowledge From Seniors

Abdullah bin Ukaim narrates that Omar ؓ used to say, "Remember that the most truthful words are those of Allah, the best way of life is that of Muhammad ﷺ and the worst of matters are those that have been fabricated matters that have been made part of Deen when they are not. Take note of the fact that people will always remain in good stead as long as their knowledge comes to them from their seniors." (Ibn Abdul Birr in Jami). Bilal bin Yahya reports that Omar ؓ said, "I know exactly when

people will remain righteous and when they will start to degenerate. When the knowledge of Deen will stem from juniors, the seniors will disregard them and degeneration will start. However, when knowledge will stem from the seniors and the juniors will follow them, both groups will be rightly guided." (Ibn Abdul Birr in Jami). Abdullah bin Mas'ood ؓ said. "People will always remain righteous and steadfast as long as their knowledge of Deen comes to them from the Sahabah of Rasulullah ﷺ and from their seniors. However, as soon as it starts coming from their juniors, they will all be destroyed." (Tabrani in Kabeer and Awsat, Haythami, Ibn Abdul Birr in Jami). Abdullah bin Mas'ood ؓ said, "People will always remain in good stead as long as they acquire their knowledge of Deen from their seniors. As soon they start acquiring it from their juniors and sinners, they will all be destroyed." (Ibn Abdul Birr in Jami). Abdullah bin Mas'ood ؓsays, "You people will remain in good stead as long as the knowledge of Deen remains in the custody of your seniors. As soon as it is entrusted to the juniors, they will start to regard the seniors as fools." (Ibn Abdul Birr in Jami)

Mu'awiya ؓ and Omar ؓ Both Warn Against Acquiring Knowledge From People who are not Worthy of It

Mu'awiya ؓ said, "Verily the most effective tool for leading people astray is a man who recites the Qur'an without understanding it and then proceeds to teach it to children, slaves and women who in turn use it to argue with the scholars." (Ibn Abdul Birr in Jami). Omar bin Khattab ؓ said, "I do not fear for this Ummah a Mu'min whose Iman restrains him nor a sinner whose sinful life is manifest. However, what I do fear for them is a man who learns the Qur'an until his tongue is fluent with it but then interprets the Qur'an in a manner it should not be interpreted." (Ibn Abdul Birr in Jami)

Uqba bin Amir ؓ Emphasizes to his Children to Accept Ahadeeth only from Reliable Sources

When Uqba bin Amir ؓ was on his deathbed, he advised his sons saying, "Dear sons! I forbid you from 3 things. Never accept a Hadith of Rasulullah ﷺ except from a reliable person, never ask for loans even though you may have to wear coarse clothing and never take to writing poetry because it will distract your hearts from the Qur'an." (Tabrani, Haythami)

The Sermon Omar ؓ Delivered at Jabiya About Acquiring Knowledge from the Scholars of the Sahabah

Abdullah bin Abbas ؓ narrates that it was at Jabiya that Omar ؓ delivered a sermon to the people saying, "Whoever has any queries about the Qur'an should go to Ubay bin Ka'b ؓ, whoever has any queries about inheritance should go to Zaid bin Thabit ؓ, whoever has any queries about Fiqh should go to Mu'adh bin Jabal ؓ and whoever requires money should come to me because Allah has given me authority over it and entrusted me with its distribution." (Tabrani in Awsat, Haythami)

Salutations and glad tidings for the Student: Rasulullah ﷺ Welcomes Safwan bin Assal ؓ

The narration as passed at the beginning of the chapter in which Safwan bin Assal Muradi ؓ says, "I once came to Rasulullah ﷺ in the Masjid as he was reclining in his red shawl. 'O Rasulullah ﷺ!' I said, 'I have come to seek knowledge.' Rasulullah ﷺ exclaimed, 'Welcome to the seeker of knowledge! Verily out of the love for what the person seeking knowledge is out to seek, the angels encircle him with their wings and then mount each other until they reach the sky above the earth.'"

Abu Sa'eed Khudri ◈ Welcomes Some Students

Abu Harun narrates that whenever they went to Abu Sa'eed Khudri ◈, he would say, "Welcome to the people about whom Rasulullah ﷺ gave us forceful instructions! Rasulullah ﷺ said, 'People are your followers and men will come from far-off places to acquire an understanding of Deen from you. When they come to you, it is my emphatic instruction to you to treat them well." (Tirmidhi). Another narration states that Abu Sa'eed Khudri ◈ quoted Rasulullah ﷺ as saying, "People will come from the East to learn from you. It is my emphatic instruction that when they come to you, you must treat them well." Abu Harun narrates that whenever Abu Sa'eed Khudri ◈ saw them, he would say, "Welcome to the people about whom Rasulullah ﷺ gave us emphatic instructions!" (Tirmidhi and Ibn Majah, Hakim). Another narration (Ibn Jareer, Ibn Asakir) adds that part of Rasulullah ﷺ's instruction was, "Teach them that which Allah has taught you." Yet another narration states that Rasulullah ﷺ said, "Soon people will come to you from the ends of the earth to ask you about your Deen. When they arrive, accommodate them and teach them and it is my emphatic instruction that you must treat them well." Yet another narration states that Rasulullah ﷺ added, "Teach them and say to them, 'Welcome! Welcome! Come closer!'" (Ibn Asakir in Kanzul Ummal). Whenever the young students came to Abu Sa'eed Khudri ◈, he would say, "Welcome to the people about whom Rasulullah ﷺ gave us forceful instructions! Rasulullah ﷺ gave us instructions to accommodate them in our gatherings and to make them understand the Ahadeeth because you people are our successors and are the ones who will narrate Ahadeeth after us." Amongst the things Abu Sa'eed Khudri ◈ used to say to the new students was, "If there is anything you do not understand, do ask me to explain it to you because I prefer you leaving here after understanding rather than leaving without understanding." (Ibn Najjar in Kanzul Ummal)

Abu Hurairah ◈ Welcomes Students

Isma'el reports that so many of them once went to visit Hasan that they filled his house. Pulling his legs together, he said, "So many of uswent to visit Abu Hurairah ◈ that we filled his house. Pulling his legs together, he said, 'So many of us once went to visit Rasulullah ﷺ that we filled his house. Rasulullah ﷺ was lying down on his side, but when he saw us, he pulled his legs together and said, 'After my demise, people of various nationalities shall soon come to you in search of knowledge. You should welcome them, greet them and teach them.' By Allah! We have met such people after the Sahabah who neither welcomed us, greeted us nor taught us anything. All they did when we went to them was to act harshly with us." (Ibn Majah)

Abu Darda ◈ Smiles When Narrating Ahadeeth

Ummu Darda ◈ says, "Whenever Abu Darda ◈ narrated Ahadeeth to people, he would always smile. I once said to him, 'I fear that people would regard you to be a fool' He explained, 'Rasulullah ﷺ also smiled whenever he narrated Ahadeeth.'" (Ahmad, Tabrani in Kabeer, Haythami)

Gatherings of knowledge and being in the company of Ulema: Rasulullah ﷺ Encourages the Gatherings of Knowledge and the Sahabah sit in Groups Around Him

Abdullah bin Abbas ◈ narrates that Rasulullah ﷺ was once asked, "O Rasulullah ﷺ! Which of our companions are best?" Rasulullah ﷺ replied, "The person who reminds you of Allah when you look at him, whose speech increases your knowledge and whose deeds remind you of the Hereafter." (Abu Ya'la,

Mundhiri). Qurra ◈ reports that when Rasulullah ﷺ sat in a gathering, the Sahabah would sit in groups around him to learn and teach, asking Rasulullah ﷺ when they needed to." (Bazzar)

The Gatherings of the Sahabah After the Fajr Salah

Yazid Raqashi says that after narrating Ahadeeth to them, Anas ◈ would say, "By Allah! This Hadith has not been learnt as you people learn when people gather around a person who lectures to them. What used to happen is that the Sahabah used to sit in groups after the Fajr salah to recite the Qur'an and learn the compulsory and optional aspects of Deen." (Majma'uz Zawa'id)

Rasulullah ﷺ sits with a Gathering of the Sahabah that Included Many Poor People

Abu Sa'eed Khudri ◈ relates, "I was sitting with a group of Muhajirin amongst whom were people who because of poverty had so little clothing that they were hiding behind each other. A Qari was busy reciting the Qur'an and we were all busy listening to Allah's Book. Rasulullah ﷺ arrived and said, 'All praise is for Allah who has created in my Ummah people with whom I have been instructed to remain with.' The group faced Rasulullah ﷺ, who recognized none of them besides myself. Rasulullah ﷺ said, 'O impoverished Muhajirin, listen to the good news that you will have perfect light on the Day of Judgment. You will enter Jannah half a day before the rich, equal to 500 years.'" (Bayhaqi in Al Bidayah wan Nihayah, Abu Nu'aym in Hilya)

Rasulullah ﷺ prefers the Gathering of Knowledge to the Gathering of Dhikr

Abdullah bin Amr ◈ narrates that Rasulullah ﷺ once passed by 2 gatherings in his Masjid. While the people in one gathering were making Du'a to Allah and concentrating on this, the other was learning and teaching Fiqh. Rasulullah ﷺ remarked, "While both gatherings are doing excellent work, the one is superior to the other. As for the one, they are making Du'a to Allah and concentrating on this. If Allah wills, He shall grant them what they ask and if He wills, He may refuse them. As for the others, they are learning and teaching the ignorant and I have been sent as a teacher." Rasulullah ﷺ therefore sat with this second group. (Ibn Abdul Birr in Jami, Darmi)

Abu Musa Ash'ari ◈ and Omar ◈ sit One Night in a Gathering of Knowledge

Abu Bakr bin Abu Musa narrates that Abu Musa ◈ once went to Omar ◈ after Isha. "What brings you here?" Omar ◈ asked. "I have come to speak with you," Abu Musa ◈ replied. "At this hour?" Omar ◈ remarked. When Abu Musa ◈ informed Omar ◈ that it was an important matter of Fiqh that he needed to discuss, Omar ◈ satand 2 men discussed for a long while. Abu Musa ◈ said, "What about the Tahajjud salah, O Amirul Mu'minin?" Omar ◈ replied, "It was in salah that I had been engaged when you arrived." (Abdur Razzaq, Ibn Abi Shaybah in Kanzul Ummal)

The Incident of Jundub Bajali with Ubay bin Ka'b ◈ Concerning Seeking Knowledge

Jundub bin Abdullah Bajali says, "When I arrived in Madinah to seek knowledge, I entered the Masjid of Rasulullah ﷺ where I saw people engaged in discussions in various groups. Passing by the groups, I eventually arrived at a group in which there sat a pale man wearing 2 pieces of cloth and who appeared to have just arrived from a journey. I heard him say, 'I swear by the Rabb of the Kabah that the people in authority have been destroyed and I am not sorry for them!' This he repeated several times. I then sat down with him and he continued to narrate Ahadeeth for some time. When he got up to leave, I asked the people who he was. They said, 'He is the leader of the Muslims! He is Ubay bin Ka'b ﷺ.' I then followed him to his house, which I discovered was in a crumbling state. I also discovered that he was very strict, had severed all ties with this world and was a man of habit. When I greeted him, he replied to my greeting and asked me where I came from. When I informed him that I was from Iraq, he remarked, 'Iraqis are people who ask even more questions than I do.' This remark made me very angry and I immediately fell to my knees, raised my hands like this before my face and faced the Qibla saying, 'O Allah! It is to You that I complain. We have spent our wealth, tired our bodies and rode our conveyances in search of knowledge. However, when we meet them, they are inhospitable and make remarks about us!' Ubay ﷺ started to weep and tried to pacify me saying, 'Oh dear! I did not mean to offend you. I really did not mean to offend you.' He then said, 'O Allah! I make a promise with You that if you keep me alive until Friday, I shall definitely state what I heard Rasulullah ﷺ say without fearing reproach from anyone.' After he said that, I left him and waited for Friday. I left my room that Thursday for something, I found the streets jammed with people. I could see crowd of people on very street I took. 'What is the matter with the people?' I asked. 'You must be a stranger here?' the people asked. I confirmed that I was, they said, 'The leader of the Muslims Ubay bin Ka'b ﷺ has passed away.' I later met Abu Musa Ash'ari ﷺ in Iraq and related to him the incident of Ubay ﷺ, he sighed, 'How tragic! If only he had lived so that you could have reported his words to us!'" *(Ibn Sa'd)*

Imran bin Husain ﷺ Narrates Ahadeeth in the Masjid of Basra

Hilal bin Yasaf says, "When I arrived in Basra and entered the Masjid, I saw an old man with white hair and a white beard leaning against a pillar and narrating Ahadeeth to a group of people. When I enquired about the man, I was informed that he was Imran bin Husain ﷺ." *(Ibn Sa'd)*

People Flock to the Door of Abdullah bin Abbas ﷺ, who Taught Them all Aspects of Deeni Knowledge

Abu Salih says, "I have seen such a large gathering around Abdullah bin Abbas ﷺ that if the entire tribe of the Quraish boasted about such numbers, they would be the envy of all. I have seen so many people flock to him that the street could not even contain them and none was able to move forward or backward. When I went in and informed him about all the people at his door, he instructed me to fetch some water for him to perform wudhu. He then performed wudhu and sat down saying, 'Go outside and announce that whoever wishes to ask about the Qur'an and its words and meaning should come in.' When I went out and made the announcement, the people who entered filled the room as well as the entire house. In addition to informing them about everything they asked, he also told them much more. 'Now allow your brothers the opportunity,' he said. When these people had left, he instructed me again saying, 'Go outside and announce that whoever wishes to ask about the Tafseer of the Qur'an and its interpretation should come in.' When I went out and made the announcement, the people who entered filled the room as well as the entire house. In addition to informing them about everything they asked, he also told them much more. 'Now allow your brothers the opportunity,' he said. When they had left, he again instructed, 'Go outside and announce that whoever wishes to ask about what is Halal and Haram and about Fiqh

should come in.' When I went out and made the announcement, the people who entered filled the room as well as the entire house. In addition to informing them about everything they asked, he also told them much more. 'Now allow your brothers the opportunity,' he said. When these people had left, he instructed me again saying, 'Go outside and announce that whoever wishes to ask about inheritance and the likes thereof should come in.' When I went out and made the announcement, the people who entered filled the room as well as the entire house. In addition to informing them about everything they asked, he also told them much more. 'Now allow your brothers the opportunity,' he said. When they had left, he instructed, 'Go and announce that whoever wishes to ask about Arabic, poetry and rare words should come in.' When I went out and made the announcement, the people who entered filled the room as well as the entire house. He also told them much more. If the entire tribe of the Quraish boasted about such numbers, they would really be the envy of all because I have never seen such a large gathering around any person." *(Abu Nu'aym in Hilya, Hakim)*

Abdullah bin Mas'ood ﷺ Praises the Gatherings of Knowledge

Abdullah bin Mas'ood ﷺ once said, "The best of all gatherings is the one in which matters of wisdom are discussed." *(Tabrani in Kabeer, Haythami)*. Another narration states that Abdullah bin Mas'ood ﷺ said, "The best of all gatherings is the one in which matters of wisdom are disseminated and in which Allah's mercy is anticipated." *(Ibn Abdul Birr in Jami)*. Abdullah bin Mas'ood ﷺ also said, "People with Taqwa are the chiefs, the jurists are the leaders and attending their gatherings is a means of increasing one's Iman and knowledge." *(Tabrani, Haythami)*

The Statements of Abu Juhaifa ﷺ and Abu Darda ﷺ in this Regard

Abu Juhaifa ﷺ always used to say, "Sit in the company of the seniors, associate with the Ulema and mingle with the wise." *(Ibn Abdul Birr in Jami)*. Abu Darda ﷺ said, "It is the deep understanding a person has that will make him accompany and stay in contact with men of knowledge." *(Ibn Abdul Birr in Jami)*. In another narration, Abu Darda ﷺ added sitting in their gatherings. *(Abu Nu'aym in Hilya)*

Sahl bin Sa'd Sa'idi ﷺ Gets Angry with People who Fooled Around in his Gathering

Abu Hazim says, "Sahl bin Sa'd Sa'idi ﷺ was narrating the Ahadeeth of Rasulullah ﷺ to a group of his people when some of them started turning to each other and talking. This made Sahl ﷺ angry and he said, 'Look at them! Some of them are turning to talk to each other when I am narrating to them what my eyes have seen and my ears have heard. I swear by Allah that I shall leave them and never return to them ever again!' 'Where will you go?' I asked. 'I shall go to wage Jihad in the Path of Allah,' came the reply. 'How will you fight in Jihad,' I submitted, 'because of your old age you are unable to ride a horse, strike a blow with a sword or even use a spear.' 'O Abu Hazim,' he said, 'I shall stand amongst the ranks of the soldiers to be struck by a stray arrow or rock by which Allah shall bless me with martyrdom.'" *(Tabrani in Kabeer, Haythami)*

The conduct of Ulema and students: Rasulullah ﷺ's Kind Address to a Youngster who Requested Permission to Fornicate

Abu Umama ﷺ narrates that a youngster from the Quraish once approached Rasulullah ﷺ with the request, "O Rasulullah ﷺ! Do permit me to fornicate." The Sahabah turned to him and started rebuking him saying, "Don't say that! Don't say that!"

'Bring him closer," Rasulullah ﷺ said. When the youngster went close to Rasulullah ﷺ, Rasulullah ﷺ asked, "Would you like someone to fornicate with your mother?" "By Allah!" the youngster exclaimed, "I would never tolerate it! May Allah sacrifice me for you, O Rasulullah ﷺ!" "Then," Rasulullah ﷺ explained, "Other people will also not want anyone to fornicate with their mothers." Rasulullah ﷺ continued, "Would you then like someone to fornicate with your daughter?" "By Allah!" the youngster exclaimed again, "I would never tolerate it! May Allah sacrifice me for you, O Rasulullah ﷺ!" "Then," Rasulullah ﷺ said, "Other people will also not want anyone to fornicate with their daughters." Rasulullah ﷺ asked further, "Would you like someone to fornicate with your sister?" Again the youngster exclaimed "By Allah! I would never tolerate it! May Allah sacrifice me for you, O Rasulullah ﷺ!" "Then other people will also not want others to fornicate with their sisters," Rasulullah ﷺ said. Again Rasulullah ﷺ asked, "Would you like someone to fornicate with your paternal aunt?" Again the youngster exclaimed "By Allah! I would never tolerate it! May Allah sacrifice me for you, O Rasulullah ﷺ!" "Then other people will also not want anyone to fornicate with their paternal aunts. Would you like someone to fornicate with your maternal aunt?" "By Allah! I would never tolerate it! May Allah sacrifice me for you, O Rasulullah ﷺ!" the youngster exclaimed. "Other people will also not want people to fornicate with their maternal aunts," Rasulullah ﷺ said. Rasulullah ﷺ then placed his hand on the youngster's chest and prayed, "O Allah! Forgive his sins, purify his heart and keep him chaste." The youngster's attention never again swayed in that direction. *(Tabrani, Ahmad, Haythami)*

Rasulullah ﷺ Repeats Himself Thrice to Make Himself Understood

Abu Umama ﷺ says, "When Rasulullah ﷺ spoke something of importance, he would repeat himself thrice so that he would be understood." *(Tabrani in Kabeer, Haythami)*

Aisha ﷺ Instructs Ibn Abi Sa'ib to hold Fast to 3 Factors when Teaching

Sha'bi narrates that Aisha ﷺ once said to the lecturer of Madinah Ibn Abi Sa'ib, "You must obey me in 3 factors; otherwise I shall oppose you strongly." Ibn Abi Sa'ib said, "I shall most definitely obey you, O Ummul Mu'mineen! What are they?" Aisha ﷺ said, "(1) Refrain from going out of your way to rhyme your Du'as because Rasulullah ﷺ and the Sahabah never did. (2) You should deliver a lecture once every week. If you do not want to do only once, you may do so twice or otherwise thrice at the most because you should never allow people to become tired of the Qur'an. (3) I never want to find you going to people who are engaged in some discussion and then you cut short their talk by starting your lecture. Rather leave them to talk and you start your lecture only when they approach you and ask you to talk." *(Ahmad, Haythami, Abu Ya'la)*

The Conduct of Abdullah bin Mas'ood ﷺ when teaching

Shaqiq bin Salama narrates that Abdullah bin Mas'ood ﷺ once came to them and said, "I know well that you people are sitting here but the only thing that prevents me from coming out to you every time is the fear of you getting tired. It was the practice of Rasulullah ﷺ to consider us when delivering lectures for fear of ever tiring us out." *(Ibn Abdul Birr in Jami).* A'mash narrates that Abdullah bin Mas'ood ﷺ once passed by a man delivering a lecture, he said, "O lecturer! Do not make the people pessimistic of Allah's mercy." *(Tabrani in Kabeer, Haythami)*

Ali ﷺ describes a true scholar

Ali ﷺ once said, "Should I not inform you who a true scholar is. He is one who neither makes people pessimistic of Allah's mercy nor grants them the license to disobey Allah. At the same time, he does not allow them to feel that they are immune from Allah's punishment. He is one who does not turn his attention to something else, thereby neglecting the Qur'an. There is no good in the Ibada that is devoid of the relevant knowledge, no good in the knowledge that is devoid of understanding and piety and no good in the recitation of the Qur'an that is devoid of thought." *(Ibn Dharis, Abu Nu'aym in Hilya, Ibn Asakir in Kanzul Ummal, lsti'ab, Ibn Abdul Birr)*

Rasulullah ﷺ's Words to Mu'adh bin Jabal ﷺ and Abu Musa Ash'ari ﷺ When Dispatching Them to Yemen

Abdullah bin Omar ﷺ narrates that when Rasulullah ﷺ sent Mu'adh bin Jabal ﷺ and Abu Musa Ash'ari ﷺ to Yemen, he addressed them saying, "Assist each other, work together, tell the people good things and do not make them averse to the Deen." When Mu'adh ﷺ delivered a lecture to the people, he encouraged them towards Islam, developing a deep understanding of Deen and the Qur'an. He also said, "I can inform you about those destined for Jannah and those destined for Jahannam. A person is destined for Jannah when people speak good of him and destined for Jahannam when they have no good to speak of him." *(Tabrani, Haythami)*

The Statement of Abu Sa'eed ﷺ Concerning the Gatherings of the Sahabah and the Statement of Abdullah bin Omar ﷺ Concerning the True Alim

Abu Sa'eed Khudri ﷺ said, "When the Sahabah sat together, their discussion always concerned Deen unless one of them was reciting a Surah or having someone else recite a Surah." *(Hakim).* Abdullah bin Omar ﷺ said, "A man can never occupy a respectable position as a scholar unless he is not jealous of those above him, does not look down on those beneath him and does not seek a price for his knowledge." *(Abu Nu'aym in Hilya)*

The Statement of Omar ﷺ Concerning the Conduct of an Alim

Omar ﷺ said, "Acquire knowledge and teach the people. Learn also the respect that goes with it. Humble yourself before those you learn from as well as before those you teach, and never be arrogant Ulema. In this manner, your ignorance will be unable to stand up to your knowledge." *(Ibn Abdul Birr in Jami, Ahmad in Zuhd, Bayhaqi, Ibn Abi Shaybah)*

The Statement of Ali ﷺ Concerning the Conduct of Students

Ali ﷺ said, "Amongst the rights of an Alim is that you should not pose too many questions to him, you should not press him to give answers and should not pressurize him if he chooses to ignore something. Also amongst his rights is that you should not hold his clothing and compel him to teach when he is tired, you should never point your finger at him, never hint at him with your eyes and never question his gatherings. You should also never wait for him to slip up and if he does, you should wait for him to correct himself and accept his excuse for the error. Never tell him that someone else opposes his opinion, never disclose his secrets, never gossip to him about anyone and always maintain his honor in his presence and his absence. While you may greet people collectively, greet him specially and sit in front of him. If he has any need, beat others in serving him and never tire him by sitting too long with him. He is like a date palm by which you ought to wait for some benefit to fall to you at any time. The

Alim occupies the status of a person who is fasting while fighting in Jihad in the Path of Allah and when he passes away, a void is created in Islam that can never be filled until the Day of Judgment. Also 70,000 high-ranking angels of the heavens escort the student of Deen." *(Murhibi and Ibn Abdul Birr in Jami, Kanzul Ummal, Muntakhab Kanzul Ummal, Khateeb in Jami)*

The Conduct of Thabit Bunani with His Teacher Anas

Jamila the slave woman of Anas who mothered some of his children says, "Whenever Thabit came to Anas , Anas would instruct me to bring him some perfume to apply to his hands saying, 'Ibn Ummu Thabit (Thabit) will not be satisfied until he kisses my hands.'" *(Abu Ya'la, Haythami)*

The Conduct of Abdullah bin Abbas with Omar and His Awe for Him

Abdullah bin Abbas says, "For many years I had wanted to ask Omar bin Khattab about an incident but it was my awe for him that prevented me from doing so. The opportunity eventually came when he lagged behind the rest of the people on a journey for Hajj or Umra because he needed to attend to the call of nature. It was in a place called Arak in Marruz Zahran and I was alone with him when he had completed. 'O Amirul Mu'minin!' I said, 'For many years I had wanted to ask you about an incident but my awe for you prevented me from doing so.' 'Do not do that,' he said, 'Whenever you need to know anything, feel free to ask me. If I know anything, I shall inform you and if I do not, I shall tell you that I know nothing about it and you may ask someone who does.' I then asked, 'Who are the 2 women that Allah speaks about who acted together against Rasulullah ?' 'They were Aisha and Hafsa ,' Omar replied. The narration continues to relate the inciden. *(Ibn Abdul Birr in Jami)*

The Awe Sa'eed bin Musayib had for Sa'd bin Abi Waqqas

Sa'eed bin Musayib says, "I once said to Sa'd bin Malik (Abi Waqqas) , 'I wish to pose certain questions to you, but I stand in too much awe of you.' 'Dear son of my brother,' he said, 'do not stand in awe of me. If you feel that I know anything, feel free to ask me.' I then asked, 'What was it that Rasulullah said to Ali when he appointed him as his deputy during the expedition to Tabuk?' Sa'd replied, 'Rasulullah said, 'O Ali! Does it not please you to know that your status with me is like that of Harun with Musa .'" *(Ibn Abdul Birr in Jami, Ibn Sa'd)*

Jubair bin Mut'im Responds to a Question by saying, "I have no Knowledge on the Subject"

Uthman bin Abdullah bin Mowhab narrates that Jubair bin Mut'im was passing through an oasis when the people questioned him about a matter of inheritance. Jubair responded by saying, "I have no knowledge on the subject. You maysend someone with me and I will enquire about it on your behalf." The people sent someone with him and Jubair posed the question to Omar . Omar remarked, "Whoever wishes to be an Alim with keen understanding should do as Jubair bin Mut'im has done. When asked about something he did not know, he said, 'Allah knows best.'" *(Ibn Sa'd in Kanzul Ummal)*

The Conduct of Abdullah bin Omar in his Teaching

Mujahid reports that when Abdullah bin Omar was once questioned about an aspect of children's inheritance, he replied, "I do not know." "What prevents you from replying?" someone asked. His reply was, "When Abdullah bin Omar was asked about something he did not know, he replied by saying, 'I do not know.'" *(Ibn Abdul Birr in Isti'ab)*. Urwa reports that when Abdullah bin Omar was questioned about something he had no knowledge of, he replied by saying, "I have no knowledge on the subject." As the man turned to leave, Abdullah bin Omar said to himself, "When Abdullah bin Omar was questioned about something he had no knowledge of, he replied by saying, 'I have no knowledge on the subject.'" *(Ibn Sa'd)*. Uqba bin Muslim says, "I stayed with Abdullah bin Omar for 34 months and on many occasions when he was questioned about something, he would reply by saying, 'I do not know.' He would then turn to me saying, 'Do you know what those people wanted by asking me about something I had no knowledge of? They intended making our backs a bridge to Jahannam.'" *(Ibn Abdul Birr in Jami)*. Nafi narrates that a man once posed a question to Abdullah bin Omar . Abdullah bin Omar lowered his head and did not respond for such a long time that the man thought his question had not been heard. "May Allah have mercy on you," the man said, "Did you not hear my question?" Abdullah bin Omar replied by saying, "I certainly did hear it. However, it seems like you people feel that Allah will not question us about the things you ask us about. May Allah have mercy on you! Leave us to think about your question. If we have a reply, we will inform you, otherwise we shall tell you that we do not know." *(Ibn Sa'd)*

Statements of Abdullah bin Mas'ood , Ali and Abdullah bin Abbas About an Alim Conceding that he does not Know

Abdullah bin Mas'ood once said, "O people! When a person is questioned about something he has knowledge about, he should give the reply and if he does not have the knowledge, he should say, 'Allah knows best'. To say 'Allah knows best' in reply to something one does not know is also an integral part of knowledge. Addressing His Nabi , Allah says:

قُلْ مَا أَسْأَلُكُمْ عَلَيْهِ مِنْ أَجْرٍ وَمَا أَنَا مِنَ الْمُتَكَلِّفِينَ (86)

Say (O Muhammad): "No wage I ask of you for this (Qur'an), nor am I one of the Mutakallifoon (who pretend and fabricate things that do not exist). (Sad:86) (Ibn Abdul Birr in Jami)

Abdullah bin Bashir states that when Ali bin Abi Talib was once asked a question, he replied by saying, "I have no knowledge on the subject." He then said, "What a great source of comfort! I was questioned about something I did know and I conceded that I did not know." *(Sa'd bin Nasr in Kanzul Ummal, Darmi in Kanzul Ummal)*. Abdullah bin Abbas said, "When an Alim forsakes the statement 'I do not know', then he has reached his point of destruction." Another narration also states that Abdullah bin Abbas said, "When an Alim omits using the statement 'I do not know', then he has reached his point of destruction." *(Abu Dawud and Malik in Jami Bayanil Ilm)*

The Conduct of Omar , Ali and Uthman When Teaching

Makhul reports that when Omar noticed that the people were getting tired as he narrated Ahadeeth to them, he would occupy them with planting trees. *(Ibn Sam'ani in Kanzul Ummal)*. Abdullah bin Mus'ab narrates that Omar bin Khattab said, "Do not pay more than 40 Awqiya as dowry, even though the bride may be the daughter of Dhul Udda Qais bin Husain Harithi. If anyone pays more, I shall deposit the surplus into the state treasury." A tall woman with a flat nose then stood up from the women's row saying, "You do not have the authority to do that." "Why not?" asked Omar . She replied, "Because Allah declares: وَآتَيْتُمْ إِحْدَاهُنَّ قِنْطَارًا فَلَا تَأْخُذُوا مِنْهُ شَيْئًا

... and you have given one of them a heap of gold (i.e. a great

amount) as Mahr, take not the least bit of it back ...(An-Nisa:20) To this, Omar 🙵 remarked, "The lady is right and the man is wrong." *(Ibn Abdul Birr in Jami).* Muhammad bin Ka'b Qurazi 🙵 narrates that a man once posed a question to Ali 🙵, to which he gave a reply. "O Amirul Mu'minin!" the man said, "That is not the answer." He then proceeded to give the correct answer, to which Ali 🙵 conceded, "You are right and I was wrong." He then recited the verse: وَفَوْقَ كُلِّ ذِي عِلْمٍ عَلِيمٌ (76) *...but over all those endowed with knowledge is the All-Knowing (Allah). (Yusuf:76) (Ibn Abdul Birr in Jami, Ibn Jareer in Kanzul Ummal)*

Sa'eed bin Musayib says, "Omar bin Khattab 🙵 and Uthman bin Affan 🙵 used to debate a question so strongly that a spectator would be convinced that they could never be reconciled. However, they always parted ways most cordially as if nothing had transpired between them." *(Khateeb in Kanzul Ummal).* For a person to forsake attending a gathering of knowledge so that a group of people may acquire knowledge.

The Incident of Uqba bin Amir 🙵 and His Tribe When They came to Rasulullah ﷺ

Uqba bin Amir 🙵 relates, "I arrived riding with 12 members of my tribe to see Rasulullah ﷺ. When we had tied our camels, Mustahab companions said, 'Who will tend to the camels so that the rest of us could go and receive enlightenment from Rasulullah ﷺ? When we return, we will then convey to him what we heard from Rasulullah ﷺ.' I assumed the responsibility for a few days until the thought occurred to me that I may be fooling myself because my companions were hearing from Nabi ﷺ what I was not hearing and they were learning from him what I was not learning. I therefore presented myself one day leaving the others to tend to the camels. There I heard someone say that Nabi ﷺ said, 'The person who performs a complete wudhu shall be free of sins as he was on the day his mother gave birth to him.' This impressed me tremendously. Omar bin Khattab 🙵 then said, 'If you think that is impressive, you will be even more impressed if you had heard what was said before that.' 'Repeat it for me,' I pleaded, 'May I be sacrificed for you!' He said, 'Rasulullah ﷺ said that if a person dies without ascribing partners to Allah, Allah shall open for him all 8 gates of Jannah so that he may enter from whichever gate he pleases.' Rasulullah ﷺ came out to us and I sat in front of him. He turned his face away from me several times. He did it for the 4th time, I asked, 'O Nabi of Allah ﷺ! May my parents be sacrificed for you! Why do you turn your face away from me?' Rasulullah ﷺ turned to me saying, 'Do you prefer one or 12?' Realizing what he meant, I returned to my companions." *(Ibn Asakir in Kanzul Ummal, Abu Nu'aym in Hilya)*

The Incident of Uthman bin Abul Aas 🙵 and His Tribe When They came to Nabi ﷺ

Uthman bin Abul Aas 🙵 reports, "I arrived with the delegation of the Thaqif tribe when they came to see Rasulullah ﷺ. We were changing our clothes at Rasulullah ﷺ's door when it was asked, 'Who will hold our animals for us?' Each one of us wanted to go to Rasulullah ﷺ and did not want to stay behind. Because I was the youngest of them all, I said, 'If it pleases you, I shall hold your camels for you on condition that you make a promise to Allah that you will wait here for me when you come out.' They made the promise and then went in to see Rasulullah ﷺ. When they came out, they said, 'Come! Let us go.' 'Where to?' I asked. 'Home,' they replied. I protested saying, 'I have left my home to come right here to Rasulullah's door just to return without seeing him after you had made me the promise you well

acknowledge?!' 'Then hurry,' they said, 'because we have already done all the questioning for you. There is nothing that we have not asked Rasulullah ﷺ about' I then went in and said, 'O Rasulullah ﷺ! Pray to Allah to grant me a deep understanding of the Deen and to teach me.' 'What was it you said?' Rasulullah ﷺ asked. When I repeated my request, Rasulullah ﷺ remarked, 'You have asked me for something that none of your companions have asked. Go! You are now their Amir and the Amir of all of your tribe's people who come to you.'" The Hadith still continues further. *(Tabrani, Haythami)* In another narration, Uthman bin Abul Aas 🙵 states that when he entered, Rasulullah ﷺ had a copy of the Qur'an with him. This Rasulullah ﷺ gave to him when he asked to have it. *(Tabrani)*

Learning, teaching and rehearsing the knowledge of Deen and questions that are appropriate and inappropriate: The Sahabah Rehearse in Rasulullah ﷺ's Gathering and ask Questions

Anas 🙵 says, "When we used to sit with Rasulullah ﷺ as he narrated Ahadeeth to us, we would sometimes number as many as 60. Then when Rasulullah ﷺ needed to leave for some need, we would rehearse amongst ourselves, repeating what Rasulullah ﷺ said one after the other so that it was firmly rooted in to hearts by the time we left." *(Abu Ya'la, Haythami).* Abu Musa Ash'ari 🙵 says, "After Rasulullah ﷺ performed the Fajr salah, we would turn towards him. Some of us would then ask him about the Qur'an, others about inheritance and others about dreams." *(Tabrani in Kabeer, Haythami)*

The Words of Fudhala bin Ubaid 🙵 to his Companions in this Regard

When his companions used to come to him, Fudhala bin Ubaid 🙵 would say to them, "Learn and teach each other, convey glad tidings and increase your knowledge. May Allah increase you in all good, love you and love all those who love you. Rehearse the lessons you have learnt because the reward for the last one is as great as that of the first. You should also add Istighfar to your discussions." *(Tabrani in Kabeer, Haythami)*

Statements of Abu Sa'eed 🙵, Ali 🙵, Abdullah bin Mas'ood 🙵 and Abdullah bin Abbas 🙵 Concerning what was Learnt

Abu Nadhra says that when they once requested Abu Sa'eed Khudri 🙵 to write down Ahadeeth for them, he said, "I shall never write it for you and never make it like the Qur'an. You should learn the Ahadeeth from us as we had learnt from Rasulullah ﷺ by memory and not in writing." Abu Sa'eed Khudri 🙵 also used to say, "Rehearse the Ahadeeth amongst yourselves because this reinforces the memory." *(Tabrani in Awsat, Haythami).* Another narration quotes Abu Sa'eed Khudri 🙵 as saying, "Rehearse the Ahadeeth amongst yourselves because this revives the memory." *(Hakim, Ibn Abdul Birr in Jami).* Ali 🙵 said, "Rehearse the Ahadeeth amongst yourselves because if you do not do this, you will forget them." *(Hakim)* Another narration states that Ali 🙵 also added, "Keep visiting each other." *(Ibn Abi Shaybah, Ibn Abdul Birr in Jami).* Abdullah bin Mas'ood 🙵 said, "Rehearse the Ahadeeth amongst yourselves because this keeps it alive." *(Hakim).* Another narration quotes Abdullah bin Mas'ood 🙵 as saying, "Rehearsing Deeni knowledge and the Ahadeeth reaps the reward of Nafl salah." *(Ibn Abdul Birr in Isti'ab).* Abdullah bin Abbas 🙵 said, "I prefer rehearsing the knowledge of Deen for a part of the night to engaging in Ibada throughout the night." *(Ibn Abdul Birr in Isti'ab)*

Omar ؓ asks Ali ؓ 3 Questions and is Overjoyed with the Replies

Abdullah bin Omar ؓ narrates that Omar ؓ once addressed Ali ؓ saying, "O Abul Hasan! There were times when you were present with Rasulullah ﷺ when we were not and there were times when we were present with Rasulullah ﷺ when you were not. I have 3 questions to pose to you. Do you know anything about them?" "What are they?" Ali ؓ asked. Omar ؓ said, "Is it possible that a man likes another when he has seen no good in him or dislikes a man when he has seen no bad in him?" "That is certainly possible," Ali ؓ replied, "Rasulullah ﷺ once said, 'All souls had been gathered together in metaphysical realm where they met and associated. Those that got to know each other there, bond in this world and those who were detached there remain detached here.'" "That was one question to which we have a reply," Omar ؓ said, "the 2nd question is that when speaking about something, a man sometimes remembers and sometimes forgets." Ali ؓ responded by saying, "Rasulullah ﷺ said, 'Every heart has clouds passing over it just as clouds pass across the moon. While the moon is shining, a cloud passes across it, causing the light to vanish, but it again shines through once the cloud has passed. Similarly, when a man is busy speaking, one of the clouds passes across (his heart), causing him to forget. Then when it passes by, he is once again able to remember." "That was 2 questions," Omar ؓ said, "Now what about a man who sees dreams, some of which are true and others false." Ali ؓ said, "I have a reply for that as well. I heard Rasulullah ﷺ say, 'Whenever any male/female falls into a deep sleep, their soul rises up to the Arsh of Allah. Those that awaken after reaching the Arsh have true dreams and those that awaken before reaching the Arsh have false dreams." Omar ؓ remarked, "These were 3 answers that I was looking for. I thank Allah that I have found them before my death." *(Tabrani in Awsat, Haythami)*

Omar ؓ Questions Abdullah bin Abbas ؓ About the Differences Amongst the Ummah

Ibrahim Taymi narrates that Omar ؓ was alone one day when he started thinking to himself. He then sent for Abdullah bin Abbas ؓ and asked him, "How will this Ummah have differences between them when their Book is one, their Nabi ﷺ is one and their Qibla is one?" "O Amirul Mu'minin!" Abdullah bin Abbas said, "When the Qur'an was revealed to us, we recited it knowing exactly for what reason every verse was revealed. However, after us there shall come many nations who will recite the Qur'an without knowing why the various verses were revealed. Every nation will therefore have its own opinion about every verse. When this happens, they will naturally have differences between them and when differences crop up, they will start to fight each other." In his grief over this Omar ؓ rebuked Abdullah bin Abbas ؓ, who then left. Omar ؓ however realized the truth of what Abdullah bin Abbas ؓ said and again called for him. When Abdullah bin Abbas ؓ arrived, Omar ؓ said to him, "Do repeat what you have said." *(Sa'eed bin Mansur, Bayhaqi, Khateeb in Kanzul Ummal)*

Omar ؓ Questions the Sahabah About a Particular Verse and is Impressed by the Reply that Abdullah bin Abbas ؓ gave

Abdullah bin Abbas ؓ narrates, "Omar ؓ once said, 'I recited a verse last night that kept me awake. The verse is:

أَيَوَدُّ أَحَدُكُمْ أَنْ تَكُونَ لَهُ جَنَّةٌ مِنْ نَخِيلٍ وَأَعْنَابٍ تَجْرِي مِنْ تَحْتِهَا الْأَنْهَارُ لَهُ فِيهَا مِنْ كُلِّ الثَّمَرَاتِ وَأَصَابَهُ الْكِبَرُ وَلَهُ ذُرِّيَّةٌ ضُعَفَاءُ فَأَصَابَهَا إِعْصَارٌ فِيهِ نَارٌ فَاحْتَرَقَتْ كَذَلِكَ يُبَيِّنُ اللَّهُ لَكُمُ الْآيَاتِ لَعَلَّكُمْ تَتَفَكَّرُونَ (266)

Would any of you wish to have a garden with date-palms and vines, with rivers flowing underneath, and all kinds of fruits for him therein, while he is stricken with old age, and his children are weak (not able to look after themselves), then it is struck with a fiery whirlwind, so that it is burnt? Thus does Allah make clear His Ayat (proofs, evidences, verses) to you that you may give thought. (Al-Baqara:266)

'What does it refer to?' Omar ؓ wanted to know. When some people responded by saying, 'Allah knows best', Omar ؓ said, 'I know well that Allah knows best, but I have asked because if any of you know anything about it or have heard anything about it, he should inform me about what he has heard.' Everyone was silent. Omar ؓ noticed me whispering something and said. 'Dear son of my brother! Say your piece and do not undermine yourself.' 'It is actions that are being referred to,' I said. 'What makes you say that actions are being referred to?' I said, 'It was something that came to my heart which I stated.' Omar ؓ left me and started explaining it himself. He said, 'You are right, dear son of my brother. It is actions that are being referred to. A man is most in need of his orchard when he is old and when he has many dependents. He is in need of his actions on the Day of Judgment. You are right, dear son of my brother.'" *(Abd bin Humaid, Ibn Mundhir in Kanzul Ummal, Hakim)*

Omar ؓ Questions Abdullah bin Abbas ؓ About some Difficulty he was Experiencing with Surah Nasr

Abdullah bin Abbas ؓ says, "Because Omar used to allow me in with the veterans of Badr, Abdur Rahman bin Auf ؓ objected saying, 'Why do you allow this youngster in with us when we have children his age?' Omar ؓ replied, 'He is of a caliber that you will soon come to know.' Omar ؓ therefore summoned them one day and called for me as well. I believe that he called them that day only to show me off to them. He said, 'What comments do you have about the following verses:

إِذَا جَاءَ نَصْرُ اللَّهِ وَالْفَتْحُ (1) وَرَأَيْتَ النَّاسَ يَدْخُلُونَ فِي دِينِ اللَّهِ أَفْوَاجًا (2) فَسَبِّحْ بِحَمْدِ رَبِّكَ وَاسْتَغْفِرْهُ إِنَّهُ كَانَ تَوَّابًا (3) *When comes the Help of Allah (to you, O Muhammad ﷺ) against your enemies) and the conquest (of Makkah), and you see that the people enter Allah's religion (Islam) in crowds, So glorify the Praises of your Lord, and ask for His Forgiveness. Verily, He is the One Who accepts the repentance and forgives. (An-Nasr)*

Some said, "Allah is commanding us to praise him and seek His forgiveness when His help arrives and when he grants us victory.' Others conceded that they were unable to comment and others remained silent. Omar ؓ said to me, 'O son of Abbas! Do you share that view?' When I declared that I did not, he asked, 'Then what have you to say?' I replied, 'The Surah speaks of the demise of Rasulullah ﷺ that Allah is informing him about. Allah is saying to Rasulullah ﷺ: 'When Allah's help and victory, namely the Conquest of Makkah, come and you see people entering the Deen of Allah in large numbers, this is an indication that your demise is imminent. At this stage, you should glorify the praises of your Rabb and seek forgiveness from Him. He is the Greatest Acceptor of repentance.' Omar ؓ said, 'That is what I understood.'" *(Sa'eed bin Mansur, Ibn Sa'd, Abu Ya'la, Ibn Jareer, Ibn Mundhir, Tabrani, Ibn Mardway, Abu Nu'aym and Bayhaqi in Dala'il, Kanzul Ummal, Abu Nu'aym in Hilya)*

Another narration quotes that Abdullah bin Abbas ؓ said, "Because Omar ؓ used to consult with me together with the senior Sahabah of Rasulullah ﷺ, Abdur Rahman bin Auf ؓ objected saying, 'Why do you consult him with us ...'" The rest of the narration is like the one above. *(Hakim by Dhahabi)*

Omar ⌐ and Abdullah bin Abbas ⌐ Discuss a Verse and an Incident with Ali ⌐

Abdullah bin Abbas ⌐ reports that he once asked Omar about the verse: يَا أَيُّهَا الَّذِينَ آمَنُوا لَا تَسْأَلُوا عَنْ أَشْيَاءَ إِنْ تُبْدَ لَكُمْ تَسُؤْكُمْ

O you who believe! Ask not about things which, if made plain to you, may cause you trouble. But if you ask about them while the Qur'an is being revealed, they will be made plain to you...(Al-Ma'ida:101)

Omar ⌐ explained, "When some people from amongst the Muhajirin had certain doubts about their lineage, they said, 'We wish that Allah would reveal verses of the Qur'an concerning our lineage.' It was then that Allah revealed the verse you have just recited." Omar ⌐ then asked Abdullah bin Abbas ⌐ about Ali bin Abi Talib ⌐ saying, "I know that if that companion of yours assumes the post of Khilafa, he will be abstinent. However, I fear that he should not be carried away by self-importance." "What are you saying, O Amirul Mu'minin?" Abdullah bin Abbas ⌐ exclaimed, "You are well aware of (the virtues of) our companion. By Allah! He has never changed or spoiled after the demise of Rasulullah ⌐ and has never offended Rasulullah ⌐ as long as he stayed with Rasulullah ⌐." Omar ⌐ asked, "And what about Abu Jahal's daughter that he wanted to marry while Fatima ⌐ was still his wife and did this not upset Rasulullah ⌐?" Abdullah bin Abbas ⌐ replied by arguing, "Concerning the decisive error Adam ⌐ made, Allah says: فَنَسِيَ وَلَمْ نَجِدْ لَهُ عَزْمًا

(115) *... but he forgot, and We found on his part no firm will-power. (TaHa:115)*

Similarly, our companion was not determined to offend Rasulullah ⌐. The idea was merely a thought that no person is capable of driving out of the mind. In addition to this, people with a deep understanding and profound knowledge of Allah's Deen are also prone to err sometimes. They retract and repent as soon as they are alerted." Omar ⌐ said, "A person will be sorely mistaken if he thinks that he will ever be able to dive and reach the depths of knowledge and wisdom with people like you." *(Zubair bin Bakkar in Muwaffaqiyat, Mintakhab Kanzul Ummal)*

Abdullah bin Omar ⌐ asks Aisha about a Hadith that Abu Hurairah ⌐ reported about attending funerals

Sa'd bin Abi Waqqas ⌐ reports that he was once sitting with Abdullah bin Omar ⌐ when Khabbab came there saying, "O Abdullah bin Omar ⌐! Have you heard what Abu Hurairah ⌐ saying? He claims to have heard Rasulullah ⌐ say, 'When a person accompanies a funeral bier from the house, performs the Janaza salah and then follows it until it has been buried, he will receive the reward of 2 Qirats, each Qirat being equal to Mount Uhud in magnitude. As for the person who returns after performing the Janaza salah, he shall have a reward equal in magnitude to Mount Uhud'." Abdullah bin Omar ⌐ sent Khabbab to Aisha ⌐ with instructions to verify the words of Abu Hurairah ⌐ and to then report what she said back to him. In the meantime, Abdullah bin Omar ⌐ took a handful of pebbles from the ground and kept turning them over in his hand until Khabbab returned. When Aisha ⌐ confirmed what Abu Hurairah ⌐ said, Abdullah bin Omar ⌐ threw the pebbles down saying, "We have lost a great number of Qirats." *(Muslim in Targheeb wat Tarheeb)*. Abu Hurairah ⌐ also said, "We the poor men of Suffa had neither plantations nor trade in the marketplaces to distract us from being with Rasulullah ⌐. All I did was to seek a word from Rasulullah ⌐ to teach me or a morsel to feed me. I therefore heard a lot that others did not hear." To this, Abdullah bin Omar ⌐ remarked, "O Abu Hurairah! You stayed more with Rasulullah ⌐

than we did and therefore know more Ahadeeth than us." *(Hakim, Ibn Sa'd)*

The Statement of Abdullah bin Abbas ⌐ Concerning How Few Questions the Sahabah Posed to Rasulullah ⌐

Abdullah bin Abbas ⌐ said, "I have never seen people better than the Sahabah of Rasulullah ⌐. Until he passed away, they did not ask him more than 13 questions, all of which appear in the Qur'an. Some of these are: "They (the Sahabah) ask you O Rasulullah ⌐ about the sacred months", "They ask you about wine and gambling", "They ask you about orphans", "They ask you about menstruation", "They ask you about the spoils of war", "They ask you about what they should spend". The Sahabah questioned Rasulullah ⌐ only about matters that were of benefit to them." Abdullah bin Abbas ⌐ stated further, "The first beings to perform Tawaf of the Kabah were the angels. Between the Hajar Aswad and the Rukn Yamani are the graves of several Ambiya ⌐. When any of these Ambiya ⌐ was harassed by his people, he left them to worship Allah here until he passed away." *(Tabrani, Haythami, Bazzar in Al Itqan)*

The Women of the Ansar ask Rasulullah ⌐ Questions About Deen and Ummu Sulaim ⌐ asks About Wet Dreams

Aisha ⌐ said, "The women of the Ansar were the best of women. Modesty did not prevent them from asking questions about Deen and attaining a deep understanding of Deen." *(Ibn Abdul Birr in Jami)*. Ummu Sulaim ⌐ narrates that she was sitting next to Rasulullah ⌐'s wife Ummu Salamah ⌐ when she asked, "O Rasulullah ⌐! Should a woman have a bath if she dreams that her husband is having intercourse with her?" "Shame on you, O Ummu Sulaim!" Ummu Salamah ⌐ cried out, "You have disgraced all women in front of Rasulullah ⌐!" Ummu Sulaim ⌐ responded by saying, "Allah does not shy away from the truth and rather than remaining in darkness about the matters we find difficulty with, we must ask Rasulullah ⌐." Rasulullah ⌐ replied to the question by saying, "Bless you, O Ummu Sulaim! The woman should take a bath if she finds any semen." "O Rasulullah ⌐!" Ummu Salamah ⌐ exclaimed, "Do women also have semen?" "Then how else do her children resemble her?" Rasulullah ⌐ asked, "Women are but offshoots of men." *(Ibn Abdul Birr in Jami)*

The Consequences of Asking Too Many Questions and Abdullah bin Mas'ood ⌐'s Condemnation of the Same

Sa'd ⌐ said, "People used to question each other about certain matters that Rasulullah ⌐ mentioned and would then question Rasulullah ⌐ so much about it that although it had been Halal, it would eventually be declared Haram." *(Bazzar, Haythami)*. Jabir ⌐ says, "The verses of Li'an were revealed only because of the many questions that were asked." *(Bazzar, Haythami)*. When people were posing too many questions to Abdullah bin Mas'ood, he said to Harith bin Qais, "O Harith! What do you think they ask so many questions for?" Harith replied, "They want to know the answers only to forget them later with no intention of putting their knowledge into practice." Abdullah bin Mas'ood ⌐ remarked, "I swear by the Being besides Whom there is none worthy of worship that You are right!" *(Tabrani in Kabeer, Haythami)*

The Sahabah Condemn Asking about Things That have not Occurred

Abdullah bin Omar ⌐ once said, "O people! Never ask about things that have not happened because Omar ⌐ use to curse people who asked about things that have not happened." *(Ibn Abdul Birr in Jami).* Omar ⚭ said, "It is not permissible to ask about things that have not happened because Allah has already decreed everything that is still to happen." *(Ibn Abdul Birr in Jami).* Kharija bin Zaid bin Thabit narrates that his father Zaid bin Thabit ⚭ would never voice his opinion concerning anything he was asked about until he ascertained whether the matter problem had already occurred. If it did not yet occur he would not say anything and he would comment only if it had occurred. Therefore, whenever he was once asked something, he queried, "Has it already happened?" "O Abu Sa'eed," the reply would come, "it has not yet happened, but we are preparing for it." "Then leave it," he would reply. It was then only when the incident actually occurred that he would duly inform the people about what to do. *(Ibn Abdul Birr in Jami).* Masruq relates, "When I once questioned Ubay bin Ka'b ⚭ about something, he asked, 'Has this actually occurred?' When I informed him that it did not, he remarked, 'Then let us rest until it does.'" Another narration *(Ibn Sa'd)* adds that he said, "Then let us rest until it does happen. Then when it does happen, we shall be able to apply ourselves and to get a solution for you." *(Ibn Abdul Birr in Jami).* Amir narrates that when Ammar ⚭ was once questioned about something, he asked, "Has this actually occurred?" When informed that it did not, he remarked, "Then leave us until it does. Then when it happens, we shall be able to apply ourselves and to get a solution for you." *(Ibn Sa'd)*

Learning, Teaching the Qur'an and reciting it to people: Rasulullah ﷺ Encourages a Person who Earned a Profit to Learn the Qur'an

Abu Umama ⚭ narrates that a man once came to Rasulullah ﷺ and explained how much profit he had earned by buying and selling the shares of a particular tribe. "Should I not inform you about something even more profitable?" Rasulullah ﷺ asked. "Can there be anything more profitable?" the man asked. Rasulullah ﷺ replied, "For a man to learn 10 verses of the Qur'an." The man then went to learn 10 verses, which he reported to Rasulullah ﷺ. *(Tabrani, Haythami)*

Rasulullah ﷺ Teaches Ubay bin Ka'b ⚭ the Virtue of Surah Fatiha

Ubay bin Ka'b ⚭ narrates, "Rasulullah ﷺ once said to me, 'Should I not inform you of a Surah, the like of which has not been revealed in the Torah, the Zabur, the Injil or the Qur'an?' 'Certainly,' I replied. Rasulullah ﷺ said, 'I expect that you will know it before you leave through that door.' Rasulullah ﷺ then stood up and I stood up with him, as he continued speaking to me with my hand in his. I then started to slow down fearing that Rasulullah ﷺ would leave before informing me about the Surah. As we drew close to the door, I said, 'O Rasulullah ﷺ! The Surah that you promised me?' Rasulullah ﷺ asked, 'What do you recite when you stand up in salah?' I then recited Surah Fatiha. Thereafter, Rasulullah ﷺ said, 'That's it! That's it! Those are the 7 often repeated verses that I have been granted and about which Allah speaks when He says: (87) وَلَقَدْ آتَيْنَاكَ سَبْعًا مِنَ الْمَثَانِي وَالْقُرْآنَ الْعَظِيمَ *And indeed, We have bestowed upon you seven of Al-Mathani (the seven repeatedly recited Verses), (i.e. Al-Fatiha) and the Grand Qur'an. (Al-Hijr:87) (Bayhaqi in Kanzul Ummal)*

Rasulullah ﷺ Teaches the Men of Suffa

Anas ⚭ says, "Abu Talha ⚭ once arrived at the Masjid to find Rasulullah ﷺ teaching the men of Suffa with a portion of a rock tied to his belly in order to keep his back straight because of extreme hunger." *(Abu Nu'aym in Hilya)*

Rasulullah ﷺ Overhears Abu Musa Ash'ari ⚭ Reciting the Qur'an to Some People

Anas ⚭ narrates that Abu Musa Ash'ari ⚭ was once sitting at home and when some people gathered there, he started reciting the Qur'an to them. A man then went to Rasulullah ﷺ saying, "O Rasulullah ﷺ! Should I not tell something remarkable of Abu Musa ⚭? He was sitting at home when some people gathered there and he started reciting the Qur'an to them." "Can you find me a place to sit from where none of them will be able to see me?" Rasulullah ﷺ asked. "Certainly," the man said. Rasulullah ﷺ went with the man, who seated him in a place from where no one could see him. After listening to Abu Musa Ash'ari ⚭ reciting the Qur'an, Rasulullah ﷺ remarked, "He recites in one of the tunes of the family of Dawud عليه السلام." *(Abu Ya'la, Haythami, Ibn Asakir in Kanzul Ummal)*

Abu Musa Ash'ari ⚭ Teaches Qur'an in the Jami Masjid of Basra

Anas ⚭ relates, " Abu Musa Ash'ari ⚭ once sent me to Omar ⚭. Omar ⚭ asked, 'How was Ash'ari when you left?' I replied, 'He was busy teaching Qur'an to the people when I left.' Omar ⚭ remarked, 'Take note that he is an extremely intelligent man. You should however never let this reach his ears. How were the Bedouins when you left?' 'The Ash'ari people?' I asked. 'No, the people of Basra,' he replied. 'They will be extremely offended to hear that you are referring to them as Bedouins,' I remarked. Omar ⚭ said, 'Then you need not inform them. They will all remain Bedouins except for the man amongst them whom Allah blesses with the inspiration to wage Jihad in the Path of Allah." *(Ibn Sa'd).* Abu Raja Utaridi says, "Abu Musa Ash'ari ⚭ used to come around to us in this Masjid of Basra and sit in each gathering. I can still picture him wearing two white sheets as he taught the Qur'an. It was from him that I learnt the Surah Alaq. It was the first Surah revealed to Allah's Rasul Muhammad ﷺ." *(Abu Nu'aym in Hilya)*

Ali ⚭ Memorizes the Qur'an After the Demise of Rasulullah ﷺ

Ali ⚭ says, "When Rasulullah ﷺ left this world, I vowed never to remove my shawl from my back (would not rest) until I had memorized what was contained between the 2 covers of the Qur'an. I therefore did not remove the shawl until I had memorized the entire Qur'an." *(Abu Nu'aym in Hilya)*

Abdullah bin Omar ⚭ Learns Surah Baqarah in 4 Years

Maymun ⚭ reports that Abdullah bin Omar ⚭ learnt Surah Baqarah in 4 years. *(Ibn Sa'd)*

Salman ⚭ recites Surah Yusuf to People in the Masjid of Mada'in

A man from the Ashja tribe narrates that when the people of Mada'in heard that Salman ⚭ was in the Masjid, they continued arriving there until almost 1,000 people had gathered. Salman ⚭ stood up and bade the people to sit down. When they were all seated, he started reciting Surah Yusuf. The people then started dispersing and leaving until there were only about 100 people left. Salman ⚭ became very angry and said, "You want an enchanting lecture, but when I recite the Book of Allah to you, you start to leave!?" *(Abu Nu'aym in Hilya)*

Abdullah bin Mas'ood ⚭ Teaches Qur'an to the People and Encourages Them to Learn

Whenever Abdullah bin Mas'ood ⚭ taught a verse of the Qur'an to someone, he would say, "This verse is better than everything upon which the sun rises and everything upon the surface of the earth. He would then say this for every verse of the

Qur'an. Another narration states that when people arrived at his house every morning, Abdullah bin Mas'ood ؓ would bade them to sit down and then passing by each person learning the Qur'an, he would ask them which verse they had reached. When they informed him, he would then teach them the next verse and say, "Learn it because it is better for you than everything between the heavens and the earth. In fact, for a person to even look at a verse of the Qur'an written somewhere outside the Qur'an is better than everything between the heavens and the earth." He would then proceed to the next person and tell him the same thing, until he had said it to each one of them. *(Tabrani, Haythami)*. Abdullah bin Mas'ood ؓ used to say to the people, "Ensure that you stick to this Qur'an because it is Allah's tablecloth laden with food. Whoever is capable of taking anything from Allah's tablecloth should do so. Knowledge is acquired only through studies." *(Bazzar, Haythami)*. Another narration states that Abdullah bin Mas'ood ؓ said, "Verily this Qur'an is Allah's tablecloth laden with food. Whoever is capable of learning anything from it should do so because the house most deprived of any good is the one that has nothing of the Allah's Book within it. Indeed, the house with nothing of Allah's Book in it is like a deserted house with none to occupy it and Saitan leaves the house in which he hears Surah Baqarah." *(Abu Nu'aym in Hilya)*

Omar ؓ Instructs a Man to Leave his Door to Study the Qur'an

Hasan narrates that Omar ؓ said to a man who very often came to his door, "Go and study the Book of Allah." The man left and Omar ؓ actually started to miss him. When Omar ؓ met him again, Omar ؓ almost rebuked him, the man said, "I have found in the Book of Allah such things that have made me independent of being at Omar ؓ's door." *(Ibn Abi Shaybah in Kanzul Ummal)*

What Amount of the Qur'an Should Every Muslim Learn?

Omar ؓ said, "It is necessary for every Muslim man to learn 6 Surahs, 2 Surahs for the Fajr salah, 2 Surahs for the Maghrib salah and 2 Surahs for the Isha salah." *(Abdur Razzaq in Kanzul Ummal)*. Miswar bin Makhrama ؓ says that he heard Omar ؓ say, "Learn Surah Baqarah, Surah Nisa, Surah Ma'ida, Surah Hajj and Surah Noor because they contain the Fara'idh." *(Hakim, Bayhaqi)*. Haritha bin Mudarrib narrates that Omar ؓ wrote to them with instructions to learn Surah Nisa, Surah Ahzab and Surah Noor. *(Abu Ubaid)*. Another narration states that Omar ؓ said, "Learn Surah Bara'ah, teach Surah Noor to your women and give them silver jewellery to wear." *(Sa'eed bin Mansur, Abu Shaikh, Baihaqi in Kanzul Ummal)*

What a Person should do when it is Difficult to Learn the Qur'an

Abu Raihana ؓ reports that he once complained to Rasulullah ﷺ that it was difficult for him to learn the Qur'an and that what he learnt escaped his memory. Rasulullah ﷺ advised him saying, "Do not take on more than you can manage and perform Nafl salah in abundance." Umaira reports, " Abu Raihana came to Asqalan where he used to perform Sejdah in abundance." *(Abdul Ghafir bin Salama Himsi in Tarikh, Isabah)*

Specializing in the Qur'an

Qaradha bin Ka'b ؓ reports that when they were leaving for Iraq, Omar ؓ accompanied them to a place called Sirar. There Omar ؓ performed wudhu and said, "Do you know why I have walked with you?" "Yes," they replied, "you have walked with us because we are the Sahabah of Rasulullah ﷺ." Omar ؓ said, "I have come to tell you that you are headed for a region where the people are humming with the recitation of the Qur'an just as bees are constantly humming. Do not preoccupy them by narrating Ahadeeth before them. They should occupy themselves with the Qur'an alone and narrate few Ahadeeth of Rasulullah ﷺ. Proceed and I shall be with you." When Qaradha ؓ arrived at there (in Iraq) and the people asked him to narrate Ahadeeth to them, he said, "Omar bin Khattab ؓ has prohibited us." *(Hakim by Dhahabi)*. Another narration states that Omar ؓ said, "Do not preoccupy them with Ahadeeth for it will prevent them from mastering the Qur'an." Yet another narration states that Omar ؓ asked the Sahabah, "Do you know why I have walked with you?" They replied, "You have walked with us because you wish to see us off and to honor us." Omar ؓ said, "In addition to that, I have come for another purpose as well. I have come to tell you that you are headed for a region where..." The rest of the narration is like the one above. *(Ibn Abdul Birr in Jami, Ibn Sa'd)*

Omar ؓ Reproaches Sabigh for Questioning the Mutashabih Verses of the Qur'an

A freed slave of Abdullah bin Omar ؓ narrates that an Iraqi called Sabigh in the Muslim army was questioning certain Mutashabih verses of the Qur'an and continued doing so until he reached Egypt. From there, Amr bin Al Aas ؓ sent him to Omar bin Khattab ؓ. A messenger brought the letter to Omar ؓ and after he had read it, he asked, "Where is the man?" "He is still on the carriage," replied the messenger. Omar ؓ instructed, "Go see if he is still there because I will punish you very severely if he has escaped." When Sabigh came, Omar ؓ said to him, "What are your questions?" When he stated his case, Omar ؓ asked Abdullah bin Omar ؓ for a branch of a date palm. He then beat the man until his back was marked. Omar ؓ then left him until his wounds healed. Thereafter, he repeated the treatment and again left him to recover. When Omar ؓ called him back for more of the same, Sabigh pleaded with him saying, "O Amirul Mu'minin! If you wish to kill me, do so in a nice manner and if you intend to cure me, then I swear by Allah that I have already been cured." Omar ؓ then permitted him to return to his land but sent a letter with him to Abu Musa Ash'ari ؓ stating that none of the Muslims should associate with him. When this became unbearable for him, Abu Musa Ash'ari ؓ wrote back to Omar ؓ stating that Sabigh had truly reformed. It was only then that Omar ؓ permitted the people to associate with him. *(Darmi, Ibn Abdil Hakam, Ibn Asakir.* Sulaiman bin Yasir states that a man from the Banu Tamim called Sabigh bin Isl once arrived in Madinah. He had many books and always questioned the Mutashabih verses of the Qur'an. When Omar ؓ heard about this, he sent for Sabigh while keeping some branches of the date palm ready for him. When he arrived, Omar ؓ asked him who he was. "I am the servant of Allah, Sabigh," came the reply. "And I am the servant of Allah, Omar!" Omar ؓ retorted. Omar ؓ then motioned him (to come forward) and started beating him with the branches until his head was injured and blood started to drip down his face. Sabigh then cried out, "Enough, O Amirul Mu'minin! By Allah! That which was in my head has now disappeared." *(Darmi in Kanzul Ummal)*. Another narration adds that Abu Uthman said, "Omar ؓ then wrote to instruct us not to associate with Sabigh. Therefore, if he ever arrived, we would all disperse, even if we were 100 people." *(Khateeb, Ibn Asakir, Dar Qutni)*. Whereas Sabigh was despised amongst his people after he had once been their leader. *(Ibn Ambari, Isma'eli in Isabah)*

The Incident Between Omar ؓ and Some People from Egypt

Hasan narrates that when some people met Abdullah bin

Omar ﷺ in Egypt, they said, "We have come across some matters in the Qur'an that we have been instructed to carry out when they cannot be carried out. We wish to meet the Amirul Mu'minin to ask him about this." Therefore, when Abdullah bin Omar ﷺ arrived in Madinah, these people arrived with him. Abdullah bin Omar ﷺ then went to Omar ﷺ saying, "O Amirul Mu'minin! Some people met me in Egypt and said, 'We have come across some matters in the Qur'an that we have been instructed to carry out when they cannot be carried out.' They therefore wished to meet you in this regard." Omar ﷺ asked for them to be brought before him and when they came, he called the one closest to him. Omar ﷺ asked him, "I ask you to tell me in the name of Allah and by the right Islam has upon you whether you have read the entire Qur'an." When the man replied that he did, Omar ﷺ further asked, "Have you then gathered it all in your heart?" When he replied in the negative, Omar ﷺ continued, "Have you then gathered it all in your sight?" When he again admitted that he did not, Omar ﷺ asked, "Have you then memorized it all? Have you put it all into practice?" Omar ﷺ then questioned each one of them in a like manner and after he had finished with the last of them, he said, "Omar's mother should have rather lost him! Do you expect me to make every person steadfast on the Book of Allah?! Your Rabb knows well that we slip up." He then recited the verse:

إِنْ تَجْتَنِبُوا كَبَائِرَ مَا تُنْهَوْنَ عَنْهُ نُكَفِّرْ عَنْكُمْ سَيِّئَاتِكُمْ وَنُدْخِلْكُمْ مُدْخَلًا كَرِيمًا (31)

If you avoid the great sins which you are forbidden to do, We shall remit from you your (small) sins, and admit you to a Noble Entrance (i.e. Paradise). (An-Nisa:31)

Omar ﷺ then asked them, "Do the people of Madinah know why you have come." "No," they replied. Omar ﷺ then said, "Had they known, I would have taught them a lesson with you." *(Ibn Jareer in Kanzul Ummal)*

Dislike for Accepting Remuneration for Teaching the Qur'an: Rasulullah ﷺ's Advice to Ubadah ﷺ and Ubay ﷺ

Ubadah bin Samit ﷺ says, "Because Rasulullah ﷺ was very occupied, he would hand over to one of us any person who migrated so that we may teach him the Qur'an. Rasulullah ﷺ once placed in my care a person who stayed in my house, ate meals with me and whom I taught the Qur'an. When he returned home, he felt that he owed me something and therefore gave me a bow as a gift. I had never seen a bow made of better wood nor more flexible. I however went to Rasulullah ﷺ and asked him his opinion. Rasulullah ﷺ said, "It is a burning ember that you are hanging between your shoulders." *(Tabrani, Bayhaqi in Kanzul Ummal, Hakim by Dhahabi)*. Ubay bin Ka'b ﷺ once taught a Surah to a man who gave him a garment or a shawl as a gift. When he informed Rasulullah ﷺ about this, Rasulullah ﷺ remarked, "If you wear it, you will be wearing a garment of fire." *(Abd bin Humaid in Kanzul Ummal, Ibn Majah, Ruyani, Bayhaqi)*. Another narration states that when Ubay ﷺ taught the Qur'an to a man, he gave him a bow as a gift. *(Sa'eed bin Mansur in Kanzul Ummal)*. Tufail bin Amr ﷺ says, "When Ubay ﷺ taught me the Qur'an, I gave him a bow as a gift. When he went to Rasulullah ﷺ the next morning with the bow hanging around his neck, Rasulullah ﷺ asked, "Who gave you this bow, O Ubay?" Ubay ﷺ replied, "It was Tufail bin Amr Dowsi to whom I had taught the Qur'an." Rasulullah ﷺ remarked, "You are hanging it around your neck when it is a spark from Jahannam?!" "O Rasulullah ﷺ!" Ubay ﷺ said, "But we even eat from their food." Rasulullah ﷺ said, "There is no harm in eating the food that was prepared for others and which you ate by being there.

However, if the food is prepared specially for you and you eat from it, you will be eating from your share of the Hereafter, because of which you will have less there." *(Baghawi, Ibn Asakir in Kanzul Ummal, Tabrani, Haythami)*

Rasulullah ﷺ's Words to Awf bin Malik ﷺ and Another Sahabi

Awf bin Malik ﷺ reports that there was a man with him to whom he had taught the Qur'an. When the man gave him a bow as a gift, he mentioned it to Rasulullah ﷺ. Rasulullah ﷺ remarked, "O Awf! Do you want to meet Allah while carrying an ember of Jahannam on your back?" *(Tabrani in Kabeer in Kanzul Ummal, Haythami)*. Muthanna bin Wa'il says, "When I went to Abdullah bin Busr ﷺ, he passed his hand over my head and I held him by the forearm. Just then someone asked him about remuneration for a teacher and he replied, 'A man once came to Rasulullah ﷺ, carrying a bow over his shoulder. Rasulullah ﷺ was very impressed by the bow and remarked, 'What an excellent bow! Did you buy it?' 'No,' the man replied, 'Someone gave it to me as a gift because I had taught his child the Qur'an.' Rasulullah ﷺ said, 'Do you want Allah to hang a bow of fire around your neck?' 'Not at all!' the man replied. 'Then return it,' Rasulullah ﷺ asked." *(Tabrani in Kabeer, Haythami)*

Omar ﷺ Disapproves accepting Remuneration to Teach the Qur'an

Usair bin Amr narrates that the news once reached Omar bin Khattab ﷺ that Said ﷺ said, "I shall include those who teach the Qur'an amongst the people who receive an allowance of 2,000." To this Omar ﷺ remarked, "Oh dear! Oh dear! Are people being paid for teaching the Book of Allah?!" Sa'eed bin Ibrahim narrates that Omar ﷺ wrote to one of his governors saying, "Give people an allowance for teaching the Qur'an." The governor wrote back saying, "You have written to say that people should be given an allowance for teaching the Qur'an, but then such people will start to teach the Qur'an whose only inclination would be to be enlisted and thereby receive a state allowance like the soldiers of the national army." Omar ﷺ then wrote back saying, "Rather give people an allowance by merit of them being family and companions of Rasulullah ﷺ." *(Abu Ubaid in Kanzul Ummal)*. Mujahid narrates that Omar bin Khattab ﷺ addressed the people saying, "O men of knowledge and men of the Qur'an! Do not accept remuneration for imparting your knowledge and for teaching the Qur'an because then even adulterers will beat you to Jannah." *(Khateeb in Kanzul Ummal)*

(Note: Since there are also Ahadeeth permitting the acceptance of remuneration for teaching the Qur'an, a person may do so if he has no other option. While it is best not to accept remuneration, if a person does accept remuneration, he should accept it as remuneration for his time and not for his teaching.)

Fear of differences arising once the Qur'an spread amongst different people: The Fear that Abdullah bin Abbas ﷺ had About This and the Incident with Omar ﷺ

Abdullah bin Abbas ﷺ narrates, "I was sitting with Omar bin Khattab ﷺ when a letter came to him from Kufa, informing him how much Qur'an the people had learnt. 'Allahu Akbar!' Omar ﷺ exclaimed out of happiness. May Allah have mercy on him. 'They will soon start to have differences,' I remarked. 'What are you saying!' Omar ﷺ exclaimed, 'How would you know that?' Because he got so angry, I left and went home. A while later, he sent for me, but I made an excuse. He however sent a message saying that I have no option but to come. When I got there, he said, 'There was something that you had said What was it?.' 'I seek Allah's forgiveness,' I said, 'I shall never repeat what I said.'

It was only when Omar ﷺ forced me to repeat my words that I said, 'A letter came to you stating how much Qur'an the people had learnt, to which I said that they will soon start to have differences.' 'How did you come to learn this?' he asked. I replied, "I read the verse:

وَمِنَ النَّاسِ مَنْ يُعْجِبُكَ قَوْلُهُ فِي الْحَيَاةِ الدُّنْيَا وَيُشْهِدُ اللَّهَ عَلَى مَا فِي قَلْبِهِ وَهُوَ أَلَدُّ الْخِصَامِ (204) وَإِذَا تَوَلَّى سَعَى فِي الْأَرْضِ لِيُفْسِدَ فِيهَا وَيُهْلِكَ الْحَرْثَ وَالنَّسْلَ وَاللَّهُ لَا يُحِبُّ الْفَسَادَ (205)

(205) And of mankind there is he whose speech may please you (O Muhammad ﷺ), in this worldly life, and he calls Allah to witness as to that which is in his heart, yet he is the most quarrelsome of the opponents. And when he turns away (from you "O Muhammad ﷺ "), his effort in the land is to make mischief therein and to destroy the crops and the cattle, and Allah likes not mischief. (Al-Baqara:204-205)

When this happens, men of the Qur'an will be unable to contain themselves. I then read the verse:

وَإِذَا قِيلَ لَهُ اتَّقِ اللَّهَ أَخَذَتْهُ الْعِزَّةُ بِالْإِثْمِ فَحَسْبُهُ جَهَنَّمُ وَلَبِئْسَ الْمِهَادُ (206) وَمِنَ النَّاسِ مَنْ يَشْرِي نَفْسَهُ ابْتِغَاءَ مَرْضَاةِ اللهِ وَاللَّهُ رَءُوفٌ بِالْعِبَادِ (207)

And when it is said to him, "Fear Allah", he is led by arrogance to (more) crime. So enough for him is Hell, and worst indeed is that place to rest! And of mankind is he who would sell himself, seeking the Pleasure of Allah. And Allah is full of Kindness to (His) slaves. (Al-Baqara:206-207).

To this, Omar ﷺ remarked, 'I swear by Allah that you are right." (Hakim by Dhahabi)

Incident About the Fear Abdullah bin Abbas ﷺ had in This Regard

Abdullah bin Ubaid bin Umair ﷺ reports that Abdullah bin Abbas ﷺ said, "I was with Omar when he caught hold of my hand and said; 'I think that the Qur'an has now spread amongst the masses.' 'I do not like that too much, O Amirul Mu'minin,' I remarked. Omar ﷺ pulled his hand away saying, 'And why not?' 'Because,' I started to explain, 'when they all start to learn the Qur'an without proper understanding, they will start to advocate their own opinions. Once they do this, they will start to dispute and once the disputes start, they will start killing each other.' Omar ﷺ then sat aside and left me alone. Only Allah knows the anxiety I endured during the rest of that day. It was only the following afternoon that his messenger came to inform me that the Amirul Mu'minin was calling me. When I got there, Omar ﷺ asked, 'What was it that you said?' After I had repeated my words to him, he said, 'I had also understood the same but I had been concealing this from the people." (Hakim)

The Advice of Omar bin Khattab ﷺ

Kinana Adawi narrates that Omar ﷺ wrote to the commanders of his armies to send him a list of all the men who were Huffadh of the Qur'an so that he could dispatch them to the ends of the empire to teach the Qur'an. Abu Musa Ash'ari ﷺ wrote back to Omar ﷺ stating that the Huffadh with him numbered just over 300. Omar ﷺ's reply to him was as follows:

"In the name of Allah the Most Kind, the Most Merciful
From the servant of Allah Omar to the servant of Allah Qais and all the Huffadh with him. Peace be upon you all This Qur'an is a great source of reward and honor for you and shall be a treasure for you in the Hereafter. You should therefore follow its dictates and never allow it to follow yours (by distorting its interpretation to suit your desires) because the person whose dictates the Qur'an is forced to follow shall have it shoved on to his neck to throw him into Jahannam. As for the one who follows the Qur'an, the Qur'an shall lead him to Jannatul*

Firdous. So as far as you can, let it be an intercessor for you and never let it be a complainant against you. The person for whom the Qur'an intercedes shall enter Jannah and the one against whom the Qur'an complains shall surely enter Jahannam. Always bear in mind that the Qur'an is a fountainhead of guidance, a flower of knowledge and the final scripture from the Most Merciful. It is by this Qur'an that Allah opens blind eyes, deaf ears and locked hearts.' You must also bear in mind that when a man wakes up at night, brushes his teeth with a Miswak, performs wudhu, says 'Allahu Akbar' and then recites the Qur'an, an angel places his mouth on the person's mouth and says, 'Recite, recite. You are doing an excellent thing and it is most excellent for you.' If he performs wudhu without using the Miswak, the angel protects him and does nothing else. Behold! Recitation of the Qur'an in salah is a protected treasure and an ordained excellence. You should therefore do as much of it as you possibly can. Salah is a celestial light, zakah is a symbol, patience is an illumination, fasting is a shield and the Qur'an is a proof either for you or against you. You should therefore honor the Qur'an and never cause it disgrace because Allah will honor the one who honors the Qur'an and will disgrace the one who brings it disgrace. You also ought to know that the person who recites the Qur'an, memorizes it, practices on it am abides by its injunctions shall have his Du'as accepted by Allah. If Allah pleases, He may accept them in this word, and if He wills, he may reserve them as a treasure for the Hereafter. What remains with Allah is better and more lasting for those who have Iman and who rely on their Rabb." (Ibn Zanjway in Kanzul Ummal)

The Advice of Abu Musa Ash'ari ﷺ

Abu Kinana reports that when Abu Musa Ash'ari ﷺ gathered together the Huffadh of the army he commanded, they numbered close to 300. Abu Musa ﷺ lectured to them about the greatness of the Qur'an saying, "Verily this Qur'an shall be either a source of reward for you or a burden in the Hereafter. You should therefore follow the dictates of the Qur'an and never force it to follows yours because the one who follows the Qur'an shall be with it in the gardens of Jannah while the one who forces the Qur'an to follow his desires shall have it shoved on his neck and it will throw him into Jahannam." (Abu Nu'aym in Hilya). Abul Aswad Daly reports that Abu Musa Ash'ari ﷺ once gathered all the Qurra, emphasizing that none but the Huffadh should come to him. It was approximately 300 men who came to him. He addressed them saying, "You men are the Qurra of the city and should therefore never allow the passage of time to harden your hearts as it happened to the Ahlul Kitab. A Surah had been revealed that we thought resembled Surah Bara'ah in length and in the stern subject matter it contained. A verse from it which I had memorized stated that if man had 2 valleys of gold he would seek to have a 3rd and it would only be the sand of his grave that would be able to fill his belly. Thereafter, another Surah was revealed which we thought resembled the Musabbihat because it begins with the words …..(Sabbaha Lillah). The verse from it that I had memorized is: يَا أَيُّهَا الَّذِينَ آمَنُوا لِمَ تَقُولُونَ مَا لَا تَفْعَلُونَ (2)

O you who believe! Why do you say that which you do not do? (As-Saff:2)

Testimony will be taken for everything you do and will be asked about it on the Day of Judgment." (Abu Nu'aym in Hilya)

The Advice of Abdullah bin Mas'ood ﷺ

Abdullah bin Mas'ood ﷺ once addressed the people of Kufa. After greeting them with Salam and instructing them to observe

Taqwa, he said, "Never dispute about the Qur'an and never oppose each other concerning it because there are no discrepancies in the Qur'an, it will never be completely forgotten and constant repetition of the Qur'an will never exhaust one. Do you not see that the restrictions, the Fara'idh and Allah's explicit commands in the Shari'ah of Islam are one? It would be said that the Qur'an has discrepancies if a part of it commands an act which another part forbids. Every part of the Qur'an rather complements the rest of it. I am convinced that such deep understanding and knowledge shall surface amongst you people that surpass all other people. If a camel could take me to a person who has more knowledge of what has been revealed to Muhammad ﷺ than I have, I shall certainly go to him to increase the knowledge I have. I know well that while the entire Qur'an would be recited to Rasulullah ﷺ once every year, it was recited to Rasulullah ﷺ twice during the year that he passed away. Every Ramadhan ﷺ Jibra'el ﷺ would recite the Qur'an to Rasulullah ﷺ and Rasulullah ﷺ would recite to him. Whenever I recited Qur'an to Rasulullah, he would approve of my recitation, therefore whoever recites Qur'an in the manner that I recite, should not turn away and forsake it. In a like manner, whoever recites the Qur'an in another authentic manner should also not turn away and forsake it because whoever rejects anyone of the various manners of recitation will reject them all." *(Ibn Asakir in Kanzul Ummal)*. A student of Abdullah bin Mas'ood ﷺ from Hamdan narrates that before Abdullah bin Mas'ood ﷺ left for Madinah, he gathered all his students together and said, "By Allah! I am convinced that such religiousness, deep understanding of Deen and knowledge of the Qur'an shall surface amongst you people that surpass that of all other Muslims..." The narration continues until it states that he said, "Verily there are no discrepancies in the Qur'an, neither does the Qur'an ever age or lose its dignity by continuous repetition." *(Ahmad, Haythami)*. Abdullah bin Mas'ood ﷺ also said, "It is only befitting that a man of the Qur'an be recognized by his nights when he is engaged in Ibadah, when others are asleep, by his days spent fasting when others are eating, by his sorrow pondering about his plight in the Hereafter when others are rejoicing, by his weeping when others are laughing, by his silence when others are socializing and by his humility when others are behaving arrogantly. It is befitting of a man of the Qur'an to be weeping and sorrowful, wise and tolerant, knowledgeable and composed. It does not behave a man of the Qur'an to be rude, negligent, overexcited, rowdy and short-tempered." Abdullah bin Mas'ood ﷺ said, "Do your best to be a listener rather than speaking and take careful note when you hear Allah say, 'O you who have Iman!' because it is only something good that you are being instructed to do or something evil that you are being prohibited from." *(Abu Nu'aym in Hilya)*.

A Bedouin Questions Rasulullah ﷺ about Judgment when he was Busy Narrating Ahadeeth

Abu Hurairah ﷺ narrates that Rasulullah ﷺ was busy narrating Ahadeeth when a Bedouin arrived and asked, "When will Judgment take place?" When Rasulullah ﷺ continued narrating, some of the Sahabah said that Rasulullah ﷺ was not giving a reply because he heard the man but did not like the question. Others said that Rasulullah ﷺ did not hear the man at all. When Rasulullah ﷺ had completed narrating Ahadeeth, he asked, "Where is the Bedouin?" "Here am I over here!" the man said. Rasulullah ﷺ then said, "Wait for Judgment when a time arrives in which trusts are misappropriated." "How will they be misappropriated?" the man asked. Rasulullah ﷺ replied, "Wait for Judgment when authority is placed in the hands of unworthy

people." *(Bukhari)*

Wabisa ﷺ Propagates a Hadith of Rasulullah ﷺ in Conformance with the Instruction Rasulullah ﷺ gave in his Farewell Sermon

Standing before the people in the largest Masjid of Riqqa during the days of Eidul Fitr and Eidul Adha, Wabisa ﷺ used to say, "I was present with Rasulullah ﷺ during the Farewell Hajj when he addressed the people saying, 'O people! Which month is most sacred?' 'This month of Dhul Hijjah is,' the people replied. Rasulullah ﷺ asked further, 'O people! Which city is most sacred?' 'This city of Makkah is,' the people replied. Rasulullah ﷺ then declared, 'Until the day you meet your Rabb, your blood, your wealth and your honor are as sacred to you as this day, this month and this city are. Have I conveyed the message?' 'You certainly have,' the people replied. Rasulullah ﷺ then raised his hands to the sky saying, 'You be the witness, O Allah.' Thereafter, he said, 'Those of you present here should pass the message on to those who are absent.' Do come closer so that I may convey to you what Rasulullah ﷺ said to us." *(Bazzar, Haythami)*

Abu Umama ﷺ Instructs his Students to Propagate

Makhul says, "Ibn Abu Zakariyya, Sulaiman bin Habib and I once went to Abu Umama ﷺ in Hims. After we had greeted him with the words of Salam, he said, 'This sitting of yours here is a means Allah has used for the Deen to reach you and will also be Allah's evidence against you if you do not propagate it. Rasulullah ﷺ propagated, so you too should propagate." Saleem bin Amir says, "When we would sit with Abu Ubadah ﷺ and he narrated to us many Ahadeeth of Rasulullah ﷺ, he would say to us after he had completed, 'Have you understood? Now propagate as it has been propagated to you.'" *(Tabrani in Kabeer, Haythami)*

Rasulullah ﷺ's Du'a for Those who Narrate his Ahadeeth and Teach Them to the People

Abdullah bin Abbas ﷺ narrates that Rasulullah ﷺ prayed, "O Allah! Shower Your mercy on my successors." "O Rasulullah ﷺ!" the Sahabah asked, "Who are your successors?" Rasulullah ﷺ replied, "Those who will come after me, who will narrate my Ahadeeth and teach to the people." *(Tabrani in Targheeb wat Tarheeb, Ibn Najjar, Khatib in Sharfus Sahabah, Kanzul Ummal)*

Abu Hurairah ﷺ Narrates Ahadeeth in the Masjid of Rasulullah ﷺ Before the Jumu'ah Salah

Asim bin Muhammad narrates from his father that he saw Abu Hurairah ﷺ come to the Masjid of Rasulullah ﷺ on the day of Jumu'ah. Standing and holding the 2 knobs of the pulpit, he said, "Abul Qasim Rasulullah ﷺ the truthful and veritable narrated to us..." He then continued to narrate Ahadeeth until he heard the door of the Imam's room open as the Imam emerged to lead the salah. He then sat down. *(Hakim by Dhahabi)*

The Difficulty Omar ﷺ, Uthman ﷺ and Ali ﷺ Experienced Narrating Ahadeeth

Aslam reports that they used to ask Omar ﷺ to narrate Ahadeeth to them, he would say, "I fear that I may add a word or omit a word because Rasulullah ﷺ said, 'The person who intentionally lies about me is headed for Jahannam." *(Ahmad, Ibn Abi, Uqaili, Abu Nu'aym in Ma'rifah, Kanzul Ummal)*. Abdur Rahman bin Hatib says, "I have not seen any of the Sahabah narrate Ahadeeth as well and as thoroughly as Uthman ﷺ. However, he was a man who was extremely reluctant to narrate

Ahadeeth." *(Ibn Sa'd, Ibn Asakir in Muntakhab Kanzul Ummal)*. Uthman ﷺ used to say, "What prevents me from narrating Ahadeeth from Rasulullah ﷺ is not the fact that I was not one of those Sahabah with the best memories. What prevents me is that I can testify that I heard Rasulullah ﷺ say, 'Whoever attributes anything to me that I never stated should prepare for his abode in Jahannam.'" Another narration quotes Rasulullah ﷺ's words as, "Whoever speaks lies about me should prepare for a house in Jahannam." *(Ahmad, Abu Ya'la, Bazzar, Haythami)*. Ali ﷺ said, "When narrating Ahadeeth to you, I prefer falling from the sky rather than stating something that Rasulullah ﷺ never said. However, when speaking to you about matters between us, then precautions need not be so strict because wars are won by strategy." *(Bukhari, Muslim in Kanzul Ummal)*

The Difficulty Abdullah bin Mas'ood ﷺ faced to Narrate Ahadeeth

Amr bin Maymun reports that sometimes an entire year would pass by without Abdullah bin Mas'ood ﷺ narrating a single Hadith. When he narrated a Hadith one day, he started to shiver and perspiration beaded up on his forehead. He said, "Rasulullah ﷺ said something like that or stated similar words." *(Hakim by Dhahabi)*. Masruq reports, "Abdullah bin Mas'ood ﷺ started to narrate a Hadith one day, but as soon as he said, 'Rasulullah ﷺ said,' he started to shake so much that his clothing shook. He then added, 'Rasulullah ﷺ said something to the effect or something similar.'" *(Ibn Abdul Birr in Jami, Isabah)*

Abu Darda ﷺ, Anas ﷺ and Abdullah bin Omar ﷺ use the Words "Something like that or Something similar" when narrate Ahadeeth

Abu Idris Khowlani says, "I noticed that whenever Abu Darda ﷺ completed narrating Ahadeeth, he would add, 'Rasulullah ﷺ said that, something similar to that or something resembling that.'" *(Tabrani, Haythami, Abu Ya'la, Ruyani, Ibn Asakir in Kanzul Ummal)*. Muhammad bin Sirin narrates that whenever Anas bin Malik ﷺ narrated Ahadeeth from Rasulullah ﷺ, he would end with the words, "It was something like this that Rasulullah said." *(Ibn Abdul Birr in Jami)*. Rasulullah ﷺ said, "Anas bin Malik ﷺ narrated few Ahadeeth from Rasulullah ﷺ, but when he did, he would end with the words, "It was something like this that Rasulullah ﷺ said." *(Ahmad, Abu Ya'la, Hakim in Kanzul Ummal)*. Abu Ja'far Muhammad bin Ali says, "There was no companion of Rasulullah ﷺ more cautious of adding anything to or omitting anything from the Ahadeeth of Rasulullah ﷺ than Abdullah bin Omar ﷺ." *(Ibn Sa'd)*. Sha'bi says, "I sat in the company of Abdullah bin Omar ﷺ for an entire year without hearing him narrate anything from Rasulullah ﷺ." *(Ibn Sa'd)*

The Dependence of Imran bin Husain ﷺ's Memory and Narration of Ahadeeth

Imran bin Husain ﷺ said, "I have heard many Ahadeeth from Rasulullah ﷺ which I have memorized. All that prevents me from narrating them is that some of my companions may differ with me in the narration." *(Tabrani in Kabeer, Haythami)*. Mutarraf reports that Imran bin Husain ﷺ said to him, "O Mutarraf! By Allah! I am certain that if I chose to do so, I could narrate Ahadeeth from Rasulullah ﷺ for 2 days continuously without repeating a single Hadith. What makes me reluctant to do so and makes me disapprove of doing such a thing is that although I was there when many Sahabah of Muhammad ﷺ were there and I also heard what they heard, they confuse the sequence of the words when they narrate." Imran bin Husain ﷺ would say, "If I were to narrate to you what Rasulullah ﷺ said, I am certain that I will be accurate." When he quoted the words of Rasulullah

ﷺ, Imran bin Husain ﷺ would do so with great certainty and say, "1 heard Rasulullah ﷺ say..." *(Tabrani, Haythami)*

Suhaib ﷺ's Reluctance to say, "Rasulullah ﷺ said"

Sulaiman bin Abu Abdullah reports that he heard Suhaib ﷺ say, "By Allah! I shall never intentionally narrate Ahadeeth to you saying that it is what Rasulullah ﷺ said. However, I shall gladly relate to you what I experienced in the expeditions I participated in with Rasulullah ﷺ. Then again, I shall never say, 'Rasulullah ﷺ said'." *(Ibn Sa'd in Muntakhab Kanzul Ummal)*

Wathila bin Asqa ﷺ Narrates only the Intended Meaning of the Ahadeeth

Makhul relates, "Abul Azhar and I once went to Wathila bin Asqa ﷺ and said, 'O Abu Asqa! Narrate to us a Hadith that you heard from Rasulullah ﷺ without any uncertain words, and without any additions or omissions.' Wathila ﷺ asked, 'Has any of you recited any part of the Qur'an last night?' 'Yes,' we replied, 'But since we are not Huffadh, we tend to add a Wawa or an Alif.' Wathila ﷺ remarked, 'And that is the Qur'an which you have still not mastered when it has been in your midst for such a long time. When you feel that you are adding or omitting letters to it, what about the Ahadeeth that we had perhaps heard only once from Rasulullah ﷺ? It is sufficient for you that we narrate only their intended meanings to you." *(Ibn Abdul Birr in Jami)*

Omar ﷺ censures Those Sahabah who Narrated Plenty of Ahadeeth

Ibrahim bin Abdur Rahman bin Auf relates, "By Allah! Before he passed away, Omar sent messengers to various distant places to summon Sahabah such as Abdullah bin Hudhafa ﷺ, Abu Darda ﷺ, Abu Dhar ﷺ and Uqba bin Amir ﷺ. When they had gathered, he said to them, 'What Ahadeeth have you people spread to even the far distant lands?' 'Are you forbidding us from narrating them?' they asked. 'No,' Omar ﷺ replied, 'I just want you to remain with me. By Allah! I do not want you to part from me (here in Madinah) for as long as I live because we know best which of your narrations we shall accept and which ones we will not.' They therefore did not part from Omar ﷺ until he passed away." *(Ibn Asakir in Kanzul Ummal)*. Ibrahim bin Abdur Rahman relates that Omar ﷺ sent for Abdullah bin Mas'ood ﷺ, Abu Mas'ood Ansari ﷺ and Abu Darda ﷺ and said to them, "What are the Ahadeeth that you are so frequently narrating to the people?" He then confined them to Madinah until he was martyred. *(Tabrani, Haythami, Ibn Sa'd)*

The Difficulty Zaid bin Arqam ﷺ Experienced with Narrating Ahadeeth in His Old Age

Ibn Abu Awfa ﷺ reports that when they used to request Zaid bin Arqam ﷺ to narrate the Ahadeeth of Rasulullah ﷺ to them, he would say, "We have aged and have begun to forget. Narrating the Ahadeeth of Rasulullah ﷺ is a very serious matter (which cannot be taken lightly)." *(Ibn Asakir in Kanzul Ummal)*

Statements of Mu'adh ﷺ, Abu Darda ﷺ and Anas ﷺ Attaching More Importance to Practice Than to Theory

Mu'adh ﷺ *(Ibn Abi Khatib)* and Abu Darda ﷺ *(Ibn Asakir)* both said, "Learn as much as you wish to learn but Allah will place no benefit in your knowledge until you practice what you know." Anas ﷺ said, "Learn as much as you please, but I swear by Allah that you will not be rewarded for your knowledge until you put it into practice." *(Abul Hasan bin Akhram in Amali, Jami'us Saghir)*. Abdur Rahman bin Ghanam says, "10 Sahabah of Rasulullah ﷺ informed me that they were learning in the Masjid of Quba when Rasulullah ﷺ came to them and said, 'Learn...'" The remainder of the words is like the narration above. *(Ibn Abdul Birr in Jami)*

Rasulullah ﷺ's Words to a Man in this Regard and the Statement of Omar ◈

Ali ◈ reports that a man came to Rasulullah ﷺ and said, "O Rasulullah ﷺ! What will satisfy the evidence that ignorance will hold against me?" "Knowledge," Rasulullah ﷺ replied. "And what will satisfy the evidence that knowledge will hold against me?" he asked. Rasulullah ﷺ's reply was, "Action." *(Khateeb in Kanzul Ummal)*. Omar ◈ said, "Study the Book of Allah and you will be known for it. Practice on its teachings and you will be amongst worthy bearers." *(Ibn Abi Shaybah in Kanzul Ummal)*

The Statements of Ali ◈ in this Regard

Ali ◈ said, "Study and you will be known for it. Practice on your knowledge and you will be amongst its worthy bearers because soon a time will come when 9o% of the truth will be rejected and the only person who will be saved will be one who remains anonymous and aloof from people. Such people are the beacons of guidance and the lanterns of knowledge. They are not hasty; do not promote immoral behavior or immoral speech." *(Ahmad in Zuhd, Abu Ubaid, Dinowri in Gharib, Ibn Asakir in Kanzul Ummal)*. Ali ◈ once said, "O men of knowledge! Practice on your knowledge because only that person is an Alim whose knowledge is followed by practice and whose practice conforms with his knowledge. Some shall soon come whose knowledge will not even transcend their collar-bones. Their private lives will contradict their public lives just as their actions will contradict their knowledge. They will sit in groups, boasting to each other and will get angry if anyone sitting in their group had to leave to sit with another group. The actions of such people will not even transcend their gatherings on its way to reach Allah." *(Ibn Abdul Birr in Jami, Kanzul Ummal)*

Abdullah bin Mas'ood ◈ emphasizes Knowledge with Action

Abdullah bin Mas'ood ◈ said, "O people! Study, but whoever studies should practice what he learns." *(Tabrani, Haythami, Abu Nu'aym in Hilya)*. Abdullah bin Ukaim says, "It was in this very Masjid that I heard Abdullah bin Mas'ood ◈ begin his speech with an oath as he said, 'Your Rabb shall be Alone with everyone of you just as you see the 14th moon all by itself. Allah will say, 'O son of Adam! What deceived you about me? O son of Adam! How did you respond to the Ambiya? O son of Adam! Did you practice on your knowledge?'" Adi bin Adi narrates that Abdullah bin Mas'ood ◈ repeated the following words: "Destruction be to the person who does not acquire knowledge. Still, if Allah wills, Allah shall educate him. However, 7 times destruction will be to the person who has the knowledge but does not practice." *(Ibn Abdul Birr in Jami)*. Abdullah bin Mas'ood ◈ said, "Everyone has fantastic words to say but only those will be successful whose deeds are consistent with their words. The one whose deeds contradict his words shall have only himself to blame." *(Ibn Abdul Birr in Jami)*. It was also Abdullah bin Mas'ood ◈ who said, "People are in need of anyone who is occupied in Allah. People are also in need of that person's knowledge who practices on his knowledge;" *(Ibn Abdul Birr in Jami, Kanzul Ummal)*

Abu Darda ◈ Fears that on the Day of Judgment he will be Questioned About How Much he Practiced on His Knowledge

Luqman bin Amir narrates that Abu Darda ◈ used to say, "What I fear most about Allah on the Day of Judgment is that he would call me in front of all creation saying, 'O Uwaymir!' Then when I respond by saying, 'I am at Your service, O my Rabb!', Allah shall ask, 'Did you practice on your knowledge?" *(Bayhaqi in Targheeb wat Tarheeb, Abu Nu'aym in Hilya)*. Abu Darda ◈ also said, "What I fear most is that I should be asked on the Day of Judgment, 'O Uwaymir! Did you acquire knowledge or remain ignorant?' If I reply that I had acquired knowledge, every verse containing a command and every verse containing an admonition shall claim their rights. The verses containing commands will ask, 'Did you carry out (what was commanded)?' and every verse containing an admonition will ask, 'Did you take heed to the admonition?' I seek Allah's protection from knowledge that does not benefit, from desires that are not sated and from Du'as that are not answered." *(Abu Nu'aym in Hilya)*. Abu Darda ◈ said, "None can possess Taqwa until he has knowledge and one can attain beauty through knowledge only if one practices on it." *(Abu Nu'aym in his Hilya Adi reported from Abdullah bin Mas'ood)*. Abu Darda ◈ also said, "The worst of people in Allah's sight on the Day of Judgment shall be that person with knowledge whose knowledge does not benefit him which he does not practice on." *(Abu Nu'aym in Hilya)*

Mu'adh bin Jabal ◈ and Anas ◈ Encourage Combining Knowledge with Practice

Mu'adh bin Jabal ◈ said, "No person will be able to move his feet on the Day of Judgment until he is questioned about 4 things; (1) about how he used his body, (2) about how he spent his life, (3) about how earned and spent his wealth and (4) about how he practiced on his knowledge." *(Ibn Abdul Birr in Jami)*. Mu'adh bin Jabal ◈ also said, "Learn as much as you want but Allah shall not reward you for it until you practice on your knowledge." *(Ibn Abdul Birr in Jami, Abu Nu'aym in Hilya)*. Anas ◈ said, "Learn as much as you want to learn but Allah shall not reward you for it until you practice on your knowledge: While the objective of true Ulema when acquiring knowledge is to remember and practice, the objective of foolish people when acquiring knowledge is to relate it to others without practicing." *(Ibn Abdul Birr in Jami)*

The Encouragement Ubay bin Ka'b ◈ to Follow the Sunnah and the Ways of the Pious Predecessors and Rejecting Bid'ah

Ubay bin Ka'b ◈ said, "Hold fast to the straight path and the Sunnah because Allah shall never punish a person who is steadfast on the straight path and the Sunnah and whose tears then flow from his eyes out of fear for Allah when he thinks of Allah. When a person who is steadfast on the straight path and the Sunnah thinks of Allah and his hairs stand on end out of fear for Allah, is just like a tree with dry leaves. Just as its leaves fall off when a strong wind blows, all his sins fall off him in the same manner. Moderation when doing something for the pleasure of Allah and according to the Sunnah is better than exerting oneself in something that is not for the pleasure of Allah and against the Sunnah. You should check well that your deeds conform with the pattern of the Ambiya ﷺ and their Sunnah, regardless of whether the deeds be an exerted effort or something done in moderation." *(Lalka'ee in Kanzul Ummal, Abu Nu'aym in Hilya)*

The Encouragement Omar ◈ and Abdullah bin Mas'ood ◈ Gave in this Regard

Sa'eed bin Musayyib narrates that when Omar ◈ arrived back in Madinah, he addressed the people saying, "O people! The

Sunan have been demonstrated to you and the Fara'idh has been ordained for you. You have therefore been left on a clear and distinct path which you will be able to follow with ease unless people lead you to the right and to the left (lead you astray)." (Ibn Abdul Birr in Jami). When lecturing the people every Thursday, Abdullah bin Mas'ood ❀ would say, "There are only 2 matters of importance. One is a way of life and the other is speech. While the best and truest of speech is that of Allah, the best way of life is that of Muhammad ❀. Everything newly introduced into the Deen is a Bid'ah and every Bid'ah is a means of leading people astray. Behold! Prolonged periods of stagnation should never pass over you, causing your hearts to harden and distant hopes should never make you negligent of the Hereafter because everything still pending is nearby and something far off is that which is never to come." (Ibn Abdul Birr in Jami). Abdullah bin Mas'ood ❀ said, "Moderation in Sunnah is better than exerting oneself in Bid'ah. (Hakim by Dhahabi, Abu Nu'aym in Hilya)

The Encouragement Imran bin Husain ❀ Gave in this Regard

Imran bin Husain ❀ said, "The Qur'an was revealed and Rasulullah ❀ demonstrated his way of life which we emulated. You people must follow us because if you do not, you shall go astray." (Ahmad, Haythami). Imran bin Husain ❀ once said to someone who insisted on following only the Qur'an, "You are a fool! Do you find any verse of the Qur'an telling you that there are 4 Rakats in Zuhr and that the Qira'ah should be silent?" He then proceeded to enumerate the other salats, zakah and other injunctions of Deen, saying, "Are the details of these found in the Qur'an. While the Book of Allah only briefly mentions these things, the Sunnah explains the details." (Ibn Abdul Birr in Jami)

Abdullah bin Mas'ood ❀ Encourages Following the Sahabah

Abdullah bin Mas'ood ❀ said, "Whoever wishes to follow anyone, should follow the companions of Muhammad ❀ because from amongst the entire Ummah, their hearts are most righteous, their knowledge is deepest, they are the least pretentious, they are most unswerving in example and their religious condition is best. Allah had selected them to be the companions of His Nabi ❀ and to establish His Deen. You should acknowledge their worth and follow in their footsteps because they had been fixed on upright guidance." (Ibn Abdul Birr in Jami, Abu Nu'aym in Hilya)

Hudhaifa ❀ Encourages the Qurra to Follow in the Footsteps of Those Who Preceded Them

Hudhaifa ❀ said, "O assembly of Qurra! Fear Allah and follow the Path of those before you. I swear by my life that if you follow them, you will go very far ahead and if you forsake their path to go this way, you will have gone far astray." (Ibn Abdul Birr in Jami, Ibn Abi Shayba, Ibn Asakir in Kanzul Ummal)

Sa'd bin Abi Waqqas ❀ Tells his son, "We are the Leaders to be Followed"

Mus'ab bin Sa'd reports that whenever his father (Sa'd bin Abi Waqqas ❀) led the salah in congregation, he would make it brief together with performing the Ruku and Sejdah properly. However, when performing salah at home by himself, he would prolong the Ruku, the Sejdah and the salah. He would then say, "Dear son! We (the Sahabah) are the leaders to be followed."(Tabrani, Haythami). Abdullah bin Mas'ood ❀ said, "Follow and do not introduce" and his statement about Abu Bakr ❀ and Omar ❀ Abdullah bin Mas'ood ❀ said, "Follow and do not introduce new ways as everything has been done for you, Rasulullah ❀ and the Sahabah have already made the process to

follow." (Tabrani, Haythami). Abdullah bin Mas'ood ❀ said, "An integral part of Sunnah is to love Abu Bakr ❀ and Omar ❀ and to acknowledge their worth." (Ibn Abdul Birr in Jami)

Ali ❀ Forbids People From Following Living People

Ali ❀ said, "Be careful not to emulate people because while a man can be doing the deeds of the people of Jannah, he can change according to the knowledge of Allah and then start doing the actions of the people of Jahannam. When he dies, he becomes an inmate of Jahannam. It may also happen that while a man can be doing the actions of the people of Jahannam, he can change according to the knowledge of Allah and then start doing the deeds of the people of Jannah. When he then dies, he becomes a worthy dweller of Jannah. If it is absolutely necessary for you follow someone, let it be those who have died as practicing Mu'minin and not those who are alive." (Ibn Abdul Birr in Jami)

Abdullah bin Mas'ood ❀ Reproaches a Group who Opposed the Sunnah by Changing the Method of Dhikr

Abul Bakhtari says that someone once informed Abdullah bin Mas'ood ❀ about a group of people who sat in the Masjid after Maghrib when one of them would tell the others to recite "Allahu Akbar" in a particular manner, to recite "SubhanAllah" in a particular manner and to recite "Al Hamdu Lillah" in a particular manner. "Do they then do as he says?" Abdullah bin Mas'ood ❀ asked. When the person confirmed that they did, Abdullah bin Mas'ood ❀ told him, "Inform me when you see them gathering again." When the person informed him afterwards, Abdullah bin Mas'ood ❀ then came to this group, wearing his high hat, and sat with them. When he heard what they were saying, he, being the stern man that he was, stood up and said, "I am Abdullah bin Mas'ood. By Allah, besides Whom there is none worthy of worship! Verily you people have certainly perpetrated a terrible wrong by carrying out this act of Bid'ah! Have you then superseded the companions of Muhammad ❀ in knowledge?" A person named Ma'dad said, "By Allah! We never intended to perpetrate a wrong with this new act, nor have we superseded the companions of Muhammad ❀ in knowledge." Amr bin Utba said, "O Abu Abdur Rahman! We seek forgiveness from Allah." Thereupon Abdullah bin Mas'ood ❀ told them, "It is compulsory for you to follow the path of Rasulullah ❀ and the Sahabah and to strictly adhere to it. By Allah! If you will do so, you will have advanced far ahead and if you start swerving to the left and right, you will stray far off." (Abu Nu'aym in Hilya). Another narration states: "The news reached Abdullah bin Mas'ood ❀ that a group of people were sitting in the Masjid between Maghrib and Isha..." The rest of the narration is like the one above. The only difference is in these words: "Abdullah bin Mas'ood ❀ said to them, "You people have certainly perpetrated a terrible wrong by carrying out this act of Bid'ah, otherwise we the companions of Muhammad ❀ must have strayed." Amr bin Utba bin Farqad said, "O Abdullah bin Mas'ood ❀! We seek forgiveness from Allah and we repent to Him." Abdullah bin Mas'ood ❀ then ordered them to disperse. (Tabrani). Another narration states that when Abdullah bin Mas'ood ❀ saw 2 groups in the Masjid of Kufa, he stood between the 2 and asked, "Which of you 2 was before the other?" The one group said that they were first, Abdullah bin Mas'ood ❀ ordered the other group to join them, thereby combining the 2 into one. (Tabrani, Haythami)

An authentic shortened narration (Tabrani) states that Abdullah bin Mas'ood ❀ approached them covering his face and said, "Whoever recognizes me will have recognized me. As for those who do not recognize me, I am Abdullah bin Mas'ood. Are you people more rightly guided than the companions of Muhammad ﷺ?" The narrator says that Abdullah bin Mas'ood ؓ also may have added, "You people are definitely clinging to the tail of deviation." Amr Ibn Salama says that they were sitting at the door of Abdullah bin Mas'ood ؓ's home between Maghrib and Isha when Abu Musa Ash'ari ؓ came to the house and said to Abdullah bin Mas'ood ؓ, "Come with me, O Abu Abdur Rahman." When Abdullah bin Mas'ood ؓ came out from the house, he asked, "O Abu Musa! What brings you here at this hour?" Abu Musa Ash'ari ؓ replied, "By Allah! The only thing that brings me here is something that I have seen which frightens me, yet it seems so good. There is a group sitting in the Masjid with a person instructing them to recite 'Subhanallah' in a particular manner and to recite 'Al Hamdu Lillah' in a particular manner." Amr bin Salama says that they accompanied Abdullah bin Mas'ood ؓ to the Masjid. When he arrived there, Abdullah bin Mas'ood ؓ told the people, "You have wandered astray so fast! Even while the companions of Muhammad ﷺ are still alive in your midst, when his wives are still young and when his clothing and utensils are still as they were! Count your evil deeds, for I stand surety for Allah that your good deeds will be counted." *(Tabrani in Kabeer, Haythami)*

The Statement of Abdullah bin Zubair ؓ When his Son Sat with a Group Who Became Ecstatic as They Engaged in Dhikr

Aamir who was the son of Abdullah bin Zubair ؓ narrates that he once came to his father, who asked him, "Where have you been?" The son replied, "I found a group of people better than whom I have not seen. When they engage in Dhikr, one of them trembles and grows overjoyed until he falls unconscious out of fear for Allah. I am late because I was sitting with them." Abdullah bin Zubair ؓ instructed his son saying, "Never sit with them again!" When he detected that this did not make an impression on his son, he added, "I have seen Rasulullah ﷺ recite the Qur'an, and I have seen Abu Bakr ؓ and Omar ؓ reciting the Qur'an. Nothing like this ever happened to them. Do you think that these people fear Allah more than Abu Bakr ؓ and Omar ؓ?" The son, Amir says, "I realized that what he said was true, after which I abandoned these people." *(Abu Nu'aym in Hilya)*

Sila bin Harith ؓ and Abdullah bin Mas'ood ؓ Admonish People who Related Stories in the Masjid

Abu Salih Sa'eed bin Abdul Rahman narrates that Anz Nujaibi was once standing and relating stories in the Masjid when a Sahabi by the name of Sila bin Harith Ghifari ؓ said to him, "By Allah! We have scarcely left Rasulullah ﷺ's time and have not even severed ties with our kin, yet you and your kind have already stood up in our midst to commit such acts of Bid'ah." *(Tabrani in Kabeer, Haythami, Bukhari, Baghawi, Muhammad bin Rabee, Ibn Sakan, Isabah)*. Amr bin Zurara says, "I was relating stories in the Masjid when Abdullah bin Mas'ood ؓ stood up and said, 'O Amr! You have started a misleading Bid'ah! Are you more rightly guided than the companions of Muhammad ﷺ?' I then saw everyone dispersing from around me until I was left all alone." *(Tabrani, Haythami)*

Statements of Omar ؓ Abstaining From Opinions that do not Conform to the Qur'an and Ahadeeth

Ibn Shihab reports that Omar ؓ was standing on the pulpit and addressed the people saying, "O people! Accurate opinions came only from Rasulullah ﷺ because Allah used to guide him. What comes from us are but assumptions and pretences." *(Ibn*

Abdul Birr in Jami) Another narration states that Omar then added: (28) وَإِنَّ الظَّنَّ لَا يُغْنِي مِنَ الْحَقِّ شَيْئًا

... They follow but a guess, and verily, guess is no substitute for the truth. (An-Najm:28) (Ibn Abi Hatim, Bayhaqi in Kanzul Ummal).

Sadaqah bin Abu Abdullah reports that Omar bin Khattab ؓ used to say, "Those who wish to exercise their personal opinions are the enemies of the Sunnah. They are too lazy to learn the Sunnah and it escapes their memory even when they do learn it. When questioned, they are too shy to admit that they do not know and therefore use their intellect to challenge the Sunnah. You should beware of such people." *(Ibn Abdul Birr in Jami)*. Omar ؓ also said, "The Sunnah is that which Allah and His Rasul ﷺ have determined. You should never make your mistaken opinion a Sunnah." *(Ibn Abdul Birr in Jami)*. Amr bin Dinar states that someone asked Omar ؓ whether Allah guided him in the judgments he passed, he replied, "Do not say that! That was a specialty of Rasulullah ﷺ." *(Ibn Mundhir in Kanzul Ummal)*

The Statements of Abdullah bin Mas'ood ؓ and Abdullah bin Abbas ؓ in this Regard

Sha'bi narrates that Abdullah bin Mas'ood ؓ said, "Beware of asking, 'What is you opinion? What is you opinion?' Because those before you were destroyed because they asked, 'What is you opinion? What is you opinion?' You should also not judge one thing by another because your feet will then slip after being firm. In addition to this, whenever any of you are asked about something that he does not know, he should say, 'Allah knows best,' because this constitutes a third of knowledge." *(Tabrani, Haythami)*. Abdullah bin Mas'ood ؓ once said, "Every year is followed by a year that is worse. While no year is essentially worse than another, no nation is essentially worse than another. However, what will happen is that when your Ulema and righteous ones leave the world, such people will come about who will analyze matters using their personal opinions, because of which they will destroy and perforate Islam." *(Tabrani in Kabeer, Ibn Abdul Birr in Jami)*. Abdullah bin Abbas ؓ said, "The basis of Islam and the Shari'a is Allah's Book and the Sunnah of Rasulullah ﷺ. Whoever says anything else based on his personal opinion, I cannot say whether he will find this amongst his good deeds or his sins." *(Ibn Abdul Birr in Jami)*. Ata narrates from his father that when a Sahabi was questioned about something, he said, "I am too shy before my Rabb to use my personal opinion in commenting on a matter that affects the Ummah of Muhammad ﷺ." *(Ibn Abdul Birr in Jami)*

The ijtihad of the Sahabah: Mu'adh bin Jabal ؓ Tells Rasulullah ﷺ that he will Practice Ijtihad Without Compromising on Diligence

Mu'adh bin Jabal ؓ narrates that when Rasulullah ﷺ sent him to Yemen, Rasulullah ﷺ asked him, "How will you pass judgment when a case comes before you?" "I shall pass judgment by Allah's Book." Mu'adh replied. Rasulullah ﷺ asked further, "And what if you do not find the solution in the Book of Allah?" "Then," Mu'adh ؓ said, "I shall judge by the Sunnah of Allah's Rasul ﷺ." Again Rasulullah ﷺ asked, "And what if you do not find the solution in the Sunnah of Allah's Rasul ﷺ?" Mu'adh ؓ replied by saying, "I shall then practice Ijtihad without compromising on carefulness." Rasulullah ﷺ then placed his hand on Mu'adh ؓ's chest saying, "All praise belongs to Allah Who inspired the colony of Rasulullah ﷺ and which pleases Rasulullah ﷺ." *(Abu Dawud, Tirmidhi, Darmi in Mishkatul Masabeth)*

The Concern Abu Bakr and Omar had for Matters They were Unaware of

Muhammad bin Sirin says, "After Rasulullah ﷺ there was none more concerned about not knowing something than Abu Bakr ؓ. After Abu Bakr ؓ there was none more concerned about not knowing than Omar ؓ. When Abu Bakr ؓ needed to pass a verdict and could not find a verse of the Qur'an or a narration of Rasulullah ﷺ that applied directly to the situation, he would say, 'I shall practice Ijtihad. If it is correct, it is from Allah and if it is wrong it is my error and I seek Allah's forgiveness for it." *(Ibn Sa'd, Ibn Abdul Birr in Jami, Kanzul Ummal)*

Omar ؓ's Letter to Shuraih in this Regard

Shuraih narrates that Omar ؓ wrote to him saying, "When a matter presents itself before you, pass your verdict according to the Book of Allah. If the matter is not mentioned in the Book of Allah, pass your verdict according to what Rasulullah ﷺ directed. If such a matter presents itself that is neither in the Book of Allah about which Rasulullah ﷺ has issued no directives, then pass your verdict by that about which the Ulema are unanimous. If such matter presents itself that is neither in the Book of Allah, about which Rasulullah ﷺ has issued no directives and about which no scholar has commented then you have 1 of 2 choices. If you prefer to practice Ijtihad, you may proceed. If you prefer, you may desist from doing so. In my opinion, desisting is the best course for you." *(Ibn Abdul Birr in Jami)*

The Statement of Abdullah bin Mas'ood ؓ Concerning Ijtihad

Abdullah bin Mas'ood ؓ said, "When any of you has to pass a verdict, he should pass his verdict according to the Book of Allah. If the matter is not mentioned in the Book of Allah, he should pass his verdict as Rasulullah ﷺ had done. If such a matter presents itself that is neither in the Book of Allah, about which Rasulullah ﷺ has not passed a verdict, then he should pass his verdict of the righteous scholars. If such a matter presents itself that is neither in the Book of Allah and about which neither Rasulullah ﷺ nor the righteous scholars have passed verdicts, he should practice Ijtihad. He must be firm on his verdict without embarrassment about it." Abdullah bin Mas'ood ؓ also said, "He should then practice Ijtihad and when stating his verdict, he must never say 'I think...' or 'I fear that...' because what is Halal is clear and what is Haram is also clear. Between the 2 are doubtful matters and you should forsake that which gives you doubts for that which does not." *(Ibn Abdul Birr in Jami)*

The Ijtihad of Abdullah bin Abbas ؓ and Ubay bin Ka'b ؓ

Abdullah bin Abu Yazid reports that when Abdullah bin Abbas ؓ was questioned about anything and the reply was to be found in the Qur'an, he would state what was in the Qur'an. If it was not found in the Qur'an but Rasulullah ﷺ had spoken about it, he would say what Rasulullah ﷺ said. If it was not found in the Qur'an and Rasulullah ﷺ had not spoken about it, but Abu Bakr ؓ or Omar ؓ had mentioned it, he would say what Abu Bakr ؓ or Omar ؓ said. However, if it was not found in the Qur'an and if Rasulullah ﷺ, Abu Bakr ؓ and Omar ؓ had not spoken about it, he would practice Ijtihad." *(Ibn Abdul Birr in Jami Bayanil Ilm, Ibn Sa'd)*. Another narration states that Abdullah bin Abbas ؓ said, "When we receive validation to an injunction, we would not equate anything else to it and would readily practice it." *(Ibn Abdul Birr in Jami Bayanil Ilm)*. Masruq narrates that when he once questioned Ubay bin Ka'b ؓ about something, Ubay ؓ asked, "Has it already happened?" When he was informed that it had not happened, he said, "Then grant us respite until it happens

and then when it does, we will be able to practice Ijtihad." *(Ibn Abdul Birr in Jami Bayanil Ilm)*

Exercising caution when issuing Fatawa and the Sahabah who used to issue Fatawa: The Statement of Abdur Rahman bin Abu Layla ؓ Concerning the Cautiousness of the Sahabah

Abdur Rahman bin Abu Laila says, "I met 120 Sahabah of Rasulullah ﷺ in the Masjid. When any of them narrated a Hadith, he wished that his brother (another Sahabi) had done it for him and when he issued a Fatwa, he also wished that his brother had done it for him." *(Ibn Abdul Birr in Jami Bayanil Ilm, Ibn Sa'd)*

Statements of Abdullah bin Mas'ood ؓ, Hudhaifa ؓ and Omar ؓ in this Regard

Abdullah bin Mas'ood ؓ said, "It is only a madman who will immediately issue a Fatwa for everything he is asked." The same statement has been reported from Abdullah bin Abbas ؓ. *(Ibn Abdul Birr in Jami Bayanil Ilm, Tabrani, Haythami)*. Hudhaifa ؓ said, "It is only one of 3 persons who would issue Fatawa; a man who knows which verses of the Qur'an abrogate injunctions of Deen and which have been abrogated, a leader who has no alternative and a affected fool." *(Ibn Abdul Birr in Jami Bayanil Ilm)*. Ibn Sirin narrates that Omar ؓ said to Abu Mas'ood Uqba bin Omar ؓ, "I was not informed that you issue Fatawa to people! The person blessed with the privileges of leadership should bear its burden of issuing Fatawa." *(Ibn Abdul Birr in Jami Bayanil Ilm)* Omar ؓ added, "You are not a governor so you need not issue Fatawa." *(Ibn Abdul Birr in Jami Bayanil Ilm)*

The Cautiousness of Zaid bin Arqam ؓ and Bara ؓ in this Regard

Abu Minhal says, "When I questioned Zaid bin Arqam ؓ and Bara ؓ about selling gold and silver, each one of them told me to ask the other, saying, 'He is better than me and has more knowledge.'" The narration further discusses trading in gold and silver. *(Ibn Abdul Birr in Jami Bayanil Ilm)*. Abu Husain says, "Everyone issues Fatawa on matters that had they been posed to Omar ؓ, he would have gathered all the veterans of Badr to consult before issuing a Fatwa." *(Ibn Asakir in Kanzul Ummal)*

Abu Bakr ؓ, Omar ؓ, Uthman ؓ and Abdur Rahman bin Auf ؓ issue Fatawa During the Time of Rasulullah ﷺ

When Abdullah bin Omar ؓ was asked who used to issue Fatawa during the time of Rasulullah ﷺ, he replied. "Abu Bakr ؓ and Omar ؓ. I do not know of anyone else." *(Ibn Sa'd)*. Qasim bin Muhammad says that Abu Bakr ؓ, Omar ؓ, Uthman ؓ and Ali ؓ used to issue Fatawa during the time of Rasulullah ﷺ. *(Ibn Sa'd)*. Fudhail bin Abu Abdullah bin Dinar narrates from his father that Abdur Rahman bin Auf ؓ, Abu Bakr ؓ, Omar ؓ and Uthman ؓ were amongst those who issued Fatawa during the time of Rasulullah ﷺ which they heard from Rasulullah ﷺ. *(Ibn Sa'd, Ibn Asakir in Muntakhab Kanzul Ummaid)*

Abu Musa Ash'ari ؓ Tells the People not to ask him Anything While Abdullah bin Mas'ood ؓ is Alive

Abu Atiya Hamdani reports that he was once sitting with Abdullah bin Mas'ood ؓ when a person came to ask him a question. "Have you asked anyone else?" Abdullah bin Mas'ood ؓ enquired. "Yes," the man replied, "I have asked Abu Musa Ash'ari ؓ." The man then informed Abdullah bin Mas'ood ؓ about Abu Musa Ash'ari ؓ's reply. Abdullah ؓ gave a reply that contradicted that of Abu Musa Ash'ari ؓ and then left. When this was brought to the attention of Abu Musa Ash'ari ؓ, he said, "Do not ask me about anything when this great scholar is in your midst." (Ibn Sa'd, Abu Nu'aym in Hilya). Those who issued Fatawa during the Time of Rasulullah ﷺ and the time of the Khulafa Rashideen. Sahl bin Abu Khaithama reports that during the time of Rasulullah ﷺ, 3 Sahabah from the Muhajirin and 3 Sahabah from the Ansar were authorized to issue Fatawa. They were Omar رضي الله عنه, Uthman رضي الله عنه, Ali رضي الله عنه from the Muhajirin and Ubay bin Ka'b رضي الله عنه, Mu'adh bin Jabal رضي الله عنه and Zaid bin Thabit رضي الله عنه from the Ansar. (Ibn Sa'd). Masrooq reports that from amongst the Sahabah of Rasulullah ﷺ, those who issued Fatawa were Omar رضي الله عنه, Ali رضي الله عنه, Abdullah bin Mas'ood رضي الله عنه, Zaid bin Thabit رضي الله عنه, Ubay bin Ka'b رضي الله عنه and Abu Musa Ash'ari رضي الله عنه. (Ibn Sa'd). Qabisa bin Duaib bin Halhala reports, "During the time of Omar رضي الله عنه, Zaid bin Thabit رضي الله عنه remained the chief authority of the judiciary of Madinah, as well as the chief authority of issuing Fatawa, Qira'ah and dissolution of estates. He maintained this position during the time of Uthman رضي الله عنه and for as long as Ali رضي الله عنه remained in Madinah as Khalifa before moving the capital to Kufa. Thereafter, he kept the post for a further 5 years until Mu'awiya رضي الله عنه became the Khalifa in the year 40 AH. Even after this, he remained instated in the position until he passed away in the year 45 AH." (Ibn Sa'd). Ata bin Yasir reports that both Omar رضي الله عنه and Uthman رضي الله عنه used to call for Abdullah bin Abbas رضي الله عنه to consult with and would also consult with the veterans of the Battle of Badr. Until the day he passed away, Abdullah bin Abbas رضي الله عنه used to issue Fatawa during the time of Omar رضي الله عنه and Uthman رضي الله عنه. (Ibn Sa'd). Ziyad bin Mina narrates that amongst those Sahabah who issued Fatawa and narrated were Abdullah bin Abbas رضي الله عنه, Abdullah bin Omar رضي الله عنه, Abu Sa'eed Khudri رضي الله عنه, Abu Hurairah رضي الله عنه, Abdullah Amr bin Al Aas رضي الله عنه, Jabir bin Abdullah رضي الله عنه, Rafi bin Khudaij رضي الله عنه, Salama bin Akwa رضي الله عنه, Abu Waqid Laythi رضي الله عنه and Abdullah bin Buhaina رضي الله عنه. This they continued doing from the time Uthman رضي الله عنه passed away until their deaths. Amongst them, the ones who issued the bulk of the Fatawa were Abdullah bin Abbas رضي الله عنه, Abdullah bin Omar رضي الله عنه, Abu Sa'eed Khudri رضي الله عنه, Abu Hurairah رضي الله عنه and Jabir bin Abdullah رضي الله عنه. (Ibn Sa'd). Qasim relates, "During the Khilafa of Abu Bakr رضي الله عنه, Omar رضي الله عنه, Uthman رضي الله عنه and until the time she passed away (may Allah shower his mercy on her), my aunt Aisha رضي الله عنها used to issue Fatawa by herself. I used to stay with her and she showed extreme affection towards me." (Ibn Sa'd)

The Statement of Abu Dhar رضي الله عنه Concerning the Vast Knowledge of the Sahabah

Abu Dhar رضي الله عنه said, "Rasulullah ﷺ left us with so much knowledge that even when a bird fluttered its wings in the sky, it would remind us of something he had taught us." (Ahmad). Another narration adds that Rasulullah ﷺ said, "Everything that draws one closer to Jannah and that takes one further from Jahannam has been explained to you (Sahabah)." (Tabrani. Ahmad confirmed by Haythami, Ibn Sa'd)

The Narration of Amr bin Al Aas رضي الله عنه About what he Memorized from Rasulullah ﷺ and the Narration of Aisha About the Knowledge of Abu Bakr رضي الله عنه

Amr bin Al Aas رضي الله عنه says, "I have learnt 1,000 similitudes from Rasulullah ﷺ." (Ahmad, Haythami). Aisha رضي الله عنها says, "Whenever they (the Sahabah) disagreed about anything, my father Abu Bakr رضي الله عنه would come forth with a Hadith that would satisfy them all and settle the dispute. When it was asked where Rasulullah ﷺ was to be buried, no one could be found who had any relevant knowledge. It was then that Abu Bakr رضي الله عنه said, 'I heard Rasulullah ﷺ say, 'Whenever a Nabi عليه السلام passed away, he was buried beneath the place he laid at the time he passed away.' Similarly, when the Sahabah posed divergent opinions about the

inheritance of Rasulullah ﷺ, they could find none with relevant knowledge. It was Abu Bakr رضي الله عنه who said, 'I heard Rasulullah ﷺ say, 'We the assembly of Ambiya عليهم السلام do not leave behind any inheritance. Everything we leave behind is donated as Sadaqa." (Baghawi, Ibn Asakir in Muntakhab Kanzul Ummal)

The Statements of Abdullah bin Mas'ood رضي الله عنه and Hudhaifa رضي الله عنه about the Knowledge of Omar رضي الله عنه

Abu Wa'il narrates that Abdullah bin Mas'ood رضي الله عنه said, "If the knowledge of Omar رضي الله عنه was placed on one pan of a scale and the knowledge of all on earth was placed on the other, the knowledge of Omar رضي الله عنه would outweigh the rest." A'mash says, "I found it difficult to accept this, so I mentioned it to Ibrahim, who said, 'Why do you find this difficult to accept when I can swear by Allah that Abdullah bin Mas'ood رضي الله عنه said something even more profound than this. He said, 'In my estimation, 90% of knowledge left the world with the demise of Omar رضي الله عنه." (Tabrani, Haythami, Ibn Sa'd). In a lengthy narration concerning the demise of Omar رضي الله عنه, Abdullah bin Mas'ood رضي الله عنه stated, "From all of us, it was Omar رضي الله عنه who possessed the most knowledge about Allah, who recited the Book of Allah the most and who had the deepest understanding of Allah 's Deen." (Tabrani in Majma'uz Zawa'id). Hudhaifa رضي الله عنه said, "In comparison to the knowledge of Omar رضي الله عنه, the knowledge of all other people seems like it could be buried in a little hole." (Ibn Sa'd). A man from Madinah said, "When I was presented before Omar bin Khattab رضي الله عنه, learned scholars appeared to be little children before him. His understanding and knowledge towered above theirs." (Ibn Sa'd)

Rasulullah ﷺ Declares that Ali رضي الله عنه was the Most Learned Sahabah and the Statement of Ali رضي الله عنه About His Knowledge of the Qur'an

Abu Is'haq narrates that when Rasulullah ﷺ got Ali رضي الله عنه married to Fatima رضي الله عنها, she said to Rasulullah ﷺ, "You have married me to a man whose eyesight is weak and whose stomach is big." Rasulullah ﷺ responded by saying, "I have married you to him because from all my companions, he was the first to accept Islam, he has the most knowledge and is the most tolerant." (Tabrani, Haythami). Rasulullah ﷺ said to Fatima رضي الله عنها, "Are you not pleased that I have married you to the person who was the first of my Ummah to accept Islam, is the one with the most knowledge and is the most tolerant?" (Tabrani, Ahmad, Haythami). Ali رضي الله عنه said, "By Allah! I know precisely about what every verse of the Qur'an was revealed, where it was revealed and concerning whom it was revealed. My Rabb has blessed me with a perceptive heart and an eloquent tongue." (Ibn Sa'd). Sa'eed bin Musayib reports that Omar رضي الله عنه used to seek Allah's protection against any intricate problem which had to be resolved without the help of Ali رضي الله عنه. (Ibn Sa'd)

The Knowledge of Abdullah bin Mas'ood رضي الله عنه

Masruq narrates that Abdullah bin Mas'ood رضي الله عنه said, "I know the precise circumstances surrounding the revelation of every chapter of the Qur'an. If I knew of a person more knowledgeable than myself, I would certainly go to him if a camel or any other conveyance could take me to him." Masruq says, "I sat in the company of many Sahabah of Muhammad ﷺ and found them to be like barriers. While some barrier may quench the thirst of one man, others may quench the thirst of 2 men, others the thirst of 10 and others will quench the thirst of 100 men. Then there are oceans that can cater for all the people on earth if they had to settle there. I found Abdullah bin Mas'ood رضي الله عنه to be such an ocean." (Ibn Sa'd). Zaid bin Wahab narrates that Abdullah bin Mas'ood رضي الله عنه arrived one day at a place where Omar رضي الله عنه was sitting.

When he saw Abdullah bin Mas'ood approach, Omar said, "He is a coffer filled to the brim with the knowledge and understanding of Deen." Omar made mention of Abdullah bin Mas'ood saying, "He is a coffer filled to the brim with the knowledge. I give preference to the people of Qadisiya over myself concerning him by sending him to teach them rather than keeping him behind with me in Madinah." *(Ibn Sa'd)*

The Statement of Ali Concerning his Knowledge and the Knowledge of Abdullah bin Mas'ood, Abu Musa Ash'ari, Ammar, Hudhaifa and Salman

Abul Bakhtari narrates that they once approached Ali with the request to inform them about the Sahabah of Rasulullah. "Which of them would like to know about?" Ali asked. "Tell us about Abdullah bin Mas'ood," they replied. Ali said, "He learnt the Qur'an and the Sunnah and reached the apex of knowledge. This is sufficient for you to gauge the extent of his knowledge." "Tell us about Abu Musa Ash'ari," they asked next. Ali said, "He had been thoroughly dyed in knowledge before coming out of the dye." The men asked further, "Then tell us about Ammar bin Yasir." Ali said, "He is a Mu'min who remembers well after being reminded about something he had forgotten." "Now tell us about Hudhaifa," they asked. Ali's reply was: "Of all the Sahabah, he best knew who the Munafiqin were." When they asked about Abu Dhar, Ali said, "He acquired a substantial amount of knowledge but was unable to disseminate it." The men further asked, "Tell us about Salman." Ali said, "He acquired the knowledge of the previous Ambiya as well as the knowledge of the final Nabi. He is an ocean whose bottom cannot be reached and he is also one of us, the household of Rasulullah." "O Amirul Mu'minin!" the men then asked, "Now tell us about yourself." Ali said, "It was this that you had intended asking from the outset! Whenever I asked Rasulullah anything, I would receive a reply and whenever I remained silent, I would be informed." *(Ibn Sa'd)*

The Statement of Abdullah bin Mas'ood Concerning the Knowledge of Mu'adh bin Jabal

Abdullah bin Mas'ood said, "Mu'adh bin Jabal is certainly an Ummah who was Qanit and Hanif (one inclined towards the truth and adverse to all false creeds). He is definitely not from the Mushrikin." The narrator says, "I thought that Abdullah bin Mas'ood had perhaps made an error because Allah says in the Qur'an: إِنَّ إِبْرَاهِيمَ كَانَ أُمَّةً قَانِتًا لِلَّهِ حَنِيفًا وَلَمْ يَكُ مِنَ الْمُشْرِكِينَ (120) شَاكِرًا لِأَنْعُمِهِ اجْتَبَاهُ وَهَدَاهُ إِلَى صِرَاطٍ مُسْتَقِيمٍ (121)

Verily, Ibrahim was an Ummah (leader having all the good righteous qualities), or a nation, obedient to Allah, Hanifa (to worship none but Allah), and he was not one of those who were Al-Mushrikoon (polytheists, idolaters, disbelievers in the Oneness of Allah, and those who joined partners with Allah). (He was) thankful for His (Allah's) Graces. He (Allah) chose him (as an intimate friend) and guided him to a Straight Path (Islamic Monotheism). (An-Nahl:120-121)

However, when Abdullah bin Mas'ood repeated his words to me, I knew that he meant what he was saying. I therefore remained silent. He then asked, 'Do you know what the meaning of 'Ummah' and 'Qanit' is?' When I submitted that Allah knows best, he explained, 'Ummah in this context refers to a person who teaches good things and 'Qanit' refers to a person who obeys Allah and His Rasul. That is exactly how Mu'adh bin Jabal was. He taught people everything that was good and was obedient to Allah and to Allah's Rasul." *(Ibn Sa'd)*

Statements of Masruq Concerning the Knowledge of the Sahabah

Masruq says, "I examined the Sahabah carefully and found that all their knowledge could be found in 6 of them; namely Omar, Ali, Abdullah bin Mas'ood, Mu'adh bin Jabal, Abu Darda and Zaid bin Thabit. After closely examining these 6, I discovered that all their knowledge could be found in Ali and Abdullah bin Mas'ood." *(Ibn Sa'd)*. Masruq also said, "When I arrived in Madinah and enquired about the Sahabah, I discovered that amongst those with the most profound knowledge was Zaid bin Thabit." *(Ibn Sa'd)*

The Knowledge of Abdullah bin Abbas

Masruq reports that Abdullah bin Mas'ood once said, "If Abdullah bin Abbas were our age, none of us would be able to equal even a tenth of his knowledge." Another narration adds that Abdullah bin Mas'ood said, "Abdullah bin Abbas is an excellent commentator of the Qur'an." *(Ibn Sa'd)*. Mujahid reports that Abdullah bin Abbas used to be called an ocean because of the great amount of knowledge he possessed. *(Ibn Sa'd)*. Laith bin Abu Sulaim says that he once said to Tawus, "Why have you attached yourself to this youngster Abdullah bin Abbas instead of the senior Sahabah of Rasulullah?" Tawus replied. "I have seen seventy Sahabah who favored the opinion of Abdullah bin Abbas, whenever a difference of opinion arose in any matter." *(Ibn Sa'd)*. Amir the son of Sa'd bin Abi Waqqas reports that his father said, "I have never seen as quick-witted, as intelligent, as knowledgeable and as tolerant as Abdullah bin Abbas. I saw that when an intricate problem arose, Omar bin Khattab would call for him and say, 'Be prepared! A most complicated problem is coming your way.' Omar would then accept his opinion on the matter even though he would be surrounded by veterans of the Battle of Badr both from the Muhajirin and the Ansar." *(Ibn Sa'd)*. Abu Zinad narrates that Abdullah bin Abbas was suffering from high fever when Omar bin Khattab came to visit him. Omar said, "Your illness has certainly posed a great obstacle to us. Nevertheless it is only from Allah that we seek help." *(Ibn Sa'd)*. Talha bin Ubaidulla said, "Abdullah bin Abbas has been blessed with deep understanding, intelligence and tremendous knowledge. I have not seen Omar bin Khattab give precedence to any other person's opinion over his." *(Ibn Sa'd)*. Muhammad the son of Ubay bin Ka'b says that Abdullah bin Abbas was once present when Ubay bin Ka'b stood up and said, "This youth will soon become the most learned scholar of this Ummah. Together with being blessed with intelligence and deep understanding, Rasulullah also prayed to Allah to grant him a sound understanding of Deen." *(Ibn Sa'd)*. Tawus says, "Abdullah bin Abbas towered above others in knowledge just as a tall palm tree towers above shorter ones." *(Ibn Sa'd)*. Abu Wa'il says, "A friend and I performed Hajj at a time when Abdullah bin Abbas was the Amir of Hajj. When he started reciting Surah Noor and commenting on it, my friend remarked, 'Oh SubhanAllah! What great knowledge is emerging from this man's head! Even the Turks would accept Islam if they had to hear this.'" Another narration adds that Abu Wa'il himself said. "I have never seen or heard anyone speak as he does! Even the Persians and Romans would accept Islam if they heard him." *(Ibn Sa'd)*. Abdullah bin Abbas relates, "When I went to Omar bin Khattab one day, he asked me a question that Ya'la bin Umaya had written to him about from Yemen. After I had given him the answer, Omar remarked, 'I testify that you are certainly most eligible to speak on behalf of Rasulullah's household.'" *(Ibn Sa'd)*. Ata says, "While some people used to approach Abdullah bin Abbas ؓ to ask about poetry, others went to him to ask about ancestry and still others referred to him to ask about the battles that the Arabs fought and about their history. He was able to give each group of people due attention and gave them detailed replies to their satisfaction." *(Ibn Sa'd)*

Ubaidullah bin Abdullah bin Utba says, "Abdullah bin Abbas ؓ surpassed all other people in his qualities. He excelled others in his knowledge of past events in the deep understanding with which he gave his opinion to people who consulted with him, in his level of tolerance and in his huge magnanimity. None knew the Ahadeeth of Rasulullah ﷺ and the verdicts of Abu Bakr ؓ, Omar ؓ and Uthman ؓ better than he. None gave opinions as deeply thought of as he and there was also none who better knew poetry and Arabic as he did. In addition to all of this, his knowledge was also most profound in the commentary of the Qur'an, in mathematics and in the laws of inheritance. I have also not seen anyone else as knowledgeable about the past events as he was, nor anyone who gave an opinion more dependable than his when people are most in need of one. Sometimes he would sit all day discussing nothing besides Fiqh, while on other days; he would discuss nothing besides the commentary of the Qur'an. Then there were days when he sat and discussed only the battles of Rasulullah ﷺ, while on other days, he discussed only poetry or only the history of the Arabs. I have never seen any scholar sit before him without surrendering himself to him. I have also seen no one asking him a question without receiving the relevant information from him." *(Ibn Sa'd)*. Abdullah bin Abbas ؓ says, "I used to remain close to the senior Muhajirin and Ansar Sahabah and ask them about the battles Rasulullah ﷺ fought and the revelation that pertained to them. Whenever I went to any one of them, they became overjoyed because I am related to Rasulullah ﷺ. Ubay bin Ka'b ؓ was one of the Sahabah with the soundest knowledge. When I asked him one day about the Surahs that were revealed in Madinah, he informed me that 27 Surahs were revealed in Madinah and all the rest in Makkah." *(Ibn Sa'd)*. Ikrama says, "I heard Amr bin Al Aas ؓ say, 'From all of us, it is Abdullah bin Abbas who has the most knowledge of the previous scriptures and also understands best those matters that the Qur'an and Ahadeeth are not explicit about.' When I informed Abdullah bin Abbas ؓ about what Amr bin Al Aas ؓ had said, he remarked, 'He himself has tremendous knowledge because he used to ask Rasulullah ﷺ about matters that were Halal and Haram." *(Ibn Sa'd)*. Aisha ؓ was once looking at a group of people gathered around Abdullah bin Abbas ؓ during the days of Hajj, asking him about the rites of Hajj. She remarked, "Of those (Sahabah) still alive, he knows the rites of Hajj best." *(Ibn Sa'd)*

What People said at the Demise of Abdullah bin Abbas ؓ

When the news of Abdullah bin Abbas ؓ's death reached Jabir ؓ, he hit his one hand on the other and said, "The most knowledgeable and most tolerant of all people has passed away. By his demise, this Ummah has been afflicted with a calamity that can never be redressed." *(Ibn Sa'd)*. Upon the demise of Abdullah bin Abbas ؓ, Rafi bin Khudaij ؓ remarked, "All the people between East and West were dependent on him who has passed away today." *(Ibn Sa'd)*. Abu Kulthum narrates that when Abdullah bin Abbas ؓ was buried, Ibn Hanafiya said, "Today the sage of this Ummah has passed away." *(Ibn Sa'd)*

The Knowledge of Abdullah bin Omar ؓ, Ubadah ؓ, Shaddad bin Aws ؓ and Abu Sa'eed Khudri ؓ

Amr bin Dinar says, "Abdullah bin Omar ؓ was regarded as one of the young Fuqaha." *(Ibn Sa'd)*. Khalid bin Ma'dan says,

"From amongst the Sahabah of Rasulullah ﷺ, there are none left in Sham whose knowledge is more dependable, who have a deeper understanding and who are more beloved to the people than Ubadah bin Samit ؓ and Shaddad bin Aws ؓ." *(Ibn Sa'd)*. Handhala reports from his teachers that none had better understanding of Deen than Abu Sa'eed Khudri ؓ." *(Ibn Sa'd)*

The Knowledge of Abu Hurairah ؓ

Abu Za'eeza'a who was Marwan bin Hakam's scribe reports, "Marwan once summoned Abu Hurairah ؓ and, seating me behind his chair, he started questioning Abu Hurairah as I wrote everything down. After a complete year had passed, Marwan again sent for Abu Hurairah ؓ and, seating him behind a screen, started asking him the same questions. Abu Hurairah ؓ replied to the questions just as he did the previous year without adding, deleting or even misplacing a single word." *(Hakim by Dhahabi)*

The Knowledge of Ummul Mu'minin Aisha ؓ

Abu Musa Ash'ari ؓ says, "Whenever the Sahabah of Rasulullah ﷺ had doubts about anything, they referred it to Aisha ؓ and always found the answer with her." *(Ibn Sa'd)*. Qabisa bin Dhuwaib says, "Aisha ؓ was one of the most knowledgeable personalities and even the senior Sahabah of Rasulullah ﷺ consulted with her." *(Ibn Sa'd)*. Abu Salamah says, "I have not seen anyone with more knowledge of the Sunnah practices of Rasulullah ﷺ than Aisha ؓ. I have also not seen anyone offer a better opinion when an opinion was sought and seen no one with more knowledge of the circumstances surrounding the revelation of any verse or with more knowledge of the laws of inheritance." *(Ibn Sa'd)*. When someone asked Masruq whether Aisha ؓ was proficient in the laws of inheritance, he replied, "I swear by the Being Who controls my life that she certainly was! In fact, I saw the senior Sahabah of Rasulullah ﷺ ask her about inheritance." *(Ibn Sa'd, Tabrani, Haythami)*. Mahmud bin Labid says, "Although all the pure wives of Rasulullah ﷺ knew many Ahadeeth, none knew as much as Aisha ؓ and Ummu Salama ؓ. In fact Aisha ؓ used to issue Fatawa during the period of Omar ؓ and Uthman ؓ. This she continued doing until she passed away. May Allah shower His mercy on her. Senior Sahabah of Rasulullah ﷺ such as Omar ؓ and Uthman ؓ after him used to send messengers to her to ask about Sunnah practices." *(Ibn Sa'd)*. Mu'awiya ؓ said, "I have never seen a speaker as well-spoken, as eloquent and as intelligent as Aisha ؓ." *(Tabrani, Haythami)*. Urwa ؓ says, "I have not seen a woman as knowledgeable in medicine, Fiqh and poetry as Aisha ؓ." *(Tabrani, Haythami)*. Urwa ؓ once said to his aunt Aisha ؓ, "I am more astonished about you the more I think about you! When I find you to be one of those most proficient in Islamic jurisprudence, I ask myself what was there to prevent you from being such when you were the wife of Rasulullah ﷺ; and the daughter of Abu Bakr ؓ? Then when I find you to be one of those most knowledgeable about the history of the Arabs and about their lineage and poetry, I ask myself what was there to prevent you from being such when your father knew most about the Quraish? However, what surprises me is that I also find you to be most proficient in medicine. Where did you learn this from?" Aisha ؓ held Urwa ؓ's hand and said, "When Rasulullah ﷺ's illness worsened, Arab and non-Arab physicians sent many medicines and prescriptions for him, from whom I learnt medicine." *(Bazzar, Ahmad, Tabrani in Kabeer and Awsat)*. Another narration states that she said, "When I used these to treat Rasulullah ﷺ, I learnt all about it." *(Ahmad, Haythami)*

The Statement of Abdullah bin Mas'ood ﷺ Concerning Those Ulema who are Attached to Allah and Those who are Evil

Abdullah bin Mas'ood ﷺ said to his students, "Be people who are the fountainheads of knowledge, who are beacons of guidance, who spend most of the time at home, who are lanterns of the night, whose hearts remain fresh and young and who wear old clothes. Thus you will be known to the inhabitants of the heavens while remaining anonymous to the inhabitants of earth." *(Ibn Abdul Birr in Jami)*. Ali ﷺ states, "In this manner, you will be known to the inhabitants of the heavens while the inhabitants of earth will rave about you." *(Abu Nu'aym in Hilya)*

The Statement of Abdullah bin Abbas ﷺ Concerning the Ulema who are Attached to Allah

Wahab bin Munabbih narrates that when Abdullah bin Abbas ﷺ was informed that some people were debating about predestination at Bab Bani Sahm, he quickly got up and, handing his staff over to Ikrama, he placed one hand on the staff and the other on Tawus. When he reached the group, they made way for him and welcomed him. Abdullah bin Abbas ﷺ however did not sit down and asked them to inform him of their lineage so that he may recognize who they were. When they did so, he addressed them saying, "Do you not know that Allah has servants whom fear for Him has driven them to silence even though they are neither handicapped nor dumb? On the contrary, they are people who are Ulema, orators and people of high status. They are well acquainted with the way Allah deals with sinners but whenever they think of the greatness of Allah, they lose their minds, their hearts are torn apart and their tongues stop functioning. When they recover from this state, they hasten to perform good deeds that will purify them. While they regard themselves as people who neglect their duties to Allah, they are really the intelligent ones with the most strength (to do good). Although they regard themselves as wrong-doers and sinners, they are really righteous and innocent. What distinguishes them is they never regard anything as being too much to do for Allah, they are never satisfied to do only a little for Him and they are never too proud of the deeds they do for Him. Wherever you meet them, they will be filled with concern, in awe of Allah and ever fearing (that they should not displease) Him." Abdullah bin Abbas ﷺ left and returned to his gathering. *(Abu Nu'aym in Hilya)*

Statements of Abdullah bin Mas'ood ﷺ and Abdullah bin Abbas ﷺ Concerning evil Ulema

Abdullah bin Mas'ood ﷺ said, "If the men of knowledge would safeguard their knowledge and give it only to those who are worthy, they would lead the people of their times. However, they have handed it over to men of this world only to receive a portion of the world and have therefore fallen in the eyes of these people. I have heard Rasulullah ﷺ say, 'Whoever narrows all his worries to the one worry for the Hereafter, Allah will take care of all his other worries. On the other hand, whoever has been confounded by the worries of this world, Allah cares not in which valley he destroys himself." *(Ibn Asakir in Kanzul Ummal, Ibn Abdul Birr in Jami)*. Sufian bin Uyayna reports that Abdullah bin Abbas ﷺ said, "If the bearers of knowledge uphold it as it ought to be upheld and in a befitting manner, Allah, His angels and the pious ones will love them. In addition to this, people will stand in awe of them. However, they seek the wealth of this world with their knowledge, because of which Allah detests them and they have no status in the eyes of the people." *(Ibn Abdul Birr in Jami)*. Abdullah bin Mas'ood ﷺ said, "What will happen to you when such a calamity overtakes you because of which

your youngsters start to age, your elders grow older and such practices are regarded as being Sunnah that when an attempt is made to change them, people will say about the act is truly Sunnah, 'This is something very strange!'" When someone asked Abdullah bin Mas'ood ﷺ when such a time would come, he replied, "When the trustworthy ones amongst you will be few while your leaders will be plenty, when the Fuqaha amongst you will be few while those reciting the Qur'an will be plenty, when the knowledge of Deen will be sought for motives other than the benefit of Deen and when worldly gain will be the motivation behind carrying out acts of the Hereafter." Another narration states that Abdullah bin Mas'ood ﷺ said, "When a fabricated Sunnah becomes such a norm in society, when an effort is made to change it, people will say, 'The Sunnah has been changed!'" The narration also adds that the time will be "when your Fuqaha will be few and your leaders will hoard wealth." *(Abdur Razzaq in Targheeb wat Tarheeb, Ibn Abdul Birr in Jami)*

The Statements of Abu Dhar ﷺ Ka'b ﷺ and Ali ﷺ Concerning Acquiring the Knowledge of Deen for Worldly Motives

Abu Dhar ﷺ said, "You should understand well that these Ahadeeth ought to be learnt solely for the pleasure of Allah. When a person learns them solely for worldly gain, he will not even smell the fragrance of Jannah." *(Ibn Abdul Birr in Jami)*. Omar ﷺ once asked Ka'b ﷺ who was learned in the previous scriptures, "What can remove knowledge from the hearts of Ulema after they have studied and memorized it?" Ka'b replied, "It will be reed and asking people for one's needs that will remove it." *(Ibn Abdul Birr in Jami)*. When Ali ﷺ once spoke about certain tribulations that will occur towards the end of time, Omar ﷺ asked, "When will this occur, O Ali?" Ali ﷺ replied, "When the knowledge of Deen will be sought for motives other than the benefit of Deen, when knowledge will be sought for reasons other than to practice and when worldly gain will be the motivation behind carrying out acts of the Hereafter." *(Abdur Razzaq in Targheeb wat Tarheeb)*

What Omar ﷺ Feared for the Ummah From Evil Ulema

Omar ﷺ once addressed the people saying, "I fear 2 people for you, the person who misinterprets the Qur'an and a person who is vying with his brother for kingdom." *(Ibn Abdul Birr in Jami, Ibn Abi Shaybah in Kanzul Ummal)*. Hasan narrates that when a delegation from Basra that included Ahnaf bin Qais came to Omar ﷺ, he granted them all leave, except for Ahnaf ﷺ, whom he kept back for an entire year. Thereafter, Omar ﷺ said to Ahnaf ﷺ, "Do you know why I kept you back? Rasulullah ﷺ warned us against well-spoken hypocrites and I feared that you should not be one. InshaAllah, (I am now confident that) you are not one of them." *(Ibn Sa'd, Abu Ya'la)*. Abu Uthman says that he heard Omar ﷺ say from the pulpit, "Beware of the hypocritical Alim." "How will a hypocrite become an Alim?" the people asked. Omar ﷺ replied, "He will be a person who speaks what is right but then does what is wrong." *(Bayhaqi, Ibn Najjar)*. Omar ﷺ also said, "We always maintained that the one to destroy this Ummah will be a hypocrite with an educated tongue." *(Firyabi, Abu Ya'la, Nasr, Ibn Asakir in Kanzul Ummal)*. Abu Uthman Nahdi reports that he heard Omar ﷺ say from the pulpit, "I fear most for this Ummah is the hypocritical Alim." "How will a hypocrite be an Alim, O Amirul Mu'minin'?" the people asked. Omar ﷺ replied, "He will be a person whose tongue will be educated but whose heart and actions will be ignorant." *(Musaddad, Firyabi in Kanzul Ummal)*

Hudhaifa ❀ and Abdullah bin Mas'ood ❀ warn the Ulema Against Frequenting the Doors of the Rulers

Hudhaifa ❀ said, "Beware of the places of tribulation!" "O Abu Abdullah!" someone asked. "What are the places of tribulation?" Abdullah bin Mas'ood ❀ replied, "The doors of the rulers. When any of you enters the door of a ruler, he confirms as truth the lies he speaks and praises him for what he is not." *(Ibn Abdul Birr in Jami)*. Abdullah bin Mas'ood ❀ said, "At the doors of the rulers lie tribulations just as certainly as there are camels at the place where camels rest. I swear by the Being Who controls my life that as much of their wealth you receive, so much of your Deen will they behave m exchange." *(Ibn Abdul Birr in Jami)*

What Rasulullah ❀ Meant When he Stated that Deeni Knowledge will be Lifted

Awf bin Malik Ashja'ee ❀ reports that Rasulullah ❀ looked to the sky one day and said, "There shall come a time when Deeni knowledge will be lifted, off the surface of the earth." A man from the Ansar called Labid ❀ asked, "O Rasulullah ❀! How will this knowledge be lifted when it is recorded in script and safeguarded in people's hearts'?" Rasulullah ❀ remarked. "I was of the opinion that you were one of the most perceptive people in Madinah." Rasulullah ❀ then proceeded to explain how the Jew and the Christians deviated from the path even though Allah's scripture was with them. The narrator says that when he met Shaddad bin Aws ❀ and narrated the Hadith of Awf ❀ to him, he said, "Awf ❀ has spoken the truth. Shall I not inform you about the first thing to be lifted?" When the narrator begged to be informed, Shaddad ❀ said, "It is devotion. It will be so completely removed that you will not find a single person with any devotion." *(Hakim, Bazzar, Tabrani in Majmu'az Zawa'id)*. Another narration adds that a person by the name of Ziyad bin Labid ❀ who was from the Ansar asked, "O Rasulullah ❀! How will it be lifted from us when we have the Book of Allah with us. which we teach to our wives and children'?" *(Ibn Abdul Birr in Jami)*. Yet another narration states that Shaddad ❀ asked. "Do you know what is meant by knowledge being lifted'?" When the narrator submitted that he did not know, Shaddad ❀ said, "It refers to the leaving of the containers of knowledge, the Ulema. And do you know which knowledge will be the first to be lifted'?" When the narrator again submitted that he did not know. Shaddad ❀ said, "It is devotion. It will be so completely removed that you will not find a single person with any devotion." *(Ibn Abdul Birr in Jami, Hakim, Tabrani in Majma'us Zawa'id)*. A similar narration from Abu Darda ❀ states that Rasulullah ❀ said, "Of what benefit was the Torah and the Injil that were with the Jews and the Christians'?" A narration from Wahshi ❀ mentions that Rasulullah ❀ said, "They (the Jews and Christians) did not pay any attention to their scriptures." *(Tabrani)* Yet another narration from Ibn Labid ❀ quotes Rasulullah ❀ as saying, "They however did not benefit from it (their scriptures) at all." *(Hakim)*

Statements of Abdullah bin Mas'ood ❀ and Abdullah bin Abbas ❀ Concerning the Lifting of Knowledge and the Statement Abdullah bin Abbas ❀ Made When Zaid ❀ Passed Away

Abdullah bin Mas'ood ❀ once asked: "Do you know how Islam will dwindle'?" The people replied, "Just as the dye on clothing fades or as an animal loses its fat or as a Dirham deteriorates when it is hidden away for too long." Abdullah bin Mas'ood ❀ replied, "That also happens, but the most serious cause will be the death of the Ulema." *(Tabrani in Kabeer, Haythami)*. Sa'eed bin Musayib says, "I attended the funeral of Zaiel bin Thabit ❀. After he had been buried, Abdullah bin Abbas ❀ said, "O you people! Whoever wishes to know how knowledge leaves us, should know that it is like this that knowledge leaves. I swear by Allah that a great deal of knowledge has just left us today." *(Tabrani, Haythami)*. Ammar bin Abu Ammar says, "When Zaid bin Thabit ❀ passed away, we sat with Abdullah bin Abbas ❀ in the shade of a building. He said, "It is like this that knowledge leaves. A great deal of knowledge has just been buried today." Another narration states that as he pointed his finger to the grave, Abdullah bin Abbas ❀ said, "It is like this that knowledge leaves. When a man passes away who knows something that no one else knows, his knowledge leaves with him." Yet another narration states that Abdullah bin Abbas ❀ once asked, "Do you know how knowledge will leave? It is by the Ulema leaving the surface of the earth." *(Majma'uz Zawa'id)*. Abdullah bin Mas'ood ❀ said, "I strongly believe that it is by committing sins that a man forgets the knowledge he once learnt." *(Abu Nu'aym in Hilya, Majmauz Zawa'id, Targheeb wat Tarheeb)*. Qasim reports that Abdullah bin Mas'ood ❀ said. "The problem with knowledge is forgetting." *(Ibn Abi Shaybah in Jami'ul Ilm)*. Propagating one's knowledge even if one does not practice and seeking protection from knowledge that is not beneficial

The Statement of Hudhaifa ❀ Concerning Propagating Knowledge

Jabir bin Abdullah ❀ narrates that Hudhaifa ❀ said to them, "We have been given this knowledge to bear and we therefore pass it on to you even though we do not practice on it." *(Bayhaqi, Ibn Asakir in Kanzul Ummal)*

Rasulullah ❀ seeks Protection from Knowledge that does not Benefit

Abu Hurairah ❀ narrates that when Rasulullah ❀ made Du'a, he said, "O Allah! I seek Your protection from 4 things; from knowledge that is not beneficial, from a heart that does not submit, from a soul that is never satiated and from a Du'a that is not answered." *(Hakim by Dhahabi)*

The chapter concerning the fervor the Sahabah had for Dhikr and the encouragement they gave towards it. It highlights the fervor that Nabi ﷺ and the Sahabah had for the Dhikr of Allah. It discusses how they were regular with it every morning and evening, during days and nights, and on journey and at home.

Rasulullah ﷺ says, "One should use Tongue that Engages in Dhikr"

Thowban ؓ narrates that they were once on a journey with Rasulullah ﷺ when some of the Muhajirin said, "If we only knew what type of wealth is good now that Allah has revealed verses of the Qur'an about gold and silver condemning those who hoard it without paying the zakah due on it." Um'ar ؓ said, "If you wish, I can ask Rasulullah ﷺ on your behalf." With their permission, Um'ar ؓ went off and Thowban ؓ followed him hurriedly on his camel. "O Rasulullah ﷺ!" Um'ar ؓ started, "Since Allah has revealed verses about gold and silver, the Muhajirin are asking, 'If only we knew what type of wealth is good now that Allah has revealed verses of the Qur'an about gold and sliver.'" Rasulullah ﷺ replied by saying, "One should adapt as the best of wealth a tongue that engages in Dhikr, a grateful heart and a Mu'min wife who will help one in carrying out acts of Iman." Another narration states Rasulullah ﷺ said, "...and a wife that will assist one in prospering one's life in the Hereafter." *(Abu Nu'aym in Hilya, Ahmad, Tirmidhi, Ibn Majah)*. Ali ؓ reports that Rasulullah ﷺ thrice repeated the words, "Destruction to gold! Destruction to silver!" This he said after Allah revealed the verse: وَالَّذِينَ يَكْنِزُونَ الذَّهَبَ وَالْفِضَّةَ وَلَا يُنْفِقُونَهَا فِي سَبِيلِ اللّهِ فَبَشِّرْهُمْ بِعَذَابٍ أَلِيمٍ

(34) *...And those who hoard up gold and silver (Al-Kanz: the money, the Zakat of which has not been paid), and spend it not in the Way of Allah, -announce unto them a painful torment. (At-Tauba:34).* Because this weighed heavily on the Sahabah, they asked, "What type of wealth should we adopt?" Then Um'ar ؓ offered to pose the question to Rasulullah ﷺ as mentioned in the narration above. The rest of the narration is the same, only in greater brevity. *(Abdur Razzaq in Tafsir Ibn Kathir)*

The meaning of Rasulullah ﷺ's words: "The Mufarridun are in Lead"

Abu Hurairah ؓ narrates that Rasulullah ﷺ was traveling on the road to Makkah when he passed by a mountain called Humdan. Rasulullah ﷺ then said, "This is Humdan. Continue traveling because the Mufarridun are in the lead." "O Rasulullah ﷺ!" the Sahabah enquired, "Who are the Mufarridun?" Rasulullah replied, "Those who abundantly engage in Dhikr." *(Muslim)*. When the Sahabah asked who the Mufarridun were, Rasulullah ﷺ replied, "Those who are intoxicated by the Dhikr of Allah. Dhikr then unburdens them of their sins so that they meet Allah without any burden on the Day of Judgment." *(Tirmidhi in Targheeb wat Tarheeb, Tabrani in Majma'uz Zawa'id)*. Rasulullah ﷺ says, "Whoever wishes to eat from the gardens of Jannah should engage in Dhikr in Abundance" Mu'adh bin Jabal ؓ reports that as they were once traveling with Rasulullah ﷺ, he asked, "Where are those in the lead?" The Sahabah replied, "While some people have gone ahead, others are still at the back." Rasulullah ﷺ said, "Where are those in the lead who are intoxicated by the Dhikr of Allah? Whoever wishes to eat from the gardens of Jannah should engage in Dhikr in abundance." *(Tabrani, Haythami)*

Rasulullah ﷺ Informs us that the Best of Allah's Servants are Those who Engage Abundantly in Dhikr

Abu Sa'eed Khudri ؓ narrates that Rasulullah ﷺ was once asked, "Which of Allah's servants shall have the highest status with Allah on the Day of Judgment?" Rasulullah ﷺ replied, "Those who engage abundantly in Dhikr." "O Rasulullah ﷺ!" Abu Sa'eed Khudri asked, "Are they even better than the person who fights in the Path of Allah?" Rasulullah ﷺ's reply was, "Even if the warrior has to strike the Kuffar and Mushrikin with his sword until it breaks and he is dyed in blood, those who abundantly engage in Dhikr will still be a stage above him." *(Tirmidhi, Bayhaqi in Targheeb wat Tarheeb)*

The Dhikr of Allah Earns the Greatest Rewards and is most Effective in Securing Deliverance from Jahannam

Jabir ؓ reports that Rasulullah ﷺ said, "A man can do no action more effective in saving him from Jahannam than Dhikr." Someone asked, "Not even Jihad in the Path of Allah?" Rasulullah ﷺ replied, "Not even Jihad in the Path of Allah unless one fights until his sword breaks." *(Tabrani in Sagheer and Aswat by Mundhiri, Haythami, Majma'uz Zawa'id)*. Mu'adh bin Anas ؓ narrates that someone once asked Rasulullah ﷺ which form of Jihad carried the most reward. Rasulullah ﷺ replied, "The Jihad of those people who engage most in the Dhikr of Allah." The Sahabi then asked Rasulullah ﷺ about whose salah, zakah, Hajj and Sadaqah carried the most reward. Each time Rasulullah ﷺ replied that it was the action of those people who engage most in the Dhikr of Allah. Abu Bakr ؓ then said to Um'ar ؓ, "O Abu Hafs! Those who engage in Dhikr have taken all the good." Rasulullah ﷺ himself confirmed this statement saying, "Yes that it true." *(Ahmad, Tabrani, Haythami)*

Rasulullah ﷺ says, "Let your Tongue be Moist with Dhikr of Allah"

Abdullah bin Busr ؓ reports that a man once came to Rasulullah ﷺ saying, "O Rasulullah ﷺ! The Nafl acts of Islam are too many for me. Inform me of something that I may constantly adhere to." Rasulullah ﷺ replied, "Let your tongue remain moist with the Dhikr of Allah." *(Tirmidhi, Hakim, Ibn Majah, Ibn Hibban in Targheeb wat Targheeb)*. Malik bin Makhamir reports that Mu'adh bin Jabal ؓ once said to them, "The last words with which I parted from Rasulullah ﷺ as I left for Yemen were that I asked, 'Which deeds are most beloved to Allah?' Rasulullah ﷺ replied, "That you die while your tongue is moist with the Dhikr of Allah." *(Tabrani, Haythami)* Another narration states that Mu'adh ؓ asked, 'Tell me which deed is best and which takes one closest to Allah." *(Bazzar, Ibn Abi Dunya, Ibn Hibban in Targheeb wat Targheeb, Ibn Najjar in Kanzul Ummal)*

The Encouragement Um'ar ؓ, Uthman ؓ and Abdullah bin Mas'ood ؓ gave Towards Dhikr

Um'ar ؓ said, "Do not preoccupy yourself with discussing people because it is a cause of misfortune. You had rather engage constantly in the Dhikr of Allah." *(Ibn Abi Dunya)* Another narration states that Um'ar ؓ said, "Engage constantly in the Dhikr of Allah because it is a cure. At the same time, avoid discussing people because it is a disease." *(Ibn Abi Dunya, Ahmad, Hanad in Kanzul Ummal)*. Uthman ؓ said, "Had our hearts been pure, we would never tire with the Dhikr of Allah." *(Ibn Mubarak in Zuhd, Kanzul Ummal)*. Abdullah bin Mas'ood ؓ said, "Engage abundantly in the Dhikr of Allah and it matters not if you do not associate with anyone apart from those who can assist you in Dhikr." *(Bayhaqi in Kanzul Ummal)*

The Encouragement Salman 🙂 and Abu Darda 🙂 Towards Dhikr

Salman 🙂 once said that if a man spends an entire night giving away slave women with fair complexions and another man spends the night reciting the Book of Allah and engaging in Dhikr, the latter is the better of the two. *(Abu Nu'aym in Hilya)*

Ahmad bin Habib bin Ubaid narrates that a man approached Abu Darda 🙂 and asked for some advice. Abu Darda 🙂 said, "Remember Allah during times of ease and Allah will remember you during your times of hardship. Whenever you are impressed by anything of this world, consider what it is soon to become." *(Ahmad in Safwatus Safwa)*. Abu Darda 🙂 once said, "Shall I not inform you of the best of all deeds, which is most beloved to your Master and will elevate your rank the most? It is better than being killed and killing the enemy in Jihad and even better than giving Dirhams and Dinars in charity." When the people begged to know what it was, Abu Darda 🙂 said, "The Dhikr of Allah because it is the greatest act." *(Abu Nu'aym in Hilya)*. Abu Darda 🙂 also said, 'Those whose tongues are ever moist with the Dhikr of Allah will enter Jannah laughingly." *(Abu Nu'aym in Hilya)*

The Encouragement Mu'adh bin Jabal 🙂 and Abdullah bin Amr 🙂 gave Towards Dhikr

Mu'adh bin Jabal 🙂 said, "A person can do no action more effective in saving himself from Allah's punishment than engaging in Allah's Dhikr." "O Abu Abdur Rahman!" someone asked, "Not even Jihad in the Path of Allah?" "No," Mu'adh 🙂 replied, "Unless he fights until even his sword breaks. This is because Allah in His Book: وَلَذِكْرُ اللَّهِ أَكْبَرُ

... (without doubt) the Dhikr of Allah is greatest (greater than other forms of worship that are devoid of Allah's remembrance)... (Al-Ankabut:45) (Abu Nu'aym in Hilya)

Abdullah bin Amr 🙂 said, "Engaging in the Dhikr of Allah in the mornings and evenings is better than breaking swords in the Path of Allah and giving donating large sums of wealth in charity." *(Ibn Abi Shaybah in Kanzul Ummal)*.

Rasulullah 🙂 Prefers the Dhikr of Allah to Setting Slaves Free

Anas 🙂 narrates that Rasulullah 🙂 said, "I prefer sitting with a group of people engaged in Allah's Dhikr between Fajr and sunrise to setting free 4 slaves from the progeny of Isma'el 🙂, even though the blood money of each one of them is worth 12,000. I prefer sitting with a group of people engaged in Allah's Dhikr between Asr and sunset to setting free 4 slaves from the progeny of Isma'el 🙂, even though the blood money of each one of them is worth 12,000." *(Abu Ya'la, Haythami)*. Anas narrates that Rasulullah 🙂 said, 'The person who performs his Asr salah and remains sitting to dictate words of worth until the evening is better than the one who frees 8 slaves from the progeny of Isma'el 🙂." *(Ahmad, Abu Ya'la)*. Rasulullah 🙂 said, "I prefer sitting with a group of people engaged in Allah's Dhikr between Fajr and sunrise to everything upon which the sun rises." *(Abu Ya'la, Haythami)*

Rasulullah 🙂 Prefers Dhikr to Donating Pure-Bred Horses to Mujahidin and to Setting Slaves Free

Sahl bin Sa'd Sa'idi 🙂 narrates that Rasulullah 🙂 said, "More than providing thorough red horses to be used in the Path of Allah, I would love to rather attend the Fajr salah and then sit to engage in the Dhikr of Allah until sunrise." *(Tabrani in Kabeer and Awsat, Majma'uz Zawa'id)*. Abbas bin Abdul Muttalib 🙂 narrates that Rasulullah 🙂 said, "I prefer sitting to engage in Allah's Dhikr from the time of the Fajr salah until sunrise to setting free 4 slaves from the progeny of Isma'el 🙂." *(Bazzar)*. Rasulullah 🙂 said, "I prefer performing the Fajr salah and then sitting to engage in Allah's Dhikr until sunrise rather than racing a horse in the Path of Allah until sunrise." *(Tabrani, Haythami)*

Rasulullah 🙂 Ranks the Recitation of 'SubhanAllah', "Al Hamdulillah", "La Ilaha Illalah" and "Allahu Akbar" higher than Everything in the World

Abu Hurairah 🙂 narrates that Rasulullah 🙂 said, "Rather than having everything over which the sun rises, I prefer reciting 'SubhanAllah', 'Al Hamdulillah', 'La Ilaaha IllAllah' and 'Allahu Akbar."(Muslim, Tirmidhi in Targheeb wat Tarheeb). Abu Umamah 🙂 reports that Rasulullah 🙂 said, "I prefer sitting and reciting 'Allahu Akbar', 'Al Hamdulillah', 'SubhanAllah', and 'La Ilaha IllAllah' until sunrise rather than setting free 2 slaves from the progeny of Isma'el 🙂. I prefer reciting them after Asr until sunset rather than setting free 4 slaves from the progeny of Isma'el 🙂." *(Ahmad)*. Rasulullah 🙂 said, "I prefer sitting until sunrise and engaging in Dhikr of Allah by reciting 'Allahu Akbar', 'La Ilaha IllAllah' and 'SubhanAllah' rather than setting free 4 slaves from the progeny of Isma'el. I prefer engaging in Allah's Dhikr from the Asr salah until sunset rather than setting free many slaves from the progeny of Isma'el 🙂." *(Ahmad, Tabrani, Haythami)*.

The Fervor Abdullah bin Mas'ood 🙂 had for Dhikr

Abdullah bin Mas'ood 🙂 said, "Rather than providing pure-bred horses for Jihad from morning to night, I prefer engaging m the Dhikr of Allah from morning to night." *(Tabrani, Haythami)*. Abu Ubaidah bin Abdullah bin Mas'ood says, "It was difficult for Abdullah bin Mas'ood 🙂 to say anything that was not the Dhikr of Allah." *(Tabrani in Kabeer, Haythami)*. Abdullah bin Mas'ood 🙂 would be upset to hear anyone talking between dawn and the Fajr salah. It was after the Fajr salah that Abdullah bin Mas'ood 🙂 approached a group of people who were busy talking in the Masjid. He forbade them from talking saying, "You have come here to perform salah. You may therefore either perform your salah or remain silent." *(Tabrani, Haythami)*.

The Fervor Abu Darda 🙂 and Mu'adh 🙂 had for Dhikr

Abu Darda 🙂 said, "I love more to recite 'Allahu Akbar' 100 times than spending 100 gold coins in Sadaqah." *(Abu Nu'aym in Hilya)*. Mu'adh bin Jabal 🙂 said, "Rather than providing pure-bred horses for Jihad in the Path of Allah from morning to night, I prefer engaging in the Dhikr of Allah from morning to night." *(Abu Nu'ayn in Hilya)*

The Fervor Anas 🙂, Abu Moosa Ash'ari 🙂 and Abdullah bin Um'ar 🙂 had for Dhikr

Anas bin Malik 🙂 reports that they were on a journey with Abu Moosa Ash'ari 🙂 when he heard people talking and having eloquent discussions. "O Anas," he said, "what benefit is there for me in that. Come, let us engage in the Dhikr of our Rabb because it seems like those people can even skin a person with their tongues." The rest of the narration has passed in the chapter discussing Iman in the Hereafter. *(Abu Nu'ayn in Hilya)*. Mu'adh bin Abdullah bin Rafi reports that he was once present in a gathering with Abdullah bin Um'ar 🙂, Abdullah bin Ja'far 🙂 and Abdullah bin Abu Umairah 🙂. Abdullah bin Abu Umairah 🙂 related to them that he had heard Mu'adh bin Jabal 🙂 say that he heard Rasulullah 🙂 say, "There are 2 phrases, one of which rises no less than the height of Allah's throne, while the other fills the atmosphere between the heavens and the earth. They are 'La Ilaha

IllAllah' and 'Allahu Akbar'." Abdullah bin Um'ar ؓ then confirmed with Abdullah bin Abu Umairah ؓ saying, "Did you really hear him say that?" "Yes," came the reply. Abdullah bin Um'ar ؓ then started weeping so much that his beard was drenched in his tears. He said, "These are 2 phrases that are very dear to me and which I recite very often." *(Tabrani, Mundhiri, Haythami).* Jareeri reports, "When Anas ؓ entered into the state of Ihram from Dhatul Irq, we heard him say nothing other than the Dhikr of Allah until he came out of Ihram. He said to me, 'Dear son of my brother! That is what Ihram is like.'" *(Ibn Sa'd)*

The Virtue on the Day of Judgment of Those Participating in the Gatherings of Dhikr

Abu Sa'eed Khudri ؓ narrates from Rasulullah ﷺ that on the Day of Judgment, Allah will say, "The people of this assembly will soon learn who the people of honor are." "O Rasulullah ﷺ!" someone asked, "Who are the people of honor?" Rasulullah ﷺ replied, "Those who join the gatherings of Dhikr." *(Ahmad, Abu Ya'la, Ibn Hibban, Bayhaqi in Targheeb wat Tarheeb, Haythami)*

The Incident of an Expedition that Rasulullah ﷺ Dispatched and how he rated People Engaged in Dhikr Above Them

Um'ar ؓ narrates that Rasulullah ﷺ once dispatched an expedition to Najd that won a large booty and returned very quickly. Someone who was not part of the expedition remarked, "I have never before seen any expedition return so quickly and win so much booty as this expedition did!" Rasulullah ﷺ said, "Should I not inform you of people who return even quicker with and even greater booty? They are people who attend the Fajr salah and remain seated in their places, engaging themselves in Dhikr until sunrise. Then they perform 2 Rakats salah before returning home. Such people have a quicker return and a greater booty than those of the expedition." *(Ibn Zanjway, Tirmidhi in Kanzul Ummal, Bazzar, Haythami)*

Rasulullah ﷺ sits with People Engaged in Dhikr after the Revelation of a Verse of the Qur'an

Abdur Rahman bin Sahl bin Hunaif ؓ narrates that Rasulullah ﷺ was in one of his rooms when Allah revealed the verse: وَاصْبِرْ نَفْسَكَ مَعَ الَّذِينَ يَدْعُونَ رَبَّهُمْ بِالْغَدَاةِ وَالْعَشِيِّ يُرِيدُونَ وَجْهَهُ *And keep yourself (O Muhammad ﷺ) patiently with those who call on their Lord (i.e. your companions who remember their Lord with glorification, praising in prayers, etc., and other righteous deeds, etc.) morning and afternoon, seeking His Face,...(Al-Kahaf:28).* Rasulullah ﷺ left the room in search of such people and found a group engaged in the Dhikr of Allah. Amongst the group were some men who had disheveled hair, others whose skin was chapped and others with only one cloth to wear. When he saw them, Rasulullah ﷺ sat with them saying, "All praise is for Allah who has created within my Ummah people with whom I have been instructed to remain with." *(Tabrani in Tafsir ibn Kathir)*

Rasulullah ﷺ sits in a Gathering Including Abdullah bin Rawaha ؓ

Abdullah bin Abbas ؓ narrates that Rasulullah ﷺ once passed by Abdullah bin Rawaha ؓ as he was busy advising some of his companions. Rasulullah ﷺ said, "Listen well! You are the people with whom Allah has instructed me to remain with." Rasulullah ﷺ then recited the verse:
وَاصْبِرْ نَفْسَكَ مَعَ الَّذِينَ يَدْعُونَ رَبَّهُمْ بِالْغَدَاةِ وَالْعَشِيِّ يُرِيدُونَ وَجْهَهُ وَلَا تَعْدُ عَيْنَاكَ عَنْهُمْ تُرِيدُ زِينَةَ الْحَيَاةِ الدُّنْيَا وَلَا تُطِعْ مَنْ أَغْفَلْنَا قَلْبَهُ عَنْ ذِكْرِنَا وَاتَّبَعَ هَوَاهُ وَكَانَ أَمْرُهُ فُرُطًا (28)

And keep yourself (O Muhammad ﷺ) patiently with those who call on their Lord (i.e. your companions who remember their Lord with glorification, praising in prayers, etc., and other righteous deeds, etc.) morning and afternoon, seeking His Face, and let not your eyes overlook them, desiring the pomp and glitter of the life of the world; and obey not him whose heart We have made heedless of Our Remembrance, one who follows his own lusts and whose affair (deeds) has been lost. (Al-Kahaf:28)

Rasulullah ﷺ then continued, "Behold! As many of you are sitting here, so many angels are also present with you. When you say 'SubhanAllah', they also say 'SubhanAllah'. When you say 'Al Hamdu Lillah', they also say 'Al Hamdu Lillah' and when you say 'Allahu Akbar', they also say 'Allahu Akbar'. They then ascend to their Rabb and although He knows more than them, they say, 'O our Rabb! When Your servants said 'SubhanAllah', we also said 'SubhanAllah', when they said 'Allahu Akbar', we also said 'Allahu Akbar' and when they said 'Al Hamdu Lillah', we also said 'Al Hamdu Lillah'. Allah then says, 'O my angels! I make you witness that I have forgiven them.' 'But some of them were sinners,' the angels add. Allah says, 'They are a group with whom no associate is deprived." *(Tabrani in his Sagheer, Haythami)*

Rasulullah ﷺ sits with a Group that Included Salman ؓ

Thabit Bunani narrates that Salman ؓ was part of a group engaged in Dhikr when Rasulullah ﷺ passed by. When they stopped, Rasulullah ﷺ asked them what they were saying. 'O Rasulullah ﷺ!" they submitted, "We were engaged in Dhikr." Rasulullah ﷺ then said, "Continue saying what you had been saying. When I noticed Allah's mercy descending on you, I wished to join you." Rasulullah ﷺ then added, "All praise is for Allah who has created within my Ummah people with whom I have been instructed to remain with." *(Abu Nu'aym in Hilya)*

Rasulullah ﷺ sits in a Gathering of Dhikr and tells the Participants to Eat From the Gardens of Jannah

Jabir ؓ reports that Rasulullah ﷺ once came to them and said, "O people! Verily Allah has many groups of angels who descend and remain with the gatherings of Dhikr on earth. You should therefore eat from the gardens of Jannah." "Where are the gardens of Jannah?" the Sahabah asked. Rasulullah ﷺ replied, "They are the gatherings of Dhikr. You should spend your mornings or evenings in the Dhikr of Allah and remind yourselves about Him. The person who wishes to know his status in Allah's estimation should see what Allah's status is in his estimation. Because Allah grants a servant only that status in His sight that the servant grants to Allah in his sight" *(Ibn Abi Dunya, Abu Ya'la, Bazzar, Tabrani, Hakim and Bayhaqi in Targheeb wat Tarheeb, Haythami).* Jabir bin Samurah ؓ reports that after performing the Fajr salah, Rasulullah ﷺ used to sit and remain engaged in Dhikr until sunrise. *(Tabrani in Sagheer, Haythami)*

Rasulullah ﷺ's Statement on the rewards of the Dhikr Gatherings

Abdullah bin Amr ؓ narrates that he asked Rasulullah ﷺ on the rewards for the gatherings of Dhikr. Rasulullah ﷺ replied, "The rewards for the gatherings of Dhikr shall be Jannah; Jannah." *(Ahmad, Tabrani, Haythami).* Abdullah bin Mas'ood ؓ said, "The gatherings of Dhikr are the life of knowledge and create humility in the heart." *(Ibn Asakir in Kanzul Ummal)*

Rasulullah ﷺ says that Expiation for the Sins of a Gathering is to recite "Subhana Kallahumma wa Bihamdik"

Aisha ؓ narrates that after every gathering and salah, Rasulullah ﷺ used to say something. When I asked him about it, he said, 'If what you spoke was good, these words shall seal (preserve) them until the Day of Judgment and if you spoke evil, they shall serve as expiation; the words are:

سُبْحَانَكَ اللَّهُمَّ وَبِحَمْدِكَ لَا إِلَهَ إِلَّا أَنْتَ أَسْتَغْفِرُكَ وَأَتُوبُ إِلَيْكَ

"You are Pure, O Allah and it is Your praises that we sing. There is none worthy of worship but You, I beg Your forgiveness and repent to You." (Ibn Abi Dunya, Nasa'ee, Hakim, Bayhaqi). Abu Barza ؓ reports that at the end of every gathering just before he stood up, Rasulullah ﷺ would recite:

سُبْحَانَكَ اللَّهُمَّ وَبِحَمْدِكَ أَشْهَدُ أَنْ لَا إِلَهَ إِلَّا أَنْتَ أَسْتَغْفِرُكَ وَأَتُوبُ إِلَيْكَ

"You are Pure, O Allah and it is Your praises that we sing. I testify there is none worthy of worship but You, I beg Your forgiveness and repent to You."

"O Rasulullah ﷺ" someone asked, *"You are saying something that you had not been saying previously."* Rasulullah ﷺ replied, *"It is expiation for the sins of a gathering."* (Abu Dawud). Another narration quotes the Du'a with additional words:

سُبْحَانَكَ اللَّهُمَّ وَبِحَمْدِكَ أَشْهَدُ أَنْ لَا إِلَهَ إِلَّا أَنْتَ أَسْتَغْفِرُكَ وَأَتُوبُ إِلَيْكَ عَمِلْتُ سُوءً وَظَلَمْتُ نَفْسِي فَاغْفِرْ لِي فَإِنَّهُ لَا يَغْفِرُ الذُّنُوبَ إِلَّا أَنْتَ

"You are Pure, O Allah and it is Your praises that we sing. I testify there is none worthy of worship but You, I beg Your forgiveness and repent to You. I have sinned and wronged myself, so forgive me because none but You can forgive sins." (Nasa'ee, Hakim, Tabrani in Targheeb wat Tarheeb)

Rasulullah ﷺ and Abdullah bin Amr ؓ Encourage the Recitation of the Du'a after a Gathering

Zubair bin Awwam ؓ reports that they once said, "O Rasulullah ﷺ! When we leave your gatherings, we find that we start discussing matters of the Period of Ignorance." Rasulullah ﷺ advised them saying, "Whenever you sit in gatherings in which you fear for yourselves (that you may have discussed what was wrong), then ensure that you recite at the end:

سُبْحَانَكَ اللَّهُمَّ وَبِحَمْدِكَ أَشْهَدُ أَنْ لَا إِلَهَ إِلَّا أَنْتَ أَسْتَغْفِرُكَ وَأَتُوبُ إِلَيْكَ

'You are Pure, O Allah and it is Your praises that we sing. I testify there is none worthy of worship but You, I beg Your forgiveness and repent to You.'

By reciting this, the sins you may have committed in the gathering will be atoned for.' (Tabrani in Sagheer and Awsat, Haythami). Abdullah bin Amr bin Al Aas ؓ said, "There are certain words that, if recited thrice after a gathering, will atone for anything wrong said in the gathering whether the gathering be one of righteousness or not. When they are recited after a Dhikr gathering or any other gathering of virtue, they serve as a seal, just as a letter is sealed." He continued to mention the words, which the same as the Du'a stated in the above narration of Aisha ؓ. (Abu Dawood, Ibn Hibban in Targheeb waf Tarheeb)

The Advice of Rasulullah ﷺ to Abu Dhar ؓ on Qur'an Recitation

Abu Dhar ؓ narrates that when he once asked Rasulullah ﷺ for advice, Rasulullah ﷺ said, "Hold fast to Taqwa because it is the basis of every act." When Abu Dhar ؓ requested for more advice, Rasulullah ﷺ added, "Be particular about reciting the Qur'an because it is a light for you on earth and a treasure for you in the heavens." (Ibn Hibban in Targheeb wat Tarheeb)

Rasulullah ﷺ Recites a Portion of the Qur'an Every Night

Aws bun Hudhaifa Thaqafi says, "When we came to Rasulullah ﷺ as a delegation from the Thaqif, those of us who belonged to the Ahlaf stayed with Mughiera bin Shu'ba ؓ while those who belonged to the Banu Malik were accommodated in Rasulullah ﷺ's tent. Rasulullah ﷺ would come to address us

every day after the Isha salah and because he remained standing for so long, he would lean on one leg and then on the other. Much of what he told us concerned the problems he experienced with the Quraish. He said, 'We were regarded as weak in Makkah, but we had our own back from them after coming to Madinah. Victory then took turns between our and their camps.' One night Rasulullah ﷺ came to us later than he usually did. 'O Rasulullah ﷺ!' we asked, 'Tonight you have come to us later than you usually do'?" Rasulullah ﷺ explained, 'Because I was unable to complete my fixed daily portions of the Qur'an, I did not want to leave until I had completed.' The next morning, we asked companions about how Rasulullah ﷺ divided the portions of the Qur'an that he recited. They explained that Rasulullah ﷺ divided the Qur'an into 7 parts, consisting of 3 Surahs (Fatiha to Al Imran), 5 Surahs (Nisa to Anfal), 7 Surahs (Tauba to Hijr), 9 Surahs (Nahl to Noor), 11 Surahs (Furqan to Fatir), 13 Surahs (Yaseen to Fatah) and the Mufassal Surahs (Hujurat to Nas)." (Tayalisi, Ahmad, Ibn Jareer, Tabrani, Abu Nu'aym in Kanzul Ummal, Abu Dawud). Mughiera bin Shu'ba ؓ narrates that Rasulullah ﷺ was at a place between Makkah and Madinah when a man sought permission to see him. Rasulullah ﷺ did not give permission and explained, "I did not complete the daily fixed portion of the Qur'an that I always recite and am unable to give anything else preference over it (he may see me after I have completed)." (Ibn Abu Dawud in Masahif, Kanzul Ummal)

The Fervor Um'ar ؓ had for the Recitation of the Qur'an and How he Used to ask Abu Musa Ash'ari ؓ to Recite the Qur'an

Abu Salama reports that when Um'ar bin Khattab ؓ used to say to Abu Musa Ash'ari ؓ, "Remind us about our Rabb", he would start reciting the Qur'an. (Abu Nu'aym in Hilya, Ibn Sa'd). Habib bin Abu Marzug says, "The report reached us that Abu Musa Ash'ari ؓ used to recite the Qur'an in a most excellent voice and would do so when Um'ar ؓ would say to him, 'Remind us of our Rabb.'" Abu Nadhra narrates that Abu Musa Ash'ari ؓ used to start reciting the Qur'an when Um'ar ؓ would say to him, "Make us yearn for our Rabb." When the people reminded him that it was time for salah, Um'ar ؓ would say, "Are we not in salah already (because the purpose of salah is to remember Allah)'?" Abdullah bin Abbas ؓ reports that whenever Um'ar ؓ entered the house he would open up the pages of the Qur'an and recite it. (Ibn Abu Dawud in Kanzul Ummal)

The Fervor Uthman ؓ had for Reciting the Qur'an

Uthman ؓ used to say, "I would not like a single day or night to pass without looking into the Book of Allah i.e. recite the Qur'an by looking." (Ahmad in Zuhd, Ibn Asakir in Kanzul Ummal). Uthman ؓ said, "Had your hearts been pure, you would never get enough of the speech of Allah." (Ahmad in Zuhd, Ibn Asakir in Kanzul Ummal). Hasan says, "Amirul Mu'mineen Uthman bin Affan ؓ said, 'Had our hearts been pure, we would never get enough of the speech of Allah and I would not like a single day pass by without looking into the Qur'an.' When Uthman ؓ passed away, the pages of his Qur'an were in tatters as he used to look into it so often." (Bayhaqi in Asma was Sifat)

The Fervor that Abdullah bin Mas'ood ؓ, Abdullah bin Um'ar ؓ and Ikrama bin Abu Jahal ؓ had for Reciting the Qur'an

Abdullah bin Mas'ood ؓ said, "Always look into the Qur'an when reciting because it facilitates easier contemplation." (Ibn Abu Dawud in Kanzul Ummal). Habib bin Shahid narrates that when Nafi was asked about what Abdullah bin Um'ar ؓ used to do at home, he replied, "Something that others would not manage. He would perform wudhu for every salah and recite from the Qur'an between every 2 salats." *(Ibn Sa'd)*. Ibn Abu Mulaika narrates that Ikrama bin Abu Jahal ؓ used to place the Qur'an on his face and weep saying, "The speech of my Rabb! The Book of my Rabb!" *(Hakim)*. Abdullah bin Um'ar ؓ said, "The reward of 10 good deeds is recorded every time a person sends salutations to Nabi ﷺ. When any of you returns home from the marketplace, he should open the Qur'an and recite it because for every letter that he recites, he will receive the reward of 10 good deeds." He stated, "Verily for every letter Allah shall record for him the reward of 10 good deeds. I am not saying that this reward is for الم *Alif-Lam-Mim*, but the reward of 10 good deeds are recorded for ا *Alif*, another 10 for the ل *Lam* and another 10 for م *Mim*" *(Ibn Abu Dawud in Kanzul Ummal)*

Rasulullah ﷺ Advises Uqba bin Amir Juhani ؓ to Recite Surah Ikhlas and the Mu'awwadhatain (Surah Falaq and Nas) Every Night

Uqba bin Amir Juhani ؓ narrates that he once met Rasulullah ﷺ, who said to him, "O Uqba bin Amir! Maintain ties of kinship with those who sever them, give to those who deprive you and forgive those who do you wrong." When he met Rasulullah ﷺ again afterwards, Rasulullah ﷺ said, "O Uqba bin Amir! Should I not inform you of a few Surahs, the likes of which Allah has neither revealed in the Torah, the Zabur or in the Injil. Not a single night should pass you by without you reciting them. They are *Surah Ikhlas, Surah Falaq and Surah Nas*." Uqba ؓ says, "After Rasulullah ﷺ had instructed me to do this, not a night has passed by without me reciting these Surahs because it is only appropriate that I should never omit them after receiving the instruction from Rasulullah ﷺ." *(Ibn Asakir in Kanzul Ummal)*. Aisha ؓ reports that whenever Rasulullah ﷺ lay down to sleep, he would place his palms next to each other, recite Surah Ikhlas and Surah Falaq and then blow into them. Thereafter, he would pass his hands over as much of his body as he could reach, beginning with his head, face and front portion of his body. This he would repeat thrice. *(Nasa'ee)*. When he lay down to sleep, Rasulullah ﷺ used to blow into his palms after reciting the complete Surahs Ikhas, Falaq and Nas. He would then pass his hands over his face, his arms, his chest and as far over his body as his arms would reach. Aisha ؓ reports further that when his illness intensified, Rasulullah ﷺ would ask her to do it for him. *(Ibn Najjar in Kanzul Ummal, Jam'ul Fawa'id, Bukhari, Muslim, Abu Dawud, Tirmidhi, Ibn Majah)*

What Rasulullah ﷺ Used to Recite Before going to Sleep

Jabir ؓ narrates that Rasulullah ﷺ would not go to sleep until he had recited Surah Alif Lam Mim Sajdah and Surah Mulk. Tawus mentioned that these two Surahs rate 70 virtues higher than the other Surahs of the Qur'an. *(Tirmidhi in Jam'ul Fawa'id)*. Irbadh bin Sariya ؓ narrates that when he lay down, Rasulullah ﷺ would recite the Musabbihat (surahs begin with "Sabbaha" or "Yusabbihu") before sleeping. He would say, "In these Surahs is a verse that is better than 1,000 verses." *(Tirmidhi, Abu Dawud)*. Aisha ؓ reports that Rasulullah ﷺ would not go to sleep until he had recited Surah ZOmar and Surah Bani Isra'el. *(Tirmidhi in Jam'ul Fawa'id)*. Farwah bin Naufal ؓ reports that he approached Rasulullah ﷺ with the request, "O Rasulullah ﷺ! Teach me something to recite when I lie down to sleep." Rasulullah ﷺ said, 'Recite *Surah Kafirun* because it is pardon from Shirk." *(Tirmidhi)*

The Statement of Abdullah bin Mas'ood ؓ Concerning the Recitation of Surah Mulk and the Statement of Abdullah bin Um'ar ؓ Concerning the Recitation of Surahs Baqarah, Al Imran and Nisa

Abdullah bin Mas'ood ؓ said, "When the angels of punishment approach a person in the grave from his feet, the feet will say, 'You have no approach from our side because he used to recite Surah Mulk.' When they then approach him from his chest, the chest will say, 'You have no approach from my side because he used to recite Surah Mulk.' Thereafter, when they approach him from his head, the head will say, 'You have no approach from my side because he used to recite Surah Mulk.' In this manner, Surah Mulk protects a person from punishment in the grave. In fact, the Torah states that wh6ever will recite Surah Mulk at night has multiplied his rewards and carried out an act of extreme virtue." *(Hakim)*. Another narration briefly states that Abdullah bin Mas'ood ؓ said, "Allah will protect from the punishment in the grave every person who recites Surah Mulk every night. During the time of Rasul ﷺ, we used to call it the 'protector' and it is also stated in one of the scriptures of Allah that whoever will recite Surah Mulk at night has multiplied his rewards and carried out an act of extreme virtue." *(Nasa'ee in Targheeb wal Tarheeb, Bayhaqi in Kitab Adhabil Qabr, Kanzul Ummal)*. Omar ؓ said, "The person who recites Surah Surah Al-Imran and Surah Nisa in a single night shall be recorded as one of the obedient ones." *(Abu Ubaidah, Sa'eed bin Mansur, Abd bin Humaid, Bayhaqi in Shu'sbul Iman, Kanzul Ummal)*

Rasulullah ﷺ Teaches Jubair bin Mut'im ؓ to Recite the 5 last Surahs of the Qur'an

Jubair bin Mut'im ؓ narrates that Rasulullah ﷺ once said to him, "O Jubair! When you travel on a journey, would you like your position to be the best from all your companions and would you like to be the one with the most provisions?" "Certainly!" Jubair ؓ replied, "May my parents be sacrificed for you!" Rasulullah ﷺ said, "Then recite these 5 Surahs: *Surah Kafirun, Surah Nasr, Surah Ikhlas, Surah Falaq and Surah Nas*. Begin each Surah with بِسْمِ اللهِ الرَّحْمٰنِ الرَّحِيْمِ *Bismillah herrah maner Rahim* and end your recitation with بِسْمِ اللهِ الرَّحْمٰنِ الرَّحِيْمِ *Bismillah herrah maner Rahim*." Jubair ؓ continues the narration saying, "Although I was a wealthy person, I was always the most poorly clad on a journey and with the least provisions. However, ever since I started reciting what Rasulullah ﷺ taught me, I was always in the best position and with the most provisions until I turned from the journey." *(Abu Ya'la, Haythami)*

Rasulullah ﷺ Teaches Abdullah bin Khubaib ؓ to Recite Surah Ikhlas and the Mu'awwadhatain Every Morning and Evening

Abdullah bin Khubaib ؓ narrates, "It was an extremely dark and rainy night when we went out in search of Rasulullah ﷺ to lead us in salah. When we met him, he said, 'Recite!' When I said nothing, Rasulullah ﷺ repeated, 'Recite!' When I again failed to respond, he said for the third time, 'Recite!' 'O Rasulullah ﷺ!' I submitted, 'What should I recite?' Rasulullah ﷺ replied, 'Recite *Surah Ikhlas* and the Mu'awwadhatain (Falaq and Nas). Recite them thrice every morning and evening and they will protect you from everything." *(Abu Dawud, Tirmidhi in Adhkar of Nawawi)*

The Statement of Ali ؓ Concerning the Recitation of Surah Ikhlas after the Fajr Salah

Ali ؓ said, 'When a person recites Surah Ikhlas 10 times after the Fajr salah, he will commit no sin all of that day even though Saitan may try his utmost (to get him to sin)." *(Sa'eed bin Mansur, Ibn Darees in Kanzul Ummal)*

What Rasulullah ﷺ and Ali ؓ said About Ayatul Kursi

Ali ؓ reports, "Rasulullah ﷺ was on the wooden step of that pulpit when I heard him say, 'When a person recites Ayatul Kursi after every salah, there is nothing but death that prevents him from entering Jannah. When a person recites it when he goes to bed, Allah will safeguard his house, the houses of his neighbors and all the houses in his vicinity." (Bayhaqi in Shu'abul Iman, Kanzul Ummal). Ali ؓ also said, "I do not think that a person born as a Muslim or who has any intelligence would ever spend the night without reciting the verse: Ayatul Kursi. If only you people knew its worth! It has been granted to your Nabi ﷺ from the treasures beneath the very Throne of Allah and no Nabi عليه السلام before him has ever received it. I never pass a single night without reciting it thrice, once in the 2 Rakats after Isha, once in my Witr salah and once when I lie down to sleep." (Abu Ubaid, Ibn Abi Shaybah, Darmi in Kanzul Ummal)

The Statements of Ali ؓ, Uthman ؓ and Abdullah bin Mas'ood ؓ on the Recitation of Verses of Surah Baqara and Surah Al Imran

Ali ؓ said, "I do not think that a person who has any intelligence would ever spend the night without reciting the concluding verses of Surah Baqarah because they are from the treasures beneath the very Throne of Allah." (Darmi, Musaddad, Muhammad bin Nasr, Ibn Darees, Ibn Mardway in Kanzul Ummal). Uthman ؓ said, "Whoever recites the concluding verses of Surah Al-Imran at night shall receive the reward of spending the night in Ibadah." (Darmi in Kanzul Ummal). Abdullah bin Mas'ood ؓ said, "If a person recites 10 verses of Surah Baqarah in his home, no Saitan shall ever enter that home all night. The verses are the 4 verses at the beginning, Aayatul Kursi together with the 2 verses that follow it and the concluding 3 verses of Surah Baqarah." (Tabrani, Haythami)

The Incident of Ubay bin Ka'b ؓ and a Jin Concerning Ayatul Kursi

Ubay bin Ka'b ؓ had 2 silos of dates and in keeping check on them, he discovered that the dates were decreasing. When he stood on guard one night, he discovered a creature that resembled a young boy. When Ubay ؓ greeted him with Salam, the creature replied to the Salam. "Give me you hand," Ubay ؓ instructed. When the creature did so, Ubay ؓ saw that its hand was that of a dog's and was also covered with dog's hair. "Such is the appearance of the Jinn," Ubay ؓ said. The Jinn said, "All of the Jinn world knows well that there is none more powerful than I." Ubay ؓ asked, "Then what makes you do this (steal from my silo)." The Jinn replied, "I have heard that you are a person who loved to give Sadaqa, so I wished to have some of your food." Ubay ؓ asked further, "What can protect us (humans) from the likes of you?" The Jinn replied, "It is that verse called Ayatul Kursi which appears in Surah Baqarah. Whoever recites it in the evening shall be protected from us until the morning and whoever recites it in the morning shall be protected from us until the evening." Ubay ؓ went early the next morning to Rasulullah ﷺ and informed him about the incident. Rasulullah ﷺ remarked, "The wretch actually spoke the truth." (Nasa'ee, Hakim, Tabrani, Abu Nu'aym, Bayhaqi, Sa'eed bin Mansur in Kanzul Ummal)

The Incident of Abdullah bin Busr ؓ and a Group of Jinn and the Verse of the Qur'an he Recited

Abdullah bin Busr ؓ says, "When I left Hims, the night gave me shelter on a piece of ground where the Jinn of the area came to me. I however recited the verse of Surah A'raf: إِنَّ رَبَّكُمُ اللَّهُ الَّذِي خَلَقَ السَّمَاوَاتِ وَالْأَرْضَ فِي سِتَّةِ أَيَّامٍ ثُمَّ اسْتَوَى عَلَى الْعَرْشِ يُغْشِي اللَّيْلَ

النَّهَارَ يَطْلُبُهُ حَثِيثًا وَالشَّمْسَ وَالْقَمَرَ وَالنُّجُومَ مُسَخَّرَاتٍ بِأَمْرِهِ أَلَا لَهُ الْخَلْقُ وَالْأَمْرُ تَبَارَكَ اللَّهُ رَبُّ الْعَالَمِينَ (54) *Indeed your Lord is Allah, Who created the heavens and the earth in Six Days, and then He Istawa (rose over) the Throne (really in a manner that suits His Majesty). He brings the night as a cover over the day, seeking it rapidly, and (He created) the sun, the moon, the stars subjected to His Command. Surely, His is the Creation and Commandment. Blessed be Allah, the Lord of the Alameen (mankind, jinns and all that exists)! (Al-A'raf:54).* Some of them said to the others, 'Look after him until the morning.' The following morning, I then took to my conveyance and left." (Tabrani, Haythami)

Ala bin Jalaj instructed Sons to do when They Place him in Grave

Ala bin Jalaj once said to his sons, "When you place me to rest in my grave, please say: بسم الله و على ملة رسول الله
'In the name of Allah and upon the creed of Rasulullah ﷺ'
Thereafter, I want you to gently cover me with sand and recite the beginning and the end of Surah Baqarah at my head-side. I have seen that Abdullah bin Omar ؓ liked to do this." (Ibn Asakir in Kanzul Ummal). The statement of Ali ؓ concerning the verse سبحان ربك رب العزة عما يصيفون "Subhanaka Rabbaka Rabbal Izzate Amma Yasifun" and Ibn Awf ؓ recites Ayatul Kursi in all the corners of his house. Ali ؓ said, "Whoever wishes to have his deeds weighed in a large scale should thrice recite:
سُبْحَانَ رَبِّكَ رَبِّ الْعِزَّةِ عَمَّا يَصِفُونَ (180) وَسَلَامٌ عَلَى الْمُرْسَلِينَ (181) وَالْحَمْدُ لِلَّهِ رَبِّ الْعَالَمِينَ (182) *Glorified be your Lord, the Lord of Honor and Power! (He is free) from what they attribute unto Him! And peace be on the Messengers! And all the praise and thanks be to Allah, Lord of the Alameen (mankind, jinns and all that exists) (As-Saffat:180-182) (Ibn Zanjway in Kanzul Ummal)*

Abdullah bin Ubaid bin Umair narrates that whenever Abdur Rahman bin Auf ؓ entered his house, he would recite Aayatul Kursi in all the corners of the house." (Abu Ya'la, Haythami)

Rasulullah ﷺ says that the Person Most Fortunate to Receive his Intercession will be the One who Recites the Kalima La Ilaha IllAllah with Complete Sincerity

Abu Hurairah ؓ reports that he once asked Rasulullah ﷺ, "O Rasulullah ﷺ! Who will be most fortunate to receive your intercession on the Day of Judgment?" "O Abu Hurairah!", Rasulullah ﷺ said, "I knew that because of your keenness for Ahadeeth, none would have asked this question before you. The person most fortunate to receive my intercession on the Day of Judgment will be the one who recites لا اله الا الله 'La Ilaha IllAllah' with complete sincerity of the heart." (Bukhari in Targheeb wat Tarheeb). Zadi bin Arqam ؓ reports that Rasulullah ﷺ said, "Whoever recites لا اله الا الله 'La Ilaha IllAllah' with sincerity shall enter Jannah." Someone asked, "What is meant by sincerity?" Rasulullah ﷺ replied, "That the Kalima should prevent one from acts that Allah has forbidden." (Tabrani in Awsat, Targheeb wat Tarheeb)

Allah Informs Musa عليه السلام on the virtue of لا اله الا الله 'La Ilaha IllAllah'

Abu Sa'eed Khudri ؓ reports from Rasulullah ﷺ that Musa عليه السلام once requested Allah saying, "O my Rabb! Teach me something by which I may engage in Your Dhikr and supplicate to you." Allah's reply to him was, لا اله الا الله "La Ilaha IllAllah'." "O my Rabb!" Musa submitted, "But all of Your creation says this." Allah repeated, "Say لا اله الا الله 'La Ilaha IllAllah'." Musa then said, "What I want is something exclusively for myself." Allah said, "O Musa! If all the 7 heavens and 7 earths are placed on one pan of the scale and لا اله الا الله 'La Ilaha IllAllah' on the other, لا اله الا الله 'La Ilaha IllAllah' would outweigh the rest." *(Nasa'ee, Ibn Hibban, Hakim in Targheeb wat Tarheeb).* Allah said, "If all the 7 heavens and their inhabitants apart from Myself together with the 7 earths are placed on one pan of the scale and 'لا اله الا الله 'La Ilaha IllAllah' on the other, لا اله الا الله 'La Ilaha IllAllah' would outweigh them all." *(Abu Ya'la, Haythami)*

Rasulullah ﷺ Speaks About the Advice of Nuh عليه السلام to his Sons

Abdullah bin Omar ؓ reports that Rasulullah ﷺ once said, "Should I not inform you of the advice that Nuh عليه السلام gave to his sons?" When the Sahabah asked to know, Rasulullah ﷺ said, "Advising his sons, Nuh عليه السلام said, 'Dear sons! I strongly advise you to carry out 2 things and forbid you from another 2. I advise you repeat the words لا اله الا الله 'La Ilaha IllAllah' because if these words are placed on one pan of a scale and all the heavens and earths are placed on the other, these words will outweigh the rest. In fact, if all of them form a ring to try to stop it, the Kalima will break right through them to reach Allah. I also advise you to repeat the words سبحان الله العظيم و بحمده 'SubhanAllahil Azeem wa Bihamdihi' because it is the words of worship used by all of creation and it is by virtue of these words that sustenance is distributed. The 2 things that I forbid you from is Shirk and pride because they both prevent one from reaching Allah.'" One of the Sahabah asked, "O Rasulullah ﷺ! Is it a sign pride that a person prepares food and invites a group of people for a meal or that he wears clean and neat clothing?" Rasulullah replied, 'That is not pride. Pride is when a person regards others as being foolish and looks down on them." *(Bazzar, Haythami, Hakim in Targheeb wat Tarheeb).* Rasulullah ﷺ said, "If the heavens and the earth and everything they contain were made into a ring and لا اله الا الله 'La Ilaha IllAllah' placed on top of it, it would shatter them all beneath its weight." *(Hakim in Targheeb wat Tarheeb)*

Rasulullah ﷺ gives the Glad Tidings of Jannah for the Sahabah who Recited the Kalima with him in a Gathering

Ya'la bin Shaddad reports, "Ubadah bin Samit ؓ was also present to confirm the report of my father Shaddad bin Aws ؓ when he said, 'We were with Rasulullah ﷺ when he asked whether there were any people of the Ahlul Kitab amongst us. When we informed him that there were none, Rasulullah ﷺ instructed that the door be shut. He said, 'Raise your hands and say لا اله الا الله 'La Ilaha IllAllah'. After we had raised our hands for a while (reciting the Kalima), Rasulullah ﷺ said, 'Al Hamdu Lillah! O Allah! You have sent me with this Kalima, instructed me to believe in it and promised me Jannah in return. Verily, You never go back on Your word.' Addressing us Rasulullah ﷺ then said, 'Glad tidings for you! Allah has forgiven you all." *(Tabrani in Targheeb wat Tarheeb, Haythami)*

Rasulullah ﷺ says that لا اله الا الله 'La Ilaha IllAllah' is the Best of all Good Deeds

Abu Dhar ؓ narrates that he requested Rasulullah ﷺ for advice, Rasulullah ﷺ said, 'When you commit a sin, follow it up with a good deed to erase it" "O Rasulullah ﷺ!" Abu Dhar ؓ asked, "Is the recitation of لا اله الا الله 'La Ilaha IllAllah' one of the good deeds?" Rasulullah ﷺ replied, "It is in fact the best of all good deeds." *(Ahmad, Haythami)*

Omar ؓ and Ali ؓ say 'La Ilaha IllAllah' is "The Word of Taqwa"

When Omar bin Khattab ؓ once saw some people reciting لا

'La Ilaha IllAllah' and الله اكبر 'Allahu Akbar', he exclaimed, "That's it! I swear by the Rabb of the Kabah! That's it!" "What is it?" someone asked. Omar ؓ replied, "That is the 'word of Taqwa' that they (the Sahabah) were most deserving and worthy of (ref Fatah:26)" *(Ibn Khusru in Kanzul Ummal).* Ali ؓ also stated that it was the Kalima لا اله الا الله 'La Ilaha IllAllah' that Allah refers to in the verse: وَأَلْزَمَهُمْ كَلِمَةَ التَّقْوَى ... *and made them stick to the word of piety (i.e. none has the right to be worshipped but Allah)...* (Al-Fath:26) *(Abdur Razzaq, Ibn Jareer, Ibn Mundhir, Ibn Abi Hatim, Hakim, Bayhaqi in Asma, Kanzul Ummal)*

Another narration adds that the words 'Allahu Akbar' are also part of the 'word of Taqwa'. *(Ibn Jareer in Kanzul Ummal)*

Dhikr of سبحان الله 'SubhanAllah', الحمد لِلَّه 'Al Hamdulillah', لا اله الا الله 'La Ilaha IllAllah, الله اكبر 'Allahu Akbar' and لاحولول ولا قوة الا بالله 'La Howla wa La Quwwata Illa Billah' Rasulullah Mentions that These Adhkar are the 'Everlasting Good Deeds'

Abu Sa'eed Khudri ؓ narrates that Rasulullah ﷺ once said to them, "Carry out the everlasting good deeds in abundance." When someone asked Rasulullah ﷺ what the everlasting good deeds are, Rasulullah ﷺ replied, "Recitation of الله اكبر 'Allahu Akbar', لا اله الا الله 'La Ilaha IllAllah', سبحان الله 'SubhanAllah', 'Al Hamdulillah' and لاحولول ولا قوة الا بالله 'La Howla wa La Quwwata Illa Billah'." *(Ahmad, Abu Ya'la, Nasa'ee, Ibn Hibban, Hakim in Targheeb wat Tarheeb, Haythami)*

Rasulullah ﷺ Mentions that These Adhkar serve as Protection from Jahannam

Abu Hurairah ؓ reports that Rasulullah ﷺ said, "Take up your shields." "O Rasulullah ﷺ!" the Sahabah asked, "Has the enemy come?" "No," Rasulullah ﷺ replied, "I am referring to your shields against Jahannam. You should recite سبحان الله 'SubhanAllah', الحمد لِلَّه 'Al Hamdulillah' and الله اكبر 'Allahu Akbar' because they shall be ahead of you and behind on the Day of Judgment to protect you and they are the 'everlasting good deeds'". *(Nasa'ee, Hakim, Bayhaqi).* Another narration states that Rasulullah ﷺ mentioned, 'They are the saviors." *(Hakim)* Yet another narration adds the words لاحولول ولا قوة الا بالله 'La Howla wa La Quwwata Illa Billah'." *(Tabrani in Awsat, Targheeb wat Tarheeb).* Anas ؓ states that Rasulullah ﷺ said, "Verily they shall be ahead of you, they are the saviors, they shall be behind and they are the 'everlasting good deeds'." *(Tabrani, Haythani)*

Rasulullah ﷺ Mentions that the Rewards for These Adhkar are as Huge as Mount Uhud

Imran bin Husain ؓ narrates that Rasulullah ﷺ said, 'Does any of you have the ability to do actions as huge as mount Uhud every day?" "O Rasulullah ﷺ!" the Sahabah said, "Who has the ability to do actions as huge as mount Uhud every day?" "All of you do," Rasulullah ﷺ replied. When the Sahabah asked how this was possible, Rasulullah ﷺ explained, سبحان الله 'SubhanAllah' is larger than mount Uhud الحمد لِلَّه 'Al Hamdulillah' is larger than mount Uhud, لا اله الا الله 'La Ilaha IllAllah' is larger than mount Uhud and الله اكب 'Allahu Akbar' is larger than mount Uhud." *(Ibn Abi Dunya, Nasa'ee, Tabrani, Bazzar, Haythami, Mundhiri)*

Rasulullah ﷺ Speaks About the Plants of Jannah and his Instruction to Eat to one's Fill in the Gardens of Jannah

Abu Hurairah ؓ narrates that he was busy planting something when Rasulullah ﷺ passed by. "O Abu Hurairah!"

Rasulullah ﷺ called out, "What are you planting?" When Abu Hurairah ؓ informed him that he was planting some plants, Rasulullah ﷺ said, "Should I not inform you of plants that are better than these? They are سبحان الله 'SubhanAllah' لِلّهِ الحمد 'Al Hamdulillah', لا اله الا الله 'La Ilaha IllAllah' and الله اكبر 'Allahu Akbar'. A tree in Jannah is planted for you in exchange for every one of these phrases." (Ibn Majah, Hakim in Targheeb wat Tarheeb). Abu Hurairah ؓ narrates that Rasulullah ﷺ said, "When you pass through the gardens of Jannah, eat to your fill there." "O Rasulullah ﷺ!" the Sahabah asked, "What are the gardens of Jannah?" "The Masajid," Rasulullah ﷺ replied. "How does one eat to one's fill?" the Sahabah asked. Rasulullah ﷺ replied, "By reciting 'Subhanallah', 'Al Humdulillah', 'La Ilaha Illallah' and 'Allahu Akbar'."(Tirmidhi in Targheeb wat Tarheeb)

Rasulullah ﷺ Speaks About Words of Dhikr that Shakes Off Sins

Anas ؓ narrates that Rasulullah ﷺ caught hold of a branch and shook it, but the leaves did not fall off. When he shook it again, the leaves still did not fall, but when he did so for the third time, the leaves fell off. Rasulullah ﷺ said, "Verily الله 'SubhanAllah', لِلّهِ الحمد 'Al Hamdulillah', لا اله الا الله 'La Ilaha IllAllah' and الله اكبر 'Allahu Akbar' shake off sins just as the leaves of a tree fall."(Ahmad in Targheeb wat Tarheeb, Tirmidhi)

Rasulullah ﷺ Teaches Dhikr to a Bedouin

Sa'd bin Abi Waqqas ؓ narrates that a Bedouin once came to Rasulullah ﷺ with the request, "Do teach me something that I may recite." Rasulullah ﷺ told him to recite:

لَا إِلَهَ إِلَّا اللهُ وَحْدَهُ لَاشَرِيْكَ لَهُ اللهُ أَكْبَرْ كَبِيْرًا وَالْحَمْدُ لِلّهِ كَثِيْرًا وَسُبْحَانَ اللهِ رَبِّ الْعَالَمِيْنَ لَا حَوْلَ وَلَا قُوَّةَ إِلَّا بِاللهِ الْعَزِيْزِ الْحَكِيْمِ

The man said, "That was for my Rabb. Now what about myself?" Rasulullah ﷺ then told him to recite: اللَّهُمَّ اغْفِرْ لِيْ وَارْحَمْنِيْ وَاهْدِنِيْ وَارْزُقْنِيْ 'O Allah! Forgive me, shower Your mercy on me, guide me and provide for me.'

Another narration adds the words وعافني 'and grant me safety'. Another narration states that Rasulullah ﷺ also said, "These words combine both your life in this world as well as your life in the Hereafter. (Muslim). Another narration states that the Bedouin asked, 'O Rasulullah ﷺ! I have done my best to memorize the Qur'an but am unable to do so. Please tell me of something that will earn me the same rewards of learning the Qur'an." Rasulullah ﷺ then told him to recite:

سُبْحَانَ اللهِ وَالْحَمْدُ لِلّهِ وَلَا إِلَهَ إِلَّا اللهُ وَاللهُ أَكْبَرْ

The Bedouin said the words, counting them with his fingers. He then said, "O Rasulullah! This is for my Rabb, but what about me?" Rasulullah then told him to recite:

اللَّهُمَّ اغْفِرْ لِيْ وَارْحَمْنِيْ وَعَافِنِيْ وَارْزُقْنِيْ وَاهْدِنِيْ

'O Allah! Forgive me, shower Your mercy on me, grant me safety, provide for me and guide me'

When the Bedouin had left, Rasulullah ﷺ remarked, "The Bedouin has left with his hands full of good." (Ibn Abi Dunya). Rasulullah ﷺ also added the words لاحول ولا قوة الا با الله (Bayhaqi in Targheeb wat Tarheeb, Abu Dawud)

Rasulullah ﷺ Informs Abu Dhar ؓ put the Words that are most Beloved to Allah

Abu Dhar ؓ narrates that Rasulullah ﷺ once said him, "Should I not inform you of those words that Allah loves most?" "O Rasulullah ﷺ!" Abu Dhar ؓ submitted, "Please do inform me of the words that Allah loves most." Rasulullah ﷺ said, "The words that Allah loves most are: سبحان الله وبحمده 'SubhanAllahi wa Bihamdihi." (Muslim, Nasa'ee) Another narration states that the words arc سبحان ربي وبحمده 'Subhana Rabbi wa Bihamdihi'. (Tirmidhi). Yet another narration states that when Rasulullah ﷺ was asked about which words Allah loves most, he replied, 'The words that Allah chose for His angels or for His bondsmen; سبحان الله و بحده 'SubhanAllahi wa Bihamdihi'." (Muslim)

Rasulullah ﷺ Speaks about the Tremendous Reward of Reciting the Kalima

Abu Talha ؓ reports that Rasulullah ﷺ said, "Whoever says لا اله الا الله 'La Ilaha IllAllah' shall enter Jannah or Rasulullah ﷺ said Jannah shall become binding on him. As for the one who recites سبحان الله وبحمده 'SubhanAllahi wa Bihamdihi' 100 times, Allah shall record for him 124,000 good deeds." "O Rasulullah ﷺ" the Sahabah said, "Then none of us will ever be destroyed," "Why not," Rasulullah ﷺ said, "when one of you will appear on the Day of Judgment with so many good deeds that would crush a mountain beneath its weight, but the bounties he enjoyed will come and claim all of it as repayment. It will only be for Allah to extend His mercy by which the person will be able to enter Jannah." (Hakim in Targheeb wat Tarheeb). Sa'd ؓ narrates that Rasulullah ﷺ asked, "Is any of you unable to earn the reward of 1,000 good deeds every day?" One of the Sahabah asked, "How can any of us earn the reward of 1,000 good deeds?" Rasulullah ﷺ replied, 'When he recites سبحان الله 'SubhanAllah' 100 times, the reward of 1,000 good deeds is recorded to his credit or 1,000 sins are written off." (Muslim, Tirmidhi, Nasa'ee in Targheeb wat Tarheeb, Ibn Abi Shaybah, Ahmad, Abd bin Humaid, Ibn Hibban, Abu Nu'aym, Kanzul Ummal).

Rasulullah ﷺ Speaks About the Tremendous Virtue of Reciting لَاحَوْلَ وَلَا قُوَّةَ إِلَّا بِاللهِ 'La Howla wa La Quwwata Illa Billah'

Qais bin Sa'd bin Ubadah ؓ relates, "My father placed me in the care of Rasulullah ﷺ to be of service to him. One day after I had performed 2 Rakats salah, Rasulullah ﷺ once came to me and, nudging me with his foot, said, 'Should I not inform you of a door from amongst the doors of Jannah?' When I asked to be informed, Rasulullah said, 'It is to recite لَاحَوْلَ وَلَا قُوَّةَ إِلَّا بِاللهِ 'La Howla wa La Quwwata Illa Billah'." (Hakim in Targheeb wat Tarheeb). Abu Dhar ؓ narrates, "I had been walking behind Rasulullah ﷺ when he said to me, 'Should I not inform you treasure from amongst the treasures of Jannah?' When I asked to be informed, Rasulullah ﷺ said, 'It is to recite لَاحَوْلَ وَلَا قُوَّةَ إِلَّا بِاللهِ 'La Howla wa La Quwwata Illa Billah'." (Ibn Majah, Ibn Abi Dunya, Ibn Hibban in Targheeb wat Tarheeb). Abdullah bin Sa'd bin Abi Waqqas ؓ narrates that Abu Ayub Ansari ؓ once said to him, "Should I not teach you some words that Rasulullah ﷺ taught me?" "Certainly, dear uncle," Abdullah replied. Abu Ayub ؓ then said, "When Rasulullah ﷺ came to stay with me, he once asked me, 'O Abu Ayub! Should I not inform you of some words from the treasures of Jannah?' 'Why, of course,' I replied, 'May my parents be sacrificed for you!' Rasulullah ﷺ said, 'Abundantly recite لَاحَوْلَ وَلَا قُوَّةَ إِلَّا بِاللهِ 'La Howla wa La Quwwata Illa Billah'."' (Tabrani, Haythami)

The Statement of Ibrahim عليه السلام Regarding لَاحَوْلَ وَلَا قُوَّةَ إِلَّا بِاللهِ 'La Uowla wa La Quwwata Illa Billah'

Abu Ayub Ansari ؓ reports that when Rasulullah ﷺ was taken on the journey of Mi'raj, he passed by Ibrahim عليه السلام, who asked, "Who is this with you, O Jibra'el عليه السلام?" "This is Muhammad ﷺ," Jibra'el عليه السلام replied. Ibrahim عليه السلام then said, "O Muhammad ﷺ! Inform your Ummah to acquire the plants of

Jannah in abundance because the soil of Jannah is extremely fertile; and its land is very vast." 'What are the plants of Jannah?" Rasulullah ﷺ asked. Ibrahim replied, لَاحَوْلَ وَلَا قُوَّةَ إِلَّا بِاللهِ "'La Howla wa La Quwwata Illa Billah,.." (Ahmad, Ibn Abi Dunya, Ibn Hibban in Targheeb wat Tarheeb, Haythami) Another adds that before addressing Rasulullah ﷺ, Ibrahim عليه السلام first greeted Rasulullah ﷺ and welcomed him. (Tabrani). The statement of Abdullah bin Abbas ؓ about لَاحَوْلَ وَلَا قُوَّةَ إِلَّا بِاللهِ 'La Howla wa La Quwwata Illa Billah' what Imran ؓ had to say about the virtues of praising Allah. Abdullah bin Abbas ؓ said, "Whoever says بسم الله 'Bismillah' has thought of Allah, whoever says لله الحمد 'Al Hamdulillah' has thanked of Allah, whoever says الله اكبر 'Allahu Akbar' has revered Allah, whoever says لا اله الا الله 'La Ilaha IllAllah' has expressed the oneness of Allah and whoever says لَاحَوْلَ وَلَا قُوَّةَ إِلَّا بِاللهِ 'La Howla wa La Quwwata Illa Billah' has submitted himself to Allah and these words will be an adornment and a treasure for him in Jannah." (Abu Nu'yam in Hilya). Mutarraf reports that Imran ؓ once said to him, "Should I not inform you of a Hadith today which ah will make a source of benefit for you even after this day? You should note that the best of Allah's bondsmen on the Day of Judgment shall be those who praised Him most excessively." (Ahmad, Haythami)

Ali ؓ's Explanation of the terms الحَمْدُ لِلّهِ 'Al Hamdulillah' and سُبْحَانَ اللهِ 'SubhanAllah'

Abdullah bin Abbas ؓ narrates that Omar ؓ asked, "While we know what is meant by سُبْحَانَ اللهِ 'SubhanAllah' and لَا إِلَهَ إِلَّا اللهُ 'La Ilaha Illallah', what is الحَمْدُ لِلّهِ 'Al Hamdulillah'?" Ali ؓ replied by saying, "It is a phrase that Allah chose for Himself and which He loves that it be said." (Ibn Abi Hatim). Abu Dhabian narrates that Ibn Kawwa once asked Ali ؓ about the phrase 'SubhanAllah', to which Ali ؓ replied, "It is a phrase that Allah has chosen for Himself and which proclaims His purity from all evil." (Askari in Amthal, Abul Hasan Bakali, Kanzul Ummal)

Omar ؓ Lessens the Punishment for a Person who Engaged in Tasbih as he was Being Lashed

When Omar ؓ once had 2 men lashed, one of them said, بسم الله 'Bismillah' while the other said, سُبْحَانَ اللهِ 'SubhanAllah'. Omar ؓ exclaimed, "Shame on you! Ease the lashing of the one who said, 'SubhanAllah' because Tasbih can find a grounding only in the heart of a Mu'min." (Bayhaqi in Kanzul Ummal)

Abdullah bin Mas'ood ؓ Interprets the Verse 'The Pure Word climbs up to Him"

Abdullah bin Mas'ood ؓ once said, "Whenever I relate a Hadith to you, I substantiate it with a verse of the Qur'an. When a person recites, سُبْحَانَ اللهِ 'SubhanAllah', الحَمْدُ لِلّهِ 'Al Hamdulillah', لا اله الا الله 'La llaha IllAllah', 'Allahu Akbar' and 'TabarakAllah', an angel takes hold of the words, thrusts it beneath his wings and then starts ascending (to the heavens). Every group of angels he passes en route seek forgiveness for the person who recited these words. He eventually presents them before the countenance of Ar-Rahman," In substantiation Abdullah bin Mas'ood ؓ then recited the verse: إِلَيْهِ يَصْعَدُ الْكَلِمُ الطَّيِّبُ وَالْعَمَلُ الصَّالِحُ يَرْفَعُهُ

...To Him ascend (all) the goodly words, and the righteous deeds exalt it (the goodly words i.e. the goodly words are not accepted by Allah unless and until they are followed by good deeds)... (Fatir:10) (Tabrani, Haythami, Hakim in Targheeb wat Tarheeb)

Rasulullah ﷺ Teaches Juwayriya a Comprehensive Dhikr

Juwayriya ؓ narrates that Rasulullah ﷺ once left her room and when he returned after midmorning, he found her still sitting where she was. Rasulullah ﷺ asked, "Did you remain sitting in this position from the time I left you?" When she informed him that she had, Rasulullah ﷺ said, "After leaving you, I recited 4 phrases 3 times, which, if weighed against what you had been reciting since the morning, it would outweigh it. The words are: سُبْحَانَ اللهِ وَبِحَمْدِهِ عَدَدَ خَلْقِهِ وَرِضَا نَفْسِهِ وَزِنَةَ عَرْشِهِ وَمِدَادَ كَلِمَاتِهِ

"I express Allah's purity and praise Him as much as all of His creation, as much as pleases Him, as much as is the weight of His throne and as much as are all of His words (attributes and bounties)." (Muslim, Abu Dawud, Tirmidhi, Nasa'ee, Ibn Majah) Another narration quotes the words as: سُبْحَانَ اللهِ عَدَدَ خَلْقِهِ سَبْحَانَ اللهِ رِضَاءَ نَفْسِهِ۔ سُبْحَانَ اللهِ زِنَةَ عَرْشِهِ، سُبْحَانَ اللهِ مِدَادَ كَلِمَاتِهِ "I express Allah's purity as much as are His creation. I express Allah's purity as much as pleases Him. I express Allah's purity as much as is the weight of His throne and I express Allah's purity as much as are all of His words (attributes and bounties)." (Muslim). Yet another narration states that the words 'Al Hamdulillah' الحَمْدُ لِلّهِ should be recited in the same manner (substitute the words سُبْحَانَ اللهِ 'SubhanAllah' with the words الحَمْدُ لِلّهِ 'Al Hamdulillah' in the above Du'a). A narration of Nasa'ee (Targheeb wat Tarheeb) quotes the words of the Du'a as: سُبْحَانَ اللهِ وَبِحَمْدِهِ وَلَا إِلَهَ إِلَّا اللهُ وَاللهُ أَكْبَرُ، عَدَدَ خَلْقِهِ وَرِضَا نَفْسِهِ، وَزِنَةَ عَرْشِهِ وَمِدَادَ كَلِمَاتِهِ

Rasulullah ﷺ Teaches a Comprehensive Dhikr to a Sahabiya

Sa'd bin Abi Waqqas ؓ reports that when he once accompanied Rasulullah ﷺ to see a particular lady, they found her reciting Tasbih, using some date seeds or pebbles to count on. Rasulullah ﷺ said, "Should I not inform you of something easier and better for you?" Rasulullah ﷺ then recited the Du'a: سُبْحَانَ اللهِ عَدَدَ مَاخَلَقَ فِي السَّمَاءِ سُبْحَانَ اللهِ عَدَدَ مَاخَلَقَ فِي الْأَرْضِ سُبْحَانَ اللهِ عَدَدَ مَا بَيْنَ ذَلِكَ

Rasulullah ﷺ then told her to recite the same for اَللهُ أَكْبَر 'Allahu Akbar', الحَمْدُ لِلّهِ 'Al Hamdulillah', لَا إِلَهَ إِلَّا اللهُ 'La Ilaha IllAllah' and لَاحَوْلَ وَلَا قُوَّةَ إِلَّا بِاللهِ 'La Howla wa La Quwwata Illa Billah' (i.e. these words should substitute the words سُبْحَانَ اللهِ 'SubhanaAllah' in the above Du'a). (Abu Dawud, Tirmidhi, Nasa'ee, Ibn Hibban, Hakim in Targheeb wat Tarheeb)

Rasulullah ﷺ Teaches a Comprehensive Dhikr to Abu Umamah ؓ

Abu Umamah ؓ narrates that when Rasulullah ﷺ saw him moving his lips one day, Rasulullah ﷺ asked, "O Abu Umama! What are you reciting causing your lips to move like that?" "I am engaged in the Dhikr of Allah," he replied. Rasulullah ﷺ said, "Should I not inform you of a Dhikr that is better than your making Dhikr day and night?" When Abu Umamah ؓ asked to be informed, Rasulullah ﷺ told him to recite: سُبْحَانَ اللهِ عَدَدَ مَاخَلَقَ، سُبْحَانَ اللهِ مِلَا مَا خَلَقَ سُبْحَانَ اللهِ عَدَدَ مَا فِى الأرْض سُبْحَانَ اللهِ مَلَا مَا فِى الأرض وَالسَّمَاءِ، سُبْحَانَ اللهِ عَدَدَ مَاأحْصَى كِتَابَه سُبْحَانَ اللهِ مَلَا مَا أحْصَى كِتَابَه سُبْحَانَ اللهِ عَدَدَ كُلِّ شَىءٍ سُبْحَانَ اللهِ مَلَا كُلَّ شَىءٍ الحَمْدُ للهِ عَدَدَ مَا خَلَقَ وَالحَمْدُ للهِ مِلَا مَاخَلَقَ وَالحَمْدُ للهِ عَدَدَ مَا أحْصَى كِتَابَه وَالحَمْدُ للهِ مَلَا مَاأحْصَى كِتَابَه، وَالحَمْدُ للهِ عَدَدَ كُلّ شَىءٍ، وَالحَمْدُ للهِ مَلَا كُلّ شَىءٍ

"I express the purity of Allah as much as He has created. I express the purity of Allah as much as it takes to fill everything He has created. I express the purity of Allah as much as everything on earth. I express the purity of Allah much as everything on earth and in the heavens. I express the purity of Allah as much as everything that His Book units. I express the purity of Allah as much as it takes to 1 everything that His Book counts. I express the purity of ah as much as everything there is. I express the purity of Allah as much as it takes to fill everything there is. I praise Allah as much as He has created. I praise Allah as much as it takes to fill everything He has created. I praise Allah as much as everything on earth and in the heavens. I praise Allah as much as it takes to fill everything on earth and in the heavens. I praise Allah as much as everything that His Book counts. I praise Allah as much as it takes to fill everything that His Book counts. I praise Allah as much as everything there is. I praise Allah as much as it takes to fill everything there is." (Ahmad, Ibn Abi Dunya, Nasa'ee, Ibn Khuzaima, Ibn Hibban, Hakim). Rasulullah ﷺ also said to Abu Umamah ؓ, "Should I not inform you of something that if you say it, you will be unable to earn the same rewards even if you have to tire yourself day and night (in Ibada)." The same narration goes on to report the same Dhikr with the addition that he recites the same for اللهُ أَكْبَرُ 'Allahu Akbar' (i.e. the phrase اللهُ أَكْبَرُ 'Allahu Akbar' should substitute the phrase سُبْحَانَ الله 'Subhanallah' in the above Du'a). (Tabrani in Targheeb wat Tarheeb). Rasulullah ﷺ said, "Should I not inform you of something that is better than engaging in Dhikr day and night?" The rest of the Hadith is then mentioned in brief. Rasulullah ﷺ then advised Abu Umamah ؓ to learn these words and to teach it to everyone else. (Tabrani, Haythami)

Rasulullah ﷺ Teaches Abu Darda ؓ a Comprehensive Dhikr

Abu Darda ؓ narrates that when Rasulullah ﷺ saw him moving his lips one day, Rasulullah ﷺ asked, "O Abu Darda! What are you reciting?" "I am engaged in the Dhikr of Allah," he replied. Rasulullah ﷺ said, "Should I inform you of a Dhikr that is better than your making from night to day and from day to night?" When Abu Darda asked to be informed, Rasulullah ﷺ told him to recite:

سُبْحَانَ اللهِ عَدَدَ مَا خَلَقَ، سُبْحَانَ اللهِ عَدَدَ كُلِّ شَيْءٍ سُبْحَانَ اللهِ مِلْءُ مَا أَحْصَى كِتَابُهُ وَالْحَمْدُ للهِ عَدَدَ مَا خَلَقَ وَالْحَمْدُ للهِ مَلْءَ مَا خَلَقَ وَالْحَمْدُ للهِ مَلْءَ مَا أَحْصَى كِتَابُهُ

"I express the purity of Allah as much as He has created. I express the purity of Allah as much as everything on earth. I express the purity of Allah as much as everything there is. I express the purity of Allah as much as everything that His Book counts. I praise Allah as much as He has created. I praise Allah as much as it takes to fill everything He has created. I praise Allah as much as it takes to fill everything that His Book counts." (Tabrani, Bazzar, Haythami)

Rasulullah ﷺ Praises the Words that a Sahabi said in a Gathering

Anas ؓ reports that he was sitting with Rasulullah ﷺ in a gathering when a Sahabi arrived and greeted Rasul ﷺ saying, اَلسَّلَامُ عَلَيْكُمْ وَرَحْمَةُ اللهِ وَبَرَكَاتُهُ 'As Salamu Alaikum wa Rahmatullahi wa Barakatuh'. Rasulullah ﷺ replied to his greeting by saying, وَعَلَيْكُمُ السَّلَامُ وَرَحْمَةُ اللهِ وَبَرَكَاتُهُ 'Was Alaykumus Salam wa Rahmatullahi wa Barakatuh'. When the Sahabi then sat down, he said: الْحَمْدُ للهِ حَمْدًا كَثِيرًا طَيِّبًا مُبَارَكًا فِيهِ كَمَا يُحِبُّ رَبُّنَا أَنْ يُحْمَدَ وَيَنْبَغِي لَهُ "I praise Allah tremendously with praises that are pure and blessed as our Rabb would like to be praised and as He deserves to be praised." "What did you say?" Rasulullah ﷺ asked. When the Sahabah repeated his words, Rasulullah ﷺ remarked, "I swear by the Being Who controls my life that 10 angels raced, each one of the angels eager to record what you said. However, none of them knew how to record it, so when they took it up to the One to Whom all honor belongs, He said,

'Record it exactly as my servant said it.'" (Ahmad in Targheeb wat Tarheeb). Another narration (Nasa'ee, Ibn Hibban) records the words of the Dhikr as: الْحَمْدُ الْحَمْدُ للهِ حَمْدًا كَثِيرًا طَيِّبًا مُبَارَكًا فِيهِ كَمَا يَكَمَا يَحِبُّ رَبَّنَا وَيَرْضَى

Abu Ayub Ansari ؓ narrates that Rasulullah ﷺ once heard someone recite: الْحَمْدُ للهِ حَمْدًا كَثِيرًا طَيِّبًا مُبَارَكًا فِيهِ "Who said those words?" Rasulullah ﷺ enquired. Thinking that he had annoyed Rasulullah ﷺ's ears with something he did not like, the man remained silent "Who was it?" Rasulullah ﷺ repeated, "Because what he said was very correct" The man then said, "It was I who said it with the expectation of being rewarded, O Rasulullah ﷺ." Rasulullah ﷺ then told him, "I swear by the Being Who controls my life! I saw 13 angels racing to see which of them would be the first to present your words to Allah." (Tabrani in Targheeb wat Tarheeb)

Omar ؓ's Words when he saw a Man using a Rosary to Engage in Tasbih

Sa'eed bin Jubair reports that when Omar ؓ once saw a man reciting Tasbih on a rosary, he remarked, "It would suffice him to say: سُبْحَانَ اللهِ مِلْأَ السَّمَاوَاتِ (وَمِلْأَ الْأَرْضِ) وَمَلْأَ مَاشَاءَ مِنْ شَيْءٍ بَعْدُ 'I express Allah's purity as much as it takes to fill the heavens and as much as it takes to fill the earth and everything else that Allah wills'
He should say: الْحَمْدُ للهِ مِلْأَ السَّمَاوَاتِ وَ(مِلْأَ) الْأَرْضِ وَمِلْأَ مَاشَاءَ مِنْ شَيْءٍ بَعْدُ 'I praise Allah as much as it takes to fill the heavens and as much as it takes to fill the earth and everything else that Allah wills'
In addition to this, he may also say: اللهُ أَكْبَر مِلْأَ السَّمَاوَاتِ وَالْأَرْضِ وَمِلْأَ مَاشَاءَ مِنْ شَيْءٍ بَعْدُ 'I express Allah's greatness as much as it takes to fill the heavens and as much as it takes to fill the earth and everything else that Allah wills'' (Ibn Abi Shaybah in Kanzul Ummal)

Rasulullah ﷺ Teaches the poor Sahabah Specific Adhkar by Which to Earn Great Rewards

Abu Hurairah ؓ narrates that the poor Muhajirin once approached Rasulullah ﷺ saying, "The wealthy ones have taken the elevated positions and everlasting bounties!" "Why do you say that?" Rasulullah ﷺ asked. They explained, "They perform salah just as we perform salah and they fast just as we fast, but they also donate in Sadaqah, which we cannot do, and they set slaves free, which we are also incapable of doing." Rasulullah ﷺ said, "Should I then not teach you something by which you may catch up with those ahead of you and beat those who are still behind? None will then be better than you except those who do the same as you do." "Please do tell us," the Sahabah entreated. Rasulullah ﷺ then told them to recite سُبْحَانَ اللهِ 'SubhanAllah' 33 times, اللهُ أَكْبَرُ 'Allahu Akbar' 33 times and الْحَمْدُ للهِ 'Al Hamdulillah' 33 after every salah. The poor Muhajirin then returned to Rasulullah ﷺ (after a while) saying, "Our wealthy brothers have heard about what we are doing and they are now doing the same." To this, Rasulullah ﷺ remarked, "That is the grace of Allah which He bestows on whomsoever He wills." (One of the narrators by the name of) Sumay says, "When I reported the Hadith to someone in my family, the person told me that I was mistaken because my teacher must have told me that while سُبْحَانَ اللهِ 'SubhanAllah' and الْحَمْدُ للهِ 'Al Hamdulillah' are to be recited 33 times each, اللهُ أَكْبَرُ 'Allahu Akbar' is to be recited 34 times. I then returned to my teacher Abu Salih and informed him about this. He took my hand and recited, سُبْحَانَ الله 'SubhanAllah',

'Al Hamdulillah' and أَكْبَرُ اللهُ 'Allahu Akbar'. Thereafter, he again recited, اللهُ سُبْحَانَ 'SubhanAllah', لِلهِ الْحَمْدُ 'Al Hamdulillah' and اللهُ أَكْبَرُ 'Allahu Akbar' until he had done so 33 times to indicate that each Dhikr be recited 33 times only." (Bukhari, Muslim). Abu Hurairah reports that Abu Dhar once said, "O Rasulullah! The wealthy ones have taken he rewards." The narration then continues like the one above except that in this narration, Rasulullah instructed to recite أَكْبَرُ اللهُ 'Allahu Akbar' 33 times, اللهِ الْحَمْدُ 'Al Hamdulillah' 33 times, اللهِ سُبْحَانَ 'SubhanAllah' 33 times after every salah. Thereafter, Rasulullah told him that he should end off the Dhikr by once reciting:

لَاإِلَهَ إِلَّا اللهُ وَحْدَهُ لَاشَرِيْكَ لَهُ لَهُ الْمُلْكُ وَلَهُ الْحَمْدُ وَهُوَ عَلَى كُلِّ شَيْءٍ قَدِيْرٌ

Rasulullah informed Abu Dhar that if he recited this, all his sins will be forgiven even if though they may be as many as the foam on the ocean. (Abu Dawud). Rasulullah also said, "Once you have performed your salah, them to recite اللهِ سُبْحَانَ 'SubhanAllah' 33 times, لِلهِ الْحَمْدُ 'Al Hamdulillah' 33 times and اللهُ 'Allahu Akbar' 34 times. Thereafter, recite اللهُ إِلَّا إِلَهَ لَا 'La Ilaha IllAllah' 10 times." (Tirmidhi in Targheeb wat Tarheeb, Ibn Asakir, Abu Dawud in Kanzul Ummal, Tayalisi, Bukhari in Adab, Bazzar in Majma'uz Zawa'id)

Rasulullah Teaches Abu Darda Some Adhkar to be Recited After Every Salah

Ummu Darda narrates that a man came to Abu Darda, he asked the man, "Will you be staying over so that we may send your animal for grazing or will you be leaving, in which case we shall give it some fodder to eat?" The man informed him that he would be leaving, Abu Darda said, "I shall then give you some provisions that had I any provisions better than them, I would have certainly given them instead. I once went to Rasulullah and said, 'The wealthy ones have taken the benefits of this world as well as the Hereafter. They perform salah just as we perform salah and they fast just as we fast, but they also donate in Sadaqah, which we cannot do.' Rasulullah said, 'Should I then not teach you something by which anyone ahead of you will be unable to beat you again and those who are still behind you will be unable to catch up with you unless they do the same as you do?' Rasulullah then told me to recite اللهُ سُبْحَانَ 'Subhanallah' 33 times, لِلهِ الْحَمْدُ 'Al Hamdulillah' 33 times and أَكْبَرُ اللهُ 'Allahu Akbar' 34 times after every salah." (Ahmad, Bazzar, Tabrani in Majma'uz Zawa'id, Abdur Razzaq). Qatadah reports that some poor Mu'minin said, "O Rasulullah! The wealthy ones have taken all the rewards. They are able to donate in Sadaqah, while we cannot and they are able to spend in good causes, which we are also incapable of doing." Rasulullah asked, "Tell me if the wealth of this world will be able to reach the heavens if they are stacked one on top of another?" "Certainly not, O Rasulullah," they replied. Rasulullah then said, 'Should I not inform you of something that has its roots on earth but its branches in the heavens? It is that you recite 10 times after every salah, إِلَّا إِلَهَ لَا اللهُ 'La Ilaha IllAllah', أَكْبَرُ اللهُ 'Allahu Akbar', اللهُ سُبْحَانَ 'SubhanAllah' and الْحَمْدُ لِلهِ 'Al Hamdulillah'.'" (Abdur Razzaq, Ibn Zanjway in Kanzul Ummal)

Rasulullah Teaches Ali and Fatima a Dhikr to Recite After Salah and Before Sleeping

Ali reports that when he married Fatima, Rasulullah sent with her a blanket, a leather pillow filled with the balk of a date palm, two grinding stones, a water bag and two earthen jars. Ali one day said to Fatima, "By Allah! Continuously drawing water from the well has caused my chest to start hurting.

Allah has sent some prisoners to your father, so please go to him and request him for a servant." Fatima agreed saying, "By Allah! Continuous grinding has also caused my hands to be calloused." She therefore went to her father Rasulullah, who asked her, "What brings you here, dearest daughter?" Feeling too embarrassed to put her quest forward, Fatima said, "I have come to greet you." When she returned and Ali asked her what had happened, she said, "I was too shy to ask him." The couple then went together to Rasulullah. Ali spoke. "O Rasulullah!" he said, "Continuously drawing water from the well has caused my chest to start hurting." Fatima then said, "By Allah! Continuous grinding has also caused my hands to be calloused. Since Allah has sent some prisoners and wealth to you, could you please give us a servant." Rasulullah said, "By Allah! I cannot give you something and leave the men of Suffa with their bellies caving in with hunger. Since I have nothing to spend on them, I intend selling the slaves and spending the money on the men of Suffa." The couple returned home. Rasulullah later went to see then at a time when they had already retired to bed. Their blanket was so small that when they covered their heads, their feet would be exposed and when they covered their feet, their heads remained uncovered. They were about to jump out of bed when Rasulullah arrived, but he bade them to remain as they were. Rasulullah asked, "Shall I not inform you of something better than what you asked of me today?" When they begged to know, Rasulullah said, "It is some words that Jibra'el has taught me. After every salah, you should recite اللهِ سُبْحَانَ 'Subhanallah' 10 times, لِلهِ الْحَمْدُ 'Al Hamdulillah' 10 times and اللهِ أَكْبَرُ 'Allahu Akbar' 10 times. Then, when you go to bed, recite اللهِ سُبْحَانَ 'Subhanallah' 33 times, لِلهِ الْحَمْدُ 'Al Hamdulillah' 33 times and اللهِ أَكْبَرُ 'Allahu Akbar' 34 times." Ali says, "By Allah! I have never omitted this practice ever since I heard it from Rasulullah." "Not even on the eve of the Battle of Siffin?" Ibn Kawwa asked. "May Allah strike you down, O people of Iraq!" Ali said, "Not even on the eve of the Battle of Siffin." (Ahmad, Bukhari, Muslim, Abu Dawud, Tirmidhi in Targheeb wat Tarheeb, Ibn Sa'd, Humaidi, Ibn Abi Shaybah, Abdur Razzaq, Adani, Ibn Jareer, Hakim, Nasa'ee, Ibn Majah in Kanzul Ummal)

Another narration states that Rasulullah said to Ali and Fatima, "Should I not tell you of something that is better for you than a servant? Recite اللهِ سُبْحَانَ 'Subhanallah' 33 times, لِلهِ الْحَمْدُ 'Al Hamdulillah' 33 times and أَكْبَرُ اللهُ 'Allahu Akbar' 34 times after every salah. Then recite the same 100 Adhkar when you retire to bed." (Ibn Abi Shaybah in Kanzul Ummal). Ummu Salamah narrates that Fatima once approached Rasulullah to tell about the difficulty she was having with her domestic chores. "O Rasulullah!" she said, "My hands have developed calluses by grinding grain in the grinding stones and with making dough." Rasulullah said to her, "If Allah intends to give you something; it would come to you itself. I shall however inform you of something better. When you go to bed, recite 'SubhanAllah' 33 times, 'Al Hamdulillah' 33 times 'Allahu Akbar' 34 times. This makes a complete 100 and is better for you than a servant. After the Fajr salah, you should recite 10 times:

لَاإِلَهَ إِلَّا اللهُ وَحْدَهُ لَاشَرِيْكَ لَهُ لَهُ الْمُلْكُ وَلَهُ الْحَمْدُ يُحْيِ وَيُمِيْتُ بِيَدِهِ الْخَيْرُ وَهُوَ عَلَى كُلِّ شَيْءٍ قَدِيْرٌ

This should again be recited 10 times after the Maghrib salah. Every time these words are recited, the reward of 10 deeds are recorded and ten sins are effaced. Each one virtuous as freeing a slave from the progeny of Ishma'el and every sin committed that day apart from will be forgiven. The words وَحْدَهُ اللهُ إِلَّا إِلَهَ لَا لَهُ لَاشَرِيْكَ offer protection from every Saitan and evil from the time you recite it in the morning until you again recite it in the evening." *(Ahmad, Tabrani in Majma'uz Zawa'id)*

What Rasulullah ﷺ used to Recite After Salah

Jabir ﷺ narrates that after performing salah, Rasulullah ﷺ used to recite:

لاَإِلٰهَ إِلاَّ اللهُ وَحْدَهُ لاَشَرِيْكَ لَهُ لَهُ الْمُلْكُ وَلَهُ الْحَمْدُ يُحْيِي وَيُمِيْتُ وَهُوَ عَلَى كُلِّ شَيْءٍ قَدِيْرٌ، اَللّٰهُمَّ لاَ مَانِعَ لِمَا أَعْطَيْتَ وَلاَمُعْطِيَ لِمَا مَنَعْتَ وَلاَ رَادَّ لِمَا قَضَيْتَ وَلاَ يَنْفَعُ ذَالْجَدِّ مِنْكَ الْجَدُّ

"There is none worthy of worship but the One Allah Who has no partner, to Him belongs all kingdoms and to Him belongs all praise. He gives life and death and has power over everything. O Allah! There is none to prevent what You give and none to give what You prevent. None can overturn what You decree and even the wealth of the wealthy ones cannot help them against You."
(Bazzar, Haythami, Tabrani)

Adhkar for the Morning and Evening

Abdul Hamid whose mother served one of the daughters of Rasulullah ﷺ narrates from Rasulullah ﷺ's daughter that Rasulullah ﷺ taught her to recite this Du'a in the morning:

سُبْحَانَ اللهِ وَبِحَمْدِهِ وَلاَقُوَّةَ إِلاَّ بِاللهِ مَاشَاءَ اللهُ كَانَ وَمَا لَمْ يَشَأْ لَمْ يَكُنْ أَعْلَمُ أَنَّ اللهَ عَلَى كُلِّ شَيْءٍ قَدِيْرٌ وَأَنَّ اللهَ قَدْ أَحَاطَ بِكُلِّ شَيْءٍ عِلْمًا

Rasulullah ﷺ stated that whoever recites this Dhikr in the morning shall be protected until the evening and whoever recites it in the evening will be protected until the morning. *(Abu Dawud, Nasa'ee, Ibnus Sunni in Tuhfatudh Dhakirin)*. Abu Darda ﷺ reports *(Abu Dawud)* that Allah will alleviate all worries of a person's if he recites the following Dhikr 7 times morning and evening, regardless of whether he recites it with sincerity or not:

حَسْبِيَ اللهُ لاَ إِلٰهَ إِلاَّ هُوَ عَلَيْهِ تَوَكَّلْتُ وَهُوَ رَبُّ الْعَرْشِ الْعَظِيْمِ

The Dhikr to be Recited in the Marketplaces and Other Places Where People are Negligent of Allah

Ismah ﷺ narrates that Rasulullah ﷺ said, "The action Allah loves most is Subhaiul Hadith and the action that Allah hates most is Tahrif." "O Rasulullah ﷺ!" the Sahabah asked, "What is Subhaiul Hadith?" Rasulullah ﷺ explained, 'When a man is engaged in Tasbih at a time when everyone else is engaged in worldly discussions." "O Rasulullah ﷺ!" the Sahabah asked further, "And what is Tahrif?" Rasulullah ﷺ replied, 'When people are enjoying prosperity but when their neighbors or companions ask them about their condition, they complain that they are suffering hardship."*(Tabrani in Targheeb wat Tarheeb, Haythami)*. Abu Idris Khowlani reports that Mu'adh ﷺ once said to them, "When you associate with people, it is inevitable that they would engage in worldly discussions. When you see that they have become negligent of Allah, that is the time when you should devote your complete attention to your Rabb. A narrator named Walid says that when he mentioned this to Abdur Rahman bin Yazid bin Jabir, he remarked, "That is quite right because Abu Talha Hakim bin Dinar informed me that according to the Sahabah, the sign of an accepted Du'a is when a person turns his complete attention to Allah at a time when others are negligent of Allah." *(Abu Nu'aym in Hilya)*. Abu Qilaba narrates that when two men met in the marketplace, one said to the other, "Come, let us seek forgiveness from Allah while the rest of the people are negligent of Allah." They then did this. After one of them passed away, the other saw him in a dream and said, "Do you know that Allah had forgiven us the night we met in the marketplace?" *(Ibn Abi Dunya in Targheeb wat Tarheeb)*

Rasulullah ﷺ Instructs Some People for Whom he Provided Transport for Hajj to Engage in the Dhikr of Allah When They Mount

Abu Las Khuza'ee ﷺ says, "Rasulullah ﷺ once provided us with a Zakah camel to go for Hajj. 'O Rasulullah ﷺ!' we said, 'We do not think that this camel will be able to carry us.' Rasulullah ﷺ said, 'Because there is a Saitan in the hump of every camel, you ought to engage in the Dhikr of Allah every time you mount them, as Allah has commanded you. You may then use them for yourselves because they can carry only by the permission of Allah." *(Ahmad, Tabrani, Haythami, Isabah)*

Rasulullah ﷺ's Words to Abdullah Abbas ﷺ When he let Him Ride Behind him on the Same Animal

Abdullah bin Abbas ﷺ narrates that Rasulullah ﷺ once let him ride behind him on his animal. When he was seated on the animal, Rasulullah recited اللهُ أَكْبَرُ 'Allahu Akbar' thrice, سُبْحَانَ الله 'SubhanAllah' thrice and لاَ إِلٰهَ إِلاَّ اللهُ 'La Ilaha IllAllah' once. Rasulullah ﷺ leaned against Abdullah bin Abbas ﷺ and smiled, turned to him and said, "When a person mounts his conveyance and does as I have done, Allah turns to him and smiles down on him just as I have smiled to you." *(Ahmad, Haythami)*

Rasulullah ﷺ Teaches a Sahabi Riding Behind him on the Same Animal What Dhikr to Recite When the Animal Falls

Usamah ﷺ narrates that he was sitting behind Rasulullah ﷺ on a camel when the camel tripped. "May Saitan be destroyed!" Usamah ﷺ exclaimed. Rasulullah ﷺ corrected him saying, "Do not say 'May Saitan be destroyed!' because this fills him with so much pride that he swells to the size of a house and says, 'It happened through my power!' You should rather say, 'Bismillah' because Saitan is then reduced to the size of a fly." *(Tabrani, Hathami)*. Abu Tamima Hujaimi narrates that someone who was once sitting behind Rasulullah ﷺ on the same animal said, "I was sitting behind Rasulullah ﷺ on his donkey when it tripped..." The narration then continues like the one above, but ends with Rasulullah ﷺ saying, "... Saitan says, 'I toppled her with my power. However, if you say 'Bismilllah', Saitan becomes so humiliated that he shrinks to a size smaller than a fly." *(Ahmad)*

Rasulullah ﷺ's Words When Mounting an Elevated Place and the Words of the Sahabah When Reaching Their Destination

Anas ﷺ narrates that whenever Rasulullah ﷺ mounted an elevated place (when traveling), he would say:

اَللّٰهُمَّ لَكَ الشَّرَفُ عَلَى كُلِّ شَرَفٍ وَلَكَ الْحَمْدُ عَلَى كُلِّ حَالٍ

"O Allah! All prominence belongs to You on every prominent place and all praise belongs to You in every condition." *(Ahmad, Abu Ya'la, Haythami)*

Anas ﷺ reports that whenever they reached a destination, they recited سُبْحَانَ الله 'SubhanAllah' until they had untied their carriages. *(Tabrani in Awsat, Haythami)*

What Abdullah bin Mas'ood ﷺ used to say when Leaving the House

Awf reports that whenever Abdullah bin Mas'ood ﷺ left the house, he used to recite: بِسْمِ اللهِ تَوَكَّلْتُ عَلَى اللهِ وَلاَ حَوْلَ وَلاَقُوَّةَ إِلاَّ بِاللهِ
"I leave in the name of Allah. I trust only in Allah and there is no power (to do good) and no might (to abstain from evil) but with Allah."

Ka'b Qurazi says that the Du'a for traveling is found in the Qur'an where Allah says:

وَقَالَ ارْكَبُوا فِيهَا بِسْمِ اللَّهِ مَجْرَاهَا وَمُرْسَاهَا إِنَّ رَبِّي لَغَفُورٌ رَحِيمٌ (41)

And he (Nooh (Noah)) said: "Embark therein, in the Name of Allah will be its moving course and its resting anchorage. Surely, my Lord is Oft-Forgiving, Most Merciful." (Hud:41)

He then recited the Du'a: توكات على الله ("I trust only in Allah"). (Tabrani, Haythami)

Ubay bin Ka'b Informs Rasulullah that he Wishes to Devote All his Time for Dhikr to Sending Salutations to Rasulullah

Ubay bin Ka'b narrates that after 2/3rd of the night had passed, Rasulullah stood up and addressed the people saying, "O people! Engage in the Dhikr of Allah. Engage in the Dhikr of Allah. The thing that shall shake everything during the blowing of the trumpet has almost already arrived and will be followed by the one riding behind it the second blowing of the trumpet. Death has arrived with all its terrors." It was then that Ubay bin Ka'b said, "O Rasulullah! I send salutations to you (recite Durud) in abundance. How .much of the time I spend for Dhikr and Du'a should I devote to sending salutations to you?" "As much as you please," Rasulullah replied. "A quarter?" Ubay asked. "As much as you please," Rasulullah replied, "but it will be better if you devoted more time." "Half then?" Ubay asked further. Again Rasulullah said, "As much as you please, but it will be better if you devoted more time." Ubay asked, "What about two-thirds?" "As much as you please, but it will be better if you devoted more time," Rasulullah repeated. Ubay finally said, "I shall devote all my time." "In that case," Rasulullah said, "All your worries will be taken care and you will be forgiven." (Ahmad, Ibn Munee, Rooyani, Hakim, Bayhaqi, Sa'eed bin Mansur, Abd bin Humaid in Kanzul Ummal, Tirmidhi, Tabrani in Targheeb wat Tarheeb, Abu Nu'aym in Kanzul Ummal)

The Incident of Rasulullah with Abdur Rahman bin Auf and his Statement Concerning Durud

Abdur Rahman bin Auf says, "4 or 5 of us would remain with Rasulullah day and night so that we could be of assistance to him when he needed. It was at a time when Rasulullah had left his room that I came to him. I followed him as he entered an orchard belonging to one of the leaders of the Ansar. Rasulullah started performing salah and remained so long in Sejdah that I started weeping at the thought of his soul having left him. Rasulullah raised his head and called for me. 'What is the matter?' Rasulullah asked. 'O Rasulullah!' I submitted, 'You remained so long in Sejdah that I started saying to myself, 'Allah has taken the soul of Rasul and I shall never see him ever again.' Rasulullah said, 'I prostrated out of gratitude for what Allah has granted me for my Ummah. Whoever sends salutations to me once, Allah will record the reward of 10 good deeds to his account and remove 10 sins from his record." (Abu Ya'la, Ibn Abi Dunya). Rasulullah also said, "Jibra'el has just come to me saying, 'Should I not convey to you the good news that Allah says, 'Whoever sends salutations to you, I shall send salutations to him and whoever sends greetings of peace for you, I shall send greetings of peace for him.'" Rasulullah also said, "It was out of gratitude for this that I prostrated." (Ahmad, Hakim in Targheeb wat Tarheeb, Haythami).

Rasulullah States the Virtue of Sending Salutations to Him

Abu Talha Ansari reports that Rasulullah was in an extremely good mood one morning and his happiness could actually be seen on his face. "O Rasulullah!" The Sahabah said, "You seem to be in such a good mood today that your happiness can clearly be seen on your face." "I certainly am," Rasulullah confirmed, " a messenger from my Rabb came to

me today saying, 'Whoever of your Ummah sends salutations to you once, Allah will record the reward of 10 good deeds to his account, will remove 10 sins from his record, will elevate his stages by 10 and will shower as much mercies on him in response.'" (Ahmad, Nasa'ee in Targheeb wat Tarheeb, Abdur Razzaq in Kanzul Ummal). Ka'b bin Ujrah narrates that Rasulullah once instructed them to present themselves at the pulpit. When they did so and Rasulullah ascended the first step, he said, "Amin." When he then ascended the 2nd step, he again said, "Amin" and then again said "Amin" when he ascended the 3rd step. After Rasulullah had descended from the pulpit, the Sahabah asked, "O Rasulullah! We have heard you say something today that we have never before heard you say." Rasulullah explained, "Jibra'el came to me and said, 'Far removed from Allah's mercy is the person who finds the month of Ramadhan without being forgiven!' To this I said 'Amin'. When I then ascended the 2nd step, he said, 'Far removed from Allah's mercy is the person before whom your name mentioned and he fails to sends salutations to you!' To this I also said 'Amin'. When I then ascended the 3rd step, he said, 'Far removed from Allah's mercy is the person whose both parents or one parent gets old in his presence and they do not enter him into Jannah (by his service to them)!' To this I said 'Amin'." (Hakim, Ibn Hibban, Bazzar, Ibn Khuzaima, Tabrani in Targhbbed wat Tarheeb, Haythami)

Rasulullah States that the Most Miserly Person is One who does not Send salutations to him When his Name is Mentioned

Abu Dhar narrates that when he went out one day to Rasulullah, Rasulullah was saying, "Should I not inform you of the most miserly person?" "Please do, O Rasulullah!" the Sahabah asked. Rasulullah said, "The one in whose presence my name is mentioned and he still does not sends salutations to me. This definitely makes him the most miserly of all people." (Ibn Abu Asim in Kitabus Salah, Targheeb wat Tarheeb)

Rasulullah Teaches the Sahabah how to Send Salutations to Him

Abu Mas'ood narrates that Rasulullah once came to sit with them as they sat with Sa'd bin Ubadah. It was then that Bashir bin Sa'd who as the father of Nu'man bin Bashir asked, "O Rasulullah! Allah has instructed us to send salutations to you, so how should we send salutations to you, O Rasulullah?" Rasulullah then remained silent for such a long while that we wished we had never asked him. Thereafter, he told us to say:

اللّٰهُمَّ صَلِّ عَلَى مُحَمَّدٍ وَعَلَى ال مُحَمَّدٍ كَمَا صَلَّيْتَ عَلَى إِبْرِهِيْمَ عَلَى مُحَمَّدٍ وَعَلَى ال مُحَمَّدٍ كَمَا بَارَكْتَ عَلَى إِبْرِهِيْمَ فِي الْعَالَمِيْنَ إِنَّكَ حَمِيْدٌ مَّجِيْدٌ

"O Allah! Shower your special mercies on Muhammad and on the family of Muhammad just as you have showered your mercies on Ibrahim. O Allah! Bless Muhammad and the family of Muhammad just as you have blessed Ibrahim in the universe. Verily You are Most Praiseworthy, Most Honorable."

Rasulullah said, "To convey greetings of peace (Salams) to me, you are taught how to do it by reciting the Tashahhud." (Malik, Ibn Abi Shaybah, Muslim, Abu Dawud, Tirmidhi, Nasa'ee, Abdur Razzaq, Abd bin Humaid in Kanzul Ummal)

Abdullah bin Mas'ood Teaches the Method of Sending Salutations to Rasulullah

Abdullah bin Mas'ood said (Ibn Majah in Targheeb wat Tarheeb), "When you send salutations to Rasulullah, do so properly because you do not know that your salutations will be presented to Rasulullah." When the people then asked

Abdullah bin Mas'ood ⬥ to teach them how to send salutations to Rasulullah ﷺ, he told them to recite:

اَللّٰهُمَّ اجْعَلْ صَلَوَاتِكَ وَرَحْمَتَكَ وَبَرَكَاتِكَ عَلَى سَيِّدِ الْمُرْسَلِيْنَ، وَإِمَامِ الْمُتَّقِيْنَ، وَخَاتَمِ النَّبِيِّيْنَ مُحَمَّدٍ عَبْدِكَ وَرَسُوْلِكَ إِمَامِ الْخَيْرِ، وَقَائِدِ الْخَيْرِ وَرَسُوْلِ الرَّحْمَةِ اللّٰهُمَّ ابْعَثْهُ مَقَامًا مَحْمُوْدًا يَغْبِطُهُ بِهِ الْأَوَّلُوْنَ وَالْآخِرُوْنَ اللّٰهُمَّ صَلِّ عَلَى مُحَمَّدٍ وَعَلَى الِ مُحَمَّدٍ كَمَا صَلَّيْتَ عَلَى اِبْرَاهِيْمَ وَعَلَى الِ اِبْرَاهِيْمَ اِنَّكَ حَمِيْدٌ مَجِيْدٌ اللّٰهُمَّ بَارِكْ عَلَى مُحَمَّدٍ وَعَلَى الِ مُحَمَّدٍ كَمَا بَارَكْتَ عَلَى اِبْرَاهِيْمَ وَعَلَى الِ اِبْرَاهِيْمَ اِنَّكَ حَمِيْدٌ مَجِيْدٌ

The Durud that Ali ⬥ taught people to recite has already passed.

The Statements of Abu Bakr ⬥ and Omar ⬥ Concerning Sending Salutations to Rasulullah ﷺ

Abu Bakr ⬥ said, "Sending salutations to Rasulullah ﷺ eradicates sins more effectively than water extinguishes fire and sending Salams to Rasulullah ﷺ is more rewarding than setting slaves free. Having love for Rasulullah ﷺ is more rewarding than both setting slaves free and wielding a sword in the Path of Allah." (Khatib, Isfahani in Kannzul Ummal). Omar bin Khattab ⬥ said, 'Du'as remain suspended between the heaven and the earth and no part of it ascends until you send salutations to Nabi ﷺ." (Tirmidhi, Ibn Rahway). Omar ⬥ said, "All Du'as are stopped just short of the heavens until salutations are sent to Nabi ﷺ. It is only when salutations are sent to Nabi ﷺ that the Du'a is raised." (Rahway, Hafidh Iraqi in Kanzul Ummal)

The Statements of Ali ⬥ and Abdullah bin Abbas ⬥ Concerning Sending Salutations to Nabi ﷺ

Ali ⬥ said, "Every Du'a is held back until salutations are sent to Muhammad ﷺ." (Tabrani in Awsat, Bayhaqi, Ubaidullah Eeshi and Rahawi in Kanzul Ummal). Ali ⬥ said, "The person who sends salutations to Nabi ﷺ 100 times on a Friday will have so much celestial light on his face on the Day of Judgment that people will wonder what great deed he carried out." (Bayhaqi in Kanzul Ummal). Abdullah bin Abbas ⬥ said, "It is not proper to send salutations to anyone other than the Ambiya (عليه السلام). (Abdur Razzaq in Kanzul Ummal). Abdullah bin Abbas ⬥ also said, "For anyone to send salutations to anyone else is inappropriate unless it be to one of the Ambiya عليه السلام." (Tabrani, Haythami)

The Narration of Abdullah bin Omar ⬥ on the Istighfar Rasulullah ﷺ Made in a Single Sitting

Abdullah bin Omar ⬥ says that in a single sitting, they would count Rasulullah ﷺ recite the following Istighfar 100 times: رَبِّ اغْفِرْلِيْ وَتُبْ عَلَيَّ اِنَّكَ اَنْتَ التَّوَّابُ الرَّحِيْمُ

"O my Rabb! Forgive me and accept my repentance, verily you are the Forgiving and Merciful." (Abu Dawud, Tirmidhi)

Rasulullah ﷺ's Words to Hudhaifa ⬥ on his Sharp Tongue

Hudhaifa ⬥ narrates that when he once complained to Rasulullah ﷺ about his sharp tongue, Rasulullah ﷺ said, "How far you are from Istighfar? I seek forgiveness from Allah 100 times daily." (Abu Nu'aym in Hilya, Ibn Abi Shaybah in Kanzul Ummal). Hudhaifa ⬥ went to Rasulullah ﷺ and said, "O Rasulullah ﷺ! My tongue is extremely sharp towards my family and I fear that it may enter me into Jahannam." The rest of the Hadith is as above. (Abu Nu'aym in Hilya)

Rasulullah ﷺ's Seeking Forgiveness 70 times a Day

Anas ⬥ says, "Rasulullah ﷺ was on a journey when he said, 'Seek forgiveness from Allah.' We all engaged in Istighfar. Rasulullah ﷺ said, 'Complete this 70 times.' When we complied, Rasulullah ﷺ said, 'When a male or female servant seeks

forgiveness from Allah 70 times a day, Allah forgives 700 of his sins. Destroyed is that servant who commits more than 700 sins during any day and night.'" (Ibn Abi Dunya, Bayhaqi, Isfahani in Targheeb wat Tarheeb, Ibn Najjar, Kanzul Ummal)

The Incident of Ali ⬥ with Rasulullah ﷺ Concerning Istighfar

Ali bin Rabe'ah narrates that Ali ⬥ allowed him to ride behind him on his animal as he went to the outskirts of Harra. Ali ⬥ then raised his head to the sky and said:

اَللّٰهُمَّ! اغْفِرْلِيْ ذُنُوْبِيْ! اِنَّهُ لَا يَغْفِرُ الذُّنُوْبَ اَحَدٌ غَيْرُكَ

'O Allah! Forgive my sins because none forgives sins but You' Thereafter, he turned to me and laughed. 'O Amirul Mu'minin!' I asked, 'You have sought forgiveness from your Rabb and then turned to me to laugh?' He explained, 'Rasulullah ﷺ allowed me to ride behind him on his animal as he went to the outskirts of Harra. Rasulullah ﷺ then raised his head to the sky and said:

اَللّٰهُمَّ! اغْفِرْلِيْ ذُنُوْبِيْ! اِنَّهُ لَا يَغْفِرُ الذُّنُوْبَ اَحَدٌ غَيْرُكَ

'O Allah! Forgive my sins because none forgives sins but You' Thereafter, he turned to me and laughed. 'O Rasulullah ﷺ!' I asked, 'You have sought forgiveness from your Rabb and then turned to me to laugh?' Rasulullah ﷺ explained, 'I am laughing because Allah laughed in His happiness to know at His servant is well aware of the fact that none but He can forgive.'" (Ibn Abi Shaybah, Ibn Munee in Kanzul Ummal)

The Narration of Abu Hurairah ⬥ Concerning the Excessive Istighfar of Rasulullah ﷺ

Abu Hurairah ⬥ says, "I have never seen anyone after Rasulullah ﷺ who more excessively recited: اَسْتَغْفِرُ اللهَ وَاَتُوْبُ اِلَيْهِ 'I seek forgiveness from Allah and repent to Him.'" (Abu Ya'la, Ibn Asakir in Kanzul Ummal)

Rasulullah ﷺ Teaches a Du'a of Istighfar to a Man who had Committed Many Sins

Jabir bin Abdullah ⬥ narrates that a man once came to Rasulullah ﷺ saying, "Alas! How many are my sins! Alas! How many are my sins!" When he repeated himself twice or thrice, Rasulullah ﷺ addressed him saying, "You should rather say:

اَللّٰهُمَّ مَغْفِرَتُكَ اَوْسَعُ مِنْ ذُنُوْبِيْ وَرَحْمَتُكَ اَرْجَى عِنْدِيْ مِنْ عَمَلِيْ

"O Allah! Your forgiveness is greater than my sins and I have more hope in Your mercy than I have in my deeds."

When the man recited the Du'a, Rasulullah ﷺ asked him to repeat it. After he had repeated it once, Rasulullah ﷺ bade him to repeat it yet again. After repeating it once more, Rasulullah ﷺ said to him, "You may now leave because Allah has forgiven all your sins." (Hakim in Kanzul Ummal)

Omar ⬥, Ali ⬥ and Abu Darda ⬥ Encourage People to Istighfar

Hannad narrates that when Omar ⬥ overheard someone saying, " اَسْتَغْفِرُ اللهَ وَاَتُوْبُ اِلَيْهِ ('I seek forgiveness from Allah and repent to Him')", Omar ⬥ addressed him saying, "Is that All? Why do you not follow it up with its partner: فَا غْفِرْلِيْ وَتُبْ عَلَيَّ ('So do forgive me and accept my repentance')" (Ahmad in Zuhd, Kanzul Ummal). Sha'bi reports that Ali ⬥ said, "I am surprised at the person who destroys himself when salvation is at hand." "What is the salvation?" someone asked. "It is Istighfar," came the reply. (Denowri in Kanzul Ummal). Abu Darda ⬥ said, "Glad tidings for the person who finds in his record of deeds even a little bit of Istighfar." (Ibn Abi Shaybah in Kanzul Ummal)

The Statement of Abdullah bin Mas'ood ⬥ Concerning Istighfar

Abdullah bin Mas'ood ⬥ mentioned that a person will be

forgiven for the sin of fleeing from the battlefield if he recites the following thrice: اَسْتَغْفِرُ اللهَ الَّذِي لاَ إِلَهَ إِلاَّ هُوَ الْحَيُّ الْقَيُّوْمُ وَأَتُوْبُ إِلَيْهِ

"I seek forgiveness from Allah. There is no deity but He Who is the Living and the One Who maintains everything. It is Him to Whom I repent." (Tabrani, Haythami)

Abdullah bin Mas'ood ❧ once said, "If you people knew my sins, not even 2 of you would walk behind me and you would rather throw sand on my head. I would be happy if Allah forgave one of my sins even though I am called by name of Abdullah bin Rowtha (Abdullah, son of dung)." *(Hakim by Dhahabi)*

The Statements of Abu Hurairah ❧ and Bara ❧ on Istighfar

Abu Hurairah ❧ once said, "Every day I seek Allah's forgiveness and repent to him 12,000 times and this is in proportion to the debt I owe Allah." *(Abu Nu'aym in Hilya)* He also said, "This is in proportion to my sins." A man once asked Bara ❧ about the verse: وَلَا تُلْقُوا بِأَيْدِيكُمْ إِلَى التَّهْلُكَةِ

...and do not throw yourselves into destruction (by not spending your wealth in the Cause of Allah)... (Al-Baqara:195)
The question he asked was, "O Abu Amara! Does this refer to a person who fights the enemy until he is killed?" "No," Bara ❧ replied, "It refers to a person who sins and then says that Allah will never forgive him." *(Hakim in Targheeb wat Tarheeb)*

Rasulullah ﷺ's Statement About Those who Love Each Other for the Pleasure of Allah

Abu Darda ❧ narrates that Rasulullah ﷺ said, "Allah shall raise some people on the Day of Judgment whose faces will be shining with resplendence. They will be sitting on thrones of pearls and will be the envy of all people. They will however neither be martyrs nor Ambiya." Sitting on his knees, a Bedouin asked, "Do describe them for us, O Rasulullah ﷺ so that we may recognize them." Rasulullah ﷺ replied, "They will be people from different tribes and from different places who love each other for the pleasure of Allah and gather together to engage in the Dhikr of Allah." *(Tabrani)*. Amr bin Abasa ❧ reports that he heard Rasulullah ﷺ say, "There shall be people on the right hand side of Ar Rahman (Allah) - and both His sides are the right - who will neither be Ambiya الْعَلَيْهِ not martyrs. The radiance from their faces will dazzle onlookers and even the Ambiya and the martyrs will envy them because of their status and close position to Allah." "Who will they be, O Rasulullah ﷺ?" someone asked. Rasulullah ﷺ replied, "They are a group of people from various tribes who gather for the Dhikr of Allah and who select good words just as a person eating dates selects the best of dates." *(Tabrani in Targheeb wat Tarheeb, Haythami)*

Rasulullah ﷺ's Words to the Sahabah When Sat Down to Discuss the Days of Ignorance and the Bounty of Iman

Anas bin Malik ❧ narrates that Rasulullah ﷺ came to some Sahabah who were engaged in a discussion. They said, 'We were busy discussing the ignorance and deviation we were in and how Allah then guided us." Rasulullah ﷺ was impressed and commended saying, "You have done well. Remain as you are and do just as you are doing." *(Tabrani in Awsat, Haythami)*

Statements of Aisha ❧ and Abdullah bin Abbas ❧ About Speaking of Omar ❧ and Sending Salutations to Rasulullah ﷺ

Abdullah bin Abbas ❧ said, "Speak about Omar bin Khattab ❧ as speaking about him is speaking about justice, and speaking about justice is speaking of Allah." *(Ibn Asakir in Muntakhab Kanzul Ummal)*. Aisha ❧ said, "Adorn your gatherings by sending salutations to Rasulullah ﷺ and speaking of Omar bin Khattab ❧." *(Ibn Asakir in Muntakhab Kanzul Ummal)*

Rasulullah ﷺ Describes the Friends of Allah

Abdullah bin Abbas ❧ narrates that when someone asked Rasulullah ﷺ who the friends of Allah (the Awliya) are, Rasulullah ﷺ replied, 'Those people who remind you of Allah when you look at them." *(Bazzar, Haythami)*

Rasulullah ﷺ's Words to Handhala ❧ and Abu Hurairah ❧

Handhala Usaidi ❧ who was one of Rasuluiah ﷺ's scribes narrates, "We were once with Rasulullah ﷺ when we spoke of Jannah and Jahannam with so much conviction that it seemed to appear before our very eyes. I then went to my wife and children with whom I started laughing and playing. However, when I thought of the state of mind I had been in with Rasulullah ﷺ, I left the house. I then met Abu Bakr ❧, to whom I said, 'O Abu Bakr! I have become a Munafiq.' 'Why do you say that?' he asked. I explained, 'When we are with Nabi ﷺ and he speaks to us about Jannah and Jahannam, it seems as if it is before our very eyes. However, when we leave his presence and become engrossed with our wives, children and occupations, we forget' Abu Bakr ❧ remarked, 'But we do the same.' I then approached Rasulullah ﷺ and mentioned this to him. Rasulullah ﷺ said, 'O Handhala! If you can be with your families as you are when you are with me, the angels will actually shake hands with you on your beds and on the street. O Handhala! There are times for this and times for that." *(Hasan bin Sufian, Abu Nu'aym)*. Rasulullah ﷺ said to him, "If you could remain at all times as you are when you are with me, the angels will even shade you with their wings." *(Tayalisi in Kanzul Ummal)*. Abu Hurairah ❧ narrates that he once said, "O Rasulullah ﷺ! When we are with you, our hearts are softened; we detach ourselves from this world and yearn for the Hereafter." Rasulullah ﷺ remarked, "If after leaving me you remain as you are when with me, the angels will visit you and shake hands with you in the streets. On the other hand, if you do not sin, Allah will create a creation that sins until their sins reach the heights of the sky. They will then seek forgiveness from Allah and He will forgive them all their sins without any concern." *(Ibn Najjar in Kanzul Ummal)*

Abdullah bin Omar ❧ Would Think of Allah While Performing Tawaf

Urwa bin Zubair ❧ says, "We were performing tawaf when I extended to Abdullah bin Omar ❧ my proposal to marry his daughter, he remained silent and offered no reply. 'Had he been happy,' I said to myself, 'he would have certainly given me a reply. By Allah! I shall never speak to him about it ever again.' It so happened that he reached Madinah before me and when I returned, I first went to the Masjid of Rasulullah ﷺ where I greeted Rasulullah ﷺ and fulfilled the rights owed to him. I then went to Abdullah bin Omar ❧. He welcomed me most warmly and asked when I had arrived. When I informed him that I had just arrived, he said, 'Were you asking me about Sauda bint Abdullah (my daughter) at a time when we were performing Tawaf and could think of Allah before our very eyes? Were you unable to meet me on any other occasion?' 'It just happened to take place at that time,' I replied. 'Well,' he asked, 'what have you to say today (are you still willing to marry her)?' 'I am now even more eager,' I replied. Abdullah bin Omar ❧ then called his 2 sons Salim and Abdullah and married me to his daughter." *(Abu Ny'aym in Hilya, Ibn Sa'd)*

Making Dhikr silently and audibly: The Statement of Rasulullah ﷺ Regarding the Virtue of Silent Dhikr

Aisha ﷺ narrates from Rasulullah ﷺ that the salah performed after brushing the teeth with a Miswak is 70 times superior to the salah performed without using the Miswak. Rasulullah ﷺ also said, "Verily the virtue of the secret Dhikr that is inaudible is 70 times superior to audible Dhikr. When Allah gathers all of creation on the Day of Judgment for reckoning, the recording angels will present everything that they recorded and have in writing. 'Look carefully to see if this person has anything else to his account.' 'O our Rabb!' the angels will submit, 'There is nothing that we had knowledge of that we have not taken cognizance of and put in writing.' Allah will then say to the person being questioned, 'I have something hidden with Me that no other knows of and I shall be rewarding you for it. It is the Dhikr that you made in secret." (Abu Ya'la, Haythami)

The Burial of a Person who use to Raise his Voice When Making Dhikr and the Burial of Abdullah Dhul Bijadain ﷺ

Jabir ﷺ narrates, "We once saw a fire in Baqee, the graveyard of Madinah and we got to the grave, Rasulullah ﷺ was already there. 'Hand over the body to me,' Rasulullah ﷺ instructed. Removing the body from the grave from the side of the legs, we made it over to Rasulullah ﷺ and when we looked at it, we realized that was the person who used to raise his voice when making Dhikr." (Abu Dawud in Jam'ul Fawa'id, Abu Nu'aym in Hilya). Muhammad bin Ibrahim Taymi narrates that Bijadain ('the one with 2 striped blankets') was a Sahabi by the name of Abdullah ﷺ. He belonged to the Muzaina tribe and was an orphan in the care of his uncle. Although his uncle was very good to him, when he heard that Abdullah ﷺ had accepted Islam, he took away from him everything that he had given him, even his clothing. When Abdullah ﷺ then went to his mother, she cut a striped blanket into 2 pieces for him, half of which he used to cover his lower body while the other half was used to cover the upper part of his body. Thereafter, when he went to Rasulullah ﷺ, Rasulullah ﷺ said to him, "You are Abdullah Dhul Bijadain ('the one 2 striped blankets). Stay at my door at all times." He therefore remained at Rasulullah ﷺ's door at all times. Because Abdullah ﷺ used to raise his voice when engaging in Dhikr, Omar ﷺ once remarked, "Is he showing off?" Rasulullah ﷺ however dispelled the allegation saying, "He is in fact one of those who sigh deeply and are greatly affected by the Dhikr they make." Taymi related further from Abdullah bin Mas'ood ﷺ who says, "It was in the middle of the night during the expedition to Tabuk that I got up and noticed some activity at a fire on the edge of the camp. When I pursued the light, I saw Abu Bakr ﷺ and Omar ﷺ with Abdullah Dhul Bijadain who had passed away. They had already dug a grave for him and Rasulullah ﷺ was standing inside the grave. After the burial, Rasulullah ﷺ prayed, 'O Allah! I have been pleased with him, You also be pleased with him." (Isabah, Baghawi, Ibn Mandah, Ahmad). Uqba bin Amir ﷺ states, "It was with regard to a person called Abdullah Dhul Bijadain ﷺ that Rasulullah ﷺ said, "Indeed, he is one who sighs very deeply." This Rasulullah ﷺ said because Abdullah Dhul Bijadain used to engage in Dhikr abundantly by reciting the Qur'an and making Du'a and all this he did in an audible voice."

What Rasulullah ﷺ said to Safiya ﷺ When he saw her Using Date Seeds to Count her Tasbihat

Safiya ﷺ narrates that Rasulullah ﷺ once came to her when she had 4,000 date seeds in front of her, which she was using to count her tasbihat. Rasulullah ﷺ said, "Should I not tell you of something greater that all the tasbihat you have recited?" "Please do 1 me," she said. Rasulullah ﷺ then told her to recite:

سُبْحَانَ اللهِ عَدَدَ خَلْقِهِ "I glorify Allah as much as all of His creation" (Tirmidhi). Another narration quotes the Dhikr in the following words: سُبْحَانَ اللهِ عَدَدَ مَا خَلَقَ مِنْ شَيْءٍ "I glorify Allah as much as everything that He has created" (Hakim in Targheeb wat Tarheeb). Several similar narrations have already passed in the chapter discussing comprehensive Adhkar.

Abu Safiya ﷺ, Abu Hurairah ﷺ and Sa'd ﷺ use Stones to Count Their Tasbihat

It is reported that Abu Safiya ﷺ who was one of Rasulullah ﷺ's freed slaves used to spread a leather tablecloth and send for a basket of stones. He would then age in Tasbih until midday (counting on the stones), after which the stones would be taken away. After performing the Zuhr salah, he would again engage in tasbih until the evening. (Baghawi in Al Bidayah wan Nihayah). Yunus bin Ubaid narrates from his mother that she saw a man from the Muhajirin called Abu Safiya ﷺ who used stones to count his tasbihat. (Baghawi, Bukhari in Isabah, Ibn Sa'd). It is reported that Abu Hurairah ﷺ had a string on which 2,000 knots were tied. He would not go to sleep until he had recited Tasbih on them. (Abu Nu'aym in Hilya). Abu Nadhra narrates that an old man from the Banu Tufawa tribe related, "I was the guest of Abu Hurairah ﷺ in Madinah and have never seen any of the Sahabah who exerted themselves in Ibada as much as he nor any of them who cared more for his guests than he. During the time I spent with him, I one day saw him on his bench with a bag full of stones or date seeds. As he sat there reciting tasbihat, his Abyssinian slave woman sat beneath him and whenever he completed what was in the bag, he gave it to her and she collected everything back. She then refilled the bag and gave it to him." The rest of the narration continues further. (Abu Dawud). Hakim bin Daylami reports that Sa'd (bin Abi Waqqas) ﷺ used stones to count his tasbihat. (Ibn Sa'd)

The Etiquette of Dhikr and Compounding Good Deeds

Abdullah bin Omar ﷺ said, "If possible, you should engage in Dhikr only when you are in a state of purity." (Ibn Jareer in Kanzul Ummal). Abu Uthman Nahdi reports that Abu Hurairah ﷺ said, "I have been told that Allah grants a servant the reward of as much as a million good deeds for a single good deed." He then said, "In fact, I have heard Rasulullah ﷺ say that Allah gives the rewards of as much as 2,000,000 good deeds." He then recited the verse: (40) يُضَاعِفْهَا وَيُؤْتِ مِنْ لَدُنْهُ أَجْرًا عَظِيمًا

... if there is any good (done), He doubles it, and gives from Him a great reward. (An-Nisa:40)

Then he added, "If Allah speaks of a 'tremendous ward', who can measure its magnitude?" Abu Uthman says that he asked Abu Hurairah ﷺ, "I have heard that according to you, the reward of a good deed multiplied as much as 1,000,000 times." To this, Hurairah ﷺ said, "Why do you find that surprising when I swear by Allah that I heard Rasulullah ﷺ say..." The rest of the narration is like the one above. (Ahmad, Bazzar in Majma'uz Zawa'id)

The Chapter Concerning the Du'as that the Sahabah Made

This chapter highlights how Nabi ﷺ and the Sahabah sobbed before Allah when making Du'a. It discusses the reasons and the times when they made Du'a and describes their Du'as.

Rasulullah ﷺ Teaches Some Sahabah the Etiquette of Making Du'a

Mu'adh bin Jabal ؓ narrates that Rasulullah ﷺ once passed by a person who was making Du'a saying, 'O Allah! Grant me patience." Rasulullah ﷺ addressed the man saying, "You have asked Allah for difficulty, now ask Him for safety." Rasulullah ﷺ then passed by another Mu'minin who was making Du'a saying, "O Allah! I ask you for the perfect bounty." "O son of Adam," Rasulullah ﷺ asked, "Do you know what the perfect bounty is?" The man's response was, "O Rasulullah ﷺ! I only made Du'a hoping for the best." Rasulullah ﷺ explained, "The perfect bounty is to gain entry into Jannah and to be rescued from Jahannam." Thereafter, passed by yet another person making Du'a, saying, "O Dhul Jalali wal Ikram!" Addressing this person, Rasulullah ﷺ said, "Your Du'a has been accepted, so ask what you need." *(Ibn Abi Shaybah in Kanzul Ummal)*

The Incident of Rasulullah ﷺ and a Man who was Making Du'a for his Punishment to be Brought Forward

Anas bin Malik ؓ narrates that Rasulullah ﷺ went to visit a man who was suffering so much that he had lost a lot of weight and looked like a defeathered baby bird. "Is there any Du'a that you have been making to Allah?" Rasulullah ﷺ asked. The man informed Rasulullah ﷺ that the Du'a he always made was, "O Allah! Please bring forward to this world whatever punishment is due to me in the Hereafter." Rasulullah ﷺ told him, "Why do you rather not say: رَبَّنَا آتِنَا فِي الدُّنْيَا حَسَنَةً وَفِي الْآخِرَةِ حَسَنَةً وَقِنَا عَذَابَ النَّارِ (201)

Our Lord! Give us in this world that which is good and in the Hereafter that which is good, and save us from the torment of the Fire! (Al-Baqarah:201)

The man then made the Du'a and was cured. *(Ibn Abi Shaybah, Ibn Najjar in Kanzul Ummal)*

Rasulullah ﷺ Refuses to make Du'a for Bashir bin Khasasia ؓ to Die Before Him

Bashir bin Khasasia ؓ reports that Rasulullah ﷺ said to him, "Thank Allah for bringing you from the Rabe'ah Khath'am tribe and all wing you to accept Islam at the hands of His Rasul ﷺ." "O Rasulullah ﷺ!" Bashir ؓ said, "Pray to Allah to allow me to die before you." Rasulullah ﷺ refused, "I shall not make that Du'a for anyone." *(Abu Nu'aym in Muntakhab Kanzul Ummal)*

Rasulullah ﷺ Begins with Himself When Making Du'a and Avoids Rhyming

Ubay bin Ka'b ؓ says, "Whenever making Du'a for anyone, Rasulullah ﷺ always began with asking for himself. When speaking of Musa one day, Rasulullah ﷺ remarked, 'May Allah shower His mercy on Musa ؈. Had he been more patient, he would have seen even stranger things from his companion. He said: إِنْ سَأَلْتُكَ عَنْ شَيْءٍ بَعْدَهَا فَلَا تُصَاحِبْنِي قَدْ بَلَغْتَ مِنْ لَدُنِّي عُذْرًا (76)

If I ask you anything after this, keep me not in your company, you have received an excuse from me. (Al-Kahaf:76) *(Ibn Abi Shaybah, Abu Dawud, Nasa'ee, Tirmidhi in Kanzul Ummal)*

Abu Ayub Ansari ؓ reports that whenever Rasulullah ﷺ made Du'a, he began with himself. *(Tabrani in Majmua'uz Zawa'id)*. Aisha ؓ once said to Ibn Abu Sa'ib who was the

lecturer of Madinah, "Refrain from going out to rhyme your Du'a because I have seen Rasulullah ﷺ and the Sahabah and none of them did this." *(Ibn Abi Shaybah in Kanzul Ummal)*

Um'ar ؓ Teaches the Etiquette of Du'a to a Man and the Du'a Abdullah bin Mas'ood ؓ Used to Make Just Before Dawn

When Um'ar ؓ overheard a man making Du'a to be protected from tests, he remarked, "O Allah! I seek Your protection from his words." He then addressed the man saying, "Are you asking your Rabb not to grant you a family and wealth?" Another narration states that Um'ar ؓ said, "Do you want your Rabb not to grant you wealth and children? Whoever seeks protection from tests should seek protection from tests that lead people astray." *(Ibn Abi Shaybah, Abu Ubaid in Kanzul Ummal)*. Muharib bin Dithar narrates that his uncle said, "I used to pass by the house of Abdullah bin Mas'ood ؓ just before dawn and would hear him make Du'a saying, 'O Allah! You have called me and I have come. You have given me a command and I have obeyed. This is now the time before dawn, so do forgive me.' When I met Abdullah bin Mas'ood ؓ, I told him about this Du'a that I heard him say. He said, 'Verily Ya'qub ؈ postponed making Du'a for his sons until pre-dawn." *(Tabrani, Haythami)*

Rasulullah ﷺ Raises Hands and Passes Them Over the Face

Um'ar ؓ says, "Whenever he made Du'a, Rasulullah ﷺ raised his hands and after completing, he would pass them over his face." *(Hakim)*. Another narration states that when raising his hands to make Du'a, Rasulullah ﷺ would not drop them until he passed them over his face (upon completing the Du'a). *(Tirmidhi)*. Um'ar ؓ also said, "I saw Rasulullah ﷺ making Du'a at Ahjaruz Zayt with his palms towards his face and when he completed, he passed them over his face." *(Abdul Ghani in Idahul Ashkal, Kanzul Ummal)*. Aisha ؓ says, "Rasulullah ﷺ used to raise his hands for so long when making Du'a that I would get tired." *(Ahmad, Haythami)*. Another narration adds that Rasulullah ﷺ made Du'a saying, "O Allah! I am but a human. Please do not punish me for verbally abusing or hurting anyone." *(Abdur Razzaq in Kanzul Ummal)*. Rasulullah ﷺ said, "O Allah! I am but a human so please do not punish me. If I have hurt any Mu'min or verbally abused him, then please not punish me for it" *(Bukhari in Adab)*

How Rasulullah ﷺ Curses the Coalition of Armies and the Practice of Abdullah bin Omar ؓ and Abdullah bin Zubair ؓ

Urwa ؓ narrates that Rasulullah ﷺ once passed by a tribe of Bedouins who had accepted Islam and whose settlement the coalition of Kuffar armies had destroyed. Raising his hands and extending them before his face, Rasulullah ﷺ cursed the coalition. "May my parents be sacrificed for you, O Rasulullah ﷺ!" one of the Bedouins said, "Extend your hands even further." Rasulullah ﷺ then extended his hands further from his face without raising them higher towards the sky. *(Abdur Razzaq in Kanzul Ummal)*. Abu Nu'aym Wahab reports that he saw both Abdullah bin Omar ؓ and Abdullah bin Zubair ؓ pass their hands over their faces after making Du'a. *(Bukhari in Adab)*

Rasulullah ﷺ says 'Amin' to the Du'as of Zaid ؓ, Abu Hurairah ؓ and Others

Qais Madani narrates that when a man came to ask Zaid bin Thabit ؓ something, he said to the man, "Go to Abu Hurairah ؓ because it once happened at Abu Hurairah someone else and I were in the Masjid engaging in Dhikr and making Du'a when Rasulullah ﷺ came to sit with us. When we fell silent, Rasulullah asked us to continue doing what we had been doing. My companion and I then started making Du'a before Abu Hurairah ﷺ and Rasulullah ﷺ said 'Amin' to our Du'as. Abu Hurairah ﷺ then started making Du'a and said, 'O Allah! I ask You for everything that my 2 companions have asked for as well as knowledge that I shall never forget.' When Rasulullah ﷺ said 'Amin', my companion and I said, 'O Rasulullah ﷺ! We also ask for knowledge that we shall never forget.' Rasulullah ﷺ said, 'The man of the Daus tribe (Abu Hurairah ﷺ) has beaten you to it.'" (Tabrani in Awsat, Majma'uz Zawa'id)

Omar ﷺ Makes Du'a and Requests the People to say 'Amin' and the Du'a he Made During the 'Year of Ashes'

Jami bin Shaddad narrates from a relative that he once heard Omar ﷺ say, "I want you people to say 'Amin' to 3 Du'as that I am going to make." He then proceeded to make Du'a saying, "O Allah! I am weak so please strengthen me. O Allah! I am stern, so please soften me. O Allah! I am miserly so please make me generous." (Ibn Sa'd). Sa'ib bin Yazid reports that it was early one morning during the Year of Ashes, the year in which Madinah experienced a crippling drought that he saw Omar ﷺ humbling himself before Allah, wearing simple clothing and a shawl that barely reached his knees. He was seeking Allah's forgiveness in a loud voice as his tears flowed on to his cheeks. Rasulullah ﷺ's uncle Abbas bin Abdul Muttalib ﷺ was standing on his right side as he faced the Qibla and raised his hands as he sobbed before his Rabb. The people also made Du'a as he made Du'a, after which he took Abbas ﷺ's hand and said, 'O Allah! Do accept the intercession of Rasulullah ﷺ's uncle on our behalf." Abbas ﷺ then stood beside Omar ﷺ for a very long time, his eyes flowing with tears as he made Du'a to Allah (Ibn Sa'd)

Omar ﷺ sits with a Group in the Masjid as They all Make Du'a One After the Other

Abu Sa'eed who was the freed slave of Usaid reports, "Omar ﷺ used to patrol the Masjid at night and remove from there everyone besides the person engaged in salah. Once he passed by a group of Sahabah amongst whom was Ubay bin Ka'b ﷺ, he asked, 'Who are you men?' Ubay ﷺ replied, 'We are members of your family, O Amirul Mu'minin.' 'What kept you behind after the salah?' Omar ﷺ asked. When they informed him that they had been engaged in Dhikr, Omar ﷺ sat with them. He then said to the person closest to him, 'Take the lead in making Du'a.' The man started making Du'a and when he had completed Omar ﷺ asked each person to make Du'a until he came to me, who was sitting next to him. 'Come on,' he said me. I was tongue-tied and started to shiver so much until he could actually feel me shake. He then said, 'Say something even if you have to only say, 'O Allah forgive me. O Allah! Have mercy on me.' Omar ﷺ started making Du'a and there was none who wept more than him. Then he said, 'That is enough. You may all disperse.'" (Ibn Sa'd)

The Du'a of Habib bin Maslama ﷺ and Nu'man bin Muqarrin ﷺ

Abu Hurairah ﷺ narrates that Habib bin Maslama Fahri ﷺ was a person whose Du'as were always accepted. When he was once appointed commander of an army and after making the necessary preparations, he was facing the Roman army when he said to the others, "I have heard Rasulullah ﷺ say, 'When a group assembles and they all say 'Aamin' as one of them makes Du'a, Allah certainly accepts the Du'a.'" He then duly praised Allah and said, "O Allah! Protect our blood and still grant us the reward of martyrs." He was still making Du'a when the commander of the Roman army entered Habib ﷺ's tent to

surrender (Tabrani, Haythami). In the chapter discussing the yearning that the Sahabah had for martyrdom and the Du'as they made for, in it the narration has already passed in which Nu'man bin Muqarrin ﷺ said, "I am to make a Du'a to Allah which I stress that every person say 'Amin' to. He then made the Du'a saying O Allah! Grant Nu'man martyrdom today with your assistance to the Muslims and make them victorious." Another narration adds that the others then said 'Amin' to the Du'a. (Tabri, Haythami, Hakim)

Dhul Bijadain ﷺ Used to Raise his Voice When Making Du'a

Uqba bin Amir ﷺ states, "Rasulullah ﷺ said about Abdullah Dhul Bijadain ﷺ that, 'Indeed, he is one who sighs very deeply.' This Rasulullah ﷺ said because Abdullah Dhul Bijadain ﷺ used to engage in Dhikr abundantly by reciting the Qur'an and making Du'a and all this he did in an audible voice." (Ahmad, Tabrani, Haythami, Ibn Jareer in Tafsir of Ibn Kathir)

Rasulullah ﷺ Requests Omar ﷺ for Du'as and Abu Umama Requests Rasulullah ﷺ for Du'as

Omar ﷺ narrates that he once requested Rasulullah ﷺ for permission to perform Umra, Rasulullah ﷺ said, 'Dear brother! After permission, he said do not forget us in your Du'as." Omar ﷺ says, "Those words gave me more joy than even the entire world could not." (Abu Dawud, Tirmidhi, Ibn Sa'd). Abu Umama Bahili ﷺ says, "Rasulullah ﷺ came to us, we wished that he would make Du'a. He said, 'O Allah forgive us, have mercy on us, be pleased with us, accept from us, enter us into Jannah, save us from Jahannam and mend all our affairs." When we wished that he would make more Du'a, he said, "I have ready included all your affairs (in Du'a)." (Ibn Abi Shaybah in Kanzul Ummal)

The Incident of a Man Rolling in the hot Sands and Rasulullah ﷺ's Request to him to Make Du'a for his Brothers

Talha bin Ubaidullah ﷺ narrates that a Sahabi once removed his excess clothing and then started to roll in the hot sand, saying to himself, "Taste the fire of Jahannam. You lie like a corpse in the night without engaging in Ibada and waste time during the day!" As he was doing this, he happened to see Rasulullah ﷺ under the shade of a tree. He then approached Rasulullah ﷺ and excused himself saying, "My Nafs got the better of me." "In fact," Rasulullah ﷺ said, "the doors of the heavens have all been thrown open for you and the angels are boasting about you." Rasulullah ﷺ then addressed the other Sahabah saying, "Take your journey's provisions from your brother, ask him for Du'as." When one of the Sahabah asked the Sahabi to make Du'a for him, Rasulullah ﷺ added, "Include them all in your Du'a." The Sahabi prayed, "O Allah! Make Taqwa their journey's provision and guide them in all their affairs." "O Allah!" Rasulullah ﷺ said in between, "Guide him to continue making Du'a." The Sahabi then concluded by saying, "O Allah! Make Jannah their final destination." (Ibn Abi Dunya in Kanzul Ummal). Buraida ﷺ reports that Rasulullah ﷺ was traveling somewhere when he came across a Sahabi rolling from his back to his belly in the hot sand as he chided himself saying, "O Nafs! You hope for Jannah when you sleep at night and waste your time during the day!" When he had regained his composure, he approached the Sahabah. Rasulullah ﷺ then instructed the Sahabah to request him for Du'as and when they did, the Sahabi prayed, "O Allah! Guide them in all their affairs." "Pray some more," the Sahabah requested. He then said, "O Allah! Make Taqwa their journey's provisions." The Sahabah again asked for more Du'as. This time, Rasulullah ﷺ also asked him to make more Du'a for them and prayed to Allah to inspire him. The Sahabi then said, "O Allah! Make Jannah their final destination." *(Tabrani, Haythami, Abu Nu'aym in Kanzul Ummal)*

Rasulullah ﷺ Requests those who Meet Uwais Qarni for Du'as

Asir bin Jabir narrates that when Omar ﷺ requested Uwais Qarni to seek forgiveness on his behalf, Uwais asked, "How can I seek forgiveness on your behalf when you are a companion of Rasulullah ﷺ?" Omar ﷺ replied, "I have heard Rasulullah ﷺ say, 'Verily the best of all the Tabi'een (Muslims who have met the Sahabah) shall be a man called Uwais." *(Ibn Sa'd)*. Rasulullah ﷺ also added, "Whoever meets Uwais, must request him to seek forgiveness on your behalf." *(Muslim in Isabah)*

Anas ﷺ Makes Du'a for his Companions Upon Their Request

Abdullah bin Rumi narrates that Anas bin Malik ﷺ was in Zawiya close to Basra when someone said to him, "Some of your brothers from Basra have come to you so that you may make Du'a for them." Anas ﷺ made Du'a saying, "O Allah! Forgive us and shower Your mercy on us. Grant us the best this world, the best of the Hereafter and save us from Jahannam." When they requested for more Du'a, Anas ﷺ repeated the Du'a and then said, "If you have been granted this, you have been granted the best of this world and the Hereafter." *(Bukhari in Adab)*

The Incident of Omar ﷺ and a Habitual Drinker to Whom he Wrote a Letter and then made Du'a, after Which the Man Stopped Drinking

Yazid bin Asam reports that a man from Sham was a fierce warrior and would often be in the company of Omar ﷺ. When Omar ﷺ did not see him for a while, he asked about him. "O Amirul Mu'minin!" someone informed him, "He has taken to drink." Omar ﷺ sent for his scribe and wrote the following letter addressed to the man:

Peace be on you. Before you do I praise Allah besides Whom there is none worthy of worship. Allah is also the Forgiver of sins, Acceptor of repentance, Severe in punishment, and All Powerful. There is none worthy of worship but Him, and all shall return to Him after death.

Thereafter, Omar ﷺ turned to the people around him saying, "Pray to Allah that He turns your brother's heart towards Him and that He accepts his repentance." When the man received the letter and he read it, he started repeating the words: "The Forgiver of sins, Acceptor of repentance, Severe in punishment. Allah has warned me of His punishment and also promised to forgive me." *(Ibn Abi Hatim)*. After repeating several times, the man started to weep and gave up drinking most admirably. When this news reached Omar ﷺ, the Amirul Mu'minin addressed the people saying, 'This is what you ought to do when you see that your brother has slipped. Correct him, give him conviction in Allah's Mercy, pray to Allah to forgive him and never be Saitan's accomplices against him by lowing him to continue and to lose hope in Allah's mercy." *(Abu Nu'aym in Tafsir Ibn Kathir)*

Words with which Du'a is Started

Rasulullah ﷺ tells Abu Aiash ﷺ and another Sahabi that they have called Allah by His 'Ismul A'zam' Buraida ﷺ narrates that Rasulullah ﷺ once overheard a Sahabi making Du'a saying:

اللَّهُمَّ إِنِّي أَسْأَلُكَ بِأَنِّي أَشْهَدُ أَنَّكَ أَنْتَ اللهُ لَا إِلَهَ إِلَّا أَنْتَ الأَحَدُ الصَّمَدُ الَّذِي لَمْ يَلِدْ وَلَمْ يُولَدْ وَلَمْ يَكُنْ لَهُ كُفُوًا أَحَدٌ

"O Allah! I beg from You on account of the fact that I testify that You are that Allah besides Whom there is none worthy of worship. You are The One and The Independent Who has no children, Who is not the child of anyone and Who has no equal."

To this, Rasulullah ﷺ remarked, "You have begged from Allah using His Ismul A'zam (The Most Majestic name) with which anything asked for is granted and with which any Du'a is accepted." *(Abu Dawud, Tirmidhi, Ibn Majah, Ibn Hibban, Hakim in Targheeb wat Tarheeb, Nasa'ee, Nawawi's Adhkar)*. Mu'adh bin Jabal ﷺ narrates that Rasulullah ﷺ once overheard a Sahabi making Du'a saying: يا ذا الجلال والكرام Rasulullah ﷺ told him saying, "Your Du'a has been accepted, so ask (what you want)." *(Tirmidhi in Targheeb wat Tarheeb)*. Anas bin Malik ﷺ narrates that Rasulullah ﷺ once passed by Abu Aiash Zaid bin Samit Zuraqi ﷺ while he was performing salah and making the Du'a: اللَّهُمَّ إِنِّي أَسْأَلُكَ بِأَنَّ لَكَ الْحَمْدُ لَا إِلَهَ إِلَّا أَنْتَ يَاحَنَّانُ يَامَنَّانُ يَابَدِيعُ السَّمَاوَاتِ وَالأَرْضِ، يَاذَا الْجَلَالِ وَالإِكْرَام

"O Allah! I beg from You on account of You being worthy of all praise and that there is none worthy of worship but You. O The Loving! O The One Who Bestows all bounties! O the Creator of the heavens and the earth! O The Honorable and Generous!"

To this, Rasulullah ﷺ remarked, "You have begged from Allah using His 'Ismul A'zam (Glorious Name) with which any Du'a is accepted and with which anything asked for is granted." *(Ahmad, Ibn Majah)*. Abu Dawud, Nasa'ee, Hakim, Ibn Hibban states that Abu Aiash ﷺ also added the words: " يا حي يا قيوم In another narration he added, "I ask You for Jannah and seek Your protection from Jahannam." *(Hakim in Targheeb wat Tarheeb)*

Rasulullah ﷺ gives Some Gold as a Gift to a Bedouin who Praised Allah Most Beautifully

Anas ﷺ reports that Rasulullah ﷺ once passed by a Bedouin who was making the following Du'a in his salah:

بَامَنْ لَانَرَاهُ الْعُيُونَ وَلَانُخَالِطُهُ الظُّنُونَ وَلَا تَغَيِّرُهُ الْخَوَادَتُ وَلَا يَخْشَى الدَّوَائِرَ يَعْلَمُ مَنَاقِيلَ الْجِبَالَ وَمَكَايِيْلَ الْبِخَارِ وَعَدَدَ قَطْرِ الأَمْطَارِ وَعَدَدَ وَرَقَ الأَشْجَارَ وَعَدَدَ مَا أَطْلَم عليه الليل وأشرق عليه النَّهَارُ وَمَا نُوَّارِي مِنْ سَمَاءٍ سَمَاءً وَلَا فَرْصٍ أَرْضَاءَ وَلَا بِغَيْرِ مَا فِءِ فَعْرُه وَلَا جَبَلٍ مَا فِي وَغَرْه – اجْعَلَ خَيْرَ عَمَرِي احِيَاهُ وَخَيْرَ عَمَلِي خَوَاتِيْمَهُ وَخَيْرَ أَيَّامِي يَوْمَ الْقَاكَ فِيْهِ فَوَكَّلَ رَسُوْلَ الله

"O The One Whom eyes cannot see, Who cannot be imagined, who is beyond description, Who is unaffected by happenings, Who cannot be overwhelmed by the vicissitudes of time, Who knows the weight of the mountains, the volume of the oceans, the number of falling raindrops, the number of leaves on the trees and everything upon which the night darkens and upon which the day brightens. No sky can hide another from Him, no surface of the earth can hide another from Him, no ocean can hide anything within its depths from Him and no mountain can conceal from Him anything within its rocks. Make the last part of my life the best, make the best of my deeds the last and make my best day be the one in which I meet You."

Rasulullah ﷺ asked someone to bring the Bedouin to as soon as he completed his salah. Rasulullah ﷺ had given some gold from a certain mine and when the Bedouin came before him after he had completed his salah, Rasulullah ﷺ handed over the gold to him saying, "Which tribe do you belong to, dear Bedouin?" The Bedouin informed Rasulullah ﷺ that he belonged to the Banu Amir bin Sasa'h tribe, Rasulullah ﷺ asked, "Do you know why I gave you this gold as a gift?" "Because of the family ties between us, O Rasulullah ﷺ," the Bedouin surmised. Rasulullah ﷺ said, 'While family ties have a right, I gave you the gold because of the manner in which you praise Allah." *(Tabrani, Haythami)*

The Du'a Rasulullah ﷺ Made Before Aisha ﷺ in Which he Included the Ismul A'zam

Aisha ﷺ narrates, "I once heard Rasulullah ﷺ make Du'a

saying, 'O Allah! I beg from You using that pure and blessed name of Yours which You love best and which you love to be taken, with which anything asked for is granted, with which you shower Your mercy when it is requested and with which You remove difficulties when asked to.' One day, Rasulullah ﷺ said to me, 'O Aisha! Do you know that Allah has informed me of the name by which any Du'a is accepted?' 'May my parents be sacrificed for you, O Rasulullah ﷺ!' I said, 'Do teach it to me.' Rasulullah ﷺ replied, 'It would be inappropriate for me to teach it to you.' I then stepped aside and sat down for awhile. Thereafter, I stood up, kissed his head and asked, 'O Rasulullah ﷺ! Please teach it to me.' Again Rasulullah ﷺ said, 'It would be inappropriate for me to teach it to you, O Aisha because it would be inappropriate for you to use it to ask for anything of this world.'" Aisha ؓ narrates further. She says, "I then got up to make wudhu, after which I performed 2 Rakats salah. Thereafter, I made Du'a saying:

اَللَّهُمَّ إِنِّى أَدْعُوكَ اللهِ وَأَدْعُوكَ الرَّحْمَنَ وَأَدْعُوكَ البَرَّ الرَّحِيمَ وَأَدْعُوكَ بِأَسْمَائِكَ الْحُسْنَى كُلِّهَا مَاعَلِمْتُ مِنْهَا وَمَالَمْ أَعْلَمْ أَنْ تَغْفِرَ لِيْ وَتَرْحَمَنِي

"O Allah! I call to You as Allah. I call to You as the Most Merciful. I call to You as the Most Pure and Most Kind. I call to You by all Your beautiful names that I know and those that I do not know, beseeching You to forgive me and shower Your mercy on me."

Rasulullah ﷺ then started to laugh saying, "It is amongst the names that you have mentioned." *(Ibn Majah)*

How Rasulullah ﷺ Started and Ended his Du'as

Salama bin Akwa ؓ narrates *(Ahmad, Tabrani, Haythami, Ibn Abi Shaybah in Kanzul Ummal)* that every Du'a he heard Rasulullah ﷺ started with the words: سُبْحَانَ رَبِّيَ الْعَلِيَّ الْأَعْلَى الْوَهَّابَ

Anas ؓ says, "Even if Rasulullah ﷺ had to make 100 Du'as, he would always say at the beginning, in the middle and at the end: رَبَّنَا اتِنَا فِي الدُّنْيَا حَسَنَةً وَفِي الاخِرَةِ حَسَنَةً وَقِنَا عَذَابَ النَّارِ

"Our Rabb! Grant us the best in this world, the best in the Ahereafter and save us from the fire of Jahannam." *(Ibn Najjar in Kanzul Ummal)*

Rasulullah ﷺ and 2 Men who Performed Salah and Made Du'a

Fudhala bin Ubaid ؓ narrates that Rasulullah ﷺ was sitting in the Masjid one day when a man entered, performed salah and made Du'a saying, "O Allah! Forgive me and have mercy on me." Rasulullah ﷺ said, "Dear Musalli! You have been too hasty. When sitting down after performing salah, first praise Allah as He deserves to be praised and then send salutations to me before making Du'a." Another Sahabi then came to perform salah. After completing his salah, he praised Allah and sent salutations to Rasulullah ﷺ. Rasulullah ﷺ then said to him, "O Musalli! Now make Du'a and it will be accepted." *(Abu Dawud, Tirmidhi, Nasa'ee, Ibn Hibban, Ibn Khuzaima in Targheeb wat Tarheeb, Tabrani in Majma'uz Zawa'id)*

Abdullah bin Mas'ood ؓ Advises to Begin Du'a with Praising Allah

Abdullah bin Mas'ood ؓ said, "When any of you intends making Du'a, he should commence by praising Allah as He deserves to be praised. Thereafter, he should send salutations to Nabi ﷺ before asking his need because in this manner it is more likely that his needs will be fulfilled." *(Tabrani, Haythami)*

Rasulullah ﷺ Prays for the Forgiveness of his Ummah at Arafat

Abbas bin Mirdas ؓ reports that during the evening Rasulullah ﷺ spent at Arafat; he made Du'a that Allah forgive and have mercy on his Ummah. After making Du'a for a very long time, Allah revealed to him saying, "I agree to your request all will be forgiven except for injustices people do to each other. I shall forgive all the sins that relate to them and I." "O my Rabb!" Rasulullah ﷺ pleaded, "You are capable of replacing the wronged one with that which is better than the wrong done to him and then forgiving the wrong-doer." Rasulullah ﷺ received no response to this Du'a that evening, but when he repeated the Du'a on the morning that he was at Muzdalifah, Allah said to him, "I have now forgiven them as well." Rasulullah ﷺ smiled at this, the Sahabah asked, "O Rasulullah ﷺ! You are smiling at a time when you usually do not smile at the time of Tahajjud." Rasulullah ﷺ explained, "I am smiling at Allah's enemy Iblees. When he came to know that Allah has accepted my Du'a for my Ummah, he fell to the ground, calling for woe and destruction to himself and then poured sand on his head." *(Bayhaqi)*

Rasulullah ﷺ's Du'a for his Ummah, After Which Allah Informed Him that Allah would Please Him with the Outcome of his Ummah

Abdullah bin Amr ؓ narrates that Rasulullah ﷺ once recited the words of Ibrahim عليه السلام when he aid:

رَبِّ إِنَّهُنَّ أَضْلَلْنَ كَثِيرًا مِنَ النَّاسِ فَمَنْ تَبِعَنِي فَإِنَّهُ مِنِّي وَمَنْ عَصَانِي فَإِنَّكَ غَفُورٌ رَحِيمٌ (36)

O my Lord! They have indeed led astray many among mankind. But whoso follows me, he verily is of me. And whoso disobeys me, - still You are indeed Oft-Forgiving, Most Merciful. (Ibrahim:36)

Rasulullah ﷺ then recited the following words of Isa:

إِنْ تُعَذِّبْهُمْ فَإِنَّهُمْ عِبَادُكَ وَإِنْ تَغْفِرْ لَهُمْ فَإِنَّكَ أَنْتَ الْعَزِيزُ الْحَكِيمُ (118)

If You punish them, they are Your slaves, and if You forgive them, verily You, only You are the All-Mighty, the All-Wise (Al-Ma'ida:118)

Rasulullah ﷺ made Du'a to Allah saying, "O Allah! My Ummah! O Allah! My Ummah! O Allah! My Ummah!" Rasulullah ﷺ then started to weep. Although Allah knows all, He sent Jibra'el عليه السلام to ask Rasulullah ﷺ what was making him weep. When Jibra'el عليه السلام came to ask, Rasulullah ﷺ informed him about what he had been saying. After Jibra'el عليه السلام had reported back Allah instructed Jibra'el saying, "Go to Muhammad ﷺ and tell him, 'We shall soon please you regarding to your Ummah and will not disappoint you.'" *(Ibn Wahab in Tafsir Ibn Kathir)*

The Du'a Rasulullah ﷺ Made for Ummah and his Du'a for Aisha ؓ

Anas ؓ narrates that Rasulullah ﷺ once made the following Du'a for his Ummah, "O Allah! Turn their hearts to your obedience and engulf them from the back with Your mercy." *(Tabrani, Haythami)*. Aisha ؓ says that when she noticed that Rasulullah ﷺ was in a very good mood one day, she said to him, "O Rasulullah ﷺ! Make Du'a to Allah for me." Rasulullah ﷺ prayed, "O Allah! Forgive Aisha's every past and future sin, those that were apparent and those that were secret." This made Aisha ؓ so happy that her head fell into her lap as she chuckled about it. "Does my Du'a make you happy?" Rasulullah ﷺ asked her. She replied, "How can I not rejoice about your Du'a?" Rasulullah ﷺ then said, "By Allah! This is the Du'a I make for Ummah in every salah." *(Tabrani, Haythami)*

Rasulullah ﷺ's Du'a for Abu Bakr ؓ and Omar ؓ

Anas ؓ reports that Rasulullah ﷺ made Du'a saying, "O Allah! Include Abu Bakr in my rank on the Day of Judgment." *(Abu Nu'aym in Hilya in Muntakhab Kanzul Ummal)*. Khabbab ؓ narrates that Rasulullah ﷺ made Du'a, "O Allah! Strengthen Islam with the one whom You love more between Omar bin

Khattab and Abu Jahal bin Hisham." *(Nasa'ee, Ahmad, Tirmidhi, Ibn Sa'd)*. Aisha ؓ reports that Rasulullah ﷺ made Du'a, "O Allah! Grant Islam strength with Omar bin Khattab especially." *(Ibn Majah, Hakim, Bayhaqi)*. Abdullah bin Mas'ood ؓ narrates that Rasulullah ﷺ made Du'a, "O Allah! Assist Islam through Omar." *(Tabrani, Ahmad in Muntakhab Kanzul Ummal)*

The Du'as Rasulullah ﷺ Made for Uthman ؓ

Zaid bin Aslam ؓ narrates that when Uthman ؓ sent a reddish colored camel to Rasulullah ﷺ, Rasulullah ﷺ prayed to Allah saying, "O Allah! Allow him to pass speedily across the bridge of Sirat." *(Ibn Asakir)*. Abu Sa'eed Khudri ؓ states at Rasulullah ﷺ thrice said, "O Allah! I am pleased with Uthman, You also be pleased with him." *(Abu Nu'aym)*. Abdullah bin Mas'ood ؓ narrates that Rasulullah ﷺ made Du'a saying, "O Allah! Forgive Uthman's past and future sins, those that he committed secretly and openly, privately or in public." *(Tabrani, Abu Nu'aym in Hilya, Ibn Asakir in Muntakhab Kanzul Ummal)*

The Du'as Rasulullah ﷺ made for Ali ؓ

Ali ؓ says, "I was experiencing severe pain, so I went to Rasulullah ﷺ. He put me where he stood, threw a portion of his shawl over me and started performing salah. He said, 'You are now well, O son of Abu Talib. Your ailment has been cured. Whatever I have asked Allah for myself, I have asked the same for you and I have been granted whatever I have asked for. I have been informed that there shall be no prophet after me.'" Ali ؓ says, "When I then got up, it seemed as if I had not had any pain at all." *(Ibn Abi Asim, Ibn Jareer, Tabrani, Ibn Shahin in Sunnah, Muntakhab Kanzul Ummal)*. Zaid bin Yuthay, Sa'eed bin Wahab and Amr bin Dhi Murr all report that they heard Ali ؓ say, "It is in the name of Allah that I ask very person to stand up who heard Rasulullah ﷺ say something at Ghadir Khum, place between Makkah and Madinah." 13 Sahabah stood up and they all testified that they heard Rasulullah ﷺ say, "Am I not closer to the Mu'minin than they are to themselves?" When the Sahabah admitted that he really was, Rasulullah ﷺ took hold of Ali ؓ's hand saying, "This man should be the friend of anyone who claims that I am his friend." Rasulullah ﷺ made Du'a for Ali saying, "O Allah! Befriend those who befriend him, be the enemy of those who are his enemies, love those who love him, despise who despise him, assist those who assist him and do not assist those who fail to assist him."*(Bazzar, Haythami)*. Abdullah bin Abbas ؓ states that Rasulullah ﷺ made Du'a for Ali ؓ saying, "O Allah! Assist him and assist others through him, have mercy on him and have mercy on others through him, help him and help others through him. O Allah! Befriend those who are his friends and be the enemy of those who are his enemies." *(Tabrani in Muntakhab Kanzul Ummal)*. Ali ؓ reports that Rasulullah ﷺ made Du'a for him saying, "O Allah! Keep his tongue firm on the truth and guide his heart." *(Hakim)*. Abdullah bin Abbas ؓ narrates that Rasulullah ﷺ's Du'a for Ali ؓ was, "O Allah! Guide him in passing judgment." *(Hakim in Muntakhab Kanzul Ummal)*

The Du'as Rasulullah ﷺ Made for Sa'd bin Abi Waqqas ؓ and Zubair bin Awwam ؓ

Abu Bakr ؓ narrates that the Du'a Rasulullah ﷺ made for Said bin Abi Waqqas ؓ was, "O Allah! Make his arrows travel straight, accept his Du'as and love him." *(Ibn Asakir, Ibn Najjar)*. Sa'd ؓ himself narrates that Rasulullah ﷺ made Du'a for him saying, "O Allah! Accept the Du'a of Sa'd whenever he makes Du'a to You." *(Tirmidhi, Ibn Hibban, Hakim in*

Muntakhab Kanzul Ummal). Zubair bin Awwam ؓ reports that Rasulullah ﷺ made Du'a for him, for his children and for his progeny. *(Abu Ya'la, Ibn Asakir in Muntakhab Kanzul Ummal)*

The Du'as Rasulullah ﷺ Made for the Members of His Family

Ummu Salamah ؓ who was the wife of Rasulullah ﷺ narrates that Rasulullah ﷺ once told Fatima ؓ to come to him with her husband and her two sons. When they arrived, Rasulullah ﷺ threw over them a blanket that Ummu Salamah ؓ was sitting on, which they had received as booty from Khaibar. Rasulullah ﷺ then prayed to Allah saying, "O Allah! This is the family of Muhammad. Shower Your mercy and blessings on the family of Muhammad just as You have showered them on the family of Ibrahim ﷺ. Verily You are most worthy of praise, Most Majestic." *(Abu Ya'la, Haythami, Tirmidhi)*. Abu Ammar narrates that he was once sitting with Wathila bin Asqa ؓ when some people started to revile Ali ؓ. When they had left, Wathila ؓ said to Abu Ammar, "Sit down and I shall inform about the personality whom they had been reviling. I was once with Rasulullah ﷺ when Ali ؓ, his wife Fatima ؓ, and his 2 sons Hasan ؓ and Husain ؓ arrived. Rasulullah ﷺ threw a blanket over them all and said, 'O Allah! These are the members of my household. Remove all (physical and spiritual) impurity from them and cleanse them thoroughly.' 'O Rasulullah ﷺ!' I asked, 'Make this Du'a for me as well.' 'It is for you as well,' Rasulullah ﷺ said. By Allah! More than all my deeds, it is in this Du'a that I have the most trust to attain my salvation." Another narration states that he said, "It is in this that I have the most trust to secure my salvation." *(Tabrani, Haythami)*. Ali ؓ narrates that he once went to Rasulullah ﷺ, who had spread out a shawl on the ground. When Rasulullah ﷺ, Ali ؓ, Fatima ؓ, Hasan ؓ and Husain ؓ were all seated on the shawl, Rasulullah ﷺ took hold of the ends and tied it above them. He then said, "O Allah! You be pleased with them just as I am pleased with them." *(Tabrani, Haythami)*

The Du'as Rasulullah ﷺ made for Hasan ؓ and Husain ؓ

Abdullah bin Mas'ood ؓ narrates that Rasulullah ﷺ made Du'a for Hasan ؓ and Husain ؓ saying, "O Allah! I love them, so You love them. Whoever loves them, loves me too." *(Bazzar, Haythami)*. Abu Hurairah ؓ reports that Rasulullah ﷺ made Du'a for Hasan ؓ and Husain ؓ saying, "O Allah! I love them, so You love them." *(Bazzar)*. Usama ؓ states that Rasulullah ﷺ added, "...and love those who love them." The beginning of this narration adds that Rasulullah ﷺ said, "These are my children just as they the children of my daughter." *(Nasa'ee, Ibn Hibban in Muntakhab Kanzul Ummal)*. Yet another narration from Abu Hurairah ؓ like he one above states that Rasulullah ﷺ added at then end of he Du'a, "...and O Allah! detest those who detest them." *(Ibn Abi Shaybah, Tayalisi in Muntakhab Kanzul Ummal)*. Abu Hurairah ؓ, Sa'eed bin Zaid ؓ and Aisha ؓ all narrate that Rasulullah ﷺ once made Du'a saying, "O Allah! I love Hasan, so You love him too and love all those who love him as well." *(Bukhari, Muslim in Muntakhab Kanzul Ummal)*. A narration from Muhammad bin Sirin states that Rasulullah ﷺ once made Du'a for Hasan ؓ saying, "O Allah! Keep him safe and keep others safe through him." *(Ibn Asakir in Muntakhab kanzul Ummal)*. Bara ؓ says, "I once saw Rasulullah ﷺ carrying Husain ؓ on his shoulders saying, 'O Allah! I love him, so You love him too.'" *(Bukhari, Muslim, Tirmidhi, Ibn Majah, Nasa'ee in Muntakhab Kanzul Ummal)*

The Du'as Rasulullah ﷺ made for Abbas ؓ and for his Children

Abdullah bin Abbas ؓ narrates that Rasulullah ﷺ once made

Du'a saying, "O Allah! Forgive the open and secret sins of Abbas and his children. O Allah! You be his successor to tend to matters in his family after his death." *(Tirmidhi, Abu Ya'la)*. Abu Hurairah ؓ narrates that Rasulullah ﷺ once made Du'a saying, "O Allah! Forgive the open and secret, the public and the private sins of Abbas and any other sins that he or his progeny may commit until the Day of Judgment." *(Ibn Asakir)*. Asim narrates from his father that Rasulullah ﷺ once said, "Abbas is my father's brother and therefore just like my father and what is left of my forefathers. O Allah! Forgive his sins for him, accept his good deeds, overlook his evil acts and restore righteousness to his progeny." *(Ibn Asakir in Muntakhab Kanzul Ummal)*. Abu Usaid Sa'idi ؓ narrates that Rasulullah ﷺ once said to Abbas ؓ, "You and your children should not leave the house in the morning until I come to you because there is something I need to do." They therefore waited for Rasulullah ﷺ and it was only after midmorning that Rasulullah ﷺ managed to arrive. When Rasulullah ﷺ arrived, he greeted them with the words السلام عليكم to which they replied "عَلَيْهِ السَّلَام وَرَحْمَةُ اللهِ وبركاته" "How was your morning?" Rasulullah ﷺ asked. "We praise Allah (for it)," they replied. Rasulullah ﷺ then instructed them to gather together and to sit close to each other. When they managed to do so, Rasulullah ﷺ threw his shawl over all of them and made Du'a saying, "O my Rabb! Here is my uncle, who is just like my father and here are the members of my household. Shelter them against the fire of Jahannam just as I am sheltering them with this shawl of mine." To this Du'a, the doorstep and all the walls of the house said, "Amin! Amin! Amin!" *(Tabrani, Haythami, Bayhaqi, Ibn Majah in Al Bidayah wan Nihayah, Abu Nu'aym in Dalail)*. Abdullah bin Abbas ؓ narrates that when he once stayed in the room of his aunt Maymuna ؓ, he kept the water ready for Rasulullah ﷺ to perform wudhu. "Who put this water here?" Rasulullah ﷺ asked, When Maymuna ؓ informed Rasulullahﷺ that it was Abdullah ؓ, Rasulullah ﷺ made Du'a for him saying, "O Allah! Grant him deep understanding of Deen and teach him the interpretation of the Qur'an." *(Ibn Abi Shaybah)*. Another narration quotes the Du'a as, "O Allah! Teach him the Qur'an and grant him deep understanding of the Deen." *(Ibn Najjar in Muntakhab Kanzul Ummal)*. Yet another narration quotes the words as, "O Allah! Teach him wisdom (the Sunnah) and the interpretation of the Qur'an." *(Ibn Majah, Ibn Sa'd, Tabrani)*. A narration from Abdullah bin Omar ؓ states that Rasulullah ﷺ's words were, 'O Allah! Bless him and spread the Deen through him." *(Abu Nu'aym in Hilya, Muntakhab Kanzul Ummal)*

The Du'as Rasulullah ﷺ Made for Ja'far ؓ and his Children and for Zaid bin Haritha ؓ and Abdullah bin Rawaha ؓ

Abdullah bin Ja'far ؓ reports that Rasulullah ﷺ once made Du'a saying, "O Allah! You be Ja'far ؓ's successor in caring for his children." *(Ahmad, Ibn Asakir, Tabrani)*. Another narration states that the Du'a Rasulullah ﷺ made was, "O Allah! You be Ja'far ؓ's successor in caring for his family and bless his son Abdullah in trade." Rasulullah ﷺ repeated this Du'a thrice. *(Tayalisi, Ibn Sa'd, Ahmad)*. Sha'bi states that after Ja'far ؓ was martyred at Balqa during the Battle of Mu'ta, Rasulullah ﷺ made Du'a saying, "O Allah! You be Ja'far ؓ's successor in caring for his family better than You would be a successor to any of Your righteous servants." *(Ibn Abi Shaybah in Muntakhab Kanzul Ummal, Ibn Sa'd)*. Abu Maisara narrates that when Rasulullah ﷺ received the news of the martyrdom of Zaid bin Haritha ؓ, Ja'far ؓ and Abdullah bin Rawaha ؓ, he got up to speak about them. Starting with Zaid ؓ, Rasulullah ﷺ said, "O Allah! Forgive Zaid. O Allah! Forgive Zaid. O Allah! Forgive Ja'far and

Abdullah bin Rawaha." *(Ibn Sa'd)*

The Du'as Rasulullah ﷺ Made for the Family Yasir ؓ, for Abu Salamah ؓ and for Usama bin Zaid ؓ

Uthman bin Affan ؓ narrates that Rasulullah ﷺ once made Du'a saying, "O Allah! Forgive the family of Yasir although you have already forgiven them." *(Ahmad, Ibn Sa'd)*. Aisha ؓ reports that Rasulullah ﷺ once made Du'a saying, "O Allah! Bless Ammar ؓ, the son of Yasir ؓ." The Hadith still continues further. *(Ibn Asakir in Muntakhab Kanzul Ummal)*. Ummu Salamah ؓ reports that Rasulullah ﷺ once made Du'a saying, "O Allah! Forgive Abu Salama, elevate his rank amongst those close to You and be his successor amongst those of his family who are left behind. Forgive us also, O Rabb of the universe and together with expanding his grave, fill it with light as well." *(Ahmad, Muslim, Abu Dawud in Muntakhab Kanzul Ummal)*. Usama bin Zaid ؓ says, "Rasulullah ﷺ used to put me on his thigh and then put Hasan bin Ali ؓ on his left thigh. Rasulullah ﷺ would hug us and say, "O Allah! I am compassionate towards the 2 of them, You be compassionate towards them." *(Ahmad, Abu Ya'la, Nasa'ee, Ibn Hibban)*. Rasulullah ﷺ would say, "O Allah! I love the 2 of them, You love them also." *(Ibn Sa'd)*. Usama ؓ relates, "When Rasulullah ﷺ's illness became severe, I returned to Madinah after camping with the Muslim army in nearby Juruf and those with me also returned. Rasulullah ﷺ was unable to speak when I entered his room and when he repeatedly placed his hand on me and lifted it, I realized that he was making Du'a." *(Ahmad, Tirmidhi, Tabrani in Kanzul Ummal, Muntakhab Kanzul Ummal)*

The Du'as Rasulullah ﷺ Made for Amr bin Al Aas ؓ, Hakim bin Hizam ؓ, Jareer ؓ and for the Family of Busr ؓ

Jabir ؓ reports that Rasulullah ﷺ thrice made Du'a saying, "O Allah! Forgive Amr bin Al Aas because whenever I request him for charity, he always brings it to me." *(Ibn Adi in Muntakhab Kanzul Ummal, Tabrani)*. Hakim bin Hizam ؓ narrates that Rasulullah ﷺ once made Du'a for him saying, "O Allah! Bless him in trade." *(Tabrani)* Another narration explains that (this happened) when Rasulullah ﷺ sent Hakim ؓ to purchase a sacrificial animal for a Dinar. After purchasing it, he sold it for 2 Dinars. Thereafter, he bought another for a Dinar and returned with the animal and a Dinar to Rasulullah ﷺ. Rasulullah ﷺ then made Du'a that Hakim ؓ be blessed in trade and instructed him to donate the Dinar in Sadaqa. *(Abdur Razzaq, Ibn Abi Shaybah in Muntakhab Kanzul Ummal)*. Jareer ؓ says, "When I once mentioned to Rasulullah ﷺ that I could never remain steady on horseback, he placed his hand on my chest until I could actually see its imprint on my chest. He then made Du'a saying, 'O Allah! Make him steady and also make him one who is rightly guided and who guides others aright.' Thereafter, I never once fell off a horse." *(Tabrani)*. In another narration, Jareer ؓ says, "Rasulullah ﷺ once said to me, 'Why do you not relieve me of Dhu Khalasa'?' Dhu Khalsa was a building of the Khath'am tribe and was referred to as the Yemeni Kabah during the Period of ignorance. 'O Rasulullah ﷺ!' I submitted, 'I am a person who cannot remain steady on horseback...' The rest of the narration is like the one above. *(Ibn Abi Shaybah in Muntakhab Kanzul Ummal)*. Abdullah bin Busr ؓ relates, "My father and I were sitting by the door of our house when Rasulullah ﷺ arrived on his mule. 'O Rasulullah ﷺ!' my father said, 'Why don't you alight to have something to eat and make Du'a for blessings?' Rasulullah ﷺ then alighted, ate something and made Du'a saying, 'O Allah! Have mercy on them, forgive them and bless them in their sustenance." *(Ibn Asakir).* Abdullah bin Busr ♦ said, "We then always saw a tremendous supply of sustenance coming from Allah.'" *(Tabrani in Muntakhab Kanzul Ummal)*

The Du'as Rasulullah ﷺ Made for Bara bin Ma'rur ♦, Sa'd bin Ubadah ♦ and Abu Qatada ♦

Nadhla bin Amr Ghifari ♦ reports, "When a man from the Ghifar tribe came to Rasulullah ﷺ and Rasulullah ﷺ asked him what his name was, he replied that it was Muhan meaning 'the disgraced one'. Rasulullah ﷺ said, 'You are now Mukrim 'the honored one'.' When Rasulullah ﷺ arrived in Madinah, he also led the Janaza salah for Bara bin Ma'rur ♦. Rasulullah ﷺ made Du'a for him saying, 'O Allah! Shower Your special mercy on Bara bin Ma'rur. Do not be unapproachable to him on the Day of Judgment and enter him into Jannah, which You already have decreed.'" *(Ibn Mandah, Ibn Asakir in Muntakhab Kanzul Ummal).* Ibn Abu Qatadah ♦ reports that the person for whom Rasulullah ﷺ led the Janaza salah when he arrived in Madinah was Bara bin Ma'rur ♦. Rasulullah ﷺ went with the Sahabah and when they formed a row in front of Bara ♦'s body, Rasulullah ﷺ made Du'a saying, "O Allah! Forgive him, have mercy on him and be pleased with him, even though You have already done this." *(Ibn Sa'd).* Qais bin Sa'd ♦ narrates that Rasulullah ﷺ once made Du'a saying, "O Allah! Shower Your special mercy on the family of Sa'd bin Ubadah and forgive them." *(Abu Dawud in Muntakhab Kanzul Ummal).* Abu Qatadah ♦ relates, "We were with Rasulullah ﷺ on a journey when because of exhaustion he started to lean to one side of his animal. I held him up with my hand until he woke up. Later he again started to lean to one side, I again supported him until he awoke. He made Du'a saying, 'O Allah! Look after Abu Qatadah as he has looked after me tonight.' He addressed me saying, 'We have certainly given you a lot of difficulty.'" *(Abu Nu'aym in Muntakhab Kanzul Ummal)*

The Du'as Rasulullah ﷺ made for Anas bin Malik ♦ and for Others

Anas ♦ reports that Ummu Sulaim ♦ requested Rasulullah ﷺ to make Du'a for him, Rasulullah ﷺ said, "O Allah! Grant him plenty of wealth and children and bless him in them." *(Abu Nu'aym in Muntakhab Kanzul Ummal).* Abu Darda ♦ narrates that a man called Harmala ♦ once came to Rasulullah ﷺ. Pointing to his tongue, he said, "O Rasulullah ﷺ! Iman is still here while hypocrisy lurks here." He pointed towards his heart. He continued, "I think but a little of Allah." Rasulullah ﷺ made Du'a for him saying, "O Allah! Grant him a tongue that makes Dhikr and a heart that is grateful. Allow him to love those whom I love and let all his affairs have a good ending." *(Tabrani, Haythami).* Talib ♦ narrates that when he requested Rasulullah ﷺ to make Du'a for him, Rasulullah said, "I will do so when permission is granted by Allah." Rasulullah ﷺ then waited awhile before he made Du'a saying, "O Allah! Forgive Talib and have mercy on him. O Allah! Forgive Talib and have mercy on him. O Allah! Forgive Talib and have mercy on him." *(Tabrani, Haythami, Ibn Sa'd).* Abu Musa Ash'ari ♦ narrates that Rasulullah ﷺ made Du'a saying, "O Allah! Elevate your little servant Abu Amir above the majority of people on the Day of Judgment." *(Ibn Sa'd, Tabrani in Muntakhab Kanzul Ummal).* Hassan bin Shaddad ♦ narrates, "When my mother arrived with a delegation to meet Rasulullah ﷺ, she said, 'O Rasulullah ﷺ! I have come with this delegation for your Du'a so that this son of mine becomes big and good.' Rasulullah ﷺ performed wudhu and, passing the leftover water over my face, said, "O Allah! Bless her in this child and make him big and good.'" *(Abu Nu'aym in Muntakhab Kanzul Ummal)*

The Du'as Rasulullah ﷺ Made for the Weak Sahabah

Abu Hurairah ♦ narrates that after making the Salam, Rasulullah ﷺ was still facing the Qibla when he raised his head and made Du'a saying, "O Allah! Free Salama bin Hisham, Aiash bin Abu Rabe'ah, Walid bin Walid and all the other weak Muslim who are unable to formulate an escape route and have no way out of Makkah." *(Bazzar, Haythami, Ibn Sa'd).* It was after raising his head from a Rakah of the Fajr salah that Rasulullah ﷺ made Du'a saying, "O Allah! Rescue Walid bin Walid, Salama bin Hisham, Aiash bin Abu Rabe'ah and the other oppressed Muslims in Makkah. O Allah! Severely trample the Mudhar tribe underfoot and afflict them with drought as the people were afflicted during the time of Yusuf السلام." *(Ibn Sa'd)*

The Du'as Rasulullah ﷺ Recited When Bidding Farewell Saying: "I Place Your Deen in Allah's Custody..."

Qaz'ah narrates that Abdullah bin Omar ♦ once said to him, "Come. Let me bid you farewell as Rasulullah ﷺ bid me farewell. Rasulullah ﷺ said: أَسْتَوْدِعُ اللهَ دِينَكَ وَأَمَانَتَكَ وَخَوَاتِيْمَ عَمَلِكَ
"I place your Deen, your trustworthiness and the results of all your deeds in Allah's custody" (Abu Dawud)

Abdullah bin Omar ♦ would always say to a person embarking on a journey, "Come close to me so that 1 may bid you farewell as Rasulullah ﷺ bid me farewell." He would then recite the Du'a quoted above. *(Tirmidhi)*

Rasulullah ﷺ's Words to a Sahabi who Informed him that he Intended Leaving on a Journey

Anas ♦ reports that a Sahabi came to Rasulullah ﷺ saying, "O Rasulullah! I intend embarking on a journey, so do give me some provision (Du'as). Rasulullah ﷺ said, "May Allah make Taqwa your provision." When he asked for more Du'a, Rasulullah ﷺ said, "May Allah also forgive your sins." "May my parents be sacrificed for you, O Rasulullah ﷺ!" the Sahabi said, "Do give me more." Rasulullah ﷺ said, "And may Allah make it easy for you to acquire good wherever you may be." *(Tirmidhi)*

Rasulullah ﷺ's Words When Bidding Farewell to Qatadah Rahawi ♦ and Another Sahabi

Qatadah Rahawi ♦ says, "When Rasulullah ﷺ appointed me as leader of my people, I held his hand as he bade me farewell. Rasulullah ﷺ said: جَعَلَ اللهُ التَّقْوَى زَادَكَ! وَغَفَرَ ذَنْبَكَ! وَوَجَّهَكَ لِلْخَيْرِ حَيْثُمَا تَوَجَّهْتَ *"May Allah make Taqwa your provision, forgive your sins and lead you towards good wherever you may be" (Tabrani, Bazzar, Haythami)*

Abu Hurairah ♦ narrates that a man said, "O Rasulullah ﷺ! I wish to undertake a journey, so please give me some advice." Rasulullah ﷺ said, "Ensure that you always adopt Taqwa and recite 'Allahu Akbar' when ascending any slope." As the man was leaving, Rasulullah ﷺ made Du'a: اللّهُمَّ اطْوِ لَهُ الْبُعْدَ! وَهَوِّنْ عَلَيْهِ السَّفَرَ *"O Allah! Shorten the distance for him and make the journey easy for him" (Tirmidhi)*

The Du'as Rasulullah ﷺ Recited When Taking Food or Drink and When Wearing Clothing

Abu Umamah ♦ reports that when Nabi ﷺ lifted the tablecloth off the ground (after eating), he would recite: الْحَمْدُ للهِ (حَمْدًا) كَثِيرًا طَيِّبًا مُبَارَكًا فِيهِ غَيْرَ مَكْفِيٍّ وَلاَ مُوَدَّعٍ وَلاَ مُسْتَغْنًى عَنْهُ رَبَّنَا! *"All praise that is most abundant, pure and blessed belongs to Allah but is (of course) insufficient (to praise Him adequately). O our Rabb, we are unable to stop praising You and will never be independent of doing so either" (Bukhari, Abu Dawud, Tirmidhi)*

Abu Sa'eed Khudri ﷺ reports that whenever Rasulullah ate or drank, he would recite: الْحَمْدُ لِلّهِ الَّذِيْ أَطْعَمَنَا وَسَقَانَا وَجَعَلَنَا مِنَ الْمُسْلِمِيْنَ "All praise belongs to Allah Who has given us food and drink and has made us amongst the Muslims" (Tirmidhi, Abu Dawud in Jam'ul Fawa'id). Abu Sa'eed Khudri ﷺ reports that whenever Rasulullah ﷺ wore a new garment, he would take the name of the garment (Qamees, turban, shawl....) and recite this Du'a: اللّهُمَّ لَكَ الْحَمْدُ أَنْتَ كَسَوْتَنِيْ هَذَا أَسْأَلُكَ خَيْرَهُ وَخَيْرَ مَاصُنِعَ لَهُ وَأَعُوْذُبِكَ مِنْ شَرِّهِ وَشَرِّ مَا صُنِعَ لَهُ "O Allah All praise belongs to You for giving me this (Qamees, turban, shawl, etc.) to wear. I ask You for the good of it and the good for which it was made and ask Your protection from the evil of it and the evil for which it was made" (Tirmidhi, Abu Dawud in Jam'ul Fawa'id)

The Du'as Rasulullah ﷺ Recited When Sighting the New Moon and When Noticing Thunder, Clouds or Wind

Talha ﷺ narrates that when Rasulullah ﷺ sighted the new moon, he would recite:

اللّهُمَّ! أَهِلَّهُ عَلَيْنَا بِالْيُمْنِ وَالْإِيْمَانِ، وَالسَّلَامَةِ، وَالْإِسْلَامِ رَبِّيْ وَرَبُّكَ الله

"O Allah! Let this new moon rise over us with good fortune, Iman, safety and Islam. (O moon) My Rabb and yours is Allah" (Tirmidhi). A narration of Abdullah bin Omar ﷺ quotes the words of the Du'a as follows: اللهُ أَكْبَرُ اللّهُمَّ! أَهِلَّهُ عَلَيْنَا بِالْأَمْنِ وَالْإِيْمَانِ وَالسَّلَامَةِ وَالْإِسْلَامِ وَالتَّوْفِيْقِ لِمَا تُحِبُّ وَتَرْضَى رَبُّنَا وَرَبُّكَ الله "Allah is the Greatest! O Allah! Let this moon rise over us with peace, security, serenity, Islam and inspiration to do that which you love and approve of. (O moon) Our Rabb and yours is Allah" (Ibn Asakir in Kanzul Ummal, Tabrani, Haythami)

Rafi bin Khadij ﷺ reports that whenever Rasulullah ﷺ saw the new moon, he would remark, "The moon of good and virtue." He would then recite the following Du'a thrice:

اللّهُمَّ! إِنِّيْ أَسْأَلُكَ مِنْ خَيْرِ هَذَا الشَّهْرِ وَخَيْرِ الْقَدَرِ وَأَعُوْذُبِكَ مِنْ شَرِّهِ

"O Allah! I ask You for the good of this month and for the best of destinies and I seek Protection from evil" (Tabrani, Haythami)

The Du'as Rasulullah ﷺ Recited during Thunder, Clouds and Wind

Abdullah bin Omar ﷺ reports that when Rasulullah ﷺ heard thunderclaps, he recited:

اللّهُمَّ! لَاتَقْتُلْنَا بِغَضَبِكَ وَلَا تُهْلِكْنَا بِعَوَابِكَ وَعَافِنَا قَبْلَ ذَلِكَ

"O Allah! Let not Your wrath kill us, let not Your punishment destroy us but rather grant us safety before that" (Tirmidhi in Jam'ul Fawa'id)

Aisha ﷺ narrates that whenever the wind blew violently, Rasulullah ﷺ would say:

اللّهُمَّ! إِنِّيْ أَسْأَلُكَ خَيْرَهَا وَخَيْرَ مَا فِيْهَا وَخَيْرَ مَا أُرْسِلَتْ بِهِ، وَأَعُوْذُبِكَ مِنْ شَرِّهَا وَشَرِّ مَا فِيْهَا وَشَرِّ مَا أُرْسِلَتْ بِهِ

"O Allah! I ask You for the good, the good in it and the good it has been sent for. I also seek Your protection from its evil, the evil in it and the evil (punishment) it has been sent for" (Bukhari, Muslim, Tirmidhi)

Aisha ﷺ also reports that whenever Rasulullah ﷺ noticed a cloud forming on the horizon, he would leave what he was doing, In fact, if he was performing salah, he would shorten it. He would then recite the Du'a: اللّهُمَّ! إِنِّيْ أَعُوْذُبِكَ مِنْ شَرِّهَا "O Allah! I seek Your protection from its evil" If rain then fell, he would say: اللّهُمَّ صَيِّبًا هَنِيئًا "O Allah! Make this a pleasant downpour" (Abu Dawud in Jam'ul Fawa'id)

Aisha ﷺ narrates that when Rasulullah ﷺ noticed a dense cloud in the sky, he would forsake everything he was doing, even

salah, He would then turn to the cloud and say:

اللّهُمَّ! إِنَّا نَعُوْذُبِكَ مِنْ شَرِّمَا أُرْسِلَ بِهِ "O Allah! We seek Your protection from the evil (punishment) with which it has been sent" However, if it happened to rain, he would recite the following Du'a twice or thrice: اللّهُمَّ صَيِّبًا نَافِعًا "O Allah! Make this a beneficial downpour" (Ibn Abi Shaybah in Kanzul Ummal)

Salama bin Akwa ﷺ reports that when the wind blew fiercely, Rasulullah ﷺ would say: اللّهُمَّ! لَقْحًا لَاعَقِيْمًا "O Allah! Make it a wind that is fruitful and not one that is destructive" (Tabrani, Haythami)

Some General Du'as that Rasulullah ﷺ Made

Abdullah bin Mas'ood ﷺ narrates that Rasulullah ﷺ used to make Du'a saying: اللّهُمَّ! إِنِّي أَسْأَلُكَ الْهُدَى وَالتُّقَى وَالْعَفَافَ وَالْغِنَى "O Allah! I ask you for guidance, Taqwa, chastity and independence" (Muslim)

Abu Musa Ash'ari ﷺ reports that one of the Du'as Rasulullah ﷺ often recited was:

اللّهُمَّ غْفِرْلِيْ خَطِيْئَتِيْ وَجَهْلِيْ، وَإِسْرَافِيْ فِيْ أَمْرِيْ، وَمَا أَنْتَ أَعْلَمُ بِهِ مِنِّي! اللّهُمَّ غْفِرْلِيْ جِدِّيْ وَهَزْلِيْ وَخَطَئِيْ وَعَمْدِيْ وَكُلُّ ذَلِكَ عِنْدِيْ اللّهُمَّ غْفِرْلِيْ مَا قَدَّمْتُ وَمَا أَخَّرْتُ وَمَا أَسْرَرْتُ وَمَا أَعْلَنْتُ وَمَا أَنْتَ أَعْلَمُ بِهِ مِنِّي! أَنْتَ الْمُقَدِّمُ وَأَنْتَ الْمُؤَخِّرُ وَأَنْتَ عَلَى كُلِّ شَيْءٍ قَدِيْرٌ

"O Allah! Forgive my sins, my acts of ignorance, the excesses I commit in my affairs and everything else that You know better than 1. O Allah! Forgive the wrong I do in earnestness, in jest, in error and on purpose, all of which I am guilty of. O Allah! Forgive my past sins, my future sins, those that I have done secretly, those I have committed openly and all others that You know better than 1. You are the one Who promotes and relegates (people in status) and You have power over all things" (Muslim, Bukhari). Abu Hurairah ﷺ narrates that Rasulullah ﷺ used to make the following Du'a:

اللّهُمَّ! أَصْلِحْ لِيْ دِيْنِيَ الَّذِيْ هُوَ عِصْمَةُ أَمْرِيْ وَأَصْلِحْ لِيْ دُنْيَايَ الَّتِيْ فِيْهَا مَعَاشِيْ، وَأَصْلِحْ لِيْ آخِرَتِيَ الَّتِيْ فِيْهَا مَعَادِيْ، وَاجْعَلِ الْحَيَاةَ زِيَادَةً لِيْ فِيْ كُلِّ خَيْرٍ وَاجْعَلِ الْمَوْتَ رَاحَةً لِيْ مِنْ كُلِّ شَرٍّ

"O Allah! Set right the affairs of my Deen in which lies the safety of all my affairs, set right my worldly affairs in which lies my livelihood and set right the affairs of my Hereafter to which I shall be returning. Make life a means for me to progress in every good and make death a means for me to be relieved of every evil" (Muslim)

Abdullah bin Abbas ﷺ reports that Rasulullah ﷺ used to make the following Du'a: اللّهُمَّ! لَكَ أَسْلَمْتُ، وَبِكَ آمَنْتُ وَعَلَيْكَ تَوَكَّلْتُ، وَإِلَيْكَ أَنَبْتُ وَبِكَ خَاصَمْتُ اللّهُمَّ إِنِّيْ أَعُوْذُ بِعِزَّتِكَ لَا إِلَهَ إِلَّا أَنْتَ أَنْ تُضِلَّنِيْ أَنْتَ الْحَيُّ الَّذِيْ (لَا يَمُوْتُ) وَالْجِنُّ وَالْإِنْسُ يَمُوْتُوْنَ "O Allah! To You do I submit, in You do I believe, in You I trust, to You do I turn and with You do I challenge (my opposition). O Allah! Because there is none worthy of worship but You, I seek protection with Your honor against me being misguided. You are the Ever Living Who will never die while man and Jinn will surely die" (Muslim, Bukhari)

Ummu Salama narrates that the Du'a Rasulullah ﷺ most often made was: يَامُقَلِّبَ الْقُلُوْبِ ثَبِّتْ قَلْبِيْ عَلَى دِيْنِكَ "O the One Who turns hearts! Keep my heart steadfast on Your Deen" (Tirmidhi)

Aisha ﷺ narrates that another of the Du'as that Rasulullah ﷺ used to make was:

اللّهُمَّ! عَافِنِيْ فِيْ جَسَدِيْ وَعَافِنِيْ فِيْ بَصَرِيْ، وَاجْعَلْهُ الْوَارِثَ مِنِّيْ لَا إِلَهَ إِلَّا أَنْتَ الْحَلِيْمُ الْكَرِيْمُ سُبْحَانَ اللهِ رَبِّ الْعَرْشِ الْعَظِيْمِ، وَالْحَمْدُ للهِ رَبِّ الْعَالَمِيْنَ

"O Allah! Grant me well-being in my body and well-being in my sight and make them my beneficiaries. There is none worthy of worship but You the Most Forbearing and Most Magnanimous. Glorified is Allah the Rabb of the Grand Throne. All praise belongs to Allah the Rabb of the universe" (Tirmidhi)

Abdullah bin Abbas ؓ narrates that one of the Du'as Rasulullah ﷺ used to make was:

رَبِّ أَعِنِّي وَلَا تُعِنْ عَلَيَّ وَانْصُرْنِي وَلَا تَنْصُرْ عَلَيَّ وَامْكُرْ لِيْ وَلَا تَمْكُرْ عَلَيَّ وَاهْدِنِي وَيَسِّرْ هُدَايَ، وَانْصُرْنِي عَلَى مَنْ بَغَى عَلَيَّ رَبِّ اجْعَلْنِي لَكَ شَاكِرًا لَكَ ذَاكِرًا لَكَ رَاهِبًا لَكَ مِطْوَاعًا إِلَيْكَ مُخِيبًا – أَوْ مُنِيبًا تَقَبَّلْ تَوْبَتِي وَاغْسِلْ حَوْبَتِي وَأَجِبْ دَعْوَتِي وَثَبِّتْ حُجَّتِي وَاهْدِ قَلْبِي وَسَدِّدْ لِسَانِي وَاسْلُلْ سَخِيمَةَ قَلْبِي

"O my Rabb! Assist me and do not assist others against me. Help me and do not help others against me. Plan in my favor and do not plan against me. Guide me and make guidance easy for me and assist me against those who oppose me. O my Rabb! Make me one who is grateful to You, who remembers You, who is not wary of You, who obeys you and who turns towards You. Accept my repentance, wash away my sins, accept my Du'a, make my testimony firm, guide my heart, steer my tongue and remove ill feeling from my heart" (Abu Dawud, Ibn Majah, Tirmidhi)

Abdullah bin Mas'ood ؓ narrates that amongst the Du'as that Rasulullah ﷺ made was:

اَللَّهُمَّ! إِنَّا نَسْأَلُكَ مُوْجِبَاتِ رَحْمَتِكَ وَعَزَائِمَ مَغْفِرَتِكَ وَالسَّلَامَةَ مِنْ كُلِّ إِثْمٍ وَالْغَنِيْمَةَ مِنْ كُلِّ بِرٍّ وَالْفَوْزَ بِالْجَنَّةِ وَالنَّجَاةَ مِنَ النَّارِ

"O Allah! We beg You for everything that attracts Your mercy and forgiveness. We also beg You for safety from every sin, for inspiration to do every good, for the success of Jannah and safety from Jahannam." (Hakim, Nawawi's Kitabul Adhkar)

Abdullah bin Amr ؓ narrates that Rasulullah ﷺ used to make Du'a saying:

اَللَّهُمَّ! غَفِرْلَنَا ذُنُوْبَنَا وَظُلْمَنَا وَهَزْلَنَا وَجِدَّنَا وَعَمْدَنَا وَكُلُّ ذَلِكَ عِنْدَنَا

"O Allah! Forgive the sins and wrong we do in jest, in earnestness and on purpose, all of which we are guilty of" (Ahmad, Tabrani, Haythami)

Imran bin Husain ؓ narrates that the Du'a Rasulullah ﷺ made most frequently was: اَللَّهُمَّ! غَفِرْلِيْ مَا أَخْطَأْتُ وَمَا تَعَمَّدْتُ وَمَا أَسْرَرْتُ وَمَا أَعْلَنْتُ وَمَا جَهِلْتُ وَمَا تَعَمَّدْتُ

"O Allah! Forgive the wrongs I do in error and on purpose, those that I have done secretly and those I have committed openly, those committed in ignorance and those done intentionally" (Ahmad, Tabrani, Bazzar, Haythami)

Aisha ؓ says that Rasulullah ﷺ used to make Du'a saying: اَللَّهُمَّ! أَحْسَنْتَ خَلْقِي فَأَحْسِنْ خُلُقِي

"O Allah! Make my character beautiful just as You have made my appearance beautiful" (Ahmad, Abu Ya'la, Haythami)

Ummu Salama reports that Rasulullah ﷺ used to say: رَبِّ اغْفِرْ وَارْحَمْ وَاهْدِنِي السَّبِيْلَ الْأَقْوَمَ

"O my Rabb! Forgive me, have mercy on me and guide me to the most upright path" (Ahmad, Abu Ya'la, Haythami)

Anas bin Malik says that يَاوَلِيَّ الْإِسْلَامِ وَأَهْلِهِ ثَبِّتْنِيْ بِهِ حَتَّى أَلْقَاكَ "O Defender of Islam and the Muslims Rasulullah ﷺ used to make Du'a saying:! Keep me steadfast on Islam until the day I meet You" (Tabrani, Haythami)

Busr bin Abu Artat Qurashi ؓ reports that he heard Rasulullah ﷺ make the following Du'a:

اَللَّهُمَّ! أَحْسِنْ عَاقِبَتَنَا فِي الْأُمُوْرِ كُلِّهَا وَأَجِرْنَا مِنْ خِزْيِ الدُّنْيَا وَعَذَابِ الْآخِرَةِ

"O Allah! Conclude all our affairs in a most beautiful manner and save us from disgrace in this world as well as the punishment of the Hereafter" (Ahmad)

Another narration adds that Rasulullah ﷺ said, 'Whoever recites this Du'a will die before being put through tribulations.' (Tabrani, Haythami)

Abu Sirma ؓ narrates that Rasulullah ﷺ used to say:

اَللَّهُمَّ إِنِّي أَسْأَلُكَ غِنَايَ وَغِنِيَّ مَوْلَايَ

"O Allah! I ask You to grant independence to me and to all those associated with me" (Ahmad, Tabrani, Haythami)

Thowban ؓ narrates that Rasulullah ﷺ used to make Du'a saying:

اَللَّهُمَّ! إِنِّيْ أَسْأَلُكَ الطَّيِّبَاتِ وَتَرْكَ الْمُنْكَرَاتِ وَحُبَّ الْمَسَاكِيْنِ، وَأَنْ تَثُوبَ عَلَيَّ وَإِنْ أَرَدْتَ بِعِبَادِكَ فِتْنَةً أَنْ تَقْبِضَنِيْ غَيْرَ مَفْتُوْنٍ

"O Allah! I ask You for all that is lawful, for the resolve to stay away from evil, for the love of the poor and to accept my repentance. When You intend putting Your servants through tribulation, I ask You to take me away without undergoing any of it" (Bazzar, Haythami)

Aisha narrates that one of the Du'as Rasulullah ﷺ used to make was: اَللَّهُمَّ اجْعَلْ أَوْسَعَ رِزْقِكَ عَلَيَّ عِنْدَ كِبَرِ سِنِّي وَانْقِطَاعِ عُمْرِيْ "O Allah! Allocate the greatest quantity of the sustenance you give me to my old age and to the period just before my death" (Tabrani, Haythami)

Rasulullah ﷺ's Preference for Comprehensive Du'as and his Teaching Them to Aisha ؓ

Aisha ؓ says, "Rasulullah ﷺ loved making comprehensive Du'as and would make them rather than any other." (Ibn Abi Shaybah in Kanzul Ummal). Aisha ؓ also reports that she was busy performing salah when (her father) Abu Bakr ؓ came to tell Rasulullah ﷺ something that she was unable to hear. "O Aisha!" Rasulullah ﷺ said to her, "Ensure that you make comprehensive Du'as. When she had completed the salah, Aisha ؓ asked Rasulullah ﷺ about this and he advised her to make the following Du'a:

اَللَّهُمَّ! إِنِّي أَسْأَلُكَ مِنَ الْخَيْرِ كُلِّهِ عَاجِلِهِ وَآجِلِهِ مَا عَلِمْتُ مِنْهُ وَمَالَمْ أَعْلَمْ وَأَعُوْذُبِكَ مِنَ الشَّرِّ كُلِّهِ عَاجِلِهِ وَآجِلِهِ مَا عَلِمْتُ مِنْهُ وَمَالَمْ أَعْلَمْ وَأَسْأَلُكَ الْجَنَّةَ وَمَا قَرَّبَ إِلَيْهَا مِنْ قَوْلٍ أَوْ عَمَلٍ (وَأَعُوْذُبِكَ مِنَ النَّارِ وَمَا قَرَّبَ إِلَيْهَا مِنْ قَوْلٍ أَوْ عَمَلٍ) وَأَسْأَلُكَ مِنْ خَيْرِ مَا سَأَلَكَ مِنْهُ عَبْدُكَ وَرَسُوْلُكَ مُحَمَّدٌ صلى الله عليه وسلم وَأَسْتَعِيْذُكَ مِمَّا اسْتَعَاذَ مِنْهُ عَبْدُكَ وَرَسُوْلُكَ مُحَمَّدٌ صلى الله عليه وسلم : وَأَسْأَلُكَ مَا قَضَيْتَ لِيْ مِنْ أَمْرٍ أَنْ تَجْعَلَ عَاقِبَتَهُ رُشْدًا

"O Allah! I ask You for all good that is immediate and that is still to come, whether I am aware of it or not. I seek Your protection from all evil that is immediate and that is still to come, whether I am aware of it or not. I ask You for Jannah and every word and deed that will take me closer to it. I also seek Your protection from Jahannam and every word and deed that will take me closer to it. I ask You for every good that Your servant and Rasul Muhammad ﷺ asked You for and I seek Your protection from everything that Your servant and Rasul Muhammad ﷺ sought Your protection from. I also beseech You to make the outcome be good of everything that You have decreed for me" (Hakim in Kanzul Ummal, Ahmad, Ibn Majah, Adhkar of Nawawi). Aisha ؓ says, "I was busy performing salah when Nabi ﷺ entered the room, He needed something and because I was delaying him, 'he said, 'O Aisha! You ought to make Du'a that is concise and comprehensive.' When I completed, I asked, 'O Rasulullah ﷺ! What Du'a is concise and comprehensive?'" Rasulullah ﷺ then taught her the Du'a quoted above. (Bukhari in Adab)

Rasulullah ﷺ Teaches a Comprehensive Du'a to Abu Umamah ؓ and to Some Other Sahabah ؓ

Abu Umamah ؓ says that because Rasulullah ﷺ made so many Du'as, they were unable to remember them, they therefore said to him one day, "O Rasulullah ﷺ! You make so many Du'as, that we are unable to remember them." Rasulullah ﷺ said, "Should I not teach you a Du'a that incorporates all of them?" Rasulullah ﷺ then told them to recite:

اللَّهُمَّ إِنَّا نَسْأَلُكَ مِنْ خَيْرِ مَاسَأَلَكَ مِنْهُ نَبِيُّكَ مُحَمَّدٌ صلى الله عليه وسلم، وَنَعُوْذُكَ مِنْ شَرِّ مَااسْتَعَاذَ مِنْهُ نَبِيُّكَ مُحَمَّدٌ صلى الله عليه وسلم، وَأَنْتَ الْمُسْتَعَانُ وَعَلَيْكَ الْبَلَاغُ وَلَا حَوْلَ وَلَاقُوَّةَ إِلَّا بِاللهِ

"We ask You for every good that Your Nabi Muhammad ﷺ asked You for and we seek Your protection from everything that Your Nabi Muhammad ﷺ sought Your protection from. It is only from You that help can be sought and only You can conclude all matters because there is no power or might but from Allah" (Tirmidhi, Bukhari in Adab)

Asking for Allah's protection: Factors From Which Rasulullah ﷺ Used to Ask for Allah's Protection

Anas ؓ reports that Rasulullah ﷺ used to make Du'a saying:
اللَّهُمَّ إِنِّى أَعُوْذُكَ مِنَ الْعَجْزِ وَالْكَسَلِ وَالْجُبْنِ وَالْهَرَمِ وَالْبُخْلِ وَأَعُوْذُكَ مِنْ عَذَابِ الْقَبْرِ وَأَعُوْذُكَ مِنْ فِتْنَةِ الْمَحْيَا وَالْمَمَاتِ

"O Allah! I seek Your protection from helplessness, laziness, cowardice, extreme old age and miserliness. I also seek Your protection from punishment in the grave and from the tribulations of life and death"

Another narration adds the words: وَضَلَعِ الدَّيْنِ وَغَلَبَةِ الرِّجَالِ
"....(and I seek Your protection from) the burden of debts and from the tyranny of men" (Bukhari, Muslim)

Aisha ؓ reports that Rasulullah ﷺ used to include the following words: اللَّهُمَّ إِنِّى أَعُوْذُكَ مِنْ شَرِّ مَاعَمِلْتُ وَمِنْ شَرِّ مَالَمْ أَعْمَلْ
"O Allah! I seek Your protection from the evil of what I do and from the evil of what I do not do" (Muslim)

Abdullah bin Omar ؓ narrates that amongst the Du'as that Rasulullah ﷺ made was:
اللَّهُمَّ إِنِّى أَعُوْذُكَ مِنْ زَوَالِ نِعْمَتِكَ وَتَحَوُّلِ عَافِيَتِكَ وَفُجْأَةِ نِقْمَتِكَ وَجَمِيْعِ سَخَطِكَ

"O Allah! I seek Your protection from losing Your bounties, from a reverse in well-being, from sudden calamities and from all forms of Your wrath"

Zaid bin Arqam ؓ once said to the people, "I am telling you only what Rasulullah ﷺ used to tell us," (He then proceeded to teach them the following Du'a:)
اللَّهُمَّ إِنِّى أَعُوْذُكَ مِنَ الْعَجْزِ وَالْكَسَلِ وَالْجُبْنِ وَالْبُخْلِ وَالْهَمِّ وَعَذَابِ الْقَبْرِ . اللَّهُمَّ اٰتِ نَفْسِي تَقْوَاهَا وَزَكِّهَا أَنْتَ خَيْرُ مَنْ زَكَّاهَا أَنْتَ وَلِيُّهَا وَمَوْلَاهَا . اللَّهُمَّ إِنِّى أَعُوْذُكَ مِنْ عِلْمٍ لَا يَنْفَعُ وَمِنْ قَلْبٍ لَايَخْشَعُ وَمِنْ نَفْسٍ لَاتَشْبَعُ وَمِنْ دَعْوَةٍ لَايُسْتَجَابُ لَهَا

"O Allah! I seek Your protection from helplessness, laziness, cowardice, miserliness and from punishment in the grave. O Allah! Grant Taqwa to my Nafs and purify it because You are the best of those who purify it. You are its Protector and Master. O Allah! I seek Your protection from knowledge that does not benefit, from a heart that does not fear (displeasing You), from a Nafs that is never satiated and from Du'as that are not accepted"

Aisha ؓ reports that Rasulullah ﷺ used the following words:
اللَّهُمَّ إِنِّى أَعُوْذُكَ مِنْ فِتْنَةِ النَّارِ وَعَذَابِ النَّارِ وَمِنْ شَرِّ الْغِنَى وَالْفَقْرِ
"O Allah! I seek Your protection from the tribulation of Jahannam, from its punishment and from the evils of both wealth and poverty" (Tirmidhi, Abu Dawud, Ibn Majah, Nasa'ee)

Qutba bin Malik ؓ reports that Rasulullah ﷺ used the following Du'a: اللَّهُمَّ إِنِّى أَعُوْذُكَ مِنْ مُنْكَرَاتِ الْأَخْلَاقِ وَالْأَعْمَالِ وَالْأَهْوَاءِ
"O Allah! I seek Your protection from character, actions and desires that are evil" (Tirmidhi)

Anas ؓ narrates that Rasulullah ﷺ used to make Du'a saying: اللَّهُمَّ إِنِّى أَعُوْذُكَ مِنَ الْبَرَصِ وَالْجُنُوْنِ وَالْجُذَامِ وَسَيِّئِ الْأَسْقَامِ
"O Allah! I seek Your protection from leprosy, insanity and all debilitating diseases" (Abu Dawud, Nasa'ee)

Abu Yasar ؓ who was also a Sahabi reports that Rasulullah

ﷺ used to make Du'a saying:
اللَّهُمَّ إِنِّى أَعُوْذُكَ مِنَ الْهَدْمِ وَأَعُوْذُكَ مِنَ التَّرَدِّي، وَأَعُوْذُكَ مِنَ الْغَرَقِ وَالْحَرَقِ وَالْهَرَمِ، وَأَعُوْذُكَ أَنْ يَتَخَبَّطَنِيَ الشَّيْطَانُ عِنْدَ الْمَوْتِ وَأَعُوْذُكَ أَنْ أَمُوْتَ فِي سَبِيْلِكَ مُدْبِرًا وَأَعُوْذُكَ أَنْ أَمُوْتَ لَدِيْغًا

"O Allah! I seek Your protection from being crushed, from falling, from drowning, from being burnt and from extreme old age. I also beseech You to protect me from being driven insane by Saitan at the time of death, from dying in Your path while fleeing from the battlefield and from dying from the bite of a poisonous creature" (Abu Dawud, Nasa'ee)

Abu Hurairah ؓ reports that Rasulullah ﷺ used to make the following Du'a:
اللَّهُمَّ إِنِّى أَعُوْذُكَ مِنَ الْجُوْعِ فَإِنَّهُ بِئْسَ الضَّجِيْعُ وَأَعُوْذُكَ مِنَ الْخِيَانَةِ فَإِنَّهَا بِئْسَتِ الْبِطَانَةُ

"O Allah! I seek Your protection from starvation because it is the worst of companions and I seek Your protection from treachery because it is the worst of confidantes" (Abu Dawud, Nasa'ee in Kitabul Adhkar)

Another narration states that Rasulullah ﷺ used say in his Du'as: اللَّهُمَّ إِنِّى أَعُوْذُكَ مِنَ الشِّقَاقِ وَالنِّفَاقِ وَسُوْءِ الْأَخْلَاقِ
"O Allah! I seek Your protection from disputes, hypocrisy and bad character" (Abu Dawud, Nasa'ee in Taysirul Wusul)

Anas ؓ reports that Rasulullah ﷺ used to recite this Du'a:
اللَّهُمَّ إِنِّى أَعُوْذُكَ مِنَ الْعَجْزِ وَالْكَسَلِ وَأَعُوْذُكَ مِنَ الْقَسْوَةِ وَالْغَفْلَةِ وَالْعَيْلَةِ وَالذِّلَّةِ وَالْمَسْكَنَةِ، وَأَعُوْذُكَ مِنَ الْفُسُوْقِ وَالشِّقَاقِ وَالنِّفَاقِ وَالسُّمْعَةِ وَالرِّيَاءِ وَأَعُوْذُكَ مِنَ الصَّمَمِ وَالْبَكَمِ وَالْجُنُوْنِ وَالْجُذَامِ وَسَيِّئِ الْأَسْقَامِ

O Allah! I seek Your protection from helplessness, laziness, hard-heartedness, negligence, poverty, disgrace and destitution. I seek Your protection from sinfulness, disputes, hypocrisy, boastfulness and ostentation. I also seek Your protection from being deaf, dumb, insane and from contracting leprosy or any other debilitating diseases" (Tabrani in Saghir, Haythami)

Uqba bin Amir ؓ narrates that Rasulullah ﷺ I used to make the following Du'a:
اللَّهُمَّ إِنِّى أَعُوْذُكَ مِنْ يَوْمِ السُّوْءِ وَمِنْ لَيْلَةِ السُّوْءِ، وَمِنْ سَاعَةِ السُّوْءِ وَمِنْ صَاحِبِ السُّوْءِ وَمِنْ جَارِ السُّوْءِ فِي دَارِ الْمُقَامَةِ

"O Allah! I seek Your protection from a terrible day, a terrible night, a terrible moment, a terrible companion and from a terrible neighbor to my permanent residence" (Tabrani, Haythami)

Omar ؓ narrates that Rasulullah ﷺ used to seek Allah's protection from 5 factors with the following words:
اللَّهُمَّ إِنِّى أَعُوْذُكَ مِنَ الْبُخْلِ وَالْجُبْنِ وَفِتْنَةِ الصَّدْرِ وَعَذَابِ الْقَبْرِ وَسُوْءِ الْعُمْرِ
"O Allah! I seek Your protection miserliness, cowardice, corruption of the heart, punishment in the grave and extreme old age" (Ahmad, Ibn Abi Shaybah, Abu Dawud, Nasa'ee)

Omar ؓ reports that Rasulullah ﷺ used the following words to secure Allah's protection for (his grandsons) Hasan and Husain:
أُعِيْذُكُمَا بِكَلِمَاتِ اللهِ التَّامَّةِ مِنْ كُلِّ شَيْطَانٍ وَهَامَّةٍ وَمِنْ كُلِّ عَيْنٍ لَامَّةٍ
"In the complete and perfect attributes of Allah I ask protection for the 2 of you from every Saitan and harmful creature and from every evil eye" (Abu Nu'aym in Kanzul Ummal)

Securing protection from the Jinn: The Words Rasulullah ﷺ Used on the Night the Jinn Plotted Against Him

Abu Tayah narrates that he once asked Abdur Rahman bin Khambash Taymi ؓ who was an old man by then, "Did you meet Rasulullah ﷺ?" When the Sahabi confirmed that he did, Abu Tayah asked, "What did Rasulullah ﷺ do the night the jinn plotted against him?" Abdur Rahman ؓ explained, "That night many jinn came down from their mountains and valleys to (attack) Rasulullah ﷺ. Amongst them was a particular Saitan who carried a flame in his hand with the intention of burning the blessed face of Rasulullah ﷺ. Bur Jibra'el came down to Rasulullah ﷺ saying, 'O Muhammad ﷺ! Say something!' 'What shall I say?' Rasulullah ﷺ asked. Jibra'el عليه السلام then told Rasulullah ﷺ to recite this words:

أَعُوذُ بِكَلِمَاتِ اللهِ التَّامَّةِ مِنْ شَرِّمَا خَلَقَ وَذَرَأَ وَبَرَأَ وَمِنْ شَرِّمَا يَنْزِلُ مِنَ السَّمَاء وَمِنْ شَرِّمَا يَعْرُجُ فِيهَا وَمِنْ شَرِّ فِتَنِ اللَّيْلِ وَالنَّهَارِ – وَمِنْ شَرِّ كُلِّ طَارِقٍ إِلاَّ طَارِقًا يَطْرُقُ بِخَيْرٍ يَارَحْمَنُ

'In the complete and perfect attributes of Allah do I ask protection from the evil of everything He has created and dispersed and form the evil of everything descending from the sky and going up into it. I also seek protection from the evil of the trials of the day and night and from every occurrence except those that bring good. O The Most Merciful. It is to You that I plead'

After Rasulullah ﷺ recited the Du'a, the flame was extinguished and Allah defeated them." *(Ahmad, Abu Ya'la in Targheeb wat Tarheeb, Nasa'ee, Ibn Abi Shaybah in Kanzul Ummal)*

Ubay bin Ka'b ﷺ says that he was with Rasulullah ﷺ when a Bedouin came and said, "O Nabi of Allah ﷺ! I have a brother who is suffering." "What is it that hurts him." Rasulullah ﷺ asked. When the man explained that his brother was affected by the Jinn, Rasulullah ﷺ told him to bring his brother to him. When the man came, Rasulullah ﷺ seated the man in front of him and recited the following to secure protection for him (against the Jinn):

• Surah Fatiha
• the first 4 verses of Surah Baqarah
• the verse of Al-Baqarah: وَإِلَهُكُمْ إِلَهٌ وَاحِدٌ لَا إِلَهَ إِلَّا هُوَ الرَّحْمَنُ الرَّحِيمُ (163)
• Ayatul Kursi
• 3 verses at the end of Surah Baqarah.
• The verse of Al Imran: شَهِدَ اللَّهُ أَنَّهُ لَا إِلَهَ إِلَّا هُوَ وَالْمَلَائِكَةُ وَأُولُو الْعِلْمِ قَائِمًا بِالْقِسْطِ لَا إِلَهَ إِلَّا هُوَ الْعَزِيزُ الْحَكِيمُ (18)
• The verse of Al-A'raf: إِنَّ رَبَّكُمُ اللَّهُ الَّذِي خَلَقَ السَّمَاوَاتِ وَالْأَرْضَ فِي سِتَّةِ أَيَّامٍ ثُمَّ اسْتَوَى عَلَى الْعَرْشِ يُغْشِي اللَّيْلَ النَّهَارَ يَطْلُبُهُ حَثِيثًا وَالشَّمْسَ وَالْقَمَرَ وَالنُّجُومَ مُسَخَّرَاتٍ بِأَمْرِهِ أَلَا لَهُ الْخَلْقُ وَالْأَمْرُ تَبَارَكَ اللَّهُ رَبُّ الْعَالَمِينَ (54)
• The concluding verses of Surah Mu'minin: فَتَعَالَى اللَّهُ الْمَلِكُ الْحَقُّ لَا إِلَهَ إِلَّا هُوَ رَبُّ الْعَرْشِ الْكَرِيمِ (116)
• The verse of Jinn: وَأَنَّهُ تَعَالَى جَدُّ رَبِّنَا مَا اتَّخَذَ صَاحِبَةً وَلَا وَلَدًا (3)
• 10 verses from the beginning of Surah Saffat.
• 3 verses at the end of Surah Hashar
• Surah Ikhlas
• Surah Falaq and Surah Nas

After Rasulullah ﷺ recited these before him the man then stood up as if he had never had any ailment whatsoever. *(Ahmad, Hakim, Tirmidhi in Kanzul Ummal)*

The Du'a Rasulullah ﷺ Taught Khalid bin Walid ﷺ to Recite to Dispel What he saw in his Dreams

Abu Umamah ﷺ narrates that Khalid bin Walid ﷺ once told Rasulullah ﷺ about the frightening dreams that he saw, which prevented him from performing salah at night. "O Khalid bin Walid ﷺ!" Rasulullah ﷺ said, "Should I not teach you some words that if you say thrice, Allah will dispel these dreams from you?" "May my parents be sacrificed for you, O Rasulullah ﷺ!" Khalid ﷺ exclaimed, "Do inform me because it was precisely for

this reason that I told you about this." Rasulullah ﷺ then told him to recite the following Du'a:

أَعُوذُ بِكَلِمَاتِ اللهِ التَّامَّةِ مِنْ غَضَبِهِ وَعِقَابِهِ وَشَرِّ عِبَادِهِ وَمِنْ هَمَزَاتِ الشَّيَاطِينَ وَأَنْ يَحْضُرُونَ

"I seek protection in the complete and perfect attributes of Allah from His wrath, His punishment and from the evil of His servants. I also seek His protection from the whispering of the Saiatin and from them approaching me"

Aisha ﷺ relates further that it was not even a few nights later that Khalid ﷺ came back to Rasulullah ﷺ saying, "May my parents be sacrificed for you, O Rasulullah ﷺ! I swear by the Being Who has sent you with the truth that when I thrice completed the words you taught me, Allah dispelled the condition I was suffering from. I now do not even fear entering a lion's den night" *(Tabrani in Targheeb wat Tarheeb, Haythami).* Abdullah bin Amr ﷺ mentioned that the above Du'a should be recited whenever a dream scares a person. He therefore used to teach the Du'a to those children of his who were of an understanding age. As for those who had not' yet reached the age of understanding, he would write the Du'a down on a piece of paper and tie it around their necks. *(Nasa'ee, Abu Dawud, Hakim, Tirmidhi).* Another narration states that Khalid bin Wa1eed ﷺ often woke up frightened from his sleep. When he mentioned this to Rasulullah ﷺ, Rasulullah ﷺ advised him that as soon as he awoke, he should recite بِسْمِ اللهِ Bismillah, followed by the Du'a quoted above. *(Nasa'ee, Malik in Mu'atta).* When Walid bin Walid ﷺ told Rasulullah ﷺ that he often felt fearful, Rasulullah advised him to recite the above Du'a when he retired to bed. *(Ahmad in Targheeb wat Tarheeb)*

Rasulullah ﷺ teaches the Du'a When Experiencing Difficulty

Ali ﷺ says, "Rasulullah ﷺ instructed me to recite the fo11owing Du'a whenever I faced any difficulty: لَا إِلَهَ إِلَّا اللهُ الْحَلِيمُ الْكَرِيمُ سُبْحَانَ اللهِ وَتَبَارَكَ اللهُ رَبِّ الْعَرْشِ الْعَظِيمِ وَالْحَمْدُ لِلَّهِ رَبِّ الْعَالَمِينَ

"There is none worthy of worship but Allah the Most Forbearing and Most Magnanimous. Glorified and Blessed is A11ah the Rabb of the Glorious throne. All praise belongs to Allah the Rabb of the universe" *(Ahmad, Nasa'ee, Ibn Jareer, Ibn Hibban in Kanzul Ummal, Hakim in Tuhfatudh Dhakirin)*

A narration of the type has already been quoted in the chapter discussing how Adhkar were taught.

The Du'as Rasulullah ﷺ Recited When Faced with Difficulty and the Du'a he Taught the Family of Abdul Muttalib

Anas ﷺ reports that whenever Rasulullah ﷺ was faced with any difficulty, he used to recite: يَاحَيُّ قَيُّومُ بِرَحْمَتِكَ أَسْتَغِيثُ

"O The Ever Living and Controller, it is by Your mercy that I seek assistance" *(Ibn Najjar in Kanzul Ummal)*

Asma bint Umais ﷺ narrates that whenever Rasulullah ﷺ was perturbed about something or when he was faced with some difficulty, he would recite: اَللهُ اللهُ رَبِّي لَا أُشْرِكُ بِهِ شَيْئًا

"Allah! Allah is my Rabb and I shall not ascribe any as partner to Him" *(Ibn Jareer)*

Asma ﷺ says that Rasulullah ﷺ taught her to the above Du'a when in difficulty. *(Ibn Jareer, Ibn Abi Shaybah in Kanzul Ummal).* Abdullah bin Abbas ﷺ reports that they were inside a room when Rasulullah ﷺ held on to the door-frame and told them, "O family of Abdul Muttalib! When you face any difficulties or hardships, say: اَللهُ اللهُ رَبُّنَا لَانُشْرِكُ بِهِ شَيْئًا

"Allah! Allah is our Rabb and we shall not ascribe any as partner to Him" *(Tabrani, Haythami)*

Another narration quotes with the words: اَللهُ اللهُ لَاشَرِيكَ لَهُ

"Allah! Allah has no partner" (Ibn Jareer in Kanzul Ummal)

Abdullah bin Abbas ؓ narrates that Rasulullah ﷺ used to recite the following Du'a during times of difficulty:

لاَإِلهَ إِلاَّ اللهُ الْعَظِيْمُ الْحَلِيْمُ، لاَإِلهَ إِلاَّ اللهُ رَبُّ الْعَرْشِ الْعَظِيْمِ. لاَ إِلهَ إِلاَّ اللهُ رَبُّ السَّمَاوَاتِ وَرَبُّ الْأَرْضِ وَرَبُّ الْعَرْشِ الْكَرِيْمِ

"There is none worthy of worship but Allah the Most Honored and The Most Forbearing. There is none worthy of worship but Allah the Rabb of the Glorious throne. There is none worthy of worship but Allah the Rabb of the heavens, the Rabb of the earth and the Rabb of the Majestic Throne" (Bukhari, Muslim in Tuhfatudh Dhakirin)

Thowban ؓ reports that whenever something alarmed Rasulullah ﷺ, he would say: اَللهُ اللهُ رَبِّي لاَ أُشْرِكُ بِهِ شَيْئًا

"Allah! Allah is my Rabb and I shall not ascribe any as partner to Him" (Ibn Asakir in Kanzul Ummal)

The Du'as of Abu Darda ؓ and Abdullah bin Abbas ؓ to be Relieved of Difficulties

Abu Darda ؓ once mentioned that whether with sincerity or not, when a person recites the following Du'a seven times, Allah will alleviate all his worries:

حَسْبِيَ اللهُ لاَ إِلهَ إِلاَّ هُوَ عَلَيْهِ تَوَكَّلْتُ وَهُوَ رَبُّ الْعَرْشِ الْعَظِيْمِ

"Allah is enough for me to alleviate all my worries). There is none worthy of worship but He. In Him do I pin my trust and He is the Rabb of the Glorious Throne" (Hakim in Kanzul Ummal)

It is reported then whenever Abdullah bin Abbas ؓ recited the following Du'a, it was accepted, whether he recited it for any anxiety or worry or for fear of any ruler:

أَسْأَلُكَ بِلاَ إِلهَ إِلاَّ أَنْتَ رَبَّ السَّمَاوَاتِ السَّبْعِ وَرَبَّ الْعَرْشِ الْعَظِيْمِ – وَأَسْأَلُكَ بِلاَ إِلهَ إِلاَّ أَنْتَ رَبَّ السَّمَاوَاتِ السَّبْعِ وَرَبَّ الْعَرْشِ الْكَرِيْمِ وَأَسْأَلُكَ بِلاَ إِلهَ إِلاَّ أَنْتَ رَبَّ السَّمَاوَاتِ السَّبْعِ وَالْأَرَضِيْنَ السَّبْعِ وَمَا فِيْهِنَّ وَمَا فِيْهِنَّ إِنَّكَ عَلَى كُلِّ شَيْءٍ قَدِيْرٌ

"I ask You on the strength of my belief that there is none worthy of worship but You, the Rabb of the 7 heavens and Rabb of the Glorious Throne. I ask You on the strength of my belief that there is none worthy of worship but You, the Rabb of the seven heavens and Rabb of the Honored Throne. I ask You on the strength of my belief that there is none worthy of worship but You, the Rabb of the seven heavens and seven earths and everything in them. Verily You have power over all things"

It is after saying this that a person should ask Allah for what he needs. *(Bukhari in Adab)*

Rasulullah ﷺ Teaches a Du'a and Abdullah bin Ja'far ؓ Teaches the Same to his Daughter

Ali ؓ reports that Rasulullah ﷺ taught him to recite the following Du'a before a tyrannical ruler and whenever one faces:

لاَ إِلهَ إِلاَّ اللهُ الْحَلِيْمُ الْكَرِيْمُ سُبْحَانَ اللهِ رَبِّ السَّمَاوَاتِ السَّبْعِ وَرَبِّ الْعَرْشِ الْعَظِيْمِ، وَالْحَمْدُ لِلهِ رَبِّ الْعَالَمِيْنَ إِنِّي أَعُوْذُكَ مِنْ شَرِّ عِبَادِكَ

"There is none worthy of worship but Allah The Most Forbearing and The Most Magnanimous. Pure is Allah The Rabb of the seven heavens and Rabb of the Majestic Throne. All praise belongs to Allah the Rabb of the universe. O Allah! I seek Your protection from the evil of Your servants" (Khara'iti in Makarimul Akhlaq, Kanzul Ummal)

Abu Rafi narrates that when Abdullah bin Ja'far ؓ (under duress) married his daughter to the notorious governor Hajjaj bin Yusuf, he advised her to recite the following Du'a whenever Hajjaj came to her:

لاَ إِلهَ إِلاَّ اللهُ الْحَلِيْمُ لكَرِيْمُ سُبْحَانَ اللهِ رَبِّ الْعَرْشِ الْعَظِيْمِ ، وَالْحَمْدُ لِلهِ رَبِّ الْعَالَمِيْنَ

"There is none worthy of worship but Allah The Most Forbearing and The Most Magnanimous. Pure is Allah The Rabb of the Majestic Throne. All praise belongs to Allah the Rabb of the universe"

He believed that it was this Du'a that Rasulullah ﷺ always cited whenever he was worried about something. As a result of her reciting this Du'a Hajjaj was unable to get close to her. *(Ibn Asakir in Kanzul Ummal)*

Abdullah bin Abbas ؓ Teaches a Du'a

Abdullah bin Abbas ؓ said, "When you appear before a fearsome ruler and you fear that he may tyrannize you, then recite the following Du'a 3 times:

اَللهُ أَكْبَرُ اللهُ أَكْبَرُ اللهُ أَعَزُّ مِنْ خَلْقِهِ جَمِيْعًا اللهُ أَعَزُّ مِمَّا أَخَافُ وَأَحْذَرُ أَعُوْذُ بِاللهِ الَّذِيْ لاَ إِلهَ إِلاَّ هُوَ، الْمُمْسِكُ السَّمَاوَاتِ السَّبْعِ أَنْ يَقَعْنَ عَلَى الْأَرْضِ إِلاَّ بِإِذْنِهِ مِنْ شَرِّ عَبْدِكَ فُلاَنٍ وَجُنُوْدِهِ وَأَتْبَاعِهِ وَأَشْيَاعِهِش مِنَ الْجِنِّ وَالْإِنْسِ، اَللَّهُمَّ كُنْ لِيْ جَارًا مِنْ شَرِّهِمْ جَلَّ ثَنَاؤُكَ وَعَزَّ جَارُكَ وَتَبَارَكَ اسْمُكَ وَلاَ إِلهَ غَيْرُكَ

"Mightier than all of the creation and Mightier than anything I fear and am apprehensive about. I seek the protection of that Allah besides whom there is none worthy of worship, the One Who holds the seven skies from falling to the earth without His permission. I seek Your protection from this servant of Yours, from his army, his followers and all his partisans from amongst Jinn and mankind. O Allah! Be my Protector against their evil. Exalted are Your praises, mighty is Your protection, blessed is Your name and there is none worthy of worship but You"' (Ibn Abi Shaybah, as quoted in Kanzul Ummanl, Tabrani, Haythami, Bukhari in Adab)

Abdullah bin Mas'ood ؓ Teaches such a Du'a

Abdullah bin Mas'ood ؓ said that if a person has a ruler whom he fears for his arrogance and oppression, he should recite:

اَللَّهُمَّ رَبَّ السَّمَاوَاتِ السَّبْعِ وَرَبَّ الْعَرْشِ الْعَظِيْمِ : كُنْ لِي جَارًا مِنْ فُلاَنٍ وَأَشْيَاعِهِ مِنَ الْجِنِّ وَالْإِنْسِ أَنْ يَفْرُطُوا عَلَيَّ وَأَنْ يَطْغَوْا عَزَّ جَارُكَ وَجَلَّ ثَنَاؤُكَ وَلاَ إِلهَ غَيْرُكَ

"O Allah Rabb of the seven heavens and Rabb of the Glorious Throne. Be my Protector from this servant of Yours, from his armies and all his partisans from amongst Jinn and mankind. O Allah! You protect me from their oppression and tyranny. Mighty is Your protection, exalted are Your praises and there is none worthy of worship but You'

Abdullah bin Mas'ood ؓ said that when one recites this Du'a, the tyrant will be unable to do anything unpleasant to him. *(Ibn Abi Shaybah, Ibn Jareer in Kanzul Ummal, Bukhari).*

In another narration, Abdullah bin Mas'ood ؓ said, "If you fear a tyrannical ruler, say..." The words of the Du'a are as quoted above, but with the words: كُنْ لِيْ جَارًا مِنْ شَرِّ

"Be my Protector against..."

After this, the name of the tyrant is to be mentioned. Thereafter, the Du'a continues as follows:

وَشَرِّ الْجِنِّ وَالْإِنْسِ، وَأَتْبَاعِهِمْ أَنْ يَفْرُطَ عَلَيَّ أَحَدٌ مِنْهُمْ عَزَّ جَارُكَ وَجَلَّ ثَنَاؤُكَ وَلاَ إِلهَ غَيْرُكَ

"... .and from the evil of the Jinn, of mankind and all their followers. I seek Your protection against any of them harming me. Mighty is Your protection, exalted are Your praises and there is none worthy of worship but You" (Tabrani, Haythami)

The Chapter Concerning the Lectures of the Sahabah

This chapter highlights how Nabi ﷺ and the Sahabah addressed the people in Jumu'ah sermons, when in congregation, on the occasions of Hajj and Umrah and on various other occasions. It discusses how they motivated the people to carry out the commands of Allah, even though these seemed to oppose experience and what was apparent. It further discusses how they made people abstain from this world and its temporary pleasures and yearn for the Hereafter and its eternal delights. Those firmly stationed every category of the Ummah whether rich, poor or prominent on the consciousness that they should fulfill the commands coming to them from Allah and Rasulullah ﷺ even if it meant spending their very lives and all their wealth. It clear that they did not build people's conviction on the temporary and short-lived wealth and resources of this world.

The First Lecture that Rasulullah ﷺ Delivered

Abu Salama bin Abdur Rahman bin Auf ﷺ narrates that when Rasulullah ﷺ stood up to deliver a sermon in Madinah for the first time, he began by duly praising Allah. He then said, "O people! Send your good deeds ahead to the Hereafter by Allah! You must know that each one of you shall definitely die, leaving his flock of goats without a shepherd. There will then neither be any interpreter or negotiator to come between him and his Rabb when his Rabb will ask him, 'Have my messengers not come to you and conveyed the message to you? Have I not granted you wealth and blessed you with favors? Now with the guidance and means at your disposal what good deeds have you sent ahead?' The man will then look to his right and left, but will see nothing. He will then look in front of him but will see nothing but Jahannam. Therefore, whoever can save himself from Jahannam even by giving a piece of a date as Sadaqa should do so. Whoever cannot afford even this, should at least say a good word because every good deed is rewarded ten fold up to 700 fold. May Allah's peace, mercy and blessings be upon Allah's messenger." Rasulullah ﷺ then delivered another sermon saying, "I praise Allah to Whom belongs all praise. We seek Allah's protection from the evil of our souls and from our evil actions. There is none to mislead the one whom Allah guides and there is none to guide the one whom Allah does not guide. I testify that there is none worthy of worship but the One Allah Who has no partner. The best of all speech is the Book of Allah and successful is the person whose heart Allah has decorated with it, whom Allah guides to Islam after kufr and who chooses it rather than all other talks. Apart from it being the most beautiful speech, it is also the most effective. Love those who love Allah and love Allah with all your heart. Never grow weary of Allah's Book and His Dhikr because your hearts will then harden. From what deeds Allah has chosen and selected, He has named the recitation of the Qur'an as the best of all good deeds, the best of all acts of worship, the most relevant of all speech and of all that explains what is lawful and unlawful. You should therefore worship Allah without ascribing any partners to Him. Fear Him as He ought to be feared and let everything righteous that you speak with your mouths be sincerely for Allah. Love each other for the pleasure of Allah and always remember that Allah hates does not like that any pledge made with Him should be broken. May Allah's peace, mercy and blessings be upon you all." *(Bayhaqi in Al Bidayah wan Nihayah)*

Rasulullah ﷺ's Jumu'ah Sermon

Sa'eed bin Abdur Rahman Jumhi narrates that from the narrations he received, the sermon that Rasulullah ﷺ delivered in the locality of the Banu Salim bin Auf on the occasion of the first Jumu'ah salah in Madinah was:

"All praise belongs to Allah! I praise Him, seek His assistance, seek His forgiveness and His guidance. I believe in Him, do not reject His Divinity and accept as an enemy all those who do reject His Divinity. I testify that there is none worthy of worship but the One and Only Allah Who has no partner. I also testify that Muhammad ﷺ is His servant and Rasul, whom Allah has sent with guidance, light and advice at a time when there was a cessation in the chain of prophets; a time when knowledge was little, people were astray, time was coming to an end, Judgment was drawing near and the world was coming to an end. Whoever obeys Allah and His Rasul ﷺ is rightly guided and whoever disobeys them has gone astray, has been negligent and strayed far off the right path. I advise you to adopt Taqwa because the best advice a Muslim can give to another Muslim is to encourage him towards the Hereafter and to instruct him to adopt Taqwa. Take heed to the warnings that Allah has given you about Himself because there is no better advice nor any better reminder. Whoever adopts Taqwa with true fear for displeasing his Rabb, his Taqwa will be his true helping hand in everything he seeks for the Hereafter. Whoever sets right all private and public affairs between his Rabb and himself solely to please Allah, shall always be fondly remembered in this world and shall have a vast treasure after death at a time when a person is most in need of the deeds he did in the past. Every person who did not do this shall wish that there was a very large distance between him and his actions. Allah warns you of Himself and Allah is Most Gentle towards His bondsmen. Allah is always true to His word and He fulfils His promises without going back on them, because He says: (29) مَا يُبَدَّلُ الْقَوْلُ لَدَيَّ وَمَا أَنَا بِظَلَّامٍ لِلْعَبِيدِ

The Sentence that comes from Me cannot be changed, and I am not unjust (to the least) to the slaves. (Qaf:29)

Fear disobeying Allah in your private and public matters of this world and the Hereafter because whoever fears Allah, Allah shall wipe out their sins and grant them an immense reward. Whoever fears Allah shall succeed most remarkably. Taqwa protects against Allah's anger, it protects against Allah's punishment, it protects against Allah's wrath, it illuminates faces, it pleases your Rabb and it elevates stages. Take your share of rewards and never be negligent in securing Allah's mercy. Allah has taught you His Book and chalked out for you a pattern of life to ascertain which of you are sincere and who are not. Do good to others just as Allah does good to you, declare your enmity with those who are Allah's enemies and fight them for the pleasure of Allah as you ought to do. It is Allah Who has chosen you and called you Muslims. Jihad takes place so that those who are destroyed are destroyed after seeing proof and those who survive live on after seeing a proof. There is no power or might without Allah, so carry out Allah's Dhikr in abundance and know well what is to happen after today. Whoever sets right the matters between himself and Allah, Allah shall see to all matters between him and other people because it is Allah Who makes decisions for people and they cannot pass decisions against Him. While Allah prevails over people, they cannot prevail over Him. Allah is the Greatest and there is no power without Allah the Most Honorable." *(Ibn Jareer in Al Bidayah wan Nihayah, Qurtubi in his Tafsir)*

The Lecture Rasulullah ﷺ Delivered During one of the Battles

A Sahabi by the name of Hirar ؓ reports that they were with Rasulullah ﷺ in a battle and it was when they were about to engage the enemy in combat that Rasulullah ﷺ delivered a lecture. After duly praising Allah, Rasulullah ﷺ said, "You are enjoying bounties in green, yellow and red and every other shade and even have this in your camps. When you meet with the enemy, you should advance step by step because whenever a person launches an attack in the Path of Allah, two damsels from the wide-eyed damsels of Jannah hurry towards him. If he is martyred, Allah forgives all his sins with the first drop of blood that falls. The 2 damsels then wipe the dust from his face and say to him, 'Your time has now come.' He then ponds by telling them, 'Your time has also come.'" *(Tabrani, Bazzar, Haythami)*

The Sermon Rasulullah ﷺ Delivered When he Stopped at Hijr En-route to Tabuk

Jabir ؓ narrates that during the expedition to Tabuk, Rasulullah ﷺ stopped at Hijr, the place where the nation of Salih was destroyed and addressed the Sahabah saying, "O people! Do not ask your Nabi for miracles because here lays the nation of Salih ﷺ who asked their Nabi to raise a pregnant she-camel for them from a mountain. He complied and she would arrive by that wide road to drink water. On the day she drank, she would consume all their water and the amount of milk they would get from her on that day would be as much as on the day when she did not drink when the other animals had their turn. She would then return by the same wide road. But they hamstrung her. Allah gave them only 3 days to repent. The promise of Allah is true and a terrible scream came, which destroyed all of them except for one of them who happened to be in the Haram. It was the Haram that saved him from Allah's punishment." "O Rasulullah ﷺ!" The Sahabah asked, "Who was he?" Rasulullah ﷺ replied, 'He was Abu Righal." *(Tabrani, Bazzar, Ahmad, Haythami)*

Sermon Rasulullah ﷺ delivered on the Expedition to Tabuk

Hasan bin Ali ؓ reports that during the expedition to Tabuk, Rasulullah ﷺ mounted the pulpit and after praising Allah, he said, "O people! I instruct you to do only that which Allah instructs me and I forbid you only from that which Allah forbids me. You should pursue the most moderate manner of seeking your livelihood because I swear by the Being Who controls the life of Abul Qasim (myself) that your sustenance searches for each one of you just as his death searches for him. When finding sustenance becomes difficult for any of you, look for it in the obedience of Allah." *(Tabrani in Targheeb wat Tarheeb)*

The Sermon Rasulullah ﷺ delivered when Makkah was Conquered

Abdullah bin Amr ؓ says, "When Madinah was conquered, Rasulullah ﷺ announced that everyone should lay down their arms except for the people of the Banu Khuza'h tribe, who were allowed to use their weapons against the people of the Banu Bakr tribe because they were at risk from them. This permission remained until Rasulullah ﷺ had performed the Asr salah, after which he instructed them to also lay down their arms. The following day however, a man from the Banu Khuza'h tribe met someone from the Banu Bakr tribe in Muzdalifa and killed him. When the news reached Rasulullah ﷺ, I saw him leaning against the Kabah as he stood up and addressed the people saying, 'Verily Allah's greatest enemy is the person who kills in the Haram, who kills someone who was no threat to his life or who kills in revenge for something done during the period of ignorance.' A man then stood up and claimed that a particular child was his. Rasulullah ﷺ's response to this was, 'One cannot randomly lay claim to a child in Islam because the practices of the period of ignorance have all come to an end. A child belongs to the biological father and the one who commits adultery shall have that which is most blunt.' 'What is that which is most blunt?' the Sahabah asked. Rasulullah ﷺ replied, 'Stones, the person will be stoned to death.' Rasulullah ﷺ then proceeded to say, 'No salah can be performed after the Fajr salah until sunrise and no salah after the Asr salah until sunset. A woman can also not be married at the same time to the person married to either her paternal or maternal aunt.'" *(Tabrani, Haythami)*

Sermon Rasulullah ﷺ Delivered When Makkah was Conquered

Abdullah bin Omar ؓ reports that Rasulullah ﷺ was standing on the steps leading to the Kabah when he praised Allah and said, "All praise belongs to Allah Who has fulfilled His promise, assisted His servant and defeated the hordes by Himself. Take note that a person killed with whipping or beating with a stick falls in the category of manslaughter, for which the blood money is 100 camels, 40 of which must be pregnant. You should also take note that every act of pride and murder during the period of ignorance now lie trampled beneath my 2 feet. All that I shall be restoring to those who had been doing it are the services of tending to the House of Allah and of providing water to the people performing Hajj." *(Ibn Majah)*. Abdullah bin Omar ؓ narrates that Rasulullah ﷺ was riding his camel Qaswa as he performed Tawaf of the Kabah. He was using the opposite end of his stick to touch the corners of the Kabah and wherever he tried to make the camel sit inside the Masjidul Haram, it would be where people already had their hands already occupied. Rasulullah ﷺ therefore left with the camel to the channel where water drained and it was there that the camel was made to sit. Sitting on his camel, Rasulullah ﷺ then started to address the people. After duly praising Allah, he said, "O people! Allah has eliminated the things you took pride in during the period of ignorance and the pride you took in your forefathers. There are now only 2 types of people. One is the righteous person with Taqwa who is honored in the sight of Allah and the other is the sinful wretch who is insignificant in Allah's sight. Allah says:

يَا أَيُّهَا النَّاسُ إِنَّا خَلَقْنَاكُمْ مِنْ ذَكَرٍ وَأُنْثَى وَجَعَلْنَاكُمْ شُعُوبًا وَقَبَائِلَ لِتَعَارَفُوا إِنَّ أَكْرَمَكُمْ عِنْدَ اللَّهِ أَتْقَاكُمْ إِنَّ اللَّهَ عَلِيمٌ خَبِيرٌ (13)

O mankind! We have created you from a male and a female, and made you into nations and tribes, that you may know one another. Verily, the most honorable of you with Allah is that (believer) who has At-Taqwa (i.e. one of the Muttaqun - pious). Verily, Allah is All-Knowing, All-Aware. (Al-Hujurat:13)

Rasulullah ﷺ then concluded by saying, "That is all I have to say for now. I seek Allah's forgiveness for myself and for you all." *(Ibn Abi Hatim, Abd bin Humaid in Tafsir Ibn Kathir)*

The Sermons Rasulullah ﷺ delivered for the Month of Ramadhan: The Epic Sermon Rasulullah ﷺ delivered upon the Arrival of Ramadhan, as narrated by Salman ؓ

Salman ؓ reports that on the last day of Sha'ban, Rasulullah ﷺ addressed the Sahabah saying, "O people! A great and blessed month is dawning upon you. It is a month that includes a day that is better than 1,000 months. Allah has made fasting compulsory in this month and standing in Tarawih salah an act of tremendous merit. Whoever carries out an act of virtue (Nafl) during this month will receive the reward of carrying out a Fardh during any other month and whoever carries out a Fardh act during this month will receive the reward of carrying out 70 Fardh acts during any other month. It is a month of patience and the reward for patience is Jannah. It is also a month of sympathy and a month when the sustenance of a Mu'min is increased. Whoever provides something for a fasting person to terminate his fast shall receive the reward of the fasting without his reward being diminished in the least." "O Rasulullah ﷺ!" the Sahabah '" submitted, "Not all of us can afford something to give a fasting person to terminate his fast." Rasulullah ﷺ consoled them saying, "Allah shall grant this reward to any person who gives a fasting person even a single date or a sip of water or milk to drink. It is a month that has mercy at the beginning, forgiveness in the middle and emancipation from Jahannam at the end. For the person who makes work light for his slaves during this month, Allah will forgive him and free him from Jahannam. In this month, you should endeavor to do 4 things in abundance. 2 of these will please your Rabb while you cannot do without the other 2. The 2 that will please your Rabb are to recite the Shahadah 'La Ilaha IllAllah' and to seek Allah's forgiveness. As for the 2 without which you cannot do, it is to beg Allah for Jannah and to seek protection from Jahannam. Whoever gives the fasting person something to drink to end the fast, Allah shall give him such a drink from my pond after which he shall never be thirsty ever again." *(Ibn Khuzaimah in Targheeb wat Tarheeb, Bayhaqi, Ibn Hibban, Ibn Najjar in Kanzul Ummal)*

The Lecture Rasulullah ﷺ gave Stating that the Sins of Muslims are Forgiven on the First Night of Ramadhan

Anas ﷺ reports that when Ramadhan drew close, Rasulullah ﷺ addressed them briefly at the time of Maghrib. Rasulullah ﷺ said, "Ramadhan is arriving, so welcome it. Take note that on the first night of Ramadhan there is not a soul from the people of the Qibla who is not forgiven." *(Ibn Najjar in Kanzul Ummal)*

The Lecture Rasulullah ﷺ gave Stating that the Saiatin are Chained and that Du'as are Accepted During Ramadhan

Ali ﷺ reports that on the first night of Ramadhan, Rasulullah ﷺ stood up to address the Sahabah. After duly praising Allah, he said, "Allah has seen to your enemy from the Jinn and promised to accept your Du'as. Allah says: ادْعُونِي أَسْتَجِبْ لَكُمْ

...Invoke Me, (i.e. believe in My Oneness (Islamic Monotheism)) (and ask Me for anything) I will respond to your (invocation)... (Ghafir:60)

Allah has appointed 7 angels to guard every rebellious Saitan and Saitan is therefore unable to escape until the end of Ramadhan. Take note also that the doors of the heavens are wide open from the first night of Ramadhan until the end and all Du'as in this month are accepted." Ali ﷺ says further, "When the first of the last 10 nights of Ramadhan arrived, Rasulullah ﷺ would tighten his loincloth, leave his wives, sit in I'tikaf and spend all night in Ibadah." Someone asked Ali ﷺ what he meant by tightening the loincloth, he said that Rasulullah ﷺ would separate from his wives during that period. *(Isfahani in Kanzul Ummal)*

The Lecture Rasulullah ﷺ gave on the Importance of Jumu'ah Salah

Jabir ﷺ reports that once Rasulullah ﷺ addressed them saying, "O people! Repent to Allah before you die and hasten to do good deeds before you become too busy. Join the ties between you and your Rabb by engaging in abundant Dhikr and by giving Sadaqa in abundance. You will then be given sustenance, assistance and you will be compensated for your losses. Take note that Allah has made the Jumu'ah salah compulsory for you

in this place, on this day, in this month and in this year until the Day of Judgment. Whoever regards it as trivial and rejects it and therefore neglects it during my lifetime or after my death in the presence of a just or unjust Imam, then may Allah not set his affairs in order and may Allah not bless him in anything. No salah, zakah, Hajj, fast or good deed of his will ever be accepted until he repents and Allah will certainly forgive anyone who repents to Him. Take note that no woman may lead a man in salah, no Bedouin may lead a Muhajir and no sinner may lead a righteous person unless forced to do so by a tyrannical ruler whose sword to lash is feared." *(Ibn Majah, Tabrani in Targheeb wat Tarheeb)*. Jabir bin Abdullah ﷺ narrates that it was on a Friday that Rasulullah stood up and addressed them saying, "When a person lives a mile away from Madinah and does not attend the Jumu'ah salah, Allah will seal his heart so that no good can ever enter." On the next Friday, Rasulullah ﷺ said, "When a person lives 2 miles away from Madinah and does not attend the Jumu'ah salah, Allah will seal his heart." On the Friday after that, Rasulullah ﷺ said, "When a person lives 3 miles away from Madinah and does not attend the Jumu'ah salah, Allah will seal his heart." *(Abu Ya'la in Targheeb wat Tarheeb)*

The Lectures Rasulullah ﷺ Delivered on the Occasion of Hajj

Abdullah bin Abbas ﷺ narrates that on the occasion of the farewell Hajj, Rasulullah ﷺ addressed the Sahabah saying, "Saitan has lost hope in being worshipped in your land but he is satisfied with having you obey him in other sins that you regard as trivial. O people, you should always be on your guard. I have left with you 2 things with which you will never go astray as long as you hold fast to them. They are Allah's Book and the Sunnah of your Nabi ﷺ. Every Muslim is the brother of another Muslim and all Muslims are brothers. The wealth of a Muslim is not permissible for another unless he willingly gives it to him. Never oppress others and never become Kuffar after my death by striking the necks of each other by killing each other." *(Hakim)*. Abdullah bin Abbas ﷺ narrates that it was in Masjidul Khaif in Mina that Rasulullah ﷺ addressed them. After praising Allah as he deserves to be praised, Rasulullah ﷺ said, "Allah will set right the affairs of the person whose prime concern is the Hereafter, Allah win also grant him self-sufficiency and the world will humble itself before him. As for the person, whose prime concern is this world, Allah will scatter his affairs, place poverty in front of him and all he will get of this world will be what has been predestined for him." *(Tabrani, Abu Bakr Khaffaf, Ibn Najjar in Kanzul Ummal)*. Abdullah bin Omar ﷺ narrates that it was in Masjidul Khaif in Mina that Rasulullah ﷺ addressed them saying, 'May Allah always keep fresh the person who after hearing my words, narrates it to his brother. There are 3 things that the heart of a Muslim will never betray; sincerely carrying out good deeds for Allah, wishing well for the Muslim leadership and remaining within the ranks of the Muslim majority because their Du'as will always be there for all of them." *(Ibn Najjar in Kanzul Ummal)*

In a lengthy Hadith describing the method in which Rasulullah ﷺ performed Hajj, Jabir ﷺ reports that after he had passed Muzdalifa to reach Arafat, Rasulullah ﷺ found that a tent had already been pitched for him at Namira. It was there that Rasulullah ﷺ then camped. When the sun had crossed the meridian, Rasulullah ﷺ had a carriage placed on Qaswa and then went to Bat Wadi where he addressed the people saying, "Verily your blood and your wealth are scared to all of you just as this day is sacred, as this month is sacred and as this city is sacred. Take note that everything that took place during the period of ignorance is now trampled beneath my 2 feet. All blood money due during the period of ignorance is also waived and the first that I wish to waive is that of the son of Rabe'ah bin Harith whom the Hudhail tribe killed while he was still a suckling infant with the Banu Sa'd tribe. All the interest due during the period of ignorance is also waived and the first that I wish to waive is that which was due to Abbas bin Abdul Muttalib. Every bit of it has now been written off. Fear Allah with regard to your women because it is by a license from Allah that you have taken them in your marriage and it is with His words that you have made cohabitation with them lawful for yourselves. They owe it to you not to allow anyone you disapprove of to enter your home. If they do this, you should punish them in a manner that does not injure them in any way. On the other hand, you owe it to them to provide food and attire for them within reason. I am leaving with you something with which you will never go astray if you hold fast to it - the Book of Allah. You will also be questioned about me on the Day of Judgment. What response will you offer?" The Sahabah replied, "We shall testify that you have conveyed the message, given excellent advice and fulfilled your responsibility." Pointing his index finger towards the sky and lowering it towards the people, Rasulullah ﷺ thrice repeated, "O Allah! You be Witness! O Allah! You be Witness!" *(Muslim in Al Bidayah wan Nihayah, Abu Dawud, Ibn Majah in Kanzul Ummal).* Abdullah bin Abbas ﷺ narrates that it was on the day of Nahr (10th of Dhul Hijjah) that Rasulullah ﷺ delivered a sermon to the people. "O people!" Rasulullah ﷺ asked, "What day is this?" "It is a sacred day," the Sahabah replied. Rasulullah ﷺ asked further, "And what city is this?" "This is a sacred city," the Sahabah responded. When Rasulullah ﷺ further asked them what month it was, they replied that the month was also a sacred one. Rasulullah ﷺ then emphasized, "Verily, your blood, your wealth and your honor are as sacred to you as this day, this city and this month." After repeating this several times, Rasulullah ﷺ looked to the sky and said, "O Allah! Have I conveyed the message? O Allah! Have I conveyed the message?" Abdullah bin Abbas ﷺ says, "I swear by the Being Who controls my life that an emphatic piece of advice that Rasulullah ﷺ gave to the Ummah was that he said, 'Those of you present here should convey the message to those who are not present and you should never become Kuffar after my death by striking the necks of each other by killing each other." *(Bukhari in Al Bidayah wan Nihayah, Ahmad, Ibn Abi Shaybah, Ibn Majah, Tabrani, Baghawi in Kanzul Ummal)*

Jareer ﷺ narrates that after asking him to keep the people quiet on the occasion of the Farewell Hajj, Rasulullah ﷺ addressed them saying, "After I have been keeping watch over you, never become Kuffar after my death by striking the necks of each other by killing each other." *(Ahmad in Al Bidayah wan Nihayah).* Ummul Husain ﷺ reports that when she performed the farewell Hajj with Rasulullah ﷺ she saw Usama ﷺ and Bilal ﷺ with Rasulullah ﷺ. One of them was holding the reins of his camel while the other was holding his shawl aloft to shade Rasulullah ﷺ from the sun until he had pelted the last Jamarah. Rasulullah ﷺ then said many things, amongst which Ummul Husain ﷺ heard him say, "Even if an Abyssinian slave with amputated limbs has to become your ruler, you should listen to and obey him if he leads you by the Book of Allah." *(Muslim in Al Bidayah wan Nihayah, Nasa'ee in Kanzul Ummal, Ibn Sa'd).* Abu Umamah ﷺ narrates that on the occasion of the Farewell Hajj, he heard Rasulullah ﷺ say the following in his sermon: "Allah has granted every rightful person his right. Therefore, no bequest can be made for an heir, a child will belong to the biological father and the adulterer will be stoned. Their reckoning will nevertheless be Allah's prerogative. The curse of Allah perpetuating until the Day of Judgment shall fall on the person who claims to be the child of anyone other than his father and on the slave who claims to be the property of anyone other than his master. A woman my also not spend from the house without the permission of her husband." Someone asked, "O Rasulullah ﷺ! Can she not even give food away without his permission?" Rasulullah ﷺ replied, "Certainly not because food is the best of our wealth." Rasulullah ﷺ then continued to say, "Items given on loan must be returned, animals lent to give milk must also be returned, debts must be paid and the guarantor must settle the penalty." *(Ahmad, Tirmidhi, Abu Dawud, Nasa'ee, Ibn Majah).* The lecture was delivered in Mina on the day of Nahr (10th of Dhul Hijjah). *(Abu Dawud).* Abu Umamah ﷺ also reports that Rasulullah ﷺ was on a camel called Jad'a with his feet in the stirrups and standing high so that people could hear him. Rasulullah ﷺ then said at the top of his voice, "Can you not hear?" "O Rasulullah ﷺ!" someone from the gathering asked, "What is it that you wish to advise us?" Rasulullah ﷺ said, "Worship your Rabb, perform your five Fardh salats, fast for your month of Ramadhan, obey your leader and you will enter the Jannah of your Rabb." *(Ahmad, Tirmidhi in Al Bidayah wan Nihayah).* Abdur Rahman bin Mu'adh Taymi ﷺ relates, "We were at Mina when Rasulullah ﷺ addressed us. We listened attentively and could therefore hear him clearly even though we were in our camps. Rasulullah ﷺ started teaching the people the rites of Hajj. When Rasulullah ﷺ reached the Jamarat, he placed both fingers in his ears and announced that only small pebbles be used to pelt. Thereafter, he instructed the Muhajirin to camp at the front of the Khaif Masjid and the Ansar to camp at the rear. The rest of the people then set up their own camps." *(Abu Dawud, Ibn Sa'd, Ahmad, Nasa'ee).* Rafi bin Amr Muzani ﷺ said that at Mina during midmorning when he saw Rasulullah ﷺ deliver a sermon on a brown mule. Ali ﷺ was amplifying what Rasulullah ﷺ said and some people were standing, others were sitting. *(Abu Dawud in Al Bidayah wan Nihayah)*

Abu Hurra Raqashi reports from his uncle ﷺ who was holding the reins of Rasulullah ﷺ's camel during the middle days of the days of Tashriq. As he was busy warding the people away from Rasulullah ﷺ, Rasulullah ﷺ was addressing the people saying, "O people! Do you know in which month you are? Do you know in which day you are? Do you know in which city you are?" The Sahabah replied, "We are in a sacred day, a sacred month and a sacred city." Rasulullah ﷺ then said, "Now remember that until the day you meet Allah, your blood, your wealth and your honor are as sacred to you as the sacredness of this day in this month and in this city." Rasulullah ﷺ said further, "Listen attentively to what I say and you will live well. Behold! Never oppress! Behold! Never oppress! Behold! Never oppress! The wealth of a Muslim is not permissible without his consent. Take note that all blood money, other monies and prejudices that took place during the period of ignorance are now trampled beneath my 2 feet until the Day of Judgment. The first blood money that I wish to waive is that of the son of Rabe'ah bin Harith whom the Hudhail tribe killed while he was still a suckling infant with the Banu Laith tribe, also take note that all the interest due during the period of ignorance is also waived and the first that I wish to waive is that which was due to Abbas bin Abdul Muttalib. Creditors have back only the amounts they lent and no interest. Do not oppress and you will not be oppressed. Take note of the fact that time has revolved to return to the way it had been when Allah created the heavens and the earth."

Rasulullah ﷺ then recited the verse:

إِنَّ عِدَّةَ الشُّهُورِ عِنْدَ اللَّهِ اثْنَا عَشَرَ شَهْرًا فِي كِتَابِ اللَّهِ يَوْمَ خَلَقَ السَّمَاوَاتِ وَالْأَرْضَ مِنْهَا أَرْبَعَةٌ حُرُمٌ ذَلِكَ الدِّينُ الْقَيِّمُ فَلَا تَظْلِمُوا فِيهِنَّ أَنْفُسَكُمْ

Verily, the number of months with Allah is twelve months (in a year), so was it ordained by Allah on the Day when He created the heavens and the earth; of them four are Sacred, (i.e. the 1st, the 7th, the 11th and the 12th months of the Islamic calendar). That is the right religion, so wrong not yourselves therein...(At-Tauba:36)

Rasulullah ﷺ continued, "Listen! Never become Kuffar after my death by striking the necks of each other. 'Remember that Saitan has given up hope of being worshipped by people performing salah, but he does his best to cause disputes between you. You should also fear Allah with regard to your wives because they are like captives with you with no powers of authority. You owe any rights to them just as they owe rights to you. The rights they owe you are that they should not allow anyone else to sleep in your bed and they should not allow into your house anyone whom you disapprove of. If you fear that they are being rebellious, you should advise them, then if they do not respond you should separate your beds and if this is also fruitless then you may punish them without causing them any injury. The right you owe them is that you provide their food and clothing within reason. It is by a license from Allah that you have taken them in your marriage and it is with His words that you have made cohabitation with them lawful for yourselves. Also bear in mind that the person who has something kept in trust with him should return it to the one who has trusted him with it." Rasulullah ﷺ then spread out his hands and said, "Have I conveyed the message? Have I conveyed the message? Those present here should convey the message to those who are absent because it is a fact that many recipients of a message are more fortunate to understand the message than the one who has heard it." Humaid reports that when this narration reached Hasan, he remarked, "By Allah! The Sahabah have conveyed the message to people who have been extremely fortunate to have received the Deen." *(Ahmad, Baghawi, Bawardi, Ibn Mardway in Kanzul Ummal).* Abdullah bin Omar ؓ reports a narration similar to the one above but with an addition at the beginning. It states that Rasulullah ﷺ was at Mina during the middle days of the days of Tashriq while performing the farewell Hajj when Allah revealed the Surah:...... *(Surah Nasr).* Realizing that this would indeed be his farewell to the people, Rasulullah ﷺ had a carriage saddled to his camel Qaswa, mounted it and then stood waiting for the people at Aqaba. When a considerable number of Muslims had gathered, Rasulullah ﷺ duly praised Allah and then said, "O people! All blood monies due during the period of ignorance have been waived..." The narration then continues as above, until Rasulullah ﷺ said, "...O people! Saitan has given up hope of being worshipped in is region until the end of time, but he is satisfied with you committing sins that you think nothing of. You should therefore guard your Deen against such seemingly trivial sins." The narration also adds that Rasulullah ﷺ said, "I am leaving with you something with which you will never go tray if you hold fast to it. It is the Book of Allah, so practice on it" The narration ends with the words, 'Those resent here should convey the message to those who are absent because there shall be no Nabi after me and no Ummah after you." Rasulullah then raised his hands saying, "O Allah! You be Witness!" *(Bazzar in Al Bidayah wan Nihayah).* Jabir bin Abdullah ؓ narrates that it was during the days of Tashriq that Rasulullah ﷺ delivered his farewell sermon to the Sahabah saying, "O people! Verily your

Rabb is One and your father is one. Take note that the Arab is not superior to the non-Arab just as the non-Arab is not superior to the Arab. Whites are not superior to blacks and blacks are not superior to whites unless it (the superiority) is by virtue of Taqwa. This is because the most honored in the sight of Allah is the one with the most Taqwa regardless of his nationality or color. Have I conveyed the message?" "You have indeed, O Rasulullah ﷺ!" the Sahabah replied. Rasulullah ﷺ then added, 'Those present here should then convey the message to those who are absent." *(Bayhaqi in Targheeb wat Tarheeb).* Abdullah bin Mas'ood ؓ reports that Rasulullah ﷺ was standing on the carriage of a camel with cut ears in Arafat when he addressed the people saying, "Do you know in which month you are? Do you know in which day you are? Do you know in which city you are?" The Sahabah replied, "We are in a sacred day, a sacred month, and a sacred city." Rasulullah ﷺ then said, "Now remember that your blood, your wealth and your honor are as sacred to you as the sacredness of this day in this month and in this city. Remember that I shall be going ahead of you to the pond and will boast about your numbers to the other nations. Please do not blacken my face, do not embarrass me by doing evil. Listen well! While I shall be rescuing many people from Jahannam, many of them will be taken away from me. 'O my Rabb!' I will say, 'But they are my Ummah.' Allah will reply by saying, 'You do not know what innovations they had introduced to the Deen after your demise." *(Bayhaqi in Kanzul Ummal)*

Rasulullah ﷺ's Lecture about Dajjal, Musaylama, Ya'jooj and Ma'jooj and sinkings: Rasulullah ﷺ's Lecture About Dajjal as Reported by Abdullah bin Omar ؓ

Abdullah bin Omar ؓ says, "We were discussing during the farewell Hajj whether it was really to be Rasulullah ﷺ's farewell or not. It was during this farewell Hajj that Rasulullah ﷺ delivered a sermon in which he deliberated at length about Masih Dajjal. He also said, 'There was not a single Nabi who did not warn his Ummah about Dajjal. Nuh and all the Ambiya after him warned about Dajjal but there is still something about him that you do not know, which you ought to know. It is the (Dajjal is one-eyed) your Rabb is not one-eyed." *(Ahmad, Haythami)*

Rasulullah ﷺ's Lecture About Dajjal as Reported by Safina ؓ

Safina ؓ narrates that Rasulullah ﷺ delivered a sermon to them in which he said, "There has not been a single Nabi before me who has not warned his Ummah about Dajjal. He has no left eye and a large growth from the comer of his right eye covers its iris. The word "......" Kafir will be written between his eyes and with him will be two valleys. While one valley will appear to be Jannah, the other will appear to be Jahannam whereas in reality the Jannah will be Jahannam and the Jahannam will be Jannah. He will also have 2 angels with him who will resemble two of the Ambiya عليهم السلام. One of them will be on his right and the other on his left. This will be a great test for the people. Dajjal will ask them, 'Am I not your Rabb who gives life and death?' 'You are lying,' one of them will say. However, no one will be able to hear this besides the other angel, who will confirm the words of the first angel saying, 'You are right.' This statement will however be heard by all the people, who will naturally assume that the angels are confirming the words of Dajjal. This will also be a great test. He will then travel to Madinah, but will not be allowed entry there. 'This,' he will say, 'is the city of that man (Rasulullah ﷺ).' From there, he will leave for Sham where Allah will destroy him at a place called Afiq." *(Ahmad, Tabrani, Haythami)*

Rasulullah ﷺ's Third Lecture About Dajjal

Junada bin Abu Umayya Azdi narrates that he went with a companion to one of the Sahabah and asked "Tell us a Hadith that you heard from Rasulullah ﷺ about Dajjal." The Sahabi said, "Rasulullah ﷺ once delivered a sermon saying, 'I am warning you about Dajjal! I am warning you about Dajjal! I am warning you about Dajjal! There is not a Nabi who did not warn his Ummah about Dajjal and, O Ummah, he is certainly amongst you. He has curly hair, is brown in complexion and his left eye is wiped out. He will have with him a Jannah, a Jahannam, a mountain of bread, and a river of water. He will be able to make it rain, he will be unable to make a tree grow and while he will have the power to kill one soul, he will not have the power over any others. He will stay on earth for 40 days, during which he will reach every place of water. He will however be unable to approach 4 Masajid; the Masjidul Haram, the Masjid of Madinah, the Masjid of Tur and Masjidul Aqsa. You should never be in doubt about Dajjal thinking him to be Allah because your Rabb is not one-eyed." *(Ahmad, Haythami)*

Rasulullah ﷺ's Lecture on Dajjal as Narrated by Abu Umamah ﷺ

Abu Umamah Bahili ﷺ reports that Rasulullah ﷺ once delivered a lengthy sermon, most of which concerned Dajjal. Rasulullah ﷺ spoke about him until the end of the sermon. Amongst the things he mentioned was, "Verily Allah has not sent a single Nabi who did not warn his Ummah about Dajjal. Since I am the last Nabi and you are the last Ummah, there is not doubt that he will emerge amongst you. If he emerges while I am with you, I shall be the advocate of every Muslim against him. However, if he emerges after my demise, then every person will have to be own advocate. Still, Allah shall be my successor over every Muslim. He will emerge from the road between Iraq and Sham and cause widespread anarchy to his right and to his left. You need to be steadfast, O servants of Allah because he will begin by claiming that he is a prophet and that no prophets will come after him. He will then advance his claim by saying, 'I am your Rabb.' However, you will not be seeing your Rabb before death. The word "....." Kafir will be written between his eyes, which every Mu'min will be able to read. Whoever of you meets him should spit on his face and recite the opening verses of Surah Kahaf. He will even be given the ability to kill one person and then bring him back to life. He will however be unable to do more than this or given this power over anyone else. Another test he will present will be that he will have a Jannah and a Jahannam, The Jahannam will however be Jannat while the Jahannam will actually be the Jannah. Whoever is tested with his Jahannam should close his eyes and ask for Allah's help. It will then become cool and comfortable for him just as the fire became cool and comfortable for Ibrahim. Another of his tests will be when he will pass by a tribe that will believe him and have faith in him. He will then make Du'a for them, as a result of which rain will fall the same day, vegetation will sprout the same day and on that very day, their animals will return in the evening in larger numbers than they had been and fatter. Their bellies would be bigger and their udders will be fuller. Thereafter, he will pass by another tribe that will reject him and refuse to believe him. He will in turn curse them, because of which all their animals will die and not a single animal will return to them. His days on earth will be 40, the first of which will be like a year, the next like a month, another like a week another like other days and the last of his days will be like a mirage when a man will be at the gate of a city in the morning and evening will arrive before he can even reach the other gate." "O Rasulullah ﷺ!" the Sahabah asked, "How will we perform salah during those short days?" Rasulullah ﷺ replied, "You will have to estimate and perform salah according to your estimation based on longer days." *(Hakim by Dhahabi)*

Rasulullah ﷺ's Lecture Stating how Dajjal will be Prevented from Entering Makkah and Madinah

Jabir ﷺ narrates that Rasulullah ﷺ stood on the pulpit and said, "O people! I have not gathered you for some news coming from the heavens..." He then discuss the incident of the spy for Dajjal. Rasulullah ﷺ then said, "He is Masih Dajjal for whom the earth will be folded in 40 days and he will travel everywhere) except for Tayba. Tayba is Madinah, which will have an angel at every entrance with a drawn sword to prevent his entry. The same will be the case for Makkah." *(Abu Ya'la, Haythami)*

The Sermon Rasulullah ﷺ delivered on the Eclipse and Dajjal

Tha'laba bin Abbad Abdi from Basra reports that he was once present for a lecture that Samura bin Jundub ﷺ delivered. Samura ﷺ narrated a Hadith from Rasulullah ﷺ and also narrated the Hadith of the solar eclipse. He said that it was when Rasulullah ﷺ was sitting after the second Rakah of the salah for an eclipse that the eclipse ended. Rasulullah ﷺ then made Salam to end the salah, praised Allah and testified to his being Allah's servant and messenger. Thereafter, Rasulullah ﷺ said, "O people! In the name of Allah do I ask you to tell me if I have been negligent in conveying any part of the messages that my Rabb sent me with." Several Sahabah then stood up and said, "We testify that you have certainly conveyed the messages of your Rabb, that you have been well-wisher for your Ummah and have fulfilled your responsibility." Rasulullah ﷺ then continued. He said, "Some people think that the eclipse of the sun and the moon and the changing of the rising positions of the stars occur because of the death of a great man on earth. They are wrong. These occurrences are signs that Allah shows His servants to test which of them are the ones who will be stirred by this to repent from kufr and sin. By Allah! For as long as I have been standing here performing salah, I have seen everything that is going to happen to you in this world and in the Hereafter. By Allah! Judgment will not arrive until 30 liars emerge, the last of them being the one-eyed Dajjal whose left eye will appear to be wiped out, like the eye of Abu Tahya." Abu Tahya was an old man of the Ansar who at that time was sitting between Rasulullah ﷺ and the room of Aisha ﷺ. Rasulullah ﷺ continued, "When Dajjal emerges, he will claim to be Allah. Whoever believes him and follows him will receive no benefit from any good deed he has ever done previously. On the other hand, whoever refuses to believe him and rejects his claim will never be punished for any sin he had done previously. He will soon make his appearance in every land except for the Haram and Baytul Maqdas. He will barricade the Mu'minin inside Baytul Maqdas, after which a catastrophic earthquake will take place. Thereafter, Allah will destroy him. Eventually a time will arrive as the Muslims and Kuffar do battle when even the foundation of walls and the roots of trees will call to the Muslims saying, 'Here is a Jew. Kill him!' or 'Here is a Kafir. Come and kill him!' This will however not take place until you see occurrences that will strike you with so much terror that you will ask each other, 'Has your Nabi ﷺ spoken anything about this'? It will also not take place until some mountains move from their places. Thereafter, everything shall perish when Judgment arrives." Tha'laba says, "Afterwards, I again heard Samura ﷺ narrate the same Hadith in another sermon without misplacing even a single word." *(Ahmad)*. Another narration states that

Rasulullah ﷺ said, "Whoever holds fast to Allah and says, 'Allah is my Rabb Who is Ever Living and will never die', he will suffer no punishment. On the other hand, the one who tells Dajjal 'You are my Rabb' will be punished." *(Bazzar, Haythami)*

The Lecture Rasulullah ﷺ delivered Concerning Musailama Kadhab

Abu Bakra ؓ says, "People had been saying a lot about Musailama before Rasulullah ﷺ made a statement about him. Rasulullah ﷺ stood up to deliver a lecture saying, "Regarding this man that you people have been speaking so much about, he is one of the 30 great liars who will appear before Judgment. There shall not be a single town that will not be swept up in the awe of Masih Dajjal." *(Ahmad, Tabrani, Haythami)* Another states that Rasulullah ﷺ added, "...except for the city of Madinah that will have 2 angels at each of its entrances who will be repelling this awe from the city." *(Hakim)*

The Lecture Rasulullah ﷺ delivered about the Ya'juj and Ma'juj and the Sinking of the Earth

Khalid bin Abdullah bin Harmala reports from his aunt that Rasulullah ﷺ once delivered a lecture when he had a bandage tied around his head because of a scorpion's bite. Rasulullah ﷺ said, "While you people say that no enemy is left, you will continue fighting enemies until the Ya'juj and Ma'juj emerge. They will have broad faces, tiny eyes and reddish hair and they will come scampering down every hill. In fact, their faces will appear to look like shields covered with hide." *(Ahmad, Tabrani, Haythami)*. Baqira ؓ who was the wife of Qa'qa ؓ says, "I was sitting in the rows of the women when I heard Rasulullah ﷺ deliver a lecture. Pointing with his left hand, Rasulullah ﷺ said, 'O people! When you hear of the earth sinking in that direction (west), then Judgment has arrived." *(Ahmad, Tabrani, Haythami)*

Rasulullah ﷺ's Lecture Condemning Backbiting

Bara ؓ narrates that Rasulullah ﷺ delivered a lecture in such a high pitch that even the young ladies sitting in seclusion in the inner rooms of their homes could hear him. Rasulullah ﷺ said, "O assembly of those who have accepted Iman with their tongues without it entering their hearts! Never backbite about the Muslims and never search for their faults because Allah will search for the faults of the person who searches for the faults of his brother. Remember that when Allah searches for the faults of a person, he will be humiliated while sitting in the inner recesses of his home." *(Abu Ya'la, Haythami)*. Rasulullah ﷺ added, "Never harm the Mu'minin, and never search their faults as Allah will expose the faults of the person who searches for the faults of his brother." *(Tabrani, Haythami, Bayhaqi in Kanzul Ummal)*

The Lecture Rasulullah ﷺ delivered about Enjoining Good and Forbidding Evil

Aisha ؓ said, "Rasulullah ﷺ came to my room one day and I could see from his face that something had happened. He proceeded to make wudhu and without speaking to anyone, he went to the Masjid. I pressed my ear to the wall to hear what he had to say. After sitting on the pulpit and praising Allah, Rasulullah ﷺ said, 'O people! Allah says, 'Enjoin good and forbid evil before the time arrives when you pray to Me and I will not respond; you will ask from Me and I will not grant you and you will ask Me for assistance and I will not assist you." Rasulullah ﷺ then descended from the pulpit without saying anything else." *(Ibn Majah, Ibn Hibban in Targheeb wat Tarheeb, Ahmad, Bazzar in Majma'uz Zawa'id)*

Rasulullah ﷺ's Lecture Warning Against Bad Character

Abdullah bin Omar ؓ reports that Rasulullah ﷺ once delivered a lecture to them saying, "Stay away from oppression because oppression will assume the form of compounded darkness on the Day of Judgment. You must avoid lewdness, lewd behavior and especially greed because those before you were destroyed on account of this very greed. It was when this greed instructed them to sever family ties that they did it, when it instructed them to be miserly, they did it and when it instructed them to commit sin, they did that as well." A person then stood up and asked, "O Rasulullah ﷺ! Which act of Islam is the best?" Rasulullah replied, "That Muslims remain safe from your tongue and your hand." The same man or another then asked, "And which Hijrah (migration) is best?" Rasulullah ﷺ replied, "To migrate from (to forsake) that which your Rabb dislikes. There are 2 types of Hijrah; the Hijrah of the city-dweller and the Hijrah of the country-dweller. Hijrah of the country-dweller is that while still living in the countryside, he should "respond to the call for Jihad when called and obey when he is given a command. The Hijrah of the city-dweller is a greater test and more rewarding because he has to forsake his hometown." *(Hakim, Abu Dawud, Tabrani in Targheeb wat Tarheeb)* Yet another narration states that Rasulullah ﷺ added, "Avoid misappropriating trusts because it is the worst of confidantes."

Rasulullah ﷺ's Lecture Condemning Major Sins

Ayman bin Khuraim ؓ reports that Rasulullah ﷺ once delivered a lecture saying, "O people! False testimony has been equated to ascribing partners to Allah." After repeating this thrice, Rasulullah ﷺ recited the verse:

$$فَاجْتَنِبُوا الرِّجْسَ مِنَ الْأَوْثَانِ وَاجْتَنِبُوا قَوْلَ الزُّورِ (30)$$

So shun the abomination (worshipping) of idol, and shun lying speech (false statements)...(Al-Hajj:30) (Ahmad, Tirmidhi, Baghawi, Abu Nu'aym in Kanzul Ummal)

Anas bin Malik ؓ narrates that when delivering a sermon one day, Rasulullah ﷺ spoke about interest and emphasizing its evil, he said, "A Dirham that a person receives through interest is more sinful in Allah's sight than committing adultery 36 times as a Muslim. The worst of all interest is dishonoring a Muslim." *(Ibn Abi Dunya in Targheeb wat Tarheeb)*. Abu Musa Ash'ari ؓ reports that in his lecture to the Sahabah one day, Rasulullah ﷺ said, "O people! Refrain from Shirk because it is more subtle than the crawling of an ant." "O Rasulullah ﷺ" someone then asked, "How can we refrain from Shirk when it is more subtle than the crawling of an ant?" Rasulullah ﷺ replied, 'Say, 'O Allah! I seek Your protection from knowingly committing Shim and we seek Your forgiveness from that which we do without knowing." *(Ibn Abi Shaybah in Kanzul Ummal)*

Rasulullah ﷺ's Lecture Concerning Gratitude

Nu'man bin Bashir ؓ reports that it was while standing on the pulpit that Rasulullah ﷺ said, "Whoever is ungrateful for a little will be ungrateful for a lot and whoever does not express gratitude to people will not express gratitude to Allah. Speaking about Allah's bounties denote gratitude while not doing so is tantamount to ingratitude. Unity is a mercy while disunity is a punishment." Abu Umama Bahili then remarked, 'Stick to the larger group who follow the ways of Rasulullah ﷺ and the Sahabah." When someone asked him what the larger group was, he replied, "Do you not recite the verse of Surah Noor that states:

$$فَإِنْ تَوَلَّوْا فَإِنَّمَا عَلَيْهِ مَا حُمِّلَ وَعَلَيْكُمْ مَا حُمِّلْتُمْ$$

...if you turn away, he (Messenger Muhammad SAW) is only

responsible for the duty placed on him (i.e. to convey Allah's Message) and you for that placed on you... (An-Nur:54) (Abdullah bin Ahmad, Bazzar, Tabrani, Haythami)

Abu Dhar ؓ reports that he heard Rasulullah ﷺ recite the following in his sermon: اعْمَلُوا آلَ دَاوُودَ شُكْرًا وَقَلِيلٌ مِنْ عِبَادِيَ الشَّكُورُ (13)
...O family of Dawud (David), with thanks!" But few of My slaves are grateful. (Saba:13)

Rasulullah ﷺ then proceeded to say, "Whoever is given 3 things has been given what was given to Dawood ؑ; the ability to fear of Allah in private and in public, the ability to be just when angry and when not and the ability to spend moderately when poor and when wealthy." (Ibn Najjar in Kanzul Ummal)

Rasulullah ﷺ's Lecture Concerning the Goodness of life

Ali ؓ narrates that Rasulullah ﷺ once said in a lecture, "There is no good in life except for the one who listens and remembers and for the Alim who speaks the truth. O people! You are going through a period of truce. However, you are moving swiftly ahead. Do you not see night and day are making every new thing old, every distant thing near and bringing along everything that has been promised? You should therefore prepare to exert yourselves for the racecourse (plains of resurrection) that is still far off." Miqdad ؓ then asked, "O Nabi of Allah ﷺ! What is this period of truce?" Rasulullah ﷺ replied, "It is a period of test and separation. However, when matters become confusing to you like the phases of a dark night when everything seems alike, then you should hold fast to the Qur'an because it is an intercessor whose intercession is accepted and an advocate whose word is always taken. The Qur'an will lead to Jannah whoever places it ahead of him and it will push into Jahannam whoever puts it behind his back. The Qur'an is a guide to the best of ways, it is decisive without being insignificant and has both an inner dimension as well as an exterior dimension. The inner dimension is the commands of the Shari'ah and the exterior is the conviction. Its depth is immense, its wonders are countless and Ulema can never have enough of it. It is Allah's strong rope, it is the straight path and the unquestionable truth about which the Jinn could not help but exclaim: إِنَّا سَمِعْنَا قُرْآنًا عَجَبًا (1) يَهْدِي إِلَى الرُّشْدِ فَآمَنَّا بِهِ ...Verily! We have heard a wonderful Recital (this Qur'an)! It guides to the Right Path, and we have believed therein... (Al-Jinn:1-2). Whoever speaks by the Qur'an is true, whoever acts on it will be rewarded, whoever passes judgment by it is just and whoever practices its teachings will be guided to the right path. It contains lights of guidance, beacons of wisdom and guides towards the proof for all truths."(Askari in Kanzul Ummal)

Rasulullah ﷺ's Lecture Concerning Abstinence from the World

Husain bin Ali ؓ narrates that he once saw Rasulullah ﷺ stand up to deliver a lecture to the Sahabah. Rasulullah ﷺ said, "O people! By the way we lead our lives; it appears as if death has been ordained only for others and that it is only the duty of others to embrace the truth. It appears as if the deceased people we see off to their graves are merely going on a little journey from which they will soon return, yet we eat up their legacy as if we will live forever after them. We have forgotten every lesson and feel safe from every calamity. Glad tidings for the person whose own faults preoccupy him from searching for the faults of others and glad tidings for the person whose earnings are pure, whose private life is a righteous one, whose public life is good and who is steadfast on the path he treads. Glad tidings also for the person who humbles himself before Allah even though he does not suffer any deficiencies within himself, who spends from

what he earns without sinning, who associates with men of understanding and wisdom and who is compassionate towards downtrodden and poor people. Glad tidings for the one who spends in Sadaqah his excess wealth, holds back his excess talk and is comfortable with practicing the Sunnah without ever resorting to Bid'ah." Rasulullah then dismounted. (Abu Nu'aym in Hilya). In another similar narration (Ibn Asakir in Kanzul Ummal), Anas ؓ states that Rasulullah ﷺ was on his camel Adba and that he added, "We eat their legacy while their corpses are still in their houses.' This narration also adds that Rasulullah ﷺ said, "Glad tidings for the person who follows the Sunnah and never transgresses it to go towards any Bid'ah." Yet another narration (Bazzar, Haythami) adds that Rasulullah ﷺ said, "Glad tidings for the person who associates with men of understanding, avoids people with doubts and who practice Bid'ah. His public life is a righteous one and people are safe from his evil." Aisha ؓ narrates that Rasulullah ﷺ was on the pulpit and the Sahabah were sitting around him when he said, "O people! Be shy to do wrong in front of Allah as you ought to be shy." "O Rasulullah ﷺ!" someone asked, "Are we to be shy in front of Allah?" Rasulullah ﷺ replied, "Whoever amongst you is shy, should not pass a single night without his death before his eyes. He should protect his abdomen and whatever it contains (heart, stomach, liver, etc) and his head and whatever organs it is host to (eyes, ears, tongue, etc). He should remember death and decomposition and forsake the pleasures of this world." (Tabrani in Awsat, Tirmidhi, Targheeb wat Tarheeb)

Rasulullah ﷺ's Lecture Concerning Resurrection

Abdullah bin Abbas ؓ reports that he heard Rasulullah ﷺ deliver the following lecture from the pulpit: "You will meet your Rabb barefooted, naked, uncircumcised and on foot." Another narration states that Rasulullah ﷺ stood up amongst the Sahabah and said, "O people! You will not be barefooted, naked and uncircumcised when you are resurrected before Allah." Rasulullah ﷺ then recited the verse:

كَمَا بَدَأْنَا أَوَّلَ خَلْقٍ نُعِيدُهُ وَعْدًا عَلَيْنَا إِنَّا كُنَّا فَاعِلِينَ (104)
...as We began the first creation, We shall repeat it, (it is) a promise binding upon Us. Truly, We shall do it. (Al-Ambiya:104)

Rasulullah ﷺ then continued. He said, 'Verily the first of creation to be clothed will be Ibrahim ؑ. Thereafter, some men from my Ummah will be caught and taken to the left. 'O my Rabb!' I will plead, 'they are my companions.' Allah will then say, 'You have no idea what innovations they had introduced after you.' I will then say what one of Allah's pious servants (Isa ؑ) will say:

وَكُنْتُ عَلَيْهِمْ شَهِيدًا مَا دُمْتُ فِيهِمْ فَلَمَّا تَوَفَّيْتَنِي كُنْتَ أَنْتَ الرَّقِيبَ عَلَيْهِمْ وَأَنْتَ عَلَى كُلِّ شَيْءٍ شَهِيدٌ (117) إِنْ تُعَذِّبْهُمْ فَإِنَّهُمْ عِبَادُكَ وَإِنْ تَغْفِرْ لَهُمْ فَإِنَّكَ أَنْتَ الْعَزِيزُ الْحَكِيمُ (118)
...and I was a witness over them while I dwelt amongst them, but when You took me up, You were the Watcher over them, and You are a Witness to all things. (This is a great admonition and warning to the Christians of the whole world). "If You punish them, they are Your slaves, and if You forgive them, verily You, only You are the All-Mighty, the All-Wise." (Al-Ma'ida:117-118)

It will then be said to me, 'Verily they had turned on their heels and become Murtad as soon as you left them which was what happened to many Arab tribes.'" Another narration adds that Rasulullah ﷺ will then say, "Take them far away! Take them far away!" (Bukhari, Muslim in Targheeb wat Tarheeb)

Rasulullah ﷺ's Lecture Concerning Predestination

Ali ؓ reports that Rasulullah ﷺ once mounted the pulpit and after duly praising Allah, he said, "Allah has written a register with the names and lineages of all the people destined for Jannah. The register has already been totaled and no person will be added or deleted from it until the Day of Judgment. Allah has also written a register with the names and lineages of all the people destined for Jahannam. The register has already been totaled and no person will be added or deleted from it until the Day of Judgment. Regardless of what the person destined for Jannah does, his concluding actions will be those of the people of Jannah. Regardless of what the person destined for Jahannam does, his concluding actions will be those of the people of Jahannam. A fortunate person destined for Jannah can sometimes be treading the Path of the unfortunate ones destined for Jahannam so much so that it will be said, 'He seems to be one of those destined for Jahannam. Nay! It seems that he actually is one of them.' His good fortune then finds him and rescues him by placing him on the path to Jannah. An unfortunate person destined for Jahannam can also sometimes be treading the Path of the fortunate ones destined for Jannah so much so that it will be said, 'He seems to be one of them destined for Jannah. Nay! It seems that he actually is one of them.' However, his ill fortune then removes him from this path and places him on the path to Jahannam. Whoever has been registered as a fortunate person in the Lowhul Mahfudh will not be removed from this world until he carries out actions that qualify him for good fortune, even though he does such an act a split second before his death. Conversely, whoever has been registered as an unfortunate person in the Lowhul Mahfudh will not be removed from this world until carries out actions that qualify him for ill fortune, even though he does such an act a split second before his death. Actions are judged according to those done at the end." *(Tabrani in Awsat, Abu Sahl Jandisafuri in Kanzul Ummal, Haythami)*

Rasulullah ﷺ's Lecture about the Benefit of Being Related to Him

Abu Sa'eed Khudri ؓ reports Rasulullah ﷺ said from the pulpit, "What is the matter with some people who say that being related to me will be of no benefit on the Day of Judgment? By Allah! My relatives are attached to me in this world as well as in the Hereafter. O people! I shall go to the pond of Kowthar ahead of you on the Day of Judgment where some people will call for me and tell me their names and father's names. I will say to them, 'Although I know your lineage to be part of my own, but you people had introduced innovations after I left the world and turned back on your heels from the true Deen." *(Ibn Najjar in Kanzul Ummal, Ahmad in Tafsir Ibn Kathir)*

Rasulullah ﷺ's Lecture Concerning Leaders and Rulers

Abu Sa'eed Khudri ؓ narrates that Rasulullah ﷺ mentioned the following in one of his lectures: "Take note that I shall soon be called to Allah and will have to respond. Such leaders will then assume authority over you who will do things that you are familiar with and well acquainted with. Obeying them will be true obedience. You will live with this status quo for some time until some other leaders take control after them. These leaders will do things that you will not be familiar with. Those who will lead them in wrong and will be their advisors in doing wrong will be destroyed and will destroy others as well. While you may associate with them physically but you must disassociate from their evil activities. You must also testify to the good of those who do good and to the evil of the wrong-doers." *(Tabrani, Haythami)*. Abu Humaid Sa'idi ؓ narrates that Rasulullah ﷺ once appointed someone as collector of zakah and when he returned after completing his collection, he said, "O Rasulullah ﷺ! This is for you and this is what has been given to me as a gift." Rasulullah ﷺ said to him, "Why do you rather not sit in your father's or mother's home and see whether or not you are given any gifts?" That night after salah, Rasulullah ﷺ stood up to deliver a lecture. After reciting the Shahada and duly praising Allah, he said, "What is the matter with some collectors whom we appoint and who then return to say, 'This amount is from the collection and this amount is what has been gifted to me.' Why does he rather not sit in his father's or mother's home and see whether or not he is given any gifts? I swear by the Being Who controls my life that when any of you embezzles any wealth, he will arrive carrying it on his neck on the Day of Judgment. If it was a camel that he took, he will bring it bellowing, if it was a cow, he will bring it mooing and if it were a goat, he will bring it bleating. I have now conveyed the message." Abu Humaid ؓ says, "Rasulullah ﷺ then lifted his so high that we could see the whites of his armpits. Zaid bin Thabit ؓ heard the lecture with me, so you may ask him." *(Bukhari, Muslim, Abu Dawud, Ahmad in Jami'us Saghir)*

Rasulullah ﷺ's Lecture about the Ansar

Abu Qatadah ؓ reports that he heard Rasulullah ﷺ say the following about the Ansar from the pulpit: "Listen well! While all other people are like my outer garments, the Ansar are like my inner garments. If everyone walked down one valley and the Ansar walked down another, I would follow the Ansar down their valley. Had it not been for the virtue of Hijrah, I would have wanted to be one of them. Whoever assumes authority over the Ansar should be good towards the righteous ones amongst them and overlook the sinful ones amongst them. Whoever sets the Ansar will have upset that which is between these two sides." Rasulullah ﷺ then pointed towards himself. *(Ahmad, Haythami)*. Ka'b bin Malik ؓ who was one of the 3 men whose repentance was accepted (who missed Tabuk expedition), was informed by one of the Sahabah that Rasulullah ﷺ once came out of his room with a bandage tied around his head. He then delivered a lecture saying, "O assembly of Muhajirin! Whereas your numbers will continue to increase as more people make Hijra, the population of the Ansar will not increase any more than they are today. The Ansar are my personal trunk with whom I have taken shelter. You should therefore honor the honorable ones amongst them and overlook the sinful ones." *(Ahmad, Haythami)*

Miscellaneous Lectures of Rasulullah ﷺ

Abu Bakr ؓ reports that Rasulullah ﷺ was on the wooden pulpit when he said, "Save yourselves from Jahannam even if it be with a piece of a date that you give in Sadaqa because Sadaqa straightens crookedness, repels a bad death and benefits a hungry person just as much as it does a person with a full stomach." *(Abu Ya'la, Bazzar in Targheeb wat Tarheeb)*. Amir bin Rabe'ah reports from his father ؓ that he heard Rasulullah ﷺ say the following in his sermon, "For as long as a person continues sending salutations to me, the angels continue making Du'a for his forgiveness." *(Ahmad, Ibn Abi Shaybah, Ibn Majah in Targheeb wat Tarheeb)*. Abdullah bin Amr ؓ narrates that Rasulullah ﷺ once delivered a lecture to them saying, "Whoever wishes to be saved from Jahannam and to be allowed entry into Jannah should meet his death at a time when he has Iman in Allah and in the Last Day and should deal with people in a manner that he likes them to deal with him." *(Ibn Jareer in Kanzul Ummal)*. Anas ؓ relates, "Rasulullah ﷺ once delivered a lecture the like of which I have never heard before. He said, 'If you people knew what I know, you would laugh less and cry more.' The Sahabah then covered their heads as they out weeping." Another narration states that when Rasulullah ﷺ heard thing about some of the Sahabah, he delivered a lecture saying, "Jannah and Jahannam have been shown to me and I have never seen such bliss and such terror to this day. If you people knew what I know, you would laugh less cry more." There was not a day weightier on the Sahabah than that day and they all covered their heads as they burst out weeping. *(Bukhari, Muslim in Targheeb wat Tarheeb).* Abu Sa'eed Khudri ؓ reports that Rasulullah ﷺ was delivering a lecture when he recited the verse:

إِنَّهُ مَنْ يَأْتِ رَبَّهُ مُجْرِمًا فَإِنَّ لَهُ جَهَنَّمَ لَا يَمُوتُ فِيهَا وَلَا يَحْيَا (74)

Verily! Whoever comes to his Lord as a Mujrim (criminal, polytheist, disbeliever in the Oneness of Allah and His Messengers, sinner, etc.), then surely, for him is Hell, therein he will neither die nor live. (TaHa:74)

Rasulullah ﷺ then said, "Those who deserve to be there forever shall neither die in Jahannam nor shall they live a life worth living. As for those who do not deserve to be there forever, Jahannam will burn them for awhile, after which intercessors will intercede on their behalf. They will then be grouped and taken to bathe in a river called *Hayat or Hayawan* where they will flourish just as grass flourishes in the silt that floodwater carries." *(Ibn Abi Hatim in Tafsir Ibn Kathir).* Abu Hurairah ؓ narrates that Rasulullah ﷺ once delivered a lecture saying, "O people! Entertain good thoughts about the Rabb of the universe because Allah treats his servants according to their expectations of Him." *(Ibn Abi Dunya, Ibn Najjar in Kanzul Ummal).* Abu Zuhair Thaqafi ؓ narrates that he heard Rasulullah ﷺ say in a lecture, "O people! Soon you will be able to distinguish the people of Jannah from the people of Jahannam or the good from the bad." "O Rasulullah ﷺ!" someone asked, "How will we be able to do that?" Rasulullah ﷺ replied, "By your praise and your criticism (of the person after his death) because you are witnesses to the behavior each other." *(Hakim by Dhahabi).* Tha'laba ؓ reports that Rasulullah ﷺ once stood up to deliver a lecture in which he instructed the payment of Sadaqatul Fitr. He detailed that it should be a San of dates or a Saa of barley for every person, whether a minor, an adult, a free person or a slave. *(Hasan bin Sufian, Abu Nu'aym in Kanzul Ummal)*

Rasulullah ﷺ's Comprehensive Lecture at Tabuk

Uqba bin Amir Juhani ؓ reports that when they left with Rasulullah ﷺ for Tabuk, they were a day away from their destination when Rasulullah ﷺ and the Sahabah fell asleep one night and did not get up until the sun had already raised the length of a spear above the horizon. "O Bilal!" Rasulullah ﷺ said, "Did I not tell you to check for us when dawn arrives and then awaken us for Fajr?" Bilal ؓ submitted, "O Rasulullah ﷺ! The same sleep that whisked you away whisked me away as well." Rasulullah ﷺ moved a little distance away and then led the Qadha salah. Thereafter, he duly praised Allah before saying, "Indeed the most truthful speech is Allah's Book and the most secure handhold is the Kalimah of Taqwa. The best of creeds is the creed of Ibrahim ؑ, the best of ways is the Sunnah of Muhammad ﷺ, the most honorable dialogue is the Dhikr of Allah and the best narrative is this Qur'an. The best of matters are the most resolute ones, while the worst of them are the fabricated ones. The best guidance is the guidance of the Ambiya ؑ, the best death is that of the martyrs and the blindest of blindness is to go astray after receiving guidance. The best knowledge is that

which is beneficial, the best directive is that which is followed and the worst blindness is the blindness of the heart. The upper (giving) hand is better than the lower (receiving) hand and that wealth which is sufficient though little is better than that which is plenty, but which makes the owner negligent of Allah. The worst time to ask to be excused is at the time of death and the worst regret will be on the Day of Judgment. There are some people who perform their salats only after its time and there are others who make Dhikr while totally detached from the consciousness of Allah. The worst sin is the lying tongue, the best wealth is contentment of heart and the best of provisions is Taqwa. The fountainhead of wisdom is fear for Allah and the best thing to have its roots in the heart is conviction. Being doubtful stems from Kufr, wailing on the occasion of death is an act from the period of ignorance, stealing from the booty is from the mounds of Jahannam and hoarded wealth shall be hot branding irons. Poetry is the flutes of Iblis, wine is the root of all sin, women are the traps of Saitan and youth is a branch of insanity.

The worst of all forms of earning are earnings from interest and the worst of things to consume is the wealth of orphans. The fortunate person is he who takes a lesson from what happens to others and the unfortunate person is he who was unfortunate from the time he was in the belly of his mother. Each one of you shall be ending up in a place measuring four arm's lengths, a matters is evaluated by the way it ends and actions are judged by those that take place at the end of a person's life. The worst of narrations are those that are lies and everything that is pending is really close by. Verbally abusing a Mu'min is a grave sin, killing a Mu'min is equal to kufr, eating his flesh (backbiting about him) is to insolently disobey Allah and his wealth is as sacred as his blood. The person who falsely swears in Allah's name, Allah will make him a liar. Allah will forgive those who forgive, will overlook the faults of those who overlook the faults of others and will reward the one who swallows anger. Allah will compensate the person who exercises patience when afflicted with a calamity and for the person who seeks fame for his good deeds, Allah will announce it to the people on the Day of Judgment, making them aware of his selfish intentions. Allah will multiply the rewards of those who persevere in fulfilling Allah's commands and punish those who disobey them. O Allah forgive me and my Ummah. O Allah forgive me and my Ummah. O Allah forgive me and my Ummah. I seek Allah's pardon for myself and for all of you." *(Bayhaqi in Dala'if, Ibn Asakir in Tarikh, Abu Nasr Sajzi in Kitabul Ibanah, Ibn Abi Shaybah, Abu Nu'aym in Hilya, Qudha'i in Shihab, Askari, Daylami in Suyuti's Jami'us Sagheer, Manawi in Faidhul Qadeer, Hakim in Zadul Ma'ad)*

Another Comprehensive Lecture from Rasulullah ﷺ

Ayadh bin Himar Mujashi'e ؓ narrates that Rasulullah ﷺ said, "From the knowledge I have today, my Rabb has instructed me to educate you about that which you have no knowledge. Allah says, 'All the wealth I have given My servants is lawful and I have created all my servants as people with the inherent inclination to follow the true Deen without swerving. However, the Saiatin have approached them, deviated them from their Deen, made unlawful for them what I have made lawful and instructed them to ascribe partners to Me when I have given no justification for it.'" Rasulullah ﷺ continued, "Before I was sent as a Rasul, Allah looked at all the people on earth and became angry with the Arabs and non-Arabs alike because they had all resorted to Shirk, except for a few remaining members of the Ahlul Kitab who had remained steadfast on their Deen without altering any part of it. Allah said to me, 'I am sending you to test you and to test others by you see whether they will accept your message. I shall also a reveal a scripture to you that water will not be able to wash off and which you will be able to recite in your sleep and when awake.' Allah then commanded me to set the Quraish alight by igniting the call to Islam amongst them. 'O my Rabb!' I said, 'They will then trample my head and make it a piece of bread to be consumed.' Allah however said, 'I shall remove them from Makkah just as they removed you. Fight them and We shall fight by your side, spend on them and We will spend on you, dispatch an army against them and We will dispatch an army of angels 5 times larger. Use those who obey you to fight those who disobey you.'" Rasulullah ﷺ continued to say, 'The people of Jannah are of 3 categories; (1) the just ruler whom Allah inspires to do good and who spends in Sadaqa, (2) the soft hearted person who is compassionate towards every relative and every Muslim and (3) the chaste and poor person with a family who still donates in Sadaqa. The people of Jahannam fall into 5 categories; (1) the weakling who has no intelligence and who follows blindly, (2) those who (in the pursuit of illicit activities) do not ever seek a family or wealth, (3) the traitor whose greed cannot be concealed and who will endeavor to betray no matter how slight the chance, (4) the person who cannot pass a single day or night without deceiving a person with regard to his family and wealth." (5) When describing the 5th type of person, Rasulullah ﷺ mentioned the traits of miserliness, lying, bad character and rudeness. *(Ahmad in Tafsir Ibn Kathir)*

A Comprehensive Lecture of Rasulullah ﷺ as Narrated by Abu Sa'eed Khudri ؓ

Abu Sa'eed Khudri ؓ narrates, "It was after he had led the Asr salah that Rasulullah ﷺ stood up to deliver a lecture. There is nothing to occur until the Day of Judgment that he did not inform us about. Whoever remembered what he said remembers it and whoever forgot it, forgot it. Amongst the things he mentioned was: 'This world is lush and sweet. Allah has appointed you as His deputies in the world and is watching how you conduct yourselves. You should be wary of the world and of women because the first trial of the Bani Isra'el that they failed involved women. Remember that the children of Adam علیه السلام are of different categories. There are those who are born as Mu'minin, live as Mu'minin and die as Mu'minin. Then there are those who are born Kuffar, live as Kuffar and die as Kuffar. There are also those who are born as Mu'minin, live as Mu'minin but then die as Kuffar. Another group is those who are born as Kuffar, live as Kuffar but then die as Mu'minin. Take note! Anger is a coal that ignites in the belly of a man. Do you not see the redness in the eyes of an angry person and the swelling of his veins? When any of you experiences this, he must take to the ground. He must take to the ground (sit or lie down). Remember that the best of people is he who is slow to anger and quick to please and the worst of people is he who is quick to anger and slow to please. As for those whose temper takes time to flare but also long to abate and those whose anger flare quickly and also abate quickly, these 2 are alike because each has one good and one bad quality. Remember also that the best trader is he who is considerate in settling debts as well as in claiming them while the worst of traders is he who is inconsiderate when settling and when claiming debts. As for the one who is considerate when settling but inconsiderate when claiming and the one who is considerate when claiming but inconsiderate when settling, they are both on par with an evil quality and a good quality each. Take note that every traitor will have a flag (denoting his treachery) on the Day of Judgment which will be proportionate to the degree of his treachery. Remember that the worst of treachery is when a ruler betrays his subjects. Listen well! Fear for the people must never stop a person from speaking the truth when he knows it because the best of Jihad is speaking the truth in front of a tyrant. Remember also that all that is left of this world in comparison to what has already passed is like what is left of this day compared to what has already passed of it." *(Ahmad, Tirmidhi, Hakim, Bayhaqi in Jami'us Saghir, Manawi)*

A Comprehensive Lecture of Rasulullah ﷺ as Narrated by Omar ؓ

Sa'ib bin Mahjan was from Sham and had met many Sahabah. He reports that when Omar ؓ arrived in Sham, he in his address to the people praised Allah, advised the people, reminded them of their responsibilities, enjoined good and forbade evil. He then said, "Rasulullah ﷺ once delivered a lecture to us just as I am doing here before you. After instructing us to adopt Taqwa, to maintain family ties and to reconcile our differences, he said, 'You must remain united by listening to your leaders and obeying them because Allah's help is with the united mainstream. Saitan is with the loner and stays far from a pair. A man must never be in seclusion with a non-Mahram woman because Saitan is then the third person. A sign of a Muslim with Iman is that he is dismayed by his sins and pleased by his good deeds while the sign of a hypocrite is that he is not dismayed by his sins and not pleased by his good deeds. When he carries out a good deed, he does not hope for reward from Allah and when he commits a sin, he does not fear Allah's punishment far it. Be moderate in seeking your livelihood because Allah has assumed responsibility for your sustenance. Every person will complete every action he is destined to carry out, so seek Allah's assistance in your actions because He removes and retains whatever event of destiny He pleases and the 'Mother of all Books' (the Lowhul Mahfudh) is with Him.'" Omar ؓ then concluded his lecture by saying,' "May Allah shower His special mercy on our Nabi Muhammad ﷺ and on his family. May peace and Allah's mercy be on him. Peace be to you all." *(Ibn Mardway, Bayhaqi in Shu'abul Iman, Ibn Asakir in Kanzul Ummal)*

Rasulullah ﷺ's Final Sermon

Mu'awiya bin Abu Sufian ؓ reports that during his final illness, Rasulullah ﷺ instructed the Sahabah saying, "Pour over me 7 water bags of waters drawn from several wells so that I may go to the people and advise them." Consequently, with a bandage tied his head, Rasulullah ﷺ managed to leave his room and mounted the pulpit. After duly praising Allah, Rasulullah ﷺ said, "A servant from amongst Allah's servants has been asked to choose between this world and what is with Allah and he has chosen that which is with Allah." None of the Sahabah besides Abu Bakr ؓ understood this statement. He therefore burst out crying and said, "May our parents and our children be sacrificed for you O Rasulullah ﷺ!" Rasulullah ﷺ consoled him saying, "Take it easy. The best all my companions and the one who assisted me the most the son of Abu Quhafa (Abu Bakr ؓ). All these doors leading to the Masjid must be closed except for the door of Abu Bakr because I see celestial light emerging from it." *(Tabrani in Awsat, Kabeer, Majma'uz Zawa'id)*. Ayub bin Bashir ؓ narrates that during his illness, Rasulullah ﷺ requested for water to be poured over him. The narration then proceeds like the one above, but adds that the first thing Rasulullah ﷺ mentioned after praising Allah was the martyrs of the Battle of Uhud. Rasulullah ﷺ sought Allah's forgiveness for them and made Du'a for them. Thereafter, he said, "O assembly of Muhajirin!

Whereas your numbers will continue to increase as more people make Hijra, the population of the Ansar will not increase any more than they are today. The Ansar are my personal trunk with whom I have taken shelter. You should therefore honor the honorable ones amongst them and overlook the sinful ones. O people! A servant from amongst Allah's servants has been asked to choose between this world and what is with Allah and he has chosen that which is with Allah." Form all the Sahabah, it was only Abu Bakr ◈ who understood this statement and therefore burst out crying. *(Bayhaqi in Al Bidayah wan Nihayah)*

Abu Sa'eed Khudri ◈ narrates, "Rasulullah ◈ delivered a lecture saying, 'Allah has asked a servant from amongst His servants to choose between this world and what is with Allah and he has chosen that which is with Allah." When Abu Bakr ◈ burst out crying, we all wondered why he should be weeping over some servant of Allah that Rasulullah ◈ was speaking about. What the rest of us did not understand was that the servant given this choice was none other than Rasulullah ◈ and Abu Bakr ◈ knew this well. Rasulullah ◈ then said, "The person who did me the most favors through his friendship and wealth is Abu Bakr. If I were to choose a bosom friend other than my Rabb, I would have chosen Abu Bakr ◈. He is nonetheless my close companion in Islam and in the love for Islam. Every door leading to the Masjid must be sealed except for the door of Abu Bakr ◈." *(Ahmad, Bukhari, Muslim in Al Bidayah wan Nihayah)*. Abdullah bin Abbas ◈ narrates that during the illness with which he passed away, Rasulullah ◈ came out of his room with his head wrapped in an oily bandage. With a shawl draped over his shoulders, Rasulullah ◈ sat on the pulpit. The narration then recounts the sermon quoted above together with the advice Rasulullah gave about the Ansar. The narration concludes to state that this was the final sermon that Rasulullah ◈ ever delivered. *(Bukhari in Al Bidayah wan Nihayah, Ibn Sa'd)*. Ka'b bin Malik ◈ who was one of the 3 men whose repentance was accepted who missed Tabuk expedition relates that Rasulullah ◈ once came out of his room and after duly praising Allah and seeking forgiveness on behalf of the martyrs of the Battle of Uhud, he said, "O assembly of Muhajirin! Whereas your numbers will continue to increase as more people make Hijra, the population of the Ansar will not increase any more than they are today. The Ansar are my personal trunk with whom I have taken shelter. You should therefore honor the honorable ones amongst them and overlook the sinful ones." *(Tabrani, Haythami)*. This was the last sermon that Rasulullah ◈ ever delivered. *(Tabrani, Haythami, Hakim by Dhahabi)*. Abu Salmah bin Abdur Rahman narrates that he heard from both Abu Hurairah ◈ and Abdullah bin Abbas ◈ that the last sermon they heard Rasulullah ◈ deliver was when he said, "Verily the person 'Who guards these 5 Fardh salats in congregation will be the first to pass over the Bridge of Sirat like a flash of lightning. Allah shall also resurrect him amongst the first group of those who followed the Deen. In addition to this, for every day and night that he guarded his salats, he will have the reward of 1,000 martyrs killed in the Path of Allah." *(Tabrani in Awsat, Haythami)*

The Lecture Rasulullah ◈ delivered from Fajr Until Maghrib

Abu Zaid Ansari ◈ relates, "Rasulullah ◈ led us in the Fajr salah and then delivered a lecture to us until Zuhr. He then dismounted the pulpit and led the Zuhr salah. Thereafter, he delivered a lecture until Asr, after which he again dismounted to lead the Asr salah. He then mounted the pulpit again and delivered a lecture until Maghrib. In these lectures, Rasulullah ◈ related to us everything that was still to happen. Those of us who

remembered the most of these lectures are therefore the most knowledgeable." *(Hakim by Dhahabi)*

Rasulullah ◈'s Condition at the Time of Delivering a Lecture

Jabir ◈ reports that when Rasulullah ◈ delivered a lecture, his eyes would redden, his voice would get louder and when necessary his anger would be intense as if he were warning an army that the enemy was attacking them that morning or evening. He would then hold up his index and middle finger and say, "My coming and Judgment are like these 2 as close as they are." Rasulullah ◈ would then also add, "The best guidance is that of Muhammad ◈, the worst of matters are those that have been fabricated and every Bid'ah is a means of misguidance. The wealth a person leaves behind after his death shall be for his family and the debts and little children he leaves behind shall be mine and will be my responsibility." *(Ibn Sa'd, Bayhaqi in Asma was Sifat, Muslim)*

The Lectures that Rasulullah ◈'s Successor Abu Bakr Siddiq ◈ delivered When he Assumed the Office of Khilafa

Urwa ◈ reports that when Abu Bakr ◈ assumed the office of Khilafa, he delivered a lecture to the people. After duly praising Allah, he said, "O people! I have been placed in charge of your affairs whereas I am not best amongst you. The Qur'an has already been revealed and Nabi ◈ has already chalked out his ways. He taught us that the best of intelligence is Taqwa and that the most foolish of all foolishness is to sin. The powerful amongst you are weak in my sight until I am able to reclaim rights he owes (to the weak ones he oppressed) and the weakest is powerful in my sight until I can restore his right taken by the powerful ones. O people! I am a follower and not one to fabricate new practices in Deen. Do assist me when I do right and straighten me when I stray. This much I have to say and I seek Allah's pardon for myself and for you." *(Ibn Sa'd, Mahamili in Kanzul Ummal)*. Abdullah bin Ukaim ◈ narrates that when the Muslims pledged allegiance to Abu Bakr ◈, he ascended the pulpit and, sitting a step beneath the step where Rasulullah ◈ usually sat, he praised Allah and said, "O people! You should know that the best of intelligence..." The Hadith continues like the one above, with the following addition at the end: "Take stock of yourselves before your reckoning takes place on the Day of Judgment. Whenever a nation forsakes Jihad in the Path of Allah, Allah smites them with poverty and whenever immorality prevails in a nation, Allah afflicts them all with a common calamity. Obey me as long as I obey Allah and as soon as I disobey Allah and His Rasul ◈, you need not obey me any more. This much I have to say and I seek Allah's pardon for myself and for you." *(Deenowri in Kanzul Ummal)*. Hasan narrates a narration similar to the one above, but with the addition that Abu Bakr ◈ said, "The most foolish of all foolishness is sin. Take note that to me truthfulness is a great trust and lying is grave treachery." After Abu Bakr ◈'s statement "I am not the best amongst you", Hasan says, "By Allah! He was the best of them and none would have contested the fact. However, he made the statement because a true Mu'min always humbles himself." This narration also states that Abu Bakr ◈ added, "I wish that one of you would have relieved me of this responsibility." To this, Hasan comments, "By Allah! He truly meant this." Abu Bakr ◈ then said further, "If you people wish that I fill the position for which Allah used revelation to steer His Nabi ◈, then you should know that I do not enjoy that privilege. I am but an ordinary human being, so please do watch over me." *(Bayhaqi)*. Hasan also reports that Abu Bakr ◈ delivered a lecture saying, "By

Allah! I am not the best of you. I have always disliked this post and have always wished that one of you would relieve me of it. Do you think that I can practice the ways of Rasulullah ﷺ precisely as he did with you? This I am unable to do because Rasulullah ﷺ was safeguarded from doing wrong by revelation and while he had an angel with him, I have a Saitan who keeps coming to me. You should therefore stay away from me when I am angry so that I harm neither your hide nor your hair. Remember to keep watch over me. When I remain steadfast on Deen, then assist me but when I stray, then correct me." Hasan says, "By Allah! This was a sermon the like of which he never delivered again." (*Abu Dhar Harawi, Ibn Rahway in Kanzul Ummal*). Another narration states that Abu Bakr ؓ also added "I am but a human being who does right and makes mistakes as well. When I do right, I want you to praise Allah and when I err, I want you to correct me." (*Abu Dhar Hawari in Kanzul Ummal*)

Qais bin Abu Hazim reports that he was sitting with Rasulullah ﷺ's Khalifa Abu Bakr ؓ a month after Rasulullah ﷺ passed away... The narration continues until he says that the people were gathered with the call "As Salatu jami'ah", after which Abu Bakr ؓ mounted the pulpit, which was a little platform made for him to deliver lectures on. This was the first sermon that Abu Bakr ؓ delivered in Islam after becoming Khalifa. After praising Allah, he said, "O people! I had wished that someone else could relieve me of this post. If you people want to charge me with following the Sunnah of your Nabi ﷺ (to the fullest), you should know that I do not fully have the ability to do so because Rasulullah ﷺ was protected from Saitan and revelation from the heavens used to come to him." (*Ahmad, Haythami*). Already quoted earlier was the following lecture in which Abu Bakr ؓ said, "O people! There are people who entered into Islam willingly and those who entered unwillingly. However, they are now all in Allah's protection and His neighbors. Therefore, if it is possible that Allah does not find you guilty of wronging anyone in His protection, then make sure that you do so. I also have a Saitan with me so when you see me angry, stay away from me so that I may not harm even your hair or your skin. O people! Keep watch over the income of your slaves because flesh nourished with Haram cannot enter Jannah. Hear this well! Inspect me with your eyes and assist me when I do good. However should I deviate, then do correct me. Obey me as long as I obey Allah and disobey me if I disobey Allah. Asim bin Adi narrates that it was a day after Rasulullah ﷺ had passed away that Abu Bakr ؓ sent a caller to announce that the expedition of Usama ؓ must proceed. The announcement was, "Behold! Not a single member of Usama's army should remain behind in Madinah - without proceeding to the military rendezvous at Juruf." Abu Bakr then stood up amongst the people to deliver a lecture. After duly praising Allah, he said, "O people! I am a human just like you. I however do not know whether you would expect me to do what only Rasulullah ﷺ could do. Allah had selected Muhammad ﷺ from all in the universe and safeguarded him against all disasters. I am only a follower and not one to start anything new. Therefore, if I remain steadfast on Deen, you should follow me and if I stray, you must correct me. Rasulullah ﷺ was taken from this world without any member of the Ummah seeking redress for a lash given unjustly or anything even less than this. Remember that I have a Saitan that comes to me, so when he does, you should keep away from me so that I never harm your hide or hair. You pass through every morning and evening with a lifespan that is hidden from you. Therefore, if you can, you must spend every moment of this life doing good deeds. This you can of course not do without

Allah's help. You should compete with each other in doing good while your lifespan still allows you grace and before it brings all your deeds to an end one day. You must beware not to be like some people who had forgotten their deaths and did all their actions for others. Exert yourselves! Exert yourselves! Rush! Rush! Hasten to salvation! Hasten to salvation! Do this because behind you is a speedy hunter, which is very quick. Fear death and take lesson from the deaths of your forefathers, children and brothers. Never envy the living for anything other than that for which you would envy the dead." (*Tabari in Tarikh*). Sa'eed bin Abu Maryam says that he was informed that when Abu Bakr ؓ became the Khalifa, he mounted the pulpit. After duly praising Allah, he said, "By Allah! Had it not been for your affairs being ruined with us your midst, I would have preferred that this responsibility be placed around the neck of the person I detest the most so that he could have no peace. Remember that the most ill-fortuned people in this world and in the Hereafter are the kings." When the people looked up and started at him, Abu Bakr ؓ said, "Take it easy! You people are too hasty. A person never becomes king of as place before Allah knows the kingdom well and the person spends half his life. Fear and worry then take charge of him and he comes greedy for what the people have, while ignoring at he has with him. His life then becomes straightened even though he eats the best and wears the best. Eventually when his shadow dwindles and his life is taken, he reaches Allah's court. Allah will then take him to task most severely and is unlikely to forgive him. Remember that it is the poor ones who will be forgiven! Remember that it is the poor who will be forgiven! Remember that it is the poor ones who will be forgiven!" (*Ibn Zanjway in Kitabul Amwal, Kinzal Ummal*)

Abu Bakr ؓ's Lecture about Taqwa and Acting for the Hereafter

Abdullah bin Ukaim reports that Rasulullah ﷺ once delivered a lecture to them saying, "I emphatically advise you to adopt Taqwa, to praise Allah as He deserves to be praised, to combine both hope and fear of Allah and that you be persistent in begging from Allah. Allah has praised Zakariyya عليه السلام and his family when He says: إِنَّهُمْ كَانُوا يُسَارِعُونَ فِي الْخَيْرَاتِ وَيَدْعُونَنَا رَغَبًا وَرَهَبًا وَكَانُوا لَنَا خَاشِعِينَ (90) *Verily, they used to hasten on to do good deeds, and they used to call on Us with hope and fear, and used to humble themselves before Us.* (Al-Anbiya:90)

O servants of Allah, you must know that Allah has taken your souls as security against the rights you owe Him. He has also taken a pledge from you (to fulfill these rights) and has bought from you this temporary little world for what is eternal and much more. This Book of Allah that you have is such that its wonders will never cease and its light will never be extinguished. You must therefore believe its words, heed its advices and glean sight from it for the day of complete darkness. You have been created only for worshipping Allah. The honorable angel Kiraman Katibin have been appointed over you to record your actions and they are aware of the actions you do. O servants of Allah! You must also know that you spend every morning and evening within a fixed lifespan that you have no knowledge of. If you are able to be doing deeds that please Allah when your lifespan comes to an end, you must do so. You will however be unable to do this without Allah's help. Compete in good deeds while your lifespans allow you grace and before they terminate, causing you to return to the worst of your actions. There have been people who have sacrificed their lives for others and forgotten about themselves. I want to stop you from being like them. Rush! Rush! Hasten to salvation! Hasten to salvation! Do this because behind you is a speedy hunter, which is very quick." *(Abu Nu'aym in Hilya, Ibn Abi Shaybah, Hannad, Hakim, Bayhaqi, Ibn Abi Dunya in Qisarul Amal, Kanzul Ummal)*

Abu Bakr ☙ Talks About Taqwa and Taking Lessons from the Past

Amr bin Dinar reports that Abu Bakr ☙ once said the following in one of his lectures: "My advice to you in your conditions of poverty and hunger is to fear Allah, to praise Him as He deserves to be praised and to seek His pardon because He is most Forgiving." The rest of the narration is like the one above narrated by Abdullah bin Ukaim. The following addition has however been reported: "You ought to remember that by being sincere in everything you do, you will be obeying your Rabb as well as safeguarding what reward is yours. You must pay what is due from you during the days that you have been given to make your advance payment i.e. in this world and ensure that you also send Nawafil ahead of you to the Hereafter because you will then collect all the advance payments you had made at a time when you will be in dire need for it. O servants of Allah! You should also ponder about those who lived before you. Where were they yesterday and where they today? Where are the kings who had erected monuments on earth and had cities built? People have forgotten about them and their feats have also been forgotten. They are non-entities today and because of their injustice, their dwellings now lie in ruins after Allah had destroyed them while they lie in the darkness of the grave. Do you hear any of them or even a whimper from them? Where are all the friends and brothers that you knew? They have reached the actions they sent ahead and it is either good fortune or ill-fortune that has become their lot. Allah has no family ties with any creation because of which He would give them some good or avert any evil from them. This will happen purely due to obedience to Him and by carrying out His commands. There is no good in the good that is followed by entry into Jahannam and there is no difficulty in the difficulty that is followed by entry into Jannah. This much I have to say and I seek Allah's pardon for myself and for all of you." *(Abu Nu'aym in Hilya).* Nu'aym bin Namha narrates that a lecture of Abu Bakr ☙ included the following: "Do you not know that you spend mornings and evenings within the confines of your lifespans..." The narration then continues like the narration of Abdullah bin Ukaim, but with the addition: "There is no good in the speech that is not said with the intention of pleasing Allah, there is no good in the wealth that is not spent in the Path of Allah, there is no good in the person whose foolishness dominates his forbearance and there is no good in the person who fears the condemnation of a critic when carrying out a command of Allah. *(Abu Nu'aym in Hilya, Tabrani Tafsir ibn Kathir)*

The Narration of Tabari Concerning Abu Bakr ☙'s Lecture About Taqwa and About Taking Lessons From the Past

Asim bin Adi reports a lecture that Abu Bakr ☙ delivered. While the first part is like the one already narrated, this narration states that Abu Bakr ☙ stood up again and after praising Allah yet again, he said, "Verily Allah accepts only those actions done solely to please Him, so ensure that your intention for all your actions solely for Him. You must know that every act that you do sincerely for Allah represents an act of obedience, a sin that you have been saved from, an installment that you have paid towards the Hereafter and an advance payment that you send ahead from these transitory days to others that are eternal. It will therefore be there for the time when you will most in need of it. O servants of Allah! Take lessons from those who have died from amongst you and think about those who had lived before you. Where were

they yesterday and where are they today? Where are all the tyrants? Where are those who were famous in battle, in conquests and whenever wars raged? Time has humbled them, their bones have decayed and people have stopped talking about them. Remember that indecent women are for indecent men and indecent men are for indecent women. Where are the kings who had erected monuments on earth and had cities built? They are far away, have been forgotten about and are non-entities today. Listen well! While their passions have long been cut off and they have passed on, their sins will still remain theirs but their worldly possessions have gone to others. We have been left as their successors and we will be saved only if we take lesson from them. However, if we allow ourselves to be deceived, we will be just like them. Where are all the handsome and attractive people who were so enamored by their youth? They have become dust and now regret their overindulgence. Where are those who erected cities, fortified them with high walls and built spectacular wonders? They had left it all behind for their successors. So there are their dwellings standing in ruins while they arc in the darkness of their graves. Do you hear any of them or even a whimper from them? Where are all the children and brothers that you knew? Their prescribed terms caught up with them so they reached the actions they sent ahead to the Hereafter and have settled there. They now live after death in either a place of ill fortune or a place of good fortune. Listen well! Allah has no family ties with any creation because of which He would give them some good or avert any evil from them. This will happen purely due to obedience to Him and by carrying out His commands. Remember that you are servants who will be rewarded and whatever is with Allah can be attained only by being obedient to Him. There is no good in the good that is followed by entry into Jahannam and there is no difficulty in the difficulty that is followed by entry into Jannah." *(Tabari)*

A Comprehensive Lecture that Abu Bakr ☙ Delivered

Musa bin Ugba reports that when he delivered a lecture, Abu Bakr ☙ would say, "All praise belongs to Allah the Rabb of the universe. I praise Him, seek his assistance and ask Him for honor after death because my death and yours have drawn very close. I testify that there is none worthy of worship but the One and Only Allah and I testify that Muhammad ﷺ is the servant and Rasul of Allah. Allah sent him with the truth, as a giver of glad tidings, a warner and an illuminating lantern. Allah sent him to warn the living and so that the proof may be established against the Kuffar. Whoever obeys Allah and His Rasul ﷺ has been rightly guided and whoever disobeys them has strayed far off the path. I strongly advise you to adopt Taqwa and to hold fast to Allah's commands that He has ordained for you and to which He has directed you. The most comprehensive guidance of Islam after the Kalima of sincerity is to listen and obey the people whom Allah has appointed to take charge of your affairs (leaders). The person who obeys the leader who enjoins good and forbids evil shall be successful and has fulfilled his responsibility. I must also warn you against following your desires. Successful is the person who is saved from his whims, from greed and from anger. You must also stay away from pride, for what pride can one have when one is created from sand and shall be returning to sand where worms shall consume his body? What pride can he have when he is alive today and shall be dead tomorrow? Act from day to day and from hour to hour, save yourselves from the curse of the oppressed one and count yourselves amongst the dead. Persevere, because all actions are achieved through perseverance and be vigilant because vigilance is truly beneficial. Continue carrying out good deeds because such deeds are accepted, beware of the punishment that Allah has warned you about and hasten to the mercy that Allah has promised you. Make an effort to understand and Allah will make you understand, make an effort to stay away from wrong and Allah will save you from it. Allah has explained to you what it was that destroyed those before you and what it was that caused others to be rescued. Allah has also detailed what is Halal and what is Haram and which actions He likes and which ones He does not like. Remember that I shall never compromise on what ensures our and my welfare. It is Allah from Whom we seek assistance because there is no power or might except with Allah. Listen well! Whenever you do something sincerely for Allah, you are obeying Allah, safeguarding your share of rewards in the Hereafter and becoming the envy of others. The deeds you carry out apart from the Fara'idh, you will be sending ahead of you to the Hereafter as Nawafil and there you will receive back in full every advance payment you made and given your reward at a time when you will be most in need of it. O servants of Allah! You must also think about your friends and brothers who have passed on. They have reached the actions they sent ahead and there that they shall abide. After their deaths, they have now settled either in a place of good fortune or one of ill fortune. Allah has no partner and no family ties with any creation because of which He would give them some good or avert any evil from them. This will happen purely due to obedience to Him and by carrying out His commands. There is no good in the good that is followed by entry into Jahannam and there is no difficulty in the difficulty that is followed by entry into Jannah. This much I have to say and I seek Allah's pardon for myself and for all of you. Send salutations to your Nabi ﷺ. May peace be on him as well as Allah's mercy and blessings." *(Ibn Abi Dunya in Kitabul Hadhr, Ibn Asakir in Kanzul Ummal)*

Abu Bakr ؓ Lectured About the Condition in the Hereafter of the Person who was Ungrateful for the Bounties of Allah

Yazid bin Harun reports that Abu Bakr ؓ once delivered a lecture saying, "On the Day of Judgment a person will be brought forward upon whom Allah had showered His bounties. Allah had given him plenty of sustenance and a healthy body, yet he was ungrateful for these bounties and did not thank Allah by being obedient to Allah. He will be made to stand before Allah and asked, "What have you done for this day? What deeds have you sent ahead for yourself?" Finding that he had not carried out any good deed, he will weep so much that all his tears would be exhausted. He will then be taunted and humiliated so much for not obeying Allah that he will start to cry tears of blood. Thereafter, he will again be taunted and humiliated so much that he will start biting his nails and eventually eat his hands up to the elbows. Then too, he will be further taunted and humiliated so much for not obeying Allah that he will scream and cry so much that eyeballs will pop out and fall to his cheeks. Each eye will then be 3 miles long and 3 miles wide. Yet again will be taunted and humiliated so much that he will cry, my Rabb! Send me to Jahannam and relieve me of standing here.' It is about this that Allah says: أَنَّهُ مَنْ يُحَادِدِ اللَّهَ وَرَسُولَهُ فَأَنَّ لَهُ نَارَ جَهَنَّمَ خَالِدًا فِيهَا ذَلِكَ الْخِزْيُ الْعَظِيمُ

(63) *...whoever opposes and shows hostility to Allah and His Messenger (ﷺ), certainly for him will be the Fire of Hell to abide therein. That is extreme disgrace. (At-Tauba:63) (Abu Sheikh in Kanzul Ummal)*

Various Lectures that Abu Bakr ؓ Delivered

Muhammad bin Ibrahim bin Harith narrates that Abu Bakr ؓ once delivered a lecture to the people saying, "I swear by the Being Who controls my life that if you have Taqwa and do good deeds, it will not be long before the time arrives when you will eat bread and butter to your fill." *(Ibn Abi Dunya, Deenowri in Kanzul Ummal)*. Zubair ؓ narrates that Abu Bakr ؓ once delivered a lecture saying, "O people! Have shame before Allah. I swear by the Being Who controls my life that out of shame before my Rabb I always have a cloth covering my head whenever I go out to relieve myself." *(Abu Nu'aym in Hilya, Ibn Mubarak, Rustah, Ibn Abi Shaybah, Khara'iti in Kanzul Ummal)*. Ibn Shihab reports that during one of his sermons, Abu Bakr Siddiq ؓ said, "Have shame before Allah. I swear by Allah that out of shame before my Rabb, since the day I pledged allegiance to Rasulullah ﷺ, I have always had a cloth covering my head whenever I go out to relieve myself." *(Ibn Hibban in Rowdhatul Uqala, Kanzul Ummal)*. Abu Bakr ؓ once stood on the pulpit and started to weep, saying, "It was during the first year that Rasulullah ﷺ stood on the pulpit and started to weep. He then said, 'Ask Allah for forgiveness and well-being because well-being is the best thing that a person can be granted after conviction." *(Tirmidhi, Nasa'ee in Targheeb wat Tarheeb)*. Aws ؓ narrates that Abu Bakr ؓ once delivered a sermon saying, "It was during the first year that Rasulullah ﷺ stood where I am standing and said, 'Ask Allah for forgiveness and well-being because well-being is the best thing that a person can be granted after conviction. You must also ensure that you adhere to speaking the troth because it is coupled with righteousness and the two will lead to Jannah. You must also ensure that you refrain from lying because it is coupled with sinfulness and the two will lead to Jahannam. Never foster jealousy between you, never have hatred for each other, never sever family ties and never turn your backs to each other. O servants of Allah! You must rather be brothers as Allah has commanded you.'" *(Ahmad, Nasa'ee, Ibn Hibban, Hakim in Kanzul Ummal)*

Abu Bakr bin Muhammad bin Amr bin Hazm reports that Abu Bakr Siddiq ؓ once delivered a lecture to them saying, "Rasulullah ﷺ once told us to seek Allah's protection from hypocritical humility. When the Sahabah asked what insincere humility was, Rasulullah ﷺ explained that it occurred when the body appeared to be humble but there lurked hypocrisy in the heart." *(Hakim, Askari, Bayhaqi in Kanzul Ummal)*. Abul Aliya narrates that Abu Bakr ؓ once delivered a lecture to them saying, "Rasulullah ﷺ once said, "The traveler will perform 2 Rakahs salah while the resident will perform 4. While Makkah is my place of birth, Madinah is my place of migration. Therefore, when I leave for Makkah from Dhul Hulaifa, I shall perform 2 Rakahs salah until I return (to Madinah)." *(Abu Nu'aym in Hilya, Ibn Jareer in Kanzul Ummal)*. Abu Dhamra narrates that Abu Bakr ؓ praised Allah and then said, "You people will soon be conquering Sham. You will then arrive in a fertile land where you shall fill yourselves with bread and olive oil. Masajid will also be built for you there. You should therefore never let Allah know that you go to these Masajid only in vanity because they are built expressly for Allah's remembrance." *(Ahmad in Zuhd, Kanzul Ummal)*. Anas ؓ reports, "When Abu Bakr ؓ delivered lectures to us, he would mention how man is created. He would say, 'When he is born, man has to twice pass through the urinary passage.' He would make this point clear until each of us would regard himself as being impure thereby expelling pride from our hearts." *(Ibn Abi Shaybah in Kanzul Ummal)*. In the chapter discussing Jihad, the lectures of Abu Bakr ؓ have already passed in which he encourages the Muslims to fight the Murtaddin, to fight in Jihad and to march against the Romans. His lecture to the Muslims before they marched to Sham has also been reported there. His lectures have also been quoted in the chapter discussing the importance that the Sahabah gave to unity. Here, his lecture warning against conflict has been quoted, as well as his lecture confirming the demise of Rasulullah ﷺ and concerning holding fast to Deen. Also quoted is his lecture about Khilafa being for the Quraish, his lecture in which he excused himself from being the Khalifa, his lecture about refusing to pledge allegiance and his lecture about the qualities of a Khalifa. The chapter discussing enjoining good and forbidding evil also quotes his lecture that explains the meaning of the verse: لَا يَضُرُّكُم

مَن ضَلَّ إِذَا اهْتَدَيْتُم...*If you follow the right guidance and enjoin what is right (Islamic Monotheism and all that Islam orders one to do) and forbid what is wrong (polytheism, disbelief and all that Islam has forbidden) no hurt can come to you...* (Al-Ma'ida:105)

The Lectures of Amirul Mu'mineen Omar bin Khattab ؓ After Burying Abu Bakr ؓ

Humaid bin Hilal reports from someone who was present for the burial of Abu Bakr ؓ that after Omar ؓ had finished with the burial, he dusted off the sand from his hands. Standing where he was, he then delivered a lecture saying, "Allah is testing you with me and me with you by making me your leader and has kept me alive after my 2 companions: Rasulullah ﷺ and Abu Bakr ؓ. By Allah! It will never be that any of your matters are presented before me to be settled and is then done by anyone other than myself. It will also never happen that something happens in my absence and I am then negligent in settling it with integrity. When people behave well, I shall be good to them, but when they do evil, I shall punish them." The man reporting the narration says, "By Allah! This was exactly what Omar ؓ did until the day he departed from this world." *(Ibn Sa'd)*

His Lecture the Day he Became the Khalifa

Sha'bi narrates that when Omar ؓ became the Khalifa, he ascended the pulpit and said, "Allah should never see me considering myself worthy of sitting where Abu Bakr ؓ sat." He then climbed a step lower and .after duly praising Allah, he said, "Recite the Qur'an and you will be noted for it. Practice its teachings and you will be amongst its bearers. Weigh yourselves before you are weighed and beautify yourselves with good deeds for the great presentation on the day you will be presented before Allah and nothing of yours will be hidden from Him. Remember that no one has such a right over you that compel you to obey him while disobeying Allah. Take note that in respect of the wealth of Allah (public funds); I regard myself to be like the guardian of an orphan. I shall stay away from it if I have sufficient means and will use it within reason if I am ever in need of it." *(Deenowri in Kanzul Ummal, Fadha'ili in Riyadhun Nudhra)*. Omar ؓ said the following in his sermon: 'Take reckoning of yourselves before your reckoning is taken on the Day of Judgment, because the reckoning you take of yourself is easier. Weigh yourselves before you are weighed for the great presentation on the day you will be presented before Allah and nothing of yours will be hidden from Him."*(Ibn Mubarak, Sa'eed bin Mansur, Ahmad in Zuhd, Ibn Abi Shaybah in Kanzul Ummal)*

The Lecture Omar ؓ gave About How he Knew the Conditions of People and About other Matters

Abul Firas reports that Omar ؓ once delivered a lecture

saying, "O people! We knew you people well when Rasulullah ﷺ was in our midst because it was a time when revelation descended and Allah used to inform us about your condition. Take note however that Rasulullah ﷺ has left and revelation has ceased. Therefore, we now get to know you only in the manner we shall be stating to you: Whoever displays good behavior; we shall think good of him and love him for the good. On the other hand, whoever displays evil behavior; we shall think negatively of him and dislike him for his evil ways. Your secret affairs lie between you and your Rabb and only He can judge you by them. There was a time when I was certain that whoever recited the Qur'an did so to please Allah and to attain what (reward) is with Him. However, I have since come to realize that lately some people recite the Qur'an to attain that which is with the people. You must therefore aspire to please only Allah when reciting the Qur'an and when carrying out any good deeds. Take note also that I do not dispatch my governors to you to beat you or to take away your wealth. I am sending them only to educate you in your Deen and in the Sunnah practices. Whoever receives treatment other than this, should take the matter up with me and I swear by the Being Who controls my life that reparation shall be done. You must never hit Muslims because this will humiliate them and never prevent them from returning home after their shifts in guarding the state borders because this will cast them into difficulty. You should not deny them their rights because this would lead them to show ingratitude. Do not make them set up camp in a dense forest because this would lead to their destruction when they fall prey to the enemy taking advantage of the cover." *(Ahmad, Ibn Sa'd, Musaddad, Ibn Khuzaima, Hakim, Bayhaqi in Kanzul Ummal, Haythami, Hakim by Dhahabi)*

Omar ؓ Delivers a lecture Preventing People from Making Dowries Expensive and From Openly Stating who is a Martyr

Ibnul Ajfa reports that Omar ؓ once said the following in his lecture: "Take note that you should not inflate the dowries of your women because had this been an act of honor in this world and an act of Taqwa in Allah's sight, Nabi ﷺ would have been most entitled to it. However, Rasulullah ﷺ never gave any of his wives a dowry of more 12 Awqiya and did not receive more than this as dowry for any of his daughters either. What is happening is that some of you inflate the dowry so much that the husband when unable to pay fosters hatred for her in his heart, saying, 'It is because of you that I have been burdened with water-bag hung around my neck.' Another aspect I wish to discuss is that when someone is killed in your battles, you say that he has been killed as a martyr or has died as a martyr. However, it is very possible that in the interests of conducting trade, he has stored away some gold or silver at the back of his animal or in his carriage. You should therefore not make such bold statements but rather say what Rasulullah ﷺ used to say; Whoever is killed or dies in the Path of Allah shall be in Jannah." *(Abdur Razzaq, Tayalisi, Ahmad, Darmi, Tirmidhi, Abu Dawud, Nasa'ee, Ibn Majah)*. Masruq narrates that Omar ؓ once mounted the pulpit and said, "O people! What is this inflation of dowries for your women when the dowries common amongst Rasulullah ﷺ and his Sahabah were in the region of 400 Dirhams and less. Had inflated dowries been a sigh of Taqwa in Allah's sight or a mark of honor, you people would have never beaten Rasulullah ﷺ and his Sahabah to it, they would have been first to implement it." *(Sa'eed bin Mansur, Abu Ya'la in Kanzul Ummal)*.

The Lecture of Omar ؓ Prohibiting Discussions on Predestination

Omar ؓ was in Jabiya when he delivered a lecture. After

duly praising Allah, he said, "There can be none to mislead the one whom Allah guides and none can guide the one whom Allah misleads." A priest who was in front of Omar ؓ then said something in Persian. When Omar ؓ asked a translator to translate what he had said, the translator said, "He is of the opinion that Allah does not mislead anyone." "You are wrong, O enemy Allah!" Omar ؓ exclaimed, "It was Allah Who created you, Who misled you and will enter you into Jahannam if He so pleases. Had you not entered into a treaty with the Muslims, I would have had you executed." Omar ؓ said, "When Allah created Adam, He spread out his progeny. Allah then recorded who the people of Jannah shall be and the actions they will carry out. Thereafter, Allah also recorded who the people Jahannam shall be and the actions they will carry out and said, 'These are for Jannah and those for Jahannam.' The people then dispersed on earth and now they dispute about predestination." *(Abu Dawud in Kitabul Qadariya, Ibn Jareer, Ibn Abi Hatim)*. Abdur Rahman bin Abza narrates that someone reported to Omar ؓ that some people were disputing about predestination, he stood up to deliver a lecture saying, "O people! The nations before you were destroyed when they disputed about predestination. I swear by the Being Who controls Omar's life that if I have to hear about any 2 persons disputing about predestination, I shall have them both executed." The people stopped disputing predestination and no one discussed until a group in Sham started to dispute during the time of Hajjaj." *(Laika'ee, Ibn Asakir in Kanzul Ummal)*

His Lecture at Jabiya

Bahili narrates that when he arrived in Sham, Omar ؓ stood up to deliver a lecture in Jabiya. He said, "Learn the Qur'an and you will be noted for it. Practice its teachings and you will be amongst its bearers. Remember that no person who has a right over you has reached such a status that compels you to obey him while disobeying Allah. You should also take note that speaking the truth and advising a senior can never draw your death any closer nor distance any of your sustenance. Remember that there is a barrier between a servant and his sustenance. If he is patient, his sustenance will come to him but if he charges towards it, not caring whether he is earning Halal or Haram, he will rupture the barrier and find nothing more than his sustenance that has been predestined for him. Train your horses, practice archery, use the Miswak, live lives of simplicity and avoid the behavior of the non-Arabs. Avoid the company of tyrants, never allow a cross to be raised in your midst and never sit at a table where wine is served. You must also not enter public baths without a lower garment and never permit your women to enter them because none of this is permissible. After entering the lands of the non-Arabs and entering into a pact with them, avoid earning your living in any manner that will prevent you from returning to your land because you will soon be required to return. A void bringing humiliation to yourselves and ensure that you stay with Arab animals and that you take them wherever you go. Remember that wine can be made from 3 substances; from raisins, honey and dates. When any of these ferments and therby becomes intoxicating, they are regarded as wine and are not permissible. You must also take note that there are 3 types of person whom Allah shall not purify, shall not even look at with mercy and will not allow to be brought close to Him. They shall be inflicted with a painful punishment. (1) The person who pledges allegiance to his leader solely for worldly gain. He is loyal to the pledge only if he receives some worldly benefit, otherwise (2) The person who leaves with his merchandise after the Asr salah and falsely swears in the name of Allah that he purchased it at a certain price

which he did not. Because of this oath, he then manages to sell the goods. (3) A person who owns a watering place in a parched land and refuses water to travelers *(Targheeb wat Tarheeb))*. Verbally abusing a Muslim is a grave sin and physically abusing him leads to kufr. It is not permissible to sever relations with your Muslim brother for more than 3 days. The person who approaches a sorcerer, a fortune-teller or an astrologer and then believes what they say has disbelieved what has been revealed to Muhammad ﷺ." *(Adani in Kanzul Ummal)*

A Most Comprehensive Lecture that Omar ؓ Delivered at Jabiya

Musa bin Uqba reports that the following is the lecture that Omar delivered at Jabiya:

"After praising Allah and sending salutations to Rasulullah ﷺ, I wish to advise you to fear that Allah Who shall remain alive forever while everything else shall perish. It is by obedience to Him that His friends are honored and it is by disobeying Him that His enemies wander astray. None has any excuse for carrying out a misdeed that he regards as an act of virtue just as there is no excuse for the person who does not carry out an act of virtue, thinking it to be a misdeed. The matters that most need the attention of a ruler are those duties that his subjects owe to Allah. These are the responsibilities of Deen that Allah has guided them carry out. Our duty (as rulers) is only to instruct you to do those acts of obedience that Allah has commanded you to do and to forbid you from carrying out those acts of disobedience that Allah has forbidden you from.. Furthermore, we need to establish the commands of Allah amongst those of you who are nearby and those far off without a concern for those who wish to bend the truth. I am aware of the fact that there are many people who entertain hopes in their Deen, saying that they will perform salah with those who perform salah, that they will strive in Jihad with the Mujahidin and adopt the prestige of making Hijra. They however do this without fulfilling the rights of these acts. Remember that Iman is not achieved by mere superficial dressing. There are times for salah that Allah has specified and they will not be correct at any other times. The time for the Fajr salah is when night draws to an end and food and drink become Haram for the fasting person. Give this salah its due share of the Qur'an; recite lengthy portions of the Qur'an during this salah. The time for the Zuhr salah starts when the heat is intense and the sun crosses the meridian. It then lasts until your shadow equals your height. This is usually the time when a person takes his siesta. In winter however, it should be performed. When the sun shines on your right eyebrow after crossing the meridian i.e. wait a while even after it crosses. The salah should be performed with all the necessary conditions that Allah has stipulated in the wudhu, the Ruku and the Sejdah. These have been ordained so that one does not sleep through the salah and is not unaware and oblivious of what he is doing. The time for the Asr salah is while the sun is still bright and clear and before it starts to turn yellow. It is equal to the time in which a person rides a slow camel for 2 Farsakh (6 miles) before the sun sets. Now the time for the Maghrib salah starts when the sun sets and the fasting person terminates his fast and the time for the Isha salah starts when the night becomes completely dark. This is between the time that the redness in the sky disappears and a third of the night passes. May Allah never awaken the person who sleeps before that without performing his salah. These are the times of the salats, as Allah says: (103) إِنَّ الصَّلَاةَ كَانَتْ عَلَى الْمُؤْمِنِينَ كِتَابًا مَوْقُوتًا *Verily, the prayer is enjoined on the believers at fixed hours. (An-Nisa:103)*

There are people who claim that they have migrated when

they have actually not done so because the true Muhajir is he who migrates away from sin. Then there are those who aim that they have waged Jihad whereas true Jihad in the Path of Allah is fighting the enemy and refraining from haram. There have also been people who fight well in battle but in doing so they have no intention of attaining rewards nor do they remember pleasing Allah. Being killed is merely one of the many means of death and every slain person will be judged according to the reasons for which he was killed, he will therefore be regarded as a martyr only if he was killed while attempting to uplift the Deen of Allah. There are those who fight because they are naturally courageous and who therefore come to the rescue of those they know and those they do not know. Then there are those who are naturally so cowardly that they will surrender their own parents to the enemy whereas even a dog will bark in defense of its family. Remember that fasting is an extremely sacred act and causing any harm to the Muslims should also be avoided while fasting just as eating, drinking and sensual pleasures are forbidden. This is a complete fast. Remember also that the zakah that Rasulullah ﷺ has made Fardh by the instruction of Allah should be paid with a happy heart and must never be regarded as a favor to the recipient. Understand the advices you are given because the ransacked person is one whose Deen is ransacked. The fortunate person is he who learns from the experiences of others while the unfortunate one has been decreed as such since the time he was in his mother's womb. The worst of things are those that have been fabricated. Remember that moderation in practicing the Sunnah is better than exerting oneself in practicing Bid'ah. Indeed, people have a natural dislike for their rulers, so I seek Allah's protection from Him finding me or you with malice ingrained within us. I also seek Allah's protection from Him finding us following our whims and giving preference to this world over the Hereafter. I fear that you should incline to the ways of those who oppress themselves, so you should never content yourselves to be with those who have been granted wealth. Hold fast to this Qur'an because it is filled with light and healing powers, whereas everything else is filled only with misfortune. I have fulfilled my responsibilities to your affairs that Allah has made me responsible for and I have advised you in your best interests. We have fixed your allowances from the state treasury, prepared your armed forces, stipulated the places where you will be engaging in military operations and specified the locations of your military camps. We have even been very accommodating in the shares of the booty you receive from the battles you fight. You therefore have no objections to present before Allah. In fact, objections can well be brought against you. I have had my say and seek Allah's forgiveness for myself and for you all." (Kanzul Ummal)

Another narration states that Omar ؓ appointed Ali ؓ as his deputy and then left Madinah by horseback so that he could travel faster. When he reached Jabiya, he dismounted and delivered an eloquent lecture there. Amongst the things he said was the following: "O people! Ensure that your private lives are in order and your public lives will automatically follow suit. Work for your Hereafter and your matters in this world will be seen by Allah. Remember that no man has a living father between himself and Adam عليه السلام who can be of assistance to him at the time of death, neither has he any pact with Allah that will ensure his salvation. The person who wished to have the path to Jannah made apparent to him should stick with the greater body of united Muslims because Saitan ways preys on the lonesome individual and stays far from two united persons. None of you should ever be alone with a non-Mahram woman because Saitan

will be the 3rd person with them encouraging them to sin. The true Mu'min is he whose good deeds please him and whose sins bother him." The narrator states that this was Omar ؓ's lecture that he has condensed into few words. (Al Bidayah wan Nihayah)

Omar ؓ's Lecture at Jabiya which he quoted from Rasulullah ﷺ

Abdullah bin Omar ؓ reports that in his lecture to the people at Jabiya, Omar bin Khattab ؓ said, 'Just as I am standing before you here, Rasulullah ﷺ once stood up to address us saying, 'Accept this advice to treat my Sahabah well as well as those to come after them and then those after them. Thereafter a time will come when lying will be so widespread that a person will be prepared to offer testimony before being even asked to do so. Whoever wishes to attain to the very heart of Jannah must stick with the greater body of united Muslims because Saitan always preys on the lonely individual while staying far from 2 united persons. None of you should ever be alone with a (non-Mahram) woman because Saitan will be the 3rd person with them. The person whose good deeds please him and whose sins bother him is a true Mu'min." (Ahmad). Suwaid bin Ghafala narrates that in an address to the people at Jabiya, Omar bin Khattab ؓ said, "Rasulullah ﷺ forbade men from wearing silken garments unless it be an insignificant quantity such as the equivalent of 3 or 4 fingers." Omar ؓ indicated with his hand to clarify. (Ahmad)

Omar ؓ's Lecture at Jabiya when he Intended to Return when the Plague Broke Out

In his report detailing Omar ؓ's arrival in Sham after the outbreak of the plague in Amwas at the end of the year 17 AH, Saif reports that it was just before his departure back to Madinah that Omar ؓ addressed the people in the month of Dhul Hijjah. After duly praising Allah, Omar ؓ said, "Listen well! I have been entrusted to your affairs and. have fulfilled my responsibilities towards your affairs as commanded by Allah. By the will of Allah, we have exercised justice between you as far as your shares of the booty are concerned and as far as your military camps and sites of battle are concerned. We have conveyed to you everything you are entitled to, amassed armed forces for you, separated your borders, built towns for you and generously given you your shares of the booty and everything you fought for in Sham. We have allotted your rations, allowances and shares of the booty. If anyone knows of anything worth doing, he should inform us and we shall InshaAllah comply. There is no strength to do good except with Allah." (Al Bidayah wan Nihayah)

Two Lectures that Omar ؓ delivered when he Became Khalifa and his Explanation of the Rights his Subjects have Over Him

Urwa bin Zubair ؓ and others have ported after duly praising Allah; Omar ؓ reminded the people about the greatness of Allah and bout the Day of Judgment. Thereafter, he said, "O people! 'I have been appointed over you and I would have never accepted the post had it not been for the hope that I may develop into one who is the best for you, the strongest for you and the most powerful for you when tackling matters of importance to you. Merely waiting for reckoning concerning my administration of your rights is enough to worry and depress Omar because it will be judged how I took up the matters, how I handled them and how I have been treating you. It is from my Rabb that I seek assistance because Omar ؓ has neither any strength nor strategy if the mercy, assistance and help of Allah was not there for him." (Ibn Jareer Tabari in Tarikh). Another narration states that Omar ؓ said the following in his lecture: "Allah has appointed me to be in charge of your affairs. Although I know what is most beneficial for you from all that which is before you, I still seek Allah's help in making the decision. I beseech Allah to watch over me when doing this just as He watches over me at other times. I also ask Him to inspire me to exercise justice when distributing things amongst you as He has commanded me to do. I am merely an average Muslim and a weak servant unless Allah comes to my aid. The post of Khilafa that I have been entrusted with will not alter my character in any way, InshaAllah because I understand well that all dignity belongs to Allah and His servants have no stake to it. None of you should therefore say that Omar has changed since becoming the Khalifa. I know what truly lies within me and I will come forward to inform you of it, I will not defend my wrongs. Therefore, any person who has a need, who feels wronged or wants to object about any facet of my character, should come to me (to redress matters) because I am merely a normal person amongst you and am prone to err. You should adhere to Taqwa in your private and public lives and when dealing with affairs that are sacred and that impact upon your honor. At the same time, ensure that you fulfill the duties that are binding upon you. None of you should ever goad others into bringing their cases to me thinking that I will certainly rule in their favor because no pact exists between me and anyone else forcing me to rule in his favor. I love you to be on the right and hate to rebuke you. You are a people whose majority resides in Allah's cities and people living in cities usually have no plantations or milk-giving animals. They therefore have no access to these necessities apart from what Allah brings to them. Allah has promised you tremendous honor and I shall be questioned about the trust given to me and about the post I occupy. InshaAllah, I shall personally tend to matters that are before me without appointing anyone else to do it. I cannot tend to matters that are far from me without the assistance of trustworthy persons who are well-wishers to the masses. I shall never entrust my duties to anyone else apart from such trustworthy and well-wishing men."(Ibn Jareer Tabari in Tarikh)

Omar ؓ's Lecture Concerning Wishing Well for his Subjects and the Rights They have Over Him

After praising Allah and sending salutations to Rasulullah ﷺ, Omar ؓ once said the following in his lecture, "O people! Some instances of greed lead to poverty and some instances of losing hope lead to independence. You people stockpile food that you will never eat and entertain hopes that you will never reach whereas in this place of deception you have been granted respite to live only until the time of your death. During the time of Rasulullah ﷺ, you were apprehended by means of revelation. Therefore whoever hid something evil was apprehended for what he hid and whoever made something public was apprehended for that. However nowadays you must make public your best behavior because only Allah knows what is in your heart. Whoever makes something evil apparent to us and then claims that what is in his heart is good, we shall not believe him. We shall therefore have a good opinion of only those people whose public behavior is good and not of those whose public behavior is evil. Remember that in so any cases, the miserliness coupled with greed is a sign of hypocrisy, so make sure that you spend generously in Sadaqa. Allah says: أَنفِقُوا خَيْرًا لِّأَنفُسِكُمْ وَمَن يُوقَ شُحَّ نَفْسِهِ (16) فَأُولَٰئِكَ هُمُ الْمُفْلِحُونَ ...and spend in charity, that is better for yourselves. And whosoever is saved from his own covetousness, then they are the successful ones. (At-Taghabun:16)

O people! Make your places of eternal residence good, reconcile matters between yourselves, fear Allah your Rabb and

never allow your women to wear the fine white Egyptian cloth because since it does not conceal well, it reveals the features of the body. O people! I wish that I attain salvation without any sin against me nor any rewards in my favor. I also hope that, InshaAllah, I am always able to exercise what is right, whether I live for a long while or for a short period amongst you. I also hope that every Muslim receives the wealth due to him from Allah's riches, even though he may be sitting in his house, without him having to do anything or even tiring himself for a single day. Ensure that you set right the wealth that Allah has blessed you with by ensuring that you earn only what is Halal. Remember that a little done with gentleness is better than a lot done with harshness. Being killed is a means of death that both the righteous and sinful attain while the martyr is the one who intends earning rewards from Allah. When any of you intends purchasing a camel, he should look for one that is tall and large and then strike it with his staff. If he then finds that it is bright, he should buy it." (Ibn Jareer in Tarikh)

The lecture Omar ؓ Delivered Concerning Allah's Bounties on the Muslims and Encouragement to Express Gratitude for the Same

Urwa ؓ and others have narrated that in one of his lectures, Omar ؓ said, "Indeed Allah is Pure and free from all blemishes and it is necessary for you to express gratitude to Him by praising Him. Without your asking for or aspiring for them, Allah has shown you many proofs of the honor that He has bestowed upon you in this world as well as in the Hereafter. When you were nothing, Allah created you as human beings for Himself and for worshipping Him even though He had all the power to make you into a creation of a much inferior type. He has placed the rest of creation at your service, something that He has not done for any other creation. In addition to this Allah says:

سَخَّرَ لَكُم مَّا فِي السَّمَاوَاتِ وَمَا فِي الْأَرْضِ وَأَسْبَغَ عَلَيْكُمْ نِعَمَهُ ظَاهِرَةً وَبَاطِنَةً

...(Allah) has subjected for you whatsoever is in the heavens and whatsoever is in the earth, and has completed and perfected His Graces upon you, (both) apparent (i.e Islamic Monotheism, and the lawful pleasures of this world, including health, good looks, etc.) and hidden (i.e. Ones Faith in Allah (of Islamic Monotheism)... (Luqman:20)

Allah also carries you on land and at sea and provides your sustenance so that you may be grateful. Furthermore, Allah has blessed you with hearing and sight. Amongst the bounties that Allah has bestowed upon you are those that He has blessed all mankind with as well as those that He has granted only to those belonging to your Deen. All of these bounties, be they the universal ones as well as the exclusive ones, have all fallen to your lands, during your time and amongst your kind. Each of these bounties given to a single individual is such that if given to all of mankind, they would get tired showing gratitude for it and fulfilling the rights of this gratitude would be much too difficult for them unless Allah assists them and they do so with Iman in Allah and His Rasul ﷺ. You have been appointed as vicegerents on earth and have authority over its people. Allah has assisted your Deen and apart from 2 groups of people, there remains no other group that is opposed to your Deen. The first of the 2 is the group of people who have been made subservient to Islam and the Muslims and who pay the Jizyah as they are the Dhimmi people non-Muslims living in a Muslim country. They labor at their occupations, toil hard and spend the sweat on their brows. While they have the responsibility of doing the hard work, the benefits of their efforts come to you. The second group comprises of those people who are waiting day and night for

Allah's armies to attack them and whose hearts Allah has filled with terror. They have no sanctuary, no place of safety and nowhere to run to from where they can be saved. Allah's armies have started military offensives against them and set up camp in their territory. With the permission of Allah, you are enjoying good lives, an abundance of wealth, a steady stream of reinforcements and impregnable borders. In addition to all of this, you have the priceless bounty of collective well-being, better than which the Ummah as a whole has never had since the dawn of Islam, Only Allah is to be praised that at the same time, you are enjoying military victories in every country. The gratitude of the grateful ones, the Dhikr of those engaged in Dhikr and all the efforts of those exerting themselves can scarcely fulfill the rights of the gratitude owing to Allah for these bounties that cannot be counted and which cannot be appreciated to their fullest extent. Of course, this is possible only with the assistance, mercy and grace of Allah. We ask Allah besides Whom there is none worthy of worship and Who has granted us all of this, that He blesses us with the ability to obey Him and to hasten to do everything that will please Him. O servants of Allah! Think about Allah's bounties when alone and even in your gatherings of 2 persons to have Allah's bounties completed upon you. Allah said to Musa: أَخْرِجْ قَوْمَكَ مِنَ الظُّلُمَاتِ إِلَى النُّورِ وَذَكِّرْهُمْ بِأَيَّامِ اللَّهِ

...bring out your people from darkness into light, and make them remember the annals of Allah... (Ibrahim:5)

Allah also said to Muhammad ﷺ: وَاذْكُرُوا إِذْ أَنْتُمْ قَلِيلٌ مُسْتَضْعَفُونَ فِي الْأَرْضِ

And remember when you were few and were reckoned weak in the land... (Al-Anfal:26)

At the time when you were regarded as weak on earth and deprived of worldly wealth, you would have been in an excellent condition had you been believing in and taking solace from some truth together with the recognition of Allah and His Deen, hoping all the time to have success after death. However at that time you led the harshest of lives and were most ignorant of Allah. It may have been best if this Deen that came to your rescue had come with no worldly gains and with only a security for your Hereafter, to which you will eventually be returning. Then in the difficult lives you were leading, you would have been more covetous over your fortune ensuring that nothing else overwhelms it. That being as it is, what has happened is that Allah has combined for you the bounties of this world as well as the honor of the Hereafter. Therefore, whoever wishes that these 2 factors be combined for him, I wish to remind him of that Allah Who can come between a man and his own heart. He must act on every right he realizes he owes to Allah, he must defeat his soul to obey Allah and together with being overjoyed with Allah's bounties, he must also fear that they must never be overturned and lost. There is nothing more effective in taking bounties away than ingratitude for them. Gratitude ensures that bounties are safe from change and is a means for them to increase and to grow. It is a duty from Allah upon me to instruct you (to do good) and to forbid you (from evil)." *(Ibn Jareer in Tarikh)*

The Lecture Omar ؓ delivered Discussing the Battle of Uhud

Ibn Kulaib narrates that it was on a Friday that Omar ؓ addressed the people. He recited a portion of Surah Al-Imran until he reached the verse: إِنَّ الَّذِينَ تَوَلَّوْا مِنْكُمْ يَوْمَ الْتَقَى الْجَمْعَانِ

Those of you who turned back on the day the two hosts met (i.e. the battle of Uhud)... (Al-Imran:155)

Omar ؓ then commented, "After we had been defeated in the Battle of Uhud, I ran up the mountain, leaping as if I were a mountain goat. When the people started saying that Muhammad ﷺ had been martyred, I announced that I would kill anyone who made that statement. We then regrouped on the mountain and Allah revealed the verse: إِنَّ الَّذِينَ تَوَلَّوْا مِنْكُمْ يَوْمَ الْتَقَى الْجَمْعَانِ

Those of you who turned back on the day the two hosts met (i.e. the battle of Uhud)... (Al-Imran:155) (Ibn Jareer)

Another narration from Ibn Kulaib states that as he recited Surah Al-Imran on the pulpit, Omar ؓ said, "This Surah discusses the Battle of Uhud. When we dispersed from around Rasulullah during the Battle of Uhud and I had climbed up the mountain, I heard a Jew announce that Rasulullah ﷺ had been martyred. I then declared, 'I shall personally execute any person who says that Rasulullah ﷺ has been martyred!' When I then had a proper look, I saw Rasulullah ﷺ and saw the Muslims regrouping around him. It was then that the verse was revealed: وَمَا مُحَمَّدٌ إِلَّا رَسُولٌ قَدْ خَلَتْ مِنْ قَبْلِهِ الرُّسُلُ أَفَإِنْ مَاتَ أَوْ قُتِلَ انْقَلَبْتُمْ عَلَى أَعْقَابِكُمْ وَمَنْ يَنْقَلِبْ عَلَى عَقِبَيْهِ فَلَنْ يَضُرَّ اللَّهَ شَيْئًا وَسَيَجْزِي اللَّهُ الشَّاكِرِينَ (144)

Muhammad (ﷺ) is no more than a Messenger, and indeed (many) Messengers have passed away before him. If he dies or is killed, will you then turn back on your heels (as disbelievers)? And he who turns back on his heels, not the least harm will he do to Allah, and Allah will give reward to those who are grateful. (Al-Imran:144) (Ibn Mundhir in Kanzul Ummal)

Various Lectures that Omar ؓ Delivered

Abdullah bin Adi bin Khiyar reports that he heard Omar ؓ deliver the following lecture from the pulpit: 'When a servant humbles himself for the pleasure of Allah, Allah elevates his status saying, 'Rise in status! May Allah elevate you.' While such a person sees himself as a degraded person, he is very much revered by the people. On the other hand, when a person has pride, and transgresses, Allah breaks him and floors him, saying, 'Be disgraced! May Allah degrade you!' While such a person sees himself as a great person, he is so humiliated in the eyes of the people that they regard him as being lower than a pig." *(Abu Ubaid, Kkra'iti, Sabuni, Abdur Razzaq in Kanzul Ummal).* Abu Sa'eed Khudri ؓ reports that Omar ؓ once delivered a lecture saying, "It may happen that I forbid you from things that are of benefit to you and instruct you to do things that hold no benefit for you. Amongst the last verses to be revealed were those forbidding interest and because of other commitments Rasulullah ﷺ passed away without explaining the finer details of interest. You people should therefore forsake all transactions that give you doubts about the involvement of interest and rather opt for those that do not give you doubts." *(Khatib in Kanzul Ummal).* Aswad bin Yazid narrates that Omar ؓ once delivered a lecture saying, "Whoever intends performing Hajj should enter into the state of Ihram only from the Miqat (the designated places to enter with Ihram). These various places as designated by Rasulullah ﷺ are: Dhul Hulaifa for the residents of Madinah and for its non-residents who happen to be passing by it. For the residents of Sham and for its non-residents happen to be passing by it, the Miqat is Juhfah. Qarn is the Miqat for the residents of Najd and for its non-residents who happen to be passing by it. Yalamlam is the Miqat for the residents of Yemen, while Dhatul Iraq is the Miqat for the people of Iraq and others (in that direction)." *(Ibnud Diya in Kanzul Ummal).* Abdullah bin Abbas ؓ narrates that while discussing Rajm (stoning an adulterer) in his lecture, Omar ؓ said, "Never be deceived about it because is definitely a penalty from amongst those that Allah has ordained. Take note of the fact that Rasulullah ﷺ had people stoned and we have also done so after him. Had it not en for people remarking that Omar adds to Allah's book things that are not part of it, I would have attached a footnote to the Qur'an stating that Omar bin Khattab, Abdur Rahman bin Auf and many others testify that Rasulullah ﷺ had people stoned and they have also done so after him. Remember that after you there shall come people who will refuse to believe in Rajm, in Dajjal, in intercession in the Hereafter, in punishment in the grave and that people will be removed from Jahannam after being burnt there." *(Ahmad, Abu Ya'la, Abu Ubaid).* Sa'eed bin Musayib narrates that when Omar ؓ left Mina after his stay in Makkah, he sat his camel down at Abtah, where he made a mound with the loose sand. Thereafter, he cast a portion of his garment over the mound and then leaned against it. He then raised his hands and made Du'a saying, "O Allah! I am growing old, my strength is dwindling and my subjects have all dispersed far and wide. Do call me to You while I am not guilty of sinning nor have I been negligent in any duty." When Omar ؓ reached Madinah, he addressed the people saying, "O people! The Fara'idh has been ordained for you, the Sunnah have been shown to you and you have been left on a clear path." He hit his right hand on the left and added, "Unless you sway people to the right and left and lead them astray. Beware that you never destroy yourselves because of the verse of Rajm and never let anyone say that we do not find 2 penalties in Allah's Book (we find only the one for lashing a fornicator and not the one for stoning an adulterer). I saw Rasulullah ﷺ having people stoned and we have done so after him. Had it not been for people remarking that Omar ؓ adds new things to Allah's book, I would have written in a footnote of the Qur'an the verse that we used to recite while the words of the verse were abrogated, the law still remained. It reads that if a married man or woman commits adultery, both must be stoned." Sa'eed says, "The month of Dhul Hijjah had hardly passed by when Omar ؓ was stabbed and passed away." *(Malik, Ibn Sa'd, Musaddad, Hakim in Kanzul Ummal).*

Ma'dan bin Abu Talha Ya'muri reports that it was on a Friday that Omar ؓ once stood on the pulpit and praised Allah. He then spoke of Rasulullah ﷺ and Abu Bakr ؓ before saying, "I have seen a dream that I feel means nothing other than the approach of my death. I saw that a red rooster twice pecked at me. When I related the dream to Asma bint Umais, she informed me that a non-Arab will kill me. Although people now want me to appoint a successor, you must remember that Allah will never destroy His Deen nor the role of vicegerency on earth for which He sent his Nabi ﷺ. If anything happens to me suddenly, the consultative assembly to decide which of them will be the Khalifa shall comprise of 6 men with whom Rasulullah ﷺ was pleased when he left this world. They are Uthman ؓ, Ali ؓ, Zubair ؓ, Talha ؓ, Abdur Rahman bin Auf ؓ and Sa'd bin Abi Waqqas ؓ. You people must listen to and obey whichever of them you pledge allegiance to. I know well that some people will criticize this matter and these are the very ones against whom I personally fought for the sake of Islam. In doing so they will be joining the ranks of the enemies of Allah and the misguided Kuffar because they will be assisting the cause of these Kuffar. I am leaving behind nothing more important in my estimation than the matter of the Kalala, the person who dies without leaving behind any ascendants or descendants. I swear by Allah that since the time I joined the company of Rasulullah ﷺ, he was not as strict with me about any matter as he was about the matter of the Kalala. In fact, Rasulullah ﷺ even poked his finger in my chest and said, "The verse of Surah Nisa [verse 176: "They (the Sahabah) seek a ruling from you (O Muhammad ﷺ). Say, "Allah shall issue a ruling to you concerning the person who leaves neither ascendants (parents or grandparents) nor descendants

(children or grandchildren). If a man passes away without any children, but has a sister, then she will inherit 1/2 of what he leaves. If she dies, he will inherit all of her wealth if she has no children. If they (the heirs) are 2 or more sisters, then they will inherit 2/3rd of what he leaves. If they (the heirs) are a few brothers and sisters, then the male will inherit the similar share of 2 females. Allah explains to you the laws of Shari'ah so that you do not go astray. Allah is Knower of all things"] revealed in summer is enough for you in this regard.' If I live long enough, I shall certainly be passing a law concerning the Kalala that every learned and unlettered person will understand. I also make Allah Witness to the fact that every governor whom I have sent to the various cities has been sent expressly for the purpose of educating the people about their Deen, about the Sunnah practices of their Nabi ﷺ and to bring to my attention maters that otherwise go unnoticed. I would also like to bring to your notice something about two plants that you eat from, namely garlic and onions. They are foul-smelling in my estimation and I swear that I have seen that when Rasulullah ﷺ smelled them on anyone, he would give the instruction for the person to be taken by the hand and led out of the Masjid as far as Baqee. If a person has to eat them, he must first eliminate the smell by cooking." Omar ؓ delivered this on a Friday and it was on a Wednesday just 4 days before the end of Dhul Hijjah that he was stabbed." *(Tayalisi, Ibn Sa'd, Ibn Abi Shaybah, Ahmaf, Ibn Hibban, Muslim, Nasa'ee, Abu Awana, Abu Ya'la in Kanzul Ummal)*

Yasar bin Marur narrates that Omar ؓ once addressed them saying, "O people! Rasulullah built this Masjid when we the Muhajirin and Ansar were with him. When the crowds become excessive, everyone of you should make Sejdah on the back of his brother (in front of him)." When Omar ؓ saw some people performing their salah in the streets, he instructed them to perform salah inside the Masjid. *(Tabrani, Ahmad, Shashi, Bayhaqi, Sa'eed bin Mansur in Kanzul Ummal).* Abdullah bin Omar ؓ narrates that when he was appointed Khalifa, Omar ؓ addressed the people saying, "Rasulullah ﷺ permitted Mut'ah for us for 3 days only, after which it was declared Haram. By Allah! I find out that any married man has committed Mut'ah, I shall have him stoned to death unless he brings forth 4 witnesses to testify that Rasulullah ﷺ permitted it after it was made Haram. In the same manner, if I find any other (non-married) Muslim committing Mut'ah, I will have him lashed 1000 lashes unless he brings forth 4 witnesses to testify that Rasulullah ﷺ permitted it after it was made Haram." *(Ibn Asakir, Sa'eed bin Mansur, Tammam in Kanzul Ummal).* Abdullah bin Sa'eed reports from his grandfather who heard Omar ؓ say from the pulpit, "O assembly of Muslims! Very Allah has granted you so many non-Arab women and children as booty that He did not grant to either Rasulullah ﷺ or to Abu Bakr ؓ. I also know that many men engage in sexual relations with these women (who are their slaves and they are therefore within their legal right to have relations with them). Therefore, if any of you have children from any of these non-Arab (slave) women, he must not sell her because if he does so, the possibility exists that without him knowing, a person may engage in intercourse with a woman who is his Mahram." *(Bayhaqi in Kanzul Ummal).* Ma'rur or Ibn Ma'rur Tamimi reports, "Omar bin Khattab ؓ was on the pulpit, sitting on a step beneath that on which Rasulullah ﷺ sat when I heard him say, 'I emphatically advise you to adopt Taqwa and to listen to and obey those who are entrusted to take charge of your affairs (your leaders)." *(Ibn Jareer in Kanzul Ummal).* Abu Hurairah ؓ narrates that Omar bin Khattab ؓ used to say the following in his lectures: "The most successful of you all is he who is safeguarded against his passions, anger and greed and who is inspired to always be truthful in his speech. It is such truthfulness that draws one towards all virtue. The person who lies will always sin and such sin will ultimately destroy him. Beware of sin! Why should one sin when he has been created from sand and who will return to sand and while he is alive today, he will be dead tomorrow? Do your deeds from day to day, avoid the curse of the oppressed and count yourself amongst the dead." (Bayhaqi in Kanzul Ummal). Qabisa narrates that he heard Omar ؓ say from the pulpit, "Whoever has no mercy will not be shown any, whoever does not forgive will not be forgiven, whoever does not repent will' not have his repentance accepted and whoever does not abstain (from sin) will not be saved (from punishment)." (Bukhari in Adab, Ibn Khuzaima, Ja'far Firyabi in Kanzul Ummal). Urwa ؓ reports that Omar ؓ once said in his lecture, "Know well that greed leads to poverty and that losing hope leads to independence because when a person loses hope in something, he becomes independent of it." (Abu Nu'aym in Hilya, Ibn Mubarak in Kanzul Ummal)

Abdullah bin Khirash reports that his uncle heard Omar ؓ say in a lecture, "O Allah! Rescue us with Your rope and keep us steadfast on your Deen." (Abu Nu'aym in Hilya) Another narration states that Omar ؓ also added, "...and provide for us from Your grace." (Ahmad in Zuhd, Ruyani, Lalka'ee, Ibn Asakir in Kanzul Ummal). Abu Sa'eed narrates that Omar ؓ once delivered a lecture saying, "Verily Allah had granted certain concessions to His Nabi ﷺ as He pleased (because of which Rasulullah ﷺ was allowed to perform Umrah with the same Ihram he originally donned only for Hajj. This is not permitted for the Ummah). Rasulullah ﷺ has now passed on and you people must complete your Hajj and Umrah as Allah has commanded (ref. Al-Baqara:196) and you must ensure that you safeguard the chastity of your women." (Ahmad). Abdullah bin Zubair says that heard Omar ؓ say in his lecture that he heard Rasulullah ﷺ say, "Whoever (from amongst the males) wears silk in this world will not be given any to wear in the hereafter." (Ahmad). Abu Ubaid who was the freed slave of Abdur Rahman bin Auf ؓ reports that he once attended the Eid salah led by Omar ؓ. Without any Adhan or Iqama being called out, Omar ؓ led the salah before delivering the lecture. He then said in his lecture, "O people! Rasulullah ﷺ forbade fasting on 2 days. The one is the day in which you break from your fasting, which is the day of Eid (Eidul Fitr). The other is the day in which you eat from your sacrificial animals (Eidul Adha)." (Ahmad). Alqama bin Waqqas Laithi ؓ narrates that he heard Omar ؓ say the following in his lecture to the people: "I have heard Rasulullah ﷺ say, 'Actions are judged according to their intentions and a man will have what he had intended. Therefore, whoever migrated for the pleasure of Allah and His Rasul ﷺ, his migration will be for Allah and His Rasul ﷺ. As for the one who migrated for worldly gain or to wed a woman, his migration shall be for that towards which he migrated.'" (Ahmad). Sulaiman bin Yasar reports that it was during the period of drought that Omar ؓ addressed the people saying, "O people! Fear Allah from within yourselves and in all those personal matters that are hidden from the people. While I have been put to test with (being Khalifa over) you, you have been put to test with me. I do not know whether this (drought) is because Allah is angry with me and not with you, and not me or whether Allah is angry with all of us. Come! Let us pray to Allah so that Allah may correct our hearts, have mercy on us and remove this drought from us." Omar ؓ and the people were seen with their arms raised as they made Du'a to Allah and wept for some time before he descended from the pulpit. (Ibn Sa'd). Abu

Uthman Nahdi says, "I was sitting beneath Omar ؓ's pulpit as he said, 'I heard Rasulullah ﷺ say, 'What I fear most from the Ummah is the Munafiq with an eloquent tongue." (Ahmad).

The Lectures of Amirul Mu'minin Uthman bin Affan ؓ

Ibrahim bin Abdur Rahman Makhzumi reports at when the people had pledged allegiance to Uthman bin Affan ؓ, he stood up to deliver a lecture. After duly praising Allah, he said, "O people! The first rung of the ladder is most difficult and there will still be many more days to come after this one. If I live longer, you shall have lectures that are properly prepared. Although we have never been speakers, Allah shall soon teach us." (Ibn Sa'd). Badr bin Uthman reports from his uncle that when the other members of the consultative assembly pledged allegiance to Uthman ؓ, he left for the Masjid in great consternation. He then went to the pulpit of Rasulullah ﷺ, from where he addressed the people. After duly praising Allah and sending salutations to Rasulullah ﷺ, he said, "You are in a place from where you shall soon be leaving and you have but a short duration of your lives ahead. You should therefore beat your deaths by doing as much good as you possibly can because death will certainly come to you, whether by day or night. Remember that this world is deception through and through. Allah says: فَلَا

تَغُرَّنَّكُمُ الْحَيَاةُ الدُّنْيَا وَلَا يَغُرَّنَّكُم بِاللَّهِ الْغَرُورُ (33)

...let not then this (worldly) present life deceive you, nor let the chief deceiver (Satan) deceive you about Allah. (Luqman:33)
Learn lessons from those who have passed on and then be resolute without giving way to negligence because death will never neglect you. Where are all those sons of this world and its brothers who inhabited the earth, left landmarks and who enjoyed it for an extensive period of time? Did the world not fling them aside? Throw the world aside just as Allah has done and seek the Hereafter. Allah has drawn a similitude for the world and the Hereafter, which is the better of the two. Allah says:

وَاضْرِبْ لَهُم مَّثَلَ الْحَيَاةِ الدُّنْيَا كَمَاءٍ أَنزَلْنَاهُ مِنَ السَّمَاءِ فَاخْتَلَطَ بِهِ نَبَاتُ الْأَرْضِ فَأَصْبَحَ هَشِيمًا تَذْرُوهُ الرِّيَاحُ وَكَانَ اللَّهُ عَلَى كُلِّ شَيْءٍ مُّقْتَدِرًا (45) الْمَالُ وَالْبَنُونَ زِينَةُ الْحَيَاةِ الدُّنْيَا وَالْبَاقِيَاتُ الصَّالِحَاتُ خَيْرٌ عِندَ رَبِّكَ ثَوَابًا وَخَيْرٌ أَمَلًا (46)

And put forward to them the example of the life of this world, it is like the water (rain) which We send down from the sky, and the vegetation of the earth mingles with it, and becomes fresh and green. But it becomes dry and broken pieces, which the winds scatter. And Allah is Able to do everything. Wealth and children are the adornment of the life of this world. But the good righteous deeds (five compulsory prayers, deeds of Allah's obedience, good and nice talk, remembrance of Allah with glorification, praises and thanks, etc.), that last, are better with your Lord for rewards and better in respect of hope. (Al-Kahf:45-46)

The people then went up to him and pledged their allegiance to him. (Ibn Jareer in Tarikh). Utba narrates that after he became the Khalifa, Uthman ؓ addressed the people saying, "I have been made responsible for this task and have accepted it. Take note of the fact that I am a follower of the Deen and not one to introduce new things. Listen well! After the Book of Allah and the Sunnah of Rasulullah ﷺ, you people have 3 rights over me: (1) That I follow that which are unanimous about, that you have been practicing and that has a precedent amongst those before me (during the periods of Rasulullah ﷺ, Abu Bakr ؓ and Omar ؓ); (2) that I follow the ways of the righteous ones in matters that you may have not been accustomed to doing; (3) that I restrain my hand from you except in matters that necessitate punishment.

Remember that this world is a lush place that has been made desirable to people, because of which so many people are inclined towards it. You should therefore not be inclined towards the world and should never place your trust in it because it is not dependable. Bear in mind also that this world will never leave anyone besides the one who leaves it first." *(Ibn Jareer)*

Various Lectures that Uthman ﷺ Delivered

Mujahid reports that Uthman bin Affan ﷺ once delivered a lecture saying, "O son of Adam عليه السلام! You must know that the angel of death who has been appointed to take your life has always been leaving you to go to others as long as you have been in this world. It now appears that he is skipping all the others out and is now stalking you. You must therefore take your precautions and prepare for him, never be unmindful of him because he is never unmindful of you. O son of Adam عليه السلام! Remember that if you are unmindful of yourself and do not prepare, no one else will prepare for you. Meeting Allah is inevitable, so take charge of your Nafs and do not hand it over to others. Peace be upon you all." *(Dinowri in Mujalasa, Ibn Asakir in Kanzul Ummal)*. Hasan narrates that in an address to the people, Uthman ﷺ started by praising Allah and then said, "O people! Adopt Taqwa because Taqwa is a great asset. Verily the greatest of all the intelligent people is the one who controls his Nafs and acts for his life after death. Glean from Allah's light some light for the darkness of the grave and every person should fear that he be raised blind when he was sighted in this world. Concise words suffice for a wise person and it is only the deaf who have to be shouted to from a distant place. Remember that the person who has Allah with him need not fear anything. On the other hand, what hope can there be for the person who has Allah up against him?" *(Dinowri, Ibn Asakir in Kanzul Ummal)*. Hasan narrates that he saw Uthman ﷺ delivering the following lecture from the pulpit: "O people! Fear Allah in your private affairs because I heard Rasulullah ﷺ say, 'I swear by the Being Who controls the life of Muhammad that whenever a person does an act in private, Allah dons him with such garments in public such will be peoples impression of him. Therefore, if the act is good, the garment will be good and if the act is evil, so too will the garment be." He then recited: وَرِيشًا وَلِبَاسُ التَّقْوَى ذَلِكَ خَيْرٌ ذَلِكَ

...and as an adornment, and the raiment of righteousness that is better... (Al-A'raf:26)

Uthman ﷺ recited the word رياشا and not ريشا (as recited in the most popular mode of recitation). *(Ibn Jareer, Ibn Abi Hatim in Kanzul Ummal)* Abad bin Zahir says that he heard Uthman ﷺ deliver a lecture saying, "By Allah! We were with Rasulullah ﷺ all the time, whether at home or on journey. Rasulullah ﷺ would visit our ill, accompany our funeral processions, fight battles with us and take care of our needs whether he had a little with him or plenty. Nowadays some people teach us certain things about Rasulullah ﷺ whereas they have perhaps never even seen him." *(Ahmad, Bazzar, Mirwazi, Shashi, Abu Ya'la, Sa'eed bin Mansur in Kanzul Ummal)* Another narration adds that a person named A'yan bin Imra'atul Farazdaq addressed Uthman ﷺ saying, "O Na'shal (Na'shal was the name of an Egyptian with very long beard. Those who opposed Uthman would call him this name)! You have changed many things in Deen." "Who is that man?" Uthman ﷺ asked. When the people named him as A'yan, others sprung to attack him. A man from the Banu Laith however managed to ward the people off him and took him to his house." *(Ahmad, Abu Ya'la in Majma'uz Zawa'id)*. Malik narrates that he heard Uthman ﷺ say the following in his lecture: 'Never burden young children with the task of earning because when you do so, they tend to steal. You should also not delegate the responsibility of earning to a slave woman who does not know a craft because when you do this, she will earn by her charms (as a prostitute). You should remain chaste when Allah has kept you chaste and eat only those foods that are good for you." *(Shafi'ee, Bayhaqi in Kanzul Ummal)*. Zaid bin Silt narrates that Uthman ﷺ was referring to backgammon when he heard him say from the pulpit, "O people! Stay away from gambling because I have been informed that this is to be found in some of your homes. Whoever has this in his house must either burn or break it." On another occasion, Uthman ﷺ mentioned the following from the pulpit, "O people! I have already spoken to you about backgammon but I see that you have not removed it from your homes. I have therefore decided to have firewood collected and to then dispatch people to set fire to the houses in which these games are to be found." *(Bayhaqi in Kanzul Ummal)*. Salim the freed slave of Abdur Rahman Humaid reports that Uthman bin Affan ﷺ performed salah in full in Mina and then addressed the people saying, "O people! The true Sunnah is that of Rasulullah and his 2 companions: Abu Bakr ﷺ and Omar ﷺ, all of whom performed 2 Rakats for Zuhr, Asr and Isha at Mina. However, because many new people are performing Hajj this year, I am performing 4 Rakats salah because I fear that they will regard it as Sunnah to always perform 2 Rakats salah." *(Bayhaqi, Ibn Asakir in Kanzul Ummal)*. Qutaiba bin Muslim narrates, "Hajjaj bin Yusuf addressed us and spoke of the grave. He then said, 'It is a place of solitude and a place of loneliness.' He repeated this so much that he then burst out crying and made everyone around him weep as well. He continued, 'I heard Amirul Mu'minin Abdul Malik bin Marwan say that he heard Marwan say in a lecture, 'Uthman ﷺ addressed us saying Rasulullah ﷺ always wept whenever he saw a grave or spoke about the grave." *(Ibn Asakir in Kanzul Ummal)*. Sa'eed bin Musayib narrates that he heard Uthman ﷺ say this address from the pulpit: "I used to buy dates from a tribe of the Jews called the Banu Qaynuqa and then sell it at a profit. Rasulullah ﷺ learnt that I was doing this, he said, "O Uthman! Weigh the dates when you purchase them and them weigh them again when you resell." *(Ahmad)*. Hasan reports that he was present when Uthman ﷺ instructed from the pulpit that all dangerous dogs should be killed and pigeons (used for sport) should be slaughtered. *(Ahmad)*

The Final Lecture that Uthman ﷺ Delivered

Badr bin Uthman reports from his uncle that in the final lecture that Uthman ﷺ delivered in public was when he said, "Verily Allah has granted you this world so that you may use it to acquire the Hereafter and not for you to attach yourselves to it. Whereas this world will come to an end, the Hereafter shall be forever, so never allow what is temporary to make you arrogant and never allow it to distract you from that which is everlasting. Give preference to that which is eternal to that which is transitory because this world will certainly come to an end while you will have to return to Allah in the Hereafter. Fear Allah because Taqwa is a shield against His punishment and a means to draw close to Him. Take precautions against Allah changing your conditions (removing your bounties), remain united with the Muslims and never break up into splinter groups. He then recited: وَاذْكُرُوا نِعْمَةَ اللَّهِ عَلَيْكُمْ إِذْ كُنْتُمْ أَعْدَاءً فَأَلَّفَ بَيْنَ قُلُوبِكُمْ فَأَصْبَحْتُمْ بِنِعْمَتِهِ إِخْوَانًا

...and remember Allah's Favor on you, for you were enemies one to another but He joined your hearts together, so that, by His Grace... (Al-Imran:103) (Ibn Jareer)

The First Lecture of Amirul Mu'minin Ali bin Abi Talib

Ali bin Husain narrates that when he was appointed Kalifa, Ali started his first lecture by praising Allah. Thereafter, he said, "Verily Allah has revealed a scripture that is a guide and which makes distinct what is good and what is not. You must therefore hold fast to what is good and abstain from what is evil. When you carry out the Fara'idh for Allah, Allah will carry you into Jannah. Allah has made many things sacred, and these are no secret. He has however made the sanctity of a Muslim more sacred than anything else and bonded the Muslims by sincerity and Towhid. The true Muslim is he from whose tongue and hands other people are safe unless it be done rightfully to seek punishment when Allah's laws are broken. It is not permissible to harm any Muslim unless it becomes necessary when he transgresses Allah's laws. Hasten to do good deeds before the universal occurrence (Judgment) and before the individual occurrence as well, which is the death of each one of you. Many people have passed ahead of you and Judgment is driving you from behind. Travel lightly without sins and you will meet those who have passed away because deceased people are waiting for those after them. Install the fear of Allah into His bondsmen with regard to abusing His other bondsmen and lands because you will be questioned even with regard to tracts of land and animals. Obey Allah and never disobey Him. Seize the opportunity to do good whenever you see it, avoid evil when you see it and remember the time when you were few in number and regarded as weak in the lands." *(Ibn Jareer)*

His Lecture Concerning the Value of a Person's Tribe

Ali once delivered a lecture saying, "A man's tribe is more valuable to him than he is to his tribe. If he restrains his hand from assisting them, he will be restraining but one hand. However, if they restrain their hands, they will be restraining many hands together with the love, protection and assistance they have to offer him. In fact, it often happens that a person becomes angry with another only because of the tribe he belongs to. I can cite to you so many verses of the Qur'an in this regard." He then recited the verse: لَوْ أَنَّ لِي بِكُمْ قُوَّةً أَوْ آوِي إِلَى رُكْنٍ شَدِيدٍ (80)

He (Lut) said, "Would that I had strength (men) to overpower you, or that I could betake myself to some powerful support (to resist you)." (Hud:80)

Ali then continued to explain, "The strong pillar is a tribe that Lut did not have in the place he resided. I swear by the Being besides Whom there is no deity that after Lut, Allah sent every Nabi as a member of a strong tribe." Ali then recited the following verse with regard to Shu'aib : وَإِنَّا لَنَرَاكَ فِينَا ضَعِيفًا

(His people said, 'O Shu'aib!) we consider you to be a weakling among us.' This they said because Shu'aib was blind. However, they then added: وَلَوْلَا رَهْطُكَ لَرَجَمْنَاكَ

...were it not for your family, we should certainly have stoned you... (Hud:91). Ali said, "I swear by the Being besides whom there is no deity that rather than fear the supremacy of their Rabb, these people were afraid of Shu'aib's tribe."*(Abu Sheikh in Kanzul Ummal)*

His Lecture When Ramadhan Arrived

Sha'bi reports that whenever Ramadhan arrived, Ali would deliver a lecture and say, "This is that blessed month in which fasting has been made obligatory while standing at night in salah has not. One must beware of saying that he will fast only if a particular person fasts and will not fast if a particular person

does not. Remember well that fasting is not only abstaining from food and drink but abstaining from lies, falsehood and kufr. Bear in mind that you must never bring the month forward. Fast only when you see the new moon of Ramadhan and stop fasting when you see the new moon (of Shawwal). However if it is overcast and you cannot see the new moon, then complete the month as 30 days." Ali used to say this after the Fajr and Asr salats. *(Husain bin Yahya Qattan, Bayhaqi in Kanzul Ummal)*

His Lecture Concerning the Grave and its Condition

After commencing with the praises of Allah in one of his lectures, Ali proceeded to speak about death. He said, "O servants of Allah! By Allah! There is no escape from death. If you stand still for it, it will seize you and if you flee from it, it will still find you. Hasten to salvation! Hasten to salvation! Be quick! Be quick! Behind you is a speedy pursuer, which is the grave. Beware of its pressure, intense darkness and loneliness. Remember well that the grave may either be a pit of Jahannam or a garden from amongst the gardens if Jannah. Bear in mind that the grave calls out three times every day saying, 'I am the home of darkness! I am the home of worms! I am the home of loneliness! Do not forget also that what is to come afterwards is even worse. There is Jahannam with extremely hot fires, a tremendous dept, decorations of iron and Malik as its custodian. In there shall be no part of Allah's mercy. After this there is Jannah, which is as wide as the heavens and the earth and which has been prepared for those with Taqwa. May Allah make us and all of' you amongst those with Taqwa and save us and all of you from a most painful punishment." *(Sabuni in Mi'atain, Ibn Asakir in Kanzul Ummal)*. Asbagh bin Nabata reports that Ali one day ascended the pulpit and after duly praising Allah, he spoke about death. The rest of the narration is similar to the one above, but after the words "I am the home of worms!", it adds that Ali then said, "Remember that after this shall come a day in which even a youngster will turn white, a grown man will break down and every expectant mother will abort her child. You will see people in a state of intoxication but they will not really be intoxicated. The fact is that (they will be in this condition because) the punishment of Allah will be extreme." Another narration states that Ali then burst out crying and the Muslims around him also wept. *(Al Bidayah wan Nihayah)*

His Lecture Concerning the World, the Grave and the Hereafter

Salih Ijli reports that Ali bin Abi Talib once addressed the people. After praising Allah and conveying salutations to Rasulullah, he said, "O servants of Allah! Never allow this worldly life to deceive you because it is a place of light difficulties, it is famous for its transitory nature and well-recognized for its treachery. Everything in it shall come to an end and is continuously assed on from person to person. The one who goes down to tap its resources cannot remain safe from its evil and even while its people enjoy prosperity and happiness, they are still involved in its calamities and deception. Living a good life in this world is condemned and its prosperity does not last. Its people are only its practice targets that it fires at with its arrows and eventually destroys with death. Dear servants of Allah! You and all that is with you in this world are following the same path as those who have passed on before you. They had lives longer than yours, they were more powerful than you, they constructed more buildings than you and their landmarks had weathered the times. However, their voices have been silenced and extinguished after their long sojourn. Their bodies have decomposed, their homes lie empty and their landmarks have been wiped out. They have exchanged their fortified palaces, their luxurious beds and their scattered cushions for rocks and stones stacked in their muddy and boxed graves dug in the wilderness, fortified with sand only. Although the graveyard may be close to a town, its inhabitants are still estranged and even though it may be in the very midst of an inhabited place, its inhabitants are extremely lonely as the people of the town engage in their activities. They feel no affinity with other inhabitants and do not even engage in mutual neighborly relations despite being so close to each other. How can they really have any relations when decomposition has ground them to dust and rocks and mud have consumed their bodies. After once being vibrant with life, they now lay dead and after once seeking good lives, they are now reduced to decayed bones. Their friends were pained as they took to live in the sand and undertook a 'Journey from which there is no return. Farfetched! Farfetched indeed (is the thought of returning to this world)! Never will they return! The request to return is merely a statement they make without any hope for a response because behind them is a impregnable barrier until the day when they are resurrected. You people will also be experiencing the loneliness and decay that they have experienced in the realm of the dead. You will be placed in trust in that resting place and that safety deposit box will take charge of you. What will your condition be when all matters will draw to an end, when everything contained in the graves will be raised, when everything contained in the heart will be exposed and you will be standing before your honored King to have everything laid bare. Hearts will then flutter out of fear because of past sins. All veils and shrouds will then be torn apart and all your faults and secrets will be exposed. He then recited the following verses:

الْيَوْمَ تُجْزَى كُلُّ نَفْسٍ بِمَا كَسَبَتْ

This Day shall every person be recompensed for what he earned... (Ghafir:17)

لِيَجْزِيَ الَّذِينَ أَسَاءُوا بِمَا عَمِلُوا وَيَجْزِيَ الَّذِينَ أَحْسَنُوا بِالْحُسْنَى (31)

...He may requite those who do evil with that which they have done (i.e. punish them in Hell), and reward those who do good, with what is best (i.e. Paradise). (An-Najm:31)

The book, every person's record of actions shall be given to them and you will see the sinners afraid of what is contained in them because it will condemn them to Jahannam. They will say,

وَوُضِعَ الْكِتَابُ فَتَرَى الْمُجْرِمِينَ مُشْفِقِينَ مِمَّا فِيهِ وَيَقُولُونَ يَا وَيْلَتَنَا مَالِ هَذَا الْكِتَابِ لَا يُغَادِرُ صَغِيرَةً وَلَا كَبِيرَةً إِلَّا أَحْصَاهَا وَوَجَدُوا مَا عَمِلُوا حَاضِرًا وَلَا يَظْلِمُ رَبُّكَ أَحَدًا (49)

And the Book (ones Record) will be placed (in the right hand for a believer in the Oneness of Allah, and in the left hand for a disbeliever in the Oneness of Allah), and you will see the Mujrimoon (criminals, polytheists, sinners, etc.), fearful of that which is (recorded) therein. They will say: "Woe to us! What sort of Book is this that leaves neither a small thing nor a big thing, but has recorded it with numbers!" And they will find all that they did, placed before them, and your Lord treats no one with injustice. (Al-Kahaf:49)

May Allah make us and you all practice on His Book and followers of His friends until he enters us all into the home of eternal residence by His grace. Verily He is Most Worthy of Praise, Most Majestic." *(Dinowri, Ibn Asakir in Kanzul Ummal, Muntakhab Kanzul Ummal).* Another narration states at the beginning that Ali ؓ commenced his lecture saying, "All praise belongs to Allah. I praise Allah, seek His assistance, believe in Him, rely on Him and I testify that there is none worthy of worship but the One Allah Who has no partner and that Muhammad ﷺ is His servant and Rasul. Allah sent him with

guidance and the true religion to eradicate all your ailments and to awaken you from your negligence. "Remember that you will surely die and resurrected after death, when you will be made to stand to account for your actions and be either rewarded or punished for it. You should never allow this worldly life to deceive you..." The rest of the narration is as quoted above. *(Ibn Jowzi in Safwatus Safwa)*

His Lecture Concerning Accompanying Funeral Processions

Ja'far bin Muhammad reports from his grandfather that Ali ؓ once accompanied a funeral procession. When the deceased was lowered into the grave, the family started to weep loudly. "What makes you weep?" he asked. "By Allah!" he continued, "If people could witness what the deceased has witnessed, the sight would make them forget all about the deceased. The angel of death will return to them time and time again until he leaves none of them alive." Ali ؓ then stood up and said, "O servants of Allah! I emphatically advise you to be conscious of that Allah Who has cited so many examples for you (to make you understand realities) and has specified the periods you are to live. He has granted you ears so that whatever enters them may be memorized and granted you eyes so that whatever is hidden can become apparent to you. Allah has also granted you hearts to understand the mechanics of whatever misfortunes strike it and to understand that which gives life to it (Allah's Dhikr). Allah has neither created you in vain nor diverted the Reminder (the Qur'an) from you. On the contrary, He has honored you with a shower of munificent bounties and granted you the best of gifts most generously. Allah has full knowledge of your numbers and has prepared returns for your every condition of prosperity and adversity. O servants of Allah! You must therefore inculcate Taqwa, earnestly apply yourselves to seeking the pleasure of Allah and hasten to do good deeds before the arrival of that which destroys passions and demolishes all desires death. This is necessary because the bounties of this world are short-lived and one is never safe from the sudden disasters of this world. In addition to this, the world is also deceptive, ever-changing, a worthless shelter and a shaky support. Things of this world quickly become old and after tiring out a person with his passions, it feeds him only the milk of deception. Dear servants of Allah! Take heed from the lessons you learn and from the signs and indications you observe. Hearken to warnings and take benefit from advices. It is almost as if the talons of death have dug themselves in to you and the home of sand has enveloped you. It is almost as if the most frightening scenes have taken you by surprise when the trumpet is sounded, when graves are emptied, when people are led to the plains of resurrection and made to stand for reckoning under the complete authority of the Almighty. Every soul will then have an angel to push him along to the Plains of Resurrection and also a witness to testify against him for the actions he carried out. The earth will then be illuminated by the light of its Rabb, records of deeds will be presented (to the people), the Ambiya and witnesses will be brought forward and without anyone being wronged, all matters will be decided with justice.

Cities will shake on that day, a crier will make the announcement, people will meet with Allah, the 'sin' will be exposed *(for the term 'Mutashabihat', refer to Qalam:42)* and the sun will eclipse. Wild animals will be gathered together on the plains, secrets will be exposed, the evil ones will be destroyed and hearts will tremble. Allah shall inflict the people of Jahannam with devastating fear and a terrible punishment. Jahannam will be brought forward for all to see along with its hooks, yokes, frightening screams, thunderous roars, fury and threats. Its flames will be leaping, its waters will be bubbling all over and its searing winds will be raging. Those doomed there for eternity will have no respite from it and their remorse will never end. The shackles of Jahannam can never be broken and the people there will have angels with them who will give them the news that the hospitality they will be shown will only be boiling water, entry into flaming fires, deprivation from the mercy of Allah, separation from friends and a trip to the fire of Jahannam. O servants of Allah! Fear Allah as a gentle and humble person would fear, who would flee out of fear and would heed all warnings he is given. Such a person would be on the lookout, would save himself by fleeing, would carry out good deeds for the Hereafter and take his journey's provisions along for assistance. Allah suffices as an avenger for the oppressed and One who sees everything. Allah's Book will suffice as a plaintiff and adversary for those who acted against it and Jannah will suffice as a reward for the righteous while Jahannam will suffice as retribution and punishment for the sinful. I seek Allah's forgiveness for myself and for all of you."*(Abu Nu'aym in Hilya)*

His Lecture Encouraging People to act for the Hereafter

After duly praising Allah in one of his lectures, Ali ﷺ said, "Verily this world is turning its back around and bidding farewell while the Akhirh is arriving and straining its eyes to look. Today this world is the time for the race while tomorrow it will be seen who has gone ahead. Behold! You are passing through days of hope which are followed by your death. Therefore, whoever is neglectful of doing good during the days of hope before death approaches will be at a loss. Remember that you should do deeds for Allah in anticipation for rewards just as you would do them when fearing his punishment. I have never seen a place like Jannah yet its seeker is asleep. I have also not seen a place like Jahannam, yet the one who ought to be running away from it is also asleep. Take note of the fact that whoever does not benefit from the truth will still be harmed by falsehood and the one whom guidance does not put on the straight path will certainly be led away from the straight path by misguidance. Listen well! You have been instructed to travel to the Hereafter and have been shown where to find the provisions for the journey. O people! Remember that this world is a ready commodity that both the righteous and the sinful eat of, whereas the Hereafter is true promise when the All Powerful King (Allah) shall pass judgment. While Saitan threatens you with poverty and instructs you to do lewd acts, Allah promises you His forgiveness and grace. Allah is Most Accommodating and All Knowing. O people! Do good works during your lives and you will be protected in the end. Allah has promised Jannah for those who obey Him and promised Jahannam for those who disobey Him. The screams of the people in the fire of Jahannam never subsides, the prisoners of Jahannam never escape and those with fractured limbs never have them heal. Its heat is intense, its depth immense and its drink is pus. What I fear most for you people is that you follow the dictates of your passions and that you entertain long hopes of the future. *(Dinowri, Ibn Asakir in Kanzul Ummal, Muntakhab Kanzul Ummal)* Another narration states that Ali ﷺ also added, "...because following one's passions prevents one from the truth and entertaining long hopes makes one forget the Hereafter." *(Al Bidayah wan Nihayah)*

His Lecture After the Battle at Nahrwan

Ziyad A'rabi narrates that Amirul Mu'minin Ali bin Abi Talib ﷺ once ascended the pulpit in Kufa after the scourge (of the Khawarij) and after the battle had been fought against them at Nahrwan. He started by praising Allah but he then choked on his tears and wept so much that his beard was soaked and the tears, which started running off. He then shook his beard and the droplets of tears happened to fall on some people. Ziyad says that they commonly believed that Allah forbade Jahannam from the people on whom those tears fell. Thereafter, he said, "O people! Never be amongst those people who wish for Jannah without doing any good and who postpone repentance because of their long hopes to live long. They are people who speak like the abstinent ones yet they behave like those who hanker after the world. If they are given any portion of the world, they are not satisfied and when anything is held back from them, they are not content. They fail to express gratitude for what they are given and still seek to have more. They instruct people to do what they do not themselves do and forbid people from that which they themselves do not abstain from. They love the righteous ones but do not carry out their actions and they detest the sinful ones whereas they are amongst them. The Nafs of such a person overpowers him in matters he is uncertain about to do worldly acts, the benefits of which are not certain but does not overpower him in maters he is convinced to do acts for the Hereafter, the benefits of which are guaranteed. When he achieves independence, he falls into sin, when he falls ill, he is grieved and when he suffers poverty, he loses hope and becomes weak-hearted. He takes benefit from both sin and Allah's bounties without ever being grateful when he is blessed with well-being or even being patient when afflicted with hardship. He behaves as if only others have been warned of death and that only they have been cautioned and rebuked. O targets of death! O pawns of death! O containers of disease! O spoils of time! O booty of the ages! O fruits of generations! O light of the vicissitudes of time! O muted ones at the time of litigation on the Day of Judgment! O those drowning in tribulations that have become an obstacle to them learning lessons! It is with proof and conviction that I state that no successful person can attain success without knowing himself and every destroyed person has destroyed himself. Allah says: يَا أَيُّهَا الَّذِينَ آمَنُوا قُوا أَنْفُسَكُمْ وَأَهْلِيكُمْ نَارًا

O you who believe! Ward off from yourselves and your families a Fire (Hell)... (At-Tahrim:6)

May Allah make us and you all amongst those who listen to advice and accept it and who respond with the correct action when summoned to carry it out." *(Ibn Najjar in Kanzul Ummal, Muntakhab Kanzul Ummal)*

Lecture Concerning Enjoining Good and Forbidding Evil

Yahya bin Yamur narrates that in a lecture to the people, Ali bin Abi Talib ﷺ started by praising Allah. Thereafter, he said, "O people! Those who came before you were destroyed only because when they started to sin openly and were not stopped by their priests and those attached to Allah, Allah sent His punishment to them. Behold! You must remember that enjoining good and forbidding evil neither cuts off your sustenance nor does it bring your death any closer. Allah's decisions descend from the heavens just as raindrops fan down. These decisions of Allah determine whether there will be prosperity or adversity in any aspect concerning a particular person's personal self, his family or his wealth. Therefore, when any of you suffers an adversity in any aspect of his personal self, his family or his wealth and he sees that someone else enjoys quite the opposite, this must never be a cause of tribulation for him. When a Muslim has not been overpowered by a wretched disposition, he expresses humility whenever he thinks of the adversity, whereas a person with a wretched disposition laments over it, behaving like a gambler waiting for his first win (after too many losses) that will bring him plenty of wealth and allow him to settle all the penalties he has had to bear. This also bears a similarity with the Muslim who is trustworthy. Whenever he makes Du'a to Allah, he waits for one of 2 good things to happen: either he gets what he prays for or he gets rewards in the Hereafter. What is with Allah his rewards in the Hereafter is better for him, otherwise Allah grants him some wealth, making him a person who has both family and wealth. There are 2 types of harvests: the harvest of this world and that of the Hereafter. While the harvest of this world is wealth and children, the harvest of the Hereafter is good deeds. Allah has however granted both to certain people." Sufyan bin Uyayna remarked, "Who else but Ali bin Abi Talib ؓ is capable of speaking such wonderful words?!" *(Ibn Abi Dunya, Ibn Asakir in Kanzul Ummal, Muntakhab Kanzul Ummal).* Another narration states that Ali ؓ said, "Allah's decisions descend from the heavens..." The narration continues like the one above, but adds that he also said, "(Whenever he makes Du'a to Allah, he waits for one of two good things to happen) He may either become a wealthy person with a large family, together with honor and Deen. Otherwise, Allah will grant him rewards in the Hereafter and the Hereafter is always better and everlasting. There are two types of harvests. While the harvest of this world is wealth and Taqwa, the harvest of the Hereafter is the everlasting good deeds." *(Al Bidayah wan Nihayah)*

The Lecture he delivered in Kufa

Abu Wa'il reports that in a lecture delivered in Kufa, he heard Ali ؓ say, 'O people! The person who portrays himself as a pauper will soon suffer poverty, the person who lives very long will suffer many trials and the one who does not prepare for adversities will be unable to exercise patience when afflicted. Remember also that the one who assumes a position of authority will practice favoritism and the one who does not consult with others will have regrets." After saying this, Ali ؓ would say, "Soon there shall remain of Islam naught but its name and of the Qur'an naught but its script. Behold! No person should be too shy to learn, neither should he be too shy to admit that he does not know something when asked about something he has no knowledge about. While your Masajid will be well attended during those times, your hearts and bodies will be bereft of guidance. The worst of you beneath the skies will be your learned ones who will be the source of trouble, which will return to them." A man then stood up and asked, "O Amirul Mu'minin! When will this happen?" Ali ؓ replied, "When the knowledge of Deen will rest with the demoralized ones, when the best of you will carry out indecent acts and when government will be in the hands of your youngsters. Then you should wait for Judgment." *(Bayhaqi in Kanzul Ummal)*

His Extremely Eloquent and Comprehensive Lecture

Ali ؓ once stood up to deliver a lecture saying, "All praise belongs to Allah Who has created creation, Who breaks the dawn, Who will resurrect the dead and raise all within the graves. I testify that there is none worthy of worship but Allah and I testify that Muhammad ﷺ is the servant and Rasul of Allah. I emphatically advise you to adopt Taqwa. Remember that the best means of attaining proximity to Allah is by Iman and Jihad in the Path of Allah. It is also most effectively attained by the Kalima of sincerity that is most natural, by establishing salah, which is part of the true creed, by paying zakah, which one of the

obligatory duties and by fasting during the month of Ramadhan, which happens to be a shield against Allah's punishment. Furthermore, it is attained by making Hajj at the Kaba, which eliminates poverty and obliterates sins. Fostering good family ties is also a means of attaining proximity to Allah since it causes one's wealth to increase, one's lifespan to be extended and love within the family to grow. Sadaqa should also be given in secret because it erases sin and extinguishes the wrath of your Rabb. Good deeds need also be carried out because it prevents a bad death and safeguards one against being floored by abject circumstances. Engage abundantly in Allah's Dhikr because it is the best thing to engage the tongue with. You must look forward to the promises Allah has made to the people of Taqwa because Allah's promises are the most truthful of all promises. Follow the guidance of your Nabi ﷺ because it is the best of all guidance and adopt his way of life because it is the best of practices to follow. Learn the Book of Allah because it is the best of all speeches and develop a deep understanding of Allah's Deen because it is the spring of the heart. Treat physical and spiritual illnesses with its light because the Qur'an is definitely a cure for all that hearts contain. Recite the Qur'an beautifully because it is the most beautiful of all narratives and when it is recited to you, listen attentively and remain silent so that mercy may be showered on you. When you have been inspired to study the Qur'an, practice what you have learnt so that you may receive guidance. Remember that the practicing Alim who does not practice his knowledge, he would be just like the tyrannical ignoramus who cannot be straightened because of his ignorance. In fact, I feel that the regret is more lasting and the case stronger against the Alim who forsakes his knowledge as opposed to the ignoramus who is confused in his ignorance. Both these persons are astray and destroyed. Never entertain doubts because it will plunge you into misgivings and it is such misgivings that will lead you to kufr. Do not also practice on concessions because you will then soon become too compromising and as soon as you promise on the truth, you will lose plenty. Bear in mind that it is an act of intelligence that you rely on Allah but this reliance should not be such that it leads you to deception. The person who most wishes well for himself will be the most obedient to his Rabb whereas the one who most deceived will be most disobedient to his Rabb. The son who obeys Allah will remain safe and happy while the one who disobeys Allah will remain in fear and have regrets.

Furthermore, you must also pray to Allah for conviction and always show Him your desire for well-being. In fact, conviction is the best of all things that remain entrenched within the heart. The best of all matters are those that are the most resolute while the worst of them are those that have been fabricated. Remember that every fabricated matter is a Bid'ah and every person who fabricates is engaging in Bid'ah. Such a person will be destroying the Deen because whenever he fabricates a Bid'ah, he is forsaking a Sunnah. Those truly at a loss are those whose Deen is at a loss and a have put their own souls at the losing end by obeying Allah. Verily ostentation is a part of Shirk, while sincerity is a part of good deeds and Iman. Gatherings of futility make one forget the Qur'an, are attended by Saitan and invite people to misguidance. Remaining in the company of non-Mahram women causes the heart to stray and captivates the eyes because women are indeed the traps of Saitan. Be true to Allah because Allah is with those who are true and abstain from lying because lying is the antithesis of Iman. Always bear in mind that the truth stands at the peak of salvation and honor while lying stands at the peak of destruction and devastation. Listen well! Always speak the truth and you will be known for it, practice it and you will be amongst its worthy bearers. Always return trusts to those who have entrusted goods with you. Join ties with those family members who have severed them and be gracious to those who deprive you. Fulfill the pledges you undertake with people, ensure that you exercise justice when passing judgment and never boast about your ancestors before each other. Never call each other names, never make fun of each other and never make each other angry. Assist the poor, the oppressed, those in debt, those striving in the Path of Allah, the beggars and slaves and always show mercy to widows and orphans. Make Salam common amongst you and reply to the Salam of those who greet you, using the same words or words that are better. (He then recited the verse:)

وَتَعَاوَنُوا عَلَى الْبِرِّ وَالتَّقْوَى وَلَا تَعَاوَنُوا عَلَى الْإِثْمِ وَالْعُدْوَانِ وَاتَّقُوا اللَّهَ إِنَّ اللَّهَ شَدِيدُ الْعِقَابِ (2)

...help you one another in Al-Birr and At-Taqwa (virtue, righteousness and piety); but do not help one another in sin and transgression. And fear Allah. Verily, Allah is Severe in punishment. (Al-Ma'ida:2)

Entertain guests, be good to your neighbor, visit the ill, accompany funeral processions and, O servants of Allah, behave like brothers. Furthermore, I wish to add that this world has turned its back and bid farewell, whereas the Hereafter has arrived and is straining its eyes to look. Today this world is the time for the race while tomorrow it will be seen who has gone ahead. The winner will have Jannah while at the other end is Jahannam. Behold! You are passing through days of respite which are followed by your death that is approaching very fast. Therefore, whoever does good deeds sincerely for Allah during the days of respite before his death, has really done well and will have what he hopes for. On the other hand, whoever is neglectful of doing good will be at a loss for good deeds, will have shattered hopes and will actually come to harm because of his hopes. You must do good deeds with hope of reward as well as in fear for punishment. If you are overcome with hope, then be grateful to Allah and couple it with fear. Then, if you are overcome with fear, remember Allah and couple it with hope because Allah has announced that men shall have Jannah in return for their good deeds and will have an increase in bounties for their gratitude. I have never seen a place like Jannah yet its seeker is asleep. I have also not seen a place like Jahannam, yet the one who ought to be running away from it is also asleep. I have also not seen anyone earn as much as the one who earns for the day when treasures win be accumulated, when secrets will be exposed and when all major sins are collected together. Take note of the fact that whoever does not benefit from the truth will still be harmed by falsehood and the one whom guidance does not put on the straight path will certainly be led away from the straight path by misguidance. The one whom conviction does not benefit will be harmed by doubt and the one who does not benefit from what is before him will be one-eyed when viewing something far off and even more helpless when it comes to things that are not present. You have been instructed to travel to the Hereafter and have been shown where to find the provisions for the Journey. What I fear most for you people is that you follow the dictates of your passions and that you entertain long hopes of the future. As for entertaining long hopes, it makes one forget the Hereafter, whereas following one's passions distances one from the truth. Listen well! This world has embarked on its return journey, the Hereafter has just commenced its arrival. Both these places have their sons, so as far as possible, you should endeavor to be amongst the sons of the Hereafter and not amongst the sons of this world. While today you have the opportunity for actions without reckoning, tomorrow you will face reckoning without the opportunity for actions." (Al Bidayah wan Nihayah)

His Lecture on what will Happen to the Progeny of Rasulullah ﷺ

Abu Khaira reports that he accompanied Ali ؓ to Kufa, where he ascended the pulpit and duly praised Allah. Thereafter, addressed the people saying, "What will you people do when the progeny of Rasulullah ﷺ will be attacked whilst in your midst?" The people replied by saying, "We will then display the most fearsome valor before Allah." To this, Ali ؓ remarked, "I swear by the Being Who controls my life that they will certainly be attacked whilst in your midst and you people will go out to kill them yourselves. He then recited the following couplets:
They bring him (Husain ؓ) there to Kufa in deception and then announce 'Accept his (Yazid's) call to pledge allegiance at his hands, otherwise there can be no escape or excuse'" (Tabrani)

His Lecture in which he Quotes the Words of Rasulullah ﷺ

Ibrahim Taymi reports from his father (Yazid bin Sharik) that Ali ؓ once addressed them saying, 'Whoever claims that we the family of Rasulullah ﷺ have with us something else to read other than the Book of Allah and this note, then he is grossly mistaken. All that this note contains is the ages of camels according to which zakah is paid, some laws pertaining to retribution for injuries and a statement of Rasulullah ﷺ in which he said, 'Madinah is sacred from between Mount Ayr and Mount Thowr. Whoever fabricates anything in Deen here or even gives refuge to one who does, he will have on him the curse of Allah, of the angels and of all of mankind. Allah will also not accept from him any obligatory or optional deeds until the Day of Judgment. Whoever claims that another person is his father or a slave claims that another person is his master, he will have on him the curse of Allah, of the angels and of all of mankind. Allah will not accept from him any obligatory or optional deeds until the Day of Judgment. The responsibility of all Muslims is one and the lowest of them must strive to fulfill it.'" (Ahmad)

His Lecture Concerning the Merits of Abu Bakr ؓ and Omar ؓ

Ibrahim Nakha'e reports that Alqama bin Qais once mounted the pulpit and said, "It was on this very pulpit that Ali ؓ delivered a lecture to us. After duly praising Allah and mentioning certain things, he said, 'Verily the best of all people after Rasulullah ﷺ were Abu Bakr ؓ and Omar ؓ. After them, we had initiated many new things, about which Allah shall pass judgment.'" (Ahmad). Abu Juhaifa also reports that Ali ؓ once mounted the pulpit where he commenced by praising Allah and sending salutations to Rasulullah ﷺ. Thereafter, he said, 'The best person of this Ummah after Rasulullah ﷺ was Abu Bakr ؓ and next was Omar ؓ. Allah places goodness wherever He pleases."(Ahmad). Another narration is similar to the first one quoted above, but without the words "After them, we had initiated many new things...". This narration however adds that Ali ؓ said, 'We never regarded it as farfetched to think that it was an angel who would speak with the tongue of Omar ؓ. " (Ahmad). Alqama reports that Ali ؓ once addressed them. After duly praising Allah, he said, "The news has reached me that some people regard me to be better than Abu Bakr ؓ and Omar ؓ. Had I forbidden you from this before, I would have certainly punished people for saying it. However, I do not like to punish before first announcing the prohibition. Nevertheless, whoever mentions anything of the sort after this address of mine shall be regarded as a slanderer and shall therefore suffer the penalty of a slanderer of 80 lashes. Verily the best of all people after

Rasulullah ﷺ was Abu Bakr ؓ, followed by Omar ؓ. After them, we had initiated many new things, about which Allah shall pass judgment." *(Ibn Asim, Ibn Shahin in Sunnah, Isfahani in Hujja, Ibn Asakir in Muntakhab Kanzul Ummal).* Zaid bin Wahab reports that Suwaid bin Ghafala once went to Ali ؓ when he was the Khalifa. "O Amirul Mu'minin!" Suwaid said, "I have passed by some people who were making inappropriate statements about Abu Bakr ؓ and Omar ؓ." Ali ؓ immediately sprang up, mounted the pulpit and said, "I swear by the Being Who slits the seed and created the soul that it is a venerable Mu'min who loves the 2 of them (Abu Bakr ؓ and Omar ؓ) whereas only a wretched and irreligious person will dislike them. Loving them is a means of attaining proximity to Allah while enmity for them will lead to irreligiousness. What is the matter with certain people that they speak ill of Rasulullah ﷺ's 2 brothers, his 2 ministers, his 2 companions, the 2 leaders of the Quraish and 2 fathers of the Muslims? I absolve myself of all those who speak ill of them and I shall have them punished." *(Abu Nu'aym in Hilya, Muntakhab Kanzul Ummal).* A detailed lecture in this regard has already passed in the chapter discussing defending one's pious predecessors. Ali bin Husain narrates that after Ali ؓ had returned from the Battle of Siffin, a youngster from the Banu Hashim family asked him, "O Amirul Mu'minin! I heard you say in the Jumu'ah sermon, 'O Allah! Set right our affairs as you had done for the rightly guided Khulafa.' Who were they?" Ali ؓ's eyes welled with tears as he said, "They were Abu Bakr ؓ and Omar ؓ. They were the leaders of guidance, the great scholars of Islam and the ones by whom guidance was attained after Rasulullah ﷺ. Whoever follows them will be guided to the straight path and whoever does what they did will have direction. Whoever holds fast to their ways will be amongst the group of Allah and the group of Allah are the ones who will attain success." *(Lalka'ee, Abu Talib Ishari, Nasr in Hujjah, Muntakhab Kanzul Ummal)*

Various Lectures that Ali ؓ Delivered

A scholar from the Banu Tamim tribe reports that Ali ؓ once addressed them saying, "There shall come a time when people will bite into each other and the wealthy will hold on to their wealth (refusing to spend it on others) whereas they have never been commanded to do that. In fact, Allah says: وَلَا تَنسَوُا الْفَضْلَ بَيْنَكُمْ

...and do not forget liberality between yourselves...(Al-Baqara:237)

During those times the evil ones will be regarded as honorable while the good people will be looked down upon. Furthermore, people will be buying from desperate people, whereas Rasulullah ﷺ forbade buying from people who are desperate (because they are forced to sell, even if it is at a loss). Rasulullah ﷺ also forbade sales that involve deception and the selling of fruit before it ripens." *(Ahmad).* Abu Ubaid who was the freed slave of Abdur Rahman bin Auf ؓ reports that he also attended the Eid (Eidul Adha) salah led by Ali ؓ. He led the salah before delivering the sermon, and there was neither any Adhan nor Iqama. He then said in his sermon, "O people! Verily Rasulullah ﷺ prohibited eating the meat of your sacrificial animals after three days, so do not eat it thereafter." (This prohibition was however lifted and Muslims are permitted to eat the meat after 3 days.) *(Ahmad).* Rib'ee bin Hirash reports that he heard Ali ؓ say in a lecture, "Do not lie about me because whoever lies about me shall enter Jahannam." *(Ahmad, Tayalisi).* Abu Abdur Rahman Sulami narrates that Ali ؓ said the following in his lecture: "O people! Enforce the penalties of the

Shari'ah on your slaves, whether they are married or not. When a slave woman belonging to Rasulullah ﷺ committed adultery, Rasulullah ﷺ instructed me to enforce the penalty. However, when I went to her I found that she had just started to bleed after giving birth. I therefore feared that she may lose her life if I had to lash her. When 1 reported back to Rasulullah ﷺ, he told me that my decision had been correct." *(Ahmad)*

Abdullah bin Sabt narrates that Ali ؓ once addressed them saying, "I swear by the Being Who splits the seed and creates the soul that this beard will certainly be smeared with the blood of this head, I will shortly be assassinated. The people asked, "Do inform us who he (your assassin) shall be. By Allah! We shall kill his entire family!" Ali ؓ however instructed them saying, "I ask you in the name of Allah not to kill anyone other than my assassin." The people's response was, "If you know this, why do you not appoint a successor then?" "No," Ali ؓ replied, "I prefer to rather leave you just as Rasulullah ﷺ left you (to choose your own Khalifa)." *(Ahmad).* Amr bin Ala reports that Ali ؓ once addressed the people saying, "O people! 1 swear by the Being besides Whom there is not deity that I have not decreased anything small or large from your wealth apart from this vial that the chief of a village gave me as a gift." He then removed from his sleeve a vial containing some perfume. *(Abdur Razzaq, Abu Ybaid in Amwal, Hakim in Kuna, Abu Nu'aym in Hilya, Muntakhab Kanzul Ummal).* Umair bin Abdul Malik reports that Ali ؓ once addressed them from the pulpit in Kufa saying, - "Rasulullah ﷺ would be first to notify me if I did not ask him a question about something and would always inform me about anything I asked. He once informed me about His Rabb saying, 'Allah says, 'I swear by My loftiness over My throne that when the people of any town or household or even when a lone man in the wilderness turns away from disobeying Me, which displeases Me towards obeying Me, which pleases Me, I shall turn away from him My punishment, which displeases him and focus towards him My mercy, which is sure to please him. On the contrary, when the people of any town or household or even when a lone man in the wilderness turns away from obeying Me, which pleases Me towards disobeying Me, which displeases Me, I shall turn away from him My mercy, which displeases him and focus towards him My wrath, which is sure to displease him." *(Ibn Mardway in Kanzul Ummal)*

The Lectures that Amirul Mu'minin Hasan bin Ali ؓ Delivered after the Demise of his Father

Hubaira narrates that when Ali bin Abi Talib ؓ passed away, his son Hasan ؓ stood up, mounted the pulpit and addressed the people saying, "O people! Tonight such a man has left this world whom the earlier people could not catch up with and whom the latter people will never be able to find. Whenever Rasulullah ﷺ dispatched him on an expedition, Jibra'el عليه السلام would be on his right side, Mika'el عليه السلام would be on his left side and he would not return until Allah had granted him victory. All that he left in estate was 700 Dirhams with which he intended to purchase a slave. His soul departed on the same night that Isa was raised to the heavens, which was the 27th of Ramadhan." Another narration adds that he also said, "He left neither any gold or silver apart from 700 Dirhams, which was all that was left over from his allowance." This narration however does not contain the words "His soul departed on the same night that…" *(Ibn Sa'd, Abu Nu'aym in Hilya, Ahmad).* When Ali ؓ was martyred, Hasan ؓ stood up to address the people. After duly praising Allah, he said, "By Allah! You have killed a man tonight, which is a night during which the Qur'an was revealed, during which Isa (عليه السلام) was raised to the heavens, during which Yusha bin Noon (عليه السلام) the aide to Musa (عليه السلام) as martyred and the night during which the repentance of Bani Isra'el was accepted." *(Abu Ya'la, Ibn Jareer, Ibn Asakir in Muntakhab Kanzul Ummal).* Abu Tufail reports a narration similar to the one above, but with the addition that Hasan (رضي الله عنه) also said, "Whoever knows me knows and whoever does not know me should know that I am Hasan the son of Muhammad (صلى الله عليه وسلم). He then recited the verse in which Yusuf (عليه السلام) says: وَاتَّبَعْتُ مِلَّةَ آبَائِي إِبْرَاهِيمَ وَإِسْحَاقَ وَيَعْقُوبَ

And I have followed the religion of my fathers, - Ibrahim, Ishaque and Yaqub (عليه السلام)... (Yusuf:38)

Just as Yusuf (عليه السلام) referred to his grandfathers as his fathers, so too do I refer to my grandfather Rasulullah (صلى الله عليه وسلم) as my father. "After then reciting some portions of the Qur'an, he said, "I am the son of the giver of glad tidings, I am the son of the Warner, I am the son of Nabi (صلى الله عليه وسلم), I am the son of the one who called to Allah with His permission, I am the son of the brilliant lamp and I am the son of the one who was sent as a mercy to the universe. I belong to that household which Allah had rid of all spiritual filth and had thoroughly purified. I belong to that family whom Allah has made it compulsory for others to love and to assist. Allah says in the revelation He has sent to Muhammad (صلى الله عليه وسلم):

قُل لَّا أَسْأَلُكُمْ عَلَيْهِ أَجْرًا إِلَّا الْمَوَدَّةَ فِي الْقُرْبَى

...say (O Muhammad (صلى الله عليه وسلم)): "No reward do I ask of you for this except to be kind to me for my kinship with you... (Ash-Shura:23) *(Abu Ya'la, Ibn Jareer, Ibn Asakir in Muntakhab Kanzul Ummal)*

Another narration adds that Hasan (رضي الله عنه) also said, "Rasulullah (صلى الله عليه وسلم) would hand over the flag to Ali (رضي الله عنه) and when the battle grew furious, Jibra'el would be there to fight by his side." The narrator of this report states that it was the twenty first of Ramadhan (when Ali (رضي الله عنه) passed away). *(Tabrani, Abu Ya'la, Bazzar in Majma'uz Zawa'id).* Yet another narration similar to the one of Abu Tufail adds that Hasan (رضي الله عنه) said, "I am from that family to whom Jibra'el (عليه السلام) descended and with whom he ascended." The narration also states that Hasan (رضي الله عنه) added the concluding part of the above verse when he recited: وَمَن يَقْتَرِفْ حَسَنَةً نَّزِدْ لَهُ فِيهَا حُسْنًا

...and whoever earns a good righteous deed, We shall give him an increase of good in respect thereof... (Ash-Shura:23)

He then explained carrying out a good deed in this verse refers to imbibing love for the family of Rasulullah (صلى الله عليه وسلم). *(Hakim)*

His Lecture After being Stabbed

Abu Jamila narrates that after Ali (رضي الله عنه) was assassinated, his son Hasan (رضي الله عنه) became the Khalifa. However, when he was once leading the salah, someone leapt at him and stabbed him with a dagger in his buttock. This confined him to bed for a month, after which he stood up to address the people from the pulpit. He said, "O people of Iraq! Fear Allah when it concerns us because we are both your leaders and your guests. We also belong to the household concerning whom Allah says: إِنَّمَا يُرِيدُ اللَّهُ لِيُذْهِبَ عَنكُمُ

الرِّجْسَ أَهْلَ الْبَيْتِ وَيُطَهِّرَكُمْ تَطْهِيرًا (33) *...Allah wishes only to remove Ar-Rijs (evil deeds and sins, etc.) from you, O members of the family (of the Prophet (صلى الله عليه وسلم)), and to purify you with a thorough purification. (Al-Ahzab:33).* He continued speaking until there was none to be seen in the Masjid who was not weeping. *(Tabrani, Haythami).* Hasan (رضي الله عنه) continued repeating these words until there was none in the Masjid who was not sobbing profusely. *(Ibn Abi Hatim in Tafsir Ibn Kathir)*

The Lecture he Delivered When he made Peace with Mu'awiya (رضي الله عنه)

Sha'bi reports that he was present at Nakhila when Hasan (رضي الله عنه) made peace with Mu'awiya (رضي الله عنه). Mu'awiya (رضي الله عنه) then said to him, "Now that the matter has been settled, do address the people and inform them that you have relinquished the Khilafa and handed it over to me." Hasan (رضي الله عنه) then stood on the pulpit and praised Allah. Sha'bi confirms that he personally heard the lecture. Hasan (رضي الله عنه) said, "The best of all intelligence is Taqwa and the worst of all foolishness is sin. The post of Khilafa that has been disputed between Mu'awiya (رضي الله عنه) and I may either be my right, which I have now relinquished in his favor for peace to reign amongst the Ummah and to save their blood. If this post is really the right of someone else other than me, then I have now handed it over. He then recited the verse: وَإِنْ أَدْرِي لَعَلَّهُ فِتْنَةٌ لَّكُمْ وَمَتَاعٌ إِلَى حِينٍ (111)

And I know not, perhaps it may be a trial for you, and an enjoyment for a while. (Al-Anbiya:111) (Tabrani in Kabeer, Haythami)

In another narration, Sha'bi says, "Hasan bin Ali (رضي الله عنه) addressed us at Nakhila when he made peace with Mu'awiya (رضي الله عنه). He stood up and after praising Allah, he said..." The words of this narration are like the one above, but states that after reciting the verse of the Qur'an, Hasan (رضي الله عنه) concluded by saying, "This is all I have to say. I now seek Allah's forgiveness for myself and for all of you." *(Hakim, Bayhaqi).* Yet another narration states that in this historic lecture, Hasan bin Ali (رضي الله عنه) said, "O people! Allah has guided you through the first generation of our family (Rasulullah (صلى الله عليه وسلم)) and has saved you blood from being spilled by the latter generation of our family (myself). The post of Khilafa is a temporary one and the successes of this world pass from hand to hand. Allah has said to His Nabi (صلى الله عليه وسلم): وَإِنْ أَدْرِي لَعَلَّهُ فِتْنَةٌ لَّكُمْ وَمَتَاعٌ إِلَى حِينٍ

(111)

And I know not, perhaps it may be a trial for you, and an enjoyment for a while. (Al-Anbiya:111) (Ibn Jareer in Tarikh)

The Lecture of Amirul Mu'minin Mu'awiya bin Abu Sufyan (رضي الله عنه)

Muhammad bin Ka'b Qurazi narrates that Mu'awiya bin Abu Sufyan (رضي الله عنه) delivered a lecture in Madinah saying, "O people! There is none to prevent that which Allah grants, none can grant what Allah prevents, the wealth of the wealthy cannot assist them and when Allah wishes well for a person, He grants him understanding of the Deen. I have heard Rasulullah (صلى الله عليه وسلم) speak these words from this very pulpit." *(Ibn Abdul Birr in Jami'ul Ilm).* Muhammad bin Abdur Rahman reports that he heard Mu'awiya (رضي الله عنه) deliver a lecture saying, "I have heard Rasulullah (صلى الله عليه وسلم) say, 'When Allah wishes well for a person, He grants him understanding of the Deen. While I am just the distributor (of knowledge), it is Allah Who grants it. This Ummah will always remain firm on the truth and on Allah's Deen until the Day of Judgment without being harmed by those who oppose them." *(Ibn Abdul Birr in Jami).* Umair bin Hani narrates that Mu'awiya bin Abu Sufyan (رضي الله عنه) once addressed them saying, "I heard Rasulullah (صلى الله عليه وسلم) say, 'Until the Day of Judgment, this Ummah will always remain steadfast on Allah's Deen and will not be harmed by those who oppose them or by those who do not want to assist them." Another narration states that he also said, "And they (the Ummah) shall dominate over others." Umair bin Hani says, "Malik bin Yakhamir then stood up and said, 'I heard Mu'adh bin Jabal (رضي الله عنه) say that these people (the Ummah steadfast on the Deen and dominant over others) are the people of Sham (during those times)." *(Ahmad, Abu Ya'la, Ya'qub bin Sufian).* Yunus bin Halbas Janadi reports a similar narration with the addition that Mu'awiya (رضي الله عنه) recited the wing verse (in substantiation):

يَا عِيسَى إِنِّي مُتَوَفِّيكَ وَرَافِعُكَ إِلَيَّ وَمُطَهِّرُكَ مِنَ الَّذِينَ كَفَرُوا وَجَاعِلُ الَّذِينَ اتَّبَعُوكَ فَوْقَ

الَّذِينَ كَفَرُوا إِلَى يَوْمِ الْقِيَامَةِ

...(Allah said) O Isa! I will take you and raise you to Myself and clear you (of the forged statement that Isa is Allah's son) of those who disbelieve, and I will make those who follow you (Monotheists, who worship none but Allah) superior to those who disbelieve (in the Oneness of Allah, or disbelieve in some of His Messengers, e.g. Muhammad ﷺ Isa, Moosa, etc., or in His Holy Books, e.g. the Taurat (Torah), the Injeel (Gospel), the Qur'an) till the Day of Resurrection... (Al-Imran:55) (Ibn Asakir)

Makhul reports that Mu'awiya ؓ was delivering a lecture from the pulpit when he said, "I heard Rasulullah ﷺ say, 'O people! Knowledge is attained through studies and understanding of Deen is attained through deep thought. When Allah wishes well for a person, He grants him understanding of the Deen and it is only the learned ones who truly fear Allah. There shall always be a group from my Ummah who will always remain steadfast on the truth and will dominate over others without being intimidated by those who oppose them and those who are hostile towards them. They will prevail until the Day of Judgment." (Ibn Asakir in Kanzul Ummal)

The Lectures of Amirul Mu'minin Abdullah bin Zubair ؓ on the Occassion of Hajj

Muhammad bin Abdullah reports, "I was present when Abdullah bin Zubair ؓ delivered a lecture during the occasion of Hajj. We had no idea of his presence until he appeared just before the day of Tarwiya (8th of Dhul Hijja) when people entered into the state of Ihram. He was an extremely handsome man in his middle ages, wearing 2 white garments. When he arrived, the people shouted, 'Here comes the Amirul Mu'minin!' He ascended the pulpit and greeted the people. After they replied to his greeting, he recited the most beautiful Talbiya I had ever heard. He then praised Allah and said, "You people have come as delegations to Allah from distant and different places. It is therefore necessary that Allah should honor you. Whoever has come in search of what is with Allah should know that the one who seeks Allah shall never return empty-handed. You must therefore confirm your words with deeds because deeds are the masters of words and intentions are confined to the heart. Fear Allah! Fear Allah in these days of yours because these are days during which Allah forgives sins. Remember that you have come here from various distant lands without the desire for trade, wealth or any other aspect of this world." Abdullah bin Zubair ؓ recited the Talbiya and the people recited it with him. After deliberating at length, he said, "Verily Allah states in His Book: الْحَجُّ أَشْهُرٌ مَعْلُومَاتٌ *'Hajj is the few known months' (Baqara:197).* These are 3 months, namely Shawwal, Dhul Qa'dah and 10 days of Dhul Hijja." He recited further

فَمَنْ فَرَضَ فِيهِنَّ الْحَجَّ فَلَا رَفَثَ وَلَا فُسُوقَ وَلَا جِدَالَ فِي الْحَجِّ وَمَا تَفْعَلُوا مِنْ خَيْرٍ يَعْلَمْهُ اللَّهُ وَتَزَوَّدُوا فَإِنَّ خَيْرَ الزَّادِ التَّقْوَى ...*so whosoever intends to perform Hajj therein by assuming Ihram), then he should not have sexual relations (with his wife), nor commit sin, nor dispute unjustly during the Hajj. And whatever good you do, (be sure) Allah knows it. And take a provision (with you) for the journey, but the best provision is At-Taqwa (piety, righteousness, etc.)... (Al-Baqara:197).* He then continued further to state, "Allah says: لَيْسَ عَلَيْكُمْ جُنَاحٌ أَنْ تَبْتَغُوا فَضْلًا مِنْ رَبِّكُمْ *'There shall be no sin upon you should you seek the bounty from your Rabb'.* Allah has therefore made trade permissible (during the days of Hajj). Thereafter, Allah says: فَإِذَا أَفَضْتُمْ مِنْ عَرَفَاتٍ *'When you leave Arafat...'* This is

the place where people will stay until sunset, after which they will depart (for Muzdalifa). Allah says further: فَاذْكُرُوا اللَّهَ عِنْدَ الْمَشْعَرِ الْحَرَامِ *'then remember Allah at the Mash'arul Haram (The Sacred Monument)'.* These are the mountains where people will also stay over, namely Muzdalifa. Allah states further: وَاذْكُرُوهُ كَمَا هَدَاكُمْ *'Remember Him as He had guided you'.* The next command is not general, but addressed specifically to the people of this city (Makkah) who used to depart (back to Makkah) from Muzdalifa (without going to Arafat at all), while others departed from Arafat. Slamming this act of theirs, Allah revealed the verse: ثُمَّ أَفِيضُوا مِنْ حَيْثُ أَفَاضَ النَّاسُ *Then depart from the place whence all the people depart... (Al-Baqara:199)*

Abdullah bin Zubair ؓ continued further. He said, "It was the practice of the people to boast about their forefathers after completing their Hajj. It was with regard to this that Allah revealed the verse stating:

فَاذْكُرُوا اللَّهَ كَذِكْرِكُمْ آبَاءَكُمْ أَوْ أَشَدَّ ذِكْرًا فَمِنَ النَّاسِ مَنْ يَقُولُ رَبَّنَا آتِنَا فِي الدُّنْيَا وَمَا لَهُ فِي الْآخِرَةِ مِنْ خَلَاقٍ (200) وَمِنْهُمْ مَنْ يَقُولُ رَبَّنَا آتِنَا فِي الدُّنْيَا حَسَنَةً وَفِي الْآخِرَةِ حَسَنَةً وَقِنَا عَذَابَ النَّارِ (201)

...remember Allah as you remember your forefathers or with a far more remembrance. But of mankind there are some who say: "Our Lord! Give us (Your Bounties) in this world!" and for such there will be no portion in the Hereafter. And of them there are some who say: "Our Lord! Give us in this world that which is good and in the Hereafter that which is good, and save us from the torment of the Fire!" (Al-Baqara:200-201)

These people work in this world for the good of this world as well as for the Hereafter." He then continued reciting until he reached the verse: وَاذْكُرُوا اللَّهَ فِي أَيَّامٍ مَعْدُودَاتٍ *And remember Allah during the appointed Days (10th, 11th, 12th and 13th of Dhul Hijja)... (Al-Baqara:203)* with reference to this verse, he commented, "These are the days of Tashriq. The Dhikr of Allah to be carried out during these days consist of سُبْحَانَ اللهِ 'SubhanAllah', الْحَمْدُ لِلهِ 'Al Hamdulillah', لَا إِلَهَ إِلَّا اللهُ 'La Ilaha IllAllah', اللهُ أَكْبَرُ 'Allahu Akbar' and other glorifications of Allah." Abdullah bin Zubair ؓ then spoke of the various points from where people need to enter the state of Ihram. He said, "The place from where the people of Madinah need to enter into Ihram is Dhul Hulaifa, the place from where the people of Iraq need to enter into Ihram is Aqiq, the place from where the people of Najd and Ta'if need to enter into Ihram is Qarn and the place from where the people of Yemen need to enter into Ihram Yalamlam." He then cursed the disbelievers from the Ahlul Kitab saying, "O Allah! Punish the disbelievers from the Ahlul Kitab who reject Your signs, disbelieve in our Ambiya ﷺ and who prevent others from Your path. O Allah! Punish them and give them the hearts of immoral women." He then proceeded to make many more Du'as. He then continued to say, "There are many men here whose hearts have been blinded just as their sight has been. Their ruling in the case of Tamattu Hajj is that if a person arrives from Khurasan with the Ihram for Hajj, they tell him that he may emerge from the Hajj Ihram after performing Umrah and then enter into Ihram again for his Hajj whereas the person intending Hajj may emerge from his Hajj Ihram only after performing Hajj. By Allah! This type of Tamattu is permissible only for the person in straitened circumstances." He then recited the Talbiya and the people recited it as well. The narrator says that he had not seen so many people weeping as he did on that day. (Tabrani in Kabeer, Haythami, Abu Nu'aym in Hilya)

Various Lectures that he Delivered

Hisham bin Urwa narrates that Abdullah bin Zubair ؓ said the following in his lecture: "You need to know that one performing Hajj may stay at every part of Arafah besides Batn Uma and you also need to know well that one may also stay in every part of Muzdalifa besides Batn Muhassar." *(Ibn Jareer in Tafsir)*. Abbas bin Sahl bin Sa'd Sa'idi Ansari reports that he heard Abdullah bin Zubair ؓ deliver a lecture on the pulpit in Makkah. He said, "O people! Rasulullah ﷺ used to say, 'If man is given a valley full of gold, he would want a second and when given a second, he would still want a third. There is nothing to fill man's belly besides the sand of the grave and Allah accepts the repentance of those who repent." *(Abu Nu'aym in Hilya)*. Ata bin Abi Rabah narrates that in one of his lectures, Abdullah bin Zubair ؓ said, "Rasulullah ﷺ said, 'A single salah in this Masjid of mine in Madinah is better than 1,000 salats in any other Masjid other than the Masjidul Haram. A single salah in the Masjidul Haram is 100 times superior than a salah in my Masjid." Ata says further, "That makes the rewards a 100,000 (more than in any other Masjid in the world). I therefore asked, 'O Abu Muhammad! Does this virtue apply exclusively to the Masjidul Haram or to all of the Haram?' He replied, It applies to all of the Haram because all of the Haram is a Masjid." *(Abu Dawud, Tayalisi)*. Wahab bin Kaisan a freed slave of Abdullah bin Zubair ؓ reports that he heard Abdullah bin Zubair ؓ deliver a lecture on the day of Eid. On that occasion, Abdullah bin Zubair ؓ led the salah before delivering the lecture and when he did stand up to deliver the lecture, he said, "O people! All of this performing the salah before the lecture is the way shown Allah and by Rasulullah ﷺ." *(Ahmad)*. Thabit reports that he heard Abdullah bin Zubair ؓ say the following in a lecture: "Muhammad ﷺ said, 'Whoever from amongst the males wears silk in this world will not wear it in the Hereafter." *(Ahmad)*. Abu Zubair says, "It was on this very pulpit that I heard Abdullah bin Zubair ؓ narrate some Ahadeeth. He said, 'After making the Salam after his salah, Rasulullah ﷺ used to recite:

لَا إِلَهَ إِلَّا اللهُ وَحْدَهُ لَاشَرِيْكَ لَهُ لَهُ الْمُلْكُ وَلَهُ الْحَمْدُ وَهُوَ عَلَى كُلِّ شَىْئٍ قَدِيْرٌ لَاحَوْلَ وَلَاقُوَّةَ إِلَّا بِاللهِ وَلَانَعْبُدُ إِلَّا إِيَّاهُ لَهُ النِّعْمَةُ الْفَضْلُ وَالثَّنَاءُ الْحَسَنُ لَاإِلَهَ إِلَّا اللهُ مُخْلِصِيْنَ لَهُ الدِّيْنَ وَلَوْكَرِهَ الْكَافِرُوْنَ

"There is none worthy of worship but the One Allah Who has no partner. All kingdom and all praise belong to Him and He has power over all things. There is no strength or power without Allah. We worship only Him Who bestows all bounties and grace and to Whom all good praise is due. There is none worthy of worship but Allah, for Whom all worship is to be done sincerely, even though the Kuffar detest it." (Ahmad)

Thuwair narrates that he heard Abdullah bin Zubair ؓ from the pulpit: "This is the day of Ashura (10th of Muharram) so fast because Rasulullah ﷺ gave the instruction to fast." *(Ahmad)*. Kulthum bin Hibr narrates that Abdullah bin Zubair ؓ once addressed the people saying, "O people of Makkah! I have been informed that some of you play a (gambling) game called Nardshir, whereas Allah says: يَا أَيُّهَا الَّذِينَ آمَنُوا إِنَّمَا الْخَمْرُ وَالْمَيْسِرُ وَالْأَنْصَابُ وَالْأَزْلَامُ رِجْسٌ مِنْ عَمَلِ الشَّيْطَانِ فَاجْتَنِبُوهُ لَعَلَّكُمْ تُفْلِحُونَ (90) *O you who believe! Intoxicants (all kinds of alcoholic drinks), gambling, Al-Ansab, and Al-Azlam (arrows for seeking luck or decision) are an abomination of Shaitans (Satan) handiwork. So avoid (strictly all) that (abomination) in order that you may be successful. (Al-Ma'ida:90).* I swear by Allah that I shall severely punish him by removing his hair and lashing him. I shall also hand over all his possessions (with him at the time) to the person who brings him in." *(Bukhari in Adab)*

The Lecture of Abdullah bin Mas'ood ؓ Delivered in the Presence of Rasulullah ﷺ

Abu Darda ؓ narrates that after once delivering a short lecture, Rasulullah ﷺ said, "O Abu Bakr ؓ! Stand up and deliver a lecture." Abu Bakr ؓ then delivered a lecture that was shorter than that of Rasulullah ﷺ. Rasulullah ﷺ then instructed Omar ؓ to deliver a lecture and he complied by delivering a lecture that was shorter than that of Abu Bakr ؓ. When Rasulullah ﷺ then asked another person to deliver a lecture, he was very bombastic in his speech, because of which Rasulullah ﷺ told him to step down. Rasulullah ﷺ then said, "Pretentious speech is from Saitan and well delivered speech is magical indeed." Addressing Abdullah bin Mas'ood ؓ, Rasulullah ﷺ said, "O Ibn Ummi Abd! You now deliver a lecture." Abdullah bin Mas'ood ؓ then stood up and after praising Allah, he said, "O people! Verily Allah is our Rabb, Islam is our Deen, the Qur'an is our Imam, the Kabah is our Qibla and pointing to Rasulullah ﷺ this is our Nabi ﷺ. We are pleased with what Allah and His Rasul like for us and we dislike that which Allah and is Rasul ﷺ dislike for us." To this, Rasulullah ﷺ remarked, "Ibn Ummi Abd has spoken well." *(Tabrani, Haythami)*. Sa'eed bin Jubair reports a similar narration from Abu Darda ؓ with the addition that Rasulullah ﷺ also said, "I am pleased with that which Allah is pleased with for me and for my Ummah and with that which pleases Ibn Ummi Abd. Likewise, I am displeased with that which Allah is displeased with for me and for my Ummah and with that which displeases Ibn Ummi Abd." *(Ibn Asakir)*. Another similar narration states that after Rasulullah ﷺ asked Abdullah bin Mas'ood ؓ to speak, he began by praising Allah, invoking peace and blessings on Rasulullah ﷺ and attesting to the Shahada of truth. Thereafter, he said, "We are pleased with Allah as Our Rabb, with Islam as our religion and I am pleased with that with which Allah and His Rasul ﷺ like for you." To this, Rasulullah ﷺ remarked, "I am pleased with that which Ibn Ummi Abd likes for you." *(Ibn Asakir in Muntakhab Kanzul Ummal)*

Various Lectures that he Delivered

Abul Ahwas Jushami reports that while Abdullah bin Mas'ood ؓ was delivering a lecture, he noticed a snake slithering along a wall. He immediately stopped the lecture and hit the snake with his staff until he killed it. Thereafter, he said, "I heard Rasulullah say that one who kills a snake is like the person who kills a Mushrik who deserves to be executed." *(Ahmad)*. Abu Wa'il narrates that when Uthman ؓ became the Khalifa, Abdullah bin Mas'ood ؓ traveled for 8 days from Madinah to Kufa. He then delivered a lecture in which he said, "When Amirul Mu'minin Omar bin Khattab ؓ passed away, we did not see so many people weep as on that day. We the companions of Muhammad ﷺ then gathered together and did our very best to select the one who is best from amongst us. We therefore pledged our allegiance to Amirul Mu'minin Uthman ؓ, so you should all pledge your allegiance to him as well." *(Ibn Sa'd)*

The Lectures of Utba bin Ghazwan ؓ

Khalid bin Umair Adawi reports that Utba bin Ghazwan was the governor of Basra when he addressed them. After duly praising Allah, he said, "Verily this world has already announced its termination and has speedily turned on its heels. All that is left of her is like the little residue left over in a utensil that a person tries to lick out of it. You people will certainly be moving over from here to a place that will never come to an end. You must therefore take along with you the best that you have with you because we have been informed that a stone thrown from the edge of Jahannam will continue falling for 70 years without reaching the bottom. By Allah! This Jahannam will however be filled. Does this not astonish you? We have also been informed that the distance between two of the many doorways to Jannah spans a distance of 40 years. There shall however come a day when even these doorways will be crowded with people entering into Jannah. I have seen the time when I was one of 7 people with Rasulullah ﷺ without any food between ourselves other than the leaves of trees which we continued to eat until our jaws were filled with sores. Throwing down a shawl of mine, I tore it into 2 parts. I used one part as a lower garment for myself and the other I gave to Sa'd bin Malik, who also used it as a loincloth. However, today there is none of us who has not become the governor of a city. I ask Allah to protect me from standing high in my own esteem while being humiliated in Allah's sight." *(Muslim in Targheeb wat Tarheeb).* Another narration adds that Utba ؓ concluded with the words, "There has never been a succession of leaders starting from the period of Nabuwwat that does not gradually decline until it degenerates into a monarchy. After me you shall soon experience and be tested with many different types of leaders and governors, so prepare yourselves." *(Hakim, Ibn Jowzi in Safwatus Sqfwa, Nabilsi in Dhakha'irul Mawarith, Muslim, Ibn Majah, Tirmidhi, Abu Nu'aym in Hilya).* Yet another narration states that this was the first lecture that Utba ؓ delivered in Basra. He said, "All praise belongs to Allah Whom I praise, from Whom I seek help, Who I believe in and in Whom do I rely. I testify that there is none worthy of worship but Allah and I testify that Muhammad ﷺ is the servant and Rasul of Allah. O people! Verily this world has already..." The rest of the narration is like both narrations quoted above. *(Ibn Sa'd)*

The Lectures of Hudhaifa bin Yaman ؓ

Abu Abdur Rahman Sulami reports, "I once accompanied my father for the Jumu'ah salah in Mada'in. We lived a Farsak away from the Masjid and it was during the time when Hudhaifa bin Yaman ؓ was the governor of Mada'in. He ascended the pulpit and after praising Allah, he recited the verse:

(1) اقْتَرَبَتِ السَّاعَةُ وَانْشَقَّ الْقَمَرُ *The Hour has drawn near, and the moon has been cleft asunder (the people of Makkah requested Prophet Muhammad ﷺ to show them a miracle, so he showed them the splitting of the moon). (Al-Qamar:1)*

He then continued, 'Listen well! The moon has already been split. Listen well! This world has already announced her departure. Listen well! Today (this world) is the time for the race while tomorrow it will be seen who has gotten ahead.' I then asked my father, 'What does he mean by the race'?' My father informed me that he was referring to the race to Jannah." *(Abu Nu'aym in Hilya).* Another similar narration states that Hudhaifa ؓ said, "Allah says: (1) اقْتَرَبَتِ السَّاعَةُ وَانْشَقَّ الْقَمَرُ *The Hour has drawn near, and the moon has been cleft asunder (the people of Makkah requested Prophet Muhammad ﷺ to show them a miracle, so he showed them the splitting of the moon). (Al-Qamar:1)*

Listen well! The moon has already been split..." This narration concludes with Abu Abdur Rahman Sulami saying, "I then asked my father, 'Will people be running a race tomorrow?' 'Dear son!' my father remarked, 'You do not understand. It is the race for good deeds that he is referring to.' When we attended the following Jumu'ah salah, Hudhaifa ؓ said in his lecture, "Behold! Verily Allah says: (1) اقْتَرَبَتِ السَّاعَةُ وَانْشَقَّ الْقَمَرُ

The Hour has drawn near, and the moon has been cleft asunder (the people of Makkah requested Prophet Muhammad ﷺ to show them a miracle, so he showed them the splitting of the moon).

(Al-Qamar:1)

Listen well! This world has already announced her departure. Listen well! Today (this world) is the time for the race while tomorrow it will be seen who has gone ahead. Take note that at the end is the fire of Jahannam while the race is on for those heading for Jannah." *(Ibn Jareer in Tafsir ibn Kathis, Hakim by Dhahabi).* Kurdus narrates that in a lecture in Mada'in Hudhaifa ؓ said, "O people! Closely monitor what your slaves earn. If it is Halal, you may utilize it, otherwise, discard it because I have heard Rasulullah say that no flesh nourished with Haram can ever enter Jannah." *(Abu Nu'aym in Hilya).* Hudhaifa ؓ said, "O people! Be vigilant over your slaves and ensure that you know their sources of income because the flesh nourished by Haram can never enter Jannah. Remember also that the seller, the buyer and the maker of wine are just like the one who consumes it." *(Abdur Razzaq in Kanzul Ummal)*

A Lecture of Abu Musa Ash'ari ؓ

Qasama bin Zuhair narrates that Abu Musa Ash'ari ؓ once addressed the people of Basra saying, "O people! Weep (over your sins and for fear of Jahannam). If you are unable to weep, then at least pretend to do so because the people of Jahannam will weep until their tears will come to an end. When their tears are eventually finished, they will cry blood so much that even ships will be able sail on it." *(Ibn Sa'd, Abu Nu'aym in Hilya)*

A Lecture of Abdullah bin Abbas ؓ

Shaqiq says, "When Abdullah bin Abbas ؓ was the Amir of Hajj, he delivered a lecture. He started reciting Surah Baqarah and he commented on each verse as he recited. This was so impressive that I said, 'I have never seen or heard anyone speak like this. If the Romans and Persians have to hear this, they will surely accept Islam." *(Abu Nu'aym in Hilya)*

Lectures of Abu Hurairah ؓ

Abu Yazid Madini reports that Abu Hurairah ؓ once ascended Rasulullah ﷺ's pulpit and stood step lower than that on which Rasulullah ﷺ stood. He then said, "All praise belongs to Allah Who has guided Abu Hurairah to Islam. All praise belongs to Allah Who has taught Abu Hurairah the Qur'an. All praise belongs to Allah Who has blessed Abu Hurairah with Muhammad ﷺ. All praise belongs to Allah Who has fed me leavened bread and given me fine garments to wear. All praise belongs to Allah Who has given me the hand of Ghazwan's daughter in marriage after I had been her servant to earn food to fill my belly and now I am able to annoy her just as she used to annoy me. Destruction will come to the Arabs because of the evil that has already arrived. Destruction will come to then because they will be led by mere children who will rule according to their passion and will kill in anger. Glad tidings to you, O non-Arabs! I swear by the Being Who controls my life that even if Deen is suspended on the Pleiades constellation, a group from you will certainly reach it." *(Abu Nu'aym in Hilya).* Abu Habiba narrates that he entered the house of Uthman ؓ during the period when he was besieged in it. It was then he heard Abu Hurairah ؓ seek permission to address Uthman ؓ. When permission was granted, Abu Hurairah ؓ stood up, duly praised Allah and then said, "I have heard Rasulullah ﷺ say, 'You will surely encounter plenty of tribulation and disputes after me.' 'O Rasulullah ﷺ!' someone asked, 'What do you advise us to do?' Rasulullah ﷺ replied, 'Attach yourselves with the Amir and those with him.'" Saying this, Abu Hurairah ؓ pointed towards Uthman ؓ. *(Hakim by Dhahabi)*

A Lecture of Abdullah bin Salam 🙾

Muhammad bin Yusuf bin Abdullah bin Salam reports that he once sought permission to see Hajjaj bin Yusuf and when permission was granted, he entered and greeted with Salam. Hajjaj instructed 2 men sitting close to his chair to make way and when they did, Muhammad bin Yusuf sat down. Hajjaj then said to him, "May Allah grant abundant good to your father. Do you know the narration that your father reported to Abdul Malik bin Marwan, which he heard from your grandfather Abdullah bin Salam 🙾?" "May Allah have mercy on you," Muhammad bin Yusuf remarked, "There are so many narrations. Which one is it?" Hajjaj replied, "The narration of the Egyptians when they blockaded the house of Uthman 🙾." Muhammad bin Yusuf then said, "I know that narration. When Uthman 🙾 was besieged in his house, Abdullah bin Salam 🙾 arrived and entered the house. The people gave him way until he came to Uthman 🙾 and said, 'Peace be on you, O Amirul Muminin!' 'Peace be on you too,' Uthman 🙾 replied, 'What brings you here, O Abdullah bin Salam?' Abdullah bin Salam 🙾 replied, 'I have come to remain by your side (and to fight these people) until I am either martyred or until Allah grants you victory because I estimate that these people will definitely come out to fight you. If they ever succeed in martyring you, it will be good for you but terrible for them.' To this Uthman 🙾 said, 'I ask you by the rights I have over you that you must go out to them and explain to them the error of their ways.' Abdullah bin Salam 🙾 complied and when the rebels saw him approach them, they gathered around, hoping to hear some news that would please them. Abdullah bin Salam 🙾 then stood before them to deliver a lecture. After duly praising Allah, he said, 'Verily Allah had sent Muhammad 🙼 as a giver of glad tidings and a Warner. He gave the glad tidings of Jannah to those who obeyed him and warned those who disobeyed him about the fire of Jahannam. Allah then made those who followed Rasulullah 🙼 prevail over the adherents to every other faith even though the Mushrikin detested this. From all the other chosen places of residence, Allah chose Madinah as the residence of Rasulullah 🙼 and made it the place of Hijra and the place of Iman. By Allah! Angels have been surrounding Madinah ever since Rasulullah 🙼 entered it and remain doing so to this day. Allah's sword has also remained sheathed against you because of which Muslims have not been fighting each other and remains so until this day.' 'Allah had sent Muhammad 🙼 with the truth and whoever takes guidance from him has been guided by the guidance of Allah and whoever strays has done so after matters have been made plain to him and proven beyond doubt. It is a fact that whenever a Nabi 🙼 has been martyred in the past, 70,000 warriors had lost their lives, each one being killed in retribution for the killing of the Nabi 🙼. Similarly, whenever a Khalifa has been martyred, 35,000 warriors had lost their lives, each one being killed in retribution for the killing of the Khalifa. You people should therefore never be rushed into assassinating this elderly man because I swear by Allah that the person who kills him will appear before Allah on the Day of Judgment with an amputated and paralyzed hand. Remember well that this elderly man has as many rights over you as a father has over his son.' The rebels however stood up and shouted, 'The Jew is lying! The Jew is lying!' Abdullah bin Salam 🙾 retorted by saying, 'I swear by Allah that it is you who are the liars and the ones at fault. I am not a Jew but one of the Muslims. Allah, Rasulullah 🙼 and all the Mu'minin know this fact well. It is with reference to me that Allah revealed the verse: قُلْ كَفَى بِاللّٰهِ شَهِيدًا بَيْنِي وَبَيْنَكُمْ وَمَنْ عِنْدَهُ عِلْمُ الْكِتَابِ (43)

You (O Muhammad 🙼) are not a Messenger." Say: "Sufficient for a witness between me and you is Allah and those too who have knowledge of the Scripture (such as Abdullah bin Salam and other Jews and Christians who embraced Islam)." (Ar-Ra'd:43)

Allah has also revealed another verse, which is:

قُلْ أَرَأَيْتُمْ إِنْ كَانَ مِنْ عِنْدِ اللّٰهِ وَكَفَرْتُمْ بِهِ وَشَهِدَ شَاهِدٌ مِنْ بَنِي إِسْرَائِيلَ عَلَى مِثْلِهِ فَآمَنَ وَاسْتَكْبَرْتُمْ

(O Muhammad 🙼) Say: "Tell me! If this (Qur'an) is from Allah, and you deny it, and a witness from among the Children of Israel (Abdullah bin Salam 🙾) testifies that this Qur'an is from Allah (like the Taurat (Torah)), so he believed (embraced Islam) while you are too proud (to believe)."... (Al-Ahqaf:10)

The narration then proceeds to recount the martyrdom of Uthman 🙾. (Tabrani, Haythami)

Lectures of Husain bin Ali 🙾

Muhammad bin Hasan narrates that when Omar bin Sa'd arrived with his army to confront Husain 🙾 and his party, Husain stood up to address his companions. After duly praising Allah, he said, "Matters have reached a head as you can see. Life in this world has changed and become detestable. The good of this life has turned away and passed on. All that is left of the good is the equivalent of what remains at the bottom of a utensil after the contents have been poured out. What is left of life is the worst of it like a diseased pasture that makes every grazing animal ill. Do you not see that the truth is no longer practiced on and that people do not refrain from falsehood? Every Mu'min should look forward to meeting Allah. I regard death as something most fortunate and life amongst oppressors as a source of great anguish." (Tabrani, Haythami, Ibn Jareer). Uqba bin Abul Ayraz narrates that it was at a place called Baida that Husain 🙾 addressed his companions together with the army of Hurr bin Yazid whose army had arrived to fight Husain 🙾. After raising Allah, he said, "O people! Verily Rasulullah 🙼 said, 'When a person sees a tyrannical ruler who permits what Allah has made Haram, who reneges his pledge with Allah, who contradicts the Sunnah of Allah's Rasul 🙼 and who sins and transgresses against Allah's servants and he neither acts or speaks out against such a ruler despite having the ability to do so, Allah takes it upon Himself to enter such a person into the same place He will be entering the tyrant i.e. into Jahannam.' Take note of the fact that these people (the present ruling party) have taken it upon themselves to obey Saitan, to forsake obedience to Allah, to spread corruption, to renounce the restrictions Allah has set, to show favoritism when distributing booty, to make legal what Allah has forbidden and to forbid what Allah has made lawful. I am most obliged to change all of this. O people of Kufa! Your letters had come to me and many of your messengers had also come to me with the assurance that you will never desert me or leave me in the lurch. If you fulfill this pledge of allegiance to me, you will have been rightly guided because I am Husain the son of Ali and the son of Fatima who was the daughter of Rasulullah 🙼. My life is with yours and my family is with yours, so you should follow the example in me by pledging your lives and families for mine as well. If you do not do this and choose to renege on your promise and to absolve yourselves of your pledge to loyalty, I swear by my life that I do not at all find this strange because you have done the same to my father, my brother and my cousin Muslim bin Aqil. A truly deceived person is one who is deceived by you. You people have forsaken your share to good fortune and whoever breaks his promise does so to his own loss. Allah will soon make me completely independent of you. Was Salamu Alaykum wa Rahmatullahi wa Barakatuh." (Ibn Jareer)

Lectures of Yazid bin Shajara ﷺ

Mujahid says, "Yazid bin Shajara ﷺ was one of those people whose words always materialized into action. He once addressed us saying, 'O people! Remember Allah's favors on you because Allah's favors on you are tremendous indeed. They are found in all colors and in the things we have in our homes.' He would often say, 'When people form their rows for salah and to do battle, the doors of the skies, the doors of Jannah and the doors of Jahannam open. The wide-eyed damsels of Jannah beautify themselves and watch closely. When the person steps forward, they pray, 'O Allah! Assist him' but if he turns his back, they conceal themselves from him saying, 'O Allah! Forgive him.' May my parents be sacrificed for you! Engage the enemy in full combat and do not disappoint the damsels. The first drop of blood that spills of a martyr erase every sin he has committed and it is then that 2 of his wives from Jannah descend to wipe his face saying, 'The time has come for you.' He will respond by saying, 'The time as come for you.' He will then be clothed in 100 garments which will not be woven like the garments of man, but will be the products of Jannah. (They are so fine that) If they (all 100 of them) are placed between 2 fingers, they will fit comfortably.' He also used to say, 'We have been informed that swords are really the keys to Jannah." *(Tabrani, Haythami).* Mujahid reports, "Yazid bin Shajara Rahawi ﷺ was one of the governors of Sham whom Mu'awiya ﷺ had placed in command of the armed forces. He once addressed us saying, 'O people! Remember Allah's favors on you. If only you could see the many shades of them as I do, in addition to the many things we have in our homes. 'When people stand up for salah, the doors of the skies, the doors of Jannah and the doors of Jahannam open. The wide-eyed damsels of Jannah beautify themselves and watch closely. Then when a person steps forward to do battle, they pray, 'O Allah! Keep him steadfast! O Allah! Assist him'. However, if he turns his back, they conceal themselves from him saying, 'O Allah! Forgive him! O Allah! Have mercy on him.' May my parents be sacrificed for you! Engage the enemy in full combat because when a person steps forward and is martyred the first drop of his blood that causes his sins to fall off just as the leaves of a tree fall off. 2 damsels from the wide-eyed damsels of Jannah then descend to wipe the dust off his face. 'I am yours,' he says. 'No,' they reply, 'We are yours.' He will then be clothed in 100 garments so fine that if they (all 100 of them) are placed between these 2 fingers (the index and middle fingers), they will fit comfortably. They are not woven like the garments of man, but are the clothes of Jannah. 'Your names are recorded by Allah together with details of your character traits, your qualities, the secret discussions you engage in and the gatherings you attend. Then on the Day of Judgment, it will be said to some people, 'O person! Here is your light by which you will be led to Jannah.' It will also be said to others, 'O person! There is no light for you.' Jahannam has a shore just as the ocean has a shore. This shore is however infested with insects, snakes as long as palm trees and scorpions as large as mules. When the people of Jahannam will plead for the punishment to be lightened, they will be told to go to the shore. When they go there, the insects will start biting their lips, faces and other parts of the body, because of which they will then plead to be delivered from there back to the fire of Jahannam. They will also be made to suffer from an itch so sever that they will scratch at it so much that their bones will eventually become exposed. 'O person!' it will be said to one of them, 'Does this cause you pain?' When he replies that it certainly does, he will be told, "This. is because of the pain that you caused to the Mu'minin." *(Hakim, Ibn Mubarak in Zuhd, Ibn Mai'da, Bayhaqi in Isabah)*

The Lecture of Umair bin Sa'd ﷺ

Sa'eed bin Suwaid reports that a Sahabi by the name of Umair bin Sa'd ﷺ was the governor of Hims and would say from the pulpit, "Listen well! Islam has a fortified wall and a reinforced door. The wall of Islam is justice and its door is the truth. (The adherents to) Islam will be vanquished only when this wall is demolished and when the door is torn apart. Islam will remain strong as long as the (Muslim) rulers remain firm. The firmness of the rulers is not in their killing by the sword nor by their striking with the whip, but by passing judgment according to the truth and by adhering to justice." *(Ibn Sa'd)*

The Lecture of Sa'd bin Ubaid Qari ﷺ the Father of Umair ﷺ

Sa'd bin Ubaid ﷺ once addressed the people saying, "We shall be meeting the enemy tomorrow and will be martyred. You should therefore not wash off any blood from us, shroud us, in anything other than the clothes we will be wearing." *(Ibn Sa'd)*

A Lecture of Mu'adh bin Jabal ﷺ

Salama bin Sabara reports that it was in Sham at Mu'adh bin Jabal ﷺ addressed them saying, "You are the Mu'minin and the people of Jannah. By Allah! I truly feel that Allah will admit into Jannah every perrson you take prisoner from Rome and Persia. This is because whenever they do any service for you, you say, 'You have done well! May Allah have mercy on you!' or 'You have done well! May Allah bless you!'" He then recited the verse:

$$وَيَسْتَجِيبُ الَّذِينَ آمَنُوا وَعَمِلُوا الصَّالِحَاتِ وَيَزِيدُهُمْ مِنْ فَضْلِه$$

And He (Allah) answers (the invocation of) those who believe (in the Oneness of Allah Islamic Monotheism) and do righteous good deeds, and gives them increase of His Bounty... (Ash-Shura:26) (Ibn Jareer, Ibn Abi Hatim in Tafsir Ibn Kathir)

A Lecture of Abu Darda ﷺ

Howshab Fazari reports that he heard Abu Darda ﷺ deliver a lecture from the pulpit saying, "I fear the day when my Rabb will summon me saying, 'O Uwaimir!' When I respond by saying, 'I am at Your service, O my Rabb!', Allah shall ask, How did you practice on your knowledge?' Then every verse in Allah's Book containing a command and every verse containing an admonition shall claim their rights. The verses containing commands testify that I did not carry out the command and every verse containing an admonition will testify that I did not take heed to the admonition it contained. How wiII I then be left alone?" *(Ibn Asakir in Kansul Ummal)*

Volume – 3 / Chapter – 17

The chapter Concerning the Advices of the Sahabah

This chapter discusses how Nabi ﷺ and the Sahabah advised people and accepted the advice given to them, regardless of whether they were at home or on journey. It also highlights how they turned their attention away from the material things of this world and its pleasures to focus on the bounties of the Hereafter. They so vehemently cautioned people to beware of disobeying Allah that tears flowed and arts became overawed. It appeared as if the Hereafter and the conditions on the plain of Resurrection were plain before their eyes. This chapter illustrates how they led the Ummah of Muhammad ﷺ through their advices and turned their attention towards the Creator of the heavens and the earth, severing the arteries of every open and discreet form of Shirk.

Rasulullah ﷺ's Profound Advice to Abu Dhar Ghifari ؓ

Abu Dhar ؓ reports that he once asked Rasulullah ﷺ what the scriptures revealed to Ibrahim عليه السلام contained. Rasulullah ﷺ replied, "They were full of expressions such as 'O conquering, troubled and deceived king! I have not sent you to gather the things of this world and to heap piles upon another. I have sent you to prevent the plea of the oppressed from reaching Me because I never reject such a plea even though it may come from a Kafir.' 'As long as a thinking man does not lose his senses, he should distribute his time in a few activities. He should devote some time in secret conversation with his Rabb, some time engaging in inner-inspection, some time contemplating over the creations of his Rabb and some time expressly for his needs of food and drink. The thinking man must not undertake a journey unless it be for one of three reasons; to earn provisions for the Hereafter, to set right an affair pertaining to his livelihood or to gain some pleasure that is not forbidden. It is also necessary for the thinking man to have a deep insight into his times and to be prepared for its conditions. He must also guard his tongue. Whoever judges his words by his actions will have few words to speak unless it concerns matters of importance.'" "O Rasulullah ﷺ!" Abu Dhar ؓ asked further, "What did the scriptures of Musa عليه السلام contain?" Rasulullah ﷺ replied, "It was filled with lessons such as 'I am astonished at the person who is convinced about death, yet enjoys himself. I am astonished at the person who is convinced about the fire of Jahannam, yet he continues to laugh. I am astonished at the person who is convinced about predestination, yet he still exert himself unnecessarily. I am astonished at the person who sees this world and how it keeps passing from person to person, yet he places his trust in her. I am astonished at the person who is convinced about reckoning tomorrow, yet he does not work for it.'" O, Rasulullah ﷺ!" Abu Dhar ؓ then asked, "Do advise me." Rasulullah ﷺ complied by saying, "I advise you to adopt Taqwa because it is the fountainhead of all affairs." "Do advise me further, O Rasulullah ﷺ," Abu Dhar ؓ asked. Rasulullah ﷺ said, 'Ensure that you recite the Qur'an and engage in Allah's Dhikr because this is a light for you in this world and a treasure in the hereafter." "O Rasulullah ﷺ," Abu Dhar ؓ entreated, "Give me some more advice." Rasulullah ﷺ continued, "Abstain from excessive laughter because it kills the heart and removes the light from one's face." "Do advise me further, O Rasulullah ﷺ," Abu Dhar ؓ pleaded. Rasulullah ﷺ advised him further saying, "Ensure that you participate in Jihad because it is the backbone of my Ummah." When Abu Dhar asked for more advice, Rasulullah ﷺ further stated, 'Ensure that you remain silent for extended periods because this will repel Saitan and assist you in matters of Deen."

Upon Abu Dhar ؓ's further insistence, Rasulullah ﷺ continued his advice saying, "Love the poor and keep their company." "O Rasulullah ﷺ!" Abu Dhar ؓ implored, "Please give me more advice." Rasulullah ﷺ said, "Look at those who are inferior to you and do not look at those who are superior to you because this is more conducive to you not lookng down on Allah's favors upon you." Again Abu Dhar ؓ asked, "O Rasulullah ﷺ! Advise me further." To this, Rasulullah ﷺ stated, "Speak the truth regardless of how bitter it may be." Upon yet another request from Abu Dhar ؓ, Rasulullah ﷺ's advice was, "Knowing your own faults should prevent you from finding faults in others and never be angry with others for the faults you have yourself. You will be guilty enough for finding such faults in people that you do not know exist within yourself and for becoming angry with others for the things you yourself do." Rasulullah ﷺ then placed his hand on Abu Dhar ؓ's chest and said, "O Abu Dhar! There is no intelligence like smart planning, no piety like abstinence and no family pride as excellent as good character. *(Ibn Abi Dunya in Targheeb wat Tarheeb, Abu Nu'aym in Hilya, Hasan bin Sufian, Ibn Asakir in Kanzul Ummal)*

"Do you know the Example of each one of you and his Family, Wealth and Deeds?"

Aisha ؓ narrates that Rasulullah ﷺ once said to the Sahabah, "Do you know the example of each one of you and his family, wealth and actions'?" "Allah and His Rasul ﷺ know best," the Sahabah submitted. Rasulullah ﷺ then explained, "The example of each one of you and his family, wealth and deeds is like a person with 3 brothers. When lying on his deathbed, the man summons one of his brothers and asks, 'You can see the plight I am now facing. What are you able to do for me?' This brother replies by saying, 'What I have to offer you is that I shall nurse you tirelessly and tend to all your affairs. When you pass away, I shall bathe you, shroud you and carry you along with the others. I shall be carrying you awhile and sometimes also be removing anything harmful from your path. Thereafter, when I return after the burial, I shall sing your praises whenever someone asks about you.' This brother represents his family. What do you think of him'?" "O Rasulullah ﷺ!" the Sahabah replied, "We do not see too much in what he has to offer." Rasulullah ﷺ then continued, "The man then summons the 2nd brother and asks, 'You can see the plight I am now facing. What are you able to do for me'?' This brother replies by saying, 'I have nothing to offer you unless you are alive. As soon as you die, I shall go my way and you will go yours.' This brother represents his wealth. What do you think of him?" The Sahabah replied, "O Rasulullah! We do not see too much in what he has to offer either." Rasulullah ﷺ further stated, "The man then summons the 3rd brother and asks, 'You can see the plight I am now facing. What are you able to do for me'?' This brother replies by saying, 'I shall be your companion in your grave and your friend in your loneliness. On the day when actions will be weighed, I shall sit in your scale and lend my weight to it.' This brother represents his good deeds. What do you think him'?" The Sahabah replied, "O Rasulullah ﷺ! He is the best brother and the best companion." "That," Rasulullah ﷺ remarked, "is exactly the way matters are." Abdullah bin Kurz ؓ then stood up and said, "O Rasulullah ﷺ! Do you permit me to string a few couplets concerning this'?" When Rasulullah ﷺ granted him permission, it was a mere day afterwards that he returned to Rasulullah ﷺ. He stood in front of Rasulullah ﷺ and others gathered around him, as he recited the following couplets (which mean):

'Indeed I, my family and the deeds / have sent ahead are like

the one who called his friends and said in an address to his brothers who were three.

'Do offer assistance in this matter that has befallen me a lengthy separation the outcome of which is uncertain what have you to offer in what appears to be most devastating'

One of them says, 'I am the one who will obey you in all matters before you leave however, when the separation occurs I will be unable to maintain our bond of kinship. Take what you please from me now because I will soon be taken on another precarious road if you wish to keep me, you will be unable to do so. However, you may hastily spend me before a sudden death to make some amends.'

The other then speaks whom I loved most dearly whom I had always favored over others with my affections

'The help I can offer is to do my best and to wish well for you at the time when you have the most difficulty. I can however not fight your death. Nonetheless, I shall weep and wail for you and sing your praises to all who ask about you I shall follow those accompanying your funeral procession and gently assist all those who carry you to your destination, where you will be entered I shall then return to continue with my occupations as if there had never been any friendship between us nor any love that we shared between ourselves'

This is the family of the person and the help they can offer as much as they would like, they can do no more. The other then speaks and says, 'I am that brother the like of whom you have never seen another at this time of difficulty and fear. You will find me sitting there by your grave arguing in your defense and responding to every interrogation on the day deeds are weighed, I shall be sitting in the scale that you have always endeavored to weigh down. Never forget me and recognize my status because I am most compassionate and helpful to you and will never desert you'

Such are the good deeds you carry out, had you done well, you shall meet them on the day of the meeting"

Rasulullah ﷺ and all the Sahabah started weeping at these words and whenever Abdullah bin Kurz ؓ passed by any group of Muslims, they called him to recite the poem to them. They would then burst out in tears when he did so. *(Ramhurmuzi in Amthal, Kanzul Ummal, Ja'far Firyabi in Kitabul Kuna, Ibn Abi Asim in Vahdan, Ibn Shaheen, Ibn Mandah in Sahabah, Ibn Abi Dunya in Kifala, Isabah)*

The Advices of Amirul Mu'minin Omar bin Khattab ؓ

Omar ؓ once advised a man saying, "Never allow people to distract you from yourself because you are ultimately responsible for yourself and not for them. Never spend your days wandering about because everything you do is recorded. Always carry out a good deed whenever you sin because I have never seen anything catch up with another as fast as a newly done good deed catches up with an old sin." *(Dinowri in Kanzul Ummal)*. Omar ؓ also said, "Stay away from that which causes you harm, ensure that you have righteous friends even though such people are scarce and consult those who fear Allah about all your matters." *(Bayhaqi in Kanzul Ummal)*

18 Wise Advices from the Lips of Omar ؓ

Sa'eed bin Musayib reports that there were 18 guidelines that Omar ؓ formulated for the people, everyone of which is replete with wisdom. He said,

1. When someone disobeys Allah in matter that impacts on you, you can give him no punishment worse than obeying Allah in matters that impact on him.
2. Always assume the best about your brother unless you learn something about him that you absolutely cannot reconcile.
3. Never assume the worst about any statement that a Muslim makes as long as you are able to make a favorable interpretation.
4. The person who exposes himself to slander must never rebuke anyone who holds a bad opinion of him.
5. Whoever guards his secrets will retain the choice in his hands.
6. Ensure that you keep true friends to stay under their wings because they are a source of beauty during times of prosperity and a means of protection during times of hardship.
7. Always speak the truth even though it leads to your death.
8. Never dig into matters that do not concern you.
9. Do not ask about matters that have not occurred because that which has already taken place is enough to preoccupy you from that which has not.
10. Never seek your needs from one who does not want to see your success.
11. Never treat false oaths lightly because Allah will then destroy you.
12. Never keep the company of the sinners to learn from their sinful ways.
13. Keep away from your enemy.
14. Beware even of your friends, except for the trustworthy one and none can be trustworthy unless he fears Allah.
15. Be humble when in the graveyard,
16. Submit to Allah's obedience and
17. Seek Allah's protection at the time of disobeying His commands.
18. Consult with those who fear Allah because Allah says:

إِنَّمَا يَخْشَى اللَّهَ مِنْ عِبَادِهِ الْعُلَمَاءُ

…it is only those who have knowledge among His slaves that fear Allah…(Fatir:28) (Khateeb, Ibn Asakir, Ibn Najjar in Kanzul Ummal)

Muhammad bin Shihab reports that Omar bin Khattab ؓ said, "Never delve into matters that do not concern you, keep your distance from your enemy and be cautious even of your friends unless he is a trustworthy person because nothing can compare with a trustworthy person. Never keep the company of a sinner because he will teach you his sinful ways and never disclose your secrets to him. Always consult with those who fear Allah." *(Abu Nu'aym in Hilya)*

"Men are of 3 Categories and Women are of 3 Categories"

Samura bin Jundub ؓ reports that Omar ؓ once said, "Men are of 3 categories and women are also of 3 categories. As for women, there is the woman who is chaste, is a Muslim, is gentle, loving and has many children. She assists her family against the fashions and influences of the times and does good to assist in the times against her family. It is however rare to find such a woman. The 2nd is the woman makes many demands and does nothing more than bear children. The 3rd is a parasitic yoke that Allah places around the neck of whoever He pleases and removes from the neck of whoever He pleases. As for the 3 categories of men, one is the man who is chaste, easy-going, gentle, holding intelligent opinions and always offering the best counsel. Whenever any matter arises, he consults with others and matters are always settled with his opinion. The other is the man who has no sound opinions but when any matter arises, he consults men of goood judgment and does what they advise. The 3rd man is the confused person who cannot distinguish right from wrong. He neither consults with others nor takes the opinion of someone offering guidance." *(Ibn Abi Shaybah, Ibn Abi Dunya, Kharta'iti, Bayhaqi, Ibn Asakir in Kanzul Ummal)*

His Advice to Mnaf bin Qais

Ahnaf bin Qais narrates that Omar ؓ once said to him, "O Ahnaf! The person who laughs too much roses respect and the one who jokes too much is not taken seriously. The one who talks too much, makes too many mistakes, the one who makes too many mistakes loses modesty, the one who loses modesty loses piety and the heart of the one who loses piety eventually dies." *(Tabrani in Awsat, Haythami).* Another narration states that Omar ؓ said, "The person who laughs too much loses respect, the one who jokes too much is not taken seriously and the one who indulges too much in something is known for it. The one 'Who talks too much, makes too many mistakes...'" The rest of the narration is like the one above. *(Ibn Abi Dunya, Askari, Bayhaqi in Kanzul Ummal).* "There are some servants of Allah who annihilate falsehood by staying away from it and revive the truth by speaking of it" Omar ؓ said, "There are some servants of Allah who annihilate falsehood by staying away from it and revive the truth by speaking of it. Given encouragement to do good, they are encouraged and when warned against something, they take heed. When fearing something, they are never off guard. With the power of conviction, they are able to see things they have never seen, blending these into those memories that never leave. Their fear for Allah has purified their souls and they forsake that which will leave them the pleasures of this world for that which will always remain theirs, the bounties of the Hereafter. Life is a bounty for them and death is a source of honor because they will marry the wide-eyed damsels of Jannah and served by servants of eternal youth." *(Abu Nu'aym in Hilya)*

Miscellaneous Advices that he Gave

Omar ؓ once said, "Become coffers of the Qur'an, fountains of knowledge and ask Allah for your sustenance on a day-to-day basis." Another narration states that he also added, "Remain in the company of those who repent excessively because such people have the softest hearts." *(Abu Nu'aym in Hilya).* Omar ؓ also said, "The person who fears Allah will never vent his anger and will never do as he pleases. Had it not been for the Day of Judgment, matters would have been very much different to what you see." *(Ibn Abi Dunya, Dinowri in Majalash, Hakim in Kuna, Kanzul Ummal).* It was Omar ؓ who said, "The person who is just to people despite the hardship he has to endure, will be granted success in all his endeavors. Humbling oneself in obedience to Allah is closer to righteousness than to desiring honor." *(Kara'iti in Kanzul Ummal).* Malik reports that the report reached him that Omar ؓ said, "A man's respect lies in his Taqwa, his honor, in his Deen and his manhood in his character. Courage is the antithesis of cowardice because while a courageous man will fight to defend those he knows as well those he does not know, the coward will flee from defending even his own parents. While people see respect in wealth, true honor really lies in Taqwa. I am not better than a Persian, a non-Arab or a common farmer except by virtue of Taqwa, the best will be the one with the most Taqwa." *(Ibn Abi Shaybah, Askari, Ibn Jareer, Dar Qutni, Ibn Asakir in Kanzul Ummal).* Sufian Thowri reports that Omar ؓ once wrote to Abu Musa Ash'ari ؓ saying, "Wisdom is not something that comes with age but it is a gift that Allah grants to whoever He pleases. Ensure that you always stay

away from shameful acts and evil character." *(Ibn Abi Dunya, Dinowri in Kanzul Ummal).* Omar ؓ once wrote to his son Abdullah ؓ saying, "I advise you to always adopt Taqwa because Allah will always protect the one who has Taqwa. Allah suffices for the one who trusts in Him, He rewards the one who gives Him a loan and increases His bounties on the one who is grateful. Taqwa should always be your prime objective, the foundation of all your actions and the polish of your heart. Remember that there is no deed for the one who makes no intention, there is no reward for the one who does not intend it, there is no benefit in the wealth of the one who has no compassion and there can be nothing new for the one who has nothing old." *(Ibn Abi Dunya, Abu Bakr Sowli, Ibn Asakir in Kanzul Ummal).* Ja'far bin Zabrqan reports that in a letter to one of his governors, Omar ؓ concluded with the words, 'Take stock of yourself during times of prosperity before difficulties take stock of you because the one who takes stock of himself during times of prosperity will ultimately by happy and the envy of others. As for the one who has been distracted by the world and who has made sin his occupation, he will ultimately have only regret and grief. Take heed of the advice given to you so that you may refrain from that which you are being prevented from doing." *(Bayhaqi in Zuhd, Ibn Asakir in Kanzul Ummal).* In a letter to Mu'awiya bin Abu Sufyan ؓ, Omar ؓ stated, 'Hold fast to the truth and it will reveal to you the status of the people of the truth. Ensure also that you always pass judgment by the truth. Was Salam." *(Abul Hasan Rizqawi in Juz, Kanzul Ummal)*

The Advices of Amirul Mu'minin Ali bin Abi Talib ؓ to Omar ؓ

Abdullah bin Abbas ؓ narrates that when Omar ؓ once asked Ali ؓ for advice, Ali ؓ said, "Never allow your conviction to become doubtful, your knowledge to regress to ignorance or your suspicions to transform into conviction. You must also remember that nothing of this world is really yours besides what you have received and then passed on, what you have distributed, thereby leveling the equation and the clothes you have already worn out." "O Abul Hasan!" Omar ؓ remarked, "What you have stated is indeed very true." *(Ibn Asakir in Kanzul Ummal).* Ali ؓ once said to Omar ؓ, "O Amirul Mu'minin! If you wish to meet up with your 2 companions (Rasulullah ﷺ and Abu Bakr ؓ), then curtail your hopes, eat less than your fill, shorten your loincloth, patch your upper garment and mend your shoes. By doing this, you will surely meet up with them." *(Bayhaqi in Kanzul Ummal)*

His Advice About What Goodness Really is

Ali ؓ once said, "Goodness is not when your wealth or your children increase, but when your knowledge increases, when your tolerance grows and when you excel people in worshipping your Rabb. When you do well, praise Allah and when you do wrong, seek Allah's forgiveness. There is no good in this world except for 2 persons: the person who commits a sin and then compensates for it by repenting and the person who hastens do good deeds. A deed carried out with Taqwa can never be underestimated because how can a deed that Allah accepts ever be underestimated?" *(Abu Nu'aym in Hilya, Ibn Asakir in Kanzul Ummal)*

His advices to his Son Hasan ؓ when he was Stabbed and Some Other Advices he Gave Him

Uqba bin Abu Sahba narrates that after Ali ؓ was stabbed by Ibn Muljim, his son Hasan ؓ came to him weeping. "What makes you weep, dear son?" Ali ؓ asked. Hasan ؓ replied, "Why should I not weep when you are passing the first day of the hereafter and the last day of this world?" "Dear son!" Ali advised, 'Remember 4 things plus another 4 and whatever else you do with these will never harm you." "What are they, beloved father?" Hasan ؓ enquired. Ali ؓ explained, "The greatest wealth is intelligence while the worst poverty is foolishness. Pride is the most harmful of all things and the greatest source of respect is good character." "Dear father!" Hasan ؓ said, "These are 4 factors. Do teach me the other 4." Ali ؓ then said, "Stay away from the company of the foolish because he will cause you harm even when he intends doing you good. Also stay away from the company of those who lie excessively because this will draw closer to you those who are far giving them the opportunity to harm you and will drive away those who are close to you. Do not also keep the company of a miser because he will distance himself from you at a time when you need him the most. Ensure that you do not also keep company with a sinner because he will sell you for something most insignificant." (Ibn Asakir in Kanzul Ummal). Ali ؓ once said, "Inspiration from Allah is the best guide, good character is the best companion, intelligence is the best friend, sound Deeni education is the best legacy and there is no source of loneliness more detrimental than pride." (Bayhaqi, Ibn Asakir in Kanzul Ummal). Ali ؓ said, "Do not look at who is saying something, but look at what is being said." He said, "All forms of friendship will come to an end besides the friendship that is not built on greed." (Sam'ani in Dala'il, Kanzul Ummal)

The Advices of Abu Ubaidah bin Jarrah ؓ to his Troops

Nimran bin Makhmar narrates that Abu Ubaidah bin Jarrah ؓ was walking amongst his troops as he said to them, "Listen well! There are many who keep their clothes white while soiling their Deen. Listen well! There are many who appear to be honoring themselves but actually disgracing themselves. Repel old sins by fresh good deeds because even if any of you commits as many sins as can fill the space between the heavens and the earth, a single good deed done afterwards will rise above them all and overpower them." (Abu Nu'aym in Hilya)

His Advice after being Afflicted by the Plague and his Statement about the Heart of a Mu'min

Sa'eed bin Abu Sa'eed Maqbari ؓ narrates that Abu Ubaidah bin Jarrah ؓ was struck by the plaque in Jordan and this is where his grave is situated. When this happened, he called all the Muslims present there and said, "I wish to give you such advice that if you take heed to it, you will always remain in good stead. Establish salah, pay zakah, fast during Ramadhan, give charity, perform Hajj, perform Umbra, encourage each other (to do good), wish well for your leaders and never betray them. Never allow the world to make you negligent because even if a man is granted the life of 1,000 years, he will have to encounter this juncture that you see me lying in. Allah has ordained death for mankind and they therefore have to die. The most intelligent of them is he who is most obedient to his Rabb and carries out the most good deeds for the day he returns to Allah. Was Salam Alaykum wa Rahmatullah. O Mu'adh bin Jabal! Lead the people in salah." Thereafter, Abu Ubaidah bin Jarrah ؓ passed away. Mu'adh bin Jabal ؓ then addressed the people saying, "O people! Repent sincerely to Allah for your sins because when a servant meets Allah after having repented for his sins, Allah makes it compulsory for Himself to forgive all his sins. It is only his debts that are not forgiven because a person is held in custody for his debts. Whoever has severed ties with his brother should meet him and shake hands with him because it does not befit a Muslim to sever ties with his brother for more than three days. Whoever

does sever ties for more than three days will be guilty of a major sin." (Ibn Asakir in Kanzul Ummal). Abu Ubaidah bin Jarrah ؓ once said, 'The heart of a Mu'min is like that of a sparrow, which changes so many times every day (because of which a person needs to consult with others)." (Abu Nu'aym in Hilya)

The Advices of Mu'adh bin Jabal ؓ

Muhammad bin Sirin reports that Mu'adh bin Jabal ؓ was once with his companions, who were greeting him and seeing him off. When a man then proached him and asked for some advice, Mu'adh bin Jabal ؓ said to him, "I will give you 2 advices, which if you take heed to, you will be taken care of. Remember that while you cannot do without your share of sustenance in this world, you are even more in need of your share in the Hereafter. You should therefore give preference to your share in the Hereafter over your share in this world and make such thorough arrangements for it that it remains with you wherever you go." (Abu Nu'aym in Hilya). Amr bin Maymun Awdi says, "Mu'adh bin Jabal ؓ once stood up amongst us and said, 'O Banu Awd! I am the messenger of Allah's messenger ﷺ. Remember well that all will have to return to Allah. Thereafter after reckoning, people will head either towards Jannah or Jahannam, where they will live forever and from where they will not be going anywhere else. There they will live until eternity in bodies that will never die." (Abu Nu'aym in Hilya). Mu'awiya bin Qurra narrates that Mu'adh bin Jabal ؓ once said to his son, 'Dear son! Whenever you perform salah, perform the salah of a person who is bidding farewell and never think that you will ever be returning to this world. Dear son! Remember that when a Mu'min dies, he lies between 2 excellent things; the good that he has sent ahead and the good that he leaves behind Sadaqa Jariya." (Abu Nu'aym in Hilya). Abdullah bin Salama narrates that when someone once asked Mu'adh bin Jabal ؓ to teach him, Mu'adh ؓ asked him, "Will you then obey me?" "I am most eager to obey you," the man replied. Mu'adh ؓ then advised him saying, "Fast at times and do not fast at times do not fast perpetually, perform salah at night and sleep as well, earn without sinning, die only as a Muslim and beware of the curse of the oppressed person." (Abu Nu'aym in Hilya). Mu'adh bin Jabal ؓ once said, "The person who does 3 things exposes himself to resentment. The 3 things are: Laughing without being amused, sleeping throughout the night without waking for salah and eating without being hungry." (Abu Nu'aym in Hilya). It was also Mu'adh bin Jabal ؓ who said, "When you were tested with adverse conditions, you exercised patience (and passed the test). You will soon be tested with conditions of prosperity so do exercise restraint. What I fear most for you are your women when they start wearing gold and silver bangles, the fine garments of Sham and the floral garments of Yemen. They will then exhaust wealthy men and tax the poor man with a burden he is unable to bear." (Abu Nu'aym in Hilya)

The Advices of Abdullah bin Mas'ood ؓ

Abdullah bin Mas'ood ؓ once said, "It angers me to see a man idle without doing anything for this world or for the Hereafter." (Abu Nu'aym in Hilya, Abdur Razzaq in Kanzul Ummal). Another narration states that Abdullah bin Mas'ood ؓ said, "Let me not find any of you lying like a corpse at night without waking for salah and behaving like the Qutrub insect all day." Ibn Uyayna states that the Qutrub insect is one that is sitting in one place at times and then somewhere else moving about all day long without taking a break. Like this, the man is constantly on the move in pursuit of worldly gain. (Abu Nu'aym *in Hilya).* Abdullah bin Mas'ood ⬥ also said, "The cream of is world has passed on, leaving only waste behind. Death day is therefore a gift for every Muslim." *(Abu Nu'aym in Hilya)* Another narration states that he said, "This world is like a lake at the top of a mountain, the best waters of which have departed, leaving behind only muddy remains." *(Abu Nu'aym in Hilya).* Abdullah bin Mas'ood ⬥ stated, "How wonderful are 2 things that people dislike; death and poverty! By Allah! One is affected by either one of 2 conditions, prosperity or poverty and I care not which of the 2 I am afflicted with. If it is prosperity, I can use it to sympathize with the poor by helping them. If it is poverty, I can use it exercise patience and be rewarded abundantly." *(Abu Nu'aym in Hilya).* It was also Abdullah bin Mas'ood ⬥ who said, "A person cannot reach the reality of Iman until he reaches its apex and he will be unable to reach the apex until he loves poverty more than prosperity, until he loves submission more than honor and until the one who praises him and the one who insults him are the same to him." The students of Abdullah bin Mas'ood ⬥ then explained this statement saying, "Until he prefers earning Halal and remaining in poverty to earning Haram and living in affluence; until he prefers submitting to Allah's commands to the worldly honor derived from sinning and until the person praising him in truth and the person insulting him are equal in his sight." *(Abu Nu'aym in Hilya, Ahnad in Safwatus Safwa).* Abdullah bin Mas'ood ⬥ also said, "I swear by the Being besides Whom there is none worthy of worship that when a person passes his mornings and evenings as a Muslim, the adversities that afflict him in this world will not harm him." *(Abu Nu'aym in Hilya).* Abdur Rahman bin Hujaira reports from his father that when he took a seat, Abdullah bin Mas'ood ⬥ would say, "Days and nights are passing you people by, as your lives are growing shorter, your actions are being recorded and death is waiting to strike you so very suddenly. The person who sows good deeds will soon harvest that which he will be pleased to have. However, the one who sows evil wiII harvest only regrets. Every farmer will reap only that which he plants. While the sustenance of a slow person will never bypass him, the greedy person cannot get more than what has been destined for him. The person who has anything good has been given the same by Allah and the person saved from any evil has been saved by Allah. Those with Taqwa are simple, those with deep understanding of Deen are to be followed and being in their company will only grant one more." *(Abu Nu'aym in Hilya, Ahmad in Safwatus Safwa).* Abdullah bin Mas'ood ⬥ once stated, 'Each one of you is a guest and his wealth is borrowed. While the guest has to leave sometime, a borrowed item has to be returned to the owner." *(Abu Nu'aym in Hilya).* Abdur Rahman the son of Abdullah bin Mas'ood ⬥ reports that a man once approached his father saying, "O Abu Abdur Rahman! Teach me some words that are both concise and beneficial." Abdullah bin Mas'ood ⬥ said, "Worship Allah without ascribing any partners to Him and go wherever the Qur'an takes you. When someone brings you the truth, accept it from him even though he may be someone distant or someone you dislike and when someone comes to you with falsehood, reject it though he may be someone close and beloved to you." *(Abu Nu'aym in Hilya)*

Abdullah bin Mas'ood ⬥ stated, "The truth is heavy and bitter while falsehood is light and pleasant. So many pleasures there are that give rise to nothing but tremendous sorrow." *(Abu Nu'aym in Hilya).* Abdullah bin Mas'ood ⬥ is reported to have said, "While the heart may have incredible enthusiasm and zeal to do good, it can also be greatly indifferent and lethargic. You must therefore exploit its enthusiasm and ignore its indifference."

(Abu Nu'aym in Hilya). Mundhir reports that when some non-Arab chiefs came to see Abdullah bin Mas'ood ⬥, the people were impressed by their muscular necks and glowing health. Abdullah bin Mas'ood ⬥ then said to the people, "You may see that a Kafir is physically most healthy while his heart is most ill with kufr and Shirk. You may then meet a Muslim whose body may be most ill, but his heart is most healthy. By Allah! If your hearts are ill and only your bodies are healthy, you will be lower than a dung-beetle in Allah's sight." *(Abu Nu'aym in Hilya).* Abdullah bin Mas'ood ⬥ once said, "A Mu'min cannot have any comfort without meeting Allah and whoever finds comfort only in meeting Allah has actually met Allah." *(Abu Nu'aym in Hilya).* It was also Abdullah bin Mas'ood ⬥ who said, "None of you should ever place his Deen around the neck of another person in a manner that he believes only when the other person believes and he rejects what the other person rejects, he must follow the teachings of the Qur'an and Sunnah instead. However, if he absolutely has to follow someone, he must follow someone who has passed away as a practicing Muslim because the living is never immune from corruption." Another narration states that he said, "None of you should ever be an lmma'ah." "What is an lmma'ah, O Abu Abdur Rahman?" the people asked. Abdullah bin Mas'ood ⬥ explained, "When a person says, 'I am with the people. If they are rightly guided, so shall I be and if they go astray, I shall stray as well.' Listen well! Each of you must fortify his heart so much that he will not resort to kufr even if all of mankind does." *(Abu Nu'aym in Hilya).* Abdullah bin Mas'ood ⬥ said, "I can make 3 statements on oath and there is a 4th thing that if I say it on oath as well, I would definitely not be wrong. (1) Allah will never make a person who has a share of Islam like the one who has no share of Islam. (2) When Allah is a person's friend in this world, He will never hand him over to someone else on the Day of Judgment. (3) When someone loves a nation, he will certainly arrive with them (on the Day of Judgment). (4) The 4th thing about which I would definitely not be wrong if I say it on oath is that if Allah conceals the faults of a person in this world, he will finitely do so in the Hereafter." *(Abu Nu'aym in Hilya).* Abdullah bin Mas'ood ⬥ also said, 'Whoever desires this world will do harm to his Hereafter and whoever desires the Hereafter will do harm to his world. O people! Rather let harm come to that which is temporary instead of harm coming to that which is everlasting." *(Abu Nu'aym in Hilya).* It is also reported that Abdullah bin Mas'ood ⬥ said, "Verily the most truthful of all speech is the Book of Allah, the strongest handhold is the Kalima of Taqwa, the best of creeds is the creed of Ibrahim ﷺ, the best of all ways is the Sunnah of Rasulullah ﷺ and the best guidance is the guidance of the Ambiya ﷺ. The most dignified discourse is the Dhikr of Allah, the best of narratives is the Qur'an, the best of all matters are those with the best results and the worst of them all are those that are fabricated. That which may be little but suffices is better than that which is plenty but which distracts one from Allah and the Hereafter. Coming to the rescue of a single soul is better than a kingdom in which justice cannot be upheld. The worst reproach will be when death appears, the worst regret will be on the Day of Judgment and the worst misguidance is to stray after once being rightly guided. The best wealth is the wealth of the heart, the best provisions is Taqwa, the best things to be placed in the heart is conviction, doubts stem from kufr and the worst blindness is the blindness of the heart. Intoxicants are the root of all sin, women are the traps of Saitan, youth is a branch of insanity and wailing is the act of the period of ignorance.

There are people who are the last to attend the Jumu'ah salah and who make the Dhikr of Allah only verbally (without concentration). The worst of all sins is lying, verbally abusing a Mu'min is an act of irreligiousness, physically abusing him leads to kufr and his wealth is as sacred as his life. Allah will forgive the one who forgives others, Allah will reward the one who swallows his anger, will pardon the one who pardons and will generously recompense the one who patiently endures difficulties. The worst of all earnings are earnings from interest and the worst thing to consume is the wealth of orphans. The fortunate person is he who takes advice from others while the unfortunate one is he who has been decreed such ever since he was in the belly of his mother. So much is enough for a person that affords him contentment and every person is traveling towards a place measuring only four arm's lengths. The matter of greatest concern is the Hereafter and the master of all deeds is the very last of them. The worst of all dreams are those that one lies about and the noblest of deaths is martyrdom. He who recognizes a test will be patient, he who does not will find it perplexing and Allah will destroy the one who is haughty. The one who spouses this world will be unable to gain mastery over it, the one who obeys Saitan will disobey Allah and he who disobeys Allah will be punished by Allah." (*Abu Nu'aym in Hilya*). Abdullah bin Mas'ood ﷺ once said, "When a person does things for show in this world, Allah will show his faults to people on the Day of Judgment and when one does things for people to hear about him in this world, Allah will make them hear all about his faults on the Day of Judgment. The person who acts proudly to gain status, Allah will humiliate him whereas Allah will elevate the person who is humble." (*Abu Nu'aym in Hilya*)

The Advices of Salman Farsi ﷺ

Ja'far bin Burqan reports that the report reached him that Salman Farsi ﷺ used to say, '3 persons make me laugh and 3 things make me cry. (1) I laugh at the person who entertains lengthy hopes in this world yet death is constantly searching for him. (2) The person who is negligent of death yet death is never negligent of him and (3) the person who laughs most heartily whereas he knows not whether his Rabb is angry with him or pleased. The 3 things that make me weep are separation from Muhammad ﷺ and his party, the frightening scene when the pangs of death arrive and standing before the Rabb of the universe when I know not whether I shall be heading for the fire of Jahannam or for Jannah." (*Abu Nu'aym in Hilya*). Salman ﷺ also said, 'When Allah intends destruction to come to a person, Allah strips him of modesty and you find that he becomes a person who hates people and they hate him. When this occurs, Allah takes His mercy away from him and you find that he becomes vulgar and hard-hearted. When this happens, Allah removes trustworthiness from him and you then find him to become treacherous and being treated treacherously by others. When this happens, the brace of Islam is then eventually snatched off his neck and he becomes one who is cursed by Allah and by all of creation." (*Abu Nu'aym in Hilya*). Salman ﷺ is also reported to have said, "The example of a Mu'min in this world is like a sick person who has with him his physician who knows every illness and every cure. When the person desires something that is harmful for him, the physician prevents him from taking it saying, 'Do not go near that because you will be destroying yourself if you do.' He then continues preventing him from things in this manner until the person is completely cured of his disease. In a like manner, a Mu'min desires a great number of things of comfort that others have been given and which he has not. However, Allah prevents him from it and shields it from him

until he dies, after which Allah admits him into Jannah." (*Abu Nu'aym in Hilya*). Yahya bin Sa'eed reports that Abu Darda ﷺ once wrote to Salman ﷺ, inviting him to come and stay in the blessed land of Sham. Salman ﷺ however wrote back saying, "It is not any piece of land that makes a person blessed, but it is knowledge that does. The news has reached me that you have been made a physician (a judge). Congratulations to you if you are able to cure people settle their cases justly, but if you are a fake, then beware that you do not kill a person or have a person wrongly executed, because of which you will have to enter Jahannam." As a result, whenever Abu Darda ﷺ had passed judgment between 2 persons and they were leaving his court, he would say, "By Allah! Have I been a quack? Come back and plead your cases to me all over again." (*Abu Nu'aym in Hilya*)

The Advices of Abu Darda ﷺ

Hassan bin Atia reports that Abu Darda ﷺ used to say, "You people will always remain in good stead as long as you love the righteous ones amongst you and as long as you recognize the truth when it is spoken amongst you because the one who recognizes the truth is like the one who practices it." (*Abu Nu'aym in Hilya, Bayhaqi, Ibn Asakir in Kanzul Ummal*). Abu Darda ﷺ said, 'Never compel people to do what they have not been compelled to do by Allah and never take them to task for what their Rabb would not. O son of Adam ﷺ! Worry about yourselves because the person who constantly pursues the wrong he sees in others will always be plagued by prolonged grief and frustration that never abates." (*Abu Nu'aym in Hilya*). Abu Darda ﷺ also said, "Worship Allah as if you can see Him and count yourselves amongst the dead. Remember that a little that is sufficient for you is better than plenty that makes you negligent and remember also that good deeds never age and sins are never forgotten." (*Abu Nu'aym in Hilya*). It is reported that Abu Darda ﷺ once said, "Goodness is not when your wealth or your children increase, but when your knowledge increases, when your tolerance grows and when you excel people in worshipping your Rabb. When you do well, praise Allah and when you do wrong, seek forgiveness from Allah." (*Abu Nu'aym in Hilya*). Salim bin Abul Ja'd narrates that Abu Darda ﷺ said, "One should beware that he is not hated in the hearts of the Mu'mineen without him knowing it. Do you know why this happens?" When Salim replied that he did not, Abu Darda ﷺ explained, "When a person secretly disobeys Allah, Allah casts resentment for him in the hearts of the Mu'minin and he does not even know about it." (*Abu Nu'aym in Hilya*). Abu Darda ﷺ also said, "The apex of Iman is to steadfastly fulfill the orders of Allah, to be satisfied with what Allah decrees, to be sincere in pinning one's trust in Allah and to surrender oneself completely to one's Rabb." (*Abu Nu'aym in Hilya*). It is reported that Abu Darda ﷺ also said, "Destruction be for the one who is concerned only with amassing wealth. Like a madman, his mouth is always agape looking at what others have rather than what he has. If he could help it, he would even join the day with the night to have more time to earn money. His destruction will be in the severe reckoning and intense punishment that he will be receiving." (*Abu Nu'aym in Hilya*). It was also Abu Darda ﷺ who said, "O people of Damascus! Do you have no shame? You store that which you will be unable to eat, you build that which you cannot live in and you have hopes that you cannot reach. There have been civilizations before you who amassed and hoarded their wealth, entertained lengthy hopes and constructed fortified buildings. However, their amassed treasures were destroyed, their hopes turned out to be deceptive illusions and their buildings became their graves. They were the nation of 'Ad who once filled the territory between Aden and Amman with wealth and offspring. Now who would want to buy their legacy for even 2 Dirhams?" *(Abu Nu'aym in Hilya)*. Another narration states that when Abu Darda ⬥ noticed how much the Muslims were absorbing them in building and planting trees, he stood up in their Masjid and addressed them saying, "Gather around me, O people of Damascus!" When the people had gathered, he duly praised Allah and said, "Do you have no shame..." The rest of the narration is like the one above. *(Ibn Abi Hatim in Tafsir Ibn Kathir)*. Safwan bin Amr narrates that Abu Darda ⬥ used to say, "O assembly of the wealthy! Cool off your skins, save it from Jahannam with your wealth by spending it in Sadaqah before you and us become equals in it when your death arrives. You will then only be able to look at it and we will join you in looking." He also said, "What I fear for you is a subtle desire for a bounty that will involve you in futility. This will happen when you fill yourselves with food and starve yourselves of knowledge."

Another narration states that he said, "The best of you is he who says to his companion, 'Let us fast before we die' and the worst of you is he who says to his companion, 'Let us eat, drink and pass time before we die'." Abu Darda ⬥ was once passing by some people who were building. He said to them, "You people are renovating this world when Allah desires that it is reduced to ruins. Allah shall however prevail in whatever He intends." Makhul reports that Abu Darda ⬥ used to search for ruins and when he found any, he would address it saying, "O ruins of the ruined ones! Where are those who had been inhabiting you initially?" *(Abu Nu'aym in Hilya)*. Abu Darda said, "There are 3 things that I love and which people generally hate; poverty, illness and death." *(Abu Nu'aym in Hilya)*. He also said, "I love death because of my longing to meet my Rabb. I love poverty because I can then truly humble myself before my Rabb and I love illness because it obliterates my sins." *(Abu Nu'aym in Hilya)*. Shurabil narrates that whenever Abu Darda ⬥ saw a funeral, he would say, "You are leaving in the morning and we shall be leaving in the evening. You are leaving in the evening and we shall be leaving in the morning. Death is a powerful advice, yet people are so quick to forget. One needs no advice other than death. While people leave one after another, it is only those without sense that remain behind (without taking heed)." *(Abu Nu'aym in Hilya)*. Aun bin Abdullah reports that Abu Darda ⬥ said, "The person who searches very hard for the faults of others will lose sight of himself of his own faults and the one who does not prepare for emergencies will be left helpless. If you give and take loans from people, they will do the same with you and if you leave them, they will not leave you." "Then what would you advise me to do?" Aun asked. Abu Darda replied, "Lend the one who will pay you back on the day you will be most in need on the Day of Judgment." *(Abu Nu'aym in Hilya)*. Abu Darda ⬥ also said, "The person who often thinks of death will show off less and will also be less jealous." *(Abu Nu'aym in Hilya)*. Abu Darda ⬥ is also reported to have said, "Why is it that I see you greedy for that sustenance for which Allah has already assumed responsibility on your behalf while you ruin those duties which you have been entrusted with? I know the wicked ones amongst you better than a horse specialist knows his horses. They are the ones who perform their salah after its time, who listen to the Qur'an indifferently and whose slaves are not free from them even after they have been set free." *(Abu Nu'aym in Hilya)*. It was also Abu Darda ⬥ who said, "Look for good throughout your lives and ensure that you present yourself for all Allah's breaths of mercy because there are many such breaths of

Allah's mercy, which Allah allows to strike those of His servants whom He pleases. Also ask Allah to conceal your faults and to calm your fears." *(Abu Nu'aym in Hilya)*. Abdullah bin Jubair bin Nufair reports that a man once said to Abu Darda ⬥, "Teach me something by which Allah may grant me benefit." Abu Darda ⬥ advised him saying, "There are 2, 3, 4 or rather 5 things that if a person practices upon, Allah will undertake to reward him with the highest stages. They are that you should never eat anything other than that which is pure (Halal), you should never earn anything other than that which is pure and you should never admit into your home anything other than that which is pure. Ask Allah for your sustenance day by day and when you count yourself amongst the dead each morning, it will be as if you have already met up with them. Hand your honor over to Allah so that you leave Allah to deal with anyone who ears you, abuses you or fights with you. Then when you commit any sin, seek forgiveness from Allah." *(Abu Nu'aym in Hilya)*. Abu Darda ⬥ also said, "A person remains youthful in his love for this world even though his collar bones may be meeting because of old age. This applies to everyone except those whose hearts Allah has tested for Taaqwa, and they are few indeed." *(Abu Nu'aym in Hilya, Ibn Asakir in Kanzul Ummal)*

It is reported that Abu Darda ⬥ once said, "It is with 3 factors that man can take charge of all his affairs; never complain of your calamities, never speak about your illness and never claim that you are spiritually pure." *(Abu Nu'aym in Hilya)*. Abu Darda ⬥ said, "Beware of the curse of the pressed and the curse of the orphan because both travel to Allah at night when people are fast asleep." He also said, "The person whom I hate most to oppress is the one who has none other than Allah to ask help of." *(Abu Nu'aym in Hilya)*. Ma'mar reports from a companion that Abu Darda ⬥ once wrote to Salman ⬥ saying, "Dear brother! Make the most of your health and free time before that calamity strikes which all of mankind cannot repel death. Also make the most of the Du'a of the afflicted person. Dear brother! Let the Masjid be your home because have heard Rasulullah ﷺ say, 'The Masjid is home to every person with Taqwa.' For those whose homes are the Masajid, Allah has also guaranteed happiness, contentment and a safe passage across the bridge of Sirat en route to the pleasure of his Rabb. Dear brother! Have mercy on the orphan, keep him close to you and feed him from the food that you eat. When a person once came to Rasulullah ﷺ complaining of a hard heart, I heard Rasulullah ﷺ ask him, 'Do you want your heart to soften?' When the man replied in the affirmative, Rasulullah ﷺ advised him saying, 'Keep an orphan close to you, pass your hand over his head and feed him from your own food. This will soften your heart and settle your needs.' Dear brother! Never collect that for which you will be unable to express gratitude because I have heard Rasulullah ﷺ say, 'On the Day of Judgment, that wealthy person who obeyed Allah with regards to his wealth will be brought forward. He will be in front of his wealth and it will be placed behind him. Every time, he stumbles on the bridge of Sirat, his wealth will say to him, 'Go on! You have fulfilled the rights due from you.' Thereafter, the wealthy person who did not obey Allah with regards to hi wealth will be brought forward with his wealth on his shoulders. His wealth will cause him to stumble saying, 'May you be destroyed! Why did you not obey Allah when it concerned me?' This will continue until the person will himself call for his destruction.' Dear brother! I have been informed that you have purchased a slave. I have heard Rasulullah ﷺ say, 'A person remains connected to Allah and Allah to him as long as another is not in his service because as soon as another person is in his service, reckoning becomes incumbent for him.' In fact my wife Ummu Darda requested me for a servant at a time when I was well off but I disapproved of the idea because of this reckoning that I heard about. Dear brother! Who is there to assure us that we will meet on the Day of Judgment without fear of reckoning? Dear brother! Never fall into deception about being a companion of Rasulullah ﷺ because we have lived long after him and Allah Alone knows what we have done in this time." *(Abu Nu'aym in Hilya, Ibn Asakir, Kanzul Ummal).* Abdur Rahman bin Muhammad Muharibi reports at Abu Darda ؓ once wrote to a companion of his saying, "Everything you have in this world belonged to someone else previously and will soon be going off to someone else after you. Nothing of it belongs to you apart from what you have sent ahead to the Hereafter for yourself by spending in the right causes. You should therefore give preference to yourself over even your righteous childlen because you are proceeding towards a Being Who will not accept excuses for your failure to spend correctly and your amassing of wealth will be only for those who will not even thank you for it. Your amassing of wealth is only for one of 2 persons. It may be for a person who uses it in the obedience of Allah, because of which he will have the good fortune that you had been deprived of. On the other hand it may for someone who uses it in the disobedience of Allah, in which case you will be ill-fortuned because it was you who saved it for him. By Allah! Neither of these 2 deserves to have their burdens lightened by you having to carry it on your back. You Muslims therefore should not give preference to anyone else over yourself. Hope for Allah's mercy to descend on those of them who have passed on and trust that Allah will provide for those of them who are still left alive. Was Salam." *(Abu Nu'aym in Hilya).* Abu Darda ؓ once wrote to Maslama bin Mukhallad saying, "When a person's actions conform with Allah's commands, Allah loves the person and when Allah loves him, Allah makes all of His creation love the person as well. On the contrary, when a person's actions do not conform with Allah's commands, Allah dislikes the person and when Allah dislikes him, Allah makes all of His creation dislike the person as well. *(Ibn Asakir in Kanzul Ummal).* Abu Darda ؓ also said, "There is no Islam without obedience to Allah and no good without affiliating with the broader Muslim community and without wishing well for (the Deen of) Allah, for His Khalifa and for the Mu'minin in general." *(Ibn Asakir in Kanzul Ummal)*

The Advices of Abu Dhar ؓ

Sufian Thowri narrates that Abu Dharr Ghifari ؓ once stood up near the Kaba and said, "O people! I am Jundub Ghifari. Come to this well-wishing and caring brother." When the people had gathered all around him, he said, "Tell me. If any of you wishes to undertake a journey, Will he not prepare sufficient provisions to see him through comfortably until he reaches his destination?" When the people confirmed this, he continued, "Well, then the journey to Judgment is the furthest that you will ever undertake, so do take enough provisions to see you through comfortably." The people then asked, "And what is enough to see us through comfortably?" Abu Dhar ؓ explained, "Perform a Hajj to take care of important matters, fast on an extremely hot day to take care of the very long Day of Resurrection, perform 2 Rakahs salah in the darkness of the night to take care of the loneliness of the grave and either say a good word or refrain from saying a bad word to take care of standing before Allah on that crucial day (of Judgment). Spend your wealth in Sadaqah dand you will be saved from the difficulties of the Day of Judgment. In this world you should attend only 2 types of gatherings;

gatherings to acquire the Hereafter and gatherings to seek Halal sustenance. You would not want a 3rd type of gathering because apart from not doing you any good, it will cause you harm. You should also spend your Dimams in 2 places; one should be spent on lawful expenses for your family and the other you should send ahead for your Ahereafter. You would not want a 3rd type of Dirham because apart from not doing you any good, it will cause you harm." Abu Dhar ؓ then called out at the top his voice, "O people! Greed has killed you and you will ever be able to get all that you are greedy for." *(Abu Nu'aym in Hilya).* Abdullah bin Muhammad reports that he heard a liable scholar say, "The news has reached me that Abu Dhar ؓ once said, 'O people! I am a well-wisher to you and have tremendous compassion for you. Perform salah in the darkness of the night to take care of the loneliness of the grave, fast in this world to take care of the extremely hot Day of Resurrection and spend in Sadaqa and you will be saved from the difficulties of the Day of Judgment. O people! I am a well-wisher to you and have tremendous compassion for you." *(Abu Nu'aym in Hilya).* Abu Dhar ؓ also said, 'People are born to die and buildings are built to fall into ruins. That which shall come to an end is sought with greed while that which is everlasting is being ignored. Oh how wonderful are the two things that people dislike; death and poverty." *(Abu Nu'aym in Hilya).* Hibban bin Abi Jabala reports that both Abu Dhar ؓ and Abu Darda ؓ said, "You are born to die, you build buildings to fall into ruins, you greedily hanker after that which shall come to an end while ignoring that which is everlasting. Ah! How wonderful are 3 things that people dislike; death, illness and poverty." *(Ibn Asakir in Kanzul Ummal)*

The Advices of Hudhaifa bin Yaman ؓ

Abu Tufail narrates that he heard Hudhaifa ؓ say, "O people! Do you have no questions to me? While others used to ask Rasulullah ﷺ about the good things to happen, I used to ask him about the evil. Will you not ask me about the living dead? Allah sent Muhammad who called people away from misguidance towards guidance and away from kufr towards Iman. When those who responded to his call he said, the dead were given life because of the truth that they accepted while those who were alive (physically), actually died spiritually because they adhered to falsehood. When Nubuwwah had left with the demise of Rasulullah ﷺ, there came Khilafa on the pattern of Nubuwwah, which will be followed by despotic kingship. Those who will oppose this despotism with their hearts, hands and tongues will be practicing on the complete truth. As for those who oppose it with their hearts and tongues but who restrain their hands will be leaving a branch of the truth. There will be those also who will oppose it within their hearts only while restraining their hands and tongues. Such people will be omitting two branches of the truth. Then there will be those will neither oppose it with their hearts nor their tongues let alone their hands. Such people are the living dead." *(Abu Nu'aym in Hilya)*

Hearts are of 4 Types

Hudhaifa ؓ said, 'Hearts are of 4 types: (1) the veiled heart, which is the heart of the Kafir, (2) the two-faced heart, which is the heart of the hypocrite, (3) the clear heart containing a shining lantern, which is the heart of a Mu'min and (4) the heart that contains both hypocrisy and Iman. The example of Iman is like a tree that grows bigger with pure water while the example of hypocrisy is like a blister that grows bigger with blood and pus. Therefore, the heart will be overpowered by whichever of the 2 (Iman and hypocrisy) is overwhelming." *(Abu Nu'aym in Hilya)*

His Advice Concerning Enticement and Other Matters

Hudhaifa ⁕ is also reported to have said, "The trial of temptation to do evil presents itself to the hearts of people. When the heart accepts it, a black spot appears on the heart and if the heart rejects it, a white spot appears. Whoever wishes to know whether such enticement has afflicted him or not, should assess himself. He should know that it has afflicted him when he starts regarding as Haram something that he always regarded as Halal or when he starts regarding as Halal something that he always regarded as Haram." *(Abu Nu'aym in Hilya)*. Hudhaifa ⁕ also said, "Beware of the trials of temptation which none can stand up to by himself because I swear by Allah that whenever someone tries to stand up to them by himself, it sweeps him away just as a flood sweeps dirt away. When they arrive, these trials appear to be right and the ignorant ones will even claim that they appear to be right. However, it is only when they are leaving that it becomes manifest that they were really not. When you see such trials approach, remain squatting in your homes, break your swords and cut your bowstrings." *(Abu Nu'aym in Hilya)*. Hudhaifa ⁕ said, "Verily, the trials of life have periods of repose and periods of upheaval. If you ever have the option to die when it is in repose, ensure that you do so." By the periods of repose, Hudhaifa was referring to the periods when swords are sheathed (when there is no in-fighting between the Muslims). *(Abu Nu'aym in Hilya)*. Hudhaifa ⁕ also said, "Verily, corruption stems from 3 persons; from the powerful and proficient scholar who uses the sword to annihilate everything that is presented to him, from the orator who calls people towards such corruption and from the ruler. As for the first two, such corruption will floor them flat on their faces. As for the ruler, it will keep clawing at him until it affects all those with him as well." *(Abu Nu'aym in Hilya)*. Another narration states that Hudhaifa ⁕ once said, "Even pure wine is not more effective than the trial of life in eliminating the cause to faulter the senses of a person." *(Abu Nu'aym in Hilya)*. Yet another narration quotes Hudhaifa ⁕ as saying, "There shall come a time when none shall have safety besides the person who makes a Du'a like a drowning person does." *(Abu Nu'aym in Hilya)*. A'mash reports that the news reached him that Hudhaifa ⁕ said, "The best of you is not the one who forsakes this world for the Hereafter, nor the person who forsakes the Hereafter for this world. Rather, he is the one who takes from both worlds." *(Abu Nu'aym in Hilya)*

The Advices of Ubay bin Ka'b ⁕

Abul Alia reports that when a man once asked Ubay bin Ka'b ⁕ for some advice, Ubay ⁕ said, "Make the Qur'an your guide and be satisfied to have it as your judge and arbiter because it has succeeded your Rasul ⁕ amongst you. It is an intercessor (on the Day of Judgment) whose intercession will be accepted and a witness whose testimony cannot be faulted. It speaks of you and of those before you, it judges the matters between you and together with news about you, it also contains news of those to come after you." *(Abu Nu'aym in Hilya)*. Ubay bin Ka'b ⁕ said, "Whenever a servant forsakes anything for the pleasure of Allah, Allah replaces it with something better from sources he never expected. On the other hand, when a servant looks down on something and takes it wrongly, Allah brings forth something much more serious from sources he never expects." *(Abu Nu'aym in Hilya)*. Ubay bin Ka'b ⁕ also said, "A Mu'min is in one of 4 conditions: when afflicted with difficulties, he exercises patience, when given something, he is grateful, when speaking, he is truthful, and when passing judgment, he is just. He also journeys in 5 instances of Noor (celestial light), regarding which Allah says, نور علي نور Noor upon Noor" *(Nur:35)*. His speech is Noor, his knowledge is Noor, the places he enters are filled with Noor, the places he exits from are filled with Noor and the place he will go to on the Day of Judgment will be one of Noor. On the other hand, the Kafir journeys through 5 instances of darkness. His speech is darkness, his knowledge is darkness, the places he enters are filled with darkness, the places he exits from are filled with darkness and the place he will go to on the Day of Judgment will be one of darkness." *(Abu Nu'aym in Hilya)*. Abu Basra reports that a companion of his named Jabar or Juwaibir once said, "When I went to request a slave-girl from Omar ⁕ during his Khilafa, I reached Madinah at night. Since I have been blessed with a keen mind and an eloquent tongue, when I went to Omar ⁕, I started ridiculing and demeaning this world, ending off on a note that left the world totally without value. When I had finished, a man who was sitting next to Omar ⁕ said, 'Everything you said was in order, apart from the manner in which you ridiculed this world. Do you know what this world really is? This world is our means of reaching the Hereafter. It contains our provisions for the Hereafter and all your deeds for which you will be rewarded in the Hereafter.' His subsequent speech about the world happened to be one of a person who obviously knew much more about this world than I did. 'O Amirul Mu'minin!' I asked, 'Who is this man next to you?' Omar ⁕ replied, 'He is the leader of the Muslims Ubay bin Ka'b ⁕." *(Bukhari in Adab, Muntakhab Kanzul Ummal)*. Addressing Ubay bin Ka'b ⁕, someone once asked, "O Abul Mundhir! please give me some advice." Ubay ⁕ then advised him saying, "Never delve into matters that do not concern you, stay away from your enemy and exercise caution even when it comes to your friends. Envy a living person only for that which you would envy a dead person for and never ask a need from a person who has no concern for fulfilling it for you." *(Ibn Asakir in Kanzul Ummal)*

The Advices of Zaid bin Thabit ⁕

Dinar Bahrani narrates that Zaid bin Thabit ⁕ once wrote to Ubay bin Ka'b saying, "Verily Allah has made the tongue an interpreter for the heart and has made the heart a treasure chest and a shepherd. The tongue therefore follows the instructions of the heart and as long as the heart remains in charge of the tongue, the speech emerging from the tongue will be pleasant and correct. The tongue will then make no slip-ups and blunders. There is however no tolerating person whose heart does not lead his tongue. When a person leaves his tongue to do the talking without conforming with the dictates of the heart, he cuts off his nose to embarrass himself. However, when he weighs his words with his actions, his words will always be true. People often say, 'Every miser you see is generous with words but stingy with actions.' This happens when the tongue precedes the heart. People also say, 'Can a person have any honor or manliness when he does not practice what he speaks when he knows well at the time of making the statement that it is true and that he is obliged to do as he says?' One must never look at the faults of others because the person who looks at the faults of others while not taking his own faults seriously is like a person who unnecessarily burdens himself with doing that which he has not been instructed to do. Was Salam." *(Ibn Asakir in Kanzul Ummal)*

The Advices of Abdullah bin Abbas ⁕

Abdullah bin Abbas ⁕ once said, "O sinner! Never feel that you are safe from an evil end. There are several things that are worse than the sin that you actually commit. Your failure to be embarrassed for those on your right and left when committing the sin is worse than the sin itself. Your laughing after the sin when you have no idea what Allah intends doing with you is worse than the sin itself. Your pleasure after you have successfully completed the sin is worse than the sin itself. Your anguish when unable to commit the sin is worse than successfully completing the sin itself. When committing the sin, you fear more that the wind should not blow the curtain of your door rather than fearing that Allah is watching you. This is worse than committing the sin itself. Alas! Do you know what was the slip Ayub ﷺ committed, because of which Allah afflicted him with illness and the loss of his wealth? The slip he made was that when a poor person sought his aid to avenge a wrong done to him, he neither assisted him nor did he enjoin good or forbid the oppressor from wronging him. It was for this reason that Allah afflicted Ayub ﷺ with the trial." *(Abu Nu'aym in Hilya, Ibn Asakir in Kanzul Ummal).* Abdullah bin Abbas ﷺ said, "Ensure that you fulfill the Fara'idh. Fulfill the rights owing to Him that Allah has prescribed and seek His assistance in doing so. Whenever Allah knows that a servant has a sincere intention and is aspiring for the rewards that are with Allah, Allah wards off from him all that he dislikes. Allah is the Absolute Sovereign Who does as He pleases." *(Abu Nu'aym in Hilya).* Abdullah bin Abbas ﷺ is also reported to have said, "Whether a person is a true Mu'min or a sinner, Allah has already decreed his Halal sustenance. If he is patient until it comes his way, Allah gives it to him. However, if he is impatient and takes from something Haram, Allah deducts that much from his Halal sustenance." *(Abu Nu'aym in Hilya)*

The Advices of Abdullah bin Omar ﷺ

Abdullah bin Omar ﷺ said, "Whenever a servant receives anything of this world, it reduces his status in Allah's sight even though the person may be enjoying an honorable status with Allah." *(Abu Nu'aym in Hilya).* Abdullah bin Omar ﷺ also said, "A man cannot reach the apex of Iman until he regards people as being foolish in Deen because of them preferring this world over the Hereafter." *(Abu Nu'aym in Hilya).* Mujahid reports that he was once walking with Abdullah bin Omar ﷺ when they passed by some ruins. "O ruins!" Abdullah bin Omar ﷺ said, "What has happened to your inhabitants?" "O ruins!" Mujahid repeated, "What has happened to your inhabitants?" Abdullah bin Omar ﷺ then replied, "They have left and all that has remained behind are their actions." *(Abu Nu'aym in Hilya)*

The Advices of Abdullah bin Zubair ﷺ

Wahab bin Kaisan narrates that Abdullah bin Zubair ﷺ once wrote to advise him saying, "The people of Taqwa have certain traits by which they are recognized and which they recognize within themselves. These include patience during times of adversity, happiness with Allah's decree, gratitude for bounties and submission to the commands of the Qur'an. A ruler is just like the marketplace. Only that commodity is brought to the marketplace which is popular. Therefore, if the truth is popular with a ruler, it will be brought to him and people of the truth will come to him. On the other hand, if falsehood is popular with a ruler, the people of falsehood will come to him and it is falsehood that will prevail with him." *(Abu Nu'aym in Hilya)*

The Advices of Hasan bin Ali ﷺ

Hasan bin Ali ﷺ once said, "When a person hankers after this world, it makes him sit down to make him subservient to it, whereas the person who exercises abstinence cares not who eats from it. The person who aspires for this world becomes the slave of those who possess the world. Whereas even the least of it is

sufficient for the person who does not aspire for it, having all of it will not benefit the one who hankers after it. The person whose days are the same without any spiritual progress is in great deception while the person who is better off today than he will be tomorrow whose spiritual condition worsens from day to day is at a loss. As for the person who does not monitor the damages done to himself (to his spirituality) is truly at a loss and death is really better for such a person." *(Ibn Najjar in Kanzul Ummal).* Hasan bin Ali ﷺ also said, "You should know that tolerance is a source of beauty in character and fulfilling one's promises is a sign of manliness. Haste is sign of foolishness, excessive travelling weakens a person, keeping company with wicked people is a mark to one's character and keeping company with sinful people is a source of doubts entering one's heart." *(Ibn Asakir in Kanzul Ummal).* Hasan bin Ali ﷺ is also reported to have said, "People are of 4 types. Some are those who have a great share of goodness but no good character. Then there are those who have good character but no share of goodness. There are those also who have neither any share of goodness nor good character and these are the worst of the lot. Then there are the best of them all, who are those with good character together with a great share of goodness." *(Ibn Asakir in Kanzul Ummal)*

The Advices of Shaddad bin Aws ﷺ

Ziyad bin Mahak narrates that Shaddad bin Aws ﷺ used to say, "Verily you people have seen no good apart from its causes and seen no evil apart from its causes because all of true goodness lies in Jannah and all of true evil lies in Jahannam. Verily this world is a ready commodity from which the righteous and the sinner eat equally. The Hereafter on the other hand is a place where the All Powerful Sovereign shall pass judgment. Each of these 2 places have their children, so be amongst the children of the Hereafter and do not be amongst the children of this world." Referring to Shaddad bin Aws ﷺ, Abu Darda ﷺ said, "While some people have been blessed with knowledge and not with forbearance, Abu Ya'la (Shaddad) has been blessed with both knowledge and forbearance." *(Abu Nu'aym in Hilya)*

The Advices of Jundub Bajali ﷺ

Jundub Bajali ﷺ once said, "Fear Allah and recite the Qur'an because it is light for a dark night and adornment for the day despite difficulties and poverty. When affliction strikes, let it be in your wealth rather than in your health, otherwise in your health rather than in your Deen. Remember that the true loser is he who suffers a loss in his Deen and the truly destroyed one is he whose Deen has been destroyed. Behold! There is no poverty after Jannah and no wealth after Jahannam because the prisoner of Jahannam will never be released, the injured there shall never be healed and the fire there shall never be extinguished. Remember that even a handful of blood that a Muslim drew from his brother will become an obstacle for him entering into Jannah. Whenever he tries to enter any of its gates, he will find it there to push him away. Remember also that when a person dies and is buried, it will be his belly that win be the first to decompose and emit an odor. You should therefore not add an additional stench of Haram food to the odor. Fear Allah when it concerns your wealth and avoid spilling blood." *(Bayhaqi in Kanzul Ummal)*

The Advices of Abu Umamah ﷺ on the Occasion of a Funeral

Sulaim bin Amir reports that they were in the company of Abu Umamah Bahili ﷺ when they once left the gates of Damascus to accompany a funeral procession. After performing the Janazh salah and when burying the person, Abu Umamah ﷺ

said, "O people! You are spending your mornings and evenings in a place (this world) where your good deeds and sins are being distributed." Pointing towards the grave, he then said, "You will soon be leaving for another place, which is this house of loneliness, this house of darkness, this house of worms and this house of narrowness for all apart from the one for whom Allah widens the grave. After this you will be proceeding to the various stages of the Day of Judgment and you will be experiencing them when such a command will come from Allah that will cause some faces to brighten and others to darken. As you people then proceed to another stage, people will be enveloped in extreme darkness, after which light will be handed out and every Mu'min will receive some light. The Kafir and the Munafiq will however be left alone and not given any light. It is this example that Allah cites in His Book when He says:

أَوْ كَظُلُمَاتٍ فِي بَحْرٍ لُجِّيٍّ يَغْشَاهُ مَوْجٌ مِنْ فَوْقِهِ مَوْجٌ مِنْ فَوْقِهِ سَحَابٌ ظُلُمَاتٌ بَعْضُهَا فَوْقَ بَعْضٍ إِذَا أَخْرَجَ يَدَهُ لَمْ يَكَدْ يَرَاهَا وَمَنْ لَمْ يَجْعَلِ اللَّهُ لَهُ نُورًا فَمَا لَهُ مِنْ نُورٍ (40)

Or (the state of a disbeliever) is like the darkness in a vast deep sea, overwhelmed with a great wave topped by a great wave, topped by dark clouds, darkness, one above another, if a man stretches out his hand, he can hardly see it! And he for whom Allah has not appointed light, for him there is no light. (An-Nur:40)

Just as a blind person cannot take sight from a seeing person, the Kafir and the Munafiq will be unable to take light from the Mu'min. The Munafiq men and women will then say to those who had Iman: انْظُرُونَا نَقْتَبِسْ مِنْ نُورِكُمْ قِيلَ ارْجِعُوا وَرَاءَكُمْ فَالْتَمِسُوا نُورًا

...Wait for us! Let us get something from your light!" It will be said: "Go back to your rear! Then seek a light!... (Al-Hadid:13)

Such will be the manner in which Allah will deceive the Munafiqin, as Allah says: إِنَّ الْمُنَافِقِينَ يُخَادِعُونَ اللَّهَ وَهُوَ خَادِعُهُمْ

Verily, the hypocrites seek to deceive Allah, but it is He Who deceives them... (An-Nisa:142)

When they then return to the place where the light was distributed, they find nothing and then return to where they had been. However, by then a wall with a door will have already been placed between them (separating them from the Mu'minin). Allah says about it: بَاطِنُهُ فِيهِ الرَّحْمَةُ وَظَاهِرُهُ مِنْ قِبَلِهِ الْعَذَابُ (13)

...Inside it will be (Allah's) mercy, and outside it will be torment. (Al-Hadid:13)

Sulaym bin Amir says, "The Munafiqin will then remain in deception until the light is distributed and the Munafiq is finally separated from the Mu'min." *(Ibn Abi Hatim in Tafsir Ibn Kathir, Bayhaqi in Asma was Sifat)*

His Advice to a Group that Came to See Him

Sulaiman bin Habib says, "I was with a group of people that went to see Abu Umamah ﷺ. I found him to be a frail and old man whose wit and speech belied his physical appearance. He said at the very beginning of the conversation, 'Verily this gathering of yours is Allah's message to you and His proof against you because Allah's Rasul ﷺ conveyed the message he was sent with and his Sahabah conveyed what they heard from Rasulullah ﷺ. You people should therefore also convey what you hear. There are 3 persons for whom Allah stands guarantee to either enter them into Jannah or return them home with their share of rewards and booty. The (1) person who departs in the Path of Allah. Allah stands guarantee to either enter him into Jannah or return him home with his share of rewards and booty. The (2) person who makes wudhu and then proceeds to the Masjid. Allah stands guarantee to either enter him into Jannah or return him home with his share of rewards and booty. The (3) person who enters his house with Salam." He then continued, 'There is a bridge in Jahannam with 7 smaller bridges, the central one of which will be for determining the settlement of debts. A person will be brought forward and when he reaches this central bridge, he will be asked, 'What debts do you have outstanding?' He will then be taken into custody."

Abu Umamah ﷺ then recited the verse: وَلَا يَكْتُمُونَ اللَّهَ حَدِيثًا (42)

...but they will never be able to hide a single fact from Allah. (An-Nisa:42)

The person will admit all the debts he had and will be instructed to settle them. He will plead, 'I have nothing. I do not know with what I can settle them!' The angels will be instructed to take his good deeds (to be paid to the creditors) and this will be done continuously until he is left with no good deeds at all. When his deeds are finished, the angels will be instructed to take from the sins of his creditors and stack them on him. The report has reached me that some people will appear in the Day of Judgment with mountain loads of good deeds, these deeds ill continuously be taken for those with claims against him until he is left with no good deeds at all. He will be burdened with the sins of those with claims against him until the sins reach the enormity of mountains. Refrain from lying because lying leads to sin and sin leads to Jahannam. Ensure that you are always truthful as truthfulness leads to righteousness and righteousness leads to Jannah. O people! You have become more astray than the people during the period of ignorance. While Allah has decreed that a Dinar spent in the Path of Allah equals 700 Dinars and that a Dirham spent equals 700 Dirhams, you people still hoard them in your purses. Listen well! I swear by Allah that victories have been achieved not by swords decorated with gold and silver, but by swords that had only (animal) tendons, lead and iron decorate them." *(Ibn Asakir in Kanzul Ummal)*

The Advices of Abdullah bin Busr ﷺ

Abdullah bin Busr ﷺ once said, "People with Taqwa are simple, Ulema are leaders and being in their company is not only an act of Ibada, but something more. The passage of night and day only reduce your life spans while the records of your actions are well preserved. Prepare your provisions because it is as if you have already reached your place of return the Hereafter." *(Bayhaqi, Ibn Asakir in Kanzul Ummal)*

The Chapter on the Unseen Assistance the Sahabah Received

This chapter discusses how Nabi ﷺ and the Sahabah received unseen assistance when they left the material means, held firmly on to spiritual means and when the Sahabah shared the concern that Rasulullah ﷺ had for the guidance of people and calling them towards Islam. The Sahabah filled themselves the same character traits and noble qualities of Rasulullah ﷺ.

Angels Assist the Sahabah During the Battle of Badr

Sahl bin Sa'd رضي الله عنه reports that after he had lost his eyesight, Abu Usaid رضي الله عنه said, "O son of my brother! By Allah! If you and I were at Badr and Allah restored my eyesight, I would show you the valley from where the angels came to (assist) us. Rest assured that I have absolutely no doubts or uncertainties about this." *(Bayhaqi in Al Bidayah wan Nihayah, Tabrani, Haythami)*. Urwa رضي الله عنه says, "Jibra'el عليه السلام descended during the Battle of Badr in the form of Zubair رضي الله عنه and wearing a yellow turban with a part of it hanging over his face." *(Tabrani, Haythami)*. Abbad bin Abdullah bin Zubair reports that because Zubair رضي الله عنه was wearing a yellow turban with a part of it hanging over his face, the angels also descended with yellow turbans on their heads." *(Hakim, Tabrani, Ibn Asakir in Kanzul Ummal)*. Abdullah bin Abbas رضي الله عنه says, "The striking feature of (many of) the angels during the Battle of Badr was their white turbans (while others wore yellow turbans), the ends of which they let hang behind their backs. During the Battle of Hunain, they wore green turbans. The angels however never actually fought during any of the battles apart from the Battle of Badr. What they would do was increase the numbers of the Muslims and assist them without actually killing the enemy." *(Abu Nu'aym in Dala'il)*. Ikrama reports that Rasulullah ﷺ's freed slave Abu Rafi رضي الله عنه said, "I was the slave of Abbas bin Abdul Muttalib when Islam entered our household. Abbas رضي الله عنه, (his wife) Ummu Fadhl رضي الله عنها and I all accepted Islam but because Abbas رضي الله عنه was afraid to oppose his tribe and because he was a wealthy man with a lot of his wealth invested with many people of his tribe, he concealed his Islam from them. Abu Lahab did not participate in the Battle of Badr and sent As bin Hisham bin Mughiera in his place. Many other people did the same and there was none who stayed behind without sending a representative. We felt tremendous strength and honor when we heard what had happened to the Quraish at Badr. May Allah humiliate and disgrace them!" Abu Rafi رضي الله عنه narrates further. He says, "I was a weak man who used to carve arrows in the Zamzam tent. By Allah! I was sitting and carving my arrows there one day and Ummu Fadhl رضي الله عنها was also there with me. We were rejoicing about the news that reached us when Abu Lahab arrived, dragging his feet along with great difficulty. He sat on the tent's rope with his back towards mine. It was while he was sitting there that someone announced, 'Here comes Abu Sufian bin Harith bin Abdul Muttalib who has just arrived (from the Battle of Badr).' This Abu Sufian's name was actually Mughiera. 'Come here!' Abu Lahab called out to him, 'I swear by my life that you should be having some news.' Mughiera sat by him as the people stood by. 'Dear nephew!' Abu Lahab said to him, 'Tell me what happened to the people (how were they defeated?).' Mughiera said, 'By Allah! As soon as we engaged them in combat, they started killing us as they pleased and took us prisoner as they pleased! By Allah! The blame cannot be placed on our men because the men we fought were extremely fair in complexion and they rode spotted horses that glided between the

ground and the sky. By Allah! They left nothing and nothing could stand before them." Abu Rafi رضي الله عنه says, "I then grabbed hold of the tent's rope and exclaimed, 'By Allah! Those were angels!' Abu Lahab then raised his hand and struck me hard on my face. As I stood up to him, he attacked me and struck me to the ground. He then sat on my chest and started hitting me because I was a weak man. Ummu Fadhl then stood up, took up one of the tent's supports and struck Abu Lahab so hard over the head that he sustained a horrible wound. She then said, 'Are you taking advantage of him because his master is not around?' Abu Lahab then went away feeling most humiliated. By Allah! Abu Lahab did not live even seven days more when Allah afflicted him with a form of smallpox that led to his death." In another narration, Ambiya عليه السلام Rafi رضي الله عنه adds, "Abu Lahab's sons left his body for 3 days after his death until it began to exude a foul odor. This was because the Quraish feared this form of smallpox as much as they feared a plague. Eventually, someone from the Quraish rebuked them saying, 'Shame on you two! Have you no shame?! Your father's body is rotting in the house and you are not burying him?' They excused themselves saying, 'We fear that those sores are contagious.' 'Come along,' the man offered, 'I shall assist you with it.' By Allah! They bathed the body by throwing water over it from a distance without going anywhere near it. They then carried it to the upper reaches of Makkah where they placed the body against a wall and threw stones over it." *(Ibn Is'haq in Al Bidayah wan Nihayah, Ibn Sa'd, Hakim, Tabrani, Bazzar, Haythami, Hakim, Abu Nu'aym in Dala'il)*

Angels Assist the Sahabah During the Battle of Hunain

Auf bin Abdur Rahman the freed slave of Ummu Burthun reports that a Sahabi who participated in the Battle of Hunain on the side of the Kuffar said, "When clashed with Rasulullah ﷺ (at one stage on the battlefield), the Muslims were unable to stand before us for even as long as it takes to milk a goat. Swinging our swords about, we finally came in front of Rasulullah ﷺ and were about to attack him when some strikingly handsome men appeared suddenly and said, 'May your faces be disfigured! Go back!' It was the effect of those words that we were ultimately defeated." *(Bayhaqi in Al Bidayah wan Nihayah)*. Auf A'rabi reports from Abdur Rahman the freed slave of Abu Burthun that a Sahabi who participated in the Battle of Hunain said, "When we clashed with the Sahabah of Rasulullah ﷺ (at one stage) on the battlefield of Hunain, they were unable to stand before us for even as long as it takes to milk a goat. When we had dispersed them, we started chasing after them until we reached a person riding a white mule. The person turned out to be Rasulullah ﷺ. We then saw some strikingly handsome men with Rasulullah ﷺ who said, 'May your faces be disfigured! Go back!' It was the effect of those words that we were defeated and the Muslims were able to get on top of us." *(Ibn Jareer in Tafsir Ibn Kathir)*. Jubair bin Mut'im رضي الله عنه says, "We were with Rasulullah ﷺ during the Battle of Hunain as the battle was raging. I happened to look up and saw something like a black blanket descending from the sky. It landed between the enemy and us and I noticed that it was a mass of ants that scattered about, filling the entire valley. This spelt the defeat of the enemy and we not once doubted the fact that these were angels." *(Ibn Is'haq in Al Bidayah wan Nihayah)*

Angels Assist the Sahabah During the Battle of Uhud and the Battle of Khandaq

Abdullah bin Fadhl reports that Rasulullah ﷺ gave the flag to Mus'ab bin Umair رضي الله عنه during the Battle of Uhud. When Mus'ab was martyred, an angel in the guise of Mus'ab رضي الله عنه took hold of the flag. Towards the end of the day, Rasulullah ﷺ addressed him saying, "Go ahead, O Mus'ab." The angel then turned to Rasulullah ﷺ and said, "I am not Mus'ab." Rasulullah ﷺ then realized that he was an angel sent to assist him. *(Ibn Sa'd)*. Anas ؓ says, "It is as if I am actually looking at the dust rising from the Banu Ghanam street as Jibra'el rode by at the time when Rasulullah ﷺ was marching against the Banu Quraiza tribe." *(Abu Nu'aym in Dala'il, Ibn Sa'd)*. Another narration recounts this incident of the battle against the Banu Quraiza tribe in detail. It states that after Rasulullah ﷺ had downed his weapons (after finishing the Battle of Khandaq), Jibra'el came to him. Jibra'el عليه السلام was resting against his horse's chest when Rasulullah ﷺ came out to him. With dust still covering his eyebrows, Jibra'el عليه السلام said, 'We have not yet downed our weapons after the battle. March on now against the Banu Qurayza tribe." "My companions have been through a lot of exertion. Why not give them a few days respite?" Jibra'el عليه السلام said, "You must march against them. I shall lead this horse of mine into their fortress and raze it to the ground" Jibra'el عليه السلام and the angels with him then turned and left and their dust clouds could be seen rising in the streets of the Ansar Banu Ghanam tribe. *(Ibn Sa'd)*

Angels Fight the Disbelievers and take them Prisoner During the Battle of Badr

Suhail bin Amr ؓ says, "Without doubt, it was during the Battle of Badr that I saw brilliant men riding spotted horses that glided between the ground and the sky. They were very conspicuous and were killing the Mushrikin and also taking them prisoner." *(Ibn Asakir, Waqidi in Kanzul Ummal)*. Bara ؓ and several other Sahabah report that when an Ansari Sahabi brought Abbas ؓ as a prisoner (during the Battle of Badr), Abbas ؓ said, "O Rasulullah ﷺ! It was not this man who took me prisoner." He then went on to describe the person who captured him, stating also that the person was someone whose head was bald in the front. Addressing the Ansari ؓ, Rasulullah ﷺ said, "Allah sent a noble angel to assist you." *(Ahmad, Haythami)*. A similar narration from Ali ؓ states that when an Ansari Sahabi brought Abbas ؓ as a prisoner, Abbas bin Abdul Muttalib ؓ said, "O Rasulullah ﷺ! By Allah! It was not this man who took me prisoner. The person who captured me was a man who was bald up to his temples. He was one of the most handsome men I have ever seen and was riding a spotted horse. I do not think that he is one of your men." "O Rasulullah ﷺ!" the Ansari ؓ said, "It was I who took him prisoner." Rasulullah ﷺ bade the Ansari not to insist saying, "Allah had sent a noble angel to assist you." *(Ibn Abi Shaybah, Ahmad, Ibn Jareer, Bayhaqi in Kanzul Ummal, Haythami, Ahmad, Bazzar)*. Abdullah bin Abbas ؓ reports that the person who took Abbas ؓ prisoner was Abu Yasr Ka'b bin Amr, who belonged to the Banu Salima tribe. While he was a short man, Abbas ؓ was a towering man. "O Abu Yasar," Rasulullah ﷺ asked him, "How did you manage to take Abbas prisoner?" He replied, "O Rasulullah ﷺ! A man whom I have never seen before or afterwards assisted me in capturing him." When he then proceeded to describe the person, Rasulullah ﷺ remarked, "It was indeed one of the noble angels who came to your assistance." *(Ibn Sa'd, Ahmad, Haythami, Abu Nu'aym in Dala'il)*. Abdullah bin Abbas ؓ narrates that as a Muslim was pursuing a Mushrik soldier during the Battle of Badr, he heard a whiplash from above and the voice of a horseman saying to his horse, "Forward, O Haizum!" When the Muslim looked ahead, he saw the Mushrik falling flat on his back. Upon closer inspection, he found that the Mushrik's nose was severed and his face had been deeply gashed as a result of a forceful whiplash. In fact, his

entire face had already turned blue. When this Ansari reported the matter to Rasulullah ﷺ, Rasulullah ﷺ confirmed what he said and marked, "That was an angel from the reinforcements of the 3rd heaven." On that day, 70 Mushrikin were killed and 70 were taken prisoner. *(Muslim in Al Bidayah wan Nihayah)*

A Sahabi belonging to the Banu Ghifar tribe says, "We were still Mushrikin when my cousin and I climbed on a mountain overlooking Badr to view the battle. We wished to see who will be defeated so we could join the victors to loot the others. As we sat on the mountain, we saw a cloud draw near to us and we heard the neighing of horses and a voice saying, 'Forward, O Haizum!' This caused my cousin's heart to rupture and he dies immediately. I was almost killed myself and just managed to control myself." *(Abu Nu'aym in Dala'il)*. Abu Talha ؓ relates, "We were with Rasulullah ﷺ in a battle and when we engaged the enemy in battle, I heard Rasulullah ﷺ say, 'O Master of the Day of Retribution, only You do we worship and only from You do we seek help.' I then saw many men (from the army of Mushrikin) fall down as the angels struck at them from the front and from the back." *(Abu Nu'aym in Dala'il)*. Abu Umamah reports that his father Sahl ؓ once said to him, "Dear son! During the Battle of Badr, I saw that when any of us merely pointed our swords in the direction of any Mushrik's head, the head would be severed from the body even before our swords could reach them." *(Bayhaqi in Al Bidayah wan Nihayah, Hakim in Dhahabi, Tabeani, Haythami)*. Abu Waqid Laithi ؓ says, "I would be following a man from the Mushrikin to strike him a blow with my sword, only to find his head rolling even before my sword could reach him. I then realized that it was someone else, an angel who had killed him." *(Ibn Is'haq in Al Bidayah wan Nihayah)*. The same words have been narrated from Abu Dawud Mazini ؓ who had participated in the Battle of Badr. *(Ahmad, Haythami, Abu Nu'aym in Dala'il)*. Sahl bin Abu Hathma ؓ narrates that when Abu Barzah ؓ brought 3 heads of the Mushrikin to Rasulullah ﷺ during the Battle of Badr. Rasulullah ﷺ remarked, "You have done extremely well!" "O Rasulullah ﷺ!" Abu Barzah ؓ said, "I killed 2 of them myself. As for the 3rd, I saw an extremely handsome man with a fair complexion decapitate him." Rasulullah ﷺ then named the angel whom Abu Barzah ؓ described. *(Tabrani, Haythami)*. Harith bin Simma ؓ says, "Rasulullah ﷺ was in a gorge when he asked me whether I had seen Abdur Rahman bin Auf ؓ. 'Yes, O Rasulullah ﷺ!' I replied, 'I saw him at the foot of a hill as a regiment of the Mushrikin army were about to attack him. For that reason I descended from the hill (to assist him), but I came to you when I saw you.' Rasulullah ﷺ remarked, 'Behold! The angels are fighting by his side.' I went to Abdur Rahman bin Auf ؓ and found him with the fallen bodies of 7 Mushrikin. 'You have done well!' I exclaimed, 'Did you kill all of them by yourself?' He replied, 'As for this person (pointing to Artat bin Abd Shurabil) and this other one, I did kill them myself. Others were killed by a man I have never seen.' I said, 'Allah and His Rasul ﷺ have spoken the truth.'" *(Tabrani, Bazzar, Haythami, Ibn Mandah, Abu Nu'aym in Muntakhab Kanzul Ummal)*

Jibra'el عليه السلام deals with those who Ridiculed Rasulullah ﷺ in Makkah

Abdullah bin Abbas ؓ reports that Rasulullah ﷺ was with Jibra'el عليه السلام when he passed by a group of people who started jeering at Rasulullah ﷺ saying, "There is the man who claims to be a prophet!" Jibra'el then pointed at them, as a result of which they developed marks on their bodies resembling those made by fingernails. These then became sores that emitted such a foul odor that people were unable to even go close to them. It was then that Allah revealed the verse: إِنَّا كَفَيْنَاكَ الْمُسْتَهْزِئِينَ (95) *Truly! We will suffice you against the scoffers. (Al-Hijr:95)* (Tabrani, Bazzar, Haythami)

Concerning to the verse إِنَّا كَفَيْنَاكَ الْمُسْتَهْزِئِينَ (95) *"We are enough for you against those who ridicule" (Al-Hijr:95)*, Abdullah bin Abbas states that the persons referred to are Walid bin Mughiera, Aswad bin Abd Ya'ooth, Aswad bin Muttalib Abu Zam'ah from the Asad bin Abd Uzza tribe, Harith bin Aytal Sahmi and Aas bin Wa'il Sahmi. When Jibra'el came to Rasulullah , Rasulullah complained of these people to him (and Jibra'el asked Rasulullah to point them out to him). When Rasulullah pointed Walid bin Mughiera out to him, Jibra'el pointed towards his radial artery. "Are you not going to do anything?" Rasulullah asked. "I have already taken care of him for you," Jibra'el replied. Thereafter when Rasulullah pointed Harith bin Aital out to him, Jibra'el pointed towards his belly. "Are you not going to do anything?" Rasulullah asked. "I have already taken care of him for you," Jibra'el replied. Rasulullah then pointed Aas bin Wa'il out and Jibra'el pointed towards the sole of his foot. Rasulullah again asked, "Are you not going to do anything?" Yet again Jibra'el replied, "I have already taken care of him for you." It then transpired that when Walid bin Mughiera was passing by a man from the Khuza'ah tribe who was busy sharpening an arrow, the arrow happened to cut Walid's radial artery. As for Aswad bin Muttalib, he became blind. While some say that he just became blind, others say that he was once lying beneath a tree when he suddenly started calling for his sons saying, "Will you not come to my rescue because I have been destroyed. A thorn has been pierced in my eye." They however said, "We can see nothing in your eye." It was not long after this that he became completely blind. As for Aswad bin Abd Ya'uth, he was once on a journey when blisters erupted on his head, causing him to die. Harith bin Aital was afflicted with an over secretion of yellow bile in his stomach which caused his excreta to emerge from his mouth. This led to his death. As for Aas bin Wa'il, he was walking when a thorn of the Shibriqa tree pierced his foot, causing it to swell leading to his death. (Tabrani, Haythami)

An Angel comes to the Aid of Abu Mu'liq

Anas narrates that there was a companion of Rasulullah called Abu Mu'liq . He was a trader who traded both his own goods as well as those of others. He was a person who was always engaged in Ibada and was extremely abstinent. He was out on business one day when an armed robber confronted him. "Put down your goods," the robber demanded, "because I am going to kill you." "You may have all the goods," Abu Mu'liq told him. "It is your life that I want," the robber barked. "Then permit me to perform salah," Abu Mu'liq requested. The robber laughed, "You may perform as much salah as you please." Abu Mu'liq made wudhu and started performing salah. One of the Du'as he made was: يَا وَدُودُ يَا ذَا الْعَرْشِ الْمَجِيْدِ! يَافَعَّالًا لِمَا يُرِيْدُ! أَسْئَلُكَ بِعِزَّتِكَ الَّتِي لَاتُرَامُ وَمُلْكِكَ الَّذِي لَايُضَامُ وَبِنُوْرِكَ الَّذِي مَلَأَ أَرْكَانَ عَرْشِكَ أَنْ تَكْفِيَنِي شَرَّ هَذَا اللِّصِّ يَا مُغِيْثُ أَغِثْنِي *"O The Most Loving! O Master of the Glorious Throne! O the One Who does as He pleases! By Your Honor that none can hope to have, by Your kingdom that none can harm and by Your light that fills the foundations of Your throne do I implore You to protect me from the evil of this robber. O Helper, do help me."*

When he had made this Du'a thrice, a rider suddenly appeared with a spear held high above his head. The rider thrust the spear at the robber and killed him. He then went up to the trader and asked, "Who are you?" Abu Mu'liq replied, "I am the one whom Allah has rescued through you." The rider then explained, "I am an angel of the 4th heaven. When you first made the Du'a, I heard the doors of the heavens rattle. When you made the Du'a the 2nd time, I heard the inhabitants of the heavens cry out. When you again made the Du'a for the 3rd time and it was announced that this was the Du'a of a person in distress, I sought permission from Allah to grant me the ability to kill the robber. You ought to know the good news that whoever makes wudhu, performs 4 Rakahs salah and then makes that Du'a, his Du'a will be answered whether he is in distress or not." (Ibn Abi Dunya in Mujanbad Da'wah quoted in Isabah)

An Angel Comes to the Aid of Zaid bin Haritha

Laith bin Sa'd reports that Zaid bin Haritha once rented a mule from a man from Ta'if. The man made a condition with him that Zaid should first take him where he wished. The man led Zaid to some ruins where he told him to get off. When Zaid got off, he saw many dead bodies lying there. When the man made a move to kill Zaid , Zaid requested to be allowed to perform 2 Rakahs salah. The man sneered, "You may perform your salah because all these people also performed salah but their salah did them no good." Zaid narrated, "As I performed salah, he came up to kill me. When I exclaimed, يا ارحم الراحمين ('*Yaa Arhamar Rahimeen* - O the Most merciful of those who show mercy!)!' he heard a voice calling out, 'Do not kill him' This startled him and he went to look from where the voice was coming, but he found nothing. When he approached me, I called out, '*Yaa Arhamar Rahimeen*'. After this had happened 3 times, I saw a horseman come riding. He held in his hand a steel spear that had a spark of flame rising from its head. He thrust the spear so forcefully at the man that it pierced through his body and emerged from his back. As the man fell dead, the horseman turned to me and said, 'When you called out '*Yaa Arhamar Rahimeen*' the first time, I was in the 7th heaven. When you called out '*Yaa Arhamar Rahimeen*' the 2nd time, I was in the heaven just above this world and by the time you called out '*Yaa Arhamar Rahimeen*' the 3rd time, I came to you.'" (Ibn Abdul Birr in Isti'ab)

See the angels: Aisha and some other Sahabah see Jibra'el

Aisha narrates, "Rasulullah once heard a man's voice, he jumped up very fast and went outside to meet the man. I followed him out to see (who the person was) and found a man leaning against the mane of his Turkish horse. As far as I could see, the man was Dihya Kalbi , wearing his turban with its ends hanging between his shoulders. When Rasulullah came back to my room, I asked, 'I saw you jump up very fast but when I went out to have a look, I saw that it was only Dihya Kalbi.' 'Did you see him?' Rasulullah asked in astonishment. I confirmed that I really did, Rasulullah said, 'That was Jibra'el. He came to give me the instruction to march against the Banu Quraiza.'" (Abu Nu'aym in Dala'il, Ibn Sa'd). Sa'eed bin Musayib adds that Rasulullah passed by several gatherings of Sahabah on his way to the Banu Quraiza, he asked them whether anyone had passed by them. "Yes," they replied, "Dihya Kalbi just passed by us riding a white mule and sitting on a velvet cloth." Rasulullah informed them, "That was not Dihya but Jibra'el. He has been sent to shake the fortress of the Banu Quraiza and to instill fear into their hearts." (Abu Nu'aym in dala'il)

An Ansari sees Jibra'el and speaks to him

Abdullah bin Abbas reports that Rasulullah once went to visit a man from the Ansar. Rasulullah drew near to the house, he overheard the Ansari speaking to someone inside. However, after seeking permission to enter, Rasulullah ﷺ entered the house but saw no one with the Ansari. "Did I not hear you speaking to someone?" Rasulullah ﷺ asked. "O Rasulullah ﷺ!" the Ansari replied, "I came indoors because of the extreme grief I felt when the people spoke about my high fever. Then someone came inside. By Allah! After you, I have seen none who is better company nor any who speaks better than him." Rasulullah ﷺ then said, "That was Jibra'el الله. Verily amongst you there are such people that if they take an oath in Allah's name, Allah will ensure that He fulfils their oath." *(Bazzar, Tabrani, Haythami)*

Abdullah bin Abbas ؓ sees Jibra'el الله

Abdullah bin Abbas ؓ narrates, "I was with my father when we went to Rasulullah ﷺ. There was a man whispering something to Rasulullah ﷺ, because of which Rasulullah ﷺ seemed to ignore my father. We then left and my father said to me, 'Did you notice that your cousin (Rasulullah ﷺ) was ignoring me?' 'Dear father!' I said, 'There was a man whispering something to him.' When we returned to Nabi ﷺ, my father said, 'O Rasulullah ﷺ! When I mentioned something to Abdullah, he informed me that there was a person here whispering something to you. Was there someone with you?' 'Did you see him, O Abdullah?' Rasulullah ﷺ asked. When I confirmed that I did, Rasulullah ﷺ said, 'That was Jibra'el الله. Because I was preoccupied with him, I was unable to tend to you.'" *(Ahmad, Tabrani, Haythami)*. Abbas ؓ once sent his son Abdullah ؓ to Rasulullah ﷺ for something. However, when Abdullah ؓ found someone with Rasulullah ﷺ, he returned without saying anything. When Rasulullah ﷺ later asked Abdullah bin Abbas ؓ if he had seen the man, Abdullah ؓ replied that he did. Rasulullah ﷺ then informed him that the person was Jibra'el الله. Rasulullah ﷺ also said about Abdullah bin Abbas ؓ, 'He will be blessed with tremendous knowledge but will become blind before he dies." (This was exactly what happened afterwards). *(Tabrani, Haythami)*

Irbadh bin Sariya ؓ sees an Angel in the Damascus Masjid

Urwa bin Ruwaim reports that a Sahabi by the name of Irbadh bin Sariya ؓ had become extremely old and was wishing that his soul could be taken. He would make Du'a saying, "O Allah! I have grown very old and my bones have become extremely weak. Do take me away to Yourself." He was in the Damascus Masjid one day when saw an exceptionally handsome young man whom he describes as the most handsome of men. The young man was wearing a green cloak. He addressed Irbadh ؓ saying, "What is the Du'a that you keep making'?" "Dear nephew!" Irbadh ؓ asked, "What Du'a should I be making'?" The man replied, "Say: اللَّهُمَّ حَسِّنِ الْعَمَلَ وَبَلِّغِ الْأَجَلَ
'O Allah! Make my actions good and deliver me (with safety) to my death." Irbadh ؓ asked, "And who are you? May Allah have mercy on you." The young man replied, "I am (the angel) Ruba'el, who removes grief from the hearts of Mu'mmin." *(Tabrani, Haythami)*

The Angels Greet and Shake Hands with the Sahabah

Mutarrif bin Abdullah reports that Imran bin Husain ؓ once said to him, "Listen, O Mutarrif! During the course of my illness the angels used to come to the headside of my bed to greet me, they would greet in my house and even at the entrance of the Hateem. However, this stopped after I had myself branded for medical reasons." When his wound received from the branding had healed, Mutarrif again spoke to him. This time, Imran ؓ said, "Listen, O Mutarrif! That which I had been missing has

come back to me. O Mutarrif! Do keep this a secret until after I die." *(Hakim)*. Mutarrif reports, " Imran bin Husain ؓ once said to me, 'Do you know that I used to be greeted by the angels during my illness, but this stopped when I had myself branded.' I asked, 'Were the greeting coming from your headside or from the side of your feet'?' "No, not from the side of the feet, but from the headside," he confirmed. To this, I remarked, 'I think that these greetings will certainly return before you pass away.' Some time later, Imran ؓ said to me, 'Do you know that the greetings have returned?' It was then only a short while later that he passed away." *(Ibn Sa'd)*. Qatadah reports that the angels used to shake the hands of Imran bin Husain ؓ until he had himself branded, upon which they left him. *(Ibn Sa'd)*

Speaking to the Angels

Salam bin Atiya Asadi reports that when Salman ؓ was at the point of death, a man came to see him. "Dear angel," Salman ؓ said, "Please be gentle with me." The angel replied by saying, "I am gentle with every Mu'min." *(Abu Nu'aym in Hilya)*

Hearing the Angels speak

Anas ؓ reports that Ubay bin Ka'b ؓ made a resolve saying, "I shall go to the Masjid, perform salah and praise Allah in such terms that none has ever done before." When he sat down to praise after performing his salah, he heard a loud voice behind him saying, "O Allah! All praise belongs to You and all kingdom belongs to You. All good is in Your control and all actions will return to You, whether they be done publicly or secretly. All praise belongs to You and You have power over all things. Forgive all the sins I have committed in the past and protect me in the remaining part of my life. Inspire me to do pure deeds that You will be pleased with and accept my repentance." Ubay ؓ reported the incident to Rasulullah ﷺ, he said, "That was Jibra'el الله." *(Ibn Abi Dunya in Kitabudh Dhokr, Targheeb wat Tarheeb)*

Angels Speaking on the Tongue of Omar ؓ

Abu Sa'eed Khudri ؓ reports that Rasulullah ﷺ once said, "Whoever dislikes Omar dislikes me and whoever loves Omar loves me. Verily, Allah boasts about mankind in general on the eve of the Day of Arafah, but boasts specifically about Omar. There has been a Muhaddath in the Ummah of every Nabi that Allah has sent and if there is one amongst my Ummah, he must be Omar." "O Rasulullah ﷺ!" the Sahabah enquired, "Who is a Muhaddath?" Rasulullah ﷺ explained, "He is a person on whose tongue the angels speak." *(Tabrani, Haythami)*

Angels speaking on the Tongue of Abu Mufazzir ؓ during the Siege of Bahursir

Anas bin Hulais reports, "After defeating the Persians in battle, we had laid siege to their fortress of Buharsir when one of their emissaries approached us saying, 'Our emperor asks whether any of you would be interested in an accord that would secure for us the land from our side of the Tigris River up to our mountain and secure for you the land from your side of the Tigris River up to your mountain? Are your bellies still not full? May Allah never fill your bellies!' Abu Mufazzir Aswad bin Qutba ؓ then stepped ahead of the others and addressed the emissary. Allah placed on his tongue words that neither he nor us knew anything about. The emissary then returned and we saw the people from the city leaving for Mada'in. 'O Abu Mufazzir ؓ!' we asked him, 'What did you say to him?' His reply was, 'I swear by the Being Who sent Muhammad ﷺ with the truth that I have no idea what I said. All I know is that a special tranquility descended upon me. I am sure that whatever was placed on my tongue was good.' People then questioned him in turns with the same response until Sa'd bin Abi Waqqas ♣ heard about the incident. Sa'd then came to our camp and asked, 'O Abu Mufazzir! What did you say to them? By Allah! They are all fleeing.' Abu Mufazzir ♣ gave him the same reply he had given us.' Sa'd ♣ announced that an attack be launched and the soldiers stood in battle formation as our catapults flung rocks at the enemy. Neither could anyone be seen in the town, nor did anyone emerge. Only one man came out, seeking amnesty. We granted him amnesty, he said, 'There is no one left here. What is keeping you back?' Some men scaled the walls to unlock the gates and when we entered as victors, we found nothing and no one. All we could do was to capture some people who were still leaving the town. We asked them and the man who asked for amnesty what it was that made them flee, they explained that when the emperor sent his emissary to request for a treaty, your reply was: 'There shall be any treaty between us until we eat the honey of Afrizin with the citron of Kutha.' The king said, 'Oh dear! The angels are speaking on their tongues. The angels replied on the tongues of Arabs. By Allah! Even if it were not so, these are words that Allah placed on the tongue of that man to deter us from fighting them. You should retreat to the city of Quswa." *(Ibn Jareer)*

Angels descend to Listen to the Sahabah reciting the Qur'an

Abu Sa'eed Khudri ♣ reports that one night when Usaid bin Hudhair ♣ was reciting Qur'an in his silo, his horse started to skip about. When he again started to recite, it started skipping about again. He again stopped and when he started reciting for a third time, it again did the same. Usaid ♣ says, "Because I feared that the horse would trample my son Yayha, I got up to see to her, but was surprised to find something like a cloud above my head, with what resembled many lanterns inside it. It then flew up into the sky until I was unable to see it." He went to Rasulullah ﷺ early next morning and reported the matter saying, "O Rasulullah ﷺ! I was reciting the Qur'an late last night in my silo when my horse started to skip about." "Recite, O Ibn Hudhair," Rasulullah ﷺ instructed. When Usaid ♣ started reciting, the horse started to skip about and he stopped. "Recite, O Ibn Hudhair," Rasulullah ﷺ repeated. When Usaid ♣ started reciting, the horse started to skip about again. Again Rasulullah ﷺ said, "Recite, O Ibn Hudhair." Because his son Yahya was again close to the horse and he feared it would trample him, Usaid ♣ stopped reciting and again he saw the cloud with what resembled many lanterns inside it. Again it flew up into the sky until he was unable to see it. To this, Rasulullah ﷺ remarked, 'Those were angels who were listening to you. Had you continued reciting, they would have been visible to everyone and would not have hidden themselves from view." *(Bukhari, Muslim)*. Usaid ♣ said, "When I turned, I saw something like lanterns suspended between the sky and the ground. I said, 'O Rasulullah ﷺ! After seeing that I was unable to recite any further. Rasulullah ﷺ explained, 'Those were angels who had descended to listen to you recite the Qur'an. Had you continued, you would have seen some amazing things." *(Hakim in Targheeb wat Tarheeb, Ibn Hibban, Tabrani, Bayhaqi, Unaid in Kanzul Ummal)*. Rasulullah ﷺ said, "Those were angels who had come close when they heard your voice. Had you continued reciting, they would have been visible to everyone and would not have hidden themselves from view." *(Abu Ubaid, Bukhari, Nasa'ee)*.

Angels bathe the Body of the Martyred Handhala ♣

Mahmood bin Labid reports that Handhala bin Abu Amir ♣ who belonged to the Banu Amr bin Auf tribe met Abu Sufyan bin Harb ♣ in combat during the Battle of Uhud. When Handhala ♣ had gained the upper hand, a person named Shaddad bin Aswad who was referred to as Ibn Sha'ub saw this and struck Handhala ♣ a fatal blow. Referring to Handhala ♣, Rasulullah ﷺ said to the Sahabah, "The angels are bathing your companion. Ask his family what had happened." When the Sahabah asked his wife about it, she replied, "He left as soon as he heard the call (to battle when the Muslims were being defeated) while he still needed to take a bath." When he heard this Rasulullah ﷺ said, "That was why the angels bathed him." *(Abu Nu'aym in Hilya, Ibn Is'haq in Maghazi, Saraj in Isabah, Hakim)*

The Angels bathe the Body of Sa'd bin Mu'adh ♣

Mahmud bin Labid also reports that when Sa'd bin Mu'adh ♣ was struck by an arrow in his radial artery during the Battle of Khandaq, he fell seriously ill. He was placed in the care of a lady called Rufaida. The narration then continues to the point where it states that when Rasulullah ﷺ heard about Sa'd's death, he rushed to the scene with the Sahabah. Rasulullah ﷺ walked so fast that the straps of the Sahabah's shoes started to break and their shawls fell off their shoulders. "O Rasulullah ﷺ!" they entreated, "Your walking is tiring us out." Rasulullah ﷺ explained saying, "I fear that the angels may beat us to him as they beat us to Handhala." Asim bin Omar bin Qatadah narrates that when Rasulullah ﷺ had awoken from his sleep, Jibra'el عليه السلام or another angel came to him and said, "Such a man from your Ummah passed away last night whose death brings joy to the inhabitants of the heavens because they are eager to receive him." Rasulullah ﷺ said, "I know of none other than Sa'd who became very ill yesterday evening. What has happened to Sa'd?" The Sahabah informed Rasulullah ﷺ that Sa'd ♣ had passed away and his tribesmen had transported his body to their locality. After the Fajr salah, Rasulullah ﷺ left with several Sahabah and walked so fast that the straps of the Sahabah's shoes started to break and their shawls fell off their shoulders. "O Rasulullah ﷺ!" someone said, "You are tiring the people out." Rasulullah ﷺ's reply was, "I fear that the angels may beat us to him as they beat us to Handhala." *(Ibn Sa'd)*

The Angels respect the Father of Jabir ♣

Jabir ♣ reports that when his father passed away, he lifted the cloth covering his father's face and started weeping. When the people forbade him from doing this, Rasulullah ﷺ remarked, "Whether you weep over him or not, you can do as you please, but his status is so high in Allah's sight that the angels will continue shading him with their wings until you carry the body away." *(Bukhari, Muslim in Al Bidayah wan Nihayah, Ibn Sa'd)*

The Angels Respect Sa'd bin Muadh ♣

Salama bin Aslam ♣ says, "We were standing at the door of the room waiting to enter after Rasulullah ﷺ. Although there was none in the room besides the covered body of Sa'd ♣, I saw Rasulullah ﷺ walk as if he was climbing over people's shoulders. Seeing this, I stopped in my tracks and Rasulullah ﷺ also motioned me to stop. I then stopped those behind me as well (from entering the room). After sitting awhile, Rasulullah ﷺ came out again. I then asked, 'O Rasulullah ﷺ! I saw you walk as if you were climbing over people's shoulders even though there was no one in the room.' Rasulullah ﷺ replied, 'The room was so full of angels that I was unable to sit down until one of the angels folded in one of his wings. It was only then that I managed to sit down.' Addressing the body of Sa'd ♣ Rasulullah ﷺ then said, 'Congratulations to you, O Abu Amr! Congratulations to you, O

Abu Amr! Congratulations to you, O Abu Amr!" *(Ibn Sa'd)*. Abdullah bin Omar ؓ narrates that Rasulullah ﷺ said, "For (the funeral of) Sa'd bin Mu'adh ؓ, 70,000 angels came down who had never tread upon earth before." When Sa'd ؓ was buried, Rasulullah ﷺ remarked, "SubhanAllah! If anyone could be saved from the squeezing of the grave, it would be Sa'd." *(Bazzar, Haythami, Ibn Sa'd)*. Sa'd bin Ibrahim narrates that when the funeral bier of Sa'd ؓ was being carried, some of the Munafiqin mocked, 'How light is this bier of Sa'd!" Rasulullah ﷺ then said, "To be present for the funeral of Sa'd ؓ, 70,000 angels came down who had never before set foot upon the earth." *(Ibn Sa'd)*. Hasan reports that Sa'd bin Mu'adh ؓ was a large and well-built man. Therefore, when he passed away, the Munafiqin walking behind his funeral bier scoffed, "To this day we have never seen a bier as light as this! Do you know why this is so? It is because of his ruling concerning the Banu Quraiza tribe." When this was reported to Rasulullah ﷺ, Rasulullah ﷺ said, "I swear by the Being Who controls my life that the bier was so light because the angels were carrying his bier." *(Ibn Sa'd)*

The fear for the Muslims that existed in the hearts of their enemies: The Fear of Mu'awiya bin Haida ؓ

Mu'awiya bin Haida Qashairi ؓ reports that he went to see Rasulullah ﷺ and he was brought into Rasulullah ﷺ's presence, Rasulullah ﷺ said, "Listen well! I had prayed to Allah to assist me by either afflicting you people with a drought that would uproot you or by placing fear in your hearts." Mu'awiya ؓ showed all his fingers to Rasulullah ﷺ saying, "As for me, I have sworn this many times on oath that I shall never believe in you nor follow you. The drought kept uprooting me and fear for you was placed so deep in my heart that I am now standing before you (to accept Islam)." *(Tabrani in Awsat, Haythami, Nasa'ee)*

The Fear that the Disbelievers felt During the Battle of Hunain

Sa'ib bin Yasar reports that they asked Yazid bin Amir Suwa'ee ؓ what the fear was like that Allah cast into the hearts of the Mushrikin during the Battle of Hunain. Yazid ؓ who was fighting on the side of the Mushrikin during the Battle of Hunain took some pebbles and threw them up and down on a platter, causing them to make a lot of noise. He said, 'This is the sound that we felt in our bellies." *(Bayhaqi in Al Bidayah wan Nihayah)*

Suraqa bin Malik is prevented from Reaching Rasulullah ﷺ and his Companion During the Hijra

Zaid bin Aslam and others reports that Suraqa bin Malik ؓ who was then not a Muslim thrice cast arrows to decide whether or not to pursue Rasulullah ﷺ. He then rode off in search of them and eventually caught up with them. Rasulullah ﷺ then made Du'a that the legs of Suraqa ؓ's horse should sink into the ground, and they did. Suraqa ؓ pleaded to Rasulullah ﷺ saying, "Make Du'a that Allah releases my horse and I will prevent anyone coming your way." Rasulullah ﷺ made Du'a saying, "O Allah! Release his horse if he is truthful." His horse's legs then came out of the sand. *(Ibn Sa'd)*. A narration from Umair bin Is'haq states that Suraqa ؓ pleaded, "O you 2 men! If you pray to Allah on my behalf, I shall give you an undertaking never to pursue you again. Rasulullah ﷺ and Abu Bakr ؓ made Du'a but as soon as he was freed, he did the same. When his horse again sank into the ground, he again pleaded, "If you pray to Allah on my behalf, I shall give you an undertaking never to pursue you again." This time he even offered them his provisions and horse. Rasulullah ﷺ and Abu Bakr ؓ however said to him, "All we need is for you to relieve us of yourself by abandoning your

pursuit." Suraqa ؓ agreed to do this. *(Ibn Sa'd)*. In a lengthy narration discussing the Hijra, Abu Ma'bad Khuza'ee ؓ states that Suraqa ؓ pleaded, "O Muhammad! Pray to Allah to release my horse and I will not only leave you alone, but will also send back anyone else I find behind me." Rasulullah ﷺ did as he requested and he was released to leave. When he then found some people searching for Rasulullah ﷺ, he said to them, "Go back. I have already secured this entire area and you know well how good I am at tracking." The others then all returned. *(Ibn Sa'd)*. In his account of the epic journey of Hijra, Anas bin Malik ؓ states that at one stage, Abu Bakr ؓ turned around and saw that a horseman had caught up with them, he exclaimed, "O Nabi of Allah ﷺ! A horseman has caught up with us." Rasulullah ﷺ then turned around and said, "O Allah! Drop him." The horse then dropped the rider and stood up again neighing. The rider said, "O Nabi of Allah ﷺ! You may instruct me to do as you please." Rasulullah ﷺ said, "Stay where you are without coming forward and when you return, do not allow anyone to catch up with us." Anas ؓ says, 'Whereas at the beginning of the day Suraqa ؓ was part of the effort against Rasulullah ﷺ, the end of the day found him as a weapon in the defense of Rasulullah ﷺ." The incident of Suraqa has already passed in a narration of Bara, quoted in the chapter discussing the Hijra of Rasulullah.

The Destruction of Arbad bin Qais and Amir bin Tufail

Abdullah bin Abbas ؓ narrates that Arbad bin Qais and Amir bin Tufail once arrived in Madinah and came to Rasulullah ﷺ. Rasulullah ﷺ was seated at the time, so they sat in front of him. Amir bin Tufail said, "O Muhammad! What will you give me if I accept Islam?" Rasulullah ﷺ replied, "You will have that which every Muslim has and will also share the same responsibilities." Amir then asked, "Will you appoint me as your successor if I accept Islam?" Rasulullah ﷺ replied, "That post is neither for you nor for your tribe. You may however assume command of a cavalry detachment." "I am already the commander of the cavalry of Najd." Amir said, "Give me command over the rural areas while you retain command over the urban areas." Rasulullah ﷺ however refused this. When the 2 men were then leaving, Amir said, "Behold! I swear by Allah that I shall fill this city with cavalry and infantry all fighting against you." Rasulullah ﷺ said calmly, "Allah will prevent you." When Arbad and Amir had left, Amir said to him, "O Arbad! While I distract Muhammad with some talk, you must strike him with your sword. If you kill him, the people will want nothing more than blood money because they would detest going to war. We will then easily be able to pay them the blood money." When Arbad agreed, the 2 returned to Rasulullah ﷺ. "O Muhammad ﷺ!" Amir said, "Come with me because I need to discuss something with you." Rasulullah ﷺ went with them and when they sat against a wall, Rasulullah ﷺ sat with them. Rasulullah ﷺ then remained there to talk to Amir. As Arbad placed his hand on his sword to take it out, his hand stuck fast to the handle and he was unable to remove it. He therefore delayed Amir by not striking. In the meantime, Rasulullah ﷺ turned around and when he saw what Arbad was doing, he left the 2 of them. Arbad and Amir then hastily left and when they camped at Harra Waqim, Sa'd bin Mu'adh ؓ and Usaid bin Hudhair ؓ came to them and demanded, "Get out of here, O enemies of Allah! May Allah curse you both." "O Sa'd!" Amir asked, "Who is this man with you?" Sa'd ؓ replied, "He is Usaid bin Hudhair, the scribe." The 2 left and it was when they reached a place called Raqam that Allah sent a bolt of lightning to kill Arbad. Amir continued further and he was at Khuraim when he developed a gland. Night found him at the house of a woman from the Salul tribe and as he stroked the gland on his throat, he said, "A gland like the hump of a camel in the house of a woman from the Salul." Because he disliked dying in her house, he mounted his horse and rode off. He later died as he went back on the same horse. It was with reference to the 2 of them that Allah revealed the verses:

اللَّهُ يَعْلَمُ مَا تَحْمِلُ كُلُّ أُنْثَى وَمَا تَغِيضُ الْأَرْحَامُ وَمَا تَزْدَادُ وَكُلُّ شَيْءٍ عِنْدَهُ بِمِقْدَارٍ (8) عَالِمُ الْغَيْبِ وَالشَّهَادَةِ الْكَبِيرُ الْمُتَعَالِ (9) سَوَاءٌ مِنْكُمْ مَنْ أَسَرَّ الْقَوْلَ وَمَنْ جَهَرَ بِهِ وَمَنْ هُوَ مُسْتَخْفٍ بِاللَّيْلِ وَسَارِبٌ بِالنَّهَارِ (10) لَهُ مُعَقِّبَاتٌ مِنْ بَيْنِ يَدَيْهِ وَمِنْ خَلْفِهِ يَحْفَظُونَهُ مِنْ أَمْرِ اللَّهِ إِنَّ اللَّهَ لَا يُغَيِّرُ مَا بِقَوْمٍ حَتَّى يُغَيِّرُوا مَا بِأَنْفُسِهِمْ وَإِذَا أَرَادَ اللَّهُ بِقَوْمٍ سُوءًا فَلَا مَرَدَّ لَهُ وَمَا لَهُمْ مِنْ دُونِهِ مِنْ وَالٍ (11)

Allah knows what every female bears, and by how much the wombs fall short (of their time or number) or exceed. Everything with Him is in (due) proportion. All-Knower of the unseen and the seen, the Most Great, the Most High. It is the same (to Him) whether any of you conceal his speech or declare it openly, whether he be hid by night or go forth freely by day. For each (person), there are angels in succession, before and behind him. They guard him by the Command of Allah. Verily! Allah will not change the good condition of a people as long as they do not change their state of goodness themselves (by committing sins and by being ungrateful and disobedient to Allah). But when Allah wills a people's punishment, there can be no turning back of it, and they will find besides Him no protector. (Ar-Ra'd:8-11). Abdullah bin Abbas ؓ says that it was the guardian angels acting by Allah's order who protected Rasulullah ﷺ. Referring to the death of Arbad by the bolt of lightning, Abdullah bin Abbas ؓ quoted the verse:

وَيُرْسِلُ الصَّوَاعِقَ فَيُصِيبُ بِهَا مَنْ يَشَاءُ وَهُمْ يُجَادِلُونَ فِي اللَّهِ وَهُوَ شَدِيدُ الْمِحَالِ (13)

...He (Allah) sends the thunderbolts, and therewith He strikes whom He wills, yet they (disbelievers) dispute about Allah. And He is Mighty in strength and Severe in punishment. (Ar-Ra'd:13) (Tabrani in Tafsir Ibn Kathir)

The Enemy is Defeated by the Throwing of Pebbles and Sand by Rasulullah ﷺ during the Battle of Hunain

Harith bin Badal ؓ says, "I participated against Rasulullah ﷺ in the Battle of Hunain. During the beginning when all the Sahabah apart from Abbas bin Abdul Muttalib ؓ and Abu Sufian bin Harith ؓ were trounced, Rasulullah ﷺ took a handful of earth and threw it on our faces, because of which we were defeated. It then appeared to me as if every tree and every stone was running after us." (Tabrani, Abu Nu'aym, Ibn Asakir in Kanzul Ummal, Ibn Mandah). Amr bin Sufian Thaqafi ؓ and others report, "When all the Sahabah were trounced during the Battle of Hunain, it was only Abbas ؓ and Abu Sufian bin Harith ؓ who remained with Rasulullah ﷺ. Rasulullah ﷺ took a handful of pebbles and threw it on our faces, because of which we were defeated. It appeared to me as if every stone and every tree was a horseman running after us. I spurred my horse on and fled until I entered Ta'if." (Ya'qub bin Sufian in Al Bidayah wan Nihayah)

The Enemy is Defeated by the Throwing of Pebbles by Rasulullah ﷺ during the Battle of Badr

Hakim bin Hizam ؓ says, "While fighting on the side of the Mushrikin during the Battle of Badr, we heard a sound booming from the heavens to the earth that sounded like stones falling on a platter. It was then that Rasulullah ﷺ threw some pebbles at us, because of which we were defeated." (Tabrani in Kabeer and Awsat, Haythami). Hakim bin Hizam ؓ also says, "During the Battle of Badr, Rasulullah ﷺ was instructed to take a handful of

pebbles, face us and throw it saying, 'May your faces be disfigured!' We were then defeated and Allah revealed the verse:

وَمَا رَمَيْتَ إِذْ رَمَيْتَ وَلَكِنَّ اللَّهَ رَمَى ...

And you (O Rasulullah ﷺ) threw not when you did throw but Allah threw...(Al-Anfal:17) (Tabrani in Kabeer and Awsat, Haythami)

Abdullah bin Abbas ؓ reports that Rasulullah ﷺ asked Ali ؓ to hand him a handful of pebbles. When Ali ؓ handed them over, Rasulullah ﷺ threw them into the faces of the enemy, causing the eyes of each one of them to be filled with pebbles. It was then that Allah revealed the verse:

وَمَا رَمَيْتَ إِذْ رَمَيْتَ وَلَكِنَّ اللَّهَ رَمَى

...And you (O Rasulullah ﷺ) threw not when you did throw but Allah threw...(Al-Anfal:17) (Tabrani in Kabeer and Awsat, Haythami).

Yazid bin Amir Suwa'ee ؓ reports that Rasulullah ﷺ took a handful of soil, faced the enemy and then threw it saying, "Get back! May your faces be disfigured." Later, when any of the Mushrikin met their companions, they would always complain of dust in their eyes." (Bayhaqi in Al Bidayah wan Nihayah)

The Enemy Appearing few in Number to the Muslims

Abdullah bin Mas'ood ؓ says, "The enemy appeared so few in our eyes during the Battle of Badr that my companion standing beside me said, 'Do you think that they number 70?' I said, 'I would estimate that they are only 100.' It was only when we captured one of them and questioned him that we discovered that they were 1,000 strong." (Tabrani in Majma'uz Zawa'id, Ibn Abi Hatim, Ibn Jareer in Tafsir Ibn Kathir)

Assistance by the Winds

Sa'eed bin Jubair reports that on the occasion of the Battle of Khandaq, those who marched to Madinah were Abu Sufian bin Harb and the Quraish and Kinana whom he led, Uyayna bin Hisn and the Banu Ghitfan tribe whom he led, Tulaiha and the Banu Asad tribe whom he led and Abu A'war and the Sulaim tribe whom he led. Also assisting the Mushrikin was the Jewish Banu Quraiza tribe, who actually contravened the pact they had made with the Muslims. It was with reference to this that Allah revealed the verse: وَأَنْزَلَ الَّذِينَ ظَاهَرُوهُمْ مِنْ أَهْلِ الْكِتَابِ مِنْ صَيَاصِيهِمْ

And those of the people of the Scripture (the Banu Quraizah tribe) who backed them (the disbelievers) Allah brought them down from their forts (and surrender to the Muslims)... (Al-Ahzab:26)

Jibra'el عليه السلام then appeared with the winds, which he unleashed against the Mushrikin. When Rasulullah ﷺ saw Jibra'el عليه السلام arrive, he thrice said to the Sahabah, "Behold! It is time to rejoice!" The wind tore open their tents, overturned their large pots, buried their carriages, severed the tent ropes and caused them to run about in such confusion that not one even turned to look at another. It was with reference to this that Allah revealed the verse: إِذْ جَاءَتْكُمْ جُنُودٌ فَأَرْسَلْنَا عَلَيْهِمْ رِيحًا وَجُنُودًا لَمْ تَرَوْهَا

...when there came against you hosts, and We sent against them a wind and forces that you saw not (i.e. troops of angels during the battle of Al-Ahzab (the Confederates)) (Al-Ahzab:9)

After this, Rasulullah ﷺ returned to Madinah. (Ibn Sa'd). Humaid bin Hilal narrates, "Rasulullah ﷺ had an unratified pact with the Banu Quraiza tribe. They broke the pact by assisting the Mushrikin when they marched to Madinah with an assortment of armies from various tribes. Allah however dispatched an army of angels and the wind, causing the Mushrikin to flee, but leaving the Banu Quraiza holed up in their fortress..." The narration continues to recount the battle against the Banu Quraiza. (Ibn

Sa'd). Abdullah bin Abbas ؓ narrates that the easterly wind approached the northerly wind during the night of the Battle of Ahzab and said, "Go and assist Rasulullah ﷺ." The northerly wind said, "An honorable lady doesn't travel by night." It was with the easterly wind that Rasulullah ﷺ was assisted. (Bazzar, Haythami, Ibn Abi Hatim, Ibn Jareer in Tafsir Ibn Kathir)

Enemies are Sunken into the Ground and Destroyed

Buraida ؓ reports that a man from the Mushrikin said during the Battle of Uhud, "O Allah! If Muhammad is upon the truth, let me sink into the ground." He sank into the ground. (Bazzar, Haythami). Nafi bin Asim says that the man who injured Rasulullah ﷺ's face was Abdullah bin Qami'a who belonged to the Hudhail tribe. Allah made a ram attack him and gore him with its horns until killed. (Abu Nu'aym in Dala'il)

Some Young Men from the Quraish lose their Eyesight by the Curse of Rasulullah ﷺ on the Day of Hudaybiya

Abdullah bin Mughaffal Muzani ؓ narrates, "We were with Rasulullah ﷺ at Hudaybiya ......" He then proceeds to recount the incident of the Treaty of Hudaybiya. Amongst other things, he mentions, 'While we were still there, 30 armed young men came to fight us. By the curse of Rasulullah ﷺ, Allah made them all blind in an instant and we stood up and disarmed them. When Rasulullah ﷺ asked them whether they had come after entering into some pact or whether anyone had granted them amnesty, the replied in the negative. Rasulullah ﷺ then set them free. It was then that Allah revealed the verse:

وَهُوَ الَّذِي كَفَّ أَيْدِيَهُمْ عَنْكُمْ وَأَيْدِيَكُمْ عَنْهُمْ بِبَطْنِ مَكَّةَ مِنْ بَعْدِ أَنْ أَظْفَرَكُمْ عَلَيْهِمْ وَكَانَ اللَّهُ بِمَا تَعْمَلُونَ بَصِيرًا (24)

It is He (Allah) who has withheld their hands from you and your hands from them in the midst of Makkah, after He had made you victors over them. And Allah is Ever the All-Seer of what you do. (Al-Fath:24) (Ahmad, Haythami, Nasa'ee in Tafsir Ibn Kathir)

A Man Loses his Sight by the Curse of Ali ؓ

Zadhan narrates that when Ali ؓ once narrated a Hadith, someone accused him of lying. "May I curse you if it is you who are lying?" Ali ؓ asked the man. "Go ahead and curse," the man challenged. The man had not even left the gathering when his eyesight was lost. (Tabrani, Haythami). Ammar ؓ narrates that when Ali ؓ narrated a Hadith, someone accused him of lying. The man had hardly stood up from the gathering and he was already blind because of the curse of Ali ؓ..(Abu Nu'aym in Dala'il). Zadhan narrates that when someone narrated a Hadith to Ali ؓ, Ali ؓ said, "I think that you are lying to me." When the man insisted that he was not, Ali ؓ asked, "May I curse you if you are lying?" "Go ahead and curse," the man challenged. Ali ؓ cursed the man and he had scarcely left the gathering when he became blind. (Ibn Abi Dunya in Al Bidayah wan Nihayah)

A Woman Becomes Blind by the Curse of Sa'eed bin Zaid ؓ

Abdullah bin Omar ؓ narrates that Marwan once sent some people to Sa'eed bin Zaid ؓ to discuss a claim that a woman named Arwa bint Uwais had made against him. Sa'eed ؓ exclaimed, "These people think that I have wronged her when I have heard Rasulullah ﷺ say, 'The one who usurps even a hand's span of land, will have a hand's span of all 7 earths placed as a yoke around his neck on the Day of Judgment.'" Sa'eed ؓ then prayed, "O Allah! If she is lying, let her not die until she turns blind and make her well her grave." Abdullah bin Omar ؓ says, "By Allah! She turned blind before her death and one day as she

very cautiously left her house, she fell into her well and it became her grave." (Abu Nu'aym in Hilya). Abu Bakr bin Muhammad bin Amr bin Hazam narrates that a woman named Arwa once sought judgment from Marwan bin Hakam against Sa'eed bin Zaid ؓ. Sa'eed ؓ prayed to Allah saying, "O Allah! She claims that I have wronged her. If she is lying, make her blind, throw her in her well and create a clear proof in my favor that will make it obvious to the Muslims that I did her no wrong." All this was still taking place when the valley of Aqiq flooded more heavily than ever before. The flood uncovered the boundary that Arwa and Sa'eed ؓ were disputing, making it clear that Sa'eed ؓ was justified. Merely a month later, Arwa became blind and she was walking about on the very same property when she stumbled into her well. Abu Bakr bin Muhammad says, "When we were little boys, we would hear a person say to another, 'May Allah make you blind as he made Arwa blind.' We used to think that the Arwa they were referring to was the mountain goat in the wild (because this is the literal translation of Arwa). However, we discovered that this expression referred to the curse of Sa'eed ؓ that afflicted Arwa. The people used the expression with reference to this curse of Sa'eed ؓ that Allah accepted. (Abu Nu'aym in Hilya)

A Man loses his Sight Because he Cursed Husain bin Ali ؓ

Abu Utaridi said, "Never revile Ali ؓ or any member of Rasulullah ﷺ's family because a neighbor of ours from Balhujaim once scoffed, 'Can you not see that sinner Husain bin Ali? May Allah destroy him!' His eyes were then struck with 2 spots and Allah removed his eyesight." (Tabrani, Haythami)

The Eyesight of a group of Quraish is Restored by the Du'a of Rasulullah ﷺ

Abdullah bin Abbas ؓ narrates that Rasulullah ﷺ used to recite the Qur'an in the Masjidul Haram. One day, he was reciting Qur'an loudly, which irritated some members of the Quraish so much that they got up to apprehend him. However, their hands suddenly got stuck on their necks and they became blind. They then approached Rasulullah ﷺ and pleaded to him in the name of Allah and in the name of the family ties that existed between them and him. Rasulullah ﷺ was related to every branch of the Quraish, so he prayed to Allah and their eyesight was restored to them. It was then that Allah revealed the verses:

يس (1) وَالْقُرْآنِ الْحَكِيمِ (2)......وَسَوَاءٌ عَلَيْهِمْ أَأَنْذَرْتَهُمْ أَمْ لَمْ تُنْذِرْهُمْ لَا يُؤْمِنُونَ (10)

Ya-Seen. (These letters are one of the miracles of the Quran, and none but Allah (alone) knows their meanings). By the Qur'an, full of wisdom (i.e. full of laws, evidences, and proofs)..... It is the same to them whether you warn them or you warn them not, they will not believe. (Ya-Seen:1-10)

Abdullah bin Abbas ؓ states that (despite witnessing miracle) none of the Mushrikin accepted Iman. (Abu Nu'aym in Dala'il)

Qatadah ؓ's Eye is Restored by the Du'a of Rasulullah ﷺ

Qatadah bin Nu'man ؓ says, "Rasulullah ﷺ received a bow as a gift, which he gave to me during the Battle of Uhud. I then continued firing arrows standing in front of Rasulullah ﷺ until one end of the bow broke. I however continued standing where I was in front of Rasulullah ﷺ's face, deflecting the arrows from him with my face. Whenever an arrow came towards Rasulullah ﷺ's face, I turned my own face and head to protect Rasulullah ﷺ's face. All this I was doing when I was unable to fire any arrows. The last of the arrows dislodged my eyeball, causing it to fall on to my cheek. When the enemy had dispersed, I held my eyeball in my hand and rushed with it to Rasulullah ﷺ. Seeing it, Rasulullah ﷺ's eyes filled with tears and he said, "O Allah! Qatadah protected Your Nabi with his face, so make this eye the better of the 2 and the one with sharper vision." (Rasulullah ﷺ then inserted the eye back in its socket and) That eye did turn out to be the better of the two and the one with sharper vision. *(Tabrani, Haythami, Abu Nu'aym in Dala'il, Ibn Sa'd).* Mahmood bin Labid reports from Qatadah ﷺ that when his eye was struck by an arrow during the Battle of Uhud, it fell out on to his cheek. Rasulullah ﷺ then replaced it in its socket and it became the better of his 2 eyes. *(Dar Qunti, Ibn Shajin in Isabah).* The eye turned out to be the better of the two and the one with sharper vision. *(Abu Nu'aym in Dala'il).* Asim bin Omar bin Qatadah reports that when Qatadah bin Nu'man ﷺ's eye was struck during the Battle of Uhud and it fell on to his cheek, the other Sahabah wanted to cut it off. He however refused to allow them saying, "Not until we consult with Rasulullah ﷺ." The Sahabah consulted Rasulullah ﷺ, Rasulullah ﷺ instructed them to take no action, but to rather bring Qatadah ﷺ to him. Rasulullah ﷺ then placed his palm on to the eyeball after inserting it into the eye-socket and then pressed it in. After this, Qatadah ﷺ could not even tell which eye had been wounded. *(Baghawi, Abu Ya'la in Isabah, Haythami)*

Optical Ailments are Cured by the Du'a of Rasulullah ﷺ

Ubaida narrates that when Abu Dhar ﷺ's eye was injured during the Battle of Uhud, Rasulullah ﷺ merely applied his saliva to it and it became the better of Abu Dhar ﷺ's two eyes. *(Abu Ya'la, Haythami).* Rifa'ah bin Rafi ﷺ reports, "During the Battle of Badr, an arrow pierced my eye. Rasulullah ﷺ applied some of his saliva to it and made Du'a, because of which I felt no pain or discomfort from it at all." *(Abu Nu'aym in Dala'il).* Habib bin Fuwaik narrates, "My father was taken to Rasulullah ﷺ because his eyes had become completely white and he was unable to see anything. When Rasulullah ﷺ asked him the reason for his blindness, he explained that he was taming a camel when his leg fell on a snake's egg, causing him to go blind. When Rasulullah ﷺ applied some saliva to the eye, my father was able to see instantly. In fact, I saw him thread a needle at the age of 80 even though his eyes were still white." *(Ibn Abi Shaybah in Isabah, Tabrani, Haythami, Abu Nu'aym in Dala'il)*

Zinnera ﷺ's Eyesight is Restored

Sa'eed bin Ibrahim narrates that Zinnera ﷺ was a Roman lady who accepted Islam. When she became blind, the Mushrikin told her that it was (their idols) Laat and Uzza who made her blind. When she strongly told them that she refused to believe in Laat and Uzza, Allah restored her vision. *(Fakihi, Ibn Mandah).* Anas ﷺ reports from Ummu Hani bint Abu Talib ﷺ that after Abu Bakr ﷺ bought Zinnera ﷺ's freedom, she became blind. To this, members of the Quraish remarked, "It is none other than Laat and Uzza who have taken away her eyesight." She however said, 'They lie! I swear by the house of Allah that Laat and Uzza are no good and can do no benefit." Allah then restored her eyesight. *(Muhammad bin Uthman bin Abi Shaybah in Isabah)*

The Palace of Heraclius of Rome was Shaken by the Recitation of the Kalima and Takbir

Hisham bin Aas Umawi ﷺ reports, "Another person and I were sent by the Khalifa Abu Bakr ﷺ to invite Heraclius the Emperor of Rome to Islam. We left and when we reached the Ghawta district of Damascus, we went to see Jabala bin Ayham Ghassani who ruled the area. He was sitting on his throne and sent his messenger to speak to us. We however said, 'By Allah! We will never speak to a messenger because we were sent to speak directly to the ruler. If he permits, we will speak to him, but never to a messenger. When the messenger reported this to him, he allowed us in and asked us to speak. I then addressed him and invited him to accept Islam. When I asked him what the black garments he was wearing, he replied, 'When wearing them, I vowed never to remove them until I dispelled you people from Sham.' I responded by saying, 'In this very gathering of yours do I swear by Allah that we shall definitely be taking control of Sham from you. In fact, we shall also be taking over all the lands of your Emperor, InshaAllah. Our Nabi Muhammad ﷺ informed us of this.' To this, he said, 'You are not the ones who will be doing this because they will be people who fast during the day and stand in prayer during the nights. How do you people fast?' When we informed him about it, his face darkened and he bade us to leave. He then sent a messenger with us to the Emperor Heraclius. We then left and when we drew near to the city, the person accompanying us said, 'These animals of yours cannot enter the Emperor's city. If you wish, we can give you Turkish horses or mules to ride.' 'By Allah!' we said, 'We shall enter with nothing other than these animals.' The people then sent a message to the Emperor, informing him of our refusal. He communicated back to them the Instruction to allow us in on our animals. With our swords hanging around our necks, we then entered the city and reached the Emperor's palace. As he watched us from above, we seated our animals beneath and called out لا اله الا الله الله اكبر ('La Ilaha IllAllah, Allahu Akbar')'. Allah knows that his palace then shook so much that it appeared to be a branch fluttering in the wind. He sent a message informing us that we were not to shout out any declarations of our faith and that we could now enter the palace. Upon entering, we found him sitting on his rug with the leading military commanders of Rome. Everything in gathering was red, everything around him was red and even his clothing was red. When we went up to him, he laughed and said, 'What would it cost you if you were to greet me with the words you greet each other with?' With him was his interpreter who spoke Arabic fluently and who spoke a lot. We replied by saying, 'It is neither permissible for us to greet you with the greeting we use amongst ourselves, nor it is permissible for us to greet you with the greeting you use amongst yourselves.' 'And what is the greeting you use amongst yourselves?' he enquired. When we informed him that it was السلام عليك (As Salamu Alayk), he asked, 'How do you greet your ruler?' 'With the same words,' we replied. 'And how does he reply?' he wanted to know. 'With these very words,' was our response. Heraclius then asked, 'What are your greatest words?' We replied by saying that they are, لا اله الا الله الله اكبر ('Laa Ilaha IllAllah, Allahu Akbar')'. Allah knows well that as soon as we said these words, the palace shook so much that the Emperor actually looked up. He then asked, 'These words that you have said now when the palace shook, do your buildings shake with them as well?' 'No,' we replied, 'we have never seen them produce this effect except here with you.' He then remarked, 'Even at the cost of half my kingdom, I wish that each time you say these words, they would cause everything around you to collapse on top of you,' 'Why is that?' we enquired. 'Because,' he explained, 'it would be easier and rather than denoting a sign of prophethood, it would then denote only a manmade conspiracy.' He then asked us many questions, to which we furnished details. He also asked about how we performed salah and fasted. After explaining these to him, he bade us to leave and had us shown to exquisite quarters that contained an abundance of amenities. We stayed there for 3 days and then went to see him when he sent for us one night. Upon arrival, he requested us to repeat what we had said previously and when we did, he sent for something that appeared to be a large gold-plated chest. It had many little compartments, each with its own door. He removed a piece of black silk. He opened it to reveal a red picture of a man with large eyes and a sizeable pelvic area. I have never seen anyone with a neck as long as his. He had no beard, wore two locks of hair and was one of the best-looking people Allah had created. 'Do you know who this is?' Heraclius asked us. When we admitted that we did not, he said, 'This is Adam ﷺ.' We then also realized that he had more hair than the average person. Heraclius then opened another compartment and removed a black piece of silk that contained a white picture. The person depicted had curly hair, reddish eyes, a large forehead and a striking beard. 'Do you know who this is?' he asked. When we again pleaded ignorance, he informed us that the man was Nuh ﷺ. Opening yet another compartment, he removed another black piece of silk with a picture of a man who was extremely fair in complexion. The man had beautiful eyes, a conspicuous forehead, long cheeks and a white beard. The man appeared to be smiling. 'Do you know who this is?' Heraclius asked us. When we admitted that we did not, he said, 'This is Ibrahim ﷺ.' Thereafter, he opened another compartment from which he took out a white picture. By Allah! It was a picture of Rasulullah ﷺ. 'Do you know who this is'?' he asked us. 'Of course!' we replied, 'This is Rasulullah ﷺ.' We then started to weep and Allah knows that Heraclius stood up for a while and then sat down. 'Do you swear by Allah that it is he'?' he asked. We said, 'It is he without doubt. It is as if you are seeing him in person.' Doing nothing for awhile as he looked at us, Heraclius then said, 'This was the last of the compartments. I opened it sooner than I should just to see what your reaction would be.' Heraclius then opened another compartment and removed another piece of black silk. The person depicted was very tanned and dark in complexion. His hair was very curly, his eyes deep and penetrating. He was frowning, his teeth were clenched and his lips drawn tightly together, appearing to be very angry. 'Do you know who this is?' he asked. When we conceded that we did not, he said, 'this is Musa ﷺ.' Next to this picture was one of a person resembling Musa ﷺ, except that this person's hair was oiled, his forehead was wide and his eyes were slightly squint. 'Do you know who this is?' Heraclius asked. 'No,' we replied. 'This,' he said, 'is Harun bin Imran ﷺ.' From the next compartment, Heraclius removed a piece of white silk that bore the picture of a tanned man with straight hair, who was of average height. He also appeared to be angry. 'Do you know who this is?' Heraclius asked. Again, we could not tell him. He informed us that the person depicted was Lut ﷺ. When he opened another of the compartments and removed another piece of white silk, we saw a picture of a very fair man with a reddish complexion. He had a high-bridged nose, thin cheeks and a handsome face. 'Do you know who this is'?' Heraclius asked. 'No,' we replied. This,' he said, 'is Is'haq ﷺ.'

Heraclius then opened another compartment and removed another white piece of silk that contained a picture of a person who looked very much like Is'haq, except that he had a mole on his lip. 'Do you know who this is?' Heraclius asked. When we admitted that we did not, he said, 'This is Ya'qub ﷺ.' He then opened another compartment and removed a black piece of silk bearing the picture of a fair-skinned person. The man depicted had a high-bridged nose, a handsome face and a perfect build. His face shone with radiance, humility could be seen on his face, which had a tinge of reddishness. 'Do you know who this is?'

Heraclius asked. When we again conceded that we did not know, he said, This is Isma'el, the grandfather of your Nabi ﷺ' Opening yet another compartment, he removed white piece of silk with a picture of a man who resembled Adam and whose face appeared to be the sun itself. 'Do you know who this is?' he asked. 'No,' we replied. He then informed us that the man was Yusuf ﷺ. Heraclius then opened another compartment and removed a piece of white silk that contained a picture of a man with a reddish complexion. The man had thin calves, small eyes, a large belly and was of average height. He also wore a sword around his neck. When Heraclius again asked us if we knew who the man was and we replied that we did not, he told us that this was Dawood ﷺ. From the next door that Heraclius opened, he took out a piece of white silk that bore the picture of a man with a large pelvic area and long legs. This man was riding a horse. 'Do you know who this is?' he asked. When we told him that we did not, he said, 'This is Sulaiman bin Dawood ﷺ.' Heraclius then opened another compartment and removed a black piece of silk that contained a white picture. The person depicted was youthful, sported a pitch black beard, had a lot of hair, striking eyes and a handsome face. 'Do you know who this is?' Heraclius asked. 'No,' we replied. 'This,' he said, 'is Isa bin Maryam ﷺ.' We then said to him, 'Where did you get these pictures from? We know that they depict exactly what these Ambiya looked like because we have seen the picture of our Nabi ﷺ exactly as he was. Heraclius explained, 'These pictures were given to Adam when he asked his Rabb to show him the Ambiya ﷺ from his progeny. They lay in the treasures of Adam at the place where the sun sets. Dhul Qarnain removed it from there and gave it to Daniyal ﷺ. Listen well! I swear by Allah that I prefer to forsake my kingdom to become a slave for the worst master amongst you and to die like that rather than accept Islam and be disgraced before my subjects.' He then gave us the most superb gifts and bid us farewell. We returned to Abu Bakr ﷺ and reported to him everything we had seen and everything that Heraclius had told us. Abu Bakr ﷺ started to weep as he said, 'Poor man! Had Allah willed good for him, he would have accepted Islam. Rasulullah ﷺ informed us that (the Christians like Heraclius as well as the Jews have the description of Muhammad ﷺ with them." *(Hakim in Tafsir Ibn Kathir, Kanzul Ummal, Bayhaqi, Ibn Kathirm Abu Nu'aym in Dala'il).* Jubair bin Mut'im ﷺ says, "When I was taken by some Christians to a church they pointed to some pictures and asked, 'Do you see him?' When I looked, I saw the features of Rasulullah ﷺ and his picture. I then also saw the features and picture of Abu Bakr ﷺ, who was following in the footsteps of Rasulullah ﷺ. 'Do you see his features?' they asked. 'I certainly do,' I replied. Pointing to the picture of Rasulullah ﷺ, they asked, 'Is this him?' I said, 'O Allah! That is he. I can testify that it certainly is him.' They asked, 'And do you recognize the one who is following in his footsteps?' When I replied that I did, they said, 'We can testify that he is your present leader and the Khalifa after him.'" *(Bayhaqi in Al Bidayah wan Nihayah, Bukhari in Tarikh, Abu Nu'aym in Dala'il).* Jubair ﷺ also asked, "And who is this person following him." The Christian replied, "There was a Nabi after every Nabi that came, except for this Rasulullah ﷺ. There shall be no Nabi after him, so this is his Khalifa." When Jubair ﷺ looked closer, he saw that the peon was indeed Abu Bakr ﷺ. *(Tabrani in Kabeer and Awsat, Haythami)*

The City of Hims Shakes with all the Romans Present There

Some scholars from the Ghassan and Banu Qain tribes report that as a reward for their patience during the battle for Hims, Allah caused an earthquake to shake the people of Hims. This happened when the Muslims formed their battle formations and shouted out الله اكبر *'Allahu Akbar'*. At this, the ground shook with all the Romans inside the city and its walls started to collapse. The Romans became frightened and hurried to their commanders and to those men of good judgment who had been urging them to make peace with the Muslims. They had however not listened to them and had thereby brought humiliation to themselves. When the Muslims called out الله اكبر *'Allahu Akbar'* for the second time, many houses caved in and more walls collapsed. The Romans hurried to their commanders and to the men of good judgment, who said to them, "Do you not see Allah's punishment? Accept what they are inviting you towards..." *(Ibn Jareer)*

Omar ﷺ's Voice Reaches far into the Distance and is Heard by Sariya ﷺ

Abdullah bin Omar ﷺ reports that when Omar ﷺ once dispatched an army, he appointed someone by the name of Sariya ﷺ as its commander. Omar ﷺ was one day delivering a lecture when he suddenly called out, 'The mountain, O Sariya, the mountain!" This he called out 3 times. When a messenger from the same later arrived in Madinah, Omar ﷺ asked him for a report. He said, "O Amirul Mu'minin! We were being defeated when we suddenly heard a voice thrice calling out, "The mountain, O Sariya, the mountain!" We then put our backs towards the mountain, as a result of which Allah defeated the enemy." Someone then said to Omar ﷺ, "It was you who shouted out that command." *(Bayhaqi, Lalka'l in Sharhus Sunnah, Zain Aquli in Fawa'd, Ibnul A'eabi in Karamatul Awliya, Harmala in Jan'u).* Abdullah bin Omar ﷺ reports that while Omar ﷺ was delivering a sermon, he suddenly called out, "The mountain, O Sariya, the mountain! The one who makes a wolf the shepherd of a flock has truly committed a grave injustice." The people looked at each other in surprise, but Ali ﷺ assured them that Omar ﷺ will surely have an explanation for what he had said. When they questioned Omar ﷺ after he had completed, he explained, "The vision flashed through my mind that the Mushrikin would defeat our brothers who were then passing by a mountain. If they turned towards the mountain placing it at their backs, they would have to fight from one direction only allowing them to win a victory. However, if they passed by the mountain, they would be destroyed because they would have to fight the enemy from the direction of the mountain as well. What you claim to have heard me say is my response to that situation." A month later, someone from the Muslim army came with the good news that they had heard Omar ﷺ's voice that day, because of which they turned towards the mountain and were granted a victory by Allah. *(Ibn Mardway in Isabah, Abu Nu'aym in Dala'il, Abu Abdur Rahman Sulamin in Arba'in).* Another narration states that the people asked Ali ﷺ." "Did you hear Omar ﷺ say, 'O Sariya!' while he was delivering the lecture on the pulpit?" "Shame on you people!" Ali ﷺ said, "Leave Omar alone because he always has a valid explanation for anything he does." *(Khatib, Ibn Asakir in Muntakhab Kanzul Ummal, Ibn Kathir in Al Bidayah wan Nihayah).* Omar ﷺ said, "The thought came to my heart that our Muslim army should use the mountain to defend themselves from the enemy. I therefore made the statement hoping that one of Allah's servants would convey it on my behalf." *(Abu Nu'aym in Dala'il).* Amr bin Harith reports that because Omar ﷺ was comfortable with Abdur Rahman bin Auf ﷺ, it was Abdur Rahman bin Auf ﷺ who approached Omar ﷺ saying, "The worst reprimand I can give the people in your defense is that you give them reason to attack you. You were delivering a lecture when you suddenly shouted, 'The mountain, O Sariya, the mountain!' What was this all about?" Omar ﷺ explained, "I swear by Allah that I could not help it. I saw our army fighting near a mountain as they were being attacked from the front and from the back. I could not help shouting 'The mountain, O Sariya, the mountain!' so that they retreat towards the mountain." All the people needed to do was to await a letter from Sariya ﷺ, which read, "We met the enemy on a Friday and continued fighting from the time we performed the Fajr salah until the time for the Jumu'ah salah arrived and the sun was starting to decline. It was then that we twice heard someone calling, 'The mountain, O Sariya, the mountain!' We retreated towards the mountain and continued gaining the upper hand until Allah finally defeated them." The people who had been criticizing Omar ﷺ also said, "Leave Omar ﷺ alone because he has good reason for all that he does." *(Abu Nu'aym in Dala'il).* Omar ﷺ was asked why he made the statement, he replied, "By Allah! I said only what was placed on my tongue (by Allah)." *(Waqidi in Al Bidayah wan Nihayah)*

The Voice of Abu Qirsafah ﷺ Reaches Far Off

Izza bint Aas bin Abu Qirsafah reports that the Romans once took one of Abu Qirsafah ﷺ's son prisoner. When the time arrived for every salah, Abu Qirsafah ﷺ used to climb a wall and call his son's name saying, "Salah!" His son would hear his father even though he was in Roman territory. *(Tabrani, Haythami)*

Hearing voices from the unseen: The Sahabah Hear a Voice While Bathing the Body of Rasulullah ﷺ

Abdullah bin Abbas ﷺ reports that after Rasulullah ﷺ had passed away, people bathing his body fell into a dispute. They heard a voice, the source of which they did no know. It said, 'Bathe the body of your Nabi ﷺ with his Qamis on." Rasulullah ﷺ was bathed wearing his Qamis. Aisha ﷺ states that the unknown voice said, "Bathe him with his clothes on." *(Ibn Sa'd)*

Abu Musa Ash'ari ﷺ Hears a Voice while on a Naval Expedition

Abdullah bin Abbas ﷺ reports that Nabi ﷺ once appointed Abu Musa Ash'ari ﷺ to command a naval expedition. As his vessel was traveling one night, a voice called to them from above saying, "Shall I not inform you of a decision that Allah has taken upon Himself? When a person keeps himself thirsty on a hot summer's day by fasting, then Allah takes it upon Himself to give him a drink on the Day of Judgment." *(Hakim).* Abu Burda reports that Abu Musa Ash'ari ﷺ said, "We were once out on a naval expedition when the wind was pleasant and the sails were filled. We then suddenly heard a voice calling, 'O people aboard this vessel! Stop so that I may inform you of something.' The voice called this out 7 times, I stood at the bow of the vessel and asked, 'Who are you and where do you come from? Can you not see where we are? Can we even stop?' The voice then responded by saying, 'Shall I not inform you of a decision that Allah has taken upon Himself?' 'Why not?' I replied, 'Please do inform us.' It then said, 'When a person keeps himself thirsty on a hot day by fasting solely for Allah's pleasure, then Allah takes it upon Himself to give him a drink on the Day of Judgment.'" It was therefore the habit of Abu Musa Ash'ari ﷺ to search for days that were so scorching hot that a person's skin could almost roast. He would then fast during such day. *(Abu Nu'aym in Hilya)*

People hear a Voice Reciting the Qur'an the Day Abdullah bin Abbas ﷺ Passed Away

Sa'eed bin Jubair reports, "I was present for the funeral of Abdullah bin Abbas ﷺ when he passed away in Ta'if. A white bird, the likes of which had never been seen before, then came and entered his shroud. We looked on and waited for it to emerge, but it was clear that it was not going to. When he was then buried, the following verses of the Qur'an were recited beside his grave, but no one knew who was reciting them:

يَا أَيَّتُهَا النَّفْسُ الْمُطْمَئِنَّةُ (27) ارْجِعِي إِلَى رَبِّكِ رَاضِيَةً مَرْضِيَّةً (28) فَادْخُلِي فِي عِبَادِي (29) وَادْخُلِي جَنَّتِي (30)

(It will be said to the pious): "O (you) the one in (complete) rest and satisfaction! Come back to your Lord, Well-pleased (yourself) and well-pleasing unto Him! Enter you, then, among My honored slaves, and enter you My Paradise!" (Al-Fajr:27-30) (Hakim, Tabrani, Haythami)

A similar narration from Maymun bin Mahran states, "After the same was leveled over his grave, we heard a voice but could not identify whom it was coming from" *(Abu Nu'aym in Hilya)*. Another narration adds, "When Abdullah bin Abbas ؓ passed away and his body was shrouded, a white bird arrived speedily and entered between the shroud. The people then searched for it but could not find it. Abdullah bin Abbas ؓ's freed slave Ikrama then said to them, "Are you all crazy? That was his eyesight that Rasulullah ﷺ promised will be returned to him the day he passes away." When his body was then brought to the grave and placed inside, some words were recited, which were heard by all those standing beside the grave. These were the same verses quoted above. *(Ibn Asakir in Muntakhab Kanzul Ummal)*

The Sahabah are assisted by the Jinn and by unseen voices: Khuraim bin Fatik ؓ hears the Voice of a Jinn Inviting him to Accept Iman

Abu Hurairah ؓ reports that Khuraim bin Fatik ؓ once said to Omar bin Khattab ؓ, "O Amirul Mu'minin! Should I relate to you how I entered the fold of Islam?" When Omar ؓ asked to be informed, Khuraim ؓ explained, "I was on the track of a camel of mine that I had been searching for when night enshrouded me at a place called Abraqul Gharraq. I therefore shouted at the top of my voice, 'I seek refuge with the king of this valley from the foolish ones of his people (the Jinn).' Suddenly, a voice called out the following couplets which mean:

'Shame on you! Seek refuge from Allah the Possessor of Honor, the Possessor of Esteem, Benevolence and Munificence. Recite the verses of Surah Anfal, attest to the Oneness of Allah and then have no more worries'
This made me extremely frightened and when I regained control over myself, I said the following couplets (which mean): 'What are you saying, O caller? Have you guidance with you or misguidance? If you have been guided, do explain to us what the situation is'

The caller then recited the following couplets (which mean):
'Verily the Rasul of Allah bearing all that is good is in Yathrib, calling people to salvation he instructs them to fast and to observe salah and cautions against all that is evil'

I then prodded my animal forward as I recited the following couplets (which mean):
'Guide me along, may Allah guide you. May you never suffer any hunger or nakedness and may you always remain a powerful leader. You may now not burden me further with the good you have been granted'

The Jinn then followed me, saying the following couplets (which mean):
'May Allah accompany you and keep you safe. May He also convey you to your family with your conveyance. Believe in Rasulullah ﷺ and Allah will make you successful. Assist him and my Rabb will assist you'

I then asked him, 'Who are you? May Allah have mercy on you.' He replied, 'I am Amr bin Uthal and I have been appointed by Rasulullah ﷺ as governor of all the Jinn of Najd. Your camel will be taken care of until you return to your family.' It was on a Friday that I entered Madinah. Abu Bakr Siddiq ؓ came to me saying, 'May Allah have mercy on you. Do enter because the news of you accepting Islam has already reached us.' When I informed him that I did not know how to purify myself properly, he taught me how. After purifying myself I then entered the Masjid, where I saw Rasulullah ﷺ delivering a sermon on the pulpit, appearing to be the 14th full moon in beauty and radiance. He happened to be saying, 'When a Muslim performs wudhu properly and then performs salah carefully and with concentration, Allah will surely admit him into Jannah.' Omar ؓ then said to me, 'You will have to present a witness to that Hadith, otherwise I shall have to punish you.' It was the prominent man from the Quraish Uthman bin Affan ؓ, who testified on my behalf and Omar ؓ accepted his testimony." *(Ruyani, Ibn Asakir in Kanzul Ummal)*. Another narration states that Khuraim ؓ recited the following couplets which mean:

"Guide me along, may Allah guide you, may you never suffer any hunger, O person, nor nakedness nor have to remain with any companion whom you dislike and may your rewards never end even after you die" (Abu Nu'aym in Dala'il)

Yet another narration states that Omar once said to Abdullah bin Abbas ؓ,"Relate to me a narration that is most astounding." It was then that Abdullah bin Abbas ؓ related to Omar the story of Khuraim bin Fatik Asadi ؓ, as is recounted above. *(Ibn Abi Shaybah, Abu Qasim bin Bushman in Isabah, Hakim, Tabrani, Haythami, Umawi in Ai Bidayah wan Nihayah)*

A Jinn brought the News of Rasulullah ﷺ's Prophethood to Sawad bin Qarib ؓ

Abdullah bin Omar ؓ says, "Whenever I heard Omar ؓ say, 'I think that this is like this,' it would always be exactly as he thought. However, we were once sitting together when a handsome man passed by and Omar ؓ said, 'Either my assumption has been wrong or this man is still on his religion of ignorance or he had been a fortune-teller. Bring that man to me.' When the man was brought, Omar ؓ told him what he had just mentioned. The man remarked, 'To this day have I never seen any Muslim man being confronted in this manner.' Omar ؓ then said to him, 'I command you to inform me about yourself.' The man said, 'I had been a fortune-teller during the period of ignorance.' 'What was the strangest incident that you experienced with your Jinn?' The man related, 'I was in the marketplace one day when he came to me and I could see that he was extremely scared. He recited the following couplets which mean:

'Have you not seen the Jinn and their bewilderment? Have you not seen their despondence after their retreat? And that they have now joined the ranks of young camels and their saddle blankets?'

'He is speaking the truth,' Omar ؓ said, 'I was also sleeping near the idols of the Mushrikin when someone brought a calf and slaughtered it. Just then, someone screamed so loudly that I had never before heard such a loud scream. The voice said, 'O Jalih! The matter is one of salvation and the man is an eloquent man saying, 'La Ilaha Illallhah" The people there sprang up in surprise, but I told them to remain where they were until I found out who was behind it. The voice then called out again, 'O Jalih! The matter is one of salvation and the man is an eloquent man saying, 'La Ilaha Illallah" I then left and we did not have to wait long afterwards when it was said that this referred to Rasulullah ﷺ.'" The man mentioned in the narration above was Sawad bin Qarib ؓ. (Bukhari). Muhammad bin Ka'b Qurazi reports that Omar was sitting somewhere one day when a man passed by. Someone asked, "O Amirul Mu'minin! Do you who that passer-by is?" When Omar ؓ asked who he was, the people replied, "He is Sawad bin Qarib, the man who was informed about the coming of Rasulullah ﷺ by the Jinn in his service." Omar ؓ sent for the man and when he arrived asked, "Are you Sawad bin Qarib?" When he replied in the affirmative, Omar ؓ asked, "Are you still practicing fortune-telling?" Sawad ؓ became angry and said, "O Amirul Mu'minin! No one has ever confronted me in this manner since the day I accepted Islam." "SubhanAllah!" Omar ؓ exclaimed, "There is no need to be offended because the Shirk that we were all involved in was much worse than the fortune-telling that you had been practicing. Tell me what the Jinn in your service told you about the coming of Rasulullah ﷺ." Sawad ؓ related, "O course, Amirul Mu'minin. I was half asleep and half awake one night when my Jinn came and nudged me with his foot. 'Get up, O Sawad bin Qarib,' he said, 'Hear what I have to say and make sense of it if you can. Verily, a Nabi has been sent from amongst the progeny of Luway bin Ghalib. He invites people towards Allah and towards worshipping Allah.' He then recited the following couplets which mean:

'I am surprised at the Jinn and their search and their traveling on white camels with their carriages. They descend on Makkah in search of guidance because a truthful Jinn cannot be compared to one who is a liar. You must therefore go to the chosen one from the Banu Hashim because the one in the lead cannot be compared to the one who lags behind'

I however said to him, 'Leave me to sleep because I have been very sleepy all evening.' He then returned the following night and nudged me with his foot, saying, 'Get up, O Sawad bin Qarib,' he said, 'Hear what I have to say and make sense of it if you can. Verily, a Nabi has been sent from amongst the progeny of Luway bin Ghalib. He invites people towards Allah and towards worshipping Allah.' He then recited the following couplets (which mean):

'I am surprised at the Jinn and their bewilderment and their traveling on white camels with their carriages. They descend on Makkah in search of guidance because a Mu'min Jinn cannot be compared to one who is a Kafir. You must therefore go to the chosen one from the Banu Hashim who resides amongst the hills and rocks of Makka'

Again I said to him, 'Leave me to sleep because I have been very sleepy all evening.' He returned again on the third night and nudged me with his foot, saying, 'Get up, O Sawad bin Qarib,' he said, 'Hear what I have to say and make sense of it if you can. Verily, a Nabi has been sent from amongst the progeny of Luway bin Ghalib. He invites people towards Allah and towards worshipping Allah.' He recited the following couplets:

'I am surprised at the Jnn and their searching and their traveling on white camels with their saddle blankets. They descend on Makkah in search of guidance because a pure Jinn cannot be compared to one who is impure. You must therefore go to the chosen one from the Banu Hashim and look up at Makkah's high peaks'

I then got up and said, 'Allah has certainly put my heart to test.' I then mounted the carriage on my camel and went to the great city of Makkah. There I found Rasulullah ﷺ with his companions and said to him, 'Would you hear what I have to say?' Rasulullah ﷺ bade me to come forward and speak. I then recited the following couplets which mean:

'My confidante came to me after a part of the night had passed and I had some sleep. Never has he lied to me in all my experiences with him for three nights he came, each night he said: 'A Nabi has come to you from Luway bin Ghalib'
I then rolled up the hem of my loincloth and my speedy full-cheeked camel carried me through dusty, level and distant plains I testify that there is none worthy of worship but Allah and that you are perfectly trustworthy to convey all unseen revelation.
Of all the Ambiya, you are the closest link to Allah. O son of honorable and pure people! O the best of all who walk! Command us with all that is revealed to you even though some of it may whiten our forelocks. Be an intercessor on my behalf on the day when no intercessor apart from you will be of any help to Sawad bin Qarin'

Rasulullah ﷺ and his companions became so happy with my words that the joy was evident on their faces." Omar ؓ jumped up and hugged Sawad ؓ, saying, "I had always wished to hear the story from you. Do your Jinn still come to you?" Sawad ؓ replied, "He does not come ever since I have been reciting the Qur'an, but the Qur'an is a most excellent replacement for him." Omar ؓ then himself recounted an incident, saying, "We were once with a family of the Quraish called the family Dhari, who had just slaughtered a calf. The butcher was still preparing the meat when we heard a voice from the calf's belly calling, 'O family of Dhari! The matter is one of salvation. A man is calling out in an eloquent tongue, testifying that there is none worthy of worship but Allah." (Abu Ya'la, Kara'itu in Hawatiful Jinn). A narration from Barra ؓ states that Sawad ؓ was staying in India when the Jinn came to him that night. The rest of the narration is like the one above, but adds that after Sawad ؓ recited the above couplets to Rasulullah ﷺ, Rasulullah ﷺ smiled so widely that his blessed teeth showed. Rasulullah then said, "You are successful, O Sawad!" (Ibn Asakir in Al Bidayah wan Nihayah). Yet another narration from Muhammad bin Ka'b Qurazi ؓ similar to the one he narrated above states that (after the Jinn advised him) Sawad ؓ said, "The love of Islam then penetrated my heart and I was drawn to it. The next morning, I fastened the carriage to my camel and left for Makkah. I was still on the road when I received the news that Rasulullah ﷺ had already migrated to Madinah. I therefore arrived in Madinah and when I asked for Rasulullah ﷺ, I was informed that he was in the Masjid. I then went to the Masjid and, after tying my camel up, I entered. There I found Rasulullah ﷺ sitting with many people around him. 'Would you hear what I have to say, O Rasulullah ﷺ? I asked. Abu Bakr ؓ then bade me to come closer and I kept going closer until I was right in front of Rasulullah ﷺ. 'Come,' Rasulullah ﷺ said, 'and inform me about how the Jinn in your control came to you." (Hakim, Tabrani in Majma'uz Zawa'id, Hasan bin Sufian, Bayhaqi, Bukhari in Tarikh, Baghawi, Tabrani, Bayhaqi, Ibn Abi Khaithama, Ruyani and Ibn Shahin in Isabah).

A Jinn bring the News of Rasulullah ﷺ's Nabuwwat to Abbas bin Mirdas ؓ

Abbas bin Mirdas Sulami ؓ relates, "My becoming a Muslim began when my father was on his deathbed and he made a bequest that I take care of his idol called Dimad. I therefore kept it in my house and would go to it once every day. It was at the time when Nabi ﷺ announced his Nabuwwat that I was startled by a voice I heard in the middle of the night. I rushed to Dimad for assistance, but I discovered that the voice was coming from within it. It was reciting the following couplets:

'Say to all the members of the Banu Sulaim tribe that idols and their worshippers will be destroyed and only the people of the Masjid will live on Dimad is destroyed though he was being worshipped for some time before the Book that has come to Muhammad. Verily the one from the Quraish who inherited Nabuwwat and guidance after the son of Mary am is truly the rightly guided one'

However, I did not disclose this to the people. It was after the people had returned from the Battle of Ahzab that I was sleeping one day amongst my camels on one side of Aqiq in the Dhatul Irq area. I heard a voice and suddenly saw a man appear on the feather of an ostrich. He said, "Follow the light that settled on Wednesday upon the one riding the camel Adba when he was in the locality of the people of the Banu Unaqa in Madinah." Another voice from the north replied to this one, saying the following couplets (which mean):

'Inform the Jinn that the reason for their bewilderment is that the camels have laid down their carriages and the sentinels of the heavens have begun their vigil'

I jumped up in fear, knowing that Muhammad ﷺ had already been sent on his duty. I then mounted my horse and sped off to Rasulullah ﷺ. After pledging my allegiance to him, I returned to Dimad and set him alight. Thereafter, I returned once more to Rasulullah ﷺ and recited to him the following couplets:

'By your life! There was a day when I was foolish enough to equate Dimad a partner to the Rabb of the universe. I had forsaken Rasulullah ﷺ while the Aws tribe were around him. They were his helpers, and what fine helpers they were! I was like one who forsook soft and fertile land in search of a Path of difficulties to tread upon. I believe in Allah Whom I worship to oppose those who opt for destruction. I have turned my face towards Makkah to search for the blessed Nabi of all honorable people. A Nabi who came to us after Isa speaking the truth that differentiates between the truth and falsehood. A trustworthy bearer of the Qur'an and the first intercessor. The first to be resurrected in response to the call of the angels. He rejoined the bonds of Islam after they had broken. Then made them secure until its injunctions were established. I am referring to you, O the best of all creation. You have the most noble of lineages and are truly the possessor of great honor. You were the purest of the Quraish when they rose in esteem despite their hunger, and may you be blessed as long as the centuries pass. When the Ka'b and Malik tribes name their lineages, we will still regard you as most pure in descent' (Abu Nu'aym in Dala'il)

After the first 3 couplets were told to Abbas bin Mirdas ؓ, he was filled with fear and went to his tribesmen. After narrating the incident to them, he left for Madinah with 300 of his people from the Banu Haritha tribe to see Rasulullah ﷺ. Upon seeing them enter the Masjid, Rasulullah ﷺ asked, "O Abbas! How did you come to accept Islam?" When he recounted the incident to Rasulullah ﷺ, Rasulullah ﷺ was impressed and Abbas ؓ together with his entire tribe accepted Islam. (Kara'iti in Al Bidayah wan Nihayah, Abu Nu'aym in Dala'il, Tabrani, Haythami)

A Jinn brought the News of Rasulullah ﷺ's Nabuwwat to a Woman in Madinah

Jabir bin Abdullah ؓ reports that the first news of Rasulullah ﷺ's Nabuwwat reached Madinah because of a Jinn that a particular woman from Madinah had under her control. When it arrived in the form of a white bird and perched upon a wall, she said to it, "Will you not come down so that we may converse with each other and exchange stories?" It then said to her, "A Nabi has been sent in Makkah who forbids adultery and has deprived us of rest because we can no longer eavesdrop on the conversations of the angels." (Abu Nu'aym in Dala'il, Ahmad, Tabrani, Haythami, Ibn Sa'd). Ali bin Husain reports that the first news of Rasulullah ﷺ's Nabuwwat reached Madinah because of a Jinn that a particular woman from Madinah called Fatima had under her control. It came to her one day and stood on a wall, she said, "Will you not come down?" It said to her, "No. A Nabi has been sent who forbids adultery." (Waqidi in Al Bidayah wan Nihayah)

A Jinn brought the News of Rasulullah ﷺ's Nabuwwat to a Fortune-Teller in the Vicinity of Sham

Uthman bin Affan ؓ reports, "We once left with a caravan to Sham before Rasulullah ﷺ announced his Nabuwwat. We had just entered the borders of Sham when a fortune-teller who lived there approached us and said, 'My companion (a Jinn) came to me and stood at my door.' When I asked him why he would not enter, he replied, 'I cannot. Ahmed (Rasulullah ﷺ) has made his appearance and such a matter has come that is beyond our capacity.'" Uthman ؓ continues. He says, "I then left and when I returned to Makkah, I found that Rasulullah ﷺ had already announced his Nabuwwat and was calling people towards Allah." (Waqidi in Al Bidayah wan Nihayah, Abu Nu'aym in Dala'il)

Another Incident in this Regard

Mujahid reports, "It was during the Battle of Rhodes an old man called Ibn Isa who had lived during the Period of Ignorance related to me, "I was busy pulling a cow belonging to our family when I heard a voice from its belly saying, 'O family of Dhari! The statement is clear. A well-wishing man is calling out that there is none worthy of worship but Allah." (Ahmad, Haythami)

Saitan instigates the Quraish against Rasulullah ﷺ and the Sahabah

Abdullah bin Abbas ؓ narrates that a caller from the jinn once announced from the Abu Qubais mountain in Makkah the following couplets which mean:

"May Allah efface the judgment of the Ka'b bin Fihr (Quraish) tribe (referring to the Muslims). How weak has their intelligence become?! Their religion they turn against is the religion of their revered forefathers who gave them protection. The Jinn of Busra have opposed the rest as have the men of the place of hills and date palms (Madinah). Is there any honorable man amongst you with a free spirit and who has reverence for his parents and uncles? Who would strike a blow (at the Muslims) that would teach them a lesson and free you from anxiety and grief. You shall soon see horses racing with each other to fight the (Muslim) people in the land of Tihamah"

When the news of this spread in Makkah, the Mushrikin started reciting poetry to each other, renewing their resolve to harm the Muslims. Rasulullah ﷺ remarked, 'That was a Saitan named Mis'ar who was addressing the people through the idols. May Allah disgrace him!" it was barely three days later that another voice announced form the mountain (the following couplets which mean):

"We have killed Mis'ar when he rebelled and was haughty when he undermined the truth and spread evil. I decapitated him with a sword that tears and devastates all because he blasphemed against our pure Nabi"

To this Rasulullah ﷺ commented, "That was a powerful Jinn named Samhaj, whom I named Abdullah after he believed in me.

He informed me that he had been looking for Mis'ar for the past 3 days." Ali ⚓ then remarked, "May Allah reward him well, O Rasulullah ﷺ!" (Abu Nu'aym in Dala'il, Umawi in Maghazi, Al Bidayah wan Nihayah, Fakihi in Akhbar Makkah, Isabah)

Some men from the Khath'am Tribe hear a Caller from the Jinn Informing them about Rasulullah ﷺ

Abdullah bin Mahmud reports that several men from the Khath'am tribe said, "We were idol worshippers and amongst the factors that called us towards Islam was that when we were once with an idol of ours, a group of people came to it, hoping that it would be able to settle a matter that they were disputing. Just then, a caller called out to them saying (the following couplets which mean): 'O people with bodies who vary in age from old men to young boys! Have you no intelligence that you refer your decisions to the idols? Are you all asleep in your confusion or do you not see that which is in front of me? It is a rising light that illuminates the darkness which has become visible to every onlooker in Tihama that is the Nabi and leader of all creation who has come with Islam after Kufr Ar Rahman has granted him special honor above all leaders and all prophets with his truthful speech. He is the most just of all judges who instructs people to perform salah, to fast, to do good and to foster good family ties. He cautions people against sinning, against impurities, worshipping idols and all that is Haram. He belongs to the noblest of lineages from the Banu Hashim and is announcing his Nabuwwat in the sacred city (Makkah)'
When we heard this, we dispersed immediately, went to Rasulullah ﷺ and accepted Islam." (Kara'iti in Al Bidayah wan Nihayah, Abu Nu'aym in Dala'il)

Tamim Dari ⚓ hears a Caller from the Jinn

Tamim Dari ⚓ says, "I was in Sham at the time Rasulullah ﷺ started to announce his Nabuwwat. I was out to do some work once when night caught up with me somewhere on the way. As was the custom during those times I said, 'Tonight 1 am in the protection of the (Jinn) master of this valley.' When I lay down to rest, I heard someone whom 1 could not see. He was calling out, 'Seek protection from Allah because the Jinn cannot protect anyone against Allah.' 'By Allah!' I exclaimed, 'What are you saying?' he explained, 'The Nabi of the unlettered people has made his appearance. He is the Rasul of Allah ﷺ and we performed salah behind him in Hajun, where we accepted Islam and undertook to follow him. The ploys of the Jinn to eavesdrop on the conversations of the angels and convey the news of future events to fortune-tellers is over and they are now being pelted by flaming stars when they attempt to eavesdrop. You had better go to Muhammad ﷺ who is the Nabi of the Rabb of the universe.'"
Tamim ⚓ relates further, "I went to the town of Dayr Ayub, where 1 consulted a monk and related the incident to him. His response was, "They (Jinn) have told you the truth. He (Muhammad ﷺ) will make his appearance in the Haram and the place to which he will migrate will also be a Haram. He is the best of all the Ambiya ﷺ and do not allow anyone to beat you to him.' I mustered up a11 the courage I had, went to Rasulullah ﷺ and accepted Islam." (Abu Nu'aym in Al Bidayah wan Nihayah)

Hajjaj bin Alat ⚓ accepts Islam after Hearing the Call of a Jinn

Wathila bin Asqa ⚓ reports that Hajjaj bin Alat Bahzi Sulami ⚓ was introduced to Islam when he once left for Makkah with a group of riders from his tribe. Night enveloped them when they were in a frightening valley, because of which they were terrified. "O Abu Kilab!" Hajjaj ⚓'s companions said to him,

"Get up and secure safety for yourself and for your companions. Hajjaj ⚓ therefore stood up and recited the following couplets (which mean):
"I seek protection for myself and for these companions of mine from every Jinn in this valley so that my companions and I may return home in safety"
They then heard someone recite the verse:
يَا مَعْشَرَ الْجِنِّ وَالْإِنسِ إِنِ اسْتَطَعْتُمْ أَن تَنفُذُوا مِنْ أَقْطَارِ السَّمَاوَاتِ وَالْأَرْضِ فَانفُذُوا لَا تَنفُذُونَ إِلَّا بِسُلْطَانٍ (33) *O assembly of jinns and men! If you have power to pass beyond the zones of the heavens and the earth, then pass (them)! But you will never be able to pass them, except with authority (from Allah)!* (Ar-Rahman:33)

When the party arrived in Makkah and related what had happened, the people of the Quraish exclaimed, "By Allah! O Abu Kilab, you have forsaken your religion! Those words are from that which Muhammad claims has been revealed to him." "By Allah!" Hajjaj ⚓ exclaimed, "Those are the words I heard and so did all those with me." While this discussion was taking place, Aas bin Wa'il arrived. Addressing him, the people said, "O Abu Hashim! Have you heard what Abu Kilab has to say?" When Asi bin Wa'il asked what it was, he was informed about the incident. "What is so surprising about that?" Asi remarked, "The one whom he heard there (Jinn) is the same one who tells it to Muhammad." Hajjaj ⚓ says, "This statement of his put my people off what I felt that we should accept Islam. This increased my insight into the matter. We returned home and it was after a while that I enquired about Rasulullah ﷺ and was informed that he had left Makkah for Madinah. I mounted my animal and left. I reached Rasulullah ﷺ and informed him about what I had heard, he remarked, 'By Allah! What you heard was the truth. That was definitely from the speech of my Rabb that He revealed to me. O Abu Kilab! You had heard the truth.' 'O Rasulullah ﷺ!' I said, 'Teach me Islam.' Rasulullah ﷺ made me testify my belief in the Kalima of Sincerity and said, 'Go and call your people towards that which I called you because it is the truth." (Ibn Abi Dunya in Hawatiful Jin, Ibn Asakir in Muntakhab Kanzul Ummal)

A group of Muslims are saved by the kind act of a Jinn

Ubay bin Ka'b ⚓ reports that a group of people once left for Makkah but got lost on the way. When they were close to death, they donned their burial shrouds and lay down to die. It was then that a Jinn came to them from between the trees. He said to them, "I am amongst those left who actually listened to Rasulullah ﷺ. I heard him say, 'A Mu'min is the brother of a Mu'min. He is his eyes and his guide and never leaves him in the lurch.' Here is water and this is the road." He then showed them where to find water and guided them to the road. (Abu Nu'aym in Dala'il)

The Jinn Assist the Muslims in the Battle of Khaibar

Sa'eed bin Shuiam who belonged to the Banu Saham bin Murra tribe reports that his father was with the army of Uyayna bin Hisn when they arrived to assist the Jews of Khaibar against the Muslims. His father relates further, "During the battle we heard a voice announce in Uyayna's army, 'O people! Your families are under attack!' Everyone then returned without even waiting for each other. We however did not see anyone make the announcement and feel that it could have come from nowhere other than from the heavens." (Baghawi in Isabah)

Rasulullah ﷺ Captures a Jinn

Abu Hurairah ⚓ reports that Rasulullah ﷺ said, "I was asleep one night when a Saitan came to interfere with me. I grabbed him by the throat and could actually feel the coldness of his tongue on my thumb. May Allah have mercy on Sulaiman ﷺ. Had it not been for his prayer to have a kingdom that no other can compare with, the Saitan would have been tied up this morning for you all to see." Abu Hurairah ؓ narrates that Rasulullah ﷺ said, "A rebellious Jinn escaped last night and came to disrupt my salah. Allah however granted me the ability to overpower him and I grabbed hold of him. This I did with the intention of tying him up to one of the pillars of the Masjid so that you people could all see him in the morning. However, I then recalled the Du'a of my brother Sulaiman ﷺ who said:

رَبِّ اغْفِرْ لِي وَهَبْ لِي مُلْكًا لَا يَنْبَغِي لِأَحَدٍ مِنْ بَعْدِي

…*My Lord! Forgive me, and bestow upon me a kingdom such as shall not belong to any other after me… (Sad:35).* I let him off with him feeling most humiliated." Another narration from Abu Darda ؓ states that Rasulullah ﷺ said, "Had it not been for the Du'a of our brother Sulaiman ﷺ, the jinn would have been tied up this morning and even the children of Madinah would have been able to play with him." *(Abu Nu'aym in Dala'il)*

Mu'adh bin Jabal ؓ Captures a Saitan During the Time of Rasulullah ﷺ

Buraida ؓ reports that when he heard that Mu'adh bin Jabal ؓ had captured a Saitan during the time of Rasulullah ﷺ, he approached him and asked, "I heard that you had captured a Saitan during the time of Rasulullah ﷺ." Mu'adh ؓ explained, "Yes, I did. When Rasulullah ﷺ handed over the Sadaqa dates to me, I stored them all in an upper story room of mine. When I started noticing them get less every day, I reported the matter to Rasulullah ﷺ, who said, 'That is the work of a Saitan. You must trap him.' I therefore lay in wait for him one night. When a short portion of the night had passed, the Saitan arrived in the form of an elephant. As he reached the door, he stopped and then entered through the cracks of the door in another form. Drawing close to the dates, he started making morsels out of them. It was then that I gathered my garments tightly around me and caught him red-handed. I said, 'I testify that there is none worthy of worship but Allah and I testify that Muhammad ﷺ is the servant and Rasul of Allah! O enemy of Allah! You have leapt at and taken Allah's dates whereas they are the right of the poor! I shall be taking you before Rasulullah ﷺ and he will disgrace you. He however promised me that he will never repeat what he did and I released him. When I went to Rasulullah ﷺ early next morning, Rasulullah ﷺ asked, 'What happened to your prisoner?' 'He promised that he would not return,' I replied. 'He will be returning,' Rasulullah ﷺ assured me, 'so wait up for him.' I therefore lay in ambush for him the second night as well. He then did as he had done and I also did as I had done. This time again I released him when he promised never to return. When I went early next morning to report to Rasulullah, I heard someone announce, 'Where is Mu'adh?' 'What happened to your prisoner?' Rasulullah ﷺ asked. 'He again promised that he would not return,' I replied. 'He will be returning,' Rasulullah ﷺ assured me yet again, 'so wait up for him.' I then lay in ambush for him for the third night and he returned to do as he had done previously. I also did as I had done before and said to him, 'O enemy of Allah! You had promised on 2 occasions that you would never return. This time I shall definitely be taking you before Rasulullah ﷺ and he will disgrace you.' He however pleaded to me saying, 'I am a Saitan who has a family to support. I have come all the way from Nasibin, a place then part of Sham but now part of Turkey and would not have come had I found anything closer. We had been

residing in this city of yours until your master Rasulullah ﷺ was sent as a Nabi. We however had to flee from here when 2 portions of the Qur'an were revealed. It was from then that we started living in Nasibin. Whenever these 2 portions are recited in a house, a Saitan will be unable to enter it for 3 days. I am prepared to teach you these 2 portions if you let me go.' When I agreed, he informed me that they were Ayatul Kursi and the concluding verses of Surah Baqara, starting from the words امن الرسول and finishing at the end of the Surah. Again I let him off and when I went early next morning to report to Rasulullah ﷺ, I was surprised to again hear someone announce, 'Where is Mu'adh bin Jabal?' 'What happened to your prisoner?' Rasulullah ﷺ asked. I then formed Rasulullah ﷺ that the Saitan promised not to turn and also informed him of the rest of the incident. Rasulullah ﷺ remarked, 'The wretch spoke the truth even though he is usually a great liar.' Thereafter, I always recited these 2 portions of the Qur'an over the dates and never found them to decrease ever again." *(Tabrani, Haythami, Abu Nu'aym in Dala'il)*

Abu Hurairah ؓ and Abu Ayub Ansari ؓ both Capture Saitan during the Time of Rasulullah ﷺ

Abu Hurairah ؓ reports, "Rasulullah ﷺ once appointed me to look after the zakah of Ramadhan. However, someone came and started helping himself to the food. I captured him immediately and said, 'I am going to take you to Rasulullah ﷺ.' 'I am a needy person,' he pleaded, 'I have a family and am in great poverty.' I then let him go. The next morning, Rasulullah ﷺ asked, 'O Abu Hurairah! What happened to your prisoner last night?' 'O Rasulullah ﷺ!' I explained, 'I took pity on him and let him go when he complained of his dire need and family.' Rasulullah ﷺ however said, 'He lied to you and will be back soon.' Because Rasulullah ﷺ said he would be back, I was convinced that he would. I therefore waited up for him. He then returned and again started to help himself. I caught him again and when I again threatened to take him to Rasulullah ﷺ, he pleaded to me to let him go and again complained of his poverty and family. Yet again, I felt him sorry and let him go. 'O Abu Hurairah! What happened to your prisoner last night?' Rasulullah ﷺ asked the next morning, 'O Rasulullah ﷺ!' I explained, 'I took pity on him and let him go when he complained of his dire need and family.' Rasulullah ﷺ repeated, 'He lied to you and will be back soon.' Because Rasulullah ﷺ said he would be back, I was convinced that he would and therefore waited up for him yet again. He returned and again started to help himself. I caught him and said, 'This time I will definitely be taking you to Rasulullah ﷺ. This is the last time that you will be returning after thrice promising not to.' This time he said, 'Leave me and I shall teach you some words by which Allah will grant you tremendous benefit.' 'What are they?' I enquired. He said, 'When you lie down to sleep, recite *Ayatul Kursi* from اللَّهُ لَا إِلَهَ إِلَّا هُوَ الْحَيُّ الْقَيُّومُ up to the end of the verse because you will then have a protecting angel from Allah with you all the time. No Saitan will then be able to even come close to you until the morning.' 'O Abu Hurairah!" Rasulullah ﷺ asked me the next morning, 'What happened to your prisoner last night?' 'O Rasulullah ﷺ!' I explained, 'I released him when he professed that he would teach me some words by which Allah will grant me tremendous benefit.' 'What are they?' Rasulullah ﷺ asked. I said, 'He said that when one lies down to sleep, if one recites *Aayatul Kursi* from اللَّهُ لَا إِلَهَ إِلَّا هُوَ الْحَيُّ الْقَيُّومُ from beginning to end, one will then have a protecting angel from Allah all the time. No Saitan will then be able to even come close to one until the morning.'" A narrator adds that the Sahabah were always the most desirous of all people to learn things of virtue (which was why Abu Hurairah ؓ released the Saitan on this occasion). Rasulullah ﷺ then said to Abu Hurairah ؓ, "Although he is a great liar, he has told you the truth this time. Do you know with whom you have been conversing these past 3 nights? It was a Saitan." *(Bukhari in Mishkatul Masabih).* Abu Ayub Ansari ؓ reports that he had a niche in his house in which he stored dates. When a type of Jinn started coming to steal from it, he reported the matter to Rasulullah ﷺ. Rasulullah ﷺ advised him saying, "Go back and when you see her again, say, 'Bismillah! Go and report to Rasulullah ﷺ.'" Abu Ayub ؓ then caught her, but she promised never to return. The rest of the narration is similar to the one narrated above. *(Tirmidhi in Targheeb wat Tarheeb, Abu Nu'aym in Dala'il, Tabrani, Haythami).* A similar narration has been quoted about Ubay bin Ka'b ؓ in the chapter concerning Dhikr.

Omar ؓ floors a Jinn and the Saiatin were Chained up During the Khilafah of Omar ؓ

Abu Wa'il reports that Abdullah bin Mas'ood ؓ once said, "When a Saitan once met a Sahabi and wrestled him, the Sahabi floored him and even bit his thumb. The Saitan then pleaded, 'Leave me and I will teach you a verse that causes any of us to run away as soon as we hear it.' When the Sahabi released him, the Saitan refused to teach it to him. The Sahabi then again wrestled him and floored him yet again and again bit his finger. Again the Saitan begged to be released, promising to teach the Sahabi the verse. However, when the Sahabi told the Saitan to inform him of the verse, he still refused. It was after the third wrestling bout that the Saitan said, 'It is the verse in Surah Baqarah from اللَّهُ لَا إِلَهَ إِلَّا هُوَ الْحَيُّ الْقَيُّومُ up to the end of the verse.'"

"O Abu Abdur Rahman!" someone asked Abdullah bin Mas'ood ؓ, "Who was the Sahabi?" Abdullah bin Mas'ood ؓ replied, "Who else but Omar ؓ." *(Tabrani).* In another narration, Abdullah bin Mas'ood ؓ said, "When a man from the companions of Rasulullah ﷺ met a man from the Jinn and they wrestled, the human floored the Jinn. The Jinn asked for another wrestling bout and this time the human floored him yet again. The human then asked, 'You appear to be extremely feeble and pale and your forearms resemble those of a dog. Are all of you Jinn like this?' 'No, By Allah!' the Jinn replied, 'Some of us are very powerfully built. Wrestle me for the third time and if you manage to floor me again, I shall teach you something that will be of great benefit to you.' The human fought him again and after flooring him, said, 'Come tell me what it is.' 'Do you recite Ayatul Kursi?' the Jinn enquired. When the human told him that he did, the Jinn said, 'Whenever you recite it in your house, every Saitan vacates the house, braying like a donkey and will not enter again until the morning.'" "O Abu Abdur Rahman!" someone asked Abdullah bin Mas'ood ؓ, "Who was that companion of Rasulullah ﷺ?" Abdullah bin Mas'ood ؓ frowned, turned to the person and replied, "Who else could he be but Omar ؓ." *(Tabrani, Haythami, Abu Nu'aym in Dala'il).* Mujahid says, "We were always told that the Saiatin were chained up during the Khilafa of Omar ؓ. It was only after his martyrdom that they were released." *(Ibn Asakir in Muntakhab Kanzul Ummal)*

Abdullah bin Zubair ؓ Rebukes a Jinn

Amir bin Abdullah bin Zubair ؓ reports that Abdullah bin Zubair ؓ was returning from Umrah with a group of people belonging to the Quraish. They were at Yanasib when they noticed a man sitting beneath a tree. Abdullah bin Zubair ؓ went up to him and greeted him with Salam. The man paid no heed to him and gave only a feeble reply. When Abdullah bin Zubair ؓ alighted from his animal, the man did not move and Abdullah bin Zubair ؓ had to ask him to move from the shade. The man reluctantly complied. Abdullah bin Zubair ؓ himself says, "I then sat down and, holding him by the arm, I asked who he was. 'I am a man from the Jinn,' came the reply. He had hardly spoken the words when every hair on my body stood on end. I then pulled at him saying, 'You are a man from the Jinn and have the audacity to appear before me like this?!' I noticed that he had the legs of an animal and when I rebuked him, he started to become meek. I further said, 'You behave so impudently before me when you are a Dhimmi?' He then fled. When my companions arrived, they asked, 'Where is the man who was with you?' 'He was a man from amongst the Jinn,' I replied, 'and he ran away.' Everyone of them then fell from his animal and I had to take them all and tie them to their animals. I then led them for Hajj without any of them returning to their complete sense." *(Ibn Mubarak).* Abu Sulaiman Darani reports that it was a moonlit night when Abdullah bin Zubair ؓ went out on his animal and camped at Tabuk. As he turned around (after alighting), he saw an old man with white hair and a white beard sitting on his animal. Abdullah bin Zubair ؓ lunged at the man and he moved off the animal. Abdullah bin Zubair ؓ then mounted the camel and rode off. The man then called out, "O Ibn Zubair! By Allah! Had even a hair's breadth of fear for me entered your heart tonight, I would have driven you insane." Abdullah bin Zubair ؓ replied, "Should fear for you enter my heart? O accursed?!" *(Al Bidayah wan Nihayah)*

Abu Dhar ؓ hears the Tasbih of some Pebbles in the Hands of his Companions

Suwaid bin Zaid reports, "When I once saw Abu Dhar ؓ sitting alone in the Masjid, I took advantage of the opportunity and went to sit beside him. When I mentioned Uthman ؓ to him, he said, 'Never say anything about Uthman ؓ unless it is good because of something about him that I saw with Rasulullah ﷺ. I used to search for the moments when Rasulullah ﷺ was alone so that I could learn from him. When I went to Rasulullah ﷺ one day, I found that he had already left home, so I followed him. Rasulullah ﷺ sat down somewhere and I sat down with him. 'O Abu Dhar!' Rasulullah ﷺ asked, 'What brings you here?' 'Allah and His Rasul ﷺ,' I replied. Abu Bakr ؓ then arrived and sat down on Rasulullah ﷺ's right side. 'O Abu Bakr!' Rasulullah ﷺ asked, 'What brings you here?' 'Allah and His Rasul ﷺ,' he replied. Omar ؓ then arrived and sat down on Abu Bakr ؓ's right side. 'What brings you here, O Omar?' Rasulullah ﷺ asked. 'Allah and His Rasul ﷺ,' he replied. Uthman ؓ then arrived and sat down on Omar ؓ's right side. 'What brings you here, O Uthman?' Rasulullah ﷺ asked. 'Allah and His Rasul ﷺ,' he replied. Rasulullah ﷺ then picked up 7 or 9 pebbles that engaged in Tasbih in his hand so audibly that we could hear them sounding like the humming of bees. Rasulullah ﷺ then put them down and they stopped humming. He then put them in Abu Bakr ؓ's hand and again they engaged in Tasbih so audibly that we could hear them sounding like the humming of bees. Abu Bakr then put them down and they stopped humming. Thereafter, Rasulullah ﷺ put them in Uthman ؓ's hand and again they engaged in Tasbih so audibly that we could hear them sounding like the humming of bees. When Uthman ؓ put them down, they stopped humming. *(Bazzar, Haythami).* Another narration adds that Abu Dhar ؓ said, "Rasulullah ﷺ then put them in Omar ؓ's hand and again they engaged in Tasbih so audibly that I could hear them sounding like the humming of bees. Omar 🕮 then put them down and they stopped humming." The end of this narration adds that Rasulullah 🕮 remarked, "This denotes the successors of Nubuwwah." *(Bayhaqi in Al Bidayah wan Nihayah, Abu Nu'aym in Dala'il)* Another narration adds that Rasulullah 🕮 gave the pebbles to Ali 🕮 and (after engaging in Tasbih) they stopped only after he had put them down. *(Tabrani in Awsat, Haythami).* Abu Dhar 🕮 said, "Every person sitting in the gathering heard the Tasbih from each from the 4 Khulafa. Then Rasulullah 🕮 gave the pebbles in our hands (those of us apart from the 4) and they did not engage in Tasbih in any of our hands." *(Tabrani in Majma'uz Zawa'id, Abu Nu'aym in Dala'il)*

Abdullah bin Mas'ood 🕮 hears the Tasbih of Food

Abdullah bin Mas'ood 🕮 once said, "We viewed the miracles of Rasulullah 🕮 as a source of blessings, while you people only see them as threats to the Kuffar. One such miracle occurred when we were once with Rasulullah 🕮 on a journey when water ran short. Rasulullah 🕮 asked for left-over water to be brought and the people brought whatever little amount of water they had in a container. Rasulullah 🕮 placed his hand in the container and announced, 'Come and get water that is pure and blessed. The blessings are of course from Allah.' I then actually saw water gushing forth from between Rasulullah 🕮's fingers. Another miracle occurred when we could actually hear food engaging in Tasbih as it was being eaten." *(Bukhari, Tirmidhi in Al Bidayah wan Nihayah).* The chapter on the Du'as Rasulullah 🕮 made for Abbas 🕮, a narration is quoted: "To this Du'a, the doorstep and all the walls of the house said, 'Amin! Amin! Amin!'" *(Tabrani, Bayhaqi, Abu Nu'aym in Dala'il, Ibn Majah)*

The Sahabah hear the Sobbing of a Tree Trunk

Jabir bin Abdullah 🕮 reports that Rasulullah 🕮 used to lean on a date palm when standing to deliver the sermon on Fridays. Someone from the Ansar made a suggestion saying, "O Rasulullah 🕮! Should we not make a pulpit for you?" "If you wish to," Rasulullah 🕮 replied. They then built a pulpit and when Friday arrived, Rasulullah 🕮 went towards the pulpit. The palm against which Rasulullah 🕮 used to lean then screamed like a little child. Rasulullah 🕮 descended from the pulpit and embraced the palm, which continued sobbing like a little child being pacified. Jabir 🕮 says that the palm wept because of the Dhikr that it used to hear when Rasulullah 🕮 leaned against, which it could no longer hear. *(Bukhari in Al Bidayah wan Nihayah).* Another narration states that when the pulpit was built and Rasulullah 🕮 was standing upon it, the Sahabah heard the trunk of the palm make a sound like that of a camel. It was only when Rasulullah 🕮 went up to it and placed his hand on it that it stopped. *(Bukhari, Ahmad, Bazzar).* Yet another narration states that after the pulpit was made and Rasulullah 🕮 was standing upright upon it, the trunk started to shake and sob like a camel. Everyone in the Masjid could hear it and it was only when Rasulullah 🕮 descended the pulpit and embraced it that it calmed down and remained silent. *(Ahmad in Al Bidayah wan Nihayah, Ibn Abdul Birr in Jami).* A different narration states that Rasulullah 🕮 said, "Had I not taken it into my arms, it would have wept until the Day of Judgment." *(Abu Nu'aym in Dala'il).* In his account of the construction of the pulpit, Anas 🕮 says, "When Rasulullah 🕮 went towards the pulpit instead of the tree trunk, I heard it start to sob like someone longing for another. It then continued to sob until Rasulullah 🕮 descended from the pulpit, walked over to it and embraced it. Then only was it pacified." *(Ahmad).* Another narration from Anas 🕮 adds that

whenever Hasan narrated this Hadith, he would weep and say, "O servants of Allah! When a piece of wood can sob out of its longing for Rasulullah 🕮 because of his esteemed status in Allah's sight, you people ought to long to meet him even more." *(Baghawi, Abu Nu'aym in Al Bidayah wan Nihayah, Ibn Abdul Birr in Jami).* An extended narration adds that Rasulullah 🕮 said, "I swear by the Being Who controls the life of Muhammad! Had I not embraced it, it would have remained like this until the Day of Judgment out of its longing for Allah's Rasul 🕮." Rasulullah 🕮 then had it buried. *(Abu Ya'la, Tirmidhi in Al Bidayah wan Nihayah. Narrations have been Ubay bin Ka'b, Sahl bin Sa'd, Abdullah bin Abbas, Abdullah bin Omar, Abu Sa'eed Khudri, Aisha and Ummu Salama in Al Bidayah wan Nihayah)*

Salman 🕮 and Abu Darda 🕮 hear the Tasbih of a Plate of Food

Abul Bakhtari reports that Salman 🕮 was with Abu Darda 🕮 when the latter was busy lighting a fire beneath his pot. Abu Darda 🕮 suddenly heard a sound coming from the pot, which then loudly engaged in Tasbih in the voice of a child. The pot fell down, toppled over and then returned to where it had been without spilling any of its contents. "O Salman!" Abu Darda 🕮 called out, "Look at this astonishing thing! Look at something that neither you nor your father have ever seen!" Salman 🕮 remarked, "Had you remained silent, you would have heard something from the great signs of Allah." *(Abu Nu'aym in Hilya).* Qais narrates that Abu Darda 🕮 wrote to Salman or Salman 🕮 wrote to Abu Darda 🕮, they would remind each other about the miracle of the plate. Qais says, "It was common knowledge between us that the two were once busy eating, the plate and all the food it contained engaged in Tasbih." *(Abu Nu'aym in Hilya)*

Abdullah bin Amr 🕮 hears the Voice of a Fire

Ja'far bin Abu Imran reports that Abdullah bin Amr bin Al Aas 🕮 heard the fire say, "Me as well." When someone asked him what this meant, he explained, "I swear by the Being Who controls my life that even fire seeks Allah's protection from being returned to the fire of Jahannam." *(Abu Nu'aym in Hilya)*

Omar 🕮 hears the Words of a Devout Youngster

Yahya bin Ayub Khuza'i narrates that he heard from someone that there lived a youngster during the time of Omar 🕮 who was extremely devoted to worship and was always in the Masjid. Omar 🕮 was very impressed with him. The youngster had a very old father and would visit his father every day after performing the Isha salah. However, his road passed by the door of a woman who used to flaunt her charms by the roadside because she had become infatuated with him. As he passed by one night, she made a persistent effort to seduce him until he followed her. As she entered through her door and he was about to do the same, he remembered Allah. The evil intention vanished and the following verse of the Qur'an came to his tongue:(201) إِنَّ الَّذِينَ اتَّقَوْا إِذَا مَسَّهُمْ طَائِفٌ مِنَ الشَّيْطَانِ تَذَكَّرُوا فَإِذَا هُمْ مُبْصِرُونَ

Verily, those who are Al-Muttaqoon (the pious), when an evil thought comes to them from Shaitan (Satan), they remember (Allah), and (indeed) they then see (aright). (Al-A'raf:201)

The youngster immediately fell unconscious. The woman then called for her maidservant and with her help, the two of them carried him to his door. He was made to sit and his father's door was knocked. When his father came out to look for him, he found him unconscious in the doorway. He summoned for some of his family members and they together carried him inside the house. When the youngster regained consciousness after a considerable part if the night had passed, his father asked, "Dear son! How' are you?" "I am well," came the reply. When his father then asked him in the name of Allah what had happened, he informed his father about the incident. "Dear son," the father asked, "What was the verse you recited?" When the youngster recited the verse he had recited at the time, he again fell unconscious. Although the people tried to revive him, this time he had passed away. It was still night when they bathed him, shrouded him and buried him. It was only the following morning that the people informed Omar ؓ about it. Omar ؓ immediately went to console the father. "Why did you not inform me (of the funeral)?" Omar ؓ enquired. "O Amirul Mu'minin!" the father replied, "It happened during the night and we did not wish to disturb you." Omar ؓ then told them to accompany him to the grave and when they arrived there, Omar ؓ addressed the youngster by his name and recited the verse: وَلِمَنْ خَافَ مَقَامَ رَبِّهِ جَنَّتَان

(46) *But for him who (the true believer of Islamic Monotheism who performs all the duties ordained by Allah and His Messenger Muhammad ﷺ, and keeps away (abstain) from all kinds of sin and evil deeds prohibited in Islam and) fears the standing before his Lord, there will be 2 Gardens (i.e. in Paradise). (Ar-Rahman:46)*

The youngster responded twice from within the grave saying, "O Omar! My Rabb has already given me both these gardens in Jannah." *(Hakim in Kanzul Ummal, Ibn Asakir in Tafsir Ibn Kathir).* Another narration states that the youngster said, "Dear uncle! Go to Omar, convey my Salams to him and ask him what the reward will be for the person who fears standing before his Rabb." The end of this narration states that Omar ؓ went to the youngster's grave and said, "You shall have 2 gardens of Jannah. You shall have 2 gardens of Jannah." *(Bayhaqi in Kanzul Ummal)*

Omar ؓ hears the Speech of People Buried in Baqi Gharqad

Muhammad bin Himiar reports that when Omar ؓ once passed by Baqi Gharqad, the graveyard of Madinah, he said, "As Salamnu Alaykum, O people of the graves! The news from our side is that your spouses have remarried, others are occupying your homes, and your wealth has already been distributed." A voice then replied saying, "The news from our side is that we have found the good deeds we had sent ahead, we have seen the profits of the charity we spend and have lost out on that which we have left behind without spending in charity." *(Ibn Abi Dunya, Ibn Sam'ani in Kanzul Ummal)*

The Sahabah see People being Punished

Abdullah bin Omar ؓ narrates, "I was passing by the fringe of the plain of Badr when I was surprised to see a man emerge from a hole. He had a chain tied around his neck and was calling out, 'O Abdullah! Give me a drink! O Abdullah! Give me a drink! O Abdullah! Give me a drink!' I did not know whether he recognized me or whether he was just calling me as Arabs call people by addressing any person as Abdullah i.e. O servant of Allah. Just then another man came out of the hole. This man had a whip in his hand and he said to me, 'O Abdullah! Do not give him anything to drink because he is a Kafir.' The man then hit the first one and he returned into the hole. I then rushed back to Rasulullah ﷺ and when I reported it to him, he asked, 'Did you actually see him?' When I confirmed that I did, Rasulullah ﷺ explained, 'That was Allah's enemy Abu Jahal and that shall be his punishment until the Day of Judgment." *(Tabrani, Haythami)*

The Incident of Zaid bin Kharija ؓ

Sa'eed bin Musaib reports that the Ansari Zaid bin Kharija ؓ who belonged to the Banu Harith bin Khazraj tribe passed away during the Khilafa of Uthman bin Affan ؓ. After wrapping him in the burial shroud, the people heard some movement in his chest. He then started to speak, saying, "Ahmad! It is the name of Ahmad (Rasulullah ﷺ) that is written in the Lowhul Mahfudh. He spoke the truth. Abu Bakr Siddiq ؓ spoke the truth. Though he was a frail man, he was strong when it concerned Allah's commands. Such is it written in the Lowhul Mahfudh. He spoke the truth. Omar bin Khattab ؓ spoke the truth. He was powerful and trustworthy, just as it is written in the Lowhul Mahfoodh. He spoke the truth. Uthman bin Affan ؓ spoke the truth and is following in the pattern of the others. 4 years have passed and the other 2 to come will come with trials. The strong will then devour the weak and Judgment will take place. There shall soon come some startling news about your armies. And the well of Aris! What about the well of Aris?" Sa'eed reports further that a man belonging to the Banu Khatma tribe then passed away and after he was wrapped in his shroud, some movement was also heard from his chest. He then spoke and said, "Verily the man from the Banu Harith bin Khazraj tribe spoke the truth. He spoke the truth." *(Bayhaqi in Al Bidayah wan Nihayah, Ibn Abi Dunya).* Nu'man bin Bashir ؓ narrates that Zaid bin Kharija ؓ was walking in one of the alleyways of Madinah some time between the Zuhr and Asr salahs when he suddenly dropped down dead. He was taken to his family and shrouded with two sheets and a blanket. It was between the Maghrib and Isha salahs that the women of the Ansar gathered around his body and started to cry loudly. They then heard a voice say from beneath the blanket, "Be silent, O people!" When this was heard for a second time, the blanket was removed from his face and chest. He then said, "Muhammad ﷺ is the prophet of Allah, the unlettered Nabi and the seal of all Ambiya. Such is it written in the Lowhul Mahfudh." A while later, he again spoke and said, "He spoke the truth. Abu Bakr Siddiq ؓ spoke the truth. He was the strong and trustworthy. Though he was a frail man, he was strong when it concerned Allah's commands. Such is it written in the Lowhul Mahfudh." A while later he again spoke. This time he thrice said, "He spoke the truth. The one in the middle spoke the truth. He is the servant of Allah and the Amirul Mu'minin who never feared the reproach of those who reproach when acting for the pleasure of Allah. It was he who prevented the strong from devouring the weak. Such is it written in the Lowhul Mahfudh." A little later, he said, "Uthman is the Amirul Mu'minin. He is compassionate towards the Mu'minin and while 2 years (of peace) have already passed, another 4 still remain. People will then start to dispute, no unity will be left and even the trees will weep (meaning that the sanctity of things will be violated). Judgment will draw close and people will devour (the property and rights of) each other." *(Tabrani).* Another narration, Nu'man bin Bashir ؓ says, "When Zaid bin Kharija ؓ passed away, I was waiting for Uthman to come, thinking that he would perform 2 Rakahs salah. Just then, Zaid ؓ moved the shroud from his face and said, 'As Salamnu Alaykum! As Salamnu Alaykum!' Because the people of the house were busy talking and I was performing salah, I exclaimed, 'SubhanAllah! SubhanAllah!' Zaid ؓ then said to the people, 'Be silent! Be silent!'" The rest of the narration is like the one above. *(Tabrani in Kabeer and Awsat, Haythami).* Another narration states that Zaid ؓ's corpse said, "The one in the middle is the strongest of the three. He never feared the reproach of those who reproach when acting for the pleasure of Allah and he never instructed the strong to devour the weak. He is the servant of

Allah and the Amirul Mu'minin. He spoke the truth. He spoke the truth. Such is it written in the Lowhul Mahfudh." Thereafter, he said further, "Uthman is the Amirul Mu'minin. He forgives a great deal of the sins people commit. While 2 years (of peace) have already passed, another 4 still remain. People will then start to dispute and people will devour (the property and rights of) each other. No unity will be left and even brave heroes will weep. The Mu'minin will then start to retrogress. Such has it been decreed and recorded in Allah's Book. O people! Turn towards your Amir, listen to him and obey him because the blood of the person who becomes a ruler shall not be safe. Allah's decree has ordained and finalized. Allahu Akbar! Here is Jannah and here is Jahannam and all the Ambiya and the Siddiqin convey their Salams to you. O Abdullah bin Rawaha ؓ! Have you seen my father Kharija and Sa'd, both of whom were martyred in the Battle of Uhud?" Finally, before his voice fell silent, he recited the verse: كَلَّا إِنَّهَا لَظَى (15) نَزَّاعَةً للشَّوَى (16) تَدْعُوا مَنْ أَدْبَرَ وَتَوَلَّى (17) وَجَمَعَ فَأَوْعَى (18) *By no means! Verily, it will be the Fire of Hell! Taking away (burning completely) the head skin! Calling: "(O Kafir (O disbeliever in Allah, His angels, His Book, His Messengers, Day of Resurrection and in Al-Qadar (Divine Preordainments), O Mushrik (O polytheist, disbeliever in the Oneness of Allah)) (all) such as turn their backs and turn away their faces (from Faith) (picking and swallowing them up from that great gathering of mankind (on the Day of Resurrection) just as a bird picks up a food-grain from the earth with its beak and swallows it up). And collect (wealth) and hide it (from spending it in the Cause of Allah) (Al-Ma'arij:15-18)*

Another narration adds that Zaid ؓ also said, "And this is Ahmad Rasulullah ﷺ. May Allah's peace, mercy and blessings be showered on you, O Rasulullah ﷺ." *(Bayhaqi, Ibn Abi Dunya in Al Bidayah wan Nihayah, Ibn Mandah, Abu Nu'aym in Isabah)*. Nu'man bin Bashir ؓ says, "When a man from amongst us (Ansar) called Zaid bin Kharija ؓ passed away, we shrouded him and I stood up to perform salah. Just then I heard some noises and when I turned to look, I was surprised to see the body move. It then started to speak, saying, 'The strongest of them (the Khulafa) was the middle one. He was Allah's servant and the Amirul Mu'minin Omar ؓ. He was strong in his commands and in enforcing the commands of Allah. Amirul Mu'minin Uthman bin Affan ؓ. He is pure and chaste and forgives a great deal of the sins people commit. While 2 nights (years of peace) have already passed, another four still remain. People will then start to dispute and no unity will be left. O people! Turn towards your leader, listen to him and obey him. Here is Rasulullah ﷺ and Ibn Rawaha ؓ. Addressing Abdullah bin Rawaha ؓ, he then asked what has become of my father Kharija bin Zaid?'" Thereafter, before his voice fell silent, he added, "The well of Aris has been seized unjustly." *(Tabrani, Haythami, Hashim bin Ammar in Kitabul Ba'th, Al Bidayah wan Nihayah)*

Bringing the dead back to life: The Incident of a Woman from the Muhajirin and her Son

Anas bin Malik ؓ says, "When we once went to visit an ailing youngster of the Ansar, he happened to pass away very quickly. We closed his eyes and drew a sheet over his face. One of us said to his mother, 'Look forward to the rewards from Allah for exercising patience upon the death of your son.' 'Has he passed away?' she asked. When we confirmed that he had, she raised her hands to the heavens and made Du'a saying, 'O Allah! I have believed In You and migrated to Your Rasul ﷺ. Whenever I have been afflicted with any calamity, I have made Du'a to You and

You have always removed it. O Allah! I am now begging You not to burden me with this calamity.' The youngster then came back to life, removed the sheet from his face and when we sat down to eat, he ate with us." *(Ibn Abi Dunya)* Another narration states that the lady was Ummu Sa'ib and that she was extremely old and blind. *(Bayhaqi)*. Abdullah bin Aun narrates that Anas ؓ once said, "I have witnessed 3 occurrences in this Ummah that would have been unmatched by any other nation had they occurred amongst the Bani Isra'el." "O Abu Hamza!" the people around Anas said, "What are these occurrences?" Anas ؓ related, "We were on the Suffa with Rasulullah ﷺ when a lady who had just made Hijra arrived with her son who had already come of age. Rasulullah ﷺ attached the lady to the other ladies and the boy to us. It was not long thereafter that the boy was affected by the disease that afflicted the people of Madinah. After an illness of a few days, the boy passed away. Rasulullah ﷺ closed the boy's eyes and instructed that burial arrangements be made. We were just about to bathe him when Rasulullah ﷺ instructed me saying, 'O Anas! Go and inform his mother.' When I informed her, she came and sat by the boy's feet. Holding his 2 feet, she made Du'a to Allah saying, 'O Allah! I happily submitted to You and vehemently opposed the idols. I then migrated out of my yearning for You. O Allah! Do not let the idol-worshippers rejoice at my expense and do not burden me with a calamity that I am unable to bear.'" Anas ؓ says further, "By Allah! She had hardly ended her Du'a when the boy's feet started to move and he threw the sheet off his face. He then lived on until Rasulullah ﷺ passed away and until his mother also passed away... " The narration continues further and will be related later on. *(Bayhaqi in Al Bidayah wan Nihayah, Abu Nu'aym in Dala'il)*

The Incident of the Martyrs of the Battle of Uhud

Abu Nadhra reports that Jabir bin Abdullah ؓ said, "The night before the Battle of Uhud was fought, my father called for me and said, 'I feel that I will certainly be amongst the very first companions of Rasulullah ﷺ to be killed. By Allah! Of all the people I am leaving behind, there is none after Rasulullah ﷺ whom I love more than you. However, I have several debts, so do settle them for me. I would also like to advise you to treat your sisters well.' The next morning, my father was the first to be martyred and I buried him with another person in the same grave. However, it did not appeal to me later on to leave him in a grave with someone else. I therefore exhumed his body six months later and found to my surprise that everything apart from his ears were exactly as they were on the day I laid him to rest." *(Hakim)*. Another narration states that Jabir ؓ said, "After 6 months had passed, I could not allow myself to rest until I buried my father in a grave of his own. I therefore exhumed the body from the grave and found to my surprise that apart from a tiny portion of his earlobe, the ground had not eaten any part of his body." *(Ibn Sa'd)*. Yet another narration states that Jabir ؓ added, "I noticed nothing different about him apart from a few strands of hair from his beam that had been touching the ground." *(Ibn Sa'd in Al Bidayah wan Nihayah)*. Abu Zubair reports that Jabir ؓ said, "When Mu'awiya ؓ intended digging a canal, we were told to move the bodies of our martyrs who had been martyred at Uhud. Although this was 40 years afterwards after their deaths, their bodies were still supple and their limbs could still be bent." *(Ibn Sa'd)*. Another narration states that Jabir ؓ said, "When their bodies were exhumed after forty ears, they were still fresh and their limbs were still pliable." *(Abu Nu'aym in Dala'il, Kanzul Ummal)*. Some scholars from the Ansar say, "When Mu'awiya ؓ was digging the canal that passed by the martyrs of Uhud, it happened to burst its banks. We hurried there and exhumed the bodies of Amr bin Jamooh ♦ and Abdullah ♦. They both wore 2 sheets of cloth that covered their faces, while their feet were covered with some plants. As we removed the bodies from the graves, they were so supple and pliable that it appeared as if they had been buried only yesterday." *(Ibn Is'haq in Maghazi, Fat'hul Bari)*. In a lengthy narration, Jabir ♦ says, "it was during the Khilafa of Mu'awiya bin Abu Sufyan ♦ that a man came to me saying, 'O Jabir bin Abdullah! By Allah! Some of Mu'awiya's laborers have dug into your father's grave, causing some of his body to become exposed.' When I went there, I discovered that his body was exactly as it was when I buried him. The only parts that were not unscathed were of course those that were wounded in the battle. I then buried him again." *(Ahmad in Wafa'ul Wafa, Darmi in Awjaz)*. Abdur Rahman bin Abdullah bin Abdur Rahman bin Sa'sa'a reports that Amr bin Jamooh Sulami ♦ and Abdullah bin Amr Sulami ♦ were both martyred during the Battle of Uhud and shared one grave. Because floodwaters passed by their grave, it eventually eroded their grave and the grave was subsequently dug up so that their bodies could be moved from there. Their bodies were however found to be unchanged, appearing as if they had been buried just the day before. When one of them was wounded (in the battle), he placed his hand on the wound and was buried in this posture. When his hand was then moved off the wound (as the grave changed) and placed by his side, it returned to its former position. There was a time lapse of 46 years between the Battle of Uhud and the day their grave was dug up. *(Malik in Awjaz)*. Abdullah bin Amr ♦ was of reddish complexion, bald and not very tall whereas Amr bin Jamooh ♦ was a tall man. They were both recognized by these features and buried in one grave. Floodwaters however ran by their grave and eventually started to enter it. The bodies were therefore exhumed, still shrouded in a black and white striped sheet. Abdullah ♦ was wounded on the face and his hand was covering the wound. When his hand was moved off the wound, blood poured out of it but as soon as the hand was replaced, the blood stopped. Jabir ♦ says, "When I saw my father in his grave, he appeared to be sleeping because his appearance had not changed in the least bit." "And did you see his shroud?" someone asked. Jabir ♦ replied, "He was buried in a black and white striped sheet which covered his face, while his feet were covered with the rue plant. We found the sheet to be exactly as it had been and the rue plant also exactly as it had been, even though there had been a time lapse of 46 years." *(Ibn Sa'd)*. Jabir ♦ says, "When Mu'awiya ♦ started to dig the canal near the martyrs of Uhud 40 years after the battle, we were summoned to move them from their graves. We went there and while we were busy exhuming the bodies, a spade accidentally hit the foot of Hamzah ♦. Blood then actually started to pour out of the wound." *(Bayhaqi in Al Bidayah wan Nihayah)* Another narration states that when a spade hit the foot of Hamza, it started to bleed even though it was after forty years (of being buried). *(Abu Nu'aym in Dala'il)*. In his Wafa'ul Wafa, Sheikh Samhodi states that this incident occurred 3 times *(Awjaz)*; once after 6 months, again after 40 years the canal was dug and again after 46 years when floodwaters started to enter the grave. This conclusion is based on the many narrations supporting each of the 3 occasions. He states that this is a clear miracle of the Sahabah and has been repeated.

The Fragrance of Musk drifts from the Grave of Sa'd bin Mu'adh ♦

Muhammad bin Shurabil narrates that one of the Sahabah took a handful of sand from the grave of Sa'd bin Mu'adh ♦ and when he opened his fist, they saw to their surprise that it was musk. To this Rasulullah ﷺ exclaimed, "SubhanAllah! SubhanAllah!" and the joy was clearly visible on his face. *(Abu Nu'aym in Ma'rifa, Kanzul Ummal)*. Another narration states, "Someone took a handful of sand from the grave of Sa'd bin Mu'adh ♦ and then left. When he looked at it afterwards, he discovered that it was actually musk. *(Ibn Sa'd)*. Abu Sa'eed Khudri ♦ says, "I was amongst those who dug the grave of Sa'd bin Mu'adh ♦. Each time we shoveled out some sand, the fragrance of musk wafted on to us. This continued until we reached to the bottom of the grave." *(Ibn Sa'd)*

Martyred Sahabah are raised to the heavens: Amir bin Fuhaira ♦ is Lifted to the Sky

Urwa ♦ reports that after many Sahabah were martyred at Bir Ma'oona and Amr bin Umayya ♦ was taken prisoner, Amir bin Tufail pointed to one of the martyrs and asked, "Who is that?" When Amr ♦ informed him that the man was Amir bin Fuhaira ♦, Amir bin Tufail remarked, "After he was killed, I actually saw him being lifted so high into the skies that I eventually saw the sky between him and the ground. Thereafter, he was brought back down again." When the news of the massacre was brought to Rasulullah ﷺ by revelation, he informed the Sahabah about the deaths of the martyrs, saying, "Verily your companions have been martyred. They have however made a request to their Rabb saying, 'O our Rabb! Inform our brother on our behalf that we are pleased with You and that You are pleased with us.'" Amongst those who were martyred on that day were Urwa bin Asma bin Silt ♦ and Mundhir bin Amr ♦, after whom Urwa bin Zubair ♦ and Mundhir bin Zubair ♦ were named. *(Bukhari, Bayhaqi, Abu Nu'aym in Hilya)*. Another narration states that the person who killed Amir bin Fuhaira ♦ was a man named Jabbar bin Sulma Kalbi. When he stabbed Amir with his spear, Amir ♦ shouted, 'I swear by the Rabb of the Kabah that I am successful!" Some time after the incident took place, Jabbar asked some of the Sahabah what success Amir ♦ was referring to. When they explained that he was referring to the success of Jannah, he exclaimed, "By Allah! He must be right." Jabbar then also accepted Islam. May Allah be pleased with him. *(Waqidi)*. Urwa reports that because the body of Amir bin Fuhaira ♦ could not be found afterwards, the Sahabah were convinced that the angels had buried him. *(Musa bin Uqba in Maghazi, Al Bidayah wan Nihayah, Abu Nu'aym in Hilya)* Another narration states that Rasulullah ﷺ said, "The angels buried him and his soul was taken to the Illiyyeen (the place where the souls of the righteous are taken)." *(Abu Nu'aym in Dala'il, Ibn Sad)*. It is also reported that speaking about one of the Sahabah (martyred in the battle) Amir bin Tufail used to say, "When he was killed, he was lifted so high between the earth and the sky that I could see the sky beneath him." He was then informed that the person was Amir bin Fuhaira ♦. *(Abu Nu'aym in Hilya, Dala'il, Ibn Sa'd)*

The Body of Khubaib bin Adi ♦ is Protected

Arm bin Umayyah ♦ relates, "Rasulullah ﷺ sent me alone as a spy to the Quraish. I came to the pole where Khubaib ♦ was crucified and, keeping a lookout for spies from the Quraish; I climbed up the pole and untied the body. When he fell to the ground, I scurried away a short distance in case anyone's attention was drawn there. When the coast was clear I then went back but was unable to see Khubaib ♦. It appeared as if the earth had taken his body in and no trace was found of his body to this day." *(Ahmad, Tabrani, Haythami, Bayhaqi, in Al Bidayah wan Nihayah, Abu Nu'aym in Dala'il, Isabah)*. Dahhak narrates that

Rasulullah ﷺ dispatched Miqdad ؓ and Zubair ؓ to remove the body of Khubaib ؓ from the pole upon which he was crucified. When the two reached Tan'im, they found 40 drunk around the pole. They then took the body down and when Zubair ؓ loaded it on his horse, it was still fresh and had not started to decompose in the least. The Mushrikin were warned however and Zubair ؓ was forced to offload the body when the Mushrikin gained on them. The ground then immediately took his body in. It is because of this that Khubaib ؓ was called 'Bali'ul Ardh,' 'the one whom the ground took in. *(Abu Yusuf in Kitabul Lata'if, Isabah)*

The Body of Ala bin Hadhrami ؓ is Protected

Anas ؓ once said, "I have witnessed 3 occurrences in this Ummah that would have been unmatched by any other nation had they occurred amongst the Bani Isra'el."... The beginning of the narration has been quoted before. Another portion of the narration states, "It was only a short while later that Ala ؓ passed away. We then dug a grave for him, bathed him and buried him. After we had finished burying him, a man came and asked who the deceased was. 'He is the best of people,' we replied, 'he is Ibnul Hadhrami.' The man said, 'This ground casts bodies to the surface. Why do you not move him a mile or two away to some ground that accommodates bodies well.' We said, 'It is certainly not fitting reward for our companion to expose him to wild animals that will devour his body.' We then undertook to exhume the body, but when we reached the bottom of the grave, we found that he was not there. We saw to our amazement that as far as the eyes could see, the grave was filled with sparkling light. We therefore covered the grave again and left." *(Bayhaqi in Al Bidayah wan Nihayah).* Another narration from Abu Hurairah ؓ states, "When he passed away, we buried him in soft sand but we had not gone far when it occurred to us that wild animals would come and eat the body. We therefore returned, but could not find him anywhere." *(Tabrani, Haythami, Abu Nu'aym in Dala'il).* Abu Hurairah ؓ reports, "We then dug a grave for him with our swords without making a recess inside within which to fit the body. After burying him and proceeding further, one of the Sahabah said, 'We dug a grave without making a recess in it' When we then returned to make the recess, we were unable to find the site of his grave." *(Ibn Sa'd)*

The Body of Asim bin Thabit ؓ is Protected

The incident of Khubaib bin Adi ؓ has been quoted in details. The narration from Abu Hurairah ؓ states that Rasulullah ﷺ once sent an expedition under the command of Asim bin Thabit bin Aflah ؓ. The narration goes on further to state that Asim ؓ said, "As for myself, I shall never surrender into the custody of a Kafir." He had in fact taken a pledge with Allah that neither would he touch any Mushrik nor will any of them ever touch him. Further on the narration states that because Asim ؓ had killed one of the leaders of the Quraish during the Battle of Badr, the Quraish sent some people to bring a portion of his body to them which they may recognize as his. However, Allah sent a swarm of wasps to his body and they protected him from these people. It was because of this that he was called "Hami'ud Dabr," 'The one who was protected by a swarm of wasps'. *(Bukhari, Muslim in Isabah).* Urwa ؓ also states that the Mushrikin were about to cut off his head to send to the other Mushrikin in Makkah, Allah sent a swarm of wasps flying into their faces, which stung them and prevented them from severing his head. *(Abu Nu'aym in Dala'il)*

Wild animals are made subservient to the Sahabah and talk to them: Rasulullah ﷺ Speaks to Wolves and they Submit to Him

Hamza bin Abu Usaid ؓ reports that Rasulullah ﷺ once went to the graveyard of Baqi for the funeral of an Ansari. There however lay in the path, a wolf with its forelegs stretched out across the path. Rasulullah ﷺ said, "This wolf has come in search of its share, so give it to him." "What is your advice, O Rasulullah ﷺ?" the Sahabah asked. Rasulullah ﷺ said, "One goat should be given from each year from every grazing flock of 40 or more goats." "That still leaves plenty behind," the Sahabah remarked. Rasulullah ﷺ then made a gesture to the wolf to leave them, and it left. *(Bayhaqi).* Mutalib bin Abdullah bin Hantab reports that Rasulullah ﷺ was in Madinah one day when a wolf arrived and stood before him. Rasulullah ﷺ said, "This is the delegate of the wild animals to you. (He comes with the proposition that) If you wish to fix a portion (of your flocks) to give to them, they will take no more than that However, if you wish, you could leave them to be as they are and continue guarding against them. In that case, whatever they take from you will be their sustenance." "O Rasulullah ﷺ!" the Sahabah submitted, "We do not like the idea of fixing a portion for them." Rasulullah ﷺ then made a gesture with his 3 fingers to the wolf, telling it to leave them and it left with a howl. *(Waqidi).* A man from the Juhaina tribe narrates that a delegation from the wolves numbering almost a hundred once arrived at a time when Rasulullah ﷺ was performing salah and sat down waiting for him. Rasulullah ﷺ then said to the Sahabah, "This is a delegation from the wolves that have come with the proposition that you fix a share of your flocks for them, in which case the rest of your flocks will be safe from them." When the Sahabah, raised the issue of their poverty that they would be unable to afford the proposition, Rasulullah ﷺ told them to then send the wolves back. The wolves all left howling. *(Abu Nu'aym, Bayhaqi, Bazzar in Al Bidayah wan Nihayah)*

A Lion is Submissive to Rasulullah ﷺ's Freed slave Safina ؓ

Rasulullah ﷺ's freed slave Safina ؓ says, "I was once on board a ship when it shipwrecked. I managed to cling on to one of its planks, which carried me to a dense forest. A lion lived in the forest and when it saw me it started coming towards me to attack me. I however addressed it saying, "O Abu Harith! I am the freed slave of Rasulullah ﷺ." It immediately lowered its head as it came closer and continued nudging me with its shoulder until I was clear of the forest and on a main road. It then purred a gesture I interpreted as a word of farewell. That was the last I saw of it. *(Hakim by Dhahabi, Bukhari in Tarikh, Abu Nu'aym in Hilya and Dala'il, Ibn Mandah in Al Bidayah wan Nihayah, Tabrani in Majma'uz Zawa'id).* In another narration, Safina ؓ says, "We were once at sea when we were shipwrecked. When we managed to make our way to land we were lost and did not know the road when we suddenly beheld a lion that came before us. As my companions retreated, I went towards it and said, 'I am Safina, a companion of Rasulullah ﷺ and we have lost our way.' The lion then walked ahead of me until we reached the main road. Thereafter, it nudged me as if to point the road to me, but I sensed that it meant to bid us farewell." *(Bazzar, Tabrani, Haythami).* Ibn Munkadir reports that Rasulullah ﷺ's freed slave Safina ؓ was in Roman territory when he either became separated from the rest of the army or was taken prisoner. As he was searching for the army, he was suddenly confronted by a lion. He addressed the lion saying, "O Abu Harith! I am Rasulullah ﷺ's freed slave." He explained his situation and the lion came closer, with its tail wagging until it stood beside him.

The lion led him and each time the lion heard a sound of another animal, it would charge towards it scaring it away and then return to walk by Safina ﷺ's side. This continued until it brought him to the army, and it returned. *(Bayhaqi in Al Bidayah wan Nihayah)*

A Lion is Submissive to Abdullah bin Omar ﷺ

Wahab bin Aban Qurashi narrates that Abdullah bin Omar ﷺ was traveling on a journey when they saw a crowd of people standing by the road. "What is the matter with those people?" Abdullah ﷺ enquired. "There is a lion on the road frightening them," came the reply. Abdullah ﷺ got off his animal, walked up to the lion and held its ears. He twisted its ears, slapped its nape and moved it off the road. He said to himself, "Rasulullah ﷺ did not lie to you. I heard Rasulullah ﷺ say, 'Only that which man fears will be given the upper hand over him and if he fears none besides Allah, Allah will not allow anything to gain the upper hand over him. Man is handed over to that which he entertains hopes and if he pins his hopes in none other than Allah, Allah will not hand him over to anyone."*(Ibn Asakir in Kanzul Ummal)*

Auf bin Malik ﷺ speaks to a Lion

Auf bin Malik ﷺ reports, "I was sleeping in a church in Ariha, which was then already a Masjid in which salah was performed. When I awoke, I was shocked to see a lion also in the church walking towards me. I stood up in fear and rushed for my weapons when the lion said, 'Leave that alone. I have only been sent with a message for you.' 'Who sent the message?' I asked. The lion replied, 'Allah sent me to inform you that the extensively traveling Mu'awiya shall be amongst the dwellers of Jannah.' 'Which Mu'awiya is this?' I asked. 'The son of Abu Sufian,' came the reply." *(Tabrani, Haythami)*

A Wolf speaks to a Shepherd and Informs him About Rasulullah ﷺ

Abu Sa'eed Khudri ﷺ reports that .a wolf once attacked a goat and took it away. The shepherd however went after it and wrestled it from the wolf. The wolf then sat down on its tail and said, "Do you not fear Allah? You snatch away from me the sustenance that Allah has brought to me!" "How astonishing!" the shepherd exclaimed, "A wolf speaking like a human!" "Should I tell you of something even more astonishing?" the wolf asked, "Muhammad ﷺ is in Yathrib informing people of events that have occurred in the past." The shepherd then led his goats into Madinah, where he gathered them all in a corner of the town. He then went to Rasulullah ﷺ and related the incident to him. Rasulullah ﷺ had the announcement "As Salatu Jami'ah" made and when the people had gathered in the Masjid, he left his room for the Masjid. Rasulullah ﷺ then instructed the shepherd to relate the incident to the people and when he was done, Rasulullah ﷺ remarked, "He has spoken the truth. I swear by the Being Who controls the life of Muhammad ﷺ that Judgment will not come until wild animals talk with humans, until people speak with the ends of their whips and their shoe straps and until a man's thighs inform him about what his wife had been doing in his absence." *(Ahmad, Tirmidhi, Bayhaqi, Hakim, Hakim in Al Bidayah wan Nihayah)*. A similar incident occurred with Abu Sufyan bin Harb ﷺ and Safwan bin Umayyah ﷺ. They saw a wolf chasing after a deer but as soon as the deer entered the precincts of the Haram, the wolf broke off the chase. The 2 men expressed surprise at this, the wolf said, "More surprising than this is that Muhammad bin Abdullah ﷺ is in Madinah calling you towards Jannah while you are calling him towards Jahannam." To this Abu Sufyan ﷺ remarked, "I swear by Lat and Uzza that if you had to mention this in Makkah, the people would certainly forsake the city and head for Madinah." *(Ibn Wahab in Al Bidayah wan Nihayah)*

Waters are made subservient to the Sahabah: The River Nile of Egypt is made Subservient to Omar ﷺ

Qais bin Hajjaj reports from his teacher that after Egypt was conquered by the Muslims, the people approached the governor Amr bin Al Aas ﷺ when the month of Bu'na (month in Egyptian calendar) started. "O governor!," they said, "There is a ritual we carry out for our Nile without which it will not flow." "What is the ritual?" Amr ﷺ enquired. They then explained, "After twelve days of this month have passed, we look for a virgin living with her parents. After satisfying her parents with a vast sum of money, we adorn her with the best of jewels and clothing and then throw her into the Nile." "This cannot happen in Islam," Amr ﷺ told them, "Islam wipes out all rituals that take place before it." It so happened that the Nile did not flow and although the people stayed in Egypt all through the months of Bu'na, Abib and Masra, they eventually decided to leave Egypt. Amr ﷺ wrote a letter to Omar ﷺ and informed him about the situation. Omar wrote back to Amr ﷺ saying, "Your course of action was correct because Islam does indeed wipe out all that is practiced before it. I have enclosed a note with this letter that you should throw into the Nile as soon as the letter reaches you." The letter reached Amr ﷺ, he opened the note and found that the following was written on it:
"From Allah's servant Omar the Amirul Mu'minin
To the Nile of the Egyptian people
If you flow by your own accord, then you need not flow. However, if it is the One and All Powerful that makes you flow, then we ask the One and All Powerful to make you flow."

Amr ﷺ threw the note into the Nile a day before the day of Salib. The Egyptians were preparing to leave the country because it was only with the Nile that their affairs could run properly. On the morning of the day of Salib, the people found that the Nile was already flowing sixteen arm's length high. In this manner, Allah cut out this evil ritual of the Egyptian people. *(Ibn Abdul Hakam in Futuh Misr, Abu Sheikh in Adhma and Ibn Asakir in Muntakhab Kanzul Ummal, Lalka'ee in Tqfsir Ibn Kathir)*

The Ocean is made to Submit to Abu Raihana ﷺ

Urwa A'ma who was a freed slave of the Banu Sa'd tribe reports that Abu Raihana ﷺ was traveling by sea. He was busy mending a few notebooks of his when his needle fell into the ocean. He said, "O Rabb! I beg You in all earnestness to return my needle to me." His needle surfaces immediately and he was able to pick it up. *(Ibrahim bin Junaid in Kitabul Awliya, Isabah)*

The Ocean is made to Submit to Ala bin Hadhrami ﷺ

Abu Hurairah ﷺ reports, "I followed Ala bin Hadhrami ﷺ when Rasulullah ﷺ dispatched him to Bahrain. I witnessed 3 incidents with him and I cannot tell which of them was most astonishing: When we stood by the shore on one occasion, he said, 'Recite Bismillah and lunge into the ocean.' We recited Bismillah, lunged in and crossed the sea without even the hooves of our animals getting wet. On the return journey, we had to pass through an arid plain and had no water with us. When we brought this to his attention, he performed 2 Rakats salah and then made Du'a. There suddenly appeared a cloud the size of a shield, which rained down so heavily on us that we had enough water to drink and to give to our animals. When he passed away, we buried him in some soft sand, but after traveling a short distance, it occurred to us that wild animals would be able to easily dig up the grave and eat up the body. We therefore returned, but did not find his body in the grave." *(Abu Nu'aym in Hilya)*. Another narration states that Abu Hurairah ؓ added, "When Ibn Muka'bir the Persian governor saw us, he exclaimed, 'Never! By Allah! We can never fight such people!' He then boarded one of his ships and returned to Persia." *(Abu Nu'aym in Hilya, Tabrani, Haythami)*. Anas ؓ once said, "I have witnessed 3 occurrences in this Ummah that would have been unmatched by any other nation had they occurred amongst the Bani Isra'el....." The narration then continues to the point where Anas ؓ says, "Omar ؓ then prepared an army and appointed Ala bin Hadhrami ؓ as its commander. I was also one of the soldiers of this army and when we reached the place where we were to fight, we discovered that the enemy had been forewarned about our arrival. They fled the area and also destroyed every sign of water, because of which we and our animals experienced tremendous difficulty. It was an extremely hot Friday and as soon as the sun had crossed its meridian, Ala ؓ led us in 2 Rakats of salah. Thereafter, he stretched his arms out to make Du'a for rain. We could see nothing in the sky but he had hardly lowered his hands when Allah sent a wind and formed a cloud. The cloud rained so much that even the ponds and valleys were filled with water. We were able to drink water and give our animals to drink as well. When we caught up with the enemy, they had already crossed the gulf and reached an island. Standing on the shore of the Gulf, Ala ؓ said: يَا عَلِيُّ يَا عَظِيْمُ يَا حَلِيْمُ يَا كَرِيْمُ

Thereafter, he instructed us saying, 'Cross over with the name of Allah!' We then crossed over without even the hooves of our animals getting wet. It was only a short while later that we managed to attack the enemy on the island. We killed many of them, took many prisoners and many slaves as well. We then returned to the shore of the gulf, Ala ؓ said the same words and again we crossed over without even the hooves of our animals getting wet...." The narration still continues further. *(Baihaqi)*. Another narration quotes the Du'a of Ala ؓ with these words:

'O The All Knowing! O Most Forbearing! O The Most Exalted! O The Most High! We are Your servants. We are out in Your path, fighting Your enemy. Shower rains on us so that we may drink from it and make wudhu with it. And when we leave, do not grant any one else a share from it.' *(Bukhari in Tarikh)*
Yet another narration states that he added: إِجْعَلْ لَنَا سَبِيْلاً إِلَى عَدُوّكَ
'Forge for us a path to get to your enemy.' *(Bahr in Al Bidayah wan Nihayah)*

It is also reported that when the Sahabah entered the water, it barely reached their saddle blankets. *(Abu Nu'aym in Hilya)*. Another narration states that Abu Bakr ؓ dispatched Ala bin Hadhrami ؓ to fight the Murtaddin in Bahrain. The narration also describes how the camels carrying the army's provisions, their tents and drink ran away and then returned with everything they were carrying. The narration also mentions how Allah created a large pond of clear water right beside the Muslims and how they actually engaged the Murtaddin in battle. *(Ibn Jareer in Al Bidayah wan Nihayah)*. There is also a narration which states that Ala ؓ said to the Muslims, "Come with us to Darin to fight the enemy there. The Muslims were quick to respond to his call and he led them to the shore of the sea, thinking that they would board some ships. However, when Ala ؓ realized that the distance was too great and that the enemy would be long gone by the time they reached there with ships, he plunged into the water with his horse as he recited:

يَاأَرْحَمَ الرَّاحِمِين! يَاحَكِمُ! يَاكَرِيْمُ! يَا أَحَدُ! يَا صَمَدُ! يَا حَيُّ! يَا مُحْيِي! يَا قَيُّوْمُ!
يَا ذَالْجَلَالِ وَالإِكْرَامُ! لاَ إِلَهَ إِلاَّ أَنْتَ يَا رَبَّنَا!

He then instructed the others to recite the same words and to plunge into the water. They did as he bade them and, by the permission of Allah, they all crossed the gulf, walking as if there was only a shallow film of water over soft sand, which did not even submerge the hooves of their camels or reach the knees of their horses. The distance they covered would have taken an entire day and night by ship. When they reached the opposite shore, they fought the enemy, overpowered them and collected plenty of booty. They then returned and again crossed the gulf to where they had been. All this transpired within the space of a single day. *(Al Bidayah wan Nihayah, Ibn Jareer)*

The Tigris river is Subjugated for the Muslims During the Conquest of Mada'in

Ibn Rufail reports that the town of Bahursir was on the nearer bank of the Tigris River. When S'ad ؓ set up camp there, he searched for boats to take the Muslim army across the river to the town on the opposite bank. He was however unable to find any and discovered that the Persians had assembled all the boats together and taken them away. He therefore stayed on in Bahursir for several days of the month of Safar. Although the Muslims expressed their willingness to cross the river without boats, he refused to allow it, fearing for their safety. In fact, even when some Kuffar pointed out to him a crossing point in the river that would take them to the centre of the valley, S'ad ؓ was doubtful and refused to act. In the meantime, the water level was rising. S'ad ؓ then saw a dream that the horses of the Muslims dived into the water and crossed over the river even though the water level had risen extremely high. The interpretation of this dream made him resolve to cross the river. He therefore gathered the Muslims together and after duly praising Allah, he said, "Your enemy has been saved from you because of this river that prevents you from reaching them. They however are at liberty to get to you whenever they wish by boarding their boats and attacking you. You have of course the advantage of not having to worry about an attack from behind. I have therefore resolved to cross the river to get to them." The Muslims said in one voice, "May Allah grant you and us the resolve to do what is right. Let us do it." S'ad ؓ then prepared the army for the crossing. He first made an announcement saying, "Who will spearhead the crossing for us and secure the gorge for us so that the others may join them there and so that the enemy cannot prevent them from reaching the opposite bank?" Asim bin Arm ؓ volunteered for the task and he was followed by another six hundred brave men. S'ad ؓ appointed Asim ؓ as their commander and he led them to the bank of the Tigris. Standing at the bank, Asim said, "Who will volunteer with me to secure the gorge from the enemy?" 60 of them volunteered and Asim ؓ divided them into two groups; one group on mares and the other on stallions so that the swimming would be easier for the horses. They then plunged into the Tigris. When S'ad ؓ saw Asim ؓ at the gorge, ready to give them cover, he permitted the rest of the army to dive into the water. He instructed them to recite: نَسْتَعِيْنُ بِاللهِ وَنَتَوَكَّلُ عَلَيْهِ وَحَسْبُنَا
اللهُ وَنِعْمَ الْوَكِيْلُ لاَحَوْلَ وَلاَقُوَّةَ إِلاَّ بِاللهِ الْعَلِيّ الْعَظِيْمِ
"We seek help from Allah and rely only on Him. Allah is Sufficient for us and is the best of Defenders. There is no power or might except with Allah The Elevated, the Most High"

The bulk of the army waded behind each other over the deep waters, even as the Tigris was frothing with foam and was black in color (because of its depth and swift currents). The Muslims were even busy talking to each other as they crossed in pairs, just as people would talk to each other while walking over dry land. They caught the Persians totally by surprise by doing what they did not expect at all. The Persians were therefore forced to abandon the place in a hurry and did not even have time to take their belonging with them. It was in the month of Safar during the year 16 AH. that the Muslims entered the town and took possession of all of the 3,000,000,000 left behind in the rooms of the Emperor and all that the Emperor Shirway and those after him had amassed. *(Abu Nu'aym in Dala'il, Tarikh of Tabari, Al Bidayah wan Nihayah).* Abu Bakr bin Hafs bin Omar reports that the person traveling with Sa'd ؓ over the water was Salman Farsi ؓ. As their horses swam across, Sa'd ؓ was saying, "Allah is sufficient for us and He is the best of Defenders. By Allah! Allah will definitely assist His friends, make His Deen vanquish all others and defeat His enemies if the wrongs and sins of the army do not exceed their good deeds." Salman ؓ then remarked, "By Allah! Although Islam is new, the waters have been made subservient to the Muslims just as the land has been made such. I swear by the Being Who controls the life of Salman that the Muslims shall leave the waters in large droves just as they have entered." The Muslims then skimmed across the water, as if the only the banks and no water was visible. In fact, the Muslims were speaking more than if they were walking on land. Just as Salman ؓ said, they all emerged safely without anyone drowning and without even losing anything. *(Abu Nu'aym in Dala'il, Tabari).* Abu Uthman Nahdi says, "Everyone of the Muslims crossed over safely, except for a man from Bariq who was called Gharqada. He happened to slip off his brown horse and it is as if I can still picture his horse shake off her sweat from her mane as the man floated on the water. Qa'qa bin Arm ؓ then turned his horse towards the man, caught hold of his arm and pulled him across. No belongings of the Muslims were also lost apart from a cup that was tied with an old rope. When the rope snapped, the waters carried the cup away. Teasing the owner of the cup, another Muslim swimming with him said, 'Fate had to have your cup.' The owner however replied by saying, 'By Allah! I am convinced that Allah would not take away only my cup from all of the army.' It then happened that one of the soldiers guarding the gorge happened to see the cup as the winds and waves carried it to the shore. Using his spear, he managed to retrieve it and then took it to the army as they came across. He then announced for the owner, who was there to receive it." *(Abu Nu'aym in Dala'il, Ibn Jareer).* Umair Sa'idi reports that when Sa'd ؓ led the army into the Tigris, they went in as pairs. Salman ؓ was Sa'd ؓ's companion, traveling by his side through the water. Sa'd ؓ recited the verse: (38) ذَلِكَ تَقْدِيرُ الْعَزِيزِ الْعَلِيمِ *That is the Decree of the All-Mighty, the All-Knowing. (Ya Seen:38)* The water was turbulent and while the horses were able to stand up straight, whenever they became tired, a mound would appear for them to rest upon, as if they were on dry land. There was never an incident more astonishing than this in the history of Mada'in. It was a day when the water was abundant and it was therefore referred to as 'The Day of Mounds'. *(Ibn Jareer)* Another narration clarifies this point when it states that because a mound would appear for them to rest every time any of them grew weary; the day was referred to as 'The Day of Mounds'. *(Abu Nu'aym in Dala'il).* Qais bin Abu Hazim ؓ says, "When we entered the Tigris, it was filled to the brim. However (by Allah's doing), when a horseman stood at the point where the water was at its deepest, it reached only up to his reins." *(Ibn Jareer, Abu Nu'aym in Dala'il).* Habib bin Suhban reports that one of the Muslims by the name of Hujr bin Adi said to the others, "What prevents you from crossing over to the enemy? Is it this little droplet?" Here he was referring to the Tigris. He then

recited the verse: وَمَا كَانَ لِنَفْسٍ أَنْ تَمُوتَ إِلَّا بِإِذْنِ اللّٰهِ كِتَابًا مُؤَجَّلًا *And no person can ever die except by Allah's Leave and at an appointed term... (Al-Imran:145)*

He then plunged into the Tigris with his horse and, seeing him, the others followed suit. When the enemy saw them, they exclaimed, 'Madmen!" and ran away. *(Ibn Abi Hatim in Tafsir Ibn Kathir).* Habib bin Suhban Abu Malik narrates that when the Persians saw the Muslims crossing the Tigris the day they conquered Mada'in, they called out in Persian, "Mad devils are coming!" They then said to each other, "By Allah! It is not humans that you are fighting against, but Jinn!" In this way, they were defeated. *(Abu Nu'aym in Dala'il, Ibn Jareer).* A'mash reports from a companion of his that when they reached the Tigris River, the water level was very high and the Kuffar had already crossed over. One of the Muslims said, "Bismillah!" and then plunged into the water with his horse. The horse rode over the water. The other Muslims then all said "Bismillah" and plunged into the water. Their horses also rode above the water. Seeing them, the Kuffar exclaimed, "Madmen! Madman!" They then all fled. *(Bayhaqi in Al Bidayah wan Nihayah)*

A Fire obeys Tamim Dari ؓ

Mu'awiya bin Harmal reports, "When I arrived in Madinah, Tamim Dari ؓ took me home to eat. Although I ate hungrily, I did not seem to get enough because of the extreme hunger I was suffering on account of remaining 3 days in the Masjid without eating anything. We were sitting together one day when a fire emerging from Harra, a rocky terrain near Madinah. Omar ؓ then came to Tamim ؓ saying, 'Go and see to that fire!' 'Who am I and what am 'I'?' Tamim ؓ said. Omar ؓ however insisted until Tamim ؓ went with him. Mu'awiya reports that he followed them as they proceeded to the fire where Tamim ؓ rounded up the fire with his bare hands until it returned into the gap it had come out from, with Tamim ؓ behind it. Omar ؓ then remarked, 'The one who has witnessed this can never be like the one who has not because it serves to boost one's Iman.'" *(Abu Nu'aym in Dala'il, Bayhaqi in Al Bidayah wan Nihayah).* Mu'awiya bin Harmal says, "I once went to Omar ؓ saying, 'O Amirul Mu'minin! I have come to repent before being caught for fighting by the side of Masailama Kadhab.' 'Who are you?' Omar ؓ asked. 'I am Mu'awiya bin Harmal, Musailama's son-in-law,' I replied. He then said to me, 'Go and stay with the best person in Madinah.' I then went to stay with Tamim Dari ؓ. We were busy talking one day when a fire emerged from Harra. Omar ؓ came to Tamim ؓ, saying, 'Go, O Tamim!' Humbling himself, Tamim ؓ said, 'Who am I? Are you not afraid that my inner self may become exposed?' He then got up and pushed the fire back through the door it came out from. He even went through the door behind it and later came out without the fire harming him in the least. *(Bagawi, Isabah).* Another narration states that Omar ؓ said to Tamim ؓ, "It is for emergencies like this that we keep you hidden, O Abu Ruqaya." *(Abu Nu'aym in Dala'il)*

Light appears for Hasan ؓ and Husain ؓ

Abu Hurairah ؓ reports, "We were once performing the Isha salah behind Rasulullah ﷺ when Hasan ؓ and Husain ؓ jumped on Rasulullah ﷺ's back as he prostrated in Sejda. When he got up from Sejda, Rasulullah ﷺ gently lowered them off his back but as soon as he went back into Sejda, they again jumped on his back. When Rasulullah ﷺ finally completed the salah, he put them to sit on his lap. I then got up and offered, 'O Rasulullah ﷺ! Should I take them back home?' Just then a streak of lightning flashed and Rasulullah ﷺ said to the 2 boys, 'You had better be going to your mother.' The light of the lightning then remained to guide them home on that very dark night until they entered their mother's house." *(Ahmad, Bazzar, Haythami, Bayhaqi in Al Bidayah wan Nihayah).* Abu Hurairah ؓ says, "Rasulullah ﷺ loved his grandson Hasan ؓ very much. Hasan ؓ was with Rasulullah ﷺ on a dark night, when the boy said, 'Should I now return to my mother?' 'Should I go with him, O Rasulullah ﷺ?' I offered. 'you need not,' Rasulullah ﷺ replied. Just then a flash of lightning streaked across the sky and Hasan ؓ walked in its light until he reached his mother." *(Abu Nu'aym in Dala'il)*

Light Appears for Qatadah bin Nu'man ؓ from a Branch

In a narration discussing the special moment of the day of Jumu'a, Abu Sa'eed Khudri ؓ reports that there was a heavy storm that night and when Rasulullah ﷺ emerged for the Isha salah, a streak of lightning flashed. In its light, Rasulullah ﷺ saw Qatadah bin Nu'man ؓ. "How did you come in the darkness, O Qatada?" Rasulullah ﷺ asked. Qatadah replied, "O Rasulullah ﷺ! I knew that there will be few people attending the salah tonight, so I wished to be here." Rasulullah ﷺ then said to him, "Stay where you are after the salah until I come pass you." When Rasulullah ﷺ turned after the salah, Rasulullah ﷺ gave Qatadaha ؓ branch of a date palm saying, "Take this. It will light up 10 arm's lengths in front of you and the behind you, When you then enter your house and see a black figure in the comer of the house, hit it with this branch because it is a Saitan." *(Ahmad, Bazzar, Haythami).* Qatadah ؓ says, "Rasulullah ﷺ gave me the branch of a date palm and said, 'Verily a Shaitan went to your family after you left. You must therefore take this branch and continue holding it until you reach your house. You must then grab him in the corner of your house and hit him with this branch. When I then left the Masjid, the branch lit up brilliantly like a candle and I used its light to reach my home. My family was all asleep and when I looked in a comer, I saw a hedgehog. I continued hitting it until it left the house." *(Tabrani, Haythami)*

A light Appears for Usaid bin Hudhair ؓ and Abbad bin Bishr ؓ

Anas ؓ reports that when 2 companions of Rasulullah ﷺ left his company one night, lights appeared in front of them like 2 lanterns. When their paths split, a light went with each one of them and stayed with them until they reached their homes. *(Bukhari).* Anas ؓ narrates that Usaid bin Hudhair ؓ and another Sahabi from amongst the Ansar once happened to be discussing a need of theirs with Rasulullah ﷺ when a considerable portion of the night passed them by. When they eventually left Rasulullah ﷺ to return home, the night was extremely dark. Each one of them was carrying a staff with him and one of their staffs suddenly lit up so that the 2 of them could walk in its light. When their paths split, the other person's staff also lit up and both of them were able to reach their homes in the light of the own staffs. *(Abdur Razzaq).* This happened to Usaid bin Hudhair ؓ and Abbad bin Bishr ؓ. *(Bukhari in Tarikh, Bayhaqi, Tabrani in Al Bidayah wan Nihayah, Haythami, Abu Nu'aym in Dala'il)*

Light Appears from the Fingers of Hamza bin Amr Aslami ؓ

Hamza bin Amr Aslami ؓ says, "We were with Rasulullah ﷺ during one extremely dark night. When we left, my fingers started to shine so brightly and for so long that the others were able to round up their conveyances and whatever they had dropped." *(Bukhari in Tarikh, Bayhaqi, Tabrani in Al Bidayah wan Nihayah, Haythami, Abu Nu'aym in Dala'il).* Hamza bin

Amr ؓ says, "We were in Tabuk when some of the Munafiqin made Rasulullah ﷺ's camel bolt. As a result of this, some of his luggage fell off. All 5 of my fingers then lit up and in its light I was able to pick up everything that had fallen, such as a whip, a rope and other such items." *(Ibn Sa'd)*

A Staff lights up for Abu Abs ؓ

Zaid bin Abu Abs narrates that his father Abu Abs ؓ used to return to the locality of the Banu Haritha tribe after every salah that he performed behind Rasulullah ﷺ. It was an extremely dark and rainy night once when he left the Masjid and his staff suddenly lit up so much that he managed to reach the Banu Haritha locality. Abu Abs ؓ was a veteran of the Battle of Badr. *(Bayhaqi in Al Bidayah wan Nihayah, Abu Nu'aym in Dala'il, Hakim).* Another narration states that Rasulullah ﷺ gave Abu Abs bin Jabr ؓ a staff after his eyesight had become very weak. Rasulullah ﷺ told him to use the light from it to walk in and it used to light up a considerably area for him. *(Isabah)*

A Whip Lights up for Tufail bin Amr Dowsi ؓ

Tufail bin Amr Dowsi ؓ was a Sahabi for whom Rasulullah ﷺ made Du'a so that his whip would shine brightly. He used to use the light of the whip to see in the darkness. *(Ibn Mandah, Ibn Asakir in Kanzul Ummal).* The incident of Tufail bin Amr Dowsi ؓ has already been quoted in the chapter discussing Da'wah. In that narration, Tufail ؓ says that he then went to his people and was at a valley from which he could see the people present there when a light radiated from between his eyes like a lantern. He then prayed, "O Allah! Not on my face because my people will think that this is a form of punishment affecting my face because I had left my religion." He narrates further, "The light then moved to the top of my whip. The people present then showed each other the light on my whip which resembled a suspended lantern as I descended the valley towards them." Abdullah bin Abbas ؓ reports that his father Abbas bin Abdul Muttalib ؓ would often say, "Whenever I treat someone well, I see a light appear between him and I and whenever I treat someone badly, I see darkness between him and I. You must therefore ensure that you treat people well and do good because this saves you from an evil death." *(Ibn Asakir in Kanzul Ummal)*

The Clouds Shade the Sahabah

A freed slave of Ka'b ؓ says, "We were once on a journey with Miqdad bin Aswad ؓ, Amr bin Abasa ؓ and Shafi bin Habib Hudhali ؓ. Amr bin Abasa ؓ went out to graze the animals one day and it was midday when I went to see him. I noticed to my surprise that a cloud was shading him and never parted from him, it went wherever he went. When I brought this to his notice, he said, 'If I ever find out that you have informed anyone about this, there would be serious .problems between us.' By Allah! I then never disclosed this to anyone until after he had passed away." *(Abu Nu'aym in Isabah)*

Rain falls by the Du'a of Rasulullah ﷺ

Anas ؓ reports that Rasulullah ﷺ was delivering a sermon from the pulpit on a Friday when a man entered the Masjid from a door that was directly in front of Rasulullah ﷺ. "O Rasulullah ﷺ!" the man said, "Our animals have been destroyed and all our avenues to earning a living have been cut off because of the drought. Do pray to Allah to send us rains." Rasulullah ﷺ raised his hands and made Du'a saying, "O Allah! Give us rain. O Allah! Give us rain. O Allah! Give us rain." Anas ؓ says, "By Allah! We could not see any cloud, any semblance of a cloud or anything else in the sky. There were no houses or buildings between us and the Sila mountain to obstruct our view and we clearly saw a cloud the size of a shield rise from behind the mountain. When it reached the centre of the sky, it spread out and started to rain. By Allah! We did not even see the sun for the next 6 days." The following Friday, Rasulullah ﷺ was again standing and delivering the sermon when the man came in front of Rasulullah ﷺ saying, 'O Rasulullah ﷺ! Our animals have been destroyed and all our avenues (to earning a living) have been cut off because of the floods. Do pray to Allah to stop the rains.' Rasulullah ﷺ then raised his hands and prayed, 'O Allah! Send the rains around us and not upon us. O Allah! Send them on the higher grounds, on the mountains and in the areas where trees and vegetation grow.' The rain stopped immediately and we were walking in the sun when we left the Masjid." In another narration, Anas ﷺ says, "I then saw the clouds scatter to the right and the left, and it continued raining everywhere else except on Madinah itself." In another narration, he says, "When Rasulullah ﷺ raised his hands; we could not see a trace of cloud in the sky. I swear by the Being Who controls my life that Rasulullah ﷺ had barely dropped his hands when clouds the size of mountains had gathered. By the time Rasulullah ﷺ descended from the pulpit, I could see water dripping from his beard." (Bukhari, Muslim, Abu Dawood, Ahmad in Al Bidayah wan Nihayah, Abu Nu'aym in Dala'il, Ibn Sa'd). Abu Lubaba bin Abdul Mundhir ﷺ reports that Rasulullah ﷺ was delivering a sermon from the pulpit one Friday when he made Du'a saying, "O Allah! Send us rain." Abu Lubaba ﷺ then said, "O Rasulullah ﷺ! The dates are already in the granaries." To this, Rasulullah added, "O Allah! Give us rain until Abu Lubaba has to remove his clothes and plug the gutter of his storage with his loincloth." Although there were no clouds in the sky, a heavy rain started to fall and the Ansar went to Abu Lubaba ﷺ saying, "O Abu Lubaba! The sky will never hold up until you do as Rasulullah ﷺ mentioned." Abu Lubaba ﷺ then removed his clothes and plugged the gutter of his storage with his loincloth." It was only then that the rain stopped. (Abu Nu'aym in Dala'il, Bayhaqi in Al Bidayah wan Nihayah). In the chapter discussing the hardships that Rasulullah ﷺ and the Sahabah bore, the narration has already been quoted stating that Rasulullah ﷺ then raised his hands to the heavens to make Du'a and had not yet lowered his hands when clouds started gathering in the sky. First a drizzle fell and then the rains came pouring down. The Sahabah filled whatever containers they had and when we left the place, we discovered that the rain had not fallen further than the area where the army was camped." (Ibn Jareer, Bazzar, Tabrani). Abdullah bin Abu Bakr bin Aiash bin Sahal reports that on one morning when the Sahabah had no water with them, they took the matter to Rasulullah ﷺ. Rasulullah ﷺ made Du'a to Allah, upon which Allah sent a cloud. The cloud brought so much rain that the people could satisfy themselves and were able to carry away enough water to tend to all their needs. (Abu Nu'aym in Dala'il)

Rains fall by the Du'a of Omar ﷺ

Khawwat bin Jubair narrates that when a severe drought afflicted the people during the time of Omar ﷺ, he took them out of the town and led them in 2 Rakats salah. Thereafter, he overturned his shawl, bringing the right side on the left and vice versa. He then stretched out his arms and made Du'a saying, "O Allah! We beg Your forgiveness and ask You to send us rain." Omar ﷺ had not yet moved from his place when rain started to fall. Some days later, some Bedouins arrived in Madinah. They went to Omar ﷺ and explained that they were in their valley on a

certain day and at a certain time when some clouds covered them and they heard a voice from the cloud say to them, "O Abu Hafs (Omar ﷺ)! Help has come to you. O Abu Hafs! Help has come to you." (Ibn Abi Dunya, Ibn Asakir in Kanzul Ummal). Malik Dar narrates that when a drought afflicted the people during the time of Omar ﷺ, someone went to Rasulullah ﷺ's grave and said, "O Rasulullah ﷺ! Beseech Allah to send rain to your Ummah because they are being devastated. The man then saw Rasulullah ﷺ in a dream in which Rasulullah ﷺ said to him, "Go to Omar and convey my Salams to him. Inform him that rain will soon come and that he should continue applying his intelligence." When the man conveyed the message to Omar ﷺ, the Amirul Mu'minin started to weep as he said, "O my Rabb! I am applying all I have, but some matters are beyond me." (Bayhaqi in Kanzul Ummal, Al Bidayah wan Nihayah)

Abdur Rahman bin Ka'b bin Malik reports that the Year of Ashes of drought brought starvation to the people of Madinah and its surroundings, causing much devastation. It was so severe that wild animals started coming into towns in search of food and people would actually not slaughter their goats seeing the poor condition of the animals even though they were so much in need of eating them. While all this was happening, Omar ﷺ did not think of seeking food aid from the other territories such as Egypt, Iraq and Sham until Bilal bin Harith Muzani ﷺ arrived one day and sought permission to see Omar ﷺ. "I am Rasulullah ﷺ's messenger to you," he said, "Rasulullah ﷺ says to you, 'I have always known you to be an intelligent person and you have always remained such. What has happened to you now?" "When did you see the dream of Rasulullah ﷺ?" Omar ﷺ asked. "Last night," came the reply. Omar ﷺ left and then had the announcement "As Salatu Jami'ah!" made. When the people had gathered he then led them in 2 Rakats salah, after which he addressed them saying, "O people! I ask you in the name of Allah to tell me whether you think I would do something that is not the best for you." "Never," they all replied in one voice. He then related to them what Bilal bin Harith ﷺ said to him, to which the people's response was: "Bilal is right. You should seek aid from Allah and from people as well." This was the solution that Omar ﷺ was up to this point unable to fathom. He therefore started sending messengers to the various territories. "Allahu Akbar!" Omar ﷺ exclaimed, "The calamity is drawing to an end and will soon be alleviated. Calamities are removed from people when they are inspired to ask from Allah." His message to the governors of the other Muslim territories was, "Assist the people of Madinah because they have reached the peak of suffering." Omar ﷺ also took the people out to perform Salatul Istisqa, a special salah to pray for rain. Abbas ﷺ walked with him and after delivering a brief lecture, he led the people in salah. Omar ﷺ then knelt down and made Du'a saying, "O Allah! Only You do we worship and only from You do we seek assistance. O Allah! Forgive us, have mercy on us and be pleased with us." He then left. It then rained so much that as the people were returning home, they had to wade through pools of water. Another narration adds that when a family of Bedouins from the Muzaina tribe requested their father to slaughter a goat for them to eat, he told them that the goats were not worth eating. They however insisted and when he eventually slaughtered it and removed the skin, all he saw inside were red bones and no meat. To this he exclaimed, "O Muhammad ﷺ pray for your Ummah." In a dreamlike state, he then saw Rasulullah ﷺ come to him and say, 'Rejoice with the news of rain. Go to Omar, convey my Salams to him and say, 'Your pledge with me is still strong and you have always been one who fulfils his pledges. O Omar! Apply your intelligence. Apply your intelligence." He then went to Omar ؓ and when he arrived at the door, he said to Omar ؓ's slave, "Seek entry for the messenger of Rasulullah ﷺ...." The narration is then similar to the one above. *(Ibn Jareer)*

Rain falls by Du'a of Mu'awiya ؓ and Yazid bin Aswad Jurashi ؓ

Sulaiman bin Amir Khaba'iri narrated that when a drought struck, Mu'awiya bin Abu Sufyan ؓ went out of the town with the people of Damascus to make Du'a for rain. When Mu'awiya ؓ sat on the pulpit, he asked, "Where is Yazid bin Aswad Jurashi ؓ?" The people called for Yazid ؓ and he came forward, climbing over people's shoulders. By Mu'awiya ؓ's commend, he also mounted the pulpit and sat a step below Mu'awiya ؓ. Mu'awiya ؓ then made Du'a saying, "O Allah! Today we are making the best and most virtuous amongst us an intercessor before You. O Allah! We are making Yazid bin Aswad Jurashi ؓ our intercessor before You. O Yazid! Raise your hands before Allah. Yazid them raised his hands and so did all the people present. It was almost immediately that a cloud wafted into the sky from the west, a wind blew and so much rain fell that the people were almost unable to reach home. *(Ibn Sa'd)*

Rain falls by the Du'a of Anas ؓ

Thumama bin Abdullah reports that the keeper of one of Anas ؓ's orchards once came to him during the summer months, complaining of a shortage of water. Anas ؓ sent for some water, made wudhu and performed salah. "Do you see anything (any clouds)?" Anas ؓ asked him. "I see nothing," the man replied. Anas ؓ then returned to his room and performed salah again. This happened three or 4 times, after which the man informed Anas that he could see a cloud the size of a bird's wing. Anas ؓ then continued performing salah and making Du'a until the keeper eventually came to him saying, "The sky became overcast and rain has fallen." Anas ؓ then said to him, "Take the horse that Bishr bin Shaghaf sent and see up to which point the rain fell" The man did as told and saw to his surprise that the rain did not fall further than the areas of Musayyirin and Ghadban where Anas ؓ's properties were located. The rain did not fall any further than Anas's land. *(Ibn Sa'd)*

Rain falls by the Du'a of Hujr bin Adi ؓ

While being held captive by Mu'awiya ؓ's forces Hujr bin Adi ؓ one day needed to have a bath. He therefore said to the guard, "Give me the water I am to drink so that I may purify myself and you need not give me my share tomorrow." The guard refused saying, "I fear that you may then die of thirst and Mu'awiya ؓ would kill me for it." Hujr ؓ then made Du'a to Allah and a cloud rained down on him, allowing him to have as much water as he required. Seeing this his companions requested him to make Du'a for their freedom. He however made Du'a saying, "O Allah! Choose for us what is best between freedom and martyrdom." As a result, Hujr ؓ and all his companions were martyred. *(Ibrahim bin Junaid in Kitabul Awliya, Isabah)*

Rain falls on the Graves of a Tribe of the Ansar Because of a Prior Du'a that Rasulullah ﷺ had made for Them

Hasan reports that a tribe of the Ansar were blessed with a Du'a that Rasulullah ﷺ had made for them, as a result a cloud would rain upon the grave of any of them who passed away. One of their freed slaves passed away, they said, "Today we shall see the truth of Rasulullah ﷺ's statement that the freed slave of a tribe is one of them." After they had buried the man, a cloud appeared and rained on his grave as well. *(Ibn Asakir in Kanzul Ummal)*

Receiving Drink from a Bucket Suspended from the Sky

Uthman bin Qasim narrates that when Ummu Ayman ؓ migrated to Madinah, she reached a place called Munsarif by the evening, which was just before Rowha. She had been fasting that day and was extremely thirsty, but had no water. When the thirst became unbearable, a bucket of water suspended from a white rope was lowered down to her from the sky. She took hold of it and drank to her fill. Thereafter, she would always say, "I never felt thirsty after that incident. In fact, I would even go out during midday on extremely hot days while fasting, but would not get thirsty after that drink. Fasting during very hot days therefore never made me thirsty." *(Ibn Sa'd)*

The Blessings in Water where Rasulullah ﷺ put his Hand and Saliva

Anas bin Malik ؓ says, "The time for Asr had arrived and I saw people looking for water to make wudhu, but were unable to find any. When some water was brought for Rasulullah ﷺ to make wudhu, he placed his hand in the utensil and instructed the people to make wudhu from it. I then actually saw water gushing forth from beneath Rasulullah ﷺ's fingers and every single person was able to make wudhu from that water." *(Bukhari, Muslim, Tirmidhi, Nasa'ee, Ahmad)*. Anas ؓ says, "When the Adhan was called out for salah, everyone who lived close to the Masjid got up (to go home to make wudhu), while all those living far from the Masjid remained behind. A stone basin was brought to Rasulullah ﷺ but it was too small for him to open his hand in it. Rasulullah ﷺ therefore kept his fingers closed, placed it in the water and then told the people there to make wudhu. As the water flowed from Rasulullah ﷺ's fingers all of them were able to make wudhu." When someone asked Anas ؓ how many they were, he replied that they were 80 or more. *(Tirmidhi, Bukhari)*. Anas ؓ reports that a utensil was brought to Rasulullah ﷺ when he was in a place called Zowra. He then placed his hand in the utensil and water started to flow from his fingers. The people were then able to make wudhu with the water. When Anas ؓ was asked how many they were, he replied that they were 300 or close to 300. *(Bukhari, Muslim, Ahmad in Al Bidayah wan Nihayah, Abu Ny'aym in Dala'il, Ibn Sa'd)*. Bara bin Azib ؓ says, 'We were 1,400 people at Hudaybiya and although Hudaybiya is itself a well, we drew so much water from it that not a drop of water was left. Rasulullah ﷺ then sat on the rim of the well, made Du'a for water, gargled his mouth and then spat the water out into the well. A short while later, we were able to draw so much water that we were satisfied and even our animals were satisfied." *(Bukhari in Al Bidayah wan Nihayah, Abu Nu'aym in Dala'il. The incident of Treaty of Hudaybiya has already been quoted before. Jabir bin Abdullah ؓ reports that the Sahabah suffered a shortage of water during their stay at Hudaybiya and only Rasulullah ﷺ had a leather bag of water with him from which he made wudhu. The Sahabah were close to tears when they came to Rasulullah ﷺ, because of which he asked, "What is the matter?" They replied, "We have no water with which to make wudhu or to drink. All the water there is that which is before you." Rasulullah ﷺ placed his hand in the bag and water started to flow from between his fingers like a spring. The Sahabah had enough to make wudhu and to drink. When someone asked Bara ؓ how many they were, he replied, "It would have been enough even if we were 100,000. We were 1,500 however." *(Bukhari, Muslim in Al Bidayah wan Nihayah, Abu Nu'aym in Dala'il, Ibn Sa'd in Tabaqat)*. Abdullah bin Mas'ood ؓ says, "We were with Rasulullah ﷺ on a journey when the time for salah arrived. We had only a little water with us and Rasulullah ﷺ asked for it and poured it into a dish. He then placed his hand into the dish and water started to gush from between his fingers. He then announced, 'Come to make wudhu and get the blessings from Allah.' The Sahabah arrived and they all made wudhu. I beat them all to the water and drank some because Rasulullah ﷺ said that it was blessings from Allah." *(Abu Nu'aym in Dala'il, Bukhari in Al Bidayah wan Nihayah)*

Blessings in the Water that was Poured in Rasulullah ﷺ's Utensil

Abdullah bin Mas'ood ؓ says, "We were with Rasulullah ﷺ on a journey when he asked whether we had any water with us. 'Yes,' I replied, 'I have some water in the container I use for wudhu.' Rasulullah ﷺ asked me to bring it and I did. Rasulullah ﷺ then told us to have small sips from it, after which he made wudhu with it. When there was only a drop of water inside, Rasulullah ﷺ said, 'O Abu Qatada! Look after this because it will soon be big news.' When the afternoon grew unbearably hot and Rasulullah ﷺ checked on the Sahabah, they said, 'O Rasulullah ﷺ! The thirst is killing us and we will soon be destroyed.' 'No destruction will come to you,' Rasulullah ﷺ assured them. Rasulullah ﷺ then called for me to bring the container and when I did, Rasulullah ﷺ said to me, 'Now open my container.' I opened Rasulullah ﷺ's container, gave it to him and he poured the water into it. He then started to give the people to drink, but when they began to crowd around him, he said, 'O people! Be considerate, do not push. All of you will have to his heart's content.' Everyone had their fill to drink and eventually it was only Rasulullah ﷺ and myself left. Rasulullah ﷺ poured some water out for me saying, 'You drink, O Abu Qatada.' 'You drink first, O Rasulullah ﷺ,' I insisted. Rasulullah ﷺ said, 'The one serving drinks to people is the last to drink.' Rasulullah ﷺ drank after me and there was still as much water left in my container as there had been. The people on that day who drank from the water numbered 700." *(Abu Nu'aym in Dala'il, Ahmad, Muslim in Al Bidayah wan Nihayah)*

Blessings in the Water with which Rasulullah ﷺ washed his Face and Hands

In a narration discussing combining salahs during the expedition to Tabuk, Mu'adh bin Jabal ؓ reports, 'Rasulullah ﷺ said to us, 'You will InshaAllah arrive at the spring of Tabuk tomorrow at midmorning only. Whoever arrives there early should not touch the water until I arrive.' By the time we reached the spring, 2 men had already beat us to it. The spring flowed very thinly, actually resembling the strap of a shoe. Rasulullah ﷺ then asked the 2 men, 'Did you have any of the water?' When they replied that they did, Rasulullah ﷺ rebuked them very sternly. By Rasulullah ﷺ's instruction some people scooped water up little by little in their hands until they had collected a bit. Rasulullah ﷺ washed his hands and face with the water and then returned it to the spring. Water then immediately started to gush forth from the spring and everyone was able to satisfy themselves. It was then that Rasulullah ﷺ said to me, 'O Mu'adh! Should you live long enough, you will soon see this entire area filled with gardens.'" *(Muslim in Al Bidayah wan Nihayah)*

Blessings in Water when Rasulullah ﷺ Touched its Container

Imran bin Husain ؓ reports, "We were on a journey with Rasulullah ﷺ..." The narration continues to the point where he says, "It then reached a stage when we became extremely thirsty. During the course of our journey, we came across a woman sitting on her camel with her legs hanging down between 2 large waterbags. 'Where is the water?' we asked. 'There is no water,' she replied. We then asked further, 'How far must your family

travel to fetch water?' 'A day and a night,' came the reply. When we then told her that she would have to come before Rasulullah ﷺ, she asked, 'What is Rasulullah ﷺ?' We did not allow her to do or say anything more until we had presented her before Rasulullah ﷺ. She however told him only as much as she told us, apart from telling him that her child was an orphan. Rasulullah ﷺ then sent for her 2 waterbags and passed his hand over them. Although we were 40 thirsty men, we all drank to our fill from them and we also filled every waterbag and utensil we had until they were on bursting point. Rasulullah ﷺ then instructed us to bring whatever we had and we complied by gathering together all the bread and dates we had which we handed over to the woman. When she went to her tribe, she said to them, 'I have just met with someone who is either the greatest of magicians or truly a Nabi as his companions claim. By virtue of this woman, Allah then guided all the people on the hillside and together with her, they all became Muslims." Another narration states that Rasulullah ﷺ then said to her, "Take this with you to your family and remember that we have not diminished your water in the least, but it was Allah Who gave us water to drink." *(Bukhari, Muslim in Al Bidayah wan Nihayah, Abu Nu'aym, Dala'il)*

Blessings in Water When Some Stones were Thrown into it that Had been in the Hands of Rasulullah ﷺ

Ziyad bin Harith Suda'ee ؓ relates, "I was with Rasulullah ﷺ on a journey when he asked me whether I had any water with me. 'I do have a little,' I replied, 'but it will not be enough for you.' 'Pour it into a utensil and then bring it to me,' Rasulullah ﷺ said. When I did so, Rasulullah ﷺ placed his hand into the water and I saw a fountain gush forth from between each of his fingers. Rasulullah ﷺ said, 'Had I not been too shy to ask more of my Rabb, we could have been drinking water like this all the time. Go and announce to my companions that whoever wishes to have water should come and fetch as much as he pleases.'" Ziyad ؓ reports that when a delegation from his tribe came to Rasulullah ﷺ to announce that they had accepted Islam and were prepared to follow him, they also said, "O Rasulullah ﷺ! We have a well provides adequately for us during winter and we then settle around it. When summer arrives, the water is not sufficient for us and we disperse in the vicinity to other watering places. We are unfortunately unable to do this any longer because everyone around us have become our enemies because we are now Muslims. Do pray to Allah to make our water sufficient for us." Rasulullah ﷺ sent for 7 stones and when these were brought, he scattered them in his hands and made a Du'a. Rasulullah ﷺ said, 'When you reach your well, take the name of Allah and throw these stones in one by one." They did what Rasulullah ﷺ told them, the water became so abundant that they were unable to see the depth of the well. *(Abu Nu'aym in Dala'il, Bayhaqi, Ahmad, Abu Dawud, Tirmidhi, Ibn Majah in al Bidayah wan Nihayah)*

Blessings in the water that Husain bin Ali ؓ Drank

Abu Awn reports that when Husain bin Ali ؓ went from Madinah to Makkah, he passed by Ibn Muti who was digging a well. The narration later mentions that Ibn Muti said to Husain ؓ, "I have drained this well to fix it but there are still times when the buckets come out empty. Would you please make Du'a that Allah blesses it." Husain ؓ asked for some of its water and when it was brought in a bucket, he took some in his mouth, gargled his mouth and then returned it to the well. After this, the water of the well not only increased, but also became sweeter. *(Ibn Sa'd)*

Blessings in the Food of the Mujahidin by the Du'a of Rasulullah ﷺ

Abu Amrah Ansari ؓ reports that they were with Rasulullah ﷺ on a military expedition when they started to feel extreme hunger. The Sahabah then sought permission from Rasulullah ﷺ to slaughter some of their camels, saying, "Allah will then grant us the strength to reach our destination." However, when Omar ؓ noticed that Rasulullah ﷺ was about to grant permission to slaughter the animals, he intervened by saying, "O Rasulullah ﷺ! What will happen to us if we have to meet the enemy tomorrow while we are both hungry and without transport? If you agree, O Rasulullah ﷺ, you could rather ask everyone to bring whatever remaining provisions they have and after collecting all together, you could pray to Allah to bless it. By our Du'a Allah will certainly bless us and grant us the strength to reach our destination." Rasulullah ﷺ then called for all the remaining provisions. While some people brought only a handful of food, others managed to bring a little more. The most that anyone brought was a Saa of dates. After he had collected all the food together, Rasulullah ﷺ stood up and made Du'a for some time. Thereafter, he summoned the army to come with their utensils and instructed them to take from the food in handfuls. After everyone had filled their utensils, the food was still as much as it had been. This made Rasulullah ﷺ smile so widely that his teeth actually showed. He then said, "I testify that there is none worthy of worship but Allah and I testify that I am the Rasul of Allah. When a person meets Allah after believing in this, he will be screened against the fire of Jahannam on the Day of Judgment." *(Ahmad, Nasa'ee in Al Bidayah wan Nihayah, Ibn Sa'd, Abu Nu'aym in Dala'il, Muslim).* In another narration, Abu Khunais Ghifari ؓ reports that they were with Rasulullah ﷺ on an expedition to Tihama and it was at a place called Usfan that the Sahabah approached Rasulullah ﷺ... The narration continues like the one above without the part stating that Rasulullah ﷺ smiled. Thereafter, it states that after Rasulullah ﷺ gave the command to leave, it started raining and Rasulullah ﷺ together with the Sahabah dismounted and drank from the water of the skies. *(Bazzar, Bayhaqi in Al Bidayah wan Nihayah, Tabrani in Awsat, Majwa'uz Zawa'id, Hakim in Isabah).* Abu Hurairah ؓ and Abu Sa'eed Khudri ؓ both report that when the Sahabah suffered extreme hunger during the expedition to Tabuk, they approached Rasulullah ﷺ saying, "O Rasulullah ﷺ! Do permit us to slaughter the camels we use for drawing water so that we can have some food and oil." "You may do so," Rasulullah ﷺ permitted. It was then that Omar ؓ intervened..." The rest of the narration is like the one above narrated by Abu Amrah ؓ. *(Abu Nu'aym in Dala'il, Muslim in Al Bidayah wan Nihayah).* Salamah ؓ reports, "We were with Rasulullah ﷺ in the Battle of Khaibar when he instructed us to gather all our provisions of dates together. Rasulullah ﷺ then spread out a leather tablecloth, on which we spread the provisions out. I then calculated and studied the pile, finally estimating it to be the size of a sitting goat. We numbered 1,400 on that day and after we had all eaten, I again calculated and studied the pile and again estimated it to be the size of a sitting goat." The narration then continues to mention an incident of blessing in their water. *(Abu Ya'la)* In another narration, Salamah ؓ says, "We then ate to our fill and also filled our satchels. *(Muslim in Al Bidayah wan Nihayah)*

Blessings in Food after Rasulullah ﷺ Places his Hand over it While the Trench was being Dug

Abdullah bin Abbas ؓ reports that when Rasulullah ﷺ was busy with the digging of the trench, the Sahabah as well as Rasulullah ﷺ had rocks tied to their bellies because of the extreme hunger they were suffering. Seeing this situation, Rasulullah ﷺ asked, "Do you know of someone who can feed us a single meal?" When someone replied that they knew of such a person, Rasulullah ﷺ said, "Since there is no alternative, come and lead us to him." When they went to the Sahabi's house, he happened to be out digging his portion of the trench. His wife sent a message to him saying, "Come quickly because Rasulullah ﷺ has come to see us." The Sahabi rushed back, saying, "May my parents be sacrificed for you O Rasulullah ﷺ!" The Sahabi had a goat and a kid and he quickly went to slaughter the goat. Rasulullah ﷺ however said to him, "What will the kid do then without the goat." The Sahabi then slaughtered the kid while his wife took some flour, pressed into dough and made some bread. When the pot was ready with the meat, she made some Tharid in a bowl and then served it to Rasulullah ﷺ and the Sahabah. Rasulullah ﷺ placed his finger into the food and said, "Bismillah. O Allah! Bless this food." He then bade the Sahabah to eat and although they ate to their fill, they could eat only a 1/3rd of the food, leaving the other 2/3rd behind. Rasulullah ﷺ then sent the 10 Sahabah with him away with the instruction to send another 10. They therefore left and when the next 10 Sahabah arrived they also ate to their fill. Rasulullah ﷺ then got up and made Du'a for the man of the house, praying for him and his family to be blessed. Rasulullah ﷺ then left for the trench, saying to the Sahabah, "Let us go to Salman." Salman ؓ had encountered a large boulder, which he had not the strength to shift. Rasulullah ﷺ's instruction was, "Leave me to be the first to strike at it." Rasulullah ﷺ then recited "Bismillah" and struck the boulder, causing a 1/3rd of it to break off. To this, Rasulullah ﷺ exclaimed, "Allah Akbar! By the Rabb of the Kabah! The palaces of Sham!" Thereafter, Rasulullah ﷺ struck the boulder a 2nd time, causing another 1/3rd of it to break off. To this, Rasulullah ﷺ exclaimed, "Allah Akbar! By the Rabb of the Kabah! The palaces of Persia!" It was then that the Munafiqin scoffed, 'We are busy digging a trench to safeguard ourselves, yet he is promising us the palaces of Persia and Rome!" *(Tabrani in A Bidayah wan Nihayah, Haythami).* In the chapter discussing spending in the Path of Allah, the narration of Jabir ؓ has already passed in which it is stated that Rasulullah ﷺ fed all the Sahabah digging the trench from a Saa of barley flour and a little goat. Although they numbered 1,000 or close to 1,000, they all managed to eat to their fill, leaving the food as much as it had originally been.

Blessings in a Plate of Thareed Served to Rasulullah ﷺ

Samurah bin Jundub ؓ narrates that they were once with Rasulullah ﷺ when a plate of Tharid was served. Rasulullah ﷺ and all the Sahabah there ate and continued eating until it was almost time for Zuhr. They ate in turns, a group eating and then standing up to allow others to eat after them. Someone then asked Samurah ؓ, "Was more food being served all the time?" Samurah ؓ replied, "Not from the earth, but definitely from the heavens." When someone asked whether more food was served, Samurah ؓ replied, "What would be the special part? The only place from where more food was served was from there." He pointed to the skies. *(Ahmad, Tirmidhi, Nasa'ee in Al Bidayah wan Nihayah, Abu Nu'aym in Dala'il)*

Blessings in the Food Rasulullah ﷺ prepared for the Men of Suffa

Wathila bin Asqa ؓ says, "I was one of the men of Suffa when Rasulullah ﷺ once sent for some bread, which he broke into a dish. He then added some boiling water and fat to it. Thereafter, he started to stir the mixture and then mixed it vigorously before bringing the sides together to make it into a little heap. When this was done, he said, 'Go and bring me 10 people, the 10th one being yourself.' When I had brought them, Rasulullah ﷺ said, 'Eat, but ensure that you eat from beneath because blessings descend from the top.' They all then ate until, they were full." *(Ahmad, Haythami, Ibn Majah)*. Wathila bin Asqa ؓ says, "I was one of the men of Suffa and when my other companions once complained to me about their severe hunger, they requested, 'O Wathila! Go to Rasulullah ﷺ and ask him to please give us some food to eat' I then approached Rasulullah ﷺ saying, 'O Rasulullah ﷺ! My companions are complaining of extreme hunger.' Rasulullah ﷺ then asked Aisha whether she had any food with her. 'O Rasulullah ﷺ!' she submitted, 'All I have are a few pieces of bread.' Rasulullah ﷺ asked her to bring it and when she brought them along in a leather bag, Rasulullah ﷺ sent for a plate. After emptying the bread in the plate, Rasulullah ﷺ started making Tharid with his own hands. As he made it, the food started to increase until the entire plate was full. Rasulullah ﷺ then said, 'O Wathila! Go and bring me 10 people, the 10th one being yourself.' I then went out and brought 9 of them, the 10th one being myself. Rasulullah ﷺ said, 'Sit down and eat with the name of Allah. However, ensure that you eat from the sides and not from the top because blessings descend from the top.' They all then ate until they were full. They then got up and left, with the plate as full as it had been. Rasulullah ﷺ then started mixing the Tharid by hand and again it increased until the plate was even more full. 'O Wathila!' Rasulullah ﷺ said, 'Go and bring me another 10 of your companions.' When I brought them, Rasulullah ﷺ bade them to sit and they also ate to their fill. They then got up and left and Rasulullah ﷺ instructed me to bring another 10. When I brought them, the same transpired. Rasulullah ﷺ then asked, 'Are there any more people left?' When I informed Rasulullah that there were still 10 people left, he asked me to bring them as well. When I brought them, Rasulullah ﷺ bade them to sit and they also ate to their fill. They then got up and left, with the plate still as full as it had been. Then Rasulullah ﷺ said, 'O Wathila! Now take this to Aisha.'" Another narration states that the men of Suffa numbered 20 at the time. This narration mentions that some bread and milk was also served. *(Tabrani, Haythami, Abu Nu'aym in Dala'il)*

Blessings in the Food that Fatima ؓ Sent for her Father ﷺ

Jabir ؓ reports that Rasulullah ﷺ had once not had anything to eat for several days. When the hunger became unbearable, he went around to the rooms of his wives, but found no food with any of them. He then went to Fatima ؓ and said, "Dear daughter! Have you anything for me to eat because I am very hungry." She replied, "May my parents be sacrificed for you! I swear by Allah that I have nothing." However, when Rasulullah ﷺ had left, a neighbor of Fatima ؓ sent her 2 pieces of bread and a piece of meat. After receiving it from the neighbor, she placed the food in one of her platters, saying, "By Allah! I shall give this to Rasulullah ﷺ rather keeping it for myself and my family." This she said despite the fact that she and her family themselves were desperately in need of food. She then sent Hasan ؓ and Husain ؓ to call Rasulullah ﷺ and when Rasulullah ﷺ returned, she said, "May my parents be sacrificed for you! Allah has sent something that I have reserved for you." "Bring it then, dear daughter," Rasulullah ﷺ said. Fatima ؓ herself narrates further. She says, "When I then brought the platter and uncovered it, I found that it was filled with bread and meat I was stunned to see this and immediately realized that this was blessings from Allah. I then praised Allah and sent salutations to His Rasul ﷺ. I then placed it before Rasulullah ﷺ and when he saw it, he praised Allah and

asked, 'Where did you get this from, dear daughter?' 'Dear father,' I replied, 'It is from Allah because Allah provides for whomsoever He wills without counting.' Rasulullah ﷺ then again praised Allah saying, Dearest daughter! All praise belongs to Allah Who had made you like the leader of all the women of the Bani Isra'el (Mariam عليها السلام) because whenever she was questioned about the sustenance Allah provided for her, she would respond by saying, 'It is from Allah because Allah provides for whomsoever He wills without counting.' 'Rasulullah ﷺ then sent for Ali ؓ and together with him, Ali ؓ, myself, Hasan ؓ, Husain ؓ and all the wives and household of Rasulullah ﷺ ate to their fill. The platter still remained as full as it had been and Rasulullah ﷺ told me to give it to all the neighbors. Allah had indeed placed blessings and abundant goodness in the food." *(Abu Ya'la in Tafsir Ibn Kathir)*. In the chapter discussing the Da'wah that Rasulullah ﷺ gave to the Banu Hashim, Ali ؓ relates, "They were close to 40 people and Rasulullah ﷺ served them food equal to just a Mudd. They all ate to their fill, they left as much food as there had been. Rasulullah ﷺ then gave them to drink from a container and although they all drank to their fill, they left as much drink as there had been. This was done for 3 consecutive days, after which Rasulullah ﷺ invited them to believe in Allah." In the chapter on the hardships that the Sahabah endured, such several incidents of the men of Suffa have been recounted, as reported by Abu Hurairah ؓ and others. In the chapters on hosting guests and spending in the Path of Allah, other incidents were related, depicting the blessings in the food that people like Abu Talha ؓ and Abu Bakr ؓ served their guests. The incident of the marriage of Zainab ؓ showed great blessings in food.

Blessings in Butter and Barley in the Story of Ummu Sharek ؓ

Abu Hurairah ؓ reports that a lady from the Dows tribe called Ummu Sharek ؓ became a Muslim in Ramadhan. The narration then goes on to describe her migration, how a Jew accompanied her and how he refused to give her any water to drink until she became a Jew. She then fell asleep and saw someone giving her something to drink in her dream. As a result, her thirst was quenched when she awoke. When she reported the incident to Rasulullah ﷺ, he proposed for her hand in marriage, but, considering herself inadequate as a spouse for Rasulullah ﷺ, she declined saying, "Rather marry me to whomsoever you please." Rasulullah ﷺ then married her to Zaid and instructed that she be given 30 Saa of barley. Rasulullah ﷺ then instructed the couple to eat from it but never to weigh it. Ummu Sharik ؓ had a little container of butter which she had intended to give Rasulullah ﷺ as a gift. She instructed her maidservant to take it to Rasulullah ﷺ and after she had emptied it into Rasulullah ﷺ's container, Rasulullah ﷺ told her that when taking it back, she should hang it up without tying the mouth. When Ummu Sharek ؓ arrived and found the bag full of butter, she asked her servant, "Did I not instruct you to take this to Rasulullah ﷺ?" "But I did," replied the servant. When the incident was reported to Rasulullah ﷺ, he instructed them never to tie the mouth. The bag then continued giving butter until Ummu Sharek ؓ mistakenly tied the mouth one day because of which the butter also finished. When after a long time the people weighed the barley, they discovered that it still weighed 30 Saa, meaning that it had not depleted in the least despite being used for many years. *(Bayhaqi in Al Bidayah wan Nihayah)*. Yahya bin Sa'eed reports that when Ummu Sharek Dowsiya ؓ migrated, she met up with a Jew and his wife on the road. She had been fasting but the Jew warned his wife that if she gave Ummu Sharek ؓ anything to drink, he would punish her most severely. Ummu Sharek ؓ therefore spent the night thirsty. She found a bucket of water and a bag upon her chest, from which she drank. When she then awakened the Jewish couple to continue the journey by night, the Jew noted, "I hear the voice of a woman who had had something to drink." "By Allah!" Ummu Sharek ؓ remarked, "It was not your wife who gave me a drink." Ummu Sharek ؓ had with her a little container of butter. The narration then continues to describe the blessings in the butter. *(Ibn Sa'd)*

Blessings in half a Wasaq of Barley that Rasulullah ﷺ gave

Jabir ؓ reports that a man once approached Rasulullah ﷺ to ask for some food. Rasulullah ﷺ gave him half a wasaq of barley from which the man, his wife and his servant ate for a long period of time until they eventually weighed it, after which it came to an end. Rasulullah ﷺ said to them, "Had you not weighed it, it would have lasted for as long as you continued to eat from it." *(Ahmad in Al Bidayah wan Nihayah)*

Blessings in the Barley that Rasulullah ﷺ gave to Naufal bin Harith ؓ

Naufal bin Harith bin Abdul Muttalib ؓ narrates, "When I requested Rasulullah ﷺ for assistance in getting married, Rasulullah ﷺ got me married but when he looked for something to give me, he could find nothing. Rasulullah ﷺ deputed Abu Rafi ؓ and Abu Ayub ؓ to pawn his armor with a Jew for 30 Saa of barley. Rasulullah ﷺ handed the barley over to me and after eating from it for half a year, we decided to weigh it. We found that it was as much as it had been when we brought it. Upon mentioning it to Rasulullah ﷺ, he remarked, 'Had you not weighed it, you would have eaten from it for as long as you lived.'"*(Hakim, Bayhaqi in Al Bidayah wan Nihayah)*

The blessings in some Barley left in Aisha ؓ's Shelf after the Demise of Rasulullah ﷺ

Aisha ؓ says, "When Rasulullah ﷺ passed away, I had nothing to eat apart from some barley stored on a shelf of mine. I continued eating from it for a very long time until I weighed it one day. It was only then that it came to an end." *(Bukhari, Muslim, Tirmidhi in Targheeb wat Tarheeb)*

Blessings in the Dates that Jabir ؓ's Father left Because of a Du'a that Rasulullah ﷺ Made

Jabir ؓ states, "Because my father had many debts when he passed away, I approached Rasulullah ﷺ saying, 'My father had left some debts for me to settle, but I have nothing apart from the produce that his orchard yields. This is however not enough to remove the years of debts due. Please come with me so that the creditors do not treat me too harshly." Rasulullah ﷺ accompanied him and walked around one of the heaps of dates and made Du'a. He then walked around another heap and made Du'a. Rasulullah ﷺ then told the creditors to take what was due to them and he paid them all off in full. Despite giving them, there was still as much left over as had been given to them all. *(Bukhari in Al Bidayah wan Nihayah, Ibn Sa'd)*. Another narration states that Jabir ؓ said, "Rasulullah ﷺ sat on the heap and told me to call the creditors. Rasulullah ﷺ then continued weighing and giving the creditors until Allah settled my father's debts. By Allah! I was prepared to have all my father's debts settled even if it meant that I would not have a single date to take back to my sisters. Allah kept the entire heap of dates so intact that when I looked at the heap Rasulullah ﷺ was sitting on, it seemed as if not even a single date had been reduced from it." *(Abu Nu'aym in Dala'il)*

Blessings in Dates as the Trench was being Dug

The daughter of Bashir bin Sa'd ؓ who was also the sister of Nu'man bin Bashir ؓ reports, "My mother Amra bint Rawaha ؓ once called for me and placed a handful of dates in my garment saying, 'Dear daughter! Take this lunch to your father and uncle Abdullah bin Rawaha ؓ.' While looking for my father and uncle, I happened to pass by Rasulullah ﷺ, who asked, 'Come here, dear daughter. What is that with you?' I replied by saying, 'O Rasulullah ﷺ! These are some dates that my mother has sent as lunch for my father Bashir bin Sa'd and my uncle Abdullah bin Rawaha.' Rasulullah ﷺ then asked me for them and when I poured them out into his hands, they barely filled them. Rasulullah ﷺ then asked for a cloth, spread it out and then threw the dates on it causing them to scatter about. He then said to someone who was with him, 'Announce to all the people digging the trench that they should come for lunch.' When everyone had gathered by Rasulullah ﷺ and started eating from the dates, they started to multiply so much that when everyone had left, the dates were still falling off the sides of the cloth." *(Abu Nu'aym in Dala'il, Ibn Is'haq in Al Bidayah wan Nihayah)*

Blessings in 7 Dates During the Expedition to Tabuk

Irbadh ؓ relates, "Whether at home or on journey, I always stood guard at Rasulullah ﷺ's door. We were at Tabuk one night when we had to leave on some emergency and by the time we returned, Rasulullah ﷺ and the others with him had already eaten supper. Rasulullah ﷺ asked us where we had been all night and when I informed him, Ju'al bin Suraqa and Abdullah bin Mughaffal Muzani ؓ also arrived. The 3 of us were extremely hungry, so Rasulullah ﷺ went to Ummu Salama ؓ's tent to look for something for us to eat. When he found nothing there, he called for Bilal ؓ and asked him whether he had anything. When Bilal ؓ shook a leather bag, he managed to gather 7 dates. Rasulullah ﷺ placed the dates in a plate, placed his hand over it and recited Bismillah. He then said, 'Eat with the name of Allah.' As we ate, I counted each one I ate and kept the stone in my other hand. In this manner, I counted a total of 54 dates. My 2 companions did as I did, eating 50 dates each. When we had stopped eating, all 7 dates were still there. Rasulullah ﷺ then told Bilal ؓ to return the dates to the bag. The following day, Rasulullah ﷺ again placed the dates in a plate and said, 'Eat with the name of Allah.' This time we were 10 people and again we all ate to our fill. When we had finished, the same 7 dates still remained as they had been. Rasulullah ﷺ then said, 'Had I not been shy before my Rabb, we would have eaten from these same dates until we all returned to Madinah.' When we returned to Madinah, a child from Madinah came up to Rasulullah ﷺ. Rasulullah ﷺ gave him the dates and he went away sucking on them." *(Ibn Asakir in Al Bidayah wan Nihayah)*

Blessings in the Bag of Provisions that Rasulullah ﷺ gave to Abu Hurairah ؓ

Abu Hurairah ؓ says, 'There were 3 such calamities that afflicted me as a Muslim, the magnitude of which I had never experienced before. (1) The demise of Rasulullah ﷺ when I was still an inadequate companion of his, (2) the assassination of Uthman ؓ and (3) the bag to carry provisions for a journey." "What was the bag to carry provisions, O Abu Hurairah ؓ?" someone asked. Abu Hurairah ؓ explained, "We were once with Rasulullah ﷺ on a journey when Rasulullah ﷺ asked me whether I had anything with me. 'I have some dates in my bag of provisions,' I replied. 'Bring them here,' Rasulullah ﷺ said. When I removed the dates from the bag and gave them to him,

Rasulullah ﷺ touched them and made Du'a. He then instructed me to call 10 people and when I did, they all ate from the dates until they were full. Thereafter, another 10 came and ate to their fill. In this manner, the entire army ate and the same number of dates remained in my bag. Rasulullah ﷺ then said, 'O Abu Hurairah! Whenever you want to take any dates from the bag, put your hand in and take some but never overturn it.' I then continued eating from the bag throughout the lifetime of Rasulullah ﷺ, the lifetime of Abu Bakr ﷺ, the lifetime of Omar ﷺ and the lifetime of Uthman ﷺ. However, when Uthman ﷺ was martyred, everything I had was stolen, including the bag of provisions. Should I not tell you how much I ate from it? I ate more than 2 wasaq (~ 845 lbs) from it." *(Bayhaqi, in Al Bidayah wan Nihayah, Abu Nu'aym in Dala'il, Tirmidhi)*

Blessings in Anas ﷺ's Produce by virtue of Rasulullah ﷺ's Du'a

Anas ﷺ says, "My mother once took me before Rasulullah ﷺ and said, 'O Rasulullah ﷺ! Please make Du'a for this little servant of yours.' Rasulullah ﷺ made Du'a saying, 'O Allah! Grant him abundance in wealth and children, give him a long life and forgive his sins.' I have already buried 2 less than 1,000 of my children or 2 more than 1,000 of them and the fruit from my orchards are plucked twice a year. I have lived long enough to fill my heart. Anas passed away at Basra in 93AH at the age of 103 and I am now looking forward to the 4th Du'a for my sins to be forgiven." *(Ibn Sa'd)*. Anas ﷺ says, " My mother Ummu Sulaim ﷺ once said, 'O Rasulullah ﷺ! Make Du'a for Anas.' Rasulullah ﷺ therefore prayed, 'O Allah! Increase his wealth and children and bless him in them.' Not counting my grandchildren, I have already buried 125 of my children and my orchards bear twice a year, whereas there are no orchards in the area that bear fruit twice a year." *(Abu Nu'aym in Kanzul Ummal)*

Blessings in the Butter of Ummu Malik Bahzia ﷺ from the Ansar

Jabir ﷺ reports that Ummu Malik Bahzia ﷺ used to give Rasulullah ﷺ butter in a little bag that she had. Her sons once asked her for some gravy to eat, she went to the bag in which she gave Rasulullah ﷺ the butter and although it was previously emptied, she found butter inside. The bag then continued to give butter to make gravy for her sons until she squeezed it one day upon which the butter finished. She went to Rasulullah ﷺ and reported the incident, after which he asked, "Did you squeeze it?" She confirmed that she did, Rasulullah ﷺ remarked, "Had you left it alone without squeezing, it would have given you butter forever." *(Ahmad in Al Bidayah wan Nihayah)*. Ummu Malik ﷺ narrates that she once brought a little bag of butter as a gift for Rasulullah ﷺ. By Rasulullah ﷺ's instruction, Bilal ﷺ squeezed out the butter into some container and then returned the bag to Ummu Malik ﷺ. When she returned home, she discovered that the bag was still full. She therefore returned to Rasulullah ﷺ and said, "O Rasulullah ﷺ! Has some revelation descended concerning me?" "Why do you ask, O Ummu Malik?" Rasulullah ﷺ questioned. "Why did you return my gift?" was her response. Rasulullah ﷺ sent for Bilal ﷺ and asked him about it. Bilal ﷺ replied, "I swear by the Being Who sent you with the truth that I squeezed the bag until I started feeling ashamed to squeeze any more." Rasulullah ﷺ said, "Congratulations to you, O Ummu Malik! Allah has given your reward in advance." Rasulullah ﷺ taught her to recite *'SubhanAllah'*, *'Al Hamdulillah'* and *'Allahu Akbar'* 10 times each after every salah. *(Tabrani, Haythami, Abu Nu'aym in Dala'il, Ibn Abi Asim, Muslim in Isabah)*

Blessings in the Butter of Ummu Aws ﷺ

Ummu Aws Bahzia ﷺ narrates that she made some butter, poured it into a little bag and then gave the butter as a gift to Rasulullah ﷺ. Rasulullah ﷺ accepted the gift, took out the butter into his container, made Du'a for Allah to bless her and then returned the bag to her. Ummu Aws ﷺ saw that the bag was still full and thought that Rasulullah ﷺ did not accept her gift. She therefore returned screaming to Rasulullah ﷺ. Rasulullah ﷺ told the Sahabah to explain to her what had happened after which she understood. She then continued eating from the bag throughout the lifetime of Nabi ﷺ, throughout the Khilafa of Abu Bakr ﷺ, throughout the Khilafa of Omar ﷺ, throughout the Khilafa of Uthman ﷺ and until the time when there arose a dispute between Ali ﷺ and Mu'awiya ﷺ. *(Tabrani, Ibn Mandah, Ibn Sakan in Isabah, Haythami, Bayhaqi in Al Bidayah wan Nihayah)*

Blessings in the Butter of Ummu Sulaim ﷺ

Anas ﷺ reports that his mother Ummu Sulaim ﷺ had a goat which she milked and she collected all the butter from the goat's milk in a little bag. When the bag was full, she sent it with a girl in her care to Rasulullah ﷺ, saying, "Dear daughter! Take this bag to Rasulullah ﷺ, so that he may use it to make his gravy." The girl took it to Rasulullah ﷺ and said, "O Rasulullah ﷺ! Here is some butter that Ummu Sulaim has sent for you." Rasulullah ﷺ gave the Sahabah the instruction to empty the bag out (into one of his containers) and when this was done, the bag was returned to the girl. Ummu Sulaim ﷺ was inside her room when the girl returned and hung the bag onto a nail. When Ummu Sulaim ﷺ came out, she saw the bag so fun of butter that it was actually dripping out. "Dear daughter!" Ummu Sulaim ﷺ called out, "Did I not tell you to take this to Rasulullah ﷺ?" The girl replied by saying, "But I have done so. You may go and ask Rasulullah ﷺ if you do not believe me." Ummu Sulaim ﷺ went with the girl to Rasulullah ﷺ and asked, "O Rasulullah ﷺ! I had sent her with a bag full of butter for you." "She did come with it," Rasulullah ﷺ replied. Ummu Sulaim ﷺ exclaimed, "I swear by the Being Who sent you with the truth and with the true religion that the bag is still full of butter that it is actually dripping!" To this, Rasulullah ﷺ remarked, "O Ummu Sulaim! Are you surprised that Allah could feed you as you had fed His Nabi? Eat from it and feed others." Ummu Sulaim ﷺ says, "I returned home and distributed the butter in a large jug and in several other containers, leaving some in the bag. This was sufficient for us to make gravy for a month or two." *(Abu Ya'la in Al Bidayah wan Nihayah, Tabrani, Abu Ya'la, Haythami, Abu Nu'aym in Dala'il, Isabah)*

Blessings in the Butter of Ummu Sharek ﷺ

Ummu Sharek ﷺ reports that she had with her a little bag in which she gave Rasulullah ﷺ some butter as a gift. One day when her children asked her for some butter and she had none, she went to the bag to have a look and was surprised to see that butter was flowing from it. She poured out some for them and the family then ate from it for a long while afterwards. It was only when she one day went to see how much remained and poured all out that it finished. When she reported this to Rasulullah ﷺ, he remarked, "Did you turn it upside down? Had you not done this, it would have lasted you a very long time." *(Ibn Sa'd)*. Another narration from Yahya bin Sa'eed states that Ummu Sharek ﷺ used to lend her little bag to whoever came to her. When a man once approached here to sell it to him, she told him that there was now nothing left in it. She then blew into it and left it in the sun (so that all the remnants could melt and be extracted) when she was astonished to see that it was again full of butter. People therefore referred to Ummu Sharek ﷺ's bag of butter as one of the signs of Allah. (Ibn Sa'd). Other narrations about Ummu Sharek 🌼 have already been quoted above.

Blessings in the Butter of Hamza bin Amr Aslami 🌼

Hamza bin Amr 🌼 relates, "Rasulullah 🌼's companions took turns in preparing food for his other companions and someone different would bring the food each night. When my turn came one night, I prepared the food but neglected to close the mouth of the bag that contained the butter. As I was about to take the food to Rasulullah 🌼, the bag fell and all the butter spilled out. 'Did Rasulullah 🌼's food have to spill by my hands?' I lamented. When I took the food Rasulullah 🌼 called me to also partake, but I refused saying, 'I really wouldn't manage to eat, O Rasulullah 🌼 because the food was too little.' When I returned home, I was shocked to hear the bag making the sound of droplets filling. 'Stop!' I said, 'Whatever was left over has already spilled out.' However, when I went over to have a look, I discovered that the bag was filled to its chest. I then took it to Rasulullah 🌼 and informed him about it, to which he remarked, 'Had you left it as is, it would have filled to its mouth, after which you could have closed it.'" (Tabrani in Majma'uz Zawa'id). Concerning the expedition to Tabuk in which Rasulullah 🌼 said to him, "Had you left it as is, the entire valley would have been flowing with butter." Hamza bin Amr 🌼 relates, "When Rasulullah 🌼 left for the expedition to Tabuk, I was in charge of the bag containing the butter. I once looked at the bag as I prepared Rasulullah 🌼's food, I noticed that there was very little butter in it. I placed the bag in the sun and fell asleep. I was awakened by the sound of liquid filling in the bag, I grabbed the bag by its head. Seeing me Rasulullah 🌼 remarked, "Had you left it, the entire valley would have been flowing with butter." (Abu Nu'aym in Dala'il)

Blessings in the Goat of Khabbab bin Arat 🌼 After Rasulullah 🌼 had milked Her

Khabbab bin Arat 🌼's daughter reports, "When my father left on an expedition, he left us nothing apart from a goat. His instruction was that whenever we needed to have it milked, we should take it to the men of Suffa. When we then took it to them, we found Rasulullah 🌼 sitting there. Rasulullah 🌼 took the goat, fastened her and then started to milk her. 'Bring me the largest utensil you have,' Rasulullah 🌼 asked. I went home and the largest I could find was the utensil in which we kneaded dough. When I brought it to Rasulullah 🌼, he milked the goat until he had filled the utensil. He then said to us, 'Take this milk, drink from it and give it to your neighbors to drink as well. Bring her to me whenever you wish to milk her." We then continued taking the goat to Rasulullah 🌼 and until my father returned, we had plenty of milk. When my father returned and tied her up to milk her, she gave only that amount of milk as she had been giving previously. 'You have ruined our goat!' my mother remarked. 'What do you mean?' my father asked. My mother explained, 'We used to fill this utensil with milk.' 'Who was doing the milking?' my father enquired. When my mother informed him that Rasulullah 🌼 did the milking, my father remarked, 'Are you equating me with Rasulullah 🌼? By Allah! His hands are much more blessed than mine.'" (Ibn Sa'd).

Blessings in the Meat of Mas'ood bin Khalid 🌼

Mas'ood bin Khalid 🌼 says, "I once sent a goat to Rasulullah 🌼 and then had to leave to do something. Rasulullah 🌼 sent a portion of the meat back to my family and when I returned to my wife Ummu Khunas 🌼, I found some meat with them. 'O Ummu Khunas!' I asked, 'What meat is this?' She replied by saying,

'Your friend Rasulullah 🌼 has sent back a piece of the meat from the goat you sent to him.' 'Then why do you not feed it to your family?' I asked. 'I have already fed them,' she replied, 'This is what was left over.' This surprised me because sometimes even 1 or 2 goats are not sufficient for them." (Tabrani, Haythami)

Blessings in the Meat of Khalid bin Abdul Uzza 🌼

Khalid bin Abdul Uzza 🌼 slaughtered a goat and sent to Rasulullah 🌼. Rasulullah 🌼 and the Sahabah ate it and sent what was left over back to Khalid 🌼. Khalid 🌼 had a very large family, they all managed to eat from it and still have leftovers. (Ya'qub bin Sufian, Hasan bin Sufian, Nasa'ee in Isabah)

Rasulullah 🌼 receives Food from the Heavens

Salama bin Nufail 🌼 reports that he once asked Rasulullah 🌼 whether he received food from the heavens. When Rasulullah 🌼 replied that he did, Salamah 🌼 asked, 'Does anything stay over from it?" "Yes," Rasulullah 🌼 replied. "Then what happens to it?" I asked further. "It is then lifted back to the heavens," came the reply. (Ibn Sa'd). Salama bin Nufail Sakuni 🌼 reports that one day while they, the Sahabah, were sitting with Rasulullah 🌼, a man arrived and asked, "O Nabi of Allah 🌼! Is food brought to you from the heavens" Rasulullah 🌼 replied, "Food is brought to me in a steaming pot." "Is any food left over afterwards?" the man questioned further. When Rasulullah 🌼 replied in the affirmative, the man asked, "Then what happens to it?" "It is then lifted back to the heavens," Rasulullah 🌼 replied. Rasulullah 🌼 then continued to say, "It has been revealed to me that I shall be remaining with you for only a short while and that after me, you people will also remain alive for a short while. You will live until a time arrives when because of the strife to be witnessed you will ask, 'How much longer are we to live?' You will then fragment into many groups and start destroying each other. There will be plenty of deaths before Judgment, after which will follow several years of earthquakes." (Hakim). Someone asked Rasulullah 🌼 whether he received food from Jannah. (Isabah)

The Sahabah are Sustained by a Gigantic Sea Creature after Suffering Extreme Hunger

In a lengthy narration reported by Jabir bin Abdullah 🌼, he says, "When the men complained of their extreme hunger to Rasulullah 🌼, he said, 'Allah shall certainly provide some food for you.' When we reached the sea shore, a massive wave threw a large creature out. We made a fire beside it, cooked some of it and roasted part of it. We then ate until we could eat no more." Jabir 🌼 then named 5 other Sahabah and stated that the 5 of them together with himself went into the eye socket of the creature and none was even able to see them until they emerged. They then took a rib of the creature and stood it up like a bow. Thereafter, they selected the tallest person sitting upon the largest camel and the biggest carriage and the man was able to pass beneath the rib without even lowering his head. (Muslim). Jabir 🌼 also reports, "Rasulullah 🌼 once dispatched a regiment of 300 men under the command of Abu Ubaidah bin Jarrah 🌼. I was amongst the men and we were sent to a coastal area. We were still traveling when our provisions came to an end. Abu Ubaidah 🌼 instructed us to gather together all that was left of the provisions and when it was done, it amounted to only 2 satchels of dates. He rationed it to us little by little until it was almost finished and we then received only a single date each for the day." "Of what use was a single date," one of the narrators asked Jabir 🌼. Jabir 🌼 replied, "When the rations were finished, we missed even that single date." Jabir 🌼 then continued the story saying, "We then reached the sea shore, where we were surprised to see a fish lying on the ground which was the size of a hill. The army then ate from this fish for 18 days. Abu Ubaidah ؓ then had 2 of the ribs placed upright, had a carriage strapped to a camel and then passed the camel and carriage beneath the ribs. The camel passed through without touching the ribs." *(Malik, Bukhari, Muslim in Al Bidayah wan Nihayah).* Jabir states, "Rasulullah ﷺ dispatched 300 of us under the command of Abu Ubaidah bin Jarrah ؓ to ambush one of the Quraish's caravans. When our provisions ran out we started to suffer such extreme hunger that we resorted to eating leaves. It was for this reason that this army was known as the Army of Leaves. Someone then slaughtered 3 camels to feed the army, after which he slaughtered another 3 and then another 3 until Abu Ubaidah ؓ stopped him because it was depriving them of transport. It was then that the sea threw out a fish called Ambar, from which we ate for half a month and from which we even derived oil. This eventually restored our strength..." The narration then goes or to mention the incident of the fish's ribs. *(Bukhari, Muslim in Al Bidayah wan Nihayah, Abu Nu'aym in Dala'il).* Jabir ؓ also says, "Rasulullah ﷺ dispatched us under the command of Abu Ubaidah bin Jarrah ؓ to intercept a caravan belonging to the Quraish. Rasulullah ﷺ gave us a bag of dates as the journey's provisions because he had nothing else to give us. Abu Ubaidah ؓ would therefore give us a daily ration of one date each." When someone asked Jabir ؓ how they managed with one date, he replied, "We would suck on it like a child does and then drink water. It would then suffice for us throughout the day and night. We then also used our staffs to knock leaves off trees, which we would then wet and eat. When we arrived on the sea shore, we saw something resembling a gigantic bank. When we observed closely, we realized that it was actually it fish called Anbar. Abu Ubaidah ؓ's initial reaction was to say that it was carrion, but he then changed his mind and said, 'No! We are the envoys of Rasulullah ﷺ, we are out in the Path of Allah and have reached the point of desperation. You may therefore eat.' Although we numbered 300, we lived off the fish for a month until we even started to put on weight. We used large containers to scoop up oil from its eye sockets and would cut off from it pieces of meat as large as bulls. Abu Ubaidah ؓ once took 13 men and seated them in the eye socket. He also took one of its ribs, stood it erect and then passed beneath it the tallest man, seated on a carriage on the largest camel. We took large chunks of meat with us as provisions for our journey and when we arrived in Madinah, we reported the incident to Rasulullah ﷺ. Rasulullah ﷺ remarked, 'It was your sustenance that Allah had taken out for you (from the ocean). Do you have any of it with you to give us to eat?' We then sent some for Rasulullah ﷺ and he ate it." *(Bayhaqi in Al Bidayah wan Nihayah, Muslim, Abu Dawood, Abu Zubair, Ibn Sa'd, Tabrani in Kanzul Ummal)*

A Sababi and his wife are Sustained from a Source they Never Expected

Abu Hurairah ؓ reports that a Sahabi once came home but when he saw the great hunger his family was experiencing, he was unable to bear it and left and went outdoors. Seeing this, is wife went to the grindstone and set it up and then went to the oven and lit it. She then made Du'a saying, "O Allah! Provide for us." When she then looked, she saw that the mixing bowl was full of dough and when she had a look at the oven, she saw that it was full of bread. Her husband returned and asked, "Did you receive anything after I had left?" "Yes," she replied, "from our Rabb." He then went to the grindstone and lifted it because of which it stopped grinding and producing flour. When the incident

was reported to Rasulullah ﷺ, he remarked, "Had he not lifted it, it would have continued grinding until the Day of Judgment." *(Ahmad).* His wife's Du'a was: "O Allah! Provide for us what we can grind, knead and make into bread. The bowl then suddenly filled with bread, the grindstone started to grind and the oven was full of roasted grains. Her husband returned and asked, "Do you have anything to eat?" "Allah has provided sustenance for us," she replied. He then lifted the grindstone and swept what was around it causing it to stop grinding. Rasulullah ﷺ said about this, "Had you left it, it would have continued grinding until the Day of Judgment." *(Ahmad, Bazzar, Tabrani, Haythami, Bayhaqi).* Abu Hurairah ؓ also reports that when a very poor man from the Ansar once left home, his wife said, "If I start to turn my grindstone and place some palm fronds in my oven, my neighbors will hear the grindstone and see the smoke and think that we have some food whereas we have nothing but extreme hunger." She then lit the oven and stood by the grindstone and started to grind. When her husband returned and heard the grindstone grinding, he asked, "What are you grinding?" She then stood up to open the door for him and informed him about what she had been doing. When the two entered- the room, they found the grindstone turning and flour pouring from it. Every utensil in their house was filled with flour. She then went to the oven with her husband in trail and found it full of bread. When the incident was reported to Rasulullah ﷺ, he asked, "What then happened to the grindstone?" The husband replied, "I lifted it up and shook it out." Rasulullah ﷺ remarked, "Had you left it, it would have continued grinding throughout my life." Rasulullah ﷺ said, "It would have continued grinding throughout your lives." *(Al Bidayah wan Nihayah)*

Rasulullah ﷺ, Abu Bakr ؓ and a Bedouin Family Receive Sustenance from an Unexpected Source

Abu Bakr ؓ says, "I once left Makkah with Rasulullah ﷺ and we traveled until we reached the locality of an Arab tribe. Rasulullah ﷺ saw a house that was detached from the rest and headed towards it. When we dismounted our animals, we found that there was none but a woman there. 'O servant of Allah!' she said, 'I am a lone woman with none living with me. You two had rather go to the chief of the tribe if you wish to be hosted.' Rasulullah ﷺ however gave her no reply. It was already evening and just then her son arrived with her goats from grazing. 'Dear son!' she said, 'Take this goat and a knife to those two men and tell them that your mother wants them to slaughter the goat, eat from it and send some for us to eat.' When the boy came to Rasulullah ﷺ, he said, 'Take this knife back and fetch me a bowl.' The boy said, 'This goat stays away from the grazing ground and therefore has no milk.' 'Go on (and fetch the bowl),' Rasulullah ﷺ bade the boy. When the boy brought the bowl, Rasulullah ﷺ placed his hand on the goat's teats and milked her until the bowl was full. Rasulullah ﷺ then instructed the boy to take the bowl to his mother and she drank until she was satisfied. The boy brought the bowl back and Rasulullah ﷺ told him to take the goat back and bring another. Rasulullah ﷺ then did the same and gave me to drink. When another goat was brought, Rasulullah ﷺ milked it and this time, he drank it. We then stayed for the night and then left. The woman then named Rasulullah ﷺ Mubarak ('The Blessed One') and her goats increased so much in number that she brought them to Madinah to sell. When I happened to pass by them, the son recognized me and said, 'Dear mother! There is the man who was with Mubarak.' She got up before me and said, 'O servant of Allah! Who was that man with you?' 'Don't you know who he is?' I asked. When she declared that she did not, I informed her that he is Nabi ﷺ. Upon her request, I then took her to Rasulullah ﷺ. Rasulullah ﷺ gave her a meal to eat and also gave her some cheese and wares that Bedouins use as a gift. He also gave her many more gifts and clothing. She then accepted Islam." *(Bayhaqi, Ibn Asakir in Kanzul Ummal)*

Rasulullah ﷺ and Abu Bakr ؓ receive Milk from a Goat that had not yet Mated

Abdullah bin Mas'ood ؓ reports, "I was grazing goats for Uqba bin Abu Mu'it when Rasulullah ﷺ and Abu Bakr ؓ passed by me. 'Dear boy!' Rasulullah ﷺ said, 'Have you any milk for us to drink?' 'Yes,' I replied, 'but I have only been placed in trust, I do not own the goats and have no permission to give the milk away.' Rasulullah ﷺ asked, 'Are there any she-goats that have not mated yet?' I then brought such a goat and when Rasulullah ﷺ passed his hand over her teats, milk started to descend and he milked her. He then drank from the container of milk and gave Abu Bakr ؓ some to drink as well. Rasulullah ﷺ then addressed the teat saying, 'Now contract' and it contracted. Thereafter, I approached Rasulullah ﷺ with the request, 'O Rasulullah ﷺ! Teach me something of this speech.' Rasulullah ﷺ then passed his hand over my head saying, 'Dear lad! May Allah shower mercy on you because you shall be a learned and well taught person." *(Ahmad)* Another narration states that Abdullah bin Mas'ood ؓ brought Rasulullah ﷺ a goat that was under a year old. Rasulullah ﷺ tied her legs and made Du'a as he passed his hand over her teats. Abu Bakr ؓ then brought a dish and Rasulullah ﷺ milked her in it. He gave Abu Bakr ؓ to drink before drinking some himself. *(Bayhaqi in Al Bidayah wan Nihayah)*

Khabbab ؓ and his Companions are Sustained from Unexpected Sources

Khabbab ؓ says, "It was during one of the expeditions on which Rasulullah ﷺ sent us that we became extremely thirsty because we had no water with us. All of a sudden, one of our companion's camel sat down and we saw her udders so full of milk that it appeared to be a water bag. We all then drank from her milk." *(Tabrani, Haythami)*

Khubaib ؓ receives Grapes from Unseen Sources when he was held Prisoner

After she had accepted Islam, Mawiya ؓ the freed slave of Hujair bin Abu Ihab reports, "When Khubaib ؓ was held prisoner in our house in Makkah, I peeped at him through a crack in the door and saw that he was eating from a bunch of grapes that was the size of a head. This was at a time when I knew that grapes could not be had anywhere." *(Ibn Is'haq in Isabah)*

Two companions of Rasulullah ﷺ are Fed from Unseen Sources

Salim bin Abul Ja'd ؓ reports that when Rasulullah ﷺ dispatched 2 men for some task, they said, "O Rasulullah ﷺ! We have nothing to take with as provisions for the journey." Rasulullah ﷺ then told them to find a water bag and when they brought one, he further instructed them to fill it with water and then tie up the mouth. Thereafter, Rasulullah ﷺ told them to proceed to a particular place where Allah will provide for them. When they proceeded to the place, the water bag opened by itself and they found goat's milk and cream inside. This they ate and drank until they could have no more. *(Ibn Sa'd)*

The Incident of Uthman bin Affan ؓ

Abdullah bin Salam ؓ narrates, "I went to Uthman ؓ when he was imprisoned in his house. 'A warm welcome to my brother,' he said. He then said, 'Last night I saw Rasulullah ﷺ by this window. 'O Uthman!' he said, 'Have they surrounded you?' When I replied in the affirmative, Rasulullah ﷺ further asked, 'And have they made you thirsty?' When I confirmed this, Rasulullah ﷺ held out a bucket of water from which I drank to my fill. In fact, I actually felt the coolness of the water on my chest and between my shoulders. Rasulullah ﷺ then said, 'If you wish, you may be assisted against them or alternatively, you may terminate your fast with us.' I chose to rather terminate my fast with them.' Uthman ؓ was then martyred that very day." *(Ibn Abi Dunya in Al Bidayah wan Nihayah)*. The incident of Ummu Sharek ؓ has already passed in which she was given water to drink in a dream and then woke up with her thirst quenched.

Wealth from unseen sources: Miqdad bin Aswad ؓ receives Money from Unseen Sources

Duba'ah bint Zubair ؓ who was married to Miqdad bin Aswad ؓ says, "People used to relieve themselves only every 2 or 3 days and would then pass stool just as camels do because of their meager diet. Miqdad ؓ went out to relieve himself one day and when he reached Hajaba near Baqi Gharqad and sat down to relieve himself in an uninhabited area. As he sat there, a large rat emerged from a hole with a Dinar. The rat then went back and forth brining Dinar after Dinar until it had brought 17 Dinars. Miqdad ؓ took the Dinars to Rasulullah ﷺ and informed him of the incident. 'Did you put your hand into the hole to remove the Dinars?' Rasulullah ﷺ asked. Miqdad ؓ replied, 'I swear by the Being Who sent you with the truth that I did not' 'Then there shall be no Sadaqa due from you. May Allah bless you in it.' Allah then blessed them so much that they finished only when I saw bags of silver in Miqdad ؓ's house." *(Abu Nu'aym in Dala'il)*

Wealth comes to Sa'ib bin Aqra ؓ and other Muslims from Unseen Sources

Sa'ib bin Aqra ؓ reports, "When Omar ؓ appointed me governor of Mada'in, I was once sitting in the throne room of the Persian Emperor when I noticed a figurine pointing its finger in a particular direction. The thought then occurred to me that it was pointing towards a treasure, so I dug at the spot and discovered a huge treasure. I then wrote to Omar ؓ to inform him of the incident and told him that it amounted to booty that Allah had given to me without the help of the other Muslims. Omar ؓ however wrote back to tell me that since I was governor of the Muslims, I should distribute the treasure amongst the Muslims." *(Khatib in Kanzul Ummal)*. Sha'bi reports that Sa'ib ؓ joined in the Conquest of Mihrijan and when he entered the chambers of Hurmuzan, he saw a lime figure of a deer with its foreleg outstretched. He said, "I swear by Allah that this is pointing towards something." After investigation, he found the treasure of Hurmuzan that included several bags of gems. *(Isabah)*

An incident of Abu Umamah ؓ in this Regard

Abdur Rahman bin Yazid bin Jabir reports that a slave woman of Abu Umamah ؓ who was a Christian once related to him, "Abu Umamah ؓ loved to spend in Sadaqa and would actually save money to do so. He would never send a beggar away empty-handed, even though it meant giving him an onion, a date or anything else to eat if that was all he could afford. A beggar once came to him at a time when he had nothing but 3 Dinars with him. When the beggar asked for something, Abu Umamah ؓ gave him a Dinar. Another beggar then came and he gave him the second Dinaf. A third beggar also came and Abu Umamah ؓ gave him the last Dinar. This made me very angry and I protested, 'You have left nothing for us?' He then put his head down and had his afternoon nap. When Adhan was called out for the Zuhr salah, I woke him up. He performed wudhu and then left for the Masjid. Because he was fasting, I felt sorry for him and took a loan to prepare supper for him and to light a lamp. When I then went to make his bed, I was surprised to find some gold coins there. I counted three hundred of them and said, 'He did what he did only because he could rely on what he had left behind.' He returned after the Isha salah and when he saw the supper and the light, he smiled, saying, 'This is the bounty of Allah.' I remained standing by him as he finished his supper, after which I said, 'May Allah have mercy on you. You had left all that money in a place where it could have easily gotten lost without even telling me so that I could use it. 'What money?' he enquired, 'I had left nothing behind.' When I then lifted the bedding and he saw it, he was overjoyed. I then got up, cut off my cross and accepted Islam." Ibn Jabir says, "I saw her (Abu Umamah ﷺ's slave woman) in the Masjid of Damascus where she was busy teaching the women Qur'an, the Sunnah, the Fara'idh and educating them about Deen." *(Abu Nu'aym in Hilya)*

Blessings in the money Rasulullah ﷺ gave Salman ﷺ to purchase his freedom

In a lengthy narration discussing how he accepted Islam, Salman ﷺ says, "When I was still left owing something, a gold nugget resembling a fowl's eggs came to Rasulullah ﷺ from some mine. 'What has happened to the Persian Mukatab slave?' When I was called before Rasulullah ﷺ, he said, "Take this, O Salman, and pay the balance of your debt off.' I said, 'How will this meager amount payoff the amount due from me?' 'Take it,' Rasulullah ﷺ insisted, 'because it will surely payoff what you owe.' I then took it and I swear by the Being Who controls my life that when it was weighed, it amounted to 40 Awqiya. I was therefore able to pay them off in full and become a free man." *(Ahmad)*. In another narration, Salman ﷺ says, "When I said 'How will this (meager amount) payoff the amount due from me?' Rasulullah ﷺ turned the gold around on his tongue and then said, 'Take it pay them off all the 40 Awqiya due to them.'" *(Ahmad, Tabrani, Haythami, Ibn Sa'd, Bazzar)*

Blessings in the Wealth of Urwa Bariqi ﷺ because of the Du'a of Rasulullah ﷺ

Urwa Bariqi ﷺ reports, "When Rasulullah ﷺ met a trade caravan, he gave me a Dinar to purchase a goat. I managed to purchase 2 goats for the Dinar and when I met someone, I sold him one of the goats for a Dinar. I then returned to Rasulullah ﷺ with a Dinar and a goat. Rasulullah ﷺ then made Du'a saying, 'May Allah bless you in your trade.' Now because of this Du'a if I have to stand in the Kunasa marketplace in Kufa, I will not return home without earning a profit of 40,000." Another narration states that he said, "I saw times when I stood in the Kunasa marketplace in Kufa and returned home with a profit of 40,000 Dinars." *(Abu Nu'aym in Dala'il, Isabah)*. Yet another narration states that because of Rasulullah ﷺ's Du'a for him, even if Urwa ﷺ had to buy sand, he would make a profit out of it. *(Abdur Razzaq, Ibn Abu Shaybah in Kanzul Ummal)*

Blessings in the Wealth of Abdullah bin Hisham ﷺ because of the Du'a of Rasulullah ﷺ

Abu Aqil reports that his grandfather Abdullah bin Hisham ﷺ would take him out to the marketplace, where he would buy some grains to resell. Abdullah bin Zubair ﷺ and Abdullah bin Omar ﷺ would then meet him and say, "Please make us partners in your business because Rasulullah ﷺ made Du'a for you to be blessed." He would then make them partners and it was often that he would earn a profit of a camel, which he would then send home. *(Bukhari in Al Bidayah wan Nihayah)*

Abdullah bin Unais ﷺ Recovers from a Head wound through Rasulullah ﷺ's Saliva

Abdullah bin Unais ﷺ says, "The Jew Mustanir bin Rizam struck my face with his bent staff made from the show hat tree. The wound fractured my skull and exposed it. I then went to show it to Rasulullah ﷺ, who opened it up and applied his saliva to it. It healed immediately and so effectively that when I then looked at it, I could see nothing of the wound." *(Tabrani, Haythami)*

Mukhallad bin Uqba ﷺ's boil Deals by the Saliva of Rasulullah ﷺ

Mukhallad bin Uqba ﷺ reports, "I went to Rasulullah ﷺ at a time when I had a boil on my palm. 'O Rasulullah ﷺ!' I said, 'This boil has developed on my palm which hinders me holding a sword properly and from holding the reins of my animal.' Rasulullah ﷺ bade me to come closer and when I did, he opened up my palm and applied some of his saliva to it. He then placed his hand on the boil and continued rubbing it with his palm until I could see no trace of it." *(Tabrani, Haythami)*

Abiadh bin Hammal ﷺ is Cured of a Ringworm Infection by the Touch and Du'a of Rasulullah ﷺ

Abadh bin Hammal Maribi ﷺ reports that he once had a ringworm infection on his face, which covered his entire nose. Rasulullah ﷺ sent for him and passed his blessed hand over his face, after which no trace of the infection remained. *(Abu Nu'aym in Dala'il, Ibn Sa'd)*

Rafi bin Khudaij ﷺ is Cured of Stomach Pain by the Touch of Rasulullah ﷺ

Rafi bin Khudaij ﷺ relates, "I once went to Rasulullah ﷺ at a time when a large pot of meat was being cooked. A delicious piece of fat caught my eye, so I took it and quickly ate it up. I then remained ill for a complete year. When I mentioned this to Rasulullah ﷺ, he said, "7 people had their hearts in that piece of fat." Rasulullah ﷺ then passed his hand over my stomach and I vomited it out as a green lump. I swear by the Being Who sent Rasulullah ﷺ with the truth that to this day, I have never had any stomach pains." *(Abu Nu'aym in Dala'il)*

Ali ﷺ is cured by the Du'a of Rasulullah ﷺ

Ali ﷺ reports, "I was ill one day when I happened to pass by Rasulullah ﷺ saying, 'O Allah! If my death is near, do grant me relief from this illness by death. If my death is for a later time, then relieve me of this illness and if it be a test, do grant me the perseverance.' Rasulullah ﷺ then asked me, 'what was it you were saying?' When I repeated my words, Rasulullah ﷺ gave me a little kick saying, 'O Allah! Cure him.' I never had cause to complain of any pain after that day." *(Abu Nu'aym in Dala'il)*. In the chapter on Da'wah, the narration of Sahl ﷺ has passed, which states that during the Battle of Khaibar, Rasulullah ﷺ applied some of his blessed saliva onto Ali ﷺ's eyes and prayed for him. His eyed were immediately cured and it appeared as if he had never suffered any pain at all. In the chapter discussing Nusra, the narration of Bara ﷺ has also passed detailing how Abdullah bin Atik ﷺ broke his leg when he went to kill Abu Rafi. Abdullah bin Atik ﷺ says, "When I got back to Rasulullah ﷺ and informed him about the events, he asked me to stretch out my leg. When I did so, he passed his hand over my leg and it was cured so well that it felt as if nothing was ever wrong with it."

Handhala bin Hadhim ☙ heals the ill through the Blessings he received from Rasulullah ﷺ

Handhala bin Hadhim ☙ says, "I accompanied my grandfather with a delegation to Rasulullah ﷺ. My grandfather said, 'O Rasulullah ﷺ! I have several sons and grandsons, some of whom have beards while others do not. This is the youngest of them all.' Rasulullah ﷺ then asked me to come closer, passed his hand over my head and made Du'a saying, 'May Allah bless you.'" One of the narrators Dhaial says, "I saw a man with a swollen face and a goat with inflamed teats brought to Handhala ☙. All he did was pass his hand over them saying, 'In the name of Allah and with the blessings of the place where Rasulullah ﷺ placed his palm.' The inflammation would then instantly disappear." (Tabrani, Ahmad in Majma'uz Zawa'id). Dhaial said, "I saw that when a man with an inflamed face was brought to Handhala ☙, he applied some saliva on his hand, recited 'Bismillah' and placed his hand on the man's head. He passed his hand over the inflamed area as he said, 'With the blessings of the place where Rasulullah ﷺ placed his palm.' The inflammation would instantly disappear." (Ahmad, Hasan bin Sufian, Tabrani, Abu Ya'la, Ya'qub bin Sufian, Minjaniqi in Isabah, Ibn Sa'd)

A Camel of Abdullah bin Qurt ☙ is cured by his Du'a

Abdullah bin Qurt ☙ reports, "Because my camel started to walk extremely slowly and sat down because of exhaustion as I rode with Khalid bin Walid ☙, I intended to abandon it. I however made Du'a to Allah and Allah made it stand up straight so that I could ride it once again." (Tabrani, Haythami)

Khalid bin Walid ☙ is Unaffected by the Poison he Drinks

Abu Safar reports that when Khalid bin Walid ☙ arrived in Hira, he stayed with the Persian governor. Some people however warned him saying, "Be careful that the non-Muslims do not give you poison to drink." Khalid ☙ then asked them to bring the poison and when they did, he took it and swallowed it, saying, "Bismillah". The poison had no effect on him whatsoever. (Abu Ya'la, Tabrani in Majma'uz Zawa'id, Abu Nu'aym in Dala'il). Another narration states that when the poison was brought to Khalid ☙, he placed it on his palm, recited "Bismillah" and then swallowed it. It did him no harm at all. (Abu Ya'la in Isabah). Dhul Jowshan Dhibabi ☙ and others report that Amr bin Buqaila had his servant with him, who carried a little bag around his waist. Khalid ☙ took the bag, emptied the contents onto his palm and asked Amr what is was. Amr replied, "I swear by Allah that this is poison that kills in an instant" "Why do you carry poison around with you?" Khalid ☙ asked. "Because," Amr explained, "I feared that you people would not be as I expected, in which case I would rather commit suicide because death is more beloved to me than bringing disgrace to my people and countrymen." Khalid ☙ then said to him, "No soul can die until its term is up." He then recited the Du'a:

بِسْمِ اللهِ خَيْرِ الأَسْمَاءِ رَبِّ الأَرْضِ وَالسَّمَاءِ الَّذِي لَيْسَ يَضُرُّ مَعَ اسْمِهِ دَاءٌ الرَّحْمَانِ الرَّحِيْمِ

"In the name of Allah, which is the best of names, the Rabb of the earth and the heavens, with Whose name no disease can cause any harm. He is the Most Kind and Most Merciful."

The people leapt forward to try to stop Khalid ☙, but he beat them and swallowed the poison which did him no harm. To this, Amr remarked, "O assembly of Arabs! I swear by Allah that you will be able to control any land you please as long as someone from this generation (the Sahabah) are amongst you." He then returned to the people of Hira saying, "To this day have I not seen anything more inviting." (Ibn Jareer)

Heat and Cold have no effect on Ali ☙ by the Du'a of Rasulullah ﷺ

Abdur Rahman bin Abu Laila reports, "Ali ☙ used to walk about during winter wearing only his loincloth and an upper garment, both made from thin material. Then in summer he would wear a padded cloak and thick clothing. Some people therefore asked me to request my father to ask Ali ☙ about this because he usually spoke to him at nights. I therefore spoke to my father saying, 'Dear father! The people have noticed something about the Amirul Mu'minin that they find strange.' When my father asked what it was, I explained, 'In the scorching heat, he comes out wearing a padded cloak and thick clothing without a bother and during icy cold days he comes out wearing only 2 light garments. He seems not to bother about the cold or to protect himself against it. Have you heard anything about it? The people have asked me to request you to enquire about this when you speak to him at night' My father then discussed this with Ali ☙ at night. 'O Amirul Mu'minin!' he said, 'The people wish to ask you something.' 'What is that?' Ali ☙ asked. My father said, 'In the scorching heat, you come out wearing a padded cloak and thick clothing without a bother and during icy cold days you come out wearing only 2 light garments. You seem not to bother about the cold or to protect yourself against it.' 'Were you not with us at Khaibar, O Abu Laila?' Ali ☙ asked. 'By Allah!' my father replied, 'Of course I was with you.' Ali ☙ then explained, 'Rasulullah ﷺ sent Abu Bakr ☙ to lead the army, but he was unable to conquer the fortress and he returned to Rasulullah ﷺ. Rasulullah ﷺ then sent Omar ☙ to lead the army, but he was also unable to conquer the fortress and he returned to Rasulullah ﷺ. Thereafter, Rasulullah ﷺ announced, 'I shall now hand the flag over to someone who loves Allah and His Rasul ﷺ and who never flees the battlefield. Allah will grant victory at his hands.' Rasulullah ﷺ then sent for me and when I arrived, I was suffering so much pain in my eye that I could see nothing. Rasulullah ﷺ applied his saliva to my eye (because of which it was cured) and then made Du'a saying, 'O Allah! Protect him against heat and cold.' After that Du'a, heat and cold have never affected me." (Ibn Abi Shaybah, Ahmad, Ibn Majah, Bazzar, Ibn Jareer, Tabrani, Hakim, Bayhaqi in Muntakhab Kanzul Ummal). Ali ☙ also states, "Rasulullah ﷺ spat in his palm and applied the saliva to my eyes, saying, 'O Allah! Remove all heat and cold from him.' I swear by the Being Who sent Rasulullah ﷺ with the truth that to this day I have never felt either of the 2 (heat and cold).'" (Abu Nu'aym in Dala'il, Tabrani, Haythami). Suwaid bin Ghafala ☙ says, "When we once met Ali ☙ wearing 2 light garments during winter, we said to him, 'Do not be deceived by our land because it is extremely cold, unlike the land you come from.' His reply was, 'I was a person who used to feel extremely cold. When Rasulullah ﷺ sent me to lead the assault at Khaibar, I told him about the pain in my eyes and he applied some of his saliva to my eyes. Thereafter, I never experienced any pain in my eyes, neither did I ever feel any heat or any cold.'" (Tabrani, Bazzar, Haythami)

The Cold has no effect on the Sahabah one Night by the Du'a of Rasulullah ﷺ

Bilal ☙ reports, "I called out the Fajr Adhan one icy winter morning but no one came for salah. I then called out the Adhan again, but still no one arrived. 'What is the matter with them, O Bilal?' Rasulullah ﷺ enquired. 'May my parents be sacrificed for you!' I said, 'The cold must be too challenging for them.'

Rasulullah ﷺ then made Du'a saying, 'O Allah! Take the cold away from them.' I then saw the people arrive for the Fajr and Duha (midmorning) salah with great ease and comfort." *(Abu Nu'aym in Dala'il, Bayhaqi in Al Bidayah wan Nihayah)*. A narration from Hudhaifa ؓ discussing the Battle of Khandaq also highlights the same point.

The Effects of Hunger are Removed from Fatima ؓ

Imran bin Husain ؓ reports, "I was sitting with Rasulullah ﷺ when Fatima ؓ arrived and stood facing towards him. 'Come closer, O Fatima,' Rasulullah ﷺ said. When she moved a little closer, Rasulullah ﷺ bade her to come even closer. When she moved a little more, Rasulullah ﷺ asked her to come even closer. She then stood right in front of him. I could see that her face had become extremely pale and all the blood seemed to have left it. Rasulullah ﷺ spread out his fingers and placed his hand on her chest. He then lifted her head and prayed, 'O Allah The One Who satiates the hungry, Who fulfils needs and who elevates the lowly ones! Do not allow Fatima the daughter of Muhammad ﷺ to suffer hunger.' I saw the paleness caused by her hunger disappear from her face and the blood return to her cheeks. I asked her about it later, she said, 'Imran, I have never experienced hunger after that day." *(Tabrani, Haythami, Abu Nu'aym in Dala'il)*

The Effects of Old Age are Reversed for Abu Zaid Ansari ؓ Through the Du'a of Rasulullah ﷺ

Abu Zaid Ansari ؓ narrates that Rasulullah ﷺ once told him to draw closer and when he did, Rasulullah ﷺ passed his hand over his head saying, "O Allah! Grant him good looks and perpetuate his looks." Abu Zaid ؓ then lived to over 100 years and until his death, he had only a few strands of white hairs on his beard and his face remained youthful without any wrinkles. *(Ahmad in Al Bidayah wan Nihayah)*. Abu Zaid ؓ says, "Rasulullah ﷺ asked for some water and I brought him a cupful. There was a strand of hair in the water and when I removed it, Rasulullah ﷺ made Du'a saying, 'O Allah! Grant him good looks.'" The narrator of the report Abu Nuhaik says that when he saw Abu Zaid ؓ at the age of 94, he had not a single white hair on his beard. *(Ahmad in Isabah, Ibn Hibban, Hakim)*. At the age of 93, Abu Zaid ؓ had not a single white hair on either his head or his beard. *(Abu Nu'aym in Dala'il)*

The Effects of Old Age are Removed from the Face of Qatadah bin Milhan ؓ Through the Touch of Rasulullah ﷺ

Abul A'la says, "I was with Qatadah bin Milhan ؓ at the place where he passed away. When someone passed by at the back of the room, I saw his reflection on the face of Qatadah ؓ. Rasulullah ﷺ once passed his hand over Qatadah ؓ's face because of which his face appeared to be oiled every time I looked at him." *(Ahmad in Al Bidayah wan Nihayah)*. Hayan bin Umair reports, "Rasulullah ﷺ passed his hand over the face of Qatadah bin Milhan ؓ, because of which every part of his body showed signs of ageing as he grew older except for his face. I was present at the time of his death and when a woman passed by behind me, I saw her reflection on his face just as I would have seen it in a mirror." *(Ibn Shahin in Isabah)*

The Effects of Old Age are Reversed for Nabigha Ja'di ؓ Through the Du'a of Rasulullah ﷺ

Nabigha Ja'di ؓ reports that he once recited the following couplet before Rasulullah ﷺ:

"While our honor and status have reached the skies we still aspire to transcend to greater heights"

"And where do these greater heights lead to, O Abu Laila?" Rasulullah ﷺ asked. "To Jannah, "came the reply. To this, Rasulullah ﷺ remarked, "That's right, InshaAllah." Nabigha ؓ then recited the following couplets as well:

"There is no good in tolerance when it does not have some hasty deeds that protect the best of them from being polluted. There is also no good in haste when it does not have some perseverance to complete a deed after commencing it"

Rasulullah ﷺ commended him saying, "You have spoken well. May Allah never allow your teeth to fall out" A narrator by the name of Ya'la says, "I saw Nabigha ؓ when he was over 100 years of age, yet none of his teeth had fallen out." *(Abu Nu'aym in Dala'il, Bayhaqi, Bazzar in Al Bidayah wan Nihayah)*. Abdullah bin Jarad reports that Nabigha Ja'di ؓ said, "When I recited to Rasulullah ﷺ the couplet 'While our honor and status...' Rasulullah ﷺ became angry and asked, "And where do these greater heights lead to, O Abu Laila?' 'To Jannah,' I replied. To this, Rasulullah ﷺ remarked, 'That's alright, InshaAllah. Recite to me another of your couplets.' I then recited to him "There is no good in tolerance..." (the 2 couplets quoted above). Rasulullah ﷺ then commended me saying, 'You have spoken well. May Allah never allow your teeth to fall out.'" Abdullah bin Jarad says, "I saw that Nabigha ؓ's teeth (even as an old man) were as white as hailstones and not one of them had even broken or become crooked." *(Hasan bin Sufian, Abu Nu'aym in Tarikh Isfahan, Shirazi in his Alqab, Khattabi's Gharibul Hadith, Marhabi's Kitabul Ilm, Dar Qutni's Al Mu'talafwal Mukhtalaf, Ibn Sakan's Sahabah)*. Another narration adds, 'Throughout his life, he always had the best set of teeth. Whenever a tooth fell out, it was replaced by another and he lived to very old age." *(Isabah)*

Eradicating the Effect of Trauma to Ummu Is'haq ؓ

Ummu Is'haq ؓ relates, "I was migrating to Rasulullah ﷺ in Madinah with my brother when he said, 'Sit here, O Ummu Is'haq because I have forgotten my money in Makkah.' I said, 'I fear that my wretch husband will harm you.' He confidently replied, 'InshaAllah, he will never be able to.' I stayed there for a few days when a man passed by who recognized me but whose name I do not know. 'O Ummu Is'haq!' he said, 'What keeps you here?' 'I am waiting for my brother,' I replied. 'You have no brother after this day,' he said, 'Your husband has killed him.' I made myself strong and finally arrived in Madinah. I went to Rasulullah ﷺ at a time when he was busy making wudhu and stood before him. 'O Rasulullah ﷺ!' I said, 'My brother Is'haq has been murdered.' I noticed that Rasulullah ﷺ bent down (towards the water) while making wudhu. Rasulullah ﷺ then took a handful of water and sprinkled it on my face." A narrator named Bashar reports that his grandmother said, "By the blessing of this water whenever Ummu Is'haq ؓ was struck by a calamity, her tears never ran down her cheeks even though her eyes would well up with them." *(Abu Ny'aym in Dala'il, Bukhari in Tarikh, Abu Ya'la in Isabah)*. Ummu Is'haq ؓ also said, "I said, 'O Rasulullah ﷺ! I keep weeping about the murder of my brother Is'haq.' Rasulullah ﷺ then took a handful of water and sprinkled it on my face." Ummu Hakim says, "Even when enormous tragedies struck Ummu Is'haq ؓ you would see tears well up in her eyes, but they never flowed on to her cheeks." *(Isabah, Hafidh on Bashar)*.

Protection from Rain by Du'a

Abdullah bin Abbas ؓ reports, "Omar bin Khattab ؓ asked us to ride with him to the countryside where his tribe resided. We left and Ubay bin Ka'b ؓ and I were behind the others. A cloud started to thunder and rain started to pour, Ubay ﷺ made Du'a saying, 'O Allah! Avert its harm from us.' We caught up with the rest, their carriages were soaking wet while we were dry. Omar ﷺ asked, 'Did the rain that fell on us not fall on you?' I replied, 'Abu Mundhir Ubay ﷺ prayed to Allah to avert the harm from us.' 'Why did you not pray for us as well?' Omar ﷺ remarked." *(Ibn Abi Dunya, Ibn Asakir in Muntakhab Kanzul Ummal)*

A Branch is Turned into a Sword

Zaid bin Aslam ﷺ and others have narrated that when Ukasha bin Mihsin ﷺ's sword broke during the Battle of Badr, Rasulullah ﷺ gave him a branch, which transformed into a sturdy and sparkling sword while in his hand. *(Ibn Sa'd)*

Wine Becomes Vinegar by Du'a

Khaithama reports that a man once came to Khalid bin Walid ﷺ with a casket of wine. Khalid ﷺ made Du'a saying, "O Allah! Transform it into honey." The wine turned into honey. When a man passed by Khalid bin Walid ﷺ with a casket of wine, Khalid ﷺ asked him what it was. When the man lied and said that it was vinegar, Khalid ﷺ said, 'May Allah make it vinegar." The people then looked at it, they found that it was vinegar even though it had been wine. *(Ibn Abi Dunya in Isabah).* When a man passed by Khalid bin Walid ﷺ with a casket of wine, Khalid ﷺ asked him what it was. When the man lied and said that it was honey, Khalid ﷺ said, "May Allah make it vinegar." The man then returned to his friends and said, "I have brought you wine that no Arab has drunk before." When he opened the casket, he found that it was full of vinegar. To this, he remarked, "By Allah! The Du'a of Khalid has struck it." *(Al Bidayah wan Nihayah)*

Prisoners are Rescued from Captivity: The Incident of Awf bin Malik Ashja'ee ﷺ

Muhammad bin Is'haq reports that Malik Ashja'ee ﷺ once came to Rasulullah ﷺ and said, "My son Awf has been taken captive." Rasulullah ﷺ then sent a message to Awf ﷺ that he should profusely recite: *'La Howla wa La Quwwata Illa Billah'.* When the messenger conveyed the message to Awf, he continuously recited: *'La Howla wa La Quwwata Illa Billah'.* Awf ﷺ was tied with leather straps. The straps eventually broke and he walked free. As he came out, he found a camel belonging to his captors and rode it away. As he rode further, he found their other camels grazing. He then screamed out to them and rounded them all up. His father was alerted of his arrival only when he called out at the door. "By the Rabb of the Kabah!" his father exclaimed, "Can that be Awf?!" "O dear!" his mother sighed, "Awf is suffering the pain of the straps, it cannot be him!" His father and servant leapt towards the door, where Awf had already filled the yard with camels. Awf ﷺ then related his experience to his father together with the details of how he came by the camels. His father then went to Rasulullah ﷺ and related to him what had happened to Awf and how he brought the camels along. "Do as you please with the camels," Rasulullah ﷺ advised, "and treat them as you treat your own camels." It was then that Allah revealed the verse:

وَمَنْ يَتَّقِ اللَّهَ يَجْعَلْ لَهُ مَخْرَجًا (2) وَيَرْزُقْهُ مِنْ حَيْثُ لَا يَحْتَسِبُ وَمَنْ يَتَوَكَّلْ عَلَى اللَّهِ فَهُوَ حَسْبُهُ

...He (Allah) will make a way for him to get out (from every difficulty). And He will provide him from (sources) he never could imagine. And whosoever puts his trust in Allah, then He will suffice him... (At-Talaq:2-3) *(Adam bin Abu Ayas in his Tafsir, Targheeb wat Tarheeb, Ibn Abi Hatim in Tafsir Ibn*

Kathir). Whenever Awf ﷺ's father went to Rasulullah ﷺ, he lamented about the situation his son was in and the difficulty he was suffering. Rasulullah ﷺ advised him to exercise patience, saying, "Allah shall soon create an escape for him." *(Ibn Jareer)*

What Happened to 2 Persons who Disobeyed Rasulullah ﷺ

Abbas bin Sahl bin Sa'd Sa'idi reports that when Rasulullah ﷺ was passing by the area of Hijr where the Thamud tribe were destroyed, he dismounted and the Sahabah drew water from the well that was there. When they were done, Rasulullah ﷺ instructed the Sahabah saying, "Do not drink from this water, do not make wudhu with it for salah and if any dough was made with it, it should be fed to the animals. In addition to this, none of you should leave the camp tonight unless accompanied by another." All of the Sahabah complied with the instruction except for 2 of them, both of whom belonged to the Banu Sa'ida tribe. While one left the camp to relieve himself, the other went out in search of his camel. The one who went out to relieve himself was throttled by a Jinn and the other who was searching for his camel was swept up by a tempest and thrown between the 2 mountains of the Banu Tay tribe in Yemen. When Rasulullah ﷺ was informed of this, he said, "Did I not forbid you all from leaving the camp unless accompanied by another?" Rasulullah ﷺ then made Du'a for the one who was throttled and he was cured. The other Sahabi rejoined Rasulullah ﷺ at Tabuk. Another narration states the Banu Tay tribe sent him back to Rasulullah ﷺ after Rasulullah ﷺ had returned to Madinah. *(Ibn Is'haq in Al Bidayah wan Nihayah, Abu Nu'aym in Dala'il)*

What Happened to Jahja Ghifari Because he Harmed Uthman ﷺ

Abdullah bin Omar ﷺ reports that Uthman ﷺ was delivering a sermon from the pulpit when Jahja Ghifari ﷺ stood up, grabbed Uthman ﷺ's staff and struck his knee so hard that the staff broke and Uthman ﷺ's knee was seriously injured. Within the same year, Allah afflicted Jahja ﷺ with a disease that affected his arm and actually ate away the flesh. He passed away with this condition. *(Abu Nu'aym in Dala'il).* Another narration states that Jahja bin Sa'eed Ghifari ﷺ once confronted Uthman ﷺ, snatched his stick from his hand and struck him so hard on his knee that the stick broke. The people were outraged, but Uthman ﷺ merely got off the pulpit and went home. Allah then afflicted Jahja Ghifari ﷺ's knee with a disease that killed him before the year had ended. *(Ibnus Sakan, Bawardi in Isabah)*

What Happened to a Man who hurt Sa'd ﷺ During the Battle of Qadisiya

Abdul Malik bin Umair reports that a Muslim man once came up to Sa'd bin Abi Waqqas ﷺ and directed the following couplets at him (which mean):

"We fight until Allah sends his assistance whereas Sa'd clings on to the gate of Qadisiya when we return, many of our wives have become widows whereas no wife of Sa'd's has been widowed"

When Sa'd ﷺ heard this, he raised his hands and made Du'a saying, "O Allah! You restrain his hand and tongue against me in a manner You see fit." It then happened that during the Battle of Qadisiya, the man was struck by an arrow, his tongue was cut out, his hand was cut off and he was killed. *(Abu Nu'aym in Dala'il).* Another narration quotes the same 2 couplets, but the first line of the couplets read:

"Do you not see that Allah has sent His assistance?"

It states further that when Sa'd ﷺ heard the man's words, he remarked, "May his tongue and hand be paralyzed." It then occurred that an arrow struck the man's mouth, rendering him dumb, after which his hand was cut off in the battle. During the fighting Sa'd ﷺ asked the others to carry him to the gate of the city and when he was carried there, his back was exposed, revealing many injuries. In this way, the people came to know that he was truly excused from fighting and they regarded him as such, knowing with certainty that he was not a coward as the man had claimed. *(Tabrani, Haythami)*

A Previously quoted Incident in this Regard Concerning Sa'd ﷺ

In the chapter entitled "Getting Annoyed for the Sake of One's Elders", the narration of Amir bin Sa'd has passed which states that Sa'd bin Abi Waqqas ﷺ cursed a man who was speaking ill of Ali ﷺ, Talha ﷺ and Zubair ﷺ. As a result of his curse a Bactrian camel then came running and the people gave her way until she trampled the man and killed him." Another narration from Qais bin Abu Hazim speaks about how Sa'd cursed a person who reviled Ali ﷺ. In the narration, Qais says, "We had not yet dispersed when the animal started sinking in the ground and it threw him off. He landed head first on the stones, causing him to die as his head burst open." Sa'eed bin Musayib states that an infuriated camel then ran through the people and it reached the man who spoke ill of the Sahabah, it struck him down, sat on him and continued crushing him between its chest and the ground until it broke his body into bits. Sa'eed says, "I saw people running up to Sa'd ﷺ, saying, 'Congratulations on the acceptance of your Du'a.'" *(Abu Nu'aym in Dala'il)*

What Happened to Ziyad due to the Du'a of Abdullah bin Omar ﷺ

Ibn Showdhab reports that when Abdullah bin Omar ﷺ heard that Ziyad wanted governorship over Hijaz, he disapproved of his being governor. He therefore made Du'a, saying, "O Allah! Verily you make the killing of whomsoever You wish a means of atoning for their sins. Therefore grant death to Ziyad the son of Sumaya without him being killed." A devastating infection then started on Ziyad's thumb and he died before the next Friday arrived. *(Ibn Asakir in Muntakhab Kanzul Ummal)*

What Happened to the Person who Harmed Husain ﷺ

Ibn Wa'il or Abu Wa'il who was present at Karbala reports, "A man then stood up and said, 'Is Husain amongst you?' When the people replied that he was, the man remarked, 'The good news is that you will be ending up in Jahannam!' Husain ﷺ replied, 'I have been given the good news of a Merciful Rabb and an intercessor Rasulullah ﷺ whose intercession is certainly accepted.' 'Who are you?' the people asked the man. He informed them that he was Ibn Juwaira or Ibn Juwaiza. Husain ﷺ then made Du'a saying, 'O Allah! Take him in pieces to Jahannam!' Just then, his animal bolted and when the man fell off, his foot got caught in the stirrup. By Allah! As the animal ran off there was eventually nothing of the man apart from his leg." *(Tabrani, Haythami)*. Kalbi reports that Husain ﷺ was drinking water when a man shot an arrow at him, which paralyzed his jaw. "May Allah never quench your thirst!" Husain ﷺ said. Unable to quench his thirst the man then drank so much water that his stomach actually burst. *(Tabrani, Haythami)*. Ubaidulla bin Ziyad's doorkeeper reports, "After Ubaidulla had martyred Husain ﷺ, I entered the palace behind. A flame suddenly leapt into Ubaidullah's face and he had to shield it with his sleeve. 'Did you see that?' Ubaidulla asked the doorkeeper. When I replied that I did, he told me to keep it a secret." *(Tabrani, Haythami)*. Sufian reports from his grandmother that there were 2 men from the Ju'fi tribe who participated in the martyrdom of Husain ﷺ. The private organ of

one of them became so grotesquely large that he had to fold it, while the other would suffer such great thirst that he would finish a large jar of water in a gulp. Sufyan says that he also saw that the son of one of them was insane. *(Tabrani, Haythami)*. A'mash narrates that when a man once defecated on the grave of Husain ﷺ, his entire family was struck with insanity, leprosy, white liver and poverty. *(Tabrani, Haythami)*

Fresh Blood Rains Down during the "Year of Jama'ah"

Rabe'ah bin Qusait reports, "I was with Amr bin Al Aas ﷺ during the "Year of Jama'ah" the year in which the armies of Ali ﷺ and Mu'awiya ﷺ clashed in battle. The army was returning when there came a downpour of fresh blood. I saw myself holding up a utensil that was filled with blood and everyone knew that this was the blood of each other that they had spilled. Amr bin Al Aas ﷺ then stood up, duly praised Allah and said, 'O people! Mend your relationship with Allah and even if these 2 mountains have to collide you will not be harmed in the least.'" *(Ibn Asakir in Kanzul Ummal)*

Blood is Discovered Beneath Stones when Husain ﷺ was Martyred

Zuhri reports, "Abdul Malik once said to me, 'If you can tell me what was the sign of Husain ﷺ's martyrdom, you can truly be called a great scholar.' I replied, 'Fresh blood was found beneath every stone lifted in Baytul Maqdas.' Abdul Malik then said to me, 'You and I are contemporaries in this narration." *(Tabrani, Haythami)*. He says, "The day Husain ﷺ was martyred, every stone lifted in Sham gave way to blood." *(Tabrani, Haythami)*

The Sky Turns Red and Eclipses the Day Husain ﷺ was Martyred

Ummu Hakim ﷺ says, "I was still a little girl when Husain ﷺ was martyred. For a few days afterwards, the sky remained the color of a blood clot." *(Tabrani, Haythami)*. Abu Qubail says, "When Husain ﷺ was martyred, the sun eclipsed so extraordinarily that stars were visible at noon and we really thought' that Judgment had arrived." *(Tabrani, Haythami)*. In his *Al Bidayah wan Nihayah*, Allama Ibn Kathir has cited all the above narrations apart from the first as weak, categorizing them as fabrications of the Shias. Allah knows best.

The Jinn mourn the death of Omar ﷺ

Malik bin Dinar reports that when Omar ﷺ was martyred, a voice of a Jinn was heard coming from the Tabala mountains in Yemen. It recited the following couplets which mean:

"I stand at the service of whoever wished to weep over (the adherents to) Islam because their destruction is imminent even though much time has not yet elapsed.
This world is leaving with all its good and those people have lost interest in this world who aspire for the hereafter"

When the people looked to see where the voice came from, they could see no one. *(Hakim)*. Ma'ruf Mowsili narrates that he heard a voice reciting some couplets when Omar ﷺ was martyred. The narration then proceeds to quote the above 2 couplets. *(Abu Nu'aym in Dala'il, Tabrani in Majma'uz Zawa'id)*. Aisha ﷺ says, "Although I could see no one, I heard someone lamenting the death of Omar ﷺ one night as he recited the followings:

"May Allah reward the Amirul Mu'minin with the best rewards and may Allah's hand bless the skin that has been ripped apart (O Amirul Mu'minin) Whoever walks or rides to achieve the accomplishments you have attained to catch up with what you have accomplished in the past, he will surely be beaten. You have accomplished tremendous feats but then left behind such tragedies, the buds of which have

still to bloom" (Ibn Sa'd)

Sulaiman bin Yasar reports that the Jinn mourned the death of Omar ؓ by reciting the following couplets (which mean):

"Peace be on the Amirul Mu'minin and may Allah's hand bless the skin that has been ripped apart

(O Amirul Mu'minin) You have accomplished tremendous feats but then left behind such tragedies, the buds of which have still to bloom. Whoever walks or rides to achieve the accomplishments you have attained to catch up with what you have accomplished in the past, he will surely be beaten.

The martyrdom of such a personality in Madinah has caused darkness to loom over the earth. After this, can the acacia tree ever allow its branches to sway in the breeze?" (Ibn Sa'd)

Aisha ؓ quotes the above 4 couplets in a different sequence, but then adds another couplet (which means):

"(O Amirul Mu'minin) May my Rabb meet you with salutations in Jannah and with the garments of Firdous that never tear" (Abu Nu'aym in Dala'il)

The Jinn mourn the Death of Husain bin Ali ؓ

Ummul Mu'minin Ummu Salamah ؓ says, "The Jinn were heard bewailing the death of Husain bin Ali ؓ." (Tabrani, Haythami). Another narration states that Ummu Salamah ؓ once said, "Since the demise of Rasulullah ﷺ, I have never heard the Jinn lament the death of anyone as I hear them do tonight. I think that my son Husain ؓ is now deceased." She then instructed her maid servant to make enquiries, after which she learnt that Husain ؓ had been martyred. She further reports that a lady from the Jinn was then heard reciting the following couplets (which mean):

"O my eye! Take careful note of my exertion because (if I do not) who will weep after me over that group of people whose deaths lead them to tyrants in the service of mere slaves" (Tabrani, Haythami)

Ummul Mu'minin Maymuna ؓ says, "The Jinn were heard lamenting the death of Husain bin Ali ؓ" (Tabrani, Haythami)

Abu Musa ؓ sees Rasulullah ﷺ in a Dream

Abu Musa Ash'ari ؓ says, "I saw myself at place where there were many roads. All the roads started to vanish until there was only one left. I then took the road, which led me to a mountain. On top of the mountain stood Rasulullah ﷺ, with Abu Bakr ؓ beside him. Rasulullah ﷺ was gesturing to Omar ؓ to come there. I then said to myself, 'Inna Lillahi wa Inna Ilayhi Raji'un! I swear by Allah that Amirul Mu'minin will be leaving this world.'" To this, Anas ؓ said, "Why do you not write to Amirul Mu'minin about this." Abu Musa ؓ replied, "I cannot inform him of his own death." (Ibn Sa'd)

Uthman ؓ sees Nabi ﷺ in a Dream

Kathir bin Silt narrates, "On the day Uthman ؓ was martyred, he happened to fall asleep during the day. He then woke up and said, 'I would inform you of something had it not been for people saying that Uthman wishes to stir trouble.' 'May Allah mend your affairs,' we said, 'Please do inform us because we will not say what other people say.' He then related, 'I saw Rasulullah ﷺ in the sleep I just had and he said to me, 'You will be with us this Friday." (Hakim by Dhahabi) Another narration adds that that very day was Friday. (Ibn Sa'd, Abu Ya'la, Haythami). Abdullah bin Omar ؓ reports that Uthman ؓ related to them one morning that he saw Nabi ﷺ telling him in a dream, "O Uthman! Terminate your fast with us." Uthman ؓ therefore fasted that day and it was on that very day that he was martyred. (Hakim by Dhahabi, Abu Ya'la, Bazzar in Majma'uz Zawa'id, Ibn Sa'd). Muslim Abu Sa'eed who was a freed slave of Uthman bin Affan ؓ says, "Uthman ؓ set 20 slaves free and then asked for a pair of trousers, which he wore, even though he never wore trousers at any time before Islam or after becoming a Muslim. He then said, 'Last night I saw Rasulullah ﷺ, Abu Bakr ؓ and Omar ؓ. They said to me, 'Be patient because you will terminate your fast with us tomorrow evening.' He asked for his Qur'an and opened it before him (to recite). He was later martyred with the Qur'an still in front of him." (Abdullah, Abu Ya'la, Haythami, Majma'uz Zawa'id, Ibn Sa'd)

Ali ؓ sees Nabi ﷺ in a Dream

Hasan ؓ or Husain ؓ reports that their father Ali ؓ once said, "I met my beloved friend Nabi ﷺ in a dream and when I complained of the problems I am having with the people of Iraq after he had left this world, he promised me deliverance from them in the near future." It was barely 3 days later that he passed away. (Adani). Abu Salih says, "Ali ؓ once said, 'I saw Nabi ﷺ in a dream and complained to him about the way in which his Ummah are falsifying me and harming me. When I started to cry, Rasulullah ﷺ said, 'Do not cry, O Ali. Turn around.' When I turned around, I saw 2 men: Ali's assassin Ibn Muljim and his accomplice bound in fetters, whose heads were being crushed by boulders. Each time, their heads were crushed, they were then restored, after which the process continued.' The following day, I was proceeding on my way to meet Ali ؓ as I did every day, but as I was passing by the place where butchers gathered, I met some people who informed me that the Amirul Mu'minin had been assassinated." (Abu Ya'la in Muntakhab Kanzul Ummal)

Hasan bin Ali ؓ sees Nabi ﷺ in a Dream

Filfila Ju'fi reports that he heard Hasan bin Ali ؓ say, "I saw in a dream that Nabi ﷺ was holding on to the Arsh. I then saw that Abu Bakr ؓ was holding on to Nabi ﷺ's waist, that Omar ؓ was holding on to Abu Bakr ؓ's waist and that Uthman ؓ was holding on to Omar ؓ's waist. Then I saw blood extending from the sky to the earth." When Hasan ؓ was relating this dream, there happened to be some members of the Shia sect with him, who then asked, "Did you not see Ali ؓ?" Hasan ؓ replied, "There is none I would not have loved to see holding Nabi ﷺ's waist more than Ali ؓ. Nevertheless, that was the dream that I saw..." (Tabrani in Awsat and Kabeer, Haythami). Hasan ؓ once said, "O people! I saw a most remarkable thing in my dream last night. I saw the Rabb the Most High upon the Arsh. Rasulullah ﷺ then arrived and stood by one of the feet of the Arsh. Thereafter, Abu Bakr ؓ arrived and placed his hand upon Rasulullah ﷺ's shoulder. He was followed by Omar ؓ, who placed his hand upon Abu Bakr ؓ's shoulder, after which Uthman ؓ arrived and placed his hand upon Omar ؓ's shoulder. Uthman ؓ then gestured with his hand and said, 'O my Rabb! Ask Your servants why they killed me.' Two downpipes of blood then started to flow from the sky to the earth." Someone reported this to Ali ؓ, saying, "Do you not see what your son Hasan ؓ is saying?" Ali ؓ's reply was, "He is only relating what he saw." Another narration states that Hasan ؓ added, "I shall not fight again after the dream that I saw..." The narration then proceeds like the one above, but with the difference that he said, "I then saw Uthman ؓ with his hand upon Omar ؓ's shoulder. Thereafter, I saw a lot of blood behind them. 'What is this?' I enquired. I was then informed that this was the blood of Uthman ؓ, for which he was asking redress from Allah." (Abu Ya'la, Haythami)

Abdullah bin Abbas sees Nabi in a Dream

Abdullah bin Abbas reports, "In my afternoon sleep, I saw Rasulullah with disheveled hair and with a glass in his hand. 'What is this glass for?' I asked. 'The blood of Husain and his companions. I have been picking it up all day.' When we then saw the date, we found it to be the same day in which Husain was martyred." *(Khateeb in Tarikh, Ibn Abdul Birr in Isti'ab)*

Abbas and his Son Abdullah see Omar in their Dreams

Abbas bin Abdul Muttalib says, "I was the neighbor of Omar bin Khattab and have never seen anyone better than him. His nights were spent in salah and his days were spent fasting and tending to the needs of people. When he passed away, I asked Allah to show him to me in a dream. In a dream one night I saw him coming form the marketplace of Madinah with his shawl draped over his neck. After exchanging greetings, I asked, 'How are you?' 'I am well,' he replied. 'What did you find?' I asked. He replied, 'My reckoning is now over. Had I not found a Merciful Rabb, my honor would have fallen.'" *(Abu Nu'aym in Hilya)*. Abbas relates, "Omar bin Khattab was my very good friend. After he passed away, I made Du'a to Allah for a complete year to show me Omar in a dream. The year had just come to an end when I saw him wiping perspiration from his forehead. 'O Amirul Mu'minin!' I said, 'How did your Rabb treat you?' 'My reckoning is now over,' he replied, 'Had I not found a Forgiving and Merciful Rabb, I would have fallen in honor.'" *(Ibn Sa'd)*. Abdullah bin Abbas says, "I made Du'a to Allah for a year to show me Omar bin Khattab in a dream. When I saw him in a dream, I asked, 'How was your experience?' He replied, 'I found a Most Forgiving and Merciful Rabb. Had it not been for His mercy, I would have fallen in honor.'" *(Ibn Sa'd)*

Abdullah bin Omar and an Ansari see Omar in a Dream

Abdullah bin Omar says, "There was nothing I wanted more than to know what had happened to Omar in the next life. I then saw a palace in a dream and when I asked whom it belonged to, I was informed that it belonged to Omar bin Khattab. He then came out of the palace wearing a shawl, appearing as if he had just taken a bath. 'What has happened to you?' I asked. 'I have been well,' he replied, 'but had I not found a Forgiving Rabb, I would have fallen in honor.' He then asked, 'How long ago did I separate from you?' 'It is 12 years now,' I replied. He then said, 'I have just now returned from my reckoning.'" *(Abu Nu'aym in Hilya)*. Salim bin Abdullah reports that he once heard an Ansari say, "I had always prayed to Allah to show me Omar bin Khattab in a dream. It was after 10 years that I did see him wiping perspiration from his brow. 'O Amirul Mu'minin!' I said, 'What has happened to you?' He replied by saying, 'I have just completed my reckoning and had it not been for the mercy of my Rabb, I would surely have been destroyed.'" *(Ibn Sa'd)*

Abdur Rahman bin Auf sees Omar in a Dream

Abdur Rahman bin Auf was returning from Hajj when he set up camp and fell asleep at a place called Suqia. When he woke up, he said, "I just saw Omar in a dream. He walked up to me and used his foot to nudge my wife Ummu Kulthum bint Uqba who was asleep beside me. This woke her up and he then went away. As the others went out in search of him, I also got my clothing, dressed and went out to search with them. Although I was the first to catch up with him, I swear by Allah that I found him only after I had thoroughly exhausted myself. 'O Amirul Mu'minin!' I said, 'You have really made it difficult for the people to keep up with you. By Allah! One can only catch up with you after thoroughly exhausting themselves. In fact, it was only after I had thoroughly exhausted myself that I managed to catch up with you.' To this, he said, 'But I do not think that I had been going fast at all.' I swear by the Being Who controls the life of Abdur Rahman that this (lead over the rest of us) was because of his deeds." *(Ibn Sa'd)*

Abdullah bin Salam sees Salman in a Dream

Abdullah bin Salam reports that Salman once said to him, "Dear brother! Whichever of us dies first should make an attempt to see his brother." "Is such a thing possible?" Abdullah asked. Salman replied, "Certainly. After death the soul of a Mu'min is free to roam wherever it wills on earth, whereas the soul of a Kafir is locked in captivity." Abdullah bin Salam says, "Salman passed away and I was lying on my bed one afternoon when I happened to fall asleep. Salman then appeared in my dream and greeted me saying, 'As Salamu Alayka wa Rahmatullah.' I responded by saying, 'As Salamu Alayka wa Rahmatullah, O Abu Abdullah. How have you found your destination?' He replied, 'It is excellent. Hold fast to Tawakkul because Tawakkul is a most excellent virtue! Hold fast to Tawakkul because Tawakkul is a most excellent virtue! Hold fast to Tawakkul because Tawakkul is a most excellent virtue!'" *(Ibn Sa'd)*. When Abdullah saw Salman in a dream, he asked, "How are you faring, O Abu Abdullah?" "I am well," came the reply. "Which deed did you find to be most virtuous?" Abdullah asked. Salman replied, 'I have found Tawakkul to be most remarkable." *(Abu Nu'aym in Hilya)*

Auf bin Malik sees Abdur Rahman bin Auf in a Dream

Auf bin Malik relates, "I saw a leather tent and a green pasture in a dream. Around the tent there sat goats that ruminated and excreted Ajwa dates. When I asked whom the tent belonged to, I was informed that it belonged to Abdur Rahman bin Auf. We then waited for him to emerge and when he did, he said, 'O Auf! This is what Allah has given me because of the Qur'an. If you look yonder over that valley, you will see things that your eyes have never seen before, that your ears have never heard of and the thought of which has never crossed your heart. Allah has prepared it for Abu Darda because he used to shove the world away with both his hands and chest.'" *(Abu Nu'aym in Hilya)*

Abdullah bin Amr bin Haram sees Mubashir bin Abdul Mundhir in a Dream

Abdullah bin Amr bin Haram says, "Before the Battle of Uhud I saw Mubashir bin Abdul Mundhir in a dream. He said to me, 'You will coming to us in a few days.' 'Where are you?' I enquired. He replied, 'In Jannah where we are able to roam wherever we please.' I then asked him, 'Were you not killed in the Battle of Badr?' 'Yes,' he replied, 'but we were then brought back to life...'" When this was reported to Rasulullah, he remarked, 'Such is martyrdom, O Abu Jabir." *(Hakim)*

The Chapter on the Reasons behind the Unseen Assistance that the Sahabah Received

This chapter discusses the reasons why Nabi ﷺ and the Sahabah received unseen assistance, how they adhered to these and turned their gazes away from the material means and the temporary commodities of this world.

The Narration of Abdur Rahman bin Auf ؓ about how the Sahabah found Good in Difficulties and Hardships

Abdur Rahman bin Auf ؓ says, "Islam came with many hardships and difficulties, but we always found the best of the good in things that seem unpleasant. When we left Makkah with Rasulullah ﷺ, we found status and victory. Then we marched to Badr. Allah describes it in the words:

وَإِنَّ فَرِيقًا مِنَ الْمُؤْمِنِينَ لَكَارِهُونَ (5) يُجَادِلُونَكَ فِي الْحَقِّ بَعْدَمَا تَبَيَّنَ كَأَنَّمَا يُسَاقُونَ إِلَى الْمَوْتِ وَهُمْ يَنْظُرُونَ (6) وَإِذْ يَعِدُكُمُ اللَّهُ إِحْدَى الطَّائِفَتَيْنِ أَنَّهَا لَكُمْ وَتَوَدُّونَ أَنَّ غَيْرَ ذَاتِ الشَّوْكَةِ تَكُونُ لَكُمْ

...and verily, a party among the believers disliked it; Disputing with you concerning the truth after it was made manifest, as if they were being driven to death, while they were looking (at it). And (remember) when Allah promised you (Muslims) one of the two parties (of the enemy i.e. either the army or the caravan) that it should be yours, you wished that the one not armed (the caravan) should be yours... (Al-Anfal:5-7)

The party without strength refers to (the caravan of) the Quraish. Allah then gave us status and victory in this. We therefore found the best of the good in such things that seemed most unpleasant." *(Bazzar, Haythami)*

The Letter Abu Bakr ؓ wrote to Khalid bin Walid ؓ in this Regard

In his narration discussing the time when Khalid bin Walid ؓ was finished with the Battle of Yamama, Muhammad bin Is'haq bin Yasar continues to narrate that Khalid bin Walid ؓ was still camped at Yamama when Abu Bakr ؓ wrote a letter to him saying:

"From the servant of Allah Abu Bakr
To Khalid bin Walid, the Muhajirin and Ansar with him and all those who follow them with devotion
Salamu Alaykum
Before you do I praise that Allah besides Whom there is none worthy of worship. All praise belongs to Allah Who has fulfilled His promise, assisted his servant, honored His friend, humiliated His enemy and defeated the opposing- armies by Himself. That Allah besides Whom there is none worthy of worship declares:

وَعَدَ اللَّهُ الَّذِينَ آمَنُوا مِنْكُمْ وَعَمِلُوا الصَّالِحَاتِ لَيَسْتَخْلِفَنَّهُمْ فِي الْأَرْضِ كَمَا اسْتَخْلَفَ الَّذِينَ مِنْ قَبْلِهِمْ وَلَيُمَكِّنَنَّ لَهُمْ دِينَهُمُ الَّذِي ارْتَضَى لَهُمْ وَلَيُبَدِّلَنَّهُمْ مِنْ بَعْدِ خَوْفِهِمْ أَمْنًا يَعْبُدُونَنِي لَا يُشْرِكُونَ بِي شَيْئًا وَمَنْ كَفَرَ بَعْدَ ذَلِكَ فَأُولَئِكَ هُمُ الْفَاسِقُونَ (55)

Allah has promised those among you who believe, and do righteous good deeds, that He will certainly grant them succession to (the present rulers) in the earth, as He granted it to those before them, and that He will grant them the authority to practice their religion, that which He has chosen for them (Islam). He will surely give them in exchange a safe security after their fear (provided) they (believers) worship Me and do not associate anything (in worship) with Me. But whoever disbelieved after this, they are the Fasiqoon (rebellious, disobedient to Allah). (An-Nur:55)

This is a promise from Allah, which will never be broken and a statement in which there can be no doubt. Allah has made Jihad compulsory on the Mu'minin. He says: كُتِبَ عَلَيْكُمُ الْقِتَالُ وَهُوَ كُرْهٌ لَكُمْ

Jihad (holy fighting in Allah's Cause) is ordained for you (Muslims) though you dislike it... (Al-Baqara:216)

You must therefore seek to have Allah's promise to you fulfilled by fulfilling the necessary requirements. Obey Him in all that He has made compulsory for you even though you my have to undergo difficulty, tolerate calamities, undertake arduous journeys or even suffer losses to your wealth and health. These are all insignificant in comparison to the tremendous rewards from Allah. May Allah shower His mercy on you all! Fight in the Path of Allah whether you are enjoying prosperity or poverty and strive with your wealth and lives. Abu Bakr ؓ then included relevant verses of the Qur'an. I have given Khalid bin Walid the command to march to Iraq and to remain there until he receives my next command. You should all march with him and not cling heavily to the ground because this is a path in which Allah grants immense rewards for those whose intentions are good and who aspire for good. When you arrive in Iraq, remain there until further instructions from me. May Allah take care of all our and your concerns for this world and the Hereafter. *Was Salamu Alaykum wa Rahmatullahi wa Barakatuh."* (Bayhaqi in Sunan)

Narrations concerning the difficulties and hardships that the Sahabah bore have already been quoted in the chapter discussing enduring difficulties and hardships, the chapter discussing Hijra, the chapter discussing Nusra, the chapter discussing Jihad and several others, which provide much detail.

Carrying out Orders even Though they Appeared to Contradict what was Apparent

Utba bin Abd Sulami ؓ reports that when Rasulullah ﷺ instructed the Sahabah to stand up and fight in battle, they responded by saying, "Certainly, O Rasulullah ﷺ! We will not tell you what the Bani Isra'el told Musa, when they said:

فَاذْهَبْ أَنْتَ وَرَبُّكَ فَقَاتِلَا إِنَّا هَاهُنَا قَاعِدُونَ (24)

So go you and your Lord and fight you two, we are sitting right here. (Al-Ma'ida:24)

You and your Rabb go ahead, O Muhammad ﷺ, and we will be there to fight right beside you." *(Ahmad, Haythami).* A similar statement of Miqdad ؓ has passed in the chapter of Jihad, as reported by Ibn Abi Hatim, Ibn Mardway and others. Also quoted earlier is the statement of Sa'd bin Ubadah ؓ who said, "I swear by the Being Who controls my life! If you command us to ride our animals into the sea, we shall readily do so and if you command us to travel to (the distant city of) Barkul Ghimad in Yemen, we shall certainly do so." The statement of Sa'd bin Mu'adh ؓ has also passed, when he said to Rasulullah ﷺ, "I swear by the Being Who has honored you and revealed the Qur'an to you that although I have never traveled the road and have no knowledge about it, we shall definitely travel with you even if you were to travel up to Barkul Ghimad which lies in Yemen. We shall also not be like those people who said to Musa السلام, 'You and your Rabb both go ahead and fight. We shall remain sitting here.' We shall rather say, 'You and your Rabb both go ahead and fight. We shall be there right behind you.' You had possibly left for a purpose after which Allah intended you to do something else. Look into the matter that Allah intends you to do and then do it. You may join ties with whoever you please, severe ties with whoever you please, initiate hostilities towards whoever you please, enter into peace treaties with whoever you please and take as much of our wealth as you please." It was with reference to this statement of Sa'd ؓ that Allah revealed the following verse of the Qur'an: كَمَا أَخْرَجَكَ رَبُّكَ مِنْ بَيْتِكَ بِالْحَقِّ وَإِنَّ فَرِيقًا

مِنَ الْمُؤْمِنِينَ لَكَارِهُونَ (5)

As your Lord caused you (O Muhammad ﷺ) to go out from your home with the truth, and verily, a party among the believers disliked it (Al-Anfal:5)

Sa'd ؓ also said to Rasulullah ﷺ, "Take as much of our wealth as you please and leave as much as you please but what you take from us is more beloved to us than what you leave. Our wills are subservient to the commands you give us."

The incident of Amirul Mu'minin Ali ؓ and a Fortune Teller: Trust in Allah and Disbelieve in what the People of Falsehood Propagate

Abdullah bin Auf bin Ahmar reports that when Ali ؓ was leaving Ambar to go to Nahrwan, Musafir bin Auf bin Ahmar said to him, "O Amirul Mu'minin! Do not leave right now, but leave after three portions of the day have passed." "Why is that?" Ali ؓ enquired. Musafir replied, "If you leave right now, you and your companions will come to harm. However, if you leave in the time I have suggested to you, you will be successful, victorious, earn plenty of booty and achieve your objectives." Ali ؓ remarked, "Neither did Muhammad ﷺ have a fortune teller, nor do we need any after him. Do you know what is in the belly of this horse of mine?" "I will be able to know by my calculations," came the reply. Ali ؓ then asserted, "Whoever believes you disbelieves in the Qur'an because Allah says:

إِنَّ اللَّهَ عِنْدَهُ عِلْمُ السَّاعَةِ وَيُنَزِّلُ الْغَيْثَ وَيَعْلَمُ مَا فِي الْأَرْحَامِ

Verily, Allah! With Him (Alone) is the knowledge of the Hour, He sends down the rain, and knows that which is in the wombs... (Luqman:34)

Muhammad ﷺ never claimed to know what you claim to know. Do you claim to possess the knowledge of what good or harm will come to someone who travels in any given hour?" "Yes, I do," he replied. Ali ؓ then said, "Whoever believes you seems to have no need for Allah to avert harm from his way. Furthemore, the one who does not travel because of your instruction has handed over his affairs to you rather than to his Rabb. This is because you claim that you are able to show him that hour in which no harm will come to the person who travels in it. I fear that the person who believes in your word is just like the one who ascribes a counterpart and partner to Allah. O Allah! There is no evil foreboding except that which You decree, there is no good except that which You ordain and there is none worthy of worship but You. O Musafir! We do not believe in what you say. In fact, we shall oppose you and travel in the very hour that you are stopping us from." Ali ؓ then addressed the people saying, "O people! Be warned against studying the stars' unless it be for the purpose of navigating in the darkness of land and sea. The astrologer is like a Kafir and the Kafir shall end up in Jahannam. (He then addressed Musafir saying,) By Allah! If the news ever reaches me that you are still practicing and implementing your findings in astrology, I shall have you imprisoned for as long I live and as long as you live. I shall also deprive you of all state allowances for as long as I am in authority." Ali ؓ then marched in the very hour that Musafir was stopping him from and then marched to Nahrwan, where he defeated the enemy. Thereafter, he said, "Had we set out during the time that he advised us to and attained victory, people would have said, 'Amirul Mu'minin left at the time that the fortune teller advised because of which he was victorious.' Neither did Muhammad ﷺ have a fortune teller, nor do we need any after him. Despite this, Allah has given us victory over the emperors of Rome and Persia and various other lands. O people! Trust in Allah and rely only on Him because with Him you will need no other." *(Harith and Khateeb in Kitabun Nujum, Kanzul Ummal)*

Incidents of Amirul Mu'minin Omar bin Khattab ؓ Seeking Honor where Allah has Placed Honor

Tariq bin Ziyad reports that when Omar ؓ was traveling to Sham, Abu Ubaidah bin Jarrah ؓ was accompanying him. When they arrived at a point where they had to wade across, Omar ؓ alighted from his camel, removed his leather socks and threw them over his shoulders. He then took hold of the reins of the camel and waded through. "O Amirul Mu'minin!" Abu Ubaidah ؓ said, "Are you doing that?! Do you also remove your leather socks, throw them over your shoulders, take hold of the reins of the camel and then wade through?! I would not like the people of that city (where we are headed) to see you like this." "O, Oh!" Omar ؓ exclaimed, "Had anyone other than Abu Ubaidah made such a statement, I would have made him a lesson for the Ummah of Muhammad ﷺ. We were once amongst the lowest of people, but Allah gave us honor because of Islam. As soon as we start to seek honor in avenues other than that in which Allah has granted us honor, Allah will then humiliate us." *(Hakim by Dhahabi)*. Another narration states that when Omar ؓ arrived in Sham and was to be received by the army, he was wearing his loincloth, leather socks and a turban. He was holding the head of his camel and wading across some water. Someone then said, "O Amirul Mu'minin! The army and the general of Sham's army are here to meet you and you are in this condition?" Omar ؓ remarked, 'We are a nation whom Allah has given honor through Islam, so we shall not seek honor in other avenues." *(Hakim)*. Yet another narration states that Abu Ubaidah bin Jarrah ؓ said to Omar ؓ, "O Amirul Mu'minin! You have done something that the people of these parts regard as a something degrading. You have removed your socks, led your camel while on foot and waded through water on foot." Omar ؓ struck Abu Ubaidah bin Jarrah ؓ on the chest and said, "O dear! If only someone other than you had made that statement, O Abu Ubaidah! You Arabs were the smallest in number and the most degraded of people before Allah gave you honor through Islam. When you start to seek honor in anything else other than Islam, Allah will certainly degrade you." *(Hakim, Abu Nu'aym in Hilya, Ibn Mubarak, Hannad, Bayhaqi in Muntakhab Kanzul Ummal)*

Qais narrates that when Omar ؓ arrived in Sham and was received by the people, he was riding a camel. "O Amirul Mu'minin!" someone said, "If only you would ride a Turkish horse because the leaders and prominent people of the city would be meeting you." To this, Omar ؓ remarked, "I do not see your honor lying here in the things of this world, but pointing to the sky, everything comes from there. Let my camel go." *(Abu Nu'aym in Hilya)*. Abul Aliya Shami reports that Omar ؓ arrived in Jabiya from the Aleppo road, riding a brown camel. The bald part of his head shone in the sun because he wore neither a hat nor a turban. Since there were no stirrups, his legs dangled loosely on either side of the carriage. His saddle blanket when he rode was a woolen blanket made in Ambijan, which doubled as a bedding when he camped. His satchel was striped cloth filled with the barn: of a date palm, which doubled as his pillow when he was not riding. He wore a thick white cotton Qamis which was patched and torn on the side. "Send the leader of these people to me," Omar ؓ commanded. When the people sent for the head priest, Omar ؓ said to him, "Please wash my Qamis, mend it and borrow me a Qamis or some clothing. A Qamis made from Kaitan, a very fine and expensive cloth was then brought to Omar ؓ. "What is this?" Omar ؓ enquired. When the people told him that it was Kattan, he asked, "And what is Kaitan?" After they explained to him what it was, he removed his Qamis and it was washed and patched. When it was returned to him, he took off the Kaftan one and wore his own. The head priest then said to him, "Because you are the king of the Arabs, it is not befitting that you ride a camel in these parts. If you ride a Turkish horse and wear some other clothing, it would command more respect in the eyes of the Romans. Omar ؓ however said, "We are people who have been given respect because of Islam and do not wish any substitute." A Turkish horse was brought and rather than a saddle or carriage, a mere saddle blanket was thrown over it. Omar ؓ rode it but when it started to walk he called out, "Stop it! Stop it! I have never seen people riding a Saitan before this because riding it brings pride in the rider." Omar ؓ's camel was brought and he rode it. *(Ibn Abi Dunya in Al Bidayah wan Nihayah)*

Giving Consideration to the Dhimmi Community when in a Position of Honor

Abu Nuhaik and Abdullah bin Handhala report; "We were with Salman ؓ in an army when someone recited Surah Maryam. Another man, probably a Jew then started to vilify Maryam عليها السلام and her son Isa عليه السلام. We then assaulted the man and hit him until he was bleeding. Since every person who was wronged in any way complained to Salman ؓ, this man also complained to him even though he had never done so before. Salman ؓ therefore approached us and asked why we had assaulted the man. 'We were reciting Surah Maryam,' we explained, 'when he started to vilify Maryam عليها السلام and her son Isa عليه السلام.' Salman ؓ rebuked us saying, 'Then why did you make him listen to it? Did you not hear what Allah says? Allah says:

وَلَا تَسُبُّوا الَّذِينَ يَدْعُونَ مِنْ دُونِ اللَّهِ فَيَسُبُّوا اللَّهَ عَدْوًا بِغَيْرِ عِلْمٍ

And insult not those whom they (disbelievers) worship besides Allah, lest they insult Allah wrongfully without knowledge...(Al-An'am:108)

O assembly of Arabs! Did you not have the worst of religions, the most inhospitable of lands and the worst lives? Did Allah not then grant you honor and give you in abundance? Do you now wish to pick on people because Allah had given you honor? By Allah! You must stop this, otherwise Allah shall take away everything in your hands and give it to someone else.' Salman ؓ then started to teach us. He said, "Perform Nafl salah between the Maghrib and Isha salahs because by reciting extra Qur'an during these Rakahs this will lighten the fixed daily recitations of the Qur'an that he recites. It will also safeguard against wasting time during the beginning of the night because this time-wasting destroys one's Hereafter." *(Abu Nu'aym in Hilya)*

Taking a Lesson from those who have Forsaken Allah's Commands

Jubair bin Nufair ؓ says, "When Cyprus was conquered, its inhabitants were separated from each other, because of which they cried for each other. I then saw Abu Darda ؓ sitting alone and weeping. 'O Abu Darda ؓ,' I said, 'What makes you weep on a day in which Allah has granted honor to Islam and its adherents?' 'Shame on you, O Jubair,' he said, 'How disgraced is that nation in the sight of Allah who forsake His commands! These people were once a powerful and victorious nation who possessed sovereignty. However, once they abandoned Allah's commands, they were degraded to the state you can now see." *(Abu Nu'aym in Hilya)*. Abu Darda ؓ added, "They were then degraded to the state you can now see. They became obsessed with taking others as their slaves and as soon as a nation takes to this obsession, Allah has no need for them." *(Ibn Jareer)*

Mu'adh ؓ told Omar ؓ made the Intention solely for Allah and making the Hereafter the Objective

Ibn Abu Maryam reports that when Omar ؓ once passed by Mu'adh bin Jabal ؓ, he asked, "What are the factors that will hold the foundations of this Ummah steady?" Mu'adh ؓ replied, 'There are 3 factors and they will ensure salvation. (1) Sincerity, which is the nature upon which Allah has created people, (2) salah, which is a fundamental pillar of Deen and (3) obedience to the Muslim leader, in which lies one's protection." "What you say is true," Omar ؓ acknowledged. When Omar ؓ had passed by, Mu'adh ؓ turned to those sitting with him and said, "O Omar! Your time is better than those afterwards because great disputes shall arise after you. Then addressing those with him, he said, Omar ؓ will be living on for only a short while." *(Ibn Jareer in Kanzul Ummal)*

The Incident of Amir bin Abd Qais in this Regard

Abu Abdah Ambari reports that when the Muslims arrived as conquerors in Mada'in and were gathering the booty together, a man arrived with a dish full of precious gems and handed it over to the person in charge of the distribution of the booty. Those with him exclaimed, "We have never seen anything like this! Let alone equaling the value of everything else we have gathered, all of it does not even come close to the value of this!" They then asked the man, "Have you taken anything from this?" "Listen well!" he said to them, "By Allah! Had it not been for the fear of Allah, I would not have brought this to you in the first place." When they realized that this was a very special person, they asked who he was. "By Allah!" he responded, "I shall not inform you for you to praise me, nor shall I inform anyone else for them to praise me falsely. I prefer to rather praise Allah and be content with His rewards." One of the people however followed the man to his companions and asked them who he was. He turned out to be none other than Amir bin Abd e Qays. *(Ibn Jareer)*

Sa'd ؓ and Jabir ؓ attest to the Integrity of the Army at Qadsiya

Muhammad, Talha, Muhallab and several others reports that Said bin Abi Waqqas ؓ said on the occasion of the Battle of Qadisiya, "By Allah! This army is a truly trustworthy one. Had it not been for the excellence that the veterans of Badr have already been noted for, I would swear by Allah that the men in this army also have the same excellence. After closely examining many groups of people, I found that they were deficient in distributing booty. I have however neither seen nor heard of such deficiencies in this army." *(Ibn Jareer)*. Jabir bin Abdullah ؓ said, "I swear in the name of Allah besides Whom there is none worthy of worship that we found no one amongst the army fighting at Qadisiya who desired the world together with the Hereafter. We did however have doubts about 3 of them from amongst the many thousands, but they also turned out to be most trustworthy and abstinent. They are Tulayha bin Khuwailid ؓ, Amr bin Ma'dikarib ؓ and Qais bin Makshuh ؓ." *(Ibn Jareer)*

Omar ؓ's Statement about those who Brought to him the Jewels and Sword of the Persian Emperor

Qais Ijli narrates that when the Persian Emperor's sword, belt and jewels were brought to Omar ؓ, he remarked, "Those who have brought this must truly be trustworthy people." To this, Ali ؓ pointed out, 'It is because you are trustworthy that your subjects are also trustworthy." *(Ibn Jareer)*

The Letter Omar ؓ wrote to Amr bin Al Aas ؓ Concerning seeking assistance from Allah

Zaid bin Aslam ؓ reports that when Omar ؓ felt that Egypt was taking too long to conquer, he wrote the following letter to Amr bin Al Aas ؓ who led the military operations in Egypt:

"It surprises me to see how long it is taking you to conquer Egypt. You are already fighting there for several years now. The only reason for this is because you people have started to do things differently and have developed love for this world just as your enemy has. Allah assists people only when their intentions are sincere. I am sending 4 persons to you and am informing you that as far as I know, each of them is worth a thousand others, unless they are also affected by that which affects others. When this letter reaches you, I want you to address the people, to encourage them to fight the enemy, to be steadfast and to correct their intentions. Keep these four ahead of all the others and command the army to attack the enemy all at once like a single person. The attack should take place just after midday on Friday because this is the time when Allah's mercy descends and Du'as are accepted. Everyone should cry before Allah and beg His assistance against the enemy." When the letter reached Amr ♦, he gathered the army, read the letter out to them and then sent for the four men. He placed them in front of the others, commanded everyone to make wudhu, to perform 2 Rakats salah, to turn to Allah and to beg Him for assistance. When this was done, Allah granted them victory. Another narration states that when Amr bin Al Aas ♦ felt that it was taking too long for him to conquer Egypt, he wrote to Omar ♦ to ask fore reinforcements. Omar ♦ sent 4,000 troops, with a commander appointed over every thousand troops. Omar also wrote to Arm bin Al Aas ♦ saying: "I have sent you 4,000 troops as reinforcements and appointed a commander for every thousand troops. The commander of every thousand troops is a man who is himself equivalent to 1,000 troops; they are Zubair bin Awam ♦, Miqdad bin Aswad bin Amr ♦, Ubadah bin Samit ♦ and Maslama bin Mukhallad ♦. Remember that you have 12,000 troops with you and an army of 12,000 can never be defeated for want of numbers." *(Ibn Abdul Hakam in Kanzul Ummal)*

The Letter Omar ♦ wrote to the Commanders in Sham in this Regard

Iyadh Ash'ari reports that he was present during the Battle of Yarmuk where there were 5 commanders over the Muslim army because the 5 armies had merged there to fight together; the 5 were: Abu Ubaidah ♦, Yazid bin Abu Sufyan ♦, Shurabil bin Hasana ♦, Khalid bin Walid ♦ and Iyadh ♦ who is not the one reporting this narration. Omar ♦'s instruction was that Abu Ubaidah ♦ should be the commander-in-chief if a battle took place. The army wrote a letter to Omar ♦ informing him that death was coming towards them because the enemy outnumbered them and he should reinforce them with more troops.

Omar ♦ replied to their letter by writing

"Your letter requesting me for reinforcements has reached me. I shall therefore refer you to one who is a more powerful helper and who has a ready army. He is Allah. Ask Him for assistance because Muhammad ﷺ was assisted at Badr when his forces were less than yours." *(Kanzul Ummal)*. Another narration states that Omar ♦ added, "When this letter reaches you, I want you to fight them without writing back to me," The narrator says, "We then fought them and defeated all of them within a distance of 4 Farsak (~12 miles). We also earned a large amount of booty. When we discuss the matter, Iyadh ♦ proposed that we exchange 10 of the enemy prisoners for each one of ours. Abu Ubaidah ♦ then asked for someone to race him. A youngster volunteered saying, 'I would like to, if you don't mind.' The youngster managed to beat Abu Ubaidah ♦ and I watched him trail behind on his barebacked horse with his two locks of hair flying furiously behind him." *(Ahmad, Haythami, Tafsir Ibn Kathir)*

The Muslims seek Allah's Assistance using the Qur'an during the Battle of Qadisiya

Muhammad, Talha and Ziyad all report that after leading the Zuhr salah, Sa'd ♦ instructed a youngster to recite the Surah of Jihad (Surah Anfal). The youngster was from amongst the Qurra, learned scholars of the Qur'an and Omar ♦ had appointed him to be with Sa'd ♦ all the time. All the Muslims there had learnt the Surah of Jihad and when the youngster recited it to the soldiers beside him, soon it was recited in the entire regiment. This lighted up the hearts and eyes of the Muslims and they all derived tranquility from reciting it. Another narration states that because the Muslims had learnt the Surah of Jihad, Sa'd ♦ commanded them to recite it to each other. *(Ibn Jareer)*

Rasulullah ﷺ teaches the Sahabah to Seek Allah's Assistance through the Verses of the Qur'an

Ibrahim bin Harith Tamimi ♦ reports that Rasulullah ﷺ once sent them on an expedition and instructed them to recite the following verse every morning and evening: أَفَحَسِبْتُمْ أَنَّمَا خَلَقْنَاكُمْ عَبَثًا

Did you think that We had created you in play (without any purpose)… (Al-Mu'minun:115)

When they recited the verse, they earned plenty of booty and remained safe. *(Abu Nu'aym in ma'rifa, Ibn Mandah in Kanzul Ummal, Isabah)*

Sa'd ♦ Commands the Muslims to seek Allah's Assistance by reciting "Allahu Akbar" and "La Howla wa La Quwwata Illa Billah" during the Battle of Badr of Qadisiya

Muhammad, Talha and Ziyad all report that Sa'd ♦ commanded the Muslims saying, "Remain in your positions and do not move until after you have performed the Zuhr salah. When I call out 'Allahu Akbar', you should all also say 'Allahu Akbar' and then start preparation for the battle. Remember that the words 'Allahu Akbar' was not granted to any nation before you and it was granted to you to give you strength. When you then hear me call out 'Allahu Akbar' for the second time, you should again call out the same and complete your preparations. Thereafter when I call out 'Allahu Akbar' for the third time, you should again call out the same and those on horseback should proceed to the battlefield and launch the offensive to give courage to the infantry. When I then call out 'Allahu Akbar' for the fourth time, you must all assault the enemy and engage them in close combat. You should also then recite: لَاحَوْلَ وَلَا قُوَّةَ إِلَّا بِاللهِ *('La Howla wa La Quwwata Illa Billah,).'* *(Ibn Jareer)*. Another narration states that when the Qurra had completed reciting the verses of Jihad, Sa'd ♦ called out الله أكبر *'Allahu Akbar'*. Those closest to him then also called out the Takbir الله أكبر *('Allahu Akbar')* and in this manner, the rest of them called out the Takbir by hearing it from the others. The soldiers were then mobilized and started preparing. When the second Takbir was called out, the preparations were rounded up and when الله أكبر *'Allahu Akbar'* was called out for the third time, the most courageous ones confronted the enemy and started the battle. The narration still continues further. *(Ibn Jareer)*

Seeking Allah's Assistance through the Agency of Rasulullah ﷺ's Hair

Ja'far bin Abdullah bin Hakam reports that when Khalid bin Walid ♦ lost his hat during the Battle of Yarmuk, he gave the order for it to be found. When the people failed to find it, he again gave the command for them to search for it. This time, they managed to find it. It happened to be an old hat, so Khalid ♦ explained. He said, "When Rasulullah ﷺ performed Umrah and had his hair shaved off, people raced around him to get some of it. I managed to beat them to the forelocks and kept it in this hat. Whenever I participate in battle with these hairs on me, I am always granted victory." *(Tabrani, Abu Ya'la, Haythami, Hakim, Abu Nu'aym in Dala'il)*. Khalid bin Walid ؓ had a hat in which were the hairs of Rasulullah ﷺ. Khalid ؓ used to say, 'Whenever I confront an enemy with this hat on my head, I am always granted victory." *(Abu Nu'yam in Kanzul Ummal)*

Competing with each other in Doing Good Deeds

Shaqiq says, "We started off the Battle of Qadisiya at the beginning of the day and the time for Zuhr had arrived by the time we returned from the battlefield. Since the Mu'adhin was injured, all the others wanted the opportunity to call out the Adhan. They were all so keen that they were close to coming to blows with their swords. Sa'd ؓ then drew lots and the opportunity fell to the lot of someone, who then called out the Adhan." *(Ibn Jareer)*

Nothing of the glamor and glitter of this world: The Incident of Mughiera bin Shu'ba ؓ and the Persian Ruler Dhul Hajibain

Ma'qal bin Yasar ؓ reports a lengthy narration concerning the conquest of Isfahan which took place under the command of Nu'man bin Muqarrin ؓ. Part of the narration states that when Nu'man ؓ and his army arrived at Isfahan, there was a river separating him from the city. Nu'man ؓ sent Mughiera bin Shu'ba ؓ as an envoy. The Persian ruler of the area was Dhul Hajibain. He consulted with his courtiers saying, "Do you think that I should sit before him in battledress or with the pomp and splendor of a king?" When they advised him to rather sit with the pomp and ceremony of a king, he did so. He sat on his throne, placed his crown upon his head and was surrounded by 2 rows of his courtiers dressed in velvet and wearing earrings and bangles. When Mughiera ؓ arrived, he walked briskly with his head lowered. He carried a spear and shield with him and started poking holes in the carpet upon which the courtiers stood in their rows. In this way, he tore the carpet so that the people may take it as an ill omen, an apprehension that their kingdom will also be torn apart. Addressing Mughiera ؓ, Dhul Hajibain said, "You Arabs have been afflicted with starvation and hardships, because of which you have left your land and come here. If you please, we shall supply you with grains and you may return to your land." Mughiera ؓ then started to talk. After duly praising Allah, he said, "We, the Arab people, used to consume carrion and although others wielded power over us, we never wielded power over anyone. Allah then raised a Nabi from amongst us, who was amongst our most noble people, of the highest lineage and the most truthful. He promised us that these lands will fall to us and we have always found his promises to be true. Now that I have seen the exquisite garments you have here and the fine luxuries, I do not think that any of the people with me will want to leave without them." The narration still continues further. *(Hakim, Tabrani, Haythami)*

The Incidents of Rib'ee ؓ, Hudhaifa ؓ and Mughiera ؓ with Rustam at Qadisiya

Muhammad ﷺ, Talha, Amr and Ziyad all reports that Sa'd bin Abi Waqqas ؓ sent for Mughiera ؓ and few others and said to them, "I intend sending you to the people of Persia. What have you to say about it?" They all said in one voice, "We shall do as you command and do no more. If a situation arises concerning which there are no directives from you, we shall look for what is best and most beneficial for the people and discuss that with them." Sa'd ؓ then said to them, "Such is the behavior of

intelligent and experienced people. Go and get ready." Rib'ee bin Amir ؓ then said, 'The non-Arabs have their own peculiar ideas and etiquette and if we all go to them, they will feel that we are placing them on a pedestal. Do not send more than one person." When the other agreed with this, Rib'ee ؓ volunteered to go first. Sa'd then sent him and Rib'ee ؓ left to meet Rustam in his cantonment. However, the sentries at the bridge stopped Rib'ee ؓ and sent a message to Rustam, informing him of the arrival. Rustam consulted with some leaders of Persia, asking, "What are your opinions? Should we boast only about our military superiority or should we make them feel worthless by displaying our wealth and riches?" They were all unanimous about making the Muslims seem worthless, so they made a display of their opulent commodities; they laid out exquisite carpets and cushions and spared nothing in their effort. A golden throne was made for Rustam and he dressed most lavishly. Expensive rugs and cushions woven with gold thread were also laid out. Rib'ee ؓ arrived on his short, long-haired horse, carrying a shining sword. His scabbard was a pouch made of old cloth and his spear was tied with a leather strap. He also carried a shield made of cow's hide, the face of which had round patches of red leather that resembled bread. He also carried his bow and arrows with him. When he came to the court and reached the first of the rugs, he was told to alight from his horse. He however rode the horse on the rug and alighted only when it stood properly on the rug. He then tore up two cushions, pierced the horse's reins through them and tied the horse up. All this while, the people there were unable to stop him. Rib'ee ؓ knew well that they were displaying everything to him to make him feel inferior, so he wished to get the upper hand over them because of which he did what he did to show them that their wealth held no attraction for him. The armor Rib'ee ؓ was wearing flowed over him like a dam and he wore the hide of a camel over it like a cloak. He had made a hole in the hide, drew it over his head and tied it about his waist with a cord made from plant fibers. Rib'ee ؓ was amongst the hairiest of all Arabs and his hair was tied with the leather reins of a camel. His hair was separated into four locks that stood like the horns of a mountain goat. The people told him to put down his weapons, to which he replied, "I have not come here by my own accord, so you cannot instruct me to drop my weapons. It is you who have sent for me, so if you do not want me to come as I please, I might as well go back." When this was reported to Rustam, he said, "Allow him in. He is but one person." Rib'ee ؓ arrived, leaning on his spear that had a sharp head. He took short steps and tore the rugs and cushions with the spear as he walked. There was no cushion or rug that he did not ruin, leaving them all torn and tattered after him.

When he came up to Rustam, the sentries surrounded him. Rib'ee ؓ then sat on the ground and stuck his spear into the rug. "What made you do that?" they asked, Rib'ee ؓ replied, "We do not like to sit on those decorated places of yours." Rustam then addressed Rib'ee ؓ saying, "What brings you here?" "Allah has sent us," Rib'ee ؓ replied, "Allah has sent us to remove whoever He wills from servitude to man and to lead him to the servitude of Allah. Allah has sent us to remove them from the narrowness of this world towards its vastness and from the oppression of other religions towards the justice of Islam." The narration then continues, as has been quoted in the chapter discussing the Da'wah that the Sahabah gave during the Khilafa of Omar ؓ. The narration proceeds to state that Rustam said to the courtiers when they criticized Rib'ee ؓ's appearance, "Shame on you! Do not look at clothing but rather look at the prudence, the speech and the personality. The Arabs care little for clothing and food but are covetous about their lineage. They do not dress like you and have different tastes." The Persians then approached Rib'ee ◈ to have a look at his weapons, regarding them to be inferior. He said to them, "Do you wish to show me your military prowess and I shall show you mine?" He then drew his sword from his cloth pouch and it flashed like a flame of fire. "Sheath it!" they called out in terror. He then sheathed his sword. They then fired arrows at his shield while he fired arrows at theirs. Their shield was shattered while his shield remained intact. He then addressed them saying, "O Persians! While you have given great importance to food and drink, we treat it with little ceremony." He then went back after giving them time (three days) to consider their position. The following day, the Persians sent a message saying that they wanted the same person sent back to them. Sa'd ◈ however sent Hudhaifa bin Mihsin ◈. He also arrived in simple attire as Rib'ee ◈ wore. When he also came to the first rug, he was told to alight from his animal. He however said, "That I would have done if I had come to you for my own needs. Ask your king whether I have come for his need or for mine. If he says that it is for my own need, he is lying and I shall return and leave you alone. However, if he says that it is for his own need, then I shall come as I please." Rustam instructed the sentries to allow Hudhaifa ◈ in and he rode up to Rustam who was seated on his throne. "You may get off your animal," Rustam said. "I shall not," Hudhaifa ◈ replied. When he saw that Hudhaifa ◈ would not get off the animal, Rustam asked, "What is the matter that you have come and not your companion who came yesterday?" Hudhaifa ◈ replied, "Our leader wishes to treat us equally in favorable and adverse conditions. It is my turn today." "What brings you people here?" Rustam asked. Hudhaifa ◈ replied, "Allah has favored us with His religion and shown us His signs until we realized that it was the truth even though we had been opposed to it. He then commanded us to invite people to one of 3 options. We shall accept any of the three options they choose. Either you accept Islam and we shall leave you alone. Otherwise, you may choose to pay the Jizya and we shall stand in your defense whenever the need arises. The next option is battle." "Do we have a few days to enter into an agreement?" Rustam asked. Hudhaifa ◈ replied, "You have 3 days which started yesterday."

When Rustam received from Hudhaifa nothing more than he got from Rib'ee ◈, he sent him away and addressed his companions saying, "Shame on you people! Do you not see what I see? The first man came to us yesterday and defeated us on our premises. He degraded what we were enamored with, stood his horse on our opulence and even tied his horse to it. He took a good omen from what he did and returned to his people, taking some of our soil with him. That was apart from his superior intelligence. Today this other man arrived and stood over us, also taking a good omen from it by taking our land after expelling us from it." Rustam however infuriated the others and they also angered him by refusing to listen to him. The following day, the Persians again asked for someone to be sent to them and this time, Mughiera bin Shu'ba ◈ was sent. (Ibn Jareer). When Mughiera ◈ reached the bridge to cross over into Persian territory, he was halted by the sentries who first sought permission from Rustam to allow him in. The Persians, however, did not leave out any of the pomp and ceremony in their effort to make the Arabs feel inferior. Therefore, when Mughiera ◈ arrived, the Persians still boasted their opulence. They wore crowns, garments woven from gold threads and carpets were laid out the distance that an arrow traveled. The only way to reach the king was over this length of carpet. Mughiera ◈ who also wore 4

locks of hair walked up to Rustam and sat with him on his throne and cushion. The courtiers sprang up, grabbed at him and brought him down, even hitting him mildly. Mughiera ◈ addressed them saying, "We have always heard that you people were intelligent, but I do not think that there is any nation more foolish than you. We Arabs treat each other as equals and do not make slaves of each other unless circumstances of war demand. I had always thought that you people also practice equality amongst yourselves just as we do. Rather than doing what you just did, it would have been better if you just told me that some of you prevail as masters over others. If sitting beside Rustam was not palatable to you, we will then not do so again. I would have not come to you had you not sent for me, but today I can see that your sovereignty is soon to vanish and that you will be vanquished because no power can survive with such a way of life and with such a mentality." Hearing this common people shouted, "The Arab is right!" To this, the leaders remarked, "By Allah! He has made a statement towards which our slaves will always be referring us! May Allah destroy our elders! How foolish were they to regard these Arabs as insignificant, they should have realized the threat and wiped them out a long time ago." The narration also mentions the questions Rustam asked and the replies Mughiera ◈ gave him. (Ibn Jareer)

Thabit bin Aqram ◈ said to Abu Hurairah ◈ about Paying no Heed to the Numbers of the Enemy and Their Resources on the Occasion of the Battle of Mu'ta

Abu Hurairah ◈ reports, "I participated in the Battle of Mu'ta. When the Mushrikin arrived, we saw what none of us could ever hope to match. Their numbers were overwhelming, as were their weapons, their horses, their velvet, silk and gold. The sight actually made my eyes squint. It was then that Thabit bin Aqram ◈ said, 'O Abu Hurairah! It appears that you are seeing an overwhelming opponent?' 'I certainly am,' I replied. He then said, 'You were not with us at Badr. It is not with large numbers that we are assisted but by the power of Allah.'" (Bayhaqi in Al Bidayah wan Nihayah, Waqidi in Isabah)

The Letter Abu Bakr ◈ wrote to Amr bin Al Aas ◈ in this Regard

Abdullah bin Amr bin Al Aas ◈ reports that Abu Bakr ◈ wrote the following letter to Amr bin Al Aas ◈:
"Salamun Alaik
Your letter detailing the enormous force that the Romans have gathered has reached me. When we were with Nabi ﷺ, Allah never assisted us with large numbers and a large concentration of troops. There were times when we fought with Rasulullah ﷺ with only 2 horses and our condition was so poor that we had to share camels. When we were with Rasulullah ﷺ in the Battle of Uhud, we had only one horse, which Rasulullah ﷺ rode. Despite this, Allah granted us victory and assistance against our enemies. O Amr! Remember that the one who is most obedient to Allah is the one who most detests sin. Obey Allah and command your companions to obey Allah as well." (Tayalisi in Kanzul Ummal, Tabrani in Awsat, Haythami)

The Statement of Khalid bin Walid ◈ about this on the Occasion of the Battle of Yarmuk

Ubadah ◈ and Khalid ◈ both report that a men once said to Khalid, "The Romans are so many and the Muslims so few!" To this, Khalid ◈ remarked, "The Muslims are so many and the Romans so few! An army is large only when they received Allah's assistance and they are few when Allah does not assist them. Numbers do not matter. By Allah! I wish that my horse Ashqar recovers from his injury, incurred because of the long and speedy journey from Iraq to Sham and that the Romans were double in number." *(Ibn Jareer)*

The Statement of one of the Apostates on the Valor of the Sahabah

Zuhri reports that after Abu Bakr ﷺ assumed the office of Khilafa, some Arabs left the fold of Islam. Abu Bakr ﷺ then personally marched against them, but when he reached a watering place near Baqi, he sensed that the safety of Madinah would be jeopardized. He therefore returned to Madinah and placed Allah's Sword Khalid bin Walid bin Mughiera ﷺ in command of an army. Others were recruited to join him and Abu Bakr ﷺ's instruction to him was to march to the locality of the Mudhar tribe, where he was to wage war against all those who forsook Islam. He was then to march to Yamama to fight Musailama Kadhab, false prophet. Khalid ﷺ left and it so happened that he first fought Tulaiha Kadhab Asadi, another false prophet, who was joined by Uyayna bin Hisn bin Hudhaifa Fazari. Allah gave the Muslims victory. When Tulaiha saw how badly defeated his troops were, he exclaimed, "Shame on you! Why are you being defeated so?" One of his men replied saying, "I shall inform you of the reason for our defeat. There is not a single man amongst us who does not want his companion to be killed before him. On the other hand, we are fighting people who would love to be killed before their companions." Tulaiha was a furious fighter and martyred both Ukasha bin Mihsin ﷺ and Ibn Aqram ﷺ on that day. However, when the truth dawned on Tulaiha, he left the battlefield on foot and went on to accept Islam and enter into the Ihram for Umrah. The narration still goes on. *(Bayhaqi)*

The Statement the King of Alexandria made to Amr bin Al Aas ﷺ in this Regard

Amr bin Al Aas ﷺ says, "I was the commander of the Muslim army that marched to Alexandria. The king of the city made a request saying, 'Send out one of your men to me so that I can speak to him and he can speak to me.' 'None but I shall go to him,' I said and I left. Both he and I had a translator and two stages were set up for us. 'Who are you people?' he asked. My reply was: 'We are Arabs. We are people accustomed to thorns and acacia trees (not lush gardens). We are also the custodians of Allah's House. We had the most inhospitable of lands, led the harshest of lives, ate carrion and looted each other. We led the worst of lives anyone could ever lead until a man emerged from amongst us. He was not the most prominent of us, neither was he the wealthiest. He told us that he was Allah's Nabi and commanded us to do things that we did not know about. He also forbade us from doing what we had been doing and what our forefathers had been doing. We therefore opposed him, falsified him and refused to accept his words. Eventually people from outside came out and said to him, 'We believe in you, we believe what you say, are prepared to follow you and to fight whoever fights you. He therefore went to them. We then went after him and fought him, but he prevailed over us and defeated us. He then turned to the other Arabs around him and defeated them as well. If those behind me know what luxurious lives you people lead, every' one of them would come here to you and join you in it.' The king laughed and said, 'Your prophet told you the truth. Our prophets also came to us with the same message your prophet brought and we remained steadfast on their teachings until kings started to preside over us. Their behavior with us conformed with their whims rather than to the teachings of the prophets. If you people adhere to the teachings of your prophet, you will prevail over everyone you engage in battle and you will

defeat anyone who tries to attack you. However, as soon as you do what we did by forsaking the teachings of the prophets and by acting on your desires, you will become just like us. You will then neither be more than us in number nor any stronger.'" Amr bin Al Aas ﷺ says, "I have not spoken to anyone afterwards who gave me any better advice than he." *(Tabrani, Haythami, Abu Ya'la)*

A Roman Leader's Statement to Heraclius Concerning the Reasons for Triumphs of the Sahabah

Abu Is'haq reports that no enemy could stand his ground before any of the Sahabah for even the time it took between two successive squeezes of a camel's teats when it is milked. Heraclius was in Antioch at the time when his Roman army returned defeated from a battle against the Muslims. "Shame on you!" Heraclius said to them, "Tell me about those people you were fighting against. Are they not humans like you?" "They certainly are," the men replied. "Then were you more in number or were their numbers more?" "On every occasion we were several times more in number than they," came the reply. "Then what is the matter," Heraclius asked, "Why were you still defeated?" An elderly leader explained. He said, 'It is because they stand in salah all night, they fast all day, they fulfill their promises, they enjoin good, they forbid from evil and are just towards each other. It is also because we drink wine, we fornicate, we do what is prohibited, we break our promises, we rob, we oppress, we enjoin what to forbidden, prohibit people from acts that please Allah and we spread anarchy on earth." Heraclius said, "You are telling the truth." *(Ahmad bin Marwan Maliki in Mujalasa, Al Bidayah wan Nihayah, Ibn Asakir)*

A Christian Arab Describes the Sahabah to the Commander of Damascus

Yahya bin Yahya Ghassani reports that two men from his tribe reported, "When the Muslims set up camp outside Jordan, we talked amongst ourselves that Damascus would soon be under siege. We therefore went to do our business in Damascus before that happened. We were still there when the commander of Damascus sent for us. When we came before him, he asked, 'Are you two Arabs?' When we replied in the affirmative, he asked further, 'Are you Christians?' 'Yes,' we replied. He then said, 'One of you will have to spy on them to learn about their intentions. The other will stay behind to look after his companion's belongings.' One of us then went and stayed with the Muslims for some time before returning. He said, 'I have come to you from people who are thin and who ride fine horses. They are monks by night, brave horsemen by day and can even attach feathers to their arrows, carve them out by themselves and straighten their spears to perfection. If you were to speak to someone sitting beside you, he would be unable to hear you because they were always reciting the Qur'an and engaging in Dhikr in loud voices." The commander then turned to his companions and said, "Such people have come to you against whom you can offer no resistance." *(Al Bidayah wan Nihayah, Ibn Asakir)*

A Christian Arab Describes the Sahabah to Qubuqalar

Urwa ﷺ reports that when the 2 armies confronted each other during the Battle of Yarmuk, Qubuqalar, the Roman general sent for an Arab man whom the narrator believes was a man from the Yazid bin Haidan family of the Qudha'ah tribe. His was known as Ibn Huzarif. Qubuqalar's instruction to the man was, "Infiltrate the ranks of these people, stay with them for day and a night and then report their condition to me." Because he was Arab, he blended into the Muslim army undetected and stayed with them for a day and a night. When he then returned, Qubuqalar asked him what he had found out. He replied, "They are monks by night and valiant horsemen by day. Even if their king's son had to steal, they would amputate his hand and should he commit adultery, he will be stoned so that the law is enforced." To this, Qubuqalar remarked, "If what you say is true, then being underground is better than clashing with them above the ground. I wish that Allah would leave me alone with them, without assisting either me against them or them against me (in which case our larger numbers would win the day)." *(Ibn Jareer)*

A Persian Spy Describes the Sahabah to Rustam

Ibn Rufail narrates that when Rustam camped at Najaf, he sent a spy from there to the Muslim army. The spy infiltrated their ranks so well at Qadisiya that he appeared to be one of them. He saw them brushing with the Miswak before every salah, performing salah and then dispersing to their respective tents. He then returned and informed Rustam about their condition and about the lives they led. Rustam interrogated him thoroughly, even asking what it was that the Sahabah ate. To this the spy replied, "By Allah! Although I stayed with them an entire night, I did not see them eat anything. All I saw them do was to suck on some sticks in the evening, when they went to sleep and just before dawn. Rustam then proceeded and when he camped somewhere between Hisn and Atiq, he happened to cross paths with the Muslim army. Sa'd's Mu'addhin had just called out the Adhan for the Fajr salah and Rustam saw them all preparing. He then instructed the Persians to mount their animals. When they asked him the reason, he said, "Did you not see that when the announcement was made amongst your enemy, they all started to prepare to fight you." The spy corrected him saying, "They are only preparing for salah." Rustam then said the following words in Persian, the translation of which is: "A voice came to me in the morning. It was the voice of Omar, talking to those Arabs and teaching them some wisdom." After they had crossed the river, they again happened to cross paths as Sa'd's Muaddhin called out the Adhan for salah. Sa'd then led them in salah. This time, Rustam remarked, "Omar has now eaten my liver." *(Ibn Jareer)*

A Roman Describes the Sahabah to Heraclius

Abu Zahra Qushairi reports from a man of the Qushair tribe that as Heraclius was leaving for Constantinople, he met with a Roman who had been held captive by the Muslims and who had subsequently escaped. "Tell me about these people," Heraclius asked the man. The man said, "I shall describe them to you as if you are actually looking at them. They are valiant horsemen by day, monks by night and they never take anything from their non-Muslim subjects without paying its full price. They never see anyone without first greeting with Salam and they remain glued to anyone they meet in combat until the matter is settled." To this, Heraclius remarked, 'If what you say is true, they will certainly be the inheritors of this land beneath my feet." *(Ibn Jareer)*

Comment that the Emperor of China made about the Sahabah

The Emperor of Persia Yazdgird once wrote to the Emperor of China to seek reinforcements. Addressing the Persian envoy, the Chinese Emperor said, "I know well that it is the duty of any Emperor to assist another against those who are overpowering him. However, I want you to describe to me these people who are driving you out of your lands because I gather from what you said that they are fewer in number than you. From what you have described to me, people as few as them cannot overpower an adversary as many as you unless there is tremendous good in them and rot within you." "You may ask me whatever you please about them," the envoy said. The Emperor then asked, "Do they fulfill their promises?" "Yes," the envoy replied. The next question was, "What do they tell you before they engage you in combat?" "They invite us to accept one of three options. We either accept their religion, in which case they treat us as they treat each other. Otherwise, we may accept to pay the Jizya and thus receive their protection. The final option is to face them in battle." The Emperor then asked, "How obedient are they towards their leaders." "They are the most obedient of all people towards their leaders," came the reply. The Emperor further asked, "What do they regard as lawful and what do they regard as unlawful?" When the envoy gave him a detailed reply, the Emperor asked, "And do they forbid what has been made lawful for them or make lawful what has been forbidden for them?" "This they do not do," the envoy replied. The Emperor then said, "Such a nation will never be destroyed as long as they regard what is lawful as lawful and what is unlawful as unlawful." The next question the Emperor asked was about the clothing the Sahabah wore. When the envoy described it to him, he then asked about the modes of transport the Sahabah used. The envoy described the Arab horses that the Sahabah used in detail, after which the Emperor remarked, "Those make excellent fortresses." The envoy then went on to describe the camels that they used and even explained how they sit and then get up with their loads. The Emperor (who had probably never seen a camel before) notes, "That is common with all animals that have long necks." The Chinese Emperor then wrote back to Yazdgird saying, "It is not ignorance of my duty that prevents me from sending to your aid an army so large that while the first of it is in (the Persian city of) Marw, the last is still here in China. However, the description of these people whom your envoy has described to me tells me that if they had to come up against a mountain, they would certainly shatter it. If they are left to advance and retain their qualities, they will soon remove me from my kingship. Enter into a treaty with them and be content to abide by the clauses of the treaty. You should however never attack them as long as they do not attack you." *(Ibn Jareer)*

This is the last narration that I wish to include in this book.

الْحَمْدُ لِلَّهِ الَّذِيْ هَدَانَا لِهَذَا وَمَا كُنَّا لِنَهْتَدِيَ لَوْلَا أَنْ هَدَانَا اللهُ

All praise is for Allah, Who has guided us to this because we would never have been rightly guided had Allah not guided us.

اللَّهُمَّ لَوْ لَا أَنْتَ مَا اهْتَدَيْنَا وَلَاتَصَدَّقْنَا وَلَاصَلَّيْنَا
فَأَنْزِلْنْ سَكِيْنَة عَلَيْنَا إِذَا أَرَادُوْا فِتْنَة أَبَيْنَا

"O Allah! Had it not been for you, we would never have been guided neither would we have given charity or performed salah so shower Your peace upon us whenever they (the Kuffar) intend any acts of anarchy, we will oppose them"

With these words this book Hayatus Sahabah ("The Lives of the Sahabah") is completed by the hand of the weak servant Muhammad Yusuf. May Allah safeguard him. This is Wednesday 10th Muharram, 1379.

Translated by:
Abdul Hye, PhD
Houston, Texas.
Rabia-2 19, 1429 / April 25, 2008

Glossary of Terms

AH: "After Hijra", if preceded by a number, this denotes a specific year of the Islamic calendar.

Hereafter: Refer to the period after people have been brought back to life on the Day of Judgment.

Aliha: see Ilah

Alim (plural - **Ulema**): Means "a learned man".

Amin: An expression said at the end of a Du'a, meaning, "O Allah! Accept this Du'a."

Ayah (plural - **Ayat**): Means "a sign", the verse of the Qur'an

Ayatul Kursi: Translated as 'Verse of the Throne', this is the name of verse #255 of Surah Baqarah.

Abdul Muttalib: The paternal grandfather of Rasulullah ﷺ.

Abu Bakr: Abu Bakr ؓ was the most eminent of the Sahabah, the father-in-law of Rasulullah ﷺ and the first Khalifa.

Abu-: A prefix meaning "father of".

Adhan: Call made before every Fardh salah to inform Muslims that salah will soon take place.

Ahadeeth: see **Hadith**

Ahlul Kitab: Means "People of the Book" and refers to the Jews and the Christians as they received books: the Torah and the Injil from Allah.

Ahzab: see Battle of Ahzab

Ali ؓ: He was one of the most eminent Sahabah, the son-in-law and cousin of Rasulullah ﷺ and the 4th Khalifa.

Al-Ameen: A title given to Rasulullah ﷺ even before he announced his Prophethood. It means "the Trustworthy".

Allah: He is the One and Only being worthy of worship Who has no partners or children and is unlike anything we know. He is the Creator and Sustainer of all creation and controls everything in the universe. Only He knows, sees and hears everything and will only be seen by the people of Jannah. Non-Muslims refer Him as "the God of the Muslims".

Allahu Akbar: An Arabic expression as "Allah is the Greatest". This expression is referred to as the "Takbir"

Ambiya: see Nabi

Amanah: Translated as "trust" and refers to something given as a trust to keep until the owner wants it back.

Amir: The word means "leader" and may refer to any Muslim leader or commander appointed to lead others.

Amirul Mu'minin: Means "Leader of the Mu'minin" and is a title reserved for someone who leads the Muslims.

Ansar: Means "helpers", refers to those Muslims during the time of Rasulullah ﷺ who were inhabitants of Madinah and who helped the Muhajirin who migrated to Madinah.

Ansari: see **Ansar**

Asr: One of the 5 Fardh salahs, performed between late afternoon and sunset.

Aws: One of the 2 prominent tribes of the Ansar. The other was the Khazraj tribe.

Awqiya: The equivalent of 40 Dirhams, with one Dirham equal to approximately 3.1g of silver.

Badr: A place approximately 100 miles south of Madinah where the Muslim army led by Rasulullah ﷺ fought the disbelievers in the first battle that the Muslims ever fought. Although only 313 in number and extremely short of arms and transport, the Muslims defeated the disbelieves; who numbered more than 1,000 and were fully armed. This battle took place 2 years after Rasulullah ﷺ migrated to Madinah.

Bani Isra'el: Literally translated as "The children of Isra'el". Isra'el was the title of Ya'qub ؑ, who was the son of Is'haq ؑ and the grandson of Ibrahim ؑ. So the Bani Isra'el are the descendants of Ya'qub ؑ.

Baqi: Also known as Jannatul Baqi. This is the graveyard of Madinah.

Barzak: The stage of existence between the time when a person passes away until the time when he is resurrected on the Day of Judgment. It is commonly referred to as a person's "existence in the grave".

Battle of Ahzab: Also called the 'Battle of the Trench' or the 'Battle of Khandaq' which was fought in 5AH. When the combined armies of the Jews and various disbelieving tribes decided to attack Madinah, the Sahabah dug a trench around the city to keep them at bay. The word "Ahzab" refers to many groups or armies, while the word "Khandaq" means "trench."

Battle of Badr: see Badr

Battle of Tabuk: see Tabuk

Battle of Uhud: see Uhud

Bay'ah: A pledge of allegiance, referring to the pledge people take at the hand of their leader, vowing to remain loyal to him.

Baytul Mal: The public treasury of a Muslim country.

Baytul Maqdas or **Baytul Muqaddas** (Al Quds/Jerusalem): This city is famous in the Muslim world because the Masjidul Aqsa is located.

Bid'ah: Act or a belief that is not part of Islam, but understood as such.

-bin- : This word appearing between 2 names means "the son of. Muhammad bin Abdullah means "Muhammad the son of Abdullah."

-bint- : This word appearing between 2 names means "the daughter of". Aisha bint Abu Bakr means "Aisha the daughter to Abu Bakr".

Bismillah: The act of reciting "Bismillah" or "Bismillcwhir Rahmanir Raheem" (In the name of Allah, The Beneficent, The Merciful).

Book of Allah: see Qur'an

Bridge of Sirrat: This is a bridge across Jahannam, which every person will have to cross on the Day of Judgment. Those who fall off will remain either permanently or temporarily in Jahannam, while those destined for Jannah will cross over speedily and enter Jannah.

Bukhari: The most authoritative compilation of Ahadeeth.

Conquest of Makkah: This refers to the time when the Muslims under Rasulullah ﷺ marched into Makkah and captured the city without a war. This occurred in the 8th year after the Hijrah.

Dajjal: Literally translated as "great deceiver". He is referred to in the present Bible as "man of sin" or "the lawless one" (2 Thessalonians 2:8-11). Rasulullah ﷺ mentioned that he will appear before the Day of Judgment and lead the non-believers against the Muslims. Isa ؑ will eventually kill him.

Da'wah: The word literally refers to an invitation, it is specifically used to describe the act of inviting people towards Islam.

Day of Judgment: Also known as the Last Day. On this day the world will come to an end and everything besides Allah will die.

Deen: This refers to the religion of Islam, it is used to refer to any true religion of the past, which Allah taught man through His Ambiya. The religions of the previous prophets are also referred to as Islam because they all taught people to surrender to Allah.

Deeni: Related to the Deen, e.g. Deeni matters would refer to matters related to the Deen.

Dhikr: This word refers to the remembrance of Allah. It is often used for the formal repetition of words by which Allah is remembered, such as repeating the words "*La Ilaha Illalah*" ("There is none worthy of worship but Allah") or "*Allahu Akbar*" ("Allah is the Greatest").

Dhimmi: A non-Muslim citizen of a Muslim country.

Dhul Hijjah: The 12th and last month of the Islamic calendar.

Dhul Qa'dah: The 11th month of the Islamic calendar.

Dinar: A coin made of pure gold that was used as a form of currency. It was equal to approximately 4.25g of gold.

Dirham: A coin made of pure silver that was used as a form of currency. It is equal to approximately 3.1g of silver.

Du'a: A supplication or prayer to Allah.

Dunya: Arabic term for this world and also commonly used everything worldly. The term is also used to refer to the life of this world.

Durud: Refers to sending salutations to Rasulullah ﷺ by reciting certain formulations, which invoke Allah to shower Mercies on Rasulullah ﷺ

Fajr: One of the 5 Fardh salahs, performed between dawn and sunrise.

Fardh (plural- **Fara'idh**): Those acts that are obligatory for a Muslim to perform and are clearly mentioned in the Qur'an.

Farsakh: A unit of length equivalent to approximately 3 miles.

Fatawa: see Fatwa

Fatwa (plural - **Fatawa**): A ruling or verdict passed by a Mufti stating the legal status of an act.

Fay: The booty received from conquered lands when the enemy surrenders without a fight.

Fiqh: Islamic jurisprudence.

Fir'oun: Translated as "Pharaoh". In Qur'anic terms, it refers to the king of Egypt during the time of Musa ﷺ.

Fitnah: The term is used very broadly to refer to temptation, trial, chaos and dissension.

Fuqaha (plural of Faqih): A term used for the recognised jurists of Islam, who were experts in the science and philosophy of Islamic law. It refers to the 4 famous Imams of the 4 schools of jurisprudence.

Ghilaf of the Kabah: This is the black drape that covers the Kabah.

Hafidh (plural - Huffadh): One who has memorised the entire Qur'an.

Haji: A person performing or who has already performed Hajj.

Hadith (plural - Ahadeeth): The words or actions of Rasulullah ﷺ, which are narrated by his companions.

Hajar Aswad: Translated as "the black Stone". It is a stone mounted on the comer of the Kabah closest to the door. It is highly revered and it is from this point that people begin their Tawaf.

Hajj: The pilgrimage of Muslims that occurs during the month of Dhul Hijjah. The pilgrims are required to abide by certain restrictions and visit specific sites in and around Makkah, carrying out specific acts. It is obligatory only for those Muslims who have the means to perform. The pilgrimage to the Kabah that the disbelievers used to perform before the coming of Rasulullah ﷺ was also called Hajj.

Halal: Something that is lawful in the Shari'ah.

Haram: Something that the Shari'ah clearly declares unlawful.

Hatem: A short semi-circular wall around one side of the Kabah.

Hidayah: The Arabic term for guidance, especially the guidance Allah gives people to do good.

Hijaz: Western province of Saudi Arabia bordering the Red Sea, Makkah and Madinah. Ta'if and the Red Sea port of Jeddah are included.

Hijrah: To migrate from one place to another for the pleasure of Allah. Hijrah is compulsory when it is difficult or impossible for a Muslim to practice Islam in the place where he lives. The term Hijrah also refers specifically to the migration of Rasulullah ﷺ from Makkah to Madinah. It is from this event that the Islamic calendar begins, which corresponds to the year 622AD of the Gregorian calendar.

Huffadh: see **Hafidh**

Hudaybiya: A place close to Makkah where the Treaty of Hudaybiya was signed by Rasulullah ﷺ with the disbelievers of Makkah. This occurred 6 years after the Hijra when the disbelievers refused the Muslims entry into Makkah to perform Umrah. Although the clauses of the treaty favored the disbelievers, it was the Muslims who abided by them. Within 1.5 years the disbelievers violated the treaty. This violation led to the Conquest of Makkah in the year 8AH.

Hypocrite (known as Munafiq): A person who is a Kafir but pretends to be a Muslim. Where Ahadeeth refer to specific hypocrites, these will be those hypocrites who lived in Madinah during the time of Rasulullah ﷺ.

Ibadah: An act of worship e.g. salah, Hajj, charity, etc.

Iblis: see **Saitan**

Ijtihad: Refers to applying one's mind to the references of the Shari'ah to deduce laws that are not explicitly stated. This is the work of a person whose proficiency in Islamic jurisprudence in not questionable.

Iman: Normally translated as "belief" or "faith". Iman means believing in Towhid and the Risala of Rasulullah ﷺ together with everything else that Rasulullah ﷺ taught. Iman is complete only when a person verbally admits this belief. The Iman of nations that lived before the coming of Rasulullah ﷺ required belief in Towhid together with the Risala of the Nabi (prophet) of their time and whatever he taught them.

Inna Lillahi wa Inna Dayhi Raji'un: Translated as "To Allah we belong and to Him shall we return". Although this expression is usually used when a person passes away, it is also used to indicate surprise and when some unfortunate event occurs.

InshaAllah: Translated as "If Allah wills". It is commonly used by Muslims when they intend to do something in future. The English equivalent would be "God willing".

Iqama: A call similar to the Adhan but given before the salah begins.

Isha: One of the 5 Fardh salahs. It is performed at night between the time when all light has vanished from the horizon and the time of dawn.

Islam: The meaning is "to surrender" or "to submit" to Allah's commands. It is the religion taught by Muhammad ﷺ and by all the prophets.

Ismul A'zam: Translation is "The Most Majestic Name". When a person makes Du'a with this name of Allah, it is definitely accepted.

Istighfar: The act of asking forgiveness from Allah.

Istinja: The act of cleaning one's private areas after relieving oneself.

I'tikaf: Refers to a person's stay in the Masjid for a period of time without coming out at all during this time.

Jamara: One of 3 pillars in Mina representing the Saitan which people pelt during Hajj as one of the obligatory requirements.

Jahannam: Translated as "hell" or "hellfire". This is a physical place where people will be punished after the Day of Judgment.

Jannah (plural - Jannat): Translated as "paradise". It is a physical place of happiness where people with Iman will live forever after the Day of Judgment.

Jannat: see **jannah**.

Jibra'el ﷺ: The angel Gabriel. He is the leader of all the angels and was responsible for bringing revelation to Allah's prophets.

Jihad: Usually translated as a "holy war", the word "Jihad" means "to make an effort" or "to exert oneself". Although a physical battle between the Muslims and the nonbelievers is called Jihad, any other effort that a Muslim makes to propagate Deen is called Jihad.

Jinn: A creation of Allah and they are made from fire. They can assume any form, have amazing powers and are invisible to the human eye.

Jizya: A sum of money that the non-Muslim citizens of a Muslim country pay to the government in exchange for security and other privileges.

Jummua: Friday congregational prayer.

Kafir (plural - Kafirun or Kuffar): Translated as "disbeliever" or "rejecter of faith". This term refers to any person who does not have Iman. Jews and Christians may be referred to as Kafirun. All Mushrikun may be called Kafirun, all Kafirun cannot be called Mushrikun.

Kabah: Referred to as "Baytullah" ("Allah's House"), the Kabah is a cube-shaped building situated in the Masjidul Haram in the city of Makkah. It is towards the Kabah that Muslims face during salah.

Kaffara: A penalty that one has to pay for committing acts of sin such as breaking oaths, etc. It varies according to the sin.

Kalima: The testimony of belief that Muslims recite to confirm their Iman. The words of the Kalima are "*La Ilaha Illal Lahu Muhammadur Rasulullah*" ("There is none worthy of worship but Allah and Muhammad ﷺ is the Rasul (messenger) of Allah").

Khadija: The first wife of Rasulullah ﷺ who assisted Islam and passed away in Makkah before Rasulullah ﷺ migrated to Madinah.

Khalifa (plural - Khulafa): A title used for the leader of the Muslims. The title was first used for Abu Bakr ﷺ, who succeeded Rasulullah ﷺ as the leader of the Muslims. The word 'Caliph' is commonly used.

Khandaq: see Battle of Ahzab

Kharaj: The Zakah due on crops.

Khaibar: A place where the Jews of Madinah took residence after being expelled from Madinah for betraying the Muslims. It is located about 100 miles north of Madinah.

Khazraj: One of the 2 tribes of the Ansar. The other was the Aws tribe.

Khilafa: Term of serving as Khalifa/position of being the Khalifa.

Khulafa: see **Khalifa**

Khulafa Rashidin: The term is translated as 'the rightly guided Khulafa'. It refers to Abu Bakr ﷺ, Omar ﷺ, Uthman ﷺ and Ali ﷺ.

Kisra: The emperor of the Persian Empire.

Kuffar: see **Kafir**

Kufr: Translated as "disbelief". Kufr is the opposite of Iman.

La Ilaha IllAllah: The first part of the Kalimah, translated as "There is none worthy of worship but Allah". see **Kalimah and Iman**

Lat: One of the idols that the Arab disbelievers worshipped during the Period of Ignorance.

Laylatul Qadr ("The night of Power"): This is an unspecified night during the Ramadhan of each year in which a person carrying out an act of Ibada will receive the reward of doing the act for 1,000 months. The virtues of this night are mentioned in Surah Qadr (Surah 97).

Lowhul Mahfudh: Translated as the "Protected Tablet". It is a book in the heavens where Allah has recorded every event that has taken place and that will take place.

Madinah: A city in Arabia. Rasulullah ﷺ migrated to Madinah after he was compelled to leave Makkah and he lived there until his demise. He is buried in Madinah.

Maghrib: One of the 5 Fardh salahs. It is performed between sunset and the period when all light vanishes from the horizon.

Mahr: The dowry that is paid to the bride upon marriage.

Mahram (plural - **Maharim**): Someone whom one is not allowed to marry, such as one's father, mother, brother, sister, etc. A list of Maharim is mentioned in verses 22, 23 and 24 of Surah Nisa (Surah 4). One who is allowed to marry is referred to as a non-Mahram.

Makkah: A city in Arabia where Rasulullah ﷺ was born. It is also referred to as Bakka. The Kaba is situated in this city.

Mala'ikah: The term for the angels. It is the plural of 'Malak'.

Maqam of Ibrahim ﷺ: It is called "Station of Ibrahim". It is the rock which Allah provided to Ibrahim ﷺ to stand and build the Kabah.

Marwa: see **Safa.**

Masjid (plural - **Masajid**): Normally referred to as a mosque, a Masjid is a place where Muslims perform their salah in congregation.

Masjidul Haram: The Masjid surrounding the Kabah.

Masjidun Nabawi: Translated as "Masjid of Rasulullah ﷺ", it is the Masjid in Madinah that was built during the time of Rasulullah and where his grave is today.

Mayta: Translated as "carrion", refers to the meat of animals that die without being slaughtered in the name of Allah as well as the meat of a limb that is removed from a living animal.

Men of Suffa: see **Suffa**

Mina: A place situated approximately 3 miles outside **Makkah.** People performing Hajj spend most of their time here.

Mithqal (plural: **Mathaqeel**): One Mithqal equals to 4.4g of silver

Mu'adhin: The person who calls out the Adhan. See **Adhan**

Mubahala: When 2 conflicting parties collectively make Du'a to Allah that He should destroy the party that is wrong.

Mudd: One Mudd is equal to 800g.

Muhajir (plural - **Muhajirin**): A person who makes Hijrah i.e. who migrates for the pleasure of Allah. It is generally used to refer to the first Muslims who migrated from Makkah to Madinah.

Muhajirin: see **Muhajir**

Muhammad ﷺ: The last Nabi (prophet) whom Allah sent to mankind. He was born in Makkah in 570AD and passed away in Madinah in 632AD. All Muslims follow his teachings.

Muharram: The 1st month of the Islamic calendar. Mujahid (plural - Mujahidun/Mujahidin): Refers to a person fighting in Jihad, it also refers to a Muslim who is engaged in any effort to propagate Islam.

Mujahidin: see **Mujahid**

Mu'min (plural - **Mu'minun or Mu'minin**): A person who has Iman.

Mu'minat: feminine of Mu'minin and Mu'minun. Mu'minin: see **Mu'min**

Mu'minun: see **Mu'min**

Munafiq (plural- **Munafiqin**): see hypocrite

Murtad (plural - **Murtaddin**): Translated as an apostate or renegade. A Murtad is a Muslim who forsakes Islam either by adopting another religion, by rejecting a fundamental of Islam or by doing or saying anything that removes him/her from the fold of Islam.

Murtaddin: see **Murtad**

Musafir: Commonly refers to "a traveler"

Mushrik (plural - **Mushrikin**): A person who commits shirk.

Mushrikin: see **Mushrik**

Muslim: (plural - **Muslims**): The word means "one who has surrendered his will to Allah". It refers to a person who follows Islam.

Nabi (plural - **Ambiya**): A prophet whom Allah sends to guide people. The term Nabi is identical with Rasul.

Nabi: Refers to **Rasulullah** ﷺ

Nafl (plural - **Nawafil**): Optional worship and not enforced by the Shari'ah. Doing it will earn reward while it will not be sinful to omit it.

Nafs: Translated as the 'soul', the term more specifically refers to the evil dimension of the soul.

Nawafil: see **Nafl**

Non-Mahram: see **Mahram**

Nubuwwah: Synonym of Risalah, see **Risalah**

Period of Ignorance: This refers to the period in Arabia before Rasulullah ﷺ brought the message of Islam.

Qari (plural - **Qumm**): A person who is proficient in reciting the Qur'an.

Qafeez: A unit of weight with one Qafeez equal to 19.2kg.

Qamis: A long, loose tailored upper garment.

Qibla: The direction a person faces when praying, which is towards the Kabah in Makkah.

Qira'ah: Refers to the recitation of the Qur'an.

Qisas: The punishment set to persons who inflict such wounds to others that can be inflicted to them in exactly the same manner.

Judgment: see Day of **Judgment**

Qiyamul Layl: Translated as "standing during the night" especially performing the Tahajjud salah.

Qur'an: The final divine scripture which Allah revealed to Rasulullah ﷺ in the Arabic language.

Quraish: The Arab tribe that dominated Makkah during the time of Rasulullah ﷺ. Rasulullah ﷺ belonged to this tribe.

Qumut: see **Qari**

Rabb: Normally translated as "Lord", it refers to the Being Who creates, nurtures, sustains, controls and owns the entire creation.

Rajab: The 7th month of the Islamic calendar.

Rakah: A unit of salah.

Ramadhan: The 9th month of the Islamic calendar for fasting.

Rasul (plural - **Rusul**): Translated as messenger, the term always refers to a Nabi (prophet) of Allah.

Rasulullah: Means "The messenger of Allah" and is used by Muslims to refer to Allah's final Rasul (prophet) Muhammad.

Risalah: Refers to a person's position as Allah's prophet and is translated as **Risalat** "prophethood". For a person's Iman to be valid, s/he has to believe in the Risalah of Rasulullah ﷺ i.e. s/he has to believe that Rasulullah ﷺ is Allah's final messenger. For the people before Rasulullah, it was necessary for them to believe in the Risalah of the Nabi (prophet) whom Allah sent during their time.

Ruku: The bowing posture in salah which precedes the prostration.

Rusul: see **Rasul**

Sa: One Sa is equal to approximately 3.2kg.

Sacred Months: These are the months of Dhul Qa'dah, Dhul Hijjah, Muharram and Rajab.

Sadaqa: Charity given for the pleasure of Allah other than zakah.

Sa'ee: One of the rituals of Hajj and Umrah in which a person has to walk back and forth 7 times between the hills of Safa and Marwa near Kabah.

Safa and Marwa: 2 hills close to the Kaba. Muslims performing Hajj and Umrah are required to walk between these hills 7 times.

Safar: The 2nd month of the Islamic calendar.

Sahabah: The companions of Rasulullah ﷺ. The term refers to any person who saw Rasulullah ﷺ and who lived and died as a Muslim.

Sahabi: Singular of Sahabah. see **Sahabah**

Sajdah: Sajdah refers to prostrating before Allah in salah. The act denotes placing the forehead on the ground as a sign of total submission and humility in front of Allah.

Sehri: A meal a person eats before dawn to start the fasting for the day.

Sham: Translated as Sham, it refers to a large area of the Middle East including parts of Sham, Palestine, Jordan and Lebanon.

Shahada: A testimony of belief similar to the Kalima but stated with these words: "*Ash Hadu Alla Ilaha IllAllahu wa Ash Hadu Anna Muhammadan Abduhu wa Rasuluh*" ("I testify that there is none worthy of worship but Allah and I testify that Muhammad ﷺ is His servant and Rasul (messenger)"). see **Kalima**

Saitan (plural - **Saiatin**): It refers to the devil Satan, who is a Jinn. It is also used for all other individuals from Jinn and mankind who create mischief among people. He is also referred to as **Iblees**.

Shari'ah: The code of law that governs the lives of Muslims.

Shirk: Translated as "polytheism", opposite of Towhid. It refers to worshipping many deities, whether Allah is included among these or not. It also includes attrbuting such qualities to others, which belong to Allah alone. It will be said that a person is committing "Shirk" if s/he believes that a being besides Allah can see and hear everything. A person who commits "Shirk" is called a Mushrik.

Siddiq (plural - **Siddiqin**): Translated as "one who is extremely truthful". It is used for people who were closest to the Ambiya and who accepted the message of the Ambiya without hesitation. This title is also used for the Ambiya themselves.

Siddiqin: see **Siddiq Sirat:** see **Bridge of Sirat**

SubhanAllah: Translated as "Glory be to Allah" which is said to express that Allah is totally without any partners.

Suffa: A raised platform in the Masjid of Rasulullah where the "men of Suffa" lived. They were poor Muslims who had neither family nor homes nor occupations in Madinah. Their number varied with time.

Sunan: see **Sunnah**

Sunnah (plural - **Sunan**): Means "practice" of Rasulullah ﷺ.

Surah: A chapter of the Qur'an. There are 114 Surahs in the Qur'an.

Tabi'een: Muslims who saw the Sahabah.

Tabligh: This term refers to propagating Islam.

Tabuk: A place 450 miles from Madinah where the Muslims camped to meet a large Roman army. The Roman army failed to appear and the Muslims consolidated their control over the region. Although no battle took place, the expedition is known as the 'Battle of Tabuk' took place in the 9th year after the Hijra. It was the final expedition which Rasulullah ﷺ personally led and the journey proved to be very tedious because of the extremely long journey and scorching heat.

Tahajjud: A non-obligatory salah performed between the Isha and Fajr salahs, preferably just before dawn. It has big rewards.

Takbir: see "**Allahu Akbar**"

Talbiya: A short Arabic sentence that people continuously recite while performing Hajj and Umrah.

Taqdir: Refers to predestination, one of the core beliefs of a Muslim that everything good and bad has been predestined by Allah. Allah has given man a choice to do good or bad, the outcome is determined by Allah.

Taqwa: Commonly translated as "fear for Allah", the word drives a person to carry out all Allah's commands and to stay away from everything that Allah has prohibited.

Tasbih (plural - **Tasbihat**): The term refers to glorifying Allah using words like "SubhanAllah" ("Glory be to Allah").

Tasbihat: see **Tasbih**

Tashahud: A Du'a recited while sitting after every 2 Rakahs of salah.

Tauba: Repentance.

Tawaf: Walking around the Kaba 7 times in an anti-clockwise direction.

Tawakkul: Refers to placing one's trust in Allah and to rely only on Allah under all circumstances.

Tayamum: A form of ablution instead of Wudhu and Ghusl. One may perform Tayamum only when water is completely unavailable, inaccessible or sick. It comprises of striking one's hands on sand and passing the hands over the entire face and arms.

Thareed: A dish prepared when bread is broken into curried meat.

Towhid: Translated as "Oneness of Allah" or "Islamic monotheism". Towhid refers to worshipping Allah Only.

Treaty of Hudaibiya: see **Hudaibiya**

Uhud: A mountain ouside Madinah, the site where the Battle of Uhud took place 3 years after Rasulullah ﷺ migrated to Madinah. The

Muslims numbered about 1,000 while the Kuffar numbered over 3,000. Rasulullah ﷺ suffered some injuries during this battle.

Ulema: see **Alim**

Omar ؓ (Omar bin Khattab): He was one of the most eminent Sahabah, the father-in-law of Rasulullah ﷺ and the 2nd Khalifa of Islam.

Ummah: Means "nation". The Ummah of Rasulullah ﷺ refers to the followers of Rasulullah.

Ummahatul Mu'minin: see **Ummul Mu'minin**

Ummu- : A prefix meaning "mother of". Ummu Abdullah means "The mother of Abdullah".

Ummul Mu'minin (plural: **Ummahatul Mu'minin**): A title used for the wives of Rasulullah ﷺ. It is translated as "Mother of the Believers".

Uthman ؓ (Uthman bin Affan ؓ): He was one of the most eminent Sahabah, the son-in-1aw of Rasulullah ﷺ and the 3rd Khalifa of Islam.

Uzza: An idol the Mushrikin worshipped during the Period of Ignorance.

Wahi: Refers to the revelation that Allah sent to His Ambiya (prophets)

Walima: A meal hosted by the groom to celebrate his marriage.

Wasaq: A unit of weight with one Wasaq being equal to 192kg.

Wudhu: An act to purify oneself before salah and other acts of worship.

Ya'jooj and Ma'jooj: Translated as Gog and Magog. Authentic Ahadeeth say that they are powerful human tribes with large numbers. They are trapped behind a wall that the king Dhul Qarnayn erected (see verses 92-99 of Surah 18) and they will appear only before Judgment.

Yathrib: The name of Madinah used before Rasulullah ﷺ arrived there.

Zakah: Referred to as a "poor due". Muslims who possess a specific minimum amount of wealth for an entire year need to pay zakah to the poor, which is calculated at 2.5% of their surplus wealth.

Zuhr: One of the 5 Fardh salahs. It is performed between midday and late afternoon.

Glossary of Symbols

ﷵ "*Alaihes Salam*", means "Peace be upon him" and is used as a term of respect and a prayer after the names of prophets and angels.

ؓ "*Radhi Yallahu Anhu*", means "May Allah be pleased with him", used as a term of respect and prayer after the name of any male Sahahah.

ؓ "*Radhi Yallahu Anhum*", means "May Allah be pleased with them", a term of respect and prayer after the name of Sahabah.

ؓ "*Radhi Yallahu Anha*", means "May Allah be pleased with her", used as a term of respect and prayer after the name of any female Sahabah.

ﷺ "*Sallallahu Alayhi wa Sallam*", used after the name of Rasulullah ﷺ, means "May Allah shower mercy and peace on him" i.e. on Rasulullah.

رحمة الله Read as "*Rahima Hullah*", means "May Allah have mercy on him", a term of respect and prayer after the name of any pious person.

ﷻ Read as "*Subhanahu wa Ta'ala*", means "The most Sublime and Exalted", used after the name of Allah.

Qiblah Direction

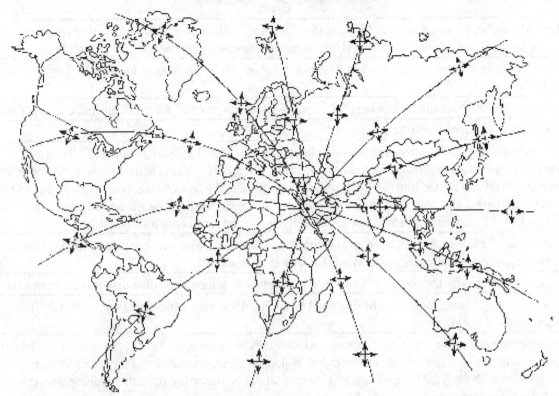

Prophets mentioned in the Qur'an
(Links between prophets may or may not indicate direct descendants)

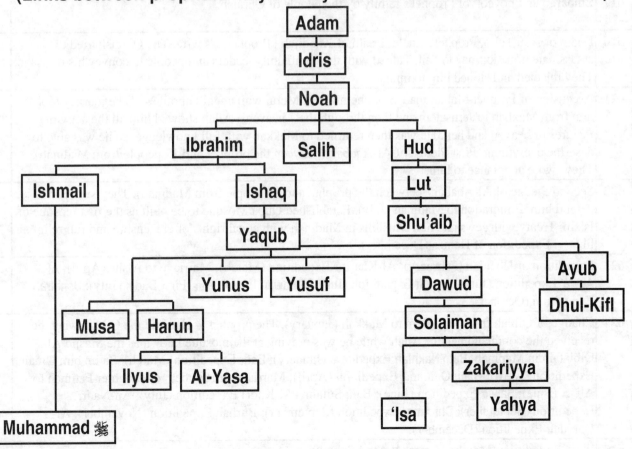

Life of Prophet Muhammad ﷺ

Year	Event	Age
570	Birth of Prophet Muhammad ﷺ at Makkah (March / April). His father Abdullah died several months before he was born. He was raised by Halimah as wet-mother according to Makkah's tradition.	0
576	Death of Aminah (Prophet ﷺ's mother). Halimah returned Muhammad ﷺ to his grandfather Abd Al-Muttalib.	6
578	Death of Abd Al-Muttalib. Muhammad ﷺ grew up under the protective care of his uncle Abu Talib.	8
582	Journey to Syria with uncle Abu Talib.	12
582 -94	Worked as a shepherd for his uncle and also later as a merchant. He lived a simple life. He was compassionate to the poor, widow and orphans. He volunteered in many activities for the community. People of Makkah named him 'Al-Siddiq (the Truthful)' and 'Al-Ameen (the Trustworthy)' due to his honesty and good character. Acted as a business service agent for Khadijah, a wealthy business woman of Makkah. Muhammad ﷺ carried her goods to the north and returned with a profit.	12-24
595	Impressed by Muhammad ﷺ's honesty and character, Khadijah (who was a widow) proposed for marriage and eventually they got married. He was 25, she was 40.	25
609	Kabah was rebuilt by the people of Quraish. Muhammad ﷺ helped to resolve disputes between tribes.	39
610	First revelation came (August) to Muhammad ﷺ at Cave Hira with a message (verses 96:1-5) from Allah by the Angel Gabriel.	40
610 -13	Received several verses during this period and later they were compiled to become part of the Islamic sacred scripture 'The Qur'an'. He was belittled, ridiculed, then persecuted and physically attacked by the people of Makkah for his message of 'Oneness' of Allah, departing from the traditional tribal ways, including idol worshipping at the Kabah.	40-43
615	Emigration of Muslims to Abyssinia to avoid sufferings and persecution from the people of Makkah. The king Negus offered asylum to Muslims.	45
617 -20	Embargo and boycott of Prophet's family by the people of Quraish.	47-50
620	Death of Abu Talib, Prophet's uncle. Death of Khadijah , Prophet ﷺ's wife. The Quraish tried to assassinate him. **Journey to Taif**. Talked with the community leaders and people to convey his message. They rejected and stoned him to injury.	50
621	Ascension of Prophet Muhammad ﷺ on the night of Meraj with angel Gibrail عليه السلام. The journey took him from Makkah to Jerusalem and then through the 7 heavens. Allah showed him all the activities, features of heaven and hell. He was then returned to Makkah with full knowledge, so he was able to describe everything. First Pledge of Al-Aqabah (between the prophet and 12 people from Madinah). They swore allegiance to him.	51
622	Second Pledge of Al-Aqabah (between the prophet and 75 people from Madinah). They swore to defend him. Emigration to Madinah (July). Established Quba Mosque to be built as the first mosque of Islam. Treaty with Jews and non-Muslims in Madinah with equal rights of citizenship and full religious liberty. Expedition of Hamza (December).	52
623	Expedition of Ubaidah (February); Al-Kharrar Expedition (March); Marriage to Aisha (April); **Al-Abwa'** Expedition (June); **Buwat** Expedition (July); **Safawan** Expedition (First Badr) (July); **Ushairah** Expedition (October).	53
624	Change of Qiblah from Jerusalem to Makkah (January). The prophet ﷺ changed the Qiblah when he received the commandment of Allah while he was praying at the mosque known as the Masjid Al-Qiblatain in Madinah. **Batn Nakhlah** Expedition (January); **Badr** Expedition (March). Salim bim Umair Expedition (April); Banu Qainuqa' Expedition (April); Marriage of Prophet ﷺ's daughter Fatimah to Ali ؓ (June); **Sawiq** Expedition (June); Bani Sulaim (Al-Kudr) Expedition (July); An-Nadri Expedition (September); **Dhi Amar** Expedition (September); Burhan Expedition (November); Al-Qaradah Expedition (December).	54
625	**Uhud** Expedition (March); **Hamra' Al-Asad** Expedition (April)	55

626	Abu Salamah Expedition (July); Abdullah bin Unais Expedition (July); Dhatur-Riqa' Expedition (July); Al-Mundhir bin Amr (August); Raji Expedition (August); **Daumatul-Jandal** Expedition (August); Banu An-Nadir Expedition (September).	56
627	**Banu Mustaliq** Expedition (January); **Ahzab** Expedition (Trench around Madinah to defend the city) (February - March); **Banu Quraiza** Expedition (April); **Second Badr** Expedition (May); Al-Qurata Expedition (June); **Banu Lihyan** Expedition (August); **Dhu Qarad** Expedition (August); Ghamr Expedition (August); Dhul-Qassah Expedition (September); Dhul Qassah (Abu Ubaidah) Expedition (September); Zaid bin Harith 5 Edpeditions (August/627 - February/628).	57
628	Daumatil-Jandal (Abdul Rahman bin Awf) Expedition (January); Fadak Expedition (January); Khaibar: (Abdullah bin Atik) Expedition (February), (Abdullah bin Rawaha) Expedition (March); 'Urainah Expedition (March); Ad-Damri Expedition; **Treaty of Hudaibiyah** between the Quraish of Makkah and Muslims (April). The Prophet Muhammad ﷺ and Muslims returned to Madinah without Umrah as a part of the treaty with a provision to return to Makkah next year for Umrah. Makkans breached the treaty a year later. Invitation letters to Kings and world leaders (April - May) of Abyssinia, Bahrain, Persia, Jerusalem (Roman King), Alexandria, Oman, Yamamah, Damascus. Khaibar Expedition (May - June).	58
629	Turabah (Omar bin Khattab) Expedition (January); Najd Expedition (Abu Bakr) (January); Fadak Expedition (Bashir bin Sa'd) (January); Mayf'ah Expedition (January); Yamn and Jabar Expedition (January). **Performance of missed Umrah** (Umratul-Qada') (April). Banu Sulaim Expedition (May); Kadid and Fadak Expedition (July); Al-Asadi Expedition (August); Dhat Atla Expedition (August); Mutah Expedition (October); Dhatus-Salasil Expedition (November); Al-Khabt Expedition (December)	59
630	Abu Qatadah Expedition (January); **Victory of Makkah** (January); The Prophet ﷺ entered Makkah with 10,000 Muslims without any bloodshed. The Makkans joined the Muslims after they saw no revenge or retaliation rather he announced general amnesty to all the enemies and treated the citizens of the city with generosity. Nakhlah (Khalid bin Al-Walid) Expedition (January); Suwa-Banu Hudhail (Amr bin Al-'Aas) Expedition (January); Al-Mushallal (Sa'd bin Zaid) Expedition (January); Banu Jadhimah (Khalid bin Al-Walid) Expedition (February). **Hunain** Expedition (February); **At-Ta'if** Expedition (February). Birth of Ibrahim (Prophet ﷺ 's son) (March); Banu Tamim Expedition (May); Tabalah Expedition (June); Dahhak Al-Kilabi Expedition (July); Jeddah Expedition (August); Ali bin Abi Talib (August); Al-Asadi Expedition (August). Death of Negus, King of Abyssinia (October). **Tabuk** Expedition (October - December).	60
631	Death of Ibrahim (Prophet ﷺ 's son) (January). Hajj Pilgrimage led by Abu Bakr (March). Najran Expedition by Khalid bin Al-Walid (July).	61
632	Yemen Expedition, Ali (January); Last Revelation (February - March). **Farewell Pilgrimage** to Makkah and thousands of Muslims joined (February - March). **Last Sermon at Arafat** (**March**); Usamah Expedition (June).	62
632	Death of Prophet Muhammad ﷺ (June). He was buried in the mosque in Madinah. During the last 10 years of his life, he ➤ destroyed idolatry in Arabia; ➤ raised the status of women to complete legal equality with men; ➤ stopped drunkenness and immorality in the society; ➤ made people live with faith, sincerity and honesty; transformed the nation from the ignorance of darkness into fully knowledgeable societies. ➤ transformed a society from all forms of injustice into universal human brotherhood as obedient servants of Allah. Within 100 years, Islam and his way of life had spread from the remote corners of Arabia to as far east as Indo-China and as far west as Morocco, France, and Spain. He is the Last messenger for the entire world from the Same Allah of Ibrahim ﷺ, Musa ﷺ, and 'Isa ﷺ. The Qur'an is the Final Revelation..	62+

Expeditions Prophet ﷺ participated are in Bold

Prophet ﷺ's letters to Rulers and Leaders

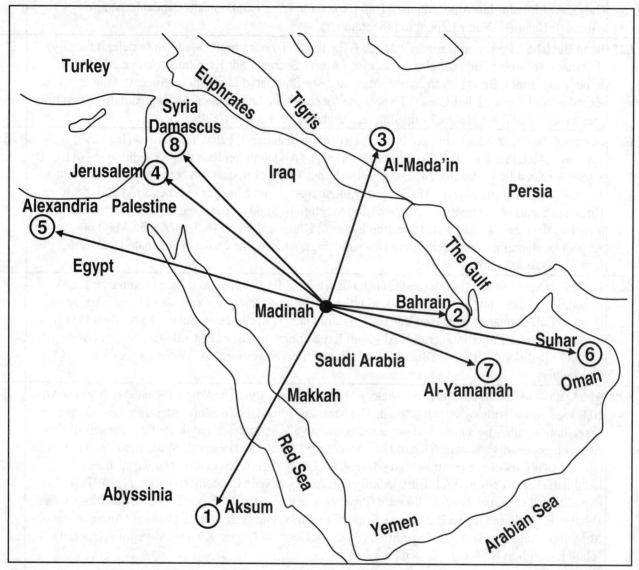

Prophet ﷺ's Letter

Seal of the Prophet ﷺ

#	City	Ruler / Country
1	Aksum	King Negus / Abyssinia
2	Bahrain	Al-Mundhir bin Sawa / Bahrain
3	Al-Mada'in	Chosroes / Persia
4	Jerusalem	Hercules, Caesar / Rome
5	Alexandria	Al-Muqawqis / Egypt
6	Suhar	Jayfar, 'Abd, sons of Al-Julandi / Oman
7	Yamamah	Hawdhah bin Ali / Al-Yamamah
8	Damascus	Al-Harith bin Abi Shamr Al-Gassani / Syria

Everyday Useful Books, CDs / DVDs

 Qur'an

 Faza'il -e- A'maal

 Da'wah Etiquette

 Basics of Islam

 Du'a Organizer

 Price of Paradise

 Hajj & Umrah Organizer

 Islamic Organizations In North America

Da'wah / Comparative Religion

Where Do You Stand ?	What Every Woman Should Know	¿Y usted en qué cree?

Comparative Religion
(English, Arabic, Spanish)

Educational DVDs

 Allah's Universe

 Prophets of the Qur'an

 Life of Prophet Muhammad ﷺ

 Scholars of Islam

 Price of Paradise

 Jerusalem

 Hajj & Umrah

For more information about these books, CDs, DVDs,
Please contact
wheredoyoustand.net; finalrevelation.net
P.O. Box – 890071, Houston, TX 77289
281-488-3191
a6h@yahoo.com

Notes: